Peterson's®
Two-Year
Colleges
2017

About Peterson's®

Peterson's® provides the accurate, dependable, high-quality education content and guidance you need to succeed. No matter where you are on your academic or professional path, you can rely on Peterson's publications and its online information at **www.petersons.com** for the most up-to-date education exploration data, expert test-prep tools, and top-notch career success resources—everything you need to achieve your goals.

For more information, contact Peterson's, 3 Columbia Circle, Suite 205, Albany, NY 12203-5158;
800-338-3282 Ext. 54229; or visit us online at **www.petersons.com**.

Previous editions published as *Peterson's Annual Guide to Undergraduate Study* © 1970, 1971, 1972, 1973, 1974, 1975, 1976, 1977, 1978, 1979, 1980, 1981, 1982 and as *Peterson's Two-Year Colleges* © 1983, 1984, 1985, 1986, 1987, 1988, 1989, 1990, 1991, 1992, 1993, 1994, 1995, 1996, 1997, 1998, 1999, 2000, 2001, 2002, 2003, 2004, 2005, 2006, 2007, 2008, 2009, 2010, 2011, 2012, 2013, 2014, 2015

Peterson's makes reasonable efforts to obtain accurate, complete, and timely data from reliable sources. Nevertheless, Peterson's and the third-party data suppliers make no representation or warranty, either expressed or implied, as to the accuracy, timeliness, or completeness of the data or the results to be obtained from using the data, including, but not limited to, its quality, performance, merchantability, or fitness for a particular purpose, non-infringement or otherwise.

Neither Peterson's nor the third-party data suppliers warrant, guarantee, or make any representations that the results from using the data will be successful or will satisfy users' requirements. The entire risk to the results and performance is assumed by the user.

NOTICE: Certain portions of or information contained in this book have been submitted and paid for by the educational institution identified, and such institutions take full responsibility for the accuracy, timeliness, completeness and functionality of such content. Such portions or information include (i) each display ad in the "Profiles" section from pages 49 through 355 that comprises a half or full page of information covering a single educational institution, and (ii) each two-page description in the "Featured Two-Year Colleges" section from pages 362 through 377.

ISSN 0894-9328
ISBN: 978-0-7689-4090-9

Printed in the United States of America

10 9 8 7 6 5 4 3 2 1   18 17 16

Forty-seventh Edition

Contents

A Note from the Peterson's® Editors

For more than 50 years, Peterson's has given students and parents the most comprehensive, up-to-date information on undergraduate institutions in the United States. Peterson's researches the data published in *Peterson's Two-Year Colleges* each year. The information is furnished by the colleges and is accurate at the time of publishing.

This guide also features advice and tips on the college search and selection process, such as how to decide if a two-year college is right for you, how to approach transferring to another college, and what's in store for adults returning to college. If you seem to be getting more, not less, anxious about choosing and getting into the right college, *Peterson's Two-Year Colleges* provides just the right help, giving you the information you need to make important college decisions and ace the admission process.

Opportunities abound for students, and this guide can help you find what you want in a number of ways:

"What You Need to Know About Two-Year Colleges" outlines the basic features and advantages of two-year colleges. "Surviving Standardized Tests" gives an overview of the common examinations students take prior to attending college. "Who's Paying for This? Financial Aid Basics" provides guidelines for financing your college education. "Frequently Asked Questions About Transferring" takes a look at the two-year college scene from the perspective of a student who is looking toward the day when he or she may pursue additional education at a four-year institution. "Returning to School: Advice for Adult Students" is an analysis of the pros and cons (mostly pros) of returning to college after already having begun a professional career. "Coming to America: Tips for International Students Considering Study in the U.S." is an article written particularly for students overseas who are considering a U.S. college education. "Community Colleges and the Green Economy" offers information on some exciting "green" programs at community colleges throughout the United States, as well as two insightful essays by Mary F. T. Spilde, President, Lane Community College and Tom Sutton, Director of Wind Energy and Technical Services, Kalamazoo Valley Community College. Finally, "How to Use This Guide" gives details on the data in this guide: what terms mean and why they're here.

- If you already have specifics in mind, such as a particular institution or major, turn to the easy-to-use **Two-Year Colleges At-a-Glance Chart** or **Indexes.** You can look up a particular feature—location and programs offered—or use the alphabetical index and immediately find the colleges that meet your criteria.

- For information about particular colleges, turn to the **Profiles of Two-Year Colleges** section. Here, our comprehensive college profiles are arranged alphabetically by state. They provide a complete picture of need-to-know information about every accredited two-year college—from admission to graduation, including expenses, financial aid, majors, and campus safety. All the information you need to apply is placed together at the conclusion of each college **Profile.** Display ads, which appear near some of the institutions' profiles, have been provided and paid for by those colleges or universities that wished to supplement their profile data with additional information about their institution.

- In addition, two-page narrative descriptions, which appear in the **Featured Two-Year Colleges** section, are paid for and written by college officials and offer great detail about each college. They are edited to provide a consistent format across entries for your ease of comparison.

Peterson's publishes a full line of books—education exploration, test prep, financial aid, and career preparation. Peterson's publications can be found at high school guidance offices, college libraries and career centers, and your local bookstore and library. Peterson's books are also available at www.petersonsbooks.com.

We welcome any comments or suggestions you may have about this publication. Your feedback will help us make educational dreams possible for you—and others like you.

Colleges will be pleased to know that Peterson's helped you in your selection. Admissions staff members are more than happy to answer questions, address specific problems and help in any way they can. The editors at Peterson's wish you great success in your college search.

NOTICE: Certain portions of or information contained in this book have been submitted and paid for by the educational institution identified, and such institutions take full responsibility for the accuracy, timeliness, completeness and functionality of such content. Such portions or information include (i) each display ad in the "Profiles" section from pages 49 through 355 that comprises a half or full page of information covering a single educational institution, and (ii) each two-page description in the "Featured Two-Year Colleges" section from pages 362 through 377.

The College Admissions Process: An Overview

What You Need to Know About Two-Year Colleges

David R. Pierce

Two-year colleges—better known as community colleges—are often called "the people's colleges." With their open-door policies (admission is open to individuals with a high school diploma or its equivalent), community colleges provide access to higher education for millions of Americans who might otherwise be excluded from higher education. Community college students are diverse and of all ages, races, and economic backgrounds. While many community college students enroll full-time, an equally large number attend on a part-time basis so they can fulfill employment and family commitments as they advance their education.

Community colleges can also be referred to as either technical or junior colleges, and they may either be under public or independent control. What unites two-year colleges is that they are regionally accredited, postsecondary institutions, whose highest credential awarded is the associate degree. With few exceptions, community colleges offer a comprehensive curriculum, which includes transfer, technical, and continuing education programs.

IMPORTANT FACTORS IN A COMMUNITY COLLEGE EDUCATION

The student who attends a community college can count on receiving high-quality instruction in a supportive learning community. This setting frees the student to pursue his or her own goals, nurture special talents, explore new fields of learning, and develop the capacity for lifelong learning.

From the student's perspective, four characteristics capture the essence of community colleges:

1. They are community-based institutions that work in close partnership with high schools, community groups, and employers in extending high-quality programs at convenient times and places.

2. Community colleges are cost effective. Annual tuition and fees at public community colleges average approximately half those at public four-year colleges and less than 15 percent of private four-year institutions. In addition, since most community colleges are generally close to their students' homes, these students can also save a significant amount of money on the room, board, and transportation expenses traditionally associated with a college education.

3. Community colleges provide a caring environment, with faculty members who are expert instructors, known for excellent teaching and meeting students at the point of their individual needs, regardless of age, sex, race, current job status, or previous academic preparation. Community colleges join a strong curriculum with a broad range of counseling and career services that are intended to assist students in making the most of their educational opportunities.

4. Many offer comprehensive programs, including transfer curricula in such liberal arts programs as chemistry, psychology, and business management, that lead directly to a baccalaureate degree and career programs that prepare students for employment or assist those already employed in upgrading their skills. For those students who need to strengthen their academic skills, community colleges also offer a wide range of developmental programs in mathematics, languages, and learning skills, designed to prepare the student for success in college studies.

GETTING TO KNOW YOUR TWO-YEAR COLLEGE

The first step in determining the quality of a community college is to check the status of its accreditation. Once you have established that a community college is appropriately accredited, find out as much as you can about the programs and services it has to offer. Much of that information can be found in materials the college provides. However, the best way to learn about a college is to visit in person.

During a campus visit, be prepared to ask a lot of questions. Talk to students, faculty members, administrators, and counselors about the college and its programs, particularly those in which you have a special interest. Ask about available certificates and associate degrees. Don't be shy. Do what you can to dig below the surface. Ask college officials about the transfer rate to four-year colleges. If a college emphasizes student services, find out what particular assistance is offered, such as educational or career guidance. Colleges are eager to provide you with the information you need to make informed decisions.

COMMUNITY COLLEGES CAN SAVE YOU MONEY

If you are able to live at home while you attend college, you will certainly save money on room and board, but it does cost something to commute. Many two-year colleges offer you instruction in your own home through online learning programs or through home study courses that can save both time and money. Look into all the options, and be sure to add up all the costs of attending various colleges before deciding which is best for you.

FINANCIAL AID

Many students who attend community colleges are eligible for a range of federal financial aid programs, state aid, and on-campus jobs. Your high school counselor or the financial aid officer at a community college will also be able to help you. It is in your interest to apply for financial aid months in advance of the date you intend to start your college program, so find out early what assistance is available to you. While many community colleges are able to help students who make a last-minute decision to attend college, either through short-term loans or emergency grants, if you are considering entering college and think you might need financial aid, it is best to find out as much as you can as early as you can.

WORKING AND GOING TO SCHOOL

Many two-year college students maintain full-time or part-time employment while they earn their degrees. Over the years, a steadily growing number of students have chosen to attend community colleges while they fulfill family and employment responsibilities. To enable these students to balance the demands of home, work, and school, most community colleges offer classes at night and on weekends.

For the full-time student, the usual length of time it takes to obtain an associate degree is two years. However, your length of study will depend on the course load you take: the fewer credits you earn each term, the longer it will take you to earn a degree. To assist you in moving more quickly toward earning your degree, many community colleges now award credit through examination or for equivalent knowledge gained through relevant life experiences. Be certain to find out the credit options that are available to you at the college in which you are interested. You may discover that it will take less time to earn a degree than you first thought.

PREPARATION FOR TRANSFER

Studies have repeatedly shown that students who first attend a community college and then transfer to a four-year college or university do at least as well academically as the students who entered the four-year institutions as freshmen. Most community colleges have agreements with nearby four-year institutions to make transfer of credits easier. If you are thinking of transferring, be sure to meet with a counselor or faculty adviser before choosing your courses. You will want to map out a course of study with transfer in mind. Make sure you also find out the credit-transfer requirements of the four-year institution you might want to attend.

ATTENDING A TWO-YEAR COLLEGE IN ANOTHER REGION

Although many community colleges serve a specific county or district, they are committed (to the extent of their ability) to the goal of equal educational opportunity without regard to economic status, race, creed, color, sex, or national origin. Independent two-year colleges recruit from a much broader geographical area—throughout the United States and, increasingly, around the world.

Although some community colleges do provide on-campus housing for their students, most do not. However, even if on-campus housing is not available, most colleges do have housing referral services.

NEW CAREER OPPORTUNITIES

Community colleges realize that many entering students are not sure about the field in which they want to focus their studies or the career they would like to pursue. Often, students discover fields and careers they never knew existed. Community colleges have the resources to help students identify areas of career interest and to set challenging occupational goals.

Once a career goal is set, you can be confident that a community college will provide job-relevant, technical education. About half of the students who take courses for credit at community colleges do so to prepare for employment or to acquire or upgrade skills for their current job. Especially helpful in charting a career path is the assistance of a counselor or a faculty adviser, who can discuss job opportunities in your chosen field and help you map out your course of study.

In addition, since community colleges have close ties to their communities, they are in constant contact with leaders in business, industry, organized labor, and public life. Community colleges work with these individuals and their organizations to prepare students for direct entry into the world of work. For example, some community colleges have established partnerships with local businesses and industries to provide specialized training programs. Some also provide the academic portion of apprenticeship training, while others offer extensive job-shadowing and cooperative education opportunities. Be sure to examine all of the career-preparation opportunities offered by the community colleges in which you are interested.

David R. Pierce is the former President of the American Association of Community Colleges.

Surviving Standardized Tests

WHAT ARE STANDARDIZED TESTS?

Colleges and universities in the United States use tests to help evaluate applicants' readiness for admission or to place them in appropriate courses. The tests that are most frequently used by colleges are the ACT® of American College Testing, Inc., and the College Board's SAT®. In addition, the Educational Testing Service (ETS) offers the TOEFL® test, which evaluates the English-language proficiency of nonnative speakers. The tests are offered at designated testing centers located at high schools and colleges throughout the United States and U.S. territories and at testing centers in various countries throughout the world.

Upon request, special accommodations for students with documented visual, hearing, physical, or learning disabilities are available. Examples of special accommodations include tests in Braille or large print and such aids as a reader, recorder, magnifying glass, or sign language interpreter. Additional testing time may be allowed in some instances. Contact the appropriate testing program or your guidance counselor for details on how to request special accommodations.

THE ACT®

The ACT® is a standardized college entrance examination that measures knowledge and skills in English, mathematics, reading comprehension, and science reasoning and the application of these skills to future academic tasks. The ACT® consists of four multiple-choice tests.

Test 1: English
- 75 questions, 45 minutes
- Usage and mechanics
- Rhetorical skills

Test 2: Mathematics
- 60 questions, 60 minutes
- Pre-algebra
- Elementary algebra
- Intermediate algebra
- Coordinate geometry
- Plane geometry
- Trigonometry

Test 3: Reading
- 40 questions, 35 minutes
- Prose fiction
- Humanities
- Social studies
- Natural sciences

Test 4: Science
- 40 questions, 35 minutes
- Data representation
- Research summary
- Conflicting viewpoints

Each section is scored from 1 to 36 and is scaled for slight variations in difficulty. Students are not penalized for incorrect responses. The composite score is the average of the four scaled scores. The ACT® Plus Writing includes the four multiple-choice tests and a writing test, which measures writing skills emphasized in high school English classes and in entry-level college composition courses.

To prepare for the ACT®, ask your guidance counselor for a free guidebook, "Preparing for the ACT®," or download it at www.act.org/aap/pdf/Preparing-for-the-ACT.pdf. Besides providing general test-preparation information and additional test-taking strategies, this guidebook provides full-length practice tests, including a Writing test, information about the optional Writing Test, strategies to prepare for the tests, and what to expect on test day.

DON'T FORGET TO . . .

- ❑ Take the SAT® or ACT® before application deadlines.
- ❑ Note that test registration deadlines precede test dates by about six weeks.
- ❑ Register to take the TOEFL® test if English is not your native language and you are planning on studying at a North American college.
- ❑ Contact the College Board or American College Testing, Inc., in advance if you need special accommodations when taking tests.

The redesigned SAT®, which saw its first test-takers in the spring of 2016, has these sections: Evidence-Based Reading and Writing, Math, and the Essay. It is based on 1600 points—the top scores for the Math section and the Evidence-Based Reading and Writing section will be 800, and the Essay score is reported separately.

Evidence-based Reading Test
* 52 questions; 65 minutes
* Passages in U.S. and world literature, history/social studies, and science
   •Paired passages
   •Lower and higher text complexities
   •Words in context, command of evidence, and analysis

Writing and Language Test
* 44 questions; 35 minutes
* Passages in careers, history/social studies, humanities, and science
* Argument, informative/explanatory, and nonfiction narrative passages
* Words in context, grammar, expression of ideas, and analysis

Mathematics Test

* One no-calculator section (25 minutes)

* One calculator section (55 minutes)

* Content includes algebra, problem solving and data analysis, advanced math, area and volume calculations, trigonometric functions, and lines, triangles, and circles using theorems.

Essay (Optional)

* 50 minutes

- Argument passage written for a general audience

- Analysis of argument in passage using text evidence

- Score: 3–12 (Reading: 1–4 scale, Analysis: 1–4 scale, Writing: 1–4 scale)

According to the College Board's website, the "Eight Key Changes" are the following:

- **Relevant Words in Context:** Students need to interpret the meaning of words based on the context of the passage in which they appear. The focus is on "relevant" words—not obscure ones.

- **Command of Evidence:** In addition to demonstrating writing skills, students need to show that they're able to interpret, synthesize, and use evidence found in a wide range of sources.

- **Essay Analyzing a Source:** Students read a passage and explain how the author builds an argument, supporting support their claims with actual data from the passage.

- **Math Focused on Three Key Areas:** Problem Solving and Data Analysis (using ratios, percentages, and proportional reasoning to solve problems in science, social science, and career contexts), the Heart of Algebra (mastery of linear equations and systems), and Passport to Advanced Math (more complex equations and the manipulation they require).

- **Problems Grounded in Real-World Contexts:** All of the questions are grounded in the real world, directly related to work performed in college.

- **Analysis in Science and in Social Studies:** Students need to apply reading, writing, language, and math skills to answer questions in contexts of science, history, and social studies.

- **Founding Documents and Great Global Conversation:** Students will find an excerpt from one of the Founding Documents—such as the Declaration of Independence, the Constitution, and the Bill of Rights—or a text from the "Great Global Conversation" about freedom, justice, and human dignity.

- **No Penalty for Wrong Answers:** Students earn points for the questions they answer correctly.

Check out the College Board's website at https://collegereadiness.collegeboard.org for the most up-to-date information.

Top 10 Ways Not to Take the Test
10. Cramming the night before the test.
9. Not becoming familiar with the directions before you take the test.
8. Not becoming familiar with the format of the test before you take it.
7. Not knowing how the test is graded.
6. Spending too much time on any one question.
5. Second-guessing yourself.
4. Not checking spelling, grammar, and sentence structure in essays.
3. Writing a one-paragraph essay.
2. Forgetting to take a deep breath to keep from—
1. Losing It!

SAT SUBJECT TESTS™

Subject Tests are required by some institutions for admission and/or placement in freshman-level courses. Each Subject Test measures one's knowledge of a specific subject and the ability to apply that knowledge. Students should check with each institution for its specific requirements. In general, students are required to take three Subject Tests (one English, one mathematics, and one of their choice).

Subject Tests are given in the following areas: biology, chemistry, Chinese, French, German, Italian, Japanese, Korean, Latin, literature, mathematics, modern Hebrew, physics, Spanish, U.S. history, and world history. These tests are 1 hou long and are primarily multiple-choice tests. Three Subject Tests may be taken on one test date.

Scored like the current SAT®, students gain a point for each correct answer and lose a fraction of a point for each incorrect answer. The raw scores are then converted to scaled scores that range from 200 to 800.

THE TOEFL® INTERNET-BASED TEST (IBT)

The Test of English as a Foreign Language Internet-Based Test (TOEFL® iBT) is designed to help assess a student's grasp of English if it is not the student's first language. Performance on the TOEFL® test may help interpret scores on the critical reading sections of the SAT®. The test consists of four integrated sections: speaking, listening, reading, and writing. The TOEFL® iBT emphasizes integrated skills. The paper-based versions of the TOEFL® will continue to be administered in certain countries where the Internet-based version has not yet been introduced. For further information, visit www.toefl.org.

WHAT OTHER TESTS SHOULD I KNOW ABOUT?

The AP® Program

This program allows high school students to try college-level work and build valuable skills and study habits in the process. Subject matter is explored in more depth in AP courses than in other high school classes. A qualifying score on an AP test—which varies from school to school—can earn you college credit or advanced placement. Getting qualifying grades on enough exams can even earn you a full year's credit and sophomore standing at more than 1,500 higher-education institutions. There are more than thirty AP courses across multiple subject areas, including art history, biology, and computer science. Speak to your guidance counselor for information about your school's offerings.

College-Level Examination Program (CLEP®)

The CLEP enables students to earn college credit for what they already know, whether it was learned in school, through independent study, or through other experiences outside of the classroom. More than 2,900 colleges and universities now award credit for qualifying scores on one or more of the 33 CLEP exams. The exams, which are 90 minutes in length and are primarily multiple choice, are administered at participating colleges and universities. For more information, check out the website at www.collegeboard.com/clep.

WHAT CAN I DO TO PREPARE FOR THESE TESTS?

Know what to expect. Get familiar with how the tests are structured, how much time is allowed, and the directions for each type of question. Get plenty of rest the night before the test and eat breakfast that morning.

There are a variety of products, from books to software to videos, available to help you prepare for most standardized tests. Find the learning style that suits you best. As for which products to buy, there are two major categories— those created by the test-makers and those created by private companies. The best approach is to talk to someone who has been through the process and find out which product or products he or she recommends.

Some students report significant increases in scores after participating in coaching programs. Longer-term programs (40 hours) seem to raise scores more than short-term programs (20 hours), but beyond 40 hours, score gains are minor. Math scores appear to benefit more from coaching than critical reading scores.

Resources

There is a variety of ways to prepare for standardized tests—find a method that fits your schedule and your budget. But you should definitely prepare. Far too many students walk into these tests cold, either because they find standardized tests frightening or annoying or they just haven't found the time to study. The key is that these exams are standardized. That means these tests are largely the same from administration to administration; they always test the same concepts. They have to, or else you couldn't compare the scores of people who took the tests on different dates. The numbers or words may change, but the underlying content doesn't.

So how do you prepare? At the very least, you should review relevant material, such as math formulas and commonly used vocabulary words, and know the directions for each question type or test section. You should take at least one practice test and review your mistakes so you don't make them again on the test day. Beyond that, you know best how much preparation you need. You'll also find lots of material in libraries or bookstores to help you: books and software from the test- makers and from other publishers (including Peterson's) or live courses that range from national test-preparation companies to teachers at your high school who offer classes.

Who's Paying for This? Financial Aid Basics

A college education can be expensive—costing more than $150,000 for four years at some of the higher priced private colleges and universities. Even at the lower-cost state colleges and universities, the cost of a four-year education can approach $60,000. Determining how you and your family will come up with the necessary funds to pay for your education requires planning, perseverance, and learning as much as you can about the options that are available to you. But before you get discouraged, College Board statistics show that 53 percent of full-time students attend four-year public and private colleges with tuition and fees less than $9,000, while 20 percent attend colleges that have tuition and fees more than $36,000. College costs tend to be less in the western states and higher in New England.

Paying for college should not be looked at as a four-year financial commitment. For many families, paying the total cost of a student's college education out of current income and savings is usually not realistic. For families that have planned ahead and have financial savings established for higher education, the burden is a lot easier. But for most, meeting the cost of college requires the pooling of current income and assets and investing in longer-term loan options. These family resources, together with financial assistance from state, federal, and institutional sources, enable millions of students each year to attend the institution of their choice.

FINANCIAL AID PROGRAMS

There are three types of financial aid:

1. Gift-aid—Scholarships and grants are funds that do not have to be repaid.

2. Loans—Loans must be repaid, usually after graduation; the amount you have to pay back is the total you've borrowed plus any accrued interest. This is considered a source of self-help aid.

3. Student employment—Student employment is a job arranged for you by the financial aid office. This is another source of self-help aid.

The federal government has four major grant programs—the Federal Pell Grant, the Federal Supplemental Educational Opportunity Grant, Academic Competitiveness Grants (ACG), and National SMART (Science and Mathematics Access to Retain Talent) grants. ACG and SMART grants are limited to students who qualify for a Pell Grant and are awarded to a select group of students. Overall, these grants are targeted to low-to-moderate income families with significant financial need. The federal government also sponsors a student employment program called the Federal Work-Study Program, which offers jobs both on and off campus, and several loan programs, including those for students and for parents of undergraduate students.

There are two types of student loan programs: subsidized and unsubsidized. The subsidized Federal Direct Loan and the Federal Perkins Loan are need-based, government-subsidized loans. Students who borrow through these programs do not have to pay interest on the loan until after they graduate or leave school. The unsubsidized Federal Direct Loan and the Federal Direct PLUS Loan Program are not based on need, and borrowers are responsible for the interest while the student is in school. These loans are administered by different methods. Once you choose your college, the financial aid office will guide you through this process.

After you've submitted your financial aid application and you've been accepted for admission, each college will send you a letter describing your financial aid award. Most award letters show estimated college costs, how much you and your family are expected to contribute, and the amount and types of aid you have been awarded. Most students are awarded aid from a combination of sources and programs. Hence, your award is often called a financial aid "package."

SOURCES OF FINANCIAL AID

Millions of students and families apply for financial aid each year. Financial aid from all sources exceeds $143 billion per year. The largest single source of aid is the federal government, which will award more than $100 billion this year.

The next largest source of financial aid is found in the college and university community. Most of this aid is awarded to students who have a demonstrated need based on the Federal Methodology. Some institutions use a different formula, the Institutional Methodology (IM), to award their own funds in conjunction with other forms of aid. Institutional aid may be either need-based or non-need based. Aid that is not based on need is usually awarded for a student's academic performance (merit awards), specific talents or abilities, or to attract the type of students a college seeks to enroll.

Another source of financial aid is from state government. All states offer grant and/or scholarship aid, most of which is need-based. However, more and more states are offering substantial merit-based aid programs. Most state programs award aid only to students attending college in their home state.

Other sources of financial aid include:

- Private agencies
- Foundations
- Corporations
- Clubs
- Fraternal and service organizations

- Civic associations
- Unions
- Religious groups that award grants, scholarships, and low-interest loans
- Employers that provide tuition reimbursement benefits for employees and their children

More information about these different sources of aid is available from high school guidance offices, public libraries, college financial aid offices, directly from the sponsoring organizations, and online at www.petersons.com/college-search/scholarship-search.aspx.

HOW NEED-BASED FINANCIAL AID IS AWARDED

When you apply for aid, your family's financial situation is analyzed using a government-approved formula called the Federal Methodology. This formula looks at five items:

1. Demographic information of the family
2. Income of the parents
3. Assets of the parents
4. Income of the student
5. Assets of the student

This analysis determines the amount you and your family are expected to contribute toward your college expenses, called your Expected Family Contribution, or EFC. If the EFC is equal to or more than the cost of attendance at a particular college, then you do not demonstrate financial need. However, even if you don't have financial need, you may still qualify for aid, as there are grants, scholarships, and loan programs that are not need-based.

If the cost of your education is greater than your EFC, then you do demonstrate financial need and qualify for assistance. The amount of your financial need that can be met varies from school to school. Some are able to meet your full need, while others can only cover a certain percentage of need. Here's the formula:

Cost of Attendance
− Expected Family Contribution
= Financial Need

The EFC remains constant, but your need will vary according to the costs of attendance at a particular college. In general, the higher the tuition and fees at a particular college, the higher the cost of attendance will be. Expenses for books and supplies, room and board, transportation, and other miscellaneous items are included in the overall cost of attendance. It is important to remember that you do not have to be low-income to qualify for financial aid. Many middle and upper-middle income families qualify for need-based financial aid.

APPLYING FOR FINANCIAL AID

Every student must complete the Free Application for Federal Student Aid (FAFSA) to be considered for financial aid. The FAFSA is available from your high school guidance office, many public libraries, colleges in your area, or directly from the U.S. Department of Education.

Students are encouraged to apply for federal student aid on the Web. The electronic version of the FAFSA can be accessed at http://www.fafsa.ed.gov.

The NEW Federal Student Aid ID

In order for a student to complete the online FAFSA®, he or she will need a Federal Student Aid (FSA) ID. You can get this online at https://fsaid.ed.gov/npas/index.htm. Since May 2015, the FSA ID has replaced the previously used PIN system. Parents of dependent students also need to obtain their own FSA ID in order to sign their child's FAFSA® electronically online.

The FSA ID can be used to access several federal aid-related websites, including FAFSA.gov and StudentLoans.gov. It consists of a username and password and can be used to electronically sign Federal Student Aid documents, access your personal records, and make binding legal obligations. The FSA ID is beneficial in several ways:

- It removes your personal identifiable personally identifiable information (PII), such as your Social Security number, from your log-in credentials.
- It creates a more secure and efficient way to verify your information when you log in to access to your federal student aid information online.
- It gives you the ability to easily update your personal information.
- It allows you to easily retrieve your username and password by requesting a secure code be sent to your e-mail address or by answering challenge questions.

It's relatively simple to create an FSA ID and should only take a few minutes. In addition, you will have an opportunity to link your current Federal Student Aid PIN (if you already have one) to your FSA ID. The final step is to confirm your e-mail address. You will receive a secure code to the e-mail address you provided when you set up your FSA ID. Once you retrieve the code from your e-mail account and enter it—to confirm your e-mail address is valid—you will be able to use this e-mail address instead of your username to log in to any of the federal aid-related websites, making the log-in process EVEN simpler for you and your parents.

When you initially create your FSA ID, your information will need to be verified with the Social Security Administration. This process can take anywhere from one to three days. For that reason, it's a good idea to take care of setting up your FSA ID as early as possible, so it will be all set when you are ready to begin completing your FAFSA.

IMPORTANT NOTE: Since your FSA ID provides access to your personal information and is used to sign online documents, it's imperative that you protect this ID. Don't share it with *anyone* or write it down in an insecure location—you could place yourself at great risk for identify theft.

If Every College You're Applying to for Fall 2017 Requires the FAFSA

then it's pretty simple: Complete the FAFSA after October 1, 2016, being certain to send it in before any college-imposed deadlines. (Students will now be permitted to send in the 2017–18 FAFSA before January 1, 2017.) Beginning with the 2017–18 FAFSA, students will be required to report income information from an earlier tax year. For example, on the 2017–18 FAFSA, students (and parents, as appropriate) will report their 2015 income information, rather than their 2016 income information.

After you send in your FAFSA, you'll receive a Student Aid Report (SAR) that includes all of the information you reported and shows your EFC. If you provided an e-mail address, the SAR is sent to you electronically; otherwise, you will receive a SAR or SAR Acknowledgment in the mail, which lists your FAFSA information but may require you to make any corrections on the FAFSA website. Be sure to review the SAR, checking to see if the information you reported is accurately represented. If you used estimated numbers to complete the FAFSA, you may have to resubmit the SAR with any corrections to the data. The college(s) you have designated on the FAFSA will receive the information you reported and will use that data to make their decision.

The CSS/Financial Aid PROFILE®

To award their own funds, some colleges require an additional application, the CSS/Financial Aid PROFILE® form. The PROFILE asks supplemental questions that some colleges and awarding agencies feel provide a more accurate assessment of the family's ability to pay for college. It is up to the college to decide whether it will use only the FAFSA or both the FAFSA and the PROFILE. PROFILE applications are available from the high school guidance office and on the Web. Both the paper application and the website list those colleges and programs that require the PROFILE application.

If a College Requires the PROFILE

Step 1: Register for the CSS/Financial Aid PROFILE in the fall of your senior year in high school. You can apply for the PROFILE online at http://profileonline.collegeboard.com/prf/index.jsp. Registration information with a list of the colleges that require the PROFILE is available in most high school guidance offices. There is a fee for using the Financial Aid PROFILE application ($25 for the first college, which includes the $9 application fee, and $16 for each additional college). You must pay for the service by credit card when you register. If you do not have a credit card, you will be billed. A limited number of fee waivers are automatically granted to first-time applicants based on the financial information provided on the PROFILE.

Step 2: Fill out your customized CSS/Financial Aid PROFILE. Once you register, your application will be immediately available online and will have questions that all students must complete, questions which must be completed by the student's parents (unless the student is independent and the colleges or programs selected do not require parental information), and *may* have supplemental questions needed by one or more of your schools or programs. If required, those will be found in Section Q of the application.

In addition to the PROFILE application you complete online, you may also be required to complete a Business/ Farm Supplement via traditional paper format. Completion of this form is not a part of the online process. If this form is required, instructions on how to download and print the supplemental form are provided. If your biological or adoptive parents are separated or divorced and your colleges and programs require it, your noncustodial parent may be asked to complete the Noncustodial PROFILE.

Once you complete and submit your PROFILE application, it will be processed and sent directly to your requested colleges and programs.

IF YOU DON'T QUALIFY FOR NEED-BASED AID

If you are not eligible for need-based aid, you can still find ways to lessen your burden.

Here are some suggestions:

- Search for merit scholarships. You can start at the initial stages of your application process. College merit awards are increasingly important as more and more colleges award these to students they especially want to attract. As a result, applying to a college at which your qualifications put you at the top of the entering class may give you a larger merit award. Another source of aid to look for is private scholarships that are given for special skills and talents. Additional information can be found at www.finaid.org.

- Seek employment during the summer and the academic year. The student employment office at your college can help you locate a school-year job. Many colleges and local businesses have vacancies remaining after they have hired students who are receiving Federal Work-Study Program financial aid.

- Borrow through the unsubsidized Federal Direct Loan program. This is generally available to all students. The terms and conditions are similar to the subsidized loans. The biggest difference is that the borrower is responsible for the interest while still in college, although the government permits students to delay paying the interest right away and add the accrued interest to the total amount owed. You must file the FAFSA to be considered.

- After you've secured what you can through scholarships, working, and borrowing, you and your parents will be expected to meet your share of the college bill (the Expected Family Contribution). Many colleges offer monthly payment plans that spread the cost over the academic year. If the monthly payments are too high, parents can borrow through the Federal Direct PLUS Loan Program, through one of the many private education loan programs available, or through home equity loans and lines of credit. Families seeking assistance in financing college expenses should inquire at the financial aid office about what programs are available at the college. Some families seek the advice of professional financial advisers and tax consultants.

Frequently Asked Questions About Transferring

Muriel M. Shishkoff

Among the students attending two-year colleges are a large number who began their higher education knowing they would eventually transfer to a four-year school to obtain their bachelor's degree. There are many reasons why students go this route. Upon graduating from high school, some simply do not have definite career goals. Although they don't want to put their education on hold, they prefer not to pay exorbitant amounts in tuition while trying to "find themselves." As the cost of a university education escalates—even in public institutions—the option of spending the freshman and sophomore years at a two-year college looks attractive to many students. Others attend a two-year college because they are unable to meet the initial entrance standards—a specified grade point average (GPA), standardized test scores, or knowledge of specific academic subjects—required by the four-year school of their choice. Many such students praise the community college system for giving them the chance to be, academically speaking, "born again." In addition, students from other countries often find that they can adapt more easily to language and cultural changes at a two-year school before transferring to a larger, more diverse four-year college.

If your plan is to attend a two-year college with the ultimate goal of transferring to a four-year school, you will be pleased to know that the increased importance of the community college route to a bachelor's degree is recognized by all segments of higher education. As a result, many two-year schools have revised their course outlines and established new courses in order to comply with the programs and curricular offerings of the universities. Institutional improvements to make transferring easier have also proliferated at both the two-and four-year levels. The generous transfer policies of the Pennsylvania, New York, and Florida state university systems, among others, reflect this attitude; these systems accept all credits from students who have graduated from accredited community colleges.

If you are interested in moving from a two-year college to a four-year school, the sooner you make up your mind that you are going to make the switch, the better position you will be to transfer successfully (that is, without having wasted valuable time and credits). The ideal point at which to make such a decision is **before** you register for classes at your two-year school; a counselor can help you plan your course work with an eye toward fulfilling the requirements needed for your major course of study.

Naturally, it is not always possible to plan your transferring strategy that far in advance, but keep in mind that the key to a successful transfer is **preparation,** and preparation takes time—time to think through your objectives and time to plan the right classes to take.

As students face the prospect of transferring from a two-year to a four-year school, many thoughts and concerns about this complicated and often frustrating process race through their minds. Here are answers to the questions that are most frequently asked by transferring students.

Q Does every college and university accept transfer students?

A Most four-year institutions accept transfer students, but some do so more enthusiastically than others. Graduating from a community college is an advantage at, for example, Arizona State University and the University of Massachusetts Boston; both accept more community college transfer students than traditional freshmen. At the University at Albany, SUNY, graduates of two-year transfer programs within the State University of New York System are given priority for upper-division (i.e., junior-and senior-level) vacancies.

Schools offering undergraduate work at the upper division only are especially receptive to transfer applications. On the other hand, some schools accept only a few transfer students; others refuse entrance to sophomores or those in their final year. Princeton University requires an "excellent academic record and particularly compelling reasons to transfer." Check the catalogs of several colleges for their transfer requirements before you make your final choice.

Q Do students who go directly from high school to a four-year college do better academically than transfer students from community colleges?

A On the contrary: some institutions report that transfers from two-year schools who persevere until graduation do *better* than those who started as freshmen in a four-year college.

Q Why is it so important that my two-year college be accredited?

A Four-year colleges and universities accept transfer credits only from schools formally recognized by a regional, national, or professional educational agency. This accreditation signifies that an institution or program of study meets or exceeds a minimum level of educational quality necessary for meeting stated educational objectives.

Q After enrolling at a four-year school, may I still make up necessary courses at a community college?

A Some institutions restrict credit after transfer to their own facilities. Others allow students to take a limited number of transfer courses after matriculation, depending on the subject matter. A few provide opportunities for cross-registration or dual enrollment, which means taking classes on more than one campus.

Q What do I need to do to transfer?

A First, send for your high school and college transcripts. Having chosen the school you wish to transfer to, check its admission requirements against your transcripts. If you find that you are admissible, file an application as early as possible before the deadline. Part of the process will be asking your former schools to send official transcripts to the admission office, i.e., not the copies you used in determining your admissibility.

Plan your transfer program with the head of your new department as soon as you have decided to transfer. Determine the recommended general education pattern and necessary preparation for your major. At your present school, take the courses you will need to meet transfer requirements for the new school.

Q What qualifies me for admission as a transfer student?

A Admission requirements for most four-year institutions vary. Depending on the reputation or popularity of the school and program you wish to enter, requirements may be quite selective and competitive. Usually, you will need to show satisfactory test scores, an academic record up to a certain standard, and completion of specific subject matter.

Transfer students can be eligible to enter a four-year school in a number of ways: by having been eligible for admission directly upon graduation from high school, by making up shortcomings in grades (or in subject matter not covered in high school) at a community college, or by satisfactory completion of necessary courses or credit hours at another postsecondary institution. Ordinarily, students coming from a community college or from another four-year institution must meet or exceed the receiving institution's standards for freshmen and show appropriate college-level course work taken since high school. Students who did not graduate from high school can present proof of proficiency through results on the the GED® Test, the HiSET® Exam, or another state-approved high school equivalency test.

Q Are exceptions ever made for students who don't meet all the requirements for transfer?

A Extenuating circumstances, such as disability, low family income, refugee or veteran status, or athletic talent, may permit the special enrollment of students who would not otherwise be eligible but who demonstrate the potential for academic success. Consult the appropriate office—the Educational Opportunity Program, the disabled students' office, the athletic department, or the academic dean—to see whether an exception can be made in your case.

Q How far in advance do I need to apply for transfer?

A Some schools have a rolling admission policy, which means that they process transfer applications as they are received, all year long. With other schools, you must apply during the priority filing period, which can be up to a year before you wish to enter. Check the date with the admission office at your prospective campus.

Q Is it possible to transfer courses from several different institutions?

A Institutions ordinarily accept the courses that they consider transferable, regardless of the number of accredited schools involved. However, there is the danger of exceeding the maximum number of credit hours that can be transferred from all other schools or earned through credit by examination, extension courses, or correspondence courses. The limit placed on transfer credits varies from school to school, so read the catalog carefully to avoid taking courses you won't be able to use. To avoid duplicating courses, keep attendance at different campuses to a minimum.

Q What is involved in transferring from a semester system to a quarter or trimester system?

A In the semester system, the academic calendar is divided into two equal parts. The quarter system is more aptly named trimester, since the academic calendar is divided into three equal terms (not counting a summer session). To convert semester units into quarter units or credit hours, simply multiply the semester units by one and a half. Conversely, multiply quarter units by two thirds to come up with semester units. If you are used to a semester system of fifteen- to sixteen-week courses, the ten-week courses of the quarter system may seem to fly by.

Q Why might a course be approved for transfer credit by one four-year school but not by another?

A The beauty of postsecondary education in the United States lies in its variety. Entrance policies and graduation requirements are designed to reflect and serve each institution's mission. Because institutional policies vary so widely, schools may interpret the subject matter of a course from quite different points of view. Given that the granting of transfer credit indicates that a course is viewed as being, in effect, parallel to one offered by the receiving institution, it is easy to see how this might be the case at one university and not another.

Q Must I take a foreign language to transfer?

A Foreign language proficiency is often required for admission to a four-year institution; such proficiency also often figures in certain majors or in the general education pattern. Often, two or three years of a single language in high school will do the trick. Find out if scores received on Advanced Placement (AP®) examinations, placement examinations given by the foreign language department, or SAT Subject Tests™ will be accepted in lieu of college course work.

Q Will the school to which I'm transferring accept pass/no pass, pass/fail, or credit/no credit grades in lieu of letter grades?

A Usually, a limit is placed on the number of these courses you can transfer, and there may be other restrictions as well. If you want to use other-than-letter grades for the fulfillment of general education requirements or lower-division (freshman and sophomore) preparation for the major, check with the receiving institution.

Q Which is more important for transfer—my grade point average or my course completion pattern?

A Some schools believe that your past grades indicate academic potential and overshadow prior preparation for a specific degree program. Others require completion of certain introductory courses before transfer to prepare you for upper-division work in your major. In any case, appropriate course selection will cut down the time to graduation and increase your chances of making a successful transfer.

Q What happens to my credits if I change majors?

A If you change majors after admission, your transferable course credit should remain fairly intact. However, because you may need extra or different preparation for your new major, some of the courses you've taken may now be useful only as electives. The need for additional lower-level preparation may mean you're staying longer at your new school than you originally planned. On the other hand, you may already have taken courses that count toward your new major as part of the university's general education pattern.

Excerpted (and updated) from *Transferring Made Easy: A Guide to Changing Colleges Successfully,* by Muriel M. Shishkoff, © 1991 by Muriel M. Shishkoff (published by Peterson's).

Returning to School: Advice for Adult Students

Sandra Cook, Ph.D.
Associate Vice President for Enrollment Management,
San Diego State University

Many adults think for a long time about returning to school without taking any action. One purpose of this article is to help the "thinkers" finally make some decisions by examining what is keeping them from action. Another purpose is to describe not only some of the difficulties and obstacles that adult students may face when returning to school but also tactics for coping with them.

If you have been thinking about going back to college, and believing that you are the only person your age contemplating college, you should know that approximately 7 million adult students are currently enrolled in higher education institutions. This number represents 50 percent of total higher education enrollments. The majority of adult students are enrolled at two-year colleges.

There are many reasons why adult students choose to attend a two-year college. Studies have shown that the three most important criteria that adult students consider when choosing a college are location, cost, and availability of the major or program desired. Most two-year colleges are public institutions that serve a geographic district, making them readily accessible to the community. Costs at most two-year colleges are far less than at other types of higher education institutions. For many students who plan to pursue a bachelor's degree, completing their first two years of college at a community college is an affordable means to that end. If you are interested in an academic program that will transfer to a four-year institution, most two-year colleges offer the "general education" courses that compose most freshman and sophomore years. If you are interested in a vocational or technical program, two-year colleges excel in providing this type of training.

SETTING THE STAGE

There are three different "stages" in the process of adults returning to school. The first stage is uncertainty. Do I really want to go back to school? What will my friends or family think? Can I compete with those 18-year-old whiz kids? Am I too old? The second stage is choice. Once the decision to return has been made, you must choose where you will attend. There are many criteria to use in making this decision. The third stage is support. You have just added another role to your already-too-busy life. There are, however, strategies that will help you accomplish your goals—perhaps not without struggle, but with grace and humor nonetheless. Let's look at each of these stages.

UNCERTAINTY

Why are you thinking about returning to school? Is it to

- fulfill a dream that had to be delayed?
- become more educationally well-rounded?
- fill an intellectual void in your life?

These reasons focus on personal growth.

If you are returning to school to

- meet people and make friends
- attain and enjoy higher social status and prestige among friends, relatives, and associates
- understand/study a cultural heritage
- have a medium in which to exchange ideas

You are interested in social and cultural opportunities.

If you are like most adult students, you want to

- qualify for a new occupation
- enter or reenter the job market
- increase earnings potential
- qualify for a more challenging position in the same field of work

You are seeking career growth.

Understanding the reasons why you want to go back to school is an important step in setting your educational goals and will help you to establish some criteria for selecting a college. However, don't delay your decision because you have not been able to clearly define your motives. Many times, these aren't clear until you have already begun the process, and they may change as you move through your college experience.

Assuming you agree that additional education will benefit you, what is it that keeps you from returning to school? You may have a litany of excuses running through your mind:

- I don't have time.
- I can't afford it.
- I'm too old to learn.
- My friends will think I'm crazy.

- I'll be older than the teachers and other students.
- My family can't survive without me to take care of them every minute.
- I'll be X years old when I finish.
- I'm afraid.
- I don't know what to expect.

And that is just what these are—excuses. You can make school, like anything else in your life, a priority or not. If you really want to return, you can. The more you understand your motivation for returning to school and the more you understand what excuses are keeping you from taking action, the easier your task will be.

If you think you don't have time: The best way to decide how attending class and studying can fit into your schedule is to keep track of what you do with your time each day for several weeks. Completing a standard time-management grid (each day is plotted out by the half hour) is helpful for visualizing how your time is spent. For each 3-credit-hour class you take, you will need to find 3 hours for class plus 6 to 9 hours for reading-studying-library time. This study time should be spaced evenly throughout the week, not loaded up on one day. It is not possible to learn or retain the material that way. When you examine your grid, see where there are activities that could be replaced with school and study time. You may decide to give up your bowling league or some time in front of the TV. Try not to give up sleeping, and don't cut out every moment of free time. Here are some suggestions that have come from adults who have returned to school:

- Enroll in a time-management workshop. It helps you rethink how you use your time.
- Don't think you have to take more than one course at a time. You may eventually want to work up to taking more, but consider starting with one. (It is more than you are taking now!)
- If you have a family, start assigning to them those household chores that you usually do—and don't redo what they do.
- Use your lunch hour or commuting time for reading.

If you think you cannot afford it: As mentioned earlier, two-year colleges are extremely affordable. If you cannot afford the tuition, look into the various financial aid options. Most federal and state funds are available to full- and part-time students. Loans are also available. While many people prefer not to accumulate a debt for school, these same people will think nothing of taking out a loan to buy a car. After five or six years, which is the better investment? Adult students who work should look into whether their company has a tuition-reimbursement policy. There are also private scholarships, available through foundations, service organizations, and clubs, that are focused on adult learners. Your public library, the Web, and a college financial aid adviser are three excellent sources for reference materials regarding financial aid.

If you think you are too old to learn: This is pure myth. A number of studies have shown that adult learners perform as well as, or better than, traditional-age students.

If you are afraid your friends will think you're crazy: Who cares? Maybe they will, maybe they won't. Usually, they will admire your courage and be just a little jealous of your ambition (although they'll never tell you that). Follow your dreams, not theirs.

If you are concerned because the teachers or students will be younger than you: Don't be. The age differences that may be apparent in other settings evaporate in the classroom. If anything, an adult in the classroom strikes fear into the hearts of some 18-year-olds because adults have been known to be prepared, ask questions, be truly motivated, and be there to learn!

If you think your family will have a difficult time surviving while you are in school: If you have done everything for them up to now, they might struggle. Consider this an opportunity to help them become independent and self-sufficient. Your family can only make you feel guilty if you let them. You are not abandoning them; you are becoming an educational role model. When you are happy and working toward your goals, everyone benefits. Admittedly, it sometimes takes time for them to realize this. For single parents, there are schools that offer support groups, child care, and cooperative babysitting.

If you're appalled at the thought of being X years old when you graduate in Y years: How old will you be in Y years if you don't go back to school?

If you are afraid or don't know what to expect: Know that these are natural feelings when one encounters any new situation. Adult students find that their fears usually dissipate once they begin classes. Fear of trying is usually the biggest roadblock to the reentry process.

No doubt you have dreamed up a few more reasons for not making the decision to return to school. Keep in mind that what you are doing is making up excuses, and you are using these excuses to release you from the obligation to make a decision about your life. The thought of returning to college can be scary. Anytime anyone ventures into unknown territory, there is a risk, but taking risks is a necessary component of personal and professional growth. It is your life, and you alone are responsible for making the decisions that determine its course. Education is an investment in your future.

CHOICE

Once you have decided to go back to school, your next task is to decide where to go. If your educational goals are well defined (e.g., you want to pursue a degree in order to change careers), then your task is a bit easier. But even if your educational goals are still evolving, do not defer your return. Many students who enter higher education with a specific major in mind change that major at least once.

Most students who attend a public two-year college choose the community college in the district in which they live. This is generally the closest and least expensive option if the school offers the programs you want. If you are planning to begin your education at a two-year college and then transfer to a four-year school, there are distinct advantages to choosing your four-year school early. Many community and four-year colleges have "articulation" agreements that designate what credits from the two-year school will transfer to the four-year college and how. Some four-year institutions accept an associate degree as equivalent to the freshman and sophomore years, regardless of the courses you have taken. Some four-year schools accept two-year college work only on a course-by-course basis. If you can identify which school you will transfer to, you can know in advance exactly how your two-year credits will apply, preventing an unexpected loss of credit or time.

Each institution of higher education is distinctive. Your goal in choosing a college is to come up with the best student-institution fit—matching your needs with the offerings and characteristics of the school. The first step in choosing a college is to determine what criteria are most important to you in attaining your educational goals. Location, cost, and program availability are the three main factors that influence an adult student's college choice. In considering location, don't forget that some colleges have conveniently located branch campuses. In considering cost, remember to explore your financial aid options before ruling out an institution because of its tuition. Program availability should include not only the major in which you are interested, but also whether or not classes in that major are available when you can take them.

Some additional considerations beyond location, cost, and programs are:

- Does the school have a commitment to adult students and offer appropriate services, such as child care, tutoring, and advising?
- Are classes offered at times when you can take them?
- Are there academic options for adults, such as credit for life or work experience, credit by examination (including CLEP), credit for military service, or accelerated programs?
- Is the faculty sensitive to the needs of adult learners?

Once you determine which criteria are vital in your choice of an institution, you can begin to narrow your choices. There are myriad ways for you to locate the information you desire. Many newspapers publish a "School Guide" several times a year in which colleges and universities advertise to an adult student market. In addition, schools themselves publish catalogs, class schedules, and promotional materials that contain much of the information you need, and they are yours for the asking. Many colleges sponsor information sessions and open houses that allow you to visit the campus and ask questions. An appointment with an adviser is a good way to assess the fit between you and the institution. Be sure to bring your questions with you to your interview.

SUPPORT

Once you have made the decision to return to school and have chosen the institution that best meets your needs, take some additional steps to ensure your success during your crucial first semester. Take advantage of institutional support and build some social support systems of your own. Here are some ways of doing just that:

- Plan to participate in any orientation programs. These serve the threefold purpose of providing you with a great deal of important information, familiarizing you with the campus and its facilities, and giving you the opportunity to meet and begin networking with other students.
- Take steps to deal with any academic weaknesses. Take mathematics and writing placement tests if you have reason to believe you may need some extra help in these areas. It is not uncommon for adult students to need a math refresher course or a program to help alleviate math anxiety. Ignoring a weakness won't make it go away.
- Look into adult reentry programs. Many institutions offer adults workshops focusing on ways to improve study skills, textbook reading, test-taking, and time-management skills.
- Build new support networks by joining an adult student organization, making a point of meeting other adult students through workshops, or actively seeking out a "study buddy" in each class—that invaluable friend who shares and understands your experience.
- Incorporate your new status as "student" into your family life. Doing your homework with your children at a designated "homework time" is a valuable family activity and reinforces the importance of education.
- Make sure you take a reasonable course load in your first semester. It is far better to have some extra time on your hands and to succeed magnificently than to spend the entire semester on the brink of a breakdown. Also, whenever possible, try to focus your first courses not only on requirements, but also on areas of personal interest.
- Faculty members, advisers, and student affairs personnel are there to help you during difficult times—let them assist you as often as necessary.

After completing your first semester, you will probably look back in wonder at why you thought going back to school was so imposing. Certainly, it's not without its occasional exasperations. But, as with life, keeping things in perspective and maintaining your sense of humor make the difference between just coping and succeeding brilliantly.

Coming to America: Tips for International Students Considering Study in the U.S.

Introduction: Why Study in the United States?

Are you thinking about going to a college or university in the United States? If you're looking at this book, you probably are! All around the world, students like you, pursuing higher education, are considering that possibility. They envision themselves on modern, high-tech campuses in well-known cities, surrounded by American students, taking classes and having fun. A degree from a U.S. school would certainly lead to success and fortune, either back in your home country or perhaps even in the United States, wouldn't it?

It can be done—but becoming a student at a college or university in the U.S. requires academic talent, planning, time, effort, and money. While there may be only a small number of institutions of higher learning in your country, there are more than 2,900 four-year colleges and universities in the United States. Choosing one, being accepted, and then traveling and becoming a student in America is a big undertaking.

If this is your dream, here is some helpful information and expert tips from professionals who work with international students at colleges and universities throughout the United States.

Timing and Planning

The journey to a college or university in the U.S. often starts years in advance. Most international students choose to study in the U.S. because of the high quality of academics. Your family may also have a lot of input on this decision, too.

"We always tell students they should be looking in the sophomore year, visiting in the junior year, and applying in the senior year," says Father Francis E. Chambers, OSA, D.Min., Associate Director of International Admission at Villanova University. He stresses that prospective students need to be taking challenging courses in the years leading up to college. "We want to see academic rigor. Most admission decisions are based on the first six semesters—senior year is too late."

Heidi Gregori-Gahan, Assistant Provost for International Programs at the University of Southern Indiana agrees that it's important to start early. "Plan ahead and do your homework. There is so much to choose from—so many schools, programs, degrees, and experiences. It can be overwhelming."

While students in some countries may pay an agent to help them get into a school in the United States, Gregori-Gahan often directs potential international students to EducationUSA (http://educationusa.state.gov), a U.S. State Department network of over 400 international student advising centers in more than 170 countries. "They are there to provide unbiased information about studying in the United States and help you understand the process and what you need to do."

Two to three years of advance planning is also recommended by Daphne Durham, who has been an international student adviser at Harvard, Suffolk University, Valdosta State University, and the University of Georgia. She points out that the academic schedule in other countries is often different than that of the United States, so you need to synchronize your calendar accordingly.

You will have to take several tests in order to gain admission to a U.S. school, so it's important to know when those tests are given in your country, then register and take them so your scores will be available when you apply. Even if you have taken English in school, you will probably have to take The Test of English as a Foreign Language (TOEFL®), but some schools also accept the International English Language Testing Sytem (IELTS). You will probably also have to take the SAT® or ACT® tests, which are achievement or aptitude tests, and are usually required of all students applying for admission, not just international students.

"Make sure you understand how the international admissions process works at the school or schools you want to attend," says Durham. "What test scores are needed and when? Does the school have a fixed calendar or rolling admissions?" Those are just some of the many factors that can impact your application and could make a difference in when you are able to start school.

"Every university is unique in what's required and what they need to do. Even navigating each school's different website can be challenging," explains Gregori-Gahan.

Searching for Schools

This book contains information on thousands of four-year colleges and universities, and it will be a valuable resource for you in your search and application process. But with so many options, how do you decide which school you should attend?

"Where I find a big difference with international students is if their parents don't recognize the school, they don't apply to the school," says Fr. Chambers. "They could be overlooking a lot of great schools. They have to look outside the box."

The school Gregori-Gahan represents is in Evansville, Indiana, and it probably isn't familiar to students abroad. "Not many people have heard of anything beyond New York and California and maybe Florida. I like to tell students that this is 'real America.' But happy international students on our campus have recruited others to come here."

She points out that Internet technology has made a huge difference in the search process for international students. Websites full of information, live chat, webinars, virtual tours, and admission interviews via Skype have made it easier for potential students to connect with U.S. institutions, get more information, and be better able to visualize the campus.

One thing than will help narrow your search for a school is knowing specifically what you want to study. You need to know what the course of study is called in the United States, what it means, and what is required in order to study that subject. You also need to consider your future plans. What are your goals and objectives? What do you plan to do after earning your degree?

"If you're going to overcome the hurdles and get to a U.S. school, you have to have a directed path chosen," says Durham.

The other thing that could help your search process is finding a school that is a good fit.

Fit Is Important

You want your clothing and shoes to fit you properly and be comfortable, so a place where you will spend four or more years of your life studying should also be comfortable and appropriate for you. So how can you determine if a particular school is a good fit?

"We really recommend international students visit first. Yes, there are websites and virtual tours, but there's still nothing that beats an in-person visit," says Fr. Chambers. He estimates that 50 to 60 percent of Villanova's international students visited the campus before enrolling.

"It can be hard to get a sense of a place—you're so far away and you're probably not going to set foot on campus until you arrive," says Gregori-Gahan. "There is a high potential for culture shock."

You need to ask yourself what is important to you in a campus environment, then do some homework to ensure that the schools you are considering meet those needs. Here are some things to consider when it comes to fit:

- **Location:** Is it important for you to be in a well-known city or is a part of the United States that is unfamiliar a possibility? "Look at geographic areas, but also cost of living," recommends Durham. "Be sure to factor in transportation costs also, especially if you plan to return to your home country regularly."
- **Student population:** Some small schools have just 1,000 students while larger ones may have 30,000 students or more.
- **Familiar faces:** Is it important for you to be at a school with others from your home nation or region?

- **Climate:** Some students want a climate similar to where they live now, but others are open and curious about seasons and weather conditions they may not have ever experienced. "We do have four seasons here," says Gregori-Gahan. "Sometimes students who come here from tropical regions are concerned about the winters. The first snow is so exciting, but after that, students may not be aware of how cold it really is."
- **Amenities:** Do you want to find your own housing or choose a school where the majority of students live on campus? Is there public transportation available or is it necessary to walk or have a bicycle or car? Does the school or community have access to things that are important to you culturally and meet the traditions you want to follow?
- **Campus size:** Some campuses are tightly compacted into a few city blocks, but others cover hundreds of acres of land. "International students are amazed by how green and spacious our campus is, with blooming flowers, trees, and lots of grass," says Gregori-Gahan.
- **Academic offerings:** Does this school offer the program you want to study? Can you complete it in four years or perhaps sooner? What sort of internship and career services are available?
- **Finances:** Can you afford to attend this school? Is there any sort of financial assistance available for international students?
- **Support services:** Durham suggests students look carefully at each school's offerings for international students. "Does the school have online guidance for getting your visa? Is ESL tutoring available? Does the school offer host family or community friend programs?" She also suggests you look for campus support groups for students from your country or region.

Looking at the listings and reading the in-depth descriptions in this book can help you search for a school that is a good fit for you.

Government Requirements

The one thing that every international student must have in order to study in the United States is a student visa. Having accurate advice and following all the necessary steps regarding the visa process is essential to being able to enter this country and start school.

As you schedule your tests and application deadlines, you must also consider how long it will take to get your visa. This varies depending on where you live; in some countries, extensive background checks are required. The subject you plan to study can also impact your visa status; it does help to have a major rather than be undeclared. The U.S. State Department website, http://travel.state.gov/content/visas/english/study-exchange.html, can give you an idea of how long it will take.

In addition to the visa, you will also need a Form I-20, which is a U.S. government immigration form. You must have that form when you get to the United States.

"It's very different from being a tourist. You need to be prepared to meet with an immigration officer and be interviewed about your college," explains Durham. "Where you are going, why you are going, where the school is located, what you are studying, and so on."

You also need to keep in mind that there are reporting requirements once you are a student in the U.S. Every semester, your adviser has to report to the government to confirm that you are enrolled in and attending school in order for you to stay in the United States.

Finances

Part of the visa process includes having the funds to pay for the cost of your schooling and support yourself. Finances are a huge hurdle in the process of becoming a college student in the United States.

"It's crucial. So many foreign systems offer 'free' higher education to students. How is your family going to handle the ongoing expense of attending college for four years or longer in the United States?" Durham reiterates that planning ahead is key because there are so many details. Student loans require a U.S.-based cosigner. Each school has its own financial aid deadlines. You have to factor in your own government's requirements, such currency exchange and fund transfers.

The notion that abundant funds are available to assist international students is not true. Sometimes state schools may offer diversity waivers or there may be special scholarship opportunities for international students. But attending school in the U.S. is still a costly venture.

"We do offer financial aid to international students, but they still have to be able to handle a large portion of the costs. Full-need scholarships are not likely," explained Fr. Chambers. "Sometimes students think that once they get here, it will all work out and the funds will be there. But the scenario for the first year has to be repeated each year they are on campus.

Once You Arrive…

You've taken your tests, researched schools, found a good fit, applied, got accepted, arranged the financing, gotten your visa and I-20, and made it to the campus in the United States. Now what?

You can expect the school where you have enrolled to be welcoming and helpful, but within reason. If you arrive on a weekend, or at a time outside of the time when international students are scheduled to arrive, the assistance you need may not be available to you.

Every school offers different levels of assistance to international students. For instance, Villanova offers a full-service office that can assist students with everything from visas, to employment, to finding a place for students to stay over breaks.

Fr. Chambers attends the international student orientation session to greet the students he's worked with through the recruitment and application process. "But I rarely see an international student after that. I think that bodes well for them being integrated into the entire university."

"Those of us who work with international students are really working to help them adjust," says Gregori-Gahan. "International students get here well before school starts so they can get over jet lag. We have orientation sessions and pair them with peer advisers who help them navigate the first few days, and we assure them that we are there for them."

Students should be open to their new setting, but they should be prepared that things may not be at all how they had envisioned during their planning and searching process. "While you may think you'll meet lots of Americans, don't underestimate the importance of community with your traditional home culture and people," says Durham.

Don't Make These Mistakes

The journey to college attendance in the United States is a long one, with many steps. The experts warn about mistakes to avoid along the way.

"Not reading through everything thoroughly and not understanding what the program of study really is and what will it cost. You have to be really clear on the important details," says Gregori-Gahan.

"Every school does things differently," cautions Fr. Chambers. "International students must be aware of that as they are applying."

Durham stresses that going to school in the United States is too big a decision to leave to someone else. "Students need to know about their school—they have to be in charge of their application."

"It involves a lot of work to be successful and happy and not surprised by too many things," Gregori-Gahan says.

Hopefully now, you are more informed and better prepared to pursue your dream of studying at a college or university in the United States.

Community Colleges and the Green Economy

Community colleges are a focal point for state and national efforts to create a green economy and workforce. As the United States transforms its economy into a "green" one, community colleges are leading the way—filling the need for both educated technicians whose skills can cross industry lines as well as those technicians who are able to learn new skills as technologies evolve.

President Obama extolled community colleges as "the unsung heroes of America's education system," essential to our country's success in the "global competition to lead in the growth of industries of the twenty-first century." With the support of state governments, and, more importantly, local and international business partners, America's community colleges are rising to meet the demands of the new green economy. Community colleges are training individuals to work in fields such as renewable energy, energy efficiency, wind energy, green building, and sustainability. The programs are as diverse as the campuses housing them.

Here is a quick look at just some of the exciting "green" programs available at community colleges throughout the United States.

At Mesalands Community College in Tucumcari, New Mexico, the North American Wind Research and Training Center provides state-of-the-art facilities for research and training qualified technicians in wind energy technology to help meet the need for an estimated 170,000 new positions in the industry by 2030. The Center includes a facility for applied research in collaboration with Sandia National Laboratories—the first-ever such partnership between a national laboratory and a community college. It also provides associate degree training for wind energy technicians, meeting the fast-growing demand for "windsmiths" in the western part of the country—jobs that pay $45,000–$60,000 per year. For more information, visit http://www.mesalands.edu.

Cape Cod Community College (CCCC) in Massachusetts has become one of the nation's leading colleges in promoting and integrating sustainability and green practices throughout all campus operations and technical training programs. Ten years ago, Cape Wind Associates, Cape Cod's first wind farm, provided $50,000 to jumpstart CCCC's wind technician program—considered a state model for community-based clean energy workforce development and education. In addition, hundreds of CCCC students have earned associate degrees in environmental technology and environmental studies, as well as certificate programs in coastal zone management, environmental site assessment, solar thermal technology, and more. Visit http://www.capecod.edu/web/natsci/env/programs for more information.

At Oakland Community College in Michigan, more than 350 students are enrolled in the college's Renewable Energies and Sustainable Living program and its related courses. Students gain field experience refurbishing public buildings with renewable materials, performing energy audits for the government, and working with small businesses and hospitals to reduce waste and pollution. To learn more, visit http://www.oaklandcc.edu/est/.

Portland Community College (PCC) in Portland, Oregon, offers associate degree and certificate options in Renewable Energy Systems (RES) training, preparing technicians for solar power, wind power, fuel cell, and other renewable energy fields. Students can earn an Associate in Applied Science (A.A.S.) degree or a One-Year Certificate in EET: Renewable Energy Systems. PCC's Microelectronic Technology Department offers an A.A.S. degree and a Certificate of Completion (COC) in Solar Voltaic Manufacturing Technology. The COC provides an orientation in solar manufacturing for those who have no prior education or experience in the field, which enables students to obtain entry-level jobs in this industry and eventually complete their A.A.S. degree.

Central Carolina Community College (CCCC) in Pittsboro, North Carolina, has been leading the way in "green" programs for more than a decade. It offered a sustainable agriculture class at its Chatham campus in 1996 and soon became the first community college in the nation to offer an Associate in Applied Science degree in sustainable agriculture and the first in North Carolina to offer an associate degree in biofuels. In addition, it was the first North Carolina community college to offer a North American Board of Certified Energy Practitioners (NABCEP)–approved solar PV panel installation course as part of its green building/renewable energy program. CCC also offers an associate degree in sustainable technology, a Natural Chef culinary arts program, an ecotourism certificate, and certificates in other green programs. For more information about Central Carolina Community College's green programs, visit http://www.cccc.edu/green.

At Metropolitan Community College in Omaha, Nebraska, the Continuing Education Department in partnership with Pro-Train is offering green/renewable energy/sustainability online training courses. The courses are designed to provide students with the workforce skills necessary for many in-demand green-collar occupations. Green/Renewable Energy courses include Building Energy Efficient Level, Fundamentals of Solar Hot Water Heating, Green Building Sales (or Technical)

Professional, and more. Sustainability Green Supply Chain Training courses include Alternative Energy Operations, Carbon Strategies, Green Building for Contractors, and Sustainability 101.

Visit www.theknowledgebase.org/metropolitan/.

At Cascadia Community College in Bothell, Washington, thanks to a grant from Puget Sound Energy (PSE), students in the Energy Informatics class designed a kiosk screen that shows the energy usage and solar generation at the local 21 Acres Center for Local Food and Sustainable Living. The PSE grant supports the classroom materials for renewable energy education and the Web-based monitoring software that allows students and interested community members to track how much energy is being generated as the weather changes. For more information, visit http://www.cascadia.edu/Default.aspx.

At Grand Rapids Community College, the federally funded Pathways to Prosperity program has successfully prepared low-income residents for jobs in fields such as renewable energy. More than 200 people have completed the program, which began in 2010 thanks to a $4-million grant from the Department of Labor, and found jobs in industries ranging from energy-efficient building construction to alternative energy and sustainable manufacturing. For additional information, check out http://cms.grcc.edu/workforce-training/pathways-prosperity.

Established in 2008, the Green Institute at Heartland Community College in Normal, Illinois, supports a wide range of campus initiatives, educational programs, and community activities that are related to sustainability, energy conservation, renewable energy, recycling, retro-commissioning, and other environmental technologies. For more information, visit http://www.heartland.edu/greenInstitute/.

Most of California's 112 community colleges offer some type of green-tech classes. These include photovoltaic panel installation and repair, green construction practices, and biotechnology courses leading to careers in agriculture, medicine, and environmental forensics. Visit http://www.californiacommunity colleges.cccco.edu/ProgramstoWatch/MoreProgramstoWatch/GreenTechnology.aspx.

Linn-Benton Community College (LBCC) in Albany, Oregon, is now offering training for the Oregon Green Technology Certificate. Oregon Green Tech is a federally funded program that is designed to prepare entry-level workers with foundational skills for a variety of industries associated with or in support of green jobs. Students learn skills in green occupations that include green energy production; manufacturing, construction, installation, monitoring, and repair of equipment for solar, wind, wave, and bio-energy; building retro-fitting; process recycling; hazardous materials removal work; and more. LBCC is one of ten Oregon community colleges to provide training for the Green Technology Certificate, offered through the Oregon Consortium and Oregon Workforce Alliance. Visit http://www.linnbenton.edu for additional information.

The Santa Fe Community College Sustainable Technology Center in New Mexico offers several green jobs training programs along with various noncredit courses. It also provides credit programs from certificates in green building systems, environmental technology training, and solar energy training as well as an Associate in Applied Science (A.A.S.) degree in environmental technology. For more information, go online to http://www.sfcc.edu/sustainable_technologies_center.

In Colorado, Red Rocks Community College (RRCC) offers degree and certificate programs in renewable energy (solar photovoltaic, solar thermal, and wind energy technology), energy and industrial maintenance, energy operations and process technology, environmental technology, water quality management, and energy audit. RRCC has made a commitment to the national challenge of creating and sustaining a green workforce and instructs students about the issues of energy, environmental stewardship, and renewable resources across the college curriculum. For more information, visit http://www.rrcc.edu/green/.

At GateWay Community College in Phoenix, Arizona, graduates of the Environmental Science program now work for the U.S. Geological Survey (USGS), the Arizona Department of Environmental Quality (ADEQ), the Occupational Safety and Health Administration (OSHA), and municipalities across the state and region, as well as private consultants and environmental organizations. For additional information, check out http://www.gatewaycc.edu/environment.

During the past 4.5 years, 17 Illinois community colleges and their partners have created 35 certificate and degree programs to prepare students for careers in green industry sectors. Over 185 courses were created and piloted, online and on-site, in communities across Illinois. The courses were created using open-source materials, with the intent to be shared with other colleges and universities through the Department of Labor's Trade Adjustment Assistance Community College and Career Training (TAACCCT) Grant Program repository.

Next you'll find two essays about other green community college programs. The first essay was written by the president of Lane Community College in Eugene, Oregon, about the role Lane and other community colleges are playing in creating a workforce for the green economy. Then, read a first-hand account of the new Wind Turbine Training Program at Kalamazoo Valley Community College in Kalamazoo, Michigan—a program that has more applicants than spaces and one whose students are being hired BEFORE they even graduate. It's clear that there are exciting "green" programs at community colleges throughout the United States.

The Role of Community Colleges in Creating a Workforce for the Green Economy

by Mary F.T. Spilde, President
Lane Community College

Community colleges are expected to play a leadership role in educating and training the workforce for the green economy.

Due to close connections with local and regional labor markets, colleges assure a steady supply of skilled workers by developing and adapting programs to respond to the needs of business and industry. Further, instead of waiting for employers to create job openings, many colleges are actively engaged in local economic development to help educate potential employers to grow their green business opportunities and to participate in the creation of the green economy.

As the green movement emerges there has been confusion about what constitutes a green job. It is now clear that many of the green jobs span several economic sectors such as renewable energy, construction, manufacturing, transportation and agriculture. It is predicted that there will be many middle skill jobs requiring more than a high school diploma but less than a bachelor's degree. This is precisely the unique role that community colleges play. Community colleges develop training programs, including pre-apprenticeship, that ladder the curriculum to take lower skilled workers through a relevant and sequenced course of study that provides a clear pathway to career track jobs. As noted in *Going Green: The Vital Role of Community Colleges in Building a Sustainable Future and Green Workforce* by the National Council for Workforce Education and the Academy for Educational Development, community colleges are strategically positioned to work with employers to redefine skills and competencies needed by the green workforce and to create the framework for new and expanded green career pathways.

While there will be new occupations such as solar and wind technologists, the majority of the jobs will be in the energy management sector—retrofitting the built environment. For example, President Obama called for retrofitting more than 75 percent of federal buildings and more than 2 million homes to make them more energy-efficient. The second major area for growth will be the "greening" of existing jobs as they evolve to incorporate green practices. Both will require new knowledge, skills and abilities. For community colleges, this means developing new programs that meet newly created industry standards and adapting existing programs and courses to integrate green skills. The key is to create a new talent pool of environmentally conscious, highly skilled workers.

These two areas show remarkable promise for education and training leading to high wage/high demand jobs:

- Efficiency and energy management: There is a need for auditors and energy efficiency experts to retrofit existing buildings. Consider how much built environment we have in this country, and it's not difficult to see that this is where the vast amount of jobs are now and will be in the future.
- Greening of existing jobs: There are few currently available jobs that environmental sustainability will not impact. Whether it is jobs in construction, such as plumbers, electricians, heating and cooling technicians, painters, and building supervisors, or chefs, farmers, custodians, architects, automotive technicians and interior designers, all will need to understand how to lessen their impact on the environment.

Lane Community College offers a variety of degree and certificate programs to prepare students to enter the energy efficiency fields. Lane has offered an Energy Management program since the late 1980s—before it was hip to be green! Students in this program learn to apply basic principles of physics and analysis techniques to the description and measurement of energy in today's building systems, with the goal of evaluating and recommending alternative energy solutions that will result in greater energy efficiency and energy cost savings. Students gain a working understanding of energy systems in today's built environment and the tools to analyze and quantify energy efficiency efforts. The program began with an emphasis in residential energy efficiency/solar energy systems and has evolved to include commercial energy efficiency and renewable energy system installation technology.

The Renewable Energy Technician program is offered as a second-year option within the Energy Management program. Course work prepares students for employment designing and installing solar electric and domestic hot water systems. Renewable Energy students, along with Energy Management students, take a first-year curriculum in commercial energy efficiency giving them a solid background that includes residential energy efficiency, HVAC systems, lighting, and physics and math. In the second year, Renewable Energy students diverge from the Energy Management curriculum and take course work that starts with two courses in electricity fundamentals and one course in energy economics. In the following terms, students learn to design, install, and develop a thorough understanding of photovoltaics and domestic hot water systems.

Recent additions to Lane's offerings are Sustainability Coordinator and Water Conservation Technician degrees. Both programs were added to meet workforce demand.

Lane graduates find employment in a wide variety of disciplines and may work as facility managers, energy auditors, energy program coordinators, or control system specialists, for such diverse employers as engineering firms, public and private utilities, energy equipment companies, and departments of energy and as sustainability leaders within public and private sector organizations.

Lane Community College also provides continuing education for working professionals. The Sustainable Building Advisor (SBA) Certificate Program is a nine-month, specialized training program for working professionals. Graduate are able to advise employers or clients on strategies and tools for implementing sustainable building practices. Benefits from participating in the SBA program often include saving long-term building operating costs; improving the environmental, social, and economic viability of the region; and reducing environmental impacts and owner liability—not to mention the chance to improve one's job skills in a rapidly growing field.

The Building Operators Certificate is a professional development program created by The Northwest Energy Efficiency

Council. It is offered through the Northwest Energy Education Institute at Lane. The certificate is designed for operations and maintenance staff working in public or private commercial buildings. It certifies individuals in energy and resource-efficient operation of building systems at two levels: Level I–Building System Maintenance and Level II–Equipment Troubleshooting and Maintenance.

Lane Community College constantly scans the environment to assess workforce needs and develop programs that provide highly skilled employees. Lane, like most colleges, publishes information in its catalog on workforce demand and wages so that students can make informed decisions about program choice.

Green jobs will be a large part of a healthy economy. Opportunities will abound for those who take advantage of programs with a proven record of connecting with employers and successfully educating students to meet high skills standards.

Establishing a World-Class Wind Turbine Technician Academy

by Thomas Sutton, Director of Wind Energy and Technical Services
Kalamazoo Valley Community College

When Kalamazoo Valley Community College (KVCC) decided it wanted to become involved in the training of utility-grade technicians for wind-energy jobs, early on the choice was made to avoid another "me too" training course.

Our program here in Southwest Michigan, 30 miles from Lake Michigan, had to meet industry needs and industry standards.

It was also obvious from the start that the utility-grade or large wind industry had not yet adopted any uniform training standards in the United States.

Of course, these would come, but why should the college wait when European standards were solidly established and working well in Germany, France, Denmark and Great Britain?

As a result, in 2009, KVCC launched its Wind Turbine Technician Academy, the first of its kind in the United States. The noncredit academy runs 8 hours a day, five days a week, for twenty-four weeks of intense training in electricity, mechanics, wind dynamics, safety, and climbing. The college developed this program rather quickly—in eight months—to fast-track individuals into this emerging field.

KVCC based its program on the training standards forged by the Bildungszentrum fur Erneuerebare Energien (BZEE)—the Renewable Energy Education Center. Located in Husum, Germany, the BZEE was created and supported by major wind-turbine manufacturers, component makers, and enterprises that provide operation and maintenance services.

As wind-energy production increased throughout Europe, the need for high-quality, industry-driven, international standards emerged. The BZEE has become the leading trainer for wind-turbine technicians across Europe and now in Asia.

With the exception of one college in Canada, the standards were not yet available in North America. When Kalamazoo Valley realized it could be the first college or university in the United States to offer this training program—that was enough motivation to move forward.

For the College to become certified by the BZEE, it needed to hire and send an electrical instructor and a mechanical instructor to Germany for six weeks of "train the trainer." The instructors not only had to excel in their respective fields, they also needed to be able to climb the skyscraper towers supporting megawatt-class turbines—a unique combination of skills to possess. Truly, individuals who fit this job description don't walk through the door everyday—but we found them! Amazingly, we found a top mechanical instructor who was a part-time fireman and comfortable with tall ladder rescues and a skilled electrical instructor who used to teach rappelling off the Rockies to the Marine Corps.

In addition to employing new instructors, the College needed a working utility-grade nacelle that could fit in its training lab that would be located in the KVCC Michigan Technical Education Center. So one of the instructors traveled to Denmark and purchased a 300-kilowatt turbine.

Once their own training was behind them and the turbine was on its way from the North Sea, the instructors quickly turned to crafting the curriculum necessary for our graduates to earn both an academy certificate from KVCC and a certification from the BZEE.

Promoting the innovative program to qualified potential students across the country was the next step. News releases were published throughout Michigan, and they were also picked up on the Internet. Rather quickly, KVCC found itself with more than 500 requests for applications for a program built for 16 students.

Acceptance into the academy includes a medical release, a climbing test, reading and math tests, relevant work experience, and, finally, an interview. Students in the academy's pioneer class, which graduated in spring 2010, ranged in age from their late teens to early 50s. They hailed from throughout Michigan, Indiana, Ohio, and Illinois as well as from Puerto Rico and Great Britain.

The students brought with them degrees in marketing, law, business, science, and architecture, as well as entrepreneurial experiences in several businesses, knowledge of other languages, military service, extensive travel, and electrical, computer, artistic, and technical/mechanical skills.

Kalamazoo Valley's academy has provided some high-value work experiences for the students in the form of two collaborations with industry that has allowed them to maintain and/or repair actual utility-grade turbines, including those at the 2.5 megawatt size. This hands-on experience will add to the attractiveness of the graduates in the market place. Potential employers were recently invited to an open house where they could see the lab and meet members of this pioneer class.

The College's Turbine Technician Academy has also attracted a federal grant for $550,000 to expand its program through additional equipment purchases. The plan is to erect our own climbing tower. Climbing is a vital part of any valid program, and yet wind farms cannot afford to shut turbines down just for climb-training. The funds were put to use engineering, fabricating, and erecting a wind training tower that incorporated all of the necessary components to teach competency-based work at heights safety training.

When the students are asked what best distinguishes the Kalamazoo Valley program, their answers point to the experienced instructors and the working lab, which is constantly changing to offer the best training experiences. Students also consistently report that the hands-on field experience operating and maintaining the five large turbines during the course has set them apart at companies where they work.

Industry continues to tell us that community colleges need to offer fast-track training programs of this caliber if the nation is to reach the U.S. Department of Energy's goal of 20 percent renewable energy by 2030. This would require more than 1,500 new technicians each year.

The Wind Turbine Technician Academy continues the process improvements as directed by industry input. The academy not only holds the BZEE certification, it is also one of the few American Wind Energy Association (AWEA) Seal of Approval schools in the nation.

With that in mind, KVCC plans to host several BZEE orientation programs for other community colleges in order to encourage them to consider adopting the European training standards and start their own programs.

Meanwhile, applications are continuing to stream in from across the country for the next Wind Turbine Technician Academy program at Kalamazoo Valley Community College. For more information about the program, visit http://www.kvccgrovescenter.com/career/wtta.

How to Use This Guide

*P*eterson's *Two-Year Colleges 2017* contains a wealth of information for anyone interested in colleges offering associate degrees. This section details the criteria that institutions must meet to be included in this guide and provides information about research procedures used by Peterson's.

QUICK-REFERENCE CHART

The **Two-Year Colleges At-a-Glance Chart** is a geographically arranged table that lists colleges by name and city within the state, or country in which they are located. Areas listed include the United States, Canada, and other countries; the institutions are included because they are accredited by recognized U.S. accrediting bodies (see **Criteria for Inclusion** section).

The At-a-Glance chart contains basic information that enables you to compare institutions quickly according to broad characteristics such as degrees awarded, enrollment, application requirements, financial aid availability, and numbers of sports and majors offered. A dagger (†) after the institution's name indicates that an institution has an entry in the **Featured Two-Year Colleges** section.

Column 1: Degrees Awarded

C= *college transfer associate degree:* the degree awarded after a "university-parallel" program, equivalent to the first two years of a bachelor's degree.

T= *terminal associate degree:* the degree resulting from a one- to three-year program providing training for a specific occupation.

B= *bachelor's degree (baccalaureate):* the degree resulting from a liberal arts, science, professional, or preprofessional program normally lasting four years, although in some cases an accelerated program can be completed in three years.

M= *master's degree:* the first graduate (postbaccalaureate) degree in the liberal arts and sciences and certain professional fields, usually requiring one to two years of full-time study.

D= *doctoral degree* (research/scholarship, professional practice, or other)

Column 2: Institutional Control

Private institutions are designated as one of the following:

Ind = *independent* (nonprofit)

I-R = *independent-religious:* nonprofit; sponsored by or affiliated with a particular religious group or having a nondenominational or interdenominational religious orientation.

Prop = *proprietary* (profit-making)

Public institutions are designated by the source of funding, as follows:

Fed = *federal*

St = *state*

Comm = *commonwealth* (Puerto Rico)

Terr = *territory* (U.S. territories)

Cou = *county*

Dist = *district:* an administrative unit of public education, often having boundaries different from units of local government.

City = *city*

St-L = *state and local:* local may refer to county, district, or city.

St-R = *state-related:* funded primarily by the state but administratively autonomous.

Column 3: Student Body

M= *men only* (100% of student body)

PM = *coed, primarily men*

W= *women only* (100% of student body)

PW = *coed, primarily women*

M/W = *coeducational*

Column 4: Undergraduate Enrollment

The figure shown represents the number of full-time and part-time students enrolled in undergraduate degree programs as of fall 2015.

Columns 5–7: Enrollment Percentages

Figures are shown for the percentages of the fall 2015 undergraduate enrollment made up of students attending part-time (column 5) and students 25 years of age or older (column 6). Also listed is the percentage of students in the last graduating class who completed a college-transfer associate program and went directly on to four-year colleges (column 7).

For columns 8 through 15, the following letter codes are used: Y = yes; N = no; R = recommended; S = for some.

Columns 8–10: Admission Policies

The information in these columns shows whether the college has an open admission policy (column 8) whereby virtually all applicants are accepted without regard to standardized test scores, grade average, or class rank; whether a high school equivalency certificate is accepted in place of a high school diploma for admission consideration (column 9); and whether a high school transcript (column 10) is required as part of the application process. In column 10, the combination of the codes R and S indicates that a high school transcript is recommended for all applicants (R) or required for some (S).

Columns 11–12: Financial Aid

These columns show which colleges offer the following types of financial aid: need-based aid (column 11) and part-time jobs (column 12), including those offered through the federal government's Federal Work-Study program.

Columns 13–15: Services and Facilities

These columns show which colleges offer the following: career counseling (column 13) on either an individual or group basis, job placement services (column 14) for individual students, and college-owned or -operated housing facilities (column 16) for noncommuting students.

Column 16: Sports

This figure indicates the number of sports that a college offers at the intramural and/or intercollegiate levels.

Column 17: Majors

This figure indicates the number of major fields of study in which a college offers degree programs.

PROFILES OF TWO-YEAR COLLEGES AND SPECIAL MESSAGES

The **Profiles of Two-Year Colleges** contain basic data in capsule form for quick review and comparison. The following outline of the **Profile** format shows the section headings and the items that each section covers. Any item that does not apply to a particular college or for which no information was supplied is omitted from that college's **Profile.** Display ads, which appear near some of the institution's profiles, have been provided and paid for by those colleges that chose to supplement their profile with additional information. A star ★ next to the name of a school signifies that the school is one of the "Featured Two-Year Colleges," with a two-page in-depth description in that section of this guide and may also have an expanded profile on Peterson's website at www.petersons/com.

Bulleted Highlights

The bulleted highlights section features important information, for quick reference and comparison. The number of possible bulleted highlights that an ideal **Profile** would have if all questions were answered in a timely manner follow. However, not every institution provides all of the information necessary to fill out every bulleted line. In such instances, the line will not appear.

First Bullet

Institutional control: Private institutions are designated as independent (nonprofit), proprietary (profit-making), or independent, with a specific religious denomination or affiliation. Nondenominational or interdenominational religious orientation is possible and would be indicated.

Public institutions are designated by the source of funding. Designations include federal, state, province, commonwealth

(Puerto Rico), territory (U.S. territories), county, district (an administrative unit of public education, often having boundaries different from units of local government), city, state and local (local may refer to county, district, or city), or state-related (funded primarily by the state but administratively autonomous).

Religious affiliation is also noted here.

Institutional type: Each institution is classified as one of the following:

>   *Primarily two-year college:* Awards baccalaureate degrees, but the vast majority of students are enrolled in two-year programs.
>
>   *Four-year college:* Awards baccalaureate degrees; may also award associate degrees; does not award graduate (postbaccalaureate) degrees.
>
>   *Upper-level institution:* Awards baccalaureate degrees, but entering students must have at least two years of previous college-level credit; may also offer graduate degrees.
>
>   *Comprehensive institution:* Awards baccalaureate degrees; may also award associate degrees; offers graduate degree programs, primarily at the master's, specialist's, or professional level, although one or two doctoral programs may be offered.
>
>   *University:* Offers four years of undergraduate work plus graduate degrees through the doctorate in more than two academic or professional fields.

Founding date: If the year an institution was chartered differs from the year when instruction actually began, the earlier date is given.

System or administrative affiliation: Any coordinate institutions or system affiliations are indicated. An institution that has separate colleges or campuses for men and women but shares facilities and courses is termed a coordinate institution. A formal administrative grouping of institutions, either private or public, of which the college is a part, or the name of a single institution with which the college is administratively affiliated, is a system.

Second Bullet

Setting: Schools are designated as urban (located within a major city), suburban (a residential area within commuting distance of a major city), small-town (a small but compactly settled area not within commuting distance of a major city), or rural (a remote and sparsely populated area). The phrase *easy access to...* indicates that the campus is within an hour's drive of the nearest major metropolitan area that has a population greater than 500,000.

Third Bullet

Endowment: The total dollar value of funds and/or property donated to the institution or the multicampus educational system of which the institution is a part.

Fourth Bullet

Student body: An institution is coed (coeducational—admits men and women), primarily (80 percent or more) women, primarily men, women only, or men only.

Undergraduate students: Represents the number of full-time and part-time students enrolled in undergraduate degree programs as of fall 2015. The percentage of full-time undergraduates and the percentages of men and women are given.

Category Overviews

Undergraduates

For fall 2015, the number of full- and part-time undergraduate students is listed. This list provides the number of states and U.S. territories, including the District of Columbia and Puerto Rico (or for Canadian institutions, provinces and territories), and other countries from which undergraduates come. Percentages of undergraduates who are part-time or full-time students; transfers in; live on campus; out-of-state; Black or African American, non-Hispanic/Latino; Hispanic/Latino; Asian, non-Hispanic/Latino; Native Hawaiian or other Pacific Islander, non-Hispanic/Latino; American Indian or Alaska Native, non-Hispanic/Latino are given.

Retention: The percentage of freshmen (or, for upper-level institutions, entering students) who returned the following year for the fall term.

Freshmen

Admission: Figures are given for the number of students who applied for fall 2015 admission, the number of those who were admitted, and the number who enrolled. Freshman statistics include the average high school GPA; the percentage of freshmen who took the SAT® and received critical reading, writing, and math scores above 500, above 600, and above 700; as well as the percentage of freshmen taking the ACT® who received a composite score of 18 or higher.

Faculty

Total: The total number of faculty members; the percentage of full-time faculty members as of fall 2015; and the percentage of full-time faculty members who hold doctoral/first professional/ terminal degrees.

Student-faculty ratio: The school's estimate of the ratio of matriculated undergraduate students to faculty members teaching undergraduate courses.

Majors

This section lists the major fields of study offered by the college.

Academics

Calendar: Most colleges indicate one of the following: 4-1-4, 4-4-1, or a similar arrangement (two terms of equal length plus an abbreviated winter or spring term, with the numbers referring to months); semesters; trimesters; quarters; 3-3 (three courses for each of three terms); modular (the academic year is divided into small blocks of time; courses of varying lengths are assembled according to individual programs); or standard year (for most Canadian institutions).

Degrees: This names the full range of levels of certificates, diplomas, and degrees, including prebaccalaureate, graduate, and professional, that are offered by this institution:

Associate degree: Normally requires at least two but fewer than four years of full-time college work or its equivalent.

Bachelor's degree (baccalaureate): Requires at least four years but not more than five years of full-time college-level work or its equivalent. This includes all bachelor's degrees in which the normal four years of work are completed in three years and bachelor's degrees conferred in a five-year cooperative (work-study plan) program. A cooperative plan provides for alternate class attendance and employment in business, industry, or government. This allows students to combine actual work experience with their college studies.

Master's degree: Requires the successful completion of a program of study of at least the full-time equivalent of one but not more than two years of work beyond the bachelor's degree.

Doctoral degree (doctorate; research/scholarship, professional, or other): The highest degree in graduate study. The doctoral degree classification includes Doctor of Education, Doctor of Juridical Science, Doctor of Public Health, Doctor of Philosophy, Doctor of Podiatry, Doctor of Veterinary Medicine, and many more.

Post-master's certificate: Requires completion of an organized program of study of 24 credit hours beyond the master's degree but does not meet the requirements of academic degrees at the doctoral level.

Special study options: Details are next given here on study options available at each college:

Accelerated degree program: Students may earn a bachelor's degree in three academic years.

Academic remediation for entering students: Instructional courses designed for students deficient in the general competencies necessary for a regular postsecondary curriculum and educational setting.

Adult/continuing education programs: Courses offered for nontraditional students who are currently working or are returning to formal education.

Advanced placement: Credit toward a degree awarded for acceptable scores on College Board Advanced Placement (AP®) tests.

Cooperative (co-op) education programs: Formal arrangements with off-campus employers allowing students to combine work and study in order to gain degree-related experience, usually extending the time required to complete a degree.

Distance learning: For-credit courses that can be accessed off-campus via cable television, the Internet, satellite, DVD, correspondence course, or other media.

Double major: A program of study in which a student concurrently completes the requirements of two majors.

English as a second language (ESL): A course of study designed specifically for students whose native language is not English.

***External* degree programs:** A program of study in which students earn credits toward a degree through a combination of independent study, college courses, proficiency examinations, and personal experience. External degree programs require minimal or no classroom attendance.

Freshmen honors college: A separate academic program for talented freshmen.

Honors programs: Any special program for very able students offering the opportunity for educational enrichment, independent study, acceleration, or some combination of these.

Independent study: Academic work, usually undertaken outside the regular classroom structure, chosen or designed by the student with departmental approval and instructor supervision.

Internships: Any short-term, supervised work experience usually related to a student's major field, for which the student earns academic credit. The work can be full-or part-time, on or off-campus, paid or unpaid.

Off-campus study: A formal arrangement with one or more domestic institutions under which students may take courses at the other institution(s) for credit.

Part-time degree program: Students may earn a degree through part-time enrollment in regular session (daytime) classes or evening, weekend, or summer classes.

Self-designed major: Program of study based on individual interests, designed by the student with the assistance of an adviser.

Services for LD students: Special help for learning-disabled students with resolvable difficulties, such as dyslexia.

Study abroad: An arrangement by which a student completes part of the academic program studying in another country. A college may operate a campus abroad or it may have a cooperative agreement with other U.S. institutions or institutions in other countries.

Summer session for credit: Summer courses through which students may make up degree work or accelerate their program.

Tutorials: Undergraduates can arrange for special in-depth academic assignments (not for remediation) working with faculty members one-on-one or in small groups.

ROTC: Army, Naval, or Air Force Reserve Officers' Training Corps programs offered either on campus, at a branch campus [designated by a (b)], or at a cooperating host institution [designated by (c)].

Unusual degree programs: Nontraditional programs such as a 3-2 degree program, in which three years of liberal arts study is followed by two years of study in a professional field at another institution (or in a professional division of the same institution), resulting in two bachelor's degrees or a bachelor's and a master's degree.

Library

The name of the college's main library, plus the number of other libraries on campus will appear followed by: *Books:* number of physical and digital/electronic books; *Serial titles:* number of physical and digital/electronic serial titles; and the number of *Databases.* Also included here (if provided by the school) are the number of "Weekly public service hours" and study area information—the number of hours and days of the week open and if students can reserve study rooms.

Student Life

Housing options: The institution's policy about whether students are permitted to live off-campus or are required to live on campus for a specified period; whether freshmen-only, coed, single-sex, cooperative, and disabled student housing options are available; whether campus housing is leased by the school and/or provided by a third party; whether freshman applicants are given priority for college housing. The phrase *college housing not available* indicates that no college-owned or -operated housing facilities are provided for undergraduates and that noncommuting students must arrange for their own accommodations.

Activities and organizations: Lists information on drama-theater groups, choral groups, marching bands, student-run campus newspapers, student-run radio stations, and social organizations (sororities, fraternities, eating clubs, etc.) and how many are represented on campus.

Campus security: Campus safety measures including 24-hour emergency response devices (telephones and alarms) and patrols by trained security personnel, student patrols, late-night transport-escort service, and controlled dormitory access (key, security card, etc.).

Student services: Information provided indicates services offered to students by the college, such as legal services, health clinics, personal-psychological counseling, and women's centers.

Athletics

Membership in one or more of the following athletic associations is indicated by initials.

NCAA: National Collegiate Athletic Association

NAIA: National Association of Intercollegiate Athletics

NCCAA: National Christian College Athletic Association

NJCAA: National Junior College Athletic Association

USCAA: United States Collegiate Athletic Association

CIS: Canadian Interuniversity Sports

The overall NCAA division in which all or most intercollegiate teams compete is designated by a roman numeral I, II, or III. All teams that do not compete in this division are listed as exceptions.

Sports offered by the college are divided into two groups: intercollegiate (**M** or **W** following the name of each sport indicates that it is offered for men or women or **M/W** if the sport is offered for both men and women) and intramural. An **s** in parentheses following an **M, W or M/W** for an intercollegiate sport indicates that athletic scholarships (or grants-in-aid) are offered for men and/or women in that sport, and a c indicates a club team as opposed to a varsity team.

Standardized Tests

The most commonly required standardized tests are the ACT®, SAT®, and SAT Subject Tests™. These and other standardized tests may be used for selective admission, as a basis for counseling or course placement, or for both purposes. This section notes if a test is used for admission or placement and whether it is required, required for some, or recommended.

In addition to the ACT and SAT, the following standardized entrance and placement examinations are referred to by their initials:

ABLE: Adult Basic Learning Examination

ACT ASSET: ACT Assessment of Skills for Successful Entry and Transfer

ACT PEP: ACT Proficiency Examination Program

CAT: California Achievement Tests

CELT: Comprehensive English Language Test

CPAt: Career Programs Assessment

CPT: Computerized Placement Test

DAT: Differential Aptitude Test

LSAT: Law School Admission Test

MAPS: Multiple Assessment Program Service

MCAT: Medical College Admission Test

MMPI: Minnesota Multiphasic Personality Inventory

OAT: Optometry Admission Test

PAA: Prueba de Aptitud Académica (Spanish-language version of the SAT)

PCAT: Pharmacy College Admission Test

PSAT/NMSQT: Preliminary SAT National Merit Scholarship Qualifying Test

SCAT: Scholastic College Aptitude Test

SRA: Scientific Research Association (administers verbal, arithmetical, and achievement tests)

TABE: Test of Adult Basic Education

TASP: Texas Academic Skills Program

TOEFL: Test of English as a Foreign Language (for international students whose native language is not English)

WPCT: Washington Pre-College Test

Costs

Costs are given for the 2016–17 academic year or for the 2015–16 academic year if 2016–17 figures were not yet available. Annual expenses may be expressed as a comprehensive fee (including full-time tuition, mandatory fees, and college room and board) or as separate figures for full-time tuition, fees, room and board, or room only. For public institutions where tuition differs according to residence, separate figures are given for area or state residents and for nonresidents. Part-time tuition is expressed in terms of a per-unit rate (per credit, per semester hour, etc.) as specified by the institution.

The tuition structure at some institutions is complex in that freshmen and sophomores may be charged a different rate from that for juniors and seniors, a professional or vocational division may have a different fee structure from the liberal arts division of the same institution, or part-time tuition may be prorated on a sliding scale according to the number of credit hours taken. Tuition and fees may vary according to academic program, campus/location, class time (day, evening, weekend), course/credit load, course level, degree level, reciprocity agreements, and student level. Room and board charges are reported as an average for one academic year and may vary according to the board plan selected, campus/location, type of housing facility, or student level. If no college-owned or college-operated housing facilities are offered, the phrase *college housing not available* will appear in the Housing section of the Student Life paragraph.

Tuition payment plans that may be offered to undergraduates include tuition prepayment, installment payments, and deferred payment. A tuition prepayment plan gives a student the option of locking in the current tuition rate for the entire term of enrollment by paying the full amount in advance rather than year by year. Colleges that offer such a prepayment plan may also help the student to arrange financing.

The availability of full or partial undergraduate tuition waivers to minority students, children of alumni, employees or their children, adult students, and senior citizens may be listed.

Financial Aid

The number of Federal Work Study and/or part-time jobs and average earnings are listed. Financial aid deadlines are given as well.

Applying

Application and admission options include the following:

Early admission: Highly qualified students may matriculate before graduating from high school.

Early action plan: An admission plan that allows students to apply and be notified of an admission decision well in advance of the regular notification dates. If accepted, the candidate is not committed to enroll; students may reply to the offer under the college's regular reply policy.

Early decision plan: A plan that permits students to apply and be notified of an admission decision (and financial aid offer, if applicable) well in advance of the regular notification date. Applicants agree to accept an offer of admission and to withdraw their applications from other colleges. Candidates who are not accepted under early decision are automatically considered with the regular applicant pool, without prejudice.

Deferred entrance: The practice of permitting accepted students to postpone enrollment, usually for a period of one academic term or year.

Application fee: The fee required with an application is noted. This is typically nonrefundable, although under certain specified conditions it may be waived or returned.

Requirements: Other application requirements are grouped into three categories: required for all, required for some, and recommended. They may include an essay, standardized test scores, a high school transcript, a minimum high school grade point average (expressed as a number on a scale of 0 to 4.0, where 4.0 equals A, 3.0 equals B, etc.), letters of recommendation, an interview on campus or with local alumni, and, for certain types of schools or programs, special requirements such as a musical audition or an art portfolio.

Application deadlines and notification dates: Admission application deadlines and dates for notification of acceptance or rejection are given either as specific dates or as **rolling** and **continuous.** Rolling means that applications are processed as they are received, and qualified students are accepted as long as there are openings. Continuous means that applicants are notified of acceptance or rejection as applications are processed up until the date indicated or the actual beginning of classes. The application deadline and the notification date for transfers are given if they differ from the dates for freshmen. Early decision and early action application deadlines and notification dates are also indicated when relevant.

Admissions Contact

The name, title, and phone number of the person to contact for application information are given at the end of the Profile. The admission office address is listed in most cases. Toll-free phone numbers may also be included. The admission office fax number and e-mail address, if available, are listed, provided the school wanted them printed for use by prospective students. Finally, the URL of the institution's Web site is provided.

Additional Information

Each college that has a **Featured Two-Year College Close-Up** in the guide will have a cross-reference appended to the Profile, referring you directly to the page number of that **Featured Two-Year College Close-Up.**

Institutional Changes Since *Peterson's® Two-Year Colleges 2016*

Here you will find an alphabetical listing of institutions that have recently closed, merged with other institutions, or changed their name or status.

FEATURED TWO-YEAR COLLEGES

These narrative descriptions provide an inside look at certain colleges, shifting the focus to a variety of other factors that should also be considered. The descriptions provide a wealth of information that is crucial in the college decision-making equation—such as tuition, financial aid, academic programs, and life on campus. Prepared exclusively by college officials, the descriptions are designed to help give students a better sense of the individuality of each institution, in terms that include campus environment, student activities, and lifestyle. Such quality-of-life intangibles can be the deciding factors in the college selection process. The absence of any college or university does not constitute an editorial decision on the part of Peterson's. In essence, these descriptions are an open forum for colleges, on a voluntary basis, to communicate their particular message to prospective students. The colleges included have paid a fee to Peterson's to provide this information. The Close-Ups in the **Featured Two-Year Colleges** section are edited to provide a generally consistent format across entries for your ease of comparison.

INDEXES

Associate Degree Programs at Two-and Four-Year Colleges

These indexes present hundreds of undergraduate fields of study that are currently offered most widely according to the colleges' responses on *Peterson's Annual Survey of Undergraduate Institutions*. The majors appear in alphabetical order, each followed by an alphabetical list of the schools that offer an associate-level program in that field. Liberal Arts and Studies indicates a general program with no specified major. The terms used for the majors are those of the U.S. Department of Education Classification of Instructional Programs (CIPs). Many institutions, however, use different terms. Readers should refer to the **Featured Two-Year Colleges** two-page descriptions in this book for the school's exact terminology. In addition, although the term "major" is used in this guide, some colleges may use other terms, such as "concentration," "program of study," or "field."

DATA COLLECTION PROCEDURES

The data contained in the **Profiles** of Two-Year Colleges and **Indexes** were researched in winter and spring 2016 through *Peterson's Annual Survey of Undergraduate Institutions*. Questionnaires were sent to the more than 1,950 colleges that meet the outlined inclusion criteria. All data included in this edition have been submitted by officials (usually admission and financial aid officers, registrars, or institutional research personnel) at the colleges themselves. All usable information received in time for publication has been included. The omission of any particular item from the **Profiles** of Two-Year Colleges and **Indexes** listing signifies either that the item is not applicable to that institution or that data were not available. Because of the comprehensive editorial review that takes place in our offices and because all material comes directly from college officials, Peterson's has every reason to believe that the information presented in this guide is accurate at the time of printing. However, students should check with a specific college or university at the time of application to verify such figures as tuition and fees, which may have changed since the publication of this volume.

CRITERIA FOR INCLUSION IN THIS BOOK

Peterson's Two-Year Colleges 2017 covers accredited institutions in the United States, U.S. territories, and other countries that award the associate degree as their most popular undergraduate offering (a few also offer bachelor's, master's, or doctoral degrees). The term two-year college is the commonly used designation for institutions that grant the associate degree, since two years is the normal duration of the traditional associate degree program. However, some programs may be completed in one year, others require three years, and, of course, part-time programs may take a consid-

erably longer period. Therefore, "two-year college" should be understood as a conventional term that accurately describes most of the institutions included in this guide but which should not be taken literally in all cases. Also included are some non-degree-granting institutions, usually branch campuses of a multicampus system, which offer the equivalent of the first two years of a bachelor's degree, transferable to a bachelor's degree–granting institution.

To be included in this guide, an institution must have full accreditation or be a candidate for accreditation (preaccreditation) status by an institutional or specialized accrediting body recognized by the U.S. Department of Education or the Council for Higher Education Accreditation (CHEA). Institutional accrediting bodies, which review each institution as a whole, include the six regional associations of schools and colleges (Middle States, New England, North Central, Northwest, Southern, and Western), each of which is responsible for a specified portion of the United States and its territories. Other institutional accrediting bodies are national in scope and accredit specific kinds of institutions (e.g., Bible colleges, independent colleges, and rabbinical and Talmudic schools). Program registration by the New York State Board of Regents is considered to be the equivalent of institutional accreditation, since the board requires that all programs offered by an institution meet its standards before recognition is granted. This guide also includes institutions outside the United States that are accredited by these U.S. accrediting bodies. There are recognized specialized or professional accrediting bodies in more than forty different fields, each of which is authorized to accredit institutions or specific programs in its particular field. For specialized institutions that offer programs in one field only, we designate this to be the equivalent of institutional accreditation. A full explanation of the accrediting process and complete information on recognized, institutional (regional and national), and specialized accrediting bodies can be found online at www.chea.org or at www.ed.gov/admins/finaid/accred/index.html.

Quick-Reference Chart

Two-Year Colleges At-a-Glance

This chart includes the names and locations of accredited two-year colleges in the United States, Canada, and other countries and shows institutions' responses to the *Peterson's Annual Survey of Undergraduate Institutions*. If an institution submitted incomplete data, one or more columns opposite the institution's name is blank. A dagger after the school name indicates that the institution has one or more entries in the *Featured Two-Year Colleges* section. If a school does not appear, it did not report any of the information.

Y—Yes; N—No; R—Recommended; S—For Some

College	Location	Degrees Awarded	Institutional Control	Student Body	Undergraduate Enrollment	Percent Attending Part-Time	Percent 25 Years of Age or Older	Percent of Grads Going on to Four-Year Colleges	High School Equivalency Certificate Accepted	Open Admissions	High School Transcript Required	Need-Based Aid Available	Part-Time Jobs Available	Career Counseling Services Available	Job Placement Services Available	College Housing Available	Number of Sports Offered	Number of Majors Offered
UNITED STATES																		
Alabama																		
Bevill State Community College	Jasper	C,T	St	M/W	3,609	49	25	18	Y	Y	Y		Y	Y	Y	Y		13
Community College of the Air Force	Maxwell Gunter AFB	T	Fed	M/W	286,450		34		Y	Y	Y			Y		N	12	49
Gadsden State Community College	Gadsden	C,T	St	M/W	5,018	49	33	11	Y	Y	Y	Y	Y	Y	Y	Y	4	23
George C. Wallace Community College	Dothan	C,T	St	M/W	4,769	55	39		Y	Y	Y	Y	Y	Y	Y	Y	2	28
H. Councill Trenholm State Community College	Montgomery	T	St	M/W	1,401		38		Y	Y	Y		Y	Y	Y			18
James H. Faulkner State Community College	Bay Minette	C,T	St	M/W	3,323	36	39		Y	Y	Y	Y	Y	Y	Y	Y	6	18
Jefferson State Community College	Birmingham	C,T	St	M/W	8,826	68	31		Y	Y	S	Y	Y	Y	Y	N		19
J. F. Drake State Community and Technical College	Huntsville	C,T	St	M/W	996	51	48		Y	Y	Y	Y	Y	Y	Y	N		13
Lurleen B. Wallace Community College	Andalusia	C,T	St	M/W	1,732	40	19		Y	Y	Y	Y	Y	Y	Y		3	10
Marion Military Institute	Marion	C	St	M/W	457	2	1		N	Y	Y	Y	Y			Y	10	4
Northeast Alabama Community College	Rainsville	C,T	St	M/W	2,704	56	24		Y	Y	Y		Y		Y	N		11
Northwest-Shoals Community College	Muscle Shoals	C	St	M/W	3,667	55	25	12	Y	Y	Y	Y	Y	Y	Y	N	3	16
Reid State Technical College	Evergreen	T	St	M/W	571	56	65		Y				Y	Y	Y	N		4
Alaska																		
Alaska Career College	Anchorage	T	Prop	M/W									Y					1
Ilisagvik College	Barrow	C	St	M/W	271		56		Y	Y	Y			Y	Y	Y	1	7
University of Alaska Anchorage, Kenai Peninsula College	Soldotna	C,T,B	St	M/W	2,733				Y	Y	Y	Y	Y			Y		9
University of Alaska, Prince William Sound College	Valdez	C,T	St	M/W			74		Y	Y	Y	Y	Y	Y		Y		3
University of Alaska Southeast, Sitka Campus	Sitka	C,T,B,M	St	M/W	1,552													3
American Samoa																		
American Samoa Community College	Pago Pago	C,T,B	Terr	M/W	1,285	45	12	0	Y	Y		Y	Y	Y	Y	N	8	25
Arizona																		
Arizona Western College	Yuma	C,T	St-L	M/W	7,514	65	30		Y			Y	Y	Y	Y	Y	7	67
Carrington College-Mesa	Mesa	T	Prop	M/W	633	10	43		N	Y	Y	Y				N		5
Carrington College-Phoenix North	Phoenix	T	Prop	M/W	676		29			Y	Y	Y			Y	N		6
Carrington College-Phoenix West	Phoenix	T	Prop	M/W	346	23	63		Y	Y	Y	Y				N		6
Carrington College-Tucson	Tucson		Prop	M/W	357		32		N	Y	Y					N		2
Chandler-Gilbert Community College	Chandler	C,T	St-L	M/W	14,654	71						Y	Y	Y	Y	N	6	37
Cochise County Community College District	Douglas	C,T	St-L	M/W	4,509	60	13	46	Y			R,S	Y	Y	Y	Y	3	50
CollegeAmerica-Flagstaff	Flagstaff	C,T,B	Ind	M/W	205													
Eastern Arizona College	Thatcher	C,T	St-L	M/W	6,379	72	53	3	Y			R	Y	Y	Y	Y	10	52
Estrella Mountain Community College	Avondale	C,T	St-L	M/W	9,164	67		0	Y				Y	Y	Y	N	2	2
Mesa Community College	Mesa	C,T	St-L	M/W	22,000													
Mohave Community College	Kingman	C,T	St	M/W	4,360	78	47		Y				Y			N		34
Penn Foster College	Scottsdale	C,T,B	Prop	M/W	24,527					Y	Y	Y				N		23
Phoenix College	Phoenix	C,T	Cou	M/W	12,676													
Scottsdale Community College	Scottsdale	C,T	St-L	M/W	10,083	73	30		Y			Y	Y	Y		N	12	22
Tohono O'odham Community College	Sells	C,T	Pub	M/W	206	57	74	25				Y		Y		Y	1	
Arkansas																		
Arkansas Northeastern College	Blytheville	C,T	St	M/W	1,425	62												
NorthWest Arkansas Community College	Bentonville	C,T	St	M/W	7,744		32		Y	Y	Y	Y	Y	Y	Y	N	6	24
University of Arkansas Community College at Batesville	Batesville	C,T	St	M/W	1,315	43												
University of Arkansas Community College at Hope	Hope	C,T	St	M/W	1,360	51												
University of Arkansas Community College at Morrilton	Morrilton	C,T	St	M/W	2,042	34	35		Y	Y	Y	Y	Y	Y	Y	N	5	18
California																		
Academy of Couture Art	Beverly Hills	C,T,B	Prop	M/W					Y	Y	S	Y	Y			N		2
American Academy of Dramatic Arts-Los Angeles	Hollywood	C	Ind	M/W	282													
American River College	Sacramento	C,T	Dist	M/W	33,821		55		Y			Y	Y	Y	Y	N	12	74
Antelope Valley College	Lancaster	C,T	Dist	M/W	13,820		37		Y		R	Y	Y	Y	Y	N	12	66
Cañada College	Redwood City	C,T	Dist	M/W	5,433	93			Y	Y	R	Y	Y	Y	Y	N	5	45
Carrington College-Citrus Heights	Citrus Heights	T	Prop	M/W	568	8	42			Y	Y							10
Carrington College-Pleasant Hill	Pleasant Hill	T	Prop	M/W	616	16	48			Y	Y							13
Carrington College-Pomona	Pomona	T	Prop	M/W	406	32				Y								5
Carrington College-Sacramento	Sacramento	T	Prop	M/W	1,272	18	0			Y	Y							11
Carrington College-San Jose	San Jose	T	Prop	M/W	791	7	45			Y	Y					N		13
Carrington College-San Leandro	San Leandro	T	Prop	M/W	478	9	31			Y	Y					N		8
Carrington College-Stockton	Stockton	T	Prop	M/W	583	6	28			Y								1
Cerritos College	Norwalk	C,T	Dist	M/W	19,780	74	46		Y			Y	Y	Y	Y	N	14	82
Citrus College	Glendora	C	Dist	M/W	12,780	61			Y	Y	Y	Y	Y	Y	Y		10	59
Coastline Community College	Fountain Valley	C	Dist	M/W	11,431	78	72		Y		R	Y	Y	Y				1
College of Marin	Kentfield	C,T	Dist	M/W	6,000													
College of the Canyons	Santa Clarita	C,T	Dist	M/W	16,989		35		Y		R	Y	Y	Y	Y	N	11	56
College of the Desert	Palm Desert	C,T	Dist	M/W	9,259	61												
Columbia College	Sonora	C,T	Dist	M/W	2,424	70	38		Y	Y	R	Y	Y	Y	Y	N	2	32
Deep Springs College	Deep Springs	C	Ind	CM	28													
Feather River College	Quincy	C,T	Dist	M/W	1,782	64	22	33	Y			Y	Y	Y	Y	Y	9	29

35

This chart includes the names and locations of accredited two-year colleges in the United States, Canada, and other countries and shows institutions' responses to the *Peterson's Annual Survey of Undergraduate Institutions*. If an institution submitted incomplete data, one or more columns opposite the institution's name is blank. A dagger after the school name indicates that the institution has one or more entries in the *Featured Two-Year Colleges* section. If a school does not appear, it did not report any of the information.

Legend: Y—Yes; N—No; R—Recommended; S—For Some

Column headers (left to right): Degrees Awarded [College Transfer Associate (C); Terminal Associate (T); Bachelor's (B); Master's (M); Doctoral (D)] | Institutional Control | Student Body (Men, Primarily Men, Women, Primarily Women, Coed) | Undergraduate Enrollment | Percent Attending Part-Time | Percent 25 Years of Age or Older | Percent of Grads Going on to Four-Year Colleges | High School Equivalency Certificate Accepted | Open Admissions | High School Transcript Required | Need-Based Aid Available | Part-Time Jobs Available | Career Counseling Available | Job Placement Services Available | College Housing Available | Number of Sports Offered | Number of Majors Offered

Institution	Location	Deg	Ctrl	Body	Enroll	%PT	%25+	→4yr	HSEq	Open	HSTr	Need	PTJob	Career	JobPl	Hous	Sports	Majors
FIDM/Fashion Institute of Design & Merchandising, Los Angeles Campus†	Los Angeles	C,T,B	Prop	M/W	2,814	10	16		N	Y	Y		Y	Y	Y	N		15
FIDM/Fashion Institute of Design & Merchandising, Orange County Campus	Irvine	C,T	Prop	PW	92	7	5		N	Y	Y			Y	Y	N		6
FIDM/Fashion Institute of Design & Merchandising, San Diego Campus	San Diego	C,T	Prop	PW	119	5	11		N	Y	Y			Y	Y	N		3
Fullerton College	Fullerton	C,T	Dist	M/W	24,613	67	18		Y				Y	Y	Y	N	13	75
Golden West College	Huntington Beach	C,T	Dist	M/W	12,394	65												
Los Angeles Mission College	Sylmar	C,T	Dist	M/W	10,191	77												
Los Angeles Trade-Technical College	Los Angeles	C,T	Dist	M/W	13,194	68	47				R	Y	Y	Y	Y	N	3	29
Los Angeles Valley College	Valley Glen	C,T	Dist	M/W	17,957	41			Y		R	Y	Y	Y	Y	N	18	57
MiraCosta College†	Oceanside	C,T	Dist	M/W	14,687	66												
Mt. San Antonio College	Walnut	C,T	Dist	M/W	4,690	45			Y		S		Y	Y	Y	N	15	77
Norco College	Norco	C,T	Dist	M/W	9,399				Y							N		7
Ohlone College	Fremont	C,T	Dist	M/W	11,318	72												
Orange Coast College	Costa Mesa	C,T	Dist	M/W	21,930	61	28		Y			Y	Y	Y	Y	N	14	89
Oxnard College	Oxnard	C	Dist	M/W	7,006	72	34		Y	Y	R	Y	Y	Y		N	5	37
Palomar College	San Marcos	C	Dist	M/W	25,244		37		Y				Y	Y	Y	N	14	95
Pasadena City College	Pasadena	C,T	Dist	M/W	27,050	59	28		Y				Y	Y	Y	N	13	74
Rio Hondo College	Whittier	C,T	Dist	M/W					Y				Y	Y	Y	N	11	4
San Diego Miramar College	San Diego	C	Dist	M/W	10,650													
San Joaquin Delta College	Stockton	C,T	Dist	M/W	17,213		31		Y				Y	Y	Y	N	18	57
San Joaquin Valley College	Bakersfield	T	Prop	M/W	864	47			N	Y	S			Y	Y	N		9
San Joaquin Valley College	Chula Vista	T	Prop	M/W	61	87												1
San Joaquin Valley College	Fresno	T	Prop	M/W	1,019	41				Y								8
San Joaquin Valley College	Hanford	T	Prop	M/W	275	45												4
San Joaquin Valley College	Hesperia	T	Prop	M/W	804	41												7
San Joaquin Valley College	Lancaster	T	Prop	M/W	328	43												7
San Joaquin Valley College	Ontario	T	Prop	M/W	994	49			N	Y				Y	Y	N		10
San Joaquin Valley College	Rancho Cordova	T	Prop	M/W	158	80			N	Y				Y	Y	N		1
San Joaquin Valley College	Salida	T	Prop	M/W	465	46			N	Y				Y	Y			6
San Joaquin Valley College	Temecula	T	Prop	M/W	728	52												6
San Joaquin Valley College	Visalia	T	Prop	M/W	1,294	56			N	Y	S	Y		Y	Y	N		16
San Joaquin Valley College-Fresno Aviation Campus	Fresno	T	Prop	PM	130	62			N	Y	S			Y	Y	N		1
San Joaquin Valley College-Online	Visalia	T	Prop	M/W	1,005	75			N	Y				Y	Y			8
Sierra College	Rocklin	C,T	Dist	M/W	18,758	74	35		Y			Y	Y	Y	Y	Y	13	61
Victor Valley College	Victorville	C,T	Dist	M/W			31		Y			Y	Y	Y	Y	N	12	41

Colorado

Institution	Location	Deg	Ctrl	Body	Enroll	%PT	%25+	→4yr	HSEq	Open	HSTr	Need	PTJob	Career	JobPl	Hous	Sports	Majors
Arapahoe Community College	Littleton	C,T	St	M/W	9,616	80	41		Y				Y	Y	Y	N		28
CollegeAmerica-Denver	Denver	T,B	Ind	M/W	321		59							Y		N		5
Colorado Northwestern Community College	Rangely	C,T	St	M/W	1,178	54	24		Y	Y	Y	Y	Y	Y	Y	Y	11	14
Community College of Aurora	Aurora	C,T	St	M/W	6,943	82					S	Y	Y	Y	Y	N		13
Community College of Denver	Denver	C,T	St	M/W	10,296	76												
Front Range Community College	Westminster	C,T	St	M/W	18,761	70	42		Y				Y	Y	Y	N		27
IBMC College	Fort Collins	T	Prop	M/W	1,020		67		Y	Y	Y	Y	Y	Y	Y	N		14
IntelliTec College	Grand Junction	C	Prop	M/W														
Lamar Community College	Lamar	C,T	St	M/W	839	50	16		Y	Y			Y	Y	Y	Y	7	29
Morgan Community College	Fort Morgan	C,T	St	M/W	1,647	77			Y		R		Y	Y	Y	N		26
Northeastern Junior College	Sterling	C,T	St	M/W	1,776	45	21		Y		R	Y	Y	Y	Y	Y	15	44
Otero Junior College	La Junta	C,T	St	M/W	1,449	32		11	Y		R	Y	Y	Y	Y	Y	7	24
Pueblo Community College	Pueblo	C,T	St	M/W	6,203	63	54	3	Y				Y	Y	Y	N		36
Trinidad State Junior College	Trinidad	C,T	St	M/W	1,783	51												

Connecticut

Institution	Location	Deg	Ctrl	Body	Enroll	%PT	%25+	→4yr	HSEq	Open	HSTr	Need	PTJob	Career	JobPl	Hous	Sports	Majors
Asnuntuck Community College	Enfield	C,T	St	M/W	1,571	60	39		Y	Y	Y	Y		Y			N		9
Gateway Community College	New Haven	C,T	St	M/W	8,201	68												
Goodwin College	East Hartford	C,T,B	Ind	M/W	3,440	82												
Housatonic Community College	Bridgeport	C,T	St	M/W	5,369				Y	Y	Y	Y	Y	Y	Y			23
Manchester Community College	Manchester	C,T	St	M/W	6,891	65	31		Y	Y	Y	Y	Y	Y		N	4	31
Naugatuck Valley Community College	Waterbury	C,T	St	M/W	6,976	66	36		Y	Y	Y	Y	Y	Y	Y	N		32
Norwalk Community College	Norwalk	C,T	St	M/W	6,054	65			Y	Y	Y	Y	Y	Y	Y	N		34
St. Vincent's College	Bridgeport	C,T,B	I-R	M/W	675	93	69				Y	Y	Y	Y	Y	N		5
Three Rivers Community College	Norwich	C,T	St	M/W	4,259	67	41		Y	Y	R	Y	Y	Y	Y	N	2	35
Tunxis Community College	Farmington	C,T	St	M/W	4,079	61	38	24	Y	Y	Y		Y	Y	Y	N		19

Delaware

Institution	Location	Deg	Ctrl	Body	Enroll	%PT	%25+	→4yr	HSEq	Open	HSTr	Need	PTJob	Career	JobPl	Hous	Sports	Majors
Delaware Technical & Community College, Terry Campus	Dover	C,T	St	M/W	2,955	57												

Florida

Institution	Location	Deg	Ctrl	Body	Enroll	%PT	%25+	→4yr	HSEq	Open	HSTr	Need	PTJob	Career	JobPl	Hous	Sports	Majors
Chipola College	Marianna	C,T,B	St	M/W	2,147	60	37		Y	Y	Y	Y	Y	Y	Y	N	4	19
College of Business and Technology-Cutler Bay Campus	Cutler Bay	C	Prop	M/W	112		77		Y	Y	Y			Y	Y			5
College of Business and Technology-Flagler Campus	Miami	C	Prop	M/W	304		80		Y	Y	Y			Y	Y			5
College of Business and Technology-Hialeah Campus	Hialeah	C	Prop	PM	212		83		Y	Y	Y			Y	Y			2
College of Business and Technology-Main Campus	Miami	C,B	Prop	M/W	9		84		Y	Y	Y			Y	Y			8
College of Business and Technology-Miami Gardens	Miami Gardens	C,B	Prop	M/W	90		73		Y	Y	Y			Y	Y			5
College of Central Florida	Ocala	C,T,B	St-L	M/W	7,931	62	39		Y	Y	Y		Y	Y	Y	N	5	75
Daytona State College	Daytona Beach	C,T,B	St	M/W	13,598	59	43		Y	Y	Y		Y	Y	Y	N	9	52
Florida Gateway College	Lake City	C,T,B	St	M/W	2,912	71												
Florida SouthWestern State College	Fort Myers	C,T,B	St-L	M/W	15,742	66	28		Y	Y	Y		Y	Y		Y	5	40

This chart includes the names and locations of accredited two-year colleges in the United States, Canada, and other countries and shows institutions' responses to the *Peterson's Annual Survey of Undergraduate Institutions.* If an institution submitted incomplete data, one or more columns opposite the institution's name is blank. A dagger after the school name indicates that the institution has one or more entries in the *Featured Two-Year Colleges* section. If a school does not appear, it did not report any of the information.

Column key: Y—Yes; N—No; R—Recommended; S—For Some

Degrees Awarded: College Transfer Associate (C); Terminal Associate (T); Bachelor's (B); Master's (M); Doctoral (D)
Institutional Control: County, District, City; Independent; Federal, State, Commonwealth, Territory; Independent-Religious; Men, Primarily Men; Women, Primarily Women; Coed

Name	Location	Degrees Awarded	Institutional Control	Student Body	Undergraduate Enrollment	Percent Attending Part-Time	Percent 25 Years of Age or Older	Percent of Grads Going on to Four-Year Colleges	HS Equivalency Certificate Accepted	HS Transcript Required	Open Admissions	Need-Based Aid Available	Part-Time Jobs Available	Career Counseling Available	Job Placement Services Available	College Housing Available	Number of Sports Offered	Number of Majors Offered
Florida State College at Jacksonville	Jacksonville	C,T,B	St	M/W	25,514	69												
Gulf Coast State College	Panama City	C,T,B	St	M/W	5,858	62	42		Y	Y	Y	Y	Y	Y	Y	N	4	43
Hillsborough Community College	Tampa	C,T	St	M/W	26,571	60	36		Y	Y	Y	Y	Y	Y	Y	N	5	36
Miami Dade College	Miami	C,T,B	St-L	M/W	62,332	60	32		Y	Y	Y	Y	Y	Y	Y	N	4	191
Pasco-Hernando State College	New Port Richey	C,T,B	St	M/W	10,206	61												
Pensacola State College	Pensacola	C,B	St	M/W	9,840	63	38		Y	Y	Y	Y	Y	Y	Y	N	16	98
Seminole State College of Florida	Sanford	C,T,B	St-L	M/W	17,741	66	42	32	Y	Y	Y	Y	Y	Y	Y	N	3	50
Southeastern College-Jacksonville	Jacksonville	T	Prop	M/W	125	46								Y	Y			
Southeastern College-West Palm Beach	West Palm Beach	T	Prop	M/W	678	57									Y			15
Southern Technical College	Orlando	C	Prop	M/W	1,445													
South Florida State College	Avon Park	C,T,B	St	M/W	2,659	66	28		Y	Y	Y	Y	Y	Y	Y	Y	6	165
Tallahassee Community College	Tallahassee	C,T,B	St-L	M/W	12,445	54	22		Y	Y	Y	Y	Y	Y	Y	N	6	38
Ultimate Medical Academy Clearwater	Clearwater	T	Ind	M/W										Y	Y	N		1
Ultimate Medical Academy Online	Clearwater	T	Ind	M/W										Y	Y	N		7
Ultimate Medical Academy Tampa	Tampa	T	Ind	M/W										Y	Y	N		2

Georgia

Name	Location	Degrees Awarded	Institutional Control	Student Body	Undergraduate Enrollment	Percent Attending Part-Time	Percent 25 Years of Age or Older	Percent of Grads Going on to Four-Year Colleges	HS Equivalency Certificate Accepted	HS Transcript Required	Open Admissions	Need-Based Aid Available	Part-Time Jobs Available	Career Counseling Available	Job Placement Services Available	College Housing Available	Number of Sports Offered	Number of Majors Offered
Albany Technical College	Albany	T	St	M/W	3,331	54						Y		Y	Y			17
Athens Technical College	Athens	T	St	M/W	4,199	77						Y	Y	Y	Y			27
Atlanta Technical College	Atlanta	T	St	M/W	3,789	63						Y		Y	Y			11
Augusta Technical College	Augusta	T	St	M/W	4,490	64						Y	Y	Y	Y			24
Bainbridge State College	Bainbridge	C,T,B	St	M/W	2,401			37		Y	S	Y	Y	Y	Y	Y	2	33
Central Georgia Technical College	Warner Robins	T	St	M/W	7,832	66						Y	Y	Y	Y			27
Chattahoochee Technical College	Marietta	T	St	M/W	9,817	70						Y	Y	Y	Y			22
Coastal Pines Technical College	Waycross	T	St	M/W	2,445	76						Y		Y	Y			11
Columbus Technical College	Columbus	T	St	M/W	3,800	74						Y	Y	Y	Y			24
Darton State College	Albany	C,T,B	St	M/W	5,620	54												
Emory University, Oxford College	Oxford	C	I-R	M/W	936		0	99	N	N	Y	Y	Y	Y	Y	Y	9	1
Georgia Highlands College	Rome	C,T,B	St	M/W	5,748	53	21		N	Y	Y	Y	Y	Y		N	12	35
Georgia Military College	Milledgeville	C,B	Pub	M/W	7,876	40	32		Y	Y	S	Y		Y		Y	10	26
Georgia Northwestern Technical College	Rome	T	St	M/W	5,874	69						Y	Y	Y	Y		N	13
Georgia Piedmont Technical College	Clarkston	T	St	M/W	3,908	76						Y		Y	Y		N	27
Gordon State College	Barnesville	C,T,B	St	M/W	4,084		21		Y	Y	Y	Y	Y	Y	Y	Y	4	44
Gupton-Jones College of Funeral Service	Decatur	T	Ind	M/W	149													
Gwinnett Technical College	Lawrenceville	T	St	M/W	6,959	76						Y		Y	Y		N	27
Interactive College of Technology	Chamblee	T	Prop	M/W	312		80					Y	Y	Y				5
Interactive College of Technology	Gainesville	T	Prop	M/W										Y				
Lanier Technical College	Oakwood	T	St	M/W	3,646	73						Y		Y	Y		N	21
North Georgia Technical College	Clarkesville	T	St	M/W	2,665	64						Y		Y	Y			10
Oconee Fall Line Technical College	Sandersville	T	St	M/W	1,569	72						Y		Y	Y			5
Ogeechee Technical College	Statesboro	T	St	M/W	2,068	63						Y		Y	Y		N	24
Savannah Technical College	Savannah	T	St	M/W	4,196	67						Y		Y	Y		N	16
Southeastern Technical College	Vidalia	T	St	M/W	1,667	74						Y		Y	Y		N	13
Southern Crescent Technical College	Griffin	T	St	M/W	4,867	64						Y		Y	Y	Y	N	23
Southern Regional Technical College	Thomasville	T	St	M/W	3,490	68						Y		Y	Y	Y	N	11
South Georgia Technical College	Americus	T	St	M/W	1,668	50						Y		Y	Y			15
West Georgia Technical College	Waco	T	St	M/W	6,431	71						Y		Y	Y	Y	N	17
Wiregrass Georgia Technical College	Valdosta	T	St	M/W	3,708	77						Y	Y	Y			N	15

Guam

Name	Location	Degrees Awarded	Institutional Control	Student Body	Undergraduate Enrollment	Percent Attending Part-Time	Percent 25 Years of Age or Older	Percent of Grads Going on to Four-Year Colleges	HS Equivalency Certificate Accepted	HS Transcript Required	Open Admissions	Need-Based Aid Available	Part-Time Jobs Available	Career Counseling Available	Job Placement Services Available	College Housing Available	Number of Sports Offered	Number of Majors Offered
Guam Community College	Mangilao	T	Terr	M/W	2,458	60												

Hawaii

Name	Location	Degrees Awarded	Institutional Control	Student Body	Undergraduate Enrollment	Percent Attending Part-Time	Percent 25 Years of Age or Older	Percent of Grads Going on to Four-Year Colleges	HS Equivalency Certificate Accepted	HS Transcript Required	Open Admissions	Need-Based Aid Available	Part-Time Jobs Available	Career Counseling Available	Job Placement Services Available	College Housing Available	Number of Sports Offered	Number of Majors Offered
Hawaii Tokai International College	Kapolei	C,T	Ind	M/W	79	1		85	N	Y	Y	Y				Y		1
Leeward Community College	Pearl City	C,T	St	M/W	7,942	58	29	37	Y	Y	S	Y	Y	Y	Y	N	3	14

Idaho

Name	Location	Degrees Awarded	Institutional Control	Student Body	Undergraduate Enrollment	Percent Attending Part-Time	Percent 25 Years of Age or Older	Percent of Grads Going on to Four-Year Colleges	HS Equivalency Certificate Accepted	HS Transcript Required	Open Admissions	Need-Based Aid Available	Part-Time Jobs Available	Career Counseling Available	Job Placement Services Available	College Housing Available	Number of Sports Offered	Number of Majors Offered
Carrington College-Boise	Boise	T	Prop	M/W	420	10	58		N	Y		Y		Y	Y	N		9
College of Southern Idaho	Twin Falls	T	St-L	M/W	8,473	72												
Eastern Idaho Technical College	Idaho Falls	T	St	M/W	725		59		Y	Y	Y	Y	Y	Y	Y	N		14

Illinois

Name	Location	Degrees Awarded	Institutional Control	Student Body	Undergraduate Enrollment	Percent Attending Part-Time	Percent 25 Years of Age or Older	Percent of Grads Going on to Four-Year Colleges	HS Equivalency Certificate Accepted	HS Transcript Required	Open Admissions	Need-Based Aid Available	Part-Time Jobs Available	Career Counseling Available	Job Placement Services Available	College Housing Available	Number of Sports Offered	Number of Majors Offered
City Colleges of Chicago, Olive-Harvey College	Chicago	C,T	St-L	M/W	3,465	62	39		Y	Y	S	Y	Y	Y	Y	N	3	18
Coyne College	Chicago	C,T	Prop	M/W	522	59		0			S			Y	Y			
Danville Area Community College	Danville	C,T	St-L	M/W	2,692	60	35		Y	Y	S	Y	Y	Y	Y	N	5	31
Elgin Community College	Elgin	C,T	St-L	M/W	11,285	67	42		Y		S		Y	Y	Y	N	8	35
Fox College	Bedford Park	T	Priv	M/W	360											N		7
Harper College	Palatine	C,T	St-L	M/W	14,957													
Highland Community College	Freeport	C,T	St-L	M/W	1,804	49	30		Y	Y	R,S	Y		Y		N	6	26
Illinois Central College	East Peoria	C,T	St-L	M/W	9,704	64	29		Y		Y	Y	Y	Y	Y	Y	11	62
Illinois Eastern Community Colleges, Frontier Community College	Fairfield	C,T	St-L	M/W	2,229	57			Y	Y	Y	Y	Y	Y	Y	N	3	15
Illinois Eastern Community Colleges, Lincoln Trail College	Robinson	C,T	St-L	M/W	1,010	58	36		Y	Y	Y	Y	Y	Y	Y	N	3	14
Illinois Eastern Community Colleges, Olney Central College	Olney	C,T	St-L	M/W	1,295	53	36		Y	Y	Y	Y	Y	Y	Y	N	3	16
Illinois Eastern Community Colleges, Wabash Valley College	Mount Carmel	C,T	St-L	M/W	4,274	88	50		Y	Y	Y	Y	Y	Y	Y	N	3	20
Kankakee Community College	Kankakee	C,T	St-L	M/W	3,306	63	35		Y	Y	Y	Y	Y	Y	Y	N	5	42
Kaskaskia College	Centralia	C,T	St-L	M/W	4,472	67	35		Y	Y	Y	Y	Y	Y	Y	N	9	43
Kishwaukee College	Malta	C,T	St-L	M/W	4,475	55												

This chart includes the names and locations of accredited two-year colleges in the United States, Canada, and other countries and shows institutions' responses to the *Peterson's Annual Survey of Undergraduate Institutions*. If an institution submitted incomplete data, one or more columns opposite the institution's name is blank. A dagger after the school name indicates that the institution has one or more entries in the *Featured Two-Year Colleges* section. If a school does not appear, it did not report any of the information.

Y—Yes; N—No; R—Recommended; S—For Some

Degrees Awarded: Bachelor's (B), Master's (M), Doctoral (D), College Transfer Associate (C), Terminal Associate (T)

Institutional Control: County/District/City (Dist), Federal, State and Local (St-L), State (St), Independent (Ind), Independent-Religious (I-R), Proprietary (Prop)

College	Location	Degrees	Control	Student Body	Undergrad Enrollment	% Part-Time	% Grads to 4-Yr	% 25+	Open Admissions	HS Equiv Accepted	HS Transcript Req	Need-Based Aid	Part-Time Jobs	Career Counseling	Job Placement	College Housing	Sports	Majors
Lake Land College	Mattoon	C,T	St-L	M/W	6,351	56			Y			R	Y	Y	Y	Y	N	9	37
Lewis and Clark Community College	Godfrey	C,T	Dist	M/W	8,179				Y			R	Y	Y	Y	Y	N	7	28
McHenry County College	Crystal Lake	C,T	St-L	M/W	6,567	63	31		Y			R	Y	Y	Y	Y	N	6	27
Moraine Valley Community College	Palos Hills	C	St-L	M/W	15,016	57	23	82	Y	Y	R	R	Y	Y	Y	Y	N	11	58
Northwestern College-Chicago Campus	Chicago	C,T	Prop	M/W	1,082	56													
Oakton Community College	Des Plaines	C,T	Dist	M/W	9,363		39		Y	Y	R	Y		Y		Y	N	10	30
Rend Lake College	Ina	C,T	St	M/W	2,189	45	47		Y	Y	Y	Y	Y	Y	Y	Y	N	6	37
Richland Community College	Decatur	C,T	Dist	M/W	3,005	68	57		Y	Y	Y	Y	Y	Y	Y	N			28
Rock Valley College	Rockford	C,T	Dist	M/W	6,937	55	32		Y		Y	Y	Y	Y	Y	Y	N	9	32
Shawnee Community College	Ullin	C,T	St-L	M/W	1,819	56	27		Y	Y	Y	Y	Y	Y	Y	Y	N	4	30
South Suburban College	South Holland	C,T	St-L	M/W	4,401		43		Y	Y	Y	Y	Y	Y		Y	N	5	23
Southwestern Illinois College	Belleville	C,T	Dist	M/W	10,545	56			Y	Y	Y	Y	Y	Y	Y	N			
Spoon River College	Canton	C,T	St	M/W	1,665	56	30		Y	Y	Y	Y	Y	Y	Y	Y	N	4	47
Vet Tech Institute at Fox College	Tinley Park	T	Priv	M/W	164					Y							N		1
Indiana																		
Ancilla College	Donaldson	C,T	I-R	M/W	504	24	2		Y	Y	Y	Y	Y	Y	Y	Y	Y	12	25
International Business College	Indianapolis	T	Prop		354					Y		Y					Y		11
Ivy Tech Community College-Bloomington	Bloomington	C,T	St	M/W	6,107	67	54		Y		Y	Y	Y	Y	Y				46
Ivy Tech Community College-Central Indiana	Indianapolis	C,T	St	M/W	19,104	72	47		Y		Y	Y	Y	Y	Y	N	6	54
Ivy Tech Community College-Columbus	Columbus	C,T	St	M/W	2,865	73	48		Y		Y	Y	Y	Y	Y	N		50
Ivy Tech Community College-East Central	Muncie	C,T	St	M/W	5,943	57	41		Y		Y	Y	Y	Y	Y	N		56
Ivy Tech Community College-Kokomo	Kokomo	C,T	St	M/W	2,847	63	51		Y		Y	Y	Y	Y	Y	N		49
Ivy Tech Community College-Lafayette	Lafayette	C,T	St	M/W	5,060	58	45		Y		Y	Y	Y	Y	Y	N		61
Ivy Tech Community College-North Central	South Bend	C,T	St	M/W	5,253	69	51		Y		Y	Y	Y	Y	Y	N		42
Ivy Tech Community College-Northeast	Fort Wayne	C,T	St	M/W	7,660	69	45		Y		Y	Y	Y	Y	Y	N		44
Ivy Tech Community College-Northwest	Gary	C,T	St	M/W	8,166	67	51		Y		Y	Y	Y	Y	Y	N		42
Ivy Tech Community College-Richmond	Richmond	C,T	St	M/W	2,182	71	54		Y		Y	Y	Y	Y	Y	N	1	48
Ivy Tech Community College-Southeast	Madison	C,T	St	M/W	2,314	68	44		Y		Y	Y	Y	Y	Y	N		32
Ivy Tech Community College-Southern Indiana	Sellersburg	C,T	St	M/W	4,750	80	52		Y		Y	Y	Y	Y	Y	N		50
Ivy Tech Community College-Southwest	Evansville	C,T	St	M/W	5,142	75	53		Y		Y	Y	Y	Y	Y	N		61
Ivy Tech Community College-Wabash Valley	Terre Haute	C,T	St	M/W	4,364	67	45		Y		Y	Y	Y	Y	Y	N	2	62
Vet Tech Institute at International Business College	Fort Wayne	T	Priv	M/W	147											Y		1
Vet Tech Institute at International Business College	Indianapolis	T	Priv	M/W	147					Y						Y		1
Vincennes University	Vincennes	C,T,B	St	M/W	18,711	69	32		Y	Y	Y	Y	Y			Y	7	124
Iowa																		
Des Moines Area Community College	Ankeny	C,T	St-L	M/W	22,324	60													
Hawkeye Community College	Waterloo	C,T	St-L	M/W	5,370	52	29		Y	Y	Y	Y	Y	Y	Y	N	9	41
Iowa Central Community College	Fort Dodge	C,T	St-L	M/W	5,634	48	16		Y	Y	R,S	Y	Y	Y	Y	Y	16	35
Iowa Lakes Community College	Estherville	C,T	St-L	M/W	2,340													
Northeast Iowa Community College	Calmar	C,T	St-L	M/W	4,865	69	35		Y		R	Y	Y	Y	Y	N	7	29
North Iowa Area Community College	Mason City	C	St-L	M/W	2,955	52												
St. Luke's College	Sioux City	C,T,B	Ind	M/W	241	47	40	25	N	Y	Y	Y	Y	Y		N		4
Southeastern Community College	West Burlington	C	St-L	M/W	2,868	55	22		Y			Y	Y	Y		Y	6	29
Western Iowa Tech Community College	Sioux City	C,T	St	M/W	6,152	63	21		Y		R	Y	Y	Y		Y	8	56
Kansas																		
Allen Community College	Iola	C,T	St-L	M/W	2,383		20		Y	Y	Y	Y	Y	Y	Y	Y	12	65
Barton County Community College	Great Bend	C,T	St-L	M/W	5,292	63			Y	Y	R	Y	Y	Y	Y	Y	15	101
Cloud County Community College	Concordia	C,T	St-L	M/W	2,294		33		Y	Y	Y	Y	Y	Y	Y	Y	8	19
Dodge City Community College	Dodge City	C,T	St-L	M/W	1,779				Y		Y	Y	Y	Y	Y	Y	13	70
Donnelly College	Kansas City	C,T,B	I-R	M/W	262	25	34	11	Y	Y	R	Y	Y	Y	Y	Y		4
Hesston College	Hesston	C,T,B	I-R	M/W	409	13	13		Y	Y	Y	Y	Y	Y	Y	Y	9	13
Hutchinson Community College	Hutchinson	C,T	St-L	M/W	5,546	61	27	75	Y	Y	Y	Y		Y	Y	N	12	58
Manhattan Area Technical College	Manhattan	C,T	St-L	M/W	870	54	30		Y	Y	Y				Y	N		24
Kentucky																		
Beckfield College	Florence	T,B	Prop	M/W	605		69		Y	Y		Y		Y	Y	N		5
Elizabethtown Community and Technical College	Elizabethtown	C,T	St	M/W	7,353	62	46			Y	S			Y	Y	N		24
Gateway Community and Technical College	Florence	C,T	St	M/W	4,592	73			Y	Y	Y			Y	Y	N		15
Hopkinsville Community College	Hopkinsville	C,T	St	M/W	3,120	60			Y	Y	R	Y	Y	Y	Y	N	5	14
Interactive College of Technology	Newport	T	Prop	M/W						Y								
Maysville Community and Technical College	Maysville	C,T	St	M/W	3,478	58												
Owensboro Community and Technical College	Owensboro	C,T	St	M/W	3,981	63	36	14	Y	Y	Y	Y	Y	Y	Y	N		28
Somerset Community College	Somerset	C,T	St	M/W	1,210	28	49		Y	Y	Y	Y	Y			N		18
Spencerian College	Louisville	T,B	Prop	M/W	497	43			Y	Y	Y	Y	Y		Y	Y		8
Spencerian College-Lexington	Lexington	T	Prop	M/W	74		60			Y	Y	Y	Y		Y			3
Sullivan College of Technology and Design	Louisville	C,T,B	Prop	M/W	365	38												
Louisiana																		
Bossier Parish Community College	Bossier City	C	St	M/W	6,623	44	57		Y	Y			Y	Y	Y	N	10	35
Delgado Community College	New Orleans	C,T	St	M/W	18,698	58												
ITI Technical College	Baton Rouge	T	Prop	M/W							Y			Y	Y	N		8
Louisiana Delta Community College	Monroe	C,T	St	M/W	4,933	54												
McCann School of Business & Technology	Monroe	T	Prop	M/W	576	22												
Nunez Community College	Chalmette	C,T	St	M/W	2,629	67	52		Y		S	Y	Y	Y	Y	N	2	9
Southern University at Shreveport	Shreveport	C,T	St	M/W	3,174	39	32			Y	Y	Y	Y	Y	Y	Y	3	36
South Louisiana Community College	Lafayette	C,T	St	M/W	6,332	46												
Sowela Technical Community College	Lake Charles	C,T	St	M/W	3,722	52	24		Y	Y	Y		Y		Y	N		12

This chart includes the names and locations of accredited two-year colleges in the United States, Canada, and other countries and shows institutions' responses to the *Peterson's Annual Survey of Undergraduate Institutions*. If an institution submitted incomplete data, one or more columns opposite the institution's name is blank. A dagger after the school name indicates that the institution has one or more entries in the *Featured Two-Year Colleges* section. If a school does not appear, it did not report any of the information.

Degrees Awarded: College Transfer Associate (C); Terminal Associate (T); Bachelor's (B), Master's (M), Doctoral (D)

Institutional Control: County, District City; Federal, State and Local, State-Related; Independent, Independent-Religious, Proprietary, Territory, Commonwealth

Student Body: Men, Primarily Men, Women, Primarily Women, Coed

Y—Yes; N—No; R—Recommended; S—For Some

Institution	Location	Degrees	Control	Student Body	Undergrad Enrollment	% Part-Time	% 25+	% Grads to 4-Yr Colleges	HS Equiv. Accepted	HS Transcript Req.	Open Admissions	Need-Based Aid	Part-Time Jobs	Career Counseling	Job Placement	College Housing	Sports	Majors
Maine																		
Beal College	Bangor	T	Prop	M/W	464	22	53		Y	Y	Y	Y		Y	Y	N		11
Central Maine Community College	Auburn	C,T	St	M/W	2,984	58	34		N	Y	Y	Y	Y	Y	Y	Y	6	23
Kennebec Valley Community College	Fairfield	C,T	St	M/W	2,451	70	50		Y	Y	Y	Y	Y	Y	Y	N	7	31
The Landing School	Arundel	C,T	Ind	M/W	81											Y		3
Maine College of Health Professions	Lewiston	T	Ind	M/W	199	70	58		N	Y	Y	Y				Y		3
Southern Maine Community College	South Portland	C,T	St	M/W	6,045	57	39		Y	Y	Y	Y	Y	Y	Y	Y	10	28
Washington County Community College	Calais	C,T	St	M/W	374		40		Y	Y	Y	Y	Y			Y	1	12
York County Community College	Wells	C,T	St	M/W	1,758	73	44		Y	Y	Y	Y	Y	Y		N	6	20
Maryland																		
Anne Arundel Community College	Arnold	C,T	St-L	M/W	14,689	71	35		Y		Y	Y	Y	Y	Y	N	11	47
Carroll Community College	Westminster	C,T	St-L	M/W	3,549	63	27		Y		Y		Y	Y	Y	N		33
Cecil College	North East	C	Cou	M/W	2,591	61	33		Y		Y	Y	Y	Y	Y	N	8	42
Chesapeake College	Wye Mills	C,T	St-L	M/W	2,069	63	35		Y	Y	Y	Y	Y	Y	Y	N	5	24
College of Southern Maryland	La Plata	C,T	St-L	M/W	8,411	63												
Community College of Baltimore County	Baltimore	C,T	Cou	M/W	22,399	71					Y	Y					N	8	56
Frederick Community College	Frederick	C,T	St-L	M/W	6,197	67	35		Y		R		Y	Y	Y	N	7	32
Garrett College	McHenry	C,T	St-L	M/W	711	23	16		Y	Y	Y	Y	Y	Y	Y	Y	8	13
Hagerstown Community College	Hagerstown	C,T	St-L	M/W	4,276	75	33		Y		S	Y	Y	Y	Y		12	29
Harford Community College	Bel Air	C,T	St-L	M/W	6,520	63	29	58	Y			Y	Y	Y	Y		13	58
Howard Community College	Columbia	C,T	St-L	M/W	9,920	62	37		Y		S	Y	Y	Y	Y	N	6	48
Montgomery College	Rockville	C,T	St-L	M/W	25,320	65	30	51	Y		R	Y	Y	Y	Y		9	44
Wor-Wic Community College	Salisbury	C,T	St-L	M/W	3,137	72	42		Y		R		Y	Y	Y	N		24
Massachusetts																		
Benjamin Franklin Institute of Technology	Boston	C,T,B	Ind	M/W	493	13												
Berkshire Community College	Pittsfield	C,T	St	M/W	2,111	66	40		Y	Y	Y	Y	Y	Y	Y	N	6	20
Bunker Hill Community College	Boston	C,T	St	M/W	14,047	70			Y	Y	Y	Y	Y	Y	Y	N	4	59
Dean College	Franklin	C,T,B	Ind	M/W	1,292	17	1		N	Y	Y	Y	Y	Y	Y	Y	8	19
Greenfield Community College	Greenfield	C,T	St	M/W	2,127	64												
Holyoke Community College	Holyoke	C,T	St	M/W	6,285	53	33		Y		Y		Y	Y	Y	N	8	25
Massachusetts Bay Community College	Wellesley Hills	C,T	St	M/W	4,859	66	49		Y	Y		Y	Y	Y	Y	N	9	35
Middlesex Community College	Bedford	C,T	St	M/W	9,205	62												
Mount Wachusett Community College	Gardner	C,T	St	M/W	4,074	61			Y	Y	Y	Y	Y	Y	Y	N	8	29
Northern Essex Community College	Haverhill	C,T	St	M/W	6,628	67	35		Y	Y	Y	Y	Y	Y	Y	N	9	64
North Shore Community College	Danvers	C,T	St	M/W	6,961	65	40	45	Y	Y	S	Y	Y	Y	Y	N	2	40
Quincy College	Quincy	C,T	City	M/W	4,732	61	47		Y		Y	Y	Y	Y	Y	N	3	20
Quinsigamond Community College	Worcester	C,T	St	M/W	8,064	62	39		Y	Y	Y	Y	Y	Y	Y	N	8	53
Springfield Technical Community College	Springfield	C,T	St	M/W	6,286	57	40		Y	Y	Y	Y	Y	Y	Y	N	8	55
Michigan																		
Delta College	University Center	C,T	Dist	M/W	9,291	63	31		Y		R	Y	Y	Y	Y	N	5	63
Grand Rapids Community College	Grand Rapids	C,T	Dist	M/W	14,926	70	36		Y		Y	Y	Y	Y	Y	N	6	44
Kalamazoo Valley Community College	Kalamazoo	C,T	St-L	M/W	11,113													
Kellogg Community College	Battle Creek	C,T	St-L	M/W	5,081	75	44		Y		S	Y	Y	Y	Y	N	5	42
Keweenaw Bay Ojibwa Community College	Baraga	C,T	Cou	M/W	77	44						Y					N		4
Kirtland Community College	Roscommon	C,T	Dist	M/W	1,628	68	44		Y	Y		Y	Y	Y	Y	N	3	26
Macomb Community College	Warren	C,T	Dist	M/W	22,182	69	36		Y			Y	Y	Y	Y	N	11	72
Monroe County Community College	Monroe	C,T	Cou	M/W														
Montcalm Community College	Sidney	C,T	St-L	M/W	1,832	71												
Mott Community College	Flint	C,T	Dist	M/W	8,617	74	42		Y		Y	Y	Y	Y	Y	N	7	46
Muskegon Community College	Muskegon	C,T	St-L	M/W	4,506	67			Y	Y	Y	Y	Y	Y	Y	N	8	43
Northwestern Michigan College	Traverse City	C,T,B	St-L	M/W	4,609	56												
Saginaw Chippewa Tribal College	Mount Pleasant	C,T	Ind	M/W	122	68						Y					N		3
St. Clair County Community College	Port Huron	C,T	St-L	M/W	3,730	62			Y		Y	Y	Y	Y	Y	N	5	27
Schoolcraft College	Livonia	C,T,B	Dist	M/W	11,687	73	34		Y	Y	R,S	Y	Y	Y	Y	N	8	37
Southwestern Michigan College	Dowagiac	C,T	St-L	M/W	2,348	52	22		Y	Y	Y	Y	Y			Y	7	25
Wayne County Community College District	Detroit	C,T	St-L	M/W	16,654	81	42		Y	Y	Y	Y	Y	Y	Y	N	5	47
Minnesota																		
Alexandria Technical and Community College	Alexandria	C,T	St	M/W	2,702	50	20		Y	Y	Y	Y	Y			Y	4	25
Anoka-Ramsey Community College	Coon Rapids	C,T	St	M/W	9,294	62			Y	Y	S	Y	Y	Y	Y	N	11	25
Anoka Technical College	Anoka	C,T	St	M/W	2,027	56			Y	Y	Y	Y	Y	Y	Y	N		21
Central Lakes College	Brainerd	C,T	St	M/W	4,274			32	Y	Y	Y	Y	Y	Y	Y	Y	8	30
Century College	White Bear Lake	C,T	St	M/W	8,921	59	41		Y	Y	Y	Y	Y	Y		N	14	46
Duluth Business University	Duluth	T,B	Prop	PW	182	43												
Dunwoody College of Technology	Minneapolis	T,B	Ind	PM	1,094	18	48		N	Y		Y	Y	Y	Y	N		26
Hennepin Technical College	Brooklyn Park	C,T	St	M/W	5,676	65	59		Y		R	Y	Y	Y	Y	N		35
Lake Superior College	Duluth	C,T	St	M/W	5,050	58	41		Y		Y	Y	Y	Y	Y	N	1	34
Mesabi Range College	Virginia	C,T	St	M/W	1,373		37		Y		Y	Y	Y	Y	Y	Y	7	16
Minneapolis Business College	Roseville	T	Prop	M/W	231							Y					Y		9
Minneapolis Community and Technical College	Minneapolis	C,T	St	M/W	9,465	66												
Minnesota State College-Southeast Technical	Winona	C,T	St	M/W	2,003	56	49		Y	Y	Y	Y	Y			N		27
Minnesota State Community and Technical College-Detroit Lakes	Detroit Lakes	C,T	St	M/W	6,391	58								Y		N		17
Minnesota State Community and Technical College-Moorhead	Moorhead	C	St	M/W	6,391	58								Y		N		21
Minnesota State Community and Technical College-Wadena	Wadena	C,T	St	M/W	6,391	58								Y		N		4

This chart includes the names and locations of accredited two-year colleges in the United States, Canada, and other countries and shows institutions' responses to the *Peterson's Annual Survey of Undergraduate Institutions*. If an institution submitted incomplete data, one or more columns opposite the institution's name is blank. A dagger after the school name indicates that the institution has one or more entries in the *Featured Two-Year Colleges* section. If a school does not appear, it did not report any of the information.

Y—Yes; N—No; R—Recommended; S—For Some

Institution	Location	Degrees Awarded	Institutional Control	Student Body	Undergraduate Enrollment	Percent Attending Part-Time	Percent 25 Years of Age or Older	Percent of Grads Going on to Four-Year Colleges	High School Equivalency Certificate Accepted	High School Transcript Required	Open Admissions	Need-Based Aid Available	Part-Time Jobs Available	Career Counseling Available	Job Placement Services Available	College Housing Available	Number of Sports Offered	Number of Majors Offered
Minnesota West Community and Technical College	Pipestone	C,T	St	M/W	3,182				Y	Y	Y	Y	Y				7	42
Normandale Community College	Bloomington	C,T	St	M/W														
North Hennepin Community College	Brooklyn Park	C,T	St	M/W	6,847	70			Y	Y	R	Y	Y	Y	Y	N	10	31
Northland Community and Technical College	Thief River Falls	C,T	St	M/W	3,573				Y	Y	Y	Y	Y	Y		N	13	63
Northwest Technical College	Bemidji	T	St	M/W	1,114	70	56		Y	Y	Y	Y			N	Y		16
Rainy River Community College	International Falls	C,T	St	M/W	278	18	54		Y	Y	R	Y	Y	Y	Y	Y	16	5
Ridgewater College	Willmar	C,T	St	M/W	3,563				Y	Y	Y	Y	Y	Y	Y	N	9	51
Riverland Community College	Austin	C,T	St	M/W	3,014													
Mississippi																		
Copiah-Lincoln Community College	Wesson	C,T	St-L	M/W	3,157	21	6		Y	Y	Y	Y	Y	Y	Y	Y	8	42
Hinds Community College	Raymond	C,T	St-L	M/W	11,514	36	35			Y	Y	Y	Y	Y	Y	Y	14	59
Itawamba Community College	Fulton	C,T	St-L	M/W	5,611	36	10		Y	Y	Y	Y	Y	Y	Y	Y	7	55
Meridian Community College	Meridian	C,T	St-L	M/W	3,381	27	30		Y	Y	Y	Y	Y	Y	Y	Y	10	13
Missouri																		
Cottey College	Nevada	C,B	Ind	CW	317	1	1	95		Y	Y	Y	Y		Y	4	8
Crowder College	Neosho	C,T	St-L	M/W	5,710	54	30		Y	Y	Y	Y	Y	Y	Y	Y	4	46
Culinary Institute of St. Louis at Hickey College	St. Louis	T	Priv	M/W	95					Y					Y			1
East Central College	Union	C,T	Dist	M/W	3,222	53	27		Y	Y	Y	Y	Y	Y		N	3	32
Jefferson College	Hillsboro	C,T	Dist	M/W	4,705	51			Y	Y	Y	Y	Y	Y	Y	Y	6	37
Metro Business College	Jefferson City	T	Prop	PW	142		62			Y			Y	Y	N		5	
Ozarks Technical Community College	Springfield	C,T	Dist	M/W	13,614				Y	Y	Y	Y	Y	Y				34
Pinnacle Career Institute	Kansas City	T	Prop	M/W	147													
Ranken Technical College	St. Louis	C,T,B	Ind	PM	1,743		34		Y	Y	Y	Y	Y	Y	Y			12
St. Charles Community College	Cottleville	C,T	St	M/W	6,865	50	25		Y	Y	R,S	Y	Y	Y		N	3	43
St. Louis Community College	St. Louis	C,T	Pub	M/W	18,902	60	40		Y	Y	S			Y	Y	N	5	
State Fair Community College	Sedalia	C,T	Dist	M/W	4,983	50												
Vet Tech Institute at Hickey College	St. Louis	T	Priv	M/W	167										Y		1	
Montana																		
Dawson Community College	Glendive	C,T	St-L	M/W	304	47	21	24	Y	Y	Y	Y	Y	Y	Y	Y	10	12
Great Falls College Montana State University	Great Falls	C,T	St	M/W	1,657	55	34	36	Y	Y	Y	Y	Y	Y				15
Nebraska																		
Mid-Plains Community College	North Platte	C,T	Dist	M/W	2,235	65	31		Y	Y	Y	Y	Y	Y	Y	Y	5	18
Nebraska Indian Community College	Macy	C,T	Fed	M/W	120	55												
Southeast Community College, Lincoln Campus	Lincoln	C,T	Dist	M/W	9,193		34		Y	Y	Y	Y	Y	Y	Y	N	6	24
Southeast Community College, Milford Campus	Milford	T	Dist	PM	9,193		34		Y	Y	Y	Y	Y	Y	Y	Y	6	14
Nevada																		
Carrington College-Las Vegas	Las Vegas	T	Prop	M/W	370	19	62			Y	Y					N		2
Carrington College-Reno	Reno	T	Prop	M/W	327	21	66			Y	Y					N		1
Great Basin College	Elko	C,T,B	St	M/W	3,127	70	39		Y			Y	Y	Y		N		35
Truckee Meadows Community College	Reno	C,T	St	M/W	11,085	73	39	34	Y			Y	Y	Y		N		53
Western Nevada College	Carson City	C,T,B	St	M/W	3,839	64	45	68	Y	Y	S	Y	Y	Y		N	2	19
New Hampshire																		
Lakes Region Community College	Laconia	C,T	St	M/W	1,179	58										N		
River Valley Community College	Claremont	C,T	St	M/W	1,009	77	53			Y	Y	Y	Y			N		16
St. Joseph School of Nursing	Nashua	C,T	Ind	M/W	144	56	76		N	Y	Y					N		1
White Mountains Community College	Berlin	C,T	St	M/W	1,001	69	29				Y	Y	Y			N		21
New Jersey																		
Camden County College†	Blackwood	C,T	St-L	M/W	11,263	50	37		Y	Y	S	Y	Y	Y	Y	N	5	45
County College of Morris	Randolph	C,T	Cou	M/W	8,026	51	21		Y	Y	Y	Y	Y	Y		N	11	35
Cumberland County College	Vineland	C,T	St-L	M/W	3,844													
Hudson County Community College	Jersey City	C,T	St-L	M/W	9,051	35	34		Y			Y	Y	Y	Y	N		31
Mercer County Community College	Trenton	C,T	St-L	M/W	7,979	61	30		Y	Y	Y	Y	Y	Y	Y	N	9	51
Middlesex County College	Edison	C,T	Cou	M/W	11,673				Y	Y	Y	Y	Y	Y	Y	N	7	40
Ocean County College	Toms River	C,T	Cou	M/W	8,663	47	21		Y		S	Y	Y			N	12	20
Raritan Valley Community College	Branchburg	C,T	St-L	M/W	8,099	59	25			Y	Y	Y	Y	Y		N	5	57
Rowan College at Burlington County	Pemberton	C,T	Cou	M/W	8,762		33		Y	Y	R	Y	Y	Y		N	6	63
Salem Community College	Carneys Point	C,T	Cou	M/W	1,107	46												
New Mexico																		
Carrington College-Albuquerque	Albuquerque	T	Prop	M/W	442	10	51			Y			Y					3
Central New Mexico Community College	Albuquerque	C,T	St	M/W	25,888	69	43		Y			Y	Y	Y	Y	N		64
New Mexico Junior College	Hobbs	C,T	St-L	M/W	3,222		52		Y			Y	Y	Y		Y	10	52
San Juan College	Farmington	C,T	St	M/W	5,692	53	55		Y	Y	Y	Y	Y	Y		N	8	53
Southwestern Indian Polytechnic Institute	Albuquerque	C,T	Fed	M/W	402	14	39	1	N	Y	Y	Y	Y	Y	Y	Y	3	12
University of New Mexico-Gallup	Gallup	C,T	St	M/W	2,473	53	41		Y	Y	S	Y	Y	Y		N		20
New York																		
American Academy of Dramatic Arts-New York	New York	T	Ind	M/W	261			0	N	Y	Y	Y	Y			Y		1
The Belanger School of Nursing	Schenectady	C,T	Ind	PW	127	75	65				Y	Y				N	1	1
Berkeley College-White Plains Campus	White Plains	C,T,B	Prop	M/W	467	8	22		N	Y	Y	Y	Y			Y	4	7
Borough of Manhattan Community College of the City University of New York	New York	C,T	St-L	M/W	27,309	34	25		Y	Y	Y	Y	Y	Y	Y	N	4	35
Cayuga County Community College	Auburn	C,T	St-L	M/W	4,430	59	40	41	Y	Y	Y	Y	Y	Y	Y	Y	7	35

This chart includes the names and locations of accredited two-year colleges in the United States, Canada, and other countries and shows institutions' responses to the *Peterson's Annual Survey of Undergraduate Institutions*. If an institution submitted incomplete data, one or more columns opposite the institution's name is blank. A dagger after the school name indicates that the institution has one or more entries in the *Featured Two-Year Colleges* section. If a school does not appear, it did not report any of the information.

Y—Yes; N—No; R—Recommended; S—For Some

Institution	Location	Degrees Awarded	Institutional Control	Student Body	Undergraduate Enrollment	Percent Attending Part-Time	Percent 25 Years of Age or Older	Percent of Grads Going on to Four-Year Colleges	High School Equivalency Certificate Accepted	Open Admissions	High School Transcript Required	Need-Based Aid Available	Part-Time Jobs Available	Career Counseling Available	Job Placement Services Available	College Housing Available	Number of Sports Offered	Number of Majors Offered
Clinton Community College	Plattsburgh	C,T	St-L	M/W	1,245	31	26	39	Y	Y	Y	Y	Y	Y	Y	Y	4	17
Cochran School of Nursing	Yonkers	T	Ind	PW	89	87	81		N	Y	Y	Y		Y		N		1
The College of Westchester	White Plains	C,T,B	Prop	M/W	1,067	21	41		N	Y	Y	Y	Y	Y	Y	N		8
Columbia-Greene Community College	Hudson	C,T	St-L	M/W	1,777	60	28			Y	Y	Y	Y	Y	Y	N	10	18
Corning Community College	Corning	C,T	St-L	M/W	3,972	51	21		Y	Y	Y	Y	Y	Y	Y	Y	7	64
Dutchess Community College	Poughkeepsie	C,T	St-L	M/W	9,544	55	15		Y	Y	Y	Y	Y	Y	Y	Y	6	31
Erie Community College	Buffalo	C,T	St-L	M/W	2,577	24	42		Y	Y	Y	Y	Y	Y	Y	N	10	16
Erie Community College, North Campus	Williamsville	C,T	St-L	M/W	5,551	33	34		Y	Y	Y	Y	Y	Y	Y	N	10	31
Erie Community College, South Campus	Orchard Park	C,T	St-L	M/W	3,894	43	22		Y	Y	Y	Y	Y	Y	Y	N	10	21
Fashion Institute of Technology†	New York	C,T,B,M	St-L	PW	9,392	21	19		N	Y	Y	Y	Y	Y	Y	Y	7	23
Finger Lakes Community College	Canandaigua	C,T	St-L	M/W	6,761	56	31		Y	Y	Y	Y	Y	Y	Y	Y	9	57
Fiorello H. LaGuardia Community College of the City University of New York	Long Island City	C,T	St-L	M/W	19,332	45	34	48	Y	Y	Y	Y	Y	Y	Y	N	7	43
Genesee Community College	Batavia	C,T	St-L	M/W	6,521	56	34		Y	Y	Y	Y	Y	Y	Y	Y	13	91
Helene Fuld College of Nursing	New York	C,T,B	Ind	PW	354	74	90		Y	Y	Y	Y						1
Herkimer County Community College	Herkimer	C,T	St-L	M/W	3,019	42	27			Y	Y	Y	Y	Y	Y	Y	13	29
Island Drafting and Technical Institute	Amityville	C,T	Prop	PM	112		32	0	Y	Y	R		Y	Y	Y	N		8
Jamestown Business College	Jamestown	T,B	Prop	M/W	318	1	34		N	Y	Y	Y		Y	Y	N	8	4
Jamestown Community College	Jamestown	C,T	St-L	M/W	3,038	27	28	65	Y	Y	Y	Y	Y	Y	Y	Y	10	28
Jefferson Community College	Watertown	C,T	St-L	M/W	3,880	45			N	Y	Y	Y	Y	Y	Y	Y	6	35
Kingsborough Community College of the City University of New York	Brooklyn	C,T	St-L	M/W	17,495	42												
Long Island Business Institute	Flushing	C	Prop	PW	590	20	58	0	N	Y	Y			Y	Y	N		7
Mohawk Valley Community College	Utica	C,T	St-L	M/W	6,675	46	29		Y		S	Y	Y	Y	Y	Y	13	48
Monroe Community College	Rochester	C,T	St-L	M/W	14,586	39	40		Y	Y	Y	Y	Y	Y	Y	Y	18	67
Nassau Community College	Garden City	C,T	St-L	M/W	22,308	40												
Niagara County Community College	Sanborn	C,T	St-L	M/W	6,133	40	21		Y	Y	Y	Y	Y	Y	Y	Y	10	42
Onondaga Community College	Syracuse	C,T	St-L	M/W	11,886	50	21		Y	Y	Y	Y	Y	Y	Y	Y	14	37
Phillips Beth Israel School of Nursing	New York	C,T,B	Ind	M/W	254	87	65		N	Y	Y	Y		Y		N		3
Plaza College	Forest Hills	C,T,B	Prop	M/W	726													
Queensborough Community College of the City University of New York	Bayside	C,T	St-L	M/W	15,493	40	22		Y	Y	Y	Y	Y	Y	Y	N	11	41
Rockland Community College	Suffern	C,T	St-L	M/W	7,434	44												
St. Joseph's College of Nursing	Syracuse	T	I-R	M/W	273	39				Y	Y	Y		Y	Y	Y		1
Schenectady County Community College	Schenectady	C,T	St-L	M/W	6,151	64	30		Y	Y	Y	Y	Y	Y	Y	N	6	21
State University of New York College of Technology at Alfred	Alfred	C,T,B	St	M/W	3,699	9	14		Y	Y	Y	Y	Y	Y	Y	Y	17	56
Sullivan County Community College	Loch Sheldrake	C,T	St-L	M/W	1,596	49	23	38	Y	Y	Y	Y	Y	Y	Y	Y	13	37
Tompkins Cortland Community College	Dryden	C,T	St-L	M/W	3,085	29	27		Y	Y	Y	Y	Y	Y	Y	Y	22	36
Trocaire College	Buffalo	T,B	Ind	PW	1,369	55	48	0	N	Y	Y	Y	Y	Y	Y	N		15
Ulster County Community College	Stone Ridge	C,T	St-L	M/W	3,540	50												
Westchester Community College †	Valhalla	C,T	St-L	M/W	12,966	46	27		Y	Y	Y	Y	Y	Y	Y	N	11	50
Wood Tobe-Coburn School	New York	T	Prop	M/W	411				N	Y		Y				N		9
North Carolina																		
Alamance Community College	Graham	C,T	St	M/W	4,420	40	45		Y	Y	Y	Y	Y	Y	Y	N	4	28
Caldwell Community College and Technical Institute	Hudson	C,T	St	M/W	3,805	61	62		Y	Y	Y	Y	Y	Y	Y	N	4	28
Cape Fear Community College	Wilmington	C,T	St	M/W	8,851	55	43		Y	Y	S	Y	Y	Y	Y	N	6	38
Carolinas College of Health Sciences	Charlotte	T	Pub	M/W	474	88	51		N	N	S	Y	Y	Y	Y	Y		3
Carteret Community College	Morehead City	C,T	St	M/W	1,872	57												
Catawba Valley Community College	Hickory	C,T	St	M/W	4,571	59	29		Y	Y	Y	Y	Y	Y	Y	N	4	41
Cleveland Community College	Shelby	C,T	St	M/W	2,990	66			Y	Y	Y	Y	Y	Y	Y	N		27
College of The Albemarle	Elizabeth City	C,T	St	M/W	2,052	65	56		Y	Y	Y	Y	Y	Y	Y	N	14	26
Craven Community College	New Bern	C,T	St	M/W	3,012	60			Y	Y	Y	Y	Y	Y	Y	N		36
Fayetteville Technical Community College	Fayetteville	C,T	St	M/W	11,546	61	57	21	Y	Y	S	Y	Y	Y	Y	N	6	54
Forsyth Technical Community College	Winston-Salem	C,T	St	M/W	9,148	59												
Guilford Technical Community College	Jamestown	C,T	St-L	M/W	12,430	53												
Halifax Community College	Weldon	C,T	St-L	M/W	1,154	42	50				Y	Y	Y			N		17
Haywood Community College	Clyde	C,T	St-L	M/W	2,127													
James Sprunt Community College	Kenansville	C,T	St	M/W	1,195	59	32	1	Y	Y	Y	Y	Y	Y	Y	N	1	17
Johnston Community College	Smithfield	C,T	St	M/W	3,969	57			Y	Y	Y	Y	Y	Y	Y	N	1	13
King's College	Charlotte	T	Prop	M/W	395											Y		9
Lenoir Community College	Kinston	C,T	St	M/W	2,757	61	34		Y	Y	Y	Y	Y	Y	Y	N	3	36
Living Arts College	Raleigh	B	Prop	M/W	578		33		N	Y	Y		Y	Y	Y	Y		6
Martin Community College	Williamston	C,T	St	M/W	890				Y	Y	Y	Y	Y	Y	Y	N		20
Mitchell Community College	Statesville	C,T	St	M/W	3,024	62	19		Y	Y	Y	Y	Y	Y	Y	N		34
Montgomery Community College	Troy	C,T	St	M/W	818	66	38		Y	Y	Y	Y	Y	Y	Y	N		13
Piedmont Community College	Roxboro	C,T	St	M/W	1,321				Y	Y	S	Y	Y	Y	Y	N	1	23
Randolph Community College	Asheboro	C,T	St	M/W	2,670	63	29	52	Y	Y		Y	Y		Y	N		28
Richmond Community College	Hamlet	C,T	St	M/W	2,531	54	40		Y	Y		Y	Y	Y	Y	N		23
Rockingham Community College	Wentworth	C,T	St	M/W	1,866	62			Y	Y		Y	Y	Y	Y	N	4	20
Rowan-Cabarrus Community College	Salisbury	C,T	St	M/W	5,158		44		Y	Y		Y	Y	Y	Y	N		24
South Piedmont Community College	Polkton	C,T	St	M/W	2,658	72												
Wayne Community College	Goldsboro	C,T	St-L	M/W	3,837	53	45		Y	Y	Y	Y	Y	Y	Y	N	1	33
Western Piedmont Community College	Morganton	C,T	St	M/W	2,933				Y	Y	Y	Y	Y	Y	Y	N	1	40
North Dakota																		
Bismarck State College	Bismarck	C,T,B	St	M/W	4,078	44	36		Y	Y	Y	Y	Y	Y	Y	Y	7	38
Dakota College at Bottineau	Bottineau	C,T	St	M/W	852													
Lake Region State College	Devils Lake	C,T	St	M/W	1,918	72			Y	Y	S	Y	Y	Y	Y	Y	8	15
Williston State College	Williston	C,T	St	M/W	1,038	42	24		Y	Y	Y	Y	Y	Y	Y	Y	5	15

This chart includes the names and locations of accredited two-year colleges in the United States, Canada, and other countries and shows institutions' responses to the *Peterson's Annual Survey of Undergraduate Institutions*. If an institution submitted incomplete data, one or more columns opposite the institution's name is blank. A dagger after the school name indicates that the institution has one or more entries in the *Featured Two-Year Colleges* section. If a school does not appear, it did not report any of the information.

Y—Yes; N—No; R—Recommended; S—For Some

Institution	City	Degrees Awarded	Institutional Control	Student Body	Undergraduate Enrollment	Percent Women	Percent Attending Part-Time	Percent of Grads Going on to Four-Year Colleges	Percent 25 Years of Age or Older	High School Equivalency Certificate Accepted	High School Transcript Required	Open Admissions	Need-Based Aid Required	Part-Time Jobs Available	Career Counseling Available	Job Placement Services Available	College Housing Available	Number of Sports Offered	Number of Majors Offered
Ohio																			
The Art Institute of Cincinnati	Cincinnati	T,B	Ind	M/W	34	12													
Beckfield College	Cincinnati	C	Prop	M/W															
Bowling Green State University-Firelands College	Huron	C,T,B	St	M/W	2,260	51	34			Y	Y	Y	Y	Y	Y	Y	N	5	25
Bradford School	Columbus	T	Prop	M/W	443										Y			N		5
Central Ohio Technical College	Newark	T	St	M/W	3,566	73	39			Y	Y	S	Y	Y	Y	Y	N	5	28
Chatfield College	St. Martin	C,T	I-R	M/W	396	50	54			Y	Y				Y	Y	N		1
Cincinnati State Technical and Community College	Cincinnati	C,T	St	M/W	9,630	70	46			Y	Y	Y	Y	Y	Y	Y	N	4	63
Columbus Culinary Institute at Bradford School	Columbus	T	Priv	M/W	150											Y				1
Davis College	Toledo	T	Prop	M/W	159	79	67			N	Y	Y	Y	Y	Y	Y	N		12
Eastern Gateway Community College	Steubenville	C,T	St-L	M/W	3,024	60	35			Y	Y	S	Y	Y	Y	Y	N	1	21
Edison Community College	Piqua	C,T	St	M/W	3,133	74	48			Y	Y	Y		Y	Y	Y	N	3	39
ETI Technical College of Niles	Niles	T	Prop	M/W	124	50	45	24		Y	Y	Y			Y	Y	N		9
Good Samaritan College of Nursing and Health Science	Cincinnati	T,B	Prop	M/W	353	64													
Hocking College	Nelsonville	C,T	St	M/W	4,094														
International College of Broadcasting	Dayton	C,T	Prop	M/W						Y	Y	Y		Y				N		2
Kent State University at Ashtabula	Ashtabula	C,B	St	M/W	2,285	50	44			Y	Y	Y	Y	Y	Y	Y	N	1	22
Kent State University at East Liverpool	East Liverpool	C,B,M	St	M/W	1,245	44	39			Y	Y	Y	Y	Y	Y	Y	N		13
Kent State University at Salem	Salem	C,B	St	M/W	1,738	34	35			Y	Y	Y	Y	Y	Y	Y	N	5	21
Kent State University at Trumbull	Warren	C,B	St	M/W	2,579	36	40			Y	Y	Y	Y	Y	Y	Y	N		22
Kent State University at Tuscarawas	New Philadelphia	C,B	St	M/W	2,146	38	34			Y	Y	Y	Y	Y	Y	Y	N	2	21
Lakeland Community College	Kirtland	C,T	St-L	M/W	7,941	66	38			Y	Y	Y	Y	Y	Y	Y	N	6	39
Lorain County Community College	Elyria	C,T	St-L	M/W	11,520	73	40			Y	Y	S	Y	Y	Y	Y	N	6	72
Northwest State Community College	Archbold	C,T	St	M/W	3,614	80													
Ohio Business College	Hilliard	T	Prop	M/W															
Ohio Business College	Sandusky	C	Prop	M/W	265	36													
Ohio Business College	Sheffield Village	T	Prop	M/W	350					Y	Y	Y		Y	Y	Y	N		12
The Ohio State University Agricultural Technical Institute	Wooster	C,T	St	M/W	757	7													
Ohio Technical College	Cleveland	T	Prop	M/W	1,072			18							Y		N			7
Owens Community College	Toledo	C,T	St	M/W	12,572	66													
School of Advertising Art	Kettering	T	Prop	M/W	168	2	2	2		N	Y				Y	Y	N		1
Stark State College	North Canton	C,T	St-R	M/W	12,645	73	53				Y		Y	Y	Y	Y	N		49
Terra State Community College	Fremont	C,T	St	M/W	2,603	68													
Trumbull Business College	Warren	T	Prop	M/W	159	35	74			Y	Y		Y	Y	Y	Y	N		7
University of Cincinnati Blue Ash College	Cincinnati	C,T	St	M/W	5,065	36	22			Y	Y	Y	Y	Y	Y	Y	N		36
University of Cincinnati Clermont College	Batavia	C,T,B	St	M/W	3,099	42													
Vet Tech Institute at Bradford School	Columbus	T	Priv	M/W	163											Y				1
Oklahoma																			
Carl Albert State College	Poteau	C,T	St	M/W	2,276	38	36			Y		Y	Y	Y	Y	Y	Y	6	24
Clary Sage College	Tulsa	T	Prop	PW	621		51			Y	Y	Y			Y	Y	N		4
Community Care College	Tulsa	T	Ind	PW	1,002		52			Y	Y	Y		Y	Y	Y	N		12
Oklahoma City Community College	Oklahoma City	C,T	St	M/W	13,334	66	37			Y		S	Y	Y	Y	Y	N	8	61
Oklahoma State University Institute of Technology	Okmulgee	C,T,B	St	M/W	2,476	29	29			Y	Y	Y	Y	Y			Y	7	25
Oklahoma State University, Oklahoma City	Oklahoma City	C,T,B	St	M/W	5,963	69	43			Y	Y	S	Y	Y	Y	Y	N		47
Oklahoma Technical College	Tulsa	T	Ind	M/W	310		50			Y	Y			Y	Y	Y	N		4
Seminole State College	Seminole	C,T	St	M/W	1,827	44	36			Y		Y	Y	Y	Y	Y	Y	7	27
Southwestern Oklahoma State University at Sayre	Sayre	C,T	St-L	M/W			37			Y		Y	Y	Y	Y	Y	Y		8
Tulsa Community College	Tulsa	C,T	St	M/W	16,708	66	41			Y		Y	Y	Y	Y	Y	N	5	55
Oregon																			
Central Oregon Community College	Bend	C,T	Dist	M/W	6,073	59	47			Y				Y	Y	Y	Y	12	56
Oregon Coast Community College	Newport	C,T	Pub	M/W	503	58	44	34		Y					Y		N		5
Rogue Community College	Grants Pass	C,T	St-L	M/W	4,954	62	48			Y	Y		Y	Y	Y	Y	Y	5	27
Southwestern Oregon Community College	Coos Bay	C,T	St-L	M/W	2,338	52	38			Y		S	Y	Y	Y		Y	13	12
Sumner College	Portland	T	Prop	PW	261		65				Y			Y	Y	Y	N		3
Treasure Valley Community College	Ontario	C,T	St-L	M/W	2,170	56	46			Y				Y	Y	Y	Y	9	30
Umpqua Community College	Roseburg	C,T	St-L	M/W	2,046	53													
Pennsylvania																			
Antonelli Institute	Erdenheim	T	Prop	M/W	188					Y	Y		Y	Y			Y		2
Bradford School	Pittsburgh	T	Prop	M/W	413						Y		Y				Y		11
Bucks County Community College	Newtown	C,T	Cou	M/W	8,611	66	30	47		Y	Y	Y	Y	Y	Y	Y	N	10	53
Butler County Community College	Butler	C,T	Cou	M/W	3,573		29			Y	Y	Y	Y	Y	Y	Y	N	6	62
Cambria-Rowe Business College	Indiana	C,T	Prop	M/W	93	1													
Career Training Academy	Lower Burrell	T	Prop	PW							Y	Y			Y		N		3
Career Training Academy	Pittsburgh	T	Prop	M/W	70														
Commonwealth Technical Institute	Johnstown	T	St	M/W	222														
Community College of Allegheny County	Pittsburgh	C,T	Cou	M/W	17,148	65													
Community College of Philadelphia	Philadelphia	C,T	St-L	M/W	34,337		53	64		Y	Y	S		Y	Y	Y	N	7	35
Harrisburg Area Community College	Harrisburg	C,T	St-L	M/W	19,121	71	41			Y		S	Y	Y	Y		N	5	72
Hussian College, School of Art	Philadelphia	B	Prop	M/W	83	1				N	Y			Y	Y				2
JNA Institute of Culinary Arts	Philadelphia	T	Prop	M/W	59														
Lackawanna College	Scranton	C,T	Ind	M/W	1,679	31				Y	Y	Y	Y	Y	Y	Y	Y	9	32
Lehigh Carbon Community College	Schnecksville	C,T	St-L	M/W	6,738	62	31	52		Y		S	Y	Y	Y	Y	N	7	62
Luzerne County Community College	Nanticoke	C,T	Cou	M/W	5,788	55	36			Y		R	Y	Y	Y	Y	N	10	74
Manor College	Jenkintown	C,T	I-R	M/W	696	39	26	60		N	Y		Y	Y	Y		Y	2	17
Montgomery County Community College	Blue Bell	C,T	Cou	M/W	12,372	69	36	60		Y	Y		Y	Y	Y	Y	N	13	55
New Castle School of Trades	New Castle	T	Ind	PM	503		0				Y		Y	Y			Y		7
Northampton Community College	Bethlehem	C,T	St-L	M/W	10,269	55	33	70		Y	Y	R,S	Y	Y	Y	Y	Y	10	63

This chart includes the names and locations of accredited two-year colleges in the United States, Canada, and other countries and shows institutions' responses to the *Peterson's Annual Survey of Undergraduate Institutions*. If an institution submitted incomplete data, one or more columns opposite the institution's name is blank. A dagger after the school name indicates that the institution has one or more entries in the *Featured Two-Year Colleges* section. If a school does not appear, it did not report any of the information.

Legend: Y—Yes; N—No; R—Recommended; S—For Some

Column key — Degrees Awarded: College Transfer Associate (C), Terminal Associate (T), Bachelor's (B), Master's (M), Doctoral (D).

Institution	City	Degrees Awarded	Institutional Control	Student Body	Undergraduate Enrollment	Percent Attending Part-Time	Percent of Grads Going on to Four-Year Colleges	Percent 25 Years of Age or Older	High School Equivalency Certificate Accepted	Open Admissions	High School Transcript Required	Need-Based Aid Available	Part-Time Jobs Available	Career Counseling Available	Job Placement Services Available	College Housing Available	Number of Sports Offered	Number of Majors Offered
Penn State DuBois	DuBois	C,T,B	St-R	M/W	602	17	18		N	Y	Y	Y	Y			N	7	127
Penn State Fayette, The Eberly Campus	Lemont Furnace	C,T,B	St-R	M/W	704	16	18		N	Y	Y	Y	Y			N	11	124
Penn State Mont Alto	Mont Alto	C,T,B	St-R	M/W	893	26	20		N	Y	Y	Y	Y			Y	10	120
Penn State Shenango	Sharon	C,T,B	St-R	M/W	508	45	49		N	Y	Y	Y	Y			N	7	124
Pennsylvania Highlands Community College	Johnstown	C	St-L	M/W	2,456	65			Y			Y	Y	Y	Y	N	7	26
Pennsylvania Institute of Technology	Media	C,T	Ind	M/W	596	49	40		Y	Y	Y	Y	Y	Y	Y	N	1	14
Pittsburgh Institute of Aeronautics	Pittsburgh	C,T	Ind	PM	368		30		Y	Y	R		Y	Y	Y	N		4
Pittsburgh Technical Institute	Oakdale	T	Prop	M/W	1,936		15		Y		Y		Y	Y	Y		5	17
Reading Area Community College	Reading	C,T	Cou	M/W	4,090	77	34		Y	Y	R,S	Y	Y	Y	Y	N		36
The Restaurant School at Walnut Hill College	Philadelphia	T,B	Prop	M/W	429		12	2	Y	Y	Y	Y		Y	Y	Y		4
South Hills School of Business & Technology	State College	T	Prop	M/W	630	9												
Thaddeus Stevens College of Technology	Lancaster	C,T	St	M/W	823		14	0	N	Y	Y			Y	Y	Y	5	20
University of Pittsburgh at Titusville	Titusville	C,T	St-R	M/W	388	19	14			Y	Y	Y	Y	Y	Y	Y	13	13
Vet Tech Institute	Pittsburgh	T	Prop	M/W	372					Y			Y		Y	Y		1
Westmoreland County Community College	Youngwood	C,T	Cou	M/W	5,517	54	34		Y			Y	Y	Y	Y	N	8	78
Williamson College of the Trades	Media	T	Ind	CM	270		0		N	Y	Y	Y		Y	Y	Y	13	8
Puerto Rico																		
Humacao Community College	Humacao	T,B	Ind	M/W	554	21	32	0	Y	Y	Y	Y	Y	Y	Y	N		13
Rhode Island																		
Community College of Rhode Island	Warwick	C,T	St	M/W	16,195	70	38		Y	Y		Y	Y	Y	Y	N	8	47
South Carolina																		
Aiken Technical College	Graniteville	C,T	St-L	M/W	2,357	71	41		Y	Y	R	Y	Y	Y	Y	N		20
Denmark Technical College	Denmark	C,T	St	M/W	1,043	37	60	5	Y	Y	Y	Y	Y	Y	Y	N	2	10
Forrest College	Anderson	C,T	Prop	M/W	99	14	60			Y	Y	Y	Y	Y	Y	N		10
Greenville Technical College	Greenville	C,T	St	M/W	12,280	61	38		Y	Y	Y	Y	Y	Y	Y	N	7	32
Horry-Georgetown Technical College	Conway	C,T	St-L	M/W	7,660	62												
Midlands Technical College	Columbia	C,T	St-L	M/W	10,946	54	37	35	Y		R	Y	Y	Y	Y	N	7	50
Spartanburg Community College	Spartanburg	C,T	St	M/W	4,928	55	20		Y	Y	Y	Y	Y	Y	Y	N		19
Spartanburg Methodist College	Spartanburg	C,T	I-R	M/W	771	1	1	80	N	Y	Y	Y	Y	Y	Y	Y	12	5
Technical College of the Lowcountry	Beaufort	C,T	St	M/W	2,332	71	0				Y	Y	Y			N		19
Tri-County Technical College	Pendleton	C,T	St	M/W	6,128	44	19		Y	Y		Y	Y			N	2	20
Trident Technical College	Charleston	C,T	St-L	M/W	16,139	55												
University of South Carolina Salkehatchie	Allendale	C,T	St	M/W	1,076													
University of South Carolina Union	Union	C,B	St	M/W	757		33		N	Y	Y	Y	Y			N	2	5
Williamsburg Technical College	Kingstree	C,T	St	M/W	693		28		Y	Y	Y	Y	Y			N		5
South Dakota																		
Lake Area Technical Institute	Watertown	T	St	M/W	1,846	16	16		Y	Y	Y	Y	Y	Y	Y	N	6	26
Mitchell Technical Institute	Mitchell	T	St	M/W	1,262	32	27		Y	Y	Y	Y	Y	Y	Y	Y	6	28
Sisseton-Wahpeton College	Sisseton	C,T	Fed	M/W	165	39												
Southeast Technical Institute	Sioux Falls	T	St	M/W	2,047	36	29		N	Y	Y	Y	Y	Y	Y	Y	3	54
Western Dakota Technical Institute	Rapid City	T	St	M/W	876	22												
Tennessee																		
Cleveland State Community College	Cleveland	C,T	St	M/W	3,522	49	28	60	Y	Y	Y	Y	Y	Y	Y	N	8	13
Dyersburg State Community College	Dyersburg	C,T	St	M/W	2,857	57	32				Y	Y	Y	Y	Y		8	20
Fountainhead College of Technology	Knoxville	C,T,B	Prop	M/W	180													
Jackson State Community College	Jackson	C,T	St	M/W	4,926													
John A. Gupton College	Nashville	C,T	Ind	M/W	120	42	51		N	Y	Y		Y		Y	Y		1
Motlow State Community College	Tullahoma	C,T	St	M/W	3,901	50												
Nashville State Community College	Nashville	C,T	St	M/W	10,192		55		Y	Y	Y	Y	Y	Y	Y	N		66
Roane State Community College	Harriman	C,T	St	M/W	5,832	60												
Southwest Tennessee Community College	Memphis	C,T	St	M/W	10,167	59	37	0	Y	Y	Y	Y	Y	Y	Y	N	3	31
Volunteer State Community College	Gallatin	C,T	St	M/W	8,068	47	27		Y	Y	Y	Y	Y	Y	Y	N	20	20
Walters State Community College	Morristown	C,T	St	M/W	5,947	46	18		Y	Y	Y	Y	Y	Y	Y	N	5	20
Texas																		
Alvin Community College	Alvin	C,T	St-L	M/W	5,116		0				S	Y	Y	Y	Y	N	2	55
Amarillo College	Amarillo	C,T	St-L	M/W			36		Y		Y	Y	Y	Y	Y	N	5	83
Austin Community College District	Austin	C,T	St-L	M/W	41,574		41		Y	Y	Y	Y	Y	Y	Y	N	3	93
Blinn College	Brenham	C,T	St-L	M/W	19,780	48	14		Y	Y	Y	Y	Y	Y	Y	Y	10	34
Brookhaven College	Farmers Branch	C,T	Cou	M/W	12,509	83	46		Y			Y	Y	Y	Y	N	5	27
Cedar Valley College	Lancaster	C,T	St	M/W	6,953	78												
Central Texas College	Killeen	C,T	St-L	M/W	19,562	78			Y	Y	Y	Y	Y	Y	Y	Y	5	49
Coastal Bend College	Beeville	C,T	Cou	M/W	3,776	64												
Collin County Community College District	McKinney	C,T	St-L	M/W	28,187	67	30		Y	S	Y	Y	Y	Y	Y	N	2	49
Dallas Institute of Funeral Service	Dallas	C,T	Ind	M/W	141		52		Y	Y	Y					N		1
El Centro College	Dallas	C,T	Cou	M/W	10,101	77												
Galveston College	Galveston	C,T	St-L	M/W	2,071	76	37		Y	Y	S	Y	Y	Y	Y	Y	4	32
Houston Community College	Houston	C,T	St-L	M/W	56,522	70	48		Y	Y	S	Y	Y	Y	Y	N		77
Interactive College of Technology	Houston	T	Prop	M/W									Y					
Interactive College of Technology	Houston	T	Prop	M/W							Y							
Interactive College of Technology	Pasadena	T	Prop	M/W									Y					
KD Conservatory College of Film and Dramatic Arts	Dallas	C,T	Prop	M/W	236													
Kilgore College	Kilgore	C,T	St-L	M/W	5,666	60	28		Y	Y	Y	Y	Y	Y	Y	Y	8	60
Lone Star College-CyFair	Cypress	C,T	St-L	M/W	20,510	71	26		Y	Y		Y	Y	Y		N		30
Lone Star College-Kingwood	Kingwood	C,T	St-L	M/W	12,764	70	31		Y	Y		Y	Y	Y		N		17

This chart includes the names and locations of accredited two-year colleges in the United States, Canada, and other countries and shows institutions' responses to the *Peterson's Annual Survey of Undergraduate Institutions*. If an institution submitted incomplete data, one or more columns opposite the institution's name is blank. A dagger after the school name indicates that the institution has one or more entries in the *Featured Two-Year Colleges* section. If a school does not appear, it did not report any of the information.

Y—Yes; N—No; R—Recommended; S—For Some

Column legend (angled headers):
- Degrees Awarded: College Transfer Associate (C), Terminal Associate (T), Bachelor's (B), Master's (M), Doctoral (D)
- Institutional Control: County District City, Federal, State and Local, State-Related, Independent, Independent-Religious, Proprietary, Commonwealth, Territory
- Student Body: Men, Primarily Men, Women, Primarily Women, Coed

Name	City	Degrees	Control	Student Body	Undergrad Enroll	% Part-Time	% 25+	% Grads→4-Yr	Open Admissions	HS Equiv. Cert. Accepted	HS Transcript Required	Need-Based Aid	Part-Time Jobs	Career Counseling	Job Placement	College Housing	Majors	Sports
Lone Star College-Montgomery	Conroe	C,T	St-L	M/W	13,826	70	31			Y	Y		Y	Y	Y	N		14
Lone Star College-North Harris	Houston	C,T	St-L	M/W	17,001	72	39			Y	Y		Y	Y	Y	Y	15	22
Lone Star College-Tomball	Tomball	C,T	St-L	M/W	8,880	71	34			Y	Y		Y	Y	Y	N		15
Lone Star College-University Park	Houston	C,T	St-L	M/W	10,951	71	29				R		Y	Y	Y	N		4
Navarro College	Corsicana	C,T	St-L	M/W	9,478	62	22			Y	Y	Y	Y	Y	Y	Y	7	46
North Central Texas College	Gainesville	C,T	St-L	M/W	9,618	68	24	2	Y	Y	Y	Y	Y	Y		Y	15	42
Northwest Vista College	San Antonio	C,T	St-L	M/W	13,218	68	72		Y	Y	Y	Y		Y		N	4	19
Odessa College	Odessa	C,T	St-L	M/W	5,096	68	25			Y	Y			Y	Y	Y	11	55
Palo Alto College	San Antonio	C,T	St-L	M/W	8,376	82												
Panola College	Carthage	C,T	St-L	M/W	2,675	50	32				R,S	Y	Y	Y	Y	Y	7	48
Paris Junior College	Paris	C,T	St-L	M/W	4,999	59	23			Y	Y	Y	Y	Y	Y	Y	10	62
St. Philip's College	San Antonio	C,T	Dist	M/W	10,514	85	40		Y	Y	Y	Y		Y	Y	N	5	68
San Jacinto College District	Pasadena	C,T	St-L	M/W	28,326	77	29	44	Y	Y	Y			Y	Y	N	11	80
Southwest Texas Junior College	Uvalde	C,T	St-L	M/W				19	Y	Y	Y	Y	Y	Y	Y		8	14
Tarrant County College District	Fort Worth	C,T	Cou	M/W	50,595	69	36					Y	Y	Y	Y	N	6	42
Temple College	Temple	C,T	Dist	M/W	5,200	66												
Texarkana College	Texarkana	C,T	St-L	M/W	4,165					Y	Y	Y	Y	Y	Y	Y	6	41
Texas State Technical College	Waco	C,T	St	M/W	10,689	56	29	10	Y	Y	Y	Y	Y	Y	Y	Y	7	38
Trinity Valley Community College	Athens	C,T	St-L	M/W	5,172	48												
Tyler Junior College	Tyler	C,T	St-L	M/W	10,934	45	25			Y	Y		Y	Y	Y	Y	11	87
Vet Tech Institute of Houston	Houston	T	Prop	M/W	216											N		1
Victoria College	Victoria	C,T	Cou	M/W	4,051	72	34			Y	Y	Y	Y	Y	Y	N	4	14
Weatherford College	Weatherford	C,T	St-L	M/W	4,528	23				Y	Y	S	Y	Y	Y	Y	5	18
Western Texas College	Snyder	C,T	St-L	M/W	2,125	74	11	31	Y	Y	Y	Y	Y	Y	Y	Y	12	37
Utah																		
AmeriTech College	Draper		Prop	M/W														
LDS Business College	Salt Lake City	C,T	I-R	M/W	2,191	27	21			Y	Y	Y	Y	Y	Y	N		41
Nightingale College	Ogden	B	Prop	M/W						Y	Y	Y		Y				
Salt Lake Community College	Salt Lake City	C,T	St	M/W	28,814	73	36		Y				Y	Y	Y	N	6	69
Vermont																		
Landmark College	Putney	T,B	Ind	M/W	514	4												
New England Culinary Institute	Montpelier	C,B	Prop	M/W	422		32		N	Y	Y	Y	Y	Y	Y	Y		3
Virginia																		
Central Virginia Community College	Lynchburg	C,T	St	M/W	4,433	21			Y	Y			Y	Y	Y	N		19
Dabney S. Lancaster Community College	Clifton Forge	C,T	St	M/W		29					R	Y	Y			N	2	17
John Tyler Community College	Chester	C,T	St	M/W	10,035	75	35			Y	R	R	Y	Y	Y	N	3	18
J. Sargeant Reynolds Community College	Richmond	C,T	St	M/W	10,887	72	40	3	Y	Y	Y	Y	Y	Y	Y	N		38
New River Community College	Dublin	C,T	St	M/W	4,345	54	40		Y		S	Y	Y	Y	Y	N	4	29
Northern Virginia Community College	Annandale	C,T	St	M/W	76,868													
Piedmont Virginia Community College	Charlottesville	C,T	St	M/W	5,554	78												
Rappahannock Community College	Glenns	C,T	St-L	M/W	3,566					Y			Y	Y			1	11
Southwest Virginia Community College	Richlands	C,T	St	M/W	2,546	53	26		Y	Y	Y		Y	Y		N		12
Tidewater Community College	Norfolk	C,T	St	M/W	25,927	50			Y				Y	Y	Y	N	5	26
Virginia Western Community College	Roanoke	C,T	St	M/W	8,632	71	32		Y	Y	R,S	Y	Y			N	3	25
Wytheville Community College	Wytheville	C,T	St	M/W	2,915	28			Y			Y	Y	Y		N	1	21
Washington																		
Bellingham Technical College	Bellingham	C,T	St	M/W	2,864	61			Y			S	Y	Y	Y	N		25
Big Bend Community College	Moses Lake	C,T	St	M/W	2,016	28	28		Y			S	S	Y	Y	Y	4	17
Carrington College-Spokane	Spokane	T	Prop	M/W	413	51				Y	Y	Y				N		3
Cascadia College	Bothell	C,T,B	St	M/W	2,759				Y							N	3	4
Clark College	Vancouver	C,T	St	M/W	10,477	52	34							Y	Y	N	8	37
Lower Columbia College	Longview	C,T	St	M/W	3,152	48												
Northwest School of Wooden Boatbuilding	Port Hadlock	T	Ind	M/W														
Olympic College	Bremerton	C,T,B	St	M/W	7,881	47			Y			S	Y	Y	Y	Y	8	27
Renton Technical College	Renton	C,T,B	St	M/W	3,359	63						S	S	Y	Y	N		30
Wenatchee Valley College	Wenatchee	C,T	St-L	M/W	3,218	27				Y		S	Y	Y	Y	Y	10	39
Whatcom Community College	Bellingham	C,T	St	M/W	6,233													
West Virginia																		
Blue Ridge Community and Technical College	Martinsburg	C,T	St	M/W	5,552	80	49		Y	Y	Y			Y	Y	N		25
Mountain State College	Parkersburg	T	Prop	M/W	176	1	55					Y	Y	Y	Y	N		7
Potomac State College of West Virginia University	Keyser	C,T,B	St	M/W	1,475	22	11		Y	Y	Y	Y	Y	Y	Y	Y	10	54
West Virginia Junior College-Bridgeport	Bridgeport	C,T	Prop	M/W	389													
Wisconsin																		
Blackhawk Technical College	Janesville	C,T	Dist	M/W	2,249	58	54	0	Y	Y	Y	Y	Y	Y	Y	N		20
Chippewa Valley Technical College	Eau Claire	C,T	Dist	M/W	6,017	66				Y	S	Y	Y	Y	Y	N		31
Fox Valley Technical College	Appleton	T	St-L	M/W	10,894	77	45		Y	Y	Y	Y	Y	Y	Y	N	2	55
Gateway Technical College	Kenosha	T	St-L	M/W	8,740	83				Y	Y	Y	Y	Y		N		38
Moraine Park Technical College	Fond du Lac	C,T	Dist	M/W	6,613													
Northcentral Technical College	Wausau	C,T	Dist	M/W	4,513	67	50		Y	Y	Y	Y	Y	Y	Y	Y		36
University of Wisconsin-Fond du Lac	Fond du Lac	C	St	M/W	626													
University of Wisconsin-Fox Valley	Menasha	C,T	St	M/W	1,797	42												
University of Wisconsin-Sheboygan	Sheboygan	C	St	M/W	769	60												
University of Wisconsin-Waukesha	Waukesha	C,B	St	M/W	2,239	52												
Waukesha County Technical College	Pewaukee	T	St-L	M/W	7,928	79	54			Y		Y	Y	Y	Y	N		40
Wisconsin Indianhead Technical College	Shell Lake	T	Dist	M/W	2,894	61	55			Y						N		25

This chart includes the names and locations of accredited two-year colleges in the United States, Canada, and other countries and shows institutions' responses to the *Peterson's Annual Survey of Undergraduate Institutions*. If an institution submitted incomplete data, one or more columns opposite the institution's name is blank. A dagger after the school name indicates that the institution has one or more entries in the *Featured Two-Year Colleges* section. If a school does not appear, it did not report any of the information.

Y—Yes; N—No; R—Recommended; S—For Some

		Degrees Awarded	Institutional Control	Student Body	Undergraduate Enrollment	Percent Attending Part-Time	Percent 25 Years of Age or Older	Percent of Grads Going on to Four-Year Colleges	Open Admissions	High School Equivalency Certificate Accepted	High School Transcript Required	Need-Based Aid Available	Part-Time Jobs Available	Career Counseling Available	Job Placement Services Available	College Housing Available	Number of Sports Offered	Number of Majors Offered
Wyoming																		
Casper College	Casper	C,T	St-L	M/W	3,680	53	33		Y	Y		Y	Y	Y	Y	Y	Y	10	100
Central Wyoming College	Riverton	C,T	St-L	M/W	2,186	67	34	48	Y			R	Y	Y	Y	Y	Y	17	54
Eastern Wyoming College	Torrington	C,T	St-L	M/W	1,715	67						R	Y	Y	Y	Y		4	42
Laramie County Community College	Cheyenne	C,T	Dist	M/W	4,148	57	40		Y	Y		S	Y	Y	Y			11	62
Northwest College	Powell	C,T	St-L	M/W	1,697	42	23		Y	Y		Y	Y	Y	Y		Y	10	61
Sheridan College	Sheridan	C,T	St-L	M/W	4,307	68	32		Y			R,S	Y	Y	Y		Y	10	43
Western Wyoming Community College	Rock Springs	C,T	St-L	M/W	3,293	65	6		Y	Y		R	Y	Y	Y	Y	Y	5	84
OTHER COUNTRIES																		
Mexico																		
Westhill University	Sante Fe	T,B,M	Ind	M/W	1,206														
Palau																		
Palau Community College	Koror	C,T	Terr	M/W	627	45			Y	Y		Y	Y	Y	Y	Y	Y	7	14

Profiles
of Two-Year
Colleges

ALABAMA

Alabama Southern Community College
Monroeville, Alabama

Freshman Application Contact Alabama Southern Community College, PO Box 2000, Monroeville, AL 36461. *Phone:* 251-575-3156 Ext. 8252. *Website:* http://www.ascc.edu/.

Bevill State Community College
Jasper, Alabama

- **State-supported** 2-year, founded 1969, part of Alabama Community College System
- **Rural** 245-acre campus with easy access to Birmingham
- **Endowment** $148,610
- **Coed,** 3,609 undergraduate students, 51% full-time, 62% women, 38% men

Undergraduates 1,838 full-time, 1,771 part-time. 15% Black or African American, non-Hispanic/Latino; 1% Hispanic/Latino; 0.4% Asian, non-Hispanic/Latino; 0.2% American Indian or Alaska Native, non-Hispanic/Latino; 0.9% Two or more races, non-Hispanic/Latino; 1% Race/ethnicity unknown. *Retention:* 56% of full-time freshmen returned.
Freshmen *Admission:* 937 enrolled.
Faculty *Total:* 286, 41% full-time, 12% with terminal degrees. *Student/faculty ratio:* 17:1.
Majors Administrative assistant and secretarial science; child-care and support services management; computer and information sciences; drafting and design technology; electrician; emergency medical technology (EMT paramedic); general studies; heating, ventilation, air conditioning and refrigeration engineering technology; industrial electronics technology; legal assistant/paralegal; liberal arts and sciences/liberal studies; registered nursing/registered nurse; tool and die technology.
Academics *Calendar:* semesters. *Degree:* certificates and associate. *Special study options:* academic remediation for entering students, adult/continuing education programs, advanced placement credit, cooperative education, distance learning, honors programs, off-campus study, part-time degree program, services for LD students, summer session for credit.
Library *Books:* 113,246 (physical); *Serial titles:* 3,563 (physical); *Databases:* 15.
Student Life *Housing Options:* coed. Campus housing is university owned. *Activities and Organizations:* drama/theater group, choral group, Student Government Association, Campus Ministries, Circle K, Outdoorsmen Club, Students Against Destructive Decisions. *Campus security:* 24-hour emergency response devices.
Costs (2015–16) *Tuition:* state resident $2760 full-time, $115 per credit hour part-time; nonresident $5520 full-time, $230 per credit hour part-time. Full-time tuition and fees vary according to course load and program. Part-time tuition and fees vary according to course load and program. *Required fees:* $711 full-time. *Room and board:* $1850. Room and board charges vary according to board plan and location. *Payment plan:* installment. *Waivers:* employees or children of employees.
Financial Aid Of all full-time matriculated undergraduates who enrolled in 2014, 88 Federal Work-Study jobs (averaging $1807).
Applying *Options:* electronic application, early admission, deferred entrance. *Required:* high school transcript. *Application deadlines:* rolling (freshmen), rolling (transfers).
Freshman Application Contact Bevill State Community College, 1411 Indiana Avenue, Jasper, AL 35501. *Phone:* 205-387-0511 Ext. 5813. *Website:* http://www.bscc.edu/.

Bishop State Community College
Mobile, Alabama

Freshman Application Contact Bishop State Community College, 351 North Broad Street, Mobile, AL 36603-5898. *Phone:* 251-405-7000. *Toll-free phone:* 800-523-7235.
Website: http://www.bishop.edu/.

Calhoun Community College
Decatur, Alabama

Freshman Application Contact Admissions Office, Calhoun Community College, PO Box 2216, Decatur, AL 35609-2216. *Phone:* 256-306-2593.

Toll-free phone: 800-626-3628. *Fax:* 256-306-2941. *E-mail:* admissions@calhoun.edu.
Website: http://www.calhoun.edu/.

Central Alabama Community College
Alexander City, Alabama

Freshman Application Contact Ms. Donna Whaley, Central Alabama Community College, 1675 Cherokee Road, Alexander City, AL 35011-0699. *Phone:* 256-234-6346 Ext. 6232. *Toll-free phone:* 800-634-2657. *Website:* http://www.cacc.edu/.

Chattahoochee Valley Community College
Phenix City, Alabama

Freshman Application Contact Chattahoochee Valley Community College, 2602 College Drive, Phenix City, AL 36869-7928. *Phone:* 334-291-4929. *Website:* http://www.cv.edu/.

Community College of the Air Force
Maxwell Gunter Air Force Base, Alabama

- **Federally supported** 2-year, founded 1972, part of Air University
- **Suburban** campus
- **Coed,** 286,450 undergraduate students, 100% full-time, 19% women, 81% men

Undergraduates 286,450 full-time.
Freshmen *Admission:* 15,726 applied, 15,726 admitted, 15,726 enrolled.
Faculty *Total:* 6,144, 100% full-time.
Majors Aeronautics/aviation/aerospace science and technology; airframe mechanics and aircraft maintenance technology; air traffic control; apparel and textile marketing management; atmospheric sciences and meteorology; automobile/automotive mechanics technology; avionics maintenance technology; biomedical technology; cardiovascular technology; clinical/medical laboratory technology; commercial and advertising art; communications technology; construction engineering technology; criminal justice/law enforcement administration; dental assisting; dental laboratory technology; dietetics; educational/instructional technology; educational leadership and administration; electrical, electronic and communications engineering technology; environmental health; environmental studies; finance; fire science/firefighting; health/health-care administration; hematology technology; hotel/motel administration; human resources management; industrial technology; legal assistant/paralegal; logistics, materials, and supply chain management; management information systems; medical radiologic technology; mental health counseling; metallurgical technology; music performance; nuclear medical technology; occupational safety and health technology; office management; ophthalmic laboratory technology; parks, recreation and leisure; pharmacy technician; physical therapy technology; physiology; public relations/image management; purchasing, procurement/acquisitions and contracts management; security and loss prevention; social work; surgical technology.
Academics *Calendar:* continuous. *Degrees:* certificates and associate (courses conducted at 125 branch locations worldwide for members of the U.S. Air Force). *Special study options:* academic remediation for entering students, adult/continuing education programs, advanced placement credit, distance learning, independent study, internships, off-campus study.
Library Air Force Library Service.
Student Life *Housing:* college housing not available. *Campus security:* 24-hour emergency response devices and patrols. *Student services:* health clinic, personal/psychological counseling, legal services.
Athletics *Intramural sports:* badminton W, basketball M/W, bowling M/W, cross-country running M/W, football M, golf M/W, racquetball M/W, softball M/W, table tennis M/W, tennis M/W, volleyball M/W, weight lifting M/W.
Standardized Tests *Required:* Armed Services Vocational Aptitude Battery (ASVAB) (for admission).
Applying *Options:* electronic application. *Required:* high school transcript, interview, military physical, good character, criminal background check. *Application deadlines:* rolling (freshmen), rolling (transfers). *Notification:* continuous (freshmen), continuous (transfers).
Freshman Application Contact Ms. Gwendolyn Ford, Chief of Admissions Flight, Community College of the Air Force, Community College of the Air Force, 100 South Turner Boulevard, Maxwell Air Force Base, Maxwell -

Gunter AFB, AL 36114-3011. *Phone:* 334-649-5081. *Fax:* 334-649-5015. *E-mail:* gwendolyn.ford@us.af.mil. *Website:* http://www.au.af.mil/au/ccaf/.

Enterprise State Community College
Enterprise, Alabama

Director of Admissions Mr. Gary Deas, Associate Dean of Students/Registrar, Enterprise State Community College, PO Box 1300, Enterprise, AL 36331-1300. *Phone:* 334-347-2623 Ext. 2233. *E-mail:* gdeas@eocc.edu. *Website:* http://www.escc.edu/.

Fortis College
Mobile, Alabama

Admissions Office Contact Fortis College, 7033 Airport Boulevard, Mobile, AL 36608. *Toll-free phone:* 855-4-FORTIS. *Website:* http://www.fortis.edu/.

Fortis College
Montgomery, Alabama

Admissions Office Contact Fortis College, 3470 Eastdale Circle, Montgomery, AL 36117. *Toll-free phone:* 855-4-FORTIS. *Website:* http://www.fortis.edu/.

Fortis College
Montgomery, Alabama

Admissions Office Contact Fortis College, 3736 Atlanta Highway, Montgomery, AL 36109. *Toll-free phone:* 855-4-FORTIS. *Website:* http://www.fortis.edu/.

Fortis Institute
Birmingham, Alabama

Admissions Office Contact Fortis Institute, 100 London Parkway, Suite 150, Birmingham, AL 35211. *Toll-free phone:* 855-4-FORTIS. *Website:* http://www.fortis.edu/.

Gadsden State Community College
Gadsden, Alabama

- **State-supported** 2-year, founded 1965, part of Alabama Community College System
- **Small-town** 275-acre campus with easy access to Birmingham
- **Coed,** 5,018 undergraduate students, 51% full-time, 60% women, 40% men

Undergraduates 2,576 full-time, 2,442 part-time. Students come from 8 states and territories; 45 other countries; 19% Black or African American, non-Hispanic/Latino; 3% Hispanic/Latino; 0.5% Asian, non-Hispanic/Latino; 0.1% Native Hawaiian or other Pacific Islander, non-Hispanic/Latino; 1% American Indian or Alaska Native, non-Hispanic/Latino; 3% Two or more races, non-Hispanic/Latino; 0.9% Race/ethnicity unknown; 2% international; 6% transferred in; 2% live on campus.

Freshmen *Admission:* 1,190 enrolled.

Faculty *Total:* 303, 49% full-time. *Student/faculty ratio:* 17:1.

Majors Accounting technology and bookkeeping; administrative assistant and secretarial science; child-care and support services management; civil engineering technology; clinical/medical laboratory technology; communication and journalism related; computer and information sciences; court reporting; criminal justice/police science; drafting and design technology; electrical, electronic and communications engineering technology; emergency medical technology (EMT paramedic); general studies; heating, ventilation, air conditioning and refrigeration engineering technology; industrial mechanics and maintenance technology; legal assistant/paralegal; liberal arts and sciences/liberal studies; manufacturing engineering technology; radiologic technology/science; registered nursing/registered nurse; sales, distribution, and marketing operations; substance abuse/addiction counseling; tool and die technology.

Academics *Calendar:* semesters. *Degree:* certificates and associate. *Special study options:* academic remediation for entering students, adult/continuing education programs, advanced placement credit, cooperative education, distance learning, English as a second language, external degree program, honors programs, internships, part-time degree program, services for LD students, study abroad, summer session for credit. *ROTC:* Army (b).

Library Meadows Library plus 2 others. *Books:* 79,933 (physical), 62,846 (digital/electronic); *Databases:* 75.

Student Life *Housing Options:* coed. Campus housing is university owned. *Activities and Organizations:* drama/theater group, choral group, National Society of Leadership and Success, Student Government Association, Circle K, International Club, Cardinal Spirit Club. *Campus security:* 24-hour patrols. *Student services:* personal/psychological counseling.

Athletics Member NJCAA. *Intercollegiate sports:* basketball M(s)/W(s), softball W(s), tennis M(s), volleyball W(s).

Costs (2015–16) *Tuition:* state resident $2760 full-time, $115 per credit hour part-time; nonresident $5520 full-time, $230 per credit hour part-time. Full-time tuition and fees vary according to reciprocity agreements. Part-time tuition and fees vary according to reciprocity agreements. *Required fees:* $456 full-time, $19 per credit hour part-time. *Room and board:* $3600. *Waivers:* minority students, adult students, senior citizens, and employees or children of employees.

Applying *Options:* electronic application, early admission, deferred entrance. *Required:* high school transcript. *Application deadlines:* rolling (freshmen), rolling (transfers).

Freshman Application Contact Mrs. Jennie Dobson, Admissions and Records, Gadsden State Community College, PO Box 227, 1001 George Wallace Drive, Gadsden, AL 35902-0227. *Phone:* 256-549-8210. *Toll-free phone:* 800-226-5563. *Fax:* 256-549-8205. *E-mail:* info@gadsdenstate.edu. *Website:* http://www.gadsdenstate.edu/.

George Corley Wallace State Community College
Selma, Alabama

Director of Admissions Ms. Sunette Newman, Registrar, George Corley Wallace State Community College, PO Box 2530, Selma, AL 36702. *Phone:* 334-876-9305. *Website:* http://www.wccs.edu/.

George C. Wallace Community College
Dothan, Alabama

- **State-supported** 2-year, founded 1949, part of The Alabama Community College System
- **Rural** 258-acre campus
- **Coed,** 4,769 undergraduate students, 45% full-time, 65% women, 35% men

Undergraduates 2,161 full-time, 2,608 part-time. Students come from 12 states and territories; 4% are from out of state; 29% Black or African American, non-Hispanic/Latino; 2% Hispanic/Latino; 0.7% Asian, non-Hispanic/Latino; 0.1% Native Hawaiian or other Pacific Islander, non-Hispanic/Latino; 0.6% American Indian or Alaska Native, non-Hispanic/Latino; 1% Two or more races, non-Hispanic/Latino; 0.1% Race/ethnicity unknown; 47% transferred in.

Freshmen *Admission:* 747 applied, 747 admitted.

Faculty *Total:* 229, 57% full-time. *Student/faculty ratio:* 19:1.

Majors Accounting; administrative assistant and secretarial science; autobody/collision and repair technology; automobile/automotive mechanics technology; business administration and management; cabinetmaking and millwork; carpentry; clinical/medical laboratory technology; computer and information sciences; computer science; criminal justice/police science; drafting and design technology; electrical, electronic and communications engineering technology; electrician; emergency medical technology (EMT paramedic); heating, air conditioning, ventilation and refrigeration maintenance technology; heating, ventilation, air conditioning and refrigeration engineering technology; industrial mechanics and maintenance technology; licensed practical/vocational nurse training; machine tool technology; medical/clinical assistant; medical radiologic technology; physical therapy technology; radiologic technology/science; registered nursing/registered nurse; respiratory care therapy; tool and die technology; welding technology.

Academics *Calendar:* semesters. *Degree:* certificates, diplomas, and associate. *Special study options:* academic remediation for entering students, adult/continuing education programs, advanced placement credit, cooperative education, distance learning, English as a second language, independent study, off-campus study, part-time degree program.

Library Learning Resources Centers.

Student Life *Housing:* college housing not available. *Activities and Organizations:* drama/theater group, student-run newspaper. *Campus security:* 24-hour patrols. *Student services:* personal/psychological counseling.

Athletics Member NJCAA. *Intercollegiate sports:* baseball M(s), softball W(s).

Standardized Tests *Recommended:* SAT or ACT (for admission).

Costs (2016–17) *Tuition:* state resident $3450 full-time, $115 per credit hour part-time; nonresident $6900 full-time, $230 per credit hour part-time. Full-time tuition and fees vary according to reciprocity agreements. Part-time tuition and fees vary according to reciprocity agreements. *Required fees:* $810 full-time, $27 per credit hour part-time. *Waivers:* senior citizens and employees or children of employees.
Financial Aid Of all full-time matriculated undergraduates who enrolled in 2014, 82 Federal Work-Study jobs (averaging $1975).
Applying *Options:* early admission. *Required:* high school transcript. *Application deadlines:* rolling (freshmen), rolling (transfers).
Freshman Application Contact Mr. Keith Saulsberry, Director, Enrollment Services/Registrar, George C. Wallace Community College, 1141 Wallace Drive, Dothan, AL 36303. *Phone:* 334-983-3521 Ext. 2470. *Toll-free phone:* 800-543-2426. *Fax:* 334-983-3600. *E-mail:* ksaulsberry@wallace.edu. *Website:* http://www.wallace.edu/.

H. Councill Trenholm State Community College
Montgomery, Alabama

- **State-supported** 2-year, founded 1962, part of Alabama Community College System
- **Urban** 83-acre campus with easy access to Montgomery
- **Coed,** 1,401 undergraduate students

Undergraduates Students come from 2 states and territories; 61% Black or African American, non-Hispanic/Latino; 0.6% Hispanic/Latino; 1% Asian, non-Hispanic/Latino; 0.1% Native Hawaiian or other Pacific Islander, non-Hispanic/Latino; 0.2% American Indian or Alaska Native, non-Hispanic/Latino; 0.1% Two or more races, non-Hispanic/Latino; 0.1% Race/ethnicity unknown. *Retention:* 53% of full-time freshmen returned.
Freshmen *Admission:* 1,173 applied, 338 admitted.
Faculty *Total:* 97, 55% full-time, 18% with terminal degrees. *Student/faculty ratio:* 15:1.
Majors Accounting technology and bookkeeping; administrative assistant and secretarial science; automotive engineering technology; child-care and support services management; computer and information sciences; culinary arts; dental assisting; diagnostic medical sonography and ultrasound technology; drafting and design technology; electrician; emergency medical technology (EMT paramedic); graphic communications related; heating, ventilation, air conditioning and refrigeration engineering technology; industrial mechanics and maintenance technology; machine tool technology; manufacturing engineering technology; medical/clinical assistant; radiologic technology/science.
Academics *Calendar:* semesters. *Degree:* certificates, diplomas, and associate. *Special study options:* academic remediation for entering students, adult/continuing education programs, advanced placement credit, cooperative education, distance learning, external degree program, independent study, internships, part-time degree program, services for LD students, summer session for credit.
Library Trenholm State Learning Resources plus 2 others. *Books:* 9,761 (physical), 36,949 (digital/electronic); *Serial titles:* 75 (physical), 58 (digital/electronic); *Databases:* 18. Weekly public service hours: 103.
Student Life *Activities and Organizations:* Student Government Association, College Ambassadors, National Society of Leadership and Science, SkillsUSA–VICA. *Campus security:* 24-hour patrols. *Student services:* personal/psychological counseling.
Standardized Tests *Required for some:* ACT (for admission).
Costs (2016–17) *Tuition:* state resident $3432 full-time, $117 per credit hour part-time; nonresident $6240 full-time, $234 per credit hour part-time. *Required fees:* $780 full-time, $26 per credit hour part-time. *Payment plan:* installment. *Waivers:* senior citizens and employees or children of employees.
Applying *Options:* electronic application, early admission. *Required:* high school transcript. *Application deadlines:* rolling (freshmen), rolling (out-of-state freshmen), rolling (transfers).
Freshman Application Contact Mrs. Tennie McBryde, Registrar, H. Councill Trenholm State Community College, Montgomery, AL 36108. *Phone:* 334-420-4306. *Toll-free phone:* 866-753-4544. *Fax:* 334-420-4201. *E-mail:* tmcbryde@trenholmstate.edu. *Website:* http://www.trenholmstate.edu/.

ITT Technical Institute
Bessemer, Alabama

Freshman Application Contact Director of Recruitment, ITT Technical Institute, 6270 Park South Drive, Bessemer, AL 35022. *Phone:* 205-497-5700. *Toll-free phone:* 800-488-7033. *Website:* http://www.itt-tech.edu/.

ITT Technical Institute
Madison, Alabama

Freshman Application Contact Director of Recruitment, ITT Technical Institute, 9238 Madison Boulevard, Suite 500, Madison, AL 35758. *Phone:* 256-542-2900. *Toll-free phone:* 877-210-4900. *Website:* http://www.itt-tech.edu/.

ITT Technical Institute
Mobile, Alabama

Freshman Application Contact Director of Recruitment, ITT Technical Institute, Office Mall South, 3100 Cottage Hill Road, Building 3, Mobile, AL 36606. *Phone:* 251-472-4760. *Toll-free phone:* 877-327-1013. *Website:* http://www.itt-tech.edu/.

James H. Faulkner State Community College
Bay Minette, Alabama

- **State-supported** 2-year, founded 1965, part of Alabama Community College System
- **Small-town** 105-acre campus
- **Coed,** 3,323 undergraduate students, 64% full-time, 63% women, 37% men

Undergraduates 2,139 full-time, 1,184 part-time. 3% are from out of state; 9% live on campus.
Freshmen *Admission:* 988 enrolled.
Faculty *Total:* 227, 38% full-time, 2% with terminal degrees. *Student/faculty ratio:* 15:1.
Majors Administrative assistant and secretarial science; agricultural economics; business administration and management; commercial and advertising art; computer and information sciences; criminal justice/law enforcement administration; dental assisting; environmental engineering technology; general studies; hospitality administration; landscaping and groundskeeping; legal assistant/paralegal; liberal arts and sciences/liberal studies; licensed practical/vocational nurse training; mass communication/media; parks, recreation and leisure facilities management; registered nursing/registered nurse; surgical technology.
Academics *Calendar:* semesters. *Degree:* certificates and associate. *Special study options:* academic remediation for entering students, adult/continuing education programs, advanced placement credit, cooperative education, honors programs, internships, part-time degree program, services for LD students.
Library Austin R. Meadows Library plus 3 others. *Books:* 66,811 (physical); *Serial titles:* 2,924 (physical); *Databases:* 67. Weekly public service hours: 40.
Student Life *Housing Options:* men-only, women-only. Campus housing is university owned. *Activities and Organizations:* drama/theater group, student-run newspaper, choral group, Student Government Association, Pow-Wow Leadership Society, Phi Theta Kappa, Association of Computational Machinery, Phi Beta Lambda, national fraternities. *Campus security:* 24-hour emergency response devices and patrols, controlled dormitory access. *Student services:* personal/psychological counseling.
Athletics Member NJCAA. *Intercollegiate sports:* baseball M(s), basketball M(s)/W(s), golf M(s), softball W(s), tennis M(s)/W(s), volleyball W(s). *Intramural sports:* basketball M, tennis M/W, volleyball M/W.
Costs (2016–17) *Tuition:* state resident $4320 full-time, $115 per hour part-time; nonresident $7770 full-time, $230 per hour part-time. Full-time tuition and fees vary according to course level, course load, program, and student level. Part-time tuition and fees vary according to course level, course load, program, and student level. *Required fees:* $850 full-time, $29 per hour part-time, $29 per hour part-time. *Room and board:* $5800. Room and board charges vary according to board plan and housing facility. *Waivers:* employees or children of employees.
Applying *Options:* early admission, deferred entrance. *Required:* high school transcript. *Application deadlines:* rolling (freshmen), rolling (transfers). *Notification:* continuous until 8/18 (freshmen), continuous until 8/18 (transfers).
Freshman Application Contact Ms. Carmelita Mikkelsen, Director of Admissions and High School Relations, James H. Faulkner State Community College, 1900 Highway 31 South, Bay Minette, AL 36507. *Phone:* 251-580-2213. *Toll-free phone:* 800-231-3752. *Fax:* 251-580-2285. *E-mail:* cmikkelsen@faulknerstate.edu. *Website:* http://www.faulknerstate.edu/.

Jefferson Davis Community College
Brewton, Alabama

Director of Admissions Ms. Robin Sessions, Registrar, Jefferson Davis Community College, PO Box 958, Brewton, AL 36427-0958. *Phone:* 251-867-4832.
Website: http://www.jdcc.edu/.

Jefferson State Community College
Birmingham, Alabama

- **State-supported** 2-year, founded 1965, part of Alabama Community College System
- **Suburban** 351-acre campus with easy access to Birmingham
- **Endowment** $1.2 million
- **Coed,** 8,826 undergraduate students, 32% full-time, 61% women, 39% men

Undergraduates 2,842 full-time, 5,984 part-time. Students come from 28 states and territories; 56 other countries; 2% are from out of state; 22% Black or African American, non-Hispanic/Latino; 4% Hispanic/Latino; 2% Asian, non-Hispanic/Latino; 0.1% Native Hawaiian or other Pacific Islander, non-Hispanic/Latino; 0.3% American Indian or Alaska Native, non-Hispanic/Latino; 3% Two or more races, non-Hispanic/Latino; 2% international; 11% transferred in. *Retention:* 49% of full-time freshmen returned.
Freshmen *Admission:* 4,380 applied, 1,639 enrolled. *Average high school GPA:* 2.9.
Faculty *Total:* 442, 8% with terminal degrees. *Student/faculty ratio:* 20:1.
Majors Accounting technology and bookkeeping; administrative assistant and secretarial science; child-care and support services management; clinical/medical laboratory technology; computer and information sciences; construction engineering technology; criminal justice/police science; emergency medical technology (EMT paramedic); engineering technology; fire services administration; funeral service and mortuary science; general studies; hospitality administration; liberal arts and sciences/liberal studies; office management; physical therapy technology; radiologic technology/science; registered nursing/registered nurse; veterinary/animal health technology.
Academics *Calendar:* semesters. *Degree:* certificates and associate. *Special study options:* academic remediation for entering students, adult/continuing education programs, advanced placement credit, distance learning, English as a second language, honors programs, independent study, internships, part-time degree program, services for LD students, summer session for credit. *ROTC:* Army (c), Air Force (c).
Library Jefferson State Libraries plus 4 others. *Books:* 74,316 (physical), 353,430 (digital/electronic); *Serial titles:* 279 (physical); *Databases:* 60. Weekly public service hours: 62.
Student Life *Housing:* college housing not available. *Activities and Organizations:* choral group, Student Government Association, Phi Theta Kappa, Sigma Kappa Delta, Jefferson State Ambassadors, Students in Free Enterprise (SIFE). *Campus security:* 24-hour patrols.
Costs (2016–17) *Tuition:* state resident $4440 full-time, $148 per semester hour part-time; nonresident $7950 full-time, $265 per semester hour part-time. Full-time tuition and fees vary according to course load. Part-time tuition and fees vary according to course load. *Waivers:* senior citizens and employees or children of employees.
Applying *Options:* electronic application, early admission, deferred entrance. *Required for some:* high school transcript. *Application deadlines:* rolling (freshmen), rolling (out-of-state freshmen), rolling (transfers). *Notification:* continuous (freshmen), continuous (out-of-state freshmen), continuous (transfers).
Freshman Application Contact Mrs. Lillian Owens, Director of Admissions and Retention, Jefferson State Community College, 2601 Carson Road, Birmingham, AL 35215-3098. *Phone:* 205-853-1200 Ext. 7990. *Toll-free phone:* 800-239-5900. *Fax:* 205-856-6070.
E-mail: lowens@jeffstateonline.com.
Website: http://www.jeffstateonline.com/.

J. F. Drake State Community and Technical College
Huntsville, Alabama

- **State-supported** 2-year, founded 1961, part of Alabama Community College System
- **Urban** 6-acre campus
- **Coed,** 996 undergraduate students, 49% full-time, 57% women, 43% men

Undergraduates 484 full-time, 512 part-time. Students come from 2 states and territories; 11% transferred in. *Retention:* 41% of full-time freshmen returned.
Freshmen *Admission:* 996 admitted, 242 enrolled.
Faculty *Total:* 79, 39% full-time. *Student/faculty ratio:* 15:1.
Majors Automotive engineering technology; business administration and management; computer and information sciences; culinary arts; drafting and design technology; electrical, electronic and communications engineering technology; electrician; heating, ventilation, air conditioning and refrigeration engineering technology; industrial electronics technology; licensed practical/vocational nurse training; medical/clinical assistant; salon/beauty salon management; tool and die technology.
Academics *Calendar:* semesters. *Degree:* certificates and associate. *Special study options:* academic remediation for entering students, cooperative education, distance learning, English as a second language, internships, part-time degree program, services for LD students.
Library S.C. O'Neal Library and Technology Center.
Student Life *Housing:* college housing not available. *Activities and Organizations:* Phi Beta Lambda, SkillsUSA, Phi Theta Kappa, National Technical Honor Society. *Campus security:* 24-hour patrols.
Costs (2015–16) *Tuition:* Full-time tuition and fees vary according to course load. Part-time tuition and fees vary according to course load. *Waivers:* senior citizens and employees or children of employees.
Financial Aid *Average indebtedness upon graduation:* $6687.
Applying *Options:* electronic application, deferred entrance. *Required:* high school transcript. *Application deadlines:* rolling (freshmen), rolling (transfers). *Notification:* continuous (freshmen), continuous (transfers).
Freshman Application Contact Mrs. Kristin Treadway, Assistant Director of Admissions, J. F. Drake State Community and Technical College, Huntsville, AL 35811. *Phone:* 256-551-3111. *Toll-free phone:* 888-413-7253.
E-mail: kristin.treadway@drakestate.edu.
Website: http://www.drakestate.edu/.

J F Ingram State Technical College
Deatsville, Alabama

Admissions Office Contact J F Ingram State Technical College, 5375 Ingram Rd, Deatsville, AL 36022.
Website: http://www.istc.edu/.

Lawson State Community College
Birmingham, Alabama

Freshman Application Contact Mr. Jeff Shelley, Director of Admissions and Records, Lawson State Community College, 3060 Wilson Road, SW, Birmingham, AL 35221-1798. *Phone:* 205-929-6361. *Fax:* 205-923-7106.
E-mail: jshelley@lawsonstate.edu.
Website: http://www.lawsonstate.edu/.

Lurleen B. Wallace Community College
Andalusia, Alabama

- **State-supported** 2-year, founded 1969, part of Alabama Community College System
- **Small-town** 200-acre campus
- **Coed,** 1,732 undergraduate students, 60% full-time, 55% women, 45% men

Undergraduates 1,034 full-time, 698 part-time. Students come from 5 states and territories; 4 other countries; 3% are from out of state; 23% Black or African American, non-Hispanic/Latino; 1% Hispanic/Latino; 0.3% Asian, non-Hispanic/Latino; 0.6% American Indian or Alaska Native, non-Hispanic/Latino; 1% Two or more races, non-Hispanic/Latino; 0.8% Race/ethnicity unknown; 0.1% international; 18% transferred in.
Freshmen *Admission:* 492 enrolled.
Faculty *Total:* 104, 52% full-time, 5% with terminal degrees. *Student/faculty ratio:* 18:1.
Majors Administrative assistant and secretarial science; child-care and support services management; computer and information sciences; diagnostic medical sonography and ultrasound technology; emergency medical technology (EMT paramedic); forest technology; general studies; industrial

electronics technology; liberal arts and sciences/liberal studies; registered nursing/registered nurse.

Academics *Calendar:* semesters. *Degree:* certificates and associate. *Special study options:* academic remediation for entering students, cooperative education, distance learning, honors programs, independent study, part-time degree program, summer session for credit.

Library Lurleen B. Wallace Library plus 3 others. Students can reserve study rooms.

Student Life *Housing:* college housing not available. *Activities and Organizations:* drama/theater group, choral group, Student Government Association, Student Ambassadors, Campus Civitan, Christian Student Ministries, Saints Angels. *Student services:* personal/psychological counseling.

Athletics Member NJCAA. *Intercollegiate sports:* baseball M(s), basketball M(s)/W(s), softball W(s).

Standardized Tests *Required for some:* ACT Compass for some technical programs.

Costs (2015–16) *Tuition:* state resident $3450 full-time, $115 per credit hour part-time; nonresident $6900 full-time, $230 per credit hour part-time. Full-time tuition and fees vary according to course load. Part-time tuition and fees vary according to course load. *Required fees:* $870 full-time, $29 per credit hour part-time. *Payment plan:* installment. *Waivers:* senior citizens and employees or children of employees.

Financial Aid Of all full-time matriculated undergraduates who enrolled in 2014, 103 Federal Work-Study jobs.

Applying *Options:* electronic application. *Required:* high school transcript. *Application deadlines:* rolling (freshmen), rolling (out-of-state freshmen), rolling (transfers).

Freshman Application Contact Lurleen B. Wallace Community College, PO Box 1418, Andalusia, AL 36420-1418. *Phone:* 334-881-2273. *Website:* http://www.lbwcc.edu/.

Marion Military Institute

Marion, Alabama

- **State-supported** 2-year, founded 1842, part of Alabama Community College System
- **Rural** 130-acre campus with easy access to Birmingham
- **Coed,** 457 undergraduate students, 98% full-time, 21% women, 79% men

Undergraduates 449 full-time, 8 part-time. Students come from 36 states and territories; 54% are from out of state; 21% Black or African American, non-Hispanic/Latino; 9% Hispanic/Latino; 2% Asian, non-Hispanic/Latino; 0.4% Native Hawaiian or other Pacific Islander, non-Hispanic/Latino; 0.7% American Indian or Alaska Native, non-Hispanic/Latino; 5% Two or more races, non-Hispanic/Latino; 1% Race/ethnicity unknown; 4% transferred in; 100% live on campus. *Retention:* 41% of full-time freshmen returned.

Freshmen *Admission:* 904 applied, 275 admitted, 275 enrolled. *Test scores:* SAT critical reading scores over 500: 70%; SAT math scores over 500: 76%; ACT scores over 18: 88%; SAT critical reading scores over 600: 20%; SAT math scores over 600: 27%; ACT scores over 24: 39%; SAT critical reading scores over 700: 1%; SAT math scores over 700: 2%; ACT scores over 30: 4%.

Faculty *Total:* 38, 53% full-time. *Student/faculty ratio:* 17:1.

Majors Biological and physical sciences; engineering; general studies; liberal arts and sciences/liberal studies.

Academics *Calendar:* semesters. *Degree:* associate. *Special study options:* academic remediation for entering students, English as a second language, services for LD students. *ROTC:* Army (b), Air Force (c).

Library Baer Memorial Library.

Student Life *Housing:* on-campus residence required through sophomore year. *Options:* coed, men-only. Campus housing is university owned. *Activities and Organizations:* drama/theater group, choral group, marching band, Honor Guard, White Knights Precision Drill Team, Swamp Foxes, Marching Band, Scabbard and Blade. *Campus security:* 24-hour patrols. *Student services:* health clinic, personal/psychological counseling.

Athletics Member NJCAA. *Intercollegiate sports:* baseball M(s), basketball M(s), softball W(s), tennis M(s)/W(s). *Intramural sports:* basketball M/W, football M/W, soccer M/W, softball M/W, table tennis M/W, ultimate Frisbee M/W, volleyball M/W, water polo M/W.

Standardized Tests *Required:* SAT or ACT (for admission).

Costs (2015–16) *Tuition:* state resident $6000 full-time; nonresident $12,000 full-time. *Required fees:* $2778 full-time. *Room and board:* $4450. *Waivers:* employees or children of employees.

Financial Aid Of all full-time matriculated undergraduates who enrolled in 2014, 29 Federal Work-Study jobs (averaging $210).

Applying *Options:* electronic application, deferred entrance. *Application fee:* $30. *Required:* high school transcript, minimum 2.0 GPA. *Application deadlines:* rolling (freshmen), rolling (transfers). *Notification:* continuous (freshmen), continuous (transfers).

Freshman Application Contact Mrs. Brittany Crawford, Director of Admissions, Marion Military Institute, 1101 Washington Street, Marion, AL 36756. *Phone:* 800-664-1842. *Toll-free phone:* 800-664-1842. *Fax:* 334-683-2383. *E-mail:* bcrawford@marionmilitary.edu. *Website:* http://www.marionmilitary.edu/.

Northeast Alabama Community College

Rainsville, Alabama

- **State-supported** 2-year, founded 1963, part of Alabama Community College System
- **Rural** 117-acre campus
- **Coed,** 2,704 undergraduate students, 44% full-time, 61% women, 39% men

Undergraduates 1,193 full-time, 1,511 part-time. Students come from 3 states and territories; 2% Black or African American, non-Hispanic/Latino; 8% Hispanic/Latino; 0.8% Asian, non-Hispanic/Latino; 3% American Indian or Alaska Native, non-Hispanic/Latino; 1% Race/ethnicity unknown; 13% transferred in.

Freshmen *Admission:* 590 enrolled.

Faculty *Total:* 148, 28% full-time, 5% with terminal degrees. *Student/faculty ratio:* 22:1.

Majors Administrative assistant and secretarial science; business administration and management; business/commerce; child-care and support services management; computer and information sciences; drafting and design technology; emergency medical technology (EMT paramedic); industrial electronics technology; industrial mechanics and maintenance technology; medical/clinical assistant; registered nursing/registered nurse.

Academics *Calendar:* semesters. *Degree:* certificates and associate. *Special study options:* academic remediation for entering students, accelerated degree program, adult/continuing education programs, advanced placement credit, cooperative education, distance learning, double majors, English as a second language, honors programs, independent study, internships, part-time degree program, services for LD students, summer session for credit.

Library Cecil B. Word Learning Resources Center. *Books:* 62,979 (physical), 47,085 (digital/electronic); *Serial titles:* 95 (physical); *Databases:* 49. Weekly public service hours: 58; students can reserve study rooms.

Student Life *Housing:* college housing not available. *Activities and Organizations:* drama/theater group, choral group. *Campus security:* 24-hour emergency response devices. *Student services:* personal/psychological counseling.

Costs (2015–16) *Tuition:* state resident $3450 full-time, $115 per credit hour part-time; nonresident $6900 full-time, $230 per credit hour part-time. *Required fees:* $870 full-time, $29 per credit hour part-time, $29 per credit hour part-time. *Waivers:* senior citizens and employees or children of employees.

Financial Aid Of all full-time matriculated undergraduates who enrolled in 2014, 40 Federal Work-Study jobs (averaging $2500).

Applying *Required:* high school transcript. *Application deadlines:* rolling (freshmen), rolling (out-of-state freshmen), rolling (transfers). *Notification:* continuous (freshmen), continuous (out-of-state freshmen), continuous (transfers).

Freshman Application Contact Northeast Alabama Community College, PO Box 159, Rainsville, AL 35986-0159. *Phone:* 256-228-6001 Ext. 2325. *Website:* http://www.nacc.edu/.

Northwest-Shoals Community College

Muscle Shoals, Alabama

- **State-supported** 2-year, founded 1963, part of Alabama Community College System
- **Small-town** 210-acre campus
- **Endowment** $734,778
- **Coed,** 3,667 undergraduate students, 45% full-time, 57% women, 43% men

Undergraduates 1,638 full-time, 2,029 part-time. Students come from 3 states and territories; 2 other countries; 15% Black or African American, non-Hispanic/Latino; 5% Hispanic/Latino; 0.5% Asian, non-Hispanic/Latino; 0.1% Native Hawaiian or other Pacific Islander, non-Hispanic/Latino; 1% American Indian or Alaska Native, non-Hispanic/Latino; 0.3% Two or more races, non-Hispanic/Latino; 3% Race/ethnicity unknown; 0.4% international; 4% transferred in.

Freshmen *Admission:* 701 applied, 701 admitted, 701 enrolled.

Faculty *Total:* 153, 51% full-time, 5% with terminal degrees. *Student/faculty ratio:* 25:1.

Majors Administrative assistant and secretarial science; child-care and support services management; child development; computer and information sciences; criminal justice/police science; drafting and design technology; emergency medical technology (EMT paramedic); environmental engineering technology; general studies; industrial electronics technology; industrial mechanics and maintenance technology; liberal arts and sciences/liberal studies; medical/clinical assistant; multi/interdisciplinary studies related; registered nursing/registered nurse; salon/beauty salon management.

Academics *Calendar:* semesters. *Degree:* certificates and associate. *Special study options:* academic remediation for entering students, accelerated degree program, adult/continuing education programs, advanced placement credit, cooperative education, distance learning, honors programs, independent study, internships, part-time degree program, services for LD students, summer session for credit.

Library Larry W. McCoy Learning Resource Center. *Books:* 61,250 (physical), 38,196 (digital/electronic); *Databases:* 2. Weekly public service hours: 59.

Student Life *Housing:* college housing not available. *Activities and Organizations:* choral group, Student Government Association, Science Club, Phi Theta Kappa, Baptist Campus Ministry, Northwest-Shoals Singers. *Campus security:* 24-hour emergency response devices.

Athletics *Intramural sports:* basketball M/W, football M/W, tennis M/W.

Costs (2016–17) *Tuition:* state resident $3450 full-time, $115 per credit hour part-time; nonresident $6900 full-time, $230 per credit hour part-time. Full-time tuition and fees vary according to course load. Part-time tuition and fees vary according to course load. *Required fees:* $841 full-time, $27 per credit hour part-time. *Waivers:* senior citizens and employees or children of employees.

Financial Aid Of all full-time matriculated undergraduates who enrolled in 2015, 31 Federal Work-Study jobs (averaging $1554). *Financial aid deadline:* 6/1.

Applying *Options:* electronic application. *Required:* high school transcript. *Application deadlines:* rolling (freshmen), rolling (transfers). *Notification:* continuous (transfers).

Freshman Application Contact Mr. Tom Carter, Assistant Dean of Recruitment, Admissions and Financial Aid, Northwest-Shoals Community College, PO Box 2545, Muscle Shoals, AL 35662. *Phone:* 256-331-5263. *Fax:* 256-331-5366. *E-mail:* tom.carter@nwscc.edu. *Website:* http://www.nwscc.edu/.

Reid State Technical College
Evergreen, Alabama

- **State-supported** 2-year, founded 1966, part of Alabama Community College System
- **Rural** 26-acre campus
- **Coed,** 571 undergraduate students, 44% full-time, 60% women, 40% men

Undergraduates 250 full-time, 321 part-time. Students come from 2 states and territories; 1% are from out of state; 52% Black or African American, non-Hispanic/Latino; 0.4% Hispanic/Latino; 0.2% Asian, non-Hispanic/Latino; 1% American Indian or Alaska Native, non-Hispanic/Latino; 0.9% Two or more races, non-Hispanic/Latino.

Freshmen *Admission:* 75 applied, 75 admitted, 75 enrolled.

Faculty *Total:* 30, 80% full-time, 3% with terminal degrees. *Student/faculty ratio:* 12:1.

Majors Administrative assistant and secretarial science; child-care and support services management; computer and information sciences; electrical, electronic and communications engineering technology.

Academics *Calendar:* semesters. *Degree:* certificates and associate. *Special study options:* academic remediation for entering students, adult/continuing education programs, double majors, independent study, internships, part-time degree program, services for LD students, summer session for credit.

Library Edith A. Gray Library.

Student Life *Housing:* college housing not available. *Activities and Organizations:* Student Government Association, Phi Beta Lambda, National Vocational-Technical Society, Ambassadors, Who's Who. *Campus security:* 24-hour emergency response devices, day and evening security guard. *Student services:* personal/psychological counseling.

Costs (2016–17) *Tuition:* state resident $4212 full-time, $117 per credit part-time; nonresident $8424 full-time, $234 per credit part-time. Full-time tuition and fees vary according to course load and program. Part-time tuition and fees vary according to course load and program. *Required fees:* $1080 full-time, $30 per credit part-time. *Waivers:* senior citizens and employees or children of employees.

Financial Aid Of all full-time matriculated undergraduates who enrolled in 2014, 35 Federal Work-Study jobs (averaging $1500).

Applying *Options:* early admission. *Required:* high school transcript. *Application deadlines:* rolling (freshmen), rolling (transfers).

Freshman Application Contact Dr. Alesia Stuart, Public Relations/Marketing/Associate Dean of Workforce Development, Reid State Technical College, Evergreen, AL 36401-0588. *Phone:* 251-578-1313 Ext. 108. *E-mail:* akstuart@rstc.edu. *Website:* http://www.rstc.edu/.

Remington College–Mobile Campus
Mobile, Alabama

Freshman Application Contact Remington College–Mobile Campus, 828 Downtowner Loop West, Mobile, AL 36609-5404. *Phone:* 251-343-8200. *Toll-free phone:* 800-560-6192. *Website:* http://www.remingtoncollege.edu/.

Shelton State Community College
Tuscaloosa, Alabama

Freshman Application Contact Ms. Sharon Chastine, Secretary to the Associate Dean of Student Services Enrollment, Shelton State Community College, 9500 Old Greensboro Road, Tuscaloosa, AL 35405. *Phone:* 205-391-2309. *Fax:* 205-391-3910. *E-mail:* schastine@sheltonstate.edu. *Website:* http://www.sheltonstate.edu/.

Snead State Community College
Boaz, Alabama

Freshman Application Contact Dr. Jason Watts, Chief Academic Officer, Snead State Community College, PO Box 734, Boaz, AL 35957-0734. *Phone:* 256-840-4118. *Fax:* 256-593-7180. *E-mail:* jwatts@snead.edu. *Website:* http://www.snead.edu/.

Southern Union State Community College
Wadley, Alabama

Freshman Application Contact Admissions Office, Southern Union State Community College, PO Box 1000, Roberts Street, Wadley, AL 36276. *Phone:* 256-395-5157. *E-mail:* info@suscc.edu. *Website:* http://www.suscc.edu/.

Virginia College in Huntsville
Huntsville, Alabama

Freshman Application Contact Director of Admission, Virginia College in Huntsville, 2021 Drake Avenue SW, Huntsville, AL 35801. *Phone:* 256-533-7387. *Fax:* 256-533-7785. *Website:* http://www.vc.edu/.

Virginia College in Mobile
Mobile, Alabama

Admissions Office Contact Virginia College in Mobile, 3725 Airport Boulevard, Suite 165, Mobile, AL 36608. *Website:* http://www.vc.edu/.

Virginia College in Montgomery
Montgomery, Alabama

Admissions Office Contact Virginia College in Montgomery, 6200 Atlanta Highway, Montgomery, AL 36117-2800. *Website:* http://www.vc.edu/.

Wallace State Community College
Hanceville, Alabama

Director of Admissions Jennifer Hill, Director of Admissions, Wallace State Community College, PO Box 2000, 801 Main Street, Hanceville, AL 35077-2000. *Phone:* 256-352-8278. *Toll-free phone:* 866-350-9722. *Website:* http://www.wallacestate.edu/.

ALASKA

Alaska Career College
Anchorage, Alaska

- **Proprietary** 2-year
- **Urban** 20-acre campus
- **Coed**

Majors Business administration and management.

Academics *Calendar:* continuous. *Degree:* certificates, diplomas, and associate.
Applying *Notification:* continuous (freshmen), continuous (out-of-state freshmen), continuous (transfers), rolling (early decision plan 1), rolling (early decision plan 2), rolling (early action).
Freshman Application Contact Alaska Career College, 1415 East Tudor Road, Anchorage, AK 99507.
Website: http://www.alaskacareercollege.edu/.

Alaska Christian College
Soldotna, Alaska

Admissions Office Contact Alaska Christian College, 35109 Royal Place, Soldotna, AK 99669.
Website: http://www.akcc.org/.

Charter College
Anchorage, Alaska

Director of Admissions Ms. Lily Sirianni, Vice President, Charter College, 2221 East Northern Lights Boulevard, Suite 120, Anchorage, AK 99508. *Phone:* 907-277-1000. *Toll-free phone:* 888-200-9942.
Website: http://www.chartercollege.edu/.

Ilisagvik College
Barrow, Alaska

- **State-supported** 2-year, founded 1995
- **Rural** 7-acre campus
- **Endowment** $4.7 million
- **Coed,** 271 undergraduate students

Undergraduates Students come from 1 other state; 1% are from out of state; 2% Black or African American, non-Hispanic/Latino; 2% Hispanic/Latino; 7% Asian, non-Hispanic/Latino; 4% Native Hawaiian or other Pacific Islander, non-Hispanic/Latino; 63% American Indian or Alaska Native, non-Hispanic/Latino; 2% Race/ethnicity unknown; 3% international; 10% live on campus.
Freshmen *Admission:* 17 applied, 17 admitted.
Faculty *Total:* 35, 31% full-time. *Student/faculty ratio:* 7:1.
Majors Accounting technology and bookkeeping; American Indian/Native American studies; business administration and management; fire science/firefighting; health services/allied health/health sciences; liberal arts and sciences/liberal studies; office management.
Academics *Calendar:* semesters. *Degree:* certificates, diplomas, and associate. *Special study options:* academic remediation for entering students, cooperative education, distance learning, double majors, English as a second language, independent study, internships, off-campus study, part-time degree program, services for LD students, summer session for credit.
Library Tuzzy Consortium Library. *Books:* 43,561 (physical), 56,345 (digital/electronic); *Serial titles:* 150 (physical). Weekly public service hours: 60; students can reserve study rooms.
Student Life *Housing Options:* coed. Campus housing is leased by the school. *Activities and Organizations:* Student Government, Barrow Camera Club, Ilisagvik Green Team, Aglaun Literary Journal. *Campus security:* 24-hour emergency response devices and patrols, controlled dormitory access. *Student services:* personal/psychological counseling.
Athletics *Intramural sports:* basketball M/W.
Standardized Tests *Recommended:* ACCUPLACER.
Costs (2016–17) *Tuition:* state resident $125 per credit part-time; nonresident $125 per year part-time. Full-time tuition and fees vary according to course load and program. Part-time tuition and fees vary according to course load and program. *Required fees:* $60 per term part-time, $60 per term part-time. *Room and board:* Room and board charges vary according to housing facility. *Payment plans:* installment, deferred payment. *Waivers:* senior citizens and employees or children of employees.
Applying *Options:* deferred entrance. *Required:* high school transcript, minimum 2.0 GPA. *Required for some:* copy of Alaska Native Shareholder/Native American Tribal Affiliation card for Natives. *Application deadlines:* 8/14 (freshmen), 8/14 (transfers). *Notification:* continuous (freshmen), continuous (transfers).
Freshman Application Contact Tennessee Judkins, Recruiter, Ilisagvik College, PO Box 749, Barrow, AK 99723. *Phone:* 907-852-1772. *Toll-free phone:* 800-478-7337. *Fax:* 907-852-1789.
E-mail: tennessee.judkins@ilisagvik.edu.
Website: http://www.ilisagvik.edu/.

University of Alaska Anchorage, Kenai Peninsula College
Soldotna, Alaska

- **State-supported** primarily 2-year, founded 1964, part of University of Alaska System
- **Rural** 360-acre campus
- **Coed,** 2,733 undergraduate students

Majors Business administration and management; digital communication and media/multimedia; early childhood education; elementary education; emergency medical technology (EMT paramedic); human services; liberal arts and sciences/liberal studies; occupational safety and health technology; psychology.
Academics *Calendar:* semesters. *Degrees:* certificates, associate, and bachelor's. *Special study options:* academic remediation for entering students, adult/continuing education programs, advanced placement credit, cooperative education, distance learning, double majors, English as a second language, part-time degree program, services for LD students.
Library Kenai Peninsula College Library.
Student Life *Housing Options:* coed. Campus housing is university owned. *Campus security:* 24-hour emergency response devices. *Student services:* health clinic.
Standardized Tests *Required:* ACT, SAT or ACCUPLACER (for admission).
Costs (2015–16) *Tuition:* state resident $5568 full-time, $183 per credit hour part-time; nonresident $16,488 full-time, $649 per credit hour part-time. Full-time tuition and fees vary according to course load, degree level, location, and program. Part-time tuition and fees vary according to course load, degree level, location, and program. No tuition increase for student's term of enrollment. *Required fees:* $1153 full-time. *Room and board:* $9290; room only: $7040. Room and board charges vary according to board plan. *Payment plan:* installment. *Waivers:* senior citizens and employees or children of employees.
Applying *Options:* electronic application. *Application fee:* $40. *Required:* high school transcript. *Application deadlines:* rolling (freshmen), rolling (transfers).
Freshman Application Contact Mrs. Julie Cotterell, Admission and Student Records Coordinator, University of Alaska Anchorage, Kenai Peninsula College, 156 College Road, Soldotna, AK 99669-9798. *Phone:* 907-262-0311. *Toll-free phone:* 877-262-0330. *E-mail:* jmcotterell@kpc.alaska.edu.
Website: http://www.kpc.alaska.edu/.

University of Alaska Anchorage, Kodiak College
Kodiak, Alaska

Freshman Application Contact University of Alaska Anchorage, Kodiak College, 117 Benny Benson Drive, Kodiak, AK 99615-6643. *Phone:* 907-486-1235. *Toll-free phone:* 800-486-7660.
Website: http://www.koc.alaska.edu/.

University of Alaska Anchorage, Matanuska-Susitna College
Palmer, Alaska

Freshman Application Contact Ms. Sandra Gravley, Student Services Director, University of Alaska Anchorage, Matanuska-Susitna College, PO Box 2889, Palmer, AK 99645-2889. *Phone:* 907-745-9712. *Fax:* 907-745-9747. *E-mail:* info@matsu.alaska.edu.
Website: http://www.matsu.alaska.edu/.

University of Alaska, Prince William Sound College
Valdez, Alaska

- **State-supported** 2-year, founded 1978, part of University of Alaska System
- **Small-town** campus
- **Endowment** $62,630
- **Coed**

Undergraduates Students come from 1 other state; 2 other countries; 13% are from out of state; 2% live on campus.
Freshmen *Admission:* 120 applied, 93 admitted. *Average high school GPA:* 2.75.
Faculty *Student/faculty ratio:* 5:1.
Majors Administrative assistant and secretarial science; liberal arts and sciences/liberal studies; mental health counseling.

Academics *Calendar:* semesters. *Degree:* certificates, diplomas, and associate. *Special study options:* academic remediation for entering students, adult/continuing education programs, advanced placement credit, cooperative education, distance learning, double majors, English as a second language, independent study, internships, services for LD students, summer session for credit.

Library Valdez Consortium Library.

Student Life *Housing Options:* coed. Campus housing is university owned. *Activities and Organizations:* drama/theater group, Student Association, Phi Theta Kappa Honor Society, Archery Team/Club. *Campus security:* student patrols, controlled dormitory access, housing manager supervision. *Student services:* personal/psychological counseling.

Standardized Tests *Recommended:* SAT or ACT (for admission), ACCUPLACER.

Costs (2016–17) *One-time required fee:* $40. *Tuition:* state resident $4032 full-time, $168 per credit part-time; nonresident $4032 full-time, $168 per credit part-time. *Required fees:* $350 full-time, $100 per term part-time. *Room and board:* room only: $2527. Room and board charges vary according to housing facility. *Payment plans:* installment, deferred payment. *Waivers:* senior citizens and employees or children of employees.

Applying *Options:* electronic application, early admission. *Application fee:* $25. *Required:* high school transcript. *Application deadlines:* rolling (freshmen), rolling (out-of-state freshmen), rolling (transfers).

Freshman Application Contact Dr. Denise Runge, Academic Affairs, University of Alaska, Prince William Sound College, PO Box 97, Valdez, AK 99686-0097. *Phone:* 907-834-1600. *Toll-free phone:* 800-478-8800. *Fax:* 907-834-1691. *E-mail:* drunge@pwscc.edu.
Website: http://www.pwsc.alaska.edu/.

University of Alaska Southeast, Ketchikan Campus

Ketchikan, Alaska

Freshman Application Contact Admissions Office, University of Alaska Southeast, Ketchikan Campus, 2600 7th Avenue, Ketchikan, AK 99901-5798. *Phone:* 907-225-6177. *Toll-free phone:* 888-550-6177. *Fax:* 907-225-3895. *E-mail:* ketch.info@uas.alaska.edu.
Website: http://www.ketch.alaska.edu/.

University of Alaska Southeast, Sitka Campus

Sitka, Alaska

- **State-supported** primarily 2-year, founded 1962, part of University of Alaska System
- **Small-town** campus
- **Coed**

Undergraduates Students come from 10 states and territories; 2 other countries.

Faculty *Student/faculty ratio:* 13:1.

Academics *Calendar:* semesters. *Degrees:* certificates, diplomas, associate, bachelor's, and master's. *Special study options:* academic remediation for entering students, adult/continuing education programs, advanced placement credit, cooperative education, distance learning, double majors, English as a second language, independent study, internships, off-campus study, part-time degree program, services for LD students, study abroad, summer session for credit.

Library Egan Library.

Student Life *Campus security:* 24-hour emergency response devices.

Costs (2015–16) *One-time required fee:* $50. *Tuition:* state resident $4224 full-time, $176 per credit part-time; nonresident $4224 full-time, $176 per credit part-time. Full-time tuition and fees vary according to degree level, location, and program. Part-time tuition and fees vary according to degree level, location, and program. *Required fees:* $856 full-time, $36 per credit part-time. *Room and board:* room only: $4800. Room and board charges vary according to housing facility.

Applying *Options:* electronic application, early admission, deferred entrance. *Application fee:* $35. *Required:* high school transcript, minimum 2.0 GPA. *Required for some:* essay or personal statement.

Freshman Application Contact Ms. Teal Gordon, Admissions Representative, University of Alaska Southeast, Sitka Campus, UAS Sitka, 1332 Seward Ave., Sitka, AK 99835. *Phone:* 907-747-7726. *Toll-free phone:* 800-478-6653. *Fax:* 907-747-7731. *E-mail:* ktgordon@uas.alaska.edu.
Website: http://www.uas.alaska.edu/.

AMERICAN SAMOA

American Samoa Community College

Pago Pago, American Samoa

- **Territory-supported** primarily 2-year, founded 1969
- **Rural** 20-acre campus
- **Endowment** $3.1 million
- **Coed**, 1,285 undergraduate students, 55% full-time, 67% women, 33% men

Undergraduates 705 full-time, 580 part-time. Students come from 5 other countries; 0.7% Asian, non-Hispanic/Latino; 90% Native Hawaiian or other Pacific Islander, non-Hispanic/Latino; 9% international; 0.2% transferred in. *Retention:* 100% of full-time freshmen returned.

Freshmen *Admission:* 425 applied, 425 admitted, 385 enrolled. *Test scores:* SAT critical reading scores over 500: 17%; SAT math scores over 500: 19%; SAT writing scores over 500: 14%; SAT critical reading scores over 600: 5%; SAT math scores over 600: 2%; SAT writing scores over 600: 2%.

Faculty *Total:* 82, 78% full-time, 9% with terminal degrees. *Student/faculty ratio:* 20:1.

Majors Accounting; agricultural business and management; agriculture; architectural drafting and CAD/CADD; art; autobody/collision and repair technology; automobile/automotive mechanics technology; business administration and management; civil engineering; construction trades; criminal justice/safety; education; electrical, electronic and communications engineering technology; family and consumer economics related; forensic science and technology; health services/allied health/health sciences; human services; liberal arts and sciences/liberal studies; marine science/merchant marine officer; music; natural resources/conservation; office occupations and clerical services; political science and government; pre-law studies; welding technology.

Academics *Calendar:* semesters. *Degrees:* certificates, associate, and bachelor's. *Special study options:* academic remediation for entering students, adult/continuing education programs, cooperative education, double majors, English as a second language, honors programs, independent study, internships, off-campus study, part-time degree program, services for LD students, student-designed majors, summer session for credit. *ROTC:* Army (b).

Library ASCC Learning Resource Center/Library plus 1 other. *Books:* 40,000 (physical); *Serial titles:* 236 (physical). Weekly public service hours: 42.

Student Life *Housing:* college housing not available. *Activities and Organizations:* student-run newspaper, Student Government Association, Phi Theta Kappa, ASCC Research Foundation Student Club, Fa'aSamoa (Samoan culture) Club, Journalism Club. *Campus security:* 24-hour patrols. *Student services:* personal/psychological counseling.

Athletics *Intramural sports:* basketball M/W, football M/W, golf M/W, rugby M, soccer M, tennis M/W, track and field M/W, volleyball M/W.

Standardized Tests *Recommended:* SAT (for admission), ACT (for admission), SAT or ACT (for admission), SAT and SAT Subject Tests or ACT (for admission), SAT Subject Tests (for admission).

Costs (2016–17) *Tuition:* territory resident $3300 full-time, $110 per credit part-time; nonresident $3600 full-time, $120 per credit part-time. Full-time tuition and fees vary according to course load. Part-time tuition and fees vary according to course load. *Required fees:* $250 full-time, $120 per term part-time. *Payment plan:* installment. *Waivers:* employees or children of employees.

Financial Aid Of all full-time matriculated undergraduates who enrolled in 2014, 591 applied for aid, 591 were judged to have need. 1 Federal Work-Study job (averaging $870). *Average percent of need met:* 62%. *Average financial aid package:* $6724. *Average need-based gift aid:* $5898.

Applying *Options:* electronic application, early admission, deferred entrance. *Application deadline:* rolling (freshmen). *Notification:* continuous (freshmen).

Freshman Application Contact Elizabeth Leuma, Admissions Officer, American Samoa Community College, PO Box 2609, Pago Pago 96799, American Samoa. *Phone:* 684-699-9155 Ext. 411. *Fax:* 684-699-1083.
Website: http://www.amsamoa.edu/.

ARIZONA

Arizona Automotive Institute

Glendale, Arizona

Director of Admissions Director of Admissions, Arizona Automotive Institute, 6829 North 46th Avenue, Glendale, AZ 85301-3597. *Phone:* 623-

934-7273 Ext. 211. *Toll-free phone:* 800-321-5861 (in-state); 800-321-5961 (out-of-state). *Fax:* 623-937-5000. *E-mail:* info@azautoinst.com. *Website:* http://www.aai.edu/.

Arizona College
Glendale, Arizona

Freshman Application Contact Admissions Department, Arizona College, 4425 West Olive Avenue, Suite 300, Glendale, AZ 85302-3843. *Phone:* 602-222-9300. *E-mail:* lhicks@arizonacollege.edu. *Website:* http://www.arizonacollege.edu/.

Arizona Western College
Yuma, Arizona

- **State and locally supported** 2-year, founded 1962, part of Arizona State Community College System
- **Rural** 640-acre campus
- **Coed,** 7,514 undergraduate students, 35% full-time, 57% women, 43% men

Undergraduates 2,653 full-time, 4,861 part-time. Students come from 28 states and territories; 34 other countries; 7% are from out of state; 3% Black or African American, non-Hispanic/Latino; 70% Hispanic/Latino; 0.7% Asian, non-Hispanic/Latino; 0.4% Native Hawaiian or other Pacific Islander, non-Hispanic/Latino; 1% American Indian or Alaska Native, non-Hispanic/Latino; 1% Two or more races, non-Hispanic/Latino; 4% Race/ethnicity unknown; 3% international; 7% live on campus.
Freshmen *Admission:* 1,645 enrolled.
Faculty *Total:* 543, 20% full-time, 13% with terminal degrees. *Student/faculty ratio:* 21:1.
Majors Accounting; agricultural business and management; agriculture; American Indian/Native American studies; architectural technology; automobile/automotive mechanics technology; automotive engineering technology; biology/biological sciences; business administration and management; CAD/CADD drafting/design technology; carpentry; chemistry; civil engineering technology; communication; community health and preventive medicine; computer and information sciences; computer graphics; construction engineering technology; construction management; criminal justice/law enforcement administration; crop production; culinary arts; data entry/microcomputer applications; dramatic/theater arts; early childhood education; electrical, electronic and communications engineering technology; elementary education; emergency medical technology (EMT paramedic); engineering; English; environmental science; family and consumer sciences/human sciences; fine/studio arts; fire science/firefighting; general studies; geology/earth science; health and physical education/fitness; heating, air conditioning, ventilation and refrigeration maintenance technology; heating, ventilation, air conditioning and refrigeration engineering technology; history; homeland security; hospitality administration; industrial technology; law enforcement investigation and interviewing; legal assistant/paralegal; logistics, materials, and supply chain management; manufacturing engineering technology; massage therapy; mathematics; music; parks, recreation and leisure facilities management; philosophy; physics; plumbing technology; political science and government; prenursing studies; psychology; radio and television broadcasting technology; radiologic technology/science; registered nursing/registered nurse; secondary education; social sciences; solar energy technology; Spanish; sport and fitness administration/management; water quality and wastewater treatment management and recycling technology; welding engineering technology.
Academics *Calendar:* semesters. *Degree:* certificates and associate. *Special study options:* academic remediation for entering students, adult/continuing education programs, advanced placement credit, cooperative education, distance learning, English as a second language, honors programs, independent study, part-time degree program, services for LD students, summer session for credit.
Library Arizona Western College and NAU-Yuma Library. *Books:* 82,935 (physical), 35,543 (digital/electronic); *Serial titles:* 4,100 (physical); *Databases:* 39,599. Students can reserve study rooms.
Student Life *Housing Options:* coed, men-only, women-only. Campus housing is university owned. *Activities and Organizations:* drama/theater group, student-run newspaper, radio and television station, choral group, Student Government Association, Spirit Squad, Dance Team, Matador Ambassadors, Presidential Leadership Society. *Campus security:* 24-hour emergency response devices and patrols, student patrols, late-night transport/escort service, controlled dormitory access. *Student services:* health clinic, personal/psychological counseling.
Athletics Member NJCAA. *Intercollegiate sports:* baseball M(s), basketball M(s)/W(s), football M(s), soccer M(s)/W(s), softball W(s), volleyball W(s). *Intramural sports:* cheerleading M(c)/W(c).
Standardized Tests *Required for some:* SAT or ACT (for admission).

Costs (2016–17) *Tuition:* state resident $2400 full-time, $80 per credit part-time; nonresident $9390 full-time, $313 per credit part-time. Full-time tuition and fees vary according to course load, program, and reciprocity agreements. Part-time tuition and fees vary according to course load, program, and reciprocity agreements. *Room and board:* $6464; room only: $2240. Room and board charges vary according to board plan and housing facility. *Payment plan:* installment. *Waivers:* senior citizens and employees or children of employees.
Financial Aid Of all full-time matriculated undergraduates who enrolled in 2014, 350 Federal Work-Study jobs (averaging $1500). 100 state and other part-time jobs (averaging $1800).
Applying *Options:* electronic application, early admission, deferred entrance. *Application deadlines:* rolling (freshmen), rolling (out-of-state freshmen), rolling (transfers).
Freshman Application Contact Nicole D. Harral, Interim Director of Admissions/Registrar, Arizona Western College, PO Box 929, Yuma, AZ 85366. *Phone:* 928-344-7600. *Toll-free phone:* 888-293-0392. *Fax:* 928-344-7543. *E-mail:* nicole.harral@azwestern.edu. *Website:* http://www.azwestern.edu/.

Brown Mackie College–Phoenix
Phoenix, Arizona

Freshman Application Contact Brown Mackie College–Phoenix, 13430 North Black Canyon Highway, Suite 190, Phoenix, AZ 85029. *Phone:* 602-337-3044. *Toll-free phone:* 866-824-4793. *Website:* http://www.brownmackie.edu/phoenix/.

Brown Mackie College–Tucson
Tucson, Arizona

Freshman Application Contact Brown Mackie College–Tucson, 4585 East Speedway Boulevard, Suite 204, Tucson, AZ 85712. *Phone:* 520-319-3300. *Website:* http://www.brownmackie.edu/tucson/.

Carrington College–Mesa
Mesa, Arizona

- **Proprietary** 2-year, founded 1977, part of Carrington Colleges Group, Inc.
- **Suburban** campus
- **Coed,** 633 undergraduate students, 90% full-time, 82% women, 18% men

Undergraduates 572 full-time, 61 part-time. 2% are from out of state; 6% Black or African American, non-Hispanic/Latino; 35% Hispanic/Latino; 2% Asian, non-Hispanic/Latino; 0.9% Native Hawaiian or other Pacific Islander, non-Hispanic/Latino; 15% American Indian or Alaska Native, non-Hispanic/Latino; 3% Two or more races, non-Hispanic/Latino; 0.3% Race/ethnicity unknown; 13% transferred in.
Freshmen *Admission:* 78 enrolled.
Faculty *Total:* 36, 17% full-time. *Student/faculty ratio:* 37:1.
Majors Dental hygiene; medical office management; physical therapy technology; respiratory care therapy; respiratory therapy technician.
Academics *Calendar:* semesters. *Degree:* certificates and associate.
Student Life *Housing:* college housing not available.
Costs (2015–16) *Tuition:* $14,265 full-time. Full-time tuition and fees vary according to program. *Required fees:* $679 full-time.
Applying *Required:* essay or personal statement, high school transcript, interview.
Freshman Application Contact Carrington College–Mesa, 1001 West Southern Avenue, Suite 130, Mesa, AZ 85210. *Website:* http://carrington.edu/.

Carrington College–Phoenix North
Phoenix, Arizona

- **Proprietary** 2-year, founded 1976, part of Carrington Colleges Group, Inc.
- **Urban** campus
- **Coed,** 676 undergraduate students, 100% full-time, 86% women, 14% men

Undergraduates 676 full-time. 3% are from out of state; 4% Black or African American, non-Hispanic/Latino; 61% Hispanic/Latino; 1% Asian, non-Hispanic/Latino; 0.4% Native Hawaiian or other Pacific Islander, non-Hispanic/Latino; 9% American Indian or Alaska Native, non-Hispanic/Latino; 1% Two or more races, non-Hispanic/Latino; 1% Race/ethnicity unknown; 14% transferred in.
Freshmen *Admission:* 139 enrolled.
Faculty *Total:* 20, 70% full-time. *Student/faculty ratio:* 37:1.

Majors Massage therapy; medical office management; occupational therapy; radiologic technology/science; registered nursing/registered nurse; respiratory care therapy.
Academics *Calendar:* continuous. *Degree:* certificates and associate.
Student Life *Housing:* college housing not available.
Costs (2015–16) *Tuition:* $14,265 full-time. Full-time tuition and fees vary according to program. No tuition increase for student's term of enrollment. *Required fees:* $679 full-time. *Payment plans:* tuition prepayment, installment.
Applying *Required:* essay or personal statement, high school transcript, interview.
Freshman Application Contact Carrington College–Phoenix North, 8503 North 27th Avenue, Phoenix, AZ 85051.
Website: http://carrington.edu/.

Carrington College–Phoenix West
Phoenix, Arizona

- **Proprietary** 2-year, part of Carrington Colleges Group, Inc.
- **Urban** campus
- **Coed,** 346 undergraduate students, 77% full-time, 63% women, 37% men

Undergraduates 266 full-time, 80 part-time. 2% are from out of state; 7% Black or African American, non-Hispanic/Latino; 36% Hispanic/Latino; 6% Asian, non-Hispanic/Latino; 0.9% Native Hawaiian or other Pacific Islander, non-Hispanic/Latino; 6% American Indian or Alaska Native, non-Hispanic/Latino; 2% Two or more races, non-Hispanic/Latino; 5% Race/ethnicity unknown; 14% transferred in.
Freshmen *Admission:* 22 enrolled.
Faculty *Total:* 43, 33% full-time. *Student/faculty ratio:* 12:1.
Majors Clinical/medical laboratory technology; hospital and health-care facilities administration; medical radiologic technology; occupational therapist assistant; registered nursing/registered nurse; respiratory therapy technician.
Academics *Calendar:* semesters. *Degree:* certificates and associate.
Student Life *Housing:* college housing not available.
Costs (2016–17) *Tuition:* $52,594 per degree program part-time. Full-time tuition and fees vary according to program.
Applying *Required:* essay or personal statement, high school transcript, interview.
Freshman Application Contact Carrington College–Phoenix West, 2701 West Bethany Home Road, Phoenix, AZ 85017.
Website: http://carrington.edu/.

Carrington College–Tucson
Tucson, Arizona

- **Proprietary** 2-year, founded 1984, part of Carrington Colleges Group, Inc.
- **Suburban** campus
- **Coed,** 357 undergraduate students, 100% full-time, 81% women, 19% men

Undergraduates 357 full-time. 4% Black or African American, non-Hispanic/Latino; 69% Hispanic/Latino; 0.6% Asian, non-Hispanic/Latino; 0.3% Native Hawaiian or other Pacific Islander, non-Hispanic/Latino; 5% American Indian or Alaska Native, non-Hispanic/Latino; 1% Two or more races, non-Hispanic/Latino; 1% Race/ethnicity unknown; 11% transferred in.
Freshmen *Admission:* 91 enrolled.
Faculty *Total:* 12, 50% full-time. *Student/faculty ratio:* 45:1.
Majors Clinical/medical laboratory technology; medical office management.
Academics *Calendar:* semesters modular courses are offered. *Degree:* certificates.
Student Life *Housing:* college housing not available. *Student services:* personal/psychological counseling, legal services.
Costs (2015–16) *Tuition:* $14,265 full-time. Full-time tuition and fees vary according to program. *Required fees:* $679 full-time.
Applying *Required:* essay or personal statement, high school transcript, interview.
Freshman Application Contact Carrington College–Tucson, 201 North Bonita Avenue, Suite 101, Tucson, AZ 85745.
Website: http://carrington.edu/.

Central Arizona College
Coolidge, Arizona

Freshman Application Contact Dr. James Moore, Dean of Records and Admissions, Central Arizona College, 8470 North Overfield Road, Coolidge, AZ 85128. *Phone:* 520-494-5261. *Toll-free phone:* 800-237-9814. *Fax:* 520-426-5083. *E-mail:* james.moore@centralaz.edu.
Website: http://www.centralaz.edu/.

Chandler-Gilbert Community College
Chandler, Arizona

- **State and locally supported** 2-year, founded 1985, part of Maricopa County Community College District System
- **Suburban** 188-acre campus with easy access to Phoenix
- **Coed,** 14,654 undergraduate students, 29% full-time, 53% women, 47% men

Undergraduates 4,193 full-time, 10,461 part-time. 4% Black or African American, non-Hispanic/Latino; 22% Hispanic/Latino; 5% Asian, non-Hispanic/Latino; 0.3% Native Hawaiian or other Pacific Islander, non-Hispanic/Latino; 2% American Indian or Alaska Native, non-Hispanic/Latino; 3% Two or more races, non-Hispanic/Latino; 13% Race/ethnicity unknown; 0.7% international; 1% transferred in.
Freshmen *Admission:* 1,188 enrolled.
Faculty *Total:* 628, 21% full-time. *Student/faculty ratio:* 25:1.
Majors Accounting; accounting technology and bookkeeping; airline pilot and flight crew; business administration and management; business administration, management and operations related; business/commerce; business, management, and marketing related; computer and information sciences; computer and information sciences and support services related; computer programming; computer programming (vendor/product certification); computer systems analysis; computer systems networking and telecommunications; criminal justice/safety; data entry/microcomputer applications; data modeling/warehousing and database administration; dietetic technology; dietitian assistant; dramatic/theater arts; electromechanical technology; elementary education; fine/studio arts; general studies; information technology; kinesiology and exercise science; liberal arts and sciences and humanities related; liberal arts and sciences/liberal studies; lineworker; massage therapy; mechanic and repair technologies related; music management; organizational behavior; physical sciences; psychology; registered nursing/registered nurse; social work; visual and performing arts.
Academics *Calendar:* semesters. *Degree:* certificates, diplomas, and associate. *Special study options:* academic remediation for entering students, advanced placement credit, English as a second language, freshman honors college, honors programs, independent study, part-time degree program, services for LD students, study abroad, summer session for credit.
Library Chandler-Gilbert Community College Library.
Student Life *Housing:* college housing not available. *Activities and Organizations:* student-run newspaper, radio station, choral group. *Campus security:* 24-hour emergency response devices and patrols, late-night transport/escort service. *Student services:* personal/psychological counseling.
Athletics Member NJCAA. *Intercollegiate sports:* baseball M, basketball M/W, golf M/W, soccer M/W, softball W, volleyball W.
Costs (2015–16) *Tuition:* state resident $2016 full-time, $84 per credit hour part-time; nonresident $7800 full-time, $325 per credit hour part-time. Full-time tuition and fees vary according to reciprocity agreements. Part-time tuition and fees vary according to reciprocity agreements. *Required fees:* $30 full-time, $15 per term part-time. *Payment plans:* installment, deferred payment. *Waivers:* employees or children of employees.
Applying *Options:* electronic application.
Freshman Application Contact Ryan Cain, Coordinator of Enrollment Services, Chandler-Gilbert Community College, 2626 East Pecos Road, Chandler, AZ 85225-2479. *Phone:* 480-732-7044.
E-mail: ryan.cain@cgc.edu.
Website: http://www.cgc.maricopa.edu/.

Cochise County Community College District
Douglas, Arizona

- **State and locally supported** 2-year, founded 1962
- **Rural** 607-acre campus with easy access to Tucson
- **Coed,** 4,509 undergraduate students, 40% full-time, 53% women, 47% men

Undergraduates 1,786 full-time, 2,723 part-time. Students come from 10 states and territories; 1 other country; 7% are from out of state; 6% Black or African American, non-Hispanic/Latino; 48% Hispanic/Latino; 2% Asian, non-Hispanic/Latino; 0.5% Native Hawaiian or other Pacific Islander, non-Hispanic/Latino; 0.7% American Indian or Alaska Native, non-Hispanic/Latino; 3% Two or more races, non-Hispanic/Latino; 2% Race/ethnicity unknown; 0.6% international; 18% transferred in; 2% live on campus. *Retention:* 63% of full-time freshmen returned.
Freshmen *Admission:* 1,949 applied, 1,949 admitted, 798 enrolled. *Average high school GPA:* 2.65.
Faculty *Total:* 325, 26% full-time. *Student/faculty ratio:* 17:1.
Majors Administrative assistant and secretarial science; adult and continuing education; agricultural business and management; air and space operations technology; airline pilot and flight crew; air transportation related; art;

automobile/automotive mechanics technology; avionics maintenance technology; biology/biological sciences; building construction technology; business administration and management; chemistry; computer and information systems security; computer programming; computer science; computer systems networking and telecommunications; criminal justice/police science; culinary arts; digital communication and media/multimedia; dramatic/theater arts; early childhood education; economics; electrical; electronic and communications engineering technology; elementary education; emergency medical technology (EMT paramedic); engineering; English; equestrian studies; fire science/firefighting; general studies; health and physical education/fitness; humanities; information science/studies; intelligence; journalism; logistics, materials, and supply chain management; mathematics; mechatronics, robotics, and automation engineering; music; philosophy; physics; psychology; registered nursing/registered nurse; respiratory care therapy; social sciences; social work; speech communication and rhetoric; transportation and materials moving related; welding technology.

Academics *Calendar:* semesters. *Degrees:* certificates and associate (profile includes campuses in Douglas and Sierra Vista AZ). *Special study options:* academic remediation for entering students, adult/continuing education programs, advanced placement credit, cooperative education, distance learning, English as a second language, honors programs, independent study, internships, part-time degree program, services for LD students, summer session for credit.

Library Charles Di Peso plus 1 other. *Books:* 68,901 (physical), 40,762 (digital/electronic); *Serial titles:* 16 (physical); *Databases:* 11. Weekly public service hours: 61.

Student Life *Housing Options:* coed, special housing for students with disabilities. Campus housing is university owned. *Activities and Organizations:* drama/theater group, choral group, The Art Club, Table Top Games, Cochise Pride, Student Nurses Association, American Sign Language Club, national sororities. *Campus security:* 24-hour emergency response devices and patrols, late-night transport/escort service. *Student services:* personal/psychological counseling.

Athletics Member NJCAA. *Intercollegiate sports:* baseball M(s), basketball M(s)/W(s), soccer W(s).

Costs (2016–17) *Tuition:* state resident $2370 full-time, $79 per credit hour part-time; nonresident $7500 full-time, $250 per credit hour part-time. Full-time tuition and fees vary according to course load, program, and reciprocity agreements. Part-time tuition and fees vary according to course load, program, and reciprocity agreements. *Room and board:* $6564. Room and board charges vary according to housing facility. *Payment plan:* installment. *Waivers:* senior citizens and employees or children of employees.

Financial Aid Of all full-time matriculated undergraduates who enrolled in 2014, 1,300 applied for aid, 1,121 were judged to have need. 72 Federal Work-Study jobs (averaging $5437). In 2014, 22 non-need-based awards were made. *Average financial aid package:* $5876. *Average need-based loan:* $3658. *Average need-based gift aid:* $3730. *Average non-need-based aid:* $1666. *Financial aid deadline:* 6/15.

Applying *Options:* electronic application, deferred entrance. *Required for some:* high school transcript. *Recommended:* high school transcript. *Application deadlines:* rolling (freshmen), rolling (out-of-state freshmen), rolling (transfers). *Notification:* continuous (freshmen), continuous (out-of-state freshmen), continuous (transfers).

Freshman Application Contact Ms. Debbie Quick, Director of Admissions and Records, Cochise County Community College District, 4190 West Highway 80, Douglas, AZ 85607-6190. *Phone:* 520-515-3640. *Toll-free phone:* 800-593-9567. *Fax:* 520-515-5452. *E-mail:* quickd@cochise.edu. *Website:* http://www.cochise.edu/.

Coconino Community College
Flagstaff, Arizona

Freshman Application Contact Veronica Hipolito, Director of Student Services, Coconino Community College, 2800 South Lone Tree Road, Flagstaff, AZ 86001. *Phone:* 928-226-4334 Ext. 4334. *Toll-free phone:* 800-350-7122. *Fax:* 928-226-4114. *E-mail:* veronica.hipolito@coconino.edu. *Website:* http://www.coconino.edu/.

CollegeAmerica–Flagstaff
Flagstaff, Arizona

- **Independent** primarily 2-year
- **Small-town** campus
- **Coed**

Undergraduates 205 full-time. 1% Black or African American, non-Hispanic/Latino; 11% Hispanic/Latino; 60% American Indian or Alaska Native, non-Hispanic/Latino; 0.5% Two or more races, non-Hispanic/Latino.

Faculty *Student/faculty ratio:* 15:1.

Academics *Calendar:* quarters modules. *Degrees:* associate and bachelor's. *Special study options:* academic remediation for entering students, internships.

Library Main Library plus 1 other.

Applying *Required:* essay or personal statement, high school transcript, interview, references.

Freshman Application Contact CollegeAmerica–Flagstaff, 399 South Malpais Lane, Flagstaff, AZ 86001. *Phone:* 928-213-6060 Ext. 1402. *Toll-free phone:* 800-622-2894.
Website: http://www.collegeamerica.edu/.

CollegeAmerica–Phoenix
Phoenix, Arizona

Admissions Office Contact CollegeAmerica–Phoenix, 9801 North Metro Parkway East, Phoenix, AZ 85051. *Toll-free phone:* 800-622-2894.
Website: http://www.collegeamerica.edu/.

Diné College
Tsaile, Arizona

Freshman Application Contact Mrs. Louise Litzin, Registrar, Diné College, PO Box 67, Tsaile, AZ 86556. *Phone:* 928-724-6633. *Toll-free phone:* 877-988-DINE. *Fax:* 928-724-3349. *E-mail:* louise@dinecollege.edu. *Website:* http://www.dinecollege.edu/.

Eastern Arizona College
Thatcher, Arizona

- **State and locally supported** 2-year, founded 1888, part of Arizona State Community College System
- **Small-town** campus
- **Endowment** $4.3 million
- **Coed**, 6,379 undergraduate students, 28% full-time, 54% women, 46% men

Undergraduates 1,783 full-time, 4,596 part-time. Students come from 19 other countries; 4% are from out of state; 3% Black or African American, non-Hispanic/Latino; 20% Hispanic/Latino; 1% Asian, non-Hispanic/Latino; 0.4% Native Hawaiian or other Pacific Islander, non-Hispanic/Latino; 7% American Indian or Alaska Native, non-Hispanic/Latino; 0.9% Two or more races, non-Hispanic/Latino; 3% Race/ethnicity unknown; 0.8% international; 37% transferred in; 5% live on campus.

Freshmen *Admission:* 623 applied, 623 admitted.

Faculty *Total:* 362, 26% full-time, 8% with terminal degrees. *Student/faculty ratio:* 18:1.

Majors Anthropology; art; art teacher education; automobile/automotive mechanics technology; biology/biological sciences; business administration and management; business, management, and marketing related; business operations support and secretarial services related; business teacher education; chemistry; civil engineering technology; commercial and advertising art; cosmetology; criminal justice/law enforcement administration; criminal justice/police science; diesel mechanics technology; drafting and design technology; dramatic/theater arts; early childhood education; elementary education; emergency medical technology (EMT paramedic); English; entrepreneurship; environmental biology; fire science/firefighting; foreign languages and literatures; forestry; geology/earth science; health and physical education/fitness; health/medical preparatory programs related; history; industrial electronics technology; industrial mechanics and maintenance technology; information science/studies; liberal arts and sciences/liberal studies; machine shop technology; mathematics; mining technology; multi/interdisciplinary studies related; music; pharmacy technician; physics; political science and government; premedical studies; pre-pharmacy studies; psychology; registered nursing/registered nurse; secondary education; sociology; technology/industrial arts teacher education; welding technology; wildlife biology.

Academics *Calendar:* semesters. *Degree:* certificates and associate. *Special study options:* academic remediation for entering students, adult/continuing education programs, advanced placement credit, cooperative education, distance learning, double majors, independent study, internships, part-time degree program, services for LD students, study abroad, summer session for credit.

Library Alumni Library.

Student Life *Housing Options:* men-only, women-only. Campus housing is university owned. *Activities and Organizations:* drama/theater group, choral group, marching band, Latter-Day Saints Student Association, Criminal Justice Student Association, Multicultural Council, Phi Theta Kappa, Mark Allen Dorm Club. *Campus security:* 24-hour emergency response devices, late-night transport/escort service, controlled dormitory access, 20-hour patrols by trained security personnel. *Student services:* personal/psychological counseling.

Athletics Member NJCAA. *Intercollegiate sports:* baseball M(s), basketball M(s)/W(s), football M(s), golf M/W, softball W(s), volleyball W(s). *Intramural sports:* basketball M/W, racquetball M/W, swimming and diving M/W, table tennis M/W, tennis M/W, volleyball M/W.

Costs (2015–16) *Tuition:* state resident $2080 full-time, $100 per credit hour part-time; nonresident $9580 full-time, $235 per credit hour part-time. Full-time tuition and fees vary according to program. Part-time tuition and fees vary according to program. *Room and board:* $6125. Room and board charges vary according to board plan. *Waivers:* senior citizens and employees or children of employees.

Financial Aid Of all full-time matriculated undergraduates who enrolled in 2015, 1,619 applied for aid, 1,419 were judged to have need, 65 had their need fully met. In 2015, 102 non-need-based awards were made. *Average percent of need met:* 28%. *Average financial aid package:* $6336. *Average need-based gift aid:* $6053. *Average non-need-based aid:* $3309.

Applying *Options:* electronic application, early admission, deferred entrance. *Recommended:* high school transcript. *Application deadlines:* rolling (freshmen), rolling (transfers). *Notification:* continuous (freshmen).

Freshman Application Contact Suzette Udall, Records Assistant, Eastern Arizona College, 615 North Stadium Avenue, Thatcher, AZ 85552-0769. *Phone:* 928-428-8904. *Toll-free phone:* 800-678-3808. *Fax:* 928-428-3729. *E-mail:* admissions@eac.edu. *Website:* http://www.eac.edu/.

Estrella Mountain Community College
Avondale, Arizona

- **State and locally supported** 2-year, founded 1992, part of Maricopa County Community College District System
- **Urban** campus with easy access to Phoenix
- **Coed,** 9,164 undergraduate students, 33% full-time, 59% women, 41% men

Undergraduates 3,015 full-time, 6,149 part-time. 9% Black or African American, non-Hispanic/Latino; 47% Hispanic/Latino; 4% Asian, non-Hispanic/Latino; 0.2% Native Hawaiian or other Pacific Islander, non-Hispanic/Latino; 1% American Indian or Alaska Native, non-Hispanic/Latino; 2% Two or more races, non-Hispanic/Latino; 4% Race/ethnicity unknown; 0.2% international.

Freshmen *Admission:* 791 applied, 791 admitted.

Faculty *Student/faculty ratio:* 22:1.

Majors General studies; liberal arts and sciences/liberal studies.

Academics *Calendar:* semesters. *Degree:* certificates and associate. *Special study options:* academic remediation for entering students, adult/continuing education programs, advanced placement credit, cooperative education, distance learning, English as a second language, honors programs, independent study, part-time degree program, services for LD students, summer session for credit. *ROTC:* Air Force (c).

Library Estrella Mountain Library.

Student Life *Housing:* college housing not available. *Activities and Organizations:* Phi Theta Kappa, Men Of Color Association (MOCA), Movimiento Estudiantil Chicano de Aztlan (MEChA), Savings and Investment Club. *Campus security:* 24-hour emergency response devices and patrols, late-night transport/escort service. *Student services:* personal/psychological counseling.

Athletics *Intercollegiate sports:* cross-country running M/W, golf M/W.

Applying *Options:* electronic application.

Freshman Application Contact Estrella Mountain Community College, 3000 North Dysart Road, Avondale, AZ 85392. *Phone:* 623-935-8812. *Website:* http://www.estrellamountain.edu/.

Fortis College
Phoenix, Arizona

Admissions Office Contact Fortis College, 555 North 18th Street, Suite 110, Phoenix, AZ 85006. *Toll-free phone:* 855-4-FORTIS. *Website:* http://www.fortis.edu/.

GateWay Community College
Phoenix, Arizona

Freshman Application Contact Director of Admissions and Records, GateWay Community College, 108 North 40th Street, Phoenix, AZ 85034. *Phone:* 602-286-8200. *Fax:* 602-286-8200. *E-mail:* enroll@gatewaycc.edu. *Website:* http://www.gatewaycc.edu/.

Glendale Community College
Glendale, Arizona

Freshman Application Contact Ms. Mary Blackwell, Dean of Enrollment Services, Glendale Community College, 6000 West Olive Avenue, Glendale, AZ 85302. *Phone:* 623-435-3305. *Fax:* 623-845-3303. *E-mail:* admissions.recruitment@gccaz.edu. *Website:* http://www.gc.maricopa.edu/.

Golf Academy of America
Chandler, Arizona

Admissions Office Contact Golf Academy of America, 2031 N. Arizona Avenue, Suite 2, Chandler, AZ 85225. *Website:* http://www.golfacademy.edu/.

ITT Technical Institute
Phoenix, Arizona

Freshman Application Contact Director of Recruitment, ITT Technical Institute, 10220 North 25th Avenue, Suite 100, Phoenix, AZ 85021. *Phone:* 602-749-7900. *Toll-free phone:* 877-221-1132. *Website:* http://www.itt-tech.edu/.

ITT Technical Institute
Phoenix, Arizona

Freshman Application Contact Director of Recruitment, ITT Technical Institute, 1840 North 95th Avenue, Suite 132, Phoenix, AZ 85037. *Phone:* 623-474-7900. *Toll-free phone:* 800-210-1178. *Website:* http://www.itt-tech.edu/.

ITT Technical Institute
Tucson, Arizona

Freshman Application Contact Director of Recruitment, ITT Technical Institute, 1455 West River Road, Tucson, AZ 85704. *Phone:* 520-408-7488. *Toll-free phone:* 800-870-9730. *Website:* http://www.itt-tech.edu/.

Mesa Community College
Mesa, Arizona

- **State and locally supported** 2-year, founded 1965, part of Maricopa County Community College District System
- **Urban** 160-acre campus with easy access to Phoenix
- **Coed**

Academics *Calendar:* semesters. *Degree:* certificates and associate. *Special study options:* academic remediation for entering students, adult/continuing education programs, advanced placement credit, cooperative education, distance learning, English as a second language, freshman honors college, honors programs, independent study, off-campus study, part-time degree program, services for LD students, student-designed majors, study abroad, summer session for credit. *ROTC:* Army (c), Air Force (c).

Library Information Commons.

Student Life *Campus security:* 24-hour emergency response devices and patrols, student patrols.

Athletics Member NJCAA.

Costs (2015–16) *Tuition:* state resident $2016 full-time; nonresident $7800 full-time. Full-time tuition and fees vary according to course load and reciprocity agreements. Part-time tuition and fees vary according to course load and reciprocity agreements. *Required fees:* $30 full-time.

Applying *Options:* electronic application, early admission, deferred entrance.

Freshman Application Contact Dr. Barbara Boros, Dean, Enrollment Services, Mesa Community College, 1833 West Southern Avenue, Mesa, AZ 85202-4866. *Phone:* 480-461-7342. *Toll-free phone:* 866-532-4983. *Fax:* 480-844-3117. *E-mail:* admissionsandrecords@mesacc.edu. *Website:* http://www.mesacc.edu/.

Mohave Community College
Kingman, Arizona

- **State-supported** 2-year, founded 1971
- **Small-town** 160-acre campus
- **Coed,** 4,360 undergraduate students, 22% full-time, 65% women, 35% men

Undergraduates 938 full-time, 3,422 part-time. Students come from 19 states and territories; 5% are from out of state; 1% Black or African American, non-Hispanic/Latino; 21% Hispanic/Latino; 2% Asian, non-Hispanic/Latino; 0.8% Native Hawaiian or other Pacific Islander, non-Hispanic/Latino; 2% American Indian or Alaska Native, non-Hispanic/Latino; 3% Two or more races, non-Hispanic/Latino; 2% Race/ethnicity unknown.
Freshmen *Admission:* 436 enrolled.
Faculty *Total:* 309, 26% full-time. *Student/faculty ratio:* 13:1.
Majors Accounting; art; automobile/automotive mechanics technology; building/construction finishing, management, and inspection related; business administration and management; computer and information sciences related; computer programming (specific applications); computer science; criminal justice/police science; culinary arts; dental assisting; dental hygiene; drafting and design technology; education; emergency medical technology (EMT paramedic); English; fire science/firefighting; heating, air conditioning, ventilation and refrigeration maintenance technology; history; information technology; legal assistant/paralegal; liberal arts and sciences/liberal studies; mathematics; medical/clinical assistant; personal and culinary services related; pharmacy technician; physical therapy technology; psychology; registered nursing/registered nurse; sociology; substance abuse/addiction counseling; surgical technology; truck and bus driver/commercial vehicle operation/instruction; welding technology.
Academics *Calendar:* semesters. *Degree:* certificates and associate. *Special study options:* academic remediation for entering students, adult/continuing education programs, cooperative education, distance learning, English as a second language, independent study, part-time degree program, summer session for credit.
Library Mohave Community College Library.
Student Life *Housing:* college housing not available. *Activities and Organizations:* Art Club, Phi Theta Kappa, Computer Club (MC4), Science Club, Student Government. *Campus security:* late-night transport/escort service.
Costs (2015–16) *Tuition:* state resident $2430 full-time, $81 per credit hour part-time; nonresident $8505 full-time, $284 per credit hour part-time. Full-time tuition and fees vary according to program. Part-time tuition and fees vary according to program. *Required fees:* $210 full-time, $7 per credit hour part-time. *Payment plans:* installment, deferred payment. *Waivers:* employees or children of employees.
Applying *Options:* electronic application, early admission, deferred entrance. *Application deadlines:* rolling (freshmen), rolling (transfers). *Notification:* continuous (freshmen), continuous (transfers).
Freshman Application Contact Mrs. Ana Masterson, Dean of Student Services, Mohave Community College, 1971 Jagerson Avenue, Kingman, AZ 86409. *Phone:* 928-757-0803. *Toll-free phone:* 888-664-2832. *Fax:* 928-757-0808. *E-mail:* amasterson@mohave.edu.
Website: http://www.mohave.edu/.

Northland Pioneer College
Holbrook, Arizona

Freshman Application Contact Ms. Suzette Willis, Coordinator of Admissions, Northland Pioneer College, PO Box 610, Holbrook, AZ 86025. *Phone:* 928-536-6271. *Toll-free phone:* 800-266-7845. *Fax:* 928-536-6212. *Website:* http://www.npc.edu/.

Paradise Valley Community College
Phoenix, Arizona

Freshman Application Contact Paradise Valley Community College, 18401 North 32nd Street, Phoenix, AZ 85032-1200. *Phone:* 602-787-7020. *Website:* http://www.pvc.maricopa.edu/.

The Paralegal Institute at Brighton College
Scottsdale, Arizona

Freshman Application Contact Patricia Yancy, Director of Admissions, The Paralegal Institute at Brighton College, 2933 West Indian School Road, Drawer 11408, Phoenix, AZ 85061-1408. *Phone:* 602-212-0501. *Toll-free*

phone: 800-354-1254. *Fax:* 602-212-0502.
E-mail: paralegalinst@mindspring.com.
Website: http://www.theparalegalinstitute.edu/.

Penn Foster College
Scottsdale, Arizona

- **Proprietary** primarily 2-year
- **Coed,** 24,527 undergraduate students

Undergraduates Students come from 50 states and territories; 5 other countries.
Faculty *Total:* 203, 20% full-time, 5% with terminal degrees.
Majors Accounting; building construction technology; business administration and management; computer and information sciences; computer installation and repair technology; criminal justice/law enforcement administration; early childhood education; engineering technology; fashion merchandising; finance; graphic design; health/health-care administration; health information/medical records technology; hospitality administration; human resources management; industrial electronics technology; legal assistant/paralegal; marketing/marketing management; marketing research; medical/clinical assistant; retail management; roofing; veterinary/animal health technology.
Academics *Calendar:* continuous. *Degrees:* certificates, associate, and bachelor's. *Special study options:* academic remediation for entering students, accelerated degree program, distance learning, external degree program, independent study, off-campus study, part-time degree program, services for LD students.
Library Penn Foster College Online Library.
Student Life *Housing:* college housing not available. *Activities and Organizations:* Online Community-Hosted Academic Interest Groups.
Costs (2016–17) *Tuition:* $79 per credit part-time. Part-time tuition and fees vary according to course load and program. *Payment plan:* installment.
Applying *Options:* electronic application. *Application fee:* $75. *Required:* high school transcript, computer with Internet access. *Application deadlines:* rolling (freshmen), rolling (out-of-state freshmen).
Freshman Application Contact Admissions, Penn Foster College, 14300 North Northsight Boulevard, Suite 120, Scottsdale, AZ 85260. *Phone:* 888-427-1000. *Toll-free phone:* 800-471-3232.
Website: http://www.pennfostercollege.edu/.

Phoenix College
Phoenix, Arizona

- **County-supported** 2-year, founded 1920, part of Maricopa County Community College District System
- **Urban** 58-acre campus
- **Coed**

Undergraduates 3,421 full-time, 9,255 part-time. 11% Black or African American, non-Hispanic/Latino; 41% Hispanic/Latino; 3% Asian, non-Hispanic/Latino; 0.2% Native Hawaiian or other Pacific Islander, non-Hispanic/Latino; 3% American Indian or Alaska Native, non-Hispanic/Latino; 0.1% Two or more races, non-Hispanic/Latino; 0.1% Race/ethnicity unknown; 0.5% international. *Retention:* 60% of full-time freshmen returned.
Faculty *Student/faculty ratio:* 17:1.
Academics *Calendar:* semesters. *Degree:* certificates, diplomas, and associate. *Special study options:* academic remediation for entering students, adult/continuing education programs, advanced placement credit, cooperative education, distance learning, English as a second language, freshman honors college, honors programs, independent study, internships, off-campus study, part-time degree program, services for LD students, study abroad, summer session for credit. *ROTC:* Army (c), Navy (c), Air Force (c).
Library Fannin Library.
Student Life *Campus security:* 24-hour emergency response devices and patrols, student patrols, late-night transport/escort service.
Athletics Member NCAA, NJCAA. All NCAA Division II.
Costs (2015–16) *Tuition:* area resident $2016 full-time, $84 per credit hour part-time; state resident $8784 full-time, $366 per credit hour part-time. Full-time tuition and fees vary according to reciprocity agreements. Part-time tuition and fees vary according to course load and reciprocity agreements. *Required fees:* $30 full-time, $15 per term part-time.
Financial Aid Of all full-time matriculated undergraduates who enrolled in 2014, 220 Federal Work-Study jobs (averaging $4800).
Applying *Options:* electronic application, early admission, deferred entrance.
Freshman Application Contact Ms. Brenda Stark, Director of Admissions, Registration, and Records, Phoenix College, 1202 West Thomas Road, Phoenix, AZ 85013. *Phone:* 602-285-7503. *Fax:* 602-285-7813.
E-mail: kathy.french@pcmail.maricopa.edu.
Website: http://www.pc.maricopa.edu/.

Pima Community College
Tucson, Arizona

Freshman Application Contact Terra Benson, Director of Admissions and Registrar, Pima Community College, 4905B East Broadway Boulevard, Tucson, AZ 85709-1120. *Phone:* 520-206-4640. *Fax:* 520-206-4790.
E-mail: tbenson@pima.edu.
Website: http://www.pima.edu/.

Pima Medical Institute
Mesa, Arizona

Freshman Application Contact Pima Medical Institute, 2160 S. Power Road, Mesa, AZ 85209. *Phone:* 480-898-9898.
Website: http://www.pmi.edu/.

Pima Medical Institute
Mesa, Arizona

Freshman Application Contact Admissions Office, Pima Medical Institute, 957 South Dobson Road, Mesa, AZ 85202. *Phone:* 480-644-0267 Ext. 225.
Toll-free phone: 800-477-PIMA (in-state); 888-477-PIMA (out-of-state).
Website: http://www.pmi.edu/.

Pima Medical Institute
Tucson, Arizona

Freshman Application Contact Admissions Office, Pima Medical Institute, 3350 East Grant Road, Tucson, AZ 85716. *Phone:* 520-326-1600 Ext. 5112.
Toll-free phone: 800-477-PIMA (in-state); 888-477-PIMA (out-of-state).
Website: http://www.pmi.edu/.

The Refrigeration School
Phoenix, Arizona

Freshman Application Contact Ms. Heather Haskell, The Refrigeration School, 4210 East Washington Street. *Phone:* 602-275-7133. *Toll-free phone:* 888-943-4822. *Fax:* 602-267-4811. *E-mail:* info@rsiaz.edu.
Website: http://www.refrigerationschool.com/.

Rio Salado College
Tempe, Arizona

Freshman Application Contact Laurel Redman, Director, Instruction Support Services and Student Development, Rio Salado College, 2323 West 14th Street, Tempe 85281. *Phone:* 480-517-8563. *Toll-free phone:* 800-729-1197. *Fax:* 480-517-8199. *E-mail:* admission@riomail.maricopa.edu.
Website: http://www.rio.maricopa.edu/.

Scottsdale Community College
Scottsdale, Arizona

- **State and locally supported** 2-year, founded 1969, part of Maricopa County Community College District System
- **Urban** 160-acre campus with easy access to Phoenix
- **Coed,** 10,083 undergraduate students, 27% full-time, 53% women, 47% men

Undergraduates 2,745 full-time, 7,338 part-time. Students come from 36 states and territories; 36 other countries; 4% are from out of state; 5% Black or African American, non-Hispanic/Latino; 15% Hispanic/Latino; 3% Asian, non-Hispanic/Latino; 0.3% Native Hawaiian or other Pacific Islander, non-Hispanic/Latino; 5% American Indian or Alaska Native, non-Hispanic/Latino; 2% Two or more races, non-Hispanic/Latino; 8% Race/ethnicity unknown; 1% international; 46% transferred in.
Faculty *Total:* 570, 30% full-time, 15% with terminal degrees. *Student/faculty ratio:* 17:1.
Majors Accounting; administrative assistant and secretarial science; business administration and management; criminal justice/law enforcement administration; culinary arts; dramatic/theater arts; electrical, electronic and communications engineering technology; environmental design/architecture; equestrian studies; fashion merchandising; finance; hospitality administration; hotel/motel administration; information science/studies; interior design; mathematics; medical administrative assistant and medical secretary; photography; public administration; real estate; registered nursing/registered nurse; special products marketing.
Academics *Calendar:* semesters. *Degree:* certificates, diplomas, and associate. *Special study options:* academic remediation for entering students,

adult/continuing education programs, advanced placement credit, cooperative education, English as a second language, honors programs, internships, off-campus study, part-time degree program, services for LD students, study abroad, summer session for credit.
Library Scottsdale Community College Library.
Student Life *Housing:* college housing not available. *Activities and Organizations:* drama/theater group, student-run newspaper, radio station, choral group, Student Leadership Forum, International Community Club, Phi Theta Kappa, Music Industry Club, SCC ASID-Interior Design group. *Campus security:* 24-hour emergency response devices and patrols, student patrols, late-night transport/escort service, 24-hour automatic surveillance cameras. *Student services:* personal/psychological counseling.
Athletics Member NCAA, NJCAA. All NCAA Division II. *Intercollegiate sports:* baseball M, basketball M/W, cross-country running M/W, football M, golf M/W, soccer M/W, softball W, volleyball W. *Intramural sports:* archery M/W, badminton M/W, basketball M/W, racquetball M/W, track and field M/W, volleyball M/W.
Costs (2015–16) *Tuition:* area resident $1260 full-time; state resident $2520 full-time, $84 per credit part-time; nonresident $9750 full-time, $325 per credit part-time. Full-time tuition and fees vary according to program and reciprocity agreements. Part-time tuition and fees vary according to program and reciprocity agreements. *Required fees:* $30 full-time, $15 per term part-time. *Payment plans:* installment, deferred payment. *Waivers:* employees or children of employees.
Financial Aid Of all full-time matriculated undergraduates who enrolled in 2014, 75 Federal Work-Study jobs (averaging $2000). *Financial aid deadline:* 7/15.
Applying *Options:* electronic application, early admission. *Application deadline:* rolling (freshmen). *Notification:* continuous (freshmen).
Freshman Application Contact Ms. Fran Vitale, Director of Admissions and Records, Scottsdale Community College, 9000 East Chaparral Road, Scottsdale, AZ 85256. *Phone:* 480-423-6133. *Fax:* 480-423-6200.
E-mail: fran.Vitale@scottsdalecc.edu.
Website: http://www.scottsdalecc.edu/.

Sessions College for Professional Design
Tempe, Arizona

Freshman Application Contact Ms. Mhelanie Hernandez, Director of Admissions, Sessions College for Professional Design, 350 South Mill Avenue, Suite B-104, Tempe, AZ 85281. *Phone:* 480-212-1704. *Toll-free phone:* 800-258-4115. *E-mail:* admissions@sessions.edu.
Website: http://www.sessions.edu/.

South Mountain Community College
Phoenix, Arizona

Director of Admissions Dean of Enrollment Services, South Mountain Community College, 7050 South Twenty-fourth Street, Phoenix, AZ 85040. *Phone:* 602-243-8120.
Website: http://www.southmountaincc.edu/.

Southwest Institute of Healing Arts
Tempe, Arizona

Director of Admissions Katie Yearous, Student Advisor, Southwest Institute of Healing Arts, 1100 East Apache Boulevard, Tempe, AZ 85281. *Phone:* 480-994-9244. *Toll-free phone:* 888-504-9106. *E-mail:* joannl@swiha.net.
Website: http://www.swiha.org/.

Tohono O'odham Community College
Sells, Arizona

- **Public** 2-year, founded 1998
- **Rural** 42-acre campus
- **Endowment** $314,747
- **Coed,** 206 undergraduate students, 43% full-time, 55% women, 45% men

Undergraduates 89 full-time, 117 part-time. Students come from 7 states and territories; 2% are from out of state; 6% Black or African American, non-Hispanic/Latino; 4% Hispanic/Latino; 82% American Indian or Alaska Native, non-Hispanic/Latino; 2% Two or more races, non-Hispanic/Latino; 10% live on campus. *Retention:* 43% of full-time freshmen returned.
Freshmen *Admission:* 19 enrolled.
Faculty *Total:* 48, 35% full-time, 21% with terminal degrees. *Student/faculty ratio:* 10:1.

Majors Business administration and management; child development; computer systems analysis; early childhood education; human services; liberal arts and sciences/liberal studies.

Academics *Calendar:* semesters. *Degree:* certificates, diplomas, and associate. *Special study options:* academic remediation for entering students, adult/continuing education programs, cooperative education, double majors, part-time degree program, services for LD students, summer session for credit.

Library Tohono O'odham Community College Library plus 2 others. *Books:* 12,865 (physical), 54 (digital/electronic). Weekly public service hours: 40.

Student Life *Housing:* on-campus residence required through sophomore year. *Options:* coed, men-only, women-only. Campus housing is university owned. *Activities and Organizations:* Student Senate, AISES, Archery Club, Chess Club. *Campus security:* 24-hour patrols. *Student services:* personal/psychological counseling.

Athletics Member NJCAA. *Intercollegiate sports:* basketball M(s)/W(s).

Costs (2015–16) *Tuition:* state resident $2070 full-time, $69 per credit hour part-time; nonresident $3696 full-time, $69 per credit hour part-time. Full-time tuition and fees vary according to class time, course level, course load, degree level, location, program, and student level. Part-time tuition and fees vary according to class time, course level, course load, degree level, location, program, and student level. *Required fees:* $20 full-time, $10 per course part-time. *Room and board:* $2400. *Payment plan:* installment. *Waivers:* employees or children of employees.

Applying *Required:* high school transcript.

Freshman Application Contact Jennifer Hill, Admissions, Tohono O'odham Community College, PO Box 3129, Sells, AZ 85634. *Phone:* 520-383-8401. *E-mail:* jhill@tocc.edu. *Website:* http://www.tocc.edu/.

Universal Technical Institute
Avondale, Arizona

Freshman Application Contact Director of Admission, Universal Technical Institute, 10695 West Pierce Street, Avondale, AZ 85323. *Phone:* 623-245-4600. *Toll-free phone:* 800-510-5072. *Fax:* 623-245-4601. *Website:* http://www.uti.edu/.

Yavapai College
Prescott, Arizona

Freshman Application Contact Mrs. Sheila Jarrell, Admissions, Registration, and Records Manager, Yavapai College, 1100 East Sheldon Street, Prescott, AZ 86301-3297. *Phone:* 928-776-2107. *Toll-free phone:* 800-922-6787. *Fax:* 928-776-2151. *E-mail:* registration@yc.edu. *Website:* http://www.yc.edu/.

ARKANSAS

Arkansas Northeastern College
Blytheville, Arkansas

- **State-supported** 2-year, founded 1975
- **Small-town** 80-acre campus with easy access to Memphis
- **Endowment** $187,500
- **Coed**

Undergraduates 538 full-time, 887 part-time. Students come from 4 states and territories; 17% are from out of state; 30% Black or African American, non-Hispanic/Latino; 4% Hispanic/Latino; 0.6% Asian, non-Hispanic/Latino; 0.1% Native Hawaiian or other Pacific Islander, non-Hispanic/Latino; 0.4% American Indian or Alaska Native, non-Hispanic/Latino; 1% Two or more races, non-Hispanic/Latino; 6% transferred in. *Retention:* 50% of full-time freshmen returned.

Academics *Calendar:* semesters. *Degree:* certificates and associate. *Special study options:* academic remediation for entering students, adult/continuing education programs, advanced placement credit, distance learning, double majors, part-time degree program, summer session for credit.

Library Adams/Vines Library.

Student Life *Campus security:* 24-hour patrols.

Costs (2015–16) *Tuition:* area resident $1820 full-time, $65 per credit hour part-time; state resident $2100 full-time, $75 per credit hour part-time; nonresident $3500 full-time, $125 per credit hour part-time. Full-time tuition and fees vary according to course load. Part-time tuition and fees vary according to course load. *Required fees:* $330 full-time, $10 per credit hour part-time, $25 per term part-time. *Payment plans:* installment, deferred payment.

Financial Aid Of all full-time matriculated undergraduates who enrolled in 2014, 42 Federal Work-Study jobs (averaging $2500).

Applying *Options:* deferred entrance. *Recommended:* high school transcript.

Freshman Application Contact Arkansas Northeastern College, PO Box 1109, Blytheville, AR 72316. *Phone:* 870-762-1020. *Fax:* 870-763-1654. *Website:* http://www.anc.edu/.

Arkansas State University–Beebe
Beebe, Arkansas

Freshman Application Contact Mr. Ronald Hudson, Coordinator of Student Recruitment, Arkansas State University–Beebe, PO Box 1000, Beebe, AR 72012. *Phone:* 501-882-8860. *Toll-free phone:* 800-632-9985. *E-mail:* rdhudson@asub.edu. *Website:* http://www.asub.edu/.

Arkansas State University Mid-South
West Memphis, Arkansas

Freshman Application Contact Jeremy Reece, Director of Admissions, Arkansas State University Mid-South, 2000 West Broadway, West Memphis, AR 72301. *Phone:* 870-733-6786. *Toll-free phone:* 866-733-6722. *Fax:* 870-733-6719. *E-mail:* jreece@midsouthcc.edu. *Website:* http://www.asumidsouth.edu/.

Arkansas State University–Mountain Home
Mountain Home, Arkansas

Freshman Application Contact Ms. Delba Parrish, Admissions Coordinator, Arkansas State University–Mountain Home, 1600 South College Street, Mountain Home, AR 72653. *Phone:* 870-508-6180. *Fax:* 870-508-6287. *E-mail:* dparrish@asumh.edu. *Website:* http://www.asumh.edu/.

Arkansas State University–Newport
Newport, Arkansas

Freshman Application Contact Arkansas State University–Newport, 7648 Victory Boulevard, Newport, AR 72112. *Phone:* 870-512-7800. *Toll-free phone:* 800-976-1676. *Website:* http://www.asun.edu/.

Baptist Health College Little Rock
Little Rock, Arkansas

Admissions Office Contact Baptist Health College Little Rock, 11900 Colonel Glenn Road, Suite 100, Little Rock, AR 72210-2820. *Website:* http://www.bhclr.edu/.

Black River Technical College
Pocahontas, Arkansas

Director of Admissions Director of Admissions, Black River Technical College, 1410 Highway 304 East, Pocahontas, AR 72455. *Phone:* 870-892-4565. *Website:* http://www.blackrivertech.edu/.

Bryan University
Rogers, Arkansas

Admissions Office Contact Bryan University, 3704 W. Walnut Street, Rogers, AR 72756. *Website:* http://www.bryanu.edu/.

College of the Ouachitas
Malvern, Arkansas

Freshman Application Contact Mrs. Shanea Nelson, Student Success Coordinator, College of the Ouachitas, One College Circle, Malvern, AR 72104. *Phone:* 501-337-5000 Ext. 1177. *Toll-free phone:* 800-337-0266. *Fax:* 501-337-9382. *E-mail:* snelson@coto.edu. *Website:* http://www.coto.edu/.

Cossatot Community College of the University of Arkansas
De Queen, Arkansas

Freshman Application Contact Mrs. Tommi Cobb, Admissions Coordinator, Cossatot Community College of the University of Arkansas, 183 College Drive, DeQueen, AR 71832. *Phone:* 870-584-4471 Ext. 1158. *Toll-free phone:* 800-844-4471. *Fax:* 870-642-5088. *E-mail:* tcobb@cccua.edu. *Website:* http://www.cccua.edu/.

Crowley's Ridge College
Paragould, Arkansas

Freshman Application Contact Amanda Drake, Director of Admissions, Crowley's Ridge College, 100 College Drive, Paragould, AR 72450-9731. *Phone:* 870-236-6901. *Toll-free phone:* 800-264-1096. *Fax:* 870-236-7748. *E-mail:* njoneshi@crc.pioneer.paragould.ar.us. *Website:* http://www.crc.edu/.

East Arkansas Community College
Forrest City, Arkansas

Freshman Application Contact Ms. Sharon Collier, Director of Enrollment Management/Institutional Research, East Arkansas Community College, 1700 Newcastle Road, Forrest City, AR 72335-2204. *Phone:* 870-633-4480. *Toll-free phone:* 877-797-3222. *Fax:* 870-633-3840. *E-mail:* dadams@eacc.edu. *Website:* http://www.eacc.edu/.

ITT Technical Institute
Little Rock, Arkansas

Freshman Application Contact Director of Recruitment, ITT Technical Institute, 10800 Financial Centre Parkway, Suite 100, Little Rock, AR 72211. *Phone:* 501-565-5550. *Toll-free phone:* 800-359-4429. *Website:* http://www.itt-tech.edu/.

Jefferson Regional Medical Center School of Nursing
Pine Bluff, Arkansas

Admissions Office Contact Jefferson Regional Medical Center School of Nursing, 1600 West 40th Avenue, Pine Bluff, AR 71603. *Website:* http://www.jrmc.org/.

National Park College
Hot Springs, Arkansas

Director of Admissions Dr. Allen B. Moody, Director of Institutional Services/Registrar, National Park College, 101 College Drive, Hot Springs, AR 71913. *Phone:* 501-760-4222. *E-mail:* bmoody@npcc.edu. *Website:* http://www.np.edu/.

North Arkansas College
Harrison, Arkansas

Freshman Application Contact Mrs. Charla Jennings, Director of Admissions, North Arkansas College, 1515 Pioneer Drive, Harrison, AR 72601. *Phone:* 870-391-3221. *Toll-free phone:* 800-679-6622. *Fax:* 870-391-3339. *E-mail:* charlam@northark.edu. *Website:* http://www.northark.edu/.

NorthWest Arkansas Community College
Bentonville, Arkansas

- **State-supported** 2-year, founded 1989
- **Suburban** 77-acre campus
- **Coed,** 7,744 undergraduate students

Undergraduates Students come from 21 states and territories; 2% are from out of state; 2% Black or African American, non-Hispanic/Latino; 16% Hispanic/Latino; 3% Asian, non-Hispanic/Latino; 0.3% Native Hawaiian or other Pacific Islander, non-Hispanic/Latino; 2% American Indian or Alaska Native, non-Hispanic/Latino; 3% Two or more races, non-Hispanic/Latino; 5% Race/ethnicity unknown; 2% international. *Retention:* 55% of full-time freshmen returned.

Freshmen *Average high school GPA:* 2.97. *Test scores:* ACT scores over 18: 74%; ACT scores over 24: 17%; ACT scores over 30: 1%.
Faculty *Total:* 470, 31% full-time. *Student/faculty ratio:* 18:1.
Majors Accounting; business administration and management; commercial and advertising art; computer programming; criminal justice/law enforcement administration; criminal justice/safety; culinary arts; data processing and data processing technology; drafting and design technology; early childhood education; education; electrical, electronic and communications engineering technology; emergency medical technology (EMT paramedic); environmental science; finance; fire services administration; health information/medical records technology; homeland security, law enforcement, firefighting and protective services related; legal assistant/paralegal; liberal arts and sciences/liberal studies; occupational safety and health technology; physical therapy; registered nursing/registered nurse; respiratory care therapy.
Academics *Calendar:* semesters. *Degree:* certificates and associate. *Special study options:* academic remediation for entering students, accelerated degree program, adult/continuing education programs, advanced placement credit, cooperative education, distance learning, double majors, English as a second language, honors programs, independent study, internships, part-time degree program, services for LD students, student-designed majors, study abroad, summer session for credit. *ROTC:* Army (c), Air Force (c).
Library Pauline Whitaker Library plus 1 other.
Student Life *Housing:* college housing not available. *Activities and Organizations:* drama/theater group, student-run newspaper, choral group, Student Advisory Activity Council, Gamma Beta Phi, Phi Beta Lambda, Student Nurses Association, Students in Free Enterprise (SIFE). *Campus security:* 24-hour emergency response devices and patrols. *Student services:* personal/psychological counseling.
Athletics *Intramural sports:* basketball M(c)/W(c), bowling M(c)/W(c), golf M(c), soccer M(c)/W(c), softball M(c)/W(c), volleyball W(c).
Costs (2015–16) *Tuition:* area resident $2250 full-time, $75 per credit hour part-time; state resident $3675 full-time, $123 per credit hour part-time; nonresident $3750 full-time, $125 per credit hour part-time. *Required fees:* $958 full-time, $29 per credit hour part-time, $55 per term part-time. *Payment plan:* installment. *Waivers:* senior citizens and employees or children of employees.
Applying *Options:* electronic application. *Application fee:* $10. *Required:* high school transcript. *Application deadline:* rolling (freshmen). *Notification:* continuous (freshmen).
Freshman Application Contact NorthWest Arkansas Community College, One College Drive, Bentonville, AR 72712. *Phone:* 479-636-9222. *Toll-free phone:* 800-995-6922. *Fax:* 479-619-4116. *E-mail:* admissions@nwacc.edu. *Website:* http://www.nwacc.edu/.

Ozarka College
Melbourne, Arkansas

Freshman Application Contact Ms. Dylan Mowery, Director of Admissions, Ozarka College, PO Box 10, Melbourne, AR 72556. *Phone:* 870-368-7371 Ext. 2013. *Toll-free phone:* 800-821-4335. *E-mail:* dmmowery@ozarka.edu. *Website:* http://www.ozarka.edu/.

Phillips Community College of the University of Arkansas
Helena, Arkansas

Director of Admissions Mr. Lynn Boone, Registrar, Phillips Community College of the University of Arkansas, PO Box 785, Helena, AR 72342-0785. *Phone:* 870-338-6474. *Website:* http://www.pccua.edu/.

Pulaski Technical College
North Little Rock, Arkansas

Freshman Application Contact Mr. Clark Atkins, Director of Admissions, Pulaski Technical College, 3000 West Scenic Drive, North Little Rock, AR 72118. *Phone:* 501-812-2734. *Fax:* 501-812-2316. *E-mail:* catkins@pulaskitech.edu. *Website:* http://www.pulaskitech.edu/.

Remington College–Little Rock Campus
Little Rock, Arkansas

Director of Admissions Brian Maggio, Director of Recruitment, Remington College–Little Rock Campus, 19 Remington Drive, Little Rock, AR 72204. *Phone:* 501-312-0007. *Fax:* 501-225-3819. *E-mail:* brian.maggio@remingtoncollege.edu. *Website:* http://www.remingtoncollege.edu/.

Rich Mountain Community College

Mena, Arkansas

Director of Admissions Dr. Steve Rook, Dean of Students, Rich Mountain Community College, 1100 College Drive, Mena, AR 71953. *Phone:* 479-394-7622 Ext. 1400.
Website: http://www.rmcc.edu/.

Shorter College

North Little Rock, Arkansas

Director of Admissions Mr. Keith Hunter, Director of Admissions, Shorter College, 604 Locust Street, North Little Rock, AR 72114-4885. *Phone:* 501-374-6305.
Website: http://www.shortercollege.edu/.

South Arkansas Community College

El Dorado, Arkansas

Freshman Application Contact Dr. Stephanie Tully-Dartez, Director of Enrollment Services, South Arkansas Community College, PO Box 7010, El Dorado, AR 71731-7010. *Phone:* 870-864-7142. *Toll-free phone:* 800-955-2289. *Fax:* 870-864-7109. *E-mail:* dinman@southark.edu.
Website: http://www.southark.edu/.

Southeast Arkansas College

Pine Bluff, Arkansas

Freshman Application Contact Ms. Barbara Dunn, Director of Admissions, Southeast Arkansas College, 1900 Hazel Street, Pine Bluff, AR 71603. *Phone:* 870-543-5957. *Toll-free phone:* 888-SEARK TC (in-state); 888-SEARC TC (out-of-state). *Fax:* 870-543-5957. *E-mail:* bdunn@seark.edu.
Website: http://www.seark.edu/.

Southern Arkansas University Tech

Camden, Arkansas

Freshman Application Contact Mrs. Beverly Ellis, Admissions Analyst, Southern Arkansas University Tech, PO Box 3499, Camden, AR 71711-1599. *Phone:* 870-574-4558. *Fax:* 870-574-4478. *E-mail:* bellis@sautech.edu.
Website: http://www.sautech.edu/.

University of Arkansas Community College at Batesville

Batesville, Arkansas

- **State-supported** 2-year, part of University of Arkansas System
- **Small-town** campus
- **Coed**

Undergraduates 750 full-time, 565 part-time. Students come from 2 states and territories; 3% Black or African American, non-Hispanic/Latino; 5% Hispanic/Latino; 0.9% Asian, non-Hispanic/Latino; 0.2% Native Hawaiian or other Pacific Islander, non-Hispanic/Latino; 0.9% American Indian or Alaska Native, non-Hispanic/Latino; 4% Two or more races, non-Hispanic/Latino; 0.4% Race/ethnicity unknown; 0.2% international; 4% transferred in. *Retention:* 60% of full-time freshmen returned.
Faculty *Student/faculty ratio:* 19:1.
Academics *Calendar:* semesters. *Degree:* certificates and associate. *Special study options:* academic remediation for entering students, adult/continuing education programs, advanced placement credit, cooperative education, distance learning, double majors, English as a second language, external degree program, independent study, internships, off-campus study, part-time degree program, services for LD students, student-designed majors, summer session for credit.
Library University of Arkansas Community College at Batesville Library.
Student Life *Campus security:* trained security officers during hours of operation, security cameras, emergency alerts systems.
Standardized Tests *Recommended:* ACT (for admission), ACT, ACT ASSET, ACT Compass, and SAT tests are all accepted for admissions purposes. Minimum reading scores must be met for admission to the colleges.
Financial Aid Of all full-time matriculated undergraduates who enrolled in 2014, 49 Federal Work-Study jobs (averaging $1311).
Applying *Options:* electronic application. *Required:* high school transcript, Composite score of 15 or higher on ACT; or a Reading score of 63 or higher on the Compass test.
Freshman Application Contact Ms. Amy Foree, Enrollment Specialist, University of Arkansas Community College at Batesville, PO Box 3350,

Batesville, AR 72503. *Phone:* 870-612-2113. *Toll-free phone:* 800-508-7878. *Fax:* 870-612-2129. *E-mail:* amy.foree@uaccb.edu.
Website: http://www.uaccb.edu/.

University of Arkansas Community College at Hope

Hope, Arkansas

- **State-supported** 2-year, founded 1966, part of University of Arkansas System
- **Rural** 60-acre campus
- **Coed**

Undergraduates 666 full-time, 694 part-time. Students come from 5 states and territories; 7% are from out of state; 37% Black or African American, non-Hispanic/Latino; 7% Hispanic/Latino; 0.4% Asian, non-Hispanic/Latino; 0.1% Native Hawaiian or other Pacific Islander, non-Hispanic/Latino; 0.8% American Indian or Alaska Native, non-Hispanic/Latino; 0.2% Two or more races, non-Hispanic/Latino; 6% transferred in. *Retention:* 42% of full-time freshmen returned.
Faculty *Student/faculty ratio:* 15:1.
Academics *Calendar:* semesters. *Degree:* certificates, diplomas, and associate. *Special study options:* academic remediation for entering students, accelerated degree program, advanced placement credit, distance learning, double majors, independent study, internships, off-campus study, part-time degree program, services for LD students, summer session for credit.
Library University of Arkansas Community College at Hope Library.
Student Life *Campus security:* 24-hour emergency response devices, on-campus security during class hours.
Standardized Tests *Recommended:* SAT or ACT (for admission), ACT Compass.
Costs (2015–16) *Tuition:* area resident $1860 full-time, $61 per credit part-time; state resident $2040 full-time, $66 per credit part-time; nonresident $4080 full-time, $131 per credit part-time. *Required fees:* $520 full-time, $15 per term part-time, $8 per term part-time.
Financial Aid Of all full-time matriculated undergraduates who enrolled in 2014, 943 were judged to have need. *Average indebtedness upon graduation:* $2625.
Applying *Options:* early admission. *Required:* high school transcript.
Freshman Application Contact University of Arkansas Community College at Hope, PO Box 140, Hope, AR 71802. *Phone:* 870-772-8174.
Website: http://www.uacch.edu/.

University of Arkansas Community College at Morrilton

Morrilton, Arkansas

- **State-supported** 2-year, founded 1961, part of University of Arkansas System
- **Rural** 79-acre campus
- **Coed,** 2,042 undergraduate students, 66% full-time, 59% women, 41% men

Undergraduates 1,354 full-time, 688 part-time. Students come from 9 states and territories; 6 other countries; 0.5% are from out of state; 10% Black or African American, non-Hispanic/Latino; 6% Hispanic/Latino; 0.7% Asian, non-Hispanic/Latino; 0.5% American Indian or Alaska Native, non-Hispanic/Latino; 5% Two or more races, non-Hispanic/Latino; 0.4% Race/ethnicity unknown; 2% international; 13% transferred in.
Freshmen *Admission:* 1,202 applied, 799 admitted, 574 enrolled. *Average high school GPA:* 2.96. *Test scores:* ACT scores over 18: 70%; ACT scores over 24: 16%.
Faculty *Total:* 75, 83% full-time, 12% with terminal degrees. *Student/faculty ratio:* 24:1.
Majors Autobody/collision and repair technology; automobile/automotive mechanics technology; business/commerce; child development; commercial and advertising art; computer and information sciences; computer technology/computer systems technology; criminal justice/law enforcement administration; drafting and design technology; education (multiple levels); forensic science and technology; general studies; heating, air conditioning, ventilation and refrigeration maintenance technology; industrial mechanics and maintenance technology; liberal arts and sciences/liberal studies; petroleum technology; registered nursing/registered nurse; surveying technology.
Academics *Calendar:* semesters. *Degree:* certificates and associate. *Special study options:* academic remediation for entering students, advanced placement credit, cooperative education, distance learning, double majors, independent study, internships, part-time degree program, services for LD students, summer session for credit.

Library E. Allen Gordon Library. *Books:* 20,368 (physical), 145,145 (digital/electronic); *Serial titles:* 45 (physical); *Databases:* 27. Weekly public service hours: 66; students can reserve study rooms.
Student Life *Housing:* college housing not available. *Activities and Organizations:* drama/theater group, Student Activities Board, Phi Theta Kappa, Petroleum Students Organization, Student Nursing Association, Computer Information Systems Club. *Campus security:* 24-hour emergency response devices, late-night transport/escort service, campus alert system through phone call, text message, and/or e-mail. *Student services:* personal/psychological counseling.
Athletics *Intramural sports:* basketball M/W, football M/W, table tennis M/W, ultimate Frisbee M/W, volleyball M/W.
Standardized Tests *Recommended:* SAT or ACT (for admission), ACT Compass.
Costs (2015–16) *Tuition:* area resident $2535 full-time, $85 per credit hour part-time; state resident $2745 full-time, $92 per credit hour part-time; nonresident $3840 full-time, $128 per credit hour part-time. Full-time tuition and fees vary according to course load and program. Part-time tuition and fees vary according to course load and program. *Required fees:* $1040 full-time, $34 per credit hour part-time, $10 per term part-time. *Payment plan:* installment. *Waivers:* senior citizens and employees or children of employees.
Financial Aid Of all full-time matriculated undergraduates who enrolled in 2015, 1,178 applied for aid, 1,028 were judged to have need, 31 had their need fully met. In 2015, 45 non-need-based awards were made. *Average percent of need met:* 44%. *Average financial aid package:* $6082. *Average need-based loan:* $1686. *Average need-based gift aid:* $3161. *Average non-need-based aid:* $1033.
Applying *Options:* electronic application, early admission, deferred entrance. *Required:* high school transcript. *Required for some:* immunization records, prior college transcript(s). *Application deadlines:* rolling (freshmen), rolling (transfers). *Notification:* continuous (freshmen), continuous (transfers).
Freshman Application Contact Ms. Terry McCoy, Coordinator of Recruitment, University of Arkansas Community College at Morrilton, 1537 University Boulevard, Morrilton, AR 72110. *Phone:* 501-977-2053. *Toll-free phone:* 800-264-1094. *Fax:* 501-977-2123. *E-mail:* mullins@uaccm.edu. *Website:* http://www.uaccm.edu/.

CALIFORNIA

Academy of Couture Art
Beverly Hills, California

- **Proprietary** primarily 2-year
- **Urban** campus with easy access to Los Angeles
- **Coed**

Undergraduates *Retention:* 75% of full-time freshmen returned.
Faculty *Total:* 4, 75% full-time.
Majors Apparel and textile manufacturing; fashion/apparel design.
Academics *Degrees:* associate and bachelor's. *Special study options:* double majors, English as a second language.
Library Main Library plus 1 other.
Student Life *Housing:* college housing not available. *Campus security:* 24-hour emergency response devices and patrols.
Standardized Tests *Recommended:* SAT or ACT (for admission).
Costs (2016–17) *One-time required fee:* $100. *Tuition:* $26,664 full-time, $621 per credit part-time. Full-time tuition and fees vary according to class time, course level, course load, degree level, location, program, reciprocity agreements, and student level. Part-time tuition and fees vary according to class time, course level, course load, degree level, location, program, reciprocity agreements, and student level. No tuition increase for student's term of enrollment. *Required fees:* $3120 full-time. *Payment plans:* tuition prepayment, installment.
Applying *Options:* electronic application, early admission. *Application fee:* $40. *Required:* essay or personal statement, interview. *Required for some:* high school transcript.
Freshman Application Contact Academy of Couture Art, 8484 Wilshire Boulevard, Suite 730, Beverly Hills, CA 90211. *Phone:* 310-360-8888. *Website:* http://www.academyofcoutureart.edu/.

Advanced College
South Gate, California

Admissions Office Contact Advanced College, 13180 Paramount Boulevard, South Gate, CA 90280.
Website: http://www.advancedcollege.edu/.

Advanced Computing Institute
Los Angeles, California

Admissions Office Contact Advanced Computing Institute, 3470 Wilshire Boulevard 11th Floor, Los Angeles, CA 90010-3911.
Website: http://www.advancedcomputinginstitute.edu/.

Advanced Training Associates
El Cajon, California

Admissions Office Contact Advanced Training Associates, 1810 Gillespie Way, Suite 104, El Cajon, CA 92020. *Toll-free phone:* 800-720-2125.
Website: http://www.advancedtraining.edu/.

Allan Hancock College
Santa Maria, California

Freshman Application Contact Ms. Adela Esquivel Swinson, Director of Admissions and Records, Allan Hancock College, 800 South College Drive, Santa Maria, CA 93454-6399. *Phone:* 805-922-6966 Ext. 3272. *Toll-free phone:* 866-342-5242. *Fax:* 805-922-3477.
Website: http://www.hancockcollege.edu/.

American Academy of Dramatic Arts–Los Angeles
Hollywood, California

- **Independent** 2-year, founded 1974
- **Urban** 4-acre campus with easy access to Los Angeles
- **Endowment** $1.7 million
- **Coed**

Undergraduates 282 full-time. Students come from 36 states and territories; 26 other countries; 54% are from out of state; 7% Black or African American, non-Hispanic/Latino; 10% Hispanic/Latino; 1% Asian, non-Hispanic/Latino; 0.4% Native Hawaiian or other Pacific Islander, non-Hispanic/Latino; 0.8% American Indian or Alaska Native, non-Hispanic/Latino; 14% Two or more races, non-Hispanic/Latino; 25% international; 0.7% transferred in.
Faculty *Student/faculty ratio:* 12:1.
Academics *Calendar:* semesters. *Degree:* certificates, diplomas, and associate. *Special study options:* internships, services for LD students.
Library Bryn Morgan Library.
Student Life *Campus security:* 24-hour emergency response devices, 8-hour patrols by trained security personnel.
Costs (2016–17) *Tuition:* $32,440 full-time. *Required fees:* $750 full-time.
Financial Aid Of all full-time matriculated undergraduates who enrolled in 2014, 15 Federal Work-Study jobs (averaging $2000).
Applying *Options:* electronic application, deferred entrance. *Application fee:* $50. *Required:* essay or personal statement, high school transcript, 2 letters of recommendation, interview, audition. *Recommended:* minimum 2.0 GPA.
Freshman Application Contact Steven Hong, Director of Admissions, American Academy of Dramatic Arts–Los Angeles, 1336 North La Brea Avenue, Hollywood, CA 90028. *Phone:* 323-464-2777 Ext. 103. *Toll-free phone:* 800-222-2867. *E-mail:* shong@aada.edu.
Website: http://www.aada.edu/.

American Career College
Anaheim, California

Director of Admissions Susan Pailet, Senior Executive Director of Admission, American Career College, 1200 North Magnolia Avenue, Anaheim, CA 92801. *Phone:* 714-952-9066. *Toll-free phone:* 877-832-0790.
E-mail: info@americancareer.com.
Website: http://americancareercollege.edu/.

American Career College
Los Angeles, California

Director of Admissions Tamra Adams, Director of Admissions, American Career College, 4021 Rosewood Avenue, Los Angeles, CA 90004-2932. *Phone:* 323-668-7555. *Toll-free phone:* 877-832-0790.
E-mail: info@americancareer.com.
Website: http://americancareercollege.edu/.

American Career College
Ontario, California

Director of Admissions Juan Tellez, Director of Admissions, American Career College, 3130 East Sedona Court, Ontario, CA 91764. *Phone:* 951-739-0788. *Toll-free phone:* 877-832-0790.
E-mail: info@amerciancareer.com.
Website: http://americancareercollege.edu/.

American Medical Sciences Center
Glendale, California

Admissions Office Contact American Medical Sciences Center, 225 West Broadway, Suite 115, Glendale, CA 91204-5108.
Website: http://www.amsc.edu/.

American River College
Sacramento, California

- **District-supported** 2-year, founded 1955, part of Los Rios Community College District System
- **Suburban** 153-acre campus
- **Coed,** 33,821 undergraduate students

Majors Accounting; administrative assistant and secretarial science; adult development and aging; advertising; American Sign Language (ASL); anthropology; apparel and textile marketing management; art; autobody/collision and repair technology; automobile/automotive mechanics technology; biological and physical sciences; biology/biotechnology laboratory technician; business administration and management; business/commerce; carpentry; child development; computer programming; computer science; computer systems networking and telecommunications; culinary arts; data entry/microcomputer applications; data modeling/warehousing and database administration; diesel mechanics technology; drafting and design technology; dramatic/theater arts; drywall installation; electrical, electronic and communications engineering technology; electrician; emergency medical technology (EMT paramedic); engineering; engineering technology; English; family systems; fashion/apparel design; fire science/firefighting; food service systems administration; funeral service and mortuary science; geography; geography related; home health aide/home attendant; human services; industrial electronics technology; interior design; international relations and affairs; journalism; landscaping and groundskeeping; legal assistant/paralegal; liberal arts and sciences/liberal studies; mathematics; music; music management; natural resources management and policy; network and system administration; nursing assistant/aide and patient care assistant/aide; parks, recreation and leisure; photography; physical sciences; plant nursery management; psychology; radio, television, and digital communication related; real estate; registered nursing/registered nurse; respiratory care therapy; restaurant, culinary, and catering management; retailing; sales, distribution, and marketing operations; sheet metal technology; sign language interpretation and translation; small business administration; social sciences; sport and fitness administration/management; substance abuse/addiction counseling; theater design and technology; welding technology.

Academics *Calendar:* semesters. *Degree:* certificates and associate. *Special study options:* academic remediation for entering students, adult/continuing education programs, advanced placement credit, cooperative education, English as a second language, part-time degree program, services for LD students, summer session for credit.

Student Life *Housing:* college housing not available. *Activities and Organizations:* drama/theater group, student-run newspaper. *Campus security:* 24-hour emergency response devices and patrols, student patrols, late-night transport/escort service. *Student services:* health clinic, personal/psychological counseling, women's center.

Athletics *Intercollegiate sports:* baseball M, basketball M/W, cross-country running M/W, football M, golf M/W, soccer M/W, softball W, swimming and diving M/W, tennis M/W, track and field M/W, volleyball W, water polo M/W. *Intramural sports:* basketball M/W.

Costs (2015–16) *Tuition:* state resident $0 full-time; nonresident $4800 full-time, $200 per unit part-time. Full-time tuition and fees vary according to course load. Part-time tuition and fees vary according to course load. *Required fees:* $1104 full-time, $46 per unit part-time. *Payment plan:* installment.

Applying *Options:* early admission, deferred entrance. *Application deadlines:* rolling (freshmen), rolling (transfers).

Freshman Application Contact American River College, 4700 College Oak Drive, Sacramento, CA 95841-4286. *Phone:* 916-484-8171.
Website: http://www.arc.losrios.edu/.

Antelope Valley College
Lancaster, California

- **District-supported** 2-year, founded 1929, part of California Community College System
- **Suburban** 135-acre campus with easy access to Los Angeles
- **Endowment** $3.7 million
- **Coed,** 13,820 undergraduate students

Freshmen *Admission:* 4,341 applied, 4,341 admitted.
Faculty *Total:* 622, 28% full-time, 8% with terminal degrees.
Majors Accounting technology and bookkeeping; administrative assistant and secretarial science; aircraft powerplant technology; airframe mechanics and aircraft maintenance technology; American Sign Language (ASL); animation, interactive technology, video graphics and special effects; anthropology; apparel and textiles; applied horticulture/horticulture operations; art; autobody/collision and repair technology; automobile/automotive mechanics technology; biological and physical sciences; business administration and management; business/commerce; child-care provision; computer graphics; computer programming; computer systems networking and telecommunications; criminal justice/police science; data entry/microcomputer applications; desktop publishing and digital imaging design; drafting and design technology; electrical/electronics equipment installation and repair; electrician; engineering technology; English; family and consumer sciences/human sciences; fire prevention and safety technology; geography; geology/earth science; health and physical education/fitness; heating, air conditioning, ventilation and refrigeration maintenance technology; heating, ventilation, air conditioning and refrigeration engineering technology; history; humanities; industrial production technologies related; information technology; interior design; kinesiology and exercise science; landscaping and groundskeeping; liberal arts and sciences/liberal studies; mathematics; medical/clinical assistant; music; philosophy; photographic and film/video technology; photography; physical sciences; physics; political science and government; pre-engineering; radiologic technology/science; real estate; registered nursing/registered nurse; respiratory care therapy; sales, distribution, and marketing operations; sign language interpretation and translation; small business administration; social sciences; sociology; speech communication and rhetoric; teacher assistant/aide; visual and performing arts; welding technology; wildland/forest firefighting and investigation.

Academics *Calendar:* semesters. *Degree:* certificates and associate. *Special study options:* academic remediation for entering students, adult/continuing education programs, advanced placement credit, cooperative education, distance learning, English as a second language, external degree program, honors programs, independent study, part-time degree program, services for LD students, student-designed majors, study abroad, summer session for credit. *ROTC:* Army (c), Navy (c), Air Force (c).

Library Antelope Valley College Library. *Books:* 51,894 (physical), 154,754 (digital/electronic); *Serial titles:* 10 (physical), 22,330 (digital/electronic); *Databases:* 52. Weekly public service hours: 152; students can reserve study rooms.

Student Life *Housing:* college housing not available. *Activities and Organizations:* drama/theater group, student-run newspaper, choral group. *Campus security:* 24-hour emergency response devices and patrols, late-night transport/escort service. *Student services:* health clinic, personal/psychological counseling.

Athletics *Intercollegiate sports:* baseball M, basketball M/W, cross-country running M/W, football M, golf M, sand volleyball W, soccer W, softball W, tennis W, track and field M/W, volleyball W. *Intramural sports:* basketball M/W, golf M/W, swimming and diving M/W, tennis M/W, volleyball M/W, weight lifting M/W.

Costs (2016–17) *Tuition:* state resident $1104 full-time, $46 per credit part-time; nonresident $6768 full-time, $236 per credit part-time. *Required fees:* $40 full-time, $20 per term part-time. *Payment plan:* installment.

Applying *Options:* electronic application, early admission. *Recommended:* high school transcript. *Application deadlines:* rolling (freshmen), rolling (out-of-state freshmen), rolling (transfers). *Notification:* continuous (freshmen), continuous (out-of-state freshmen), continuous (transfers).

Freshman Application Contact Welcome Center, Antelope Valley College, 3041 West Avenue K, SSV Building, Lancaster, CA 93536. *Phone:* 661-722-6300 Ext. 6331.
Website: http://www.avc.edu/.

APT College
Carlsbad, California

Director of Admissions Monica Hoffman, Director of Admissions/Registrar, APT College, 5751 Palmer Way, Suite D, PO Box 131717, Carlsbad, CA 92013. *Phone:* 800-431-8488. *Toll-free phone:* 800-431-8488. *Fax:* 888-431-8588. *E-mail:* aptc@aptc.com.
Website: http://www.aptc.edu/.

Ashdown College of Health Sciences
Redlands, California

Admissions Office Contact Ashdown College of Health Sciences, 101 E. Redlands Boulevard, Suite 285, Redlands, CA 92373.
Website: http://ashdowncollege.edu/.

Aviation & Electronic Schools of America
Colfax, California

Freshman Application Contact Admissions Office, Aviation & Electronic Schools of America, 111 South Railroad Street, PO Box 1810, Colfax, CA 95713-1810. *Phone:* 530-346-6792. *Toll-free phone:* 800-345-2742. *Fax:* 530-346-8466. *E-mail:* aesa@aesa.com.
Website: http://www.aesa.com/.

Bakersfield College
Bakersfield, California

Freshman Application Contact Bakersfield College, 1801 Panorama Drive, Bakersfield, CA 93305-1299. *Phone:* 661-395-4301.
Website: http://www.bakersfieldcollege.edu/.

Barstow Community College
Barstow, California

Freshman Application Contact Barstow Community College, 2700 Barstow Road, Barstow, CA 92311-6699. *Phone:* 760-252-2411 Ext. 7236.
Website: http://www.barstow.edu/.

Berkeley City College
Berkeley, California

Freshman Application Contact Dr. May Kuang-chi Chen, Vice President of Student Services, Berkeley City College, 2050 Center Street, Berkeley, CA 94704. *Phone:* 510-981-2820. *Fax:* 510-841-7333.
E-mail: mrivas@peralta.edu.
Website: http://www.berkeleycitycollege.edu/.

Blake Austin College
Vacaville, California

Admissions Office Contact Blake Austin College, 611-K Orange Drive, Vacaville, CA 95687.
Website: http://www.blakeaustincollege.edu/.

Brightwood College, Bakersfield Campus
Bakersfield, California

Freshman Application Contact Brightwood College, Bakersfield Campus, 1914 Wible Road, Bakersfield, CA 93304. *Phone:* 661-836-6300. *Toll-free phone:* 800-935-1857.
Website: http://www.brightwood.edu/.

Brightwood College, Chula Vista Campus
Chula Vista, California

Freshman Application Contact Brightwood College, Chula Vista Campus, 555 Broadway, Chula Vista, CA 91910. *Phone:* 877-473-3052. *Toll-free phone:* 800-935-1857.
Website: http://www.brightwood.edu/.

Brightwood College, Fresno Campus
Fresno, California

Freshman Application Contact Brightwood College, Fresno Campus, 44 Shaw Avenue, Fresno, CA 93612. *Phone:* 559-325-5100. *Toll-free phone:* 800-935-1857.
Website: http://www.brightwood.edu/.

Brightwood College, Modesto Campus
Modesto, California

Freshman Application Contact Brightwood College, Modesto Campus, 5172 Kiernan Court, Modesto, CA 95368. *Phone:* 209-543-7000. *Toll-free phone:* 800-935-1857.
Website: http://www.brightwood.edu/.

Brightwood College, North Hollywood Campus
North Hollywood, California

Freshman Application Contact Ms. Renee Codner, Director of Admissions, Brightwood College, North Hollywood Campus, 6180 Laurel Canyon Boulevard, Suite 101, North Hollywood, CA 91606. *Phone:* 818-763-2563 Ext. 240. *Toll-free phone:* 800-935-1857. *E-mail:* rcodner@mariccollege.edu.
Website: http://www.brightwood.edu/.

Brightwood College, Palm Springs Campus
Palm Springs, California

Freshman Application Contact Brightwood College, Palm Springs Campus, 2475 East Tahquitz Canyon Way, Palm Springs, CA 92262. *Phone:* 760-778-3540. *Toll-free phone:* 800-935-1857.
Website: http://www.brightwood.edu/.

Brightwood College, Riverside Campus
Riverside, California

Freshman Application Contact Brightwood College, Riverside Campus, 4040 Vine Street, Riverside, CA 92507. *Phone:* 951-276-1704. *Toll-free phone:* 800-935-1857.
Website: http://www.brightwood.edu/.

Brightwood College, Sacramento Campus
Sacramento, California

Freshman Application Contact Brightwood College, Sacramento Campus, 4330 Watt Avenue, Suite 400, Sacramento, CA 95821. *Phone:* 916-649-8168. *Toll-free phone:* 800-935-1857.
Website: http://www.brightwood.edu/.

Brightwood College, San Diego Campus
San Diego, California

Freshman Application Contact Brightwood College, San Diego Campus, 9055 Balboa Avenue, San Diego, CA 92123. *Phone:* 858-279-4500. *Toll-free phone:* 800-935-1857.
Website: http://www.brightwood.edu/.

Brightwood College, Vista Campus
Vista, California

Freshman Application Contact Brightwood College, Vista Campus, 2022 University Drive, Vista, CA 92083. *Phone:* 760-630-1555. *Toll-free phone:* 800-935-1857.
Website: http://www.brightwood.edu/.

Bryan College
Gold River, California

Freshman Application Contact Bryan College, 2339 Gold Meadow Way, Suite 111, Gold River, CA 95670. *Phone:* 916-649-2400. *Toll-free phone:* 866-649-2400.
Website: http://www.bryancollege.edu/.

Bryan University
Los Angeles, California

Admissions Office Contact Bryan University, 3580 Wilshire Boulevard, Los Angeles, CA 90010.
Website: http://losangeles.bryanuniversity.edu/.

Butte College
Oroville, California

Freshman Application Contact Mr. Brad Zuniga, Director of Recruitment, Outreach and New Student Orientation, Butte College, 3536 Butte Campus Drive, Oroville, CA 95965-8399. *Phone:* 530-895-2948. *Website:* http://www.butte.edu/.

Cabrillo College
Aptos, California

Freshman Application Contact Tama Bolton, Director of Admissions and Records, Cabrillo College, 6500 Soquel Drive, Aptos, CA 95003-3194. *Phone:* 831-477-3548. *Fax:* 831-479-5782. *E-mail:* tabolton@cabrillo.edu. *Website:* http://www.cabrillo.edu/.

Cambridge Junior College
Yuba City, California

Freshman Application Contact Admissions Office, Cambridge Junior College, 990-A Klamath Lane, Yuba City, CA 95993. *Phone:* 530-674-9199. *Fax:* 530-671-7319. *Website:* http://www.cambridge.edu/.

Cañada College
Redwood City, California

- **District-supported** 2-year, founded 1968, part of San Mateo County Community College District System
- **Suburban** 131-acre campus with easy access to San Francisco, San Jose
- **Endowment** $150,000
- **Coed,** 5,433 undergraduate students, 7% full-time, 63% women, 37% men

Undergraduates 406 full-time, 5,027 part-time. 2% are from out of state; 3% Black or African American, non-Hispanic/Latino; 36% Hispanic/Latino; 10% Asian, non-Hispanic/Latino; 2% Native Hawaiian or other Pacific Islander, non-Hispanic/Latino; 0.2% American Indian or Alaska Native, non-Hispanic/Latino; 17% Two or more races, non-Hispanic/Latino; 2% Race/ethnicity unknown; 5% international.

Freshmen *Admission:* 394 applied, 470 enrolled.

Faculty *Total:* 241, 34% full-time. *Student/faculty ratio:* 16:1.

Majors Accounting technology and bookkeeping; administrative assistant and secretarial science; animation, interactive technology, video graphics and special effects; anthropology; apparel and textile manufacturing; archeology; art; biological and physical sciences; biology/biological sciences; business administration and management; chemistry; child-care provision; computer science; computer systems networking and telecommunications; dramatic/theater arts; economics; education; engineering; English; fashion/apparel design; geography; health and physical education/fitness; history; humanities; human services; interior design; international relations and affairs; legal assistant/paralegal; liberal arts and sciences/liberal studies; linguistics; mathematics; medical/clinical assistant; music; network and system administration; philosophy; physics; political science and government; psychology; radiologic technology/science; retailing; small business administration; sociology; Spanish; speech communication and rhetoric; sport and fitness administration/management.

Academics *Calendar:* semesters. *Degree:* certificates and associate. *Special study options:* academic remediation for entering students, accelerated degree program, adult/continuing education programs, advanced placement credit, cooperative education, distance learning, double majors, English as a second language, honors programs, independent study, internships, part-time degree program, services for LD students, study abroad, summer session for credit. *ROTC:* Army (c), Navy (c), Air Force (c).

Library *Books:* 25,000 (physical), 230,000 (digital/electronic); *Serial titles:* 40 (physical), 20,000 (digital/electronic); *Databases:* 45. Weekly public service hours: 64; students can reserve study rooms.

Student Life *Housing:* college housing not available. *Activities and Organizations:* drama/theater group, choral group, Phi Theta Kappa, DREAMers Club, Community First, Glee Club, Civil Liberties Club. *Campus security:* 24-hour emergency response devices and patrols, late-night transport/escort service, 12-hour patrols by trained security personnel. *Student services:* health clinic, personal/psychological counseling.

Athletics *Intercollegiate sports:* baseball M, basketball M, golf W, soccer M/W, tennis W.

Costs (2016–17) *Tuition:* state resident $1380 full-time, $46 per unit part-time; nonresident $8070 full-time, $269 per unit part-time. Full-time tuition and fees vary according to course load. Part-time tuition and fees vary according to course load. *Required fees:* $56 full-time, $28 per term part-time. *Payment plan:* installment.

Financial Aid Of all full-time matriculated undergraduates who enrolled in 2014, 40 Federal Work-Study jobs (averaging $2026).

Applying *Options:* electronic application. *Recommended:* high school transcript. *Application deadlines:* rolling (freshmen), rolling (transfers).

Freshman Application Contact Cañada College, 4200 Farm Hill Boulevard, Redwood City, CA 94061-1099. *Phone:* 650-306-3125. *Website:* http://www.canadacollege.edu/.

Carrington College–Citrus Heights
Citrus Heights, California

- **Proprietary** 2-year, part of Carrington Colleges Group, Inc.
- **Coed,** 568 undergraduate students, 92% full-time, 83% women, 17% men

Undergraduates 521 full-time, 47 part-time. 6% Black or African American, non-Hispanic/Latino; 18% Hispanic/Latino; 4% Asian, non-Hispanic/Latino; 2% Native Hawaiian or other Pacific Islander, non-Hispanic/Latino; 2% American Indian or Alaska Native, non-Hispanic/Latino; 6% Two or more races, non-Hispanic/Latino; 1% Race/ethnicity unknown; 0.4% international; 13% transferred in.

Freshmen *Admission:* 32 enrolled.

Faculty *Total:* 25, 44% full-time. *Student/faculty ratio:* 34:1.

Majors Accounting technology and bookkeeping; business administration and management; criminal justice/safety; dental assisting; health/health-care administration; medical/clinical assistant; medical insurance/medical billing; pharmacy technician; surgical technology; veterinary/animal health technology.

Academics *Degree:* certificates and associate.

Student Life *Housing:* college housing not available.

Costs (2015–16) *Tuition:* $32,266 full-time. *Required fees:* $1653 full-time.

Applying *Required:* essay or personal statement, high school transcript, interview.

Freshman Application Contact Carrington College–Citrus Heights, 7301 Greenback Lane, Suite A, Citrus Heights, CA 95621. *Website:* http://carrington.edu/.

Carrington College–Pleasant Hill
Pleasant Hill, California

- **Proprietary** 2-year, founded 1997, part of Carrington Colleges Group, Inc.
- **Coed,** 616 undergraduate students, 84% full-time, 85% women, 15% men

Undergraduates 519 full-time, 97 part-time. 1% are from out of state; 12% Black or African American, non-Hispanic/Latino; 28% Hispanic/Latino; 14% Asian, non-Hispanic/Latino; 2% Native Hawaiian or other Pacific Islander, non-Hispanic/Latino; 1% American Indian or Alaska Native, non-Hispanic/Latino; 2% Two or more races, non-Hispanic/Latino; 4% Race/ethnicity unknown; 0.5% international; 17% transferred in.

Freshmen *Admission:* 40 enrolled.

Faculty *Total:* 36, 53% full-time. *Student/faculty ratio:* 22:1.

Majors Criminal justice/police science; dental assisting; health and medical administrative services related; health/health-care administration; health information/medical records technology; massage therapy; medical/clinical assistant; medical insurance/medical billing; pharmacy technician; physical therapy technology; respiratory therapy technician; security and loss prevention; veterinary/animal health technology.

Academics *Calendar:* semesters. *Degree:* certificates and associate.

Student Life *Housing:* college housing not available.

Costs (2016–17) *Tuition:* $34,166 per degree program part-time. Full-time tuition and fees vary according to program. Part-time tuition and fees vary according to program.

Applying *Required:* essay or personal statement, high school transcript, interview. *Notification:* continuous (freshmen).

Freshman Application Contact Carrington College–Pleasant Hill, 380 Civic Drive, Suite 300, Pleasant Hill, CA 94523. *Website:* http://carrington.edu/.

Carrington College–Pomona
Pomona, California

- **Proprietary** 2-year
- **Coed,** 406 undergraduate students, 68% full-time, 89% women, 11% men

Undergraduates 278 full-time, 128 part-time. 28% are from out of state; 4% Black or African American, non-Hispanic/Latino; 64% Hispanic/Latino; 3% Asian, non-Hispanic/Latino; 0.5% Native Hawaiian or other Pacific Islander, non-Hispanic/Latino; 0.5% American Indian or Alaska Native, non-Hispanic/Latino; 0.7% Two or more races, non-Hispanic/Latino; 0.5% Race/ethnicity unknown; 14% transferred in.

Freshmen *Admission:* 22 enrolled.

Faculty *Total:* 17, 88% full-time. *Student/faculty ratio:* 20:1.

Majors Dental assisting; medical/clinical assistant; medical insurance/medical billing; pharmacy technician; veterinary/animal health technology.
Academics *Degree:* certificates and associate.
Costs (2016–17) *Tuition:* $34,166 per degree program part-time. Full-time tuition and fees vary according to program. Part-time tuition and fees vary according to program.
Applying *Notification:* continuous (freshmen).
Freshman Application Contact Carrington College–Pomona, 901 Corporate Center Drive, Suite 300, Pomona, CA 91768. *Toll-free phone:* 877-206-2106. *Website:* http://carrington.edu/.

Carrington College–Sacramento
Sacramento, California

- **Proprietary** 2-year, founded 1967, part of Carrington Colleges Group, Inc.
- **Coed,** 1,272 undergraduate students, 82% full-time, 89% women, 11% men

Undergraduates 1,048 full-time, 224 part-time. 6% are from out of state; 10% Black or African American, non-Hispanic/Latino; 26% Hispanic/Latino; 12% Asian, non-Hispanic/Latino; 2% Native Hawaiian or other Pacific Islander, non-Hispanic/Latino; 1% American Indian or Alaska Native, non-Hispanic/Latino; 4% Two or more races, non-Hispanic/Latino; 8% Race/ethnicity unknown; 10% transferred in.
Freshmen *Admission:* 60 enrolled.
Faculty *Total:* 80, 45% full-time. *Student/faculty ratio:* 16:1.
Majors Dental assisting; dental hygiene; health/health-care administration; licensed practical/vocational nurse training; medical administrative assistant and medical secretary; medical/clinical assistant; medical insurance/medical billing; medical office management; pharmacy technician; registered nursing/registered nurse; veterinary/animal health technology.
Academics *Calendar:* semesters. *Degree:* certificates and associate.
Standardized Tests *Required:* Entrance test administered by Carrington College California (for admission).
Costs (2016–17) *Tuition:* $44,490 per degree program part-time. Full-time tuition and fees vary according to program. Part-time tuition and fees vary according to program.
Applying *Required:* essay or personal statement, high school transcript, interview. *Application deadline:* rolling (freshmen).
Freshman Application Contact Carrington College–Sacramento, 8909 Folsom Boulevard, Sacramento, CA 95826.
Website: http://carrington.edu/.

Carrington College–San Jose
San Jose, California

- **Proprietary** 2-year, founded 1999, part of Carrington Colleges Group, Inc.
- **Coed,** 791 undergraduate students, 93% full-time, 88% women, 12% men

Undergraduates 739 full-time, 52 part-time. 1% are from out of state; 3% Black or African American, non-Hispanic/Latino; 49% Hispanic/Latino; 18% Asian, non-Hispanic/Latino; 3% Native Hawaiian or other Pacific Islander, non-Hispanic/Latino; 0.4% American Indian or Alaska Native, non-Hispanic/Latino; 4% Two or more races, non-Hispanic/Latino; 0.3% Race/ethnicity unknown; 0.8% international; 11% transferred in.
Freshmen *Admission:* 25 enrolled.
Faculty *Total:* 51, 43% full-time. *Student/faculty ratio:* 24:1.
Majors Allied health and medical assisting services related; criminal justice/safety; dental assisting; dental hygiene; health/health-care administration; licensed practical/vocational nurse training; medical/clinical assistant; medical insurance/medical billing; medical office management; pharmacy technician; security and loss prevention; surgical technology; veterinary/animal health technology.
Academics *Calendar:* semesters. *Degree:* certificates and associate.
Student Life *Housing:* college housing not available.
Standardized Tests *Required:* institutional entrance test (for admission).
Costs (2015–16) *Tuition:* $17,603 full-time. Full-time tuition and fees vary according to program. Part-time tuition and fees vary according to program. *Required fees:* $760 full-time.
Applying *Required:* essay or personal statement, high school transcript, interview.
Freshman Application Contact Carrington College–San Jose, 5883 Rue Ferrari, Suite 125, San Jose, CA 95138.
Website: http://carrington.edu/.

Carrington College–San Leandro
San Leandro, California

- **Proprietary** 2-year, founded 1986, part of Carrington Colleges Group, Inc.
- **Coed,** 478 undergraduate students, 91% full-time, 90% women, 10% men

Undergraduates 436 full-time, 42 part-time. 1% are from out of state; 18% Black or African American, non-Hispanic/Latino; 47% Hispanic/Latino; 13% Asian, non-Hispanic/Latino; 2% Native Hawaiian or other Pacific Islander, non-Hispanic/Latino; 0.8% American Indian or Alaska Native, non-Hispanic/Latino; 3% Two or more races, non-Hispanic/Latino; 0.6% Race/ethnicity unknown; 0.8% international; 14% transferred in.
Freshmen *Admission:* 32 enrolled.
Faculty *Total:* 23, 52% full-time. *Student/faculty ratio:* 28:1.
Majors Dental assisting; health and medical administrative services related; health/health-care administration; medical/clinical assistant; medical insurance/medical billing; pharmacy technician; security and loss prevention; veterinary/animal health technology.
Academics *Calendar:* semesters. *Degree:* certificates and associate.
Student Life *Housing:* college housing not available.
Standardized Tests *Required:* Entrance test administered by Carrington Colleges California (for admission).
Costs (2015–16) *Tuition:* $17,603 full-time. Full-time tuition and fees vary according to program. Part-time tuition and fees vary according to program. *Required fees:* $760 full-time.
Applying *Required:* essay or personal statement, high school transcript, interview. *Application deadline:* rolling (freshmen).
Freshman Application Contact Carrington College–San Leandro, 15555 East 14th Street, Suite 500, San Leandro, CA 94578.
Website: http://carrington.edu/.

Carrington College–Stockton
Stockton, California

- **Proprietary** 2-year
- **Coed,** 583 undergraduate students, 94% full-time, 89% women, 11% men

Undergraduates 550 full-time, 33 part-time. 8% Black or African American, non-Hispanic/Latino; 51% Hispanic/Latino; 10% Asian, non-Hispanic/Latino; 2% Native Hawaiian or other Pacific Islander, non-Hispanic/Latino; 0.5% American Indian or Alaska Native, non-Hispanic/Latino; 3% Two or more races, non-Hispanic/Latino; 1% Race/ethnicity unknown; 15% transferred in.
Freshmen *Admission:* 54 enrolled.
Faculty *Total:* 16, 44% full-time. *Student/faculty ratio:* 56:1.
Majors Veterinary/animal health technology.
Academics *Degree:* certificates and associate.
Costs (2015–16) *Tuition:* $32,266 full-time. Full-time tuition and fees vary according to program. Part-time tuition and fees vary according to program. *Required fees:* $1653 full-time.
Freshman Application Contact Carrington College–Stockton, 1313 West Robinhood Drive, Suite B, Stockton, CA 95207.
Website: http://carrington.edu/.

Casa Loma College–Van Nuys
Los Angeles, California

Admissions Office Contact Casa Loma College–Van Nuys, 6725 Kester Avenue, Los Angeles, CA 91405.
Website: http://www.casalomacollege.edu/.

Cerritos College
Norwalk, California

- **District-supported** 2-year, founded 1956, part of California Community College System
- **Suburban** 140-acre campus with easy access to Los Angeles
- **Coed,** 19,780 undergraduate students, 26% full-time, 57% women, 43% men

Undergraduates 5,107 full-time, 14,673 part-time. Students come from 32 other countries; 1% are from out of state; 3% Black or African American, non-Hispanic/Latino; 71% Hispanic/Latino; 9% Asian, non-Hispanic/Latino; 0.6% Native Hawaiian or other Pacific Islander, non-Hispanic/Latino; 5% American Indian or Alaska Native, non-Hispanic/Latino; 2% Two or more races, non-Hispanic/Latino; 5% Race/ethnicity unknown; 2% international; 3% transferred in. *Retention:* 61% of full-time freshmen returned.
Freshmen *Admission:* 36,863 applied, 32,371 admitted, 3,056 enrolled.
Faculty *Total:* 845, 32% full-time.
Majors Accounting; administrative assistant and secretarial science; alternative fuel vehicle technology; animation, interactive technology, video

graphics and special effects; anthropology; architectural engineering technology; art; audiology and speech-language pathology; autobody/collision and repair technology; automobile/automotive mechanics technology; biological and physical sciences; biology/biological sciences; biomedical technology; broadcast journalism; business administration and management; cabinetmaking and millwork; chemistry; cinematography and film/video production; computer programming; computer science; computer systems analysis; computer systems networking and telecommunications; cooking and related culinary arts; cosmetology; court reporting; criminal justice/police science; dance; data entry/microcomputer applications; dental hygiene; drafting and design technology; dramatic/theater arts; economics; electrical, electronic and communications engineering technology; English; fashion/apparel design; food technology and processing; French; geography; geology/earth science; German; Hispanic-American, Puerto Rican, and Mexican-American/Chicano studies; history; human services; industrial technology; insurance; international relations and affairs; journalism; kindergarten/preschool education; kinesiology and exercise science; legal administrative assistant/secretary; legal assistant/paralegal; liberal arts and sciences/liberal studies; machine tool technology; manufacturing engineering technology; marketing/marketing management; mathematics; medical/clinical assistant; music; pharmacy; philosophy; photography; physical education teaching and coaching; physical sciences related; physical therapy; physics; plastics and polymer engineering technology; political science and government; pre-engineering; psychology; real estate; registered nursing/registered nurse; religious studies; small business administration; sociology; Spanish; speech communication and rhetoric; sport and fitness administration/management; technology/industrial arts teacher education; visual and performing arts; welding technology; women's studies; zoology/animal biology.

Academics *Calendar:* semesters. *Degree:* associate. *Special study options:* academic remediation for entering students, advanced placement credit, distance learning, double majors, English as a second language, honors programs, independent study, part-time degree program, services for LD students, study abroad, summer session for credit.

Library Wilford Michael Library. *Books:* 117,647 (physical), 13,466 (digital/electronic); *Serial titles:* 155 (physical), 138,332 (digital/electronic); *Databases:* 66. Weekly public service hours: 71; students can reserve study rooms.

Student Life *Housing:* college housing not available. *Activities and Organizations:* drama/theater group, student-run newspaper, radio station, choral group, Psi Beta (psychology club), Phi Beta (PBL), Phi Theta Kappa (honor society), Wilderness Club, Where People Make Difference (WPMD radio). *Campus security:* 24-hour emergency response devices and patrols, late-night transport/escort service. *Student services:* health clinic, personal/psychological counseling, women's center, legal services.

Athletics Member NJCAA. *Intercollegiate sports:* baseball M, basketball M/W, cross-country running M/W, football M, golf M, soccer M/W, softball W, swimming and diving M/W, tennis M/W, track and field M/W, volleyball W, water polo M, wrestling M. *Intramural sports:* cheerleading M/W.

Costs (2016–17) *Tuition:* state resident $0 full-time; nonresident $4972 full-time, $259 per unit part-time. Full-time tuition and fees vary according to course load. Part-time tuition and fees vary according to course load. *Required fees:* $1346 full-time, $46 per unit part-time, $342 per term part-time.

Financial Aid Of all full-time matriculated undergraduates who enrolled in 2014, 180 Federal Work-Study jobs (averaging $3000). 89 state and other part-time jobs (averaging $2734).

Applying *Options:* electronic application, early admission, deferred entrance. *Application deadlines:* rolling (freshmen), rolling (transfers).

Freshman Application Contact Cerritos College, 11110 Alondra Boulevard, Norwalk, CA 90650-6298. *Phone:* 562-860-2451 Ext. 2102. *Website:* http://www.cerritos.edu/.

Cerro Coso Community College
Ridgecrest, California

Freshman Application Contact Mrs. Heather Ootash, Counseling/Matriculation Coordinator, Cerro Coso Community College, 3000 College Heights Boulevard, Ridgecrest, CA 93555. *Phone:* 760-384-6291. *Fax:* 760-375-4776. *E-mail:* hostash@cerrocoso.edu. *Website:* http://www.cerrocoso.edu/.

Chabot College
Hayward, California

Director of Admissions Paulette Lino, Director of Admissions and Records, Chabot College, 25555 Hesperian Boulevard, Hayward, CA 94545-5001. *Phone:* 510-723-6700. *Website:* http://www.chabotcollege.edu/.

Chaffey College
Rancho Cucamonga, California

Freshman Application Contact Erlinda Martinez, Coordinator of Admissions, Chaffey College, 5885 Haven Avenue, Rancho Cucamonga, CA 91737-3002. *Phone:* 909-652-6610. *E-mail:* erlinda.martinez@chaffey.edu. *Website:* http://www.chaffey.edu/.

Charter College
Canyon Country, California

Admissions Office Contact Charter College, 19034 Soledad Canyon Road, Canyon Country, CA 91351. *Website:* http://www.chartercollege.edu/.

Citrus College
Glendora, California

- **District-supported** 2-year, founded 1915, part of California Community College System
- **Small-town** 104-acre campus with easy access to Los Angeles
- **Coed,** 12,780 undergraduate students, 39% full-time, 53% women, 47% men

Undergraduates 4,921 full-time, 7,859 part-time. 4% Black or African American, non-Hispanic/Latino; 61% Hispanic/Latino; 8% Asian, non-Hispanic/Latino; 0.1% Native Hawaiian or other Pacific Islander, non-Hispanic/Latino; 0.2% American Indian or Alaska Native, non-Hispanic/Latino; 3% Two or more races, non-Hispanic/Latino; 0.7% Race/ethnicity unknown; 4% international.

Freshmen *Admission:* 11,388 applied, 11,388 admitted, 2,183 enrolled.

Faculty *Total:* 509, 30% full-time. *Student/faculty ratio:* 30:1.

Majors Administrative assistant and secretarial science; art; automobile/automotive mechanics technology; behavioral sciences; biological and physical sciences; biology/biological sciences; business administration and management; business/commerce; child development; computer and information sciences related; computer graphics; computer science; construction trades related; cosmetology; criminal justice/law enforcement administration; criminal justice/police science; dance; dance related; data processing and data processing technology; dental assisting; diesel mechanics technology; drafting and design technology; dramatic/theater arts; electrical, electronic and communications engineering technology; engineering; engineering technology; English; English language and literature related; French; German; health and physical education/fitness; history; hydrology and water resources science; Japanese; journalism; liberal arts and sciences/liberal studies; library and archives assisting; library and information science; licensed practical/vocational nurse training; mathematics; mechanical engineering/mechanical technology; modern languages; music; natural sciences; photography; physical education teaching and coaching; physical sciences; psychology; public administration; real estate; recording arts technology; registered nursing/registered nurse; security and loss prevention; social sciences; sociology; Spanish; speech communication and rhetoric; visual and performing arts; water quality and wastewater treatment management and recycling technology.

Academics *Calendar:* semesters. *Degree:* certificates, diplomas, and associate. *Special study options:* academic remediation for entering students, advanced placement credit, cooperative education, distance learning, double majors, English as a second language, honors programs, part-time degree program, services for LD students, study abroad, summer session for credit.

Library Hayden Library.

Student Life *Activities and Organizations:* drama/theater group, student-run newspaper, choral group, Student Government, Alpha Gamma Sigma (AGS), Veterans Network, International Friendship Club, Citrus Business Association (CBA). *Campus security:* 24-hour patrols, student patrols, late-night transport/escort service. *Student services:* health clinic, personal/psychological counseling, legal services.

Athletics *Intercollegiate sports:* baseball M, basketball M/W, cross-country running M/W, football M, golf M/W, soccer M/W, softball W, swimming and diving W, volleyball W, water polo M/W.

Costs (2015–16) *Tuition:* state resident $1380 full-time, $46 per unit part-time; nonresident $8100 full-time, $224 per unit part-time. Full-time tuition and fees vary according to course load. Part-time tuition and fees vary according to course load. *Required fees:* $87 full-time.

Financial Aid Of all full-time matriculated undergraduates who enrolled in 2014, 141 Federal Work-Study jobs (averaging $5500).

Applying *Options:* electronic application, early decision. *Required:* high school transcript. *Application deadline:* rolling (freshmen).

Freshman Application Contact Admissions and Records, Citrus College, Glendora, CA 91741-1899. *Phone:* 626-914-8511. *Fax:* 626-914-8613. *E-mail:* admissions@citruscollege.edu.
Website: http://www.citruscollege.edu/.

City College of San Francisco
San Francisco, California

Freshman Application Contact Ms. Mary Lou Leyba-Frank, Dean of Admissions and Records, City College of San Francisco, 50 Phelan Avenue, San Francisco, CA 94112-1821. *Phone:* 415-239-3291. *Fax:* 415-239-3936. *E-mail:* mleyba@ccsf.edu.
Website: http://www.ccsf.edu/.

Coastline Community College
Fountain Valley, California

- **District-supported** 2-year, founded 1976, part of Coast Community College District System
- **Urban** campus with easy access to Orange County
- **Coed,** 11,431 undergraduate students, 22% full-time, 41% women, 59% men

Undergraduates 2,488 full-time, 8,943 part-time. 12% Black or African American, non-Hispanic/Latino; 28% Hispanic/Latino; 22% Asian, non-Hispanic/Latino; 0.5% Native Hawaiian or other Pacific Islander, non-Hispanic/Latino; 0.8% American Indian or Alaska Native, non-Hispanic/Latino; 4% Two or more races, non-Hispanic/Latino; 2% Race/ethnicity unknown.
Freshmen *Admission:* 900 enrolled.
Faculty *Total:* 282, 15% full-time. *Student/faculty ratio:* 32:1.
Majors Liberal arts and sciences/liberal studies.
Academics *Calendar:* semesters. *Degree:* certificates and associate. *Special study options:* academic remediation for entering students, accelerated degree program, adult/continuing education programs, advanced placement credit, cooperative education, distance learning, double majors, English as a second language, external degree program, honors programs, independent study, internships, off-campus study, part-time degree program, services for LD students, study abroad, summer session for credit.
Library Coastline Virtual Library plus 1 other.
Student Life *Housing:* college housing not available. *Campus security:* 24-hour emergency response devices. *Student services:* health clinic, personal/psychological counseling.
Costs (2015–16) *Tuition:* state resident $1104 full-time, $46 per unit part-time; nonresident $6648 full-time, $231 per unit part-time. No tuition increase for student's term of enrollment. *Required fees:* $32 full-time.
Financial Aid Of all full-time matriculated undergraduates who enrolled in 2014, 8,176 applied for aid, 7,655 were judged to have need, 3 had their need fully met. 37 Federal Work-Study jobs (averaging $4000). *Average percent of need met:* 13%. *Average financial aid package:* $4227. *Average need-based loan:* $2930. *Average need-based gift aid:* $4156. *Financial aid deadline:* 8/15.
Applying *Options:* electronic application, early admission. *Recommended:* high school transcript. *Application deadlines:* rolling (freshmen), rolling (transfers).
Freshman Application Contact Jennifer McDonald, Director of Admissions and Records, Coastline Community College, 11460 Warner Avenue, Fountain Valley, CA 92708-2597. *Phone:* 714-241-6163.
Website: http://www.coastline.edu/.

College of Alameda
Alameda, California

Freshman Application Contact College of Alameda, 555 Ralph Appezzato Memorial Parkway, Alameda, CA 94501-2109. *Phone:* 510-748-2204.
Website: http://alameda.peralta.edu/.

College of Marin
Kentfield, California

- **District-supported** 2-year, founded 1926, part of California Community College System
- **Suburban** 410-acre campus with easy access to San Francisco
- **Coed**

Undergraduates 7% Black or African American, non-Hispanic/Latino; 25% Hispanic/Latino; 8% Asian, non-Hispanic/Latino; 0.3% Native Hawaiian or other Pacific Islander, non-Hispanic/Latino; 0.2% American Indian or Alaska Native, non-Hispanic/Latino; 5% Two or more races, non-Hispanic/Latino; 2% Race/ethnicity unknown; 1% international.
Academics *Calendar:* semesters. *Degree:* certificates and associate. *Special study options:* academic remediation for entering students, advanced placement credit, cooperative education, distance learning, double majors, English as a second language, part-time degree program, services for LD students, summer session for credit.
Library Main Library plus 1 other.
Student Life *Campus security:* 24-hour emergency response devices and patrols.
Costs (2015–16) *Tuition:* state resident $1380 full-time, $46 per credit hour part-time; nonresident $7530 full-time, $205 per credit hour part-time. Full-time tuition and fees vary according to course load. Part-time tuition and fees vary according to course load.
Applying *Options:* electronic application, early admission.
Freshman Application Contact College of Marin, 835 College Avenue, Kentfield, CA 94904. *Phone:* 415-485-9414.
Website: http://www.marin.edu/.

College of San Mateo
San Mateo, California

Director of Admissions Mr. Henry Villareal, Dean of Admissions and Records, College of San Mateo, 1700 West Hillsdale Boulevard, San Mateo, CA 94402-3784. *Phone:* 650-574-6590. *E-mail:* csmadmission@smccd.edu.
Website: http://www.collegeofsanmateo.edu/.

College of the Canyons
Santa Clarita, California

- **District-supported** 2-year, founded 1969, part of California Community College System
- **Suburban** 224-acre campus with easy access to Los Angeles
- **Coed,** 16,989 undergraduate students

Undergraduates Students come from 44 other countries; 1% are from out of state.
Faculty *Total:* 724, 24% full-time.
Majors Accounting technology and bookkeeping; administrative assistant and secretarial science; animation, interactive technology, video graphics and special effects; architectural drafting and CAD/CADD; art; athletic training; automobile/automotive mechanics technology; biological and physical sciences; building/construction site management; business administration and management; child-care provision; cinematography and film/video production; clinical/medical laboratory technology; computer science; computer systems networking and telecommunications; criminal justice/police science; dramatic/theater arts; English; fire prevention and safety technology; French; geography; geology/earth science; graphic design; health and physical education/fitness; history; hospitality administration; hotel/motel administration; humanities; interior design; journalism; legal assistant/paralegal; liberal arts and sciences/liberal studies; manufacturing engineering technology; mathematics; music; musical theater; parks, recreation and leisure; philosophy; photography; physics; political science and government; pre-engineering; psychology; real estate; registered nursing/registered nurse; restaurant, culinary, and catering management; sales, distribution, and marketing operations; sign language interpretation and translation; small business administration; social sciences; sociology; Spanish; speech communication and rhetoric; surveying technology; water quality and wastewater treatment management and recycling technology; welding technology.
Academics *Calendar:* semesters. *Degree:* certificates and associate. *Special study options:* academic remediation for entering students, accelerated degree program, adult/continuing education programs, advanced placement credit, cooperative education, distance learning, double majors, English as a second language, honors programs, internships, part-time degree program, services for LD students, study abroad, summer session for credit.
Library College of the Canyons Library. *Books:* 136,581 (digital/electronic).
Student Life *Housing:* college housing not available. *Activities and Organizations:* drama/theater group, choral group. *Campus security:* 24-hour emergency response devices, late-night transport/escort service. *Student services:* health clinic, personal/psychological counseling, women's center.
Athletics *Intercollegiate sports:* baseball M, basketball M/W, cross-country running M/W, football M, golf M/W, ice hockey M(c), soccer M/W, softball W, swimming and diving M/W, track and field M/W, volleyball W.
Costs (2016–17) *Tuition:* state resident $1154 full-time, $46 per credit hour part-time. Full-time tuition and fees vary according to course load. Part-time tuition and fees vary according to course load. *Required fees:* $50 full-time.
Financial Aid Of all full-time matriculated undergraduates who enrolled in 2014, 90 Federal Work-Study jobs (averaging $2978).

Applying *Options:* electronic application. *Recommended:* high school transcript. *Application deadlines:* rolling (freshmen), rolling (transfers). *Notification:* continuous (freshmen), continuous (transfers).

Freshman Application Contact Dr. Jasmine Ruys, Director, Admissions and Records and Online Services, College of the Canyons, 26455 Rockwell Canyon Road, Santa Clarita, CA 91355. *Phone:* 661-362-3280. *Fax:* 661-254-7996. *E-mail:* jasmine.ruys@canyons.edu. *Website:* http://www.canyons.edu/.

College of the Desert
Palm Desert, California

- **District-supported** 2-year, founded 1959, part of California Community College System
- **Small-town** 160-acre campus
- **Coed**

Undergraduates 3,629 full-time, 5,630 part-time. 8% are from out of state; 4% Black or African American, non-Hispanic/Latino; 65% Hispanic/Latino; 3% Asian, non-Hispanic/Latino; 0.2% Native Hawaiian or other Pacific Islander, non-Hispanic/Latino; 0.3% American Indian or Alaska Native, non-Hispanic/Latino; 2% Two or more races, non-Hispanic/Latino; 1% Race/ethnicity unknown; 2% international; 4% transferred in. *Retention:* 75% of full-time freshmen returned.

Faculty *Student/faculty ratio:* 29:1.

Academics *Calendar:* semesters. *Degree:* certificates, diplomas, and associate. *Special study options:* academic remediation for entering students, adult/continuing education programs, distance learning, double majors, English as a second language, freshman honors college, honors programs, independent study, part-time degree program, services for LD students, study abroad, summer session for credit.

Library College of the Desert Library.

Student Life *Campus security:* 24-hour emergency response devices and patrols, late-night transport/escort service.

Athletics Member NJCAA.

Applying *Options:* electronic application.

Freshman Application Contact College of the Desert, 43-500 Monterey Avenue, Palm Desert, CA 92260-9305. *Phone:* 760-346-8041 Ext. 7441. *Website:* http://www.collegeofthedesert.edu/.

College of the Redwoods
Eureka, California

Freshman Application Contact Director of Enrollment Management, College of the Redwoods, 7351 Tompkins Hill Road, Eureka, CA 95501-9300. *Phone:* 707-476-4100. *Toll-free phone:* 800-641-0400. *Fax:* 707-476-4400. *Website:* http://www.redwoods.edu/.

College of the Sequoias
Visalia, California

Freshman Application Contact Ms. Lisa Hott, Director for Admissions, College of the Sequoias, 915 South Mooney Boulevard, Visalia, CA 93277-2234. *Phone:* 559-737-4844. *Fax:* 559-737-4820. *Website:* http://www.cos.edu/.

College of the Siskiyous
Weed, California

Freshman Application Contact Recruitment and Admissions, College of the Siskiyous, 800 College Avenue, Weed, CA 96094-2899. *Phone:* 530-938-5555. *Toll-free phone:* 888-397-4339. *E-mail:* admissions-weed@siskyous.edu. *Website:* http://www.siskiyous.edu/.

Columbia College
Sonora, California

- **District-supported** 2-year, founded 1968, part of Yosemite Community College District System
- **Rural** 200-acre campus
- **Endowment** $312,432
- **Coed**, 2,424 undergraduate students, 30% full-time, 57% women, 43% men

Undergraduates 717 full-time, 1,707 part-time. Students come from 2 states and territories; 1% are from out of state; 2% Black or African American, non-Hispanic/Latino; 16% Hispanic/Latino; 2% Asian, non-Hispanic/Latino; 0.4% Native Hawaiian or other Pacific Islander, non-Hispanic/Latino; 2% American Indian or Alaska Native, non-Hispanic/Latino; 2% Two or more races, non-Hispanic/Latino; 1% Race/ethnicity unknown; 12% transferred in.

Freshmen *Admission:* 464 enrolled.

Faculty *Total:* 51, 86% full-time, 33% with terminal degrees. *Student/faculty ratio:* 19:1.

Majors Administrative assistant and secretarial science; art; automobile/automotive mechanics technology; biological and physical sciences; biology/biological sciences; business administration and management; business/commerce; child-care provision; computer science; cooking and related culinary arts; emergency medical technology (EMT paramedic); English; environmental science; fire science/firefighting; forestry; geography related; geology/earth science; health and physical education/fitness; health services/allied health/health sciences; hotel/motel administration; humanities; human services; information technology; liberal arts and sciences/liberal studies; mathematics; medical administrative assistant and medical secretary; music; natural resources/conservation; photography; physical sciences; restaurant, culinary, and catering management; speech communication and rhetoric.

Academics *Calendar:* semesters. *Degree:* certificates, diplomas, and associate. *Special study options:* academic remediation for entering students, cooperative education, distance learning, English as a second language, independent study, off-campus study, part-time degree program, services for LD students, summer session for credit.

Library Columbia College Library plus 1 other. *Books:* 40,828 (physical), 19,501 (digital/electronic); *Serial titles:* 4,151 (physical); *Databases:* 75. Weekly public service hours: 50; students can reserve study rooms.

Student Life *Housing:* college housing not available. *Activities and Organizations:* drama/theater group, student-run newspaper, choral group, Associated Students (leadership and governance), Veterans Club, Debate Club. *Campus security:* 24-hour emergency response devices and patrols, late-night transport/escort service. *Student services:* health clinic, personal/psychological counseling.

Athletics Member NJCAA. *Intercollegiate sports:* basketball M, volleyball W.

Costs (2016–17) *Tuition:* state resident $0 full-time; nonresident $6406 full-time. Full-time tuition and fees vary according to course load. Part-time tuition and fees vary according to course load. *Required fees:* $1150 full-time.

Financial Aid Of all full-time matriculated undergraduates who enrolled in 2010, 2,616 applied for aid, 2,232 were judged to have need. 29 Federal Work-Study jobs (averaging $1672). In 2010, 30 non-need-based awards were made. *Average non-need-based aid:* $100.

Applying *Options:* electronic application, early admission. *Recommended:* high school transcript. *Application deadlines:* rolling (freshmen), rolling (transfers). *Notification:* continuous (freshmen), continuous (transfers).

Freshman Application Contact Admissions Office, Columbia College, 11600 Columbia College Drive, Sonora, CA 95370. *Phone:* 209-588-5231. *Fax:* 209-588-5337. *E-mail:* ccadmissions@yosemite.edu. *Website:* http://www.gocolumbia.edu/.

Community Christian College
Redlands, California

Freshman Application Contact Mr. Enrique D. Melendez, Assistant Director of Admissions, Community Christian College, 251 Tennessee Street, Redlands, CA 92373. *Phone:* 909-222-9556. *Fax:* 909-335-9101. *E-mail:* emelendez@cccollege.edu. *Website:* http://www.cccollege.edu/.

Concorde Career College
Garden Grove, California

Freshman Application Contact Chris Becker, Director, Concorde Career College, 12951 Euclid Street, Suite 101, Garden Grove, CA 92840. *Phone:* 714-703-1900. *Fax:* 714-530-4737. *E-mail:* cbecker@concorde.edu. *Website:* http://www.concorde.edu/.

Concorde Career College
North Hollywood, California

Freshman Application Contact Madeline Volker, Director, Concorde Career College, 12412 Victory Boulevard, North Hollywood, CA 91606. *Phone:* 818-766-8151. *Fax:* 818-766-1587. *E-mail:* mvolker@concorde.edu. *Website:* http://www.concorde.edu/.

Concorde Career College
San Bernardino, California

Admissions Office Contact Concorde Career College, 201 East Airport Drive, San Bernardino, CA 92408.
Website: http://www.concorde.edu/.

Concorde Career College
San Diego, California

Admissions Office Contact Concorde Career College, 4393 Imperial Avenue, Suite 100, San Diego, CA 92113.
Website: http://www.concorde.edu/.

Contra Costa College
San Pablo, California

Freshman Application Contact Admissions and Records Office, Contra Costa College, San Pablo, CA 94806. *Phone:* 510-235-7800 Ext. 7500. *Fax:* 510-412-0769. *E-mail:* a&r@contracosta.edu.
Website: http://www.contracosta.edu/.

Copper Mountain College
Joshua Tree, California

Freshman Application Contact Greg Brown, Executive Vice President for Academic and Student Affairs, Copper Mountain College, 6162 Rotary Way, Joshua Tree, CA 92252. *Phone:* 760-366-3791. *Toll-free phone:* 866-366-3791. *Fax:* 760-366-5257. *E-mail:* gbrown@cmccd.edu.
Website: http://www.cmccd.edu/.

Cosumnes River College
Sacramento, California

Freshman Application Contact Admissions and Records, Cosumnes River College, 8401 Center Parkway, Sacramento, CA 95823-5799. *Phone:* 916-691-7411.
Website: http://www.crc.losrios.edu/.

Crafton Hills College
Yucaipa, California

Director of Admissions Larry Aycock, Admissions and Records Coordinator, Crafton Hills College, 11711 Sand Canyon Road, Yucaipa, CA 92399-1799. *Phone:* 909-389-3663. *E-mail:* laycock@craftonhills.edu.
Website: http://www.craftonhills.edu/.

Cuesta College
San Luis Obispo, California

Freshman Application Contact Cuesta College, PO Box 8106, San Luis Obispo, CA 93403-8106. *Phone:* 805-546-3130 Ext. 2262.
Website: http://www.cuesta.edu/.

Cuyamaca College
El Cajon, California

Freshman Application Contact Ms. Susan Topham, Dean of Admissions and Records, Cuyamaca College, 900 Rancho San Diego Parkway, El Cajon, CA 92019-4304. *Phone:* 619-660-4302. *Fax:* 619-660-4575.
E-mail: susan.topham@gcccd.edu.
Website: http://www.cuyamaca.net/.

Cypress College
Cypress, California

Freshman Application Contact Admissions Office, Cypress College, 9200 Valley View, Cypress, CA 90630-5897. *Phone:* 714-484-7346. *Fax:* 714-484-7446. *E-mail:* admissions@cypresscollege.edu.
Website: http://www.cypresscollege.edu/.

De Anza College
Cupertino, California

Freshman Application Contact De Anza College, 21250 Stevens Creek Boulevard, Cupertino, CA 95014-5793. *Phone:* 408-864-8292.
Website: http://www.deanza.fhda.edu/.

Deep Springs College
Deep Springs, California

- **Independent** 2-year, founded 1917
- **Rural** 3000-acre campus
- **Endowment** $18.0 million
- **Men only**

Undergraduates 28 full-time. Students come from 14 states and territories; 3 other countries; 83% are from out of state; 4% Hispanic/Latino; 14% Asian, non-Hispanic/Latino; 4% Two or more races, non-Hispanic/Latino; 14% international; 50% transferred in; 100% live on campus. *Retention:* 93% of full-time freshmen returned.
Faculty *Student/faculty ratio:* 4:1.
Academics *Calendar:* 6 7-week terms. *Degree:* associate. *Special study options:* distance learning, independent study, internships, services for LD students, summer session for credit.
Library Deep Springs College.
Student Life *Campus security:* 24-hour emergency response devices, late-night transport/escort service.
Standardized Tests *Required for some:* SAT or ACT (for admission).
Applying *Required:* essay or personal statement, high school transcript, 2 letters of recommendation, interview.
Freshman Application Contact Jack Davis, Chair, Applications Committee, Deep Springs College, HC 72, Box 45001, Dyer, NV 89010-9803. *Phone:* 760-872-2000. *Fax:* 760-874-0314. *E-mail:* apcom@deepsprings.edu.
Website: http://www.deepsprings.edu/.

Diablo Valley College
Pleasant Hill, California

Freshman Application Contact Ileana Dorn, Director of Admissions and Records, Diablo Valley College, Pleasant Hill, CA 94523-1529. *Phone:* 925-685-1230 Ext. 2330. *Fax:* 925-609-8085. *E-mail:* idorn@dvc.edu.
Website: http://www.dvc.edu/.

East Los Angeles College
Monterey Park, California

Freshman Application Contact Mr. Jeremy Allred, Associate Dean of Admissions, East Los Angeles College, 1301 Avenida Cesar Chavez, Monterey Park, CA 91754. *Phone:* 323-265-8801. *Fax:* 323-265-8688.
E-mail: allredjp@elac.edu.
Website: http://www.elac.edu/.

East San Gabriel Valley Regional Occupational Program & Technical Center
West Covina, California

Admissions Office Contact East San Gabriel Valley Regional Occupational Program & Technical Center, 1501 West Del Norte Avenue, West Covina, CA 91790.
Website: http://www.esgvrop.org/.

El Camino College
Torrance, California

Director of Admissions Mr. William Mulrooney, Director of Admissions, El Camino College, 16007 Crenshaw Boulevard, Torrance, CA 90506-0001. *Phone:* 310-660-3418. *Toll-free phone:* 866-ELCAMINO. *Fax:* 310-660-6779. *E-mail:* wmulrooney@elcamino.edu.
Website: http://www.elcamino.edu/.

Empire College
Santa Rosa, California

Freshman Application Contact Ms. Dahnja Barker, Admissions Officer, Empire College, 3035 Cleveland Avenue, Santa Rosa, CA 95403. *Phone:* 707-546-4000. *Toll-free phone:* 877-395-8535. *Website:* http://www.empcol.edu/.

Evergreen Valley College
San Jose, California

Freshman Application Contact Evergreen Valley College, 3095 Yerba Buena Road, San Jose, CA 95135-1598. *Phone:* 408-270-6423. *Website:* http://www.evc.edu/.

Feather River College
Quincy, California

- **District-supported** 2-year, founded 1968, part of California Community College System
- **Rural** 150-acre campus
- **Endowment** $39,354
- **Coed,** 1,782 undergraduate students, 36% full-time, 47% women, 53% men

Undergraduates 636 full-time, 1,146 part-time. Students come from 27 states and territories; 3 other countries; 15% are from out of state; 13% Black or African American, non-Hispanic/Latino; 20% Hispanic/Latino; 5% Asian, non-Hispanic/Latino; 1% Native Hawaiian or other Pacific Islander, non-Hispanic/Latino; 3% American Indian or Alaska Native, non-Hispanic/Latino; 0.7% Two or more races, non-Hispanic/Latino; 5% Race/ethnicity unknown; 2% international; 16% transferred in; 32% live on campus.
Freshmen *Admission:* 354 enrolled.
Faculty *Total:* 106, 24% full-time, 12% with terminal degrees. *Student/faculty ratio:* 20:1.
Majors Accounting technology and bookkeeping; administrative assistant and secretarial science; agriculture; anthropology; biology/biological sciences; business/commerce; child-care provision; computer programming; cooking and related culinary arts; corrections and criminal justice related; English; environmental studies; foods, nutrition, and wellness; health and physical education/fitness; history; horse husbandry/equine science and management; humanities; kinesiology and exercise science; liberal arts and sciences/liberal studies; licensed practical/vocational nurse training; mathematics; natural resources/conservation; parks, recreation and leisure; physical sciences; political science and government; social sciences; sociology; visual and performing arts; wildlife, fish and wildlands science and management.
Academics *Calendar:* semesters plus summer and winter terms. *Degree:* certificates, diplomas, and associate. *Special study options:* academic remediation for entering students, adult/continuing education programs, advanced placement credit, cooperative education, distance learning, double majors, English as a second language, independent study, part-time degree program, services for LD students, summer session for credit.
Library Feather River College Library. *Books:* 22,000 (physical), 130,000 (digital/electronic); *Serial titles:* 68 (physical), 28,376 (digital/electronic); *Databases:* 35. Weekly public service hours: 61; students can reserve study rooms.
Student Life *Housing Options:* coed. Campus housing is provided by a third party. *Activities and Organizations:* drama/theater group, Phi Theta Kappa Honor Society, International Cultural Club, Horse Show Team, Student Environmental Association, Student Alliance for Equity. *Campus security:* student patrols, part-time private security company patrols. *Student services:* health clinic.
Athletics *Intercollegiate sports:* baseball M, basketball M/W, cross-country running W, equestrian sports M(s)/W(s), football M, sand volleyball W, soccer M/W, softball W, track and field W, volleyball W.
Standardized Tests *Recommended:* ACCUPLACER.
Costs (2015–16) *Tuition:* state resident $1380 full-time, $46 per credit part-time; nonresident $7410 full-time, $247 per credit part-time. Full-time tuition and fees vary according to course load. Part-time tuition and fees vary according to course load. *Required fees:* $81 full-time, $2 per credit part-time, $18 per term part-time. *Room and board:* room only: $5350. Room and board charges vary according to housing facility. *Payment plan:* installment.
Financial Aid Of all full-time matriculated undergraduates who enrolled in 2014, 22 Federal Work-Study jobs (averaging $750). 103 state and other part-time jobs (averaging $1504).
Applying *Options:* electronic application.
Freshman Application Contact Mrs. Leslie Mikesell, Director of Admissions and Records, Feather River College, 570 Golden Eagle Avenue, Quincy, CA

95971. *Phone:* 530-283-0202 Ext. 285. *Toll-free phone:* 800-442-9799. *E-mail:* info@frc.edu. *Website:* http://www.frc.edu/.

 ## FIDM/Fashion Institute of Design & Merchandising, Los Angeles Campus
Los Angeles, California

- **Proprietary** 4-year, founded 1969, part of FIDM/Fashion Institute of Design & Merchandising
- **Urban** campus
- **Coed,** 2,814 undergraduate students, 90% full-time, 88% women, 12% men

Undergraduates 2,525 full-time, 289 part-time. Students come from 49 states and territories; 58 other countries; 34% are from out of state; 5% Black or African American, non-Hispanic/Latino; 22% Hispanic/Latino; 11% Asian, non-Hispanic/Latino; 1% Native Hawaiian or other Pacific Islander, non-Hispanic/Latino; 0.5% American Indian or Alaska Native, non-Hispanic/Latino; 3% Two or more races, non-Hispanic/Latino; 6% Race/ethnicity unknown; 17% international; 16% transferred in. *Retention:* 92% of full-time freshmen returned.
Freshmen *Admission:* 1,419 applied, 699 admitted, 471 enrolled. *Average high school GPA:* 2.9.
Faculty *Total:* 252, 29% full-time. *Student/faculty ratio:* 20:1.
Majors Apparel and textile manufacturing; apparel and textile marketing management; business, management, and marketing related; cinematography and film/video production; costume design; design and visual communications; fashion/apparel design; fashion merchandising; graphic design; industrial and product design; interdisciplinary studies; interior design; logistics, materials, and supply chain management; marketing/marketing management; metal and jewelry arts.
Academics *Calendar:* quarters. *Degrees:* associate and bachelor's (also includes Orange County Campus). *Special study options:* academic remediation for entering students, accelerated degree program, adult/continuing education programs, advanced placement credit, cooperative education, distance learning, English as a second language, independent study, internships, off-campus study, part-time degree program, services for LD students, study abroad, summer session for credit.
Library FIDM Los Angeles Campus Library. *Books:* 31,280 (physical), 2,576 (digital/electronic); *Serial titles:* 231 (physical); *Databases:* 35. Students can reserve study rooms.
Student Life *Housing:* college housing not available. *Activities and Organizations:* Cross-Cultural Student Alliance, Fashion Industry Club, Phi Theta Kappa Honor Society, Student Council, FIDM MODE Magazine. *Campus security:* 24-hour emergency response devices and patrols, late-night transport/escort service. *Student services:* personal/psychological counseling.
Standardized Tests *Recommended:* SAT or ACT (for admission).
Costs (2015–16) *Tuition:* $28,965 full-time. Full-time tuition and fees vary according to program. Part-time tuition and fees vary according to program. *Required fees:* $965 full-time. *Payment plan:* installment. *Waivers:* employees or children of employees.
Financial Aid Of all full-time matriculated undergraduates who enrolled in 2014, 88 Federal Work-Study jobs (averaging $2935).
Applying *Options:* electronic application, deferred entrance. *Application fee:* $225. *Required:* essay or personal statement, high school transcript, minimum 2.5 GPA, 3 letters of recommendation, interview, major-determined project. *Application deadlines:* rolling (freshmen), rolling (out-of-state freshmen), rolling (transfers).
Freshman Application Contact Ms. Susan Aronson, Executive Director of Admissions, FIDM/Fashion Institute of Design & Merchandising, Los Angeles Campus, 919 South Grand Avenue, Los Angeles, CA 90015. *Phone:* 213-624-1200 Ext. 5400. *Toll-free phone:* 800-624-1200. *E-mail:* saronson@fidm.edu. *Website:* http://www.fidm.edu/.

See next page for display ad and page 368 for the College Close-Up.

FIDM/Fashion Institute of Design & Merchandising, Orange County Campus
Irvine, California

- **Proprietary** 2-year, founded 1981, part of FIDM/Fashion Institute of Design & Merchandising
- **Urban** campus with easy access to Los Angeles
- **Coed, primarily women,** 92 undergraduate students, 93% full-time, 96% women, 4% men

Undergraduates 86 full-time, 6 part-time. Students come from 11 states and territories; 5 other countries; 12% are from out of state; 5% Black or African

American, non-Hispanic/Latino; 20% Hispanic/Latino; 14% Asian, non-Hispanic/Latino; 2% Native Hawaiian or other Pacific Islander, non-Hispanic/Latino; 2% Two or more races, non-Hispanic/Latino; 10% Race/ethnicity unknown; 9% international; 38% transferred in.
Freshmen *Admission:* 164 applied, 95 admitted, 54 enrolled. *Average high school GPA:* 2.9.
Faculty *Total:* 19, 21% full-time. *Student/faculty ratio:* 10:1.
Majors Apparel and textile marketing management; design and visual communications; fashion/apparel design; fashion merchandising; graphic design; interior design.
Academics *Calendar:* quarters. *Degree:* associate. *Special study options:* academic remediation for entering students, accelerated degree program, adult/continuing education programs, advanced placement credit, cooperative education, distance learning, English as a second language, independent study, internships, part-time degree program, services for LD students, study abroad, summer session for credit.
Library FIDM Orange County Campus Library. *Books:* 4,009 (physical), 2,576 (digital/electronic); *Serial titles:* 42 (physical); *Databases:* 35. Students can reserve study rooms.
Student Life *Housing:* college housing not available. *Activities and Organizations:* Cross-Cultural Student Alliance, Fashion Industry Club, Phi Theta Kappa (national honor society), Student Council, FIDM MODE Magazine. *Campus security:* 24-hour emergency response devices, late-night transport/escort service. *Student services:* personal/psychological counseling.
Standardized Tests *Recommended:* SAT or ACT (for admission).
Costs (2015–16) *Tuition:* $28,965 full-time. Full-time tuition and fees vary according to program. Part-time tuition and fees vary according to program. *Required fees:* $965 full-time. *Payment plan:* installment. *Waivers:* employees or children of employees.
Applying *Options:* electronic application, deferred entrance. *Application fee:* $225. *Required:* essay or personal statement, high school transcript, minimum 2.5 GPA, 3 letters of recommendation, interview, entrance project. *Application deadlines:* rolling (freshmen), rolling (out-of-state freshmen), rolling (transfers).
Freshman Application Contact Mr. Michael Mirabella, Admissions, FIDM/Fashion Institute of Design & Merchandising, Orange County Campus, 17590 Gillette Avenue, Irvine, CA 92614-5610. *Phone:* 949-851-6200 Ext. 1750. *Toll-free phone:* 888-974-3436.
Website: http://www.fidm.edu/.

FIDM/Fashion Institute of Design & Merchandising, San Diego Campus
San Diego, California

- **Proprietary** 2-year, founded 1985, part of FIDM/Fashion Institute of Design & Merchandising
- **Urban** campus
- **Coed, primarily women,** 119 undergraduate students, 95% full-time, 94% women, 6% men

Undergraduates 113 full-time, 6 part-time. Students come from 15 states and territories; 4 other countries; 21% are from out of state; 4% Black or African American, non-Hispanic/Latino; 29% Hispanic/Latino; 5% Asian, non-Hispanic/Latino; 0.8% Native Hawaiian or other Pacific Islander, non-Hispanic/Latino; 3% American Indian or Alaska Native, non-Hispanic/Latino; 6% Two or more races, non-Hispanic/Latino; 4% Race/ethnicity unknown; 3% international; 28% transferred in.
Freshmen *Admission:* 154 applied, 87 admitted, 61 enrolled. *Average high school GPA:* 2.9. *Test scores:* ACT scores over 18: 100%; ACT scores over 24: 40%; ACT scores over 30: 10%.
Faculty *Total:* 20, 10% full-time. *Student/faculty ratio:* 14:1.
Majors Design and visual communications; fashion/apparel design; fashion merchandising.
Academics *Calendar:* quarters. *Degree:* associate. *Special study options:* academic remediation for entering students, accelerated degree program, adult/continuing education programs, advanced placement credit, cooperative education, distance learning, English as a second language, independent study, internships, part-time degree program, services for LD students, study abroad, summer session for credit.
Library FIDM San Diego Campus Library. *Books:* 7,305 (physical), 2,576 (digital/electronic); *Serial titles:* 118 (physical); *Databases:* 35. Students can reserve study rooms.
Student Life *Housing:* college housing not available. *Activities and Organizations:* Cross-Cultural Student Alliance, Fashion Industry Club, Phi Theta Kappa (national honor society), Student Council, FIDM MODE Magazine. *Campus security:* 24-hour emergency response devices and patrols. *Student services:* personal/psychological counseling.
Standardized Tests *Recommended:* SAT or ACT (for admission).
Costs (2015–16) *Tuition:* $28,965 full-time. Full-time tuition and fees vary according to program. Part-time tuition and fees vary according to program. *Required fees:* $965 full-time. *Payment plan:* installment. *Waivers:* employees or children of employees.

L.A.

S.D.

O.C.

S.F.

FIDM. Creative careers begin here.

Applying *Options:* electronic application, deferred entrance. *Application fee:* $225. *Required:* essay or personal statement, high school transcript, minimum 2.5 GPA, 3 letters of recommendation, interview, major-determined project. *Application deadlines:* rolling (freshmen), rolling (out-of-state freshmen), rolling (transfers).
Freshman Application Contact Ms. Denise Baca, Campus Director, FIDM/Fashion Institute of Design & Merchandising, San Diego Campus, 350 Tenth Avenue, San Diego, CA 92101. *Phone:* 619-235-2049. *Toll-free phone:* 800-243-3436. *E-mail:* dbaca@fidm.edu.
Website: http://www.fidm.edu/.

Folsom Lake College
Folsom, California

Freshman Application Contact Admissions Office, Folsom Lake College, 10 College Parkway, Folsom, CA 95630. *Phone:* 916-608-6500.
Website: http://www.flc.losrios.edu/.

Foothill College
Los Altos Hills, California

Freshman Application Contact Ms. Shawna Aced, Registrar, Foothill College, Admissions and Records, 12345 El Monte Road, Los Altos Hills, CA 94022. *Phone:* 650-949-7771. *E-mail:* acedshawna@hda.edu.
Website: http://www.foothill.edu/.

Fremont College
Cerritos, California

Freshman Application Contact Natasha Dawson, Director of Admissions, Fremont College, 18000 Studebaker Road, Suite 900A, Cerritos, CA 90703. *Phone:* 562-809-5100. *Toll-free phone:* 800-373-6668. *Fax:* 562-809-5100. *E-mail:* info@fremont.edu.
Website: http://www.fremont.edu/.

Fremont College
Los Angeles, California

Admissions Office Contact Fremont College, 3440 Wilshire Boulevard, 10th Floor, Los Angeles, CA 90010. *Toll-free phone:* 800-373-6668.
Website: http://www.fremont.edu/.

Fresno City College
Fresno, California

Freshman Application Contact Office Assistant, Fresno City College, 1101 East University Avenue, Fresno, CA 93741-0002. *Phone:* 559-442-4600 Ext. 8604. *Fax:* 559-237-4232. *E-mail:* fcc.admissions@fresnocitycollege.edu.
Website: http://www.fresnocitycollege.edu/.

Fullerton College
Fullerton, California

- **District-supported** 2-year, founded 1913, part of California Community College System
- **Suburban** 79-acre campus with easy access to Los Angeles
- **Coed,** 24,613 undergraduate students, 33% full-time, 51% women, 49% men

Undergraduates 8,145 full-time, 16,468 part-time. 2% Black or African American, non-Hispanic/Latino; 54% Hispanic/Latino; 14% Asian, non-Hispanic/Latino; 0.4% Native Hawaiian or other Pacific Islander, non-Hispanic/Latino; 0.3% American Indian or Alaska Native, non-Hispanic/Latino; 3% Two or more races, non-Hispanic/Latino; 3% Race/ethnicity unknown; 1% international. *Retention:* 64% of full-time freshmen returned.
Freshmen *Admission:* 4,052 enrolled.
Faculty *Student/faculty ratio:* 29:1.
Majors Accounting technology and bookkeeping; administrative assistant and secretarial science; anthropology; apparel and textile marketing management; apparel and textiles; applied horticulture/horticulture operations; architectural technology; area studies related; art; astronomy; automobile/automotive mechanics technology; biological and physical sciences; biology/biological sciences; biomedical technology; building/construction site management; building/home/construction inspection; business administration and management; carpentry; chemical technology; chemistry; child-care provision; computer science; construction trades related; cosmetology; criminal justice/police science; dance; drafting and design technology; dramatic/theater arts; economics; electrical/electronics equipment installation and repair; engineering; English; environmental studies; ethnic, cultural minority, gender, and group studies related; fashion/apparel design; foods, nutrition, and wellness; foreign languages and literatures; geography; geology/earth science; graphic and printing equipment operation/production; graphic design; hazardous materials management and waste technology; health and physical education/fitness; health/medical preparatory programs related; history; humanities; information technology; interior design; international business/trade/commerce; journalism; landscaping and groundskeeping; legal administrative assistant/secretary; legal assistant/paralegal; liberal arts and sciences/liberal studies; mass communication/media; mathematics; mechanical engineering/mechanical technology; microbiology; music; parks, recreation and leisure; philosophy; physics; plant nursery management; political science and government; psychology; radio and television; real estate; recording arts technology; religious studies; sales, distribution, and marketing operations; small business administration; sociology; speech communication and rhetoric; sport and fitness administration/management; technology/industrial arts teacher education.
Academics *Calendar:* semesters. *Degree:* certificates and associate. *Special study options:* academic remediation for entering students, adult/continuing education programs, advanced placement credit, cooperative education, English as a second language, honors programs, part-time degree program, services for LD students, study abroad, summer session for credit. *ROTC:* Army (c), Navy (c), Air Force (c).
Library William T. Boyce Library.
Student Life *Housing:* college housing not available. *Activities and Organizations:* drama/theater group, student-run newspaper, radio station. *Student services:* health clinic, personal/psychological counseling, women's center, legal services.
Athletics *Intercollegiate sports:* badminton W, baseball M, basketball M/W, cross-country running M/W, football M, golf W, soccer M/W, softball W, swimming and diving M/W, tennis M/W, track and field M/W, volleyball W, water polo M/W.
Financial Aid *Financial aid deadline:* 6/30.
Applying *Options:* electronic application, early admission. *Application deadlines:* rolling (freshmen), rolling (transfers).
Freshman Application Contact Fullerton College, 321 East Chapman Avenue, Fullerton, CA 92832-2095. *Phone:* 714-992-7076.
Website: http://www.fullcoll.edu/.

Gavilan College
Gilroy, California

Freshman Application Contact Gavilan College, 5055 Santa Teresa Boulevard, Gilroy, CA 95020-9599. *Phone:* 408-848-4754.
Website: http://www.gavilan.edu/.

Glendale Career College
Glendale, California

Admissions Office Contact Glendale Career College, 240 North Brand Boulevard, Lower Level, Glendale, CA 91203.
Website: http://www.glendalecareer.com/.

Glendale Community College
Glendale, California

Freshman Application Contact Ms. Sharon Combs, Dean, Admissions, and Records, Glendale Community College, 1500 North Verdugo Road, Glendale, CA 91208. *Phone:* 818-240-1000 Ext. 5910. *E-mail:* scombs@glendale.edu.
Website: http://www.glendale.edu/.

Golden West College
Huntington Beach, California

- **District-supported** 2-year, founded 1966, part of Coast Community College District System
- **Suburban** 122-acre campus with easy access to Los Angeles
- **Endowment** $7.6 million
- **Coed**

Undergraduates 4,394 full-time, 8,000 part-time. 1% are from out of state; 2% Black or African American, non-Hispanic/Latino; 32% Hispanic/Latino; 28% Asian, non-Hispanic/Latino; 0.5% Native Hawaiian or other Pacific Islander, non-Hispanic/Latino; 0.3% American Indian or Alaska Native, non-Hispanic/Latino; 4% Two or more races, non-Hispanic/Latino; 1% Race/ethnicity unknown; 2% international. *Retention:* 71% of full-time freshmen returned.
Faculty *Student/faculty ratio:* 33:1.

Academics *Calendar:* semesters plus summer session. *Degree:* certificates and associate. *Special study options:* academic remediation for entering students, adult/continuing education programs, advanced placement credit, cooperative education, distance learning, English as a second language, external degree program, honors programs, independent study, internships, part-time degree program, services for LD students, student-designed majors, study abroad, summer session for credit. *ROTC:* Air Force (c).
Library Golden West College Library plus 1 other.
Student Life *Campus security:* 24-hour emergency response devices and patrols, late-night transport/escort service.
Athletics Member NJCAA.
Costs (2015–16) *Tuition:* state resident $1104 full-time, $46 per unit part-time; nonresident $6648 full-time, $278 per unit part-time. Full-time tuition and fees vary according to course load and program. Part-time tuition and fees vary according to course load and program. *Required fees:* $72 full-time, $36 per term part-time.
Applying *Options:* early admission. *Required for some:* essay or personal statement. *Recommended:* high school transcript.
Freshman Application Contact Golden West College, PO Box 2748, 15744 Golden West Street, Huntington Beach, CA 92647-2748. *Phone:* 714-892-7711 Ext. 58965.
Website: http://www.goldenwestcollege.edu/.

Golf Academy of America
Carlsbad, California

Director of Admissions Ms. Deborah Wells, Admissions Coordinator, Golf Academy of America, 1950 Camino Vida Roble, Suite 125, Carlsbad, CA 92008. *Phone:* 760-414-1501. *Toll-free phone:* 800-342-7342.
E-mail: sdga@sdgagolf.com.
Website: http://www.golfacademy.edu/.

Grossmont College
El Cajon, California

Freshman Application Contact Admissions Office, Grossmont College, 8800 Grossmont College Drive, El Cajon, CA 92020-1799. *Phone:* 619-644-7186.
Website: http://www.grossmont.edu/.

Gurnick Academy of Medical Arts
San Mateo, California

Admissions Office Contact Gurnick Academy of Medical Arts, 2121 South El Camino Real, Building C 2000, San Mateo, CA 94403.
Website: http://www.gurnick.edu/.

Hartnell College
Salinas, California

Director of Admissions Director of Admissions, Hartnell College, 411 Central Avenue, Salinas, CA 93901. *Phone:* 831-755-6711. *Fax:* 831-759-6014.
Website: http://www.hartnell.edu/.

ICDC College
Huntington Park, California

Admissions Office Contact ICDC College, 6812 Pacific Boulevard, Huntington Park, CA 33409.
Website: http://icdccollege.edu/.

Imperial Valley College
Imperial, California

Freshman Application Contact Imperial Valley College, 380 East Aten Road, PO Box 158, Imperial, CA 92251-0158. *Phone:* 760-352-8320 Ext. 200.
Website: http://www.imperial.edu/.

Institute of Technology
Clovis, California

Admissions Office Contact Institute of Technology, 564 W. Herndon Avenue, Clovis, CA 93612.
Website: http://www.it-colleges.edu/.

Irvine Valley College
Irvine, California

Director of Admissions Mr. John Edwards, Director of Admissions, Records, and Enrollment Services, Irvine Valley College, 5500 Irvine Center Drive, Irvine, CA 92618. *Phone:* 949-451-5416.
Website: http://www.ivc.edu/.

ITT Technical Institute
Lathrop, California

Freshman Application Contact Director of Recruitment, ITT Technical Institute, 16916 South Harlan Road, Lathrop, CA 95330. *Phone:* 209-858-0077. *Toll-free phone:* 800-346-1786.
Website: http://www.itt-tech.edu/.

ITT Technical Institute
National City, California

Freshman Application Contact Director of Recruitment, ITT Technical Institute, 401 Mile of Cars Way, Suite 100, National City, CA 91950. *Phone:* 619-327-1800. *Toll-free phone:* 800-883-0380.
Website: http://www.itt-tech.edu/.

ITT Technical Institute
Oakland, California

Freshman Application Contact Director of Recruitment, ITT Technical Institute, 1200 Clay Street, Suite 200, Oakland, CA 94612. *Phone:* 510-553-2800. *Toll-free phone:* 877-442-5833.
Website: http://www.itt-tech.edu/.

ITT Technical Institute
Orange, California

Freshman Application Contact Director of Recruitment, ITT Technical Institute, 4000 West Metropolitan Drive, Suite 100, Orange, CA 92868. *Phone:* 714-941-2400.
Website: http://www.itt-tech.edu/.

ITT Technical Institute
Oxnard, California

Freshman Application Contact Director of Recruitment, ITT Technical Institute, 2051 Solar Drive, Suite 150, Oxnard, CA 93036. *Phone:* 805-988-0143. *Toll-free phone:* 800-530-1582.
Website: http://www.itt-tech.edu/.

ITT Technical Institute
Rancho Cordova, California

Freshman Application Contact Director of Recruitment, ITT Technical Institute, 10863 Gold Center Drive, Rancho Cordova, CA 95670-6034. *Phone:* 916-851-3900. *Toll-free phone:* 800-488-8466.
Website: http://www.itt-tech.edu/.

ITT Technical Institute
San Bernardino, California

Freshman Application Contact Director of Recruitment, ITT Technical Institute, 670 East Carnegie Drive, San Bernardino, CA 92408. *Phone:* 909-806-4600. *Toll-free phone:* 800-888-3801.
Website: http://www.itt-tech.edu/.

ITT Technical Institute
San Dimas, California

Freshman Application Contact Director of Recruitment, ITT Technical Institute, 650 West Cienega Avenue, San Dimas, CA 91773. *Phone:* 909-971-2300. *Toll-free phone:* 800-414-6522.
Website: http://www.itt-tech.edu/.

ITT Technical Institute
Sylmar, California

Freshman Application Contact Director of Recruitment, ITT Technical Institute, 12669 Encinitas Avenue, Sylmar, CA 91342-3664. *Phone:* 818-364-5151. *Toll-free phone:* 800-363-2086 (in-state); 800-636-2086 (out-of-state). *Website:* http://www.itt-tech.edu/.

ITT Technical Institute
Torrance, California

Freshman Application Contact Director of Recruitment, ITT Technical Institute, 2555 West 190th Street, Suite 125, Torrance, CA 90504. *Phone:* 310-965-5900. *Website:* http://www.itt-tech.edu/.

Lake Tahoe Community College
South Lake Tahoe, California

Freshman Application Contact Office of Admissions and Records, Lake Tahoe Community College, One College Drive, South Lake Tahoe, CA 96150. *Phone:* 530-541-4660 Ext. 211. *Fax:* 530-541-7852. *E-mail:* admissions@ltcc.edu. *Website:* http://www.ltcc.edu/.

Laney College
Oakland, California

Freshman Application Contact Mrs. Barbara Simmons, District Admissions Officer, Laney College, 900 Fallon Street, Oakland, CA 94607-4893. *Phone:* 510-466-7369. *Website:* http://www.laney.edu/.

Las Positas College
Livermore, California

Director of Admissions Mrs. Sylvia R. Rodriguez, Director of Admissions and Records, Las Positas College, 3000 Campus Hill Drive, Livermore, CA 94551. *Phone:* 925-373-4942. *Website:* http://www.laspositascollege.edu/.

Lassen Community College District
Susanville, California

Freshman Application Contact Mr. Chris J. Alberico, Registrar, Lassen Community College District, Highway 139, PO Box 3000, Susanville, CA 96130. *Phone:* 530-257-6181. *Website:* http://www.lassencollege.edu/.

Laurus College
San Luis Obispo, California

Admissions Office Contact Laurus College, 81 Higuera Street, Suite 110, San Luis Obispo, CA 93401. *Website:* http://www.lauruscollege.edu/.

Learnet Academy
Los Angeles, California

Admissions Office Contact Learnet Academy, 3251 West 6th Street, 2nd Floor, Los Angeles, CA 90020. *Website:* http://www.learnet.edu/.

Long Beach City College
Long Beach, California

Director of Admissions Mr. Ross Miyashiro, Dean of Admissions and Records, Long Beach City College, 4901 East Carson Street, Long Beach, CA 90808-1780. *Phone:* 562-938-4130. *Website:* http://www.lbcc.edu/.

Los Angeles City College
Los Angeles, California

Freshman Application Contact Elaine Geismar, Director of Student Assistance Center, Los Angeles City College, 855 North Vermont Avenue, Los Angeles, CA 90029-3590. *Phone:* 323-953-4340. *Website:* http://www.lacitycollege.edu/.

Los Angeles County College of Nursing and Allied Health
Los Angeles, California

Freshman Application Contact Admissions Office, Los Angeles County College of Nursing and Allied Health, 1237 North Mission Road, Los Angeles, CA 90033. *Phone:* 323-226-4911. *Website:* http://www.ladhs.org/wps/portal/CollegeOfNursing.

Los Angeles Harbor College
Wilmington, California

Freshman Application Contact Los Angeles Harbor College, 1111 Figueroa Place, Wilmington, CA 90744-2397. *Phone:* 310-233-4091. *Website:* http://www.lahc.edu/.

Los Angeles Mission College
Sylmar, California

- **District-supported** 2-year, founded 1974, part of Los Angeles Community College District System, California Community Colleges
- **Urban** 33-acre campus with easy access to Los Angeles
- **Coed**

Undergraduates 2,338 full-time, 7,853 part-time. 2% are from out of state; 3% Black or African American, non-Hispanic/Latino; 76% Hispanic/Latino; 5% Asian, non-Hispanic/Latino; 0.1% Native Hawaiian or other Pacific Islander, non-Hispanic/Latino; 0.2% American Indian or Alaska Native, non-Hispanic/Latino; 1% Two or more races, non-Hispanic/Latino; 2% Race/ethnicity unknown; 1% international; 9% transferred in. *Retention:* 71% of full-time freshmen returned.
Academics *Calendar:* semesters. *Degree:* certificates and associate. *Special study options:* academic remediation for entering students, adult/continuing education programs, advanced placement credit, distance learning, double majors, English as a second language, honors programs, independent study, internships, off-campus study, part-time degree program, services for LD students, study abroad, summer session for credit.
Library Los Angeles Mission College Library.
Student Life *Campus security:* 24-hour emergency response devices and patrols, late-night transport/escort service.
Financial Aid Of all full-time matriculated undergraduates who enrolled in 2013, 40 Federal Work-Study jobs (averaging $4000).
Applying *Options:* early admission.
Freshman Application Contact Los Angeles Mission College, 13356 Eldridge Avenue, Sylmar, CA 91342-3245. *Website:* http://www.lamission.edu/.

Los Angeles Pierce College
Woodland Hills, California

Director of Admissions Ms. Shelley L. Gerstl, Dean of Admissions and Records, Los Angeles Pierce College, 6201 Winnetka Avenue, Woodland Hills, CA 91371-0001. *Phone:* 818-719-6448. *Website:* http://www.piercecollege.edu/.

Los Angeles Southwest College
Los Angeles, California

Director of Admissions Dan W. Walden, Dean of Academic Affairs, Los Angeles Southwest College, 1600 West Imperial Highway, Los Angeles, CA 90047-4810. *Phone:* 323-242-5511. *Website:* http://www.lasc.edu/.

Los Angeles Trade-Technical College

Los Angeles, California

- **District-supported** 2-year, founded 1925, part of Los Angeles Community College District System
- **Urban** 25-acre campus
- **Coed,** 13,194 undergraduate students, 32% full-time, 51% women, 49% men

Undergraduates 4,160 full-time, 9,034 part-time.

Freshmen *Admission:* 342 enrolled.

Faculty *Total:* 443, 45% full-time.

Majors Accounting; architectural engineering technology; automobile/automotive mechanics technology; business administration and management; carpentry; chemical engineering; commercial and advertising art; computer engineering technology; computer programming; construction engineering technology; cosmetology; culinary arts; drafting and design technology; electrical, electronic and communications engineering technology; engineering; fashion/apparel design; fashion merchandising; heating, air conditioning, ventilation and refrigeration maintenance technology; heavy equipment maintenance technology; hydrology and water resources science; industrial technology; information science/studies; labor and industrial relations; liberal arts and sciences/liberal studies; pipefitting and sprinkler fitting; real estate; registered nursing/registered nurse; transportation and materials moving related; welding technology.

Academics *Calendar:* semesters. *Degree:* certificates, diplomas, and associate. *Special study options:* academic remediation for entering students, adult/continuing education programs, advanced placement credit, cooperative education, English as a second language, part-time degree program, services for LD students, summer session for credit.

Library Los Angeles Trade-Technical College Library. *Books:* 2,640 (physical), 6,799 (digital/electronic); *Serial titles:* 93 (physical), 41 (digital/electronic); *Databases:* 48. Weekly public service hours: 52.

Student Life *Housing:* college housing not available. *Campus security:* 24-hour patrols, student patrols, late-night transport/escort service. *Student services:* health clinic, personal/psychological counseling, women's center.

Athletics *Intercollegiate sports:* basketball M/W, swimming and diving M/W, volleyball M/W.

Applying *Options:* electronic application. *Recommended:* high school transcript. *Application deadline:* 9/7 (freshmen).

Freshman Application Contact Los Angeles Trade-Technical College, 400 West Washington Boulevard, Los Angeles, CA 90015-4108. *Phone:* 213-763-7127.

Website: http://www.lattc.edu/.

Los Angeles Valley College

Valley Glen, California

- **District-supported** 2-year, founded 1949, part of Los Angeles Community College District System
- **Suburban** 105-acre campus with easy access to Los Angeles
- **Coed,** 17,957 undergraduate students

Undergraduates Students come from 20 states and territories; 21 other countries; 5% Black or African American, non-Hispanic/Latino; 50% Hispanic/Latino; 8% Asian, non-Hispanic/Latino; 0.2% Native Hawaiian or other Pacific Islander, non-Hispanic/Latino; 2% Two or more races, non-Hispanic/Latino; 4% Race/ethnicity unknown; 0.7% international. *Retention:* 84% of full-time freshmen returned.

Majors Accounting; administrative assistant and secretarial science; art; banking and financial support services; biology/biological sciences; biomedical technology; chemistry; child development; cinematography and film/video production; commercial and advertising art; computer installation and repair technology; computer programming; criminal justice/police science; dramatic/theater arts; drawing; economics; electrical/electronics equipment installation and repair; engineering; English; ethnic, cultural minority, gender, and group studies related; fire science/firefighting; foreign languages and literatures; French; geography; geology/earth science; German; health and physical education/fitness; Hebrew; history; industrial electronics technology; Italian; journalism; kindergarten/preschool education; liberal arts and sciences/liberal studies; machine tool technology; manufacturing engineering technology; mass communication/media; mathematics; mechanical drafting and CAD/CADD; music; music management; office management; philosophy; physics; political science and government; psychology; radio and television; real estate; registered nursing/registered nurse; respiratory care therapy; rhetoric and composition; sales, distribution, and marketing operations; sculpture; sociology; Spanish; special education–early childhood; theater design and technology.

Academics *Calendar:* semesters. *Degree:* certificates and associate. *Special study options:* academic remediation for entering students, adult/continuing education programs, cooperative education, distance learning, double majors, English as a second language, honors programs, independent study, internships, part-time degree program, services for LD students, student-designed majors, summer session for credit.

Library Los Angeles Valley Library.

Student Life *Housing:* college housing not available. *Activities and Organizations:* drama/theater group, student-run newspaper, radio station, choral group. *Campus security:* 24-hour emergency response devices and patrols, student patrols, late-night transport/escort service. *Student services:* health clinic, personal/psychological counseling, women's center, legal services.

Athletics Member NJCAA. *Intercollegiate sports:* baseball M, basketball M/W, cross-country running M/W, football M, soccer W, softball W, swimming and diving M/W, track and field M/W, volleyball M/W, water polo M/W. *Intramural sports:* badminton M/W, basketball M/W, cross-country running M/W, fencing M/W, football M, golf M/W, gymnastics M/W, skiing (cross-country) M/W, skiing (downhill) M/W, soccer M/W, swimming and diving M/W, tennis M/W, track and field M/W, volleyball M/W, water polo M/W, wrestling M.

Financial Aid Of all full-time matriculated undergraduates who enrolled in 2014, 65 Federal Work-Study jobs (averaging $4000).

Applying *Options:* electronic application, early admission. *Recommended:* high school transcript. *Application deadlines:* rolling (freshmen), rolling (transfers).

Freshman Application Contact Los Angeles Valley College, 5800 Fulton Avenue, Valley Glen, CA 91401. *Phone:* 818-947-5518.

Website: http://www.lavc.edu/.

Los Medanos College

Pittsburg, California

Freshman Application Contact Ms. Gail Newman, Director of Admissions and Records, Los Medanos College, 2700 East Leland Road, Pittsburg, CA 94565-5197. *Phone:* 925-439-2181 Ext. 7500.

Website: http://www.losmedanos.net/.

Mendocino College

Ukiah, California

Freshman Application Contact Mendocino College, 1000 Hensley Creek Road, Ukiah, CA 95482-0300. *Phone:* 707-468-3103.

Website: http://www.mendocino.edu/.

Merced College

Merced, California

Freshman Application Contact Ms. Cherie Davis, Associate Registrar, Merced College, 3600 M Street, Merced, CA 95348-2898. *Phone:* 209-384-6188. *Fax:* 209-384-6339.

Website: http://www.mccd.edu/.

Merritt College

Oakland, California

Freshman Application Contact Ms. Barbara Simmons, District Admissions Officer, Merritt College, 12500 Campus Drive, Oakland, CA 94619-3196. *Phone:* 510-466-7369. *E-mail:* hperdue@peralta.cc.ca.us.

Website: http://www.merritt.edu/.

★ MiraCosta College

Oceanside, California

- **District-supported** 2-year, founded 1934, part of California Community College System
- **Suburban** 131-acre campus with easy access to San Diego
- **Endowment** $5.0 million
- **Coed**

Undergraduates 5,024 full-time, 9,663 part-time. 2% are from out of state; 3% Black or African American, non-Hispanic/Latino; 33% Hispanic/Latino; 6% Asian, non-Hispanic/Latino; 0.5% Native Hawaiian or other Pacific Islander, non-Hispanic/Latino; 0.3% American Indian or Alaska Native, non-Hispanic/Latino; 7% Two or more races, non-Hispanic/Latino; 2% Race/ethnicity unknown; 1% international.

Faculty *Student/faculty ratio:* 23:1.

Academics *Calendar:* semesters. *Degree:* certificates, diplomas, and associate. *Special study options:* academic remediation for entering students, accelerated degree program, adult/continuing education programs, advanced placement credit, cooperative education, distance learning, double majors, English as a second language, honors programs, independent study, internships, part-time degree program, services for LD students, student-designed majors, study abroad, summer session for credit.

Library MiraCosta College Library.

Student Life *Campus security:* 24-hour emergency response devices, student patrols, late-night transport/escort service, trained security personnel during class hours.

Costs (2015–16) *Tuition:* state resident $1104 full-time, $46 per unit part-time; nonresident $5904 full-time, $246 per unit part-time. Full-time tuition and fees vary according to course load. Part-time tuition and fees vary according to course load. *Required fees:* $48 full-time.

Applying *Options:* electronic application, early admission, deferred entrance.

Freshman Application Contact Jane Sparks, Interim Director of Admissions and Records, MiraCosta College, One Barnard Drive, Oceanside, CA 92057. *Phone:* 760-795-6620. *Toll-free phone:* 888-201-8480. *E-mail:* admissions@miracosta.edu. *Website:* http://www.miracosta.edu/.

See this page for display ad and page 372 for the College Close-Up.

Mission College
Santa Clara, California
Director of Admissions Daniel Sanidad, Dean of Student Services, Mission College, 3000 Mission College Boulevard, Santa Clara, CA 95054-1897. *Phone:* 408-855-5139. *Website:* http://www.missioncollege.edu/.

Modesto Junior College
Modesto, California
Freshman Application Contact Ms. Martha Robles, Dean of Student Services and Support, Modesto Junior College, 435 College Avenue, Modesto, CA 95350. *Phone:* 209-575-6470. *Fax:* 209-575-6859. *E-mail:* mjcadmissions@mail.yosemite.cc.ca.us. *Website:* http://www.mjc.edu/.

Monterey Peninsula College
Monterey, California
Director of Admissions Ms. Vera Coleman, Registrar, Monterey Peninsula College, 980 Fremont Street, Monterey, CA 93940-4799. *Phone:* 831-646-4007. *E-mail:* vcoleman@mpc.edu. *Website:* http://www.mpc.edu/.

Moorpark College
Moorpark, California
Freshman Application Contact Ms. Katherine Colborn, Registrar, Moorpark College, 7075 Campus Road, Moorpark, CA 93021-2899. *Phone:* 805-378-1415. *Website:* http://www.moorparkcollege.edu/.

Moreno Valley College
Moreno Valley, California
Freshman Application Contact Jamie Clifton, Director, Enrollment Services, Moreno Valley College, 16130 Lasselle Street, Moreno Valley, CA 92551. *Phone:* 951-571-6293. *E-mail:* admissions@mvc.edu. *Website:* http://www.mvc.edu/.

Mt. San Antonio College
Walnut, California
- **District-supported** 2-year, founded 1946, part of California Community College System
- **Suburban** 421-acre campus with easy access to Los Angeles
- **Coed,** 28,991 undergraduate students, 9% full-time, 8% women, 8% men

Undergraduates 2,577 full-time, 2,113 part-time. 4% Black or African American, non-Hispanic/Latino; 62% Hispanic/Latino; 17% Asian, non-Hispanic/Latino; 0.3% Native Hawaiian or other Pacific Islander, non-Hispanic/Latino; 0.2% American Indian or Alaska Native, non-Hispanic/Latino; 3% Two or more races, non-Hispanic/Latino; 0.7% Race/ethnicity unknown; 2% international. *Retention:* 79% of full-time freshmen returned.

Freshmen *Admission:* 4,690 enrolled.

Faculty *Total:* 1,247, 31% full-time. *Student/faculty ratio:* 26:1.

Majors Accounting; administrative assistant and secretarial science; advertising; agricultural business and management; agriculture; airframe mechanics and aircraft maintenance technology; airline pilot and flight crew; air traffic control; animal sciences; apparel and textiles; architectural engineering technology; avionics maintenance technology; biological and physical sciences; building/construction finishing, management, and inspection related; business administration and management; business teacher education; child development; civil engineering technology; commercial and advertising art; computer and information sciences; computer engineering technology; computer graphics; computer science; corrections; criminal justice/police science; dairy science; data processing and data processing technology; drafting and design technology; drafting/design engineering technologies related; electrical, electronic and communications engineering technology; emergency medical technology (EMT paramedic); engineering technology; English language and literature related; family and consumer sciences/human sciences; fashion merchandising; finance; fire science/firefighting; forest technology; health and physical education/fitness; heating, air conditioning, ventilation and refrigeration maintenance technology; horticultural science; hotel/motel administration; humanities; industrial and product design; industrial radiologic technology; interior design; journalism; kindergarten/preschool education; landscape architecture; legal administrative assistant/secretary; legal assistant/paralegal; machine tool technology; marketing/marketing management; materials science; mathematics; medical administrative assistant and medical secretary; mental health counseling; music; occupational safety and health technology; ornamental horticulture; parks, recreation and leisure; parks, recreation and leisure facilities management; photography; physical sciences related; pre-engineering; quality control technology; radio and television; real estate; registered nursing/registered nurse; respiratory care therapy; sign language interpretation and translation; social sciences; surveying technology; transportation and materials moving related; visual and performing arts; welding technology; wildlife, fish and wildlands science and management.

Academics *Calendar:* semesters. *Degree:* certificates, diplomas, and associate. *Special study options:* academic remediation for entering students, adult/continuing education programs, advanced placement credit, cooperative education, distance learning, double majors, English as a second language, honors programs, independent study, part-time degree program, services for LD students, study abroad, summer session for credit. *ROTC:* Army (b), Air Force (b).

Library Learning Resources Center. *Books:* 75,587 (physical), 82,336 (digital/electronic); *Databases:* 113. Students can reserve study rooms.

Student Life *Housing:* college housing not available. *Activities and Organizations:* drama/theater group, student-run radio station, choral group, Alpha Gamma Sigma, Muslim Student Association, Student Government, Asian Student Association, Kasama-Filipino Student Organization. *Campus security:* 24-hour emergency response devices and patrols, late-night transport/escort service. *Student services:* health clinic, personal/psychological counseling, women's center.

Athletics *Intercollegiate sports:* badminton W, baseball M, basketball M/W, cheerleading M/W, cross-country running M/W, football M, golf M/W, soccer M/W, softball W, swimming and diving M/W, tennis M/W, track and field M/W, volleyball M/W, water polo M/W, wrestling M.

Costs (2015–16) *Tuition:* state resident $1288 full-time, $46 per unit part-time; nonresident $7364 full-time, $273 per unit part-time. Full-time tuition and fees vary according to course load and program. Part-time tuition and fees vary according to course load and program. *Required fees:* $60 full-time, $60 per term part-time.

Applying *Options:* electronic application, early admission, deferred entrance. *Required for some:* high school transcript. *Notification:* continuous (freshmen), continuous (transfers).

Freshman Application Contact Dr. George Bradshaw, Dean of Enrollment Management, Mt. San Antonio College, Walnut, CA 91789. *Phone:* 909-274-5570 Ext. 4505.

Website: http://www.mtsac.edu/.

Mt. San Jacinto College
San Jacinto, California

Freshman Application Contact Mt. San Jacinto College, 1499 North State Street, San Jacinto, CA 92583-2399. *Phone:* 951-639-5212.

Website: http://www.msjc.edu/.

MTI College
Sacramento, California

Freshman Application Contact Director of Admissions, MTI College, 5221 Madison Avenue, Sacramento, CA 95841. *Phone:* 916-339-1500. *Fax:* 916-339-0305.

Website: http://www.mticollege.edu/.

Napa Valley College
Napa, California

Director of Admissions Mr. Oscar De Haro, Vice President of Student Services, Napa Valley College, 2277 Napa-Vallejo Highway, Napa, CA 94558-6236. *Phone:* 707-253-3000. *Toll-free phone:* 800-826-1077.

E-mail: odeharo@napavalley.edu.

Website: http://www.napavalley.edu/.

National Career College
Panorama City, California

Admissions Office Contact National Career College, 14355 Roscoe Boulevard, Panorama City, CA 91402.

Website: http://www.nccusa.edu/.

National Polytechnic College
Commerce, California

Admissions Office Contact National Polytechnic College, 6630 Telegraph Road, Commerce, CA 90040.

Website: http://www.npcollege.edu/.

Norco College
Norco, California

- **District-supported** 2-year, founded 2010
- **Urban** 141-acre campus with easy access to Los Angeles
- **Coed,** 9,399 undergraduate students

Undergraduates 6% Black or African American, non-Hispanic/Latino; 57% Hispanic/Latino; 6% Asian, non-Hispanic/Latino; 3% Native Hawaiian or other Pacific Islander, non-Hispanic/Latino; 0.3% American Indian or Alaska Native, non-Hispanic/Latino; 3% Two or more races, non-Hispanic/Latino; 0.5% Race/ethnicity unknown.

Faculty *Total:* 271, 25% full-time.

Majors Accounting; business/commerce; computer programming; early childhood education; engineering technology; marketing/marketing management; real estate.

Academics *Degree:* certificates and associate. *Special study options:* academic remediation for entering students, distance learning, English as a second language, honors programs, services for LD students, summer session for credit.

Student Life *Housing:* college housing not available.

Applying *Options:* electronic application. *Application deadlines:* rolling (freshmen), rolling (transfers). *Notification:* continuous (freshmen), continuous (transfers).

Freshman Application Contact Mark DeAsis, Director, Enrollment Services, Norco College, 2001 Third Street, Norco, CA 92860.

E-mail: admissionsnorco@norcocollege.edu.

Website: http://www.norcocollege.edu/.

North-West College
West Covina, California

Admissions Office Contact North-West College, 2121 West Garvey Avenue, West Covina, CA 91790.

Website: http://www.nw.edu/.

Ohlone College
Fremont, California

- **District-supported** 2-year, founded 1967, part of California Community College System
- **Suburban** 530-acre campus with easy access to San Jose
- **Coed**

Undergraduates 3,211 full-time, 8,138 part-time. Students come from 11 states and territories; 40 other countries; 0.2% are from out of state; 4% Black or African American, non-Hispanic/Latino; 18% Hispanic/Latino; 30% Asian, non-Hispanic/Latino; 0.7% Native Hawaiian or other Pacific Islander, non-Hispanic/Latino; 0.2% American Indian or Alaska Native, non-Hispanic/Latino; 5% Two or more races, non-Hispanic/Latino; 19% Race/ethnicity unknown; 3% international; 13% transferred in. *Retention:* 55% of full-time freshmen returned.

Faculty *Student/faculty ratio:* 27:1.

Academics *Calendar:* semesters. *Degrees:* certificates and associate (profile includes campuses in Fremont and Newark CA). *Special study options:* academic remediation for entering students, adult/continuing education programs, advanced placement credit, cooperative education, distance

learning, double majors, English as a second language, external degree program, honors programs, internships, off-campus study, part-time degree program, services for LD students, student-designed majors, study abroad, summer session for credit. *ROTC:* Army (c), Air Force (c).
Library Ohlone College Library plus 1 other.
Student Life *Campus security:* 24-hour emergency response devices and patrols, late-night transport/escort service.
Costs (2015–16) *Tuition:* state resident $1162 full-time, $46 per unit part-time; nonresident $6730 full-time, $278 per unit part-time. Full-time tuition and fees vary according to course load, program, and reciprocity agreements. Part-time tuition and fees vary according to course load, program, and reciprocity agreements. *Required fees:* $58 full-time.
Financial Aid Of all full-time matriculated undergraduates who enrolled in 2014, 35 Federal Work-Study jobs (averaging $1800).
Applying *Options:* early admission. *Required for some:* high school transcript.
Freshman Application Contact Ohlone College, 43600 Mission Boulevard, Fremont, CA 94539-5884. *Phone:* 510-659-6107.
Website: http://www.ohlone.edu/.

Orange Coast College
Costa Mesa, California

- **District-supported** 2-year, founded 1947, part of Coast Community College District System
- **Suburban** 164-acre campus with easy access to Los Angeles
- **Endowment** $14.8 million
- **Coed,** 21,930 undergraduate students, 39% full-time, 48% women, 52% men

Undergraduates 8,620 full-time, 13,310 part-time. Students come from 69 other countries; 2% are from out of state; 2% Black or African American, non-Hispanic/Latino; 24% Hispanic/Latino; 22% Asian, non-Hispanic/Latino; 0.3% Native Hawaiian or other Pacific Islander, non-Hispanic/Latino; 0.2% American Indian or Alaska Native, non-Hispanic/Latino; 9% Two or more races, non-Hispanic/Latino; 3% Race/ethnicity unknown; 7% international; 6% transferred in.
Freshmen *Admission:* 2,609 enrolled.
Faculty *Total:* 650, 37% full-time. *Student/faculty ratio:* 35:1.
Majors Accounting; accounting technology and bookkeeping; aircraft powerplant technology; airframe mechanics and aircraft maintenance technology; airline flight attendant; animation, interactive technology, video graphics and special effects; anthropology; apparel and textile manufacturing; apparel and textile marketing management; applied horticulture/horticulture operations; architectural technology; art; audiology and speech-language pathology; aviation/airway management; biology/biological sciences; business administration and management; business/commerce; cardiovascular technology; chemistry; child-care and support services management; child-care provision; cinematography and film/video production; clinical/medical laboratory technology; commercial and advertising art; computer graphics; computer installation and repair technology; computer programming; computer science; construction trades; cooking and related culinary arts; culinary arts; dance; dance related; dental assisting; diagnostic medical sonography and ultrasound technology; dietetic technology; dramatic/theater arts; economics; electrical/electronics equipment installation and repair; electrocardiograph technology; electroneurodiagnostic/electroencephalographic technology; elementary education; engineering technologies and engineering related; family and consumer sciences/human sciences; fashion/apparel design; foods, nutrition, and wellness; foreign languages and literatures; geography; geology/earth science; health and physical education/fitness; health services/allied health/health sciences; history; hotel/motel administration; humanities; interior design; international business/trade/commerce; journalism; kinesiology and exercise science; liberal arts and sciences/liberal studies; machine tool technology; marine transportation related; mass communication/media; mathematics; medical/clinical assistant; mental health counseling; merchandising, sales, and marketing operations related (general); music; philosophy; photographic and film/video technology; photography; physical fitness technician; physics; political science and government; pre-engineering; psychology; real estate; recording arts technology; religious studies; respiratory care therapy; restaurant, culinary, and catering management; retail management; sales, distribution, and marketing operations; social sciences; sociology; Spanish; special education–early childhood; speech communication and rhetoric; tourism and travel services marketing; welding technology.
Academics *Calendar:* semesters plus summer session. *Degree:* certificates and associate. *Special study options:* academic remediation for entering students, adult/continuing education programs, advanced placement credit, cooperative education, distance learning, double majors, English as a second language, external degree program, freshman honors college, honors programs, internships, off-campus study, part-time degree program, services

for LD students, student-designed majors, study abroad, summer session for credit. *ROTC:* Army (c), Air Force (c).
Library Main Library plus 1 other. *Books:* 106,838 (physical), 19,874 (digital/electronic); *Serial titles:* 109 (physical), 4 (digital/electronic); *Databases:* 53. Weekly public service hours: 64; students can reserve study rooms.
Student Life *Housing:* college housing not available. *Activities and Organizations:* drama/theater group, student-run newspaper, choral group, Architecture Club, Circle K, Doctors of Tomorrow, Speech, Theater, and Debate, Vietnamese Student Association. *Campus security:* 24-hour emergency response devices and patrols, student patrols, late-night transport/escort service. *Student services:* health clinic, personal/psychological counseling, legal services.
Athletics *Intercollegiate sports:* baseball M, basketball M/W, bowling M(c)/W(c), crew M/W, cross-country running M/W, football M, golf M/W, soccer M/W, softball W, swimming and diving M/W, tennis M/W, track and field M/W, volleyball W, water polo M/W.
Costs (2016–17) *Tuition:* state resident $1326 full-time, $46 per unit part-time; nonresident $6338 full-time, $246 per unit part-time. Full-time tuition and fees vary according to program. Part-time tuition and fees vary according to program. *Required fees:* $900 full-time, $140 per term part-time. *Payment plan:* installment.
Financial Aid Of all full-time matriculated undergraduates who enrolled in 2014, 108 Federal Work-Study jobs (averaging $3000). *Financial aid deadline:* 5/28.
Applying *Options:* electronic application. *Application deadlines:* rolling (freshmen), rolling (transfers). *Notification:* continuous (freshmen), continuous (transfers).
Freshman Application Contact Efren Galvan, Director of Admissions, Records and Enrollment Technology, Orange Coast College, 2701 Fairview Road, Costa Mesa, CA 92926. *Phone:* 714-432-5774.
E-mail: egalvan@occ.cccd.edu.
Website: http://www.orangecoastcollege.edu/.

Oxnard College
Oxnard, California

- **District-supported** 2-year, founded 1975, part of Ventura County Community College District System
- **Urban** 119-acre campus
- **Endowment** $5.8 million
- **Coed,** 7,006 undergraduate students, 28% full-time, 54% women, 46% men

Undergraduates 1,958 full-time, 5,048 part-time. Students come from 3 states and territories; 3% Black or African American, non-Hispanic/Latino; 65% Hispanic/Latino; 6% Asian, non-Hispanic/Latino; 0.2% Native Hawaiian or other Pacific Islander, non-Hispanic/Latino; 0.3% American Indian or Alaska Native, non-Hispanic/Latino; 0.2% Two or more races, non-Hispanic/Latino; 0.4% Race/ethnicity unknown; 13% transferred in. *Retention:* 73% of full-time freshmen returned.
Freshmen *Admission:* 1,088 enrolled.
Faculty *Total:* 230, 38% full-time. *Student/faculty ratio:* 30:1.
Majors Administrative assistant and secretarial science; anthropology; art; autobody/collision and repair technology; automobile/automotive mechanics technology; biology/biological sciences; business administration and management; child development; computer and information systems security; computer systems networking and telecommunications; culinary arts; dental hygiene; economics; English; environmental engineering technology; environmental studies; family and community services; fine/studio arts; fire prevention and safety technology; fire science/firefighting; fire services administration; heating, air conditioning, ventilation and refrigeration maintenance technology; history; hotel/motel administration; legal assistant/paralegal; marketing/marketing management; mathematics; philosophy; political science and government; psychology; radio and television; restaurant/food services management; sociology; Spanish; speech communication and rhetoric; substance abuse/addiction counseling; web page, digital/multimedia and information resources design.
Academics *Calendar:* semesters. *Degree:* certificates, diplomas, and associate. *Special study options:* academic remediation for entering students, accelerated degree program, advanced placement credit, distance learning, double majors, English as a second language, honors programs, independent study, part-time degree program, services for LD students, summer session for credit.
Library Oxnard College Library. *Books:* 47,874 (physical), 141,577 (digital/electronic); *Serial titles:* 422 (physical), 9 (digital/electronic); *Databases:* 12. Students can reserve study rooms.
Student Life *Housing:* college housing not available. *Activities and Organizations:* drama/theater group, student-run television station. *Campus security:* 24-hour patrols, late-night transport/escort service. *Student services:* health clinic, personal/psychological counseling, women's center.

Athletics *Intercollegiate sports:* baseball M, basketball M/W, cross-country running M/W, soccer M/W, softball W.
Costs (2015–16) *Tuition:* state resident $0 full-time; nonresident $8164 full-time, $230 per unit part-time. *Required fees:* $1338 full-time, $46 per unit part-time. *Payment plan:* installment.
Financial Aid Of all full-time matriculated undergraduates who enrolled in 2014, 80 Federal Work-Study jobs (averaging $3000).
Applying *Options:* electronic application, early admission. *Recommended:* high school transcript. *Application deadlines:* rolling (freshmen), rolling (transfers). *Notification:* continuous (freshmen), continuous (transfers).
Freshman Application Contact Mr. Joel Diaz, Registrar, Oxnard College, 4000 South Rose Avenue, Oxnard, CA 93033-6699. *Phone:* 805-986-5843. *Fax:* 805-986-5943. *E-mail:* jdiaz@vcccd.edu.
Website: http://www.oxnardcollege.edu/.

Palomar College
San Marcos, California

- **District-supported** 2-year, founded 1946, part of California Community College System
- **Suburban** 156-acre campus with easy access to San Diego
- **Coed,** 25,244 undergraduate students, 100% full-time, 47% women, 53% men

Undergraduates 25,244 full-time.
Faculty *Total:* 1,305, 21% full-time. *Student/faculty ratio:* 21:1.
Majors Accounting technology and bookkeeping; administrative assistant and secretarial science; advertising; airline pilot and flight crew; animation, interactive technology, video graphics and special effects; apparel and textile marketing management; archeology; architectural drafting and CAD/CADD; architectural technology; art; astronomy; autobody/collision and repair technology; automobile/automotive mechanics technology; aviation/airway management; biological and physical sciences; biology/biological sciences; broadcast journalism; building/home/construction inspection; business administration and management; business/commerce; cabinetmaking and millwork; carpentry; ceramic arts and ceramics; chemistry; child-care and support services management; child-care provision; commercial and advertising art; computer graphics; computer programming; computer systems networking and telecommunications; construction trades related; dance; dental assisting; design and visual communications; desktop publishing and digital imaging design; diesel mechanics technology; drafting and design technology; dramatic/theater arts; drawing; drywall installation; economics; education; electrical/electronics drafting and CAD/CADD; electrician; emergency medical technology (EMT paramedic); English; family and community services; family and consumer sciences/human sciences; fashion/apparel design; film/cinema/video studies; fire prevention and safety technology; foreign languages and literatures; forensic science and technology; French; geography; geography related; geology/earth science; graphic and printing equipment operation/production; graphic design; homeland security; humanities; information technology; insurance; interior design; international business/trade/commerce; journalism; kinesiology and exercise science; legal studies; liberal arts and sciences/liberal studies; library and archives assisting; masonry; mathematics; medical administrative assistant and medical secretary; metal and jewelry arts; music; parks, recreation and leisure; photographic and film/video technology; pre-engineering; psychology; public administration; radio and television; real estate; registered nursing/registered nurse; sculpture; sheet metal technology; sign language interpretation and translation; social sciences; sociology; special education–early childhood; speech communication and rhetoric; substance abuse/addiction counseling; water quality and wastewater treatment management and recycling technology; web page, digital/multimedia and information resources design; welding technology; women's studies.
Academics *Calendar:* semesters. *Degree:* certificates and associate. *Special study options:* academic remediation for entering students, advanced placement credit, cooperative education, distance learning, English as a second language, internships, part-time degree program, services for LD students, summer session for credit.
Library Palomar College Library.
Student Life *Housing:* college housing not available. *Activities and Organizations:* drama/theater group, student-run newspaper, radio and television station, choral group, SNAP (Student Nursing Association of Palomar College), Alpha Omega Rho Chapter of Phi Theta Kappa (international honor society), Active Minds, Student Veterans Organization, MEChA (Chicano organization). *Campus security:* 24-hour emergency response devices and patrols, student patrols, late-night transport/escort service. *Student services:* health clinic, personal/psychological counseling.
Athletics *Intercollegiate sports:* baseball M, basketball M/W, football M, golf M, soccer M/W, softball W, swimming and diving M/W, tennis M/W, track and field M/W, volleyball M/W, water polo M/W, wrestling M. *Intramural sports:* basketball M/W, bowling M, golf M, skiing (downhill) M/W, soccer M, softball W, tennis M, volleyball M, water polo M, wrestling M.

Costs (2016–17) *Tuition:* state resident $1104 full-time, $46 per unit part-time; nonresident $6288 full-time, $262 per unit part-time. *Required fees:* $60 full-time, $1 per unit part-time, $19 per term part-time.
Applying *Options:* electronic application. *Application deadlines:* rolling (freshmen), rolling (transfers). *Notification:* continuous (freshmen), continuous (transfers).
Freshman Application Contact Dr. Kendyl Magnuson, Director of Enrollment Services, Palomar College, 1140 W Mission Road, San Marcos, CA 92069. *Phone:* 760-744-1150 Ext. 2171. *Fax:* 760-744-2932.
E-mail: kmagnuson@palomar.edu.
Website: http://www.palomar.edu/.

Palo Verde College
Blythe, California

Freshman Application Contact Diana Rodriguez, Vice President of Student Services, Palo Verde College, 1 College Drive, Blythe, CA 92225. *Phone:* 760-921-5428. *Fax:* 760-921-3608. *E-mail:* diana.rodriguez@paloverde.edu.
Website: http://www.paloverde.edu/.

Pasadena City College
Pasadena, California

- **District-supported** 2-year, founded 1924, part of California Community College System
- **Urban** 55-acre campus with easy access to Los Angeles
- **Coed,** 27,050 undergraduate students, 41% full-time, 52% women, 48% men

Undergraduates 11,068 full-time, 15,982 part-time. Students come from 20 states and territories; 150 other countries; 1% are from out of state; 4% Black or African American, non-Hispanic/Latino; 50% Hispanic/Latino; 24% Asian, non-Hispanic/Latino; 0.1% Native Hawaiian or other Pacific Islander, non-Hispanic/Latino; 0.1% American Indian or Alaska Native, non-Hispanic/Latino; 11% Two or more races, non-Hispanic/Latino; 0.7% Race/ethnicity unknown; 4% international; 9% transferred in. *Retention:* 78% of full-time freshmen returned.
Freshmen *Admission:* 5,189 enrolled.
Faculty *Total:* 1,099, 32% full-time. *Student/faculty ratio:* 25:1.
Majors Accounting; accounting technology and bookkeeping; administrative assistant and secretarial science; animation, interactive technology, video graphics and special effects; anthropology; architecture; art; audiology and speech-language pathology; automobile/automotive mechanics technology; biochemistry; biological and physical sciences; biology/biological sciences; broadcast journalism; building/home/construction inspection; business administration and management; business automation/technology/data entry; chemistry; child development; cinematography and film/video production; classics and classical languages; computer/information technology services administration related; computer science; computer technology/computer systems technology; construction trades; cosmetology; cosmetology, barber/styling, and nail instruction; criminal justice/law enforcement administration; dance; data entry/microcomputer applications related; dental assisting; dental hygiene; dental laboratory technology; desktop publishing and digital imaging design; digital communication and media/multimedia; drafting and design technology; dramatic/theater arts; electrical and electronic engineering technologies related; electrical and electronics engineering; engineering technology; fashion/apparel design; fashion merchandising; fire prevention and safety technology; food service and dining room management; graphic and printing equipment operation/production; graphic design; history; hospitality administration; humanities; industrial electronics technology; international business/trade/commerce; international/global studies; legal assistant/paralegal; liberal arts and sciences/liberal studies; library science related; licensed practical/vocational nurse training; machine shop technology; marketing/marketing management; mathematics; mechanical engineering; medical/clinical assistant; medical insurance/medical billing; medical office assistant; photography; photojournalism; psychology; radio and television; radio and television broadcasting technology; radiologic technology/science; registered nursing/registered nurse; sociology; Spanish; speech communication and rhetoric; theater design and technology; welding technology.
Academics *Calendar:* semesters. *Degree:* certificates, diplomas, and associate. *Special study options:* academic remediation for entering students, adult/continuing education programs, advanced placement credit, distance learning, double majors, English as a second language, honors programs, independent study, internships, part-time degree program, services for LD students, study abroad, summer session for credit.
Library Pasadena City College Library plus 1 other. *Books:* 133,975 (physical), 35,619 (digital/electronic); *Databases:* 56. Weekly public service hours: 54; students can reserve study rooms.

Student Life *Housing:* college housing not available. *Activities and Organizations:* drama/theater group, student-run newspaper, choral group, marching band, AGS Honor Society, TROPA, Candela Salsa, International Students, Ujima. *Campus security:* 24-hour emergency response devices and patrols, late-night transport/escort service, cadet patrols. *Student services:* health clinic, personal/psychological counseling.

Athletics *Intercollegiate sports:* badminton M/W, baseball M, basketball M/W, cheerleading W(c), cross-country running M/W, football M, soccer M/W, softball W, swimming and diving M/W, tennis M/W, track and field M/W, volleyball W, water polo W. *Intramural sports:* water polo M(c).

Costs (2016–17) *Tuition:* state resident $1152 full-time, $46 per unit part-time; nonresident $6180 full-time, $262 per unit part-time. *Required fees:* $48 full-time, $24 per hour part-time.

Applying *Options:* electronic application. *Application deadlines:* rolling (freshmen), rolling (transfers). *Notification:* continuous (freshmen), continuous (transfers).

Freshman Application Contact Pasadena City College, 1570 East Colorado Boulevard, Pasadena, CA 91106-2041. *Phone:* 626-585-7614. *Fax:* 626-585-7915.

Website: http://www.pasadena.edu/.

Pima Medical Institute
Chula Vista, California

Freshman Application Contact Admissions Office, Pima Medical Institute, 780 Bay Boulevard, Suite 101, Chula Vista, CA 91910. *Phone:* 619-425-3200. *Toll-free phone:* 800-477-PIMA (in-state); 888-477-PIMA (out-of-state). *Website:* http://www.pmi.edu/.

Platt College
Alhambra, California

Director of Admissions Mr. Detroit Whiteside, Director of Admissions, Platt College, 1000 South Fremont A9W, Alhambra, CA 91803. *Phone:* 323-258-8050. *Toll-free phone:* 888-866-6697 (in-state); 888-80-PLATT (out-of-state). *Website:* http://www.plattcollege.edu/.

Platt College
Ontario, California

Director of Admissions Ms. Jennifer Abandonato, Director of Admissions, Platt College, 3700 Inland Empire Boulevard, Suite 400, Ontario, CA 91764. *Phone:* 909-941-9410. *Toll-free phone:* 888-80-PLATT. *Website:* http://www.plattcollege.edu/.

Porterville College
Porterville, California

Director of Admissions Ms. Judy Pope, Director of Admissions and Records/Registrar, Porterville College, 100 East College Avenue, Porterville, CA 93257-6058. *Phone:* 559-791-2222. *Website:* http://www.pc.cc.ca.us/.

Professional Golfers Career College
Temecula, California

Freshman Application Contact Mr. Gary Gilleon, Professional Golfers Career College, 26109 Ynez Road, Temecula, CA 92591. *Phone:* 951-719-2994 Ext. 1021. *Toll-free phone:* 800-877-4380. *Fax:* 951-719-1643. *E-mail:* garygilleon@golfcollege.edu. *Website:* http://www.golfcollege.edu/.

Reedley College
Reedley, California

Freshman Application Contact Admissions and Records Office, Reedley College, 995 North Reed Avenue, Reedley, CA 93654. *Phone:* 559-638-0323. *Fax:* 559-637-2523. *Website:* http://www.reedleycollege.edu/.

Rio Hondo College
Whittier, California

- **District-supported** 2-year, founded 1960, part of California Community College System
- **Suburban** 128-acre campus with easy access to Los Angeles
- **Coed**

Faculty *Total:* 560, 34% full-time.

Majors Business teacher education; criminal justice/law enforcement administration; liberal arts and sciences/liberal studies; registered nursing/registered nurse.

Academics *Calendar:* semesters. *Degree:* certificates and associate. *Special study options:* academic remediation for entering students, adult/continuing education programs, advanced placement credit, English as a second language, honors programs, part-time degree program, services for LD students, study abroad, summer session for credit. *ROTC:* Army (c), Navy (c), Air Force (c).

Library Library and Learning Resource Center plus 1 other. *Books:* 88,245 (physical); *Serial titles:* 104 (physical); *Databases:* 12. Weekly public service hours: 68; students can reserve study rooms.

Student Life *Housing:* college housing not available. *Activities and Organizations:* drama/theater group, student-run newspaper, radio station, choral group. *Campus security:* 24-hour patrols, late-night transport/escort service. *Student services:* health clinic, personal/psychological counseling, women's center, legal services.

Athletics *Intercollegiate sports:* baseball M, basketball M/W, cross-country running M/W, soccer M/W, softball W, swimming and diving M/W, tennis M/W, track and field M/W, volleyball W, water polo M/W, wrestling M.

Costs (2015–16) *Tuition:* state resident $1104 full-time, $46 per credit part-time; nonresident $4800 full-time, $200 per credit part-time. Full-time tuition and fees vary according to course load. Part-time tuition and fees vary according to course load. *Required fees:* $72 full-time.

Financial Aid Of all full-time matriculated undergraduates who enrolled in 2014, 150 Federal Work-Study jobs (averaging $3200). 35 state and other part-time jobs (averaging $3200). *Financial aid deadline:* 5/1.

Applying *Application deadlines:* rolling (freshmen), rolling (transfers). *Notification:* continuous (freshmen), continuous (transfers).

Freshman Application Contact Rio Hondo College, 3600 Workman Mill Road, Whittier, CA 90601-1699. *Phone:* 562-692-0921 Ext. 3415. *Website:* http://www.riohondo.edu/.

Riverside City College
Riverside, California

Freshman Application Contact Joy Chambers, Dean of Enrollment Services, Riverside City College, Riverside, CA 92506. *Phone:* 951-222-8600. *Fax:* 951-222-8037. *E-mail:* admissionsriverside@rcc.edu. *Website:* http://www.rcc.edu/.

Sacramento City College
Sacramento, California

Director of Admissions Mr. Sam T. Sandusky, Dean, Student Services, Sacramento City College, 3835 Freeport Boulevard, Sacramento, CA 95822-1386. *Phone:* 916-558-2438. *Website:* http://www.scc.losrios.edu/.

Saddleback College
Mission Viejo, California

Freshman Application Contact Admissions Office, Saddleback College, 28000 Marguerite Parkway, Mission Viejo, CA 92692. *Phone:* 949-582-4555. *Fax:* 949-347-8315. *E-mail:* earaiza@saddleback.edu. *Website:* http://www.saddleback.edu/.

Sage College
Moreno Valley, California

Admissions Office Contact Sage College, 12125 Day Street, Building L, Moreno Valley, CA 92557-6720. *Toll-free phone:* 888-755-SAGE. *Website:* http://www.sagecollege.edu/.

The Salvation Army College for Officer Training at Crestmont
Rancho Palos Verdes, California

Freshman Application Contact Capt. Brian Jones, Director of Curriculum, The Salvation Army College for Officer Training at Crestmont, 30840

Hawthorne Boulevard, Rancho Palos Verdes, CA 90275. *Phone:* 310-544-6442. *Fax:* 310-265-6520.
Website: http://www.crestmont.edu/.

San Bernardino Valley College
San Bernardino, California

Director of Admissions Ms. Helena Johnson, Director of Admissions and Records, San Bernardino Valley College, 701 South Mount Vernon Avenue, San Bernardino, CA 92410-2748. *Phone:* 909-384-4401.
Website: http://www.valleycollege.edu/.

San Diego City College
San Diego, California

Freshman Application Contact Ms. Lou Humphries, Registrar/Supervisor of Admissions, Records, Evaluations and Veterans, San Diego City College, 1313 Park Boulevard, San Diego, CA 92101-4787. *Phone:* 619-388-3474. *Fax:* 619-388-3505. *E-mail:* lhumphri@sdccd.edu.
Website: http://www.sdcity.edu/.

San Diego Mesa College
San Diego, California

Freshman Application Contact Ms. Cheri Sawyer, Admissions Supervisor, San Diego Mesa College, 7250 Mesa College Drive, San Diego, CA 92111. *Phone:* 619-388-2686. *Fax:* 619-388-2960. *E-mail:* csawyer@sdccd.edu.
Website: http://www.sdmesa.edu/.

San Diego Miramar College
San Diego, California

- **District-supported** 2-year, founded 1969, part of San Diego Community College District System
- **Suburban** 120-acre campus
- **Coed**

Academics *Calendar:* semesters. *Degree:* certificates and associate. *Special study options:* academic remediation for entering students, accelerated degree program, adult/continuing education programs, advanced placement credit, cooperative education, distance learning, double majors, English as a second language, honors programs, independent study, part-time degree program, services for LD students, student-designed majors, study abroad, summer session for credit.
Library Miramar College Library.
Student Life *Campus security:* 24-hour emergency response devices and patrols.
Costs (2015–16) *Tuition:* state resident $1380 full-time, $46 per credit hour part-time; nonresident $5790 full-time, $193 per credit hour part-time. No tuition increase for student's term of enrollment. *Required fees:* $38 full-time, $19 per term part-time.
Applying *Options:* electronic application.
Freshman Application Contact Ms. Dana Stack, Admissions Supervisor, San Diego Miramar College, 10440 Black Mountain Road, San Diego, CA 92126-2999. *Phone:* 619-536-7854. *E-mail:* dstack@sdccd.edu.
Website: http://www.sdmiramar.edu/.

San Joaquin Delta College
Stockton, California

- **District-supported** 2-year, founded 1935, part of California Community College System
- **Urban** 165-acre campus with easy access to Sacramento
- **Coed,** 17,213 undergraduate students

Undergraduates Students come from 20 states and territories; 0.2% are from out of state; 8% Black or African American, non-Hispanic/Latino; 45% Hispanic/Latino; 12% Asian, non-Hispanic/Latino; 0.6% Native Hawaiian or other Pacific Islander, non-Hispanic/Latino; 0.4% American Indian or Alaska Native, non-Hispanic/Latino; 5% Two or more races, non-Hispanic/Latino; 0.6% Race/ethnicity unknown; 0.2% international. *Retention:* 77% of full-time freshmen returned.
Faculty *Total:* 544, 41% full-time. *Student/faculty ratio:* 27:1.
Majors Accounting; agricultural business and management; agricultural mechanization; agriculture; animal sciences; anthropology; art; automobile/automotive mechanics technology; biology/biological sciences; broadcast journalism; business administration and management; chemistry; civil engineering technology; commercial and advertising art; comparative literature; computer science; construction engineering technology; corrections;

criminal justice/police science; crop production; culinary arts; dance; dramatic/theater arts; economics; electrical, electronic and communications engineering technology; engineering; engineering related; engineering technology; English; family and consumer sciences/human sciences; fashion merchandising; fire science/firefighting; geology/earth science; heating, air conditioning, ventilation and refrigeration maintenance technology; history; humanities; journalism; liberal arts and sciences/liberal studies; licensed practical/vocational nurse training; machine tool technology; mathematics; mechanical engineering/mechanical technology; music; natural resources management and policy; natural sciences; ornamental horticulture; philosophy; photography; physical education teaching and coaching; physical sciences; political science and government; psychology; registered nursing/registered nurse; religious studies; rhetoric and composition; social sciences; sociology.
Academics *Calendar:* semesters. *Degree:* certificates and associate. *Special study options:* academic remediation for entering students, adult/continuing education programs, advanced placement credit, cooperative education, distance learning, English as a second language, honors programs, independent study, part-time degree program, services for LD students, summer session for credit.
Library Goleman Library plus 1 other.
Student Life *Housing:* college housing not available. *Activities and Organizations:* drama/theater group, student-run newspaper, radio station, choral group. *Campus security:* 24-hour emergency response devices and patrols, late-night transport/escort service. *Student services:* personal/psychological counseling, legal services.
Athletics Member NJCAA. *Intercollegiate sports:* baseball M, basketball M/W, cross-country running M/W, fencing M/W, football M, golf M/W, soccer M/W, softball W, swimming and diving M/W, tennis M/W, track and field M/W, volleyball W, water polo M/W, wrestling M. *Intramural sports:* badminton M/W, basketball M/W, bowling M/W, soccer M/W, swimming and diving M/W, tennis M/W, ultimate Frisbee M/W, volleyball M/W, weight lifting M/W.
Costs (2016–17) *Tuition:* state resident $1380 full-time; nonresident $7950 full-time.
Financial Aid Of all full-time matriculated undergraduates who enrolled in 2014, 12,032 applied for aid, 10,833 were judged to have need, 24 had their need fully met. 163 Federal Work-Study jobs (averaging $2872). *Average percent of need met:* 32%. *Average financial aid package:* $5410. *Average need-based loan:* $2845. *Average need-based gift aid:* $5151.
Applying *Options:* electronic application, early admission. *Application deadlines:* rolling (freshmen), rolling (transfers). *Notification:* continuous (freshmen), continuous (transfers).
Freshman Application Contact Ms. Karen Sea, Registrar, San Joaquin Delta College, 5151 Pacific Avenue, Stockton, CA 95207. *Phone:* 209-954-6127. *E-mail:* ksea@deltacollege.edu.
Website: http://www.deltacollege.edu/.

San Joaquin Valley College
Bakersfield, California

- **Proprietary** 2-year, founded 1977, part of San Joaquin Valley College
- **Suburban** campus with easy access to Bakersfield
- **Coed,** 864 undergraduate students, 100% full-time, 68% women, 32% men

Undergraduates 864 full-time. 5% Black or African American, non-Hispanic/Latino; 57% Hispanic/Latino; 3% Asian, non-Hispanic/Latino; 0.2% Native Hawaiian or other Pacific Islander, non-Hispanic/Latino; 1% American Indian or Alaska Native, non-Hispanic/Latino; 0.9% Two or more races, non-Hispanic/Latino; 3% Race/ethnicity unknown; 3% international.
Faculty *Total:* 57, 40% full-time. *Student/faculty ratio:* 25:1.
Majors Business administration and management; corrections; heating, ventilation, air conditioning and refrigeration engineering technology; homeland security, law enforcement, firefighting and protective services related; medical/clinical assistant; medical insurance/medical billing; pharmacy technician; respiratory care therapy; surgical technology.
Academics *Calendar:* continuous. *Degree:* certificates and associate.
Student Life *Activities and Organizations:* CAMA Club, RACT Club, Business Club, Student Council, National Technical Honor Society.
Costs (2015–16) *Tuition:* $16,785 full-time. No tuition increase for student's term of enrollment. *Payment plan:* installment. *Waivers:* employees or children of employees.
Applying *Required for some:* essay or personal statement, high school transcript, interview. *Application deadlines:* rolling (freshmen), rolling (transfers). *Notification:* continuous (freshmen), continuous (transfers).
Freshman Application Contact Enrollment Services Director, San Joaquin Valley College, 201 New Stine Road, Bakersfield, CA 93309. *Phone:* 661-834-0126. *Toll-free phone:* 866-544-7898. *Fax:* 661-834-8124.
E-mail: admissions@sjvc.edu.
Website: http://www.sjvc.edu/campuses/central-california/bakersfield.

San Joaquin Valley College
Chula Vista, California

- **Proprietary** 2-year, founded 2012
- **Urban** campus with easy access to San Diego
- **Coed,** 61 undergraduate students, 100% full-time, 89% women, 11% men

Undergraduates 61 full-time. 2% Black or African American, non-Hispanic/Latino; 16% Hispanic/Latino; 15% Asian, non-Hispanic/Latino; 2% Native Hawaiian or other Pacific Islander, non-Hispanic/Latino; 7% Two or more races, non-Hispanic/Latino; 2% Race/ethnicity unknown; 3% international.

Faculty *Total:* 11, 45% full-time. *Student/faculty ratio:* 9:1.

Majors Dental hygiene.

Academics *Calendar:* continuous. *Degree:* associate.

Costs (2015–16) *Tuition:* $28,825 full-time. No tuition increase for student's term of enrollment. *Payment plan:* installment. *Waivers:* employees or children of employees.

Freshman Application Contact San Joaquin Valley College, 333 H Street, Suite 1065, Chula Vista, CA 91910.

Website: http://www.sjvc.edu/campuses/southern-california/san-diego.

San Joaquin Valley College
Fresno, California

- **Proprietary** 2-year, part of San Joaquin Valley College
- **Urban** campus with easy access to Fresno
- **Coed,** 1,019 undergraduate students, 100% full-time, 76% women, 24% men

Undergraduates 1,019 full-time. 4% Black or African American, non-Hispanic/Latino; 57% Hispanic/Latino; 5% Asian, non-Hispanic/Latino; 0.7% Native Hawaiian or other Pacific Islander, non-Hispanic/Latino; 1% American Indian or Alaska Native, non-Hispanic/Latino; 5% Two or more races, non-Hispanic/Latino; 2% Race/ethnicity unknown; 2% international.

Faculty *Total:* 55, 35% full-time. *Student/faculty ratio:* 33:1.

Majors Corrections; heating, ventilation, air conditioning and refrigeration engineering technology; medical/clinical assistant; medical office assistant; office occupations and clerical services; pharmacy technician; surgical technology; veterinary/animal health technology.

Academics *Calendar:* continuous. *Degree:* certificates and associate.

Student Life *Housing:* college housing not available. *Activities and Organizations:* Associated Student Body, American Medical Technologists, State and County Dental Assistants Association, Arts and Entertainment.

Costs (2015–16) *Tuition:* $15,897 full-time. Full-time tuition and fees vary according to location and program. No tuition increase for student's term of enrollment. *Payment plans:* tuition prepayment, installment. *Waivers:* employees or children of employees.

Applying *Required for some:* essay or personal statement, 1 letter of recommendation, interview. *Application deadlines:* rolling (freshmen), rolling (transfers). *Notification:* continuous (freshmen), continuous (transfers).

Freshman Application Contact Enrollment Services Director, San Joaquin Valley College, 295 East Sierra Avenue, Fresno, CA 93710. *Phone:* 559-448-8282. *Fax:* 559-448-8250. *E-mail:* admissions@sjvc.edu.

Website: http://www.sjvc.edu/campuses/central-california/fresno/.

San Joaquin Valley College
Hanford, California

- **Proprietary** 2-year
- **Small-town** campus with easy access to Fresno
- **Coed,** 275 undergraduate students, 100% full-time, 85% women, 15% men

Undergraduates 275 full-time. 4% Black or African American, non-Hispanic/Latino; 62% Hispanic/Latino; 1% Asian, non-Hispanic/Latino; 1% American Indian or Alaska Native, non-Hispanic/Latino; 4% Two or more races, non-Hispanic/Latino; 2% Race/ethnicity unknown; 4% international.

Faculty *Total:* 6, 67% full-time. *Student/faculty ratio:* 59:1.

Majors Criminal justice/law enforcement administration; medical/clinical assistant; medical insurance/medical billing; office occupations and clerical services.

Academics *Calendar:* continuous. *Degree:* certificates and associate.

Costs (2015–16) *Tuition:* $15,603 full-time. No tuition increase for student's term of enrollment. *Payment plans:* tuition prepayment, installment. *Waivers:* employees or children of employees.

Freshman Application Contact Ms., San Joaquin Valley College, 215 West 7th Street, Hanford, CA 93230.

Website: http://www.sjvc.edu/campuses/central-california/hanford/.

San Joaquin Valley College
Hesperia, California

- **Proprietary** 2-year, part of San Joaquin Valley College
- **Suburban** campus with easy access to San Bernadino
- **Coed,** 679 undergraduate students, 118% full-time, 87% women, 32% men

Undergraduates 804 full-time. 12% Black or African American, non-Hispanic/Latino; 53% Hispanic/Latino; 1% Asian, non-Hispanic/Latino; 0.7% Native Hawaiian or other Pacific Islander, non-Hispanic/Latino; 1% American Indian or Alaska Native, non-Hispanic/Latino; 6% Two or more races, non-Hispanic/Latino; 2% Race/ethnicity unknown; 1% international.

Faculty *Total:* 40, 25% full-time. *Student/faculty ratio:* 34:1.

Majors Criminal justice/law enforcement administration; heating, air conditioning, ventilation and refrigeration maintenance technology; industrial technology; medical/clinical assistant; medical insurance/medical billing; office occupations and clerical services; pharmacy technician.

Academics *Calendar:* continuous. *Degree:* certificates and associate.

Costs (2015–16) *Tuition:* $16,953 full-time. No tuition increase for student's term of enrollment. *Payment plans:* tuition prepayment, installment. *Waivers:* employees or children of employees.

Freshman Application Contact San Joaquin Valley College, 9331 Mariposa Road, Hesperia, CA 92344.

Website: http://www.sjvc.edu/campuses/southern-california/victor-valley/.

San Joaquin Valley College
Lancaster, California

- **Proprietary** 2-year, founded 2012, part of San Joaquin Valley College
- **Suburban** campus
- **Coed,** 328 undergraduate students, 100% full-time, 73% women, 27% men

Undergraduates 328 full-time. 21% Black or African American, non-Hispanic/Latino; 52% Hispanic/Latino; 1% Asian, non-Hispanic/Latino; 2% Native Hawaiian or other Pacific Islander, non-Hispanic/Latino; 0.6% American Indian or Alaska Native, non-Hispanic/Latino; 9% Two or more races, non-Hispanic/Latino; 2% Race/ethnicity unknown; 2% international.

Faculty *Total:* 18, 11% full-time. *Student/faculty ratio:* 45:1.

Majors Corrections; heating, air conditioning, ventilation and refrigeration maintenance technology; industrial mechanics and maintenance technology; medical/clinical assistant; medical office assistant; office occupations and clerical services; pharmacy technician.

Academics *Calendar:* continuous. *Degree:* certificates and associate.

Costs (2015–16) *Tuition:* $16,684 full-time. No tuition increase for student's term of enrollment. *Payment plans:* tuition prepayment, installment. *Waivers:* employees or children of employees.

Freshman Application Contact San Joaquin Valley College, 42135 10th Street West, Lancaster, CA 93534.

Website: http://www.sjvc.edu/campuses/southern-california/antelope-valley/.

San Joaquin Valley College
Ontario, California

- **Proprietary** 2-year, part of San Joaquin Valley College
- **Urban** campus with easy access to Los Angeles
- **Coed,** 994 undergraduate students, 100% full-time, 57% women, 43% men

Undergraduates 994 full-time. 6% Black or African American, non-Hispanic/Latino; 61% Hispanic/Latino; 6% Asian, non-Hispanic/Latino; 2% Native Hawaiian or other Pacific Islander, non-Hispanic/Latino; 0.3% American Indian or Alaska Native, non-Hispanic/Latino; 5% Two or more races, non-Hispanic/Latino; 2% Race/ethnicity unknown; 2% international.

Faculty *Total:* 97, 35% full-time. *Student/faculty ratio:* 18:1.

Majors Construction management; corrections; dental hygiene; heating, air conditioning, ventilation and refrigeration maintenance technology; industrial mechanics and maintenance technology; medical/clinical assistant; medical office assistant; office occupations and clerical services; pharmacy technician; respiratory care therapy.

Academics *Calendar:* continuous. *Degree:* certificates and associate.

Student Life *Housing:* college housing not available. *Activities and Organizations:* Students in Free Enterprise (SIFE), Associated Student Body, Fitness Club, Ambassador Club, Diversity Club.

Costs (2015–16) *Tuition:* $17,985 full-time. Full-time tuition and fees vary according to location and program. No tuition increase for student's term of enrollment. *Payment plans:* tuition prepayment, installment. *Waivers:* employees or children of employees.

Applying *Required for some:* essay or personal statement, interview. *Application deadlines:* rolling (freshmen), rolling (transfers). *Notification:* continuous (freshmen), continuous (transfers).
Freshman Application Contact Enrollment Services Director, San Joaquin Valley College, 4580 Ontario Mills Parkway, Ontario, CA 91764. *Phone:* 909-948-7582. *Fax:* 909-948-3860. *E-mail:* admissions@sjvc.edu.
Website: http://www.sjvc.edu/campuses/southern-california/ontario/.

San Joaquin Valley College
Rancho Cordova, California

- **Proprietary** 2-year, part of San Joaquin Valley College
- **Suburban** campus with easy access to Sacramento
- **Coed,** 158 undergraduate students, 100% full-time, 53% women, 47% men

Undergraduates 158 full-time. 2% Black or African American, non-Hispanic/Latino; 10% Hispanic/Latino; 18% Asian, non-Hispanic/Latino; 4% Native Hawaiian or other Pacific Islander, non-Hispanic/Latino; 6% Two or more races, non-Hispanic/Latino; 4% Race/ethnicity unknown; 4% international.
Faculty *Total:* 12, 42% full-time. *Student/faculty ratio:* 22:1.
Majors Respiratory therapy technician.
Academics *Calendar:* continuous. *Degree:* certificates and associate.
Student Life *Housing:* college housing not available. *Activities and Organizations:* Associated Student Body, Diversity Committee.
Costs (2015–16) *Tuition:* $24,250 full-time. Full-time tuition and fees vary according to location and program. No tuition increase for student's term of enrollment. *Payment plans:* tuition prepayment, installment. *Waivers:* employees or children of employees.
Applying *Required for some:* essay or personal statement, interview. *Application deadlines:* rolling (freshmen), rolling (transfers). *Notification:* continuous (freshmen), continuous (transfers).
Freshman Application Contact Enrollment Services Director, San Joaquin Valley College, 11050 Olson Drive, Suite 210, Rancho Cordova, CA 95670. *Phone:* 916-638-7582. *Fax:* 916-638-7553. *E-mail:* admissions@sjvc.edu.
Website: http://www.sjvc.edu/campuses/northern-california/rancho-cordova/.

San Joaquin Valley College
Salida, California

- **Proprietary** 2-year, part of San Joaquin Valley College
- **Suburban** campus
- **Coed,** 465 undergraduate students, 100% full-time, 74% women, 26% men

Undergraduates 465 full-time. Students come from 1 other state; 3% Black or African American, non-Hispanic/Latino; 47% Hispanic/Latino; 6% Asian, non-Hispanic/Latino; 2% Native Hawaiian or other Pacific Islander, non-Hispanic/Latino; 0.2% American Indian or Alaska Native, non-Hispanic/Latino; 6% Two or more races, non-Hispanic/Latino; 2% Race/ethnicity unknown; 3% international.
Faculty *Total:* 29, 28% full-time. *Student/faculty ratio:* 31:1.
Majors Industrial technology; massage therapy; medical/clinical assistant; medical office assistant; office occupations and clerical services; pharmacy technician.
Academics *Calendar:* continuous. *Degree:* certificates and associate.
Student Life *Activities and Organizations:* Associated Student Body, Book Club.
Costs (2015–16) *Tuition:* $15,478 full-time. Full-time tuition and fees vary according to location and program. No tuition increase for student's term of enrollment. *Payment plans:* tuition prepayment, installment. *Waivers:* employees or children of employees.
Applying *Required for some:* essay or personal statement, interview. *Application deadlines:* rolling (freshmen), rolling (transfers). *Notification:* continuous (freshmen), continuous (transfers).
Freshman Application Contact Enrollment Services Director, San Joaquin Valley College, 5380 Pirrone Road, Salida, CA 95368. *Phone:* 209-543-8800. *Fax:* 209-543-8320. *E-mail:* admissions@sjvc.edu.
Website: http://www.sjvc.edu/campuses/northern-california/modesto/.

San Joaquin Valley College
Temecula, California

- **Proprietary** 2-year, part of San Joaquin Valley College
- **Urban** campus with easy access to Los Angeles
- **Coed,** 728 undergraduate students, 100% full-time, 73% women, 27% men

Undergraduates 728 full-time. 7% Black or African American, non-Hispanic/Latino; 40% Hispanic/Latino; 6% Asian, non-Hispanic/Latino; 2%

Native Hawaiian or other Pacific Islander, non-Hispanic/Latino; 1% American Indian or Alaska Native, non-Hispanic/Latino; 6% Two or more races, non-Hispanic/Latino; 2% Race/ethnicity unknown; 5% international.
Faculty *Total:* 43, 30% full-time. *Student/faculty ratio:* 32:1.
Majors Heating, air conditioning, ventilation and refrigeration maintenance technology; medical/clinical assistant; medical office assistant; office occupations and clerical services; pharmacy technician; respiratory care therapy.
Academics *Calendar:* continuous. *Degree:* certificates and associate.
Costs (2015–16) *Tuition:* $17,452 full-time. No tuition increase for student's term of enrollment. *Payment plans:* tuition prepayment, installment. *Waivers:* employees or children of employees.
Freshman Application Contact Ms. Robyn Whiles, Enrollment Services Director, San Joaquin Valley College, 27270 Madison Avenue, Suite 103, Temecula, CA 92590. *Phone:* 559-651-2500. *E-mail:* admissions@sjvc.edu.
Website: http://www.sjvc.edu/campuses/southern-california/temecula/.

San Joaquin Valley College
Visalia, California

- **Proprietary** 2-year, founded 1977, part of San Joaquin Valley College
- **Suburban** campus with easy access to Fresno
- **Coed,** 1,294 undergraduate students, 100% full-time, 70% women, 30% men

Undergraduates 1,294 full-time. 2% Black or African American, non-Hispanic/Latino; 54% Hispanic/Latino; 6% Asian, non-Hispanic/Latino; 0.5% Native Hawaiian or other Pacific Islander, non-Hispanic/Latino; 0.9% American Indian or Alaska Native, non-Hispanic/Latino; 4% Two or more races, non-Hispanic/Latino; 2% Race/ethnicity unknown; 3% international.
Faculty *Total:* 101, 42% full-time. *Student/faculty ratio:* 21:1.
Majors Business/commerce; computer and information sciences and support services related; corrections; dental hygiene; health and medical administrative services related; heating, ventilation, air conditioning and refrigeration engineering technology; human resources management; industrial technology; licensed practical/vocational nurse training; medical administrative assistant and medical secretary; medical/clinical assistant; medical office assistant; pharmacy technician; physician assistant; registered nursing/registered nurse; respiratory care therapy.
Academics *Calendar:* continuous. *Degree:* certificates and associate. *Special study options:* academic remediation for entering students.
Library SJVC Visalia Campus Library.
Student Life *Housing:* college housing not available. *Activities and Organizations:* Associated Student Body, Students in Free Enterprise (SIFE), American Medical Technologists, National and Technical Honor Society. *Campus security:* late-night transport/escort service, full-time security personnel.
Costs (2015–16) *Tuition:* $19,480 full-time. No tuition increase for student's term of enrollment. *Payment plan:* installment. *Waivers:* employees or children of employees.
Applying *Required for some:* essay or personal statement, high school transcript, interview. *Application deadlines:* rolling (freshmen), rolling (transfers). *Notification:* continuous (freshmen), continuous (transfers).
Freshman Application Contact Susie Topjian, Enrollment Services Director, San Joaquin Valley College, 8400 West Mineral King Boulevard, Visalia, CA 93291. *Phone:* 559-651-2500. *Fax:* 559-734-9048.
E-mail: admissions@sjvc.edu.
Website: http://www.sjvc.edu/campuses/central-california/visalia/.

San Joaquin Valley College–Fresno Aviation Campus
Fresno, California

- **Proprietary** 2-year, part of San Joaquin Valley College
- **Urban** campus with easy access to Fresno
- **Coed, primarily men,** 130 undergraduate students, 100% full-time, 5% women, 95% men

Undergraduates 130 full-time. 2% Black or African American, non-Hispanic/Latino; 34% Hispanic/Latino; 11% Asian, non-Hispanic/Latino; 0.8% Native Hawaiian or other Pacific Islander, non-Hispanic/Latino; 0.8% American Indian or Alaska Native, non-Hispanic/Latino; 6% Two or more races, non-Hispanic/Latino; 2% Race/ethnicity unknown; 4% international.
Faculty *Total:* 8, 38% full-time. *Student/faculty ratio:* 26:1.
Majors Airframe mechanics and aircraft maintenance technology.
Academics *Calendar:* semesters. *Degree:* associate.
Student Life *Housing:* college housing not available. *Activities and Organizations:* RC Club (radio controlled airplane).

Costs (2015–16) *Tuition:* $13,620 full-time. No tuition increase for student's term of enrollment. *Payment plans:* tuition prepayment, installment. *Waivers:* employees or children of employees.

Applying *Required for some:* essay or personal statement, high school transcript, interview. *Application deadlines:* rolling (freshmen), rolling (transfers). *Notification:* continuous (freshmen), continuous (transfers).

Freshman Application Contact Enrollment Services Coordinator, San Joaquin Valley College–Fresno Aviation Campus, 4985 East Anderson Avenue, Fresno, CA 93727. *Phone:* 559-453-0123. *Fax:* 599-453-0133. *E-mail:* admissions@sjvc.edu.

Website: http://www.sjvc.edu/campuses/central-california/fresno-aviation/.

San Joaquin Valley College–Online
Visalia, California

- **Proprietary** 2-year, part of San Joaquin Valley College
- **Suburban** campus
- **Coed,** 1,005 undergraduate students, 100% full-time, 85% women, 15% men

Undergraduates 1,005 full-time. 32% Black or African American, non-Hispanic/Latino; 17% Hispanic/Latino; 2% Asian, non-Hispanic/Latino; 0.1% Native Hawaiian or other Pacific Islander, non-Hispanic/Latino; 0.9% American Indian or Alaska Native, non-Hispanic/Latino; 5% Two or more races, non-Hispanic/Latino; 5% Race/ethnicity unknown; 0.6% international.

Faculty *Total:* 50, 22% full-time. *Student/faculty ratio:* 42:1.

Majors Business administration and management; construction management; human resources management; information technology; medical/clinical assistant; medical insurance coding; medical office management; office occupations and clerical services.

Academics *Calendar:* continuous. *Degree:* certificates and associate.

Costs (2015–16) *Tuition:* $14,645 full-time. No tuition increase for student's term of enrollment. *Payment plans:* tuition prepayment, installment. *Waivers:* employees or children of employees.

Applying *Options:* electronic application. *Required for some:* essay or personal statement, interview. *Application deadlines:* rolling (freshmen), rolling (transfers). *Notification:* continuous (freshmen), continuous (transfers).

Freshman Application Contact Enrollment Services Director, San Joaquin Valley College–Online, 8344 West Mineral King Avenue, Visalia, CA 93291. *E-mail:* admissions@sjvc.edu.

Website: http://www.sjvc.edu/online-programs/.

San Jose City College
San Jose, California

Freshman Application Contact Mr. Carlo Santos, Director of Admissions/Registrar, San Jose City College, 2100 Moorpark Avenue, San Jose, CA 95128-2799. *Phone:* 408-288-3707. *Fax:* 408-298-1935.

Website: http://www.sjcc.edu/.

Santa Ana College
Santa Ana, California

Freshman Application Contact Mrs. Christie Steward, Admissions Clerk, Santa Ana College, 1530 West 17th Street, Santa Ana, CA 92706-3398. *Phone:* 714-564-6053.

Website: http://www.sac.edu/.

Santa Barbara Business College
Bakersfield, California

Admissions Office Contact Santa Barbara Business College, 5300 California Avenue, Bakersfield, CA 93309.

Website: http://www.sbbcollege.edu/.

Santa Barbara Business College
Santa Maria, California

Admissions Office Contact Santa Barbara Business College, 303 East Plaza Drive, Santa Maria, CA 93454.

Website: http://www.sbbcollege.edu/.

Santa Barbara City College
Santa Barbara, California

Freshman Application Contact Ms. Allison Curtis, Director of Admissions and Records, Santa Barbara City College, Santa Barbara, CA 93109. *Phone:* 805-965-0581 Ext. 2352. *Fax:* 805-962-0497. *E-mail:* admissions@sbcc.edu. *Website:* http://www.sbcc.edu/.

Santa Monica College
Santa Monica, California

Freshman Application Contact Santa Monica College, 1900 Pico Boulevard, Santa Monica, CA 90405-1628. *Phone:* 310-434-4774.

Website: http://www.smc.edu/.

Santa Rosa Junior College
Santa Rosa, California

Freshman Application Contact Ms. Freyja Pereira, Director, Admissions, Records and Enrollment Services, Santa Rosa Junior College, 1501 Mendocino Avenue, Santa Rosa, CA 95401. *Phone:* 707-527-4512. *Fax:* 707-527-4798. *E-mail:* adminfo@santarosa.edu.

Website: http://www.santarosa.edu/.

Santiago Canyon College
Orange, California

Freshman Application Contact Tuyen Nguyen, Admissions and Records, Santiago Canyon College, 8045 East Chapman Avenue, Orange, CA 92869. *Phone:* 714-628-4902.

Website: http://www.sccollege.edu/.

Shasta College
Redding, California

Director of Admissions Dr. Kevin O'Rorke, Dean of Enrollment Services, Shasta College, PO Box 496006, 11555 Old Oregon Trail, Redding, CA 96049-6006. *Phone:* 530-242-7669.

Website: http://www.shastacollege.edu/.

Sierra College
Rocklin, California

- **District-supported** 2-year, founded 1936, part of California Community College System
- **Suburban** 327-acre campus with easy access to Sacramento
- **Coed,** 18,758 undergraduate students, 26% full-time, 56% women, 44% men

Undergraduates 4,874 full-time, 13,884 part-time. Students come from 27 states and territories; 10 other countries; 0.7% are from out of state; 18% transferred in; 1% live on campus. *Retention:* 68% of full-time freshmen returned.

Freshmen *Admission:* 24,000 applied, 24,000 admitted, 4,444 enrolled.

Faculty *Total:* 870, 18% full-time. *Student/faculty ratio:* 25:1.

Majors Accounting; administrative assistant and secretarial science; agriculture; American Sign Language (ASL); animal/livestock husbandry and production; apparel and textile manufacturing; apparel and textile marketing management; applied horticulture/horticulture operations; architectural drafting and CAD/CADD; art; automobile/automotive mechanics technology; biological and physical sciences; biology/biological sciences; business administration and management; business/commerce; cabinetmaking and millwork; chemistry; child development; commercial photography; computer and information sciences and support services related; computer installation and repair technology; computer programming; computer systems networking and telecommunications; construction trades; corrections; criminal justice/police science; data entry/microcomputer applications; digital communication and media/multimedia; electrical/electronics equipment installation and repair; engineering; English; equestrian studies; fire science/firefighting; forestry; general studies; geology/earth science; graphic design; hazardous materials management and waste technology; health and physical education/fitness; industrial electronics technology; information technology; liberal arts and sciences/liberal studies; licensed practical/vocational nurse training; manufacturing engineering technology; mathematics; mechanical drafting and CAD/CADD; music; network and system administration; parks, recreation and leisure; philosophy; physics; psychology; real estate; registered nursing/registered nurse; rhetoric and composition; sales, distribution, and marketing operations; small business administration; social sciences; visual and performing arts; web page, digital/multimedia and information resources design; women's studies.

Academics *Calendar:* semesters. *Degree:* certificates and associate. *Special study options:* academic remediation for entering students, accelerated degree program, advanced placement credit, distance learning, double majors, English as a second language, honors programs, independent study, internships, off-campus study, part-time degree program, services for LD students, study abroad, summer session for credit.

Library Leary Resource Center plus 1 other.

Student Life *Housing Options:* coed. Campus housing is university owned. *Activities and Organizations:* drama/theater group, student-run newspaper, choral group, Drama Club, Student Government, Art Club, Band, Aggie Club. *Campus security:* 24-hour emergency response devices and patrols, late-night transport/escort service. *Student services:* health clinic, personal/psychological counseling.

Athletics *Intercollegiate sports:* baseball M, basketball M/W, football M, golf M/W, soccer W, softball W, swimming and diving M/W, tennis M/W, volleyball W, water polo M/W, wrestling M. *Intramural sports:* archery M/W, badminton M/W, basketball M/W, tennis M/W, volleyball M/W.

Costs (2015–16) *Tuition:* state resident $1380 full-time, $46 per credit hour part-time; nonresident $5790 full-time, $193 per credit hour part-time. Full-time tuition and fees vary according to course load. Part-time tuition and fees vary according to course load. *Required fees:* $46 full-time, $19 per term part-time. *Room and board:* $3700. *Payment plan:* installment.

Financial Aid Of all full-time matriculated undergraduates who enrolled in 2013, 112 Federal Work-Study jobs (averaging $4400). 14 state and other part-time jobs (averaging $4644). *Average financial aid package:* $5779. *Average need-based loan:* $3726. *Average need-based gift aid:* $5309.

Applying *Options:* electronic application, early admission. *Application deadline:* rolling (freshmen). *Notification:* continuous (freshmen), continuous (transfers).

Freshman Application Contact Sierra College, 5000 Rocklin Road, Rocklin, CA 95677-3397. *Phone:* 916-660-7341.

Website: http://www.sierracollege.edu/.

Skyline College
San Bruno, California

Freshman Application Contact Terry Stats, Admissions Office, Skyline College, 3300 College Drive, San Bruno, CA 94066-1698. *Phone:* 650-738-4251. *E-mail:* stats@smccd.net.

Website: http://skylinecollege.edu/.

Solano Community College
Fairfield, California

Freshman Application Contact Solano Community College, 4000 Suisun Valley Road, Fairfield, CA 94534. *Phone:* 707-864-7000 Ext. 4313.

Website: http://www.solano.edu/.

South Coast College
Orange, California

Director of Admissions South Coast College, 2011 West Chapman Avenue, Orange, CA 92868. *Toll-free phone:* 877-568-6130.

Website: http://www.southcoastcollege.com/.

Southwestern College
Chula Vista, California

Freshman Application Contact Director of Admissions and Records, Southwestern College, 900 Otay Lakes Road, Chula Vista, CA 91910-7299. *Phone:* 619-421-6700 Ext. 5215. *Fax:* 619-482-6489.

Website: http://www.swccd.edu/.

Spartan College of Aeronautics and Technology
Inglewood, California

Freshman Application Contact Admissions Office, Spartan College of Aeronautics and Technology, 8911 Aviation Boulevard, Inglewood, CA 90301. *Phone:* 866-451-0818. *Toll-free phone:* 866-451-0818.

Website: http://www.spartan.edu/.

Stanbridge College
Irvine, California

Admissions Office Contact Stanbridge College, 2041 Business Center Drive, Irvine, CA 92612.

Website: http://www.stanbridge.edu/.

Taft College
Taft, California

Freshman Application Contact Nichole Cook, Admissions/Counseling Technician, Taft College, 29 Emmons Park Drive, Taft, CA 93268-2317. *Phone:* 661-763-7790. *Fax:* 661-763-7758. *E-mail:* ncook@taftcollege.edu.

Website: http://www.taftcollege.edu/.

Unitek College
Fremont, California

Admissions Office Contact Unitek College, 4670 Auto Mall Parkway, Fremont, CA 94538.

Website: http://www.unitekcollege.edu/.

Valley College of Medical Careers
West Hills, California

Admissions Office Contact Valley College of Medical Careers, 8399 Topanga Canyon Boulevard, Suite 200, West Hills, CA 91304.

Website: http://www.vcmc.edu/.

Ventura College
Ventura, California

Freshman Application Contact Ms. Susan Bricker, Registrar, Ventura College, 4667 Telegraph Road, Ventura, CA 93003-3899. *Phone:* 805-654-6456. *Fax:* 805-654-6357. *E-mail:* sbricker@vcccd.net.

Website: http://www.venturacollege.edu/.

Victor Valley College
Victorville, California

- **District-supported** 2-year, founded 1961, part of California Community College System
- **Small-town** 253-acre campus with easy access to Los Angeles
- **Coed**

Undergraduates 3% are from out of state. *Retention:* 61% of full-time freshmen returned.

Faculty *Student/faculty ratio:* 26:1.

Majors Administrative assistant and secretarial science; agricultural teacher education; art; automobile/automotive mechanics technology; biological and physical sciences; biology/biological sciences; building/construction finishing, management, and inspection related; business administration and management; business/commerce; child-care and support services management; child development; computer and information sciences; computer programming (specific applications); computer science; construction engineering technology; criminal justice/police science; dramatic/theater arts; electrical, electronic and communications engineering technology; fire prevention and safety technology; fire science/firefighting; food technology and processing; horticultural science; humanities; information science/studies; kindergarten/preschool education; liberal arts and sciences/liberal studies; management information systems; mathematics; music; natural sciences; ornamental horticulture; physical sciences; real estate; registered nursing/registered nurse; respiratory care therapy; science technologies related; social sciences; teacher assistant/aide; trade and industrial teacher education; vehicle maintenance and repair technologies related; welding technology.

Academics *Calendar:* semesters. *Degree:* certificates, diplomas, and associate. *Special study options:* academic remediation for entering students, accelerated degree program, advanced placement credit, cooperative education, distance learning, double majors, English as a second language, honors programs, independent study, internships, off-campus study, part-time degree program, services for LD students, study abroad, summer session for credit.

Library Learning Resource Center.

Student Life *Housing:* college housing not available. *Activities and Organizations:* drama/theater group, student-run newspaper, choral group, Black Student Union, Drama Club, Rugby, Phi Theta Kappa. *Campus security:* 24-hour emergency response devices and patrols, late-night

transport/escort service, part-time trained security personnel. *Student services:* health clinic, personal/psychological counseling.
Athletics Member NCAA, NJCAA. *Intercollegiate sports:* baseball M, basketball M/W, cross-country running M/W, football M, golf M, soccer M/W, softball W, tennis M/W, track and field M/W, volleyball W, wrestling M. *Intramural sports:* rock climbing M/W.
Costs (2015–16) *Tuition:* state resident $1104 full-time, $46 per credit part-time; nonresident $5904 full-time, $200 per credit part-time. *Required fees:* $10 full-time. *Payment plan:* installment.
Financial Aid *Average need-based loan:* $6168. *Average need-based gift aid:* $3707.
Applying *Application deadline:* rolling (freshmen). *Notification:* continuous (freshmen).
Freshman Application Contact Ms. Greta Moon, Director of Admissions and Records (Interim), Victor Valley College, 18422 Bear Valley Road, Victorville, CA 92395. *Phone:* 760-245-4271. *Fax:* 760-843-7707.
E-mail: moong@vvc.edu.
Website: http://www.vvc.edu/.

West Coast Ultrasound Institute
Beverly Hills, California
Admissions Office Contact West Coast Ultrasound Institute, 291 S. La Cienega Boulevard, Suite 500, Beverly Hills, CA 90211.
Website: http://wcui.edu/.

West Hills Community College
Coalinga, California
Freshman Application Contact Sandra Dagnino, West Hills Community College, 300 Cherry Lane, Coalinga, CA 93210-1399. *Phone:* 559-934-3203. *Toll-free phone:* 800-266-1114. *Fax:* 559-934-2830.
E-mail: sandradagnino@westhillscollege.com.
Website: http://www.westhillscollege.com/.

West Hills Community College–Lemoore
Lemoore, California
Admissions Office Contact West Hills Community College–Lemoore, 555 College Avenue, Lemoore, CA 93245.
Website: http://www.westhillscollege.com/.

West Los Angeles College
Culver City, California
Director of Admissions Mr. Len Isaksen, Director of Admissions, West Los Angeles College, 9000 Overland Avenue, Culver City, CA 90230-3519.
Phone: 310-287-4255.
Website: http://www.lacolleges.net/.

West Valley College
Saratoga, California
Freshman Application Contact Ms. Barbara Ogilive, Supervisor, Admissions and Records, West Valley College, 14000 Fruitvale Avenue, Saratoga, CA 95070-5698. *Phone:* 408-741-4630.
E-mail: barbara_ogilvie@westvalley.edu.
Website: http://www.westvalley.edu/.

Woodland Community College
Woodland, California
Admissions Office Contact Woodland Community College, 2300 East Gibson Road, Woodland, CA 95776.
Website: http://www.yccd.edu/woodland/.

Yuba College
Marysville, California
Director of Admissions Dr. David Farrell, Dean of Student Development, Yuba College, 2088 North Beale Road, Marysville, CA 95901-7699. *Phone:* 530-741-6705.
Website: http://www.yccd.edu/.

COLORADO

Aims Community College
Greeley, Colorado
Freshman Application Contact Ms. Susie Gallardo, Admissions Technician, Aims Community College, Box 69, 5401 West 20th Street, Greeley, CO 80632-0069. *Phone:* 970-330-8008 Ext. 6624.
E-mail: wgreen@chiron.aims.edu.
Website: http://www.aims.edu/.

Arapahoe Community College
Littleton, Colorado
- **State-supported** 2-year, founded 1965, part of Colorado Community College and Occupational Education System
- **Suburban** 52-acre campus with easy access to Denver
- **Coed,** 9,616 undergraduate students, 20% full-time, 56% women, 44% men

Undergraduates 1,907 full-time, 7,709 part-time. 5% are from out of state; 3% Black or African American, non-Hispanic/Latino; 15% Hispanic/Latino; 3% Asian, non-Hispanic/Latino; 0.2% Native Hawaiian or other Pacific Islander, non-Hispanic/Latino; 0.7% American Indian or Alaska Native, non-Hispanic/Latino; 4% Two or more races, non-Hispanic/Latino; 4% Race/ethnicity unknown; 1% international.
Freshmen *Admission:* 1,981 applied, 1,981 admitted, 866 enrolled.
Faculty *Total:* 493, 21% full-time. *Student/faculty ratio:* 19:1.
Majors Accounting technology and bookkeeping; architectural engineering technology; automobile/automotive mechanics technology; building/construction site management; business administration and management; clinical/medical laboratory technology; computer and information sciences; computer systems networking and telecommunications; criminal justice/law enforcement administration; emergency medical technology (EMT paramedic); engineering technology; funeral service and mortuary science; game and interactive media design; general studies; graphic design; health and physical education/fitness; health information/medical records technology; interior design; journalism; legal assistant/paralegal; liberal arts and sciences and humanities related; liberal arts and sciences/liberal studies; music technology; physical therapy technology; registered nursing/registered nurse; retailing; science technologies related; telecommunications technology.
Academics *Calendar:* semesters. *Degree:* certificates, diplomas, and associate. *Special study options:* academic remediation for entering students, accelerated degree program, adult/continuing education programs, advanced placement credit, cooperative education, distance learning, double majors, English as a second language, external degree program, independent study, internships, off-campus study, part-time degree program, services for LD students, study abroad, summer session for credit. *ROTC:* Army (c), Navy (c), Air Force (c).
Library Weber Center for Learning Resources plus 1 other.
Student Life *Housing:* college housing not available. *Activities and Organizations:* drama/theater group, student-run newspaper, choral group, Student Veteran Association, Phi Theta Kappa, History Club, Jewelry Club, ASID (American Society of Interior Designers). *Campus security:* 24-hour emergency response devices and patrols, late-night transport/escort service. *Student services:* personal/psychological counseling.
Standardized Tests *Recommended:* ACT (for admission), SAT or ACT (for admission).
Costs (2015–16) *Tuition:* state resident $3915 full-time, $131 per credit hour part-time; nonresident $16,062 full-time, $535 per credit hour part-time. Full-time tuition and fees vary according to program. Part-time tuition and fees vary according to program. *Required fees:* $264 full-time. *Payment plan:* installment. *Waivers:* employees or children of employees.
Financial Aid Of all full-time matriculated undergraduates who enrolled in 2014, 100 Federal Work-Study jobs (averaging $4200). 200 state and other part-time jobs (averaging $4200).
Applying *Options:* electronic application, early admission, deferred entrance. *Application deadlines:* rolling (freshmen), rolling (out-of-state freshmen), rolling (transfers). *Notification:* continuous (freshmen), continuous (out-of-state freshmen), continuous (transfers).
Freshman Application Contact Arapahoe Community College, 5900 South Santa Fe Drive, PO Box 9002, Littleton, CO 80160-9002. *Phone:* 303-797-5623.
Website: http://www.arapahoe.edu/.

Bel–Rea Institute of Animal Technology
Denver, Colorado

Director of Admissions Ms. Paulette Kaufman, Director, Bel–Rea Institute of Animal Technology, 1681 South Dayton Street, Denver, CO 80247. *Phone:* 303-751-8700. *Toll-free phone:* 800-950-8001.
E-mail: admissions@bel-rea.com.
Website: http://www.bel-rea.com/.

CollegeAmerica–Colorado Springs
Colorado Springs, Colorado

Freshman Application Contact CollegeAmerica–Colorado Springs, 2020 North Academy Boulevard, Colorado Springs, CO 80909. *Phone:* 719-637-0600. *Toll-free phone:* 800-622-2894.
Website: http://www.collegeamerica.edu/.

CollegeAmerica–Denver
Denver, Colorado

- **Independent** primarily 2-year, founded 1962
- **Urban** campus
- **Coed,** 321 undergraduate students

Faculty *Student/faculty ratio:* 15:1.
Majors Accounting; accounting and business/management; computer technology/computer systems technology; health/health-care administration; medical/health management and clinical assistant.
Academics *Calendar:* continuous. *Degrees:* associate and bachelor's. *Special study options:* academic remediation for entering students, accelerated degree program, cooperative education.
Student Life *Housing:* college housing not available.
Freshman Application Contact Admissions Office, CollegeAmerica–Denver, 1385 South Colorado Boulevard, Denver, CO 80222. *Phone:* 303-300-8740 Ext. 7020. *Toll-free phone:* 800-622-2894.
Website: http://www.collegeamerica.edu/.

CollegeAmerica–Fort Collins
Fort Collins, Colorado

Director of Admissions Ms. Anna DiTorrice-Mull, Director of Admissions, CollegeAmerica–Fort Collins, 4601 South Mason Street, Fort Collins, CO 80525. *Phone:* 970-223-6060 Ext. 8002. *Toll-free phone:* 800-622-2894.
Website: http://www.collegeamerica.edu/.

Colorado Academy of Veterinary Technology
Colorado Springs, Colorado

Admissions Office Contact Colorado Academy of Veterinary Technology, 2766 Janitell Road, Colorado Springs, CO 80906.
Website: http://www.coloradovettech.com/.

Colorado Northwestern Community College
Rangely, Colorado

- **State-supported** 2-year, founded 1962, part of Colorado Community College and Occupational Education System
- **Rural** 150-acre campus
- **Coed,** 1,178 undergraduate students, 46% full-time, 59% women, 41% men

Undergraduates 538 full-time, 640 part-time. 18% are from out of state; 1% Black or African American, non-Hispanic/Latino; 6% Hispanic/Latino; 1% American Indian or Alaska Native, non-Hispanic/Latino; 7% Two or more races, non-Hispanic/Latino; 7% Race/ethnicity unknown; 1% international; 10% transferred in; 24% live on campus. *Retention:* 49% of full-time freshmen returned.
Freshmen *Admission:* 601 applied, 601 admitted, 177 enrolled.
Faculty *Total:* 104, 41% full-time. *Student/faculty ratio:* 12:1.
Majors Accounting; aircraft powerplant technology; airline pilot and flight crew; banking and financial support services; cosmetology; dental hygiene; early childhood education; emergency medical technology (EMT paramedic); equestrian studies; general studies; liberal arts and sciences/liberal studies; natural resources/conservation; registered nursing/registered nurse; small business administration.

Academics *Calendar:* semesters. *Degree:* certificates and associate. *Special study options:* academic remediation for entering students, adult/continuing education programs, advanced placement credit, distance learning, double majors, independent study, internships, part-time degree program, services for LD students, student-designed majors, summer session for credit.
Library Colorado Northwestern Community College Library–Rangely plus 1 other.
Student Life *Housing:* on-campus residence required for freshman year. *Options:* coed. Campus housing is university owned. Freshman applicants given priority for college housing. *Activities and Organizations:* student-run newspaper, choral group. *Campus security:* student patrols, late-night transport/escort service. *Student services:* personal/psychological counseling.
Athletics Member NJCAA. *Intercollegiate sports:* baseball M(s), basketball M(s)/W(s), softball W(s), volleyball W(s). *Intramural sports:* basketball M/W, football M/W, golf M/W, racquetball M/W, skiing (cross-country) M/W, skiing (downhill) M/W, softball M/W, table tennis M/W, tennis M/W, volleyball M/W.
Standardized Tests *Recommended:* ACT (for admission).
Costs (2015–16) *Tuition:* state resident $4210 full-time, $206 per credit hour part-time; nonresident $6999 full-time, $223 per credit hour part-time. Full-time tuition and fees vary according to program. Part-time tuition and fees vary according to program. *Required fees:* $295 full-time, $8 per credit hour part-time, $13 per term part-time. *Room and board:* $6654; room only: $2356. Room and board charges vary according to board plan and housing facility. *Payment plan:* installment.
Applying *Options:* electronic application, early admission, deferred entrance. *Required:* high school transcript. *Required for some:* essay or personal statement, 3 letters of recommendation, interview. *Application deadlines:* rolling (freshmen), rolling (out-of-state freshmen), rolling (transfers). *Notification:* continuous (freshmen), continuous (out-of-state freshmen), continuous (transfers).
Freshman Application Contact Colorado Northwestern Community College, 500 Kennedy Drive, Rangely, CO 81648-3598. *Phone:* 970-675-3285. *Toll-free phone:* 800-562-1105.
Website: http://www.cncc.edu/.

Colorado School of Healing Arts
Lakewood, Colorado

Freshman Application Contact Colorado School of Healing Arts, 7655 West Mississippi Avenue, Suite 100, Lakewood, CO 80220. *Phone:* 303-986-2320. *Toll-free phone:* 800-233-7114. *Fax:* 303-980-6594.
Website: http://www.csha.net/.

Colorado School of Trades
Lakewood, Colorado

Freshman Application Contact Colorado School of Trades, 1575 Hoyt Street, Lakewood, CO 80215-2996. *Phone:* 303-233-4697 Ext. 44. *Toll-free phone:* 800-234-4594.
Website: http://www.schooloftrades.edu/.

Community College of Aurora
Aurora, Colorado

- **State-supported** 2-year, founded 1983, part of Colorado Community College System
- **Suburban** campus with easy access to Denver
- **Coed,** 6,943 undergraduate students, 18% full-time, 59% women, 41% men

Undergraduates 1,259 full-time, 5,684 part-time. 20% Black or African American, non-Hispanic/Latino; 22% Hispanic/Latino; 5% Asian, non-Hispanic/Latino; 0.3% Native Hawaiian or other Pacific Islander, non-Hispanic/Latino; 0.5% American Indian or Alaska Native, non-Hispanic/Latino; 5% Two or more races, non-Hispanic/Latino; 5% Race/ethnicity unknown; 3% international.
Freshmen *Admission:* 688 enrolled.
Faculty *Student/faculty ratio:* 20:1.
Majors Accounting technology and bookkeeping; child development; cinematography and film/video production; criminal justice/law enforcement administration; emergency medical technology (EMT paramedic); fire science/firefighting; general studies; heavy equipment maintenance technology; liberal arts and sciences and humanities related; liberal arts and sciences/liberal studies; management information systems; office management; science technologies related.
Academics *Calendar:* semesters. *Degree:* certificates and associate. *Special study options:* academic remediation for entering students, adult/continuing education programs, cooperative education, distance learning, English as a second language, external degree program, independent study, internships, off-

campus study, part-time degree program, services for LD students, summer session for credit.

Student Life *Housing:* college housing not available. *Activities and Organizations:* drama/theater group. *Campus security:* late-night transport/escort service. *Student services:* women's center.

Costs (2015–16) *Tuition:* state resident $3142 full-time, $131 per credit hour part-time; nonresident $12,860 full-time, $535 per credit hour part-time. Full-time tuition and fees vary according to course load, location, program, and reciprocity agreements. Part-time tuition and fees vary according to course load, location, program, and reciprocity agreements. *Required fees:* $396 full-time, $37 per credit hour part-time. *Payment plan:* installment. *Waivers:* employees or children of employees.

Applying *Required for some:* high school transcript.

Freshman Application Contact Community College of Aurora, 16000 East CentreTech Parkway, Aurora, CO 80011-9036. *Phone:* 303-360-4701. *Website:* http://www.ccaurora.edu/.

Community College of Denver
Denver, Colorado

- **State-supported** 2-year, founded 1970, part of Colorado Community College System
- **Urban** 124-acre campus
- **Coed**

Undergraduates 2,514 full-time, 7,782 part-time. 2% are from out of state; 13% Black or African American, non-Hispanic/Latino; 26% Hispanic/Latino; 5% Asian, non-Hispanic/Latino; 0.2% Native Hawaiian or other Pacific Islander, non-Hispanic/Latino; 1% American Indian or Alaska Native, non-Hispanic/Latino; 4% Two or more races, non-Hispanic/Latino; 13% Race/ethnicity unknown; 4% international. *Retention:* 53% of full-time freshmen returned.

Faculty *Student/faculty ratio:* 25:1.

Academics *Calendar:* semesters. *Degree:* certificates and associate. *Special study options:* academic remediation for entering students, accelerated degree program, adult/continuing education programs, advanced placement credit, cooperative education, distance learning, double majors, English as a second language, external degree program, freshman honors college, honors programs, independent study, internships, off-campus study, part-time degree program, services for LD students, study abroad, summer session for credit. *ROTC:* Army (c).

Library Auraria Library.

Student Life *Campus security:* 24-hour emergency response devices and patrols, late-night transport/escort service.

Costs (2015–16) *Tuition:* state resident $2998 full-time, $125 per credit hour part-time; nonresident $12,296 full-time, $512 per credit hour part-time. Full-time tuition and fees vary according to course load, location, program, and reciprocity agreements. Part-time tuition and fees vary according to course load, location, program, and reciprocity agreements.

Applying *Options:* electronic application, early admission, deferred entrance.

Freshman Application Contact Mr. Michael Rusk, Dean of Students, Community College of Denver, PO Box 173363, Campus Box 201, Denver, CO 80127-3363. *Phone:* 303-556-6325. *Fax:* 303-556-2431. *E-mail:* enrollment_services@ccd.edu. *Website:* http://www.ccd.edu/.

Concorde Career College
Aurora, Colorado

Admissions Office Contact Concorde Career College, 111 North Havana Street, Aurora, CO 80010. *Website:* http://www.concorde.edu/.

Ecotech Institute
Aurora, Colorado

Admissions Office Contact Ecotech Institute, 1400 South Abilene Street, Aurora, CO 80012. *Website:* http://www.ecotechinstitute.com/.

Everest College
Colorado Springs, Colorado

Director of Admissions Director of Admissions, Everest College, 1815 Jet Wing Drive, Colorado Springs, CO 80916. *Phone:* 719-630-6580. *Toll-free phone:* 888-741-4270. *Fax:* 719-638-6818. *Website:* http://www.everest.edu/.

Everest College
Thornton, Colorado

Freshman Application Contact Admissions Office, Everest College, 9065 Grant Street, Thornton, CO 80229. *Phone:* 303-457-2757. *Toll-free phone:* 888-741-4270. *Fax:* 303-457-4030. *Website:* http://www.everest.edu/.

Front Range Community College
Westminster, Colorado

- **State-supported** 2-year, founded 1968, part of Community Colleges of Colorado System
- **Suburban** 90-acre campus with easy access to Denver
- **Endowment** $457,964
- **Coed**, 18,761 undergraduate students, 30% full-time, 57% women, 43% men

Undergraduates 5,575 full-time, 13,186 part-time. Students come from 45 states and territories; 24 other countries; 2% are from out of state; 2% Black or African American, non-Hispanic/Latino; 14% Hispanic/Latino; 3% Asian, non-Hispanic/Latino; 0.2% Native Hawaiian or other Pacific Islander, non-Hispanic/Latino; 0.8% American Indian or Alaska Native, non-Hispanic/Latino; 4% Two or more races, non-Hispanic/Latino; 4% Race/ethnicity unknown; 2% international; 9% transferred in. *Retention:* 56% of full-time freshmen returned.

Freshmen *Admission:* 5,304 applied, 5,304 admitted, 2,348 enrolled.

Faculty *Total:* 1,014, 24% full-time. *Student/faculty ratio:* 20:1.

Majors Accounting technology and bookkeeping; animation, interactive technology, video graphics and special effects; applied horticulture/horticulture operations; architectural engineering technology; automobile/automotive mechanics technology; business administration and management; CAD/CADD drafting/design technology; computer and information sciences; computer systems networking and telecommunications; early childhood education; energy management and systems technology; general studies; health information/medical records technology; heating, ventilation, air conditioning and refrigeration engineering technology; holistic health; hospitality administration; interior design; legal assistant/paralegal; liberal arts and sciences and humanities related; liberal arts and sciences/liberal studies; medical office assistant; registered nursing/registered nurse; science technologies related; sign language interpretation and translation; veterinary/animal health technology; welding technology; wildlife, fish and wildlands science and management.

Academics *Calendar:* semesters. *Degree:* certificates and associate. *Special study options:* academic remediation for entering students, advanced placement credit, cooperative education, distance learning, double majors, English as a second language, freshman honors college, honors programs, independent study, internships, off-campus study, part-time degree program, services for LD students, student-designed majors, study abroad, summer session for credit. *ROTC:* Army (c), Air Force (c).

Library College Hill Library plus 2 others. *Books:* 57,957 (physical), 12,255 (digital/electronic); *Databases:* 33.

Student Life *Housing:* college housing not available. *Activities and Organizations:* drama/theater group, student-run newspaper, Student Government Association, Student Colorado Registry of Interpreters for the Deaf, Students in Free Enterprise (SIFE), Gay-Straight Alliance, Recycling Club. *Campus security:* 24-hour emergency response devices and patrols, late-night transport/escort service. *Student services:* personal/psychological counseling.

Costs (2015–16) *Tuition:* state resident $3132 full-time, $131 per credit hour part-time; nonresident $12,850 full-time, $535 per credit hour part-time. Full-time tuition and fees vary according to program. Part-time tuition and fees vary according to program. *Required fees:* $395 full-time, $395 per year part-time. *Payment plan:* installment. *Waivers:* employees or children of employees.

Applying *Options:* electronic application, early admission, deferred entrance.

Freshman Application Contact Ms. Miori Gidley, Registrar, Front Range Community College, Westminster, CO 80031. *Phone:* 303-404-5000. *Fax:* 303-439-2614. *E-mail:* miori.gidley@frontrange.edu. *Website:* http://www.frontrange.edu/.

Heritage College
Denver, Colorado

Freshman Application Contact Admissions Office, Heritage College, 4704 Harlan Street, Suite 100, Denver, CO 80212. *Toll-free phone:* 888-334-7339. *Website:* http://www.heritagecollege.edu/.

IBMC College
Colorado Springs, Colorado

Director of Admissions Michelle Squibb, Admissions Representative, IBMC College, 6805 Corporate Drive, Suite 100, Colorado Springs, CO 80919. *Phone:* 719-596-7400. *Toll-free phone:* 800-748-2282. *Website:* http://www.ibmc.edu/.

IBMC College
Fort Collins, Colorado

- **Proprietary** 2-year, founded 1987
- **Suburban** campus with easy access to Denver
- **Coed,** 1,020 undergraduate students, 100% full-time, 85% women, 15% men
- 92% of applicants were admitted

Undergraduates 1,020 full-time. 2% are from out of state; 1% Black or African American, non-Hispanic/Latino; 20% Hispanic/Latino; 0.5% Asian, non-Hispanic/Latino; 0.2% Native Hawaiian or other Pacific Islander, non-Hispanic/Latino; 0.6% American Indian or Alaska Native, non-Hispanic/Latino; 1% Two or more races, non-Hispanic/Latino. *Retention:* 72% of full-time freshmen returned.
Freshmen *Admission:* 1,064 applied, 977 admitted, 355 enrolled.
Faculty *Total:* 115, 40% full-time, 3% with terminal degrees. *Student/faculty ratio:* 10:1.
Majors Accounting technology and bookkeeping; aesthetician/esthetician and skin care; business administration and management; computer support specialist; cosmetology; barber/styling, and nail instruction; dental assisting; hair styling and hair design; legal administrative assistant/secretary; legal assistant/paralegal; massage therapy; medical administrative assistant and medical secretary; medical/clinical assistant; nail technician and manicurist; office occupations and clerical services.
Academics *Calendar:* continuous. *Degree:* certificates, diplomas, and associate. *Special study options:* accelerated degree program, adult/continuing education programs, cooperative education, honors programs, internships, summer session for credit.
Library IBMC College plus 8 others.
Student Life *Housing:* college housing not available. *Activities and Organizations:* Alpha Beta Kappa, Circle of Hope, Relay for Life, Peer Mentoring, Peer Tutor.
Standardized Tests *Required:* Wonderlic aptitude test (for admission).
Costs (2015–16) *One-time required fee:* $100. *Tuition:* $12,240 full-time. Full-time tuition and fees vary according to course load and program. Part-time tuition and fees vary according to course load and program. No tuition increase for student's term of enrollment. *Payment plans:* tuition prepayment, installment. *Waivers:* children of alumni and employees or children of employees.
Financial Aid Of all full-time matriculated undergraduates who enrolled in 2015, 1,085 applied for aid, 944 were judged to have need, 701 had their need fully met. *Average percent of need met:* 72%. *Average financial aid package:* $7500. *Average need-based loan:* $4270. *Average need-based gift aid:* $3222. *Average indebtedness upon graduation:* $94.
Applying *Options:* electronic application. *Application fee:* $50. *Required:* high school transcript, interview. *Application deadlines:* rolling (freshmen), rolling (out-of-state freshmen).
Freshman Application Contact Mr. Jeremy Shoup, Admissions and Marketing Coordinator, IBMC College, 3842 South Mason Street, Fort Collins, CO 80525. *Phone:* 970-223-2669. *Toll-free phone:* 800-495-2669. *E-mail:* jshoup@ibmc.edu. *Website:* http://www.ibmc.edu/.

IntelliTec College
Colorado Springs, Colorado

Director of Admissions Director of Admissions, IntelliTec College, 2315 East Pikes Peak Avenue, Colorado Springs, CO 80909. *Phone:* 719-632-7626. *Toll-free phone:* 800-748-2282. *Website:* http://www.intelliteccollege.edu/.

IntelliTec College
Grand Junction, Colorado

- **Proprietary** 2-year
- **Small-town** campus
- **Coed**

Faculty *Student/faculty ratio:* 22:1.
Academics *Calendar:* continuous. *Degree:* certificates, diplomas, and associate.

Costs (2015–16) *Tuition:* $23,151 full-time. Full-time tuition and fees vary according to class time, course load, degree level, location, program, and reciprocity agreements. Part-time tuition and fees vary according to class time. No tuition increase for student's term of enrollment. *Required fees:* $480 full-time.
Applying *Required:* high school transcript, interview.
Freshman Application Contact Admissions, IntelliTec College, 772 Horizon Drive, Grand Junction, CO 81506. *Phone:* 970-245-8101. *Toll-free phone:* 800-748-2282. *Fax:* 970-243-8074. *Website:* http://www.intelliteccollege.edu/.

IntelliTec College
Pueblo, Colorado

Admissions Office Contact IntelliTec College, 3673 Parker Boulevard, Pueblo, CO 81008. *Toll-free phone:* 800-748-2282. *Website:* http://www.intelliteccollege.edu/.

ITT Technical Institute
Aurora, Colorado

Freshman Application Contact Director of Recruitment, ITT Technical Institute, 14001 East Iliff Avenue, Suite 118, Aurora, CO 80014. *Phone:* 303-695-6317. *Toll-free phone:* 877-832-8460. *Website:* http://www.itt-tech.edu/.

Lamar Community College
Lamar, Colorado

- **State-supported** 2-year, founded 1937, part of Colorado Community College and Occupational Education System
- **Small-town** 125-acre campus
- **Endowment** $51,729
- **Coed,** 839 undergraduate students, 50% full-time, 55% women, 45% men

Undergraduates 419 full-time, 420 part-time. Students come from 31 states and territories; 3 other countries; 9% are from out of state; 8% Black or African American, non-Hispanic/Latino; 22% Hispanic/Latino; 0.2% Asian, non-Hispanic/Latino; 1% American Indian or Alaska Native, non-Hispanic/Latino; 3% Two or more races, non-Hispanic/Latino; 2% Race/ethnicity unknown; 3% international; 6% transferred in; 20% live on campus.
Freshmen *Admission:* 457 applied, 457 admitted, 142 enrolled.
Faculty *Total:* 55, 29% full-time. *Student/faculty ratio:* 19:1.
Majors Accounting; agricultural business and management; agriculture; agronomy and crop science; animal sciences; animal training; biological and physical sciences; biology/biological sciences; business administration and management; computer programming; computer science; computer typography and composition equipment operation; construction trades; cosmetology; criminal justice/safety; data processing and data processing technology; emergency medical technology (EMT paramedic); entrepreneurship; equestrian studies; farm and ranch management; history; information science/studies; liberal arts and sciences/liberal studies; licensed practical/vocational nurse training; management information systems; marketing/marketing management; medical office computer specialist; pre-engineering; registered nursing/registered nurse.
Academics *Calendar:* semesters. *Degree:* certificates, diplomas, and associate. *Special study options:* academic remediation for entering students, adult/continuing education programs, advanced placement credit, cooperative education, distance learning, double majors, English as a second language, independent study, internships, part-time degree program, services for LD students, student-designed majors, summer session for credit.
Library Learning Resources Center.
Student Life *Housing:* on-campus residence required for freshman year. *Options:* coed. Campus housing is university owned. *Campus security:* 24-hour emergency response devices and patrols, student patrols, late-night transport/escort service, controlled dormitory access. *Student services:* health clinic, personal/psychological counseling.
Athletics Member NJCAA. *Intercollegiate sports:* baseball M(s), basketball M(s)/W(s), equestrian sports M(s)/W(s), golf M(s), soccer M(c), softball W(s), volleyball W(s).
Costs (2015–16) *Tuition:* state resident $3132 full-time, $131 per credit hour part-time; nonresident $5352 full-time, $223 per credit hour part-time. Full-time tuition and fees vary according to course load, program, and reciprocity agreements. Part-time tuition and fees vary according to course load, program, and reciprocity agreements. *Required fees:* $414 full-time. *Room and board:* $6070; room only: $1950. *Payment plan:* installment. *Waivers:* employees or children of employees.

Applying *Options:* electronic application, early admission. *Application deadlines:* 9/16 (freshmen), 9/16 (transfers).
Freshman Application Contact Director of Admissions, Lamar Community College, 2401 South Main Street, Lamar, CO 81052-3999. *Phone:* 719-336-1592. *Toll-free phone:* 800-968-6920. *E-mail:* admissions@lamarcc.edu. *Website:* http://www.lamarcc.edu/.

Lincoln College of Technology
Denver, Colorado

Freshman Application Contact Lincoln College of Technology, 11194 East 45th Avenue, Denver, CO 80239. *Phone:* 800-347-3232 Ext. 43032. *Website:* http://www.lincolnedu.com/campus/denver-co/.

Morgan Community College
Fort Morgan, Colorado

- **State-supported** 2-year, founded 1967, part of Colorado Community College and Occupational Education System
- **Small-town** 20-acre campus with easy access to Denver
- **Coed,** 1,647 undergraduate students, 23% full-time, 65% women, 35% men

Undergraduates 374 full-time, 1,273 part-time. Students come from 8 states and territories; 2% Black or African American, non-Hispanic/Latino; 18% Hispanic/Latino; 0.5% Asian, non-Hispanic/Latino; 0.1% Native Hawaiian or other Pacific Islander, non-Hispanic/Latino; 0.3% American Indian or Alaska Native, non-Hispanic/Latino; 1% Two or more races, non-Hispanic/Latino; 7% Race/ethnicity unknown; 1% international. *Retention:* 52% of full-time freshmen returned.
Freshmen *Admission:* 172 enrolled.
Faculty *Total:* 147, 22% full-time. *Student/faculty ratio:* 15:1.
Majors Agribusiness; agricultural business technology; agricultural/farm supplies retailing and wholesaling; airline pilot and flight crew; animation, interactive technology, video graphics and special effects; autobody/collision and repair technology; automobile/automotive mechanics technology; business administration and management; child-care provision; emergency medical technology (EMT paramedic); farm and ranch management; general studies; health aide; liberal arts and sciences and humanities related; liberal arts and sciences/liberal studies; licensed practical/vocational nurse training; manufacturing engineering technology; massage therapy; medical/clinical assistant; medical office assistant; nursing assistant/aide and patient care assistant/aide; phlebotomy technology; physical therapy technology; registered nursing/registered nurse; science technologies related; welding technology.
Academics *Calendar:* semesters. *Degree:* certificates and associate. *Special study options:* academic remediation for entering students, adult/continuing education programs, advanced placement credit, distance learning, double majors, internships, part-time degree program, services for LD students, summer session for credit.
Library Learning Resource Center.
Student Life *Housing:* college housing not available. *Activities and Organizations:* student-run newspaper.
Costs (2015–16) *Tuition:* state resident $3132 full-time, $131 per credit hour part-time; nonresident $12,850 full-time, $535 per credit hour part-time. Full-time tuition and fees vary according to course load, program, and reciprocity agreements. Part-time tuition and fees vary according to course load, program, and reciprocity agreements. *Required fees:* $344 full-time, $13 per credit hour part-time, $13 per term part-time. *Payment plan:* installment.
Applying *Options:* electronic application, early admission, deferred entrance. *Recommended:* high school transcript. *Application deadlines:* rolling (freshmen), rolling (transfers).
Freshman Application Contact Ms. Kim Maxwell, Morgan Community College, 920 Barlow Road, Fort Morgan, CO 80701-4399. *Phone:* 970-542-3111. *Toll-free phone:* 800-622-0216. *Fax:* 970-867-6608. *E-mail:* kim.maxwell@morgancc.edu. *Website:* http://www.morgancc.edu/.

Northeastern Junior College
Sterling, Colorado

- **State-supported** 2-year, founded 1941, part of Colorado Community College and Occupational Education System
- **Small-town** 65-acre campus
- **Endowment** $5.6 million
- **Coed,** 1,776 undergraduate students, 55% full-time, 56% women, 44% men

Undergraduates 981 full-time, 795 part-time. Students come from 31 states and territories; 5 other countries; 8% are from out of state; 7% Black or African American, non-Hispanic/Latino; 12% Hispanic/Latino; 0.5% Asian, non-Hispanic/Latino; 0.1% Native Hawaiian or other Pacific Islander, non-Hispanic/Latino; 0.8% American Indian or Alaska Native, non-Hispanic/Latino; 3% Two or more races, non-Hispanic/Latino; 7% Race/ethnicity unknown; 0.4% international; 4% transferred in; 25% live on campus. *Retention:* 59% of full-time freshmen returned.
Freshmen *Admission:* 1,608 applied, 1,608 admitted, 414 enrolled. *Average high school GPA:* 2.81.
Faculty *Total:* 77, 64% full-time, 5% with terminal degrees. *Student/faculty ratio:* 21:1.
Majors Accounting; agricultural business and management; agricultural teacher education; agriculture; agronomy and crop science; animal sciences; anthropology; art; art history, criticism and conservation; automobile/automotive mechanics technology; biology/biological sciences; business administration and management; chemistry; child development; communication; cosmetology; criminal justice/police science; dramatic/theater arts; economics; elementary education; emergency medical technology (EMT paramedic); English; equestrian studies; farm and ranch management; fine/studio arts; geography; geology/earth science; history; journalism; liberal arts and sciences/liberal studies; licensed practical/vocational nurse training; marketing/marketing management; mathematics; music; natural sciences; philosophy; physical education teaching and coaching; physical sciences; political science and government; pre-engineering; psychology; registered nursing/registered nurse; social sciences; sociology.
Academics *Calendar:* semesters. *Degree:* certificates and associate. *Special study options:* academic remediation for entering students, accelerated degree program, adult/continuing education programs, advanced placement credit, cooperative education, distance learning, double majors, English as a second language, honors programs, independent study, internships, part-time degree program, services for LD students, summer session for credit.
Library Monahan Library. *Books:* 26,613 (physical), 90,000 (digital/electronic); *Serial titles:* 88 (physical), 137 (digital/electronic); *Databases:* 8. Weekly public service hours: 66.
Student Life *Housing:* on-campus residence required for freshman year. *Options:* coed, women-only. Campus housing is university owned. Freshman applicants given priority for college housing. *Activities and Organizations:* drama/theater group, choral group, Associated Student Government, Post Secondary Agriculture (PAS), Crossroads, NJC Ambassadors, Business Club. *Campus security:* 24-hour emergency response devices, late-night transport/escort service, controlled dormitory access. *Student services:* health clinic, personal/psychological counseling.
Athletics Member NCAA, NJCAA. All NCAA Division I. *Intercollegiate sports:* baseball M(s), basketball M(s)/W(s), equestrian sports M(s)/W(s), golf M(s)/W(s), soccer M(s), softball W(s), volleyball W(s). *Intramural sports:* badminton M/W, baseball M/W, basketball M/W, bowling M/W, cheerleading M/W, football M, golf M/W, racquetball M/W, soccer M/W, softball M/W, tennis M/W, ultimate Frisbee M/W, volleyball M/W, weight lifting M/W.
Costs (2015–16) *Tuition:* state resident $3708 full-time, $131 per credit hour part-time; nonresident $5274 full-time, $196 per credit hour part-time. Full-time tuition and fees vary according to course load. Part-time tuition and fees vary according to course load. *Required fees:* $576 full-time, $23 per credit hour part-time, $13 per term part-time. *Room and board:* $6566; room only: $2978. Room and board charges vary according to board plan and housing facility. *Payment plan:* installment. *Waivers:* senior citizens and employees or children of employees.
Applying *Options:* electronic application, early admission, deferred entrance. *Recommended:* high school transcript. *Application deadlines:* rolling (freshmen), rolling (out-of-state freshmen), rolling (transfers). *Notification:* continuous until 8/1 (freshmen), continuous (out-of-state freshmen), continuous until 8/1 (transfers).
Freshman Application Contact Adam Kunkel, Director of Admission, Northeastern Junior College, 100 College Avenue, Sterling, CO 80751-2399. *Phone:* 970-521-7000. *Toll-free phone:* 800-626-4637. *Fax:* 970-521-6715. *E-mail:* adam.kunkel@njc.edu. *Website:* http://www.njc.edu/.

Otero Junior College
La Junta, Colorado

- **State-supported** 2-year, founded 1941, part of Colorado Community College System
- **Rural** 40-acre campus
- **Endowment** $1.5 million
- **Coed,** 1,449 undergraduate students

Undergraduates Students come from 20 states and territories; 10 other countries; 9% are from out of state; 3% Black or African American, non-Hispanic/Latino; 32% Hispanic/Latino; 0.8% Asian, non-Hispanic/Latino; 0.5% Native Hawaiian or other Pacific Islander, non-Hispanic/Latino; 1% American Indian or Alaska Native, non-Hispanic/Latino; 6% Race/ethnicity unknown; 3% international. *Retention:* 53% of full-time freshmen returned.
Faculty *Student/faculty ratio:* 19:1.

Majors Administrative assistant and secretarial science; agricultural business and management; automobile/automotive mechanics technology; biological and physical sciences; biology/biological sciences; business administration and management; child development; comparative literature; data processing and data processing technology; dramatic/theater arts; elementary education; history; humanities; kindergarten/preschool education; legal administrative assistant/secretary; liberal arts and sciences/liberal studies; mathematics; medical administrative assistant and medical secretary; modern languages; political science and government; pre-engineering; psychology; registered nursing/registered nurse; social sciences.

Academics *Calendar:* semesters. *Degree:* certificates and associate. *Special study options:* academic remediation for entering students, adult/continuing education programs, advanced placement credit, distance learning, external degree program, honors programs, internships, part-time degree program, summer session for credit.

Library Wheeler Library.

Student Life *Housing:* on-campus residence required for freshman year. *Options:* men-only, women-only. Campus housing is university owned. *Activities and Organizations:* drama/theater group, student-run newspaper, choral group. *Campus security:* 24-hour patrols, late-night transport/escort service.

Athletics Member NJCAA. *Intercollegiate sports:* baseball M(s), basketball M(s)/W(s), golf M(s)/W(s), soccer M(s)/W(s), softball W(s), volleyball W(s), wrestling M(s). *Intramural sports:* basketball M/W, volleyball M/W.

Costs (2015–16) *Tuition:* state resident $3132 full-time; nonresident $5363 full-time. Full-time tuition and fees vary according to course load. Part-time tuition and fees vary according to course load. *Required fees:* $278 full-time. *Room and board:* $6306. Room and board charges vary according to board plan and housing facility. *Payment plans:* installment, deferred payment. *Waivers:* senior citizens.

Financial Aid Of all full-time matriculated undergraduates who enrolled in 2014, 30 Federal Work-Study jobs (averaging $2000). 100 state and other part-time jobs (averaging $2000).

Applying *Options:* electronic application, early admission. *Recommended:* high school transcript. *Application deadlines:* 8/15 (freshmen), 8/15 (transfers). *Notification:* continuous (freshmen), continuous (transfers).

Freshman Application Contact Mrs. Lauren Berg, Registrar, Otero Junior College, 1802 Colorado Avenue, La Junta, CO 81050. *Phone:* 719-384-6831. *Fax:* 719-384-6933. *E-mail:* lauren.berg@ojc.edu. *Website:* http://www.ojc.edu/.

Pikes Peak Community College
Colorado Springs, Colorado

Freshman Application Contact Pikes Peak Community College, 5675 South Academy Boulevard, Colorado Springs, CO 80906-5498. *Phone:* 719-540-7041. *Toll-free phone:* 866-411-7722. *Website:* http://www.ppcc.edu/.

Pima Medical Institute
Aurora, Colorado

Admissions Office Contact Pima Medical Institute, 13750 E. Mississippi Avenue, Aurora, CO 80012. *Toll-free phone:* 800-477-PIMA. *Website:* http://www.pmi.edu/.

Pima Medical Institute
Colorado Springs, Colorado

Freshman Application Contact Pima Medical Institute, 3770 Citadel Drive North, Colorado Springs, CO 80909. *Phone:* 719-482-7462. *Website:* http://www.pmi.edu/.

Pima Medical Institute
Denver, Colorado

Freshman Application Contact Admissions Office, Pima Medical Institute, 7475 Dakin Street, Denver, CO 80221. *Phone:* 303-426-1800. *Toll-free phone:* 800-477-PIMA (in-state); 888-477-PIMA (out-of-state). *Website:* http://www.pmi.edu/.

Pueblo Community College
Pueblo, Colorado

- **State-supported** 2-year, founded 1933, part of Colorado Community College System
- **Urban** 35-acre campus
- **Endowment** $1.1 million
- **Coed**, 6,203 undergraduate students, 37% full-time, 55% women, 45% men

Undergraduates 2,281 full-time, 3,922 part-time. Students come from 23 states and territories; 2 other countries; 4% are from out of state; 4% Black or African American, non-Hispanic/Latino; 28% Hispanic/Latino; 0.7% Asian, non-Hispanic/Latino; 0.1% Native Hawaiian or other Pacific Islander, non-Hispanic/Latino; 3% American Indian or Alaska Native, non-Hispanic/Latino; 3% Two or more races, non-Hispanic/Latino; 5% Race/ethnicity unknown; 0.5% international; 7% transferred in. *Retention:* 55% of full-time freshmen returned.

Freshmen *Admission:* 2,075 applied, 2,075 admitted, 724 enrolled.

Faculty *Total:* 427, 26% full-time. *Student/faculty ratio:* 16:1.

Majors Accounting technology and bookkeeping; animation, interactive technology, video graphics and special effects; autobody/collision and repair technology; automobile/automotive mechanics technology; business administration and management; business automation/technology/data entry; communications technology; computer and information sciences; cooking and related culinary arts; cosmetology; criminal justice/law enforcement administration; dental assisting; dental hygiene; early childhood education; electrical, electronic and communications engineering technology; electromechanical and instrumentation and maintenance technologies related; emergency medical technology (EMT paramedic); engineering technology; fire science/firefighting; general studies; liberal arts and sciences and humanities related; liberal arts and sciences/liberal studies; library and archives assisting; machine shop technology; manufacturing engineering technology; medical office management; occupational therapist assistant; physical therapy technology; psychiatric/mental health services technology; radiologic technology/science; registered nursing/registered nurse; respiratory care therapy; science technologies related; surgical technology; web page, digital/multimedia and information resources design; welding technology.

Academics *Calendar:* semesters. *Degree:* certificates and associate. *Special study options:* academic remediation for entering students, accelerated degree program, advanced placement credit, cooperative education, distance learning, double majors, English as a second language, honors programs, independent study, internships, part-time degree program, services for LD students, summer session for credit.

Library PCC Library.

Student Life *Housing:* college housing not available. *Activities and Organizations:* drama/theater group, choral group, Phi Theta Kappa, Welding Club, Culinary Arts Club, Performing Arts Club, Art Club. *Campus security:* 24-hour emergency response devices and patrols, late-night transport/escort service. *Student services:* health clinic, personal/psychological counseling.

Costs (2015–16) *Tuition:* state resident $4722 full-time, $157 per credit hour part-time; nonresident $15,371 full-time, $512 per credit hour part-time. Full-time tuition and fees vary according to location, program, and reciprocity agreements. Part-time tuition and fees vary according to location, program, and reciprocity agreements. *Required fees:* $1199 full-time, $20 per credit hour part-time, $56 per term part-time. *Payment plans:* installment, deferred payment.

Financial Aid Of all full-time matriculated undergraduates who enrolled in 2013, 84 Federal Work-Study jobs (averaging $3500). 254 state and other part-time jobs (averaging $3500). *Average financial aid package:* $5647.

Applying *Options:* electronic application, early admission, deferred entrance. *Application deadlines:* rolling (freshmen), rolling (out-of-state freshmen), rolling (transfers). *Notification:* continuous until 9/1 (freshmen), continuous until 9/1 (out-of-state freshmen), continuous until 9/1 (transfers).

Freshman Application Contact Mrs. Barbara Benedict, Director of Admissions and Records, Pueblo Community College, 900 West Orman Avenue, Pueblo, CO 81004. *Phone:* 719-549-3039. *Toll-free phone:* 888-642-6017. *Fax:* 719-549-3012. *E-mail:* barbara.benedict@pueblocc.edu. *Website:* http://www.pueblocc.edu/.

Red Rocks Community College
Lakewood, Colorado

Freshman Application Contact Admissions Office, Red Rocks Community College, 13300 West 6th Avenue, Lakewood, CO 80228-1255. *Phone:* 303-914-6360. *Fax:* 303-914-6919. *E-mail:* admissions@rrcc.edu. *Website:* http://www.rrcc.edu/.

Redstone College–Denver
Broomfield, Colorado

Freshman Application Contact Redstone College–Denver, 10851 West 120th Avenue, Broomfield, CO 80021. *Phone:* 303-466-7383. *Toll-free phone:* 877-801-1025.
Website: http://www.redstone.edu/.

Trinidad State Junior College
Trinidad, Colorado

- **State-supported** 2-year, founded 1925, part of Colorado Community College and Occupational Education System
- **Small-town** 17-acre campus
- **Coed**

Undergraduates 882 full-time, 901 part-time. Students come from 33 states and territories; 8 other countries; 13% are from out of state; 2% Black or African American, non-Hispanic/Latino; 41% Hispanic/Latino; 0.7% Asian, non-Hispanic/Latino; 0.1% Native Hawaiian or other Pacific Islander, non-Hispanic/Latino; 1% American Indian or Alaska Native, non-Hispanic/Latino; 2% Two or more races, non-Hispanic/Latino; 8% Race/ethnicity unknown; 1% international; 8% transferred in; 12% live on campus. *Retention:* 60% of full-time freshmen returned.
Faculty *Student/faculty ratio:* 13:1.
Academics *Calendar:* semesters. *Degree:* certificates, diplomas, and associate. *Special study options:* academic remediation for entering students, accelerated degree program, adult/continuing education programs, advanced placement credit, cooperative education, distance learning, double majors, English as a second language, independent study, internships, part-time degree program, services for LD students, student-designed majors, summer session for credit.
Library Freudenthal Memorial Library.
Student Life *Campus security:* 24-hour emergency response devices, trained security personnel patrol after campus hours.
Athletics Member NJCAA.
Costs (2015–16) *One-time required fee:* $25. *Tuition:* state resident $3915 full-time, $131 per credit hour part-time; nonresident $6703 full-time, $223 per credit hour part-time. Full-time tuition and fees vary according to course load, location, program, and reciprocity agreements. Part-time tuition and fees vary according to course load, location, program, and reciprocity agreements. *Required fees:* $615 full-time, $10 per credit hour part-time. *Room and board:* $5884. Room and board charges vary according to board plan.
Applying *Options:* deferred entrance. *Required:* high school transcript.
Freshman Application Contact Bernadine DeGarbo, Student Services Administrative Assistant, Trinidad State Junior College, 600 Prospect Street, Trinidad, CO 81082. *Phone:* 719-846-5621. *Toll-free phone:* 800-621-8752. *Fax:* 719-846-5620. *E-mail:* bernadine.degarbo@trinidadstate.edu.
Website: http://www.trinidadstate.edu/.

CONNECTICUT

Asnuntuck Community College
Enfield, Connecticut

- **State-supported** 2-year, founded 1972, part of Connecticut State Colleges & Universities (CSCU)
- **Suburban** 36-acre campus
- **Endowment** $137,046
- **Coed,** 1,571 undergraduate students, 40% full-time, 53% women, 47% men

Undergraduates 622 full-time, 949 part-time. 8% are from out of state; 9% Black or African American, non-Hispanic/Latino; 9% Hispanic/Latino; 3% Asian, non-Hispanic/Latino; 0.2% American Indian or Alaska Native, non-Hispanic/Latino; 3% Two or more races, non-Hispanic/Latino; 3% Race/ethnicity unknown; 12% transferred in. *Retention:* 59% of full-time freshmen returned.
Freshmen *Admission:* 451 applied, 451 admitted, 325 enrolled.
Faculty *Total:* 30. *Student/faculty ratio:* 15:1.
Majors Accounting technology and bookkeeping; banking and financial support services; criminal justice/police science; engineering science; engineering technology; general studies; liberal arts and sciences/liberal studies; management information systems; psychiatric/mental health services technology.
Academics *Calendar:* semesters. *Degree:* certificates and associate. *Special study options:* academic remediation for entering students, adult/continuing education programs, advanced placement credit, cooperative education,

distance learning, double majors, English as a second language, independent study, internships, part-time degree program, services for LD students, student-designed majors, summer session for credit.
Library ACTC Library plus 1 other.
Student Life *Housing:* college housing not available. *Activities and Organizations:* student-run radio station. *Campus security:* late-night transport/escort service.
Standardized Tests *Required:* Basic Skills Assessment, ACCUPLACER (for admission).
Costs (2016–17) *Tuition:* state resident $3600 full-time, $150 per credit hour part-time; nonresident $10,800 full-time, $450 per credit hour part-time. *Required fees:* $432 full-time. *Payment plan:* installment.
Applying *Options:* deferred entrance. *Application fee:* $20. *Required:* high school transcript. *Application deadlines:* rolling (freshmen), rolling (transfers). *Notification:* continuous (freshmen), continuous (transfers).
Freshman Application Contact Timothy St. James, Director of Enrollment Management, Asnuntuck Community College, 170 Elm Street, Enfield, CT 06082-3800. *Phone:* 860-253-3087. *Fax:* 860-253-3014.
E-mail: tstjames@asnuntuck.edu.
Website: http://www.asnuntuck.edu/.

Capital Community College
Hartford, Connecticut

Freshman Application Contact Ms. Jackie Phillips, Director of the Welcome and Advising Center, Capital Community College, 950 Main Street, Hartford, CT 06103. *Phone:* 860-906-5078. *Toll-free phone:* 800-894-6126.
E-mail: jphillips@ccc.commnet.edu.
Website: http://www.ccc.commnet.edu/.

Gateway Community College
New Haven, Connecticut

- **State-supported** 2-year, founded 1992, part of Connecticut Community –Technical College System
- **Urban** 5-acre campus with easy access to New York City
- **Coed**

Undergraduates 2,590 full-time, 5,611 part-time. 26% Black or African American, non-Hispanic/Latino; 22% Hispanic/Latino; 4% Asian, non-Hispanic/Latino; 0.2% American Indian or Alaska Native, non-Hispanic/Latino; 2% Two or more races, non-Hispanic/Latino; 4% Race/ethnicity unknown; 0.5% international; 9% transferred in.
Faculty *Student/faculty ratio:* 17:1.
Academics *Calendar:* semesters. *Degree:* certificates and associate. *Special study options:* academic remediation for entering students, adult/continuing education programs, advanced placement credit, distance learning, English as a second language, external degree program, independent study, internships, off-campus study, part-time degree program, services for LD students, summer session for credit.
Library Gateway Community College Library plus 2 others.
Student Life *Campus security:* late-night transport/escort service.
Athletics Member NJCAA.
Financial Aid Of all full-time matriculated undergraduates who enrolled in 2014, 69 Federal Work-Study jobs (averaging $3092). 69 state and other part-time jobs (averaging $1772).
Applying *Options:* early admission, deferred entrance. *Application fee:* $20. *Required:* high school transcript. *Required for some:* essay or personal statement, interview.
Freshman Application Contact Mr. Joseph Carberry, Director of Enrollment Management, Gateway Community College, 20 Church Street, New Haven, CT 06510. *Phone:* 203-285-2011. *Toll-free phone:* 800-390-7723. *Fax:* 203-285-2018. *E-mail:* jcarberry@gatewayct.edu.
Website: http://www.gwcc.commnet.edu/.

Goodwin College
East Hartford, Connecticut

- **Independent** primarily 2-year, founded 1999
- **Suburban** 660-acre campus with easy access to Hartford
- **Coed**

Undergraduates 612 full-time, 2,828 part-time. 3% are from out of state; 22% Black or African American, non-Hispanic/Latino; 17% Hispanic/Latino; 2% Asian, non-Hispanic/Latino; 0.1% Native Hawaiian or other Pacific Islander, non-Hispanic/Latino; 0.3% American Indian or Alaska Native, non-Hispanic/Latino; 2% Two or more races, non-Hispanic/Latino; 0.2% Race/ethnicity unknown; 0.1% international; 14% transferred in. *Retention:* 62% of full-time freshmen returned.
Faculty *Student/faculty ratio:* 10:1.

Academics *Calendar:* semesters. *Degrees:* certificates, associate, and bachelor's. *Special study options:* academic remediation for entering students, adult/continuing education programs, advanced placement credit, distance learning, double majors, English as a second language, internships, off-campus study, part-time degree program, services for LD students, summer session for credit.

Library Hoffman Family Library.

Student Life *Campus security:* 24-hour emergency response devices, late-night transport/escort service, evening security patrolman.

Costs (2015–16) *Tuition:* $19,500 full-time, $690 per credit hour part-time. Full-time tuition and fees vary according to course load and program. Part-time tuition and fees vary according to course load and program. *Required fees:* $900 full-time.

Applying *Options:* electronic application, early admission, deferred entrance. *Application fee:* $50. *Required:* essay or personal statement, high school transcript, minimum 2.0 GPA, medical exam. *Recommended:* 2 letters of recommendation, interview.

Freshman Application Contact Mr. Nicholas Lentino, Assistant Vice President for Admissions, Goodwin College, One Riverside Drive, East Hartford, CT 06118. *Phone:* 860-727-6765. *Toll-free phone:* 800-889-3282. *Fax:* 860-291-9550. *E-mail:* nlentino@goodwin.edu. *Website:* http://www.goodwin.edu/.

Housatonic Community College
Bridgeport, Connecticut

- **State-supported** 2-year, founded 1965, part of Connecticut State Colleges & Universities (CSCU)
- **Urban** 4-acre campus with easy access to New York City
- **Coed,** 5,369 undergraduate students

Undergraduates 31% Black or African American, non-Hispanic/Latino; 30% Hispanic/Latino; 3% Asian, non-Hispanic/Latino; 0.1% Native Hawaiian or other Pacific Islander, non-Hispanic/Latino; 0.1% American Indian or Alaska Native, non-Hispanic/Latino; 2% Two or more races, non-Hispanic/Latino; 1% Race/ethnicity unknown.

Faculty *Total:* 352, 21% full-time. *Student/faculty ratio:* 13:1.

Majors Accounting; administrative assistant and secretarial science; art; avionics maintenance technology; business administration and management; child development; clinical/medical laboratory technology; commercial and advertising art; computer typography and composition equipment operation; criminal justice/law enforcement administration; data processing and data processing technology; environmental studies; humanities; human services; journalism; liberal arts and sciences/liberal studies; mathematics; mental health counseling; physical therapy; pre-engineering; public administration; social sciences; substance abuse/addiction counseling.

Academics *Calendar:* semesters. *Degree:* certificates and associate. *Special study options:* academic remediation for entering students, adult/continuing education programs, advanced placement credit, cooperative education, distance learning, double majors, English as a second language, honors programs, independent study, internships, part-time degree program, services for LD students, summer session for credit. *ROTC:* Army (c).

Library Housatonic Community College Library. *Books:* 53,000 (physical), 29,000 (digital/electronic); *Databases:* 60. Students can reserve study rooms.

Student Life *Activities and Organizations:* drama/theater group, student-run newspaper, Student Senate, Association of Latin American Students, Community Action Network, Drama Club, Phi Theta Kappa. *Campus security:* 24-hour emergency response devices, late-night transport/escort service. *Student services:* health clinic, personal/psychological counseling, women's center.

Costs (2015–16) *Tuition:* state resident $4052 full-time, $150 per semester hour part-time; nonresident $12,116 full-time, $450 per semester hour part-time. *Required fees:* $432 full-time. *Payment plan:* installment. *Waivers:* senior citizens and employees or children of employees.

Financial Aid Of all full-time matriculated undergraduates who enrolled in 2014, 70 Federal Work-Study jobs (averaging $2850).

Applying *Options:* electronic application, deferred entrance. *Application fee:* $20. *Required:* high school transcript. *Required for some:* interview. *Application deadlines:* rolling (freshmen), rolling (transfers). *Notification:* continuous (freshmen), continuous (transfers).

Freshman Application Contact Mr. Earl Graham, Director of Admissions, Housatonic Community College, 900 Lafayette Boulevard, Bridgeport, CT 06604-4704. *Phone:* 203-332-5102. *E-mail:* egraham@hcc.commnet.edu. *Website:* http://www.hctc.commnet.edu/.

Manchester Community College
Manchester, Connecticut

- **State-supported** 2-year, founded 1963, part of Connecticut State Colleges & Universities (ConnSCU)
- **Small-town** campus
- **Coed,** 6,891 undergraduate students, 35% full-time, 53% women, 47% men

Undergraduates 2,383 full-time, 4,508 part-time. 16% Black or African American, non-Hispanic/Latino; 19% Hispanic/Latino; 5% Asian, non-Hispanic/Latino; 0.2% Native Hawaiian or other Pacific Islander, non-Hispanic/Latino; 0.2% American Indian or Alaska Native, non-Hispanic/Latino; 2% Two or more races, non-Hispanic/Latino; 6% Race/ethnicity unknown; 0.1% international; 12% transferred in. *Retention:* 66% of full-time freshmen returned.

Freshmen *Admission:* 2,758 applied, 2,739 admitted, 1,163 enrolled.

Faculty *Total:* 486, 22% full-time. *Student/faculty ratio:* 16:1.

Majors Accounting; administrative assistant and secretarial science; business administration and management; clinical/medical laboratory technology; commercial and advertising art; criminal justice/law enforcement administration; dramatic/theater arts; engineering science; fine/studio arts; general studies; hotel/motel administration; human services; industrial engineering; industrial technology; information science/studies; journalism; kindergarten/preschool education; legal administrative assistant/secretary; legal assistant/paralegal; liberal arts and sciences/liberal studies; management information systems; marketing/marketing management; medical administrative assistant and medical secretary; music; occupational therapist assistant; physical therapy technology; respiratory care therapy; social work; speech communication and rhetoric; surgical technology; teacher assistant/aide.

Academics *Calendar:* semesters. *Degree:* certificates and associate. *Special study options:* adult/continuing education programs, part-time degree program.

Student Life *Housing:* college housing not available.

Athletics Member NJCAA. *Intercollegiate sports:* baseball M, basketball M/W, soccer M/W, softball W.

Costs (2015–16) *Tuition:* state resident $3600 full-time, $150 per credit hour part-time; nonresident $10,800 full-time, $450 per credit hour part-time. *Required fees:* $452 full-time. *Payment plan:* installment. *Waivers:* senior citizens and employees or children of employees.

Financial Aid *Financial aid deadline:* 8/13.

Applying *Options:* electronic application. *Required:* high school transcript.

Freshman Application Contact Director of Admissions, Manchester Community College, PO Box 1046, Manchester, CT 06045-1046. *Phone:* 860-512-3210. *Fax:* 860-512-3221. *Website:* http://www.manchestercc.edu/.

Middlesex Community College
Middletown, Connecticut

Freshman Application Contact Mensimah Shabazz, Director of Admissions, Middlesex Community College, Middletown, CT 06457-4889. *Phone:* 860-343-5742. *Fax:* 860-344-3055. *E-mail:* mshabazz@mxcc.commnet.edu. *Website:* http://www.mxcc.commnet.edu/.

Naugatuck Valley Community College
Waterbury, Connecticut

- **State-supported** 2-year, founded 1992, part of Connecticut State Colleges & Universities (CSCU)
- **Urban** 110-acre campus
- **Coed,** 6,976 undergraduate students, 34% full-time, 57% women, 43% men

Undergraduates 2,362 full-time, 4,614 part-time. Students come from 5 states and territories; 1 other country; 0.2% are from out of state; 10% Black or African American, non-Hispanic/Latino; 26% Hispanic/Latino; 3% Asian, non-Hispanic/Latino; 0.2% Native Hawaiian or other Pacific Islander, non-Hispanic/Latino; 0.2% American Indian or Alaska Native, non-Hispanic/Latino; 2% Two or more races, non-Hispanic/Latino; 4% Race/ethnicity unknown; 0.2% international; 7% transferred in. *Retention:* 65% of full-time freshmen returned.

Freshmen *Admission:* 2,253 applied, 1,905 admitted, 1,434 enrolled.

Faculty *Total:* 457, 23% full-time. *Student/faculty ratio:* 17:1.

Majors Accounting technology and bookkeeping; aeronautics/aviation/aerospace science and technology; art; automobile/automotive mechanics technology; behavioral sciences; business administration and management; business/commerce; computer engineering technology; criminal justice/police science; digital communication and media/multimedia; early childhood education; electrical, electronic and communications engineering technology; engineering science; engineering technology; environmental engineering technology; finance; fire services administration; general studies; horticultural science; hospitality administration; hotel/motel administration; legal assistant/paralegal; liberal arts and sciences/liberal studies; marketing/marketing management; medical radiologic technology; physical sciences related; physical therapy technology; psychiatric/mental health services technology; registered nursing/registered nurse; respiratory care therapy; restaurant/food services management; substance abuse/addiction counseling.

Academics *Calendar:* semesters. *Degree:* certificates and associate. *Special study options:* academic remediation for entering students, accelerated degree program, adult/continuing education programs, advanced placement credit, cooperative education, distance learning, English as a second language, external degree program, independent study, internships, off-campus study, part-time degree program, services for LD students, summer session for credit.

Library Max R. Traurig Learning Resource Center. *Books:* 38,400 (physical); *Serial titles:* 108 (physical); *Databases:* 12. Weekly public service hours: 65; students can reserve study rooms.

Student Life *Housing:* college housing not available. *Activities and Organizations:* drama/theater group, student-run newspaper, choral group, Student Senate, Choral Society, Automotive Technician Club, Human Service Club, Legal Assistant Club. *Campus security:* 24-hour emergency response devices and patrols, late-night transport/escort service, security escort service. *Student services:* personal/psychological counseling, women's center.

Standardized Tests *Required:* ACCUPLACER (for admission).

Costs (2015–16) *Tuition:* state resident $4072 full-time, $150 per credit hour part-time; nonresident $12,136 full-time, $450 per credit hour part-time. Part-time tuition and fees vary according to course load. *Required fees:* $472 full-time. *Payment plan:* installment. *Waivers:* senior citizens and employees or children of employees.

Financial Aid Of all full-time matriculated undergraduates who enrolled in 2014, 70 Federal Work-Study jobs (averaging $1942). 16 state and other part-time jobs (averaging $1660).

Applying *Options:* electronic application, deferred entrance. *Application fee:* $20. *Required:* high school transcript. *Required for some:* interview. *Application deadlines:* rolling (freshmen), rolling (transfers). *Notification:* continuous (freshmen), continuous (transfers).

Freshman Application Contact Linda Stango, Director of Admissions, Naugatuck Valley Community College, Waterbury, CT 06708. *Phone:* 203-575-8016. *Fax:* 203-596-8766. *E-mail:* lstango@nvcc.commnet.edu. *Website:* http://www.nvcc.commnet.edu/.

Northwestern Connecticut Community College
Winsted, Connecticut

Freshman Application Contact Admissions Office, Northwestern Connecticut Community College, Park Place East, Winsted, CT 06098-1798. *Phone:* 860-738-6330. *Fax:* 860-738-6437. *E-mail:* admissions@nwcc.commnet.edu. *Website:* http://www.nwcc.commnet.edu/.

Norwalk Community College
Norwalk, Connecticut

- **State-supported** 2-year, founded 1961, part of Connecticut State Colleges & Universities (CSCU)
- **Suburban** 30-acre campus with easy access to New York City
- **Coed,** 6,054 undergraduate students, 35% full-time, 57% women, 43% men

Undergraduates 2,134 full-time, 3,920 part-time. 1% are from out of state; 18% Black or African American, non-Hispanic/Latino; 33% Hispanic/Latino; 4% Asian, non-Hispanic/Latino; 0.2% Native Hawaiian or other Pacific Islander, non-Hispanic/Latino; 0.1% American Indian or Alaska Native, non-Hispanic/Latino; 1% Two or more races, non-Hispanic/Latino; 5% Race/ethnicity unknown; 2% international; 6% transferred in. *Retention:* 58% of full-time freshmen returned.

Freshmen *Admission:* 877 enrolled.

Faculty *Total:* 334, 31% full-time. *Student/faculty ratio:* 20:1.

Majors Accounting; administrative assistant and secretarial science; architectural engineering technology; art; business administration and management; commercial and advertising art; computer and information systems security; computer systems networking and telecommunications; construction engineering technology; criminal justice/law enforcement administration; early childhood education; engineering science; finance; fine/studio arts; fire science/firefighting; general studies; graphic design; hotel/motel administration; human services; information science/studies; information technology; interior design; kinesiology and exercise science; legal assistant/paralegal; liberal arts and sciences/liberal studies; marketing/marketing management; medical office management; parks,

recreation and leisure; psychology; registered nursing/registered nurse; respiratory care therapy; restaurant/food services management; speech communication and rhetoric; web page, digital/multimedia and information resources design.

Academics *Calendar:* semesters. *Degree:* certificates and associate. *Special study options:* academic remediation for entering students, advanced placement credit, cooperative education, distance learning, English as a second language, independent study, internships, part-time degree program, services for LD students, summer session for credit.

Library Everett I. L. Baker Library.

Student Life *Housing:* college housing not available. *Activities and Organizations:* drama/theater group, student-run newspaper, choral group, Student World Assembly, Accounting Club, Literature Club, Art Club, Phi Theta Kappa. *Campus security:* late-night transport/escort service, all buildings secured each evening, foot patrols and vehicle patrols by security from 7 a.m. to 11 p.m.. *Student services:* personal/psychological counseling, women's center.

Costs (2015–16) *Tuition:* state resident $3600 full-time, $150 per credit hour part-time; nonresident $10,800 full-time, $450 per credit hour part-time. *Required fees:* $452 full-time. *Payment plan:* installment. *Waivers:* senior citizens and employees or children of employees.

Financial Aid Of all full-time matriculated undergraduates who enrolled in 2012, 53 Federal Work-Study jobs (averaging $2800). 20 state and other part-time jobs (averaging $2800).

Applying *Options:* electronic application, deferred entrance. *Required:* high school transcript, 4 math courses, 3 science courses, 2 labs, immunization form.

Freshman Application Contact Mr. Curtis Antrum, Admissions Counselor, Norwalk Community College, 188 Richards Avenue, Norwalk, CT 06854-1655. *Phone:* 203-857-7060. *Fax:* 203-857-3335. *E-mail:* admissions@ncc.commnet.edu. *Website:* http://www.ncc.commnet.edu/.

Quinebaug Valley Community College
Danielson, Connecticut

Freshman Application Contact Dr. Toni Moumouris, Director of Admissions, Quinebaug Valley Community College, 742 Upper Maple Street, Danielson, CT 06239. *Phone:* 860-774-1130 Ext. 318. *Fax:* 860-774-7768. *E-mail:* qu_isd@commnet.edu. *Website:* http://www.qvcc.commnet.edu/.

St. Vincent's College
Bridgeport, Connecticut

- **Independent** primarily 2-year, founded 1991, affiliated with Roman Catholic Church
- **Urban** campus with easy access to New York City
- **Endowment** $4.4 million
- **Coed,** 675 undergraduate students, 7% full-time, 87% women, 13% men

Undergraduates 50 full-time, 625 part-time. Students come from 4 states and territories; 1 other country; 1% are from out of state; 12% Black or African American, non-Hispanic/Latino; 13% Hispanic/Latino; 2% Asian, non-Hispanic/Latino; 0.3% American Indian or Alaska Native, non-Hispanic/Latino; 15% Race/ethnicity unknown; 21% transferred in.

Freshmen *Admission:* 14 enrolled. *Average high school GPA:* 2.93. *Test scores:* SAT critical reading scores over 500: 25%; SAT math scores over 500: 50%; SAT writing scores over 500: 50%; SAT critical reading scores over 600: 25%.

Faculty *Total:* 74, 28% full-time, 16% with terminal degrees. *Student/faculty ratio:* 10:1.

Majors General studies; health/health-care administration; medical/clinical assistant; radiologic technology/science; registered nursing/registered nurse.

Academics *Calendar:* semesters. *Degrees:* certificates, associate, and bachelor's. *Special study options:* academic remediation for entering students, adult/continuing education programs, advanced placement credit, distance learning, internships, part-time degree program, summer session for credit.

Library Daniel T. Banks Health Science Library. *Books:* 1,500 (physical), 84,000 (digital/electronic); *Serial titles:* 81 (physical); *Databases:* 5. Weekly public service hours: 40; students can reserve study rooms.

Student Life *Housing:* college housing not available. *Activities and Organizations:* Radiography Club, Student Nurses Association, SALUTE (veterans national honor society), Phi Theta Kappa (honor society). *Campus security:* 24-hour emergency response devices and patrols, late-night transport/escort service.

Standardized Tests *Required for some:* SAT or ACT (for admission). *Recommended:* SAT or ACT (for admission).

Costs (2016–17) *Tuition:* $14,520 full-time, $605 per credit hour part-time. Full-time tuition and fees vary according to course load. Part-time tuition and fees vary according to course load. *Required fees:* $350 full-time, $350 per year part-time. *Payment plan:* installment. *Waivers:* employees or children of employees.

Financial Aid Of all full-time matriculated undergraduates who enrolled in 2014, 64 applied for aid, 58 were judged to have need, 7 had their need fully met. *Average percent of need met:* 40%. *Average financial aid package:* $8235. *Average need-based loan:* $3883. *Average need-based gift aid:* $4765. *Average indebtedness upon graduation:* $18,805.

Applying *Required:* high school transcript. *Recommended:* minimum 3.0 GPA.

Freshman Application Contact Mr. Joseph Marrone, Director of Admissions, St. Vincent's College, 2800 Main Street, Bridgeport, CT 06606-4292. *Phone:* 203-576-5515. *Toll-free phone:* 800-873-1013. *Fax:* 203-576-5318.
E-mail: jmarrone@stvincentscollege.edu.
Website: http://www.stvincentscollege.edu/.

Three Rivers Community College
Norwich, Connecticut

- **State-supported** 2-year, founded 1963, part of Connecticut State Colleges & Universities (CSCU)
- **Suburban** 40-acre campus with easy access to Hartford
- **Coed,** 4,259 undergraduate students, 33% full-time, 58% women, 42% men

Undergraduates 1,407 full-time, 2,852 part-time. Students come from 5 states and territories; 1% are from out of state; 8% Black or African American, non-Hispanic/Latino; 15% Hispanic/Latino; 4% Asian, non-Hispanic/Latino; 0.3% Native Hawaiian or other Pacific Islander, non-Hispanic/Latino; 0.6% American Indian or Alaska Native, non-Hispanic/Latino; 4% Two or more races, non-Hispanic/Latino; 4% Race/ethnicity unknown; 0.2% international; 7% transferred in. *Retention:* 56% of full-time freshmen returned.

Freshmen *Admission:* 860 enrolled.

Faculty *Total:* 277, 25% full-time. *Student/faculty ratio:* 17:1.

Majors Accounting; accounting technology and bookkeeping; airframe mechanics and aircraft maintenance technology; architectural drafting and CAD/CADD; architectural engineering technology; banking and financial support services; business/commerce; child-care and support services management; civil engineering technology; computer engineering technology; construction management; criminal justice/police science; e-commerce; education; electrical, electronic and communications engineering technology; engineering science; engineering technology; entrepreneurship; environmental engineering technology; fine/studio arts; fire services administration; general studies; graphic design; hospitality administration; kinesiology and exercise science; laser and optical technology; liberal arts and sciences/liberal studies; management information systems; manufacturing engineering technology; marketing/marketing management; mechanical engineering/mechanical technology; nuclear/nuclear power technology; psychiatric/mental health services technology; registered nursing/registered nurse; sport and fitness administration/management.

Academics *Calendar:* semesters. *Degrees:* certificates and associate (engineering technology programs are offered on the Thames Valley Campus; liberal arts, transfer and career programs are offered on the Mohegan Campus). *Special study options:* adult/continuing education programs, part-time degree program.

Library Three Rivers Community College Learning Resource Center plus 1 other.

Student Life *Housing:* college housing not available. *Activities and Organizations:* student-run newspaper. *Campus security:* 24-hour emergency response devices, late-night transport/escort service, 14-hour patrols by trained security personnel.

Athletics *Intramural sports:* baseball M(c)/W(c), golf M(c)/W(c).

Costs (2015–16) *Tuition:* state resident $3600 full-time, $150 per credit hour part-time; nonresident $10,800 full-time, $450 per credit hour part-time. Full-time tuition and fees vary according to course load and reciprocity agreements. Part-time tuition and fees vary according to course load and reciprocity agreements. *Required fees:* $472 full-time, $84 per credit hour part-time. *Payment plan:* installment. *Waivers:* senior citizens and employees or children of employees.

Financial Aid Of all full-time matriculated undergraduates who enrolled in 2010, 1,135 applied for aid, 967 were judged to have need, 266 had their need fully met. *Average percent of need met:* 48%. *Average financial aid package:* $2631. *Average need-based loan:* $3308. *Average need-based gift aid:* $2409.

Applying *Options:* electronic application, early admission, deferred entrance. *Recommended:* high school transcript. *Application deadlines:* rolling (freshmen), rolling (transfers). *Notification:* continuous (freshmen), continuous (transfers).

Freshman Application Contact Admissions Office, Three Rivers Community College, CT. *Phone:* 860-215-9296.
E-mail: admissions@trcc.commnet.edu.
Website: http://www.trcc.commnet.edu/.

Tunxis Community College
Farmington, Connecticut

- **State-supported** 2-year, founded 1969, part of Connecticut State Colleges & Universities (CSCU)
- **Suburban** 12-acre campus with easy access to Hartford
- **Coed,** 4,079 undergraduate students, 39% full-time, 56% women, 44% men

Undergraduates 1,594 full-time, 2,485 part-time. Students come from 6 states and territories; 2% are from out of state; 7% Black or African American, non-Hispanic/Latino; 19% Hispanic/Latino; 4% Asian, non-Hispanic/Latino; 0.0% Native Hawaiian or other Pacific Islander, non-Hispanic/Latino; 0.2% American Indian or Alaska Native, non-Hispanic/Latino; 5% Race/ethnicity unknown; 0.1% international. *Retention:* 61% of full-time freshmen returned.

Freshmen *Admission:* 831 enrolled.

Faculty *Total:* 239, 28% full-time, 12% with terminal degrees. *Student/faculty ratio:* 17:1.

Majors Accounting; administrative assistant and secretarial science; art; business administration and management; commercial and advertising art; corrections; criminal justice/law enforcement administration; data processing and data processing technology; dental hygiene; design and applied arts related; engineering; engineering technology; forensic science and technology; human services; information science/studies; kindergarten/preschool education; liberal arts and sciences/liberal studies; marketing/marketing management; medical administrative assistant and medical secretary.

Academics *Calendar:* semesters. *Degree:* certificates and associate. *Special study options:* academic remediation for entering students, adult/continuing education programs, cooperative education, distance learning, double majors, English as a second language, honors programs, independent study, internships, part-time degree program, services for LD students, summer session for credit.

Library Tunxis Community College Library. Students can reserve study rooms.

Student Life *Housing:* college housing not available. *Activities and Organizations:* drama/theater group, student-run newspaper, Phi Theta Kappa, Student American Dental Hygiene Association (SADHA), Human Services Club, Student Newspaper, Criminal Justice Club. *Campus security:* 24-hour emergency response devices.

Costs (2015–16) *Tuition:* state resident $3432 full-time, $143 per semester hour part-time; nonresident $10,296 full-time, $429 per semester hour part-time. *Required fees:* $434 full-time, $124 per term part-time. *Payment plan:* installment. *Waivers:* senior citizens and employees or children of employees.

Applying *Options:* deferred entrance. *Application fee:* $20. *Required:* high school transcript. *Application deadlines:* rolling (freshmen), rolling (out-of-state freshmen), rolling (transfers). *Notification:* continuous (freshmen), continuous (out-of-state freshmen), continuous (transfers).

Freshman Application Contact Ms. Tamika Davis, Director of Admissions, Tunxis Community College, 271 Scott Swamp Road, Farmington, CT 06032. *Phone:* 860-773-1494. *Fax:* 860-606-9501.
E-mail: pmccluskey@tunxis.edu.
Website: http://www.tunxis.edu/.

DELAWARE

Delaware College of Art and Design
Wilmington, Delaware

Freshman Application Contact Ms. Allison Gullo, Delaware College of Art and Design, 600 North Market Street, Wilmington, DE 19801. *Phone:* 302-622-8867 Ext. 111. *Fax:* 302-622-8870. *E-mail:* agullo@dcad.edu.
Website: http://www.dcad.edu/.

Delaware Technical & Community College, Jack F. Owens Campus
Georgetown, Delaware

Freshman Application Contact Ms. Claire McDonald, Admissions Counselor, Delaware Technical & Community College, Jack F. Owens Campus, PO Box 610, Georgetown, DE 19947. *Phone:* 302-856-5400. *Fax:* 302-856-9461.
Website: http://www.dtcc.edu/.

Delaware Technical & Community College, Stanton/Wilmington Campus
Newark, Delaware

Freshman Application Contact Ms. Rebecca Bailey, Admissions Coordinator, Wilmington, Delaware Technical & Community College, Stanton/Wilmington Campus, 333 Shipley Street, Wilmington, DE 19713. *Phone:* 302-571-5343. *Fax:* 302-577-2548.
Website: http://www.dtcc.edu/.

Delaware Technical & Community College, Terry Campus
Dover, Delaware

- **State-supported** 2-year, founded 1972, part of Delaware Technical and Community College System
- **Small-town** campus
- **Coed**

Undergraduates 1,285 full-time, 1,670 part-time. 29% Black or African American, non-Hispanic/Latino; 6% Hispanic/Latino; 2% Asian, non-Hispanic/Latino; 0.1% Native Hawaiian or other Pacific Islander, non-Hispanic/Latino; 0.4% American Indian or Alaska Native, non-Hispanic/Latino; 3% Two or more races, non-Hispanic/Latino; 2% Race/ethnicity unknown; 0.8% international. *Retention:* 52% of full-time freshmen returned.
Academics *Calendar:* semesters. *Degree:* certificates, diplomas, and associate. *Special study options:* part-time degree program.
Student Life *Campus security:* 24-hour emergency response devices, late-night transport/escort service.
Athletics Member NJCAA.
Financial Aid Of all full-time matriculated undergraduates who enrolled in 2014, 50 Federal Work-Study jobs (averaging $1500).
Applying *Options:* electronic application, early admission, deferred entrance. *Application fee:* $10. *Required for some:* high school transcript.
Freshman Application Contact Mrs. Maria Harris, Admissions Officer, Delaware Technical & Community College, Terry Campus, 100 Campus Drive, Dover, DE 19904. *Phone:* 302-857-1020. *Fax:* 302-857-1296.
E-mail: terry-info@dtcc.edu.
Website: http://www.dtcc.edu/.

DISTRICT OF COLUMBIA

Graduate School USA
Washington, District of Columbia

Admissions Office Contact Graduate School USA, 600 Maryland Avenue, SW, Washington, DC 20024.
Website: http://www.graduateschool.edu/.

Radians College
Washington, District of Columbia

Admissions Office Contact Radians College, 1025 Vermont Avenue, NW, Suite 200, Washington, DC 20005.
Website: http://www.radianscollege.edu/.

FLORIDA

Academy for Nursing and Health Occupations
West Palm Beach, Florida

Admissions Office Contact Academy for Nursing and Health Occupations, 5154 Okeechobee Boulevard, Suite 201, West Palm Beach, FL 33417.
Website: http://www.apnho.com/.

Advance Science Institute
Hialeah, Florida

Admissions Office Contact Advance Science Institute, 3750 W. 12 Avenue, Hialeah, FL 33012.
Website: http://www.asimedschool.com/.

American Medical Academy
Miami, Florida

Admissions Office Contact American Medical Academy, 12215 SW 112 Street, Miami, FL 33186-4830.
Website: http://www.ama.edu/.

ATA Career Education
Spring Hill, Florida

Admissions Office Contact ATA Career Education, 7351 Spring Hill Drive, Suite 11, Spring Hill, FL 34606.
Website: http://www.atafl.edu/.

Aviator College of Aeronautical Science & Technology
Fort Pierce, Florida

Admissions Office Contact Aviator College of Aeronautical Science & Technology, 3800 St. Lucie Boulevard, Fort Pierce, FL 34946.
Website: http://aviator.edu/FlightSchool/.

Broward College
Fort Lauderdale, Florida

Freshman Application Contact Mr. Willie J. Alexander, Associate Vice President for Student Affairs/College Registrar, Broward College, 225 East Las Olas Boulevard, Fort Lauderdale, FL 33301. *Phone:* 954-201-7471. *Fax:* 954-201-7466. *E-mail:* walexand@broward.edu.
Website: http://www.broward.edu/.

Brown Mackie College–Miami
Miramar, Florida

Freshman Application Contact Brown Mackie College–Miami, 3700 Lakeside Drive, Miramar, FL 33027. *Phone:* 305-341-6600. *Toll-free phone:* 866-505-0335.
Website: http://www.brownmackie.edu/miami/.

Burnett International College
Boynton Beach, Florida

Admissions Office Contact Burnett International College, 1903 South Congress Avenue, Boynton Beach, FL 33426-6591.
Website: http://www.burnett.edu/.

Cambridge Institute of Allied Health and Technology
Delray Beach, Florida

Admissions Office Contact Cambridge Institute of Allied Health and Technology, 5150 Linton Boulevard, Suite 340, Delray Beach, FL 33484.
Website: http://www.cambridgehealth.edu/.

Chipola College
Marianna, Florida

- **State-supported** primarily 2-year, founded 1947
- **Rural** 105-acre campus
- **Coed**, 2,147 undergraduate students, 40% full-time, 63% women, 37% men

Undergraduates 863 full-time, 1,284 part-time. Students come from 7 states and territories; 6 other countries; 8% are from out of state; 14% Black or African American, non-Hispanic/Latino; 0.7% Hispanic/Latino; 0.7% Asian, non-Hispanic/Latino; 0.1% Native Hawaiian or other Pacific Islander, non-Hispanic/Latino; 1% American Indian or Alaska Native, non-Hispanic/Latino; 4% Two or more races, non-Hispanic/Latino; 1% Race/ethnicity unknown; 7% transferred in.

Freshmen *Admission:* 212 enrolled. *Average high school GPA:* 2.5. *Test scores:* SAT critical reading scores over 500: 16%; SAT math scores over 500: 36%; ACT scores over 18: 81%; SAT critical reading scores over 600: 4%; SAT math scores over 600: 12%; ACT scores over 24: 25%; ACT scores over 30: 3%.

Faculty *Total:* 127, 31% full-time, 13% with terminal degrees. *Student/faculty ratio:* 24:1.

Majors Accounting; agriculture; agronomy and crop science; art; biological and physical sciences; business administration and management; clinical laboratory science/medical technology; computer and information sciences related; computer science; education; finance; liberal arts and sciences/liberal studies; mass communication/media; mathematics teacher education; pre-engineering; registered nursing/registered nurse; science teacher education; secondary education; social work.

Academics *Calendar:* semesters. *Degrees:* certificates, associate, and bachelor's. *Special study options:* academic remediation for entering students, adult/continuing education programs, advanced placement credit, distance learning, honors programs, independent study, part-time degree program, services for LD students, summer session for credit.

Library Chipola Library.

Student Life *Housing:* college housing not available. *Activities and Organizations:* drama/theater group, student-run newspaper, choral group, Drama/Theater Group. *Campus security:* night security personnel.

Athletics Member NJCAA. *Intercollegiate sports:* baseball M(s), basketball M(s)/W(s), softball W(s).

Costs (2015–16) *Tuition:* state resident $3060 full-time, $102 per semester hour part-time; nonresident $8891 full-time, $296 per semester hour part-time. Full-time tuition and fees vary according to degree level. Part-time tuition and fees vary according to degree level. *Required fees:* $40 full-time.

Applying *Options:* early admission. *Required:* high school transcript. *Application deadlines:* rolling (freshmen), rolling (transfers). *Notification:* continuous (freshmen), continuous (transfers).

Freshman Application Contact Mrs. Kathy L. Rehberg, Registrar, Chipola College, 3094 Indian Circle, Marianna, FL 32446-3065. *Phone:* 850-718-2233. *Fax:* 850-718-2287. *E-mail:* rehbergk@chipola.edu. *Website:* http://www.chipola.edu/.

City College
Altamonte Springs, Florida

Director of Admissions Ms. Kimberly Bowden, Director of Admissions, City College, 177 Montgomery Road, Altamonte Springs, FL 32714. *Phone:* 352-335-4000. *Fax:* 352-335-4303. *E-mail:* kbowden@citycollege.edu. *Website:* http://www.citycollege.edu/.

City College
Fort Lauderdale, Florida

Freshman Application Contact City College, 2000 West Commercial Boulevard, Suite 200, Fort Lauderdale, FL 33309. *Phone:* 954-492-5353. *Toll-free phone:* 866-314-5681. *Website:* http://www.citycollege.edu/.

City College
Gainesville, Florida

Freshman Application Contact Admissions Office, City College, 7001 Northwest 4th Boulevard, Gainesville, FL 32607. *Phone:* 352-335-4000. *Website:* http://www.citycollege.edu/.

City College
Miami, Florida

Freshman Application Contact Admissions Office, City College, 9300 South Dadeland Boulevard, Suite PH, Miami, FL 33156. *Phone:* 305-666-9242. *Fax:* 305-666-9243. *Website:* http://www.citycollege.edu/.

College of Business and Technology–Cutler Bay Campus
Cutler Bay, Florida

- **Proprietary** 2-year
- **Urban** campus with easy access to Miami
- **Coed,** 112 undergraduate students, 100% full-time, 77% women, 23% men

Undergraduates 112 full-time. Students come from 1 other state; 29% Black or African American, non-Hispanic/Latino; 56% Hispanic/Latino; 3% Asian, non-Hispanic/Latino; 0.9% Native Hawaiian or other Pacific Islander, non-Hispanic/Latino; 0.9% Two or more races, non-Hispanic/Latino; 3% Race/ethnicity unknown.

Freshmen *Admission:* 19 enrolled.

Faculty *Total:* 18, 22% full-time, 17% with terminal degrees. *Student/faculty ratio:* 13:1.

Majors Accounting; business administration and management; electrical/electronics maintenance and repair technology related; health information/medical records technology; medical/clinical assistant.

Academics *Calendar:* semesters. *Degree:* certificates, diplomas, and associate. *Special study options:* academic remediation for entering students, accelerated degree program, adult/continuing education programs, cooperative education, independent study, part-time degree program.

Library CBT College–Cutler Bay Library. *Books:* 2,501 (physical); *Serial titles:* 24 (physical); *Databases:* 70.

Student Life *Campus security:* security guard patrol, local police department patrol.

Costs (2016–17) *Tuition:* $11,952 full-time. *Required fees:* $1400 full-time. *Payment plan:* installment.

Applying *Options:* electronic application. *Application fee:* $25. *Required:* high school transcript, interview.

Freshman Application Contact College of Business and Technology–Cutler Bay Campus, 19151 South Dixie Highway, Cutler Bay, FL 33157. *Phone:* 305-273-4499 Ext. 1100. *Website:* http://www.cbt.edu/.

College of Business and Technology–Flagler Campus
Miami, Florida

- **Proprietary** 2-year
- **Urban** campus
- **Coed,** 304 undergraduate students, 100% full-time, 7% women, 93% men

Undergraduates 304 full-time. Students come from 2 states and territories; 13 other countries; 0.7% Black or African American, non-Hispanic/Latino; 96% Hispanic/Latino; 2% Race/ethnicity unknown; 0.7% international.

Freshmen *Admission:* 65 enrolled.

Faculty *Total:* 32, 34% full-time, 3% with terminal degrees. *Student/faculty ratio:* 17:1.

Majors Accounting; business administration and management; computer systems networking and telecommunications; electrical/electronics maintenance and repair technology related; heating, ventilation, air conditioning and refrigeration engineering technology.

Academics *Calendar:* semesters. *Degree:* certificates, diplomas, and associate. *Special study options:* academic remediation for entering students, adult/continuing education programs, cooperative education, English as a second language, independent study, part-time degree program.

Library CBT College–Flagler Library. *Books:* 1,432 (physical); *Serial titles:* 16 (physical); *Databases:* 70.

Student Life *Housing:* college housing not available. *Campus security:* security guard patrol, local police department patrol.

Costs (2016–17) *Tuition:* $11,952 full-time. *Required fees:* $1400 full-time. *Payment plan:* installment.

Applying *Options:* electronic application. *Application fee:* $25. *Required:* high school transcript, interview.

Freshman Application Contact College of Business and Technology–Flagler Campus, 8230 West Flagler Street, Miami, FL 33144. *Phone:* 305-273-4499 Ext. 1100. *Website:* http://www.cbt.edu/.

College of Business and Technology–Hialeah Campus

Hialeah, Florida

- **Proprietary** 2-year
- **Urban** campus with easy access to Miami
- **Coed, primarily men,** 212 undergraduate students, 100% full-time, 3% women, 97% men

Undergraduates 212 full-time. Students come from 2 states and territories; 9 other countries; 3% Black or African American, non-Hispanic/Latino; 96% Hispanic/Latino; 0.5% Race/ethnicity unknown.

Freshmen *Admission:* 83 enrolled.

Faculty *Total:* 28, 29% full-time, 7% with terminal degrees. *Student/faculty ratio:* 14:1.

Majors Electrical/electronics maintenance and repair technology related; heating, ventilation, air conditioning and refrigeration engineering technology.

Academics *Calendar:* semesters. *Degree:* certificates, diplomas, and associate. *Special study options:* academic remediation for entering students, accelerated degree program, adult/continuing education programs, cooperative education, English as a second language, independent study, part-time degree program.

Library CBT College–Hialeah Library. *Books:* 1,006 (physical); *Serial titles:* 7 (physical); *Databases:* 70.

Student Life *Campus security:* local police department patrols.

Costs (2016–17) *Tuition:* $11,952 full-time. *Required fees:* $1400 full-time. *Payment plan:* installment.

Applying *Options:* electronic application. *Application fee:* $25. *Required:* high school transcript, interview.

Freshman Application Contact College of Business and Technology–Hialeah Campus, 935 West 49 Street, Hialeah, FL 33012. *Phone:* 305-273-4499 Ext. 1100.

Website: http://www.cbt.edu/.

College of Business and Technology–Main Campus

Miami, Florida

- **Proprietary** primarily 2-year, founded 1988
- **Urban** campus
- **Coed,** 9 undergraduate students, 100% full-time, 44% women, 56% men

Undergraduates 9 full-time. Students come from 1 other state; 2 other countries; 11% Black or African American, non-Hispanic/Latino; 56% Hispanic/Latino; 11% American Indian or Alaska Native, non-Hispanic/Latino; 11% international.

Faculty *Total:* 3, 33% full-time, 100% with terminal degrees. *Student/faculty ratio:* 5:1.

Majors Accounting; business administration and management; computer graphics; computer systems networking and telecommunications; graphic design; heating, air conditioning, ventilation and refrigeration maintenance technology; medical/clinical assistant; system, networking, and LAN/WAN management.

Academics *Calendar:* semesters. *Degrees:* certificates, diplomas, associate, and bachelor's. *Special study options:* academic remediation for entering students, accelerated degree program, adult/continuing education programs, cooperative education, English as a second language, independent study, part-time degree program.

Library CBT College–Main Campus Library. *Books:* 1,100 (physical); *Serial titles:* 7 (physical); *Databases:* 70.

Student Life *Campus security:* security guard posted at main entrance, local police department.

Costs (2016–17) *Tuition:* $11,952 full-time. *Required fees:* $1400 full-time. *Payment plan:* installment.

Applying *Options:* electronic application. *Application fee:* $25. *Required:* high school transcript, interview.

Freshman Application Contact Ms., College of Business and Technology–Main Campus, 8700 West Flagler Street, Suite 420, Miami, FL 33174. *Phone:* 305-273-4499 Ext. 1100.

Website: http://www.cbt.edu/.

College of Business and Technology–Miami Gardens

Miami Gardens, Florida

- **Proprietary** primarily 2-year
- **Urban** campus
- **Coed,** 90 undergraduate students, 100% full-time, 59% women, 41% men

Undergraduates 90 full-time. Students come from 2 states and territories; 6 other countries; 27% Black or African American, non-Hispanic/Latino; 59% Hispanic/Latino; 1% Asian, non-Hispanic/Latino; 1% Native Hawaiian or other Pacific Islander, non-Hispanic/Latino; 9% Race/ethnicity unknown; 1% international.

Freshmen *Admission:* 13 enrolled.

Faculty *Total:* 14, 14% full-time, 14% with terminal degrees. *Student/faculty ratio:* 15:1.

Majors Business administration and management; computer systems networking and telecommunications; electrical/electronics maintenance and repair technology related; graphic design; medical/clinical assistant.

Academics *Calendar:* semesters. *Degrees:* certificates, diplomas, associate, and bachelor's. *Special study options:* academic remediation for entering students, accelerated degree program, adult/continuing education programs, cooperative education, independent study, part-time degree program.

Library CBT College–Miami Gardens Library. *Books:* 1,234 (physical); *Serial titles:* 16 (physical); *Databases:* 70.

Student Life *Campus security:* security guard posted at main entrance, local police department.

Costs (2016–17) *Tuition:* $11,952 full-time. *Required fees:* $1400 full-time. *Payment plan:* installment.

Applying *Options:* electronic application. *Application fee:* $25. *Required:* high school transcript, interview.

Freshman Application Contact College of Business and Technology–Miami Gardens, 5190 NW 167 Street, Miami Gardens, FL 33014. *Phone:* 305-273-4499 Ext. 1100.

Website: http://www.cbt.edu/.

College of Central Florida

Ocala, Florida

- **State and locally supported** primarily 2-year, founded 1957, part of Florida Community College System
- **Small-town** 139-acre campus
- **Endowment** $65.4 million
- **Coed,** 7,931 undergraduate students, 38% full-time, 63% women, 37% men

Undergraduates 3,036 full-time, 4,895 part-time. 16% are from out of state.

Freshmen *Admission:* 4,416 applied, 2,430 admitted, 1,503 enrolled.

Faculty *Total:* 374, 37% full-time, 10% with terminal degrees.

Majors Accounting technology and bookkeeping; advertising; agribusiness; agriculture; animal sciences; architecture; art; biology/biological sciences; business administration and management; business administration, management and operations related; business/commerce; chemistry; clinical laboratory science/medical technology; computer and information sciences; construction engineering technology; criminal justice/law enforcement administration; criminology; dental assisting; drafting and design technology; dramatic/theater arts; early childhood education; economics; elementary education; emergency medical technology (EMT paramedic); engineering; engineering technology; English; environmental studies; equestrian studies; family and consumer sciences/human sciences; fire science/firefighting; foreign languages and literatures; forestry; health information/medical records technology; health/medical preparatory programs related; health services/allied health/health sciences; history; humanities; human services; information technology; interior architecture; journalism; landscaping and groundskeeping; legal assistant/paralegal; liberal arts and sciences and humanities related; liberal arts and sciences/liberal studies; library and information science; marketing/marketing management; mathematics; medical radiologic technology; music; music teacher education; occupational therapy; office management; parks, recreation and leisure; philosophy; physical education teaching and coaching; physical therapy; physical therapy technology; physics; pre-law studies; premedical studies; pre-pharmacy studies; pre-veterinary studies; psychology; registered nursing/registered nurse; religious studies; restaurant, culinary, and catering management; secondary education; social sciences; social work; sociology; special education; statistics; veterinary/animal health technology.

Academics *Calendar:* semesters. *Degrees:* certificates, diplomas, associate, and bachelor's. *Special study options:* academic remediation for entering students, adult/continuing education programs, advanced placement credit, cooperative education, distance learning, English as a second language, freshman honors college, honors programs, independent study, internships, part-time degree program, services for LD students, summer session for credit.

Library Clifford B. Stearns Learning Resources Center. *Books:* 75,935 (physical), 43,910 (digital/electronic); *Databases:* 152. Students can reserve study rooms.

Student Life *Housing:* college housing not available. *Activities and Organizations:* drama/theater group, student-run newspaper, choral group, Inspirational Choir, Model United Nations, Performing Arts, Phi Theta Kappa (PTK), Student Nurses Association. *Campus security:* 24-hour emergency response devices and patrols, student patrols, late-night transport/escort service. *Student services:* personal/psychological counseling.

Athletics Member NJCAA. *Intercollegiate sports:* baseball M(s), basketball M(s)/W(s), softball W(s), volleyball W(s). *Intramural sports:* bowling M/W.

Standardized Tests *Recommended:* SAT (for admission), ACT (for admission), SAT or ACT (for admission), SAT and SAT Subject Tests or ACT (for admission), SAT Subject Tests (for admission).

Costs (2015–16) *Tuition:* state resident $3213 full-time, $107 per credit hour part-time; nonresident $12,656 full-time, $422 per credit hour part-time. Full-time tuition and fees vary according to course level, degree level, program, and student level. Part-time tuition and fees vary according to course level, degree level, program, and student level. *Waivers:* employees or children of employees.

Applying *Options:* electronic application, early admission. *Application fee:* $30. *Required:* high school transcript. *Application deadlines:* rolling (freshmen), rolling (transfers). *Notification:* continuous (freshmen), continuous (transfers).

Freshman Application Contact Ms. Devona Sewell, Registrar, Admission and Records, College of Central Florida, 3001 SW College Road, Ocala, FL 34474. *Phone:* 352-237-2111 Ext. 1398. *Fax:* 352-873-5882.
E-mail: sewelld@cf.edu.
Website: http://www.cf.edu/.

Concorde Career Institute
Jacksonville, Florida

Admissions Office Contact Concorde Career Institute, 7259 Salisbury Road, Jacksonville, FL 32256.
Website: http://www.concorde.edu/.

Concorde Career Institute
Miramar, Florida

Admissions Office Contact Concorde Career Institute, 10933 Marks Way, Miramar, FL 33025.
Website: http://www.concorde.edu/.

Concorde Career Institute
Orlando, Florida

Admissions Office Contact Concorde Career Institute, 3444 McCrory Place, Orlando, FL 32803.
Website: http://www.concorde.edu/.

Concorde Career Institute
Tampa, Florida

Admissions Office Contact Concorde Career Institute, 4202 West Spruce Street, Tampa, FL 33607.
Website: http://www.concorde.edu/.

Daytona College
Ormond Beach, Florida

Admissions Office Contact Daytona College, 469 South Nova Road, Ormond Beach, FL 32174-8445.
Website: http://www.daytonacollege.edu/.

Daytona State College
Daytona Beach, Florida

- **State-supported** primarily 2-year, founded 1958, part of Florida Community College System
- **Suburban** 100-acre campus with easy access to Orlando
- **Endowment** $11.4 million
- **Coed,** 13,598 undergraduate students, 41% full-time, 61% women, 39% men

Undergraduates 5,544 full-time, 8,054 part-time. Students come from 8 other countries; 3% are from out of state; 13% Black or African American, non-Hispanic/Latino; 14% Hispanic/Latino; 2% Asian, non-Hispanic/Latino; 0.2% Native Hawaiian or other Pacific Islander, non-Hispanic/Latino; 0.4% American Indian or Alaska Native, non-Hispanic/Latino; 2% Two or more races, non-Hispanic/Latino; 2% Race/ethnicity unknown; 0.4% international; 5% transferred in.

Freshmen *Admission:* 4,328 applied, 1,856 admitted, 1,683 enrolled. *Test scores:* SAT critical reading scores over 500: 39%; SAT math scores over 500: 38%; SAT writing scores over 500: 25%; ACT scores over 18: 61%; SAT critical reading scores over 600: 11%; SAT math scores over 600: 6%; SAT writing scores over 600: 5%; ACT scores over 24: 11%; SAT critical reading scores over 700: 1%; SAT math scores over 700: 1%; SAT writing scores over 700: 1%; ACT scores over 30: 1%.

Faculty *Total:* 876, 34% full-time, 16% with terminal degrees. *Student/faculty ratio:* 17:1.

Majors Accounting; administrative assistant and secretarial science; architectural engineering technology; automobile/automotive mechanics technology; biology teacher education; business administration and management; child development; communications technology; computer and information sciences related; computer engineering; computer engineering related; computer graphics; computer/information technology services administration related; computer programming; computer programming (specific applications); computer science; computer systems networking and telecommunications; computer technology/computer systems technology; criminal justice/law enforcement administration; criminal justice/police science; culinary arts; dental hygiene; drafting and design technology; electrical, electronic and communications engineering technology; elementary education; emergency medical technology (EMT paramedic); engineering; fire science/firefighting; health information/medical records administration; hospitality administration; hotel/motel administration; human services; industrial radiologic technology; industrial technology; information technology; interior design; kindergarten/preschool education; legal assistant/paralegal; machine shop technology; mathematics teacher education; medical administrative assistant and medical secretary; occupational therapist assistant; photographic and film/video technology; physical therapy; plastics and polymer engineering technology; radio and television; registered nursing/registered nurse; respiratory care therapy; robotics technology; secondary education; special education–early childhood; tourism and travel services management.

Academics *Calendar:* semesters. *Degrees:* certificates, diplomas, associate, bachelor's, and postbachelor's certificates. *Special study options:* academic remediation for entering students, adult/continuing education programs, advanced placement credit, cooperative education, distance learning, double majors, English as a second language, external degree program, freshman honors college, honors programs, independent study, internships, off-campus study, part-time degree program, services for LD students, study abroad, summer session for credit. *ROTC:* Army (c), Air Force (c).

Library Mary Karl Memorial Learning Resources Center plus 1 other. *Books:* 65,000 (physical), 170,000 (digital/electronic); *Serial titles:* 250 (physical); *Databases:* 100. Weekly public service hours: 68; students can reserve study rooms.

Student Life *Housing:* college housing not available. *Activities and Organizations:* drama/theater group, student-run newspaper, choral group, Phi Theta Kappa International Honors Society, Student Government Association, Student Occupational Therapy Club, Massage Therapy Club, Student Paralegal Club, national fraternities, national sororities. *Campus security:* 24-hour emergency response devices and patrols, late-night transport/escort service. *Student services:* personal/psychological counseling, women's center.

Athletics Member NJCAA. *Intercollegiate sports:* baseball M(s), basketball M(s)/W(s), golf W(s), softball W(s), volleyball W(s). *Intramural sports:* basketball M/W, football M/W, soccer M/W, table tennis M/W, tennis M/W.

Costs (2015–16) *Tuition:* state resident $1901 full-time, $79 per credit hour part-time; nonresident $7621 full-time, $318 per credit hour part-time. Full-time tuition and fees vary according to course load and degree level. Part-time tuition and fees vary according to course load and degree level. *Required fees:* $543 full-time, $23 per credit hour part-time. *Payment plan:* installment.

Financial Aid Of all full-time matriculated undergraduates who enrolled in 2014, 3,802 applied for aid, 3,212 were judged to have need. 194 Federal Work-Study jobs (averaging $1978). 1 state and other part-time job (averaging $2500). *Average need-based gift aid:* $4312.

Applying *Options:* electronic application, early admission, deferred entrance. *Required:* high school transcript. *Application deadlines:* rolling (freshmen), rolling (transfers). *Notification:* continuous (freshmen), continuous (transfers).

Freshman Application Contact Dr. Karen Sanders, Director of Admissions and Recruitment, Daytona State College, 1200 International Speedway Boulevard, Daytona Beach, FL 32114. *Phone:* 386-506-3050.
E-mail: sanderk@daytonastate.edu.
Website: http://www.daytonastate.edu/.

Eastern Florida State College
Cocoa, Florida

Freshman Application Contact Ms. Stephanie Burnette, Registrar, Eastern Florida State College, 1519 Clearlake Road, Cocoa, FL 32922-6597. *Phone:* 321-433-7271. *Fax:* 321-433-7172.
E-mail: cocoaadmissions@brevardcc.edu.
Website: http://www.easternflorida.edu/.

Everest University
Orange Park, Florida

Freshman Application Contact Admissions Office, Everest University, 805 Wells Road, Orange Park, FL 32073. *Phone:* 904-264-9122.
Website: http://www.everest.edu/.

Florida Career College
Miami, Florida

Director of Admissions Mr. David Knobel, President, Florida Career College, 1321 Southwest 107 Avenue, Suite 201B, Miami, FL 33174. *Phone:* 305-553-6065. *Toll-free phone:* 888-852-7272.
Website: http://www.careercollege.edu/.

Florida College of Natural Health
Maitland, Florida

Freshman Application Contact Admissions Office, Florida College of Natural Health, 2600 Lake Lucien Drive, Suite 140, Maitland, FL 32751. *Phone:* 407-261-0319. *Toll-free phone:* 800-393-7337.
Website: http://www.fcnh.com/.

Florida College of Natural Health
Miami, Florida

Director of Admissions Admissions Coordinator, Florida College of Natural Health, 7925 Northwest 12th Street, Suite 201, Miami, FL 33126. *Phone:* 305-597-9599. *Toll-free phone:* 800-599-9599. *Fax:* 305-597-9110.
Website: http://www.fcnh.com/.

Florida College of Natural Health
Pompano Beach, Florida

Freshman Application Contact Admissions Office, Florida College of Natural Health, 2001 West Sample Road, Suite 100, Pompano Beach, FL 33064. *Phone:* 954-975-6400. *Toll-free phone:* 800-541-9299.
Website: http://www.fcnh.com/.

Florida Gateway College
Lake City, Florida

- **State-supported** primarily 2-year, founded 1962, part of Florida Community College System
- **Small-town** 132-acre campus with easy access to Jacksonville
- **Coed**

Undergraduates 831 full-time, 2,081 part-time. Students come from 2 states and territories; 11% Black or African American, non-Hispanic/Latino; 5% Hispanic/Latino; 1% Asian, non-Hispanic/Latino; 0.4% American Indian or Alaska Native, non-Hispanic/Latino; 0.7% Two or more races, non-Hispanic/Latino; 0.9% Race/ethnicity unknown; 0.1% international; 3% transferred in.
Faculty *Student/faculty ratio:* 14:1.
Academics *Calendar:* semesters. *Degrees:* certificates, diplomas, associate, bachelor's, and postbachelor's certificates. *Special study options:* academic remediation for entering students, accelerated degree program, adult/continuing education programs, advanced placement credit, cooperative education, distance learning, English as a second language, honors programs, independent study, off-campus study, part-time degree program, services for LD students, summer session for credit.
Library Wilson S. Rivers Library and Media Center.
Student Life *Campus security:* 24-hour emergency response devices and patrols.
Costs (2015–16) *Tuition:* state resident $2368 full-time, $103 per credit hour part-time; nonresident $11,747 full-time, $392 per credit hour part-time. Full-time tuition and fees vary according to course level, course load, degree level, program, reciprocity agreements, and student level. Part-time tuition and fees vary according to course level, course load, degree level, program, reciprocity agreements, and student level. *Required fees:* $731 full-time. *Payment plans:* installment, deferred payment.
Applying *Options:* electronic application. *Required for some:* high school transcript.
Freshman Application Contact Admissions, Florida Gateway College, 149 SE College Place, Lake City, FL 32025-8703. *Phone:* 386-755-4236.
E-mail: admissions@fgc.edu.
Website: http://www.fgc.edu/.

Florida Keys Community College
Key West, Florida

Director of Admissions Ms. Cheryl A. Malsheimer, Director of Admissions and Records, Florida Keys Community College, 5901 College Road, Key West, FL 33040-4397. *Phone:* 305-296-9081 Ext. 201.
Website: http://www.fkcc.edu/.

The Florida School of Traditional Midwifery
Gainseville, Florida

Freshman Application Contact Admissions Office, The Florida School of Traditional Midwifery, 810 East University Avenue, 2nd Floor, Gainesville, FL 32601. *Phone:* 352-338-0766. *Fax:* 352-338-2013.
E-mail: info@midwiferyschool.org.
Website: http://www.midwiferyschool.org/.

Florida SouthWestern State College
Fort Myers, Florida

- **State and locally supported** primarily 2-year, founded 1962, part of Florida College System
- **Urban** 413-acre campus
- **Endowment** $731,365
- **Coed,** 15,742 undergraduate students, 34% full-time, 61% women, 39% men

Undergraduates 5,389 full-time, 10,353 part-time. Students come from 42 states and territories; 20 other countries; 2% are from out of state; 11% Black or African American, non-Hispanic/Latino; 27% Hispanic/Latino; 2% Asian, non-Hispanic/Latino; 0.2% Native Hawaiian or other Pacific Islander, non-Hispanic/Latino; 0.3% American Indian or Alaska Native, non-Hispanic/Latino; 2% Two or more races, non-Hispanic/Latino; 5% Race/ethnicity unknown; 2% international; 3% transferred in; 2% live on campus. *Retention:* 65% of full-time freshmen returned.
Freshmen *Admission:* 5,525 applied, 4,500 admitted, 2,979 enrolled. *Average high school GPA:* 2.95. *Test scores:* SAT critical reading scores over 500: 38%; SAT math scores over 500: 32%; SAT critical reading scores over 600: 8%; SAT math scores over 600: 4%.
Faculty *Total:* 601, 30% full-time, 36% with terminal degrees. *Student/faculty ratio:* 27:1.
Majors Accounting technology and bookkeeping; architectural technology; biology/biotechnology laboratory technician; biology teacher education; business administration and management; business administration, management and operations related; cardiovascular technology; child-care provision; civil engineering technology; community health services counseling; computer programming; computer systems networking and telecommunications; criminal justice/law enforcement administration; dental hygiene; drafting and design technology; early childhood education; elementary education; emergency medical technology (EMT paramedic); English/language arts teacher education; fire prevention and safety technology; forensic science and technology; health information/medical records technology; homeland security, law enforcement, firefighting and protective services related; information technology; legal assistant/paralegal; liberal arts and sciences/liberal studies; management information systems; mathematics teacher education; medical radiologic technology; network and system administration; operations management; opticianry; physical therapy technology; registered nursing/registered nurse; respiratory care therapy; respiratory therapy technician; science teacher education; substance abuse/addiction counseling; turf and turfgrass management; web page, digital/multimedia and information resources design.
Academics *Calendar:* semesters. *Degrees:* certificates, associate, and bachelor's. *Special study options:* academic remediation for entering students, accelerated degree program, advanced placement credit, cooperative education, distance learning, double majors, English as a second language, honors programs, independent study, internships, off-campus study, part-time degree program, services for LD students, study abroad, summer session for credit.

Library Richard H. Rush Library. *Books:* 43,740 (physical), 163,580 (digital/electronic); *Databases:* 172. Weekly public service hours: 79.
Student Life *Housing Options:* coed. Campus housing is university owned. *Activities and Organizations:* drama/theater group, choral group. *Campus security:* 24-hour emergency response devices and patrols, late-night transport/escort service, controlled dormitory access, Rave Guardian app for students, faculty, and staff.
Athletics Member NJCAA. *Intercollegiate sports:* baseball M, softball W. *Intramural sports:* basketball M/W, soccer M/W, volleyball M/W.
Costs (2015–16) *Tuition:* state resident $2436 full-time, $81 per credit hour part-time; nonresident $9750 full-time, $325 per credit hour part-time. Full-time tuition and fees vary according to degree level. Part-time tuition and fees vary according to degree level. *Required fees:* $965 full-time, $32 per credit hour part-time. *Room and board:* $9000; room only: $6000. *Payment plan:* installment. *Waivers:* employees or children of employees.
Financial Aid Of all full-time matriculated undergraduates who enrolled in 2014, 3,887 applied for aid, 3,311 were judged to have need, 68 had their need fully met. In 2014, 166 non-need-based awards were made. *Average percent of need met:* 47%. *Average financial aid package:* $6172. *Average need-based loan:* $3461. *Average need-based gift aid:* $5119. *Average non-need-based aid:* $2588.
Applying *Options:* electronic application, early admission, deferred entrance. *Application fee:* $30. *Required:* high school transcript. *Application deadlines:* 8/17 (freshmen), 8/17 (transfers). *Notification:* continuous (freshmen), continuous (transfers).
Freshman Application Contact FSW Admissions, Florida SouthWestern State College, 8099 College Parkway, Fort Myers, FL 33919. *Phone:* 239-489-9054. *Fax:* 239-489-9094. *E-mail:* admissions@fsw.edu.
Website: http://www.fsw.edu/.

Florida State College at Jacksonville
Jacksonville, Florida

- **State-supported** primarily 2-year, founded 1963, part of Florida College System
- **Urban** 844-acre campus
- **Endowment** $44.6 million
- **Coed**

Undergraduates 7,819 full-time, 17,695 part-time. 25% Black or African American, non-Hispanic/Latino; 7% Hispanic/Latino; 4% Asian, non-Hispanic/Latino; 0.5% Native Hawaiian or other Pacific Islander, non-Hispanic/Latino; 0.3% American Indian or Alaska Native, non-Hispanic/Latino; 2% Two or more races, non-Hispanic/Latino; 12% Race/ethnicity unknown; 0.8% international; 6% transferred in.
Faculty *Student/faculty ratio:* 21:1.
Academics *Calendar:* semesters. *Degrees:* certificates, diplomas, associate, and bachelor's. *Special study options:* academic remediation for entering students, accelerated degree program, adult/continuing education programs, advanced placement credit, cooperative education, distance learning, double majors, English as a second language, honors programs, independent study, internships, off-campus study, part-time degree program, services for LD students, study abroad, summer session for credit. *ROTC:* Navy (c).
Library Florida State College at Jacksonville Library and Learning Commons plus 7 others.
Student Life *Campus security:* 24-hour emergency response devices and patrols, late-night transport/escort service.
Athletics Member NJCAA.
Costs (2015–16) *Tuition:* state resident $2518 full-time, $105 per credit hour part-time; nonresident $9632 full-time, $402 per credit hour part-time. Full-time tuition and fees vary according to degree level and program. Part-time tuition and fees vary according to degree level and program. *Required fees:* $360 full-time.
Applying *Options:* electronic application, early admission, deferred entrance. *Application fee:* $25. *Required for some:* high school transcript.
Freshman Application Contact Dr. Peter Biegel, Registrar, Florida State College at Jacksonville, 501 West State Street, Jacksonville, FL 32202. *Phone:* 904-632-5112. *Toll-free phone:* 888-873-1145. *E-mail:* pbiegel@fscj.edu.
Website: http://www.fscj.edu/.

Florida Technical College
DeLand, Florida

Freshman Application Contact Mr. Bill Atkinson, Director, Florida Technical College, 1199 South Woodland Boulevard, 3rd Floor, DeLand, FL 32720. *Phone:* 386-734-3303. *Fax:* 386-734-5150.
Website: http://www.ftccollege.edu/.

Florida Technical College
Orlando, Florida

Director of Admissions Ms. Jeanette E. Muschlitz, Director of Admissions, Florida Technical College, 12900 Challenger Parkway, Orlando, FL 32826. *Phone:* 407-678-5600. *Toll-free phone:* 888-574-2082.
Website: http://www.ftccollege.edu/.

Fortis College
Cutler Bay, Florida

Admissions Office Contact Fortis College, 19600 South Dixie Highway, Suite B, Cutler Bay, FL 33157. *Toll-free phone:* 855-4-FORTIS.
Website: http://www.fortis.edu/.

Fortis College
Largo, Florida

Admissions Office Contact Fortis College, 6565 Ulmerton Road, Largo, FL 33771. *Toll-free phone:* 855-4-FORTIS.
Website: http://www.fortis.edu/.

Fortis College
Orange Park, Florida

Admissions Office Contact Fortis College, 700 Blanding Boulevard, Suite 16, Orange Park, FL 32065. *Toll-free phone:* 855-4-FORTIS.
Website: http://www.fortis.edu/.

Fortis College
Winter Park, Florida

Freshman Application Contact Admissions Office, Fortis College, 1573 West Fairbanks Avenue, Suite 100, Winter Park, FL 32789. *Phone:* 407-843-3984. *Toll-free phone:* 855-4-FORTIS. *Fax:* 407-843-9828.
Website: http://www.fortis.edu/.

Fortis Institute
Fort Lauderdale, Florida

Admissions Office Contact Fortis Institute, 4850 W. Oakland Park Boulevard, Suite 200, Fort Lauderdale, FL 33313. *Toll-free phone:* 855-4-FORTIS.
Website: http://www.fortis.edu/.

Fortis Institute
Palm Springs, Florida

Director of Admissions Campus Director, Fortis Institute, 1630 South Congress Avenue, Palm Springs, FL 33461. *Phone:* 561-304-3466. *Toll-free phone:* 855-4-FORTIS. *Fax:* 561-304-3471.
Website: http://www.fortis.edu/.

Fortis Institute
Pensacola, Florida

Admissions Office Contact Fortis Institute, 4081 East Olive Road, Suite B, Pensacola, FL 32514. *Toll-free phone:* 855-4-FORTIS.
Website: http://www.fortis.edu/.

Fortis Institute
Port St. Lucie, Florida

Admissions Office Contact Fortis Institute, 9022 South US Highway 1, Port St. Lucie, FL 34952. *Toll-free phone:* 855-4-FORTIS.
Website: http://www.fortis.edu/.

Golf Academy of America
Apopka, Florida

Admissions Office Contact Golf Academy of America, 510 South Hunt Club Boulevard, Apopka, FL 32703.
Website: http://www.golfacademy.edu/.

Gulf Coast State College
Panama City, Florida

- **State-supported** primarily 2-year, founded 1957, part of Florida College System
- **Urban** 80-acre campus
- **Endowment** $30.5 million
- **Coed,** 5,858 undergraduate students, 38% full-time, 62% women, 38% men

Undergraduates 2,216 full-time, 3,642 part-time. Students come from 13 states and territories; 4% are from out of state; 12% Black or African American, non-Hispanic/Latino; 6% Hispanic/Latino; 3% Asian, non-Hispanic/Latino; 0.8% American Indian or Alaska Native, non-Hispanic/Latino; 4% Two or more races, non-Hispanic/Latino; 3% Race/ethnicity unknown; 0.2% international; 3% transferred in.
Freshmen *Admission:* 878 enrolled.
Faculty *Total:* 293, 37% full-time. *Student/faculty ratio:* 19:1.
Majors Accounting technology and bookkeeping; animation, interactive technology, video graphics and special effects; automation engineer technology; business administration and management; business administration, management and operations related; CAD/CADD drafting/design technology; child-care provision; civil engineering technology; communications technology; computer/information technology services administration related; computer programming; computer programming (vendor/product certification); computer systems networking and telecommunications; construction engineering technology; criminal justice/law enforcement administration; dental hygiene; diagnostic medical sonography and ultrasound technology; digital arts; digital communication and media/multimedia; early childhood education; electrical, electronic and communications engineering technology; emergency medical technology (EMT paramedic); engineering technology; fire prevention and safety technology; forensic science and technology; health services/allied health/health sciences; hospitality administration; liberal arts and sciences/liberal studies; management information systems; manufacturing engineering technology; medical administrative assistant and medical secretary; medical radiologic technology; music technology; network and system administration; nuclear medical technology; office management; physical therapy technology; registered nursing/registered nurse; respiratory care therapy; restaurant, culinary, and catering management; surgical technology; transportation/mobility management; web page, digital/multimedia and information resources design.
Academics *Calendar:* semesters. *Degrees:* certificates, associate, and bachelor's. *Special study options:* academic remediation for entering students, accelerated degree program, adult/continuing education programs, advanced placement credit, cooperative education, distance learning, double majors, English as a second language, external degree program, honors programs, independent study, off-campus study, part-time degree program, services for LD students, summer session for credit.
Library Gulf Coast State College Library. *Books:* 51,515 (physical), 48,473 (digital/electronic); *Serial titles:* 12,778 (physical), 31,595 (digital/electronic); *Databases:* 152.
Student Life *Housing:* college housing not available. *Activities and Organizations:* drama/theater group, student-run newspaper, television station, choral group. *Campus security:* 24-hour patrols, late-night transport/escort service, patrols by trained security personnel during campus hours. *Student services:* personal/psychological counseling.
Athletics Member NJCAA. *Intercollegiate sports:* baseball M(s), basketball M(s)/W(s), softball W(s), volleyball W(s).
Costs (2016–17) *Tuition:* state resident $2370 full-time, $99 per credit hour part-time; nonresident $8635 full-time, $360 per credit hour part-time. Full-time tuition and fees vary according to degree level. Part-time tuition and fees vary according to degree level. *Required fees:* $620 full-time, $26 per credit hour part-time.
Financial Aid Of all full-time matriculated undergraduates who enrolled in 2014, 145 Federal Work-Study jobs (averaging $3200). 60 state and other part-time jobs (averaging $2600).
Applying *Options:* electronic application, early admission, deferred entrance. *Application fee:* $20. *Required:* high school transcript. *Application deadlines:* rolling (freshmen), rolling (transfers). *Notification:* continuous (freshmen).
Freshman Application Contact Mrs. Donna Newell, Application Process Specialist, Gulf Coast State College, 5230 West U.S. Highway 98, Panama City, FL 32401. *Phone:* 850-769-1551 Ext. 2936. *Fax:* 850-913-3308. *E-mail:* dnewell@gulfcoast.edu. *Website:* http://www.gulfcoast.edu/.

Heritage Institute
Fort Myers, Florida

Admissions Office Contact Heritage Institute, 6630 Orion Drive, Fort Myers, FL 33912.
Website: http://www.heritage-education.com/.

Heritage Institute
Jacksonville, Florida

Admissions Office Contact Heritage Institute, 4130 Salisbury Road, Suite 1100, Jacksonville, FL 32216.
Website: http://www.heritage-education.com/.

Hillsborough Community College
Tampa, Florida

- **State-supported** 2-year, founded 1968, part of Florida College System
- **Urban** campus with easy access to Tampa, Clearwater, St. Petersburg
- **Coed,** 26,571 undergraduate students, 40% full-time, 57% women, 43% men

Undergraduates 10,566 full-time, 16,005 part-time. Students come from 38 states and territories; 135 other countries; 0.8% are from out of state; 17% Black or African American, non-Hispanic/Latino; 26% Hispanic/Latino; 3% Asian, non-Hispanic/Latino; 0.2% Native Hawaiian or other Pacific Islander, non-Hispanic/Latino; 0.5% American Indian or Alaska Native, non-Hispanic/Latino; 3% Two or more races, non-Hispanic/Latino; 11% Race/ethnicity unknown; 3% international; 27% transferred in.
Freshmen *Admission:* 4,781 enrolled.
Faculty *Total:* 1,452, 21% full-time, 15% with terminal degrees. *Student/faculty ratio:* 23:1.
Majors Accounting technology and bookkeeping; aquaculture; architectural engineering technology; biology/biotechnology laboratory technician; business administration and management; child-care and support services management; cinematography and film/video production; computer programming (specific applications); computer systems analysis; computer technology/computer systems technology; criminal justice/law enforcement administration; dental hygiene; diagnostic medical sonography and ultrasound technology; dietitian assistant; electrical, electronic and communications engineering technology; emergency medical technology (EMT paramedic); engineering technology; environmental control technologies related; executive assistant/executive secretary; fire prevention and safety technology; hospitality administration; legal assistant/paralegal; liberal arts and sciences/liberal studies; management information systems and services related; medical radiologic technology; nuclear medical technology; operations management; opticianry; optometric technician; psychiatric/mental health services technology; registered nursing/registered nurse; respiratory care therapy; restaurant, culinary, and catering management; restaurant/food services management; special education–individuals with hearing impairments; veterinary/animal health technology.
Academics *Calendar:* semesters. *Degree:* certificates and associate. *Special study options:* academic remediation for entering students, advanced placement credit, cooperative education, distance learning, English as a second language, honors programs, independent study, internships, off-campus study, part-time degree program, services for LD students, study abroad, summer session for credit. *ROTC:* Army (c), Air Force (c).
Library Dale Mabry Library plus 5 others. *Books:* 123,613 (physical), 54,967 (digital/electronic); *Databases:* 103.
Student Life *Housing Options:* Campus housing is provided by a third party. *Activities and Organizations:* drama/theater group, student-run newspaper, radio station, choral group. *Campus security:* 24-hour emergency response devices and patrols, late-night transport/escort service. *Student services:* personal/psychological counseling.
Athletics Member NJCAA. *Intercollegiate sports:* baseball M(s), basketball M(s)/W(s), softball W(s), tennis W(s), volleyball W(s).
Standardized Tests *Required:* PERT, CPT, FCLEPT, ACT or SAT for degree-seeking students (for admission).
Costs (2015–16) *Tuition:* state resident $2505 full-time, $104 per credit hour part-time; nonresident $9111 full-time, $380 per credit hour part-time. *Payment plan:* installment. *Waivers:* employees or children of employees.
Applying *Options:* electronic application, early admission. *Required:* high school transcript. *Application deadlines:* rolling (freshmen), rolling (out-of-state freshmen), rolling (transfers).
Freshman Application Contact Ms. Jennifer Young, College Registrar, Hillsborough Community College, PO Box 31127, Tampa, FL 33631-3127. *Phone:* 813-259-6565. *E-mail:* jyoung92@hccfl.edu. *Website:* http://www.hccfl.edu/.

ITT Technical Institute
Fort Lauderdale, Florida

Freshman Application Contact Director of Recruitment, ITT Technical Institute, 3401 South University Drive, Fort Lauderdale, FL 33328. *Phone:* 954-476-9300. *Toll-free phone:* 800-488-7797. *Website:* http://www.itt-tech.edu/.

ITT Technical Institute
Fort Myers, Florida

Freshman Application Contact Director of Recruitment, ITT Technical Institute, 13500 Powers Court, Suite 100, Fort Myers, FL 33912. *Phone:* 239-603-8700. *Toll-free phone:* 877-485-5313.
Website: http://www.itt-tech.edu/.

ITT Technical Institute
Hialeah, Florida

Freshman Application Contact Director of Recruitment, ITT Technical Institute, 5901 NW 183rd Street, Suite 100, Hialeah, FL 33015. *Phone:* 305-477-3080. *Toll-free phone:* 877-216-8352.
Website: http://www.itt-tech.edu/.

ITT Technical Institute
Jacksonville, Florida

Freshman Application Contact Director of Recruitment, ITT Technical Institute, 7011 A.C. Skinner Parkway, Suite 140, Jacksonville, FL 32256. *Phone:* 904-573-9100. *Toll-free phone:* 800-318-1264.
Website: http://www.itt-tech.edu/.

ITT Technical Institute
Lake Mary, Florida

Freshman Application Contact Director of Recruitment, ITT Technical Institute, 1400 South International Parkway, Lake Mary, FL 32746. *Phone:* 407-936-0600. *Toll-free phone:* 866-489-8441.
Website: http://www.itt-tech.edu/.

ITT Technical Institute
Pensacola, Florida

Freshman Application Contact Director of Recruiting, ITT Technical Institute, 6913 North 9th Avenue, Pensacola, FL 32504. *Phone:* 850-483-5700. *Toll-free phone:* 877-290-8248.
Website: http://www.itt-tech.edu/.

ITT Technical Institute
Tallahassee, Florida

Freshman Application Contact Director of Recruitment, ITT Technical Institute, 2639 North Monroe Street, Building A, Suite 100, Tallahassee, FL 32303. *Phone:* 850-422-6300. *Toll-free phone:* 877-230-3359.
Website: http://www.itt-tech.edu/.

ITT Technical Institute
Tampa, Florida

Freshman Application Contact Director of Recruitment, ITT Technical Institute, 4809 Memorial Highway, Tampa, FL 33634-7350. *Phone:* 813-885-2244. *Toll-free phone:* 800-825-2831.
Website: http://www.itt-tech.edu/.

Key College
Dania Beach, Florida

Director of Admissions Mr. Ronald H. Dooley, President and Director of Admissions, Key College, 225 East Dania Beach Boulevard, Dania Beach, FL 33004. *Phone:* 954-581-2223 Ext. 23. *Toll-free phone:* 877-421-6149.
Website: http://www.keycollege.edu/.

Lake-Sumter State College
Leesburg, Florida

Freshman Application Contact Ms. Bonnie Yanick, Enrollment Specialist, Lake-Sumter State College, 9501 U.S. Highway 441, Leesburg, FL 34788-8751. *Phone:* 352-365-3561. *Fax:* 352-365-3553. *E-mail:* admissinquiry@lscc.edu.
Website: http://www.lssc.edu/.

Lincoln College of Technology
West Palm Beach, Florida

Director of Admissions Mr. Kevin Cassidy, Director of Admissions, Lincoln College of Technology, 2410 Metrocentre Boulevard, West Palm Beach, FL 33407. *Phone:* 561-842-8324 Ext. 117. *Fax:* 561-842-9503.
Website: http://www.lincolnedu.com/.

Lincoln Technical Institute
Fern Park, Florida

Admissions Office Contact Lincoln Technical Institute, 7275 Estapona Circle, Fern Park, FL 32730.
Website: http://www.lincolnedu.com/.

Management Resources College
Miami, Florida

Admissions Office Contact Management Resources College, 10 NW LeJeune Road, Miami, FL 33126.
Website: http://www.mrc.edu/.

Medtech College
Orlando, Florida

Admissions Office Contact Medtech College, 1900 N. Alafaya Trail, Orlando, FL 32826-4906.
Website: http://www.medtech.edu.

Meridian College
Sarasota, Florida

Admissions Office Contact Meridian College, 7020 Professional Parkway East, Sarasota, FL 34240.
Website: http://www.meridian.edu/.

★ Miami Dade College
Miami, Florida

- **State and locally supported** primarily 2-year, founded 1960, part of Florida College System
- **Urban** campus
- **Endowment** $182.3 million
- **Coed,** 62,332 undergraduate students, 40% full-time, 58% women, 42% men

Undergraduates 24,716 full-time, 37,616 part-time. Students come from 43 states and territories; 178 other countries; 0.4% are from out of state; 15% Black or African American, non-Hispanic/Latino; 69% Hispanic/Latino; 1% Asian, non-Hispanic/Latino; 0.1% American Indian or Alaska Native, non-Hispanic/Latino; 0.4% Two or more races, non-Hispanic/Latino; 3% Race/ethnicity unknown; 6% international; 2% transferred in.
Freshmen *Admission:* 22,005 applied, 22,005 admitted, 11,807 enrolled.
Faculty *Total:* 2,608, 28% full-time, 23% with terminal degrees. *Student/faculty ratio:* 27:1.
Majors Accounting technology and bookkeeping; administrative assistant and secretarial science; aeronautics/aviation/aerospace science and technology; agriculture; airline pilot and flight crew; air traffic control; American studies; anthropology; architectural drafting and CAD/CADD; architectural engineering technology; architectural technology; art; Asian studies; audiology and speech-language pathology; automation engineer technology; aviation/airway management; banking and financial support services; behavioral sciences; biology/biological sciences; biology teacher education; biomedical technology; biotechnology; business administration and management; business administration, management and operations related; business automation/technology/data entry; CAD/CADD drafting/design technology; chemistry; chemistry teacher education; child-care provision; child development; cinematography and film/video production; civil engineering technology; clinical/medical laboratory technology; commercial and advertising art; community health services counseling; comparative literature; computer engineering technology; computer graphics; computer installation and repair technology; computer programming; computer programming (specific applications); computer programming (vendor/product certification); computer science; computer software technology; computer support specialist; computer systems networking and telecommunications; computer technology/computer systems technology; construction engineering technology; cooking and related culinary arts; corrections; corrections and criminal justice related; court reporting; criminal justice/law enforcement administration; criminal justice/police science; culinary arts; customer service

support/call center/teleservice operation; dance; dental hygiene; diagnostic medical sonography and ultrasound technology; dietetics; dietetic technology; drafting and design technology; dramatic/theater arts; early childhood education; economics; education; education related; education (specific levels and methods) related; electrical and electronic engineering technologies related; electrical, electronic and communications engineering technology; electrician; elementary education; emergency medical technology (EMT paramedic); engineering; engineering related; engineering technology; English; entrepreneurship; environmental engineering technology; environmental science; finance; fire prevention and safety technology; fire science/firefighting; food science; forensic science and technology; forestry; French; funeral service and mortuary science; general studies; geology/earth science; German; health information/medical records administration; health information/medical records technology; health/medical preparatory programs related; health professions related; health services/allied health/health sciences; heating, air conditioning, ventilation and refrigeration maintenance technology; heating, ventilation, air conditioning and refrigeration engineering technology; histologic technician; histologic technology/histotechnologist; history; homeland security, law enforcement, firefighting and protective services related; horticultural science; hospitality administration; hotel/motel administration; humanities; human services; industrial technology; information science/studies; information technology; interior design; international relations and affairs; Italian; journalism; kindergarten/preschool education; landscaping and groundskeeping; Latin American studies; legal administrative assistant/secretary; legal assistant/paralegal; liberal arts and sciences/liberal studies; logistics, materials, and supply chain management; management information systems; manufacturing engineering technology; marketing/marketing management; massage therapy; mass communication/media; mathematics; mathematics teacher education; medical/clinical assistant; medical radiologic technology; middle school education; music; music performance; music teacher education; music technology; natural sciences; network and system administration; nonprofit management; nuclear medical technology; office management; operations management; ophthalmic technology; opticianry; ornamental horticulture; parks, recreation and leisure; pharmacy technician; philosophy; phlebotomy technology; photographic and film/video technology; photography; physical education teaching and coaching; physical sciences; physical therapy technology; physician assistant; physics; physics teacher education; pipefitting and sprinkler fitting; plant nursery management; plumbing technology; political science and government; Portuguese; pre-engineering; psychology; public administration; radio and television; radio and television broadcasting technology; radiologic technology/science; real estate; recording arts technology; registered nursing/registered nurse; respiratory care therapy; respiratory therapy technician; restaurant, culinary, and catering management; restaurant/food services management; science teacher education; security and loss prevention; sheet metal technology; sign language interpretation and translation; social sciences; social work; sociology; Spanish; special education; special education–individuals with hearing impairments; substance abuse/addiction counseling; teacher assistant/aide; telecommunications technology; theater design and technology; tourism and travel services management; veterinary/animal health technology; web page, digital/multimedia and information resources design.

Academics *Calendar:* 16-16-6-6. *Degrees:* certificates, associate, bachelor's, and postbachelor's certificates. *Special study options:* academic remediation for entering students, accelerated degree program, adult/continuing education programs, advanced placement credit, cooperative education, distance learning, English as a second language, freshman honors college, honors programs, independent study, internships, off-campus study, part-time degree program, services for LD students, study abroad, summer session for credit. *ROTC:* Army (b), Air Force (b).

Library Miami Dade College Learning Resources plus 9 others. *Books:* 289,116 (physical), 61,305 (digital/electronic); *Serial titles:* 128 (physical), 357 (digital/electronic); *Databases:* 125. Weekly public service hours: 69; students can reserve study rooms.

Student Life *Housing:* college housing not available. *Activities and Organizations:* drama/theater group, student-run newspaper, radio and television station, choral group, Student Government Association, Phi Theta Kappa, Phi Beta Lambda (business), Future Educators of America Professional, Kappa Delta Pi Honor Society (education), national fraternities. *Campus security:* 24-hour emergency response devices and patrols, late-night transport/escort service, Emergency Mass Notification System (EMNS), campus sirens and public address systems, In Case of Crisis smart phone application. *Student services:* health clinic, personal/psychological counseling.

Athletics Member NCAA, NJCAA. All NCAA Division I. *Intercollegiate sports:* baseball M(s), basketball M(s)/W(s), softball W(s), volleyball W(s).

Costs (2015–16) *One-time required fee:* $30. *Tuition:* state resident $1987 full-time, $83 per credit hour part-time; nonresident $7947 full-time, $331 per credit hour part-time. Full-time tuition and fees vary according to course load, degree level, and program. Part-time tuition and fees vary according to course load, degree level, and program. *Required fees:* $851 full-time, $35 per credit hour part-time. *Waivers:* employees or children of employees.

Financial Aid Of all full-time matriculated undergraduates who enrolled in 2014, 800 Federal Work-Study jobs (averaging $5000). 125 state and other part-time jobs (averaging $5000).

Applying *Options:* electronic application, early admission. *Application fee:* $30. *Required:* high school transcript. *Application deadlines:* rolling (freshmen), rolling (out-of-state freshmen), rolling (transfers). *Notification:* continuous (freshmen), continuous (out-of-state freshmen), continuous (transfers).

Freshman Application Contact Ms. Ferne Creary, Interim College Registrar, Miami Dade College, 11011 SW 104th Street, Miami, FL 33176. *Phone:* 305-237-2206. *Fax:* 305-237-2532. *E-mail:* fcreary@mdc.edu. *Website:* http://www.mdc.edu/.

See previous page for display ad and page 370 for the College Close-Up.

North Florida Community College
Madison, Florida

Freshman Application Contact Mr. Bobby Scott, North Florida Community College, 325 Northwest Turner Davis Drive, Madison, FL 32340. *Phone:* 850-973-9450. *Toll-free phone:* 866-937-6322. *Fax:* 850-973-1697. *Website:* http://www.nfcc.edu/.

Northwest Florida State College
Niceville, Florida

Freshman Application Contact Ms. Karen Cooper, Director of Admissions, Northwest Florida State College, 100 College Boulevard, Niceville, FL 32578. *Phone:* 850-729-4901. *Fax:* 850-729-5206. *E-mail:* cooperk@nwfsc.edu. *Website:* http://www.nwfsc.edu/.

Orion College
Plantation, Florida

Admissions Office Contact Orion College, 51 North State Road 7, Plantation, FL 33317. *Toll-free phone:* 888-331-9957. *Website:* http://www.orioncollege.org/.

Pasco-Hernando State College
New Port Richey, Florida

- **State-supported** primarily 2-year, founded 1972, part of Florida College System
- **Suburban** 142-acre campus with easy access to Tampa
- **Coed**

Undergraduates 4,004 full-time, 6,202 part-time. Students come from 50 states and territories; 7 other countries; 2% are from out of state; 4% Black or African American, non-Hispanic/Latino; 14% Hispanic/Latino; 2% Asian, non-Hispanic/Latino; 0.2% Native Hawaiian or other Pacific Islander, non-Hispanic/Latino; 0.4% American Indian or Alaska Native, non-Hispanic/Latino; 3% Two or more races, non-Hispanic/Latino; 2% Race/ethnicity unknown; 0.2% international. *Retention:* 53% of full-time freshmen returned.

Faculty *Student/faculty ratio:* 26:1.

Academics *Calendar:* semesters. *Degrees:* certificates, diplomas, associate, and bachelor's. *Special study options:* academic remediation for entering students, accelerated degree program, adult/continuing education programs, advanced placement credit, cooperative education, distance learning, double majors, honors programs, independent study, internships, off-campus study, part-time degree program, services for LD students, summer session for credit. *ROTC:* Army (c).

Library Alric Pottberg Library plus 1 other.

Student Life *Campus security:* Security Personnel while college classes are being held.

Athletics Member NJCAA.

Standardized Tests *Recommended:* SAT and SAT Subject Tests or ACT (for admission), PERT.

Financial Aid Of all full-time matriculated undergraduates who enrolled in 2014, 83 Federal Work-Study jobs (averaging $3201).

Applying *Options:* electronic application. *Application fee:* $25. *Required:* high school transcript.

Freshman Application Contact Ms. Estela Carrion, Director of Admissions and Student Records, Pasco-Hernando State College, 10230 Ridge Road, New Port Richey, FL 34654-5199. *Phone:* 727-816-3261. *Toll-free phone:* 877-TRY-PHSC. *Fax:* 727-816-3389. *E-mail:* carrioe@phsc.edu. *Website:* http://www.phsc.edu/.

Pensacola State College
Pensacola, Florida

- **State-supported** primarily 2-year, founded 1948, part of Florida College System
- **Urban** 130-acre campus
- **Coed,** 9,840 undergraduate students, 37% full-time, 60% women, 40% men

Undergraduates 3,592 full-time, 6,248 part-time. Students come from 16 states and territories; 1% are from out of state; 14% Black or African American, non-Hispanic/Latino; 6% Hispanic/Latino; 3% Asian, non-Hispanic/Latino; 0.3% Native Hawaiian or other Pacific Islander, non-Hispanic/Latino; 0.8% American Indian or Alaska Native, non-Hispanic/Latino; 5% Two or more races, non-Hispanic/Latino; 2% Race/ethnicity unknown; 0.4% international; 2% transferred in.

Freshmen *Admission:* 1,489 enrolled.

Faculty *Total:* 599, 30% full-time, 6% with terminal degrees. *Student/faculty ratio:* 21:1.

Majors Accounting; accounting technology and bookkeeping; administrative assistant and secretarial science; agricultural business and management; agriculture; art; art teacher education; biochemistry; biology/biological sciences; botany/plant biology; building/property maintenance; business administration and management; business administration, management and operations related; business/commerce; chemical technology; chemistry; child-care and support services management; child-care provision; civil engineering technology; commercial and advertising art; communications technology; computer and information sciences; computer and information sciences related; computer and information systems security; computer engineering; computer programming; computer programming (specific applications); computer programming (vendor/product certification); computer science; computer systems analysis; construction engineering technology; consumer services and advocacy; cooking and related culinary arts; criminal justice/law enforcement administration; cyber/computer forensics and counterterrorism; dental hygiene; diagnostic medical sonography and ultrasound technology; dietetics; drafting and design technology; dramatic/theater arts; early childhood education; education; electrical, electronic and communications engineering technology; elementary education; emergency medical technology (EMT paramedic); engineering; engineering technology; English; executive assistant/executive secretary; food service systems administration; foods, nutrition, and wellness; forensic science and technology; geology/earth science; graphic design; hazardous materials management and waste technology; health/health-care administration; health information/medical records administration; health information/medical records technology; history; homeland security related; hospitality administration; hotel/motel administration; hotel, motel, and restaurant management; information science/studies; journalism; landscaping and groundskeeping; legal administrative assistant/secretary; legal assistant/paralegal; liberal arts and sciences/liberal studies; management information systems; management information systems and services related; management science; mathematics; medical radiologic technology; music; music teacher education; natural resources management and policy; nursing assistant/aide and patient care assistant/aide; nursing science; ornamental horticulture; pharmacy technician; philosophy; photography; physical therapy technology; physics; pre-dentistry studies; pre-law studies; premedical studies; prenursing studies; pre-pharmacy studies; pre-veterinary studies; psychology; registered nursing/registered nurse; restaurant, culinary, and catering management; sociology; special education; telecommunications technology; veterinary/animal health technology.

Academics *Calendar:* semesters. *Degrees:* certificates, diplomas, associate, and bachelor's. *Special study options:* academic remediation for entering students, adult/continuing education programs, advanced placement credit, cooperative education, distance learning, double majors, English as a second language, external degree program, honors programs, independent study, part-time degree program, services for LD students, summer session for credit. *ROTC:* Army (b).

Library Edward M. Chadbourne Library plus 3 others.

Student Life *Housing:* college housing not available. *Activities and Organizations:* drama/theater group, student-run newspaper, choral group, Student Government Association, Health Occupations Students of America (HOSA), SkillsUSA, African-American Student Association, Forestry Club. *Campus security:* 24-hour emergency response devices and patrols, late-night transport/escort service. *Student services:* health clinic, personal/psychological counseling.

Athletics Member NJCAA. *Intercollegiate sports:* baseball M(s), basketball M(s)/W(s), softball W(s), volleyball W. *Intramural sports:* archery M/W, badminton M/W, basketball M/W, bowling M/W, cross-country running M/W, gymnastics M/W, racquetball M/W, sailing M/W, swimming and diving M/W, tennis M/W, track and field M/W, volleyball M/W, weight lifting M/W, wrestling M.

Costs (2015–16) *Tuition:* $105 per credit hour part-time; state resident $2510 full-time, $105 per credit hour part-time; nonresident $10,075 full-time, $420 per credit hour part-time. Full-time tuition and fees vary according to degree level. Part-time tuition and fees vary according to degree level. *Payment plan:* deferred payment. *Waivers:* senior citizens and employees or children of employees.

Financial Aid Of all full-time matriculated undergraduates who enrolled in 2014, 120 Federal Work-Study jobs (averaging $3000).

Applying *Options:* electronic application, early admission. *Application fee:* $30. *Required:* high school transcript. *Application deadlines:* 8/30 (freshmen), 8/30 (transfers). *Notification:* continuous until 8/30 (freshmen), continuous until 8/30 (transfers).

Freshman Application Contact Susan Desbrow, Registrar, Pensacola State College, 1000 College Boulevard, Pensacola, FL 32504. *Phone:* 850-484-1605. *Fax:* 850-484-1020. *E-mail:* kdutremble@pensacolastate.edu. *Website:* http://www.pensacolastate.edu/.

Praxis Institute
Miami, Florida

Admissions Office Contact Praxis Institute, 1850 SW 8th Street, 4th Floor, Miami, FL 33135.
Website: http://the-praxisinstitute.com/.

Professional Hands Institute
Miami, Florida

Admissions Office Contact Professional Hands Institute, 10 NW 42 Avenue, Suite 200, Miami, FL 33126.
Website: http://prohands.edu/.

Remington College–Heathrow Campus
Heathrow, Florida

Admissions Office Contact Remington College–Heathrow Campus, 500 International Parkway, Heathrow, FL 32746. *Toll-free phone:* 800-560-6192. *Website:* http://www.remingtoncollege.edu/.

SABER College
Miami, Florida

Admissions Office Contact SABER College, 3990 W. Flagler Street, Suite 103, Miami, FL 33134.
Website: http://www.sabercollege.com/.

St. Johns River State College
Palatka, Florida

Director of Admissions Dean of Admissions and Records, St. Johns River State College, 5001 Saint Johns Avenue, Palatka, FL 32177-3897. *Phone:* 386-312-4032. *Fax:* 386-312-4289.
Website: http://www.sjrstate.edu/.

Seminole State College of Florida
Sanford, Florida

- **State and locally supported** primarily 2-year, founded 1966
- **Small-town** 200-acre campus with easy access to Orlando
- **Endowment** $14.6 million
- **Coed,** 17,741 undergraduate students, 34% full-time, 56% women, 44% men

Undergraduates 5,995 full-time, 11,746 part-time. Students come from 21 states and territories; 0.2% are from out of state; 16% Black or African American, non-Hispanic/Latino; 23% Hispanic/Latino; 3% Asian, non-Hispanic/Latino; 0.3% Native Hawaiian or other Pacific Islander, non-Hispanic/Latino; 0.2% American Indian or Alaska Native, non-Hispanic/Latino; 3% Two or more races, non-Hispanic/Latino; 1% Race/ethnicity unknown; 2% international; 7% transferred in.

Freshmen *Admission:* 4,587 applied, 2,941 admitted, 2,720 enrolled.

Faculty *Total:* 798, 26% full-time, 22% with terminal degrees. *Student/faculty ratio:* 26:1.

Majors Accounting; administrative assistant and secretarial science; architectural engineering technology; automobile/automotive mechanics technology; banking and financial support services; building/construction finishing, management, and inspection related; business administration and management; child development; civil engineering technology; computer and information sciences and support services related; computer and information sciences related; computer and information systems security; computer engineering related; computer engineering technology; computer graphics; computer hardware engineering; computer/information technology services administration related; computer programming; computer programming related; computer programming (specific applications); computer programming (vendor/product certification); computer software and media applications related; computer software engineering; computer systems networking and telecommunications; construction engineering technology; criminal justice/law enforcement administration; data entry/microcomputer applications; data entry/microcomputer applications related; data modeling/warehousing and database administration; data processing and data processing technology; drafting and design technology; electrical, electronic and communications engineering technology; emergency medical technology (EMT paramedic); finance; fire science/firefighting; industrial technology; information science/studies; information technology; interior design; legal assistant/paralegal; liberal arts and sciences/liberal studies; marketing/marketing management; network and system administration; physical therapy; registered nursing/registered nurse; respiratory care therapy; telecommunications technology; web/multimedia management and webmaster; web page, digital/multimedia and information resources design; word processing.

Academics *Calendar:* semesters. *Degrees:* certificates, diplomas, associate, bachelor's, and postbachelor's certificates. *Special study options:* academic remediation for entering students, accelerated degree program, adult/continuing education programs, advanced placement credit, cooperative education, distance learning, double majors, English as a second language, external degree program, honors programs, independent study, internships, part-time degree program, services for LD students, study abroad, summer session for credit. *ROTC:* Army (b).

Library Seminole State Library at Sanford Lake Mary plus 3 others. *Books:* 67,023 (physical), 145,374 (digital/electronic); *Serial titles:* 520 (physical), 18,003 (digital/electronic); *Databases:* 130. Weekly public service hours: 60; students can reserve study rooms.

Student Life *Housing:* college housing not available. *Activities and Organizations:* drama/theater group, student-run newspaper, choral group, Phi Beta Lambda, Phi Theta Kappa, Student Government Association, Sigma Phi Gamma, Hispanic Student Association. *Campus security:* 24-hour emergency response devices and patrols, late-night transport/escort service. *Student services:* personal/psychological counseling.

Athletics Member NJCAA. *Intercollegiate sports:* baseball M(s), golf W(s), softball W(s).

Standardized Tests *Recommended:* SAT (for admission), ACT (for admission), SAT or ACT (for admission), SAT and SAT Subject Tests or ACT (for admission), SAT Subject Tests (for admission), CPT, PERT.

Costs (2015–16) *Tuition:* state resident $3131 full-time, $104 per credit hour part-time; nonresident $11,456 full-time, $382 per credit hour part-time. Full-time tuition and fees vary according to course level, course load, degree level, and program. Part-time tuition and fees vary according to course level, course load, degree level, and program. *Payment plan:* deferred payment. *Waivers:* senior citizens and employees or children of employees.

Applying *Options:* electronic application, early admission, deferred entrance. *Required:* high school transcript, minimum 2.0 GPA. *Application deadlines:* rolling (freshmen), rolling (transfers). *Notification:* continuous (freshmen), continuous (transfers).

Freshman Application Contact Ms. Pamela Mennechey, Associate Vice President - Student Recruitment and Enrollment, Seminole State College of Florida, Sanford, FL 32773-6199. *Phone:* 407-708-2050. *Fax:* 407-708-2395. *E-mail:* admissions@scc-fl.edu.
Website: http://www.seminolestate.edu/.

Southeastern College–Jacksonville
Jacksonville, Florida

- **Proprietary** 2-year
- **Urban** campus
- **Coed,** 125 undergraduate students, 54% full-time, 86% women, 14% men

Undergraduates 67 full-time, 58 part-time. 47% Black or African American, non-Hispanic/Latino; 6% Hispanic/Latino; 2% Asian, non-Hispanic/Latino; 2% Two or more races, non-Hispanic/Latino.

Freshmen *Admission:* 58 enrolled.

Academics *Calendar:* quarters. *Degree:* certificates, diplomas, and associate.

Costs (2015–16) *Tuition:* $16,784 full-time. *Required fees:* $1600 full-time.

Financial Aid Of all full-time matriculated undergraduates who enrolled in 2014, 157 applied for aid, 157 were judged to have need, 157 had their need fully met. 2 Federal Work-Study jobs (averaging $2282).

Applying *Application fee:* $55.

Freshman Application Contact Southeastern College–Jacksonville, 6700 Southpoint Parkway, Suite 400, Jacksonville, FL 32216.
Website: http://www.sec.edu/.

Southeastern College–West Palm Beach

West Palm Beach, Florida

- **Proprietary** 2-year
- **Urban** campus
- **Coed,** 678 undergraduate students, 43% full-time, 81% women, 19% men

Undergraduates 292 full-time, 386 part-time. 32% Black or African American, non-Hispanic/Latino; 34% Hispanic/Latino; 1% Asian, non-Hispanic/Latino; 0.3% American Indian or Alaska Native, non-Hispanic/Latino; 0.7% Two or more races, non-Hispanic/Latino; 2% Race/ethnicity unknown; 0.1% international.

Freshmen *Admission:* 543 enrolled.

Majors Aesthetician/esthetician and skin care; business, management, and marketing related; computer and information sciences and support services related; computer systems networking and telecommunications; emergency medical technology (EMT paramedic); health professions related; licensed practical/vocational nurse training; massage therapy; medical/clinical assistant; medical insurance coding; medical insurance/medical billing; parks, recreation and leisure facilities management; pharmacy technician; salon/beauty salon management; surgical technology.

Academics *Degree:* certificates, diplomas, and associate.

Costs (2015–16) *Tuition:* $16,784 full-time, $699 per credit hour part-time. Full-time tuition and fees vary according to course load and program. Part-time tuition and fees vary according to course load and program. *Required fees:* $1600 full-time.

Applying *Application fee:* $55. *Required:* high school transcript.

Freshman Application Contact Admissions Office, Southeastern College–West Palm Beach, 2081 Vista Parkway, West Palm Beach, FL 33411. *Website:* http://www.sec.edu/.

Southern Technical College

Orlando, Florida

- **Proprietary** 2-year
- **Urban** 1-acre campus with easy access to Greater Orlando
- **Coed**

Undergraduates 1,445 full-time. 40% Black or African American, non-Hispanic/Latino; 27% Hispanic/Latino; 0.6% Asian, non-Hispanic/Latino; 0.4% Native Hawaiian or other Pacific Islander, non-Hispanic/Latino; 0.6% American Indian or Alaska Native, non-Hispanic/Latino; 0.9% Two or more races, non-Hispanic/Latino; 2% Race/ethnicity unknown; 0.1% international.

Faculty *Student/faculty ratio:* 25:1.

Academics *Calendar:* quarters. *Degree:* diplomas and associate. *Special study options:* academic remediation for entering students, advanced placement credit, distance learning, independent study, summer session for credit.

Library STC Library.

Student Life *Campus security:* evening security guard.

Applying *Required:* self attestation at time of application that student has met admissions criteria of high school diploma or GED completion.

Freshman Application Contact Mr. Robinson Elie, Director of Admissions, Southern Technical College, 1485 Florida Mall Avenue, Orlando, FL 32809. *Phone:* 407-438-6000. *Toll-free phone:* 877-347-5492. *E-mail:* relie@southerntech.edu. *Website:* http://www.southerntech.edu/.

Southern Technical College

Tampa, Florida

Director of Admissions Admissions, Southern Technical College, 3910 Riga Boulevard, Tampa, FL 33619. *Phone:* 813-630-4401. *Toll-free phone:* 877-347-5492. *Website:* http://www.southerntech.edu/locations/tampa/.

South Florida State College

Avon Park, Florida

- **State-supported** primarily 2-year, founded 1965, part of Florida State College System
- **Rural** 228-acre campus with easy access to Tampa, St. Petersburg, Orlando
- **Endowment** $5.8 million
- **Coed,** 2,659 undergraduate students, 34% full-time, 62% women, 38% men

Undergraduates 900 full-time, 1,759 part-time. 3% are from out of state; 10% Black or African American, non-Hispanic/Latino; 32% Hispanic/Latino; 2% Asian, non-Hispanic/Latino; 0.2% Native Hawaiian or other Pacific Islander, non-Hispanic/Latino; 0.3% American Indian or Alaska Native, non-Hispanic/Latino; 2% Two or more races, non-Hispanic/Latino; 1% Race/ethnicity unknown; 2% international; 1% transferred in.

Freshmen *Admission:* 655 applied, 355 admitted, 342 enrolled. *Average high school GPA:* 3.12.

Faculty *Total:* 145, 45% full-time, 18% with terminal degrees. *Student/faculty ratio:* 16:1.

Majors Accounting; accounting technology and bookkeeping; actuarial science; advertising; aerospace, aeronautical and astronautical/space engineering; agribusiness; agricultural economics; agricultural engineering; agricultural teacher education; agriculture; American studies; animal sciences; anthropology; applied mathematics; architecture; art; art history, criticism and conservation; art teacher education; astronomy; atmospheric sciences and meteorology; audiology and speech-language pathology; banking and financial support services; biochemistry; biological and physical sciences; biology/biological sciences; biomedical technology; botany/plant biology; business administration and management; business administration, management and operations related; business/commerce; business/managerial economics; business teacher education; chemical engineering; chemistry; chemistry related; city/urban, community and regional planning; civil engineering; civil engineering technology; clinical laboratory science/medical technology; computer and information sciences; computer engineering; computer engineering technology; computer programming; construction engineering technology; criminal justice/law enforcement administration; criminal justice/safety; dental hygiene; dietetics; dramatic/theater arts; early childhood education; economics; electrical and electronics engineering; electrical, electronic and communications engineering technology; elementary education; emergency medical technology (EMT paramedic); engineering; engineering science; engineering technology; English; English/language arts teacher education; entomology; environmental/environmental health engineering; environmental science; family and consumer sciences/home economics teacher education; finance; fine/studio arts; fire prevention and safety technology; food science; foreign languages and literatures; foreign language teacher education; forensic science and technology; forestry; French; general studies; geography; geology/earth science; gerontology; graphic design; health/health-care administration; health information/medical records administration; health services/allied health/health sciences; health teacher education; history; horticultural science; hospitality administration; humanities; human resources management; industrial engineering; information science/studies; insurance; international business/trade/commerce; international relations and affairs; jazz/jazz studies; journalism; kinesiology and exercise science; landscaping and groundskeeping; legal assistant/paralegal; liberal arts and sciences and humanities related; liberal arts and sciences/liberal studies; linguistics; management information systems; management science; manufacturing engineering technology; marine biology and biological oceanography; marketing/marketing management; materials engineering; mathematics; mathematics teacher education; mechanical engineering; medical microbiology and bacteriology; medical radiologic technology; middle school education; multi/interdisciplinary studies related; music; music history, literature, and theory; music performance; music teacher education; music theory and composition; music therapy; network and system administration; nuclear engineering; occupational therapy; ocean engineering; office management; operations management; parks, recreation and leisure facilities management; pharmacy; philosophy; philosophy and religious studies related; physics; physics related; plant sciences; political science and government; psychology; public administration; public relations/image management; radio and television; real estate; registered nursing/registered nurse; religious studies; respiratory care therapy; rhetoric and composition; science teacher education; secondary education; social psychology; social sciences; social science teacher education; social work; sociology; soil science and agronomy; Spanish; special education; special education–individuals with emotional disturbances; special education–individuals with intellectual disabilities; special education–individuals with specific learning disabilities; special education–individuals with vision impairments; speech communication and rhetoric; statistics; surveying technology; systems engineering; trade and industrial teacher education; transportation/mobility management; vocational rehabilitation counseling; water, wetlands, and marine resources management; zoology/animal biology.

Academics *Calendar:* semesters. *Degrees:* certificates, diplomas, associate, and bachelor's. *Special study options:* academic remediation for entering students, adult/continuing education programs, advanced placement credit, cooperative education, distance learning, English as a second language, internships, part-time degree program, services for LD students, summer session for credit.

Library Learning Resource Center.

Student Life *Housing Options:* Campus housing is provided by a third party. *Activities and Organizations:* drama/theater group, student-run newspaper, choral group, Phi Theta Kappa, Phi Beta Lambda, Performing Arts Club, Anime and Gaming Club, Basketball Club. *Campus security:* 24-hour emergency response devices and patrols, late-night transport/escort service. *Student services:* personal/psychological counseling.

Athletics Member NJCAA. *Intercollegiate sports:* baseball M(s), cross-country running W(s), softball W(s), volleyball W(s). *Intramural sports:* basketball M(c)/W(c), soccer M(c)/W(c).
Costs (2016–17) *One-time required fee:* $15. *Tuition:* state resident $105 per credit hour part-time; nonresident $394 per credit hour part-time. Full-time tuition and fees vary according to course level, course load, degree level, and program. Part-time tuition and fees vary according to course level, course load, degree level, and program. *Room and board:* $5920; room only: $2000. *Payment plan:* installment. *Waivers:* employees or children of employees.
Applying *Options:* electronic application, early admission, deferred entrance. *Application fee:* $15. *Required:* high school transcript. *Application deadline:* rolling (freshmen). *Notification:* continuous (freshmen).
Freshman Application Contact Ms. Mary Puckorius, Admissions Coordinator, South Florida State College, 600 West College Drive, Avon Park, FL 33825. *Phone:* 863-784-7416.
Website: http://www.southflorida.edu/.

Sullivan and Cogliano Training Center
Miami Gardens, Florida

Admissions Office Contact Sullivan and Cogliano Training Center, 4760 North West 167th Street, Miami Gardens, FL 33014.
Website: http://www.sctrain.edu/.

Tallahassee Community College
Tallahassee, Florida

- **State and locally supported** primarily 2-year, founded 1966, part of Florida College System
- **Suburban** 214-acre campus
- **Endowment** $10.0 million
- **Coed,** 12,445 undergraduate students, 46% full-time, 53% women, 47% men

Undergraduates 5,740 full-time, 6,705 part-time. Students come from 24 states and territories; 79 other countries; 1% are from out of state; 30% Black or African American, non-Hispanic/Latino; 12% Hispanic/Latino; 1% Asian, non-Hispanic/Latino; 0.1% Native Hawaiian or other Pacific Islander, non-Hispanic/Latino; 0.2% American Indian or Alaska Native, non-Hispanic/Latino; 4% Two or more races, non-Hispanic/Latino; 2% Race/ethnicity unknown; 1% international; 9% transferred in. *Retention:* 59% of full-time freshmen returned.
Freshmen *Admission:* 5,511 applied, 2,828 admitted, 2,288 enrolled.
Faculty *Total:* 568, 33% full-time, 72% with terminal degrees. *Student/faculty ratio:* 22:1.
Majors Accounting technology and bookkeeping; CAD/CADD drafting/design technology; commercial and advertising art; computer graphics; computer programming; computer programming (specific applications); computer systems networking and telecommunications; construction engineering technology; corrections; criminal justice/law enforcement administration; criminal justice/police science; dental assisting; dental hygiene; diagnostic medical sonography and ultrasound technology; drafting and design technology; early childhood education; emergency medical technology (EMT paramedic); entrepreneurship; environmental science; fire science/firefighting; health information/medical records technology; homeland security related; information technology; legal assistant/paralegal; liberal arts and sciences/liberal studies; manufacturing engineering technology; masonry; medical radiologic technology; nursing assistant/aide and patient care assistant/aide; office management; pharmacy technician; physical fitness technician; registered nursing/registered nurse; respiratory care therapy; security and loss prevention; surgical technology; web page, digital/multimedia and information resources design; welding technology.
Academics *Calendar:* semesters. *Degrees:* certificates, associate, and bachelor's. *Special study options:* academic remediation for entering students, accelerated degree program, adult/continuing education programs, advanced placement credit, distance learning, English as a second language, external degree program, honors programs, independent study, off-campus study, part-time degree program, services for LD students, study abroad, summer session for credit. *ROTC:* Army (c), Navy (c), Air Force (c).
Library Tallahassee Community College Library. Weekly public service hours: 68; students can reserve study rooms.
Student Life *Housing:* college housing not available. *Activities and Organizations:* drama/theater group, student-run newspaper, choral group, Student Government Association, International Student Organization, Phi Theta Kappa, Model United Nations, Honors Council. *Campus security:* 24-hour emergency response devices and patrols, late-night transport/escort service. *Student services:* personal/psychological counseling.

Athletics Member NJCAA. *Intercollegiate sports:* baseball M(s), basketball M(s)/W(s), softball W(s). *Intramural sports:* basketball M/W, football M/W, soccer M/W, softball M/W, volleyball M/W.
Costs (2015–16) *Tuition:* state resident $3025 full-time, $101 per credit hour part-time; nonresident $11,288 full-time, $387 per credit hour part-time. Full-time tuition and fees vary according to course load. Part-time tuition and fees vary according to course load. *Payment plans:* installment, deferred payment. *Waivers:* employees or children of employees.
Financial Aid Of all full-time matriculated undergraduates who enrolled in 2014, 4,508 applied for aid, 3,203 were judged to have need. 77 Federal Work-Study jobs (averaging $2662). *Average financial aid package:* $4019. *Average need-based gift aid:* $3855.
Applying *Options:* electronic application, early admission, deferred entrance. *Required:* high school transcript. *Application deadlines:* 8/1 (freshmen), 8/1 (transfers).
Freshman Application Contact Student Success Center, Tallahassee Community College, 444 Appleyard Drive, Tallahassee, FL 32304-2895. *Phone:* 850-201-8555. *E-mail:* admissions@tcc.fl.edu.
Website: http://www.tcc.fl.edu/.

Ultimate Medical Academy Clearwater
Clearwater, Florida

- **Independent** 2-year
- **Urban** campus with easy access to Tampa
- **Coed**

Majors Health services/allied health/health sciences.
Academics *Calendar:* continuous. *Degree:* diplomas and associate. *Special study options:* distance learning, services for LD students.
Student Life *Housing:* college housing not available.
Applying *Required:* high school transcript.
Freshman Application Contact Ultimate Medical Academy Clearwater, 1255 Cleveland Street, Clearwater, FL 33756. *Toll-free phone:* 888-205-8685.
Website: http://www.ultimatemedical.edu/.

Ultimate Medical Academy Online
Clearwater, Florida

- **Independent** 2-year
- **Urban** campus
- **Coed**

Majors Health/health-care administration; health information/medical records technology; health services/allied health/health sciences; human services; medical administrative assistant and medical secretary; medical insurance/medical billing; pharmacy technician.
Academics *Calendar:* continuous. *Degree:* diplomas and associate. *Special study options:* distance learning, services for LD students.
Student Life *Housing:* college housing not available.
Applying *Options:* electronic application.
Freshman Application Contact Online Admissions Department, Ultimate Medical Academy Online, 1255 Cleveland Street, Clearwater, FL 33756. *Phone:* 888-209-8848. *Toll-free phone:* 888-205-2510.
E-mail: onlineadmissions@ultimatemedical.edu.
Website: http://www.ultimatemedical.edu/.

Ultimate Medical Academy Tampa
Tampa, Florida

- **Independent** 2-year
- **Urban** campus
- **Coed**

Majors Health services/allied health/health sciences; nursing science.
Academics *Calendar:* continuous. *Degree:* diplomas and associate. *Special study options:* distance learning, services for LD students.
Student Life *Housing:* college housing not available.
Freshman Application Contact Ultimate Medical Academy Tampa, 9309 N. Florida Avenue, Suite 100, Tampa, FL 33612. *Toll-free phone:* 888-205-2510.
Website: http://www.ultimatemedical.edu/.

Universal Career School
Sweetwater, Florida

Admissions Office Contact Universal Career School, 10720 W. Flagler Street, Suite 21, Sweetwater, FL 33174.
Website: http://www.ucs.edu/.

Virginia College in Fort Pierce
Fort Pierce, Florida

Admissions Office Contact Virginia College in Fort Pierce, 2810 South Federal Highway, Fort Pierce, FL 34982-6331.
Website: http://www.vc.edu/.

Virginia College in Jacksonville
Jacksonville, Florida

Admissions Office Contact Virginia College in Jacksonville, 5940 Beach Boulevard, Jacksonville, FL 32207.
Website: http://www.vc.edu/.

Virginia College in Pensacola
Pensacola, Florida

Admissions Office Contact Virginia College in Pensacola, 312 East Nine Mile Road, Suite 34, Pensacola, FL 32514.
Website: http://www.vc.edu/.

WyoTech Daytona
Ormond Beach, Florida

Admissions Office Contact WyoTech Daytona, 470 Destination Daytona Lane, Ormond Beach, FL 32174. *Toll-free phone:* 800-881-2AMI.
Website: http://www.wyotech.edu/.

GEORGIA

Albany Technical College
Albany, Georgia

- **State-supported** 2-year, founded 1961, part of Technical College System of Georgia
- **Coed,** 3,331 undergraduate students, 46% full-time, 63% women, 37% men

Undergraduates 1,537 full-time, 1,794 part-time. 1% are from out of state; 79% Black or African American, non-Hispanic/Latino; 1% Hispanic/Latino; 0.1% Asian, non-Hispanic/Latino; 0.1% American Indian or Alaska Native, non-Hispanic/Latino; 0.8% Two or more races, non-Hispanic/Latino. *Retention:* 55% of full-time freshmen returned.
Freshmen *Admission:* 616 enrolled.
Majors Accounting; adult development and aging; child development; computer and information sciences; corrections and criminal justice related; culinary arts; drafting and design technology; electrical and electronic engineering technologies related; forest technology; hotel/motel administration; human development and family studies related; industrial technology; manufacturing engineering technology; marketing/marketing management; medical radiologic technology; pharmacy technician; tourism and travel services management.
Academics *Calendar:* quarters. *Degree:* certificates, diplomas, and associate. *Special study options:* distance learning.
Library Albany Technical College Library and Media Center.
Student Life *Housing:* college housing not available.
Costs (2016–17) *Tuition:* state resident $89 per credit hour part-time; nonresident $178 per credit hour part-time.
Applying *Options:* early admission. *Application fee:* $23. *Required:* high school transcript.
Freshman Application Contact Albany Technical College, 1704 South Slappey Boulevard, Albany, GA 31701. *Phone:* 229-430-3520. *Toll-free phone:* 877-261-3113.
Website: http://www.albanytech.edu/.

Andrew College
Cuthbert, Georgia

Freshman Application Contact Ms. Bridget Kurkowski, Director of Admission, Andrew College, 413 College Street, Cuthbert, GA 39840. *Phone:* 229-732-5986. *Toll-free phone:* 800-664-9250. *Fax:* 229-732-2176.
E-mail: admissions@andrewcollege.edu.
Website: http://www.andrewcollege.edu/.

Athens Technical College
Athens, Georgia

- **State-supported** 2-year, founded 1958, part of Technical College System of Georgia
- **Suburban** campus
- **Coed,** 4,199 undergraduate students, 23% full-time, 65% women, 35% men

Undergraduates 970 full-time, 3,229 part-time. 1% are from out of state; 22% Black or African American, non-Hispanic/Latino; 6% Hispanic/Latino; 3% Asian, non-Hispanic/Latino; 0.1% Native Hawaiian or other Pacific Islander, non-Hispanic/Latino; 0.1% American Indian or Alaska Native, non-Hispanic/Latino; 0.5% Two or more races, non-Hispanic/Latino; 5% Race/ethnicity unknown; 0.9% international. *Retention:* 56% of full-time freshmen returned.
Freshmen *Admission:* 707 enrolled.
Majors Accounting; administrative assistant and secretarial science; biology/biotechnology laboratory technician; child development; clinical laboratory science/medical technology; communications technology; computer programming; computer systems networking and telecommunications; criminal justice/law enforcement administration; dental assisting; dental hygiene; diagnostic medical sonography and ultrasound technology; electrical, electronic and communications engineering technology; emergency medical technology (EMT paramedic); hotel/motel administration; information science/studies; legal assistant/paralegal; licensed practical/vocational nurse training; logistics, materials, and supply chain management; marketing/marketing management; medical radiologic technology; physical therapy; registered nursing/registered nurse; respiratory care therapy; surgical technology; tourism and travel services management; veterinary/animal health technology.
Academics *Calendar:* quarters. *Degree:* certificates, diplomas, and associate. *Special study options:* distance learning.
Student Life *Housing:* college housing not available.
Costs (2016–17) *Tuition:* state resident $89 per credit hour part-time; nonresident $178 per credit hour part-time.
Financial Aid Of all full-time matriculated undergraduates who enrolled in 2014, 34 Federal Work-Study jobs (averaging $3090).
Applying *Options:* early admission. *Application fee:* $20. *Required:* high school transcript.
Freshman Application Contact Athens Technical College, 800 US Highway 29 North, Athens, GA 30601-1500. *Phone:* 706-355-5008.
Website: http://www.athenstech.edu/.

Atlanta Metropolitan State College
Atlanta, Georgia

Freshman Application Contact Ms. Audrey Reid, Director, Office of Admissions, Atlanta Metropolitan State College, 1630 Metropolitan Parkway, SW, Atlanta, GA 30310-4498. *Phone:* 404-756-4004. *Fax:* 404-756-4407.
E-mail: admissions@atlm.edu.
Website: http://www.atlm.edu/.

Atlanta Technical College
Atlanta, Georgia

- **State-supported** 2-year, founded 1945, part of Technical College System of Georgia
- **Coed,** 3,789 undergraduate students, 37% full-time, 65% women, 35% men

Undergraduates 1,413 full-time, 2,376 part-time. 0.5% are from out of state; 91% Black or African American, non-Hispanic/Latino; 2% Hispanic/Latino; 0.7% Asian, non-Hispanic/Latino; 0.2% Native Hawaiian or other Pacific Islander, non-Hispanic/Latino; 0.3% American Indian or Alaska Native, non-Hispanic/Latino; 2% Two or more races, non-Hispanic/Latino; 0.3% Race/ethnicity unknown; 0.9% international. *Retention:* 55% of full-time freshmen returned.
Freshmen *Admission:* 604 enrolled.
Majors Accounting; child development; computer programming; culinary arts; dental hygiene; health information/medical records technology; hotel/motel administration; information technology; legal assistant/paralegal; marketing/marketing management; tourism and travel services management.
Academics *Calendar:* quarters. *Degree:* certificates, diplomas, and associate. *Special study options:* distance learning, study abroad.
Student Life *Housing:* college housing not available.
Costs (2016–17) *Tuition:* state resident $89 per credit hour part-time; nonresident $178 per credit hour part-time.

Applying *Options:* early admission. *Application fee:* \$25. *Required:* high school transcript.

Freshman Application Contact Atlanta Technical College, 1560 Metropolitan Parkway, SW, Atlanta, GA 30310. *Phone:* 404-225-4455. *Website:* http://www.atlantatech.edu/.

Augusta Technical College
Augusta, Georgia

- **State-supported** 2-year, founded 1961, part of Technical College System of Georgia
- **Urban** campus
- **Coed,** 4,490 undergraduate students, 36% full-time, 57% women, 43% men

Undergraduates 1,631 full-time, 2,859 part-time. 4% are from out of state; 49% Black or African American, non-Hispanic/Latino; 3% Hispanic/Latino; 2% Asian, non-Hispanic/Latino; 0.1% Native Hawaiian or other Pacific Islander, non-Hispanic/Latino; 0.4% American Indian or Alaska Native, non-Hispanic/Latino; 2% Two or more races, non-Hispanic/Latino; 2% Race/ethnicity unknown; 0.2% international. *Retention:* 58% of full-time freshmen returned.

Freshmen *Admission:* 900 enrolled.

Majors Accounting; administrative assistant and secretarial science; biotechnology; business administration and management; cardiovascular technology; child development; computer programming; computer systems networking and telecommunications; criminal justice/safety; culinary arts; e-commerce; electrical, electronic and communications engineering technology; emergency medical technology (EMT paramedic); fire science/firefighting; information science/studies; marketing/marketing management; mechanical engineering/mechanical technology; medical radiologic technology; occupational therapist assistant; parks, recreation and leisure facilities management; pharmacy technician; respiratory care therapy; respiratory therapy technician; surgical technology.

Academics *Calendar:* quarters. *Degree:* certificates, diplomas, and associate. *Special study options:* distance learning.

Library Information Technology Center.

Student Life *Housing:* college housing not available.

Costs (2016–17) *Tuition:* state resident \$89 per credit hour part-time; nonresident \$176 per credit hour part-time.

Applying *Options:* early admission. *Application fee:* \$25. *Required:* high school transcript.

Freshman Application Contact Augusta Technical College, 3200 Augusta Tech Drive, Augusta, GA 30906. *Phone:* 706-771-4150. *Website:* http://www.augustatech.edu/.

Bainbridge State College
Bainbridge, Georgia

- **State-supported** primarily 2-year, founded 1972, part of University System of Georgia
- **Small-town** 160-acre campus
- **Coed,** 2,401 undergraduate students, 34% full-time, 69% women, 31% men

Undergraduates 818 full-time, 1,583 part-time. Students come from 3 states and territories; 2 other countries; 3% are from out of state; 50% Black or African American, non-Hispanic/Latino; 4% Hispanic/Latino; 0.4% Asian, non-Hispanic/Latino; 0.2% American Indian or Alaska Native, non-Hispanic/Latino; 0.9% Two or more races, non-Hispanic/Latino; 1% Race/ethnicity unknown; 0.3% international.

Freshmen *Admission:* 425 admitted.

Faculty *Total:* 138, 45% full-time, 23% with terminal degrees.

Majors Accounting; administrative assistant and secretarial science; agribusiness; agriculture; art; biology/biological sciences; business administration and management; business teacher education; chemistry; criminal justice/law enforcement administration; data processing and data processing technology; drafting and design technology; dramatic/theater arts; education; electrical, electronic and communications engineering technology; elementary education; English; family and consumer sciences/human sciences; health information/medical records technology; health teacher education; history; information science/studies; kindergarten/preschool education; liberal arts and sciences/liberal studies; licensed practical/vocational nurse training; marketing/marketing management; mathematics; political science and government; psychology; registered nursing/registered nurse; rhetoric and composition; sociology; welding technology.

Academics *Calendar:* semesters. *Degrees:* certificates, associate, and bachelor's. *Special study options:* academic remediation for entering students, advanced placement credit, distance learning, double majors, honors programs, independent study, part-time degree program, services for LD students, study abroad, summer session for credit.

Library Bainbridge State College Library. *Books:* 43,778 (physical), 27,020 (digital/electronic); *Serial titles:* 207 (physical), 2,011 (digital/electronic); *Databases:* 279. Weekly public service hours: 50; students can reserve study rooms.

Student Life *Housing:* college housing not available. *Activities and Organizations:* choral group, Adult Learners Student Organization, BANS, LPN Club, Honors, Student Government Association. *Campus security:* 24-hour patrols. *Student services:* personal/psychological counseling.

Athletics *Intramural sports:* table tennis M/W, volleyball M/W.

Standardized Tests *Required for some:* SAT or ACT (for admission), ACT Compass.

Costs (2015–16) *Tuition:* state resident \$2181 full-time, \$91 per credit hour part-time; nonresident \$8256 full-time, \$344 per credit hour part-time. Full-time tuition and fees vary according to course load and program. Part-time tuition and fees vary according to course load and program. *Required fees:* \$1046 full-time, \$523 per term part-time. *Waivers:* senior citizens and employees or children of employees.

Applying *Options:* electronic application, early admission. *Required for some:* high school transcript, minimum 1.8 GPA, 3 letters of recommendation, interview, immunizations/waivers, medical records, criminal background check. *Application deadlines:* rolling (freshmen), rolling (transfers). *Notification:* continuous (freshmen), continuous (transfers).

Freshman Application Contact Ms. Melanie Cleveland, Director of Admission, Bainbridge State College, 2500 East Shotwell Street, Bainbridge, GA 39819. *Phone:* 229-243-6922. *Toll-free phone:* 866-825-1715 (in-state); 888-825-1715 (out-of-state). *Fax:* 229-248-2525. *E-mail:* melanie.cleveland@bainbridge.edu. *Website:* http://www.bainbridge.edu/.

Brown College of Court Reporting
Atlanta, Georgia

Admissions Office Contact Brown College of Court Reporting, 1900 Emery Street NW, Suite 200, Atlanta, GA 30318. *Website:* http://www.bccr.edu/.

Brown Mackie College–Atlanta
Atlanta, Georgia

Freshman Application Contact Brown Mackie College–Atlanta, 4370 Peachtree Road, NE, Atlanta, GA 30319. *Phone:* 404-799-4500. *Website:* http://www.brownmackie.edu/atlanta/.

Central Georgia Technical College
Warner Robins, Georgia

- **State-supported** 2-year, founded 1966, part of Technical College System of Georgia
- **Suburban** campus
- **Coed,** 7,832 undergraduate students, 34% full-time, 63% women, 37% men

Undergraduates 2,649 full-time, 5,183 part-time. 2% are from out of state; 53% Black or African American, non-Hispanic/Latino; 3% Hispanic/Latino; 0.9% Asian, non-Hispanic/Latino; 0.2% American Indian or Alaska Native, non-Hispanic/Latino; 1% Two or more races, non-Hispanic/Latino; 1% Race/ethnicity unknown; 0.4% international. *Retention:* 51% of full-time freshmen returned.

Freshmen *Admission:* 1,588 enrolled.

Majors Accounting; administrative assistant and secretarial science; adult development and aging; banking and financial support services; business administration and management; cabinetmaking and millwork; cardiovascular technology; carpentry; child-care and support services management; child development; clinical/medical laboratory technology; computer programming; computer systems networking and telecommunications; criminal justice/safety; dental hygiene; drafting and design technology; e-commerce; electrical, electronic and communications engineering technology; hotel/motel administration; industrial technology; information science/studies; legal assistant/paralegal; marketing/marketing management; medical radiologic technology; tourism and travel services management; veterinary/animal health technology; web page, digital/multimedia and information resources design.

Academics *Calendar:* quarters. *Degree:* certificates, diplomas, and associate. *Special study options:* distance learning.

Student Life *Housing:* college housing not available.

Costs (2016–17) *Tuition:* state resident \$89 per credit hour part-time; nonresident \$178 per credit hour part-time.

Financial Aid Of all full-time matriculated undergraduates who enrolled in 2014, 175 Federal Work-Study jobs (averaging \$2000). *Financial aid deadline:* 9/1.

Applying *Options:* early admission. *Application fee:* $25. *Required:* high school transcript.
Freshman Application Contact Central Georgia Technical College, 80 Cohen Walker Drive, Warner Robins, GA 31088. *Phone:* 770-531-6332. *Toll-free phone:* 866-430-0135.
Website: http://www.centralgatech.edu/.

Chattahoochee Technical College
Marietta, Georgia

- **State-supported** 2-year, founded 1961, part of Technical College System of Georgia
- **Suburban** campus
- **Coed,** 9,817 undergraduate students, 30% full-time, 55% women, 45% men

Undergraduates 2,902 full-time, 6,915 part-time. 0.5% are from out of state; 29% Black or African American, non-Hispanic/Latino; 10% Hispanic/Latino; 2% Asian, non-Hispanic/Latino; 0.1% Native Hawaiian or other Pacific Islander, non-Hispanic/Latino; 0.6% American Indian or Alaska Native, non-Hispanic/Latino; 2% Two or more races, non-Hispanic/Latino; 1% Race/ethnicity unknown; 1% international. *Retention:* 54% of full-time freshmen returned.
Freshmen *Admission:* 1,984 enrolled.
Majors Accounting; administrative assistant and secretarial science; automobile/automotive mechanics technology; biomedical technology; business administration and management; child development; civil engineering technology; computer and information systems security; computer programming; computer systems networking and telecommunications; criminal justice/safety; culinary arts; drafting and design technology; electrical, electronic and communications engineering technology; fire science/firefighting; horticultural science; information science/studies; logistics, materials, and supply chain management; marketing/marketing management; medical radiologic technology; parks, recreation and leisure facilities management; web page, digital/multimedia and information resources design.
Academics *Calendar:* quarters. *Degree:* certificates, diplomas, and associate. *Special study options:* distance learning.
Student Life *Housing:* college housing not available.
Costs (2016–17) *Tuition:* state resident $89 per credit hour part-time; nonresident $178 per credit hour part-time.
Financial Aid Of all full-time matriculated undergraduates who enrolled in 2014, 40 Federal Work-Study jobs (averaging $2500).
Applying *Options:* early admission. *Application fee:* $20. *Required:* high school transcript.
Freshman Application Contact Chattahoochee Technical College, 980 South Cobb Drive, SE, Marietta, GA 30060. *Phone:* 770-757-3408.
Website: http://www.chattahoocheetech.edu/.

Coastal Pines Technical College
Waycross, Georgia

- **State-supported** 2-year, part of Technical College System of Georgia
- **Small-town** campus
- **Coed,** 2,445 undergraduate students, 24% full-time, 60% women, 40% men

Undergraduates 599 full-time, 1,846 part-time. 0.5% are from out of state; 28% Black or African American, non-Hispanic/Latino; 5% Hispanic/Latino; 0.7% Asian, non-Hispanic/Latino; 0.1% Native Hawaiian or other Pacific Islander, non-Hispanic/Latino; 0.3% American Indian or Alaska Native, non-Hispanic/Latino; 2% Two or more races, non-Hispanic/Latino; 0.5% Race/ethnicity unknown; 0.3% international. *Retention:* 59% of full-time freshmen returned.
Freshmen *Admission:* 408 enrolled.
Majors Administrative assistant and secretarial science; child development; clinical/medical laboratory technology; computer systems networking and telecommunications; computer technology/computer systems technology; criminal justice/police science; forest technology; information science/studies; occupational safety and health technology; respiratory therapy technician; surgical technology.
Academics *Calendar:* quarters. *Degree:* certificates, diplomas, and associate. *Special study options:* distance learning.
Student Life *Housing:* college housing not available.
Costs (2016–17) *Tuition:* state resident $89 per credit hour part-time; nonresident $178 per credit hour part-time.

Applying *Options:* early admission. *Application fee:* $20. *Required:* high school transcript.
Freshman Application Contact Coastal Pines Technical College, 1701 Carswell Avenue, Waycross, GA 31503. *Phone:* 912-338-5251. *Toll-free phone:* 877-ED-AT-OTC.
Website: http://www.coastalpines.edu/.

Columbus Technical College
Columbus, Georgia

- **State-supported** 2-year, founded 1961, part of Technical College System of Georgia
- **Urban** campus
- **Coed,** 3,800 undergraduate students, 26% full-time, 64% women, 36% men

Undergraduates 981 full-time, 2,819 part-time. 14% are from out of state; 45% Black or African American, non-Hispanic/Latino; 6% Hispanic/Latino; 2% Asian, non-Hispanic/Latino; 0.5% Native Hawaiian or other Pacific Islander, non-Hispanic/Latino; 0.5% American Indian or Alaska Native, non-Hispanic/Latino; 3% Two or more races, non-Hispanic/Latino; 2% Race/ethnicity unknown; 0.1% international. *Retention:* 52% of full-time freshmen returned.
Freshmen *Admission:* 606 enrolled.
Majors Accounting; administrative assistant and secretarial science; automobile/automotive mechanics technology; child development; computer engineering related; computer systems networking and telecommunications; dental hygiene; diagnostic medical sonography and ultrasound technology; drafting and design technology; electrical, electronic and communications engineering technology; emergency medical technology (EMT paramedic); health information/medical records technology; horticultural science; industrial technology; information science/studies; machine tool technology; mechanical engineering/mechanical technology; medical office management; medical radiologic technology; pharmacy technician; registered nursing/registered nurse; respiratory therapy technician; surgical technology; web page, digital/multimedia and information resources design.
Academics *Calendar:* quarters. *Degree:* certificates, diplomas, and associate. *Special study options:* distance learning.
Library Columbus Technical College Library.
Student Life *Housing:* college housing not available.
Costs (2016–17) *Tuition:* state resident $89 per credit hour part-time; nonresident $178 per credit hour part-time.
Financial Aid Of all full-time matriculated undergraduates who enrolled in 2014, 6 Federal Work-Study jobs (averaging $2000).
Applying *Options:* early admission. *Application fee:* $20. *Required:* high school transcript.
Freshman Application Contact Columbus Technical College, 928 Manchester Expressway, Columbus, GA 31904-6572. *Phone:* 706-649-1901.
Website: http://www.columbustech.edu/.

Darton State College
Albany, Georgia

- **State-supported** primarily 2-year, founded 1965, part of University System of Georgia
- **Urban** 185-acre campus
- **Endowment** $1.9 million
- **Coed**

Undergraduates 2,577 full-time, 3,043 part-time. Students come from 29 states and territories; 6 other countries; 3% are from out of state; 45% Black or African American, non-Hispanic/Latino; 3% Hispanic/Latino; 1% Asian, non-Hispanic/Latino; 0.1% Native Hawaiian or other Pacific Islander, non-Hispanic/Latino; 0.3% American Indian or Alaska Native, non-Hispanic/Latino; 0.8% Two or more races, non-Hispanic/Latino; 0.5% Race/ethnicity unknown; 0.1% international; 12% transferred in. *Retention:* 40% of full-time freshmen returned.
Faculty *Student/faculty ratio:* 25:1.
Academics *Calendar:* semesters. *Degrees:* certificates, associate, bachelor's, and postbachelor's certificates. *Special study options:* academic remediation for entering students, accelerated degree program, adult/continuing education programs, advanced placement credit, cooperative education, distance learning, double majors, English as a second language, honors programs, independent study, off-campus study, part-time degree program, services for LD students, summer session for credit. *ROTC:* Army (c).
Library Weatherbee Learning Resources Center.
Student Life *Campus security:* 24-hour emergency response devices and patrols, student patrols, late-night transport/escort service, controlled dormitory access.
Athletics Member NJCAA.

Standardized Tests *Required:* non-traditional students must take the ACT Compass test (for admission). *Required for some:* SAT or ACT (for admission), SAT Subject Tests (for admission). *Recommended:* SAT or ACT (for admission), SAT Subject Tests (for admission).

Applying *Options:* electronic application, deferred entrance. *Application fee:* $20. *Required:* minimum 2.0 GPA, proof of immunization. *Required for some:* high school transcript.

Freshman Application Contact Darton State College, 2400 Gillionville Road, Albany, GA 31707-3098. *Phone:* 229-430-6740. *Toll-free phone:* 866-775-1214.

Website: http://www.darton.edu/.

East Georgia State College
Swainsboro, Georgia

Freshman Application Contact East Georgia State College, 131 College Circle, Swainsboro, GA 30401-2699. *Phone:* 478-289-2017.

Website: http://www.ega.edu/.

Emory University, Oxford College
Oxford, Georgia

- **Independent Methodist** 2-year, founded 1836
- **Small-town** 150-acre campus with easy access to Atlanta
- **Endowment** $48.7 million
- **Coed,** 936 undergraduate students, 100% full-time, 57% women, 43% men

Undergraduates 932 full-time, 4 part-time. Students come from 46 states and territories; 20 other countries; 75% are from out of state; 8% Black or African American, non-Hispanic/Latino; 7% Hispanic/Latino; 27% Asian, non-Hispanic/Latino; 0.1% Native Hawaiian or other Pacific Islander, non-Hispanic/Latino; 4% Two or more races, non-Hispanic/Latino; 3% Race/ethnicity unknown; 16% international; 99% live on campus. *Retention:* 93% of full-time freshmen returned.

Freshmen *Admission:* 9,734 applied, 3,760 admitted, 485 enrolled. *Average high school GPA:* 3.55. *Test scores:* SAT critical reading scores over 500: 100%; SAT math scores over 500: 99%; SAT writing scores over 500: 99%; ACT scores over 18: 100%; SAT critical reading scores over 600: 79%; SAT math scores over 600: 83%; SAT writing scores over 600: 86%; ACT scores over 24: 98%; SAT critical reading scores over 700: 24%; SAT math scores over 700: 49%; SAT writing scores over 700: 34%; ACT scores over 30: 52%.

Faculty *Total:* 90, 80% with terminal degrees. *Student/faculty ratio:* 12:1.

Majors Liberal arts and sciences/liberal studies.

Academics *Calendar:* semesters. *Degree:* associate. *Special study options:* advanced placement credit, independent study, internships, off-campus study, services for LD students, study abroad, summer session for credit. *ROTC:* Army (c), Navy (c), Air Force (c).

Library Hoke O'Kelly Library. *Books:* 84,104 (physical), 704,535 (digital/electronic).

Student Life *Housing:* on-campus residence required through sophomore year. *Options:* coed, women-only, special housing for students with disabilities. Campus housing is university owned. Freshman campus housing is guaranteed. *Activities and Organizations:* drama/theater group, student-run newspaper, choral group, Residence Hall Association, Intramurals/Junior Varsity Sports, Student Government Association, Student Admissions Association, Volunteer Oxford. *Campus security:* 24-hour emergency response devices and patrols, student patrols, late-night transport/escort service, controlled dormitory access. *Student services:* health clinic, personal/psychological counseling.

Athletics Member NJCAA. *Intercollegiate sports:* basketball M, soccer W, tennis M/W. *Intramural sports:* badminton M/W, baseball M(c), basketball M/W, football M, soccer M/W, swimming and diving M/W, tennis M/W, ultimate Frisbee M/W, volleyball M/W.

Standardized Tests *Required:* SAT or ACT (for admission).

Costs (2016–17) *Comprehensive fee:* $55,260 includes full-time tuition ($42,600), mandatory fees ($654), and room and board ($12,006). Part-time tuition: $1775 per credit hour. *Room and board:* college room only: $7788. *Waivers:* employees or children of employees.

Financial Aid Of all full-time matriculated undergraduates who enrolled in 2014, 225 Federal Work-Study jobs (averaging $1600).

Applying *Options:* electronic application, early admission, early decision, deferred entrance. *Application fee:* $75. *Required:* essay or personal statement, high school transcript, 1 letter of recommendation. *Recommended:* minimum 3.0 GPA, 2 letters of recommendation. *Application deadlines:* 1/1 (freshmen), 3/15 (transfers). *Early decision deadline:* 11/1 (for plan 1), 1/1

(for plan 2). *Notification:* continuous until 4/1 (freshmen), 4/30 (transfers), 12/15 (early decision plan 1), 2/15 (early decision plan 2).

Freshman Application Contact Emory University, Oxford College, 100 Hamill Street, PO Box 1328, Oxford, GA 30054. *Phone:* 770-784-8328. *Toll-free phone:* 800-723-8328.

Website: http://oxford.emory.edu/.

Everest Institute
Norcross, Georgia

Admissions Office Contact Everest Institute, 1750 Beaver Ruin Road, Suite 500, Norcross, GA 30093.
Website: http://www.everest.edu/.

Fortis College
Smyrna, Georgia

Admissions Office Contact Fortis College, 2108 Cobb Parkway, Smyrna, GA 30080. *Toll-free phone:* 855-4-FORTIS.
Website: http://www.fortis.edu/.

Georgia Highlands College
Rome, Georgia

- **State-supported** primarily 2-year, founded 1970, part of University System of Georgia
- **Suburban** 226-acre campus with easy access to Atlanta
- **Endowment** $36,933
- **Coed,** 5,748 undergraduate students, 47% full-time, 63% women, 37% men

Undergraduates 2,681 full-time, 3,067 part-time. Students come from 16 states and territories; 49 other countries; 1% are from out of state; 17% Black or African American, non-Hispanic/Latino; 11% Hispanic/Latino; 1% Asian, non-Hispanic/Latino; 0.1% Native Hawaiian or other Pacific Islander, non-Hispanic/Latino; 0.2% American Indian or Alaska Native, non-Hispanic/Latino; 3% Two or more races, non-Hispanic/Latino; 0.4% Race/ethnicity unknown; 9% transferred in. *Retention:* 62% of full-time freshmen returned.

Freshmen *Admission:* 2,388 applied, 1,925 admitted, 1,378 enrolled. *Average high school GPA:* 2.9. *Test scores:* SAT critical reading scores over 500: 30%; SAT math scores over 500: 23%; SAT writing scores over 500: 21%; ACT scores over 18: 68%; SAT critical reading scores over 600: 6%; SAT math scores over 600: 3%; SAT writing scores over 600: 3%; ACT scores over 24: 9%; SAT critical reading scores over 700: 1%.

Faculty *Total:* 277, 44% full-time, 21% with terminal degrees. *Student/faculty ratio:* 21:1.

Majors Agriculture; art; biology/biological sciences; business administration and management; chemistry; clinical laboratory science/medical technology; computer and information sciences; criminal justice/police science; dental hygiene; economics; education; English; foreign languages and literatures; general studies; geology/earth science; health information/medical records administration; history; human services; information science/studies; journalism; liberal arts and sciences/liberal studies; mathematics; music; philosophy; physician assistant; physics; political science and government; pre-engineering; pre-pharmacy studies; pre-physical therapy; psychology; registered nursing/registered nurse; respiratory therapy technician; sociology; speech communication and rhetoric.

Academics *Calendar:* semesters. *Degrees:* associate and bachelor's. *Special study options:* academic remediation for entering students, advanced placement credit, cooperative education, distance learning, double majors, honors programs, independent study, part-time degree program, services for LD students, study abroad, summer session for credit.

Library Georgia Highlands College Library–Floyd Campus. *Books:* 80,541 (physical), 94,529 (digital/electronic); *Serial titles:* 103 (physical), 37,000 (digital/electronic); *Databases:* 353. Weekly public service hours: 56; students can reserve study rooms.

Student Life *Housing:* college housing not available. *Activities and Organizations:* student-run newspaper, Highlands Association of Nursing Students, Green Highlands, Black Awareness Society, Political Science Association, Phi Theta Kappa. *Campus security:* 24-hour emergency response devices and patrols, emergency phone/email alert system. *Student services:* personal/psychological counseling.

Athletics Member NJCAA. *Intercollegiate sports:* baseball M(s)/W(s), basketball M(s)/W(s), softball M(s)/W(s). *Intramural sports:* basketball M/W, cheerleading M/W, football M/W, golf M/W, skiing (downhill) M/W, table tennis M/W, tennis M/W, ultimate Frisbee M/W, volleyball M/W, weight lifting M/W.

Standardized Tests *Required:* ACT Compass (for admission). *Recommended:* SAT or ACT (for admission), SAT and SAT Subject Tests or ACT (for admission).

Costs (2016–17) *Tuition:* state resident $3115 full-time, $91 per credit hour part-time; nonresident $9190 full-time, $344 per credit hour part-time. Full-time tuition and fees vary according to course load and location. Part-time tuition and fees vary according to course load and location. *Required fees:* $934 full-time, $347 per term part-time. *Payment plan:* installment. *Waivers:* senior citizens and employees or children of employees.

Financial Aid Of all full-time matriculated undergraduates who enrolled in 2014, 50 Federal Work-Study jobs (averaging $3500).

Applying *Options:* electronic application, deferred entrance. *Application fee:* $30. *Required:* high school transcript, minimum 2.0 GPA. *Application deadlines:* rolling (freshmen), rolling (out-of-state freshmen), rolling (transfers). *Notification:* continuous (freshmen), continuous (out-of-state freshmen), continuous (transfers).

Freshman Application Contact Sandie Davis, Director of Admissions, Georgia Highlands College, 3175 Cedartown Highway, Rome, GA 30161. *Phone:* 706-295-6339. *Toll-free phone:* 800-332-2406. *Fax:* 706-295-6341. *E-mail:* sdavis@highlands.edu. *Website:* http://www.highlands.edu/.

Georgia Military College
Milledgeville, Georgia

- **Public** primarily 2-year, founded 1879
- **Small-town** campus
- **Endowment** $1.5 million
- **Coed,** 7,876 undergraduate students, 60% full-time, 60% women, 40% men

Undergraduates 4,754 full-time, 3,122 part-time. Students come from 37 states and territories; 11 other countries; 3% are from out of state; 44% Black or African American, non-Hispanic/Latino; 6% Hispanic/Latino; 2% Asian, non-Hispanic/Latino; 1% American Indian or Alaska Native, non-Hispanic/Latino; 0.7% Two or more races, non-Hispanic/Latino; 5% Race/ethnicity unknown; 0.2% international; 0.5% transferred in; 3% live on campus. *Retention:* 56% of full-time freshmen returned.

Freshmen *Admission:* 1,850 enrolled.

Faculty *Total:* 381, 31% full-time. *Student/faculty ratio:* 23:1.

Majors Biology/biological sciences; business administration and management; business/commerce; computer and information systems security; computer science; criminal justice/law enforcement administration; early childhood education; English; general studies; health services/allied health/health sciences; health teacher education; history; homeland security; information technology; legal assistant/paralegal; logistics, materials, and supply chain management; management information systems; mass communication/media; mathematics; middle school education; political science and government; prenursing studies; psychology; secondary education; social work; sociology.

Academics *Calendar:* quarters. *Degrees:* associate and bachelor's. *Special study options:* academic remediation for entering students, advanced placement credit, cooperative education, distance learning, double majors, independent study, off-campus study, part-time degree program, services for LD students, student-designed majors, study abroad, summer session for credit. *ROTC:* Army (b).

Library Sibley Cone Library plus 1 other. *Books:* 38,125 (physical), 57,769 (digital/electronic); *Serial titles:* 52 (physical); *Databases:* 331. Weekly public service hours: 68.

Student Life *Housing:* on-campus residence required through sophomore year. *Options:* coed. Campus housing is university owned. Freshman campus housing is guaranteed. *Activities and Organizations:* drama/theater group, student-run newspaper, choral group, Student Government Association, Alpha Phi Omega National Service Fraternity, Phi Theta Kappa, Drama Club, Biology Club. *Campus security:* 24-hour emergency response devices and patrols, controlled dormitory access. *Student services:* health clinic.

Athletics Member NJCAA. *Intercollegiate sports:* cross-country running M/W, football M(s), golf M/W, riflery M/W, soccer M(s)/W(s), softball W(s). *Intramural sports:* badminton M/W, basketball M/W, golf M/W, softball M/W, tennis M/W, volleyball M/W.

Costs (2016–17) *Tuition:* state resident $5445 full-time, $121 per quarter hour part-time; nonresident $5445 full-time, $121 per quarter hour part-time. Full-time tuition and fees vary according to location. Part-time tuition and fees vary according to location. *Required fees:* $683 full-time, $14 per quarter hour part-time, $14 per quarter hour part-time. *Room and board:* $7500; room only: $3150. Room and board charges vary according to location. *Waivers:* senior citizens and employees or children of employees.

Financial Aid Of all full-time matriculated undergraduates who enrolled in 2012, 6,554 applied for aid, 6,132 were judged to have need, 282 had their need fully met. 121 Federal Work-Study jobs (averaging $1614). In 2012, 61 non-need-based awards were made. *Average percent of need met:* 47%.

Average financial aid package: $9567. *Average need-based loan:* $3189. *Average need-based gift aid:* $4626. *Average non-need-based aid:* $2226.

Applying *Options:* electronic application, early admission, deferred entrance. *Application fee:* $35. *Required for some:* high school transcript, interview. *Application deadlines:* rolling (freshmen), rolling (out-of-state freshmen), rolling (transfers).

Freshman Application Contact Georgia Military College, 201 East Greene Street, Old Capitol Building, Milledgeville, GA 31061-3398. *Phone:* 478-387-4890. *Toll-free phone:* 800-342-0413. *Website:* http://www.gmc.edu/.

Georgia Northwestern Technical College
Rome, Georgia

- **State-supported** 2-year, founded 1962, part of Technical College System of Georgia
- **Small-town** campus with easy access to Atlanta
- **Coed,** 5,874 undergraduate students, 31% full-time, 63% women, 37% men

Undergraduates 1,803 full-time, 4,071 part-time. 2% are from out of state; 9% Black or African American, non-Hispanic/Latino; 10% Hispanic/Latino; 0.8% Asian, non-Hispanic/Latino; 0.3% American Indian or Alaska Native, non-Hispanic/Latino; 2% Two or more races, non-Hispanic/Latino; 0.7% international. *Retention:* 55% of full-time freshmen returned.

Freshmen *Admission:* 929 enrolled.

Majors Accounting; child development; computer programming; criminal justice/safety; environmental engineering technology; fire science/firefighting; information science/studies; legal assistant/paralegal; marketing/marketing management; medical office management; respiratory therapy technician; surgical technology; web page, digital/multimedia and information resources design.

Academics *Calendar:* quarters. *Degree:* certificates, diplomas, and associate. *Special study options:* distance learning.

Student Life *Housing:* college housing not available.

Costs (2016–17) *Tuition:* state resident $89 per credit hour part-time; nonresident $178 per credit hour part-time.

Applying *Options:* early admission. *Application fee:* $15. *Required:* high school transcript.

Freshman Application Contact Georgia Northwestern Technical College, One Maurice Culberson Drive, Rome, GA 30161. *Phone:* 706-295-6933. *Toll-free phone:* 866-983-GNTC. *Website:* http://www.gntc.edu/.

Georgia Piedmont Technical College
Clarkston, Georgia

- **State-supported** 2-year, founded 1961, part of Technical College System of Georgia
- **Suburban** campus
- **Coed,** 3,908 undergraduate students, 24% full-time, 65% women, 35% men

Undergraduates 927 full-time, 2,981 part-time. 0.3% are from out of state; 82% Black or African American, non-Hispanic/Latino; 2% Hispanic/Latino; 2% Asian, non-Hispanic/Latino; 0.1% Native Hawaiian or other Pacific Islander, non-Hispanic/Latino; 0.2% American Indian or Alaska Native, non-Hispanic/Latino; 2% Two or more races, non-Hispanic/Latino; 0.2% Race/ethnicity unknown; 0.9% international. *Retention:* 57% of full-time freshmen returned.

Freshmen *Admission:* 405 enrolled.

Majors Accounting; administrative assistant and secretarial science; automobile/automotive mechanics technology; business/commerce; clinical/medical laboratory technology; computer engineering technology; computer programming; computer systems networking and telecommunications; criminal justice/safety; drafting and design technology; electrical, electronic and communications engineering technology; electromechanical technology; engineering technology; heating, ventilation, air conditioning and refrigeration engineering technology; industrial technology; information science/studies; instrumentation technology; legal administrative assistant/secretary; legal assistant/paralegal; machine tool technology; marketing/marketing management; medical/clinical assistant; operations management; ophthalmic laboratory technology; opticianry; surgical technology; telecommunications technology.

Academics *Calendar:* quarters. *Degree:* certificates, diplomas, and associate. *Special study options:* distance learning.

Student Life *Housing:* college housing not available.

Costs (2016–17) *Tuition:* state resident $89 per credit hour part-time; nonresident $178 per credit hour part-time.

Financial Aid Of all full-time matriculated undergraduates who enrolled in 2010, 7,200 applied for aid, 7,100 were judged to have need. 145 Federal

Work-Study jobs (averaging $4000). *Average financial aid package:* $4500. *Average need-based gift aid:* $4500.
Applying *Options:* early admission. *Application fee:* $20. *Required:* high school transcript.
Freshman Application Contact Georgia Piedmont Technical College, 495 North Indian Creek Drive, Clarkston, GA 30021-2397. *Phone:* 404-297-9522 Ext. 1229.
Website: http://www.gptc.edu/.

Gordon State College
Barnesville, Georgia

- **State-supported** primarily 2-year, founded 1852, part of University System of Georgia
- **Small-town** 235-acre campus with easy access to Atlanta
- **Coed,** 4,084 undergraduate students

Undergraduates Students come from 9 states and territories; 1 other country; 0.1% are from out of state.
Freshmen *Admission:* 2,480 applied, 1,068 admitted.
Faculty *Total:* 202, 59% full-time, 49% with terminal degrees. *Student/faculty ratio:* 21:1.
Majors Art; astronomy; biological and biomedical sciences related; biology teacher education; business administration and management; chemistry; communication; computer science; criminal justice/safety; dental services and allied professions related; dramatic/theater arts; early childhood education; elementary education; English; English as a second/foreign language (teaching); English/language arts teacher education; environmental science; foreign languages and literatures; forestry; general studies; health and physical education/fitness; health information/medical records administration; health/medical preparatory programs related; history; history teacher education; human services; information technology; liberal arts and sciences/liberal studies; mathematics; mathematics teacher education; middle school education; music; physics; political science and government; pre-engineering; pre-occupational therapy; pre-pharmacy studies; pre-physical therapy; psychology; radiologic technology/science; registered nursing/registered nurse; secondary education; social work; sociology.
Academics *Calendar:* semesters. *Degrees:* certificates, associate, and bachelor's. *Special study options:* academic remediation for entering students, accelerated degree program, adult/continuing education programs, advanced placement credit, cooperative education, distance learning, double majors, honors programs, internships, off-campus study, part-time degree program, services for LD students, study abroad, summer session for credit.
Library Hightower Library. *Books:* 103,423 (physical), 35,999 (digital/electronic); *Serial titles:* 401 (physical), 87,985 (digital/electronic); *Databases:* 325. Weekly public service hours: 73.
Student Life *Housing:* on-campus residence required for freshman year. *Options:* coed. Campus housing is university owned. Freshman applicants given priority for college housing. *Activities and Organizations:* drama/theater group, student-run newspaper, choral group, Campus Activity Board, Student Government Association, Earth Wind Fire (science club), Student African American Brotherhood (SAAB), Swazi Step Team. *Campus security:* 24-hour emergency response devices and patrols, student patrols, late-night transport/escort service, controlled dormitory access, Resident Assistants and Resident Directors in housing, parking patrol. *Student services:* health clinic, personal/psychological counseling.
Athletics Member NJCAA. *Intercollegiate sports:* baseball M, basketball M, soccer M/W, softball W.
Standardized Tests *Required for some:* SAT and SAT Subject Tests or ACT (for admission).
Costs (2015–16) *Tuition:* state resident $2451 full-time; nonresident $9058 full-time. *Required fees:* $1100 full-time. *Room and board:* $8101; room only: $5290. Room and board charges vary according to board plan and housing facility. *Payment plan:* installment.
Financial Aid Of all full-time matriculated undergraduates who enrolled in 2014, 75 Federal Work-Study jobs (averaging $1850).
Applying *Options:* electronic application, early admission, deferred entrance. *Application fee:* $30. *Required:* high school transcript, letters of recommendation. *Application deadlines:* rolling (freshmen), rolling (transfers).
Freshman Application Contact Gordon State College, 419 College Drive, Barnesville, GA 30204-1762. *Phone:* 678-359-5021. *Toll-free phone:* 800-282-6504.
Website: http://www.gordonstate.edu/.

Gupton-Jones College of Funeral Service
Decatur, Georgia

- **Independent** 2-year, founded 1920, part of Pierce Mortuary Colleges, Inc.
- **Suburban** 3-acre campus with easy access to Atlanta
- **Coed**

Academics *Calendar:* quarters. *Degree:* associate. *Special study options:* distance learning, summer session for credit.
Library Russell Millison Library.
Applying *Options:* electronic application. *Application fee:* $50. *Required:* high school transcript, health certificate. *Recommended:* minimum 3.0 GPA.
Freshman Application Contact Ms. Felicia Smith, Registrar, Gupton-Jones College of Funeral Service, 5141 Snapfinger Woods Drive, Decatur, GA 30035-4022. *Phone:* 770-593-2257. *Toll-free phone:* 800-848-5352.
Website: http://www.gupton-jones.edu/.

Gwinnett College
Lilburn, Georgia

Admissions Office Contact Gwinnett College, 4230 Highway 29, Suite 11, Lilburn, GA 30047.
Website: http://www.gwinnettcollege.edu/.

Gwinnett Technical College
Lawrenceville, Georgia

- **State-supported** 2-year, founded 1984, part of Technical College System of Georgia
- **Suburban** 88-acre campus
- **Coed,** 6,959 undergraduate students, 24% full-time, 59% women, 41% men

Undergraduates 1,659 full-time, 5,300 part-time. 1% are from out of state; 35% Black or African American, non-Hispanic/Latino; 13% Hispanic/Latino; 7% Asian, non-Hispanic/Latino; 0.2% Native Hawaiian or other Pacific Islander, non-Hispanic/Latino; 0.3% American Indian or Alaska Native, non-Hispanic/Latino; 3% Two or more races, non-Hispanic/Latino; 6% Race/ethnicity unknown; 1% international. *Retention:* 58% of full-time freshmen returned.
Freshmen *Admission:* 883 enrolled.
Faculty *Total:* 404, 25% full-time. *Student/faculty ratio:* 25:1.
Majors Accounting; administrative assistant and secretarial science; automobile/automotive mechanics technology; building/construction finishing, management, and inspection related; business administration and management; computer programming; computer science; computer systems networking and telecommunications; drafting and design technology; electrical, electronic and communications engineering technology; emergency medical technology (EMT paramedic); horticultural science; hotel/motel administration; information science/studies; interior design; machine tool technology; management information systems; marketing/marketing management; medical/clinical assistant; medical radiologic technology; ornamental horticulture; photography; physical therapy; physical therapy technology; respiratory care therapy; tourism and travel services management; veterinary/animal health technology.
Academics *Calendar:* semesters. *Degree:* certificates, diplomas, and associate. *Special study options:* distance learning, English as a second language, part-time degree program, services for LD students, summer session for credit.
Library Gwinnett Technical College Library plus 1 other.
Student Life *Housing:* college housing not available. *Campus security:* 24-hour emergency response devices and patrols. *Student services:* personal/psychological counseling.
Costs (2016–17) *Tuition:* state resident $89 per credit hour part-time; nonresident $178 per credit hour part-time.
Financial Aid Of all full-time matriculated undergraduates who enrolled in 2014, 20 Federal Work-Study jobs (averaging $2100).
Applying *Options:* electronic application, early admission. *Application fee:* $20. *Required:* high school transcript.
Freshman Application Contact Gwinnett Technical College, 5150 Sugarloaf Parkway, Lawrenceville, GA 30043-5702. *Phone:* 678-762-7580 Ext. 434.
Website: http://www.gwinnetttech.edu/.

Interactive College of Technology
Chamblee, Georgia

- **Proprietary** 2-year, part of Interactive Learning Systems
- **Suburban** 14-acre campus
- **Coed,** 312 undergraduate students

Faculty *Student/faculty ratio:* 25:1.

Majors Accounting technology and bookkeeping; administrative assistant and secretarial science; computer and information sciences; computer and information sciences and support services related; management information systems.

Academics *Calendar:* semesters. *Degree:* certificates, diplomas, and associate. *Special study options:* academic remediation for entering students, accelerated degree program, adult/continuing education programs, advanced placement credit, double majors, English as a second language, independent study, internships, part-time degree program.

Applying *Application fee:* $50. *Required:* high school transcript, interview. *Application deadlines:* rolling (freshmen), rolling (transfers).

Freshman Application Contact Director of Admissions, Interactive College of Technology, 5303 New Peachtree Road, Chamblee, GA 30341. *Phone:* 770-216-2960. *Toll-free phone:* 800-447-2011. *Fax:* 770-216-2988. *Website:* http://ict.edu/.

Interactive College of Technology
Gainesville, Georgia

- **Proprietary** 2-year
- **Small-town** campus
- **Coed**

Academics *Calendar:* semesters. *Degree:* certificates, diplomas, and associate. *Special study options:* academic remediation for entering students, cooperative education, distance learning, English as a second language, internships.

Applying *Required:* high school transcript, interview.

Freshman Application Contact Interactive College of Technology, 2323-C Browns Bridge Road, Gainesville, GA 30504. *Website:* http://ict.edu/.

Interactive College of Technology
Morrow, Georgia

Admissions Office Contact Interactive College of Technology, 1580 Southlake Parkway, Suite C, Morrow, GA 30260. *Website:* http://ict.edu/.

ITT Technical Institute
Atlanta, Georgia

Freshman Application Contact Director of Recruitment, ITT Technical Institute, 485 Oak Place, Suite 800, Atlanta, GA 30349. *Phone:* 404-765-4600. *Toll-free phone:* 877-488-6102 (in-state); 877-788-6102 (out-of-state). *Website:* http://www.itt-tech.edu/.

ITT Technical Institute
Duluth, Georgia

Freshman Application Contact Director of Recruitment, ITT Technical Institute, 10700 Abbotts Bridge Road, Suite 190, Duluth, GA 30097. *Phone:* 678-957-8510. *Toll-free phone:* 866-489-8818. *Website:* http://www.itt-tech.edu/.

ITT Technical Institute
Kennesaw, Georgia

Freshman Application Contact Director of Recruitment, ITT Technical Institute, 2065 ITT Tech Way, Kennesaw, GA 30144. *Phone:* 770-426-2300. *Toll-free phone:* 877-231-6415. *Website:* http://www.itt-tech.edu/.

Lanier Technical College
Oakwood, Georgia

- **State-supported** 2-year, founded 1964, part of Technical College System of Georgia
- **Coed,** 3,646 undergraduate students, 27% full-time, 59% women, 41% men

Undergraduates 984 full-time, 2,662 part-time. 9% Black or African American, non-Hispanic/Latino; 14% Hispanic/Latino; 2% Asian, non-Hispanic/Latino; 0.2% Native Hawaiian or other Pacific Islander, non-Hispanic/Latino; 0.4% American Indian or Alaska Native, non-Hispanic/Latino; 2% Two or more races, non-Hispanic/Latino; 0.1% Race/ethnicity unknown; 1% international. *Retention:* 56% of full-time freshmen returned.

Freshmen *Admission:* 853 enrolled.

Majors Accounting; administrative assistant and secretarial science; banking and financial support services; child development; computer and information systems security; computer programming; computer science; computer systems networking and telecommunications; criminal justice/safety; drafting and design technology; electrical, electronic and communications engineering technology; fire science/firefighting; health professions related; industrial technology; information science/studies; interior design; marketing/marketing management; medical radiologic technology; occupational safety and health technology; surgical technology; web page, digital/multimedia and information resources design.

Academics *Calendar:* quarters. *Degree:* certificates, diplomas, and associate. *Special study options:* distance learning.

Student Life *Housing:* college housing not available.

Costs (2016–17) *Tuition:* state resident $89 per credit hour part-time; nonresident $178 per credit hour part-time.

Applying *Options:* early admission. *Application fee:* $15. *Required:* high school transcript.

Freshman Application Contact Lanier Technical College, 2990 Landrum Education Drive, PO Box 58, Oakwood, GA 30566. *Phone:* 770-531-6332. *Website:* http://www.laniertech.edu/.

Lincoln College of Technology
Marietta, Georgia

Admissions Office Contact Lincoln College of Technology, 2359 Windy Hill Road, SE, Suite 280, Marietta, GA 30067-8645. *Website:* http://www.lincolnedu.com/campus/marietta-ga.

Medtech College
Atlanta, Georgia

Admissions Office Contact Medtech College, 4501 Circle 75 Parkway, Suite C-3180, Atlanta, GA 30339. *Website:* http://www.medtech-atlanta.com/atlanta-marietta-ga/.

Miller-Motte Technical College
Augusta, Georgia

Admissions Office Contact Miller-Motte Technical College, 621 NW Frontage Road, Augusta, GA 30907. *Toll-free phone:* 866-297-0267. *Website:* http://www.miller-motte.edu/.

Miller-Motte Technical College
Columbus, Georgia

Admissions Office Contact Miller-Motte Technical College, 1800 Box Road, Columbus, GA 31907. *Website:* http://www.miller-motte.edu/.

Miller-Motte Technical College
Macon, Georgia

Admissions Office Contact Miller-Motte Technical College, 175 Tom Hill Sr. Boulevard, Macon, GA 31210. *Toll-free phone:* 866-297-0267. *Website:* http://www.miller-motte.edu/.

North Georgia Technical College
Clarkesville, Georgia

- **State-supported** 2-year, founded 1943, part of Technical College System of Georgia
- **Coed,** 2,665 undergraduate students, 36% full-time, 59% women, 41% men

Undergraduates 970 full-time, 1,695 part-time. 2% are from out of state; 7% Black or African American, non-Hispanic/Latino; 5% Hispanic/Latino; 0.9% Asian, non-Hispanic/Latino; 0.5% American Indian or Alaska Native, non-Hispanic/Latino; 1% Two or more races, non-Hispanic/Latino; 2% Race/ethnicity unknown; 0.2% international. *Retention:* 59% of full-time freshmen returned.
Freshmen *Admission:* 629 enrolled.
Majors Administrative assistant and secretarial science; computer systems networking and telecommunications; criminal justice/safety; culinary arts; heating, ventilation, air conditioning and refrigeration engineering technology; horticultural science; industrial technology; parks, recreation and leisure facilities management; turf and turfgrass management; web page, digital/multimedia and information resources design.
Academics *Calendar:* quarters. *Degree:* certificates, diplomas, and associate. *Special study options:* distance learning.
Costs (2016–17) *Tuition:* state resident $89 per credit hour part-time; nonresident $178 per credit hour part-time.
Applying *Options:* early admission. *Application fee:* $20. *Required:* high school transcript.
Freshman Application Contact North Georgia Technical College, 1500 Georgia Highway 197, North, PO Box 65, Clarkesville, GA 30523. *Phone:* 706-754-7724.
Website: http://www.northgatech.edu/.

Oconee Fall Line Technical College
Sandersville, Georgia

- **State-supported** 2-year, part of Technical College System of Georgia
- **Coed,** 1,569 undergraduate students, 28% full-time, 62% women, 38% men

Undergraduates 434 full-time, 1,135 part-time. 48% Black or African American, non-Hispanic/Latino; 2% Hispanic/Latino; 0.4% Asian, non-Hispanic/Latino; 0.1% American Indian or Alaska Native, non-Hispanic/Latino; 0.9% Two or more races, non-Hispanic/Latino; 0.4% Race/ethnicity unknown; 0.2% international. *Retention:* 61% of full-time freshmen returned.
Freshmen *Admission:* 317 enrolled.
Majors Accounting; administrative assistant and secretarial science; child development; computer systems networking and telecommunications; information science/studies.
Academics *Calendar:* quarters. *Degree:* certificates, diplomas, and associate. *Special study options:* distance learning.
Student Life *Housing:* college housing not available.
Costs (2016–17) *Tuition:* state resident $89 per credit hour part-time; nonresident $178 per credit hour part-time.
Applying *Options:* early admission. *Application fee:* $20. *Required:* high school transcript.
Freshman Application Contact Oconee Fall Line Technical College, 1189 Deepstep Road, Sandersville, GA 31082. *Phone:* 478-553-2050. *Toll-free phone:* 877-399-8324.
Website: http://www.oftc.edu/.

Ogeechee Technical College
Statesboro, Georgia

- **State-supported** 2-year, founded 1989, part of Technical College System of Georgia
- **Small-town** campus
- **Coed,** 2,068 undergraduate students, 37% full-time, 68% women, 32% men

Undergraduates 759 full-time, 1,309 part-time. 0.9% are from out of state; 38% Black or African American, non-Hispanic/Latino; 3% Hispanic/Latino; 0.7% Asian, non-Hispanic/Latino; 0.1% Native Hawaiian or other Pacific Islander, non-Hispanic/Latino; 0.3% American Indian or Alaska Native, non-Hispanic/Latino; 2% Two or more races, non-Hispanic/Latino; 0.2% international. *Retention:* 63% of full-time freshmen returned.
Freshmen *Admission:* 336 enrolled.
Majors Accounting; administrative assistant and secretarial science; agribusiness; automobile/automotive mechanics technology; banking and financial support services; child development; computer systems networking and telecommunications; construction trades; culinary arts; dental hygiene; forest technology; funeral service and mortuary science; health

information/medical records technology; hotel/motel administration; information science/studies; interior design; legal assistant/paralegal; marketing/marketing management; opticianry; tourism and travel services management; veterinary/animal health technology; water quality and wastewater treatment management and recycling technology; wildlife, fish and wildlands science and management; wood science and wood products/pulp and paper technology.
Academics *Calendar:* quarters. *Degree:* certificates, diplomas, and associate. *Special study options:* distance learning.
Student Life *Housing:* college housing not available.
Costs (2016–17) *Tuition:* state resident $89 per credit hour part-time; nonresident $178 per credit hour part-time.
Applying *Options:* early admission. *Application fee:* $20. *Required:* high school transcript.
Freshman Application Contact Ogeechee Technical College, One Joe Kennedy Boulevard, Statesboro, GA 30458. *Phone:* 912-871-1600. *Toll-free phone:* 800-646-1316.
Website: http://www.ogeecheetech.edu/.

SAE Institute Atlanta
Atlanta, Georgia

Admissions Office Contact SAE Institute Atlanta, 215 Peachtree Street, Suite 300, Atlanta, GA 30303.
Website: http://www.sae.edu/.

Savannah Technical College
Savannah, Georgia

- **State-supported** 2-year, founded 1929, part of Technical College System of Georgia
- **Urban** campus
- **Coed,** 4,196 undergraduate students, 33% full-time, 62% women, 38% men

Undergraduates 1,390 full-time, 2,806 part-time. 2% are from out of state; 46% Black or African American, non-Hispanic/Latino; 8% Hispanic/Latino; 2% Asian, non-Hispanic/Latino; 0.3% Native Hawaiian or other Pacific Islander, non-Hispanic/Latino; 0.4% American Indian or Alaska Native, non-Hispanic/Latino; 2% Two or more races, non-Hispanic/Latino; 0.3% Race/ethnicity unknown; 0.8% international. *Retention:* 55% of full-time freshmen returned.
Freshmen *Admission:* 693 enrolled.
Majors Accounting; administrative assistant and secretarial science; automobile/automotive mechanics technology; child development; computer systems networking and telecommunications; criminal justice/safety; culinary arts; electrical, electronic and communications engineering technology; fire science/firefighting; heating, ventilation, air conditioning and refrigeration engineering technology; hotel/motel administration; industrial technology; information technology; marketing/marketing management; surgical technology; tourism and travel services management.
Academics *Calendar:* quarters. *Degree:* certificates, diplomas, and associate. *Special study options:* distance learning.
Student Life *Housing:* college housing not available.
Costs (2016–17) *Tuition:* state resident $89 per credit hour part-time; nonresident $178 per credit hour part-time.
Applying *Options:* early admission. *Application fee:* $20. *Required:* high school transcript.
Freshman Application Contact Savannah Technical College, 5717 White Bluff Road, Savannah, GA 31405. *Phone:* 912-443-5711. *Toll-free phone:* 800-769-6362.
Website: http://www.savannahtech.edu/.

Southeastern Technical College
Vidalia, Georgia

- **State-supported** 2-year, founded 1989, part of Technical College System of Georgia
- **Coed,** 1,667 undergraduate students, 26% full-time, 72% women, 28% men

Undergraduates 429 full-time, 1,238 part-time. 0.3% are from out of state; 28% Black or African American, non-Hispanic/Latino; 7% Hispanic/Latino; 0.2% Asian, non-Hispanic/Latino; 0.1% Native Hawaiian or other Pacific Islander, non-Hispanic/Latino; 0.1% American Indian or Alaska Native, non-Hispanic/Latino; 0.6% Two or more races, non-Hispanic/Latino. *Retention:* 52% of full-time freshmen returned.
Freshmen *Admission:* 329 enrolled.
Majors Accounting; administrative assistant and secretarial science; child development; computer systems networking and telecommunications; criminal

justice/safety; dental hygiene; design and visual communications; electrical, electronic and communications engineering technology; information science/studies; marketing/marketing management; medical radiologic technology; respiratory therapy technician; web page, digital/multimedia and information resources design.

Academics *Calendar:* quarters. *Degree:* certificates, diplomas, and associate. *Special study options:* distance learning.

Student Life *Housing:* college housing not available.

Costs (2016–17) *Tuition:* state resident $89 per credit hour part-time; nonresident $178 per credit hour part-time.

Applying *Options:* early admission. *Application fee:* $20. *Required:* high school transcript.

Freshman Application Contact Southeastern Technical College, 3001 East First Street, Vidalia, GA 30474. *Phone:* 912-538-3121. *Website:* http://www.southeasterntech.edu/.

Southern Crescent Technical College
Griffin, Georgia

- **State-supported** 2-year, founded 1965, part of Technical College System of Georgia
- **Small-town** campus
- **Coed,** 4,867 undergraduate students, 36% full-time, 65% women, 35% men

Undergraduates 1,764 full-time, 3,103 part-time. 0.3% are from out of state; 43% Black or African American, non-Hispanic/Latino; 4% Hispanic/Latino; 1% Asian, non-Hispanic/Latino; 0.1% Native Hawaiian or other Pacific Islander, non-Hispanic/Latino; 0.2% American Indian or Alaska Native, non-Hispanic/Latino; 0.5% Two or more races, non-Hispanic/Latino; 1% Race/ethnicity unknown; 0.3% international. *Retention:* 53% of full-time freshmen returned.

Freshmen *Admission:* 866 enrolled.

Majors Accounting; administrative assistant and secretarial science; automobile/automotive mechanics technology; business administration and management; child development; computer and information systems security; computer programming; computer systems networking and telecommunications; criminal justice/safety; drafting and design technology; electrical, electronic and communications engineering technology; emergency medical technology (EMT paramedic); heating, ventilation, air conditioning and refrigeration engineering technology; horticultural science; industrial technology; legal assistant/paralegal; manufacturing engineering technology; marketing/marketing management; medical radiologic technology; pharmacy technician; respiratory therapy technician; surgical technology; web page, digital/multimedia and information resources design.

Academics *Calendar:* quarters. *Degree:* certificates, diplomas, and associate. *Special study options:* distance learning.

Library Griffin Technical College Library.

Costs (2016–17) *Tuition:* state resident $89 per credit hour part-time; nonresident $178 per credit hour part-time.

Applying *Options:* early admission. *Application fee:* $20. *Required:* high school transcript.

Freshman Application Contact Southern Crescent Technical College, 501 Varsity Road, Griffin, GA 30223. *Phone:* 770-646-6160. *Website:* http://www.sctech.edu/.

Southern Regional Technical College
Thomasville, Georgia

- **State-supported** 2-year, founded 1963, part of Technical College System of Georgia
- **Coed,** 3,490 undergraduate students, 32% full-time, 65% women, 35% men

Undergraduates 1,122 full-time, 2,368 part-time. 1% are from out of state; 33% Black or African American, non-Hispanic/Latino; 6% Hispanic/Latino; 0.4% Asian, non-Hispanic/Latino; 0.3% American Indian or Alaska Native, non-Hispanic/Latino; 1% Two or more races, non-Hispanic/Latino; 0.5% Race/ethnicity unknown; 0.6% international. *Retention:* 39% of full-time freshmen returned.

Freshmen *Admission:* 439 enrolled.

Majors Accounting; administrative assistant and secretarial science; agricultural mechanization; child development; computer systems networking and telecommunications; criminal justice/safety; information science/studies; medical radiologic technology; registered nursing/registered nurse; respiratory care therapy; surgical technology.

Academics *Calendar:* quarters. *Degree:* certificates, diplomas, and associate. *Special study options:* distance learning.

Student Life *Housing:* college housing not available.

Costs (2016–17) *Tuition:* state resident $89 per credit hour part-time; nonresident $178 per credit hour part-time.

Applying *Options:* electronic application, early admission. *Application fee:* $25. *Required:* high school transcript.

Freshman Application Contact Southern Regional Technical College, 15689 US 19 North, Thomasville, GA 31792. *Phone:* 229-225-5089. *Website:* http://www.southwestgatech.edu/.

South Georgia State College
Douglas, Georgia

Freshman Application Contact South Georgia State College, 100 West College Park Drive, Douglas, GA 31533-5098. *Phone:* 912-260-4409. *Toll-free phone:* 800-342-6364. *Website:* http://www.sgc.edu/.

South Georgia Technical College
Americus, Georgia

- **State-supported** 2-year, founded 1948, part of Technical College System of Georgia
- **Coed,** 1,668 undergraduate students, 50% full-time, 46% women, 54% men

Undergraduates 833 full-time, 835 part-time. 6% are from out of state; 52% Black or African American, non-Hispanic/Latino; 3% Hispanic/Latino; 0.7% Asian, non-Hispanic/Latino; 0.2% American Indian or Alaska Native, non-Hispanic/Latino; 0.1% Race/ethnicity unknown; 0.2% international. *Retention:* 64% of full-time freshmen returned.

Freshmen *Admission:* 470 enrolled.

Majors Accounting; administrative assistant and secretarial science; child development; computer systems networking and telecommunications; criminal justice/safety; culinary arts; drafting and design technology; electrical, electronic and communications engineering technology; heating, ventilation, air conditioning and refrigeration engineering technology; horticultural science; industrial technology; information science/studies; legal assistant/paralegal; manufacturing engineering technology; marketing/marketing management.

Academics *Calendar:* quarters. *Degree:* certificates, diplomas, and associate. *Special study options:* distance learning.

Costs (2016–17) *Tuition:* state resident $89 per credit hour part-time; nonresident $178 per credit hour part-time.

Applying *Options:* early admission. *Application fee:* $25. *Required:* high school transcript.

Freshman Application Contact South Georgia Technical College, 900 South Georgia Tech Parkway, Americus, GA 31709. *Phone:* 229-931-2299. *Website:* http://www.southgatech.edu/.

Virginia College in Augusta
Augusta, Georgia

Admissions Office Contact Virginia College in Augusta, 2807 Wylds Road Extension, Suite B, Augusta, GA 30909. *Website:* http://www.vc.edu/.

Virginia College in Columbus
Columbus, Georgia

Admissions Office Contact Virginia College in Columbus, 5601 Veterans Parkway, Columbus, GA 31904. *Website:* http://www.vc.edu/.

Virginia College in Macon
Macon, Georgia

Admissions Office Contact Virginia College in Macon, 1901 Paul Walsh Drive, Macon, GA 31206. *Website:* http://www.vc.edu/.

Virginia College in Savannah
Savannah, Georgia

Admissions Office Contact Virginia College in Savannah, 14045 Abercorn Street, Suite 1503, Savannah, GA 31419. *Website:* http://www.vc.edu/.

West Georgia Technical College
Waco, Georgia

- **State-supported** 2-year, founded 1966, part of Technical College System of Georgia
- **Coed,** 6,431 undergraduate students, 29% full-time, 65% women, 35% men

Undergraduates 1,881 full-time, 4,550 part-time. 2% are from out of state; 30% Black or African American, non-Hispanic/Latino; 4% Hispanic/Latino; 1% Asian, non-Hispanic/Latino; 0.2% Native Hawaiian or other Pacific Islander, non-Hispanic/Latino; 0.4% American Indian or Alaska Native, non-Hispanic/Latino; 2% Two or more races, non-Hispanic/Latino; 1% Race/ethnicity unknown; 0.4% international. *Retention:* 55% of full-time freshmen returned.
Freshmen *Admission:* 1,217 enrolled.
Majors Accounting; administrative assistant and secretarial science; automobile/automotive mechanics technology; child development; computer systems networking and telecommunications; criminal justice/safety; electrical, electronic and communications engineering technology; fire science/firefighting; health information/medical records technology; industrial technology; information science/studies; marketing/marketing management; medical radiologic technology; pharmacy technician; plastics and polymer engineering technology; social work; web page, digital/multimedia and information resources design.
Academics *Calendar:* quarters. *Degree:* certificates, diplomas, and associate. *Special study options:* distance learning.
Student Life *Housing:* college housing not available.
Costs (2016–17) *Tuition:* state resident $89 per credit hour part-time; nonresident $178 per credit hour part-time.
Financial Aid Of all full-time matriculated undergraduates who enrolled in 2014, 68 Federal Work-Study jobs (averaging $800).
Applying *Options:* early admission. *Application fee:* $24. *Required:* high school transcript.
Freshman Application Contact West Georgia Technical College, 176 Murphy Campus Boulevard, Waco, GA 30182. *Phone:* 770-537-5719. *Website:* http://www.westgatech.edu/.

Wiregrass Georgia Technical College
Valdosta, Georgia

- **State-supported** 2-year, founded 1963, part of Technical College System of Georgia
- **Suburban** campus
- **Coed,** 3,708 undergraduate students, 23% full-time, 64% women, 36% men

Undergraduates 871 full-time, 2,837 part-time. 1% are from out of state; 32% Black or African American, non-Hispanic/Latino; 5% Hispanic/Latino; 0.6% Asian, non-Hispanic/Latino; 0.1% Native Hawaiian or other Pacific Islander, non-Hispanic/Latino; 0.3% American Indian or Alaska Native, non-Hispanic/Latino; 1% Two or more races, non-Hispanic/Latino; 0.3% Race/ethnicity unknown; 0.4% international. *Retention:* 49% of full-time freshmen returned.
Freshmen *Admission:* 484 enrolled.
Majors Accounting; administrative assistant and secretarial science; banking and financial support services; child development; computer and information systems security; computer programming; computer systems networking and telecommunications; criminal justice/safety; drafting and design technology; e-commerce; fire science/firefighting; machine tool technology; marketing/marketing management; medical radiologic technology; web page, digital/multimedia and information resources design.
Academics *Calendar:* quarters. *Degree:* certificates, diplomas, and associate. *Special study options:* distance learning.
Student Life *Housing:* college housing not available.
Costs (2016–17) *Tuition:* state resident $89 per credit hour part-time; nonresident $178 per credit hour part-time.
Applying *Options:* early admission. *Application fee:* $25. *Required:* high school transcript.
Freshman Application Contact Wiregrass Georgia Technical College, 4089 Val Tech Road, Valdosta, GA 31602. *Phone:* 229-468-2278. *Website:* http://www.wiregrass.edu/.

GUAM

Guam Community College
Mangilao, Guam

- **Territory-supported** 2-year, founded 1977
- **Small-town** 33-acre campus
- **Endowment** $8.8 million
- **Coed**

Undergraduates 989 full-time, 1,469 part-time. 2% Black or African American, non-Hispanic/Latino; 0.4% Hispanic/Latino; 39% Asian, non-Hispanic/Latino; 55% Native Hawaiian or other Pacific Islander, non-Hispanic/Latino; 0.1% American Indian or Alaska Native, non-Hispanic/Latino; 0.6% Race/ethnicity unknown; 0.7% international; 1% transferred in.
Faculty *Student/faculty ratio:* 15:1.
Academics *Calendar:* semesters. *Degree:* certificates, diplomas, and associate. *Special study options:* academic remediation for entering students, adult/continuing education programs, advanced placement credit, cooperative education, double majors, English as a second language, honors programs, independent study, internships, off-campus study, part-time degree program, services for LD students, summer session for credit. *ROTC:* Army (c).
Library Learning Resource Center.
Student Life *Campus security:* 12-hour patrols by trained security personnel.
Costs (2015–16) *Tuition:* territory resident $3120 full-time, $130 per credit hour part-time; nonresident $3720 full-time, $155 per credit hour part-time. *Required fees:* $294 full-time, $147 per term part-time. *Payment plans:* installment, deferred payment.
Financial Aid Of all full-time matriculated undergraduates who enrolled in 2014, 83 Federal Work-Study jobs (averaging $940).
Applying *Options:* early admission. *Required:* high school transcript.
Freshman Application Contact Mr. Patrick L. Clymer, Registrar, Guam Community College, PO Box 23069 GMF, Barrigada, GU 96921. *Phone:* 671-735-5561. *Fax:* 671-735-5531. *E-mail:* patrick.clymer@guamcc.edu. *Website:* http://www.guamcc.edu/.

HAWAII

Hawaii Community College
Hilo, Hawaii

Director of Admissions Mrs. Tammy M. Tanaka, Admissions Specialist, Hawaii Community College, 200 West Kawili Street, Hilo, HI 96720-4091. *Phone:* 808-974-7661.
Website: http://www.hawcc.hawaii.edu/.

Hawaii Tokai International College
Kapolei, Hawaii

- **Independent** 2-year, founded 1992, part of Tokai University Educational System
- **Suburban** 7-acre campus with easy access to Honolulu
- **Coed,** 79 undergraduate students, 100% full-time, 49% women, 51% men

Undergraduates 79 full-time. Students come from 3 states and territories; 3 other countries; 23% are from out of state; 8% Asian, non-Hispanic/Latino; 3% Native Hawaiian or other Pacific Islander, non-Hispanic/Latino; 82% international; 90% live on campus. *Retention:* 94% of full-time freshmen returned.
Freshmen *Admission:* 49 applied, 43 admitted, 22 enrolled. *Average high school GPA:* 3.1.
Faculty *Total:* 17, 35% full-time, 35% with terminal degrees. *Student/faculty ratio:* 5:1.
Majors Liberal arts and sciences/liberal studies.
Academics *Calendar:* quarters. *Degree:* certificates, diplomas, and associate. *Special study options:* academic remediation for entering students, advanced placement credit, English as a second language, part-time degree program, study abroad, summer session for credit.
Library Library and Learning Center plus 1 other. *Books:* 6,487 (physical); *Serial titles:* 32 (physical); *Databases:* 4. Weekly public service hours: 68; students can reserve study rooms.
Student Life *Housing Options:* men-only, women-only, special housing for students with disabilities. Campus housing is university owned. Freshman applicants given priority for college housing. *Activities and Organizations:* International Coffee Hour, Chess Club, Hula Club, Yoga Club, Phi Theta Kappa International Honor Society. *Campus security:* 24-hour emergency

response devices and patrols, controlled dormitory access. *Student services:* personal/psychological counseling.

Standardized Tests *Required for some:* TOEFL for international students.

Costs (2016–17) *One-time required fee:* $20. *Comprehensive fee:* $20,925 includes full-time tuition ($11,550), mandatory fees ($675), and room and board ($8700). Part-time tuition: $475 per credit hour. Part-time tuition and fees vary according to course load. *Room and board:* Room and board charges vary according to board plan and housing facility.

Applying *Options:* electronic application, deferred entrance. *Application fee:* $50. *Required:* essay or personal statement, high school transcript, minimum 2.5 GPA. *Required for some:* interview. *Recommended:* 1 letter of recommendation. *Application deadlines:* rolling (freshmen), rolling (out-of-state freshmen), rolling (transfers). *Notification:* continuous (freshmen), continuous (out-of-state freshmen), continuous (transfers).

Freshman Application Contact Mr. Darrell Kicker, Director of Admissions and Recruitment, Hawaii Tokai International College, 91-971 Farrington Highway, Kapolei, HI 96707. *Phone:* 808-983-4202. *Fax:* 808-983-4107. *E-mail:* admissions@tokai.edu. *Website:* http://www.hawaiitokai.edu/.

Honolulu Community College
Honolulu, Hawaii

Freshman Application Contact Admissions Office, Honolulu Community College, 874 Dillingham Boulevard, Honolulu, HI 96817. *Phone:* 808-845-9129. *E-mail:* honcc@hawaii.edu. *Website:* http://www.honolulu.hawaii.edu/.

Kapiolani Community College
Honolulu, Hawaii

Freshman Application Contact Kapiolani Community College, 4303 Diamond Head Road, Honolulu, HI 96816-4421. *Phone:* 808-734-9555. *Website:* http://www.kapiolani.hawaii.edu/.

Kauai Community College
Lihue, Hawaii

Freshman Application Contact Mr. Leighton Oride, Admissions Officer and Registrar, Kauai Community College, 3-1901 Kaumualii Highway, Lihue, HI 96766. *Phone:* 808-245-8225. *Fax:* 808-245-8297. *E-mail:* arkauai@hawaii.edu. *Website:* http://kauai.hawaii.edu/.

Leeward Community College
Pearl City, Hawaii

- **State-supported** 2-year, founded 1968, part of University of Hawaii System
- **Suburban** 49-acre campus with easy access to Honolulu
- **Coed,** 7,942 undergraduate students, 42% full-time, 60% women, 40% men

Undergraduates 3,296 full-time, 4,646 part-time. Students come from 13 other countries; 0.8% are from out of state; 2% Black or African American, non-Hispanic/Latino; 11% Hispanic/Latino; 37% Asian, non-Hispanic/Latino; 12% Native Hawaiian or other Pacific Islander, non-Hispanic/Latino; 0.3% American Indian or Alaska Native, non-Hispanic/Latino; 26% Two or more races, non-Hispanic/Latino; 1% Race/ethnicity unknown; 0.5% international; 7% transferred in. *Retention:* 65% of full-time freshmen returned.

Freshmen *Admission:* 2,013 applied, 2,013 admitted, 1,404 enrolled.

Faculty *Total:* 283, 63% full-time. *Student/faculty ratio:* 23:1.

Majors Accounting; administrative assistant and secretarial science; American Indian/Native American studies; automobile/automotive mechanics technology; business administration and management; computer and information sciences; cooking and related culinary arts; desktop publishing and digital imaging design; education (specific levels and methods) related; health information/medical records technology; liberal arts and sciences/liberal studies; natural sciences; plant sciences; radio and television broadcasting technology.

Academics *Calendar:* semesters. *Degree:* certificates and associate. *Special study options:* academic remediation for entering students, advanced placement credit, cooperative education, distance learning, English as a second language, honors programs, independent study, internships, off-campus study, part-time degree program, services for LD students, study abroad, summer session for credit. *ROTC:* Air Force (c).

Student Life *Housing:* college housing not available. *Activities and Organizations:* drama/theater group, student-run newspaper, choral group, Soccer Club, Japan Circle, Future Teachers Club, Campus Crusade For Christ,

4n Tongues (Hip Hop). *Campus security:* 24-hour emergency response devices and patrols, late-night transport/escort service. *Student services:* health clinic, personal/psychological counseling.

Athletics *Intramural sports:* soccer M/W, tennis M/W, volleyball M/W.

Costs (2015–16) *Tuition:* state resident $2880 full-time, $120 per credit hour part-time; nonresident $7872 full-time, $328 per credit hour part-time. Full-time tuition and fees vary according to course level and course load. Part-time tuition and fees vary according to course level and course load. *Required fees:* $55 full-time, $28 per term part-time. *Payment plan:* installment. *Waivers:* senior citizens and employees or children of employees.

Applying *Options:* electronic application, early admission. *Application fee:* $25. *Required for some:* high school transcript. *Application deadlines:* 7/15 (freshmen), 7/15 (transfers). *Notification:* continuous (freshmen), continuous (transfers).

Freshman Application Contact Ms. Sheryl Higa, Assistant Registrar, Leeward Community College, 96-045 Ala Ike, Pearl City, HI 96782-3393. *Phone:* 808-455-0643. *Website:* http://www.leeward.hawaii.edu/.

Remington College–Honolulu Campus
Honolulu, Hawaii

Director of Admissions Louis LaMair, Director of Recruitment, Remington College–Honolulu Campus, 1111 Bishop Street, Suite 400, Honolulu, HI 96813. *Phone:* 808-942-1000. *Fax:* 808-533-3064. *E-mail:* louis.lamair@remingtoncollege.edu. *Website:* http://www.remingtoncollege.edu/.

University of Hawaii Maui College
Kahului, Hawaii

Freshman Application Contact Mr. Stephen Kameda, Director of Admissions and Records, University of Hawaii Maui College, 310 Kaahumanu Avenue, Kahului, HI 96732. *Phone:* 808-984-3267. *Toll-free phone:* 800-479-6692. *Fax:* 808-984-3872. *E-mail:* skameda@hawaii.edu. *Website:* http://maui.hawaii.edu/.

Windward Community College
Kaneohe, Hawaii

Director of Admissions Geri Imai, Registrar, Windward Community College, 45-720 Keaahala Road, Kaneohe, HI 96744-3528. *Phone:* 808-235-7430. *E-mail:* gerii@hawaii.edu. *Website:* http://www.windward.hawaii.edu/.

IDAHO

Brown Mackie College–Boise
Boise, Idaho

Freshman Application Contact Brown Mackie College–Boise, 9050 West Overland Road, Suite 100, Boise, ID 83709. *Phone:* 208-321-8800. *Website:* http://www.brownmackie.edu/boise/.

Carrington College–Boise
Boise, Idaho

- **Proprietary** 2-year, founded 1980, part of Carrington Colleges Group, Inc.
- **Coed,** 420 undergraduate students, 90% full-time, 86% women, 14% men

Undergraduates 380 full-time, 40 part-time. 15% are from out of state; 2% Black or African American, non-Hispanic/Latino; 15% Hispanic/Latino; 8% Asian, non-Hispanic/Latino; 0.2% Native Hawaiian or other Pacific Islander, non-Hispanic/Latino; 2% American Indian or Alaska Native, non-Hispanic/Latino; 2% Two or more races, non-Hispanic/Latino; 0.2% Race/ethnicity unknown; 19% transferred in.

Freshmen *Admission:* 22 enrolled.

Faculty *Total:* 56, 36% full-time. *Student/faculty ratio:* 12:1.

Majors Dental assisting; dental hygiene; massage therapy; medical/clinical assistant; medical insurance/medical billing; medical office management; pharmacy technician; physical therapy technology; registered nursing/registered nurse.

Academics *Calendar:* semesters. *Degree:* certificates and associate.

Student Life *Housing:* college housing not available.

Costs (2016–17) *Tuition:* $58,183 per degree program part-time. Full-time tuition and fees vary according to program. Part-time tuition and fees vary according to program.
Applying *Required:* essay or personal statement, high school transcript, interview, institutional entrance test.
Freshman Application Contact Carrington College–Boise, 1122 North Liberty Street, Boise, ID 83704.
Website: http://carrington.edu/.

College of Southern Idaho
Twin Falls, Idaho

- State and locally supported 2-year, founded 1964
- Small-town 287-acre campus
- Coed

Undergraduates 2,402 full-time, 6,071 part-time. 4% are from out of state; 0.8% Black or African American, non-Hispanic/Latino; 22% Hispanic/Latino; 0.9% Asian, non-Hispanic/Latino; 0.5% Native Hawaiian or other Pacific Islander, non-Hispanic/Latino; 0.9% American Indian or Alaska Native, non-Hispanic/Latino; 1% Two or more races, non-Hispanic/Latino; 3% Race/ethnicity unknown; 0.8% international; 4% live on campus.
Faculty *Student/faculty ratio:* 21:1.
Academics *Calendar:* semesters. *Degree:* certificates and associate. *Special study options:* academic remediation for entering students, adult/continuing education programs, advanced placement credit, cooperative education, distance learning, English as a second language, honors programs, independent study, internships, part-time degree program, services for LD students, summer session for credit.
Library College of Southern Idaho Library.
Student Life *Campus security:* 24-hour emergency response devices and patrols, controlled dormitory access.
Athletics Member NJCAA.
Costs (2015–16) *Tuition:* area resident $2880 full-time, $120 per credit hour part-time; state resident $3880 full-time, $170 per credit hour part-time; nonresident $6720 full-time, $280 per credit hour part-time. Full-time tuition and fees vary according to course load. Part-time tuition and fees vary according to course load. *Room and board:* $5540; room only: $2500. Room and board charges vary according to board plan.
Applying *Application fee:* $10. *Required:* high school transcript. *Required for some:* interview.
Freshman Application Contact Director of Admissions, Registration, and Records, College of Southern Idaho, PO Box 1238, Twin Falls, ID 83303-1238. *Phone:* 208-732-6232. *Toll-free phone:* 800-680-0274. *Fax:* 208-736-3014.
Website: http://www.csi.edu/.

College of Western Idaho
Nampa, Idaho

Freshman Application Contact College of Western Idaho, 6056 Birch Lane, Nampa, ID 83687.
Website: http://cwidaho.cc/.

Eastern Idaho Technical College
Idaho Falls, Idaho

- State-supported 2-year, founded 1970
- Small-town 40-acre campus
- Endowment $881,885
- Coed, 725 undergraduate students

Undergraduates Students come from 1 other state; 1% are from out of state; 0.4% Black or African American, non-Hispanic/Latino; 14% Hispanic/Latino; 0.6% Asian, non-Hispanic/Latino; 1% American Indian or Alaska Native, non-Hispanic/Latino; 2% Race/ethnicity unknown.
Faculty *Student/faculty ratio:* 8:1.
Majors Accounting; administrative assistant and secretarial science; automobile/automotive mechanics technology; computer systems networking and telecommunications; diesel mechanics technology; electrician; fire science/firefighting; legal assistant/paralegal; marketing/marketing management; medical/clinical assistant; registered nursing/registered nurse; surgical technology; web page, digital/multimedia and information resources design; welding technology.
Academics *Calendar:* semesters. *Degree:* certificates and associate. *Special study options:* academic remediation for entering students, adult/continuing education programs, advanced placement credit, English as a second language, part-time degree program, services for LD students, summer session for credit.
Library Richard and Lila Jordan Library plus 1 other.

Student Life *Housing:* college housing not available. *Campus security:* 24-hour emergency response devices and patrols, controlled dormitory access.
Standardized Tests *Required for some:* ACT Compass, ACT ASSET, or CPT.
Costs (2015–16) *One-time required fee:* $15. *Tuition:* state resident $2234 full-time, $103 per credit part-time; nonresident $8550 full-time, $205 per credit part-time. Full-time tuition and fees vary according to course load and program. Part-time tuition and fees vary according to course load and program. *Required fees:* $1645 full-time, $103 per credit hour part-time, $15 per term part-time.
Financial Aid Of all full-time matriculated undergraduates who enrolled in 2014, 37 Federal Work-Study jobs (averaging $1176). 11 state and other part-time jobs (averaging $1619).
Applying *Options:* electronic application, deferred entrance. *Application fee:* $10. *Required:* high school transcript, interview. *Required for some:* essay or personal statement. *Application deadline:* rolling (freshmen).
Freshman Application Contact Hailey Mack, Career Placement and Recruiting Coordinator, Eastern Idaho Technical College, 1600 South 25th East, Idaho Falls, ID 83404. *Phone:* 208-524-5337 Ext. 35337. *Toll-free phone:* 800-662-0261. *Fax:* 208-524-0429.
E-mail: hailey.mack@my.eitc.edu.
Website: http://www.eitc.edu/.

ITT Technical Institute
Boise, Idaho

Freshman Application Contact Director of Recruitment, ITT Technical Institute, 12302 West Explorer Drive, Boise, ID 83713-1529. *Phone:* 208-322-8844. *Toll-free phone:* 800-666-4888.
Website: http://www.itt-tech.edu/.

North Idaho College
Coeur d'Alene, Idaho

Freshman Application Contact North Idaho College, 1000 West Garden Avenue, Coeur d Alene, ID 83814-2199. *Phone:* 208-769-3303. *Toll-free phone:* 877-404-4536 Ext. 3311. *E-mail:* admit@nic.edu.
Website: http://www.nic.edu/.

ILLINOIS

Ambria College of Nursing
Hoffman Estates, Illinois

Admissions Office Contact Ambria College of Nursing, 5210 Trillium Boulevard, Hoffman Estates, IL 60192.
Website: http://www.ambria.edu/.

Black Hawk College
Moline, Illinois

Freshman Application Contact Ms. Gabriella Hurtado, Recruitment Coordinator/Admissions Advisor, Black Hawk College, 6600-34th Avenue, Moline, IL 61265. *Phone:* 309-796-5341. *Toll-free phone:* 800-334-1311.
E-mail: ghurtado@bhc.edu.
Website: http://www.bhc.edu/.

Carl Sandburg College
Galesburg, Illinois

Director of Admissions Ms. Carol Kreider, Dean of Student Support Services, Carl Sandburg College, 2400 Tom L. Wilson Boulevard, Galesburg, IL 61401-9576. *Phone:* 309-341-5234.
Website: http://www.sandburg.edu/.

City Colleges of Chicago, Harold Washington College
Chicago, Illinois

Freshman Application Contact Admissions Office, City Colleges of Chicago, Harold Washington College, 30 East Lake Street, Chicago, IL 60601-2449. *Phone:* 312-553-6010.
Website: http://hwashington.ccc.edu/.

City Colleges of Chicago, Harry S. Truman College
Chicago, Illinois

Freshman Application Contact City Colleges of Chicago, Harry S. Truman College, 1145 West Wilson Avenue, Chicago, IL 60640-5616. *Phone:* 773-907-4000 Ext. 1112.
Website: http://www.trumancollege.edu/.

City Colleges of Chicago, Kennedy-King College
Chicago, Illinois

Freshman Application Contact Admissions Office, City Colleges of Chicago, Kennedy-King College, 6301 South Halstead Street, Chicago, IL 60621. *Phone:* 773-602-5062. *Fax:* 773-602-5055.
Website: http://kennedyking.ccc.edu/.

City Colleges of Chicago, Malcolm X College
Chicago, Illinois

Freshman Application Contact Ms. Kimberly Hollingsworth, Dean of Student Services, City Colleges of Chicago, Malcolm X College, 1900 West Van Buren Street, Chicago, IL 60612-3145. *Phone:* 312-850-7120. *Fax:* 312-850-7119. *E-mail:* khollingsworth@ccc.edu.
Website: http://malcolmx.ccc.edu/.

City Colleges of Chicago, Olive-Harvey College
Chicago, Illinois

- **State and locally supported** 2-year, founded 1970, part of City Colleges of Chicago
- **Urban** 67-acre campus
- **Coed,** 3,465 undergraduate students, 38% full-time, 61% women, 39% men

Undergraduates 1,322 full-time, 2,143 part-time. 69% Black or African American, non-Hispanic/Latino; 14% Hispanic/Latino; 6% Asian, non-Hispanic/Latino; 0.1% American Indian or Alaska Native, non-Hispanic/Latino; 2% Two or more races, non-Hispanic/Latino; 3% Race/ethnicity unknown; 0.1% international. *Retention:* 39% of full-time freshmen returned.
Freshmen *Admission:* 413 enrolled.
Faculty *Total:* 157, 34% full-time. *Student/faculty ratio:* 23:1.
Majors Accounting; biological and physical sciences; business administration and management; child-care provision; crisis/emergency/disaster management; diesel mechanics technology; engineering science; fine/studio arts; general studies; homeland security; human development and family studies; information technology; liberal arts and sciences/liberal studies; logistics, materials, and supply chain management; manufacturing engineering technology; registered nursing/registered nurse; respiratory care therapy; web page, digital/multimedia and information resources design.
Academics *Calendar:* semesters. *Degree:* certificates and associate. *Special study options:* academic remediation for entering students, accelerated degree program, adult/continuing education programs, advanced placement credit, cooperative education, distance learning, English as a second language, independent study, internships, part-time degree program, services for LD students, summer session for credit.
Library Olga-Haley Library-Learning Resource Center. *Books:* 41,551 (physical).
Student Life *Housing:* college housing not available. *Activities and Organizations:* drama/theater group. *Campus security:* 24-hour emergency response devices and patrols. *Student services:* personal/psychological counseling, women's center.
Athletics Member NJCAA. *Intercollegiate sports:* baseball M, basketball M/W, volleyball W.
Costs (2016–17) *Tuition:* area resident $3506 full-time, $137 per credit hour part-time; state resident $8126 full-time, $436 per credit hour part-time; nonresident $11,906 full-time, $554 per credit hour part-time. Full-time tuition and fees vary according to course load. Part-time tuition and fees vary according to course load. *Payment plan:* installment. *Waivers:* employees or children of employees.
Financial Aid Of all full-time matriculated undergraduates who enrolled in 2014, 150 Federal Work-Study jobs (averaging $3900).

Applying *Options:* electronic application, early admission, deferred entrance. *Required for some:* high school transcript. *Application deadlines:* rolling (freshmen), rolling (out-of-state freshmen), rolling (transfers). *Notification:* continuous (freshmen), continuous (out-of-state freshmen), continuous (transfers).
Freshman Application Contact Mr. Dorian Thomas, Registrar, City Colleges of Chicago, Olive-Harvey College, 10001 South Woodlawn Avenue, Room 1405, Chicago, IL 60628. *Phone:* 773-291-6384. *E-mail:* dthomas236@ccc.edu.
Website: http://oliveharvey.ccc.edu/.

City Colleges of Chicago, Richard J. Daley College
Chicago, Illinois

Freshman Application Contact City Colleges of Chicago, Richard J. Daley College, 7500 South Pulaski Road, Chicago, IL 60652-1242. *Phone:* 773-838-7606.
Website: http://daley.ccc.edu/.

City Colleges of Chicago, Wilbur Wright College
Chicago, Illinois

Freshman Application Contact Ms. Amy Aiello, Assistant Dean of Student Services, City Colleges of Chicago, Wilbur Wright College, Chicago, IL 60634. *Phone:* 773-481-8207. *Fax:* 773-481-8185. *E-mail:* aaiello@ccc.edu.
Website: http://wright.ccc.edu/.

College of DuPage
Glen Ellyn, Illinois

Freshman Application Contact College of DuPage, IL.
E-mail: admissions@cod.edu.
Website: http://www.cod.edu/.

College of Lake County
Grayslake, Illinois

Freshman Application Contact Director, Student Recruitment, College of Lake County, Grayslake, IL 60030-1198. *Phone:* 847-543-2383. *Fax:* 847-543-3061.
Website: http://www.clcillinois.edu/.

Coyne College
Chicago, Illinois

- **Proprietary** 2-year
- **Urban** campus
- **Coed,** 522 undergraduate students, 100% full-time, 25% women, 75% men

Undergraduates 522 full-time. Students come from 2 states and territories; 2% are from out of state; 36% Black or African American, non-Hispanic/Latino; 44% Hispanic/Latino; 0.8% Asian, non-Hispanic/Latino; 0.8% American Indian or Alaska Native, non-Hispanic/Latino; 4% Two or more races, non-Hispanic/Latino.
Freshmen *Admission:* 24 enrolled.
Academics *Calendar:* continuous. *Degree:* certificates, diplomas, and associate. *Special study options:* academic remediation for entering students, accelerated degree program, cooperative education, internships, off-campus study.
Library Coyne College Resource Center plus 1 other. *Books:* 2,500 (physical), 200 (digital/electronic).
Student Life *Campus security:* security guard during class times.
Standardized Tests *Required for some:* SAT or ACT (for admission), Wonderlic aptitude test.
Applying *Required:* interview, minimum Wonderlic Assessement score of 13, ACT score of 15, SAT score of 1800, or a degree from an accredited institution. *Required for some:* essay or personal statement, high school transcript, 1 letter of recommendation.
Freshman Application Contact Coyne College, 330 North Green Street, Chicago, IL 60607. *Phone:* 773-577-8100 Ext. 8102. *Toll-free phone:* 800-707-1922.
Website: http://www.coynecollege.edu/.

Danville Area Community College
Danville, Illinois

- **State and locally supported** 2-year, founded 1946, part of Illinois Community College Board
- **Small-town** 50-acre campus
- **Coed,** 2,692 undergraduate students, 40% full-time, 55% women, 45% men

Undergraduates 1,070 full-time, 1,622 part-time. Students come from 5 states and territories; 1 other country; 1% are from out of state; 15% Black or African American, non-Hispanic/Latino; 5% Hispanic/Latino; 1% Asian, non-Hispanic/Latino; 0.2% Native Hawaiian or other Pacific Islander, non-Hispanic/Latino; 0.5% American Indian or Alaska Native, non-Hispanic/Latino; 0.7% Two or more races, non-Hispanic/Latino; 8% Race/ethnicity unknown; 25% transferred in. *Retention:* 55% of full-time freshmen returned.

Freshmen *Admission:* 370 enrolled.

Faculty *Total:* 167, 41% full-time, 11% with terminal degrees. *Student/faculty ratio:* 17:1.

Majors Accounting technology and bookkeeping; agricultural business and management; autobody/collision and repair technology; automobile/automotive mechanics technology; business automation/technology/data entry; CAD/CADD drafting/design technology; child-care provision; computer programming (specific applications); computer systems networking and telecommunications; corrections; criminal justice/police science; electrician; energy management and systems technology; engineering; executive assistant/executive secretary; fire science/firefighting; floriculture/floristry management; general studies; health information/medical records technology; industrial electronics technology; industrial mechanics and maintenance technology; juvenile corrections; landscaping and groundskeeping; liberal arts and sciences/liberal studies; manufacturing engineering technology; medical administrative assistant and medical secretary; radiologic technology/science; registered nursing/registered nurse; selling skills and sales; teacher assistant/aide; turf and turfgrass management.

Academics *Calendar:* semesters. *Degree:* certificates and associate. *Special study options:* academic remediation for entering students, adult/continuing education programs, advanced placement credit, cooperative education, distance learning, double majors, English as a second language, independent study, internships, part-time degree program, services for LD students, summer session for credit.

Student Life *Housing:* college housing not available. *Activities and Organizations:* drama/theater group, choral group, Phi Theta Kappa International Honor Society, The Guild, Powerhouse Collegian Ministry, Rad Tech Club, Ag Club. *Campus security:* 24-hour emergency response devices and patrols. *Student services:* personal/psychological counseling.

Athletics Member NJCAA. *Intercollegiate sports:* baseball M(s), basketball M(s)/W(s), cheerleading W, cross-country running M(s)/W(s), softball W(s).

Costs (2015–16) *Tuition:* area resident $3600 full-time, $130 per credit hour part-time; state resident $6000 full-time, $200 per credit hour part-time; nonresident $6000 full-time, $200 per credit hour part-time. Full-time tuition and fees vary according to program. Part-time tuition and fees vary according to program. *Required fees:* $600 full-time, $20 per credit hour part-time. *Payment plan:* installment. *Waivers:* senior citizens and employees or children of employees.

Financial Aid Of all full-time matriculated undergraduates who enrolled in 2011, 60 Federal Work-Study jobs (averaging $3000). 100 state and other part-time jobs (averaging $3000).

Applying *Options:* early admission, deferred entrance. *Required:* high school transcript. *Application deadlines:* rolling (freshmen), rolling (transfers).

Freshman Application Contact Mr. Nick Catlett, Coordinator of Recruitment, Danville Area Community College, 2000 East Main Street, Danville, IL 61832-5199. *Phone:* 217-443-8864. *Fax:* 217-443-8337. *E-mail:* ncatlett@dacc.edu.

Website: http://www.dacc.edu/.

Elgin Community College
Elgin, Illinois

- **State and locally supported** 2-year, founded 1949, part of Illinois Community College Board
- **Suburban** 145-acre campus with easy access to Chicago
- **Coed,** 11,285 undergraduate students, 33% full-time, 55% women, 45% men

Undergraduates 3,780 full-time, 7,505 part-time. Students come from 4 states and territories; 15 other countries; 0.2% are from out of state; 5% Black or African American, non-Hispanic/Latino; 37% Hispanic/Latino; 6% Asian, non-Hispanic/Latino; 0.1% Native Hawaiian or other Pacific Islander, non-Hispanic/Latino; 0.2% American Indian or Alaska Native, non-Hispanic/Latino; 2% Two or more races, non-Hispanic/Latino; 3% Race/ethnicity unknown; 0.4% international; 4% transferred in. *Retention:* 77% of full-time freshmen returned.

Freshmen *Admission:* 1,357 enrolled.

Majors Accounting; administrative assistant and secretarial science; animation, interactive technology, video graphics and special effects; automobile/automotive mechanics technology; baking and pastry arts; biological and physical sciences; biology/biotechnology laboratory technician; business administration and management; CAD/CADD drafting/design technology; clinical/medical laboratory technology; computer and information systems security; criminal justice/police science; culinary arts; data entry/microcomputer applications; design and visual communications; engineering; entrepreneurship; executive assistant/executive secretary; fine/studio arts; fire science/firefighting; graphic design; health and physical education/fitness; heating, air conditioning, ventilation and refrigeration maintenance technology; industrial mechanics and maintenance technology; legal assistant/paralegal; liberal arts and sciences/liberal studies; machine tool technology; marketing/marketing management; music; physical therapy technology; radiologic technology/science; registered nursing/registered nurse; restaurant, culinary, and catering management; retailing; social work.

Academics *Calendar:* semesters. *Degree:* certificates, diplomas, and associate. *Special study options:* academic remediation for entering students, accelerated degree program, advanced placement credit, cooperative education, distance learning, double majors, English as a second language, honors programs, independent study, internships, off-campus study, part-time degree program, services for LD students, study abroad, summer session for credit.

Library Renner Academic Library & Learning Resources.

Student Life *Housing:* college housing not available. *Activities and Organizations:* drama/theater group, student-run newspaper, choral group, Phi Theta Kappa Honor Society, Organization of Latin American Students, Asian Filipino Club, Amnesty International, Student Government. *Campus security:* grounds patrolled daily 7 a.m.-11 p.m. during the academic year. *Student services:* personal/psychological counseling, legal services.

Athletics Member NJCAA. *Intercollegiate sports:* baseball M(s), basketball M(s)/W(s), cross-country running M(s)/W(s), golf M(s), soccer M(s)/W(s), softball W(s), tennis M(s)/W(s), volleyball W(s).

Costs (2015–16) *Tuition:* area resident $3570 full-time, $119 per credit hour part-time; state resident $13,035 full-time, $434 per credit hour part-time; nonresident $14,934 full-time, $498 per credit hour part-time. *Required fees:* $10 full-time, $5 per term part-time. *Payment plan:* installment. *Waivers:* senior citizens.

Applying *Options:* electronic application. *Required for some:* high school transcript, specific departmental requirements. *Application deadlines:* rolling (freshmen), rolling (transfers). *Notification:* continuous (freshmen), continuous (transfers).

Freshman Application Contact Admissions, Recruitment, and Student Life, Elgin Community College, 1700 Spartan Drive, Elgin, IL 60123. *Phone:* 847-214-7414. *E-mail:* admissions@elgin.edu.

Website: http://www.elgin.edu/.

Fox College
Bedford Park, Illinois

- **Private** 2-year, founded 1932
- **Suburban** campus
- **Coed,** 360 undergraduate students
- 68% of applicants were admitted

Freshmen *Admission:* 742 applied, 504 admitted.

Majors Accounting technology and bookkeeping; administrative assistant and secretarial science; dental hygiene; medical/clinical assistant; occupational therapist assistant; physical therapy technology; veterinary/animal health technology.

Academics *Calendar:* semesters. *Degree:* diplomas and associate. *Special study options:* accelerated degree program, internships.

Student Life *Housing:* college housing not available.

Freshman Application Contact Admissions Office, Fox College, 6640 South Cicero, Bedford Park, IL 60638. *Phone:* 708-444-4500.

Website: http://www.foxcollege.edu/.

Harper College
Palatine, Illinois

- **State and locally supported** 2-year, founded 1965, part of Illinois Community College Board
- **Suburban** 200-acre campus with easy access to Chicago
- **Coed**

Undergraduates Students come from 9 states and territories; 1% are from out of state; 5% Black or African American, non-Hispanic/Latino; 16%

Hispanic/Latino; 11% Asian, non-Hispanic/Latino; 0.9% Native Hawaiian or other Pacific Islander, non-Hispanic/Latino; 0.1% American Indian or Alaska Native, non-Hispanic/Latino; 9% Two or more races, non-Hispanic/Latino; 4% Race/ethnicity unknown.
Faculty *Student/faculty ratio:* 8:1.
Academics *Calendar:* semesters. *Degree:* certificates and associate. *Special study options:* academic remediation for entering students, accelerated degree program, adult/continuing education programs, advanced placement credit, cooperative education, distance learning, English as a second language, honors programs, independent study, internships, part-time degree program, services for LD students, study abroad, summer session for credit.
Library Harper College Library.
Student Life *Campus security:* 24-hour emergency response devices and patrols, late-night transport/escort service.
Athletics Member NJCAA.
Costs (2015–16) *Tuition:* area resident $3413 full-time, $114 per credit hour part-time; state resident $11,123 full-time, $371 per credit hour part-time; nonresident $13,388 full-time, $446 per credit hour part-time. Full-time tuition and fees vary according to course load and program. Part-time tuition and fees vary according to course load and program. No tuition increase for student's term of enrollment. *Required fees:* $619 full-time, $16 per credit hour part-time. *Payment plans:* installment, deferred payment.
Financial Aid Of all full-time matriculated undergraduates who enrolled in 2013, 2,811 applied for aid, 2,310 were judged to have need, 594 had their need fully met. In 2013, 108. *Average percent of need met:* 50. *Average financial aid package:* $5084. *Average need-based loan:* $3050. *Average need-based gift aid:* $4747. *Average non-need-based aid:* $2118.
Applying *Options:* electronic application, early admission, deferred entrance. *Application fee:* $25. *Required:* high school transcript.
Freshman Application Contact Admissions Office, Harper College, 1200 West Algonquin Road, Palatine, IL 60067. *Phone:* 847-925-6700. *Fax:* 847-925-6044. *E-mail:* admissions@harpercollege.edu.
Website: http://goforward.harpercollege.edu/.

Heartland Community College
Normal, Illinois

Freshman Application Contact Ms. Candace Brownlee, Director of Student Recruitment, Heartland Community College, 1500 West Raab Road, Normal, IL 61761. *Phone:* 309-268-8041. *Fax:* 309-268-7992.
E-mail: candace.brownlee@heartland.edu.
Website: http://www.heartland.edu/.

Highland Community College
Freeport, Illinois

- **State and locally supported** 2-year, founded 1962, part of Illinois Community College Board
- **Rural** 240-acre campus
- **Coed,** 1,804 undergraduate students, 51% full-time, 61% women, 39% men

Undergraduates 924 full-time, 880 part-time. 3% are from out of state; 9% Black or African American, non-Hispanic/Latino; 3% Hispanic/Latino; 1% Asian, non-Hispanic/Latino; 0.1% Native Hawaiian or other Pacific Islander, non-Hispanic/Latino; 2% American Indian or Alaska Native, non-Hispanic/Latino; 4% Two or more races, non-Hispanic/Latino; 2% Race/ethnicity unknown; 3% transferred in.
Freshmen *Admission:* 862 applied, 862 admitted, 404 enrolled.
Faculty *Total:* 120, 40% full-time, 8% with terminal degrees. *Student/faculty ratio:* 17:1.
Majors Accounting; administrative assistant and secretarial science; autobody/collision and repair technology; automobile/automotive mechanics technology; biological and physical sciences; business administration and management; child-care provision; early childhood education; emergency medical technology (EMT paramedic); engineering; equestrian studies; general studies; graphic design; health information/medical records technology; heavy equipment maintenance technology; hospitality administration; industrial technology; information technology; liberal arts and sciences/liberal studies; mathematics teacher education; medical/clinical assistant; registered nursing/registered nurse; special education; teacher assistant/aide; web page, digital/multimedia and information resources design; welding technology.
Academics *Calendar:* semesters. *Degree:* certificates and associate. *Special study options:* academic remediation for entering students, adult/continuing education programs, advanced placement credit, cooperative education, distance learning, English as a second language, external degree program, honors programs, independent study, internships, part-time degree program, services for LD students, student-designed majors, summer session for credit.
Library Clarence Mitchell Library.

Student Life *Housing:* college housing not available. *Activities and Organizations:* drama/theater group, student-run newspaper, radio station, choral group, Phi Theta Kappa, Royal Scots, Prairie Wind, Intramurals, Collegiate Choir. *Campus security:* 24-hour emergency response devices and patrols. *Student services:* personal/psychological counseling.
Athletics Member NJCAA. *Intercollegiate sports:* baseball M(s), basketball M(s)/W(s), bowling M(s)/W(s), golf M(s)/W(s), softball W(s), volleyball W(s). *Intramural sports:* basketball M/W, volleyball M/W.
Costs (2015–16) *Tuition:* area resident $3690 full-time, $123 per credit hour part-time; state resident $5910 full-time, $197 per credit hour part-time; nonresident $6180 full-time, $206 per credit hour part-time. Full-time tuition and fees vary according to program and reciprocity agreements. Part-time tuition and fees vary according to program and reciprocity agreements. *Required fees:* $600 full-time, $19 per credit hour part-time, $15 per term part-time. *Payment plans:* installment, deferred payment. *Waivers:* minority students, senior citizens, and employees or children of employees.
Financial Aid Of all full-time matriculated undergraduates who enrolled in 2014, 771 applied for aid, 668 were judged to have need. 44 Federal Work-Study jobs (averaging $1703). 77 state and other part-time jobs (averaging $1607). In 2014, 32 non-need-based awards were made. *Average percent of need met:* 37%. *Average financial aid package:* $6079. *Average need-based loan:* $6732. *Average need-based gift aid:* $5553. *Average non-need-based aid:* $4401.
Applying *Options:* electronic application, early admission, deferred entrance. *Required for some:* high school transcript, 1 letter of recommendation. *Recommended:* high school transcript. *Application deadlines:* rolling (freshmen), rolling (transfers).
Freshman Application Contact Mr. Jeremy Bradt, Director, Enrollment and Records, Highland Community College, 2998 West Pearl City Road, Freeport, IL 61032. *Phone:* 815-235-6121 Ext. 3500. *Fax:* 815-235-6130.
E-mail: jeremy.bradt@highland.edu.
Website: http://www.highland.edu/.

Illinois Central College
East Peoria, Illinois

- **State and locally supported** 2-year, founded 1967, part of Illinois Community College Board
- **Suburban** 430-acre campus
- **Coed,** 9,704 undergraduate students, 36% full-time, 55% women, 45% men

Undergraduates 3,475 full-time, 6,229 part-time. Students come from 22 states and territories; 4 other countries; 1% are from out of state; 11% Black or African American, non-Hispanic/Latino; 5% Hispanic/Latino; 2% Asian, non-Hispanic/Latino; 0.2% Native Hawaiian or other Pacific Islander, non-Hispanic/Latino; 0.3% American Indian or Alaska Native, non-Hispanic/Latino; 3% Two or more races, non-Hispanic/Latino; 0.2% Race/ethnicity unknown; 4% transferred in. *Retention:* 68% of full-time freshmen returned.
Freshmen *Admission:* 4,829 applied, 1,961 admitted, 1,052 enrolled. *Test scores:* ACT scores over 18: 62%; ACT scores over 24: 14%; ACT scores over 30: 1%.
Faculty *Total:* 548, 32% full-time, 11% with terminal degrees. *Student/faculty ratio:* 18:1.
Majors Accounting; accounting technology and bookkeeping; administrative assistant and secretarial science; agricultural business and management; agricultural/farm supplies retailing and wholesaling; agricultural mechanics and equipment technology; agricultural production; animal/livestock husbandry and production; animation, interactive technology, video graphics and special effects; applied horticulture/horticulture operations; automobile/automotive mechanics technology; banking and financial support services; business administration and management; child-care provision; clinical/medical laboratory technology; community health services counseling; computer programming; computer systems networking and telecommunications; construction engineering technology; corrections; criminal justice/police science; crop production; culinary arts; data entry/microcomputer applications; dental hygiene; diesel mechanics technology; electrical, electronic and communications engineering technology; emergency medical technology (EMT paramedic); energy management and systems technology; engineering; fire science/firefighting; forensic science and technology; general studies; graphic design; health and physical education/fitness; heating, air conditioning, ventilation and refrigeration maintenance technology; industrial technology; juvenile corrections; legal assistant/paralegal; liberal arts and sciences/liberal studies; library and archives assisting; manufacturing engineering technology; mechanical engineering/mechanical technology; mental health counseling; occupational therapist assistant; physical therapy technology; platemaking/imaging; psychiatric/mental health services technology; radiologic technology/science; real estate; registered nursing/registered nurse; respiratory care therapy; retailing; robotics technology; security and loss prevention; sign language

interpretation and translation; substance abuse/addiction counseling; surgical technology; teacher assistant/aide; web/multimedia management and webmaster; web page, digital/multimedia and information resources design; welding technology.

Academics *Calendar:* semesters. *Degree:* certificates and associate. *Special study options:* academic remediation for entering students, adult/continuing education programs, advanced placement credit, English as a second language, honors programs, independent study, internships, part-time degree program, services for LD students, summer session for credit.

Library Illinois Central College Library plus 2 others.

Student Life *Housing Options:* Campus housing is provided by a third party. *Activities and Organizations:* drama/theater group, student-run newspaper, radio station, choral group. *Campus security:* 24-hour emergency response devices and patrols, late-night transport/escort service. *Student services:* health clinic, personal/psychological counseling.

Athletics Member NJCAA. *Intercollegiate sports:* baseball M(s), basketball M(s)/W(s), cross-country running M(s)/W(s), golf M(s), soccer M(s)/W(s), softball W(s), volleyball W(s), weight lifting M/W. *Intramural sports:* basketball M/W, bowling M/W, football M/W, softball M/W, ultimate Frisbee M/W, volleyball M/W.

Costs (2015–16) *Tuition:* area resident $3240 full-time, $135 per credit hour part-time; state resident $6960 full-time, $290 per credit hour part-time; nonresident $8040 full-time, $335 per credit hour part-time. Full-time tuition and fees vary according to course load. Part-time tuition and fees vary according to course load. *Room and board:* Room and board charges vary according to housing facility. *Payment plan:* installment. *Waivers:* senior citizens and employees or children of employees.

Financial Aid Of all full-time matriculated undergraduates who enrolled in 2011, 6,521 applied for aid, 5,525 were judged to have need.

Applying *Options:* electronic application, early admission. *Required:* high school transcript. *Application deadlines:* rolling (freshmen), rolling (out-of-state freshmen), rolling (transfers). *Notification:* continuous (freshmen), continuous (out-of-state freshmen), continuous (transfers).

Freshman Application Contact Angela Dreessen, Dean of Student Success, Illinois Central College, 1 College Drive, East Peoria, IL 61635-0001. *Phone:* 309-694-5323.

Website: http://www.icc.edu/.

Illinois Eastern Community Colleges, Frontier Community College

Fairfield, Illinois

- **State and locally supported** 2-year, founded 1976, part of Illinois Eastern Community Colleges System
- **Rural** 8-acre campus
- **Coed,** 2,229 undergraduate students

Undergraduates 1% are from out of state; 0.7% Black or African American, non-Hispanic/Latino; 0.9% Hispanic/Latino; 0.6% Asian, non-Hispanic/Latino; 0.3% American Indian or Alaska Native, non-Hispanic/Latino; 0.4% Race/ethnicity unknown.

Faculty *Total:* 95, 6% full-time. *Student/faculty ratio:* 23:1.

Majors Automobile/automotive mechanics technology; biological and physical sciences; business automation/technology/data entry; construction trades; corrections; emergency care attendant (EMT ambulance); engineering; executive assistant/executive secretary; fire science/firefighting; general studies; health information/medical records technology; liberal arts and sciences/liberal studies; quality control technology; registered nursing/registered nurse; sport and fitness administration/management.

Academics *Calendar:* semesters. *Degree:* certificates and associate. *Special study options:* academic remediation for entering students, adult/continuing education programs, advanced placement credit, cooperative education, distance learning, double majors, English as a second language, external degree program, independent study, part-time degree program, services for LD students, student-designed majors, summer session for credit.

Library Learning Resource Center plus 1 other.

Student Life *Housing:* college housing not available.

Athletics Member NJCAA. *Intercollegiate sports:* golf M/W, squash W, volleyball W.

Costs (2016–17) *Tuition:* area resident $2656 full-time, $83 per semester hour part-time; state resident $8589 full-time, $268 per semester hour part-time; nonresident $10,580 full-time, $331 per semester hour part-time. *Required fees:* $490 full-time, $15 per semester hour part-time, $5 per term part-time. *Payment plan:* installment. *Waivers:* senior citizens and employees or children of employees.

Applying *Options:* early admission, deferred entrance. *Required:* high school transcript. *Application deadlines:* rolling (freshmen), rolling (transfers). *Notification:* continuous (freshmen), continuous (transfers).

Freshman Application Contact Ms. Mary Johnston, Coordinator of Registration and Records, Illinois Eastern Community Colleges, Frontier Community College, Frontier Drive, Fairfield, IL 62837. *Phone:* 618-842-3711 Ext. 4111. *Toll-free phone:* 877-464-3687. *Fax:* 618-842-6340. *E-mail:* johnstonm@iecc.edu.

Website: http://www.iecc.edu/fcc/.

Illinois Eastern Community Colleges, Lincoln Trail College

Robinson, Illinois

- **State and locally supported** 2-year, founded 1969, part of Illinois Eastern Community Colleges System
- **Rural** 120-acre campus
- **Coed,** 1,010 undergraduate students, 42% full-time, 60% women, 40% men

Undergraduates 427 full-time, 583 part-time. 5% are from out of state; 3% Black or African American, non-Hispanic/Latino; 1% Hispanic/Latino; 2% Asian, non-Hispanic/Latino; 0.3% American Indian or Alaska Native, non-Hispanic/Latino; 0.2% Race/ethnicity unknown.

Freshmen *Admission:* 163 enrolled.

Faculty *Total:* 64, 25% full-time. *Student/faculty ratio:* 17:1.

Majors Biological and physical sciences; business automation/technology/data entry; computer systems networking and telecommunications; construction trades; corrections; general studies; health information/medical records administration; liberal arts and sciences/liberal studies; mechanical engineering/mechanical technology; medical/clinical assistant; quality control technology; sport and fitness administration/management; teacher assistant/aide; telecommunications technology.

Academics *Calendar:* semesters. *Degree:* certificates and associate. *Special study options:* academic remediation for entering students, adult/continuing education programs, advanced placement credit, cooperative education, distance learning, double majors, English as a second language, external degree program, independent study, internships, part-time degree program, services for LD students, student-designed majors, summer session for credit.

Library Eagleton Learning Resource Center plus 1 other.

Student Life *Housing:* college housing not available. *Activities and Organizations:* drama/theater group, choral group, national fraternities.

Athletics Member NJCAA. *Intercollegiate sports:* baseball M(s), basketball M(s)/W(s), softball W(s). *Intramural sports:* baseball M, basketball M, softball W.

Costs (2016–17) *Tuition:* area resident $2656 full-time, $83 per semester hour part-time; state resident $8589 full-time, $268 per semester hour part-time; nonresident $10,580 full-time, $331 per semester hour part-time. *Required fees:* $490 full-time, $15 per semester hour part-time, $5 per term part-time. *Payment plan:* installment. *Waivers:* senior citizens and employees or children of employees.

Applying *Options:* early admission, deferred entrance. *Required:* high school transcript. *Application deadlines:* rolling (freshmen), rolling (transfers). *Notification:* continuous (freshmen), continuous (transfers).

Freshman Application Contact Ms. Megan Scott, Director of Admissions, Illinois Eastern Community Colleges, Lincoln Trail College, 11220 State Highway 1, Robinson, IL 62454. *Phone:* 618-544-8657 Ext. 1137. *Toll-free phone:* 866-582-4322. *Fax:* 618-544-7423. *E-mail:* scottm@iecc.edu.

Website: http://www.iecc.edu/ltc/.

Illinois Eastern Community Colleges, Olney Central College

Olney, Illinois

- **State and locally supported** 2-year, founded 1962, part of Illinois Eastern Community Colleges System
- **Rural** 128-acre campus
- **Coed,** 1,295 undergraduate students, 47% full-time, 60% women, 40% men

Undergraduates 612 full-time, 683 part-time. 1% are from out of state; 1% Black or African American, non-Hispanic/Latino; 0.6% Hispanic/Latino; 1% Asian, non-Hispanic/Latino; 0.4% American Indian or Alaska Native, non-Hispanic/Latino; 0.2% Race/ethnicity unknown; 0.1% international.

Freshmen *Admission:* 206 enrolled.

Faculty *Total:* 97, 44% full-time. *Student/faculty ratio:* 14:1.

Majors Accounting; autobody/collision and repair technology; automobile/automotive mechanics technology; biological and physical sciences; business administration and management; business automation/technology/data entry; culinary arts; engineering; general studies; human resources management; industrial mechanics and maintenance technology; information technology; liberal arts and sciences/liberal studies; medical administrative assistant and medical secretary; medical radiologic technology; registered nursing/registered nurse.

Academics *Calendar:* semesters. *Degree:* certificates and associate. *Special study options:* academic remediation for entering students, adult/continuing education programs, advanced placement credit, cooperative education, distance learning, double majors, English as a second language, external degree program, independent study, internships, part-time degree program, services for LD students, student-designed majors, summer session for credit.
Library Anderson Learning Resources Center plus 1 other.
Student Life *Housing:* college housing not available. *Activities and Organizations:* drama/theater group, student-run newspaper, choral group.
Athletics Member NJCAA. *Intercollegiate sports:* baseball M(s), basketball M(s)/W(s), softball W(s). *Intramural sports:* baseball M, basketball M/W, softball W.
Costs (2016–17) *Tuition:* area resident $2656 full-time, $83 per semester hour part-time; state resident $8589 full-time, $268 per semester hour part-time; nonresident $10,580 full-time, $331 per semester hour part-time. *Required fees:* $490 full-time, $15 per semester hour part-time, $5 per term part-time. *Payment plan:* installment. *Waivers:* senior citizens and employees or children of employees.
Applying *Options:* early admission, deferred entrance. *Required:* high school transcript. *Application deadlines:* rolling (freshmen), rolling (transfers). *Notification:* continuous (freshmen), continuous (transfers).
Freshman Application Contact Mr. Adam Greathouse, Assistant Dean for Student Services, Illinois Eastern Community Colleges, Olney Central College, 305 North West Street, Olney, IL 62450. *Phone:* 618-395-7777 Ext. 2005. *Toll-free phone:* 866-622-4322. *Fax:* 618-392-5212.
E-mail: greathousea@iecc.edu.
Website: http://www.iecc.edu/occ/.

Illinois Eastern Community Colleges, Wabash Valley College

Mount Carmel, Illinois

- **State and locally supported** 2-year, founded 1960, part of Illinois Eastern Community Colleges System
- **Rural** 40-acre campus
- **Coed,** 4,274 undergraduate students, 12% full-time, 31% women, 69% men

Undergraduates 530 full-time, 3,744 part-time. 3% are from out of state; 2% Black or African American, non-Hispanic/Latino; 0.7% Hispanic/Latino; 1% Asian, non-Hispanic/Latino; 0.3% American Indian or Alaska Native, non-Hispanic/Latino; 0.2% Race/ethnicity unknown.
Freshmen *Admission:* 255 enrolled.
Faculty *Total:* 80, 44% full-time. *Student/faculty ratio:* 34:1.
Majors Agricultural business and management; agricultural production; biological and physical sciences; business administration and management; business automation/technology/data entry; child development; diesel mechanics technology; energy management and systems technology; engineering; executive assistant/executive secretary; general studies; industrial technology; legal assistant/paralegal; liberal arts and sciences/liberal studies; machine tool technology; manufacturing engineering technology; mining technology; radio and television; social work; sport and fitness administration/management.
Academics *Calendar:* semesters. *Degree:* certificates and associate. *Special study options:* academic remediation for entering students, adult/continuing education programs, advanced placement credit, cooperative education, distance learning, double majors, English as a second language, external degree program, independent study, internships, part-time degree program, services for LD students, student-designed majors, summer session for credit.
Library Bauer Media Center plus 1 other.
Student Life *Housing:* college housing not available. *Activities and Organizations:* drama/theater group, student-run newspaper, radio and television station, choral group.
Athletics Member NJCAA. *Intercollegiate sports:* baseball M(s), basketball M(s)/W(s), softball W(s). *Intramural sports:* baseball M, basketball M/W, softball W.
Costs (2016–17) *Tuition:* area resident $2656 full-time, $83 per semester hour part-time; state resident $8589 full-time, $268 per semester hour part-time; nonresident $10,580 full-time, $331 per semester hour part-time. *Required fees:* $490 full-time. *Payment plan:* installment. *Waivers:* senior citizens and employees or children of employees.
Applying *Options:* early admission, deferred entrance. *Required:* high school transcript. *Application deadlines:* rolling (freshmen), rolling (transfers). *Notification:* continuous (freshmen), continuous (transfers).
Freshman Application Contact Mrs. Tiffany Cowger, Assistant Dean for Student Services, Illinois Eastern Community Colleges, Wabash Valley College, 2200 College Drive, Mt. Carmel, IL 62863. *Phone:* 618-262-8641 Ext. 3101. *Toll-free phone:* 866-982-4322. *Fax:* 618-262-8647.
E-mail: cowgert@iecc.edu.
Website: http://www.iecc.edu/wvc/.

Illinois Valley Community College

Oglesby, Illinois

Freshman Application Contact Mr. Mark Grzybowski, Director of Admissions and Records, Illinois Valley Community College, Oglesby, IL 61348. *Phone:* 815-224-0437. *Fax:* 815-224-3033.
E-mail: mark_grzybowski@ivcc.edu.
Website: http://www.ivcc.edu/.

ITT Technical Institute

Arlington Heights, Illinois

Freshman Application Contact Director of Recruitment, ITT Technical Institute, 3800 North Wilke Road, Suite 100, Arlington Heights, IL 60004. *Phone:* 847-454-1800.
Website: http://www.itt-tech.edu/.

ITT Technical Institute

Oak Brook, Illinois

Freshman Application Contact Director of Recruitment, ITT Technical Institute, 800 Jorie Boulevard, Suite 100, Oak Brook, IL 60523. *Phone:* 630-472-7000. *Toll-free phone:* 877-488-0001.
Website: http://www.itt-tech.edu/.

ITT Technical Institute

Orland Park, Illinois

Freshman Application Contact Director of Recruitment, ITT Technical Institute, 11551 184th Place, Orland Park, IL 60467. *Phone:* 708-326-3200.
Website: http://www.itt-tech.edu/.

John A. Logan College

Carterville, Illinois

Director of Admissions Mr. Terry Crain, Dean of Student Services, John A. Logan College, 700 Logan College Road, Carterville, IL 62918-9900. *Phone:* 618-985-3741 Ext. 8382. *Fax:* 618-985-4433. *E-mail:* terrycrain@jalc.edu.
Website: http://www.jalc.edu/.

John Wood Community College

Quincy, Illinois

Freshman Application Contact Mr. Lee Wibbell, Director of Admissions, John Wood Community College, Quincy, IL 62305-8736. *Phone:* 217-641-4339. *Fax:* 217-224-4208. *E-mail:* admissions@jwcc.edu.
Website: http://www.jwcc.edu/.

Joliet Junior College

Joliet, Illinois

Freshman Application Contact Ms. Jennifer Kloberdanz, Director of Admissions and Recruitment, Joliet Junior College, 1215 Houbolt Road, Joliet, IL 60431. *Phone:* 815-729-9020 Ext. 2414. *E-mail:* admission@jjc.edu.
Website: http://www.jjc.edu/.

Kankakee Community College

Kankakee, Illinois

- **State and locally supported** 2-year, founded 1966, part of Illinois Community College Board
- **Small-town** 185-acre campus with easy access to Chicago
- **Endowment** $6.5 million
- **Coed,** 3,306 undergraduate students, 37% full-time, 62% women, 38% men

Undergraduates 1,222 full-time, 2,084 part-time. Students come from 17 states and territories; 7 other countries; 1% are from out of state; 14% Black or African American, non-Hispanic/Latino; 12% Hispanic/Latino; 1% Asian, non-Hispanic/Latino; 0.1% Native Hawaiian or other Pacific Islander, non-Hispanic/Latino; 0.5% American Indian or Alaska Native, non-Hispanic/Latino; 1% Two or more races, non-Hispanic/Latino; 4% Race/ethnicity unknown; 0.2% international; 2% transferred in. *Retention:* 68% of full-time freshmen returned.
Freshmen *Admission:* 1,260 applied, 1,260 admitted, 334 enrolled. *Average high school GPA:* 2.9. *Test scores:* ACT scores over 18: 65%; ACT scores over 24: 13%.

Faculty *Total:* 245, 24% full-time, 5% with terminal degrees. *Student/faculty ratio:* 14:1.

Majors Administrative assistant and secretarial science; agriculture; applied horticulture/horticulture operations; art; automobile/automotive mechanics technology; biology/biological sciences; business administration and management; chemistry; clinical/medical laboratory technology; construction management; criminal justice/law enforcement administration; criminal justice/police science; desktop publishing and digital imaging design; drafting and design technology; early childhood education; education; elementary education; emergency medical technology (EMT paramedic); engineering; English; general studies; heating, air conditioning, ventilation and refrigeration maintenance technology; history; industrial electronics technology; legal assistant/paralegal; mathematics; mathematics teacher education; medical/clinical assistant; medical office assistant; physical therapy technology; physics; political science and government; psychology; radiologic technology/science; registered nursing/registered nurse; respiratory care therapy; secondary education; sociology; special education; teacher assistant/aide; visual and performing arts; welding technology.

Academics *Calendar:* semesters. *Degrees:* certificates, diplomas, and associate (also offers continuing education program with significant enrollment not reflected in profile). *Special study options:* academic remediation for entering students, advanced placement credit, distance learning, English as a second language, honors programs, independent study, internships, off-campus study, part-time degree program, services for LD students, student-designed majors, study abroad, summer session for credit. *ROTC:* Army (c).

Library Kankakee Community College Learning Resource Center.

Student Life *Housing:* college housing not available. *Activities and Organizations:* drama/theater group, Phi Theta Kappa, Hort, Student Nursing, Gay-Straight Alliance, Student Advisory Council. *Campus security:* 24-hour patrols, late-night transport/escort service.

Athletics Member NJCAA. *Intercollegiate sports:* baseball M(s), basketball M(s)/W(s), soccer M(s), softball W(s), volleyball W(s).

Costs (2015–16) *Tuition:* area resident $3660 full-time, $122 per credit hour part-time; state resident $8700 full-time, $290 per credit hour part-time; nonresident $17,340 full-time, $578 per credit hour part-time. *Required fees:* $420 full-time. *Payment plan:* installment. *Waivers:* senior citizens and employees or children of employees.

Financial Aid Of all full-time matriculated undergraduates who enrolled in 2014, 70 Federal Work-Study jobs (averaging $1100). *Financial aid deadline:* 10/1.

Applying *Options:* electronic application, early admission. *Required:* high school transcript. *Application deadlines:* rolling (freshmen), rolling (out-of-state freshmen), rolling (transfers). *Notification:* continuous (freshmen), continuous (out-of-state freshmen), continuous (transfers).

Freshman Application Contact Ms. Kim Harpin, Director of Support Services, Kankakee Community College, 100 College Drive, Kankakee, IL 60901. *Phone:* 815-802-8472. *Fax:* 815-802-8472.
E-mail: kharpin@kcc.edu.
Website: http://www.kcc.edu/.

Kaskaskia College
Centralia, Illinois

- **State and locally supported** 2-year, founded 1966, part of Illinois Community College Board
- **Rural** 195-acre campus with easy access to St. Louis
- **Endowment** $6.0 million
- **Coed**, 4,472 undergraduate students, 33% full-time, 58% women, 42% men

Undergraduates 1,458 full-time, 3,014 part-time. Students come from 9 states and territories; 1 other country; 1% are from out of state; 8% Black or African American, non-Hispanic/Latino; 1% Hispanic/Latino; 0.5% Asian, non-Hispanic/Latino; 0.4% American Indian or Alaska Native, non-Hispanic/Latino; 2% Two or more races, non-Hispanic/Latino; 0.3% Race/ethnicity unknown; 0.1% international; 16% transferred in.

Freshmen *Admission:* 265 applied, 265 admitted, 265 enrolled.

Faculty *Total:* 206, 37% full-time, 6% with terminal degrees. *Student/faculty ratio:* 21:1.

Majors Accounting; agriculture; animal sciences; applied horticulture/horticulture operations; architectural drafting and CAD/CADD; autobody/collision and repair technology; automobile/automotive mechanics technology; biological and physical sciences; business automation/technology/data entry; business/commerce; carpentry; child-care provision; clinical/medical laboratory technology; construction management; cosmetology; criminal justice/law enforcement administration; culinary arts; dental assisting; electrical, electronic and communications engineering technology; electrician; emergency medical technology (EMT paramedic); engineering; executive assistant/executive secretary; general studies; health information/medical records technology; heating, air conditioning, ventilation and refrigeration maintenance technology; industrial mechanics and maintenance technology; information science/studies; juvenile corrections; liberal arts and sciences/liberal studies; mathematics teacher education; music; network and system administration; occupational therapist assistant; physical therapy technology; radiologic technology/science; registered nursing/registered nurse; respiratory care therapy; robotics technology; teacher assistant/aide; veterinary/animal health technology; web/multimedia management and webmaster; welding technology.

Academics *Calendar:* semesters. *Degree:* certificates and associate. *Special study options:* academic remediation for entering students, accelerated degree program, adult/continuing education programs, cooperative education, distance learning, double majors, honors programs, independent study, internships, off-campus study, part-time degree program, services for LD students, study abroad, summer session for credit. *ROTC:* Army (c).

Library Kaskaskia College Library. *Books:* 17,571 (physical), 12,675 (digital/electronic); *Serial titles:* 58 (physical); *Databases:* 37. Weekly public service hours: 49.

Student Life *Housing:* college housing not available. *Activities and Organizations:* drama/theater group, student-run newspaper, choral group, Student Nurse Organization, Veteran's Student Organization, Criminal Justice Club, Respiratory Care Club, Student Radiography Club. *Campus security:* 24-hour emergency response devices and patrols, late-night transport/escort service. *Student services:* personal/psychological counseling.

Athletics Member NJCAA. *Intercollegiate sports:* baseball M(s), basketball M(s)/W(s), cheerleading M(s)/W(s), cross-country running M(s)/W(s), golf M(s)/W(s), soccer W(s), softball W(s), tennis M(s), volleyball W(s).

Standardized Tests *Recommended:* ACT (for admission).

Costs (2015–16) *Tuition:* area resident $3680 full-time, $115 per credit hour part-time; state resident $6944 full-time, $217 per credit hour part-time; nonresident $12,640 full-time, $395 per credit hour part-time. Full-time tuition and fees vary according to program. Part-time tuition and fees vary according to program. *Required fees:* $480 full-time, $16 per credit hour part-time. *Payment plan:* installment. *Waivers:* senior citizens and employees or children of employees.

Financial Aid Of all full-time matriculated undergraduates who enrolled in 2015, 1,170 applied for aid, 925 were judged to have need, 40 had their need fully met. 30 Federal Work-Study jobs (averaging $3913). 20 state and other part-time jobs (averaging $2147). In 2015, 33 non-need-based awards were made. *Average percent of need met:* 35%. *Average financial aid package:* $5668. *Average need-based gift aid:* $4526. *Average non-need-based aid:* $3073.

Applying *Options:* electronic application, early admission, deferred entrance. *Required:* high school transcript. *Required for some:* interview. *Application deadlines:* rolling (freshmen), rolling (transfers). *Notification:* continuous (freshmen), continuous (transfers).

Freshman Application Contact Jan Ripperda, Manager of Records and Registration, Kaskaskia College, 27210 College Road, Centralia, IL 62801. *Phone:* 618-545-3041. *Toll-free phone:* 800-642-0859. *Fax:* 618-532-1990.
E-mail: jripperda@kaskaskia.edu.
Website: http://www.kaskaskia.edu/.

Kishwaukee College
Malta, Illinois

- **State and locally supported** 2-year, founded 1967, part of Illinois Community College Board
- **Rural** 120-acre campus with easy access to Chicago
- **Coed**

Undergraduates 2,030 full-time, 2,445 part-time. 17% Black or African American, non-Hispanic/Latino; 11% Hispanic/Latino; 2% Asian, non-Hispanic/Latino; 0.1% Native Hawaiian or other Pacific Islander, non-Hispanic/Latino; 0.6% American Indian or Alaska Native, non-Hispanic/Latino; 5% Two or more races, non-Hispanic/Latino; 1% Race/ethnicity unknown; 7% transferred in.

Academics *Calendar:* semesters. *Degree:* certificates, diplomas, and associate. *Special study options:* academic remediation for entering students, adult/continuing education programs, advanced placement credit, cooperative education, distance learning, double majors, English as a second language, external degree program, freshman honors college, honors programs, independent study, internships, off-campus study, part-time degree program, services for LD students, study abroad, summer session for credit.

Library Kishwaukee College Library.

Student Life *Campus security:* 24-hour emergency response devices and patrols.

Athletics Member NJCAA.

Costs (2015–16) *Tuition:* area resident $3570 full-time, $119 per credit hour part-time; state resident $9330 full-time, $311 per credit hour part-time; nonresident $15,030 full-time, $501 per credit hour part-time. Full-time tuition and fees vary according to program and reciprocity agreements. Part-time tuition and fees vary according to program and reciprocity agreements.

Required fees: $420 full-time, $12 per credit hour part-time. *Payment plans:* installment, deferred payment.
Financial Aid *Average indebtedness upon graduation:* $4375.
Applying *Options:* electronic application, early admission, deferred entrance. *Required for some:* high school transcript. *Recommended:* high school transcript, Transcripts from all other colleges or universities previously attended.
Freshman Application Contact Mr. Bryce Law, Coordinator-Student Outreach and Orientation, Kishwaukee College, 21193 Malta Road, Malta, IL 60150. *Phone:* 815-825-2086 Ext. 2351.
E-mail: bryce.law@kishwaukeecollege.edu.
Website: http://www.kishwaukeecollege.edu/.

Lake Land College
Mattoon, Illinois

- **State and locally supported** 2-year, founded 1966, part of Illinois Community College Board
- **Rural** 308-acre campus
- **Endowment** $2.7 million
- **Coed,** 6,351 undergraduate students, 44% full-time, 52% women, 48% men

Undergraduates 2,809 full-time, 3,542 part-time. 1% are from out of state; 0.6% transferred in. *Retention:* 89% of full-time freshmen returned.
Freshmen *Admission:* 1,101 enrolled.
Faculty *Total:* 191, 61% full-time, 5% with terminal degrees. *Student/faculty ratio:* 21:1.
Majors Accounting technology and bookkeeping; administrative assistant and secretarial science; agricultural business and management; agricultural mechanization; agricultural production; architectural engineering technology; automobile/automotive mechanics technology; biological and physical sciences; business administration and management; child-care and support services management; civil engineering technology; computer programming (specific applications); computer systems networking and telecommunications; corrections; criminal justice/police science; dental hygiene; desktop publishing and digital imaging design; drafting and design technology; electrical, electronic and communications engineering technology; electromechanical technology; executive assistant/executive secretary; general studies; graphic and printing equipment operation/production; human services; industrial technology; information technology; legal administrative assistant/secretary; liberal arts and sciences/liberal studies; marketing/marketing management; medical administrative assistant and medical secretary; office management; physical therapy technology; printing press operation; radio and television; registered nursing/registered nurse; social work; telecommunications technology.
Academics *Calendar:* semesters. *Degree:* certificates and associate. *Special study options:* academic remediation for entering students, accelerated degree program, adult/continuing education programs, cooperative education, distance learning, English as a second language, external degree program, honors programs, internships, part-time degree program, services for LD students, summer session for credit.
Library Virgil H. Judge Learning Resource Center plus 1 other.
Student Life *Housing:* college housing not available. *Activities and Organizations:* student-run newspaper, radio station, choral group, Agriculture Production and Management Club, Cosmetology Club, Agriculture Transfer Club, Phi Theta Kappa, Civil Engineering Technology Club. *Campus security:* 24-hour patrols. *Student services:* personal/psychological counseling.
Athletics Member NJCAA. *Intercollegiate sports:* baseball M(s), basketball M(s)/W(s), cheerleading W, softball W(s), tennis M(s)/W, volleyball W(s). *Intramural sports:* basketball M/W, bowling M/W, golf M/W, soccer M/W, softball M/W, volleyball M/W.
Standardized Tests *Recommended:* ACT (for admission).
Costs (2015–16) *Tuition:* area resident $2775 full-time, $93 per credit hour part-time; state resident $6599 full-time, $220 per credit hour part-time; nonresident $12,400 full-time, $413 per credit hour part-time. *Required fees:* $684 full-time, $23 per credit hour part-time. *Payment plan:* deferred payment. *Waivers:* senior citizens and employees or children of employees.
Financial Aid Of all full-time matriculated undergraduates who enrolled in 2014, 120 Federal Work-Study jobs (averaging $1400).
Applying *Options:* electronic application, early admission. *Recommended:* high school transcript. *Application deadlines:* rolling (freshmen), rolling (transfers). *Notification:* continuous (freshmen), continuous (transfers).
Freshman Application Contact Mr. Jon VanDyke, Dean of Admissions Services, Lake Land College, Mattoon, IL 61938-9366. *Phone:* 217-234-5378. *E-mail:* admissions@lakeland.cc.il.us.
Website: http://www.lakelandcollege.edu/.

Lewis and Clark Community College
Godfrey, Illinois

- **District-supported** 2-year, founded 1970, part of Illinois Community College Board
- **Small-town** 275-acre campus with easy access to St. Louis
- **Coed,** 8,179 undergraduate students

Majors Accounting; administrative assistant and secretarial science; art; automobile/automotive mechanics technology; biological and physical sciences; business administration and management; CAD/CADD drafting/design technology; child-care provision; computer graphics; computer programming; computer systems networking and telecommunications; criminal justice/law enforcement administration; dental hygiene; engineering; fire science/firefighting; general studies; kinesiology and exercise science; legal administrative assistant/secretary; legal assistant/paralegal; liberal arts and sciences/liberal studies; library and archives assisting; manufacturing engineering technology; massage therapy; medical administrative assistant and medical secretary; occupational therapist assistant; radio and television; registered nursing/registered nurse; web page, digital/multimedia and information resources design.
Academics *Calendar:* semesters. *Degree:* certificates and associate. *Special study options:* academic remediation for entering students, adult/continuing education programs, advanced placement credit, cooperative education, distance learning, double majors, English as a second language, independent study, internships, off-campus study, part-time degree program, services for LD students, summer session for credit. *ROTC:* Army (b).
Library Reid Memorial Library. *Books:* 50,000 (physical), 123 (digital/electronic); *Serial titles:* 65 (physical), 12,000 (digital/electronic); *Databases:* 44. Weekly public service hours: 56; students can reserve study rooms.
Student Life *Housing:* college housing not available. *Activities and Organizations:* student-run newspaper, radio station, choral group. *Campus security:* 24-hour emergency response devices and patrols. *Student services:* health clinic, personal/psychological counseling.
Athletics Member NJCAA. *Intercollegiate sports:* baseball M, basketball M/W(s), golf M, soccer M(s)/W, softball W, tennis M(s)/W(s), volleyball W(s).
Financial Aid Of all full-time matriculated undergraduates who enrolled in 2014, 69 Federal Work-Study jobs (averaging $5700). 84 state and other part-time jobs (averaging $5700).
Applying *Options:* early admission, deferred entrance. *Required for some:* interview. *Recommended:* high school transcript. *Application deadlines:* rolling (freshmen), rolling (transfers). *Notification:* continuous (freshmen), continuous (transfers).
Freshman Application Contact Lewis and Clark Community College, 5800 Godfrey Road, Godfrey, IL 62035-2466. *Phone:* 618-468-5100. *Toll-free phone:* 800-YES-LCCC.
Website: http://www.lc.edu/.

Lincoln College
Lincoln, Illinois

Director of Admissions Gretchen Bree, Director of Admissions, Lincoln College, 300 Keokuk Street, Lincoln, IL 62656-1699. *Phone:* 217-732-3155 Ext. 256. *Toll-free phone:* 800-569-0558. *E-mail:* gbree@lincolncollege.edu.
Website: http://www.lincolncollege.edu/.

Lincoln College of Technology
Melrose Park, Illinois

Admissions Office Contact Lincoln College of Technology, 8317 W. North Avenue, Melrose Park, IL 60160.
Website: http://www.lincolnedu.com/.

Lincoln Land Community College
Springfield, Illinois

Freshman Application Contact Mr. Ron Gregoire, Executive Director of Admissions and Records, Lincoln Land Community College, 5250 Shepherd Road, PO Box 19256, Springfield, IL 62794-9256. *Phone:* 217-786-2243. *Toll-free phone:* 800-727-4161. *Fax:* 217-786-2492.
E-mail: ron.gregoire@llcc.edu.
Website: http://www.llcc.edu/.

MacCormac College
Chicago, Illinois

Director of Admissions Mr. David Grassi, Director of Admissions, MacCormac College, 506 South Wabash Avenue, Chicago, IL 60605-1667. *Phone:* 312-922-1884 Ext. 102.
Website: http://www.maccormac.edu/.

McHenry County College
Crystal Lake, Illinois

- **State and locally supported** 2-year, founded 1967, part of Illinois Community College Board
- **Suburban** 168-acre campus with easy access to Chicago
- **Coed,** 6,567 undergraduate students, 37% full-time, 54% women, 46% men

Undergraduates 2,460 full-time, 4,107 part-time. 0.8% are from out of state; 2% Black or African American, non-Hispanic/Latino; 14% Hispanic/Latino; 2% Asian, non-Hispanic/Latino; 0.2% Native Hawaiian or other Pacific Islander, non-Hispanic/Latino; 0.2% American Indian or Alaska Native, non-Hispanic/Latino; 2% Two or more races, non-Hispanic/Latino; 7% Race/ethnicity unknown; 0.2% international.
Freshmen *Admission:* 1,719 applied, 1,719 admitted, 1,144 enrolled. *Average high school GPA:* 2.25.
Faculty *Total:* 360, 27% full-time, 70% with terminal degrees. *Student/faculty ratio:* 20:1.
Majors Accounting; administrative assistant and secretarial science; animation, interactive technology, video graphics and special effects; applied horticulture/horticulture operations; biological and physical sciences; business administration and management; child-care provision; commercial photography; computer systems networking and telecommunications; construction management; criminal justice/police science; emergency medical technology (EMT paramedic); engineering; fine/studio arts; fire science/firefighting; general studies; health and physical education/fitness; information technology; liberal arts and sciences/liberal studies; music; occupational therapist assistant; operations management; registered nursing/registered nurse; restaurant, culinary, and catering management; robotics technology; selling skills and sales; special education.
Academics *Calendar:* semesters. *Degree:* certificates and associate. *Special study options:* academic remediation for entering students, accelerated degree program, adult/continuing education programs, advanced placement credit, cooperative education, distance learning, English as a second language, independent study, internships, part-time degree program, services for LD students, study abroad, summer session for credit.
Library McHenry County College Library. *Books:* 44,867 (physical), 1,388 (digital/electronic); *Serial titles:* 132 (physical), 16,018 (digital/electronic); *Databases:* 70.
Student Life *Housing:* college housing not available. *Activities and Organizations:* drama/theater group, student-run newspaper, radio station, choral group, Phi Theta Kappa, Student Senate, Equality Club, Writer's Block, Latinos Unidos. *Campus security:* 24-hour emergency response devices and patrols, late-night transport/escort service. *Student services:* personal/psychological counseling.
Athletics Member NJCAA. *Intercollegiate sports:* baseball M(s), basketball M(s)/W(s), soccer M(s), softball W(s), tennis M(s)/W(s), volleyball W(s).
Costs (2016–17) *Tuition:* area resident $3030 full-time, $101 per credit hour part-time; state resident $10,416 full-time, $347 per credit hour part-time; nonresident $12,958 full-time, $432 per credit hour part-time. Full-time tuition and fees vary according to course load. Part-time tuition and fees vary according to course load. *Required fees:* $284 full-time, $9 per credit hour part-time, $7 per term part-time. *Payment plan:* installment. *Waivers:* senior citizens and employees or children of employees.
Financial Aid Of all full-time matriculated undergraduates who enrolled in 2014, 200 Federal Work-Study jobs (averaging $3700). 130 state and other part-time jobs (averaging $2000).
Applying *Options:* electronic application, early admission, deferred entrance. *Application fee:* $15. *Recommended:* high school transcript. *Application deadlines:* rolling (freshmen), rolling (out-of-state freshmen), rolling (transfers). *Notification:* continuous (freshmen), continuous (out-of-state freshmen), continuous (transfers).
Freshman Application Contact Kellie Carper-Sowiak, Manager of New Student Transitions, McHenry County College, 8900 US Highway 14, Crystal Lake, IL 60012-2761. *Phone:* 815-455-8670.
E-mail: admissions@mchenry.edu.
Website: http://www.mchenry.edu/.

Midwestern Career College
Chicago, Illinois

Admissions Office Contact Midwestern Career College, 20 North Wacker Drive #3800, Chicago, IL 60606.
Website: http://www.mccollege.edu/.

Moraine Valley Community College
Palos Hills, Illinois

- **State and locally supported** 2-year, founded 1967, part of Illinois Community College Board
- **Suburban** 294-acre campus with easy access to Chicago
- **Endowment** $13.3 million
- **Coed,** 15,016 undergraduate students, 43% full-time, 52% women, 48% men

Undergraduates 6,393 full-time, 8,623 part-time. 0.2% are from out of state; 9% Black or African American, non-Hispanic/Latino; 23% Hispanic/Latino; 3% Asian, non-Hispanic/Latino; 0.1% Native Hawaiian or other Pacific Islander, non-Hispanic/Latino; 0.3% American Indian or Alaska Native, non-Hispanic/Latino; 2% Two or more races, non-Hispanic/Latino; 9% Race/ethnicity unknown; 2% international; 3% transferred in. *Retention:* 66% of full-time freshmen returned.
Freshmen *Admission:* 2,250 enrolled. *Test scores:* ACT scores over 18: 63%; ACT scores over 24: 16%; ACT scores over 30: 2%.
Faculty *Total:* 959, 20% full-time, 10% with terminal degrees. *Student/faculty ratio:* 21:1.
Majors Administrative assistant and secretarial science; automobile/automotive mechanics technology; baking and pastry arts; biological and physical sciences; biology/biological sciences; business administration and management; business/commerce; child-care provision; computer and information sciences; computer and information systems security; computer graphics; computer science; criminal justice/law enforcement administration; criminal justice/police science; design and visual communications; early childhood education; elementary education; emergency medical technology (EMT paramedic); engineering; English; fire prevention and safety technology; fire science/firefighting; health information/medical records technology; heating, air conditioning, ventilation and refrigeration maintenance technology; history; hospitality administration; human resources management; industrial electronics technology; instrumentation technology; liberal arts and sciences/liberal studies; management information systems; manufacturing engineering technology; mathematics; mathematics teacher education; mechanical engineering/mechanical technology; movement and mind-body therapies and education related; music; parks, recreation and leisure facilities management; physics; political science and government; polysomnography; psychology; radiologic technology/science; registered nursing/registered nurse; respiratory care therapy; restaurant, culinary, and catering management; retailing; science teacher education; small business administration; sociology; special education; substance abuse/addiction counseling; surveying technology; system, networking, and LAN/WAN management; teacher assistant/aide; tourism and travel services management; visual and performing arts; web/multimedia management and webmaster.
Academics *Calendar:* semesters. *Degree:* certificates and associate. *Special study options:* academic remediation for entering students, accelerated degree program, adult/continuing education programs, advanced placement credit, cooperative education, distance learning, double majors, English as a second language, honors programs, independent study, internships, off-campus study, part-time degree program, services for LD students, study abroad, summer session for credit.
Library *Books:* 64,610 (physical), 493 (digital/electronic); *Serial titles:* 314 (physical), 55 (digital/electronic); *Databases:* 63.
Student Life *Housing:* college housing not available. *Activities and Organizations:* drama/theater group, student-run newspaper, choral group, Student Newspaper, Speech Team, Alliance of Latin American Students, Phi Theta Kappa, Arab Student Union. *Campus security:* 24-hour emergency response devices and patrols, late-night transport/escort service, campus police department, safety and security programs. *Student services:* personal/psychological counseling, women's center.
Athletics Member NJCAA. *Intercollegiate sports:* baseball M(s), basketball M(s)/W(s), cross-country running M(s)/W(s), golf M(s), soccer M(s)/W(s), softball W(s), tennis M(s)/W(s), volleyball W(s). *Intramural sports:* badminton M/W, basketball M/W, cheerleading W, soccer M/W, ultimate Frisbee M/W, volleyball M/W.
Costs (2015–16) *Tuition:* area resident $3996 full-time, $116 per credit hour part-time; state resident $8916 full-time, $280 per credit hour part-time; nonresident $10,326 full-time, $327 per credit hour part-time. *Required fees:* $516 full-time, $17 per credit hour part-time, $3 per term part-time. *Payment plan:* installment. *Waivers:* senior citizens and employees or children of employees.

Applying *Options:* electronic application, early admission, deferred entrance. *Recommended:* high school transcript. *Application deadlines:* rolling (freshmen), rolling (transfers). *Notification:* continuous (freshmen), continuous (transfers).
Freshman Application Contact Mr. Andrew Sarata, Director, Admissions and Recruitment, Moraine Valley Community College, 9000 West College Parkway, Palos Hills, IL 60465-0937. *Phone:* 708-974-5357. *Fax:* 708-974-0681. *E-mail:* sarataa@morainevalley.edu.
Website: http://www.morainevalley.edu/.

Morrison Institute of Technology
Morrison, Illinois

Freshman Application Contact Mrs. Tammy Pruis, Admission Secretary, Morrison Institute of Technology, 701 Portland Avenue, Morrison, IL 61270. *Phone:* 815-772-7218. *Fax:* 815-772-7584.
E-mail: admissions@morrison.tec.il.us.
Website: http://www.morrisontech.edu/.

Morton College
Cicero, Illinois

Freshman Application Contact Morton College, 3801 South Central Avenue, Cicero, IL 60804-4398. *Phone:* 708-656-8000 Ext. 401.
Website: http://www.morton.edu/.

Northwestern College–Bridgeview Campus
Bridgeview, Illinois

Admissions Office Contact Northwestern College–Bridgeview Campus, 7725 South Harlem Avenue, Bridgeview, IL 60645. *Toll-free phone:* 888-205-2283.
Website: http://www.nc.edu/locations/bridgeview-campus/.

Northwestern College–Chicago Campus
Chicago, Illinois

- **Proprietary** 2-year, founded 1902
- **Urban** 3-acre campus with easy access to Chicago, IL
- **Coed**

Undergraduates 472 full-time, 610 part-time. 2% are from out of state; 40% Black or African American, non-Hispanic/Latino; 21% Hispanic/Latino; 1% Asian, non-Hispanic/Latino; 0.2% Native Hawaiian or other Pacific Islander, non-Hispanic/Latino; 2% American Indian or Alaska Native, non-Hispanic/Latino; 8% Two or more races, non-Hispanic/Latino; 6% Race/ethnicity unknown.
Academics *Calendar:* quarters. *Degrees:* certificates and associate (profile includes branch campuses in Bridgeview and Naperville, IL). *Special study options:* academic remediation for entering students, cooperative education, honors programs, independent study, internships, part-time degree program, summer session for credit.
Library Edward G. Schumacher Memorial Library.
Standardized Tests *Recommended:* SAT or ACT (for admission).
Costs (2015–16) *Tuition:* $20,925 full-time, $465 per quarter hour part-time. *Required fees:* $370 full-time.
Applying *Options:* electronic application. *Application fee:* $25. *Required:* high school transcript.
Freshman Application Contact Northwestern College–Chicago Campus, 4829 North Lipps Avenue, Chicago, IL 60630. *Phone:* 708-233-5000. *Toll-free phone:* 888-205-2283.
Website: http://www.nc.edu/locations/chicago-campus/.

Oakton Community College
Des Plaines, Illinois

- **District-supported** 2-year, founded 1969, part of Illinois Community College Board
- **Suburban** 193-acre campus with easy access to Chicago
- **Coed,** 9,363 undergraduate students

Majors Accounting technology and bookkeeping; administrative assistant and secretarial science; architectural drafting and CAD/CADD; automobile/automotive mechanics technology; banking and financial support services; biological and physical sciences; building/construction finishing, management, and inspection related; child-care provision; clinical/medical laboratory technology; computer programming; criminal justice/police science; electrical, electronic and communications engineering technology; engineering; fire science/firefighting; graphic design; health information/medical records administration; heating, ventilation, air conditioning and refrigeration engineering technology; information technology; liberal arts and sciences/liberal studies; manufacturing engineering technology; marketing/marketing management; mechanical engineering/mechanical technology; music; operations management; physical therapy technology; real estate; registered nursing/registered nurse; sales, distribution, and marketing operations; social work; substance abuse/addiction counseling.
Academics *Calendar:* semesters. *Degree:* certificates and associate. *Special study options:* academic remediation for entering students, adult/continuing education programs, advanced placement credit, distance learning, English as a second language, honors programs, independent study, internships, off-campus study, part-time degree program, services for LD students, study abroad, summer session for credit.
Library Oakton Community College Library plus 1 other.
Student Life *Housing:* college housing not available. *Activities and Organizations:* drama/theater group, student-run newspaper, choral group. *Campus security:* 24-hour emergency response devices and patrols, student patrols, late-night transport/escort service. *Student services:* health clinic, personal/psychological counseling.
Athletics Member NJCAA. *Intercollegiate sports:* baseball M, basketball M/W, cross-country running M/W, soccer M/W, softball W, tennis M/W, track and field M/W, volleyball W. *Intramural sports:* basketball M/W, cheerleading W, soccer M, table tennis M/W, volleyball M/W.
Costs (2016–17) *Tuition:* area resident $2845 full-time; state resident $7639 full-time; nonresident $9673 full-time. Full-time tuition and fees vary according to course load. Part-time tuition and fees vary according to course load. *Payment plans:* installment, deferred payment. *Waivers:* employees or children of employees.
Applying *Options:* electronic application. *Application fee:* $25. *Required for some:* interview. *Recommended:* high school transcript. *Application deadlines:* rolling (freshmen), rolling (transfers). *Notification:* continuous (freshmen), continuous (transfers).
Freshman Application Contact Ms. Nicci Cisarik, Admissions Specialist, Oakton Community College, 1600 East Golf Road, Des Plaines, IL 60016-1268. *Phone:* 847-635-1913. *Fax:* 847-635-1890.
E-mail: ncisarik@oakton.edu.
Website: http://www.oakton.edu/.

Parkland College
Champaign, Illinois

Freshman Application Contact Mr. Tim Wendt, Director of Enrollment Services, Parkland College, Champaign, IL 61821-1899. *Phone:* 217-351-2482. *Toll-free phone:* 800-346-8089. *Fax:* 217-353-2640.
E-mail: admissions@parkland.edu.
Website: http://www.parkland.edu/.

Prairie State College
Chicago Heights, Illinois

Freshman Application Contact Jaime Miller, Director of Admissions, Prairie State College, 202 South Halsted Street, Chicago Heights, IL 60411. *Phone:* 708-709-3513. *E-mail:* jmmiller@prairiestate.edu.
Website: http://www.prairiestate.edu/.

Rend Lake College
Ina, Illinois

- **State-supported** 2-year, founded 1967, part of Illinois Community College Board
- **Rural** 350-acre campus
- **Coed,** 2,189 undergraduate students, 55% full-time, 56% women, 44% men

Undergraduates 1,198 full-time, 991 part-time. *Retention:* 66% of full-time freshmen returned.
Freshmen *Admission:* 530 enrolled.
Faculty *Total:* 215, 31% full-time. *Student/faculty ratio:* 15:1.
Majors Administrative assistant and secretarial science; agricultural mechanics and equipment technology; agricultural mechanization; agricultural production; applied horticulture/horticulture operations; architectural drafting and CAD/CADD; automobile/automotive mechanics technology; barbering; biological and physical sciences; child-care provision; clinical/medical laboratory technology; computer technology/computer systems technology; cosmetology; criminal justice/police science; culinary arts; drafting and design technology; e-commerce; electrical, electronic and communications engineering technology; electrician; emergency medical technology (EMT paramedic); engineering; fine/studio arts; graphic design; health information/medical records technology; heavy equipment maintenance

technology; industrial mechanics and maintenance technology; liberal arts and sciences/liberal studies; manufacturing engineering technology; medical radiologic technology; medical staff services technology; mining technology; occupational therapist assistant; petroleum technology; plant sciences; special education; veterinary/animal health technology; welding technology.

Academics *Calendar:* semesters. *Degree:* certificates and associate. *Special study options:* academic remediation for entering students, adult/continuing education programs, advanced placement credit, cooperative education, distance learning, double majors, English as a second language, honors programs, independent study, internships, off-campus study, part-time degree program, services for LD students, study abroad, summer session for credit.

Library Learning Resource Center plus 1 other. *Books:* 13,804 (physical), 20,616 (digital/electronic); *Serial titles:* 1,627 (physical), 32,458 (digital/electronic); *Databases:* 21,087.

Student Life *Housing:* college housing not available. *Activities and Organizations:* drama/theater group, student-run newspaper, choral group. *Campus security:* 24-hour emergency response devices and patrols, late-night transport/escort service.

Athletics Member NJCAA. *Intercollegiate sports:* baseball M(s), basketball M(s)/W(s), golf M(s)/W(s), softball W(s), tennis W(s), volleyball W(s).

Standardized Tests *Required:* SAT or ACT (for admission), ACT Compass or ACCUPLACER (for admission).

Costs (2016–17) *Tuition:* area resident $3750 full-time, $110 per credit hour part-time; nonresident $6000 full-time, $200 per credit hour part-time. Full-time tuition and fees vary according to course level, course load, program, and reciprocity agreements. Part-time tuition and fees vary according to course level, course load, program, and reciprocity agreements. *Required fees:* $450 full-time, $15 per credit hour part-time. *Payment plan:* installment. *Waivers:* senior citizens and employees or children of employees.

Financial Aid Of all full-time matriculated undergraduates who enrolled in 2014, 133 Federal Work-Study jobs (averaging $1000). 174 state and other part-time jobs (averaging $940).

Applying *Options:* electronic application, deferred entrance. *Required:* high school transcript. *Application deadlines:* 8/18 (freshmen), 8/18 (transfers).

Freshman Application Contact Mr. Jason Swann, Dean of Admissions and Enrollment Management, Rend Lake College, 468 North Ken Gray Parkway, Ina, IL 62846-9801. *Phone:* 618-437-5321 Ext. 1265. *Toll-free phone:* 800-369-5321. *Fax:* 618-437-5677. *E-mail:* swannj@rlc.edu. *Website:* http://www.rlc.edu/.

Richland Community College
Decatur, Illinois

- **District-supported** 2-year, founded 1971, part of Illinois Community College Board
- **Small-town** 117-acre campus
- **Coed,** 3,005 undergraduate students, 32% full-time, 60% women, 40% men

Undergraduates 951 full-time, 2,054 part-time. Students come from 25 states and territories; 2% are from out of state; 16% Black or African American, non-Hispanic/Latino; 1% Hispanic/Latino; 1% Asian, non-Hispanic/Latino; 0.2% Native Hawaiian or other Pacific Islander, non-Hispanic/Latino; 0.6% American Indian or Alaska Native, non-Hispanic/Latino; 4% Race/ethnicity unknown; 0.8% transferred in. *Retention:* 57% of full-time freshmen returned.

Freshmen *Admission:* 602 applied, 397 admitted. *Average high school GPA:* 2.15. *Test scores:* ACT scores over 18: 50%; ACT scores over 24: 8%; ACT scores over 30: 1%.

Faculty *Total:* 203, 37% full-time, 7% with terminal degrees. *Student/faculty ratio:* 15:1.

Majors Accounting; administrative assistant and secretarial science; agricultural business and management; automobile/automotive mechanics technology; biological and physical sciences; business administration and management; child development; computer and information sciences related; computer graphics; computer programming (specific applications); construction engineering technology; criminal justice/police science; data entry/microcomputer applications; data entry/microcomputer applications related; drafting and design technology; electrical, electronic and communications engineering technology; fire science/firefighting; food technology and processing; industrial technology; information science/studies; insurance; legal administrative assistant/secretary; liberal arts and sciences/liberal studies; medical administrative assistant and medical secretary; pre-engineering; registered nursing/registered nurse; surgical technology; word processing.

Academics *Calendar:* semesters. *Degree:* certificates and associate. *Special study options:* academic remediation for entering students, adult/continuing education programs, advanced placement credit, distance learning, English as a second language, freshman honors college, honors programs, part-time degree program, services for LD students, student-designed majors, summer session for credit.

Library Kitty Lindsay Library. *Books:* 29,388 (physical), 15 (digital/electronic); *Serial titles:* 975 (physical); *Databases:* 28. Students can reserve study rooms.

Student Life *Housing:* college housing not available. *Activities and Organizations:* student-run newspaper, Phi Theta Kappa, Media Club, InterVarsity Christian Fellowship, X-Ray Vision, Practical Nursing Club. *Campus security:* 24-hour emergency response devices and patrols. *Student services:* personal/psychological counseling.

Standardized Tests *Recommended:* ACT (for admission).

Costs (2016–17) *Tuition:* area resident $3744 full-time, $119 per credit hour part-time; state resident $5445 full-time, $201 per credit hour part-time; nonresident $462 per credit part-time. Full-time tuition and fees vary according to program and reciprocity agreements. Part-time tuition and fees vary according to program and reciprocity agreements. *Required fees:* $324 full-time, $2 per credit part-time. *Payment plan:* installment. *Waivers:* senior citizens and employees or children of employees.

Financial Aid Of all full-time matriculated undergraduates who enrolled in 2014, 43 Federal Work-Study jobs (averaging $1339). 129 state and other part-time jobs (averaging $578).

Applying *Options:* early admission. *Required:* high school transcript. *Application deadlines:* rolling (freshmen), rolling (transfers).

Freshman Application Contact Ms. Catherine Sebok, Director of Admissions and Records, Richland Community College, Decatur, IL 62521. *Phone:* 217-875-7200 Ext. 558. *Fax:* 217-875-7783. *E-mail:* csebok@richland.edu. *Website:* http://www.richland.edu/.

Rockford Career College
Rockford, Illinois

Director of Admissions Ms. Barbara Holliman, Director of Admissions, Rockford Career College, 1130 South Alpine Road, Suite 100, Rockford, IL 61108. *Phone:* 815-965-8616 Ext. 16. *Website:* http://www.rockfordcareercollege.edu/.

Rock Valley College
Rockford, Illinois

- **District-supported** 2-year, founded 1964, part of Illinois Community College Board
- **Suburban** 217-acre campus with easy access to Chicago
- **Coed,** 6,937 undergraduate students, 45% full-time, 56% women, 44% men

Undergraduates 3,138 full-time, 3,799 part-time. 9% Black or African American, non-Hispanic/Latino; 15% Hispanic/Latino; 2% Asian, non-Hispanic/Latino; 0.1% Native Hawaiian or other Pacific Islander, non-Hispanic/Latino; 0.4% American Indian or Alaska Native, non-Hispanic/Latino; 2% Two or more races, non-Hispanic/Latino; 1% Race/ethnicity unknown; 0.3% international; 3% transferred in. *Retention:* 68% of full-time freshmen returned.

Freshmen *Admission:* 957 enrolled.

Faculty *Total:* 461, 34% full-time.

Majors Accounting; administrative assistant and secretarial science; automobile/automotive mechanics technology; avionics maintenance technology; business administration and management; child development; computer engineering technology; computer science; computer systems networking and telecommunications; construction engineering technology; criminal justice/law enforcement administration; dental hygiene; drafting/design engineering technologies related; electrical, electronic and communications engineering technology; electrician; energy management and systems technology; fire science/firefighting; graphic and printing equipment operation/production; human services; industrial and product design; industrial technology; liberal arts and sciences/liberal studies; marketing/marketing management; pre-engineering; quality control technology; registered nursing/registered nurse; respiratory care therapy; sheet metal technology; sport and fitness administration/management; surgical technology; tool and die technology; welding technology.

Academics *Calendar:* semesters. *Degree:* certificates and associate. *Special study options:* academic remediation for entering students, adult/continuing education programs, advanced placement credit, cooperative education, distance learning, English as a second language, honors programs, independent study, internships, part-time degree program, services for LD students, student-designed majors, study abroad, summer session for credit.

Library Educational Resource Center.

Student Life *Housing:* college housing not available. *Activities and Organizations:* drama/theater group, student-run newspaper, choral group, Black Student Alliance, Phi Theta Kappa, Adults on Campus, Inter-Varsity Club, Christian Fellowship. *Campus security:* 24-hour emergency response devices and patrols, late-night transport/escort service. *Student services:* personal/psychological counseling.

Athletics Member NJCAA. *Intercollegiate sports:* baseball M, basketball M/W, golf M, soccer M/W, softball W, squash W, tennis M/W, volleyball W. *Intramural sports:* skiing (downhill) M/W.

Costs (2016–17) *Tuition:* area resident $2730 full-time, $91 per credit hour part-time; state resident $7620 full-time, $254 per credit hour part-time; nonresident $14,460 full-time, $482 per credit hour part-time. Full-time tuition and fees vary according to course load. Part-time tuition and fees vary according to course load. *Required fees:* $314 full-time. *Payment plans:* installment, deferred payment. *Waivers:* employees or children of employees.

Financial Aid Of all full-time matriculated undergraduates who enrolled in 2014, 120 Federal Work-Study jobs (averaging $1800).

Applying *Required:* high school transcript.

Freshman Application Contact Mr. Patrick Peyer, Director, Student Retention and Success, Rock Valley College, 3301 North Mulford Road, Rockford, IL 61008. *Phone:* 815-921-4103. *Toll-free phone:* 800-973-7821. *E-mail:* p.peyer@rockvalleycollege.edu. *Website:* http://www.rockvalleycollege.edu/.

SAE Institute Chicago
Chicago, Illinois

Admissions Office Contact SAE Institute Chicago, 820 North Orleans Street, Chicago, IL 60610-3132.
Website: http://www.sae.edu/.

Sauk Valley Community College
Dixon, Illinois

Freshman Application Contact Sauk Valley Community College, 173 Illinois Route 2, Dixon, IL 61021. *Phone:* 815-288-5511 Ext. 378. *Website:* http://www.svcc.edu/.

Shawnee Community College
Ullin, Illinois

- **State and locally supported** 2-year, founded 1967, part of Illinois Community College Board
- **Rural** 163-acre campus
- **Coed,** 1,819 undergraduate students, 44% full-time, 61% women, 39% men

Undergraduates 801 full-time, 1,018 part-time. Students come from 3 states and territories; 2% are from out of state; 15% Black or African American, non-Hispanic/Latino; 2% Hispanic/Latino; 0.6% Asian, non-Hispanic/Latino; 0.1% American Indian or Alaska Native, non-Hispanic/Latino; 2% Race/ethnicity unknown; 12% transferred in. *Retention:* 55% of full-time freshmen returned.

Freshmen *Admission:* 633 applied, 633 admitted, 115 enrolled.

Faculty *Total:* 169, 24% full-time, 4% with terminal degrees. *Student/faculty ratio:* 13:1.

Majors Accounting; administrative assistant and secretarial science; agricultural business and management; agriculture; agronomy and crop science; animal sciences; automobile/automotive mechanics technology; biological and physical sciences; business administration and management; business automation/technology/data entry; child development; clinical/medical laboratory technology; computer graphics; computer systems networking and telecommunications; cosmetology; criminal justice/police science; electrical, electronic and communications engineering technology; health information/medical records technology; human services; information science/studies; legal administrative assistant/secretary; liberal arts and sciences/liberal studies; medical administrative assistant and medical secretary; occupational therapist assistant; registered nursing/registered nurse; sheet metal technology; social work; veterinary/animal health technology; welding technology; wildlife, fish and wildlands science and management.

Academics *Calendar:* semesters. *Degree:* certificates, diplomas, and associate. *Special study options:* academic remediation for entering students, accelerated degree program, adult/continuing education programs, advanced placement credit, cooperative education, distance learning, double majors, English as a second language, external degree program, independent study, internships, off-campus study, part-time degree program, services for LD students, summer session for credit.

Library Shawnee Community College Library.

Student Life *Housing:* college housing not available. *Activities and Organizations:* drama/theater group, choral group, Phi Theta Kappa, Phi Beta Lambda, Music Club, Student Senate, Future Teachers Organization. *Campus security:* 24-hour patrols. *Student services:* personal/psychological counseling.

Athletics Member NJCAA. *Intercollegiate sports:* baseball M(s), basketball M(s)/W(s), softball W(s). *Intramural sports:* weight lifting M/W.

Standardized Tests *Required for some:* ACT (for admission). *Recommended:* ACT (for admission).

Costs (2015–16) *Tuition:* area resident $2376 full-time, $99 per hour part-time; state resident $3936 full-time, $164 per hour part-time; nonresident $3984 full-time, $166 per hour part-time. *Payment plans:* installment, deferred payment. *Waivers:* senior citizens and employees or children of employees.

Financial Aid Of all full-time matriculated undergraduates who enrolled in 2014, 60 Federal Work-Study jobs (averaging $2000). 50 state and other part-time jobs (averaging $2000).

Applying *Options:* electronic application, early admission, deferred entrance. *Required:* high school transcript. *Application deadlines:* rolling (freshmen), rolling (out-of-state freshmen), rolling (transfers). *Notification:* continuous (freshmen), continuous (out-of-state freshmen), continuous (transfers).

Freshman Application Contact Mrs. Erin King, Recruiter/Advisor, Shawnee Community College, 8364 Shawnee College Road, Ullin, IL 62992. *Phone:* 618-634-3200. *Toll-free phone:* 800-481-2242. *Fax:* 618-634-3300. *E-mail:* erink@shawneecc.edu. *Website:* http://www.shawneecc.edu/.

Solex College
Wheeling, Illinois

Freshman Application Contact Solex College, 350 East Dundee Road, Wheeling, IL 60090.
Website: http://www.solex.edu/.

Southeastern Illinois College
Harrisburg, Illinois

Freshman Application Contact Dr. David Nudo, Director of Counseling, Southeastern Illinois College, 3575 College Road, Harrisburg, IL 62946-4925. *Phone:* 618-252-5400 Ext. 2430. *Toll-free phone:* 866-338-2742. *Website:* http://www.sic.edu/.

South Suburban College
South Holland, Illinois

- **State and locally supported** 2-year, founded 1927, part of Illinois Community College Board
- **Suburban** campus with easy access to Chicago
- **Coed,** 4,401 undergraduate students, 37% full-time, 68% women, 32% men

Undergraduates 1,614 full-time, 2,787 part-time. 6% are from out of state; 62% Black or African American, non-Hispanic/Latino; 16% Hispanic/Latino; 0.3% Asian, non-Hispanic/Latino; 1% American Indian or Alaska Native, non-Hispanic/Latino; 2% Two or more races, non-Hispanic/Latino; 2% Race/ethnicity unknown; 0.2% international. *Retention:* 20% of full-time freshmen returned.

Freshmen *Average high school GPA:* 2.33.

Faculty *Total:* 444, 28% full-time. *Student/faculty ratio:* 14:1.

Majors Accounting; accounting technology and bookkeeping; architectural drafting and CAD/CADD; biological and physical sciences; building/home/construction inspection; CAD/CADD drafting/design technology; child-care provision; construction engineering technology; court reporting; criminal justice/safety; electrical, electronic and communications engineering technology; executive assistant/executive secretary; fine/studio arts; information technology; kinesiology and exercise science; legal assistant/paralegal; liberal arts and sciences/liberal studies; nursing administration; occupational therapist assistant; office management; radiologic technology/science; small business administration; social work.

Academics *Calendar:* semesters. *Degree:* certificates and associate. *Special study options:* academic remediation for entering students, adult/continuing education programs, advanced placement credit, cooperative education, distance learning, English as a second language, honors programs, internships, off-campus study, part-time degree program, services for LD students, study abroad, summer session for credit.

Library South Suburban College Library plus 1 other. *Books:* 21,333 (physical), 1,973 (digital/electronic); *Serial titles:* 58 (physical); *Databases:* 24. Weekly public service hours: 60; students can reserve study rooms.

Student Life *Housing:* college housing not available. *Activities and Organizations:* drama/theater group, choral group. *Campus security:* 24-hour emergency response devices and patrols.

Athletics Member NJCAA. *Intercollegiate sports:* baseball M, basketball M/W, soccer M/W, softball W, volleyball W.

Costs (2015–16) *Tuition:* area resident $4050 full-time; state resident $9990 full-time; nonresident $11,640 full-time. Full-time tuition and fees vary according to course load and reciprocity agreements. Part-time tuition and fees vary according to course load and reciprocity agreements. *Required fees:* $533 full-time. *Payment plan:* installment. *Waivers:* senior citizens and employees or children of employees.

Financial Aid Of all full-time matriculated undergraduates who enrolled in 2014, 3,631 applied for aid, 3,328 were judged to have need. 121 Federal Work-Study jobs (averaging $1750). In 2014, 63 non-need-based awards were made. *Average need-based gift aid:* $5420. *Average non-need-based aid:* $650.

Applying *Options:* early admission, deferred entrance. *Required:* high school transcript. *Required for some:* essay or personal statement. *Recommended:* essay or personal statement, minimum 2.0 GPA. *Application deadlines:* rolling (freshmen), rolling (transfers). *Notification:* continuous (freshmen), continuous (transfers).

Freshman Application Contact Ms. Tiffane Jones, Admissions, South Suburban College, 15800 South State Street, South Holland, IL 60473. *Phone:* 708-596-2000 Ext. 2158. *E-mail:* admissionsquestions@ssc.edu. *Website:* http://www.ssc.edu/.

Southwestern Illinois College
Belleville, Illinois

- **District-supported** 2-year, founded 1946, part of Illinois Community College Board
- **Suburban** 341-acre campus with easy access to St. Louis
- **Endowment** $7.1 million
- **Coed**

Undergraduates 4,591 full-time, 5,954 part-time. Students come from 13 states and territories; 1% are from out of state; 24% Black or African American, non-Hispanic/Latino; 4% Hispanic/Latino; 2% Asian, non-Hispanic/Latino; 0.4% Native Hawaiian or other Pacific Islander, non-Hispanic/Latino; 0.5% American Indian or Alaska Native, non-Hispanic/Latino; 4% Race/ethnicity unknown; 5% transferred in.

Faculty *Student/faculty ratio:* 15:1.

Academics *Calendar:* semesters. *Degree:* certificates, diplomas, and associate. *Special study options:* academic remediation for entering students, accelerated degree program, adult/continuing education programs, advanced placement credit, cooperative education, distance learning, double majors, English as a second language, internships, off-campus study, part-time degree program, services for LD students, study abroad, summer session for credit. *ROTC:* Army (c), Air Force (c).

Library Southwestern Illinois College Library.

Student Life *Campus security:* 24-hour emergency response devices and patrols, late-night transport/escort service.

Athletics Member NJCAA.

Standardized Tests *Required for some:* ACT (for admission), ACT ASSET or ACT Compass.

Costs (2015–16) *Tuition:* area resident $3270 full-time, $109 per credit hour part-time; state resident $11,970 full-time, $399 per credit hour part-time; nonresident $15,600 full-time, $520 per credit hour part-time. Full-time tuition and fees vary according to program and reciprocity agreements. Part-time tuition and fees vary according to program and reciprocity agreements. *Required fees:* $150 full-time, $5 per credit hour part-time.

Financial Aid Of all full-time matriculated undergraduates who enrolled in 2014, 170 Federal Work-Study jobs (averaging $1537). 179 state and other part-time jobs (averaging $1004).

Applying *Options:* electronic application, early admission, deferred entrance. *Required:* high school transcript.

Freshman Application Contact Ms. Michelle Birk, Dean of Enrollment Services, Southwestern Illinois College, 2500 Carlyle Ave, Belleville, IL 62221. *Phone:* 618-235-2700 Ext. 5400. *Toll-free phone:* 866-942-SWIC. *Fax:* 618-222-9768. *E-mail:* michelle.birk@swic.edu. *Website:* http://www.swic.edu/.

Spoon River College
Canton, Illinois

- **State-supported** 2-year, founded 1959, part of Illinois Community College Board
- **Rural** 160-acre campus
- **Endowment** $1.5 million
- **Coed,** 1,665 undergraduate students, 44% full-time, 59% women, 41% men

Undergraduates 739 full-time, 926 part-time. 9% Black or African American, non-Hispanic/Latino; 3% Hispanic/Latino; 0.7% Asian, non-Hispanic/Latino; 0.5% American Indian or Alaska Native, non-Hispanic/Latino; 0.5% Two or more races, non-Hispanic/Latino; 0.2% Race/ethnicity unknown; 0.2% international; 11% transferred in. *Retention:* 59% of full-time freshmen returned.

Freshmen *Admission:* 215 applied, 894 admitted, 412 enrolled. *Test scores:* ACT scores over 18: 67%; ACT scores over 24: 18%; ACT scores over 30: 2%.

Faculty *Total:* 122, 30% full-time. *Student/faculty ratio:* 14:1.

Majors Accounting; administrative assistant and secretarial science; agricultural business and management; agricultural mechanics and equipment technology; agricultural mechanization; agricultural teacher education; art; biological and physical sciences; biology/biological sciences; botany/plant biology; business administration and management; business teacher education; chemistry; child development; computer and information systems security; computer programming (specific applications); criminal justice/law enforcement administration; criminal justice/police science; dramatic/theater arts; education; electrical, electronic and communications engineering technology; English; finance; general studies; graphic design; health professions related; history; industrial technology; information science/studies; kindergarten/preschool education; legal administrative assistant/secretary; liberal arts and sciences/liberal studies; mass communication/media; mathematics; medical administrative assistant and medical secretary; physical education teaching and coaching; physical sciences; physics; political science and government; pre-engineering; psychology; registered nursing/registered nurse; rhetoric and composition; social sciences; sociology; truck and bus driver/commercial vehicle operation/instruction; web page, digital/multimedia and information resources design.

Academics *Calendar:* semesters. *Degree:* certificates and associate. *Special study options:* academic remediation for entering students, accelerated degree program, adult/continuing education programs, advanced placement credit, distance learning, English as a second language, freshman honors college, honors programs, internships, part-time degree program, services for LD students, summer session for credit. *ROTC:* Army (b).

Library Library/Learning Resource Center. *Books:* 15,193 (physical); *Serial titles:* 869 (physical); *Databases:* 28.

Student Life *Housing:* college housing not available. *Activities and Organizations:* drama/theater group, student-run newspaper, Student Government Association, PEEPS, Intramural Athletics, Habitat for Humanity, Drama Club. *Campus security:* 24-hour emergency response devices, night patrol by trained security personnel. *Student services:* personal/psychological counseling.

Athletics Member NJCAA. *Intercollegiate sports:* baseball M(s), cross-country running M(s)/W(s), softball W(s), track and field M(s)/W(s).

Costs (2015–16) *Tuition:* area resident $4200 full-time, $140 per credit hour part-time; state resident $9240 full-time, $308 per credit hour part-time; nonresident $10,020 full-time, $334 per credit hour part-time. Full-time tuition and fees vary according to course load and location. Part-time tuition and fees vary according to course load and location. *Required fees:* $600 full-time, $20 per credit hour part-time. *Waivers:* employees or children of employees.

Financial Aid Of all full-time matriculated undergraduates who enrolled in 2013, 44 Federal Work-Study jobs (averaging $1735).

Applying *Options:* electronic application, early admission, deferred entrance. *Required:* high school transcript. *Application deadlines:* rolling (freshmen), rolling (transfers). *Notification:* continuous (freshmen), continuous (transfers).

Freshman Application Contact Ms. Missy Wilkinson, Dean of Student Services, Spoon River College, 23235 North County 22, Canton, IL 61520-9801. *Phone:* 309-649-6305. *Toll-free phone:* 800-334-7337. *Fax:* 309-649-6235. *E-mail:* info@spoonrivercollege.edu. *Website:* http://www.src.edu/.

Taylor Business Institute
Chicago, Illinois

Director of Admissions Mr. Rashed Jahangir, Taylor Business Institute, 318 West Adams, Chicago, IL 60606. *Website:* http://www.tbiil.edu/.

Tribeca Flashpoint College
Chicago, Illinois

Admissions Office Contact Tribeca Flashpoint College, 28 North Clark Street, Chicago, IL 60602. *Website:* http://www.tribecaflashpoint.edu/.

Triton College
River Grove, Illinois

Freshman Application Contact Ms. Mary-Rita Moore, Dean of Admissions, Triton College, 2000 Fifth Avenue, River Grove, IL 60171. *Phone:* 708-456-0300 Ext. 3679. *Fax:* 708-583-3162. *E-mail:* mpatrice@triton.edu. *Website:* http://www.triton.edu/.

Vatterott College
Fairview Heights, Illinois

Admissions Office Contact Vatterott College, 110 Commerce Lane, Fairview Heights, IL 62208. *Toll-free phone:* 888-202-2636.
Website: http://www.vatterott.edu/.

Vatterott College
Quincy, Illinois

Admissions Office Contact Vatterott College, 3609 North Marx Drive, Quincy, IL 62305.
Website: http://www.vatterott.edu/.

Vet Tech Institute at Fox College
Tinley Park, Illinois

- **Private** 2-year, founded 2006
- **Suburban** campus
- **Coed,** 164 undergraduate students
- **65%** of applicants were admitted

Freshmen *Admission:* 349 applied, 226 admitted.
Majors Veterinary/animal health technology.
Academics *Calendar:* semesters. *Degree:* associate. *Special study options:* accelerated degree program, internships.
Student Life *Housing:* college housing not available.
Freshman Application Contact Admissions Office, Vet Tech Institute at Fox College, 18020 South Oak Park Avenue, Tinley Park, IL 60477. *Phone:* 888-884-3694. *Toll-free phone:* 888-884-3694.
Website: http://chicago.vettechinstitute.edu/.

Waubonsee Community College
Sugar Grove, Illinois

Freshman Application Contact Joy Sanders, Admissions Manager, Waubonsee Community College, Route 47 at Waubonsee Drive, Sugar Grove, IL 60554. *Phone:* 630-466-7900 Ext. 5756. *Fax:* 630-466-6663.
E-mail: admissions@waubonsee.edu.
Website: http://www.waubonsee.edu/.

Worsham College of Mortuary Science
Wheeling, Illinois

Director of Admissions President, Worsham College of Mortuary Science, 495 Northgate Parkway, Wheeling, IL 60090-2646. *Phone:* 847-808-8444.
Website: http://www.worshamcollege.com/.

INDIANA

Ancilla College
Donaldson, Indiana

- **Independent Roman Catholic** 2-year, founded 1937
- **Rural** 63-acre campus
- **Endowment** $5.9 million
- **Coed,** 504 undergraduate students, 76% full-time, 55% women, 45% men

Undergraduates 382 full-time, 122 part-time. Students come from 14 states and territories; 9 other countries; 11% are from out of state; 13% Black or African American, non-Hispanic/Latino; 11% Hispanic/Latino; 0.6% Asian, non-Hispanic/Latino; 5% Two or more races, non-Hispanic/Latino; 4% international; 14% transferred in; 24% live on campus. *Retention:* 49% of full-time freshmen returned.
Freshmen *Admission:* 720 applied, 447 admitted, 213 enrolled. *Average high school GPA:* 2.59. *Test scores:* SAT critical reading scores over 500: 21%; SAT math scores over 500: 15%; SAT critical reading scores over 600: 4%; SAT math scores over 600: 1%.
Faculty *Total:* 49, 33% full-time, 8% with terminal degrees. *Student/faculty ratio:* 16:1.
Majors Agriculture; behavioral sciences; biological and physical sciences; business administration and management; business administration, management and operations related; computer and information sciences; criminal justice/safety; culinary arts related; data processing and data processing technology; early childhood education; elementary education; English; environmental studies; general studies; health services/allied health/health sciences; history; hospitality administration related; kinesiology and exercise science; logistics, materials, and supply chain management; mass communication/media; registered nursing/registered nurse; religious studies related; secondary education; speech communication and rhetoric; theology and religious vocations related.
Academics *Calendar:* semesters. *Degree:* certificates and associate. *Special study options:* academic remediation for entering students, adult/continuing education programs, advanced placement credit, cooperative education, distance learning, double majors, independent study, internships, part-time degree program, services for LD students, student-designed majors, summer session for credit.
Library Gerald J. Ball Library. *Books:* 22,226 (physical), 3,767 (digital/electronic); *Serial titles:* 51 (physical); *Databases:* 45. Weekly public service hours: 64; students can reserve study rooms.
Student Life *Housing Options:* coed. Campus housing is university owned. Freshman applicants given priority for college housing. *Activities and Organizations:* Student Government Association, Ancilla Student Ambassadors, FFA, Phi Theta Kappa, Leaders for Life. *Campus security:* 24-hour emergency response devices and patrols, late-night transport/escort service, controlled dormitory access. *Student services:* personal/psychological counseling.
Athletics Member NJCAA. *Intercollegiate sports:* baseball M(s), basketball M(s)/W(s), bowling M(s)/W(s), cheerleading M(s)/W(s), cross-country running M(s)/W(s), golf M(s)/W(s), lacrosse M(s), soccer M(s)/W(s), softball W(s), tennis M(s)/W(s), volleyball W(s), wrestling M(s). *Intramural sports:* basketball M/W, softball M/W, volleyball M/W.
Standardized Tests *Recommended:* SAT or ACT (for admission).
Costs (2016–17) *Comprehensive fee:* $23,830 includes full-time tuition ($14,700), mandatory fees ($230), and room and board ($8900). Full-time tuition and fees vary according to course load and program. Part-time tuition: $490 per credit hour. Part-time tuition and fees vary according to course load and program. *Required fees:* $55 per term part-time. *Payment plan:* installment. *Waivers:* employees or children of employees.
Financial Aid Of all full-time matriculated undergraduates who enrolled in 2015, 407 applied for aid, 383 were judged to have need. 23 Federal Work-Study jobs (averaging $1808). *Average need-based loan:* $2897. *Average need-based gift aid:* $1432. *Financial aid deadline:* 2/28.
Applying *Options:* electronic application. *Required:* high school transcript. *Application deadlines:* rolling (freshmen), rolling (out-of-state freshmen), rolling (transfers).
Freshman Application Contact Mr. Eric Wignall, Vice President of Enrollment Management, Ancilla College, PO Box 1, 9601 Union Road, Donaldson, IN 46513. *Phone:* 574-936-8898 Ext. 339. *Toll-free phone:* 866-ANCILLA. *Fax:* 574-935-1773. *E-mail:* admissions@ancilla.edu.
Website: http://www.ancilla.edu/.

Brightwood College, Hammond Campus
Hammond, Indiana

Freshman Application Contact Brightwood College, Hammond Campus, 7833 Indianapolis Boulevard, Hammond, IN 46324. *Phone:* 219-844-0100. *Toll-free phone:* 800-935-1857.
Website: http://www.brightwood.edu/.

Brightwood College, Indianapolis Campus
Indianapolis, Indiana

Freshman Application Contact Director of Admissions, Brightwood College, Indianapolis Campus, 4200 South East Street, Indianapolis, IN 46227. *Phone:* 317-782-0315.
Website: http://www.brightwood.edu/.

Brown Mackie College–Fort Wayne
Fort Wayne, Indiana

Freshman Application Contact Brown Mackie College–Fort Wayne, 3000 East Coliseum Boulevard, Fort Wayne, IN 46805. *Phone:* 260-484-4400. *Toll-free phone:* 866-433-2289.
Website: http://www.brownmackie.edu/fortwayne/.

Brown Mackie College–Indianapolis
Indianapolis, Indiana

Freshman Application Contact Brown Mackie College–Indianapolis, 1200 North Meridian Street, Suite 100, Indianapolis, IN 46204. *Phone:* 317-554-8300. *Toll-free phone:* 866-255-0279.
Website: http://www.brownmackie.edu/indianapolis/.

Brown Mackie College–Merrillville
Merrillville, Indiana

Freshman Application Contact Brown Mackie College–Merrillville, 1000 East 80th Place, Suite 205M, Merrillville, IN 46410. *Phone:* 219-769-3321. *Toll-free phone:* 800-258-3321.
Website: http://www.brownmackie.edu/merrillville/.

Brown Mackie College–Michigan City
Michigan City, Indiana

Freshman Application Contact Brown Mackie College–Michigan City, 1001 East US Highway 20, Michigan City, IN 46360. *Phone:* 219-877-3100. *Toll-free phone:* 800-519-2416.
Website: http://www.brownmackie.edu/michigancity/.

Brown Mackie College–South Bend
South Bend, Indiana

Freshman Application Contact Brown Mackie College–South Bend, 3454 Douglas Road, South Bend, IN 46635. *Phone:* 574-237-0774. *Toll-free phone:* 800-743-2447.
Website: http://www.brownmackie.edu/southbend/.

College of Court Reporting
Hobart, Indiana

Freshman Application Contact Ms. Nicky Rodriquez, Director of Admissions, College of Court Reporting, 111 West Tenth Street, Suite 111, Hobart, IN 46342. *Phone:* 219-942-1459 Ext. 222. *Toll-free phone:* 866-294-3974. *Fax:* 219-942-1631. *E-mail:* nrodriquez@ccr.edu.
Website: http://www.ccr.edu/.

Fortis College
Indianapolis, Indiana

Freshman Application Contact Mr. Alex Teitelbaum, Vice President Systems and Administration, Fortis College, 9001 N. Wesleyan Road, Suite 101, Indianapolis, IN 46268. *Phone:* 410-633-2929. *Toll-free phone:* 855-4-FORTIS. *E-mail:* kbennett@edaff.com.
Website: http://www.fortis.edu/.

International Business College
Indianapolis, Indiana

- **Proprietary** 2-year, founded 1889
- **Suburban** campus
- **Coed,** 354 undergraduate students
- 71% of applicants were admitted

Freshmen *Admission:* 825 applied, 583 admitted.
Majors Accounting technology and bookkeeping; administrative assistant and secretarial science; computer programming; computer systems networking and telecommunications; dental assisting; graphic design; hotel/motel administration; legal administrative assistant/secretary; legal assistant/paralegal; medical/clinical assistant; veterinary/animal health technology.
Academics *Calendar:* semesters. *Degree:* diplomas and associate. *Special study options:* accelerated degree program, internships.
Freshman Application Contact Admissions Office, International Business College, 7205 Shadeland Station, Indianapolis, IN 46256. *Phone:* 317-813-2300. *Toll-free phone:* 800-589-6500.
Website: http://www.ibcindianapolis.edu/.

ITT Technical Institute
Fort Wayne, Indiana

Freshman Application Contact Director of Recruitment, ITT Technical Institute, 2810 Dupont Commerce Court, Fort Wayne, IN 46825. *Phone:* 260-497-6200. *Toll-free phone:* 800-866-4488.
Website: http://www.itt-tech.edu/.

ITT Technical Institute
Merrillville, Indiana

Freshman Application Contact Director of Recruitment, ITT Technical Institute, 8488 Georgia Street, Merrillville, IN 46410. *Phone:* 219-738-6100. *Toll-free phone:* 877-418-8134.
Website: http://www.itt-tech.edu/.

ITT Technical Institute
Newburgh, Indiana

Freshman Application Contact Director of Recruitment, ITT Technical Institute, 10999 Stahl Road, Newburgh, IN 47630. *Phone:* 812-858-1600. *Toll-free phone:* 800-832-4488.
Website: http://www.itt-tech.edu/.

Ivy Tech Community College–Bloomington
Bloomington, Indiana

- **State-supported** 2-year, founded 2001, part of Ivy Tech Community College System
- **Coed,** 6,107 undergraduate students, 33% full-time, 63% women, 37% men

Undergraduates 2,017 full-time, 4,090 part-time. 1% are from out of state; 3% Black or African American, non-Hispanic/Latino; 3% Hispanic/Latino; 1% Asian, non-Hispanic/Latino; 0.5% American Indian or Alaska Native, non-Hispanic/Latino; 2% Two or more races, non-Hispanic/Latino; 28% Race/ethnicity unknown; 2% international; 5% transferred in. *Retention:* 41% of full-time freshmen returned.
Freshmen *Admission:* 2,141 applied, 2,141 admitted, 825 enrolled.
Faculty *Total:* 409, 21% full-time. *Student/faculty ratio:* 20:1.
Majors Accounting technology and bookkeeping; administrative assistant and secretarial science; biotechnology; building/property maintenance; business administration and management; business automation/technology/data entry; cabinetmaking and millwork; child-care and support services management; computer and information sciences; computer science; computer systems networking and telecommunications; criminal justice/safety; data modeling/warehousing and database administration; drafting and design technology; early childhood education; education; electrical, electronic and communications engineering technology; electrician; emergency medical technology (EMT paramedic); engineering technology; executive assistant/executive secretary; fine/studio arts; general studies; heating, air conditioning, ventilation and refrigeration maintenance technology; hospitality administration; human services; industrial technology; informatics; information science/studies; information technology; legal assistant/paralegal; liberal arts and sciences/liberal studies; library and archives assisting; logistics, materials, and supply chain management; machine tool technology; manufacturing engineering technology; mechanic and repair technologies related; mechanics and repair; medical/health management and clinical assistant; medical radiologic technology; network and system administration; pipefitting and sprinkler fitting; psychiatric/mental health services technology; registered nursing/registered nurse; respiratory care therapy; tool and die technology.
Academics *Calendar:* semesters. *Degree:* certificates and associate. *Special study options:* academic remediation for entering students, adult/continuing education programs, advanced placement credit, distance learning, external degree program, internships, part-time degree program, services for LD students, summer session for credit.
Student Life *Activities and Organizations:* Student Government, Phi Theta Kappa. *Campus security:* late-night transport/escort service.
Costs (2015–16) *Tuition:* state resident $3995 full-time, $133 per credit hour part-time; nonresident $7872 full-time, $262 per credit hour part-time. *Required fees:* $120 full-time, $60 per term part-time. *Payment plans:* installment, deferred payment. *Waivers:* senior citizens and employees or children of employees.
Financial Aid Of all full-time matriculated undergraduates who enrolled in 2014, 51 Federal Work-Study jobs (averaging $3259).
Applying *Options:* electronic application, deferred entrance. *Required:* high school transcript. *Required for some:* interview. *Application deadlines:* rolling (freshmen), rolling (transfers). *Notification:* continuous (freshmen), continuous (transfers).
Freshman Application Contact Mr. Neil Frederick, Assistant Director of Admissions, Ivy Tech Community College–Bloomington, 200 Daniels Way, Bloomington, IN 47404. *Phone:* 812-330-6026. *Toll-free phone:* 888-IVY-LINE. *Fax:* 812-332-8147. *E-mail:* nfrederi@ivytech.edu.
Website: http://www.ivytech.edu/.

Ivy Tech Community College–Central Indiana
Indianapolis, Indiana

- **State-supported** 2-year, founded 1963, part of Ivy Tech Community College System
- **Urban** 10-acre campus
- **Coed,** 19,104 undergraduate students, 28% full-time, 55% women, 45% men

Undergraduates 5,270 full-time, 13,834 part-time. 2% are from out of state; 23% Black or African American, non-Hispanic/Latino; 8% Hispanic/Latino; 3% Asian, non-Hispanic/Latino; 0.1% Native Hawaiian or other Pacific Islander, non-Hispanic/Latino; 0.2% American Indian or Alaska Native, non-Hispanic/Latino; 3% Two or more races, non-Hispanic/Latino; 11% Race/ethnicity unknown; 0.7% international; 5% transferred in. *Retention:* 48% of full-time freshmen returned.
Freshmen *Admission:* 3,549 enrolled.
Faculty *Total:* 946, 20% full-time. *Student/faculty ratio:* 23:1.
Majors Accounting technology and bookkeeping; automobile/automotive mechanics technology; biotechnology; building/property maintenance; business administration and management; business automation/technology/data entry; cabinetmaking and millwork; carpentry; child-care and support services management; child development; computer and information sciences; computer science; criminal justice/safety; data modeling/warehousing and database administration; design and visual communications; drafting and design technology; early childhood education; education; electrical, electronic and communications engineering technology; electrician; executive assistant/executive secretary; general studies; health information/medical records technology; heating, air conditioning, ventilation and refrigeration maintenance technology; hospitality administration related; human services; industrial production technologies related; industrial technology; informatics; information science/studies; information technology; legal assistant/paralegal; liberal arts and sciences/liberal studies; logistics, materials, and supply chain management; machine shop technology; machine tool technology; manufacturing engineering technology; masonry; mechanics and repair; medical/clinical assistant; medical/health management and clinical assistant; medical radiologic technology; network and system administration; occupational safety and health technology; occupational therapist assistant; painting and wall covering; pipefitting and sprinkler fitting; psychiatric/mental health services technology; registered nursing/registered nurse; respiratory care therapy; sheet metal technology; surgical technology; tool and die technology; transportation/mobility management.
Academics *Calendar:* semesters. *Degree:* certificates and associate. *Special study options:* academic remediation for entering students, adult/continuing education programs, advanced placement credit, cooperative education, distance learning, English as a second language, internships, off-campus study, part-time degree program, services for LD students, summer session for credit.
Student Life *Housing:* college housing not available. *Activities and Organizations:* student-run newspaper, Student Government, Phi Theta Kappa, Human Services Club, Administrative Office Assistants Club, Radiology Club. *Campus security:* 24-hour emergency response devices and patrols, late-night transport/escort service. *Student services:* personal/psychological counseling.
Athletics *Intramural sports:* baseball M, basketball M/W, cheerleading W, golf M/W, softball W, volleyball M/W.
Costs (2015–16) *Tuition:* state resident $3995 full-time, $131 per credit hour part-time; nonresident $7872 full-time, $262 per credit hour part-time. *Required fees:* $120 full-time, $60 per term part-time. *Payment plans:* installment, deferred payment. *Waivers:* senior citizens and employees or children of employees.
Financial Aid Of all full-time matriculated undergraduates who enrolled in 2014, 92 Federal Work-Study jobs (averaging $3766).
Applying *Options:* electronic application, early admission, deferred entrance. *Required:* high school transcript. *Required for some:* interview. *Application deadlines:* rolling (freshmen), rolling (transfers). *Notification:* continuous (freshmen), continuous (transfers).
Freshman Application Contact Ms. Tracy Funk, Director of Admissions, Ivy Tech Community College–Central Indiana, 50 West Fall Creek Parkway North Drive, Indianapolis, IN 46208-4777. *Phone:* 317-921-4371. *Toll-free phone:* 888-IVYLINE. *Fax:* 317-917-5919. *E-mail:* tfunk@ivytech.edu. *Website:* http://www.ivytech.edu/.

Ivy Tech Community College–Columbus
Columbus, Indiana

- **State-supported** 2-year, founded 1963, part of Ivy Tech Community College System
- **Small-town** campus with easy access to Indianapolis
- **Coed,** 2,865 undergraduate students, 27% full-time, 60% women, 40% men

Undergraduates 781 full-time, 2,084 part-time. 1% are from out of state; 2% Black or African American, non-Hispanic/Latino; 3% Hispanic/Latino; 0.5% Asian, non-Hispanic/Latino; 0.1% American Indian or Alaska Native, non-Hispanic/Latino; 1% Two or more races, non-Hispanic/Latino; 24% Race/ethnicity unknown; 1% international; 3% transferred in. *Retention:* 46% of full-time freshmen returned.
Freshmen *Admission:* 423 enrolled.
Faculty *Total:* 283, 19% full-time. *Student/faculty ratio:* 18:1.
Majors Accounting technology and bookkeeping; administrative assistant and secretarial science; agriculture; automobile/automotive mechanics technology; building/property maintenance; business administration and management; business automation/technology/data entry; cabinetmaking and millwork; child-care and support services management; computer and information sciences; computer science; criminal justice/safety; data modeling/warehousing and database administration; dental assisting; design and visual communications; drafting and design technology; early childhood education; education; electrical and power transmission installation; electrical, electronic and communications engineering technology; emergency medical technology (EMT paramedic); engineering technology; executive assistant/executive secretary; general studies; heating, air conditioning, ventilation and refrigeration maintenance technology; hospitality administration; human services; industrial technology; informatics; information science/studies; information technology; interior design; legal assistant/paralegal; liberal arts and sciences/liberal studies; library and archives assisting; logistics, materials, and supply chain management; machine tool technology; manufacturing engineering technology; masonry; mechanic and repair technologies related; mechanics and repair; medical/clinical assistant; medical/health management and clinical assistant; medical radiologic technology; pipefitting and sprinkler fitting; pre-engineering; psychiatric/mental health services technology; robotics technology; surgical technology; tool and die technology.
Academics *Calendar:* semesters. *Degree:* certificates and associate. *Special study options:* academic remediation for entering students, adult/continuing education programs, advanced placement credit, distance learning, internships, part-time degree program, services for LD students, summer session for credit.
Student Life *Housing:* college housing not available. *Activities and Organizations:* Student Government, Phi Theta Kappa, LPN Club. *Campus security:* late-night transport/escort service, trained evening security personnel, escort service.
Costs (2015–16) *Tuition:* state resident $3995 full-time, $133 per credit hour part-time; nonresident $7872 full-time, $262 per credit hour part-time. *Required fees:* $120 full-time, $60 per term part-time. *Payment plans:* installment, deferred payment. *Waivers:* senior citizens and employees or children of employees.
Financial Aid Of all full-time matriculated undergraduates who enrolled in 2014, 26 Federal Work-Study jobs (averaging $1694).
Applying *Options:* electronic application, early admission, deferred entrance. *Required:* high school transcript. *Required for some:* interview. *Application deadlines:* rolling (freshmen), rolling (transfers). *Notification:* continuous (freshmen), continuous (transfers).
Freshman Application Contact Alisa Deck, Director of Admissions, Ivy Tech Community College–Columbus, 4475 Central Avenue, Columbus, IN 47203-1868. *Phone:* 812-374-5129. *Toll-free phone:* 888-IVY-LINE. *Fax:* 812-372-0331. *E-mail:* adeck@ivytech.edu. *Website:* http://www.ivytech.edu/.

Ivy Tech Community College–East Central
Muncie, Indiana

- **State-supported** 2-year, founded 1968, part of Ivy Tech Community College System
- **Suburban** 15-acre campus with easy access to Indianapolis
- **Coed,** 5,943 undergraduate students, 43% full-time, 62% women, 38% men

Undergraduates 2,571 full-time, 3,372 part-time. 10% are from out of state; 6% Black or African American, non-Hispanic/Latino; 4% Hispanic/Latino; 0.7% Asian, non-Hispanic/Latino; 0.3% American Indian or Alaska Native, non-Hispanic/Latino; 3% Two or more races, non-Hispanic/Latino; 7% Race/ethnicity unknown; 0.2% international; 5% transferred in. *Retention:* 47% of full-time freshmen returned.

Freshmen *Admission:* 1,118 enrolled.

Faculty *Total:* 566, 20% full-time. *Student/faculty ratio:* 18:1.

Majors Accounting technology and bookkeeping; administrative assistant and secretarial science; agriculture; automobile/automotive mechanics technology; building/property maintenance; business administration and management; carpentry; computer and information sciences; computer science; computer systems networking and telecommunications; construction trades; construction trades related; criminal justice/safety; data modeling/warehousing and database administration; dental assisting; dental hygiene; drafting and design technology; early childhood education; education; electrical, electronic and communications engineering technology; electrician; energy management and systems technology; engineering technology; executive assistant/executive secretary; general studies; health information/medical records technology; heating, air conditioning, ventilation and refrigeration maintenance technology; hospitality administration; hospitality administration related; human services; industrial mechanics and maintenance technology; industrial production technologies related; industrial technology; informatics; information science/studies; information technology; interior design; kinesiology and exercise science; legal assistant/paralegal; liberal arts and sciences/liberal studies; library and archives assisting; logistics, materials, and supply chain management; machine shop technology; machine tool technology; manufacturing engineering technology; masonry; medical/clinical assistant; medical/health management and clinical assistant; medical radiologic technology; network and system administration; painting and wall covering; physical therapy technology; pipefitting and sprinkler fitting; registered nursing/registered nurse; surgical technology; tool and die technology.

Academics *Calendar:* semesters. *Degree:* certificates and associate. *Special study options:* academic remediation for entering students, adult/continuing education programs, advanced placement credit, distance learning, internships, part-time degree program, services for LD students.

Student Life *Housing:* college housing not available. *Activities and Organizations:* Business Professionals of America, SkillsUSA–VICA, Student Government, Phi Theta Kappa, Human Services Club.

Costs (2015–16) *Tuition:* state resident $3995 full-time, $133 per credit hour part-time; nonresident $7872 full-time, $262 per credit hour part-time. *Required fees:* $120 full-time, $60 per term part-time. *Payment plans:* installment, deferred payment. *Waivers:* senior citizens and employees or children of employees.

Financial Aid Of all full-time matriculated undergraduates who enrolled in 2014, 65 Federal Work-Study jobs (averaging $2666).

Applying *Options:* electronic application, early admission, deferred entrance. *Required:* high school transcript. *Required for some:* interview. *Application deadlines:* rolling (freshmen), rolling (transfers). *Notification:* continuous (freshmen), continuous (transfers).

Freshman Application Contact Ms. Mary Lewellen, Ivy Tech Community College–East Central, 4301 South Cowan Road, Muncie, IN 47302-9448. *Phone:* 765-289-2291 Ext. 1391. *Toll-free phone:* 888-IVY-LINE. *Fax:* 765-289-2292. *E-mail:* mlewelle@ivytech.edu. *Website:* http://www.ivytech.edu/.

Ivy Tech Community College–Kokomo

Kokomo, Indiana

- **State-supported** 2-year, founded 1968, part of Ivy Tech Community College System
- **Small-town** 20-acre campus with easy access to Indianapolis
- **Coed,** 2,847 undergraduate students, 37% full-time, 61% women, 39% men

Undergraduates 1,046 full-time, 1,801 part-time. 5% Black or African American, non-Hispanic/Latino; 3% Hispanic/Latino; 0.7% Asian, non-Hispanic/Latino; 1% American Indian or Alaska Native, non-Hispanic/Latino; 2% Two or more races, non-Hispanic/Latino; 19% Race/ethnicity unknown; 0.7% international; 5% transferred in. *Retention:* 47% of full-time freshmen returned.

Freshmen *Admission:* 471 enrolled.

Faculty *Total:* 329, 23% full-time. *Student/faculty ratio:* 15:1.

Majors Accounting technology and bookkeeping; administrative assistant and secretarial science; agriculture; automobile/automotive mechanics technology; building/construction site management; building/property maintenance; business administration and management; communication and journalism related; computer and information sciences; computer science; computer systems networking and telecommunications; construction trades related; criminal justice/safety; data modeling/warehousing and database administration; dental assisting; dental hygiene; design and visual communications; drafting and design technology; early childhood education; education; electrical, electronic and communications engineering technology; electrician; emergency medical technology (EMT paramedic); engineering technology; executive assistant/executive secretary; general studies; health aide; health information/medical records technology; heating, air conditioning,

ventilation and refrigeration maintenance technology; human services; industrial production technologies related; industrial technology; informatics; information science/studies; information technology; legal assistant/paralegal; liberal arts and sciences/liberal studies; library and archives assisting; machine shop technology; machine tool technology; manufacturing engineering technology; mechanic and repair technologies related; mechanics and repair; medical/clinical assistant; network and system administration; physical therapy technology; registered nursing/registered nurse; surgical technology; tool and die technology.

Academics *Calendar:* semesters. *Degree:* certificates and associate. *Special study options:* academic remediation for entering students, adult/continuing education programs, advanced placement credit, distance learning, internships, part-time degree program, services for LD students, summer session for credit.

Student Life *Housing:* college housing not available. *Activities and Organizations:* student-run newspaper, Student Government, Collegiate Secretaries International, Licensed Practical Nursing Club, Phi Theta Kappa. *Campus security:* 24-hour emergency response devices, late-night transport/escort service. *Student services:* personal/psychological counseling.

Costs (2015–16) *Tuition:* state resident $3995 full-time, $133 per credit hour part-time; nonresident $7872 full-time, $262 per credit hour part-time. *Required fees:* $120 full-time. *Payment plans:* installment, deferred payment. *Waivers:* senior citizens and employees or children of employees.

Financial Aid Of all full-time matriculated undergraduates who enrolled in 2014, 45 Federal Work-Study jobs (averaging $1829).

Applying *Options:* electronic application, early admission. *Required:* high school transcript. *Required for some:* interview. *Application deadlines:* rolling (freshmen), rolling (transfers). *Notification:* continuous (freshmen), continuous (transfers).

Freshman Application Contact Mr. Mike Federspill, Director of Admissions, Ivy Tech Community College–Kokomo, 1815 East Morgan Street, Kokomo, IN 46903-1373. *Phone:* 765-459-0561 Ext. 233. *Toll-free phone:* 888-IVY-LINE. *Fax:* 765-454-5111. *E-mail:* mfedersp@ivytech.edu. *Website:* http://www.ivytech.edu/.

Ivy Tech Community College–Lafayette

Lafayette, Indiana

- **State-supported** 2-year, founded 1968, part of Ivy Tech Community College System
- **Suburban** campus with easy access to Indianapolis
- **Coed,** 5,060 undergraduate students, 42% full-time, 57% women, 43% men

Undergraduates 2,144 full-time, 2,916 part-time. 1% are from out of state; 4% Black or African American, non-Hispanic/Latino; 8% Hispanic/Latino; 2% Asian, non-Hispanic/Latino; 0.1% Native Hawaiian or other Pacific Islander, non-Hispanic/Latino; 0.3% American Indian or Alaska Native, non-Hispanic/Latino; 2% Two or more races, non-Hispanic/Latino; 15% Race/ethnicity unknown; 1% international; 10% transferred in. *Retention:* 54% of full-time freshmen returned.

Freshmen *Admission:* 982 enrolled.

Faculty *Total:* 439, 22% full-time. *Student/faculty ratio:* 15:1.

Majors Accounting; accounting technology and bookkeeping; agriculture; automobile/automotive mechanics technology; biotechnology; building/property maintenance; business administration and management; business automation/technology/data entry; cabinetmaking and millwork; carpentry; chemical technology; child-care and support services management; clinical/medical laboratory technology; computer and information sciences; computer science; computer systems networking and telecommunications; criminal justice/safety; data modeling/warehousing and database administration; dental assisting; drafting and design technology; early childhood education; education; electrical, electronic and communications engineering technology; electrician; executive assistant/executive secretary; general studies; health aide; health information/medical records technology; heating, air conditioning, ventilation and refrigeration maintenance technology; human services; industrial production technologies related; industrial technology; informatics; information science/studies; information technology; ironworking; legal assistant/paralegal; liberal arts and sciences/liberal studies; library and archives assisting; lineworker; machine tool technology; manufacturing engineering technology; masonry; mechanical engineering/mechanical technology; mechanic and repair technologies related; mechanics and repair; medical/clinical assistant; medical/health management and clinical assistant; painting and wall covering; pipefitting and sprinkler fitting; pre-engineering; psychiatric/mental health services technology; quality control and safety technologies related; quality control technology; registered nursing/registered nurse; respiratory care therapy; robotics technology; sheet metal technology; surgical technology; telecommunications technology; tool and die technology.

Academics *Calendar:* semesters. *Degree:* certificates and associate. *Special study options:* academic remediation for entering students, advanced placement credit, distance learning, internships, part-time degree program, services for LD students, summer session for credit.

Student Life *Housing:* college housing not available. *Activities and Organizations:* student-run newspaper, Student Government, Phi Theta Kappa, LPN Club, Accounting Club, Student Computer Technology Association. *Student services:* personal/psychological counseling.

Costs (2015–16) *Tuition:* state resident $3995 full-time, $133 per credit hour part-time; nonresident $7872 full-time, $262 per credit hour part-time. *Required fees:* $120 full-time. *Payment plans:* installment, deferred payment. *Waivers:* senior citizens and employees or children of employees.

Financial Aid Of all full-time matriculated undergraduates who enrolled in 2014, 65 Federal Work-Study jobs (averaging $2222). 1 state and other part-time job (averaging $2436).

Applying *Options:* electronic application. *Required:* high school transcript. *Required for some:* interview. *Application deadlines:* rolling (freshmen), rolling (transfers). *Notification:* continuous (freshmen), continuous (transfers).

Freshman Application Contact Mr. Ivan Hernanadez, Director of Admissions, Ivy Tech Community College–Lafayette, 3101 South Creasy Lane, PO Box 6299, Lafayette, IN 47903. *Phone:* 765-269-5116. *Toll-free phone:* 888-IVY-LINE. *Fax:* 765-772-9293. *E-mail:* ihernand@ivytech.edu. *Website:* http://www.ivytech.edu/.

Ivy Tech Community College–North Central
South Bend, Indiana

- **State-supported** 2-year, founded 1968, part of Ivy Tech Community College System
- **Suburban** 4-acre campus
- **Coed,** 5,253 undergraduate students, 31% full-time, 63% women, 37% men

Undergraduates 1,635 full-time, 3,618 part-time. 2% are from out of state; 13% Black or African American, non-Hispanic/Latino; 13% Hispanic/Latino; 1% Asian, non-Hispanic/Latino; 0.1% Native Hawaiian or other Pacific Islander, non-Hispanic/Latino; 0.4% American Indian or Alaska Native, non-Hispanic/Latino; 3% Two or more races, non-Hispanic/Latino; 11% Race/ethnicity unknown; 2% international; 5% transferred in. *Retention:* 45% of full-time freshmen returned.

Freshmen *Admission:* 728 enrolled.

Faculty *Total:* 415, 26% full-time. *Student/faculty ratio:* 14:1.

Majors Accounting technology and bookkeeping; automobile/automotive mechanics technology; biotechnology; building/property maintenance; business administration and management; business automation/technology/data entry; cabinetmaking and millwork; carpentry; child-care and support services management; clinical/medical laboratory technology; computer and information sciences; criminal justice/safety; design and visual communications; early childhood education; educational/instructional technology; electrical, electronic and communications engineering technology; electrician; emergency medical technology (EMT paramedic); executive assistant/executive secretary; general studies; heating, air conditioning, ventilation and refrigeration maintenance technology; hospitality administration; human services; industrial production technologies related; industrial technology; interior design; ironworking; legal assistant/paralegal; liberal arts and sciences/liberal studies; library and archives assisting; machine tool technology; masonry; mechanic and repair technologies related; mechanics and repair; medical/clinical assistant; painting and wall covering; pipefitting and sprinkler fitting; registered nursing/registered nurse; robotics technology; sheet metal technology; telecommunications technology; tool and die technology.

Academics *Calendar:* semesters. *Degree:* certificates and associate. *Special study options:* academic remediation for entering students, adult/continuing education programs, advanced placement credit, distance learning, English as a second language, internships, off-campus study, part-time degree program, services for LD students, summer session for credit.

Student Life *Housing:* college housing not available. *Activities and Organizations:* Phi Theta Kappa, student government, LPN Club. *Campus security:* 24-hour emergency response devices and patrols, late-night transport/escort service, security during open hours. *Student services:* personal/psychological counseling, women's center.

Costs (2015–16) *Tuition:* state resident $3995 full-time, $133 per credit hour part-time; nonresident $7872 full-time, $262 per credit hour part-time. *Required fees:* $120 full-time. *Payment plans:* installment, deferred payment. *Waivers:* senior citizens and employees or children of employees.

Financial Aid Of all full-time matriculated undergraduates who enrolled in 2014, 100 Federal Work-Study jobs (averaging $1538).

Applying *Options:* electronic application, early admission, deferred entrance. *Required:* high school transcript. *Required for some:* interview. *Application*

deadlines: rolling (freshmen), rolling (transfers). *Notification:* continuous (freshmen), continuous (transfers).

Freshman Application Contact Ms. Janice Austin, Director of Admissions, Ivy Tech Community College–North Central, 220 Dean Johnson Boulevard, South Bend, IN 46601-3415. *Phone:* 574-289-7001 Ext. 5326. *Toll-free phone:* 888-IVY-LINE. *Fax:* 574-236-7177. *E-mail:* jaustin@ivytech.edu. *Website:* http://www.ivytech.edu/.

Ivy Tech Community College–Northeast
Fort Wayne, Indiana

- **State-supported** 2-year, founded 1969, part of Ivy Tech Community College System
- **Urban** 22-acre campus
- **Coed,** 7,660 undergraduate students, 31% full-time, 53% women, 47% men

Undergraduates 2,409 full-time, 5,251 part-time. 1% are from out of state; 11% Black or African American, non-Hispanic/Latino; 6% Hispanic/Latino; 2% Asian, non-Hispanic/Latino; 0.1% Native Hawaiian or other Pacific Islander, non-Hispanic/Latino; 0.4% American Indian or Alaska Native, non-Hispanic/Latino; 3% Two or more races, non-Hispanic/Latino; 14% Race/ethnicity unknown; 1% international; 7% transferred in. *Retention:* 46% of full-time freshmen returned.

Freshmen *Admission:* 1,320 enrolled.

Faculty *Total:* 541, 25% full-time. *Student/faculty ratio:* 15:1.

Majors Accounting technology and bookkeeping; agriculture; automobile/automotive mechanics technology; building/property maintenance; business administration and management; business automation/technology/data entry; cabinetmaking and millwork; child-care and support services management; computer and information sciences; computer science; construction trades; construction trades related; criminal justice/safety; data modeling/warehousing and database administration; drafting and design technology; early childhood education; electrical, electronic and communications engineering technology; electrician; executive assistant/executive secretary; heating, air conditioning, ventilation and refrigeration maintenance technology; hospitality administration; hospitality administration related; human services; industrial production technologies related; industrial technology; ironworking; legal assistant/paralegal; liberal arts and sciences/liberal studies; library and archives assisting; machine tool technology; manufacturing engineering technology; masonry; massage therapy; mechanics and repair; medical/clinical assistant; occupational safety and health technology; painting and wall covering; pipefitting and sprinkler fitting; psychiatric/mental health services technology; registered nursing/registered nurse; respiratory care therapy; robotics technology; sheet metal technology; tool and die technology.

Academics *Calendar:* semesters. *Degree:* certificates and associate. *Special study options:* adult/continuing education programs, advanced placement credit, distance learning, English as a second language, internships, part-time degree program, services for LD students, summer session for credit.

Student Life *Housing:* college housing not available. *Activities and Organizations:* student-run newspaper, Student Government, LPN Club, Phi Theta Kappa. *Campus security:* 24-hour emergency response devices and patrols, late-night transport/escort service.

Costs (2015–16) *Tuition:* state resident $3995 full-time, $133 per credit hour part-time; nonresident $7872 full-time, $262 per credit hour part-time. *Required fees:* $120 full-time. *Payment plans:* installment, deferred payment. *Waivers:* senior citizens and employees or children of employees.

Financial Aid Of all full-time matriculated undergraduates who enrolled in 2014, 40 Federal Work-Study jobs (averaging $4041).

Applying *Options:* early admission. *Required:* high school transcript. *Required for some:* interview. *Application deadlines:* rolling (freshmen), rolling (transfers). *Notification:* continuous (freshmen), continuous (transfers).

Freshman Application Contact Robyn Boss, Director of Admissions, Ivy Tech Community College–Northeast, 3800 North Anthony Boulevard, Ft. Wayne, IN 46805-1489. *Phone:* 260-480-4211. *Toll-free phone:* 888-IVY-LINE. *Fax:* 260-480-2053. *E-mail:* rboss1@ivytech.edu. *Website:* http://www.ivytech.edu/.

Ivy Tech Community College–Northwest
Gary, Indiana

- **State-supported** 2-year, founded 1963, part of Ivy Tech Community College System
- **Urban** 13-acre campus with easy access to Chicago
- **Coed,** 8,166 undergraduate students, 33% full-time, 60% women, 40% men

Undergraduates 2,673 full-time, 5,493 part-time. 3% are from out of state; 22% Black or African American, non-Hispanic/Latino; 15% Hispanic/Latino; 0.9% Asian, non-Hispanic/Latino; 0.1% Native Hawaiian or other Pacific

Islander, non-Hispanic/Latino; 0.2% American Indian or Alaska Native, non-Hispanic/Latino; 2% Two or more races, non-Hispanic/Latino; 15% Race/ethnicity unknown; 0.2% international; 7% transferred in. *Retention:* 44% of full-time freshmen returned.
Freshmen *Admission:* 1,421 enrolled.
Faculty *Total:* 536, 24% full-time. *Student/faculty ratio:* 17:1.
Majors Accounting technology and bookkeeping; automobile/automotive mechanics technology; building/construction finishing, management, and inspection related; building/property maintenance; business administration and management; business automation/technology/data entry; cabinetmaking and millwork; carpentry; child-care and support services management; computer and information sciences; construction trades; criminal justice/safety; drafting and design technology; early childhood education; electrical, electronic and communications engineering technology; electrician; executive assistant/executive secretary; funeral service and mortuary science; general studies; heating, air conditioning, ventilation and refrigeration maintenance technology; hospitality administration; human services; industrial technology; ironworking; legal assistant/paralegal; liberal arts and sciences/liberal studies; library and archives assisting; machine tool technology; masonry; mechanic and repair technologies related; mechanics and repair; medical/clinical assistant; occupational safety and health technology; painting and wall covering; pipefitting and sprinkler fitting; psychiatric/mental health services technology; registered nursing/registered nurse; respiratory care therapy; sheet metal technology; surgical technology; telecommunications technology; tool and die technology.
Academics *Calendar:* semesters. *Degree:* certificates and associate. *Special study options:* academic remediation for entering students, adult/continuing education programs, advanced placement credit, distance learning, internships, part-time degree program, services for LD students, summer session for credit.
Student Life *Housing:* college housing not available. *Activities and Organizations:* Phi Theta Kappa, LPN Club, Computer Club, Student Government, Business Club. *Campus security:* 24-hour emergency response devices, late-night transport/escort service.
Costs (2015–16) *Tuition:* state resident $3995 full-time, $133 per credit hour part-time; nonresident $7872 full-time, $262 per credit hour part-time. *Required fees:* $120 full-time. *Waivers:* senior citizens and employees or children of employees.
Financial Aid Of all full-time matriculated undergraduates who enrolled in 2014, 74 Federal Work-Study jobs (averaging $2131).
Applying *Options:* electronic application, deferred entrance. *Required:* high school transcript. *Required for some:* interview. *Application deadlines:* rolling (freshmen), rolling (transfers). *Notification:* continuous (freshmen), continuous (transfers).
Freshman Application Contact Ms. Twilla Lewis, Associate Dean of Student Affairs, Ivy Tech Community College–Northwest, 1440 East 35th Avenue, Gary, IN 46409-499. *Phone:* 219-981-1111 Ext. 2273. *Toll-free phone:* 888-IVY-LINE. *Fax:* 219-981-4415. *E-mail:* tlewis@ivytech.edu. *Website:* http://www.ivytech.edu/.

Ivy Tech Community College–Richmond
Richmond, Indiana

- **State-supported** 2-year, founded 1963, part of Ivy Tech Community College System
- **Small-town** 23-acre campus with easy access to Indianapolis
- **Coed,** 2,182 undergraduate students, 29% full-time, 66% women, 34% men

Undergraduates 639 full-time, 1,543 part-time. 1% are from out of state; 4% Black or African American, non-Hispanic/Latino; 2% Hispanic/Latino; 0.1% Asian, non-Hispanic/Latino; 0.1% Native Hawaiian or other Pacific Islander, non-Hispanic/Latino; 0.2% American Indian or Alaska Native, non-Hispanic/Latino; 2% Two or more races, non-Hispanic/Latino; 18% Race/ethnicity unknown; 0.6% international; 5% transferred in. *Retention:* 37% of full-time freshmen returned.
Freshmen *Admission:* 398 enrolled.
Faculty *Total:* 198, 20% full-time. *Student/faculty ratio:* 19:1.
Majors Accounting technology and bookkeeping; agriculture; automobile/automotive mechanics technology; building/property maintenance; business administration and management; business automation/technology/data entry; cabinetmaking and millwork; child-care and support services management; computer and information sciences; computer science; construction trades; construction trades related; criminal justice/safety; data modeling/warehousing and database administration; early childhood education; education; electrical, electronic and communications engineering technology; electrician; emergency medical technology (EMT paramedic); engineering technology; executive assistant/executive secretary; general studies; heating, air conditioning, ventilation and refrigeration maintenance technology; human services; industrial production technologies related; industrial technology; informatics; information science/studies; information technology; legal assistant/paralegal; liberal arts and sciences and

humanities related; liberal arts and sciences/liberal studies; library and archives assisting; logistics, materials, and supply chain management; machine shop technology; machine tool technology; manufacturing engineering technology; mechanics and repair; medical/clinical assistant; medical/health management and clinical assistant; medical radiologic technology; network and system administration; pipefitting and sprinkler fitting; psychiatric/mental health services technology; registered nursing/registered nurse; respiratory care therapy; robotics technology; tool and die technology.
Academics *Calendar:* semesters. *Degree:* certificates and associate. *Special study options:* academic remediation for entering students, adult/continuing education programs, advanced placement credit, distance learning, independent study, internships, off-campus study, part-time degree program, services for LD students, summer session for credit.
Student Life *Housing:* college housing not available. *Activities and Organizations:* student-run newspaper, Student Government, Phi Theta Kappa, LPN Club, CATS 2000, Business Professionals of America. *Campus security:* 24-hour emergency response devices, late-night transport/escort service. *Student services:* personal/psychological counseling.
Athletics *Intramural sports:* softball M/W.
Costs (2015–16) *Tuition:* state resident $3995 full-time, $133 per credit hour part-time; nonresident $7872 full-time, $262 per credit hour part-time. *Required fees:* $120 full-time. *Payment plans:* installment, deferred payment. *Waivers:* senior citizens and employees or children of employees.
Financial Aid Of all full-time matriculated undergraduates who enrolled in 2014, 14 Federal Work-Study jobs (averaging $3106). 1 state and other part-time job (averaging $3380).
Applying *Options:* electronic application, early admission. *Required:* high school transcript. *Required for some:* interview. *Application deadlines:* rolling (freshmen), rolling (transfers). *Notification:* continuous (freshmen), continuous (transfers).
Freshman Application Contact Christine Seger, Director of Admissions, Ivy Tech Community College–Richmond, 2325 Chester Boulevard, Richmond, IN 47374-1298. *Phone:* 765-966-2656 Ext. 1212. *Toll-free phone:* 888-IVY-LINE. *Fax:* 765-962-8741. *E-mail:* crethlake@ivytech.edu. *Website:* http://www.ivytech.edu/.

Ivy Tech Community College–Southeast
Madison, Indiana

- **State-supported** 2-year, founded 1963, part of Ivy Tech Community College System
- **Small-town** 5-acre campus with easy access to Louisville
- **Coed,** 2,314 undergraduate students, 32% full-time, 67% women, 33% men

Undergraduates 739 full-time, 1,575 part-time. 6% are from out of state; 0.8% Black or African American, non-Hispanic/Latino; 2% Hispanic/Latino; 0.2% Asian, non-Hispanic/Latino; 0.3% American Indian or Alaska Native, non-Hispanic/Latino; 0.8% Two or more races, non-Hispanic/Latino; 16% Race/ethnicity unknown; 0.2% international; 3% transferred in. *Retention:* 53% of full-time freshmen returned.
Freshmen *Admission:* 358 enrolled.
Faculty *Total:* 226, 22% full-time. *Student/faculty ratio:* 15:1.
Majors Accounting technology and bookkeeping; administrative assistant and secretarial science; business administration and management; business automation/technology/data entry; child-care and support services management; computer and information sciences; computer science; criminal justice/safety; data modeling/warehousing and database administration; drafting and design technology; early childhood education; education; electrical, electronic and communications engineering technology; executive assistant/executive secretary; general studies; human services; industrial technology; informatics; information science/studies; information technology; legal assistant/paralegal; liberal arts and sciences/liberal studies; library and archives assisting; licensed practical/vocational nurse training; logistics, materials, and supply chain management; manufacturing engineering technology; medical/clinical assistant; medical/health management and clinical assistant; medical radiologic technology; network and system administration; psychiatric/mental health services technology; registered nursing/registered nurse.
Academics *Calendar:* semesters. *Degree:* certificates and associate. *Special study options:* academic remediation for entering students, advanced placement credit, distance learning, internships, part-time degree program, services for LD students, summer session for credit.
Student Life *Housing:* college housing not available. *Activities and Organizations:* Student Government, Phi Theta Kappa, LPN Club. *Campus security:* 24-hour emergency response devices.
Costs (2015–16) *Tuition:* state resident $3995 full-time, $133 per credit hour part-time; nonresident $7872 full-time, $262 per credit hour part-time. *Required fees:* $120 full-time, $60 per term part-time. *Payment plans:* installment, deferred payment. *Waivers:* senior citizens and employees or children of employees.

Financial Aid Of all full-time matriculated undergraduates who enrolled in 2014, 26 Federal Work-Study jobs (averaging $1696).

Applying *Options:* electronic application. *Required:* high school transcript. *Required for some:* interview. *Application deadlines:* rolling (freshmen), rolling (transfers). *Notification:* continuous (freshmen), continuous (transfers).

Freshman Application Contact Ms. Cindy Hutcherson, Assistant Director of Admission/Career Counselor, Ivy Tech Community College–Southeast, 590 Ivy Tech Drive, Madison, IN 47250-1881. *Phone:* 812-265-2580 Ext. 4142. *Toll-free phone:* 888-IVY-LINE. *Fax:* 812-265-4028.
E-mail: chutcher@ivytech.edu.
Website: http://www.ivytech.edu/.

Ivy Tech Community College–Southern Indiana
Sellersburg, Indiana

- **State-supported** 2-year, founded 1968, part of Ivy Tech Community College System
- **Small-town** 63-acre campus with easy access to Louisville
- **Coed,** 4,750 undergraduate students, 20% full-time, 52% women, 48% men

Undergraduates 972 full-time, 3,778 part-time. 8% are from out of state; 5% Black or African American, non-Hispanic/Latino; 2% Hispanic/Latino; 0.4% Asian, non-Hispanic/Latino; 0.1% Native Hawaiian or other Pacific Islander, non-Hispanic/Latino; 0.2% American Indian or Alaska Native, non-Hispanic/Latino; 2% Two or more races, non-Hispanic/Latino; 31% Race/ethnicity unknown; 0.3% international; 6% transferred in. *Retention:* 48% of full-time freshmen returned.

Freshmen *Admission:* 1,014 enrolled.

Faculty *Total:* 275, 21% full-time. *Student/faculty ratio:* 19:1.

Majors Accounting technology and bookkeeping; administrative assistant and secretarial science; automobile/automotive mechanics technology; building/property maintenance; business administration and management; business automation/technology/data entry; cabinetmaking and millwork; carpentry; child-care and support services management; clinical/medical laboratory technology; computer and information sciences; computer science; computer systems networking and telecommunications; data modeling/warehousing and database administration; design and visual communications; drafting and design technology; early childhood education; education; electrical, electronic and communications engineering technology; electrician; energy management and systems technology; engineering technology; executive assistant/executive secretary; general studies; heating, air conditioning, ventilation and refrigeration maintenance technology; human services; industrial technology; informatics; information science/studies; information technology; kinesiology and exercise science; legal assistant/paralegal; liberal arts and sciences/liberal studies; library and archives assisting; logistics, materials, and supply chain management; machine tool technology; manufacturing engineering technology; masonry; mechanics and repair; medical/clinical assistant; medical/health management and clinical assistant; network and system administration; physical therapy technology; pipefitting and sprinkler fitting; psychiatric/mental health services technology; registered nursing/registered nurse; respiratory care therapy; sheet metal technology; telecommunications technology; tool and die technology.

Academics *Calendar:* semesters. *Degree:* certificates and associate. *Special study options:* academic remediation for entering students, adult/continuing education programs, advanced placement credit, cooperative education, distance learning, internships, part-time degree program, services for LD students, summer session for credit.

Student Life *Housing:* college housing not available. *Activities and Organizations:* Phi Theta Kappa, Practical Nursing Club, Medical Assistant Club, Accounting Club, Student Government. *Campus security:* late-night transport/escort service.

Costs (2015–16) *Tuition:* state resident $3995 full-time, $133 per credit hour part-time; nonresident $7872 full-time, $262 per credit hour part-time. *Required fees:* $120 full-time, $60 per term part-time. *Payment plans:* installment, deferred payment. *Waivers:* senior citizens and employees or children of employees.

Financial Aid Of all full-time matriculated undergraduates who enrolled in 2014, 20 Federal Work-Study jobs (averaging $5007). 1 state and other part-time job (averaging $6080).

Applying *Options:* electronic application, early admission, deferred entrance. *Required:* high school transcript. *Required for some:* interview. *Application deadlines:* rolling (freshmen), rolling (transfers). *Notification:* continuous (freshmen), continuous (transfers).

Freshman Application Contact Ben Harris, Director of Admissions, Ivy Tech Community College–Southern Indiana, 8204 Highway 311, Sellersburg, IN 47172-1897. *Phone:* 812-246-3301 Ext. 4137. *Toll-free phone:* 888-IVY-LINE. *Fax:* 812-246-9905. *E-mail:* bharris88@ivytech.edu.
Website: http://www.ivytech.edu/.

Ivy Tech Community College–Southwest
Evansville, Indiana

- **State-supported** 2-year, founded 1963, part of Ivy Tech Community College System
- **Suburban** 15-acre campus
- **Coed,** 5,142 undergraduate students, 25% full-time, 49% women, 51% men

Undergraduates 1,280 full-time, 3,862 part-time. 6% are from out of state; 7% Black or African American, non-Hispanic/Latino; 3% Hispanic/Latino; 0.8% Asian, non-Hispanic/Latino; 0.1% Native Hawaiian or other Pacific Islander, non-Hispanic/Latino; 0.3% American Indian or Alaska Native, non-Hispanic/Latino; 2% Two or more races, non-Hispanic/Latino; 21% Race/ethnicity unknown; 0.4% international; 4% transferred in. *Retention:* 54% of full-time freshmen returned.

Freshmen *Admission:* 1,007 enrolled.

Faculty *Total:* 344, 25% full-time. *Student/faculty ratio:* 18:1.

Majors Accounting technology and bookkeeping; administrative assistant and secretarial science; agriculture; automobile/automotive mechanics technology; biotechnology; boilermaking; building/property maintenance; business administration and management; business automation/technology/data entry; cabinetmaking and millwork; carpentry; child-care and support services management; computer and information sciences; computer science; construction/heavy equipment/earthmoving equipment operation; criminal justice/safety; data modeling/warehousing and database administration; design and visual communications; drafting and design technology; early childhood education; education; electrical, electronic and communications engineering technology; electrician; emergency medical technology (EMT paramedic); energy management and systems technology; engineering technology; executive assistant/executive secretary; general studies; graphic design; heating, air conditioning, ventilation and refrigeration maintenance technology; hospitality administration; human services; industrial production technologies related; industrial technology; informatics; information science/studies; information technology; interior design; ironworking; legal assistant/paralegal; liberal arts and sciences/liberal studies; library and archives assisting; logistics, materials, and supply chain management; machine tool technology; manufacturing engineering technology; masonry; mechanic and repair technologies related; mechanics and repair; medical/clinical assistant; medical/health management and clinical assistant; network and system administration; painting and wall covering; pipefitting and sprinkler fitting; pre-engineering; psychiatric/mental health services technology; registered nursing/registered nurse; robotics technology; sheet metal technology; surgical technology; telecommunications technology; tool and die technology.

Academics *Calendar:* semesters. *Degree:* certificates and associate. *Special study options:* academic remediation for entering students, advanced placement credit, cooperative education, distance learning, independent study, internships, part-time degree program, services for LD students, summer session for credit.

Student Life *Housing:* college housing not available. *Activities and Organizations:* Student Government, Phi Theta Kappa, LPN Club, National Association of Industrial Technology, Design Club. *Campus security:* late-night transport/escort service.

Costs (2015–16) *Tuition:* state resident $3995 full-time, $133 per credit hour part-time; nonresident $7872 full-time, $262 per credit hour part-time. *Required fees:* $120 full-time, $60 per term part-time. *Payment plans:* installment, deferred payment. *Waivers:* senior citizens and employees or children of employees.

Financial Aid Of all full-time matriculated undergraduates who enrolled in 2014, 65 Federal Work-Study jobs (averaging $2264).

Applying *Options:* electronic application, early admission, deferred entrance. *Required:* high school transcript. *Required for some:* interview. *Application deadlines:* rolling (freshmen), rolling (transfers). *Notification:* continuous (freshmen), continuous (transfers).

Freshman Application Contact Ms. Denise Johnson-Kincade, Director of Admissions, Ivy Tech Community College–Southwest, 3501 First Avenue, Evansville, IN 47710-3398. *Phone:* 812-429-1430. *Toll-free phone:* 888-IVY-LINE. *Fax:* 812-429-9878. *E-mail:* ajohnson@ivytech.edu.
Website: http://www.ivytech.edu/.

Ivy Tech Community College–Wabash Valley
Terre Haute, Indiana

- **State-supported** 2-year, founded 1966, part of Ivy Tech Community College System
- **Suburban** 55-acre campus with easy access to Indianapolis
- **Coed,** 4,364 undergraduate students, 33% full-time, 54% women, 46% men

Undergraduates 1,441 full-time, 2,923 part-time. 5% are from out of state; 4% Black or African American, non-Hispanic/Latino; 2% Hispanic/Latino; 0.5% Asian, non-Hispanic/Latino; 0.2% American Indian or Alaska Native, non-Hispanic/Latino; 2% Two or more races, non-Hispanic/Latino; 14% Race/ethnicity unknown; 0.5% international; 3% transferred in. *Retention:* 54% of full-time freshmen returned.
Freshmen *Admission:* 449 enrolled.
Faculty *Total:* 287, 34% full-time. *Student/faculty ratio:* 19:1.
Majors Accounting technology and bookkeeping; agricultural mechanization; agriculture; airframe mechanics and aircraft maintenance technology; automobile/automotive mechanics technology; biomedical sciences; building/property maintenance; business administration and management; cabinetmaking and millwork; carpentry; chemical technology; clinical/medical laboratory technology; computer and information sciences; computer science; computer systems networking and telecommunications; construction/heavy equipment/earthmoving equipment operation; criminal justice/safety; data modeling/warehousing and database administration; design and visual communications; drafting and design technology; early childhood education; education; electrical, electronic and communications engineering technology; electrician; emergency medical technology (EMT paramedic); energy management and systems technology; engineering technology; executive assistant/executive secretary; general studies; health aide; health information/medical records technology; heating, air conditioning, ventilation and refrigeration maintenance technology; human services; industrial production technologies related; industrial technology; informatics; information science/studies; information technology; ironworking; legal assistant/paralegal; liberal arts and sciences/liberal studies; library and archives assisting; logistics, materials, and supply chain management; machine shop technology; machine tool technology; manufacturing engineering technology; masonry; mechanics and repair; medical/clinical assistant; medical/health management and clinical assistant; medical radiologic technology; network and system administration; occupational safety and health technology; office management; painting and wall covering; pipefitting and sprinkler fitting; quality control and safety technologies related; registered nursing/registered nurse; respiratory care therapy; sheet metal technology; surgical technology; tool and die technology.
Academics *Calendar:* semesters. *Degree:* certificates and associate. *Special study options:* academic remediation for entering students, adult/continuing education programs, advanced placement credit, distance learning, internships, part-time degree program, services for LD students, summer session for credit.
Student Life *Housing:* college housing not available. *Activities and Organizations:* Student Government, Phi Theta Kappa, LPN Club, National Association of Industrial Technology. *Campus security:* 24-hour emergency response devices. *Student services:* personal/psychological counseling, women's center.
Athletics *Intramural sports:* basketball M/W, volleyball M/W.
Costs (2015–16) *Tuition:* state resident $3995 full-time, $133 per credit hour part-time; nonresident $7872 full-time, $262 per credit hour part-time. *Required fees:* $120 full-time. *Payment plans:* installment, deferred payment. *Waivers:* senior citizens and employees or children of employees.
Financial Aid Of all full-time matriculated undergraduates who enrolled in 2014, 51 Federal Work-Study jobs (averaging $2110). 1 state and other part-time job (averaging $2963).
Applying *Options:* electronic application, early admission, deferred entrance. *Required:* high school transcript. *Required for some:* interview. *Application deadlines:* rolling (freshmen), rolling (transfers). *Notification:* continuous (freshmen), continuous (transfers).
Freshman Application Contact Mr. Michael Fisher, Director of Admissions, Ivy Tech Community College–Wabash Valley, 7999 U.S. Highway 41 South, Terre Haute, IN 47802-4898. *Phone:* 812-298-2300. *Toll-free phone:* 888-IVY-LINE. *Fax:* 812-298-2291. *E-mail:* mfisher@ivytech.edu. *Website:* http://www.ivytech.edu/.

Lincoln College of Technology
Indianapolis, Indiana

Director of Admissions Ms. Cindy Ryan, Director of Admissions, Lincoln College of Technology, 7225 Winton Drive, Building 128, Indianapolis, IN 46268. *Phone:* 317-632-5553.
Website: http://www.lincolnedu.com/.

Medtech College
Ft. Wayne, Indiana

Admissions Office Contact Medtech College, 7230 Engle Road, Ft. Wayne, IN 46804.
Website: http://www.medtech.edu/.

Medtech College
Greenwood, Indiana

Admissions Office Contact Medtech College, 1500 American Way, Greenwood, IN 46143.
Website: http://www.medtech.edu/.

Medtech College
Indianapolis, Indiana

Admissions Office Contact Medtech College, 6612 East 75th Street, Suite 300, Indianapolis, IN 46250-2865.
Website: http://www.medtech.edu/.

Mid-America College of Funeral Service
Jeffersonville, Indiana

Freshman Application Contact Mr. Richard Nelson, Dean of Students, Mid-America College of Funeral Service, 3111 Hamburg Pike, Jeffersonville, IN 47130-9630. *Phone:* 812-288-8878. *Toll-free phone:* 800-221-6158. *Fax:* 812-288-5942. *E-mail:* macfs@mindspring.com.
Website: http://www.mid-america.edu/.

Vet Tech Institute at International Business College
Fort Wayne, Indiana

- **Private** 2-year, founded 2005
- **Suburban** campus
- **Coed,** 147 undergraduate students
- 54% of applicants were admitted

Freshmen *Admission:* 317 applied, 171 admitted.
Majors Veterinary/animal health technology.
Academics *Calendar:* semesters. *Degree:* associate. *Special study options:* accelerated degree program, internships.
Freshman Application Contact Admissions Office, Vet Tech Institute at International Business College, 5699 Coventry Lane, Fort Wayne, IN 46804. *Phone:* 800-589-6363. *Toll-free phone:* 800-589-6363.
Website: http://ftwayne.vettechinstitute.edu/.

Vet Tech Institute at International Business College
Indianapolis, Indiana

- **Private** 2-year, founded 2007
- **Suburban** campus
- **Coed,** 147 undergraduate students
- 51% of applicants were admitted

Freshmen *Admission:* 390 applied, 198 admitted.
Majors Veterinary/animal health technology.
Academics *Calendar:* semesters. *Degree:* associate. *Special study options:* accelerated degree program, internships.
Freshman Application Contact Admissions Office, Vet Tech Institute at International Business College, 7205 Shadeland Station, Indianapolis, IN 46256. *Phone:* 800-589-6500. *Toll-free phone:* 800-589-6500.
Website: http://indianapolis.vettechinstitute.edu/.

Vincennes University
Vincennes, Indiana

- **State-supported** primarily 2-year, founded 1801
- **Small-town** 160-acre campus
- **Coed,** 18,711 undergraduate students, 31% full-time, 46% women, 54% men

Undergraduates 5,773 full-time, 12,938 part-time. Students come from 40 states and territories; 15 other countries; 19% are from out of state; 12% Black or African American, non-Hispanic/Latino; 3% Hispanic/Latino; 0.6% Asian, non-Hispanic/Latino; 0.2% Native Hawaiian or other Pacific Islander, non-Hispanic/Latino; 0.2% American Indian or Alaska Native, non-

Hispanic/Latino; 3% Two or more races, non-Hispanic/Latino; 8% Race/ethnicity unknown; 0.6% international; 45% live on campus. *Retention:* 52% of full-time freshmen returned.

Freshmen *Admission:* 4,860 admitted, 2,889 enrolled.

Majors Accounting technology and bookkeeping; administrative assistant and secretarial science; agricultural business and management; agricultural engineering; agriculture; aircraft powerplant technology; airline pilot and flight crew; American Sign Language (ASL); anthropology; applied horticulture/horticulture operations; architectural drafting and CAD/CADD; art; art teacher education; art therapy; autobody/collision and repair technology; automobile/automotive mechanics technology; behavioral sciences; biochemistry; biological and biomedical sciences related; biological and physical sciences; biology/biological sciences; biotechnology; building/home/construction inspection; business administration and management; business/commerce; chemistry; chemistry related; chemistry teacher education; child-care and support services management; child-care provision; civil engineering; commercial and advertising art; communications technology; computer and information sciences; computer/information technology services administration related; computer programming; computer science; computer systems networking and telecommunications; construction trades; corrections and criminal justice related; cosmetology; criminal justice/police science; culinary arts; design and applied arts related; diesel mechanics technology; dietetics; dramatic/theater arts; early childhood education; economics; education; electrical, electronic and communications engineering technology; elementary education; emergency medical technology (EMT paramedic); engineering technology; English; English/language arts teacher education; family and consumer sciences/home economics teacher education; family and consumer sciences/human sciences; fashion merchandising; finance; fire science/firefighting; food science; foreign languages and literatures; foreign languages related; funeral service and mortuary science; geology/earth science; graphic and printing equipment operation/production; health and physical education/fitness; health information/medical records technology; history; hospitality administration; hotel/motel administration; industrial technology; journalism; legal assistant/paralegal; liberal arts and sciences/liberal studies; manufacturing engineering technology; marketing/marketing management; massage therapy; mathematics; mathematics teacher education; mechanical drafting and CAD/CADD; mechanical engineering/mechanical technology; medical radiologic technology; music; music teacher education; natural resources/conservation; nuclear medical technology; ophthalmic and optometric support services and allied professions related; parks, recreation and leisure; pharmacy technician; philosophy; photojournalism; physical education teaching and coaching; physical sciences; physical therapy technology; political science and government; pre-dentistry studies; premedical studies; pre-pharmacy studies; pre-veterinary studies; psychology; public relations/image management; radio and television broadcasting technology; recording arts technology; registered nursing/registered nurse; restaurant, culinary, and catering management; robotics technology; science teacher education; secondary education; securities services administration; security and loss prevention; sheet metal technology; social work; sociology; special education; sport and fitness administration/management; surgical technology; surveying technology; teacher assistant/aide; theater design and technology; tool and die technology; web/multimedia management and webmaster; woodworking.

Academics *Calendar:* semesters. *Degrees:* certificates, associate, and bachelor's. *Special study options:* academic remediation for entering students, accelerated degree program, adult/continuing education programs, advanced placement credit, distance learning, double majors, English as a second language, external degree program, freshman honors college, honors programs, independent study, internships, off-campus study, part-time degree program, services for LD students, student-designed majors, summer session for credit. *ROTC:* Army (b), Air Force (c).

Library Shake Learning Resource Center.

Student Life *Housing:* on-campus residence required for freshman year. *Options:* coed, men-only, women-only, special housing for students with disabilities. Campus housing is university owned. Freshman campus housing is guaranteed. *Activities and Organizations:* drama/theater group, student-run newspaper, radio and television station, choral group, national fraternities, national sororities. *Campus security:* 24-hour emergency response devices and patrols, student patrols, late-night transport/escort service, controlled dormitory access, surveillance cameras. *Student services:* health clinic, personal/psychological counseling.

Athletics Member NJCAA. *Intercollegiate sports:* baseball M, basketball M/W, bowling M, cross-country running M/W, golf M, track and field M/W, volleyball W.

Costs (2015–16) *Tuition:* state resident $5374 full-time, $2294 per year part-time; nonresident $12,710 full-time, $5227 per year part-time. Full-time tuition and fees vary according to course level, course load, location, program, reciprocity agreements, and student level. Part-time tuition and fees vary according to course level, course load, location, program, reciprocity

agreements, and student level. *Room and board:* $8732. Room and board charges vary according to board plan, gender, and housing facility. *Payment plan:* installment. *Waivers:* senior citizens and employees or children of employees.

Applying *Options:* electronic application, early admission, deferred entrance. *Application fee:* $20. *Required:* high school transcript. *Required for some:* interview. *Application deadlines:* rolling (freshmen), rolling (transfers). *Notification:* continuous until 8/1 (freshmen), continuous (transfers).

Freshman Application Contact Vincennes University, 1002 North First Street, Vincennes, IN 47591-5202. *Phone:* 812-888-4313. *Toll-free phone:* 800-742-9198.

Website: http://www.vinu.edu/.

IOWA

Brown Mackie College–Quad Cities
Bettendorf, Iowa

Freshman Application Contact Brown Mackie College–Quad Cities, 2119 East Kimberly Road, Bettendorf, IA 52722. *Phone:* 563-344-1500. *Toll-free phone:* 888-420-1652.

Website: http://www.brownmackie.edu/quad-cities/.

Clinton Community College
Clinton, Iowa

Freshman Application Contact Mr. Gary Mohr, Executive Director of Enrollment Management and Marketing, Clinton Community College, 1000 Lincoln Boulevard, Clinton, IA 52732-6299. *Phone:* 563-336-3322. *Toll-free phone:* 800-462-3255. *Fax:* 563-336-3350. *E-mail:* gmohr@eicc.edu.

Website: http://www.eicc.edu/ccc/.

Des Moines Area Community College
Ankeny, Iowa

- **State and locally supported** 2-year, founded 1966, part of Iowa Area Community Colleges System
- **Small-town** 362-acre campus
- **Endowment** $11.1 million
- **Coed**

Undergraduates 8,947 full-time, 13,377 part-time. Students come from 47 states and territories; 69 other countries; 6% Black or African American, non-Hispanic/Latino; 6% Hispanic/Latino; 4% Asian, non-Hispanic/Latino; 0.1% Native Hawaiian or other Pacific Islander, non-Hispanic/Latino; 0.4% American Indian or Alaska Native, non-Hispanic/Latino; 2% Two or more races, non-Hispanic/Latino; 4% Race/ethnicity unknown; 0.8% international. *Retention:* 58% of full-time freshmen returned.

Faculty *Student/faculty ratio:* 33:1.

Academics *Calendar:* semesters. *Degrees:* certificates, diplomas, and associate (profile also includes information from the Boone, Carroll, Des Moines, and Newton campuses). *Special study options:* academic remediation for entering students, adult/continuing education programs, advanced placement credit, cooperative education, distance learning, English as a second language, honors programs, off-campus study, part-time degree program, services for LD students, student-designed majors, summer session for credit.

Library DMACC District Library plus 4 others.

Student Life *Campus security:* 24-hour emergency response devices and patrols, late-night transport/escort service.

Athletics Member NJCAA.

Standardized Tests *Required for some:* SAT or ACT (for admission), ACT Compass.

Costs (2015–16) *Tuition:* state resident $3913 full-time, $143 per credit hour part-time; nonresident $7826 full-time, $286 per credit hour part-time. Full-time tuition and fees vary according to course load and reciprocity agreements. Part-time tuition and fees vary according to course load and reciprocity agreements. *Room and board:* room only: $4400. Room and board charges vary according to location.

Financial Aid Of all full-time matriculated undergraduates who enrolled in 2014, 377 Federal Work-Study jobs (averaging $1055).

Applying *Options:* electronic application, early admission, deferred entrance. *Required for some:* high school transcript, interview.

Freshman Application Contact Mr. Michael Lentsch, Director of Enrollment Management, Des Moines Area Community College, 2006 South Ankeny Boulevard, Ankeny, IA 50021-8995. *Phone:* 515-964-6216. *Toll-free phone:* 800-362-2127. *Fax:* 515-964-6391. *E-mail:* mjleutsch@dmacc.edu.

Website: http://www.dmacc.edu/.

Ellsworth Community College
Iowa Falls, Iowa

Director of Admissions Mrs. Nancy Walters, Registrar, Ellsworth Community College, 1100 College Avenue, Iowa Falls, IA 50126-1199. *Phone:* 641-648-4611. *Toll-free phone:* 800-ECC-9235.
Website: http://www.iavalley.cc.ia.us/ecc/.

Hawkeye Community College
Waterloo, Iowa

- **State and locally supported** 2-year, founded 1966
- **Rural** 320-acre campus
- **Endowment** $2.1 million
- **Coed,** 5,370 undergraduate students, 48% full-time, 56% women, 44% men

Undergraduates 2,566 full-time, 2,804 part-time. Students come from 7 states and territories; 1% are from out of state; 11% Black or African American, non-Hispanic/Latino; 4% Hispanic/Latino; 1% Asian, non-Hispanic/Latino; 0.2% Native Hawaiian or other Pacific Islander, non-Hispanic/Latino; 0.2% American Indian or Alaska Native, non-Hispanic/Latino; 2% Two or more races, non-Hispanic/Latino; 0.5% international; 31% transferred in.
Freshmen *Admission:* 3,693 applied, 2,566 admitted, 1,025 enrolled. *Test scores:* ACT scores over 18: 49%; ACT scores over 24: 16%; ACT scores over 30: 3%.
Faculty *Total:* 342, 35% full-time, 9% with terminal degrees. *Student/faculty ratio:* 18:1.
Majors Accounting; agricultural/farm supplies retailing and wholesaling; agricultural power machinery operation; animal/livestock husbandry and production; autobody/collision and repair technology; automobile/automotive mechanics technology; carpentry; child-care provision; civil engineering technology; clinical/medical laboratory technology; commercial photography; computer/information technology services administration related; computer systems networking and telecommunications; criminal justice/police science; dental hygiene; desktop publishing and digital imaging design; diesel mechanics technology; digital communication and media/multimedia; electrical, electronic and communications engineering technology; electromechanical technology; emergency medical technology (EMT paramedic); energy management and systems technology; executive assistant/executive secretary; fire science/firefighting; golf course operation and grounds management; hospitality administration; human resources management; interior design; landscaping and groundskeeping; liberal arts and sciences/liberal studies; machine tool technology; medical administrative assistant and medical secretary; medical insurance coding; multi/interdisciplinary studies related; natural resources management and policy; occupational therapist assistant; physical therapy technology; registered nursing/registered nurse; respiratory care therapy; sales, distribution, and marketing operations; web page, digital/multimedia and information resources design.
Academics *Calendar:* semesters. *Degree:* certificates, diplomas, and associate. *Special study options:* academic remediation for entering students, accelerated degree program, adult/continuing education programs, advanced placement credit, cooperative education, distance learning, English as a second language, external degree program, part-time degree program, services for LD students, study abroad, summer session for credit. *ROTC:* Army (c).
Library Hawkeye Community College Library. *Books:* 25,186 (physical), 152,062 (digital/electronic); *Serial titles:* 171 (physical), 46 (digital/electronic); *Databases:* 33. Weekly public service hours: 70; students can reserve study rooms.
Student Life *Housing:* college housing not available. *Activities and Organizations:* drama/theater group, choral group, Student Senate, Phi Theta Kappa, Student Ambassadors, Chorus, Natural Resources. *Campus security:* 24-hour patrols. *Student services:* health clinic, personal/psychological counseling, women's center.
Athletics Member NJCAA. *Intramural sports:* badminton M/W, basketball M/W, bowling M/W, football M/W, golf M/W, soccer M/W, softball M/W, table tennis M/W, volleyball M/W.
Standardized Tests *Required:* ACT Compass or the equivalent from ACT or accredited college course(s) (for admission). *Required for some:* ACT (for admission).
Costs (2015–16) *Tuition:* state resident $4256 full-time, $152 per credit hour part-time; nonresident $4956 full-time, $177 per credit hour part-time. *Required fees:* $210 full-time, $8 per credit hour part-time. *Payment plan:* installment.
Applying *Options:* electronic application, deferred entrance. *Required:* high school transcript. *Application deadlines:* rolling (freshmen), rolling (out-of-state freshmen), rolling (transfers). *Notification:* continuous (freshmen), continuous (out-of-state freshmen), continuous (transfers).
Freshman Application Contact Ms. Holly Grimm-See, Associate Director, Admissions and Recruitment, Hawkeye Community College, PO Box 8015,

Waterloo, IA 50704-8015. *Phone:* 319-296-4277. *Toll-free phone:* 800-670-4769. *Fax:* 319-296-2505. *E-mail:* holly.grimm-see@hawkeyecollege.edu. *Website:* http://www.hawkeyecollege.edu/.

Indian Hills Community College
Ottumwa, Iowa

Freshman Application Contact Mrs. Jane Sapp, Admissions Officer, Indian Hills Community College, 525 Grandview Avenue, Building #1, Ottumwa, IA 52501-1398. *Phone:* 641-683-5155. *Toll-free phone:* 800-726-2585. *Website:* http://www.ihcc.cc.ia.us/.

Iowa Central Community College
Fort Dodge, Iowa

- **State and locally supported** 2-year, founded 1966
- **Small-town** 110-acre campus
- **Coed,** 5,634 undergraduate students, 52% full-time, 50% women, 50% men

Undergraduates 2,956 full-time, 2,678 part-time. Students come from 38 states and territories; 28 other countries; 9% are from out of state; 9% Black or African American, non-Hispanic/Latino; 8% Hispanic/Latino; 1% Asian, non-Hispanic/Latino; 0.2% Native Hawaiian or other Pacific Islander, non-Hispanic/Latino; 0.6% American Indian or Alaska Native, non-Hispanic/Latino; 1% Two or more races, non-Hispanic/Latino; 6% Race/ethnicity unknown; 1% international; 3% transferred in; 18% live on campus.
Freshmen *Admission:* 1,092 applied, 1,247 enrolled.
Faculty *Total:* 416, 21% full-time. *Student/faculty ratio:* 19:1.
Majors Accounting; administrative assistant and secretarial science; airline pilot and flight crew; automobile/automotive mechanics technology; aviation/airway management; biological and physical sciences; broadcast journalism; business administration and management; business teacher education; carpentry; clinical/medical laboratory technology; community organization and advocacy; computer engineering technology; criminal justice/police science; data processing and data processing technology; drafting and design technology; education; electrical, electronic and communications engineering technology; hospitality and recreation marketing; industrial radiologic technology; journalism; liberal arts and sciences/liberal studies; licensed practical/vocational nurse training; machine tool technology; mass communication/media; medical/clinical assistant; occupational therapy; physical therapy; radio and television; registered nursing/registered nurse; science teacher education; social work; sociology; telecommunications technology; welding technology.
Academics *Calendar:* semesters. *Degree:* certificates, diplomas, and associate. *Special study options:* academic remediation for entering students, adult/continuing education programs, advanced placement credit, cooperative education, distance learning, English as a second language, independent study, internships, part-time degree program, services for LD students, study abroad, summer session for credit.
Library Iowa Central Community College Library plus 1 other. Students can reserve study rooms.
Student Life *Housing Options:* men-only, women-only. Campus housing is university owned. *Activities and Organizations:* drama/theater group, student-run newspaper, radio station, choral group, marching band, Student Senate, BPA, Phi Beta Lambda. *Campus security:* 24-hour emergency response devices and patrols, student patrols, late-night transport/escort service, controlled dormitory access. *Student services:* health clinic, personal/psychological counseling.
Athletics Member NJCAA. *Intercollegiate sports:* baseball M(s), basketball M(s)/W(s), bowling M(s)/W(s), cheerleading M(s)/W(s), cross-country running M/W, football M(s), golf M(s)/W(s), rugby M(c), soccer M(s)/W(s), softball W(s), swimming and diving M/W, tennis M(s)/W(s), volleyball W(s), wrestling M(s). *Intramural sports:* basketball M/W, football M, golf M/W, softball W, table tennis M/W, tennis M/W, volleyball M/W, weight lifting M, wrestling M.
Costs (2015–16) *Tuition:* state resident $4564 full-time, $163 per credit hour part-time; nonresident $6650 full-time, $238 per credit hour part-time. Full-time tuition and fees vary according to course load and program. Part-time tuition and fees vary according to course load and program. *Required fees:* $420 per term part-time. *Room and board:* $6350; room only: $4098. *Payment plan:* installment.
Applying *Options:* electronic application, early admission, deferred entrance. *Required for some:* high school transcript, interview. *Recommended:* high school transcript. *Application deadlines:* rolling (freshmen), rolling (out-of-state freshmen), rolling (transfers). *Notification:* continuous (freshmen), continuous (out-of-state freshmen), continuous (transfers).
Freshman Application Contact Mrs. Sue Flattery, Enrollment Management Secretary, Iowa Central Community College, One Triton Circle, Fort Dodge,

IA 50501. *Phone:* 515-574-1010 Ext. 2402. *Toll-free phone:* 800-362-2793. *Fax:* 515-576-7207. *E-mail:* flattery@iowacentral.com. *Website:* http://www.iccc.cc.ia.us/.

Iowa Lakes Community College
Estherville, Iowa

- **State and locally supported** 2-year, founded 1967, part of Iowa Community College System
- **Small-town** 20-acre campus
- **Endowment** $6.5 million
- **Coed**

Undergraduates 1,090 full-time, 1,250 part-time. Students come from 37 states and territories; 10 other countries; 6% Black or African American, non-Hispanic/Latino; 7% Hispanic/Latino; 0.6% Asian, non-Hispanic/Latino; 0.3% Native Hawaiian or other Pacific Islander, non-Hispanic/Latino; 1% American Indian or Alaska Native, non-Hispanic/Latino; 0.1% Two or more races, non-Hispanic/Latino; 3% Race/ethnicity unknown; 2% international; 37% live on campus. *Retention:* 54% of full-time freshmen returned.
Faculty *Student/faculty ratio:* 18:1.
Academics *Calendar:* semesters. *Degree:* certificates, diplomas, and associate. *Special study options:* academic remediation for entering students, accelerated degree program, adult/continuing education programs, advanced placement credit, cooperative education, distance learning, English as a second language, honors programs, independent study, internships, part-time degree program, services for LD students, summer session for credit.
Library Iowa Lakes Community College Library plus 2 others.
Student Life *Campus security:* 24-hour emergency response devices, student patrols.
Athletics Member NJCAA.
Costs (2015–16) *Tuition:* state resident $5676 full-time, $160 per credit hour part-time; nonresident $6028 full-time, $171 per credit hour part-time. Full-time tuition and fees vary according to program and reciprocity agreements. Part-time tuition and fees vary according to program and reciprocity agreements. *Required fees:* $17 per credit hour part-time. *Room and board:* Room and board charges vary according to board plan and location.
Applying *Options:* electronic application. *Required for some:* interview.
Freshman Application Contact Iowa Lakes Community College, IA. *Phone:* 712-362-7923 Ext. 7923. *Toll-free phone:* 800-521-5054.
E-mail: info@iowalakes.edu.
Website: http://www.iowalakes.edu/.

Iowa Western Community College
Council Bluffs, Iowa

Freshman Application Contact Ms. Tori Christie, Director of Admissions, Iowa Western Community College, 2700 College Road, Box 4-C, Council Bluffs, IA 51502. *Phone:* 712-325-3288. *Toll-free phone:* 800-432-5852.
E-mail: admissions@iwcc.edu.
Website: http://www.iwcc.edu/.

Kaplan University, Cedar Falls
Cedar Falls, Iowa

Freshman Application Contact Kaplan University, Cedar Falls, 7009 Nordic Drive, Cedar Falls, IA 50613. *Phone:* 319-277-0220.
Toll-free phone: 866-527-5268 (in-state); 800-527-5268 (out-of-state).
Website: http://www.kaplanuniversity.edu/.

Kaplan University, Cedar Rapids
Cedar Rapids, Iowa

Freshman Application Contact Kaplan University, Cedar Rapids, 3165 Edgewood Parkway, SW, Cedar Rapids, IA 52404. *Phone:* 319-363-0481.
Toll-free phone: 866-527-5268 (in-state); 800-527-5268 (out-of-state).
Website: http://www.kaplanuniversity.edu/.

Kaplan University, Des Moines
Urbandale, Iowa

Freshman Application Contact Kaplan University, Des Moines, 4655 121st Street, Urbandale, IA 50323. *Phone:* 515-727-2100.
Toll-free phone: 866-527-5268 (in-state); 800-527-5268 (out-of-state).
Website: http://www.kaplanuniversity.edu/.

Kirkwood Community College
Cedar Rapids, Iowa

Freshman Application Contact Kirkwood Community College, PO Box 2068, Cedar Rapids, IA 52406-2068. *Phone:* 319-398-5517. *Toll-free phone:* 800-332-2055.
Website: http://www.kirkwood.edu/.

Marshalltown Community College
Marshalltown, Iowa

Freshman Application Contact Ms. Deana Inman, Director of Admissions, Marshalltown Community College, 3700 South Center Street, Marshalltown, IA 50158-4760. *Phone:* 641-752-7106. *Toll-free phone:* 866-622-4748. *Fax:* 641-752-8149.
Website: http://www.marshalltowncommunitycollege.com/.

Muscatine Community College
Muscatine, Iowa

Freshman Application Contact Gary Mohr, Executive Director of Enrollment Management and Marketing, Muscatine Community College, 152 Colorado Street, Muscatine, IA 52761-5396. *Phone:* 563-336-3322. *Toll-free phone:* 800-351-4669. *Fax:* 563-336-3350. *E-mail:* gmohr@eicc.edu.
Website: http://www.eicc.edu/general/muscatine/.

Northeast Iowa Community College
Calmar, Iowa

- **State and locally supported** 2-year, founded 1966, part of Iowa Area Community Colleges System
- **Rural** 210-acre campus
- **Coed,** 4,865 undergraduate students, 31% full-time, 57% women, 43% men

Undergraduates 1,485 full-time, 3,380 part-time. 14% are from out of state; 4% Black or African American, non-Hispanic/Latino; 2% Hispanic/Latino; 0.7% Asian, non-Hispanic/Latino; 0.5% Native Hawaiian or other Pacific Islander, non-Hispanic/Latino; 0.5% American Indian or Alaska Native, non-Hispanic/Latino; 5% Two or more races, non-Hispanic/Latino; 3% Race/ethnicity unknown; 4% transferred in. *Retention:* 63% of full-time freshmen returned.
Freshmen *Admission:* 1,107 applied, 878 admitted, 621 enrolled.
Faculty *Total:* 354, 33% full-time, 6% with terminal degrees. *Student/faculty ratio:* 14:1.
Majors Accounting; administrative assistant and secretarial science; agribusiness; agricultural and food products processing; agricultural power machinery operation; agricultural production; automobile/automotive mechanics technology; business administration and management; business automation/technology/data entry; clinical/medical laboratory technology; computer programming (specific applications); construction trades; cosmetology; crop production; dairy husbandry and production; desktop publishing and digital imaging design; electrical, electronic and communications engineering technology; electrician; emergency medical technology (EMT paramedic); energy management and systems technology; fire science/firefighting; health information/medical records technology; liberal arts and sciences/liberal studies; plumbing technology; radiologic technology/science; registered nursing/registered nurse; respiratory care therapy; sales, distribution, and marketing operations; social work.
Academics *Calendar:* semesters. *Degree:* certificates, diplomas, and associate. *Special study options:* academic remediation for entering students, adult/continuing education programs, advanced placement credit, cooperative education, distance learning, double majors, external degree program, honors programs, internships, off-campus study, part-time degree program, services for LD students, summer session for credit.
Library Wilder Resource Center and Burton Payne Library plus 2 others.
Student Life *Housing:* college housing not available. *Activities and Organizations:* student-run newspaper, choral group, national fraternities, national sororities. *Campus security:* security personnel on weeknights. *Student services:* personal/psychological counseling.
Athletics *Intramural sports:* basketball M/W, bowling M/W, football M, golf M/W, skiing (downhill) M/W, softball M/W, volleyball M/W.
Costs (2015–16) *Tuition:* state resident $4312 full-time, $154 per credit hour part-time; nonresident $4312 full-time, $154 per credit hour part-time. Full-time tuition and fees vary according to course load and program. Part-time tuition and fees vary according to course load and program. *Required fees:* $364 full-time, $13 per credit hour part-time. *Payment plan:* installment. *Waivers:* employees or children of employees.

Applying *Options:* electronic application. *Recommended:* high school transcript.
Freshman Application Contact Ms. Brynn McConnell, Admissions Representative, Northeast Iowa Community College, Calmar, IA 52132. *Phone:* 563-562-3263 Ext. 307. *Toll-free phone:* 800-728-CALMAR. *Fax:* 563-562-4369. *E-mail:* mcconnellb@nicc.edu.
Website: http://www.nicc.edu/.

North Iowa Area Community College
Mason City, Iowa

- **State and locally supported** 2-year, founded 1918, part of Iowa Community College System
- **Rural** 500-acre campus
- **Coed**

Undergraduates 1,420 full-time, 1,535 part-time. 3% Black or African American, non-Hispanic/Latino; 5% Hispanic/Latino; 1% Asian, non-Hispanic/Latino; 0.3% American Indian or Alaska Native, non-Hispanic/Latino; 1% Two or more races, non-Hispanic/Latino; 0.3% Race/ethnicity unknown; 1% international.
Faculty *Student/faculty ratio:* 13:1.
Academics *Calendar:* semesters. *Degree:* certificates, diplomas, and associate. *Special study options:* academic remediation for entering students, advanced placement credit, cooperative education, distance learning, English as a second language, honors programs, internships, part-time degree program, services for LD students, student-designed majors, study abroad, summer session for credit.
Student Life *Campus security:* student patrols, late-night transport/escort service, controlled dormitory access.
Athletics Member NJCAA.
Costs (2015–16) *Tuition:* state resident $4013 full-time, $133 per semester hour part-time; nonresident $6019 full-time, $200 per semester hour part-time. Full-time tuition and fees vary according to course load. Part-time tuition and fees vary according to course load. *Required fees:* $780 full-time, $26 per semester hour part-time. *Room and board:* $6518. Room and board charges vary according to housing facility.
Financial Aid Of all full-time matriculated undergraduates who enrolled in 2014, 125 Federal Work-Study jobs (averaging $2000). 4 state and other part-time jobs (averaging $2000).
Applying *Options:* electronic application. *Required for some:* high school transcript.
Freshman Application Contact Ms. Rachel McGuire, Director of Enrollment Services, North Iowa Area Community College, 500 College Drive, Mason City, IA 50401. *Phone:* 641-422-4104. *Toll-free phone:* 888-GO NIACC Ext. 4245. *Fax:* 641-422-4385. *E-mail:* request@niacc.edu.
Website: http://www.niacc.edu/.

Northwest Iowa Community College
Sheldon, Iowa

Director of Admissions Ms. Lisa Story, Director of Enrollment Management, Northwest Iowa Community College, 603 West Park Street, Sheldon, IA 51201-1046. *Phone:* 712-324-5061 Ext. 115. *Toll-free phone:* 800-352-4907. *E-mail:* lstory@nwicc.edu.
Website: http://www.nwicc.edu/.

St. Luke's College
Sioux City, Iowa

- **Independent** primarily 2-year, founded 1967, part of UnityPoint Health
- **Rural** 3-acre campus with easy access to Omaha
- **Endowment** $1.0 million
- **Coed,** 241 undergraduate students, 53% full-time, 89% women, 11% men

Undergraduates 128 full-time, 113 part-time. Students come from 19 states and territories; 3 other countries; 39% are from out of state; 3% Black or African American, non-Hispanic/Latino; 7% Hispanic/Latino; 2% Asian, non-Hispanic/Latino; 0.8% American Indian or Alaska Native, non-Hispanic/Latino; 2% Two or more races, non-Hispanic/Latino; 8% Race/ethnicity unknown; 9% transferred in. *Retention:* 100% of full-time freshmen returned.
Freshmen *Admission:* 15 applied, 12 admitted, 9 enrolled. *Average high school GPA:* 3.32.
Faculty *Total:* 47, 51% full-time, 6% with terminal degrees. *Student/faculty ratio:* 7:1.
Majors Health services/allied health/health sciences; radiologic technology/science; registered nursing/registered nurse; respiratory care therapy.

Academics *Calendar:* semesters. *Degrees:* certificates, associate, and bachelor's. *Special study options:* advanced placement credit, distance learning, summer session for credit.
Library St. Luke's College. *Books:* 2,950 (physical); *Serial titles:* 63 (physical); *Databases:* 31. Weekly public service hours: 58; students can reserve study rooms.
Student Life *Housing:* college housing not available. *Campus security:* 24-hour emergency response devices and patrols, late-night transport/escort service. *Student services:* health clinic, personal/psychological counseling.
Standardized Tests *Required:* SAT or ACT (for admission).
Costs (2016–17) *Tuition:* $18,900 full-time, $525 per credit part-time. Full-time tuition and fees vary according to course load, degree level, and program. Part-time tuition and fees vary according to course load, degree level, and program. *Required fees:* $1560 full-time. *Payment plans:* installment, deferred payment. *Waivers:* employees or children of employees.
Financial Aid Of all full-time matriculated undergraduates who enrolled in 2015, 87 applied for aid, 87 were judged to have need. 7 Federal Work-Study jobs (averaging $1357). 3 state and other part-time jobs (averaging $1500). *Average percent of need met:* 80%. *Average financial aid package:* $10,078. *Average need-based loan:* $4565. *Average need-based gift aid:* $4830. *Average indebtedness upon graduation:* $11,405.
Applying *Options:* electronic application. *Application fee:* $50. *Required:* essay or personal statement, high school transcript, minimum 2.5 GPA, interview. *Application deadline:* 8/1 (freshmen). *Notification:* continuous (transfers).
Freshman Application Contact Ms. Sherry McCarthy, Admissions Coordinator, St. Luke's College, 2720 Stone Park Boulevard, Sioux City, IA 51104. *Phone:* 712-279-3149. *Toll-free phone:* 800-352-4660 Ext. 3149. *Fax:* 712-233-8017. *E-mail:* sherry.mccarthy@stlukescollege.edu.
Website: http://stlukescollege.edu/.

Scott Community College
Bettendorf, Iowa

Freshman Application Contact Mr. Gary Mohr, Executive Director of Enrollment Management and Marketing, Scott Community College, 500 Belmont Road, Bettendorf, IA 52722-6804. *Phone:* 563-336-3322. *Toll-free phone:* 800-895-0811. *Fax:* 563-336-3350. *E-mail:* gmohr@eicc.edu. *Website:* http://www.eicc.edu/scc/.

Southeastern Community College
West Burlington, Iowa

- **State and locally supported** 2-year, founded 1968, part of Iowa Department of Education Division of Community Colleges
- **Small-town** 160-acre campus
- **Coed,** 2,868 undergraduate students, 45% full-time, 58% women, 42% men

Undergraduates 1,280 full-time, 1,588 part-time. 15% are from out of state; 6% Black or African American, non-Hispanic/Latino; 5% Hispanic/Latino; 1% Asian, non-Hispanic/Latino; 0.5% American Indian or Alaska Native, non-Hispanic/Latino; 3% Two or more races, non-Hispanic/Latino; 2% Race/ethnicity unknown; 1% international; 2% transferred in; 4% live on campus.
Freshmen *Admission:* 1,055 applied, 891 admitted, 410 enrolled. *Average high school GPA:* 2.95. *Test scores:* ACT scores over 18: 75%; ACT scores over 24: 20%; ACT scores over 30: 2%.
Faculty *Total:* 129, 47% full-time, 9% with terminal degrees. *Student/faculty ratio:* 16:1.
Majors Accounting; administrative assistant and secretarial science; agricultural business and management; agronomy and crop science; artificial intelligence; automobile/automotive mechanics technology; biomedical technology; business administration and management; child development; computer programming; construction engineering technology; cosmetology; criminal justice/law enforcement administration; drafting and design technology; electrical, electronic and communications engineering technology; emergency medical technology (EMT paramedic); engineering related; industrial radiologic technology; information science/studies; liberal arts and sciences/liberal studies; licensed practical/vocational nurse training; machine tool technology; mechanical engineering/mechanical technology; medical/clinical assistant; registered nursing/registered nurse; respiratory care therapy; substance abuse/addiction counseling; trade and industrial teacher education; welding technology.
Academics *Calendar:* semesters. *Degree:* certificates, diplomas, and associate. *Special study options:* adult/continuing education programs, part-time degree program.
Library Yohe Memorial Library.

Student Life *Housing Options:* coed, men-only, special housing for students with disabilities. Campus housing is university owned. *Campus security:* controlled dormitory access, night patrols by trained security personnel.

Athletics Member NJCAA. *Intercollegiate sports:* baseball M(s), basketball M(s), softball W(s), volleyball W(s). *Intramural sports:* basketball M, bowling M/W, softball M/W, volleyball M/W, weight lifting M/W.

Costs (2015–16) *Tuition:* state resident $4740 full-time, $158 per credit hour part-time; nonresident $4890 full-time, $163 per credit hour part-time. Full-time tuition and fees vary according to course load, program, and reciprocity agreements. Part-time tuition and fees vary according to course load, program, and reciprocity agreements. *Required fees:* $50 full-time. *Room and board:* $6216. Room and board charges vary according to board plan and housing facility. *Payment plan:* installment. *Waivers:* employees or children of employees.

Financial Aid Of all full-time matriculated undergraduates who enrolled in 2014, 1,178 applied for aid, 1,119 were judged to have need. In 2014, 16 non-need-based awards were made. *Average financial aid package:* $6092. *Average need-based loan:* $3058. *Average need-based gift aid:* $4520. *Average non-need-based aid:* $2166.

Applying *Options:* early admission, deferred entrance.

Freshman Application Contact Ms. Stacy White, Admissions, Southeastern Community College, 1500 West Agency Road, West Burlington, IA 52655-0180. *Phone:* 319-752-2731 Ext. 8137. *Toll-free phone:* 866-722-4692. *E-mail:* admoff@scciowa.edu. *Website:* http://www.scciowa.edu/.

Southwestern Community College
Creston, Iowa

Freshman Application Contact Ms. Lisa Carstens, Admissions Coordinator, Southwestern Community College, 1501 West Townline Street, Creston, IA 50801. *Phone:* 641-782-7081 Ext. 453. *Toll-free phone:* 800-247-4023. *Fax:* 641-782-3312. *E-mail:* carstens@swcciowa.edu. *Website:* http://www.swcciowa.edu/.

Vatterott College
Des Moines, Iowa

Freshman Application Contact Mr. Dana Smith, Co-Director, Vatterott College, 7000 Fleur Drive, Suite 290, Des Moines, IA 50321. *Phone:* 515-309-9000. *Toll-free phone:* 888-553-6627. *Fax:* 515-309-0366. *Website:* http://www.vatterott.edu/.

Western Iowa Tech Community College
Sioux City, Iowa

- **State-supported** 2-year, founded 1966, part of Iowa Department of Education Division of Community Colleges
- **Suburban** 143-acre campus
- **Endowment** $1.7 million
- **Coed,** 6,152 undergraduate students, 37% full-time, 57% women, 43% men

Undergraduates 2,292 full-time, 3,860 part-time. Students come from 30 states and territories; 8 other countries; 10% are from out of state; 3% Black or African American, non-Hispanic/Latino; 15% Hispanic/Latino; 2% Asian, non-Hispanic/Latino; 0.2% Native Hawaiian or other Pacific Islander, non-Hispanic/Latino; 2% American Indian or Alaska Native, non-Hispanic/Latino; 2% Two or more races, non-Hispanic/Latino; 11% Race/ethnicity unknown; 0.7% international; 4% transferred in; 5% live on campus. *Retention:* 52% of full-time freshmen returned.

Freshmen *Admission:* 689 enrolled. *Test scores:* ACT scores over 18: 74%; ACT scores over 24: 12%; ACT scores over 30: 1%.

Faculty *Total:* 518, 15% full-time, 7% with terminal degrees. *Student/faculty ratio:* 16:1.

Majors Accounting; accounting technology and bookkeeping; administrative assistant and secretarial science; agricultural/farm supplies retailing and wholesaling; animation, interactive technology, video graphics and special effects; architectural engineering technology; autobody/collision and repair technology; automobile/automotive mechanics technology; biomedical technology; business administration and management; business automation/technology/data entry; carpentry; child-care provision; cinematography and film/video production; commercial photography; computer/information technology services administration related; computer programming (specific applications); criminal justice/police science; crisis/emergency/disaster management; dental assisting; desktop publishing and digital imaging design; electrician; emergency medical technology (EMT paramedic); energy management and systems technology; finance; fire science/firefighting; game and interactive media design; heating, air conditioning, ventilation and refrigeration maintenance technology; human

resources management; industrial mechanics and maintenance technology; interior design; legal assistant/paralegal; liberal arts and sciences/liberal studies; licensed practical/vocational nurse training; mechanical drafting and CAD/CADD; medical administrative assistant and medical secretary; medical/clinical assistant; medical office management; motorcycle maintenance and repair technology; multi/interdisciplinary studies related; musical instrument fabrication and repair; nursing assistant/aide and patient care assistant/aide; pharmacy technician; physical fitness technician; physical therapy technology; recording arts technology; registered nursing/registered nurse; retailing; sales, distribution, and marketing operations; securities services administration; surgical technology; teacher assistant/aide; telecommunications technology; veterinary/animal health technology; web page, digital/multimedia and information resources design; welding technology.

Academics *Calendar:* semesters. *Degree:* certificates, diplomas, and associate. *Special study options:* academic remediation for entering students, accelerated degree program, advanced placement credit, cooperative education, distance learning, double majors, English as a second language, honors programs, independent study, internships, off-campus study, part-time degree program, services for LD students, student-designed majors, study abroad, summer session for credit.

Library Western Iowa Tech Community College Library Services plus 1 other. *Books:* 17,232 (physical), 12,438 (digital/electronic). Weekly public service hours: 60.

Student Life *Housing Options:* coed. Campus housing is university owned. *Activities and Organizations:* drama/theater group, choral group, Shakespeare Overseas Traveling Club, Habitat for Humanity, Anime Club, Leadership Academy, Police Science Club. *Campus security:* 24-hour emergency response devices and patrols, controlled dormitory access. *Student services:* personal/psychological counseling.

Athletics *Intramural sports:* basketball M/W, bowling M/W, football M/W, rugby M/W, soccer M/W, softball M/W, volleyball M/W, wrestling M/W.

Standardized Tests *Recommended:* ACT (for admission), SAT or ACT (for admission).

Costs (2015–16) *Tuition:* state resident $4100 full-time, $139 per credit hour part-time; nonresident $4130 full-time, $140 per credit hour part-time. *Required fees:* $944 full-time, $32 per credit hour part-time. *Room and board:* $5355; room only: $3069.

Financial Aid Of all full-time matriculated undergraduates who enrolled in 2014, 148 Federal Work-Study jobs (averaging $1000). 2 state and other part-time jobs (averaging $2500).

Applying *Options:* electronic application, early admission, deferred entrance. *Recommended:* high school transcript. *Application deadlines:* rolling (freshmen), rolling (out-of-state freshmen), rolling (transfers). *Notification:* continuous (freshmen), continuous (out-of-state freshmen), continuous (transfers).

Freshman Application Contact Ms. Lora Vander Zwaag, Registrar, Western Iowa Tech Community College, 4647 Stone Avenue, Sioux City, IA 51106. *Phone:* 712-274-6400. *Toll-free phone:* 800-352-4649 Ext. 6403. *Fax:* 712-274-6441. *E-mail:* lora.vanderzwaag@witcc.edu. *Website:* http://www.witcc.edu/.

KANSAS

Allen Community College
Iola, Kansas

- **State and locally supported** 2-year, founded 1923, part of Kansas State Board of Regents
- **Small-town** 88-acre campus
- **Coed,** 2,383 undergraduate students

Faculty *Student/faculty ratio:* 22:1.

Majors Accounting; administrative assistant and secretarial science; agricultural production; architecture; art; athletic training; banking and financial support services; biology/biological sciences; business administration and management; business/commerce; business teacher education; chemistry; child development; computer science; computer systems networking and telecommunications; criminal justice/law enforcement administration; data processing and data processing technology; drafting and design technology; dramatic/theater arts; economics; electrical and electronics engineering; electrical, electronic and communications engineering technology; elementary education; emergency medical technology (EMT paramedic); engineering; engineering technology; equestrian studies; family and consumer sciences/human sciences; farm and ranch management; forestry; general studies; geography; health aide; health and physical education/fitness; history; home health aide/home attendant; hospital and health-care facilities administration; humanities; industrial technology; information science/studies;

journalism; language interpretation and translation; library and information science; mathematics; music; nuclear/nuclear power technology; nursing assistant/aide and patient care assistant/aide; parks, recreation and leisure facilities management; philosophy; physical therapy; physics; political science and government; pre-dentistry studies; pre-law studies; premedical studies; pre-pharmacy studies; pre-veterinary studies; psychology; religious studies; rhetoric and composition; secondary education; social work; sociology; technology/industrial arts teacher education; writing.

Academics *Calendar:* semesters. *Degree:* certificates and associate. *Special study options:* academic remediation for entering students, adult/continuing education programs, cooperative education, distance learning, English as a second language, independent study, internships, part-time degree program, services for LD students, student-designed majors, summer session for credit.

Library Learning Resource Center plus 1 other.

Student Life *Housing Options:* men-only, women-only. Campus housing is university owned. *Activities and Organizations:* drama/theater group, student-run newspaper, choral group, Intramurals, Student Senate, Theatre, Phi Theta Kappa. *Student services:* personal/psychological counseling.

Athletics Member NJCAA. *Intercollegiate sports:* baseball M(s), basketball M(s)/W(s), cheerleading M(s)/W(s), cross-country running M(s)/W(s), golf M(s), soccer M(s)/W(s), softball W(s), track and field M(s)/W(s), volleyball W(s). *Intramural sports:* basketball M/W, football M/W, soccer M/W, softball M/W, table tennis M/W, tennis M/W, volleyball M/W.

Costs (2016–17) *Tuition:* state resident $1920 full-time; nonresident $1920 full-time. *Required fees:* $1120 full-time. *Room and board:* $4830.

Financial Aid Of all full-time matriculated undergraduates who enrolled in 2008, 510 applied for aid, 411 were judged to have need, 384 had their need fully met. 40 Federal Work-Study jobs (averaging $2600). 112 state and other part-time jobs (averaging $2600). In 2008, 22 non-need-based awards were made. *Average percent of need met:* 80%. *Average financial aid package:* $4738. *Average need-based loan:* $2482. *Average need-based gift aid:* $3257. *Average non-need-based aid:* $1241.

Applying *Options:* electronic application, early admission, deferred entrance. *Required:* high school transcript. *Application deadlines:* 8/24 (freshmen), 8/24 (transfers). *Notification:* continuous (freshmen), continuous (transfers).

Freshman Application Contact Rebecca Bilderback, Director of Admissions, Allen Community College, 1801 North Cottonwood, Iola, KS 66749. *Phone:* 620-365-5116 Ext. 267. *Fax:* 620-365-7406.
E-mail: bilderback@allencc.edu.
Website: http://www.allencc.edu/.

Barton County Community College
Great Bend, Kansas

- **State and locally supported** 2-year, founded 1969, part of Kansas Board of Regents
- **Rural** 140-acre campus
- **Coed,** 5,292 undergraduate students, 37% full-time, 49% women, 51% men

Undergraduates 1,978 full-time, 3,314 part-time. 13% Black or African American, non-Hispanic/Latino; 10% Hispanic/Latino; 4% Asian, non-Hispanic/Latino; 0.9% Native Hawaiian or other Pacific Islander, non-Hispanic/Latino; 0.7% American Indian or Alaska Native, non-Hispanic/Latino; 2% Two or more races, non-Hispanic/Latino; 2% Race/ethnicity unknown; 0.5% international; 8% live on campus.

Freshmen *Admission:* 2,646 enrolled.

Faculty *Total:* 233, 30% full-time, 3% with terminal degrees. *Student/faculty ratio:* 25:1.

Majors Accounting; administrative assistant and secretarial science; agricultural business and management; agriculture; anthropology; architecture; art; athletic training; automobile/automotive mechanics technology; banking and financial support services; biology/biological sciences; business administration and management; chemistry; child-care and support services management; chiropractic assistant; clinical/medical laboratory technology; computer/information technology services administration related; computer programming (specific applications); computer science; computer systems networking and telecommunications; corrections; criminal justice/police science; crop production; cytotechnology; dance; dental hygiene; dietitian assistant; dramatic/theater arts; early childhood education; economics; elementary education; emergency care attendant (EMT ambulance); emergency medical technology (EMT paramedic); engineering technology; English; financial planning and services; fire science/firefighting; forestry; funeral service and mortuary science; general studies; geology/earth science; graphic design; hazardous materials management and waste technology; health aides/attendants/orderlies related; health and medical administrative services related; health information/medical records administration; history; home health aide/home attendant; homeland security, law enforcement, firefighting and protective services related; human resources management; human resources management and services related; industrial production technologies

related; information science/studies; journalism; kinesiology and exercise science; liberal arts and sciences/liberal studies; licensed practical/vocational nurse training; livestock management; logistics, materials, and supply chain management; marketing/marketing management; mathematics; medical administrative assistant and medical secretary; medical/clinical assistant; medical insurance coding; medical office assistant; medical transcription; medication aide; military studies; modern languages; music; nursing assistant/aide and patient care assistant/aide; occupational therapy; optometric technician; pharmacy; pharmacy technician; philosophy; phlebotomy technology; physical education teaching and coaching; physical sciences; physical therapy; physical therapy technology; physician assistant; physics; political science and government; pre-dentistry studies; pre-engineering; pre-law studies; premedical studies; pre-veterinary studies; psychology; public administration; radiologic technology/science; registered nursing/registered nurse; religious studies; respiratory care therapy; secondary education; social work; sociology; speech communication and rhetoric; sport and fitness administration/management; wildlife, fish and wildlands science and management.

Academics *Calendar:* semesters. *Degree:* certificates and associate. *Special study options:* academic remediation for entering students, accelerated degree program, adult/continuing education programs, advanced placement credit, cooperative education, distance learning, double majors, English as a second language, external degree program, honors programs, independent study, internships, part-time degree program, services for LD students, summer session for credit. *ROTC:* Army (b).

Library Barton County Community College Library.

Student Life *Housing Options:* coed, special housing for students with disabilities. Campus housing is university owned. Freshman campus housing is guaranteed. *Activities and Organizations:* drama/theater group, student-run newspaper, choral group, Danceline, Business Professionals, Psychology Club, Agriculture Club, Cougarettes. *Campus security:* 24-hour emergency response devices and patrols. *Student services:* health clinic, personal/psychological counseling.

Athletics Member NJCAA. *Intercollegiate sports:* baseball M(s), basketball M(s)/W(s), cheerleading M(s)/W(s), cross-country running M(s)/W(s), golf M(s)/W(s), soccer M(s)/W(s), softball W(s), tennis M(s)/W(s), track and field M(s)/W(s), volleyball W(s), wrestling M(s). *Intramural sports:* basketball M/W, bowling M/W, football M/W, golf M/W, softball M/W, swimming and diving M/W, table tennis M/W, tennis M/W, track and field M/W, volleyball M/W.

Costs (2015–16) *Tuition:* state resident $2040 full-time, $68 per credit hour part-time; nonresident $2970 full-time, $99 per credit hour part-time. Full-time tuition and fees vary according to course load. Part-time tuition and fees vary according to course load. *Required fees:* $960 full-time, $32 per credit hour part-time. *Room and board:* $7705. Room and board charges vary according to board plan. *Payment plans:* installment, deferred payment. *Waivers:* senior citizens and employees or children of employees.

Applying *Options:* electronic application, early admission. *Recommended:* high school transcript. *Application deadlines:* rolling (freshmen), rolling (transfers).

Freshman Application Contact Ms. Tana Cooper, Director of Admissions and Promotions, Barton County Community College, 245 Northeast 30th Road, Great Bend, KS 67530. *Phone:* 620-792-9241. *Toll-free phone:* 800-722-6842. *Fax:* 620-786-1160. *E-mail:* admissions@bartonccc.edu. *Website:* http://www.bartonccc.edu/.

Brown Mackie College–Kansas City
Lenexa, Kansas

Freshman Application Contact Brown Mackie College–Kansas City, 9705 Lenexa Drive, Lenexa, KS 66215. *Phone:* 913-768-1900. *Toll-free phone:* 800-635-9101.
Website: http://www.brownmackie.edu/kansascity/.

Brown Mackie College–Salina
Salina, Kansas

Freshman Application Contact Brown Mackie College–Salina, 2106 South 9th Street, Salina, KS 67401. *Phone:* 785-825-5422. *Toll-free phone:* 800-365-0433.
Website: http://www.brownmackie.edu/salina/.

Bryan University
Topeka, Kansas

Admissions Office Contact Bryan University, 1527 SW Fairlawn Road, Topeka, KS 66604.
Website: http://www.bryanu.edu/.

Butler Community College
El Dorado, Kansas

Freshman Application Contact Mr. Glenn Lygrisse, Interim Director of Enrollment Management, Butler Community College, 901 South Haverhill Road, El Dorado, KS 67042. *Phone:* 316-321-2222. *Fax:* 316-322-3109. *E-mail:* admissions@butlercc.edu. *Website:* http://www.butlercc.edu/.

Cloud County Community College
Concordia, Kansas

- **State and locally supported** 2-year, founded 1965, part of Kansas Community College System
- **Rural** 35-acre campus
- **Coed,** 2,294 undergraduate students

Undergraduates Students come from 17 states and territories; 13 other countries; 8% are from out of state. *Retention:* 56% of full-time freshmen returned.
Faculty *Total:* 306, 19% full-time. *Student/faculty ratio:* 20:1.
Majors Administrative assistant and secretarial science; agricultural business and management; agricultural/farm supplies retailing and wholesaling; business administration and management; business, management, and marketing related; child-care and support services management; child development; criminal justice/police science; graphic design; journalism; legal assistant/paralegal; liberal arts and sciences/liberal studies; mechanic and repair technologies related; office occupations and clerical services; radio and television broadcasting technology; registered nursing/registered nurse; system, networking, and LAN/WAN management; teacher assistant/aide; web page, digital/multimedia and information resources design.
Academics *Calendar:* semesters. *Degree:* certificates, diplomas, and associate. *Special study options:* academic remediation for entering students, adult/continuing education programs, advanced placement credit, cooperative education, distance learning, honors programs, internships, part-time degree program, services for LD students, summer session for credit.
Student Life *Activities and Organizations:* drama/theater group, student-run newspaper, radio station, choral group. *Campus security:* 24-hour emergency response devices. *Student services:* health clinic.
Athletics Member NJCAA. *Intercollegiate sports:* baseball M(s), basketball M(s)/W(s), cross-country running M(s)/W(s), soccer M(s), softball W(s), tennis M(s)/W(s), track and field M(s)/W(s), volleyball W(s). *Intramural sports:* baseball M, basketball M/W, softball W, volleyball M/W.
Costs (2015–16) *Tuition:* area resident $2070 full-time, $69 per credit hour part-time; state resident $2220 full-time, $74 per credit hour part-time; nonresident $2370 full-time, $79 per credit hour part-time. Full-time tuition and fees vary according to course level, course load, location, reciprocity agreements, and student level. Part-time tuition and fees vary according to course level, course load, location, reciprocity agreements, and student level. *Required fees:* $750 full-time. *Room and board:* $5800. Room and board charges vary according to board plan and housing facility. *Payment plan:* installment. *Waivers:* senior citizens and employees or children of employees.
Financial Aid Of all full-time matriculated undergraduates who enrolled in 2014, 122 Federal Work-Study jobs (averaging $800).
Applying *Options:* early admission, deferred entrance. *Required:* high school transcript. *Application deadlines:* 9/11 (freshmen), 9/11 (transfers). *Notification:* continuous (freshmen), continuous (transfers).
Freshman Application Contact Cloud County Community College, 2221 Campus Drive, PO Box 1002, Concordia, KS 66901-1002. *Phone:* 785-243-1435 Ext. 213. *Toll-free phone:* 800-729-5101. *Website:* http://www.cloud.edu/.

Coffeyville Community College
Coffeyville, Kansas

Freshman Application Contact Stacia Meek, Admissions Counselor/Marketing Event Coordinator, Coffeyville Community College, 400 West 11th Street, Coffeyville, KS 67337-5063. *Phone:* 620-252-7100. *Toll-free phone:* 877-51-RAVEN. *E-mail:* staciam@coffeyville.edu. *Website:* http://www.coffeyville.edu/.

Colby Community College
Colby, Kansas

Freshman Application Contact Ms. Nikol Nolan, Admissions Director, Colby Community College, Colby, KS 67701-4099. *Phone:* 785-462-3984 Ext. 5496. *Toll-free phone:* 888-634-9350. *Fax:* 785-460-4691. *E-mail:* admissions@colbycc.edu. *Website:* http://www.colbycc.edu/.

Cowley County Community College and Area Vocational–Technical School
Arkansas City, Kansas

Freshman Application Contact Ms. Lory West, Director of Admissions, Cowley County Community College and Area Vocational–Technical School, PO Box 1147, Arkansas City, KS 67005. *Phone:* 620-441-5594. *Toll-free phone:* 800-593-CCCC. *Fax:* 620-441-5350. *E-mail:* admissions@cowley.edu. *Website:* http://www.cowley.edu/.

Dodge City Community College
Dodge City, Kansas

- **State and locally supported** 2-year, founded 1935, part of Kansas State Board of Regents
- **Small-town** 143-acre campus
- **Coed,** 1,779 undergraduate students, 54% full-time, 45% women, 55% men

Undergraduates 957 full-time, 822 part-time. 9% Black or African American, non-Hispanic/Latino; 39% Hispanic/Latino; 1% Asian, non-Hispanic/Latino; 0.1% Native Hawaiian or other Pacific Islander, non-Hispanic/Latino; 1% American Indian or Alaska Native, non-Hispanic/Latino; 2% Two or more races, non-Hispanic/Latino; 0.1% Race/ethnicity unknown; 20% live on campus.
Faculty *Total:* 201, 29% full-time. *Student/faculty ratio:* 12:1.
Majors Accounting; administrative assistant and secretarial science; agricultural business and management; agricultural economics; agricultural mechanization; agronomy and crop science; animal sciences; art; athletic training; automobile/automotive mechanics technology; behavioral sciences; biological and physical sciences; biology/biological sciences; broadcast journalism; business administration and management; chemistry; child development; clinical laboratory science/medical technology; communications technology; computer programming; computer science; construction engineering technology; cosmetology; criminal justice/law enforcement administration; data processing and data processing technology; dramatic/theater arts; education; electrical, electronic and communications engineering technology; elementary education; engineering; engineering technology; English; equestrian studies; farm and ranch management; finance; fire science/firefighting; forestry; health information/medical records administration; history; humanities; hydrology and water resources science; industrial technology; information science/studies; journalism; legal administrative assistant/secretary; liberal arts and sciences/liberal studies; licensed practical/vocational nurse training; marketing/marketing management; mass communication/media; mathematics; medical administrative assistant and medical secretary; music; music teacher education; physical education teaching and coaching; physical sciences; physical therapy; physics; political science and government; pre-engineering; pre-pharmacy studies; psychology; radio and television; real estate; registered nursing/registered nurse; respiratory care therapy; rhetoric and composition; social sciences; social work; welding technology; wildlife biology.
Academics *Calendar:* semesters. *Degree:* certificates and associate. *Special study options:* academic remediation for entering students, adult/continuing education programs, advanced placement credit, cooperative education, distance learning, English as a second language, external degree program, internships, off-campus study, part-time degree program, services for LD students, summer session for credit.
Library Learning Resource Center. Students can reserve study rooms.
Student Life *Housing:* on-campus residence required for freshman year. *Options:* men-only, women-only. Campus housing is university owned. Freshman applicants given priority for college housing. *Activities and Organizations:* student-run radio station, choral group. *Campus security:* 24-hour emergency response devices and patrols, late-night transport/escort service, controlled dormitory access. *Student services:* personal/psychological counseling.
Athletics Member NJCAA. *Intercollegiate sports:* baseball M(s), basketball M(s)/W(s), cheerleading M(s)/W(s), cross-country running M(s)/W(s), football M(s), golf M(s)/W(s), soccer M(s)/W(s), softball W(s), track and field M(s)/W(s), volleyball W(s). *Intramural sports:* basketball M/W, bowling M/W, racquetball M/W, volleyball M/W, weight lifting M/W.
Standardized Tests *Recommended:* ACT (for admission), SAT or ACT (for admission).
Costs (2016–17) *One-time required fee:* $50. *Tuition:* area resident $900 full-time, $30 per credit part-time; state resident $1410 full-time, $47 per credit part-time; nonresident $1650 full-time, $55 per credit part-time. *Required fees:* $1800 full-time, $40 per credit hour part-time, $25 per term part-time. *Room and board:* $6386. Room and board charges vary according to board plan. *Payment plans:* installment, deferred payment. *Waivers:* senior citizens and employees or children of employees.

Applying *Options:* electronic application, early admission, deferred entrance. *Required:* high school transcript. *Application deadlines:* rolling (freshmen), rolling (out-of-state freshmen), rolling (transfers). *Notification:* continuous (freshmen), continuous (out-of-state freshmen), continuous (transfers). **Freshman Application Contact** Dodge City Community College, 2501 North 14th Avenue, Dodge City, KS 67801-2399. *Phone:* 620-225-1321. *Website:* http://www.dc3.edu/.

Donnelly College
Kansas City, Kansas

- **Independent Roman Catholic** primarily 2-year, founded 1949
- **Urban** 4-acre campus
- **Coed,** 262 undergraduate students, 75% full-time, 68% women, 32% men

Undergraduates 196 full-time, 66 part-time. Students come from 2 states and territories; 24 other countries; 34% are from out of state; 29% Black or African American, non-Hispanic/Latino; 48% Hispanic/Latino; 5% Asian, non-Hispanic/Latino; 5% Two or more races, non-Hispanic/Latino; 5% international; 2% transferred in; 13% live on campus. *Retention:* 37% of full-time freshmen returned.
Freshmen *Admission:* 73 enrolled.
Faculty *Total:* 49, 45% full-time. *Student/faculty ratio:* 10:1.
Majors Computer and information systems security; elementary education; liberal arts and sciences/liberal studies; nonprofit management.
Academics *Calendar:* semesters. *Degrees:* certificates, associate, and bachelor's. *Special study options:* academic remediation for entering students, advanced placement credit, distance learning, English as a second language, external degree program, honors programs, independent study, part-time degree program, services for LD students, summer session for credit.
Library Trant Memorial Library plus 1 other.
Student Life *Housing Options:* men-only, women-only. Campus housing is university owned and is provided by a third party. *Activities and Organizations:* Organization of Student Leadership, Student Ambassadors, Healthy Student Task Force, Men's Soccer Club, Women's Soccer Club. *Campus security:* 24-hour emergency response devices. *Student services:* personal/psychological counseling.
Standardized Tests *Recommended:* ACT (for admission).
Costs (2015–16) *Comprehensive fee:* $14,362 includes full-time tuition ($6822), mandatory fees ($102), and room and board ($7438). Full-time tuition and fees vary according to course level, degree level, and program. Part-time tuition and fees vary according to course level. *Room and board:* Room and board charges vary according to housing facility. *Waivers:* employees or children of employees.
Applying *Options:* electronic application, early admission, deferred entrance. *Recommended:* high school transcript. *Application deadlines:* rolling (freshmen), rolling (transfers).
Freshman Application Contact Ms. Sydney Beeler, Vice President of Enrollment and Student Affairs, Donnelly College, 608 North 18th Street, Kansas City, KS 66102. *Phone:* 913-621-8713. *Fax:* 913-621-8719. *E-mail:* admissions@donnelly.edu. *Website:* http://www.donnelly.edu/.

Flint Hills Technical College
Emporia, Kansas

Freshman Application Contact Admissions Office, Flint Hills Technical College, 3301 West 18th Avenue, Emporia, KS 66801. *Phone:* 620-341-1325. *Toll-free phone:* 800-711-6947. *Website:* http://www.fhtc.edu/.

Fort Scott Community College
Fort Scott, Kansas

Director of Admissions Mrs. Mert Barrows, Director of Admissions, Fort Scott Community College, 2108 South Horton, Fort Scott, KS 66701. *Phone:* 620-223-2700 Ext. 353. *Toll-free phone:* 800-874-3722. *Website:* http://www.fortscott.edu/.

Garden City Community College
Garden City, Kansas

Freshman Application Contact Office of Admissions, Garden City Community College, 801 Campus Drive, Garden City, KS 67846. *Phone:* 620-276-9531. *Toll-free phone:* 800-658-1696. *Fax:* 620-276-9650. *E-mail:* admissions@gcccks.edu. *Website:* http://www.gcccks.edu/.

Heritage College
Wichita, Kansas

Admissions Office Contact Heritage College, 2800 South Rock Road, Wichita, KS 67210. *Toll-free phone:* 888-334-7339. *Website:* http://www.heritagecollege.edu/.

Hesston College
Hesston, Kansas

- **Independent Mennonite** primarily 2-year, founded 1909
- **Small-town** 50-acre campus with easy access to Wichita
- **Coed,** 409 undergraduate students, 87% full-time, 62% women, 38% men

Undergraduates 356 full-time, 53 part-time. Students come from 33 states and territories; 14 other countries; 54% are from out of state; 6% Black or African American, non-Hispanic/Latino; 11% Hispanic/Latino; 2% Asian, non-Hispanic/Latino; 0.2% American Indian or Alaska Native, non-Hispanic/Latino; 3% Two or more races, non-Hispanic/Latino; 0.2% Race/ethnicity unknown; 11% international; 11% transferred in; 72% live on campus. *Retention:* 76% of full-time freshmen returned.
Freshmen *Admission:* 522 applied, 337 admitted, 167 enrolled. *Average high school GPA:* 3.45. *Test scores:* SAT critical reading scores over 500: 48%; SAT math scores over 500: 44%; SAT writing scores over 500: 30%; ACT scores over 18: 87%; SAT critical reading scores over 600: 17%; SAT math scores over 600: 20%; SAT writing scores over 600: 11%; ACT scores over 24: 35%; SAT math scores over 700: 9%; SAT writing scores over 700: 2%; ACT scores over 30: 8%.
Faculty *Total:* 56, 57% full-time, 16% with terminal degrees. *Student/faculty ratio:* 9:1.
Majors Aeronautics/aviation/aerospace science and technology; airline pilot and flight crew; air traffic control; biblical studies; business administration and management; computer/information technology services administration related; early childhood education; general studies; kindergarten/preschool education; liberal arts and sciences/liberal studies; pastoral studies/counseling; registered nursing/registered nurse; youth ministry.
Academics *Calendar:* semesters. *Degrees:* associate and bachelor's. *Special study options:* academic remediation for entering students, adult/continuing education programs, advanced placement credit, cooperative education, double majors, English as a second language, independent study, internships, part-time degree program, services for LD students, summer session for credit.
Library Mary Miller Library.
Student Life *Housing:* on-campus residence required through sophomore year. *Options:* men-only, women-only. Campus housing is university owned. Freshman campus housing is guaranteed. *Activities and Organizations:* drama/theater group, student-run newspaper, choral group, Peace and Service Club, Intramural Sports, Ministry Assistants. *Campus security:* 24-hour emergency response devices, controlled dormitory access. *Student services:* health clinic, personal/psychological counseling, women's center.
Athletics Member NJCAA. *Intercollegiate sports:* baseball M(s), basketball M(s)/W(s), cross-country running M(s)/W(s), golf M, soccer M(s)/W(s), softball W(s), tennis M(s)/W(s), volleyball W(s). *Intramural sports:* basketball M/W, golf M(c)/W(c), soccer M/W, ultimate Frisbee M/W, volleyball M/W.
Standardized Tests *Required:* SAT or ACT (for admission).
Costs (2015–16) *Comprehensive fee:* $36,034 includes full-time tuition ($24,824), mandatory fees ($410), and room and board ($10,800). Full-time tuition and fees vary according to course load and program. Part-time tuition: $1034 per credit hour. Part-time tuition and fees vary according to course load. *Payment plans:* installment, deferred payment. *Waivers:* employees or children of employees.
Financial Aid Of all full-time matriculated undergraduates who enrolled in 2014, 120 Federal Work-Study jobs (averaging $800).
Applying *Options:* electronic application, early admission, deferred entrance. *Application fee:* $15. *Required:* high school transcript, 2 letters of recommendation. *Required for some:* interview. *Application deadlines:* rolling (freshmen), rolling (out-of-state freshmen), rolling (transfers).
Freshman Application Contact Rachel Swartzendruber-Miller, Vice President of Admissions, Hesston College, Hesston, KS 67062. *Phone:* 620-327-8206. *Toll-free phone:* 800-995-2757. *Fax:* 620-327-8300. *E-mail:* admissions@hesston.edu. *Website:* http://www.hesston.edu/.

Highland Community College
Highland, Kansas

Director of Admissions Ms. Cheryl Rasmussen, Vice President of Student Services, Highland Community College, 606 West Main Street, Highland, KS 66035. *Phone:* 785-442-6020. *Fax:* 785-442-6106. *Website:* http://www.highlandcc.edu/.

Hutchinson Community College
Hutchinson, Kansas

- **State and locally supported** 2-year, founded 1928, part of Kansas Board of Regents
- **Small-town** 47-acre campus with easy access to Wichita
- **Coed,** 5,546 undergraduate students, 39% full-time, 55% women, 45% men

Undergraduates 2,149 full-time, 3,397 part-time. Students come from 45 states and territories; 6 other countries; 9% are from out of state; 8% Black or African American, non-Hispanic/Latino; 9% Hispanic/Latino; 0.7% Asian, non-Hispanic/Latino; 0.1% Native Hawaiian or other Pacific Islander, non-Hispanic/Latino; 1% American Indian or Alaska Native, non-Hispanic/Latino; 0.3% Two or more races, non-Hispanic/Latino; 7% Race/ethnicity unknown; 0.7% international; 6% transferred in; 8% live on campus.

Freshmen *Admission:* 1,206 applied, 1,206 admitted, 1,004 enrolled. *Average high school GPA:* 3.1. *Test scores:* ACT scores over 18: 74%; ACT scores over 24: 20%; ACT scores over 30: 2%.

Faculty *Total:* 406, 27% full-time, 4% with terminal degrees. *Student/faculty ratio:* 16:1.

Majors Administrative assistant and secretarial science; agricultural mechanics and equipment technology; agriculture; architectural drafting and CAD/CADD; autobody/collision and repair technology; automobile/automotive mechanics technology; biology/biological sciences; biology/biotechnology laboratory technician; business and personal/financial services marketing; business/commerce; carpentry; child-care and support services management; clinical/medical laboratory technology; communications technology; computer and information sciences; computer systems analysis; computer systems networking and telecommunications; criminal justice/police science; design and visual communications; drafting and design technology; drama and dance teacher education; education; electrical, electronic and communications engineering technology; electrical/electronics equipment installation and repair; emergency medical technology (EMT paramedic); engineering; English; family and consumer sciences/human sciences; farm and ranch management; fire science/firefighting; foreign languages and literatures; graphic communications; health information/medical records technology; legal assistant/paralegal; liberal arts and sciences/liberal studies; machine tool technology; manufacturing engineering technology; mathematics; mechanical drafting and CAD/CADD; medical radiologic technology; natural resources management and policy; pharmacy technician; physical sciences; physical therapy technology; psychology; radio and television broadcasting technology; radiologic technology/science; registered nursing/registered nurse; respiratory care therapy; respiratory therapy technician; retailing; social sciences; speech communication and rhetoric; sport and fitness administration/management; surgical technology; visual and performing arts; web page, digital/multimedia and information resources design; welding technology.

Academics *Calendar:* semesters. *Degree:* certificates and associate. *Special study options:* academic remediation for entering students, advanced placement credit, cooperative education, distance learning, double majors, English as a second language, honors programs, independent study, internships, part-time degree program, services for LD students, summer session for credit.

Library John F. Kennedy Library plus 1 other. *Books:* 41,545 (physical), 14,112 (digital/electronic); *Serial titles:* 203 (physical); *Databases:* 28. Weekly public service hours: 69.

Student Life *Housing Options:* men-only, women-only. Campus housing is university owned. *Activities and Organizations:* drama/theater group, student-run newspaper, choral group, CKI (Circle K), Social Dance Club, SPARK (non-denominational religious group), DragonLAN, Chess Club. *Campus security:* 24-hour emergency response devices and patrols, student patrols, late-night transport/escort service, controlled dormitory access. *Student services:* health clinic, personal/psychological counseling.

Athletics Member NJCAA. *Intercollegiate sports:* baseball M(s), basketball M(s)/W(s), cheerleading M(s)/W(s), cross-country running M(s)/W(s), football M(s), golf M(s), soccer W(s), softball W(s), track and field M(s)/W(s), volleyball W(s). *Intramural sports:* basketball M/W, football M/W, soccer M/W, table tennis M/W, tennis M/W, volleyball M/W.

Costs (2016–17) *Tuition:* area resident $2368 full-time, $74 per credit hour part-time; state resident $2688 full-time, $84 per credit hour part-time; nonresident $3680 full-time, $124 per credit hour part-time. *Required fees:* $608 full-time, $19 per credit hour part-time. *Room and board:* $5600. Room and board charges vary according to board plan and housing facility. *Payment plan:* installment. *Waivers:* employees or children of employees.

Applying *Options:* electronic application, early admission, deferred entrance. *Required:* high school transcript. *Required for some:* interview. *Application deadlines:* rolling (freshmen), rolling (out-of-state freshmen), rolling (transfers). *Notification:* continuous (freshmen), continuous (out-of-state freshmen), continuous (transfers).

Freshman Application Contact Mr. Corbin Strobel, Director of Admissions, Hutchinson Community College, 1300 North Plum, Hutchinson, KS 67501. *Phone:* 620-665-3536. *Toll-free phone:* 888-GO-HUTCH. *Fax:* 620-665-3301. *E-mail:* strobelc@hutchcc.edu.
Website: http://www.hutchcc.edu/.

Independence Community College
Independence, Kansas

Freshman Application Contact Ms. Brittany Thornton, Admissions Coordinator, Independence Community College, PO Box 708, 1057 W. College Avenue, Independence, KS 673001. *Phone:* 620-332-5495. *Toll-free phone:* 800-842-6063. *Fax:* 620-331-0946. *E-mail:* bthornton@indycc.edu.
Website: http://www.indycc.edu/.

Johnson County Community College
Overland Park, Kansas

Director of Admissions Dr. Charles J. Carlsen, President, Johnson County Community College, 12345 College Boulevard, Overland Park, KS 66210-1299. *Phone:* 913-469-8500 Ext. 3806.
Website: http://www.johnco.cc.ks.us/.

Kansas City Kansas Community College
Kansas City, Kansas

Freshman Application Contact Dr. Denise McDowell, Dean of Enrollment Management/Registrar, Kansas City Kansas Community College, Admissions Office, 7250 State Avenue, Kansas City, KS 66112. *Phone:* 913-288-7694. *Fax:* 913-288-7648. *E-mail:* dmcdowell@kckcc.edu.
Website: http://www.kckcc.edu/.

Labette Community College
Parsons, Kansas

Freshman Application Contact Ms. Tammy Fuentez, Director of Admission, Labette Community College, 200 South 14th Street, Parsons, KS 67357-4299. *Phone:* 620-421-6700. *Toll-free phone:* 888-522-3883. *Fax:* 620-421-0180.
Website: http://www.labette.edu/.

Manhattan Area Technical College
Manhattan, Kansas

- **State and locally supported** 2-year, founded 1965
- **Rural** 18-acre campus
- **Coed,** 870 undergraduate students, 46% full-time, 50% women, 50% men

Undergraduates 404 full-time, 466 part-time. Students come from 8 states and territories; 0.8% are from out of state; 5% Black or African American, non-Hispanic/Latino; 7% Hispanic/Latino; 2% Asian, non-Hispanic/Latino; 0.3% Native Hawaiian or other Pacific Islander, non-Hispanic/Latino; 0.6% American Indian or Alaska Native, non-Hispanic/Latino; 5% Two or more races, non-Hispanic/Latino; 1% Race/ethnicity unknown; 0.1% international; 12% transferred in. *Retention:* 23% of full-time freshmen returned.

Freshmen *Admission:* 62 admitted, 62 enrolled. *Test scores:* ACT scores over 18: 72%; ACT scores over 24: 17%; ACT scores over 30: 2%.

Faculty *Total:* 84, 33% full-time, 5% with terminal degrees. *Student/faculty ratio:* 12:1.

Majors Accounting technology and bookkeeping; administrative assistant and secretarial science; autobody/collision and repair technology; automobile/automotive mechanics technology; biology/biotechnology laboratory technician; building/construction finishing, management, and inspection related; building/property maintenance; CAD/CADD drafting/design technology; carpentry; clinical/medical laboratory technology; computer systems networking and telecommunications; computer technology/computer systems technology; drafting and design technology; electrical and power transmission installation; electrical and power transmission installation related; heating, air conditioning, ventilation and refrigeration maintenance technology; heating, ventilation, air conditioning and refrigeration engineering technology; licensed practical/vocational nurse training; management information systems; medical office assistant; multi/interdisciplinary studies related; network and system administration; registered nursing/registered nurse; welding technology.

Academics *Calendar:* semesters. *Degree:* certificates and associate. *Special study options:* academic remediation for entering students, adult/continuing education programs, advanced placement credit, cooperative education, distance learning, double majors, honors programs, internships, part-time degree program, services for LD students, student-designed majors, summer session for credit.

Library MATC Library. *Books:* 2,031 (physical), 3,665 (digital/electronic); *Databases:* 42. Weekly public service hours: 50.

Student Life *Housing:* college housing not available. *Campus security:* late-night transport/escort service, evening security guards.

Standardized Tests *Required:* SAT, ACT or ACT Compass (for admission).

Costs (2015–16) *Tuition:* state resident $3895 full-time, $100 per credit hour part-time; nonresident $3895 full-time, $100 per credit hour part-time. Full-time tuition and fees vary according to program. Part-time tuition and fees vary according to program. *Required fees:* $1000 full-time, $30 per credit hour part-time. *Payment plan:* installment. *Waivers:* employees or children of employees.

Applying *Options:* electronic application. *Application fee:* $40. *Required:* high school transcript. *Required for some:* essay or personal statement, 3 letters of recommendation, interview, specific admission criteria for pre-allied health programs, Class A CDL for electric power and distribution program. *Application deadlines:* rolling (freshmen), rolling (out-of-state freshmen), rolling (transfers).

Freshman Application Contact Mr. Neil Ross, Director of Admissions, Manhattan Area Technical College, 3136 Dickens Avenue, Manhattan, KS 66503. *Phone:* 785-320-4554. *Toll-free phone:* 800-352-7575. *Fax:* 785-587-2804. *E-mail:* neilross@manhattantech.edu.
Website: http://www.manhattantech.edu/.

National American University
Overland Park, Kansas

Freshman Application Contact Admissions Office, National American University, 10310 Mastin Street, Overland Park, KS 66212.
Website: http://www.national.edu/.

Neosho County Community College
Chanute, Kansas

Freshman Application Contact Ms. Lisa Last, Dean of Student Development, Neosho County Community College, 800 West 14th Street, Chanute, KS 66720. *Phone:* 620-431-2820 Ext. 213. *Toll-free phone:* 800-729-6222. *Fax:* 620-431-0082. *E-mail:* llast@neosho.edu.
Website: http://www.neosho.edu/.

North Central Kansas Technical College
Beloit, Kansas

Freshman Application Contact Ms. Judy Heidrick, Director of Admissions, North Central Kansas Technical College, PO Box 507, 3033 US Highway 24, Beloit, KS 67420. *Toll-free phone:* 800-658-4655.
E-mail: jheidrick@ncktc.tec.ks.us.
Website: http://www.ncktc.edu/.

Northwest Kansas Technical College
Goodland, Kansas

Admissions Office Contact Northwest Kansas Technical College, PO Box 668, 1209 Harrison Street, Goodland, KS 67735. *Toll-free phone:* 800-316-4127.
Website: http://www.nwktc.edu/.

Pinnacle Career Institute
Lawrence, Kansas

Admissions Office Contact Pinnacle Career Institute, 1601 West 23rd Street, Suite 200, Lawrence, KS 66046-2743. *Toll-free phone:* 877-241-3097.
Website: http://www.pcitraining.edu/.

Pratt Community College
Pratt, Kansas

Freshman Application Contact Ms. Theresa Ziehr, Office Assistant, Student Services, Pratt Community College, 348 Northeast State Road 61, Pratt, KS 67124. *Phone:* 620-450-2217. *Toll-free phone:* 800-794-3091. *Fax:* 620-672-5288. *E-mail:* theresaz@prattcc.edu.
Website: http://www.prattcc.edu/.

Salina Area Technical College
Salina, Kansas

Admissions Office Contact Salina Area Technical College, 2562 Centennial Road, Salina, KS 67401.
Website: http://www.salinatech.edu/.

Seward County Community College and Area Technical School
Liberal, Kansas

Director of Admissions Dr. Gerald Harris, Dean of Student Services, Seward County Community College and Area Technical School, PO Box 1137, Liberal, KS 67905-1137. *Phone:* 620-624-1951 Ext. 617. *Toll-free phone:* 800-373-9951.
Website: http://www.sccc.edu/.

Vatterott College
Wichita, Kansas

Admissions Office Contact Vatterott College, 8853 37th Street North, Wichita, KS 67226.
Website: http://www.vatterott.edu/.

Wichita Area Technical College
Wichita, Kansas

Freshman Application Contact Mr. Andy McFayden, Director, Admissions, Wichita Area Technical College, 4004 N. Webb Road, Suite 100, Wichita, KS 67226 . *Phone:* 316-677-9400. *Fax:* 316-677-9555. *E-mail:* info@watc.edu.
Website: http://www.watc.edu/.

Wichita Technical Institute
Wichita, Kansas

Admissions Office Contact Wichita Technical Institute, 2051 S. Meridian Avenue, Wichita, KS 67213.
Website: http://www.wti.edu/.

KENTUCKY

Ashland Community and Technical College
Ashland, Kentucky

Freshman Application Contact Ashland Community and Technical College, 1400 College Drive, Ashland, KY 41101-3683. *Phone:* 606-326-2008. *Toll-free phone:* 800-928-4256.
Website: http://www.ashland.kctcs.edu/.

ATA College
Louisville, Kentucky

Freshman Application Contact Admissions Office, ATA College, 10180 Linn Station Road, Suite A200, Louisville, KY 40223. *Phone:* 502-371-8330. *Fax:* 502-371-8598.
Website: http://www.ata.edu/.

Beckfield College
Florence, Kentucky

- **Proprietary** primarily 2-year, founded 1984
- **Suburban** campus
- **Coed**, 605 undergraduate students

Majors Business administration and management; computer systems networking and telecommunications; legal assistant/paralegal; medical office management; registered nursing/registered nurse.

Academics *Calendar:* quarters. *Degrees:* certificates, diplomas, associate, bachelor's, and postbachelor's certificates.

Student Life *Housing:* college housing not available.

Applying *Application fee:* $150.
Freshman Application Contact Mrs. Leah Boerger, Director of Admissions, Beckfield College, 16 Spiral Drive, Florence, KY 41042. *Phone:* 859-371-9393. *E-mail:* lboerger@beckfield.edu.
Website: http://www.beckfield.edu/.

Big Sandy Community and Technical College
Prestonsburg, Kentucky

Director of Admissions Jimmy Wright, Director of Admissions, Big Sandy Community and Technical College, One Bert T. Combs Drive, Prestonsburg, KY 41653-1815. *Phone:* 606-886-3863. *Toll-free phone:* 888-641-4132. *E-mail:* jimmy.wright@kctcs.edu.
Website: http://www.bigsandy.kctcs.edu/.

Bluegrass Community and Technical College
Lexington, Kentucky

Freshman Application Contact Mrs. Shelbie Hugle, Director of Admission Services, Bluegrass Community and Technical College, 470 Cooper Drive, Lexington, KY 40506. *Phone:* 859-246-6216. *Toll-free phone:* 800-744-4872 (in-state); 866-744-4872 (out-of-state). *E-mail:* shelbie.hugle@kctcs.edu.
Website: http://www.bluegrass.kctcs.edu/.

Brown Mackie College–Hopkinsville
Hopkinsville, Kentucky

Freshman Application Contact Brown Mackie College–Hopkinsville, 4001 Fort Cambell Boulevard, Hopkinsville, KY 42240. *Phone:* 270-886-1302. *Toll-free phone:* 800-359-4753.
Website: http://www.brownmackie.edu/Hopkinsville/.

Brown Mackie College–Louisville
Louisville, Kentucky

Freshman Application Contact Brown Mackie College–Louisville, 3605 Fern Valley Road, Louisville, KY 40219. *Phone:* 502-968-7191. *Toll-free phone:* 800-999-7387.
Website: http://www.brownmackie.edu/louisville/.

Brown Mackie College–Northern Kentucky
Fort Mitchell, Kentucky

Freshman Application Contact Brown Mackie College–Northern Kentucky, 309 Buttermilk Pike, Fort Mitchell, KY 41017. *Phone:* 859-341-5627. *Toll-free phone:* 800-888-1445.
Website: http://www.brownmackie.edu/northernkentucky/.

Daymar College
Bellevue, Kentucky

Freshman Application Contact Ms. Cathy Baird, Director of Admissions, Daymar College, 119 Fairfield Avenue, Bellevue, KY 41073. *Phone:* 859-291-0800. *Toll-free phone:* 877-258-7796. *Fax:* 859-491-7500.
Website: http://www.daymarcollege.edu/.

Daymar College
Bowling Green, Kentucky

Freshman Application Contact Mrs. Traci Henderson, Admissions Director, Daymar College, 2421 Fitzgerald Industrial Drive, Bowling Green, KY 42101. *Phone:* 270-843-6750. *Toll-free phone:* 877-258-7796. *E-mail:* thenderson@daymarcollege.edu.
Website: http://www.daymarcollege.edu/.

Daymar College
Madisonville, Kentucky

Admissions Office Contact Daymar College, 1105 National Mine Drive, Madisonville, KY 42431. *Toll-free phone:* 877-258-7796.
Website: http://www.daymarcollege.edu/.

Daymar College
Owensboro, Kentucky

Freshman Application Contact Ms. Vickie McDougal, Director of Admissions, Daymar College, 3361 Buckland Square, Owensboro, KY 42301. *Phone:* 270-926-4040. *Toll-free phone:* 877-258-7796. *Fax:* 270-685-4090. *E-mail:* info@daymarcollege.edu.
Website: http://www.daymarcollege.edu/.

Elizabethtown Community and Technical College
Elizabethtown, Kentucky

- **State-supported** 2-year, founded 1966, part of Kentucky Community and Technical College System
- **Small-town** 80-acre campus
- **Endowment** $655,000
- **Coed,** 7,353 undergraduate students, 38% full-time, 53% women, 47% men

Undergraduates 2,822 full-time, 4,531 part-time. Students come from 17 states and territories; 0.5% are from out of state; 7% Black or African American, non-Hispanic/Latino; 3% Hispanic/Latino; 0.9% Asian, non-Hispanic/Latino; 0.2% Native Hawaiian or other Pacific Islander, non-Hispanic/Latino; 0.4% American Indian or Alaska Native, non-Hispanic/Latino; 3% Two or more races, non-Hispanic/Latino; 3% Race/ethnicity unknown; 3% transferred in.
Freshmen *Admission:* 1,218 enrolled.
Faculty *Total:* 302, 47% full-time. *Student/faculty ratio:* 22:1.
Majors Automobile/automotive mechanics technology; business administration and management; child-care provision; computer and information sciences; criminal justice/law enforcement administration; data processing and data processing technology; dental hygiene; diesel mechanics technology; electrician; engineering technology; executive assistant/executive secretary; fire science/firefighting; industrial electronics technology; industrial mechanics and maintenance technology; interdisciplinary studies; liberal arts and sciences/liberal studies; medical administrative assistant and medical secretary; medical radiologic technology; quality control and safety technologies related; registered nursing/registered nurse; respiratory care therapy; social work; teacher assistant/aide; welding technology.
Academics *Calendar:* semesters. *Degree:* certificates, diplomas, and associate. *Special study options:* academic remediation for entering students, advanced placement credit, cooperative education, distance learning, internships, off-campus study, part-time degree program, services for LD students, summer session for credit.
Library ECTC Media Center.
Student Life *Housing:* college housing not available. *Activities and Organizations:* student-run newspaper. *Campus security:* late-night transport/escort service.
Standardized Tests *Recommended:* ACT (for admission).
Costs (2015–16) *Tuition:* state resident $4410 full-time; nonresident $15,450 full-time. *Payment plan:* installment. *Waivers:* senior citizens and employees or children of employees.
Applying *Options:* electronic application. *Required for some:* high school transcript. *Application deadlines:* rolling (freshmen), rolling (transfers). *Notification:* continuous (freshmen), continuous (transfers).
Freshman Application Contact Elizabethtown Community and Technical College, 620 College Street Road, Elizabethtown, KY 42701. *Phone:* 270-706-8800. *Toll-free phone:* 877-246-2322.
Website: http://www.elizabethtown.kctcs.edu/.

Galen College of Nursing
Louisville, Kentucky

Admissions Office Contact Galen College of Nursing, 1031 Zorn Avenue, Suite 400, Louisville, KY 40207. *Toll-free phone:* 877-223-7040.
Website: http://www.galencollege.edu/.

Gateway Community and Technical College
Florence, Kentucky

- **State-supported** 2-year, founded 1961, part of Kentucky Community and Technical College System
- **Suburban** campus with easy access to Cincinnati
- **Coed,** 4,592 undergraduate students, 27% full-time, 50% women, 50% men

Undergraduates 1,223 full-time, 3,369 part-time. 8% Black or African American, non-Hispanic/Latino; 3% Hispanic/Latino; 0.7% Asian, non-Hispanic/Latino; 0.1% Native Hawaiian or other Pacific Islander, non-Hispanic/Latino; 0.3% American Indian or Alaska Native, non-Hispanic/Latino; 2% Two or more races, non-Hispanic/Latino; 2% Race/ethnicity unknown.
Freshmen *Admission:* 1,318 applied, 1,055 admitted, 398 enrolled. *Average high school GPA:* 2.05.
Faculty *Total:* 257, 35% full-time. *Student/faculty ratio:* 18:1.
Majors Business administration and management; CAD/CADD drafting/design technology; computer and information sciences; criminal justice/law enforcement administration; early childhood education; educational/instructional technology; engineering technology; fire science/firefighting; general studies; health professions related; industrial technology; manufacturing engineering technology; office occupations and clerical services; registered nursing/registered nurse; teacher assistant/aide.
Academics *Calendar:* semesters. *Degree:* certificates, diplomas, and associate. *Special study options:* academic remediation for entering students, cooperative education, distance learning, internships, part-time degree program, services for LD students, summer session for credit.
Library Main Library plus 3 others.
Student Life *Housing:* college housing not available. *Activities and Organizations:* National Technical Honor Society, Student Government Association, Speech Team, American Criminal Justice Association, Phi Theta Kappa. *Campus security:* 24-hour emergency response devices, campus security during hours of operation. *Student services:* personal/psychological counseling.
Standardized Tests *Required:* ACT or ACT Compass (for admission).
Costs (2015–16) *Tuition:* state resident $3528 full-time, $147 per credit hour part-time; nonresident $12,360 full-time, $515 per credit hour part-time. Full-time tuition and fees vary according to course load. Part-time tuition and fees vary according to course load. *Required fees:* $40 per term part-time. *Payment plan:* installment. *Waivers:* senior citizens and employees or children of employees.
Applying *Options:* electronic application, early admission, deferred entrance. *Required:* high school transcript. *Application deadlines:* rolling (freshmen), rolling (out-of-state freshmen), rolling (transfers). *Notification:* continuous (freshmen), continuous (out-of-state freshmen), continuous (transfers).
Freshman Application Contact Gateway Community and Technical College, 500 Technology Way, Florence, KY 41042. *Phone:* 859-442-4176. *E-mail:* andre.washington@kctcs.edu.
Website: http://www.gateway.kctcs.edu/.

Hazard Community and Technical College
Hazard, Kentucky

Freshman Application Contact Director of Admissions, Hazard Community and Technical College, 1 Community College Drive, Hazard, KY 41701-2403. *Phone:* 606-487-3102. *Toll-free phone:* 800-246-7521. *Website:* http://www.hazard.kctcs.edu/.

Henderson Community College
Henderson, Kentucky

Freshman Application Contact Ms. Teresa Hamiton, Admissions Counselor, Henderson Community College, 2660 South Green Street, Henderson, KY 42420-4623. *Phone:* 270-827-1867 Ext. 354. *Toll-free phone:* 800-696-9958. *Website:* http://www.henderson.kctcs.edu/.

Hopkinsville Community College
Hopkinsville, Kentucky

- **State-supported** 2-year, founded 1965, part of Kentucky Community and Technical College System
- **Small-town** 69-acre campus with easy access to Nashville
- **Coed,** 3,120 undergraduate students, 40% full-time, 63% women, 37% men

Undergraduates 1,245 full-time, 1,875 part-time. 22% Black or African American, non-Hispanic/Latino; 9% Hispanic/Latino; 1% Asian, non-Hispanic/Latino; 0.8% Native Hawaiian or other Pacific Islander, non-Hispanic/Latino; 0.5% American Indian or Alaska Native, non-Hispanic/Latino; 4% Two or more races, non-Hispanic/Latino; 2% Race/ethnicity unknown; 0.2% international; 7% transferred in. *Retention:* 43% of full-time freshmen returned.
Freshmen *Admission:* 273 enrolled.
Faculty *Total:* 158, 36% full-time. *Student/faculty ratio:* 12:1.
Majors Administrative assistant and secretarial science; agricultural production; business administration and management; child-care provision; computer and information sciences; criminal justice/law enforcement administration; electrical, electronic and communications engineering technology; executive assistant/executive secretary; human services; industrial technology; liberal arts and sciences/liberal studies; multi/interdisciplinary studies related; registered nursing/registered nurse; social work.
Academics *Calendar:* semesters. *Degree:* certificates, diplomas, and associate. *Special study options:* academic remediation for entering students, advanced placement credit, cooperative education, distance learning, honors programs, independent study, part-time degree program, services for LD students, summer session for credit.
Library Learning Resource Center.
Student Life *Housing:* college housing not available. *Activities and Organizations:* student-run newspaper, Ag Tech, Amateur Radio, Ballroom Dance, Baptist Campus Ministries, Black Men United. *Campus security:* 24-hour emergency response devices, late-night transport/escort service, security provided by trained security personnel during hours of normal operation.
Athletics *Intramural sports:* basketball M, football M, golf M, table tennis M/W, volleyball M/W.
Costs (2015–16) *Tuition:* state resident $4410 full-time, $147 per credit hour part-time; nonresident $15,450 full-time, $515 per credit hour part-time. Full-time tuition and fees vary according to reciprocity agreements. Part-time tuition and fees vary according to reciprocity agreements. *Required fees:* $360 full-time, $12 per credit hour part-time. *Payment plan:* installment. *Waivers:* senior citizens and employees or children of employees.
Financial Aid Of all full-time matriculated undergraduates who enrolled in 2014, 30 Federal Work-Study jobs (averaging $1500). *Financial aid deadline:* 6/30.
Applying *Options:* electronic application, deferred entrance. *Recommended:* high school transcript. *Application deadlines:* rolling (freshmen), rolling (out-of-state freshmen), rolling (transfers). *Notification:* continuous (freshmen), continuous (out-of-state freshmen), continuous (transfers).
Freshman Application Contact Ms., Hopkinsville Community College, KY. *Phone:* 270-707-3811. *Toll-free phone:* 866-534-2224. *Website:* http://hopkinsville.kctcs.edu/.

Interactive College of Technology
Newport, Kentucky

- **Proprietary** 2-year, founded 1980, part of Interactive Learning Systems
- **Small-town** campus with easy access to Cincinnati
- **Coed**

Academics *Calendar:* semesters. *Degree:* certificates, diplomas, and associate. *Special study options:* academic remediation for entering students, distance learning, internships, part-time degree program.
Freshman Application Contact Diana Mamas, Interactive College of Technology, 76 Carothers Road, Newport, KY 41071. *Phone:* 859-282-8989. *Fax:* 859-282-8475. *E-mail:* dmamas@ict.edu. *Website:* http://ict.edu/.

ITT Technical Institute
Louisville, Kentucky

Freshman Application Contact Director of Recruitment, ITT Technical Institute, 4420 Dixie Highway, Suite 230, Louisville, KY 40216. *Phone:* 502-327-7424. *Toll-free phone:* 888-790-7427. *Website:* http://www.itt-tech.edu/.

Jefferson Community and Technical College
Louisville, Kentucky

Freshman Application Contact Ms. Melanie Vaughan-Cooke, Admissions Coordinator, Jefferson Community and Technical College, Louisville, KY 40202. *Phone:* 502-213-4000. *Fax:* 502-213-2540.
Website: http://www.jefferson.kctcs.edu/.

Madisonville Community College
Madisonville, Kentucky

Director of Admissions Mr. Jay Parent, Registrar, Madisonville Community College, 2000 College Drive, Madisonville, KY 42431-9185. *Phone:* 270-821-2250.
Website: http://www.madisonville.kctcs.edu/.

Maysville Community and Technical College
Maysville, Kentucky

- **State-supported** 2-year, founded 1967, part of Kentucky Community and Technical College System
- **Rural** 12-acre campus
- **Coed**

Undergraduates 1,466 full-time, 2,012 part-time. 3% Black or African American, non-Hispanic/Latino; 1% Hispanic/Latino; 0.2% Asian, non-Hispanic/Latino; 0.1% Native Hawaiian or other Pacific Islander, non-Hispanic/Latino; 0.2% American Indian or Alaska Native, non-Hispanic/Latino; 1% Two or more races, non-Hispanic/Latino; 1% Race/ethnicity unknown; 0.1% international.
Academics *Calendar:* semesters. *Degree:* certificates, diplomas, and associate. *Special study options:* academic remediation for entering students, adult/continuing education programs, advanced placement credit, cooperative education, distance learning, English as a second language, external degree program, honors programs, independent study, internships, off-campus study, part-time degree program, services for LD students, summer session for credit.
Library Finch Library.
Student Life *Campus security:* student patrols, evening parking lot security.
Costs (2015–16) *Tuition:* state resident $3528 full-time; nonresident $12,360 full-time. Full-time tuition and fees vary according to reciprocity agreements. Part-time tuition and fees vary according to reciprocity agreements. *Payment plans:* installment, deferred payment.
Financial Aid Of all full-time matriculated undergraduates who enrolled in 2014, 30 Federal Work-Study jobs (averaging $1960).
Applying *Options:* electronic application, early admission. *Required:* high school transcript.
Freshman Application Contact Maysville Community and Technical College, 1755 US 68, Maysville, KY 41056. *Phone:* 606-759-7141.
Website: http://www.maysville.kctcs.edu/.

Maysville Community and Technical College
Morehead, Kentucky

Director of Admissions Patee Massie, Registrar, Maysville Community and Technical College, 609 Viking Drive, Morehead, KY 40351. *Phone:* 606-759-7141 Ext. 66184.
Website: http://www.maysville.kctcs.edu/.

Medtech College
Lexington, Kentucky

Admissions Office Contact Medtech College, 1648 McGrathiana Parkway, Suite 200, Lexington, KY 40511.
Website: http://www.medtech.edu/.

Owensboro Community and Technical College
Owensboro, Kentucky

- **State-supported** 2-year, founded 1986, part of Kentucky Community and Technical College System
- **Suburban** 102-acre campus
- **Coed**, 3,981 undergraduate students, 37% full-time, 57% women, 43% men

Undergraduates 1,459 full-time, 2,522 part-time. Students come from 21 states and territories; 4% are from out of state; 3% Black or African American, non-Hispanic/Latino; 2% Hispanic/Latino; 0.5% Asian, non-Hispanic/Latino; 0.1% Native Hawaiian or other Pacific Islander, non-Hispanic/Latino; 0.1% American Indian or Alaska Native, non-Hispanic/Latino; 2% Two or more races, non-Hispanic/Latino; 0.5% Race/ethnicity unknown; 0.2% international.
Retention: 52% of full-time freshmen returned.
Freshmen *Admission:* 566 enrolled.
Faculty *Total:* 161, 51% full-time, 9% with terminal degrees. *Student/faculty ratio:* 21:1.
Majors Agricultural production; applied horticulture/horticulture operations; automobile/automotive mechanics technology; business administration and management; child-care provision; computer and information sciences; construction trades; criminal justice/law enforcement administration; diesel mechanics technology; dramatic/theater arts; electrical and electronic engineering technologies related; electrician; emergency medical technology (EMT paramedic); executive assistant/executive secretary; fine/studio arts; fire science/firefighting; health and medical administrative services related; human services; liberal arts and sciences/liberal studies; machine shop technology; mechanics and repair; medical administrative assistant and medical secretary; multi/interdisciplinary studies related; precision production trades; radiologic technology/science; registered nursing/registered nurse; surgical technology; veterinary/animal health technology.
Academics *Calendar:* semesters. *Degree:* certificates, diplomas, and associate. *Special study options:* academic remediation for entering students, adult/continuing education programs, advanced placement credit, cooperative education, distance learning, double majors, English as a second language, external degree program, honors programs, independent study, off-campus study, part-time degree program, services for LD students, student-designed majors, study abroad, summer session for credit. *ROTC:* Army (b).
Library Main Campus Library. *Books:* 25,322 (physical), 294,387 (digital/electronic); *Serial titles:* 16 (physical); *Databases:* 52. Weekly public service hours: 52.
Student Life *Housing:* college housing not available. *Activities and Organizations:* drama/theater group, choral group, Student Government Association. *Campus security:* 24-hour emergency response devices, late-night transport/escort service.
Standardized Tests *Recommended:* SAT or ACT (for admission).
Costs (2016–17) *Tuition:* state resident $4410 full-time, $147 per credit hour part-time; nonresident $15,450 full-time, $515 per credit hour part-time. Full-time tuition and fees vary according to course load and reciprocity agreements. Part-time tuition and fees vary according to course load and reciprocity agreements. *Required fees:* $240 full-time, $8 per credit hour part-time. *Payment plan:* installment. *Waivers:* senior citizens and employees or children of employees.
Financial Aid Of all full-time matriculated undergraduates who enrolled in 2015, 30 Federal Work-Study jobs. *Financial aid deadline:* 4/1.
Applying *Options:* electronic application. *Required:* high school transcript. *Application deadlines:* rolling (freshmen), rolling (transfers). *Notification:* continuous (freshmen), continuous (transfers).
Freshman Application Contact Ms. Barbara Tipmore, Director of Counseling Services, Owensboro Community and Technical College, 4800 New Hartford Road, Owensboro, KY 42303. *Phone:* 270-686-4530. *Toll-free phone:* 866-755-6282. *E-mail:* barb.tipmore@kctcs.edu.
Website: http://www.owensboro.kctcs.edu/.

Somerset Community College
Somerset, Kentucky

- **State-supported** 2-year, founded 1965, part of Kentucky Community and Technical College System
- **Small-town** 70-acre campus
- **Coed**, 7,504 undergraduate students, 12% full-time, 9% women, 7% men

Undergraduates 866 full-time, 344 part-time. *Retention:* 60% of full-time freshmen returned.
Freshmen *Admission:* 1,282 applied, 1,282 admitted, 1,210 enrolled.
Faculty *Total:* 340, 54% full-time. *Student/faculty ratio:* 18:1.
Majors Aircraft powerplant technology; business administration and management; child-care provision; clinical/medical laboratory assistant; computer and information sciences; criminal justice/law enforcement

administration; engineering technology; executive assistant/executive secretary; industrial mechanics and maintenance technology; liberal arts and sciences/liberal studies; medical administrative assistant and medical secretary; medical radiologic technology; multi/interdisciplinary studies related; physical therapy technology; registered nursing/registered nurse; respiratory care therapy; surgical technology; teacher assistant/aide.
Academics *Calendar:* semesters. *Degree:* certificates, diplomas, and associate. *Special study options:* academic remediation for entering students, adult/continuing education programs, advanced placement credit, distance learning, part-time degree program, summer session for credit.
Library Somerset Community College Library.
Student Life *Housing:* college housing not available. *Activities and Organizations:* drama/theater group, student-run newspaper.
Costs (2015–16) *Tuition:* state resident $4410 full-time, $147 per credit hour part-time; nonresident $15,450 full-time, $515 per credit hour part-time. Full-time tuition and fees vary according to course load. Part-time tuition and fees vary according to course load. *Required fees:* $240 full-time. *Payment plan:* installment. *Waivers:* senior citizens and employees or children of employees.
Applying *Options:* electronic application, early admission. *Required:* high school transcript. *Application deadlines:* 8/14 (freshmen), 8/14 (transfers). *Notification:* continuous (freshmen), continuous (transfers).
Freshman Application Contact Director of Admission, Somerset Community College, 808 Monticello Street, Somerset, KY 42501-2973. *Phone:* 606-451-6630. *Toll-free phone:* 877-629-9722. *E-mail:* somerset-admissions@kctcs.edu. *Website:* http://www.somerset.kctcs.edu/.

Southcentral Kentucky Community and Technical College
Bowling Green, Kentucky
Director of Admissions Mark Garrett, Chief Student Affairs Officer, Southcentral Kentucky Community and Technical College, 1845 Loop Drive, Bowling Green, KY 42101. *Phone:* 270-901-1114. *Toll-free phone:* 800-790-0990.
Website: http://www.bowlinggreen.kctcs.edu/.

Southeast Kentucky Community and Technical College
Cumberland, Kentucky
Freshman Application Contact Southeast Kentucky Community and Technical College, 700 College Road, Cumberland, KY 40823-1099. *Phone:* 606-589-2145 Ext. 13018. *Toll-free phone:* 888-274-SECC. *Website:* http://www.southeast.kctcs.edu/.

Spencerian College
Louisville, Kentucky
- **Proprietary** primarily 2-year, founded 1892
- **Urban** 10-acre campus
- **Coed,** 497 undergraduate students, 57% full-time, 88% women, 12% men
Undergraduates 284 full-time, 213 part-time. 18% Black or African American, non-Hispanic/Latino; 3% Hispanic/Latino; 1% Asian, non-Hispanic/Latino; 13% Two or more races, non-Hispanic/Latino; 6% Race/ethnicity unknown; 1% live on campus.
Freshmen *Admission:* 82 enrolled.
Faculty *Total:* 91, 48% full-time.
Majors Clinical laboratory science/medical technology; clinical/medical laboratory technology; massage therapy; medical insurance coding; radiologic technology/science; registered nursing/registered nurse; respiratory care therapy; surgical technology.
Academics *Calendar:* quarters. *Degrees:* certificates, diplomas, associate, and bachelor's. *Special study options:* distance learning, internships, summer session for credit.
Library Spencerian College Learning Resource Center.
Student Life *Housing Options:* coed. Campus housing is university owned.
Costs (2015–16) *Comprehensive fee:* $28,545 includes full-time tuition ($17,940), mandatory fees ($1680), and room and board ($8925). Full-time tuition and fees vary according to class time, degree level, and program. Part-time tuition: $299 per credit hour. Part-time tuition and fees vary according to class time, degree level, and program. *Required fees:* $60 per course part-time. *Room and board:* college room only: $5940. Room and board charges vary according to housing facility. *Waivers:* employees or children of employees.
Applying *Application fee:* $50. *Required:* high school transcript. *Required for some:* essay or personal statement, interview, specific selective admission

criteria for some medical programs. *Notification:* continuous (freshmen), continuous (out-of-state freshmen), continuous (transfers).
Freshman Application Contact Spencerian College, 4627 Dixie Highway, Louisville, KY 40216. *Phone:* 502-447-1000 Ext. 7808. *Toll-free phone:* 800-264-1799.
Website: http://www.spencerian.edu/.

Spencerian College–Lexington
Lexington, Kentucky
- **Proprietary** 2-year, founded 1997, part of The Sullivan University System, Inc.
- **Urban** campus with easy access to Louisville
- **Coed,** 74 undergraduate students, 81% full-time, 77% women, 23% men
Undergraduates 60 full-time, 14 part-time. Students come from 2 states and territories; 1% are from out of state.
Freshmen *Average high school GPA:* 2.5.
Faculty *Total:* 29, 69% full-time. *Student/faculty ratio:* 3:1.
Majors Clinical/medical laboratory technology; medical office management; radiologic technology/science.
Academics *Calendar:* quarters. *Degree:* certificates, diplomas, and associate. *Special study options:* academic remediation for entering students, cooperative education, independent study, part-time degree program, services for LD students, summer session for credit.
Library Spencerian College Library.
Student Life *Housing Options:* men-only, women-only. Campus housing is leased by the school. *Activities and Organizations:* student-run newspaper. *Campus security:* 24-hour emergency response devices.
Standardized Tests *Required for some:* ACT ASSET.
Costs (2016–17) *One-time required fee:* $50. *Tuition:* $17,940 full-time, $299 per credit hour part-time. Full-time tuition and fees vary according to class time, course load, program, and student level. Part-time tuition and fees vary according to class time, course load, program, and student level. *Required fees:* $1700 full-time, $1700 per year part-time. *Room only:* $5760. *Payment plans:* tuition prepayment, installment, deferred payment. *Waivers:* employees or children of employees.
Applying *Application fee:* $50. *Required:* high school transcript, interview. *Application deadline:* rolling (freshmen).
Freshman Application Contact Spencerian College–Lexington, 2355 Harrodsburg Road, Lexington, KY 40504. *Phone:* 859-223-9608 Ext. 5430. *Toll-free phone:* 800-456-3253.
Website: http://www.spencerian.edu/.

Sullivan College of Technology and Design
Louisville, Kentucky
- **Proprietary** primarily 2-year, founded 1961, part of The Sullivan University System, Inc.
- **Suburban** 10-acre campus with easy access to Louisville
- **Coed**
Undergraduates 228 full-time, 137 part-time. Students come from 3 states and territories; 13% are from out of state; 12% Black or African American, non-Hispanic/Latino; 0.3% Hispanic/Latino; 2% Asian, non-Hispanic/Latino; 0.5% Native Hawaiian or other Pacific Islander, non-Hispanic/Latino; 0.3% American Indian or Alaska Native, non-Hispanic/Latino; 13% Two or more races, non-Hispanic/Latino; 4% Race/ethnicity unknown; 5% transferred in.
Faculty *Student/faculty ratio:* 9:1.
Academics *Calendar:* quarters. *Degrees:* associate and bachelor's. *Special study options:* academic remediation for entering students, accelerated degree program, adult/continuing education programs, advanced placement credit, double majors, independent study, internships, part-time degree program, services for LD students, summer session for credit.
Library Sullivan College of Technology and Design Library plus 1 other.
Student Life *Campus security:* late-night transport/escort service, controlled dormitory access, patrols by trained security personnel while classes are in session.
Standardized Tests *Required:* ACT Compass or ACT or SAT Language and Math scores in place of Compass results (for admission). *Recommended:* SAT or ACT (for admission).
Costs (2015–16) *Comprehensive fee:* $32,005 includes full-time tuition ($20,460), mandatory fees ($1735), and room and board ($9810). Full-time tuition and fees vary according to course load, degree level, and program. Part-time tuition and fees vary according to course load, degree level, and program. No tuition increase for student's term of enrollment. *Room and board:* Room and board charges vary according to board plan.

Applying *Options:* electronic application, deferred entrance. *Application fee:* $50. *Required:* high school transcript, interview, COMPASS Exam or ACT/SAT Scores.

Freshman Application Contact Ms. Heather Wilson, Director of Admissions, Sullivan College of Technology and Design, 3901 Atkinson Square Drive, Louisville, KY 40218. *Phone:* 502-456-6509 Ext. 8220. *Toll-free phone:* 800-884-6528. *Fax:* 502-456-2341. *E-mail:* hwilson@sctd.edu. *Website:* http://www.sctd.edu/.

West Kentucky Community and Technical College

Paducah, Kentucky

Freshman Application Contact Ms. Debbie Smith, Admissions Counselor, West Kentucky Community and Technical College, 4810 Alben Barkley Drive, Paducah, KY 42001. *Phone:* 270-554-3266. *E-mail:* debbie.smith@kctcs.edu. *Website:* http://www.westkentucky.kctcs.edu/.

LOUISIANA

Baton Rouge Community College

Baton Rouge, Louisiana

Director of Admissions Nancy Clay, Interim Executive Director for Enrollment Services, Baton Rouge Community College, 201 Community College Drive, Baton Rouge, LA 70806. *Phone:* 225-216-8700. *Toll-free phone:* 800-601-4558. *Website:* http://www.mybrcc.edu/.

Baton Rouge School of Computers

Baton Rouge, Louisiana

Freshman Application Contact Admissions Office, Baton Rouge School of Computers, 10425 Plaza Americana, Baton Rouge, LA 70816. *Phone:* 225-923-2524. *Toll-free phone:* 888-920-BRSC. *Fax:* 225-923-2979. *E-mail:* admissions@brsc.net. *Website:* http://www.brsc.edu/.

Blue Cliff College–Shreveport

Shreveport, Louisiana

Freshman Application Contact Blue Cliff College–Shreveport, 8731 Park Plaza Drive, Shreveport, LA 71105. *Toll-free phone:* 800-516-6597. *Website:* http://www.bluecliffcollege.edu/.

Bossier Parish Community College

Bossier City, Louisiana

- **State-supported** 2-year, founded 1967, part of Louisiana Community and Technical College System
- **Urban** 64-acre campus with easy access to Shreveport
- **Coed,** 6,623 undergraduate students, 56% full-time, 64% women, 36% men

Undergraduates 3,741 full-time, 2,882 part-time. 3% are from out of state; 38% Black or African American, non-Hispanic/Latino; 6% Hispanic/Latino; 0.6% Asian, non-Hispanic/Latino; 0.2% Native Hawaiian or other Pacific Islander, non-Hispanic/Latino; 1% American Indian or Alaska Native, non-Hispanic/Latino; 2% Two or more races, non-Hispanic/Latino; 4% Race/ethnicity unknown; 0.2% international; 4% transferred in. *Retention:* 50% of full-time freshmen returned.

Freshmen *Admission:* 4,220 applied, 3,833 admitted, 1,116 enrolled. *Average high school GPA:* 2.63. *Test scores:* SAT critical reading scores over 500: 20%; SAT math scores over 500: 30%; SAT writing scores over 500: 20%.

Faculty *Total:* 286, 47% full-time, 8% with terminal degrees. *Student/faculty ratio:* 23:1.

Majors Administrative assistant and secretarial science; audiovisual communications technologies related; business/commerce; child-care provision; computer/information technology services administration related; construction engineering; construction engineering technology; criminal justice/safety; culinary arts; drafting and design technology; dramatic/theater arts; education; educational/instructional technology; emergency medical technology (EMT paramedic); engineering; foods, nutrition, and wellness; general studies; hospital and health-care facilities administration; industrial mechanics and maintenance technology; industrial technology; information science/studies; liberal arts and sciences and humanities related; liberal arts and sciences/liberal studies; medical/clinical assistant; music; natural sciences; occupational therapist assistant; petroleum technology; pharmacy technician; physical therapy; physical therapy technology; recording arts technology; registered nursing/registered nurse; respiratory care therapy; visual and performing arts related.

Academics *Calendar:* semesters. *Degree:* certificates, diplomas, and associate. *Special study options:* academic remediation for entering students, adult/continuing education programs, advanced placement credit, distance learning, double majors, part-time degree program, services for LD students, summer session for credit.

Library Bossier Parish Community College Library.

Student Life *Housing:* college housing not available. *Activities and Organizations:* drama/theater group, student-run newspaper, choral group. *Campus security:* student patrols. *Student services:* personal/psychological counseling.

Athletics Member NJCAA. *Intercollegiate sports:* baseball M(s), basketball M(s), soccer W, softball W(s). *Intramural sports:* badminton M/W, bowling M/W, football M, racquetball M, softball M, table tennis M/W, volleyball M/W.

Costs (2015–16) *Tuition:* state resident $139 per credit hour part-time; nonresident $334 per credit hour part-time. Full-time tuition and fees vary according to course load, location, and program. Part-time tuition and fees vary according to course load, location, and program. *Required fees:* $24 per credit hour part-time, $30 per term part-time. *Payment plan:* deferred payment. *Waivers:* employees or children of employees.

Financial Aid Of all full-time matriculated undergraduates who enrolled in 2014, 3,011 applied for aid, 2,756 were judged to have need, 73 had their need fully met. In 2014, 2 non-need-based awards were made. *Average percent of need met:* 43%. *Average financial aid package:* $9958. *Average need-based loan:* $2103. *Average need-based gift aid:* $1715. *Average non-need-based aid:* $500.

Applying *Options:* early admission. *Application fee:* $15.

Freshman Application Contact Mr. Richard Cockerham, Registrar, Bossier Parish Community College, 6220 East Texas Street, Bossier City, LA 71111. *Phone:* 318-678-6093. *Fax:* 318-678-6390. *Website:* http://www.bpcc.edu/.

Cameron College

New Orleans, Louisiana

Admissions Office Contact Cameron College, 2740 Canal Street, New Orleans, LA 70119. *Website:* http://www.cameroncollege.com/.

Central Louisiana Technical Community College

Alexandria, Louisiana

Director of Admissions Ms. Janice Bolden, Vice Chancellor of Student Services, Enrollment Management and College Registrar, Central Louisiana Technical Community College, 4311 South MacArthur Drive, Alexandria, LA 71302. *Phone:* 800-351-7611. *Website:* http://www.cltcc.edu/.

Delgado Community College

New Orleans, Louisiana

- **State-supported** 2-year, founded 1921, part of Louisiana Community and Technical College System
- **Urban** 57-acre campus
- **Endowment** $2.0 million
- **Coed**

Undergraduates 7,906 full-time, 10,792 part-time. Students come from 20 states and territories; 45% Black or African American, non-Hispanic/Latino; 8% Hispanic/Latino; 3% Asian, non-Hispanic/Latino; 0.1% Native Hawaiian or other Pacific Islander, non-Hispanic/Latino; 0.4% American Indian or Alaska Native, non-Hispanic/Latino; 2% Two or more races, non-Hispanic/Latino; 7% Race/ethnicity unknown; 0.8% international. *Retention:* 57% of full-time freshmen returned.

Faculty *Student/faculty ratio:* 42:1.

Academics *Calendar:* semesters. *Degree:* certificates and associate. *Special study options:* academic remediation for entering students, advanced placement credit, cooperative education, distance learning, double majors, English as a second language, honors programs, off-campus study, part-time degree program, services for LD students, summer session for credit. *ROTC:* Army (c), Air Force (c).

Library Moss Memorial Library.
Student Life *Campus security:* 24-hour patrols, late-night transport/escort service.
Athletics Member NJCAA.
Financial Aid Of all full-time matriculated undergraduates who enrolled in 2014, 308 Federal Work-Study jobs (averaging $1375).
Applying *Options:* electronic application. *Application fee:* $25. *Required for some:* high school transcript. *Recommended:* high school transcript, proof of immunization.
Freshman Application Contact Ms. Gwen Boute, Director of Admissions, Delgado Community College, 615 City Park Avenue, New Orleans, LA 70119. *Phone:* 504-671-5010. *Fax:* 504-483-1895. *E-mail:* enroll@dcc.edu.
Website: http://www.dcc.edu/.

Delta School of Business and Technology
Lake Charles, Louisiana

Freshman Application Contact Jeffery Tibodeaux, Director of Admissions, Delta School of Business and Technology, 517 Broad Street, Lake Charles, LA 70601. *Phone:* 337-439-5765.
Website: http://www.deltatech.edu/.

Fletcher Technical Community College
Schriever, Louisiana

Director of Admissions Admissions Office, Fletcher Technical Community College, 1407 Highway 311, Schriever, LA 70395. *Phone:* 985-857-3659.
Website: http://www.fletcher.edu/.

Fortis College
Baton Rouge, Louisiana

Director of Admissions Ms. Sheri Kirley, Associate Director of Admissions, Fortis College, 9255 Interline Avenue, Baton Rouge, LA 70809. *Phone:* 225-248-1015. *Toll-free phone:* 855-4-FORTIS.
Website: http://www.fortis.edu/.

ITI Technical College
Baton Rouge, Louisiana

- **Proprietary** 2-year, founded 1973
- **Suburban** 10-acre campus
- **Coed**

Majors Computer technology/computer systems technology; drafting and design technology; electrical, electronic and communications engineering technology; information science/studies; information technology; instrumentation technology; manufacturing engineering technology; office occupations and clerical services.
Academics *Calendar:* quarters. *Degree:* certificates and associate. *Special study options:* internships.
Library ITI Technical College Library.
Student Life *Housing:* college housing not available. *Campus security:* electronic alarm devices during non-business hours, security cameras 24-hours.
Costs (2015–16) *Tuition:* Tuition and fees vary according to program. Contact school for costs.
Applying *Required:* high school transcript, interview.
Freshman Application Contact Mr. Shawn Norris, Admissions Director, ITI Technical College, 13944 Airline Highway, Baton Rouge, LA 70817. *Phone:* 225-752-4230 Ext. 261. *Toll-free phone:* 888-211-7165. *Fax:* 225-756-0903. *E-mail:* snorris@iticollege.edu.
Website: http://www.iticollege.edu/.

ITT Technical Institute
Baton Rouge, Louisiana

Freshman Application Contact Director of Recruitment, ITT Technical Institute, 14111 Airline Highway, Suite 101, Baton Rouge, LA 70817. *Phone:* 225-754-5800. *Toll-free phone:* 800-295-8485.
Website: http://www.itt-tech.edu/.

ITT Technical Institute
St. Rose, Louisiana

Freshman Application Contact Director of Recruitment, ITT Technical Institute, 140 James Drive East, St. Rose, LA 70087. *Phone:* 504-463-0338. *Toll-free phone:* 866-463-0338.
Website: http://www.itt-tech.edu/.

Louisiana Culinary Institute
Baton Rouge, Louisiana

Admissions Office Contact Louisiana Culinary Institute, 10550 Airline Highway, Baton Rouge, LA 70816. *Toll-free phone:* 877-533-3198.
Website: http://www.louisianaculinary.com/.

Louisiana Delta Community College
Monroe, Louisiana

- **State-supported** 2-year, part of Louisiana Community and Technical College System
- **Rural** 70-acre campus with easy access to Monroe, LA
- **Coed**

Undergraduates 2,259 full-time, 2,674 part-time. Students come from 23 states and territories; 2% are from out of state; 36% Black or African American, non-Hispanic/Latino; 4% Hispanic/Latino; 0.4% Asian, non-Hispanic/Latino; 0.1% Native Hawaiian or other Pacific Islander, non-Hispanic/Latino; 0.2% American Indian or Alaska Native, non-Hispanic/Latino; 1% Two or more races, non-Hispanic/Latino; 8% Race/ethnicity unknown; 0.1% international; 5% transferred in.
Faculty *Student/faculty ratio:* 19:1.
Academics *Calendar:* semesters. *Degree:* certificates, diplomas, and associate. *Special study options:* academic remediation for entering students, accelerated degree program, advanced placement credit, distance learning, double majors, internships, part-time degree program, services for LD students, summer session for credit.
Standardized Tests *Required:* SAT or ACT (for admission), ACT Compass (for admission).
Applying *Required:* high school transcript.
Freshman Application Contact Ms. Kathy Gardner, Interim Dean of Enrollment Services, Louisiana Delta Community College, 7500 Millhaven Dr, Monroe, LA 71203. *Phone:* 318-345-9261. *Toll-free phone:* 866-500-LDCC.
Website: http://www.ladelta.edu/.

Louisiana State University at Eunice
Eunice, Louisiana

Freshman Application Contact Ms. Gracie Guillory, Director of Financial Aid, Louisiana State University at Eunice, PO Box 1129, Eunice, LA 70535-1129. *Phone:* 337-550-1282. *Toll-free phone:* 888-367-5783.
Website: http://www.lsue.edu/.

McCann School of Business & Technology
Monroe, Louisiana

- **Proprietary** 2-year, founded 1985, part of Delta Career Education Corporation
- **Small-town** campus with easy access to Shreveport
- **Coed**

Undergraduates 450 full-time, 126 part-time. Students come from 2 states and territories; 1% are from out of state; 71% Black or African American, non-Hispanic/Latino; 0.7% Hispanic/Latino; 0.2% Asian, non-Hispanic/Latino; 0.3% American Indian or Alaska Native, non-Hispanic/Latino; 2% Two or more races, non-Hispanic/Latino; 0.2% Race/ethnicity unknown. *Retention:* 80% of full-time freshmen returned.
Faculty *Student/faculty ratio:* 20:1.
Academics *Calendar:* quarters. *Degree:* diplomas and associate. *Special study options:* academic remediation for entering students, adult/continuing education programs, advanced placement credit, cooperative education, double majors, independent study, internships.
Library Library & Information Resources Network.
Student Life *Campus security:* 24-hour emergency response devices, late-night transport/escort service, evening security guard.
Standardized Tests *Required:* SLE-Wonderlic Scholastic Level Exam; Math Proficiency Exam; English Proficiency Exam (for admission).

Applying *Options:* deferred entrance. *Application fee:* $40. *Required:* high school transcript, interview.

Freshman Application Contact Mrs. Susan Boudreaux, Admissions Office, McCann School of Business & Technology, 2319 Louisville Avenue, Monroe, LA 71201. *Phone:* 318-323-2889. *Toll-free phone:* 800-923-1947. *Fax:* 318-324-9883. *E-mail:* susan.boudreaux@careertc.edu. *Website:* http://www.mccann.edu/.

McCann School of Business & Technology
Shreveport, Louisiana

Admissions Office Contact McCann School of Business & Technology, 1227 Shreveport-Barksdale Highway, Shreveport, LA 71105. *Website:* http://www.mccann.edu/.

Northshore Technical Community College
Bogalusa, Louisiana

Director of Admissions Admissions Office, Northshore Technical Community College, 1710 Sullivan Drive, Bogalusa, LA 70427. *Phone:* 985-732-6640. *Website:* http://www.northshorecollege.edu/.

Northwest Louisiana Technical College
Minden, Louisiana

Director of Admissions Ms. Helen Deville, Admissions Office, Northwest Louisiana Technical College, 9500 Industrial Drive, Minden, LA 71055. *Phone:* 318-371-3035. *Toll-free phone:* 800-529-1387. *Fax:* 318-371-3155. *Website:* http://www.nwltc.edu/.

Nunez Community College
Chalmette, Louisiana

- **State-supported** 2-year, founded 1992, part of Louisiana Community and Technical College System
- **Suburban** 20-acre campus with easy access to New Orleans
- **Endowment** $1.2 million
- **Coed,** 2,629 undergraduate students, 33% full-time, 62% women, 38% men

Undergraduates 878 full-time, 1,751 part-time. Students come from 3 states and territories; 34% Black or African American, non-Hispanic/Latino; 6% Hispanic/Latino; 2% Asian, non-Hispanic/Latino; 0.2% Native Hawaiian or other Pacific Islander, non-Hispanic/Latino; 0.5% American Indian or Alaska Native, non-Hispanic/Latino; 2% Two or more races, non-Hispanic/Latino; 14% Race/ethnicity unknown; 0.2% international.

Freshmen *Admission:* 244 enrolled. *Average high school GPA:* 2.09.

Faculty *Total:* 99, 47% full-time. *Student/faculty ratio:* 23:1.

Majors Business/commerce; child-care provision; culinary arts; education; general studies; industrial technology; kindergarten/preschool education; legal assistant/paralegal; liberal arts and sciences and humanities related.

Academics *Calendar:* semesters. *Degree:* certificates, diplomas, and associate. *Special study options:* academic remediation for entering students, adult/continuing education programs, advanced placement credit, cooperative education, distance learning, double majors, independent study, internships, off-campus study, part-time degree program, services for LD students, student-designed majors, summer session for credit.

Library Nunez Community College Library.

Student Life *Housing:* college housing not available. *Campus security:* late-night transport/escort service, security cameras. *Student services:* health clinic, personal/psychological counseling.

Athletics *Intramural sports:* basketball M, football M/W.

Standardized Tests *Recommended:* ACT (for admission).

Costs (2015–16) *Tuition:* state resident $3335 full-time; nonresident $6834 full-time. Full-time tuition and fees vary according to course load and location. Part-time tuition and fees vary according to course load and location. *Required fees:* $689 full-time. *Payment plan:* installment. *Waivers:* senior citizens and employees or children of employees.

Financial Aid Of all full-time matriculated undergraduates who enrolled in 2014, 70 Federal Work-Study jobs (averaging $1452).

Applying *Options:* electronic application, early admission, deferred entrance. *Application fee:* $20. *Required for some:* high school transcript. *Application deadlines:* rolling (freshmen), rolling (transfers).

Freshman Application Contact Mrs. Becky Maillet, Nunez Community College, 3710 Paris Road, Chalmette, LA 70043. *Phone:* 504-278-6477. *E-mail:* bmaillet@nunez.edu. *Website:* http://www.nunez.edu/.

Remington College–Baton Rouge Campus
Baton Rouge, Louisiana

Director of Admissions Monica Butler-Johnson, Director of Recruitment, Remington College–Baton Rouge Campus, 10551 Coursey Boulevard, Baton Rouge, LA 70816. *Phone:* 225-236-3200. *Fax:* 225-922-3250. *E-mail:* monica.johnson@remingtoncollege.edu. *Website:* http://www.remingtoncollege.edu/.

Remington College–Lafayette Campus
Lafayette, Louisiana

Freshman Application Contact Remington College–Lafayette Campus, 303 Rue Louis XIV, Lafayette, LA 70508. *Phone:* 337-981-4010. *Toll-free phone:* 800-560-6192. *Website:* http://www.remingtoncollege.edu/.

Remington College–Shreveport
Shreveport, Louisiana

Freshman Application Contact Mr. Marc Wright, Remington College–Shreveport, 2106 Bert Kouns Industrial Loop, Shreveport, LA 71118. *Phone:* 318-671-4000. *Website:* http://www.remingtoncollege.edu/.

River Parishes Community College
Gonzales, Louisiana

Director of Admissions Ms. Allison Dauzat, Dean of Students and Enrollment Management, River Parishes Community College, 925 West Edenborne Parkway, Gonzales, LA 70737. *Phone:* 225-675-8270. *Fax:* 225-675-5478. *E-mail:* adauzat@rpcc.cc.la.us. *Website:* http://www.rpcc.edu/.

South Central Louisiana Technical College
Morgan City, Louisiana

Director of Admissions Ms. Melanie Henry, Admissions Office, South Central Louisiana Technical College, 900 Youngs Road, Morgan City, LA 70380. *Phone:* 504-380-2436. *Fax:* 504-380-2440. *Website:* http://www.scl.edu/.

Southern University at Shreveport
Shreveport, Louisiana

- **State-supported** 2-year, founded 1964, part of Southern University System
- **Urban** 103-acre campus
- **Endowment** $619,644
- **Coed,** 3,174 undergraduate students, 61% full-time, 64% women, 36% men

Undergraduates 1,922 full-time, 1,252 part-time. Students come from 5 states and territories; 1 other country; 28% are from out of state; 88% Black or African American, non-Hispanic/Latino; 0.4% Hispanic/Latino; 0.2% Asian, non-Hispanic/Latino; 0.1% American Indian or Alaska Native, non-Hispanic/Latino; 0.3% Two or more races, non-Hispanic/Latino; 6% international; 8% transferred in; 7% live on campus. *Retention:* 45% of full-time freshmen returned.

Freshmen *Admission:* 424 enrolled. *Average high school GPA:* 2. *Test scores:* ACT scores over 18: 8%.

Faculty *Total:* 123, 55% full-time, 9% with terminal degrees. *Student/faculty ratio:* 27:1.

Majors Accounting; accounting technology and bookkeeping; avionics maintenance technology; banking and financial support services; biology/biological sciences; business/commerce; cardiovascular technology; chemistry; clinical/medical laboratory technology; computer science; criminal justice/law enforcement administration; dental hygiene; electrical, electronic and communications engineering technology; general studies; health information/medical records administration; health information/medical records technology; hospitality administration; hotel/motel administration; human services; kindergarten/preschool education; legal assistant/paralegal; liberal arts and sciences and humanities related; mathematics; mechanical engineering/mechanical technology; medical radiologic technology; mental health counseling; physical therapy technology; public administration; radiologic technology/science; registered nursing/registered nurse; respiratory care therapy; robotics technology; sociology; surgical technology; teacher assistant/aide; tourism and travel services management.

Academics *Calendar:* semesters. *Degree:* certificates and associate. *Special study options:* academic remediation for entering students, accelerated degree program, adult/continuing education programs, advanced placement credit, cooperative education, distance learning, honors programs, internships, off-campus study, part-time degree program, student-designed majors, summer session for credit. *ROTC:* Army (c).

Library Library/Learning Resources Center plus 1 other.

Student Life *Housing Options:* coed. Campus housing is provided by a third party. *Activities and Organizations:* drama/theater group, student-run newspaper, choral group, Afro-American Society, SUSLA Gospel Choir, Student Center Board, Allied Health, Engineering Club. *Campus security:* 24-hour patrols, controlled dormitory access. *Student services:* personal/psychological counseling.

Athletics Member NJCAA. *Intercollegiate sports:* basketball M(s)/W(s). *Intramural sports:* basketball M/W, cheerleading M/W, soccer M.

Standardized Tests *Required for some:* SAT or ACT (for admission). *Recommended:* ACT (for admission).

Applying *Required:* high school transcript.

Freshman Application Contact Ms. Danielle Anderson, Admissions Advisor, Southern University at Shreveport, 3050 Martin Luther King Jr. Drive, Shreveport, LA 71107. *Phone:* 318-670-9211. *Toll-free phone:* 800-458-1472. *Fax:* 318-670-6483. *E-mail:* danderson@susla.edu.
Website: http://www.susla.edu/.

South Louisiana Community College
Lafayette, Louisiana

- **State-supported** 2-year, part of Louisiana Community and Technical College System
- **Small-town** campus
- **Endowment** $846,166
- **Coed**

Undergraduates 3,436 full-time, 2,896 part-time. Students come from 12 states and territories; 17 other countries; 1% are from out of state; 35% Black or African American, non-Hispanic/Latino; 3% Hispanic/Latino; 2% Asian, non-Hispanic/Latino; 0.1% Native Hawaiian or other Pacific Islander, non-Hispanic/Latino; 0.5% American Indian or Alaska Native, non-Hispanic/Latino; 2% Two or more races, non-Hispanic/Latino; 5% Race/ethnicity unknown; 0.8% international; 7% transferred in. *Retention:* 55% of full-time freshmen returned.

Faculty *Student/faculty ratio:* 25:1.

Academics *Calendar:* semesters. *Degree:* certificates, diplomas, and associate. *Special study options:* academic remediation for entering students, advanced placement credit, distance learning, double majors, English as a second language, independent study, internships, part-time degree program, services for LD students, summer session for credit.

Costs (2015–16) *Tuition:* state resident $3335 full-time, $139 per credit hour part-time; nonresident $6940 full-time, $289 per credit hour part-time. Full-time tuition and fees vary according to course load and program. Part-time tuition and fees vary according to course load and program. *Required fees:* $639 full-time, $28 per credit hour part-time, $15 per term part-time.

Applying *Options:* electronic application. *Required:* high school transcript.

Freshman Application Contact Director of Admissions, South Louisiana Community College, 1101 Bertrand Drive, Lafayette, LA 70506. *Phone:* 337-521-8953. *E-mail:* admissions@solacc.edu.
Website: http://www.solacc.edu/.

Sowela Technical Community College
Lake Charles, Louisiana

- **State-supported** 2-year, founded 1938, part of Louisiana Community and Technical College System
- **Urban** 84-acre campus
- **Endowment** $383,426
- **Coed,** 3,722 undergraduate students, 48% full-time, 41% women, 59% men
- 100% of applicants were admitted

Undergraduates 1,796 full-time, 1,926 part-time. Students come from 11 states and territories; 8 other countries; 2% are from out of state; 22% Black or African American, non-Hispanic/Latino; 3% Hispanic/Latino; 0.8% Asian, non-Hispanic/Latino; 0.7% American Indian or Alaska Native, non-Hispanic/Latino; 3% Two or more races, non-Hispanic/Latino; 10% Race/ethnicity unknown; 2% international; 10% transferred in. *Retention:* 49% of full-time freshmen returned.

Freshmen *Admission:* 978 applied, 978 admitted, 707 enrolled. *Average high school GPA:* 2.8.

Faculty *Total:* 165, 56% full-time, 7% with terminal degrees. *Student/faculty ratio:* 22:1.

Majors Accounting technology and bookkeeping; administrative assistant and secretarial science; aircraft powerplant technology; commercial and advertising art; computer programming; computer systems networking and telecommunications; criminal justice/safety; culinary arts; drafting and design technology; general studies; instrumentation technology; liberal arts and sciences and humanities related.

Academics *Calendar:* semesters. *Degree:* certificates, diplomas, and associate. *Special study options:* academic remediation for entering students, accelerated degree program, adult/continuing education programs, advanced placement credit, distance learning, double majors, internships, off-campus study, part-time degree program, services for LD students, summer session for credit.

Library Library and Learning Resource Center plus 2 others. *Books:* 8,318 (physical), 11,838 (digital/electronic). Weekly public service hours: 50; students can reserve study rooms.

Student Life *Housing:* college housing not available. *Activities and Organizations:* student-run newspaper, choral group, SkillsUSA, Student Government Association (SGA), Phi Theta Kappa, Criminal Justice Club, Astronomy Club. *Campus security:* security guard on duty. *Student services:* personal/psychological counseling.

Costs (2015–16) *Tuition:* state resident $3335 full-time, $139 per credit hour part-time; nonresident $6762 full-time, $282 per credit hour part-time. Full-time tuition and fees vary according to course load, program, and reciprocity agreements. Part-time tuition and fees vary according to course load, program, and reciprocity agreements. *Required fees:* $742 full-time, $35 per credit hour part-time, $5 per term part-time. *Payment plans:* installment, deferred payment. *Waivers:* employees or children of employees.

Applying *Options:* electronic application, early admission. *Required:* high school transcript, proof of immunization, proof of Selective Service status. *Application deadlines:* rolling (freshmen), rolling (transfers). *Notification:* continuous (freshmen), continuous (transfers).

Freshman Application Contact Office of Admissions, Sowela Technical Community College, 3820 Senator J. Bennett Johnston Avenue, Lake Charles, LA 70616. *Phone:* 337-421-6550. *Toll-free phone:* 800-256-0483. *Fax:* 337-491-2663.
Website: http://www.sowela.edu/.

Virginia College in Baton Rouge
Baton Rouge, Louisiana

Admissions Office Contact Virginia College in Baton Rouge, 9501 Cortana Place, Baton Rouge, LA 70815.
Website: http://www.vc.edu/.

Virginia College in Shreveport/Bossier City
Bossier City, Louisiana

Admissions Office Contact Virginia College in Shreveport/Bossier City, 2950 East Texas Street, Suite C, Bossier City, LA 71111.
Website: http://www.vc.edu/.

MAINE

Beal College
Bangor, Maine

- **Proprietary** 2-year, founded 1891
- **Small-town** 4-acre campus
- **Coed,** 464 undergraduate students, 78% full-time, 66% women, 34% men

Undergraduates 363 full-time, 101 part-time. Students come from 1 other state; 0.9% Black or African American, non-Hispanic/Latino; 1% Hispanic/Latino; 0.6% Asian, non-Hispanic/Latino; 0.2% Native Hawaiian or other Pacific Islander, non-Hispanic/Latino; 2% American Indian or Alaska Native, non-Hispanic/Latino; 4% Race/ethnicity unknown; 10% transferred in. *Retention:* 60% of full-time freshmen returned.
Freshmen *Admission:* 93 enrolled.
Faculty *Total:* 40, 20% full-time, 3% with terminal degrees. *Student/faculty ratio:* 30:1.
Majors Accounting; administrative assistant and secretarial science; business administration and management; criminal justice/law enforcement administration; health information/medical records technology; human resources management; human services; medical/clinical assistant; medical office assistant; substance abuse/addiction counseling; welding technology.
Academics *Calendar:* modular. *Degree:* certificates, diplomas, and associate. *Special study options:* accelerated degree program, adult/continuing education programs, advanced placement credit, internships, part-time degree program, summer session for credit.
Library Beal College Library.
Student Life *Housing:* college housing not available. *Activities and Organizations:* student-run newspaper.
Applying *Options:* deferred entrance. *Application fee:* $30. *Required:* essay or personal statement, high school transcript, 1 letter of recommendation, interview, entrance exam, immunizations. *Application deadlines:* rolling (freshmen), rolling (transfers).
Freshman Application Contact Sierra Kennedy, Admissions Assistant, Beal College, 99 Farm Road, Bangor, ME 04401. *Phone:* 207-947-4591. *Toll-free phone:* 800-660-7351. *Fax:* 207-947-0208.
E-mail: admissions@bealcollege.edu.
Website: http://www.bealcollege.edu/.

Central Maine Community College
Auburn, Maine

- **State-supported** 2-year, founded 1964, part of Maine Community College System
- **Small-town** 135-acre campus
- **Endowment** $800,000
- **Coed,** 2,984 undergraduate students, 42% full-time, 55% women, 45% men

Undergraduates 1,263 full-time, 1,721 part-time. Students come from 12 states and territories; 1 other country; 5% are from out of state; 6% Black or African American, non-Hispanic/Latino; 2% Hispanic/Latino; 2% Asian, non-Hispanic/Latino; 0.1% Native Hawaiian or other Pacific Islander, non-Hispanic/Latino; 0.8% American Indian or Alaska Native, non-Hispanic/Latino; 2% Two or more races, non-Hispanic/Latino; 10% Race/ethnicity unknown; 0.6% international; 7% transferred in; 8% live on campus.
Freshmen *Admission:* 2,430 applied, 711 admitted, 629 enrolled.
Faculty *Total:* 209, 26% full-time, 1% with terminal degrees. *Student/faculty ratio:* 17:1.
Majors Accounting; administrative assistant and secretarial science; automobile/automotive mechanics technology; biology/biological sciences; building construction technology; business administration and management; civil engineering technology; construction trades related; criminal justice/law enforcement administration; criminal justice/safety; early childhood education; electromechanical technology; graphic and printing equipment operation/production; graphic communications; human services; liberal arts and sciences/liberal studies; licensed practical/vocational nurse training; machine tool technology; medical/clinical assistant; multi/interdisciplinary studies related; network and system administration; physical fitness technician; registered nursing/registered nurse.
Academics *Calendar:* semesters. *Degree:* certificates, diplomas, and associate. *Special study options:* academic remediation for entering students, accelerated degree program, adult/continuing education programs, advanced placement credit, cooperative education, distance learning, English as a second language, independent study, internships, part-time degree program, services for LD students, summer session for credit.

Library Central Maine Community College Library. *Books:* 18,068 (physical); *Serial titles:* 117 (physical); *Databases:* 129. Weekly public service hours: 60; students can reserve study rooms.
Student Life *Housing Options:* coed, men-only, women-only. Campus housing is university owned. Freshman applicants given priority for college housing. *Activities and Organizations:* drama/theater group. *Campus security:* 24-hour emergency response devices, student patrols, controlled dormitory access, night patrols by police.
Athletics Member USCAA. *Intercollegiate sports:* baseball M, basketball M/W, golf M/W, soccer M/W, softball W. *Intramural sports:* volleyball M/W.
Standardized Tests *Recommended:* SAT (for admission), SAT and SAT Subject Tests or ACT (for admission), SAT Subject Tests (for admission).
Costs (2016–17) *Tuition:* state resident $2700 full-time, $1350 per year part-time; nonresident $5400 full-time, $2700 per year part-time. Full-time tuition and fees vary according to course load and program. Part-time tuition and fees vary according to course load and program. *Required fees:* $1050 full-time, $35 per credit hour part-time. *Room and board:* $8916; room only: $4150. Room and board charges vary according to housing facility. *Payment plan:* installment. *Waivers:* employees or children of employees.
Financial Aid Of all full-time matriculated undergraduates who enrolled in 2014, 89 Federal Work-Study jobs (averaging $1200). *Financial aid deadline:* 8/1.
Applying *Options:* electronic application, deferred entrance. *Application fee:* $20. *Required:* high school transcript. *Recommended:* essay or personal statement. *Application deadlines:* rolling (freshmen), rolling (transfers). *Notification:* continuous (freshmen), continuous (transfers).
Freshman Application Contact Ms. Joan Nichols, Admissions Assistant, Central Maine Community College, 1250 Turner Street, Auburn, ME 04210. *Phone:* 207-755-5273. *Toll-free phone:* 800-891-2002. *Fax:* 207-755-5493.
E-mail: enroll@cmcc.edu.
Website: http://www.cmcc.edu/.

Eastern Maine Community College
Bangor, Maine

Freshman Application Contact Mr. W. Gregory Swett, Director of Admissions, Eastern Maine Community College, 354 Hogan Road, Bangor, ME 04401. *Phone:* 207-974-4680. *Toll-free phone:* 800-286-9357. *Fax:* 207-974-4683. *E-mail:* admissions@emcc.edu.
Website: http://www.emcc.edu/.

Kaplan University, Lewiston
Lewiston, Maine

Freshman Application Contact Kaplan University, Lewiston, 475 Lisbon Street, Lewiston, ME 04240. *Phone:* 207-333-3300. *Toll-free phone:* 866-527-5268 (in-state); 800-527-5268 (out-of-state).
Website: http://www.kaplanuniversity.edu/.

Kaplan University, South Portland
South Portland, Maine

Freshman Application Contact Kaplan University, South Portland, 265 Western Avenue, South Portland, ME 04106. *Phone:* 207-774-6126. *Toll-free phone:* 866-527-5268 (in-state); 800-527-5268 (out-of-state).
Website: http://www.kaplanuniversity.edu/.

Kennebec Valley Community College
Fairfield, Maine

- **State-supported** 2-year, founded 1970, part of Maine Community College System
- **Small-town** campus
- **Endowment** $2.8 million
- **Coed,** 2,451 undergraduate students, 30% full-time, 64% women, 36% men

Undergraduates 724 full-time, 1,727 part-time. Students come from 15 states and territories; 2% are from out of state; 0.8% Black or African American, non-Hispanic/Latino; 1% Hispanic/Latino; 0.6% Asian, non-Hispanic/Latino; 0.8% American Indian or Alaska Native, non-Hispanic/Latino; 1% Two or more races, non-Hispanic/Latino; 7% Race/ethnicity unknown; 8% transferred in.
Freshmen *Admission:* 364 enrolled.
Faculty *Total:* 43, 95% full-time.
Majors Accounting technology and bookkeeping; agroecology and sustainable agriculture; biology/biotechnology laboratory technician; building construction technology; child development; cooking and related culinary arts; diagnostic medical sonography and ultrasound technology; drafting/design

engineering technologies related; electrical, electronic and communications engineering technology; electrical/electronics maintenance and repair technology related; electrician; emergency medical technology (EMT paramedic); health information/medical records technology; heating, ventilation, air conditioning and refrigeration engineering technology; industrial mechanics and maintenance technology; liberal arts and sciences/liberal studies; lineworker; machine tool technology; management information systems; marketing/marketing management; medical administrative assistant and medical secretary; medical/clinical assistant; mental and social health services and allied professions related; multi/interdisciplinary studies related; occupational therapist assistant; physical therapy technology; radiologic technology/science; registered nursing/registered nurse; respiratory care therapy; welding technology; wood science and wood products/pulp and paper technology.

Academics *Calendar:* semesters. *Degree:* certificates, diplomas, and associate. *Special study options:* academic remediation for entering students, accelerated degree program, adult/continuing education programs, advanced placement credit, distance learning, external degree program, independent study, internships, part-time degree program, services for LD students, summer session for credit.

Library Lunder Library plus 2 others.

Student Life *Housing:* college housing not available. *Activities and Organizations:* choral group, Phi Theta Kappa, National Society for Leadership and Success, Student Senate, Respiratory Therapy Club, KV Federal Nurses Association. *Campus security:* evening security patrol. *Student services:* personal/psychological counseling.

Athletics *Intercollegiate sports:* ice hockey M/W. *Intramural sports:* basketball M/W, bowling M/W, golf M/W, soccer M/W, softball M/W, volleyball M/W.

Standardized Tests *Required for some:* HESI nursing exam, HOBET for allied health programs, ACCUPLACER. *Recommended:* SAT or ACT (for admission).

Costs (2015–16) *One-time required fee:* $30. *Tuition:* state resident $2700 full-time, $90 per credit hour part-time; nonresident $5400 full-time, $180 per credit hour part-time. *Required fees:* $610 full-time, $3 per credit hour part-time. *Payment plan:* installment. *Waivers:* senior citizens and employees or children of employees.

Financial Aid Of all full-time matriculated undergraduates who enrolled in 2014, 1,971 applied for aid, 1,768 were judged to have need, 16 had their need fully met. In 2014, 11 non-need-based awards were made. *Average percent of need met:* 51%. *Average financial aid package:* $6827. *Average need-based loan:* $3025. *Average need-based gift aid:* $5176. *Average non-need-based aid:* $2090.

Applying *Options:* electronic application, deferred entrance. *Application fee:* $20. *Required:* essay or personal statement, high school transcript. *Required for some:* interview. *Application deadlines:* rolling (freshmen), rolling (transfers). *Notification:* continuous (freshmen), continuous (transfers).

Freshman Application Contact Mr. Crichton McKenna, Assistant Director of Admissions, Kennebec Valley Community College, 92 Western Avenue, Fairfield, ME 04937-1367. *Phone:* 207-453-5155. *Toll-free phone:* 800-528-5882. *Fax:* 207-453-5011. *E-mail:* admissions@kvcc.me.edu. *Website:* http://www.kvcc.me.edu/.

The Landing School
Arundel, Maine

- **Independent** 2-year, founded 1978
- **Rural** 4-acre campus with easy access to Portland, ME and Boston, MA
- **Coed**
- 68% of applicants were admitted

Undergraduates 81 full-time. Students come from 41 states and territories; 8 other countries; 75% are from out of state; 1% Black or African American, non-Hispanic/Latino; 2% Hispanic/Latino; 1% Two or more races, non-Hispanic/Latino; 2% international. *Retention:* 84% of full-time freshmen returned.

Faculty *Student/faculty ratio:* 9:1.

Academics *Calendar:* continuous. *Degree:* diplomas and associate. *Special study options:* academic remediation for entering students, adult/continuing education programs, cooperative education, internships, services for LD students.

Library S/V Patience Learning Resource Center.

Student Life *Campus security:* 24-hour emergency response devices.

Costs (2015–16) *Tuition:* $20,107 full-time. Full-time tuition and fees vary according to program. *Required fees:* $1000 full-time. *Room only:* Room and board charges vary according to housing facility. *Payment plans:* tuition prepayment, installment, deferred payment.

Applying *Options:* electronic application, early admission, deferred entrance. *Required:* essay or personal statement, high school transcript, 3 letters of recommendation, interview.

Freshman Application Contact Kristin Potter, Admissions Representative, The Landing School, 286 River Road, Arundel, ME 04046. *Phone:* 207-985-7976. *E-mail:* info@landingschool.edu. *Website:* http://www.landingschool.edu/.

Maine College of Health Professions
Lewiston, Maine

- **Independent** 2-year, founded 1891
- **Urban** campus
- **Coed,** 199 undergraduate students, 30% full-time, 89% women, 11% men

Undergraduates 60 full-time, 139 part-time. Students come from 3 states and territories; 2% are from out of state; 0.5% Hispanic/Latino; 2% Asian, non-Hispanic/Latino; 0.5% Native Hawaiian or other Pacific Islander, non-Hispanic/Latino; 1% American Indian or Alaska Native, non-Hispanic/Latino; 3% live on campus.

Freshmen *Admission:* 12 applied, 3 admitted, 3 enrolled. *Average high school GPA:* 3.67. *Test scores:* SAT critical reading scores over 700: 34%.

Faculty *Total:* 25, 72% full-time, 4% with terminal degrees. *Student/faculty ratio:* 10:1.

Majors Nuclear medical technology; radiologic technology/science; registered nursing/registered nurse.

Academics *Calendar:* semesters. *Degree:* associate. *Special study options:* advanced placement credit, off-campus study, services for LD students, summer session for credit.

Library Gerrish True Health Sciences Library plus 1 other.

Student Life *Housing Options:* coed. Campus housing is university owned. *Activities and Organizations:* Student Communication Council, Student Government, Student Nurses Association. *Campus security:* 24-hour emergency response devices and patrols, late-night transport/escort service, controlled dormitory access. *Student services:* health clinic, personal/psychological counseling.

Standardized Tests *Required:* SAT or ACT (for admission). *Required for some:* HESI Entrance Exam for nursing, ACCUPLACER.

Costs (2016–17) *Tuition:* $9310 full-time. *Required fees:* $1590 full-time. *Room only:* $2350. *Waivers:* employees or children of employees.

Financial Aid Of all full-time matriculated undergraduates who enrolled in 2010, 5 applied for aid, 4 were judged to have need. *Average financial aid package:* $17,200. *Average need-based loan:* $4000. *Average need-based gift aid:* $7700.

Applying *Application fee:* $50. *Required:* essay or personal statement, high school transcript, high school or college-level algebra, second math, biology, chemistry. *Application deadline:* 1/15 (freshmen). *Notification:* 3/15 (freshmen).

Freshman Application Contact Ms. Erica Watson, Admissions Director, Maine College of Health Professions, 70 Middle Street, Lewiston, ME 04240. *Phone:* 207-795-2843. *Fax:* 207-795-2849. *E-mail:* watsoner@cmhc.org. *Website:* http://www.mchp.edu/.

Northern Maine Community College
Presque Isle, Maine

Freshman Application Contact Ms. Nancy Gagnon, Admissions Secretary, Northern Maine Community College, 33 Edgemont Drive, Presque Isle, ME 04769-2016. *Phone:* 207-768-2785. *Toll-free phone:* 800-535-6682. *Fax:* 207-768-2848. *E-mail:* ngagnon@nmcc.edu. *Website:* http://www.nmcc.edu/.

Southern Maine Community College
South Portland, Maine

- **State-supported** 2-year, founded 1946, part of Maine Community College System
- **Suburban** 80-acre campus
- **Coed,** 6,045 undergraduate students, 43% full-time, 52% women, 48% men

Undergraduates 2,618 full-time, 3,427 part-time. Students come from 25 states and territories; 19 other countries; 4% are from out of state; 6% Black or African American, non-Hispanic/Latino; 3% Hispanic/Latino; 2% Asian, non-Hispanic/Latino; 0.1% Native Hawaiian or other Pacific Islander, non-Hispanic/Latino; 0.6% American Indian or Alaska Native, non-Hispanic/Latino; 2% Two or more races, non-Hispanic/Latino; 4% Race/ethnicity unknown; 0.4% international; 8% transferred in; 5% live on campus. *Retention:* 55% of full-time freshmen returned.

Freshmen *Admission:* 1,251 enrolled.

Faculty *Total:* 427, 25% full-time. *Student/faculty ratio:* 18:1.

Majors Agroecology and sustainable agriculture; automobile/automotive mechanics technology; biotechnology; business administration and management; cardiovascular technology; computer engineering technology; computer science; culinary arts; dietetic technology; digital communication and media/multimedia; drafting and design technology; early childhood education; electrical, electronic and communications engineering technology; emergency medical technology (EMT paramedic); fire science/firefighting; health information/medical records technology; heating, air conditioning, ventilation and refrigeration maintenance technology; liberal arts and sciences and humanities related; machine tool technology; marine biology and biological oceanography; materials engineering; medical/clinical assistant; plumbing technology; pre-engineering; radiologic technology/science; registered nursing/registered nurse; respiratory care therapy; surgical technology.

Academics *Calendar:* semesters. *Degree:* certificates and associate. *Special study options:* academic remediation for entering students, advanced placement credit, distance learning, double majors, English as a second language, honors programs, independent study, internships, off-campus study, part-time degree program, services for LD students, study abroad, summer session for credit.

Library Southern Maine Community College Library. *Books:* 20,586 (physical), 30,783 (digital/electronic); *Serial titles:* 1,026 (physical), 23,074 (digital/electronic); *Databases:* 34. Weekly public service hours: 68; students can reserve study rooms.

Student Life *Housing Options:* coed. Campus housing is university owned. *Activities and Organizations:* drama/theater group, student-run newspaper, choral group, Student Senate. *Campus security:* 24-hour emergency response devices and patrols, student patrols, late-night transport/escort service, controlled dormitory access. *Student services:* personal/psychological counseling.

Athletics Member USCAA. *Intercollegiate sports:* baseball M, basketball M/W, golf M/W, soccer M/W, softball W. *Intramural sports:* cheerleading M(c)/W, cross-country running M(c)/W(c), ice hockey M(c), rock climbing M(c)/W(c), soccer M/W, volleyball M/W.

Standardized Tests *Recommended:* SAT or ACT (for admission).

Costs (2015–16) *Tuition:* state resident $2700 full-time, $90 per credit part-time; nonresident $5400 full-time, $180 per credit part-time. *Required fees:* $950 full-time, $30 per credit hour part-time, $25 per term part-time. *Room and board:* $8788. *Payment plan:* installment. *Waivers:* senior citizens and employees or children of employees.

Financial Aid Of all full-time matriculated undergraduates who enrolled in 2014, 130 Federal Work-Study jobs (averaging $1500).

Applying *Options:* electronic application. *Application fee:* $20. *Required:* high school transcript. *Application deadlines:* rolling (freshmen), rolling (out-of-state freshmen), rolling (transfers). *Notification:* continuous (freshmen), continuous (out-of-state freshmen), continuous (transfers).

Freshman Application Contact Amy Lee, Director of Enrollment Services, Southern Maine Community College, 2 Fort Road, South, Portland, ME 04106. *Phone:* 207-741-5800. *Toll-free phone:* 877-282-2182. *Fax:* 207-741-5760. *E-mail:* alee@smccme.edu.
Website: http://www.smccme.edu/.

Washington County Community College
Calais, Maine

- **State-supported** 2-year, founded 1969, part of Maine Community College System
- **Rural** 40-acre campus
- **Coed,** 374 undergraduate students

Undergraduates Students come from 4 states and territories; 1 other country; 3% are from out of state. *Retention:* 63% of full-time freshmen returned.

Faculty *Student/faculty ratio:* 11:1.

Majors Automobile/automotive mechanics technology; business administration and management; child development; computer installation and repair technology; construction engineering technology; engineering technology; marine maintenance and ship repair technology; mechanic and repair technologies related; medical/clinical assistant; multi/interdisciplinary studies related; parks, recreation, leisure, and fitness studies related; teacher assistant/aide.

Academics *Calendar:* semesters. *Degree:* certificates, diplomas, and associate. *Special study options:* academic remediation for entering students, adult/continuing education programs, advanced placement credit, cooperative education, distance learning, double majors, external degree program, independent study, internships, off-campus study, part-time degree program, services for LD students, study abroad.

Library Washington County Technical College Library.

Student Life *Housing Options:* coed. *Activities and Organizations:* choral group. *Campus security:* 24-hour emergency response devices. *Student services:* personal/psychological counseling.

Athletics *Intramural sports:* basketball M/W.

Costs (2015–16) *Tuition:* $135 per credit hour part-time; state resident $2700 full-time, $90 per credit hour part-time; nonresident $5400 full-time, $180 per credit hour part-time. Full-time tuition and fees vary according to course load and program. Part-time tuition and fees vary according to course load and program. *Required fees:* $830 full-time. *Room and board:* $5340; room only: $3770. *Payment plan:* installment. *Waivers:* minority students, senior citizens, and employees or children of employees.

Financial Aid Of all full-time matriculated undergraduates who enrolled in 2014, 269 applied for aid, 269 were judged to have need.

Applying *Options:* deferred entrance. *Application fee:* $20. *Required:* essay or personal statement, high school transcript, interview. *Recommended:* minimum 2.0 GPA. *Application deadline:* rolling (freshmen). *Notification:* continuous (freshmen).

Freshman Application Contact Washington County Community College, One College Drive, Calais, ME 04619. *Phone:* 207-454-1000. *Toll-free phone:* 800-210-6932.
Website: http://www.wccc.me.edu/.

York County Community College
Wells, Maine

- **State-supported** 2-year, founded 1994, part of Maine Community College System
- **Small-town** 84-acre campus with easy access to Boston
- **Endowment** $559,868
- **Coed,** 1,758 undergraduate students, 27% full-time, 64% women, 36% men

Undergraduates 466 full-time, 1,292 part-time. Students come from 12 states and territories; 2% are from out of state; 0.9% Black or African American, non-Hispanic/Latino; 2% Hispanic/Latino; 1% Asian, non-Hispanic/Latino; 0.1% Native Hawaiian or other Pacific Islander, non-Hispanic/Latino; 0.7% American Indian or Alaska Native, non-Hispanic/Latino; 2% Two or more races, non-Hispanic/Latino; 14% Race/ethnicity unknown; 0.4% international; 27% transferred in. *Retention:* 58% of full-time freshmen returned.

Freshmen *Admission:* 560 applied, 327 admitted, 210 enrolled.

Faculty *Total:* 152, 16% full-time, 12% with terminal degrees. *Student/faculty ratio:* 13:1.

Majors Accounting; animation, interactive technology, video graphics and special effects; architectural drafting and CAD/CADD; business administration and management; computer science; construction trades related; criminal justice/safety; culinary arts; drafting and design technology; early childhood education; education; health information/medical records technology; health services/allied health/health sciences; human services; liberal arts and sciences/liberal studies; machine tool technology; medical/clinical assistant; multi/interdisciplinary studies related; network and system administration; veterinary/animal health technology.

Academics *Calendar:* semesters. *Degree:* certificates and associate. *Special study options:* academic remediation for entering students, adult/continuing education programs, advanced placement credit, cooperative education, distance learning, internships, off-campus study, part-time degree program, services for LD students, summer session for credit.

Library Library and Learning Resource Center plus 1 other. *Books:* 12,399 (physical); *Serial titles:* 1,625 (physical); *Databases:* 28. Weekly public service hours: 57; students can reserve study rooms.

Student Life *Housing:* college housing not available. *Activities and Organizations:* Student Senate, Phi Theta Kappa, Criminal Justice Club. *Campus security:* 24-hour emergency response devices, late-night transport/escort service.

Athletics *Intramural sports:* basketball M/W, ice hockey M/W, soccer M/W, softball M/W, ultimate Frisbee M/W, volleyball M/W.

Costs (2015–16) *Tuition:* state resident $2700 full-time, $90 per credit part-time; nonresident $5400 full-time, $180 per credit part-time. Full-time tuition and fees vary according to course level and course load. Part-time tuition and fees vary according to course level and course load. *Required fees:* $780 full-time. *Payment plan:* installment. *Waivers:* senior citizens and employees or children of employees.

Financial Aid Of all full-time matriculated undergraduates who enrolled in 2014, 232 applied for aid, 197 were judged to have need, 3 had their need fully met. In 2014, 12 non-need-based awards were made. *Average percent of need met:* 45%. *Average financial aid package:* $6573. *Average need-based loan:* $3070. *Average need-based gift aid:* $5586. *Average non-need-based aid:* $905. *Average indebtedness upon graduation:* $11,034.

Applying *Options:* electronic application. *Required:* high school transcript, interview. *Application deadlines:* rolling (freshmen), rolling (transfers).

Freshman Application Contact Fred Quistgard, Director of Admissions, York County Community College, 112 College Drive, Wells, ME 04090. *Phone:* 207-216-4406 Ext. 311. *Toll-free phone:* 800-580-3820. *Fax:* 207-641-0837.
Website: http://www.yccc.edu/.

MARSHALL ISLANDS

College of the Marshall Islands
Majuro, Marshall Islands, Marshall Islands

Freshman Application Contact Ms. Rosita Capelle, Director of Admissions and Records, College of the Marshall Islands, PO Box 1258, Majuro, MH 96960, Marshall Islands. *Phone:* 692-625-6823. *Fax:* 692-625-7203.
E-mail: cmiadmissions@cmi.edu.
Website: http://www.cmi.edu/.

MARYLAND

Allegany College of Maryland
Cumberland, Maryland

Freshman Application Contact Ms. Cathy Nolan, Director of Admissions and Registration, Allegany College of Maryland, Cumberland, MD 21502. *Phone:* 301-784-5000 Ext. 5202. *Fax:* 301-784-5220.
E-mail: cnolan@allegany.edu.
Website: http://www.allegany.edu/.

Anne Arundel Community College
Arnold, Maryland

- **State and locally supported** 2-year, founded 1961
- **Suburban** 230-acre campus with easy access to Baltimore and Washington, DC
- **Coed**, 14,689 undergraduate students, 29% full-time, 59% women, 41% men

Undergraduates 4,257 full-time, 10,432 part-time. Students come from 21 states and territories; 92 other countries; 15% are from out of state; 18% Black or African American, non-Hispanic/Latino; 7% Hispanic/Latino; 4% Asian, non-Hispanic/Latino; 0.3% Native Hawaiian or other Pacific Islander, non-Hispanic/Latino; 0.4% American Indian or Alaska Native, non-Hispanic/Latino; 4% Two or more races, non-Hispanic/Latino; 7% Race/ethnicity unknown; 1% international; 29% transferred in.
Freshmen *Admission:* 2,361 enrolled. *Test scores:* SAT critical reading scores over 500: 53%; SAT math scores over 500: 69%; SAT writing scores over 500: 49%; ACT scores over 18: 73%; SAT critical reading scores over 600: 12%; SAT math scores over 600: 24%; SAT writing scores over 600: 13%; ACT scores over 24: 29%; SAT math scores over 700: 1%; SAT writing scores over 700: 2%; ACT scores over 30: 11%.
Faculty *Total:* 1,266, 21% full-time, 9% with terminal degrees. *Student/faculty ratio:* 13:1.
Majors Accounting technology and bookkeeping; architectural drafting and CAD/CADD; business administration and management; business administration, management and operations related; business/commerce; chemistry teacher education; child-care and support services management; clinical/medical laboratory technology; communications technologies and support services related; computer and information sciences; computer and information systems security; computer systems networking and telecommunications; criminal justice/law enforcement administration; criminal justice/police science; early childhood education; electrical and electronics engineering; electrical, electronic and communications engineering technology; engineering; English/language arts teacher education; entrepreneurship; fire prevention and safety technology; gerontology; graphic design; health and physical education/fitness; health information/medical records technology; hotel/motel administration; legal assistant/paralegal; liberal arts and sciences and humanities related; liberal arts and sciences/liberal studies; management information systems; management information systems and services related; mathematics; mathematics teacher education; mechatronics, robotics, and automation engineering; medical administrative assistant and medical secretary; medical radiologic technology; multi/interdisciplinary studies related; occupational safety and health technology; physical therapy technology; physics teacher education; pre-law studies; psychiatric/mental health services technology; public health; registered nursing/registered nurse; Spanish language teacher education; substance abuse/addiction counseling; surgical technology.
Academics *Calendar:* semesters. *Degree:* certificates and associate. *Special study options:* academic remediation for entering students, accelerated degree program, adult/continuing education programs, advanced placement credit, cooperative education, distance learning, English as a second language, freshman honors college, honors programs, independent study, internships,

part-time degree program, services for LD students, summer session for credit. *ROTC:* Army (c), Air Force (c).
Library Andrew G. Truxal Library plus 1 other.
Student Life *Housing:* college housing not available. *Activities and Organizations:* drama/theater group, student-run newspaper, choral group, Drama Club, Student Association, Black Student Union, International Student Association, Chemistry Club. *Campus security:* 24-hour emergency response devices and patrols, student patrols, late-night transport/escort service. *Student services:* health clinic, personal/psychological counseling.
Athletics Member NJCAA. *Intercollegiate sports:* baseball M(s), basketball M(s)/W(s), cross-country running W, golf M, lacrosse M(s)/W(s), soccer M/W(s), softball W, volleyball W. *Intramural sports:* weight lifting M/W.
Costs (2015–16) *Tuition:* area resident $3150 full-time, $105 per credit hour part-time; state resident $6060 full-time, $202 per credit hour part-time; nonresident $10,710 full-time, $357 per credit hour part-time. Full-time tuition and fees vary according to program. Part-time tuition and fees vary according to program. *Required fees:* $770 full-time, $26 per credit hour part-time. *Payment plans:* installment, deferred payment. *Waivers:* adult students, senior citizens, and employees or children of employees.
Applying *Options:* electronic application, early admission, deferred entrance. *Required:* high school transcript. *Application deadlines:* rolling (freshmen), rolling (out-of-state freshmen), rolling (transfers). *Notification:* continuous (freshmen), continuous (out-of-state freshmen), continuous (transfers).
Freshman Application Contact Mr. Thomas McGinn, Director of Enrollment Development and Admissions, Anne Arundel Community College, 101 College Parkway, Arnold, MD 21012-1895. *Phone:* 410-777-2240. *Fax:* 410-777-2246. *E-mail:* 4info@aacc.edu.
Website: http://www.aacc.edu/.

Baltimore City Community College
Baltimore, Maryland

Freshman Application Contact Baltimore City Community College, 2901 Liberty Heights Avenue, Baltimore, MD 21215-7893. *Phone:* 410-462-8311. *Toll-free phone:* 888-203-1261.
Website: http://www.bccc.edu/.

Brightwood College, Baltimore Campus
Baltimore, Maryland

Freshman Application Contact Brightwood College, Baltimore Campus, 1520 South Caton Avenue, Baltimore, MD 21227. *Phone:* 410-644-6400. *Toll-free phone:* 800-935-1857.
Website: http://www.brightwood.edu/.

Brightwood College, Beltsville Campus
Beltsville, Maryland

Freshman Application Contact Brightwood College, Beltsville Campus, 4600 Powder Mill Road, Beltsville, MD 20705. *Phone:* 301-937-8448. *Toll-free phone:* 800-935-1857.
Website: http://www.brightwood.edu/.

Brightwood College, Towson Campus
Towson, Maryland

Freshman Application Contact Brightwood College, Towson Campus, 803 Glen Eagles Court, Towson, MD 21286. *Phone:* 410-296-5350. *Toll-free phone:* 800-935-1857.
Website: http://www.brightwood.edu/.

Carroll Community College
Westminster, Maryland

- **State and locally supported** 2-year, founded 1993, part of Maryland Higher Education Commission
- **Suburban** 80-acre campus with easy access to Baltimore
- **Endowment** $5.7 million
- **Coed**, 3,549 undergraduate students, 37% full-time, 61% women, 39% men

Undergraduates 1,297 full-time, 2,252 part-time. Students come from 6 states and territories; 20 other countries; 3% are from out of state; 4% Black or African American, non-Hispanic/Latino; 4% Hispanic/Latino; 2% Asian, non-Hispanic/Latino; 0.3% American Indian or Alaska Native, non-Hispanic/Latino; 2% Two or more races, non-Hispanic/Latino; 2% Race/ethnicity unknown; 0.2% international; 6% transferred in.
Freshmen *Admission:* 737 applied, 737 admitted, 737 enrolled.

Faculty *Total:* 263, 30% full-time, 6% with terminal degrees. *Student/faculty ratio:* 14:1.

Majors Accounting technology and bookkeeping; administrative assistant and secretarial science; architectural drafting and CAD/CADD; art; business administration and management; chemistry teacher education; child-care and support services management; computer engineering; computer graphics; criminal justice/police science; early childhood education; education; electrical and electronics engineering; elementary education; emergency medical technology (EMT paramedic); English/language arts teacher education; forensic science and technology; general studies; health information/medical records technology; health professions related; kinesiology and exercise science; legal studies; liberal arts and sciences/liberal studies; licensed practical/vocational nurse training; management information systems; mathematics teacher education; multi/interdisciplinary studies related; music; physical therapy technology; psychology; registered nursing/registered nurse; Spanish language teacher education; theater design and technology.

Academics *Calendar:* semesters plus winter and summer sessions. *Degree:* certificates and associate. *Special study options:* academic remediation for entering students, advanced placement credit, distance learning, English as a second language, honors programs, independent study, internships, part-time degree program, services for LD students, summer session for credit.

Library Carroll Community College Library plus 1 other. *Books:* 41,599 (physical), 695 (digital/electronic); *Serial titles:* 2,491 (physical), 18,070 (digital/electronic); *Databases:* 44.

Student Life *Housing:* college housing not available. *Activities and Organizations:* drama/theater group, choral group, Student Government Organization, S.T.E.M. Club, Campus Activities Board, Service Learning Club, Early Childhood Education Club. *Campus security:* 24-hour emergency response devices, late night security escort to vehicle in parking lot.

Costs (2015–16) *Tuition:* area resident $4524 full-time, $151 per credit hour part-time; state resident $6576 full-time, $219 per credit hour part-time; nonresident $9168 full-time, $306 per credit hour part-time. *Payment plan:* deferred payment. *Waivers:* senior citizens and employees or children of employees.

Financial Aid Of all full-time matriculated undergraduates who enrolled in 2014, 43 Federal Work-Study jobs (averaging $2002).

Applying *Options:* electronic application. *Required:* high school transcript. *Application deadlines:* rolling (freshmen), rolling (out-of-state freshmen), rolling (transfers). *Notification:* continuous (freshmen), continuous (out-of-state freshmen), continuous (transfers).

Freshman Application Contact Ms. Candace Edwards, Director of Admissions, Carroll Community College, 1601 Washington Road, Westminster, MD 21157. *Phone:* 410-386-8405. *Toll-free phone:* 888-221-9748. *Fax:* 410-386-8446. *E-mail:* cedwards@carrollcc.edu. *Website:* http://www.carrollcc.edu/.

Cecil College
North East, Maryland

- **County-supported** 2-year, founded 1968
- **Small-town** 159-acre campus with easy access to Baltimore
- **Coed,** 2,591 undergraduate students, 39% full-time, 61% women, 39% men

Undergraduates 1,003 full-time, 1,588 part-time. Students come from 11 states and territories; 15 other countries; 11% are from out of state; 10% Black or African American, non-Hispanic/Latino; 5% Hispanic/Latino; 1% Asian, non-Hispanic/Latino; 0.5% American Indian or Alaska Native, non-Hispanic/Latino; 3% Two or more races, non-Hispanic/Latino; 0.5% Race/ethnicity unknown; 0.5% international; 4% transferred in. *Retention:* 56% of full-time freshmen returned.

Freshmen *Admission:* 458 applied, 458 admitted, 452 enrolled.

Faculty *Total:* 311, 16% full-time, 5% with terminal degrees. *Student/faculty ratio:* 13:1.

Majors Administrative assistant and secretarial science; aeronautics/aviation/aerospace science and technology; air traffic control; animation, interactive technology, video graphics and special effects; applied horticulture/horticulture operations; biology/biological sciences; biotechnology; business administration and management; business/commerce; business/corporate communications; chemistry; child-care and support services management; commercial photography; criminal justice/police science; design and visual communications; drawing; education; electrical, electronic and communications engineering technology; elementary education; emergency medical technology (EMT paramedic); English/language arts teacher education; financial planning and services; fine/studio arts; fire science/firefighting; general studies; health services/allied health/health sciences; horse husbandry/equine science and management; human resources management; liberal arts and sciences/liberal studies; logistics, materials, and supply chain management; management information systems; marketing/marketing management; mathematics; office management; photography; physics; purchasing, procurement/acquisitions and contracts

management; registered nursing/registered nurse; secondary education; transportation and materials moving related; transportation/mobility management; web page, digital/multimedia and information resources design.

Academics *Calendar:* semesters. *Degree:* certificates and associate. *Special study options:* academic remediation for entering students, accelerated degree program, adult/continuing education programs, advanced placement credit, cooperative education, distance learning, double majors, English as a second language, independent study, internships, off-campus study, part-time degree program, services for LD students, summer session for credit.

Library Cecil County Veterans Memorial Library.

Student Life *Housing:* college housing not available. *Activities and Organizations:* drama/theater group, Student Government, Non-Traditional Student Organization, Student Nurses Association, national fraternities. *Campus security:* 24-hour emergency response devices, late-night transport/escort service, armed patrols from 6:30 a.m. until 7:00 p.m.. *Student services:* personal/psychological counseling, women's center.

Athletics Member NJCAA. *Intercollegiate sports:* baseball M(s), basketball M(s)/W(s), cheerleading W, lacrosse M(c), soccer M(s)/W(s), softball W(s), tennis W(s), volleyball W(s).

Costs (2015–16) *Tuition:* area resident $3000 full-time, $100 per credit hour part-time; state resident $5700 full-time, $190 per credit hour part-time; nonresident $7050 full-time, $235 per credit hour part-time. *Required fees:* $362 full-time. *Payment plan:* deferred payment. *Waivers:* senior citizens and employees or children of employees.

Applying *Options:* electronic application, early admission, deferred entrance. *Required:* high school transcript. *Application deadlines:* rolling (freshmen), rolling (out-of-state freshmen), rolling (transfers). *Notification:* continuous (freshmen), continuous (out-of-state freshmen), continuous (transfers).

Freshman Application Contact Dr. Diane Lane, Cecil College, One Seahawk Drive, North East, MD 21901-1999. *Phone:* 410-287-1002. *Fax:* 410-287-1001. *E-mail:* dlane@cecil.edu. *Website:* http://www.cecil.edu/.

Chesapeake College
Wye Mills, Maryland

- **State and locally supported** 2-year, founded 1965
- **Rural** 170-acre campus with easy access to Baltimore and Washington, DC
- **Endowment** $3.7 million
- **Coed,** 2,069 undergraduate students, 37% full-time, 66% women, 34% men

Undergraduates 773 full-time, 1,296 part-time. 17% Black or African American, non-Hispanic/Latino; 4% Hispanic/Latino; 1% Asian, non-Hispanic/Latino; 0.1% Native Hawaiian or other Pacific Islander, non-Hispanic/Latino; 0.8% American Indian or Alaska Native, non-Hispanic/Latino; 2% Two or more races, non-Hispanic/Latino; 2% Race/ethnicity unknown; 1% international; 16% transferred in. *Retention:* 43% of full-time freshmen returned.

Freshmen *Admission:* 541 enrolled.

Faculty *Total:* 127, 43% full-time, 19% with terminal degrees. *Student/faculty ratio:* 17:1.

Majors Accounting technology and bookkeeping; business administration and management; business/commerce; child-care and support services management; computer and information sciences and support services related; computer and information systems security; computer science; corrections and criminal justice related; early childhood education; education; elementary education; emergency medical technology (EMT paramedic); engineering-related technologies; general studies; hospitality administration; legal assistant/paralegal; liberal arts and sciences and humanities related; liberal arts and sciences/liberal studies; mathematics teacher education; medical radiologic technology; mental and social health services and allied professions related; physical therapy; physics teacher education; registered nursing/registered nurse.

Academics *Calendar:* semesters. *Degree:* certificates and associate. *Special study options:* academic remediation for entering students, adult/continuing education programs, advanced placement credit, cooperative education, distance learning, English as a second language, honors programs, independent study, internships, part-time degree program, services for LD students, summer session for credit.

Library Learning Resource Center.

Student Life *Housing:* college housing not available. *Activities and Organizations:* drama/theater group. *Campus security:* 24-hour patrols. *Student services:* personal/psychological counseling, women's center.

Athletics Member NJCAA. *Intercollegiate sports:* baseball M, basketball M/W, soccer M, softball W, volleyball W.

Costs (2015–16) *Tuition:* area resident $3450 full-time, $115 per credit hour part-time; state resident $5490 full-time, $183 per credit hour part-time; nonresident $7800 full-time, $260 per credit hour part-time. *Required fees:* $1045 full-time, $34 per credit hour part-time, $25 per term part-time.

Payment plan: installment. *Waivers:* senior citizens and employees or children of employees.

Financial Aid Of all full-time matriculated undergraduates who enrolled in 2014, 32 Federal Work-Study jobs (averaging $1482).

Applying *Options:* electronic application, early admission, deferred entrance. *Required:* high school transcript. *Application deadlines:* rolling (freshmen), rolling (out-of-state freshmen), rolling (transfers). *Notification:* continuous (freshmen), continuous (out-of-state freshmen), continuous (transfers).

Freshman Application Contact Ms. Marci Leach, Director of Student Recruitment and Outreach, Chesapeake College, PO Box 8, Wye Mills, MD 21679-0008. *Phone:* 410-822-5400. *Fax:* 410-827-5875.
E-mail: mleach@chesapeake.edu.
Website: http://www.chesapeake.edu/.

College of Southern Maryland
La Plata, Maryland

- **State and locally supported** 2-year, founded 1958
- **Rural** 175-acre campus with easy access to Washington, DC
- **Coed**

Undergraduates 3,087 full-time, 5,324 part-time. 26% Black or African American, non-Hispanic/Latino; 6% Hispanic/Latino; 3% Asian, non-Hispanic/Latino; 0.3% Native Hawaiian or other Pacific Islander, non-Hispanic/Latino; 0.5% American Indian or Alaska Native, non-Hispanic/Latino; 5% Two or more races, non-Hispanic/Latino; 2% Race/ethnicity unknown; 0.4% international; 7% transferred in.

Faculty *Student/faculty ratio:* 19:1.

Academics *Calendar:* semesters. *Degree:* certificates and associate. *Special study options:* academic remediation for entering students, accelerated degree program, adult/continuing education programs, advanced placement credit, cooperative education, distance learning, honors programs, independent study, part-time degree program, services for LD students, study abroad, summer session for credit.

Library College of Southern Maryland Library.

Student Life *Campus security:* 24-hour emergency response devices and patrols.

Athletics Member NJCAA.

Financial Aid Of all full-time matriculated undergraduates who enrolled in 2013, 2,067 applied for aid, 1,496 were judged to have need, 10 had their need fully met. In 2013, 12. *Average percent of need met:* 35. *Average financial aid package:* $5727. *Average need-based loan:* $3115. *Average need-based gift aid:* $5347. *Average non-need-based aid:* $1090.

Applying *Options:* electronic application, early admission, deferred entrance. *Recommended:* high school transcript.

Freshman Application Contact Admissions Department, College of Southern Maryland, PO Box 910, La Plata, MD 20646-0910. *Phone:* 301-934-2251. *Toll-free phone:* 800-933-9177. *Fax:* 301-934-7698.
E-mail: askme@csmd.edu.
Website: http://www.csmd.edu/.

Community College of Baltimore County
Baltimore, Maryland

- **County-supported** 2-year, founded 1957
- **Suburban** 350-acre campus with easy access to Baltimore
- **Coed,** 22,399 undergraduate students, 29% full-time, 60% women, 40% men

Undergraduates 6,454 full-time, 15,945 part-time. 40% Black or African American, non-Hispanic/Latino; 5% Hispanic/Latino; 6% Asian, non-Hispanic/Latino; 0.2% Native Hawaiian or other Pacific Islander, non-Hispanic/Latino; 0.4% American Indian or Alaska Native, non-Hispanic/Latino; 4% Two or more races, non-Hispanic/Latino; 0.5% Race/ethnicity unknown; 4% international.

Freshmen *Admission:* 4,157 enrolled.

Faculty *Total:* 1,282, 34% full-time, 9% with terminal degrees.

Majors Accounting technology and bookkeeping; administrative assistant and secretarial science; aeronautics/aviation/aerospace science and technology; applied horticulture/horticulture operations; architectural drafting and CAD/CADD; automobile/automotive mechanics technology; biological and physical sciences; building/construction finishing, management, and inspection related; building/construction site management; business administration and management; business/commerce; chemistry teacher education; child-care and support services management; clinical/medical laboratory technology; commercial and advertising art; computer and information sciences; computer and information systems security; computer engineering; computer systems networking and telecommunications; criminal justice/police science; dental hygiene; early childhood education; education; electrical and electronics engineering; elementary education; emergency medical technology (EMT paramedic); engineering; engineering technologies

and engineering related; funeral service and mortuary science; geography; heating, ventilation, air conditioning and refrigeration engineering technology; hotel/motel administration; hydraulics and fluid power technology; legal assistant/paralegal; liberal arts and sciences and humanities related; liberal arts and sciences/liberal studies; management information systems; massage therapy; mathematics teacher education; medical administrative assistant and medical secretary; medical informatics; medical radiologic technology; occupational safety and health technology; occupational therapy; parks, recreation and leisure; parks, recreation, leisure, and fitness studies related; physics teacher education; psychiatric/mental health services technology; registered nursing/registered nurse; respiratory care therapy; sign language interpretation and translation; Spanish language teacher education; substance abuse/addiction counseling; surveying technology; veterinary/animal health technology; visual and performing arts.

Academics *Calendar:* semesters. *Degree:* certificates and associate. *Special study options:* academic remediation for entering students, advanced placement credit, cooperative education, distance learning, English as a second language, honors programs, independent study, internships, off-campus study, part-time degree program, services for LD students, study abroad, summer session for credit.

Student Life *Housing:* college housing not available. *Activities and Organizations:* drama/theater group, student-run newspaper, choral group. *Campus security:* 24-hour emergency response devices and patrols, late-night transport/escort service.

Athletics Member NJCAA. *Intercollegiate sports:* baseball M(s), basketball M(s)/W(s), cross-country running W(s), lacrosse M(s)/W(s), soccer M(s)/W(s), softball W(s), track and field W(s), volleyball W(s).

Standardized Tests *Recommended:* SAT or ACT (for admission).

Costs (2015–16) *Tuition:* area resident $3390 full-time, $113 per credit part-time; state resident $6480 full-time, $216 per credit part-time; nonresident $9720 full-time, $324 per credit part-time. Full-time tuition and fees vary according to course load. Part-time tuition and fees vary according to course load. *Required fees:* $862 full-time. *Payment plan:* installment. *Waivers:* employees or children of employees.

Applying *Options:* electronic application. *Required:* high school transcript. *Application deadlines:* rolling (freshmen), rolling (out-of-state freshmen), rolling (transfers).

Freshman Application Contact Ms. Diane Drake, Director of Admissions, Community College of Baltimore County, 7201 Rossville Boulevard, Baltimore, MD 21237-3899. *Phone:* 443-840-4392.
E-mail: ddrake@ccbcmd.edu.
Website: http://www.ccbcmd.edu/.

Fortis College
Landover, Maryland

Admissions Office Contact Fortis College, 4351 Garden City Drive, Landover, MD 20785. *Toll-free phone:* 855-4-FORTIS.
Website: http://www.fortis.edu/.

Frederick Community College
Frederick, Maryland

- **State and locally supported** 2-year, founded 1957
- **Small-town** 100-acre campus with easy access to Baltimore and Washington, DC
- **Endowment** $13.0 million
- **Coed,** 6,197 undergraduate students, 33% full-time, 56% women, 44% men

Undergraduates 2,057 full-time, 4,140 part-time. 2% are from out of state; 14% Black or African American, non-Hispanic/Latino; 11% Hispanic/Latino; 5% Asian, non-Hispanic/Latino; 0.4% American Indian or Alaska Native, non-Hispanic/Latino; 4% Two or more races, non-Hispanic/Latino; 0.3% Race/ethnicity unknown; 0.6% international; 3% transferred in. *Retention:* 45% of full-time freshmen returned.

Freshmen *Admission:* 1,297 enrolled.

Faculty *Total:* 531, 19% full-time, 15% with terminal degrees. *Student/faculty ratio:* 11:1.

Majors Accounting; art; biology/biological sciences; building/construction finishing, management, and inspection related; business administration and management; chemistry; child development; computer science; criminal justice/law enforcement administration; drafting and design technology; early childhood education; education; elementary education; emergency medical technology (EMT paramedic); engineering; fire science/firefighting; general studies; human services; information technology; legal assistant/paralegal; liberal arts and sciences/liberal studies; mathematics; mathematics teacher education; medical administrative assistant and medical secretary; medical/clinical assistant; nuclear medical technology; political science and government; psychology; registered nursing/registered nurse; respiratory care therapy; Spanish language teacher education; surgical technology.

Academics *Calendar:* semesters. *Degree:* certificates and associate. *Special study options:* academic remediation for entering students, adult/continuing education programs, advanced placement credit, cooperative education, distance learning, English as a second language, external degree program, freshman honors college, honors programs, independent study, internships, off-campus study, part-time degree program, services for LD students, study abroad, summer session for credit.

Library FCC Library. *Books:* 12,000 (physical), 186 (digital/electronic); *Serial titles:* 2,068 (physical); *Databases:* 25. Students can reserve study rooms.

Student Life *Housing:* college housing not available. *Activities and Organizations:* drama/theater group, student-run newspaper. *Campus security:* 24-hour emergency response devices and patrols, late-night transport/escort service. *Student services:* personal/psychological counseling, women's center.

Athletics Member NJCAA. *Intercollegiate sports:* baseball M, basketball M/W, golf M/W, lacrosse M/W, soccer M/W, softball W, volleyball W.

Costs (2015–16) *Tuition:* area resident $4166 full-time, $116 per credit hour part-time; state resident $8246 full-time, $252 per credit hour part-time; nonresident $10,946 full-time, $342 per credit hour part-time. *Required fees:* $20 per credit hour part-time, $57 per semester part-time. *Payment plans:* installment, deferred payment. *Waivers:* senior citizens.

Financial Aid Of all full-time matriculated undergraduates who enrolled in 2014, 25 Federal Work-Study jobs (averaging $1368). 14 state and other part-time jobs (averaging $2715).

Applying *Options:* electronic application. *Recommended:* high school transcript. *Application deadlines:* rolling (freshmen), rolling (transfers). *Notification:* continuous (freshmen), continuous (transfers).

Freshman Application Contact Ms. Lisa A. Freel, Director of Admissions, Frederick Community College, 7932 Opossumtown Pike, Frederick, MD 21702. *Phone:* 301-846-2468. *Fax:* 301-624-2799.
E-mail: admissions@frederick.edu.
Website: http://www.frederick.edu/.

Garrett College
McHenry, Maryland

- **State and locally supported** 2-year, founded 1966
- **Rural** 62-acre campus
- **Coed,** 711 undergraduate students, 77% full-time, 52% women, 48% men

Undergraduates 549 full-time, 162 part-time. Students come from 14 states and territories; 7 other countries; 19% are from out of state; 26% Black or African American, non-Hispanic/Latino; 2% Hispanic/Latino; 0.2% Asian, non-Hispanic/Latino; 0.2% American Indian or Alaska Native, non-Hispanic/Latino; 4% Two or more races, non-Hispanic/Latino; 0.2% Race/ethnicity unknown; 2% international; 7% transferred in; 24% live on campus.

Freshmen *Admission:* 1,159 applied, 820 admitted, 184 enrolled. *Average high school GPA:* 2.63. *Test scores:* SAT critical reading scores over 500: 20%; SAT math scores over 500: 38%; SAT writing scores over 500: 34%; ACT scores over 18: 75%; SAT critical reading scores over 600: 10%; SAT math scores over 600: 15%; SAT writing scores over 600: 2%; ACT scores over 24: 25%.

Faculty *Total:* 84, 29% full-time, 7% with terminal degrees. *Student/faculty ratio:* 13:1.

Majors Business administration and management; business automation/technology/data entry; business/commerce; corrections; early childhood education; education; electrical and electronics engineering; elementary education; liberal arts and sciences and humanities related; liberal arts and sciences/liberal studies; management information systems; sport and fitness administration/management; wildlife, fish and wildlands science and management.

Academics *Calendar:* semesters. *Degree:* certificates and associate. *Special study options:* academic remediation for entering students, adult/continuing education programs, advanced placement credit, cooperative education, distance learning, double majors, external degree program, honors programs, independent study, internships, part-time degree program, services for LD students, summer session for credit.

Library Learning Resource Center. *Books:* 31,225 (physical), 35,243 (digital/electronic); *Serial titles:* 119 (physical); *Databases:* 21. Weekly public service hours: 64.

Student Life *Housing Options:* coed, special housing for students with disabilities. Campus housing is university owned and leased by the school. *Activities and Organizations:* SGA, International Students Club, CRU, SING (Students in Need Group), Rock Climbing Wall (open sessions). *Campus security:* 24-hour emergency response devices and patrols, controlled dormitory access. *Student services:* health clinic, personal/psychological counseling.

Athletics Member NJCAA. *Intercollegiate sports:* baseball M(s), basketball M(s)/W(s), golf M, softball W(s), volleyball W(s). *Intramural sports:* basketball M/W, cheerleading M(c)/W(c), football M/W, ultimate Frisbee M/W.

Standardized Tests *Recommended:* SAT or ACT (for admission).

Costs (2016–17) *Tuition:* area resident $2884 full-time, $103 per credit hour part-time; state resident $6300 full-time, $225 per credit hour part-time; nonresident $7420 full-time, $265 per credit hour part-time. Full-time tuition and fees vary according to program and reciprocity agreements. Part-time tuition and fees vary according to program and reciprocity agreements. *Required fees:* $896 full-time, $32 per credit hour part-time, $25 per term part-time. *Room and board:* $7400; room only: $5400. Room and board charges vary according to board plan and housing facility. *Payment plans:* installment, deferred payment. *Waivers:* senior citizens and employees or children of employees.

Financial Aid Of all full-time matriculated undergraduates who enrolled in 2014, 593 applied for aid, 517 were judged to have need, 49 had their need fully met. 43 Federal Work-Study jobs (averaging $926). 13 state and other part-time jobs (averaging $1059). In 2014, 71 non-need-based awards were made. *Average percent of need met:* 54%. *Average financial aid package:* $7316. *Average need-based loan:* $2949. *Average need-based gift aid:* $4768. *Average non-need-based aid:* $3547.

Applying *Options:* electronic application, early admission, deferred entrance. *Required:* high school transcript. *Application deadlines:* rolling (freshmen), rolling (out-of-state freshmen), rolling (transfers). *Notification:* continuous (freshmen), continuous (out-of-state freshmen), continuous (transfers).

Freshman Application Contact Mrs. Rachelle Davis, Director of Admissions, Garrett College, 687 Mosser Road, McHenry, MD 21541. *Phone:* 301-387-3044. *Toll-free phone:* 866-55-GARRETT.
E-mail: admissions@garrettcollege.edu.
Website: http://www.garrettcollege.edu/.

Hagerstown Community College
Hagerstown, Maryland

- **State and locally supported** 2-year, founded 1946
- **Suburban** 319-acre campus with easy access to Baltimore and Washington, DC
- **Coed,** 4,276 undergraduate students, 25% full-time, 62% women, 38% men

Undergraduates 1,090 full-time, 3,186 part-time. 9% Black or African American, non-Hispanic/Latino; 6% Hispanic/Latino; 2% Asian, non-Hispanic/Latino; 0.2% Native Hawaiian or other Pacific Islander, non-Hispanic/Latino; 0.2% American Indian or Alaska Native, non-Hispanic/Latino; 4% Two or more races, non-Hispanic/Latino; 2% Race/ethnicity unknown; 1% international; 8% transferred in.

Freshmen *Admission:* 793 enrolled.

Faculty *Total:* 232, 34% full-time, 6% with terminal degrees. *Student/faculty ratio:* 16:1.

Majors Accounting technology and bookkeeping; animation, interactive technology, video graphics and special effects; biology/biotechnology laboratory technician; business administration and management; business/commerce; child-care and support services management; commercial and advertising art; computer and information sciences; computer and information systems security; criminal justice/police science; dental hygiene; early childhood education; education; elementary education; emergency medical technology (EMT paramedic); engineering; engineering technologies and engineering related; English/language arts teacher education; industrial technology; instrumentation technology; liberal arts and sciences and humanities related; liberal arts and sciences/liberal studies; management information systems; mechanical engineering/mechanical technology; medical radiologic technology; psychiatric/mental health services technology; registered nursing/registered nurse; transportation/mobility management; web page, digital/multimedia and information resources design.

Academics *Calendar:* semesters. *Degree:* certificates and associate. *Special study options:* academic remediation for entering students, accelerated degree program, adult/continuing education programs, advanced placement credit, cooperative education, distance learning, English as a second language, honors programs, independent study, internships, off-campus study, part-time degree program, services for LD students, summer session for credit.

Library William Brish Library.

Student Life *Activities and Organizations:* drama/theater group, student-run newspaper, choral group, Phi Theta Kappa, Robinwood Players Theater Club, Association of Nursing Students, Radiography Club, Art and Design Club. *Campus security:* 24-hour patrols, student patrols. *Student services:* personal/psychological counseling.

Athletics Member NJCAA. *Intercollegiate sports:* baseball M(s), basketball M(s)/W(s), cross-country running M(s)/W(s), golf M/W, soccer M(s)/W, softball W(s), track and field M(s)/W(s), volleyball W(s). *Intramural sports:* cheerleading M/W, golf M/W, lacrosse M/W, table tennis M/W, tennis M/W.

Costs (2015–16) *Tuition:* area resident $3042 full-time, $117 per credit hour part-time; state resident $4758 full-time, $183 per credit hour part-time; nonresident $6266 full-time, $241 per credit hour part-time. Full-time tuition and fees vary according to course load, program, and reciprocity agreements. Part-time tuition and fees vary according to course load, program, and reciprocity agreements. *Required fees:* $522 full-time, $12 per credit hour part-time, $30 per term part-time. *Payment plan:* installment. *Waivers:* senior citizens and employees or children of employees.

Financial Aid Of all full-time matriculated undergraduates who enrolled in 2014, 823 applied for aid, 688 were judged to have need, 32 had their need fully met. 42 Federal Work-Study jobs (averaging $2400). 176 state and other part-time jobs (averaging $2969). In 2014, 29 non-need-based awards were made. *Average percent of need met:* 47%. *Average financial aid package:* $6244. *Average need-based loan:* $3149. *Average need-based gift aid:* $4705. *Average non-need-based aid:* $834.

Applying *Options:* electronic application, early admission, deferred entrance. *Required for some:* high school transcript. *Application deadlines:* rolling (freshmen), rolling (out-of-state freshmen), rolling (transfers). *Notification:* continuous (freshmen), continuous (out-of-state freshmen), continuous (transfers).

Freshman Application Contact Mr. Kevin L. Crawford, Assistant Director, Recruiting, Admissions, Records and Registration, Hagerstown Community College, 11400 Robinwood Drive, Hagerstown, MD 21742-6514. *Phone:* 240-500-2412. *Fax:* 301-791-9165. *E-mail:* klcrawford@hagerstowncc.edu. *Website:* http://www.hagerstowncc.edu/.

Harford Community College
Bel Air, Maryland

- **State and locally supported** 2-year, founded 1957
- **Small-town** 331-acre campus with easy access to Baltimore
- **Coed,** 6,520 undergraduate students, 37% full-time, 57% women, 43% men

Undergraduates 2,395 full-time, 4,125 part-time. 15% Black or African American, non-Hispanic/Latino; 5% Hispanic/Latino; 2% Asian, non-Hispanic/Latino; 0.2% Native Hawaiian or other Pacific Islander, non-Hispanic/Latino; 0.4% American Indian or Alaska Native, non-Hispanic/Latino; 3% Two or more races, non-Hispanic/Latino; 0.8% Race/ethnicity unknown; 1% international.

Freshmen *Admission:* 1,150 enrolled. *Test scores:* SAT critical reading scores over 500: 59%; SAT math scores over 500: 73%; SAT critical reading scores over 600: 19%; SAT math scores over 600: 24%; SAT critical reading scores over 700: 1%; SAT math scores over 700: 2%.

Faculty *Total:* 344, 29% full-time, 13% with terminal degrees. *Student/faculty ratio:* 21:1.

Majors Accounting; administrative assistant and secretarial science; advertising; agribusiness; agriculture; anthropology; biology/biological sciences; business administration and management; chemistry; chemistry teacher education; civil drafting and CAD/CADD; computer and information sciences; computer science; criminal justice/police science; digital arts; early childhood education; education; education (specific levels and methods) related; education (specific subject areas) related; electroneurodiagnostic/electroencephalographic technology; elementary education; engineering; engineering technology; English; English/language arts teacher education; entrepreneurship; environmental engineering technology; environmental science; fine/studio arts; general studies; graphic design; history; human resources management; information science/studies; interior design; international relations and affairs; legal assistant/paralegal; marketing/marketing management; mass communication/media; mathematics; mathematics teacher education; medical office assistant; music; philosophy; photography; physics; physics teacher education; political science and government; psychology; registered nursing, nursing administration, nursing research and clinical nursing related; social work; sociology; Spanish language teacher education; special education; special education–early childhood; special education–elementary school; teacher assistant/aide; theater design and technology.

Academics *Calendar:* semesters. *Degree:* certificates, diplomas, and associate. *Special study options:* academic remediation for entering students, adult/continuing education programs, advanced placement credit, cooperative education, distance learning, double majors, English as a second language, honors programs, independent study, internships, part-time degree program, services for LD students, student-designed majors, study abroad, summer session for credit.

Library Harford Community College Library.

Student Life *Activities and Organizations:* drama/theater group, student-run newspaper, radio station, choral group, Phi Theta Kappa, Student Nurses Association, Gamers Guild, Actor's Guild, Future Educators of America. *Campus security:* 24-hour patrols, late-night transport/escort service. *Student services:* personal/psychological counseling.

Athletics Member NJCAA. *Intercollegiate sports:* baseball M(s), basketball M(s)/W(s), cross-country running M(s)/W(s), golf M(s), lacrosse M(s)/W(s), soccer M(s)/W(s), softball W(s), tennis M(s)/W(s), volleyball W(s). *Intramural sports:* badminton M/W, basketball M/W, cheerleading M(c)/W(c), football M/W, soccer M/W, softball M/W, swimming and diving M/W, tennis M/W, volleyball M/W.

Costs (2016–17) *Tuition:* area resident $3480 full-time, $116 per credit hour part-time; state resident $6090 full-time, $203 per credit hour part-time; nonresident $8700 full-time, $290 per credit hour part-time. *Required fees:* $696 full-time, $23 per credit hour part-time. *Payment plan:* installment. *Waivers:* senior citizens and employees or children of employees.

Financial Aid Of all full-time matriculated undergraduates who enrolled in 2014, 1,478 applied for aid, 1,066 were judged to have need. 78 Federal Work-Study jobs (averaging $1842).

Applying *Options:* electronic application. *Application deadlines:* rolling (freshmen), rolling (transfers). *Notification:* continuous (transfers).

Freshman Application Contact Jennifer Starkey, Enrollment Services Associate - Admissions, Harford Community College, 401 Thomas Run Road, Bel Air, MD 21015-1698. *Phone:* 443-412-2311. *Fax:* 443-412-2169. *E-mail:* jestarkey@harford.edu. *Website:* http://www.harford.edu/.

Howard Community College
Columbia, Maryland

- **State and locally supported** 2-year, founded 1966
- **Suburban** 122-acre campus with easy access to Baltimore and Washington, DC
- **Coed,** 9,920 undergraduate students, 38% full-time, 56% women, 44% men

Undergraduates 3,729 full-time, 6,191 part-time. Students come from 5 states and territories; 111 other countries; 0.4% are from out of state; 29% Black or African American, non-Hispanic/Latino; 9% Hispanic/Latino; 11% Asian, non-Hispanic/Latino; 0.3% Native Hawaiian or other Pacific Islander, non-Hispanic/Latino; 0.3% American Indian or Alaska Native, non-Hispanic/Latino; 4% Two or more races, non-Hispanic/Latino; 3% Race/ethnicity unknown; 4% international.

Freshmen *Admission:* 3,320 applied, 3,265 admitted, 1,671 enrolled.

Faculty *Total:* 805, 24% full-time, 19% with terminal degrees. *Student/faculty ratio:* 15:1.

Majors Accounting; art; biological and physical sciences; biomedical technology; biotechnology; business administration and management; cardiovascular technology; child development; clinical laboratory science/medical technology; computer and information sciences related; computer graphics; computer/information technology services administration related; computer science; computer systems networking and telecommunications; criminal justice/law enforcement administration; design and applied arts related; diagnostic medical sonography and ultrasound technology; dramatic/theater arts; electrical, electronic and communications engineering technology; elementary education; emergency medical technology (EMT paramedic); engineering; environmental studies; financial planning and services; general studies; health teacher education; information science/studies; information technology; kindergarten/preschool education; legal administrative assistant/secretary; liberal arts and sciences/liberal studies; licensed practical/vocational nurse training; medical administrative assistant and medical secretary; music; nuclear medical technology; office management; photography; physical sciences; physical therapy technology; premedical studies; pre-pharmacy studies; registered nursing/registered nurse; secondary education; social sciences; sport and fitness administration/management; substance abuse/addiction counseling; telecommunications technology; theater design and technology.

Academics *Calendar:* semesters. *Degree:* certificates and associate. *Special study options:* academic remediation for entering students, adult/continuing education programs, advanced placement credit, cooperative education, distance learning, double majors, English as a second language, external degree program, freshman honors college, honors programs, internships, off-campus study, part-time degree program, services for LD students, study abroad, summer session for credit.

Library Howard Community College Library.

Student Life *Housing:* college housing not available. *Activities and Organizations:* drama/theater group, student-run newspaper, radio station, choral group, Phi Theta Kappa, Nursing Club, Black Leadership Organization, Student Newspaper, Student Government Association. *Campus security:* 24-hour emergency response devices and patrols, late-night transport/escort service. *Student services:* personal/psychological counseling.

Athletics Member NJCAA. *Intercollegiate sports:* basketball M/W, cross-country running M/W, lacrosse M/W, soccer M/W, track and field M/W, volleyball W. *Intramural sports:* basketball M/W.

Standardized Tests *Required for some:* SAT or ACT (for admission).

Financial Aid Of all full-time matriculated undergraduates who enrolled in 2013, 571 applied for aid, 477 were judged to have need. In 2013, 31 non-need-based awards were made. *Average percent of need met:* 22%. *Average financial aid package:* $3871. *Average need-based loan:* $2525. *Average need-based gift aid:* $4032. *Average non-need-based aid:* $1288.

Applying *Options:* electronic application, early admission, deferred entrance. *Application fee:* $25. *Required for some:* essay or personal statement, high school transcript, minimum 3.2 GPA, 2 letters of recommendation. *Application deadlines:* rolling (freshmen), rolling (out-of-state freshmen), rolling (transfers). *Notification:* continuous (freshmen), continuous (out-of-state freshmen), continuous (transfers).

Freshman Application Contact Ms. Christine Palmer, Assistant Director of Admissions, Howard Community College, 10901 Little Patuxent Parkway, Columbia, MD 21044-3197. *Phone:* 443-518-4599. *Fax:* 443-518-4589. *E-mail:* admissions@howardcc.edu. *Website:* http://www.howardcc.edu/.

ITT Technical Institute
Owings Mills, Maryland

Freshman Application Contact Director of Recruitment, ITT Technical Institute, 11301 Red Run Boulevard, Owings Mills, MD 21117. *Phone:* 443-394-7115. *Toll-free phone:* 877-411-6782. *Website:* http://www.itt-tech.edu/.

Kaplan University, Hagerstown Campus
Hagerstown, Maryland

Freshman Application Contact Kaplan University, Hagerstown Campus, 18618 Crestwood Drive, Hagerstown, MD 21742-2797. *Phone:* 301-739-2680 Ext. 217. *Toll-free phone:* 866-527-5268 (in-state); 800-527-5268 (out-of-state). *Website:* http://www.kaplanuniversity.edu/.

Lincoln College of Technology
Columbia, Maryland

Admissions Office Contact Lincoln College of Technology, 9325 Snowden River Parkway, Columbia, MD 21046. *Website:* http://www.lincolnedu.com/.

Montgomery College
Rockville, Maryland

- **State and locally supported** 2-year, founded 1946
- **Suburban** 333-acre campus with easy access to Washington, DC
- **Endowment** $22.4 million
- **Coed,** 25,320 undergraduate students, 35% full-time, 53% women, 47% men

Undergraduates 8,890 full-time, 16,430 part-time. Students come from 21 states and territories; 159 other countries; 3% are from out of state; 27% Black or African American, non-Hispanic/Latino; 23% Hispanic/Latino; 11% Asian, non-Hispanic/Latino; 0.3% Native Hawaiian or other Pacific Islander, non-Hispanic/Latino; 0.3% American Indian or Alaska Native, non-Hispanic/Latino; 3% Two or more races, non-Hispanic/Latino; 0.1% Race/ethnicity unknown; 10% international; 4% transferred in.

Freshmen *Admission:* 10,408 applied, 10,408 admitted, 3,571 enrolled.

Faculty *Total:* 1,452, 35% full-time, 33% with terminal degrees. *Student/faculty ratio:* 18:1.

Majors Accounting technology and bookkeeping; American Sign Language (ASL); animation, interactive technology, video graphics and special effects; applied horticulture/horticulture operations; architectural drafting and CAD/CADD; art; automobile/automotive mechanics technology; biology/biotechnology laboratory technician; building/construction finishing, management, and inspection related; business/commerce; chemistry teacher education; child-care provision; commercial and advertising art; commercial photography; communications technologies and support services related; computer and information sciences; computer and information systems security; computer technology/computer systems technology; criminal justice/police science; crisis/emergency/disaster management; data entry/microcomputer applications; diagnostic medical sonography and ultrasound technology; early childhood education; elementary education; engineering; English/language arts teacher education; fire prevention and safety technology; geography; health information/medical records technology; hotel/motel administration; interior design; legal assistant/paralegal; liberal arts and sciences and humanities related; liberal arts and sciences/liberal studies; mathematics teacher education; medical radiologic technology; physical therapy technology; physics teacher education; psychiatric/mental

health services technology; registered nursing/registered nurse; Spanish language teacher education; speech communication and rhetoric; surgical technology; web page, digital/multimedia and information resources design.

Academics *Calendar:* semesters. *Degree:* certificates and associate. *Special study options:* academic remediation for entering students, adult/continuing education programs, advanced placement credit, cooperative education, distance learning, double majors, English as a second language, external degree program, honors programs, independent study, internships, off-campus study, part-time degree program, services for LD students, study abroad, summer session for credit. *ROTC:* Air Force (c).

Library Montgomery College Library plus 3 others. *Books:* 226,690 (physical), 21,883 (digital/electronic); *Serial titles:* 847 (physical), 61,709 (digital/electronic); *Databases:* 128. Weekly public service hours: 71; students can reserve study rooms.

Student Life *Activities and Organizations:* drama/theater group, student-run newspaper, choral group, Math Club, International Club, Anime Society Club, Animation and Video Game Club, Sports Clubs. *Campus security:* 24-hour emergency response devices and patrols, late-night transport/escort service. *Student services:* personal/psychological counseling, women's center.

Athletics Member NJCAA. *Intercollegiate sports:* baseball M, basketball M/W, soccer M/W, softball W, tennis M/W, track and field M/W, volleyball W. *Intramural sports:* baseball M, basketball M/W, cheerleading W, cross-country running M, soccer M/W, softball W, tennis M/W, track and field M/W, volleyball W.

Costs (2015–16) *Tuition:* area resident $3304 full-time, $118 per credit hour part-time; state resident $6748 full-time, $241 per credit hour part-time; nonresident $9296 full-time, $332 per credit hour part-time. Full-time tuition and fees vary according to course load. Part-time tuition and fees vary according to course load. *Required fees:* $1109 full-time, $40 per credit hour part-time. *Payment plan:* installment. *Waivers:* senior citizens and employees or children of employees.

Financial Aid Of all full-time matriculated undergraduates who enrolled in 2014, 217 Federal Work-Study jobs (averaging $3469).

Applying *Options:* electronic application, early admission, deferred entrance. *Application fee:* $25. *Recommended:* high school transcript, interview. *Application deadlines:* rolling (freshmen), rolling (out-of-state freshmen), rolling (transfers). *Notification:* continuous (freshmen), continuous (out-of-state freshmen), continuous (transfers).

Freshman Application Contact Montgomery College, 51 Mannakee Street, Rockville, MD 20850. *Phone:* 240-567-5036. *Website:* http://www.montgomerycollege.edu/.

Prince George's Community College
Largo, Maryland

Freshman Application Contact Ms. Vera Bagley, Director of Admissions and Records, Prince George's Community College, 301 Largo Road, Largo, MD 20774-2199. *Phone:* 301-322-0801. *Fax:* 301-322-0119. *E-mail:* enrollmentservices@pgcc.edu. *Website:* http://www.pgcc.edu/.

Wor-Wic Community College
Salisbury, Maryland

- **State and locally supported** 2-year, founded 1976
- **Small-town** 202-acre campus
- **Endowment** $14.8 million
- **Coed,** 3,137 undergraduate students, 28% full-time, 65% women, 35% men

Undergraduates 864 full-time, 2,273 part-time. Students come from 15 states and territories; 3% are from out of state; 23% Black or African American, non-Hispanic/Latino; 4% Hispanic/Latino; 1% Asian, non-Hispanic/Latino; 0.1% Native Hawaiian or other Pacific Islander, non-Hispanic/Latino; 0.3% American Indian or Alaska Native, non-Hispanic/Latino; 4% Two or more races, non-Hispanic/Latino; 2% Race/ethnicity unknown; 0.4% international; 7% transferred in.

Freshmen *Admission:* 1,083 applied, 1,083 admitted, 613 enrolled.

Faculty *Total:* 168, 41% full-time, 16% with terminal degrees. *Student/faculty ratio:* 16:1.

Majors Accounting technology and bookkeeping; administrative assistant and secretarial science; biological and physical sciences; business administration and management; business/commerce; child-care and support services management; computer and information sciences; computer systems analysis; criminal justice/police science; early childhood education; education; electrical, electronic and communications engineering technology; elementary education; emergency medical technology (EMT paramedic); engineering technologies and engineering related; environmental engineering technology; hospitality administration; liberal arts and sciences and humanities related; liberal arts and sciences/liberal studies; medical radiologic technology;

occupational therapist assistant; physical therapy technology; registered nursing/registered nurse; substance abuse/addiction counseling.

Academics *Calendar:* semesters. *Degree:* certificates and associate. *Special study options:* academic remediation for entering students, accelerated degree program, adult/continuing education programs, advanced placement credit, distance learning, double majors, English as a second language, honors programs, independent study, internships, part-time degree program, services for LD students, summer session for credit.

Library Patricia M. Hazel Media Center plus 4 others. *Databases:* 72.

Student Life *Housing:* college housing not available. *Activities and Organizations:* drama/theater group, Anime Club, Criminal Justice Club, Role Playing Game Association, Veterans and Military Association, Alpha Nu Omicron (PTK). *Campus security:* 24-hour emergency response devices, late-night transport/escort service, patrols by trained security personnel 9 a.m. to midnight. *Student services:* personal/psychological counseling.

Costs (2015–16) *Tuition:* area resident $3090 full-time, $103 per credit part-time; state resident $6930 full-time, $231 per credit part-time; nonresident $8520 full-time, $284 per credit part-time. *Required fees:* $510 full-time, $17 per credit part-time. *Payment plan:* installment. *Waivers:* senior citizens and employees or children of employees.

Applying *Options:* electronic application, early admission. *Recommended:* high school transcript. *Application deadlines:* rolling (freshmen), rolling (transfers).

Freshman Application Contact Mr. Richard Webster, Director of Admissions, Wor-Wic Community College, 32000 Campus Drive, Salisbury, MD 21804. *Phone:* 410-334-2895. *Fax:* 410-334-2954.
E-mail: admissions@worwic.edu.
Website: http://www.worwic.edu/.

MASSACHUSETTS

★ Bay State College
Boston, Massachusetts

Freshman Application Contact Kimberly Odusami, Director of Admissions, Bay State College, 122 Commonwealth Avenue, Boston, MA 02116. *Phone:* 617-217-9186. *Toll-free phone:* 800-81-LEARN.
E-mail: admissions@baystate.edu.
Website: http://www.baystate.edu/.

See below for display ad and page 362 for the College Close-Up.

Benjamin Franklin Institute of Technology
Boston, Massachusetts

- **Independent** primarily 2-year, founded 1908
- **Urban** 3-acre campus
- **Coed**

Undergraduates 428 full-time, 65 part-time. 29% Black or African American, non-Hispanic/Latino; 21% Hispanic/Latino; 9% Asian, non-Hispanic/Latino; 0.2% Native Hawaiian or other Pacific Islander, non-Hispanic/Latino; 0.4% American Indian or Alaska Native, non-Hispanic/Latino; 3% Two or more races, non-Hispanic/Latino; 6% Race/ethnicity unknown; 0.8% international.

Academics *Calendar:* semesters. *Degrees:* certificates, associate, and bachelor's. *Special study options:* academic remediation for entering students, adult/continuing education programs, advanced placement credit, cooperative education, English as a second language, internships, off-campus study, part-time degree program, services for LD students, summer session for credit.

Library Lufkin Memorial Library.

Student Life *Campus security:* 24-hour emergency response devices.

Athletics Member NJCAA.

Standardized Tests *Recommended:* SAT or ACT (for admission).

Costs (2015–16) *Comprehensive fee:* $32,815 includes full-time tuition ($16,950), mandatory fees ($1265), and room and board ($14,600). Full-time tuition and fees vary according to course load, degree level, and program. Part-time tuition: $707 per credit hour. Part-time tuition and fees vary according to course load, degree level, and program. *Room and board:* Room and board charges vary according to housing facility.

Financial Aid *Average percent of need met:* 45. *Average financial aid package:* $11,677. *Average need-based gift aid:* $8581.

Applying *Options:* electronic application, deferred entrance. *Application fee:* $25. *Required:* high school transcript. *Recommended:* essay or personal statement, minimum 2.0 GPA, interview.

Freshman Application Contact Ms. Brittainy Johnson, Associate Director of Admissions, Benjamin Franklin Institute of Technology, Boston, MA 02116. *Phone:* 617-423-4630 Ext. 122. *Toll-free phone:* 877-400-BFIT. *Fax:* 617-482-3706.
E-mail: bjohnson@bfit.edu.
Website: http://www.bfit.edu/.

Berkshire Community College

Pittsfield, Massachusetts

- **State-supported** 2-year, founded 1960, part of Massachusetts Public Higher Education System
- **Rural** 180-acre campus with easy access to Hartford, CT; Albany, NY
- **Coed,** 2,111 undergraduate students, 34% full-time, 60% women, 40% men

Undergraduates 721 full-time, 1,390 part-time. Students come from 4 states and territories; 6 other countries; 3% are from out of state; 7% Black or African American, non-Hispanic/Latino; 7% Hispanic/Latino; 2% Asian, non-Hispanic/Latino; 0.2% Native Hawaiian or other Pacific Islander, non-Hispanic/Latino; 0.3% American Indian or Alaska Native, non-Hispanic/Latino; 1% Two or more races, non-Hispanic/Latino; 4% Race/ethnicity unknown; 0.3% international; 4% transferred in.

Freshmen *Admission:* 434 applied, 434 admitted, 434 enrolled.

Faculty *Total:* 176, 32% full-time. *Student/faculty ratio:* 15:1.

Majors Business administration and management; business automation/technology/data entry; business/commerce; community organization and advocacy; computer and information sciences; criminal justice/safety; electrical, electronic and communications engineering technology; engineering; environmental studies; fire science/firefighting; health professions related; hospitality administration; human services; international/global studies; liberal arts and sciences/liberal studies; medical insurance coding; physical therapy technology; registered nursing/registered nurse; respiratory care therapy; visual and performing arts.

Academics *Calendar:* semesters. *Degree:* certificates and associate. *Special study options:* academic remediation for entering students, accelerated degree program, adult/continuing education programs, advanced placement credit, cooperative education, distance learning, English as a second language, freshman honors college, honors programs, independent study, internships, off-campus study, part-time degree program, services for LD students, summer session for credit.

Library Jonathan Edwards Library.

Student Life *Housing:* college housing not available. *Activities and Organizations:* drama/theater group, choral group, Mass PIRG, Student Nurse Organization, Student Senate, Diversity Club, LPN Organization. *Campus security:* 24-hour emergency response devices and patrols, late-night transport/escort service. *Student services:* personal/psychological counseling.

Athletics *Intramural sports:* basketball M/W, cross-country running M/W, soccer M/W, track and field M/W, weight lifting M/W, wrestling M/W.

Costs (2015–16) *Tuition:* state resident $1248 full-time; nonresident $12,480 full-time. *Required fees:* $8484 full-time.

Financial Aid Of all full-time matriculated undergraduates who enrolled in 2014, 1,545 applied for aid, 1,393 were judged to have need. 154 Federal Work-Study jobs (averaging $541). 130 state and other part-time jobs (averaging $666). In 2014, 168 non-need-based awards were made. *Average financial aid package:* $5582. *Average need-based loan:* $1498. *Average need-based gift aid:* $4277. *Average non-need-based aid:* $519.

Applying *Options:* electronic application, deferred entrance. *Required:* high school transcript. *Application deadlines:* rolling (freshmen), rolling (out-of-state freshmen), rolling (transfers). *Notification:* continuous (freshmen), continuous (out-of-state freshmen), continuous (transfers).

Freshman Application Contact Ms. Tina Schettini, Enrollment Services, Berkshire Community College, 1350 West Street, Pittsfield, MA 01201-5786. *Phone:* 413-236-1635. *Toll-free phone:* 800-816-1233. *Fax:* 413-496-9511. *E-mail:* tschetti@berkshirecc.edu. *Website:* http://www.berkshirecc.edu/.

Bristol Community College

Fall River, Massachusetts

Freshman Application Contact Ms. Shilo Henriques, Dean of Admissions, Bristol Community College, 777 Elsbree Street, Fall River, MA 02720. *Phone:* 508-678-2811 Ext. 2947. *Fax:* 508-730-3265. *E-mail:* shilo.henriques@bristolcc.edu. *Website:* http://www.bristolcc.edu/.

Bunker Hill Community College

Boston, Massachusetts

- **State-supported** 2-year, founded 1973
- **Urban** 21-acre campus
- **Endowment** $4.3 million
- **Coed,** 14,047 undergraduate students, 30% full-time, 57% women, 43% men

Undergraduates 4,191 full-time, 9,856 part-time. 26% Black or African American, non-Hispanic/Latino; 24% Hispanic/Latino; 10% Asian, non-Hispanic/Latino; 0.2% Native Hawaiian or other Pacific Islander, non-Hispanic/Latino; 0.3% American Indian or Alaska Native, non-Hispanic/Latino; 4% Two or more races, non-Hispanic/Latino; 6% Race/ethnicity unknown; 6% international.

Freshmen *Admission:* 6,185 applied, 4,787 admitted, 1,678 enrolled.

Faculty *Total:* 768, 20% full-time. *Student/faculty ratio:* 17:1.

Majors Accounting; art; bioengineering and biomedical engineering; biology/biological sciences; biotechnology; business administration and management; business administration, management and operations related; business operations support and secretarial services related; cardiovascular technology; chemistry; clinical/medical laboratory technology; computer and information sciences and support services related; computer and information systems security; computer/information technology services administration related; computer programming; computer programming (specific applications); computer science; computer systems networking and telecommunications; criminal justice/law enforcement administration; criminal justice/police science; culinary arts; data entry/microcomputer applications; design and visual communications; diagnostic medical sonography and ultrasound technology; dramatic/theater arts; early childhood education; education; electrical/electronics maintenance and repair technology related; emergency medical technology (EMT paramedic); engineering; English; entrepreneurship; finance; fine arts related; fire prevention and safety technology; foreign languages and literatures; general studies; health information/medical records administration; history; hospitality administration; hospitality administration related; human services; international business/trade/commerce; legal assistant/paralegal; mass communication/media; mathematics; medical administrative assistant and medical secretary; medical radiologic technology; music; operations management; physics; psychology; registered nursing/registered nurse; respiratory therapy technician; sociology; speech communication and rhetoric; sport and fitness administration/management; tourism and travel services management; web page, digital/multimedia and information resources design.

Academics *Calendar:* semesters. *Degree:* certificates and associate. *Special study options:* academic remediation for entering students, accelerated degree program, advanced placement credit, cooperative education, distance learning, English as a second language, external degree program, honors programs, independent study, internships, part-time degree program, services for LD students, study abroad, summer session for credit.

Library Bunker Hill Community College Library. *Books:* 43,792 (physical), 62,257 (digital/electronic); *Serial titles:* 91 (physical), 42 (digital/electronic); *Databases:* 106. Weekly public service hours: 86; study areas open 24 hours, 5&-7 days a week.

Student Life *Housing:* college housing not available. *Activities and Organizations:* drama/theater group, student-run radio station, choral group, Alpha Kappa Mu Honor Society, Asian-Pacific Students Association, Music Club, Latinos Unidos Club, Haitian Students Club. *Campus security:* 24-hour emergency response devices and patrols, late-night transport/escort service. *Student services:* health clinic, personal/psychological counseling.

Athletics Member NJCAA. *Intercollegiate sports:* baseball M, basketball M/W, soccer M/W, volleyball W. *Intramural sports:* basketball M/W, soccer M/W, volleyball M/W.

Costs (2016–17) *Tuition:* state resident $576 full-time, $24 per credit hour part-time; nonresident $5520 full-time, $230 per credit hour part-time. Full-time tuition and fees vary according to course load, program, and reciprocity agreements. Part-time tuition and fees vary according to course load, program, and reciprocity agreements. *Required fees:* $3312 full-time, $138 per credit hour part-time. *Payment plan:* installment. *Waivers:* minority students, senior citizens, and employees or children of employees.

Financial Aid Of all full-time matriculated undergraduates who enrolled in 2010, 135 Federal Work-Study jobs (averaging $2376).

Applying *Options:* electronic application. *Required:* high school transcript. *Application deadlines:* rolling (freshmen), rolling (transfers). *Notification:* continuous (freshmen), continuous (transfers).

Freshman Application Contact Vanessa Whaley Rowley, Director of Enrollment Management and Admissions, Bunker Hill Community College, 250 New Rutherford Avenue, Boston, MA 02129. *Phone:* 617-228-3398. *Fax:* 617-228-3481. *E-mail:* admissions@bhcc.mass.edu. *Website:* http://www.bhcc.mass.edu/.

Cape Cod Community College

West Barnstable, Massachusetts

Freshman Application Contact Director of Admissions, Cape Cod Community College, 2240 Iyannough Road, West Barnstable, MA 02668-1599. *Phone:* 508-362-2131 Ext. 4311. *Toll-free phone:* 877-846-3672. *Fax:* 508-375-4089. *E-mail:* admiss@capecod.edu. *Website:* http://www.capecod.edu/.

Dean College
Franklin, Massachusetts

- **Independent** primarily 2-year, founded 1865
- **Small-town** 100-acre campus with easy access to Boston, Providence
- **Endowment** $38.9 million
- **Coed,** 1,292 undergraduate students, 83% full-time, 52% women, 48% men

Undergraduates 1,069 full-time, 223 part-time. Students come from 31 states and territories; 16 other countries; 47% are from out of state; 14% Black or African American, non-Hispanic/Latino; 5% Hispanic/Latino; 3% Asian, non-Hispanic/Latino; 0.1% Native Hawaiian or other Pacific Islander, non-Hispanic/Latino; 0.3% American Indian or Alaska Native, non-Hispanic/Latino; 3% Two or more races, non-Hispanic/Latino; 20% Race/ethnicity unknown; 10% international; 6% transferred in; 89% live on campus. *Retention:* 70% of full-time freshmen returned.
Freshmen *Admission:* 2,646 applied, 1,806 admitted, 454 enrolled. *Average high school GPA:* 2.5. *Test scores:* SAT critical reading scores over 500: 22%; SAT math scores over 500: 17%; SAT writing scores over 500: 20%; SAT critical reading scores over 600: 4%; SAT math scores over 600: 3%; SAT writing scores over 600: 2%; SAT critical reading scores over 700: 1%; SAT writing scores over 700: 1%.
Faculty *Total:* 151, 21% full-time, 25% with terminal degrees. *Student/faculty ratio:* 16:1.
Majors Arts, entertainment, and media management; athletic training; biology/biological sciences; business administration and management; criminal justice/safety; dance; dramatic/theater arts; early childhood education; English; environmental studies; general studies; health and wellness; history; liberal arts and sciences/liberal studies; mass communication/media; mathematics; psychology; sociology; sport and fitness administration/management.
Academics *Calendar:* semesters. *Degrees:* certificates, diplomas, associate, and bachelor's. *Special study options:* adult/continuing education programs, advanced placement credit, cooperative education, distance learning, double majors, English as a second language, honors programs, independent study, internships, off-campus study, part-time degree program, services for LD students, student-designed majors, study abroad, summer session for credit.
Library E. Ross Anderson Library.
Student Life *Housing Options:* coed, men-only, women-only, special housing for students with disabilities. Campus housing is university owned. Freshman campus housing is guaranteed. *Activities and Organizations:* student-run radio station, National Society of Leadership and Success, Student Activities Committee, Residence Hall Association, International Student Association, Phi Theta Kappa. *Campus security:* 24-hour emergency response devices and patrols, late-night transport/escort service, controlled dormitory access. *Student services:* health clinic, personal/psychological counseling.
Athletics Member NJCAA. *Intercollegiate sports:* baseball M(s), basketball M(s)/W(s), football M(s), golf M, lacrosse M(s)/W(s), soccer M(s)/W(s), softball W(s), volleyball W(s). *Intramural sports:* basketball M, football M, golf M, lacrosse M, soccer M, volleyball M/W.
Standardized Tests *Recommended:* SAT or ACT (for admission).
Costs (2015–16) *Comprehensive fee:* $50,920 includes full-time tuition ($35,420), mandatory fees ($300), and room and board ($15,200). Full-time tuition and fees vary according to class time, course load, and program. Part-time tuition: $313 per credit. Part-time tuition and fees vary according to class time, course load, and program. *Required fees:* $25 per term part-time. *Room and board:* college room only: $9600. Room and board charges vary according to housing facility. *Payment plan:* installment. *Waivers:* employees or children of employees.
Applying *Options:* electronic application, early admission, early action, deferred entrance. *Required:* high school transcript. *Required for some:* audition for performing arts majors. *Recommended:* essay or personal statement, minimum 2.0 GPA, 1 letter of recommendation, interview. *Application deadlines:* rolling (freshmen), 12/1 (early action). *Notification:* continuous (freshmen), 1/15 (early action).
Freshman Application Contact Iris P. Godes, Assistant Vice President of Enrollment Services and Dean of Admissions, Dean College, 99 Main Street, Franklin, MA 02038. *Phone:* 508-541-1547. *Toll-free phone:* 877-TRY-DEAN. *Fax:* 508-541-8726. *E-mail:* igodes@dean.edu.
Website: http://www.dean.edu/.

FINE Mortuary College, LLC
Norwood, Massachusetts

Freshman Application Contact Dean Marsha Wise, Admissions Office, FINE Mortuary College, LLC, 150 Kerry Place, Norwood, MA 02062. *Phone:* 781-762-1211. *Fax:* 781-762-7177. *E-mail:* mwise@fine-ne.com.
Website: http://www.fine-ne.com/.

Greenfield Community College
Greenfield, Massachusetts

- **State-supported** 2-year, founded 1962, part of Commonwealth of Massachusetts Department of Higher Education
- **Small-town** 120-acre campus
- **Coed**

Undergraduates 758 full-time, 1,369 part-time. 8% are from out of state; 3% Black or African American, non-Hispanic/Latino; 7% Hispanic/Latino; 4% Asian, non-Hispanic/Latino; 0.6% American Indian or Alaska Native, non-Hispanic/Latino; 3% Two or more races, non-Hispanic/Latino; 4% Race/ethnicity unknown; 11% transferred in. *Retention:* 60% of full-time freshmen returned.
Faculty *Student/faculty ratio:* 13:1.
Academics *Calendar:* semesters. *Degree:* certificates and associate. *Special study options:* academic remediation for entering students, adult/continuing education programs, advanced placement credit, cooperative education, distance learning, double majors, English as a second language, independent study, internships, part-time degree program, services for LD students, summer session for credit.
Library Greenfield Community College Library.
Student Life *Campus security:* 24-hour emergency response devices and patrols, late-night transport/escort service.
Standardized Tests *Required for some:* Psychological Corporation Practical Nursing Entrance Examination.
Costs (2015–16) *Tuition:* state resident $624 full-time; nonresident $6744 full-time. Full-time tuition and fees vary according to class time, course load, and program. Part-time tuition and fees vary according to class time, course load, and program. *Required fees:* $4334 full-time.
Applying *Options:* electronic application. *Required for some:* high school transcript, interview.
Freshman Application Contact Ms. Colleen Kucinski, Assistant Director of Admission, Greenfield Community College, 1 College Drive, Greenfield, MA 01301-9739. *Phone:* 413-775-1000. *Fax:* 413-773-5129.
E-mail: admission@gcc.mass.edu.
Website: http://www.gcc.mass.edu/.

Holyoke Community College
Holyoke, Massachusetts

- **State-supported** 2-year, founded 1946, part of Massachusetts Public Higher Education System
- **Small-town** 135-acre campus
- **Endowment** $13.2 million
- **Coed,** 6,285 undergraduate students, 47% full-time, 61% women, 39% men

Undergraduates 2,956 full-time, 3,329 part-time. Students come from 15 states and territories; 1% are from out of state; 6% Black or African American, non-Hispanic/Latino; 24% Hispanic/Latino; 2% Asian, non-Hispanic/Latino; 0.1% Native Hawaiian or other Pacific Islander, non-Hispanic/Latino; 0.5% American Indian or Alaska Native, non-Hispanic/Latino; 3% Two or more races, non-Hispanic/Latino; 4% Race/ethnicity unknown; 0.7% international; 8% transferred in.
Freshmen *Admission:* 1,416 enrolled.
Faculty *Total:* 486, 27% full-time, 26% with terminal degrees. *Student/faculty ratio:* 16:1.
Majors Accounting technology and bookkeeping; administrative assistant and secretarial science; art; biology/biological sciences; biotechnology; business administration and management; chemistry; child-care and support services management; computer programming (specific applications); criminal justice/safety; engineering; environmental control technologies related; health and physical education/fitness; health services/allied health/health sciences; hospitality administration related; liberal arts and sciences and humanities related; liberal arts and sciences/liberal studies; mathematics; medical radiologic technology; music; physics; registered nursing/registered nurse; social work; sport and fitness administration/management; veterinary/animal health technology.
Academics *Calendar:* semesters. *Degree:* certificates and associate. *Special study options:* academic remediation for entering students, adult/continuing education programs, advanced placement credit, cooperative education, distance learning, double majors, English as a second language, external degree program, honors programs, independent study, internships, off-campus study, part-time degree program, services for LD students, student-designed majors, study abroad, summer session for credit. *ROTC:* Army (c), Air Force (c).
Library Holyoke Community College Library plus 1 other. *Books:* 62,093 (physical), 42,000 (digital/electronic); *Serial titles:* 36 (physical), 36,306 (digital/electronic); *Databases:* 125. Weekly public service hours: 65; students can reserve study rooms.

Student Life *Housing:* college housing not available. *Activities and Organizations:* drama/theater group, student-run newspaper, radio station, Drama Club, Japanese Anime Club, Student Senate, LISA Club, STRIVE. *Campus security:* 24-hour emergency response devices and patrols, late-night transport/escort service. *Student services:* health clinic, personal/psychological counseling, women's center.

Athletics Member NJCAA. *Intercollegiate sports:* baseball M, basketball M/W, cross-country running M/W, golf M/W, soccer M/W, softball W, track and field M/W, volleyball W.

Costs (2015–16) *One-time required fee:* $65. *Tuition:* state resident $576 full-time, $168 per credit hour part-time; nonresident $5520 full-time, $370 per credit hour part-time. Full-time tuition and fees vary according to course load. Part-time tuition and fees vary according to course load. *Required fees:* $3590 full-time, $95 per term part-time. *Payment plan:* installment. *Waivers:* senior citizens and employees or children of employees.

Applying *Options:* electronic application, early admission, deferred entrance. *Required:* high school transcript. *Recommended:* interview. *Application deadlines:* rolling (freshmen), rolling (transfers). *Notification:* continuous (freshmen), continuous (transfers).

Freshman Application Contact Ms. Renee Tastad, Director of Admissions and Transfer Affairs, Holyoke Community College, Admission Office, Holyoke, MA 01040. *Phone:* 413-552-2321. *Fax:* 413-552-2045. *E-mail:* admissions@hcc.edu. *Website:* http://www.hcc.edu/.

ITT Technical Institute
Norwood, Massachusetts

Freshman Application Contact Director of Recruitment, ITT Technical Institute, 333 Providence Highway, Norwood, MA 02062. *Phone:* 781-278-7200. *Toll-free phone:* 800-879-8324. *Website:* http://www.itt-tech.edu/.

ITT Technical Institute
Wilmington, Massachusetts

Freshman Application Contact Director of Recruitment, ITT Technical Institute, 200 Ballardvale Street, Suite 200, Wilmington, MA 01887. *Phone:* 978-658-2636. *Toll-free phone:* 800-430-5097. *Website:* http://www.itt-tech.edu/.

Labouré College
Boston, Massachusetts

Director of Admissions Ms. Gina M. Morrissette, Director of Admissions, Labouré College, 2120 Dorchester Avenue, Boston, MA 02124-5698. *Phone:* 617-296-8300. *Website:* http://www.laboure.edu/.

Massachusetts Bay Community College
Wellesley Hills, Massachusetts

- **State-supported** 2-year, founded 1961
- **Suburban** 84-acre campus with easy access to Boston
- **Coed,** 4,859 undergraduate students, 34% full-time, 54% women, 46% men

Undergraduates 1,648 full-time, 3,211 part-time. Students come from 16 states and territories; 94 other countries; 1% are from out of state; 17% Black or African American, non-Hispanic/Latino; 16% Hispanic/Latino; 5% Asian, non-Hispanic/Latino; 0.2% Native Hawaiian or other Pacific Islander, non-Hispanic/Latino; 0.4% American Indian or Alaska Native, non-Hispanic/Latino; 8% Race/ethnicity unknown; 2% international; 5% transferred in. *Retention:* 53% of full-time freshmen returned.

Freshmen *Admission:* 1,605 applied, 1,605 admitted, 973 enrolled.

Faculty *Total:* 316, 24% full-time. *Student/faculty ratio:* 18:1.

Majors Accounting; animal physiology; automobile/automotive mechanics technology; bioinformatics; biological and biomedical sciences related; biology/biotechnology laboratory technician; business administration and management; business/commerce; community health and preventive medicine; computer and information sciences and support services related; computer and information systems security; computer/information technology services administration related; computer science; criminal justice/law enforcement administration; early childhood education; electrical and electronic engineering technologies related; electrical, electronic and communications engineering technology; elementary education; engineering technologies and engineering related; engineering technology; English; environmental control technologies related; general studies; hospitality administration; human services; international business/trade/commerce; international/global studies; legal assistant/paralegal; liberal arts and sciences/liberal studies; mathematics; mechanical engineering/mechanical technology; network and system administration; radiologic technology/science; registered nursing/registered nurse; social sciences.

Academics *Calendar:* semesters. *Degree:* certificates and associate. *Special study options:* academic remediation for entering students, adult/continuing education programs, advanced placement credit, cooperative education, distance learning, honors programs, internships, part-time degree program, services for LD students, summer session for credit.

Library Perkins Library.

Student Life *Housing:* college housing not available. *Activities and Organizations:* drama/theater group, student-run newspaper, Student Government Association, Latino Student Organization, New World Society Club, Mass Bay Players, Student Occupational Therapy Association. *Campus security:* 24-hour emergency response devices and patrols. *Student services:* health clinic, personal/psychological counseling.

Athletics Member NJCAA. *Intercollegiate sports:* baseball M, basketball M/W, cross-country running M/W, golf M/W, soccer M/W, softball W, tennis M/W, volleyball W. *Intramural sports:* ice hockey M, soccer M/W.

Costs (2016–17) *Tuition:* state resident $576 full-time, $24 per credit part-time; nonresident $5520 full-time, $230 per credit part-time. Full-time tuition and fees vary according to class time, program, and reciprocity agreements. Part-time tuition and fees vary according to class time, program, and reciprocity agreements. *Required fees:* $3920 full-time, $160 per credit part-time, $40 per term part-time. *Payment plan:* installment. *Waivers:* senior citizens and employees or children of employees.

Financial Aid Of all full-time matriculated undergraduates who enrolled in 2014, 59 Federal Work-Study jobs (averaging $1840).

Applying *Options:* electronic application, deferred entrance. *Application deadlines:* rolling (freshmen), rolling (transfers). *Notification:* continuous (freshmen), continuous (transfers).

Freshman Application Contact Ms. Lisa Slavin, Director of Admissions, Massachusetts Bay Community College, 50 Oakland Street, Wellesley Hills, MA 02481. *Phone:* 781-239-2500. *Fax:* 781-239-1047. *E-mail:* lslavin@massbay.edu. *Website:* http://www.massbay.edu/.

Massasoit Community College
Brockton, Massachusetts

Freshman Application Contact Michelle Hughes, Director of Admissions, Massasoit Community College, 1 Massasoit Boulevard, Brockton, MA 02302-3996. *Phone:* 508-588-9100. *Toll-free phone:* 800-CAREERS. *Website:* http://www.massasoit.mass.edu/.

Middlesex Community College
Bedford, Massachusetts

- **State-supported** 2-year, founded 1970, part of Massachusetts Public Higher Education System
- **Suburban** 200-acre campus with easy access to Boston
- **Coed**

Undergraduates 3,537 full-time, 5,668 part-time. 7% Black or African American, non-Hispanic/Latino; 18% Hispanic/Latino; 11% Asian, non-Hispanic/Latino; 0.1% Native Hawaiian or other Pacific Islander, non-Hispanic/Latino; 0.2% American Indian or Alaska Native, non-Hispanic/Latino; 2% Two or more races, non-Hispanic/Latino; 0.7% Race/ethnicity unknown; 1% international.

Academics *Calendar:* semesters. *Degree:* certificates and associate. *Special study options:* academic remediation for entering students, accelerated degree program, adult/continuing education programs, advanced placement credit, cooperative education, distance learning, English as a second language, honors programs, independent study, internships, off-campus study, part-time degree program, services for LD students, study abroad, summer session for credit. *ROTC:* Air Force (c).

Library Main Library plus 1 other.

Student Life *Campus security:* 24-hour emergency response devices and patrols.

Standardized Tests *Required for some:* CPT.

Costs (2015–16) *Tuition:* state resident $4464 full-time; nonresident $9408 full-time. Full-time tuition and fees vary according to course load and reciprocity agreements. Part-time tuition and fees vary according to course load, program, and reciprocity agreements. *Required fees:* $50 full-time.

Financial Aid Of all full-time matriculated undergraduates who enrolled in 2014, 68 Federal Work-Study jobs (averaging $2200).

Applying *Options:* electronic application, early admission. *Required for some:* essay or personal statement, high school transcript, 3 letters of recommendation, interview.
Freshman Application Contact Middlesex Community College, 591 Springs Road, Bedford, MA 01730-1655. *Phone:* 978-656-3211. *Toll-free phone:* 800-818-3434.
Website: http://www.middlesex.mass.edu/.

Mount Wachusett Community College
Gardner, Massachusetts

- **State-supported** 2-year, founded 1963, part of Massachusetts Public Higher Education System
- **Small-town** 270-acre campus with easy access to Boston
- **Endowment** $352,291
- **Coed,** 4,074 undergraduate students, 39% full-time, 65% women, 35% men

Undergraduates 1,599 full-time, 2,475 part-time. 8% Black or African American, non-Hispanic/Latino; 15% Hispanic/Latino; 2% Asian, non-Hispanic/Latino; 0.2% Native Hawaiian or other Pacific Islander, non-Hispanic/Latino; 0.6% American Indian or Alaska Native, non-Hispanic/Latino; 2% Two or more races, non-Hispanic/Latino; 2% Race/ethnicity unknown; 0.4% international; 6% transferred in.
Freshmen *Admission:* 1,781 applied, 1,780 admitted, 796 enrolled. *Average high school GPA:* 2.56.
Faculty *Total:* 396, 19% full-time, 16% with terminal degrees. *Student/faculty ratio:* 13:1.
Majors Allied health and medical assisting services related; alternative and complementary medical support services related; art; automobile/automotive mechanics technology; biotechnology; business administration and management; business/commerce; child-care and support services management; child development; clinical/medical laboratory technology; computer and information sciences; computer graphics; corrections; criminal justice/law enforcement administration; dental hygiene; energy management and systems technology; environmental studies; fire prevention and safety technology; general studies; health information/medical records administration; human services; legal assistant/paralegal; liberal arts and sciences/liberal studies; medical/clinical assistant; physical therapy technology; plastics and polymer engineering technology; radio and television broadcasting technology; registered nursing/registered nurse; web page, digital/multimedia and information resources design.
Academics *Calendar:* semesters. *Degree:* certificates, diplomas, and associate. *Special study options:* academic remediation for entering students, accelerated degree program, adult/continuing education programs, advanced placement credit, cooperative education, distance learning, double majors, English as a second language, honors programs, independent study, internships, part-time degree program, services for LD students, study abroad, summer session for credit. *ROTC:* Army (c).
Library LaChance Library. *Books:* 40,000 (physical), 1,400 (digital/electronic); *Serial titles:* 27 (physical); *Databases:* 78. Weekly public service hours: 57; students can reserve study rooms.
Student Life *Housing:* college housing not available. *Activities and Organizations:* drama/theater group, student-run newspaper, Otaku Anime Club, Dental Hygienist Club, ESL Club, Student Government Association, Student Nurses Association. *Campus security:* 24-hour emergency response devices and patrols, late-night transport/escort service. *Student services:* health clinic, personal/psychological counseling.
Athletics *Intramural sports:* badminton M/W, basketball M/W, football M/W, soccer M/W, softball M/W, table tennis M/W, volleyball M/W, water polo M/W.
Costs (2015–16) *Tuition:* state resident $600 full-time, $25 per credit hour part-time; nonresident $5520 full-time, $230 per credit hour part-time. Full-time tuition and fees vary according to program and reciprocity agreements. Part-time tuition and fees vary according to program and reciprocity agreements. *Required fees:* $4588 full-time, $177 per credit hour part-time, $170 per term part-time. *Payment plan:* installment. *Waivers:* senior citizens and employees or children of employees.
Financial Aid Of all full-time matriculated undergraduates who enrolled in 2014, 47 Federal Work-Study jobs (averaging $2228).
Applying *Options:* electronic application, early admission. *Required:* high school transcript. *Required for some:* 2 letters of recommendation. *Recommended:* interview. *Application deadlines:* rolling (freshmen), rolling (transfers). *Notification:* continuous (freshmen), continuous (transfers).
Freshman Application Contact Ms. Marcia Rosbury-Henne, Dean of Admissions and Enrollment, Mount Wachusett Community College, 444 Green Street, Gardner, MA 01440-1378. *Phone:* 978-632-6600 Ext. 337. *Fax:* 978-630-9558. *E-mail:* admissions@mwcc.mass.edu.
Website: http://www.mwcc.mass.edu/.

Northern Essex Community College
Haverhill, Massachusetts

- **State-supported** 2-year, founded 1960
- **Suburban** 106-acre campus with easy access to Boston
- **Endowment** $4.2 million
- **Coed,** 6,628 undergraduate students, 33% full-time, 61% women, 39% men

Undergraduates 2,219 full-time, 4,409 part-time. Students come from 6 states and territories; 14% are from out of state; 4% Black or African American, non-Hispanic/Latino; 41% Hispanic/Latino; 2% Asian, non-Hispanic/Latino; 0.4% Native Hawaiian or other Pacific Islander, non-Hispanic/Latino; 0.2% American Indian or Alaska Native, non-Hispanic/Latino; 1% Two or more races, non-Hispanic/Latino; 1% Race/ethnicity unknown; 0.6% international.
Retention: 59% of full-time freshmen returned.
Freshmen *Admission:* 2,056 applied, 2,040 admitted, 1,330 enrolled.
Faculty *Total:* 624, 18% full-time.
Majors Accounting; administrative assistant and secretarial science; biology/biological sciences; business administration and management; business/commerce; business teacher education; civil engineering technology; commercial and advertising art; computer and information sciences; computer engineering technology; computer graphics; computer programming; computer programming related; computer programming (specific applications); computer science; computer systems networking and telecommunications; computer typography and composition equipment operation; criminal justice/law enforcement administration; dance; data processing and data processing technology; dental assisting; dramatic/theater arts; education; electrical, electronic and communications engineering technology; elementary education; emergency medical technology (EMT paramedic); engineering science; finance; general studies; health information/medical records administration; history; hotel/motel administration; human services; industrial radiologic technology; international relations and affairs; journalism; kindergarten/preschool education; legal assistant/paralegal; liberal arts and sciences/liberal studies; logistics, materials, and supply chain management; machine tool technology; marketing/marketing management; materials science; medical administrative assistant and medical secretary; medical transcription; mental health counseling; music; parks, recreation and leisure; physical education teaching and coaching; political science and government; psychology; public health; radiologic technology/science; real estate; registered nursing/registered nurse; respiratory care therapy; respiratory therapy technician; science technologies; sign language interpretation and translation; sport and fitness administration/management; telecommunications technology; tourism and travel services management; web/multimedia management and webmaster; web page, digital/multimedia and information resources design.
Academics *Calendar:* semesters. *Degree:* certificates and associate. *Special study options:* academic remediation for entering students, adult/continuing education programs, advanced placement credit, cooperative education, distance learning, double majors, English as a second language, freshman honors college, honors programs, independent study, internships, off-campus study, part-time degree program, services for LD students, study abroad, summer session for credit. *ROTC:* Air Force (c).
Library Bentley Library. *Books:* 45,155 (physical), 10,012 (digital/electronic); *Serial titles:* 2,623 (physical), 3,108 (digital/electronic); *Databases:* 67.
Student Life *Housing:* college housing not available. *Activities and Organizations:* drama/theater group, student-run newspaper. *Campus security:* 24-hour emergency response devices and patrols.
Athletics Member NJCAA. *Intercollegiate sports:* baseball M, basketball M/W, softball W, volleyball M/W. *Intramural sports:* basketball M/W, cross-country running M/W, football M/W, lacrosse M/W, soccer M/W, volleyball M/W, weight lifting M/W.
Standardized Tests *Required for some:* Psychological Corporation Aptitude Test for practical nursing.
Costs (2016–17) *Tuition:* state resident $600 full-time, $25 per credit hour part-time; nonresident $6384 full-time, $266 per credit hour part-time. Full-time tuition and fees vary according to program and reciprocity agreements. Part-time tuition and fees vary according to program and reciprocity agreements. *Required fees:* $3960 full-time, $165 per credit hour part-time. *Payment plan:* installment. *Waivers:* employees or children of employees.
Financial Aid Of all full-time matriculated undergraduates who enrolled in 2014, 74 Federal Work-Study jobs (averaging $1759).
Applying *Options:* early admission. *Application fee:* $25. *Required:* high school transcript. *Application deadlines:* rolling (freshmen), rolling (out-of-state freshmen), rolling (transfers). *Notification:* continuous (freshmen), continuous (out-of-state freshmen), continuous (transfers).
Freshman Application Contact Northern Essex Community College, 100 Elliott Street, Haverhill, MA 01830. *Phone:* 978-556-3616.
Website: http://www.necc.mass.edu/.

North Shore Community College
Danvers, Massachusetts

- **State-supported** 2-year, founded 1965
- **Suburban** campus with easy access to Boston
- **Endowment** $7.4 million
- **Coed,** 6,961 undergraduate students, 35% full-time, 61% women, 39% men

Undergraduates 2,437 full-time, 4,524 part-time. Students come from 12 states and territories; 8 other countries; 2% are from out of state; 9% Black or African American, non-Hispanic/Latino; 23% Hispanic/Latino; 4% Asian, non-Hispanic/Latino; 0.2% American Indian or Alaska Native, non-Hispanic/Latino; 2% Two or more races, non-Hispanic/Latino; 3% Race/ethnicity unknown; 0.1% international; 8% transferred in.

Freshmen *Admission:* 3,733 applied, 2,181 admitted, 1,244 enrolled.

Faculty *Total:* 486, 28% full-time, 18% with terminal degrees. *Student/faculty ratio:* 17:1.

Majors Accounting; administrative assistant and secretarial science; airline pilot and flight crew; biology/biotechnology laboratory technician; business administration and management; child development; computer and information sciences related; computer engineering technology; computer graphics; computer programming; computer programming (specific applications); computer science; criminal justice/law enforcement administration; culinary arts; data entry/microcomputer applications; engineering science; fire science/firefighting; foods, nutrition, and wellness; gerontology; health professions related; hospitality administration; information science/studies; interdisciplinary studies; kindergarten/preschool education; legal administrative assistant/secretary; legal assistant/paralegal; liberal arts and sciences/liberal studies; marketing/marketing management; medical administrative assistant and medical secretary; medical radiologic technology; mental health counseling; occupational therapy; physical therapy technology; pre-engineering; registered nursing/registered nurse; respiratory care therapy; substance abuse/addiction counseling; tourism and travel services management; veterinary/animal health technology; web page, digital/multimedia and information resources design.

Academics *Calendar:* semesters. *Degree:* certificates and associate. *Special study options:* academic remediation for entering students, accelerated degree program, adult/continuing education programs, advanced placement credit, cooperative education, distance learning, English as a second language, honors programs, independent study, internships, part-time degree program, services for LD students, summer session for credit.

Library Learning Resource Center plus 2 others.

Student Life *Housing:* college housing not available. *Activities and Organizations:* drama/theater group, student-run newspaper, Program Council, Student Government, Performing Arts, Student Newspaper, Phi Theta Kappa, national fraternities. *Campus security:* 24-hour emergency response devices and patrols, late-night transport/escort service. *Student services:* health clinic, personal/psychological counseling, women's center.

Athletics *Intramural sports:* basketball M/W, soccer M/W.

Costs (2015–16) *Tuition:* state resident $600 full-time, $25 per credit hour part-time; nonresident $6168 full-time, $257 per credit hour part-time. Full-time tuition and fees vary according to program. Part-time tuition and fees vary according to program. *Required fees:* $3936 full-time, $164 per credit hour part-time. *Payment plan:* installment. *Waivers:* senior citizens and employees or children of employees.

Financial Aid Of all full-time matriculated undergraduates who enrolled in 2009, 1,658 applied for aid, 1,438 were judged to have need, 23 had their need fully met. 123 Federal Work-Study jobs (averaging $1359). In 2009, 11 non-need-based awards were made. *Average percent of need met:* 18%. *Average financial aid package:* $6856. *Average need-based loan:* $1639. *Average need-based gift aid:* $2522. *Average non-need-based aid:* $614.

Applying *Options:* electronic application, early admission, deferred entrance. *Required for some:* essay or personal statement, high school transcript, interview. *Application deadlines:* rolling (freshmen), rolling (transfers). *Notification:* continuous (freshmen), continuous (transfers).

Freshman Application Contact Mrs. Gissel Lopez, Academic Counselor, North Shore Community College, Danvers, MA 01923. *Phone:* 978-762-4000 Ext. 2108. *Fax:* 978-762-4015. *E-mail:* gilopez@northshore.edu. *Website:* http://www.northshore.edu/.

Quincy College
Quincy, Massachusetts

- **City-supported** 2-year, founded 1958
- **Suburban** 2-acre campus with easy access to Boston
- **Endowment** $112,021
- **Coed,** 4,732 undergraduate students, 39% full-time, 67% women, 33% men

Undergraduates 1,844 full-time, 2,888 part-time. Students come from 18 states and territories; 1% are from out of state; 25% Black or African American, non-Hispanic/Latino; 7% Hispanic/Latino; 6% Asian, non-Hispanic/Latino; 0.1% Native Hawaiian or other Pacific Islander, non-Hispanic/Latino; 0.3% American Indian or Alaska Native, non-Hispanic/Latino; 2% Two or more races, non-Hispanic/Latino; 9% Race/ethnicity unknown; 8% international; 0.3% transferred in. *Retention:* 53% of full-time freshmen returned.

Freshmen *Admission:* 624 enrolled.

Faculty *Total:* 352, 19% full-time. *Student/faculty ratio:* 18:1.

Majors Accounting; biology/biotechnology laboratory technician; business administration and management; clinical/medical laboratory technology; computer science; criminal justice/law enforcement administration; early childhood education; electromechanical technology; elementary education; exercise physiology; fine arts related; general studies; health services administration; human services; legal assistant/paralegal; liberal arts and sciences/liberal studies; natural sciences; physical therapy technology; registered nursing/registered nurse; securities services administration.

Academics *Calendar:* semesters. *Degree:* certificates and associate. *Special study options:* academic remediation for entering students, adult/continuing education programs, advanced placement credit, distance learning, English as a second language, external degree program, independent study, internships, part-time degree program, services for LD students, summer session for credit.

Library Anselmo Library plus 1 other. *Books:* 10,543 (physical), 240,593 (digital/electronic); *Serial titles:* 12 (physical), 1,922 (digital/electronic); *Databases:* 52.

Student Life *Housing:* college housing not available. *Activities and Organizations:* drama/theater group, student-run newspaper, Student Government Association, Computer Club, Campus Newspaper, Drama Club, Chess Club. *Campus security:* 24-hour emergency response devices.

Athletics *Intramural sports:* basketball M/W, soccer M/W, volleyball M/W.

Costs (2015–16) *Tuition:* state resident $5040 full-time, $210 per credit part-time; nonresident $5040 full-time, $210 per credit part-time. Full-time tuition and fees vary according to course load and program. Part-time tuition and fees vary according to course load, program, and reciprocity agreements. *Required fees:* $484 full-time, $12 per credit part-time, $98 per term part-time. *Payment plan:* installment. *Waivers:* senior citizens and employees or children of employees.

Applying *Options:* electronic application, early admission, deferred entrance. *Application fee:* $30. *Required:* high school transcript. *Application deadlines:* rolling (freshmen), rolling (transfers). *Notification:* continuous (freshmen).

Freshman Application Contact Quincy College, 1250 Hancock Street, Quincy, MA 02169. *Phone:* 617-984-1710. *Toll-free phone:* 800-698-1700. *Website:* http://www.quincycollege.edu/.

Quinsigamond Community College
Worcester, Massachusetts

- **State-supported** 2-year, founded 1963, part of Massachusetts System of Higher Education
- **Urban** 57-acre campus with easy access to Boston
- **Endowment** $429,289
- **Coed,** 8,064 undergraduate students, 38% full-time, 58% women, 42% men

Undergraduates 3,040 full-time, 5,024 part-time. Students come from 21 states and territories; 22 other countries; 2% are from out of state; 13% Black or African American, non-Hispanic/Latino; 18% Hispanic/Latino; 4% Asian, non-Hispanic/Latino; 0.1% Native Hawaiian or other Pacific Islander, non-Hispanic/Latino; 0.4% American Indian or Alaska Native, non-Hispanic/Latino; 2% Two or more races, non-Hispanic/Latino; 5% Race/ethnicity unknown; 0.4% international; 7% transferred in.

Freshmen *Admission:* 3,865 applied, 2,205 admitted, 1,639 enrolled.

Faculty *Total:* 582, 24% full-time, 14% with terminal degrees. *Student/faculty ratio:* 16:1.

Majors Alternative and complementary medicine related; automobile/automotive mechanics technology; bioengineering and biomedical engineering; biomedical technology; biotechnology; business administration and management; business/commerce; chemistry; community health and preventive medicine; computer and information sciences; computer and information systems security; computer engineering technology; computer graphics; computer programming (specific applications); computer science;

computer systems analysis; criminal justice/police science; data modeling/warehousing and database administration; deaf studies; dental hygiene; dental services and allied professions related; directing and theatrical production; electrical, electronic and communications engineering technology; electromechanical technology; elementary education; emergency medical technology (EMT paramedic); energy management and systems technology; engineering technologies and engineering related; environmental science; executive assistant/executive secretary; fire services administration; game and interactive media design; general studies; health information/medical records technology; health services/allied health/health sciences; hospitality administration; human services; kindergarten/preschool education; laser and optical technology; liberal arts and sciences/liberal studies; manufacturing engineering technology; medical administrative assistant and medical secretary; music; occupational therapist assistant; pre-pharmacy studies; psychology; radiologic technology/science; registered nursing/registered nurse; respiratory care therapy; restaurant/food services management; telecommunications technology; trade and industrial teacher education; web page, digital/multimedia and information resources design.

Academics *Calendar:* semesters. *Degree:* certificates and associate. *Special study options:* academic remediation for entering students, accelerated degree program, advanced placement credit, cooperative education, distance learning, double majors, English as a second language, honors programs, independent study, internships, off-campus study, part-time degree program, services for LD students, summer session for credit. *ROTC:* Army (c).

Library Alden Library plus 1 other. *Books:* 57,682 (physical), 88,865 (digital/electronic); *Serial titles:* 54 (physical), 65,124 (digital/electronic); *Databases:* 75. Weekly public service hours: 67; students can reserve study rooms.

Student Life *Housing:* college housing not available. *Activities and Organizations:* drama/theater group, student-run newspaper, Academic-Related Clubs, Phi Theta Kappa, Student Senate, Anime Club, Psi Beta Club. *Campus security:* 24-hour emergency response devices and patrols, late-night transport/escort service. *Student services:* personal/psychological counseling.

Athletics Member NJCAA. *Intercollegiate sports:* baseball M, basketball M/W, softball W. *Intramural sports:* basketball M/W, cheerleading W(c), soccer M/W, table tennis M/W, ultimate Frisbee M/W, volleyball M/W.

Costs (2016–17) *Tuition:* state resident $576 full-time, $24 per credit part-time; nonresident $5520 full-time, $230 per credit part-time. Full-time tuition and fees vary according to course load and program. Part-time tuition and fees vary according to course load and program. *Required fees:* $4866 full-time, $164 per credit part-time, $355 per term part-time. *Payment plan:* installment. *Waivers:* senior citizens and employees or children of employees.

Applying *Options:* electronic application. *Application fee:* $20. *Required:* high school transcript. *Required for some:* interview. *Application deadlines:* rolling (freshmen), rolling (out-of-state freshmen), rolling (transfers). *Notification:* continuous (freshmen), continuous (out-of-state freshmen), continuous (transfers).

Freshman Application Contact Quinsigamond Community College, 670 West Boylston Street, Worcester, MA 01606-2092. *Phone:* 508-854-4576. *Website:* http://www.qcc.edu/.

Roxbury Community College
Roxbury Crossing, Massachusetts

Director of Admissions Nancy Santos, Director, Admissions, Roxbury Community College, 1234 Columbus Avenue, Roxbury Crossing, MA 02120-3400. *Phone:* 617-541-5310. *Website:* http://www.rcc.mass.edu/.

Salter College
Chicopee, Massachusetts

Admissions Office Contact Salter College, 645 Shawinigan Drive, Chicopee, MA 01020. *Website:* http://www.saltercollege.com/.

Salter College
West Boylston, Massachusetts

Admissions Office Contact Salter College, 184 West Boylston Street, West Boylston, MA 01583. *Website:* http://www.saltercollege-us.com/.

Springfield Technical Community College
Springfield, Massachusetts

- **State-supported** 2-year, founded 1967
- **Urban** 34-acre campus
- **Coed,** 6,286 undergraduate students, 43% full-time, 57% women, 43% men

Undergraduates 2,715 full-time, 3,571 part-time. Students come from 10 states and territories; 3% are from out of state; 16% Black or African American, non-Hispanic/Latino; 29% Hispanic/Latino; 3% Asian, non-Hispanic/Latino; 0.1% Native Hawaiian or other Pacific Islander, non-Hispanic/Latino; 0.5% American Indian or Alaska Native, non-Hispanic/Latino; 2% Two or more races, non-Hispanic/Latino; 0.4% Race/ethnicity unknown; 0.8% international; 7% transferred in.

Freshmen *Admission:* 3,139 applied, 2,704 admitted, 1,342 enrolled.

Faculty *Total:* 474, 30% full-time. *Student/faculty ratio:* 15:1.

Majors Accounting; administrative assistant and secretarial science; animation, interactive technology, video graphics and special effects; architectural engineering; automobile/automotive mechanics technology; automotive engineering technology; biology/biological sciences; biotechnology; building/construction finishing, management, and inspection related; business administration and management; business/commerce; chemistry; civil engineering technology; clinical/medical laboratory technology; commercial and advertising art; commercial photography; computer and information systems security; computer engineering technology; computer programming (specific applications); computer science; criminal justice/police science; dental hygiene; diagnostic medical sonography and ultrasound technology; early childhood education; electrical, electronic and communications engineering technology; electromechanical technology; elementary education; engineering; fine/studio arts; fire prevention and safety technology; heating, ventilation, air conditioning and refrigeration engineering technology; landscaping and groundskeeping; laser and optical technology; liberal arts and sciences/liberal studies; marketing/marketing management; massage therapy; mathematics; mechanical engineering/mechanical technology; medical administrative assistant and medical secretary; medical/clinical assistant; medical insurance coding; occupational therapist assistant; physical therapy technology; physics; premedical studies; radio and television broadcasting technology; radiologic technology/science; recording arts technology; registered nursing/registered nurse; respiratory care therapy; secondary education; small business administration; sport and fitness administration/management; surgical technology; telecommunications technology.

Academics *Calendar:* semesters. *Degree:* certificates and associate. *Special study options:* academic remediation for entering students, adult/continuing education programs, advanced placement credit, cooperative education, distance learning, English as a second language, honors programs, independent study, internships, off-campus study, part-time degree program, services for LD students, summer session for credit.

Library Springfield Technical Community College Library. *Books:* 45,975 (physical), 9,970 (digital/electronic); *Serial titles:* 159 (physical), 12 (digital/electronic); *Databases:* 93. Weekly public service hours: 61.

Student Life *Housing:* college housing not available. *Activities and Organizations:* drama/theater group, student-run newspaper, Phi Theta Kappa, Campus Civitian Club, Tech Times (student newspaper), Dental Hygiene Club, Landscape Design Club. *Campus security:* 24-hour emergency response devices and patrols, late-night transport/escort service. *Student services:* health clinic, personal/psychological counseling.

Athletics Member NJCAA. *Intercollegiate sports:* basketball M/W, golf M, soccer M/W, wrestling M. *Intramural sports:* basketball M/W, cross-country running M/W, golf M/W, skiing (cross-country) M/W, volleyball M/W, weight lifting M/W.

Standardized Tests *Required for some:* SAT (for admission).

Costs (2015–16) *Tuition:* state resident $750 full-time, $25 per credit part-time; nonresident $7260 full-time, $242 per credit part-time. Full-time tuition and fees vary according to course load and reciprocity agreements. Part-time tuition and fees vary according to course load and reciprocity agreements. No tuition increase for student's term of enrollment. *Required fees:* $4686 full-time, $149 per credit part-time, $108 per term part-time. *Payment plan:* installment. *Waivers:* senior citizens and employees or children of employees.

Applying *Options:* electronic application. *Required:* high school transcript. *Required for some:* interview. *Application deadlines:* rolling (freshmen), rolling (transfers). *Notification:* continuous (freshmen), continuous (transfers).

Freshman Application Contact Mr. LaRue Pierce, Dean of Students, Springfield Technical Community College, Springfield, MA 01105. *Phone:* 413-781-7822 Ext. 4868. *E-mail:* lapierce@stcc.edu. *Website:* http://www.stcc.edu/.

Urban College of Boston
Boston, Massachusetts

Director of Admissions Dr. Henry J. Johnson, Director of Enrollment Services/Registrar, Urban College of Boston, 178 Tremont Street, Boston, MA 02111. *Phone:* 617-348-6353.
Website: http://www.urbancollege.edu/.

MICHIGAN

Alpena Community College
Alpena, Michigan

Freshman Application Contact Mr. Mike Kollien, Director of Admissions, Alpena Community College, 665 Johnson, Alpena, MI 49707. *Phone:* 989-358-7339. *Toll-free phone:* 888-468-6222. *Fax:* 989-358-7540.
E-mail: kollienm@alpenacc.edu.
Website: http://www.alpenacc.edu/.

Bay de Noc Community College
Escanaba, Michigan

Freshman Application Contact Bay de Noc Community College, 2001 North Lincoln Road, Escanaba, MI 49829-2511. *Phone:* 906-786-5802 Ext. 1276. *Toll-free phone:* 800-221-2001.
Website: http://www.baycollege.edu/.

Bay Mills Community College
Brimley, Michigan

Freshman Application Contact Ms. Elaine Lehre, Admissions Officer, Bay Mills Community College, 12214 West Lakeshore Drive, Brimley, MI 49715. *Phone:* 906-248-3354. *Toll-free phone:* 800-844-BMCC. *Fax:* 906-248-3351.
Website: http://www.bmcc.edu/.

Delta College
University Center, Michigan

- **District-supported** 2-year, founded 1961
- **Rural** 640-acre campus
- **Endowment** $19.5 million
- **Coed,** 9,291 undergraduate students, 37% full-time, 54% women, 46% men

Undergraduates 3,432 full-time, 5,859 part-time. Students come from 4 states and territories; 1 other country; 8% Black or African American, non-Hispanic/Latino; 6% Hispanic/Latino; 0.9% Asian, non-Hispanic/Latino; 0.7% American Indian or Alaska Native, non-Hispanic/Latino; 0.1% Two or more races, non-Hispanic/Latino; 3% Race/ethnicity unknown; 0.2% international; 4% transferred in.
Freshmen *Admission:* 1,471 applied, 1,471 admitted, 1,471 enrolled.
Faculty *Total:* 531, 40% full-time. *Student/faculty ratio:* 22:1.
Majors Accounting technology and bookkeeping; administrative assistant and secretarial science; architectural engineering technology; automobile/automotive mechanics technology; building/construction finishing, management, and inspection related; building/property maintenance; business administration and management; carpentry; chemical technology; child-care provision; computer and information sciences related; computer and information systems security; computer installation and repair technology; computer programming; computer systems networking and telecommunications; construction engineering technology; corrections; criminal justice/police science; dental assisting; dental hygiene; diagnostic medical sonography and ultrasound technology; electrical and power transmission installation; electrician; energy management and systems technology; environmental engineering technology; fine/studio arts; fire prevention and safety technology; fire science/firefighting; fire services administration; general studies; heating, air conditioning, ventilation and refrigeration maintenance technology; industrial mechanics and maintenance technology; journalism; legal assistant/paralegal; liberal arts and sciences/liberal studies; machine shop technology; manufacturing engineering technology; marketing/marketing management; mechanical engineering/mechanical technology; medical administrative assistant and medical secretary; medical radiologic technology; merchandising; peace studies and conflict resolution; physical therapy technology; pipefitting and sprinkler fitting; plumbing technology; precision metal working related; precision production related; radio and television; registered nursing/registered

nurse; respiratory care therapy; retailing; salon/beauty salon management; security and loss prevention; sheet metal technology; small business administration; sport and fitness administration/management; surgical technology; technology/industrial arts teacher education; tool and die technology; water quality and wastewater treatment management and recycling technology; web/multimedia management and webmaster; welding technology.
Academics *Calendar:* semesters. *Degree:* certificates and associate. *Special study options:* academic remediation for entering students, adult/continuing education programs, advanced placement credit, cooperative education, distance learning, double majors, freshman honors college, honors programs, independent study, internships, off-campus study, part-time degree program, services for LD students, study abroad, summer session for credit.
Library Library Learning Information Center. *Books:* 56,452 (physical); *Serial titles:* 289 (physical); *Databases:* 32. Weekly public service hours: 71.
Student Life *Housing:* college housing not available. *Activities and Organizations:* drama/theater group, student-run newspaper, choral group, DECA, Phi Theta Kappa, DCSNA (student nursing association), Physical Therapy Assistant (PTA) Club, Inter-Varsity Christian Fellowship. *Campus security:* 24-hour emergency response devices, student patrols, late-night transport/escort service. *Student services:* personal/psychological counseling.
Athletics Member NJCAA. *Intercollegiate sports:* baseball M(s), basketball M(s)/W(s), golf M, soccer W(s), softball W(s).
Costs (2015–16) *Tuition:* area resident $2509 full-time, $97 per credit hour part-time; state resident $4134 full-time, $159 per credit hour part-time; nonresident $8034 full-time, $309 per credit hour part-time. Full-time tuition and fees vary according to course load. Part-time tuition and fees vary according to course load. *Required fees:* $80 full-time, $40 per term part-time. *Payment plan:* installment. *Waivers:* senior citizens and employees or children of employees.
Financial Aid Of all full-time matriculated undergraduates who enrolled in 2014, 115 Federal Work-Study jobs (averaging $2307). 67 state and other part-time jobs (averaging $2214).
Applying *Options:* electronic application, early admission, deferred entrance. *Required for some:* essay or personal statement. *Recommended:* high school transcript. *Application deadlines:* rolling (freshmen), rolling (transfers).
Freshman Application Contact Mr. Zachary Ward, Director of Admissions and Recruitment, Delta College, 1961 Delta Road, University Center, MI 48710. *Phone:* 989-686-9590. *Fax:* 989-667-2202.
E-mail: admit@delta.edu.
Website: http://www.delta.edu/.

Glen Oaks Community College
Centreville, Michigan

Freshman Application Contact Ms. Beverly M. Andrews, Director of Admissions/Registrar, Glen Oaks Community College, 62249 Shimmel Road, Centreville, MI 49032-9719. *Phone:* 269-294-4249. *Toll-free phone:* 888-994-7818. *Fax:* 269-467-4114. *E-mail:* thowden@glenoaks.edu.
Website: http://www.glenoaks.edu/.

Gogebic Community College
Ironwood, Michigan

Freshman Application Contact Ms. Kim Zeckovich, Director of Admissions, Marketing, and Public Relations, Gogebic Community College, E4946 Jackson Road, Ironwood, MI 49938. *Phone:* 906-932-4231 Ext. 347. *Toll-free phone:* 800-682-5910. *Fax:* 906-932-2339. *E-mail:* jeanneg@gogebic.edu.
Website: http://www.gogebic.edu/.

Grand Rapids Community College
Grand Rapids, Michigan

- **District-supported** 2-year, founded 1914, part of Michigan Department of Education
- **Urban** 35-acre campus
- **Endowment** $30.8 million
- **Coed,** 14,926 undergraduate students, 30% full-time, 52% women, 48% men

Undergraduates 4,493 full-time, 10,433 part-time. Students come from 10 states and territories; 23 other countries; 1% are from out of state; 9% Black or African American, non-Hispanic/Latino; 11% Hispanic/Latino; 4% Asian, non-Hispanic/Latino; 0.1% Native Hawaiian or other Pacific Islander, non-Hispanic/Latino; 0.6% American Indian or Alaska Native, non-Hispanic/Latino; 2% Two or more races, non-Hispanic/Latino; 4% Race/ethnicity unknown; 0.2% international; 8% transferred in. *Retention:* 58% of full-time freshmen returned.

Freshmen *Admission:* 9,001 applied, 2,856 enrolled. *Average high school GPA:* 2.9. *Test scores:* ACT scores over 18: 71%; ACT scores over 24: 18%; ACT scores over 30: 1%.

Faculty *Total:* 914, 27% full-time. *Student/faculty ratio:* 21:1.

Majors Architectural technology; architecture; art; automobile/automotive mechanics technology; business administration and management; chemistry; child-care and support services management; computer and information sciences; computer and information systems security; computer programming; computer programming (specific applications); computer support specialist; computer systems networking and telecommunications; corrections; criminal justice/law enforcement administration; criminal justice/police science; culinary arts; dental hygiene; electrical, electronic and communications engineering technology; elementary education; engineering; English; fashion merchandising; foreign languages and literatures; forestry; geology/earth science; heating, air conditioning, ventilation and refrigeration maintenance technology; industrial technology; journalism; landscaping and groundskeeping; liberal arts and sciences/liberal studies; library and information science; licensed practical/vocational nurse training; medical administrative assistant and medical secretary; music; music teacher education; physical education teaching and coaching; plastics and polymer engineering technology; quality control technology; recording arts technology; registered nursing/registered nurse; restaurant, culinary, and catering management; secondary education; welding technology.

Academics *Calendar:* semesters. *Degree:* certificates and associate. *Special study options:* academic remediation for entering students, adult/continuing education programs, advanced placement credit, cooperative education, distance learning, English as a second language, honors programs, independent study, internships, off-campus study, part-time degree program, services for LD students, study abroad, summer session for credit.

Library Arthur Andrews Memorial Library.

Student Life *Housing:* college housing not available. *Activities and Organizations:* drama/theater group, student-run newspaper, choral group, Student Congress, Phi Theta Kappa, Hispanic Student Organization, Student Gamers Association, Foreign Affairs Club. *Campus security:* 24-hour emergency response devices, late-night transport/escort service. *Student services:* personal/psychological counseling.

Athletics Member NJCAA. *Intercollegiate sports:* baseball M(s), basketball M(s)/W(s), cross-country running M/W, golf M(s), softball W(s), volleyball W(s).

Standardized Tests *Recommended:* SAT or ACT (for admission).

Costs (2015–16) *Tuition:* area resident $3240 full-time, $108 per contact hour part-time; state resident $6960 full-time, $232 per contact hour part-time; nonresident $10,320 full-time, $344 per contact hour part-time. Full-time tuition and fees vary according to course load and program. Part-time tuition and fees vary according to course load and program. *Required fees:* $459 full-time, $15 per contact hour part-time, $90 per term part-time. *Payment plan:* installment. *Waivers:* employees or children of employees.

Financial Aid Of all full-time matriculated undergraduates who enrolled in 2008, 6,142 applied for aid, 4,896 were judged to have need, 1,012 had their need fully met. In 2008, 96 non-need-based awards were made. *Average financial aid package:* $4850. *Average need-based loan:* $2764. *Average need-based gift aid:* $3984. *Average non-need-based aid:* $1051.

Applying *Options:* electronic application, early admission, deferred entrance. *Required:* high school transcript. *Application deadline:* 8/30 (freshmen). *Notification:* continuous (freshmen), continuous (transfers).

Freshman Application Contact Ms. Diane Patrick, Director of Admissions, Grand Rapids Community College, Grand Rapids, MI 49503-3201. *Phone:* 616-234-4100. *Fax:* 616-234-4005. *E-mail:* dpatrick@grcc.edu. *Website:* http://www.grcc.edu/.

Henry Ford College
Dearborn, Michigan

Freshman Application Contact Admissions Office, Henry Ford College, 5101 Evergreen Road, Dearborn, MI 48128-1495. *Phone:* 313-845-6403. *Toll-free phone:* 800-585-HFCC. *Fax:* 313-845-6464. *E-mail:* enroll@hfcc.edu. *Website:* http://www.hfcc.edu/.

ITT Technical Institute
Canton, Michigan

Freshman Application Contact Director of Recruitment, ITT Technical Institute, 1905 South Haggerty Road, Canton, MI 48188-2025. *Phone:* 784-397-7800. *Toll-free phone:* 800-247-4477. *Website:* http://www.itt-tech.edu/.

ITT Technical Institute
Dearborn, Michigan

Freshman Application Contact Director of Recruitment, ITT Technical Institute, 19855 Outer Drive, West Bldg-LL, Dearborn, MI 48124. *Phone:* 313-278-5208. *Toll-free phone:* 800-605-0801. *Website:* http://www.itt-tech.edu/.

ITT Technical Institute
Swartz Creek, Michigan

Freshman Application Contact Director of Recruitment, ITT Technical Institute, 6359 Miller Road, Swartz Creek, MI 48473. *Phone:* 810-628-2500. *Toll-free phone:* 800-514-6564. *Website:* http://www.itt-tech.edu/.

ITT Technical Institute
Troy, Michigan

Freshman Application Contact Director of Recruitment, ITT Technical Institute, 1522 East Big Beaver Road, Troy, MI 48083-1905. *Phone:* 248-524-1800. *Toll-free phone:* 800-832-6817. *Website:* http://www.itt-tech.edu/.

ITT Technical Institute
Wyoming, Michigan

Freshman Application Contact Director of Recruitment, ITT Technical Institute, 1980 Metro Court SW, Wyoming, MI 49519. *Phone:* 616-406-1200. *Toll-free phone:* 800-632-4676. *Website:* http://www.itt-tech.edu/.

Jackson College
Jackson, Michigan

Freshman Application Contact Mr. Daniel Vainner, Registrar, Jackson College, 2111 Emmons Road, Jackson, MI 49201. *Phone:* 517-796-8425. *Toll-free phone:* 888-522-7344. *Fax:* 517-796-8446. *E-mail:* admissions@jccmi.edu. *Website:* http://www.jccmi.edu/.

Kalamazoo Valley Community College
Kalamazoo, Michigan

- **State and locally supported** 2-year, founded 1966
- **Suburban** 187-acre campus
- **Coed**

Undergraduates 1% are from out of state.

Academics *Calendar:* semesters. *Degree:* certificates and associate. *Special study options:* academic remediation for entering students, advanced placement credit, cooperative education, distance learning, English as a second language, honors programs, independent study, internships, off-campus study, part-time degree program, services for LD students, student-designed majors, summer session for credit. *ROTC:* Army (c).

Library Kalamazoo Valley Community College Library.

Student Life *Campus security:* 24-hour emergency response devices and patrols.

Athletics Member NJCAA.

Standardized Tests *Required:* ACT (for admission).

Financial Aid Of all full-time matriculated undergraduates who enrolled in 2014, 65 Federal Work-Study jobs (averaging $1920).

Applying *Required:* high school transcript.

Freshman Application Contact Kalamazoo Valley Community College, PO Box 4070, Kalamazoo, MI 49003-4070. *Phone:* 269-488-4207. *Website:* http://www.kvcc.edu/.

Kellogg Community College
Battle Creek, Michigan

- **State and locally supported** 2-year, founded 1956, part of Michigan Department of Education
- **Urban** 120-acre campus
- **Coed,** 5,081 undergraduate students, 25% full-time, 66% women, 34% men

Undergraduates 1,268 full-time, 3,813 part-time. Students come from 2 states and territories; 8 other countries; 9% Black or African American, non-Hispanic/Latino; 5% Hispanic/Latino; 2% Asian, non-Hispanic/Latino; 0.6%

American Indian or Alaska Native, non-Hispanic/Latino; 0.1% Two or more races, non-Hispanic/Latino; 9% Race/ethnicity unknown; 0.3% international; 4% transferred in.

Freshmen *Admission:* 436 applied, 436 admitted, 436 enrolled.

Faculty *Total:* 447, 19% full-time, 5% with terminal degrees. *Student/faculty ratio:* 12:1.

Majors Accounting; accounting technology and bookkeeping; administrative assistant and secretarial science; animation, interactive technology, video graphics and special effects; business administration and management; CAD/CADD drafting/design technology; child-care and support services management; community organization and advocacy; computer engineering technology; computer graphics; computer programming; computer programming (specific applications); computer software and media applications related; computer technology/computer systems technology; corrections; criminal justice/law enforcement administration; criminal justice/police science; criminal justice/safety; data entry/microcomputer applications; data entry/microcomputer applications related; dental hygiene; drafting and design technology; elementary education; emergency medical technology (EMT paramedic); executive assistant/executive secretary; general studies; heating, air conditioning, ventilation and refrigeration maintenance technology; human services; industrial technology; legal administrative assistant/secretary; legal assistant/paralegal; liberal arts and sciences/liberal studies; machine tool technology; manufacturing engineering technology; medical administrative assistant and medical secretary; medical radiologic technology; physical therapy technology; pipefitting and sprinkler fitting; registered nursing/registered nurse; web page, digital/multimedia and information resources design; welding technology; word processing.

Academics *Calendar:* semesters. *Degree:* certificates and associate. *Special study options:* academic remediation for entering students, accelerated degree program, adult/continuing education programs, advanced placement credit, cooperative education, distance learning, double majors, English as a second language, freshman honors college, honors programs, independent study, internships, off-campus study, part-time degree program, services for LD students, summer session for credit.

Library Emory W. Morris Learning Resource Center.

Student Life *Housing:* college housing not available. *Activities and Organizations:* drama/theater group, student-run newspaper, choral group, Tech Club, Phi Theta Kappa, Student Nurses Association, Crude Arts Club, Art League. *Campus security:* 24-hour emergency response devices and patrols, late-night transport/escort service.

Athletics Member NJCAA. *Intercollegiate sports:* baseball M(s), basketball M(s)/W(s), soccer W, softball W(s), volleyball W(s).

Standardized Tests *Required for some:* ACT (for admission), SAT or ACT (for admission).

Costs (2016–17) *Tuition:* area resident $2388 full-time; state resident $3870 full-time; nonresident $5538 full-time. Full-time tuition and fees vary according to program. Part-time tuition and fees vary according to program. *Required fees:* $312 full-time. *Payment plan:* installment. *Waivers:* senior citizens and employees or children of employees.

Financial Aid Of all full-time matriculated undergraduates who enrolled in 2014, 41 Federal Work-Study jobs (averaging $2251). 43 state and other part-time jobs (averaging $2058).

Applying *Options:* electronic application, early admission. *Required for some:* high school transcript, minimum 2.0 GPA. *Application deadlines:* rolling (freshmen), rolling (transfers). *Notification:* continuous (freshmen), continuous (transfers).

Freshman Application Contact Ms. Meredith Stravers, Director of Admissions, Kellogg Community College, 450 North Avenue, Battle Creek, MI 49017. *Phone:* 269-965-3931 Ext. 2644. *Fax:* 269-965-4133. *E-mail:* straversm@kellogg.edu. *Website:* http://www.kellogg.edu/.

Keweenaw Bay Ojibwa Community College
Baraga, Michigan

- **County-supported** 2-year
- **Rural** campus
- **Coed,** 77 undergraduate students, 56% full-time, 69% women, 31% men

Undergraduates 43 full-time, 34 part-time. Students come from 1 other state.

Freshmen *Admission:* 16 enrolled.

Majors American Indian/Native American studies; early childhood education; environmental science; liberal arts and sciences/liberal studies.

Academics *Calendar:* semesters. *Degree:* associate.

Student Life *Housing:* college housing not available.

Applying *Application fee:* $20. *Required:* high school transcript.

Freshman Application Contact Ms. Megan Shanahan, Admissions Officer, Keweenaw Bay Ojibwa Community College, 111 Beartown Road, Baraga, MI 49908. *Phone:* 909-353-4600. *E-mail:* megan@kbocc.org. *Website:* http://www.kbocc.edu/.

Kirtland Community College
Roscommon, Michigan

- **District-supported** 2-year, founded 1966
- **Rural** 180-acre campus
- **Coed,** 1,628 undergraduate students, 32% full-time, 58% women, 42% men

Undergraduates 520 full-time, 1,108 part-time. Students come from 4 states and territories; 1 other country; 1% Black or African American, non-Hispanic/Latino; 2% Hispanic/Latino; 0.5% Asian, non-Hispanic/Latino; 1% American Indian or Alaska Native, non-Hispanic/Latino; 1% Two or more races, non-Hispanic/Latino; 2% Race/ethnicity unknown; 0.1% international.

Freshmen *Admission:* 603 applied, 603 admitted, 185 enrolled. *Test scores:* ACT scores over 18: 53%; ACT scores over 24: 7%; ACT scores over 30: 1%.

Faculty *Total:* 128, 26% full-time. *Student/faculty ratio:* 18:1.

Majors Administrative assistant and secretarial science; art; automobile/automotive mechanics technology; business administration and management; cardiovascular technology; cosmetology; criminal justice/law enforcement administration; criminal justice/police science; electrical, electronic and communications engineering technology; electromechanical technology; emergency medical technology (EMT paramedic); general studies; graphic design; health information/medical records technology; heating, air conditioning, ventilation and refrigeration maintenance technology; information science/studies; liberal arts and sciences/liberal studies; licensed practical/vocational nurse training; management information systems; medical administrative assistant and medical secretary; medical/clinical assistant; pharmacy technician; registered nursing/registered nurse; robotics technology; surgical technology; welding technology.

Academics *Calendar:* semesters. *Degree:* certificates and associate. *Special study options:* academic remediation for entering students, adult/continuing education programs, advanced placement credit, cooperative education, distance learning, honors programs, independent study, internships, part-time degree program, services for LD students, summer session for credit.

Library Kirtland Community College Library. *Books:* 33,972 (physical), 140,479 (digital/electronic); *Databases:* 89. Weekly public service hours: 48; students can reserve study rooms.

Student Life *Housing:* college housing not available. *Campus security:* 24-hour emergency response devices, student patrols, late-night transport/escort service, campus warning siren, uniformed armed police officers, RAVE alert system (text, email, voice).

Athletics Member NJCAA. *Intercollegiate sports:* bowling M(s)/W(s), cross-country running M(s)/W(s), golf M(s)/W(s).

Standardized Tests *Recommended:* SAT or ACT (for admission).

Costs (2015–16) *Tuition:* area resident $3150 full-time, $105 per contact hour part-time; state resident $4380 full-time, $146 per contact hour part-time; nonresident $7050 full-time, $235 per contact hour part-time. *Required fees:* $575 full-time, $18 per contact hour part-time, $35 per term part-time. *Payment plan:* installment. *Waivers:* senior citizens and employees or children of employees.

Financial Aid Of all full-time matriculated undergraduates who enrolled in 2014, 50 Federal Work-Study jobs (averaging $1253). 28 state and other part-time jobs (averaging $1647).

Applying *Options:* electronic application. *Application deadlines:* rolling (freshmen), rolling (transfers). *Notification:* continuous until 8/22 (freshmen), continuous until 8/22 (transfers).

Freshman Application Contact Ms. Michelle Vyskocil, Dean of Student Services, Kirtland Community College, 10775 North Saint Helen Road, Roscommon, MI 48653. *Phone:* 989-275-5000 Ext. 248. *Fax:* 989-275-6789. *E-mail:* registrar@kirtland.edu. *Website:* http://www.kirtland.edu/.

Lake Michigan College
Benton Harbor, Michigan

Freshman Application Contact Mr. Louis Thomas, Lead Admissions Specialist, Lake Michigan College, 2755 East Napier Avenue, Benton Harbor, MI 49022-1899. *Phone:* 269-927-6584. *Toll-free phone:* 800-252-1LMC. *Fax:* 269-927-6718. *E-mail:* thomas@lakemichigancollege.edu. *Website:* http://www.lakemichigancollege.edu/.

Lansing Community College
Lansing, Michigan

Freshman Application Contact Ms. Tammy Grossbauer, Director of Admissions/Registrar, Lansing Community College, 1121 - Enrollment Services, PO BOX 40010, Lansing, MI 48901. *Phone:* 517-483-1200. *Toll-free phone:* 800-644-4LCC. *Fax:* 517-483-1170. *E-mail:* grossbt@lcc.edu. *Website:* http://www.lcc.edu/.

Macomb Community College
Warren, Michigan

- **District-supported** 2-year, founded 1954, part of Michigan Public Community College System
- **Suburban** 384-acre campus with easy access to Detroit
- **Endowment** $21.3 million
- **Coed**, 22,182 undergraduate students, 31% full-time, 53% women, 47% men

Undergraduates 6,894 full-time, 15,288 part-time. Students come from 4 states and territories; 11% Black or African American, non-Hispanic/Latino; 3% Hispanic/Latino; 4% Asian, non-Hispanic/Latino; 0.1% Native Hawaiian or other Pacific Islander, non-Hispanic/Latino; 0.5% American Indian or Alaska Native, non-Hispanic/Latino; 2% Two or more races, non-Hispanic/Latino; 9% Race/ethnicity unknown; 2% international. *Retention:* 56% of full-time freshmen returned.
Freshmen *Admission:* 3,435 enrolled.
Faculty *Total:* 1,002, 20% full-time, 11% with terminal degrees. *Student/faculty ratio:* 27:1.
Majors Accounting; administrative assistant and secretarial science; agriculture; architectural drafting and CAD/CADD; automobile/automotive mechanics technology; automotive engineering technology; biology/biological sciences; business administration and management; business automation/technology/data entry; business/commerce; cabinetmaking and millwork; chemistry; child-care and support services management; civil engineering technology; commercial and advertising art; computer programming; computer programming (specific applications); construction engineering technology; criminal justice/law enforcement administration; criminal justice/police science; culinary arts; drafting and design technology; drafting/design engineering technologies related; electrical, electronic and communications engineering technology; electrical/electronics equipment installation and repair; electromechanical technology; emergency medical technology (EMT paramedic); energy management and systems technology; engineering related; finance; fire prevention and safety technology; forensic science and technology; general studies; graphic and printing equipment operation/production; heating, air conditioning, ventilation and refrigeration maintenance technology; heating, ventilation, air conditioning and refrigeration engineering technology; industrial mechanics and maintenance technology; industrial technology; international/global studies; legal assistant/paralegal; legal studies; liberal arts and sciences/liberal studies; machine tool technology; manufacturing engineering technology; marketing/marketing management; mathematics; mechanical drafting and CAD/CADD; mechanical engineering/mechanical technology; mechanic and repair technologies related; medical/clinical assistant; mental health counseling; metallurgical technology; music performance; occupational therapist assistant; operations management; physical therapy technology; plastics and polymer engineering technology; plumbing technology; pre-engineering; quality control and safety technologies related; quality control technology; registered nursing/registered nurse; respiratory care therapy; robotics technology; sheet metal technology; social psychology; speech communication and rhetoric; surgical technology; surveying technology; tool and die technology; veterinary/animal health technology; welding technology.
Academics *Calendar:* semesters. *Degree:* certificates and associate. *Special study options:* academic remediation for entering students, adult/continuing education programs, advanced placement credit, cooperative education, English as a second language, honors programs, internships, off-campus study, part-time degree program, services for LD students, student-designed majors, summer session for credit.
Library Library of South Campus.
Student Life *Housing:* college housing not available. *Activities and Organizations:* drama/theater group, Phi Beta Kappa, Adventure Unlimited, Alpha Rho Rho, SADD. *Campus security:* 24-hour emergency response devices and patrols, late-night transport/escort service, security phones in parking lots, surveillance cameras. *Student services:* health clinic, personal/psychological counseling.
Athletics Member NJCAA. *Intercollegiate sports:* baseball M(s), basketball M(s), cross-country running M(s)/W(s), soccer M(s), softball W(s), track and field M(s)/W(s), volleyball W(s). *Intramural sports:* baseball M, basketball M, bowling M/W, cross-country running M/W, football M/W, skiing (cross-country) M/W, skiing (downhill) M/W, volleyball M/W.

Costs (2015–16) *Tuition:* area resident $2914 full-time, $94 per credit hour part-time; state resident $4960 full-time, $160 per credit hour part-time; nonresident $6386 full-time, $206 per credit hour part-time. Full-time tuition and fees vary according to course load. Part-time tuition and fees vary according to course load. *Required fees:* $255 full-time, $5 per credit hour part-time, $50 per term part-time. *Waivers:* employees or children of employees.
Applying *Options:* early admission, deferred entrance. *Application deadlines:* rolling (freshmen), rolling (transfers).
Freshman Application Contact Mr. Brian Bouwman, Coordinator of Admissions and Transfer Credit, Macomb Community College, 14500 East 12 Mile Road, Warren, MI 48088-3896. *Phone:* 586-445-7246. *Toll-free phone:* 866-MACOMB1. *Fax:* 586-445-7140. *E-mail:* stevensr@macomb.edu. *Website:* http://www.macomb.edu/.

Manthano Christian College
Westland, Michigan

Admissions Office Contact Manthano Christian College, 6420 N. Newburgh, Westland, MI 48185-1919.
Website: http://www.manthanochristian.org.

MIAT College of Technology
Canton, Michigan

Admissions Office Contact MIAT College of Technology, 2955 South Haggerty Road, Canton, MI 48188.
Website: http://www.miat.edu/.

Mid Michigan Community College
Harrison, Michigan

Freshman Application Contact Jennifer Casebeer, Admissions Specialist, Mid Michigan Community College, 1375 South Clare Avenue, Harrison, MI 48625-9447. *Phone:* 989-386-6661. *E-mail:* apply@midmich.edu. *Website:* http://www.midmich.edu/.

Monroe County Community College
Monroe, Michigan

- **County-supported** 2-year, founded 1964, part of Michigan Department of Education
- **Small-town** 150-acre campus with easy access to Detroit, Toledo
- **Coed**

Undergraduates Students come from 3 other countries; 4% are from out of state.
Academics *Calendar:* semesters. *Degree:* certificates and associate. *Special study options:* academic remediation for entering students, advanced placement credit, distance learning, independent study, part-time degree program, services for LD students, summer session for credit.
Library Campbell Learning Resource Center.
Student Life *Campus security:* police patrols during open hours.
Standardized Tests *Required:* ACT, ACT Compass (for admission). *Required for some:* ACT (for admission). *Recommended:* ACT (for admission).
Costs (2015–16) *Tuition:* area resident $2638 full-time, $120 per contact hour part-time; state resident $4270 full-time, $197 per contact hour part-time; nonresident $4702 full-time, $217 per contact hour part-time. Full-time tuition and fees vary according to reciprocity agreements. Part-time tuition and fees vary according to reciprocity agreements. *Required fees:* $204 full-time, $35 per term part-time.
Applying *Options:* early admission, deferred entrance. *Required:* high school transcript, Baseline cut scores on ACT or COMPASS.
Freshman Application Contact Mr. Mark V. Hall, Director of Admissions and Guidance Services, Monroe County Community College, 1555 South Raisinville Road, Monroe, MI 48161. *Phone:* 734-384-4261. *Toll-free phone:* 877-YES-MCCC. *Fax:* 734-242-9711. *E-mail:* mhall@monroeccc.edu. *Website:* http://www.monroeccc.edu/.

Montcalm Community College
Sidney, Michigan

- **State and locally supported** 2-year, founded 1965, part of Michigan Department of Education
- **Rural** 240-acre campus with easy access to Grand Rapids
- **Coed**

Undergraduates 538 full-time, 1,294 part-time. 0.4% Black or African American, non-Hispanic/Latino; 1% Hispanic/Latino; 0.2% Asian, non-Hispanic/Latino; 0.6% American Indian or Alaska Native, non-

Hispanic/Latino; 2% Two or more races, non-Hispanic/Latino; 7% Race/ethnicity unknown; 0.1% international; 15% transferred in.

Faculty *Student/faculty ratio:* 16:1.

Academics *Calendar:* semesters. *Degree:* certificates and associate. *Special study options:* academic remediation for entering students, adult/continuing education programs, advanced placement credit, cooperative education, distance learning, double majors, independent study, internships, off-campus study, part-time degree program, services for LD students, study abroad, summer session for credit.

Library Montcalm Community College Library.

Financial Aid Of all full-time matriculated undergraduates who enrolled in 2013, 444 were judged to have need.

Applying *Options:* electronic application, early admission, deferred entrance. *Recommended:* high school transcript.

Freshman Application Contact Ms. Debra Alexander, Associate Dean of Student Services, Montcalm Community College, 2800 College Drive, SW, Sidney, MI 48885. *Phone:* 989-328-1276. *Toll-free phone:* 877-328-2111. *E-mail:* admissions@montcalm.edu. *Website:* http://www.montcalm.edu/.

Mott Community College
Flint, Michigan

- **District-supported** 2-year, founded 1923
- **Urban** 32-acre campus with easy access to Detroit
- **Endowment** $40.1 million
- **Coed,** 8,617 undergraduate students, 26% full-time, 59% women, 41% men

Undergraduates 2,230 full-time, 6,387 part-time. Students come from 36 states and territories; 19% Black or African American, non-Hispanic/Latino; 4% Hispanic/Latino; 0.6% Asian, non-Hispanic/Latino; 0.1% Native Hawaiian or other Pacific Islander, non-Hispanic/Latino; 0.6% American Indian or Alaska Native, non-Hispanic/Latino; 4% Two or more races, non-Hispanic/Latino; 4% Race/ethnicity unknown; 0.4% international; 2% transferred in.

Freshmen *Admission:* 1,549 enrolled.

Faculty *Total:* 454, 31% full-time, 11% with terminal degrees. *Student/faculty ratio:* 18:1.

Majors Accounting technology and bookkeeping; architectural engineering technology; automation engineer technology; automobile/automotive mechanics technology; baking and pastry arts; biology/biological sciences; business administration and management; business/commerce; child-care provision; cinematography and film/video production; communications technology; community health services counseling; computer programming; computer programming (specific applications); computer systems networking and telecommunications; corrections; criminal justice/police science; culinary arts; dental assisting; dental hygiene; drafting and design technology; early childhood education; electrical, electronic and communications engineering technology; emergency medical technology (EMT paramedic); engineering technologies and engineering related; entrepreneurship; fire prevention and safety technology; food service systems administration; general studies; graphic design; heating, ventilation, air conditioning and refrigeration engineering technology; histologic technician; liberal arts and sciences/liberal studies; marketing/marketing management; mechanical engineering/mechanical technology; medical radiologic technology; music technology; occupational therapist assistant; photography; physical therapy technology; precision production related; registered nursing/registered nurse; respiratory care therapy; salon/beauty salon management; sign language interpretation and translation; visual and performing arts.

Academics *Calendar:* semesters. *Degree:* certificates and associate. *Special study options:* academic remediation for entering students, accelerated degree program, adult/continuing education programs, advanced placement credit, cooperative education, distance learning, double majors, English as a second language, honors programs, independent study, internships, part-time degree program, services for LD students, summer session for credit.

Library Charles Stewart Mott Library. *Books:* 45,948 (physical), 64,921 (digital/electronic); *Serial titles:* 295 (digital/electronic); *Databases:* 78.

Student Life *Housing:* college housing not available. *Activities and Organizations:* choral group, Otaku Club, Respiratory Care Student Society, Physical Therapist Assistants, Occupational Therapist Assistants, Transitions Cosmetology, national fraternities, national sororities. *Campus security:* 24-hour emergency response devices and patrols, student patrols, late-night transport/escort service, closed-circuit TV surveillance, whistle alert program, 3P Campaign: Prevent, Protect, and Prosecute Violence Against Women. *Student services:* health clinic, personal/psychological counseling.

Athletics Member NJCAA. *Intercollegiate sports:* baseball M(s), basketball M(s)/W(s), cross-country running M(s)/W(s), golf M(s), softball W(s), volleyball W(s). *Intramural sports:* cheerleading W(c).

Costs (2016–17) *Tuition:* area resident $3910 full-time, $130 per contact hour part-time; state resident $5504 full-time, $183 per contact hour part-time;

nonresident $7842 full-time, $261 per contact hour part-time. Full-time tuition and fees vary according to course load. Part-time tuition and fees vary according to course load. *Required fees:* $657 full-time, $17 per contact hour part-time, $130 per term part-time. *Payment plan:* installment. *Waivers:* senior citizens and employees or children of employees.

Financial Aid Of all full-time matriculated undergraduates who enrolled in 2011, 16,668 applied for aid, 15,858 were judged to have need, 810 had their need fully met. 7,449 Federal Work-Study jobs (averaging $6303). In 2011, 95 non-need-based awards were made. *Average percent of need met:* 79%. *Average financial aid package:* $21,292. *Average need-based loan:* $3019. *Average need-based gift aid:* $3471. *Average non-need-based aid:* $2356.

Applying *Options:* electronic application, early admission, deferred entrance. *Required:* high school transcript. *Application deadline:* 8/31 (freshmen). *Notification:* continuous (transfers).

Freshman Application Contact Ms. Regina Broomfield, Supervisor of Admissions Operations - Outreach and Recruitment, Mott Community College, 1401 East Court Street, Flint, MI 48503. *Phone:* 810-762-0358. *Toll-free phone:* 800-852-8614. *Fax:* 810-232-9442. *E-mail:* regina.broomfield@mcc.edu. *Website:* http://www.mcc.edu/.

Muskegon Community College
Muskegon, Michigan

- **State and locally supported** 2-year, founded 1926, part of Michigan Department of Education
- **Small-town** 112-acre campus with easy access to Grand Rapids
- **Coed,** 4,506 undergraduate students, 33% full-time, 56% women, 44% men

Undergraduates 1,488 full-time, 3,018 part-time. Students come from 4 states and territories; 9% Black or African American, non-Hispanic/Latino; 3% Hispanic/Latino; 0.8% Asian, non-Hispanic/Latino; 0.1% Native Hawaiian or other Pacific Islander, non-Hispanic/Latino; 0.9% American Indian or Alaska Native, non-Hispanic/Latino; 4% Two or more races, non-Hispanic/Latino; 5% Race/ethnicity unknown; 0.4% international. *Retention:* 59% of full-time freshmen returned.

Freshmen *Admission:* 802 applied, 802 admitted, 802 enrolled.

Faculty *Total:* 324, 26% full-time. *Student/faculty ratio:* 19:1.

Majors Accounting; administrative assistant and secretarial science; advertising; anthropology; applied mathematics; art; art history, criticism and conservation; art teacher education; automobile/automotive mechanics technology; biology/biotechnology laboratory technician; biomedical technology; business administration and management; business machine repair; chemical engineering; child development; commercial and advertising art; criminal justice/law enforcement administration; data processing and data processing technology; design and applied arts related; developmental and child psychology; drafting and design technology; economics; education; electrical, electronic and communications engineering technology; electromechanical technology; elementary education; engineering technology; finance; hospitality administration; hospitality and recreation marketing; hotel/motel administration; industrial technology; information science/studies; legal administrative assistant/secretary; liberal arts and sciences/liberal studies; machine tool technology; marketing/marketing management; medical administrative assistant and medical secretary; parks, recreation and leisure; registered nursing/registered nurse; special products marketing; transportation and materials moving related; welding technology.

Academics *Calendar:* semesters. *Degree:* associate. *Special study options:* academic remediation for entering students, adult/continuing education programs, cooperative education, honors programs, part-time degree program, student-designed majors, summer session for credit.

Library Hendrik Meijer and Technology Center.

Student Life *Housing:* college housing not available. *Activities and Organizations:* drama/theater group, student-run newspaper, choral group, Respiratory Therapy, Hispanic Student Organization, Black Student Alliance, International Club, Rotaract. *Campus security:* 24-hour emergency response devices, on-campus security officer. *Student services:* personal/psychological counseling.

Athletics Member NJCAA. *Intercollegiate sports:* baseball M, basketball M(s)/W(s), golf M/W, softball W, tennis M/W, volleyball W(s), wrestling M. *Intramural sports:* basketball M/W, skiing (downhill) M(c)/W(c).

Costs (2015–16) *Tuition:* area resident $3960 full-time, $99 per contact hour part-time; state resident $7360 full-time, $184 per contact hour part-time; nonresident $10,240 full-time, $256 per contact hour part-time. *Required fees:* $1163 full-time, $25 per contact hour part-time, $35 per term part-time. *Payment plan:* deferred payment. *Waivers:* senior citizens.

Financial Aid Of all full-time matriculated undergraduates who enrolled in 2014, 250 Federal Work-Study jobs (averaging $2500). 50 state and other part-time jobs (averaging $2500).

Applying *Options:* electronic application, early admission, deferred entrance. *Required:* high school transcript. *Application deadlines:* rolling (freshmen), rolling (transfers). *Notification:* continuous (freshmen), continuous (transfers).
Freshman Application Contact Mr. Johnathon Skidmore, Senior Clerk 1 Admissions, Muskegon Community College, 221 South Quarterline Road, Muskegon, MI 49442-1493. *Phone:* 231-777-0366. *Toll-free phone:* 866-711-4622. *E-mail:* johnathon.skidmore@muskegoncc.edu.
Website: http://www.muskegoncc.edu/.

North Central Michigan College
Petoskey, Michigan

Director of Admissions Ms. Julieanne Tobin, Director of Enrollment Management, North Central Michigan College, 1515 Howard Street, Petoskey, MI 49770-8717. *Phone:* 231-439-6511. *Toll-free phone:* 888-298-6605. *E-mail:* jtobin@ncmich.edu.
Website: http://www.ncmich.edu/.

Northwestern Michigan College
Traverse City, Michigan

- **State and locally supported** primarily 2-year, founded 1951
- **Small-town** 180-acre campus
- **Coed**

Undergraduates 2,011 full-time, 2,598 part-time. Students come from 19 states and territories; 21 other countries; 2% are from out of state; 11% transferred in. *Retention:* 61% of full-time freshmen returned.
Faculty *Student/faculty ratio:* 18:1.
Academics *Calendar:* semesters. *Degrees:* certificates, associate, and bachelor's. *Special study options:* academic remediation for entering students, adult/continuing education programs, advanced placement credit, cooperative education, distance learning, honors programs, independent study, internships, part-time degree program, services for LD students, summer session for credit.
Library Mark and Helen Osterlin Library plus 1 other.
Student Life *Campus security:* 24-hour emergency response devices and patrols, student patrols, late-night transport/escort service, controlled dormitory access, well-lit campus.
Financial Aid Of all full-time matriculated undergraduates who enrolled in 2014, 58 Federal Work-Study jobs (averaging $2068). 39 state and other part-time jobs (averaging $1718).
Applying *Options:* electronic application, early admission, deferred entrance. *Application fee:* $20. *Required for some:* high school transcript. *Recommended:* minimum 2.0 GPA.
Freshman Application Contact Catheryn Claerhout, Director of Admissions, Northwestern Michigan College, 1701 E. Front Street, Traverse City, MI 49686. *Phone:* 231-995-1034. *Toll-free phone:* 800-748-0566.
E-mail: c.claerhout@nmc.edu.
Website: http://www.nmc.edu/.

Oakland Community College
Bloomfield Hills, Michigan

Freshman Application Contact Stephan M. Linden, Registrar, Oakland Community College, 2480 Opdyke Road, Bloomfield Hills, MI 48304-2266. *Phone:* 248-341-2192. *Fax:* 248-341-2099.
E-mail: smlinden@oaklandcc.edu.
Website: http://www.oaklandcc.edu/.

Saginaw Chippewa Tribal College
Mount Pleasant, Michigan

- **Independent** 2-year, founded 1998
- **Small-town** campus
- **Coed,** 122 undergraduate students, 32% full-time, 65% women, 35% men

Undergraduates 39 full-time, 83 part-time. 2% Black or African American, non-Hispanic/Latino; 2% Hispanic/Latino; 80% American Indian or Alaska Native, non-Hispanic/Latino; 0.8% Two or more races, non-Hispanic/Latino; 2% Race/ethnicity unknown.
Freshmen *Admission:* 23 enrolled.
Faculty *Total:* 18, 39% full-time, 17% with terminal degrees. *Student/faculty ratio:* 7:1.
Majors American Indian/Native American studies; business/commerce; liberal arts and sciences/liberal studies.

Academics *Calendar:* semesters. *Degree:* associate. *Special study options:* part-time degree program.
Student Life *Housing:* college housing not available.
Costs (2016–17) *Tuition:* $1560 full-time, $60 per contact hour part-time. Full-time tuition and fees vary according to class time, course level, course load, degree level, location, program, and student level. Part-time tuition and fees vary according to class time, course level, course load, degree level, location, program, and student level. *Required fees:* $650 full-time, $25 per credit hour part-time. *Payment plans:* installment, deferred payment.
Applying *Required:* high school transcript.
Freshman Application Contact Ms. Amanda Flaugher, Admissions Officer/Registrar/Financial Aid, Saginaw Chippewa Tribal College, 2274 Enterprise Drive, Mount Pleasant, MI 48858. *Phone:* 989-775-4123. *Fax:* 989-775-4528. *E-mail:* flaugher.amanda@sagchip.org.
Website: http://www.sagchip.edu/.

St. Clair County Community College
Port Huron, Michigan

- **State and locally supported** 2-year, founded 1923, part of Michigan Department of Education
- **Small-town** 25-acre campus with easy access to Detroit
- **Coed,** 3,730 undergraduate students, 38% full-time, 60% women, 40% men

Undergraduates 1,399 full-time, 2,331 part-time. 3% Black or African American, non-Hispanic/Latino; 3% Hispanic/Latino; 0.4% Asian, non-Hispanic/Latino; 0.9% American Indian or Alaska Native, non-Hispanic/Latino; 2% Two or more races, non-Hispanic/Latino; 4% Race/ethnicity unknown; 0.1% international. *Retention:* 59% of full-time freshmen returned.
Freshmen *Admission:* 579 enrolled.
Faculty *Total:* 254, 29% full-time. *Student/faculty ratio:* 19:1.
Majors Accounting technology and bookkeeping; automation engineer technology; business/commerce; child-care and support services management; commercial and advertising art; computer programming; computer systems networking and telecommunications; corrections; criminal justice/law enforcement administration; data processing and data processing technology; drafting and design technology; electrical, electronic and communications engineering technology; emergency medical technology (EMT paramedic); energy management and systems technology; engineering; executive assistant/executive secretary; fire science/firefighting; health information/medical records technology; liberal arts and sciences/liberal studies; manufacturing engineering technology; marketing/marketing management; massage therapy; medical radiologic technology; office management; registered nursing/registered nurse; web/multimedia management and webmaster; welding engineering technology.
Academics *Calendar:* semesters. *Degree:* certificates and associate. *Special study options:* academic remediation for entering students, adult/continuing education programs, advanced placement credit, cooperative education, distance learning, honors programs, independent study, part-time degree program, services for LD students, summer session for credit.
Library Main Library plus 1 other.
Student Life *Housing:* college housing not available. *Activities and Organizations:* drama/theater group, student-run newspaper, radio station, Phi Theta Kappa, Marketing and Management Club, Gay-Straight Alliance, Criminal Justice Club. *Campus security:* 24-hour emergency response devices, late-night transport/escort service, patrols by security until 10 p.m.. *Student services:* personal/psychological counseling.
Athletics Member NJCAA. *Intercollegiate sports:* baseball M(s), basketball M(s)/W(s), golf M, softball W(s), volleyball W(s).
Costs (2016–17) *Tuition:* area resident $3689 full-time, $105 per contact hour part-time; state resident $6758 full-time, $204 per contact hour part-time; nonresident $9672 full-time, $298 per contact hour part-time. Full-time tuition and fees vary according to course load and location. Part-time tuition and fees vary according to course load and location. *Required fees:* $154 full-time, $14 per contact hour part-time. *Payment plan:* deferred payment. *Waivers:* senior citizens and employees or children of employees.
Applying *Options:* electronic application, early admission. *Required:* high school transcript. *Application deadlines:* rolling (freshmen), rolling (transfers).
Freshman Application Contact St. Clair County Community College, 323 Erie Street, PO Box 5015, Port Huron, MI 48061-5015. *Phone:* 810-989-5501. *Toll-free phone:* 800-553-2427.
Website: http://www.sc4.edu/.

Schoolcraft College
Livonia, Michigan

- **District-supported** primarily 2-year, founded 1961, part of Michigan Department of Education
- **Suburban** campus with easy access to Detroit
- **Coed,** 11,687 undergraduate students, 27% full-time, 54% women, 46% men

Undergraduates 3,148 full-time, 8,539 part-time. 14% Black or African American, non-Hispanic/Latino; 4% Hispanic/Latino; 4% Asian, non-Hispanic/Latino; 0.1% Native Hawaiian or other Pacific Islander, non-Hispanic/Latino; 0.7% American Indian or Alaska Native, non-Hispanic/Latino; 3% Two or more races, non-Hispanic/Latino; 7% Race/ethnicity unknown; 1% international; 25% transferred in. *Retention:* 64% of full-time freshmen returned.

Freshmen *Admission:* 2,174 enrolled.

Faculty *Total:* 538, 18% full-time. *Student/faculty ratio:* 25:1.

Majors Accounting technology and bookkeeping; biomedical technology; business administration and management; business automation/technology/data entry; business/commerce; child development; computer graphics; computer programming; computer programming (specific applications); criminal justice/police science; culinary arts; drafting and design technology; education; electrical, electronic and communications engineering technology; emergency medical technology (EMT paramedic); engineering; environmental engineering technology; executive assistant/executive secretary; fine arts related; fire science/firefighting; foods and nutrition related; general studies; health information/medical records technology; health services/allied health/health sciences; homeland security, law enforcement, firefighting and protective services related; manufacturing engineering technology; marketing/marketing management; massage therapy; metallurgical technology; pre-pharmacy studies; radio and television broadcasting technology; recording arts technology; registered nursing/registered nurse; salon/beauty salon management; small business administration; web page, digital/multimedia and information resources design; welding technology.

Academics *Calendar:* semesters. *Degrees:* certificates, associate, and bachelor's. *Special study options:* academic remediation for entering students, accelerated degree program, adult/continuing education programs, advanced placement credit, distance learning, English as a second language, honors programs, independent study, internships, part-time degree program, services for LD students, study abroad, summer session for credit.

Library Bradner Library. Students can reserve study rooms.

Student Life *Housing:* college housing not available. *Activities and Organizations:* drama/theater group, student-run newspaper, choral group, Phi Theta Kappa, The Schoolcraft Connection Newspaper, Student Activities Board, Project Playhem Gaming Club, Otaku Anime Japanese Animation Club. *Campus security:* 24-hour emergency response devices and patrols, late-night transport/escort service. *Student services:* personal/psychological counseling, women's center.

Athletics Member NJCAA. *Intercollegiate sports:* baseball M, basketball M(s)/W(s), bowling M/W, cross-country running M/W, golf M, soccer M(s)/W(s), softball W, volleyball W(s).

Costs (2015–16) *Tuition:* area resident $2880 full-time, $96 per semester hour part-time; state resident $4170 full-time, $139 per semester hour part-time; nonresident $6150 full-time, $205 per semester hour part-time. *Required fees:* $684 full-time, $20 per credit hour part-time, $42 per term part-time. *Payment plans:* installment, deferred payment. *Waivers:* senior citizens and employees or children of employees.

Financial Aid Of all full-time matriculated undergraduates who enrolled in 2014, 42 Federal Work-Study jobs (averaging $1722).

Applying *Options:* electronic application, early admission, deferred entrance. *Required for some:* high school transcript. *Recommended:* high school transcript. *Application deadlines:* rolling (freshmen), rolling (transfers).

Freshman Application Contact Ms. Nicole Wilson-Fennell, Registrar, Schoolcraft College, 18600 Haggerty Road, Livonia, MI 48152-2696. *Phone:* 734-462-4683. *Fax:* 734-462-4553. *E-mail:* gotoSC@schoolcraft.edu. *Website:* http://www.schoolcraft.edu/.

Southwestern Michigan College
Dowagiac, Michigan

- **State and locally supported** 2-year, founded 1964
- **Rural** 240-acre campus
- **Coed,** 2,348 undergraduate students, 48% full-time, 58% women, 42% men

Undergraduates 1,122 full-time, 1,226 part-time. Students come from 11 states and territories; 2 other countries; 15% are from out of state; 12% Black or African American, non-Hispanic/Latino; 6% Hispanic/Latino; 1% Asian, non-Hispanic/Latino; 0.1% Native Hawaiian or other Pacific Islander, non-Hispanic/Latino; 1% American Indian or Alaska Native, non-Hispanic/Latino; 5% Two or more races, non-Hispanic/Latino; 3% Race/ethnicity unknown; 0.2% international; 32% transferred in; 20% live on campus. *Retention:* 56% of full-time freshmen returned.

Freshmen *Admission:* 2,352 applied, 2,333 admitted, 638 enrolled.

Faculty *Total:* 149, 34% full-time, 21% with terminal degrees. *Student/faculty ratio:* 18:1.

Majors Accounting technology and bookkeeping; agricultural production; automation engineer technology; automobile/automotive mechanics technology; business administration and management; carpentry; computer programming; computer systems networking and telecommunications; criminal justice/safety; early childhood education; engineering technology; fire science/firefighting; general studies; graphic design; health information/medical records technology; industrial mechanics and maintenance technology; industrial production technologies related; liberal arts and sciences/liberal studies; machine tool technology; medical/clinical assistant; prenursing studies; professional, technical, business, and scientific writing; registered nursing/registered nurse; social work; sport and fitness administration/management.

Academics *Calendar:* semesters. *Degree:* certificates and associate. *Special study options:* academic remediation for entering students, accelerated degree program, adult/continuing education programs, advanced placement credit, cooperative education, English as a second language, independent study, internships, part-time degree program, services for LD students, summer session for credit.

Library Fred L. Mathews Library. *Books:* 22,905 (physical), 365 (digital/electronic); *Serial titles:* 12 (physical); *Databases:* 17. Weekly public service hours: 61; students can reserve study rooms.

Student Life *Housing Options:* coed. Campus housing is university owned. *Activities and Organizations:* drama/theater group, choral group, Advocates for All, Business Club, Criminal Justice Club, Rock Climbing Club, STEM Club. *Campus security:* 24-hour emergency response devices and patrols, controlled dormitory access, day and evening police patrols.

Athletics *Intramural sports:* basketball M/W, football M/W, rock climbing M/W, soccer M/W, softball M/W, tennis M/W, volleyball M/W.

Costs (2015–16) *Tuition:* area resident $2938 full-time, $113 per contact hour part-time; state resident $3816 full-time, $147 per contact hour part-time; nonresident $4154 full-time, $160 per contact hour part-time. *Required fees:* $1190 full-time, $46 per contact hour part-time. *Room and board:* $8700; room only: $5980. *Payment plan:* installment. *Waivers:* employees or children of employees.

Financial Aid Of all full-time matriculated undergraduates who enrolled in 2014, 125 Federal Work-Study jobs (averaging $1000). 75 state and other part-time jobs (averaging $1000).

Applying *Options:* electronic application, deferred entrance. *Required:* high school transcript. *Required for some:* interview. *Application deadlines:* rolling (freshmen), rolling (transfers). *Notification:* continuous (freshmen), continuous (transfers).

Freshman Application Contact Ms. Angela Palsak, Executive Director of Student Services, Southwestern Michigan College, Dowagiac, MI 49047. *Phone:* 269-782-1000 Ext. 1310. *Toll-free phone:* 800-456-8675. *Fax:* 269-782-1331. *E-mail:* apalsak@swmich.edu. *Website:* http://www.swmich.edu/.

Washtenaw Community College
Ann Arbor, Michigan

Freshman Application Contact Washtenaw Community College, 4800 East Huron River Drive, PO Box D-1, Ann Arbor, MI 48106. *Phone:* 734-973-3315. *Website:* http://www.wccnet.edu/.

Wayne County Community College District
Detroit, Michigan

- **State and locally supported** 2-year, founded 1967
- **Urban** campus
- **Coed,** 16,654 undergraduate students, 19% full-time, 65% women, 35% men

Undergraduates 3,137 full-time, 13,517 part-time. 58% Black or African American, non-Hispanic/Latino; 2% Hispanic/Latino; 0.7% Asian, non-Hispanic/Latino; 0.1% Native Hawaiian or other Pacific Islander, non-Hispanic/Latino; 0.3% American Indian or Alaska Native, non-Hispanic/Latino; 10% Two or more races, non-Hispanic/Latino; 7% Race/ethnicity unknown; 0.4% international; 15% transferred in.

Freshmen *Admission:* 2,992 enrolled.

Faculty *Student/faculty ratio:* 24:1.

Majors Accounting technology and bookkeeping; aircraft powerplant technology; airframe mechanics and aircraft maintenance technology; autobody/collision and repair technology; automobile/automotive mechanics technology; biomedical technology; building/property maintenance; business administration and management; CAD/CADD drafting/design technology; child-care and support services management; computer and information sciences and support services related; computer numerically controlled (CNC) machinist technology; computer programming; corrections; criminal justice/police science; data modeling/warehousing and database administration; dental hygiene; digital communication and media/multimedia; e-commerce; electrical and electronic engineering technologies related; electrical, electronic and communications engineering technology; electromechanical technology; elementary education; emergency medical technology (EMT paramedic); fire prevention and safety technology; food service systems administration; game and interactive media design; heating, air conditioning, ventilation and refrigeration maintenance technology; heavy/industrial equipment maintenance technologies related; legal assistant/paralegal; liberal arts and sciences/liberal studies; machine tool technology; manufacturing engineering technology; mortuary science and embalming; network and system administration; office management; pharmacy technician; physician assistant; pre-engineering; psychiatric/mental health services technology; registered nursing/registered nurse; social work; surgical technology; system, networking, and LAN/WAN management; veterinary/animal health technology; web/multimedia management and webmaster; welding technology.

Academics *Calendar:* semesters. *Degree:* certificates and associate. *Special study options:* academic remediation for entering students, adult/continuing education programs, advanced placement credit, cooperative education, distance learning, English as a second language, honors programs, internships, part-time degree program, services for LD students, study abroad, summer session for credit.

Library Learning Resource Center plus 5 others.

Student Life *Housing:* college housing not available. *Campus security:* 24-hour emergency response devices.

Athletics Member NJCAA. *Intercollegiate sports:* basketball M/W, bowling M/W, cross-country running M/W, golf M, volleyball W.

Costs (2015–16) *Tuition:* area resident $2545 full-time; state resident $2812 full-time; nonresident $3539 full-time. *Required fees:* $268 full-time. *Waivers:* senior citizens and employees or children of employees.

Financial Aid Of all full-time matriculated undergraduates who enrolled in 2014, 239 Federal Work-Study jobs (averaging $2360). 147 state and other part-time jobs (averaging $1200).

Applying *Options:* electronic application, early admission, deferred entrance. *Required:* high school transcript. *Application deadlines:* rolling (freshmen), rolling (transfers).

Freshman Application Contact Mr. Adrian Phillips, District Associate Vice Chancellor of Student Services, Wayne County Community College District, 801 West Fort Street, Detroit, MI 48226-9975. *Phone:* 313-496-2820. *Fax:* 313-962-1643. *E-mail:* aphilli1@wcccd.edu. *Website:* http://www.wcccd.edu/.

West Shore Community College
Scottville, Michigan

Freshman Application Contact Wendy Fought, Director of Admissions, West Shore Community College, PO Box 277, 3000 North Stiles Road, Scottville, MI 49454-0277. *Phone:* 231-843-5503. *Fax:* 231-845-3944. *E-mail:* admissions@westshore.edu. *Website:* http://www.westshore.edu/.

MICRONESIA

College of Micronesia–FSM
Kolonia Pohnpei, Federated States of Micronesia, Micronesia

Freshman Application Contact Rita Hinga, Student Services Specialist, College of Micronesia–FSM, PO Box 159, Kolonia Pohnpei, FM 96941-0159, Micronesia. *Phone:* 691-320-3795 Ext. 15. *E-mail:* rhinga@comfsm.fm. *Website:* http://www.comfsm.fm/.

MINNESOTA

Alexandria Technical and Community College
Alexandria, Minnesota

- **State-supported** 2-year, founded 1961, part of Minnesota State Colleges and Universities System
- **Small-town** 98-acre campus
- **Coed,** 2,702 undergraduate students, 50% full-time, 49% women, 51% men

Undergraduates 1,355 full-time, 1,347 part-time. Students come from 21 states and territories; 1 other country; 4% are from out of state; 0.5% Black or African American, non-Hispanic/Latino; 4% Hispanic/Latino; 0.4% Asian, non-Hispanic/Latino; 0.2% Native Hawaiian or other Pacific Islander, non-Hispanic/Latino; 0.2% American Indian or Alaska Native, non-Hispanic/Latino; 2% Two or more races, non-Hispanic/Latino; 1% Race/ethnicity unknown; 0.1% international; 20% transferred in.

Freshmen *Admission:* 512 enrolled.

Faculty *Total:* 95, 72% full-time, 3% with terminal degrees. *Student/faculty ratio:* 21:1.

Majors Accounting; automation engineer technology; business administration and management; clinical/medical laboratory technology; commercial and advertising art; computer systems networking and telecommunications; criminal justice/police science; diesel mechanics technology; early childhood education; fashion merchandising; human services; information science/studies; interior design; legal administrative assistant/secretary; legal assistant/paralegal; liberal arts and sciences/liberal studies; mechanical drafting and CAD/CADD; medical administrative assistant and medical secretary; multi/interdisciplinary studies related; office management; physical fitness technician; pre-engineering; registered nursing/registered nurse; sales, distribution, and marketing operations; speech-language pathology assistant.

Academics *Calendar:* semesters. *Degree:* certificates, diplomas, and associate. *Special study options:* academic remediation for entering students, advanced placement credit, distance learning, double majors, independent study, internships, part-time degree program, services for LD students, student-designed majors, summer session for credit.

Library Learning Resource Center. *Books:* 7,582 (physical), 13,367 (digital/electronic); *Serial titles:* 24 (physical); *Databases:* 14. Weekly public service hours: 51; students can reserve study rooms.

Student Life *Housing Options:* Campus housing is provided by a third party. *Activities and Organizations:* Student Senate, Intercultural Club, Trapshooting League, GAT (Gamers of Alex Tech), Book Club. *Campus security:* student patrols, late-night transport/escort service, security cameras inside and outside. *Student services:* personal/psychological counseling.

Athletics *Intramural sports:* basketball M/W, football M/W, softball M/W, volleyball M/W.

Costs (2016–17) *Tuition:* state resident $4817 full-time; nonresident $4817 full-time. *Required fees:* $585 full-time. *Payment plan:* deferred payment. *Waivers:* senior citizens and employees or children of employees.

Financial Aid Of all full-time matriculated undergraduates who enrolled in 2014, 94 Federal Work-Study jobs (averaging $1871).

Applying *Options:* electronic application, early admission, deferred entrance. *Application fee:* $20. *Required:* high school transcript. *Required for some:* interview. *Recommended:* interview. *Application deadlines:* rolling (freshmen), rolling (out-of-state freshmen), rolling (transfers). *Notification:* continuous (freshmen), continuous (out-of-state freshmen), continuous (transfers).

Freshman Application Contact Danielle Meinert, Information Center Manager, Alexandria Technical and Community College, 1601 Jefferson Street, Alexandria, MN 56308. *Phone:* 320-762-4600. *Toll-free phone:* 888-234-1222. *Fax:* 320-762-4501. *E-mail:* info@alextech.edu. *Website:* http://www.alextech.edu/.

Anoka-Ramsey Community College
Coon Rapids, Minnesota

- **State-supported** 2-year, founded 1965, part of Minnesota State Colleges and Universities System
- **Suburban** 103-acre campus with easy access to Minneapolis-St. Paul
- **Coed,** 9,294 undergraduate students, 38% full-time, 60% women, 40% men

Undergraduates 3,577 full-time, 5,717 part-time. 8% transferred in. *Retention:* 57% of full-time freshmen returned.

Freshmen *Admission:* 1,226 enrolled.

Faculty *Total:* 261, 47% full-time. *Student/faculty ratio:* 33:1.

Majors Accounting; accounting technology and bookkeeping; biology/biological sciences; biomedical technology; business administration and management; business/commerce; community health and preventive medicine; computer science; computer systems networking and telecommunications; creative writing; dramatic/theater arts; environmental science; fine/studio arts; health services/allied health/health sciences; holistic health; human resources management; interdisciplinary studies; liberal arts and sciences/liberal studies; music; pharmacy technician; physical fitness technician; physical therapy technology; pre-engineering; registered nursing/registered nurse; sales, distribution, and marketing operations.

Academics *Calendar:* semesters. *Degree:* certificates and associate. *Special study options:* academic remediation for entering students, accelerated degree program, advanced placement credit, cooperative education, distance learning, double majors, English as a second language, honors programs, independent study, internships, off-campus study, part-time degree program, services for LD students, study abroad, summer session for credit. *ROTC:* Air Force (c).

Library Coon Rapids Campus Library plus 1 other. *Books:* 39,271 (physical), 14,795 (digital/electronic); *Serial titles:* 94 (physical), 44 (digital/electronic); *Databases:* 30. Weekly public service hours: 63.

Student Life *Housing:* college housing not available. *Activities and Organizations:* drama/theater group, student-run newspaper, choral group, Student Senate, Swing Dance Club, Concert Choir, Anime Association, Concert Band. *Campus security:* 24-hour emergency response devices, late-night transport/escort service. *Student services:* personal/psychological counseling.

Athletics Member NJCAA. *Intercollegiate sports:* baseball M, basketball M/W, soccer M/W, softball W, volleyball W. *Intramural sports:* badminton M/W, baseball M/W, basketball M/W, bowling M/W, football M/W, golf M/W, ice hockey M/W, soccer M/W, softball M/W, tennis M/W, volleyball M/W.

Costs (2016–17) *Tuition:* state resident $4349 full-time, $145 per credit part-time; nonresident $4349 full-time, $145 per credit part-time. Full-time tuition and fees vary according to course load and program. Part-time tuition and fees vary according to course load and program. *Required fees:* $674 full-time, $22 per credit part-time. *Payment plans:* installment, deferred payment. *Waivers:* senior citizens and employees or children of employees.

Applying *Options:* electronic application, early admission, deferred entrance. *Required for some:* high school transcript. *Application deadlines:* rolling (freshmen), rolling (out-of-state freshmen), rolling (transfers). *Notification:* continuous (freshmen), continuous (out-of-state freshmen), continuous (transfers).

Freshman Application Contact Admissions Department, Anoka-Ramsey Community College, 11200 Mississippi Boulevard NW, Coon Rapids, MN 55433-3470. *Phone:* 763-433-1300. *Fax:* 763-433-1521.
E-mail: admissions@anokaramsey.edu.
Website: http://www.anokaramsey.edu/.

Anoka Technical College
Anoka, Minnesota

- **State-supported** 2-year, founded 1967, part of Minnesota State Colleges and Universities System
- **Small-town** 25-acre campus with easy access to Minneapolis-St. Paul
- **Coed,** 2,027 undergraduate students, 44% full-time, 59% women, 41% men

Undergraduates 885 full-time, 1,142 part-time. 9% Black or African American, non-Hispanic/Latino; 4% Hispanic/Latino; 4% Asian, non-Hispanic/Latino; 0.1% Native Hawaiian or other Pacific Islander, non-Hispanic/Latino; 0.5% American Indian or Alaska Native, non-Hispanic/Latino; 3% Two or more races, non-Hispanic/Latino; 1% Race/ethnicity unknown; 0.1% international; 19% transferred in. *Retention:* 55% of full-time freshmen returned.

Freshmen *Admission:* 265 enrolled.

Faculty *Total:* 97, 54% full-time. *Student/faculty ratio:* 19:1.

Majors Accounting; administrative assistant and secretarial science; architectural drafting and CAD/CADD; automobile/automotive mechanics technology; biomedical technology; computer numerically controlled (CNC) machinist technology; computer technology/computer systems technology; court reporting; developmental services worker; electrical, electronic and communications engineering technology; golf course operation and grounds management; health information/medical records technology; landscaping and groundskeeping; legal administrative assistant/secretary; mechanical drafting and CAD/CADD; medical administrative assistant and medical secretary; medical/clinical assistant; occupational therapist assistant; office management; surgical technology; welding technology.

Academics *Calendar:* semesters. *Degree:* certificates, diplomas, and associate. *Special study options:* academic remediation for entering students, advanced placement credit, cooperative education, distance learning, double majors, English as a second language, internships, part-time degree program, services for LD students.

Library Anoka Technical College Library. Weekly public service hours: 59.

Student Life *Housing:* college housing not available. *Campus security:* 24-hour emergency response devices, late-night transport/escort service. *Student services:* personal/psychological counseling.

Costs (2016–17) *Tuition:* state resident $5010 full-time, $167 per credit part-time; nonresident $5010 full-time, $167 per credit part-time. Full-time tuition and fees vary according to course load, program, and reciprocity agreements. Part-time tuition and fees vary according to course load, program, and reciprocity agreements. *Required fees:* $575 full-time, $19 per credit part-time. *Payment plan:* installment. *Waivers:* senior citizens and employees or children of employees.

Applying *Options:* electronic application, deferred entrance. *Required:* high school transcript. *Required for some:* interview.

Freshman Application Contact Enrollment Services, Anoka Technical College, 1355 West Highway 10, Anoka, MN 55303. *Phone:* 763-576-7710. *E-mail:* enrollmentservices@anokatech.edu.
Website: http://www.anokatech.edu/.

Central Lakes College
Brainerd, Minnesota

- **State-supported** 2-year, founded 1938, part of Minnesota State Colleges and Universities System
- **Small-town** campus
- **Endowment** $7.3 million
- **Coed,** 4,274 undergraduate students, 39% full-time, 55% women, 45% men

Undergraduates 1,680 full-time, 2,594 part-time. Students come from 32 states and territories; 0.3% are from out of state; 3% Black or African American, non-Hispanic/Latino; 2% Hispanic/Latino; 0.7% Asian, non-Hispanic/Latino; 0.1% Native Hawaiian or other Pacific Islander, non-Hispanic/Latino; 1% American Indian or Alaska Native, non-Hispanic/Latino; 3% Two or more races, non-Hispanic/Latino; 4% Race/ethnicity unknown; 0.1% international. *Retention:* 58% of full-time freshmen returned.

Faculty *Total:* 155, 58% full-time. *Student/faculty ratio:* 20:1.

Majors Accounting; administrative assistant and secretarial science; applied horticulture/horticulture operations; business administration and management; child-care and support services management; commercial and advertising art; computer systems networking and telecommunications; computer technology/computer systems technology; conservation biology; criminalistics and criminal science; criminal justice/police science; criminal justice/safety; developmental and child psychology; diesel mechanics technology; engineering; horticultural science; industrial electronics technology; industrial engineering; kindergarten/preschool education; legal administrative assistant/secretary; liberal arts and sciences/liberal studies; machine tool technology; marketing/marketing management; mechanical drafting and CAD/CADD; medical administrative assistant and medical secretary; natural resources/conservation; photographic and film/video technology; registered nursing/registered nurse; robotics technology; welding technology.

Academics *Calendar:* semesters. *Degree:* certificates, diplomas, and associate. *Special study options:* academic remediation for entering students, advanced placement credit, distance learning, English as a second language, external degree program, independent study, internships, off-campus study, part-time degree program, services for LD students, summer session for credit.

Library Learning Resource Center.

Student Life *Housing:* college housing not available. *Activities and Organizations:* drama/theater group, student-run newspaper, choral group. *Campus security:* 24-hour emergency response devices and patrols, student patrols, late-night transport/escort service. *Student services:* personal/psychological counseling.

Athletics Member NJCAA. *Intercollegiate sports:* baseball M, basketball M/W, football M, golf M/W, softball W, volleyball W. *Intramural sports:* basketball M/W, bowling M/W, football M, golf M/W, softball M/W, tennis M/W, volleyball M/W.

Costs (2015–16) *Tuition:* state resident $4773 full-time, $159 per credit part-time; nonresident $4773 full-time, $159 per credit part-time. Full-time tuition and fees vary according to course load and program. Part-time tuition and fees vary according to course load and program. *Required fees:* $611 full-time, $21 per credit part-time. *Payment plan:* installment. *Waivers:* senior citizens and employees or children of employees.

Applying *Options:* electronic application, deferred entrance. *Application fee:* $20. *Required:* high school transcript. *Application deadlines:* rolling (freshmen), rolling (out-of-state freshmen), rolling (transfers).

Freshman Application Contact Ms. Rose Tretter, Central Lakes College, 501 West College Drive, Brainerd, MN 56401-3904. *Phone:* 218-855-8036. *Toll-free phone:* 800-933-0346. *Fax:* 218-855-8220. *E-mail:* cdaniels@clcmn.edu. *Website:* http://www.clcmn.edu/.

Century College
White Bear Lake, Minnesota

- **State-supported** 2-year, founded 1970, part of Minnesota State Colleges and Universities System
- **Suburban** 170-acre campus with easy access to Minneapolis-St. Paul
- **Coed,** 8,921 undergraduate students, 41% full-time, 55% women, 45% men

Undergraduates 3,696 full-time, 5,225 part-time. Students come from 38 states and territories; 49 other countries; 6% are from out of state; 11% Black or African American, non-Hispanic/Latino; 8% Hispanic/Latino; 18% Asian, non-Hispanic/Latino; 0.1% Native Hawaiian or other Pacific Islander, non-Hispanic/Latino; 0.5% American Indian or Alaska Native, non-Hispanic/Latino; 5% Two or more races, non-Hispanic/Latino; 0.7% Race/ethnicity unknown; 2% international; 43% transferred in.
Freshmen *Admission:* 2,913 applied, 2,913 admitted, 1,246 enrolled.
Faculty *Total:* 360, 49% full-time. *Student/faculty ratio:* 22:1.
Majors Accounting; administrative assistant and secretarial science; animation, interactive technology, video graphics and special effects; building/property maintenance; business administration and management; CAD/CADD drafting/design technology; cinematography and film/video production; commercial photography; computer and information systems security; computer science; computer systems networking and telecommunications; computer technology/computer systems technology; cosmetology; criminal justice/police science; criminal justice/safety; cyber/computer forensics and counterterrorism; dental assisting; dental hygiene; e-commerce; education; emergency medical technology (EMT paramedic); energy management and systems technology; fine/studio arts; graphic design; greenhouse management; health services/allied health/health sciences; heating, air conditioning, ventilation and refrigeration maintenance technology; homeland security, law enforcement, firefighting and protective services related; horticultural science; human services; information science/studies; interior design; landscaping and groundskeeping; language interpretation and translation; liberal arts and sciences/liberal studies; marketing/marketing management; medical administrative assistant and medical secretary; multi/interdisciplinary studies related; music; orthotics/prosthetics; pre-engineering; radiologic technology/science; registered nursing/registered nurse; substance abuse/addiction counseling; teacher assistant/aide; web page, digital/multimedia and information resources design.
Academics *Calendar:* semesters. *Degree:* certificates, diplomas, and associate. *Special study options:* academic remediation for entering students, advanced placement credit, distance learning, double majors, English as a second language, honors programs, independent study, internships, part-time degree program, services for LD students, student-designed majors, summer session for credit. *ROTC:* Air Force (c).
Library Century College Library. *Books:* 57,925 (physical), 168,505 (digital/electronic); *Serial titles:* 407 (physical), 50 (digital/electronic); *Databases:* 69. Weekly public service hours: 65; students can reserve study rooms.
Student Life *Housing:* college housing not available. *Activities and Organizations:* drama/theater group, student-run newspaper, choral group, Asian Student Association, Student Senate, Phi Theta Kappa, Planning Activities Committee, Anime Club. *Campus security:* late-night transport/escort service, day patrols. *Student services:* health clinic, personal/psychological counseling.
Athletics Member NJCAA. *Intercollegiate sports:* baseball M, soccer M/W, softball W. *Intramural sports:* archery M/W, badminton M/W, basketball M/W, bowling M/W, football M/W, golf M/W, ice hockey M/W, skiing (downhill) M/W, soccer M/W, softball M/W, table tennis M/W, ultimate Frisbee M/W, volleyball M/W.
Costs (2015–16) *Tuition:* state resident $4818 full-time, $161 per semester hour part-time; nonresident $4818 full-time, $161 per semester hour part-time. Full-time tuition and fees vary according to class time, program, and reciprocity agreements. Part-time tuition and fees vary according to class time, program, and reciprocity agreements. *Required fees:* $573 full-time, $19 per semester hour part-time. *Payment plan:* installment. *Waivers:* senior citizens and employees or children of employees.
Financial Aid Of all full-time matriculated undergraduates who enrolled in 2014, 81 Federal Work-Study jobs (averaging $2763). 85 state and other part-time jobs (averaging $2646).
Applying *Options:* electronic application, deferred entrance. *Application fee:* $20. *Required:* high school transcript. *Application deadlines:* rolling (freshmen), rolling (transfers).
Freshman Application Contact Katy Melek, Interim Assistant Admissions Director, Century College, 3300 Century Avenue North, White Bear Lake, MN 55110. *Phone:* 651-779-5744. *Toll-free phone:* 800-228-1978. *Fax:* 651-773-1796. *E-mail:* admissions@century.edu.
Website: http://www.century.edu/.

Dakota County Technical College
Rosemount, Minnesota

Freshman Application Contact Mr. Patrick Lair, Admissions Director, Dakota County Technical College, 1300 East 145th Street, Rosemount, MN 55068. *Phone:* 651-423-8399. *Toll-free phone:* 877-YES-DCTC. *Fax:* 651-423-8775. *E-mail:* admissions@dctc.mnscu.edu.
Website: http://www.dctc.edu/.

Duluth Business University
Duluth, Minnesota

- **Proprietary** primarily 2-year, founded 1891
- **Urban** 2-acre campus
- **Coed, primarily women**

Undergraduates 103 full-time, 79 part-time. Students come from 6 states and territories; 24% are from out of state; 2% Black or African American, non-Hispanic/Latino; 0.5% Asian, non-Hispanic/Latino; 0.5% Native Hawaiian or other Pacific Islander, non-Hispanic/Latino; 2% American Indian or Alaska Native, non-Hispanic/Latino.
Academics *Calendar:* quarters. *Degrees:* diplomas, associate, and bachelor's.
Applying *Application fee:* $35.
Freshman Application Contact Mr. Mark Traux, Director of Admissions, Duluth Business University, 4724 Mike Colalillo Drive, Duluth, MN 55807. *Phone:* 218-722-4000. *Toll-free phone:* 800-777-8406. *Fax:* 218-628-2127. *E-mail:* markt@dbumn.edu.
Website: http://www.dbumn.edu/.

Dunwoody College of Technology
Minneapolis, Minnesota

- **Independent** primarily 2-year, founded 1914
- **Urban** 12-acre campus with easy access to Minneapolis-St. Paul
- **Endowment** $23.8 million
- **Coed, primarily men,** 1,094 undergraduate students, 82% full-time, 14% women, 86% men

Undergraduates 898 full-time, 196 part-time. 2% are from out of state; 6% Black or African American, non-Hispanic/Latino; 2% Hispanic/Latino; 6% Asian, non-Hispanic/Latino; 0.8% American Indian or Alaska Native, non-Hispanic/Latino; 2% Two or more races, non-Hispanic/Latino; 5% Race/ethnicity unknown; 0.1% international. *Retention:* 100% of full-time freshmen returned.
Freshmen *Admission:* 741 applied, 501 admitted, 188 enrolled. *Average high school GPA:* 2.52.
Faculty *Total:* 128, 63% full-time, 13% with terminal degrees. *Student/faculty ratio:* 10:1.
Majors Architectural drafting and CAD/CADD; architectural technology; architecture; autobody/collision and repair technology; automobile/automotive mechanics technology; building/construction site management; business administration and management; CAD/CADD drafting/design technology; computer science; computer systems networking and telecommunications; construction management; desktop publishing and digital imaging design; electrical, electronic and communications engineering technology; electrical/electronics drafting and CAD/CADD; electrician; graphic design; heating, air conditioning, ventilation and refrigeration maintenance technology; heating, ventilation, air conditioning and refrigeration engineering technology; industrial technology; interior design; medical radiologic technology; printing press operation; robotics technology; tool and die technology; web page, digital/multimedia and information resources design; welding technology.
Academics *Calendar:* semesters. *Degrees:* certificates, associate, and bachelor's. *Special study options:* academic remediation for entering students, cooperative education, distance learning, independent study, internships, study abroad, summer session for credit.
Library Learning Resource Center and Design Library. *Books:* 1,313 (physical), 155,893 (digital/electronic); *Serial titles:* 131 (physical); *Databases:* 24. Students can reserve study rooms.
Student Life *Housing:* college housing not available. *Activities and Organizations:* Phi Theta Kappa, Historic Green, Dunwoody Motorsports Club, Architectural Institute of America Student Chapter, Professional Association for Design. *Campus security:* 24-hour emergency response devices, late-night transport/escort service. *Student services:* personal/psychological counseling, women's center.
Standardized Tests *Required for some:* SAT or ACT (for admission).
Costs (2016–17) *Tuition:* $17,400 full-time, $580 per credit part-time. Full-time tuition and fees vary according to course load, degree level, and program. Part-time tuition and fees vary according to course load, degree level, and program. *Required fees:* $1690 full-time, $1400 per term part-time. *Payment plan:* installment. *Waivers:* employees or children of employees.

Financial Aid Of all full-time matriculated undergraduates who enrolled in 2014, 799 applied for aid, 722 were judged to have need, 24 had their need fully met. 27 Federal Work-Study jobs (averaging $3266). 24 state and other part-time jobs (averaging $4477). In 2014, 20 non-need-based awards were made. *Average percent of need met:* 30%. *Average financial aid package:* $7627. *Average need-based loan:* $3714. *Average need-based gift aid:* $5210. *Average non-need-based aid:* $2248. *Average indebtedness upon graduation:* $9798.

Applying *Options:* electronic application. *Application fee:* $50. *Required:* essay or personal statement, high school transcript. *Required for some:* minimum 3.0 GPA, resumé. *Recommended:* minimum 2.5 GPA, interview. *Application deadlines:* rolling (freshmen), rolling (out-of-state freshmen), rolling (transfers). *Notification:* continuous (freshmen), continuous (out-of-state freshmen), continuous (transfers).

Freshman Application Contact Cynthia Olson, Director of Admissions, Dunwoody College of Technology, 818 Dunwoody Boulevard, Minneapolis, MN 55403. *Phone:* 612-374-5800. *Toll-free phone:* 800-292-4625. *Website:* http://www.dunwoody.edu/.

Fond du Lac Tribal and Community College
Cloquet, Minnesota

Freshman Application Contact Kathie Jubie, Admissions Representative, Fond du Lac Tribal and Community College, 2101 14th Street, Cloquet, MN 55720. *Phone:* 218-879-0808. *Toll-free phone:* 800-657-3712. *E-mail:* admissions@fdltcc.edu. *Website:* http://www.fdltcc.edu/.

Hennepin Technical College
Brooklyn Park, Minnesota

- **State-supported** 2-year, founded 1972, part of Minnesota State Colleges and Universities System
- **Suburban** 100-acre campus with easy access to Minneapolis-St. Paul
- **Coed,** 5,676 undergraduate students, 35% full-time, 39% women, 61% men

Undergraduates 2,004 full-time, 3,672 part-time. 22% Black or African American, non-Hispanic/Latino; 7% Hispanic/Latino; 10% Asian, non-Hispanic/Latino; 0.2% Native Hawaiian or other Pacific Islander, non-Hispanic/Latino; 0.7% American Indian or Alaska Native, non-Hispanic/Latino; 3% Two or more races, non-Hispanic/Latino; 3% Race/ethnicity unknown; 0.3% international; 17% transferred in.

Freshmen *Admission:* 1,987 applied, 1,987 admitted, 612 enrolled.

Faculty *Total:* 235, 49% full-time. *Student/faculty ratio:* 21:1.

Majors Accounting; administrative assistant and secretarial science; architectural drafting and CAD/CADD; autobody/collision and repair technology; automation engineer technology; automobile/automotive mechanics technology; business administration and management; CAD/CADD drafting/design technology; carpentry; child development; computer numerically controlled (CNC) machinist technology; computer programming; computer systems networking and telecommunications; dental assisting; desktop publishing and digital imaging design; drafting/design engineering technologies related; electrical, electronic and communications engineering technology; fire science/firefighting; graphic design; greenhouse management; heating, air conditioning, ventilation and refrigeration maintenance technology; hydraulics and fluid power technology; landscaping and groundskeeping; licensed practical/vocational nurse training; machine tool technology; management information systems; manufacturing engineering technology; medical administrative assistant and medical secretary; medium/heavy vehicle and truck technology; photography; plastics and polymer engineering technology; recording arts technology; tool and die technology; urban forestry; web page, digital/multimedia and information resources design.

Academics *Calendar:* semesters. *Degree:* certificates, diplomas, and associate. *Special study options:* academic remediation for entering students, adult/continuing education programs, advanced placement credit, cooperative education, distance learning, double majors, English as a second language, independent study, internships, part-time degree program, services for LD students, student-designed majors, summer session for credit.

Library Hennepin Technical College Library plus 1 other. *Books:* 10,633 (physical), 204,824 (digital/electronic); *Databases:* 39. Weekly public service hours: 60.

Student Life *Housing:* college housing not available. *Activities and Organizations:* Student Senate, Pangea, Images, SkillsUSA. *Campus security:* late-night transport/escort service, security service. *Student services:* personal/psychological counseling.

Costs (2016–17) *Tuition:* state resident $5130 full-time, $155 per credit part-time; nonresident $5130 full-time, $155 per credit part-time. Full-time tuition and fees vary according to program. Part-time tuition and fees vary according to program. *Required fees:* $476 full-time, $16 per credit part-time. *Payment plan:* installment. *Waivers:* senior citizens and employees or children of employees.

Financial Aid Of all full-time matriculated undergraduates who enrolled in 2014, 72 Federal Work-Study jobs (averaging $3000).

Applying *Options:* electronic application. *Recommended:* high school transcript. *Application deadlines:* rolling (freshmen), rolling (transfers). *Notification:* continuous (freshmen), continuous (transfers).

Freshman Application Contact Admissions, Hennepin Technical College, 9000 Brooklyn Boulevard, Brooklyn Park, MN 55445. *Phone:* 763-488-2415. *Toll-free phone:* 800-345-4655 (in-state); 800-645-4655 (out-of-state). *Fax:* 763-550-2113. *E-mail:* info@hennepintech.edu. *Website:* http://www.hennepintech.edu/.

Herzing University
Minneapolis, Minnesota

Freshman Application Contact Ms. Shelly Larson, Director of Admissions, Herzing University, 5700 West Broadway, Minneapolis, MN 55428. *Phone:* 763-231-3155. *Toll-free phone:* 800-596-0724. *Fax:* 763-535-9205. *E-mail:* info@mpls.herzing.edu. *Website:* http://www.herzing.edu/minneapolis.

Hibbing Community College
Hibbing, Minnesota

Freshman Application Contact Admissions, Hibbing Community College, 1515 East 25th Street, Hibbing, MN 55746. *Phone:* 218-262-7200. *Toll-free phone:* 800-224-4HCC. *Fax:* 218-262-6717. *E-mail:* admissions@hibbing.edu. *Website:* http://www.hcc.mnscu.edu/.

The Institute of Production and Recording
Minneapolis, Minnesota

Freshman Application Contact The Institute of Production and Recording, 300 North 1st Avenue, Suite 500, Minneapolis, MN 55401. *Website:* http://www.ipr.edu/.

Inver Hills Community College
Inver Grove Heights, Minnesota

Freshman Application Contact Mr. Casey Carmody, Admissions Representative, Inver Hills Community College, 2500 East 80th Street, Inver Grove Heights, MN 55076-3224. *Phone:* 651-450-3589. *Fax:* 651-450-3677. *E-mail:* admissions@inverhills.edu. *Website:* http://www.inverhills.edu/.

Itasca Community College
Grand Rapids, Minnesota

Freshman Application Contact Ms. Candace Perry, Director of Enrollment Services, Itasca Community College, Grand Rapids, MN 55744. *Phone:* 218-322-2340. *Toll-free phone:* 800-996-6422. *Fax:* 218-327-4350. *E-mail:* iccinfo@itascacc.edu. *Website:* http://www.itascacc.edu/.

ITT Technical Institute
Brooklyn Center, Minnesota

Freshman Application Contact Director of Recruitment, ITT Technical Institute, 6120 Earle Brown Drive, Suite 100, Brooklyn Center, MN 55430. *Phone:* 763-549-5900. *Toll-free phone:* 800-216-8883. *Website:* http://www.itt-tech.edu/.

Lake Superior College
Duluth, Minnesota

- **State-supported** 2-year, founded 1995, part of Minnesota State Colleges and Universities System
- **Urban** 105-acre campus
- **Coed,** 5,050 undergraduate students, 42% full-time, 58% women, 42% men

Undergraduates 2,108 full-time, 2,942 part-time. Students come from 28 states and territories; 6 other countries; 15% are from out of state; 4% Black or African American, non-Hispanic/Latino; 3% Hispanic/Latino; 1% Asian, non-Hispanic/Latino; 0.1% Native Hawaiian or other Pacific Islander, non-Hispanic/Latino; 2% American Indian or Alaska Native, non-Hispanic/Latino; 4% Two or more races, non-Hispanic/Latino; 1% Race/ethnicity unknown; 0.1% international; 39% transferred in.

Freshmen *Admission:* 1,062 applied, 1,062 admitted, 700 enrolled.

Faculty *Total:* 251, 39% full-time, 6% with terminal degrees. *Student/faculty ratio:* 21:1.

Majors Accounting; airline pilot and flight crew; architectural drafting and CAD/CADD; automobile/automotive mechanics technology; building construction technology; business administration and management; business automation/technology/data entry; CAD/CADD drafting/design technology; civil engineering technology; clinical/medical laboratory technology; computer numerically controlled (CNC) machinist technology; computer technology/computer systems technology; dental hygiene; electrical, electronic and communications engineering technology; electrician; fine/studio arts; fire prevention and safety technology; health services/allied health/health sciences; legal administrative assistant/secretary; legal assistant/paralegal; liberal arts and sciences/liberal studies; management information systems; mechanical drafting and CAD/CADD; medical administrative assistant and medical secretary; multi/interdisciplinary studies related; network and system administration; office management; physical therapy technology; radiologic technology/science; registered nursing/registered nurse; respiratory care therapy; sheet metal technology; surgical technology; web page, digital/multimedia and information resources design.

Academics *Calendar:* semesters. *Degree:* certificates, diplomas, and associate. *Special study options:* academic remediation for entering students, advanced placement credit, distance learning, double majors, independent study, internships, part-time degree program, services for LD students, study abroad, summer session for credit.

Library Harold P. Erickson Library. Students can reserve study rooms.

Student Life *Housing:* college housing not available. *Activities and Organizations:* choral group. *Campus security:* 24-hour emergency response devices, late-night transport/escort service. *Student services:* personal/psychological counseling.

Athletics Member NJCAA. *Intercollegiate sports:* soccer M/W.

Costs (2015–16) *Tuition:* state resident $4418 full-time; nonresident $8835 full-time. Full-time tuition and fees vary according to course load, program, and reciprocity agreements. Part-time tuition and fees vary according to course load, program, and reciprocity agreements. *Required fees:* $721 full-time. *Payment plans:* installment, deferred payment. *Waivers:* senior citizens and employees or children of employees.

Financial Aid Of all full-time matriculated undergraduates who enrolled in 2014, 53 Federal Work-Study jobs (averaging $2720). 145 state and other part-time jobs (averaging $2720).

Applying *Options:* electronic application. *Application fee:* $20. *Required:* high school transcript. *Application deadlines:* rolling (freshmen), rolling (transfers). *Notification:* continuous (freshmen), continuous (transfers).

Freshman Application Contact Ms. Melissa Leno, Director of Admissions, Lake Superior College, 2101 Trinity Road, Duluth, MN 55811. *Phone:* 218-733-5903. *Toll-free phone:* 800-432-2884. *E-mail:* enroll@lsc.edu. *Website:* http://www.lsc.edu/.

Leech Lake Tribal College
Cass Lake, Minnesota

Freshman Application Contact Ms. Shelly Braford, Recruiter, Leech Lake Tribal College, PO Box 180, 6945 Littlewolf Road NW, Cass Lake, MN 56633. *Phone:* 218-335-4200 Ext. 4270. *Fax:* 218-335-4217. *E-mail:* shelly.braford@lltc.edu. *Website:* http://www.lltc.edu/.

Mesabi Range College
Virginia, Minnesota

- **State-supported** 2-year, founded 1918, part of Minnesota State Colleges and Universities System
- **Small-town** 30-acre campus
- **Coed,** 1,373 undergraduate students

Undergraduates Students come from 6 states and territories; 2 other countries; 4% are from out of state; 6% Black or African American, non-Hispanic/Latino; 0.4% Hispanic/Latino; 0.7% Asian, non-Hispanic/Latino; 3% American Indian or Alaska Native, non-Hispanic/Latino; 8% Race/ethnicity unknown; 10% live on campus.

Faculty *Total:* 165. *Student/faculty ratio:* 24:1.

Majors Administrative assistant and secretarial science; business/commerce; computer graphics; computer/information technology services administration related; computer programming related; computer programming (specific applications); computer software and media applications related; computer systems networking and telecommunications; electrical/electronics equipment installation and repair; human services; information technology; instrumentation technology; liberal arts and sciences/liberal studies; pre-engineering; substance abuse/addiction counseling; web page, digital/multimedia and information resources design.

Academics *Calendar:* semesters. *Degree:* certificates, diplomas, and associate. *Special study options:* academic remediation for entering students, adult/continuing education programs, advanced placement credit, cooperative education, distance learning, independent study, internships, off-campus study, part-time degree program, services for LD students, student-designed majors, study abroad, summer session for credit.

Library Mesabi Library.

Student Life *Housing Options:* coed. Campus housing is provided by a third party. *Activities and Organizations:* drama/theater group, student-run newspaper, choral group, Student Senate, Human Services Club, Career Program Clubs, Student Life Club, Gaming Club. *Student services:* personal/psychological counseling.

Athletics Member NJCAA. *Intercollegiate sports:* baseball M, basketball M/W, football M, golf M/W, softball W, volleyball W. *Intramural sports:* basketball M/W, ice hockey M/W, volleyball M/W.

Costs (2015–16) *Tuition:* state resident $4740 full-time, $158 per credit part-time; nonresident $5910 full-time, $197 per credit part-time. Full-time tuition and fees vary according to reciprocity agreements. Part-time tuition and fees vary according to reciprocity agreements. *Required fees:* $582 full-time, $19 per hour part-time. *Room and board:* room only: $4036. *Payment plan:* installment. *Waivers:* senior citizens.

Financial Aid Of all full-time matriculated undergraduates who enrolled in 2011, 168 Federal Work-Study jobs (averaging $1227). 82 state and other part-time jobs (averaging $1380).

Applying *Options:* electronic application, early admission, deferred entrance. *Application fee:* $20. *Required:* high school transcript. *Application deadlines:* rolling (freshmen), rolling (transfers). *Notification:* continuous (freshmen), continuous (transfers).

Freshman Application Contact Ms. Brenda Kochevar, Enrollment Services Director, Mesabi Range College, Virginia, MN 55792. *Phone:* 218-749-0314. *Toll-free phone:* 800-657-3860. *Fax:* 218-749-0318. *E-mail:* b.kochevar@mesabirange.edu. *Website:* http://www.mesabirange.edu/.

Minneapolis Business College
Roseville, Minnesota

- **Proprietary** 2-year, founded 1874
- **Suburban** campus with easy access to Minneapolis-St. Paul
- **Coed,** 231 undergraduate students
- 87% of applicants were admitted

Freshmen *Admission:* 379 applied, 331 admitted.

Majors Accounting technology and bookkeeping; administrative assistant and secretarial science; computer programming; computer systems networking and telecommunications; graphic design; hotel/motel administration; legal administrative assistant/secretary; legal assistant/paralegal; medical/clinical assistant.

Academics *Calendar:* semesters. *Degree:* diplomas and associate. *Special study options:* accelerated degree program, internships.

Freshman Application Contact Admissions Office, Minneapolis Business College, 1711 West County Road B, Roseville, MN 55113. *Phone:* 651-636-7406. *Toll-free phone:* 800-279-5200. *Website:* http://www.minneapolisbusinesscollege.edu/.

Minneapolis Community and Technical College

Minneapolis, Minnesota

- **State-supported** 2-year, founded 1965, part of Minnesota State Colleges and Universities System
- **Urban** 22-acre campus
- **Coed**

Undergraduates 3,210 full-time, 6,255 part-time. 31% Black or African American, non-Hispanic/Latino; 10% Hispanic/Latino; 6% Asian, non-Hispanic/Latino; 0.1% Native Hawaiian or other Pacific Islander, non-Hispanic/Latino; 2% American Indian or Alaska Native, non-Hispanic/Latino; 8% Two or more races, non-Hispanic/Latino; 2% Race/ethnicity unknown; 1% international.

Academics *Calendar:* semesters. *Degree:* certificates, diplomas, and associate. *Special study options:* academic remediation for entering students, accelerated degree program, adult/continuing education programs, advanced placement credit, distance learning, English as a second language, honors programs, independent study, internships, off-campus study, part-time degree program, services for LD students, study abroad, summer session for credit.

Library Minneapolis Community and Technical College Library plus 1 other.

Student Life *Campus security:* 24-hour emergency response devices and patrols, late-night transport/escort service.

Costs (2015–16) *Tuition:* state resident $4658 full-time; nonresident $4658 full-time. Full-time tuition and fees vary according to course load and program. Part-time tuition and fees vary according to course load and program. *Required fees:* $692 full-time.

Applying *Options:* electronic application, early admission, deferred entrance. *Application fee:* $20. *Required:* high school transcript.

Freshman Application Contact Minneapolis Community and Technical College, 1501 Hennepin Avenue, Minneapolis, MN 55403. *Phone:* 612-659-6200. *Toll-free phone:* 800-247-0911.
E-mail: admissions.office@minneapolis.edu.
Website: http://www.minneapolis.edu/.

Minneapolis Media Institute

Edina, Minnesota

Admissions Office Contact Minneapolis Media Institute, 4100 West 76th Street, Edina, MN 55435. *Toll-free phone:* 800-236-4997.
Website: http://www.mediainstitute.edu/.

Minnesota School of Business–Brooklyn Center

Brooklyn Center, Minnesota

Freshman Application Contact Minnesota School of Business–Brooklyn Center, 5910 Shingle Creek Parkway, Brooklyn Center, MN 55430.
Website: http://www.msbcollege.edu/.

Minnesota School of Business–Plymouth

Plymouth, Minnesota

Freshman Application Contact Minnesota School of Business–Plymouth, 1455 Country Road 101 North, Plymouth, MN 55447.
Website: http://www.msbcollege.edu/.

Minnesota State College–Southeast Technical

Winona, Minnesota

- **State-supported** 2-year, founded 1992, part of Minnesota State Colleges and Universities System
- **Small-town** 132-acre campus with easy access to Minneapolis-St. Paul
- **Coed,** 2,003 undergraduate students, 44% full-time, 60% women, 40% men

Undergraduates 875 full-time, 1,128 part-time. 29% are from out of state; 6% Black or African American, non-Hispanic/Latino; 4% Hispanic/Latino; 2% Asian, non-Hispanic/Latino; 0.1% Native Hawaiian or other Pacific Islander, non-Hispanic/Latino; 0.7% American Indian or Alaska Native, non-Hispanic/Latino; 3% Two or more races, non-Hispanic/Latino; 0.4% Race/ethnicity unknown; 0.3% international; 13% transferred in. *Retention:* 32% of full-time freshmen returned.

Freshmen *Admission:* 633 admitted, 252 enrolled. *Average high school GPA:* 2.7.

Faculty *Total:* 106, 59% full-time, 4% with terminal degrees. *Student/faculty ratio:* 16:1.

Majors Accounting; accounting technology and bookkeeping; administrative assistant and secretarial science; autobody/collision and repair technology; biomedical technology; business administration and management; CAD/CADD drafting/design technology; carpentry; computer programming; computer systems networking and telecommunications; computer technology/computer systems technology; cosmetology; criminal justice/safety; early childhood education; electrical, electronic and communications engineering technology; heating, air conditioning, ventilation and refrigeration maintenance technology; industrial mechanics and maintenance technology; legal administrative assistant/secretary; massage therapy; medical administrative assistant and medical secretary; multi/interdisciplinary studies related; radiologic technology/science; registered nursing/registered nurse; retailing; sales, distribution, and marketing operations; selling skills and sales; web page, digital/multimedia and information resources design.

Academics *Calendar:* semesters. *Degree:* certificates, diplomas, and associate. *Special study options:* distance learning, double majors, internships.

Library Learning Resource Center.

Student Life *Housing:* college housing not available. *Activities and Organizations:* student-run newspaper. *Campus security:* 24-hour emergency response devices, late-night transport/escort service.

Costs (2016–17) *Tuition:* state resident $5019 full-time, $167 per credit part-time; nonresident $5019 full-time, $167 per credit part-time. Full-time tuition and fees vary according to program. Part-time tuition and fees vary according to program. *Required fees:* $598 full-time, $22 per credit part-time. *Payment plan:* installment. *Waivers:* senior citizens and employees or children of employees.

Financial Aid Of all full-time matriculated undergraduates who enrolled in 2014, 834 applied for aid, 752 were judged to have need, 14 had their need fully met. In 2014, 35 non-need-based awards were made. *Average percent of need met:* 39%. *Average financial aid package:* $7112. *Average need-based loan:* $3470. *Average need-based gift aid:* $4757. *Average non-need-based aid:* $1835.

Applying *Options:* electronic application. *Application fee:* $20. *Required:* high school transcript. *Recommended:* interview. *Application deadlines:* rolling (freshmen), rolling (out-of-state freshmen), rolling (transfers). *Notification:* continuous (freshmen), continuous (out-of-state freshmen), continuous (transfers).

Freshman Application Contact Admissions, SE Technical, Minnesota State College–Southeast Technical, 1250 Homer Road, PO Box 409, Winona, MN 55987. *Phone:* 877-853-8324. *Toll-free phone:* 800-372-8164. *Fax:* 507-453-2715. *E-mail:* enrollmentservices@southeastmn.edu.
Website: http://www.southeastmn.edu/.

Minnesota State Community and Technical College

Fergus Falls, Minnesota

Freshman Application Contact Ms. Carrie Brimhall, Dean of Enrollment Management, Minnesota State Community and Technical College, Fergus Falls, MN 56537-1009. *Phone:* 218-736-1528. *Toll-free phone:* 877-450-3322. *E-mail:* carrie.brimhall@minnesota.edu.
Website: http://www.minnesota.edu/.

Minnesota State Community and Technical College–Detroit Lakes

Detroit Lakes, Minnesota

- **State-supported** 2-year, founded 1966
- **Small-town** campus
- **Coed,** 6,391 undergraduate students, 42% full-time, 59% women, 41% men

Undergraduates 2,658 full-time, 3,733 part-time. 18% Black or African American, non-Hispanic/Latino; 7% Hispanic/Latino; 4% Asian, non-Hispanic/Latino; 0.2% Native Hawaiian or other Pacific Islander, non-Hispanic/Latino; 1% American Indian or Alaska Native, non-Hispanic/Latino; 2% Two or more races, non-Hispanic/Latino; 0.3% international.

Freshmen *Admission:* 1,071 enrolled.

Faculty *Total:* 276, 56% full-time.

Majors Accounting; administrative assistant and secretarial science; architectural technology; autobody/collision and repair technology; automotive engineering technology; computer and information systems security; dental assisting; early childhood education; engineering technology; entrepreneurship; information technology; legal assistant/paralegal; marine maintenance and ship repair technology; marketing/marketing management; nursing practice; radiologic technology/science; web page, digital/multimedia and information resources design.

Academics *Calendar:* semesters. *Degree:* certificates and associate.

Student Life *Housing:* college housing not available.

Athletics Member NJCAA.

Costs (2016–17) *Tuition:* state resident $4824 full-time, $161 per credit hour part-time; nonresident $4824 full-time, $161 per credit hour part-time. Full-time tuition and fees vary according to location and program. Part-time tuition and fees vary according to location and program. *Required fees:* $514 full-time. *Waivers:* senior citizens and employees or children of employees.

Applying *Application fee:* $20. *Required:* high school transcript, immunization record.

Freshman Application Contact Minnesota State Community and Technical College–Detroit Lakes, 900 Highway 34, E, Detroit Lakes, MN 56501. *Phone:* 218-846-3777. *Toll-free phone:* 800-492-4836.

Website: http://www.minnesota.edu/.

Minnesota State Community and Technical College–Moorhead

Moorhead, Minnesota

- **State-supported** 2-year
- **Small-town** campus
- **Coed,** 6,391 undergraduate students, 42% full-time, 59% women, 41% men

Undergraduates 2,658 full-time, 3,733 part-time. 18% Black or African American, non-Hispanic/Latino; 7% Hispanic/Latino; 4% Asian, non-Hispanic/Latino; 0.2% Native Hawaiian or other Pacific Islander, non-Hispanic/Latino; 1% American Indian or Alaska Native, non-Hispanic/Latino; 2% Two or more races, non-Hispanic/Latino; 0.3% international.

Freshmen *Admission:* 1,071 enrolled.

Faculty *Total:* 276, 56% full-time.

Majors Accounting; administrative assistant and secretarial science; automotive engineering technology; biology/biological sciences; business administration and management; carpentry; computer programming; construction management; criminal justice/law enforcement administration; dental assisting; dental hygiene; diesel mechanics technology; engineering; graphic design; human resources development; information technology; mechanical drafting and CAD/CADD; medical administrative assistant and medical secretary; nursing practice; plumbing technology; sign language interpretation and translation.

Academics *Calendar:* semesters. *Degree:* certificates and associate.

Student Life *Housing:* college housing not available.

Costs (2016–17) *Tuition:* state resident $4824 full-time, $161 per credit hour part-time; nonresident $4824 full-time, $161 per credit hour part-time. Full-time tuition and fees vary according to location and program. Part-time tuition and fees vary according to location and program. *Required fees:* $514 full-time. *Waivers:* senior citizens and employees or children of employees.

Applying *Application fee:* $20. *Required:* high school transcript, immunization record.

Freshman Application Contact Minnesota State Community and Technical College–Moorhead, 1900 28th Avenue, South, Moorhead, MN 56560. *Phone:* 218-846-3777. *Toll-free phone:* 800-426-5603.

Website: http://www.minnesota.edu/.

Minnesota State Community and Technical College–Wadena

Wadena, Minnesota

- **State-supported** 2-year
- **Small-town** campus
- **Coed,** 6,391 undergraduate students, 42% full-time, 59% women, 41% men

Undergraduates 2,658 full-time, 3,733 part-time. 18% Black or African American, non-Hispanic/Latino; 7% Hispanic/Latino; 4% Asian, non-Hispanic/Latino; 0.2% Native Hawaiian or other Pacific Islander, non-Hispanic/Latino; 1% American Indian or Alaska Native, non-Hispanic/Latino; 2% Two or more races, non-Hispanic/Latino; 0.3% international.

Freshmen *Admission:* 1,071 enrolled.

Faculty *Total:* 276, 56% full-time.

Majors Electrical and power transmission installation related; medical administrative assistant and medical secretary; network and system administration; nursing practice.

Academics *Calendar:* semesters. *Degree:* certificates and associate.

Student Life *Housing:* college housing not available.

Costs (2016–17) *Tuition:* state resident $4824 full-time; nonresident $4824 full-time. Full-time tuition and fees vary according to location and program. Part-time tuition and fees vary according to location and program. *Required fees:* $414 full-time. *Waivers:* senior citizens and employees or children of employees.

Applying *Application fee:* $20. *Required:* high school transcript, immunization record.

Freshman Application Contact Minnesota State Community and Technical College–Wadena, 405 Colfax Avenue, SW, PO Box 566, Wadena, MN 56482. *Phone:* 218-736-1544. *Toll-free phone:* 800-247-2007.

Website: http://www.minnesota.edu/.

Minnesota West Community and Technical College

Pipestone, Minnesota

- **State-supported** 2-year, founded 1967, part of Minnesota State Colleges and Universities System
- **Rural** campus
- **Coed,** 3,182 undergraduate students, 36% full-time, 57% women, 43% men

Undergraduates 1,153 full-time, 2,029 part-time. 11% are from out of state; 5% Black or African American, non-Hispanic/Latino; 6% Hispanic/Latino; 3% Asian, non-Hispanic/Latino; 0.1% Native Hawaiian or other Pacific Islander, non-Hispanic/Latino; 0.9% American Indian or Alaska Native, non-Hispanic/Latino; 2% Two or more races, non-Hispanic/Latino; 5% Race/ethnicity unknown. *Retention:* 60% of full-time freshmen returned.

Freshmen *Average high school GPA:* 2.62.

Faculty *Total:* 146, 66% full-time. *Student/faculty ratio:* 21:1.

Majors Accounting; administrative assistant and secretarial science; agribusiness; agricultural and food products processing; agricultural/farm supplies retailing and wholesaling; agricultural production; agriculture; agronomy and crop science; automobile/automotive mechanics technology; biology/biotechnology laboratory technician; business administration and management; business/commerce; child-care and support services management; clinical/medical laboratory technology; computer and information systems security; computer engineering technology; computer science; computer systems networking and telecommunications; computer technology/computer systems technology; criminal justice/police science; dental assisting; diesel mechanics technology; electrical and power transmission installation; electrical and power transmission installation related; electrician; energy management and systems technology; hospital and healthcare facilities administration; human services; hydraulics and fluid power technology; information technology; liberal arts and sciences and humanities related; liberal arts and sciences/liberal studies; lineworker; manufacturing engineering technology; medical administrative assistant and medical secretary; medical/clinical assistant; medical insurance coding; plumbing technology; radiologic technology/science; registered nursing/registered nurse; robotics technology; surgical technology.

Academics *Calendar:* semesters. *Degrees:* certificates, diplomas, and associate (profile contains information from Canby, Granite Falls, Jackson, and Worthington campuses). *Special study options:* academic remediation for entering students, advanced placement credit, cooperative education, distance learning, double majors, external degree program, honors programs, independent study, internships, part-time degree program, services for LD students, summer session for credit.

Library Library and Academic Resource Center plus 4 others.

Student Life *Activities and Organizations:* choral group.

Athletics Member NJCAA. *Intercollegiate sports:* baseball M, basketball M/W, cheerleading W, football M, softball W, volleyball W, wrestling M.

Standardized Tests *Required:* ACCUPLACER (for admission).

Costs (2015–16) *One-time required fee:* $20. *Tuition:* state resident $5490 full-time, $172 per credit part-time; nonresident $5490 full-time, $172 per credit part-time. Full-time tuition and fees vary according to program and reciprocity agreements. Part-time tuition and fees vary according to program and reciprocity agreements. *Required fees:* $565 full-time, $18 per credit part-time. *Payment plan:* installment. *Waivers:* senior citizens and employees or children of employees.

Financial Aid Of all full-time matriculated undergraduates who enrolled in 2014, 1,844 applied for aid. 191 Federal Work-Study jobs (averaging $1633). 147 state and other part-time jobs (averaging $1278).

Applying *Options:* electronic application. *Application fee:* $20. *Required:* high school transcript. *Application deadlines:* rolling (freshmen), rolling (transfers).

Freshman Application Contact Ms. Crystal Strouth, College Registrar, Minnesota West Community and Technical College, 1450 Collegeway, Worthington, MN 56187. *Phone:* 507-372-3451. *Toll-free phone:* 800-658-2330. *Fax:* 507-372-5803. *E-mail:* crystal.strouth@mnwest.edu.

Website: http://www.mnwest.edu/.

National American University
Bloomington, Minnesota

Freshman Application Contact Ms. Jennifer Michaelson, Admissions Assistant, National American University, 321 Kansas City Street, Rapid City, SD 57201. *Phone:* 605-394-4827. *Toll-free phone:* 866-628-6387. *E-mail:* jmichaelson@national.edu. *Website:* http://www.national.edu/.

National American University
Brooklyn Center, Minnesota

Freshman Application Contact Admissions Office, National American University, 6200 Shingle Creek Parkway, Suite 130, Brooklyn Center, MN 55430. *Website:* http://www.national.edu/.

Normandale Community College
Bloomington, Minnesota

- **State-supported** 2-year, founded 1968, part of Minnesota State Colleges and Universities System
- **Suburban** 90-acre campus with easy access to Minneapolis-St. Paul
- **Coed**

Academics *Calendar:* semesters. *Degree:* certificates and associate. *Special study options:* academic remediation for entering students, adult/continuing education programs, advanced placement credit, cooperative education, distance learning, English as a second language, external degree program, independent study, internships, off-campus study, part-time degree program, services for LD students, student-designed majors, study abroad, summer session for credit.
Library Library plus 1 other.
Student Life *Campus security:* 24-hour emergency response devices, student patrols, late-night transport/escort service.
Costs (2015–16) *Tuition:* state resident $5736 full-time; nonresident $5736 full-time. *Required fees:* $891 full-time. *Payment plans:* installment, deferred payment.
Applying *Options:* electronic application, deferred entrance. *Application fee:* $20. *Required for some:* high school transcript, GED is also accepted for admission.
Freshman Application Contact Admissions Office, Normandale Community College, 9700 France Avenue South, Bloomington, MN 55431. *Phone:* 952-358-8201. *Toll-free phone:* 800-481-5412. *Fax:* 952-358-8230. *E-mail:* information@normandale.edu. *Website:* http://www.normandale.edu/.

North Hennepin Community College
Brooklyn Park, Minnesota

- **State-supported** 2-year, founded 1966, part of Minnesota State Colleges and Universities System
- **Suburban** 80-acre campus with easy access to Minneapolis-St. Paul
- **Endowment** $952,413
- **Coed**, 6,847 undergraduate students, 30% full-time, 58% women, 42% men

Undergraduates 2,055 full-time, 4,792 part-time. Students come from 26 states and territories; 36 other countries.
Freshmen *Admission:* 5,306 applied, 4,318 admitted, 1,114 enrolled.
Faculty *Total:* 291, 45% full-time.
Majors Accounting; accounting technology and bookkeeping; biology/biological sciences; business administration and management; chemistry; clinical/medical laboratory technology; computer science; construction management; creative writing; criminal justice/police science; criminal justice/safety; dramatic/theater arts; education; entrepreneurship; finance; fine/studio arts; graphic design; health and physical education/fitness; health services/allied health/health sciences; histologic technician; human services; legal assistant/paralegal; liberal arts and sciences/liberal studies; management information systems; marketing/marketing management; mathematics; multi/interdisciplinary studies related; music; physical education teaching and coaching; pre-engineering; registered nursing/registered nurse.
Academics *Calendar:* semesters. *Degree:* certificates and associate. *Special study options:* academic remediation for entering students, accelerated degree program, adult/continuing education programs, advanced placement credit, distance learning, double majors, English as a second language, external degree program, honors programs, independent study, internships, off-campus study, part-time degree program, services for LD students, student-designed majors, study abroad, summer session for credit. *ROTC:* Army (c), Navy (c), Air Force (c).

Library Learning Resource Center.
Student Life *Housing:* college housing not available. *Activities and Organizations:* drama/theater group, choral group, Student Anime Game Club, Hmong Student Club, Muslim Student Association, Multicultural Student Club, Soccer Club. *Campus security:* 24-hour emergency response devices, student patrols, late-night transport/escort service. *Student services:* personal/psychological counseling.
Athletics *Intramural sports:* basketball M/W, bowling M/W, football M/W, ice hockey M(c)/W(c), lacrosse M/W, soccer M/W, softball M/W, table tennis M/W, volleyball M/W, weight lifting M/W.
Costs (2015–16) *Tuition:* state resident $3962 full-time, $165 per credit part-time; nonresident $3962 full-time, $165 per credit part-time. Full-time tuition and fees vary according to location and program. Part-time tuition and fees vary according to location and program. *Required fees:* $421 full-time, $18 per credit part-time, $18 per credit part-time. *Payment plan:* installment. *Waivers:* senior citizens and employees or children of employees.
Applying *Options:* electronic application, early admission, deferred entrance. *Application fee:* $20. *Recommended:* high school transcript. *Application deadlines:* rolling (freshmen), rolling (transfers). *Notification:* continuous (freshmen), continuous (transfers).
Freshman Application Contact Mr. Sean Olson, Associate Director of Admissions and Outreach, North Hennepin Community College, 7411 85th Avenue North, Brooklyn Center, MN 55445. *Phone:* 763-424-0724. *Toll-free phone:* 800-818-0395. *Fax:* 763-493-0563. *E-mail:* solson2@nhcc.edu. *Website:* http://www.nhcc.edu/.

Northland Community and Technical College
Thief River Falls, Minnesota

- **State-supported** 2-year, founded 1965, part of Minnesota State Colleges and Universities System
- **Small-town** 239-acre campus
- **Coed**, 3,573 undergraduate students, 39% full-time, 57% women, 43% men

Undergraduates 1,389 full-time, 2,184 part-time. 7% Black or African American, non-Hispanic/Latino; 6% Hispanic/Latino; 2% Asian, non-Hispanic/Latino; 2% American Indian or Alaska Native, non-Hispanic/Latino; 3% Two or more races, non-Hispanic/Latino; 0.8% Race/ethnicity unknown; 0.9% international.
Freshmen *Admission:* 1,200 applied, 1,200 admitted.
Faculty *Total:* 150, 61% full-time, 7% with terminal degrees. *Student/faculty ratio:* 21:1.
Majors Accounting; accounting technology and bookkeeping; administrative assistant and secretarial science; aeronautics/aviation/aerospace science and technology; agricultural economics; agricultural mechanics and equipment technology; agriculture; agronomy and crop science; airframe mechanics and aircraft maintenance technology; architectural drafting and CAD/CADD; architectural engineering technology; autobody/collision and repair technology; automation engineer technology; automobile/automotive mechanics technology; avionics maintenance technology; business administration and management; CAD/CADD drafting/design technology; carpentry; child-care provision; computer support specialist; computer systems networking and telecommunications; criminal justice/police science; criminology; customer service management; dietetic technology; electrician; emergency medical technology (EMT paramedic); entrepreneurship; farm and ranch management; fire prevention and safety technology; fire science/firefighting; health services/allied health/health sciences; heating, air conditioning, ventilation and refrigeration maintenance technology; homeland security, law enforcement, firefighting and protective services related; liberal arts and sciences/liberal studies; licensed practical/vocational nurse training; logistics, materials, and supply chain management; machine shop technology; manufacturing engineering technology; marketing/marketing management; mass communication/media; medical administrative assistant and medical secretary; medical insurance coding; medical office assistant; nursing assistant/aide and patient care assistant/aide; occupational therapist assistant; office management; operations management; pharmacy technician; phlebotomy technology; physical therapy technology; plumbing technology; radiologic technology/science; registered nursing/registered nurse; respiratory care therapy; sales, distribution, and marketing operations; signal/geospatial intelligence; special products marketing; surgical technology; teacher assistant/aide; truck and bus driver/commercial vehicle operation/instruction; vehicle maintenance and repair technologies related; welding technology.
Academics *Calendar:* semesters. *Degree:* certificates, diplomas, and associate. *Special study options:* academic remediation for entering students, adult/continuing education programs, advanced placement credit, cooperative education, distance learning, double majors, internships, off-campus study, part-time degree program, services for LD students, summer session for credit.

Library Northland Community and Technical College Library plus 1 other. *Books:* 24,000 (physical), 19,000 (digital/electronic); *Serial titles:* 55 (physical); *Databases:* 47. Weekly public service hours: 82; students can reserve study rooms.

Student Life *Housing:* college housing not available. *Activities and Organizations:* student-run radio station, choral group, Student Senate, PAMA, AD Nursing, PN Nursing, Fire Tech. *Campus security:* student patrols, late-night transport/escort service. *Student services:* personal/psychological counseling, women's center.

Athletics Member NJCAA. *Intercollegiate sports:* baseball M, basketball M/W, football M, softball W, volleyball W, wrestling M. *Intramural sports:* basketball M/W, bowling M/W, golf M/W, ice hockey M/W, racquetball M/W, rock climbing M/W, soccer M/W, softball M/W, volleyball M/W, weight lifting M/W.

Costs (2015–16) *Tuition:* state resident $4950 full-time, $165 per credit hour part-time; nonresident $4950 full-time, $165 per credit hour part-time. Full-time tuition and fees vary according to course load, program, and reciprocity agreements. Part-time tuition and fees vary according to course load, program, and reciprocity agreements. *Required fees:* $611 full-time, $19 per credit hour part-time. *Payment plan:* installment. *Waivers:* senior citizens and employees or children of employees.

Financial Aid Of all full-time matriculated undergraduates who enrolled in 2011, 98 Federal Work-Study jobs (averaging $2701). 68 state and other part-time jobs (averaging $2839).

Applying *Options:* electronic application, early admission, deferred entrance. *Application fee:* $20. *Required:* high school transcript. *Application deadlines:* 8/24 (freshmen), 8/24 (transfers). *Notification:* continuous (freshmen), continuous (transfers).

Freshman Application Contact Mrs. Nicki Carlson, Director of Enrollment Management, Northland Community and Technical College, 1101 Highway One East, Thief River Falls, MN 56701. *Phone:* 218-683-8546. *Toll-free phone:* 800-959-6282. *Fax:* 218-683-8980. *E-mail:* nicki.carlson@northlandcollege.edu. *Website:* http://www.northlandcollege.edu/.

Northwest Technical College
Bemidji, Minnesota

- **State-supported** 2-year, founded 1993, part of Minnesota State Colleges and Universities System
- **Small-town** campus
- **Coed,** 1,114 undergraduate students, 30% full-time, 69% women, 31% men

Undergraduates 336 full-time, 778 part-time. 7% are from out of state; 2% Black or African American, non-Hispanic/Latino; 2% Hispanic/Latino; 0.4% Asian, non-Hispanic/Latino; 0.3% Native Hawaiian or other Pacific Islander, non-Hispanic/Latino; 8% American Indian or Alaska Native, non-Hispanic/Latino; 7% Two or more races, non-Hispanic/Latino; 2% Race/ethnicity unknown; 0.3% international; 13% transferred in; 4% live on campus. *Retention:* 49% of full-time freshmen returned.

Freshmen *Admission:* 104 enrolled.

Faculty *Total:* 73, 38% full-time. *Student/faculty ratio:* 14:1.

Majors Accounting; administrative assistant and secretarial science; automobile/automotive mechanics technology; business administration and management; child-care and support services management; computer systems networking and telecommunications; dental assisting; energy management and systems technology; engine machinist; industrial safety technology; industrial technology; licensed practical/vocational nurse training; manufacturing engineering technology; medical administrative assistant and medical secretary; registered nursing/registered nurse; sales, distribution, and marketing operations.

Academics *Calendar:* semesters. *Degree:* certificates, diplomas, and associate. *Special study options:* part-time degree program.

Library Northwest Technical College Learning Enrichment Center.

Student Life *Housing Options:* coed, special housing for students with disabilities. Campus housing is provided by a third party.

Costs (2015–16) *Tuition:* state resident $5190 full-time, $173 per credit part-time; nonresident $5190 full-time, $173 per credit part-time. Full-time tuition and fees vary according to location, program, and reciprocity agreements. Part-time tuition and fees vary according to location, program, and reciprocity agreements. *Required fees:* $290 full-time, $10 per credit part-time. *Room and board:* $7690. Room and board charges vary according to board plan and housing facility. *Payment plan:* installment. *Waivers:* senior citizens and employees or children of employees.

Applying *Options:* electronic application. *Application fee:* $20. *Required:* high school transcript.

Freshman Application Contact Ms. Kari Kantack-Miller, Diversity and Enrollment Representative, Northwest Technical College, 905 Grant Avenue,

Southeast, Bemidji, MN 56601. *Phone:* 218-333-6645. *Toll-free phone:* 800-942-8324. *Fax:* 218-333-6694. *E-mail:* kari.kantack@ntcmn.edu. *Website:* http://www.ntcmn.edu/.

Pine Technical and Community College
Pine City, Minnesota

Freshman Application Contact Pine Technical and Community College, 900 4th Street SE, Pine City, MN 55063. *Phone:* 320-629-5100. *Toll-free phone:* 800-521-7463. *Website:* http://www.pine.edu/.

Rainy River Community College
International Falls, Minnesota

- **State-supported** 2-year, founded 1967, part of Minnesota State Colleges and Universities System
- **Small-town** 80-acre campus
- **Coed,** 278 undergraduate students, 82% full-time, 58% women, 42% men

Undergraduates 229 full-time, 49 part-time. 15% Black or African American, non-Hispanic/Latino; 3% Hispanic/Latino; 1% Asian, non-Hispanic/Latino; 6% American Indian or Alaska Native, non-Hispanic/Latino; 7% international.

Faculty *Total:* 25, 40% full-time. *Student/faculty ratio:* 15:1.

Majors Administrative assistant and secretarial science; biological and physical sciences; business administration and management; liberal arts and sciences/liberal studies; pre-engineering.

Academics *Calendar:* semesters. *Degree:* certificates, diplomas, and associate. *Special study options:* academic remediation for entering students, adult/continuing education programs, advanced placement credit, cooperative education, honors programs, independent study, internships, part-time degree program, services for LD students, summer session for credit.

Library Rainy River Community College Library.

Student Life *Housing Options:* special housing for students with disabilities. Campus housing is university owned. *Activities and Organizations:* drama/theater group, Anishinaabe Student Coalition, Student Senate, Black Student Association. *Campus security:* 24-hour emergency response devices, late-night transport/escort service, controlled dormitory access. *Student services:* personal/psychological counseling.

Athletics Member NJCAA. *Intercollegiate sports:* basketball M/W, ice hockey W, softball W, volleyball W. *Intramural sports:* archery M/W, badminton M/W, baseball M, bowling M/W, cheerleading M/W, cross-country running M/W, ice hockey M, skiing (cross-country) M/W, skiing (downhill) M/W, swimming and diving M/W, table tennis M/W, tennis M/W, volleyball M/W, weight lifting M/W.

Applying *Options:* electronic application, early admission, deferred entrance. *Application fee:* $20. *Recommended:* high school transcript. *Application deadlines:* rolling (freshmen), rolling (out-of-state freshmen), rolling (transfers). *Notification:* continuous (freshmen), continuous (out-of-state freshmen), continuous (transfers).

Freshman Application Contact Ms. Berta Hagen, Registrar, Rainy River Community College, 1501 Highway 71, International Falls, MN 56649. *Phone:* 218-285-2207. *Toll-free phone:* 800-456-3996. *Fax:* 218-285-2314. *E-mail:* berta.hagen@rainyriver.edu. *Website:* http://www.rainyriver.edu/.

Ridgewater College
Willmar, Minnesota

- **State-supported** 2-year, founded 1961, part of Minnesota State Colleges and Universities System
- **Small-town** 83-acre campus
- **Coed,** 3,563 undergraduate students, 56% full-time, 54% women, 46% men

Undergraduates 2,002 full-time, 1,561 part-time.

Faculty *Total:* 173, 62% full-time.

Majors Accounting; administrative assistant and secretarial science; agribusiness; agricultural production; agriculture; agronomy and crop science; animal/livestock husbandry and production; autobody/collision and repair technology; automobile/automotive mechanics technology; biology/biological sciences; business administration and management; carpentry; chemistry; commercial photography; computer programming; computer science; computer systems networking and telecommunications; computer technology/computer systems technology; cosmetology; criminal justice/police science; crop production; dairy husbandry and production; desktop publishing and digital imaging design; digital communication and media/multimedia; early childhood education; electrical, electronic and communications engineering technology; electrician; electromechanical technology; health information/medical records technology; instrumentation technology; legal administrative assistant/secretary; liberal arts and sciences and humanities related; liberal arts and sciences/liberal studies; machine tool technology; marketing/marketing management; mechanical drafting and CAD/CADD; medical administrative assistant and medical secretary; medical/clinical assistant; network and system administration; radiologic technology/science; recording arts technology; registered nursing/registered nurse; sales, distribution, and marketing operations; selling skills and sales; teacher assistant/aide; telecommunications technology; therapeutic recreation; tool and die technology; veterinary/animal health technology; web page, digital/multimedia and information resources design; welding technology.

Academics *Calendar:* semesters. *Degree:* certificates, diplomas, and associate. *Special study options:* academic remediation for entering students, advanced placement credit, cooperative education, distance learning, internships, off-campus study, part-time degree program, services for LD students, student-designed majors, study abroad, summer session for credit.

Student Life *Housing:* college housing not available. *Campus security:* 24-hour emergency response devices. *Student services:* personal/psychological counseling.

Athletics Member NJCAA. *Intercollegiate sports:* baseball M, basketball M/W, football M, soccer M, softball W, volleyball W, wrestling M. *Intramural sports:* basketball M/W, football M, golf M/W, softball M/W, weight lifting M/W.

Costs (2016–17) *Tuition:* state resident $4839 full-time, $161 per credit part-time; nonresident $4839 full-time, $161 per credit part-time. Full-time tuition and fees vary according to course load and reciprocity agreements. Part-time tuition and fees vary according to course load and reciprocity agreements. *Required fees:* $567 full-time, $19 per credit part-time. *Waivers:* senior citizens.

Financial Aid Of all full-time matriculated undergraduates who enrolled in 2014, 350 Federal Work-Study jobs (averaging $3000). 133 state and other part-time jobs (averaging $2400).

Applying *Options:* electronic application. *Application fee:* $20. *Required:* high school transcript. *Required for some:* interview.

Freshman Application Contact Ms. Linda Duering, Admissions Assistant, Ridgewater College, 2101 15th Avenue NW, Willmar, MN 56201. *Phone:* 320-222-5976. *Toll-free phone:* 800-722-1151.
E-mail: linda.duering@ridgewater.edu.
Website: http://www.ridgewater.edu/.

Riverland Community College
Austin, Minnesota

- **State-supported** 2-year, founded 1940, part of Minnesota State Colleges and Universities System
- **Small-town** 187-acre campus
- **Coed**

Undergraduates 1,249 full-time, 1,765 part-time. Students come from 16 states and territories; 23 other countries; 3% are from out of state; 5% Black or African American, non-Hispanic/Latino; 11% Hispanic/Latino; 1% Asian, non-Hispanic/Latino; 0.2% Native Hawaiian or other Pacific Islander, non-Hispanic/Latino; 0.3% American Indian or Alaska Native, non-Hispanic/Latino; 2% Two or more races, non-Hispanic/Latino; 0.5% Race/ethnicity unknown; 1% international; 2% live on campus. *Retention:* 52% of full-time freshmen returned.

Academics *Calendar:* semesters. *Degree:* certificates, diplomas, and associate. *Special study options:* academic remediation for entering students, adult/continuing education programs, advanced placement credit, distance learning, double majors, English as a second language, independent study, internships, off-campus study, part-time degree program, services for LD students, study abroad, summer session for credit.

Library Riverland Community College Library plus 2 others.

Student Life *Campus security:* late-night transport/escort service.

Athletics Member NJCAA.

Financial Aid Of all full-time matriculated undergraduates who enrolled in 2014, 1,133 applied for aid. 132 Federal Work-Study jobs (averaging $3000). 88 state and other part-time jobs (averaging $3000). *Average indebtedness upon graduation:* $7167.

Applying *Options:* electronic application, early admission. *Application fee:* $20. *Required:* high school transcript.

Freshman Application Contact Riverland Community College, 1900 8th Avenue, NW, Austin, MN 55912. *Phone:* 507-433-0600. *Toll-free phone:* 800-247-5039.
Website: http://www.riverland.edu/.

Rochester Community and Technical College
Rochester, Minnesota

Director of Admissions Mr. Troy Tynsky, Director of Admissions, Rochester Community and Technical College, 851 30th Avenue, SE, Rochester, MN 55904-4999. *Phone:* 507-280-3509.
Website: http://www.rctc.edu/.

St. Cloud Technical & Community College
St. Cloud, Minnesota

Freshman Application Contact Ms. Jodi Elness, Admissions Office, St. Cloud Technical & Community College, 1540 Northway Drive, St. Cloud, MN 56303. *Phone:* 320-308-5089. *Toll-free phone:* 800-222-1009. *Fax:* 320-308-5981. *E-mail:* jelness@sctcc.edu.
Website: http://www.sctcc.edu/.

Saint Paul College–A Community & Technical College
St. Paul, Minnesota

Freshman Application Contact Ms. Sarah Carrico, Saint Paul College–A Community & Technical College, 235 Marshall Avenue, Saint Paul, MN 55102. *Phone:* 651-846-1424. *Toll-free phone:* 800-227-6029. *Fax:* 651-846-1703. *E-mail:* admissions@saintpaul.edu.
Website: http://www.saintpaul.edu/.

South Central College
North Mankato, Minnesota

Freshman Application Contact Ms. Beverly Herda, Director of Admissions, South Central College, 1920 Lee Boulevard, North Mankato, MN 56003. *Phone:* 507-389-7334. *Fax:* 507-388-9951.
Website: http://southcentral.edu/.

Vermilion Community College
Ely, Minnesota

Freshman Application Contact Mr. Todd Heiman, Director of Enrollment Services, Vermilion Community College, 1900 East Camp Street, Ely, MN 55731-1996. *Phone:* 218-365-7224. *Toll-free phone:* 800-657-3608.
Website: http://www.vcc.edu/.

White Earth Tribal and Community College
Mahnomen, Minnesota

Admissions Office Contact White Earth Tribal and Community College, 102 3rd Street NE, Mahnomen, MN 56557.
Website: http://www.wetcc.edu/.

MISSISSIPPI

Antonelli College
Hattiesburg, Mississippi

Freshman Application Contact Mrs. Karen Gautreau, Director, Antonelli College, 1500 North 31st Avenue, Hattiesburg, MS 39401. *Phone:* 601-583-4100. *Fax:* 601-583-0839. *E-mail:* admissionsh@antonellicollege.edu.
Website: http://www.antonellicollege.edu/.

Antonelli College
Jackson, Mississippi

Freshman Application Contact Antonelli College, 2323 Lakeland Drive, Jackson, MS 39232. *Phone:* 601-362-9991.
Website: http://www.antonellicollege.edu/.

Blue Cliff College–Gulfport
Gulfport, Mississippi

Admissions Office Contact Blue Cliff College–Gulfport, 12251 Bernard Parkway, Gulfport, MS 39503.
Website: http://www.bluecliffcollege.edu/.

Coahoma Community College
Clarksdale, Mississippi

Freshman Application Contact Mrs. Wanda Holmes, Director of Admissions and Records, Coahoma Community College, Clarksdale, MS 38614-9799.
Phone: 662-621-4205. *Toll-free phone:* 866-470-1CCC.
Website: http://www.ccc.cc.ms.us/.

Copiah-Lincoln Community College
Wesson, Mississippi

- **State and locally supported** 2-year, founded 1928, part of Mississippi Community College Board
- **Rural** 525-acre campus with easy access to Jackson
- **Endowment** $2.5 million
- **Coed,** 3,157 undergraduate students, 79% full-time, 63% women, 37% men

Undergraduates 2,509 full-time, 648 part-time. Students come from 6 states and territories; 1% are from out of state; 42% Black or African American, non-Hispanic/Latino; 1% Hispanic/Latino; 0.3% Asian, non-Hispanic/Latino; 0.3% American Indian or Alaska Native, non-Hispanic/Latino; 0.2% Two or more races, non-Hispanic/Latino; 1% Race/ethnicity unknown; 6% transferred in; 30% live on campus.
Freshmen *Admission:* 692 enrolled.
Faculty *Total:* 138.
Majors Accounting; agribusiness; agricultural business and management; agricultural business and management related; agricultural economics; agricultural/farm supplies retailing and wholesaling; agriculture; architecture; art teacher education; biological and physical sciences; biology/biological sciences; business administration and management; chemistry; child development; civil engineering technology; clinical/medical laboratory technology; computer programming; cosmetology; criminal justice/police science; data processing and data processing technology; drafting and design technology; economics; education; electrical, electronic and communications engineering technology; elementary education; engineering; English; family and consumer sciences/home economics teacher education; farm and ranch management; food technology and processing; forestry; health teacher education; history; industrial radiologic technology; journalism; liberal arts and sciences/liberal studies; library and information science; music teacher education; physical education teaching and coaching; registered nursing/registered nurse; special products marketing; trade and industrial teacher education.
Academics *Calendar:* semesters. *Degree:* certificates and associate. *Special study options:* academic remediation for entering students, adult/continuing education programs, advanced placement credit, honors programs, part-time degree program, student-designed majors, summer session for credit.
Library Oswalt Memorial Library.
Student Life *Housing Options:* Campus housing is university owned. *Activities and Organizations:* drama/theater group, student-run newspaper, radio station, choral group, marching band. *Campus security:* 24-hour patrols. *Student services:* health clinic, personal/psychological counseling.
Athletics Member NJCAA. *Intercollegiate sports:* baseball M(s), basketball M(s)/W(s), football M(s), golf M/W, softball W, tennis M/W, track and field M. *Intramural sports:* basketball M/W, football M, golf M/W, tennis M/W, volleyball M/W.
Costs (2015–16) *Tuition:* state resident $2390 full-time, $120 per semester hour part-time; nonresident $4390 full-time, $205 per semester hour part-time. *Required fees:* $340 full-time. *Room and board:* $3750; room only: $1550. Room and board charges vary according to board plan and housing facility. *Waivers:* senior citizens and employees or children of employees.
Financial Aid Of all full-time matriculated undergraduates who enrolled in 2014, 125 Federal Work-Study jobs (averaging $1000).
Applying *Options:* early admission. *Required:* high school transcript. *Application deadlines:* rolling (freshmen), rolling (transfers).
Freshman Application Contact Ms. Gay Langham, Student Records Manager, Copiah-Lincoln Community College, PO Box 649, Wesson, MS 39191-0457. *Phone:* 601-643-8307. *E-mail:* gay.langham@colin.edu. *Website:* http://www.colin.edu/.

East Central Community College
Decatur, Mississippi

Director of Admissions Ms. Donna Luke, Director of Admissions, Records, and Research, East Central Community College, PO Box 129, Decatur, MS 39327-0129. *Phone:* 601-635-2111 Ext. 206. *Toll-free phone:* 877-462-3222. *Website:* http://www.eccc.edu/.

East Mississippi Community College
Scooba, Mississippi

Director of Admissions Ms. Melinda Sciple, Admissions Officer, East Mississippi Community College, PO Box 158, Scooba, MS 39358-0158. *Phone:* 662-476-5041. *Website:* http://www.eastms.edu/.

Hinds Community College
Raymond, Mississippi

- **State and locally supported** 2-year, founded 1917, part of Mississippi Community College Board
- **Small-town** 671-acre campus
- **Coed,** 11,514 undergraduate students, 64% full-time, 61% women, 39% men

Undergraduates 7,344 full-time, 4,170 part-time. Students come from 29 states and territories; 22 other countries; 3% are from out of state; 55% Black or African American, non-Hispanic/Latino; 2% Hispanic/Latino; 0.8% Asian, non-Hispanic/Latino; 0.2% American Indian or Alaska Native, non-Hispanic/Latino; 2% Two or more races, non-Hispanic/Latino; 3% Race/ethnicity unknown; 0.1% international; 89% transferred in. *Retention:* 48% of full-time freshmen returned.
Freshmen *Admission:* 2,661 enrolled. *Test scores:* ACT scores over 18: 38%; ACT scores over 24: 5%.
Faculty *Total:* 819, 46% full-time. *Student/faculty ratio:* 19:1.
Majors Accounting technology and bookkeeping; administrative assistant and secretarial science; aeronautics/aviation/aerospace science and technology; agribusiness; agricultural mechanization related; airframe mechanics and aircraft maintenance technology; applied horticulture/horticultural business services related; architectural engineering technology; arts, entertainment, and media management related; aviation/airway management; banking and financial support services; child-care provision; clinical/medical laboratory technology; computer and information systems security; computer installation and repair technology; computer programming; computer systems networking and telecommunications; corrections and criminal justice related; court reporting; dental assisting; diagnostic medical sonography and ultrasound technology; diesel mechanics technology; digital communication and media/multimedia; drafting and design technology; electrical, electronic and communications engineering technology; electrical/electronics equipment installation and repair; electrician; emergency medical technology (EMT paramedic); fashion merchandising; game and interactive media design; general studies; geographic information science and cartography; graphic design; health and medical administrative services related; health information/medical records technology; heating, air conditioning, ventilation and refrigeration maintenance technology; hospitality administration; institutional food workers; landscaping and groundskeeping; legal assistant/paralegal; logistics, materials, and supply chain management; marketing/marketing management; medical/clinical assistant; multi/interdisciplinary studies related; photographic and film/video technology; physical therapy technology; plant protection and integrated pest management; plumbing technology; poultry science; radio and television broadcasting technology; radiologic technology/science; real estate; registered nursing/registered nurse; respiratory care therapy; sign language interpretation and translation; surgical technology; telecommunications technology; tourism and travel services management; veterinary/animal health technology.
Academics *Calendar:* semesters. *Degrees:* certificates and associate (profile includes Raymond, Jackson Academic and Technical Center, Jackson Nursing-Allied Health Center, Rankin, Utica, and Vicksburg campus locations). *Special study options:* academic remediation for entering students, accelerated degree program, adult/continuing education programs, advanced placement credit, cooperative education, distance learning, double majors, freshman honors college, honors programs, independent study, internships, part-time degree program, services for LD students, study abroad, summer session for credit. *ROTC:* Army (b).
Library McLendon Library plus 5 others. *Books:* 128,296 (physical), 173,588 (digital/electronic); *Databases:* 83. Students can reserve study rooms.
Student Life *Housing Options:* coed, men-only, women-only, special housing for students with disabilities. Campus housing is university owned. *Activities and Organizations:* drama/theater group, student-run newspaper, choral group, marching band. *Campus security:* 24-hour emergency response devices and

patrols, late-night transport/escort service, controlled dormitory access. *Student services:* personal/psychological counseling, legal services.
Athletics Member NJCAA. *Intercollegiate sports:* baseball M(s), basketball M(s)/W(s), cheerleading M(s)/W(s), football M(s), golf M(s), soccer M(s)/W(s), softball W(s), tennis M(s)/W(s), track and field M(s)/W(s). *Intramural sports:* basketball M/W, bowling M/W, cross-country running M/W, football M/W, golf M/W, softball M/W, swimming and diving M/W, tennis M/W, ultimate Frisbee M/W, volleyball M/W.
Standardized Tests *Required for some:* SAT and SAT Subject Tests or ACT (for admission).
Costs (2015–16) *Tuition:* state resident $2400 full-time, $100 per semester hour part-time; nonresident $5000 full-time, $200 per semester hour part-time. Part-time tuition and fees vary according to course load. *Required fees:* $100 full-time, $50 per term part-time. *Room and board:* $3960. Room and board charges vary according to housing facility. *Payment plan:* installment. *Waivers:* senior citizens and employees or children of employees.
Financial Aid Of all full-time matriculated undergraduates who enrolled in 2014, 300 Federal Work-Study jobs (averaging $1250). 200 state and other part-time jobs (averaging $1000).
Applying *Required:* high school transcript.
Freshman Application Contact Hinds Community College, PO Box 1100, Raymond, MS 39154-1100. *Phone:* 601-857-3280. *Toll-free phone:* 800-HINDSCC.
Website: http://www.hindscc.edu/.

Holmes Community College
Goodman, Mississippi

Director of Admissions Dr. Lynn Wright, Dean of Admissions and Records, Holmes Community College, PO Box 369, Goodman, MS 39079-0369. *Phone:* 601-472-2312 Ext. 1023. *Toll-free phone:* 800-HOLMES-4.
Website: http://www.holmescc.edu/.

Itawamba Community College
Fulton, Mississippi

- **State and locally supported** 2-year, founded 1947, part of Mississippi State Board for Community and Junior Colleges
- **Small-town** 300-acre campus
- **Coed,** 5,611 undergraduate students, 64% full-time, 60% women, 40% men

Undergraduates 3,605 full-time, 2,006 part-time. *Retention:* 70% of full-time freshmen returned.
Freshmen *Admission:* 1,204 enrolled.
Faculty *Total:* 353, 47% full-time. *Student/faculty ratio:* 19:1.
Majors Accounting; administrative assistant and secretarial science; agricultural business and management; art; art teacher education; biological and physical sciences; biology/biological sciences; business administration and management; chemistry; civil engineering technology; computer and information sciences; computer science; construction engineering technology; criminal justice/police science; data processing and data processing technology; developmental and child psychology; drafting and design technology; economics; education; electrical, electronic and communications engineering technology; elementary education; English; family and consumer sciences/home economics teacher education; family and consumer sciences/human sciences; fashion/apparel design; forest technology; health information/medical records administration; history; human services; journalism; keyboard instruments; kindergarten/preschool education; liberal arts and sciences/liberal studies; library and information science; marketing/marketing management; mathematics; medical radiologic technology; modern languages; music; music teacher education; percussion instruments; physical education teaching and coaching; political science and government; pre-engineering; psychology; public administration; registered nursing/registered nurse; respiratory care therapy; rhetoric and composition; science teacher education; social sciences; social work; sociology; trade and industrial teacher education; woodwind instruments.
Academics *Calendar:* semesters. *Degree:* certificates and associate. *Special study options:* academic remediation for entering students, adult/continuing education programs, cooperative education, distance learning, English as a second language, honors programs, part-time degree program, services for LD students, summer session for credit. *ROTC:* Army (b).
Student Life *Housing Options:* Campus housing is university owned. *Activities and Organizations:* drama/theater group, student-run newspaper, choral group, marching band.
Athletics Member NJCAA. *Intercollegiate sports:* basketball M(s)/W(s), football M(s), golf M(s), tennis M(s)/W(s), track and field M. *Intramural sports:* badminton M/W, basketball M/W, football M/W, golf M/W, tennis M/W, volleyball M/W.

Costs (2016–17) *Tuition:* state resident $2500 full-time, $120 per semester hour part-time; nonresident $4700 full-time, $120 per semester hour part-time. *Required fees:* $120 full-time, $120 per semester part-time. *Room and board:* $3510; room only: $1500. Room and board charges vary according to board plan and housing facility. *Payment plan:* installment. *Waivers:* employees or children of employees.
Financial Aid Of all full-time matriculated undergraduates who enrolled in 2013, 230 Federal Work-Study jobs (averaging $2500).
Applying *Options:* electronic application, early admission. *Required:* high school transcript. *Application deadlines:* rolling (freshmen), rolling (transfers). *Notification:* continuous (freshmen), continuous (transfers).
Freshman Application Contact Mr. Larry Boggs, Director of Student Recruitment and Scholarships, Itawamba Community College, 602 West Hill Street, Fulton, MS 38843. *Phone:* 601-862-8252.
E-mail: laboggs@iccms.edu.
Website: http://www.iccms.edu/.

Jones County Junior College
Ellisville, Mississippi

Director of Admissions Mrs. Dianne Speed, Director of Admissions and Records, Jones County Junior College, 900 South Court Street, Ellisville, MS 39437-3901. *Phone:* 601-477-4025.
Website: http://www.jcjc.edu/.

Meridian Community College
Meridian, Mississippi

- **State and locally supported** 2-year, founded 1937, part of Mississippi Community College Board
- **Small-town** 91-acre campus
- **Endowment** $12.7 million
- **Coed,** 3,381 undergraduate students, 73% full-time, 68% women, 32% men

Undergraduates 2,453 full-time, 928 part-time. Students come from 16 states and territories; 3% are from out of state; 43% Black or African American, non-Hispanic/Latino; 1% Hispanic/Latino; 0.7% Asian, non-Hispanic/Latino; 2% American Indian or Alaska Native, non-Hispanic/Latino; 6% Race/ethnicity unknown; 0.7% international; 12% live on campus. *Retention:* 51% of full-time freshmen returned.
Freshmen *Admission:* 657 enrolled.
Faculty *Total:* 209, 74% full-time, 4% with terminal degrees. *Student/faculty ratio:* 18:1.
Majors Administrative assistant and secretarial science; child-care provision; clinical/medical laboratory technology; dental hygiene; drafting and design technology; electrical, electronic and communications engineering technology; emergency medical technology (EMT paramedic); fire science/firefighting; machine tool technology; marketing/marketing management; registered nursing/registered nurse; respiratory care therapy; telecommunications technology.
Academics *Calendar:* semesters. *Degree:* certificates and associate. *Special study options:* academic remediation for entering students, accelerated degree program, adult/continuing education programs, advanced placement credit, cooperative education, distance learning, double majors, English as a second language, freshman honors college, honors programs, independent study, internships, part-time degree program, services for LD students, summer session for credit.
Library L. O. Todd Library. *Books:* 49,345 (physical), 63,815 (digital/electronic); *Databases:* 13.
Student Life *Housing Options:* coed, men-only, women-only. Campus housing is university owned. *Activities and Organizations:* drama/theater group, student-run radio station, choral group, Phi Theta Kappa, VICA (Vocational Industrial Clubs of America), Health Occupations Students of America, Organization of Student Nurses, Distributive Education Clubs of America. *Campus security:* 24-hour patrols by law enforcement officers. *Student services:* personal/psychological counseling.
Athletics Member NJCAA. *Intercollegiate sports:* baseball M(s), basketball M(s)/W(s), cross-country running M(s)/W(s), golf M(s), soccer M(s)/W(s), softball W(s), tennis M(s)/W(s), track and field M(s)/W(s). *Intramural sports:* basketball M/W, cross-country running M/W, swimming and diving M/W, tennis M/W, volleyball M/W.
Standardized Tests *Recommended:* ACT (for admission).
Costs (2015–16) *Tuition:* state resident $2100 full-time, $100 per credit hour part-time; nonresident $3380 full-time, $157 per credit hour part-time. Full-time tuition and fees vary according to program. Part-time tuition and fees vary according to program. *Required fees:* $230 full-time, $6 per credit hour part-time, $25 per term part-time. *Room and board:* $3878. Room and board charges vary according to housing facility. *Waivers:* employees or children of employees.

Applying *Options:* early admission. *Required:* high school transcript, minimum 2.0 GPA. *Application deadlines:* rolling (freshmen), rolling (out-of-state freshmen), rolling (transfers). *Notification:* continuous (freshmen), continuous (out-of-state freshmen), continuous (transfers).
Freshman Application Contact Ms. Angela Payne, Director of Admissions, Meridian Community College, 910 Highway 19 North, Meridian, MS 39307. *Phone:* 601-484-8357. *Toll-free phone:* 800-MCC-THE-1. *E-mail:* apayne@meridiancc.edu. *Website:* http://www.meridiancc.edu/.

Miller-Motte Technical College
Gulfport, Mississippi

Admissions Office Contact Miller-Motte Technical College, 12121 Highway 49 North, Gulfport, MS 39503. *Toll-free phone:* 866-297-0267. *Website:* http://www.miller-motte.edu/.

Mississippi Delta Community College
Moorhead, Mississippi

Freshman Application Contact Mississippi Delta Community College, PO Box 668, Highway 3 and Cherry Street, Moorhead, MS 38761-0668. *Phone:* 662-246-6302. *Website:* http://www.msdelta.edu/.

Mississippi Gulf Coast Community College
Perkinston, Mississippi

Freshman Application Contact Mrs. Nichol Green, Director of Admissions, Mississippi Gulf Coast Community College, PO Box 548, Perkinston, MS 39573. *Phone:* 601-928-6264. *Fax:* 601-928-6345. *Website:* http://www.mgccc.edu/.

Northeast Mississippi Community College
Booneville, Mississippi

Freshman Application Contact Office of Enrollment Services, Northeast Mississippi Community College, 101 Cunningham Boulevard, Booneville, MS 38829. *Phone:* 662-720-7239. *Toll-free phone:* 800-555-2154. *E-mail:* admitme@nemcc.edu. *Website:* http://www.nemcc.edu/.

Northwest Mississippi Community College
Senatobia, Mississippi

Freshman Application Contact Northwest Mississippi Community College, 4975 Highway 51 North, Senatobia, MS 38668-1701. *Phone:* 662-562-3222. *Website:* http://www.northwestms.edu/.

Pearl River Community College
Poplarville, Mississippi

Freshman Application Contact Mr. J. Dow Ford, Director of Admissions, Pearl River Community College, 101 Highway 11 North, Poplarville, MS 39470. *Phone:* 601-403-1000. *E-mail:* dford@prcc.edu. *Website:* http://www.prcc.edu/.

Southwest Mississippi Community College
Summit, Mississippi

Freshman Application Contact Mr. Matthew Calhoun, Vice President of Admissions and Records, Southwest Mississippi Community College, 1156 College Drive, Summit, MS 39666. *Phone:* 601-276-2001. *Fax:* 601-276-3888. *E-mail:* mattc@smcc.edu. *Website:* http://www.smcc.cc.ms.us/.

Virginia College in Biloxi
Biloxi, Mississippi

Admissions Office Contact Virginia College in Biloxi, 920 Cedar Lake Road, Biloxi, MS 39532. *Website:* http://www.vc.edu/.

Virginia College in Jackson
Jackson, Mississippi

Director of Admissions Director of Admissions, Virginia College in Jackson, 5841 Ridgewood Road, Jackson, MS 39211. *Phone:* 601-977-0960. *Website:* http://www.vc.edu/.

MISSOURI

American Trade School
Saint Ann, Missouri

Admissions Office Contact American Trade School, 3925 Industrial Drive, Saint Ann, MO 63074. *Website:* http://www.americantradeschool.edu/.

Brown Mackie College–St. Louis
Fenton, Missouri

Freshman Application Contact Brown Mackie College–St. Louis, #2 Soccer Park Road, Fenton, MO 63026. *Phone:* 636-651-3290. *Website:* http://www.brownmackie.edu/st-louis/.

Bryan University
Columbia, Missouri

Admissions Office Contact Bryan University, 3215 LeMone Industrial Boulevard, Columbia, MO 65201. *Toll-free phone:* 855-566-0650. *Website:* http://www.bryanu.edu/.

Concorde Career College
Kansas City, Missouri

Freshman Application Contact Deborah Crow, Director, Concorde Career College, 3239 Broadway, Kansas City, MO 64111. *Phone:* 816-531-5223. *Fax:* 816-756-3231. *E-mail:* dcrow@concorde.edu. *Website:* http://www.concorde.edu/.

Cottey College
Nevada, Missouri

- **Independent** primarily 2-year, founded 1884
- **Small-town** 51-acre campus
- **Endowment** $108.8 million
- **Women only,** 317 undergraduate students, 99% full-time

Undergraduates 314 full-time, 3 part-time. Students come from 43 states and territories; 25 other countries; 80% are from out of state; 8% Black or African American, non-Hispanic/Latino; 10% Hispanic/Latino; 2% Asian, non-Hispanic/Latino; 0.6% Native Hawaiian or other Pacific Islander, non-Hispanic/Latino; 2% American Indian or Alaska Native, non-Hispanic/Latino; 5% Two or more races, non-Hispanic/Latino; 14% international; 3% transferred in; 98% live on campus. *Retention:* 79% of full-time freshmen returned.
Freshmen *Admission:* 169 enrolled. *Average high school GPA:* 3.47. *Test scores:* SAT critical reading scores over 500: 75%; SAT math scores over 500: 55%; ACT scores over 18: 92%; SAT critical reading scores over 600: 33%; SAT math scores over 600: 10%; ACT scores over 24: 44%; SAT critical reading scores over 700: 4%; ACT scores over 30: 4%.
Faculty *Total:* 44, 82% full-time, 80% with terminal degrees. *Student/faculty ratio:* 9:1.
Majors Business administration and management; English; environmental studies; health services/allied health/health sciences; international business/trade/commerce; international relations and affairs; liberal arts and sciences/liberal studies; psychology.
Academics *Calendar:* semesters. *Degrees:* associate and bachelor's. *Special study options:* advanced placement credit, distance learning, independent study, internships, part-time degree program, services for LD students, study abroad.

Library Blanche Skiff Ross Memorial Library plus 1 other.
Student Life *Housing Options:* women-only. Campus housing is university owned. *Activities and Organizations:* drama/theater group, student-run newspaper, choral group, International Friendship Circle, Cottey Intramural Association, Ozarks Explorers Club, Inter-Varsity Club, Golden Keys. *Campus security:* 24-hour emergency response devices and patrols, late-night transport/escort service, controlled dormitory access. *Student services:* health clinic, personal/psychological counseling.
Athletics Member NJCAA. *Intercollegiate sports:* basketball W(s), cross-country running W(s), softball W(s), volleyball W(s).
Standardized Tests *Required:* SAT or ACT (for admission).
Costs (2016–17) *Comprehensive fee:* $26,950 includes full-time tuition ($18,400), mandatory fees ($900), and room and board ($7650). Part-time tuition: $125 per credit hour. Part-time tuition and fees vary according to course load. *Room and board:* college room only: $4000. Room and board charges vary according to housing facility. *Payment plan:* installment. *Waivers:* employees or children of employees.
Financial Aid Of all full-time matriculated undergraduates who enrolled in 2014, 224 applied for aid, 208 were judged to have need, 55 had their need fully met. In 2014, 54 non-need-based awards were made. *Average percent of need met:* 84%. *Average financial aid package:* $19,897. *Average need-based loan:* $3028. *Average need-based gift aid:* $16,481. *Average non-need-based aid:* $13,729. *Average indebtedness upon graduation:* $26,427.
Applying *Required:* essay or personal statement, high school transcript, 1 letter of recommendation. *Recommended:* minimum 2.6 GPA, interview.
Freshman Application Contact Ms. Judi Steege, Director of Admission, Cottey College, 1000 West Austin Boulevard, Nevada, MO 64772. *Phone:* 417-667-8181. *Toll-free phone:* 888-526-8839. *Fax:* 417-667-8103. *E-mail:* enrollmgt@cottey.edu. *Website:* http://www.cottey.edu/.

Court Reporting Institute of St. Louis
Clayton, Missouri

Freshman Application Contact Admissions Office, Court Reporting Institute of St. Louis, 7730 Carondelet Avenue, Suite 400, Clayton, MO 63105. *Phone:* 713-996-8300. *Toll-free phone:* 888-208-6780.
Website: http://www.cri.edu/st-louis-court-reporting-school.asp.

Crowder College
Neosho, Missouri

- **State and locally supported** 2-year, founded 1963, part of Missouri Coordinating Board for Higher Education
- **Rural** 608-acre campus
- **Coed,** 5,710 undergraduate students, 46% full-time, 64% women, 36% men

Undergraduates 2,638 full-time, 3,072 part-time. Students come from 12 states and territories; 6% are from out of state; 1% Black or African American, non-Hispanic/Latino; 8% Hispanic/Latino; 1% Asian, non-Hispanic/Latino; 0.4% Native Hawaiian or other Pacific Islander, non-Hispanic/Latino; 2% American Indian or Alaska Native, non-Hispanic/Latino; 2% Two or more races, non-Hispanic/Latino; 1% Race/ethnicity unknown; 1% international; 5% transferred in; 10% live on campus. *Retention:* 64% of full-time freshmen returned.
Freshmen *Admission:* 1,320 enrolled.
Faculty *Total:* 449, 21% full-time, 7% with terminal degrees. *Student/faculty ratio:* 12:1.
Majors Administrative assistant and secretarial science; agribusiness; agricultural mechanization; agriculture; art; autobody/collision and repair technology; automobile/automotive mechanics technology; biology/biological sciences; business administration and management; business automation/technology/data entry; computer systems analysis; computer systems networking and telecommunications; construction engineering technology; construction trades; drafting and design technology; dramatic/theater arts; education; electrical, electronic and communications engineering technology; elementary education; emergency medical technology (EMT paramedic); energy management and systems technology; environmental engineering technology; executive assistant/executive secretary; farm and ranch management; fire science/firefighting; general studies; health information/medical records technology; industrial technology; legal administrative assistant/secretary; liberal arts and sciences/liberal studies; manufacturing engineering technology; mass communication/media; mathematics; mathematics and computer science; medical administrative assistant and medical secretary; music; occupational therapist assistant; physical education teaching and coaching; physical sciences; pre-engineering; psychology; public relations/image management; registered nursing/registered nurse; solar energy technology; veterinary/animal health technology; welding technology.

Academics *Calendar:* semesters. *Degree:* certificates and associate. *Special study options:* academic remediation for entering students, adult/continuing education programs, advanced placement credit, cooperative education, English as a second language, freshman honors college, honors programs, independent study, part-time degree program, student-designed majors, study abroad, summer session for credit.
Library Bill & Margot Lee Library.
Student Life *Housing Options:* men-only, women-only. Campus housing is university owned. *Activities and Organizations:* drama/theater group, student-run newspaper, choral group, Phi Theta Kappa, Students in Free Enterprise (SIFE), Baptist Student Union, Student Senate, Student Ambassadors. *Campus security:* 24-hour patrols.
Athletics Member NJCAA. *Intercollegiate sports:* baseball M(s), basketball W(s), soccer M(s).
Costs (2015–16) *Tuition:* area resident $2460 full-time, $82 per credit hour part-time; state resident $3660 full-time, $122 per credit hour part-time; nonresident $3660 full-time, $122 per credit hour part-time. *Required fees:* $480 full-time, $16 per credit hour part-time. *Room and board:* $3200; room only: $2200. Room and board charges vary according to board plan and housing facility. *Payment plan:* installment. *Waivers:* senior citizens and employees or children of employees.
Financial Aid Of all full-time matriculated undergraduates who enrolled in 2014, 150 Federal Work-Study jobs (averaging $1000).
Applying *Application fee:* $25. *Required:* high school transcript. *Application deadlines:* rolling (freshmen), rolling (transfers). *Notification:* continuous (freshmen).
Freshman Application Contact Mr. Jim Riggs, Admissions Coordinator, Crowder College, Neosho, MO 64850. *Phone:* 417-451-3223 Ext. 5466. *Toll-free phone:* 866-238-7788. *Fax:* 417-455-5731. *E-mail:* jimriggs@crowder.edu. *Website:* http://www.crowder.edu/.

Culinary Institute of St. Louis at Hickey College
St. Louis, Missouri

- **Private** 2-year, founded 2009
- **Suburban** campus
- **Coed,** 95 undergraduate students
- **81% of applicants were admitted**

Freshmen *Admission:* 211 applied, 171 admitted.
Majors Cooking and related culinary arts.
Academics *Calendar:* semesters. *Degree:* associate.
Freshman Application Contact Admissions Office, Culinary Institute of St. Louis at Hickey College, 2700 North Lindbergh Boulevard, St. Louis, MO 63114. *Phone:* 314-434-2212. *Website:* http://www.ci-stl.com/.

East Central College
Union, Missouri

- **District-supported** 2-year, founded 1959
- **Rural** 207-acre campus with easy access to St. Louis
- **Endowment** $3.0 million
- **Coed,** 3,222 undergraduate students, 47% full-time, 61% women, 39% men

Undergraduates 1,508 full-time, 1,714 part-time. Students come from 3 states and territories; 1% Black or African American, non-Hispanic/Latino; 2% Hispanic/Latino; 0.5% Asian, non-Hispanic/Latino; 0.8% American Indian or Alaska Native, non-Hispanic/Latino; 0.1% Two or more races, non-Hispanic/Latino; 0.9% Race/ethnicity unknown; 0.1% international; 5% transferred in.
Freshmen *Admission:* 686 admitted, 686 enrolled.
Faculty *Total:* 231, 30% full-time, 7% with terminal degrees. *Student/faculty ratio:* 17:1.
Majors Accounting technology and bookkeeping; administrative assistant and secretarial science; automobile/automotive mechanics technology; biology/biotechnology laboratory technician; business/commerce; chemical technology; child-care and support services management; commercial and advertising art; computer systems networking and telecommunications; construction trades; construction trades related; culinary arts; drafting and design technology; education; emergency medical technology (EMT paramedic); engineering; fine/studio arts; fire science/firefighting; general studies; health information/medical records technology; heating, air conditioning, ventilation and refrigeration maintenance technology; heavy/industrial equipment maintenance technologies related; machine tool technology; medical/clinical assistant; medical radiologic technology; music; occupational therapist assistant; precision production related; registered

nursing/registered nurse; respiratory care therapy; technical teacher education; welding technology.

Academics *Calendar:* semesters. *Degree:* certificates and associate. *Special study options:* academic remediation for entering students, adult/continuing education programs, advanced placement credit, distance learning, English as a second language, honors programs, independent study, internships, off-campus study, part-time degree program, services for LD students, study abroad, summer session for credit.

Library East Central College Library. *Books:* 25,006 (physical), 186,259 (digital/electronic); *Serial titles:* 87 (physical), 3 (digital/electronic); *Databases:* 38. Weekly public service hours: 55; students can reserve study rooms.

Student Life *Housing:* college housing not available. *Activities and Organizations:* drama/theater group, student-run newspaper, choral group, AHERO Club, Art Club, Phi Theta Kappa, R&R Club, Student Government Association. *Campus security:* 24-hour emergency response devices, late-night transport/escort service. *Student services:* personal/psychological counseling.

Athletics Member NJCAA. *Intercollegiate sports:* soccer M(s), softball W(s), volleyball W(s).

Costs (2015–16) *Tuition:* area resident $1824 full-time; state resident $2664 full-time; nonresident $4032 full-time. Full-time tuition and fees vary according to program. Part-time tuition and fees vary according to program. *Required fees:* $456 full-time. *Waivers:* senior citizens and employees or children of employees.

Applying *Options:* electronic application, early admission, deferred entrance. *Required:* high school transcript. *Application deadlines:* rolling (freshmen), rolling (transfers).

Freshman Application Contact Mr. Nathaniel Mitchell, Director, Admissions, East Central College, 1964 Prairie Dell Road, Union, MO 63084. *Phone:* 636-584-6552. *E-mail:* nathaniel.mitchell@eastcentral.edu. *Website:* http://www.eastcentral.edu/.

Everest College
Springfield, Missouri

Freshman Application Contact Admissions Office, Everest College, 1010 West Sunshine Street, Springfield, MO 65807. *Phone:* 417-864-7220. *Toll-free phone:* 888-741-4270. *Fax:* 417-864-5697. *Website:* http://www.everest.edu/.

Heritage College
Kansas City, Missouri

Freshman Application Contact Admissions Office, Heritage College, 1200 East 104th Street, Suite 150, Kansas City, MO 64131. *Phone:* 816-942-5474. *Toll-free phone:* 888-334-7339. *E-mail:* info@heritage-education.com. *Website:* http://www.heritagecollege.edu/.

IHM Academy of EMS
St. Louis, Missouri

Freshman Application Contact Admissions Director, IHM Academy of EMS, 2500 Abbott Place, St. Louis, MO 63143. *Phone:* 314-768-1234. *Fax:* 314-768-1595. *E-mail:* info@ihmhealthstudies.edu. *Website:* http://www.ihmacademyofems.net/.

ITT Technical Institute
Arnold, Missouri

Freshman Application Contact Director of Recruitment, ITT Technical Institute, 1930 Meyer Drury Drive, Arnold, MO 63010. *Phone:* 636-464-6600. *Toll-free phone:* 888-488-1082. *Website:* http://www.itt-tech.edu/.

ITT Technical Institute
Earth City, Missouri

Freshman Application Contact Director of Recruitment, ITT Technical Institute, 3640 Corporate Trail Drive, Earth City, MO 63045. *Phone:* 314-298-7800. *Toll-free phone:* 800-235-5488. *Website:* http://www.itt-tech.edu/.

ITT Technical Institute
Kansas City, Missouri

Freshman Application Contact Director of Recruitment, ITT Technical Institute, 9150 East 41st Terrace, Kansas City, MO 64133. *Phone:* 816-276-1400. *Toll-free phone:* 877-488-1442. *Website:* http://www.itt-tech.edu/.

Jefferson College
Hillsboro, Missouri

- **District-supported** 2-year, founded 1963
- **Rural** 455-acre campus with easy access to St. Louis
- **Endowment** $689,969
- **Coed,** 4,705 undergraduate students, 49% full-time, 59% women, 41% men

Undergraduates 2,287 full-time, 2,418 part-time. 2% Black or African American, non-Hispanic/Latino; 0.4% Hispanic/Latino; 0.8% Asian, non-Hispanic/Latino; 0.1% Native Hawaiian or other Pacific Islander, non-Hispanic/Latino; 0.6% American Indian or Alaska Native, non-Hispanic/Latino; 5% Race/ethnicity unknown; 0.3% international.

Freshmen *Admission:* 980 enrolled.

Faculty *Total:* 353, 28% full-time, 9% with terminal degrees. *Student/faculty ratio:* 17:1.

Majors Accounting technology and bookkeeping; administrative assistant and secretarial science; automobile/automotive mechanics technology; biomedical technology; business administration and management; business/commerce; CAD/CADD drafting/design technology; child-care and support services management; computer systems networking and telecommunications; criminal justice/law enforcement administration; criminal justice/police science; culinary arts; cyber/computer forensics and counterterrorism; education; education (specific levels and methods) related; electrical, electronic and communications engineering technology; emergency medical technology (EMT paramedic); engineering; fire prevention and safety technology; health information/medical records technology; heating, air conditioning, ventilation and refrigeration maintenance technology; industrial mechanics and maintenance technology; information technology; legal administrative assistant/secretary; liberal arts and sciences/liberal studies; licensed practical/vocational nurse training; machine tool technology; manufacturing engineering technology; medical administrative assistant and medical secretary; occupational therapist assistant; office occupations and clerical services; physical therapy technology; precision production related; radiologic technology/science; registered nursing/registered nurse; veterinary/animal health technology; welding technology.

Academics *Calendar:* semesters. *Degree:* certificates, diplomas, and associate. *Special study options:* academic remediation for entering students, adult/continuing education programs, advanced placement credit, distance learning, English as a second language, freshman honors college, honors programs, internships, off-campus study, part-time degree program, services for LD students, summer session for credit.

Library Jefferson College Library plus 1 other. *Books:* 75,216 (physical), 183,744 (digital/electronic); *Serial titles:* 54 (physical), 31,939 (digital/electronic); *Databases:* 62. Weekly public service hours: 66; students can reserve study rooms.

Student Life *Housing Options:* coed. Campus housing is university owned. *Activities and Organizations:* drama/theater group, student-run newspaper, television station, choral group, Student Senate, Nursing Associations, Baptist Student Unit, Phi Theta Kappa, National Technical Honors Society, national sororities. *Campus security:* 24-hour patrols, campus police department. *Student services:* health clinic, personal/psychological counseling.

Athletics Member NJCAA. *Intercollegiate sports:* baseball M(s), basketball W(s), cheerleading M(s)/W(s), soccer M(s), softball W(s), volleyball W(s).

Costs (2016–17) *One-time required fee:* $25. *Tuition:* area resident $2910 full-time, $97 per credit hour part-time; state resident $4380 full-time, $146 per credit hour part-time; nonresident $5820 full-time, $194 per credit hour part-time. Full-time tuition and fees vary according to course load and program. Part-time tuition and fees vary according to course load and program. *Required fees:* $90 full-time, $3 per credit hour part-time, $10 per term part-time. *Room and board:* $5644. Room and board charges vary according to housing facility. *Payment plan:* installment. *Waivers:* senior citizens and employees or children of employees.

Financial Aid Of all full-time matriculated undergraduates who enrolled in 2014, 2,268 applied for aid, 1,767 were judged to have need, 59 had their need fully met. 81 Federal Work-Study jobs (averaging $1430). 98 state and other part-time jobs (averaging $1861). In 2014, 154 non-need-based awards were made. *Average percent of need met:* 56%. *Average financial aid package:* $5094. *Average need-based loan:* $3155. *Average need-based gift aid:* $2539. *Average non-need-based aid:* $1908.

Applying *Options:* electronic application, early admission. *Application fee:* $25. *Required:* high school transcript. *Application deadlines:* rolling (freshmen), rolling (transfers).

Freshman Application Contact Dr. Kimberly Harvey, Director of Student Records and Admissions Services, Jefferson College, 1000 Viking Drive, Hillsboro, MO 63050-2441. *Phone:* 636-481-3205 Ext. 3205. *Fax:* 636-789-5103. *E-mail:* admissions@jeffco.edu.
Website: http://www.jeffco.edu/.

L'Ecole Culinaire–Kansas City

Kansas City, Missouri

Admissions Office Contact L'Ecole Culinaire–Kansas City, 310 Ward Parkway, Kansas City, MO 64112-2110.
Website: http://www.lecole.edu/kansas-city/.

L'Ecole Culinaire–St. Louis

St. Louis, Missouri

Admissions Office Contact L'Ecole Culinaire–St. Louis, 9811 South Forty Drive, St. Louis, MO 63124.
Website: http://www.lecole.edu/st-louis/.

Metro Business College

Cape Girardeau, Missouri

Director of Admissions Ms. Kyla Evans, Admissions Director, Metro Business College, 1732 North Kingshighway, Cape Girardeau, MO 63701. *Phone:* 573-334-9181. *Toll-free phone:* 888-206-4545. *Fax:* 573-334-0617.
Website: http://www.metrobusinesscollege.edu/.

Metro Business College

Jefferson City, Missouri

- **Proprietary** 2-year, founded 1979
- **Suburban** campus
- **Coed, primarily women,** 142 undergraduate students

Undergraduates Students come from 1 other state; 18% Black or African American, non-Hispanic/Latino; 2% Asian, non-Hispanic/Latino; 0.7% American Indian or Alaska Native, non-Hispanic/Latino; 4% Race/ethnicity unknown.
Faculty *Total:* 11, 55% full-time. *Student/faculty ratio:* 11:1.
Majors Business administration and management; computer and information sciences related; medical administrative assistant and medical secretary; medical insurance coding; medical office assistant.
Academics *Calendar:* continuous. *Degree:* certificates and associate. *Special study options:* academic remediation for entering students, adult/continuing education programs, advanced placement credit, independent study, internships, part-time degree program, services for LD students, summer session for credit.
Student Life *Housing:* college housing not available. *Activities and Organizations:* student-run newspaper, Student Council. *Student services:* personal/psychological counseling.
Standardized Tests *Required:* Wonderlic aptitude test (for admission).
Costs (2016–17) *Tuition:* $11,250 full-time, $278 per quarter hour part-time. Full-time tuition and fees vary according to program. Part-time tuition and fees vary according to program. No tuition increase for student's term of enrollment. *Required fees:* $125 full-time. *Payment plans:* tuition prepayment, installment, deferred payment. *Waivers:* senior citizens and employees or children of employees.
Applying *Required:* essay or personal statement, high school transcript, interview.
Freshman Application Contact Ms. Cheri Chockley, Campus Director, Metro Business College, 210 El Mercado Plaza, Jefferson City, MO 65109. *Phone:* 573-635-6600. *Toll-free phone:* 888-206-4545. *Fax:* 573-635-6999. *E-mail:* cheri@metrobusinesscollege.edu.
Website: http://www.metrobusinesscollege.edu/.

Metro Business College

Rolla, Missouri

Freshman Application Contact Admissions Office, Metro Business College, 1202 East Highway 72, Rolla, MO 65401. *Phone:* 573-364-8464. *Toll-free*

phone: 888-206-4545. *Fax:* 573-364-8077.
E-mail: inforolla@metrobusinesscollege.edu.
Website: http://www.metrobusinesscollege.edu/.

Metropolitan Community College– Kansas City

Kansas City, Missouri

Freshman Application Contact Dr. Tuesday Stanley, Vice Chancellor of Student Development and Enrollment Services, Metropolitan Community College–Kansas City, 3200 Broadway, Kansas City, MO 64111-2429. *Phone:* 816-604-1253. *E-mail:* tuesday.stanley@mcckc.edu.
Website: http://www.mcckc.edu/.

Midwest Institute

Fenton, Missouri

Freshman Application Contact Admissions Office, Midwest Institute, 964 S. Highway Drive, Fenton, MO 63026. *Toll-free phone:* 800-695-5550.
Website: http://www.midwestinstitute.com/.

Midwest Institute

St. Louis, Missouri

Freshman Application Contact Admissions Office, Midwest Institute, 4260 Shoreline Drive, St. Louis, MO 63045. *Phone:* 314-344-4440. *Toll-free phone:* 800-695-5550. *Fax:* 314-344-0495.
Website: http://www.midwestinstitute.com/.

Mineral Area College

Park Hills, Missouri

Freshman Application Contact Pam Reeder, Registrar, Mineral Area College, PO Box 1000, Park Hills, MO 63601-1000. *Phone:* 573-518-2204. *Fax:* 573-518-2166. *E-mail:* preeder@mineralarea.edu.
Website: http://www.mineralarea.edu/.

Missouri College

Brentwood, Missouri

Director of Admissions Mr. Doug Brinker, Admissions Director, Missouri College, 1405 South Hanley Road, Brentwood, MO 63117. *Phone:* 314-821-7700. *Toll-free phone:* 800-216-6732. *Fax:* 314-821-0891.
Website: http://www.missouricollege.edu/.

Missouri State University–West Plains

West Plains, Missouri

Freshman Application Contact Ms. Melissa Jett, Coordinator of Admissions, Missouri State University–West Plains, 128 Garfield, West Plains, MO 65775. *Phone:* 417-255-7955. *Toll-free phone:* 888-466-7897. *Fax:* 417-255-7959. *E-mail:* melissajett@missouristate.edu.
Website: http://wp.missouristate.edu/.

Moberly Area Community College

Moberly, Missouri

Freshman Application Contact Dr. James Grant, Dean of Student Services, Moberly Area Community College, Moberly, MO 65270-1304. *Phone:* 660-263-4110 Ext. 235. *Toll-free phone:* 800-622-2070. *Fax:* 660-263-2406. *E-mail:* info@macc.edu.
Website: http://www.macc.edu/.

North Central Missouri College

Trenton, Missouri

Freshman Application Contact Megan Goodin, Admissions Assistant, North Central Missouri College, Trenton, MO 64683. *Phone:* 660-359-3948 Ext. 1410. *E-mail:* megoodin@mail.ncmissouri.edu.
Website: http://www.ncmissouri.edu/.

Ozarks Technical Community College
Springfield, Missouri

- **District-supported** 2-year, founded 1990, part of Missouri Coordinating Board for Higher Education
- **Urban** campus
- **Endowment** $2.8 million
- **Coed,** 13,614 undergraduate students, 44% full-time, 58% women, 42% men

Undergraduates 5,950 full-time, 7,664 part-time. 2% are from out of state.
Faculty *Total:* 888, 21% full-time. *Student/faculty ratio:* 22:1.
Majors Accounting; administrative assistant and secretarial science; autobody/collision and repair technology; automobile/automotive mechanics technology; business administration and management; business machine repair; computer systems networking and telecommunications; construction engineering technology; culinary arts; diesel mechanics technology; electrical, electronic and communications engineering technology; emergency medical technology (EMT paramedic); fire science/firefighting; graphic and printing equipment operation/production; health information/medical records technology; heating, air conditioning, ventilation and refrigeration maintenance technology; heavy equipment maintenance technology; hotel/motel administration; industrial technology; information science/studies; instrumentation technology; kindergarten/preschool education; liberal arts and sciences/liberal studies; machine tool technology; management information systems; mechanical drafting and CAD/CADD; occupational therapist assistant; occupational therapy; physical sciences; physical therapy technology; radio and television broadcasting technology; respiratory care therapy; turf and turfgrass management; welding technology.
Academics *Calendar:* semesters. *Degree:* certificates, diplomas, and associate. *Special study options:* academic remediation for entering students, adult/continuing education programs, cooperative education, distance learning, double majors, English as a second language, honors programs, internships, off-campus study, part-time degree program, services for LD students, summer session for credit.
Library Main Library plus 1 other.
Student Life *Housing:* college housing not available. *Activities and Organizations:* student-run newspaper, choral group, Phi Theta Kappa. *Campus security:* 24-hour emergency response devices. *Student services:* personal/psychological counseling.
Costs (2016–17) *Tuition:* area resident $2352 full-time, $98 per credit hour part-time; state resident $3528 full-time, $147 per credit hour part-time; nonresident $4704 full-time, $196 per credit hour part-time. *Required fees:* $500 full-time, $22 per credit hour part-time, $50 per term part-time. *Payment plans:* installment, deferred payment. *Waivers:* employees or children of employees.
Financial Aid Of all full-time matriculated undergraduates who enrolled in 2014, 201 Federal Work-Study jobs.
Applying *Options:* electronic application. *Required:* high school transcript. *Application deadlines:* rolling (freshmen), rolling (out-of-state freshmen), rolling (transfers). *Notification:* continuous (freshmen), continuous (out-of-state freshmen), continuous (transfers).
Freshman Application Contact Ozarks Technical Community College, 1001 E. Chestnut Expressway, Springfield, MO 65802.
Website: http://www.otc.edu/.

Pinnacle Career Institute
Kansas City, Missouri

Director of Admissions Ms. Ruth Matous, Director of Admissions, Pinnacle Career Institute, 1001 East 101st Terrace, Suite 325, Kansas City, MO 64131. *Phone:* 816-331-5700 Ext. 212. *Toll-free phone:* 877-241-3097.
Website: http://www.pcitraining.edu/.

Pinnacle Career Institute
Kansas City, Missouri

- **Proprietary** 2-year, part of Pinnacle Career Institute
- **Suburban** campus with easy access to Kansas City
- **Coed**

Undergraduates 14% Black or African American, non-Hispanic/Latino; 9% Hispanic/Latino; 0.7% American Indian or Alaska Native, non-Hispanic/Latino; 4% Two or more races, non-Hispanic/Latino; 0.7% Race/ethnicity unknown.
Academics *Calendar:* monthly modules. *Degree:* certificates, diplomas, and associate.

Applying *Options:* electronic application. *Required:* high school transcript, interview.
Freshman Application Contact Pinnacle Career Institute, 11500 NW. Ambassador, Suite 221, Kansas City, MO 64153. *Phone:* 816-331-5700. *Website:* http://www.pcitraining.edu/.

Ranken Technical College
St. Louis, Missouri

- **Independent** primarily 2-year, founded 1907
- **Urban** 10-acre campus
- **Coed, primarily men,** 1,743 undergraduate students

Majors Architectural engineering technology; autobody/collision and repair technology; automobile/automotive mechanics technology; business administration and management; carpentry; communications systems installation and repair technology; computer engineering technology; heating, air conditioning, ventilation and refrigeration maintenance technology; heavy/industrial equipment maintenance technologies related; industrial electronics technology; instrumentation technology; machine tool technology.
Academics *Calendar:* semesters. *Degrees:* certificates, associate, and bachelor's. *Special study options:* academic remediation for entering students, adult/continuing education programs, advanced placement credit, cooperative education, distance learning, independent study, internships, part-time degree program, services for LD students, summer session for credit.
Library Ashley Gray, Jr. Learning Center.
Student Life *Housing Options:* men-only, women-only. Campus housing is provided by a third party. *Activities and Organizations:* student-run newspaper. *Campus security:* 24-hour emergency response devices and patrols. *Student services:* personal/psychological counseling, women's center.
Financial Aid Of all full-time matriculated undergraduates who enrolled in 2014, 30 Federal Work-Study jobs (averaging $2000).
Applying *Options:* electronic application. *Application fee:* $25. *Required:* essay or personal statement, high school transcript, interview. *Application deadline:* rolling (freshmen). *Notification:* continuous (transfers).
Freshman Application Contact Ranken Technical College, 4431 Finney Avenue, St. Louis, MO 63113. *Phone:* 314-371-0233 Ext. 4811. *Toll-free phone:* 866-4-RANKEN.
Website: http://www.ranken.edu/.

St. Charles Community College
Cottleville, Missouri

- **State-supported** 2-year, founded 1986, part of Missouri Coordinating Board for Higher Education
- **Suburban** 228-acre campus with easy access to St. Louis
- **Endowment** $77,955
- **Coed,** 6,865 undergraduate students, 50% full-time, 56% women, 44% men

Undergraduates 3,426 full-time, 3,439 part-time. Students come from 23 states and territories; 33 other countries; 6% Black or African American, non-Hispanic/Latino; 4% Hispanic/Latino; 2% Asian, non-Hispanic/Latino; 0.1% Native Hawaiian or other Pacific Islander, non-Hispanic/Latino; 0.3% American Indian or Alaska Native, non-Hispanic/Latino; 3% Two or more races, non-Hispanic/Latino; 3% Race/ethnicity unknown; 1% international; 7% transferred in.
Freshmen *Admission:* 2,644 applied, 2,644 admitted, 1,504 enrolled.
Faculty *Total:* 380, 28% full-time, 20% with terminal degrees. *Student/faculty ratio:* 22:1.
Majors Accounting technology and bookkeeping; biology/biological sciences; chemistry; child-care and support services management; child-care provision; civil engineering; commercial and advertising art; computer programming; criminal justice/police science; drafting and design technology; dramatic/theater arts; economics; education (specific subject areas) related; emergency medical technology (EMT paramedic); engineering; English; fire science/firefighting; foreign languages and literatures; French; general studies; health information/medical records technology; history; human services; industrial technology; liberal arts and sciences/liberal studies; marketing/marketing management; mathematics; mechanical engineering; music history, literature, and theory; occupational therapist assistant; office management; philosophy; political science and government; precision production related; pre-pharmacy studies; psychology; registered nursing/registered nurse; rhetoric and composition; social work; sociology; Spanish; teacher assistant/aide; welding technology.
Academics *Calendar:* semesters. *Degree:* certificates and associate. *Special study options:* academic remediation for entering students, adult/continuing education programs, advanced placement credit, cooperative education, distance learning, double majors, English as a second language, honors programs, independent study, internships, part-time degree program, services for LD students, study abroad, summer session for credit.

Library Paul and Helen Schnare Library. *Books:* 67,926 (physical), 30,148 (digital/electronic); *Serial titles:* 348 (physical), 240,258 (digital/electronic); *Databases:* 42. Weekly public service hours: 72.

Student Life *Activities and Organizations:* drama/theater group, student-run newspaper, choral group, Phi Theta Kappa, Student Nurse Organization, GAMES Club, SAGE (Straights and Gays for Equality), Student Veterans Organization. *Campus security:* 24-hour emergency response devices and patrols, late-night transport/escort service, campus police officers on duty during normal operating hours. *Student services:* personal/psychological counseling.

Athletics Member NJCAA. *Intercollegiate sports:* baseball M(s), soccer M(s)/W(s), softball W(s).

Costs (2015–16) *Tuition:* area resident $2352 full-time, $98 per credit part-time; state resident $3528 full-time, $147 per credit part-time; nonresident $5160 full-time, $215 per credit part-time. Full-time tuition and fees vary according to course load and program. Part-time tuition and fees vary according to course load and program. *Required fees:* $120 full-time, $5 per credit part-time. *Payment plan:* installment. *Waivers:* senior citizens and employees or children of employees.

Financial Aid Of all full-time matriculated undergraduates who enrolled in 2013, 33 Federal Work-Study jobs.

Applying *Options:* electronic application, early admission, deferred entrance. *Application fee:* $10. *Required for some:* high school transcript, minimum 2.5 GPA. *Recommended:* high school transcript. *Application deadlines:* rolling (freshmen), rolling (out-of-state freshmen), rolling (transfers). *Notification:* continuous (freshmen), continuous (out-of-state freshmen), continuous (transfers).

Freshman Application Contact Ms. Kathy Brockgreitens-Gober, Dean of Enrollment Services, St. Charles Community College, 4601 Mid Rivers Mall Drive, Cottleville, MO 63376-0975. *Phone:* 636-922-8229. *Fax:* 636-922-8236. *E-mail:* regist@stchas.edu.
Website: http://www.stchas.edu/.

St. Louis College of Health Careers
Fenton, Missouri

Admissions Office Contact St. Louis College of Health Careers, 1297 North Highway Drive, Fenton, MO 63026.
Website: http://www.slchc.com/.

St. Louis College of Health Careers
St. Louis, Missouri

Freshman Application Contact Admissions Office, St. Louis College of Health Careers, 909 South Taylor Avenue, St. Louis, MO 63110-1511. *Phone:* 314-652-0300. *Toll-free phone:* 888-789-4820. *Fax:* 314-652-4825.
Website: http://www.slchc.com/.

St. Louis Community College
St. Louis, Missouri

- **Public** 2-year, part of St. Louis Community College System
- **Suburban** campus with easy access to St. Louis
- **Coed,** 18,902 undergraduate students, 40% full-time, 59% women, 41% men

Undergraduates 7,653 full-time, 11,249 part-time. Students come from 25 states and territories; 102 other countries; 2% are from out of state; 33% Black or African American, non-Hispanic/Latino; 3% Hispanic/Latino; 4% Asian, non-Hispanic/Latino; 0.1% Native Hawaiian or other Pacific Islander, non-Hispanic/Latino; 0.4% American Indian or Alaska Native, non-Hispanic/Latino; 4% Two or more races, non-Hispanic/Latino; 0.7% Race/ethnicity unknown; 1% international; 9% transferred in. *Retention:* 53% of full-time freshmen returned.

Freshmen *Admission:* 3,052 enrolled.

Faculty *Total:* 1,385, 30% full-time. *Student/faculty ratio:* 17:1.

Academics *Calendar:* semesters. *Degree:* certificates and associate. *Special study options:* academic remediation for entering students, accelerated degree program, adult/continuing education programs, advanced placement credit, distance learning, English as a second language, honors programs, independent study, internships, part-time degree program, services for LD students, study abroad, summer session for credit.

Student Life *Housing:* college housing not available. *Activities and Organizations:* drama/theater group, student-run newspaper. *Campus security:* 24-hour emergency response devices, late-night transport/escort service. *Student services:* personal/psychological counseling.

Athletics Member NJCAA. *Intercollegiate sports:* baseball M(s), basketball M(s)/W(s), soccer M(s)/W(s), softball W(s), volleyball W(s).

Costs (2015–16) *Tuition:* area resident $2700 full-time, $90 per credit part-time; state resident $4080 full-time, $136 per credit part-time; nonresident $5760 full-time, $192 per credit part-time. Full-time tuition and fees vary according to course load. Part-time tuition and fees vary according to course load. *Required fees:* $390 full-time, $13 per credit part-time. *Payment plan:* installment. *Waivers:* senior citizens and employees or children of employees.

Applying *Options:* electronic application. *Required for some:* high school transcript, interview. *Application deadlines:* rolling (freshmen), rolling (out-of-state freshmen), rolling (transfers). *Notification:* continuous (freshmen), continuous (out-of-state freshmen), continuous (transfers).

Freshman Application Contact St. Louis Community College, 300 South Broadway, St. Louis, MO 63102.
Website: http://www.stlcc.edu/.

Southeast Missouri Hospital College of Nursing and Health Sciences
Cape Girardeau, Missouri

Freshman Application Contact Southeast Missouri Hospital College of Nursing and Health Sciences, 2001 William Street, Cape Girardeau, MO 63701. *Phone:* 573-334-6825 Ext. 12.
Website: http://www.sehcollege.edu/.

State Fair Community College
Sedalia, Missouri

- **District-supported** 2-year, founded 1966, part of Missouri Coordinating Board for Higher Education
- **Small-town** 128-acre campus
- **Endowment** $12.5 million
- **Coed**

Undergraduates 2,506 full-time, 2,477 part-time. Students come from 15 states and territories; 2 other countries; 4% Black or African American, non-Hispanic/Latino; 2% Hispanic/Latino; 0.7% Asian, non-Hispanic/Latino; 0.2% Native Hawaiian or other Pacific Islander, non-Hispanic/Latino; 0.7% American Indian or Alaska Native, non-Hispanic/Latino; 6% Two or more races, non-Hispanic/Latino; 0.3% Race/ethnicity unknown; 7% transferred in. *Retention:* 59% of full-time freshmen returned.

Faculty *Student/faculty ratio:* 32:1.

Academics *Calendar:* semesters. *Degree:* certificates and associate. *Special study options:* academic remediation for entering students, adult/continuing education programs, advanced placement credit, distance learning, English as a second language, internships, off-campus study, part-time degree program, services for LD students, summer session for credit.

Library Donald C. Proctor Library.

Student Life *Campus security:* 24-hour emergency response devices, controlled dormitory access, Campus Safety Officer on campus M-Th from 11 am - 10 pm, security during evening class hours.

Athletics Member NJCAA.

Costs (2015–16) *Tuition:* area resident $3000 full-time, $100 per credit hour part-time; state resident $4200 full-time, $140 per credit hour part-time; nonresident $6000 full-time, $200 per credit hour part-time. *Required fees:* $300 full-time, $10 per credit hour part-time. *Room and board:* $6250. Room and board charges vary according to location.

Financial Aid Of all full-time matriculated undergraduates who enrolled in 2013, 87 Federal Work-Study jobs (averaging $1148).

Applying *Options:* electronic application.

Freshman Application Contact State Fair Community College, 3201 West 16th Street, Sedalia, MO 65301-2199. *Phone:* 660-596-7379. *Toll-free phone:* 877-311-7322.
Website: http://www.sfccmo.edu/.

State Technical College of Missouri
Linn, Missouri

Freshman Application Contact State Technical College of Missouri, One Technology Drive, Linn, MO 65051-9606. *Phone:* 573-897-5196. *Toll-free phone:* 800-743-TECH.
Website: http://www.statetechmo.edu/.

Texas County Technical College
Houston, Missouri

Admissions Office Contact Texas County Technical College, 6915 S. Hwy 63, Houston, MO 65483.
Website: http://www.texascountytech.edu/.

Three Rivers Community College
Poplar Bluff, Missouri

Freshman Application Contact Ms. Marcia Fields, Director of Admissions and Recruiting, Three Rivers Community College, Poplar Bluff, MO 63901. *Phone:* 573-840-9675. *Toll-free phone:* 877-TRY-TRCC.
E-mail: trytrcc@trcc.edu.
Website: http://www.trcc.edu/.

Vatterott College
Berkeley, Missouri

Director of Admissions Ann Farajallah, Director of Admissions, Vatterott College, 8580 Evans Avenue, Berkeley, MO 63134. *Phone:* 314-264-1020. *Toll-free phone:* 888-553-6627.
Website: http://www.vatterott.edu/.

Vatterott College
Joplin, Missouri

Admissions Office Contact Vatterott College, 809 Illinois Avenue, Joplin, MO 64801. *Toll-free phone:* 800-934-6975.
Website: http://www.vatterott.edu/.

Vatterott College
Kansas City, Missouri

Admissions Office Contact Vatterott College, 4131 N. Corrington Avenue, Kansas City, MO 64117. *Toll-free phone:* 888-553-6627.
Website: http://www.vatterott.edu/.

Vatterott College
St. Charles, Missouri

Director of Admissions Gertrude Bogan-Jones, Director of Admissions, Vatterott College, 3550 West Clay Street, St. Charles, MO 63301. *Phone:* 636-978-7488. *Toll-free phone:* 888-553-6627. *Fax:* 636-978-5121.
E-mail: ofallon@vatterott-college.edu.
Website: http://www.vatterott.edu/.

Vatterott College
St. Joseph, Missouri

Director of Admissions Director of Admissions, Vatterott College, 3709 Belt Highway, St. Joseph, MO 64506. *Phone:* 816-364-5399. *Toll-free phone:* 888-553-6627. *Fax:* 816-364-1593.
Website: http://www.vatterott.edu/.

Vatterott College
Springfield, Missouri

Freshman Application Contact Mr. Scott Lester, Director of Admissions, Vatterott College, 3850 South Campbell Avenue, Springfield, MO 65807. *Phone:* 417-831-8116. *Toll-free phone:* 888-553-6627. *Fax:* 417-831-5099.
E-mail: springfield@vatterott-college.edu.
Website: http://www.vatterott.edu/.

Vatterott College
Sunset Hills, Missouri

Director of Admissions Director of Admission, Vatterott College, 12900 Maurer Industrial Drive, Sunset Hills, MO 63127. *Phone:* 314-843-4200. *Toll-free phone:* 888-553-6627. *Fax:* 314-843-1709.
Website: http://www.vatterott.edu/.

Vet Tech Institute at Hickey College
St. Louis, Missouri

- **Private** 2-year, founded 2007
- **Suburban** campus
- **Coed,** 167 undergraduate students
- **58% of applicants were admitted**

Freshmen *Admission:* 474 applied, 274 admitted.
Majors Veterinary/animal health technology.

Academics *Calendar:* semesters. *Degree:* associate. *Special study options:* accelerated degree program, internships.
Freshman Application Contact Admissions Office, Vet Tech Institute at Hickey College, 2780 North Lindbergh Boulevard, St. Louis, MO 63114. *Phone:* 888-884-1459. *Toll-free phone:* 888-884-1459.
Website: http://stlouis.vettechinstitute.edu/.

WellSpring School of Allied Health
Kansas City, Missouri

Admissions Office Contact WellSpring School of Allied Health, 9140 Ward Parkway, Suite 100, Kansas City, MO 64114.
Website: http://www.wellspring.edu/.

Wentworth Military Academy and College
Lexington, Missouri

Freshman Application Contact Capt. Mike Bellis, College Admissions Director, Wentworth Military Academy and College, 1880 Washington Avenue, Lexington, MO 64067. *Phone:* 660-259-2221 Ext. 1351. *Fax:* 660-259-2677. *E-mail:* admissions@wma.edu.
Website: http://www.wma.edu/.

MONTANA

Aaniiih Nakoda College
Harlem, Montana

Director of Admissions Ms. Dixie Brockie, Registrar and Admissions Officer, Aaniiih Nakoda College, PO Box 159, Harlem, MT 59526-0159. *Phone:* 406-353-2607 Ext. 233. *Fax:* 406-353-2898. *E-mail:* dbrockie@mail.fbcc.edu.
Website: http://www.ancollege.edu/.

Blackfeet Community College
Browning, Montana

Freshman Application Contact Ms. Deana M. McNabb, Registrar and Admissions Officer, Blackfeet Community College, PO Box 819, Browning, MT 59417-0819. *Phone:* 406-338-5421. *Toll-free phone:* 800-549-7457. *Fax:* 406-338-3272.
Website: http://www.bfcc.edu/.

Chief Dull Knife College
Lame Deer, Montana

Freshman Application Contact Director of Admissions, Chief Dull Knife College, PO Box 98, 1 College Drive, Lame Deer, MT 59043-0098. *Phone:* 406-477-6215.
Website: http://www.cdkc.edu/.

Dawson Community College
Glendive, Montana

- **State and locally supported** 2-year, founded 1940
- **Rural** 300-acre campus
- **Endowment** $3.5 million
- **Coed,** 304 undergraduate students, 53% full-time, 47% women, 53% men

Undergraduates 162 full-time, 142 part-time. Students come from 20 states and territories; 5 other countries; 35% are from out of state; 4% Black or African American, non-Hispanic/Latino; 6% Hispanic/Latino; 2% Asian, non-Hispanic/Latino; 1% American Indian or Alaska Native, non-Hispanic/Latino; 2% Two or more races, non-Hispanic/Latino; 2% Race/ethnicity unknown; 3% international; 17% transferred in.
Freshmen *Admission:* 319 applied, 319 admitted, 82 enrolled.
Faculty *Total:* 33, 33% full-time, 3% with terminal degrees. *Student/faculty ratio:* 16:1.
Majors Agricultural business and management; business/commerce; childcare provision; clinical/medical social work; community psychology; computer and information sciences; computer and information sciences related; criminal justice/police science; liberal arts and sciences/liberal studies; music; substance abuse/addiction counseling; welding technology.
Academics *Calendar:* semesters. *Degree:* certificates and associate. *Special study options:* academic remediation for entering students, adult/continuing

education programs, distance learning, independent study, internships, part-time degree program, services for LD students, summer session for credit.

Library Jane Carey Memorial Library plus 1 other. *Books:* 33,477 (physical), 13,359 (digital/electronic); *Serial titles:* 81 (physical); *Databases:* 118. Weekly public service hours: 40; students can reserve study rooms.

Student Life *Housing Options:* coed. Campus housing is university owned. *Activities and Organizations:* drama/theater group, choral group, Phi Theta Kappa, Associated Student Body, Rodeo Club, Law Enforcement Club, Campus Corp. *Campus security:* 24-hour emergency response devices.

Athletics Member NJCAA. *Intercollegiate sports:* baseball M, basketball M(s)/W(s), equestrian sports M(s)/W(s), softball W. *Intramural sports:* basketball M/W, bowling M/W, golf M/W, racquetball M/W, softball M/W, table tennis M/W, tennis M/W, volleyball M/W.

Costs (2015–16) *Tuition:* area resident $1950 full-time, $65 per credit hour part-time; state resident $3345 full-time, $112 per credit hour part-time; nonresident $9195 full-time, $307 per credit hour part-time. *Required fees:* $1620 full-time, $54 per credit hour part-time. *Room and board:* $5575; room only: $2500.

Financial Aid Of all full-time matriculated undergraduates who enrolled in 2014, 138 applied for aid, 103 were judged to have need, 9 had their need fully met. 51 Federal Work-Study jobs (averaging $1917). 33 state and other part-time jobs (averaging $1583). In 2014, 29 non-need-based awards were made. *Average percent of need met:* 91%. *Average financial aid package:* $13,648. *Average need-based loan:* $2866. *Average need-based gift aid:* $4929. *Average non-need-based aid:* $803.

Applying *Options:* electronic application, deferred entrance. *Application fee:* $30. *Required:* high school transcript. *Application deadlines:* rolling (freshmen), rolling (transfers). *Notification:* continuous (freshmen), continuous (transfers).

Freshman Application Contact Mrs. Daneen Peterson, Admissions Specialist, Dawson Community College, 300 College Drive, Glendive, MT 59330. *Phone:* 406-377-9411. *Toll-free phone:* 800-821-8320. *Fax:* 406-377-8132. *E-mail:* dpeterson@dawson.edu. *Website:* http://www.dawson.edu/.

Flathead Valley Community College
Kalispell, Montana

Freshman Application Contact Ms. Marlene C. Stoltz, Admissions/Graduation Coordinator, Flathead Valley Community College, 777 Grandview Drive, Kalispell, MT 59901-2622. *Phone:* 406-756-3846. *Toll-free phone:* 800-313-3822. *E-mail:* mstoltz@fvcc.cc.mt.us. *Website:* http://www.fvcc.edu/.

Fort Peck Community College
Poplar, Montana

Director of Admissions Mr. Robert McAnally, Vice President for Student Services, Fort Peck Community College, PO Box 398, Poplar, MT 59255-0398. *Phone:* 406-768-6329. *Website:* http://www.fpcc.edu/.

Great Falls College Montana State University
Great Falls, Montana

- **State-supported** 2-year, founded 1969, part of Montana University System
- **Small-town** 40-acre campus
- **Endowment** $11,300
- **Coed,** 1,657 undergraduate students, 45% full-time, 72% women, 28% men

Undergraduates 743 full-time, 914 part-time. Students come from 27 states and territories; 1 other country; 1% are from out of state; 1% Black or African American, non-Hispanic/Latino; 5% Hispanic/Latino; 1% Asian, non-Hispanic/Latino; 0.1% Native Hawaiian or other Pacific Islander, non-Hispanic/Latino; 4% American Indian or Alaska Native, non-Hispanic/Latino; 4% Two or more races, non-Hispanic/Latino; 2% Race/ethnicity unknown; 8% transferred in. *Retention:* 39% of full-time freshmen returned.

Freshmen *Admission:* 441 applied, 421 admitted, 232 enrolled.

Faculty *Total:* 123, 40% full-time. *Student/faculty ratio:* 14:1.

Majors Accounting technology and bookkeeping; computer systems networking and telecommunications; dental hygiene; emergency medical technology (EMT paramedic); entrepreneurship; health information/medical records technology; information technology; liberal arts and sciences and humanities related; licensed practical/vocational nurse training; medical/clinical assistant; physical therapy technology; radiologic technology/science; respiratory care therapy; surgical technology; welding technology.

Academics *Calendar:* semesters. *Degree:* certificates and associate. *Special study options:* academic remediation for entering students, advanced placement credit, distance learning, double majors, independent study, internships, off-campus study, part-time degree program, services for LD students, summer session for credit.

Library Weaver Library plus 1 other.

Student Life *Activities and Organizations:* choral group, The Associated Students of Great Falls College Montana State University, Phi Theta Kappa Honorary, Physical Therapy Assistant Club, Dental Hygiene Assistant Club, Nursing Club. *Campus security:* 24-hour emergency response devices.

Costs (2015–16) *Tuition:* state resident $2496 full-time, $104 per credit part-time; nonresident $8748 full-time, $364 per credit part-time. Full-time tuition and fees vary according to course load, location, and program. Part-time tuition and fees vary according to course load, location, and program. *Required fees:* $634 full-time, $89 per credit part-time. *Payment plan:* deferred payment. *Waivers:* minority students, senior citizens, and employees or children of employees.

Financial Aid Of all full-time matriculated undergraduates who enrolled in 2013, 783 applied for aid, 708 were judged to have need, 17 had their need fully met. In 2013, 3 non-need-based awards were made. *Average percent of need met:* 71%. *Average financial aid package:* $9632. *Average need-based loan:* $3079. *Average need-based gift aid:* $5339. *Average non-need-based aid:* $400. *Average indebtedness upon graduation:* $22,219.

Applying *Options:* electronic application, early admission. *Application fee:* $30. *Required:* high school transcript, proof of immunization. *Application deadlines:* rolling (freshmen), rolling (out-of-state freshmen), rolling (transfers). *Notification:* continuous (freshmen), continuous (out-of-state freshmen), continuous (transfers).

Freshman Application Contact Mr. Joe Simonsen, Admissions, Great Falls College Montana State University, 2100 16th Avenue South, Great Falls, MT 59405. *Phone:* 406-771-4309. *Toll-free phone:* 800-446-2698. *Fax:* 406-771-2267. *E-mail:* joe.simonsen@gfcmsu.edu. *Website:* http://www.gfcmsu.edu/.

Helena College University of Montana
Helena, Montana

Freshman Application Contact Mr. Ryan Loomis, Admissions Representative/Recruiter, Helena College University of Montana, 1115 North Roberts Street, Helena, MT 59601. *Phone:* 406-447-6904. *Toll-free phone:* 800-241-4882. *Website:* http://www.umhelena.edu/.

Highlands College of Montana Tech
Butte, Montana

Admissions Office Contact Highlands College of Montana Tech, 25 Basin Creek Road, Butte, MT 59701. *Website:* http://www.mtech.edu/academics/highlands/.

Little Big Horn College
Crow Agency, Montana

Freshman Application Contact Ms. Ann Bullis, Dean of Student Services, Little Big Horn College, Box 370, 1 Forest Lane, Crow Agency, MT 59022-0370. *Phone:* 406-638-2228 Ext. 50. *Website:* http://www.lbhc.edu/.

Miles Community College
Miles City, Montana

Freshman Application Contact Mr. Haley Anderson, Admissions Representative, Miles Community College, 2715 Dickinson Street, Miles City, MT 59301. *Phone:* 406-874-6178. *Toll-free phone:* 800-541-9281. *E-mail:* andersonh@milescc.edu. *Website:* http://www.milescc.edu/.

Salish Kootenai College
Pablo, Montana

Freshman Application Contact Ms. Jackie Moran, Admissions Officer, Salish Kootenai College, PO Box 70, Pablo, MT 59855-0117. *Phone:* 406-275-4866. *Fax:* 406-275-4810. *E-mail:* jackie_moran@skc.edu. *Website:* http://www.skc.edu/.

Stone Child College
Box Elder, Montana

Director of Admissions Mr. Ted Whitford, Director of Admissions/Registrar, Stone Child College, RR1, Box 1082, Box Elder, MT 59521. *Phone:* 406-395-4313 Ext. 110. *E-mail:* uanet337@quest.ocsc.montana.edu. *Website:* http://www.stonechild.edu/.

NEBRASKA

Central Community College–Columbus Campus
Columbus, Nebraska

Freshman Application Contact Ms. Erica Leffler, Admissions/Recruiting Coordinator, Central Community College–Columbus Campus, PO Box 1027, Columbus, NE 68602-1027. *Phone:* 402-562-1296. *Toll-free phone:* 877-CCC-0780. *Fax:* 402-562-1201. *E-mail:* eleffler@cccneb.edu. *Website:* http://www.cccneb.edu/.

Central Community College–Grand Island Campus
Grand Island, Nebraska

Freshman Application Contact Michelle Lubken, Admissions Director, Central Community College–Grand Island Campus, PO Box 4903, Grand Island, NE 68802-4903. *Phone:* 308-398-7406 Ext. 406. *Toll-free phone:* 877-CCC-0780. *Fax:* 308-398-7398. *E-mail:* mlubken@cccneb.edu. *Website:* http://www.cccneb.edu/.

Central Community College–Hastings Campus
Hastings, Nebraska

Freshman Application Contact Mr. Robert Glenn, Admissions and Recruiting Director, Central Community College–Hastings Campus, PO Box 1024, East Highway 6, Hastings, NE 68902-1024. *Phone:* 402-461-2428. *Toll-free phone:* 877-CCC-0780. *E-mail:* rglenn@ccneb.edu. *Website:* http://www.cccneb.edu/.

CHI Health School of Radiologic Technology
Omaha, Nebraska

Admissions Office Contact CHI Health School of Radiologic Technology, 7500 Mercy Road, Omaha, NE 68124-9832. *Website:* http://www.chihealth.com/school-of-radiologic-technology.

ITT Technical Institute
Omaha, Nebraska

Freshman Application Contact Director of Recruitment, ITT Technical Institute, 1120 North 103rd Plaza, Suite 200, Omaha, NE 68114. *Phone:* 402-331-2900. *Toll-free phone:* 800-677-9260. *Website:* http://www.itt-tech.edu/.

Kaplan University, Lincoln
Lincoln, Nebraska

Freshman Application Contact Kaplan University, Lincoln, 1821 K Street, Lincoln, NE 68501-2826. *Phone:* 402-474-5315. *Toll-free phone:* 866-527-5268 (in-state); 800-527-5268 (out-of-state). *Website:* http://www.kaplanuniversity.edu/.

Kaplan University, Omaha
Omaha, Nebraska

Freshman Application Contact Kaplan University, Omaha, 5425 North 103rd Street, Omaha, NE 68134. *Phone:* 402-572-8500. *Toll-free phone:* 866-527-5268 (in-state); 800-527-5268 (out-of-state). *Website:* http://www.kaplanuniversity.edu/.

Little Priest Tribal College
Winnebago, Nebraska

Freshman Application Contact Little Priest Tribal College, PO Box 270, Winnebago, NE 68071. *Phone:* 402-878-2380 Ext. 112. *Website:* http://www.littlepriest.edu/.

Metropolitan Community College
Omaha, Nebraska

Freshman Application Contact Ms. Maria Vazquez, Associate Vice President for Student Affairs, Metropolitan Community College, PO Box 3777, Omaha, NE 69103-0777. *Phone:* 402-457-2430. *Toll-free phone:* 800-228-9553. *Fax:* 402-457-2238. *E-mail:* mvazquez@mccneb.edu. *Website:* http://www.mccneb.edu/.

Mid-Plains Community College
North Platte, Nebraska

- **District-supported** 2-year, founded 1973
- **Small-town** campus
- **Endowment** $6.1 million
- **Coed,** 2,235 undergraduate students, 35% full-time, 57% women, 43% men

Undergraduates 789 full-time, 1,446 part-time. Students come from 33 states and territories; 6 other countries; 10% are from out of state; 2% Black or African American, non-Hispanic/Latino; 7% Hispanic/Latino; 0.4% Asian, non-Hispanic/Latino; 0.2% Native Hawaiian or other Pacific Islander, non-Hispanic/Latino; 0.5% American Indian or Alaska Native, non-Hispanic/Latino; 2% Two or more races, non-Hispanic/Latino; 7% Race/ethnicity unknown; 1% international; 2% transferred in; 20% live on campus.

Freshmen *Admission:* 434 applied, 434 admitted.

Faculty *Total:* 305, 22% full-time, 2% with terminal degrees. *Student/faculty ratio:* 9:1.

Majors Administrative assistant and secretarial science; autobody/collision and repair technology; automobile/automotive mechanics technology; building/construction finishing, management, and inspection related; business administration and management; clinical/medical laboratory technology; commercial and advertising art; computer and information sciences; construction engineering technology; dental assisting; diesel mechanics technology; fire science/firefighting; heating, air conditioning, ventilation and refrigeration maintenance technology; liberal arts and sciences/liberal studies; licensed practical/vocational nurse training; registered nursing/registered nurse; transportation and materials moving related; welding technology.

Academics *Calendar:* semesters. *Degree:* certificates, diplomas, and associate. *Special study options:* academic remediation for entering students, accelerated degree program, adult/continuing education programs, advanced placement credit, cooperative education, distance learning, double majors, English as a second language, external degree program, independent study, internships, part-time degree program, services for LD students, summer session for credit.

Library von Riesen Library plus 1 other. *Books:* 19,824 (physical), 51,889 (digital/electronic); *Serial titles:* 53 (physical); *Databases:* 31. Weekly public service hours: 70; students can reserve study rooms.

Student Life *Housing Options:* coed, special housing for students with disabilities. Campus housing is university owned. *Activities and Organizations:* drama/theater group, choral group, Student Senate, Phi Theta Kappa, Phi Beta Lambda, Intercollegiate Athletics, MPCC Student Nurses Association, national fraternities, national sororities. *Campus security:* controlled dormitory access, patrols by trained security personnel. *Student services:* personal/psychological counseling.

Athletics Member NJCAA. *Intercollegiate sports:* baseball M(s), basketball M(s)/W(s), golf M(s), softball W(s), volleyball W(s). *Intramural sports:* baseball M, basketball M/W, softball W, volleyball W.

Standardized Tests *Required for some:* ACT Compass. *Recommended:* ACT (for admission).

Costs (2015–16) *Tuition:* state resident $2430 full-time, $81 per credit hour part-time; nonresident $3150 full-time, $105 per credit hour part-time. *Required fees:* $450 full-time, $15 per credit hour part-time. *Room and board:* $5896. Room and board charges vary according to board plan, housing facility, and location. *Payment plan:* installment. *Waivers:* senior citizens and employees or children of employees.

Financial Aid Of all full-time matriculated undergraduates who enrolled in 2014, 691 applied for aid, 564 were judged to have need, 169 had their need fully met. 38 Federal Work-Study jobs (averaging $845). In 2014, 121 non-need-based awards were made. *Average percent of need met:* 80%. *Average financial aid package:* $7021. *Average need-based loan:* $2480. *Average*

need-based gift aid: $4669. *Average non-need-based aid:* $1342. *Average indebtedness upon graduation:* $12,013.
Applying *Options:* electronic application, deferred entrance. *Required:* high school transcript. *Required for some:* 2 letters of recommendation, interview. *Application deadlines:* rolling (freshmen), rolling (out-of-state freshmen), rolling (transfers). *Notification:* continuous (freshmen), continuous (out-of-state freshmen), continuous (transfers).
Freshman Application Contact Mr. Michael Driskell, Area Recruiter, Mid-Plains Community College, 1101 Halligan Drive, North Platte, NE 69101. *Phone:* 308-535-3709. *Toll-free phone:* 800-658-4308 (in-state); 800-658-4348 (out-of-state). *Fax:* 308-534-5767. *E-mail:* driskellm@mpcc.edu. *Website:* http://www.mpcc.edu/.

Myotherapy Institute
Lincoln, Nebraska

Freshman Application Contact Admissions Office, Myotherapy Institute, 6020 South 58th Street, Lincoln, NE 68516. *Phone:* 402-421-7410. *Website:* http://www.myotherapy.edu/.

Nebraska College of Technical Agriculture
Curtis, Nebraska

Freshman Application Contact Kevin Martin, Assistant Admissions Coordinator, Nebraska College of Technical Agriculture, 404 East 7th Street, Curtis, NE 69025. *Phone:* 308-367-4124. *Toll-free phone:* 800-3CURTIS. *Website:* http://www.ncta.unl.edu/.

Nebraska Indian Community College
Macy, Nebraska

- **Federally supported** 2-year, founded 1979
- **Rural** 22-acre campus with easy access to Omaha
- **Endowment** $384,373
- **Coed**

Undergraduates 54 full-time, 66 part-time. Students come from 3 states and territories; 22% are from out of state; 14% transferred in.
Faculty *Student/faculty ratio:* 6:1.
Academics *Calendar:* semesters. *Degree:* certificates and associate. *Special study options:* academic remediation for entering students, adult/continuing education programs, double majors, independent study, internships, part-time degree program, study abroad, summer session for credit.
Library Macy Library plus 1 other.
Standardized Tests *Required:* ACT Compass testing for Math and English placement (for admission).
Costs (2015–16) *One-time required fee:* $50. *Tuition:* state resident $4080 full-time, $170 per credit hour part-time; nonresident $4080 full-time, $170 per credit hour part-time.
Applying *Required:* high school transcript, certificate of tribal enrollment if applicable.
Freshman Application Contact Troy Munhofen, Registrar, Nebraska Indian Community College, PO Box 428, Macy, NE 68039. *Phone:* 402-241-5922. *Toll-free phone:* 844-440-NICC. *Fax:* 402-837-4183. *E-mail:* tmunhofen@thenicc.edu. *Website:* http://www.thenicc.edu/.

Northeast Community College
Norfolk, Nebraska

Freshman Application Contact Ms. Tiffany Hopper, Admissions Specialist, Northeast Community College, 801 East Benjamin Avenue, PO Box 469, Norfolk, NE 68702-0469. *Phone:* 402-844-7260. *Toll-free phone:* 800-348-9033 Ext. 7260. *E-mail:* admission@northeast.edu. *Website:* http://www.northeast.edu/.

Omaha School of Massage and Healthcare of Herzing University
Omaha, Nebraska

Admissions Office Contact Omaha School of Massage and Healthcare of Herzing University, 9748 Park Drive, Omaha, NE 68127. *Website:* http://www.osmhc.com/.

Southeast Community College, Beatrice Campus
Beatrice, Nebraska

Freshman Application Contact Admissions Office, Southeast Community College, Beatrice Campus, 4771 West Scott Road, Beatrice, NE 68310. *Phone:* 402-228-3468. *Toll-free phone:* 800-233-5027. *Fax:* 402-228-2218. *Website:* http://www.southeast.edu/.

Southeast Community College, Lincoln Campus
Lincoln, Nebraska

- **District-supported** 2-year, founded 1973, part of Southeast Community College System
- **Suburban** 115-acre campus with easy access to Omaha
- **Coed,** 9,193 undergraduate students, 44% full-time, 52% women, 48% men

Undergraduates 4,086 full-time, 5,107 part-time. 7% Black or African American, non-Hispanic/Latino; 7% Hispanic/Latino; 3% Asian, non-Hispanic/Latino; 0.3% Native Hawaiian or other Pacific Islander, non-Hispanic/Latino; 1% American Indian or Alaska Native, non-Hispanic/Latino; 1% Race/ethnicity unknown.
Faculty *Total:* 707, 44% full-time. *Student/faculty ratio:* 18:1.
Majors Administrative assistant and secretarial science; automobile/automotive mechanics technology; business administration and management; child-care and support services management; clinical laboratory science/medical technology; clinical/medical laboratory technology; clinical/medical social work; commercial and advertising art; computer and information sciences; criminal justice/safety; drafting and design technology; electrical, electronic and communications engineering technology; emergency medical technology (EMT paramedic); fire science/firefighting; health/health-care administration; liberal arts and sciences/liberal studies; medical radiologic technology; network and system administration; physical therapy technology; registered nursing/registered nurse; respiratory care therapy; restaurant, culinary, and catering management; surgical technology; welding technology.
Academics *Calendar:* quarters. *Degree:* certificates, diplomas, and associate. *Special study options:* academic remediation for entering students, advanced placement credit, cooperative education, distance learning, English as a second language, independent study, internships, off-campus study, part-time degree program, services for LD students, summer session for credit.
Library Lincoln Campus Learning Resource Center. *Books:* 34,767 (physical), 34,800 (digital/electronic); *Serial titles:* 2,348 (physical), 20,505 (digital/electronic); *Databases:* 59. Weekly public service hours: 68.
Student Life *Housing:* college housing not available. *Campus security:* late-night transport/escort service.
Athletics *Intercollegiate sports:* baseball M, basketball M/W, golf M, softball W, volleyball W. *Intramural sports:* basketball M/W, football M, sand volleyball M/W, softball M/W, volleyball M/W.
Standardized Tests *Recommended:* ACT (for admission).
Costs (2015–16) *Tuition:* state resident $2723 full-time, $61 per quarter hour part-time; nonresident $3353 full-time, $75 per quarter hour part-time. Full-time tuition and fees vary according to course load. Part-time tuition and fees vary according to course load. *Required fees:* $56 full-time, $1 per quarter hour part-time. *Waivers:* employees or children of employees.
Applying *Options:* electronic application, early admission, deferred entrance. *Required:* high school transcript. *Application deadlines:* rolling (freshmen), rolling (transfers).
Freshman Application Contact Admissions Office, Southeast Community College, Lincoln Campus, 8800 O Street, Lincoln, NE 68520. *Phone:* 402-471-3333. *Toll-free phone:* 800-642-4075. *Fax:* 402-437-2404. *E-mail:* admissions@southeast.edu. *Website:* http://www.southeast.edu/.

Southeast Community College, Milford Campus
Milford, Nebraska

- **District-supported** 2-year, founded 1941, part of Southeast Community College System
- **Small-town** 50-acre campus with easy access to Omaha
- **Coed, primarily men,** 9,193 undergraduate students, 44% full-time, 52% women, 48% men

Undergraduates 4,086 full-time, 5,107 part-time. 7% Black or African American, non-Hispanic/Latino; 7% Hispanic/Latino; 3% Asian, non-Hispanic/Latino; 0.3% Native Hawaiian or other Pacific Islander, non-

Hispanic/Latino; 1% American Indian or Alaska Native, non-Hispanic/Latino; 1% Race/ethnicity unknown.

Faculty *Total:* 707, 44% full-time. *Student/faculty ratio:* 18:1.

Majors Architectural engineering technology; autobody/collision and repair technology; automobile/automotive mechanics technology; building/construction finishing, management, and inspection related; business administration and management; civil engineering technology; diesel mechanics technology; electrical, electronic and communications engineering technology; energy management and systems technology; heating, air conditioning, ventilation and refrigeration maintenance technology; machine tool technology; manufacturing engineering; network and system administration; quality control technology.

Academics *Calendar:* quarters. *Degree:* diplomas and associate. *Special study options:* academic remediation for entering students, advanced placement credit, cooperative education, distance learning, internships, part-time degree program, services for LD students, summer session for credit.

Library Milford Campus Learning Resource Center. *Books:* 34,767 (physical), 34,800 (digital/electronic); *Serial titles:* 2,348 (physical), 20,505 (digital/electronic); *Databases:* 59. Weekly public service hours: 51; students can reserve study rooms.

Student Life *Housing Options:* men-only, women-only, special housing for students with disabilities. Campus housing is university owned. *Campus security:* late-night transport/escort service, controlled dormitory access.

Athletics Member NJCAA. *Intercollegiate sports:* baseball M, basketball M/W, golf M, softball W, volleyball W. *Intramural sports:* basketball M/W, football M, sand volleyball M/W, softball M/W, volleyball M/W.

Standardized Tests *Recommended:* ACT (for admission).

Costs (2015–16) *Tuition:* state resident $2723 full-time, $61 per credit hour part-time; nonresident $3353 full-time, $75 per credit hour part-time. Full-time tuition and fees vary according to course load. Part-time tuition and fees vary according to course load. *Required fees:* $56 full-time, $1 per credit hour part-time. *Room and board:* $4647; room only: $2355. Room and board charges vary according to gender, housing facility, and location. *Waivers:* employees or children of employees.

Applying *Options:* electronic application, early admission, deferred entrance. *Required:* high school transcript. *Application deadlines:* rolling (freshmen), rolling (transfers). *Notification:* continuous (freshmen), continuous (transfers).

Freshman Application Contact Admissions Office, Southeast Community College, Milford Campus, 600 State Street, Milford, NE 68405. *Phone:* 402-761-2131. *Toll-free phone:* 800-933-7223. *Fax:* 402-761-2324. *E-mail:* admissions@southeast.edu. *Website:* http://www.southeast.edu/.

Universal College of Healing Arts
Omaha, Nebraska

Admissions Office Contact Universal College of Healing Arts, 8702 North 30th Street, Omaha, NE 68112-1810. *Website:* http://www.ucha.edu/.

Western Nebraska Community College
Sidney, Nebraska

Director of Admissions Mr. Troy Archuleta, Admissions and Recruitment Director, Western Nebraska Community College, 371 College Drive, Sidney, NE 69162. *Phone:* 308-635-6015. *Toll-free phone:* 800-222-9682. *E-mail:* rhovey@wncc.net. *Website:* http://www.wncc.net/.

NEVADA

Brightwood College, Las Vegas Campus
Las Vegas, Nevada

Freshman Application Contact Admissions Office, Brightwood College, Las Vegas Campus, 3535 West Sahara Avenue, Las Vegas, NV 89102. *Phone:* 702-368-2338. *Toll-free phone:* 800-935-1857. *Website:* http://www.brightwood.edu/.

Career College of Northern Nevada
Sparks, Nevada

Freshman Application Contact Ms. Laura Goldhammer, Director of Admissions, Career College of Northern Nevada, 1421 Pullman Drive, Sparks, NV 89434. *Phone:* 775-856-2266 Ext. 11. *Fax:* 775-856-0935. *E-mail:* lgoldhammer@ccnn4u.com. *Website:* http://www.ccnn.edu/.

Carrington College–Las Vegas
Las Vegas, Nevada

- **Proprietary** 2-year, part of Carrington Colleges Group, Inc.
- **Coed,** 370 undergraduate students, 81% full-time, 68% women, 32% men

Undergraduates 298 full-time, 72 part-time. 2% are from out of state; 18% Black or African American, non-Hispanic/Latino; 24% Hispanic/Latino; 21% Asian, non-Hispanic/Latino; 5% Native Hawaiian or other Pacific Islander, non-Hispanic/Latino; 0.8% American Indian or Alaska Native, non-Hispanic/Latino; 2% Two or more races, non-Hispanic/Latino; 3% Race/ethnicity unknown; 22% transferred in.

Freshmen *Admission:* 39 enrolled.

Faculty *Total:* 18, 33% full-time. *Student/faculty ratio:* 32:1.

Majors Physical therapy technology; respiratory therapy technician.

Academics *Degree:* certificates and associate.

Student Life *Housing:* college housing not available.

Costs (2016–17) *Tuition:* $44,582 per degree program part-time.

Applying *Required:* essay or personal statement, high school transcript, interview, institutional entrance test.

Freshman Application Contact Carrington College–Las Vegas, 5740 South Eastern Avenue, Las Vegas, NV 89119. *Website:* http://carrington.edu/.

Carrington College–Reno
Reno, Nevada

- **Proprietary** 2-year, part of Carrington Colleges Group, Inc.
- **Coed,** 327 undergraduate students, 79% full-time, 83% women, 17% men

Undergraduates 257 full-time, 70 part-time. 11% are from out of state; 0.6% Black or African American, non-Hispanic/Latino; 18% Hispanic/Latino; 8% Asian, non-Hispanic/Latino; 1% Native Hawaiian or other Pacific Islander, non-Hispanic/Latino; 0.3% American Indian or Alaska Native, non-Hispanic/Latino; 1% Two or more races, non-Hispanic/Latino; 0.9% Race/ethnicity unknown; 19% transferred in.

Freshmen *Admission:* 13 enrolled.

Faculty *Total:* 33, 36% full-time. *Student/faculty ratio:* 15:1.

Majors Registered nursing/registered nurse.

Academics *Degree:* certificates and associate.

Student Life *Housing:* college housing not available.

Costs (2016–17) *Tuition:* $50,599 per degree program part-time. Full-time tuition and fees vary according to program. Part-time tuition and fees vary according to program.

Applying *Required:* essay or personal statement, high school transcript, interview, institutional entrance test. *Notification:* continuous (freshmen).

Freshman Application Contact Carrington College–Reno, 5580 Kietzke Lane, Reno, NV 89511. *Phone:* 775-335-2900. *Website:* http://carrington.edu/.

College of Southern Nevada
Las Vegas, Nevada

Freshman Application Contact Admissions and Records, College of Southern Nevada, 6375 West Charleston Boulevard, Las Vegas, NV 89146. *Phone:* 702-651-4060. *Website:* http://www.csn.edu/.

Everest College
Henderson, Nevada

Admissions Office Contact Everest College, 170 North Stephanie Street, Henderson, NV 89074. *Toll-free phone:* 888-741-4270. *Website:* http://www.everest.edu/.

Great Basin College
Elko, Nevada

- **State-supported** primarily 2-year, founded 1967, part of Nevada System of Higher Education
- **Small-town** 45-acre campus
- **Endowment** $239,000
- **Coed,** 3,127 undergraduate students, 30% full-time, 62% women, 38% men

Undergraduates 948 full-time, 2,179 part-time. Students come from 21 states and territories; 22 other countries; 2% are from out of state; 6% transferred in; 4% live on campus. *Retention:* 62% of full-time freshmen returned.
Freshmen *Admission:* 460 applied, 460 admitted, 447 enrolled.
Faculty *Total:* 185, 37% full-time, 9% with terminal degrees. *Student/faculty ratio:* 16:1.
Majors Accounting technology and bookkeeping; biology/biological sciences; business administration and management; business/commerce; computer and information sciences; computer graphics; computer/information technology services administration related; computer systems networking and telecommunications; criminal justice/safety; data processing and data processing technology; diesel mechanics technology; early childhood education; electrical, electronic and communications engineering technology; elementary education; emergency medical technology (EMT paramedic); English; general studies; geological and earth sciences/geosciences related; human services; industrial technology; instrumentation technology; interdisciplinary studies; liberal arts and sciences/liberal studies; management science; natural resources management and policy related; office occupations and clerical services; operations management; radiologic technology/science; registered nursing/registered nurse; science technologies; secondary education; social sciences; social work; surveying technology; welding technology.
Academics *Calendar:* semesters. *Degrees:* certificates, associate, bachelor's, and postbachelor's certificates. *Special study options:* academic remediation for entering students, accelerated degree program, adult/continuing education programs, cooperative education, distance learning, double majors, English as a second language, external degree program, independent study, off-campus study, part-time degree program, services for LD students, summer session for credit.
Library Learning Resource Center. *Books:* 94,193 (physical), 250,157 (digital/electronic); *Serial titles:* 2,946 (physical), 230,872 (digital/electronic); *Databases:* 75. Weekly public service hours: 54; students can reserve study rooms.
Student Life *Housing Options:* coed, special housing for students with disabilities. Campus housing is university owned. *Campus security:* late-night transport/escort service, evening patrols by trained security personnel. *Student services:* personal/psychological counseling.
Costs (2015–16) *Tuition:* state resident $2640 full-time, $88 per unit part-time; nonresident $9450 full-time, $185 per unit part-time. Full-time tuition and fees vary according to course level, degree level, and reciprocity agreements. Part-time tuition and fees vary according to course level, degree level, and reciprocity agreements. *Required fees:* $165 full-time, $6 per unit part-time. *Room and board:* $6800. Room and board charges vary according to housing facility. *Payment plan:* installment. *Waivers:* employees or children of employees.
Financial Aid Of all full-time matriculated undergraduates who enrolled in 2015, 406 applied for aid, 356 were judged to have need, 21 had their need fully met. In 2015, 97 non-need-based awards were made. *Average financial aid package:* $2331. *Average need-based loan:* $3501. *Average need-based gift aid:* $2710. *Average non-need-based aid:* $976.
Applying *Options:* electronic application, early admission, deferred entrance. *Application fee:* $10. *Application deadlines:* rolling (freshmen), rolling (out-of-state freshmen), rolling (transfers). *Notification:* continuous (freshmen), continuous (out-of-state freshmen), continuous (transfers).
Freshman Application Contact Ms. Jan King, Director of Admissions and Registrar, Great Basin College, 1500 College Parkway, Elko, NV 89801. *Phone:* 775-753-2102. *E-mail:* jan.king@gbcnv.edu.
Website: http://www.gbcnv.edu/.

ITT Technical Institute
Henderson, Nevada

Freshman Application Contact Director of Recruitment, ITT Technical Institute, 2300 Corporate Circle, Suite 150, Henderson, NV 89074. *Phone:* 702-558-5404. *Toll-free phone:* 800-488-8459.
Website: http://www.itt-tech.edu/.

ITT Technical Institute
North Las Vegas, Nevada

Freshman Application Contact Director of Recruitment, ITT Technical Institute, 3825 W. Cheyenne Avenue, Suite 600, North Las Vegas, NV 89032. *Phone:* 702-240-0967. *Toll-free phone:* 877-832-8442.
Website: http://www.itt-tech.edu/.

Northwest Career College
Las Vegas, Nevada

Admissions Office Contact Northwest Career College, 7398 Smoke Ranch Road, Suite 100, Las Vegas, NV 89128.
Website: http://www.northwestcareercollege.edu/.

Pima Medical Institute
Las Vegas, Nevada

Freshman Application Contact Admissions Office, Pima Medical Institute, 3333 East Flamingo Road, Las Vegas, NV 89121. *Phone:* 702-458-9650 Ext. 202. *Toll-free phone:* 800-477-PIMA.
Website: http://www.pmi.edu/.

Truckee Meadows Community College
Reno, Nevada

- **State-supported** 2-year, founded 1971, part of Nevada System of Higher Education
- **Suburban** 63-acre campus
- **Endowment** $10.0 million
- **Coed,** 11,085 undergraduate students, 27% full-time, 54% women, 46% men

Undergraduates 3,015 full-time, 8,070 part-time. Students come from 23 states and territories; 7% are from out of state; 2% Black or African American, non-Hispanic/Latino; 25% Hispanic/Latino; 6% Asian, non-Hispanic/Latino; 0.1% Native Hawaiian or other Pacific Islander, non-Hispanic/Latino; 1% American Indian or Alaska Native, non-Hispanic/Latino; 4% Two or more races, non-Hispanic/Latino; 2% Race/ethnicity unknown; 0.4% international; 6% transferred in. *Retention:* 66% of full-time freshmen returned.
Freshmen *Admission:* 2,079 applied, 2,079 admitted, 1,509 enrolled.
Faculty *Total:* 551, 27% full-time. *Student/faculty ratio:* 20:1.
Majors Anthropology; architectural drafting and CAD/CADD; architecture; automobile/automotive mechanics technology; biology/biological sciences; business/commerce; chemistry; civil engineering; commercial and advertising art; computer programming (specific applications); computer systems networking and telecommunications; cooking and related culinary arts; criminal justice/police science; criminal justice/safety; dental assisting; dental hygiene; diesel mechanics technology; dietetics; drafting and design technology; elementary education; energy management and systems technology; engineering; engineering technologies and engineering related; English; entrepreneurial and small business related; environmental science; fine arts related; fire prevention and safety technology; foods, nutrition, and wellness; general studies; geology/earth science; heating, air conditioning, ventilation and refrigeration maintenance technology; history; kindergarten/preschool education; landscape architecture; legal assistant/paralegal; liberal arts and sciences/liberal studies; logistics, materials, and supply chain management; management information systems and services related; manufacturing engineering technology; mathematics; medical radiologic technology; mental health counseling; music; music performance; natural resources/conservation; philosophy; physics; psychology; registered nursing/registered nurse; science, technology and society; veterinary/animal health technology; welding technology.
Academics *Calendar:* semesters. *Degree:* certificates and associate. *Special study options:* academic remediation for entering students, accelerated degree program, adult/continuing education programs, advanced placement credit, cooperative education, distance learning, double majors, English as a second language, independent study, internships, part-time degree program, services for LD students, summer session for credit. *ROTC:* Army (c).
Library Elizabeth Sturm Library.
Student Life *Housing:* college housing not available. *Activities and Organizations:* drama/theater group, student-run newspaper, Entrepreneurship Club, International Club, Phi Theta Kappa, Student Government Association, Student Media and Broadcasting Club. *Campus security:* 24-hour emergency response devices and patrols, late-night transport/escort service. *Student services:* personal/psychological counseling.
Costs (2016–17) *Tuition:* state resident $3030 full-time, $92 per credit hour part-time; nonresident $9675 full-time, $222 per credit hour part-time. Full-time tuition and fees vary according to course load and program. Part-time tuition and fees vary according to course load and program. *Required fees:* $9

per credit hour part-time. *Payment plan:* installment. *Waivers:* employees or children of employees.

Financial Aid Of all full-time matriculated undergraduates who enrolled in 2014, 126 Federal Work-Study jobs (averaging $5000). 368 state and other part-time jobs (averaging $5000).

Applying *Options:* electronic application, early admission. *Application fee:* $10.

Freshman Application Contact Truckee Meadows Community College, 7000 Dandini Boulevard, Reno, NV 89512-3901. *Phone:* 775-673-7240. *Website:* http://www.tmcc.edu/.

Western Nevada College
Carson City, Nevada

- **State-supported** primarily 2-year, founded 1971, part of Nevada System of Higher Education
- **Small-town** 200-acre campus
- **Endowment** $250,000
- **Coed**, 3,839 undergraduate students, 36% full-time, 57% women, 43% men

Undergraduates 1,401 full-time, 2,438 part-time. Students come from 15 states and territories; 4% are from out of state; 2% Black or African American, non-Hispanic/Latino; 19% Hispanic/Latino; 2% Asian, non-Hispanic/Latino; 0.9% Native Hawaiian or other Pacific Islander, non-Hispanic/Latino; 2% American Indian or Alaska Native, non-Hispanic/Latino; 3% Two or more races, non-Hispanic/Latino; 5% Race/ethnicity unknown; 5% transferred in. *Retention:* 58% of full-time freshmen returned.

Freshmen *Admission:* 647 applied, 647 admitted, 623 enrolled.

Majors Accounting; automobile/automotive mechanics technology; building construction technology; business administration and management; business/commerce; commercial and advertising art; computer and information sciences; construction management; criminal justice/law enforcement administration; deaf studies; general studies; industrial technology; liberal arts and sciences/liberal studies; machine tool technology; management information systems; manufacturing engineering technology; physical sciences; registered nursing/registered nurse; welding technology.

Academics *Calendar:* semesters. *Degrees:* certificates, associate, and bachelor's. *Special study options:* academic remediation for entering students, adult/continuing education programs, advanced placement credit, cooperative education, distance learning, double majors, English as a second language, honors programs, independent study, internships, part-time degree program, services for LD students, summer session for credit.

Library Western Nevada College Library and Media Services plus 1 other. *Books:* 38,834 (physical), 4,544 (digital/electronic); *Serial titles:* 2,725 (physical); *Databases:* 33. Weekly public service hours: 61; students can reserve study rooms.

Student Life *Housing:* college housing not available. *Activities and Organizations:* drama/theater group, choral group, Associated Students of Western Nevada, WNC Business Club, Lone Mountain Writers, Gay-Straight Alliance, ASL Club. *Campus security:* late-night transport/escort service. *Student services:* personal/psychological counseling.

Athletics Member NJCAA. *Intercollegiate sports:* baseball M, softball W.

Standardized Tests *Recommended:* SAT or ACT (for admission).

Costs (2015–16) *Tuition:* state resident $2640 full-time, $88 per unit part-time; nonresident $9285 full-time, $185 per unit part-time. Full-time tuition and fees vary according to course level, degree level, and reciprocity agreements. Part-time tuition and fees vary according to course level, degree level, and reciprocity agreements. *Required fees:* $165 full-time, $6 per credit part-time. *Payment plan:* installment. *Waivers:* employees or children of employees.

Financial Aid Of all full-time matriculated undergraduates who enrolled in 2015, 565 applied for aid, 530 were judged to have need, 19 had their need fully met. In 2015, 88 non-need-based awards were made. *Average financial aid package:* $2644. *Average need-based loan:* $2402. *Average need-based gift aid:* $3053. *Average non-need-based aid:* $1263.

Applying *Options:* electronic application, early admission. *Application fee:* $15. *Required for some:* high school transcript. *Application deadlines:* rolling (freshmen), rolling (transfers).

Freshman Application Contact Admissions and Records, Western Nevada College, 2201 West College Parkway, Carson City, NV 89703. *Phone:* 775-445-2377. *Fax:* 775-445-3147. *E-mail:* wncc_aro@wncc.edu. *Website:* http://www.wnc.edu/.

NEW HAMPSHIRE

Great Bay Community College
Portsmouth, New Hampshire

Freshman Application Contact Mr. Matt Thornton, Admissions Coordinator, Great Bay Community College, 320 Corporate Drive, Portsmouth, NH 03801. *Phone:* 603-427-7605. *Toll-free phone:* 800-522-1194. *E-mail:* askgreatbay@ccsnh.edu. *Website:* http://www.greatbay.edu/.

Lakes Region Community College
Laconia, New Hampshire

- **State-supported** 2-year, part of Community College System of New Hampshire
- **Small-town** campus
- **Coed**

Undergraduates 490 full-time, 689 part-time. Students come from 2 other countries; 3% are from out of state; 0.5% Black or African American, non-Hispanic/Latino; 1% Hispanic/Latino; 0.5% Asian, non-Hispanic/Latino; 0.1% Native Hawaiian or other Pacific Islander, non-Hispanic/Latino; 0.5% American Indian or Alaska Native, non-Hispanic/Latino; 0.9% Two or more races, non-Hispanic/Latino; 22% Race/ethnicity unknown.

Faculty *Student/faculty ratio:* 9:1.

Academics *Calendar:* semesters accelerated terms also offered. *Degree:* associate. *Special study options:* academic remediation for entering students, adult/continuing education programs, cooperative education, distance learning, double majors, independent study, internships, part-time degree program, services for LD students, summer session for credit.

Library Hugh Bennett Library plus 1 other.

Student Life *Campus security:* 24-hour emergency response devices.

Standardized Tests *Required for some:* TEAS for nursing programs.

Applying *Options:* electronic application, deferred entrance. *Application fee:* $20. *Required:* high school transcript.

Freshman Application Contact Ms. Kathy Plummer, Admissions, Lakes Region Community College, Admissions Office, 379 Belmont Road, Laconia, NH 03246. *Phone:* 603-524-3207 Ext. 6410. *Toll-free phone:* 800-357-2992. *E-mail:* lrccinfo@ccsnh.edu. *Website:* http://www.lrcc.edu/.

Manchester Community College
Manchester, New Hampshire

Freshman Application Contact Ms. Jacquie Poirier, Coordinator of Admissions, Manchester Community College, 1066 Front Street, Manchester, NH 03102-8518. *Phone:* 603-668-6706 Ext. 283. *Toll-free phone:* 800-924-3445. *E-mail:* jpoirier@nhctc.edu. *Website:* http://www.mccnh.edu/.

Nashua Community College
Nashua, New Hampshire

Freshman Application Contact Ms. Patricia Goodman, Vice President of Student Services, Nashua Community College, Nashua, NH 03063. *Phone:* 603-882-6923 Ext. 1529. *Fax:* 603-882-8690. *E-mail:* pgoodman@ccsnh.edu. *Website:* http://www.nashuacc.edu/.

NHTI, Concord's Community College
Concord, New Hampshire

Freshman Application Contact Mr. Francis P. Meyer, Director of Admissions, NHTI, Concord's Community College, 31 College Drive, Concord, NH 03301-7412. *Phone:* 603-271-6484 Ext. 2459. *Toll-free phone:* 800-247-0179. *E-mail:* fmeyer@ccsnh.edu. *Website:* http://www.nhti.edu/.

River Valley Community College
Claremont, New Hampshire

- **State-supported** 2-year, part of Community College System of New Hampshire
- **Rural** 80-acre campus
- **Coed,** 1,009 undergraduate students, 23% full-time, 69% women, 31% men
- 77% of applicants were admitted

Undergraduates 236 full-time, 773 part-time. 6% are from out of state; 0.7% Black or African American, non-Hispanic/Latino; 2% Hispanic/Latino; 2% Asian, non-Hispanic/Latino; 1% American Indian or Alaska Native, non-Hispanic/Latino; 0.8% Two or more races, non-Hispanic/Latino; 9% Race/ethnicity unknown.
Freshmen *Admission:* 664 applied, 511 admitted, 177 enrolled.
Faculty *Total:* 112, 32% full-time, 4% with terminal degrees. *Student/faculty ratio:* 6:1.
Majors Accounting; business administration and management; clinical/medical laboratory technology; computer science; computer systems networking and telecommunications; criminal justice/law enforcement administration; early childhood education; general studies; human services; liberal arts and sciences/liberal studies; management information systems; occupational therapist assistant; physical therapy technology; registered nursing/registered nurse; respiratory care therapy; web/multimedia management and webmaster.
Academics *Calendar:* semesters. *Degree:* certificates, diplomas, and associate. *Special study options:* academic remediation for entering students, distance learning, double majors, independent study, part-time degree program, services for LD students, summer session for credit.
Library Charles Puksta Library plus 1 other.
Student Life *Housing:* college housing not available. *Activities and Organizations:* Student Government Association. *Campus security:* 24-hour emergency response devices, security personnel on campus 6:30 a.m. to 10 p.m..
Costs (2015–16) *Tuition:* $300 per credit hour part-time; state resident $6720 full-time, $200 per credit hour part-time; nonresident $15,296 full-time, $455 per credit hour part-time. Full-time tuition and fees vary according to class time, course load, and program. Part-time tuition and fees vary according to class time, course load, and program. *Required fees:* $455 full-time. *Payment plans:* installment, deferred payment. *Waivers:* senior citizens and employees or children of employees.
Financial Aid Of all full-time matriculated undergraduates who enrolled in 2014, 18 Federal Work-Study jobs (averaging $1450).
Applying *Options:* electronic application. *Application fee:* $20. *Required:* high school transcript. *Required for some:* 2 letters of recommendation, interview.
Freshman Application Contact River Valley Community College, 1 College Place, Claremont, NH 03743. *Phone:* 603-542-7744 Ext. 5323. *Toll-free phone:* 800-837-0658.
Website: http://www.rivervalley.edu/.

St. Joseph School of Nursing
Nashua, New Hampshire

- **Independent** 2-year, founded 1964, affiliated with Roman Catholic Church
- **Urban** campus with easy access to Boston, Portland
- **Coed,** 144 undergraduate students, 44% full-time, 90% women, 10% men

Undergraduates 63 full-time, 81 part-time. Students come from 3 states and territories; 9 other countries; 27% are from out of state; 24% transferred in.
Freshmen *Admission:* 5 applied, 2 admitted, 2 enrolled. *Average high school GPA:* 3.25.
Faculty *Total:* 20, 55% full-time, 100% with terminal degrees.
Majors Registered nursing, nursing administration, nursing research and clinical nursing related.
Academics *Calendar:* semesters. *Degree:* associate. *Special study options:* academic remediation for entering students, advanced placement credit, services for LD students, summer session for credit.
Student Life *Housing:* college housing not available. *Campus security:* 24-hour emergency response devices and patrols, late-night transport/escort service.
Costs (2016–17) *Tuition:* $870 per course part-time. Full-time tuition and fees vary according to course load and program. Part-time tuition and fees vary according to course load and program. *Payment plan:* installment. *Waivers:* employees or children of employees.

Applying *Options:* electronic application. *Application fee:* $50. *Required:* essay or personal statement, high school transcript, minimum 2.5 GPA, 3 letters of recommendation, interview. *Application deadline:* 7/10 (freshmen).
Freshman Application Contact Mrs. L. Nadeau, Admissions, St. Joseph School of Nursing, 5 Woodward Avenue, Nashua, NH 03060. *Toll-free phone:* 800-370-3169.
Website: http://www.sjhacademiccenter.org/.

White Mountains Community College
Berlin, New Hampshire

- **State-supported** 2-year, founded 1966, part of Community College System of New Hampshire
- **Rural** 325-acre campus
- **Coed,** 1,001 undergraduate students, 31% full-time, 61% women, 39% men

Undergraduates 310 full-time, 691 part-time. Students come from 5 states and territories; 5% are from out of state; 0.6% Black or African American, non-Hispanic/Latino; 2% Hispanic/Latino; 0.1% Asian, non-Hispanic/Latino; 0.1% Native Hawaiian or other Pacific Islander, non-Hispanic/Latino; 0.9% Two or more races, non-Hispanic/Latino; 5% Race/ethnicity unknown; 6% transferred in.
Freshmen *Admission:* 209 enrolled.
Faculty *Total:* 113, 19% full-time. *Student/faculty ratio:* 20:1.
Majors Accounting; automobile/automotive mechanics technology; baking and pastry arts; business administration and management; computer and information sciences; criminal justice/safety; culinary arts; diesel mechanics technology; early childhood education; education; environmental studies; general studies; health services/allied health/health sciences; human services; liberal arts and sciences/liberal studies; medical/clinical assistant; medical office assistant; office management; registered nursing/registered nurse; resort management; welding technology.
Academics *Calendar:* semesters. *Degree:* certificates, diplomas, and associate. *Special study options:* academic remediation for entering students, adult/continuing education programs, advanced placement credit, cooperative education, distance learning, double majors, external degree program, independent study, internships, part-time degree program, services for LD students, student-designed majors, summer session for credit.
Library Fortier Library. *Books:* 17,808 (physical); *Serial titles:* 35 (physical); *Databases:* 48. Weekly public service hours: 55; students can reserve study rooms.
Student Life *Housing:* college housing not available. *Activities and Organizations:* Student Senate.
Standardized Tests *Required for some:* TEAS for associate's degree nursing program.
Costs (2016–17) *Tuition:* state resident $6000 full-time, $200 per credit part-time; nonresident $13,500 full-time, $450 per credit part-time. Full-time tuition and fees vary according to class time, location, and program. Part-time tuition and fees vary according to class time, location, and program. *Required fees:* $510 full-time, $17 per credit part-time. *Payment plans:* installment, deferred payment. *Waivers:* senior citizens and employees or children of employees.
Applying *Required:* high school transcript. *Required for some:* letters of recommendation.
Freshman Application Contact Ms. Kristen Miller, Admissions Counselor, White Mountains Community College, 2020 Riverside Drive, Berlin, NH 03570. *Phone:* 603-342-3002. *Toll-free phone:* 800-445-4525. *Fax:* 603-752-6335. *E-mail:* kmiller@ccsnh.edu.
Website: http://www.wmcc.edu/.

NEW JERSEY

Assumption College for Sisters
Mendham, New Jersey

Freshman Application Contact Sr. Gerardine Tantsits, Academic Dean/Registrar, Assumption College for Sisters, 350 Bernardsville Road, Mendham, NJ 07945-2923. *Phone:* 973-543-6528 Ext. 228. *Fax:* 973-543-1738. *E-mail:* deanregistrar@acs350.org.
Website: http://www.acs350.org/.

Atlantic Cape Community College
Mays Landing, New Jersey

Freshman Application Contact Mrs. Linda McLeod, Assistant Director, Admissions and College Recruitment, Atlantic Cape Community College,

5100 Black Horse Pike, Mays Landing, NJ 08330-2699. *Phone:* 609-343-5009. *Fax:* 609-343-4921. *E-mail:* accadmit@atlantic.edu. *Website:* http://www.atlantic.edu/.

Bergen Community College
Paramus, New Jersey

Freshman Application Contact Admissions Office, Bergen Community College, 400 Paramus Road, Paramus, NJ 07652-1595. *Phone:* 201-447-7195. *E-mail:* admsoffice@bergen.edu. *Website:* http://www.bergen.edu/.

Brookdale Community College
Lincroft, New Jersey

Director of Admissions Ms. Kim Toomey, Registrar, Brookdale Community College, 765 Newman Springs Road, Lincroft, NJ 07738-1597. *Phone:* 732-224-2268. *Website:* http://www.brookdalecc.edu/.

★ Camden County College
Blackwood, New Jersey

- **State and locally supported** 2-year, founded 1967, part of New Jersey Commission on Higher Education
- **Suburban** 320-acre campus with easy access to Philadelphia
- **Coed,** 11,263 undergraduate students, 50% full-time, 57% women, 43% men

Undergraduates 5,646 full-time, 5,617 part-time. 20% Black or African American, non-Hispanic/Latino; 16% Hispanic/Latino; 5% Asian, non-Hispanic/Latino; 0.2% Native Hawaiian or other Pacific Islander, non-Hispanic/Latino; 1% American Indian or Alaska Native, non-Hispanic/Latino; 0.9% Two or more races, non-Hispanic/Latino; 5% Race/ethnicity unknown; 2% international; 11% transferred in.
Freshmen *Admission:* 9,430 applied, 2,073 enrolled.
Faculty *Total:* 678, 19% full-time.
Majors Accounting technology and bookkeeping; administrative assistant and secretarial science; automotive engineering technology; biology/biotechnology laboratory technician; business administration and management; cinematography and film/video production; clinical/medical laboratory technology; computer and information sciences; criminal justice/police science; dental assisting; dental hygiene; desktop publishing and digital imaging design; dietetics; dietetic technology; drafting and design technology; early childhood education; education (multiple levels); electrical, electronic and communications engineering technology; electromechanical technology; emergency medical technology (EMT paramedic); engineering science; engineering technologies and engineering related; fine/studio arts; fire prevention and safety technology; fire services administration; health information/medical records administration; health services/allied health/health sciences; industrial production technologies related; legal assistant/paralegal; liberal arts and sciences/liberal studies; management information systems; marketing/marketing management; massage therapy; mechanical engineering/mechanical technology; mechanical engineering technologies related; opticianry; radio and television broadcasting technology; registered nursing/registered nurse; rehabilitation and therapeutic professions related; sign language interpretation and translation; social work; speech communication and rhetoric; sport and fitness administration/management; substance abuse/addiction counseling; veterinary/animal health technology.
Academics *Calendar:* semesters. *Degree:* certificates and associate. *Special study options:* academic remediation for entering students, adult/continuing education programs, advanced placement credit, cooperative education, distance learning, double majors, English as a second language, external degree program, freshman honors college, honors programs, independent study, internships, off-campus study, part-time degree program, services for LD students, study abroad, summer session for credit.
Library Learning Resource Center.
Student Life *Housing:* college housing not available. *Activities and Organizations:* drama/theater group, student-run newspaper, radio station, choral group. *Campus security:* 24-hour emergency response devices, late-night transport/escort service. *Student services:* health clinic.
Athletics Member NJCAA. *Intercollegiate sports:* baseball M, basketball M/W, golf M, soccer M/W, softball W. *Intramural sports:* baseball M, basketball M/W, soccer M/W, softball W.
Costs (2015–16) *Tuition:* area resident $3210 full-time, $107 per credit part-time; state resident $3330 full-time, $111 per credit part-time; nonresident $3330 full-time, $111 per credit part-time. Full-time tuition and fees vary according to course load. Part-time tuition and fees vary according to course load. *Required fees:* $1110 full-time, $37 per credit part-time. *Payment plans:* installment, deferred payment.

Financial Aid Of all full-time matriculated undergraduates who enrolled in 2014, 117 Federal Work-Study jobs (averaging $1126).
Applying *Options:* early admission. *Required for some:* high school transcript. *Application deadlines:* rolling (freshmen), rolling (transfers).
Freshman Application Contact Donald Delaney, Director of Program Outreach, Camden County College, PO Box 200, Blackwood, NJ 08012-0200. *Phone:* 856-227-7200 Ext. 4660. *Fax:* 856-374-4916.
E-mail: ddelaney@camdencc.edu.
Website: http://www.camdencc.edu/.

See previous page for display ad and page 364 for the College Close-Up.

County College of Morris
Randolph, New Jersey

- **County-supported** 2-year, founded 1966
- **Suburban** 218-acre campus with easy access to New York City
- **Endowment** $3.1 million
- **Coed,** 8,026 undergraduate students, 49% full-time, 50% women, 50% men

Undergraduates 3,946 full-time, 4,080 part-time. Students come from 10 states and territories; 0.1% are from out of state; 5% Black or African American, non-Hispanic/Latino; 18% Hispanic/Latino; 5% Asian, non-Hispanic/Latino; 0.1% Native Hawaiian or other Pacific Islander, non-Hispanic/Latino; 0.4% American Indian or Alaska Native, non-Hispanic/Latino; 2% Two or more races, non-Hispanic/Latino; 8% Race/ethnicity unknown; 3% international; 5% transferred in. *Retention:* 70% of full-time freshmen returned.
Freshmen *Admission:* 4,198 applied, 2,574 admitted, 1,751 enrolled.
Faculty *Total:* 515, 30% full-time. *Student/faculty ratio:* 19:1.
Majors Agricultural business and management; airline pilot and flight crew; biology/biotechnology laboratory technician; business administration and management; business, management, and marketing related; chemical technology; clinical/medical laboratory technology; communication and media related; computer science; criminal justice/police science; culinary arts; design and applied arts related; electrical, electronic and communications engineering technology; engineering science; engineering technologies and engineering related; fine arts related; fire prevention and safety technology; graphic design; hospitality administration; kindergarten/preschool education; kinesiology and exercise science; liberal arts and sciences/liberal studies; management information systems; mechanical engineering/mechanical technology; multi/interdisciplinary studies related; music related; occupational therapist assistant; photography; public administration; public health; radiologic technology/science; registered nursing/registered nurse; respiratory care therapy; telecommunications technology; web page, digital/multimedia and information resources design.
Academics *Calendar:* semesters. *Degree:* certificates and associate. *Special study options:* academic remediation for entering students, accelerated degree program, advanced placement credit, cooperative education, distance learning, double majors, English as a second language, independent study, internships, services for LD students, study abroad, summer session for credit.
Library Learning Resource Center plus 1 other. *Books:* 41,877 (physical), 3,710 (digital/electronic); *Databases:* 96.
Student Life *Housing:* college housing not available. *Activities and Organizations:* drama/theater group, student-run newspaper, choral group, Phi Theta Kappa Honor Society, EOF Student Alliance, Student Nurses Association, New Social Engine, Volunteer Club. *Campus security:* 24-hour emergency response devices and patrols, late-night transport/escort service. *Student services:* health clinic, personal/psychological counseling, women's center.
Athletics Member NJCAA. *Intercollegiate sports:* baseball M(s), basketball M(s)/W(s), golf M, lacrosse M, soccer M/W(s), softball W(s), volleyball W. *Intramural sports:* badminton M, basketball M/W, bowling M/W, soccer M/W, table tennis M/W, tennis M/W, volleyball M/W.
Costs (2016–17) *Tuition:* area resident $3690 full-time, $123 per credit hour part-time; state resident $7380 full-time, $246 per credit hour part-time; nonresident $10,530 full-time, $351 per credit hour part-time. Full-time tuition and fees vary according to course load, location, and program. Part-time tuition and fees vary according to course load, location, and program. *Required fees:* $1000 full-time, $27 per credit hour part-time, $19 per course part-time. *Waivers:* senior citizens and employees or children of employees.
Financial Aid Of all full-time matriculated undergraduates who enrolled in 2014, 588 Federal Work-Study jobs (averaging $1947).
Applying *Options:* electronic application. *Application fee:* $30. *Required:* high school transcript. *Application deadlines:* rolling (freshmen), rolling (out-of-state freshmen), rolling (transfers). *Notification:* continuous (freshmen), continuous (out-of-state freshmen), continuous (transfers).
Freshman Application Contact County College of Morris, 214 Center Grove Road, Randolph, NJ 07869-2086. *Phone:* 973-328-5096.
Website: http://www.ccm.edu/.

Cumberland County College
Vineland, New Jersey

- **State and locally supported** 2-year, founded 1963, part of New Jersey Commission on Higher Education
- **Small-town** 100-acre campus with easy access to Philadelphia
- **Coed**

Undergraduates 2,298 full-time, 1,546 part-time. 23% Black or African American, non-Hispanic/Latino; 28% Hispanic/Latino; 0.8% Asian, non-Hispanic/Latino; 0.9% Native Hawaiian or other Pacific Islander, non-Hispanic/Latino; 1% American Indian or Alaska Native, non-Hispanic/Latino; 0.5% Race/ethnicity unknown; 0.1% international. *Retention:* 66% of full-time freshmen returned.
Faculty *Student/faculty ratio:* 23:1.
Academics *Calendar:* semesters. *Degree:* certificates and associate. *Special study options:* academic remediation for entering students, advanced placement credit, cooperative education, distance learning, double majors, English as a second language, honors programs, independent study, part-time degree program, services for LD students, summer session for credit.
Library Cumberland County College Library.
Student Life *Campus security:* 24-hour emergency response devices, late-night transport/escort service.
Athletics Member NJCAA.
Costs (2015–16) *Tuition:* area resident $3390 full-time, $113 per credit hour part-time; state resident $3690 full-time, $123 per credit hour part-time; nonresident $13,560 full-time, $452 per credit hour part-time. Full-time tuition and fees vary according to program and reciprocity agreements. Part-time tuition and fees vary according to program and reciprocity agreements. *Required fees:* $900 full-time, $30 per credit hour part-time.
Financial Aid Of all full-time matriculated undergraduates who enrolled in 2014, 100 Federal Work-Study jobs (averaging $500). 100 state and other part-time jobs (averaging $600).
Applying *Options:* electronic application, early admission, deferred entrance. *Required:* high school transcript.
Freshman Application Contact Ms. Anne Daly-Eimer, Director of Admissions and Registration, Cumberland County College, PO Box 1500, College Drive, Vineland, NJ 08362. *Phone:* 856-691-8600.
Website: http://www.cccnj.edu/.

Eastern International College
Belleville, New Jersey

Admissions Office Contact Eastern International College, 251 Washington Avenue, Belleville, NJ 07109.
Website: http://www.eicollege.edu/.

Eastern International College
Jersey City, New Jersey

Admissions Office Contact Eastern International College, 684 Newark Avenue, Jersey City, NJ 07306.
Website: http://www.eicollege.edu/.

Eastwick College
Hackensack, New Jersey

Admissions Office Contact Eastwick College, 250 Moore Street, Hackensack, NJ 07601.
Website: http://www.eastwickcollege.edu/.

Eastwick College
Nutley, New Jersey

Admissions Office Contact Eastwick College, 103 Park Avenue, Nutley, NJ 07110.
Website: http://www.eastwickcollege.edu/.

Eastwick College
Ramsey, New Jersey

Admissions Office Contact Eastwick College, 10 South Franklin Turnpike, Ramsey, NJ 07446.
Website: http://www.eastwickcollege.edu/.

Essex County College
Newark, New Jersey

Freshman Application Contact Ms. Marva Mack, Director of Admissions, Essex County College, 303 University Avenue, Newark, NJ 07102. *Phone:* 973-877-3119. *Fax:* 973-623-6449.
Website: http://www.essex.edu/.

Hudson County Community College
Jersey City, New Jersey

- **State and locally supported** 2-year, founded 1974
- **Urban** campus with easy access to New York City
- **Coed,** 9,051 undergraduate students, 65% full-time, 58% women, 42% men

Undergraduates 5,876 full-time, 3,175 part-time. 13% Black or African American, non-Hispanic/Latino; 57% Hispanic/Latino; 7% Asian, non-Hispanic/Latino; 0.6% Native Hawaiian or other Pacific Islander, non-Hispanic/Latino; 0.3% American Indian or Alaska Native, non-Hispanic/Latino; 2% Two or more races, non-Hispanic/Latino; 8% Race/ethnicity unknown; 0.4% international; 4% transferred in.
Freshmen *Admission:* 2,283 enrolled.
Faculty *Total:* 661, 13% full-time.
Majors Accounting; accounting technology and bookkeeping; baking and pastry arts; biological and physical sciences; business administration and management; child-care provision; computer and information sciences; computer engineering technology; computer graphics; criminal justice/police science; culinary arts; dietetic technology; electrical, electronic and communications engineering technology; emergency medical technology (EMT paramedic); engineering science; engineering technologies and engineering related; environmental studies; fine/studio arts; geographic information science and cartography; health information/medical records technology; health services/allied health/health sciences; hospitality administration; legal assistant/paralegal; liberal arts and sciences/liberal studies; licensed practical/vocational nurse training; medical/clinical assistant; medical transcription; radiologic technology/science; registered nursing/registered nurse; respiratory care therapy; social work.
Academics *Calendar:* semesters. *Degree:* certificates and associate. *Special study options:* academic remediation for entering students, advanced placement credit, distance learning, English as a second language, honors programs, independent study, internships, part-time degree program, services for LD students, summer session for credit.
Library Hudson County Community College Library plus 1 other. *Books:* 49,853 (physical), 2,881 (digital/electronic); *Serial titles:* 1,269 (physical), 750 (digital/electronic); *Databases:* 74.
Student Life *Housing:* college housing not available. *Activities and Organizations:* drama/theater group, student-run newspaper. *Campus security:* 24-hour emergency response devices, late-night transport/escort service. *Student services:* personal/psychological counseling.
Costs (2016–17) *Tuition:* area resident $4683 full-time, $116 per credit hour part-time; state resident $8163 full-time, $225 per credit hour part-time; nonresident $11,643 full-time, $348 per credit hour part-time. Full-time tuition and fees vary according to course load and program. Part-time tuition and fees vary according to course load and program. *Required fees:* $1423 full-time, $46 per credit hour part-time, $25 per term part-time. *Payment plan:* installment. *Waivers:* senior citizens and employees or children of employees.
Financial Aid Of all full-time matriculated undergraduates who enrolled in 2014, 102 Federal Work-Study jobs (averaging $3000).
Applying *Options:* electronic application. *Application fee:* $20. *Application deadlines:* 9/1 (freshmen), 9/1 (transfers). *Notification:* continuous until 9/1 (freshmen), continuous until 9/1 (transfers).
Freshman Application Contact Hudson County Community College, 70 Sip Avenue, Jersey City, NJ 07306. *Phone:* 201-360-4111.
Website: http://www.hccc.edu/.

ITT Technical Institute
Marlton, New Jersey

Freshman Application Contact Director of Recruitment, ITT Technical Institute, 9000 Lincoln Drive East, Suite 100, Marlton, NJ 08053. *Phone:* 856-396-3500. *Toll-free phone:* 877-209-5410.
Website: http://www.itt-tech.edu/.

Jersey College
Teterboro, New Jersey

Admissions Office Contact Jersey College, 546 US Highway 46, Teterboro, NJ 07608.
Website: http://www.jerseycollege.edu/.

Mercer County Community College
Trenton, New Jersey

- **State and locally supported** 2-year, founded 1966
- **Suburban** 292-acre campus with easy access to New York City, Philadelphia
- **Coed,** 7,979 undergraduate students, 39% full-time, 51% women, 49% men

Undergraduates 3,077 full-time, 4,902 part-time. Students come from 7 states and territories; 89 other countries; 1% are from out of state; 22% Black or African American, non-Hispanic/Latino; 18% Hispanic/Latino; 6% Asian, non-Hispanic/Latino; 0.2% Native Hawaiian or other Pacific Islander, non-Hispanic/Latino; 0.2% American Indian or Alaska Native, non-Hispanic/Latino; 2% Two or more races, non-Hispanic/Latino; 9% Race/ethnicity unknown; 4% international; 3% transferred in. *Retention:* 71% of full-time freshmen returned.
Freshmen *Admission:* 1,748 enrolled.
Faculty *Total:* 797. *Student/faculty ratio:* 18:1.
Majors Accounting; administrative assistant and secretarial science; airline flight attendant; airline pilot and flight crew; architectural engineering technology; art; art history, criticism and conservation; automotive engineering technology; aviation/airway management; biology/biological sciences; biology/biotechnology laboratory technician; business administration and management; ceramic arts and ceramics; chemistry; civil engineering technology; clinical/medical laboratory technology; commercial and advertising art; community organization and advocacy; computer graphics; computer science; computer systems networking and telecommunications; corrections; criminal justice/police science; culinary arts; dance; dramatic/theater arts; electrical, electronic and communications engineering technology; engineering science; fire science/firefighting; funeral service and mortuary science; health professions related; heating, ventilation, air conditioning and refrigeration engineering technology; hotel/motel administration; humanities; legal assistant/paralegal; liberal arts and sciences/liberal studies; management information systems; mass communication/media; mathematics; medical radiologic technology; music; ornamental horticulture; photography; physical therapy technology; physics; plant sciences; radio and television broadcasting technology; registered nursing/registered nurse; respiratory care therapy; sculpture; teacher assistant/aide.
Academics *Calendar:* semesters. *Degree:* certificates and associate. *Special study options:* academic remediation for entering students, accelerated degree program, adult/continuing education programs, advanced placement credit, cooperative education, distance learning, double majors, English as a second language, external degree program, independent study, internships, part-time degree program, services for LD students, student-designed majors, summer session for credit. *ROTC:* Army (c), Air Force (c).
Library Mercer County Community College Library plus 1 other.
Student Life *Housing:* college housing not available. *Activities and Organizations:* drama/theater group, student-run newspaper, radio station, choral group, Student Government Association, Student Radio Station, African-American Student Organization, Student Activities Board, Phi Theta Kappa. *Campus security:* 24-hour emergency response devices and patrols. *Student services:* personal/psychological counseling.
Athletics Member NJCAA. *Intercollegiate sports:* baseball M, basketball M(s)/W(s), golf M/W, soccer M(s)/W(s), softball W, tennis M/W, track and field M/W. *Intramural sports:* basketball M/W, skiing (downhill) M/W, softball M/W, volleyball M/W.
Costs (2015–16) *Tuition:* area resident $2856 full-time, $119 per credit hour part-time; state resident $3984 full-time, $166 per credit hour part-time; nonresident $6096 full-time, $254 per credit hour part-time. Full-time tuition and fees vary according to program and reciprocity agreements. Part-time tuition and fees vary according to program and reciprocity agreements. *Required fees:* $804 full-time, $34 per credit hour part-time. *Payment plan:* installment. *Waivers:* senior citizens and employees or children of employees.
Financial Aid Of all full-time matriculated undergraduates who enrolled in 2014, 100 Federal Work-Study jobs (averaging $1500). 12 state and other part-time jobs (averaging $1500).
Applying *Options:* electronic application, deferred entrance. *Required:* high school transcript. *Recommended:* interview. *Application deadlines:* rolling (freshmen), rolling (transfers). *Notification:* continuous (freshmen), continuous (transfers).
Freshman Application Contact Dr. L. Campbell, Dean for Student and Academic Services, Mercer County Community College, 1200 Old Trenton Road, PO Box B, Trenton, NJ 08690-1004. *Phone:* 609-586-4800 Ext. 3222. *Toll-free phone:* 800-392-MCCC. *Fax:* 609-586-6944.
E-mail: admiss@mccc.edu.
Website: http://www.mccc.edu/.

Middlesex County College

Edison, New Jersey

- **County-supported** 2-year, founded 1964
- **Suburban** 200-acre campus with easy access to New York City
- **Coed,** 11,673 undergraduate students

Undergraduates 11% Black or African American, non-Hispanic/Latino; 30% Hispanic/Latino; 14% Asian, non-Hispanic/Latino; 0.5% Native Hawaiian or other Pacific Islander, non-Hispanic/Latino; 0.4% American Indian or Alaska Native, non-Hispanic/Latino; 3% Two or more races, non-Hispanic/Latino; 7% Race/ethnicity unknown; 2% international. *Retention:* 62% of full-time freshmen returned.

Faculty *Student/faculty ratio:* 24:1.

Majors Accounting; administrative assistant and secretarial science; automotive engineering technology; biology/biotechnology laboratory technician; biotechnology; business administration and management; civil engineering technology; clinical/medical laboratory technology; communications technologies and support services related; computer and information sciences; criminal justice/police science; dental hygiene; dietitian assistant; electrical, electronic and communications engineering technology; energy management and systems technology; engineering science; engineering technologies and engineering related; environmental control technologies related; fire prevention and safety technology; geology/earth science; graphic communications related; health professions related; health services/allied health/health sciences; hotel/motel administration; industrial production technologies related; legal assistant/paralegal; liberal arts and sciences/liberal studies; marketing/marketing management; mechanical engineering/mechanical technology; mechanical engineering technologies related; medical radiologic technology; merchandising, sales, and marketing operations related (specialized); physical sciences; registered nursing/registered nurse; rehabilitation and therapeutic professions related; respiratory care therapy; small business administration; surveying technology; teacher assistant/aide; visual and performing arts.

Academics *Calendar:* semesters. *Degree:* certificates and associate. *Special study options:* academic remediation for entering students, adult/continuing education programs, advanced placement credit, cooperative education, distance learning, English as a second language, independent study, internships, off-campus study, part-time degree program, services for LD students, study abroad, summer session for credit. *ROTC:* Army (c).

Library Middlesex County College Library plus 1 other.

Student Life *Housing:* college housing not available. *Activities and Organizations:* drama/theater group, student-run newspaper, radio station, choral group. *Campus security:* 24-hour emergency response devices and patrols. *Student services:* health clinic, personal/psychological counseling.

Athletics Member NJCAA. *Intercollegiate sports:* baseball M, basketball M/W, cross-country running M/W, soccer M/W, softball W, track and field M/W, wrestling M.

Costs (2015–16) *One-time required fee:* $86. *Tuition:* area resident $4215 full-time, $106 per credit part-time; state resident $8430 full-time, $212 per credit part-time; nonresident $8430 full-time, $212 per credit part-time. *Payment plan:* installment. *Waivers:* employees or children of employees.

Financial Aid Of all full-time matriculated undergraduates who enrolled in 2014, 69 Federal Work-Study jobs (averaging $3350).

Applying *Options:* early admission, deferred entrance. *Application fee:* $25. *Required:* high school transcript. *Application deadlines:* rolling (freshmen), rolling (transfers). *Notification:* continuous (freshmen), continuous (transfers).

Freshman Application Contact Middlesex County College, 2600 Woodbridge Avenue, PO Box 3050, Edison, NJ 08818-3050. *Website:* http://www.middlesexcc.edu/.

Ocean County College

Toms River, New Jersey

- **County-supported** 2-year, founded 1964
- **Suburban** 275-acre campus with easy access to Philadelphia
- **Coed,** 8,663 undergraduate students, 53% full-time, 56% women, 44% men

Undergraduates 4,611 full-time, 4,052 part-time. Students come from 36 states and territories; 0.9% are from out of state; 5% Black or African American, non-Hispanic/Latino; 11% Hispanic/Latino; 2% Asian, non-Hispanic/Latino; 0.2% Native Hawaiian or other Pacific Islander, non-Hispanic/Latino; 0.3% American Indian or Alaska Native, non-Hispanic/Latino; 2% Two or more races, non-Hispanic/Latino; 4% Race/ethnicity unknown; 1% international; 4% transferred in. *Retention:* 69% of full-time freshmen returned.

Freshmen *Admission:* 1,842 applied, 1,842 admitted, 1,842 enrolled.

Faculty *Total:* 490, 20% full-time, 20% with terminal degrees. *Student/faculty ratio:* 25:1.

Majors Broadcast journalism; business administration and management; business/commerce; communications technologies and support services related; computer and information sciences; criminal justice/police science; engineering; engineering technologies and engineering related; environmental science; general studies; homeland security, law enforcement, firefighting and protective services related; human services; international/global studies; liberal arts and sciences/liberal studies; occupational therapist assistant; registered nursing/registered nurse; rehabilitation and therapeutic professions related; respiratory care therapy; sign language interpretation and translation; visual and performing arts.

Academics *Calendar:* semesters. *Degree:* certificates, diplomas, and associate. *Special study options:* academic remediation for entering students, accelerated degree program, adult/continuing education programs, advanced placement credit, cooperative education, distance learning, English as a second language, honors programs, internships, part-time degree program, services for LD students, study abroad, summer session for credit.

Library Ocean County College Library. *Books:* 69,761 (physical), 170,000 (digital/electronic); *Serial titles:* 290 (physical); *Databases:* 42. Weekly public service hours: 68; students can reserve study rooms.

Student Life *Housing:* college housing not available. *Activities and Organizations:* drama/theater group, student-run newspaper, radio and television station, choral group, Student Activities Board, Student Government, OCC Vikings Cheerleaders, NJ STARS Club, Speech and Theater Club. *Campus security:* 24-hour emergency response devices and patrols, late-night transport/escort service, security cameras in hallways and parking lots. *Student services:* personal/psychological counseling.

Athletics Member NJCAA. *Intercollegiate sports:* baseball M, basketball M/W, cross-country running M/W, golf M, lacrosse M, soccer M/W, softball W, tennis M/W, volleyball W. *Intramural sports:* basketball M/W, cheerleading M(c)/W(c), ice hockey M(c), sailing M(c)/W(c), soccer M/W, softball W, tennis M/W, volleyball M/W.

Standardized Tests *Required for some:* ACCUPLACER or waiver for degree-seeking students.

Costs (2016–17) *Tuition:* area resident $3360 full-time, $112 per credit part-time; state resident $4050 full-time, $135 per credit part-time; nonresident $6750 full-time, $225 per credit part-time. Full-time tuition and fees vary according to program. Part-time tuition and fees vary according to program. *Required fees:* $985 full-time, $32 per credit part-time, $20 per term part-time. *Payment plan:* installment. *Waivers:* senior citizens and employees or children of employees.

Financial Aid Of all full-time matriculated undergraduates who enrolled in 2014, 76 Federal Work-Study jobs (averaging $1300). 45 state and other part-time jobs (averaging $850).

Applying *Options:* electronic application. *Required for some:* high school transcript. *Application deadlines:* rolling (freshmen), rolling (out-of-state freshmen), rolling (transfers). *Notification:* continuous (freshmen), continuous (out-of-state freshmen), continuous (transfers).

Freshman Application Contact Ms. Sheenah Hartigan, CRM Communications Administrator, Ocean County College, College Drive, PO Box 2001, Toms River, NJ 08754-2001. *Phone:* 732-255-0400 Ext. 2189. *E-mail:* shartigan@ocean.edu. *Website:* http://www.ocean.edu/.

Passaic County Community College

Paterson, New Jersey

Freshman Application Contact Mr. Patrick Noonan, Director of Admissions, Passaic County Community College, One College Boulevard, Paterson, NJ 07505-1179. *Phone:* 973-684-6304. *Website:* http://www.pccc.cc.nj.us/.

Raritan Valley Community College

Branchburg, New Jersey

- **State and locally supported** 2-year, founded 1965
- **Suburban** 225-acre campus with easy access to New York City, Philadelphia
- **Endowment** $974,466
- **Coed,** 8,099 undergraduate students, 41% full-time, 51% women, 49% men

Undergraduates 3,361 full-time, 4,738 part-time. Students come from 14 states and territories; 0.8% are from out of state; 10% Black or African American, non-Hispanic/Latino; 20% Hispanic/Latino; 6% Asian, non-Hispanic/Latino; 0.4% Native Hawaiian or other Pacific Islander, non-Hispanic/Latino; 0.2% American Indian or Alaska Native, non-Hispanic/Latino; 2% Two or more races, non-Hispanic/Latino; 7% Race/ethnicity unknown; 2% international; 4% transferred in. *Retention:* 71% of full-time freshmen returned.

Freshmen *Admission:* 1,403 enrolled. *Test scores:* SAT critical reading scores over 500: 67%; SAT math scores over 500: 78%; SAT writing scores over 500: 60%; SAT critical reading scores over 600: 18%; SAT math scores over 600: 25%; SAT writing scores over 600: 15%; SAT critical reading scores over 700: 1%; SAT math scores over 700: 1%; SAT writing scores over 700: 1%.

Faculty *Total:* 463, 27% full-time. *Student/faculty ratio:* 21:1.

Majors Accounting related; accounting technology and bookkeeping; administrative assistant and secretarial science; animation, interactive technology, video graphics and special effects; automotive engineering technology; biotechnology; business administration and management; business/commerce; chemical technology; child-care provision; cinematography and film/video production; communication and media related; computer and information sciences and support services related; computer programming (vendor/product certification); computer systems networking and telecommunications; construction engineering technology; corrections; criminal justice/law enforcement administration; criminal justice/police science; critical incident response/special police operations; dance; dental assisting; dental hygiene; design and applied arts related; diesel mechanics technology; digital communication and media/multimedia; engineering science; engineering technologies and engineering related; English; financial planning and services; fine/studio arts; health and physical education/fitness; health information/medical records technology; health services/allied health/health sciences; heating, ventilation, air conditioning and refrigeration engineering technology; information technology; interior design; international business/trade/commerce; kindergarten/preschool education; kinesiology and exercise science; legal assistant/paralegal; liberal arts and sciences/liberal studies; lineworker; management information systems; manufacturing engineering technology; marketing/marketing management; medical/clinical assistant; meeting and event planning; multi/interdisciplinary studies related; music; opticianry; optometric technician; registered nursing/registered nurse; respiratory care therapy; restaurant, culinary, and catering management; small business administration; web page, digital/multimedia and information resources design.

Academics *Calendar:* semesters. *Degree:* certificates and associate. *Special study options:* academic remediation for entering students, adult/continuing education programs, advanced placement credit, cooperative education, distance learning, double majors, English as a second language, honors programs, independent study, internships, off-campus study, part-time degree program, services for LD students, summer session for credit. *ROTC:* Army (c), Air Force (c).

Library Evelyn S. Field Library. *Books:* 76,075 (physical), 109,201 (digital/electronic); *Databases:* 81.

Student Life *Housing:* college housing not available. *Activities and Organizations:* drama/theater group, student-run newspaper, radio station, choral group, Phi Theta Kappa, Orgullo Latino, Student Nurses Association, Business Club/SIFE, Environmental Club. *Campus security:* 24-hour emergency response devices and patrols, late-night transport/escort service, 24-hour outdoor and indoor surveillance cameras, 24-hour communication center. *Student services:* personal/psychological counseling.

Athletics Member NJCAA. *Intercollegiate sports:* baseball M(s), basketball M(s)/W(s), soccer M/W, softball W(s), volleyball W. *Intramural sports:* basketball M/W, softball M/W, volleyball M/W.

Costs (2015–16) *Tuition:* area resident $4110 full-time, $137 per credit hour part-time; state resident $5010 full-time, $167 per credit hour part-time; nonresident $5010 full-time, $167 per credit hour part-time. *Required fees:* $924 full-time, $22 per credit hour part-time, $132 per term part-time. *Payment plan:* installment. *Waivers:* employees or children of employees.

Financial Aid Of all full-time matriculated undergraduates who enrolled in 2014, 12 Federal Work-Study jobs (averaging $2500).

Applying *Required:* high school transcript.

Freshman Application Contact Mr. Daniel Palubniak, Registrar, Enrollment Services, Raritan Valley Community College, 118 Lamington Road, Branchburg, NJ 08876. *Phone:* 908-526-1200 Ext. 8206. *Fax:* 908-704-3442. *E-mail:* dpalubni@raritanval.edu. *Website:* http://www.raritanval.edu/.

Rowan College at Burlington County
Pemberton, New Jersey

- **County-supported** 2-year, founded 1966
- **Suburban** 225-acre campus with easy access to Philadelphia
- **Coed,** 8,762 undergraduate students, 49% full-time, 57% women, 43% men

Undergraduates 4,289 full-time, 4,473 part-time. Students come from 23 states and territories; 0.9% are from out of state; 20% Black or African American, non-Hispanic/Latino; 10% Hispanic/Latino; 4% Asian, non-Hispanic/Latino; 0.2% Native Hawaiian or other Pacific Islander, non-Hispanic/Latino; 0.2% American Indian or Alaska Native, non-Hispanic/Latino; 3% Two or more races, non-Hispanic/Latino; 5% Race/ethnicity unknown; 2% international.

Faculty *Student/faculty ratio:* 26:1.

Majors Accounting; agribusiness; American Sign Language (ASL); animation, interactive technology, video graphics and special effects; art; automotive engineering technology; baking and pastry arts; biological and physical sciences; biology/biological sciences; biotechnology; business administration and management; casino management; chemical engineering; chemistry; commercial and advertising art; communication disorders sciences and services related; computer graphics; computer science; construction engineering technology; criminal justice/police science; culinary arts; dental hygiene; drafting and design technology; dramatic/theater arts; education; electrical, electronic and communications engineering technology; energy management and systems technology; engineering; engineering technologies and engineering related; English; environmental science; fashion/apparel design; fire science/firefighting; food service systems administration; geological and earth sciences/geosciences related; graphic and printing equipment operation/production; graphic design; health information/medical records technology; health services/allied health/health sciences; history; hospitality administration; human services; information technology; international/global studies; journalism; legal assistant/paralegal; liberal arts and sciences/liberal studies; management information systems; mathematics; medical radiologic technology; music; philosophy; physics; psychology; registered nursing/registered nurse; respiratory care therapy; restaurant/food services management; retailing; sales, distribution, and marketing operations; sign language interpretation and translation; social sciences; sociology; sustainability studies.

Academics *Calendar:* semesters plus 2 summer terms. *Degree:* certificates and associate. *Special study options:* academic remediation for entering students, accelerated degree program, adult/continuing education programs, advanced placement credit, cooperative education, distance learning, double majors, English as a second language, honors programs, independent study, internships, part-time degree program, services for LD students, study abroad, summer session for credit.

Library William K. McDaniel Integrated Learning Resource Center plus 1 other.

Student Life *Housing:* college housing not available. *Activities and Organizations:* drama/theater group, student-run radio station, choral group, Student Government Association, Phi Theta Kappa, Dental Hygiene Club, Student Nurses Association, Radiography Club. *Campus security:* 24-hour emergency response devices and patrols, late-night transport/escort service, electronic entrances to buildings and rooms, surveillance cameras. *Student services:* personal/psychological counseling.

Athletics Member NJCAA. *Intercollegiate sports:* baseball M(s), basketball M(s)/W(s), golf M(s)/W(s), soccer M(s)/W(s), softball W(s). *Intramural sports:* archery M.

Costs (2016–17) *Tuition:* area resident $3000 full-time, $100 per credit hour part-time; state resident $3480 full-time, $116 per credit hour part-time; nonresident $5430 full-time, $181 per credit hour part-time. Full-time tuition and fees vary according to program. Part-time tuition and fees vary according to program. *Required fees:* $1065 full-time, $36 per credit hour part-time. *Payment plans:* installment, deferred payment. *Waivers:* senior citizens and employees or children of employees.

Financial Aid Of all full-time matriculated undergraduates who enrolled in 2014, 100 Federal Work-Study jobs (averaging $1200). 100 state and other part-time jobs (averaging $2000).

Applying *Options:* electronic application, early admission, deferred entrance. *Application fee:* $20. *Recommended:* high school transcript. *Application deadlines:* rolling (freshmen), rolling (out-of-state freshmen), rolling (transfers). *Notification:* continuous (freshmen), continuous (out-of-state freshmen), continuous (transfers).

Freshman Application Contact Rowan College at Burlington County, 601 Pemberton Browns Mills Road, Pemberton, NJ 08068. *Phone:* 609-894-9311 Ext. 1200. *Website:* http://www.rcbc.edu/.

Rowan College at Gloucester County
Sewell, New Jersey

Freshman Application Contact Ms. Judy Atkinson, Registrar/Admissions, Rowan College at Gloucester County, 1400 Tanyard Road, Sewell, NJ 08080. *Phone:* 856-415-2209. *E-mail:* jatkinso@gccnj.edu. *Website:* http://www.rcgc.edu/.

Salem Community College
Carneys Point, New Jersey

- **County-supported** 2-year, founded 1972
- **Small-town** campus with easy access to Philadelphia
- **Coed**

Undergraduates 602 full-time, 505 part-time. 20% are from out of state; 18% Black or African American, non-Hispanic/Latino; 5% Hispanic/Latino; 2% Asian, non-Hispanic/Latino; 0.5% Native Hawaiian or other Pacific Islander, non-Hispanic/Latino; 0.6% American Indian or Alaska Native, non-Hispanic/Latino; 4% Two or more races, non-Hispanic/Latino; 18% Race/ethnicity unknown.
Faculty *Student/faculty ratio:* 19:1.
Academics *Calendar:* semesters. *Degree:* certificates and associate. *Special study options:* academic remediation for entering students, adult/continuing education programs, advanced placement credit, cooperative education, distance learning, double majors, English as a second language, independent study, off-campus study, part-time degree program, services for LD students, summer session for credit.
Library Michael S. Cettei Memorial Library.
Student Life *Campus security:* 24-hour emergency response devices and patrols, late-night transport/escort service.
Costs (2015–16) *Tuition:* area resident $3060 full-time, $102 per credit hour part-time; state resident $3750 full-time, $125 per credit hour part-time; nonresident $4500 full-time, $150 per credit hour part-time. Full-time tuition and fees vary according to course load and program. Part-time tuition and fees vary according to course load and program. *Required fees:* $1044 full-time, $33 per credit hour part-time, $27 per term part-time.
Financial Aid Of all full-time matriculated undergraduates who enrolled in 2010, 756 applied for aid, 624 were judged to have need, 35 had their need fully met. 34 Federal Work-Study jobs (averaging $1137). In 2010, 39. *Average percent of need met:* 47. *Average financial aid package:* $4663. *Average need-based loan:* $2304. *Average need-based gift aid:* $4284. *Average non-need-based aid:* $1652.
Applying *Options:* electronic application, early admission, deferred entrance. *Application fee:* $27. *Required:* high school transcript, Basic Skills test or minimum SAT scores. Students with a minimum score of 530 in math and 540 in English on the SAT are exempt from placement testing. HS GPA of 3.0 or higher needed for placement in Gateway courses. *Required for some:* essay or personal statement.
Freshman Application Contact Kelly McShay, Director of Retention and Admissions, Salem Community College, 460 Hollywood Avenue, Carneys Point, NJ 08069. *Phone:* 856-351-2919. *E-mail:* kmcshay@salemcc.edu. *Website:* http://www.salemcc.edu/.

Sussex County Community College
Newton, New Jersey

Freshman Application Contact Mr. Todd Poltersdorf, Director of Admissions, Sussex County Community College, 1 College Hill Road, Newton, NJ 07860. *Phone:* 973-300-2253. *E-mail:* tpoltersdorf@sussex.edu. *Website:* http://www.sussex.edu/.

Union County College
Cranford, New Jersey

Freshman Application Contact Ms. Nina Hernandez, Director of Admissions, Records, and Registration, Union County College, Cranford, NJ 07016. *Phone:* 908-709-7127. *Fax:* 908-709-7125. *E-mail:* hernandez@ucc.edu. *Website:* http://www.ucc.edu/.

Warren County Community College
Washington, New Jersey

Freshman Application Contact Shannon Horwath, Associate Director of Admissions, Warren County Community College, 475 Route 57 West, Washington, NJ 07882-9605. *Phone:* 908-835-2300. *E-mail:* shorwath@warren.edu. *Website:* http://www.warren.edu/.

NEW MEXICO

Brown Mackie College–Albuquerque
Albuquerque, New Mexico

Freshman Application Contact Brown Mackie College–Albuquerque, 10500 Copper Avenue NE, Albuquerque, NM 87123. *Phone:* 505-559-5200. *Toll-free phone:* 877-271-3488.
Website: http://www.brownmackie.edu/albuquerque/.

Carrington College–Albuquerque
Albuquerque, New Mexico

- **Proprietary** 2-year, part of Carrington Colleges Group, Inc.
- **Coed,** 442 undergraduate students, 90% full-time, 86% women, 14% men

Undergraduates 399 full-time, 43 part-time. 2% are from out of state; 3% Black or African American, non-Hispanic/Latino; 56% Hispanic/Latino; 2% Asian, non-Hispanic/Latino; 0.2% Native Hawaiian or other Pacific Islander, non-Hispanic/Latino; 21% American Indian or Alaska Native, non-Hispanic/Latino; 0.5% Two or more races, non-Hispanic/Latino; 1% Race/ethnicity unknown; 24% transferred in.
Freshmen *Admission:* 43 enrolled.
Faculty *Total:* 26, 35% full-time. *Student/faculty ratio:* 28:1.
Majors Medical office management; physical therapy technology; registered nursing/registered nurse.
Academics *Degree:* certificates and associate.
Costs (2015–16) *Tuition:* $14,053 full-time. Full-time tuition and fees vary according to program. Part-time tuition and fees vary according to program. *Required fees:* $780 full-time.
Applying *Required:* essay or personal statement, high school transcript, interview, institutional entrance test.
Freshman Application Contact Carrington College–Albuquerque, 1001 Menaul Boulevard NE, Albuquerque, NM 87107. *Website:* http://carrington.edu/.

Central New Mexico Community College
Albuquerque, New Mexico

- **State-supported** 2-year, founded 1965
- **Urban** campus
- **Endowment** $1.6 million
- **Coed,** 25,888 undergraduate students, 31% full-time, 56% women, 44% men

Undergraduates 7,953 full-time, 17,935 part-time. 0.4% are from out of state; 3% Black or African American, non-Hispanic/Latino; 49% Hispanic/Latino; 2% Asian, non-Hispanic/Latino; 0.2% Native Hawaiian or other Pacific Islander, non-Hispanic/Latino; 7% American Indian or Alaska Native, non-Hispanic/Latino; 2% Two or more races, non-Hispanic/Latino; 7% Race/ethnicity unknown; 0.1% international; 5% transferred in.
Freshmen *Admission:* 5,172 applied, 5,172 admitted, 2,886 enrolled.
Faculty *Total:* 1,084, 33% full-time. *Student/faculty ratio:* 23:1.
Majors Accounting; administrative assistant and secretarial science; airframe mechanics and aircraft maintenance technology; anthropology; architectural drafting and CAD/CADD; art; automobile/automotive mechanics technology; biology/biological sciences; biotechnology; business administration and management; chemistry; clinical/medical laboratory technology; communication; computer and information sciences; computer science; construction management; cosmetology; criminal justice/law enforcement administration; criminology; culinary arts; diagnostic medical sonography and ultrasound technology; dramatic/theater arts; early childhood education; education (multiple levels); electrical, electronic and communications engineering technology; electrician; emergency medical technology (EMT paramedic); English; environmental design/architecture; fire science/firefighting; foods, nutrition, and wellness; foreign languages and literatures; general studies; geographic information science and cartography; health and physical education/fitness; health information/medical records administration; health information/medical records technology; health services/allied health/health sciences; heating, air conditioning, ventilation and refrigeration maintenance technology; history; hospitality administration; human development and family studies; Latin American studies; legal assistant/paralegal; liberal arts and sciences/liberal studies; machine tool technology; mathematics; opticianry; physics; plumbing technology; political science and government; pre-engineering; pre-law studies; psychology; radiologic technology/science; registered nursing/registered nurse; respiratory care therapy; sociology; surgical technology; surveying engineering; technology/industrial arts teacher education; vehicle maintenance and repair technologies related; veterinary/animal health technology; welding technology.

Academics *Calendar:* trimesters. *Degree:* certificates and associate. *Special study options:* academic remediation for entering students, accelerated degree program, adult/continuing education programs, advanced placement credit, cooperative education, distance learning, English as a second language, honors programs, independent study, internships, off-campus study, part-time degree program, services for LD students, summer session for credit. *ROTC:* Army (c), Navy (c), Air Force (c).
Library Main Campus Library.
Student Life *Housing:* college housing not available. *Activities and Organizations:* student-run newspaper. *Campus security:* 24-hour emergency response devices and patrols, late-night transport/escort service. *Student services:* health clinic, personal/psychological counseling.
Costs (2015–16) *Tuition:* state resident $1224 full-time, $51 per credit hour part-time; nonresident $6480 full-time, $270 per credit hour part-time. *Required fees:* $224 full-time, $6 per credit hour part-time, $40 per term part-time. *Payment plan:* installment. *Waivers:* senior citizens and employees or children of employees.
Financial Aid Of all full-time matriculated undergraduates who enrolled in 2014, 4,841 were judged to have need. 115 Federal Work-Study jobs (averaging $8000). 300 state and other part-time jobs (averaging $8000). In 2014, 3367 non-need-based awards were made. *Average non-need-based aid:* $397.
Applying *Options:* electronic application. *Application deadlines:* rolling (freshmen), rolling (out-of-state freshmen), rolling (transfers). *Notification:* continuous (freshmen), continuous (out-of-state freshmen), continuous (transfers).
Freshman Application Contact Glenn Damiani, Sr. Director, Enrollment Services, Central New Mexico Community College, Albuquerque, NM 87106. *Phone:* 505-224-3223. *E-mail:* gdamiani@cnm.edu.
Website: http://www.cnm.edu/.

Clovis Community College
Clovis, New Mexico

Freshman Application Contact Ms. Rosie Corrie, Director of Admissions and Records/Registrar, Clovis Community College, Clovis, NM 88101-8381. *Phone:* 575-769-4962. *Toll-free phone:* 800-769-1409. *Fax:* 575-769-4190. *E-mail:* admissions@clovis.edu.
Website: http://www.clovis.edu/.

Doña Ana Community College
Las Cruces, New Mexico

Freshman Application Contact Mrs. Ricci Montes, Admissions Advisor, Doña Ana Community College, MSC-3DA, Box 30001, 3400 South Espina Street, Las Cruces, NM 88003-8001. *Phone:* 575-527-7683. *Toll-free phone:* 800-903-7503. *Fax:* 575-527-7515.
Website: http://dacc.nmsu.edu/.

Eastern New Mexico University–Roswell
Roswell, New Mexico

Freshman Application Contact Eastern New Mexico University–Roswell, PO Box 6000, Roswell, NM 88202-6000. *Phone:* 505-624-7142. *Toll-free phone:* 800-243-6687 (in-state); 800-624-7000 (out-of-state).
Website: http://www.roswell.enmu.edu/.

IntelliTec College
Albuquerque, New Mexico

Admissions Office Contact IntelliTec College, 5001 Montgomery Boulevard NE, Suite A24, Albuquerque, NM 87109.
Website: http://www.intelliteccollege.edu/.

ITT Technical Institute
Albuquerque, New Mexico

Freshman Application Contact Director of Recruitment, ITT Technical Institute, 5100 Masthead Street, NE, Albuquerque, NM 87109. *Phone:* 505-828-1114. *Toll-free phone:* 800-636-1114.
Website: http://www.itt-tech.edu/.

Luna Community College
Las Vegas, New Mexico

Freshman Application Contact Ms. Henrietta Griego, Director of Admissions, Recruitment, and Retention, Luna Community College, PO Box 1510, Las Vegas, NM 87701. *Phone:* 505-454-2020. *Toll-free phone:* 800-588-7232 (in-state); 800-5888-7232 (out-of-state). *Fax:* 505-454-2588. *E-mail:* hgriego@luna.cc.nm.us.
Website: http://www.luna.edu/.

Mesalands Community College
Tucumcari, New Mexico

Director of Admissions Mr. Ken Brashear, Director of Enrollment Management, Mesalands Community College, 911 South Tenth Street, Tucumcari, NM 88401. *Phone:* 505-461-4413.
Website: http://www.mesalands.edu/.

National American University
Albuquerque, New Mexico

Freshman Application Contact Admissions Office, National American University, 10131 Coors Boulevard NW, Suite I-01, Albuquerque, NM 87114.
Website: http://www.national.edu/.

New Mexico Junior College
Hobbs, New Mexico

- **State and locally supported** 2-year, founded 1965, part of New Mexico Commission on Higher Education
- **Small-town** 185-acre campus
- **Coed**, 3,222 undergraduate students

Undergraduates Students come from 17 states and territories; 7 other countries; 10% are from out of state; 15% live on campus.
Freshmen *Average high school GPA:* 2.75.
Faculty *Total:* 120, 54% full-time. *Student/faculty ratio:* 19:1.
Majors Accounting; administrative assistant and secretarial science; agriculture; art; art teacher education; athletic training; automobile/automotive mechanics technology; biological and physical sciences; biology/biological sciences; business administration and management; business teacher education; carpentry; chemistry; clinical/medical laboratory technology; commercial and advertising art; computer graphics; computer programming; computer science; computer typography and composition equipment operation; construction engineering technology; cosmetology; criminal justice/police science; data processing and data processing technology; drafting and design technology; dramatic/theater arts; education; elementary education; emergency medical technology (EMT paramedic); engineering; English; environmental education; environmental studies; finance; fire science/firefighting; health professions related; history; legal administrative assistant/secretary; liberal arts and sciences/liberal studies; licensed practical/vocational nurse training; machine tool technology; marketing/marketing management; mathematics; medical administrative assistant and medical secretary; medical/clinical assistant; music; parks, recreation and leisure; petroleum technology; physical education teaching and coaching; real estate; registered nursing/registered nurse; trade and industrial teacher education; welding technology.
Academics *Calendar:* semesters. *Degree:* certificates and associate. *Special study options:* academic remediation for entering students, advanced placement credit, cooperative education, distance learning, internships, part-time degree program, services for LD students, summer session for credit.
Library Pannell Library.
Student Life *Housing:* on-campus residence required for freshman year. *Options:* coed. Campus housing is university owned. *Activities and Organizations:* drama/theater group, choral group, Student Nurses Association, Phi Theta Kappa, Fellowship of Christian Athletes. *Campus security:* 24-hour emergency response devices and patrols, late-night transport/escort service, controlled dormitory access. *Student services:* health clinic, personal/psychological counseling.
Athletics Member NJCAA. *Intercollegiate sports:* baseball M(s), basketball M(s)/W(s), golf M(s). *Intramural sports:* badminton M/W, basketball M/W, cross-country running M/W, football M, racquetball M/W, table tennis M/W, volleyball M/W, weight lifting M/W.
Costs (2015–16) *Tuition:* area resident $1050 full-time, $35 per credit hour part-time; state resident $1620 full-time, $54 per credit hour part-time; nonresident $1860 full-time, $62 per credit hour part-time. Full-time tuition and fees vary according to course load. Part-time tuition and fees vary according to course load. *Required fees:* $510 full-time, $17 per credit hour part-time. *Room and board:* $4700; room only: $2400. Room and board charges vary according to board plan and housing facility. *Payment plan:* deferred payment. *Waivers:* senior citizens and employees or children of employees.

Applying *Options:* electronic application, early admission, deferred entrance. *Application deadlines:* rolling (freshmen), rolling (transfers).
Freshman Application Contact New Mexico Junior College, 5317 Lovington Highway, Hobbs, NM 88240-9123. *Phone:* 575-492-2587. *Toll-free phone:* 800-657-6260.
Website: http://www.nmjc.edu/.

New Mexico Military Institute
Roswell, New Mexico

Freshman Application Contact New Mexico Military Institute, Roswell, NM 88201-5173. *Phone:* 505-624-8050. *Toll-free phone:* 800-421-5376. *Fax:* 505-624-8058. *E-mail:* admissions@nmmi.edu.
Website: http://www.nmmi.edu/.

New Mexico State University–Alamogordo
Alamogordo, New Mexico

Freshman Application Contact Ms. Elma Hernandez, Coordinator of Admissions and Records, New Mexico State University–Alamogordo, 2400 North Scenic Drive, Alamogordo, NM 88311-0477. *Phone:* 575-439-3700. *E-mail:* advisor@nmsua.nmsu.edu.
Website: http://nmsua.edu/.

New Mexico State University–Carlsbad
Carlsbad, New Mexico

Freshman Application Contact Ms. Everal Shannon, Records Specialist, New Mexico State University–Carlsbad, 1500 University Drive, Carlsbad, NM 88220. *Phone:* 575-234-9222. *Fax:* 575-885-4951.
E-mail: eshannon@nmsu.edu.
Website: http://www.cavern.nmsu.edu/.

New Mexico State University–Grants
Grants, New Mexico

Director of Admissions Ms. Irene Lutz, Campus Student Services Officer, New Mexico State University–Grants, 1500 3rd Street, Grants, NM 87020-2025. *Phone:* 505-287-7981.
Website: http://grants.nmsu.edu/.

Pima Medical Institute
Albuquerque, New Mexico

Freshman Application Contact Admissions Office, Pima Medical Institute, 4400 Cutler Avenue NE, Albuquerque, NM 87110. *Phone:* 505-881-1234. *Toll-free phone:* 800-477-PIMA (in-state); 888-477-PIMA (out-of-state). *Fax:* 505-881-5329.
Website: http://www.pmi.edu/.

Pima Medical Institute
Albuquerque, New Mexico

Freshman Application Contact Pima Medical Institute, RMTS 32, 8601 Golf Course Road, NW, Albuquerque, NM 87114. *Phone:* 505-816-0556.
Website: http://www.pmi.edu/.

San Juan College
Farmington, New Mexico

- **State-supported** 2-year, founded 1958, part of New Mexico Higher Education Department
- **Small-town** 698-acre campus
- **Endowment** $14.1 million
- **Coed,** 5,692 undergraduate students, 47% full-time, 65% women, 35% men

Undergraduates 2,674 full-time, 3,018 part-time. Students come from 52 states and territories; 33 other countries; 27% are from out of state; 9% transferred in.
Freshmen *Admission:* 1,015 applied, 1,015 admitted, 890 enrolled.
Faculty *Total:* 306, 55% full-time, 6% with terminal degrees. *Student/faculty ratio:* 23:1.
Majors Accounting technology and bookkeeping; American Indian/Native American studies; autobody/collision and repair technology; automobile/automotive mechanics technology; biology/biological sciences;

business administration and management; carpentry; chemistry; child-care provision; clinical/medical laboratory technology; commercial and advertising art; cosmetology; criminal justice/police science; data processing and data processing technology; dental hygiene; diesel mechanics technology; drafting and design technology; electrical, electronic and communications engineering technology; elementary education; emergency medical technology (EMT paramedic); engineering; engineering technology; fire science/firefighting; general studies; geology/earth science; health and physical education/fitness; health information/medical records technology; industrial mechanics and maintenance technology; industrial technology; instrumentation technology; landscaping and groundskeeping; legal assistant/paralegal; liberal arts and sciences/liberal studies; machine shop technology; mathematics; occupational safety and health technology; occupational therapist assistant; parks, recreation and leisure; physical sciences; physical therapy technology; physics; premedical studies; psychology; registered nursing/registered nurse; respiratory care therapy; secondary education; social work; solar energy technology; special education; surgical technology; theater design and technology; veterinary/animal health technology; welding technology.
Academics *Calendar:* semesters. *Degree:* certificates, diplomas, and associate. *Special study options:* academic remediation for entering students, adult/continuing education programs, advanced placement credit, cooperative education, distance learning, double majors, English as a second language, freshman honors college, honors programs, independent study, internships, part-time degree program, services for LD students, summer session for credit.
Library San Juan College Library. *Books:* 71,434 (physical), 169,102 (digital/electronic); *Serial titles:* 241 (physical), 18,076 (digital/electronic); *Databases:* 64. Weekly public service hours: 69.
Student Life *Housing:* college housing not available. *Activities and Organizations:* drama/theater group, student-run newspaper, choral group, AGAVE, SJC National Society of Leadership and Success, Psychology/PSI Beta, National Honor Society of Leadership and Success (NSLS), American Indian Science and Leadership Society (AISES), national fraternities, national sororities. *Campus security:* 24-hour emergency response devices and patrols, late-night transport/escort service. *Student services:* personal/psychological counseling.
Athletics *Intramural sports:* basketball M/W, football M/W, rock climbing M/W, soccer M/W, softball M/W, table tennis M/W, ultimate Frisbee M/W, volleyball M/W.
Costs (2016–17) *Tuition:* state resident $1104 full-time, $46 per credit hour part-time; nonresident $3504 full-time, $146 per credit hour part-time. Full-time tuition and fees vary according to reciprocity agreements. Part-time tuition and fees vary according to reciprocity agreements. *Required fees:* $370 full-time, $78 per term part-time. *Payment plans:* tuition prepayment, installment. *Waivers:* senior citizens and employees or children of employees.
Financial Aid Of all full-time matriculated undergraduates who enrolled in 2014, 150 Federal Work-Study jobs (averaging $2500). 175 state and other part-time jobs (averaging $2500).
Applying *Options:* electronic application, early admission, deferred entrance. *Application fee:* $10. *Required:* high school transcript. *Application deadlines:* rolling (freshmen), rolling (transfers). *Notification:* continuous (freshmen), continuous (transfers).
Freshman Application Contact Mrs. Abby Calcote, Enrollment Specialist, San Juan College, 4601 College Boulevard, Farmington, NM 87402. *Phone:* 505-566-3572. *Fax:* 505-566-3500. *E-mail:* calcotea@sanjuancollege.edu.
Website: http://www.sanjuancollege.edu/.

Santa Fe Community College
Santa Fe, New Mexico

Freshman Application Contact Ms. Rebecca Estrada, Director of Recruitment, Santa Fe Community College, 6401 Richards Ave, Santa Fe, NM 87508. *Phone:* 505-428-1604. *Fax:* 505-428-1468.
E-mail: rebecca.estrada@sfcc.edu.
Website: http://www.sfcc.edu/.

Southwestern Indian Polytechnic Institute
Albuquerque, New Mexico

- **Federally supported** 2-year, founded 1971
- **Suburban** 144-acre campus
- **Coed,** 402 undergraduate students, 86% full-time, 55% women, 45% men

Undergraduates 346 full-time, 56 part-time. Students come from 18 states and territories; 60% live on campus.
Freshmen *Admission:* 183 applied, 157 admitted, 103 enrolled. *Average high school GPA:* 2.11.
Faculty *Total:* 41, 56% full-time, 12% with terminal degrees. *Student/faculty ratio:* 16:1.

Majors Accounting technology and bookkeeping; business administration and management; business/commerce; early childhood education; engineering; geographic information science and cartography; institutional food workers; instrumentation technology; liberal arts and sciences/liberal studies; natural resources and conservation related; opticianry; system, networking, and LAN/WAN management.

Academics *Calendar:* trimesters. *Degree:* certificates and associate. *Special study options:* academic remediation for entering students, advanced placement credit, cooperative education, distance learning, double majors, internships, part-time degree program, services for LD students, summer session for credit.

Library Southwestern Indian Polytechnic Institute Library.

Student Life *Housing Options:* men-only, women-only. Campus housing is university owned. *Activities and Organizations:* Dance Club, Student Senate, Natural Resources, Pow-Wow Club. *Campus security:* 24-hour emergency response devices and patrols, late-night transport/escort service. *Student services:* personal/psychological counseling.

Athletics *Intramural sports:* basketball M/W, softball M/W, volleyball M/W.

Costs (2015–16) *Tuition:* The Bureau of Indian Education (BIE) provides tuition, room board, and books to students at minimal charge. *Required fees:* $1095 full-time, $290 per term part-time. *Room and board:* $675. *Payment plan:* deferred payment.

Financial Aid Of all full-time matriculated undergraduates who enrolled in 2013, 350 applied for aid, 350 were judged to have need, 4 had their need fully met. 15 Federal Work-Study jobs (averaging $774). 16 state and other part-time jobs (averaging $813). *Average percent of need met:* 22%. *Average financial aid package:* $2590. *Average need-based gift aid:* $2590.

Applying *Required:* high school transcript, Certificate of Indian Blood, physical, immunization records. *Application deadlines:* 7/30 (freshmen), 7/30 (transfers). *Notification:* continuous (freshmen).

Freshman Application Contact Southwestern Indian Polytechnic Institute, 9169 Coors, NW, Box 10146, Albuquerque, NM 87184-0146. *Phone:* 505-346-2324. *Toll-free phone:* 800-586-7474.

Website: http://www.sipi.edu/.

University of New Mexico–Gallup
Gallup, New Mexico

- **State-supported** 2-year, founded 1968, part of New Mexico Commission on Higher Education
- **Small-town** 80-acre campus
- **Coed,** 2,473 undergraduate students, 47% full-time, 62% women, 38% men

Undergraduates 1,163 full-time, 1,310 part-time. 11% are from out of state; 0.5% Black or African American, non-Hispanic/Latino; 13% Hispanic/Latino; 0.9% Asian, non-Hispanic/Latino; 76% American Indian or Alaska Native, non-Hispanic/Latino; 2% Two or more races, non-Hispanic/Latino; 0.8% Race/ethnicity unknown; 0.4% international; 4% transferred in. *Retention:* 56% of full-time freshmen returned.

Freshmen *Admission:* 2,473 enrolled.

Faculty *Student/faculty ratio:* 20:1.

Majors Accounting; administrative assistant and secretarial science; art; automobile/automotive mechanics technology; business administration and management; clinical/medical laboratory technology; community organization and advocacy; construction engineering technology; corrections; cosmetology; criminal justice/law enforcement administration; education; elementary education; general studies; kindergarten/preschool education; liberal arts and sciences/liberal studies; marketing/marketing management; physical sciences; registered nursing/registered nurse; welding technology.

Academics *Calendar:* semesters. *Degree:* certificates, diplomas, and associate. *Special study options:* academic remediation for entering students, adult/continuing education programs, advanced placement credit, cooperative education, distance learning, double majors, honors programs, independent study, internships, off-campus study, part-time degree program, services for LD students, summer session for credit.

Library Zollinger Library plus 1 other. Study areas open 24 hours, 5&-7 days a week.

Student Life *Housing:* college housing not available. *Activities and Organizations:* student-run newspaper. *Campus security:* late-night transport/escort service.

Costs (2015–16) *Tuition:* state resident $904 full-time, $75 per credit hour part-time; nonresident $2189 full-time, $183 per credit hour part-time. *Payment plan:* installment. *Waivers:* senior citizens.

Applying *Options:* electronic application. *Application fee:* $15. *Required for some:* high school transcript. *Application deadlines:* rolling (freshmen), rolling (transfers). *Notification:* continuous (freshmen), continuous (transfers).

Freshman Application Contact University of New Mexico–Gallup, 200 College Road, Gallup, NM 87301-5603. *Phone:* 505-863-7576.

Website: http://www.gallup.unm.edu/.

University of New Mexico–Los Alamos Branch
Los Alamos, New Mexico

Freshman Application Contact Mrs. Irene K. Martinez, Enrollment Representative, University of New Mexico–Los Alamos Branch, 4000 University Drive, Los Alamos, NM 87544-2233. *Phone:* 505-662-0332.

E-mail: l65130@unm.edu.

Website: http://losalamos.unm.edu/.

University of New Mexico–Taos
Taos, New Mexico

Director of Admissions Vickie Alvarez, Student Enrollment Associate, University of New Mexico–Taos, 115 Civic Plaza Drive, Taos, NM 87571. *Phone:* 575-737-6425. *E-mail:* valvarez@unm.edu.

Website: http://taos.unm.edu/.

University of New Mexico–Valencia Campus
Los Lunas, New Mexico

Director of Admissions Richard M. Hulett, Director of Admissions and Recruitment, University of New Mexico–Valencia Campus, 280 La Entrada, Los Lunas, NM 87031-7633. *Phone:* 505-277-2446.

E-mail: mhulett@unm.edu.

Website: http://www.unm.edu/~unmvc/.

NEW YORK

Adirondack Community College
Queensbury, New York

Freshman Application Contact Office of Admissions, Adirondack Community College, 640 Bay Road, Queensbury, NY 12804. *Phone:* 518-743-2264. *Toll-free phone:* 888-SUNY-ADK. *Fax:* 518-743-2200.

Website: http://www.sunyacc.edu/.

American Academy McAllister Institute of Funeral Service
New York, New York

Freshman Application Contact Mr. Norman Provost, Registrar, American Academy McAllister Institute of Funeral Service, 450 West 56th Street, New York, NY 10019-3602. *Phone:* 212-757-1190. *Toll-free phone:* 866-932-2264.

Website: http://www.funeraleducation.org/.

American Academy of Dramatic Arts–New York
New York, New York

- **Independent** 2-year, founded 1884
- **Urban** campus
- **Coed,** 261 undergraduate students, 100% full-time, 67% women, 33% men

Undergraduates 261 full-time. 53% live on campus.

Freshmen *Admission:* 520 applied, 393 admitted, 103 enrolled.

Faculty *Total:* 31, 32% full-time, 35% with terminal degrees. *Student/faculty ratio:* 13:1.

Majors Dramatic/theater arts.

Academics *Calendar:* semesters. *Degree:* certificates and associate. *Special study options:* academic remediation for entering students, honors programs.

Library Academy/CBS Library.

Student Life *Housing Options:* coed. Campus housing is leased by the school. Freshman applicants given priority for college housing. *Activities and Organizations:* national fraternities. *Campus security:* 24-hour emergency response devices and patrols, controlled dormitory access, trained security guard during hours of operation and for campus housing. *Student services:* personal/psychological counseling.

Costs (2016–17) *Tuition:* $32,440 full-time. *Required fees:* $750 full-time.

Financial Aid Of all full-time matriculated undergraduates who enrolled in 2012, 240 applied for aid, 231 were judged to have need. 50 Federal Work-Study jobs (averaging $900). 50 state and other part-time jobs (averaging $2000). In 2012, 59 non-need-based awards were made. *Average percent of need met:* 67%. *Average financial aid package:* $18,150. *Average need-based loan:* $4500. *Average need-based gift aid:* $7000. *Average non-need-based aid:* $7000. *Average indebtedness upon graduation:* $15,000. *Financial aid deadline:* 5/15.

Applying *Options:* electronic application, deferred entrance. *Application fee:* $50. *Required:* essay or personal statement, high school transcript, minimum 2.0 GPA, 2 letters of recommendation, interview, audition. *Application deadlines:* rolling (freshmen), rolling (transfers). *Notification:* continuous (freshmen), continuous (transfers).

Freshman Application Contact Kerin Reilly, Director of Admissions, American Academy of Dramatic Arts–New York, 120 Madison Avenue, New York, NY 10016. *Phone:* 212-686-9244 Ext. 333. *Toll-free phone:* 800-463-8990. *E-mail:* kreilly@aada.edu.
Website: http://www.aada.edu/.

ASA College
Brooklyn, New York

Freshman Application Contact Admissions Office, ASA College, 81 Willoughby Street, Brooklyn, NY 11201. *Phone:* 718-522-9073. *Toll-free phone:* 877-679-8772.
Website: http://www.asa.edu/.

The Belanger School of Nursing
Schenectady, New York

- **Independent** 2-year, founded 1906
- **Urban** campus
- **Coed, primarily women,** 127 undergraduate students, 25% full-time, 87% women, 13% men

Undergraduates 32 full-time, 95 part-time. Students come from 1 other state; 10% Black or African American, non-Hispanic/Latino; 3% Hispanic/Latino; 5% Asian, non-Hispanic/Latino; 0.8% Two or more races, non-Hispanic/Latino; 0.8% Race/ethnicity unknown.
Freshmen *Admission:* 2 enrolled. *Average high school GPA:* 3.2.
Faculty *Student/faculty ratio:* 6:1.
Majors Registered nursing/registered nurse.
Academics *Degree:* associate.
Student Life *Housing:* college housing not available.
Standardized Tests *Recommended:* SAT or ACT (for admission).
Costs (2015–16) *Tuition:* $9072 full-time, $6867 per year part-time. Full-time tuition and fees vary according to course level, course load, and student level. Part-time tuition and fees vary according to course level, course load, and student level. *Required fees:* $1148 full-time, $315 per credit part-time, $728 per year part-time. *Payment plan:* installment.
Applying *Required:* essay or personal statement, high school transcript, minimum 3.0 GPA, 2 letters of recommendation.
Freshman Application Contact Carolyn Lansing, Student Services Manager, The Belanger School of Nursing, 65 McClellan Street, Schenectady, NY 12304. *Phone:* 518-831-8810. *Fax:* 518-243-4470.
E-mail: lansingc@ellismedicine.org.
Website: http://www.ellismedicine.org/school-of-nursing/.

Berkeley College–White Plains Campus
White Plains, New York

- **Proprietary** primarily 2-year, founded 1945
- **Suburban** campus with easy access to New York City
- **Coed,** 467 undergraduate students, 92% full-time, 65% women, 35% men

Undergraduates 428 full-time, 39 part-time. Students come from 8 other countries; 22% are from out of state; 29% Black or African American, non-Hispanic/Latino; 23% Hispanic/Latino; 2% Asian, non-Hispanic/Latino; 0.2% American Indian or Alaska Native, non-Hispanic/Latino; 24% Race/ethnicity unknown; 7% international; 20% transferred in. *Retention:* 59% of full-time freshmen returned.
Freshmen *Admission:* 104 enrolled.
Faculty *Student/faculty ratio:* 23:1.
Majors Business administration and management; criminal justice/law enforcement administration; criminal justice/police science; fashion merchandising; health/health-care administration; health information/medical records technology; marketing/marketing management.
Academics *Calendar:* quarters. *Degrees:* associate and bachelor's. *Special study options:* academic remediation for entering students, accelerated degree program, adult/continuing education programs, advanced placement credit, cooperative education, distance learning, honors programs, independent study,

internships, off-campus study, part-time degree program, study abroad, summer session for credit.
Student Life *Housing Options:* coed. Campus housing is university owned. *Activities and Organizations:* student-run newspaper. *Campus security:* 24-hour emergency response devices, controlled dormitory access, monitored entrance with front desk security guard. *Student services:* personal/psychological counseling.
Athletics Member USCAA. *Intercollegiate sports:* basketball M/W, cross-country running M/W, soccer M/W, tennis M/W.
Costs (2016–17) *Tuition:* $23,100 full-time, $810 per credit hour part-time. Full-time tuition and fees vary according to course load. Part-time tuition and fees vary according to course load. No tuition increase for student's term of enrollment. *Required fees:* $1650 full-time, $412 per term part-time. *Room only:* $9000. *Payment plan:* installment. *Waivers:* employees or children of employees.
Applying *Options:* electronic application, deferred entrance. *Application fee:* $50. *Required:* high school transcript. *Recommended:* interview. *Application deadlines:* rolling (freshmen), rolling (out-of-state freshmen), rolling (transfers). *Notification:* continuous (freshmen), continuous (out-of-state freshmen), continuous (transfers).
Freshman Application Contact Lynn Ovimeleh, Director of High School Admissions, Berkeley College–White Plains Campus, 99 Church Street, White Plains, NY 10601. *Phone:* 914-694-1122. *Toll-free phone:* 800-446-5400.
E-mail: info@berkeleycollege.edu.
Website: http://www.berkeleycollege.edu/.

Bill and Sandra Pomeroy College of Nursing at Crouse Hospital
Syracuse, New York

Freshman Application Contact Ms. Amy Graham, Enrollment Management Supervisor, Bill and Sandra Pomeroy College of Nursing at Crouse Hospital, 765 Irving Avenue, Syracuse, NY 13210. *Phone:* 315-470-7481. *Fax:* 315-470-7925. *E-mail:* amygraham@crouse.org.
Website: http://www.crouse.org/nursing/.

Borough of Manhattan Community College of the City University of New York
New York, New York

- **State and locally supported** 2-year, founded 1963, part of City University of New York System
- **Urban** 5-acre campus
- **Coed,** 27,309 undergraduate students, 66% full-time, 57% women, 43% men

Undergraduates 18,074 full-time, 9,235 part-time. 2% are from out of state; 30% Black or African American, non-Hispanic/Latino; 40% Hispanic/Latino; 13% Asian, non-Hispanic/Latino; 0.3% American Indian or Alaska Native, non-Hispanic/Latino; 6% international; 6% transferred in.
Freshmen *Admission:* 24,438 applied, 24,143 admitted, 6,812 enrolled. *Test scores:* SAT critical reading scores over 500: 8%; SAT math scores over 500: 10%; SAT critical reading scores over 600: 1%; SAT math scores over 600: 1%.
Faculty *Total:* 1,567, 35% full-time. *Student/faculty ratio:* 24:1.
Majors Accounting; accounting technology and bookkeeping; administrative assistant and secretarial science; animation, interactive technology, video graphics and special effects; art history, criticism and conservation; biotechnology; business administration and management; community organization and advocacy; computer and information sciences; computer science; computer systems networking and telecommunications; criminal justice/law enforcement administration; criminal justice/police science; emergency medical technology (EMT paramedic); engineering; English; foreign languages and literatures; forensic science and technology; general studies; geographic information science and cartography; health information/medical records technology; history; liberal arts and sciences/liberal studies; mathematics; medical informatics; physical sciences; public health education and promotion; radio and television broadcasting technology; registered nursing/registered nurse; respiratory therapy technician; small business administration; sociology; teacher assistant/aide; visual and performing arts; web page, digital/multimedia and information resources design.
Academics *Calendar:* semesters. *Degree:* certificates and associate. *Special study options:* academic remediation for entering students, adult/continuing education programs, advanced placement credit, cooperative education, distance learning, English as a second language, honors programs, independent

study, internships, off-campus study, part-time degree program, services for LD students, study abroad, summer session for credit.
Library A. Philip Randolph Library plus 1 other. *Books:* 104,541 (physical), 220,000 (digital/electronic); *Serial titles:* 265 (physical), 75,883 (digital/electronic); *Databases:* 176. Weekly public service hours: 104; students can reserve study rooms.
Student Life *Housing:* college housing not available. *Activities and Organizations:* drama/theater group, student-run newspaper, choral group, Anime Club, Health Information Technology Club, Muslim Students Association, Organization for Student Veterans, Urban Mentors and Leaders Association. *Campus security:* 24-hour patrols. *Student services:* health clinic, personal/psychological counseling, women's center.
Athletics Member NJCAA. *Intercollegiate sports:* basketball M/W, soccer M/W, volleyball W.
Standardized Tests *Recommended:* SAT or ACT (for admission).
Costs (2016–17) *Tuition:* state resident $4800 full-time, $210 per credit part-time; nonresident $7680 full-time, $320 per credit part-time. Full-time tuition and fees vary according to course load. Part-time tuition and fees vary according to course load. *Required fees:* $369 full-time, $100 per term part-time. *Payment plans:* installment, deferred payment. *Waivers:* senior citizens and employees or children of employees.
Applying *Options:* electronic application, deferred entrance. *Application fee:* $65. *Required:* high school transcript. *Application deadlines:* rolling (freshmen), rolling (transfers). *Notification:* continuous (freshmen), continuous (transfers).
Freshman Application Contact Dr. Eugenio Barrios, Director of Enrollment Management, Borough of Manhattan Community College of the City University of New York, 199 Chambers Street, Room S-310, New York, NY 10007. *Phone:* 212-220-1265. *Toll-free phone:* 866-583-5729. *Fax:* 212-220-2366. *E-mail:* admissions@bmcc.cuny.edu.
Website: http://www.bmcc.cuny.edu/.

Bramson ORT College
Forest Hills, New York

Freshman Application Contact Admissions Office, Bramson ORT College, 69-30 Austin Street, Forest Hills, NY 11375-4239. *Phone:* 718-261-5800. *Fax:* 718-575-5119. *E-mail:* admissions@bramsonort.edu.
Website: http://www.bramsonort.edu/.

Bronx Community College of the City University of New York
Bronx, New York

Freshman Application Contact Ms. Patricia A. Ramos, Admissions Officer, Bronx Community College of the City University of New York, 2155 University Avenue, Bronx, NY 10453. *Phone:* 718-289-5888.
E-mail: admission@bcc.cuny.edu.
Website: http://www.bcc.cuny.edu/.

Broome Community College
Binghamton, New York

Freshman Application Contact Ms. Jenae Norris, Director of Admissions, Broome Community College, PO Box 1017, Upper Front Street, Binghamton, NY 13902. *Phone:* 607-778-5001. *Fax:* 607-778-5394.
E-mail: admissions@sunybroome.edu.
Website: http://www.sunybroome.edu/.

Bryant & Stratton College–Albany Campus
Albany, New York

Freshman Application Contact Mr. Robert Ferrell, Director of Admissions, Bryant & Stratton College–Albany Campus, 1259 Central Avenue, Albany, NY 12205. *Phone:* 518-437-1802 Ext. 205. *Fax:* 518-437-1048.
Website: http://www.bryantstratton.edu/.

Bryant & Stratton College–Amherst Campus
Clarence, New York

Freshman Application Contact Mr. Brian K. Dioguardi, Director of Admissions, Bryant & Stratton College–Amherst Campus, Audubon Business Center, 40 Hazelwood Drive, Amherst, NY 14228. *Phone:* 716-691-0012. *Fax:* 716-691-0012. *E-mail:* bkdioguardi@bryantstratton.edu.
Website: http://www.bryantstratton.edu/.

Bryant & Stratton College–Buffalo Campus
Buffalo, New York

Freshman Application Contact Mr. Philip J. Struebel, Director of Admissions, Bryant & Stratton College–Buffalo Campus, 465 Main Street, Suite 400, Buffalo, NY 14203. *Phone:* 716-884-9120. *Fax:* 716-884-0091.
E-mail: pjstruebel@bryantstratton.edu.
Website: http://www.bryantstratton.edu/.

Bryant & Stratton College–Greece Campus
Rochester, New York

Freshman Application Contact Bryant & Stratton College–Greece Campus, 854 Long Pond Road, Rochester, NY 14612. *Phone:* 585-720-0660.
Website: http://www.bryantstratton.edu/.

Bryant & Stratton College–Henrietta Campus
Rochester, New York

Freshman Application Contact Bryant & Stratton College–Henrietta Campus, 1225 Jefferson Road, Rochester, NY 14623. *Phone:* 585-292-5627 Ext. 101.
Website: http://www.bryantstratton.edu/.

Bryant & Stratton College–Liverpool Campus
Liverpool, New York

Freshman Application Contact Ms. Heather Macnik, Director of Admissions, Bryant & Stratton College–Liverpool Campus, 8687 Carling Road, Liverpool, NY 13090. *Phone:* 315-652-6500.
Website: http://www.bryantstratton.edu/.

Bryant & Stratton College–Orchard Park Campus
Orchard Park, New York

Freshman Application Contact Bryant & Stratton College–Orchard Park Campus, 200 Redtail Road, Orchard Park, NY 14127. *Phone:* 716-677-9500.
Website: http://www.bryantstratton.edu/.

Bryant & Stratton College–Syracuse Campus
Syracuse, New York

Freshman Application Contact Ms. Dawn Rajkowski, Director of High School Enrollments, Bryant & Stratton College–Syracuse Campus, 953 James Street, Syracuse, NY 13203-2502. *Phone:* 315-472-6603 Ext. 248. *Fax:* 315-474-4383.
Website: http://www.bryantstratton.edu/.

Cayuga County Community College
Auburn, New York

- **State and locally supported** 2-year, founded 1953, part of State University of New York System
- **Small-town** 50-acre campus with easy access to Rochester, Syracuse
- **Endowment** $13.3 million
- **Coed,** 4,430 undergraduate students, 41% full-time, 61% women, 39% men

Undergraduates 1,814 full-time, 2,616 part-time. Students come from 17 states and territories; 4 other countries; 1% are from out of state; 6% Black or African American, non-Hispanic/Latino; 4% Hispanic/Latino; 1% Asian, non-Hispanic/Latino; 0.1% Native Hawaiian or other Pacific Islander, non-Hispanic/Latino; 0.3% American Indian or Alaska Native, non-Hispanic/Latino; 2% Two or more races, non-Hispanic/Latino; 3%

Race/ethnicity unknown; 0.1% international; 4% transferred in. *Retention:* 57% of full-time freshmen returned.

Freshmen *Admission:* 1,826 applied, 1,411 admitted, 563 enrolled.

Faculty *Total:* 229, 22% full-time. *Student/faculty ratio:* 20:1.

Majors Accounting technology and bookkeeping; art; business administration and management; child-care and support services management; communication and journalism related; communications systems installation and repair technology; computer and information sciences; computer and information sciences and support services related; corrections; criminal justice/police science; drafting and design technology; education (multiple levels); electrical, electronic and communications engineering technology; fine/studio arts; game and interactive media design; general studies; geography; graphic design; health services/allied health/health sciences; humanities; information science/studies; liberal arts and sciences/liberal studies; literature related; mathematics related; mechanical engineering; mechanical engineering/mechanical technology; music related; psychology related; radio, television, and digital communication related; registered nursing/registered nurse; science technologies related; sport and fitness administration/management; telecommunications technology; wine steward/sommelier; writing.

Academics *Calendar:* semesters. *Degree:* certificates and associate. *Special study options:* academic remediation for entering students, accelerated degree program, adult/continuing education programs, advanced placement credit, cooperative education, distance learning, double majors, honors programs, independent study, internships, off-campus study, part-time degree program, services for LD students, study abroad, summer session for credit. *ROTC:* Air Force (c).

Library Norman F. Bourke Memorial Library plus 2 others. *Books:* 87,056 (physical), 150,000 (digital/electronic); *Serial titles:* 292 (physical), 60,000 (digital/electronic); *Databases:* 100. Weekly public service hours: 61; students can reserve study rooms.

Student Life *Housing Options:* coed. Campus housing is provided by a third party. *Activities and Organizations:* drama/theater group, student-run newspaper, radio and television station, choral group, Student Activity Board, Student Government, Criminal Justice Club, Tutor Club, Early Childhood Club. *Campus security:* security from 8 a.m. to 9 p.m.. *Student services:* health clinic.

Athletics Member NJCAA. *Intercollegiate sports:* basketball M/W, bowling M/W, golf M/W, soccer M/W, softball W, volleyball W. *Intramural sports:* basketball M/W, skiing (downhill) M/W, volleyball M/W.

Standardized Tests Required for some: SAT or ACT (for admission).

Costs (2015–16) *Tuition:* state resident $4326 full-time, $178 per credit hour part-time; nonresident $8652 full-time, $356 per credit hour part-time. Full-time tuition and fees vary according to course load. Part-time tuition and fees vary according to course load. *Required fees:* $396 full-time. *Payment plan:* installment. *Waivers:* senior citizens and employees or children of employees.

Financial Aid Of all full-time matriculated undergraduates who enrolled in 2014, 150 Federal Work-Study jobs (averaging $2000). 200 state and other part-time jobs (averaging $1000).

Applying *Options:* electronic application, deferred entrance. *Required:* high school transcript. *Required for some:* interview. *Application deadlines:* rolling (freshmen), rolling (transfers). *Notification:* continuous (freshmen), continuous (transfers).

Freshman Application Contact Cayuga County Community College, 197 Franklin Street, Auburn, NY 13021-3099. *Phone:* 315-255-1743 Ext. 2244. *Toll-free phone:* 866-598-8883.

Website: http://www.cayuga-cc.edu/.

Clinton Community College

Plattsburgh, New York

- **State and locally supported** 2-year, founded 1969, part of State University of New York System
- **Small-town** 100-acre campus
- **Coed,** 1,245 undergraduate students, 69% full-time, 59% women, 41% men

Undergraduates 864 full-time, 381 part-time. Students come from 12 states and territories; 22 other countries; 3% are from out of state; 7% Black or African American, non-Hispanic/Latino; 2% Hispanic/Latino; 1% Asian, non-Hispanic/Latino; 0.1% Native Hawaiian or other Pacific Islander, non-Hispanic/Latino; 0.8% American Indian or Alaska Native, non-Hispanic/Latino; 1% Two or more races, non-Hispanic/Latino; 11% Race/ethnicity unknown; 1% international; 7% transferred in; 10% live on campus. *Retention:* 63% of full-time freshmen returned.

Freshmen *Admission:* 1,206 applied, 365 admitted, 365 enrolled.

Faculty *Total:* 111, 55% full-time. *Student/faculty ratio:* 11:1.

Majors Accounting; biological and physical sciences; business administration and management; community organization and advocacy; computer/information technology services administration related; consumer merchandising/retailing management; criminal justice/law enforcement administration; criminal justice/police science; electrical, electronic and communications engineering technology; energy management and systems technology; engineering technologies and engineering related; humanities; industrial technology; liberal arts and sciences/liberal studies; physical education teaching and coaching; registered nursing/registered nurse; social sciences.

Academics *Calendar:* semesters. *Degree:* certificates and associate. *Special study options:* academic remediation for entering students, adult/continuing education programs, advanced placement credit, cooperative education, distance learning, English as a second language, external degree program, honors programs, independent study, internships, off-campus study, part-time degree program, services for LD students, student-designed majors, summer session for credit.

Library Clinton Community College Learning Resource Center plus 1 other.

Student Life *Housing Options:* coed, special housing for students with disabilities. Campus housing is provided by a third party. Freshman campus housing is guaranteed. *Activities and Organizations:* drama/theater group, student-run newspaper, choral group, Athletics, Future Human Services Professionals, PTK (honor society), Drama Club, Criminal Justice Club. *Campus security:* 24-hour emergency response devices and patrols, late-night transport/escort service, controlled dormitory access. *Student services:* health clinic, personal/psychological counseling.

Athletics Member NJCAA. *Intercollegiate sports:* baseball M, basketball M/W, soccer M/W. *Intramural sports:* volleyball M/W.

Costs (2016–17) *Tuition:* state resident $4300 full-time, $179 per credit hour part-time; nonresident $9300 full-time, $383 per credit hour part-time. Full-time tuition and fees vary according to course load and program. Part-time tuition and fees vary according to course load and program. *Required fees:* $998 full-time, $33 per credit hour part-time. *Room and board:* $9310; room only: $5170. Room and board charges vary according to board plan. *Payment plan:* installment.

Financial Aid Of all full-time matriculated undergraduates who enrolled in 2014, 45 Federal Work-Study jobs (averaging $1260).

Applying *Options:* electronic application, deferred entrance. *Required:* high school transcript. *Required for some:* essay or personal statement, 3 letters of recommendation, interview. *Application deadlines:* 8/26 (freshmen), 9/3 (transfers). *Notification:* continuous (freshmen), continuous (out-of-state freshmen), continuous (transfers).

Freshman Application Contact Clinton Community College, 136 Clinton Point Drive, Plattsburgh, NY 12901-9573. *Phone:* 518-562-4100. *Toll-free phone:* 800-552-1160.

Website: http://www.clinton.edu/.

Cochran School of Nursing

Yonkers, New York

- **Independent** 2-year, founded 1894
- **Urban** campus with easy access to New York City
- **Coed, primarily women,** 89 undergraduate students, 13% full-time, 85% women, 15% men

Undergraduates 12 full-time, 77 part-time. 17% are from out of state; 22% Black or African American, non-Hispanic/Latino; 28% Hispanic/Latino; 7% Asian, non-Hispanic/Latino; 3% Two or more races, non-Hispanic/Latino.

Freshmen *Average high school GPA:* 3.

Faculty *Total:* 11, 82% full-time. *Student/faculty ratio:* 10:1.

Majors Registered nursing/registered nurse.

Academics *Calendar:* semesters. *Degree:* associate. *Special study options:* advanced placement credit, part-time degree program.

Library Cochran School of Nursing Library. *Books:* 2,179 (physical), 545 (digital/electronic); *Serial titles:* 21 (physical), 3 (digital/electronic); *Databases:* 12.

Student Life *Housing:* college housing not available. *Campus security:* 24-hour emergency response devices and patrols, late-night transport/escort service. *Student services:* health clinic, personal/psychological counseling.

Costs (2016–17) *Tuition:* $9571 full-time, $563 per credit part-time. Full-time tuition and fees vary according to course load and student level. Part-time tuition and fees vary according to course load and student level. *Required fees:* $1486 full-time, $734 per term part-time. *Payment plan:* installment.

Applying *Options:* deferred entrance. *Application fee:* $35. *Required:* essay or personal statement, high school transcript, interview. *Application deadline:* 4/15 (freshmen). *Notification:* 4/15 (freshmen), continuous (transfers).

Freshman Application Contact Drew Thompson, Admissions Counselor, Cochran School of Nursing, 967 North Broadway, Yonkers, NY 10701. *Phone:* 914-964-4606. *Fax:* 914-964-4796.

E-mail: dthompson@riversidehealth.org.

Website: http://www.cochranschoolofnursing.us/.

The College of Westchester
White Plains, New York

- **Proprietary** primarily 2-year, founded 1915
- **Suburban** campus with easy access to New York City
- **Coed,** 1,067 undergraduate students, 79% full-time, 65% women, 35% men

Undergraduates 847 full-time, 220 part-time. Students come from 3 states and territories; 3% are from out of state; 37% Black or African American, non-Hispanic/Latino; 41% Hispanic/Latino; 2% Asian, non-Hispanic/Latino; 0.2% American Indian or Alaska Native, non-Hispanic/Latino; 2% Two or more races, non-Hispanic/Latino; 6% Race/ethnicity unknown. *Retention:* 80% of full-time freshmen returned.

Freshmen *Admission:* 779 applied, 713 admitted, 211 enrolled.

Faculty *Total:* 80, 44% full-time. *Student/faculty ratio:* 18:1.

Majors Accounting; business administration and management; computer software and media applications related; health/health-care administration; health information/medical records administration; medical/clinical assistant; network and system administration; web page, digital/multimedia and information resources design.

Academics *Calendar:* semesters. *Degrees:* certificates, associate, and bachelor's. *Special study options:* academic remediation for entering students, accelerated degree program, adult/continuing education programs, cooperative education, distance learning, double majors, honors programs, internships, part-time degree program, summer session for credit.

Library Dr. William R. Papallo Library.

Student Life *Housing:* college housing not available. *Activities and Organizations:* student-run newspaper. *Student services:* personal/psychological counseling.

Standardized Tests *Recommended:* SAT (for admission).

Costs (2016–17) *Tuition:* $20,115 full-time, $745 per credit part-time. *Required fees:* $900 full-time. *Payment plan:* installment. *Waivers:* employees or children of employees.

Applying *Options:* electronic application, deferred entrance. *Application fee:* $40. *Required:* high school transcript, interview. *Required for some:* essay or personal statement. *Application deadlines:* rolling (freshmen), rolling (out-of-state freshmen), rolling (transfers).

Freshman Application Contact Mr. Matt Curtis, Senior Director, Enrollment Management, The College of Westchester, 325 Central Avenue, PO Box 710, White Plains, NY 10602. *Phone:* 914-948-4442 Ext. 313. *Toll-free phone:* 855-403-7722. *Fax:* 914-948-5441. *E-mail:* admissions@cw.edu. *Website:* http://www.cw.edu/.

Columbia-Greene Community College
Hudson, New York

- **State and locally supported** 2-year, founded 1969, part of State University of New York System
- **Rural** 143-acre campus
- **Coed,** 1,777 undergraduate students, 40% full-time, 64% women, 36% men

Undergraduates 710 full-time, 1,067 part-time. Students come from 4 states and territories; 2 other countries; 0.3% are from out of state; 8% Black or African American, non-Hispanic/Latino; 7% Hispanic/Latino; 3% Asian, non-Hispanic/Latino; 0.2% Native Hawaiian or other Pacific Islander, non-Hispanic/Latino; 0.2% American Indian or Alaska Native, non-Hispanic/Latino; 3% Two or more races, non-Hispanic/Latino; 0.2% Race/ethnicity unknown; 0.1% international; 6% transferred in. *Retention:* 64% of full-time freshmen returned.

Freshmen *Admission:* 317 enrolled.

Faculty *Total:* 98, 46% full-time. *Student/faculty ratio:* 17:1.

Majors Accounting technology and bookkeeping; administrative assistant and secretarial science; art; automobile/automotive mechanics technology; business administration and management; business/commerce; computer and information sciences; criminal justice/law enforcement administration; cyber/computer forensics and counterterrorism; environmental studies; general studies; health and physical education/fitness; humanities; human services; information technology; liberal arts and sciences/liberal studies; medical/clinical assistant; registered nursing/registered nurse.

Academics *Calendar:* semesters. *Degree:* certificates and associate. *Special study options:* academic remediation for entering students, advanced placement credit, cooperative education, distance learning, English as a second language, honors programs, independent study, internships, part-time degree program, services for LD students, summer session for credit.

Student Life *Housing:* college housing not available. *Activities and Organizations:* student-run radio station, Criminal Justice Club, Human Services Club, Psychology Club, Student Senate, Animal Advocates. *Campus security:* 24-hour emergency response devices and patrols, student patrols,

late-night transport/escort service. *Student services:* personal/psychological counseling.

Athletics Member NCAA, NJCAA. All NCAA Division III. *Intercollegiate sports:* baseball M/W, basketball M, cross-country running M/W, golf M/W, softball W, track and field M/W, volleyball W. *Intramural sports:* badminton M/W, basketball M/W, table tennis M/W, tennis M/W, volleyball M/W.

Costs (2015–16) *Tuition:* state resident $4200 full-time, $175 per semester hour part-time; nonresident $8400 full-time, $350 per semester hour part-time. Full-time tuition and fees vary according to course load and program. Part-time tuition and fees vary according to course load and program. *Required fees:* $352 full-time, $15 per semester hour part-time, $5 per term part-time. *Payment plan:* installment. *Waivers:* senior citizens and employees or children of employees.

Applying *Required:* high school transcript. *Required for some:* interview.

Freshman Application Contact Ms. Rachel Kappel, Acting Director of Admissions, Columbia-Greene Community College, 4400 Route 23, Hudson, NY 12534. *Phone:* 518-828-4181 Ext. 3370. *Fax:* 518-822-2015. *E-mail:* rachel.kappel@sunycgcc.edu. *Website:* http://www.sunycgcc.edu/.

Corning Community College
Corning, New York

- **State and locally supported** 2-year, founded 1956, part of State University of New York System
- **Rural** 500-acre campus
- **Endowment** $521,628
- **Coed,** 3,972 undergraduate students, 49% full-time, 58% women, 42% men

Undergraduates 1,929 full-time, 2,043 part-time. Students come from 9 states and territories; 14 other countries; 7% are from out of state; 4% Black or African American, non-Hispanic/Latino; 2% Hispanic/Latino; 1% Asian, non-Hispanic/Latino; 0.1% Native Hawaiian or other Pacific Islander, non-Hispanic/Latino; 0.5% American Indian or Alaska Native, non-Hispanic/Latino; 3% Two or more races, non-Hispanic/Latino; 5% Race/ethnicity unknown; 0.2% international; 3% transferred in; 6% live on campus. *Retention:* 56% of full-time freshmen returned.

Freshmen *Admission:* 1,772 applied, 1,772 admitted, 745 enrolled. *Average high school GPA:* 3.25.

Faculty *Total:* 229, 39% full-time. *Student/faculty ratio:* 18:1.

Majors Accounting; art; autobody/collision and repair technology; automobile/automotive mechanics technology; business administration and management; CAD/CADD drafting/design technology; chemical technology; computer and information sciences; computer and information sciences and support services related; computer and information sciences related; computer/information technology services administration related; computer numerically controlled (CNC) machinist technology; computer science; computer support specialist; computer technology/computer systems technology; corrections and criminal justice related; criminal justice/police science; customer service management; digital arts; drafting/design engineering technologies related; early childhood education; education related; education (specific levels and methods) related; electrical and electronic engineering technologies related; electrical and electronics engineering; energy management and systems technology; engineering science; engineering technology; environmental science; fine arts related; fine/studio arts; graphic design; health and physical education/fitness; health and physical education related; health and wellness; health professions related; hospitality administration related; humanities; human services; information technology; liberal arts and sciences and humanities related; liberal arts and sciences/liberal studies; machine tool technology; manufacturing engineering technology; mathematics; mathematics related; mechanical drafting and CAD/CADD; mechanical engineering/mechanical technology; mechanical engineering technologies related; mechanic and repair technologies related; mechanics and repair; network and system administration; office management; office occupations and clerical services; outdoor education; parks, recreation and leisure; parks, recreation, leisure, and fitness studies related; pre-engineering; registered nursing/registered nurse; social sciences; substance abuse/addiction counseling; vehicle maintenance and repair technologies; vehicle maintenance and repair technologies related; web page, digital/multimedia and information resources design.

Academics *Calendar:* semesters. *Degree:* certificates and associate. *Special study options:* academic remediation for entering students, accelerated degree program, adult/continuing education programs, advanced placement credit, cooperative education, distance learning, double majors, English as a second language, honors programs, independent study, internships, off-campus study, part-time degree program, services for LD students, student-designed majors, study abroad, summer session for credit.

Library Arthur A. Houghton, Jr. Library. *Books:* 28,518 (physical), 185,642 (digital/electronic); *Serial titles:* 571 (physical), 27,480 (digital/electronic);

Databases: 190. Weekly public service hours: 63; students can reserve study rooms.

Student Life *Housing Options:* coed. Campus housing is university owned. *Activities and Organizations:* drama/theater group, student-run newspaper, radio station, choral group, Student Association, EQUAL, Nursing Society, Muse of Fire (theatre group), WCEB radio station. *Campus security:* 24-hour emergency response devices and patrols, late-night transport/escort service, controlled dormitory access. *Student services:* health clinic, personal/psychological counseling.

Athletics Member NJCAA. *Intercollegiate sports:* baseball M, basketball M/W, bowling M/W, soccer M/W, softball W, volleyball W. *Intramural sports:* badminton M/W, basketball M/W, soccer M/W, softball W, volleyball M/W.

Costs (2016–17) *Tuition:* state resident $4230 full-time, $177 per credit hour part-time; nonresident $8460 full-time, $354 per credit hour part-time. Part-time tuition and fees vary according to course load. *Required fees:* $544 full-time, $9 per credit hour part-time. *Room and board:* $9000; room only: $6200. Room and board charges vary according to housing facility. *Payment plan:* installment. *Waivers:* senior citizens and employees or children of employees.

Financial Aid Of all full-time matriculated undergraduates who enrolled in 2014, 264 Federal Work-Study jobs (averaging $1128).

Applying *Options:* electronic application, early admission. *Required:* high school transcript. *Required for some:* interview. *Application deadlines:* rolling (freshmen), rolling (transfers). *Notification:* continuous (freshmen), continuous (transfers).

Freshman Application Contact Corning Community College, One Academic Drive, Corning, NY 14830-3297. *Phone:* 607-962-9540. *Toll-free phone:* 800-358-7171.

Website: http://www.corning-cc.edu/.

Dutchess Community College
Poughkeepsie, New York

- **State and locally supported** 2-year, founded 1957, part of State University of New York System
- **Suburban** 130-acre campus with easy access to New York City
- **Coed,** 9,544 undergraduate students, 45% full-time, 54% women, 46% men

Undergraduates 4,283 full-time, 5,261 part-time. 11% Black or African American, non-Hispanic/Latino; 17% Hispanic/Latino; 3% Asian, non-Hispanic/Latino; 0.1% Native Hawaiian or other Pacific Islander, non-Hispanic/Latino; 0.2% American Indian or Alaska Native, non-Hispanic/Latino; 3% Two or more races, non-Hispanic/Latino; 1% Race/ethnicity unknown; 1% international; 3% transferred in; 5% live on campus.

Freshmen *Admission:* 1,853 enrolled. *Average high school GPA:* 2.5.

Faculty *Total:* 507, 25% full-time, 6% with terminal degrees. *Student/faculty ratio:* 25:1.

Majors Accounting; accounting technology and bookkeeping; airline pilot and flight crew; architectural engineering technology; art; aviation/airway management; business administration and management; child-care and support services management; clinical/medical laboratory technology; commercial and advertising art; communications systems installation and repair technology; community health services counseling; computer/information technology services administration related; computer science; construction trades related; criminal justice/police science; electrical, electronic and communications engineering technology; emergency medical technology (EMT paramedic); engineering; fire services administration; general studies; humanities; human services; information science/studies; legal assistant/paralegal; liberal arts and sciences and humanities related; liberal arts and sciences/liberal studies; physical education teaching and coaching; registered nursing/registered nurse; speech communication and rhetoric; visual and performing arts.

Academics *Calendar:* semesters. *Degree:* certificates and associate. *Special study options:* academic remediation for entering students, adult/continuing education programs, advanced placement credit, distance learning, English as a second language, freshman honors college, honors programs, internships, off-campus study, part-time degree program, services for LD students, summer session for credit.

Library Dutchess Library plus 1 other. *Books:* 88,251 (physical), 119,373 (digital/electronic); *Serial titles:* 150 (physical), 357,227 (digital/electronic); *Databases:* 70. Weekly public service hours: 70.

Student Life *Housing Options:* coed. Campus housing is university owned. *Activities and Organizations:* drama/theater group, student-run newspaper, radio station, choral group, Rap, Poetry and Music, Outdoor Adventure, Student Government Association, Gamers Club, Masquer's Guild Theatre Club. *Campus security:* 24-hour emergency response devices and patrols, late-night transport/escort service, Mass Notification System. *Student services:* health clinic, personal/psychological counseling.

Athletics Member NJCAA. *Intercollegiate sports:* baseball M, basketball M/W, cross-country running M/W, soccer M, softball W, volleyball W.

Costs (2015–16) *Tuition:* state resident $3360 full-time, $140 per credit hour part-time; nonresident $6720 full-time, $280 per credit hour part-time. *Required fees:* $447 full-time, $10 per hour part-time, $19 per term part-time. *Room and board:* $9830. Room and board charges vary according to board plan. *Payment plan:* installment. *Waivers:* senior citizens and employees or children of employees.

Applying *Options:* electronic application, early admission, deferred entrance. *Required:* high school transcript. *Application deadlines:* rolling (freshmen), rolling (transfers). *Notification:* continuous (freshmen), continuous (transfers).

Freshman Application Contact Dutchess Community College, 53 Pendell Road, Poughkeepsie, NY 12601-1595. *Phone:* 845-431-8010.

Website: http://www.sunydutchess.edu/.

Elmira Business Institute
Elmira, New York

Freshman Application Contact Ms. Lindsay Dull, Director of Student services, Elmira Business Institute, Elmira, NY 14901. *Phone:* 607-733-7177. *Toll-free phone:* 800-843-1812. *E-mail:* info@ebi-college.com. *Website:* http://www.ebi-college.com/.

Erie Community College
Buffalo, New York

- **State and locally supported** 2-year, founded 1971, part of State University of New York System
- **Urban** 1-acre campus
- **Coed,** 2,577 undergraduate students, 76% full-time, 60% women, 40% men

Undergraduates 1,965 full-time, 612 part-time. Students come from 17 states and territories; 11 other countries; 0.9% are from out of state; 31% Black or African American, non-Hispanic/Latino; 8% Hispanic/Latino; 3% Asian, non-Hispanic/Latino; 0.1% Native Hawaiian or other Pacific Islander, non-Hispanic/Latino; 1% American Indian or Alaska Native, non-Hispanic/Latino; 3% Two or more races, non-Hispanic/Latino; 13% Race/ethnicity unknown; 6% international; 5% transferred in.

Freshmen *Admission:* 2,664 applied, 1,772 admitted, 647 enrolled.

Faculty *Student/faculty ratio:* 26:1.

Majors Building/property maintenance; business administration and management; child-care and support services management; criminal justice/police science; crisis/emergency/disaster management; culinary arts; general studies; health and physical education/fitness; health and wellness; humanities; legal assistant/paralegal; liberal arts and sciences and humanities related; liberal arts and sciences/liberal studies; medical radiologic technology; registered nursing/registered nurse; substance abuse/addiction counseling.

Academics *Calendar:* semesters plus summer sessions, winter intersession. *Degree:* certificates, diplomas, and associate. *Special study options:* academic remediation for entering students, adult/continuing education programs, advanced placement credit, cooperative education, distance learning, double majors, English as a second language, honors programs, independent study, internships, part-time degree program, services for LD students, student-designed majors, study abroad, summer session for credit. *ROTC:* Army (c).

Library Leon E. Butler Library. *Books:* 22,998 (physical), 2,350 (digital/electronic); *Serial titles:* 98 (physical); *Databases:* 67. Weekly public service hours: 66; students can reserve study rooms.

Student Life *Housing:* college housing not available. *Activities and Organizations:* HPER, Muslim International Student Association, Campus Ministry, Pride Alliance. *Campus security:* 24-hour emergency response devices and patrols, late-night transport/escort service. *Student services:* health clinic, personal/psychological counseling, women's center.

Athletics Member NJCAA. *Intercollegiate sports:* baseball M, basketball M/W, bowling M/W, cheerleading W, football M, ice hockey M, lacrosse W, soccer M/W, softball W, volleyball W.

Costs (2015–16) *One-time required fee:* $75. *Tuition:* area resident $4595 full-time, $192 per credit hour part-time; state resident $9190 full-time, $384 per credit hour part-time; nonresident $9190 full-time, $384 per credit hour part-time. *Required fees:* $593 full-time, $15 per credit hour part-time, $70 per term part-time. *Payment plan:* installment. *Waivers:* senior citizens and employees or children of employees.

Applying *Options:* electronic application. *Application fee:* $25. *Required:* high school transcript. *Required for some:* interview. *Application deadlines:* rolling (freshmen), rolling (transfers). *Notification:* continuous (freshmen), continuous (transfers).

Freshman Application Contact Erie Community College, 121 Ellicott Street, Buffalo, NY 14203-2698. *Phone:* 716-851-1155. *Fax:* 716-270-2821. *E-mail:* admissions@ecc.edu. *Website:* http://www.ecc.edu/.

Erie Community College, North Campus
Williamsville, New York

- **State and locally supported** 2-year, founded 1946, part of State University of New York System
- **Suburban** 120-acre campus with easy access to Buffalo
- **Coed,** 5,551 undergraduate students, 67% full-time, 49% women, 51% men

Undergraduates 3,741 full-time, 1,810 part-time. Students come from 23 states and territories; 24 other countries; 1% are from out of state; 11% Black or African American, non-Hispanic/Latino; 4% Hispanic/Latino; 3% Asian, non-Hispanic/Latino; 0.1% Native Hawaiian or other Pacific Islander, non-Hispanic/Latino; 0.7% American Indian or Alaska Native, non-Hispanic/Latino; 2% Two or more races, non-Hispanic/Latino; 17% Race/ethnicity unknown; 5% international; 8% transferred in.
Freshmen *Admission:* 4,664 applied, 3,291 admitted, 1,217 enrolled. *Test scores:* SAT critical reading scores over 500: 90%; SAT math scores over 500: 87%; SAT critical reading scores over 600: 15%; SAT math scores over 600: 12%; SAT critical reading scores over 700: 1%; SAT math scores over 700: 1%.
Faculty *Student/faculty ratio:* 26:1.
Majors Biology/biotechnology laboratory technician; building/construction site management; business administration and management; civil engineering technology; clinical/medical laboratory technology; computer and information sciences; criminal justice/law enforcement administration; criminal justice/police science; culinary arts; dental hygiene; dietitian assistant; electrical, electronic and communications engineering technology; engineering; environmental engineering technology; environmental science; general studies; health and physical education/fitness; health and wellness; health information/medical records technology; humanities; industrial technology; liberal arts and sciences/liberal studies; mechanical engineering/mechanical technology; medical administrative assistant and medical secretary; nanotechnology; occupational therapist assistant; office management; opticianry; registered nursing/registered nurse; respiratory care therapy; restaurant/food services management.
Academics *Calendar:* semesters plus summer sessions, winter intersession. *Degree:* certificates, diplomas, and associate. *Special study options:* academic remediation for entering students, adult/continuing education programs, advanced placement credit, cooperative education, distance learning, double majors, English as a second language, honors programs, independent study, internships, part-time degree program, services for LD students, student-designed majors, study abroad, summer session for credit. *ROTC:* Army (c).
Library Richard R. Dry Memorial Library. *Books:* 49,298 (physical), 2,350 (digital/electronic); *Serial titles:* 161 (physical); *Databases:* 67. Weekly public service hours: 73.
Student Life *Housing:* college housing not available. *Activities and Organizations:* Dental Hygiene, American Public Works Association, Student Occupational Therapy Association, Anime and Gaming Club, International Student Organization. *Campus security:* 24-hour emergency response devices and patrols, late-night transport/escort service. *Student services:* health clinic, personal/psychological counseling, women's center.
Athletics Member NJCAA. *Intercollegiate sports:* baseball M, basketball M/W, bowling M/W, cheerleading W, football M, ice hockey M, lacrosse W, soccer M/W, softball W, volleyball W.
Costs (2015–16) *One-time required fee:* $75. *Tuition:* area resident $4595 full-time, $192 per credit hour part-time; state resident $9190 full-time, $384 per credit hour part-time; nonresident $9190 full-time, $384 per credit hour part-time. *Required fees:* $593 full-time, $15 per credit hour part-time, $70 per term part-time. *Payment plan:* installment. *Waivers:* senior citizens and employees or children of employees.
Applying *Options:* electronic application. *Application fee:* $25. *Required:* high school transcript. *Required for some:* interview. *Application deadlines:* rolling (freshmen), rolling (transfers). *Notification:* continuous (freshmen), continuous (transfers).
Freshman Application Contact Erie Community College, North Campus, 6205 Main Street, Williamsville, NY 14221-7095. *Phone:* 716-851-1455. *Fax:* 716-270-2961. *E-mail:* admissions@ecc.edu. *Website:* http://www.ecc.edu/.

Erie Community College, South Campus
Orchard Park, New York

- **State and locally supported** 2-year, founded 1974, part of State University of New York System
- **Suburban** 110-acre campus with easy access to Buffalo
- **Coed,** 3,894 undergraduate students, 57% full-time, 45% women, 55% men

Undergraduates 2,225 full-time, 1,669 part-time. Students come from 13 states and territories; 8 other countries; 1% are from out of state; 7% Black or African American, non-Hispanic/Latino; 4% Hispanic/Latino; 1% Asian, non-Hispanic/Latino; 0.1% Native Hawaiian or other Pacific Islander, non-Hispanic/Latino; 0.8% American Indian or Alaska Native, non-Hispanic/Latino; 3% Two or more races, non-Hispanic/Latino; 19% Race/ethnicity unknown; 1% international; 5% transferred in.
Freshmen *Admission:* 2,662 applied, 2,194 admitted, 797 enrolled. *Test scores:* SAT math scores over 500: 88%; SAT math scores over 600: 18%; SAT math scores over 700: 1%.
Faculty *Student/faculty ratio:* 26:1.
Majors Architectural engineering technology; autobody/collision and repair technology; automobile/automotive mechanics technology; business administration and management; CAD/CADD drafting/design technology; communications systems installation and repair technology; computer technology/computer systems technology; criminal justice/police science; dental laboratory technology; emergency medical technology (EMT paramedic); fire services administration; general studies; graphic and printing equipment operation/production; health and physical education/fitness; health and wellness; humanities; information technology; liberal arts and sciences/liberal studies; office management; speech communication and rhetoric; telecommunications technology.
Academics *Calendar:* semesters plus summer sessions, winter intersession. *Degree:* certificates, diplomas, and associate. *Special study options:* academic remediation for entering students, adult/continuing education programs, advanced placement credit, cooperative education, distance learning, double majors, English as a second language, honors programs, independent study, internships, part-time degree program, services for LD students, student-designed majors, study abroad, summer session for credit. *ROTC:* Army (c).
Library ECC South Campus Libarary. *Books:* 36,535 (physical), 2,350 (digital/electronic); *Serial titles:* 174 (physical); *Databases:* 67.
Student Life *Housing:* college housing not available. *Activities and Organizations:* STEM Club, Philosophy Club. *Campus security:* 24-hour emergency response devices and patrols, late-night transport/escort service. *Student services:* health clinic, personal/psychological counseling, women's center.
Athletics Member NJCAA. *Intercollegiate sports:* baseball M, basketball M/W, bowling M/W, cheerleading W, football M, ice hockey M, lacrosse W, soccer M/W, softball W, volleyball W.
Costs (2015–16) *One-time required fee:* $75. *Tuition:* area resident $4595 full-time, $192 per credit hour part-time; state resident $9190 full-time, $384 per credit hour part-time; nonresident $9190 full-time, $384 per credit hour part-time. *Required fees:* $593 full-time, $15 per credit hour part-time, $70 per term part-time. *Payment plan:* installment. *Waivers:* senior citizens and employees or children of employees.
Applying *Options:* electronic application. *Application fee:* $25. *Required:* high school transcript. *Required for some:* interview. *Application deadlines:* rolling (freshmen), rolling (transfers). *Notification:* continuous (freshmen), continuous (transfers).
Freshman Application Contact Erie Community College, South Campus, 4041 Southwestern Boulevard, Orchard Park, NY 14127-2199. *Phone:* 716-851-1655. *Fax:* 716-851-1687. *E-mail:* admissions@ecc.edu. *Website:* http://www.ecc.edu/.

Eugenio María de Hostos Community College of the City University of New York
Bronx, New York

Freshman Application Contact Mr. Roland Velez, Director of Admissions, Eugenio María de Hostos Community College of the City University of New York, 120 149th Street, Bronx, NY 10451. *Phone:* 718-319-7968. *Fax:* 718-319-7919. *E-mail:* admissions@hostos.cuny.edu. *Website:* http://www.hostos.cuny.edu/.

★ Fashion Institute of Technology
New York, New York

- **State and locally supported** comprehensive, founded 1944, part of State University of New York System
- **Urban** 5-acre campus with easy access to New York City
- **Coed, primarily women,** 9,392 undergraduate students, 79% full-time, 85% women, 15% men

Undergraduates 7,409 full-time, 1,983 part-time. 31% are from out of state; 9% Black or African American, non-Hispanic/Latino; 16% Hispanic/Latino; 11% Asian, non-Hispanic/Latino; 0.3% Native Hawaiian or other Pacific Islander, non-Hispanic/Latino; 0.2% American Indian or Alaska Native, non-Hispanic/Latino; 3% Two or more races, non-Hispanic/Latino; 1% Race/ethnicity unknown; 13% international; 9% transferred in; 21% live on campus. *Retention:* 90% of full-time freshmen returned.

Freshmen *Admission:* 4,753 applied, 1,948 admitted, 1,265 enrolled. *Average high school GPA:* 3.6.

Faculty *Total:* 970, 24% full-time. *Student/faculty ratio:* 17:1.

Majors Advertising; animation, interactive technology, video graphics and special effects; apparel and textile manufacturing; cinematography and film/video production; commercial and advertising art; commercial photography; design and applied arts related; entrepreneurial and small business related; fashion/apparel design; fashion merchandising; fashion modeling; film/cinema/video studies; fine and studio arts management; fine/studio arts; graphic design; illustration; industrial and product design; interior design; international marketing; marketing research; merchandising, sales, and marketing operations related (specialized); metal and jewelry arts; special products marketing.

Academics *Calendar:* semesters. *Degrees:* certificates, associate, bachelor's, and master's. *Special study options:* academic remediation for entering students, adult/continuing education programs, advanced placement credit, distance learning, English as a second language, honors programs, independent study, internships, part-time degree program, services for LD students, study abroad, summer session for credit.

Library Gladys Marcus Library.

Student Life *Housing Options:* coed, women-only, special housing for students with disabilities. Campus housing is university owned. Freshman applicants given priority for college housing. *Activities and Organizations:* drama/theater group, student-run newspaper, radio and television station, choral group. *Campus security:* 24-hour emergency response devices and patrols, late-night transport/escort service, controlled dormitory access. *Student services:* health clinic, personal/psychological counseling.

Athletics Member NJCAA. *Intercollegiate sports:* cross-country running M/W, soccer W, swimming and diving M/W, table tennis M/W, tennis M/W, track and field M/W, volleyball W.

Standardized Tests *Recommended:* SAT or ACT (for admission).

Costs (2015–16) *Tuition:* state resident $6470 full-time, $270 per credit hour part-time; nonresident $19,592 full-time, $816 per credit hour part-time. Full-time tuition and fees vary according to degree level. Part-time tuition and fees vary according to degree level. *Required fees:* $730 full-time. *Room and board:* $13,291; room only: $8945. Room and board charges vary according to board plan and housing facility.

Financial Aid Of all full-time matriculated undergraduates who enrolled in 2014, 4,941 applied for aid, 3,812 were judged to have need, 1,568 had their need fully met. In 2014, 188 non-need-based awards were made. *Average percent of need met:* 70%. *Average financial aid package:* $11,458. *Average need-based loan:* $3319. *Average need-based gift aid:* $5970. *Average non-need-based aid:* $582. *Average indebtedness upon graduation:* $25,162.

Applying *Options:* electronic application. *Application fee:* $50. *Required:* essay or personal statement, high school transcript. *Required for some:* portfolio for art and design programs. *Application deadlines:* 1/1 (freshmen), 1/1 (transfers). *Notification:* 4/1 (freshmen), 4/1 (transfers).

Freshman Application Contact Ms. Magda Francois, Director of Admissions and Strategic Recruitment, Fashion Institute of Technology, Seventh Avenue at 27th Street, New York, NY 10001-5992. *E-mail:* fitinfo@fitnyc.edu. *Website:* http://www.fitnyc.edu/.

See below for display ad and page 366 for the College Close-Up.

Finger Lakes Community College
Canandaigua, New York

- **State and locally supported** 2-year, founded 1965, part of State University of New York System
- **Small-town** 300-acre campus with easy access to Rochester
- **Coed,** 6,761 undergraduate students, 44% full-time, 57% women, 43% men

Undergraduates 3,003 full-time, 3,758 part-time. Students come from 12 states and territories; 4 other countries; 0.4% are from out of state; 7% Black or African American, non-Hispanic/Latino; 5% Hispanic/Latino; 0.7% Asian, non-Hispanic/Latino; 0.1% Native Hawaiian or other Pacific Islander, non-Hispanic/Latino; 0.3% American Indian or Alaska Native, non-Hispanic/Latino; 3% Two or more races, non-Hispanic/Latino; 8% Race/ethnicity unknown; 3% transferred in.

Freshmen *Admission:* 4,022 applied, 3,316 admitted, 1,272 enrolled.

Faculty *Total:* 341, 35% full-time. *Student/faculty ratio:* 22:1.

Majors Accounting; administrative assistant and secretarial science; animation, interactive technology, video graphics and special effects; architectural engineering technology; biological and physical sciences; biology/biological sciences; biology/biotechnology laboratory technician; business administration and management; chemistry; commercial and advertising art; computer and information sciences; computer science; criminal justice/law enforcement administration; criminal justice/police science; culinary arts; data processing and data processing technology; digital communication and media/multimedia; drafting and design technology; dramatic/theater arts; early childhood education; e-commerce; emergency medical technology (EMT paramedic); engineering science; environmental studies; fine/studio arts; fishing and fisheries sciences and management;

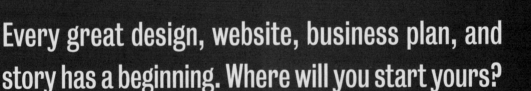

hotel/motel administration; humanities; human services; instrumentation technology; kindergarten/preschool education; legal assistant/paralegal; liberal arts and sciences/liberal studies; marketing/marketing management; mass communication/media; mathematics; mechanical engineering/mechanical technology; music; natural resources/conservation; natural resources law enforcement and protective services; natural resources management and policy; natural resources management and policy related; ornamental horticulture; physical education teaching and coaching; physics; political science and government; pre-engineering; psychology; recording arts technology; registered nursing/registered nurse; resort management; social sciences; sociology; sports studies; substance abuse/addiction counseling; tourism and travel services management; viticulture and enology.

Academics *Calendar:* semesters. *Degree:* certificates and associate. *Special study options:* academic remediation for entering students, accelerated degree program, advanced placement credit, distance learning, honors programs, internships, off-campus study, part-time degree program, services for LD students, study abroad, summer session for credit. *ROTC:* Air Force (c).

Library Charles Meder Library.

Student Life *Housing Options:* Campus housing is provided by a third party. *Activities and Organizations:* drama/theater group, student-run radio station, choral group. *Campus security:* 24-hour emergency response devices and patrols, late-night transport/escort service. *Student services:* health clinic, personal/psychological counseling, legal services.

Athletics Member NJCAA. *Intercollegiate sports:* baseball M, basketball M/W, cross-country running M/W, lacrosse M, soccer M/W, softball W, track and field M/W, volleyball W. *Intramural sports:* basketball M/W, tennis M/W, volleyball M/W.

Costs (2015–16) *Tuition:* state resident $4180 full-time, $168 per credit hour part-time; nonresident $8360 full-time, $336 per credit hour part-time. Full-time tuition and fees vary according to course load. Part-time tuition and fees vary according to course load. *Required fees:* $524 full-time, $16 per credit hour part-time. *Payment plan:* installment. *Waivers:* senior citizens and employees or children of employees.

Applying *Options:* electronic application, early admission, deferred entrance. *Application fee:* $20. *Required:* high school transcript. *Application deadlines:* 8/19 (freshmen), 8/19 (transfers).

Freshman Application Contact Ms. Bonnie B. Ritts, Director of Admissions, Finger Lakes Community College, 3325 Marvin Sands Drive, Canandaigua, NY 14424-8395. *Phone:* 585-785-1279. *Fax:* 585-785- 1734. *E-mail:* admissions@flcc.edu. *Website:* http://www.flcc.edu/.

Finger Lakes Health College of Nursing
Geneva, New York

Admissions Office Contact Finger Lakes Health College of Nursing, 196 North Street, Geneva, NY 14456. *Website:* http://www.flhcon.com/.

Fiorello H. LaGuardia Community College of the City University of New York
Long Island City, New York

- **State and locally supported** 2-year, founded 1970, part of City University of New York System
- **Urban** 10-acre campus with easy access to New York City
- **Endowment** $6.1 million
- **Coed,** 19,332 undergraduate students, 55% full-time, 57% women, 43% men

Undergraduates 10,642 full-time, 8,690 part-time. Students come from 14 states and territories; 151 other countries; 0.2% are from out of state; 15% Black or African American, non-Hispanic/Latino; 42% Hispanic/Latino; 12% Asian, non-Hispanic/Latino; 0.3% Native Hawaiian or other Pacific Islander, non-Hispanic/Latino; 0.3% American Indian or Alaska Native, non-Hispanic/Latino; 1% Two or more races, non-Hispanic/Latino; 19% Race/ethnicity unknown; 4% international; 7% transferred in.

Freshmen *Admission:* 20,608 applied, 20,608 admitted, 2,955 enrolled. **Faculty** *Total:* 1,126, 36% full-time, 30% with terminal degrees. *Student/faculty ratio:* 22:1.

Majors Accounting technology and bookkeeping; administrative assistant and secretarial science; adult development and aging; biology/biological sciences; business administration and management; civil engineering; commercial photography; computer and information sciences and support services related; computer installation and repair technology; computer programming; computer science; computer systems networking and telecommunications; criminal justice/safety; data entry/microcomputer applications; dietetic technology; digital arts; dramatic/theater arts; electrical and electronics

engineering; emergency medical technology (EMT paramedic); English; environmental science; fine/studio arts; funeral service and mortuary science; industrial and product design; legal assistant/paralegal; liberal arts and sciences/liberal studies; licensed practical/vocational nurse training; mechanical engineering; medical radiologic technology; occupational therapist assistant; philosophy; physical therapy technology; psychiatric/mental health services technology; psychology; recording arts technology; registered nursing/registered nurse; restaurant/food services management; Spanish; speech communication and rhetoric; teacher assistant/aide; tourism and travel services management; veterinary/animal health technology; visual and performing arts.

Academics *Calendar:* enhanced semester. *Degree:* certificates and associate. *Special study options:* academic remediation for entering students, accelerated degree program, adult/continuing education programs, advanced placement credit, cooperative education, distance learning, double majors, English as a second language, honors programs, independent study, internships, off-campus study, part-time degree program, services for LD students, student-designed majors, study abroad, summer session for credit.

Library Fiorello H. LaGuardia Community College Library Media Resources Center plus 1 other.

Student Life *Housing:* college housing not available. *Activities and Organizations:* drama/theater group, student-run newspaper, radio station, Bangladesh Student Association, Christian Club, Chinese Club, Web Radio, Black Student Union. *Campus security:* 24-hour emergency response devices and patrols, late-night transport/escort service. *Student services:* health clinic, personal/psychological counseling, women's center, legal services.

Athletics *Intercollegiate sports:* basketball M/W. *Intramural sports:* basketball M/W, bowling M/W, cheerleading M/W, soccer M/W, swimming and diving M/W, table tennis M/W, volleyball M/W.

Costs (2015–16) *Tuition:* state resident $4800 full-time, $210 per credit part-time; nonresident $9600 full-time, $320 per credit part-time. *Required fees:* $417 full-time, $105 per term part-time. *Payment plan:* installment. *Waivers:* senior citizens and employees or children of employees.

Financial Aid Of all full-time matriculated undergraduates who enrolled in 2012, 7,961 applied for aid, 7,741 were judged to have need, 286 had their need fully met. 352 Federal Work-Study jobs (averaging $1175). *Average percent of need met:* 45%. *Average financial aid package:* $5523. *Average need-based gift aid:* $5818.

Applying *Options:* electronic application, early admission, deferred entrance. *Application fee:* $65. *Required:* high school transcript. *Application deadlines:* rolling (freshmen), rolling (transfers). *Notification:* continuous (freshmen), continuous (transfers).

Freshman Application Contact Ms. LaVora Desvigne, Director of Admissions, Fiorello H. LaGuardia Community College of the City University of New York, RM-147, 31-10 Thomson Avenue, Long Island City, NY 11101. *Phone:* 718-482-5114. *Fax:* 718-482-5112. *E-mail:* admissions@lagcc.cuny.edu. *Website:* http://www.lagcc.cuny.edu/.

Fulton-Montgomery Community College
Johnstown, New York

Freshman Application Contact Fulton-Montgomery Community College, 2805 State Highway 67, Johnstown, NY 12095-3790. *Phone:* 518-762-4651 Ext. 8301. *Website:* http://www.fmcc.suny.edu/.

Genesee Community College
Batavia, New York

- **State and locally supported** 2-year, founded 1966, part of State University of New York System
- **Small-town** 256-acre campus with easy access to Buffalo, Rochester
- **Endowment** $4.4 million
- **Coed,** 6,521 undergraduate students, 44% full-time, 63% women, 37% men

Undergraduates 2,846 full-time, 3,675 part-time. Students come from 25 states and territories; 19 other countries; 2% are from out of state; 10% Black or African American, non-Hispanic/Latino; 5% Hispanic/Latino; 0.6% Asian, non-Hispanic/Latino; 0.1% Native Hawaiian or other Pacific Islander, non-Hispanic/Latino; 0.9% American Indian or Alaska Native, non-Hispanic/Latino; 23% Two or more races, non-Hispanic/Latino; 4% Race/ethnicity unknown; 4% international; 5% transferred in.

Freshmen *Admission:* 3,414 applied, 2,473 admitted, 988 enrolled. **Faculty** *Total:* 347, 26% full-time, 7% with terminal degrees. *Student/faculty ratio:* 18:1.

Majors Accounting; administrative assistant and secretarial science; biology/biological sciences; biology/biotechnology laboratory technician; biotechnology; business administration and management; business

administration, management and operations related; business, management, and marketing related; business operations support and secretarial services related; chemistry; civil drafting and CAD/CADD; clinical/medical laboratory technology; computer and information sciences related; computer graphics; computer installation and repair technology; computer programming related; computer science; computer software and media applications related; computer support specialist; computer systems networking and telecommunications; corrections and criminal justice related; criminal justice/law enforcement administration; criminal justice/police science; criminal justice/safety; criminology; digital arts; drafting and design technology; drafting/design engineering technologies related; dramatic/theater arts; dramatic/theater arts and stagecraft related; e-commerce; education; education (multiple levels); education related; elementary education; engineering; engineering science; entrepreneurship; fashion/apparel design; fashion merchandising; fine/studio arts; food technology and processing; foreign languages related; general studies; gerontology; graphic design; health and physical education/fitness; health and physical education related; health professions related; hospitality administration; hotel/motel administration; humanities; human services; information science/studies; kindergarten/preschool education; legal assistant/paralegal; liberal arts and sciences and humanities related; liberal arts and sciences/liberal studies; marketing/marketing management; mass communication/media; mathematics; mathematics related; medical administrative assistant and medical secretary; network and system administration; nursing practice; parks, recreation, leisure, and fitness studies related; physical education teaching and coaching; physical therapy; physical therapy technology; polysomnography; psychology; psychology related; radio and television; radio and television broadcasting technology; radio, television, and digital communication related; registered nursing, nursing administration, nursing research and clinical nursing related; registered nursing/registered nurse; respiratory care therapy; social sciences; social sciences related; social work; social work related; sports studies; substance abuse/addiction counseling; teacher assistant/aide; theater design and technology; theater/theater arts management; tourism and travel services management; tourism promotion; veterinary/animal health technology; web page, digital/multimedia and information resources design.
Academics *Calendar:* semesters. *Degree:* certificates and associate. *Special study options:* academic remediation for entering students, adult/continuing education programs, advanced placement credit, cooperative education, distance learning, double majors, English as a second language, honors programs, independent study, internships, part-time degree program, services for LD students, study abroad, summer session for credit. *ROTC:* Army (c).
Library Alfred C. OConnell Library. *Books:* 79,471 (physical), 10,879 (digital/electronic); *Serial titles:* 172 (physical), 61,458 (digital/electronic); *Databases:* 89. Weekly public service hours: 76.
Student Life *Housing Options:* special housing for students with disabilities. Campus housing is provided by a third party. *Activities and Organizations:* drama/theater group, student-run newspaper, radio station, choral group, Cougarettes Dance Team, Honor Society, Multi Cultural Communications Club, Christian Students United, Theater Group. *Campus security:* 24-hour emergency response devices and patrols, student patrols, late-night transport/escort service, controlled dormitory access. *Student services:* health clinic, personal/psychological counseling.
Athletics Member NJCAA. *Intercollegiate sports:* baseball M(s), basketball M(s)/W(s), cheerleading M/W, golf M/W, lacrosse M(s)/W, soccer M/W, softball W, swimming and diving M/W, volleyball W(s). *Intramural sports:* badminton M/W, basketball M/W, soccer M/W, tennis M/W, track and field M/W, volleyball M/W, water polo M/W.
Standardized Tests *Recommended:* ACT (for admission).
Costs (2015–16) *Tuition:* state resident $3900 full-time, $160 per credit hour part-time; nonresident $4500 full-time, $185 per credit hour part-time. Full-time tuition and fees vary according to course load. Part-time tuition and fees vary according to course load. *Required fees:* $510 full-time, $2 per credit hour part-time. *Room and board:* $8475; room only: $6200. Room and board charges vary according to board plan and housing facility. *Payment plan:* installment. *Waivers:* senior citizens and employees or children of employees.
Financial Aid Of all full-time matriculated undergraduates who enrolled in 2014, 2,629 applied for aid, 2,366 were judged to have need, 1,125 had their need fully met. 156 Federal Work-Study jobs (averaging $944). 115 state and other part-time jobs (averaging $1606). *Average percent of need met:* 83%. *Average financial aid package:* $5023. *Average need-based loan:* $3675. *Average need-based gift aid:* $3266. *Average indebtedness upon graduation:* $8995.
Applying *Options:* electronic application. *Required:* high school transcript. *Required for some:* 1 letter of recommendation. *Application deadlines:* rolling (freshmen), rolling (out-of-state freshmen), rolling (transfers). *Notification:* continuous (freshmen), continuous (out-of-state freshmen), continuous (transfers).
Freshman Application Contact Mrs. Tanya Lane-Martin, Director of Admissions, Genesee Community College, Batavia, NY 14020. *Phone:* 585-343-0055 Ext. 6413. *Toll-free phone:* 866-CALL GCC. *Fax:* 585-345-6892. *E-mail:* tmlanemartin@genesee.edu. *Website:* http://www.genesee.edu/.

Helene Fuld College of Nursing
New York, New York

- **Independent** primarily 2-year, founded 1945
- **Urban** campus
- **Coed, primarily women,** 354 undergraduate students, 26% full-time, 88% women, 12% men

Undergraduates 91 full-time, 263 part-time. Students come from 4 states and territories; 8% are from out of state; 74% Black or African American, non-Hispanic/Latino; 12% Hispanic/Latino; 6% Asian, non-Hispanic/Latino; 100% transferred in.
Faculty *Total:* 19, 84% full-time, 100% with terminal degrees. *Student/faculty ratio:* 11:1.
Majors Registered nursing/registered nurse.
Academics *Calendar:* quarters semester for BS program. *Degrees:* associate and bachelor's (program only open to licensed practical nurses). *Special study options:* accelerated degree program, part-time degree program, summer session for credit.
Library Peggy Wines Memorial Library plus 1 other.
Student Life *Campus security:* security guard during hours of operation. *Student services:* personal/psychological counseling.
Standardized Tests *Required:* Nelson Denny Reading Test (for admission).
Costs (2016–17) *Tuition:* $341 per quarter hour part-time. Full-time tuition and fees vary according to course load, degree level, and program. Part-time tuition and fees vary according to course load, degree level, and program. *Payment plan:* installment.
Applying *Options:* deferred entrance. *Application fee:* $110. *Required:* essay or personal statement, high school transcript, 2 letters of recommendation, must be Licensed Practical Nurse. *Required for some:* interview. *Application deadlines:* rolling (freshmen), rolling (out-of-state freshmen), rolling (transfers).
Freshman Application Contact Helene Fuld College of Nursing, 24 East 120th Street, New York, NY 10035. *Phone:* 212-616-7271. *Website:* http://www.helenefuld.edu/.

Herkimer County Community College
Herkimer, New York

- **State and locally supported** 2-year, founded 1966, part of State University of New York System
- **Small-town** 500-acre campus with easy access to Syracuse
- **Coed,** 3,019 undergraduate students, 58% full-time, 59% women, 41% men

Undergraduates 1,752 full-time, 1,267 part-time. Students come from 34 states and territories; 17 other countries; 4% are from out of state; 11% Black or African American, non-Hispanic/Latino; 5% Hispanic/Latino; 1% Asian, non-Hispanic/Latino; 0.5% American Indian or Alaska Native, non-Hispanic/Latino; 1% Two or more races, non-Hispanic/Latino; 1% Race/ethnicity unknown; 3% international; 7% transferred in; 19% live on campus.
Freshmen *Admission:* 793 enrolled. *Average high school GPA:* 2.52.
Faculty *Total:* 160, 32% full-time, 9% with terminal degrees. *Student/faculty ratio:* 21:1.
Majors Accounting technology and bookkeeping; art; broadcast journalism; business administration and management; child-care and support services management; community organization and advocacy; computer and information sciences; computer and information sciences and support services related; corrections; criminal justice/law enforcement administration; emergency medical technology (EMT paramedic); entrepreneurship; fashion merchandising; forensic science and technology; general studies; health and physical education related; health professions related; humanities; human resources management; international business/trade/commerce; legal administrative assistant/secretary; legal assistant/paralegal; liberal arts and sciences/liberal studies; merchandising, sales, and marketing operations related (general); parks, recreation and leisure facilities management; photographic and film/video technology; physical therapy; tourism and travel services marketing; visual and performing arts.
Academics *Calendar:* semesters. *Degree:* certificates and associate. *Special study options:* academic remediation for entering students, adult/continuing education programs, advanced placement credit, distance learning, English as a second language, honors programs, independent study, internships, part-time degree program, services for LD students, summer session for credit. *ROTC:* Army (c).

Library Herkimer County Community College Library. *Books:* 73,618 (physical), 33,173 (digital/electronic); *Serial titles:* 218 (physical), 58,707 (digital/electronic); *Databases:* 96. Weekly public service hours: 65.

Student Life *Housing Options:* coed. *Activities and Organizations:* drama/theater group, choral group, Phi Theta Kappa, Campus Christian Fellowship, International Students Association, Physical Therapy Assistants Club, Criminal Justice. *Campus security:* 24-hour emergency response devices and patrols. *Student services:* personal/psychological counseling.

Athletics Member NJCAA. *Intercollegiate sports:* baseball M, basketball M/W, cross-country running M/W, field hockey W, lacrosse M/W, soccer M/W, softball W, swimming and diving M/W, tennis M/W, track and field M/W, volleyball W. *Intramural sports:* badminton M/W, baseball M, basketball M/W, bowling M/W, lacrosse M/W, soccer M/W, softball M/W, swimming and diving M/W, tennis M/W, volleyball M/W.

Costs (2015–16) *Tuition:* state resident $3940 full-time, $139 per credit hour part-time; nonresident $7000 full-time, $278 per credit hour part-time. *Required fees:* $700 full-time, $12 per credit hour part-time, $40 per term part-time. *Room and board:* $9550. Room and board charges vary according to board plan and housing facility. *Payment plan:* installment. *Waivers:* employees or children of employees.

Financial Aid Of all full-time matriculated undergraduates who enrolled in 2014, 150 Federal Work-Study jobs (averaging $700).

Applying *Required:* high school transcript.

Freshman Application Contact Herkimer County Community College, 100 Reservoir Road, Herkimer, NY 13350. *Phone:* 315-866-0300 Ext. 8278. *Toll-free phone:* 888-464-4222 Ext. 8278.

Website: http://www.herkimer.edu/.

Hudson Valley Community College
Troy, New York

Freshman Application Contact Ms. Marie Claire Bauer, Director of Admissions, Hudson Valley Community College, 80 Vandenburgh Avenue, Troy, NY 12180-6096. *Phone:* 518-629-7309. *Toll-free phone:* 877-325-HVCC.

Website: http://www.hvcc.edu/.

Island Drafting and Technical Institute
Amityville, New York

- **Proprietary** 2-year, founded 1957
- **Suburban** campus with easy access to New York City
- **Coed, primarily men,** 112 undergraduate students, 100% full-time, 5% women, 95% men

Undergraduates 112 full-time. 11% Black or African American, non-Hispanic/Latino; 24% Hispanic/Latino; 0.9% Native Hawaiian or other Pacific Islander, non-Hispanic/Latino; 2% American Indian or Alaska Native, non-Hispanic/Latino; 6% Two or more races, non-Hispanic/Latino; 19% Race/ethnicity unknown. *Retention:* 91% of full-time freshmen returned.

Freshmen *Admission:* 44 enrolled. *Average high school GPA:* 2.5.

Faculty *Total:* 11, 45% full-time. *Student/faculty ratio:* 15:1.

Majors Architectural drafting and CAD/CADD; computer and information sciences and support services related; computer and information systems security; computer systems networking and telecommunications; computer technology/computer systems technology; electrical, electronic and communications engineering technology; mechanical drafting and CAD/CADD; network and system administration.

Academics *Calendar:* semesters. *Degree:* certificates, diplomas, and associate. *Special study options:* accelerated degree program, adult/continuing education programs, summer session for credit.

Student Life *Housing:* college housing not available.

Costs (2015–16) *Tuition:* $15,750 full-time, $525 per credit part-time. No tuition increase for student's term of enrollment. *Required fees:* $450 full-time. *Payment plan:* installment.

Applying *Options:* early admission. *Application fee:* $40. *Required:* interview. *Recommended:* high school transcript. *Notification:* continuous (freshmen).

Freshman Application Contact Larry Basile, Island Drafting and Technical Institute, 128 Broadway, Amityville, NY 11701. *Phone:* 631-691-8733 Ext. 114. *Fax:* 631-691-8738. *E-mail:* info@idti.edu.

Website: http://www.idti.edu/.

ITT Technical Institute
Albany, New York

Freshman Application Contact Director of Recruitment, ITT Technical Institute, 13 Airline Drive, Albany, NY 12205. *Phone:* 518-452-9300. *Toll-free phone:* 800-489-1191.

Website: http://www.itt-tech.edu/.

ITT Technical Institute
Getzville, New York

Freshman Application Contact Director of Recruitment, ITT Technical Institute, 2295 Millersport Highway, Getzville, NY 14068. *Phone:* 716-689-2200. *Toll-free phone:* 800-469-7593.

Website: http://www.itt-tech.edu/.

ITT Technical Institute
Liverpool, New York

Freshman Application Contact Director of Recruitment, ITT Technical Institute, 235 Greenfield Parkway, Liverpool, NY 13088-6651. *Phone:* 315-461-8000. *Toll-free phone:* 877-488-0011.

Website: http://www.itt-tech.edu/.

Jamestown Business College
Jamestown, New York

- **Proprietary** primarily 2-year, founded 1886
- **Small-town** 1-acre campus
- **Coed,** 318 undergraduate students, 99% full-time, 71% women, 29% men

Undergraduates 314 full-time, 4 part-time. Students come from 2 states and territories; 7% are from out of state; 2% Black or African American, non-Hispanic/Latino; 16% Hispanic/Latino; 0.6% Native Hawaiian or other Pacific Islander, non-Hispanic/Latino; 6% American Indian or Alaska Native, non-Hispanic/Latino; 4% Two or more races, non-Hispanic/Latino; 0.9% Race/ethnicity unknown; 10% transferred in. *Retention:* 68% of full-time freshmen returned.

Freshmen *Admission:* 98 applied, 91 admitted.

Faculty *Total:* 25, 24% full-time, 8% with terminal degrees. *Student/faculty ratio:* 23:1.

Majors Administrative assistant and secretarial science; business administration and management; medical/clinical assistant; office management.

Academics *Calendar:* quarters. *Degrees:* certificates, associate, and bachelor's. *Special study options:* advanced placement credit, double majors, off-campus study, part-time degree program, summer session for credit.

Library James Prendergast Library.

Student Life *Housing:* college housing not available. *Campus security:* 24-hour emergency response devices.

Athletics *Intramural sports:* basketball M(c)/W(c), racquetball M(c)/W(c), softball M(c)/W(c), swimming and diving M(c)/W(c), table tennis M(c)/W(c), tennis M(c)/W(c), volleyball M(c)/W(c), weight lifting M(c)/W(c).

Costs (2015–16) *One-time required fee:* $25. *Tuition:* $11,400 full-time, $317 per credit hour part-time. Full-time tuition and fees vary according to course load. Part-time tuition and fees vary according to course load. *Required fees:* $900 full-time, $150 per course part-time. *Waivers:* employees or children of employees.

Financial Aid Of all full-time matriculated undergraduates who enrolled in 2014, 316 applied for aid, 316 were judged to have need.

Applying *Application fee:* $25. *Required:* essay or personal statement, high school transcript, interview. *Application deadlines:* rolling (freshmen), rolling (transfers).

Freshman Application Contact Mrs. Brenda Salemme, Director of Admissions and Placement, Jamestown Business College, 7 Fairmount Avenue, Box 429, Jamestown, NY 14702-0429. *Phone:* 716-664-5100. *Fax:* 716-664-3144. *E-mail:* brendasalemme@jamestownbusinesscollege.edu.

Website: http://www.jamestownbusinesscollege.edu/.

Jamestown Community College
Jamestown, New York

- **State and locally supported** 2-year, founded 1950, part of State University of New York System
- **Small-town** 107-acre campus
- **Endowment** $12.5 million
- **Coed,** 3,038 undergraduate students, 73% full-time, 58% women, 42% men

Undergraduates 2,232 full-time, 806 part-time. Students come from 11 states and territories; 8 other countries; 8% are from out of state; 5% Black or African American, non-Hispanic/Latino; 8% Hispanic/Latino; 0.8% Asian, non-Hispanic/Latino; 0.2% Native Hawaiian or other Pacific Islander, non-Hispanic/Latino; 1% American Indian or Alaska Native, non-Hispanic/Latino; 3% Two or more races, non-Hispanic/Latino; 1% Race/ethnicity unknown; 0.8% international; 7% transferred in; 11% live on campus.

Freshmen *Admission:* 1,822 applied, 1,817 admitted, 929 enrolled. *Average high school GPA:* 3.25.

Faculty *Total:* 350, 25% full-time. *Student/faculty ratio:* 16:1.
Majors Accounting technology and bookkeeping; administrative assistant and secretarial science; airline pilot and flight crew; biology/biotechnology laboratory technician; business administration and management; computer and information sciences; criminal justice/law enforcement administration; criminal justice/police science; engineering; environmental science; fine/studio arts; general studies; health and physical education/fitness; health information/medical records technology; humanities; human services; information science/studies; information technology; international/global studies; liberal arts and sciences and humanities related; liberal arts and sciences/liberal studies; mechanical engineering/mechanical technology; music; occupational therapist assistant; registered nursing/registered nurse; speech communication and rhetoric; teacher assistant/aide; welding technology.
Academics *Calendar:* semesters. *Degree:* certificates and associate. *Special study options:* academic remediation for entering students, adult/continuing education programs, advanced placement credit, distance learning, honors programs, independent study, internships, off-campus study, part-time degree program, services for LD students, study abroad, summer session for credit.
Library Hultquist Library plus 1 other. *Books:* 90,517 (physical), 2,229 (digital/electronic); *Serial titles:* 653 (physical), 14 (digital/electronic); *Databases:* 86. Weekly public service hours: 63.
Student Life *Housing Options:* coed. Campus housing is university owned. *Activities and Organizations:* drama/theater group, choral group, Nursing Club, InterVarsity Christian Fellowship, Anime Club, Earth Awareness, Campus Activities Board. *Campus security:* 24-hour emergency response devices, controlled dormitory access. *Student services:* health clinic, personal/psychological counseling.
Athletics Member NJCAA. *Intercollegiate sports:* baseball M, basketball M/W, golf M/W, soccer M/W, softball W, swimming and diving M/W, volleyball W, wrestling M. *Intramural sports:* basketball M/W, bowling M/W, cross-country running M/W, softball M/W, volleyball M/W.
Standardized Tests *Required for some:* TOEFL (or equivalent) for international students.
Costs (2015–16) *One-time required fee:* $85. *Tuition:* state resident $4570 full-time, $188 per credit hour part-time; nonresident $9040 full-time, $377 per credit hour part-time. Full-time tuition and fees vary according to course load and program. Part-time tuition and fees vary according to course load and program. *Required fees:* $582 full-time, $24 per credit hour part-time. *Room and board:* $10,740; room only: $7540. Room and board charges vary according to board plan. *Payment plan:* installment. *Waivers:* employees or children of employees.
Financial Aid Of all full-time matriculated undergraduates who enrolled in 2014, 85 Federal Work-Study jobs (averaging $1500). 85 state and other part-time jobs (averaging $1300).
Applying *Options:* electronic application, deferred entrance. *Required:* high school transcript. *Application deadlines:* rolling (freshmen), rolling (out-of-state freshmen), rolling (transfers). *Notification:* continuous (freshmen), continuous (out-of-state freshmen), continuous (transfers).
Freshman Application Contact Ms. Wendy Present, Director of Admissions, Jamestown Community College, 525 Falconer Street, PO Box 20, Jamestown, NY 14702-0020. *Phone:* 716-338-1001. *Toll-free phone:* 800-388-8557. *Fax:* 716-338-1450. *E-mail:* admissions@mail.sunyjcc.edu. *Website:* http://www.sunyjcc.edu/.

Jefferson Community College
Watertown, New York

- **State and locally supported** 2-year, founded 1961, part of State University of New York System
- **Small-town** 90-acre campus with easy access to Syracuse
- **Coed,** 3,880 undergraduate students, 55% full-time, 60% women, 40% men

Undergraduates 2,153 full-time, 1,727 part-time. 7% Black or African American, non-Hispanic/Latino; 10% Hispanic/Latino; 1% Asian, non-Hispanic/Latino; 0.4% Native Hawaiian or other Pacific Islander, non-Hispanic/Latino; 0.5% American Indian or Alaska Native, non-Hispanic/Latino; 3% Two or more races, non-Hispanic/Latino; 3% Race/ethnicity unknown; 0.8% international.
Freshmen *Admission:* 882 enrolled.
Majors Accounting; accounting technology and bookkeeping; administrative assistant and secretarial science; animal/livestock husbandry and production; business administration and management; child-care and support services management; child development; community organization and advocacy; computer and information sciences; computer and information sciences and support services related; computer/information technology services

administration related; computer science; computer technology/computer systems technology; criminal justice/law enforcement administration; early childhood education; emergency medical technology (EMT paramedic); engineering; engineering science; fire prevention and safety technology; fire services administration; hospitality administration; humanities; human services; information science/studies; legal assistant/paralegal; liberal arts and sciences/liberal studies; mathematics; mechanical engineering technologies related; medical administrative assistant and medical secretary; office management; office occupations and clerical services; registered nursing/registered nurse; sport and fitness administration/management; teacher assistant/aide; tourism promotion.
Academics *Calendar:* semesters. *Degree:* certificates and associate. *Special study options:* academic remediation for entering students, advanced placement credit, cooperative education, distance learning, double majors, honors programs, independent study, internships, part-time degree program, services for LD students, student-designed majors, summer session for credit.
Library Melvil Dewey Library plus 1 other.
Student Life *Activities and Organizations:* student-run newspaper. *Campus security:* 24-hour emergency response devices and patrols. *Student services:* health clinic, personal/psychological counseling.
Athletics Member NJCAA. *Intercollegiate sports:* baseball M, basketball M/W, lacrosse M/W, soccer M/W, softball W, volleyball W.
Standardized Tests *Recommended:* SAT or ACT (for admission).
Costs (2015–16) *Tuition:* state resident $4176 full-time, $174 per credit hour part-time; nonresident $6456 full-time, $269 per credit hour part-time. Full-time tuition and fees vary according to course load, location, and program. Part-time tuition and fees vary according to course load, location, and program. *Room and board:* $10,050. Room and board charges vary according to board plan. *Payment plan:* installment. *Waivers:* senior citizens and employees or children of employees.
Financial Aid Of all full-time matriculated undergraduates who enrolled in 2009, 1,748 applied for aid. 98 Federal Work-Study jobs (averaging $1093).
Applying *Options:* electronic application, early admission, deferred entrance. *Required:* high school transcript. *Required for some:* interview. *Application deadlines:* 9/6 (freshmen), rolling (transfers). *Notification:* continuous (freshmen), continuous (transfers).
Freshman Application Contact Ms. Rosanne N. Weir, Director of Admissions, Jefferson Community College, 1220 Coffeen Street, Watertown, NY 13601. *Phone:* 315-786-2277. *Toll-free phone:* 888-435-6522. *Fax:* 315-786-2459. *E-mail:* admissions@sunyjefferson.edu. *Website:* http://www.sunyjefferson.edu/.

Kingsborough Community College of the City University of New York
Brooklyn, New York

- **State and locally supported** 2-year, founded 1963, part of City University of New York System
- **Urban** 72-acre campus with easy access to New York City
- **Coed**

Undergraduates 10,179 full-time, 7,316 part-time. Students come from 10 states and territories; 136 other countries; 1% are from out of state; 25% Black or African American, non-Hispanic/Latino; 18% Hispanic/Latino; 13% Asian, non-Hispanic/Latino; 0.5% Native Hawaiian or other Pacific Islander, non-Hispanic/Latino; 0.8% American Indian or Alaska Native, non-Hispanic/Latino; 17% Race/ethnicity unknown; 2% international; 8% transferred in. *Retention:* 66% of full-time freshmen returned.
Academics *Calendar:* semesters. *Degree:* associate. *Special study options:* academic remediation for entering students, adult/continuing education programs, advanced placement credit, distance learning, English as a second language, honors programs, independent study, internships, off-campus study, part-time degree program, services for LD students, summer session for credit.
Library Robert J. Kibbee Library.
Student Life *Campus security:* 24-hour emergency response devices and patrols.
Athletics Member NJCAA.
Costs (2015–16) *Tuition:* state resident $4800 full-time, $210 per credit part-time; nonresident $9600 full-time, $320 per credit part-time. *Required fees:* $400 full-time, $92 per term part-time.
Applying *Application fee:* $65. *Required:* high school transcript.
Freshman Application Contact Mr. Javier Morgades, Director of Admissions Information Center, Kingsborough Community College of the City University of New York, 2001 Oriental Boulevard, Brooklyn, NY 11235. *Phone:* 718-368-4600. *E-mail:* info@kbcc.cuny.edu. *Website:* http://www.kbcc.cuny.edu/.

Long Island Business Institute
Flushing, New York

- **Proprietary** 2-year, founded 1968
- **Urban** campus with easy access to New York City
- **Coed, primarily women,** 590 undergraduate students, 80% full-time, 74% women, 26% men

Undergraduates 472 full-time, 118 part-time. Students come from 2 states and territories; 19 other countries; 18% Black or African American, non-Hispanic/Latino; 19% Hispanic/Latino; 41% Asian, non-Hispanic/Latino; 0.3% Two or more races, non-Hispanic/Latino; 2% Race/ethnicity unknown; 4% international; 6% transferred in.

Freshmen *Admission:* 161 applied, 98 admitted.

Faculty *Total:* 78, 32% full-time, 4% with terminal degrees. *Student/faculty ratio:* 6:1.

Majors Accounting; business administration and management; business, management, and marketing related; court reporting; homeland security; hospitality administration related; medical office management.

Academics *Calendar:* semesters. *Degrees:* certificates and associate (information provided for Commack and Flushing campuses). *Special study options:* academic remediation for entering students, adult/continuing education programs, advanced placement credit, cooperative education, English as a second language, honors programs, independent study, part-time degree program, summer session for credit.

Library Flushing Main Campus Library.

Student Life *Housing:* college housing not available. *Activities and Organizations:* Small Business Club, Web Design Club, Investment Club, Court Reporting Alumni Association. *Campus security:* 24-hour emergency response devices.

Standardized Tests *Required:* ACT Compass, CELSA (for admission).

Costs (2016–17) *Tuition:* $13,299 full-time, $375 per credit part-time. *Required fees:* $1350 full-time, $450 per term part-time. *Payment plans:* installment, deferred payment.

Applying *Required:* high school transcript, interview. *Application deadlines:* rolling (freshmen), rolling (transfers).

Freshman Application Contact Ms. Jane Lin, Director of Admissions, Long Island Business Institute, 408 Broadway, 2nd Floor, New York, NY 10013. *Phone:* 212-226-7300. *E-mail:* jlin@libi.edu. *Website:* http://www.libi.edu/.

Mandl School
New York, New York

Admissions Office Contact Mandl School, 254 West 54th Street, 9th Floor, New York, NY 10019. *Website:* http://www.mandlschool.com/.

Memorial Hospital School of Nursing
Albany, New York

Freshman Application Contact Admissions Office, Memorial Hospital School of Nursing, 600 Northern Boulevard, Albany, NY 12204. *Website:* http://www.nehealth.com/son/.

Mildred Elley–New York City
New York, New York

Admissions Office Contact Mildred Elley–New York City, 25 Broadway, 16th Floor, New York, NY 10004-1010. *Website:* http://www.mildred-elley.edu/.

Mildred Elley School
Albany, New York

Director of Admissions Mr. Michael Cahalan, Enrollment Manager, Mildred Elley School, 855 Central Avenue, Albany, NY 12206. *Phone:* 518-786-3171 Ext. 227. *Toll-free phone:* 800-622-6327. *Website:* http://www.mildred-elley.edu/.

Mohawk Valley Community College
Utica, New York

- **State and locally supported** 2-year, founded 1946, part of State University of New York System
- **Suburban** 80-acre campus
- **Endowment** $5.6 million
- **Coed,** 6,675 undergraduate students, 54% full-time, 53% women, 47% men

Undergraduates 3,632 full-time, 3,043 part-time. Students come from 12 states and territories; 21 other countries; 0.3% are from out of state; 8% Black or African American, non-Hispanic/Latino; 9% Hispanic/Latino; 6% Asian, non-Hispanic/Latino; 0.2% Native Hawaiian or other Pacific Islander, non-Hispanic/Latino; 0.3% American Indian or Alaska Native, non-Hispanic/Latino; 3% Two or more races, non-Hispanic/Latino; 0.3% Race/ethnicity unknown; 1% international; 5% transferred in; 7% live on campus.

Freshmen *Admission:* 2,812 applied, 2,807 admitted, 1,279 enrolled. *Average high school GPA:* 2.67.

Faculty *Total:* 509, 28% full-time, 12% with terminal degrees. *Student/faculty ratio:* 18:1.

Majors Accounting technology and bookkeeping; administrative assistant and secretarial science; advertising; airframe mechanics and aircraft maintenance technology; art; banking and financial support services; business administration and management; CAD/CADD drafting/design technology; chemical technology; civil engineering technology; commercial and advertising art; commercial photography; communications systems installation and repair technology; computer and information sciences; computer and information sciences and support services related; computer and information systems security; computer programming; criminal justice/law enforcement administration; dietetic technology; digital arts; electrical, electronic and communications engineering technology; electrical/electronics maintenance and repair technology related; emergency care attendant (EMT ambulance); engineering; fire services administration; general studies; heating, air conditioning, ventilation and refrigeration maintenance technology; hotel/motel administration; humanities; human services; law enforcement investigation and interviewing; liberal arts and sciences and humanities related; liberal arts and sciences/liberal studies; mechanical engineering/mechanical technology; mechanical engineering technologies related; medical/clinical assistant; medical radiologic technology; operations management; parks, recreation and leisure facilities management; registered nursing/registered nurse; respiratory care therapy; restaurant, culinary, and catering management; semiconductor manufacturing technology; sign language interpretation and translation; substance abuse/addiction counseling; surveying technology; web page, digital/multimedia and information resources design; welding technology.

Academics *Calendar:* semesters. *Degree:* certificates and associate. *Special study options:* academic remediation for entering students, advanced placement credit, distance learning, double majors, English as a second language, honors programs, independent study, internships, off-campus study, part-time degree program, services for LD students, student-designed majors, summer session for credit. *ROTC:* Army (c), Air Force (c).

Library Mohawk Valley Community College Library plus 1 other. *Books:* 107,717 (physical), 1,580 (digital/electronic); *Serial titles:* 461 (physical), 127,697 (digital/electronic); *Databases:* 105. Weekly public service hours: 126.

Student Life *Housing Options:* coed, men-only, women-only, special housing for students with disabilities. Campus housing is provided by a third party. Freshman applicants given priority for college housing. *Activities and Organizations:* drama/theater group, student-run newspaper, Student Congress, Phi Theta Kappa, Catalyst, Program Board, Kidz-n-Coaches. *Campus security:* 24-hour emergency response devices and patrols, late-night transport/escort service, controlled dormitory access. *Student services:* health clinic, personal/psychological counseling.

Athletics Member NJCAA. *Intercollegiate sports:* baseball M, basketball M/W, bowling M/W, cross-country running M/W, golf M/W, ice hockey M, lacrosse M/W, soccer M/W, softball W, tennis M/W, track and field M/W, volleyball W. *Intramural sports:* badminton M/W, basketball M/W, volleyball M/W.

Costs (2015–16) *Tuition:* state resident $3960 full-time, $160 per credit hour part-time; nonresident $7920 full-time, $320 per credit hour part-time. *Required fees:* $656 full-time, $24 per credit hour part-time, $15 per term part-time. *Room and board:* $10,090; room only: $6140. Room and board charges vary according to board plan. *Payment plans:* installment, deferred payment. *Waivers:* senior citizens and employees or children of employees.

Financial Aid Of all full-time matriculated undergraduates who enrolled in 2014, 229 Federal Work-Study jobs (averaging $1750).

Applying *Options:* electronic application, deferred entrance. *Required for some:* high school transcript. *Recommended:* interview. *Application deadlines:* rolling (freshmen), rolling (out-of-state freshmen), rolling (transfers). *Notification:* continuous (freshmen), continuous (out-of-state freshmen), continuous (transfers).

Freshman Application Contact Mr. Nolan Snyder, Technical Assistant, Admissions, Mohawk Valley Community College, 1101 Sherman Drive, Utica, NY 13501. *Phone:* 315-792-5640. *Toll-free phone:* 800-SEE-MVCC. *Fax:* 315-792-5527. *E-mail:* nsnyder@mvcc.edu.
Website: http://www.mvcc.edu/.

Monroe Community College
Rochester, New York

- **State and locally supported** 2-year, founded 1961, part of State University of New York System
- **Suburban** 314-acre campus with easy access to Buffalo
- **Coed,** 14,586 undergraduate students, 61% full-time, 53% women, 47% men

Undergraduates 8,856 full-time, 5,730 part-time. 2% are from out of state; 20% Black or African American, non-Hispanic/Latino; 9% Hispanic/Latino; 4% Asian, non-Hispanic/Latino; 0.1% Native Hawaiian or other Pacific Islander, non-Hispanic/Latino; 0.4% American Indian or Alaska Native, non-Hispanic/Latino; 4% Two or more races, non-Hispanic/Latino; 0.4% Race/ethnicity unknown; 0.9% international. *Retention:* 53% of full-time freshmen returned.
Freshmen *Admission:* 3,272 enrolled. *Test scores:* SAT critical reading scores over 500: 40%; SAT math scores over 500: 48%; SAT writing scores over 500: 26%; ACT scores over 18: 78%; SAT critical reading scores over 600: 9%; SAT math scores over 600: 14%; SAT writing scores over 600: 4%; ACT scores over 24: 36%; SAT critical reading scores over 700: 1%; SAT math scores over 700: 2%; ACT scores over 30: 3%.
Faculty *Total:* 808, 38% full-time, 13% with terminal degrees. *Student/faculty ratio:* 23:1.
Majors Accounting; administrative assistant and secretarial science; art; automobile/automotive mechanics technology; behavioral sciences; biological and physical sciences; biology/biological sciences; biology/biotechnology laboratory technician; business administration and management; chemical engineering; chemistry; civil engineering technology; commercial and advertising art; computer and information sciences and support services related; computer and information sciences related; computer engineering related; computer engineering technology; computer science; construction engineering technology; consumer merchandising/retailing management; corrections; criminal justice/law enforcement administration; criminal justice/police science; data processing and data processing technology; dental hygiene; electrical, electronic and communications engineering technology; engineering science; environmental studies; family and consumer sciences/human sciences; fashion/apparel design; fashion merchandising; fire science/firefighting; food technology and processing; forestry; graphic and printing equipment operation/production; health information/medical records administration; heating, air conditioning, ventilation and refrigeration maintenance technology; history; hotel/motel administration; human services; industrial radiologic technology; industrial technology; information science/studies; information technology; instrumentation technology; interior design; international business/trade/commerce; landscape architecture; laser and optical technology; legal administrative assistant/secretary; liberal arts and sciences/liberal studies; marketing/marketing management; mass communication/media; mathematics; mechanical engineering/mechanical technology; music; parks, recreation and leisure; physical education teaching and coaching; physics; political science and government; pre-pharmacy studies; quality control technology; registered nursing/registered nurse; social sciences; special products marketing; telecommunications technology; tourism and travel services management.
Academics *Calendar:* semesters. *Degree:* certificates and associate. *Special study options:* academic remediation for entering students, accelerated degree program, adult/continuing education programs, advanced placement credit, cooperative education, English as a second language, honors programs, internships, off-campus study, part-time degree program, services for LD students, summer session for credit.
Library LeRoy V. Good Library.
Student Life *Housing Options:* coed, men-only, women-only. Campus housing is university owned. *Activities and Organizations:* drama/theater group, student-run newspaper, radio station, choral group, Student Newspaper, Phi Theta Kappa, Student Government. *Campus security:* 24-hour emergency response devices, late-night transport/escort service. *Student services:* health clinic, personal/psychological counseling.
Athletics Member NJCAA. *Intercollegiate sports:* baseball M(s), basketball M(s)/W(s), golf M, ice hockey M(s), lacrosse M(s), soccer M(s)/W(s), softball W, swimming and diving M(s)/W(s), tennis M/W, volleyball W. *Intramural*

sports: archery M/W, basketball M/W, bowling M/W, cheerleading W, cross-country running M/W, football M, lacrosse W, racquetball M/W, rugby M, skiing (cross-country) M/W, soccer M/W, softball M/W, swimming and diving M/W, tennis M/W, volleyball M/W.
Costs (2015–16) *Tuition:* state resident $3800 full-time, $159 per credit hour part-time; nonresident $7600 full-time, $318 per credit hour part-time. Full-time tuition and fees vary according to program. Part-time tuition and fees vary according to course load and program. *Required fees:* $604 full-time. *Room and board:* room only: $6170. Room and board charges vary according to housing facility. *Payment plan:* installment. *Waivers:* senior citizens and employees or children of employees.
Applying *Options:* electronic application, early admission. *Required:* high school transcript. *Application deadlines:* rolling (freshmen), rolling (transfers). *Notification:* continuous (freshmen), continuous (transfers).
Freshman Application Contact Ms. Christine Casalinuovo-Adams, Director of Admissions, Monroe Community College, 1000 East Henrietta Road, Rochester, NY 14623. *Phone:* 585-292-2222. *Fax:* 585-292-3860.
E-mail: admissions@monroecc.edu.
Website: http://www.monroecc.edu/.

Montefiore School of Nursing
Mount Vernon, New York

Director of Admissions Sandra Farrior, Coordinator of Student Services, Montefiore School of Nursing, 53 Valentine Street, Mount Vernon, NY 10550. *Phone:* 914-361-6472. *E-mail:* hopferadmissions@sshsw.org.
Website: http://www.montefiorehealthsystem.org/landing.cfm?id=19.

Nassau Community College
Garden City, New York

- **State and locally supported** 2-year, founded 1959, part of State University of New York System
- **Suburban** 225-acre campus with easy access to New York City
- **Coed**

Undergraduates 13,282 full-time, 9,026 part-time. Students come from 19 states and territories; 69 other countries; 0.3% are from out of state; 22% Black or African American, non-Hispanic/Latino; 23% Hispanic/Latino; 6% Asian, non-Hispanic/Latino; 0.4% Native Hawaiian or other Pacific Islander, non-Hispanic/Latino; 0.3% American Indian or Alaska Native, non-Hispanic/Latino; 6% Race/ethnicity unknown; 0.9% international; 6% transferred in. *Retention:* 32% of full-time freshmen returned.
Faculty *Student/faculty ratio:* 21:1.
Academics *Calendar:* semesters. *Degree:* certificates and associate. *Special study options:* academic remediation for entering students, adult/continuing education programs, advanced placement credit, cooperative education, distance learning, English as a second language, honors programs, internships, off-campus study, part-time degree program, services for LD students, summer session for credit.
Library A. Holly Patterson Library.
Student Life *Campus security:* 24-hour emergency response devices and patrols, late-night transport/escort service.
Athletics Member NJCAA.
Standardized Tests *Recommended:* SAT or ACT (for admission).
Costs (2015–16) *Tuition:* state resident $9070 full-time, $189 per credit hour part-time; nonresident $9070 full-time, $378 per credit hour part-time. *Required fees:* $140 full-time.
Financial Aid Of all full-time matriculated undergraduates who enrolled in 2014, 400 Federal Work-Study jobs (averaging $3000).
Applying *Options:* electronic application, deferred entrance. *Application fee:* $40. *Required:* high school transcript. *Required for some:* minimum 3.0 GPA, interview. *Recommended:* minimum 2.0 GPA.
Freshman Application Contact Mr. Craig Wright, Vice President of Enrollment Management, Nassau Community College, Garden City, NY 11530. *Phone:* 516-572-7345. *E-mail:* admissions@sunynassau.edu.
Website: http://www.ncc.edu/.

New York Career Institute
New York, New York

Freshman Application Contact Mr. Larry Stieglitz, Director of Admissions, New York Career Institute, 11 Park Place, New York, NY 10007. *Phone:* 212-962-0002 Ext. 115. *Fax:* 212-385-7574. *E-mail:* lstieglitz@nyci.edu.
Website: http://www.nyci.com/.

Niagara County Community College
Sanborn, New York

- **State and locally supported** 2-year, founded 1962, part of State University of New York System
- **Rural** 287-acre campus with easy access to Buffalo
- **Endowment** $8.9 million
- **Coed,** 6,133 undergraduate students, 60% full-time, 58% women, 42% men

Undergraduates 3,670 full-time, 2,463 part-time. Students come from 17 states and territories; 3 other countries; 1% are from out of state; 11% Black or African American, non-Hispanic/Latino; 3% Hispanic/Latino; 1% Asian, non-Hispanic/Latino; 1% American Indian or Alaska Native, non-Hispanic/Latino; 3% Race/ethnicity unknown; 7% transferred in; 4% live on campus.
Freshmen *Admission:* 2,403 applied, 2,403 admitted, 1,301 enrolled. *Average high school GPA:* 2.48.
Faculty *Total:* 360, 29% full-time, 13% with terminal degrees. *Student/faculty ratio:* 17:1.
Majors Accounting; administrative assistant and secretarial science; animal sciences; baking and pastry arts; biological and physical sciences; business administration and management; business, management, and marketing related; chemical technology; computer science; consumer merchandising/retailing management; criminal justice/law enforcement administration; culinary arts; design and applied arts related; drafting and design technology; drafting/design engineering technologies related; dramatic/theater arts; elementary education; fine/studio arts; general studies; hospitality administration; humanities; human services; information science/studies; liberal arts and sciences/liberal studies; massage therapy; mass communication/media; mathematics; medical/clinical assistant; medical radiologic technology; music; natural resources/conservation; occupational health and industrial hygiene; parks, recreation and leisure; physical education teaching and coaching; physical therapy technology; registered nursing/registered nurse; social sciences; sport and fitness administration/management; surgical technology; tourism and travel services management; web page, digital/multimedia and information resources design; wine steward/sommelier.
Academics *Calendar:* semesters. *Degree:* certificates and associate. *Special study options:* academic remediation for entering students, adult/continuing education programs, advanced placement credit, cooperative education, distance learning, double majors, honors programs, independent study, internships, off-campus study, part-time degree program, services for LD students, student-designed majors, study abroad, summer session for credit. *ROTC:* Army (c).
Library Henrietta G. Lewis Library. *Books:* 83,592 (physical); *Serial titles:* 336 (physical); *Databases:* 87. Weekly public service hours: 64.
Student Life *Housing Options:* coed. Campus housing is provided by a third party. *Activities and Organizations:* drama/theater group, student-run newspaper, radio station, choral group, Student Radio Station, Student Nurses Association, Phi Theta Kappa, Alpha Beta Gamma, Physical Education Club. *Campus security:* 24-hour emergency response devices and patrols, student patrols, late-night transport/escort service. *Student services:* health clinic, personal/psychological counseling.
Athletics Member NJCAA. *Intercollegiate sports:* baseball M, basketball M(s)/W(s), golf M/W, soccer M/W, softball W, volleyball W, wrestling M(s). *Intramural sports:* basketball M/W, ice hockey M, racquetball M/W, soccer M/W, tennis M/W.
Costs (2015–16) *Tuition:* state resident $3960 full-time, $165 per credit hour part-time; nonresident $9900 full-time, $413 per credit hour part-time. Full-time tuition and fees vary according to course load and program. Part-time tuition and fees vary according to course load and program. *Required fees:* $410 full-time. *Room and board:* $11,189; room only: $8698. Room and board charges vary according to housing facility. *Payment plan:* installment. *Waivers:* senior citizens and employees or children of employees.
Financial Aid Of all full-time matriculated undergraduates who enrolled in 2014, 5,538 applied for aid, 5,538 were judged to have need. 71 Federal Work-Study jobs (averaging $1848). 77 state and other part-time jobs (averaging $1142). *Average percent of need met:* 84%. *Average financial aid package:* $5500. *Average need-based loan:* $2977. *Average need-based gift aid:* $603.
Applying *Options:* electronic application, early admission. *Required:* high school transcript. *Required for some:* minimum 2.0 GPA. *Notification:* continuous until 8/31 (freshmen), continuous until 8/31 (transfers).
Freshman Application Contact Mr. James Trimboli, Director of Enrollment Services, Niagara County Community College, 3111 Saunders Settlement Road, Sanborn, NY 14132. *Phone:* 716-614-6200. *Fax:* 716-614-6820.
E-mail: admissions@niagaracc.suny.edu.
Website: http://www.niagaracc.suny.edu/.

North Country Community College
Saranac Lake, New York

Freshman Application Contact Enrollment Management Assistant, North Country Community College, 23 Santanoni Avenue, PO Box 89, Saranac Lake, NY 12983-0089. *Phone:* 518-891-2915 Ext. 686. *Toll-free phone:* 800-TRY-NCCC (in-state); 888-TRY-NCCC (out-of-state). *Fax:* 518-891-0898.
E-mail: info@nccc.edu.
Website: http://www.nccc.edu/.

Onondaga Community College
Syracuse, New York

- **State and locally supported** 2-year, founded 1962, part of State University of New York System
- **Suburban** 280-acre campus
- **Endowment** $10.5 million
- **Coed,** 11,886 undergraduate students, 50% full-time, 52% women, 48% men

Undergraduates 5,895 full-time, 5,991 part-time. Students come from 25 states and territories; 19 other countries; 1% are from out of state; 13% Black or African American, non-Hispanic/Latino; 5% Hispanic/Latino; 3% Asian, non-Hispanic/Latino; 0.1% Native Hawaiian or other Pacific Islander, non-Hispanic/Latino; 1% American Indian or Alaska Native, non-Hispanic/Latino; 3% Two or more races, non-Hispanic/Latino; 27% Race/ethnicity unknown; 0.4% international; 49% transferred in; 6% live on campus.
Freshmen *Admission:* 1,331 applied, 879 admitted.
Faculty *Total:* 645, 27% full-time. *Student/faculty ratio:* 24:1.
Majors Accounting; accounting technology and bookkeeping; architectural engineering technology; architectural technology; art; automobile/automotive mechanics technology; business administration and management; business/commerce; computer engineering technology; computer science; computer systems networking and telecommunications; construction engineering technology; criminal justice/law enforcement administration; criminal justice/police science; design and applied arts related; education (multiple levels); electrical and electronic engineering technologies related; electrical, electronic and communications engineering technology; engineering science; environmental engineering technology; fire prevention and safety technology; general studies; health information/medical records technology; health professions related; homeland security, law enforcement, firefighting and protective services related; hospitality administration; humanities; interior design; liberal arts and sciences and humanities related; mechanical engineering/mechanical technology; music; parks, recreation and leisure; physical therapy technology; public administration and social service professions related; radio and television; registered nursing/registered nurse; speech communication and rhetoric.
Academics *Calendar:* semesters. *Degree:* certificates, diplomas, and associate. *Special study options:* academic remediation for entering students, accelerated degree program, adult/continuing education programs, advanced placement credit, cooperative education, distance learning, double majors, English as a second language, external degree program, honors programs, internships, part-time degree program, services for LD students, study abroad, summer session for credit. *ROTC:* Air Force (c).
Library Sidney B. Coulter Library plus 1 other. *Books:* 84,742 (physical), 542 (digital/electronic); *Serial titles:* 194 (physical), 10 (digital/electronic); *Databases:* 92. Weekly public service hours: 67; students can reserve study rooms.
Student Life *Housing Options:* coed. Campus housing is provided by a third party. *Activities and Organizations:* drama/theater group, student-run newspaper, radio station, choral group. *Campus security:* 24-hour emergency response devices and patrols, controlled dormitory access. *Student services:* personal/psychological counseling.
Athletics Member NJCAA. *Intercollegiate sports:* baseball M, basketball M/W, cross-country running M/W, lacrosse M/W, soccer M/W, softball W, tennis M/W, volleyball W. *Intramural sports:* badminton M/W, basketball M/W, golf M/W, skiing (downhill) M/W, swimming and diving M/W, table tennis M/W, tennis M/W, track and field M/W, volleyball M/W.
Costs (2015–16) *Tuition:* state resident $4430 full-time, $184 per credit hour part-time; nonresident $8860 full-time, $368 per credit hour part-time. Full-time tuition and fees vary according to program. Part-time tuition and fees vary according to course load and program. *Required fees:* $584 full-time. *Room and board:* $8826. Room and board charges vary according to board plan. *Payment plan:* installment. *Waivers:* senior citizens and employees or children of employees.
Financial Aid Of all full-time matriculated undergraduates who enrolled in 2014, 5,594 applied for aid, 5,025 were judged to have need, 227 had their need fully met. 99 Federal Work-Study jobs (averaging $3161). *Average percent of need met:* 1%. *Average financial aid package:* $6747. *Average need-based loan:* $3000. *Average need-based gift aid:* $5539.

Applying *Options:* electronic application. *Required:* high school transcript. *Required for some:* minimum 2.0 GPA, interview. *Notification:* continuous (freshmen), continuous (transfers).

Freshman Application Contact Mr. Denny Nicholson, Onondaga Community College, 4585 West Seneca Turnpike, Syracuse, NY 13215. *Phone:* 315-488-2912. *Fax:* 315-488-2107. *E-mail:* admissions@sunyocc.edu. *Website:* http://www.sunyocc.edu/.

Orange County Community College
Middletown, New York

Freshman Application Contact Michael Roe, Director of Admissions and Recruitment, Orange County Community College, 115 South Street, Middletown, NY 10940. *Phone:* 845-341-4205. *Fax:* 845-343-1228. *E-mail:* apply@sunyorange.edu. *Website:* http://www.sunyorange.edu/.

Phillips Beth Israel School of Nursing
New York, New York

- **Independent** primarily 2-year, founded 1904
- **Urban** campus
- **Endowment** $750,000
- **Coed,** 254 undergraduate students, 13% full-time, 80% women, 20% men

Undergraduates 34 full-time, 220 part-time. Students come from 7 states and territories; 5 other countries; 15% are from out of state; 30% Black or African American, non-Hispanic/Latino; 14% Hispanic/Latino; 15% Asian, non-Hispanic/Latino; 7% Native Hawaiian or other Pacific Islander, non-Hispanic/Latino; 0.4% international; 35% transferred in. *Retention:* 84% of full-time freshmen returned.

Freshmen *Admission:* 67 applied, 2 admitted, 2 enrolled. *Average high school GPA:* 2.9. *Test scores:* SAT critical reading scores over 500: 100%; SAT math scores over 500: 100%.

Faculty *Total:* 30, 33% full-time, 47% with terminal degrees. *Student/faculty ratio:* 8:1.

Majors Health professions related; nursing practice; registered nursing/registered nurse.

Academics *Calendar:* semesters. *Degrees:* associate and bachelor's. *Special study options:* academic remediation for entering students, accelerated degree program, advanced placement credit, distance learning, honors programs, off-campus study, part-time degree program, services for LD students, study abroad, summer session for credit.

Library Phillips Health Science Library. *Books:* 400 (physical), 25 (digital/electronic); *Databases:* 10.

Student Life *Housing:* college housing not available. *Activities and Organizations:* student-run newspaper, choral group, Student Government Organization, National Student Nurses Association. *Campus security:* 24-hour emergency response devices. *Student services:* health clinic, personal/psychological counseling.

Standardized Tests *Recommended:* SAT (for admission).

Costs (2015–16) *Tuition:* $17,000 full-time, $525 per credit part-time. Full-time tuition and fees vary according to degree level. Part-time tuition and fees vary according to degree level. *Required fees:* $3100 full-time. *Payment plan:* installment. *Waivers:* employees or children of employees.

Financial Aid *Financial aid deadline:* 6/1.

Applying *Options:* deferred entrance. *Application fee:* $50. *Required:* essay or personal statement, high school transcript, minimum 2.5 GPA, 2 letters of recommendation, interview. *Application deadlines:* 4/1 (freshmen), 4/1 (transfers). *Notification:* continuous (freshmen), continuous (transfers).

Freshman Application Contact Mrs. Bernice Pass-Stern, Assistant Dean, Phillips Beth Israel School of Nursing, 776 Sixth Avenue, 4th Floor, New York, NY 10010-6354. *Phone:* 212-614-6176. *Fax:* 212-614-6109. *E-mail:* bstern@chpnet.org. *Website:* http://www.pbisn.edu/.

Plaza College
Forest Hills, New York

- **Proprietary** primarily 2-year, founded 1916
- **Urban** campus with easy access to New York City
- **Coed**

Academics *Calendar:* semesters. *Degrees:* certificates, associate, and bachelor's. *Special study options:* academic remediation for entering students, English as a second language, internships, services for LD students, summer session for credit.

Student Life *Campus security:* 24-hour emergency response devices.

Standardized Tests *Required:* ACT Compass (for admission).

Applying *Application fee:* $100. *Required:* essay or personal statement, interview, placement test. *Required for some:* 2 letters of recommendation.

Freshman Application Contact Dean Vanessa Lopez, Dean of Admissions, Plaza College, 118-33 Queens Boulevard, Forest Hills, NY 11375. *Phone:* 718-779-1430. *E-mail:* info@plazacollege.edu. *Website:* http://www.plazacollege.edu/.

Queensborough Community College of the City University of New York
Bayside, New York

- **State and locally supported** 2-year, founded 1958, part of City University of New York System
- **Urban** 37-acre campus with easy access to New York City
- **Coed,** 15,493 undergraduate students, 60% full-time, 54% women, 46% men

Undergraduates 9,290 full-time, 6,203 part-time. Students come from 15 states and territories; 135 other countries; 22% Black or African American, non-Hispanic/Latino; 32% Hispanic/Latino; 23% Asian, non-Hispanic/Latino; 0.8% Native Hawaiian or other Pacific Islander, non-Hispanic/Latino; 0.9% American Indian or Alaska Native, non-Hispanic/Latino; 1% Two or more races, non-Hispanic/Latino; 6% international; 7% transferred in. *Retention:* 62% of full-time freshmen returned.

Freshmen *Admission:* 3,354 enrolled.

Faculty *Total:* 955, 41% full-time. *Student/faculty ratio:* 19:1.

Majors Accounting; accounting technology and bookkeeping; administrative assistant and secretarial science; biotechnology; business administration and management; business, management, and marketing related; chemistry; clinical/medical laboratory technology; communication and journalism related; computer engineering technology; computer installation and repair technology; criminal justice/law enforcement administration; data processing and data processing technology; digital arts; electrical, electronic and communications engineering technology; engineering; engineering science; environmental design/architecture; environmental engineering technology; environmental health; fine/studio arts; forensic science and technology; general studies; health professions related; health services/allied health/health sciences; information science/studies; information technology; laser and optical technology; liberal arts and sciences/liberal studies; massage therapy; mechanical drafting and CAD/CADD; mechanical engineering/mechanical technology; medical/clinical assistant; medical office management; museum studies; musical instrument fabrication and repair; physical sciences; recording arts technology; registered nursing/registered nurse; telecommunications technology; visual and performing arts.

Academics *Calendar:* semesters. *Degree:* certificates and associate. *Special study options:* academic remediation for entering students, accelerated degree program, advanced placement credit, cooperative education, double majors, English as a second language, honors programs, internships, off-campus study, part-time degree program, services for LD students, student-designed majors, study abroad, summer session for credit. *ROTC:* Army (c).

Library The Kurt R. Schmeller Library.

Student Life *Housing:* college housing not available. *Activities and Organizations:* drama/theater group, student-run newspaper, choral group, Phi Theta kappa, Student Organization for Disability Awareness (SODA), ASAP Club, CSTEP Club, NYPIRG. *Campus security:* 24-hour patrols, late-night transport/escort service. *Student services:* health clinic, personal/psychological counseling, legal services.

Athletics Member NJCAA. *Intercollegiate sports:* baseball M, basketball M/W, cross-country running M/W, soccer M, softball W, swimming and diving M/W, track and field M/W, volleyball W. *Intramural sports:* badminton M/W, basketball M/W, football M/W, swimming and diving M/W, table tennis M/W, volleyball M/W.

Costs (2015–16) *Tuition:* state resident $4800 full-time, $210 per credit part-time; nonresident $9600 full-time, $320 per credit part-time. *Required fees:* $640 full-time, $320 per term part-time.

Applying *Options:* electronic application, deferred entrance. *Application fee:* $65. *Required:* high school transcript. *Application deadlines:* rolling (freshmen), rolling (transfers). *Notification:* continuous (freshmen), continuous (transfers).

Freshman Application Contact Mr. Anthony Davis, Director, Queensborough Community College of the City University of New York, 222-05 56th Avenue, Bayside, NY 11364. *Phone:* 718-631-6262 Ext. 1. *Fax:* 718-281-5189. *Website:* http://www.qcc.cuny.edu/.

Rockland Community College
Suffern, New York

- **State and locally supported** 2-year, founded 1959, part of State University of New York System
- **Suburban** 150-acre campus with easy access to New York City
- **Coed**

Undergraduates 4,189 full-time, 3,245 part-time. Students come from 5 states and territories; 78 other countries; 1% are from out of state; 18% Black or African American, non-Hispanic/Latino; 19% Hispanic/Latino; 5% Asian, non-Hispanic/Latino; 0.3% Native Hawaiian or other Pacific Islander, non-Hispanic/Latino; 0.2% American Indian or Alaska Native, non-Hispanic/Latino; 2% Two or more races, non-Hispanic/Latino; 17% Race/ethnicity unknown; 0.9% international; 6% transferred in. *Retention:* 70% of full-time freshmen returned.
Faculty *Student/faculty ratio:* 22:1.
Academics *Calendar:* semesters. *Degree:* certificates and associate. *Special study options:* academic remediation for entering students, accelerated degree program, adult/continuing education programs, advanced placement credit, cooperative education, distance learning, double majors, English as a second language, external degree program, freshman honors college, honors programs, independent study, internships, off-campus study, part-time degree program, services for LD students, study abroad, summer session for credit.
Library Rockland Community College Library.
Student Life *Campus security:* 24-hour emergency response devices and patrols, student patrols, late-night transport/escort service.
Athletics Member NJCAA.
Costs (2015–16) *Tuition:* state resident $4299 full-time, $180 per credit part-time; nonresident $8598 full-time, $359 per credit part-time. Full-time tuition and fees vary according to course load and program. Part-time tuition and fees vary according to course load and program. *Required fees:* $355 full-time, $13 per credit part-time. *Payment plans:* installment, deferred payment.
Financial Aid Of all full-time matriculated undergraduates who enrolled in 2014, 51 Federal Work-Study jobs (averaging $2922). *Average need-based loan:* $4364. *Average need-based gift aid:* $4125.
Applying *Options:* early admission, deferred entrance. *Application fee:* $30. *Required:* high school transcript.
Freshman Application Contact Rockland Community College, 145 College Road, Suffern, NY 10901-3699. *Phone:* 845-574-4484. *Toll-free phone:* 800-722-7666.
Website: http://www.sunyrockland.edu/.

St. Elizabeth College of Nursing
Utica, New York

Freshman Application Contact Donna Ernst, Director of Recruitment, St. Elizabeth College of Nursing, 2215 Genesee Street, Utica, NY 13501. *Phone:* 315-798-8189. *E-mail:* dernst@secon.edu.
Website: http://www.secon.edu/.

St. Joseph's College of Nursing
Syracuse, New York

- **Independent Roman Catholic** 2-year, founded 1898
- **Urban** campus
- **Coed,** 273 undergraduate students, 61% full-time, 91% women, 9% men

Undergraduates 166 full-time, 107 part-time. Students come from 2 states and territories; 20% live on campus.
Freshmen *Admission:* 42 applied, 23 admitted, 10 enrolled. *Average high school GPA:* 3. *Test scores:* SAT critical reading scores over 500: 56%; SAT math scores over 500: 50%; ACT scores over 18: 100%; ACT scores over 24: 1%.
Faculty *Total:* 30, 57% full-time. *Student/faculty ratio:* 9:1.
Majors Registered nursing/registered nurse.
Academics *Calendar:* semesters. *Degree:* associate. *Special study options:* academic remediation for entering students, adult/continuing education programs, advanced placement credit, cooperative education, internships, part-time degree program, services for LD students.
Library St. Joseph's Hospital Health Center School of Nursing Library.
Student Life *Housing Options:* coed. Campus housing is university owned. Freshman applicants given priority for college housing. *Activities and Organizations:* New York State Student Nurse's Association, Syracuse Area Black Nurses Association, Student Body Organization. *Campus security:* 24-hour patrols. *Student services:* health clinic, personal/psychological counseling.
Standardized Tests *Required:* SAT or ACT (for admission).
Costs (2016–17) *Tuition:* $16,960 full-time, $530 per credit part-time. Full-time tuition and fees vary according to program. Part-time tuition and fees vary according to program. *Required fees:* $1340 full-time. *Room only:* $5500. *Payment plan:* installment.
Applying *Options:* electronic application, deferred entrance. *Application fee:* $50. *Required:* essay or personal statement, high school transcript, minimum 3.0 GPA, 2 letters of recommendation, interview, high school or college algebra, biology and chemistry. *Application deadlines:* rolling (out-of-state freshmen), rolling (transfers). *Notification:* continuous (freshmen), continuous (out-of-state freshmen), continuous (transfers).
Freshman Application Contact Ms. Felicia Corp, Recruiter, St. Joseph's College of Nursing, 206 Prospect Avenue, Syracuse, NY 13203. *Phone:* 315-448-5040. *Fax:* 315-448-5745. *E-mail:* collegeofnursing@sjhsyr.org.
Website: http://www.sjhsyr.org/nursing/.

St. Paul's School of Nursing
Rego Park, New York

Director of Admissions Nancy Wolinski, Chairperson of Admissions, St. Paul's School of Nursing, 97-77 Queens Boulevard, Rego Park, NY 11374. *Phone:* 718-357-0500 Ext. 131. *E-mail:* nwolinski@svcmcny.org.
Website: http://www.stpaulsschoolofnursing.com/.

St. Paul's School of Nursing
Staten Island, New York

Admissions Office Contact St. Paul's School of Nursing, Corporate Commons Two, 2 Teleport Drive, Suite 203, Staten Island, NY 10311.
Website: http://www.stpaulsschoolofnursing.com/.

Samaritan Hospital School of Nursing
Troy, New York

Director of Admissions Diane Dyer, Student Services Coordinator, Samaritan Hospital School of Nursing, 2215 Burdett Avenue, Troy, NY 12180. *Phone:* 518-271-3734. *Fax:* 518-271-3303. *E-mail:* marronej@nehealth.com.
Website: http://www.nehealth.com/.

Schenectady County Community College
Schenectady, New York

- **State and locally supported** 2-year, founded 1969, part of State University of New York System
- **Urban** 50-acre campus
- **Coed,** 6,151 undergraduate students, 36% full-time, 53% women, 47% men

Undergraduates 2,235 full-time, 3,916 part-time. 14% Black or African American, non-Hispanic/Latino; 6% Hispanic/Latino; 7% Asian, non-Hispanic/Latino; 0.8% Native Hawaiian or other Pacific Islander, non-Hispanic/Latino; 1% American Indian or Alaska Native, non-Hispanic/Latino; 2% Two or more races, non-Hispanic/Latino; 2% Race/ethnicity unknown; 6% transferred in.
Freshmen *Admission:* 845 enrolled.
Majors Accounting technology and bookkeeping; avionics maintenance technology; business administration and management; business, management, and marketing related; community organization and advocacy; computer/information technology services administration related; computer programming; criminal justice/law enforcement administration; data processing and data processing technology; education; electrical, electronic and communications engineering technology; fire science/firefighting; hotel/motel administration; interdisciplinary studies; liberal arts and sciences/liberal studies; public administration and social service professions related; restaurant/food services management; science technologies related; teacher assistant/aide; transportation and materials moving related; visual and performing arts.
Academics *Calendar:* semesters. *Degree:* certificates and associate. *Special study options:* academic remediation for entering students, adult/continuing education programs, advanced placement credit, distance learning, double majors, English as a second language, honors programs, internships, off-campus study, part-time degree program, services for LD students, summer session for credit.
Library Begley Library.
Student Life *Housing:* college housing not available. *Activities and Organizations:* drama/theater group, choral group. *Campus security:* 24-hour emergency response devices and patrols, late-night transport/escort service. *Student services:* personal/psychological counseling.
Athletics Member NJCAA. *Intercollegiate sports:* baseball M, basketball M/W, bowling M/W, softball W. *Intramural sports:* soccer M/W, volleyball M/W.

Costs (2015–16) *Tuition:* state resident $3528 full-time, $147 per credit hour part-time; nonresident $7056 full-time, $294 per credit hour part-time. Full-time tuition and fees vary according to course load and program. Part-time tuition and fees vary according to course load and program. *Required fees:* $526 full-time, $22 per credit hour part-time, $4 per year part-time. *Payment plan:* installment. *Waivers:* senior citizens and employees or children of employees.
Financial Aid Of all full-time matriculated undergraduates who enrolled in 2014, 50 Federal Work-Study jobs (averaging $2400).
Applying *Options:* electronic application, early admission, deferred entrance. *Required:* high school transcript. *Application deadlines:* rolling (freshmen), rolling (transfers). *Notification:* continuous (freshmen), continuous (transfers).
Freshman Application Contact Mr. David Sampson, Director of Admissions, Schenectady County Community College, 78 Washington Avenue, Schenectady, NY 12305-2294. *Phone:* 518-381-1370.
E-mail: sampsodg@gw.sunysccc.edu.
Website: http://www.sunysccc.edu/.

State University of New York College of Technology at Alfred
Alfred, New York

- **State-supported** primarily 2-year, founded 1908, part of State University of New York System
- **Rural** 1084-acre campus with easy access to Rochester, Buffalo
- **Endowment** $4.5 million
- **Coed,** 3,699 undergraduate students, 91% full-time, 38% women, 62% men

Undergraduates 3,378 full-time, 321 part-time. Students come from 35 states and territories; 9 other countries; 4% are from out of state; 10% Black or African American, non-Hispanic/Latino; 7% Hispanic/Latino; 1% Asian, non-Hispanic/Latino; 0.1% Native Hawaiian or other Pacific Islander, non-Hispanic/Latino; 0.2% American Indian or Alaska Native, non-Hispanic/Latino; 2% Two or more races, non-Hispanic/Latino; 1% Race/ethnicity unknown; 2% international; 9% transferred in; 64% live on campus. *Retention:* 88% of full-time freshmen returned.
Freshmen *Admission:* 4,912 applied, 2,790 admitted, 1,058 enrolled. *Average high school GPA:* 3.04. *Test scores:* SAT critical reading scores over 500: 36%; SAT math scores over 500: 47%; SAT critical reading scores over 600: 8%; SAT math scores over 600: 12%; SAT critical reading scores over 700: 1%; SAT math scores over 700: 1%.
Faculty *Total:* 226, 77% full-time, 28% with terminal degrees. *Student/faculty ratio:* 18:1.
Majors Accounting technology and bookkeeping; agribusiness; agriculture; animation, interactive technology, video graphics and special effects; architectural engineering technology; architecture; autobody/collision and repair technology; automobile/automotive mechanics technology; biology/biological sciences; business administration and management; business, management, and marketing related; computer and information sciences; computer and information systems security; computer engineering technology; computer programming (specific applications); construction engineering technology; construction management; construction trades related; court reporting; criminology; culinary arts; diesel mechanics technology; drafting and design technology; electrical and power transmission installation; electrical, electronic and communications engineering technology; engineering; environmental engineering technology; environmental science; financial planning and services; forensic science and technology; general studies; graphic design; health information/medical records technology; heating, air conditioning, ventilation and refrigeration maintenance technology; heavy/industrial equipment maintenance technologies related; humanities; human resources management; human services; information science/studies; interior design; intermedia/multimedia; liberal arts and sciences and humanities related; liberal arts and sciences/liberal studies; machine shop technology; masonry; mechanical engineering/mechanical technology; radiologic technology/science; registered nursing/registered nurse; sales, distribution, and marketing operations; sport and fitness administration/management; surveying technology; system, networking, and LAN/WAN management; vehicle maintenance and repair technologies related; veterinary/animal health technology; web/multimedia management and webmaster; welding technology.
Academics *Calendar:* semesters. *Degrees:* certificates, associate, and bachelor's. *Special study options:* academic remediation for entering students, accelerated degree program, adult/continuing education programs, advanced placement credit, cooperative education, distance learning, double majors, English as a second language, honors programs, independent study, internships, off-campus study, part-time degree program, services for LD students, student-designed majors, study abroad, summer session for credit. *ROTC:* Army (c).

Library Walter C. Hinkle Memorial Library plus 1 other. *Books:* 54,671 (physical), 49,782 (digital/electronic); *Serial titles:* 253 (physical), 164,768 (digital/electronic); *Databases:* 193. Weekly public service hours: 88.
Student Life *Housing Options:* coed, men-only, women-only, special housing for students with disabilities. Campus housing is university owned. Freshman campus housing is guaranteed. *Activities and Organizations:* drama/theater group, student-run newspaper, radio station, choral group, Outdoor Recreation Club, Caribbean Student Association, Alfred Programming Board, Pioneer Woodsmen, Disaster Relief Team. *Campus security:* 24-hour emergency response devices and patrols, late-night transport/escort service, controlled dormitory access, residence hall entrance guards. *Student services:* health clinic, personal/psychological counseling.
Athletics Member NCAA, USCAA. All Division III. *Intercollegiate sports:* baseball M, basketball M/W, cross-country running M/W, football M, lacrosse M, soccer M/W, softball W, swimming and diving M/W, track and field M/W, volleyball W, wrestling M. *Intramural sports:* basketball M/W, equestrian sports M(c)/W(c), football M, golf M/W, ice hockey M(c), rock climbing M/W, soccer M/W, softball M/W, swimming and diving M/W, tennis M/W, ultimate Frisbee M/W, volleyball M/W.
Standardized Tests *Required for some:* SAT or ACT (for admission). *Recommended:* SAT or ACT (for admission).
Costs (2016–17) *One-time required fee:* $110. *Tuition:* state resident $6470 full-time, $270 per credit part-time; nonresident $9740 full-time, $406 per credit part-time. Full-time tuition and fees vary according to course load and degree level. Part-time tuition and fees vary according to course load and degree level. *Required fees:* $1587 full-time, $66 per credit part-time, $10 per credit part-time. *Room and board:* $12,010; room only: $7080. Room and board charges vary according to board plan and housing facility. *Payment plan:* installment. *Waivers:* employees or children of employees.
Financial Aid Of all full-time matriculated undergraduates who enrolled in 2015, 3,090 applied for aid, 2,790 were judged to have need, 342 had their need fully met. 235 Federal Work-Study jobs (averaging $2000). In 2015, 175 non-need-based awards were made. *Average percent of need met:* 60%. *Average financial aid package:* $11,523. *Average need-based loan:* $4196. *Average need-based gift aid:* $7414. *Average non-need-based aid:* $6090. *Average indebtedness upon graduation:* $30,200.
Applying *Options:* electronic application. *Application fee:* $50. *Required:* high school transcript, minimum 2.0 GPA, Common Application with essay on supplemental application. *Recommended:* essay or personal statement, interview. *Application deadlines:* rolling (freshmen), rolling (out-of-state freshmen), rolling (transfers). *Notification:* continuous (freshmen), continuous (out-of-state freshmen), continuous (transfers).
Freshman Application Contact Mrs. Goodrich Deborah, Associate Vice President for Enrollment Management, State University of New York College of Technology at Alfred, Huntington Administration Building, 10 Upper College Drive, Alfred, NY 14802. *Phone:* 607-587-3945. *Toll-free phone:* 800-4-ALFRED. *Fax:* 607-587-4299. *E-mail:* admissions@alfredstate.edu. *Website:* http://www.alfredstate.edu/.

Stella and Charles Guttman Community College
New York, New York

Admissions Office Contact Stella and Charles Guttman Community College, 50 West 40th Street, New York, NY 10018.
Website: http://guttman.cuny.edu/.

Suffolk County Community College
Selden, New York

Freshman Application Contact Suffolk County Community College, 533 College Road, Selden, NY 11784-2899. *Phone:* 631-451-4000.
Website: http://www.sunysuffolk.edu/.

Sullivan County Community College
Loch Sheldrake, New York

- **State and locally supported** 2-year, founded 1962, part of State University of New York System
- **Rural** 405-acre campus
- **Endowment** $750,752
- **Coed,** 1,596 undergraduate students, 51% full-time, 54% women, 46% men

Undergraduates 809 full-time, 787 part-time. Students come from 6 states and territories; 3 other countries; 2% are from out of state; 18% Black or African American, non-Hispanic/Latino; 19% Hispanic/Latino; 1% Asian, non-Hispanic/Latino; 0.1% Native Hawaiian or other Pacific Islander, non-Hispanic/Latino; 0.4% American Indian or Alaska Native, non-

Hispanic/Latino; 3% Two or more races, non-Hispanic/Latino; 5% Race/ethnicity unknown; 0.4% international; 4% transferred in; 21% live on campus.
Freshmen *Admission:* 1,524 applied, 1,396 admitted, 295 enrolled. *Average high school GPA:* 2.9.
Faculty *Total:* 100, 47% full-time, 17% with terminal degrees. *Student/faculty ratio:* 16:1.
Majors Accounting; administrative assistant and secretarial science; baking and pastry arts; business administration and management; commercial and advertising art; computer graphics; computer programming (specific applications); construction engineering technology; consumer merchandising/retailing management; criminal justice/police science; crisis/emergency/disaster management; culinary arts; data entry/microcomputer applications; electrical, electronic and communications engineering technology; elementary education; environmental studies; fire prevention and safety technology; forensic science and technology; hospitality administration; human services; information science/studies; kindergarten/preschool education; legal assistant/paralegal; liberal arts and sciences/liberal studies; marketing/marketing management; mathematics; medical/clinical assistant; parks, recreation and leisure; photography; psychology; radio and television; radio, television, and digital communication related; registered nursing/registered nurse; respiratory care therapy; science technologies related; sport and fitness administration/management; tourism and travel services management.
Academics *Calendar:* semesters. *Degree:* certificates and associate. *Special study options:* academic remediation for entering students, adult/continuing education programs, advanced placement credit, cooperative education, distance learning, double majors, honors programs, independent study, internships, off-campus study, part-time degree program, services for LD students, summer session for credit.
Library Hermann Memorial Library plus 1 other. *Books:* 55,262 (physical), 144,922 (digital/electronic); *Serial titles:* 111 (physical), 52,877 (digital/electronic); *Databases:* 116. Weekly public service hours: 62.
Student Life *Housing Options:* coed. Campus housing is provided by a third party. Freshman applicants given priority for college housing. *Activities and Organizations:* drama/theater group, student-run newspaper, Science Alliance, Black Student Union, Gay-Straight Alliance, Dance Club, Honor Society. *Campus security:* 24-hour emergency response devices and patrols, student patrols, controlled dormitory access. *Student services:* health clinic, personal/psychological counseling, legal services.
Athletics Member NJCAA. *Intercollegiate sports:* baseball M, basketball M/W, cross-country running M/W, softball W, volleyball W, wrestling M. *Intramural sports:* baseball M, basketball M/W, bowling M/W, cross-country running M/W, golf M/W, racquetball M/W, soccer M/W, softball M/W, table tennis M/W, tennis M/W, volleyball M/W, weight lifting M/W.
Costs (2016–17) *Tuition:* state resident $4674 full-time; nonresident $9348 full-time. Full-time tuition and fees vary according to program. Part-time tuition and fees vary according to program. *Required fees:* $826 full-time. *Room and board:* $9450; room only: $6150. Room and board charges vary according to board plan and housing facility. *Payment plans:* installment, deferred payment. *Waivers:* senior citizens and employees or children of employees.
Financial Aid Of all full-time matriculated undergraduates who enrolled in 2014, 941 applied for aid, 852 were judged to have need, 852 had their need fully met. 47 Federal Work-Study jobs (averaging $1072). 28 state and other part-time jobs (averaging $2439). *Average percent of need met:* 100%. *Average financial aid package:* $6012. *Average need-based loan:* $3096. *Average need-based gift aid:* $6012.
Applying *Options:* electronic application, early admission, deferred entrance. *Required:* high school transcript. *Application deadlines:* rolling (freshmen), rolling (out-of-state freshmen), rolling (transfers). *Notification:* continuous (freshmen), continuous (out-of-state freshmen), continuous (transfers).
Freshman Application Contact Ms. Sari Rosenheck, Director of Admissions and Registration Services, Sullivan County Community College, 112 College Road, Loch Sheldrake, NY 12759. *Phone:* 845-434-5750 Ext. 4200. *Toll-free phone:* 800-577-5243. *Fax:* 845-434-4806. *E-mail:* sarir@sunysullivan.edu. *Website:* http://www.sullivan.suny.edu/.

TCI–College of Technology
New York, New York
Freshman Application Contact TCI–College of Technology, 320 West 31st Street, New York, NY 10001-2705. *Phone:* 212-594-4000. *Toll-free phone:* 800-878-8246.
Website: http://www.tcicollege.edu/.

Tompkins Cortland Community College
Dryden, New York
- **State and locally supported** 2-year, founded 1968, part of State University of New York System
- **Rural** 300-acre campus
- **Coed**, 3,085 undergraduate students, 71% full-time, 56% women, 44% men

Undergraduates 2,179 full-time, 906 part-time. Students come from 19 states and territories; 38 other countries; 2% are from out of state; 13% Black or African American, non-Hispanic/Latino; 10% Hispanic/Latino; 1% Asian, non-Hispanic/Latino; 0.2% American Indian or Alaska Native, non-Hispanic/Latino; 4% Two or more races, non-Hispanic/Latino; 8% Race/ethnicity unknown; 3% international; 8% transferred in.
Freshmen *Admission:* 820 enrolled.
Faculty *Total:* 342, 18% full-time, 15% with terminal degrees. *Student/faculty ratio:* 16:1.
Majors Accounting technology and bookkeeping; administrative assistant and secretarial science; agroecology and sustainable agriculture; biology/biotechnology laboratory technician; business administration and management; child-care and support services management; commercial and advertising art; computer and information sciences; computer support specialist; construction engineering technology; creative writing; criminal justice/law enforcement administration; criminal justice/police science; culinary arts; digital communication and media/multimedia; engineering; entrepreneurship; environmental studies; hotel, motel, and restaurant management; humanities; human services; information science/studies; international business/trade/commerce; international/global studies; legal assistant/paralegal; liberal arts and sciences and humanities related; liberal arts and sciences/liberal studies; parks, recreation and leisure; parks, recreation and leisure facilities management; photographic and film/video technology; radio and television broadcasting technology; registered nursing/registered nurse; special products marketing; speech communication and rhetoric; sport and fitness administration/management; substance abuse/addiction counseling.
Academics *Calendar:* semesters. *Degree:* certificates and associate. *Special study options:* academic remediation for entering students, adult/continuing education programs, advanced placement credit, cooperative education, distance learning, double majors, English as a second language, freshman honors college, honors programs, independent study, internships, off-campus study, part-time degree program, services for LD students, study abroad, summer session for credit.
Library Gerald A. Barry Memorial Library plus 1 other.
Student Life *Housing Options:* coed. Campus housing is provided by a third party. *Activities and Organizations:* drama/theater group, College Entertainment Board, Sport Management Club, Nursing Club, Media Club, Writer's Guild. *Campus security:* 24-hour patrols, late-night transport/escort service, controlled dormitory access, armed peace officers. *Student services:* health clinic, personal/psychological counseling.
Athletics Member NJCAA. *Intercollegiate sports:* baseball M, basketball M/W, golf M/W, lacrosse M, soccer M/W, softball W, volleyball W. *Intramural sports:* archery M/W, badminton M/W, basketball M/W, bowling M/W, football M/W, golf M/W, lacrosse M/W, racquetball M/W, skiing (cross-country) M/W, skiing (downhill) M/W, soccer M/W, softball M/W, squash M/W, swimming and diving M/W, table tennis M/W, tennis M/W, ultimate Frisbee M/W, volleyball M/W, water polo M/W, weight lifting M/W, wrestling M/W.
Costs (2015–16) *Tuition:* state resident $4650 full-time, $164 per credit hour part-time; nonresident $9600 full-time, $338 per credit hour part-time. Part-time tuition and fees vary according to course load. *Required fees:* $1016 full-time, $36 per credit hour part-time, $16 per term part-time. *Room and board:* $10,380. Room and board charges vary according to board plan and housing facility. *Payment plans:* installment, deferred payment. *Waivers:* employees or children of employees.
Financial Aid Of all full-time matriculated undergraduates who enrolled in 2014, 150 Federal Work-Study jobs (averaging $1000). 150 state and other part-time jobs (averaging $1000).
Applying *Options:* electronic application, early admission, deferred entrance. *Required:* high school transcript. *Required for some:* essay or personal statement, interview. *Application deadlines:* rolling (freshmen), rolling (out-of-state freshmen), rolling (transfers). *Notification:* continuous (freshmen), continuous (out-of-state freshmen), continuous (transfers).
Freshman Application Contact Mr. Sandy Drumluk, Director of Admissions, Tompkins Cortland Community College, 170 North Street, PO Box 139, Dryden, NY 13053-0139. *Phone:* 607-844-6580. *Toll-free phone:* 888-567-8211. *Fax:* 607-844-6538. *E-mail:* admissions@tc3.edu. *Website:* http://www.TC3.edu/.

Trocaire College

Buffalo, New York

- **Independent** primarily 2-year, founded 1958
- **Urban** 1-acre campus
- **Endowment** $7.3 million
- **Coed, primarily women,** 1,369 undergraduate students, 45% full-time, 87% women, 13% men

Undergraduates 621 full-time, 748 part-time. Students come from 4 states and territories; 1 other country; 0.2% are from out of state; 13% Black or African American, non-Hispanic/Latino; 5% Hispanic/Latino; 1% Asian, non-Hispanic/Latino; 0.1% Native Hawaiian or other Pacific Islander, non-Hispanic/Latino; 1% American Indian or Alaska Native, non-Hispanic/Latino; 1% Two or more races, non-Hispanic/Latino; 9% Race/ethnicity unknown; 0.1% international; 16% transferred in.

Freshmen *Admission:* 759 applied, 382 admitted, 117 enrolled.

Faculty *Total:* 172, 24% full-time. *Student/faculty ratio:* 11:1.

Majors Business administration and management; computer systems networking and telecommunications; diagnostic medical sonography and ultrasound technology; dietetic technology; general studies; health information/medical records technology; hospitality administration; human resources management; liberal arts and sciences/liberal studies; massage therapy; medical/clinical assistant; medical informatics; radiologic technology/science; registered nursing/registered nurse; surgical technology.

Academics *Calendar:* semesters. *Degrees:* certificates, associate, and bachelor's. *Special study options:* academic remediation for entering students, adult/continuing education programs, advanced placement credit, cooperative education, distance learning, double majors, external degree program, independent study, internships, off-campus study, part-time degree program, services for LD students, study abroad, summer session for credit.

Library The Rachel R. Savarino Library plus 1 other. *Books:* 10,822 (physical), 1,308 (digital/electronic); *Databases:* 90.

Student Life *Housing:* college housing not available. *Activities and Organizations:* student-run newspaper, Student Governance Association, TroGreen, Diversity Club. *Campus security:* 24-hour emergency response devices and patrols, late-night transport/escort service. *Student services:* personal/psychological counseling.

Standardized Tests *Required:* ACCUPLACER (for admission).

Costs (2015–16) *Tuition:* $15,970 full-time, $660 per hour part-time. Full-time tuition and fees vary according to course load. Part-time tuition and fees vary according to course load. *Required fees:* $320 full-time, $27 per credit hour part-time. *Payment plan:* installment. *Waivers:* employees or children of employees.

Applying *Options:* electronic application, deferred entrance. *Required:* high school transcript. *Required for some:* essay or personal statement, 1 letter of recommendation. *Recommended:* minimum 1.9 GPA, interview. *Application deadlines:* rolling (freshmen), rolling (transfers).

Freshman Application Contact Trocaire College, 360 Choate Avenue, Buffalo, NY 14220-2094. *Phone:* 716-826-2558.

Website: http://www.trocaire.edu/.

Ulster County Community College

Stone Ridge, New York

- **State and locally supported** 2-year, founded 1961, part of State University of New York System
- **Rural** 165-acre campus
- **Endowment** $4.9 million
- **Coed**

Undergraduates 1,759 full-time, 1,781 part-time. Students come from 10 states and territories; 8 other countries; 6% transferred in.

Faculty *Student/faculty ratio:* 19:1.

Academics *Calendar:* semesters. *Degree:* certificates, diplomas, and associate. *Special study options:* academic remediation for entering students, adult/continuing education programs, advanced placement credit, cooperative education, distance learning, double majors, English as a second language, honors programs, independent study, internships, off-campus study, part-time degree program, services for LD students, student-designed majors, study abroad, summer session for credit.

Library McDonald Dewitt Library.

Student Life *Campus security:* 24-hour emergency response devices and patrols.

Athletics Member NJCAA.

Costs (2015–16) *Tuition:* state resident $159 per credit hour part-time; nonresident $318 per credit hour part-time. *Required fees:* $796 full-time, $65 per course part-time, $23 per term part-time. *Payment plans:* installment, deferred payment.

Financial Aid Of all full-time matriculated undergraduates who enrolled in 2014, 45 Federal Work-Study jobs (averaging $1000).

Applying *Options:* electronic application, early admission, deferred entrance. *Required:* high school transcript.

Freshman Application Contact Admissions Office, Ulster County Community College, 491 Cottekill Road, Stone Ridge, NY 12484. *Phone:* 845-687-5022. *Toll-free phone:* 800-724-0833.

E-mail: admissionsoffice@sunyulster.edu.

Website: http://www.sunyulster.edu/.

Utica School of Commerce

Utica, New York

Freshman Application Contact Senior Admissions Coordinator, Utica School of Commerce, 201 Bleecker Street, Utica, NY 13501-2280. *Phone:* 315-733-2300. *Toll-free phone:* 800-321-4USC. *Fax:* 315-733-9281.

Website: http://www.uscny.edu/.

★ Westchester Community College

Valhalla, New York

- **State and locally supported** 2-year, founded 1946, part of State University of New York System
- **Suburban** 218-acre campus with easy access to New York City
- **Coed,** 12,966 undergraduate students, 54% full-time, 53% women, 47% men

Undergraduates 7,062 full-time, 5,904 part-time. 6% transferred in.

Freshmen *Admission:* 4,631 applied, 4,631 admitted, 2,235 enrolled.

Faculty *Total:* 1,054, 16% full-time, 5% with terminal degrees.

Majors Accounting; administrative assistant and secretarial science; apparel and textile manufacturing; business administration and management; child development; civil engineering technology; clinical laboratory science/medical technology; clinical/medical laboratory technology; community organization and advocacy; computer and information sciences; computer and information sciences and support services related; computer and information sciences related; computer and information systems security; computer science; computer systems networking and telecommunications; consumer merchandising/retailing management; corrections; culinary arts; dance; data processing and data processing technology; design and applied arts related; dietetics; education (multiple levels); electrical, electronic and communications engineering technology; emergency medical technology (EMT paramedic); energy management and systems technology; engineering science; engineering technology; environmental control technologies related; environmental science; environmental studies; film/video and photographic arts related; finance; fine/studio arts; food technology and processing; humanities; information science/studies; international business/trade/commerce; journalism; legal assistant/paralegal; liberal arts and sciences/liberal studies; marketing/marketing management; mass communication/media; mechanical engineering/mechanical technology; public administration; registered nursing/registered nurse; respiratory care therapy; social sciences; substance abuse/addiction counseling; veterinary/animal health technology.

Academics *Calendar:* semesters. *Degree:* certificates and associate. *Special study options:* academic remediation for entering students, adult/continuing education programs, advanced placement credit, cooperative education, distance learning, double majors, English as a second language, honors programs, independent study, internships, off-campus study, part-time degree program, services for LD students, student-designed majors, study abroad, summer session for credit.

Library Harold L. Drimmer Library.

Student Life *Housing:* college housing not available. *Activities and Organizations:* drama/theater group, student-run newspaper, radio station, choral group, Deca Fashion Retail, Future Educators, Respiratory Club, Black Student Union, Diversity Action. *Campus security:* 24-hour emergency response devices and patrols, late-night transport/escort service. *Student services:* health clinic, personal/psychological counseling, women's center.

Athletics Member NJCAA. *Intercollegiate sports:* baseball M, basketball M/W, bowling M/W, golf M, soccer M, softball W, volleyball W. *Intramural sports:* badminton M/W, basketball M/W, softball M/W, swimming and diving M/W, tennis M/W, volleyball M/W, weight lifting M/W.

Costs (2016–17) *Tuition:* state resident $4280 full-time, $179 per credit hour part-time; nonresident $11,770 full-time, $493 per credit hour part-time. Full-time tuition and fees vary according to location. Part-time tuition and fees vary according to location. *Required fees:* $443 full-time. *Payment plan:* installment.

Financial Aid Of all full-time matriculated undergraduates who enrolled in 2014, 5,358 applied for aid, 4,232 were judged to have need. In 2014, 179 non-need-based awards were made. *Average financial aid package:* $3960. *Average need-based loan:* $1700. *Average need-based gift aid:* $3805. *Average non-need-based aid:* $1328.

Applying *Options:* early admission. *Application fee:* $35. *Required:* high school transcript. *Recommended:* interview.
Freshman Application Contact Ms. Gloria Leon, Director of Admissions, Westchester Community College, 75 Grasslands Road, Administration Building, Valhalla, NY 10595-1698. *Phone:* 914-606-6735. *Fax:* 914-606-6540. *E-mail:* admissions@sunywcc.edu.
Website: http://www.sunywcc.edu/.

See below for display ad and page 376 for the College Close-Up.

Wood Tobe–Coburn School
New York, New York
- **Proprietary** 2-year, founded 1879
- **Urban** campus
- **Coed,** 411 undergraduate students
- 89% of applicants were admitted

Freshmen *Admission:* 696 applied, 622 admitted.
Majors Accounting technology and bookkeeping; administrative assistant and secretarial science; computer programming; computer systems networking and telecommunications; fashion/apparel design; graphic design; hotel/motel administration; medical/clinical assistant; retailing.
Academics *Calendar:* semesters. *Degree:* diplomas and associate. *Special study options:* accelerated degree program, internships.
Student Life *Housing:* college housing not available.
Freshman Application Contact Admissions Office, Wood Tobe–Coburn School, 8 East 40th Street, New York, NY 10016. *Phone:* 212-686-9040. *Toll-free phone:* 800-394-9663.
Website: http://www.woodtobecoburn.edu/.

NORTH CAROLINA

Alamance Community College
Graham, North Carolina
- **State-supported** 2-year, founded 1959, part of North Carolina Community College System
- **Small-town** 48-acre campus
- **Endowment** $2.9 million
- **Coed,** 4,420 undergraduate students, 60% full-time, 60% women, 40% men

Undergraduates 2,654 full-time, 1,766 part-time. Students come from 7 states and territories; 4 other countries; 1% are from out of state; 21% Black or African American, non-Hispanic/Latino; 10% Hispanic/Latino; 2% Asian, non-Hispanic/Latino; 0.5% American Indian or Alaska Native, non-Hispanic/Latino; 3% Two or more races, non-Hispanic/Latino; 0.8% international; 27% transferred in.
Freshmen *Admission:* 785 applied, 785 admitted, 785 enrolled.
Faculty *Total:* 435, 26% full-time, 3% with terminal degrees. *Student/faculty ratio:* 12:1.
Majors Accounting technology and bookkeeping; animal sciences; applied horticulture/horticulture operations; automobile/automotive mechanics technology; banking and financial support services; biotechnology; business administration and management; carpentry; clinical/medical laboratory technology; commercial and advertising art; criminal justice/safety; culinary arts; electrical, electronic and communications engineering technology; executive assistant/executive secretary; heating, ventilation, air conditioning and refrigeration engineering technology; information science/studies; kindergarten/preschool education; legal administrative assistant/secretary; liberal arts and sciences/liberal studies; machine tool technology; mechanical engineering/mechanical technology; medical administrative assistant and medical secretary; medical/clinical assistant; office occupations and clerical services; registered nursing/registered nurse; retailing; teacher assistant/aide; welding technology.
Academics *Calendar:* semesters. *Degree:* certificates, diplomas, and associate. *Special study options:* academic remediation for entering students, adult/continuing education programs, cooperative education, distance learning, double majors, English as a second language, independent study, off-campus study, part-time degree program, services for LD students, summer session for credit.

Did you know that more local high school graduates choose Westchester Community College than any other institution? Learn details on more than sixty academic programs that can get you on track toward a four-year college degree or help launch your career.

914-606-6735 ▪ sunywcc.edu

Library Learning Resources Center.
Student Life *Housing:* college housing not available. *Campus security:* 24-hour emergency response devices and patrols, student patrols, late-night transport/escort service. *Student services:* personal/psychological counseling.
Athletics *Intramural sports:* basketball M/W, bowling M/W, tennis M/W, volleyball M/W.
Costs (2015–16) *Tuition:* state resident $2432 full-time; nonresident $8576 full-time. Full-time tuition and fees vary according to course load. Part-time tuition and fees vary according to course load. *Required fees:* $30 full-time. *Waivers:* senior citizens.
Financial Aid Of all full-time matriculated undergraduates who enrolled in 2010, 4,000 applied for aid, 3,000 were judged to have need. 200 Federal Work-Study jobs. *Average percent of need met:* 30%. *Average financial aid package:* $4500. *Average need-based gift aid:* $4500. *Average indebtedness upon graduation:* $2500.
Applying *Options:* electronic application. *Required:* high school transcript. *Application deadlines:* rolling (freshmen), rolling (transfers). *Notification:* continuous (freshmen), continuous (transfers).
Freshman Application Contact Ms. Elizabeth Brehler, Director for Enrollment Management, Alamance Community College, Graham, NC 27253-8000. *Phone:* 336-506-4120. *Fax:* 336-506-4264.
E-mail: brehlere@alamancecc.edu.
Website: http://www.alamancecc.edu/.

Asheville-Buncombe Technical Community College
Asheville, North Carolina

Freshman Application Contact Asheville-Buncombe Technical Community College, 340 Victoria Road, Asheville, NC 28801-4897. *Phone:* 828-254-1921 Ext. 7520.
Website: http://www.abtech.edu/.

Beaufort County Community College
Washington, North Carolina

Freshman Application Contact Mr. Gary Burbage, Director of Admissions, Beaufort County Community College, PO Box 1069, 5337 US Highway 264 East, Washington, NC 27889-1069. *Phone:* 252-940-6233. *Fax:* 252-940-6393. *E-mail:* garyb@beaufortccc.edu.
Website: http://www.beaufortccc.edu/.

Bladen Community College
Dublin, North Carolina

Freshman Application Contact Ms. Andrea Fisher, Enrollment Specialist, Bladen Community College, PO Box 266, Dublin, NC 28332. *Phone:* 910-879-5593. *Fax:* 910-879-5564. *E-mail:* acarterfisher@bladencc.edu.
Website: http://www.bladen.cc.nc.us/.

Blue Ridge Community College
Flat Rock, North Carolina

Freshman Application Contact Blue Ridge Community College, 180 West Campus Drive, Flat Rock, NC 28731. *Phone:* 828-694-1810.
Website: http://www.blueridge.edu/.

Brightwood College, Charlotte Campus
Charlotte, North Carolina

Freshman Application Contact Director of Admissions, Brightwood College, Charlotte Campus, 6070 East Independence Boulevard, Charlotte, NC 28212. *Phone:* 704-567-3700.
Website: http://www.brightwood.edu/.

Brunswick Community College
Supply, North Carolina

Freshman Application Contact Admissions Counselor, Brunswick Community College, 50 College Road, PO Box 30, Supply, NC 28462-0030. *Phone:* 910-755-7300. *Toll-free phone:* 800-754-1050. *Fax:* 910-754-9609. *E-mail:* admissions@brunswickcc.edu.
Website: http://www.brunswickcc.edu/.

Caldwell Community College and Technical Institute
Hudson, North Carolina

- **State-supported** 2-year, founded 1964, part of North Carolina Community College System
- **Small-town** 50-acre campus
- **Coed,** 3,805 undergraduate students, 39% full-time, 56% women, 44% men

Undergraduates 1,472 full-time, 2,333 part-time.
Freshmen *Admission:* 530 enrolled.
Faculty *Total:* 420, 31% full-time, 9% with terminal degrees.
Majors Accounting; automobile/automotive mechanics technology; biological and physical sciences; biomedical technology; biotechnology; business administration and management; computer programming; construction management; cosmetology; culinary arts; diagnostic medical sonography and ultrasound technology; early childhood education; e-commerce; education; electrical and electronics engineering; emergency medical technology (EMT paramedic); fine/studio arts; information technology; landscape architecture; legal assistant/paralegal; liberal arts and sciences/liberal studies; mechanical engineering/mechanical technology; medical office management; nuclear medical technology; office occupations and clerical services; physical therapy technology; radiologic technology/science; registered nursing/registered nurse.
Academics *Calendar:* semesters. *Degree:* certificates, diplomas, and associate. *Special study options:* academic remediation for entering students, adult/continuing education programs, advanced placement credit, cooperative education, distance learning, double majors, independent study, part-time degree program, services for LD students, summer session for credit.
Library Broyhill Center for Learning Resources.
Student Life *Housing:* college housing not available. *Activities and Organizations:* drama/theater group, choral group. *Campus security:* trained security personnel during hours of operation. *Student services:* personal/psychological counseling.
Athletics Member NJCAA. *Intercollegiate sports:* basketball M/W, golf M, volleyball W. *Intramural sports:* basketball M/W, tennis M/W.
Costs (2015–16) *Tuition:* state resident $1872 full-time, $72 per credit hour part-time; nonresident $6864 full-time, $264 per credit hour part-time. Full-time tuition and fees vary according to course load and program. Part-time tuition and fees vary according to course load and program. *Required fees:* $38 full-time, $9 per course part-time. *Payment plan:* installment.
Financial Aid Of all full-time matriculated undergraduates who enrolled in 2014, 69 Federal Work-Study jobs (averaging $960).
Applying *Options:* early admission. *Required:* high school transcript. *Application deadlines:* rolling (freshmen), rolling (transfers). *Notification:* continuous (freshmen), continuous (transfers).
Freshman Application Contact Carolyn Woodard, Director of Enrollment Management Services, Caldwell Community College and Technical Institute, 2855 Hickory Boulevard, Hudson, NC 28638. *Phone:* 828-726-2703. *Fax:* 828-726-2709. *E-mail:* cwoodard@cccti.edu.
Website: http://www.cccti.edu/.

Cape Fear Community College
Wilmington, North Carolina

- **State-supported** 2-year, founded 1959, part of North Carolina Community College System
- **Urban** 150-acre campus
- **Endowment** $8.8 million
- **Coed,** 8,851 undergraduate students, 45% full-time, 54% women, 46% men

Undergraduates 3,983 full-time, 4,868 part-time. Students come from 39 states and territories; 48 other countries; 6% are from out of state; 13% Black or African American, non-Hispanic/Latino; 7% Hispanic/Latino; 1% Asian, non-Hispanic/Latino; 0.3% Native Hawaiian or other Pacific Islander, non-Hispanic/Latino; 0.9% American Indian or Alaska Native, non-Hispanic/Latino; 3% Two or more races, non-Hispanic/Latino; 2% Race/ethnicity unknown; 9% transferred in.
Freshmen *Admission:* 4,453 applied, 2,392 admitted, 1,625 enrolled.
Faculty *Total:* 756, 40% full-time. *Student/faculty ratio:* 12:1.
Majors Accounting technology and bookkeeping; architectural engineering technology; automobile/automotive mechanics technology; baking and pastry arts; building/property maintenance; business administration and management; chemical technology; cinematography and film/video production; computer systems networking and telecommunications; computer technology/computer systems technology; cosmetology; criminal justice/police science; culinary arts; dental hygiene; diagnostic medical sonography and ultrasound technology; early childhood education; electrical, electronic and communications engineering technology; electrical/electronics equipment installation and repair; electromechanical and instrumentation and

maintenance technologies related; emergency medical technology (EMT paramedic); executive assistant/executive secretary; fire prevention and safety technology; hotel/motel administration; instrumentation technology; interior design; landscaping and groundskeeping; language interpretation and translation; liberal arts and sciences/liberal studies; machine shop technology; marine maintenance and ship repair technology; mechanical engineering/mechanical technology; medical office management; medical radiologic technology; nuclear/nuclear power technology; occupational therapist assistant; oceanography (chemical and physical); registered nursing/registered nurse; surgical technology.

Academics *Calendar:* semesters. *Degree:* certificates, diplomas, and associate. *Special study options:* academic remediation for entering students, adult/continuing education programs, advanced placement credit, cooperative education, distance learning, double majors, English as a second language, independent study, off-campus study, part-time degree program, services for LD students, summer session for credit.

Library Cape Fear Community College Library.

Student Life *Housing:* college housing not available. *Activities and Organizations:* student-run newspaper, choral group, Nursing Club, Dental Hygiene Club, Pineapple Guild, Phi Theta Kappa, Occupational Therapy. *Campus security:* 24-hour emergency response devices and patrols, late-night transport/escort service, armed police officers. *Student services:* personal/psychological counseling.

Athletics Member NJCAA. *Intercollegiate sports:* basketball M/W, cheerleading M/W, golf M, soccer M/W, volleyball W. *Intramural sports:* basketball M/W, table tennis M/W.

Costs (2015–16) *Tuition:* state resident $2498 full-time, $76 per credit hour part-time; nonresident $8580 full-time, $268 per credit hour part-time. Full-time tuition and fees vary according to course load. Part-time tuition and fees vary according to course load. *Required fees:* $218 full-time, $32 per credit hour part-time. *Payment plan:* installment.

Applying *Options:* electronic application, early admission. *Required for some:* high school transcript, interview. *Application deadlines:* 8/20 (freshmen), rolling (transfers). *Notification:* continuous (freshmen), continuous (transfers).

Freshman Application Contact Ms. Linda Kasyan, Director of Enrollment Management, Cape Fear Community College, 411 North Front Street, Wilmington, NC 28401-3993. *Phone:* 910-362-7054. *Toll-free phone:* 877-799-2322. *Fax:* 910-362-7080. *E-mail:* admissions@cfcc.edu. *Website:* http://www.cfcc.edu/.

Carolinas College of Health Sciences
Charlotte, North Carolina

- **Public** 2-year, founded 1990
- **Urban** 3-acre campus with easy access to Charlotte
- **Endowment** $2.2 million
- **Coed,** 474 undergraduate students, 12% full-time, 89% women, 11% men

Undergraduates 59 full-time, 415 part-time. Students come from 3 states and territories; 4% are from out of state; 9% Black or African American, non-Hispanic/Latino; 2% Hispanic/Latino; 3% Asian, non-Hispanic/Latino; 0.2% Native Hawaiian or other Pacific Islander, non-Hispanic/Latino; 0.2% American Indian or Alaska Native, non-Hispanic/Latino; 3% Two or more races, non-Hispanic/Latino; 7% Race/ethnicity unknown.

Freshmen *Admission:* 22 enrolled. *Average high school GPA:* 3.59.

Faculty *Student/faculty ratio:* 11:1.

Majors Medical radiologic technology; radiologic technology/science; registered nursing/registered nurse.

Academics *Calendar:* semesters. *Degree:* certificates, diplomas, and associate. *Special study options:* advanced placement credit, distance learning, double majors, independent study, off-campus study, services for LD students, study abroad, summer session for credit.

Library AHEC Library.

Student Life *Housing Options:* Campus housing is provided by a third party. *Campus security:* 24-hour emergency response devices and patrols, late-night transport/escort service. *Student services:* health clinic, personal/psychological counseling.

Standardized Tests *Required for some:* SAT or ACT (for admission).

Costs (2016–17) *Tuition:* state resident $13,986 full-time, $333 per credit part-time; nonresident $13,986 full-time, $333 per credit part-time. Full-time tuition and fees vary according to course load and program. Part-time tuition and fees vary according to course load and program. *Required fees:* $1270 full-time, $126 per term part-time. *Waivers:* employees or children of employees.

Financial Aid Of all full-time matriculated undergraduates who enrolled in 2014, 7 Federal Work-Study jobs (averaging $3569).

Applying *Options:* electronic application. *Application fee:* $50. *Required:* minimum 2.5 GPA. *Required for some:* high school transcript, 1 letter of recommendation, interview.

Freshman Application Contact Ms. Merritt Newman, Admissions Representative, Carolinas College of Health Sciences, 1200 Blythe Boulevard, Charlotte, NC 28203. *Phone:* 704-355-5583. *Fax:* 704-355-9336. *E-mail:* merritt.newman@carolinascollege.edu. *Website:* http://www.carolinascollege.edu/.

Carteret Community College
Morehead City, North Carolina

- **State-supported** 2-year, founded 1963, part of North Carolina Community College System
- **Small-town** 25-acre campus
- **Coed**

Undergraduates 804 full-time, 1,068 part-time. Students come from 27 states and territories; 2 other countries; 8% transferred in. *Retention:* 52% of full-time freshmen returned.

Faculty *Student/faculty ratio:* 9:1.

Academics *Calendar:* semesters. *Degrees:* certificates, diplomas, associate, and postbachelor's certificates. *Special study options:* academic remediation for entering students, adult/continuing education programs, cooperative education, distance learning, double majors, internships, part-time degree program, services for LD students, summer session for credit.

Library Michael J. Smith Learning Resource Center.

Student Life *Campus security:* late-night transport/escort service, security service from 7 am until 11:30 pm.

Standardized Tests *Recommended:* SAT or ACT (for admission).

Costs (2015–16) *Tuition:* state resident $1728 full-time, $72 per credit hour part-time; nonresident $6336 full-time, $264 per credit hour part-time. *Required fees:* $91 full-time, $24 per term part-time.

Applying *Options:* electronic application. *Required for some:* high school transcript.

Freshman Application Contact Ms. Margie Ward, Admissions Officer, Carteret Community College, 3505 Arendell Street, Morehead City, NC 28557-2989. *Phone:* 252-222-6155. *Fax:* 252-222-6265. *E-mail:* admissions@carteret.edu. *Website:* http://www.carteret.edu/.

Catawba Valley Community College
Hickory, North Carolina

- **State-supported** 2-year, founded 1960, part of North Carolina Community College System
- **Small-town** 50-acre campus with easy access to Charlotte
- **Endowment** $3.2 million
- **Coed,** 4,571 undergraduate students, 41% full-time, 58% women, 42% men

Undergraduates 1,870 full-time, 2,701 part-time. Students come from 3 states and territories; 9% Black or African American, non-Hispanic/Latino; 10% Hispanic/Latino; 9% Asian, non-Hispanic/Latino; 0.2% Native Hawaiian or other Pacific Islander, non-Hispanic/Latino; 0.8% American Indian or Alaska Native, non-Hispanic/Latino; 1% Two or more races, non-Hispanic/Latino; 2% Race/ethnicity unknown; 21% transferred in.

Freshmen *Admission:* 3,714 applied, 3,296 admitted, 830 enrolled. *Average high school GPA:* 2.73.

Faculty *Total:* 429, 32% full-time. *Student/faculty ratio:* 12:1.

Majors Accounting technology and bookkeeping; applied horticulture/horticulture operations; architectural engineering technology; automobile/automotive mechanics technology; business administration and management; commercial and advertising art; computer engineering technologies related; computer engineering technology; computer programming; computer systems networking and telecommunications; criminal justice/safety; cyber/computer forensics and counterterrorism; dental hygiene; early childhood education; electrical, electronic and communications engineering technology; electromechanical and instrumentation and maintenance technologies related; electroneurodiagnostic/electroencephalographic technology; emergency medical technology (EMT paramedic); entrepreneurship; fire prevention and safety technology; general studies; health and physical education related; health information/medical records technology; heating, air conditioning, ventilation and refrigeration maintenance technology; industrial mechanics and maintenance technology; information science/studies; information technology; liberal arts and sciences/liberal studies; machine shop technology; mechanical engineering/mechanical technology; mechatronics, robotics, and automation engineering; medical office management; medical radiologic technology; office management; photographic and film/video technology; polysomnography; radiologic technology/science; registered nursing/registered nurse; respiratory care therapy; turf and turfgrass management; welding technology.

Academics *Calendar:* semesters. *Degree:* certificates, diplomas, and associate. *Special study options:* academic remediation for entering students, adult/continuing education programs, advanced placement credit, cooperative education, distance learning, double majors, English as a second language, independent study, part-time degree program, services for LD students, student-designed majors, summer session for credit.

Library CVCC Library. *Books:* 31,890 (physical), 61 (digital/electronic); *Serial titles:* 26 (physical), 11 (digital/electronic); *Databases:* 12. Weekly public service hours: 59; students can reserve study rooms.

Student Life *Housing:* college housing not available. *Activities and Organizations:* drama/theater group, choral group, SkillsUSA, Campus Crusade for Christ, Emerging Entrepreneurs, Circle K, Phi Theta Kappa. *Campus security:* 24-hour emergency response devices, late-night transport/escort service.

Athletics Member NJCAA. *Intercollegiate sports:* baseball M, basketball M/W, cheerleading M/W, volleyball W.

Standardized Tests *Required:* TABE for Basic Law Enforcement Training (BLET); PSB for nursing, dental hygiene, EMS, electroneurodiagnostic technology, health occupations, radiography, surgical technology; TEAS for surgical technology programs (for admission).

Costs (2016–17) *Tuition:* state resident $2128 full-time, $76 per credit hour part-time; nonresident $7504 full-time, $268 per contact hour part-time. Part-time tuition and fees vary according to course load. *Required fees:* $123 full-time, $61 per contact hour part-time, $61 per term part-time. *Payment plan:* installment.

Applying *Options:* electronic application. *Required:* high school transcript. *Required for some:* 1 letter of recommendation. *Application deadlines:* rolling (freshmen), rolling (out-of-state freshmen), rolling (transfers). *Notification:* continuous (freshmen), continuous (out-of-state freshmen), continuous (transfers).

Freshman Application Contact Catawba Valley Community College, 2550 Highway 70 SE, Hickory, NC 28602-9699. *Phone:* 828-327-7000 Ext. 4618. *Website:* http://www.cvcc.edu/.

Central Carolina Community College
Sanford, North Carolina

Freshman Application Contact Mrs. Jamie Tyson Childress, Dean of Enrollment/Registrar, Central Carolina Community College, 1105 Kelly Drive, Sanford, NC 27330-9000. *Phone:* 919-718-7239. *Toll-free phone:* 800-682-8353. *Fax:* 919-718-7380.
Website: http://www.cccc.edu/.

Central Piedmont Community College
Charlotte, North Carolina

Freshman Application Contact Ms. Linda McComb, Associate Dean, Central Piedmont Community College, PO Box 35009, Charlotte, NC 28235-5009. *Phone:* 704-330-6784. *Fax:* 704-330-6136.
Website: http://www.cpcc.edu/.

Cleveland Community College
Shelby, North Carolina

- **State-supported** 2-year, founded 1965, part of North Carolina Community College System
- **Small-town** 43-acre campus with easy access to Charlotte
- **Coed,** 2,990 undergraduate students, 34% full-time, 64% women, 36% men

Undergraduates 1,029 full-time, 1,961 part-time. 22% Black or African American, non-Hispanic/Latino; 4% Hispanic/Latino; 1% Asian, non-Hispanic/Latino; 0.1% Native Hawaiian or other Pacific Islander, non-Hispanic/Latino; 0.3% American Indian or Alaska Native, non-Hispanic/Latino; 2% Two or more races, non-Hispanic/Latino; 2% Race/ethnicity unknown.

Freshmen *Admission:* 512 enrolled.

Faculty *Total:* 308, 25% full-time. *Student/faculty ratio:* 10:1.

Majors Accounting; banking and financial support services; biotechnology; business administration and management; criminal justice/safety; early childhood education; electrical, electronic and communications engineering technology; electrician; elementary education; emergency medical technology (EMT paramedic); entrepreneurship; fire prevention and safety technology; general studies; information technology; language interpretation and translation; legal administrative assistant/secretary; liberal arts and sciences and humanities related; liberal arts and sciences/liberal studies; marketing/marketing management; mechanical drafting and CAD/CADD; medical/clinical assistant; medical office management; office management;

operations management; radio and television broadcasting technology; radiologic technology/science; registered nursing/registered nurse.

Academics *Calendar:* semesters. *Degree:* certificates, diplomas, and associate. *Special study options:* academic remediation for entering students, adult/continuing education programs, advanced placement credit, cooperative education, distance learning, double majors, English as a second language, independent study, off-campus study, part-time degree program, summer session for credit.

Library Jim & Patsy Rose Library.

Student Life *Housing:* college housing not available. *Activities and Organizations:* drama/theater group, student-run television station. *Campus security:* security personnel during hours of operation. *Student services:* personal/psychological counseling.

Costs (2015–16) *Tuition:* state resident $2432 full-time; nonresident $8572 full-time. Full-time tuition and fees vary according to course load. Part-time tuition and fees vary according to course load. *Required fees:* $94 full-time.

Financial Aid Of all full-time matriculated undergraduates who enrolled in 2014, 20 Federal Work-Study jobs.

Applying *Options:* electronic application, deferred entrance. *Required:* high school transcript. *Application deadlines:* rolling (freshmen), rolling (transfers). *Notification:* continuous (freshmen), continuous (transfers).

Freshman Application Contact Cleveland Community College, 137 South Post Road, Shelby, NC 28152. *Phone:* 704-669-4139.
Website: http://www.clevelandcc.edu/.

Coastal Carolina Community College
Jacksonville, North Carolina

Freshman Application Contact Ms. Heather Calihan, Counseling Coordinator, Coastal Carolina Community College, Jacksonville, NC 28546. *Phone:* 910-938-6241. *Fax:* 910-455-2767.
E-mail: calihanh@coastal.cc.nc.us.
Website: http://www.coastalcarolina.edu/.

College of The Albemarle
Elizabeth City, North Carolina

- **State-supported** 2-year, founded 1960, part of North Carolina Community College System
- **Small-town** 40-acre campus
- **Coed,** 2,052 undergraduate students, 35% full-time, 64% women, 36% men

Undergraduates 715 full-time, 1,337 part-time. Students come from 17 states and territories; 4 other countries.

Freshmen *Admission:* 411 enrolled. *Test scores:* SAT critical reading scores over 500: 8%; SAT math scores over 500: 20%; SAT critical reading scores over 600: 1%; SAT math scores over 600: 5%.

Faculty *Total:* 122, 49% full-time.

Majors Administrative assistant and secretarial science; architectural engineering technology; art; biotechnology; business administration and management; computer engineering technology; computer programming; computer programming (specific applications); construction trades; crafts, folk art and artisanry; criminal justice/law enforcement administration; culinary arts; data entry/microcomputer applications; drafting/design engineering technologies related; dramatic/theater arts; education; information science/studies; information technology; liberal arts and sciences/liberal studies; licensed practical/vocational nurse training; marine maintenance and ship repair technology; medical administrative assistant and medical secretary; metal and jewelry arts; music; registered nursing/registered nurse; teacher assistant/aide.

Academics *Calendar:* semesters. *Degree:* certificates, diplomas, and associate. *Special study options:* academic remediation for entering students, adult/continuing education programs, advanced placement credit, cooperative education, English as a second language, part-time degree program, services for LD students, summer session for credit.

Library Learning Resources Center.

Student Life *Housing:* college housing not available. *Activities and Organizations:* drama/theater group, choral group, Phi Beta Lambda, Phi Theta Kappa. *Campus security:* 24-hour patrols. *Student services:* personal/psychological counseling.

Athletics *Intercollegiate sports:* soccer M. *Intramural sports:* archery M/W, badminton M/W, baseball M/W, basketball M/W, football M/W, golf M/W, gymnastics M/W, sailing M/W, soccer M(c), softball M/W, swimming and diving M/W, table tennis M/W, tennis M/W, volleyball M/W.

Costs (2015–16) *One-time required fee:* $147. *Tuition:* state resident $2064 full-time, $76 per credit hour part-time; nonresident $7252 full-time, $268 per credit hour part-time. Full-time tuition and fees vary according to course load, location, and program. *Payment plans:* installment, deferred payment.

Applying *Options:* electronic application, early admission, deferred entrance. *Required:* high school transcript. *Application deadlines:* rolling (freshmen), rolling (transfers). *Notification:* continuous (freshmen), continuous (transfers). **Freshman Application Contact** Angie Godfrey-Dawson, Director of Admissions/Financial Aid, College of The Albemarle, PO Box 2327, Elizabeth City, NC 27906-2327. *Phone:* 252-335-0821 Ext. 2360. *Fax:* 252-335-2011. *Website:* http://www.albemarle.edu/.

Craven Community College
New Bern, North Carolina

- **State-supported** 2-year, founded 1965, part of North Carolina Community College System
- **Suburban** 100-acre campus
- **Coed,** 3,012 undergraduate students, 40% full-time, 60% women, 40% men

Undergraduates 1,214 full-time, 1,798 part-time. 17% Black or African American, non-Hispanic/Latino; 8% Hispanic/Latino; 2% Asian, non-Hispanic/Latino; 0.2% Native Hawaiian or other Pacific Islander, non-Hispanic/Latino; 1% American Indian or Alaska Native, non-Hispanic/Latino; 4% Two or more races, non-Hispanic/Latino; 7% Race/ethnicity unknown; 2% international; 4% transferred in.

Freshmen *Admission:* 543 enrolled.

Majors Accounting; airframe mechanics and aircraft maintenance technology; automobile/automotive mechanics technology; banking and financial support services; business administration and management; computer and information systems security; computer programming (specific applications); computer systems networking and telecommunications; criminal justice/law enforcement administration; criminal justice/safety; early childhood education; electrical, electronic and communications engineering technology; electromechanical technology; elementary education; entrepreneurship; general studies; health information/medical records technology; heating, air conditioning, ventilation and refrigeration maintenance technology; hotel, motel, and restaurant management; information technology; legal administrative assistant/secretary; liberal arts and sciences and humanities related; liberal arts and sciences/liberal studies; machine shop technology; mechanical engineering/mechanical technology; medical administrative assistant and medical secretary; medical/clinical assistant; medical office management; office management; physical therapy technology; pre-engineering; registered nursing/registered nurse; special education; system, networking, and LAN/WAN management; tool and die technology; welding technology.

Academics *Calendar:* semesters. *Degree:* certificates, diplomas, and associate. *Special study options:* academic remediation for entering students, adult/continuing education programs, advanced placement credit, cooperative education, distance learning, double majors, English as a second language, honors programs, independent study, internships, part-time degree program, services for LD students, student-designed majors, study abroad, summer session for credit.

Library R. C. Godwin Memorial Library. *Books:* 25,333 (physical), 285,381 (digital/electronic); *Serial titles:* 45 (physical), 19,586 (digital/electronic); *Databases:* 86. Students can reserve study rooms.

Student Life *Housing:* college housing not available. *Activities and Organizations:* drama/theater group, choral group. *Campus security:* 24-hour patrols. *Student services:* personal/psychological counseling.

Costs (2015–16) *Tuition:* state resident $1824 full-time, $76 per credit hour part-time; nonresident $6432 full-time, $268 per credit hour part-time. Full-time tuition and fees vary according to course load. Part-time tuition and fees vary according to course load. *Required fees:* $199 full-time, $99 per term part-time. *Payment plan:* installment. *Waivers:* senior citizens.

Applying *Options:* electronic application. *Required:* high school transcript. *Application deadlines:* rolling (freshmen), rolling (out-of-state freshmen), rolling (transfers).

Freshman Application Contact Craven Community College, 800 College Court, New Bern, NC 28562-4984. *Phone:* 252-638-4597. *Website:* http://www.cravencc.edu/.

Davidson County Community College
Lexington, North Carolina

Freshman Application Contact Davidson County Community College, PO Box 1287, Lexington, NC 27293-1287. *Phone:* 336-249-8186 Ext. 6715. *Fax:* 336-224-0240. *E-mail:* admissions@davidsonccc.edu. *Website:* http://www.davidsonccc.edu/.

Durham Technical Community College
Durham, North Carolina

Director of Admissions Ms. Penny Augustine, Director of Admissions and Testing, Durham Technical Community College, 1637 Lawson Street, Durham, NC 27703-5023. *Phone:* 919-686-3619. *Website:* http://www.durhamtech.edu/.

ECPI University
Charlotte, North Carolina

Admissions Office Contact ECPI University, 4800 Airport Center Parkway, Charlotte, NC 28208. *Toll-free phone:* 844-611-0624. *Website:* http://www.ecpi.edu/.

ECPI University
Greensboro, North Carolina

Admissions Office Contact ECPI University, 7802 Airport Center Drive, Greensboro, NC 27409. *Toll-free phone:* 844-611-0702. *Website:* http://www.ecpi.edu/.

Edgecombe Community College
Tarboro, North Carolina

Freshman Application Contact Ms. Jackie Heath, Admissions Officer, Edgecombe Community College, 2009 West Wilson Street, Tarboro, NC 27886-9399. *Phone:* 252-823-5166 Ext. 254. *Website:* http://www.edgecombe.edu/.

Fayetteville Technical Community College
Fayetteville, North Carolina

- **State-supported** 2-year, founded 1961, part of North Carolina Community College System
- **Suburban** 204-acre campus with easy access to Raleigh
- **Endowment** $39,050
- **Coed,** 11,546 undergraduate students, 39% full-time, 55% women, 45% men

Undergraduates 4,509 full-time, 7,037 part-time. Students come from 46 states and territories; 42 other countries; 17% are from out of state; 39% Black or African American, non-Hispanic/Latino; 10% Hispanic/Latino; 2% Asian, non-Hispanic/Latino; 0.5% Native Hawaiian or other Pacific Islander, non-Hispanic/Latino; 2% American Indian or Alaska Native, non-Hispanic/Latino; 4% Two or more races, non-Hispanic/Latino; 2% Race/ethnicity unknown; 0.6% international; 8% transferred in.

Freshmen *Admission:* 4,028 applied, 4,028 admitted, 1,865 enrolled. *Average high school GPA:* 2.6. *Test scores:* SAT critical reading scores over 500: 33%; SAT math scores over 500: 28%; SAT writing scores over 500: 24%; ACT scores over 18: 100%; SAT critical reading scores over 600: 11%; SAT math scores over 600: 4%; ACT scores over 24: 50%.

Faculty *Total:* 556, 49% full-time, 6% with terminal degrees. *Student/faculty ratio:* 19:1.

Majors Accounting; applied horticulture/horticulture operations; architectural engineering technology; autobody/collision and repair technology; automobile/automotive mechanics technology; banking and financial support services; building/construction finishing, management, and inspection related; business administration and management; civil engineering technology; commercial and advertising art; computer and information systems security; computer programming; computer systems networking and telecommunications; cosmetology; criminal justice/safety; crisis/emergency/disaster management; culinary arts; dental hygiene; early childhood education; electrical, electronic and communications engineering technology; electrician; elementary education; emergency medical technology (EMT paramedic); fire prevention and safety technology; forensic science and technology; funeral service and mortuary science; game and interactive media design; general studies; gunsmithing; health and physical education related; heating, air conditioning, ventilation and refrigeration maintenance technology; hotel, motel, and restaurant management; human resources management; information science/studies; information technology; legal assistant/paralegal; liberal arts and sciences and humanities related; liberal arts and sciences/liberal studies; logistics, materials, and supply chain management; machine shop technology; marketing/marketing management; medical office management; office management; operations management; pharmacy technician; physical therapy technology; pre-engineering; public administration; radiologic technology/science; registered nursing/registered nurse; respiratory care therapy; speech-language pathology assistant; surgical technology; surveying technology.

Academics *Calendar:* semesters. *Degree:* certificates, diplomas, and associate. *Special study options:* academic remediation for entering students, accelerated degree program, adult/continuing education programs, advanced placement credit, cooperative education, distance learning, double majors, English as a second language, independent study, internships, off-campus study, part-time degree program, services for LD students, summer session for credit.

Library Paul H. Thompson Library plus 1 other. *Books:* 56,392 (physical), 245,000 (digital/electronic); *Serial titles:* 53 (physical), 11 (digital/electronic); *Databases:* 149.

Student Life *Housing:* college housing not available. *Activities and Organizations:* Parents for Higher Education, Phi Theta Kappa, Phi Beta Lambda, Surgical Technology Club, FTCC Game Club. *Campus security:* 24-hour emergency response devices and patrols, late-night transport/escort service, campus-wide emergency notification system. *Student services:* personal/psychological counseling.

Athletics *Intramural sports:* badminton M/W, basketball M/W, bowling M/W, football M/W, soccer M/W, tennis M/W.

Costs (2015–16) *One-time required fee:* $25. *Tuition:* state resident $2304 full-time, $72 per credit hour part-time; nonresident $8448 full-time, $264 per credit hour part-time. Full-time tuition and fees vary according to course load. Part-time tuition and fees vary according to course load. *Required fees:* $90 full-time, $45 per term part-time. *Payment plan:* installment. *Waivers:* employees or children of employees.

Financial Aid Of all full-time matriculated undergraduates who enrolled in 2014, 75 Federal Work-Study jobs (averaging $2000). *Financial aid deadline:* 6/1.

Applying *Options:* electronic application, deferred entrance. *Required for some:* essay or personal statement, high school transcript, interview. *Application deadlines:* rolling (freshmen), rolling (out-of-state freshmen), rolling (transfers). *Notification:* continuous (freshmen), continuous (out-of-state freshmen), continuous (transfers).

Freshman Application Contact Dr. Louanna Castleman, Director of Admissions, Fayetteville Technical Community College, 2201 Hull Road, PO Box 35236, Fayetteville, NC 28303. *Phone:* 910-678-0141. *Fax:* 910-678-0085. *E-mail:* castleml@faytechcc.edu.
Website: http://www.faytechcc.edu/.

Forsyth Technical Community College
Winston-Salem, North Carolina

- **State-supported** 2-year, founded 1964, part of North Carolina Community College System
- **Suburban** 38-acre campus
- **Coed**

Undergraduates 3,726 full-time, 5,422 part-time. 1% are from out of state; 29% Black or African American, non-Hispanic/Latino; 8% Hispanic/Latino; 2% Asian, non-Hispanic/Latino; 0.1% Native Hawaiian or other Pacific Islander, non-Hispanic/Latino; 0.5% American Indian or Alaska Native, non-Hispanic/Latino; 2% Two or more races, non-Hispanic/Latino; 2% Race/ethnicity unknown; 0.7% international; 26% transferred in.

Faculty *Student/faculty ratio:* 13:1.

Academics *Calendar:* semesters. *Degree:* certificates, diplomas, and associate. *Special study options:* academic remediation for entering students, adult/continuing education programs, advanced placement credit, cooperative education, distance learning, double majors, English as a second language, independent study, internships, off-campus study, part-time degree program, services for LD students, summer session for credit.

Library Forsyth Technical Community College Library plus 1 other.

Student Life *Campus security:* 24-hour emergency response devices and patrols, late-night transport/escort service.

Standardized Tests *Required:* ACT Compass (for admission).

Costs (2015–16) *Tuition:* state resident $1824 full-time, $72 per credit hour part-time; nonresident $6432 full-time, $264 per credit hour part-time. Full-time tuition and fees vary according to course load. Part-time tuition and fees vary according to course load. *Required fees:* $150 full-time, $75 per term part-time.

Financial Aid Of all full-time matriculated undergraduates who enrolled in 2014, 42 Federal Work-Study jobs (averaging $2083).

Applying *Required:* high school transcript.

Freshman Application Contact Admissions Office, Forsyth Technical Community College, 2100 Silas Creek Parkway, Winston-Salem, NC 27103-5197. *Phone:* 336-734-7556. *E-mail:* admissions@forsythtech.edu.
Website: http://www.forsythtech.edu/.

Gaston College
Dallas, North Carolina

Freshman Application Contact Terry Basier, Director of Enrollment Management and Admissions, Gaston College, 201 Highway 321 South, Dallas, NC 28034. *Phone:* 704-922-6214. *Fax:* 704-922-6443.
Website: http://www.gaston.edu/.

Guilford Technical Community College
Jamestown, North Carolina

- **State and locally supported** 2-year, founded 1958, part of North Carolina Community College System
- **Urban** 158-acre campus with easy access to Raleigh, Charlotte, Greensboro
- **Endowment** $3.4 million
- **Coed**

Undergraduates 5,783 full-time, 6,647 part-time. Students come from 19 states and territories; 0.5% are from out of state; 42% Black or African American, non-Hispanic/Latino; 7% Hispanic/Latino; 4% Asian, non-Hispanic/Latino; 0.1% Native Hawaiian or other Pacific Islander, non-Hispanic/Latino; 0.8% American Indian or Alaska Native, non-Hispanic/Latino; 2% Two or more races, non-Hispanic/Latino; 2% Race/ethnicity unknown; 1% international; 9% transferred in. *Retention:* 50% of full-time freshmen returned.

Faculty *Student/faculty ratio:* 20:1.

Academics *Calendar:* semesters. *Degree:* certificates, diplomas, and associate. *Special study options:* academic remediation for entering students, adult/continuing education programs, advanced placement credit, cooperative education, distance learning, double majors, English as a second language, external degree program, independent study, internships, off-campus study, part-time degree program, services for LD students, student-designed majors, summer session for credit. *ROTC:* Army (c), Air Force (c).

Library M. W. Bell Library plus 2 others.

Student Life *Campus security:* 24-hour emergency response devices and patrols, late-night transport/escort service.

Athletics Member NJCAA.

Applying *Options:* electronic application, early admission, deferred entrance. *Required for some:* high school transcript, interview.

Freshman Application Contact Guilford Technical Community College, PO Box 309, Jamestown, NC 27282-0309. *Phone:* 336-334-4822 Ext. 50125.
Website: http://www.gtcc.edu/.

Halifax Community College
Weldon, North Carolina

- **State and locally supported** 2-year, founded 1967, part of North Carolina Community College System
- **Rural** 109-acre campus
- **Endowment** $1.1 million
- **Coed**, 1,154 undergraduate students, 58% full-time, 62% women, 38% men

Undergraduates 666 full-time, 488 part-time. Students come from 2 states and territories; 51% Black or African American, non-Hispanic/Latino; 2% Hispanic/Latino; 0.8% Asian, non-Hispanic/Latino; 2% American Indian or Alaska Native, non-Hispanic/Latino; 2% Two or more races, non-Hispanic/Latino; 3% Race/ethnicity unknown; 37% transferred in. *Retention:* 37% of full-time freshmen returned.

Freshmen *Admission:* 241 enrolled. *Average high school GPA:* 2.5.

Faculty *Total:* 184, 35% full-time, 3% with terminal degrees. *Student/faculty ratio:* 11:1.

Majors Business administration and management; clinical/medical laboratory technology; commercial and advertising art; criminal justice/safety; dental hygiene; early childhood education; electromechanical and instrumentation and maintenance technologies related; information technology; legal assistant/paralegal; liberal arts and sciences and humanities related; liberal arts and sciences/liberal studies; medical administrative assistant and medical secretary; medical office management; mental and social health services and allied professions related; office management; registered nursing/registered nurse; welding technology.

Academics *Calendar:* semesters. *Degree:* certificates, diplomas, and associate. *Special study options:* academic remediation for entering students, cooperative education, distance learning, double majors, English as a second language, independent study, part-time degree program, services for LD students, summer session for credit.

Library Learning Resources Center plus 1 other. *Books:* 30,331 (physical), 185,334 (digital/electronic); *Serial titles:* 94 (physical), 19,584 (digital/electronic); *Databases:* 77. Weekly public service hours: 60; students can reserve study rooms.

Student Life *Housing:* college housing not available. *Activities and Organizations:* Phi Theta Kappa, PRIDE, Women of Excellence. *Campus security:* 24-hour emergency response devices, 12-hour patrols by trained security personnel. *Student services:* health clinic.
Costs (2016–17) *Tuition:* state resident $76 per credit hour part-time; nonresident $268 per credit hour part-time. Full-time tuition and fees vary according to course load. Part-time tuition and fees vary according to course load. *Payment plan:* installment.
Applying *Required:* high school transcript.
Freshman Application Contact Mr. James Washington, Director of Admissions, Halifax Community College, PO Drawer 809, Weldon, NC 27890-0809. *Phone:* 252-536-7220. *E-mail:* jwashington660@halifaxcc.edu. *Website:* http://www.halifaxcc.edu/.

Harrison College
Morrisville, North Carolina

Freshman Application Contact Mr. Jason Howanec, Vice President of Enrollment, Harrison College, 500 N. Meridian Street, Indianapolis, IN 46204. *Phone:* 800-919-2500. *E-mail:* admissions@harrison.edu. *Website:* http://www.harrison.edu/.

Haywood Community College
Clyde, North Carolina

- **State and locally supported** 2-year, founded 1964, part of North Carolina Community College System
- **Rural** 85-acre campus
- **Coed**

Academics *Calendar:* semesters. *Degree:* certificates, diplomas, and associate. *Special study options:* academic remediation for entering students, adult/continuing education programs, advanced placement credit, cooperative education, distance learning, double majors, English as a second language, honors programs, independent study, internships, part-time degree program, services for LD students, study abroad, summer session for credit.
Library Freedlander Learning Resource Center.
Student Life *Campus security:* 24-hour emergency response devices and patrols.
Financial Aid Of all full-time matriculated undergraduates who enrolled in 2014, 41 Federal Work-Study jobs (averaging $857).
Applying *Options:* electronic application. *Required:* high school transcript. *Required for some:* interview.
Freshman Application Contact Enrollment Technician, Haywood Community College, 185 Freedlander Drive, Clyde, NC 28721-9453. *Phone:* 828-627-4669. *Toll-free phone:* 866-GOTOHCC. *E-mail:* enrollment@haywood.edu. *Website:* http://www.haywood.edu/.

Isothermal Community College
Spindale, North Carolina

Freshman Application Contact Ms. Vickie Searcy, Enrollment Management Office, Isothermal Community College, PO Box 804, Spindale, NC 28160-0804. *Phone:* 828-286-3636 Ext. 251. *Fax:* 828-286-8109. *E-mail:* vsearcy@isothermal.edu. *Website:* http://www.isothermal.edu/.

ITT Technical Institute
Charlotte, North Carolina

Freshman Application Contact Director of Recruitment, ITT Technical Institute, 4135 Southstream Boulevard, Suite L100, Charlotte, NC 28217. *Phone:* 704-423-3100. *Toll-free phone:* 800-488-0173. *Website:* http://www.itt-tech.edu/.

ITT Technical Institute
High Point, North Carolina

Freshman Application Contact Director of Recruitment, ITT Technical Institute, 4050 Piedmont Parkway, Suite 110, High Point, NC 27265. *Phone:* 336-819-5900. *Toll-free phone:* 877-536-5231. *Website:* http://www.itt-tech.edu/.

James Sprunt Community College
Kenansville, North Carolina

- **State-supported** 2-year, founded 1964, part of North Carolina Community College System
- **Rural** 51-acre campus with easy access to Raleigh, Wilmington
- **Endowment** $1.2 million
- **Coed,** 1,195 undergraduate students, 41% full-time, 70% women, 30% men

Undergraduates 484 full-time, 711 part-time. Students come from 4 states and territories; 2% are from out of state; 29% Black or African American, non-Hispanic/Latino; 18% Hispanic/Latino; 0.3% Asian, non-Hispanic/Latino; 0.1% Native Hawaiian or other Pacific Islander, non-Hispanic/Latino; 0.6% American Indian or Alaska Native, non-Hispanic/Latino; 2% Two or more races, non-Hispanic/Latino; 0.1% Race/ethnicity unknown; 0.3% international; 5% transferred in.
Freshmen *Admission:* 664 applied, 655 admitted, 151 enrolled.
Faculty *Total:* 65, 48% full-time, 3% with terminal degrees. *Student/faculty ratio:* 15:1.
Majors Accounting; agribusiness; animal sciences; business administration and management; child development; commercial and advertising art; criminal justice/safety; early childhood education; elementary education; general studies; information technology; institutional food workers; liberal arts and sciences and humanities related; liberal arts and sciences/liberal studies; medical/clinical assistant; registered nursing/registered nurse; viticulture and enology.
Academics *Calendar:* semesters. *Degree:* certificates, diplomas, and associate. *Special study options:* academic remediation for entering students, accelerated degree program, advanced placement credit, cooperative education, distance learning, double majors, English as a second language, independent study, internships, part-time degree program, services for LD students, summer session for credit.
Library James Sprunt Community College Library. *Books:* 23,718 (physical), 184,606 (digital/electronic); *Serial titles:* 72 (physical), 2 (digital/electronic); *Databases:* 77. Weekly public service hours: 48.
Student Life *Housing:* college housing not available. *Activities and Organizations:* choral group, Student Nurses Association, Art Club, Alumni Association, National Technical-Vocational Honor Society, Phi Theta Kappa, national sororities. *Campus security:* day, evening, and Saturday trained security personnel. *Student services:* personal/psychological counseling.
Athletics *Intramural sports:* soccer M/W.
Costs (2016–17) *Tuition:* state resident $2432 full-time, $76 per semester hour part-time; nonresident $8576 full-time, $268 per semester hour part-time. Full-time tuition and fees vary according to course load. Part-time tuition and fees vary according to course load. *Required fees:* $70 full-time, $35 per term part-time.
Financial Aid Of all full-time matriculated undergraduates who enrolled in 2014, 35 Federal Work-Study jobs (averaging $1057).
Applying *Options:* electronic application. *Required:* high school transcript. *Application deadlines:* rolling (freshmen), rolling (out-of-state freshmen), rolling (transfers). *Notification:* continuous (freshmen), continuous (out-of-state freshmen), continuous (transfers).
Freshman Application Contact Ms. Wanda Edwards, Admissions Specialist, James Sprunt Community College, PO Box 398, 133 James Sprunt Drive, Kenansville, NC 28349. *Phone:* 910-296-6078. *Fax:* 910-296-1222. *E-mail:* wedwards@jamessprunt.edu. *Website:* http://www.jamessprunt.edu/.

Johnston Community College
Smithfield, North Carolina

- **State-supported** 2-year, founded 1969, part of North Carolina Community College System
- **Rural** 100-acre campus
- **Endowment** $4.8 million
- **Coed,** 3,969 undergraduate students, 43% full-time, 65% women, 35% men

Undergraduates 1,726 full-time, 2,243 part-time. 13% Black or African American, non-Hispanic/Latino; 12% Hispanic/Latino; 0.7% Asian, non-Hispanic/Latino; 0.3% Native Hawaiian or other Pacific Islander, non-Hispanic/Latino; 0.7% American Indian or Alaska Native, non-Hispanic/Latino; 2% Two or more races, non-Hispanic/Latino; 7% Race/ethnicity unknown; 1% international.
Freshmen *Admission:* 613 enrolled.
Majors Accounting; administrative assistant and secretarial science; business administration and management; criminal justice/police science; diesel mechanics technology; early childhood education; heating, air conditioning, ventilation and refrigeration maintenance technology; legal assistant/paralegal;

liberal arts and sciences/liberal studies; medical/clinical assistant; medical office management; office management; registered nursing/registered nurse.

Academics *Calendar:* semesters. *Degree:* certificates, diplomas, and associate. *Special study options:* academic remediation for entering students, adult/continuing education programs, advanced placement credit, cooperative education, distance learning, double majors, honors programs, independent study, part-time degree program, services for LD students, summer session for credit.

Library Johnston Community College Library plus 1 other. *Books:* 38,090 (physical), 65 (digital/electronic); *Serial titles:* 69 (physical), 11 (digital/electronic); *Databases:* 10. Weekly public service hours: 57; students can reserve study rooms.

Student Life *Housing:* college housing not available. *Campus security:* 24-hour patrols. *Student services:* personal/psychological counseling.

Athletics Member NJCAA. *Intercollegiate sports:* golf M/W.

Standardized Tests *Required:* ACCUPLACER (for admission). *Recommended:* SAT or ACT (for admission).

Costs (2016–17) *Tuition:* state resident $2432 full-time, $76 per credit part-time; nonresident $8576 full-time, $268 per credit part-time. *Required fees:* $97 full-time. *Payment plan:* installment.

Financial Aid Of all full-time matriculated undergraduates who enrolled in 2014, 35 Federal Work-Study jobs (averaging $1853).

Applying *Options:* electronic application. *Required:* high school transcript, interview. *Application deadlines:* rolling (freshmen), rolling (transfers). *Notification:* continuous (freshmen), continuous (transfers).

Freshman Application Contact Dr. Pamela J. Harrell, Vice President of Student Services, Johnston Community College, Smithfield, NC 27577-2350. *Phone:* 919-209-2048. *Fax:* 919-989-7862.
E-mail: pjharrell@johnstoncc.edu.
Website: http://www.johnstoncc.edu/.

King's College
Charlotte, North Carolina

- **Proprietary** 2-year, founded 1901
- **Suburban** campus
- **Coed,** 395 undergraduate students
- 77% of applicants were admitted

Freshmen *Admission:* 874 applied, 676 admitted.

Majors Accounting technology and bookkeeping; administrative assistant and secretarial science; computer programming; computer systems networking and telecommunications; graphic design; hotel/motel administration; legal administrative assistant/secretary; legal assistant/paralegal; medical/clinical assistant.

Academics *Calendar:* semesters. *Degree:* diplomas and associate. *Special study options:* accelerated degree program, internships.

Freshman Application Contact Admissions Office, King's College, 322 Lamar Avenue, Charlotte, NC 28204-2436. *Phone:* 704-372-0266. *Toll-free phone:* 800-768-2255.
Website: http://www.kingscollegecharlotte.edu/.

Lenoir Community College
Kinston, North Carolina

- **State-supported** 2-year, founded 1960, part of North Carolina Community College System
- **Small-town** 86-acre campus
- **Coed,** 2,757 undergraduate students, 39% full-time, 60% women, 40% men

Undergraduates 1,069 full-time, 1,688 part-time. Students come from 25 states and territories; 3 other countries; 2% are from out of state; 31% Black or African American, non-Hispanic/Latino; 10% Hispanic/Latino; 0.8% Asian, non-Hispanic/Latino; 0.8% American Indian or Alaska Native, non-Hispanic/Latino; 1% Two or more races, non-Hispanic/Latino; 0.7% international; 20% transferred in.

Freshmen *Admission:* 1,935 applied, 1,264 admitted, 336 enrolled.

Faculty *Total:* 135, 69% full-time. *Student/faculty ratio:* 15:1.

Majors Accounting; aeronautical/aerospace engineering technology; agroecology and sustainable agriculture; airline pilot and flight crew; applied horticulture/horticulture operations; autobody/collision and repair technology; automobile/automotive mechanics technology; computer engineering technology; computer systems networking and telecommunications; cosmetology; criminal justice/safety; culinary arts; elementary education; emergency medical technology (EMT paramedic); energy management and systems technology; graphic design; gunsmithing; industrial electronics technology; information technology; liberal arts and sciences and humanities related; liberal arts and sciences/liberal studies; logistics, materials, and supply

chain management; machine shop technology; marketing/marketing management; massage therapy; medical/clinical assistant; medical office management; mental and social health services and allied professions related; office management; operations management; polysomnography; public administration; radiologic technology/science; registered nursing/registered nurse; trade and industrial teacher education; welding technology.

Academics *Calendar:* semesters. *Degree:* certificates, diplomas, and associate. *Special study options:* academic remediation for entering students, adult/continuing education programs, advanced placement credit, cooperative education, distance learning, double majors, English as a second language, independent study, part-time degree program, summer session for credit.

Library Learning Resources Center plus 1 other.

Student Life *Housing:* college housing not available. *Activities and Organizations:* student-run newspaper, choral group, Student Government Association, Automotive Club, Electronics Club, Drafting Club, Cosmetology Club. *Campus security:* 24-hour emergency response devices and patrols, student patrols. *Student services:* personal/psychological counseling.

Athletics Member NJCAA. *Intercollegiate sports:* baseball M, basketball M/W, volleyball W.

Standardized Tests *Recommended:* SAT or ACT (for admission).

Costs (2016–17) *Tuition:* state resident $2280 full-time, $76 per credit part-time; nonresident $8040 full-time, $268 per credit part-time. Full-time tuition and fees vary according to course load. Part-time tuition and fees vary according to course load. *Required fees:* $119 full-time. *Waivers:* employees or children of employees.

Applying *Options:* electronic application, early admission. *Required:* high school transcript. *Application deadlines:* rolling (freshmen), rolling (transfers). *Notification:* continuous (freshmen), continuous (transfers).

Freshman Application Contact Mrs. Kim Hill, Director of Admissions, Lenoir Community College, PO Box 188, Kinston, NC 28502-0188. *Phone:* 252-527-6223 Ext. 301. *Fax:* 252-233-6895.
E-mail: krhill01@lenoircc.edu.
Website: http://www.lenoircc.edu/.

Living Arts College
Raleigh, North Carolina

- **Proprietary** primarily 2-year, founded 1992
- **Suburban** campus with easy access to Raleigh
- **Coed,** 578 undergraduate students

Undergraduates Students come from 8 states and territories; 1 other country; 1% are from out of state; 48% Black or African American, non-Hispanic/Latino; 5% Hispanic/Latino; 0.9% Asian, non-Hispanic/Latino; 0.7% American Indian or Alaska Native, non-Hispanic/Latino; 2% Two or more races, non-Hispanic/Latino; 3% Race/ethnicity unknown; 35% live on campus. *Retention:* 69% of full-time freshmen returned.

Freshmen *Admission:* 95 applied, 95 admitted.

Faculty *Total:* 53, 70% full-time, 19% with terminal degrees. *Student/faculty ratio:* 10:1.

Majors Animation, interactive technology, video graphics and special effects; cinematography and film/video production; interior design; photography; recording arts technology; web page, digital/multimedia and information resources design.

Academics *Calendar:* quarters. *Degree:* certificates, diplomas, and bachelor's. *Special study options:* cooperative education, summer session for credit.

Student Life *Housing Options:* Campus housing is university owned. Freshman applicants given priority for college housing. *Activities and Organizations:* MODIV (student council), Student Ambassadors, Firebreathers Animation Studio, NVTHS (National Vocational Technical Honor Society). *Campus security:* controlled dormitory access.

Standardized Tests *Required:* Wonderlic aptitude test (for admission).

Costs (2015–16) *Tuition:* $84,960 per degree program part-time. Full-time tuition and fees vary according to degree level. No tuition increase for student's term of enrollment. *Payment plans:* tuition prepayment, installment, deferred payment.

Applying *Options:* electronic application, early admission, early decision, early action, deferred entrance. *Application fee:* $25. *Required:* essay or personal statement, high school transcript, interview. *Required for some:* portfolio. *Application deadlines:* rolling (freshmen), rolling (out-of-state freshmen), rolling (early action). *Notification:* continuous (freshmen), continuous (out-of-state freshmen), rolling (early action).

Freshman Application Contact Julie Wenta, Director of Admissions, Living Arts College, 3000 Wakefield Crossing Drive, Raleigh, NC 27614. *Phone:* 919-488-5902. *Toll-free phone:* 800-288-7442. *Fax:* 919-488-8490.
E-mail: jwenta@living-arts-college.edu.
Website: http://www.living-arts-college.edu/.

Louisburg College
Louisburg, North Carolina

Freshman Application Contact Ms. Stephanie Tolbert, Vice President for Enrollment Management, Louisburg College, 501 North Main Street, Louisburg, NC 27549-2399. *Phone:* 919-497-3233. *Toll-free phone:* 800-775-0208. *Fax:* 919-496-1788. *E-mail:* admissions@louisburg.edu. *Website:* http://www.louisburg.edu/.

Martin Community College
Williamston, North Carolina

- **State-supported** 2-year, founded 1968, part of North Carolina Community College System
- **Rural** 65-acre campus
- **Coed,** 890 undergraduate students

Majors Accounting; administrative assistant and secretarial science; automobile/automotive mechanics technology; business administration and management; cosmetology; dietitian assistant; electrical and power transmission installation related; electromechanical technology; equestrian studies; general studies; heating, air conditioning, ventilation and refrigeration maintenance technology; heating, ventilation, air conditioning and refrigeration engineering technology; information science/studies; liberal arts and sciences and humanities related; liberal arts and sciences/liberal studies; management information systems; management information systems and services related; medical administrative assistant and medical secretary; medical/clinical assistant; physical therapy technology.

Academics *Calendar:* semesters. *Degree:* certificates, diplomas, and associate. *Special study options:* academic remediation for entering students, advanced placement credit, cooperative education, distance learning, independent study, internships, off-campus study, part-time degree program, services for LD students, summer session for credit.

Library Martin Community College Learning Resources Center.

Student Life *Housing:* college housing not available. *Activities and Organizations:* Phi Theta Kappa, Student Government Association, Alpha Beta Gamma, Physical Therapy Club, Equine Club. *Campus security:* 24-hour emergency response devices, part-time patrols by trained security personnel. *Student services:* personal/psychological counseling.

Financial Aid Of all full-time matriculated undergraduates who enrolled in 2014, 30 Federal Work-Study jobs (averaging $1200).

Applying *Options:* electronic application. *Required:* high school transcript. *Application deadlines:* rolling (freshmen), rolling (transfers). *Notification:* continuous until 8/17 (freshmen), continuous until 8/17 (transfers).

Freshman Application Contact Martin Community College, 1161 Kehukee Park Road, Williamston, NC 27892. *Phone:* 252-792-1521 Ext. 244. *Website:* http://www.martincc.edu/.

Mayland Community College
Spruce Pine, North Carolina

Director of Admissions Ms. Cathy Morrison, Director of Admissions, Mayland Community College, PO Box 547, Spruce Pine, NC 28777-0547. *Phone:* 828-765-7351 Ext. 224. *Toll-free phone:* 800-462-9526. *Website:* http://www.mayland.edu/.

McDowell Technical Community College
Marion, North Carolina

Freshman Application Contact Mr. Rick L. Wilson, Director of Admissions, McDowell Technical Community College, 54 College Drive, Marion, NC 28752. *Phone:* 828-652-0632. *Fax:* 828-652-1014. *E-mail:* rickw@mcdowelltech.edu. *Website:* http://www.mcdowelltech.edu/.

Miller-Motte College
Cary, North Carolina

Admissions Office Contact Miller-Motte College, 2205 Walnut Street, Cary, NC 27518. *Website:* http://www.miller-motte.edu/.

Miller-Motte College
Fayetteville, North Carolina

Admissions Office Contact Miller-Motte College, 3725 Ramsey Street, Suite 103A, Fayetteville, NC 28311. *Website:* http://www.miller-motte.edu/.

Miller-Motte College
Greenville, North Carolina

Admissions Office Contact Miller-Motte College, 1021 WH Smith Boulevard, Suite 102, Greenville, NC 27834. *Website:* http://www.miller-motte.edu/.

Miller-Motte College
Jacksonville, North Carolina

Admissions Office Contact Miller-Motte College, 1291 Hargett Street, Jacksonville, NC 28540. *Toll-free phone:* 866-297-0267. *Website:* http://www.miller-motte.edu/.

Miller-Motte College
Raleigh, North Carolina

Admissions Office Contact Miller-Motte College, 3901 Capital Boulevard, Suite 151, Raleigh, NC 27604-6072. *Website:* http://www.miller-motte.edu/.

Miller-Motte College
Wilmington, North Carolina

Freshman Application Contact Admissions Office, Miller-Motte College, 5000 Market Street, Wilmington, NC 28405. *Toll-free phone:* 800-784-2110. *Website:* http://www.miller-motte.edu/.

Mitchell Community College
Statesville, North Carolina

- **State-supported** 2-year, founded 1852, part of North Carolina Community College System
- **Small-town** 8-acre campus with easy access to Charlotte
- **Endowment** $14.8 million
- **Coed,** 3,024 undergraduate students, 38% full-time, 62% women, 38% men

Undergraduates 1,150 full-time, 1,874 part-time. 14% Black or African American, non-Hispanic/Latino; 9% Hispanic/Latino; 3% Asian, non-Hispanic/Latino; 0.2% Native Hawaiian or other Pacific Islander, non-Hispanic/Latino; 0.6% American Indian or Alaska Native, non-Hispanic/Latino; 1% Two or more races, non-Hispanic/Latino; 1% Race/ethnicity unknown; 0.5% international; 4% transferred in. *Retention:* 56% of full-time freshmen returned.

Freshmen *Admission:* 563 enrolled.

Majors Accounting; agribusiness; business administration and management; child-care and support services management; computer programming; computer programming (specific applications); computer systems analysis; criminal justice/law enforcement administration; early childhood education; electrical, electronic and communications engineering technology; electrician; electromechanical and instrumentation and maintenance technologies related; elementary education; engineering/industrial management; executive assistant/executive secretary; general studies; health professions related; information science/studies; information technology; kindergarten/preschool education; liberal arts and sciences and humanities related; liberal arts and sciences/liberal studies; machine shop technology; manufacturing engineering; manufacturing engineering technology; mechanical drafting and CAD/CADD; mechanical engineering/mechanical technology; mechatronics, robotics, and automation engineering; medical/clinical assistant; office management; operations management; registered nursing/registered nurse; special education–early childhood; teacher assistant/aide.

Academics *Calendar:* semesters. *Degree:* certificates, diplomas, and associate. *Special study options:* academic remediation for entering students, adult/continuing education programs, advanced placement credit, cooperative education, distance learning, English as a second language, part-time degree program, services for LD students, summer session for credit. *ROTC:* Army (c).

Library Huskins Library. *Books:* 47,381 (digital/electronic). Students can reserve study rooms.

Student Life *Housing:* college housing not available. *Activities and Organizations:* choral group. *Campus security:* late-night transport/escort service, day and evening security guards. *Student services:* personal/psychological counseling.

Costs (2016–17) *Tuition:* state resident $76 per credit hour part-time; nonresident $268 per credit hour part-time. Full-time tuition and fees vary according to course load. Part-time tuition and fees vary according to course load. *Required fees:* $1 per credit hour part-time, $18 per term part-time. *Payment plan:* installment.

Financial Aid Of all full-time matriculated undergraduates who enrolled in 2014, 30 Federal Work-Study jobs.
Applying *Required:* high school transcript. *Application deadlines:* rolling (freshmen), rolling (transfers). *Notification:* continuous (freshmen), continuous (transfers).
Freshman Application Contact Mitchell Community College, 500 West Broad Street, Statesville, NC 28677. *Phone:* 704-878-3281.
Website: http://www.mitchellcc.edu/.

Montgomery Community College
Troy, North Carolina

- **State-supported** 2-year, founded 1967, part of North Carolina Community College System
- **Rural** 159-acre campus
- **Coed,** 818 undergraduate students, 34% full-time, 63% women, 37% men

Undergraduates 277 full-time, 541 part-time. Students come from 4 states and territories; 1% are from out of state; 18% Black or African American, non-Hispanic/Latino; 13% Hispanic/Latino; 1% Asian, non-Hispanic/Latino; 1% American Indian or Alaska Native, non-Hispanic/Latino; 0.9% Two or more races, non-Hispanic/Latino; 0.1% international.
Freshmen *Admission:* 124 enrolled.
Faculty *Total:* 113, 32% full-time. *Student/faculty ratio:* 7:1.
Majors Business administration and management; criminal justice/safety; early childhood education; electrician; electromechanical and instrumentation and maintenance technologies related; forest technology; gunsmithing; heating, air conditioning, ventilation and refrigeration maintenance technology; information technology; liberal arts and sciences/liberal studies; medical/clinical assistant; mental and social health services and allied professions related; office management.
Academics *Calendar:* semesters. *Degree:* certificates, diplomas, and associate. *Special study options:* academic remediation for entering students, advanced placement credit, distance learning, English as a second language, part-time degree program, services for LD students, summer session for credit.
Library Montgomery Community College Learning Resource Center. *Books:* 18,791 (physical), 44,708 (digital/electronic); *Databases:* 71. Weekly public service hours: 55.
Student Life *Housing:* college housing not available. *Activities and Organizations:* Student Government Association, Nursing Club, Gunsmithing Society, Medical Assisting Club, Forestry Club. *Campus security:* 24-hour emergency response devices. *Student services:* personal/psychological counseling.
Costs (2015–16) *Tuition:* state resident $2432 full-time, $76 per credit hour part-time; nonresident $8576 full-time, $268 per credit hour part-time. Full-time tuition and fees vary according to course load. Part-time tuition and fees vary according to course load. *Required fees:* $105 full-time, $53 per term part-time. *Payment plan:* installment.
Financial Aid Of all full-time matriculated undergraduates who enrolled in 2014, 24 Federal Work-Study jobs (averaging $500).
Applying *Options:* electronic application, early admission, deferred entrance. *Required:* high school transcript. *Application deadlines:* rolling (freshmen), rolling (transfers). *Notification:* continuous (freshmen), continuous (transfers).
Freshman Application Contact Ms. Tavia Housley, Enrollment Specialist, Montgomery Community College, 1011 Page Street, Troy, NC 27371. *Phone:* 910-576-6222 Ext. 220. *E-mail:* housleyt@montgomery.edu.
Website: http://www.montgomery.edu/.

Nash Community College
Rocky Mount, North Carolina

Freshman Application Contact Ms. Dorothy Gardner, Admissions Officer, Nash Community College, PO Box 7488, Rocky Mount, NC 27804.
Phone: 252-451-8300. *E-mail:* dgardner@nashcc.edu.
Website: http://www.nashcc.edu/.

Pamlico Community College
Grantsboro, North Carolina

Director of Admissions Mr. Floyd H. Hardison, Admissions Counselor, Pamlico Community College, PO Box 185, Grantsboro, NC 28529-0185.
Phone: 252-249-1851 Ext. 28.
Website: http://www.pamlicocc.edu/.

Piedmont Community College
Roxboro, North Carolina

- **State-supported** 2-year, founded 1970, part of North Carolina Community College System
- **Small-town** 178-acre campus
- **Coed,** 1,321 undergraduate students, 41% full-time, 59% women, 41% men

Undergraduates 541 full-time, 780 part-time.
Freshmen *Admission:* 644 applied, 644 admitted.
Faculty *Student/faculty ratio:* 12:1.
Majors Accounting; business administration and management; child-care and support services management; cinematography and film/video production; criminal justice/safety; early childhood education; electrical and power transmission installation; electrician; electromechanical and instrumentation and maintenance technologies related; general studies; graphic communications; health professions related; historic preservation and conservation; industrial technology; information technology; liberal arts and sciences and humanities related; liberal arts and sciences/liberal studies; medical administrative assistant and medical secretary; medical/clinical assistant; medical office management; mental and social health services and allied professions related; office management; registered nursing/registered nurse.
Academics *Calendar:* semesters. *Degree:* certificates, diplomas, and associate. *Special study options:* academic remediation for entering students, adult/continuing education programs, advanced placement credit, cooperative education, distance learning, double majors, English as a second language, off-campus study, part-time degree program, summer session for credit.
Library Learning Resource Center.
Student Life *Housing:* college housing not available. *Activities and Organizations:* drama/theater group, choral group. *Campus security:* routine patrols by the local sheriff's department.
Athletics *Intramural sports:* volleyball M/W.
Costs (2015–16) *Tuition:* state resident $1728 full-time, $72 per credit hour part-time; nonresident $6336 full-time, $264 per credit hour part-time. Full-time tuition and fees vary according to course load. Part-time tuition and fees vary according to course load. *Required fees:* $115 full-time, $57 per term part-time. *Payment plan:* installment.
Financial Aid Of all full-time matriculated undergraduates who enrolled in 2014, 30 Federal Work-Study jobs (averaging $1500).
Applying *Options:* electronic application, early admission, deferred entrance. *Required for some:* high school transcript. *Application deadlines:* rolling (freshmen), rolling (transfers). *Notification:* continuous (freshmen), continuous (transfers).
Freshman Application Contact Piedmont Community College, PO Box 1197, Roxboro, NC 27573-1197. *Phone:* 336-599-1181 Ext. 2243.
Website: http://www.piedmont.cc.nc.us/.

Pitt Community College
Winterville, North Carolina

Freshman Application Contact Dr. Kimberly Williamson, Interim Coordinator of Counseling, Pitt Community College, PO Drawer 7007, Greenville, NC 27835-7007. *Phone:* 252-493-7217. *Fax:* 252-321-4612.
E-mail: pittadm@pcc.pitt.cc.nc.us.
Website: http://www.pittcc.edu/.

Randolph Community College
Asheboro, North Carolina

- **State-supported** 2-year, founded 1962, part of North Carolina Community College System
- **Small-town** 40-acre campus with easy access to Greensboro, Winston-Salem, High Point
- **Endowment** $9.8 million
- **Coed,** 2,670 undergraduate students, 37% full-time, 64% women, 36% men

Undergraduates 978 full-time, 1,692 part-time. Students come from 3 states and territories; 16 other countries; 6% Black or African American, non-Hispanic/Latino; 14% Hispanic/Latino; 0.9% Asian, non-Hispanic/Latino; 0.2% Native Hawaiian or other Pacific Islander, non-Hispanic/Latino; 1% American Indian or Alaska Native, non-Hispanic/Latino; 10% Two or more races, non-Hispanic/Latino; 0.1% Race/ethnicity unknown; 1% international; 29% transferred in. *Retention:* 76% of full-time freshmen returned.
Freshmen *Admission:* 2,611 applied, 2,611 admitted, 557 enrolled. *Average high school GPA:* 2.92.
Faculty *Total:* 254, 33% full-time. *Student/faculty ratio:* 11:1.
Majors Accounting; autobody/collision and repair technology; automobile/automotive mechanics technology; business administration and

management; commercial and advertising art; commercial photography; computer systems networking and telecommunications; cosmetology; criminal justice/safety; early childhood education; electrician; electromechanical technology; funeral service and mortuary science; human services; information technology; interior design; liberal arts and sciences and humanities related; liberal arts and sciences/liberal studies; logistics, materials, and supply chain management; machine shop technology; mechatronics, robotics, and automation engineering; medical/clinical assistant; medical office management; photographic and film/video technology; photojournalism; physical therapy technology; radiologic technology/science; registered nursing/registered nurse.

Academics *Calendar:* semesters. *Degree:* certificates, diplomas, and associate. *Special study options:* academic remediation for entering students, adult/continuing education programs, advanced placement credit, cooperative education, distance learning, double majors, English as a second language, independent study, internships, off-campus study, part-time degree program, services for LD students, summer session for credit. *ROTC:* Air Force (c).

Library R. Alton Cox Learning Resources Center. *Books:* 20,000 (physical).

Student Life *Housing:* college housing not available. *Activities and Organizations:* Student Government Association, Phi Theta Kappa, Student Nurse Association, Phi Beta Lambda, Campus Crusaders. *Campus security:* 24-hour emergency response devices, security officer during hours of operation. *Student services:* personal/psychological counseling.

Costs (2016–17) *Tuition:* state resident $2432 full-time, $76 per credit part-time; nonresident $8576 full-time, $268 per credit part-time. *Required fees:* $88 full-time, $3 per credit part-time. *Payment plan:* installment.

Applying *Options:* electronic application, deferred entrance. *Application deadlines:* rolling (freshmen), rolling (transfers). *Notification:* continuous (freshmen), continuous (transfers).

Freshman Application Contact Ms. Brandi F. Hagerman, Director of Enrollment Management/Registrar, Randolph Community College, 629 Industrial Park Avenue, Asheboro, NC 27205-7333. *Phone:* 336-633-0213. *Fax:* 336-629-9547. *E-mail:* bhagerman@randolph.edu. *Website:* http://www.randolph.edu/.

Richmond Community College
Hamlet, North Carolina

- **State-supported** 2-year, founded 1964, part of North Carolina Community College System
- **Rural** 163-acre campus
- **Coed,** 2,531 undergraduate students, 46% full-time, 67% women, 33% men

Undergraduates 1,170 full-time, 1,361 part-time. 0.5% are from out of state; 32% Black or African American, non-Hispanic/Latino; 2% Hispanic/Latino; 0.6% Asian, non-Hispanic/Latino; 9% American Indian or Alaska Native, non-Hispanic/Latino; 3% Two or more races, non-Hispanic/Latino; 11% Race/ethnicity unknown; 0.2% international; 6% transferred in.

Freshmen *Admission:* 397 enrolled.

Faculty *Student/faculty ratio:* 15:1.

Majors Accounting; business administration and management; computer engineering technology; criminal justice/safety; early childhood education; electrical and power transmission installation; electrical, electronic and communications engineering technology; electromechanical and instrumentation and maintenance technologies related; electromechanical technology; elementary education; entrepreneurship; health information/medical records technology; health professions related; heating, air conditioning, ventilation and refrigeration maintenance technology; information technology; liberal arts and sciences/liberal studies; mechanical engineering/mechanical technology; medical/clinical assistant; medical office computer specialist; medical office management; mental and social health services and allied professions related; office management; registered nursing/registered nurse.

Academics *Calendar:* semesters. *Degree:* certificates, diplomas, and associate. *Special study options:* academic remediation for entering students, adult/continuing education programs, advanced placement credit, cooperative education, distance learning, double majors, English as a second language, independent study, internships, part-time degree program, student-designed majors, summer session for credit.

Library Richmond Community College Library.

Student Life *Housing:* college housing not available. *Campus security:* 24-hour emergency response devices, security guard during hours of operation. *Student services:* personal/psychological counseling.

Costs (2015–16) *Tuition:* state resident $2368 full-time, $72 per credit hour part-time; nonresident $8512 full-time, $264 per credit hour part-time. Full-time tuition and fees vary according to course load. Part-time tuition and fees vary according to course load. *Required fees:* $78 full-time, $32 per term part-time. *Payment plan:* installment. *Waivers:* employees or children of employees.

Financial Aid Of all full-time matriculated undergraduates who enrolled in 2014, 35 Federal Work-Study jobs (averaging $2000).

Applying *Options:* electronic application, deferred entrance. *Required:* high school transcript. *Application deadlines:* rolling (freshmen), rolling (transfers). *Notification:* continuous until 8/1 (freshmen), continuous until 8/1 (transfers).

Freshman Application Contact Cayce Holmes, Registrar, Richmond Community College, PO Box 1189, 1042 W. Hamlet Avenue, Hamlet, NC 28345. *Phone:* 910-410-1737. *Fax:* 910-582-7102. *E-mail:* ccholmes@richmondcc.edu. *Website:* http://www.richmondcc.edu/.

Roanoke-Chowan Community College
Ahoskie, North Carolina

Director of Admissions Miss Sandra Copeland, Director, Counseling Services, Roanoke-Chowan Community College, 109 Community College Road, Ahoskie, NC 27910. *Phone:* 252-862-1225. *Website:* http://www.roanokechowan.edu/.

Robeson Community College
Lumberton, North Carolina

Freshman Application Contact Ms. Patricia Locklear, College Recruiter, Robeson Community College, PO Box 1420, Lumberton, NC 28359. *Phone:* 910-272-3356 Ext. 251. *Fax:* 910-618-5686. *E-mail:* plocklear@robeson.edu. *Website:* http://www.robeson.edu/.

Rockingham Community College
Wentworth, North Carolina

- **State-supported** 2-year, founded 1964, part of North Carolina Community College System
- **Rural** 257-acre campus
- **Coed,** 1,866 undergraduate students, 38% full-time, 58% women, 42% men

Undergraduates 715 full-time, 1,151 part-time. 18% Black or African American, non-Hispanic/Latino; 5% Hispanic/Latino; 0.4% Asian, non-Hispanic/Latino; 0.1% Native Hawaiian or other Pacific Islander, non-Hispanic/Latino; 0.3% American Indian or Alaska Native, non-Hispanic/Latino; 3% Two or more races, non-Hispanic/Latino; 1% Race/ethnicity unknown; 0.3% international.

Freshmen *Admission:* 362 enrolled.

Faculty *Total:* 127, 49% full-time, 7% with terminal degrees. *Student/faculty ratio:* 18:1.

Majors Accounting; agricultural and food products processing; banking and financial support services; biology/biotechnology laboratory technician; business administration and management; corrections and criminal justice related; criminal justice/police science; early childhood education; electrical, electronic and communications engineering technology; electrician; general studies; health/health-care administration; information technology; liberal arts and sciences/liberal studies; logistics, materials, and supply chain management; machine shop technology; medical office management; office management; registered nursing/registered nurse; respiratory care therapy.

Academics *Calendar:* semesters. *Degree:* certificates, diplomas, and associate. *Special study options:* academic remediation for entering students, adult/continuing education programs, advanced placement credit, cooperative education, part-time degree program, student-designed majors, summer session for credit.

Library Gerald B. James Library.

Student Life *Housing:* college housing not available. *Activities and Organizations:* student-run newspaper. *Campus security:* 24-hour emergency response devices and patrols. *Student services:* personal/psychological counseling.

Athletics Member NJCAA. *Intercollegiate sports:* baseball M, volleyball W. *Intramural sports:* table tennis M/W, tennis M/W, volleyball M/W.

Costs (2015–16) *Tuition:* state resident $2304 full-time; nonresident $8448 full-time. *Required fees:* $116 full-time.

Financial Aid Of all full-time matriculated undergraduates who enrolled in 2014, 37 Federal Work-Study jobs (averaging $2300).

Applying *Options:* electronic application, early admission, deferred entrance. *Application deadlines:* rolling (freshmen), rolling (transfers). *Notification:* continuous (freshmen), continuous (transfers).

Freshman Application Contact Mr. Derrick Satterfield, Director of Enrollment Services, Rockingham Community College, PO Box 38, Wentworth, NC 27375-0038. *Phone:* 336-342-4261 Ext. 2114. *Fax:* 336-342-1809. *E-mail:* admissions@rockinghamcc.edu. *Website:* http://www.rockinghamcc.edu/.

Rowan-Cabarrus Community College

Salisbury, North Carolina

- **State-supported** 2-year, founded 1963, part of North Carolina Community College System
- **Small-town** 100-acre campus with easy access to Charlotte
- **Coed,** 5,158 undergraduate students

Freshmen *Admission:* 3,561 applied, 3,528 admitted.
Majors Accounting; automobile/automotive mechanics technology; building/property maintenance; business administration and management; business administration, management and operations related; computer and information systems security; computer programming; cosmetology; criminal justice/law enforcement administration; early childhood education; electrical, electronic and communications engineering technology; electrician; elementary education; general studies; industrial technology; information science/studies; information technology; liberal arts and sciences/liberal studies; marketing/marketing management; medical office management; office management; radiologic technology/science; registered nursing/registered nurse; system, networking, and LAN/WAN management.
Academics *Calendar:* semesters. *Degree:* certificates, diplomas, and associate. *Special study options:* academic remediation for entering students, adult/continuing education programs, advanced placement credit, cooperative education, distance learning, English as a second language, internships, part-time degree program, services for LD students, summer session for credit.
Library Learning Resource Center.
Student Life *Housing:* college housing not available. *Campus security:* on-campus security during hours of operation. *Student services:* personal/psychological counseling.
Costs (2015–16) *Tuition:* state resident $2368 full-time, $76 per credit hour part-time; nonresident $8512 full-time, $268 per credit hour part-time. Full-time tuition and fees vary according to course load. Part-time tuition and fees vary according to course load. *Required fees:* $138 full-time, $132 per term part-time. *Payment plan:* installment. *Waivers:* employees or children of employees.
Applying *Required:* high school transcript. *Application deadlines:* rolling (freshmen), rolling (transfers).
Freshman Application Contact Mrs. Gail Cummins, Director of Admissions and Recruitment, Rowan-Cabarrus Community College, PO Box 1595, Salisbury, NC 28145-1595. *Phone:* 704-637-0760. *Fax:* 704-633-6804. *Website:* http://www.rccc.edu/.

Sampson Community College

Clinton, North Carolina

Director of Admissions Mr. William R. Jordan, Director of Admissions, Sampson Community College, PO Box 318, 1801 Sunset Avenue, Highway 24 West, Clinton, NC 28329-0318. *Phone:* 910-592-8084 Ext. 2022. *Website:* http://www.sampsoncc.edu/.

Sandhills Community College

Pinehurst, North Carolina

Freshman Application Contact Mr. Isai Robledo, Recruiter, Sandhills Community College, 3395 Airport Road, Pinehurst, NC 28374-8299. *Phone:* 910-246-5365. *Toll-free phone:* 800-338-3944. *Fax:* 910-695-3981. *E-mail:* robledoi@sandhills.edu. *Website:* http://www.sandhills.edu/.

South College–Asheville

Asheville, North Carolina

Freshman Application Contact Director of Admissions, South College–Asheville, 1567 Patton Avenue, Asheville, NC 28806. *Phone:* 828-277-5521. *Fax:* 828-277-6151. *Website:* http://www.southcollegenc.edu/.

Southeastern Community College

Whiteville, North Carolina

Freshman Application Contact Ms. Sylvia McQueen, Registrar, Southeastern Community College, PO Box 151, Whiteville, NC 28472. *Phone:* 910-642-7141 Ext. 249. *Fax:* 910-642-5658. *Website:* http://www.sccnc.edu/.

South Piedmont Community College

Polkton, North Carolina

- **State-supported** 2-year, founded 1962, part of North Carolina Community College System
- **Rural** 56-acre campus with easy access to Charlotte
- **Endowment** $27,818
- **Coed**

Undergraduates 732 full-time, 1,926 part-time. Students come from 5 states and territories; 1% are from out of state; 19% Black or African American, non-Hispanic/Latino; 11% Hispanic/Latino; 2% Asian, non-Hispanic/Latino; 0.2% Native Hawaiian or other Pacific Islander, non-Hispanic/Latino; 0.3% American Indian or Alaska Native, non-Hispanic/Latino; 2% Two or more races, non-Hispanic/Latino; 4% Race/ethnicity unknown; 2% international; 5% transferred in. *Retention:* 58% of full-time freshmen returned.
Faculty *Student/faculty ratio:* 17:1.
Academics *Calendar:* semesters. *Degree:* certificates, diplomas, and associate. *Special study options:* academic remediation for entering students, accelerated degree program, adult/continuing education programs, cooperative education, distance learning, English as a second language, independent study, internships, off-campus study, part-time degree program, services for LD students, summer session for credit.
Library Martin Learning Resource Center.
Student Life *Campus security:* 24-hour emergency response devices and patrols, evening security.
Costs (2015–16) *Tuition:* state resident $2304 full-time, $72 per semester hour part-time; nonresident $8448 full-time, $264 per semester hour part-time. Full-time tuition and fees vary according to course load. Part-time tuition and fees vary according to course load. *Required fees:* $169 full-time, $9 per semester hour part-time, $44 per term part-time.
Applying *Options:* electronic application, early admission, deferred entrance. *Required:* high school transcript.
Freshman Application Contact Ms. Amanda Secrest, Assistant Director Admissions and Testing, South Piedmont Community College, PO Box 126, Polkton, NC 28135. *Phone:* 704-290-5847. *Toll-free phone:* 800-766-0319. *E-mail:* asecrest@spcc.edu. *Website:* http://www.spcc.edu/.

Southwestern Community College

Sylva, North Carolina

Freshman Application Contact Ms. Dominique Benson, Admissions Officer, Southwestern Community College, 447 College Drive, Sylva, NC 28779. *Phone:* 828-339-4217. *Toll-free phone:* 800-447-4091 (in-state); 800-447-7091 (out-of-state). *E-mail:* d_benson@southwesterncc.edu. *Website:* http://www.southwesterncc.edu/.

Stanly Community College

Albemarle, North Carolina

Freshman Application Contact Mrs. Denise B. Ross, Associate Dean, Admissions, Stanly Community College, 141 College Drive, Albemarle, NC 28001. *Phone:* 704-982-0121 Ext. 264. *Fax:* 704-982-0255. *E-mail:* dross7926@stanly.edu. *Website:* http://www.stanly.edu/.

Surry Community College

Dobson, North Carolina

Freshman Application Contact Renita Hazelwood, Director of Admissions, Surry Community College, 630 South Main Street, Dobson, NC 27017. *Phone:* 336-386-3392. *Fax:* 336-386-3690. *E-mail:* hazelwoodr@surry.edu. *Website:* http://www.surry.edu/.

Tri-County Community College

Murphy, North Carolina

Freshman Application Contact Dr. Jason Chambers, Director of Student Services and Admissions, Tri-County Community College, 21 Campus Circle, Murphy, NC 28906-7919. *Phone:* 828-837-6810. *Fax:* 828-837-3266. *E-mail:* jchambers@tricountycc.edu. *Website:* http://www.tricountycc.edu/.

Vance-Granville Community College
Henderson, North Carolina

Freshman Application Contact Ms. Kathy Kutl, Admissions Officer, Vance-Granville Community College, PO Box 917, State Road 1126, Henderson, NC 27536. *Phone:* 252-492-2061 Ext. 3265. *Fax:* 252-430-0460. *Website:* http://www.vgcc.edu/.

Virginia College in Greensboro
Greensboro, North Carolina

Admissions Office Contact Virginia College in Greensboro, 3740 South Holden Road, Greensboro, NC 27406. *Website:* http://www.vc.edu/.

Wake Technical Community College
Raleigh, North Carolina

Director of Admissions Ms. Susan Bloomfield, Director of Admissions, Wake Technical Community College, 9101 Fayetteville Road, Raleigh, NC 27603-5696. *Phone:* 919-866-5452. *E-mail:* srbloomfield@waketech.edu. *Website:* http://www.waketech.edu/.

Wayne Community College
Goldsboro, North Carolina

- **State and locally supported** 2-year, founded 1957, part of North Carolina Community College System
- **Small-town** 175-acre campus with easy access to Raleigh
- **Endowment** $92,408
- **Coed,** 3,837 undergraduate students, 47% full-time, 60% women, 40% men

Undergraduates 1,813 full-time, 2,024 part-time. 4% are from out of state; 27% Black or African American, non-Hispanic/Latino; 8% Hispanic/Latino; 2% Asian, non-Hispanic/Latino; 0.3% Native Hawaiian or other Pacific Islander, non-Hispanic/Latino; 0.6% American Indian or Alaska Native, non-Hispanic/Latino; 0.8% Two or more races, non-Hispanic/Latino; 2% Race/ethnicity unknown; 0.3% international; 26% transferred in.
Freshmen *Admission:* 2,328 applied, 1,335 admitted, 655 enrolled.
Faculty *Total:* 333, 42% full-time, 1% with terminal degrees. *Student/faculty ratio:* 20:1.
Majors Accounting; agribusiness; agroecology and sustainable agriculture; airframe mechanics and aircraft maintenance technology; animal/livestock husbandry and production; autobody/collision and repair technology; automobile/automotive mechanics technology; biology/biotechnology laboratory technician; business administration and management; criminal justice/police science; criminal justice/safety; crisis/emergency/disaster management; dental hygiene; early childhood education; electrical, electronic and communications engineering technology; electromechanical and instrumentation and maintenance technologies related; elementary education; energy management and systems technology; forensic science and technology; forest technology; game and interactive media design; information technology; liberal arts and sciences and humanities related; liberal arts and sciences/liberal studies; machine shop technology; mechanical engineering/mechanical technology; medical/clinical assistant; medical office management; mental and social health services and allied professions related; office management; operations management; registered nursing/registered nurse; turf and turfgrass management.
Academics *Calendar:* semesters. *Degree:* certificates, diplomas, and associate. *Special study options:* academic remediation for entering students, adult/continuing education programs, advanced placement credit, cooperative education, distance learning, double majors, English as a second language, external degree program, honors programs, part-time degree program, services for LD students, summer session for credit.
Library Dr. Clyde A. Erwin, Jr. Library.
Student Life *Housing:* college housing not available. *Activities and Organizations:* choral group, Student Government Association, Phi Beta Lambda, Phi Theta Kappa, Criminal Justice Club, International Club. *Campus security:* 24-hour emergency response devices and patrols. *Student services:* personal/psychological counseling.
Athletics *Intramural sports:* football M/W.
Standardized Tests *Recommended:* SAT or ACT (for admission).
Financial Aid Of all full-time matriculated undergraduates who enrolled in 2014, 100 Federal Work-Study jobs (averaging $2000).
Applying *Options:* electronic application. *Required:* high school transcript, interview. *Application deadlines:* rolling (freshmen), rolling (out-of-state

freshmen), rolling (transfers). *Notification:* continuous (freshmen), continuous (out-of-state freshmen), continuous (transfers).
Freshman Application Contact Mrs. Jennifer P. Mayo, Associate Director of Admissions and Records, Wayne Community College, PO Box 8002, Goldsboro, NC 27533. *Phone:* 919-735-5151 Ext. 6721. *Fax:* 919-736-9425. *E-mail:* jbmayo@waynecc.edu. *Website:* http://www.waynecc.edu/.

Western Piedmont Community College
Morganton, North Carolina

- **State-supported** 2-year, founded 1964, part of North Carolina Community College System
- **Small-town** 130-acre campus
- **Coed,** 2,933 undergraduate students

Undergraduates 7% Black or African American, non-Hispanic/Latino; 5% Hispanic/Latino; 7% Asian, non-Hispanic/Latino; 0.2% Native Hawaiian or other Pacific Islander, non-Hispanic/Latino; 0.3% American Indian or Alaska Native, non-Hispanic/Latino; 0.5% Race/ethnicity unknown.
Majors Accounting; accounting technology and bookkeeping; agroecology and sustainable agriculture; animation, interactive technology, video graphics and special effects; applied horticulture/horticulture operations; building/construction finishing, management, and inspection related; business administration and management; child-care and support services management; cinematography and film/video production; civil engineering technology; clinical/medical laboratory technology; computer engineering technology; crafts, folk art and artisanry; criminal justice/law enforcement administration; criminal justice/police science; early childhood education; electrical, electronic and communications engineering technology; engineering technologies and engineering related; environmental science; executive assistant/executive secretary; game and interactive media design; information technology; legal assistant/paralegal; liberal arts and sciences and humanities related; liberal arts and sciences/liberal studies; machine shop technology; mechanical engineering/mechanical technology; medical administrative assistant and medical secretary; medical/clinical assistant; medical office management; mental and social health services and allied professions related; office management; precision production related; psychiatric/mental health services technology; registered nursing/registered nurse; sign language interpretation and translation; substance abuse/addiction counseling; surveying technology; therapeutic recreation; welding technology.
Academics *Calendar:* semesters. *Degree:* certificates, diplomas, and associate. *Special study options:* academic remediation for entering students, adult/continuing education programs, advanced placement credit, cooperative education, distance learning, double majors, English as a second language, part-time degree program, services for LD students, summer session for credit.
Student Life *Housing:* college housing not available. *Activities and Organizations:* drama/theater group. *Student services:* personal/psychological counseling.
Athletics *Intramural sports:* basketball M.
Costs (2015–16) *Tuition:* state resident $2368 full-time, $74 per credit hour part-time; nonresident $8512 full-time, $266 per credit hour part-time. *Required fees:* $145 full-time. *Payment plan:* deferred payment. *Waivers:* employees or children of employees.
Applying *Options:* electronic application. *Required:* high school transcript. *Application deadlines:* rolling (freshmen), rolling (transfers). *Notification:* continuous (freshmen), continuous (transfers).
Freshman Application Contact Susan Williams, Director of Admissions, Western Piedmont Community College, 1001 Burkemont Avenue, Morganton, NC 28655-4511. *Phone:* 828-438-6051. *Fax:* 828-438-6065. *E-mail:* swilliams@wpcc.edu. *Website:* http://www.wpcc.edu/.

Wilkes Community College
Wilkesboro, North Carolina

Freshman Application Contact Mr. Mac Warren, Director of Admissions, Wilkes Community College, PO Box 120, Wilkesboro, NC 28697. *Phone:* 336-838-6141. *Fax:* 336-838-6547. *E-mail:* mac.warren@wilkescc.edu. *Website:* http://www.wilkescc.edu/.

Wilson Community College
Wilson, North Carolina

Freshman Application Contact Mrs. Maegan Williams, Admissions Technician, Wilson Community College, Wilson, NC 27893-0305. *Phone:* 252-246-1275. *Fax:* 252-243-7148. *E-mail:* mwilliams@wilsoncc.edu. *Website:* http://www.wilsoncc.edu/.

NORTH DAKOTA

Bismarck State College
Bismarck, North Dakota

- **State-supported** primarily 2-year, founded 1939, part of North Dakota University System
- **Urban** 100-acre campus
- **Endowment** $15.1 million
- **Coed**, 4,078 undergraduate students, 56% full-time, 43% women, 57% men

Undergraduates 2,281 full-time, 1,797 part-time. Students come from 55 states and territories; 13 other countries; 25% are from out of state; 3% Black or African American, non-Hispanic/Latino; 3% Hispanic/Latino; 0.6% Asian, non-Hispanic/Latino; 0.1% Native Hawaiian or other Pacific Islander, non-Hispanic/Latino; 2% American Indian or Alaska Native, non-Hispanic/Latino; 3% Two or more races, non-Hispanic/Latino; 2% Race/ethnicity unknown; 0.3% international; 4% transferred in.

Freshmen *Admission:* 1,067 applied, 1,067 admitted, 848 enrolled. *Average high school GPA:* 3.02. *Test scores:* ACT scores over 18: 72%; ACT scores over 24: 19%; ACT scores over 30: 1%.

Faculty *Total:* 357, 37% full-time, 11% with terminal degrees. *Student/faculty ratio:* 14:1.

Majors Administrative assistant and secretarial science; agricultural business and management; autobody/collision and repair technology; automobile/automotive mechanics technology; building/home/construction inspection; business automation/technology/data entry; business/commerce; carpentry; clinical/medical laboratory technology; commercial and advertising art; computer systems networking and telecommunications; criminal justice/safety; electrical, electronic and communications engineering technology; emergency medical technology (EMT paramedic); engineering technology; environmental control technologies related; farm and ranch management; heating, air conditioning, ventilation and refrigeration maintenance technology; human services; industrial mechanics and maintenance technology; industrial production technologies related; industrial technology; instrumentation technology; legal administrative assistant/secretary; liberal arts and sciences/liberal studies; lineworker; medical administrative assistant and medical secretary; multi/interdisciplinary studies related; nuclear engineering technology; operations management; petroleum technology; public relations/image management; recording arts technology; registered nursing/registered nurse; surgical technology; surveying technology; web page, digital/multimedia and information resources design; welding technology.

Academics *Calendar:* semesters. *Degrees:* certificates, diplomas, associate, and bachelor's. *Special study options:* academic remediation for entering students, adult/continuing education programs, advanced placement credit, cooperative education, distance learning, independent study, internships, part-time degree program, services for LD students, study abroad, summer session for credit.

Library Bismarck State College Library. *Books:* 82,049 (physical), 13,580 (digital/electronic); *Serial titles:* 169 (physical), 131 (digital/electronic); *Databases:* 98. Weekly public service hours: 67; students can reserve study rooms.

Student Life *Housing Options:* coed, men-only, women-only, special housing for students with disabilities. Campus housing is university owned. *Activities and Organizations:* drama/theater group, student-run newspaper, radio station, choral group, Intramural Sports, Campus Crusade, Student Government Association, Concert/Chamber Choir, Drama Club. *Campus security:* late-night transport/escort service, controlled dormitory access. *Student services:* personal/psychological counseling.

Athletics Member NJCAA. *Intercollegiate sports:* baseball M, basketball M/W(s), golf M/W, soccer M, softball W(s), volleyball W(s). *Intramural sports:* basketball M/W, football M/W, volleyball M/W.

Standardized Tests *Recommended:* SAT or ACT (for admission).

Costs (2015–16) *Tuition:* state resident $2861 full-time, $119 per credit hour part-time; nonresident $7640 full-time, $318 per credit hour part-time. Full-time tuition and fees vary according to course level, course load, degree level, location, program, and reciprocity agreements. Part-time tuition and fees vary according to course level, course load, degree level, location, program, and reciprocity agreements. *Required fees:* $743 full-time, $31 per credit hour part-time. *Room and board:* $7151; room only: $2521. Room and board charges vary according to board plan and housing facility. *Waivers:* minority students and employees or children of employees.

Financial Aid Of all full-time matriculated undergraduates who enrolled in 2013, 1,731 applied for aid, 1,133 were judged to have need, 429 had their need fully met. In 2013, 236 non-need-based awards were made. *Average percent of need met:* 49%. *Average financial aid package:* $11,129. *Average need-based loan:* $4646. *Average need-based gift aid:* $4241. *Average non-need-based aid:* $709.

Applying *Options:* electronic application, early admission. *Application fee:* $35. *Required:* high school transcript. *Required for some:* interview. *Application deadlines:* rolling (freshmen), rolling (out-of-state freshmen), rolling (transfers). *Notification:* continuous (freshmen), continuous (out-of-state freshmen), continuous (transfers).

Freshman Application Contact Karen Erickson, Director of Admissions and Enrollment Services, Bismarck State College, PO Box 5587, Bismarck, ND 58506. *Phone:* 701-224-5424. *Toll-free phone:* 800-445-5073. *Fax:* 701-224-5643. *E-mail:* karen.erickson@bismarckstate.edu. *Website:* http://www.bismarckstate.edu/.

Cankdeska Cikana Community College
Fort Totten, North Dakota

Director of Admissions Mr. Ermen Brown Jr., Registrar, Cankdeska Cikana Community College, PO Box 269, Fort Totten, ND 58335-0269. *Phone:* 701-766-1342. *Toll-free phone:* 888-783-1463.
Website: http://www.littlehoop.edu/.

Dakota College at Bottineau
Bottineau, North Dakota

- **State-supported** 2-year, founded 1906, part of North Dakota University System
- **Rural** 35-acre campus
- **Coed**

Undergraduates Students come from 3 other countries; 23% are from out of state; 10% Black or African American, non-Hispanic/Latino; 3% Hispanic/Latino; 0.4% Asian, non-Hispanic/Latino; 0.3% Native Hawaiian or other Pacific Islander, non-Hispanic/Latino; 2% American Indian or Alaska Native, non-Hispanic/Latino; 3% Two or more races, non-Hispanic/Latino; 17% Race/ethnicity unknown; 3% international.

Faculty *Student/faculty ratio:* 10:1.

Academics *Calendar:* semesters. *Degree:* certificates, diplomas, and associate. *Special study options:* academic remediation for entering students, advanced placement credit, cooperative education, distance learning, double majors, off-campus study, part-time degree program, services for LD students, summer session for credit.

Library Dakota College at Bottineau Library plus 1 other.

Student Life *Campus security:* controlled dormitory access, security cameras.

Athletics Member NJCAA.

Standardized Tests *Required:* SAT or ACT (for admission). *Recommended:* ACT (for admission).

Financial Aid *Financial aid deadline:* 4/15.

Applying *Options:* electronic application, early admission, deferred entrance. *Application fee:* $35. *Required:* high school transcript, immunization records, previous college official transcripts, ACT or SAT scores.

Freshman Application Contact Mrs. Luann Soland, Admissions Counselor, Dakota College at Bottineau, 105 Simrall Boulevard, Bottineau, ND 58318. *Phone:* 701-228-5487. *Toll-free phone:* 800-542-6866. *Fax:* 701-228-5499. *E-mail:* luann.soland@dakotacollege.edu. *Website:* http://www.dakotacollege.edu/.

Lake Region State College
Devils Lake, North Dakota

- **State-supported** 2-year, founded 1941, part of North Dakota University System
- **Small-town** 120-acre campus
- **Coed**, 1,918 undergraduate students, 28% full-time, 54% women, 46% men

Undergraduates 535 full-time, 1,383 part-time. Students come from 30 states and territories; 8 other countries; 13% are from out of state; 4% Black or African American, non-Hispanic/Latino; 5% Hispanic/Latino; 0.8% Asian, non-Hispanic/Latino; 0.6% Native Hawaiian or other Pacific Islander, non-Hispanic/Latino; 4% American Indian or Alaska Native, non-Hispanic/Latino; 4% Two or more races, non-Hispanic/Latino; 2% Race/ethnicity unknown; 6% international; 5% transferred in; 10% live on campus.

Freshmen *Admission:* 282 applied, 281 admitted, 193 enrolled. *Test scores:* ACT scores over 18: 72%; ACT scores over 24: 17%.

Faculty *Total:* 44.

Majors Administrative assistant and secretarial science; agricultural business and management; automobile/automotive mechanics technology; business administration and management; child-care provision; computer installation and repair technology; criminal justice/police science; electrical and electronic engineering technologies related; language interpretation and translation; liberal arts and sciences/liberal studies; management information systems; merchandising, sales, and marketing operations related (general); physical fitness technician; registered nursing/registered nurse; speech-language pathology.

Academics *Calendar:* semesters. *Degree:* certificates, diplomas, and associate. *Special study options:* academic remediation for entering students, cooperative education, distance learning, double majors, English as a second language, honors programs, internships, part-time degree program, services for LD students, summer session for credit.

Library Paul Hoghaug Library. *Books:* 48,000 (physical), 18,000 (digital/electronic); *Databases:* 7.

Student Life *Housing Options:* coed, men-only, women-only. Campus housing is university owned and leased by the school. *Activities and Organizations:* drama/theater group, choral group, marching band, Student Senate, Phi Theta Kappa, Delta Epsilon Chi, Phi Theta Lambda, Student Nurse Organization. *Campus security:* 24-hour emergency response devices, controlled dormitory access. *Student services:* personal/psychological counseling.

Athletics Member NJCAA. *Intercollegiate sports:* baseball M(s), basketball M(s)/W(s), golf M(s)/W(s), softball W(s), volleyball W(s). *Intramural sports:* basketball M/W, riflery M/W, soccer M/W, volleyball M/W, weight lifting M/W.

Standardized Tests *Required for some:* SAT or ACT (for admission), ACT Compass.

Costs (2015–16) *Tuition:* state resident $3261 full-time, $136 per credit part-time; nonresident $3261 full-time, $136 per credit part-time. Full-time tuition and fees vary according to course load, location, and program. Part-time tuition and fees vary according to course load, location, and program. *Required fees:* $877 full-time, $29 per credit part-time. *Room and board:* $6055. Room and board charges vary according to board plan and housing facility. *Payment plan:* installment. *Waivers:* minority students, senior citizens, and employees or children of employees.

Financial Aid Of all full-time matriculated undergraduates who enrolled in 2015, 383 applied for aid, 306 were judged to have need, 137 had their need fully met. In 2015, 70 non-need-based awards were made. *Average percent of need met:* 80%. *Average financial aid package:* $10,502. *Average need-based loan:* $5278. *Average need-based gift aid:* $6099. *Average non-need-based aid:* $905. *Average indebtedness upon graduation:* $9405.

Applying *Options:* electronic application. *Application fee:* $35. *Required for some:* high school transcript, interview, immunization records, college transcripts. *Application deadlines:* rolling (freshmen), rolling (out-of-state freshmen), rolling (transfers). *Notification:* continuous (freshmen), continuous (out-of-state freshmen), continuous (transfers).

Freshman Application Contact Lisa Howard, Administrative Assistant, Admissions Office, Lake Region State College, 1801 College Drive North, Devils Lake, ND 58301. *Phone:* 701-662-1519. *Toll-free phone:* 800-443-1313. *Fax:* 701-662-1581. *E-mail:* lisa.howard@lrsc.edu. *Website:* http://www.lrsc.edu/.

North Dakota State College of Science
Wahpeton, North Dakota

Freshman Application Contact Ms. Barb Mund, Director of Admissions and Records, North Dakota State College of Science, 800 North 6th Street, Wahpeton, ND 58076. *Phone:* 701-671-2204. *Toll-free phone:* 800-342-4325. *Fax:* 701-671-2201. *E-mail:* barb.mund@ndscs.edu. *Website:* http://www.ndscs.edu/.

Nueta Hidatsa Sahnish College
New Town, North Dakota

Freshman Application Contact Office of Admissions, Nueta Hidatsa Sahnish College, PO Box 490, 220 8th Avenue North, New Town, ND 58763-0490. *Phone:* 701-627-4738 Ext. 295. *Website:* http://www.nhsc.edu/.

Turtle Mountain Community College
Belcourt, North Dakota

Director of Admissions Ms. Joni LaFontaine, Admissions/Records Officer, Turtle Mountain Community College, Box 340, Belcourt, ND 58316-0340. *Phone:* 701-477-5605 Ext. 217. *E-mail:* jlafontaine@tm.edu. *Website:* http://my.tm.edu/.

United Tribes Technical College
Bismarck, North Dakota

Freshman Application Contact Ms. Vivian Gillette, Director of Admissions, United Tribes Technical College, Bismarck, ND 58504. *Phone:* 701-255-3285 Ext. 1334. *Fax:* 701-530-0640. *E-mail:* vgillette@uttc.edu. *Website:* http://www.uttc.edu/.

Williston State College
Williston, North Dakota

- **State-supported** 2-year, founded 1957, part of North Dakota University System
- **Small-town** 80-acre campus
- **Endowment** $52,200
- **Coed,** 1,038 undergraduate students, 58% full-time, 61% women, 39% men

Undergraduates 603 full-time, 435 part-time. Students come from 33 states and territories; 8 other countries; 19% are from out of state; 4% Black or African American, non-Hispanic/Latino; 6% Hispanic/Latino; 0.7% Asian, non-Hispanic/Latino; 0.1% Native Hawaiian or other Pacific Islander, non-Hispanic/Latino; 3% American Indian or Alaska Native, non-Hispanic/Latino; 5% Two or more races, non-Hispanic/Latino; 4% Race/ethnicity unknown; 6% international; 20% transferred in. *Retention:* 49% of full-time freshmen returned.

Freshmen *Admission:* 294 applied, 236 admitted, 302 enrolled.

Faculty *Total:* 30, 93% full-time, 3% with terminal degrees. *Student/faculty ratio:* 23:1.

Majors Accounting technology and bookkeeping; agriculture; business administration, management and operations related; diesel mechanics technology; health information/medical records technology; liberal arts and sciences/liberal studies; licensed practical/vocational nurse training; massage therapy; multi/interdisciplinary studies related; petroleum technology; psychiatric/mental health services technology; registered nursing/registered nurse; speech-language pathology; system, networking, and LAN/WAN management; welding technology.

Academics *Calendar:* semesters. *Degree:* certificates, diplomas, and associate. *Special study options:* academic remediation for entering students, advanced placement credit, cooperative education, distance learning, double majors, independent study, part-time degree program, services for LD students, student-designed majors, study abroad, summer session for credit.

Library Williston State College Learning Commons.

Student Life *Housing Options:* coed, special housing for students with disabilities. Campus housing is university owned. *Activities and Organizations:* student-run newspaper, choral group, Phi Theta Kappa, Student Senate, Teton Activity Board, Biz-Tech, Student Nurses Organization. *Campus security:* 24-hour patrols, controlled dormitory access. *Student services:* personal/psychological counseling.

Athletics Member NJCAA. *Intercollegiate sports:* baseball M(s), basketball M(s)/W(s), ice hockey M(s), softball W(s), volleyball W(s). *Intramural sports:* basketball M/W, volleyball M/W.

Costs (2016–17) *One-time required fee:* $35. *Tuition:* state resident $2874 full-time, $111 per credit hour part-time; nonresident $2874 full-time, $111 per credit hour part-time. Full-time tuition and fees vary according to course load, location, program, and reciprocity agreements. Part-time tuition and fees vary according to course load, location, program, and reciprocity agreements. *Required fees:* $1465 full-time, $56 per credit hour part-time. *Room and board:* $9572; room only: $6000. Room and board charges vary according to board plan and housing facility. *Payment plan:* installment. *Waivers:* minority students, senior citizens, and employees or children of employees.

Applying *Options:* electronic application, deferred entrance. *Application fee:* $35. *Required:* high school transcript. *Application deadlines:* rolling (freshmen), rolling (out-of-state freshmen), rolling (transfers). *Notification:* continuous (freshmen), continuous (out-of-state freshmen), continuous (transfers).

Freshman Application Contact Ms. Brittney O'Neill, Enrollment Services Associate, Williston State College, 1410 University Avenue, Williston, ND 58801. *Phone:* 701-774-4202. *Toll-free phone:* 888-863-9455. *E-mail:* brittney.f.oneill@willistonstate.edu. *Website:* http://www.willistonstate.edu/.

NORTHERN MARIANA ISLANDS

Northern Marianas College
Saipan, Northern Mariana Islands

Freshman Application Contact Ms. Leilani M. Basa-Alam, Admission Specialist, Northern Marianas College, PO Box 501250, Saipan, MP 96950-1250. *Phone:* 670-234-3690 Ext. 1539. *Fax:* 670-235-4967. *E-mail:* leilanib@nmcnet.edu. *Website:* http://www.marianas.edu/.

OHIO

American Institute of Alternative Medicine
Columbus, Ohio

Admissions Office Contact American Institute of Alternative Medicine, 6685 Doubletree Avenue, Columbus, OH 43229.
Website: http://www.aiam.edu/.

Antonelli College
Cincinnati, Ohio

Freshman Application Contact Antonelli College, 124 East Seventh Street, Cincinnati, OH 45202. *Phone:* 513-241-4338. *Toll-free phone:* 877-500-4304.
Website: http://www.antonellicollege.edu/.

The Art Institute of Cincinnati
Cincinnati, Ohio

- **Independent** primarily 2-year, founded 1976
- **Urban** 3-acre campus with easy access to Cincinnati
- **Coed**

Undergraduates 30 full-time, 4 part-time. Students come from 3 states and territories; 27% are from out of state; 18% Black or African American, non-Hispanic/Latino. *Retention:* 90% of full-time freshmen returned.
Faculty *Student/faculty ratio:* 5:1.
Academics *Degrees:* associate and bachelor's. *Special study options:* academic remediation for entering students, accelerated degree program, advanced placement credit, cooperative education, part-time degree program, services for LD students.
Library The Art Institute of Cincinnati Library plus 1 other.
Student Life *Campus security:* 24-hour emergency response devices, SMS.
Standardized Tests *Recommended:* SAT or ACT (for admission).
Costs (2015–16) *Tuition:* $23,001 full-time, $511 per credit hour part-time. Full-time tuition and fees vary according to course load. Part-time tuition and fees vary according to course load. No tuition increase for student's term of enrollment. *Required fees:* $1017 full-time.
Applying *Options:* early admission, early decision, deferred entrance. *Application fee:* $100. *Required:* essay or personal statement, high school transcript, interview. *Recommended:* minimum 2.0 GPA, ACT or SAT score submission recommended. Placement testing is offered.
Freshman Application Contact Megan Orsburn, Admissions Assistant, The Art Institute of Cincinnati, 1171 E. Kemper Road, Cincinnati, OH 45246. *Phone:* 513-751-1206.
Website: http://www.aic-arts.edu/.

ATS Institute of Technology
Highland Heights, Ohio

Freshman Application Contact Admissions Office, ATS Institute of Technology, 325 Alpha Park, Highland Heights, OH 44143. *Phone:* 440-449-1700 Ext. 103. *E-mail:* info@atsinstitute.edu.
Website: http://www.atsinstitute.edu/cleveland/.

Beckfield College
Cincinnati, Ohio

- **Proprietary** 2-year, founded 1984
- **Suburban** campus
- **Coed**

Academics *Calendar:* quarters. *Degree:* diplomas and associate.
Freshman Application Contact Beckfield College, 225 Pictoria Drive, Suite 200, Cincinnati, OH 45246.
Website: http://www.beckfield.edu/.

Belmont College
St. Clairsville, Ohio

Director of Admissions Michael Sterling, Director of Recruitment, Belmont College, 120 Fox Shannon Place, St. Clairsville, OH 43950-9735. *Phone:* 740-695-9500 Ext. 1563. *Toll-free phone:* 800-423-1188.
E-mail: msterling@btc.edu.
Website: http://www.belmontcollege.edu/.

Bowling Green State University–Firelands College
Huron, Ohio

- **State-supported** primarily 2-year, founded 1968, part of Bowling Green State University System
- **Rural** 216-acre campus with easy access to Cleveland, Toledo
- **Coed,** 2,260 undergraduate students, 49% full-time, 64% women, 36% men

Undergraduates 1,114 full-time, 1,146 part-time. Students come from 6 states and territories; 1 other country; 1% are from out of state; 5% Black or African American, non-Hispanic/Latino; 5% Hispanic/Latino; 0.5% Asian, non-Hispanic/Latino; 0.4% American Indian or Alaska Native, non-Hispanic/Latino; 3% Two or more races, non-Hispanic/Latino; 3% Race/ethnicity unknown. *Retention:* 51% of full-time freshmen returned.
Freshmen *Admission:* 408 enrolled. *Average high school GPA:* 2.8.
Faculty *Total:* 126, 40% full-time. *Student/faculty ratio:* 20:1.
Majors Allied health and medical assisting services related; business administration and management; communications technologies and support services related; computer and information sciences and support services related; computer engineering technology; computer systems networking and telecommunications; criminal justice/safety; design and visual communications; diagnostic medical sonography and ultrasound technology; education; electrical, electronic and communications engineering technology; electromechanical technology; health information/medical records administration; health professions related; human services; industrial technology; interdisciplinary studies; liberal arts and sciences/liberal studies; management information systems and services related; manufacturing engineering technology; mechanical engineering/mechanical technology; medical radiologic technology; registered nursing/registered nurse; respiratory care therapy; social work.
Academics *Calendar:* semesters. *Degrees:* certificates, associate, and bachelor's (also offers some upper-level and graduate courses). *Special study options:* academic remediation for entering students, adult/continuing education programs, advanced placement credit, cooperative education, distance learning, double majors, honors programs, independent study, internships, part-time degree program, services for LD students, student-designed majors, study abroad, summer session for credit. *ROTC:* Army (c), Air Force (c).
Library BGSU Firelands College Library.
Student Life *Housing:* college housing not available. *Activities and Organizations:* drama/theater group, Society of Fandom and Gaming, Student Government, Student Theater Guild, Safe Space, Society of Leadership and Success. *Campus security:* 24-hour emergency response devices, late-night transport/escort service, patrols by trained security personnel.
Athletics *Intramural sports:* basketball M/W, bowling M/W, football M, table tennis M/W, volleyball M/W.
Costs (2015–16) *Tuition:* state resident $4706 full-time, $196 per credit hour part-time; nonresident $12,014 full-time, $501 per credit hour part-time. Full-time tuition and fees vary according to location. Part-time tuition and fees vary according to location. *Required fees:* $240 full-time, $9 per credit hour part-time, $120 per term part-time. *Payment plan:* installment. *Waivers:* employees or children of employees.
Applying *Options:* electronic application, early admission, deferred entrance. *Application fee:* $45. *Required:* high school transcript. *Application deadlines:* 8/6 (freshmen), 8/6 (transfers). *Notification:* continuous (freshmen), continuous (transfers).
Freshman Application Contact Debralee Divers, Director of Admissions and Financial Aid, Bowling Green State University–Firelands College, One University Drive, Huron, OH 44839-9791. *Phone:* 419-433-5560. *Toll-free phone:* 800-322-4787. *Fax:* 419-372-0604. *E-mail:* divers@bgsu.edu.
Website: http://www.firelands.bgsu.edu/.

Bradford School
Columbus, Ohio

- **Proprietary** 2-year, founded 1911
- **Suburban** campus
- **Coed,** 443 undergraduate students

Majors Cooking and related culinary arts; graphic design; medical/clinical assistant; physical therapy technology; veterinary/animal health technology.
Academics *Calendar:* semesters. *Degree:* diplomas and associate. *Special study options:* accelerated degree program, internships.
Freshman Application Contact Admissions Office, Bradford School, 2469 Stelzer Road, Columbus, OH 43219. *Phone:* 614-416-6200. *Toll-free phone:* 800-678-7981.
Website: http://www.bradfordschoolcolumbus.edu/.

Brightwood College, Dayton Campus
Dayton, Ohio

Freshman Application Contact Brightwood College, Dayton Campus, 2800 East River Road, Dayton, OH 45439. *Phone:* 937-294-6155. *Toll-free phone:* 800-935-1857.
Website: http://www.brightwood.edu/.

Brown Mackie College–Akron
Akron, Ohio

Freshman Application Contact Brown Mackie College–Akron, 755 White Pond Drive, Suite 101, Akron, OH 44320. *Phone:* 330-869-3600.
Website: http://www.brownmackie.edu/akron/.

Brown Mackie College–Cincinnati
Cincinnati, Ohio

Freshman Application Contact Brown Mackie College–Cincinnati, 1011 Glendale-Milford Road, Cincinnati, OH 45215. *Phone:* 513-771-2424. *Toll-free phone:* 800-888-1445.
Website: http://www.brownmackie.edu/cincinnati/.

Brown Mackie College–Findlay
Findlay, Ohio

Freshman Application Contact Brown Mackie College–Findlay, 1700 Fostoria Avenue, Suite 100, Findlay, OH 45840. *Phone:* 419-423-2211. *Toll-free phone:* 800-842-3687.
Website: http://www.brownmackie.edu/findlay/.

Brown Mackie College–North Canton
Canton, Ohio

Freshman Application Contact Brown Mackie College–North Canton, 4300 Munson Street NW, Canton, OH 44718-3674. *Phone:* 330-494-1214.
Website: http://www.brownmackie.edu/northcanton/.

Bryant & Stratton College–Eastlake Campus
Eastlake, Ohio

Freshman Application Contact Ms. Melanie Pettit, Director of Admissions, Bryant & Stratton College–Eastlake Campus, 35350 Curtis Boulevard, Eastlake, OH 44095. *Phone:* 440-510-1112.
Website: http://www.bryantstratton.edu/.

Bryant & Stratton College–Parma Campus
Parma, Ohio

Freshman Application Contact Bryant & Stratton College–Parma Campus, 12955 Snow Road, Parma, OH 44130-1005. *Phone:* 216-265-3151. *Toll-free phone:* 866-948-0571.
Website: http://www.bryantstratton.edu/.

Central Ohio Technical College
Newark, Ohio

- **State-supported** 2-year, founded 1971, part of Ohio Department of Higher Education
- **Small-town** 177-acre campus with easy access to Columbus
- **Endowment** $2.8 million
- **Coed,** 3,566 undergraduate students, 27% full-time, 67% women, 33% men

Undergraduates 969 full-time, 2,597 part-time. 1% are from out of state; 10% Black or African American, non-Hispanic/Latino; 2% Hispanic/Latino; 0.9% Asian, non-Hispanic/Latino; 0.3% American Indian or Alaska Native, non-Hispanic/Latino; 3% Two or more races, non-Hispanic/Latino; 8% Race/ethnicity unknown; 12% transferred in. *Retention:* 46% of full-time freshmen returned.
Freshmen *Admission:* 459 enrolled.
Faculty *Total:* 242, 24% full-time. *Student/faculty ratio:* 15:1.

Majors Accounting; advertising; architectural drafting and CAD/CADD; business administration and management; CAD/CADD drafting/design technology; civil drafting and CAD/CADD; civil engineering technology; computer graphics; computer programming; computer support specialist; criminal justice/law enforcement administration; criminal justice/police science; culinary arts; diagnostic medical sonography and ultrasound technology; early childhood education; electrical, electronic and communications engineering technology; emergency medical technology (EMT paramedic); fire science/firefighting; forensic science and technology; human services; liberal arts and sciences/liberal studies; licensed practical/vocational nurse training; manufacturing engineering technology; mechanical engineering/mechanical technology; radiologic technology/science; registered nursing/registered nurse; surgical technology; web page, digital/multimedia and information resources design.
Academics *Calendar:* semesters. *Degree:* certificates and associate. *Special study options:* academic remediation for entering students, accelerated degree program, adult/continuing education programs, advanced placement credit, cooperative education, distance learning, double majors, internships, off-campus study, part-time degree program, services for LD students, student-designed majors, summer session for credit.
Library Newark Campus Library.
Student Life *Housing:* college housing not available. *Activities and Organizations:* drama/theater group, choral group, Radiologic Technology Student Organization, Phi Theta Kappa, Society of Engineering Technology, The Human Services Committee, Digital Media Design Coshocton. *Campus security:* 24-hour emergency response devices and patrols, student patrols, late-night transport/escort service. *Student services:* personal/psychological counseling.
Athletics *Intramural sports:* badminton M/W, basketball M/W, soccer M/W, table tennis M/W, volleyball M/W.
Costs (2015–16) *One-time required fee:* $80. *Tuition:* state resident $4296 full-time, $179 per semester hour part-time; nonresident $7056 full-time, $294 per semester hour part-time. *Payment plan:* installment. *Waivers:* senior citizens and employees or children of employees.
Financial Aid Of all full-time matriculated undergraduates who enrolled in 2014, 43 Federal Work-Study jobs (averaging $4000).
Applying *Options:* electronic application, early admission, deferred entrance. *Required for some:* high school transcript. *Application deadlines:* rolling (freshmen), rolling (transfers).
Freshman Application Contact Brad Pulcini, Director of Gateway Operations, Central Ohio Technical College, 1179 University Drive, Newark, OH 43055-1767. *Phone:* 740-755-7139. *Toll-free phone:* 800-9NEWARK. *E-mail:* bpulcini@cotc.edu.
Website: http://www.cotc.edu/.

Chatfield College
St. Martin, Ohio

- **Independent** 2-year, founded 1970, affiliated with Roman Catholic Church
- **Rural** 200-acre campus with easy access to Cincinnati, Dayton
- **Endowment** $2.9 million
- **Coed,** 396 undergraduate students, 50% full-time, 76% women, 24% men

Undergraduates 197 full-time, 199 part-time. Students come from 1 other state; 62% Black or African American, non-Hispanic/Latino; 0.4% Hispanic/Latino; 0.4% Asian, non-Hispanic/Latino; 0.8% Two or more races, non-Hispanic/Latino; 3% Race/ethnicity unknown; 0.4% international; 0.8% transferred in.
Freshmen *Admission:* 204 applied, 191 admitted, 71 enrolled.
Faculty *Total:* 86, 6% full-time, 8% with terminal degrees. *Student/faculty ratio:* 8:1.
Majors Liberal arts and sciences/liberal studies.
Academics *Calendar:* semesters. *Degree:* associate. *Special study options:* academic remediation for entering students, adult/continuing education programs, advanced placement credit, internships, off-campus study, part-time degree program, summer session for credit.
Library Chatfield College Library. *Books:* 20,284 (physical), 89,098 (digital/electronic); *Serial titles:* 8 (physical); *Databases:* 47. Students can reserve study rooms.
Student Life *Housing:* college housing not available. *Activities and Organizations:* drama/theater group, student-run newspaper, choral group, Student Leadership. *Campus security:* 12-hour night patrols by security. *Student services:* personal/psychological counseling.
Costs (2015–16) *Tuition:* $9698 full-time, $373 per credit hour part-time. *Required fees:* $320 full-time, $93 per term part-time. *Payment plans:* installment, deferred payment. *Waivers:* employees or children of employees.
Financial Aid Of all full-time matriculated undergraduates who enrolled in 2014, 10 Federal Work-Study jobs (averaging $1500). 4 state and other part-time jobs (averaging $800). *Financial aid deadline:* 8/1.

Applying *Options:* early admission, deferred entrance. *Application fee:* $10. *Application deadlines:* rolling (freshmen), rolling (transfers). *Notification:* continuous (freshmen), continuous (transfers).
Freshman Application Contact Chatfield College, 20918 State Route 251, St. Martin, OH 45118-9705. *Phone:* 513-875-3344 Ext. 138.
Website: http://www.chatfield.edu/.

The Christ College of Nursing and Health Sciences
Cincinnati, Ohio

Freshman Application Contact Mr. Bradley Jackson, Admissions, The Christ College of Nursing and Health Sciences, 2139 Auburn Avenue, Cincinnati, OH 45219. *Phone:* 513-585-0016. *E-mail:* bradley.jackson@thechristcollege.edu. *Website:* http://www.thechristcollege.edu/.

Cincinnati State Technical and Community College
Cincinnati, Ohio

- **State-supported** 2-year, founded 1966, part of Ohio Board of Regents
- **Urban** 46-acre campus
- **Coed,** 9,630 undergraduate students, 30% full-time, 55% women, 45% men

Undergraduates 2,873 full-time, 6,757 part-time. 9% are from out of state; 26% Black or African American, non-Hispanic/Latino; 2% Hispanic/Latino; 2% Asian, non-Hispanic/Latino; 0.1% Native Hawaiian or other Pacific Islander, non-Hispanic/Latino; 0.4% American Indian or Alaska Native, non-Hispanic/Latino; 3% Two or more races, non-Hispanic/Latino; 5% Race/ethnicity unknown; 2% international. *Retention:* 49% of full-time freshmen returned.
Freshmen *Admission:* 1,183 enrolled.
Faculty *Total:* 963, 20% full-time, 2% with terminal degrees. *Student/faculty ratio:* 11:1.
Majors Accounting; administrative assistant and secretarial science; aeronautical/aerospace engineering technology; allied health and medical assisting services related; applied horticulture/horticultural business services related; architectural engineering technology; audiovisual communications technologies related; automobile/automotive mechanics technology; automotive engineering technology; baking and pastry arts; biology/biological sciences; biomedical technology; business administration and management; business administration, management and operations related; chemical technology; civil engineering technology; clinical/medical laboratory technology; commercial and advertising art; computer and information sciences; computer engineering technology; computer programming (specific applications); computer support specialist; computer systems analysis; crisis/emergency/disaster management; culinary arts; desktop publishing and digital imaging design; diagnostic medical sonography and ultrasound technology; dietetics; early childhood education; electrical, electronic and communications engineering technology; electromechanical technology; emergency medical technology (EMT paramedic); energy management and systems technology; engineering technologies and engineering related; entrepreneurship; environmental control technologies related; environmental engineering technology; executive assistant/executive secretary; financial planning and services; fire science/firefighting; general studies; health information/medical records technology; hospitality administration; industrial technology; information technology project management; landscaping and groundskeeping; liberal arts and sciences/liberal studies; marketing/marketing management; mechanical engineering/mechanical technology; medical office assistant; multi/interdisciplinary studies related; network and system administration; nuclear medical technology; occupational safety and health technology; occupational therapist assistant; parks, recreation, leisure, and fitness studies related; plastics and polymer engineering technology; real estate; registered nursing/registered nurse; restaurant, culinary, and catering management; sign language interpretation and translation; surgical technology; turf and turfgrass management.
Academics *Calendar:* 5 10-week terms. *Degree:* certificates and associate. *Special study options:* academic remediation for entering students, advanced placement credit, cooperative education, distance learning, double majors, English as a second language, honors programs, independent study, internships, off-campus study, part-time degree program, services for LD students, student-designed majors, summer session for credit. *ROTC:* Army (c).
Library Johnnie Mae Berry Library.
Student Life *Housing:* college housing not available. *Activities and Organizations:* Student government, Nursing Student Association, Phi Theta Kappa, American Society of Civil Engineers, Respiratory Care Club. *Campus*

security: 24-hour emergency response devices and patrols, late-night transport/escort service. *Student services:* personal/psychological counseling.
Athletics Member NJCAA. *Intercollegiate sports:* basketball M(s)/W(s), golf M/W, soccer M(s)/W(s), volleyball W.
Costs (2016–17) *Tuition:* state resident $3567 full-time, $149 per credit hour part-time; nonresident $7135 full-time, $297 per credit hour part-time. *Required fees:* $258 full-time. *Payment plan:* installment. *Waivers:* senior citizens and employees or children of employees.
Financial Aid Of all full-time matriculated undergraduates who enrolled in 2014, 100 Federal Work-Study jobs (averaging $3500).
Applying *Options:* electronic application, deferred entrance. *Required:* high school transcript.
Freshman Application Contact Ms. Gabriele Boeckermann, Director of Admission, Cincinnati State Technical and Community College, Office of Admissions, 3520 Central Parkway, Cincinnati, OH 45223-2690. *Phone:* 513-569-1550. *Toll-free phone:* 877-569-0115. *Fax:* 513-569-1562.
E-mail: adm@cincinnatistate.edu.
Website: http://www.cincinnatistate.edu/.

Clark State Community College
Springfield, Ohio

Freshman Application Contact Admissions Office, Clark State Community College, PO Box 570, Springfield, OH 45501-0570. *Phone:* 937-328-3858. *Fax:* 937-328-6133. *E-mail:* admissions@clarkstate.edu.
Website: http://www.clarkstate.edu/.

Columbus Culinary Institute at Bradford School
Columbus, Ohio

- **Private** 2-year, founded 2006
- **Suburban** campus
- **Coed,** 150 undergraduate students
- 58% of applicants were admitted

Freshmen *Admission:* 560 applied, 325 admitted.
Majors Cooking and related culinary arts.
Academics *Calendar:* semesters. *Degree:* associate.
Freshman Application Contact Admissions Office, Columbus Culinary Institute at Bradford School, 2435 Stelzer Road, Columbus, OH 43219. *Phone:* 614-944-4200. *Toll-free phone:* 877-506-5006.
Website: http://www.columbusculinary.com/.

Columbus State Community College
Columbus, Ohio

Freshman Application Contact Ms. Tari Blaney, Director of Admissions, Columbus State Community College, 550 East Spring Street, Columbus, OH 43215. *Phone:* 614-287-2669. *Toll-free phone:* 800-621-6407 Ext. 2669. *Fax:* 614-287-6019. *E-mail:* tblaney@cscc.edu.
Website: http://www.cscc.edu/.

Cuyahoga Community College
Cleveland, Ohio

Freshman Application Contact Mr. Kevin McDaniel, Director of Admissions and Records, Cuyahoga Community College, Cleveland, OH 44115. *Phone:* 216-987-4030. *Toll-free phone:* 800-954-8742. *Fax:* 216-696-2567.
Website: http://www.tri-c.edu/.

Davis College
Toledo, Ohio

- **Proprietary** 2-year, founded 1858
- **Urban** 1-acre campus with easy access to Detroit
- **Coed,** 159 undergraduate students, 21% full-time, 81% women, 19% men

Undergraduates 34 full-time, 125 part-time. Students come from 2 states and territories; 2% are from out of state; 40% Black or African American, non-Hispanic/Latino; 2% Hispanic/Latino; 0.6% American Indian or Alaska Native, non-Hispanic/Latino; 4% Race/ethnicity unknown.
Freshmen *Admission:* 27 enrolled.
Faculty *Total:* 25, 12% full-time. *Student/faculty ratio:* 7:1.
Majors Accounting related; administrative assistant and secretarial science; business administration and management; business operations support and secretarial services related; computer systems networking and telecommunications; early childhood education; graphic design; interior

design; marketing/marketing management; medical administrative assistant and medical secretary; medical/clinical assistant; medical insurance coding.

Academics *Calendar:* quarters. *Degree:* certificates, diplomas, and associate. *Special study options:* academic remediation for entering students, adult/continuing education programs, advanced placement credit, distance learning, internships, part-time degree program, summer session for credit.

Library Davis College Resource Center. *Books:* 2,108 (physical); *Serial titles:* 109 (physical).

Student Life *Housing:* college housing not available. *Campus security:* interior and exterior security cameras. *Student services:* personal/psychological counseling.

Costs (2016–17) *Tuition:* $12,600 full-time, $350 per credit hour part-time. *Required fees:* $1050 full-time, $350 per term part-time. *Payment plan:* installment. *Waivers:* employees or children of employees.

Financial Aid Of all full-time matriculated undergraduates who enrolled in 2014, 10 Federal Work-Study jobs (averaging $3500).

Applying *Options:* electronic application, early admission, deferred entrance. *Application fee:* $30. *Required:* high school transcript, interview. *Application deadlines:* rolling (freshmen), rolling (transfers). *Notification:* continuous (freshmen), continuous (transfers).

Freshman Application Contact Mr. Timothy Brunner, Davis College, 4747 Monroe Street, Toledo, OH 43623-4307. *Phone:* 419-473-2700. *Toll-free phone:* 800-477-7021. *Fax:* 419-473-2472. *E-mail:* tbrunner@daviscollege.edu. *Website:* http://daviscollege.edu/.

Daymar College
Columbus, Ohio

Freshman Application Contact Holly Hankinson, Admissions Office, Daymar College, 2745 Winchester Pike, Columbus, OH 43232. *Phone:* 740-687-6126. *Toll-free phone:* 877-258-7796. *E-mail:* hhankinson@daymarcollege.edu. *Website:* http://www.daymarcollege.edu/.

Eastern Gateway Community College
Steubenville, Ohio

- **State and locally supported** 2-year, founded 1966, part of Ohio Board of Regents
- **Small-town** 83-acre campus with easy access to Pittsburgh
- **Endowment** $448,293
- **Coed**, 3,024 undergraduate students, 40% full-time, 62% women, 38% men

Undergraduates 1,199 full-time, 1,825 part-time. Students come from 5 states and territories; 1 other country; 21% Black or African American, non-Hispanic/Latino; 2% Hispanic/Latino; 0.5% Asian, non-Hispanic/Latino; 0.1% Native Hawaiian or other Pacific Islander, non-Hispanic/Latino; 0.4% American Indian or Alaska Native, non-Hispanic/Latino; 4% Two or more races, non-Hispanic/Latino; 1% Race/ethnicity unknown; 0.1% international.

Freshmen *Admission:* 2,558 applied, 2,558 admitted, 546 enrolled.

Faculty *Total:* 219, 18% full-time. *Student/faculty ratio:* 23:1.

Majors Accounting; administrative assistant and secretarial science; business administration and management; child-care and support services management; computer engineering related; corrections; criminal justice/police science; data processing and data processing technology; dental assisting; drafting and design technology; electrical, electronic and communications engineering technology; emergency medical technology (EMT paramedic); industrial radiologic technology; industrial technology; legal administrative assistant/secretary; licensed practical/vocational nurse training; mechanical engineering/mechanical technology; medical administrative assistant and medical secretary; medical/clinical assistant; real estate; respiratory care therapy.

Academics *Calendar:* semesters. *Degree:* certificates and associate. *Special study options:* academic remediation for entering students, accelerated degree program, adult/continuing education programs, cooperative education, distance learning, double majors, off-campus study, part-time degree program, services for LD students, summer session for credit.

Library Eastern Gateway Community College Library.

Student Life *Housing:* college housing not available. *Activities and Organizations:* Student Senate, Phi Theta Kappa. *Campus security:* 24-hour emergency response devices, day and evening security.

Athletics *Intramural sports:* softball M/W.

Standardized Tests *Required for some:* SAT or ACT (for admission).

Costs (2015–16) *Tuition:* area resident $3330 full-time, $111 per credit hour part-time; state resident $3510 full-time, $117 per credit hour part-time; nonresident $4350 full-time, $145 per credit hour part-time.

Financial Aid Of all full-time matriculated undergraduates who enrolled in 2014, 30 Federal Work-Study jobs (averaging $1500).

Applying *Options:* electronic application, early admission, deferred entrance. *Application fee:* $20. *Required for some:* high school transcript. *Notification:* continuous (freshmen), continuous (out-of-state freshmen), continuous (transfers).

Freshman Application Contact Mr. Ryan Ogrodnik, Director of Admissions, Eastern Gateway Community College, 4000 Sunset Boulevard, Steubenville, OH 43952. *Phone:* 740-264-5591 Ext. 1656. *Toll-free phone:* 800-68-COLLEGE. *Fax:* 740-266-2944. *E-mail:* rogrodnik@egcc.edu. *Website:* http://www.egcc.edu/.

Edison Community College
Piqua, Ohio

- **State-supported** 2-year, founded 1973, part of Ohio Board of Regents
- **Small-town** 131-acre campus with easy access to Dayton, Columbus, Cincinnati
- **Coed**, 3,133 undergraduate students, 26% full-time, 61% women, 39% men

Undergraduates 806 full-time, 2,327 part-time. Students come from 3 states and territories; 1 other country; 1% are from out of state; 4% Black or African American, non-Hispanic/Latino; 1% Hispanic/Latino; 1% Asian, non-Hispanic/Latino; 0.2% Native Hawaiian or other Pacific Islander, non-Hispanic/Latino; 0.3% American Indian or Alaska Native, non-Hispanic/Latino; 0.9% Two or more races, non-Hispanic/Latino; 3% Race/ethnicity unknown; 4% transferred in. *Retention:* 44% of full-time freshmen returned.

Freshmen *Admission:* 688 applied, 593 admitted, 404 enrolled. *Average high school GPA:* 2.84. *Test scores:* ACT scores over 18: 79%; ACT scores over 24: 23%; ACT scores over 30: 2%.

Faculty *Total:* 178, 29% full-time, 13% with terminal degrees. *Student/faculty ratio:* 17:1.

Majors Accounting; art; biology/biological sciences; business administration and management; child development; clinical/medical laboratory technology; computer and information sciences; computer and information systems security; computer programming; computer systems networking and telecommunications; criminal justice/police science; dramatic/theater arts; economics; education; electrical, electronic and communications engineering technology; electromechanical technology; English; executive assistant/executive secretary; geology/earth science; health/medical preparatory programs related; history; human resources management; industrial technology; legal assistant/paralegal; liberal arts and sciences/liberal studies; manufacturing engineering technology; marketing/marketing management; mathematics; mechanical drafting and CAD/CADD; medical administrative assistant and medical secretary; medical/clinical assistant; medium/heavy vehicle and truck technology; philosophy and religious studies related; physical therapy technology; prenursing studies; psychology; registered nursing/registered nurse; social work; speech communication and rhetoric.

Academics *Calendar:* semesters. *Degrees:* certificates, associate, and postbachelor's certificates. *Special study options:* academic remediation for entering students, accelerated degree program, adult/continuing education programs, advanced placement credit, distance learning, double majors, English as a second language, honors programs, independent study, internships, off-campus study, part-time degree program, services for LD students, student-designed majors, summer session for credit.

Library Edison Community College Library. *Books:* 19,779 (physical), 458 (digital/electronic); *Serial titles:* 295 (physical), 215,870 (digital/electronic); *Databases:* 249. Weekly public service hours: 54; students can reserve study rooms.

Student Life *Housing:* college housing not available. *Activities and Organizations:* drama/theater group, student-run newspaper. *Campus security:* late-night transport/escort service, 18-hour patrols by trained security personnel. *Student services:* health clinic.

Athletics Member NJCAA. *Intercollegiate sports:* baseball M(s), basketball M(s)/W(s), volleyball W(s).

Standardized Tests *Required:* ACT Compass (for admission).

Costs (2015–16) *Tuition:* state resident $3609 full-time, $120 per credit hour part-time; nonresident $7219 full-time, $241 per credit hour part-time. Full-time tuition and fees vary according to class time, course level, course load, degree level, location, program, reciprocity agreements, and student level. Part-time tuition and fees vary according to class time, course level, course load, degree level, location, program, reciprocity agreements, and student level. *Required fees:* $609 full-time, $20 per credit hour part-time. *Payment plans:* installment, deferred payment. *Waivers:* senior citizens and employees or children of employees.

Financial Aid Of all full-time matriculated undergraduates who enrolled in 2014, 42 Federal Work-Study jobs (averaging $3000).

Applying *Options:* electronic application. *Required:* high school transcript. *Application deadlines:* rolling (freshmen), rolling (out-of-state freshmen), rolling (transfers).
Freshman Application Contact Ms. Loleta Collins, Director of Student Services, Edison Community College, 1973 Edison Drive, Piqua, OH 45356. *Phone:* 937-778-7983. *E-mail:* lcollins@edisonohio.edu. *Website:* http://www.edisonohio.edu/.

ETI Technical College of Niles
Niles, Ohio

- **Proprietary** 2-year, founded 1989
- **Small-town** 1-acre campus with easy access to Cleveland, Pittsburgh
- **Coed,** 124 undergraduate students, 50% full-time, 48% women, 52% men

Undergraduates 62 full-time, 62 part-time. Students come from 2 states and territories; 1% are from out of state; 23% Black or African American, non-Hispanic/Latino; 0.8% Hispanic/Latino; 0.8% Asian, non-Hispanic/Latino; 2% transferred in.
Freshmen *Admission:* 2 applied, 2 admitted, 2 enrolled. *Average high school GPA:* 2.6.
Faculty *Total:* 23, 35% full-time. *Student/faculty ratio:* 5:1.
Majors Computer/information technology services administration related; computer programming (specific applications); computer software and media applications related; data entry/microcomputer applications related; electrical and electronic engineering technologies related; electrical, electronic and communications engineering technology; legal assistant/paralegal; medical/clinical assistant; word processing.
Academics *Calendar:* semesters. *Degree:* diplomas and associate. *Special study options:* academic remediation for entering students, adult/continuing education programs, double majors, internships, part-time degree program, services for LD students.
Library Main Library plus 1 other.
Student Life *Housing:* college housing not available. *Activities and Organizations:* Student Government. *Campus security:* 24-hour emergency response devices.
Costs (2016–17) *Tuition:* $11,000 full-time, $400 per credit part-time. Full-time tuition and fees vary according to course load, degree level, and program. Part-time tuition and fees vary according to course load, degree level, and program. No tuition increase for student's term of enrollment. *Required fees:* $500 full-time, $250 per term part-time. *Payment plan:* installment. *Waivers:* employees or children of employees.
Financial Aid Of all full-time matriculated undergraduates who enrolled in 2015, 39 applied for aid, 39 were judged to have need. *Average percent of need met:* 100%. *Average financial aid package:* $9513. *Average need-based loan:* $3500. *Average need-based gift aid:* $6013.
Applying *Options:* early admission, deferred entrance. *Application fee:* $50. *Required:* high school transcript, interview. *Application deadlines:* rolling (freshmen), rolling (transfers). *Notification:* continuous (freshmen), continuous (transfers).
Freshman Application Contact Ms. Diane Marsteller, Director of Admissions, ETI Technical College of Niles, 2076 Youngstown-Warren Road, Niles, OH 44446-4398. *Phone:* 330-652-9919 Ext. 16. *Fax:* 330-652-4399. *E-mail:* dianemarsteller@eticollege.edu. *Website:* http://eticollege.edu/.

Fortis College
Centerville, Ohio

Freshman Application Contact Fortis College, 555 East Alex Bell Road, Centerville, OH 45459. *Phone:* 937-433-3410. *Toll-free phone:* 855-4-FORTIS. *Website:* http://www.fortis.edu/.

Fortis College
Cincinnati, Ohio

Admissions Office Contact Fortis College, 11499 Chester Road, Suite 200, Cincinnati, OH 45246. *Toll-free phone:* 855-4-FORTIS. *Website:* http://www.fortis.edu/.

Fortis College
Cuyahoga Falls, Ohio

Freshman Application Contact Admissions Office, Fortis College, 2545 Bailey Road, Cuyahoga Falls, OH 44221. *Phone:* 330-923-9959. *Toll-free phone:* 855-4-FORTIS. *Fax:* 330-923-0886. *Website:* http://www.fortis.edu/.

Fortis College
Ravenna, Ohio

Freshman Application Contact Admissions Office, Fortis College, 653 Enterprise Parkway, Ravenna, OH 44266. *Toll-free phone:* 855-4-FORTIS. *Website:* http://www.fortis.edu/.

Fortis College
Westerville, Ohio

Admissions Office Contact Fortis College, 4151 Executive Parkway, Suite 120, Westerville, OH 43081. *Toll-free phone:* 855-4-FORTIS. *Website:* http://www.fortis.edu/.

Gallipolis Career College
Gallipolis, Ohio

Freshman Application Contact Mr. Jack Henson, Director of Admissions, Gallipolis Career College, 1176 Jackson Pike, Suite 312, Gallipolis, OH 45631. *Phone:* 740-446-4367. *Toll-free phone:* 800-214-0452. *Fax:* 740-446-4124. *E-mail:* admissions@gallipoliscareercollege.com. *Website:* http://gallipoliscareercollege.edu/.

Good Samaritan College of Nursing and Health Science
Cincinnati, Ohio

- **Proprietary** primarily 2-year
- **Urban** campus with easy access to Cincinnati
- **Coed**

Undergraduates 128 full-time, 225 part-time. 14% are from out of state; 11% Black or African American, non-Hispanic/Latino; 3% Hispanic/Latino; 2% Asian, non-Hispanic/Latino; 0.8% Two or more races, non-Hispanic/Latino; 22% transferred in.
Faculty *Student/faculty ratio:* 7:1.
Academics *Calendar:* semesters. *Degrees:* associate and bachelor's. *Special study options:* academic remediation for entering students, advanced placement credit, cooperative education, honors programs, part-time degree program, services for LD students, summer session for credit.
Student Life *Campus security:* 24-hour emergency response devices and patrols, late-night transport/escort service.
Standardized Tests *Required:* SAT or ACT (for admission).
Costs (2015–16) *Tuition:* $13,304 full-time, $512 per credit hour part-time. *Required fees:* $1750 full-time, $80 per credit hour part-time.
Financial Aid Of all full-time matriculated undergraduates who enrolled in 2010, 155 applied for aid, 149 were judged to have need. 8 state and other part-time jobs (averaging $750). In 2010, 8. *Average percent of need met:* 68. *Average financial aid package:* $7488. *Average need-based loan:* $3477. *Average need-based gift aid:* $4260. *Average non-need-based aid:* $1100.
Applying *Options:* electronic application. *Application fee:* $40. *Required:* high school transcript, minimum 2.5 GPA, average GPA 2.25 in these high school courses: English, Math (Algebra required), Science (Chemistry required), and Social Studies.
Freshman Application Contact Admissions Office, Good Samaritan College of Nursing and Health Science, 375 Dixmyth Avenue, Cincinnati, OH 45220. *Phone:* 513-862-2743. *Fax:* 513-862-3572. *Website:* http://www.gscollege.edu/.

Herzing University
Akron, Ohio

Admissions Office Contact Herzing University, 1600 South Arlington Street, Suite 100, Akron, OH 44306. *Toll-free phone:* 800-596-0724. *Website:* http://https://www.herzing.edu/akron.

Herzing University
Toledo, Ohio

Admissions Office Contact Herzing University, 5212 Hill Avenue, Toledo, OH 43615. *Toll-free phone:* 800-596-0724. *Website:* http://www.herzing.edu/toledo.

Hocking College
Nelsonville, Ohio

- **State-supported** 2-year, founded 1968, part of Ohio Board of Regents
- **Rural** 1600-acre campus with easy access to Columbus
- **Endowment** $4.8 million
- **Coed**

Undergraduates 3,012 full-time, 1,082 part-time. Students come from 25 states and territories; 17 other countries; 3% are from out of state; 4% Black or African American, non-Hispanic/Latino; 2% Hispanic/Latino; 0.5% Asian, non-Hispanic/Latino; 0.5% American Indian or Alaska Native, non-Hispanic/Latino; 3% Two or more races, non-Hispanic/Latino; 2% Race/ethnicity unknown; 2% international; 18% live on campus. *Retention:* 44% of full-time freshmen returned.

Faculty *Student/faculty ratio:* 16:1.

Academics *Calendar:* semesters. *Degree:* certificates, diplomas, and associate. *Special study options:* academic remediation for entering students, accelerated degree program, adult/continuing education programs, advanced placement credit, cooperative education, distance learning, double majors, English as a second language, internships, off-campus study, part-time degree program, services for LD students, student-designed majors, summer session for credit. *ROTC:* Army (c).

Library Hocking College Learning Resources Center.

Student Life *Campus security:* 24-hour emergency response devices and patrols, student patrols, late-night transport/escort service, controlled dormitory access.

Costs (2015–16) *Tuition:* state resident $4390 full-time, $183 per credit hour part-time; nonresident $8780 full-time, $366 per credit hour part-time. Full-time tuition and fees vary according to course load and program. Part-time tuition and fees vary according to program. *Room and board:* $6560. Room and board charges vary according to board plan and housing facility.

Financial Aid Of all full-time matriculated undergraduates who enrolled in 2014, 125 Federal Work-Study jobs (averaging $1700). 225 state and other part-time jobs (averaging $1700).

Applying *Options:* electronic application. *Application fee:* $15. *Required:* high school transcript.

Freshman Application Contact Hocking College, 3301 Hocking Parkway, Nelsonville, OH 45764-9588. *Phone:* 740-753-3591 Ext. 7080.
Website: http://www.hocking.edu/.

Hondros College
Westerville, Ohio

Director of Admissions Ms. Carol Thomas, Operations Manager, Hondros College, 4140 Executive Parkway, Westerville, OH 43081-3855. *Phone:* 614-508-7244. *Toll-free phone:* 888-HONDROS.
Website: http://www.hondros.edu/.

International College of Broadcasting
Dayton, Ohio

- **Proprietary** 2-year, founded 1968
- **Urban** campus with easy access to Dayton
- **Coed**

Majors Audiovisual communications technologies related; radio and television broadcasting technology.

Academics *Calendar:* semesters. *Degree:* diplomas and associate. *Special study options:* academic remediation for entering students, internships, services for LD students.

Student Life *Housing:* college housing not available. *Activities and Organizations:* student-run radio station.

Standardized Tests *Required:* Wonderlic aptitude test (for admission).

Costs (2015–16) *Tuition:* $30,485 full-time. Full-time tuition and fees vary according to program. Part-time tuition and fees vary according to program. No tuition increase for student's term of enrollment. *Payment plans:* tuition prepayment, installment.

Applying *Options:* early admission. *Required:* high school transcript, interview.

Freshman Application Contact International College of Broadcasting, 6 South Smithville Road, Dayton, OH 45431-1833. *Phone:* 937-258-8251. *Toll-free phone:* 800-517-7284.
Website: http://www.icb.edu/.

ITT Technical Institute
Akron, Ohio

Freshman Application Contact Director of Recruitment, ITT Technical Institute, 3428 West Market Street, Akron, OH 44333. *Phone:* 330-865-8600. *Toll-free phone:* 877-818-0154.
Website: http://www.itt-tech.edu/.

ITT Technical Institute
Columbus, Ohio

Freshman Application Contact Director of Recruitment, ITT Technical Institute, 4717 Hilton Corporate Drive, Columbus, OH 43232-4152. *Phone:* 614-868-2000. *Toll-free phone:* 877-233-8864.
Website: http://www.itt-tech.edu/.

ITT Technical Institute
Dayton, Ohio

Freshman Application Contact Director of Recruitment, ITT Technical Institute, 3325 Stop Eight Road, Dayton, OH 45414. *Phone:* 937-264-7700. *Toll-free phone:* 800-568-3241.
Website: http://www.itt-tech.edu/.

ITT Technical Institute
Hilliard, Ohio

Freshman Application Contact Director of Recruitment, ITT Technical Institute, 3781 Park Mill Run Drive, Hilliard, OH 43026. *Phone:* 614-771-4888. *Toll-free phone:* 888-483-4888.
Website: http://www.itt-tech.edu/.

ITT Technical Institute
Maumee, Ohio

Freshman Application Contact Director of Recruitment, ITT Technical Institute, 1656 Henthorne Drive, Suite B, Maumee, OH 43537. *Phone:* 419-861-6500. *Toll-free phone:* 877-205-4639.
Website: http://www.itt-tech.edu/.

ITT Technical Institute
Norwood, Ohio

Freshman Application Contact Director of Recruitment, ITT Technical Institute, 4750 Wesley Avenue, Norwood, OH 45212. *Phone:* 513-531-8300. *Toll-free phone:* 800-314-8324.
Website: http://www.itt-tech.edu/.

ITT Technical Institute
Strongsville, Ohio

Freshman Application Contact Director of Recruitment, ITT Technical Institute, 14955 Sprague Road, Strongsville, OH 44136. *Phone:* 440-234-9091. *Toll-free phone:* 800-331-1488.
Website: http://www.itt-tech.edu/.

ITT Technical Institute
Warrensville Heights, Ohio

Freshman Application Contact Director of Recruitment, ITT Technical Institute, 24865 Emery Road, Warrensville Heights, OH 44128. *Phone:* 216-896-6500. *Toll-free phone:* 800-741-3494.
Website: http://www.itt-tech.edu/.

ITT Technical Institute
Youngstown, Ohio

Freshman Application Contact Director of Recruitment, ITT Technical Institute, 1030 North Meridian Road, Youngstown, OH 44509-4098. *Phone:* 330-270-1600. *Toll-free phone:* 800-832-5001.
Website: http://www.itt-tech.edu/.

James A. Rhodes State College
Lima, Ohio

Freshman Application Contact Traci Cox, Director, Office of Admissions, James A. Rhodes State College, Lima, OH 45804-3597. *Phone:* 419-995-8040. *E-mail:* cox.t@rhodesstate.edu. *Website:* http://www.rhodesstate.edu/.

Kent State University at Ashtabula
Ashtabula, Ohio

- **State-supported** primarily 2-year, founded 1958, part of Kent State University System
- **Small-town** 83-acre campus with easy access to Cleveland
- **Coed,** 2,285 undergraduate students, 50% full-time, 64% women, 36% men

Undergraduates 1,147 full-time, 1,138 part-time. Students come from 24 states and territories; 4 other countries; 4% are from out of state; 5% Black or African American, non-Hispanic/Latino; 3% Hispanic/Latino; 1% Asian, non-Hispanic/Latino; 0.1% Native Hawaiian or other Pacific Islander, non-Hispanic/Latino; 0.5% American Indian or Alaska Native, non-Hispanic/Latino; 2% Two or more races, non-Hispanic/Latino; 2% Race/ethnicity unknown; 0.5% international; 4% transferred in. *Retention:* 57% of full-time freshmen returned.
Freshmen *Admission:* 389 applied, 387 admitted, 252 enrolled. *Average high school GPA:* 2.82. *Test scores:* SAT critical reading scores over 500: 60%; SAT math scores over 500: 83%; SAT writing scores over 500: 22%; ACT scores over 18: 67%; SAT critical reading scores over 600: 7%; SAT math scores over 600: 17%; SAT writing scores over 600: 13%; ACT scores over 24: 14%; ACT scores over 30: 2%.
Faculty *Total:* 106, 45% full-time. *Student/faculty ratio:* 22:1.
Majors Accounting technology and bookkeeping; administrative assistant and secretarial science; aerospace, aeronautical and astronautical/space engineering; business administration and management; business/commerce; computer programming (specific applications); criminal justice/safety; English; general studies; health and medical administrative services related; health/medical preparatory programs related; hospitality administration; liberal arts and sciences and humanities related; medical radiologic technology; occupational therapist assistant; physical therapy technology; psychology; registered nursing/registered nurse; respiratory care therapy; sociology; speech communication and rhetoric; viticulture and enology.
Academics *Calendar:* semesters. *Degrees:* certificates, associate, and bachelor's (also offers some upper-level and graduate courses). *Special study options:* academic remediation for entering students, advanced placement credit, distance learning, double majors, independent study, internships, part-time degree program, services for LD students, student-designed majors, summer session for credit. *ROTC:* Army (c), Air Force (c).
Library Kent State at Ashtabula Library. *Books:* 66,090 (physical); *Serial titles:* 454 (physical).
Student Life *Housing:* college housing not available. *Activities and Organizations:* Student Government, Student Veterans Association, Student Nurses Association, Student Occupational Therapy Association, Media Club. *Campus security:* 24-hour emergency response devices.
Athletics *Intramural sports:* volleyball M/W.
Standardized Tests *Recommended:* SAT or ACT (for admission).
Costs (2015–16) *One-time required fee:* $150. *Tuition:* state resident $5664 full-time, $258 per credit hour part-time; nonresident $13,864 full-time, $620 per credit hour part-time. Full-time tuition and fees vary according to course level and course load. Part-time tuition and fees vary according to course level and course load. *Payment plan:* installment. *Waivers:* senior citizens and employees or children of employees.
Financial Aid Of all full-time matriculated undergraduates who enrolled in 2015, 587 applied for aid, 528 were judged to have need, 1 had their need fully met. In 2015, 7 non-need-based awards were made. *Average percent of need met:* 50%. *Average financial aid package:* $7409. *Average need-based loan:* $3858. *Average need-based gift aid:* $4921. *Average non-need-based aid:* $1476.
Applying *Options:* electronic application, deferred entrance. *Application fee:* $40. *Required:* high school transcript. *Application deadlines:* 8/15 (freshmen), 8/15 (transfers). *Notification:* continuous (freshmen), continuous (transfers).
Freshman Application Contact Kent State University at Ashtabula, 3300 Lake Road West, Ashtabula, OH 44004-2299. *Phone:* 440-964-4314. *Website:* http://www.ashtabula.kent.edu/.

Kent State University at East Liverpool
East Liverpool, Ohio

- **State-supported** primarily 2-year, founded 1967, part of Kent State University System
- **Small-town** 3-acre campus with easy access to Pittsburgh
- **Coed,** 1,245 undergraduate students, 56% full-time, 67% women, 33% men

Undergraduates 692 full-time, 553 part-time. Students come from 8 states and territories; 1 other country; 8% are from out of state; 6% Black or African American, non-Hispanic/Latino; 3% Hispanic/Latino; 1% Asian, non-Hispanic/Latino; 0.1% Native Hawaiian or other Pacific Islander, non-Hispanic/Latino; 0.2% American Indian or Alaska Native, non-Hispanic/Latino; 3% Two or more races, non-Hispanic/Latino; 3% Race/ethnicity unknown; 0.2% international; 5% transferred in. *Retention:* 59% of full-time freshmen returned.
Freshmen *Admission:* 120 applied, 120 admitted, 77 enrolled. *Average high school GPA:* 2.86. *Test scores:* ACT scores over 18: 67%; ACT scores over 24: 8%.
Faculty *Total:* 58, 43% full-time. *Student/faculty ratio:* 24:1.
Majors Accounting technology and bookkeeping; business/commerce; computer programming (specific applications); criminal justice/safety; English; general studies; legal assistant/paralegal; liberal arts and sciences and humanities related; occupational therapist assistant; physical therapy technology; psychology; registered nursing/registered nurse; speech communication and rhetoric.
Academics *Calendar:* semesters. *Degrees:* certificates, associate, bachelor's, and master's. *Special study options:* academic remediation for entering students, accelerated degree program, advanced placement credit, distance learning, double majors, freshman honors college, honors programs, independent study, internships, part-time degree program, services for LD students, student-designed majors, summer session for credit. *ROTC:* Army (c), Air Force (c).
Library Blair Memorial Library. *Books:* 21,499 (physical); *Serial titles:* 238 (physical).
Student Life *Housing:* college housing not available. *Activities and Organizations:* Student Government, Student Nurses Association, Environmental Club, Student Occupational Therapist Assistants, Physical Therapist Assistant Club. *Campus security:* 24-hour emergency response devices, student patrols, late-night transport/escort service. *Student services:* personal/psychological counseling.
Standardized Tests *Required for some:* SAT or ACT (for admission). *Recommended:* SAT or ACT (for admission).
Costs (2015–16) *One-time required fee:* $150. *Tuition:* state resident $5664 full-time, $258 per credit hour part-time; nonresident $13,864 full-time, $620 per credit hour part-time. Full-time tuition and fees vary according to course level and course load. Part-time tuition and fees vary according to course level and course load. *Payment plan:* installment. *Waivers:* senior citizens and employees or children of employees.
Financial Aid Of all full-time matriculated undergraduates who enrolled in 2015, 208 applied for aid, 192 were judged to have need, 2 had their need fully met. In 2015, 6 non-need-based awards were made. *Average percent of need met:* 53%. *Average financial aid package:* $7220. *Average need-based loan:* $3817. *Average need-based gift aid:* $5118. *Average non-need-based aid:* $750.
Applying *Options:* electronic application, deferred entrance. *Application fee:* $40. *Required:* high school transcript. *Application deadlines:* 8/15 (freshmen), 8/15 (transfers). *Notification:* continuous (freshmen), continuous (transfers).
Freshman Application Contact Kent State University at East Liverpool, 400 East 4th Street, East Liverpool, OH 43920-3497. *Phone:* 330-382-7415. *Website:* http://www.eliv.kent.edu/.

Kent State University at Salem
Salem, Ohio

- **State-supported** primarily 2-year, founded 1966, part of Kent State University System
- **Rural** 102-acre campus with easy access to Youngstown
- **Coed,** 1,738 undergraduate students, 66% full-time, 69% women, 31% men

Undergraduates 1,148 full-time, 590 part-time. Students come from 6 states and territories; 2% are from out of state; 3% Black or African American, non-Hispanic/Latino; 2% Hispanic/Latino; 0.7% Asian, non-Hispanic/Latino; 0.3% American Indian or Alaska Native, non-Hispanic/Latino; 2% Two or more races, non-Hispanic/Latino; 2% Race/ethnicity unknown; 1% international; 7% transferred in. *Retention:* 56% of full-time freshmen returned.

Freshmen *Admission:* 304 applied, 303 admitted, 180 enrolled. *Average high school GPA:* 3.01. *Test scores:* ACT scores over 18: 74%; ACT scores over 24: 15%; ACT scores over 30: 1%.

Faculty *Total:* 125, 31% full-time. *Student/faculty ratio:* 20:1.

Majors Accounting technology and bookkeeping; administrative assistant and secretarial science; applied horticulture/horticulture operations; biological and biomedical sciences related; business administration and management; business/commerce; computer programming (specific applications); criminal justice/safety; early childhood education; education related; English; general studies; health and medical administrative services related; human development and family studies; insurance; liberal arts and sciences and humanities related; liberal arts and sciences/liberal studies; medical radiologic technology; psychology; registered nursing/registered nurse; speech communication and rhetoric.

Academics *Calendar:* semesters. *Degrees:* certificates, associate, and bachelor's (also offers some upper-level and graduate courses). *Special study options:* academic remediation for entering students, accelerated degree program, adult/continuing education programs, advanced placement credit, cooperative education, distance learning, double majors, freshman honors college, honors programs, independent study, internships, part-time degree program, services for LD students, student-designed majors, summer session for credit. *ROTC:* Army (c), Air Force (c).

Library Kent State Salem Library. *Books:* 23,500 (physical); *Serial titles:* 4,500 (physical).

Student Life *Housing:* college housing not available. *Activities and Organizations:* Criminal Justice Club, Human Services Technology Club, Radiologic Technology Club, Student Government Association, Students for Professional Nursing. *Campus security:* 24-hour emergency response devices, late-night transport/escort service. *Student services:* personal/psychological counseling.

Athletics *Intramural sports:* basketball M/W, skiing (downhill) M/W, table tennis M/W, tennis M/W, volleyball M/W.

Standardized Tests *Required for some:* SAT or ACT (for admission). *Recommended:* SAT or ACT (for admission).

Costs (2015–16) *One-time required fee:* $150. *Tuition:* state resident $5664 full-time, $258 per credit hour part-time; nonresident $13,864 full-time, $620 per credit hour part-time. Full-time tuition and fees vary according to course level and course load. Part-time tuition and fees vary according to course level and course load. *Payment plan:* installment. *Waivers:* senior citizens and employees or children of employees.

Financial Aid Of all full-time matriculated undergraduates who enrolled in 2015, 647 applied for aid, 578 were judged to have need, 7 had their need fully met. In 2015, 33 non-need-based awards were made. *Average percent of need met:* 50%. *Average financial aid package:* $6774. *Average need-based loan:* $3885. *Average need-based gift aid:* $4791. *Average non-need-based aid:* $1265.

Applying *Options:* electronic application, deferred entrance. *Application fee:* $40. *Required:* high school transcript. *Required for some:* essay or personal statement. *Application deadlines:* 8/15 (freshmen), 8/15 (transfers). *Notification:* continuous (freshmen), continuous (transfers).

Freshman Application Contact Kent State University at Salem, 2491 State Route 45 South, Salem, OH 44460-9412. *Phone:* 330-382-7415.
Website: http://www.salem.kent.edu/.

Kent State University at Trumbull
Warren, Ohio

- **State-supported** primarily 2-year, founded 1954, part of Kent State University System
- **Suburban** 193-acre campus with easy access to Cleveland, Akron, Canton
- **Coed,** 2,579 undergraduate students, 64% full-time, 61% women, 39% men

Undergraduates 1,646 full-time, 933 part-time. Students come from 5 states and territories; 1 other country; 2% are from out of state; 8% Black or African American, non-Hispanic/Latino; 3% Hispanic/Latino; 0.9% Asian, non-Hispanic/Latino; 0.2% Native Hawaiian or other Pacific Islander, non-Hispanic/Latino; 0.1% American Indian or Alaska Native, non-Hispanic/Latino; 3% Two or more races, non-Hispanic/Latino; 3% Race/ethnicity unknown; 1% international; 8% transferred in. *Retention:* 54% of full-time freshmen returned.

Freshmen *Admission:* 469 applied, 466 admitted, 277 enrolled. *Average high school GPA:* 2.82. *Test scores:* SAT critical reading scores over 500: 100%; SAT math scores over 500: 100%; SAT writing scores over 500: 100%; ACT scores over 18: 68%; SAT critical reading scores over 600: 50%; SAT writing scores over 600: 50%; ACT scores over 24: 13%.

Faculty *Total:* 107, 49% full-time. *Student/faculty ratio:* 28:1.

Majors Accounting technology and bookkeeping; administrative assistant and secretarial science; business administration and management; business/commerce; computer programming (specific applications); criminal

justice/safety; electrical and electronic engineering technologies related; emergency medical technology (EMT paramedic); English; environmental engineering technology; general studies; health/health-care administration; industrial production technologies related; industrial technology; legal assistant/paralegal; liberal arts and sciences and humanities related; mechanical engineering/mechanical technology; psychology; public health; registered nursing/registered nurse; speech communication and rhetoric; urban forestry.

Academics *Calendar:* semesters. *Degrees:* associate and bachelor's (also offers some upper-level and graduate courses). *Special study options:* academic remediation for entering students, adult/continuing education programs, advanced placement credit, distance learning, double majors, freshman honors college, honors programs, independent study, internships, part-time degree program, services for LD students, student-designed majors, summer session for credit. *ROTC:* Army (c), Air Force (c).

Library Trumbull Campus Library. *Books:* 36,000 (physical); *Serial titles:* 347 (physical).

Student Life *Housing:* college housing not available. *Activities and Organizations:* Student Nurses Association, REACH, ENACTUS, Jurisprudence, If These Hands Could Talk (ASL). *Campus security:* 24-hour emergency response devices, late-night transport/escort service, patrols by trained security personnel during open hours. *Student services:* personal/psychological counseling.

Standardized Tests *Recommended:* SAT or ACT (for admission).

Costs (2015–16) *One-time required fee:* $150. *Tuition:* state resident $5664 full-time, $258 per credit hour part-time; nonresident $13,864 full-time, $620 per credit hour part-time. Full-time tuition and fees vary according to course level and course load. Part-time tuition and fees vary according to course level and course load. *Payment plan:* installment. *Waivers:* senior citizens and employees or children of employees.

Financial Aid Of all full-time matriculated undergraduates who enrolled in 2015, 820 applied for aid, 734 were judged to have need, 5 had their need fully met. In 2015, 33 non-need-based awards were made. *Average percent of need met:* 52%. *Average financial aid package:* $7115. *Average need-based loan:* $3787. *Average need-based gift aid:* $4700. *Average non-need-based aid:* $1209.

Applying *Options:* electronic application, deferred entrance. *Application fee:* $40. *Required:* high school transcript. *Application deadlines:* 8/15 (freshmen), 8/15 (transfers). *Notification:* continuous (freshmen), continuous (transfers).

Freshman Application Contact Kent State University at Trumbull, Warren, OH 44483. *Phone:* 330-675-8935.
Website: http://www.trumbull.kent.edu/.

Kent State University at Tuscarawas
New Philadelphia, Ohio

- **State-supported** primarily 2-year, founded 1962, part of Kent State University System
- **Small-town** 182-acre campus with easy access to Cleveland, Akron, Canton
- **Coed,** 2,146 undergraduate students, 62% full-time, 59% women, 41% men

Undergraduates 1,323 full-time, 823 part-time. Students come from 7 states and territories; 2 other countries; 2% are from out of state; 2% Black or African American, non-Hispanic/Latino; 1% Hispanic/Latino; 0.9% Asian, non-Hispanic/Latino; 0.1% Native Hawaiian or other Pacific Islander, non-Hispanic/Latino; 0.2% American Indian or Alaska Native, non-Hispanic/Latino; 2% Two or more races, non-Hispanic/Latino; 3% Race/ethnicity unknown; 0.6% international; 5% transferred in. *Retention:* 64% of full-time freshmen returned.

Freshmen *Admission:* 352 applied, 352 admitted, 244 enrolled. *Average high school GPA:* 3.1. *Test scores:* SAT critical reading scores over 500: 83%; SAT math scores over 500: 100%; SAT writing scores over 500: 50%; ACT scores over 18: 83%; SAT critical reading scores over 600: 17%; SAT math scores over 600: 25%; SAT writing scores over 600: 17%; ACT scores over 24: 24%; SAT math scores over 700: 25%; ACT scores over 30: 1%.

Faculty *Total:* 107, 44% full-time. *Student/faculty ratio:* 24:1.

Majors Accounting technology and bookkeeping; administrative assistant and secretarial science; agribusiness; business administration and management; business/commerce; CAD/CADD drafting/design technology; computer programming (specific applications); criminal justice/safety; early childhood education; education related; electrical and electronic engineering technologies related; engineering technology; English; general studies; industrial technology; liberal arts and sciences and humanities related; mechanical engineering/mechanical technology; psychology; registered nursing/registered nurse; speech communication and rhetoric; veterinary/animal health technology.

Academics *Calendar:* semesters. *Degrees:* certificates, associate, and bachelor's (also offers some upper-level and graduate courses). *Special study options:* academic remediation for entering students, accelerated degree program, adult/continuing education programs, advanced placement credit, distance learning, double majors, freshman honors college, honors programs, independent study, internships, part-time degree program, services for LD students, student-designed majors, study abroad, summer session for credit. *ROTC:* Army (c), Air Force (c).

Library Tuscarawas Campus Library. *Books:* 52,500 (physical), 12 (digital/electronic); *Serial titles:* 540 (physical).

Student Life *Housing:* college housing not available. *Activities and Organizations:* Society for Manufacturing Engineers, IEEE, Animation Imagineers, Criminology and Justice Studies Club, Student Activities Council. *Campus security:* 24-hour emergency response devices.

Athletics *Intramural sports:* basketball M/W, volleyball M/W.

Standardized Tests *Required for some:* SAT or ACT (for admission). *Recommended:* SAT or ACT (for admission).

Costs (2015–16) *One-time required fee:* $150. *Tuition:* state resident $5664 full-time, $258 per credit hour part-time; nonresident $13,864 full-time, $620 per credit hour part-time. Full-time tuition and fees vary according to course level and course load. Part-time tuition and fees vary according to course level and course load. *Payment plan:* installment. *Waivers:* senior citizens and employees or children of employees.

Financial Aid Of all full-time matriculated undergraduates who enrolled in 2015, 618 applied for aid, 533 were judged to have need, 6 had their need fully met. In 2015, 9 non-need-based awards were made. *Average percent of need met:* 52%. *Average financial aid package:* $6872. *Average need-based loan:* $3854. *Average need-based gift aid:* $4509. *Average non-need-based aid:* $3103.

Applying *Options:* electronic application, deferred entrance. *Application fee:* $40. *Required:* high school transcript. *Application deadlines:* 8/15 (freshmen), 8/15 (transfers). *Notification:* continuous (freshmen), continuous (transfers).

Freshman Application Contact Kent State University at Tuscarawas, 330 University Drive Northeast, New Philadelphia, OH 44663-9403. *Phone:* 330-339-3391 Ext. 47425. *Fax:* 330-339-3321. *E-mail:* info@tusc.kent.edu. *Website:* http://www.tusc.kent.edu/.

Lakeland Community College
Kirtland, Ohio

- **State and locally supported** 2-year, founded 1967, part of Ohio Department of Higher Education
- **Suburban** 380-acre campus with easy access to Cleveland
- **Endowment** $35,367
- **Coed,** 7,941 undergraduate students, 34% full-time, 59% women, 41% men

Undergraduates 2,675 full-time, 5,266 part-time. Students come from 5 states and territories; 14% Black or African American, non-Hispanic/Latino; 3% Hispanic/Latino; 1% Asian, non-Hispanic/Latino; 0.2% Native Hawaiian or other Pacific Islander, non-Hispanic/Latino; 0.5% American Indian or Alaska Native, non-Hispanic/Latino; 2% Two or more races, non-Hispanic/Latino; 4% Race/ethnicity unknown; 0.2% international; 5% transferred in. *Retention:* 50% of full-time freshmen returned.

Freshmen *Admission:* 3,037 applied, 764 enrolled.

Faculty *Total:* 569, 20% full-time. *Student/faculty ratio:* 17:1.

Majors Accounting; administrative assistant and secretarial science; biotechnology; business administration and management; child-care provision; civil engineering technology; clinical/medical laboratory technology; commercial and advertising art; computer engineering technology; computer programming (specific applications); computer systems analysis; computer systems networking and telecommunications; computer technology/computer systems technology; corrections; criminal justice/police science; dental hygiene; electrical, electronic and communications engineering technology; energy management and systems technology; fire prevention and safety technology; health professions related; homeland security, law enforcement, firefighting and protective services related; hospitality administration; instrumentation technology; legal assistant/paralegal; liberal arts and sciences/liberal studies; management information systems; marketing/marketing management; mechanical engineering/mechanical technology; medical radiologic technology; nuclear medical technology; ophthalmic technology; quality control technology; registered nursing/registered nurse; respiratory care therapy; restaurant, culinary, and catering management; sign language interpretation and translation; social work; surgical technology; tourism and travel services management.

Academics *Calendar:* semesters. *Degree:* certificates and associate. *Special study options:* academic remediation for entering students, adult/continuing education programs, advanced placement credit, cooperative education, distance learning, English as a second language, external degree program, independent study, internships, off-campus study, part-time degree program, services for LD students, study abroad, summer session for credit.

Library Lakeland Community College Library.

Student Life *Housing:* college housing not available. *Activities and Organizations:* drama/theater group, student-run newspaper, radio station, choral group, Campus Activities Board, Lakeland Student Government, Lakeland Signers, Gamer's Guild. *Campus security:* 24-hour emergency response devices and patrols, student patrols, late-night transport/escort service. *Student services:* health clinic, personal/psychological counseling, women's center.

Athletics Member NJCAA. *Intercollegiate sports:* baseball M(s), basketball M(s)/W(s), golf M(s), soccer M(s), softball W(s), volleyball W(s).

Standardized Tests *Required:* ACT Compass (for admission).

Costs (2015–16) *Tuition:* area resident $3287 full-time, $110 per credit hour part-time; state resident $4136 full-time, $138 per credit hour part-time; nonresident $9176 full-time, $306 per credit hour part-time. Full-time tuition and fees vary according to course load. Part-time tuition and fees vary according to course load. *Required fees:* $29 full-time, $14 per term part-time. *Payment plan:* installment. *Waivers:* senior citizens and employees or children of employees.

Financial Aid Of all full-time matriculated undergraduates who enrolled in 2014, 3,430 applied for aid, 2,659 were judged to have need, 468 had their need fully met. 65 Federal Work-Study jobs (averaging $2650). *Average percent of need met:* 56%. *Average financial aid package:* $7024. *Average need-based loan:* $3232. *Average need-based gift aid:* $5250.

Applying *Options:* electronic application, early admission, deferred entrance. *Application fee:* $15. *Required:* high school transcript. *Application deadlines:* 9/1 (freshmen), 9/1 (transfers). *Notification:* continuous until 9/1 (freshmen), continuous until 9/1 (transfers).

Freshman Application Contact Lakeland Community College, 7700 Clocktower Drive, Kirtland, OH 44094-5198. *Phone:* 440-525-7230. *Toll-free phone:* 800-589-8520.
Website: http://www.lakeland.cc.oh.us/.

Lorain County Community College
Elyria, Ohio

- **State and locally supported** 2-year, founded 1963, part of Ohio Board of Regents
- **Suburban** 280-acre campus with easy access to Cleveland
- **Endowment** $34.1 million
- **Coed,** 11,520 undergraduate students, 27% full-time, 62% women, 38% men

Undergraduates 3,138 full-time, 8,382 part-time. Students come from 16 states and territories; 21 other countries; 1% are from out of state; 9% Black or African American, non-Hispanic/Latino; 10% Hispanic/Latino; 1% Asian, non-Hispanic/Latino; 0.2% Native Hawaiian or other Pacific Islander, non-Hispanic/Latino; 0.5% American Indian or Alaska Native, non-Hispanic/Latino; 3% Two or more races, non-Hispanic/Latino; 1% Race/ethnicity unknown; 0.8% international. *Retention:* 67% of full-time freshmen returned.

Freshmen *Admission:* 1,787 applied, 1,787 admitted, 1,608 enrolled.

Faculty *Total:* 615, 20% full-time. *Student/faculty ratio:* 20:1.

Majors Accounting; administrative assistant and secretarial science; art; artificial intelligence; athletic training; biological and physical sciences; biology/biological sciences; business administration and management; chemistry; civil engineering technology; clinical/medical laboratory technology; computer and information sciences related; computer engineering technology; computer programming; computer programming related; computer programming (specific applications); computer programming (vendor/product certification); computer science; computer systems networking and telecommunications; computer technology/computer systems technology; consumer merchandising/retailing management; corrections; cosmetology; cosmetology and personal grooming arts related; criminal justice/police science; data entry/microcomputer applications; data entry/microcomputer applications related; diagnostic medical sonography and ultrasound technology; drafting and design technology; drafting/design engineering technologies related; dramatic/theater arts; education; electrical, electronic and communications engineering technology; elementary education; engineering; engineering technology; finance; fire science/firefighting; history; human services; industrial radiologic technology; industrial technology; information science/studies; information technology; journalism; kindergarten/preschool education; liberal arts and sciences/liberal studies; machine tool technology; marketing/marketing management; mass communication/media; mathematics; music; nuclear medical technology; pharmacy; physical education teaching and coaching; physical therapy technology; physics; plastics and polymer engineering technology; political science and government; pre-engineering; psychology; quality control technology; real estate; registered nursing/registered nurse; social sciences; social work; sociology; sport and fitness administration/management; surgical technology; tourism and travel services management; urban studies/affairs; word processing.

Academics *Calendar:* semesters. *Degree:* certificates and associate. *Special study options:* academic remediation for entering students, adult/continuing education programs, advanced placement credit, cooperative education, distance learning, double majors, English as a second language, external degree program, honors programs, independent study, internships, part-time degree program, services for LD students, student-designed majors, summer session for credit.
Library Learning Resource Center.
Student Life *Housing:* college housing not available. *Activities and Organizations:* drama/theater group, student-run newspaper, radio station, choral group, Phi Beta Kappa, Black Progressives, Hispanic Club, national fraternities, national sororities. *Campus security:* 24-hour emergency response devices and patrols, late-night transport/escort service. *Student services:* health clinic, personal/psychological counseling, women's center, legal services.
Athletics *Intramural sports:* archery M/W, basketball M/W, softball M/W, volleyball M/W, weight lifting M/W, wrestling M.
Costs (2015–16) *Tuition:* area resident $3077 full-time, $118 per credit hour part-time; state resident $3679 full-time, $141 per credit hour part-time; nonresident $7302 full-time, $281 per credit hour part-time. *Payment plans:* installment, deferred payment. *Waivers:* senior citizens and employees or children of employees.
Applying *Options:* early admission, deferred entrance. *Required for some:* high school transcript. *Application deadlines:* rolling (freshmen), rolling (transfers). *Notification:* continuous (freshmen), continuous (transfers).
Freshman Application Contact Lorain County Community College, 1005 Abbe Road, North, Elyria, OH 44035. *Phone:* 440-366-7622. *Toll-free phone:* 800-995-5222 Ext. 4032.
Website: http://www.lorainccc.edu/.

Marion Technical College
Marion, Ohio

Freshman Application Contact Mr. Joel Liles, Dean of Enrollment Services, Marion Technical College, 1467 Mount Vernon Avenue, Marion, OH 43302. *Phone:* 740-389-4636 Ext. 249. *Fax:* 740-389-6136.
E-mail: enroll@mtc.edu.
Website: http://www.mtc.edu/.

Miami-Jacobs Career College
Columbus, Ohio

Admissions Office Contact Miami-Jacobs Career College, 150 E. Gay Street, Columbus, OH 43215.
Website: http://www.miamijacobs.edu/.

Miami-Jacobs Career College
Dayton, Ohio

Director of Admissions Mary Percell, Vice President of Information Services, Miami-Jacobs Career College, 401 East Third Street, Dayton, OH 45402. *Phone:* 937-461-5174 Ext. 118.
Website: http://www.miamijacobs.edu/.

Miami-Jacobs Career College
Independence, Ohio

Freshman Application Contact Director of Admissions, Miami-Jacobs Career College, 6400 Rockside Road, Independence, OH 44131. *Phone:* 216-861-3222. *Toll-free phone:* 866-324-0142. *Fax:* 216-861-4517.
Website: http://www.miamijacobs.edu/.

Miami-Jacobs Career College
Sharonville, Ohio

Admissions Office Contact Miami-Jacobs Career College, 2 Crowne Pointe Courte, Suite 100, Sharonville, OH 45241.
Website: http://www.miamijacobs.edu/.

Miami-Jacobs Career College
Springboro, Ohio

Admissions Office Contact Miami-Jacobs Career College, 875 West Central Avenue, Springboro, OH 45066.
Website: http://www.miamijacobs.edu/.

Miami-Jacobs Career College
Troy, Ohio

Admissions Office Contact Miami-Jacobs Career College, 865 W. Market Street, Troy, OH 45373.
Website: http://www.miamijacobs.edu/.

Miami University Middletown
Middletown, Ohio

Freshman Application Contact Diane Cantonwine, Assistant Director of Admission and Financial Aid, Miami University Middletown, 4200 East University Boulevard, Middletown, OH 45042-3497. *Phone:* 513-727-3346. *Toll-free phone:* 866-426-4643. *Fax:* 513-727-3223.
E-mail: cantondm@muohio.edu.
Website: http://regionals.miamioh.edu/.

North Central State College
Mansfield, Ohio

Freshman Application Contact Ms. Nikia L. Fletcher, Director of Admissions, North Central State College, 2441 Kenwood Circle, PO Box 698, Mansfield, OH 44901-0698. *Phone:* 419-755-4813. *Toll-free phone:* 888-755-4899. *E-mail:* nfletcher@ncstatecollege.edu.
Website: http://www.ncstatecollege.edu/.

Northwest State Community College
Archbold, Ohio

- **State-supported** 2-year, founded 1968, part of Ohio Board of Regents
- **Rural** 80-acre campus with easy access to Toledo
- **Coed**

Undergraduates 713 full-time, 2,901 part-time. Students come from 6 states and territories; 2 other countries; 4% are from out of state; 3% Black or African American, non-Hispanic/Latino; 6% Hispanic/Latino; 0.7% Asian, non-Hispanic/Latino; 0.1% American Indian or Alaska Native, non-Hispanic/Latino; 1% Two or more races, non-Hispanic/Latino; 12% Race/ethnicity unknown; 3% transferred in.
Faculty *Student/faculty ratio:* 27:1.
Academics *Calendar:* semesters. *Degree:* certificates and associate. *Special study options:* academic remediation for entering students, adult/continuing education programs, advanced placement credit, cooperative education, distance learning, double majors, external degree program, independent study, internships, off-campus study, part-time degree program, services for LD students, student-designed majors, summer session for credit.
Library Northwest State Community College Library plus 1 other.
Student Life *Campus security:* 24-hour emergency response devices, security patrols.
Costs (2015–16) *Tuition:* state resident $3768 full-time, $157 per credit part-time; nonresident $7392 full-time, $308 per credit part-time. *Required fees:* $70 full-time, $35 per term part-time.
Financial Aid Of all full-time matriculated undergraduates who enrolled in 2014, 43 Federal Work-Study jobs (averaging $1077).
Applying *Options:* electronic application, early admission, deferred entrance. *Required:* high school transcript. *Required for some:* minimum 2.5 GPA, interview, Nursing requires the NLN PAX with a relative score greater than or equal to 50 in each of the 3 sections.
Freshman Application Contact Mrs. Amanda Potts, Director of Admissions, Northwest State Community College, 22600 State Route 34, Archbold, OH 43502. *Phone:* 419-267-1364. *Toll-free phone:* 855-267-5511. *Fax:* 419-267-3688. *E-mail:* apotts@northweststate.edu.
Website: http://www.northweststate.edu/.

Ohio Business College
Hilliard, Ohio

- **Proprietary** 2-year
- **Suburban** campus
- **Coed**

Academics *Degree:* diplomas and associate.
Costs (2015–16) *Tuition:* $8140 full-time, $225 per credit hour part-time. Full-time tuition and fees vary according to course load. Part-time tuition and fees vary according to course load.
Freshman Application Contact Ohio Business College, 4525 Trueman Boulevard, Hilliard, OH 43026. *Toll-free phone:* 800-954-4274.
Website: http://www.ohiobusinesscollege.edu/.

Ohio Business College
Sandusky, Ohio

- **Proprietary** 2-year, founded 1982
- **Small-town** 1-acre campus with easy access to Cleveland, Toledo
- **Coed**

Undergraduates 170 full-time, 95 part-time. Students come from 1 other state; 22% Black or African American, non-Hispanic/Latino; 5% Hispanic/Latino; 0.4% Asian, non-Hispanic/Latino; 0.4% American Indian or Alaska Native, non-Hispanic/Latino; 0.4% Two or more races, non-Hispanic/Latino; 2% Race/ethnicity unknown.
Faculty *Student/faculty ratio:* 8:1.
Academics *Calendar:* quarters. *Degree:* diplomas and associate. *Special study options:* academic remediation for entering students, independent study, internships, part-time degree program, summer session for credit.
Library Main Library plus 1 other.
Costs (2015–16) *Tuition:* $8140 full-time, $225 per credit hour part-time. Full-time tuition and fees vary according to course load. Part-time tuition and fees vary according to course load. No tuition increase for student's term of enrollment. *Payment plans:* tuition prepayment, installment.
Applying *Required:* Valid HS diploma or GED.
Freshman Application Contact Ohio Business College, 5202 Timber Commons Drive, Sandusky, OH 44870. *Phone:* 419-627-8345. *Toll-free phone:* 888-627-8345.
Website: http://www.ohiobusinesscollege.edu/.

Ohio Business College
Sheffield Village, Ohio

- **Proprietary** 2-year, founded 1903, part of Tri State Educational Systems
- **Suburban** campus with easy access to Cleveland
- **Coed,** 350 undergraduate students

Majors Accounting; administrative assistant and secretarial science; banking and financial support services; business administration and management; computer programming; computer software and media applications related; computer technology/computer systems technology; data entry/microcomputer applications; human resources management; legal administrative assistant/secretary; medical administrative assistant and medical secretary; web page, digital/multimedia and information resources design.
Academics *Calendar:* quarters. *Degree:* diplomas and associate. *Special study options:* academic remediation for entering students, accelerated degree program, adult/continuing education programs, advanced placement credit, double majors, external degree program, independent study, internships, part-time degree program, summer session for credit.
Library Ohio Business College Library.
Student Life *Housing:* college housing not available.
Costs (2015–16) *Tuition:* $8140 full-time, $225 per credit hour part-time. Full-time tuition and fees vary according to course load. Part-time tuition and fees vary according to course load. *Payment plan:* installment. *Waivers:* employees or children of employees.
Applying *Options:* electronic application. *Application fee:* $25. *Required:* high school transcript, interview. *Application deadline:* rolling (freshmen).
Freshman Application Contact Ohio Business College, 5095 Waterford Drive, Sheffield Village, OH 44035. *Toll-free phone:* 888-514-3126.
Website: http://www.ohiobusinesscollege.edu/.

Ohio College of Massotherapy
Akron, Ohio

Director of Admissions Mr. John Atkins, Director of Admissions and Marketing, Ohio College of Massotherapy, 225 Heritage Woods Drive, Akron, OH 44321. *Phone:* 330-665-1084 Ext. 11. *Toll-free phone:* 888-888-4325. *E-mail:* johna@ocm.edu.
Website: http://www.ocm.edu/.

The Ohio State University Agricultural Technical Institute
Wooster, Ohio

- **State-supported** 2-year, founded 1971, part of The Ohio State University
- **Small-town** 1942-acre campus with easy access to Cleveland, Columbus, Akron, Canton
- **Coed**

Undergraduates 702 full-time, 55 part-time. Students come from 8 states and territories; 2% are from out of state; 3% transferred in. *Retention:* 62% of full-time freshmen returned.
Faculty *Student/faculty ratio:* 17:1.
Academics *Calendar:* semesters. *Degree:* certificates, diplomas, and associate. *Special study options:* academic remediation for entering students, accelerated degree program, adult/continuing education programs, advanced placement credit, cooperative education, distance learning, double majors, independent study, internships, off-campus study, part-time degree program, services for LD students, student-designed majors, study abroad. *ROTC:* Army (c), Navy (c), Air Force (c).
Library Agricultural Technical Institute Library plus 1 other.
Student Life *Campus security:* 24-hour emergency response devices and patrols, controlled dormitory access.
Standardized Tests *Required for some:* SAT or ACT (for admission).
Costs (2015–16) *Tuition:* state resident $7104 full-time, $296 per credit hour part-time; nonresident $24,432 full-time, $1018 per credit hour part-time. Full-time tuition and fees vary according to course load, location, and program. Part-time tuition and fees vary according to course load, location, and program. *Room and board:* $8130; room only: $6530. Room and board charges vary according to board plan and location.
Financial Aid Of all full-time matriculated undergraduates who enrolled in 2010, 540 applied for aid, 474 were judged to have need, 25 had their need fully met. 64 Federal Work-Study jobs (averaging $2000). In 2010, 24. *Average percent of need met:* 44. *Average financial aid package:* $6859. *Average need-based loan:* $3826. *Average need-based gift aid:* $4241. *Average non-need-based aid:* $2107.
Applying *Options:* electronic application. *Application fee:* $60. *Required:* high school transcript.
Freshman Application Contact Ms. Julia Morris, Admissions Counselor, The Ohio State University Agricultural Technical Institute, 1328 Dover Road, Wooster, OH 44691. *Phone:* 330-287-1327. *Toll-free phone:* 800-647-8283 Ext. 1327. *Fax:* 330-287-1333. *E-mail:* morris.878@osu.edu.
Website: http://www.ati.osu.edu/.

Ohio Technical College
Cleveland, Ohio

- **Proprietary** 2-year, founded 1969
- **Urban** 18-acre campus
- **Coed,** 1,072 undergraduate students, 100% full-time, 5% women, 95% men

Undergraduates 1,072 full-time. Students come from 42 states and territories; 5 other countries; 47% are from out of state; 16% Black or African American, non-Hispanic/Latino; 7% Hispanic/Latino; 0.8% Asian, non-Hispanic/Latino; 0.7% American Indian or Alaska Native, non-Hispanic/Latino; 3% Two or more races, non-Hispanic/Latino; 1% Race/ethnicity unknown; 0.8% international. *Retention:* 74% of full-time freshmen returned.
Freshmen *Admission:* 334 enrolled.
Faculty *Total:* 53, 79% full-time.
Majors Autobody/collision and repair technology; automobile/automotive mechanics technology; diesel mechanics technology; high performance and custom engine technology; mechanic and repair technologies related; vehicle maintenance and repair technologies; welding technology.
Academics *Degree:* certificates, diplomas, and associate.
Library Ohio Technical College Library Resource Center plus 1 other. *Books:* 1,522 (physical); *Databases:* 6. Weekly public service hours: 40.
Student Life *Housing Options:* Campus housing is provided by a third party. *Campus security:* late-night transport/escort service. *Student services:* personal/psychological counseling.
Costs (2015–16) *Comprehensive fee:* $21,662 includes full-time tuition ($20,500) and room and board ($1162). No tuition increase for student's term of enrollment. *Room and board:* college room only: $818. *Payment plans:* tuition prepayment, installment.
Applying *Required:* high school transcript, interview.
Freshman Application Contact Ohio Technical College, 1374 East 51st Street, Cleveland, OH 44103. *Phone:* 216-881-1700. *Toll-free phone:* 800-322-7000.
Website: http://www.ohiotech.edu/.

Ohio Valley College of Technology
East Liverpool, Ohio

Freshman Application Contact Mr. Scott S. Rogers, Director, Ohio Valley College of Technology, 15258 State Route 170, East Liverpool, OH 43920. *Phone:* 330-385-1070.
Website: http://www.ovct.edu/.

Owens Community College
Toledo, Ohio

- **State-supported** 2-year, founded 1966
- **Suburban** 420-acre campus with easy access to Detroit
- **Endowment** $1.7 million
- **Coed**

Undergraduates 4,257 full-time, 8,315 part-time. Students come from 25 states and territories; 6 other countries; 3% are from out of state; 15% Black or African American, non-Hispanic/Latino; 7% Hispanic/Latino; 1% Asian, non-Hispanic/Latino; 0.4% American Indian or Alaska Native, non-Hispanic/Latino; 3% Two or more races, non-Hispanic/Latino; 2% Race/ethnicity unknown; 1% international; 0.7% transferred in.
Faculty *Student/faculty ratio:* 16:1.
Academics *Calendar:* semesters. *Degree:* certificates and associate. *Special study options:* academic remediation for entering students, accelerated degree program, adult/continuing education programs, advanced placement credit, cooperative education, distance learning, double majors, English as a second language, honors programs, independent study, internships, part-time degree program, services for LD students, study abroad, summer session for credit.
Library Owens Community College Library plus 1 other.
Student Life *Campus security:* 24-hour emergency response devices and patrols, student patrols, classroom doors that lock from the inside; campus alert system.
Athletics Member NJCAA.
Costs (2015–16) *One-time required fee:* $195. *Tuition:* state resident $4284 full-time, $167 per credit hour part-time; nonresident $8568 full-time, $334 per credit hour part-time. Full-time tuition and fees vary according to course load and reciprocity agreements. Part-time tuition and fees vary according to course load and reciprocity agreements. *Required fees:* $54 full-time, $25 per term part-time. *Payment plans:* installment, deferred payment.
Financial Aid Of all full-time matriculated undergraduates who enrolled in 2015, 2,688 applied for aid, 2,160 were judged to have need, 233 had their need fully met. In 2015, 175. *Average percent of need met:* 70. *Average financial aid package:* $6228. *Average need-based loan:* $6786. *Average need-based gift aid:* $4194. *Average non-need-based aid:* $1643.
Applying *Options:* electronic application, early admission, deferred entrance. *Application fee:* $20. *Required:* high school transcript. *Required for some:* minimum 2.0 GPA, interview, Health Technology, Peace Officer Academy, and Early Childhood Education programs require high school transcripts and standardized test scores for admission.
Freshman Application Contact Ms. Meghan L. Schmidbauer, Director, Admissions, Owens Community College, PO Box 10000, Toledo, OH 43699. *Phone:* 567-661-2155. *Toll-free phone:* 800-GO-OWENS. *Fax:* 567-661-7734. *E-mail:* meghan_schmidbauer@owens.edu.
Website: http://www.owens.edu/.

Professional Skills Institute
Maumee, Ohio

Director of Admissions Ms. Hope Finch, Director of Marketing, Professional Skills Institute, 1505 Holland Road, Maumee, OH 43537. *Phone:* 419-531-9610.

Remington College–Cleveland Campus
Cleveland, Ohio

Director of Admissions Director of Recruitment, Remington College–Cleveland Campus, 14445 Broadway Avenue, Cleveland, OH 44125. *Phone:* 216-475-7520. *Fax:* 216-475-6055.
Website: http://www.remingtoncollege.edu/.

Rosedale Bible College
Irwin, Ohio

Director of Admissions Mr. John Showalter, Director of Enrollment Services, Rosedale Bible College, 2270 Rosedale Road, Irwin, OH 43029-9501. *Phone:* 740-857-1311. *Fax:* 740-857-1577. *E-mail:* pweber@rosedale.edu.
Website: http://www.rosedale.edu/.

School of Advertising Art
Kettering, Ohio

- **Proprietary** 2-year, founded 1983
- **Suburban** 5-acre campus with easy access to Columbus
- **Coed,** 168 undergraduate students, 98% full-time, 69% women, 31% men

Undergraduates 164 full-time, 4 part-time. Students come from 4 states and territories; 11% are from out of state; 4% Black or African American, non-Hispanic/Latino; 3% Hispanic/Latino; 2% Asian, non-Hispanic/Latino; 0.6% American Indian or Alaska Native, non-Hispanic/Latino; 11% transferred in.
Retention: 81% of full-time freshmen returned.
Freshmen *Admission:* 468 applied, 277 admitted, 93 enrolled.
Faculty *Total:* 17, 59% full-time, 6% with terminal degrees. *Student/faculty ratio:* 14:1.
Majors Commercial and advertising art.
Academics *Calendar:* semesters. *Degree:* associate.
Library SAA Library.
Student Life *Housing:* college housing not available. *Activities and Organizations:* Fine Art Club. *Student services:* personal/psychological counseling.
Costs (2015–16) *Tuition:* $25,701 full-time. Full-time tuition and fees vary according to class time, course level, course load, degree level, location, program, reciprocity agreements, and student level. *Required fees:* $1310 full-time. *Payment plan:* installment. *Waivers:* employees or children of employees.
Applying *Options:* electronic application. *Required:* high school transcript, minimum 2.0 GPA, interview. *Required for some:* essay or personal statement, 2 letters of recommendation.
Freshman Application Contact Ms. Abigail Heaney, Housing & Marketing Coordinator, School of Advertising Art, 1725 East David Road, Kettering, OH 45440. *Phone:* 937-294-0592. *Toll-free phone:* 877-300-9866. *Fax:* 937-294-5869. *E-mail:* abbie@saa.edu.
Website: http://www.saa.edu/.

Sinclair Community College
Dayton, Ohio

Freshman Application Contact Ms. Sara Smith, Director and Systems Manager, Outreach Services, Sinclair Community College, 444 West Third Street, Dayton, OH 45402-1460. *Phone:* 937-512-3060. *Toll-free phone:* 800-315-3000. *Fax:* 937-512-2393. *E-mail:* ssmith@sinclair.edu.
Website: http://www.sinclair.edu/.

Southern State Community College
Hillsboro, Ohio

Freshman Application Contact Ms. Wendy Johnson, Director of Admissions, Southern State Community College, Hillsboro, OH 45133. *Phone:* 937-393-3431 Ext. 2720. *Toll-free phone:* 800-628-7722. *Fax:* 937-393-6682. *E-mail:* wjohnson@sscc.edu.
Website: http://www.sscc.edu/.

Stark State College
North Canton, Ohio

- **State-related** 2-year, founded 1970, part of University System of Ohio
- **Suburban** 34-acre campus with easy access to Cleveland
- **Endowment** $4.8 million
- **Coed,** 12,645 undergraduate students, 27% full-time, 58% women, 42% men

Undergraduates 3,451 full-time, 9,194 part-time. Students come from 17 states and territories; 3 other countries; 1% are from out of state; 11% Black or African American, non-Hispanic/Latino; 1% Hispanic/Latino; 1% Asian, non-Hispanic/Latino; 0.1% Native Hawaiian or other Pacific Islander, non-Hispanic/Latino; 0.3% American Indian or Alaska Native, non-Hispanic/Latino; 3% Two or more races, non-Hispanic/Latino; 10% Race/ethnicity unknown; 7% transferred in.
Freshmen *Admission:* 1,559 enrolled. *Test scores:* ACT scores over 18: 55%; ACT scores over 24: 10%; ACT scores over 30: 1%.
Faculty *Total:* 558, 35% full-time. *Student/faculty ratio:* 22:1.
Majors Accounting; administrative assistant and secretarial science; architectural engineering technology; automobile/automotive mechanics technology; biomedical technology; business administration and management; child development; civil engineering technology; clinical/medical laboratory technology; computer and information sciences and support services related; computer and information sciences related; computer engineering related; computer hardware engineering; computer/information technology services administration related; computer programming; computer programming related; computer programming (specific applications); computer programming (vendor/product certification); computer software and media applications related; computer software engineering; computer systems networking and telecommunications; consumer merchandising/retailing management; court reporting; data entry/microcomputer applications; data entry/microcomputer applications related; dental hygiene; drafting and design technology; environmental studies; finance; fire science/firefighting; food technology and processing; health information/medical records administration; human services; industrial technology; information technology; international

business/trade/commerce; legal administrative assistant/secretary; marketing/marketing management; mechanical engineering/mechanical technology; medical/clinical assistant; occupational therapy; operations management; physical therapy; registered nursing/registered nurse; respiratory care therapy; surveying technology; web/multimedia management and webmaster; web page, digital/multimedia and information resources design; word processing.

Academics *Calendar:* semesters. *Degree:* certificates and associate. *Special study options:* academic remediation for entering students, adult/continuing education programs, cooperative education, distance learning, double majors, external degree program, independent study, internships, off-campus study, part-time degree program, services for LD students, student-designed majors, summer session for credit.

Library Learning Resource Center plus 1 other.

Student Life *Housing:* college housing not available. *Activities and Organizations:* student-run newspaper, Phi Theta Kappa, Business Student Club, Institute of Management Accountants, Stark State College Association of Medical Assistants, Student Health Information Management Association, national fraternities, national sororities. *Campus security:* 24-hour emergency response devices and patrols, student patrols, late-night transport/escort service, patrols by trained security personnel during open hours. *Student services:* personal/psychological counseling.

Standardized Tests *Recommended:* SAT or ACT (for admission).

Costs (2015–16) *One-time required fee:* $85. *Tuition:* state resident $2796 full-time, $117 per credit hour part-time; nonresident $4980 full-time, $208 per credit hour part-time. Full-time tuition and fees vary according to course load and program. Part-time tuition and fees vary according to program. *Required fees:* $890 full-time, $37 per credit hour part-time, $30 per term part-time. *Payment plan:* installment. *Waivers:* senior citizens and employees or children of employees.

Financial Aid Of all full-time matriculated undergraduates who enrolled in 2014, 1,939 applied for aid, 1,697 were judged to have need, 6 had their need fully met. 74 Federal Work-Study jobs (averaging $2306). *Average need-based loan:* $2537. *Average need-based gift aid:* $4317.

Applying *Required:* high school transcript.

Freshman Application Contact JP Cooney, Executive Director to Recruitment, Admissions and Marketing, Stark State College, 6200 Frank Road NE, Canton, OH 44720. *Phone:* 330-494-6170 Ext. 4401. *Toll-free phone:* 800-797-8275. *E-mail:* info@starkstate.edu. *Website:* http://www.starkstate.edu/.

Stautzenberger College
Brecksville, Ohio

Admissions Office Contact Stautzenberger College, 8001 Katherine Boulevard, Brecksville, OH 44141. *Toll-free phone:* 800-437-2997. *Website:* http://www.sctoday.edu/.

Stautzenberger College
Maumee, Ohio

Director of Admissions Ms. Karen Fitzgerald, Director of Admissions and Marketing, Stautzenberger College, 1796 Indian Wood Circle, Maumee, OH 43537. *Phone:* 419-866-0261. *Toll-free phone:* 800-552-5099. *Fax:* 419-867-9821. *E-mail:* klfitzgerald@stautzenberger.com. *Website:* http://www.sctoday.edu/maumee/.

Terra State Community College
Fremont, Ohio

- **State-supported** 2-year, founded 1968, part of Ohio Board of Regents
- **Small-town** 100-acre campus with easy access to Toledo
- **Coed**

Undergraduates 822 full-time, 1,781 part-time. 4% Black or African American, non-Hispanic/Latino; 9% Hispanic/Latino; 0.4% Asian, non-Hispanic/Latino; 0.5% American Indian or Alaska Native, non-Hispanic/Latino; 0.8% Two or more races, non-Hispanic/Latino; 2% Race/ethnicity unknown; 0.4% international.

Faculty *Student/faculty ratio:* 15:1.

Academics *Calendar:* semesters. *Degree:* certificates, diplomas, and associate. *Special study options:* academic remediation for entering students, adult/continuing education programs, advanced placement credit, cooperative education, distance learning, double majors, independent study, internships, off-campus study, part-time degree program, services for LD students, student-designed majors, summer session for credit.

Library Learning Resource Center.

Student Life *Campus security:* 24-hour emergency response devices.

Costs (2015–16) *Tuition:* state resident $3876 full-time, $162 per semester hour part-time; nonresident $8160 full-time, $341 per semester hour part-time.

Required fees: $408 full-time, $17 per semester hour part-time, $10 per term part-time.

Financial Aid Of all full-time matriculated undergraduates who enrolled in 2014, 57 Federal Work-Study jobs (averaging $1450).

Applying *Options:* electronic application, early admission, deferred entrance. *Required:* high school transcript.

Freshman Application Contact Mr. Heath Martin, Director of Admissions and Enrollment Services, Terra State Community College, 2830 Napoleon Road, Fremont, OH 43420. *Phone:* 419-559-2154. *Toll-free phone:* 866-AT-TERRA. *Fax:* 419-559-2352. *Website:* http://www.terra.edu/.

Trumbull Business College
Warren, Ohio

- **Proprietary** 2-year, founded 1972
- **Small-town** 6-acre campus with easy access to Cleveland and Youngstown, OH; Pittsburgh, PA
- **Coed**, 159 undergraduate students, 65% full-time, 82% women, 18% men

Undergraduates 103 full-time, 56 part-time. Students come from 3 states and territories; 2% are from out of state; 23% Black or African American, non-Hispanic/Latino; 1% Hispanic/Latino; 3% Two or more races, non-Hispanic/Latino; 8% transferred in. *Retention:* 43% of full-time freshmen returned.

Freshmen *Admission:* 25 applied, 18 admitted, 11 enrolled.

Faculty *Total:* 39. *Student/faculty ratio:* 10:1.

Majors Accounting; administrative assistant and secretarial science; business administration and management; data processing and data processing technology; legal administrative assistant/secretary; management information systems; medical administrative assistant and medical secretary.

Academics *Calendar:* quarters. *Degree:* certificates, diplomas, and associate. *Special study options:* academic remediation for entering students, adult/continuing education programs, advanced placement credit, distance learning, part-time degree program, summer session for credit.

Student Life *Housing:* college housing not available. *Activities and Organizations:* student-run newspaper.

Financial Aid Of all full-time matriculated undergraduates who enrolled in 2014, 2 Federal Work-Study jobs. *Financial aid deadline:* 9/30.

Applying *Application fee:* $75. *Required:* high school transcript, interview. *Application deadline:* rolling (freshmen). *Notification:* continuous until 10/1 (freshmen).

Freshman Application Contact Trumbull Business College, 3200 Ridge Avenue SE, Warren, OH 44484. *Phone:* 330-369-6792. *Toll-free phone:* 888-766-1598. *Website:* http://www.trumbull.edu/.

The University of Akron Wayne College
Orrville, Ohio

Freshman Application Contact Ms. Alicia Broadus, Student Services Counselor, The University of Akron Wayne College, Orrville, OH 44667. *Phone:* 800-221-8308 Ext. 8901. *Toll-free phone:* 800-221-8308. *Fax:* 330-684-8989. *E-mail:* wayneadmissions@uakron.edu. *Website:* http://www.wayne.uakron.edu/.

University of Cincinnati Blue Ash College
Cincinnati, Ohio

- **State-supported** 2-year, founded 1967, part of University of Cincinnati System
- **Suburban** 120-acre campus
- **Endowment** $457,000
- **Coed**, 5,065 undergraduate students, 64% full-time, 58% women, 42% men

Undergraduates 3,241 full-time, 1,824 part-time. Students come from 9 states and territories; 12 other countries; 3% are from out of state; 21% Black or African American, non-Hispanic/Latino; 3% Hispanic/Latino; 3% Asian, non-Hispanic/Latino; 0.1% Native Hawaiian or other Pacific Islander, non-Hispanic/Latino; 0.3% American Indian or Alaska Native, non-Hispanic/Latino; 3% Two or more races, non-Hispanic/Latino; 7% Race/ethnicity unknown; 2% international; 11% transferred in. *Retention:* 64% of full-time freshmen returned.

Freshmen *Admission:* 1,269 enrolled. *Average high school GPA:* 2.73.

Faculty *Total:* 339, 50% full-time. *Student/faculty ratio:* 16:1.

Majors Accounting technology and bookkeeping; business administration and management; business administration, management and operations related; business/commerce; chemical technology; commercial and advertising art;

computer technology/computer systems technology; criminal justice/safety; dental hygiene; education; emergency medical technology (EMT paramedic); executive assistant/executive secretary; general studies; health/medical preparatory programs related; kindergarten/preschool education; liberal arts and sciences/liberal studies; library and information science; medical administrative assistant and medical secretary; medical/clinical assistant; medical radiologic technology; medical transcription; nuclear medical technology; personal and culinary services related; photographic and film/video technology; pre-law studies; pre-pharmacy studies; psychology; public health education and promotion; real estate; registered nursing/registered nurse; retailing; science technologies related; secondary education; social work; speech communication and rhetoric; veterinary/animal health technology.

Academics *Calendar:* semesters. *Degrees:* certificates, associate, and postbachelor's certificates. *Special study options:* academic remediation for entering students, adult/continuing education programs, advanced placement credit, distance learning, double majors, off-campus study, part-time degree program, services for LD students, study abroad, summer session for credit. *ROTC:* Army (c), Air Force (c).

Library UC Blue Ash College Library. Students can reserve study rooms.

Student Life *Housing:* college housing not available. *Campus security:* 24-hour emergency response devices and patrols, student patrols, late-night transport/escort service. *Student services:* personal/psychological counseling.

Standardized Tests *Required for some:* SAT or ACT (for admission). *Recommended:* SAT or ACT (for admission).

Costs (2016–17) *Tuition:* state resident $6010 full-time, $251 per quarter hour part-time; nonresident $14,808 full-time, $617 per credit hour part-time. Full-time tuition and fees vary according to course load, program, and reciprocity agreements. Part-time tuition and fees vary according to course load and reciprocity agreements. *Required fees:* $736 full-time. *Payment plan:* installment. *Waivers:* senior citizens and employees or children of employees.

Financial Aid Of all full-time matriculated undergraduates who enrolled in 2014, 285 Federal Work-Study jobs (averaging $2903).

Applying *Options:* electronic application, deferred entrance. *Application fee:* $50. *Required:* high school transcript. *Application deadlines:* rolling (freshmen), rolling (transfers). *Notification:* continuous (freshmen), continuous (transfers).

Freshman Application Contact University of Cincinnati Blue Ash College, 9555 Plainfield Road, Cincinnati, OH 45236-1007. *Phone:* 513-745-5700. *Website:* http://www.ucblueash.edu/.

University of Cincinnati Clermont College
Batavia, Ohio

- **State-supported** primarily 2-year, founded 1972, part of University of Cincinnati System
- **Rural** 91-acre campus with easy access to Cincinnati
- **Coed**

Undergraduates 1,788 full-time, 1,311 part-time. 5% are from out of state; 3% Black or African American, non-Hispanic/Latino; 2% Hispanic/Latino; 1% Asian, non-Hispanic/Latino; 0.1% Native Hawaiian or other Pacific Islander, non-Hispanic/Latino; 0.4% American Indian or Alaska Native, non-Hispanic/Latino; 2% Two or more races, non-Hispanic/Latino; 11% Race/ethnicity unknown; 0.4% international. *Retention:* 60% of full-time freshmen returned.

Faculty *Student/faculty ratio:* 14:1.

Academics *Calendar:* semesters. *Degrees:* certificates, associate, bachelor's, and postbachelor's certificates. *Special study options:* academic remediation for entering students, adult/continuing education programs, advanced placement credit, cooperative education, distance learning, double majors, independent study, internships, off-campus study, part-time degree program, services for LD students, student-designed majors, study abroad, summer session for credit. *ROTC:* Air Force (c).

Library UC Clermont College Library. Students can reserve study rooms.

Student Life *Campus security:* 24-hour emergency response devices and patrols.

Costs (2016–17) *Tuition:* state resident $5316 full-time, $222 per credit part-time; nonresident $12,548 full-time, $523 per credit part-time. Full-time tuition and fees vary according to course level, degree level, program, and reciprocity agreements. Part-time tuition and fees vary according to course level, degree level, program, and reciprocity agreements.

Applying *Options:* electronic application, deferred entrance. *Application fee:* $50. *Required:* high school transcript.

Freshman Application Contact Mrs. Jamie Adkins, University Services Associate, University of Cincinnati Clermont College, 4200 Clermont College Drive, Batavia, OH 45103. *Phone:* 513-732-5294. *Toll-free phone:* 866-446-2822. *Fax:* 513-732-5303. *E-mail:* jamie.adkins@uc.edu. *Website:* http://www.ucclermont.edu/.

Vatterott College
Broadview Heights, Ohio

Director of Admissions Mr. Jack Chalk, Director of Admissions, Vatterott College, 5025 East Royalton Road, Broadview Heights, OH 44147. *Phone:* 440-526-1660. *Toll-free phone:* 888-553-6627. *Website:* http://www.vatterott.edu/.

Vet Tech Institute at Bradford School
Columbus, Ohio

- **Private** 2-year, founded 2005
- **Suburban** campus
- **Coed,** 163 undergraduate students
- 33% of applicants were admitted

Freshmen *Admission:* 524 applied, 174 admitted.

Majors Veterinary/animal health technology.

Academics *Calendar:* semesters. *Degree:* associate. *Special study options:* accelerated degree program, internships.

Freshman Application Contact Admissions Office, Vet Tech Institute at Bradford School, 2469 Stelzer Road, Columbus, OH 43219. *Phone:* 800-678-7981. *Toll-free phone:* 800-678-7981. *Website:* http://columbus.vettechinstitute.edu/.

Virginia Marti College of Art and Design
Lakewood, Ohio

Freshman Application Contact Virginia Marti College of Art and Design, 11724 Detroit Avenue, Lakewood, OH 44107. *Phone:* 216-221-8584 Ext. 106. *Website:* http://www.vmcad.edu/.

Washington State Community College
Marietta, Ohio

Freshman Application Contact Ms. Rebecca Peroni, Director of Admissions, Washington State Community College, 110 Colegate Drive, Marietta, OH 45750. *Phone:* 740-374-8716. *Fax:* 740-376-0257. *E-mail:* rperoni@wscc.edu. *Website:* http://www.wscc.edu/.

Zane State College
Zanesville, Ohio

Director of Admissions Mr. Paul Young, Director of Admissions, Zane State College, 1555 Newark Road, Zanesville, OH 43701-2626. *Phone:* 740-454-2501 Ext. 1225. *Toll-free phone:* 800-686-8324. *E-mail:* pyoung@zanestate.edu. *Website:* http://www.zanestate.edu/.

OKLAHOMA

Brown Mackie College–Oklahoma City
Oklahoma City, Oklahoma

Freshman Application Contact Brown Mackie College–Oklahoma City, 7101 Northwest Expressway, Suite 800, Oklahoma City, OK 73132. *Phone:* 405-621-8000. *Toll-free phone:* 888-229-3280. *Website:* http://www.brownmackie.edu/oklahoma-city/.

Brown Mackie College–Tulsa
Tulsa, Oklahoma

Freshman Application Contact Brown Mackie College–Tulsa, 4608 South Garnett, Suite 110, Tulsa, OK 74146. *Phone:* 918-628-3700. *Toll-free phone:* 888-794-8411. *Website:* http://www.brownmackie.edu/tulsa/.

Career Point College
Tulsa, Oklahoma

Admissions Office Contact Career Point College, 3138 South Garnett Road, Tulsa, OK 74146. *Website:* http://www.careerpointcollege.edu/.

Carl Albert State College
Poteau, Oklahoma

- **State-supported** 2-year, founded 1934, part of Oklahoma State Regents for Higher Education
- **Small-town** 78-acre campus
- **Endowment** $5.7 million
- **Coed,** 2,276 undergraduate students, 62% full-time, 63% women, 37% men

Undergraduates 1,415 full-time, 861 part-time. Students come from 17 states and territories; 10 other countries; 4% Black or African American, non-Hispanic/Latino; 5% Hispanic/Latino; 0.4% Asian, non-Hispanic/Latino; 0.1% Native Hawaiian or other Pacific Islander, non-Hispanic/Latino; 22% American Indian or Alaska Native, non-Hispanic/Latino; 7% Two or more races, non-Hispanic/Latino; 1% Race/ethnicity unknown; 1% international; 12% live on campus.
Freshmen *Admission:* 783 enrolled.
Faculty *Student/faculty ratio:* 16:1.
Majors Biology/biological sciences; business administration and management; business/commerce; child development; computer and information sciences; elementary education; engineering; engineering technologies and engineering related; English; foods, nutrition, and wellness; health professions related; health services/allied health/health sciences; hotel/motel administration; management information systems; mathematics; physical education teaching and coaching; physical sciences; physical therapy technology; pre-law studies; registered nursing/registered nurse; rhetoric and composition; secondary education; social sciences; telecommunications technology.
Academics *Calendar:* semesters. *Degree:* certificates and associate. *Special study options:* academic remediation for entering students, adult/continuing education programs, cooperative education, part-time degree program.
Library Joe E. White Library.
Student Life *Housing Options:* men-only, women-only. Campus housing is university owned. *Activities and Organizations:* drama/theater group, student-run newspaper, radio station, choral group, Student Government Association, Phi Theta Kappa, Baptist Student Union, BACCHUS, Student Physical Therapist Assistant Association. *Campus security:* security guards. *Student services:* health clinic, personal/psychological counseling.
Athletics Member NJCAA. *Intercollegiate sports:* baseball M, basketball M(s)/W(s), softball M. *Intramural sports:* tennis M/W, volleyball M/W, weight lifting M.
Costs (2015–16) *Tuition:* state resident $1572 full-time, $105 per credit hour part-time; nonresident $3042 full-time, $217 per credit hour part-time. Full-time tuition and fees vary according to course load. Part-time tuition and fees vary according to course load. *Required fees:* $1185 full-time, $500 per term part-time. *Room and board:* $2111; room only: $1600. Room and board charges vary according to board plan. *Payment plan:* installment. *Waivers:* employees or children of employees.
Financial Aid Of all full-time matriculated undergraduates who enrolled in 2014, 112 Federal Work-Study jobs (averaging $2100).
Applying *Required:* high school transcript. *Application deadlines:* 8/13 (freshmen), 8/15 (transfers). *Notification:* continuous (freshmen), continuous (transfers).
Freshman Application Contact Mr. Jonathan Bradley Davis, Admission Clerk, Carl Albert State College, 1507 South McKenna, Poteau, OK 74953-5208. *Phone:* 918-647-1300. *Fax:* 918-647-1306.
Website: http://www.carlalbert.edu/.

Clary Sage College
Tulsa, Oklahoma

- **Proprietary** 2-year
- **Urban** 6-acre campus with easy access to Tulsa
- **Coed, primarily women,** 621 undergraduate students, 100% full-time, 90% women, 10% men

Undergraduates 621 full-time. Students come from 8 states and territories; 3% are from out of state; 22% Black or African American, non-Hispanic/Latino; 7% Hispanic/Latino; 1% Asian, non-Hispanic/Latino; 0.2% Native Hawaiian or other Pacific Islander, non-Hispanic/Latino; 11% American Indian or Alaska Native, non-Hispanic/Latino; 3% Two or more races, non-Hispanic/Latino; 4% Race/ethnicity unknown.
Freshmen *Admission:* 578 enrolled.
Faculty *Total:* 32, 100% full-time, 3% with terminal degrees. *Student/faculty ratio:* 19:1.
Majors Cosmetology; fashion/apparel design; interior design; massage therapy.
Academics *Calendar:* continuous. *Degree:* diplomas and associate. *Special study options:* adult/continuing education programs, distance learning, internships, part-time degree program.

Student Life *Housing:* college housing not available. *Activities and Organizations:* Student Ambassadors. *Campus security:* security guard during hours of operation.
Costs (2015–16) *Tuition:* $12,987 full-time, $6 per credit part-time. Full-time tuition and fees vary according to class time, course level, course load, degree level, location, program, reciprocity agreements, and student level. Part-time tuition and fees vary according to class time, course level, location, reciprocity agreements, and student level. *Required fees:* $1209 full-time. *Payment plans:* tuition prepayment, installment. *Waivers:* employees or children of employees.
Applying *Options:* electronic application. *Application fee:* $100. *Required:* essay or personal statement, high school transcript, interview. *Application deadlines:* rolling (freshmen), rolling (out-of-state freshmen), rolling (transfers). *Notification:* continuous (freshmen), continuous (out-of-state freshmen), continuous (transfers).
Freshman Application Contact Ms. Raye Mahlberg, Campus Director, Clary Sage College, 3131 South Sheridan, Tulsa, OK 74145. *Phone:* 918-298-8200 Ext. 1025. *E-mail:* rmahlberg@clarysagecollege.com.
Website: http://www.clarysagecollege.com/.

College of the Muscogee Nation
Okmulgee, Oklahoma

Admissions Office Contact College of the Muscogee Nation, 2170 Raven Circle, Okmulgee, OK 74447-0917.
Website: http://www.mvsktc.org/.

Comanche Nation College
Lawton, Oklahoma

Admissions Office Contact Comanche Nation College, 1608 SW 9th Street, Lawton, OK 73501.
Website: http://www.cnc.cc.ok.us/.

Community Care College
Tulsa, Oklahoma

- **Independent** 2-year, founded 1995
- **Urban** 6-acre campus
- **Coed, primarily women,** 1,002 undergraduate students, 100% full-time, 90% women, 10% men

Undergraduates 1,002 full-time. Students come from 17 states and territories; 2% are from out of state; 16% Black or African American, non-Hispanic/Latino; 6% Hispanic/Latino; 2% Asian, non-Hispanic/Latino; 17% American Indian or Alaska Native, non-Hispanic/Latino; 3% Two or more races, non-Hispanic/Latino; 3% Race/ethnicity unknown.
Freshmen *Admission:* 802 enrolled.
Faculty *Total:* 30, 93% full-time. *Student/faculty ratio:* 28:1.
Majors Accounting technology and bookkeeping; business administration, management and operations related; dental assisting; early childhood education; health and physical education/fitness; health/health-care administration; legal assistant/paralegal; medical/clinical assistant; medical insurance coding; pharmacy technician; surgical technology; veterinary/animal health technology.
Academics *Calendar:* continuous. *Degree:* diplomas and associate. *Special study options:* adult/continuing education programs, distance learning, independent study, internships, services for LD students.
Student Life *Housing:* college housing not available. *Activities and Organizations:* Student Ambassadors. *Campus security:* campus security personnel during school hours.
Costs (2015–16) *Tuition:* $12,989 full-time. Full-time tuition and fees vary according to class time, course level, course load, degree level, location, program, and reciprocity agreements. Part-time tuition and fees vary according to class time, course level, location, and reciprocity agreements. *Required fees:* $1442 full-time. *Payment plans:* tuition prepayment, installment. *Waivers:* employees or children of employees.
Applying *Options:* electronic application. *Application fee:* $100. *Required:* essay or personal statement, high school transcript, interview. *Required for some:* 1 letter of recommendation. *Application deadlines:* rolling (freshmen), rolling (out-of-state freshmen). *Notification:* continuous (freshmen), continuous (out-of-state freshmen).
Freshman Application Contact Dr. Celia Stall-Meadows, Chief Executive Officer, Community Care College, 4242 South Sheridan, Tulsa, OK 74145. *Phone:* 918-610-0027 Ext. 2022. *Fax:* 918-610-0029.
E-mail: cmeadows@communitycarecollege.edu.
Website: http://www.communitycarecollege.edu/.

Connors State College
Warner, Oklahoma

Freshman Application Contact Ms. Sonya Baker, Registrar, Connors State College, Route 1 Box 1000, Warner, OK 74469-9700. *Phone:* 918-463-6233. *Website:* http://www.connorsstate.edu/.

Eastern Oklahoma State College
Wilburton, Oklahoma

Freshman Application Contact Ms. Leah McLaughlin, Director of Admissions, Eastern Oklahoma State College, 1301 West Main, Wilburton, OK 74578-4999. *Phone:* 918-465-1811. *Toll-free phone:* 855-534-3672. *Fax:* 918-465-2431. *E-mail:* lmiller@eosc.edu. *Website:* http://www.eosc.edu/.

Heritage College
Oklahoma City, Oklahoma

Freshman Application Contact Admissions Office, Heritage College, 7202 I-35 Service Road, Oklahoma City, OK 73149. *Phone:* 405-631-3399. *Toll-free phone:* 888-334-7339. *E-mail:* info@heritage-education.com. *Website:* http://www.heritagecollege.edu/.

ITT Technical Institute
Tulsa, Oklahoma

Freshman Application Contact Director of Recruitment, ITT Technical Institute, 4500 South 129th East Avenue, Suite 152, Tulsa, OK 74134. *Phone:* 918-615-3900. *Toll-free phone:* 800-514-6535. *Website:* http://www.itt-tech.edu/.

Murray State College
Tishomingo, Oklahoma

Freshman Application Contact Murray State College, One Murray Campus, Tishomingo, OK 73460-3130. *Phone:* 580-371-2371 Ext. 171. *Website:* http://www.mscok.edu/.

Northeastern Oklahoma Agricultural and Mechanical College
Miami, Oklahoma

Freshman Application Contact Amy Ishmael, Vice President for Enrollment Management, Northeastern Oklahoma Agricultural and Mechanical College, 200 I Street, NE, Miami, OK 74354-6434. *Phone:* 918-540-6212. *Toll-free phone:* 800-464-6636. *Fax:* 918-540-6946. *E-mail:* neoadmission@neo.edu. *Website:* http://www.neo.edu/.

Northern Oklahoma College
Tonkawa, Oklahoma

Freshman Application Contact Ms. Sheri Snyder, Director of College Relations, Northern Oklahoma College, 1220 East Grand Avenue, PO Box 310, Tonkawa, OK 74653-0310. *Phone:* 580-628-6290. *Website:* http://www.noc.edu/.

Oklahoma City Community College
Oklahoma City, Oklahoma

- **State-supported** 2-year, founded 1969, part of Oklahoma State Regents for Higher Education
- **Urban** 143-acre campus with easy access to Oklahoma City
- **Endowment** $283,328
- **Coed,** 13,334 undergraduate students, 34% full-time, 58% women, 42% men

Undergraduates 4,575 full-time, 8,759 part-time. Students come from 23 states and territories; 59 other countries; 6% are from out of state; 9% Black or African American, non-Hispanic/Latino; 11% Hispanic/Latino; 4% Asian, non-Hispanic/Latino; 0.2% Native Hawaiian or other Pacific Islander, non-Hispanic/Latino; 4% American Indian or Alaska Native, non-Hispanic/Latino; 5% Two or more races, non-Hispanic/Latino; 8% international; 34% transferred in.

Freshmen *Admission:* 4,639 applied, 3,716 admitted, 2,412 enrolled. *Test scores:* ACT scores over 18: 78%; ACT scores over 24: 25%; ACT scores over 30: 3%.

Faculty *Total:* 614, 22% full-time, 13% with terminal degrees. *Student/faculty ratio:* 22:1.

Majors Administrative assistant and secretarial science; American government and politics; animation, interactive technology, video graphics and special effects; architectural drafting and CAD/CADD; art; automobile/automotive mechanics technology; automotive engineering technology; banking and financial support services; biology/biological sciences; biotechnology; broadcast journalism; business administration and management; business/commerce; chemistry; child development; cinematography and film/video production; commercial and advertising art; computer engineering technology; computer science; computer systems analysis; computer systems networking and telecommunications; cyber/electronic operations and warfare; design and applied arts related; design and visual communications; diesel mechanics technology; digital communication and media/multimedia; drafting and design technology; dramatic/theater arts; elementary education; emergency medical technology (EMT paramedic); engineering technologies and engineering related; fine/studio arts; foreign languages and literatures; game and interactive media design; general studies; geographic information science and cartography; graphic communications; health information/medical records administration; history; humanities; legal administrative assistant/secretary; liberal arts and sciences/liberal studies; literature; mass communication/media; mathematics; medical/clinical assistant; multi/interdisciplinary studies related; music; philosophy; photographic and film/video technology; physics; political science and government; pre-engineering; psychology; public relations, advertising, and applied communication; registered nursing/registered nurse; respiratory care therapy; sociology; speech-language pathology assistant; surgical technology; system, networking, and LAN/WAN management.

Academics *Calendar:* semesters. *Degree:* certificates and associate. *Special study options:* academic remediation for entering students, accelerated degree program, advanced placement credit, cooperative education, distance learning, double majors, English as a second language, honors programs, independent study, internships, part-time degree program, services for LD students, student-designed majors, summer session for credit.

Library Keith Leftwich Memorial Library. *Books:* 87,598 (physical), 11,647 (digital/electronic); *Serial titles:* 152 (physical); *Databases:* 50. Weekly public service hours: 84.

Student Life *Housing:* college housing not available. *Activities and Organizations:* drama/theater group, student-run newspaper, television station, choral group, Health Professions Association, Black Student Association, Nursing Student Association, Hispanic Organization Promoting Education (HOPE), The Gamers Guild. *Campus security:* 24-hour emergency response devices and patrols, late-night transport/escort service. *Student services:* personal/psychological counseling.

Athletics *Intramural sports:* badminton M/W, basketball M/W, football M/W, soccer M/W, table tennis M/W, ultimate Frisbee M/W, volleyball M/W, weight lifting M/W.

Standardized Tests *Required for some:* ACT (for admission). *Recommended:* ACT (for admission), SAT or ACT (for admission).

Costs (2016–17) *One-time required fee:* $25. *Tuition:* state resident $2627 full-time, $88 per credit hour part-time; nonresident $7661 full-time. Full-time tuition and fees vary according to class time and course level. Part-time tuition and fees vary according to class time and course level. *Required fees:* $764 full-time, $25 per credit hour part-time. *Payment plan:* installment. *Waivers:* senior citizens and employees or children of employees.

Applying *Options:* electronic application. *Application fee:* $30. *Required for some:* high school transcript, college and university transcripts. *Application deadlines:* rolling (freshmen), rolling (out-of-state freshmen), rolling (transfers). *Notification:* continuous (freshmen), continuous (out-of-state freshmen), continuous (transfers).

Freshman Application Contact Mrs. Mary Bodine Al-Sharif, Director of Recruitment and Admissions, Oklahoma City Community College, 7777 South May Avenue, Oklahoma City, OK 73159. *Phone:* 405-682-7743. *Fax:* 405-682-7817. *E-mail:* mary.bodineal-sharif@occc.edu. *Website:* http://www.occc.edu/.

Oklahoma State University Institute of Technology
Okmulgee, Oklahoma

- **State-supported** primarily 2-year, founded 1946, part of Oklahoma State University
- **Small-town** 160-acre campus with easy access to Tulsa
- **Endowment** $8.1 million
- **Coed,** 2,476 undergraduate students, 71% full-time, 37% women, 63% men

Undergraduates 1,770 full-time, 706 part-time. Students come from 30 states and territories; 13 other countries; 10% are from out of state; 5% Black or African American, non-Hispanic/Latino; 5% Hispanic/Latino; 0.9% Asian,

non-Hispanic/Latino; 0.1% Native Hawaiian or other Pacific Islander, non-Hispanic/Latino; 14% American Indian or Alaska Native, non-Hispanic/Latino; 9% Two or more races, non-Hispanic/Latino; 4% Race/ethnicity unknown; 0.7% international; 8% transferred in; 29% live on campus. *Retention:* 59% of full-time freshmen returned.
Freshmen *Admission:* 2,050 applied, 852 admitted, 508 enrolled. *Average high school GPA:* 2.97. *Test scores:* ACT scores over 18: 51%; ACT scores over 24: 6%.
Faculty *Total:* 168, 72% full-time, 5% with terminal degrees. *Student/faculty ratio:* 15:1.
Majors Autobody/collision and repair technology; automotive engineering technology; business/commerce; casino management; civil engineering technology; computer and information systems security; construction engineering technology; culinary arts related; diesel mechanics technology; education (multiple levels); engineering technology; graphic design; health services/allied health/health sciences; heating, air conditioning, ventilation and refrigeration maintenance technology; information technology; instrumentation technology; intermedia/multimedia; mechanical engineering/mechanical technology; mechanic and repair technologies related; multi/interdisciplinary studies related; office occupations and clerical services; orthotics/prosthetics; petroleum technology; photography; registered nursing/registered nurse.
Academics *Calendar:* trimesters. *Degrees:* associate and bachelor's. *Special study options:* academic remediation for entering students, adult/continuing education programs, advanced placement credit, distance learning, double majors, independent study, internships, part-time degree program, services for LD students, summer session for credit.
Library Oklahoma State University Institute of Technology Library. *Books:* 9,119 (physical), 141,547 (digital/electronic); *Serial titles:* 175 (physical), 80,091 (digital/electronic); *Databases:* 37. Weekly public service hours: 66; students can reserve study rooms.
Student Life *Housing:* on-campus residence required for freshman year. *Options:* coed, men-only. Campus housing is university owned. Freshman applicants given priority for college housing. *Activities and Organizations:* Phi Theta Kappa, Future Art Directors Club, Air Conditioning and Refrigeration Club, Future Chefs Association Club, Instrumentation, Society and Automation Club. *Campus security:* 24-hour emergency response devices and patrols, late-night transport/escort service, controlled dormitory access. *Student services:* health clinic, personal/psychological counseling.
Athletics *Intramural sports:* basketball M/W, football M/W, racquetball M/W, soccer M/W, softball M/W, table tennis M/W, volleyball M/W.
Standardized Tests *Required for some:* SAT or ACT (for admission). *Recommended:* ACT (for admission).
Costs (2016–17) *Tuition:* state resident $3720 full-time, $124 per credit hour part-time; nonresident $9330 full-time, $311 per credit hour part-time. Full-time tuition and fees vary according to course level, course load, location, program, and student level. Part-time tuition and fees vary according to course level, course load, location, program, and student level. *Required fees:* $1140 full-time, $38 per credit hour part-time. *Room and board:* $6370. Room and board charges vary according to board plan and housing facility. *Payment plan:* installment. *Waivers:* senior citizens and employees or children of employees.
Financial Aid Of all full-time matriculated undergraduates who enrolled in 2015, 1,857 applied for aid, 1,598 were judged to have need, 1,151 had their need fully met. In 2015, 217 non-need-based awards were made. *Average percent of need met:* 75%. *Average financial aid package:* $7600. *Average need-based loan:* $4500. *Average need-based gift aid:* $7600. *Average non-need-based aid:* $500. *Financial aid deadline:* 6/30.
Applying *Options:* deferred entrance. *Required:* high school transcript. *Application deadlines:* rolling (freshmen), rolling (out-of-state freshmen), rolling (transfers).
Freshman Application Contact Chenoa Worthington, Assistant Registrar, Oklahoma State University Institute of Technology, 1801 E 4th Street, Okmulgee, OK 74447. *Phone:* 918-293-5274. *Toll-free phone:* 800-722-4471. *Fax:* 918-293-4643. *E-mail:* chenoa.worthington@okstate.edu. *Website:* http://www.osuit.edu/.

Oklahoma State University, Oklahoma City

Oklahoma City, Oklahoma

- **State-supported** primarily 2-year, founded 1961, part of Oklahoma State University
- **Urban** 110-acre campus
- **Coed,** 5,963 undergraduate students, 31% full-time, 60% women, 40% men

Undergraduates 1,878 full-time, 4,085 part-time. Students come from 26 states and territories; 4% are from out of state; 13% Black or African American, non-Hispanic/Latino; 11% Hispanic/Latino; 3% Asian, non-Hispanic/Latino; 3% American Indian or Alaska Native, non-Hispanic/Latino; 12% Two or more races, non-Hispanic/Latino; 5% Race/ethnicity unknown; 13% transferred in.
Freshmen *Admission:* 2,412 applied, 795 admitted, 795 enrolled.
Faculty *Total:* 414, 21% full-time. *Student/faculty ratio:* 14:1.
Majors Accounting; American Sign Language (ASL); architectural drafting and CAD/CADD; architectural engineering technology; art; building/home/construction inspection; business administration and management; civil engineering technology; construction engineering technology; construction management; construction trades; criminal justice/police science; drafting and design technology; early childhood education; economics; electrical and power transmission installation; electrical, electronic and communications engineering technology; electrocardiograph technology; emergency medical technology (EMT paramedic); engineering technology; fire prevention and safety technology; fire science/firefighting; general studies; health/health-care administration; history; horticultural science; humanities; human services; illustration; information science/studies; information technology; language interpretation and translation; occupational safety and health technology; physics; pre-engineering; prenursing studies; professional, technical, business, and scientific writing; psychology; public administration and social service professions related; radiologic technology/science; registered nursing/registered nurse; sign language interpretation and translation; substance abuse/addiction counseling; surveying technology; turf and turfgrass management; veterinary/animal health technology; web page, digital/multimedia and information resources design.
Academics *Calendar:* semesters. *Degrees:* certificates, associate, and bachelor's. *Special study options:* academic remediation for entering students, advanced placement credit, distance learning, double majors, honors programs, independent study, internships, part-time degree program, services for LD students, study abroad, summer session for credit.
Library Oklahoma State University, Oklahoma City Library. *Books:* 47,903 (physical); *Serial titles:* 237 (physical); *Databases:* 72. Weekly public service hours: 73; students can reserve study rooms.
Student Life *Housing:* college housing not available. *Activities and Organizations:* OSU-OKC Chapter of the OK Student Nurse Association, Veterinary Technician Association, Hispanic Student Association, Student Leaders of Tomorrow, Student Government Association. *Campus security:* 24-hour patrols, late-night transport/escort service.
Costs (2015–16) *Tuition:* state resident $2846 full-time, $119 per credit hour part-time; nonresident $7877 full-time, $328 per credit hour part-time. Full-time tuition and fees vary according to course level, degree level, program, and student level. Part-time tuition and fees vary according to course level, degree level, program, and student level. No tuition increase for student's term of enrollment. *Required fees:* $89 full-time, $12 per term part-time, $65 per year part-time. *Payment plans:* tuition prepayment, installment. *Waivers:* senior citizens and employees or children of employees.
Applying *Options:* electronic application. *Required for some:* high school transcript. *Application deadlines:* rolling (freshmen), rolling (transfers). *Notification:* continuous (freshmen), continuous (transfers).
Freshman Application Contact Mr. Kyle Williams, Senior Director of Enrollment Management, Oklahoma State University, Oklahoma City, 900 North Portland Avenue, AD202, Oklahoma City, OK 73107. *Phone:* 405-945-9152. *Toll-free phone:* 800-560-4099. *E-mail:* wilkylw@osuokc.edu. *Website:* http://www.osuokc.edu/.

Oklahoma Technical College

Tulsa, Oklahoma

- **Independent** 2-year
- **Urban** 9-acre campus with easy access to Tulsa
- **Coed,** 310 undergraduate students, 100% full-time, 13% women, 87% men

Undergraduates 310 full-time. Students come from 8 states and territories; 5% are from out of state; 20% Black or African American, non-Hispanic/Latino; 6% Hispanic/Latino; 0.6% Native Hawaiian or other Pacific Islander, non-Hispanic/Latino; 7% American Indian or Alaska Native, non-Hispanic/Latino; 2% Two or more races, non-Hispanic/Latino; 7% Race/ethnicity unknown.
Freshmen *Admission:* 306 enrolled.
Faculty *Total:* 12, 100% full-time. *Student/faculty ratio:* 25:1.
Majors Automobile/automotive mechanics technology; diesel mechanics technology; heating, ventilation, air conditioning and refrigeration engineering technology; welding technology.
Academics *Calendar:* continuous. *Degree:* diplomas and associate. *Special study options:* adult/continuing education programs, distance learning, internships, services for LD students.
Student Life *Housing:* college housing not available. *Activities and Organizations:* Student Ambassadors. *Campus security:* campus security during school hours. *Student services:* personal/psychological counseling.

Costs (2015–16) *Tuition:* $17,223 full-time, $6 per credit part-time. Full-time tuition and fees vary according to class time, course level, course load, degree level, location, program, and student level. Part-time tuition and fees vary according to class time and degree level. *Required fees:* $2166 full-time. *Payment plans:* tuition prepayment, installment. *Waivers:* employees or children of employees.

Applying *Options:* electronic application. *Application fee:* $100. *Required:* essay or personal statement, high school transcript, interview. *Application deadlines:* rolling (freshmen), rolling (out-of-state freshmen), rolling (transfers). *Notification:* continuous (freshmen), continuous (out-of-state freshmen), continuous (transfers).

Freshman Application Contact Mr. Jeremy Cooper, Campus Director, Oklahoma Technical College, 4444 South Sheridan Road, Tulsa, OK 74145. *Phone:* 918-895-7500 Ext. 3007. *Fax:* 918-895-7885. *E-mail:* jcooper@oklahomatechnicalcollege.com. *Website:* http://www.oklahomatechnicalcollege.com/.

Platt College
Moore, Oklahoma

Admissions Office Contact Platt College, 201 North Eastern Avenue, Moore, OK 73160.
Website: http://www.plattcolleges.edu/.

Platt College
Oklahoma City, Oklahoma

Freshman Application Contact Ms. Kim Lamb, Director of Admissions, Platt College, 309 South Ann Arbor, Oklahoma City, OK 73128. *Phone:* 405-946-7799. *Fax:* 405-943-2150. *E-mail:* klamb@plattcollege.org. *Website:* http://www.plattcolleges.edu/.

Platt College
Tulsa, Oklahoma

Director of Admissions Mrs. Susan Rone, Director, Platt College, 3801 South Sheridan Road, Tulsa, OK 74145-111. *Phone:* 918-663-9000. *Fax:* 918-622-1240. *E-mail:* susanr@plattcollege.org. *Website:* http://www.plattcolleges.edu/.

Redlands Community College
El Reno, Oklahoma

Freshman Application Contact Redlands Community College, 1300 South Country Club Road, El Reno, OK 73036-5304. *Phone:* 405-262-2552 Ext. 1263. *Toll-free phone:* 866-415-6367.
Website: http://www.redlandscc.edu/.

Rose State College
Midwest City, Oklahoma

Freshman Application Contact Ms. Mechelle Aitson-Roessler, Registrar and Director of Admissions, Rose State College, 6420 Southeast 15th Street, Midwest City, OK 73110-2799. *Phone:* 405-733-7308. *Toll-free phone:* 866-621-0987. *Fax:* 405-736-0203. *E-mail:* maitson@ms.rose.cc.ok.us. *Website:* http://www.rose.edu/.

Seminole State College
Seminole, Oklahoma

- **State-supported** 2-year, founded 1931, part of Oklahoma State Regents for Higher Education
- **Small-town** 40-acre campus with easy access to Oklahoma City
- **Endowment** $3.1 million
- **Coed,** 1,827 undergraduate students, 56% full-time, 65% women, 35% men

Undergraduates 1,016 full-time, 811 part-time. Students come from 16 states and territories; 9 other countries; 4% are from out of state; 6% Black or African American, non-Hispanic/Latino; 4% Hispanic/Latino; 0.8% Asian, non-Hispanic/Latino; 0.2% Native Hawaiian or other Pacific Islander, non-Hispanic/Latino; 25% American Indian or Alaska Native, non-Hispanic/Latino; 0.5% Race/ethnicity unknown; 2% international; 5% transferred in; 8% live on campus.

Freshmen *Admission:* 495 applied, 495 admitted, 434 enrolled. *Test scores:* ACT scores over 18: 77%; ACT scores over 24: 18%; ACT scores over 30: 1%.

Faculty *Total:* 100, 37% full-time, 3% with terminal degrees. *Student/faculty ratio:* 22:1.

Majors Accounting; art; behavioral sciences; biological and biomedical sciences related; biology/biological sciences; business administration and management; business/commerce; child development; clinical/medical laboratory technology; computer science; criminal justice/law enforcement administration; criminal justice/police science; elementary education; engineering; English; fine arts related; general studies; humanities; liberal arts and sciences/liberal studies; management information systems and services related; mathematics; physical education teaching and coaching; physical sciences; pre-engineering; psychology related; registered nursing/registered nurse; social sciences.

Academics *Calendar:* semesters. *Degree:* diplomas and associate. *Special study options:* academic remediation for entering students, adult/continuing education programs, advanced placement credit, cooperative education, distance learning, double majors, English as a second language, independent study, off-campus study, part-time degree program, services for LD students, study abroad, summer session for credit.

Library Boren Library plus 1 other. *Books:* 26,841 (physical); *Serial titles:* 35 (physical), 11 (digital/electronic); *Databases:* 3.

Student Life *Housing Options:* coed. Campus housing is university owned. *Activities and Organizations:* Student Government Association, Native American Student Association, Psi Beta Honor Society, Student Nurses Association, Phi Theta Kappa. *Campus security:* 24-hour emergency response devices and patrols, student patrols, late-night transport/escort service, controlled dormitory access.

Athletics Member NJCAA. *Intercollegiate sports:* baseball M(s), basketball M(s)/W(s), cheerleading W, golf M(s)/W(s), softball W(s), tennis M(s)/W(s), volleyball W(s).

Costs (2016–17) *One-time required fee:* $15. *Tuition:* state resident $2504 full-time, $83 per credit hour part-time; nonresident $7664 full-time, $255 per credit hour part-time. Full-time tuition and fees vary according to location and program. Part-time tuition and fees vary according to location and program. *Required fees:* $1305 full-time, $44 per credit hour part-time. *Room and board:* $7070; room only: $3900. *Payment plans:* installment, deferred payment. *Waivers:* senior citizens and employees or children of employees.

Financial Aid Of all full-time matriculated undergraduates who enrolled in 2014, 21 Federal Work-Study jobs (averaging $2675).

Applying *Options:* early admission, deferred entrance. *Application fee:* $15. *Required:* high school transcript. *Application deadlines:* rolling (freshmen), rolling (transfers). *Notification:* continuous (freshmen), continuous (transfers).

Freshman Application Contact Mrs. Corey Quiett, Registrar, Seminole State College, PO Box 351, 2701 Boren Boulevard, Seminole, OK 74818-0351. *Phone:* 405-382-9501. *Fax:* 405-382-9524. *E-mail:* c.quiett@sscok.edu. *Website:* http://www.sscok.edu/.

Southwestern Oklahoma State University at Sayre
Sayre, Oklahoma

- **State and locally supported** 2-year, founded 1938, part of Southwestern Oklahoma State University
- **Rural** 6-acre campus
- **Coed**

Undergraduates 2% Black or African American, non-Hispanic/Latino; 7% Hispanic/Latino; 0.2% Asian, non-Hispanic/Latino; 3% American Indian or Alaska Native, non-Hispanic/Latino; 6% Two or more races, non-Hispanic/Latino; 3% Race/ethnicity unknown; 1% international.

Freshmen *Admission:* 34 applied, 34 admitted. *Test scores:* ACT scores over 18: 59%; ACT scores over 24: 14%; ACT scores over 30: 2%.

Faculty *Total:* 18, 78% full-time. *Student/faculty ratio:* 20:1.

Majors Business administration and management; clinical/medical laboratory technology; computer science; corrections; criminal justice/safety; general studies; medical radiologic technology; registered nursing/registered nurse.

Academics *Calendar:* semesters. *Degree:* diplomas and associate. *Special study options:* academic remediation for entering students, adult/continuing education programs, advanced placement credit, cooperative education, distance learning, independent study, part-time degree program, services for LD students, summer session for credit.

Library Oscar McMahan Library.

Student Life *Housing:* college housing not available. *Activities and Organizations:* student-run newspaper.

Standardized Tests *Required for some:* SAT or ACT (for admission).

Costs (2015–16) *Tuition:* state resident $191 per credit hour part-time; nonresident $406 per credit hour part-time. No tuition increase for student's term of enrollment. *Required fees:* $34 per credit hour part-time. *Payment plan:* installment. *Waivers:* employees or children of employees.

Applying *Options:* electronic application. *Required:* high school transcript. *Application deadlines:* rolling (freshmen), rolling (transfers).
Freshman Application Contact Ms. Kim Seymour, Registrar, Southwestern Oklahoma State University at Sayre, 409 East Mississippi Avenue, Sayre, OK 73662. *Phone:* 580-928-5533 Ext. 101. *Fax:* 580-928-1140.
E-mail: kim.seymour@swosu.edu.
Website: http://www.swosu.edu/sayre/.

Spartan College of Aeronautics and Technology
Tulsa, Oklahoma

Freshman Application Contact Mr. Mark Fowler, Vice President of Student Records and Finance, Spartan College of Aeronautics and Technology, 8820 East Pine Street, PO Box 582833, Tulsa, OK 74158-2833. *Phone:* 918-836-6886. *Toll-free phone:* 800-331-1204 (in-state); 800-331-124 (out-of-state). *Website:* http://www.spartan.edu/.

Tulsa Community College
Tulsa, Oklahoma

- **State-supported** 2-year, founded 1968, part of Oklahoma State Regents for Higher Education
- **Urban** 160-acre campus
- **Coed,** 16,708 undergraduate students, 34% full-time, 60% women, 40% men

Undergraduates 5,713 full-time, 10,995 part-time. 9% Black or African American, non-Hispanic/Latino; 8% Hispanic/Latino; 4% Asian, non-Hispanic/Latino; 0.1% Native Hawaiian or other Pacific Islander, non-Hispanic/Latino; 8% American Indian or Alaska Native, non-Hispanic/Latino; 9% Two or more races, non-Hispanic/Latino; 3% Race/ethnicity unknown; 2% international; 3% transferred in.
Freshmen *Admission:* 3,734 enrolled. *Average high school GPA:* 2.98. *Test scores:* ACT scores over 18: 76%; ACT scores over 24: 20%; ACT scores over 30: 2%.
Faculty *Total:* 867, 35% full-time. *Student/faculty ratio:* 19:1.
Majors Accounting technology and bookkeeping; aeronautical/aerospace engineering technology; air traffic control; applied horticulture/horticulture operations; biotechnology; business administration and management; business/commerce; business, management, and marketing related; child development; clinical/medical laboratory technology; communication; computer and information sciences and support services related; computer and information sciences related; computer installation and repair technology; computer science; criminal justice/police science; dental hygiene; diagnostic medical sonography and ultrasound technology; digital communication and media/multimedia; dramatic/theater arts; education; electrical, electronic and communications engineering technology; engineering-related technologies; environmental science; fine/studio arts; fire services administration; foreign languages related; general studies; graphic and printing equipment operation/production; health information/medical records technology; health/medical preparatory programs related; human resources management; interior design; international business/trade/commerce; legal assistant/paralegal; marketing/marketing management; mathematics; medical radiologic technology; multi/interdisciplinary studies related; music; nutrition sciences; occupational therapy; physical sciences; physical therapy technology; pre-engineering; prenursing studies; pre-pharmacy studies; registered nursing/registered nurse; respiratory care therapy; sign language interpretation and translation; social sciences; social work; sport and fitness administration/management; surgical technology; veterinary/animal health technology.
Academics *Calendar:* semesters. *Degree:* certificates and associate. *Special study options:* academic remediation for entering students, accelerated degree program, adult/continuing education programs, advanced placement credit, cooperative education, distance learning, English as a second language, freshman honors college, honors programs, independent study, internships, off-campus study, part-time degree program, services for LD students, student-designed majors, study abroad, summer session for credit.
Student Life *Housing:* college housing not available. *Activities and Organizations:* drama/theater group, student-run newspaper, radio station, choral group. *Campus security:* 24-hour emergency response devices and patrols, student patrols, late-night transport/escort service. *Student services:* health clinic, personal/psychological counseling, women's center.
Athletics *Intramural sports:* basketball M/W, football M/W, soccer M/W, softball M/W, volleyball M/W.
Costs (2015–16) *Tuition:* state resident $3623 full-time, $91 per credit hour part-time; nonresident $9803 full-time, $2729 per credit hour part-time. *Required fees:* $894 full-time, $30 per credit hour part-time, $5 per term part-time. *Payment plan:* installment. *Waivers:* senior citizens and employees or children of employees.

Financial Aid Of all full-time matriculated undergraduates who enrolled in 2015, 4,676 applied for aid, 3,438 were judged to have need, 245 had their need fully met. In 2015, 635 non-need-based awards were made. *Average percent of need met:* 70%. *Average financial aid package:* $3843. *Average need-based loan:* $1785. *Average need-based gift aid:* $2821. *Average non-need-based aid:* $1585.
Applying *Options:* electronic application, early admission. *Application fee:* $20. *Required:* high school transcript. *Application deadlines:* rolling (freshmen), rolling (transfers).
Freshman Application Contact Ms. Traci Heck, Dean of Enrollment Management, Tulsa Community College, 6111 East Skelly Drive, Tulsa, OK 74135. *Phone:* 918-595-3411. *E-mail:* traci.heck@tulsacc.edu. *Website:* http://www.tulsacc.edu/.

Tulsa Welding School
Tulsa, Oklahoma

Freshman Application Contact Mrs. Debbie Renee Burke, Vice President/Executive Director, Tulsa Welding School, 2545 East 11th Street, Tulsa, OK 74104. *Phone:* 918-587-6789 Ext. 2258. *Toll-free phone:* 888-765-5555. *Fax:* 918-295-6812. *E-mail:* dburke@twsweld.com. *Website:* http://www.tulsaweldingschool.com/.

Vatterott College
Tulsa, Oklahoma

Freshman Application Contact Mr. Terry Queeno, Campus Director, Vatterott College, 4343 South 118th East Avenue, Suite A, Tulsa, OK 74146. *Phone:* 918-836-6656. *Toll-free phone:* 888-553-6627. *Fax:* 918-836-9698. *E-mail:* tulsa@vatterott-college.edu. *Website:* http://www.vatterott.edu/.

Vatterott College
Warr Acres, Oklahoma

Freshman Application Contact Mr. Mark Hybers, Director of Admissions, Vatterott College, Oklahoma City, OK 73127. *Phone:* 405-945-0088 Ext. 4416. *Toll-free phone:* 888-553-6627. *Fax:* 405-945-0788. *E-mail:* mark.hybers@vatterott-college.edu. *Website:* http://www.vatterott.edu/.

Virginia College in Tulsa
Tulsa, Oklahoma

Admissions Office Contact Virginia College in Tulsa, 5124 South Peoria Avenue, Tulsa, OK 74105. *Website:* http://www.vc.edu/.

Western Oklahoma State College
Altus, Oklahoma

Freshman Application Contact Dean Chad E. Wiginton, Dean of Student Support Services, Western Oklahoma State College, 2801 North Main, Altus, OK 73521. *Phone:* 580-477-7918. *Fax:* 580-477-7716. *E-mail:* chad.wiginton@wosc.edu. *Website:* http://www.wosc.edu/.

OREGON

American College of Healthcare Sciences
Portland, Oregon

Freshman Application Contact Admissions Office, American College of Healthcare Sciences, 5940 SW Hood Avenue, Portland, OR 97239. *Phone:* 503-244-0726. *Toll-free phone:* 800-487-8839. *Fax:* 503-244-0727. *E-mail:* achs@achs.edu. *Website:* http://www.achs.edu/.

Blue Mountain Community College
Pendleton, Oregon

Director of Admissions Ms. Theresa Bosworth, Director of Admissions, Blue Mountain Community College, 2411 Northwest Carden Avenue, PO Box 100,

Pendleton, OR 97801-1000. *Phone:* 541-278-5774.
E-mail: tbosworth@bluecc.edu.
Website: http://www.bluecc.edu/.

Central Oregon Community College
Bend, Oregon

- **District-supported** 2-year, founded 1949, part of Oregon Community College Association
- **Small-town** 193-acre campus
- **Endowment** $16.7 million
- **Coed,** 6,073 undergraduate students, 41% full-time, 54% women, 46% men

Undergraduates 2,492 full-time, 3,581 part-time. Students come from 25 states and territories; 6% are from out of state; 0.6% Black or African American, non-Hispanic/Latino; 10% Hispanic/Latino; 1% Asian, non-Hispanic/Latino; 0.3% Native Hawaiian or other Pacific Islander, non-Hispanic/Latino; 2% American Indian or Alaska Native, non-Hispanic/Latino; 3% Two or more races, non-Hispanic/Latino; 13% Race/ethnicity unknown; 8% transferred in; 1% live on campus. *Retention:* 45% of full-time freshmen returned.
Freshmen *Admission:* 1,678 applied, 1,678 admitted, 809 enrolled.
Faculty *Total:* 329, 39% full-time, 16% with terminal degrees. *Student/faculty ratio:* 19:1.
Majors Accounting; airline pilot and flight crew; art; automobile/automotive mechanics technology; biological and physical sciences; biology/biological sciences; business administration and management; CAD/CADD drafting/design technology; child-care and support services management; computer and information sciences related; computer science; computer systems networking and telecommunications; cooking and related culinary arts; customer service management; dental assisting; dietetics; drafting and design technology; early childhood education; education; electrical, electronic and communications engineering technology; emergency medical technology (EMT paramedic); engineering; entrepreneurship; fire science/firefighting; fishing and fisheries sciences and management; foreign languages and literatures; forestry; forest technology; health and physical education/fitness; health information/medical records technology; hotel/motel administration; humanities; industrial technology; kinesiology and exercise science; liberal arts and sciences/liberal studies; licensed practical/vocational nurse training; management information systems; manufacturing engineering technology; marketing/marketing management; massage therapy; mathematics; medical/clinical assistant; natural resources/conservation; physical sciences; physical therapy; polymer/plastics engineering; pre-law studies; premedical studies; pre-pharmacy studies; radiologic technology/science; registered nursing/registered nurse; retailing; social sciences; speech communication and rhetoric; sport and fitness administration/management; substance abuse/addiction counseling.
Academics *Calendar:* quarters. *Degree:* certificates and associate. *Special study options:* academic remediation for entering students, cooperative education, distance learning, double majors, English as a second language, independent study, internships, part-time degree program, services for LD students, student-designed majors, study abroad, summer session for credit. *ROTC:* Army (c).
Library COCC Library plus 1 other. *Books:* 65,539 (physical), 1,409 (digital/electronic); *Serial titles:* 241 (physical), 26 (digital/electronic); *Databases:* 96. Weekly public service hours: 78.
Student Life *Housing Options:* coed. Campus housing is university owned. *Activities and Organizations:* drama/theater group, student-run newspaper, choral group, Club Sports, Student Newspaper, Criminal Justice Club, Aviation Club. *Campus security:* 24-hour emergency response devices and patrols, late-night transport/escort service, controlled dormitory access. *Student services:* personal/psychological counseling.
Athletics *Intercollegiate sports:* golf M/W. *Intramural sports:* baseball M, basketball M/W, cross-country running M/W, football M, rugby M, skiing (cross-country) M/W, skiing (downhill) M/W, soccer M/W, track and field M/W, volleyball M/W, weight lifting M/W.
Costs (2015–16) *Tuition:* area resident $4095 full-time, $91 per credit hour part-time; state resident $5400 full-time, $120 per credit hour part-time; nonresident $11,070 full-time, $246 per credit hour part-time. *Required fees:* $349 full-time, $8 per credit hour part-time. *Room and board:* $10,550. Room and board charges vary according to board plan. *Payment plan:* installment. *Waivers:* employees or children of employees.
Financial Aid Of all full-time matriculated undergraduates who enrolled in 2015, 1,769 applied for aid, 1,617 were judged to have need, 58 had their need fully met. In 2015, 9 non-need-based awards were made. *Average percent of need met:* 67%. *Average financial aid package:* $12,014. *Average need-based loan:* $3681. *Average need-based gift aid:* $5974. *Average non-need-based aid:* $2722.

Applying *Options:* electronic application. *Application fee:* $25. *Application deadlines:* rolling (freshmen), rolling (transfers). *Notification:* continuous (freshmen), continuous (transfers).
Freshman Application Contact Central Oregon Community College, 2600 Northwest College Way, Bend, OR 97703. *Phone:* 541-383-7500.
Website: http://www.cocc.edu/.

Chemeketa Community College
Salem, Oregon

Freshman Application Contact Admissions Office, Chemeketa Community College, PO Box 14009, Salem, OR 97309. *Phone:* 503-399-5001.
E-mail: admissions@chemeketa.edu.
Website: http://www.chemeketa.edu/.

Clackamas Community College
Oregon City, Oregon

Freshman Application Contact Ms. Tara Sprehe, Registrar, Clackamas Community College, 19600 South Molalla Avenue, Oregon City, OR 97045. *Phone:* 503-657-6958 Ext. 2742. *Fax:* 503-650-6654.
E-mail: pattyw@clackamas.edu.
Website: http://www.clackamas.edu/.

Clatsop Community College
Astoria, Oregon

Freshman Application Contact Ms. Monica Van Steenberg, Recruiting Coordinator, Clatsop Community College, 1651 Lexington Avenue, Astoria, OR 97103. *Phone:* 503-338-2417. *Toll-free phone:* 855-252-8767. *Fax:* 503-325-5738. *E-mail:* admissions@clatsopcc.edu.
Website: http://www.clatsopcc.edu/.

Columbia Gorge Community College
The Dalles, Oregon

Freshman Application Contact Columbia Gorge Community College, 400 East Scenic Drive, The Dalles, OR 97058. *Phone:* 541-506-6025.
Website: http://www.cgcc.cc.or.us/.

Concorde Career College
Portland, Oregon

Admissions Office Contact Concorde Career College, 1425 NE Irving Street, Portland, OR 97232.
Website: http://www.concorde.edu/.

ITT Technical Institute
Portland, Oregon

Freshman Application Contact Director of Recruitment, ITT Technical Institute, 9500 Northeast Cascades Parkway, Portland, OR 97220. *Phone:* 503-255-6500. *Toll-free phone:* 800-234-5488.
Website: http://www.itt-tech.edu/.

Klamath Community College
Klamath Falls, Oregon

Freshman Application Contact Tammi Garlock, Retention Coordinator, Klamath Community College, 7390 So. 6th Street, Klamath Falls, OR 97603. *Phone:* 541-882-3521. *Fax:* 541-885-7758. *E-mail:* garlock@klamathcc.edu.
Website: http://www.klamathcc.edu/.

Lane Community College
Eugene, Oregon

Freshman Application Contact Lane Community College, 4000 East 30th Avenue, Eugene, OR 97405-0640. *Phone:* 541-747-4501 Ext. 2686.
Website: http://www.lanecc.edu/.

Linn-Benton Community College
Albany, Oregon

Freshman Application Contact Ms. Kim Sullivan, Outreach Coordinator, Linn-Benton Community College, 6500 Pacific Boulevard, SW, Albany, OR

97321. *Phone:* 541-917-4847. *Fax:* 541-917-4838.
E-mail: admissions@linnbenton.edu.
Website: http://www.linnbenton.edu/.

Mt. Hood Community College
Gresham, Oregon

Director of Admissions Dr. Craig Kolins, Associate Vice President of Enrollment Services, Mt. Hood Community College, 26000 Southeast Stark Street, Gresham, OR 97030-3300. *Phone:* 503-491-7265.
Website: http://www.mhcc.edu/.

Oregon Coast Community College
Newport, Oregon

- **Public** 2-year, founded 1987
- **Small-town** 24-acre campus
- **Coed,** 503 undergraduate students, 42% full-time, 65% women, 35% men

Undergraduates 213 full-time, 290 part-time. 1% are from out of state; 0.8% Black or African American, non-Hispanic/Latino; 11% Hispanic/Latino; 2% Asian, non-Hispanic/Latino; 0.2% Native Hawaiian or other Pacific Islander, non-Hispanic/Latino; 3% American Indian or Alaska Native, non-Hispanic/Latino; 5% Two or more races, non-Hispanic/Latino; 3% Race/ethnicity unknown; 15% transferred in. *Retention:* 48% of full-time freshmen returned.
Freshmen *Admission:* 75 applied, 75 admitted, 75 enrolled.
Faculty *Total:* 67, 15% full-time, 15% with terminal degrees. *Student/faculty ratio:* 17:1.
Majors Criminal justice/safety; general studies; liberal arts and sciences/liberal studies; marine biology and biological oceanography; registered nursing/registered nurse.
Academics *Calendar:* quarters. *Degree:* certificates and associate. *Special study options:* academic remediation for entering students, cooperative education, distance learning, English as a second language, honors programs, internships, part-time degree program, services for LD students, summer session for credit.
Library Oregon Coast Community College Library. *Books:* 13,033 (physical), 110,699 (digital/electronic); *Serial titles:* 2,771 (physical); *Databases:* 53. Students can reserve study rooms.
Student Life *Housing:* college housing not available. *Activities and Organizations:* Psych Club, Triangle Club, Writing Club, ASG. *Campus security:* 24-hour emergency response devices.
Standardized Tests *Required for some:* nursing entrance exam.
Costs (2016–17) *Tuition:* state resident $3564 full-time, $99 per credit part-time; nonresident $7704 full-time, $214 per credit part-time. Full-time tuition and fees vary according to course load and program. Part-time tuition and fees vary according to course load and program. *Required fees:* $252 full-time, $7 per credit part-time. *Payment plan:* deferred payment. *Waivers:* senior citizens and employees or children of employees.
Applying *Options:* electronic application. *Required for some:* essay or personal statement, 2 letters of recommendation, interview.
Freshman Application Contact Student Services, Oregon Coast Community College, 400 SE College Way, Newport, OR 97366. *Phone:* 541-265-2283. *Fax:* 541-265-3820. *E-mail:* webinfo@occc.cc.or.us.
Website: http://www.oregoncoastcc.org.

Portland Community College
Portland, Oregon

Freshman Application Contact Admissions and Registration Office, Portland Community College, PO Box 19000, Portland, OR 97280. *Phone:* 503-977-8888. *Toll-free phone:* 866-922-1010.
Website: http://www.pcc.edu/.

Rogue Community College
Grants Pass, Oregon

- **State and locally supported** 2-year, founded 1970
- **Rural** 84-acre campus
- **Endowment** $9.3 million
- **Coed,** 4,954 undergraduate students, 38% full-time, 56% women, 44% men

Undergraduates 1,901 full-time, 3,053 part-time. Students come from 23 states and territories; 3 other countries; 3% are from out of state; 1% Black or African American, non-Hispanic/Latino; 15% Hispanic/Latino; 1% Asian, non-Hispanic/Latino; 0.5% Native Hawaiian or other Pacific Islander, non-Hispanic/Latino; 1% American Indian or Alaska Native, non-Hispanic/Latino;

4% Two or more races, non-Hispanic/Latino; 4% Race/ethnicity unknown; 0.1% international; 70% transferred in.
Freshmen *Admission:* 837 enrolled. *Average high school GPA:* 2.97.
Faculty *Total:* 472, 16% full-time. *Student/faculty ratio:* 14:1.
Majors Accounting technology and bookkeeping; automobile/automotive mechanics technology; business administration and management; business/commerce; child-care and support services management; computer and information sciences; computer science; computer software technology; construction engineering technology; construction trades; criminal justice/police science; diesel mechanics technology; electrical and power transmission installation; electrical, electronic and communications engineering technology; emergency medical technology (EMT paramedic); family and community services; fire prevention and safety technology; general studies; liberal arts and sciences/liberal studies; manufacturing engineering technology; marketing/marketing management; mechanics and repair; medical office computer specialist; registered nursing/registered nurse; social work; visual and performing arts; welding technology.
Academics *Calendar:* quarters. *Degree:* certificates and associate. *Special study options:* academic remediation for entering students, adult/continuing education programs, advanced placement credit, cooperative education, distance learning, double majors, English as a second language, independent study, internships, part-time degree program, services for LD students, study abroad, summer session for credit.
Library Rogue Community College Library. *Books:* 58,578 (physical), 159 (digital/electronic); *Serial titles:* 98 (physical).
Student Life *Activities and Organizations:* drama/theater group, student-run newspaper, choral group. *Campus security:* 24-hour emergency response devices and patrols, late-night transport/escort service. *Student services:* personal/psychological counseling.
Athletics *Intercollegiate sports:* soccer M/W. *Intramural sports:* badminton M/W, basketball M/W, soccer M/W, softball M/W, volleyball M/W.
Costs (2015–16) *Tuition:* state resident $3420 full-time, $95 per credit hour part-time; nonresident $4176 full-time, $116 per credit hour part-time. Full-time tuition and fees vary according to reciprocity agreements. Part-time tuition and fees vary according to reciprocity agreements. *Required fees:* $585 full-time, $5 per credit hour part-time, $135 per term part-time. *Payment plan:* installment. *Waivers:* senior citizens and employees or children of employees.
Financial Aid Of all full-time matriculated undergraduates who enrolled in 2015, 1,482 applied for aid, 1,324 were judged to have need, 41 had their need fully met. 79 Federal Work-Study jobs (averaging $3054). In 2015, 29 non-need-based awards were made. *Average percent of need met:* 84%. *Average financial aid package:* $10,714. *Average need-based loan:* $3417. *Average need-based gift aid:* $5627. *Average non-need-based aid:* $1294.
Applying *Options:* electronic application, early admission. *Application deadlines:* rolling (freshmen), rolling (out-of-state freshmen), rolling (transfers).
Freshman Application Contact Mr. John Duarte, Director of Enrollment Services, Rogue Community College, 3345 Redwood Highway, Grants Pass, OR 97527-9291. *Phone:* 541-956-7176. *Fax:* 541-471-3585.
E-mail: csullivan@roguecc.edu.
Website: http://www.roguecc.edu/.

Southwestern Oregon Community College
Coos Bay, Oregon

- **State and locally supported** 2-year, founded 1961
- **Small-town** 174-acre campus
- **Endowment** $851,280
- **Coed,** 2,338 undergraduate students, 48% full-time, 54% women, 46% men

Undergraduates 1,129 full-time, 1,209 part-time. Students come from 24 states and territories; 6 other countries; 30% are from out of state; 1% Black or African American, non-Hispanic/Latino; 9% Hispanic/Latino; 1% Asian, non-Hispanic/Latino; 0.9% Native Hawaiian or other Pacific Islander, non-Hispanic/Latino; 3% American Indian or Alaska Native, non-Hispanic/Latino; 4% Two or more races, non-Hispanic/Latino; 17% Race/ethnicity unknown; 0.9% international; 17% live on campus.
Freshmen *Admission:* 580 enrolled.
Faculty *Total:* 54. *Student/faculty ratio:* 15:1.
Majors Accounting; business administration and management; child-care provision; criminal justice/police science; criminal justice/safety; fire science/firefighting; liberal arts and sciences/liberal studies; machine tool technology; medical/clinical assistant; registered nursing/registered nurse; restaurant, culinary, and catering management; welding technology.
Academics *Calendar:* quarters. *Degree:* certificates, diplomas, and associate. *Special study options:* academic remediation for entering students, adult/continuing education programs, advanced placement credit, cooperative education, distance learning, double majors, English as a second language,

honors programs, independent study, internships, part-time degree program, services for LD students, summer session for credit.

Library Southwestern Oregon Community College Library. *Books:* 28,092 (physical), 857 (digital/electronic); *Serial titles:* 101 (physical); *Databases:* 58. Weekly public service hours: 43.

Student Life *Housing:* on-campus residence required for freshman year. *Options:* coed. Campus housing is university owned. *Activities and Organizations:* choral group. *Campus security:* 24-hour emergency response devices and patrols, late-night transport/escort service, controlled dormitory access.

Athletics Member NJCAA. *Intercollegiate sports:* baseball M(s), basketball M(s)/W(s), cheerleading M(s)/W(s), cross-country running M(s)/W(s), golf M(s)/W(s), soccer M(s)/W(s), softball W(s), swimming and diving M(s)/W(s), track and field M(s)/W(s), volleyball W(s), wrestling M(s)/W(s). *Intramural sports:* basketball M, rock climbing M/W, sand volleyball M/W, table tennis M/W, volleyball M/W.

Costs (2016–17) *One-time required fee:* $40. *Tuition:* state resident $4095 full-time, $91 per credit part-time; nonresident $4095 full-time, $91 per credit part-time. Full-time tuition and fees vary according to program. Part-time tuition and fees vary according to program. *Required fees:* $1752 full-time, $29 per credit part-time, $60 per course part-time. *Room and board:* $7478. Room and board charges vary according to board plan. *Payment plans:* installment, deferred payment. *Waivers:* senior citizens and employees or children of employees.

Applying *Options:* electronic application, early admission. *Application fee:* $40. *Required for some:* high school transcript. *Application deadlines:* rolling (freshmen), rolling (transfers). *Notification:* continuous (freshmen), continuous (transfers).

Freshman Application Contact Miss Barb Shreckengost, Admissions, Southwestern Oregon Community College, 1988 Newmark Avenue, Coos Bay, OR 97420. *Phone:* 541-888-7636. *Toll-free phone:* 800-962-2838. *E-mail:* lwells@socc.edu. *Website:* http://www.socc.edu/.

Sumner College
Portland, Oregon

- **Proprietary** 2-year, founded 1974
- **Urban** campus with easy access to Portland
- **Coed, primarily women,** 261 undergraduate students, 100% full-time, 84% women, 16% men

Undergraduates 261 full-time. 10% are from out of state; 15% Black or African American, non-Hispanic/Latino; 6% Hispanic/Latino; 7% Asian, non-Hispanic/Latino; 0.8% Race/ethnicity unknown.

Freshmen *Admission:* 261 enrolled.

Faculty *Total:* 23, 52% full-time. *Student/faculty ratio:* 15:1.

Majors Court reporting; legal assistant/paralegal; registered nursing/registered nurse.

Academics *Calendar:* quarters. *Degree:* diplomas and associate. *Special study options:* academic remediation for entering students, distance learning.

Library Main Library plus 2 others. *Books:* 800 (physical); *Serial titles:* 100 (digital/electronic); *Databases:* 2. Weekly public service hours: 50; students can reserve study rooms.

Student Life *Housing:* college housing not available.

Applying *Required:* high school transcript, interview. *Required for some:* essay or personal statement, interview.

Freshman Application Contact Sumner College, 15115 SW Sequoia Parkway, Suite 200, Portland, OR 97224. *Website:* http://www.sumnercollege.edu/.

Tillamook Bay Community College
Tillamook, Oregon

Freshman Application Contact Lori Gates, Tillamook Bay Community College, 4301 Third Street, Tillamook, OR 97141. *Phone:* 503-842-8222. *Fax:* 503-842-2214. *E-mail:* gates@tillamookbay.cc. *Website:* http://www.tbcc.cc.or.us/.

Treasure Valley Community College
Ontario, Oregon

- **State and locally supported** 2-year, founded 1962
- **Rural** 90-acre campus with easy access to Boise
- **Coed,** 2,170 undergraduate students, 44% full-time, 57% women, 43% men

Undergraduates 958 full-time, 1,212 part-time. Students come from 15 states and territories; 2 other countries; 67% are from out of state; 2% Black or African American, non-Hispanic/Latino; 25% Hispanic/Latino; 0.7% Asian, non-Hispanic/Latino; 0.3% Native Hawaiian or other Pacific Islander, non-Hispanic/Latino; 1% American Indian or Alaska Native, non-Hispanic/Latino; 3% Two or more races, non-Hispanic/Latino; 4% Race/ethnicity unknown; 0.4% international; 5% transferred in; 6% live on campus. *Retention:* 40% of full-time freshmen returned.

Freshmen *Admission:* 2,447 applied, 2,447 admitted, 455 enrolled.

Faculty *Total:* 86, 55% full-time, 79% with terminal degrees. *Student/faculty ratio:* 21:1.

Majors Agricultural business and management; agricultural economics; agriculture; agronomy and crop science; airline pilot and flight crew; animal sciences; business/commerce; carpentry; computer and information sciences; criminal justice/police science; drafting and design technology; elementary education; farm and ranch management; fire prevention and safety technology; fire science/firefighting; horse husbandry/equine science and management; horticultural science; legal administrative assistant/secretary; management information systems; medical administrative assistant and medical secretary; medical transcription; natural resources/conservation; office management; range science and management; registered nursing/registered nurse; soil science and agronomy; solar energy technology; substance abuse/addiction counseling; welding technology; wildlife, fish and wildlands science and management.

Academics *Calendar:* quarters. *Degree:* certificates and associate. *Special study options:* academic remediation for entering students, accelerated degree program, adult/continuing education programs, advanced placement credit, cooperative education, distance learning, English as a second language, honors programs, independent study, internships, off-campus study, part-time degree program, services for LD students, summer session for credit.

Library Treasure Valley Community College Library. *Books:* 28,277 (physical), 276,342 (digital/electronic); *Serial titles:* 97 (physical), 15 (digital/electronic); *Databases:* 9. Weekly public service hours: 72; study areas open 24 hours, 5&-7 days a week; students can reserve study rooms.

Student Life *Housing Options:* coed. Campus housing is university owned. *Activities and Organizations:* choral group, Phi Theta Kappa, Natural Resources, International Business Club, Circle K International (service organization), Ag Ambassadors. *Campus security:* 24-hour emergency response devices, late-night transport/escort service, controlled dormitory access, emergency response phone and computer notifications.

Athletics *Intercollegiate sports:* baseball M(s), basketball M(s)/W(s), cross-country running M(s)/W(s), soccer M(s)/W(s), softball W(s), tennis M(s)/W(s), track and field M(s)/W(s), volleyball W(s). *Intramural sports:* basketball M/W, soccer M/W, softball M/W, table tennis M/W, volleyball M/W.

Costs (2016–17) *Tuition:* state resident $4320 full-time, $96 per credit part-time; nonresident $4770 full-time, $106 per credit part-time. *Required fees:* $990 full-time, $22 per credit part-time. *Room and board:* $7069; room only: $3763. Room and board charges vary according to board plan. *Waivers:* employees or children of employees.

Financial Aid Of all full-time matriculated undergraduates who enrolled in 2014, 90 Federal Work-Study jobs (averaging $1500).

Applying *Options:* electronic application, early admission, deferred entrance. *Application deadlines:* rolling (freshmen), rolling (out-of-state freshmen), rolling (transfers). *Notification:* continuous (freshmen), continuous (out-of-state freshmen), continuous (transfers).

Freshman Application Contact Kelly Young, Office of Admissions and Student Services, Treasure Valley Community College, 650 College Boulevard, Ontario, OR 97914. *Phone:* 541-881-5822. *E-mail:* kmyoung@tvcc.cc. *Website:* http://www.tvcc.cc/.

Umpqua Community College
Roseburg, Oregon

- **State and locally supported** 2-year, founded 1964
- **Rural** 100-acre campus
- **Endowment** $7.3 million
- **Coed**

Undergraduates 971 full-time, 1,075 part-time. Students come from 15 states and territories; 1% Black or African American, non-Hispanic/Latino; 12% Hispanic/Latino; 1% Asian, non-Hispanic/Latino; 0.3% Native Hawaiian or other Pacific Islander, non-Hispanic/Latino; 2% American Indian or Alaska Native, non-Hispanic/Latino; 5% Two or more races, non-Hispanic/Latino; 3% Race/ethnicity unknown; 22% transferred in. *Retention:* 48% of full-time freshmen returned.

Faculty *Student/faculty ratio:* 14:1.

Academics *Calendar:* quarters. *Degree:* certificates and associate. *Special study options:* academic remediation for entering students, accelerated degree program, adult/continuing education programs, advanced placement credit, cooperative education, distance learning, English as a second language, honors programs, independent study, internships, part-time degree program, services for LD students, study abroad, summer session for credit.

Library Umpqua Community College Library.

Student Life *Campus security:* 24-hour emergency response devices and patrols.
Financial Aid Of all full-time matriculated undergraduates who enrolled in 2014, 120 Federal Work-Study jobs (averaging $3000).
Applying *Options:* electronic application, early admission, deferred entrance. *Application fee:* $25. *Recommended:* high school transcript.
Freshman Application Contact Admissions Office, Umpqua Community College, PO Box 967, Roseburg, OR 97470-0226. *Phone:* 541-440-7743. *Fax:* 541-440-4612.
Website: http://www.umpqua.edu/.

PENNSYLVANIA

All-State Career School–Essington Campus
Essington, Pennsylvania
Admissions Office Contact All-State Career School–Essington Campus, 50 West Powhattan Ave, Essington, PA 19029.
Website: http://www.allstatecareer.edu/.

Antonelli Institute
Erdenheim, Pennsylvania
- **Proprietary** 2-year, founded 1938
- **Suburban** 15-acre campus with easy access to Philadelphia
- **Coed,** 188 undergraduate students
- 87% of applicants were admitted

Freshmen *Admission:* 200 applied, 173 admitted.
Majors Graphic design; photography.
Academics *Calendar:* semesters. *Degree:* associate.
Financial Aid Of all full-time matriculated undergraduates who enrolled in 2014, 5 Federal Work-Study jobs (averaging $2000).
Freshman Application Contact Admissions Office, Antonelli Institute, 300 Montgomery Avenue, Erdenheim, PA 19038. *Phone:* 800-722-7871. *Toll-free phone:* 800-722-7871.
Website: http://www.antonelli.edu/.

Berks Technical Institute
Wyomissing, Pennsylvania
Freshman Application Contact Mr. Allan Brussolo, Academic Dean, Berks Technical Institute, 2205 Ridgewood Road, Wyomissing, PA 19610-1168. *Phone:* 610-372-1722. *Toll-free phone:* 866-591-8384. *Fax:* 610-376-4684. *E-mail:* abrussolo@berks.edu.
Website: http://www.berks.edu/.

Bidwell Training Center
Pittsburgh, Pennsylvania
Freshman Application Contact Admissions Office, Bidwell Training Center, 1815 Metropolitan Street, Pittsburgh, PA 15233. *Phone:* 412-322-1773. *Toll-free phone:* 800-516-1800. *E-mail:* admissions@mcg-btc.org.
Website: http://www.bidwell-training.org/.

Bradford School
Pittsburgh, Pennsylvania
- **Proprietary** 2-year, founded 1968
- **Urban** campus
- **Coed,** 413 undergraduate students
- 84% of applicants were admitted

Freshmen *Admission:* 667 applied, 559 admitted.
Majors Accounting technology and bookkeeping; administrative assistant and secretarial science; computer programming; computer systems networking and telecommunications; dental assisting; graphic design; hotel/motel administration; legal administrative assistant/secretary; legal assistant/paralegal; medical/clinical assistant; retailing.
Academics *Calendar:* semesters. *Degree:* diplomas and associate. *Special study options:* accelerated degree program, internships.
Freshman Application Contact Admissions Office, Bradford School, 125 West Station Square Drive, Pittsburgh, PA 15219. *Phone:* 412-391-6710. *Toll-free phone:* 800-391-6810.
Website: http://www.bradfordpittsburgh.edu/.

Brightwood Career Institute, Broomall Campus
Broomall, Pennsylvania
Freshman Application Contact Brightwood Career Institute, Broomall Campus, 1991 Sproul Road, Suite 42, Broomall, PA 19008. *Phone:* 610-353-3300. *Toll-free phone:* 800-935-1857.
Website: http://www.brightwoodcareer.edu/.

Brightwood Career Institute, Harrisburg Campus
Harrisburg, Pennsylvania
Freshman Application Contact Brightwood Career Institute, Harrisburg Campus, 5650 Derry Street, Harrisburg, PA 17111-3518. *Phone:* 717-558-1300. *Toll-free phone:* 800-935-1857.
Website: http://www.brightwoodcareer.edu/.

Brightwood Career Institute, Philadelphia Campus
Philadelphia, Pennsylvania
Freshman Application Contact Admissions Director, Brightwood Career Institute, Philadelphia Campus, 3010 Market Street, Philadelphia, PA 19104. *Toll-free phone:* 800-935-1857.
Website: http://www.brightwoodcareer.edu/.

Brightwood Career Institute, Philadelphia Mills Campus
Philadelphia, Pennsylvania
Freshman Application Contact Brightwood Career Institute, Philadelphia Mills Campus, 177 Franklin Mills Boulevard, Philadelphia, PA 19154. *Phone:* 215-612-6600. *Toll-free phone:* 800-935-1857.
Website: http://www.brightwoodcareer.edu/.

Brightwood Career Institute, Pittsburgh Campus
Pittsburgh, Pennsylvania
Freshman Application Contact Brightwood Career Institute, Pittsburgh Campus, 933 Penn Avenue, Pittsburgh, PA 15222. *Phone:* 412-261-2647. *Toll-free phone:* 800-935-1857.
Website: http://www.brightwoodcareer.edu/.

Bucks County Community College
Newtown, Pennsylvania
- **County-supported** 2-year, founded 1964
- **Suburban** 200-acre campus with easy access to Philadelphia
- **Endowment** $6.3 million
- **Coed,** 8,611 undergraduate students, 34% full-time, 55% women, 45% men

Undergraduates 2,927 full-time, 5,684 part-time. Students come from 9 states and territories; 0.2% are from out of state; 5% Black or African American, non-Hispanic/Latino; 6% Hispanic/Latino; 3% Asian, non-Hispanic/Latino; 0.1% Native Hawaiian or other Pacific Islander, non-Hispanic/Latino; 0.9% American Indian or Alaska Native, non-Hispanic/Latino; 3% Two or more races, non-Hispanic/Latino; 21% Race/ethnicity unknown; 77% transferred in. *Retention:* 70% of full-time freshmen returned.
Freshmen *Admission:* 4,338 applied, 4,236 admitted, 2,055 enrolled.
Faculty *Total:* 691, 22% full-time, 23% with terminal degrees. *Student/faculty ratio:* 16:1.
Majors Accounting technology and bookkeeping; art history, criticism and conservation; baking and pastry arts; biology/biotechnology laboratory technician; biology teacher education; building/home/construction inspection; business administration and management; business, management, and marketing related; cabinetmaking and millwork; chemical technology; child-care provision; cinematography and film/video production; commercial and advertising art; commercial photography; computer and information sciences; computer systems networking and telecommunications; criminal justice/safety; culinary arts; early childhood education; engineering technology; English; environmental science; food service systems administration; health professions related; history; history teacher education;

human development and family studies; humanities; industrial technology; information science/studies; journalism; kinesiology and exercise science; legal professions and studies related; liberal arts and sciences and humanities related; liberal arts and sciences/liberal studies; mathematics; mathematics teacher education; medical/clinical assistant; medical insurance coding; multi/interdisciplinary studies related; music; network and system administration; neuroscience; physical education teaching and coaching; psychology; registered nursing/registered nurse; retailing; small business administration; speech communication and rhetoric; sport and fitness administration/management; tourism and travel services management; visual and performing arts; web page, digital/multimedia and information resources design.

Academics *Calendar:* semesters. *Degree:* certificates and associate. *Special study options:* academic remediation for entering students, adult/continuing education programs, advanced placement credit, cooperative education, distance learning, English as a second language, external degree program, independent study, internships, part-time degree program, services for LD students, student-designed majors, summer session for credit.

Library Bucks County Community College Library. *Books:* 113,651 (physical), 8,387 (digital/electronic); *Serial titles:* 299 (physical), 29 (digital/electronic); *Databases:* 48. Weekly public service hours: 72; students can reserve study rooms.

Student Life *Housing:* college housing not available. *Activities and Organizations:* drama/theater group, student-run newspaper, radio and television station, choral group, Phi Theta Kappa, Kappa Beta Delta, Students Student Success, Digital Gaming, Glass Arts. *Campus security:* 24-hour emergency response devices and patrols, late-night transport/escort service. *Student services:* personal/psychological counseling, women's center.

Athletics Member NJCAA. *Intercollegiate sports:* baseball M, basketball M, equestrian sports M/W, golf M, skiing (downhill) M/W, soccer M/W, tennis M/W, volleyball W. *Intramural sports:* baseball M, basketball M/W, equestrian sports M/W, football M, tennis M/W, ultimate Frisbee M/W, volleyball M.

Costs (2015–16) *Tuition:* area resident $4050 full-time, $135 per credit hour part-time; state resident $8100 full-time, $270 per credit hour part-time; nonresident $12,150 full-time, $405 per credit hour part-time. Full-time tuition and fees vary according to program. Part-time tuition and fees vary according to program. *Required fees:* $1160 full-time, $62 per credit hour part-time. *Payment plans:* installment, deferred payment. *Waivers:* senior citizens and employees or children of employees.

Financial Aid Of all full-time matriculated undergraduates who enrolled in 2015, 150 Federal Work-Study jobs (averaging $2095).

Applying *Options:* electronic application, early admission. *Required:* high school transcript. *Required for some:* essay or personal statement, interview.

Freshman Application Contact Ms. Marlene Barlow, Director of Admissions, Bucks County Community College, Newtown, PA 18940. *Phone:* 215-968-8137. *Fax:* 215-968-8110. *E-mail:* marlene.barlow@bucks.edu. *Website:* http://www.bucks.edu/.

Butler County Community College
Butler, Pennsylvania

- **County-supported** 2-year, founded 1965
- **Rural** 300-acre campus with easy access to Pittsburgh
- **Coed,** 3,573 undergraduate students, 48% full-time, 59% women, 41% men

Undergraduates 1,706 full-time, 1,867 part-time. 1% are from out of state; 3% Black or African American, non-Hispanic/Latino; 2% Hispanic/Latino; 0.3% Asian, non-Hispanic/Latino; 0.1% American Indian or Alaska Native, non-Hispanic/Latino; 1% Two or more races, non-Hispanic/Latino; 17% Race/ethnicity unknown; 0.2% international.

Faculty Total: 351. Student/faculty ratio: 18:1.

Majors Administrative assistant and secretarial science; architectural drafting and CAD/CADD; biology/biological sciences; business administration and management; business/commerce; business, management, and marketing related; CAD/CADD drafting/design technology; civil engineering technology; computer and information sciences; computer and information systems security; computer programming (specific applications); computer technology/computer systems technology; cooking and related culinary arts; corrections; cosmetology; criminal justice/law enforcement administration; criminal justice/police science; digital communication and media/multimedia; education; electrical, electronic and communications engineering technology; elementary education; engineering; English; fine arts related; fire science/firefighting; food service systems administration; food technology and processing; general studies; health and medical administrative services related; health/health-care administration; heating, air conditioning, ventilation and refrigeration maintenance technology; homeland security; homeland security, law enforcement, firefighting and protective services related; hospitality

administration related; human resources management; instrumentation technology; kindergarten/preschool education; legal administrative assistant/secretary; machine shop technology; machine tool technology; manufacturing engineering technology; massage therapy; mathematics; mechanical drafting and CAD/CADD; medical insurance coding; medical office assistant; network and system administration; office occupations and clerical services; organizational communication; parks, recreation and leisure facilities management; photography; physical sciences; physical therapy technology; precision production trades; psychology; radiologic technology/science; registered nursing/registered nurse; robotics technology; selling skills and sales; social work related; sport and fitness administration/management; web page, digital/multimedia and information resources design.

Academics *Calendar:* semesters. *Degree:* certificates and associate. *Special study options:* academic remediation for entering students, adult/continuing education programs, advanced placement credit, cooperative education, distance learning, English as a second language, internships, part-time degree program, services for LD students, summer session for credit.

Library John A. Beck, Jr. Library. *Books:* 60,000 (digital/electronic).

Student Life *Housing:* college housing not available. *Activities and Organizations:* student-run newspaper. *Campus security:* 24-hour emergency response devices, late-night transport/escort service. *Student services:* personal/psychological counseling.

Athletics Member NJCAA. *Intercollegiate sports:* baseball M, basketball M, golf M/W, softball W, volleyball W. *Intramural sports:* basketball M/W, table tennis M/W, volleyball M/W.

Costs (2015–16) *Tuition:* area resident $4110 full-time; state resident $6990 full-time; nonresident $9870 full-time. *Required fees:* $930 full-time. *Payment plan:* installment. *Waivers:* employees or children of employees.

Financial Aid Of all full-time matriculated undergraduates who enrolled in 2015, 77 Federal Work-Study jobs (averaging $1595).

Applying *Options:* electronic application. *Application fee:* $25. *Required:* high school transcript. *Required for some:* interview. *Application deadlines:* 8/15 (freshmen), 8/15 (transfers). *Notification:* continuous until 8/15 (freshmen), continuous until 8/15 (transfers).

Freshman Application Contact Mr. Robert Morris, Director of Admissions, Butler County Community College, College Drive, PO Box 1205, Butler, PA 16003-1203. *Phone:* 724-287-8711 Ext. 344. *Toll-free phone:* 888-826-2829. *Fax:* 724-287-4961. *E-mail:* robert.morris@bc3.edu. *Website:* http://www.bc3.edu/.

Cambria-Rowe Business College
Indiana, Pennsylvania

- **Proprietary** 2-year, founded 1959
- **Small-town** 1-acre campus
- **Coed**
- 60% of applicants were admitted

Undergraduates 92 full-time, 1 part-time. 1% Asian, non-Hispanic/Latino; 1% American Indian or Alaska Native, non-Hispanic/Latino; 2% Two or more races, non-Hispanic/Latino. *Retention:* 64% of full-time freshmen returned.

Faculty *Student/faculty ratio:* 13:1.

Academics *Calendar:* quarters. *Degree:* diplomas and associate. *Special study options:* part-time degree program.

Library LIRN.

Costs (2015–16) *Comprehensive fee:* $20,625 includes full-time tuition ($13,200) and room and board ($7425). Full-time tuition and fees vary according to course level and course load. Part-time tuition: $250 per credit. Part-time tuition and fees vary according to course level and course load. *Room and board:* Room and board charges vary according to housing facility and location.

Applying *Options:* electronic application. *Application fee:* $30. *Required:* high school transcript. *Recommended:* interview.

Freshman Application Contact Mrs. Stacey Bell-Leger, Representative at Indiana Campus, Cambria-Rowe Business College, 422 South 13th Street, Indiana, PA 15701. *Phone:* 724-463-0222. *Toll-free phone:* 800-NEW-CAREER. *Fax:* 724-463-7246. *E-mail:* sbell-leger@crbc.net. *Website:* http://www.crbc.edu/.

Cambria-Rowe Business College
Johnstown, Pennsylvania

Freshman Application Contact Mrs. Riley McDonald, Admissions Representative, Cambria-Rowe Business College, 221 Central Avenue, Johnstown, PA 15902. *Phone:* 814-536-5168. *Toll-free phone:* 800-NEWCAREER. *Fax:* 814-536-5160. *E-mail:* admissions@crbc.net. *Website:* http://www.crbc.edu/.

Career Training Academy
Lower Burrell, Pennsylvania

- **Proprietary** 2-year, founded 1986
- **Coed, primarily women**

Faculty *Total:* 96. *Student/faculty ratio:* 20:1.

Majors Massage therapy; medical/clinical assistant; medical insurance coding.

Academics *Calendar:* quarters. *Degrees:* diplomas and associate (profile includes branch campuses in Monroeville and Pittsburgh, PA).

Student Life *Housing:* college housing not available. *Student services:* personal/psychological counseling.

Costs (2015–16) *Tuition:* $10,549 full-time. Full-time tuition and fees vary according to program. No tuition increase for student's term of enrollment. *Payment plans:* tuition prepayment, installment.

Applying *Application fee:* $30. *Required:* essay or personal statement, high school transcript, minimum 1.5 GPA, interview. *Application deadlines:* rolling (freshmen), rolling (transfers). *Notification:* continuous (freshmen), continuous (transfers).

Director of Admissions Ms. Tyna Pitignano, Career Training Academy, 179 Hillcrest Shopping Center, Lower Burrell, PA 15068. *Phone:* 724-337-1000. *Toll-free phone:* 866-673-7773. *E-mail:* admissions@careerta.edu. *Website:* http://www.careerta.edu/.

Career Training Academy
Monroeville, Pennsylvania

Freshman Application Contact Career Training Academy, 4314 Old William Penn Highway, Suite 103, Monroeville, PA 15146. *Phone:* 412-372-3900. *Toll-free phone:* 866-673-7773. *Website:* http://www.careerta.edu/.

Career Training Academy
Pittsburgh, Pennsylvania

- **Proprietary** 2-year
- **Suburban** campus with easy access to Pittsburgh
- **Coed**

Undergraduates 70 full-time. Students come from 1 other state; 33% Black or African American, non-Hispanic/Latino; 4% Hispanic/Latino; 1% Native Hawaiian or other Pacific Islander, non-Hispanic/Latino.

Faculty *Student/faculty ratio:* 9:1.

Academics *Calendar:* continuous. *Degree:* diplomas and associate. *Special study options:* academic remediation for entering students, advanced placement credit, cooperative education, internships, services for LD students.

Library Career Training Academy.

Student Life *Campus security:* 24-hour emergency response devices and patrols, late-night transport/escort service.

Applying *Application fee:* $30. *Required:* essay or personal statement, high school transcript, minimum 1.5 GPA, interview.

Freshman Application Contact Jaimie Vignone, Career Training Academy, 1014 West View Park Drive, Pittsburgh, PA 15229. *Phone:* 412-367-4000. *Toll-free phone:* 866-673-7773. *Fax:* 412-369-7223. *E-mail:* admission3@careerta.edu. *Website:* http://www.careerta.edu/.

Commonwealth Technical Institute
Johnstown, Pennsylvania

- **State-supported** 2-year
- **Suburban** 59-acre campus
- **Coed**

Undergraduates 222 full-time. Students come from 4 states and territories; 1% are from out of state; 7% Black or African American, non-Hispanic/Latino; 1% Asian, non-Hispanic/Latino; 0.5% Two or more races, non-Hispanic/Latino; 25% Race/ethnicity unknown. *Retention:* 74% of full-time freshmen returned.

Faculty *Student/faculty ratio:* 15:1.

Academics *Calendar:* trimesters. *Degree:* diplomas and associate. *Special study options:* academic remediation for entering students, advanced placement credit, services for LD students.

Library Commonwealth Technical Institute at the Hiram G. Andrews Center Library.

Student Life *Campus security:* 24-hour patrols, controlled dormitory access.

Costs (2015–16) *Tuition:* state resident $11,224 full-time. *Room and board:* $5490.

Financial Aid Of all full-time matriculated undergraduates who enrolled in 2011, 403 applied for aid, 259 were judged to have need. 35 Federal Work-Study jobs (averaging $1000). *Average percent of need met:* 30. *Average financial aid package:* $2500. *Average need-based gift aid:* $2500.

Applying *Required for some:* high school transcript. *Recommended:* high school transcript.

Freshman Application Contact Mr. Jason Gies, Admissions Supervisor, Commonwealth Technical Institute, Commonwealth Technical Institute @ Hiram G. Andrews Center, 727 Goucher Street, Johnstown, PA 15905. *Phone:* 814-255-8200 Ext. 0564. *Toll-free phone:* 800-762-4211. *Fax:* 814-255-8283. *E-mail:* jgies@pa.gov. *Website:* http://www.portal.state.pa.us/portal/server.pt/community/commonwealth_tech nical_institute/10361.

Community College of Allegheny County
Pittsburgh, Pennsylvania

- **County-supported** 2-year, founded 1966
- **Urban** 242-acre campus
- **Coed**

Undergraduates 6,009 full-time, 11,139 part-time. 2% are from out of state.

Academics *Calendar:* semesters. *Degree:* certificates, diplomas, and associate. *Special study options:* part-time degree program.

Library Community College of Allegheny County Library.

Student Life *Campus security:* 24-hour emergency response devices and patrols, late-night transport/escort service.

Athletics Member NJCAA.

Costs (2015–16) *Tuition:* area resident $3143 full-time, $105 per credit part-time; state resident $6285 full-time, $210 per credit part-time; nonresident $9428 full-time, $314 per credit part-time. Full-time tuition and fees vary according to program. Part-time tuition and fees vary according to program.

Applying *Options:* early decision, early action. *Recommended:* high school transcript.

Freshman Application Contact Admissions Office, Community College of Allegheny County, 808 Ridge Avenue, Pittsburgh, PA 15212. *Phone:* 412-237-2511. *Website:* http://www.ccac.edu/.

Community College of Beaver County
Monaca, Pennsylvania

Freshman Application Contact Enrollment Management, Community College of Beaver County, One Campus Drive, Monaca, PA 15061-2588. *Phone:* 724-480-3500. *Toll-free phone:* 800-335-0222. *E-mail:* admissions@ccbc.edu. *Website:* http://www.ccbc.edu/.

Community College of Philadelphia
Philadelphia, Pennsylvania

- **State and locally supported** 2-year, founded 1964
- **Urban** 14-acre campus
- **Coed**, 34,337 undergraduate students

Undergraduates Students come from 50 other countries.

Faculty *Total:* 1,050, 39% full-time.

Majors Accounting; architectural engineering technology; art; automobile/automotive mechanics technology; business administration and management; chemical technology; clinical/medical laboratory technology; computer science; construction engineering technology; criminal justice/law enforcement administration; culinary arts; dental hygiene; drafting and design technology; education; engineering; engineering technology; facilities planning and management; finance; fire science/firefighting; forensic science and technology; health information/medical records administration; health professions related; hotel/motel administration; human services; kindergarten/preschool education; liberal arts and sciences/liberal studies; medical radiologic technology; music; photography; pre-engineering; psychology; recording arts technology; registered nursing/registered nurse; respiratory care therapy; sign language interpretation and translation.

Academics *Calendar:* semesters. *Degree:* certificates, diplomas, and associate. *Special study options:* academic remediation for entering students, accelerated degree program, adult/continuing education programs, advanced placement credit, cooperative education, distance learning, English as a second language, external degree program, honors programs, independent study, internships, off-campus study, part-time degree program, services for LD students, student-designed majors, study abroad, summer session for credit. *ROTC:* Army (c).

Library Main Campus Library plus 2 others. Students can reserve study rooms.

Student Life *Housing:* college housing not available. *Activities and Organizations:* drama/theater group, student-run newspaper, choral group,

Philadelphia L.E.A.D.S, Phi Theta Kappa, Student Government Association, Vanguard Student Newspaper, Fundraising Club. *Campus security:* 24-hour emergency response devices and patrols, phone/alert systems in classrooms/buildings, electronic messages/alerts, ID required to enter buildings. *Student services:* personal/psychological counseling, women's center.

Athletics Member NJCAA. *Intercollegiate sports:* basketball M/W, cheerleading M/W, cross-country running M/W, tennis M/W, track and field M/W, volleyball W. *Intramural sports:* soccer M/W, volleyball M/W.

Costs (2015–16) *Tuition:* area resident $4440 full-time, $153 per credit hour part-time; state resident $8880 full-time, $306 per credit hour part-time; nonresident $13,320 full-time, $459 per credit hour part-time. Full-time tuition and fees vary according to course load and program. Part-time tuition and fees vary according to course load and program. *Payment plan:* installment. *Waivers:* senior citizens and employees or children of employees.

Applying *Options:* electronic application, early admission, deferred entrance. *Required for some:* high school transcript, specific entry requirements for allied health and nursing programs. *Application deadlines:* rolling (freshmen), rolling (transfers). *Notification:* continuous (freshmen), continuous (transfers). **Freshman Application Contact** Community College of Philadelphia, 1700 Spring Garden Street, Philadelphia, PA 19130-3991. *Phone:* 215-751-8010. *Website:* http://www.ccp.edu/.

Consolidated School of Business
Lancaster, Pennsylvania

Freshman Application Contact Ms. Libby Paul, Admissions Representative, Consolidated School of Business, 2124 Ambassador Circle, Lancaster, PA 17603. *Phone:* 717-394-6211. *Toll-free phone:* 800-541-8298. *Fax:* 717-394-6213. *E-mail:* lpaul@csb.edu. *Website:* http://www.csb.edu/.

Consolidated School of Business
York, Pennsylvania

Freshman Application Contact Ms. Sandra Swanger, Admissions Representative, Consolidated School of Business, 1605 Clugston Road, York, PA 17404. *Phone:* 717-764-9550. *Toll-free phone:* 800-520-0691. *Fax:* 717-764-9469. *E-mail:* sswanger@csb.edu. *Website:* http://www.csb.edu/.

Dean Institute of Technology
Pittsburgh, Pennsylvania

Director of Admissions Mr. Richard D. Ali, Admissions Director, Dean Institute of Technology, 1501 West Liberty Avenue, Pittsburgh, PA 15226-1103. *Phone:* 412-531-4433. *Website:* http://www.deantech.edu/.

Delaware County Community College
Media, Pennsylvania

Freshman Application Contact Ms. Hope Diehl, Director of Admissions and Enrollment Services, Delaware County Community College, 901 South Media Line Road, Media, PA 19063-1094. *Phone:* 610-359-5050. *Fax:* 610-723-1530. *E-mail:* admiss@dccc.edu. *Website:* http://www.dccc.edu/.

Douglas Education Center
Monessen, Pennsylvania

Freshman Application Contact Ms. Sherry Lee Walters, Director of Enrollment Services, Douglas Education Center, 130 Seventh Street, Monessen, PA 15062. *Phone:* 724-684-3684 Ext. 2181. *Toll-free phone:* 800-413-6013. *Website:* http://www.dec.edu/.

DuBois Business College
DuBois, Pennsylvania

Director of Admissions Terry Khoury, Director of Admissions, DuBois Business College, 1 Beaver Drive, DuBois, PA 15801. *Phone:* 814-371-6920. *Toll-free phone:* 800-692-6213. *Fax:* 814-371-3947. *E-mail:* dotylj@dbcollege.com. *Website:* http://www.dbcollege.edu/.

DuBois Business College
Huntingdon, Pennsylvania

Admissions Office Contact DuBois Business College, 1001 Moore Street, Huntingdon, PA 16652. *Website:* http://www.dbcollege.edu/.

DuBois Business College
Oil City, Pennsylvania

Admissions Office Contact DuBois Business College, 701 East Third Street, Oil City, PA 16301. *Website:* http://www.dbcollege.edu/.

Erie Institute of Technology
Erie, Pennsylvania

Freshman Application Contact Erie Institute of Technology, 940 Millcreek Mall, Erie, PA 16565. *Phone:* 814-868-9900. *Toll-free phone:* 866-868-3743. *Website:* http://www.erieit.edu/.

Fortis Institute
Erie, Pennsylvania

Director of Admissions Guy M. Euliano, President, Fortis Institute, 5757 West 26th Street, Erie, PA 16506. *Phone:* 814-838-7673. *Toll-free phone:* 855-4-FORTIS. *Fax:* 814-838-8642. *E-mail:* geuliano@tsbi.org. *Website:* http://www.fortis.edu/.

Fortis Institute
Forty Fort, Pennsylvania

Freshman Application Contact Admissions Office, Fortis Institute, 166 Slocum Street, Forty Fort, PA 18704. *Phone:* 570-288-8400. *Toll-free phone:* 855-4-FORTIS. *Website:* http://www.fortis.edu/.

Fortis Institute
Scranton, Pennsylvania

Director of Admissions Ms. Heather Contardi, Director of Admissions, Fortis Institute, 517 Ash Street, Scranton, PA 18509. *Phone:* 570-558-1818. *Toll-free phone:* 855-4-FORTIS. *Fax:* 570-342-4537. *E-mail:* heatherp@markogroup.com. *Website:* http://www.fortis.edu/.

Great Lakes Institute of Technology
Erie, Pennsylvania

Admissions Office Contact Great Lakes Institute of Technology, 5100 Peach Street, Erie, PA 16509. *Website:* http://www.glit.edu/.

Harcum College
Bryn Mawr, Pennsylvania

Freshman Application Contact Office of Enrollment Management, Harcum College, 750 Montgomery Avenue, Bryn Mawr, PA 19010-3476. *Phone:* 610-526-6050. *E-mail:* enroll@harcum.edu. *Website:* http://www.harcum.edu/.

Harrisburg Area Community College
Harrisburg, Pennsylvania

- **State and locally supported** 2-year, founded 1964
- **Urban** 212-acre campus
- **Coed,** 19,121 undergraduate students, 29% full-time, 63% women, 37% men

Undergraduates 5,516 full-time, 13,605 part-time. 2% are from out of state; 11% Black or African American, non-Hispanic/Latino; 10% Hispanic/Latino; 3% Asian, non-Hispanic/Latino; 0.2% Native Hawaiian or other Pacific Islander, non-Hispanic/Latino; 0.3% American Indian or Alaska Native, non-Hispanic/Latino; 3% Two or more races, non-Hispanic/Latino; 2% Race/ethnicity unknown; 2% international; 7% transferred in.

Freshmen *Admission:* 12,163 applied, 12,153 admitted, 2,561 enrolled.

Faculty *Total:* 1,091, 31% full-time, 46% with terminal degrees. *Student/faculty ratio:* 17:1.

Majors Accounting technology and bookkeeping; administrative assistant and secretarial science; adult development and aging; architectural engineering technology; architecture; automobile/automotive mechanics technology; banking and financial support services; biology/biological sciences; business administration and management; business/commerce; cardiovascular technology; chemistry; civil engineering technology; clinical/medical laboratory technology; communication and journalism related; computer and information sciences; computer and information systems security; computer science; computer systems networking and telecommunications; construction engineering technology; construction trades; criminal justice/law enforcement administration; criminal justice/police science; culinary arts; dental hygiene; design and visual communications; diagnostic medical sonography and ultrasound technology; dietetics; dramatic/theater arts; early childhood education; electrical, electronic and communications engineering technology; electrician; emergency medical technology (EMT paramedic); engineering; engineering technologies and engineering related; environmental science; environmental studies; fire science/firefighting; general studies; geographic information science and cartography; graphic design; health/health-care administration; health professions related; health services administration; heating, air conditioning, ventilation and refrigeration maintenance technology; human services; international relations and affairs; legal assistant/paralegal; mathematics; mechanical engineering/mechanical technology; mechatronics, robotics, and automation engineering; medical/clinical assistant; medical informatics; music management; nuclear medical technology; philosophy; photography; physical sciences; psychology; radiologic technology/science; real estate; registered nursing/registered nurse; respiratory care therapy; sales, distribution, and marketing operations; secondary education; social sciences; social work; structural engineering; surgical technology; visual and performing arts; viticulture and enology; web page, digital/multimedia and information resources design.

Academics *Calendar:* semesters. *Degree:* certificates, diplomas, and associate. *Special study options:* academic remediation for entering students, adult/continuing education programs, advanced placement credit, distance learning, double majors, English as a second language, honors programs, independent study, internships, part-time degree program, services for LD students, summer session for credit. *ROTC:* Army (b).

Library McCormick Library.

Student Life *Housing:* college housing not available. *Activities and Organizations:* drama/theater group, student-run newspaper, Student Government Association, Phi Theta Kappa, African-American Student Association, Mosiaco Club, Fourth Estate. *Campus security:* 24-hour emergency response devices and patrols, late-night transport/escort service.

Athletics *Intercollegiate sports:* basketball M/W, soccer M, tennis M/W. *Intramural sports:* basketball M/W, soccer M/W, swimming and diving M/W, tennis M/W, volleyball M/W.

Costs (2015–16) *Tuition:* area resident $3900 full-time, $163 per credit hour part-time; state resident $4968 full-time, $207 per credit hour part-time; nonresident $6000 full-time, $250 per credit hour part-time. Full-time tuition and fees vary according to location and program. Part-time tuition and fees vary according to location and program. *Required fees:* $1032 full-time, $48 per credit hour part-time. *Payment plan:* installment. *Waivers:* employees or children of employees.

Financial Aid Of all full-time matriculated undergraduates who enrolled in 2015, 5,159 applied for aid.

Applying *Options:* electronic application, early admission, deferred entrance. *Application fee:* $35. *Required for some:* high school transcript, 1 letter of recommendation, interview.

Freshman Application Contact Mr. Matt Huber, Director of Admissions, Harrisburg Area Community College, Harrisburg, PA 17110. *Phone:* 717-736-4138. *Toll-free phone:* 800-ABC-HACC. *Fax:* 717-231-7674. *E-mail:* admit@hacc.edu. *Website:* http://www.hacc.edu/.

Hussian College, School of Art
Philadelphia, Pennsylvania

- **Proprietary** primarily 2-year, founded 1946
- **Urban** 1-acre campus with easy access to Philadelphia
- **Coed**, 83 undergraduate students, 99% full-time, 52% women, 48% men

Undergraduates 82 full-time, 1 part-time. 20% Black or African American, non-Hispanic/Latino; 14% Hispanic/Latino; 6% Asian, non-Hispanic/Latino.

Freshmen *Admission:* 126 applied, 31 admitted, 17 enrolled. *Average high school GPA:* 2.5.

Majors Advertising; commercial and advertising art.

Academics *Calendar:* semesters. *Degree:* bachelor's. *Special study options:* independent study, internships.

Library Hussian Library. *Books:* 4,000 (physical); *Serial titles:* 15 (physical); *Databases:* 100.

Student Life *Housing Options:* Campus housing is provided by a third party. *Campus security:* 24-hour patrols.

Costs (2016–17) *Tuition:* $18,600 full-time. Full-time tuition and fees vary according to course load. Part-time tuition and fees vary according to course load. *Payment plan:* installment.

Applying *Options:* electronic application, deferred entrance. *Required:* high school transcript, interview, portfolio evaluation, creative assessment activity or portfolio development drawing workshop. *Recommended:* minimum 2.5 GPA. *Application deadlines:* rolling (freshmen), rolling (transfers). *Notification:* continuous (freshmen), continuous (transfers).

Freshman Application Contact Mr. Mark Cernero, Director of Admissions, Hussian College, School of Art, The Bourse, Suite 300, 111 South Independence Mall East, Philadelphia, PA 19106. *Phone:* 215-574-9600. *Fax:* 215-574-9800. *E-mail:* mcernero@hussianart.edu. *Website:* http://www.hussianart.edu/.

ITT Technical Institute
Harrisburg, Pennsylvania

Freshman Application Contact Director of Recruitment, ITT Technical Institute, 449 Eisenhower Boulevard, Suite 100, Harrisburg, PA 17111. *Phone:* 717-565-1700. *Toll-free phone:* 800-847-4756. *Website:* http://www.itt-tech.edu/.

ITT Technical Institute
Levittown, Pennsylvania

Freshman Application Contact Director of Recruitment, ITT Technical Institute, 311 Veterans Highway, Suite 100E, Levittown, PA 19056. *Phone:* 215-702-6300. *Toll-free phone:* 866-488-8324. *Website:* http://www.itt-tech.edu/.

ITT Technical Institute
Philadelphia, Pennsylvania

Freshman Application Contact Director of Recruiting, ITT Technical Institute, 105 South 7th Street, Suite 100, Philadelphia, PA 19106. *Phone:* 215-413-4300. *Toll-free phone:* 877-215-7835. *Website:* http://www.itt-tech.edu/.

ITT Technical Institute
Pittsburgh, Pennsylvania

Freshman Application Contact Director of Recruitment, ITT Technical Institute, 5460 Campbells Run Road, Pittsburgh, PA 15205. *Phone:* 412-446-2900. *Toll-free phone:* 800-353-8324. *Website:* http://www.itt-tech.edu/.

ITT Technical Institute
Plymouth Meeting, Pennsylvania

Freshman Application Contact Director of Recruitment, ITT Technical Institute, 220 West Germantown Pike, Suite 100, Plymouth Meeting, PA 19462. *Phone:* 610-832-3400. *Toll-free phone:* 866-902-8324. *Website:* http://www.itt-tech.edu/.

JNA Institute of Culinary Arts
Philadelphia, Pennsylvania

- **Proprietary** 2-year, founded 1988
- **Urban** campus with easy access to Philadelphia
- **Coed**

Undergraduates 59 full-time. Students come from 7 states and territories; 10% are from out of state; 57% Black or African American, non-Hispanic/Latino; 11% Hispanic/Latino; 3% Asian, non-Hispanic/Latino. *Retention:* 60% of full-time freshmen returned.

Academics *Calendar:* continuous. *Degree:* associate.

Costs (2015–16) *One-time required fee:* $75. *Tuition:* $12,650 full-time, $375 per credit hour part-time. Full-time tuition and fees vary according to program. No tuition increase for student's term of enrollment.

Freshman Application Contact Admissions Office, JNA Institute of Culinary Arts, 1212 South Broad Street, Philadelphia, PA 19146. *Website:* http://www.culinaryarts.com/.

Johnson College
Scranton, Pennsylvania

Freshman Application Contact Ms. Melissa Ide, Director of Enrollment Management, Johnson College, 3427 North Main Avenue, Scranton, PA 18508. *Phone:* 570-702-8910. *Toll-free phone:* 800-2WE-WORK. *Fax:* 570-348-2181. *E-mail:* admit@johnson.edu.
Website: http://www.johnson.edu/.

Keystone Technical Institute
Harrisburg, Pennsylvania

Freshman Application Contact Tom Bogush, Director of Admissions, Keystone Technical Institute, 2301 Academy Drive, Harrisburg, PA 17112. *Phone:* 717-545-4747. *Toll-free phone:* 800-400-3322. *Fax:* 717-901-9090. *E-mail:* info@acadcampus.com.
Website: http://www.kti.edu/.

Lackawanna College
Scranton, Pennsylvania

- **Independent** 2-year, founded 1894
- **Urban** 4-acre campus
- **Endowment** $1.9 million
- **Coed,** 1,679 undergraduate students, 69% full-time, 49% women, 51% men

Undergraduates 1,158 full-time, 521 part-time. 17% Black or African American, non-Hispanic/Latino; 8% Hispanic/Latino; 2% Asian, non-Hispanic/Latino; 0.1% Native Hawaiian or other Pacific Islander, non-Hispanic/Latino; 0.2% American Indian or Alaska Native, non-Hispanic/Latino; 2% Two or more races, non-Hispanic/Latino; 5% Race/ethnicity unknown; 0.2% international; 20% live on campus. *Retention:* 50% of full-time freshmen returned.
Freshmen *Admission:* 2,048 applied, 893 admitted, 334 enrolled. *Test scores:* SAT critical reading scores over 500: 19%; SAT math scores over 500: 23%; SAT writing scores over 500: 15%; SAT critical reading scores over 600: 2%; SAT math scores over 600: 3%; SAT writing scores over 600: 1%.
Faculty *Total:* 168, 16% full-time, 5% with terminal degrees. *Student/faculty ratio:* 16:1.
Majors Accounting; accounting technology and bookkeeping; administrative assistant and secretarial science; banking and financial support services; biology/biological sciences; biotechnology; business administration and management; business administration, management and operations related; business/commerce; cardiopulmonary technology; communications technology; computer and information sciences; criminal justice/safety; diagnostic medical sonography and ultrasound technology; early childhood education; education; emergency medical technology (EMT paramedic); environmental studies; general studies; humanities; human services; industrial electronics technology; industrial technology; legal assistant/paralegal; liberal arts and sciences/liberal studies; management information systems; mass communication/media; medical administrative assistant and medical secretary; mental health counseling; petroleum technology; speech communication and rhetoric; surgical technology.
Academics *Calendar:* semesters. *Degree:* certificates, diplomas, and associate. *Special study options:* academic remediation for entering students, adult/continuing education programs, cooperative education, double majors, English as a second language, internships, part-time degree program, services for LD students, summer session for credit. *ROTC:* Army (c), Air Force (c).
Library Seeley Memorial Library. Students can reserve study rooms.
Student Life *Housing:* on-campus residence required through sophomore year. *Options:* coed, men-only. Campus housing is university owned. *Activities and Organizations:* drama/theater group, student-run newspaper, choral group, Student Government, Student/Alumni Association, United Cultures Leadership Association, Green Falcons (sustainability action group), Sonography Club. *Campus security:* 24-hour emergency response devices and patrols, late-night transport/escort service, controlled dormitory access, patrols by college liaison staff. *Student services:* personal/psychological counseling.
Athletics Member NJCAA. *Intercollegiate sports:* baseball M(s), basketball M(s)/W(s), cheerleading W(s), cross-country running M(s)/W(s), football M(s), golf M(s)/W(s), soccer W(s), softball W(s), volleyball W(s).
Standardized Tests *Recommended:* SAT (for admission), ACT (for admission), SAT or ACT (for admission).
Costs (2015–16) *Comprehensive fee:* $22,410 includes full-time tuition ($13,400), mandatory fees ($710), and room and board ($8300). Full-time tuition and fees vary according to course load. Part-time tuition: $465 per credit. *Required fees:* $105 per term part-time. *Room and board:* college room only: $5800. *Payment plans:* installment, deferred payment. *Waivers:* employees or children of employees.

Financial Aid Of all full-time matriculated undergraduates who enrolled in 2015, 1,047 applied for aid, 984 were judged to have need, 42 had their need fully met. 82 Federal Work-Study jobs (averaging $961). 22 state and other part-time jobs (averaging $517). In 2015, 11 non-need-based awards were made. *Average percent of need met:* 50%. *Average financial aid package:* $9289. *Average need-based loan:* $3277. *Average need-based gift aid:* $6925. *Average non-need-based aid:* $2854. *Average indebtedness upon graduation:* $19,780.
Applying *Options:* electronic application, early admission, deferred entrance. *Application fee:* $30. *Required:* high school transcript, interview. *Application deadlines:* rolling (freshmen), rolling (out-of-state freshmen), rolling (transfers).
Freshman Application Contact Ms. Stacey Muchal, Associate Director of Admissions, Lackawanna College, 501 Vine Street, Scranton, PA 18509. *Phone:* 570-961-7868. *Toll-free phone:* 877-346-3552. *Fax:* 570-961-7843. *E-mail:* muchals@lackawanna.edu.
Website: http://www.lackawanna.edu/.

Lancaster County Career and Technology Center
Willow Street, Pennsylvania

Admissions Office Contact Lancaster County Career and Technology Center, 1730 Hans Herr Drive, Willow Street, PA 17584.
Website: http://www.lcctc.org/.

Lansdale School of Business
North Wales, Pennsylvania

Director of Admissions Ms. Marianne H. Johnson, Director of Admissions, Lansdale School of Business, 201 Church Road, North Wales, PA 19454-4148. *Phone:* 215-699-5700 Ext. 112. *Toll-free phone:* 800-219-0486. *Fax:* 215-699-8770. *E-mail:* mjohnson@lsb.edu.
Website: http://www.lsb.edu/.

Laurel Business Institute
Uniontown, Pennsylvania

Freshman Application Contact Mrs. Lisa Dolan, Laurel Business Institute, 11 East Penn Street, PO Box 877, Uniontown, PA 15401. *Phone:* 724-439-4900 Ext. 158. *Fax:* 724-439-3607. *E-mail:* ldolan@laurel.edu.
Website: http://www.laurel.edu/lbi/.

Laurel Technical Institute
Sharon, Pennsylvania

Freshman Application Contact Irene Lewis, Laurel Technical Institute, 200 Sterling Avenue, Sharon, PA 16146. *Phone:* 724-983-0700. *Fax:* 724-983-8355. *E-mail:* info@biop.edu.
Website: http://www.laurel.edu/lti/.

Lehigh Carbon Community College
Schnecksville, Pennsylvania

- **State and locally supported** 2-year, founded 1967
- **Suburban** 254-acre campus with easy access to Philadelphia
- **Endowment** $4.2 million
- **Coed,** 6,738 undergraduate students, 38% full-time, 60% women, 40% men

Undergraduates 2,577 full-time, 4,161 part-time. Students come from 10 states and territories; 17 other countries; 0.3% are from out of state; 6% Black or African American, non-Hispanic/Latino; 11% Hispanic/Latino; 2% Asian, non-Hispanic/Latino; 0.2% American Indian or Alaska Native, non-Hispanic/Latino; 4% Two or more races, non-Hispanic/Latino; 13% Race/ethnicity unknown; 0.4% international; 58% transferred in.
Freshmen *Admission:* 4,354 applied, 4,354 admitted, 1,405 enrolled.
Faculty *Total:* 443, 20% full-time, 5% with terminal degrees. *Student/faculty ratio:* 19:1.
Majors Accounting technology and bookkeeping; aeronautics/aviation/aerospace science and technology; airline pilot and flight crew; animation, interactive technology, video graphics and special effects; art; biology/biological sciences; biotechnology; building/construction site management; business administration and management; business/commerce; chemical technology; chemistry; computer and information sciences; computer and information systems security; computer programming; computer programming (specific applications); computer systems networking and telecommunications; construction trades; criminal justice/law enforcement

administration; criminal justice/safety; drafting and design technology; early childhood education; education; electrical, electronic and communications engineering technology; engineering; environmental science; fashion/apparel design; game and interactive media design; general studies; geographic information science and cartography; graphic design; health information/medical records technology; health services/allied health/health sciences; heating, air conditioning, ventilation and refrigeration maintenance technology; human resources management; human services; industrial electronics technology; interior design; kinesiology and exercise science; legal assistant/paralegal; liberal arts and sciences/liberal studies; manufacturing engineering technology; mathematics; mechanical engineering/mechanical technology; medical/clinical assistant; nanotechnology; occupational therapist assistant; physical sciences; physical therapy technology; psychology; public administration; radio and television broadcasting technology; recording arts technology; registered nursing/registered nurse; resort management; social work; special education; speech communication and rhetoric; sport and fitness administration/management; teacher assistant/aide; veterinary/animal health technology; web page, digital/multimedia and information resources design.

Academics *Calendar:* semesters. *Degree:* certificates, diplomas, and associate. *Special study options:* academic remediation for entering students, advanced placement credit, cooperative education, distance learning, English as a second language, external degree program, honors programs, independent study, internships, part-time degree program, services for LD students, summer session for credit. *ROTC:* Army (c).

Library Rothrock Library. *Books:* 49,146 (physical), 64,336 (digital/electronic); *Serial titles:* 268 (physical); *Databases:* 47. Weekly public service hours: 71.

Student Life *Housing:* college housing not available. *Activities and Organizations:* drama/theater group, student-run newspaper, choral group, Phi Theta Kappa, Justice Society, PSI BETA (psychology club), Student Government Association, Teacher Education Student Association (TESA). *Campus security:* 24-hour emergency response devices. *Student services:* personal/psychological counseling.

Athletics Member NJCAA. *Intercollegiate sports:* baseball M, basketball M/W, golf M/W, soccer M, softball W, volleyball W. *Intramural sports:* basketball M/W, golf M/W, table tennis M/W, volleyball M/W.

Standardized Tests *Required for some:* TEAS for nursing program.

Costs (2015–16) *Tuition:* area resident $3000 full-time, $100 per credit part-time; state resident $6270 full-time, $209 per credit part-time; nonresident $9540 full-time, $318 per credit part-time. *Required fees:* $800 full-time, $37 per credit part-time. *Payment plan:* installment. *Waivers:* senior citizens and employees or children of employees.

Applying *Options:* electronic application. *Required for some:* essay or personal statement, high school transcript, interview. *Application deadlines:* rolling (freshmen), rolling (out-of-state freshmen), rolling (transfers). *Notification:* continuous (freshmen), continuous (out-of-state freshmen), continuous (transfers).

Freshman Application Contact Ms. Nancy Kelley, Admission Representative, Lehigh Carbon Community College, 4525 Education Park Drive, Schnecksville, PA 18078. *Phone:* 610-799-1558. *Fax:* 610-799-1527. *E-mail:* admissions@lccc.edu. *Website:* http://www.lccc.edu/.

Lincoln Technical Institute
Allentown, Pennsylvania

Freshman Application Contact Admissions Office, Lincoln Technical Institute, 5151 Tilghman Street, Allentown, PA 18104-3298. *Phone:* 610-398-5301. *Website:* http://www.lincolnedu.com/.

Lincoln Technical Institute
Philadelphia, Pennsylvania

Admissions Office Contact Lincoln Technical Institute, 2180 Hornig Road, Building A, Philadelphia, PA 19116-4202. *Website:* http://www.lincolnedu.com/.

Lincoln Technical Institute
Philadelphia, Pennsylvania

Director of Admissions Mr. James Kuntz, Executive Director, Lincoln Technical Institute, 9191 Torresdale Avenue, Philadelphia, PA 19136-1595. *Phone:* 215-335-0800. *Fax:* 215-335-1443. *E-mail:* jkuntz@lincolntech.com. *Website:* http://www.lincolnedu.com/.

Luzerne County Community College
Nanticoke, Pennsylvania

- **County-supported** 2-year, founded 1966
- **Suburban** 122-acre campus with easy access to Philadelphia
- **Coed,** 5,788 undergraduate students, 45% full-time, 60% women, 40% men

Undergraduates 2,621 full-time, 3,167 part-time. 0.2% are from out of state; 5% Black or African American, non-Hispanic/Latino; 11% Hispanic/Latino; 2% Asian, non-Hispanic/Latino; 0.2% Native Hawaiian or other Pacific Islander, non-Hispanic/Latino; 0.3% American Indian or Alaska Native, non-Hispanic/Latino; 1% Two or more races, non-Hispanic/Latino; 9% Race/ethnicity unknown. *Retention:* 53% of full-time freshmen returned.

Freshmen *Admission:* 2,178 applied, 2,178 admitted, 1,286 enrolled.

Faculty *Total:* 486, 23% full-time. *Student/faculty ratio:* 17:1.

Majors Accounting; administrative assistant and secretarial science; airline pilot and flight crew; architectural engineering; architectural engineering technology; automobile/automotive mechanics technology; aviation/airway management; baking and pastry arts; banking and financial support services; biological and physical sciences; building/property maintenance; business administration and management; child-care provision; commercial and advertising art; commercial photography; computer and information sciences; computer and information sciences related; computer graphics; computer programming related; computer science; computer systems networking and telecommunications; computer technology/computer systems technology; court reporting; criminal justice/law enforcement administration; culinary arts; data entry/microcomputer applications; data processing and data processing technology; dental assisting; dental hygiene; drafting and design technology; drafting/design engineering technologies related; drawing; early childhood education; education; electrical, electronic and communications engineering technology; electrician; emergency medical technology (EMT paramedic); engineering technology; executive assistant/executive secretary; fire science/firefighting; food technology and processing; funeral service and mortuary science; general studies; graphic and printing equipment operation/production; graphic design; health and physical education/fitness; health/health-care administration; heating, air conditioning, ventilation and refrigeration maintenance technology; horticultural science; hospitality and recreation marketing; hotel/motel administration; humanities; human services; industrial and product design; international business/trade/commerce; journalism; legal assistant/paralegal; liberal arts and sciences and humanities related; liberal arts and sciences/liberal studies; mathematics; medical administrative assistant and medical secretary; painting; photography; physical education teaching and coaching; plumbing technology; pre-pharmacy studies; radio and television broadcasting technology; real estate; registered nursing/registered nurse; respiratory care therapy; social sciences; surgical technology; tourism and travel services management; tourism and travel services marketing.

Academics *Calendar:* semesters. *Degree:* certificates, diplomas, and associate. *Special study options:* academic remediation for entering students, accelerated degree program, advanced placement credit, distance learning, external degree program, internships, part-time degree program, services for LD students, summer session for credit.

Library Learning Resources Center.

Student Life *Housing:* college housing not available. *Activities and Organizations:* student-run newspaper, radio and television station, Student Government, Circle K, Nursing Forum, Science Club, SADAH. *Campus security:* 24-hour patrols.

Athletics Member NJCAA. *Intercollegiate sports:* baseball M, basketball M/W, cross-country running M/W, golf M/W, soccer M/W, softball W, volleyball W. *Intramural sports:* badminton M/W, basketball M/W, bowling M/W, softball M/W, tennis M/W, volleyball M/W.

Applying *Options:* early admission, deferred entrance. *Recommended:* high school transcript.

Freshman Application Contact Mr. Francis Curry, Director of Admissions, Luzerne County Community College, 1333 South Prospect Street, Nanticoke, PA 18634-9804. *Phone:* 570-740-0337. *Toll-free phone:* 800-377-5222 Ext. 7337. *Fax:* 570-740-0238. *E-mail:* admissions@luzerne.edu. *Website:* http://www.luzerne.edu/.

Manor College
Jenkintown, Pennsylvania

- **Independent Byzantine Catholic** 2-year, founded 1947
- **Small-town** 35-acre campus with easy access to Philadelphia
- **Endowment** $2.2 million
- **Coed,** 696 undergraduate students, 61% full-time, 74% women, 26% men

Undergraduates 426 full-time, 270 part-time. Students come from 9 states and territories; 3% are from out of state; 40% Black or African American, non-Hispanic/Latino; 9% Hispanic/Latino; 2% Asian, non-Hispanic/Latino; 1%

American Indian or Alaska Native, non-Hispanic/Latino; 4% Two or more races, non-Hispanic/Latino; 3% Race/ethnicity unknown; 16% transferred in; 11% live on campus. *Retention:* 55% of full-time freshmen returned.
Freshmen *Admission:* 1,115 applied, 618 admitted, 170 enrolled. *Average high school GPA:* 2.71. *Test scores:* SAT critical reading scores over 500: 9%; SAT math scores over 500: 9%; SAT writing scores over 500: 6%; ACT scores over 18: 20%; SAT critical reading scores over 600: 4%; SAT math scores over 600: 1%; SAT writing scores over 600: 2%; ACT scores over 24: 10%; SAT critical reading scores over 700: 1%.
Faculty *Total:* 140, 18% full-time, 34% with terminal degrees. *Student/faculty ratio:* 8:1.
Majors Accounting; business administration and management; business, management, and marketing related; communication and media related; computer programming (specific applications); criminal justice/law enforcement administration; dental assisting; dental hygiene; education (specific levels and methods) related; elementary education; health professions related; legal assistant/paralegal; liberal arts and sciences/liberal studies; marketing/marketing management; psychology; sport and fitness administration/management; veterinary/animal health technology.
Academics *Calendar:* semesters. *Degrees:* certificates, diplomas, associate, and postbachelor's certificates. *Special study options:* academic remediation for entering students, accelerated degree program, adult/continuing education programs, advanced placement credit, distance learning, double majors, honors programs, independent study, internships, part-time degree program, services for LD students, summer session for credit.
Library Basileiad Library.
Student Life *Housing Options:* coed. Campus housing is university owned. *Activities and Organizations:* choral group, Rotoract (student service organization), Vet Tech Club, Campus Activities Board, Macrinian Yearbook, Phi Theta Kappa (honor society). *Campus security:* 24-hour emergency response devices and patrols, late-night transport/escort service. *Student services:* personal/psychological counseling.
Athletics Member NJCAA. *Intercollegiate sports:* basketball M/W, soccer M/W.
Standardized Tests *Required for some:* SAT or ACT (for admission). *Recommended:* SAT or ACT (for admission).
Costs (2015–16) *Comprehensive fee:* $24,050 includes full-time tuition ($15,950), mandatory fees ($600), and room and board ($7500). Full-time tuition and fees vary according to course load and program. Part-time tuition: $599 per credit. Part-time tuition and fees vary according to course load and program. *Required fees:* $100 per term part-time. *Payment plan:* installment. *Waivers:* adult students, senior citizens, and employees or children of employees.
Financial Aid Of all full-time matriculated undergraduates who enrolled in 2009, 35 Federal Work-Study jobs (averaging $3000). 10 state and other part-time jobs (averaging $3600).
Applying *Options:* electronic application, deferred entrance. *Required:* high school transcript. *Application deadlines:* rolling (freshmen), rolling (transfers). *Notification:* continuous (freshmen), continuous (transfers).
Freshman Application Contact Stephanie Walker, Director of Admissions, Manor College, 700 Fox Chase Road, Jenkintown, PA 19046. *Phone:* 215-885-2360 Ext. 205. *Fax:* 215-576-6564. *E-mail:* swalker@manor.edu. *Website:* http://www.manor.edu/.

McCann School of Business & Technology
Hazelton, Pennsylvania
Admissions Office Contact McCann School of Business & Technology, 370 Maplewood Drive, Hazelton, PA 18202.
Website: http://www.mccann.edu/.

McCann School of Business & Technology
Lewisburg, Pennsylvania
Admissions Office Contact McCann School of Business & Technology, 7495 Westbranch Highway, Lewisburg, PA 17837.
Website: http://www.mccann.edu/.

McCann School of Business & Technology
Pottsville, Pennsylvania
Freshman Application Contact Mrs. Amelia Hopkins, Director, Pottsville Campus, McCann School of Business & Technology, 2650 Woodglen Road, Pottsville, PA 17901. *Phone:* 570-622-7622. *Fax:* 570-622-7770.
Website: http://www.mccann.edu/.

Mercyhurst North East
North East, Pennsylvania
Director of Admissions Travis Lindahl, Director of Admissions, Mercyhurst North East, 16 West Division Street, North East, PA 16428. *Phone:* 814-725-6217. *Toll-free phone:* 866-846-6042. *Fax:* 814-725-6251.
E-mail: neadmiss@mercyhurst.edu.
Website: http://northeast.mercyhurst.edu/.

Metropolitan Career Center Computer Technology Institute
Philadelphia, Pennsylvania
Freshman Application Contact Admissions Office, Metropolitan Career Center Computer Technology Institute, 100 South Broad Street, Suite 830, Philadelphia, PA 19110. *Phone:* 215-568-7861.
Website: http://www.careersinit.org/.

Montgomery County Community College
Blue Bell, Pennsylvania
- **County-supported** 2-year, founded 1964
- **Suburban** 186-acre campus with easy access to Philadelphia
- **Coed,** 12,372 undergraduate students, 31% full-time, 57% women, 43% men

Undergraduates 3,897 full-time, 8,475 part-time. Students come from 17 states and territories; 101 other countries; 0.8% are from out of state; 15% Black or African American, non-Hispanic/Latino; 6% Hispanic/Latino; 6% Asian, non-Hispanic/Latino; 0.3% Native Hawaiian or other Pacific Islander, non-Hispanic/Latino; 0.3% American Indian or Alaska Native, non-Hispanic/Latino; 3% Two or more races, non-Hispanic/Latino; 9% Race/ethnicity unknown; 2% international. *Retention:* 63% of full-time freshmen returned.
Freshmen *Admission:* 8,467 applied, 8,467 admitted, 2,771 enrolled.
Faculty *Total:* 723, 24% full-time. *Student/faculty ratio:* 19:1.
Majors Accounting; accounting technology and bookkeeping; administrative assistant and secretarial science; art; baking and pastry arts; biology/biological sciences; biotechnology; business administration and management; business/commerce; business/corporate communications; child-care and support services management; clinical/medical laboratory technology; commercial and advertising art; communications technologies and support services related; computer and information sciences; computer programming; computer systems networking and telecommunications; criminal justice/police science; culinary arts; dental hygiene; electrical, electronic and communications engineering technology; electromechanical technology; elementary education; engineering science; engineering technologies and engineering related; environmental science; fire prevention and safety technology; health and physical education/fitness; hospitality and recreation marketing; humanities; information science/studies; liberal arts and sciences/liberal studies; management information systems and services related; mathematics; mechanical engineering/mechanical technology; medical/clinical assistant; medical radiologic technology; network and system administration; physical education teaching and coaching; physical sciences; psychiatric/mental health services technology; psychology; radiologic technology/science; radio, television, and digital communication related; real estate; recording arts technology; registered nursing/registered nurse; sales, distribution, and marketing operations; secondary education; social sciences; speech communication and rhetoric; surgical technology; teacher assistant/aide; tourism and travel services marketing; web/multimedia management and webmaster.
Academics *Calendar:* semesters plus winter term. *Degree:* certificates and associate. *Special study options:* academic remediation for entering students, accelerated degree program, adult/continuing education programs, advanced placement credit, cooperative education, distance learning, English as a second language, honors programs, independent study, internships, part-time degree program, services for LD students, student-designed majors, study abroad, summer session for credit.

Library The Brendlinger Library. *Books:* 74,778 (physical); *Databases:* 41. Weekly public service hours: 75; students can reserve study rooms.

Student Life *Housing:* college housing not available. *Activities and Organizations:* drama/theater group, student-run newspaper, radio and television station, choral group, West End Student Theater (drama club), Phi Theta Kappa, Gender Sexuality Association, Thrive (Christian fellowship), Student Government. *Campus security:* 24-hour emergency response devices and patrols, late-night transport/escort service, bicycle patrol. *Student services:* health clinic, personal/psychological counseling.

Athletics Member NJCAA. *Intercollegiate sports:* baseball M, basketball M/W, soccer M/W, softball W, volleyball W. *Intramural sports:* badminton M/W, basketball M/W, bowling M/W, cross-country running M/W, football M, racquetball M/W, soccer M/W, table tennis M/W, tennis M/W, volleyball M/W, weight lifting M/W.

Costs (2015–16) *Tuition:* area resident $4020 full-time, $134 per credit part-time; state resident $8340 full-time, $268 per credit part-time; nonresident $12,660 full-time, $402 per credit part-time. Full-time tuition and fees vary according to program. Part-time tuition and fees vary according to program. *Required fees:* $900 full-time, $30 per credit part-time. *Payment plan:* deferred payment. *Waivers:* senior citizens and employees or children of employees.

Financial Aid Of all full-time matriculated undergraduates who enrolled in 2014, 60 Federal Work-Study jobs (averaging $2500).

Applying *Options:* electronic application, early admission, deferred entrance. *Required:* high school transcript. *Required for some:* interview. *Application deadline:* rolling (transfers). *Notification:* continuous (freshmen), continuous (transfers).

Freshman Application Contact Montgomery County Community College, Blue Bell, PA 19422. *Phone:* 215-641-6551. *Fax:* 215-619-7188. *E-mail:* admrec@admin.mc3.edu. *Website:* http://www.mc3.edu/.

New Castle School of Trades
New Castle, Pennsylvania

- **Independent** 2-year, founded 1945
- **Rural** 20-acre campus with easy access to Pittsburgh
- **Coed, primarily men,** 503 undergraduate students, 100% full-time, 5% women, 95% men

Undergraduates 503 full-time. Students come from 3 states and territories; 45% are from out of state.

Faculty *Total:* 46, 65% full-time, 2% with terminal degrees. *Student/faculty ratio:* 11:1.

Majors Automotive engineering technology; construction engineering technology; diesel mechanics technology; electrical, electronic and communications engineering technology; heating, ventilation, air conditioning and refrigeration engineering technology; industrial mechanics and maintenance technology; machine tool technology.

Academics *Calendar:* quarters. *Degree:* diplomas and associate. *Special study options:* part-time degree program.

Library New Castle School of Trades plus 1 other. *Books:* 600 (physical). Weekly public service hours: 60.

Student Life *Housing:* college housing not available. *Campus security:* 24-hour emergency response devices. *Student services:* personal/psychological counseling.

Standardized Tests *Required:* Wonderlic aptitude test (for admission).

Applying *Required:* high school transcript, interview. *Required for some:* essay or personal statement.

Freshman Application Contact Mr. Joe Blazak, Admissions Director, New Castle School of Trades, 4117 Pulaski Road, New Castle, PA 16101. *Phone:* 724-964-8811. *Toll-free phone:* 800-837-8299. *Fax:* 724-964-8177. *Website:* http://www.ncstrades.com/.

Northampton Community College
Bethlehem, Pennsylvania

- **State and locally supported** 2-year, founded 1967
- **Suburban** 165-acre campus with easy access to Philadelphia
- **Endowment** $42.1 million
- **Coed,** 10,269 undergraduate students, 45% full-time, 59% women, 41% men

Undergraduates 4,594 full-time, 5,675 part-time. Students come from 29 states and territories; 45 other countries; 2% are from out of state; 13% Black or African American, non-Hispanic/Latino; 20% Hispanic/Latino; 2% Asian, non-Hispanic/Latino; 0.2% Native Hawaiian or other Pacific Islander, non-Hispanic/Latino; 0.3% American Indian or Alaska Native, non-Hispanic/Latino; 3% Two or more races, non-Hispanic/Latino; 1% Race/ethnicity unknown; 1% international; 9% transferred in; 6% live on campus.

Freshmen *Admission:* 2,917 applied, 2,917 admitted, 2,085 enrolled.

Faculty *Total:* 707, 17% full-time, 13% with terminal degrees. *Student/faculty ratio:* 20:1.

Majors Accounting technology and bookkeeping; acting; administrative assistant and secretarial science; applied psychology; architectural engineering technology; athletic training; automobile/automotive mechanics technology; biology/biological sciences; biotechnology; business administration and management; business/commerce; CAD/CADD drafting/design technology; chemistry; computer and information systems security; computer installation and repair technology; computer programming; computer science; computer systems networking and telecommunications; construction management; criminal justice/safety; culinary arts; dental hygiene; diagnostic medical sonography and ultrasound technology; early childhood education; electrical, electronic and communications engineering technology; electrician; electromechanical technology; engineering; environmental science; fine/studio arts; fire science/firefighting; fire services administration; funeral service and mortuary science; general studies; graphic design; heating, air conditioning, ventilation and refrigeration maintenance technology; hotel/motel administration; industrial electronics technology; interior design; international/global studies; journalism; legal assistant/paralegal; liberal arts and sciences and humanities related; liberal arts and sciences/liberal studies; marketing/marketing management; mathematics; medical administrative assistant and medical secretary; meeting and event planning; middle school education; physics; public health education and promotion; quality control technology; radio and television broadcasting technology; radiologic technology/science; registered nursing/registered nurse; restaurant/food services management; secondary education; social work; speech communication and rhetoric; sport and fitness administration/management; teacher assistant/aide; veterinary/animal health technology; web page, digital/multimedia and information resources design.

Academics *Calendar:* semesters. *Degree:* certificates, diplomas, and associate. *Special study options:* academic remediation for entering students, adult/continuing education programs, advanced placement credit, distance learning, English as a second language, honors programs, independent study, internships, off-campus study, part-time degree program, services for LD students, student-designed majors, study abroad, summer session for credit.

Library Paul & Harriett Mack Library. *Books:* 73,078 (physical), 19,505 (digital/electronic); *Serial titles:* 276 (physical), 40,194 (digital/electronic); *Databases:* 71. Weekly public service hours: 83; students can reserve study rooms.

Student Life *Housing Options:* coed. Campus housing is university owned. *Activities and Organizations:* student-run newspaper, radio station, choral group, Phi Theta Kappa, Student Senate, College and Hospital Association of Radiologic Technologies Students (CHARTS), American Dental Hygiene Association (ADHA), International Student Organization. *Campus security:* 24-hour emergency response devices and patrols, controlled dormitory access. *Student services:* health clinic, personal/psychological counseling.

Athletics Member NJCAA. *Intercollegiate sports:* baseball M, basketball M/W, cross-country running M/W, golf M, lacrosse M, soccer M/W, softball W, tennis W, volleyball W. *Intramural sports:* basketball M/W, cheerleading M(c)/W(c), soccer M/W, volleyball M/W.

Costs (2015–16) *Tuition:* area resident $2820 full-time, $94 per credit hour part-time; state resident $5640 full-time, $188 per credit hour part-time; nonresident $8460 full-time, $282 per credit hour part-time. Full-time tuition and fees vary according to course load. Part-time tuition and fees vary according to course load. *Required fees:* $1170 full-time, $39 per credit hour part-time. *Room and board:* $8092; room only: $5000. Room and board charges vary according to board plan and housing facility. *Payment plan:* installment. *Waivers:* adult students, senior citizens, and employees or children of employees.

Financial Aid Of all full-time matriculated undergraduates who enrolled in 2015, 243 Federal Work-Study jobs (averaging $2400). 146 state and other part-time jobs (averaging $2000).

Applying *Options:* electronic application, deferred entrance. *Application fee:* $25. *Required for some:* high school transcript, minimum 2.5 GPA, interview, interview for radiography and veterinary programs. *Recommended:* high school transcript. *Application deadlines:* rolling (freshmen), rolling (out-of-state freshmen), rolling (transfers). *Notification:* continuous (freshmen), continuous (out-of-state freshmen), continuous (transfers).

Freshman Application Contact Mr. James McCarthy, Director of Admissions, Northampton Community College, 3835 Green Pond Road, Bethlehem, PA 18020-7599. *Phone:* 610-861-5506. *Fax:* 610-861-5551. *E-mail:* jrmccarthy@northampton.edu. *Website:* http://www.northampton.edu/.

Penn Commercial Business and Technical School
Washington, Pennsylvania

Director of Admissions Mr. Michael John Joyce, Director of Admissions, Penn Commercial Business and Technical School, 242 Oak Spring Road, Washington, PA 15301. *Phone:* 724-222-5330 Ext. 1. *Toll-free phone:* 888-309-7484. *E-mail:* mjoyce@penn-commercial.com. *Website:* http://www.penncommercial.net/.

Pennco Tech
Bristol, Pennsylvania

Freshman Application Contact Pennco Tech, 3815 Otter Street, Bristol, PA 19007-3696. *Phone:* 215-785-0111. *Toll-free phone:* 800-575-9399. *Website:* http://www.penncotech.com/.

Penn State DuBois
DuBois, Pennsylvania

- **State-related** primarily 2-year, founded 1935, part of Pennsylvania State University
- **Small-town** campus
- **Coed,** 602 undergraduate students, 83% full-time, 45% women, 55% men

Undergraduates 497 full-time, 105 part-time. 3% are from out of state; 2% Black or African American, non-Hispanic/Latino; 2% Hispanic/Latino; 0.6% Asian, non-Hispanic/Latino; 0.2% Native Hawaiian or other Pacific Islander, non-Hispanic/Latino; 0.4% Two or more races, non-Hispanic/Latino; 1% Race/ethnicity unknown; 0.4% international; 4% transferred in. *Retention:* 87% of full-time freshmen returned.

Freshmen *Admission:* 394 applied, 335 admitted, 163 enrolled. *Average high school GPA:* 3.13. *Test scores:* SAT critical reading scores over 500: 40%; SAT math scores over 500: 52%; SAT writing scores over 500: 22%; ACT scores over 18: 100%; SAT critical reading scores over 600: 10%; SAT math scores over 600: 12%; SAT writing scores over 600: 1%; ACT scores over 24: 33%; SAT critical reading scores over 700: 1%; SAT math scores over 700: 1%; SAT writing scores over 700: 1%.

Faculty *Total:* 58, 72% full-time, 52% with terminal degrees. *Student/faculty ratio:* 11:1.

Majors Accounting; acting; actuarial science; adult and continuing education administration; advertising; aerospace, aeronautical and astronautical/space engineering; African American/Black studies; agribusiness; agricultural and extension education; agricultural business and management related; agricultural engineering; agricultural mechanization; agriculture; agronomy and crop science; animal sciences; animal sciences related; anthropology; applied economics; archeology; architectural engineering; art; art history, criticism and conservation; art teacher education; Asian studies (East); astronomy; atmospheric sciences and meteorology; biochemistry; bioengineering and biomedical engineering; biological and biomedical sciences related; biological and physical sciences; biology/biological sciences; biology/biotechnology laboratory technician; biomedical technology; business administration and management; business/commerce; business/managerial economics; chemical engineering; chemistry; civil engineering; classics and classical languages; clinical/medical laboratory technology; communication and journalism related; communication sciences and disorders; comparative literature; computer and information sciences; computer engineering; criminal justice/law enforcement administration; economics; electrical and electronics engineering; electrical, electronic and communications engineering technology; elementary education; engineering science; English; environmental/environmental health engineering; film/cinema/video studies; finance; food science; foreign language teacher education; forest sciences and biology; forest technology; French; geography; geological and earth sciences/geosciences related; geology/earth science; German; graphic design; health/health-care administration; history; horticultural science; hospitality administration related; human development and family studies; human nutrition; industrial engineering; information science/studies; international business/trade/commerce; international relations and affairs; Italian; Japanese; Jewish/Judaic studies; journalism; kinesiology and exercise science; labor and industrial relations; landscaping and groundskeeping; Latin American studies; liberal arts and sciences/liberal studies; management information systems; marketing/marketing management; materials science; mathematics; mechanical engineering; mechanical engineering/mechanical technology; medical microbiology and bacteriology; medieval and Renaissance studies; metallurgical technology; mining and mineral engineering; music; natural resources and conservation related; natural resources/conservation; nuclear engineering; occupational therapist assistant; organizational behavior; parks, recreation and leisure facilities management; petroleum engineering; philosophy; physical therapy technology; physics; political science and government; premedical studies; psychology; registered nursing/registered

nurse; rehabilitation and therapeutic professions related; religious studies; Russian; secondary education; sociology; soil science and agronomy; Spanish; special education; speech communication and rhetoric; statistics; telecommunications technology; theater design and technology; toxicology; turf and turfgrass management; visual and performing arts; wildlife, fish and wildlands science and management; women's studies.

Academics *Calendar:* semesters. *Degrees:* certificates, associate, and bachelor's. *Special study options:* adult/continuing education programs, external degree program.

Student Life *Housing:* college housing not available.

Athletics Member NJCAA. *Intercollegiate sports:* basketball M, cross-country running M/W, golf M/W, volleyball W. *Intramural sports:* basketball M/W, football M, soccer M/W, table tennis M/W, volleyball M/W.

Standardized Tests *Required:* SAT or ACT (for admission).

Costs (2015–16) *Tuition:* state resident $12,718 full-time, $524 per credit hour part-time; nonresident $19,404 full-time, $809 per credit hour part-time. Full-time tuition and fees vary according to course level, degree level, location, program, and student level. Part-time tuition and fees vary according to course level, course load, degree level, location, program, and student level. *Required fees:* $828 full-time. *Payment plans:* installment, deferred payment. *Waivers:* senior citizens and employees or children of employees.

Financial Aid Of all full-time matriculated undergraduates who enrolled in 2014, 403 applied for aid, 359 were judged to have need, 23 had their need fully met. In 2014, 24 non-need-based awards were made. *Average percent of need met:* 66%. *Average financial aid package:* $11,553. *Average need-based loan:* $3717. *Average need-based gift aid:* $6849. *Average non-need-based aid:* $1772. *Average indebtedness upon graduation:* $43,504.

Applying *Options:* electronic application, early admission, deferred entrance. *Application fee:* $50. *Required:* high school transcript. *Required for some:* interview. *Recommended:* essay or personal statement. *Application deadlines:* rolling (freshmen), rolling (transfers). *Notification:* continuous (freshmen), continuous (transfers).

Freshman Application Contact Admissions Office, Penn State DuBois, 1 College Place, DuBois, PA 15801. *Phone:* 814-375-4720. *Toll-free phone:* 800-346-7627. *Fax:* 814-375-4784. *E-mail:* duboisinfo@psi.edu. *Website:* http://www.ds.psu.edu/.

Penn State Fayette, The Eberly Campus
Lemont Furnace, Pennsylvania

- **State-related** primarily 2-year, founded 1934, part of Pennsylvania State University
- **Small-town** campus
- **Coed,** 704 undergraduate students, 84% full-time, 58% women, 42% men

Undergraduates 592 full-time, 112 part-time. 5% are from out of state; 6% transferred in. *Retention:* 77% of full-time freshmen returned.

Freshmen *Admission:* 659 applied, 533 admitted, 193 enrolled. *Average high school GPA:* 3.19. *Test scores:* SAT critical reading scores over 500: 29%; SAT math scores over 500: 35%; SAT writing scores over 500: 18%; ACT scores over 18: 70%; SAT critical reading scores over 600: 3%; SAT math scores over 600: 7%; SAT writing scores over 600: 5%; ACT scores over 24: 10%; SAT math scores over 700: 3%; ACT scores over 30: 10%.

Faculty *Total:* 69, 64% full-time, 35% with terminal degrees. *Student/faculty ratio:* 12:1.

Majors Accounting; acting; actuarial science; adult and continuing education administration; advertising; aerospace, aeronautical and astronautical/space engineering; African American/Black studies; agribusiness; agricultural and extension education; agricultural business and management related; agricultural engineering; agricultural mechanization; agriculture; agronomy and crop science; animal sciences; animal sciences related; anthropology; applied economics; archeology; architectural engineering; architectural engineering technology; art; art history, criticism and conservation; art teacher education; Asian studies (East); astronomy; atmospheric sciences and meteorology; biochemistry; bioengineering and biomedical engineering; biological and biomedical sciences related; biological and physical sciences; biology/biological sciences; biology/biotechnology laboratory technician; biomedical technology; business administration and management; business/commerce; business/managerial economics; chemical engineering; chemistry; civil engineering; classics and classical languages; communication and journalism related; communication sciences and disorders; comparative literature; computer and information sciences; computer engineering; criminal justice/law enforcement administration; criminal justice/safety; economics; electrical and electronics engineering; electrical, electronic and communications engineering technology; elementary education; engineering science; English; environmental/environmental health engineering; film/cinema/video studies; finance; food science; foreign language teacher education; forest sciences and biology; forest technology; French; geography; geological and earth sciences/geosciences related; geology/earth science; German; graphic design; health/health-care administration; history; horticultural science; hospitality administration related; human development and family studies; human nutrition; industrial engineering; information science/studies; international relations and affairs; Italian; Japanese; Jewish/Judaic studies; journalism; kinesiology and exercise science; labor and industrial relations; landscaping and groundskeeping; Latin American studies; liberal arts and sciences/liberal studies; logistics, materials, and supply chain management; management information systems; manufacturing engineering; marketing/marketing management; materials science; mathematics; mechanical engineering; medical microbiology and bacteriology; medieval and Renaissance studies; metallurgical technology; mining and mineral engineering; natural resources and conservation related; natural resources/conservation; nuclear engineering; organizational behavior; parks, recreation and leisure facilities management; petroleum engineering; philosophy; physics; political science and government; premedical studies; psychology; registered nursing/registered nurse; rehabilitation and therapeutic professions related; religious studies; Russian; secondary education; sociology; soil science and agronomy; Spanish; special education; speech communication and rhetoric; statistics; telecommunications technology; theater design and technology; toxicology; turf and turfgrass management; visual and performing arts; women's studies.

Academics *Calendar:* semesters. *Degrees:* certificates, associate, and bachelor's. *Special study options:* adult/continuing education programs, external degree program.

Student Life *Housing:* college housing not available. *Campus security:* student patrols, 8-hour patrols by trained security personnel.

Athletics Member NJCAA. *Intercollegiate sports:* baseball M, basketball M, softball W, volleyball W. *Intramural sports:* badminton M/W, basketball M/W, cheerleading M(c)/W(c), equestrian sports M(c)/W(c), football M/W, golf M(c)/W(c), softball M/W, tennis M/W, volleyball M/W, weight lifting M/W.

Standardized Tests *Required:* SAT or ACT (for admission).

Costs (2015–16) *Tuition:* state resident $12,718 full-time, $524 per credit hour part-time; nonresident $19,404 full-time, $809 per credit hour part-time. Full-time tuition and fees vary according to course level, degree level, location, program, and student level. Part-time tuition and fees vary according to course level, course load, degree level, location, program, and student level. *Required fees:* $890 full-time. *Payment plans:* installment, deferred payment. *Waivers:* senior citizens and employees or children of employees.

Financial Aid Of all full-time matriculated undergraduates who enrolled in 2014, 523 applied for aid, 452 were judged to have need, 28 had their need fully met. In 2014, 59 non-need-based awards were made. *Average percent of need met:* 65%. *Average financial aid package:* $10,865. *Average need-based loan:* $4017. *Average need-based gift aid:* $6423. *Average non-need-based aid:* $2682. *Average indebtedness upon graduation:* $37,338.

Applying *Options:* electronic application, early admission, deferred entrance. *Application fee:* $50. *Required:* high school transcript. *Required for some:* interview. *Recommended:* essay or personal statement. *Application deadlines:* rolling (freshmen), rolling (transfers). *Notification:* continuous (freshmen), continuous (transfers).

Freshman Application Contact Admissions Office, Penn State Fayette, The Eberly Campus, 2201 University Drive, Lemont Furnace, PA 15456. *Phone:* 724-430-4130. *Toll-free phone:* 877-568-4130. *Fax:* 724-430-4175. *E-mail:* feadm@psu.edu. *Website:* http://www.fe.psu.edu/.

Penn State Mont Alto

Mont Alto, Pennsylvania

- **State-related** primarily 2-year, founded 1929, part of Pennsylvania State University
- **Small-town** campus
- **Coed,** 893 undergraduate students, 74% full-time, 57% women, 43% men

Undergraduates 661 full-time, 232 part-time. 12% are from out of state; 8% Black or African American, non-Hispanic/Latino; 5% Hispanic/Latino; 2% Asian, non-Hispanic/Latino; 0.1% Native Hawaiian or other Pacific Islander, non-Hispanic/Latino; 3% Two or more races, non-Hispanic/Latino; 0.9% Race/ethnicity unknown; 0.4% international; 4% transferred in; 26% live on campus. *Retention:* 77% of full-time freshmen returned.

Freshmen *Admission:* 688 applied, 546 admitted, 246 enrolled. *Average high school GPA:* 3.11. *Test scores:* SAT critical reading scores over 500: 43%; SAT math scores over 500: 42%; SAT writing scores over 500: 29%; ACT scores over 18: 57%; SAT critical reading scores over 600: 5%; SAT math scores over 600: 11%; SAT writing scores over 600: 2%; ACT scores over 24: 29%.

Faculty *Total:* 92, 61% full-time, 30% with terminal degrees. *Student/faculty ratio:* 11:1.

Majors Accounting; acting; actuarial science; adult and continuing education administration; advertising; aerospace, aeronautical and astronautical/space

engineering; African American/Black studies; agribusiness; agricultural and extension education; agricultural business and management related; agricultural engineering; agricultural mechanization; agriculture; agronomy and crop science; animal sciences; animal sciences related; anthropology; applied economics; archeology; architectural engineering; art; art history, criticism and conservation; art teacher education; Asian studies (East); astronomy; atmospheric sciences and meteorology; biochemistry; bioengineering and biomedical engineering; biological and biomedical sciences related; biological and physical sciences; biology/biological sciences; biology/biotechnology laboratory technician; business administration and management; business/commerce; business/managerial economics; chemical engineering; chemistry; civil engineering; classics and classical languages; communication and journalism related; communication sciences and disorders; comparative literature; computer and information sciences; computer engineering; criminal justice/law enforcement administration; economics; electrical and electronics engineering; elementary education; engineering science; English; environmental/environmental health engineering; film/cinema/video studies; finance; food science; foreign language teacher education; forest sciences and biology; forest technology; French; geography; geological and earth sciences/geosciences related; geology/earth science; German; graphic design; health/health-care administration; history; horticultural science; hospitality administration related; human development and family studies; human nutrition; industrial engineering; information science/studies; international relations and affairs; Italian; Japanese; Jewish/Judaic studies; journalism; kinesiology and exercise science; labor and industrial relations; landscaping and groundskeeping; Latin American studies; liberal arts and sciences/liberal studies; management information systems; marketing/marketing management; materials science; mathematics; mechanical engineering; medical microbiology and bacteriology; medieval and Renaissance studies; mining and mineral engineering; music; natural resources and conservation related; natural resources/conservation; nuclear engineering; occupational therapist assistant; occupational therapy; organizational behavior; parks, recreation and leisure facilities management; petroleum engineering; philosophy; physical therapy technology; physics; political science and government; premedical studies; psychology; registered nursing/registered nurse; rehabilitation and therapeutic professions related; religious studies; Russian; secondary education; sociology; soil science and agronomy; Spanish; special education; speech communication and rhetoric; statistics; theater design and technology; toxicology; turf and turfgrass management; visual and performing arts; women's studies.

Academics *Calendar:* semesters. *Degrees:* certificates, associate, and bachelor's. *Special study options:* adult/continuing education programs, external degree program. *ROTC:* Army (c).

Student Life *Housing Options:* coed, special housing for students with disabilities. Campus housing is university owned. Freshman campus housing is guaranteed. *Campus security:* 24-hour patrols, controlled dormitory access.

Athletics Member NJCAA. *Intercollegiate sports:* basketball M/W, cheerleading M/W, cross-country running M/W, golf M/W, soccer M/W, softball W, tennis M/W, volleyball W. *Intramural sports:* badminton M/W, basketball M/W, cheerleading M(c)/W(c), racquetball M/W, soccer M/W, softball W, volleyball M/W.

Standardized Tests *Required:* SAT or ACT (for admission).

Costs (2015–16) *Tuition:* state resident $12,718 full-time, $524 per credit hour part-time; nonresident $19,404 full-time, $809 per credit hour part-time. Full-time tuition and fees vary according to course level, degree level, location, program, and student level. Part-time tuition and fees vary according to course level, course load, degree level, location, program, and student level. *Required fees:* $952 full-time. *Room and board:* $10,920; room only: $5720. Room and board charges vary according to board plan, housing facility, and location. *Payment plans:* installment, deferred payment. *Waivers:* senior citizens and employees or children of employees.

Financial Aid Of all full-time matriculated undergraduates who enrolled in 2014, 618 applied for aid, 540 were judged to have need, 27 had their need fully met. In 2014, 48 non-need-based awards were made. *Average percent of need met:* 62%. *Average financial aid package:* $11,700. *Average need-based loan:* $4106. *Average need-based gift aid:* $6493. *Average non-need-based aid:* $4677. *Average indebtedness upon graduation:* $46,030.

Applying *Options:* electronic application, early admission, deferred entrance. *Application fee:* $50. *Required:* high school transcript. *Required for some:* interview. *Recommended:* essay or personal statement. *Application deadlines:* rolling (freshmen), rolling (transfers). *Notification:* continuous (freshmen), continuous (transfers).

Freshman Application Contact Admissions Office, Penn State Mont Alto, 1 Campus Drive, Mont Alto, PA 17237-9703. *Phone:* 717-749-6130. *Toll-free phone:* 800-392-6173. *Fax:* 717-749-6132. *E-mail:* psuma@psu.edu. *Website:* http://www.ma.psu.edu/.

Penn State Shenango
Sharon, Pennsylvania

- **State-related** primarily 2-year, founded 1965, part of Pennsylvania State University
- **Small-town** campus
- **Coed,** 508 undergraduate students, 55% full-time, 72% women, 28% men

Undergraduates 280 full-time, 228 part-time. 22% are from out of state; 7% Black or African American, non-Hispanic/Latino; 2% Hispanic/Latino; 0.7% Asian, non-Hispanic/Latino; 3% Two or more races, non-Hispanic/Latino; 3% Race/ethnicity unknown; 9% transferred in. *Retention:* 66% of full-time freshmen returned.

Freshmen *Admission:* 154 applied, 105 admitted, 57 enrolled. *Average high school GPA:* 3.04. *Test scores:* SAT critical reading scores over 500: 36%; SAT math scores over 500: 44%; SAT writing scores over 500: 28%; ACT scores over 18: 80%; SAT critical reading scores over 600: 3%; SAT math scores over 600: 5%; SAT writing scores over 600: 5%; ACT scores over 24: 10%.

Faculty *Total:* 44, 64% full-time, 39% with terminal degrees. *Student/faculty ratio:* 11:1.

Majors Accounting; acting; actuarial science; adult and continuing education administration; advertising; aerospace, aeronautical and astronautical/space engineering; African American/Black studies; agribusiness; agricultural and extension education; agricultural business and management related; agricultural engineering; agricultural mechanization; agriculture; agronomy and crop science; animal sciences; animal sciences related; anthropology; applied economics; archeology; architectural engineering; art; art history, criticism and conservation; art teacher education; Asian studies (East); astronomy; atmospheric sciences and meteorology; biochemistry; bioengineering and biomedical engineering; biological and biomedical sciences related; biological and physical sciences; biology/biological sciences; biology/biotechnology laboratory technician; biomedical technology; business administration and management; business/commerce; business/managerial economics; chemical engineering; chemistry; civil engineering; classics and classical languages; communication and journalism related; communication sciences and disorders; comparative literature; computer and information sciences; computer engineering; criminal justice/law enforcement administration; economics; electrical and electronics engineering; electrical, electronic and communications engineering technology; elementary education; engineering science; English; environmental/environmental health engineering; film/cinema/video studies; finance; food science; foreign language teacher education; forest sciences and biology; forest technology; French; geography; geological and earth sciences/geosciences related; geology/earth science; German; graphic design; health/health-care administration; history; horticultural science; hospitality administration related; human development and family studies; human nutrition; industrial engineering; information science/studies; international relations and affairs; Italian; Japanese; Jewish/Judaic studies; journalism; kinesiology and exercise science; labor and industrial relations; landscaping and groundskeeping; Latin American studies; liberal arts and sciences/liberal studies; logistics, materials, and supply chain management; management information systems; marketing/marketing management; materials science; mathematics; mechanical engineering; mechanical engineering/mechanical technology; medical microbiology and bacteriology; medieval and Renaissance studies; metallurgical technology; mining and mineral engineering; music; natural resources and conservation related; natural resources/conservation; nuclear engineering; organizational behavior; parks, recreation and leisure facilities management; petroleum engineering; philosophy; physical therapy technology; physics; political science and government; premedical studies; psychology; registered nursing/registered nurse; rehabilitation and therapeutic professions related; religious studies; Russian; secondary education; sociology; soil science and agronomy; Spanish; special education; speech communication and rhetoric; statistics; telecommunications technology; theater design and technology; toxicology; turf and turfgrass management; visual and performing arts; women's studies.

Academics *Calendar:* semesters. *Degrees:* certificates, associate, and bachelor's. *Special study options:* adult/continuing education programs, external degree program.

Student Life *Housing:* college housing not available.

Athletics *Intramural sports:* basketball M(c)/W, bowling M/W, football M(c), golf M/W, softball M/W, tennis M/W, volleyball M/W.

Standardized Tests *Required:* SAT or ACT (for admission).

Costs (2015–16) *Tuition:* state resident $12,474 full-time, $504 per credit hour part-time; nonresident $19,030 full-time, $793 per credit hour part-time. Full-time tuition and fees vary according to course level, degree level, location, program, and student level. Part-time tuition and fees vary according to course level, course load, degree level, location, program, and student level. *Required*

fees: $880 full-time. *Payment plans:* installment, deferred payment. *Waivers:* senior citizens and employees or children of employees.

Financial Aid Of all full-time matriculated undergraduates who enrolled in 2014, 286 applied for aid, 268 were judged to have need, 20 had their need fully met. In 2014, 15 non-need-based awards were made. *Average percent of need met:* 64%. *Average financial aid package:* $13,301. *Average need-based loan:* $4120. *Average need-based gift aid:* $7464. *Average non-need-based aid:* $2894. *Average indebtedness upon graduation:* $35,187.

Applying *Options:* electronic application, early admission, deferred entrance. *Application fee:* $50. *Required:* high school transcript. *Application deadlines:* rolling (freshmen), rolling (transfers). *Notification:* continuous (freshmen), continuous (transfers).

Freshman Application Contact Admissions Office, Penn State Shenango, 147 Shenango Avenue, Sharon, PA 16146-1537. *Phone:* 724-983-2803. *Fax:* 724-983-2820. *E-mail:* psushenango@psu.edu.
Website: http://www.shenango.psu.edu/.

Pennsylvania Highlands Community College
Johnstown, Pennsylvania

- **State and locally supported** 2-year, founded 1994
- **Small-town** campus
- **Coed,** 2,456 undergraduate students, 35% full-time, 58% women, 42% men

Undergraduates 866 full-time, 1,590 part-time. 4% Black or African American, non-Hispanic/Latino; 2% Hispanic/Latino; 2% Asian, non-Hispanic/Latino; 0.2% American Indian or Alaska Native, non-Hispanic/Latino; 2% Two or more races, non-Hispanic/Latino; 3% Race/ethnicity unknown; 4% transferred in.

Freshmen *Admission:* 400 applied, 400 admitted, 400 enrolled.

Faculty *Total:* 108, 25% full-time. *Student/faculty ratio:* 26:1.

Majors Accounting; airline pilot and flight crew; architectural drafting and CAD/CADD; business/commerce; child-care and support services management; computer and information sciences; computer science; corrections; criminal justice/law enforcement administration; early childhood education; education; emergency medical technology (EMT paramedic); engineering technologies and engineering related; environmental science; general studies; health information/medical records technology; health professions related; histologic technician; human services; lineworker; medical/clinical assistant; operations management; psychology; radiologic technology/science; radio, television, and digital communication related; welding technology.

Academics *Calendar:* semesters. *Degree:* certificates, diplomas, and associate. *Special study options:* academic remediation for entering students, adult/continuing education programs, advanced placement credit, cooperative education, distance learning, independent study, internships, part-time degree program, services for LD students, summer session for credit.

Library Mangarella Library. *Books:* 1,274 (physical), 2,192 (digital/electronic); *Databases:* 35.

Student Life *Housing:* college housing not available. *Activities and Organizations:* Student Senate Organization, Phi Theta Kappa Honor Society (PTK), National Society of Leadership and Success Organization (Sigma Alpha Pi), Black Bear Bowling Club, Anime Art Style Club. *Student services:* personal/psychological counseling.

Athletics Member NJCAA. *Intercollegiate sports:* basketball M, bowling M/W, cross-country running M/W, volleyball W. *Intramural sports:* basketball M/W, bowling M/W, cheerleading M/W, soccer M/W, table tennis M/W, volleyball M/W.

Costs (2015–16) *Tuition:* area resident $3810 full-time, $127 per credit part-time; state resident $5850 full-time, $195 per credit part-time; nonresident $8790 full-time, $293 per credit part-time. Full-time tuition and fees vary according to course load. Part-time tuition and fees vary according to course load. *Required fees:* $1860 full-time, $62 per credit part-time. *Payment plan:* installment. *Waivers:* employees or children of employees.

Financial Aid Of all full-time matriculated undergraduates who enrolled in 2014, 25 Federal Work-Study jobs (averaging $2500).

Applying *Options:* electronic application. *Application fee:* $20. *Application deadlines:* rolling (freshmen), rolling (out-of-state freshmen), rolling (transfers). *Notification:* continuous (freshmen), continuous (out-of-state freshmen), continuous (transfers).

Freshman Application Contact Mr. Jeff Maul, Admissions Officer, Pennsylvania Highlands Community College, 101 Community College Way, Johnstown, PA 15904. *Phone:* 814-262-6431. *Toll-free phone:* 888-385-7325. *Fax:* 814-269-9743. *E-mail:* jmaul@pennhighlands.edu.
Website: http://www.pennhighlands.edu/.

Pennsylvania Institute of Health and Technology
Mount Braddock, Pennsylvania

Admissions Office Contact Pennsylvania Institute of Health and Technology, 1015 Mount Braddock Road, Mount Braddock, PA 15465.
Website: http://www.piht.edu/.

Pennsylvania Institute of Technology
Media, Pennsylvania

- **Independent** 2-year, founded 1953
- **Small-town** 12-acre campus with easy access to Philadelphia
- **Coed,** 596 undergraduate students, 51% full-time, 76% women, 24% men

Undergraduates 306 full-time, 290 part-time. 62% Black or African American, non-Hispanic/Latino; 6% Hispanic/Latino; 2% Asian, non-Hispanic/Latino; 0.2% American Indian or Alaska Native, non-Hispanic/Latino; 2% Two or more races, non-Hispanic/Latino; 16% Race/ethnicity unknown.
Freshmen *Admission:* 299 enrolled.
Faculty *Total:* 74, 26% full-time. *Student/faculty ratio:* 14:1.
Majors Allied health and medical assisting services related; biomedical technology; business administration and management; communication; electrical, electronic and communications engineering technology; engineering technology; general studies; health/health-care administration; health information/medical records technology; health services/allied health/health sciences; medical office management; pharmacy technician; physical therapy technology; practical nursing, vocational nursing and nursing assistants related.
Academics *Calendar:* semesters. *Degree:* certificates and associate. *Special study options:* academic remediation for entering students, adult/continuing education programs, advanced placement credit, cooperative education, part-time degree program, summer session for credit.
Library Pennsylvania Institute of Technology Library/Learning Resource Center.
Student Life *Housing:* college housing not available. *Campus security:* 24-hour emergency response devices. *Student services:* personal/psychological counseling.
Athletics *Intramural sports:* basketball M/W.
Costs (2015–16) *Tuition:* $11,250 full-time, $375 per credit hour part-time. Full-time tuition and fees vary according to program. Part-time tuition and fees vary according to course load and program. *Required fees:* $1950 full-time, $65 per credit hour part-time. *Payment plan:* installment. *Waivers:* employees or children of employees.
Financial Aid Of all full-time matriculated undergraduates who enrolled in 2014, 15 Federal Work-Study jobs (averaging $1025). *Financial aid deadline:* 8/1.
Applying *Options:* electronic application, deferred entrance. *Application fee:* $25. *Required:* high school transcript, interview. *Required for some:* 2 letters of recommendation. *Recommended:* essay or personal statement. *Application deadlines:* 9/9 (freshmen), 9/9 (transfers). *Notification:* continuous until 9/9 (freshmen), continuous until 9/9 (transfers).
Freshman Application Contact Mr. John DeTurris, Director of Admissions, Pennsylvania Institute of Technology, 800 Manchester Avenue, Media, PA 19063-4036. *Phone:* 610-892-1543. *Toll-free phone:* 800-422-0025. *Fax:* 610-892-1510. *E-mail:* info@pit.edu.
Website: http://www.pit.edu/.

Pittsburgh Career Institute
Pittsburgh, Pennsylvania

Director of Admissions Mr. Bruce E. Jones, Director of Admission, Pittsburgh Career Institute, 421 Seventh Avenue, Pittsburgh, PA 15219-1907. *Phone:* 412-281-7083 Ext. 114. *Toll-free phone:* 888-270-6333.
Website: http://www.pci.edu/.

Pittsburgh Institute of Aeronautics
Pittsburgh, Pennsylvania

- **Independent** 2-year, founded 1929
- **Suburban** campus
- **Coed, primarily men,** 368 undergraduate students, 100% full-time, 6% women, 94% men

Undergraduates 368 full-time. Students come from 12 states and territories; 4 other countries; 35% are from out of state; 6% Black or African American, non-Hispanic/Latino; 0.8% Hispanic/Latino; 0.8% Asian, non-Hispanic/Latino; 0.5% Native Hawaiian or other Pacific Islander, non-Hispanic/Latino; 0.5% American Indian or Alaska Native, non-

Hispanic/Latino; 6% Two or more races, non-Hispanic/Latino; 0.3% Race/ethnicity unknown; 0.3% international.
Freshmen *Admission:* 85 applied, 85 admitted.
Faculty *Total:* 37, 84% full-time. *Student/faculty ratio:* 17:1.
Majors Aeronautical/aerospace engineering technology; airframe mechanics and aircraft maintenance technology; avionics maintenance technology; electrical, electronic and communications engineering technology.
Academics *Calendar:* quarters. *Degree:* associate. *Special study options:* academic remediation for entering students, advanced placement credit.
Library Technical Library.
Student Life *Housing:* college housing not available. *Student services:* personal/psychological counseling.
Applying *Options:* deferred entrance. *Application fee:* $150. *Recommended:* high school transcript, interview. *Application deadlines:* rolling (freshmen), rolling (transfers). *Notification:* continuous (freshmen), continuous (transfers).
Freshman Application Contact Steven J. Sabold, Director of Admissions, Pittsburgh Institute of Aeronautics, PO Box 10897, Pittsburgh, PA 15236-0897. *Phone:* 412-346-2100. *Toll-free phone:* 800-444-1440. *Fax:* 412-466-5013. *E-mail:* admissions@pia.edu.
Website: http://www.pia.edu/.

Pittsburgh Institute of Mortuary Science, Incorporated
Pittsburgh, Pennsylvania

Freshman Application Contact Ms. Karen Rocco, Registrar, Pittsburgh Institute of Mortuary Science, Incorporated, 5808 Baum Boulevard, Pittsburgh, PA 15206-3706. *Phone:* 412-362-8500 Ext. 105. *Fax:* 412-362-1684. *E-mail:* pims5808@aol.com.
Website: http://www.pims.edu/.

Pittsburgh Technical Institute
Oakdale, Pennsylvania

- **Proprietary** 2-year, founded 1946
- **Suburban** 180-acre campus with easy access to Pittsburgh
- **Coed,** 1,936 undergraduate students, 100% full-time, 41% women, 59% men

Undergraduates 1,936 full-time. Students come from 13 states and territories; 18% are from out of state; 11% Black or African American, non-Hispanic/Latino; 0.5% Hispanic/Latino; 0.8% Asian, non-Hispanic/Latino; 0.2% Native Hawaiian or other Pacific Islander, non-Hispanic/Latino; 0.2% American Indian or Alaska Native, non-Hispanic/Latino; 7% Two or more races, non-Hispanic/Latino; 7% Race/ethnicity unknown; 10% transferred in; 40% live on campus.
Freshmen *Admission:* 2,062 applied, 694 enrolled. *Average high school GPA:* 2.97.
Faculty *Total:* 121, 63% full-time. *Student/faculty ratio:* 16:1.
Majors Business administration and management; computer graphics; computer programming; computer technology/computer systems technology; drafting and design technology; electrical, electronic and communications engineering technology; electrical/electronics equipment installation and repair; heating, air conditioning, ventilation and refrigeration maintenance technology; homeland security, law enforcement, firefighting and protective services related; hotel/motel administration; medical/health management and clinical assistant; medical office assistant; network and system administration; registered nursing/registered nurse; surgical technology; web page, digital/multimedia and information resources design; welding technology.
Academics *Calendar:* quarters. *Degree:* certificates and associate. *Special study options:* academic remediation for entering students, advanced placement credit, cooperative education, distance learning, double majors, internships, services for LD students.
Library Library Resource Center. *Books:* 6,549 (physical), 21 (digital/electronic); *Serial titles:* 145 (physical). Weekly public service hours: 58.
Student Life *Housing Options:* coed. Campus housing is university owned and leased by the school. Freshman campus housing is guaranteed. *Activities and Organizations:* drama/theater group, American Society of Travel Agents (ASTA), DECA, Software Development Club, Gay-Straight Alliance, Drama Club. *Campus security:* 24-hour emergency response devices and patrols, controlled dormitory access. *Student services:* personal/psychological counseling.
Athletics *Intramural sports:* basketball M/W, soccer M/W, softball M/W, ultimate Frisbee M/W, volleyball M/W.
Standardized Tests *Required:* entrance exam for practical nursing certificate and nursing Associate degree (for admission).
Costs (2016–17) *Comprehensive fee:* $27,527 includes full-time tuition ($16,664), mandatory fees ($1350), and room and board ($9513). Full-time tuition and fees vary according to course load and program. No tuition increase

for student's term of enrollment. *Room and board:* college room only: $7137. Room and board charges vary according to housing facility. *Payment plans:* installment, deferred payment. *Waivers:* children of alumni and employees or children of employees.

Applying *Options:* electronic application, deferred entrance. *Required:* high school transcript. *Required for some:* essay or personal statement, criminal background check, rank in top 50-80% of class. *Recommended:* interview. *Application deadlines:* rolling (freshmen), rolling (out-of-state freshmen), rolling (transfers). *Notification:* continuous (freshmen), continuous (out-of-state freshmen), continuous (transfers).

Freshman Application Contact Ms. Nancy Goodlin, Admissions Office Assistant, Pittsburgh Technical Institute, 1111 McKee Road, Oakdale, PA 15071. *Phone:* 412-809-5100. *Toll-free phone:* 800-784-9675. *Fax:* 412-809-5351. *E-mail:* goodlin.nancy@pti.edu.
Website: http://www.pti.edu/.

Reading Area Community College
Reading, Pennsylvania

- **County-supported** 2-year, founded 1971
- **Urban** 14-acre campus with easy access to Philadelphia
- **Endowment** $10.6 million
- **Coed,** 4,090 undergraduate students, 23% full-time, 62% women, 38% men

Undergraduates 936 full-time, 3,154 part-time. 0.3% are from out of state; 11% Black or African American, non-Hispanic/Latino; 32% Hispanic/Latino; 2% Asian, non-Hispanic/Latino; 0.2% Native Hawaiian or other Pacific Islander, non-Hispanic/Latino; 0.4% American Indian or Alaska Native, non-Hispanic/Latino; 3% Two or more races, non-Hispanic/Latino; 0.6% Race/ethnicity unknown.
Freshmen *Admission:* 1,577 applied, 1,577 admitted, 825 enrolled.
Faculty *Total:* 212, 27% full-time. *Student/faculty ratio:* 18:1.
Majors Accounting; accounting and business/management; administrative assistant and secretarial science; art; business administration and management; child-care and support services management; child development; clinical/medical laboratory technology; communication and media related; computer and information sciences; computer technology/computer systems technology; creative writing; criminal justice/police science; elementary education; engineering; general studies; health information/medical records technology; health services/allied health/health sciences; industrial mechanics and maintenance technology; interdisciplinary studies; liberal arts and sciences/liberal studies; machine tool technology; medical administrative assistant and medical secretary; mental and social health services and allied professions related; occupational therapist assistant; physical sciences; physical therapy technology; psychology; registered nursing/registered nurse; respiratory care therapy; restaurant, culinary, and catering management; science technologies related; secondary education; social sciences; social work; web page, digital/multimedia and information resources design.
Academics *Calendar:* semesters. *Degree:* certificates, diplomas, and associate. *Special study options:* academic remediation for entering students, adult/continuing education programs, advanced placement credit, cooperative education, distance learning, English as a second language, honors programs, part-time degree program, services for LD students, summer session for credit.
Library Yocum Library.
Student Life *Housing:* college housing not available. *Activities and Organizations:* student-run newspaper, Student Government Association, Environment Club, Legacy Organization, Multicultural/International Club, RACC Olympics. *Campus security:* 24-hour emergency response devices, late-night transport/escort service. *Student services:* personal/psychological counseling.
Standardized Tests *Required for some:* TOEFL. *Recommended:* SAT (for admission), ACT (for admission).
Costs (2016–17) *Tuition:* area resident $3750 full-time, $125 per credit part-time; state resident $7500 full-time, $250 per credit part-time; nonresident $11,250 full-time, $375 per credit part-time. Full-time tuition and fees vary according to course load and program. Part-time tuition and fees vary according to course load and program. *Required fees:* $1560 full-time, $52 per credit part-time. *Payment plan:* installment. *Waivers:* senior citizens and employees or children of employees.
Financial Aid Of all full-time matriculated undergraduates who enrolled in 2014, 80 Federal Work-Study jobs (averaging $5400). 20 state and other part-time jobs (averaging $3300).
Applying *Options:* electronic application, early admission. *Required for some:* essay or personal statement, high school transcript, 1 letter of

recommendation, interview, background/criminal check, physical exam, proof of insurance for selective admissions programs. *Recommended:* high school transcript. *Application deadlines:* rolling (freshmen), rolling (out-of-state freshmen), rolling (transfers). *Notification:* continuous (freshmen), continuous (out-of-state freshmen), continuous (transfers).
Freshman Application Contact Ms. Debbie Hettinger, Enrollment Services Coordinator/Communications Specialist, Reading Area Community College, PO Box 1706, Reading, PA 19603-1706. *Phone:* 610-372-4721 Ext. 5130. *E-mail:* dhettinger@racc.edu.
Website: http://www.racc.edu/.

The Restaurant School at Walnut Hill College
Philadelphia, Pennsylvania

- **Proprietary** primarily 2-year, founded 1974
- **Urban** 2-acre campus
- **Coed,** 429 undergraduate students, 100% full-time, 49% women, 51% men
- **97%** of applicants were admitted

Undergraduates 429 full-time. Students come from 2 other countries; 28% are from out of state; 29% Black or African American, non-Hispanic/Latino; 6% Hispanic/Latino; 2% Asian, non-Hispanic/Latino; 0.3% American Indian or Alaska Native, non-Hispanic/Latino; 5% Two or more races, non-Hispanic/Latino; 4% Race/ethnicity unknown; 0.5% international; 10% transferred in.
Freshmen *Admission:* 174 applied, 168 admitted, 173 enrolled.
Faculty *Total:* 19, 95% full-time. *Student/faculty ratio:* 22:1.
Majors Baking and pastry arts; culinary arts; hotel/motel administration; restaurant/food services management.
Academics *Calendar:* quarters. *Degrees:* associate and bachelor's. *Special study options:* internships, part-time degree program.
Library Alumni Resource Center plus 1 other. Weekly public service hours: 61.
Student Life *Housing Options:* coed. Campus housing is leased by the school. *Activities and Organizations:* Wine Club, Book Club, Coffee and Tea Club, Craft Club, Flair Bartending. *Campus security:* 24-hour emergency response devices and patrols, student patrols, controlled dormitory access.
Standardized Tests *Recommended:* SAT or ACT (for admission).
Costs (2016–17) *One-time required fee:* $200. *Tuition:* $19,050 full-time. *Required fees:* $3850 full-time. *Room only:* $5400. Room and board charges vary according to housing facility. *Payment plans:* installment, deferred payment.
Applying *Options:* electronic application, early admission, early decision, deferred entrance. *Application fee:* $50. *Required:* essay or personal statement, high school transcript, 2 letters of recommendation, interview. *Recommended:* minimum 2.0 GPA. *Application deadline:* rolling (freshmen).
Freshman Application Contact Mr. John English, Director of Admissions, The Restaurant School at Walnut Hill College, 4207 Walnut Street, Philadelphia, PA 19104-3518. *Phone:* 267-295-2353. *Fax:* 215-222-4219. *E-mail:* jenglish@walnuthillcollege.edu.
Website: http://www.walnuthillcollege.edu/.

Rosedale Technical Institute
Pittsburgh, Pennsylvania

Freshman Application Contact Ms. Debbie Bier, Director of Admissions, Rosedale Technical Institute, 215 Beecham Drive, Suite 2, Pittsburgh, PA 15205-9791. *Phone:* 412-521-6200. *Toll-free phone:* 800-521-6262. *Fax:* 412-521-2520. *E-mail:* admissions@rosedaletech.org.
Website: http://www.rosedaletech.org/.

South Hills School of Business & Technology
Altoona, Pennsylvania

Freshman Application Contact Ms. Holly J. Emerick, Director of Admissions, South Hills School of Business & Technology, 508 58th Street, Altoona, PA 16602. *Phone:* 814-944-6134. *Fax:* 814-944-4684.
E-mail: hemerick@southhills.edu.
Website: http://www.southhills.edu/.

South Hills School of Business & Technology
State College, Pennsylvania

- **Proprietary** 2-year, founded 1970
- **Small-town** 6-acre campus
- **Coed**

Undergraduates 574 full-time, 56 part-time. 2% Black or African American, non-Hispanic/Latino; 0.6% Hispanic/Latino; 0.5% Asian, non-Hispanic/Latino; 0.3% American Indian or Alaska Native, non-Hispanic/Latino; 1% Two or more races, non-Hispanic/Latino; 0.2% international; 15% transferred in. *Retention:* 70% of full-time freshmen returned.
Faculty *Student/faculty ratio:* 13:1.
Academics *Calendar:* quarters. *Degrees:* certificates, diplomas, and associate (also includes Altoona campus). *Special study options:* advanced placement credit, internships, part-time degree program.
Library Main Library plus 1 other.
Student Life *Campus security:* 24-hour emergency response devices.
Standardized Tests *Required:* Wonderlic aptitude test (for admission).
Costs (2015–16) *Tuition:* $16,521 full-time, $459 per credit part-time. Full-time tuition and fees vary according to program. Part-time tuition and fees vary according to course load.
Applying *Options:* electronic application. *Required:* high school transcript, interview. *Required for some:* essay or personal statement, 2 letters of recommendation.
Freshman Application Contact Mr. Troy R. Otradovec, Regional Director of Admissions, South Hills School of Business & Technology, 480 Waupelani Drive, State College, PA 16801-4516. *Phone:* 814-234-7755 Ext. 2020. *Toll-free phone:* 888-282-7427. *Fax:* 814-234-0926.
E-mail: admissions@southhills.edu.
Website: http://www.southhills.edu/.

Thaddeus Stevens College of Technology
Lancaster, Pennsylvania

- **State-supported** 2-year, founded 1905
- **Urban** 33-acre campus with easy access to Philadelphia
- **Endowment** $696,058
- **Coed,** 823 undergraduate students

Undergraduates 45% live on campus. *Retention:* 79% of full-time freshmen returned.
Freshmen *Admission:* 2,673 applied, 817 admitted.
Faculty *Total:* 80, 73% full-time. *Student/faculty ratio:* 12:1.
Majors Architectural technology; autobody/collision and repair technology; automotive engineering technology; cabinetmaking and millwork; CAD/CADD drafting/design technology; carpentry; computer and information sciences and support services related; electrical and electronic engineering technologies related; electrical, electronic and communications engineering technology; engineering-related technologies; executive assistant/executive secretary; graphic communications related; heating, air conditioning, ventilation and refrigeration maintenance technology; machine shop technology; masonry; plumbing technology; respiratory care therapy; sheet metal technology; water quality and wastewater treatment management and recycling technology; welding technology.
Academics *Calendar:* semesters. *Degree:* certificates and associate. *Special study options:* academic remediation for entering students, advanced placement credit, internships, services for LD students.
Library K. W. Schuler Learning Resources Center plus 1 other. *Books:* 59,073 (physical), 1,187 (digital/electronic); *Serial titles:* 21 (physical), 2,823 (digital/electronic); *Databases:* 21. Weekly public service hours: 78; students can reserve study rooms.
Student Life *Housing Options:* men-only, women-only. Campus housing is university owned. Freshman applicants given priority for college housing. *Activities and Organizations:* Phi Theta Kappa, Student Congress, Residence Hall Council, American Institute of Architectural Students (AIAS), Society of Manufacturing Engineers (SME). *Campus security:* 24-hour emergency response devices and patrols, controlled dormitory access. *Student services:* personal/psychological counseling, women's center.
Athletics Member NCAA, NJCAA. *Intercollegiate sports:* basketball M, cross-country running M, football M, track and field M, wrestling M.
Standardized Tests *Required:* ACT, SAT, or ACT Compass (for admission).
Costs (2015–16) *Tuition:* state resident $7400 full-time, $308 per credit hour part-time. Pennsylvania residency is required for admission. *Required fees:* $30 full-time. *Room and board:* $8620; room only: $4500. Room and board charges vary according to board plan. *Payment plan:* installment. *Waivers:* employees or children of employees.

Applying *Options:* electronic application, deferred entrance. *Application fee:* $45. *Required:* essay or personal statement, high school transcript, minimum 2.0 GPA. *Required for some:* interview. *Application deadlines:* 6/30 (freshmen), 6/30 (transfers). *Notification:* continuous until 7/15 (freshmen), continuous until 7/15 (transfers).
Freshman Application Contact Ms. Amy Kwiatkowski, Thaddeus Stevens College of Technology, 750 East King Street, Lancaster, PA 17055. *Phone:* 717-391-3540. *Toll-free phone:* 800-842-3832.
E-mail: kwiatkowski@stevenscollege.edu.
Website: http://www.stevenscollege.edu/.

Triangle Tech, Bethlehem
Bethlehem, Pennsylvania

Freshman Application Contact Triangle Tech, Bethlehem, 3184 Airport Road, Bethlehem, PA 18017.
Website: http://www.triangle-tech.edu/.

Triangle Tech, DuBois
Falls Creek, Pennsylvania

Freshman Application Contact Terry Kucic, Director of Admissions, Triangle Tech, DuBois, PO Box 551, DuBois, PA 15801. *Phone:* 814-371-2090. *Toll-free phone:* 800-874-8324. *Fax:* 814-371-9227.
E-mail: tkucic@triangle-tech.com.
Website: http://www.triangle-tech.edu/.

Triangle Tech, Erie
Erie, Pennsylvania

Freshman Application Contact Admissions Representative, Triangle Tech, Erie, 2000 Liberty Street, Erie, PA 16502-2594. *Phone:* 814-453-6016. *Toll-free phone:* 800-874-8324 (in-state); 800-TRI-TECH (out-of-state).
Website: http://www.triangle-tech.edu/.

Triangle Tech, Greensburg
Greensburg, Pennsylvania

Freshman Application Contact Mr. John Mazzarese, Vice President of Admissions, Triangle Tech, Greensburg, 222 East Pittsburgh Street, Greensburg, PA 15601. *Phone:* 412-359-1000. *Toll-free phone:* 800-874-8324.
Website: http://www.triangle-tech.edu/.

Triangle Tech, Pittsburgh
Pittsburgh, Pennsylvania

Freshman Application Contact Director of Admissions, Triangle Tech, Pittsburgh, 1940 Perrysville Avenue, Pittsburgh, PA 15214-3897. *Phone:* 412-359-1000. *Toll-free phone:* 800-874-8324. *Fax:* 412-359-1012.
E-mail: info@triangle-tech.edu.
Website: http://www.triangle-tech.edu/.

Triangle Tech, Sunbury
Sunbury, Pennsylvania

Freshman Application Contact Triangle Tech, Sunbury, 191 Performance Road, Sunbury, PA 17801. *Phone:* 412-359-1000.
Website: http://www.triangle-tech.edu/.

University of Pittsburgh at Titusville
Titusville, Pennsylvania

- **State-related** 2-year, founded 1963, part of University of Pittsburgh System
- **Small-town** 10-acre campus
- **Endowment** $850,000
- **Coed,** 388 undergraduate students, 81% full-time, 65% women, 35% men

Undergraduates 313 full-time, 75 part-time. Students come from 15 states and territories; 8% are from out of state; 14% Black or African American, non-Hispanic/Latino; 4% Hispanic/Latino; 2% Asian, non-Hispanic/Latino; 2% Two or more races, non-Hispanic/Latino; 2% Race/ethnicity unknown; 4% transferred in; 57% live on campus.
Freshmen *Admission:* 160 enrolled. *Average high school GPA:* 3.1. *Test scores:* SAT critical reading scores over 500: 22%; SAT math scores over 500: 29%; SAT writing scores over 500: 23%; ACT scores over 18: 69%; SAT

critical reading scores over 600: 5%; SAT math scores over 600: 4%; SAT writing scores over 600: 4%; ACT scores over 24: 7%.

Faculty *Total:* 48, 52% full-time. *Student/faculty ratio:* 15:1.

Majors Accounting; biology/biological sciences; business/commerce; criminal justice/law enforcement administration; history related; human services; information technology; liberal arts and sciences/liberal studies; management information systems; natural sciences; physical therapy technology; psychology related; registered nursing/registered nurse.

Academics *Calendar:* semesters. *Degree:* associate. *Special study options:* academic remediation for entering students, advanced placement credit, distance learning, internships, part-time degree program, summer session for credit.

Library Haskell Memorial Library.

Student Life *Housing:* on-campus residence required through sophomore year. *Options:* coed, special housing for students with disabilities. Campus housing is university owned. Freshman campus housing is guaranteed. *Activities and Organizations:* Phi Theta Kappa, BSU, SAB, Dining Club, Diversity Club. *Campus security:* 24-hour emergency response devices and patrols, late-night transport/escort service, controlled dormitory access. *Student services:* health clinic, personal/psychological counseling.

Athletics Member NJCAA. *Intercollegiate sports:* basketball M/W, cheerleading M/W, volleyball W. *Intramural sports:* badminton M/W, basketball M/W, bowling M/W, football M/W, golf M/W, racquetball M/W, sand volleyball M/W, softball M/W, table tennis M/W, tennis M/W, ultimate Frisbee M/W, volleyball M/W, weight lifting M/W.

Standardized Tests *Required:* SAT or ACT (for admission).

Costs (2016–17) *One-time required fee:* $60. *Tuition:* state resident $10,754 full-time, $448 per credit part-time; nonresident $20,316 full-time, $846 per credit part-time. Full-time tuition and fees vary according to program. Part-time tuition and fees vary according to program. *Required fees:* $830 full-time, $135 per term part-time. *Room and board:* $10,224; room only: $5292. Room and board charges vary according to board plan. *Payment plan:* installment.

Financial Aid Of all full-time matriculated undergraduates who enrolled in 2014, 289 applied for aid, 271 were judged to have need, 16 had their need fully met. In 2014, 12 non-need-based awards were made. *Average percent of need met:* 55%. *Average financial aid package:* $11,602. *Average need-based loan:* $3661. *Average need-based gift aid:* $7633. *Average non-need-based aid:* $3050.

Applying *Required:* high school transcript, minimum 2.0 GPA. *Required for some:* essay or personal statement. *Recommended:* interview.

Freshman Application Contact Ms. Colleen R. Motter, Admissions Counselor, University of Pittsburgh at Titusville, 504 East Main Street, Titusville, PA 16354. *Phone:* 814-827-4408. *Toll-free phone:* 888-878-0462. *Fax:* 814-827-4519. *E-mail:* motter@pitt.edu. *Website:* http://www.upt.pitt.edu/.

Valley Forge Military College
Wayne, Pennsylvania

Freshman Application Contact Maj. Greg Potts, Dean of Enrollment Management, Valley Forge Military College, 1001 Eagle Road, Wayne, PA 19087-3695. *Phone:* 610-989-1300. *Toll-free phone:* 800-234-8362. *Fax:* 610-688-1545. *E-mail:* admissions@vfmac.edu. *Website:* http://www.vfmac.edu/.

Vet Tech Institute
Pittsburgh, Pennsylvania

- **Proprietary** 2-year, founded 1958
- **Urban** campus
- **Coed,** 372 undergraduate students
- 64% of applicants were admitted

Freshmen *Admission:* 497 applied, 318 admitted.

Majors Veterinary/animal health technology.

Academics *Calendar:* semesters. *Degree:* associate. *Special study options:* accelerated degree program, internships.

Freshman Application Contact Admissions Office, Vet Tech Institute, 125 7th Street, Pittsburgh, PA 15222-3400. *Phone:* 412-391-7021. *Toll-free phone:* 800-570-0693. *Website:* http://pittsburgh.vettechinstitute.edu/.

Westmoreland County Community College
Youngwood, Pennsylvania

- **County-supported** 2-year, founded 1970
- **Rural** 85-acre campus with easy access to Pittsburgh
- **Endowment** $561,298
- **Coed,** 5,517 undergraduate students, 46% full-time, 62% women, 38% men

Undergraduates 2,531 full-time, 2,986 part-time. Students come from 5 states and territories; 0.2% are from out of state; 3% Black or African American, non-Hispanic/Latino; 2% Hispanic/Latino; 0.7% Asian, non-Hispanic/Latino; 0.2% American Indian or Alaska Native, non-Hispanic/Latino; 3% Two or more races, non-Hispanic/Latino; 21% transferred in. *Retention:* 59% of full-time freshmen returned.

Freshmen *Admission:* 2,071 applied, 2,071 admitted, 1,302 enrolled.

Faculty *Total:* 389, 21% full-time. *Student/faculty ratio:* 18:1.

Majors Accounting technology and bookkeeping; administrative assistant and secretarial science; applied horticulture/horticulture operations; architectural drafting and CAD/CADD; baking and pastry arts; banking and financial support services; biology/biotechnology laboratory technician; business administration and management; business/commerce; casino management; chemical technology; child-care provision; clinical laboratory science/medical technology; clinical/medical laboratory assistant; communications systems installation and repair technology; computer and information systems security; computer numerically controlled (CNC) machinist technology; computer programming; computer programming (specific applications); computer support specialist; computer systems networking and telecommunications; corrections; criminal justice/police science; criminal justice/safety; culinary arts; data entry/microcomputer applications; data processing and data processing technology; dental assisting; dental hygiene; diagnostic medical sonography and ultrasound technology; dietetic technology; early childhood education; electrical and power transmission installation; electrical, electronic and communications engineering technology; electromechanical technology; executive assistant/executive secretary; family and community services; fire prevention and safety technology; floriculture/floristry management; food service and dining room management; graphic communications related; graphic design; health and medical administrative services related; heating, air conditioning, ventilation and refrigeration maintenance technology; homeland security, law enforcement, firefighting and protective services related; hotel/motel administration; human resources management; industrial mechanics and maintenance technology; industrial technology; legal assistant/paralegal; liberal arts and sciences/liberal studies; library and information science; licensed practical/vocational nurse training; logistics, materials, and supply chain management; machine shop technology; machine tool technology; manufacturing engineering technology; mechanical drafting and CAD/CADD; mechanical engineering/mechanical technology; mechatronics, robotics, and automation engineering; medical/clinical assistant; medical office assistant; occupational safety and health technology; phlebotomy technology; physical science technologies related; pre-engineering; radio and television broadcasting technology; radiologic technology/science; real estate; registered nursing/registered nurse; restaurant, culinary, and catering management; sales, distribution, and marketing operations; special education–elementary school; tourism and travel services management; turf and turfgrass management; web page, digital/multimedia and information resources design; welding technology; well drilling.

Academics *Calendar:* semesters. *Degree:* certificates, diplomas, and associate. *Special study options:* academic remediation for entering students, accelerated degree program, adult/continuing education programs, advanced placement credit, cooperative education, distance learning, double majors, English as a second language, honors programs, independent study, internships, off-campus study, part-time degree program, services for LD students, summer session for credit.

Library Westmoreland County Community College Learning Resources Center. *Books:* 44,422 (physical), 135,000 (digital/electronic); *Serial titles:* 84 (physical); *Databases:* 25. Weekly public service hours: 60.

Student Life *Housing:* college housing not available. *Activities and Organizations:* choral group, Phi Theta Kappa, Sigma Alpha Pi Leadership Society, Criminal Justice Fraternity, SNAP, SADAA/SADHA. *Campus security:* 24-hour emergency response devices and patrols, late-night transport/escort service, county police office on campus. *Student services:* personal/psychological counseling.

Athletics Member NJCAA. *Intercollegiate sports:* baseball M, basketball M/W, bowling M/W, cross-country running M/W, golf M/W, soccer M/W, softball W, volleyball W.

Costs (2016–17) *Tuition:* area resident $3660 full-time, $122 per credit part-time; state resident $7320 full-time, $244 per credit part-time; nonresident $10,980 full-time, $366 per credit part-time. Full-time tuition and fees vary according to course load. Part-time tuition and fees vary according to course

load. *Required fees:* $1410 full-time, $47 per credit part-time. *Payment plans:* installment, deferred payment. *Waivers:* senior citizens and employees or children of employees.
Applying *Options:* electronic application, early admission. *Application deadlines:* rolling (freshmen), rolling (out-of-state freshmen), rolling (transfers). *Notification:* continuous (freshmen), continuous (out-of-state freshmen), continuous (transfers).
Freshman Application Contact Ms. Shawna Little, Admissions Coordinator, Westmoreland County Community College, 145 Pavillon Lane, Youngwood, PA 15697. *Phone:* 724-925-4064. *Toll-free phone:* 800-262-2103. *Fax:* 724-925-4292. *E-mail:* littles@wccc.edu.
Website: http://www.wccc.edu/.

Williamson College of the Trades
Media, Pennsylvania

- **Independent** 2-year, founded 1888
- **Small-town** 222-acre campus with easy access to Philadelphia
- **Men only,** 270 undergraduate students, 100% full-time

Undergraduates 270 full-time. Students come from 9 states and territories; 24% are from out of state; 100% live on campus.
Freshmen *Admission:* 389 applied, 102 admitted, 100 enrolled. *Average high school GPA:* 2.5.
Faculty *Total:* 29. *Student/faculty ratio:* 12:1.
Majors Carpentry; construction engineering technology; electrical, electronic and communications engineering technology; energy management and systems technology; horticultural science; landscaping and groundskeeping; machine tool technology; turf and turfgrass management.
Academics *Calendar:* semesters. *Degree:* diplomas and associate. *Special study options:* academic remediation for entering students, independent study, off-campus study.
Library Shrigley Library plus 3 others.
Student Life *Housing Options:* men-only. Freshman campus housing is guaranteed. *Activities and Organizations:* student-run newspaper, choral group, Ambassadors, SkillsUSA, Jazz Band, College Newspaper, Choir. *Campus security:* evening patrols and gate security. *Student services:* health clinic, personal/psychological counseling.
Athletics Member USCAA, NJCAA. *Intercollegiate sports:* baseball M, basketball M, cross-country running M, football M, lacrosse M, soccer M, tennis M, wrestling M. *Intramural sports:* archery M, basketball M, sand volleyball M, table tennis M, ultimate Frisbee M, volleyball M, weight lifting M.
Standardized Tests *Required:* Armed Services Vocational Aptitude Battery (ASVAB) (for admission).
Costs (2016–17) *Tuition:* $0 full-time. All Williamson students attend on full scholarships covering tuition, room, board, and textbooks. *Required fees:* $800 full-time.
Financial Aid *Financial aid deadline:* 2/22.
Applying *Options:* electronic application. *Required:* essay or personal statement, high school transcript, minimum 2.0 GPA, interview, average performance or better on the Armed Services Vocational Aptitude Battery (ASVAB). *Application deadline:* 2/22 (freshmen).
Freshman Application Contact Mr. Jay Merillat, Dean of Admissions, Williamson College of the Trades, 106 South New Middletown Road, Media, PA 19063. *Phone:* 610-566-1776 Ext. 235.
E-mail: jmerillat@williamson.edu.
Website: http://www.williamson.edu/.

WyoTech Blairsville
Blairsville, Pennsylvania

Freshman Application Contact Mr. Tim Smyers, WyoTech Blairsville, 500 Innovation Drive, Blairsville, PA 15717. *Phone:* 724-459-2311. *Toll-free phone:* 888-577-7559. *Fax:* 724-459-6499. *E-mail:* tsmyers@wyotech.edu.
Website: http://www.wyotech.edu/.

YTI Career Institute–Altoona
Altoona, Pennsylvania

Admissions Office Contact YTI Career Institute–Altoona, 2900 Fairway Drive, Altoona, PA 16602.
Website: http://www.yti.edu/.

YTI Career Institute–York
York, Pennsylvania

Freshman Application Contact YTI Career Institute–York, 1405 Williams Road, York, PA 17402-9017. *Phone:* 717-757-1100 Ext. 318. *Toll-free phone:* 800-557-6335.
Website: http://www.yti.edu/.

PUERTO RICO

The Center of Cinematography, Arts and Television
Bayamon, Puerto Rico

Admissions Office Contact The Center of Cinematography, Arts and Television, 51 Dr. Veve Street, Degetau Street Corner, Bayamon, PR 00960.
Website: http://ccatmiami.com/.

Centro de Estudios Multidisciplinarios
Mayaguez, Puerto Rico

Admissions Office Contact Centro de Estudios Multidisciplinarios, Calle Cristy #56, Mayaguez, PR 00680.
Website: http://www.cempr.edu/.

Centro de Estudios Multidisciplinarios
Rio Piedras, Puerto Rico

Director of Admissions Admissions Department, Centro de Estudios Multidisciplinarios, Calle 13 #1206, Ext. San Agustin, Rio Piedras, PR 00926. *Phone:* 787-765-4210 Ext. 115. *Toll-free phone:* 877-779-CDEM.
Website: http://www.cempr.edu/.

Dewey University–Arroyo
Arroyo, Puerto Rico

Admissions Office Contact Dewey University–Arroyo, Carr. #3, Km.129.7, Barrio Palmas, Arroyo, PR 00910.
Website: http://www.dewey.edu/.

Dewey University–Bayamón
Bayamón, Puerto Rico

Admissions Office Contact Dewey University–Bayamón, Carr. #2, Km. 15.9, Parque Industrial Corujo, Hato Tejas, Bayamón, PR 00959.
Website: http://www.dewey.edu/.

Dewey University–Carolina
Carolina, Puerto Rico

Admissions Office Contact Dewey University–Carolina, Carr. #3, Km. 11, Parque Industrial de Carolina, Lote 7, Carolina, PR 00986.
Website: http://www.dewey.edu/.

Dewey University–Fajardo
Fajardo, Puerto Rico

Admissions Office Contact Dewey University–Fajardo, 267 Calle General Valero, Fajardo, PR 00910.
Website: http://www.dewey.edu/.

Dewey University–Hatillo
Hatillo, Puerto Rico

Admissions Office Contact Dewey University–Hatillo, Carr. #2 Km. 86.9 Barrio Pueblo, Hatillo, PR 00659.
Website: http://www.dewey.edu/.

Dewey University–Hato Rey
Hato Rey, Puerto Rico

Admissions Office Contact Dewey University–Hato Rey, 427 Avenida Barbosa, Hato Rey, PR 00923.
Website: http://www.dewey.edu/.

Dewey University–Juana Diaz
Juana Diaz, Puerto Rico

Admissions Office Contact Dewey University–Juana Diaz, Carr. 149, Km. 55.9, Parque Industrial Lomas, Juana Diaz, PR 00910.
Website: http://www.dewey.edu/.

Dewey University–Manati
Manati, Puerto Rico

Admissions Office Contact Dewey University–Manati, Carr. 604, Km. 49.1 Barrio Tierras Nuevas, Salientes, Manati, PR 00674. *Toll-free phone:* 866-773-3939.
Website: http://www.dewey.edu/.

Dewey University–Mayaguez
Mayaguez, Puerto Rico

Admissions Office Contact Dewey University–Mayaguez, Carr. #64 Km 6.6 Barrio Algarrobo, Mayaguez, PR 00682.
Website: http://dewey.edu/.

EDIC College
Caguas, Puerto Rico

Admissions Office Contact EDIC College, Ave. Rafael Cordero Calle Gnova Urb. Caguas Norte, Caguas, PR 00726.
Website: http://www.ediccollege.edu/.

Huertas Junior College
Caguas, Puerto Rico

Director of Admissions Mrs. Barbara Hassim López, Director of Admissions, Huertas Junior College, PO Box 8429, Caguas, PR 00726. *Phone:* 787-743-1242. *Fax:* 787-743-0203. *E-mail:* huertas@huertas.org.
Website: http://www.huertas.edu/.

Humacao Community College
Humacao, Puerto Rico

- **Independent** primarily 2-year
- **Urban** campus
- **Endowment** $865,348
- **Coed,** 554 undergraduate students, 79% full-time, 66% women, 34% men

Undergraduates 435 full-time, 119 part-time. Students come from 1 other state; 100% Hispanic/Latino. *Retention:* 61% of full-time freshmen returned.
Freshmen *Admission:* 140 applied, 124 admitted, 108 enrolled. *Average high school GPA:* 2.89.
Faculty *Total:* 27, 48% full-time, 100% with terminal degrees. *Student/faculty ratio:* 30:1.
Majors Biotechnology; business/commerce; chemical technology; computer programming (specific applications); dental assisting; electrical and electronics engineering; environmental science; executive assistant/executive secretary; health information/medical records administration; heating, ventilation, air conditioning and refrigeration engineering technology; medical administrative assistant and medical secretary; microbiology; pharmacy technician.
Academics *Calendar:* trimesters. *Degrees:* certificates, diplomas, associate, and bachelor's. *Special study options:* academic remediation for entering students, adult/continuing education programs, cooperative education, distance learning, internships, part-time degree program, services for LD students.
Library Santiago N. Manuez Educational Resources Center plus 1 other. *Books:* 6,797 (digital/electronic); *Serial titles:* 30 (digital/electronic); *Databases:* 5. Weekly public service hours: 54.
Student Life *Housing:* college housing not available. *Activities and Organizations:* Enactus Humacao Community College, Students Council. *Campus security:* 24-hour emergency response devices and patrols. *Student services:* personal/psychological counseling.
Costs (2016–17) *One-time required fee:* $140. *Tuition:* $4932 full-time, $2340 per year part-time. Full-time tuition and fees vary according to degree level. Part-time tuition and fees vary according to degree level. *Required fees:* $450 full-time. *Payment plan:* installment. *Waivers:* employees or children of employees.
Financial Aid Of all full-time matriculated undergraduates who enrolled in 2014, 64 Federal Work-Study jobs (averaging $546).
Applying *Application fee:* $15. *Required:* high school transcript, interview. *Required for some:* certificate of Immunization for students under 21 years. *Notification:* continuous (freshmen).
Freshman Application Contact Mrs. Loalis Quinones, Director of Admissions, Humacao Community College, PO Box 9139, Humacao, PR 00792, Puerto Rico. *Phone:* 787-852-1430 Ext. 225. *Fax:* 787-850-1577. *E-mail:* lquinones@hccpr.edu.
Website: http://www.hccpr.edu/.

ICPR Junior College–Hato Rey Campus
Hato Rey, Puerto Rico

Freshman Application Contact Admissions Office, ICPR Junior College–Hato Rey Campus, 558 Munoz Rivera Avenue, PO Box 190304, Hato Rey, PR 00919-0304. *Phone:* 787-753-6335.
Website: http://www.icprjc.edu/.

Ponce Paramedical College
Ponce, Puerto Rico

Admissions Office Contact Ponce Paramedical College, L-15 Acacia Street Villa Flores Urbanizacion, Ponce, PR 00731.
Website: http://www.popac.edu/.

RHODE ISLAND

Community College of Rhode Island
Warwick, Rhode Island

- **State-supported** 2-year, founded 1964
- **Urban** 205-acre campus with easy access to Boston
- **Coed,** 16,195 undergraduate students, 30% full-time, 59% women, 41% men

Undergraduates 4,836 full-time, 11,359 part-time. Students come from 17 states and territories; 4% are from out of state; 9% Black or African American, non-Hispanic/Latino; 20% Hispanic/Latino; 3% Asian, non-Hispanic/Latino; 0.5% American Indian or Alaska Native, non-Hispanic/Latino; 4% Two or more races, non-Hispanic/Latino; 4% Race/ethnicity unknown; 0.1% international.
Freshmen *Admission:* 5,617 applied, 5,593 admitted, 2,941 enrolled.
Faculty *Total:* 823, 40% full-time. *Student/faculty ratio:* 18:1.
Majors Accounting; administrative assistant and secretarial science; adult development and aging; art; banking and financial support services; biological and physical sciences; business administration and management; business/commerce; chemical technology; clinical/medical laboratory technology; computer and information sciences; computer engineering technology; computer programming (specific applications); computer support specialist; computer systems networking and telecommunications; criminal justice/police science; crisis/emergency/disaster management; dental hygiene; diagnostic medical sonography and ultrasound technology; dramatic/theater arts; electromechanical technology; engineering; fire science/firefighting; general studies; histologic technician; jazz/jazz studies; kindergarten/preschool education; legal administrative assistant/secretary; legal assistant/paralegal; liberal arts and sciences/liberal studies; licensed practical/vocational nurse training; marketing/marketing management; massage therapy; medical administrative assistant and medical secretary; mental health counseling; music; occupational therapist assistant; opticianry; physical therapy technology; radiologic technology/science; registered nursing/registered nurse; respiratory care therapy; social work; special education; substance abuse/addiction counseling; surveying engineering; web/multimedia management and webmaster.
Academics *Calendar:* semesters. *Degree:* certificates, diplomas, and associate. *Special study options:* academic remediation for entering students, adult/continuing education programs, advanced placement credit, cooperative education, distance learning, double majors, English as a second language, external degree program, honors programs, independent study, internships, off-campus study, part-time degree program, services for LD students, study abroad, summer session for credit. *ROTC:* Army (c).
Library Community College of Rhode Island Learning Resources Center plus 3 others.

Student Life *Housing:* college housing not available. *Activities and Organizations:* drama/theater group, student-run newspaper, choral group, Distributive Education Clubs of America, Players (theater group), SkillsUSA, Phi Theta Kappa, Student Government. *Campus security:* 24-hour emergency response devices and patrols. *Student services:* health clinic, personal/psychological counseling.

Athletics Member NJCAA. *Intercollegiate sports:* baseball M(s), basketball M(s)/W(s), golf M/W, soccer M(s)/W(s), softball W(s), tennis M/W, track and field M/W, volleyball W(s). *Intramural sports:* basketball M/W, volleyball M/W.

Costs (2015–16) *Tuition:* state resident $3950 full-time, $180 per credit hour part-time; nonresident $11,180 full-time, $534 per credit hour part-time. Full-time tuition and fees vary according to program. Part-time tuition and fees vary according to course load and program. *Required fees:* $316 full-time, $12 per credit hour part-time. *Payment plans:* installment, deferred payment. *Waivers:* senior citizens and employees or children of employees.

Financial Aid Of all full-time matriculated undergraduates who enrolled in 2014, 500 Federal Work-Study jobs (averaging $2500).

Applying *Options:* deferred entrance. *Application fee:* $20. *Application deadlines:* rolling (freshmen), rolling (transfers). *Notification:* continuous (freshmen).

Freshman Application Contact Community College of Rhode Island, Flanagan Campus, 1762 Louisquisset Pike, Lincoln, RI 02865-4585. *Phone:* 401-333-7490. *Fax:* 401-333-7122. *E-mail:* webadmission@ccri.edu. *Website:* http://www.ccri.edu/.

SOUTH CAROLINA

Aiken Technical College
Graniteville, South Carolina

- **State and locally supported** 2-year, founded 1972, part of South Carolina State Board for Technical and Comprehensive Education
- **Rural** 88-acre campus
- **Endowment** $4.7 million
- **Coed,** 2,357 undergraduate students, 29% full-time, 64% women, 36% men

Undergraduates 694 full-time, 1,663 part-time. 14% are from out of state; 33% Black or African American, non-Hispanic/Latino; 5% Hispanic/Latino; 1% Asian, non-Hispanic/Latino; 0.1% Native Hawaiian or other Pacific Islander, non-Hispanic/Latino; 0.7% American Indian or Alaska Native, non-Hispanic/Latino; 0.9% Two or more races, non-Hispanic/Latino; 2% Race/ethnicity unknown; 36% transferred in. *Retention:* 57% of full-time freshmen returned.

Freshmen *Admission:* 1,289 applied, 705 admitted, 571 enrolled.

Faculty *Total:* 200, 29% full-time.

Majors Accounting; administrative assistant and secretarial science; business administration and management; child-care and support services management; computer and information sciences and support services related; computer programming; computer systems networking and telecommunications; criminal justice/law enforcement administration; criminal justice/safety; data processing and data processing technology; early childhood education; electrical, electronic and communications engineering technology; industrial mechanics and maintenance technology; liberal arts and sciences/liberal studies; medical radiologic technology; multi/interdisciplinary studies related; quality control technology; radiation protection/health physics technology; registered nursing/registered nurse; sales, distribution, and marketing operations.

Academics *Calendar:* semesters. *Degree:* certificates, diplomas, and associate. *Special study options:* academic remediation for entering students, accelerated degree program, advanced placement credit, cooperative education, distance learning, double majors, independent study, internships, off-campus study, part-time degree program, services for LD students, summer session for credit.

Library Aiken Technical College Learning Resources Center. *Books:* 29,105 (physical), 133,000 (digital/electronic); *Serial titles:* 124 (physical), 391,523 (digital/electronic); *Databases:* 73. Weekly public service hours: 64; study areas open 24 hours, 5&-7 days a week; students can reserve study rooms.

Student Life *Housing:* college housing not available. *Campus security:* 24-hour emergency response devices and patrols, late-night transport/escort service. *Student services:* personal/psychological counseling.

Costs (2016–17) *Tuition:* area resident $4352 full-time; state resident $4712 full-time; nonresident $8224 full-time.

Financial Aid Of all full-time matriculated undergraduates who enrolled in 2014, 48 Federal Work-Study jobs (averaging $3000).

Applying *Options:* electronic application, deferred entrance. *Recommended:* high school transcript. *Application deadlines:* rolling (freshmen), rolling (out-of-state freshmen), rolling (transfers). *Notification:* continuous (freshmen), continuous (out-of-state freshmen), continuous (transfers).

Freshman Application Contact Jessica Moon, Director of Enrollment Services, Aiken Technical College, 2276 J. Davis Highway, Graniteville, SC 29829. *Phone:* 803-508-7262 Ext. 156. *E-mail:* moonj@atc.edu. *Website:* http://www.atc.edu/.

Brown Mackie College–Greenville
Greenville, South Carolina

Freshman Application Contact Brown Mackie College–Greenville, Two Liberty Square, 75 Beattie Place, Suite 100, Greenville, SC 29601. *Phone:* 864-239-5300. *Toll-free phone:* 877-479-8465. *Website:* http://www.brownmackie.edu/greenville/.

Central Carolina Technical College
Sumter, South Carolina

Freshman Application Contact Ms. Barbara Wright, Director of Admissions and Counseling, Central Carolina Technical College, 506 North Guignard Drive, Sumter, SC 29150. *Phone:* 803-778-6695. *Toll-free phone:* 800-221-8711. *Fax:* 803-778-6696. *E-mail:* wrightb@cctech.edu. *Website:* http://www.cctech.edu/.

Centura College
Columbia, South Carolina

Admissions Office Contact Centura College, 7500 Two Notch Road, Columbia, SC 29223. *Website:* http://www.centuracollege.edu/.

Clinton College
Rock Hill, South Carolina

Director of Admissions Robert M. Copeland, Vice President for Student Affairs, Clinton College, 1029 Crawford Road, Rock Hill, SC 29730. *Phone:* 803-327-7402. *Toll-free phone:* 877-837-9645. *Fax:* 803-327-3261. *E-mail:* rcopeland@clintonjrcollege.org. *Website:* http://www.clintoncollege.edu/.

Denmark Technical College
Denmark, South Carolina

- **State-supported** 2-year, founded 1948, part of South Carolina State Board for Technical and Comprehensive Education
- **Rural** 53-acre campus
- **Coed,** 1,043 undergraduate students, 63% full-time, 60% women, 40% men

Undergraduates 655 full-time, 388 part-time. 4% are from out of state; 92% Black or African American, non-Hispanic/Latino; 0.8% Hispanic/Latino; 0.2% Asian, non-Hispanic/Latino; 0.2% American Indian or Alaska Native, non-Hispanic/Latino; 0.4% Race/ethnicity unknown; 0.8% transferred in. *Retention:* 28% of full-time freshmen returned.

Freshmen *Admission:* 368 enrolled.

Faculty *Total:* 63, 59% full-time, 8% with terminal degrees. *Student/faculty ratio:* 20:1.

Majors Administrative assistant and secretarial science; business/commerce; child-care and support services management; criminal justice/safety; data processing and data processing technology; electromechanical technology; human services; industrial electronics technology; liberal arts and sciences/liberal studies; multi/interdisciplinary studies related.

Academics *Calendar:* semesters. *Degree:* certificates, diplomas, and associate. *Special study options:* academic remediation for entering students, adult/continuing education programs, advanced placement credit, cooperative education, distance learning, independent study, internships, off-campus study, part-time degree program, services for LD students, summer session for credit.

Library Denmark Technical College Learning Resources Center. *Books:* 9,810 (physical); *Databases:* 2. Weekly public service hours: 40; study areas open 24 hours, 5&-7 days a week; students can reserve study rooms.

Student Life *Housing Options:* men-only, women-only. Campus housing is university owned. Freshman applicants given priority for college housing. *Activities and Organizations:* choral group, Student Government Association, DTC Choir, Athletics, Phi Theta Kappa Internal Honor Society, Esquire Club (men and women). *Campus security:* 24-hour patrols, late-night transport/escort service, 24-hour emergency contact line/alarm devices. *Student services:* health clinic, personal/psychological counseling.

Athletics Member NJCAA. *Intercollegiate sports:* basketball M/W, cheerleading W. *Intramural sports:* basketball M/W.

Standardized Tests *Required:* ACT ASSET, ACCUPLACER, and TEAS (for nursing) (for admission). *Recommended:* SAT or ACT (for admission).
Costs (2015–16) *Tuition:* state resident $2616 full-time, $109 per credit hour part-time; nonresident $5232 full-time, $218 per credit hour part-time. *Required fees:* $310 full-time. *Room and board:* $3958; room only: $1932.
Financial Aid Of all full-time matriculated undergraduates who enrolled in 2014, 250 Federal Work-Study jobs (averaging $2000).
Applying *Options:* electronic application, early admission, deferred entrance. *Application fee:* $10. *Required:* high school transcript. *Required for some:* essay or personal statement, criminal background check, drug test, PPD test for LPN. *Application deadlines:* rolling (freshmen), rolling (out-of-state freshmen), rolling (transfers). *Notification:* continuous (freshmen), continuous (out-of-state freshmen), continuous (transfers).
Freshman Application Contact Ms. Kara Troy, Administrative Specialist II, Denmark Technical College, PO Box 327, 1126 Solomon Blatt Boulevard, Denmark, SC 29042. *Phone:* 803-793-5180. *Fax:* 803-793-5942.
E-mail: troyk@denmarktech.edu.
Website: http://www.denmarktech.edu/.

ECPI University
Columbia, South Carolina

Admissions Office Contact ECPI University, 250 Berryhill Road, #300, Columbia, SC 29210. *Toll-free phone:* 844-611-0668.
Website: http://www.ecpi.edu/.

ECPI University
Greenville, South Carolina

Admissions Office Contact ECPI University, 1001 Keys Drive, #100, Greenville, SC 29615. *Toll-free phone:* 844-611-0627.
Website: http://www.ecpi.edu/.

ECPI University
North Charleston, South Carolina

Admissions Office Contact ECPI University, 7410 Northside Drive, #100, North Charleston, SC 29420. *Toll-free phone:* 844-611-0642.
Website: http://www.ecpi.edu/.

Florence-Darlington Technical College
Florence, South Carolina

Director of Admissions Shelley Fortin, Vice President for Enrollment Management and Student Services, Florence-Darlington Technical College, 2715 West Lucas Street, PO Box 100548, Florence, SC 29501-0548. *Phone:* 843-661-8111 Ext. 117. *Toll-free phone:* 800-228-5745.
E-mail: shelley.fortin@fdtc.edu.
Website: http://www.fdtc.edu/.

Forrest College
Anderson, South Carolina

- **Proprietary** 2-year, founded 1946
- **Small-town** 3-acre campus
- **Endowment** $60,000
- **Coed,** 99 undergraduate students, 86% full-time, 90% women, 10% men

Undergraduates 85 full-time, 14 part-time. Students come from 1 other state; 31% Black or African American, non-Hispanic/Latino; 2% Hispanic/Latino.
Freshmen *Admission:* 17 enrolled.
Faculty *Total:* 28, 39% full-time, 11% with terminal degrees. *Student/faculty ratio:* 4:1.
Majors Accounting; business administration and management; child-care and support services management; computer installation and repair technology; computer technology/computer systems technology; legal administrative assistant/secretary; legal assistant/paralegal; medical/clinical assistant; medical office management; office management.
Academics *Calendar:* quarters. *Degree:* certificates, diplomas, and associate. *Special study options:* advanced placement credit, cooperative education, double majors, independent study, internships, part-time degree program, summer session for credit.
Library Forrest College Library plus 1 other.
Student Life *Housing:* college housing not available. *Campus security:* 24-hour emergency response devices, late-night transport/escort service.
Costs (2015–16) *Tuition:* $11,760 full-time, $245 per credit hour part-time. Full-time tuition and fees vary according to class time, course level, course load, degree level, program, reciprocity agreements, and student level. Part-time tuition and fees vary according to class time, course level, course load,

degree level, program, reciprocity agreements, and student level. *Required fees:* $375 full-time, $125 per term part-time. *Payment plan:* installment. *Waivers:* employees or children of employees.
Applying *Required:* essay or personal statement, high school transcript, interview.
Freshman Application Contact Ms. Janie Turmon, Admissions and Placement Coordinator/Representative, Forrest College, 601 East River Street, Anderson, SC 29624. *Phone:* 864-225-7653. *Fax:* 864-261-7471.
E-mail: janieturmon@forrestcollege.edu.
Website: http://www.forrestcollege.edu/.

Fortis College
Columbia, South Carolina

Admissions Office Contact Fortis College, 246 Stoneridge Drive, Suite 101, Columbia, SC 29210. *Toll-free phone:* 855-4-FORTIS.
Website: http://www.fortis.edu/.

Golf Academy of America
Myrtle Beach, South Carolina

Admissions Office Contact Golf Academy of America, 3268 Waccamaw Boulevard, Myrtle Beach, SC 29579.
Website: http://www.golfacademy.edu/.

Greenville Technical College
Greenville, South Carolina

- **State-supported** 2-year, founded 1962, part of South Carolina State Board for Technical and Comprehensive Education
- **Urban** 604-acre campus
- **Coed,** 12,280 undergraduate students, 39% full-time, 58% women, 42% men

Undergraduates 4,793 full-time, 7,487 part-time. Students come from 62 other countries; 3% are from out of state; 23% Black or African American, non-Hispanic/Latino; 8% Hispanic/Latino; 2% Asian, non-Hispanic/Latino; 0.1% Native Hawaiian or other Pacific Islander, non-Hispanic/Latino; 0.4% American Indian or Alaska Native, non-Hispanic/Latino; 3% Two or more races, non-Hispanic/Latino; 4% Race/ethnicity unknown; 0.3% international; 6% transferred in.
Freshmen *Admission:* 5,014 applied, 5,010 admitted, 2,241 enrolled.
Faculty *Total:* 817, 42% full-time, 10% with terminal degrees. *Student/faculty ratio:* 15:1.
Majors Accounting; administrative assistant and secretarial science; architectural engineering technology; automobile/automotive mechanics technology; business administration and management; child-care and support services management; clinical/medical laboratory technology; construction engineering technology; criminal justice/safety; culinary arts; data processing and data processing technology; dental hygiene; diagnostic medical sonography and ultrasound technology; electrical, electronic and communications engineering technology; electromechanical and instrumentation and maintenance technologies related; emergency medical technology (EMT paramedic); fire science/firefighting; health information/medical records technology; legal assistant/paralegal; liberal arts and sciences/liberal studies; machine tool technology; mechanical drafting and CAD/CADD; mechanical engineering/mechanical technology; mechanic and repair technologies related; medical radiologic technology; multi/interdisciplinary studies related; occupational therapist assistant; physical therapy technology; purchasing, procurement/acquisitions and contracts management; registered nursing/registered nurse; respiratory care therapy; sales, distribution, and marketing operations.
Academics *Calendar:* semesters. *Degree:* certificates, diplomas, and associate. *Special study options:* academic remediation for entering students, advanced placement credit, cooperative education, distance learning, double majors, English as a second language, honors programs, independent study, internships, part-time degree program, services for LD students, summer session for credit.
Library J. Verne Smith Library plus 3 others. *Books:* 36,932 (physical), 372,967 (digital/electronic); *Serial titles:* 143 (physical), 16 (digital/electronic); *Databases:* 30. Weekly public service hours: 67.
Student Life *Housing:* college housing not available. *Activities and Organizations:* Phi Theta Kappa, AAMLI, Cosmetology Club, Engineering Club, SGA/SAT Club. *Campus security:* 24-hour emergency response devices and patrols, late-night transport/escort service.
Athletics *Intramural sports:* badminton M(c)/W(c), basketball M(c)/W(c), football M(c)/W(c), soccer M(c)/W(c), softball M(c)/W(c), tennis M(c)/W(c), volleyball M(c)/W(c).
Standardized Tests *Recommended:* SAT, ACT ASSET, or ACT Compass.

Costs (2016–17) *Tuition:* area resident $5370 full-time; state resident $5820 full-time; nonresident $10,710 full-time. Full-time tuition and fees vary according to course load and program. Part-time tuition and fees vary according to course load and program. *Payment plans:* installment, deferred payment. *Waivers:* senior citizens.

Financial Aid Of all full-time matriculated undergraduates who enrolled in 2014, 101 Federal Work-Study jobs (averaging $2997).

Applying *Options:* electronic application, early admission, deferred entrance. *Application fee:* $35. *Required:* high school transcript. *Application deadlines:* rolling (freshmen), rolling (transfers). *Notification:* continuous until 8/18 (freshmen), continuous until 8/18 (transfers).

Freshman Application Contact Greenville Technical College, PO Box 5616, Greenville, SC 29606-5616. *Phone:* 864-250-8287. *Toll-free phone:* 800-992-1183 (in-state); 800-723-0673 (out-of-state).
Website: http://www.gvltec.edu/.

Horry-Georgetown Technical College
Conway, South Carolina

- **State and locally supported** 2-year, founded 1966, part of South Carolina State Board for Technical and Comprehensive Education
- **Small-town** campus
- **Coed**

Undergraduates 2,911 full-time, 4,749 part-time. 22% Black or African American, non-Hispanic/Latino; 4% Hispanic/Latino; 1% Asian, non-Hispanic/Latino; 0.1% Native Hawaiian or other Pacific Islander, non-Hispanic/Latino; 0.5% American Indian or Alaska Native, non-Hispanic/Latino; 2% Two or more races, non-Hispanic/Latino; 0.6% Race/ethnicity unknown; 0.2% international. *Retention:* 57% of full-time freshmen returned.

Faculty *Student/faculty ratio:* 21:1.

Academics *Calendar:* semesters. *Degree:* certificates, diplomas, and associate. *Special study options:* academic remediation for entering students, adult/continuing education programs, advanced placement credit, cooperative education, distance learning, double majors, independent study, internships, part-time degree program, services for LD students, summer session for credit.

Library Conway Campus Library.

Student Life *Campus security:* 24-hour emergency response devices and patrols.

Costs (2015–16) *Tuition:* area resident $1793 full-time, $150 per hour part-time; state resident $2250 full-time, $188 per hour part-time; nonresident $3229 full-time, $270 per hour part-time. *Required fees:* $402 full-time.

Applying *Options:* early admission. *Application fee:* $25. *Required for some:* high school transcript.

Freshman Application Contact Mr. George Swindoll, Associate Vice President for Enrollment, Development, and Registration, Horry-Georgetown Technical College, 2050 Highway 501 East, PO Box 261966, Conway, SC 29528-6066. *Phone:* 843-349-5277. *Fax:* 843-349-7501.
E-mail: george.swindoll@hgtc.edu.
Website: http://www.hgtc.edu/.

ITT Technical Institute
Columbia, South Carolina

Freshman Application Contact Director of Recruitment, ITT Technical Institute, 1628 Browning Road, Suite 180, Columbia, SC 29210. *Phone:* 803-216-6000. *Toll-free phone:* 800-242-5158.
Website: http://www.itt-tech.edu/.

ITT Technical Institute
Greenville, South Carolina

Freshman Application Contact Director of Recruitment, ITT Technical Institute, 6 Independence Pointe, Greenville, SC 29615. *Phone:* 864-288-0777. *Toll-free phone:* 800-932-4488.
Website: http://www.itt-tech.edu/.

ITT Technical Institute
North Charleston, South Carolina

Freshman Application Contact Director of Recruitment, ITT Technical Institute, 2431 West Aviation Avenue, North Charleston, SC 29406. *Phone:* 843-745-5700. *Toll-free phone:* 877-291-0900.
Website: http://www.itt-tech.edu/.

Midlands Technical College
Columbia, South Carolina

- **State and locally supported** 2-year, founded 1974, part of South Carolina State Board for Technical and Comprehensive Education
- **Suburban** 156-acre campus
- **Endowment** $6.9 million
- **Coed,** 10,946 undergraduate students, 46% full-time, 59% women, 41% men

Undergraduates 4,981 full-time, 5,965 part-time. Students come from 30 states and territories; 65 other countries; 2% are from out of state; 36% Black or African American, non-Hispanic/Latino; 4% Hispanic/Latino; 2% Asian, non-Hispanic/Latino; 0.1% Native Hawaiian or other Pacific Islander, non-Hispanic/Latino; 0.5% American Indian or Alaska Native, non-Hispanic/Latino; 3% Two or more races, non-Hispanic/Latino; 3% Race/ethnicity unknown; 10% transferred in.

Freshmen *Admission:* 5,753 applied, 3,763 admitted, 2,354 enrolled.

Faculty *Total:* 658, 34% full-time. *Student/faculty ratio:* 20:1.

Majors Accounting; administrative assistant and secretarial science; architectural engineering technology; automobile/automotive mechanics technology; building construction technology; business administration and management; business/commerce; child-care and support services management; child-care provision; civil engineering technology; clinical/medical laboratory technology; commercial and advertising art; computer and information sciences and support services related; computer installation and repair technology; computer systems networking and telecommunications; construction engineering technology; court reporting; criminal justice/safety; data processing and data processing technology; dental assisting; dental hygiene; electrical, electronic and communications engineering technology; engineering technology; gerontology; health information/medical records technology; health professions related; heating, air conditioning, ventilation and refrigeration maintenance technology; human services; industrial electronics technology; industrial mechanics and maintenance technology; legal assistant/paralegal; liberal arts and sciences/liberal studies; licensed practical/vocational nurse training; machine tool technology; mechanical drafting and CAD/CADD; mechanical engineering/mechanical technology; medical/clinical assistant; medical radiologic technology; multi/interdisciplinary studies related; nuclear medical technology; occupational therapist assistant; pharmacy technician; physical therapy technology; precision production related; precision production trades; registered nursing/registered nurse; respiratory care therapy; sales, distribution, and marketing operations; surgical technology; youth services.

Academics *Calendar:* semesters. *Degree:* certificates, diplomas, and associate. *Special study options:* academic remediation for entering students, adult/continuing education programs, advanced placement credit, cooperative education, distance learning, double majors, English as a second language, internships, part-time degree program, services for LD students, student-designed majors, summer session for credit. *ROTC:* Army (c), Navy (c), Air Force (c).

Library Midlands Technical College Library plus 5 others. *Books:* 50,329 (physical), 354,481 (digital/electronic); *Serial titles:* 295 (physical); *Databases:* 111. Weekly public service hours: 58; students can reserve study rooms.

Student Life *Housing:* college housing not available. *Activities and Organizations:* drama/theater group, student-run newspaper, Student Nurses Association, Human Services Association, Dental Hygiene Association, Health Information Management Student Association, Medical Laboratory Technology Club. *Campus security:* 24-hour emergency response devices and patrols, late-night transport/escort service.

Athletics *Intramural sports:* basketball M, bowling M/W, cross-country running M/W, football M, softball M/W, ultimate Frisbee M/W, volleyball M/W.

Standardized Tests *Required for some:* ACT ASSET. *Recommended:* SAT or ACT (for admission).

Costs (2016–17) *One-time required fee:* $35. *Tuition:* area resident $3840 full-time, $160 per credit hour part-time; state resident $4800 full-time, $200 per credit hour part-time; nonresident $11,520 full-time, $480 per credit hour part-time. Full-time tuition and fees vary according to course load. Part-time tuition and fees vary according to course load. *Required fees:* $1044 full-time, $30 per credit hour part-time, $162 per term part-time. *Payment plan:* installment. *Waivers:* senior citizens and employees or children of employees.

Financial Aid Of all full-time matriculated undergraduates who enrolled in 2011, 4,794 applied for aid, 4,160 were judged to have need, 118 had their need fully met. 154 Federal Work-Study jobs (averaging $2775). *Average percent of need met:* 13%. *Average financial aid package:* $6098. *Average need-based loan:* $3089. *Average need-based gift aid:* $4370.

Applying *Options:* electronic application, early admission, deferred entrance. *Application fee:* $35. *Recommended:* high school transcript. *Application deadline:* rolling (transfers). *Notification:* continuous (transfers).
Freshman Application Contact Ms. Sylvia Littlejohn, Director of Admissions, Midlands Technical College, PO Box 2408, Columbia, SC 29202. *Phone:* 803-738-8324. *Toll-free phone:* 800-922-8038. *Fax:* 803-790-7524. *E-mail:* admissions@midlandstech.edu. *Website:* http://www.midlandstech.edu/.

Miller-Motte Technical College
Conway, South Carolina

Admissions Office Contact Miller-Motte Technical College, 2451 Highway 501 East, Conway, SC 29526. *Toll-free phone:* 866-297-0267.
Website: http://www.miller-motte.edu/.

Miller-Motte Technical College
North Charleston, South Carolina

Freshman Application Contact Ms. Elaine Cue, Campus President, Miller-Motte Technical College, 8085 Rivers Avenue, Suite E, North Charleston, SC 29406. *Phone:* 843-574-0101. *Toll-free phone:* 800-923-4162. *Fax:* 843-266-3424. *E-mail:* juliasc@miller-mott.net.
Website: http://www.miller-motte.edu/.

Northeastern Technical College
Cheraw, South Carolina

Freshman Application Contact Mrs. Mary K. Newton, Dean of Students, Northeastern Technical College, 1201 Chesterfield Highway, Cheraw, SC 29520-1007. *Phone:* 843-921-6935. *Toll-free phone:* 800-921-7399. *Fax:* 843-921-1476. *E-mail:* mpace@netc.edu.
Website: http://www.netc.edu/.

Orangeburg-Calhoun Technical College
Orangeburg, South Carolina

Freshman Application Contact Mr. Dana Rickards, Director of Recruitment, Orangeburg-Calhoun Technical College, 3250 St Matthews Road, NE, Orangeburg, SC 29118-8299. *Phone:* 803-535-1219. *Toll-free phone:* 800-813-6519.
Website: http://www.octech.edu/.

Piedmont Technical College
Greenwood, South Carolina

Director of Admissions Mr. Steve Coleman, Director of Admissions, Piedmont Technical College, 620 North Emerald Road, PO Box 1467, Greenwood, SC 29648-1467. *Phone:* 864-941-8603. *Toll-free phone:* 800-868-5528.
Website: http://www.ptc.edu/.

Spartanburg Community College
Spartanburg, South Carolina

- **State-supported** 2-year, founded 1961, part of South Carolina State Board for Technical and Comprehensive Education
- **Suburban** 104-acre campus with easy access to Charlotte
- **Coed,** 4,928 undergraduate students, 45% full-time, 58% women, 42% men

Undergraduates 2,232 full-time, 2,696 part-time. Students come from 7 states and territories; 3 other countries; 1% are from out of state; 22% Black or African American, non-Hispanic/Latino; 7% Hispanic/Latino; 4% Asian, non-Hispanic/Latino; 0.1% Native Hawaiian or other Pacific Islander, non-Hispanic/Latino; 0.2% American Indian or Alaska Native, non-Hispanic/Latino; 2% Two or more races, non-Hispanic/Latino; 2% Race/ethnicity unknown; 9% transferred in. *Retention:* 36% of full-time freshmen returned.
Freshmen *Admission:* 961 enrolled.
Faculty *Total:* 345, 31% full-time. *Student/faculty ratio:* 16:1.
Majors Accounting; administrative assistant and secretarial science; applied horticulture/horticulture operations; automobile/automotive mechanics technology; business administration and management; clinical/medical laboratory technology; data processing and data processing technology; electrical, electronic and communications engineering technology; heating, air conditioning, ventilation and refrigeration maintenance technology; industrial electronics technology; liberal arts and sciences/liberal studies; machine tool

technology; manufacturing engineering technology; mechanical engineering/mechanical technology; medical radiologic technology; multi/interdisciplinary studies related; radiation protection/health physics technology; registered nursing/registered nurse; respiratory care therapy.
Academics *Calendar:* semesters condensed semesters plus summer sessions. *Degree:* certificates, diplomas, and associate. *Special study options:* academic remediation for entering students, adult/continuing education programs, advanced placement credit, cooperative education, distance learning, English as a second language, part-time degree program, services for LD students, summer session for credit.
Library Spartanburg Community College Library.
Student Life *Housing:* college housing not available. *Activities and Organizations:* drama/theater group, student-run newspaper. *Campus security:* 24-hour emergency response devices and patrols. *Student services:* personal/psychological counseling, women's center.
Standardized Tests *Required for some:* SAT or ACT (for admission).
Costs (2015–16) *Tuition:* area resident $4092 full-time, $171 per credit hour part-time; state resident $5110 full-time, $213 per credit hour part-time; nonresident $8372 full-time, $349 per credit hour part-time. Full-time tuition and fees vary according to course load and location. Part-time tuition and fees vary according to location. *Required fees:* $100 full-time, $50 per term part-time. *Payment plans:* installment, deferred payment. *Waivers:* senior citizens.
Financial Aid Of all full-time matriculated undergraduates who enrolled in 2014, 41 Federal Work-Study jobs (averaging $3020).
Applying *Options:* electronic application, early admission. *Application fee:* $25. *Required:* high school transcript. *Recommended:* interview. *Application deadlines:* rolling (freshmen), rolling (transfers). *Notification:* continuous (freshmen), continuous (transfers).
Freshman Application Contact Ms. Sabrina Sims, Admissions Counselor, Spartanburg Community College, PO Box 4386, Spartanburg, SC 29305. *Phone:* 864-592-4816. *Toll-free phone:* 866-591-3700. *Fax:* 864-592-4564. *E-mail:* admissions@sccsc.edu.
Website: http://www.sccsc.edu/.

Spartanburg Methodist College
Spartanburg, South Carolina

- **Independent Methodist** 2-year, founded 1911
- **Suburban** 110-acre campus with easy access to Charlotte
- **Endowment** $22.0 million
- **Coed,** 771 undergraduate students, 99% full-time, 46% women, 54% men

Undergraduates 762 full-time, 9 part-time. Students come from 13 states and territories; 2 other countries; 6% are from out of state; 33% Black or African American, non-Hispanic/Latino; 6% Hispanic/Latino; 1% Asian, non-Hispanic/Latino; 0.1% American Indian or Alaska Native, non-Hispanic/Latino; 2% Two or more races, non-Hispanic/Latino; 0.5% international; 4% transferred in; 65% live on campus.
Freshmen *Admission:* 1,261 applied, 878 admitted, 440 enrolled. *Average high school GPA:* 3.36. *Test scores:* SAT critical reading scores over 500: 16%; SAT math scores over 500: 20%; SAT writing scores over 500: 10%; ACT scores over 18: 46%; SAT critical reading scores over 600: 2%; SAT math scores over 600: 3%; SAT writing scores over 600: 1%; ACT scores over 24: 5%.
Faculty *Total:* 73, 38% full-time, 32% with terminal degrees. *Student/faculty ratio:* 19:1.
Majors Business/commerce; criminal justice/law enforcement administration; liberal arts and sciences/liberal studies; religious studies related; visual and performing arts.
Academics *Calendar:* semesters. *Degree:* associate. *Special study options:* academic remediation for entering students, advanced placement credit, English as a second language, honors programs, independent study, part-time degree program, services for LD students, summer session for credit.
Library Marie Blair Burgess Learning Resource Center plus 1 other.
Student Life *Housing Options:* coed, men-only, women-only. Campus housing is university owned. Freshman campus housing is guaranteed. *Activities and Organizations:* drama/theater group, student-run newspaper, choral group, College Christian Movement, Alpha Phi Omega, Campus Union, Fellowship of Christian Athletes, Kappa Sigma Alpha. *Campus security:* 24-hour emergency response devices and patrols, student patrols, late-night transport/escort service, controlled dormitory access. *Student services:* health clinic, personal/psychological counseling.
Athletics Member NJCAA. *Intercollegiate sports:* baseball M(s), basketball M(s)/W(s), cross-country running M(s)/W(s), golf M(s)/W(s), soccer M(s)/W(s), softball W(s), tennis M(s)/W(s), volleyball W(s), wrestling M(s). *Intramural sports:* basketball M/W, cheerleading M/W, football M/W, softball M/W, table tennis M/W, volleyball M/W.
Standardized Tests *Required:* SAT or ACT (for admission).
Costs (2016–17) *One-time required fee:* $175. *Comprehensive fee:* $26,578 includes full-time tuition ($16,538), mandatory fees ($950), and room and board ($9090). Full-time tuition and fees vary according to course load. Part-

time tuition and fees vary according to course load. *Payment plan:* installment. *Waivers:* senior citizens and employees or children of employees.

Financial Aid Of all full-time matriculated undergraduates who enrolled in 2014, 80 Federal Work-Study jobs (averaging $1600). 90 state and other part-time jobs (averaging $1600). *Financial aid deadline:* 8/30.

Applying *Options:* electronic application, deferred entrance. *Application fee:* $25. *Required:* essay or personal statement, high school transcript, minimum 2.0 GPA. *Required for some:* interview. *Recommended:* interview. *Application deadlines:* rolling (freshmen), rolling (transfers). *Notification:* continuous (freshmen), continuous (transfers).

Freshman Application Contact Mr. Daniel L. Philbeck, Vice President for Enrollment Management, Spartanburg Methodist College, 1000 Powell Mill Road, Spartanburg, SC 29301-5899. *Phone:* 864-587-4223. *Toll-free phone:* 800-772-7286. *Fax:* 864-587-4355. *E-mail:* admiss@smcsc.edu. *Website:* http://www.smcsc.edu/.

Technical College of the Lowcountry
Beaufort, South Carolina

- **State-supported** 2-year, founded 1972, part of South Carolina Technical and Comprehensive Education System
- **Small-town** 12-acre campus
- **Coed,** 2,332 undergraduate students, 29% full-time, 68% women, 32% men

Undergraduates 665 full-time, 1,667 part-time. 6% are from out of state; 35% Black or African American, non-Hispanic/Latino; 9% Hispanic/Latino; 1% Asian, non-Hispanic/Latino; 0.5% American Indian or Alaska Native, non-Hispanic/Latino; 2% Two or more races, non-Hispanic/Latino; 1% Race/ethnicity unknown; 12% transferred in.

Freshmen *Admission:* 428 enrolled.

Faculty *Student/faculty ratio:* 15:1.

Majors Administrative assistant and secretarial science; business/commerce; child-care provision; civil engineering technology; construction engineering technology; data processing and data processing technology; early childhood education; education; emergency medical technology (EMT paramedic); fire services administration; golf course operation and grounds management; hospitality administration; industrial electronics technology; legal assistant/paralegal; liberal arts and sciences and humanities related; liberal arts and sciences/liberal studies; medical radiologic technology; physical therapy technology; registered nursing/registered nurse.

Academics *Calendar:* semesters. *Degree:* certificates, diplomas, and associate. *Special study options:* academic remediation for entering students, adult/continuing education programs, advanced placement credit, distance learning, part-time degree program, summer session for credit.

Student Life *Housing:* college housing not available. *Campus security:* security during class hours.

Standardized Tests *Required:* ACT ASSET (for admission). *Recommended:* SAT and SAT Subject Tests or ACT (for admission).

Costs (2015–16) *Tuition:* area resident $3984 full-time, $166 per credit hour part-time; state resident $4584 full-time, $191 per credit hour part-time; nonresident $8880 full-time, $370 per credit hour part-time. *Required fees:* $196 full-time. *Payment plan:* installment. *Waivers:* senior citizens.

Financial Aid Of all full-time matriculated undergraduates who enrolled in 2014, 56 Federal Work-Study jobs (averaging $1700).

Applying *Options:* early admission, deferred entrance. *Application fee:* $25. *Application deadlines:* rolling (freshmen), rolling (transfers).

Freshman Application Contact Rhonda Cole, Admissions Services Manager, Technical College of the Lowcountry, 921 Ribaut Road, PO Box 1288, Beaufort, SC 29901-1288. *Phone:* 843-525-8229. *Fax:* 843-525-8285. *E-mail:* rcole@tcl.edu. *Website:* http://www.tcl.edu/.

Tri-County Technical College
Pendleton, South Carolina

- **State-supported** 2-year, founded 1962, part of South Carolina State Board for Technical and Comprehensive Education
- **Rural** 100-acre campus
- **Endowment** $21.8 million
- **Coed,** 6,128 undergraduate students, 56% full-time, 50% women, 50% men

Undergraduates 3,451 full-time, 2,677 part-time. Students come from 38 states and territories; 35 other countries; 2% are from out of state; 10% Black or African American, non-Hispanic/Latino; 4% Hispanic/Latino; 1% Asian, non-Hispanic/Latino; 0.1% Native Hawaiian or other Pacific Islander, non-

Hispanic/Latino; 0.2% American Indian or Alaska Native, non-Hispanic/Latino; 3% Two or more races, non-Hispanic/Latino; 0.8% Race/ethnicity unknown; 6% transferred in. *Retention:* 36% of full-time freshmen returned.

Freshmen *Admission:* 2,038 enrolled.

Faculty *Student/faculty ratio:* 21:1.

Majors Accounting; administrative assistant and secretarial science; business administration and management; clinical/medical laboratory technology; criminal justice/safety; data processing and data processing technology; electrical, electronic and communications engineering technology; engineering technology; heating, air conditioning, ventilation and refrigeration maintenance technology; industrial electronics technology; industrial production technologies related; liberal arts and sciences/liberal studies; machine tool technology; mechanical drafting and CAD/CADD; multi/interdisciplinary studies related; radio and television broadcasting technology; registered nursing/registered nurse; respiratory therapy technician; technical teacher education; veterinary/animal health technology.

Academics *Calendar:* semesters. *Degree:* certificates, diplomas, and associate. *Special study options:* academic remediation for entering students, adult/continuing education programs, advanced placement credit, distance learning, part-time degree program, study abroad, summer session for credit. *ROTC:* Army (c), Air Force (c).

Library Tri-County Technical College Library.

Student Life *Housing:* college housing not available. *Campus security:* 24-hour emergency response devices and patrols.

Athletics Member NJCAA. *Intercollegiate sports:* golf M, soccer M.

Applying *Options:* early admission. *Application fee:* $30. *Application deadlines:* rolling (freshmen), rolling (transfers). *Notification:* continuous (freshmen), continuous (transfers).

Freshman Application Contact Tri-County Technical College, PO Box 587, 7900 Highway 76, Pendleton, SC 29670-0587. *Phone:* 864-646-1550. *Website:* http://www.tctc.edu/.

Trident Technical College
Charleston, South Carolina

- **State and locally supported** 2-year, founded 1964, part of South Carolina State Board for Technical and Comprehensive Education
- **Urban** campus
- **Coed**

Undergraduates 7,186 full-time, 8,953 part-time. Students come from 83 other countries; 2% are from out of state; 30% Black or African American, non-Hispanic/Latino; 5% Hispanic/Latino; 2% Asian, non-Hispanic/Latino; 0.3% Native Hawaiian or other Pacific Islander, non-Hispanic/Latino; 0.6% American Indian or Alaska Native, non-Hispanic/Latino; 2% Two or more races, non-Hispanic/Latino; 2% Race/ethnicity unknown; 0.9% transferred in.

Faculty *Student/faculty ratio:* 17:1.

Academics *Calendar:* semesters. *Degree:* certificates, diplomas, and associate. *Special study options:* academic remediation for entering students, advanced placement credit, cooperative education, distance learning, double majors, English as a second language, internships, off-campus study, part-time degree program, services for LD students, study abroad, summer session for credit.

Library Learning Resource Center plus 2 others.

Student Life *Campus security:* 24-hour emergency response devices and patrols, late-night transport/escort service.

Costs (2015–16) *Tuition:* area resident $3912 full-time; state resident $4340 full-time; nonresident $7404 full-time. Full-time tuition and fees vary according to course load and program. Part-time tuition and fees vary according to course load and program.

Applying *Options:* electronic application, early admission. *Application fee:* $30. *Required for some:* high school transcript.

Freshman Application Contact Ms. Clara Martin, Admissions Director, Trident Technical College, Charleston, SC 29423-8067. *Phone:* 843-574-6326. *Fax:* 843-574-6109. *E-mail:* clara.martin@tridenttech.edu. *Website:* http://www.tridenttech.edu/.

University of South Carolina Lancaster
Lancaster, South Carolina

Freshman Application Contact Susan Vinson, Admissions Counselor, University of South Carolina Lancaster, PO Box 889, Lancaster, SC 29721. *Phone:* 803-313-7000. *Fax:* 803-313-7116. *E-mail:* vinsons@mailbox.sc.edu. *Website:* http://usclancaster.sc.edu/.

University of South Carolina Salkehatchie
Allendale, South Carolina

- **State-supported** 2-year, founded 1965, part of University of South Carolina System
- **Rural** 95-acre campus
- **Coed**

Undergraduates 5% are from out of state. *Retention:* 45% of full-time freshmen returned.

Faculty *Student/faculty ratio:* 17:1.

Academics *Calendar:* semesters. *Degree:* associate. *Special study options:* academic remediation for entering students, adult/continuing education programs, advanced placement credit, cooperative education, distance learning, independent study, internships, part-time degree program, services for LD students, study abroad, summer session for credit.

Library Salkehatchie Learning Resource Center.

Student Life *Campus security:* 24-hour emergency response devices, late-night transport/escort service.

Athletics Member NJCAA.

Standardized Tests *Required:* SAT or ACT (for admission).

Applying *Options:* electronic application. *Application fee:* $40. *Required:* high school transcript, minimum 2.0 GPA.

Freshman Application Contact Ms. Carmen Brown, Admissions Coordinator, University of South Carolina Salkehatchie, PO Box 617, Allendale, SC 29810. *Phone:* 803-584-3446. *Toll-free phone:* 800-922-5500. *Fax:* 803-584-3884. *E-mail:* cdbrown@mailbox.sc.edu. *Website:* http://uscsalkehatchie.sc.edu/.

University of South Carolina Sumter
Sumter, South Carolina

Freshman Application Contact Mr. Keith Britton, Director of Admissions, University of South Carolina Sumter, 200 Miller Road, Sumter, SC 29150-2498. *Phone:* 803-938-3882. *Fax:* 803-938-3901. *E-mail:* kbritton@usc.sumter.edu. *Website:* http://www.uscsumter.edu/.

University of South Carolina Union
Union, South Carolina

- **State-supported** primarily 2-year, founded 1965, part of University of South Carolina System
- **Small-town** campus with easy access to Charlotte
- **Coed,** 757 undergraduate students, 57% full-time, 60% women, 40% men

Undergraduates 435 full-time, 322 part-time.

Freshmen *Average high school GPA:* 3.2.

Faculty *Total:* 38, 26% full-time. *Student/faculty ratio:* 18:1.

Majors Biological and physical sciences; liberal arts and sciences/liberal studies.

Academics *Calendar:* semesters. *Degrees:* associate and bachelor's. *Special study options:* cooperative education, part-time degree program.

Library USC Union Campus Library plus 1 other.

Student Life *Housing:* college housing not available. *Activities and Organizations:* drama/theater group, choral group.

Athletics *Intramural sports:* baseball M(c), softball W(c).

Standardized Tests *Required:* SAT or ACT (for admission).

Costs (2015–16) *Tuition:* state resident $3243 full-time, $270 per credit hour part-time; nonresident $8103 full-time, $675 per credit hour part-time. Full-time tuition and fees vary according to course load, degree level, and student level. Part-time tuition and fees vary according to student level. *Required fees:* $361 full-time, $180 per term part-time. *Payment plan:* deferred payment. *Waivers:* senior citizens.

Financial Aid Of all full-time matriculated undergraduates who enrolled in 2014, 16 Federal Work-Study jobs (averaging $3400).

Applying *Options:* electronic application. *Application fee:* $40. *Required:* high school transcript. *Application deadline:* rolling (freshmen).

Freshman Application Contact Mr. Michael B. Greer, Director of Enrollment Services, University of South Carolina Union, PO Drawer 729, Union, SC 29379-0729. *Phone:* 864-424-8039. *E-mail:* tyoung@gwm.sc.edu. *Website:* http://uscunion.sc.edu/.

Virginia College in Charleston
North Charleston, South Carolina

Admissions Office Contact Virginia College in Charleston, 6185 Rivers Avenue, North Charleston, SC 29406. *Website:* http://www.vc.edu/.

Virginia College in Columbia
Columbia, South Carolina

Admissions Office Contact Virginia College in Columbia, 7201 Two Notch Road, Suite 1000, Columbia, SC 29223. *Website:* http://www.vc.edu/.

Virginia College in Florence
Florence, South Carolina

Admissions Office Contact Virginia College in Florence, 2400 David H. McLeod Boulevard, Florence, SC 29501. *Website:* http://www.vc.edu/.

Virginia College in Greenville
Greenville, South Carolina

Admissions Office Contact Virginia College in Greenville, 78 Global Drive, Suite 200, Greenville, SC 29607. *Website:* http://www.vc.edu/.

Virginia College in Spartanburg
Spartanburg, South Carolina

Admissions Office Contact Virginia College in Spartanburg, 8150 Warren H. Abernathy Highway, Spartanburg, SC 29301. *Website:* http://www.vc.edu/.

Williamsburg Technical College
Kingstree, South Carolina

- **State-supported** 2-year, founded 1969, part of South Carolina State Board for Technical and Comprehensive Education
- **Rural** 41-acre campus
- **Coed,** 693 undergraduate students, 29% full-time, 57% women, 43% men

Undergraduates 199 full-time, 494 part-time. Students come from 1 other state; 71% Black or African American, non-Hispanic/Latino; 0.7% Hispanic/Latino; 0.1% Asian, non-Hispanic/Latino; 0.3% Two or more races, non-Hispanic/Latino; 2% Race/ethnicity unknown. *Retention:* 45% of full-time freshmen returned.

Faculty *Total:* 47, 40% full-time. *Student/faculty ratio:* 14:1.

Majors Administrative assistant and secretarial science; business/commerce; child-care and support services management; interdisciplinary studies; liberal arts and sciences/liberal studies.

Academics *Calendar:* semesters. *Degree:* certificates, diplomas, and associate. *Special study options:* academic remediation for entering students, adult/continuing education programs, distance learning, part-time degree program, summer session for credit.

Library Learning Resource Center. *Books:* 18,138 (physical), 295,948 (digital/electronic); *Databases:* 58.

Student Life *Housing:* college housing not available. *Activities and Organizations:* Phi Theta Kappa, Student Government Association. *Campus security:* late-night transport/escort service. *Student services:* personal/psychological counseling.

Costs (2015–16) *Tuition:* area resident $3816 full-time, $159 per credit hour part-time; state resident $3936 full-time, $164 per credit hour part-time; nonresident $7416 full-time, $309 per credit hour part-time. *Required fees:* $192 full-time, $8 per credit hour part-time. *Payment plan:* deferred payment. *Waivers:* senior citizens and employees or children of employees.

Applying *Options:* electronic application, early admission, deferred entrance. *Required:* high school transcript. *Application deadlines:* rolling (freshmen), rolling (transfers). *Notification:* continuous (freshmen), continuous (transfers).

Freshman Application Contact Williamsburg Technical College, 601 Martin Luther King, Jr Avenue, Kingstree, SC 29556-4197. *Phone:* 843-355-4162. *Toll-free phone:* 800-768-2021. *Website:* http://www.wiltech.edu/.

York Technical College
Rock Hill, South Carolina

Freshman Application Contact Mr. Kenny Aldridge, Admissions Department Manager, York Technical College, Rock Hill, SC 29730. *Phone:* 803-327-8008. *Toll-free phone:* 800-922-8324. *Fax:* 803-981-7237. *E-mail:* kaldridge@yorktech.com. *Website:* http://www.yorktech.com/.

SOUTH DAKOTA

Lake Area Technical Institute
Watertown, South Dakota

- **State-supported** 2-year, founded 1964, part of South Dakota Department of Education
- **Small-town** 40-acre campus
- **Endowment** $2.4 million
- **Coed,** 1,846 undergraduate students, 84% full-time, 47% women, 53% men

Undergraduates 1,548 full-time, 298 part-time. Students come from 10 states and territories; 3 other countries; 5% are from out of state. *Retention:* 83% of full-time freshmen returned.

Freshmen *Admission:* 1,236 enrolled.

Faculty *Total:* 168, 60% full-time. *Student/faculty ratio:* 16:1.

Majors Agricultural business and management; aircraft powerplant technology; autobody/collision and repair technology; automobile/automotive mechanics technology; banking and financial support services; building construction technology; clinical/medical laboratory technology; computer science; construction engineering technology; construction/heavy equipment/earthmoving equipment operation; criminal justice/police science; dental assisting; diesel mechanics technology; electrical, electronic and communications engineering technology; emergency medical technology (EMT paramedic); engine machinist; environmental science; human services; machine tool technology; manufacturing engineering technology; marketing/marketing management; medical/clinical assistant; occupational therapist assistant; physical therapy technology; robotics technology; welding technology.

Academics *Calendar:* semesters. *Degree:* certificates, diplomas, and associate. *Special study options:* academic remediation for entering students, advanced placement credit, cooperative education, distance learning, double majors, English as a second language, independent study, internships, part-time degree program, services for LD students, summer session for credit.

Library Leonard H. Timmerman Library plus 1 other. *Books:* 2,500 (physical), 50,000 (digital/electronic); *Serial titles:* 32 (physical); *Databases:* 40. Weekly public service hours: 58; students can reserve study rooms.

Student Life *Housing:* college housing not available. *Activities and Organizations:* Campus Crusades, Campus Activities Board, Student Voice, Student Ambassador, SkillsUSA. *Campus security:* 24-hour emergency response devices, partnership with local police department. *Student services:* personal/psychological counseling.

Athletics *Intramural sports:* basketball M/W, bowling M/W, equestrian sports M/W, football M, softball M/W, volleyball M/W.

Standardized Tests *Required:* ACT (for admission), ACCUPLACER (for admission).

Costs (2015–16) *Tuition:* state resident $2616 full-time, $109 per credit hour part-time; nonresident $2616 full-time, $109 per credit hour part-time. Full-time tuition and fees vary according to course load and program. Part-time tuition and fees vary according to course load and program. *Required fees:* $2545 full-time. *Payment plan:* installment. *Waivers:* employees or children of employees.

Financial Aid Of all full-time matriculated undergraduates who enrolled in 2015, 1,238 applied for aid, 1,010 were judged to have need, 99 had their need fully met. 127 Federal Work-Study jobs (averaging $1840). In 2015, 60 non-need-based awards were made. *Average percent of need met:* 54%. *Average financial aid package:* $8021. *Average need-based loan:* $3906. *Average need-based gift aid:* $4966. *Average non-need-based aid:* $1527.

Applying *Options:* electronic application. *Application fee:* $25. *Required:* high school transcript. *Required for some:* essay or personal statement, 3 letters of recommendation, interview. *Application deadlines:* rolling (freshmen), rolling (out-of-state freshmen), rolling (transfers). *Notification:* continuous (freshmen), continuous (out-of-state freshmen), continuous (transfers).

Freshman Application Contact Ms. LuAnn Strait, Director of Student Services, Lake Area Technical Institute, 1201 Arrow Avenue, Watertown, SD 57201. *Phone:* 605-882-5284 Ext. 241. *Toll-free phone:* 800-657-4344. *E-mail:* straitl@lakeareatech.edu. *Website:* http://www.lakeareatech.edu/.

Mitchell Technical Institute
Mitchell, South Dakota

- **State-supported** 2-year, founded 1968, part of South Dakota Board of Regents
- **Rural** 90-acre campus
- **Coed,** 1,262 undergraduate students, 68% full-time, 34% women, 66% men

Undergraduates 852 full-time, 410 part-time. Students come from 19 states and territories; 1 other country; 10% are from out of state; 0.1% Black or African American, non-Hispanic/Latino; 2% Hispanic/Latino; 0.8% Asian, non-Hispanic/Latino; 3% American Indian or Alaska Native, non-Hispanic/Latino; 1% Two or more races, non-Hispanic/Latino; 0.1% Race/ethnicity unknown; 0.1% international; 10% transferred in.

Freshmen *Admission:* 992 applied, 542 admitted, 377 enrolled. *Average high school GPA:* 2.89. *Test scores:* ACT scores over 18: 70%; ACT scores over 24: 20%.

Faculty *Total:* 93, 86% full-time, 1% with terminal degrees. *Student/faculty ratio:* 12:1.

Majors Accounting and business/management; agricultural mechanics and equipment technology; agricultural production; automation engineer technology; building construction technology; building/property maintenance; business automation/technology/data entry; clinical/medical laboratory technology; computer support specialist; construction trades related; culinary arts; electrician; energy management and systems technology; geographic information science and cartography; heating, air conditioning, ventilation and refrigeration maintenance technology; human services; lineworker; magnetic resonance imaging (MRI) technology; medical/clinical assistant; medical office assistant; medical radiologic technology; network and system administration; radiologic technology/science; radio, television, and digital communication related; small engine mechanics and repair technology; speech-language pathology assistant; telecommunications technology; welding engineering technology.

Academics *Calendar:* semesters. *Degree:* certificates, diplomas, and associate. *Special study options:* academic remediation for entering students, advanced placement credit, cooperative education, distance learning, double majors, internships, part-time degree program, services for LD students, summer session for credit.

Library Center for Student Success. *Books:* 1,657 (physical), 929 (digital/electronic); *Databases:* 17. Weekly public service hours: 45.

Student Life *Activities and Organizations:* Student Representative Board, SkillsUSA, Post-Secondary Agricultural Students, Rodeo Club, Diversity Club. *Student services:* personal/psychological counseling.

Athletics *Intercollegiate sports:* equestrian sports M/W. *Intramural sports:* basketball M/W, bowling M/W, riflery M/W, softball M/W, volleyball M/W.

Standardized Tests *Required:* ACT (for admission), ACCUPLACER (for admission).

Costs (2015–16) *Tuition:* state resident $3270 full-time, $109 per credit hour part-time; nonresident $3270 full-time, $109 per credit hour part-time. Full-time tuition and fees vary according to course load and program. Part-time tuition and fees vary according to course load and program. *Required fees:* $2610 full-time, $87 per credit hour part-time. *Payment plan:* installment. *Waivers:* employees or children of employees.

Financial Aid Of all full-time matriculated undergraduates who enrolled in 2015, 715 applied for aid, 597 were judged to have need, 12 had their need fully met. *Average percent of need met:* 58%. *Average financial aid package:* $7632. *Average need-based loan:* $3314. *Average need-based gift aid:* $4284.

Applying *Options:* electronic application. *Required:* high school transcript. *Required for some:* essay or personal statement, interview. *Recommended:* minimum 2.0 GPA. *Application deadlines:* rolling (freshmen), rolling (out-of-state freshmen), rolling (transfers). *Notification:* continuous (freshmen), continuous (out-of-state freshmen), continuous (transfers).

Freshman Application Contact Mr. Clayton Deuter, Director of Admissions, Mitchell Technical Institute, 1800 East Spruce Street, Mitchell, SD 57301. *Phone:* 605-995-3025. *Toll-free phone:* 800-684-1969. *Fax:* 605-995-3067. *E-mail:* clayton.deuter@mitchelltech.edu. *Website:* http://www.mitchelltech.edu/.

National American University
Ellsworth AFB, South Dakota

Freshman Application Contact Admissions Office, National American University, 1000 Ellsworth Street, Suite 2400B, Ellsworth AFB, SD 57706. *Website:* http://www.national.edu/.

Sisseton-Wahpeton College

Sisseton, South Dakota

- **Federally supported** 2-year, founded 1979
- **Rural** 2-acre campus
- **Coed**

Undergraduates 101 full-time, 64 part-time. 2% are from out of state; 0.6% Black or African American, non-Hispanic/Latino; 91% American Indian or Alaska Native, non-Hispanic/Latino; 0.6% Two or more races, non-Hispanic/Latino; 0.6% transferred in.

Faculty *Student/faculty ratio:* 10:1.

Academics *Calendar:* semesters. *Degree:* certificates and associate. *Special study options:* academic remediation for entering students, adult/continuing education programs, cooperative education, double majors, internships, off-campus study, part-time degree program, summer session for credit.

Library Sisseton-Wahpeton Community College Library.

Student Life *Campus security:* 24-hour emergency response devices.

Standardized Tests *Required:* ACT Compass (for admission).

Costs (2015–16) *One-time required fee:* $540. *Tuition:* state resident $3000 full-time, $125 per credit hour part-time; nonresident $3000 full-time, $125 per credit hour part-time. No tuition increase for student's term of enrollment. *Required fees:* $590 full-time, $265 per credit hour part-time. *Room and board:* $6000; room only: $6000.

Financial Aid Of all full-time matriculated undergraduates who enrolled in 2014, 151 applied for aid, 151 were judged to have need. In 2014, 151. *Average need-based gift aid:* $800. *Average non-need-based aid:* $800.

Applying *Required:* high school transcript. *Required for some:* Certificate of Indian Blood for enrolled tribal members. *Recommended:* minimum 2.0 GPA, interview.

Freshman Application Contact Sisseton-Wahpeton College, Old Agency Box 689, Sisseton, SD 57262. *Phone:* 605-698-3966 Ext. 1180. *Website:* http://www.swc.tc/.

Southeast Technical Institute

Sioux Falls, South Dakota

- **State-supported** 2-year, founded 1968
- **Urban** 138-acre campus
- **Endowment** $768,716
- **Coed,** 2,047 undergraduate students, 64% full-time, 53% women, 47% men

Undergraduates 1,304 full-time, 743 part-time. Students come from 11 states and territories; 9% are from out of state; 4% Black or African American, non-Hispanic/Latino; 4% Hispanic/Latino; 2% Asian, non-Hispanic/Latino; 0.2% Native Hawaiian or other Pacific Islander, non-Hispanic/Latino; 2% American Indian or Alaska Native, non-Hispanic/Latino; 2% Two or more races, non-Hispanic/Latino; 2% Race/ethnicity unknown; 14% transferred in; 2% live on campus. *Retention:* 64% of full-time freshmen returned.

Freshmen *Admission:* 2,887 applied, 1,202 admitted, 416 enrolled. *Average high school GPA:* 2.5.

Faculty *Total:* 201, 44% full-time, 3% with terminal degrees. *Student/faculty ratio:* 15:1.

Majors Accounting; animation, interactive technology, video graphics and special effects; applied horticulture/horticulture operations; architectural engineering technology; autobody/collision and repair technology; automobile/automotive mechanics technology; banking and financial support services; biomedical technology; building/construction finishing, management, and inspection related; business administration and management; cardiovascular technology; child-care and support services management; child-care provision; civil engineering technology; clinical/medical laboratory science and allied professions related; clinical/medical laboratory technology; commercial and advertising art; computer and information sciences and support services related; computer and information systems security; computer/information technology services administration related; computer installation and repair technology; computer programming; computer programming related; computer software engineering; computer systems networking and telecommunications; computer technology/computer systems technology; construction engineering technology; criminal justice/police science; desktop publishing and digital imaging design; diagnostic medical sonography and ultrasound technology; diesel mechanics technology; electrical, electronic and communications engineering technology; electrical/electronics equipment installation and repair; electrician; electromechanical technology; electroneurodiagnostic/electroencephalographic technology; finance; health unit coordinator/ward clerk; heating, air conditioning, ventilation and refrigeration maintenance technology; horticultural science; industrial technology; licensed practical/vocational nurse training; marketing/marketing management; mechanical engineering/mechanical technology; medical insurance coding; merchandising, sales, and marketing operations related (general); nuclear medical technology; office occupations and clerical services; plumbing technology; registered nursing/registered nurse; surgical technology; surveying technology; turf and turfgrass management; welding technology.

Academics *Calendar:* semesters. *Degree:* certificates, diplomas, and associate. *Special study options:* academic remediation for entering students, advanced placement credit, distance learning, double majors, independent study, internships, part-time degree program, services for LD students, summer session for credit.

Library Southeast Library.

Student Life *Housing Options:* coed. Campus housing is provided by a third party. *Activities and Organizations:* VICA (Vocational Industrial Clubs of America), American Landscape Contractors Association. *Campus security:* 24-hour patrols, late-night transport/escort service, controlled dormitory access. *Student services:* personal/psychological counseling.

Athletics *Intramural sports:* basketball M/W, bowling M/W, volleyball M/W.

Standardized Tests *Required for some:* ACT (for admission). *Recommended:* ACT (for admission).

Costs (2015–16) *Tuition:* state resident $3270 full-time, $109 per credit part-time; nonresident $3270 full-time, $109 per credit part-time. Full-time tuition and fees vary according to program. Part-time tuition and fees vary according to program. *Required fees:* $3330 full-time, $111 per credit part-time, $111 per credit part-time. *Room and board:* room only: $4750. *Payment plan:* installment.

Financial Aid Of all full-time matriculated undergraduates who enrolled in 2014, 35 Federal Work-Study jobs (averaging $2550).

Applying *Options:* electronic application. *Application fee:* $35. *Required:* high school transcript, minimum 2.2 GPA. *Required for some:* interview, background check, drug screening. *Application deadlines:* rolling (freshmen), rolling (out-of-state freshmen), rolling (transfers). *Notification:* continuous (freshmen), continuous (out-of-state freshmen), continuous (transfers).

Freshman Application Contact Mr. Scott Dorman, Recruiter, Southeast Technical Institute, Sioux Falls, SD 57107. *Phone:* 605-367-4458. *Toll-free phone:* 800-247-0789. *Fax:* 605-367-8305. *E-mail:* scott.dorman@southeasttech.edu. *Website:* http://www.southeasttech.edu/.

Western Dakota Technical Institute

Rapid City, South Dakota

- **State-supported** 2-year, founded 1968
- **Small-town** 5-acre campus
- **Coed**

Undergraduates 681 full-time, 195 part-time. Students come from 10 states and territories; 3% are from out of state; 3% Black or African American, non-Hispanic/Latino; 5% Hispanic/Latino; 1% Asian, non-Hispanic/Latino; 0.9% Native Hawaiian or other Pacific Islander, non-Hispanic/Latino; 15% American Indian or Alaska Native, non-Hispanic/Latino; 0.1% Two or more races, non-Hispanic/Latino; 1% Race/ethnicity unknown; 31% transferred in. *Retention:* 53% of full-time freshmen returned.

Faculty *Student/faculty ratio:* 16:1.

Academics *Calendar:* semesters. *Degree:* certificates, diplomas, and associate. *Special study options:* academic remediation for entering students, advanced placement credit, distance learning, independent study, internships, part-time degree program, services for LD students, summer session for credit.

Library Western Dakota Technical Institute Library.

Student Life *Campus security:* 24-hour video surveillance.

Standardized Tests *Recommended:* SAT or ACT (for admission).

Costs (2015–16) *One-time required fee:* $170. *Tuition:* state resident $3924 full-time, $109 per credit hour part-time; nonresident $3924 full-time, $109 per credit hour part-time. Full-time tuition and fees vary according to course load and program. Part-time tuition and fees vary according to course load. *Required fees:* $3096 full-time, $86 per credit hour part-time. *Payment plans:* installment, deferred payment.

Financial Aid Of all full-time matriculated undergraduates who enrolled in 2014, 162 Federal Work-Study jobs (averaging $1476). *Average percent of need met:* 50. *Average financial aid package:* $8139. *Average need-based gift aid:* $5443. *Financial aid deadline:* 6/30.

Applying *Options:* electronic application. *Application fee:* $20. *Required:* high school transcript, placement test. *Required for some:* essay or personal statement, 3 letters of recommendation, interview. *Recommended:* minimum 2.0 GPA.

Freshman Application Contact Jill Elder, Admissions Coordinator, Western Dakota Technical Institute, 800 Mickelson Drive, Rapid City, SD 57703. *Phone:* 605-718-2411. *Toll-free phone:* 800-544-8765. *Fax:* 605-394-2204. *E-mail:* jill.elder@wdt.edu. *Website:* http://www.wdt.edu/.

TENNESSEE

Brightwood College, Nashville Campus
Nashville, Tennessee

Freshman Application Contact Brightwood College, Nashville Campus, 750 Envious Lane, Nashville, TN 37217. *Phone:* 615-269-9900. *Toll-free phone:* 800-935-1857.
Website: http://www.brightwood.edu/.

Chattanooga College–Medical, Dental and Technical Careers
Chattanooga, Tennessee

Freshman Application Contact Chattanooga College–Medical, Dental and Technical Careers, 248 Northgate Mall Drive, Suite 130, Chattanooga, TN 37415. *Phone:* 423-305-7781. *Toll-free phone:* 877-313-2373.
Website: http://www.chattanoogacollege.edu/.

Chattanooga State Community College
Chattanooga, Tennessee

Freshman Application Contact Brad McCormick, Director of Admissions and Records, Chattanooga State Community College, 4501 Amnicola Highway, Chattanooga, TN 37406. *Phone:* 423-697-4401 Ext. 3264. *Toll-free phone:* 866-547-3733. *Fax:* 423-697-4709.
E-mail: brad.mccormick@chattanoogastate.edu.
Website: http://www.chattanoogastate.edu/.

Cleveland State Community College
Cleveland, Tennessee

- **State-supported** 2-year, founded 1967, part of Tennessee Board of Regents
- **Suburban** 83-acre campus
- **Endowment** $7.9 million
- **Coed,** 3,522 undergraduate students, 51% full-time, 61% women, 39% men

Undergraduates 1,785 full-time, 1,737 part-time. Students come from 8 states and territories; 3 other countries; 1% are from out of state; 6% Black or African American, non-Hispanic/Latino; 4% Hispanic/Latino; 1% Asian, non-Hispanic/Latino; 0.1% Native Hawaiian or other Pacific Islander, non-Hispanic/Latino; 0.3% American Indian or Alaska Native, non-Hispanic/Latino; 1% Two or more races, non-Hispanic/Latino; 4% Race/ethnicity unknown; 0.1% international; 15% transferred in.
Freshmen *Admission:* 1,599 applied, 798 admitted, 798 enrolled. *Average high school GPA:* 3.08. *Test scores:* ACT scores over 18: 69%; ACT scores over 24: 10%.
Faculty *Total:* 174, 40% full-time, 15% with terminal degrees. *Student/faculty ratio:* 23:1.
Majors Administrative assistant and secretarial science; business administration and management; child development; community organization and advocacy; criminal justice/police science; general studies; industrial technology; kindergarten/preschool education; liberal arts and sciences and humanities related; liberal arts and sciences/liberal studies; public administration and social service professions related; registered nursing/registered nurse; science technologies related.
Academics *Calendar:* semesters. *Degree:* certificates and associate. *Special study options:* academic remediation for entering students, adult/continuing education programs, advanced placement credit, cooperative education, distance learning, double majors, external degree program, honors programs, independent study, internships, off-campus study, part-time degree program, services for LD students, summer session for credit.
Library Cleveland State Community College Library.
Student Life *Housing:* college housing not available. *Activities and Organizations:* student-run newspaper, choral group, Human Services/Social Work, Computer-Aided Design, Phi Theta Kappa, Student Nursing Association, Early Childhood Education. *Campus security:* 24-hour emergency response devices and patrols. *Student services:* personal/psychological counseling.
Athletics Member NJCAA. *Intercollegiate sports:* baseball M(s), basketball M(s)/W(s), softball W(s). *Intramural sports:* archery M/W, basketball M/W, bowling M/W, cheerleading M(c)/W(c), softball W, table tennis M/W, volleyball M/W.
Costs (2015–16) *Tuition:* state resident $3828 full-time, $152 per credit hour part-time; nonresident $15,618 full-time, $627 per credit hour part-time. Full-time tuition and fees vary according to course load. *Required fees:* $299 full-time, $14 per credit hour part-time, $27 per term part-time. *Payment plan:* deferred payment. *Waivers:* senior citizens and employees or children of employees.
Financial Aid Of all full-time matriculated undergraduates who enrolled in 2014, 52 Federal Work-Study jobs (averaging $1025).
Applying *Options:* electronic application, early admission, deferred entrance. *Application fee:* $20. *Required:* high school transcript. *Application deadlines:* rolling (freshmen), rolling (transfers). *Notification:* continuous (freshmen), continuous (transfers).
Freshman Application Contact Mrs. Suzanne Bayne, Assistant Director of Admissions and Recruitment, Cleveland State Community College, PO Box 3570, Cleveland, TN 37320-3570. *Phone:* 423-472-7141 Ext. 743. *Toll-free phone:* 800-604-2722. *Fax:* 423-614-8711.
E-mail: sbayne@clevelandstatecc.edu.
Website: http://www.clevelandstatecc.edu/.

Columbia State Community College
Columbia, Tennessee

Freshman Application Contact Mr. Joey Scruggs, Coordinator of Recruitment, Columbia State Community College, 1665 Hampshire Pike, Columbia, TN 38401. *Phone:* 931-540-2540.
E-mail: scruggs@coscc.cc.tn.us.
Website: http://www.columbiastate.edu/.

Concorde Career College
Memphis, Tennessee

Freshman Application Contact Dee Vickers, Director, Concorde Career College, 5100 Poplar Avenue, Suite 132, Memphis, TN 38137. *Phone:* 901-761-9494. *Fax:* 901-761-3293. *E-mail:* dvickers@concorde.edu.
Website: http://www.concorde.edu/.

Daymar College
Clarksville, Tennessee

Freshman Application Contact Daymar College, 2691 Trenton Road, Clarksville, TN 37040. *Phone:* 931-552-7600 Ext. 204.
Website: http://www.daymarcollege.edu/.

Daymar College
Murfreesboro, Tennessee

Admissions Office Contact Daymar College, 415 Golden Bear Court, Murfreesboro, TN 37128.
Website: http://www.daymarcollege.edu/.

Daymar College
Nashville, Tennessee

Director of Admissions Admissions Office, Daymar College, 560 Royal Parkway, Nashville, TN 37214. *Phone:* 615-361-7555. *Fax:* 615-367-2736.
Website: http://www.daymarcollege.edu/.

Dyersburg State Community College
Dyersburg, Tennessee

- **State-supported** 2-year, founded 1969, part of Tennessee Board of Regents
- **Small-town** 115-acre campus with easy access to Memphis
- **Endowment** $4.0 million
- **Coed,** 2,857 undergraduate students, 43% full-time, 65% women, 35% men

Undergraduates 1,226 full-time, 1,631 part-time. Students come from 5 states and territories; 1 other country; 23% Black or African American, non-Hispanic/Latino; 2% Hispanic/Latino; 0.7% Asian, non-Hispanic/Latino; 0.1% Native Hawaiian or other Pacific Islander, non-Hispanic/Latino; 0.4% American Indian or Alaska Native, non-Hispanic/Latino; 2% Two or more races, non-Hispanic/Latino; 0.7% Race/ethnicity unknown; 6% transferred in. *Retention:* 45% of full-time freshmen returned.
Freshmen *Admission:* 611 enrolled. *Average high school GPA:* 2.9. *Test scores:* ACT scores over 18: 64%; ACT scores over 24: 13%; ACT scores over 30: 1%.
Faculty *Total:* 182, 29% full-time, 12% with terminal degrees. *Student/faculty ratio:* 8:1.
Majors Agriculture; automation engineer technology; business administration and management; child development; computer and information systems

security; criminal justice/police science; criminal justice/safety; education; emergency medical technology (EMT paramedic); general studies; health information/medical records technology; health services/allied health/health sciences; industrial electronics technology; industrial mechanics and maintenance technology; information science/studies; liberal arts and sciences/liberal studies; medical informatics; music performance; registered nursing/registered nurse; web page, digital/multimedia and information resources design.

Academics *Calendar:* semesters. *Degree:* certificates and associate. *Special study options:* academic remediation for entering students, accelerated degree program, adult/continuing education programs, advanced placement credit, cooperative education, distance learning, double majors, honors programs, independent study, internships, off-campus study, part-time degree program, services for LD students, study abroad, summer session for credit.

Library Learning Resource Center.

Student Life *Activities and Organizations:* drama/theater group, choral group, Psychology Club, Phi Theta Kappa, Student Government, Student Nurses Association, Criminal Justice Association. *Campus security:* 24-hour emergency response devices and patrols. *Student services:* personal/psychological counseling.

Athletics Member NJCAA. *Intercollegiate sports:* baseball M(s), basketball M(s)/W(s), cheerleading M(s)/W(s), softball W(s). *Intramural sports:* basketball M/W, soccer M/W, table tennis M/W, ultimate Frisbee M/W, volleyball M/W.

Standardized Tests *Required:* SAT or ACT (for admission). *Required for some:* ACT Compass for students who are over 21.

Costs (2015–16) *Tuition:* state resident $3648 full-time, $152 per credit hour part-time; nonresident $15,048 full-time, $627 per credit hour part-time. Full-time tuition and fees vary according to course load. Part-time tuition and fees vary according to course load. *Required fees:* $299 full-time, $150 per term part-time. *Payment plan:* deferred payment. *Waivers:* senior citizens and employees or children of employees.

Financial Aid Of all full-time matriculated undergraduates who enrolled in 2014, 38 Federal Work-Study jobs (averaging $2082). 154 state and other part-time jobs (averaging $1094).

Applying *Required:* high school transcript.

Freshman Application Contact Mrs. Margaret Jones, Director of Admissions, Dyersburg State Community College, Dyersburg, TN 38024. *Phone:* 731-286-3327. *Fax:* 731-286-3325. *E-mail:* mjones@dscc.edu. *Website:* http://www.dscc.edu/.

Fortis Institute
Cookeville, Tennessee

Director of Admissions Ms. Sharon Mellott, Director of Admissions, Fortis Institute, 1025 Highway 111, Cookeville, TN 38501. *Phone:* 931-526-3660. *Toll-free phone:* 855-4-FORTIS. *Website:* http://www.fortis.edu/.

Fortis Institute
Nashville, Tennessee

Admissions Office Contact Fortis Institute, 3354 Perimeter Hill Drive, Suite 105, Nashville, TN 37211. *Toll-free phone:* 855-4-FORTIS. *Website:* http://www.fortis.edu/.

Fountainhead College of Technology
Knoxville, Tennessee

- **Proprietary** primarily 2-year, founded 1947
- **Suburban** 2-acre campus
- **Coed**

Undergraduates 180 full-time. Students come from 1 other state. *Retention:* 82% of full-time freshmen returned.

Faculty *Student/faculty ratio:* 8:1.

Academics *Calendar:* semesters. *Degrees:* associate and bachelor's. *Special study options:* accelerated degree program, distance learning, double majors, part-time degree program, summer session for credit.

Library Library and Resource Center.

Student Life *Campus security:* 24-hour emergency response devices.

Standardized Tests *Required for some:* SAT or ACT (for admission), Institutional Entrance Exam.

Applying *Required:* high school transcript, interview.

Freshman Application Contact Mr. Joel B. Southern, Director of Admissions, Fountainhead College of Technology, 10208 Technology Drive, Knoxville, TN 37932. *Phone:* 865-688-9422. *Toll-free phone:* 888-218-7335. *Fax:* 865-688-2419. *E-mail:* joel.southern@fountainheadcollege.edu. *Website:* http://www.fountainheadcollege.edu/.

Hiwassee College
Madisonville, Tennessee

Director of Admissions Jamie Williamson, Director of Admission, Hiwassee College, 225 Hiwassee College Drive, Madisonville, TN 37354. *Phone:* 423-420-1891. *Toll-free phone:* 800-356-2187. *Website:* http://www.hiwassee.edu/.

ITT Technical Institute
Chattanooga, Tennessee

Freshman Application Contact Director of Recruitment, ITT Technical Institute, 5600 Brainerd Road, Suite G-1, Chattanooga, TN 37411. *Phone:* 423-510-6800. *Toll-free phone:* 877-474-8312. *Website:* http://www.itt-tech.edu/.

ITT Technical Institute
Cordova, Tennessee

Freshman Application Contact Director of Recruitment, ITT Technical Institute, 7260 Goodlett Farms Parkway, Cordova, TN 38016. *Phone:* 901-381-0200. *Toll-free phone:* 866-444-5141. *Website:* http://www.itt-tech.edu/.

ITT Technical Institute
Knoxville, Tennessee

Freshman Application Contact Director of Recruitment, ITT Technical Institute, 9123 Executive Park Drive, Knoxville, TN 37923. *Phone:* 865-342-2300. *Toll-free phone:* 800-671-2801. *Website:* http://www.itt-tech.edu/.

ITT Technical Institute
Nashville, Tennessee

Freshman Application Contact Director of Recruitment, ITT Technical Institute, 2845 Elm Hill Pike, Nashville, TN 37214-3717. *Phone:* 615-889-8700. *Toll-free phone:* 800-331-8386. *Website:* http://www.itt-tech.edu/.

Jackson State Community College
Jackson, Tennessee

- **State-supported** 2-year, founded 1967, part of Tennessee Board of Regents
- **Suburban** 100-acre campus with easy access to Memphis
- **Coed**

Faculty *Student/faculty ratio:* 19:1.

Academics *Calendar:* semesters. *Degree:* certificates, diplomas, and associate. *Special study options:* academic remediation for entering students, accelerated degree program, adult/continuing education programs, advanced placement credit, cooperative education, distance learning, external degree program, honors programs, independent study, internships, off-campus study, part-time degree program, services for LD students, study abroad, summer session for credit. *ROTC:* Army (c).

Library Jackson State Community College Library.

Student Life *Campus security:* 24-hour patrols, late-night transport/escort service, field camera surveillance.

Athletics Member NJCAA.

Standardized Tests *Required:* SAT or ACT (for admission), ACT Compass (for admission). *Recommended:* ACT (for admission).

Costs (2015–16) *Tuition:* state resident $4560 full-time, $152 per credit hour part-time; nonresident $14,250 full-time, $475 per credit hour part-time. Full-time tuition and fees vary according to course load and program. Part-time tuition and fees vary according to course load and program. *Required fees:* $285 full-time, $9 per credit hour part-time, $30 per term part-time.

Financial Aid Of all full-time matriculated undergraduates who enrolled in 2013, 2,070 applied for aid, 1,907 were judged to have need, 46 had their need fully met. 38 Federal Work-Study jobs (averaging $1763). 14 state and other part-time jobs (averaging $1595). In 2013, 40. *Average percent of need met:* 45. *Average financial aid package:* $4961. *Average need-based loan:* $643. *Average need-based gift aid:* $4717. *Average non-need-based aid:* $3204.

Applying *Options:* electronic application. *Required for some:* high school transcript.

Freshman Application Contact Ms. Andrea Winchester, Director of High School Initiatives, Jackson State Community College, 2046 North Parkway,

Jackson, TN 38301-3797. *Phone:* 731-424-3520 Ext. 50484. *Toll-free phone:* 800-355-5722. *Fax:* 731-425-9559. *E-mail:* awinchester@jscc.edu. *Website:* http://www.jscc.edu/.

John A. Gupton College
Nashville, Tennessee

- **Independent** 2-year, founded 1946
- **Urban** 1-acre campus with easy access to Nashville
- **Endowment** $60,000
- **Coed,** 120 undergraduate students, 58% full-time, 63% women, 37% men

Undergraduates 70 full-time, 50 part-time. Students come from 5 states and territories; 10% are from out of state; 23% Black or African American, non-Hispanic/Latino; 3% Hispanic/Latino; 0.8% Asian, non-Hispanic/Latino; 18% transferred in; 11% live on campus.
Freshmen *Admission:* 15 enrolled.
Faculty *Total:* 13, 23% full-time.
Majors Funeral service and mortuary science.
Academics *Calendar:* semesters. *Degree:* certificates, diplomas, and associate. *Special study options:* part-time degree program.
Library Memorial Library plus 1 other.
Student Life *Housing Options:* coed. Campus housing is university owned. *Campus security:* controlled dormitory access, day patrols.
Standardized Tests *Required:* ACT (for admission).
Costs (2015–16) *Tuition:* $9920 full-time, $310 per semester hour part-time. Full-time tuition and fees vary according to course load. Part-time tuition and fees vary according to course load. *Required fees:* $70 full-time. *Room only:* $3600. *Payment plan:* installment.
Financial Aid *Financial aid deadline:* 6/1.
Applying *Options:* electronic application, deferred entrance. *Application fee:* $50. *Required:* essay or personal statement, high school transcript, 2 letters of recommendation. *Application deadlines:* rolling (freshmen), rolling (transfers).
Freshman Application Contact John A. Gupton College, 1616 Church Street, Nashville, TN 37203-2920. *Phone:* 615-327-3927.
Website: http://www.guptoncollege.edu/.

L'Ecole Culinaire–Memphis
Cordova, Tennessee

Admissions Office Contact L'Ecole Culinaire–Memphis, 1245 N. Germantown Parkway, Cordova, TN 38016.
Website: http://www.lecole.edu/memphis/.

Lincoln College of Technology
Nashville, Tennessee

Freshman Application Contact Ms. Tanya Smith, Director of Admissions, Lincoln College of Technology, 1524 Gallatin Road, Nashville, TN 37206. *Phone:* 615-226-3990 Ext. 71703. *Toll-free phone:* 800-228-6232. *Fax:* 615-262-8466. *E-mail:* tlegg-smith@lincolntech.com.
Website: http://www.lincolnedu.com/campus/nashville-tn.

Miller-Motte Technical College
Chattanooga, Tennessee

Admissions Office Contact Miller-Motte Technical College, 6397 Lee Highway, Suite 100, Chattanooga, TN 37421.
Website: http://www.miller-motte.edu/.

Miller-Motte Technical College
Clarksville, Tennessee

Director of Admissions Joseph Kuchno, Director of Admissions, Miller-Motte Technical College, 1820 Business Park Drive, Clarksville, TN 37040. *Phone:* 800-558-0071. *E-mail:* lisateague@hotmail.com.
Website: http://www.miller-motte.edu/.

Miller-Motte Technical College
Madison, Tennessee

Admissions Office Contact Miller-Motte Technical College, 1515 Gallatin Pike North, Madison, TN 37115.
Website: http://www.miller-motte.edu/.

Motlow State Community College
Tullahoma, Tennessee

- **State-supported** 2-year, founded 1969, part of Tennessee Board of Regents
- **Rural** 187-acre campus with easy access to Nashville
- **Endowment** $6.1 million
- **Coed**

Undergraduates 1,951 full-time, 1,950 part-time. Students come from 13 states and territories; 1% are from out of state; 9% Black or African American, non-Hispanic/Latino; 4% Hispanic/Latino; 2% Asian, non-Hispanic/Latino; 0.1% Native Hawaiian or other Pacific Islander, non-Hispanic/Latino; 0.2% American Indian or Alaska Native, non-Hispanic/Latino; 1% Two or more races, non-Hispanic/Latino; 3% Race/ethnicity unknown; 0.4% international; 9% transferred in.
Academics *Calendar:* semesters. *Degree:* certificates and associate. *Special study options:* academic remediation for entering students, accelerated degree program, adult/continuing education programs, advanced placement credit, cooperative education, distance learning, double majors, honors programs, independent study, part-time degree program, services for LD students, study abroad, summer session for credit.
Library Clayton-Glass Library.
Student Life *Campus security:* 24-hour patrols, late-night transport/escort service.
Athletics Member NJCAA.
Financial Aid Of all full-time matriculated undergraduates who enrolled in 2013, 1,773 applied for aid, 1,422 were judged to have need, 72 had their need fully met. 2 Federal Work-Study jobs (averaging $1750). In 2013, 234. *Average percent of need met:* 55. *Average financial aid package:* $5212. *Average need-based loan:* $2344. *Average need-based gift aid:* $4313. *Average non-need-based aid:* $2970.
Applying *Options:* electronic application, early admission, deferred entrance. *Application fee:* $10. *Required:* high school transcript.
Freshman Application Contact Ms. Sheri Mason, Assistant Director of Student Services, Motlow State Community College, Lynchburg, TN 37352-8500. *Phone:* 931-393-1764. *Toll-free phone:* 800-654-4877. *Fax:* 931-393-1681. *E-mail:* smason@mscc.edu.
Website: http://www.mscc.edu/.

Nashville State Community College
Nashville, Tennessee

- **State-supported** 2-year, founded 1970, part of Tennessee Board of Regents
- **Urban** 85-acre campus
- **Coed,** 10,192 undergraduate students

Undergraduates Students come from 55 other countries; 2% are from out of state; 27% Black or African American, non-Hispanic/Latino; 6% Hispanic/Latino; 3% Asian, non-Hispanic/Latino; 0.2% Native Hawaiian or other Pacific Islander, non-Hispanic/Latino; 0.3% American Indian or Alaska Native, non-Hispanic/Latino; 4% Two or more races, non-Hispanic/Latino; 0.9% Race/ethnicity unknown.
Freshmen *Average high school GPA:* 2.91.
Faculty *Student/faculty ratio:* 19:1.
Majors Accounting; administrative assistant and secretarial science; architectural engineering; architectural engineering technology; art; automobile/automotive mechanics technology; biology/biological sciences; business administration and management; chemistry; child development; civil engineering; civil engineering technology; commercial and advertising art; computer and information sciences related; computer engineering technology; computer science; computer systems networking and telecommunications; computer technology/computer systems technology; construction engineering technology; criminal justice/police science; culinary arts; design and visual communications; early childhood education; economics; electrical, electronic and communications engineering technology; elementary education; English; foreign languages related; geography; health/health-care administration; health information/medical records administration; health professions related; history; industrial engineering; industrial production technologies related; industrial technology; information science/studies; information technology; kindergarten/preschool education; kinesiology and exercise science; legal assistant/paralegal; mathematics; mechanical engineering; medical informatics; middle school education; music; nursing practice; occupational therapist assistant; occupational therapy; philosophy; photography; physics; political science and government; pre-engineering; pre-law studies; premedical studies; prenursing studies; pre-occupational therapy; pre-physical therapy; psychology; secondary education; sign language interpretation and translation; social work; sociology; special education; speech communication and rhetoric.
Academics *Calendar:* semesters. *Degree:* certificates and associate. *Special study options:* academic remediation for entering students, adult/continuing

education programs, advanced placement credit, cooperative education, distance learning, double majors, English as a second language, off-campus study, part-time degree program, services for LD students, study abroad, summer session for credit.
Library Jane G. Kisber Memorial Library. Students can reserve study rooms.
Student Life *Housing:* college housing not available. *Activities and Organizations:* drama/theater group, student-run newspaper, choral group, National Society of Leadership and Success, Occupational Therapy Club, Phi Theta Kappa, Student Government Association, Black Student Association. *Campus security:* 24-hour emergency response devices and patrols, late-night transport/escort service. *Student services:* personal/psychological counseling.
Standardized Tests *Required:* SAT or ACT (for admission).
Costs (2015–16) *Tuition:* state resident $4560 full-time, $152 per credit hour part-time; nonresident $18,110 full-time, $627 per credit hour part-time. Full-time tuition and fees vary according to course load. Part-time tuition and fees vary according to course load. *Required fees:* $10 per credit hour part-time. *Payment plan:* deferred payment. *Waivers:* senior citizens and employees or children of employees.
Financial Aid Of all full-time matriculated undergraduates who enrolled in 2015, 3,942 applied for aid, 3,514 were judged to have need, 917 had their need fully met. 188 Federal Work-Study jobs (averaging $5400). 64 state and other part-time jobs (averaging $3600). In 2015, 3 non-need-based awards were made. *Average percent of need met:* 33%. *Average financial aid package:* $6616. *Average need-based loan:* $2970. *Average need-based gift aid:* $3331. *Average non-need-based aid:* $950.
Applying *Options:* electronic application. *Application fee:* $20. *Required:* high school transcript. *Application deadlines:* rolling (freshmen), rolling (out-of-state freshmen), rolling (transfers). *Notification:* continuous (freshmen), continuous (out-of-state freshmen), continuous (transfers).
Freshman Application Contact Miss Jennifer Evernham, Coordinator of Recruitment, Nashville State Community College, 120 White Bridge Road, Nashville, TN 37209-4515. *Phone:* 615-353-3265. *Toll-free phone:* 800-272-7363. *E-mail:* jennifer.evernham@nscc.edu.
Website: http://www.nscc.edu/.

National College
Bristol, Tennessee
Freshman Application Contact National College, 1328 Highway 11 West, Bristol, TN 37620. *Phone:* 423-878-4440. *Toll-free phone:* 888-9-JOBREADY.
Website: http://www.national-college.edu/.

National College
Knoxville, Tennessee
Director of Admissions Frank Alvey, Campus Director, National College, 8415 Kingston Pike, Knoxville, TN 37919. *Phone:* 865-539-2011. *Toll-free phone:* 888-9-JOBREADY. *Fax:* 865-539-2049.
Website: http://www.national-college.edu/.

National College
Nashville, Tennessee
Director of Admissions Jerry Lafferty, Campus Director, National College, 1638 Bell Road, Nashville, TN 37211. *Phone:* 615-333-3344. *Toll-free phone:* 888-9-JOBREADY.
Website: http://www.national-college.edu/.

North Central Institute
Clarksville, Tennessee
Freshman Application Contact Dale Wood, Director of Admissions, North Central Institute, 168 Jack Miller Boulevard, Clarksville, TN 37042. *Phone:* 931-431-9700. *Toll-free phone:* 800-603-4116. *Fax:* 931-431-9771. *E-mail:* admissions@nci.edu.
Website: http://www.nci.edu/.

Northeast State Community College
Blountville, Tennessee
Freshman Application Contact Dr. Jon P. Harr, Vice President for Student Affairs, Northeast State Community College, PO Box 246, Blountville, TN 37617. *Phone:* 423-323-0231. *Toll-free phone:* 800-836-7822. *Fax:* 423-323-0240. *E-mail:* jpharr@northeaststate.edu.
Website: http://www.northeaststate.edu/.

Pellissippi State Community College
Knoxville, Tennessee
Freshman Application Contact Director of Admissions and Records, Pellissippi State Community College, PO Box 22990, Knoxville, TN 37933-0990. *Phone:* 865-694-6400. *Fax:* 865-539-7217.
Website: http://www.pstcc.edu/.

Remington College–Memphis Campus
Memphis, Tennessee
Director of Admissions Randal Hayes, Director of Recruitment, Remington College–Memphis Campus, 2710 Nonconnah Boulevard, Memphis, TN 38132. *Phone:* 901-345-1000. *Fax:* 901-396-8310. *E-mail:* randal.hayes@remingtoncollege.edu.
Website: http://www.remingtoncollege.edu/.

Remington College–Nashville Campus
Nashville, Tennessee
Director of Admissions Mr. Frank Vivelo, Campus President, Remington College–Nashville Campus, 441 Donelson Pike, Suite 150, Nashville, TN 37214. *Phone:* 615-889-5520. *Fax:* 615-889-5528. *E-mail:* frank.vivelo@remingtoncollege.edu.
Website: http://www.remingtoncollege.edu/.

Roane State Community College
Harriman, Tennessee
- **State-supported** 2-year, founded 1971, part of Tennessee Board of Regents
- **Small-town** 104-acre campus with easy access to Knoxville
- **Endowment** $8.3 million
- **Coed**

Undergraduates 2,358 full-time, 3,474 part-time. Students come from 11 states and territories; 5 other countries; 1% are from out of state; 3% Black or African American, non-Hispanic/Latino; 3% Hispanic/Latino; 0.7% Asian, non-Hispanic/Latino; 0.1% Native Hawaiian or other Pacific Islander, non-Hispanic/Latino; 0.3% American Indian or Alaska Native, non-Hispanic/Latino; 3% Two or more races, non-Hispanic/Latino; 2% Race/ethnicity unknown; 0.2% international; 4% transferred in. *Retention:* 62% of full-time freshmen returned.
Faculty *Student/faculty ratio:* 17:1.
Academics *Calendar:* semesters. *Degree:* certificates and associate. *Special study options:* academic remediation for entering students, accelerated degree program, advanced placement credit, cooperative education, distance learning, double majors, honors programs, independent study, internships, off-campus study, services for LD students, study abroad, summer session for credit. *ROTC:* Army (c), Air Force (c).
Library Roane State Community College Library plus 3 others.
Student Life *Campus security:* 24-hour patrols.
Athletics Member NJCAA.
Costs (2015–16) *Tuition:* state resident $3528 full-time; nonresident $14,592 full-time. *Required fees:* $303 full-time.
Financial Aid Of all full-time matriculated undergraduates who enrolled in 2014, 2,700 applied for aid, 2,260 were judged to have need, 202 had their need fully met. 61 Federal Work-Study jobs (averaging $1892). In 2014, 53. *Average percent of need met:* 54. *Average financial aid package:* $7143. *Average need-based loan:* $3157. *Average need-based gift aid:* $6062. *Average non-need-based aid:* $8059.
Applying *Options:* electronic application, early admission, deferred entrance. *Application fee:* $20. *Required:* high school transcript.
Freshman Application Contact Admissions Office, Roane State Community College, 276 Patton Lane, Harriman, TN 37748. *Phone:* 865-882-4523. *Toll-free phone:* 866-462-7722 Ext. 4554. *E-mail:* admissionsrecords@roanestate.edu.
Website: http://www.roanestate.edu/.

SAE Institute Nashville
Nashville, Tennessee
Admissions Office Contact SAE Institute Nashville, 7 Music Circle N, Nashville, TN 37203.
Website: http://www.sae.edu/.

Southwest Tennessee Community College
Memphis, Tennessee

- **State-supported** 2-year, founded 2000, part of Tennessee Board of Regents
- **Urban** 100-acre campus
- **Coed,** 10,167 undergraduate students, 41% full-time, 61% women, 39% men

Undergraduates 4,183 full-time, 5,984 part-time. Students come from 13 states and territories; 8 other countries; 2% are from out of state; 6% transferred in.

Freshmen *Admission:* 5,416 applied, 5,416 admitted, 2,208 enrolled.

Majors Accounting; administrative assistant and secretarial science; applied horticulture/horticultural business services related; architectural engineering technology; automobile/automotive mechanics technology; biomedical technology; business administration and management; business/commerce; clinical/medical laboratory technology; commercial and advertising art; computer engineering technology; court reporting; criminal justice/safety; dietitian assistant; electrical, electronic and communications engineering technology; electrical/electronics equipment installation and repair; fire science/firefighting; general studies; geographic information science and cartography; health professions related; heavy equipment maintenance technology; industrial technology; information technology; kindergarten/preschool education; legal assistant/paralegal; management information systems; mechanical engineering/mechanical technology; medical/clinical assistant; medical radiologic technology; physical therapy technology; registered nursing/registered nurse.

Academics *Calendar:* semesters. *Degree:* certificates and associate. *Special study options:* academic remediation for entering students, accelerated degree program, adult/continuing education programs, advanced placement credit, cooperative education, distance learning, double majors, English as a second language, internships, part-time degree program, services for LD students, student-designed majors, summer session for credit. *ROTC:* Army (c), Air Force (c).

Library Infonet Library plus 4 others.

Student Life *Housing:* college housing not available. *Activities and Organizations:* drama/theater group, student-run newspaper, choral group, Human Key Society, NAACP, Black Student Association, Honor Society, Collegiate Secretaries. *Campus security:* 24-hour emergency response devices and patrols, late-night transport/escort service. *Student services:* personal/psychological counseling.

Athletics Member NJCAA.

Financial Aid Of all full-time matriculated undergraduates who enrolled in 2014, 201 Federal Work-Study jobs (averaging $2600).

Applying *Options:* early admission, deferred entrance. *Application fee:* $10. *Required:* high school transcript. *Notification:* continuous (freshmen), continuous (transfers).

Freshman Application Contact Mrs. Vanessa Dowdy, Southwest Tennessee Community College, 5983 Macon Cove, Memphis, TN 38134. *Phone:* 901-333-4275. *Toll-free phone:* 877-717-STCC. *E-mail:* vdowdy@southwest.tn.edu. *Website:* http://www.southwest.tn.edu/.

Vatterott College
Memphis, Tennessee

Admissions Office Contact Vatterott College, 2655 Dividend Drive, Memphis, TN 38132. *Toll-free phone:* 888-553-6627. *Website:* http://www.vatterott.edu/.

Vatterott College
Memphis, Tennessee

Admissions Office Contact Vatterott College, 6991 Appling Farms Parkway, Memphis, TN 38133. *Website:* http://www.vatterott.edu/.

Virginia College in Chattanooga
Chattanooga, Tennessee

Admissions Office Contact Virginia College in Chattanooga, 721 Eastgate Loop Road, Chattanooga, TN 37411. *Website:* http://www.vc.edu/.

Virginia College in Knoxville
Knoxville, Tennessee

Admissions Office Contact Virginia College in Knoxville, 5003 North Broadway Street, Knoxville, TN 37918. *Website:* http://www.vc.edu/.

Volunteer State Community College
Gallatin, Tennessee

- **State-supported** 2-year, founded 1970, part of Tennessee Board of Regents
- **Suburban** 110-acre campus with easy access to Nashville
- **Endowment** $4.4 million
- **Coed,** 8,068 undergraduate students, 53% full-time, 60% women, 40% men

Undergraduates 4,267 full-time, 3,801 part-time. Students come from 17 states and territories; 16 other countries; 1% are from out of state; 11% Black or African American, non-Hispanic/Latino; 5% Hispanic/Latino; 1% Asian, non-Hispanic/Latino; 0.1% Native Hawaiian or other Pacific Islander, non-Hispanic/Latino; 0.4% American Indian or Alaska Native, non-Hispanic/Latino; 3% Two or more races, non-Hispanic/Latino; 2% Race/ethnicity unknown; 0.5% international; 5% transferred in.

Freshmen *Admission:* 2,896 applied, 2,896 admitted, 2,345 enrolled. *Average high school GPA:* 2.97. *Test scores:* ACT scores over 18: 58%; ACT scores over 24: 12%; ACT scores over 30: 1%.

Faculty *Total:* 411, 41% full-time, 13% with terminal degrees. *Student/faculty ratio:* 22:1.

Majors Business administration and management; child development; clinical/medical laboratory technology; computer and information sciences; criminal justice/police science; digital arts; education; fire science/firefighting; general studies; health information/medical records technology; health professions related; legal assistant/paralegal; liberal arts and sciences/liberal studies; medical informatics; medical radiologic technology; music performance; ophthalmic technology; physical therapy technology; respiratory care therapy; veterinary/animal health technology.

Academics *Calendar:* semesters. *Degree:* certificates and associate. *Special study options:* academic remediation for entering students, accelerated degree program, adult/continuing education programs, advanced placement credit, cooperative education, distance learning, double majors, English as a second language, honors programs, independent study, internships, part-time degree program, services for LD students, study abroad, summer session for credit.

Library Thigpen Library.

Student Life *Housing:* college housing not available. *Activities and Organizations:* drama/theater group, student-run newspaper, radio station, choral group, Gamma Beta Phi, Returning Woman's Organization, Phi Theta Kappa, Student Government Association, The Settler. *Campus security:* 24-hour emergency response devices and patrols, late-night transport/escort service. *Student services:* personal/psychological counseling.

Athletics Member NJCAA. *Intercollegiate sports:* baseball M(s), basketball M(s)/W(s), softball W(s).

Standardized Tests *Required for some:* SAT or ACT (for admission).

Costs (2016–17) *Tuition:* state resident $3648 full-time, $152 per credit hour part-time; nonresident $15,048 full-time, $627 per credit hour part-time. Full-time tuition and fees vary according to course load. Part-time tuition and fees vary according to course load. *Required fees:* $277 full-time, $9 per hour part-time, $26 per term part-time. *Payment plan:* deferred payment. *Waivers:* senior citizens and employees or children of employees.

Financial Aid Of all full-time matriculated undergraduates who enrolled in 2014, 2,872 applied for aid, 2,142 were judged to have need, 180 had their need fully met. 47 Federal Work-Study jobs (averaging $2125). In 2014, 49 non-need-based awards were made. *Average percent of need met:* 52%. *Average financial aid package:* $5792. *Average need-based loan:* $2963. *Average need-based gift aid:* $4590. *Average non-need-based aid:* $2277.

Applying *Options:* electronic application, early admission, deferred entrance. *Application fee:* $20. *Required:* high school transcript. *Required for some:* minimum 2.0 GPA, interview. *Application deadlines:* 8/25 (freshmen), 8/25 (transfers). *Notification:* continuous (freshmen), continuous (transfers).

Freshman Application Contact Mr. Tim Amyx, Director of Admissions, Volunteer State Community College, 1480 Nashville Pike, Gallatin, TN 37066-3188. *Phone:* 615-452-8600 Ext. 3614. *Toll-free phone:* 888-335-8722. *Fax:* 615-230-4875. *E-mail:* admissions@volstate.edu. *Website:* http://www.volstate.edu/.

Walters State Community College
Morristown, Tennessee

- **State-supported** 2-year, founded 1970, part of Tennessee Board of Regents
- **Small-town** 100-acre campus
- **Coed,** 5,947 undergraduate students, 54% full-time, 61% women, 39% men

Undergraduates 3,227 full-time, 2,720 part-time. 3% Black or African American, non-Hispanic/Latino; 3% Hispanic/Latino; 0.8% Asian, non-Hispanic/Latino; 0.2% American Indian or Alaska Native, non-Hispanic/Latino; 2% Two or more races, non-Hispanic/Latino; 0.1% Race/ethnicity unknown; 1% international; 3% transferred in.
Freshmen *Admission:* 3,707 applied, 1,622 admitted, 1,622 enrolled. *Average high school GPA:* 3.14. *Test scores:* ACT scores over 18: 69%; ACT scores over 24: 15%; ACT scores over 30: 1%.
Faculty *Total:* 372, 44% full-time, 26% with terminal degrees. *Student/faculty ratio:* 18:1.
Majors Business administration and management; child development; computer and information sciences; criminal justice/police science; criminal justice/safety; data processing and data processing technology; education; energy management and systems technology; general studies; health information/medical records technology; industrial technology; liberal arts and sciences/liberal studies; music performance; occupational therapist assistant; ornamental horticulture; physical therapy technology; registered nursing/registered nurse; respiratory care therapy; surgical technology; web page, digital/multimedia and information resources design.
Academics *Calendar:* semesters. *Degree:* certificates and associate. *Special study options:* academic remediation for entering students, accelerated degree program, advanced placement credit, cooperative education, distance learning, English as a second language, freshman honors college, honors programs, independent study, internships, off-campus study, part-time degree program, services for LD students, student-designed majors, study abroad, summer session for credit.
Library Walters State Library.
Student Life *Housing:* college housing not available. *Activities and Organizations:* drama/theater group, choral group, Baptist Collegiate Ministry, Phi Theta Kappa, Debate Club, Student Government Association, Service Learners Club. *Campus security:* 24-hour emergency response devices and patrols, late-night transport/escort service, security cameras. *Student services:* health clinic, personal/psychological counseling.
Athletics Member NJCAA. *Intercollegiate sports:* baseball M(s), basketball M(s)/W(s), golf M(s), softball W(s), volleyball W(s). *Intramural sports:* baseball M, basketball M/W.
Costs (2015–16) *Tuition:* state resident $3936 full-time, $152 per credit hour part-time; nonresident $15,336 full-time, $627 per credit hour part-time. Full-time tuition and fees vary according to course load and program. Part-time tuition and fees vary according to course load and program. *Required fees:* $288 full-time, $16 per credit hour part-time, $20 per term part-time. *Payment plan:* deferred payment. *Waivers:* senior citizens and employees or children of employees.
Financial Aid Of all full-time matriculated undergraduates who enrolled in 2014, 3,039 applied for aid, 2,553 were judged to have need, 187 had their need fully met. In 2014, 460 non-need-based awards were made. *Average percent of need met:* 56%. *Average financial aid package:* $5422. *Average need-based gift aid:* $4618. *Average non-need-based aid:* $3428.
Applying *Options:* electronic application, early admission. *Required:* high school transcript. *Application deadlines:* rolling (freshmen), rolling (transfers). *Notification:* continuous (freshmen), continuous (transfers).
Freshman Application Contact Mr. Michael Campbell, Assistant Vice President for Student Affairs, Walters State Community College, 500 South Davy Crockett Parkway, Morristown, TN 37813-6899. *Phone:* 423-585-2682. *Toll-free phone:* 800-225-4770. *Fax:* 423-585-6876.
E-mail: mike.campbell@ws.edu.
Website: http://www.ws.edu/.

West Tennessee Business College
Jackson, Tennessee

Admissions Office Contact West Tennessee Business College, 1186 Highway 45 Bypass, Jackson, TN 38343.

TEXAS

Alvin Community College
Alvin, Texas

- **State and locally supported** 2-year, founded 1949
- **Suburban** 114-acre campus with easy access to Houston
- **Coed,** 5,116 undergraduate students

Undergraduates Students come from 17 states and territories.
Faculty *Total:* 297, 36% full-time. *Student/faculty ratio:* 17:1.
Majors Accounting; administrative assistant and secretarial science; aeronautics/aviation/aerospace science and technology; art; automobile/automotive mechanics technology; biology/biological sciences; business administration and management; business/commerce; chemical technology; child development; computer engineering technology; computer programming; corrections; court reporting; criminalistics and criminal science; criminal justice/police science; criminal justice/safety; culinary arts; desktop publishing and digital imaging design; diagnostic medical sonography and ultrasound technology; drafting and design technology; dramatic/theater arts; early childhood education; electrical, electronic and communications engineering technology; electroneurodiagnostic/electroencephalographic technology; emergency medical technology (EMT paramedic); executive assistant/executive secretary; general studies; health and physical education/fitness; health services/allied health/health sciences; history; legal administrative assistant/secretary; legal assistant/paralegal; legal studies; liberal arts and sciences/liberal studies; licensed practical/vocational nurse training; marketing/marketing management; mathematics; medical administrative assistant and medical secretary; mental health counseling; middle school education; music; office occupations and clerical services; pharmacy technician; physical education teaching and coaching; physical sciences; psychiatric/mental health services technology; psychology; radio and television; registered nursing/registered nurse; respiratory care therapy; secondary education; sociology; substance abuse/addiction counseling; voice and opera.
Academics *Calendar:* semesters. *Degree:* certificates, diplomas, and associate. *Special study options:* academic remediation for entering students, accelerated degree program, adult/continuing education programs, advanced placement credit, cooperative education, distance learning, double majors, English as a second language, honors programs, independent study, internships, part-time degree program, services for LD students, student-designed majors, study abroad, summer session for credit.
Library Alvin Community College Library. *Books:* 13,600 (physical); *Serial titles:* 36 (physical). Weekly public service hours: 67.
Student Life *Housing:* college housing not available. *Activities and Organizations:* drama/theater group, student-run radio and television station, choral group. *Campus security:* 24-hour patrols, late-night transport/escort service. *Student services:* personal/psychological counseling.
Athletics Member NJCAA. *Intercollegiate sports:* baseball M(s), softball W(s).
Costs (2015–16) *Tuition:* area resident $1080 full-time, $45 per credit hour part-time; state resident $2160 full-time, $90 per credit hour part-time; nonresident $3360 full-time, $140 per credit hour part-time. Full-time tuition and fees vary according to course load and program. Part-time tuition and fees vary according to course load and program. *Required fees:* $434 full-time, $5 per credit hour part-time, $157 per term part-time. *Payment plan:* installment.
Financial Aid Of all full-time matriculated undergraduates who enrolled in 2015, 4,800 applied for aid, 1,795 were judged to have need.
Applying *Required for some:* high school transcript.
Freshman Application Contact Alvin Community College, 3110 Mustang Road, Alvin, TX 77511-4898. *Phone:* 281-756-3531.
Website: http://www.alvincollege.edu/.

Amarillo College
Amarillo, Texas

- **State and locally supported** 2-year, founded 1929
- **Urban** 1542-acre campus
- **Endowment** $37.8 million
- **Coed**

Undergraduates 5% Black or African American, non-Hispanic/Latino; 38% Hispanic/Latino; 3% Asian, non-Hispanic/Latino; 1% American Indian or Alaska Native, non-Hispanic/Latino; 0.9% Race/ethnicity unknown. *Retention:* 52% of full-time freshmen returned.
Faculty *Total:* 429, 51% full-time, 8% with terminal degrees.
Majors Accounting; administrative assistant and secretarial science; airframe mechanics and aircraft maintenance technology; architectural engineering technology; art; automobile/automotive mechanics technology; behavioral sciences; biblical studies; biology/biological sciences; broadcast journalism;

business administration and management; business teacher education; chemical technology; chemistry; child development; clinical laboratory science/medical technology; commercial and advertising art; computer engineering technology; computer programming; computer science; computer systems analysis; corrections; criminal justice/law enforcement administration; criminal justice/police science; dental hygiene; drafting and design technology; dramatic/theater arts; electrical, electronic and communications engineering technology; elementary education; emergency medical technology (EMT paramedic); engineering; English; environmental health; fine/studio arts; fire science/firefighting; funeral service and mortuary science; general studies; geology/earth science; health information/medical records administration; heating, air conditioning, ventilation and refrigeration maintenance technology; heavy equipment maintenance technology; history; industrial radiologic technology; information science/studies; instrumentation technology; interior design; journalism; laser and optical technology; legal administrative assistant/secretary; liberal arts and sciences/liberal studies; licensed practical/vocational nurse training; machine tool technology; mass communication/media; mathematics; medical administrative assistant and medical secretary; modern languages; music; music teacher education; natural sciences; nuclear medical technology; occupational therapy; photography; physical education teaching and coaching; physical sciences; physical therapy; physics; pre-engineering; pre-pharmacy studies; psychology; public relations/image management; radio and television; radiologic technology/science; real estate; registered nursing/registered nurse; religious studies; respiratory care therapy; rhetoric and composition; social sciences; social work; substance abuse/addiction counseling; telecommunications technology; tourism and travel services management; visual and performing arts.

Academics *Calendar:* semesters. *Degree:* certificates and associate. *Special study options:* academic remediation for entering students, adult/continuing education programs, advanced placement credit, cooperative education, distance learning, English as a second language, freshman honors college, honors programs, part-time degree program, services for LD students, summer session for credit.

Library Lynn Library Learning Center plus 2 others.

Student Life *Housing:* college housing not available. *Activities and Organizations:* drama/theater group, student-run newspaper, radio station, choral group, Student Government Association, College Republicans. *Campus security:* 24-hour emergency response devices, late-night transport/escort service, campus police patrol Monday through Saturday 7 a.m. to 11 p.m..

Athletics *Intramural sports:* basketball M/W, soccer M/W, softball M/W, tennis M/W, volleyball M/W.

Costs (2015–16) *Tuition:* area resident $2010 full-time, $84 per semester hour part-time; state resident $3042 full-time, $127 per semester hour part-time; nonresident $4578 full-time, $191 per credit hour part-time. Full-time tuition and fees vary according to course load. Part-time tuition and fees vary according to course load. *Payment plan:* installment. *Waivers:* senior citizens and employees or children of employees.

Financial Aid Of all full-time matriculated undergraduates who enrolled in 2014, 100 Federal Work-Study jobs (averaging $3000).

Applying *Options:* early admission, deferred entrance. *Required:* high school transcript. *Notification:* continuous (freshmen), continuous (transfers).

Freshman Application Contact Amarillo College, PO Box 447, Amarillo, TX 79178-0001. *Phone:* 806-371-5000. *Toll-free phone:* 800-227-8784. *Fax:* 806-371-5497. *E-mail:* askac@actx.edu.

Website: http://www.actx.edu/.

Angelina College

Lufkin, Texas

Freshman Application Contact Angelina College, PO Box 1768, Lufkin, TX 75902-1768. *Phone:* 936-633-5213.

Website: http://www.angelina.cc.tx.us/.

Auguste Escoffier School of Culinary Arts

Austin, Texas

Admissions Office Contact Auguste Escoffier School of Culinary Arts, 6020-B Dillard, Austin, TX 78752.

Website: http://www.escoffier.edu/.

Austin Community College District

Austin, Texas

- **State and locally supported** 2-year, founded 1972
- **Urban** campus with easy access to Austin
- **Endowment** $5.0 million
- **Coed,** 41,574 undergraduate students, 22% full-time, 55% women, 45% men

Undergraduates 9,031 full-time, 32,543 part-time. Students come from 54 states and territories; 112 other countries; 2% are from out of state; 7% Black or African American, non-Hispanic/Latino; 32% Hispanic/Latino; 5% Asian, non-Hispanic/Latino; 0.2% Native Hawaiian or other Pacific Islander, non-Hispanic/Latino; 0.8% American Indian or Alaska Native, non-Hispanic/Latino; 3% Two or more races, non-Hispanic/Latino; 4% Race/ethnicity unknown; 3% international.

Faculty *Total:* 1,868, 29% full-time. *Student/faculty ratio:* 20:1.

Majors Accounting technology and bookkeeping; administrative assistant and secretarial science; animation, interactive technology, video graphics and special effects; anthropology; Arabic; art; automobile/automotive mechanics technology; biology/biological sciences; biology/biotechnology laboratory technician; business administration and management; business/commerce; carpentry; chemistry; child development; Chinese; clinical/medical laboratory technology; commercial and advertising art; commercial photography; computer and information sciences; computer programming; computer systems networking and telecommunications; corrections; creative writing; criminal justice/police science; culinary arts; dance; dental hygiene; diagnostic medical sonography and ultrasound technology; drafting and design technology; dramatic/theater arts; early childhood education; economics; electrical, electronic and communications engineering technology; emergency medical technology (EMT paramedic); engineering; environmental engineering technology; fire prevention and safety technology; French; general studies; geographic information science and cartography; geography; geology/earth science; German; health and physical education/fitness; health information/medical records technology; health teacher education; heating, ventilation, air conditioning and refrigeration engineering technology; history; hospitality administration; human services; international business/trade/commerce; Japanese; journalism; Latin; legal assistant/paralegal; marketing/marketing management; mathematics; middle school education; music; music management; occupational therapist assistant; pharmacy technician; philosophy; physical sciences; physical therapy technology; physics; political science and government; pre-dentistry studies; premedical studies; pre-pharmacy studies; pre-veterinary studies; professional, technical, business, and scientific writing; psychology; radio and television; radiologic technology/science; real estate; registered nursing/registered nurse; rhetoric and composition; Russian; secondary education; sign language interpretation and translation; social work; sociology; Spanish; substance abuse/addiction counseling; surgical technology; surveying technology; therapeutic recreation; tourism and travel services management; veterinary/animal health technology; watchmaking and jewelrymaking; welding technology; writing.

Academics *Calendar:* semesters. *Degrees:* certificates, associate, and postbachelor's certificates. *Special study options:* academic remediation for entering students, accelerated degree program, adult/continuing education programs, advanced placement credit, cooperative education, distance learning, English as a second language, honors programs, independent study, internships, part-time degree program, services for LD students, summer session for credit. *ROTC:* Army (c), Air Force (c).

Library Main Library plus 11 others.

Student Life *Housing:* college housing not available. *Activities and Organizations:* student-run newspaper, choral group, Intramurals, Student Government Association (SGA), Phi Theta Kappa (PTK), Center for Student Political Studies (CSPS), Circle K International (CKI). *Campus security:* 24-hour emergency response devices, late-night transport/escort service, 24-hour patrols by police officers. *Student services:* personal/psychological counseling.

Athletics *Intramural sports:* basketball M/W, soccer M/W, volleyball W.

Costs (2015–16) *Tuition:* area resident $2010 full-time, $67 per credit hour part-time; state resident $8670 full-time, $289 per credit hour part-time; nonresident $10,800 full-time, $360 per credit hour part-time. Full-time tuition and fees vary according to course load. Part-time tuition and fees vary according to course load. *Required fees:* $540 full-time, $18 per credit hour part-time. *Payment plan:* installment. *Waivers:* senior citizens and employees or children of employees.

Financial Aid Of all full-time matriculated undergraduates who enrolled in 2015, 4,539 applied for aid, 3,812 were judged to have need. 181 Federal Work-Study jobs (averaging $4347). 46 state and other part-time jobs (averaging $3983). *Average need-based loan:* $3184. *Average need-based gift aid:* $3027.

Applying *Options:* electronic application. *Required:* high school transcript. *Application deadlines:* rolling (freshmen), rolling (transfers).
Freshman Application Contact Ms. Linda Kluck, Director, Admissions and Records, Austin Community College District, 5930 Middle Fiskville Road, Austin, TX 78752. *Phone:* 512-223-7503. *Fax:* 512-223-7665. *E-mail:* admission@austincc.edu.
Website: http://www.austincc.edu/.

Blinn College
Brenham, Texas

- **State and locally supported** 2-year, founded 1883
- **Small-town** 100-acre campus with easy access to Houston
- **Endowment** $29.8 million
- **Coed,** 19,780 undergraduate students, 52% full-time, 51% women, 49% men

Undergraduates 10,360 full-time, 9,420 part-time. Students come from 42 other countries; 1% are from out of state; 9% Black or African American, non-Hispanic/Latino; 19% Hispanic/Latino; 2% Asian, non-Hispanic/Latino; 0.1% Native Hawaiian or other Pacific Islander, non-Hispanic/Latino; 0.4% American Indian or Alaska Native, non-Hispanic/Latino; 3% Two or more races, non-Hispanic/Latino; 1% Race/ethnicity unknown; 0.9% international; 23% transferred in; 9% live on campus.
Freshmen *Admission:* 8,378 admitted, 8,378 enrolled.
Faculty *Total:* 648, 61% full-time. *Student/faculty ratio:* 29:1.
Majors Accounting; administrative assistant and secretarial science; agriculture; biology/biological sciences; business administration and management; chemistry; child development; comparative literature; computer science; computer systems networking and telecommunications; criminal justice/law enforcement administration; dental hygiene; dramatic/theater arts; English; fire science/firefighting; French; German; health information/medical records technology; history; industrial radiologic technology; legal administrative assistant/secretary; mass communication/media; mathematics; mental health counseling; music; philosophy; physical education teaching and coaching; physical therapy technology; physics; psychology; real estate; registered nursing/registered nurse; rhetoric and composition; Spanish.
Academics *Calendar:* semesters. *Degree:* certificates, diplomas, and associate. *Special study options:* academic remediation for entering students, adult/continuing education programs, advanced placement credit, distance learning, double majors, English as a second language, freshman honors college, part-time degree program, services for LD students, summer session for credit.
Library W. L. Moody, Jr. Library plus 1 other.
Student Life *Housing Options:* men-only, women-only. Campus housing is university owned. *Activities and Organizations:* drama/theater group, student-run newspaper, choral group, marching band, Student Government Association, Phi Theta Kappa, Baptist student ministries, Blinn Ethnic Student Organization, Circle K. *Campus security:* 24-hour emergency response devices and patrols, controlled dormitory access. *Student services:* personal/psychological counseling.
Athletics Member NJCAA. *Intercollegiate sports:* baseball M(s), basketball M(s)/W(s), cheerleading M(s)/W(s), football M(s), softball W(s), volleyball W(s). *Intramural sports:* basketball M/W, bowling M/W, football M, golf M, softball W, table tennis M/W, volleyball M/W, weight lifting M/W.
Costs (2015–16) *Tuition:* area resident $1440 full-time, $48 per credit hour part-time; state resident $3510 full-time, $117 per credit hour part-time; nonresident $6000 full-time, $200 per credit hour part-time. Full-time tuition and fees vary according to course load. Part-time tuition and fees vary according to course load. *Required fees:* $1380 full-time, $46 per credit hour part-time. *Room and board:* $6700; room only: $4400. Room and board charges vary according to board plan, gender, and housing facility. *Payment plan:* installment.
Financial Aid Of all full-time matriculated undergraduates who enrolled in 2014, 103 Federal Work-Study jobs (averaging $1985).
Applying *Options:* electronic application, early admission, deferred entrance. *Required:* high school transcript. *Application deadlines:* rolling (freshmen), rolling (transfers).
Freshman Application Contact Ms. Jennifer Bynum, Director Prospective Student Relations/ Community Outreach, Blinn College, PO Box 6030, Bryan, TX 77805-6030. *Phone:* 979-209-7640. *E-mail:* jennifer.bynum@blinn.edu.
Website: http://www.blinn.edu/.

Brazosport College
Lake Jackson, Texas

Freshman Application Contact Brazosport College, 500 College Drive, Lake Jackson, TX 77566-3199. *Phone:* 979-230-3020.
Website: http://www.brazosport.edu/.

Brightwood College, Arlington Campus
Arlington, Texas

Freshman Application Contact Brightwood College, Arlington Campus, 2241 South Watson Road, Arlington, TX 76010. *Phone:* 866-249-2074. *Toll-free phone:* 800-935-1857.
Website: http://www.brightwood.edu/.

Brightwood College, Beaumont Campus
Beaumont, Texas

Freshman Application Contact Admissions Office, Brightwood College, Beaumont Campus, 6115 Eastex Freeway, Beaumont, TX 77706. *Phone:* 409-833-2722. *Toll-free phone:* 800-935-1857.
Website: http://www.brightwood.edu/.

Brightwood College, Brownsville Campus
Brownsville, Texas

Freshman Application Contact Director of Admissions, Brightwood College, Brownsville Campus, 1900 North Expressway, Suite O, Brownsville, TX 78521. *Phone:* 956-547-8200.
Website: http://www.brightwood.edu/.

Brightwood College, Corpus Christi Campus
Corpus Christi, Texas

Freshman Application Contact Admissions Director, Brightwood College, Corpus Christi Campus, 1620 South Padre Island Drive, Suite 600, Corpus Christi, TX 78416. *Phone:* 361-852-2900.
Website: http://www.brightwood.edu/.

Brightwood College, Dallas Campus
Dallas, Texas

Freshman Application Contact Brightwood College, Dallas Campus, 12005 Ford Road, Suite 100, Dallas, TX 75234. *Phone:* 972-385-1446. *Toll-free phone:* 800-935-1857.
Website: http://www.brightwood.edu/.

Brightwood College, El Paso Campus
El Paso, Texas

Freshman Application Contact Director of Admissions, Brightwood College, El Paso Campus, 8360 Burnham Road, Suite 100, El Paso, TX 79907.
Website: http://www.brightwood.edu/.

Brightwood College, Fort Worth Campus
Fort Worth, Texas

Freshman Application Contact Director of Admissions, Brightwood College, Fort Worth Campus, 2001 Beach Street, Suite 201, Fort Worth, TX 76103. *Phone:* 817-413-2000.
Website: http://www.brightwood.edu/.

Brightwood College, Friendswood Campus
Friendswood, Texas

Freshman Application Contact Admissions Office, Brightwood College, Friendswood Campus, 3208 Farm to Market Road 528, Friendswood, TX 77546.
Website: http://www.brightwood.edu/.

Brightwood College, Houston Campus
Houston, Texas

Freshman Application Contact Admissions Office, Brightwood College, Houston Campus, 711 East Airtex Drive, Houston, TX 77073. *Phone:* 281-443-8900.
Website: http://www.brightwood.edu/.

Brightwood College, Laredo Campus
Laredo, Texas

Freshman Application Contact Admissions Office, Brightwood College, Laredo Campus, 6410 McPherson Road, Laredo, TX 78041. *Phone:* 956-717-5909. *Toll-free phone:* 800-935-1857.
Website: http://www.brightwood.edu/.

Brightwood College, McAllen Campus
McAllen, Texas

Admissions Office Contact Brightwood College, McAllen Campus, 1500 South Jackson Road, McAllen, TX 78503. *Toll-free phone:* 800-935-1857.
Website: http://www.brightwood.edu/.

Brightwood College, San Antonio Ingram Campus
San Antonio, Texas

Freshman Application Contact Admissions Office, Brightwood College, San Antonio Ingram Campus, 6441 NW Loop 410, San Antonio, TX 78238. *Phone:* 210-308-8584. *Toll-free phone:* 800-935-1857.
Website: http://www.brightwood.edu/.

Brightwood College, San Antonio San Pedro Campus
San Antonio, Texas

Freshman Application Contact Director of Admissions, Brightwood College, San Antonio San Pedro Campus, 7142 San Pedro Avenue, Suite 100, San Antonio, TX 78216. *Toll-free phone:* 800-935-1857.
Website: http://www.brightwood.edu/.

Brookhaven College
Farmers Branch, Texas

- **County-supported** 2-year, founded 1978, part of Dallas County Community College District System
- **Suburban** 200-acre campus with easy access to Dallas-Fort Worth
- **Coed,** 12,509 undergraduate students, 17% full-time, 58% women, 42% men

Undergraduates 2,125 full-time, 10,384 part-time. Students come from 34 states and territories; 79 other countries; 0.2% are from out of state; 17% Black or African American, non-Hispanic/Latino; 39% Hispanic/Latino; 11% Asian, non-Hispanic/Latino; 0.1% Native Hawaiian or other Pacific Islander, non-Hispanic/Latino; 0.4% American Indian or Alaska Native, non-Hispanic/Latino; 2% Two or more races, non-Hispanic/Latino; 2% Race/ethnicity unknown; 2% international; 8% transferred in.
Freshmen *Admission:* 5,257 enrolled.
Faculty *Total:* 573, 23% full-time. *Student/faculty ratio:* 20:1.
Majors Accounting; automobile/automotive mechanics technology; business administration and management; business/commerce; child development; computer engineering technology; computer programming; computer technology/computer systems technology; criminal justice/law enforcement administration; design and visual communications; e-commerce; education (multiple levels); emergency medical technology (EMT paramedic); executive assistant/executive secretary; general studies; geographic information science and cartography; graphic design; humanities; information science/studies; liberal arts and sciences/liberal studies; marketing/marketing management; music; office management; radiologic technology/science; registered nursing/registered nurse; secondary education; speech communication and rhetoric.
Academics *Calendar:* semesters. *Degree:* certificates and associate. *Special study options:* academic remediation for entering students, adult/continuing education programs, advanced placement credit, cooperative education, distance learning, English as a second language, honors programs, independent study, internships, off-campus study, part-time degree program, services for LD students, student-designed majors, study abroad, summer session for credit.
Library Brookhaven College Learning Resources Center plus 1 other.
Student Life *Housing:* college housing not available. *Activities and Organizations:* drama/theater group, student-run newspaper, choral group. *Campus security:* 24-hour emergency response devices and patrols, late-night transport/escort service. *Student services:* health clinic, personal/psychological counseling.
Athletics Member NJCAA. *Intercollegiate sports:* baseball M, basketball M, soccer W, volleyball W. *Intramural sports:* weight lifting M/W.

Costs (2015–16) *Tuition:* area resident $1770 full-time, $59 per credit part-time; state resident $3330 full-time, $111 per credit part-time; nonresident $5220 full-time, $174 per credit part-time. *Payment plan:* installment. *Waivers:* senior citizens and employees or children of employees.
Applying *Options:* electronic application, early admission, deferred entrance. *Required:* high school transcript. *Required for some:* HESI score, minimum GPA in prerequisite courses, completion of support courses for nursing program. *Application deadlines:* rolling (freshmen), rolling (transfers).
Freshman Application Contact Admissions Office, Brookhaven College, 3939 Valley View Lane, Farmers Branch, TX 75244-4997. *Phone:* 972-860-4883. *Fax:* 972-860-4886. *E-mail:* bhcAdmissions@dcccd.edu.
Website: http://www.brookhavencollege.edu/.

Cedar Valley College
Lancaster, Texas

- **State-supported** 2-year, founded 1977, part of Dallas County Community College District System
- **Suburban** 353-acre campus with easy access to Dallas-Fort Worth
- **Coed**

Undergraduates 1,564 full-time, 5,389 part-time. Students come from 1 other state; 1% are from out of state; 54% Black or African American, non-Hispanic/Latino; 21% Hispanic/Latino; 2% Asian, non-Hispanic/Latino; 0.1% Native Hawaiian or other Pacific Islander, non-Hispanic/Latino; 0.3% American Indian or Alaska Native, non-Hispanic/Latino; 1% Two or more races, non-Hispanic/Latino; 2% Race/ethnicity unknown; 0.1% international; 20% transferred in. *Retention:* 44% of full-time freshmen returned.
Faculty *Student/faculty ratio:* 24:1.
Academics *Calendar:* semesters. *Degree:* certificates and associate. *Special study options:* academic remediation for entering students, advanced placement credit, cooperative education, distance learning, double majors, English as a second language, internships, off-campus study, part-time degree program, services for LD students, summer session for credit.
Library Cedar Valley College Library.
Student Life *Campus security:* 24-hour emergency response devices and patrols, late-night transport/escort service.
Athletics Member NCAA, NJCAA.
Standardized Tests *Required:* SAT or ACT (for admission), TSI (for admission). *Required for some:* SAT and SAT Subject Tests or ACT (for admission).
Costs (2015–16) *Tuition:* area resident $1180 full-time, $59 per credit hour part-time; state resident $2220 full-time, $111 per credit hour part-time; nonresident $3480 full-time, $200 per credit hour part-time. Full-time tuition and fees vary according to class time, course level, course load, degree level, location, program, reciprocity agreements, and student level. Part-time tuition and fees vary according to class time, course level, course load, degree level, location, program, reciprocity agreements, and student level. No tuition increase for student's term of enrollment. *Required fees:* $59 per credit hour part-time. *Payment plans:* tuition prepayment, installment.
Applying *Required:* high school transcript, minimum 2.0 GPA.
Freshman Application Contact Admissions Office, Cedar Valley College, Lancaster, TX 75134-3799. *Phone:* 972-860-8206. *Fax:* 972-860-8207.
Website: http://www.cedarvalleycollege.edu/.

Center for Advanced Legal Studies
Houston, Texas

Freshman Application Contact Mr. James Scheffer, Center for Advanced Legal Studies, 3910 Kirby, Suite 200, Houston, TX 77098. *Phone:* 713-529-2778. *Toll-free phone:* 800-446-6931. *Fax:* 713-523-2715.
E-mail: james.scheffer@paralegal.edu.
Website: http://www.paralegal.edu/.

Central Texas College
Killeen, Texas

- **State and locally supported** 2-year, founded 1967
- **Suburban** 500-acre campus with easy access to Austin
- **Endowment** $6.4 million
- **Coed,** 19,562 undergraduate students, 22% full-time, 47% women, 53% men

Undergraduates 4,362 full-time, 15,200 part-time. 27% Black or African American, non-Hispanic/Latino; 21% Hispanic/Latino; 3% Asian, non-Hispanic/Latino; 2% Native Hawaiian or other Pacific Islander, non-Hispanic/Latino; 1% American Indian or Alaska Native, non-Hispanic/Latino; 3% Two or more races, non-Hispanic/Latino; 3% Race/ethnicity unknown; 0.3% international; 1% live on campus. *Retention:* 54% of full-time freshmen returned.

Freshmen *Admission:* 2,625 enrolled.

Faculty *Total:* 1,540, 15% full-time. *Student/faculty ratio:* 16:1.

Majors Administrative assistant and secretarial science; agriculture; aircraft powerplant technology; airline pilot and flight crew; autobody/collision and repair technology; automobile/automotive mechanics technology; biology/biological sciences; building/property maintenance; business administration and management; chemistry; child-care provision; clinical/medical laboratory technology; clinical/medical social work; commercial and advertising art; computer and information systems security; computer technology/computer systems technology; criminal justice/police science; diesel mechanics technology; drafting and design technology; dramatic/theater arts; early childhood education; emergency medical technology (EMT paramedic); engineering; environmental science; farm and ranch management; fine/studio arts; fire services administration; foreign languages and literatures; general studies; geology/earth science; graphic and printing equipment operation/production; health and physical education/fitness; heating, air conditioning, ventilation and refrigeration maintenance technology; hospitality administration; journalism; legal assistant/paralegal; liberal arts and sciences/liberal studies; licensed practical/vocational nurse training; marketing/marketing management; mathematics; music; public administration; radio and television; registered nursing/registered nurse; restaurant/food services management; social sciences; system, networking, and LAN/WAN management; telecommunications technology; welding technology.

Academics *Calendar:* semesters. *Degree:* certificates and associate. *Special study options:* academic remediation for entering students, accelerated degree program, adult/continuing education programs, advanced placement credit, distance learning, English as a second language, external degree program, internships, part-time degree program, services for LD students, student-designed majors, summer session for credit. *ROTC:* Army (b).

Library Oveta Culp Hobby Memorial Library. *Books:* 64,080 (physical), 32,555 (digital/electronic); *Serial titles:* 65,620 (physical), 32,639 (digital/electronic); *Databases:* 87.

Student Life *Housing Options:* coed. Campus housing is university owned. *Activities and Organizations:* drama/theater group, student-run newspaper, International Student Association, We Can Do It Club, Enactus, Student Nurses Association, NAACP, national fraternities. *Campus security:* 24-hour emergency response devices and patrols.

Athletics *Intramural sports:* basketball M/W, football M/W, soccer M/W, softball M/W, volleyball M/W.

Costs (2016–17) *Tuition:* area resident $2280 full-time, $76 per credit part-time; state resident $2940 full-time, $98 per credit part-time; nonresident $6420 full-time, $214 per credit part-time. Full-time tuition and fees vary according to location and program. Part-time tuition and fees vary according to location and program. *Room and board:* $5031. Room and board charges vary according to housing facility. *Payment plan:* installment. *Waivers:* senior citizens and employees or children of employees.

Financial Aid Of all full-time matriculated undergraduates who enrolled in 2014, 68 Federal Work-Study jobs (averaging $3658).

Applying *Options:* electronic application, early admission, deferred entrance. *Required:* high school transcript. *Application deadlines:* rolling (freshmen), rolling (out-of-state freshmen), rolling (transfers).

Freshman Application Contact Admissions Office, Central Texas College, PO Box 1800, Killeen, TX 76540-1800. *Phone:* 254-526-1696. *Toll-free phone:* 800-223-4760 (in-state); 800-792-3348 (out-of-state). *E-mail:* admissions@ctcd.edu. *Website:* http://www.ctcd.edu/.

Cisco College
Cisco, Texas

Freshman Application Contact Mr. Olin O. Odom III, Dean of Admission/Registrar, Cisco College, 101 College Heights, Cisco, TX 76437-9321. *Phone:* 254-442-2567 Ext. 5130. *E-mail:* oodom@cjc.edu. *Website:* http://www.cisco.edu/.

Clarendon College
Clarendon, Texas

Freshman Application Contact Ms. Martha Smith, Admissions Director, Clarendon College, PO Box 968, Clarendon, TX 79226. *Phone:* 806-874-3571 Ext. 106. *Toll-free phone:* 800-687-9737. *Fax:* 806-874-3201. *E-mail:* martha.smith@clarendoncollege.edu. *Website:* http://www.clarendoncollege.edu/.

Coastal Bend College
Beeville, Texas

- **County-supported** 2-year, founded 1965
- **Rural** 100-acre campus
- **Endowment** $514,263
- **Coed**

Undergraduates 1,353 full-time, 2,423 part-time. Students come from 2 states and territories; 1 other country; 1% are from out of state; 5% transferred in; 5% live on campus.

Faculty *Student/faculty ratio:* 13:1.

Academics *Calendar:* semesters. *Degree:* certificates and associate. *Special study options:* academic remediation for entering students, adult/continuing education programs, advanced placement credit, cooperative education, distance learning, internships, part-time degree program, services for LD students, summer session for credit.

Library Grady C. Hogue Learning Resource Center.

Student Life *Campus security:* 24-hour emergency response devices, night security.

Athletics Member NJCAA.

Financial Aid Of all full-time matriculated undergraduates who enrolled in 2014, 80 Federal Work-Study jobs (averaging $1484). 11 state and other part-time jobs (averaging $1159).

Applying *Options:* electronic application, deferred entrance. *Required:* high school transcript.

Freshman Application Contact Mrs. Tammy Adams, Director of Admissions/Registrar, Coastal Bend College, Beeville, TX 78102-2197. *Phone:* 361-354-2245. *Toll-free phone:* 866-722-2838 (in-state); 866-262-2838 (out-of-state). *Fax:* 361-354-2254. *E-mail:* tadams@coastalbend.edu. *Website:* http://www.coastalbend.edu/.

The College of Health Care Professions
Austin, Texas

Admissions Office Contact The College of Health Care Professions, 6505 Airport Boulevard, Austin, TX 78752. *Website:* http://www.chcp.edu/.

The College of Health Care Professions
Fort Worth, Texas

Admissions Office Contact The College of Health Care Professions, 4248 North Freeway, Fort Worth, TX 76137-5021. *Website:* http://www.chcp.edu/.

The College of Health Care Professions
Houston, Texas

Freshman Application Contact Admissions Office, The College of Health Care Professions, 240 Northwest Mall Boulevard, Houston, TX 77092. *Phone:* 713-425-3100. *Toll-free phone:* 800-487-6728. *Fax:* 713-425-3193. *Website:* http://www.chcp.edu/.

The College of Health Care Professions
San Antonio, Texas

Admissions Office Contact The College of Health Care Professions, 4738 NW Loop 410, San Antonio, TX 78229. *Website:* http://www.chcp.edu/.

College of the Mainland
Texas City, Texas

Freshman Application Contact Mr. Martin Perez, Director of Admissions/International Affairs, College of the Mainland, 1200 Amburn Road, Texas City, TX 77591. *Phone:* 409-933-8653. *Toll-free phone:* 888-258-8859 Ext. 8264. *E-mail:* mperez@com.edu. *Website:* http://www.com.edu/.

Collin County Community College District
McKinney, Texas

- **State and locally supported** 2-year, founded 1985
- **Suburban** 333-acre campus with easy access to Dallas-Fort Worth
- **Endowment** $10.7 million
- **Coed,** 28,187 undergraduate students, 33% full-time, 55% women, 45% men

Undergraduates 9,427 full-time, 18,760 part-time. Students come from 55 states and territories; 98 other countries; 12% Black or African American, non-Hispanic/Latino; 19% Hispanic/Latino; 9% Asian, non-Hispanic/Latino; 0.2% Native Hawaiian or other Pacific Islander, non-Hispanic/Latino; 0.5% American Indian or Alaska Native, non-Hispanic/Latino; 4% Two or more races, non-Hispanic/Latino; 0.7% Race/ethnicity unknown; 3% international; 7% transferred in. *Retention:* 53% of full-time freshmen returned.
Freshmen *Admission:* 4,579 applied, 4,579 admitted.
Faculty *Total:* 1,217, 35% full-time, 23% with terminal degrees. *Student/faculty ratio:* 23:1.
Majors Administrative assistant and secretarial science; baking and pastry arts; biology/biotechnology laboratory technician; business administration and management; business/commerce; child-care provision; child development; commercial and advertising art; computer and information sciences; computer and information systems security; computer science; criminal justice/police science; culinary arts; dental hygiene; drafting and design technology; early childhood education; electrical, electronic and communications engineering technology; electroneurodiagnostic/electroencephalographic technology; emergency medical technology (EMT paramedic); engineering; engineering technology; fire prevention and safety technology; fire science/firefighting; game and interactive media design; geographic information science and cartography; graphic design; health information/medical records technology; hospitality administration; illustration; integrated circuit design; interior design; legal assistant/paralegal; liberal arts and sciences/liberal studies; medical insurance coding; middle school education; music; music management; network and system administration; real estate; registered nursing/registered nurse; respiratory care therapy; retail management; secondary education; sign language interpretation and translation; speech communication and rhetoric; surgical technology; system, networking, and LAN/WAN management; telecommunications technology; web page, digital/multimedia and information resources design.
Academics *Calendar:* semesters. *Degree:* certificates and associate. *Special study options:* academic remediation for entering students, adult/continuing education programs, advanced placement credit, cooperative education, distance learning, English as a second language, honors programs, internships, part-time degree program, services for LD students, summer session for credit. *ROTC:* Air Force (c).
Library Collin College Library. *Books:* 223,886 (physical), 36,653 (digital/electronic); *Databases:* 168. Students can reserve study rooms.
Student Life *Housing:* college housing not available. *Activities and Organizations:* drama/theater group, choral group, Student Government, Phi Theta Kappa, Baptist Student Ministry, National Society of Leadership Success, Political Science Club. *Campus security:* 24-hour emergency response devices and patrols, late-night transport/escort service. *Student services:* personal/psychological counseling.
Athletics Member NJCAA. *Intercollegiate sports:* basketball M(s)/W(s), tennis M(s)/W(s).
Costs (2015–16) *Tuition:* area resident $960 full-time, $39 per credit hour part-time; state resident $2130 full-time, $78 per credit hour part-time; nonresident $3930 full-time, $138 per credit hour part-time. *Required fees:* $214 full-time, $7 per credit hour part-time, $2 per term part-time. *Payment plan:* installment. *Waivers:* senior citizens.
Applying *Options:* electronic application. *Required for some:* high school transcript. *Application deadlines:* rolling (freshmen), rolling (out-of-state freshmen), rolling (transfers). *Notification:* continuous (freshmen), continuous (out-of-state freshmen), continuous (transfers).
Freshman Application Contact Mr. Todd Fields, Registrar/Director of Admissions, Collin County Community College District, 2800 E. Spring Creek Parkway, Plano, TX 75074. *Phone:* 972-881-5174. *Fax:* 972-881-5175. *E-mail:* tfields@collin.edu.
Website: http://www.collin.edu/.

Commonwealth Institute of Funeral Service
Houston, Texas

Freshman Application Contact Ms. Patricia Moreno, Registrar, Commonwealth Institute of Funeral Service, 415 Barren Springs Drive, Houston, TX 77090. *Phone:* 281-873-0262. *Toll-free phone:* 800-628-1580. *Fax:* 281-873-5232. *E-mail:* p.moreno@commonwealth.edu. *Website:* http://www.commonwealth.edu/.

Concorde Career College
Dallas, Texas

Admissions Office Contact Concorde Career College, 12606 Greenville Avenue, Suite 130, Dallas, TX 75243.
Website: http://www.concorde.edu/.

Concorde Career College
Grand Prairie, Texas

Admissions Office Contact Concorde Career College, 3015 West Interstate 20, Grand Prairie, TX 75052. *Toll-free phone:* 800-693-7010.
Website: http://www.concorde.edu/.

Concorde Career College
San Antonio, Texas

Admissions Office Contact Concorde Career College, 4803 NW Loop 410, Suite 200, San Antonio, TX 78229.
Website: http://www.concorde.edu/.

Culinary Institute LeNotre
Houston, Texas

Freshman Application Contact Admissions Office, Culinary Institute LeNotre, 7070 Allensby, Houston, TX 77022-4322. *Phone:* 713-358-5070. *Toll-free phone:* 888-LENOTRE.
Website: http://www.culinaryinstitute.edu/.

Dallas Institute of Funeral Service
Dallas, Texas

- **Independent** 2-year, founded 1945, part of Pierce Mortuary Colleges, Inc.
- **Urban** 4-acre campus with easy access to Dallas-Fort Worth
- **Coed,** 141 undergraduate students, 100% full-time, 47% women, 53% men

Undergraduates 141 full-time. Students come from 7 states and territories; 11% are from out of state; 30% Black or African American, non-Hispanic/Latino; 15% Hispanic/Latino. *Retention:* 71% of full-time freshmen returned.
Freshmen *Admission:* 56 enrolled.
Faculty *Total:* 11, 45% full-time. *Student/faculty ratio:* 17:1.
Majors Funeral service and mortuary science.
Academics *Calendar:* quarters. *Degree:* certificates and associate. *Special study options:* distance learning, services for LD students.
Student Life *Housing:* college housing not available. *Campus security:* 24-hour emergency response devices.
Applying *Options:* electronic application. *Application fee:* $50. *Required:* high school transcript. *Application deadlines:* rolling (freshmen), rolling (transfers).
Freshman Application Contact Director of Admissions, Dallas Institute of Funeral Service, 3909 South Buckner Boulevard, Dallas, TX 75227. *Phone:* 214-388-5466. *Toll-free phone:* 800-235-5444. *Fax:* 214-388-0316. *E-mail:* difs@dallasinstitute.edu.
Website: http://www.dallasinstitute.edu/.

Dallas Nursing Institute
Dallas, Texas

Admissions Office Contact Dallas Nursing Institute, 12170 N. Abrams Road, Suite 200, Dallas, TX 75243.
Website: http://www.dni.edu/.

Del Mar College
Corpus Christi, Texas

Freshman Application Contact Ms. Frances P. Jordan, Director of Admissions and Registrar, Del Mar College, 101 Baldwin, Corpus Christi, TX 78404. *Phone:* 361-698-1255. *Toll-free phone:* 800-652-3357. *Fax:* 361-698-1595. *E-mail:* fjordan@delmar.edu.
Website: http://www.delmar.edu/.

Eastfield College
Mesquite, Texas

Freshman Application Contact Ms. Glynis Miller, Director of Admissions/Registrar, Eastfield College, 3737 Motley Drive, Mesquite, TX 75150-2099. *Phone:* 972-860-7010. *Fax:* 972-860-8306.
E-mail: efc@dcccd.edu.
Website: http://www.efc.dcccd.edu/.

El Centro College
Dallas, Texas

- **County-supported** 2-year, founded 1966, part of Dallas County Community College District System
- **Urban** 2-acre campus
- **Coed**

Undergraduates 2,314 full-time, 7,787 part-time. Students come from 49 other countries; 1% are from out of state; 19% Black or African American, non-Hispanic/Latino; 38% Hispanic/Latino; 3% Asian, non-Hispanic/Latino; 0.0% Native Hawaiian or other Pacific Islander, non-Hispanic/Latino; 0.3% American Indian or Alaska Native, non-Hispanic/Latino; 24% Two or more races, non-Hispanic/Latino; 2% Race/ethnicity unknown; 0.3% international; 74% transferred in. *Retention:* 39% of full-time freshmen returned.
Faculty *Student/faculty ratio:* 19:1.
Academics *Calendar:* semesters. *Degree:* certificates and associate. *Special study options:* academic remediation for entering students, adult/continuing education programs, advanced placement credit, cooperative education, distance learning, double majors, English as a second language, freshman honors college, honors programs, internships, part-time degree program, services for LD students, summer session for credit. *ROTC:* Army (c).
Library El Centro College Library.
Student Life *Campus security:* 24-hour emergency response devices and patrols, late-night transport/escort service, e-mail and text message alerts.
Applying *Required for some:* high school transcript, 1 letter of recommendation.
Freshman Application Contact Ms. Rebecca Garza, Director of Admissions and Registrar, El Centro College, Dallas, TX 75202. *Phone:* 214-860-2618. *Fax:* 214-860-2233. *E-mail:* rgarza@dcccd.edu.
Website: http://www.elcentrocollege.edu/.

El Paso Community College
El Paso, Texas

Freshman Application Contact Daryle Hendry, Director of Admissions, El Paso Community College, PO Box 20500, El Paso, TX 79998-0500. *Phone:* 915-831-2580. *E-mail:* daryleh@epcc.edu.
Website: http://www.epcc.edu/.

Everest College
Arlington, Texas

Freshman Application Contact Admissions Office, Everest College, 300 Six Flags Drive, Suite 100, Arlington, TX 76011. *Phone:* 817-652-7790. *Toll-free phone:* 888-741-4270. *Fax:* 817-649-6033.
Website: http://www.everest.edu/.

Everest College
Fort Worth, Texas

Admissions Office Contact Everest College, 4200 South Freeway, Suite 1940, Fort Worth, TX 76115.
Website: http://www.everest.edu/.

Frank Phillips College
Borger, Texas

Freshman Application Contact Ms. Michele Stevens, Director of Enrollment Management, Frank Phillips College, PO Box 5118, Borger, TX 79008-5118. *Phone:* 806-457-4200 Ext. 707. *Fax:* 806-457-4225.
E-mail: mstevens@fpctx.edu.
Website: http://www.fpctx.edu/.

Galveston College
Galveston, Texas

- **State and locally supported** 2-year, founded 1967
- **Urban** 11-acre campus with easy access to Houston
- **Coed,** 2,071 undergraduate students, 24% full-time, 62% women, 38% men

Undergraduates 504 full-time, 1,567 part-time. 13% Black or African American, non-Hispanic/Latino; 37% Hispanic/Latino; 3% Asian, non-Hispanic/Latino; 0.2% Native Hawaiian or other Pacific Islander, non-Hispanic/Latino; 0.5% American Indian or Alaska Native, non-Hispanic/Latino; 0.4% Two or more races, non-Hispanic/Latino; 3% Race/ethnicity unknown; 1% international; 12% transferred in. *Retention:* 53% of full-time freshmen returned.
Freshmen *Admission:* 238 enrolled.
Faculty *Total:* 99, 56% full-time, 22% with terminal degrees. *Student/faculty ratio:* 15:1.
Majors Administrative assistant and secretarial science; behavioral sciences; biological and physical sciences; business administration and management; computer science; criminal justice/safety; culinary arts; data entry/microcomputer applications; dramatic/theater arts; education; electromechanical technology; emergency medical technology (EMT paramedic); English; general studies; heating, air conditioning, ventilation and refrigeration maintenance technology; history; humanities; information technology; liberal arts and sciences/liberal studies; mathematics; medical administrative assistant and medical secretary; medical radiologic technology; music; natural sciences; nuclear medical technology; physical education teaching and coaching; radiologic technology/science; registered nursing/registered nurse; social sciences; social work; welding technology; word processing.
Academics *Calendar:* semesters. *Degree:* certificates and associate. *Special study options:* adult/continuing education programs, advanced placement credit, cooperative education, distance learning, internships, off-campus study, part-time degree program, services for LD students, summer session for credit.
Library David Glenn Hunt Memorial Library.
Student Life *Housing Options:* Campus housing is university owned. *Activities and Organizations:* drama/theater group, choral group, Student Government, Phi Theta Kappa, Student Nurses Association, ATTC, Hispanic Student Organization. *Campus security:* 24-hour emergency response devices and patrols, late-night transport/escort service. *Student services:* personal/psychological counseling.
Athletics Member NJCAA. *Intercollegiate sports:* baseball M(s), softball W(s). *Intramural sports:* basketball M/W, bowling M/W.
Standardized Tests *Required:* TSI or exemption test scores and documentation (for admission).
Costs (2015–16) *Tuition:* area resident $1110 full-time, $37 per credit hour part-time; state resident $1590 full-time, $53 per credit hour part-time; nonresident $3480 full-time, $116 per credit hour part-time. Full-time tuition and fees vary according to course load. Part-time tuition and fees vary according to course load. *Required fees:* $790 full-time, $20 per credit hour part-time, $95 per term part-time.
Financial Aid Of all full-time matriculated undergraduates who enrolled in 2014, 36 Federal Work-Study jobs (averaging $2000).
Applying *Required for some:* high school transcript. *Application deadlines:* rolling (freshmen), rolling (transfers). *Notification:* continuous (freshmen), continuous (transfers).
Freshman Application Contact Galveston College, 4015 Avenue Q, Galveston, TX 77550. *Phone:* 409-944-1216.
Website: http://www.gc.edu/.

Golf Academy of America
Farmers Branch, Texas

Admissions Office Contact Golf Academy of America, 1861 Valley View Lane, Suite 100, Farmers Branch, TX 75234. *Toll-free phone:* 800-342-7342.
Website: http://www.golfacademy.edu/.

Grayson College
Denison, Texas

Freshman Application Contact Charles Leslie, Enrollment Advisor, Grayson College, 6101Grayson Drive, Denison, TX 75020. *Phone:* 903-415-2532. *Fax:* 903-463-5284. *E-mail:* lesliec@grayson.edu.
Website: http://www.grayson.edu/.

Hill College
Hillsboro, Texas

Freshman Application Contact Enrollment Management, Hill College, 112 Lamar Drive, Hillsboro, TX 76645. *Phone:* 254-659-7600. *Fax:* 254-582-7591. *E-mail:* enrollmentinfo@hillcollege.edu.
Website: http://www.hillcollege.edu/.

Houston Community College
Houston, Texas

- **State and locally supported** 2-year, founded 1971
- **Urban** campus with easy access to Houston
- **Coed,** 56,522 undergraduate students, 30% full-time, 58% women, 42% men

Undergraduates 16,896 full-time, 39,626 part-time. Students come from 47 states and territories; 30% Black or African American, non-Hispanic/Latino; 32% Hispanic/Latino; 9% Asian, non-Hispanic/Latino; 0.2% Native Hawaiian or other Pacific Islander, non-Hispanic/Latino; 0.2% American Indian or Alaska Native, non-Hispanic/Latino; 2% Two or more races, non-Hispanic/Latino; 2% Race/ethnicity unknown; 10% international; 8% transferred in.
Freshmen *Admission:* 3,547 applied, 3,547 admitted.
Faculty *Total:* 2,446, 31% full-time.
Majors Accounting; animation, interactive technology, video graphics and special effects; anthropology; applied horticulture/horticulture operations; automobile/automotive mechanics technology; banking and financial support services; biology/biological sciences; biology/biotechnology laboratory technician; business administration and management; business automation/technology/data entry; business/corporate communications; cardiovascular technology; chemical technology; chemistry; child development; cinematography and film/video production; clinical/medical laboratory science and allied professions related; clinical/medical laboratory technology; commercial photography; computer engineering technology; computer programming; computer programming (specific applications); computer science; computer systems networking and telecommunications; construction engineering technology; cosmetology; court reporting; criminal justice/police science; culinary arts; desktop publishing and digital imaging design; drafting and design technology; early childhood education; education (multiple levels); emergency medical technology (EMT paramedic); energy management and systems technology; engineering science; English; fashion/apparel design; fashion merchandising; fine/studio arts; fire prevention and safety technology; general studies; health and physical education/fitness; health information/medical records technology; health services/allied health/health sciences; histologic technician; hotel/motel administration; instrumentation technology; interior design; international business/trade/commerce; legal assistant/paralegal; logistics, materials, and supply chain management; manufacturing engineering technology; marketing/marketing management; mathematics; music management; music performance; music theory and composition; network and system administration; nuclear medical technology; occupational safety and health technology; occupational therapist assistant; petroleum technology; physical therapy technology; physics; psychiatric/mental health services technology; public administration; radio and television broadcasting technology; radiologic technology/science; real estate; registered nursing/registered nurse; respiratory care therapy; secondary education; sign language interpretation and translation; speech communication and rhetoric; tourism and travel services management; turf and turfgrass management.
Academics *Calendar:* semesters. *Degree:* certificates and associate. *Special study options:* academic remediation for entering students, advanced placement credit, cooperative education, distance learning, English as a second language, honors programs, internships, part-time degree program, services for LD students, study abroad, summer session for credit. *ROTC:* Army (c), Air Force (c).
Library Houston Community College Libraries plus 18 others. *Books:* 278,187 (physical), 175,821 (digital/electronic); *Serial titles:* 415 (physical), 23,746 (digital/electronic); *Databases:* 126. Students can reserve study rooms.
Student Life *Housing:* college housing not available. *Activities and Organizations:* student-run newspaper. *Campus security:* 24-hour emergency response devices and patrols, late-night transport/escort service, crime prevention services.
Costs (2015–16) *Tuition:* area resident $1632 full-time, $411 per term part-time; state resident $3360 full-time, $843 per term part-time; nonresident $3756 full-time, $942 per term part-time. Full-time tuition and fees vary according to course load. Part-time tuition and fees vary according to course load. *Payment plan:* installment. *Waivers:* senior citizens and employees or children of employees.
Financial Aid Of all full-time matriculated undergraduates who enrolled in 2015, 54,732 applied for aid, 54,732 were judged to have need, 30,354 had

their need fully met. 739 Federal Work-Study jobs (averaging $5500). 253 state and other part-time jobs (averaging $3300). *Average percent of need met:* 78%. *Average financial aid package:* $6510. *Average need-based loan:* $3826.
Applying *Options:* electronic application. *Required for some:* high school transcript, interview. *Application deadlines:* rolling (freshmen), rolling (out-of-state freshmen), rolling (transfers).
Freshman Application Contact Ms. Mary Lemburg, Registrar, Houston Community College, 3100 Main Street, PO Box 667517, Houston, TX 77266-7517. *Phone:* 713-718-2000. *Toll-free phone:* 877-422-6111. *Fax:* 713-718-2111. *E-mail:* student.info@hccs.edu.
Website: http://www.hccs.edu/.

Howard College
Big Spring, Texas

Freshman Application Contact Ms. TaNeal Richardson, Assistant Registrar, Howard College, 1001 Birdwell Lane, Big Spring, TX 79720-3702. *Phone:* 432-264-5105. *Toll-free phone:* 866-HC-HAWKS. *Fax:* 432-264-5604. *E-mail:* trichardson@howardcollege.edu.
Website: http://www.howardcollege.edu/.

Interactive College of Technology
Houston, Texas

- **Proprietary** 2-year
- **Urban** campus
- **Coed**

Academics *Calendar:* semesters. *Degree:* certificates, diplomas, and associate. *Special study options:* academic remediation for entering students, advanced placement credit, cooperative education, distance learning, English as a second language, internships.
Applying *Required:* high school transcript, interview.
Freshman Application Contact Interactive College of Technology, 4473 I-45 N. Freeway, Airline Plaza, Houston, TX 77022.
Website: http://ict.edu/.

Interactive College of Technology
Houston, Texas

- **Proprietary** 2-year
- **Coed**

Academics *Calendar:* semesters. *Degree:* certificates, diplomas, and associate. *Special study options:* academic remediation for entering students, cooperative education, distance learning, English as a second language, internships.
Freshman Application Contact Interactive College of Technology, 6200 Hillcroft Avenue, Suite 200, Houston, TX 77081.
Website: http://ict.edu/.

Interactive College of Technology
Pasadena, Texas

- **Proprietary** 2-year
- **Coed**

Academics *Calendar:* semesters. *Special study options:* academic remediation for entering students, advanced placement credit, distance learning, English as a second language, internships, part-time degree program.
Applying *Required:* high school transcript, interview.
Freshman Application Contact Interactive College of Technology, 213 W. Southmore Street, Suite 101, Pasadena, TX 77502.
Website: http://ict.edu/.

International Business College
El Paso, Texas

Admissions Office Contact International Business College, 1155 North Zaragosa Road, El Paso, TX 79907.
Website: http://www.ibcelpaso.edu/.

International Business College
El Paso, Texas

Admissions Office Contact International Business College, 5700 Cromo Drive, El Paso, TX 79912.
Website: http://www.ibcelpaso.edu/.

ITT Technical Institute
Arlington, Texas

Freshman Application Contact Director of Recruitment, ITT Technical Institute, 551 Ryan Plaza Drive, Arlington, TX 76011. *Phone:* 817-794-5100. *Toll-free phone:* 888-288-4950.
Website: http://www.itt-tech.edu/.

ITT Technical Institute
Austin, Texas

Freshman Application Contact Director of Recruitment, ITT Technical Institute, 6330 East Highway 290, Suite 150, Austin, TX 78723. *Phone:* 512-467-6800. *Toll-free phone:* 800-431-0677.
Website: http://www.itt-tech.edu/.

ITT Technical Institute
DeSoto, Texas

Freshman Application Contact Director of Recruitment, ITT Technical Institute, 921 West Belt Line Road, Suite 181, DeSoto, TX 75115. *Phone:* 972-274-8600. *Toll-free phone:* 877-854-5728.
Website: http://www.itt-tech.edu/.

ITT Technical Institute
Houston, Texas

Freshman Application Contact Director of Recruitment, ITT Technical Institute, 15651 North Freeway, Houston, TX 77090. *Phone:* 281-873-0512. *Toll-free phone:* 800-879-6486.
Website: http://www.itt-tech.edu/.

ITT Technical Institute
Houston, Texas

Freshman Application Contact Director of Recruitment, ITT Technical Institute, 2950 South Gessner, Houston, TX 77063-3751. *Phone:* 713-952-2294. *Toll-free phone:* 800-235-4787.
Website: http://www.itt-tech.edu/.

ITT Technical Institute
Richardson, Texas

Freshman Application Contact Director of Recruitment, ITT Technical Institute, 2101 Waterview Parkway, Richardson, TX 75080. *Phone:* 972-690-9100. *Toll-free phone:* 888-488-5761.
Website: http://www.itt-tech.edu/.

ITT Technical Institute
San Antonio, Texas

Freshman Application Contact Director of Recruiting, ITT Technical Institute, 2895 NE Loop 410, San Antonio, TX 78218. *Phone:* 210-651-8500. *Toll-free phone:* 877-400-8894.
Website: http://www.itt-tech.edu/.

ITT Technical Institute
San Antonio, Texas

Freshman Application Contact Director of Recruitment, ITT Technical Institute, 5700 Northwest Parkway, San Antonio, TX 78249-3303. *Phone:* 210-694-4612. *Toll-free phone:* 800-880-0570.
Website: http://www.itt-tech.edu/.

ITT Technical Institute
Waco, Texas

Freshman Application Contact Director of Recruitment, ITT Technical Institute, 3700 S. Jack Kultgen Expressway, Suite 100, Waco, TX 76706. *Phone:* 254-523-3940. *Toll-free phone:* 877-201-7143.
Website: http://www.itt-tech.edu/.

ITT Technical Institute
Webster, Texas

Freshman Application Contact Director of Recruitment, ITT Technical Institute, 1001 Magnolia Avenue, Webster, TX 77598. *Phone:* 281-316-4700. *Toll-free phone:* 888-488-9347.
Website: http://www.itt-tech.edu/.

Jacksonville College
Jacksonville, Texas

Freshman Application Contact Danny Morris, Director of Admissions, Jacksonville College, 105 B.J. Albritton Drive, Jacksonville, TX 75766. *Phone:* 903-589-7110. *Toll-free phone:* 800-256-8522.
E-mail: admissions@jacksonville-college.org.
Website: http://www.jacksonville-college.edu/.

KD Conservatory College of Film and Dramatic Arts
Dallas, Texas

- **Proprietary** 2-year, founded 1979
- **Urban** campus
- **Coed**

Undergraduates 236 full-time. Students come from 11 states and territories; 1 other country; 5% are from out of state; 31% Black or African American, non-Hispanic/Latino; 19% Hispanic/Latino; 2% Asian, non-Hispanic/Latino; 0.4% American Indian or Alaska Native, non-Hispanic/Latino; 0.8% Two or more races, non-Hispanic/Latino; 12% Race/ethnicity unknown; 1% international. *Retention:* 69% of full-time freshmen returned.
Faculty *Student/faculty ratio:* 12:1.
Academics *Calendar:* semesters. *Degree:* associate.
Library KD Studio Library.
Student Life *Campus security:* 24-hour emergency response devices and patrols.
Costs (2015–16) *Tuition:* $14,025 full-time. No tuition increase for student's term of enrollment. *Required fees:* $550 full-time. *Payment plans:* tuition prepayment, installment.
Applying *Options:* electronic application, deferred entrance. *Required:* essay or personal statement, high school transcript, interview, AUDITION AND/OR INTERVIEW WITH PROGRAM CHAIR AND DIRECTOR OF SCHOOL.
Freshman Application Contact Mr. T. A. Taylor, Director of Education, KD Conservatory College of Film and Dramatic Arts, 2600 Stemmons Freeway, Suite 117, Dallas, TX 75207. *Phone:* 214-638-0484. *Toll-free phone:* 877-278-2283. *Fax:* 214-630-5140. *E-mail:* tataylor@kdstudio.com.
Website: http://www.kdstudio.com/.

Kilgore College
Kilgore, Texas

- **State and locally supported** 2-year, founded 1935
- **Small-town** 35-acre campus with easy access to Dallas-Fort Worth
- **Endowment** $10.0 million
- **Coed,** 5,666 undergraduate students, 40% full-time, 58% women, 42% men

Undergraduates 2,245 full-time, 3,421 part-time. Students come from 25 states and territories; 18 other countries; 2% are from out of state; 19% Black or African American, non-Hispanic/Latino; 18% Hispanic/Latino; 1% Asian, non-Hispanic/Latino; 0.5% American Indian or Alaska Native, non-Hispanic/Latino; 3% Two or more races, non-Hispanic/Latino; 0.9% Race/ethnicity unknown; 0.7% international; 6% transferred in; 7% live on campus. *Retention:* 52% of full-time freshmen returned.
Freshmen *Admission:* 988 enrolled.
Faculty *Total:* 308, 48% full-time, 7% with terminal degrees. *Student/faculty ratio:* 17:1.
Majors Accounting technology and bookkeeping; aerospace, aeronautical and astronautical/space engineering; agriculture; architecture; art; autobody/collision and repair technology; automobile/automotive mechanics technology; biological and physical sciences; business administration and management; business/commerce; chemical engineering; chemistry; child-care and support services management; child-care provision; civil engineering; commercial and advertising art; commercial photography; computer and information sciences; computer programming; computer systems networking and telecommunications; criminal justice/law enforcement administration; dance; diesel mechanics technology; drafting and design technology; dramatic/theater arts; electrical, electronic and communications engineering technology; elementary education; emergency medical technology (EMT paramedic); English; executive assistant/executive secretary; general studies;

geology/earth science; health teacher education; heating, air conditioning, ventilation and refrigeration maintenance technology; journalism; legal assistant/paralegal; mathematics; mechanical engineering; medical radiologic technology; metallurgical technology; music; occupational safety and health technology; operations management; petroleum engineering; physical education teaching and coaching; physical therapy; physical therapy technology; physics; pre-dentistry studies; pre-law studies; premedical studies; pre-pharmacy studies; pre-veterinary studies; psychology; radiologic technology/science; registered nursing/registered nurse; religious studies; social sciences; surgical technology; welding technology.

Academics *Calendar:* semesters. *Degree:* certificates and associate. *Special study options:* academic remediation for entering students, adult/continuing education programs, advanced placement credit, cooperative education, distance learning, honors programs, internships, part-time degree program, services for LD students, summer session for credit.

Library Randolph C. Watson Library plus 1 other. *Books:* 44,165 (physical), 34,163 (digital/electronic); *Serial titles:* 153 (physical), 50,534 (digital/electronic); *Databases:* 106. Weekly public service hours: 62.

Student Life *Housing Options:* coed, men-only, women-only. Campus housing is university owned. *Activities and Organizations:* drama/theater group, student-run newspaper, choral group, marching band. *Campus security:* 24-hour emergency response devices and patrols. *Student services:* health clinic, personal/psychological counseling.

Athletics Member NJCAA. *Intercollegiate sports:* basketball M(s)/W(s), football M(s), softball W(s). *Intramural sports:* basketball M/W, football M/W, racquetball M/W, soccer M/W, table tennis M/W, tennis M/W, volleyball M/W.

Costs (2015–16) *Tuition:* area resident $768 full-time, $32 per semester hour part-time; state resident $2424 full-time, $101 per semester hour part-time; nonresident $3624 full-time, $151 per semester hour part-time. Full-time tuition and fees vary according to course load and program. Part-time tuition and fees vary according to course load and program. *Required fees:* $696 full-time. *Room and board:* $4640. Room and board charges vary according to board plan and housing facility. *Payment plan:* installment. *Waivers:* employees or children of employees.

Financial Aid Of all full-time matriculated undergraduates who enrolled in 2014, 80 Federal Work-Study jobs (averaging $2500). *Financial aid deadline:* 6/1.

Applying *Options:* electronic application, early admission. *Required:* high school transcript. *Required for some:* interview. *Application deadlines:* rolling (freshmen), rolling (out-of-state freshmen), rolling (transfers).

Freshman Application Contact Kilgore College, 1100 Broadway Boulevard, Kilgore, TX 75662-3299. *Phone:* 903-983-8200.
E-mail: register@kilgore.cc.tx.us.
Website: http://www.kilgore.edu/.

Lamar Institute of Technology
Beaumont, Texas

Freshman Application Contact Admissions Office, Lamar Institute of Technology, 855 East Lavaca, Beaumont, TX 77705. *Phone:* 409-880-8354.
Toll-free phone: 800-950-6989.
Website: http://www.lit.edu/.

Lamar State College–Orange
Orange, Texas

Freshman Application Contact Kerry Olson, Director of Admissions and Financial Aid, Lamar State College–Orange, 410 Front Street, Orange, TX 77632. *Phone:* 409-882-3362. *Fax:* 409-882-3374.
Website: http://www.lsco.edu/.

Lamar State College–Port Arthur
Port Arthur, Texas

Freshman Application Contact Ms. Connie Nicholas, Registrar, Lamar State College–Port Arthur, PO Box 310, Port Arthur, TX 77641-0310. *Phone:* 409-984-6165. *Toll-free phone:* 800-477-5872. *Fax:* 409-984-6025.
E-mail: nichoca@lamarpa.edu.
Website: http://www.lamarpa.edu/.

Laredo Community College
Laredo, Texas

Freshman Application Contact Ms. Josie Soliz, Admissions Records Supervisor, Laredo Community College, Laredo, TX 78040-4395. *Phone:* 956-721-5177. *Fax:* 956-721-5493.
Website: http://www.laredo.edu/.

Lee College
Baytown, Texas

Director of Admissions Ms. Becki Griffith, Registrar, Lee College, PO Box 818, Baytown, TX 77522-0818. *Phone:* 281-425-6399.
E-mail: bgriffit@lee.edu.
Website: http://www.lee.edu/.

Lincoln College of Technology
Grand Prairie, Texas

Admissions Office Contact Lincoln College of Technology, 2915 Alouette Drive, Grand Prairie, TX 75052.
Website: http://www.lincolnedu.com/.

Lone Star College–CyFair
Cypress, Texas

- **State and locally supported** 2-year, founded 2002, part of Lone Star College
- **Suburban** campus with easy access to Houston
- **Coed,** 20,510 undergraduate students, 29% full-time, 57% women, 43% men

Undergraduates 5,964 full-time, 14,546 part-time. Students come from 65 other countries; 14% Black or African American, non-Hispanic/Latino; 43% Hispanic/Latino; 10% Asian, non-Hispanic/Latino; 0.2% American Indian or Alaska Native, non-Hispanic/Latino; 3% Two or more races, non-Hispanic/Latino; 2% Race/ethnicity unknown; 22% transferred in.

Freshmen *Admission:* 3,383 applied, 3,383 admitted, 3,383 enrolled.

Faculty *Total:* 1,103, 20% full-time, 19% with terminal degrees. *Student/faculty ratio:* 21:1.

Majors Accounting; accounting and computer science; animation, interactive technology, video graphics and special effects; business administration and management; computer and information sciences; computer science; criminal justice/law enforcement administration; dance; design and visual communications; diagnostic medical sonography and ultrasound technology; economics; education; electrical, electronic and communications engineering technology; emergency medical technology (EMT paramedic); fire science/firefighting; geographic information science and cartography; health information/medical records technology; industrial technology; information technology; liberal arts and sciences/liberal studies; logistics, materials, and supply chain management; marketing/marketing management; medical radiologic technology; music; office occupations and clerical services; radiation protection/health physics technology; registered nursing/registered nurse; sign language interpretation and translation; speech communication and rhetoric; welding technology.

Academics *Calendar:* semesters. *Degree:* certificates, diplomas, and associate. *Special study options:* academic remediation for entering students, accelerated degree program, adult/continuing education programs, advanced placement credit, cooperative education, distance learning, double majors, English as a second language, honors programs, independent study, internships, part-time degree program, services for LD students, study abroad, summer session for credit.

Library LSC–CyFair Library.

Student Life *Housing:* college housing not available. *Activities and Organizations:* drama/theater group, choral group. *Campus security:* 24-hour emergency response devices and patrols, late-night transport/escort service. *Student services:* personal/psychological counseling.

Costs (2015–16) *Tuition:* area resident $1008 full-time, $42 per credit hour part-time; state resident $2688 full-time, $112 per credit hour part-time; nonresident $3048 full-time, $127 per credit hour part-time. Full-time tuition and fees vary according to course load and program. Part-time tuition and fees vary according to course load and program. *Required fees:* $496 full-time, $18 per credit hour part-time, $32 per credit hour part-time. *Payment plans:* installment, deferred payment. *Waivers:* employees or children of employees.

Applying *Options:* electronic application, early admission.

Freshman Application Contact Admissions Office, Lone Star College–CyFair, 9191 Barker Cypress Road, Cypress, TX 77433-1383. *Phone:* 281-290-3200. *E-mail:* cfc.info@lonestar.edu.
Website: http://www.lonestar.edu/cyfair.

Lone Star College–Kingwood
Kingwood, Texas

- **State and locally supported** 2-year, founded 1984, part of Lone Star College
- **Suburban** 264-acre campus with easy access to Houston
- **Coed,** 12,764 undergraduate students, 30% full-time, 63% women, 37% men

Undergraduates 3,852 full-time, 8,912 part-time. Students come from 47 other countries; 15% Black or African American, non-Hispanic/Latino; 32% Hispanic/Latino; 4% Asian, non-Hispanic/Latino; 0.3% American Indian or Alaska Native, non-Hispanic/Latino; 3% Two or more races, non-Hispanic/Latino; 3% Race/ethnicity unknown; 24% transferred in.

Freshmen *Admission:* 1,712 applied, 1,712 admitted, 1,712 enrolled.

Faculty *Total:* 838, 16% full-time, 12% with terminal degrees. *Student/faculty ratio:* 19:1.

Majors Administrative assistant and secretarial science; business administration and management; computer and information sciences; computer science; cosmetology; criminal justice/law enforcement administration; dental hygiene; design and visual communications; education; electroneurodiagnostic/electroencephalographic technology; fire science/firefighting; interior design; marketing/marketing management; music; occupational therapy; registered nursing/registered nurse; respiratory care therapy.

Academics *Calendar:* semesters. *Degree:* certificates and associate. *Special study options:* academic remediation for entering students, accelerated degree program, adult/continuing education programs, advanced placement credit, cooperative education, distance learning, double majors, English as a second language, honors programs, independent study, internships, part-time degree program, services for LD students, study abroad, summer session for credit.

Library LSC–Kingwood Library.

Student Life *Housing:* college housing not available. *Activities and Organizations:* drama/theater group, student-run television station, choral group. *Campus security:* 24-hour emergency response devices and patrols, late-night transport/escort service. *Student services:* personal/psychological counseling.

Costs (2015–16) *Tuition:* area resident $1008 full-time, $42 per credit hour part-time; state resident $2688 full-time, $112 per credit hour part-time; nonresident $3048 full-time, $127 per credit hour part-time. Full-time tuition and fees vary according to course load and program. Part-time tuition and fees vary according to course load and program. *Required fees:* $496 full-time, $18 per credit hour part-time, $32 per term part-time. *Payment plans:* installment, deferred payment. *Waivers:* employees or children of employees.

Financial Aid Of all full-time matriculated undergraduates who enrolled in 2009, 28 Federal Work-Study jobs, 6 state and other part-time jobs. *Financial aid deadline:* 4/1.

Applying *Options:* electronic application, early admission. *Application deadlines:* rolling (freshmen), rolling (transfers).

Freshman Application Contact Admissions Office, Lone Star College–Kingwood, 20000 Kingwood Drive, Kingwood, TX 77339. *Phone:* 281-312-1525. *Fax:* 281-312-1477. *E-mail:* kingwoodadvising@lonestar.edu. *Website:* http://www.lonestar.edu/kingwood.htm.

Lone Star College–Montgomery
Conroe, Texas

- **State and locally supported** 2-year, founded 1995, part of Lone Star College
- **Suburban** campus with easy access to Houston
- **Coed,** 13,826 undergraduate students, 30% full-time, 60% women, 40% men

Undergraduates 4,199 full-time, 9,627 part-time. Students come from 52 other countries; 10% Black or African American, non-Hispanic/Latino; 29% Hispanic/Latino; 4% Asian, non-Hispanic/Latino; 0.3% American Indian or Alaska Native, non-Hispanic/Latino; 3% Two or more races, non-Hispanic/Latino; 2% Race/ethnicity unknown; 22% transferred in.

Freshmen *Admission:* 1,907 applied, 1,907 admitted, 1,907 enrolled.

Faculty *Total:* 699, 21% full-time, 16% with terminal degrees. *Student/faculty ratio:* 22:1.

Majors Accounting and business/management; automobile/automotive mechanics technology; biology/biotechnology laboratory technician; business administration and management; computer science; criminal justice/law enforcement administration; education; emergency medical technology (EMT paramedic); fire science/firefighting; human services; information technology; music; physical therapy technology; registered nursing/registered nurse.

Academics *Calendar:* semesters. *Degree:* certificates and associate. *Special study options:* academic remediation for entering students, adult/continuing education programs, advanced placement credit, cooperative education, distance learning, double majors, English as a second language, honors programs, independent study, internships, part-time degree program, services for LD students, study abroad, summer session for credit.

Library LSC–Montgomery Library.

Student Life *Housing:* college housing not available. *Activities and Organizations:* drama/theater group, student-run newspaper, choral group, Campus Crusade for Christ, Criminal Justice Club, Phi Theta Kappa, Latino-American Student Association, African-American Cultural Awareness. *Campus security:* 24-hour emergency response devices and patrols, late-night transport/escort service. *Student services:* personal/psychological counseling.

Costs (2015–16) *Tuition:* area resident $1008 full-time, $42 per credit hour part-time; state resident $2688 full-time, $112 per credit hour part-time; nonresident $3048 full-time, $127 per credit hour part-time. Full-time tuition and fees vary according to course load and program. Part-time tuition and fees vary according to course load and program. *Required fees:* $496 full-time, $18 per credit hour part-time, $32 per term part-time. *Payment plans:* installment, deferred payment. *Waivers:* employees or children of employees.

Financial Aid Of all full-time matriculated undergraduates who enrolled in 2014, 25 Federal Work-Study jobs (averaging $2500). 4 state and other part-time jobs.

Applying *Options:* electronic application, early admission. *Application deadlines:* rolling (freshmen), rolling (transfers).

Freshman Application Contact Lone Star College–Montgomery, 3200 College Park Drive, Conroe, TX 77384. *Phone:* 281-290-2721. *Website:* http://www.lonestar.edu/montgomery.

Lone Star College–North Harris
Houston, Texas

- **State and locally supported** 2-year, founded 1972, part of Lone Star College
- **Suburban** campus with easy access to Houston
- **Coed,** 17,001 undergraduate students, 28% full-time, 60% women, 40% men

Undergraduates 4,735 full-time, 12,266 part-time. Students come from 54 other countries; 28% Black or African American, non-Hispanic/Latino; 43% Hispanic/Latino; 6% Asian, non-Hispanic/Latino; 0.2% American Indian or Alaska Native, non-Hispanic/Latino; 3% Two or more races, non-Hispanic/Latino; 3% Race/ethnicity unknown; 23% transferred in.

Freshmen *Admission:* 2,470 applied, 2,470 admitted, 2,470 enrolled.

Faculty *Total:* 1,100, 17% full-time, 13% with terminal degrees. *Student/faculty ratio:* 18:1.

Majors Accounting; automobile/automotive mechanics technology; business administration and management; computer science; cosmetology; criminal justice/law enforcement administration; design and visual communications; drafting and design technology; education; educational/instructional technology; electrical, electronic and communications engineering technology; emergency medical technology (EMT paramedic); health information/medical records technology; heating, air conditioning, ventilation and refrigeration maintenance technology; industrial technology; legal assistant/paralegal; mechanical engineering; music; pharmacy technician; registered nursing/registered nurse; sign language interpretation and translation; welding technology.

Academics *Calendar:* semesters. *Degree:* certificates and associate. *Special study options:* academic remediation for entering students, adult/continuing education programs, advanced placement credit, cooperative education, distance learning, double majors, English as a second language, honors programs, independent study, internships, part-time degree program, services for LD students, study abroad, summer session for credit.

Library LSC–North Harris Library.

Student Life *Activities and Organizations:* drama/theater group, student-run newspaper, choral group, Student Government Association, Phi Theta Kappa, Ambassadors, Honors Student Organizations, Soccer Club. *Campus security:* 24-hour emergency response devices and patrols, late-night transport/escort service. *Student services:* personal/psychological counseling, women's center.

Athletics *Intramural sports:* badminton M/W, baseball M/W, basketball M/W, bowling M/W, football M/W, golf M/W, gymnastics M/W, racquetball M/W, soccer M/W, softball M/W, table tennis M/W, tennis M/W, track and field M/W, volleyball M/W, weight lifting M/W.

Costs (2015–16) *Tuition:* area resident $1008 full-time, $42 per credit hour part-time; state resident $2688 full-time, $112 per credit hour part-time; nonresident $3048 full-time, $127 per credit hour part-time. Full-time tuition and fees vary according to course load and program. Part-time tuition and fees vary according to course load and program. *Required fees:* $496 full-time, $18 per credit hour part-time, $32 per term part-time. *Payment plans:* installment, deferred payment. *Waivers:* employees or children of employees.

Applying *Options:* electronic application, early admission. *Application deadlines:* rolling (freshmen), rolling (transfers).
Freshman Application Contact Admissions Office, Lone Star College–North Harris, 2700 W. W. Thorne Drive, Houston, TX 77073-3499. *Phone:* 281-618-5410. *E-mail:* nhcounselor@lonestar.edu.
Website: http://www.lonestar.edu/northharris.

Lone Star College–Tomball
Tomball, Texas

- **State and locally supported** 2-year, founded 1988, part of Lone Star College
- **Suburban** campus with easy access to Houston
- **Coed,** 8,880 undergraduate students, 29% full-time, 63% women, 37% men

Undergraduates 2,543 full-time, 6,337 part-time. Students come from 40 other countries; 13% Black or African American, non-Hispanic/Latino; 28% Hispanic/Latino; 5% Asian, non-Hispanic/Latino; 0.3% American Indian or Alaska Native, non-Hispanic/Latino; 3% Two or more races, non-Hispanic/Latino; 3% Race/ethnicity unknown; 26% transferred in.
Freshmen *Admission:* 1,095 applied, 1,095 admitted, 1,095 enrolled.
Faculty *Total:* 392, 26% full-time, 18% with terminal degrees. *Student/faculty ratio:* 24:1.
Majors Accounting; administrative assistant and secretarial science; animation, interactive technology, video graphics and special effects; business administration and management; computer programming; computer science; criminal justice/law enforcement administration; education; electrical, electronic and communications engineering technology; industrial technology; music; registered nursing/registered nurse; surgical technology; system, networking, and LAN/WAN management; veterinary/animal health technology.
Academics *Calendar:* semesters. *Degree:* certificates and associate. *Special study options:* academic remediation for entering students, adult/continuing education programs, advanced placement credit, cooperative education, distance learning, double majors, English as a second language, honors programs, independent study, internships, part-time degree program, services for LD students, study abroad, summer session for credit.
Library LSC–Tomball Community Library.
Student Life *Housing:* college housing not available. *Activities and Organizations:* drama/theater group, student-run newspaper, choral group, Phi Theta Kappa, Occupational Therapy OTA, Veterinary Technicians Student Organization, STARS, Student Nurses Association. *Campus security:* 24-hour emergency response devices and patrols, late-night transport/escort service, trained security personnel during hours of operation. *Student services:* personal/psychological counseling.
Costs (2015–16) *Tuition:* area resident $1008 full-time, $42 per credit hour part-time; state resident $2688 full-time, $112 per credit hour part-time; nonresident $3048 full-time, $127 per credit hour part-time. Full-time tuition and fees vary according to course load and program. Part-time tuition and fees vary according to course load and program. *Required fees:* $496 full-time, $18 per credit hour part-time, $32 per term part-time. *Payment plans:* installment, deferred payment. *Waivers:* employees or children of employees.
Financial Aid Of all full-time matriculated undergraduates who enrolled in 2014, 34 Federal Work-Study jobs (averaging $3000).
Applying *Options:* electronic application, early admission. *Application deadlines:* rolling (freshmen), rolling (transfers).
Freshman Application Contact Admissions Office, Lone Star College–Tomball, 30555 Tomball Parkway, Tomball, TX 77375-4036. *Phone:* 281-351-3310. *E-mail:* tcinfo@lonestar.edu.
Website: http://www.lonestar.edu/tomball.

Lone Star College–University Park
Houston, Texas

- **State and locally supported** 2-year, founded 2010, part of Lone Star College
- **Suburban** campus with easy access to Houston
- **Coed,** 10,951 undergraduate students, 29% full-time, 57% women, 43% men

Undergraduates 3,190 full-time, 7,761 part-time. Students come from 55 other countries; 15% Black or African American, non-Hispanic/Latino; 37% Hispanic/Latino; 12% Asian, non-Hispanic/Latino; 0.2% American Indian or Alaska Native, non-Hispanic/Latino; 3% Two or more races, non-Hispanic/Latino; 4% Race/ethnicity unknown; 22% transferred in.
Freshmen *Admission:* 1,642 enrolled.
Faculty *Total:* 447, 15% full-time, 18% with terminal degrees. *Student/faculty ratio:* 30:1.
Majors Accounting; business administration and management; criminal justice/law enforcement administration; speech communication and rhetoric.

Academics *Degree:* certificates and associate. *Special study options:* academic remediation for entering students, advanced placement credit, cooperative education, distance learning, English as a second language, honors programs, independent study, internships, off-campus study, part-time degree program, services for LD students, study abroad, summer session for credit.
Student Life *Housing:* college housing not available. *Campus security:* 24-hour emergency response devices and patrols, late-night transport/escort service.
Costs (2015–16) *Tuition:* area resident $1008 full-time, $42 per credit hour part-time; state resident $2688 full-time, $112 per credit hour part-time; nonresident $3048 full-time, $127 per credit hour part-time. Full-time tuition and fees vary according to course load and program. Part-time tuition and fees vary according to course load and program. *Required fees:* $496 full-time, $18 per credit hour part-time, $32 per credit hour part-time. *Payment plans:* installment, deferred payment. *Waivers:* senior citizens and employees or children of employees.
Applying *Recommended:* high school transcript.
Freshman Application Contact Lone Star College–University Park, 20515 SH 249, Houston, TX 77070-2607. *Phone:* 281-290-2721.
Website: http://www.lonestar.edu/universitypark.

McLennan Community College
Waco, Texas

Freshman Application Contact Dr. Vivian G. Jefferson, Director, Admissions and Recruitment, McLennan Community College, 1400 College Drive, Waco, TX 76708. *Phone:* 254-299-8689. *Fax:* 254-299-8694.
E-mail: vjefferson@mclennan.edu.
Website: http://www.mclennan.edu/.

MediaTech Institute
Irving, Texas

Admissions Office Contact MediaTech Institute, 400 E. Royal Lane, Suite 100, Irving, TX 75039.
Website: http://www.mediatech.edu/.

Mountain View College
Dallas, Texas

Freshman Application Contact Ms. Glenda Hall, Director of Admissions, Mountain View College, 4849 West Illinois Avenue, Dallas, TX 75211-6599. *Phone:* 214-860-8666. *Fax:* 214-860-8570. *E-mail:* ghall@dcccd.edu.
Website: http://www.mountainviewcollege.edu/.

Navarro College
Corsicana, Texas

- **State and locally supported** 2-year, founded 1946
- **Small-town** 275-acre campus with easy access to Dallas-Fort Worth
- **Coed,** 9,478 undergraduate students, 38% full-time, 59% women, 41% men

Undergraduates 3,555 full-time, 5,923 part-time. Students come from 36 other countries; 1% are from out of state; 20% Black or African American, non-Hispanic/Latino; 19% Hispanic/Latino; 0.8% Asian, non-Hispanic/Latino; 0.3% Native Hawaiian or other Pacific Islander, non-Hispanic/Latino; 0.6% American Indian or Alaska Native, non-Hispanic/Latino; 1% Two or more races, non-Hispanic/Latino; 1% international; 25% live on campus.
Freshmen *Admission:* 1,579 enrolled.
Faculty *Total:* 533, 24% full-time, 7% with terminal degrees. *Student/faculty ratio:* 25:1.
Majors Accounting; administrative assistant and secretarial science; agricultural mechanization; art; biological and physical sciences; biology/biological sciences; business administration and management; chemistry; clinical/medical laboratory technology; commercial and advertising art; computer graphics; computer programming; computer science; consumer merchandising/retailing management; corrections; criminal justice/law enforcement administration; criminal justice/police science; data processing and data processing technology; developmental and child psychology; drafting and design technology; dramatic/theater arts; education; elementary education; engineering; English; fire science/firefighting; industrial technology; legal administrative assistant/secretary; legal assistant/paralegal; legal studies; licensed practical/vocational nurse training; marketing/marketing management; mathematics; music; occupational therapy; pharmacy; physical education teaching and coaching; physical sciences; physics; pre-engineering; psychology; registered nursing/registered nurse; rhetoric and composition; social sciences; sociology; voice and opera.

Academics *Calendar:* semesters. *Degree:* certificates, diplomas, and associate. *Special study options:* academic remediation for entering students, adult/continuing education programs, advanced placement credit, cooperative education, distance learning, freshman honors college, honors programs, part-time degree program, services for LD students, student-designed majors, summer session for credit.
Library Richard M. Sanchez Library.
Student Life *Housing Options:* Campus housing is university owned. *Activities and Organizations:* drama/theater group, choral group, marching band, Student Government Association, Phi Theta Kappa, Ebony Club, Que Pasa. *Campus security:* 24-hour emergency response devices. *Student services:* personal/psychological counseling.
Athletics Member NJCAA. *Intercollegiate sports:* baseball M(s), basketball M(s), football M(s), soccer W, softball W, volleyball W(s). *Intramural sports:* basketball M/W, bowling M/W, football M, soccer M, softball M/W, volleyball M/W.
Costs (2015–16) *Tuition:* area resident $1200 full-time, $120 per credit hour part-time; state resident $1350 full-time, $135 per credit hour part-time; nonresident $2850 full-time, $285 per credit hour part-time. Full-time tuition and fees vary according to course load. Part-time tuition and fees vary according to course load. *Required fees:* $101 per credit hour part-time. *Room and board:* $6611. Room and board charges vary according to board plan. *Payment plan:* installment. *Waivers:* employees or children of employees.
Applying *Options:* electronic application, early admission. *Required:* high school transcript.
Freshman Application Contact Tammy Adams, Registrar, Navarro College, 3200 West 7th Avenue, Corsicana, TX 75110-4899. *Phone:* 903-875-7348. *Toll-free phone:* 800-NAVARRO (in-state); 800-628-2776 (out-of-state). *Fax:* 903-875-7353. *E-mail:* tammy.adams@navarrocollege.edu.
Website: http://www.navarrocollege.edu/.

North Central Texas College
Gainesville, Texas

- **State and locally supported** 2-year, founded 1924
- **Suburban** 132-acre campus with easy access to Dallas-Fort Worth
- **Endowment** $4.3 million
- **Coed,** 9,618 undergraduate students, 32% full-time, 56% women, 44% men

Undergraduates 3,068 full-time, 6,550 part-time. Students come from 27 states and territories; 31 other countries; 1% are from out of state; 9% Black or African American, non-Hispanic/Latino; 22% Hispanic/Latino; 3% Asian, non-Hispanic/Latino; 0.1% Native Hawaiian or other Pacific Islander, non-Hispanic/Latino; 0.7% American Indian or Alaska Native, non-Hispanic/Latino; 3% Two or more races, non-Hispanic/Latino; 0.4% Race/ethnicity unknown; 1% international; 32% transferred in; 1% live on campus. *Retention:* 55% of full-time freshmen returned.
Freshmen *Admission:* 2,236 applied, 2,236 admitted, 2,236 enrolled.
Faculty *Total:* 403, 38% full-time, 9% with terminal degrees. *Student/faculty ratio:* 16:1.
Majors Administrative assistant and secretarial science; agricultural mechanization; animal/livestock husbandry and production; automobile/automotive mechanics technology; biological and physical sciences; business administration and management; business and personal/financial services marketing; computer and information sciences and support services related; computer engineering technology; computer graphics; computer/information technology services administration related; computer programming; computer programming related; computer programming (specific applications); computer programming (vendor/product certification); computer science; criminal justice/law enforcement administration; criminal justice/police science; data processing and data processing technology; drafting and design technology; electrical, electronic and communications engineering technology; emergency medical technology (EMT paramedic); engineering technology; equestrian studies; farm and ranch management; health information/medical records administration; industrial mechanics and maintenance technology; information science/studies; legal administrative assistant/secretary; legal assistant/paralegal; liberal arts and sciences/liberal studies; machine shop technology; machine tool technology; merchandising; occupational therapy; pre-engineering; real estate; registered nursing/registered nurse; retailing; sales, distribution, and marketing operations; welding technology; word processing.
Academics *Calendar:* semesters. *Degree:* certificates, diplomas, and associate. *Special study options:* academic remediation for entering students, adult/continuing education programs, advanced placement credit, cooperative education, distance learning, internships, part-time degree program, services for LD students, summer session for credit. *ROTC:* Army (c).
Library North Central Texas College Library plus 1 other.
Student Life *Housing Options:* coed. Campus housing is university owned. *Activities and Organizations:* drama/theater group, choral group, Student Nursing Association, Residence Hall Association, Cosmetology Student

Association, Student Government Association, Gainesville Program Council. *Campus security:* late-night transport/escort service, controlled dormitory access, security cameras. *Student services:* personal/psychological counseling.
Athletics Member NJCAA. *Intercollegiate sports:* baseball M(s), equestrian sports M(s)/W(s), softball W(s), tennis W(s), volleyball W(s). *Intramural sports:* archery M/W, basketball M/W, bowling M/W, field hockey M/W, football M/W, golf M/W, soccer M/W, softball M/W, swimming and diving M/W, table tennis M/W, tennis M/W, ultimate Frisbee M/W, volleyball M/W.
Costs (2016–17) *Tuition:* area resident $1824 full-time, $76 per semester hour part-time; state resident $3120 full-time, $130 per semester hour part-time; nonresident $5232 full-time, $218 per semester hour part-time. *Room and board:* $1964; room only: $850. Room and board charges vary according to housing facility. *Payment plans:* installment, deferred payment. *Waivers:* employees or children of employees.
Financial Aid Of all full-time matriculated undergraduates who enrolled in 2014, 108 Federal Work-Study jobs (averaging $1253). 29 state and other part-time jobs (averaging $392).
Applying *Options:* electronic application, early admission. *Required:* high school transcript. *Application deadlines:* rolling (freshmen), rolling (out-of-state freshmen), rolling (transfers).
Freshman Application Contact Melinda Carroll, Director of Admissions/Registrar, North Central Texas College, 1525 West California, Gainesville, TX 76240-4699. *Phone:* 940-668-7731. *Fax:* 940-668-7075.
E-mail: mcarroll@nctc.edu.
Website: http://www.nctc.edu/.

Northeast Texas Community College
Mount Pleasant, Texas

Freshman Application Contact Linda Bond, Admissions Specialist, Northeast Texas Community College, PO Box 1307, Mount Pleasant, TX 75456-1307. *Phone:* 903-434-8140. *Toll-free phone:* 800-870-0142. *E-mail:* lbond@ntcc.edu.
Website: http://www.ntcc.edu/.

North Lake College
Irving, Texas

Freshman Application Contact Admissions/Registration Office, North Lake College, 5001 North MacArthur Boulevard, Irving, TX 75038. *Phone:* 972-273-3183.
Website: http://www.northlakecollege.edu/.

Northwest Vista College
San Antonio, Texas

- **State and locally supported** 2-year, founded 1995, part of Alamo Community College District System
- **Urban** 137-acre campus with easy access to San Antonio
- **Coed,** 13,218 undergraduate students, 32% full-time, 54% women, 46% men

Undergraduates 4,235 full-time, 8,983 part-time. Students come from 24 states and territories; 7% transferred in. *Retention:* 54% of full-time freshmen returned.
Freshmen *Admission:* 2,397 enrolled.
Faculty *Total:* 876, 19% full-time. *Student/faculty ratio:* 23:1.
Majors Accounting; accounting technology and bookkeeping; administrative assistant and secretarial science; biology/biotechnology laboratory technician; business administration, management and operations related; community health and preventive medicine; computer and information sciences; computer and information sciences and support services related; computer and information systems security; computer/information technology services administration related; computer programming; computer science; criminal justice/safety; international/global studies; liberal arts and sciences/liberal studies; pre-engineering; recording arts technology; water quality and wastewater treatment management and recycling technology; web page, digital/multimedia and information resources design.
Academics *Calendar:* semesters. *Degree:* certificates and associate. *Special study options:* academic remediation for entering students, advanced placement credit, cooperative education, distance learning, double majors, English as a second language, independent study, internships, off-campus study, part-time degree program, services for LD students, study abroad, summer session for credit. *ROTC:* Army (c).
Library Redbud Learning Center. *Books:* 19,338 (physical), 233,202 (digital/electronic); *Serial titles:* 48 (physical), 33,000 (digital/electronic); *Databases:* 133. Weekly public service hours: 67.
Student Life *Housing:* college housing not available. *Activities and Organizations:* drama/theater group, Business Student Organization, Psychology Club, Neko Anime Club. *Campus security:* 24-hour emergency

response devices, student patrols, late-night transport/escort service. *Student services:* personal/psychological counseling.
Athletics *Intramural sports:* basketball M/W, cross-country running M/W, soccer M/W, volleyball M/W.
Costs (2016–17) *Tuition:* area resident $1418 full-time; state resident $3962 full-time; nonresident $7777 full-time. Full-time tuition and fees vary according to course load, location, and program. Part-time tuition and fees vary according to course load, location, and program. *Required fees:* $74 full-time. *Payment plan:* installment. *Waivers:* senior citizens and employees or children of employees.
Applying *Options:* electronic application, early admission. *Required:* high school transcript.
Freshman Application Contact Ms. Robin Sandberg, Director of Enrollment Management, Northwest Vista College, 3535 North Ellison Drive, San Antonio, TX 78251. *Phone:* 210-486-4134. *Fax:* 210-486-9091.
E-mail: rsandberg@alamo.edu.
Website: http://www.alamo.edu/nvc/.

Odessa College
Odessa, Texas
- **State and locally supported** 2-year, founded 1946
- **Urban** 87-acre campus
- **Endowment** $844,464
- **Coed,** 5,096 undergraduate students, 32% full-time, 60% women, 40% men

Undergraduates 1,609 full-time, 3,487 part-time. Students come from 26 states and territories; 2% are from out of state; 4% Black or African American, non-Hispanic/Latino; 59% Hispanic/Latino; 1% Asian, non-Hispanic/Latino; 0.1% Native Hawaiian or other Pacific Islander, non-Hispanic/Latino; 0.6% American Indian or Alaska Native, non-Hispanic/Latino; 0.7% Two or more races, non-Hispanic/Latino; 4% Race/ethnicity unknown; 1% international; 14% transferred in; 5% live on campus. *Retention:* 46% of full-time freshmen returned.
Freshmen *Admission:* 344 applied, 344 admitted.
Faculty *Total:* 190, 68% full-time, 11% with terminal degrees. *Student/faculty ratio:* 18:1.
Majors Accounting; administrative assistant and secretarial science; agriculture; art; athletic training; automobile/automotive mechanics technology; biology/biological sciences; business administration and management; chemistry; child development; clinical/medical laboratory technology; computer and information sciences; computer science; computer systems networking and telecommunications; construction engineering technology; cosmetology; criminal justice/law enforcement administration; criminal justice/police science; culinary arts; data processing and data processing technology; design and applied arts related; drafting and design technology; education; electrical, electronic and communications engineering technology; emergency medical technology (EMT paramedic); English; fire science/firefighting; geology/earth science; hazardous materials management and waste technology; heating, air conditioning, ventilation and refrigeration maintenance technology; history; human services; industrial radiologic technology; information science/studies; kindergarten/preschool education; legal administrative assistant/secretary; liberal arts and sciences/liberal studies; machine tool technology; mathematics; modern languages; music; photography; physical education teaching and coaching; physical therapy; physics; political science and government; pre-engineering; psychology; registered nursing/registered nurse; rhetoric and composition; social sciences; sociology; substance abuse/addiction counseling; teacher assistant/aide; welding technology.
Academics *Calendar:* semesters. *Degree:* certificates and associate. *Special study options:* academic remediation for entering students, adult/continuing education programs, advanced placement credit, cooperative education, distance learning, independent study, internships, part-time degree program, services for LD students, summer session for credit.
Library Murry H. Fly Learning Resources Center plus 1 other. *Books:* 29,875 (physical), 179,657 (digital/electronic); *Databases:* 76.
Student Life *Housing Options:* coed. Campus housing is provided by a third party. *Activities and Organizations:* choral group, Baptist Student Union, Student Government Association, Rodeo Club, Physical Therapy Assistant Club, American Chemical Society. *Campus security:* 24-hour emergency response devices and patrols, late-night transport/escort service, controlled dormitory access. *Student services:* personal/psychological counseling.
Athletics Member NJCAA. *Intercollegiate sports:* baseball M(s), basketball M(s)/W(s), cross-country running M(s)/W(s), golf M(s), softball W(s). *Intramural sports:* basketball M/W, bowling M/W, football M, racquetball M/W, softball M/W, table tennis M/W, volleyball M/W, weight lifting M/W.
Financial Aid Of all full-time matriculated undergraduates who enrolled in 2014, 59 Federal Work-Study jobs (averaging $1527). 8 state and other part-time jobs (averaging $1904).

Applying *Options:* electronic application, early admission, deferred entrance. *Application deadlines:* rolling (freshmen), rolling (transfers). *Notification:* continuous (freshmen), continuous (transfers).
Freshman Application Contact Ms. Tracy Avery, Director of Recruitment, Odessa College, 201 West University Avenue, Odessa, TX 79764. *Phone:* 432-335-6765. *Fax:* 432-335-6303. *E-mail:* tavery@odessa.edu.
Website: http://www.odessa.edu/.

Palo Alto College
San Antonio, Texas
- **State and locally supported** 2-year, founded 1987, part of Alamo Community College District System
- **Urban** campus
- **Coed**

Undergraduates 1,533 full-time, 6,843 part-time. Students come from 15 states and territories; 0.3% are from out of state; 3% Black or African American, non-Hispanic/Latino; 69% Hispanic/Latino; 1% Asian, non-Hispanic/Latino; 0.2% Native Hawaiian or other Pacific Islander, non-Hispanic/Latino; 0.3% American Indian or Alaska Native, non-Hispanic/Latino; 2% Two or more races, non-Hispanic/Latino; 3% Race/ethnicity unknown; 0.1% international; 34% transferred in.
Faculty *Student/faculty ratio:* 24:1.
Academics *Calendar:* semesters. *Degree:* certificates and associate. *Special study options:* academic remediation for entering students, adult/continuing education programs, cooperative education, English as a second language, part-time degree program, summer session for credit.
Library Ozuna Learning and Resource Center.
Student Life *Campus security:* 24-hour emergency response devices and patrols.
Costs (2015–16) *Tuition:* area resident $831 full-time, $6 per credit part-time; state resident $2216 full-time, $480 per credit part-time; nonresident $4292 full-time, $1172 per credit part-time.
Financial Aid Of all full-time matriculated undergraduates who enrolled in 2014, 272 Federal Work-Study jobs (averaging $2000).
Applying *Options:* early admission. *Required:* high school transcript.
Freshman Application Contact Ms. Elizabeth Aguilar-Villarreal, Director of Enrollment Management, Palo Alto College, 1400 West Villaret Boulevard, San Antonio, TX 78224. *Phone:* 210-486-3713.
E-mail: eaguilar-villarr@alamo.edu.
Website: http://www.alamo.edu/pac/.

Panola College
Carthage, Texas
- **State and locally supported** 2-year, founded 1947
- **Small-town** 35-acre campus
- **Endowment** $2.9 million
- **Coed,** 2,675 undergraduate students, 50% full-time, 68% women, 32% men

Undergraduates 1,335 full-time, 1,340 part-time. Students come from 11 states and territories; 12 other countries; 1% are from out of state; 21% Black or African American, non-Hispanic/Latino; 13% Hispanic/Latino; 0.5% Asian, non-Hispanic/Latino; 0.4% American Indian or Alaska Native, non-Hispanic/Latino; 0.5% Two or more races, non-Hispanic/Latino; 0.8% Race/ethnicity unknown; 1% international; 12% transferred in; 9% live on campus. *Retention:* 48% of full-time freshmen returned.
Freshmen *Admission:* 442 enrolled.
Faculty *Total:* 147, 47% full-time, 6% with terminal degrees. *Student/faculty ratio:* 18:1.
Majors Administrative assistant and secretarial science; agriculture; architecture; art; biology/biological sciences; business administration and management; business automation/technology/data entry; chemistry; clinical/medical laboratory technology; computer/information technology services administration related; computer science; construction engineering technology; criminology; dramatic/theater arts; early childhood education; education; electrician; English; foreign languages and literatures; forestry; general studies; geology/earth science; health information/medical records technology; health professions related; history; industrial technology; information science/studies; information technology; journalism; liberal arts and sciences and humanities related; management information systems; mathematics; medical/clinical assistant; middle school education; music; occupational therapist assistant; petroleum technology; physical education teaching and coaching; physics; pre-dentistry studies; pre-law studies; pre-pharmacy studies; pre-veterinary studies; psychology; registered nursing/registered nurse; sociology; speech communication and rhetoric; welding technology.
Academics *Calendar:* semesters. *Degree:* certificates and associate. *Special study options:* academic remediation for entering students, advanced

placement credit, cooperative education, distance learning, English as a second language, part-time degree program, services for LD students, summer session for credit.

Library M. P. Baker Library. *Books:* 25,725 (physical), 325,451 (digital/electronic); *Serial titles:* 60 (physical), 16 (digital/electronic); *Databases:* 60. Weekly public service hours: 64; study areas open 24 hours, 5&-7 days a week; students can reserve study rooms.

Student Life *Housing Options:* coed. Campus housing is university owned. *Activities and Organizations:* drama/theater group, student-run newspaper, choral group, Student Government Organization, Student Occupational Therapy Assistant Club, Baptist Student Ministries, Texas Nursing Student Association, Phi Theta Kappa. *Campus security:* controlled dormitory access, 24-hour campus police department.

Athletics Member NCAA, NJCAA. *Intercollegiate sports:* baseball M(s), basketball M(s)/W(s), equestrian sports M(s)/W(s), volleyball W(s). *Intramural sports:* basketball M/W, football M/W, table tennis M/W, volleyball M/W, weight lifting M/W.

Costs (2015–16) *Tuition:* area resident $750 full-time, $60 per semester hour part-time; state resident $2190 full-time, $108 per semester hour part-time; nonresident $3120 full-time, $279 per semester hour part-time. Full-time tuition and fees vary according to course load and reciprocity agreements. Part-time tuition and fees vary according to course load and reciprocity agreements. *Required fees:* $1440 full-time, $48 per semester hour part-time. *Room and board:* $4600. Room and board charges vary according to housing facility. *Payment plan:* deferred payment. *Waivers:* employees or children of employees.

Applying *Required for some:* high school transcript. *Recommended:* high school transcript.

Freshman Application Contact Mr. Jeremy Dorman, Registrar/Director of Admissions, Panola College, 1109 West Panola Street, Carthage, TX 75633-2397. *Phone:* 903-693-2009. *Fax:* 903-693-2031.

E-mail: bsimpson@panola.edu.

Website: http://www.panola.edu/.

Paris Junior College
Paris, Texas

- **State and locally supported** 2-year, founded 1924
- **Rural** 54-acre campus with easy access to Dallas-Fort Worth
- **Endowment** $21.2 million
- **Coed,** 4,999 undergraduate students, 41% full-time, 60% women, 40% men

Undergraduates 2,057 full-time, 2,942 part-time. Students come from 23 states and territories; 5 other countries; 3% are from out of state; 11% Black or African American, non-Hispanic/Latino; 15% Hispanic/Latino; 1% Asian, non-Hispanic/Latino; 2% American Indian or Alaska Native, non-Hispanic/Latino; 1% Two or more races, non-Hispanic/Latino; 0.1% Race/ethnicity unknown; 0.3% international; 7% transferred in; 4% live on campus.

Freshmen *Admission:* 859 applied, 859 admitted.

Faculty *Total:* 233, 38% full-time, 6% with terminal degrees. *Student/faculty ratio:* 22:1.

Majors Accounting; agricultural mechanization; agriculture; art; biological and physical sciences; biology/biological sciences; business administration and management; business automation/technology/data entry; business/commerce; business teacher education; chemistry; computer and information sciences; computer engineering technology; computer typography and composition equipment operation; cosmetology; criminal justice/safety; criminology; drafting and design technology; dramatic/theater arts; early childhood education; education; education (multiple levels); electrical, electronic and communications engineering technology; electromechanical technology; elementary education; emergency medical technology (EMT paramedic); engineering; English; foreign languages and literatures; general studies; health and physical education/fitness; health information/medical records technology; health services/allied health/health sciences; heating, air conditioning, ventilation and refrigeration maintenance technology; history; information science/studies; journalism; liberal arts and sciences/liberal studies; mathematics; medical insurance coding; metal and jewelry arts; music; nursing administration; physical sciences; physics; political science and government; pre-law studies; premedical studies; prenursing studies; pre-pharmacy studies; psychology; radiologic technology/science; registered nursing/registered nurse; rhetoric and composition; secondary education; social sciences; social work; sociology; surgical technology; system, networking, and LAN/WAN management; watchmaking and jewelrymaking; welding technology.

Academics *Calendar:* semesters. *Degree:* certificates, diplomas, and associate. *Special study options:* academic remediation for entering students,

adult/continuing education programs, advanced placement credit, cooperative education, distance learning, English as a second language, part-time degree program, services for LD students, summer session for credit.

Library Mike Rheudasil Learning Center.

Student Life *Housing Options:* men-only, women-only. Campus housing is university owned. *Activities and Organizations:* drama/theater group, student-run newspaper, choral group, Student Government Organization, Blends Club (for all ethic groups). *Campus security:* 24-hour emergency response devices and patrols, late-night transport/escort service, controlled dormitory access. *Student services:* personal/psychological counseling.

Athletics Member NJCAA. *Intercollegiate sports:* baseball M(s), basketball M(s)/W(s), golf M(s), soccer M(s)/W(s), softball W(s), volleyball W(s). *Intramural sports:* basketball M, football M, table tennis M/W, tennis M/W, volleyball M/W.

Costs (2015–16) *Tuition:* area resident $1500 full-time, $50 per credit hour part-time; state resident $2580 full-time, $86 per credit hour part-time; nonresident $3990 full-time, $133 per credit hour part-time. Full-time tuition and fees vary according to class time, course level, course load, degree level, location, program, and student level. Part-time tuition and fees vary according to class time, course level, course load, degree level, location, program, and student level. *Required fees:* $390 full-time. *Room and board:* $4924. Room and board charges vary according to board plan and housing facility. *Payment plan:* installment. *Waivers:* employees or children of employees.

Financial Aid Of all full-time matriculated undergraduates who enrolled in 2013, 54 Federal Work-Study jobs (averaging $3600). 8 state and other part-time jobs (averaging $3600).

Applying *Options:* electronic application, early admission. *Required:* high school transcript. *Application deadlines:* rolling (freshmen), rolling (out-of-state freshmen), rolling (transfers). *Notification:* continuous (freshmen), continuous (out-of-state freshmen), continuous (transfers).

Freshman Application Contact Paris Junior College, 2400 Clarksville Street, Paris, TX 75460-6298. *Phone:* 903-782-0211. *Toll-free phone:* 800-232-5804.

Website: http://www.parisjc.edu/.

Pima Medical Institute
Houston, Texas

Freshman Application Contact Mr. Christopher Luebke, Corporate Director of Admissions, Pima Medical Institute, 2160 South Power Road, Mesa, AZ 85209. *Phone:* 480-610-6063. *E-mail:* cluebke@pmi.edu.

Website: http://www.pmi.edu/.

Quest College
San Antonio, Texas

Admissions Office Contact Quest College, 5430 Fredericksburg Road, Suite 310, San Antonio, TX 78229.

Website: http://www.questcollege.edu/.

Ranger College
Ranger, Texas

Freshman Application Contact Dr. Jim Davis, Dean of Students, Ranger College, 1100 College Circle, Ranger, TX 76470. *Phone:* 254-647-3234 Ext. 110.

Website: http://www.rangercollege.edu/.

Remington College–Dallas Campus
Garland, Texas

Director of Admissions Ms. Shonda Wisenhunt, Remington College–Dallas Campus, 1800 Eastgate Drive, Garland, TX 75041. *Phone:* 972-686-7878. *Fax:* 972-686-5116. *E-mail:* shonda.wisenhunt@remingtoncollege.edu.

Website: http://www.remingtoncollege.edu/.

Remington College–Fort Worth Campus
Fort Worth, Texas

Director of Admissions Marcia Kline, Director of Recruitment, Remington College–Fort Worth Campus, 300 East Loop 820, Fort Worth, TX 76112. *Phone:* 817-451-0017. *Toll-free phone:* 800-560-6192. *Fax:* 817-496-1257. *E-mail:* marcia.kline@remingtoncollege.edu.

Website: http://www.remingtoncollege.edu/.

Remington College–Houston Southeast Campus
Webster, Texas

Director of Admissions Lori Minor, Director of Recruitment, Remington College–Houston Southeast Campus, 20985 Interstate 45 South, Webster, TX 77598. *Phone:* 281-554-1700. *Fax:* 281-554-1765.
E-mail: lori.minor@remingtoncollege.edu.
Website: http://www.remingtoncollege.edu/.

Remington College–North Houston Campus
Houston, Texas

Director of Admissions Edmund Flores, Director of Recruitment, Remington College–North Houston Campus, 11310 Greens Crossing Boulevard, Suite 300, Houston, TX 77067. *Phone:* 281-885-4450. *Fax:* 281-875-9964.
E-mail: edmund.flores@remingtoncollege.edu.
Website: http://www.remingtoncollege.edu/.

Richland College
Dallas, Texas

Freshman Application Contact Ms. Carol McKinney, Department Assistant, Richland College, 12800 Abrams Road, Dallas, TX 75243-2199. *Phone:* 972-238-6100.
Website: http://www.rlc.dcccd.edu/.

St. Philip's College
San Antonio, Texas

- **District-supported** 2-year, founded 1898, part of Alamo Community College District System
- **Urban** 68-acre campus with easy access to San Antonio
- **Coed,** 10,514 undergraduate students, 15% full-time, 56% women, 44% men

Undergraduates 1,622 full-time, 8,892 part-time. Students come from 11 other countries; 1% are from out of state; 10% Black or African American, non-Hispanic/Latino; 51% Hispanic/Latino; 3% Asian, non-Hispanic/Latino; 0.2% Native Hawaiian or other Pacific Islander, non-Hispanic/Latino; 0.4% American Indian or Alaska Native, non-Hispanic/Latino; 3% Two or more races, non-Hispanic/Latino; 2% Race/ethnicity unknown; 0.4% international; 5% transferred in.
Freshmen *Admission:* 1,228 enrolled.
Faculty *Total:* 398, 42% full-time, 10% with terminal degrees. *Student/faculty ratio:* 19:1.
Majors Accounting; administrative assistant and secretarial science; aircraft powerplant technology; airframe mechanics and aircraft maintenance technology; art; autobody/collision and repair technology; automobile/automotive mechanics technology; biology/biological sciences; biomedical technology; building/construction finishing, management, and inspection related; business administration and management; CAD/CADD drafting/design technology; chemistry; clinical/medical laboratory technology; computer and information systems security; computer systems networking and telecommunications; computer technology/computer systems technology; construction engineering technology; criminal justice/law enforcement administration; culinary arts; data entry/microcomputer applications; diesel mechanics technology; dramatic/theater arts; dramatic/theater arts and stagecraft related; early childhood education; e-commerce; economics; education; electrical/electronics equipment installation and repair; electromechanical technology; energy management and systems technology; English; environmental science; geology/earth science; health information/medical records technology; heating, air conditioning, ventilation and refrigeration maintenance technology; history; hotel/motel administration; kinesiology and exercise science; legal administrative assistant/secretary; liberal arts and sciences/liberal studies; mathematics; medical administrative assistant and medical secretary; medical radiologic technology; music; natural resources/conservation; occupational safety and health technology; occupational therapist assistant; philosophy; physical therapy technology; political science and government; pre-dentistry studies; pre-engineering; pre-law studies; premedical studies; prenursing studies; pre-pharmacy studies; psychology; respiratory care therapy; restaurant/food services management; rhetoric and composition; social work; sociology; Spanish; system, networking, and LAN/WAN management; teacher assistant/aide; telecommunications technology; welding technology.
Academics *Calendar:* semesters. *Degree:* certificates, diplomas, and associate. *Special study options:* academic remediation for entering students, adult/continuing education programs, advanced placement credit, cooperative education, distance learning, double majors, English as a second language, honors programs, independent study, internships, off-campus study, part-time degree program, services for LD students, study abroad, summer session for credit. *ROTC:* Army (c).
Library St. Philip's College Library plus 1 other. *Books:* 73,409 (physical), 36,224 (digital/electronic); *Serial titles:* 13,164 (physical), 127,142 (digital/electronic); *Databases:* 132. Weekly public service hours: 68.
Student Life *Housing:* college housing not available. *Activities and Organizations:* drama/theater group, choral group, Student Government, Future United Latino Leaders of Change, Collegiate 100. *Campus security:* 24-hour emergency response devices and patrols, late-night transport/escort service. *Student services:* health clinic.
Athletics *Intramural sports:* basketball M/W, cheerleading M/W, table tennis M/W, volleyball M/W, weight lifting M/W.
Costs (2016–17) *Tuition:* area resident $2108 full-time; state resident $5744 full-time; nonresident $11,194 full-time. Full-time tuition and fees vary according to course load and program. Part-time tuition and fees vary according to course load and program. *Required fees:* $80 full-time. *Payment plan:* installment. *Waivers:* senior citizens and employees or children of employees.
Applying *Options:* electronic application, early admission. *Required:* high school transcript. *Application deadlines:* rolling (freshmen), rolling (transfers). *Notification:* continuous (freshmen), continuous (transfers).
Freshman Application Contact Ms. Angela Molina, Coordinator, Student Success, St. Philip's College, 1801 Martin Luther King Drive, San Antonio, TX 78203-2098. *Phone:* 210-486-2403. *Fax:* 210-486-2103.
E-mail: amolina@alamo.edu.
Website: http://www.alamo.edu/spc/.

San Antonio College
San Antonio, Texas

Director of Admissions Mr. J. Martin Ortega, Director of Admissions and Records, San Antonio College, 1300 San Pedro Avenue, San Antonio, TX 78212-4299. *Phone:* 210-733-2582.
Website: http://www.alamo.edu/sac/.

San Jacinto College District
Pasadena, Texas

- **State and locally supported** 2-year, founded 1961
- **Suburban** 445-acre campus with easy access to Houston
- **Endowment** $5.8 million
- **Coed,** 28,326 undergraduate students, 23% full-time, 56% women, 44% men

Undergraduates 6,613 full-time, 21,713 part-time. Students come from 48 states and territories; 70 other countries; 1% are from out of state; 9% Black or African American, non-Hispanic/Latino; 52% Hispanic/Latino; 5% Asian, non-Hispanic/Latino; 0.1% Native Hawaiian or other Pacific Islander, non-Hispanic/Latino; 0.2% American Indian or Alaska Native, non-Hispanic/Latino; 2% Two or more races, non-Hispanic/Latino; 2% Race/ethnicity unknown; 2% international; 5% transferred in. *Retention:* 54% of full-time freshmen returned.
Freshmen *Admission:* 11,945 applied, 6,953 admitted, 5,574 enrolled. *Test scores:* SAT critical reading scores over 500: 27%; SAT math scores over 500: 33%; ACT scores over 18: 100%; SAT critical reading scores over 600: 6%; SAT math scores over 600: 5%; ACT scores over 24: 55%; SAT critical reading scores over 700: 5%; SAT math scores over 700: 4%; ACT scores over 30: 5%.
Faculty *Total:* 1,193, 41% full-time, 14% with terminal degrees. *Student/faculty ratio:* 19:1.
Majors Accounting; administrative assistant and secretarial science; agribusiness; agriculture; airline pilot and flight crew; art; autobody/collision and repair technology; automobile/automotive mechanics technology; aviation/airway management; baking and pastry arts; behavioral sciences; biology/biological sciences; business administration and management; business/commerce; chemical process technology; chemical technology; chemistry; child development; clinical/medical laboratory technology; commercial and advertising art; computer and information sciences; construction engineering technology; cosmetology; cosmetology, barber/styling, and nail instruction; criminal justice/police science; culinary arts; dance; diagnostic medical sonography and ultrasound technology; diesel mechanics technology; digital communication and media/multimedia; drafting and design technology; dramatic/theater arts; electrical and power transmission installation; electrical, electronic and communications engineering technology; emergency medical technology (EMT paramedic); engineering; English; environmental science; fire science/firefighting; food service systems administration; foreign languages and literatures; general studies;

geology/earth science; health and physical education/fitness; health information/medical records technology; heating, air conditioning, ventilation and refrigeration maintenance technology; Hispanic-American, Puerto Rican, and Mexican-American/Chicano studies; history; instrumentation technology; interior design; international business/trade/commerce; journalism; legal assistant/paralegal; management information systems; marine science/merchant marine officer; mathematics; medical/clinical assistant; music; occupational safety and health technology; optometric technician; pharmacy technician; philosophy; physical sciences; physical therapy technology; physics; political science and government; psychology; radio and television broadcasting technology; radiologic technology/science; real estate; registered nursing/registered nurse; respiratory care therapy; restaurant, culinary, and catering management; rhetoric and composition; science teacher education; secondary education; social sciences; sociology; surgical technology; welding technology.

Academics *Calendar:* semesters. *Degree:* certificates, diplomas, and associate. *Special study options:* academic remediation for entering students, accelerated degree program, adult/continuing education programs, advanced placement credit, cooperative education, distance learning, double majors, English as a second language, honors programs, off-campus study, part-time degree program, services for LD students, student-designed majors, study abroad, summer session for credit. *ROTC:* Army (c), Air Force (c).

Library Lee Davis Library plus 2 others. Students can reserve study rooms.

Student Life *Housing:* college housing not available. *Activities and Organizations:* drama/theater group, student-run newspaper, choral group, Phi Theta Kappa honor society, Nurses Association, Student Government Association, ABG Radiography, Texas Student Education Association. *Campus security:* 24-hour emergency response devices and patrols, late-night transport/escort service.

Athletics Member NJCAA. *Intercollegiate sports:* baseball M(s), basketball M(s)/W(s), soccer M(s), softball W(s), volleyball W(s). *Intramural sports:* basketball M/W, football M/W, golf M/W, soccer M/W, softball M/W, table tennis M/W, tennis M/W, volleyball M/W, weight lifting M/W.

Costs (2015–16) *Tuition:* area resident $1408 full-time, $47 per credit hour part-time; state resident $2416 full-time, $89 per credit hour part-time; nonresident $3856 full-time, $149 per credit hour part-time. Full-time tuition and fees vary according to course load. Part-time tuition and fees vary according to course load. *Required fees:* $280 full-time. *Payment plan:* installment. *Waivers:* senior citizens.

Applying *Options:* electronic application, early admission. *Required:* high school transcript. *Required for some:* interview. *Application deadlines:* rolling (freshmen), rolling (out-of-state freshmen), rolling (transfers). *Notification:* continuous (freshmen), continuous (out-of-state freshmen), continuous (transfers).

Freshman Application Contact San Jacinto College District, 4624 Fairmont Parkway, Pasadena, TX 77504-3323. *Phone:* 281-998-6150. *Website:* http://www.sanjac.edu/.

School of Automotive Machinists
Houston, Texas

Admissions Office Contact School of Automotive Machinists, 1911 Antoine Drive, Houston, TX 77055-1803. *Website:* http://www.samracing.com/.

South Plains College
Levelland, Texas

Freshman Application Contact Mrs. Andrea Rangel, Dean of Admissions and Records, South Plains College, 1401 College Avenue, Levelland, TX 78336. *Phone:* 806-894-9611 Ext. 2370. *Fax:* 806-897-3167. *E-mail:* arangel@southplainscollege.edu. *Website:* http://www.southplainscollege.edu/.

South Texas College
McAllen, Texas

Freshman Application Contact Mr. Matthew Hebbard, Director of Enrollment Services and Registrar, South Texas College, 3201 West Pecan, McAllen, TX 78501. *Phone:* 956-872-2147. *Toll-free phone:* 800-742-7822. *E-mail:* mshebbar@southtexascollege.edu. *Website:* http://www.southtexascollege.edu/.

Southwest Texas Junior College
Uvalde, Texas

- **State and locally supported** 2-year, founded 1946
- **Small-town** 97-acre campus with easy access to San Antonio
- **Coed**

Undergraduates Students come from 2 states and territories; 6 other countries; 1% Black or African American, non-Hispanic/Latino; 84% Hispanic/Latino; 0.5% Asian, non-Hispanic/Latino; 1% American Indian or Alaska Native, non-Hispanic/Latino; 0.9% Race/ethnicity unknown; 0.1% international; 9% live on campus.

Faculty *Total:* 199, 57% full-time.

Majors Agricultural mechanization; automobile/automotive mechanics technology; avionics maintenance technology; biological and physical sciences; business administration and management; computer engineering technology; cosmetology; criminal justice/law enforcement administration; data processing and data processing technology; education; engineering; farm and ranch management; liberal arts and sciences/liberal studies; teacher assistant/aide.

Academics *Calendar:* semesters. *Degree:* certificates and associate. *Special study options:* academic remediation for entering students, adult/continuing education programs, advanced placement credit, English as a second language, external degree program, honors programs, part-time degree program, summer session for credit.

Library Will C. Miller Memorial Library.

Student Life *Housing Options:* coed, women-only. Campus housing is university owned. *Activities and Organizations:* drama/theater group, student-run newspaper, Catholic Students Club, Business Administration Club. *Campus security:* 24-hour patrols, controlled dormitory access. *Student services:* health clinic, personal/psychological counseling.

Athletics *Intercollegiate sports:* basketball M/W, cross-country running M/W, equestrian sports M/W. *Intramural sports:* basketball M/W, equestrian sports M/W, football M, golf M/W, racquetball M/W, swimming and diving M/W, tennis M/W.

Financial Aid Of all full-time matriculated undergraduates who enrolled in 2014, 150 Federal Work-Study jobs (averaging $1250). 75 state and other part-time jobs (averaging $1250).

Applying *Options:* electronic application, early admission, deferred entrance. *Required:* high school transcript. *Application deadlines:* rolling (freshmen), rolling (transfers). *Notification:* continuous (freshmen), continuous (transfers).

Freshman Application Contact Southwest Texas Junior College, 2401 Garner Field Road, Uvalde, TX 78801-6297. *Phone:* 830-278-4401 Ext. 7284. *Website:* http://www.swtjc.edu/.

Tarrant County College District
Fort Worth, Texas

- **County-supported** 2-year, founded 1967
- **Urban** 667-acre campus with easy access to Dallas-Fort Worth
- **Endowment** $5.8 million
- **Coed,** 50,595 undergraduate students, 31% full-time, 58% women, 42% men

Undergraduates 15,764 full-time, 34,831 part-time. 19% Black or African American, non-Hispanic/Latino; 29% Hispanic/Latino; 6% Asian, non-Hispanic/Latino; 0.2% Native Hawaiian or other Pacific Islander, non-Hispanic/Latino; 0.5% American Indian or Alaska Native, non-Hispanic/Latino; 2% Two or more races, non-Hispanic/Latino; 1% Race/ethnicity unknown; 0.8% international.

Freshmen *Admission:* 8,233 applied, 8,233 admitted, 8,233 enrolled.

Faculty *Total:* 2,171, 31% full-time. *Student/faculty ratio:* 25:1.

Majors Accounting; administrative assistant and secretarial science; architectural engineering technology; automobile/automotive mechanics technology; avionics maintenance technology; business administration and management; clinical laboratory science/medical technology; clinical/medical laboratory technology; computer programming; computer science; construction engineering technology; consumer merchandising/retailing management; criminal justice/law enforcement administration; dental hygiene; developmental and child psychology; dietetics; drafting and design technology; educational/instructional technology; electrical, electronic and communications engineering technology; electromechanical technology; emergency medical technology (EMT paramedic); fashion merchandising; fire science/firefighting; food technology and processing; graphic and printing equipment operation/production; health information/medical records administration; heating, air conditioning, ventilation and refrigeration maintenance technology; horticultural science; industrial radiologic technology; legal assistant/paralegal; liberal arts and sciences/liberal studies; machine tool technology; marketing/marketing management; mechanical engineering/mechanical technology; mental health counseling; physical therapy; quality control technology; registered nursing/registered nurse;

respiratory care therapy; sign language interpretation and translation; surgical technology; welding technology.
Academics *Calendar:* semesters. *Degree:* certificates and associate. *Special study options:* academic remediation for entering students, adult/continuing education programs, advanced placement credit, distance learning, English as a second language, honors programs, part-time degree program, services for LD students, summer session for credit. *ROTC:* Army (c), Air Force (c).
Library *Books:* 163,235 (physical), 78,477 (digital/electronic); *Databases:* 131.
Student Life *Housing:* college housing not available. *Activities and Organizations:* drama/theater group, student-run newspaper, choral group. *Campus security:* 24-hour emergency response devices and patrols, late-night transport/escort service. *Student services:* health clinic, personal/psychological counseling.
Athletics *Intramural sports:* football M, golf M, sailing M/W, table tennis M, tennis M/W, volleyball M/W.
Costs (2015–16) *Tuition:* area resident $1320 full-time, $55 per credit hour part-time; state resident $2064 full-time, $86 per credit hour part-time; nonresident $4920 full-time, $205 per credit hour part-time. Full-time tuition and fees vary according to course load and program. Part-time tuition and fees vary according to course load and program. *Payment plans:* installment, deferred payment. *Waivers:* senior citizens and employees or children of employees.
Financial Aid Of all full-time matriculated undergraduates who enrolled in 2014, 8,364 applied for aid, 7,642 were judged to have need. 449 Federal Work-Study jobs (averaging $1678). 87 state and other part-time jobs (averaging $4160). In 2014, 60 non-need-based awards were made. *Average need-based loan:* $3346. *Average need-based gift aid:* $4432. *Average non-need-based aid:* $1592.
Applying *Options:* electronic application. *Application deadlines:* rolling (freshmen), rolling (transfers).
Freshman Application Contact Ms. Nichole Mancone, District Director of Admissions & Records, Tarrant County College District, 300 Trinity Campus Circle, Fort Worth, TX 76102-6599. *Phone:* 817-515-1581.
E-mail: nichole.mancone@tccd.edu.
Website: http://www.tccd.edu/.

Temple College
Temple, Texas

- **District-supported** 2-year, founded 1926
- **Suburban** 106-acre campus with easy access to Austin
- **Endowment** $638,964
- **Coed**

Undergraduates 1,769 full-time, 3,431 part-time. Students come from 24 states and territories; 6 other countries; 2% are from out of state; 18% Black or African American, non-Hispanic/Latino; 22% Hispanic/Latino; 2% Asian, non-Hispanic/Latino; 0.3% Native Hawaiian or other Pacific Islander, non-Hispanic/Latino; 0.7% American Indian or Alaska Native, non-Hispanic/Latino; 1% Race/ethnicity unknown; 0.1% international; 5% transferred in.
Faculty *Student/faculty ratio:* 25:1.
Academics *Calendar:* semesters. *Degree:* certificates and associate. *Special study options:* academic remediation for entering students, adult/continuing education programs, advanced placement credit, cooperative education, distance learning, English as a second language, internships, off-campus study, part-time degree program, services for LD students, study abroad, summer session for credit.
Library Hubert Dawson Library.
Student Life *Campus security:* 24-hour emergency response devices and patrols.
Athletics Member NJCAA.
Applying *Options:* electronic application, early admission. *Required:* high school transcript.
Freshman Application Contact Ms. Toni Cuellar, Director of Admissions and Records, Temple College, 2600 South First Street, Temple, TX 76504. *Phone:* 254-298-8303. *Toll-free phone:* 800-460-4636.
E-mail: carey.rose@templejc.edu.
Website: http://www.templejc.edu/.

Texarkana College
Texarkana, Texas

- **State and locally supported** 2-year, founded 1927
- **Urban** 105-acre campus
- **Coed,** 4,165 undergraduate students, 33% full-time, 62% women, 38% men

Undergraduates 1,386 full-time, 2,779 part-time. Students come from 10 states and territories; 15% are from out of state; 23% Black or African

American, non-Hispanic/Latino; 7% Hispanic/Latino; 1% Asian, non-Hispanic/Latino; 0.1% Native Hawaiian or other Pacific Islander, non-Hispanic/Latino; 0.6% American Indian or Alaska Native, non-Hispanic/Latino; 4% Two or more races, non-Hispanic/Latino; 0.6% Race/ethnicity unknown; 0.4% international; 1% live on campus.
Faculty *Total:* 183, 49% full-time. *Student/faculty ratio:* 21:1.
Majors Administrative assistant and secretarial science; agriculture; art; automobile/automotive mechanics technology; biology/biological sciences; business administration and management; business/commerce; chemistry; child-care and support services management; child development; computer and information sciences; cosmetology; criminal justice/law enforcement administration; criminal justice/safety; culinary arts; diesel mechanics technology; drafting and design technology; dramatic/theater arts; electrical, electronic and communications engineering technology; emergency medical technology (EMT paramedic); engineering; foreign languages and literatures; health aide; heating, air conditioning, ventilation and refrigeration maintenance technology; history; humanities; industrial mechanics and maintenance technology; journalism; liberal arts and sciences/liberal studies; licensed practical/vocational nurse training; marketing/marketing management; mathematics; music; pharmacy technician; physics; political science and government; real estate; registered nursing/registered nurse; social sciences; substance abuse/addiction counseling; welding technology.
Academics *Calendar:* semesters. *Degree:* certificates and associate. *Special study options:* academic remediation for entering students, adult/continuing education programs, advanced placement credit, cooperative education, distance learning, freshman honors college, honors programs, independent study, internships, part-time degree program, services for LD students, study abroad, summer session for credit.
Library Palmer Memorial Library.
Student Life *Housing Options:* coed. Campus housing is university owned. *Activities and Organizations:* drama/theater group, choral group, Black Student Association, Earth Club, Culinary Arts Club, Cultural Awareness Student Association, Cosmetology Club. *Campus security:* 24-hour patrols. *Student services:* personal/psychological counseling.
Athletics Member NJCAA. *Intramural sports:* basketball M/W, football M/W, racquetball M/W, soccer M/W, tennis M/W, volleyball M/W.
Costs (2015–16) *Tuition:* area resident $1152 full-time, $48 per semester hour part-time; state resident $2328 full-time, $97 per semester hour part-time; nonresident $3456 full-time, $144 per semester hour part-time. *Required fees:* $800 full-time, $66 per semester part-time. *Room and board:* room only: $2000.
Financial Aid Of all full-time matriculated undergraduates who enrolled in 2014, 30 Federal Work-Study jobs (averaging $3090).
Applying *Options:* electronic application, early admission, deferred entrance. *Required:* high school transcript. *Recommended:* interview for nursing program, meningitis vaccine. *Application deadlines:* rolling (freshmen), rolling (out-of-state freshmen), rolling (transfers).
Freshman Application Contact Mr. Lee Williams, Director of Admissions, Texarkana College, 2500 North Robison Road, Texarkana, TX 75599-0001. *Phone:* 903-823-3016. *Fax:* 903-823-3451.
E-mail: lee.williams@texarkanacollege.edu.
Website: http://www.texarkanacollege.edu/.

Texas Southmost College
Brownsville, Texas

Freshman Application Contact New Student Relations, Texas Southmost College, 80 Fort Brown, Brownsville, TX 78520-4991. *Phone:* 956-882-8860. *Toll-free phone:* 877-882-8721. *Fax:* 956-882-8959.
Website: http://www.utb.edu/.

Texas State Technical College
Waco, Texas

- **State-supported** 2-year, founded 1965
- **Suburban** 200-acre campus
- **Coed,** 10,689 undergraduate students, 44% full-time, 36% women, 64% men

Undergraduates 4,665 full-time, 6,024 part-time. 1% are from out of state; 7% Black or African American, non-Hispanic/Latino; 53% Hispanic/Latino; 0.7% Asian, non-Hispanic/Latino; 0.1% Native Hawaiian or other Pacific Islander, non-Hispanic/Latino; 0.3% American Indian or Alaska Native, non-Hispanic/Latino; 0.2% Two or more races, non-Hispanic/Latino; 3% Race/ethnicity unknown; 7% transferred in. *Retention:* 18% of full-time freshmen returned.
Freshmen *Admission:* 1,286 applied, 1,286 admitted.
Faculty *Total:* 283, 89% full-time, 3% with terminal degrees. *Student/faculty ratio:* 17:1.

Majors Aircraft powerplant technology; airframe mechanics and aircraft maintenance technology; airline pilot and flight crew; air traffic control; autobody/collision and repair technology; automobile/automotive mechanics technology; avionics maintenance technology; biomedical technology; chemical technology; computer and information systems security; computer programming; computer technology/computer systems technology; construction trades; culinary arts; diesel mechanics technology; drafting and design technology; educational/instructional technology; electrical, electronic and communications engineering technology; electromechanical technology; environmental engineering technology; game and interactive media design; graphic design; heating, ventilation, air conditioning and refrigeration engineering technology; instrumentation technology; laser and optical technology; manufacturing engineering technology; mechanical engineering/mechanical technology; network and system administration; nuclear/nuclear power technology; occupational safety and health technology; robotics technology; solar energy technology; surveying technology; system, networking, and LAN/WAN management; telecommunications technology; turf and turfgrass management; viticulture and enology; web page, digital/multimedia and information resources design.

Academics *Calendar:* trimesters. *Degree:* certificates and associate. *Special study options:* academic remediation for entering students, adult/continuing education programs, cooperative education, distance learning, internships, part-time degree program, services for LD students, summer session for credit.

Library Texas State Technical College-Waco Campus Library.

Student Life *Housing:* on-campus residence required for freshman year. *Options:* coed, men-only, women-only, special housing for students with disabilities. Campus housing is university owned. *Activities and Organizations:* Student Ambassador Association, SkillsUSA, Student Leadership Council, Phi Theta Kappa, Hispanic Student Association. *Campus security:* 24-hour emergency response devices and patrols, late-night transport/escort service, controlled dormitory access. *Student services:* health clinic, personal/psychological counseling, women's center.

Athletics *Intramural sports:* basketball M/W, football M, golf M/W, racquetball M/W, softball M/W, volleyball M/W, weight lifting M.

Standardized Tests *Required:* Texas Success Initiative assessment (for admission).

Costs (2016–17) *Tuition:* state resident $4386 full-time, $142 per credit hour part-time; nonresident $9660 full-time, $322 per credit hour part-time. Full-time tuition and fees vary according to class time, course load, and program. Part-time tuition and fees vary according to class time, course load, and program. *Room and board:* $5214; room only: $3780. Room and board charges vary according to board plan, housing facility, and location. *Payment plan:* installment. *Waivers:* employees or children of employees.

Applying *Options:* electronic application, early admission. *Required:* high school transcript. *Required for some:* interview. *Application deadlines:* rolling (freshmen), rolling (transfers). *Notification:* continuous (freshmen), continuous (transfers).

Freshman Application Contact Mrs. Paula Arredondo, Registrar/Director of Admission and Records, Texas State Technical College, 3801 Campus Drive, Waco, TX 76705. *Phone:* 254-867-3363. *Toll-free phone:* 800-792-8784 Ext. 2362. *E-mail:* mary.daniel@tstc.edu.
Website: http://www.tstc.edu/.

Trinity Valley Community College
Athens, Texas

- **State and locally supported** 2-year, founded 1946
- **Rural** 65-acre campus with easy access to Dallas-Fort Worth
- **Coed**

Undergraduates 2,685 full-time, 2,487 part-time. Students come from 28 states and territories; 15 other countries; 1% are from out of state; 17% Black or African American, non-Hispanic/Latino; 7% Hispanic/Latino; 0.4% Asian, non-Hispanic/Latino; 0.4% American Indian or Alaska Native, non-Hispanic/Latino; 11% Two or more races, non-Hispanic/Latino; 2% Race/ethnicity unknown; 0.3% international; 14% live on campus.

Faculty *Student/faculty ratio:* 16:1.

Academics *Calendar:* semesters. *Degree:* certificates, diplomas, and associate. *Special study options:* academic remediation for entering students, adult/continuing education programs, advanced placement credit, cooperative education, distance learning, double majors, English as a second language, honors programs, independent study, internships, part-time degree program, services for LD students, summer session for credit.

Library Ginger Murchison Learning Resource Center plus 3 others.

Student Life *Campus security:* 24-hour emergency response devices and patrols, controlled dormitory access.

Athletics Member NJCAA.

Costs (2015–16) *Tuition:* area resident $2340 full-time, $34 per semester hour part-time; state resident $4110 full-time, $93 per semester hour part-time; nonresident $4680 full-time, $112 per semester hour part-time. Full-time tuition and fees vary according to course load. Part-time tuition and fees vary

according to course load. *Required fees:* $44 per semester hour part-time. *Room and board:* $5580. Room and board charges vary according to board plan.

Financial Aid Of all full-time matriculated undergraduates who enrolled in 2014, 90 Federal Work-Study jobs (averaging $1176). 56 state and other part-time jobs (averaging $660).

Applying *Options:* electronic application, early admission. *Required:* high school transcript.

Freshman Application Contact Dr. Colette Hilliard, Dean of Enrollment Management and Registrar, Trinity Valley Community College, 100 Cardinal Drive, Athens, TX 75751. *Phone:* 903-675-6209 Ext. 209.
Website: http://www.tvcc.edu/.

Tyler Junior College
Tyler, Texas

- **State and locally supported** 2-year, founded 1926
- **Suburban** 85-acre campus
- **Endowment** $41.0 million
- **Coed,** 10,934 undergraduate students, 55% full-time, 59% women, 41% men

Undergraduates 6,007 full-time, 4,927 part-time. Students come from 39 other countries; 2% are from out of state; 22% Black or African American, non-Hispanic/Latino; 18% Hispanic/Latino; 1% Asian, non-Hispanic/Latino; 0.2% Native Hawaiian or other Pacific Islander, non-Hispanic/Latino; 0.5% American Indian or Alaska Native, non-Hispanic/Latino; 3% Two or more races, non-Hispanic/Latino; 0.8% Race/ethnicity unknown; 1% international; 7% transferred in; 10% live on campus. *Retention:* 55% of full-time freshmen returned.

Freshmen *Admission:* 10,653 applied, 10,653 admitted, 2,891 enrolled.

Faculty *Total:* 553, 55% full-time, 13% with terminal degrees. *Student/faculty ratio:* 20:1.

Majors Accounting; administrative assistant and secretarial science; art; athletic training; automobile/automotive mechanics technology; behavioral sciences; biology/biological sciences; business administration and management; CAD/CADD drafting/design technology; chemistry; child development; clinical/medical laboratory technology; commercial and advertising art; commercial photography; computer and information sciences; computer and information sciences related; computer engineering technology; computer graphics; computer programming; computer programming related; computer science; computer systems networking and telecommunications; computer technology/computer systems technology; criminalistics and criminal science; criminal justice/law enforcement administration; criminal justice/police science; criminal justice/safety; dance; data entry/microcomputer applications; dental hygiene; diagnostic medical sonography and ultrasound technology; drafting and design technology; dramatic/theater arts; economics; education (multiple levels); electromechanical technology; emergency medical technology (EMT paramedic); engineering; English literature (British and Commonwealth); environmental science; family and consumer sciences/human sciences; fire science/firefighting; foreign languages and literatures; general studies; geology/earth science; health and physical education/fitness; health/health-care administration; health information/medical records technology; heating, air conditioning, ventilation and refrigeration maintenance technology; history; industrial electronics technology; industrial radiologic technology; information technology; legal administrative assistant/secretary; legal assistant/paralegal; liberal arts and sciences/liberal studies; licensed practical/vocational nurse training; mathematics; medical administrative assistant and medical secretary; middle school education; modern languages; music; natural sciences; occupational therapist assistant; photography; physical education teaching and coaching; physical therapy technology; physics; political science and government; prenursing studies; psychology; public administration; radio and television; radiologic technology/science; registered nursing/registered nurse; respiratory care therapy; secondary education; sign language interpretation and translation; social sciences; social work; sociology; speech communication and rhetoric; substance abuse/addiction counseling; surgical technology; surveying technology; system, networking, and LAN/WAN management; welding technology.

Academics *Calendar:* semesters. *Degree:* certificates, diplomas, and associate. *Special study options:* academic remediation for entering students, accelerated degree program, adult/continuing education programs, advanced placement credit, distance learning, freshman honors college, honors programs, part-time degree program, services for LD students, study abroad, summer session for credit.

Library Vaughn Library and Learning Resource Center. *Books:* 85,418 (physical), 135,816 (digital/electronic); *Databases:* 100. Weekly public service hours: 74.

Student Life *Housing Options:* coed, men-only, women-only. Campus housing is university owned. *Activities and Organizations:* drama/theater group, student-run newspaper, choral group, marching band, Student

Government, Religious Affiliation Clubs, Phi Theta Kappa, national sororities. *Campus security:* 24-hour emergency response devices and patrols, controlled dormitory access. *Student services:* health clinic, personal/psychological counseling.

Athletics Member NJCAA. *Intercollegiate sports:* baseball M, basketball M(s)/W(s), cheerleading W(s), football M(s), golf M/W, soccer M(s)/W(s), softball W(s), tennis M(s)/W(s), volleyball W(s). *Intramural sports:* basketball M/W, cheerleading W, racquetball M/W, volleyball M/W, weight lifting M/W.

Standardized Tests *Required:* TSI (for admission).

Costs (2015–16) *Tuition:* area resident $900 full-time, $30 per credit hour part-time; state resident $2310 full-time, $77 per credit hour part-time; nonresident $2910 full-time, $97 per credit hour part-time. *Required fees:* $1602 full-time, $7 per credit hour part-time, $100 per term part-time. *Room and board:* $8320; room only: $5940. Room and board charges vary according to housing facility. *Payment plan:* installment. *Waivers:* senior citizens and employees or children of employees.

Financial Aid Of all full-time matriculated undergraduates who enrolled in 2014, 4,922 applied for aid, 4,010 were judged to have need, 73 had their need fully met. 45 Federal Work-Study jobs (averaging $1411). 27 state and other part-time jobs (averaging $2297). In 2014, 37 non-need-based awards were made. *Average percent of need met:* 56%. *Average financial aid package:* $7014. *Average need-based loan:* $3349. *Average need-based gift aid:* $5569. *Average non-need-based aid:* $2956. *Average indebtedness upon graduation:* $14,743.

Applying *Options:* electronic application, early admission. *Required:* high school transcript. *Application deadlines:* rolling (freshmen), rolling (out-of-state freshmen), rolling (transfers). *Notification:* continuous (freshmen), continuous (out-of-state freshmen), continuous (transfers).

Freshman Application Contact Ms. Janna Chancey, Director of Enrollment Management, Tyler Junior College, PO Box 9020, Tyler, TX 75711-9020. *Phone:* 903-510-3325. *Toll-free phone:* 800-687-5680. *E-mail:* jcha@tjc.edu. *Website:* http://www.tjc.edu/.

Vernon College
Vernon, Texas

Director of Admissions Mr. Joe Hite, Dean of Admissions/Registrar, Vernon College, 4400 College Drive, Vernon, TX 76384-4092. *Phone:* 940-552-6291 Ext. 2204.
Website: http://www.vernoncollege.edu/.

Vet Tech Institute of Houston
Houston, Texas

- **Proprietary** 2-year, founded 1958
- **Suburban** campus
- **Coed,** 216 undergraduate students
- **62%** of applicants were admitted

Freshmen *Admission:* 455 applied, 281 admitted.
Majors Veterinary/animal health technology.
Academics *Calendar:* semesters. *Degree:* associate. *Special study options:* accelerated degree program, internships.
Student Life *Housing:* college housing not available.
Freshman Application Contact Admissions Office, Vet Tech Institute of Houston, 4669 Southwest Freeway, Suite 100, Houston, TX 77027. *Phone:* 800-275-2736. *Toll-free phone:* 800-275-2736.
Website: http://houston.vettechinstitute.edu/.

Victoria College
Victoria, Texas

- **County-supported** 2-year, founded 1925
- **Rural** 80-acre campus
- **Coed,** 4,051 undergraduate students, 28% full-time, 65% women, 35% men

Undergraduates 1,144 full-time, 2,907 part-time. Students come from 16 states and territories; 5 other countries; 0.5% are from out of state; 6% Black or African American, non-Hispanic/Latino; 48% Hispanic/Latino; 2% Asian, non-Hispanic/Latino; 0.1% Native Hawaiian or other Pacific Islander, non-Hispanic/Latino; 0.1% American Indian or Alaska Native, non-Hispanic/Latino; 1% Two or more races, non-Hispanic/Latino; 0.6% Race/ethnicity unknown; 6% transferred in.
Freshmen *Admission:* 788 applied, 788 admitted, 703 enrolled.
Faculty *Total:* 428, 21% full-time. *Student/faculty ratio:* 11:1.
Majors Administrative assistant and secretarial science; business administration and management; chemical technology; clinical/medical laboratory technology; computer systems networking and telecommunications; criminal justice/police science; early childhood education; electrical, electronic

and communications engineering technology; emergency medical technology (EMT paramedic); fire science/firefighting; general studies; physical therapy technology; registered nursing/registered nurse; respiratory care therapy.
Academics *Calendar:* semesters. *Degree:* certificates and associate. *Special study options:* academic remediation for entering students, advanced placement credit, distance learning, English as a second language, off-campus study, part-time degree program, services for LD students, summer session for credit.
Library Victoria College/University of Houston-Victoria Library. *Books:* 166,027 (physical), 75,644 (digital/electronic); *Serial titles:* 133 (physical), 48,862 (digital/electronic); *Databases:* 124. Weekly public service hours: 76; students can reserve study rooms.
Student Life *Housing:* college housing not available. *Activities and Organizations:* choral group, Student Government Association. *Campus security:* 24-hour emergency response devices. *Student services:* personal/psychological counseling.
Athletics *Intercollegiate sports:* basketball M/W, volleyball W. *Intramural sports:* basketball M/W, sand volleyball M/W, soccer M/W, tennis M/W, volleyball M/W.
Costs (2015–16) *Tuition:* area resident $1380 full-time, $46 per credit hour part-time; state resident $2790 full-time, $93 per credit hour part-time; nonresident $3390 full-time, $113 per credit hour part-time. Full-time tuition and fees vary according to program. Part-time tuition and fees vary according to program. *Required fees:* $1260 full-time, $42 per credit hour part-time. *Payment plan:* installment. *Waivers:* employees or children of employees.
Applying *Options:* electronic application, early admission. *Required:* high school transcript. *Application deadlines:* rolling (freshmen), rolling (out-of-state freshmen), rolling (transfers).
Freshman Application Contact Missy Klimitchek, Registrar, Victoria College, 2200 E Red River, Victoria, TX 77901. *Phone:* 361-573-3291 Ext. 6407. *Toll-free phone:* 877-843-4369. *Fax:* 361-582-2525.
E-mail: registrar@victoriacollege.edu.
Website: http://www.victoriacollege.edu/.

Virginia College in Austin
Austin, Texas

Admissions Office Contact Virginia College in Austin, 14200 North Interstate Highway 35, Austin, TX 78728.
Website: http://www.vc.edu/.

Virginia College in Lubbock
Lubbock, Texas

Admissions Office Contact Virginia College in Lubbock, 5005 50th Street, Lubbock, TX 79414.
Website: http://www.vc.edu/.

Vista College
El Paso, Texas

Director of Admissions Ms. Sarah Hernandez, Registrar, Vista College, 6101 Montana Avenue, El Paso, TX 79925. *Phone:* 915-779-8031. *Toll-free phone:* 866-442-4197.
Website: http://www.vistacollege.edu/.

Wade College
Dallas, Texas

Freshman Application Contact Wade College, INFOMart, 1950 Stemmons Freeway, Suite 4080, LB 562, Dallas, TX 75207. *Phone:* 214-637-3530. *Toll-free phone:* 800-624-4850.
Website: http://www.wadecollege.edu/.

Weatherford College
Weatherford, Texas

- **State and locally supported** 2-year, founded 1869
- **Small-town** 94-acre campus with easy access to Dallas-Fort Worth
- **Coed,** 4,528 undergraduate students

Undergraduates 7% live on campus.
Faculty *Total:* 220, 43% full-time. *Student/faculty ratio:* 22:1.
Majors Administrative assistant and secretarial science; biological and physical sciences; business administration and management; computer graphics; computer programming; corrections; cosmetology; criminal justice/law enforcement administration; emergency medical technology (EMT paramedic); fire science/firefighting; information science/studies; liberal arts and sciences/liberal studies; occupational therapist assistant; pharmacy

technician; physical therapy technology; radiologic technology/science; registered nursing/registered nurse; respiratory care therapy.

Academics *Calendar:* semesters. *Degree:* certificates, diplomas, and associate. *Special study options:* academic remediation for entering students, adult/continuing education programs, cooperative education, distance learning, freshman honors college, honors programs, internships, part-time degree program, services for LD students, student-designed majors, summer session for credit. *ROTC:* Air Force (c).

Library Weatherford College Library.

Student Life *Housing Options:* coed. Campus housing is university owned. *Activities and Organizations:* drama/theater group, choral group, Black Awareness Student Organization, Criminal Justice Club, Phi Theta Kappa. *Campus security:* 24-hour emergency response devices and patrols, late-night transport/escort service. *Student services:* personal/psychological counseling.

Athletics Member NJCAA. *Intercollegiate sports:* baseball M(s), basketball M(s)/W(s), cheerleading M(s)/W(s), equestrian sports M(s)/W(s), tennis W(s).

Costs (2015–16) *Tuition:* area resident $1920 full-time, $80 per semester hour part-time; state resident $2976 full-time, $124 per semester hour part-time; nonresident $4224 full-time, $176 per semester hour part-time. Full-time tuition and fees vary according to course load and program. Part-time tuition and fees vary according to course load and program. *Room and board:* $6900; room only: $4530. Room and board charges vary according to board plan. *Payment plan:* installment. *Waivers:* senior citizens and employees or children of employees.

Applying *Options:* early admission. *Required for some:* high school transcript. *Application deadlines:* rolling (freshmen), rolling (transfers). *Notification:* continuous (freshmen), continuous (transfers).

Freshman Application Contact Mr. Ralph Willingham, Director of Admissions, Weatherford College, 225 College Park Drive, Weatherford, TX 76086-5699. *Phone:* 817-598-6248. *Toll-free phone:* 800-287-5471. *Fax:* 817-598-6205. *E-mail:* willingham@wc.edu.

Website: http://www.wc.edu/.

Western Technical College
El Paso, Texas

Freshman Application Contact Ms. Laura Pena, Director of Admissions, Western Technical College, 9451 Diana Drive, El Paso, TX 79930-2610. *Phone:* 915-566-9621. *Toll-free phone:* 800-201-9232.

E-mail: lpena@westerntech.edu.

Website: http://www.westerntech.edu/.

Western Technical College
El Paso, Texas

Freshman Application Contact Mr. Bill Terrell, Chief Admissions Officer, Western Technical College, 9624 Plaza Circle, El Paso, TX 79927. *Phone:* 915-532-3737 Ext. 117. *Fax:* 915-532-6946. *E-mail:* bterrell@wtc-ep.edu.

Website: http://www.westerntech.edu/.

Western Texas College
Snyder, Texas

- **State and locally supported** 2-year, founded 1969
- **Small-town** 165-acre campus
- **Coed,** 2,125 undergraduate students, 26% full-time, 48% women, 52% men

Undergraduates 543 full-time, 1,582 part-time. Students come from 34 states and territories; 17 other countries; 6% are from out of state; 15% Black or African American, non-Hispanic/Latino; 35% Hispanic/Latino; 0.2% Asian, non-Hispanic/Latino; 0.6% Native Hawaiian or other Pacific Islander, non-Hispanic/Latino; 0.2% American Indian or Alaska Native, non-Hispanic/Latino; 2% Two or more races, non-Hispanic/Latino; 6% international; 3% transferred in; 100% live on campus.

Freshmen *Admission:* 668 applied, 599 admitted, 368 enrolled.

Faculty *Total:* 97, 38% full-time, 5% with terminal degrees. *Student/faculty ratio:* 19:1.

Majors Accounting; administrative assistant and secretarial science; agricultural teacher education; agriculture; applied horticulture/horticulture operations; art; art teacher education; automobile/automotive mechanics technology; biology/biological sciences; business administration and management; child-care provision; computer and information sciences; computer engineering technology; computer science; corrections; criminal justice/law enforcement administration; criminal justice/police science; dramatic/theater arts; early childhood education; engineering; health and physical education/fitness; landscape architecture; liberal arts and sciences/liberal studies; licensed practical/vocational nurse training; marketing/marketing management; mass communication/media; mathematics; parks, recreation and leisure facilities management; petroleum technology; pre-law studies; premedical studies; radio and television; registered nursing/registered nurse; secondary education; social sciences; turf and turfgrass management; welding technology.

Academics *Calendar:* semesters. *Degree:* certificates and associate. *Special study options:* academic remediation for entering students, adult/continuing education programs, advanced placement credit, distance learning, independent study, internships, part-time degree program, services for LD students, student-designed majors, summer session for credit.

Library Western Texas College Resource Center. *Books:* 30,884 (physical), 28,077 (digital/electronic); *Serial titles:* 95 (physical); *Databases:* 23. Weekly public service hours: 56.

Student Life *Housing:* on-campus residence required for freshman year. *Options:* coed, men-only. Campus housing is university owned. Freshman applicants given priority for college housing. *Activities and Organizations:* drama/theater group, student-run radio station, choral group, Student Government Association, Phi Theta Kappa, Agriculture Club, Art Club, Fellowship of Christian Athletes. *Campus security:* 24-hour emergency response devices and patrols, late-night transport/escort service. *Student services:* health clinic, personal/psychological counseling.

Athletics Member NCAA, NJCAA. All NCAA Division I. *Intercollegiate sports:* baseball M(s), basketball M(s)/W(s), cross-country running M(s)/W(s), golf M(s)/W(s), soccer M(s)/W(s), softball W(s), track and field M(s)/W(s), volleyball W(s). *Intramural sports:* basketball M/W, football M, golf M/W, racquetball M/W, soccer M/W, softball M/W, table tennis M/W, volleyball M/W, weight lifting M/W.

Costs (2016–17) *Tuition:* area resident $2370 full-time, $52 per credit hour part-time; state resident $3780 full-time, $93 per credit hour part-time; nonresident $4890 full-time, $130 per credit hour part-time. Full-time tuition and fees vary according to course load, location, and program. Part-time tuition and fees vary according to course load, location, and program. *Required fees:* $450 full-time, $30 per credit hour part-time. *Room and board:* $2550. Room and board charges vary according to housing facility. *Payment plan:* installment.

Financial Aid Of all full-time matriculated undergraduates who enrolled in 2014, 19 Federal Work-Study jobs (averaging $1600).

Applying *Options:* electronic application, early admission, deferred entrance. *Required:* high school transcript. *Application deadlines:* rolling (freshmen), rolling (out-of-state freshmen), rolling (transfers). *Notification:* continuous (freshmen), continuous (out-of-state freshmen), continuous (transfers).

Freshman Application Contact Western Texas College, 6200 College Avenue, Snyder, TX 79549. *Phone:* 325-573-8511. *Toll-free phone:* 888-GO-TO-WTC.

Website: http://www.wtc.edu/.

Wharton County Junior College
Wharton, Texas

Freshman Application Contact Mr. Albert Barnes, Dean of Admissions and Registration, Wharton County Junior College, 911 Boling Highway, Wharton, TX 77488-3298. *Phone:* 979-532-6381. *E-mail:* albertb@wcjc.edu.

Website: http://www.wcjc.edu/.

UTAH

AmeriTech College
Draper, Utah

- **Proprietary** 2-year
- **Coed**

Admissions Office Contact AmeriTech College, 12257 South Business Park Drive, Suite 108, Draper, UT 84020-6545.

Website: http://www.ameritech.edu/.

Fortis College
Salt Lake City, Utah

Admissions Office Contact Fortis College, 3949 South 700 East, Suite 150, Salt Lake City, UT 84107. *Toll-free phone:* 855-4-FORTIS.

Website: http://www.fortis.edu/.

ITT Technical Institute
Murray, Utah

Freshman Application Contact Director of Recruitment, ITT Technical Institute, 920 West Levoy Drive, Murray, UT 84123. *Phone:* 801-263-3313. *Toll-free phone:* 800-365-2136.
Website: http://www.itt-tech.edu/.

LDS Business College
Salt Lake City, Utah

- **Independent** 2-year, founded 1886, affiliated with The Church of Jesus Christ of Latter-day Saints, part of Church Education System (CES) of The Church of Jesus Christ of Latter-day Saints
- **Urban** 2-acre campus with easy access to Salt Lake City
- **Endowment** $8.5 million
- **Coed**, 2,191 undergraduate students, 73% full-time, 47% women, 53% men

Undergraduates 1,589 full-time, 602 part-time. Students come from 60 other countries; 45% are from out of state; 0.2% Black or African American, non-Hispanic/Latino; 11% Hispanic/Latino; 1% Asian, non-Hispanic/Latino; 2% Native Hawaiian or other Pacific Islander, non-Hispanic/Latino; 0.5% American Indian or Alaska Native, non-Hispanic/Latino; 4% Two or more races, non-Hispanic/Latino; 3% Race/ethnicity unknown; 13% international; 34% transferred in. *Retention:* 48% of full-time freshmen returned.
Freshmen *Admission:* 878 applied, 820 admitted, 604 enrolled.
Faculty *Total:* 142, 10% full-time, 66% with terminal degrees. *Student/faculty ratio:* 25:1.
Majors Accounting; accounting and business/management; accounting technology and bookkeeping; architecture related; business administration and management; business administration, management and operations related; business, management, and marketing related; computer and information sciences; computer and information sciences and support services related; computer and information sciences related; computer and information systems security; computer/information technology services administration related; computer programming; computer programming related; computer programming (specific applications); computer science; computer software engineering; cosmetology and personal grooming arts related; data modeling/warehousing and database administration; design and applied arts related; engineering/industrial management; entrepreneurial and small business related; entrepreneurship; food service and dining room management; health information/medical records administration; health professions related; information technology; interior design; legal assistant/paralegal; liberal arts and sciences/liberal studies; logistics, materials, and supply chain management; marketing related; medical/clinical assistant; medical insurance coding; public relations, advertising, and applied communication related; restaurant, culinary, and catering management; restaurant/food services management; salon/beauty salon management; system, networking, and LAN/WAN management; vehicle maintenance and repair technologies related; web page, digital/multimedia and information resources design.
Academics *Calendar:* semesters. *Degree:* certificates and associate. *Special study options:* academic remediation for entering students, adult/continuing education programs, advanced placement credit, distance learning, English as a second language, internships, part-time degree program, services for LD students, summer session for credit. *ROTC:* Army (c), Air Force (c).
Library LDS Business College Library.
Student Life *Housing:* college housing not available. *Activities and Organizations:* choral group, DECA, Service Committee, Mentors, LDSBC Dance Co., Soccer Club. *Campus security:* 24-hour emergency response devices and patrols.
Standardized Tests *Recommended:* SAT or ACT (for admission).
Applying *Options:* electronic application, deferred entrance. *Application fee:* $35. *Required:* essay or personal statement, high school transcript, interview. *Application deadlines:* rolling (freshmen), rolling (out-of-state freshmen), rolling (transfers). *Notification:* continuous (freshmen), continuous (out-of-state freshmen), continuous (transfers).
Freshman Application Contact Miss Dawn Fellows, Assistant Director of Admissions, LDS Business College, 95 North 300 West, Salt Lake City, UT 84101-3500. *Phone:* 801-524-8146. *Toll-free phone:* 800-999-5767. *Fax:* 801-524-1900. *E-mail:* dfellows@ldsbc.edu.
Website: http://www.ldsbc.edu/.

Nightingale College
Ogden, Utah

- **Proprietary** primarily 2-year
- **Suburban** campus with easy access to Salt Lake City
- **Coed**
- 75% of applicants were admitted

Undergraduates *Retention:* 95% of full-time freshmen returned.
Freshmen *Admission:* 96 applied, 72 admitted.
Academics *Calendar:* semesters. *Degree:* diplomas and bachelor's. *Special study options:* part-time degree program.
Standardized Tests *Required:* Nightingale Entrance Exam (for admission).
Applying *Options:* electronic application, early admission. *Application fee:* $100. *Required:* essay or personal statement, high school transcript, interview.
Freshman Application Contact Nightingale College, 4155 Harrison Boulevard #100, Ogden, UT 84403.
Website: http://www.nightingale.edu/.

Provo College
Provo, Utah

Director of Admissions Mr. Gordon Peters, College Director, Provo College, 1450 West 820 North, Provo, UT 84601. *Phone:* 801-375-1861. *Toll-free phone:* 877-777-5886. *Fax:* 801-375-9728.
E-mail: gordonp@provocollege.org.
Website: http://www.provocollege.edu/.

Salt Lake Community College
Salt Lake City, Utah

- **State-supported** 2-year, founded 1948, part of Utah System of Higher Education
- **Urban** 114-acre campus with easy access to Salt Lake City
- **Endowment** $830,992
- **Coed**, 28,814 undergraduate students, 27% full-time, 51% women, 49% men

Undergraduates 7,789 full-time, 21,025 part-time. 2% Black or African American, non-Hispanic/Latino; 16% Hispanic/Latino; 4% Asian, non-Hispanic/Latino; 1% Native Hawaiian or other Pacific Islander, non-Hispanic/Latino; 0.8% American Indian or Alaska Native, non-Hispanic/Latino; 2% Two or more races, non-Hispanic/Latino; 2% Race/ethnicity unknown; 1% international; 4% transferred in.
Freshmen *Admission:* 2,992 applied, 2,992 admitted, 2,992 enrolled.
Faculty *Total:* 1,494, 23% full-time. *Student/faculty ratio:* 19:1.
Majors Accounting technology and bookkeeping; airline pilot and flight crew; architectural engineering technology; autobody/collision and repair technology; avionics maintenance technology; biology/biological sciences; biology/biotechnology laboratory technician; building/construction finishing, management, and inspection related; business administration and management; chemistry; clinical/medical laboratory technology; computer and information sciences; computer science; cosmetology; criminal justice/law enforcement administration; culinary arts; dental hygiene; design and visual communications; diesel mechanics technology; drafting and design technology; economics; electrical, electronic and communications engineering technology; engineering; engineering technology; English; entrepreneurship; environmental engineering technology; finance; general studies; geology/earth science; graphic design; health professions related; heating, air conditioning, ventilation and refrigeration maintenance technology; history; human development and family studies; humanities; industrial radiologic technology; information science/studies; information technology; instrumentation technology; international/global studies; international relations and affairs; kinesiology and exercise science; legal assistant/paralegal; marketing/marketing management; mass communication/media; medical/clinical assistant; medical radiologic technology; music; occupational therapist assistant; photographic and film/video technology; physical sciences; physical therapy technology; physics; political science and government; psychology; public health related; quality control technology; radio and television broadcasting technology; registered nursing/registered nurse; sign language interpretation and translation; social work; sociology; speech communication and rhetoric; sport and fitness administration/management; surveying technology; teacher assistant/aide; telecommunications technology; welding technology.
Academics *Calendar:* semesters. *Degree:* certificates, diplomas, and associate. *Special study options:* academic remediation for entering students, advanced placement credit, cooperative education, distance learning, double majors, English as a second language, internships, part-time degree program, services for LD students, student-designed majors, study abroad, summer session for credit. *ROTC:* Army (c), Air Force (c).
Library Markosian Library plus 2 others.

Student Life *Housing:* college housing not available. *Activities and Organizations:* drama/theater group, student-run newspaper, radio and television station, choral group, marching band. *Campus security:* 24-hour emergency response devices and patrols, late-night transport/escort service. *Student services:* health clinic, personal/psychological counseling.

Athletics Member NJCAA. *Intercollegiate sports:* baseball M(s), basketball M(s)/W(s), cheerleading M(s)/W(s), soccer M(c)/W(c), softball W(s), volleyball W(s).

Costs (2015–16) *Tuition:* state resident $3130 full-time, $130 per credit hour part-time; nonresident $10,898 full-time, $453 per credit hour part-time. *Required fees:* $439 full-time. *Payment plan:* installment. *Waivers:* senior citizens and employees or children of employees.

Financial Aid Of all full-time matriculated undergraduates who enrolled in 2014, 132 Federal Work-Study jobs (averaging $2567).

Applying *Options:* electronic application, early admission. *Application fee:* $40. *Application deadlines:* rolling (freshmen), rolling (transfers).

Freshman Application Contact Ms. Kathy Thompson, Salt Lake Community College, Salt Lake City, UT 84130. *Phone:* 801-957-4485.
E-mail: kathy.thompson@slcc.edu.
Website: http://www.slcc.edu/.

Snow College
Ephraim, Utah

Freshman Application Contact Ms. Lorie Parry, Admissions Advisor, Snow College, 150 East College Avenue, Ephraim, UT 84627. *Phone:* 435-283-7144. *Fax:* 435-283-7157. *E-mail:* snowcollege@snow.edu.
Website: http://www.snow.edu/.

Vista College
Clearfield, Utah

Admissions Office Contact Vista College, 775 South 2000 East, Clearfield, UT 84015.
Website: http://www.vistacollege.edu/.

VERMONT

Community College of Vermont
Montpelier, Vermont

Freshman Application Contact Community College of Vermont, 660 Elm Street, Montpelier, VT 05602. *Phone:* 802-654-0505. *Toll-free phone:* 800-CCV-6686.
Website: http://www.ccv.edu/.

Landmark College
Putney, Vermont

- **Independent** primarily 2-year, founded 1983
- **Small-town** 125-acre campus
- **Endowment** $19.1 million
- **Coed**

Undergraduates 494 full-time, 20 part-time. Students come from 39 states and territories; 7 other countries; 93% are from out of state; 4% Black or African American, non-Hispanic/Latino; 4% Hispanic/Latino; 2% Asian, non-Hispanic/Latino; 0.2% Native Hawaiian or other Pacific Islander, non-Hispanic/Latino; 0.2% American Indian or Alaska Native, non-Hispanic/Latino; 2% Two or more races, non-Hispanic/Latino; 14% Race/ethnicity unknown; 2% international; 15% transferred in; 95% live on campus. *Retention:* 66% of full-time freshmen returned.

Faculty *Student/faculty ratio:* 6:1.

Academics *Calendar:* semesters. *Degrees:* certificates, associate, and bachelor's. *Special study options:* academic remediation for entering students, advanced placement credit, distance learning, internships, services for LD students, study abroad, summer session for credit.

Library Landmark College Library.

Student Life *Campus security:* 24-hour emergency response devices and patrols, late-night transport/escort service, controlled dormitory access.

Standardized Tests *Required:* Cognitive and achievement tests such as the Wechsler Adult Intelligence Scale III and the Nelson Denny Reading Test are required (for admission).

Costs (2015–16) *Comprehensive fee:* $62,040 includes full-time tuition ($51,200), mandatory fees ($130), and room and board ($10,710). *Room and*

board: college room only: $5530. Room and board charges vary according to board plan and housing facility.

Financial Aid Of all full-time matriculated undergraduates who enrolled in 2010, 341 applied for aid, 243 were judged to have need, 3 had their need fully met. 85 Federal Work-Study jobs (averaging $1000). 3 state and other part-time jobs (averaging $1000). In 2010, 18. *Average percent of need met:* 45. *Average financial aid package:* $26,000. *Average need-based loan:* $4500. *Average need-based gift aid:* $21,000. *Average non-need-based aid:* $7800. *Average indebtedness upon graduation:* $6100.

Applying *Options:* electronic application, early action, deferred entrance. *Application fee:* $75. *Required:* essay or personal statement, high school transcript, diagnosis of LD and/or ADHD and cognitive testing. *Recommended:* 2 letters of recommendation, interview.

Freshman Application Contact Admissions Main Desk, Landmark College, Admissions Office, River Road South, Putney, VT 05346. *Phone:* 802-387-6718. *Fax:* 802-387-6868. *E-mail:* admissions@landmark.edu.
Website: http://www.landmark.edu/.

New England Culinary Institute
Montpelier, Vermont

- **Proprietary** primarily 2-year, founded 1980
- **Small-town** campus
- **Coed,** 422 undergraduate students, 80% full-time, 45% women, 55% men

Undergraduates 338 full-time, 84 part-time. Students come from 39 states and territories; 6 other countries; 80% are from out of state; 4% Black or African American, non-Hispanic/Latino; 6% Hispanic/Latino; 2% Asian, non-Hispanic/Latino; 0.5% Native Hawaiian or other Pacific Islander, non-Hispanic/Latino; 1% Two or more races, non-Hispanic/Latino; 11% Race/ethnicity unknown; 1% international; 80% live on campus. *Retention:* 93% of full-time freshmen returned.

Freshmen *Admission:* 249 applied, 92 admitted.

Faculty *Total:* 39, 62% full-time. *Student/faculty ratio:* 13:1.

Majors Baking and pastry arts; culinary arts; restaurant, culinary, and catering management.

Academics *Calendar:* quarters. *Degrees:* certificates, associate, and bachelor's. *Special study options:* academic remediation for entering students, accelerated degree program, advanced placement credit, cooperative education, distance learning, honors programs, internships, services for LD students.

Library New England Culinary Institute Library.

Student Life *Housing:* on-campus residence required for freshman year. *Options:* coed, men-only, women-only. Campus housing is leased by the school. Freshman applicants given priority for college housing. *Activities and Organizations:* American Culinary Federation, Slow Food, Student Council, Special Guest Lecture Series, Student Ambassadors (leadership program). *Campus security:* 24-hour emergency response devices, student patrols.

Standardized Tests *Recommended:* SAT or ACT (for admission).

Costs (2015–16) *Comprehensive fee:* $28,625 includes full-time tuition ($20,625) and room and board ($8000). Full-time tuition and fees vary according to course load, degree level, program, reciprocity agreements, and student level. Part-time tuition and fees vary according to course load, degree level, program, reciprocity agreements, and student level. *Room and board:* Room and board charges vary according to housing facility. *Payment plan:* installment. *Waivers:* employees or children of employees.

Financial Aid Of all full-time matriculated undergraduates who enrolled in 2014, 320 Federal Work-Study jobs (averaging $1000).

Applying *Options:* electronic application, early admission, deferred entrance. *Required:* high school transcript. *Required for some:* interview. *Recommended:* essay or personal statement, 2 letters of recommendation, culinary experience. *Application deadline:* rolling (freshmen).

Freshman Application Contact Adonica Williams, New England Culinary Institute, 56 College Street, Montpelier, VT 05602-3115. *Phone:* 802-225-3210. *Toll-free phone:* 877-223-6324. *Fax:* 802-225-3280.
E-mail: admissions@neci.edu.
Website: http://www.neci.edu/.

VIRGINIA

Advanced Technology Institute
Virginia Beach, Virginia

Freshman Application Contact Admissions Office, Advanced Technology Institute, 5700 Southern Boulevard, Suite 100, Virginia Beach, VA 23462. *Phone:* 757-490-1241. *Toll-free phone:* 888-468-1093.
Website: http://www.auto.edu/.

Blue Ridge Community College
Weyers Cave, Virginia

Freshman Application Contact Blue Ridge Community College, PO Box 80, Weyers Cave, VA 24486-0080. *Phone:* 540-453-2217. *Toll-free phone:* 888-750-2722.
Website: http://www.brcc.edu/.

Bryant & Stratton College–Richmond Campus
Richmond, Virginia

Freshman Application Contact Mr. David K. Mayle, Director of Admissions, Bryant & Stratton College–Richmond Campus, 8141 Hull Street Road, Richmond, VA 23235-6411. *Phone:* 804-745-2444. *Fax:* 804-745-6884. *E-mail:* tlawson@bryanstratton.edu.
Website: http://www.bryantstratton.edu/.

Bryant & Stratton College–Virginia Beach Campus
Virginia Beach, Virginia

Freshman Application Contact Bryant & Stratton College–Virginia Beach Campus, 301 Centre Pointe Drive, Virginia Beach, VA 23462. *Phone:* 757-499-7900 Ext. 173.
Website: http://www.bryantstratton.edu/.

Centra College of Nursing
Lynchburg, Virginia

Admissions Office Contact Centra College of Nursing, 905 Lakeside Drive, Suite A, Lynchburg, VA 24501.
Website: http://www.centrahealth.com/college-of-nursing.

Central Virginia Community College
Lynchburg, Virginia

- **State-supported** 2-year, founded 1966, part of Virginia Community College System
- **Suburban** 104-acre campus
- **Coed,** 4,433 undergraduate students, 33% full-time, 52% women, 48% men

Undergraduates 1,464 full-time, 2,969 part-time. Students come from 12 states and territories; 1% are from out of state; 17% Black or African American, non-Hispanic/Latino; 3% Hispanic/Latino; 2% Asian, non-Hispanic/Latino; 0.1% Native Hawaiian or other Pacific Islander, non-Hispanic/Latino; 0.4% American Indian or Alaska Native, non-Hispanic/Latino; 3% Two or more races, non-Hispanic/Latino; 0.8% Race/ethnicity unknown.
Freshmen *Admission:* 1,326 applied, 1,326 admitted.
Faculty *Total:* 302, 21% full-time. *Student/faculty ratio:* 18:1.
Majors Accounting related; business administration and management; business/commerce; business operations support and secretarial services related; computer and information sciences; criminal justice/law enforcement administration; culinary arts; design and visual communications; education; emergency medical technology (EMT paramedic); engineering; engineering technology; industrial technology; liberal arts and sciences/liberal studies; management science; medical/clinical assistant; radiologic technology/science; respiratory care therapy; science technologies.
Academics *Calendar:* semesters. *Degree:* certificates, diplomas, and associate. *Special study options:* academic remediation for entering students, advanced placement credit, cooperative education, distance learning, independent study, internships, part-time degree program, services for LD students, summer session for credit.
Library Bedford Learning Resources Center.
Student Life *Housing:* college housing not available. *Activities and Organizations:* drama/theater group. *Campus security:* 24-hour emergency response devices.
Athletics Member NJCAA.
Costs (2015–16) *Tuition:* state resident $4470 full-time, $149 per credit hour part-time; nonresident $10,293 full-time, $343 per credit hour part-time. *Payment plan:* installment. *Waivers:* senior citizens.
Financial Aid Of all full-time matriculated undergraduates who enrolled in 2014, 65 Federal Work-Study jobs (averaging $2700).
Applying *Options:* electronic application, early admission, deferred entrance. *Application deadlines:* rolling (freshmen), rolling (out-of-state freshmen), rolling (transfers). *Notification:* continuous (freshmen), continuous (out-of-state freshmen), continuous (transfers).
Freshman Application Contact Admissions Office, Central Virginia Community College, 3506 Wards Road, Lynchburg, VA 24502. *Phone:* 434-832-7633. *Toll-free phone:* 800-562-3060. *Fax:* 434-832-7793.
Website: http://www.cvcc.vccs.edu/.

Centura College
Chesapeake, Virginia

Director of Admissions Director of Admissions, Centura College, 932 Ventures Way, Chesapeake, VA 23320. *Phone:* 757-549-2121. *Toll-free phone:* 877-575-5627. *Fax:* 575-549-1196.
Website: http://www.centuracollege.edu/.

Centura College
Newport News, Virginia

Director of Admissions Victoria Whitehead, Director of Admissions, Centura College, 616 Denbigh Boulevard, Newport News, VA 23608. *Phone:* 757-874-2121. *Toll-free phone:* 877-575-5627. *Fax:* 757-874-3857. *E-mail:* admdircpen@centura.edu.
Website: http://www.centuracollege.edu/.

Centura College
Norfolk, Virginia

Director of Admissions Director of Admissions, Centura College, 7020 North Military Highway, Norfolk, VA 23518. *Phone:* 757-853-2121. *Toll-free phone:* 877-575-5627. *Fax:* 757-852-9017.
Website: http://www.centuracollege.edu/.

Centura College
North Chesterfield, Virginia

Freshman Application Contact Admissions Office, Centura College, 7914 Midlothian Turnpike, North Chesterfield, VA 23235-5230. *Phone:* 804-330-0111. *Toll-free phone:* 877-575-5627. *Fax:* 804-330-3809.
Website: http://www.centuracollege.edu/.

Centura College
Virginia Beach, Virginia

Freshman Application Contact Admissions Office, Centura College, 2697 Dean Drive, Suite 100, Virginia Beach, VA 23452. *Phone:* 757-340-2121. *Toll-free phone:* 877-575-5627. *Fax:* 757-340-9704.
Website: http://www.centuracollege.edu/.

Columbia College
Fairfax, Virginia

Admissions Office Contact Columbia College, 8300 Merrifield Avenue, Fairfax, VA 22031.
Website: http://www.ccdc.edu/.

Dabney S. Lancaster Community College
Clifton Forge, Virginia

- **State-supported** 2-year, founded 1964, part of Virginia Community College System
- **Rural** 117-acre campus
- **Endowment** $5.7 million
- **Coed**

Undergraduates Students come from 4 states and territories; 2% are from out of state; 6% Black or African American, non-Hispanic/Latino; 2% Hispanic/Latino; 0.6% Asian, non-Hispanic/Latino; 0.9% American Indian or Alaska Native, non-Hispanic/Latino; 3% Two or more races, non-Hispanic/Latino; 0.8% Race/ethnicity unknown.
Faculty *Total:* 97, 24% full-time. *Student/faculty ratio:* 16:1.
Majors Administrative assistant and secretarial science; biological and physical sciences; business administration and management; computer programming; criminal justice/law enforcement administration; data processing and data processing technology; drafting and design technology; drafting/design engineering technologies related; education; electrical, electronic and communications engineering technology; forest technology; information science/studies; legal administrative assistant/secretary; liberal arts and sciences/liberal studies; medical administrative assistant and medical

secretary; registered nursing/registered nurse; wood science and wood products/pulp and paper technology.

Academics *Calendar:* semesters. *Degree:* certificates and associate. *Special study options:* academic remediation for entering students, adult/continuing education programs, advanced placement credit, cooperative education, distance learning, honors programs, independent study, internships, part-time degree program, services for LD students, study abroad, summer session for credit.

Library DSLCC Library plus 1 other.

Student Life *Housing:* college housing not available. *Campus security:* 24-hour emergency response devices. *Student services:* personal/psychological counseling.

Athletics *Intramural sports:* basketball M/W, volleyball M/W.

Standardized Tests *Required for some:* SAT and SAT Subject Tests or ACT (for admission), SAT Subject Tests (for admission).

Costs (2015–16) *Tuition:* state resident $3492 full-time, $134 per credit part-time; nonresident $8162 full-time, $311 per credit part-time. Full-time tuition and fees vary according to reciprocity agreements. Part-time tuition and fees vary according to reciprocity agreements. *Required fees:* $276 full-time, $12 per credit part-time. *Payment plan:* installment. *Waivers:* senior citizens.

Applying *Recommended:* high school transcript.

Freshman Application Contact Mrs. Lorrie Wilhelm Ferguson, Registrar, Dabney S. Lancaster Community College, Backels Hall, Clifton Forge, VA 24422. *Phone:* 540-863-2823. *Toll-free phone:* 877-73-DSLCC. *Fax:* 540-863-2915. *E-mail:* lwferguson@dslcc.edu.
Website: http://www.dslcc.edu/.

Danville Community College
Danville, Virginia

Freshman Application Contact Cathy Pulliam, Coordinator of Student Recruitment and Enrollment, Danville Community College, 1008 South Main Street, Danville, VA 24541-4088. *Phone:* 434-797-8538. *Toll-free phone:* 800-560-4291. *E-mail:* cpulliam@dcc.vccs.edu.
Website: http://www.dcc.vccs.edu/.

Eastern Shore Community College
Melfa, Virginia

Freshman Application Contact P. Bryan Smith, Dean of Student Services, Eastern Shore Community College, 29300 Lankford Highway, Melfa, VA 23410. *Phone:* 757-789-1732. *Toll-free phone:* 877-871-8455. *Fax:* 757-789-1737. *E-mail:* bsmith@es.vccs.edu.
Website: http://www.es.vccs.edu/.

Eastern Virginia Career College
Fredericksburg, Virginia

Admissions Office Contact Eastern Virginia Career College, 10304 Spotsylvania Avenue, Suite 400, Fredericksburg, VA 22408.
Website: http://www.evcc.edu/.

ECPI University
Richmond, Virginia

Freshman Application Contact Director, ECPI University, 800 Moorefield Park Drive, Richmond, VA 23236. *Phone:* 804-330-5533. *Toll-free phone:* 844-611-0694. *Fax:* 804-330-5577. *E-mail:* agerard@ecpi.edu.
Website: http://www.ecpi.edu/.

Everest College
Chesapeake, Virginia

Admissions Office Contact Everest College, 825 Greenbrier Circle, Suite 100, Chesapeake, VA 23320.
Website: http://www.everest.edu/.

Fortis College
Norfolk, Virginia

Admissions Office Contact Fortis College, 6300 Center Drive, Suite 100, Norfolk, VA 23502. *Toll-free phone:* 855-4-FORTIS.
Website: http://www.fortis.edu/.

Fortis College
Richmond, Virginia

Admissions Office Contact Fortis College, 2000 Westmoreland Street, Suite A, Richmond, VA 23230. *Toll-free phone:* 855-4-FORTIS.
Website: http://www.fortis.edu/.

Germanna Community College
Locust Grove, Virginia

Freshman Application Contact Ms. Rita Dunston, Registrar, Germanna Community College, 10000 Germanna Point Drive, Fredericksburg, VA 22408. *Phone:* 540-891-3020. *Fax:* 540-891-3092.
Website: http://www.germanna.edu/.

Global Health College
Alexandria, Virginia

Admissions Office Contact Global Health College, 25 South Quaker Lane, 1st Floor, Alexandria, VA 22314.
Website: http://www.global.edu/.

ITT Technical Institute
Chantilly, Virginia

Freshman Application Contact Director of Recruitment, ITT Technical Institute, 14420 Albemarle Point Place, Suite 100, Chantilly, VA 20151. *Phone:* 703-263-2541. *Toll-free phone:* 888-895-8324.
Website: http://www.itt-tech.edu/.

ITT Technical Institute
Norfolk, Virginia

Freshman Application Contact Director of Recruitment, ITT Technical Institute, 5425 Robin Hood Road, Suite 100, Norfolk, VA 23513. *Phone:* 757-466-1260. *Toll-free phone:* 888-253-8324.
Website: http://www.itt-tech.edu/.

ITT Technical Institute
Richmond, Virginia

Freshman Application Contact Director of Recruitment, ITT Technical Institute, 300 Gateway Centre Parkway, Richmond, VA 23235. *Phone:* 804-330-4992. *Toll-free phone:* 888-330-4888.
Website: http://www.itt-tech.edu/.

ITT Technical Institute
Salem, Virginia

Freshman Application Contact Director of Recruitment, ITT Technical Institute, 2159 Apperson Drive, Salem, VA 24153. *Phone:* 540-989-2500. *Toll-free phone:* 877-208-6132.
Website: http://www.itt-tech.edu/.

ITT Technical Institute
Springfield, Virginia

Freshman Application Contact Director of Recruitment, ITT Technical Institute, 7300 Boston Boulevard, Springfield, VA 22153. *Phone:* 703-440-9535. *Toll-free phone:* 866-817-8324.
Website: http://www.itt-tech.edu/.

John Tyler Community College
Chester, Virginia

- **State-supported** 2-year, founded 1967, part of Virginia Community College System
- **Suburban** 160-acre campus with easy access to Richmond
- **Coed,** 10,035 undergraduate students, 25% full-time, 58% women, 42% men

Undergraduates 2,558 full-time, 7,477 part-time. Students come from 35 states and territories; 1% are from out of state; 24% Black or African American, non-Hispanic/Latino; 8% Hispanic/Latino; 3% Asian, non-Hispanic/Latino; 0.2% Native Hawaiian or other Pacific Islander, non-Hispanic/Latino; 0.5% American Indian or Alaska Native, non-

Hispanic/Latino; 4% Two or more races, non-Hispanic/Latino; 0.8% Race/ethnicity unknown; 5% transferred in.

Freshmen *Admission:* 1,328 enrolled.

Faculty *Total:* 574, 22% full-time. *Student/faculty ratio:* 18:1.

Majors Accounting related; architectural technology; business administration and management; business administration, management and operations related; child-care provision; computer and information sciences; criminal justice/law enforcement administration; emergency medical technology (EMT paramedic); engineering; funeral service and mortuary science; general studies; humanities; industrial technology; information technology; mechanical engineering technologies related; mental and social health services and allied professions related; registered nursing/registered nurse; visual and performing arts related.

Academics *Calendar:* semesters. *Degree:* certificates and associate. *Special study options:* academic remediation for entering students, adult/continuing education programs, advanced placement credit, distance learning, external degree program, honors programs, off-campus study, part-time degree program, services for LD students, study abroad, summer session for credit. *ROTC:* Army (c).

Library John Tyler Community College Learning Resource and Technology Center.

Student Life *Housing:* college housing not available. *Activities and Organizations:* drama/theater group, choral group, Phi Theta Kappa, Human Services Club, Future Teachers Club, Student Nurses' Association, Student Veteran's Organization. *Campus security:* 24-hour emergency response devices and patrols.

Athletics *Intramural sports:* basketball M(c)/W(c), golf M(c)/W(c), ultimate Frisbee M(c)/W(c).

Costs (2015–16) *Tuition:* state resident $3420 full-time, $143 per credit hour part-time; nonresident $8090 full-time, $337 per credit hour part-time. Full-time tuition and fees vary according to course load. Part-time tuition and fees vary according to course load. *Required fees:* $70 full-time, $35 per term part-time. *Payment plan:* installment. *Waivers:* senior citizens.

Applying *Options:* electronic application, early admission, deferred entrance. *Recommended:* high school transcript. *Application deadline:* rolling (freshmen). *Notification:* continuous (freshmen).

Freshman Application Contact Ms. Joy James, Director of Admissions and Records/Veterans Affairs and Registrar, John Tyler Community College, 13101 Jefferson Davis Highway, Chester, VA 23831. *Phone:* 804-706-5214. *Toll-free phone:* 800-552-3490. *Fax:* 804-796-4362. *E-mail:* jjames@jtcc.edu. *Website:* http://www.jtcc.edu/.

J. Sargeant Reynolds Community College
Richmond, Virginia

- **State-supported** 2-year, founded 1972, part of Virginia Community College System
- **Suburban** 207-acre campus with easy access to Richmond
- **Coed,** 10,887 undergraduate students, 28% full-time, 60% women, 40% men

Undergraduates 3,100 full-time, 7,787 part-time. Students come from 25 states and territories; 14 other countries; 1% are from out of state; 33% Black or African American, non-Hispanic/Latino; 3% Hispanic/Latino; 6% Asian, non-Hispanic/Latino; 0.2% Native Hawaiian or other Pacific Islander, non-Hispanic/Latino; 0.5% American Indian or Alaska Native, non-Hispanic/Latino; 7% Two or more races, non-Hispanic/Latino; 0.9% Race/ethnicity unknown; 5% transferred in. *Retention:* 44% of full-time freshmen returned.

Freshmen *Admission:* 1,495 enrolled.

Faculty *Total:* 645, 22% full-time. *Student/faculty ratio:* 18:1.

Majors Accounting related; applied horticulture/horticulture operations; architectural and building sciences; automobile/automotive mechanics technology; baking and pastry arts; biological and physical sciences; building/construction site management; business administration and management; child-care provision; clinical/medical laboratory technology; computer and information sciences; computer programming; computer systems networking and telecommunications; consumer merchandising/retailing management; cooking and related culinary arts; criminal justice/law enforcement administration; dental laboratory technology; emergency medical technology (EMT paramedic); engineering; fire science/firefighting; floriculture/floristry management; hospitality administration; hospitality administration related; hotel/motel administration; legal assistant/paralegal; liberal arts and sciences and humanities related;

licensed practical/vocational nurse training; mathematics; mental and social health services and allied professions related; opticianry; pharmacy technician; respiratory care therapy; restaurant/food services management; sign language interpretation and translation; small business administration; social sciences; substance abuse/addiction counseling; web page, digital/multimedia and information resources design.

Academics *Calendar:* semesters. *Degree:* certificates and associate. *Special study options:* academic remediation for entering students, adult/continuing education programs, advanced placement credit, distance learning, double majors, English as a second language, independent study, internships, off-campus study, part-time degree program, services for LD students, summer session for credit.

Library J. Sargeant Reynolds Community College Library plus 2 others.

Student Life *Housing:* college housing not available. *Campus security:* 24-hour emergency response devices and patrols, late-night transport/escort service, security during open hours. *Student services:* personal/psychological counseling.

Costs (2015–16) *Tuition:* state resident $3722 full-time, $147 per credit part-time; nonresident $8393 full-time, $341 per credit part-time. Full-time tuition and fees vary according to course load and program. Part-time tuition and fees vary according to course load and program. *Payment plan:* installment. *Waivers:* senior citizens.

Financial Aid Of all full-time matriculated undergraduates who enrolled in 2015, 1,060 applied for aid, 1,060 were judged to have need. *Average financial aid package:* $2260. *Average need-based gift aid:* $2260.

Applying *Options:* electronic application. *Required:* high school transcript. *Required for some:* interview, interview, criminal background check and/or drug screening, physical standard minimum. *Application deadlines:* rolling (freshmen), rolling (transfers). *Notification:* continuous (freshmen), continuous (transfers).

Freshman Application Contact Ms. Karen Pettis-Walden, Director of Admissions and Records, J. Sargeant Reynolds Community College, PO Box 85622, Richmond, VA 23285-5622. *Phone:* 804-523-5029. *Fax:* 804-371-3650. *E-mail:* kpettis-walden@reynolds.edu. *Website:* http://www.reynolds.edu/.

Lord Fairfax Community College
Middletown, Virginia

Freshman Application Contact Karen Bucher, Director of Enrollment Management, Lord Fairfax Community College, 173 Skirmisher Lane, Middletown, VA 22645. *Phone:* 540-868-7132. *Toll-free phone:* 800-906-LFCC. *Fax:* 540-868-7005. *E-mail:* kbucher@lfcc.edu. *Website:* http://www.lfcc.edu/.

Medtech College
Falls Church, Virginia

Admissions Office Contact Medtech College, 6565 Arlington Boulevard, Falls Church, VA 22042. *Website:* http://www.medtech.edu/.

Miller-Motte Technical College
Lynchburg, Virginia

Director of Admissions Ms. Betty J. Dierstein, Director, Miller-Motte Technical College, 1011 Creekside Lane, Lynchburg, VA 24502. *Phone:* 434-239-5222. *Fax:* 434-239-1069. *E-mail:* bjdierstein@miller-mott.com. *Website:* http://www.miller-motte.edu/.

Miller-Motte Technical College
Roanoke, Virginia

Admissions Office Contact Miller-Motte Technical College, 4444 Electric Road, Roanoke, VA 24018. *Website:* http://www.miller-motte.edu/.

Mountain Empire Community College
Big Stone Gap, Virginia

Freshman Application Contact Mountain Empire Community College, 3441 Mountain Empire Road, Big Stone Gap, VA 24219. *Phone:* 276-523-2400 Ext. 219. *Website:* http://www.mecc.edu/.

New River Community College
Dublin, Virginia

- **State-supported** 2-year, founded 1969, part of Virginia Community College System
- **Rural** 100-acre campus
- **Endowment** $1.9 million
- **Coed,** 4,345 undergraduate students, 46% full-time, 53% women, 47% men

Undergraduates 2,008 full-time, 2,337 part-time. Students come from 22 states and territories; 21 other countries; 3% are from out of state; 5% transferred in.

Freshmen *Admission:* 850 enrolled.

Faculty *Total:* 206, 25% full-time. *Student/faculty ratio:* 22:1.

Majors Accounting; administrative assistant and secretarial science; architectural engineering technology; automobile/automotive mechanics technology; biological and physical sciences; business administration and management; child development; community organization and advocacy; computer engineering technology; computer graphics; criminal justice/law enforcement administration; criminal justice/police science; drafting and design technology; education; electrical, electronic and communications engineering technology; engineering; forensic science and technology; general studies; information science/studies; instrumentation technology; legal assistant/paralegal; liberal arts and sciences/liberal studies; licensed practical/vocational nurse training; machine tool technology; marketing/marketing management; medical administrative assistant and medical secretary; mental and social health services and allied professions related; registered nursing/registered nurse; welding technology.

Academics *Calendar:* semesters. *Degree:* certificates, diplomas, and associate. *Special study options:* academic remediation for entering students, adult/continuing education programs, advanced placement credit, cooperative education, distance learning, double majors, external degree program, internships, part-time degree program, services for LD students, summer session for credit.

Library New River Community College Library plus 1 other.

Student Life *Housing:* college housing not available. *Activities and Organizations:* Student Government Association, Phi Beta Lambda, Instrument Society of America, Human Service Organization, Sign Language Club. *Campus security:* 24-hour patrols. *Student services:* personal/psychological counseling.

Athletics Member NJCAA. *Intercollegiate sports:* baseball M. *Intramural sports:* basketball M/W, soccer M/W, table tennis M/W.

Costs (2015–16) *Tuition:* state resident $145 per credit hour part-time; nonresident $340 per credit hour part-time. Full-time tuition and fees vary according to course load and program. Part-time tuition and fees vary according to course load and program. *Payment plans:* installment, deferred payment. *Waivers:* senior citizens.

Applying *Options:* electronic application, early admission, deferred entrance. *Required for some:* high school transcript. *Application deadlines:* rolling (freshmen), rolling (transfers). *Notification:* continuous (freshmen), continuous (transfers).

Freshman Application Contact Mrs. Tammy L. Smith, Coordinator, Admissions and Records, New River Community College, 5251 College Drive, Dublin, VA 24084. *Phone:* 540-674-3600 Ext. 4203. *Toll-free phone:* 866-462-6722. *Fax:* 540-674-3644. *E-mail:* tsmith@nr.edu. *Website:* http://www.nr.edu/.

★ Northern Virginia Community College
Annandale, Virginia

- **State-supported** 2-year, founded 1965, part of Virginia Community College System
- **Suburban** 435-acre campus with easy access to Washington, DC
- **Coed**

Undergraduates 3% are from out of state; 18% Black or African American, non-Hispanic/Latino; 19% Hispanic/Latino; 14% Asian, non-Hispanic/Latino; 10% Native Hawaiian or other Pacific Islander, non-Hispanic/Latino; 3% Two or more races, non-Hispanic/Latino; 3% Race/ethnicity unknown; 3% international.

Academics *Calendar:* semesters. *Degree:* certificates and associate. *Special study options:* academic remediation for entering students, adult/continuing education programs, advanced placement credit, cooperative education, distance learning, double majors, English as a second language, external degree program, honors programs, part-time degree program, services for LD students, study abroad, summer session for credit.

Student Life *Campus security:* 24-hour emergency response devices, campus police.

Costs (2015–16) *Tuition:* state resident $171 per credit hour part-time; nonresident $369 per credit hour part-time. Full-time tuition and fees vary according to course load. Part-time tuition and fees vary according to course load.

Applying *Options:* early admission, deferred entrance. *Required for some:* high school transcript.

Freshman Application Contact Northern Virginia Community College, 8333 Little River Turnpike, Annandale, VA 22003. *Phone:* 703-323-3195. *Website:* http://www.nvcc.edu/.

See previous page for display ad and page 374 for the College Close-Up.

Patrick Henry Community College
Martinsville, Virginia

Freshman Application Contact Mr. Travis Tisdale, Coordinator, Admissions and Records, Patrick Henry Community College, 645 Patriot Avenue, Martinsville, VA 24112. *Phone:* 276-656-0311. *Toll-free phone:* 800-232-7997. *Fax:* 276-656-0352.
Website: http://www.ph.vccs.edu/.

Paul D. Camp Community College
Franklin, Virginia

Freshman Application Contact Mrs. Trina Jones, Dean Student Services, Paul D. Camp Community College, PO Box 737, 100 N College Drive, Franklin, VA 23851. *Phone:* 757-569-6720. *E-mail:* tjones@pdc.edu. *Website:* http://www.pdc.edu/.

Piedmont Virginia Community College
Charlottesville, Virginia

- **State-supported** 2-year, founded 1972, part of Virginia Community College System
- **Suburban** 114-acre campus with easy access to Richmond
- **Endowment** $6.8 million
- **Coed**

Undergraduates 1,234 full-time, 4,320 part-time. Students come from 22 states and territories; 13% Black or African American, non-Hispanic/Latino; 5% Hispanic/Latino; 4% Asian, non-Hispanic/Latino; 0.2% Native Hawaiian or other Pacific Islander, non-Hispanic/Latino; 0.3% American Indian or Alaska Native, non-Hispanic/Latino; 4% Two or more races, non-Hispanic/Latino; 1% Race/ethnicity unknown; 0.6% international; 6% transferred in.

Faculty *Student/faculty ratio:* 19:1.

Academics *Calendar:* semesters. *Degree:* certificates and associate. *Special study options:* academic remediation for entering students, adult/continuing education programs, advanced placement credit, cooperative education, distance learning, English as a second language, honors programs, independent study, internships, part-time degree program, services for LD students, summer session for credit. *ROTC:* Army (c).

Library Jessup Library.

Student Life *Campus security:* 24-hour emergency response devices and patrols, late-night transport/escort service, establishment of Campus Police.

Costs (2015–16) *Tuition:* state resident $4445 full-time, $135 per credit hour part-time; nonresident $10,283 full-time, $311 per credit hour part-time. Full-time tuition and fees vary according to course load. Part-time tuition and fees vary according to course load. *Required fees:* $395 full-time, $13 per credit hour part-time.

Financial Aid Of all full-time matriculated undergraduates who enrolled in 2014, 35 Federal Work-Study jobs.

Applying *Options:* electronic application, early admission, deferred entrance. *Required for some:* high school transcript, Admission to programs in Nursing, Practical Nursing, Radiography, Sonography, Surgical Technology, Emergency Medical Services, Health Information Management, and Patient Admissions Coordination is competitive and/or requires completion of specific prerequisites.

Freshman Application Contact Ms. Mary Lee Walsh, Dean of Student Services, Piedmont Virginia Community College, 501 College Drive, Charlottesville, VA 22902-7589. *Phone:* 434-961-6540. *Fax:* 434-961-5425. *E-mail:* mwalsh@pvcc.edu.
Website: http://www.pvcc.edu/.

Rappahannock Community College
Glenns, Virginia

- **State and locally supported** 2-year, founded 1970, part of Virginia Community College System
- **Rural** campus
- **Coed,** 3,566 undergraduate students, 23% full-time, 62% women, 38% men

Undergraduates 821 full-time, 2,745 part-time.

Majors Accounting; administrative assistant and secretarial science; biological and physical sciences; business administration and management; business administration, management and operations related; criminal justice/law enforcement administration; criminal justice/police science; engineering technology; information science/studies; liberal arts and sciences/liberal studies; registered nursing/registered nurse.

Academics *Calendar:* semesters. *Degree:* certificates and associate. *Special study options:* academic remediation for entering students, adult/continuing education programs, distance learning, honors programs, internships, off-campus study, part-time degree program, services for LD students, summer session for credit.

Student Life *Student services:* personal/psychological counseling.

Athletics *Intercollegiate sports:* softball W.

Costs (2015–16) *Tuition:* state resident $4020 full-time, $134 per credit hour part-time; nonresident $9318 full-time, $311 per credit hour part-time. Full-time tuition and fees vary according to course load. Part-time tuition and fees vary according to course load. *Required fees:* $440 full-time. *Payment plan:* deferred payment. *Waivers:* senior citizens.

Financial Aid Of all full-time matriculated undergraduates who enrolled in 2014, 40 Federal Work-Study jobs (averaging $1015).

Applying *Options:* electronic application, early admission. *Application deadlines:* rolling (freshmen), rolling (out-of-state freshmen), rolling (transfers). *Notification:* continuous (freshmen), continuous (out-of-state freshmen), continuous (transfers).

Freshman Application Contact Ms. Felicia Packett, Admissions and Records Officer, Rappahannock Community College, 12745 College Drive, Glenns, VA 23149-0287. *Phone:* 804-758-6740. *Toll-free phone:* 800-836-9381. *Website:* http://www.rappahannock.edu/.

Richard Bland College of The College of William and Mary
Petersburg, Virginia

Freshman Application Contact Office of Admissions, Richard Bland College of The College of William and Mary, 8311 Halifax Road, Petersburg, VA 23805. *Phone:* 804-862-6100 Ext. 6249. *E-mail:* apply@rbc.edu. *Website:* http://www.rbc.edu/.

Riverside School of Health Careers
Newport News, Virginia

Admissions Office Contact Riverside School of Health Careers, 316 Main Street, Newport News, VA 23601.
Website: http://www.riversideonline.com/rshc/.

Southside Regional Medical Center Professional Schools
Colonial Heights, Virginia

Admissions Office Contact Southside Regional Medical Center Professional Schools, 430 Clairmont Court, Suite 200, Colonial Heights, VA 23834. *Website:* http://www.srmconline.com/Southside-Regional-Medical-Center/nursingeducation.aspx.

Southside Virginia Community College
Alberta, Virginia

Freshman Application Contact Mr. Brent Richey, Dean of Enrollment Management, Southside Virginia Community College, 109 Campus Drive, Alberta, VA 23821. *Phone:* 434-949-1012. *Fax:* 434-949-7863. *E-mail:* rhina.jones@sv.vccs.edu.
Website: http://www.southside.edu/.

Southwest Virginia Community College
Richlands, Virginia

- **State-supported** 2-year, founded 1968, part of Virginia Community College System
- **Rural** 100-acre campus
- **Endowment** $18.0 million
- **Coed,** 2,546 undergraduate students, 47% full-time, 61% women, 39% men

Undergraduates 1,209 full-time, 1,337 part-time. Students come from 7 states and territories; 1% are from out of state; 2% Black or African American, non-Hispanic/Latino; 0.5% Hispanic/Latino; 0.6% Asian, non-Hispanic/Latino; 0.4% American Indian or Alaska Native, non-Hispanic/Latino; 1% Two or

more races, non-Hispanic/Latino; 0.2% Race/ethnicity unknown; 29% transferred in. *Retention:* 60% of full-time freshmen returned.
Freshmen *Admission:* 367 enrolled.
Faculty *Total:* 129, 31% full-time. *Student/faculty ratio:* 23:1.
Majors Accounting related; business administration, management and operations related; business operations support and secretarial services related; child-care provision; computer and information sciences; criminal justice/law enforcement administration; electrical, electronic and communications engineering technology; emergency medical technology (EMT paramedic); liberal arts and sciences/liberal studies; mental and social health services and allied professions related; radiologic technology/science; registered nursing/registered nurse.
Academics *Calendar:* semesters. *Degree:* certificates, diplomas, and associate. *Special study options:* academic remediation for entering students, accelerated degree program, adult/continuing education programs, advanced placement credit, distance learning, double majors, honors programs, internships, off-campus study, part-time degree program, summer session for credit.
Library Southwest Virginia Community College Library. *Books:* 46,325 (physical). Students can reserve study rooms.
Student Life *Housing:* college housing not available. *Activities and Organizations:* choral group, Phi Theta Kappa, Phi Beta Lambda, Intervoice, Helping Minds Club, Project ACHEIVE. *Campus security:* 24-hour emergency response devices and patrols, student patrols, extensive security camera system. *Student services:* personal/psychological counseling.
Standardized Tests *Required:* VCCS Math and English Assessments (for admission).
Costs (2015–16) *Tuition:* state resident $4335 full-time, $145 per credit hour part-time; nonresident $10,173 full-time, $339 per credit hour part-time. Full-time tuition and fees vary according to reciprocity agreements. Part-time tuition and fees vary according to reciprocity agreements. *Required fees:* $315 full-time, $11 per credit hour part-time. *Waivers:* senior citizens.
Financial Aid Of all full-time matriculated undergraduates who enrolled in 2014, 150 Federal Work-Study jobs (averaging $1140).
Applying *Options:* electronic application, early admission, deferred entrance. *Required:* high school transcript, interview. *Application deadlines:* rolling (freshmen), rolling (transfers).
Freshman Application Contact Ms. Dionne Cook, Admissions Counselor, Southwest Virginia Community College, Box SVCC, Richlands, VA 24641. *Phone:* 276-964-7301. *Toll-free phone:* 800-822-7822. *Fax:* 276-964-7716. *E-mail:* dionne.cook@sw.edu.
Website: http://www.sw.edu/.

Standard Healthcare Services, College of Nursing
Falls Church, Virginia

Admissions Office Contact Standard Healthcare Services, College of Nursing, 1073 West Broad Street, Suite 201, Falls Church, VA 22046-4612.
Website: http://www.standardcollege.edu/.

Thomas Nelson Community College
Hampton, Virginia

Freshman Application Contact Ms. Geraldine Newson, Sr. Admission Specialist, Thomas Nelson Community College, PO Box 9407, Hampton, VA 23670-0407. *Phone:* 757-825-2800. *Fax:* 757-825-2763.
E-mail: admissions@tncc.edu.
Website: http://www.tncc.edu/.

Tidewater Community College
Norfolk, Virginia

- **State-supported** 2-year, founded 1968, part of Virginia Community College System
- **Suburban** 520-acre campus
- **Endowment** $7.1 million
- **Coed**, 25,927 undergraduate students, 37% full-time, 59% women, 41% men

Undergraduates 9,499 full-time, 16,428 part-time. 14% are from out of state; 33% Black or African American, non-Hispanic/Latino; 8% Hispanic/Latino; 4% Asian, non-Hispanic/Latino; 0.6% Native Hawaiian or other Pacific Islander, non-Hispanic/Latino; 0.5% American Indian or Alaska Native, non-Hispanic/Latino; 5% Two or more races, non-Hispanic/Latino; 0.8% Race/ethnicity unknown; 0.5% international. *Retention:* 59% of full-time freshmen returned.
Faculty *Total:* 1,420, 25% full-time. *Student/faculty ratio:* 21:1.

Majors Accounting; administrative assistant and secretarial science; advertising; automobile/automotive mechanics technology; biological and physical sciences; business administration and management; civil engineering; commercial and advertising art; computer programming; drafting and design technology; education; electrical, electronic and communications engineering technology; engineering; finance; fine/studio arts; graphic design; horticultural science; information technology; interior design; kindergarten/preschool education; legal assistant/paralegal; liberal arts and sciences/liberal studies; marketing/marketing management; music; real estate; registered nursing/registered nurse.
Academics *Calendar:* semesters. *Degree:* certificates and associate. *Special study options:* academic remediation for entering students, accelerated degree program, adult/continuing education programs, advanced placement credit, cooperative education, distance learning, English as a second language, honors programs, independent study, internships, off-campus study, part-time degree program, services for LD students, summer session for credit.
Library Main Library plus 5 others.
Student Life *Housing:* college housing not available. *Activities and Organizations:* drama/theater group, student-run newspaper. *Campus security:* 24-hour patrols. *Student services:* personal/psychological counseling, women's center.
Athletics *Intramural sports:* basketball M/W, soccer M, softball W, tennis M/W, volleyball W.
Costs (2016–17) *Tuition:* state resident $3354 full-time, $140 per credit hour part-time; nonresident $7592 full-time, $316 per credit hour part-time. *Required fees:* $884 full-time, $37 per credit hour part-time. *Payment plan:* installment. *Waivers:* senior citizens.
Financial Aid Of all full-time matriculated undergraduates who enrolled in 2014, 64 Federal Work-Study jobs (averaging $2000).
Applying *Options:* electronic application, early admission, deferred entrance. *Application deadlines:* rolling (freshmen), rolling (transfers). *Notification:* continuous (freshmen), continuous (transfers).
Freshman Application Contact Registrar, Tidewater Community College, Norfolk, VA 23510. *Phone:* 757-822-1900. *E-mail:* centralrecords@tcc.edu.
Website: http://www.tcc.edu/.

Virginia College in Richmond
Richmond, Virginia

Admissions Office Contact Virginia College in Richmond, 7200 Midlothian Turnpike, Richmond, VA 23225.
Website: http://www.vc.edu/.

Virginia Highlands Community College
Abingdon, Virginia

Freshman Application Contact Karen Cheers, Acting Director of Admissions, Records, and Financial Aid, Virginia Highlands Community College, PO Box 828, 100 VHCC Drive Abingdon, Abingdon, VA 24212. *Phone:* 276-739-2490. *Toll-free phone:* 877-207-6115.
E-mail: kcheers@vhcc.edu.
Website: http://www.vhcc.edu/.

Virginia Western Community College
Roanoke, Virginia

- **State-supported** 2-year, founded 1966, part of Virginia Community College System
- **Suburban** 70-acre campus
- **Coed**, 8,632 undergraduate students, 29% full-time, 55% women, 45% men

Undergraduates 2,527 full-time, 6,105 part-time. 2% are from out of state; 15% Black or African American, non-Hispanic/Latino; 3% Hispanic/Latino; 3% Asian, non-Hispanic/Latino; 0.1% Native Hawaiian or other Pacific Islander, non-Hispanic/Latino; 0.3% American Indian or Alaska Native, non-Hispanic/Latino; 3% Two or more races, non-Hispanic/Latino; 0.6% Race/ethnicity unknown; 0.3% international; 3% transferred in. *Retention:* 53% of full-time freshmen returned.
Freshmen *Admission:* 2,770 applied, 1,376 enrolled.
Faculty *Student/faculty ratio:* 34:1.
Majors Accounting; administrative assistant and secretarial science; art; automobile/automotive mechanics technology; biological and physical sciences; business administration and management; child development; civil engineering technology; commercial and advertising art; computer science; criminal justice/law enforcement administration; data processing and data processing technology; dental hygiene; education; electrical, electronic and communications engineering technology; engineering; industrial radiologic technology; kindergarten/preschool education; liberal arts and sciences/liberal studies; mechanical engineering/mechanical technology; mental health

counseling; pre-engineering; radio and television; radiologic technology/science; registered nursing/registered nurse.

Academics *Calendar:* semesters. *Degree:* certificates and associate. *Special study options:* academic remediation for entering students, advanced placement credit, cooperative education, distance learning, double majors, English as a second language, honors programs, independent study, internships, part-time degree program, services for LD students, summer session for credit.

Library Brown Library.

Student Life *Housing:* college housing not available. *Activities and Organizations:* drama/theater group, student-run newspaper. *Campus security:* 24-hour emergency response devices and patrols, late-night transport/escort service. *Student services:* personal/psychological counseling.

Athletics *Intramural sports:* basketball M/W, soccer M, volleyball W.

Costs (2016–17) *Tuition:* state resident $4066 full-time, $136 per credit hour part-time; nonresident $9364 full-time, $312 per credit hour part-time. *Required fees:* $633 full-time. *Payment plan:* installment. *Waivers:* senior citizens and employees or children of employees.

Applying *Options:* electronic application, early admission, deferred entrance. *Required for some:* high school transcript. *Recommended:* high school transcript. *Application deadlines:* rolling (freshmen), rolling (transfers). *Notification:* continuous (freshmen), continuous (transfers).

Freshman Application Contact Admissions Office, Virginia Western Community College, PO Box 14007, Roanoke, VA 24038. *Phone:* 540-857-7231.

Website: http://www.virginiawestern.edu/.

Wytheville Community College
Wytheville, Virginia

- **State-supported** 2-year, founded 1967, part of Virginia Community College System
- **Rural** 141-acre campus
- **Coed,** 2,915 undergraduate students, 36% full-time, 62% women, 38% men

Undergraduates 1,037 full-time, 1,878 part-time. 2% are from out of state; 4% Black or African American, non-Hispanic/Latino; 3% Hispanic/Latino; 0.8% Asian, non-Hispanic/Latino; 0.1% Native Hawaiian or other Pacific Islander, non-Hispanic/Latino; 0.3% American Indian or Alaska Native, non-Hispanic/Latino; 2% Two or more races, non-Hispanic/Latino; 0.3% Race/ethnicity unknown; 0.2% international. *Retention:* 62% of full-time freshmen returned.

Faculty *Total:* 137, 29% full-time. *Student/faculty ratio:* 23:1.

Majors Accounting; administrative assistant and secretarial science; biological and physical sciences; business administration and management; civil engineering technology; clinical/medical laboratory technology; corrections; criminal justice/law enforcement administration; criminal justice/police science; dental hygiene; drafting and design technology; education; electrical, electronic and communications engineering technology; information science/studies; liberal arts and sciences/liberal studies; machine tool technology; mass communication/media; mechanical engineering/mechanical technology; medical administrative assistant and medical secretary; physical therapy; registered nursing/registered nurse.

Academics *Calendar:* semesters. *Degree:* certificates, diplomas, and associate. *Special study options:* academic remediation for entering students, adult/continuing education programs, advanced placement credit, distance learning, external degree program, independent study, part-time degree program, services for LD students, summer session for credit.

Library Wytheville Community College Library.

Student Life *Housing:* college housing not available. *Activities and Organizations:* drama/theater group, student-run newspaper. *Campus security:* 24-hour emergency response devices and patrols.

Athletics Member NJCAA. *Intercollegiate sports:* volleyball W.

Costs (2015–16) *Tuition:* state resident $4020 full-time, $134 per credit hour part-time; nonresident $9318 full-time, $311 per credit hour part-time. *Required fees:* $360 full-time, $12 per credit hour part-time.

Financial Aid Of all full-time matriculated undergraduates who enrolled in 2014, 125 Federal Work-Study jobs (averaging $2592).

Applying *Options:* electronic application, early admission. *Required:* high school transcript. *Required for some:* interview. *Application deadlines:* rolling (freshmen), rolling (transfers). *Notification:* continuous (freshmen), continuous (transfers).

Freshman Application Contact Wytheville Community College, 1000 East Main Street, Wytheville, VA 24382-3308. *Phone:* 276-223-4701. *Toll-free phone:* 800-468-1195.

Website: http://www.wcc.vccs.edu/.

WASHINGTON

Bates Technical College
Tacoma, Washington

Director of Admissions Director of Admissions, Bates Technical College, 1101 South Yakima Avenue, Tacoma, WA 98405-4895. *Phone:* 253-680-7000. *E-mail:* registration@bates.ctc.edu.

Website: http://www.bates.ctc.edu/.

Bellevue College
Bellevue, Washington

Freshman Application Contact Morenika Jacobs, Associate Dean of Enrollment Services, Bellevue College, 3000 Landerholm Circle, SE, Bellevue, WA 98007-6484. *Phone:* 425-564-2205. *Fax:* 425-564-4065.

Website: http://www.bcc.ctc.edu/.

Bellingham Technical College
Bellingham, Washington

- **State-supported** 2-year, founded 1957, part of Washington State Board for Community and Technical Colleges
- **Suburban** 21-acre campus with easy access to Vancouver, BC; Seattle, WA
- **Coed,** 2,864 undergraduate students

Freshmen *Admission:* 2,562 applied, 2,562 admitted.

Faculty *Total:* 189, 67% full-time. *Student/faculty ratio:* 24:1.

Majors Accounting technology and bookkeeping; autobody/collision and repair technology; automobile/automotive mechanics technology; building/property maintenance; civil engineering technology; communications systems installation and repair technology; computer systems networking and telecommunications; culinary arts; data entry/microcomputer applications; diesel mechanics technology; electrician; executive assistant/executive secretary; fishing and fisheries sciences and management; heating, air conditioning, ventilation and refrigeration maintenance technology; heavy/industrial equipment maintenance technologies related; industrial mechanics and maintenance technology; instrumentation technology; legal assistant/paralegal; machine tool technology; marketing/marketing management; medical radiologic technology; registered nursing/registered nurse; surgical technology; surveying technology; welding technology.

Academics *Calendar:* quarters. *Degree:* certificates and associate. *Special study options:* academic remediation for entering students, distance learning, English as a second language, internships, part-time degree program, services for LD students, summer session for credit.

Library Bellingham Technical College Library. *Books:* 15,500 (physical), 120,000 (digital/electronic); *Serial titles:* 90 (physical); *Databases:* 13. Weekly public service hours: 70; students can reserve study rooms.

Student Life *Housing:* college housing not available. *Student services:* personal/psychological counseling.

Standardized Tests *Required:* ACCUPLACER or waiver (for admission).

Costs (2015–16) *Tuition:* state resident $3389 full-time, $102 per credit part-time; nonresident $279 per credit part-time. Full-time tuition and fees vary according to course load. Part-time tuition and fees vary according to course load. *Waivers:* employees or children of employees.

Financial Aid Of all full-time matriculated undergraduates who enrolled in 2014, 11 Federal Work-Study jobs (averaging $3876). 22 state and other part-time jobs (averaging $3171).

Applying *Options:* electronic application, early admission, deferred entrance. *Required for some:* high school transcript, prerequisite courses. *Application deadlines:* rolling (freshmen), rolling (out-of-state freshmen), rolling (transfers).

Freshman Application Contact Bellingham Technical College, 3028 Lindbergh Avenue, Bellingham, WA 98225. *Phone:* 360-752-8324.

Website: http://www.btc.edu/.

Big Bend Community College
Moses Lake, Washington

- **State-supported** 2-year, founded 1962
- **Small-town** 159-acre campus
- **Coed,** 2,016 undergraduate students, 72% full-time, 53% women, 47% men

Undergraduates 1,458 full-time, 558 part-time. 1% Black or African American, non-Hispanic/Latino; 35% Hispanic/Latino; 2% Asian, non-Hispanic/Latino; 0.6% American Indian or Alaska Native, non-

Hispanic/Latino; 2% Two or more races, non-Hispanic/Latino; 3% Race/ethnicity unknown; 0.5% international; 7% live on campus.
Freshmen *Admission:* 364 enrolled.
Faculty *Student/faculty ratio:* 22:1.
Majors Accounting technology and bookkeeping; agricultural production; airline pilot and flight crew; automobile/automotive mechanics technology; avionics maintenance technology; biomedical technology; computer programming; computer systems networking and telecommunications; early childhood education; industrial electronics technology; industrial mechanics and maintenance technology; liberal arts and sciences/liberal studies; medical/clinical assistant; medical office management; office management; registered nursing/registered nurse; welding technology.
Academics *Calendar:* quarters. *Degree:* certificates and associate. *Special study options:* academic remediation for entering students, advanced placement credit, cooperative education, distance learning, English as a second language, part-time degree program, services for LD students, summer session for credit.
Library William C. Bonaudi Library. *Books:* 37,906 (physical), 3,484 (digital/electronic); *Serial titles:* 102 (physical); *Databases:* 29. Weekly public service hours: 68; students can reserve study rooms.
Student Life *Housing Options:* coed. Campus housing is university owned. *Activities and Organizations:* choral group. *Campus security:* 24-hour emergency response devices, late-night transport/escort service, daytime security during the week, dorm security six evenings/week, Enhanced Campus Notification System, video surveillance on campus. *Student services:* personal/psychological counseling.
Athletics *Intercollegiate sports:* baseball M, basketball M/W, softball W, volleyball W.
Costs (2015–16) *Tuition:* state resident $3846 full-time, $103 per credit hour part-time; nonresident $4254 full-time, $116 per credit hour part-time. Full-time tuition and fees vary according to course load and program. Part-time tuition and fees vary according to course load and program. *Required fees:* $150 full-time, $5 per credit hour part-time. *Room and board:* $7140. *Payment plan:* installment. *Waivers:* senior citizens.
Applying *Options:* electronic application, early admission, deferred entrance. *Application fee:* $30. *Required for some:* high school transcript. *Application deadlines:* rolling (freshmen), rolling (transfers). *Notification:* continuous (freshmen), continuous (transfers).
Freshman Application Contact Candis Lacher, Associate Vice President of Student Services, Big Bend Community College, 7662 Chanute Street NE, Moses Lake, WA 98837. *Phone:* 509-793-2061. *Toll-free phone:* 877-745-1212. *Fax:* 509-793-6243. *E-mail:* admissions@bigbend.edu.
Website: http://www.bigbend.edu/.

Carrington College–Spokane
Spokane, Washington

- **Proprietary** 2-year, founded 1976, part of Carrington Colleges Group, Inc.
- **Coed,** 413 undergraduate students, 100% full-time, 86% women, 14% men

Undergraduates 413 full-time. 18% are from out of state; 2% Black or African American, non-Hispanic/Latino; 9% Hispanic/Latino; 1% Asian, non-Hispanic/Latino; 1% Native Hawaiian or other Pacific Islander, non-Hispanic/Latino; 2% American Indian or Alaska Native, non-Hispanic/Latino; 4% Two or more races, non-Hispanic/Latino; 1% Race/ethnicity unknown; 18% transferred in.
Freshmen *Admission:* 42 enrolled.
Faculty *Total:* 13, 85% full-time. *Student/faculty ratio:* 35:1.
Majors Medical administrative assistant and medical secretary; medical office management; medical radiologic technology.
Academics *Degree:* certificates and associate.
Student Life *Housing:* college housing not available.
Costs (2015–16) *Tuition:* $15,537 full-time. *Required fees:* $780 full-time.
Applying *Required:* essay or personal statement, high school transcript, interview, institutional entrance test.
Freshman Application Contact Carrington College–Spokane, 10102 East Knox Avenue, Suite 200, Spokane, WA 99206.
Website: http://carrington.edu/.

Cascadia College
Bothell, Washington

- **State-supported** primarily 2-year, founded 1999, part of Washington State Board for Community and Technical Colleges
- **Suburban** 128-acre campus
- **Coed,** 2,759 undergraduate students, 55% full-time, 49% women, 51% men

Undergraduates 1,529 full-time, 1,230 part-time. Students come from 12 states and territories; 3% Black or African American, non-Hispanic/Latino; 18% Hispanic/Latino; 15% Asian, non-Hispanic/Latino; 0.4% Native Hawaiian or other Pacific Islander, non-Hispanic/Latino; 0.8% American Indian or Alaska Native, non-Hispanic/Latino; 16% Two or more races, non-Hispanic/Latino; 17% Race/ethnicity unknown; 12% international.
Freshmen *Admission:* 2,939 applied.
Faculty *Total:* 129, 24% full-time.
Majors Liberal arts and sciences and humanities related; liberal arts and sciences/liberal studies; science technologies related; sustainability studies.
Academics *Calendar:* quarters. *Degrees:* certificates, diplomas, associate, and bachelor's. *Special study options:* academic remediation for entering students, accelerated degree program, adult/continuing education programs, advanced placement credit, cooperative education, distance learning, double majors, English as a second language, independent study, internships, off-campus study, part-time degree program, services for LD students, study abroad, summer session for credit.
Library Campus Library. *Books:* 90,000 (physical), 600,000 (digital/electronic); *Serial titles:* 600 (physical), 100,000 (digital/electronic); *Databases:* 600. Weekly public service hours: 86; students can reserve study rooms.
Student Life *Housing:* college housing not available. *Activities and Organizations:* drama/theater group, student-run newspaper. *Campus security:* 24-hour emergency response devices, late-night transport/escort service. *Student services:* personal/psychological counseling.
Athletics *Intramural sports:* basketball M/W, football M/W, soccer M/W.
Costs (2015–16) *One-time required fee:* $30. *Tuition:* state resident $3846 full-time, $103 per credit hour part-time; nonresident $4253 full-time, $116 per credit hour part-time. Full-time tuition and fees vary according to course load and program. Part-time tuition and fees vary according to course load and program. *Required fees:* $420 full-time, $11 per credit hour part-time. *Waivers:* senior citizens and employees or children of employees.
Applying *Options:* electronic application. *Application fee:* $30. *Application deadlines:* rolling (freshmen), rolling (out-of-state freshmen), rolling (transfers). *Notification:* continuous (freshmen), continuous (out-of-state freshmen), continuous (transfers).
Freshman Application Contact Ms. Erin Blakeney, Dean for Student Success, Cascadia College, 18345 Campus Way, NE, Bothell, WA 98011. *Phone:* 425-352-8000. *Fax:* 425-352-8137.
E-mail: admissions@cascadia.edu.
Website: http://www.cascadia.edu/.

Centralia College
Centralia, Washington

Freshman Application Contact Admissions Office, Centralia College, Centralia, WA 98531. *Phone:* 360-736-9391 Ext. 221. *Fax:* 360-330-7503.
E-mail: admissions@centralia.edu.
Website: http://www.centralia.edu/.

Clark College
Vancouver, Washington

- **State-supported** primarily 2-year, founded 1933, part of Washington State Board for Community and Technical Colleges
- **Urban** 101-acre campus with easy access to Portland
- **Coed,** 10,477 undergraduate students, 48% full-time, 57% women, 43% men

Undergraduates 5,035 full-time, 5,442 part-time. 4% are from out of state; 2% Black or African American, non-Hispanic/Latino; 9% Hispanic/Latino; 4% Asian, non-Hispanic/Latino; 0.1% Native Hawaiian or other Pacific Islander, non-Hispanic/Latino; 0.6% American Indian or Alaska Native, non-Hispanic/Latino; 8% Two or more races, non-Hispanic/Latino; 6% Race/ethnicity unknown; 1% international; 3% transferred in.
Freshmen *Admission:* 1,349 applied, 1,349 admitted, 1,215 enrolled.
Faculty *Student/faculty ratio:* 24:1.
Majors Accounting technology and bookkeeping; applied horticulture/horticulture operations; automobile/automotive mechanics technology; baking and pastry arts; business administration and management; business automation/technology/data entry; computer programming; computer systems networking and telecommunications; construction engineering

technology; culinary arts; data entry/microcomputer applications; dental hygiene; diesel mechanics technology; early childhood education; electrical, electronic and communications engineering technology; emergency medical technology (EMT paramedic); executive assistant/executive secretary; graphic communications; human resources management; landscaping and groundskeeping; legal administrative assistant/secretary; legal assistant/paralegal; liberal arts and sciences/liberal studies; machine tool technology; manufacturing engineering technology; medical administrative assistant and medical secretary; medical/clinical assistant; radiologic technology/science; registered nursing/registered nurse; retailing; selling skills and sales; sport and fitness administration/management; substance abuse/addiction counseling; surveying technology; telecommunications technology; web/multimedia management and webmaster; welding technology.

Academics *Calendar:* quarters. *Degrees:* certificates, diplomas, associate, and bachelor's. *Special study options:* adult/continuing education programs, part-time degree program. *ROTC:* Army (c), Air Force (c).

Library Lewis D. Cannell Library.

Student Life *Housing:* college housing not available. *Campus security:* 24-hour patrols, late-night transport/escort service, security staff during hours of operation.

Athletics *Intercollegiate sports:* baseball M, basketball M(s)/W(s), cross-country running M(s)/W(s), fencing M(c)/W(c), soccer M(s)/W(s), softball W, track and field M(s)/W(s), volleyball W(s). *Intramural sports:* basketball M/W, fencing M/W, soccer M/W, softball M/W, volleyball M/W.

Costs (2015–16) *Tuition:* area resident $3930 full-time, $105 per credit hour part-time; state resident $5337 full-time, $151 per credit hour part-time; nonresident $9333 full-time, $281 per credit hour part-time. Full-time tuition and fees vary according to course load, degree level, program, and reciprocity agreements. Part-time tuition and fees vary according to course load, degree level, program, and reciprocity agreements. *Payment plan:* installment. *Waivers:* senior citizens and employees or children of employees.

Applying *Options:* electronic application, early admission, deferred entrance. *Application fee:* $25.

Freshman Application Contact Ms. Sheryl Anderson, Director of Admissions, Clark College, Vancouver, WA 98663. *Phone:* 360-992-2308. *Fax:* 360-992-2867. *E-mail:* admissions@clark.edu. *Website:* http://www.clark.edu/.

Clover Park Technical College
Lakewood, Washington

Director of Admissions Ms. Judy Richardson, Registrar, Clover Park Technical College, 4500 Steilacoom Boulevard, SW, Lakewood, WA 98499. *Phone:* 253-589-5570. *Website:* http://www.cptc.edu/.

Columbia Basin College
Pasco, Washington

Freshman Application Contact Admissions Department, Columbia Basin College, 2600 North 20th Avenue, Pasco, WA 99301-3397. *Phone:* 509-542-4524. *Fax:* 509-544-2023. *E-mail:* admissions@columbiabasin.edu. *Website:* http://www.columbiabasin.edu/.

Edmonds Community College
Lynnwood, Washington

Freshman Application Contact Ms. Nancy Froemming, Enrollment Services Office Manager, Edmonds Community College, 20000 68th Avenue West, Lynwood, WA 98036-5999. *Phone:* 425-640-1853. *Fax:* 425-640-1159. *E-mail:* nanci.froemming@edcc.edu. *Website:* http://www.edcc.edu/.

Everest College
Tacoma, Washington

Admissions Office Contact Everest College, 2156 Pacific Avenue, Tacoma, WA 98402. *Website:* http://www.everest.edu/.

Everett Community College
Everett, Washington

Freshman Application Contact Ms. Linda Baca, Entry Services Manager, Everett Community College, 2000 Tower Street, Everett, WA 98201-1327. *Phone:* 425-388-9219. *Fax:* 425-388-9173. *E-mail:* admissions@everettcc.edu. *Website:* http://www.everettcc.edu/.

Grays Harbor College
Aberdeen, Washington

Freshman Application Contact Ms. Brenda Dell, Admissions Officer, Grays Harbor College, 1620 Edward P. Smith Drive, Aberdeen, WA 98520. *Phone:* 360-532-4216. *Toll-free phone:* 800-562-4830. *Website:* http://www.ghc.edu/.

Green River College
Auburn, Washington

Freshman Application Contact Ms. Peggy Morgan, Program Support Supervisor, Green River College, 12401 Southeast 320th Street, Auburn, WA 98092-3699. *Phone:* 253-833-9111. *Fax:* 253-288-3454. *Website:* http://www.greenriver.edu/.

Highline College
Des Moines, Washington

Freshman Application Contact Ms. Michelle Kuwasaki, Director of Admissions, Highline College, 2400 South 240th Street, Des Moines, WA 98198-9800. *Phone:* 206-878-3710 Ext. 9800. *Website:* http://www.highline.edu/.

ITT Technical Institute
Everett, Washington

Freshman Application Contact Director of Recruitment, ITT Technical Institute, 1615 75th Street SW, Everett, WA 98203. *Phone:* 425-583-0200. *Toll-free phone:* 800-272-3791. *Website:* http://www.itt-tech.edu/.

ITT Technical Institute
Seattle, Washington

Freshman Application Contact Director of Recruitment, ITT Technical Institute, 12720 Gateway Drive, Suite 100, Seattle, WA 98168-9903. *Phone:* 206-244-3300. *Toll-free phone:* 800-422-2029. *Website:* http://www.itt-tech.edu/.

ITT Technical Institute
Spokane Valley, Washington

Freshman Application Contact Director of Recruitment, ITT Technical Institute, 13518 East Indiana Avenue, Spokane Valley, WA 99216. *Phone:* 509-926-2900. *Toll-free phone:* 800-777-8324. *Website:* http://www.itt-tech.edu/.

Lake Washington Institute of Technology
Kirkland, Washington

Freshman Application Contact Shawn Miller, Registrar, Enrollment Services, Lake Washington Institute of Technology, 11605 132nd Avenue NE, Kirkland, WA 98034-8506. *Phone:* 425-739-8104. *E-mail:* info@lwtc.edu. *Website:* http://www.lwtech.edu/.

Lower Columbia College
Longview, Washington

- **State-supported** 2-year, founded 1934, part of Washington State Board for Community and Technical Colleges
- **Rural** 39-acre campus with easy access to Portland
- **Endowment** $14.9 million
- **Coed**

Undergraduates 1,633 full-time, 1,519 part-time.

Faculty *Student/faculty ratio:* 15:1.

Academics *Calendar:* quarters. *Degree:* certificates, diplomas, and associate. *Special study options:* academic remediation for entering students, adult/continuing education programs, advanced placement credit, cooperative education, distance learning, English as a second language, external degree program, independent study, internships, part-time degree program, services for LD students, student-designed majors, summer session for credit.

Library Alan Thompson Library plus 1 other.

Student Life *Campus security:* 24-hour emergency response devices and patrols.

Costs (2015–16) *Tuition:* state resident $4130 full-time, $111 per credit part-time; nonresident $4644 full-time, $125 per credit part-time. Full-time tuition and fees vary according to course load and reciprocity agreements. Part-time tuition and fees vary according to course load and reciprocity agreements. *Required fees:* $329 full-time, $7 per credit part-time.

Financial Aid Of all full-time matriculated undergraduates who enrolled in 2014, 440 Federal Work-Study jobs (averaging $708). 447 state and other part-time jobs (averaging $2415).

Applying *Options:* electronic application. *Application fee:* $30. *Recommended:* high school transcript.

Freshman Application Contact Ms. Nichole Seroshek, Director of Registration, Lower Columbia College, 1600 Maple Street, Longview, WA 98632. *Phone:* 360-442-2372. *Toll-free phone:* 866-900-2311. *Fax:* 360-442-2379. *E-mail:* registration@lowercolumbia.edu.

Website: http://www.lowercolumbia.edu/.

North Seattle College
Seattle, Washington

Freshman Application Contact Ms. Betsy Abts, Registrar, North Seattle College, Seattle, WA 98103-3599. *Phone:* 206-934-3663. *Fax:* 206-934-3671. *E-mail:* arrc@seattlecolleges.edu.

Website: http://www.northseattle.edu/.

Northwest Indian College
Bellingham, Washington

Freshman Application Contact Office of Admissions, Northwest Indian College, 2522 Kwina Road, Bellingham, WA 98226. *Phone:* 360-676-2772. *Toll-free phone:* 866-676-2772. *Fax:* 360-392-4333. *E-mail:* admissions@nwic.edu.

Website: http://www.nwic.edu/.

Northwest School of Wooden Boatbuilding
Port Hadlock, Washington

- **Independent** 2-year, founded 1980
- **Small-town** campus
- **Coed**

Faculty *Student/faculty ratio:* 12:1.

Academics *Calendar:* quarters. *Degree:* diplomas and associate.

Library School Library.

Costs (2015–16) *Tuition:* $19,400 full-time. No tuition increase for student's term of enrollment. *Required fees:* $100 full-time.

Applying *Options:* electronic application.

Freshman Application Contact Northwest School of Wooden Boatbuilding, 42 North Water Street, Port Hadlock, WA 98339. *Phone:* 360-385-4948. *Website:* http://www.nwboatschool.org/.

Olympic College
Bremerton, Washington

- **State-supported** primarily 2-year, founded 1946, part of Washington State Board for Community and Technical Colleges
- **Suburban** 33-acre campus with easy access to Seattle, Tacoma
- **Coed,** 7,881 undergraduate students

Undergraduates 5% Black or African American, non-Hispanic/Latino; 7% Hispanic/Latino; 9% Asian, non-Hispanic/Latino; 2% American Indian or Alaska Native, non-Hispanic/Latino; 2% international; 1% live on campus.

Freshmen *Admission:* 3,784 applied, 3,784 admitted.

Faculty *Total:* 493, 26% full-time.

Majors Accounting technology and bookkeeping; administrative assistant and secretarial science; business administration and management; chemical engineering; computer systems networking and telecommunications; cosmetology; crisis/emergency/disaster management; culinary arts; drafting and design technology; early childhood education; electrical and electronics engineering; electrical, electronic and communications engineering technology; engineering technology; industrial technology; information technology; liberal arts and sciences/liberal studies; marine maintenance and ship repair technology; mechanical engineering; medical/clinical assistant; mental and social health services and allied professions related; organizational leadership; photographic and film/video technology; physical sciences; physical therapy technology; registered nursing/registered nurse; substance abuse/addiction counseling; welding technology.

Academics *Calendar:* quarters. *Degrees:* certificates, diplomas, associate, and bachelor's. *Special study options:* academic remediation for entering students, adult/continuing education programs, advanced placement credit, cooperative education, distance learning, English as a second language, honors programs, independent study, internships, off-campus study, part-time degree program, services for LD students, summer session for credit.

Library Haselwood Library. Students can reserve study rooms.

Student Life *Housing Options:* coed. Campus housing is university owned. *Activities and Organizations:* drama/theater group, student-run newspaper, choral group, Gaming Club, International Club, Gay/Straight Alliace, Engineering Club, Armed Forces Club. *Campus security:* 24-hour emergency response devices and patrols, student patrols, late-night transport/escort service. *Student services:* personal/psychological counseling.

Athletics *Intercollegiate sports:* baseball M(s), basketball M(s)/W(s), cross-country running M/W, golf M(s)/W(s), softball W(s), track and field M/W, volleyball W(s). *Intramural sports:* basketball M/W, table tennis M/W, volleyball M/W.

Financial Aid Of all full-time matriculated undergraduates who enrolled in 2014, 105 Federal Work-Study jobs (averaging $2380). 31 state and other part-time jobs (averaging $2880).

Applying *Options:* electronic application. *Required for some:* essay or personal statement, high school transcript, 2 letters of recommendation. *Application deadlines:* rolling (freshmen), rolling (out-of-state freshmen), rolling (transfers).

Freshman Application Contact Ms. Nora Downard, Program Support Supervisor, Olympic College, 1600 Chester Avenue, Bremerton, WA 98337-1699. *Phone:* 360-475-7445. *Toll-free phone:* 800-259-6718. *Fax:* 360-475-7202. *E-mail:* ndownard@olympic.edu.

Website: http://www.olympic.edu/.

Peninsula College
Port Angeles, Washington

Freshman Application Contact Ms. Pauline Marvin, Peninsula College, 1502 East Lauridsen Boulevard, Port Angeles, WA 98362. *Phone:* 360-417-6596. *Toll-free phone:* 877-452-9277. *Fax:* 360-457-8100. *E-mail:* admissions@pencol.edu.

Website: http://www.pc.ctc.edu/.

Pierce College at Fort Steilacoom
Lakewood, Washington

Freshman Application Contact Admissions Office, Pierce College at Fort Steilacoom, 9401 Farwest Drive SW, Lakewood, WA 98498. *Phone:* 253-964-6501. *E-mail:* admiss1@pierce.ctc.edu.

Website: http://www.pierce.ctc.edu/.

Pierce College at Puyallup
Puyallup, Washington

Freshman Application Contact Pierce College at Puyallup, 1601 39th Avenue Southeast, Puyallup, WA 98374. *Phone:* 253-840-8400.

Website: http://www.pierce.ctc.edu/.

Pima Medical Institute
Renton, Washington

Freshman Application Contact Pima Medical Institute, 555 South Renton Village Place, Renton, WA 98057. *Phone:* 425-228-9600.

Website: http://www.pmi.edu/.

Pima Medical Institute
Seattle, Washington

Freshman Application Contact Admissions Office, Pima Medical Institute, 9709 Third Avenue NE, Suite 400, Seattle, WA 98115. *Phone:* 206-322-6100. *Toll-free phone:* 800-477-PIMA (in-state); 888-477-PIMA (out-of-state).

Website: http://www.pmi.edu/.

Renton Technical College
Renton, Washington

- **State-supported** primarily 2-year, founded 1942, part of Washington State Board for Community and Technical Colleges
- **Suburban** 30-acre campus with easy access to Seattle
- **Endowment** $818,276
- **Coed,** 3,359 undergraduate students, 37% full-time, 34% women, 66% men

Undergraduates 1,249 full-time, 2,110 part-time. Students come from 3 states and territories; 1% are from out of state; 9% Black or African American, non-Hispanic/Latino; 7% Hispanic/Latino; 13% Asian, non-Hispanic/Latino; 0.5% Native Hawaiian or other Pacific Islander, non-Hispanic/Latino; 0.8% American Indian or Alaska Native, non-Hispanic/Latino; 3% Two or more races, non-Hispanic/Latino; 26% Race/ethnicity unknown; 0.1% international; 15% transferred in. *Retention:* 67% of full-time freshmen returned.
Freshmen *Admission:* 196 enrolled.
Faculty *Total:* 244, 36% full-time. *Student/faculty ratio:* 19:1.
Majors Accounting and business/management; anesthesiologist assistant; appliance installation and repair technology; autobody/collision and repair technology; automobile/automotive mechanics technology; building/property maintenance; business automation/technology/data entry; civil drafting and CAD/CADD; computer science; computer systems networking and telecommunications; construction management; culinary arts; dental assisting; drafting and design technology; early childhood education; heating, air conditioning, ventilation and refrigeration maintenance technology; legal administrative assistant/secretary; machine tool technology; massage therapy; medical administrative assistant and medical secretary; medical/clinical assistant; medical insurance coding; musical instrument fabrication and repair; office management; ophthalmic technology; pharmacy technician; registered nursing/registered nurse; surgical technology; surveying technology; welding technology.
Academics *Calendar:* quarters. *Degrees:* certificates, diplomas, associate, and bachelor's. *Special study options:* academic remediation for entering students, adult/continuing education programs, advanced placement credit, cooperative education, distance learning, English as a second language, internships, off-campus study, part-time degree program, services for LD students, summer session for credit.
Library Renton Technical College Library.
Student Life *Housing:* college housing not available. *Campus security:* patrols by security, security system. *Student services:* personal/psychological counseling.
Standardized Tests *Required for some:* ACT ASSET, CLEP, ACT Compass.
Costs (2015–16) *Tuition:* state resident $4161 full-time, $110 per credit hour part-time; nonresident $4568 full-time, $123 per credit hour part-time. Full-time tuition and fees vary according to course load and program. Part-time tuition and fees vary according to course load and program. *Payment plan:* installment.
Applying *Options:* electronic application, early admission. *Application fee:* $30. *Required for some:* essay or personal statement, high school transcript, interview. *Application deadlines:* rolling (freshmen), rolling (out-of-state freshmen), rolling (transfers). *Notification:* continuous (freshmen), continuous (out-of-state freshmen), continuous (transfers).
Freshman Application Contact Linh Bracking, Student Success Advisor, Renton Technical College, 3000 NE 4th Street, Reton, WA 98056. *Phone:* 425-235-2352 Ext. 5543. *E-mail:* lbracking@rtc.edu.
Website: http://www.rtc.edu/.

Seattle Central College
Seattle, Washington

Freshman Application Contact Admissions Office, Seattle Central College, 1701 Broadway, Seattle, WA 98122-2400. *Phone:* 206-587-5450.
Website: http://www.seattlecentral.edu/.

Shoreline Community College
Shoreline, Washington

Freshman Application Contact Shoreline Community College, 16101 Greenwood Avenue North, Shoreline, WA 98133-5696. *Phone:* 206-546-4613.
Website: http://www.shoreline.edu/.

Skagit Valley College
Mount Vernon, Washington

Freshman Application Contact Ms. Karen Marie Bade, Admissions and Recruitment Coordinator, Skagit Valley College, 2405 College Way, Mount Vernon, WA 98273-5899. *Phone:* 360-416-7620.
E-mail: karenmarie.bade@skagit.edu.
Website: http://www.skagit.edu/.

South Puget Sound Community College
Olympia, Washington

Freshman Application Contact Ms. Heidi Dearborn, South Puget Sound Community College, 2011 Mottman Road, SW, Olympia, WA 98512-6292. *Phone:* 360-754-7711 Ext. 5358. *E-mail:* hdearborn@spcc.edu.
Website: http://www.spscc.edu/.

South Seattle College
Seattle, Washington

Director of Admissions Ms. Kim Manderbach, Dean of Student Services/Registration, South Seattle College, 6000 16th Avenue, SW, Seattle, WA 98106-1499. *Phone:* 206-764-5378. *Fax:* 206-764-7947.
E-mail: kimmanderb@sccd.ctc.edu.
Website: http://southseattle.edu/.

Spokane Community College
Spokane, Washington

Freshman Application Contact Ann Hightower-Chavez, Researcher, District Institutional Research, Spokane Community College, Spokane, WA 99217-5399. *Phone:* 509-434-5242. *Toll-free phone:* 800-248-5644. *Fax:* 509-434-5249. *E-mail:* mlee@ccs.spokane.edu.
Website: http://www.scc.spokane.edu/.

Spokane Falls Community College
Spokane, Washington

Freshman Application Contact Admissions Office, Spokane Falls Community College, Admissions MS 3011, 3410 West Fort George Wright Drive, Spokane, WA 99224. *Phone:* 509-533-3401. *Toll-free phone:* 888-509-7944. *Fax:* 509-533-3852.
Website: http://www.spokanefalls.edu/.

Tacoma Community College
Tacoma, Washington

Freshman Application Contact Enrollment Services, Tacoma Community College, 6501 South 19th Street, Tacoma, WA 98466. *Phone:* 253-566-5325. *Fax:* 253-566-6034.
Website: http://www.tacomacc.edu/.

Walla Walla Community College
Walla Walla, Washington

Freshman Application Contact Walla Walla Community College, 500 Tausick Way, Walla Walla, WA 99362-9267. *Phone:* 509-522-2500. *Toll-free phone:* 877-992-9922.
Website: http://www.wwcc.edu/.

Wenatchee Valley College
Wenatchee, Washington

- **State and locally supported** 2-year, founded 1939, part of Washington State Board for Community and Technical Colleges
- **Small-town** 56-acre campus
- **Coed,** 3,218 undergraduate students, 73% full-time, 58% women, 42% men

Undergraduates 2,334 full-time, 884 part-time. 0.8% Black or African American, non-Hispanic/Latino; 36% Hispanic/Latino; 1% Asian, non-Hispanic/Latino; 2% American Indian or Alaska Native, non-Hispanic/Latino; 3% Two or more races, non-Hispanic/Latino; 3% Race/ethnicity unknown; 0.1% international.
Freshmen *Admission:* 475 enrolled.
Majors Accounting; accounting technology and bookkeeping; administrative assistant and secretarial science; agricultural production; athletic training; automobile/automotive mechanics technology; biology/biological sciences; business administration and management; casino management; chemistry; clinical/medical laboratory assistant; clinical/medical laboratory technology; computer systems networking and telecommunications; criminal justice/police science; design and applied arts related; early childhood education; economics; education; electrical/electronics equipment installation and repair; heating, air

conditioning, ventilation and refrigeration maintenance technology; history; industrial electronics technology; kindergarten/preschool education; legal administrative assistant/secretary; liberal arts and sciences/liberal studies; licensed practical/vocational nurse training; mathematics; medical administrative assistant and medical secretary; medical/clinical assistant; music; music teacher education; natural resource recreation and tourism; office management; physical sciences; pre-engineering; radiologic technology/science; registered nursing/registered nurse; sociology; substance abuse/addiction counseling.

Academics *Calendar:* quarters. *Degree:* certificates, diplomas, and associate. *Special study options:* academic remediation for entering students, adult/continuing education programs, advanced placement credit, cooperative education, distance learning, English as a second language, external degree program, independent study, internships, part-time degree program, services for LD students, study abroad, summer session for credit.

Library John Brown Library plus 1 other.

Student Life *Housing Options:* coed. Campus housing is university owned. *Activities and Organizations:* drama/theater group, choral group. *Campus security:* 24-hour patrols, controlled dormitory access.

Athletics *Intercollegiate sports:* baseball M, basketball M(s)/W(s), soccer M/W, softball W(s), volleyball W(s). *Intramural sports:* basketball M/W, racquetball M/W, skiing (cross-country) M/W, skiing (downhill) M/W, tennis M/W, volleyball M/W, weight lifting M/W.

Costs (2016–17) *Tuition:* state resident $3801 full-time; nonresident $4234 full-time. Full-time tuition and fees vary according to course load. *Payment plan:* installment. *Waivers:* senior citizens and employees or children of employees.

Applying *Options:* electronic application, early admission, deferred entrance. *Required for some:* high school transcript. *Application deadline:* rolling (freshmen).

Freshman Application Contact Wenatchee Valley College, 1300 Fifth Street, Wenatchee, WA 98801-1799. *Phone:* 509-682-6835. *Toll-free phone:* 877-982-4968.

Website: http://www.wvc.edu/.

Whatcom Community College
Bellingham, Washington

- **State-supported** 2-year, founded 1970, part of Washington State Board for Community and Technical Colleges
- **Small-town** 52-acre campus with easy access to Vancouver
- **Endowment** $2.0 million
- **Coed**

Undergraduates Students come from 30 other countries; 5% are from out of state.

Academics *Calendar:* quarters. *Degree:* certificates, diplomas, and associate. *Special study options:* academic remediation for entering students, accelerated degree program, adult/continuing education programs, advanced placement credit, cooperative education, distance learning, English as a second language, external degree program, honors programs, independent study, internships, part-time degree program, services for LD students, student-designed majors, study abroad, summer session for credit.

Library Whatcom Community College Library.

Student Life *Campus security:* 24-hour emergency response devices.

Financial Aid Of all full-time matriculated undergraduates who enrolled in 2014, 30 Federal Work-Study jobs (averaging $3780). 80 state and other part-time jobs (averaging $3620).

Applying *Options:* electronic application.

Freshman Application Contact Entry and Advising Center, Whatcom Community College, 237 West Kellogg Road, Bellingham, WA 98226-8003. *Phone:* 360-676-2170. *Fax:* 360-676-2171. *E-mail:* admit@whatcom.ctc.edu. *Website:* http://www.whatcom.ctc.edu/.

Yakima Valley Community College
Yakima, Washington

Freshman Application Contact Ms. Denise Anderson, Registrar and Director for Enrollment Services, Yakima Valley Community College, PO Box 1647, Yakima, WA 98907-1647. *Phone:* 509-574-4702. *Fax:* 509-574-6879. *E-mail:* admis@yvcc.edu. *Website:* http://www.yvcc.edu/.

WEST VIRGINIA

Blue Ridge Community and Technical College
Martinsburg, West Virginia

- **State-supported** 2-year, founded 1974, part of Community and Technical College System of West Virginia
- **Small-town** 46-acre campus
- **Coed,** 5,552 undergraduate students, 20% full-time, 63% women, 37% men

Undergraduates 1,093 full-time, 4,459 part-time. 5% are from out of state; 9% Black or African American, non-Hispanic/Latino; 4% Hispanic/Latino; 0.8% Asian, non-Hispanic/Latino; 0.2% Native Hawaiian or other Pacific Islander, non-Hispanic/Latino; 0.4% American Indian or Alaska Native, non-Hispanic/Latino; 3% Two or more races, non-Hispanic/Latino; 0.1% Race/ethnicity unknown; 4% transferred in. *Retention:* 51% of full-time freshmen returned.

Freshmen *Admission:* 388 enrolled. *Test scores:* SAT critical reading scores over 500: 45%; SAT critical reading scores over 600: 10%.

Faculty *Total:* 180, 39% full-time, 12% with terminal degrees. *Student/faculty ratio:* 24:1.

Majors Accounting; allied health and medical assisting services related; automation engineer technology; baking and pastry arts; business administration and management; business administration, management and operations related; clinical/medical laboratory technology; computer and information systems security; criminal justice/safety; culinary arts; data entry/microcomputer applications related; electrical and electronic engineering technologies related; emergency medical technology (EMT paramedic); general studies; information technology; legal assistant/paralegal; liberal arts and sciences/liberal studies; medical/clinical assistant; multi/interdisciplinary studies related; operations management; physical therapy technology; registered nursing/registered nurse; restaurant, culinary, and catering management; science technologies related; system, networking, and LAN/WAN management.

Academics *Calendar:* semesters. *Degree:* certificates and associate. *Special study options:* academic remediation for entering students, accelerated degree program, adult/continuing education programs, advanced placement credit, double majors, English as a second language, independent study, internships, part-time degree program, services for LD students.

Student Life *Housing:* college housing not available. *Activities and Organizations:* drama/theater group, Student Leadership Academy, Drama Club, Phi Theta Kappa, SkillsUSA, Student Nurses Association, national fraternities. *Campus security:* late-night transport/escort service. *Student services:* personal/psychological counseling.

Standardized Tests *Recommended:* SAT and SAT Subject Tests or ACT (for admission).

Costs (2015–16) *Tuition:* state resident $3696 full-time, $154 per credit hour part-time; nonresident $6456 full-time, $278 per credit hour part-time. Full-time tuition and fees vary according to class time and course load. Part-time tuition and fees vary according to class time and course load. *Payment plan:* installment. *Waivers:* employees or children of employees.

Applying *Options:* deferred entrance. *Application fee:* $25. *Required:* high school transcript. *Required for some:* interview.

Freshman Application Contact Brenda K. Neal, Director of Access, Blue Ridge Community and Technical College, 13650 Apple Harvest Drive, Martinsburg, WV 25403. *Phone:* 304-260-4380 Ext. 2109. *Fax:* 304-260-4376. *E-mail:* bneal@blueridgectc.edu.

Website: http://www.blueridgectc.edu/.

BridgeValley Community and Technical College
Montgomery, West Virginia

Director of Admissions Ms. Lisa Graham, Director of Admissions, BridgeValley Community and Technical College, 619 2nd Avenue, Montgomery, WV 25136. *Phone:* 304-442-3167.

Website: http://www.bridgevalley.edu/.

BridgeValley Community and Technical College
South Charleston, West Virginia

Freshman Application Contact Mr. Bryce Casto, Vice President, Student Affairs, BridgeValley Community and Technical College, 2001 Union Carbide

Drive, South Charleston, WV 25303. *Phone:* 304-766-3140. *Fax:* 304-766-4158. *E-mail:* castosb@wvstateu.edu. *Website:* http://www.bridgevalley.edu/.

Eastern West Virginia Community and Technical College
Moorefield, West Virginia

Freshman Application Contact Learner Support Services, Eastern West Virginia Community and Technical College, HC 65 Box 402, Moorefield, WV 26836. *Phone:* 304-434-8000. *Toll-free phone:* 877-982-2322. *Fax:* 304-434-7000. *E-mail:* askeast@eastern.wvnet.edu. *Website:* http://www.eastern.wvnet.edu/.

Huntington Junior College
Huntington, West Virginia

Director of Admissions Mr. James Garrett, Educational Services Director, Huntington Junior College, 900 Fifth Avenue, Huntington, WV 25701-2004. *Phone:* 304-697-7550. *Toll-free phone:* 800-344-4522. *Website:* http://www.huntingtonjuniorcollege.com/.

Mountain State College
Parkersburg, West Virginia

- **Proprietary** 2-year, founded 1888
- **Small-town** campus
- **Coed,** 176 undergraduate students, 99% full-time, 92% women, 8% men

Undergraduates 174 full-time, 2 part-time. Students come from 2 states and territories; 3% transferred in. *Retention:* 70% of full-time freshmen returned.
Freshmen *Admission:* 28 enrolled.
Faculty *Total:* 11, 64% full-time, 36% with terminal degrees. *Student/faculty ratio:* 17:1.
Majors Accounting and business/management; administrative assistant and secretarial science; computer and information sciences; legal assistant/paralegal; medical/clinical assistant; medical transcription; substance abuse/addiction counseling.
Academics *Calendar:* quarters. *Degree:* diplomas and associate. *Special study options:* distance learning, independent study, internships, part-time degree program, services for LD students.
Library Mountain State College Library.
Student Life *Housing:* college housing not available. *Student services:* personal/psychological counseling.
Standardized Tests *Required:* CPAt (for admission).
Applying *Required:* interview.
Freshman Application Contact Ms. Judith Sutton, President, Mountain State College, 1508 Spring Street, Parkersburg, WV 26101-3993. *Phone:* 304-485-5487. *Toll-free phone:* 800-841-0201. *Fax:* 304-485-3524. *E-mail:* jsutton@msc.edu. *Website:* http://www.msc.edu/.

Mountwest Community & Technical College
Huntington, West Virginia

Freshman Application Contact Dr. Tammy Johnson, Admissions Director, Mountwest Community & Technical College, 1 John Marshall Drive, Huntington, WV 25755. *Phone:* 304-696-3160. *Toll-free phone:* 866-676-5533. *Fax:* 304-696-3135. *E-mail:* admissions@marshall.edu. *Website:* http://www.mctc.edu/.

New River Community and Technical College
Beaver, West Virginia

Director of Admissions Dr. Allen B. Withers, Vice President, Student Services, New River Community and Technical College, 280 University Drive, Beaver, WV 25813. *Phone:* 304-929-5011. *Toll-free phone:* 866-349-3739. *E-mail:* awithers@newriver.edu. *Website:* http://www.newriver.edu/.

Pierpont Community & Technical College
Fairmont, West Virginia

Freshman Application Contact Mr. Steve Leadman, Director of Admissions and Recruiting, Pierpont Community & Technical College, 1201 Locust Avenue, Fairmont, WV 26554. *Phone:* 304-367-4892. *Toll-free phone:* 800-641-5678. *Fax:* 304-367-4789. *Website:* http://www.pierpont.edu/.

Potomac State College of West Virginia University
Keyser, West Virginia

- **State-supported** primarily 2-year, founded 1901, part of West Virginia Higher Education Policy Commission
- **Small-town** 18-acre campus
- **Coed,** 1,475 undergraduate students, 78% full-time, 54% women, 46% men

Undergraduates 1,156 full-time, 319 part-time. Students come from 24 states and territories; 2 other countries; 37% are from out of state; 21% Black or African American, non-Hispanic/Latino; 3% Hispanic/Latino; 0.2% Asian, non-Hispanic/Latino; 0.2% Native Hawaiian or other Pacific Islander, non-Hispanic/Latino; 0.5% American Indian or Alaska Native, non-Hispanic/Latino; 4% Two or more races, non-Hispanic/Latino; 1% Race/ethnicity unknown; 0.6% international; 3% transferred in; 52% live on campus. *Retention:* 44% of full-time freshmen returned.
Freshmen *Admission:* 2,582 applied, 1,241 admitted, 588 enrolled. *Average high school GPA:* 2.86. *Test scores:* SAT critical reading scores over 500: 15%; SAT math scores over 500: 15%; ACT scores over 18: 60%; SAT critical reading scores over 600: 1%; SAT math scores over 600: 2%; ACT scores over 24: 19%; ACT scores over 30: 1%.
Faculty *Total:* 85, 53% full-time, 16% with terminal degrees. *Student/faculty ratio:* 22:1.
Majors Administrative assistant and secretarial science; agricultural and extension education; agricultural business and management; agriculture; agriculture and agriculture operations related; agronomy and crop science; animal sciences; biology/biological sciences; business administration and management; business automation/technology/data entry; chemistry; civil engineering; communication; computer and information sciences; criminal justice/safety; criminology; data entry/microcomputer applications related; early childhood education; economics; electrical and electronics engineering; elementary education; English; forensic science and technology; forest resources production and management; geological and earth sciences/geosciences related; geology/earth science; history; horse husbandry/equine science and management; horticultural science; hospitality administration; journalism; liberal arts and sciences/liberal studies; mathematics; mechanical engineering; medical/clinical assistant; modern languages; parks, recreation and leisure facilities management; physical education teaching and coaching; physics; political science and government; pre-dentistry studies; pre-law studies; premedical studies; prenursing studies; pre-occupational therapy; pre-pharmacy studies; pre-physical therapy; pre-veterinary studies; psychology; secondary education; social work; sociology; wildlife, fish and wildlands science and management; wood science and wood products/pulp and paper technology.
Academics *Calendar:* semesters. *Degrees:* associate and bachelor's. *Special study options:* academic remediation for entering students, adult/continuing education programs, advanced placement credit, cooperative education, distance learning, double majors, honors programs, independent study, internships, part-time degree program, services for LD students, study abroad, summer session for credit.
Library Mary F. Shipper Library.
Student Life *Housing:* on-campus residence required through sophomore year. *Options:* coed. Campus housing is university owned. Freshman applicants given priority for college housing. *Activities and Organizations:* drama/theater group, student-run newspaper, choral group, Agriculture and Forestry Club, Black Student Alliance, Gamers and Geeks Club, Campus and Community Ministries. *Campus security:* 24-hour patrols, late-night transport/escort service, controlled dormitory access. *Student services:* health clinic, personal/psychological counseling.
Athletics Member NJCAA. *Intercollegiate sports:* baseball M(s), basketball M(s)/W(s), cross-country running M(s)/W(s), lacrosse M(s)/W(s), soccer M/W, softball W(s), volleyball W(s). *Intramural sports:* basketball M/W, football M/W, soccer M/W, softball M/W, table tennis M/W, ultimate Frisbee M/W, volleyball M/W.
Standardized Tests *Recommended:* SAT or ACT (for admission).
Costs (2015–16) *Tuition:* state resident $3864 full-time, $161 per credit hour part-time; nonresident $10,080 full-time, $420 per credit hour part-time. Full-

time tuition and fees vary according to course load and degree level. Part-time tuition and fees vary according to course load and degree level. *Room and board:* $8476; room only: $4464. Room and board charges vary according to board plan and housing facility. *Payment plan:* installment. *Waivers:* senior citizens and employees or children of employees.
Financial Aid Of all full-time matriculated undergraduates who enrolled in 2014, 70 Federal Work-Study jobs (averaging $1300).
Applying *Options:* electronic application. *Required:* high school transcript. *Application deadlines:* rolling (freshmen), rolling (transfers).
Freshman Application Contact Ms. Beth Little, Director of Enrollment Services, Potomac State College of West Virginia University, 75 Arnold Street, Keyser, WV 26726. *Phone:* 304-788-6820. *Toll-free phone:* 800-262-7332 Ext. 6820. *Fax:* 304-788-6939. *E-mail:* go2psc@mail.wvu.edu.
Website: http://www.potomacstatecollege.edu/.

Southern West Virginia Community and Technical College
Mount Gay, West Virginia

Freshman Application Contact Mr. Roy Simmons, Registrar, Southern West Virginia Community and Technical College, PO Box 2900, Mt. Gay, WV 25637. *Phone:* 304-792-7160 Ext. 120. *Fax:* 304-792-7096.
E-mail: admissions@southern.wvnet.edu.
Website: http://southernwv.edu/.

Valley College
Beckley, West Virginia

Director of Admissions Kerri Cline, Admissions Director, Valley College, 120 New River Town Center, Beckley, WV 25801. *Phone:* 304-252-9547. *Toll-free phone:* 888-53LEARN. *Fax:* 304-252-1694.
Website: http://www.valley.edu/.

West Virginia Business College
Nutter Fort, West Virginia

Director of Admissions Robert Wright, Campus Director, West Virginia Business College, 116 Pennsylvania Avenue, Nutter Fort, WV 26301.
Phone: 304-624-7695. *E-mail:* info@wvbc.edu.
Website: http://www.wvbc.edu/.

West Virginia Business College
Wheeling, West Virginia

Freshman Application Contact Ms. Karen D. Shaw, Director, West Virginia Business College, 1052 Main Street, Wheeling, WV 26003. *Phone:* 304-232-0361. *Fax:* 304-232-0363. *E-mail:* wvbcwheeling@stratuswave.net.
Website: http://www.wvbc.edu/.

West Virginia Junior College–Bridgeport
Bridgeport, West Virginia

- **Proprietary** 2-year, founded 1922
- **Small-town** 3-acre campus with easy access to Pittsburgh
- **Coed**

Undergraduates 389 full-time. Students come from 4 states and territories; 0.5% Black or African American, non-Hispanic/Latino; 10% transferred in. *Retention:* 80% of full-time freshmen returned.
Faculty *Student/faculty ratio:* 15:1.
Academics *Calendar:* quarters. *Degree:* diplomas and associate. *Special study options:* cooperative education, distance learning, independent study, internships, services for LD students, summer session for credit.
Library WVJC Resource Center plus 1 other.
Student Life *Campus security:* 24-hour emergency response devices.
Standardized Tests *Recommended:* SAT or ACT (for admission).
Financial Aid Of all full-time matriculated undergraduates who enrolled in 2014, 10 Federal Work-Study jobs.
Applying *Options:* electronic application. *Application fee:* $25. *Required:* essay or personal statement, minimum 2.5 GPA, interview, Applicants are required to meet with an Admissions Representative. *Required for some:* 1 letter of recommendation. *Recommended:* high school transcript.
Freshman Application Contact Mr. Adam Pratt, High School Admissions Coordinator, West Virginia Junior College–Bridgeport, 176 Thompson Drive, Bridgeport, WV 26330. *Phone:* 304-842-4007 Ext. 112. *Toll-free phone:* 800-470-5627. *Fax:* 304-842-8191. *E-mail:* apratt@wvjcinfo.net.
Website: http://www.wvjc.edu/.

West Virginia Junior College–Charleston
Charleston, West Virginia

Freshman Application Contact West Virginia Junior College–Charleston, 1000 Virginia Street East, Charleston, WV 25301-2817. *Phone:* 304-345-2820. *Toll-free phone:* 800-924-5208.
Website: http://www.wvjc.edu/.

West Virginia Junior College–Morgantown
Morgantown, West Virginia

Freshman Application Contact Admissions Office, West Virginia Junior College–Morgantown, 148 Willey Street, Morgantown, WV 26505-5521. *Phone:* 304-296-8282.
Website: http://www.wvjcmorgantown.edu/.

West Virginia Northern Community College
Wheeling, West Virginia

Freshman Application Contact Mrs. Janet Fike, Vice President of Student Services, West Virginia Northern Community College, 1704 Market Street, Wheeling, WV 26003. *Phone:* 304-214-8837.
E-mail: jfike@northern.wvnet.edu.
Website: http://www.wvncc.edu/.

West Virginia University at Parkersburg
Parkersburg, West Virginia

Freshman Application Contact Christine Post, Associate Dean of Enrollment Management, West Virginia University at Parkersburg, 300 Campus Drive, Parkersburg, WV 26104. *Phone:* 304-424-8223 Ext. 223. *Toll-free phone:* 800-WVA-WVUP. *Fax:* 304-424-8332.
E-mail: christine.post@mail.wvu.edu.
Website: http://www.wvup.edu/.

WISCONSIN

Blackhawk Technical College
Janesville, Wisconsin

- **District-supported** 2-year, founded 1968, part of Wisconsin Technical College System
- **Small-town** 84-acre campus
- **Coed,** 2,249 undergraduate students, 42% full-time, 58% women, 42% men

Undergraduates 947 full-time, 1,302 part-time. Students come from 3 states and territories; 1% are from out of state. *Retention:* 54% of full-time freshmen returned.
Freshmen *Admission:* 312 enrolled.
Faculty *Total:* 367, 26% full-time, 2% with terminal degrees. *Student/faculty ratio:* 8:1.
Majors Accounting; administrative assistant and secretarial science; business administration and management; clinical/medical laboratory technology; computer systems networking and telecommunications; criminal justice/police science; culinary arts; diagnostic medical sonography and ultrasound technology; early childhood education; electromechanical technology; fire science/firefighting; human resources management; interdisciplinary studies; legal administrative assistant/secretary; marketing/marketing management; medical administrative assistant and medical secretary; physical therapy technology; radiologist assistant; registered nursing/registered nurse; web page, digital/multimedia and information resources design.
Academics *Calendar:* semesters. *Degree:* certificates, diplomas, and associate. *Special study options:* academic remediation for entering students, accelerated degree program, adult/continuing education programs, advanced placement credit, cooperative education, distance learning, English as a second language, independent study, internships, part-time degree program, services for LD students, student-designed majors, summer session for credit.
Library Blackhawk Technical College Library. *Books:* 12,866 (physical), 49,999 (digital/electronic); *Serial titles:* 115 (physical), 13 (digital/electronic); *Databases:* 60. Weekly public service hours: 56.
Student Life *Housing:* college housing not available. *Activities and Organizations:* student-run newspaper, Student Government Association,

Public Safety Association, Epicurean Club, Veterans Club, Phi Theta Kappa Honor Society. *Campus security:* student patrols.

Costs (2015–16) *Tuition:* state resident $3852 full-time, $128 per credit hour part-time; nonresident $5778 full-time, $193 per credit hour part-time. Full-time tuition and fees vary according to course load. Part-time tuition and fees vary according to course load. *Required fees:* $307 full-time, $6 per credit hour part-time. *Payment plan:* deferred payment. *Waivers:* senior citizens.

Financial Aid Of all full-time matriculated undergraduates who enrolled in 2014, 33 Federal Work-Study jobs (averaging $1150).

Applying *Options:* electronic application. *Application fee:* $30. *Required:* high school transcript. *Application deadlines:* rolling (freshmen), rolling (transfers). *Notification:* continuous (freshmen), continuous (transfers).

Freshman Application Contact Blackhawk Technical College, 6004 South County Road G, Janesville, WI 53546-9458. *Phone:* 608-757-7713. *Website:* http://www.blackhawk.edu/.

Bryant & Stratton College–Bayshore Campus

Glendale, Wisconsin

Admissions Office Contact Bryant & Stratton College–Bayshore Campus, 500 West Silver Spring Drive, Bayshore Town Center, Suite K340, Glendale, WI 53217.

Website: http://www.bryantstratton.edu/.

Bryant & Stratton College–Milwaukee Campus

Milwaukee, Wisconsin

Freshman Application Contact Mr. Dan Basile, Director of Admissions, Bryant & Stratton College–Milwaukee Campus, 310 West Wisconsin Avenue, Suite 500 East, Milwaukee, WI 53203-2214. *Phone:* 414-276-5200.

Website: http://www.bryantstratton.edu/.

Chippewa Valley Technical College

Eau Claire, Wisconsin

- **District-supported** 2-year, founded 1912, part of Wisconsin Technical College System
- **Suburban** 255-acre campus
- **Coed,** 6,017 undergraduate students, 34% full-time, 55% women, 45% men

Undergraduates 2,037 full-time, 3,980 part-time. 1% are from out of state; 1% Black or African American, non-Hispanic/Latino; 1% Hispanic/Latino; 3% Asian, non-Hispanic/Latino; 0.1% Native Hawaiian or other Pacific Islander, non-Hispanic/Latino; 0.8% American Indian or Alaska Native, non-Hispanic/Latino; 2% Two or more races, non-Hispanic/Latino; 9% Race/ethnicity unknown. *Retention:* 63% of full-time freshmen returned.

Freshmen *Admission:* 878 enrolled.

Faculty *Total:* 434, 51% full-time, 6% with terminal degrees.

Majors Accounting; administrative assistant and secretarial science; agricultural business and management related; applied horticulture/horticultural business services related; business administration and management; civil engineering technology; clinical/medical laboratory technology; computer programming; computer systems networking and telecommunications; criminal justice/police science; dental hygiene; diagnostic medical sonography and ultrasound technology; early childhood education; electromechanical technology; emergency medical technology (EMT paramedic); health information/medical records technology; heating, ventilation, air conditioning and refrigeration engineering technology; human resources management; industrial mechanics and maintenance technology; legal assistant/paralegal; liberal arts and sciences/liberal studies; manufacturing engineering technology; marketing/marketing management; medical radiologic technology; multi/interdisciplinary studies related; nanotechnology; operations management; physical therapy technology; registered nursing/registered nurse; respiratory care therapy; substance abuse/addiction counseling.

Academics *Calendar:* semesters. *Degree:* certificates, diplomas, and associate. *Special study options:* academic remediation for entering students, accelerated degree program, adult/continuing education programs, advanced placement credit, cooperative education, distance learning, double majors, English as a second language, honors programs, independent study, internships, part-time degree program, services for LD students, student-designed majors, summer session for credit.

Library The Learning Center. *Books:* 12,870 (physical), 310,200 (digital/electronic); *Serial titles:* 161 (physical), 17,987 (digital/electronic);

Databases: 130. Weekly public service hours: 66; students can reserve study rooms.

Student Life *Housing:* college housing not available. *Activities and Organizations:* Phi Theta Kappa, Nursing Club, Welding Club, Imagers, Cosmetology Club. *Campus security:* 24-hour emergency response devices, late-night transport/escort service, security cameras. *Student services:* health clinic, personal/psychological counseling.

Standardized Tests *Required:* ACCUPLACER (for admission). *Recommended:* ACT (for admission).

Costs (2015–16) *Tuition:* state resident $3852 full-time, $128 per credit part-time; nonresident $5778 full-time, $193 per credit part-time. Full-time tuition and fees vary according to course load and reciprocity agreements. Part-time tuition and fees vary according to course load and reciprocity agreements. *Required fees:* $307 full-time, $307 per year part-time. *Payment plans:* installment, deferred payment. *Waivers:* senior citizens.

Financial Aid Of all full-time matriculated undergraduates who enrolled in 2014, 218 Federal Work-Study jobs (averaging $875).

Applying *Options:* electronic application, early admission, deferred entrance. *Application fee:* $30. *Required for some:* high school transcript. *Application deadlines:* rolling (freshmen), rolling (transfers). *Notification:* continuous (freshmen), continuous (transfers).

Freshman Application Contact Admissions Office, Chippewa Valley Technical College, 620 W. Clairemont Avenue, Eau Claire, WI 54701. *Phone:* 715-833-6200. *Toll-free phone:* 800-547-2882. *Fax:* 715-833-6470.

E-mail: infocenter@cvtc.edu.

Website: http://www.cvtc.edu/.

College of Menominee Nation

Keshena, Wisconsin

Director of Admissions Tessa James, Admissions Coordinator, College of Menominee Nation, PO Box 1179, Keshena, WI 54135. *Phone:* 715-799-5600 Ext. 3053. *Toll-free phone:* 800-567-2344. *E-mail:* tjames@menominee.edu. *Website:* http://www.menominee.edu/.

Fox Valley Technical College

Appleton, Wisconsin

- **State and locally supported** 2-year, founded 1967, part of Wisconsin Technical College System
- **Suburban** 100-acre campus
- **Endowment** $3.3 million
- **Coed,** 10,894 undergraduate students, 23% full-time, 48% women, 52% men

Undergraduates 2,545 full-time, 8,349 part-time. Students come from 14 states and territories; 7 other countries; 0.8% are from out of state; 3% Black or African American, non-Hispanic/Latino; 4% Hispanic/Latino; 5% Asian, non-Hispanic/Latino; 0.1% Native Hawaiian or other Pacific Islander, non-Hispanic/Latino; 1% American Indian or Alaska Native, non-Hispanic/Latino; 0.5% Two or more races, non-Hispanic/Latino; 9% Race/ethnicity unknown; 0.1% international.

Freshmen *Admission:* 1,526 applied, 1,159 admitted, 940 enrolled.

Faculty *Total:* 875, 36% full-time. *Student/faculty ratio:* 11:1.

Majors Accounting; administrative assistant and secretarial science; agricultural/farm supplies retailing and wholesaling; agricultural mechanization; airline pilot and flight crew; autobody/collision and repair technology; automation engineer technology; automobile/automotive mechanics technology; avionics maintenance technology; banking and financial support services; biology/biotechnology laboratory technician; building/construction site management; business administration and management; computer programming; computer support specialist; computer systems networking and telecommunications; court reporting; criminal justice/police science; culinary arts; dental hygiene; diesel mechanics technology; early childhood education; electrical and electronic engineering technologies related; electrical, electronic and communications engineering technology; electromechanical technology; emergency medical technology (EMT paramedic); energy management and systems technology; fire protection related; fire science/firefighting; forensic science and technology; graphic communications; health information/medical records technology; homeland security related; hospitality administration; human resources management; industrial safety technology; interior design; legal assistant/paralegal; logistics, materials, and supply chain management; manufacturing engineering technology; marketing/marketing management; mechanical drafting and CAD/CADD; medical office management; meeting and event planning; multi/interdisciplinary studies related; natural resources/conservation; occupational therapist assistant; office management; professional, technical, business, and scientific writing; radio, television, and digital communication related; registered nursing/registered nurse; substance abuse/addiction counseling; web/multimedia management and webmaster; welding technology; wildland/forest firefighting and investigation.

Academics *Calendar:* semesters. *Degree:* certificates, diplomas, and associate. *Special study options:* academic remediation for entering students, accelerated degree program, advanced placement credit, cooperative education, distance learning, double majors, English as a second language, independent study, internships, off-campus study, part-time degree program, services for LD students, student-designed majors, study abroad, summer session for credit.

Library Student Success Center Library. *Books:* 7,873 (physical), 132,919 (digital/electronic); *Serial titles:* 50 (physical), 45,000 (digital/electronic); *Databases:* 85. Weekly public service hours: 65; students can reserve study rooms.

Student Life *Housing:* college housing not available. *Activities and Organizations:* student-run newspaper, Student Government Association, Phi Theta Kappa, Culinary Arts Club, Machine Tool Club, Post Secondary Agribusiness Club. *Campus security:* 24-hour emergency response devices, late-night transport/escort service, trained security personnel patrol during hours of operation. *Student services:* health clinic, personal/psychological counseling.

Athletics *Intercollegiate sports:* basketball M/W. *Intramural sports:* table tennis M/W.

Costs (2015–16) *Tuition:* state resident $3852 full-time, $128 per credit part-time; nonresident $5778 full-time, $193 per credit part-time. *Required fees:* $521 full-time, $17 per credit part-time. *Payment plan:* installment.

Applying *Options:* electronic application, early admission, deferred entrance. *Application fee:* $30. *Required:* high school transcript. *Application deadlines:* rolling (freshmen), rolling (transfers).

Freshman Application Contact Admissions Center, Fox Valley Technical College, 1825 North Bluemound Drive, PO Box 2277, Appleton, WI 54912-2277. *Phone:* 920-735-5643. *Toll-free phone:* 800-735-3882. *Fax:* 920-735-2582.

Website: http://www.fvtc.edu/.

Gateway Technical College
Kenosha, Wisconsin

- **State and locally supported** 2-year, founded 1911, part of Wisconsin Technical College System
- **Urban** 10-acre campus with easy access to Chicago, Milwaukee
- **Endowment** $3.4 million
- **Coed**, 8,740 undergraduate students, 17% full-time, 57% women, 43% men

Undergraduates 1,449 full-time, 7,291 part-time. Students come from 6 states and territories; 2% are from out of state; 11% Black or African American, non-Hispanic/Latino; 14% Hispanic/Latino; 1% Asian, non-Hispanic/Latino; 0.5% American Indian or Alaska Native, non-Hispanic/Latino; 3% Two or more races, non-Hispanic/Latino; 6% Race/ethnicity unknown; 9% transferred in. *Retention:* 62% of full-time freshmen returned.

Freshmen *Admission:* 1,296 applied, 1,276 admitted, 1,236 enrolled.

Faculty *Total:* 719, 34% full-time. *Student/faculty ratio:* 10:1.

Majors Accounting; administrative assistant and secretarial science; airline pilot and flight crew; applied horticulture/horticulture operations; architectural engineering technology; automation engineer technology; automobile/automotive mechanics technology; business administration and management; computer programming; computer support specialist; computer systems networking and telecommunications; criminal justice/police science; culinary arts; diesel mechanics technology; early childhood education; electrical, electronic and communications engineering technology; electromechanical technology; emergency medical technology (EMT paramedic); graphic design; health information/medical records technology; heating, air conditioning, ventilation and refrigeration maintenance technology; hospitality administration; industrial mechanics and maintenance technology; interdisciplinary studies; interior design; marketing/marketing management; mechanical drafting and CAD/CADD; physical therapy technology; professional, technical, business, and scientific writing; psychiatric/mental health services technology; registered nursing/registered nurse; surgical technology; surveying technology; teacher assistant/aide; transportation and highway engineering; veterinary/animal health technology; water resources engineering; web/multimedia management and webmaster.

Academics *Calendar:* semesters. *Degree:* certificates, diplomas, and associate. *Special study options:* academic remediation for entering students, advanced placement credit, cooperative education, distance learning, double majors, English as a second language, independent study, internships, off-campus study, part-time degree program, services for LD students, student-designed majors, summer session for credit.

Library Library/Learning Resources Center plus 3 others. *Books:* 22,018 (physical), 4,369 (digital/electronic); *Serial titles:* 135 (physical); *Databases:* 40. Weekly public service hours: 59.

Student Life *Housing:* college housing not available. *Activities and Organizations:* student-run newspaper, International Club, United Student Government, Outdoor Adventure Club, Team EXCEED. *Campus security:* 24-hour emergency response devices, late-night transport/escort service, patrols by trained security when open, locked/alarmed when closed. *Student services:* personal/psychological counseling.

Costs (2016–17) *Tuition:* state resident $4002 full-time; nonresident $5778 full-time. Full-time tuition and fees vary according to course level, course load, program, and reciprocity agreements. Part-time tuition and fees vary according to course level, course load, program, and reciprocity agreements. *Required fees:* $338 full-time. *Payment plan:* installment. *Waivers:* senior citizens and employees or children of employees.

Applying *Options:* electronic application, early admission, deferred entrance. *Application fee:* $30. *Required:* high school transcript. *Required for some:* interview. *Application deadlines:* rolling (freshmen), rolling (out-of-state freshmen), rolling (transfers). *Notification:* continuous (freshmen), continuous (out-of-state freshmen), continuous (transfers).

Freshman Application Contact Admissions, Gateway Technical College, 3520 30th Avenue, Kenosha, WI 53144-1690. *Phone:* 262-564-2300. *Fax:* 262-564-2301. *E-mail:* admissions@gtc.edu.

Website: http://www.gtc.edu/.

ITT Technical Institute
Greenfield, Wisconsin

Freshman Application Contact Director of Recruitment, ITT Technical Institute, 6300 West Layton Avenue, Greenfield, WI 53220-4612. *Phone:* 414-282-9494.

Website: http://www.itt-tech.edu/.

Lac Courte Oreilles Ojibwa Community College
Hayward, Wisconsin

Freshman Application Contact Ms. Annette Wiggins, Registrar, Lac Courte Oreilles Ojibwa Community College, 13466 West Trepania Road, Hayward, WI 54843-2181. *Phone:* 715-634-4790 Ext. 104. *Toll-free phone:* 888-526-6221.

Website: http://www.lco.edu/.

Lakeshore Technical College
Cleveland, Wisconsin

Freshman Application Contact Lakeshore Technical College, 1290 North Avenue, Cleveland, WI 53015. *Phone:* 920-693-1339. *Toll-free phone:* 888-GO TO LTC. *Fax:* 920-693-3561.

Website: http://www.gotoltc.com/.

Madison Area Technical College
Madison, Wisconsin

Director of Admissions Ms. Maureen Menendez, Interim Admissions Administrator, Madison Area Technical College, 1701 Wright Street, Madison, WI 53704. *Phone:* 608-246-6212. *Toll-free phone:* 800-322-6282.

Website: http://madisoncollege.edu/.

Madison Media Institute
Madison, Wisconsin

Freshman Application Contact Mr. Chris K. Hutchings, President/Director, Madison Media Institute, 2702 Agriculture Drive, Madison, WI 53718. *Phone:* 608-237-8301. *Toll-free phone:* 800-236-4997.

Website: http://www.mediainstitute.edu/.

Mid-State Technical College
Wisconsin Rapids, Wisconsin

Freshman Application Contact Ms. Carole Prochnow, Admissions Assistant, Mid-State Technical College, 500 32nd Street North, Wisconsin Rapids, WI 54494-5599. *Phone:* 715-422-5444.

Website: http://www.mstc.edu/.

Milwaukee Area Technical College

Milwaukee, Wisconsin

Freshman Application Contact Sarah Adams, Director, Enrollment Services, Milwaukee Area Technical College, 700 West State Street, Milwaukee, WI 53233-1443. *Phone:* 414-297-6595. *Fax:* 414-297-7800.
E-mail: adamss4@matc.edu.
Website: http://www.matc.edu/.

Milwaukee Career College

Milwaukee, Wisconsin

Admissions Office Contact Milwaukee Career College, 3077 N. Mayfair Road, Suite 300, Milwaukee, WI 53222.
Website: http://www.mkecc.edu/.

Moraine Park Technical College

Fond du Lac, Wisconsin

- **District-supported** 2-year, founded 1967, part of Wisconsin Technical College System
- **Small-town** 40-acre campus with easy access to Milwaukee
- **Coed**

Academics *Calendar:* semesters. *Degree:* certificates, diplomas, and associate. *Special study options:* academic remediation for entering students, accelerated degree program, adult/continuing education programs, advanced placement credit, distance learning, double majors, English as a second language, external degree program, independent study, internships, part-time degree program, services for LD students, student-designed majors, study abroad, summer session for credit.
Library Moraine Park Technical College Library/Learning Resource Center.
Student Life *Campus security:* late-night transport/escort service, Campus Security Services between 5-10 pm M-Th during the academic year. Services include night patrols.
Standardized Tests *Required:* ACT, ACCUPLACER OR ACT Compass (for admission). *Required for some:* ACT (for admission).
Costs (2015–16) *One-time required fee:* $30. *Tuition:* state resident $3947 full-time, $128 per credit hour part-time; nonresident $5920 full-time, $193 per credit hour part-time. Full-time tuition and fees vary according to program. Part-time tuition and fees vary according to program. *Required fees:* $316 full-time, $10 per credit hour part-time. *Payment plans:* installment, deferred payment.
Applying *Required:* high school transcript, interview, placement test required for all; criminal background ground check required for some. *Required for some:* interview.
Freshman Application Contact Karen Jarvis, Student Services, Moraine Park Technical College, 235 North National Avenue, Fond du Lac, WI 54935. *Phone:* 920-924-3200. *Toll-free phone:* 800-472-4554. *Fax:* 920-924-3421. *E-mail:* kjarvis@morainepark.edu.
Website: http://www.morainepark.edu/.

Nicolet Area Technical College

Rhinelander, Wisconsin

Freshman Application Contact Ms. Susan Kordula, Director of Admissions, Nicolet Area Technical College, PO Box 518, Rhinelander, WI 54501. *Phone:* 715-365-4451. *Toll-free phone:* 800-544-3039.
E-mail: inquire@nicoletcollege.edu.
Website: http://www.nicoletcollege.edu/.

Northcentral Technical College

Wausau, Wisconsin

- **District-supported** 2-year, founded 1912, part of Wisconsin Technical College System
- **Rural** 96-acre campus
- **Coed,** 4,513 undergraduate students, 33% full-time, 61% women, 39% men

Undergraduates 1,486 full-time, 3,027 part-time. 1% Black or African American, non-Hispanic/Latino; 0.4% Hispanic/Latino; 6% Asian, non-Hispanic/Latino; 0.2% Native Hawaiian or other Pacific Islander, non-Hispanic/Latino; 2% American Indian or Alaska Native, non-Hispanic/Latino; 27% Race/ethnicity unknown.
Freshmen *Admission:* 772 enrolled.
Faculty *Student/faculty ratio:* 23:1.
Majors Accounting; administrative assistant and secretarial science; agribusiness; agronomy and crop science; architectural engineering technology; automobile/automotive mechanics technology; business

administration and management; cinematography and film/video production; clinical/medical laboratory technology; computer and information sciences and support services related; computer systems analysis; computer systems networking and telecommunications; criminal justice/police science; culinary arts; dental hygiene; diesel mechanics technology; early childhood education; electromechanical technology; emergency medical technology (EMT paramedic); entrepreneurship; furniture design and manufacturing; general studies; graphic communications; manufacturing engineering technology; marketing/marketing management; mechanical drafting and CAD/CADD; medical insurance/medical billing; medical radiologic technology; mental and social health services and allied professions related; merchandising, sales, and marketing operations related (general); multi/interdisciplinary studies related; operations management; registered nursing/registered nurse; sign language interpretation and translation; substance abuse/addiction counseling; teacher assistant/aide.
Academics *Calendar:* semesters. *Degree:* certificates, diplomas, and associate. *Special study options:* academic remediation for entering students, accelerated degree program, adult/continuing education programs, advanced placement credit, cooperative education, distance learning, double majors, English as a second language, independent study, internships, off-campus study, part-time degree program, services for LD students, student-designed majors, summer session for credit.
Library Northcentral Technical College, Wausau Campus Library.
Student Life *Housing Options:* Campus housing is provided by a third party. *Campus security:* 24-hour emergency response devices, student patrols, late-night transport/escort service. *Student services:* personal/psychological counseling, women's center.
Athletics *Intramural sports:* basketball M/W, field hockey M/W, football M/W, soccer M/W, softball M/W, volleyball M/W.
Costs (2015–16) *Tuition:* state resident $4233 full-time; nonresident $6264 full-time. Full-time tuition and fees vary according to course level, course load, and program. Part-time tuition and fees vary according to course level, course load, and program. *Payment plans:* installment, deferred payment. *Waivers:* senior citizens.
Financial Aid Of all full-time matriculated undergraduates who enrolled in 2014, 366 Federal Work-Study jobs (averaging $2000).
Applying *Options:* electronic application, early admission, deferred entrance. *Application fee:* $30. *Required:* high school transcript. *Required for some:* interview. *Application deadlines:* rolling (freshmen), rolling (transfers). *Notification:* continuous (freshmen), continuous (transfers).
Freshman Application Contact Northcentral Technical College, 1000 West Campus Drive, Wausau, WI 54401-1899. *Phone:* 715-675-3331.
Website: http://www.ntc.edu/.

Northeast Wisconsin Technical College

Green Bay, Wisconsin

Freshman Application Contact Christine Lemerande, Program Enrollment Supervisor, Northeast Wisconsin Technical College, 2740 W Mason Street, PO Box 19042, Green Bay, WI 54307-9042. *Phone:* 920-498-5444. *Toll-free phone:* 888-385-6982. *Fax:* 920-498-6882.
Website: http://www.nwtc.edu/.

Southwest Wisconsin Technical College

Fennimore, Wisconsin

Freshman Application Contact Student Services, Southwest Wisconsin Technical College, 1800 Bronson Boulevard, Fennimore, WI 53809-9778. *Phone:* 608-822-2354. *Toll-free phone:* 800-362-3322. *Fax:* 608-822-6019. *E-mail:* student-services@swtc.edu.
Website: http://www.swtc.edu/.

University of Wisconsin–Baraboo/Sauk County

Baraboo, Wisconsin

Freshman Application Contact Ms. Jan Gerlach, Assistant Director of Student Services, University of Wisconsin–Baraboo/Sauk County, Baraboo, WI 53913-1015. *Phone:* 608-355-5270. *E-mail:* booinfo@uwc.edu.
Website: http://www.baraboo.uwc.edu/.

University of Wisconsin–Barron County

Rice Lake, Wisconsin

Freshman Application Contact Assistant Dean for Student Services, University of Wisconsin–Barron County, 1800 College Drive, Rice Lake, WI 54868-2497. *Phone:* 715-234-8024. *Fax:* 715-234-8024.
Website: http://www.barron.uwc.edu/.

University of Wisconsin–Fond du Lac
Fond du Lac, Wisconsin

- **State-supported** 2-year, founded 1968, part of University of Wisconsin System
- **Small-town** 182-acre campus with easy access to Milwaukee
- **Coed**

Undergraduates Students come from 3 states and territories; 1% are from out of state. *Retention:* 58% of full-time freshmen returned.
Faculty *Student/faculty ratio:* 18:1.
Academics *Calendar:* semesters. *Degree:* associate. *Special study options:* academic remediation for entering students, accelerated degree program, adult/continuing education programs, advanced placement credit, cooperative education, distance learning, independent study, off-campus study, part-time degree program, services for LD students, study abroad, summer session for credit.
Student Life *Campus security:* 24-hour emergency response devices.
Athletics Member NJCAA.
Standardized Tests *Required:* SAT or ACT (for admission).
Costs (2015–16) *One-time required fee:* $135. *Tuition:* state resident $5200 full-time; nonresident $11,734 full-time. Full-time tuition and fees vary according to course load and reciprocity agreements. Part-time tuition and fees vary according to course load and reciprocity agreements. *Required fees:* $221 full-time.
Applying *Options:* electronic application. *Required:* high school transcript.
Freshman Application Contact University of Wisconsin–Fond du Lac, 400 University Drive, Fond du Lac, WI 54935. *Phone:* 920-929-1122.
Website: http://www.fdl.uwc.edu/.

University of Wisconsin–Fox Valley
Menasha, Wisconsin

- **State-supported** 2-year, founded 1933, part of University of Wisconsin System
- **Urban** 33-acre campus
- **Coed**

Undergraduates 1,037 full-time, 760 part-time. Students come from 3 states and territories; 4 other countries; 1% are from out of state. *Retention:* 60% of full-time freshmen returned.
Faculty *Student/faculty ratio:* 20:1.
Academics *Calendar:* semesters. *Degree:* certificates and associate. *Special study options:* academic remediation for entering students, accelerated degree program, adult/continuing education programs, advanced placement credit, cooperative education, distance learning, honors programs, independent study, internships, off-campus study, part-time degree program, services for LD students, study abroad, summer session for credit.
Library UW Fox Library.
Student Life *Campus security:* 24-hour emergency response devices, late-night transport/escort service.
Athletics Member NJCAA.
Standardized Tests *Required:* ACT (for admission).
Costs (2015–16) *Tuition:* state resident $5019 full-time; nonresident $12,002 full-time. Full-time tuition and fees vary according to course load. Part-time tuition and fees vary according to course load.
Applying *Required:* high school transcript. *Required for some:* interview. *Recommended:* essay or personal statement.
Freshman Application Contact University of Wisconsin–Fox Valley, 1478 Midway Road, Menasha, WI 54952. *Phone:* 920-832-2620.
Website: http://www.uwfox.uwc.edu/.

University of Wisconsin–Manitowoc
Manitowoc, Wisconsin

Freshman Application Contact Dr. Christopher Lewis, Assistant Campus Dean for Student Services, University of Wisconsin–Manitowoc, 705 Viebahn Street, Manitowoc, WI 54220-6699. *Phone:* 920-683-4707. *Fax:* 920-683-4776. *E-mail:* christopher.lewis@uwc.edu.
Website: http://www.manitowoc.uwc.edu/.

University of Wisconsin–Marathon County
Wausau, Wisconsin

Freshman Application Contact Dr. Nolan Beck, Director of Student Services, University of Wisconsin–Marathon County, 518 South Seventh Avenue, Wausau, WI 54401-5396. *Phone:* 715-261-6238. *Toll-free phone:* 888-367-8962. *Fax:* 715-848-3568.
Website: http://www.uwmc.uwc.edu/.

University of Wisconsin–Marinette
Marinette, Wisconsin

Freshman Application Contact Ms. Cynthia M. Bailey, Assistant Campus Dean for Student Services, University of Wisconsin–Marinette, 750 West Bay Shore, Marinette, WI 54143-4299. *Phone:* 715-735-4301.
E-mail: cynthia.bailey@uwc.edu.
Website: http://www.marinette.uwc.edu/.

University of Wisconsin–Marshfield/Wood County
Marshfield, Wisconsin

Freshman Application Contact Brittany Lueth, Director of Student Services, University of Wisconsin–Marshfield/Wood County, 2000 West 5th Street, Marshfield, WI 54449. *Phone:* 715-389-6500. *Fax:* 715-384-1718.
Website: http://marshfield.uwc.edu/.

University of Wisconsin–Richland
Richland Center, Wisconsin

Freshman Application Contact Mr. John D. Poole, Assistant Campus Dean, University of Wisconsin–Richland, 1200 Highway 14 West, Richland Center, WI 53581. *Phone:* 608-647-8422. *Fax:* 608-647-2275.
E-mail: john.poole@uwc.edu.
Website: http://richland.uwc.edu/.

University of Wisconsin–Rock County
Janesville, Wisconsin

Freshman Application Contact University of Wisconsin–Rock County, 2909 Kellogg Avenue, Janesville, WI 53546-5699. *Phone:* 608-758-6523. *Toll-free phone:* 888-INFO-UWC.
Website: http://rock.uwc.edu/.

University of Wisconsin–Sheboygan
Sheboygan, Wisconsin

- **State-supported** 2-year, founded 1933, part of University of Wisconsin System
- **Small-town** 75-acre campus with easy access to Milwaukee
- **Coed**

Undergraduates 305 full-time, 464 part-time. 2% Black or African American, non-Hispanic/Latino; 2% Hispanic/Latino; 11% Asian, non-Hispanic/Latino; 0.4% American Indian or Alaska Native, non-Hispanic/Latino; 0.4% Race/ethnicity unknown.
Faculty *Student/faculty ratio:* 16:1.
Academics *Calendar:* semesters. *Degree:* associate. *Special study options:* academic remediation for entering students, adult/continuing education programs, advanced placement credit, cooperative education, distance learning, English as a second language, independent study, off-campus study, part-time degree program, services for LD students, summer session for credit.
Library University Library - Open for use by all Sheboygan County residents.
Student Life *Campus security:* 24-hour patrols by city police.
Standardized Tests *Required:* SAT or ACT (for admission).
Costs (2015–16) *Tuition:* state resident $4750 full-time, $198 per credit part-time; nonresident $11,737 full-time, $489 per credit part-time. Full-time tuition and fees vary according to course load. Part-time tuition and fees vary according to course load. *Required fees:* $354 full-time, $15 per credit part-time.
Applying *Options:* electronic application. *Application fee:* $44. *Required:* essay or personal statement, high school transcript. *Required for some:* ACT Scores required for students under age 21.
Freshman Application Contact Mrs. Elisa Carr, High School Relations and Recruitment Coordinator, University of Wisconsin–Sheboygan, One University Drive, Sheboygan, WI 53081. *Phone:* 920-459-5956. *Fax:* 920-459-6602. *E-mail:* elisa.carr@uwc.edu.
Website: http://www.sheboygan.uwc.edu/.

University of Wisconsin–Washington County
West Bend, Wisconsin

Freshman Application Contact Mr. Dan Cebrario, Associate Director of Student Services, University of Wisconsin–Washington County, Student

Services Office, 400 University Drive, West Bend, WI 53095. *Phone:* 262-335-5201. *Fax:* 262-335-5220. *E-mail:* dan.cibrario@uwc.edu. *Website:* http://www.washington.uwc.edu/.

University of Wisconsin–Waukesha
Waukesha, Wisconsin

- **State-supported** primarily 2-year, founded 1966, part of University of Wisconsin System
- **Suburban** 86-acre campus with easy access to Milwaukee
- **Coed**

Undergraduates 1,069 full-time, 1,170 part-time. Students come from 16 states and territories; 1 other country; 7% are from out of state; 4% Black or African American, non-Hispanic/Latino; 4% Hispanic/Latino; 3% Asian, non-Hispanic/Latino; 0.9% Native Hawaiian or other Pacific Islander, non-Hispanic/Latino; 0.1% American Indian or Alaska Native, non-Hispanic/Latino; 0.1% Race/ethnicity unknown; 0.1% international; 7% transferred in.
Faculty *Student/faculty ratio:* 24:1.
Academics *Calendar:* semesters. *Degrees:* associate and bachelor's. *Special study options:* academic remediation for entering students, accelerated degree program, advanced placement credit, distance learning, honors programs, internships, off-campus study, part-time degree program, services for LD students, study abroad, summer session for credit.
Library University of Wisconsin-Waukesha Library plus 1 other.
Student Life *Campus security:* late-night transport/escort service, part-time patrols by trained security personnel.
Athletics Member NJCAA.
Standardized Tests *Required:* SAT or ACT (for admission).
Costs (2015–16) *Tuition:* state resident $5091 full-time, $215 per credit part-time; nonresident $12,072 full-time, $506 per credit part-time. Full-time tuition and fees vary according to course load. Part-time tuition and fees vary according to course load. *Required fees:* $230 full-time.
Applying *Options:* electronic application, early admission, deferred entrance. *Application fee:* $44. *Required:* high school transcript. *Required for some:* interview. *Recommended:* essay or personal statement, Admission interview may be recommended.
Freshman Application Contact Ms. Deb Kusick, Sr. Admission Specialist, University of Wisconsin–Waukesha, 1500 North University Drive, Waukesha, WI 53188-2799. *Phone:* 262-521-5040. *Fax:* 262-521-5530. *E-mail:* deborah.kusick@uwc.edu. *Website:* http://www.waukesha.uwc.edu/.

Waukesha County Technical College
Pewaukee, Wisconsin

- **State and locally supported** 2-year, founded 1923, part of Wisconsin Technical College System
- **Suburban** 137-acre campus with easy access to Milwaukee
- **Coed,** 7,928 undergraduate students, 21% full-time, 49% women, 51% men

Undergraduates 1,679 full-time, 6,249 part-time. 7% Black or African American, non-Hispanic/Latino; 7% Hispanic/Latino; 2% Asian, non-Hispanic/Latino; 0.2% Native Hawaiian or other Pacific Islander, non-Hispanic/Latino; 0.5% American Indian or Alaska Native, non-Hispanic/Latino; 2% Two or more races, non-Hispanic/Latino; 3% Race/ethnicity unknown; 0.1% international.
Freshmen *Admission:* 564 enrolled.
Faculty *Total:* 864, 23% full-time. *Student/faculty ratio:* 18:1.
Majors Accounting; administrative assistant and secretarial science; architectural drafting and CAD/CADD; automation engineer technology; automobile/automotive mechanics technology; baking and pastry arts; biomedical technology; business administration and management; business administration, management and operations related; clinical/medical laboratory technology; computer programming; computer support specialist; computer systems networking and telecommunications; criminal justice/police science; dental hygiene; digital arts; early childhood education; electrical, electronic and communications engineering technology; emergency medical technology (EMT paramedic); fire science/firefighting; graphic communications; graphic design; health information/medical records technology; hotel, motel, and restaurant management; human resources management; interior design; international marketing; marketing/marketing management; mechanical drafting and CAD/CADD; medical radiologic technology; metal fabricator; multi/interdisciplinary studies related; office management; physical therapy technology; psychiatric/mental health services technology; real estate; registered nursing/registered nurse; restaurant, culinary, and catering management; surgical technology; teacher assistant/aide.
Academics *Calendar:* semesters. *Degree:* certificates, diplomas, and associate. *Special study options:* academic remediation for entering students,

accelerated degree program, adult/continuing education programs, advanced placement credit, cooperative education, distance learning, double majors, English as a second language, independent study, internships, part-time degree program, services for LD students, student-designed majors, study abroad, summer session for credit.
Student Life *Housing:* college housing not available. *Campus security:* patrols by police officers 8 a.m. to 10 p.m..
Costs (2015–16) *Tuition:* state resident $3852 full-time, $128 per credit hour part-time; nonresident $5778 full-time, $193 per credit hour part-time. Full-time tuition and fees vary according to program. Part-time tuition and fees vary according to program. *Required fees:* $231 full-time, $8 per credit hour part-time. *Payment plans:* installment, deferred payment. *Waivers:* senior citizens.
Financial Aid Of all full-time matriculated undergraduates who enrolled in 2014, 230 Federal Work-Study jobs (averaging $3574). 230 state and other part-time jobs (averaging $1018).
Applying *Options:* electronic application. *Application fee:* $30. *Required:* high school transcript. *Required for some:* interview. *Application deadlines:* rolling (freshmen), rolling (transfers).
Freshman Application Contact Waukesha County Technical College, 800 Main Street, Pewaukee, WI 53072-4601. *Phone:* 262-691-5464. *Website:* http://www.wctc.edu/.

Western Technical College
La Crosse, Wisconsin

Freshman Application Contact Ms. Jane Wells, Manager of Admissions, Registration, and Records, Western Technical College, PO Box 908, La Crosse, WI 54602-0908. *Phone:* 608-785-9158. *Toll-free phone:* 800-322-9982. *Fax:* 608-785-9094. *E-mail:* mildes@wwtc.edu. *Website:* http://www.westerntc.edu/.

Wisconsin Indianhead Technical College
Shell Lake, Wisconsin

- **District-supported** 2-year, founded 1912, part of Wisconsin Technical College System
- **Urban** 118-acre campus
- **Endowment** $3.8 million
- **Coed,** 2,894 undergraduate students, 39% full-time, 61% women, 39% men

Undergraduates 1,142 full-time, 1,752 part-time. Students come from 6 states and territories; 8% are from out of state; 0.7% Black or African American, non-Hispanic/Latino; 0.5% Hispanic/Latino; 0.4% Asian, non-Hispanic/Latino; 0.1% Native Hawaiian or other Pacific Islander, non-Hispanic/Latino; 2% American Indian or Alaska Native, non-Hispanic/Latino; 2% Two or more races, non-Hispanic/Latino; 1% Race/ethnicity unknown.
Freshmen *Admission:* 532 enrolled.
Faculty *Total:* 373, 48% full-time. *Student/faculty ratio:* 17:1.
Majors Accounting; administrative assistant and secretarial science; architectural engineering technology; business administration and management; computer installation and repair technology; computer programming; computer support specialist; computer systems networking and telecommunications; corrections; criminal justice/police science; early childhood education; emergency medical technology (EMT paramedic); finance; gerontology; health information/medical records technology; human resources management; interdisciplinary studies; marketing/marketing management; materials engineering; medical administrative assistant and medical secretary; occupational therapist assistant; office management; psychiatric/mental health services technology; registered nursing/registered nurse; web page, digital/multimedia and information resources design.
Academics *Calendar:* semesters. *Degree:* certificates, diplomas, and associate.
Student Life *Housing:* college housing not available. *Student services:* health clinic.
Costs (2015–16) *Tuition:* state resident $3852 full-time, $128 per credit part-time; nonresident $5778 full-time, $193 per credit part-time. Full-time tuition and fees vary according to course load, program, and reciprocity agreements. Part-time tuition and fees vary according to course load, program, and reciprocity agreements. *Required fees:* $408 full-time. *Payment plans:* installment, deferred payment.
Applying *Options:* electronic application. *Application fee:* $30. *Application deadline:* rolling (freshmen).
Freshman Application Contact Mr. Steve Bitzer, Vice President, Student Affairs and Campus Administrator, Wisconsin Indianhead Technical College, 2100 Beaser Avenue, Ashland, WI 54806. *Phone:* 715-468-2815 Ext. 3149. *Toll-free phone:* 800-243-9482. *Fax:* 715-468-2819. *E-mail:* steve.bitzer@witc.edu. *Website:* http://www.witc.edu/.

WYOMING

Casper College
Casper, Wyoming

- **State and locally supported** 2-year, founded 1945
- **Small-town** 200-acre campus
- **Coed**, 3,680 undergraduate students, 47% full-time, 56% women, 44% men

Undergraduates 1,719 full-time, 1,961 part-time. Students come from 37 states and territories; 17 other countries; 11% are from out of state; 1% Black or African American, non-Hispanic/Latino; 6% Hispanic/Latino; 0.9% Asian, non-Hispanic/Latino; 0.2% Native Hawaiian or other Pacific Islander, non-Hispanic/Latino; 0.5% American Indian or Alaska Native, non-Hispanic/Latino; 2% Two or more races, non-Hispanic/Latino; 3% Race/ethnicity unknown; 0.8% international; 4% transferred in; 10% live on campus.

Freshmen *Admission:* 1,063 applied, 1,063 admitted, 654 enrolled. *Average high school GPA:* 3.1. *Test scores:* ACT scores over 18: 76%; ACT scores over 24: 18%; ACT scores over 30: 1%.

Faculty *Total:* 258, 57% full-time, 23% with terminal degrees. *Student/faculty ratio:* 13:1.

Majors Accounting; accounting technology and bookkeeping; acting; administrative assistant and secretarial science; agricultural business and management; agricultural communication/journalism; agriculture; airline pilot and flight crew; animal sciences; anthropology; art; art teacher education; athletic training; autobody/collision and repair technology; automobile/automotive mechanics technology; biology/biological sciences; business administration and management; business automation/technology/data entry; chemistry; clinical laboratory science/medical technology; computer and information systems security; computer programming; construction management; construction trades; criminal justice/law enforcement administration; dance; diesel mechanics technology; drafting and design technology; economics; electrical, electronic and communications engineering technology; elementary education; emergency medical technology (EMT paramedic); energy management and systems technology; engineering; English; entrepreneurship; environmental science; fine/studio arts; fire science/firefighting; foreign languages and literatures; forensic science and technology; general studies; geographic information science and cartography; geology/earth science; graphic design; health services/allied health/health sciences; history; hospitality administration; industrial mechanics and maintenance technology; international relations and affairs; journalism; kindergarten/preschool education; legal assistant/paralegal; liberal arts and sciences/liberal studies; machine tool technology; manufacturing engineering technology; marketing/marketing management; mass communication/media; mathematics; mining technology; museum studies; music; musical theater; music performance; music teacher education; nutrition sciences; occupational therapist assistant; pharmacy technician; photography; physical education teaching and coaching; physics; political science and government; pre-dentistry studies; pre-law studies; premedical studies; pre-occupational therapy; pre-optometry; pre-pharmacy studies; pre-physical therapy; pre-veterinary studies; psychology; radiologic technology/science; range science and management; registered nursing/registered nurse; respiratory care therapy; retailing; robotics technology; social studies teacher education; social work; sociology; speech communication and rhetoric; statistics related; substance abuse/addiction counseling; technology/industrial arts teacher education; theater design and technology; web/multimedia management and webmaster; web page, digital/multimedia and information resources design; welding technology; wildlife, fish and wildlands science and management; women's studies.

Academics *Calendar:* semesters. *Degree:* certificates and associate. *Special study options:* academic remediation for entering students, accelerated degree program, advanced placement credit, cooperative education, distance learning, English as a second language, honors programs, independent study, internships, off-campus study, part-time degree program, services for LD students, summer session for credit.

Library Goodstein Foundation Library. *Books:* 66,488 (physical), 184,000 (digital/electronic); *Serial titles:* 4,300 (physical); *Databases:* 415. Weekly public service hours: 82; students can reserve study rooms.

Student Life *Housing Options:* coed. Campus housing is university owned. *Activities and Organizations:* drama/theater group, student-run newspaper, choral group, Student Senate, Student Activities Board, Agriculture Club, Theater Club, Phi Theta Kappa. *Campus security:* 24-hour emergency response devices and patrols, late-night transport/escort service. *Student services:* health clinic, personal/psychological counseling.

Athletics Member NJCAA. *Intercollegiate sports:* basketball M(s)/W(s), equestrian sports M/W, volleyball W(s). *Intramural sports:* basketball M/W, bowling M/W, football M/W, golf M/W, racquetball M/W, soccer M/W, softball M/W, tennis M/W.

Costs (2015–16) *Tuition:* state resident $1992 full-time, $83 per credit part-time; nonresident $5976 full-time, $249 per credit part-time. Part-time tuition and fees vary according to course load. *Required fees:* $648 full-time, $27 per credit part-time. *Room and board:* $6294. Room and board charges vary according to board plan and housing facility. *Payment plan:* installment. *Waivers:* senior citizens and employees or children of employees.

Financial Aid Of all full-time matriculated undergraduates who enrolled in 2014, 80 Federal Work-Study jobs (averaging $2000).

Applying *Options:* electronic application, early admission. *Required:* high school transcript. *Application deadlines:* 8/15 (freshmen), 8/15 (transfers). *Notification:* continuous until 8/15 (freshmen), continuous until 8/15 (transfers).

Freshman Application Contact Mrs. Kyla Foltz, Director of Admissions Services, Casper College, 125 College Drive, Casper, WY 82601. *Phone:* 307-268-2111. *Toll-free phone:* 800-442-2963. *Fax:* 307-268-2611. *E-mail:* kfoltz@caspercollege.edu. *Website:* http://www.caspercollege.edu/.

Central Wyoming College
Riverton, Wyoming

- **State and locally supported** 2-year, founded 1966, part of Wyoming Community College Commission
- **Small-town** 200-acre campus
- **Endowment** $17.5 million
- **Coed**, 2,186 undergraduate students, 33% full-time, 54% women, 46% men

Undergraduates 727 full-time, 1,459 part-time. Students come from 40 states and territories; 7 other countries; 13% are from out of state; 1% Black or African American, non-Hispanic/Latino; 9% Hispanic/Latino; 0.7% Asian, non-Hispanic/Latino; 0.2% Native Hawaiian or other Pacific Islander, non-Hispanic/Latino; 10% American Indian or Alaska Native, non-Hispanic/Latino; 3% Two or more races, non-Hispanic/Latino; 1% Race/ethnicity unknown; 0.4% international; 4% transferred in; 10% live on campus. *Retention:* 52% of full-time freshmen returned.

Freshmen *Admission:* 516 applied, 516 admitted, 271 enrolled. *Average high school GPA:* 3.09. *Test scores:* SAT critical reading scores over 500: 46%; SAT math scores over 500: 26%; ACT scores over 18: 71%; SAT critical reading scores over 600: 33%; SAT math scores over 600: 13%; ACT scores over 24: 18%; ACT scores over 30: 1%.

Faculty *Total:* 198, 29% full-time, 39% with terminal degrees. *Student/faculty ratio:* 12:1.

Majors Accounting; accounting technology and bookkeeping; acting; administrative assistant and secretarial science; agricultural business and management; American Indian/Native American studies; art; athletic training; automobile/automotive mechanics technology; biology/biological sciences; building/property maintenance; business administration and management; business/commerce; carpentry; commercial photography; computer science; computer technology/computer systems technology; criminal justice/law enforcement administration; culinary arts; customer service support/call center/teleservice operation; dramatic/theater arts; early childhood education; elementary education; engineering; English; entrepreneurship; environmental/environmental health engineering; environmental science; equestrian studies; fire science/firefighting; general studies; geology/earth science; graphic design; homeland security, law enforcement, firefighting and protective services related; hotel/motel administration; international/global studies; mathematics; medical office assistant; music; occupational safety and health technology; parks, recreation and leisure; parks, recreation and leisure facilities management; physical sciences; pre-law studies; psychology; radio and television; range science and management; registered nursing/registered nurse; rehabilitation and therapeutic professions related; secondary education; social sciences; teacher assistant/aide; theater design and technology; welding technology.

Academics *Calendar:* semesters. *Degree:* certificates, diplomas, and associate. *Special study options:* academic remediation for entering students, adult/continuing education programs, advanced placement credit, cooperative education, distance learning, double majors, English as a second language, honors programs, independent study, off-campus study, part-time degree program, services for LD students, summer session for credit.

Library Central Wyoming College Library. *Books:* 53,204 (physical), 5 (digital/electronic); *Serial titles:* 152 (physical), 8 (digital/electronic); *Databases:* 141. Weekly public service hours: 82.

Student Life *Housing Options:* coed. Campus housing is university owned. *Activities and Organizations:* drama/theater group, student-run radio and television station, choral group, Multi-Cultural Club, La Vida Nueva Club, Fellowship of College Christians, Quality Leaders, Science Club. *Campus security:* 24-hour emergency response devices, late-night transport/escort service, controlled dormitory access. *Student services:* personal/psychological counseling.

Athletics Member NJCAA. *Intercollegiate sports:* basketball M(s)/W(s), cross-country running M(s)/W(s), equestrian sports M(s)/W(s), golf M(s)/W(s), volleyball W(s). *Intramural sports:* badminton M/W, basketball M/W, football M/W, rock climbing M/W, skiing (cross-country) M/W, skiing (downhill) M/W, soccer M/W, softball M/W, swimming and diving M/W, table tennis M/W, tennis M/W, ultimate Frisbee M/W, volleyball M/W, weight lifting M/W.

Costs (2015–16) *Tuition:* state resident $1992 full-time, $83 per credit part-time; nonresident $5976 full-time, $249 per credit part-time. Full-time tuition and fees vary according to course load, program, and reciprocity agreements. Part-time tuition and fees vary according to course load, program, and reciprocity agreements. *Required fees:* $720 full-time, $30 per credit part-time. *Room and board:* $5130; room only: $2530. Room and board charges vary according to board plan and housing facility. *Payment plans:* installment, deferred payment. *Waivers:* senior citizens and employees or children of employees.

Financial Aid Of all full-time matriculated undergraduates who enrolled in 2014, 362 applied for aid, 285 were judged to have need. 91 Federal Work-Study jobs (averaging $2040). *Financial aid deadline:* 6/30.

Applying *Options:* electronic application, early admission, deferred entrance. *Recommended:* high school transcript. *Application deadlines:* rolling (freshmen), rolling (out-of-state freshmen), rolling (transfers).

Freshman Application Contact Mrs. Deborah Graham, Admissions Assistant, Central Wyoming College, 2660 Peck Avenue, Riverton, WY 82501-2273. *Phone:* 307-855-2061. *Toll-free phone:* 800-735-8418. *Fax:* 307-855-2065. *E-mail:* admit@cwc.edu.
Website: http://www.cwc.edu/.

Eastern Wyoming College
Torrington, Wyoming

- **State and locally supported** 2-year, founded 1948, part of Wyoming Community College Commission
- **Rural** 40-acre campus
- **Coed,** 1,715 undergraduate students, 33% full-time, 58% women, 42% men

Undergraduates 571 full-time, 1,144 part-time. 1% Black or African American, non-Hispanic/Latino; 8% Hispanic/Latino; 0.3% Asian, non-Hispanic/Latino; 0.5% Native Hawaiian or other Pacific Islander, non-Hispanic/Latino; 1% American Indian or Alaska Native, non-Hispanic/Latino; 0.8% Two or more races, non-Hispanic/Latino; 2% international.

Freshmen *Admission:* 205 enrolled.

Faculty *Total:* 68, 59% full-time. *Student/faculty ratio:* 21:1.

Majors Accounting; administrative assistant and secretarial science; agribusiness; agricultural teacher education; art; biology/biological sciences; business administration and management; business teacher education; computer systems networking and telecommunications; corrections administration; cosmetology; criminal justice/law enforcement administration; criminal justice/police science; criminal justice/safety; early childhood education; economics; elementary education; English; environmental biology; farm and ranch management; foreign languages and literatures; general studies; health/medical preparatory programs related; liberal arts and sciences/liberal studies; mathematics; mathematics teacher education; music; music teacher education; office management; physical education teaching and coaching; pre-dentistry studies; premedical studies; pre-pharmacy studies; pre-veterinary studies; range science and management; secondary education; social sciences; speech communication and rhetoric; statistics; veterinary/animal health technology; welding technology; wildlife, fish and wildlands science and management.

Academics *Calendar:* semesters. *Degree:* certificates, diplomas, and associate. *Special study options:* academic remediation for entering students, accelerated degree program, advanced placement credit, distance learning, double majors, English as a second language, independent study, internships, part-time degree program, services for LD students, student-designed majors, summer session for credit.

Library Eastern Wyoming College Library plus 1 other.

Student Life *Housing Options:* coed, men-only, women-only. Campus housing is university owned. *Activities and Organizations:* drama/theater group, student-run newspaper, choral group, Veterinary Technology Club, Rodeo Club, Student Senate, Block and Bridle Club, SkillsUSA. *Campus security:* 24-hour emergency response devices, controlled dormitory access. *Student services:* personal/psychological counseling.

Athletics Member NJCAA. *Intercollegiate sports:* basketball M/W, equestrian sports M/W, golf M, volleyball W.

Costs (2016–17) *Tuition:* state resident $1992 full-time, $83 per credit part-time; nonresident $5976 full-time, $249 per credit part-time. Full-time tuition and fees vary according to course load, location, and program. Part-time tuition and fees vary according to course load, location, and program. *Required fees:*

$648 full-time, $27 per credit part-time. *Room and board:* $6136; room only: $3292. Room and board charges vary according to housing facility. *Payment plan:* installment. *Waivers:* senior citizens and employees or children of employees.

Applying *Recommended:* high school transcript.

Freshman Application Contact Dr. Rex Cogdill, Vice President for Students Services, Eastern Wyoming College, 3200 West C Street, Torrington, WY 82240. *Phone:* 307-532-8257. *Toll-free phone:* 866-327-8996. *Fax:* 307-532-8222. *E-mail:* rex.cogdill@ewc.wy.edu.
Website: http://www.ewc.wy.edu/.

Laramie County Community College
Cheyenne, Wyoming

- **District-supported** 2-year, founded 1968, part of Wyoming Community College Commission
- **Small-town** 271-acre campus
- **Coed,** 4,148 undergraduate students, 43% full-time, 59% women, 41% men

Undergraduates 1,800 full-time, 2,348 part-time. 15% are from out of state; 3% Black or African American, non-Hispanic/Latino; 12% Hispanic/Latino; 1% Asian, non-Hispanic/Latino; 0.3% Native Hawaiian or other Pacific Islander, non-Hispanic/Latino; 1% American Indian or Alaska Native, non-Hispanic/Latino; 0.4% Two or more races, non-Hispanic/Latino; 2% Race/ethnicity unknown; 1% international; 19% transferred in; 13% live on campus.

Freshmen *Admission:* 1,831 applied, 1,831 admitted, 524 enrolled. *Average high school GPA:* 2.95. *Test scores:* ACT scores over 18: 74%; ACT scores over 24: 20%.

Faculty *Total:* 306, 36% full-time, 8% with terminal degrees. *Student/faculty ratio:* 14:1.

Majors Accounting; agribusiness; agricultural business technology; agricultural production; agriculture; anthropology; art; autobody/collision and repair technology; automobile/automotive mechanics technology; biological and physical sciences; biology/biological sciences; business administration and management; business/commerce; chemistry; computer programming; computer science; corrections; criminal justice/law enforcement administration; dental hygiene; diagnostic medical sonography and ultrasound technology; diesel mechanics technology; digital communication and media/multimedia; drafting and design technology; early childhood education; economics; education; emergency medical technology (EMT paramedic); energy management and systems technology; engineering; English; entrepreneurship; equestrian studies; fire science/firefighting; general studies; heating, air conditioning, ventilation and refrigeration maintenance technology; history; homeland security, law enforcement, firefighting and protective services related; humanities; human services; kinesiology and exercise science; legal assistant/paralegal; mass communication/media; mathematics; mechanic and repair technologies related; medical insurance coding; music; physical education teaching and coaching; physical therapy technology; political science and government; pre-law studies; pre-pharmacy studies; psychology; public administration; radiologic technology/science; registered nursing/registered nurse; religious studies; social sciences; sociology; Spanish; speech communication and rhetoric; surgical technology; wildlife, fish and wildlands science and management.

Academics *Calendar:* semesters. *Degree:* certificates, diplomas, and associate. *Special study options:* academic remediation for entering students, adult/continuing education programs, advanced placement credit, cooperative education, distance learning, double majors, English as a second language, honors programs, independent study, internships, off-campus study, part-time degree program, services for LD students, summer session for credit. *ROTC:* Army (c), Air Force (c).

Library Ludden Library.

Student Life *Housing Options:* coed. Campus housing is university owned. *Activities and Organizations:* drama/theater group, student-run newspaper, choral group, Student Government Association, Phi Theta Kappa, Block and Bridle, Student Nursing Club, SkillsUSA. *Campus security:* 24-hour emergency response devices and patrols, late-night transport/escort service, controlled dormitory access. *Student services:* health clinic, personal/psychological counseling.

Athletics Member NJCAA. *Intercollegiate sports:* basketball M(s), cheerleading M(s)/W(s), equestrian sports M(s)/W(s), soccer M(s)/W(s), volleyball W(s). *Intramural sports:* basketball M/W, equestrian sports M/W, racquetball M/W, rock climbing M/W, skiing (cross-country) M/W, soccer M/W, softball M/W, table tennis M/W, ultimate Frisbee M/W, volleyball M/W.

Costs (2016–17) *Tuition:* state resident $1992 full-time, $83 per credit hour part-time; nonresident $5976 full-time, $249 per credit hour part-time. Part-time tuition and fees vary according to course load. *Required fees:* $1152 full-time. *Room and board:* $7988. Room and board charges vary according to housing facility. *Payment plan:* installment. *Waivers:* senior citizens and employees or children of employees.

Financial Aid Of all full-time matriculated undergraduates who enrolled in 2014, 1,308 applied for aid, 1,036 were judged to have need, 150 had their need fully met. In 2014, 526 non-need-based awards were made. *Average percent of need met:* 69%. *Average financial aid package:* $6907. *Average need-based loan:* $3140. *Average need-based gift aid:* $2157. *Average non-need-based aid:* $1416.

Applying *Options:* electronic application, deferred entrance. *Required for some:* high school transcript, interview.

Freshman Application Contact Ms. Holly Bruegman, Director of Admissions, Laramie County Community College, 1400 East College Drive, Cheyenne, WY 82007. *Phone:* 307-778-1117. *Toll-free phone:* 800-522-2993 Ext. 1357. *Fax:* 307-778-1360. *E-mail:* learnmore@lccc.wy.edu. *Website:* http://www.lccc.wy.edu/.

Northwest College
Powell, Wyoming

- **State and locally supported** 2-year, founded 1946, part of Wyoming Community College System
- **Rural** 132-acre campus
- **Coed,** 1,697 undergraduate students, 58% full-time, 58% women, 42% men

Undergraduates 976 full-time, 721 part-time. Students come from 36 states and territories; 23 other countries; 21% are from out of state; 0.6% Black or African American, non-Hispanic/Latino; 8% Hispanic/Latino; 0.6% Asian, non-Hispanic/Latino; 0.2% Native Hawaiian or other Pacific Islander, non-Hispanic/Latino; 0.7% American Indian or Alaska Native, non-Hispanic/Latino; 2% Two or more races, non-Hispanic/Latino; 3% international. *Retention:* 60% of full-time freshmen returned.

Freshmen *Admission:* 320 enrolled.

Faculty *Total:* 146, 53% full-time. *Student/faculty ratio:* 12:1.

Majors Accounting; administrative assistant and secretarial science; aeronautics/aviation/aerospace science and technology; agribusiness; agricultural communication/journalism; agricultural production; agricultural teacher education; allied health and medical assisting services related; animal sciences; anthropology; archeology; art; athletic training; biology/biological sciences; broadcast journalism; business administration and management; business/commerce; CAD/CADD drafting/design technology; chemistry; cinematography and film/video production; commercial and advertising art; commercial photography; criminal justice/law enforcement administration; crop production; desktop publishing and digital imaging design; elementary education; engineering; English; equestrian studies; farm and ranch management; general studies; graphic and printing equipment operation/production; health and physical education/fitness; health/medical preparatory programs related; health services/allied health/health sciences; history; international relations and affairs; journalism; kindergarten/preschool education; liberal arts and sciences/liberal studies; mathematics; music; natural resources management and policy; parks, recreation and leisure; physics; playwriting and screenwriting; political science and government; pre-pharmacy studies; psychology; radio and television; radio and television broadcasting technology; range science and management; registered nursing/registered nurse; secondary education; social sciences; sociology; Spanish; speech communication and rhetoric; veterinary/animal health technology; visual and performing arts related; welding technology.

Academics *Calendar:* semesters. *Degree:* certificates and associate. *Special study options:* academic remediation for entering students, adult/continuing education programs, advanced placement credit, cooperative education, distance learning, double majors, English as a second language, external degree program, independent study, internships, off-campus study, part-time degree program, services for LD students, study abroad, summer session for credit.

Library John Taggart Hinckley Library.

Student Life *Housing:* on-campus residence required for freshman year. *Options:* coed, women-only, special housing for students with disabilities. Campus housing is university owned. Freshman campus housing is guaranteed. *Activities and Organizations:* drama/theater group, student-run newspaper, radio and television station, choral group. *Campus security:* 24-hour emergency response devices and patrols, late-night transport/escort service, controlled dormitory access. *Student services:* health clinic, personal/psychological counseling.

Athletics Member NJCAA. *Intercollegiate sports:* basketball M(s)/W(s), equestrian sports M(s)/W(s), soccer M(s)/W(s), volleyball W(s), wrestling M(s). *Intramural sports:* basketball M/W, football M/W, golf M/W, softball M/W, tennis M/W, ultimate Frisbee M/W, volleyball M/W.

Standardized Tests *Recommended:* SAT or ACT (for admission), ACCUPLACER.

Costs (2015–16) *Tuition:* state resident $1992 full-time, $83 per credit hour part-time; nonresident $5976 full-time, $249 per credit hour part-time. Full-time tuition and fees vary according to course load, location, and program. Part-time tuition and fees vary according to course load, location, and program.

Required fees: $797 full-time, $26 per credit hour part-time. *Room and board:* $5198. Room and board charges vary according to board plan and housing facility. *Payment plan:* installment. *Waivers:* children of alumni, senior citizens, and employees or children of employees.

Financial Aid Of all full-time matriculated undergraduates who enrolled in 2014, 115 Federal Work-Study jobs (averaging $2700). 215 state and other part-time jobs (averaging $2700).

Applying *Options:* electronic application. *Required:* high school transcript. *Required for some:* minimum 2.0 GPA. *Recommended:* minimum 2.0 GPA. *Application deadlines:* rolling (freshmen), rolling (out-of-state freshmen), rolling (transfers). *Notification:* continuous (freshmen), continuous (out-of-state freshmen), continuous (transfers).

Freshman Application Contact Mr. West Hernandez, Admissions Manager, Northwest College, 231 West 6th Street, Orendorff Building 1, Powell, WY 82435-1898. *Phone:* 307-754-6103. *Toll-free phone:* 800-560-4692. *Fax:* 307-754-6249. *E-mail:* west.hernandez@nwc.edu. *Website:* http://www.nwc.edu/.

Sheridan College
Sheridan, Wyoming

- **State and locally supported** 2-year, founded 1948, part of Wyoming Community College Commission
- **Small-town** 145-acre campus
- **Endowment** $29.6 million
- **Coed,** 4,307 undergraduate students, 32% full-time, 46% women, 54% men

Undergraduates 1,398 full-time, 2,909 part-time. Students come from 37 states and territories; 11 other countries; 18% are from out of state; 1% Black or African American, non-Hispanic/Latino; 7% Hispanic/Latino; 0.6% Asian, non-Hispanic/Latino; 0.2% Native Hawaiian or other Pacific Islander, non-Hispanic/Latino; 2% American Indian or Alaska Native, non-Hispanic/Latino; 3% Two or more races, non-Hispanic/Latino; 0.8% international; 3% transferred in; 10% live on campus. *Retention:* 59% of full-time freshmen returned.

Freshmen *Admission:* 564 enrolled.

Faculty *Total:* 217, 46% full-time, 14% with terminal degrees. *Student/faculty ratio:* 17:1.

Majors Agriculture; agriculture and agriculture operations related; animal sciences; art; biological and physical sciences; biology/biological sciences; building construction technology; business/commerce; CAD/CADD drafting/design technology; community organization and advocacy; computer and information sciences; computer and information systems security; criminal justice/safety; culinary arts; dental hygiene; diesel mechanics technology; dramatic/theater arts; early childhood education; electrical and electronic engineering technologies related; elementary education; engineering; English; environmental engineering technology; general studies; health and physical education/fitness; health services/allied health/health sciences; history; horticultural science; hospitality administration; information science/studies; machine tool technology; massage therapy; mathematics; mining technology; music; physical fitness technician; precision production related; psychology; range science and management; registered nursing/registered nurse; secondary education; surveying technology; welding technology.

Academics *Calendar:* semesters. *Degree:* certificates and associate. *Special study options:* academic remediation for entering students, accelerated degree program, advanced placement credit, cooperative education, distance learning, double majors, English as a second language, independent study, internships, off-campus study, part-time degree program, services for LD students, summer session for credit.

Library Mary Brown Kooi Library plus 1 other.

Student Life *Housing Options:* coed. Campus housing is university owned and leased by the school. *Activities and Organizations:* drama/theater group, choral group, National Society of Leadership and Success, Student Senate, Baptist Collegiate Ministries, Nursing Club, Dental Hygiene Club. *Campus security:* 24-hour emergency response devices, student patrols, controlled dormitory access, night patrols by certified officers. *Student services:* personal/psychological counseling.

Athletics Member NJCAA. *Intercollegiate sports:* basketball M(s)/W(s), cross-country running M(s)/W(s), equestrian sports M(s)/W(s), soccer M(s)/W(s), volleyball W(s). *Intramural sports:* basketball M/W, bowling M/W, football M/W, lacrosse M/W, soccer M/W, softball M/W, ultimate Frisbee M/W, volleyball M/W.

Costs (2015–16) *Tuition:* state resident $1992 full-time, $83 per credit part-time; nonresident $5976 full-time, $249 per credit part-time. Full-time tuition and fees vary according to course load, location, and reciprocity agreements. Part-time tuition and fees vary according to location and reciprocity agreements. *Required fees:* $960 full-time, $32 per hour part-time. *Room and board:* $6170. Room and board charges vary according to board plan, housing facility, and location. *Payment plan:* installment. *Waivers:* senior citizens and employees or children of employees.

Applying *Options:* electronic application, early admission, deferred entrance. *Required for some:* high school transcript. *Recommended:* high school transcript. *Application deadlines:* rolling (freshmen), rolling (out-of-state freshmen), rolling (transfers). *Notification:* continuous (freshmen), continuous (out-of-state freshmen), continuous (transfers).

Freshman Application Contact Mr. Matt Adams, Admissions Coordinator, Sheridan College, PO Box 1500, Sheridan, WY 82801-1500. *Phone:* 307-674-6446 Ext. 2005. *Toll-free phone:* 800-913-9139 Ext. 2002. *Fax:* 307-674-3373. *E-mail:* madams@sheridan.edu. *Website:* http://www.sheridan.edu/.

Western Wyoming Community College
Rock Springs, Wyoming

- **State and locally supported** 2-year, founded 1959
- **Small-town** 342-acre campus
- **Endowment** $20.2 million
- **Coed,** 3,293 undergraduate students, 35% full-time, 53% women, 47% men

Undergraduates 1,154 full-time, 2,139 part-time. Students come from 32 states and territories; 22 other countries; 8% are from out of state; 1% Black or African American, non-Hispanic/Latino; 11% Hispanic/Latino; 0.5% Asian, non-Hispanic/Latino; 0.2% Native Hawaiian or other Pacific Islander, non-Hispanic/Latino; 0.5% American Indian or Alaska Native, non-Hispanic/Latino; 2% Two or more races, non-Hispanic/Latino; 0.1% Race/ethnicity unknown; 2% international; 2% transferred in; 41% live on campus.

Freshmen *Admission:* 205 enrolled. *Average high school GPA:* 2.97.

Faculty *Total:* 313, 25% full-time. *Student/faculty ratio:* 16:1.

Majors Accounting; administrative assistant and secretarial science; anthropology; archeology; art; automobile/automotive mechanics technology; biological and physical sciences; biology/biological sciences; business administration and management; chemistry; computer and information sciences; computer programming (specific applications); computer science; criminal justice/law enforcement administration; criminology; dance; data entry/microcomputer applications; data processing and data processing technology; diesel mechanics technology; dramatic/theater arts; early childhood education; economics; education; education (multiple levels); electrical, electronic and communications engineering technology; electrical/electronics equipment installation and repair; electrician; elementary education; engineering technology; English; environmental science; forestry; general studies; geology/earth science; health/medical preparatory programs related; health services/allied health/health sciences; heavy equipment maintenance technology; history; humanities; human services; industrial electronics technology; industrial mechanics and maintenance technology; information science/studies; information technology; instrumentation technology; international relations and affairs; journalism; kinesiology and exercise science; legal administrative assistant/secretary; liberal arts and sciences/liberal studies; licensed practical/vocational nurse training; marketing/marketing management; mathematics; mechanics and repair; medical administrative assistant and medical secretary; medical/clinical assistant; medical office assistant; medical office computer specialist; mining technology; music; nursing assistant/aide and patient care assistant/aide; photography; political science and government; pre-dentistry studies; pre-engineering; pre-law studies; premedical studies; prenursing studies; pre-pharmacy studies; pre-veterinary studies; psychology; secondary education; social sciences; social work; sociology; Spanish; speech communication and rhetoric; theater design and technology; visual and performing arts; web/multimedia management and webmaster; web page, digital/multimedia and information resources design; welding technology; wildlife, fish and wildlands science and management; word processing.

Academics *Calendar:* semesters. *Degree:* certificates, diplomas, and associate. *Special study options:* academic remediation for entering students, advanced placement credit, cooperative education, distance learning, English as a second language, honors programs, independent study, internships, part-time degree program, services for LD students, summer session for credit.

Library Hay Library. *Books:* 115,615 (physical), 102,621 (digital/electronic).

Student Life *Housing Options:* coed, special housing for students with disabilities. Campus housing is university owned. *Activities and Organizations:* drama/theater group, student-run newspaper, radio station, choral group, Association of Non-Traditional Students (ANTS), Spanish Club, Residence Hall Association, International Club, Latter Day Saints Student Association. *Campus security:* 24-hour emergency response devices and patrols, late-night transport/escort service, controlled dormitory access, patrols by trained security personnel from 4 p.m. to 8 a.m., 24-hour patrols on weekends and holidays. *Student services:* personal/psychological counseling.

Athletics Member NJCAA. *Intercollegiate sports:* basketball M(s)/W(s), cheerleading M(s)/W(s), soccer M(s)/W(s), volleyball W(s), wrestling M(s).

Standardized Tests *Recommended:* SAT or ACT (for admission).

Costs (2016–17) *Tuition:* state resident $996 full-time, $83 per credit hour part-time; nonresident $2988 full-time, $249 per credit hour part-time. *Required fees:* $204 full-time, $18 per credit hour part-time, $18 per credit hour part-time. *Room and board:* Room and board charges vary according to board plan and housing facility. *Waivers:* senior citizens and employees or children of employees.

Financial Aid Of all full-time matriculated undergraduates who enrolled in 2014, 20 Federal Work-Study jobs (averaging $1500).

Applying *Options:* electronic application, early admission, deferred entrance. *Recommended:* high school transcript. *Application deadlines:* rolling (freshmen), rolling (out-of-state freshmen), rolling (transfers).

Freshman Application Contact Ms. Erin M. Grey, Director of Admissions, Western Wyoming Community College, 2500 College Drive, PO Box 428, Rock Springs, WY 82901. *Phone:* 307-382-1647. *Toll-free phone:* 800-226-1181. *Fax:* 307-382-1636. *E-mail:* admissions@wwcc.wy.edu. *Website:* http://www.wwcc.wy.edu/.

WyoTech Laramie
Laramie, Wyoming

Director of Admissions Director of Admissions, WyoTech Laramie, 4373 North Third Street, Laramie, WY 82072-9519. *Phone:* 307-742-3776. *Toll-free phone:* 888-577-7559. *Fax:* 307-721-4854. *Website:* http://www.wyotech.edu/.

CANADA

CANADA

Southern Alberta Institute of Technology
Calgary, Alberta, Canada

Freshman Application Contact Southern Alberta Institute of Technology, 1301 16th Avenue NW, Calgary, AB T2M 0L4, Canada. *Phone:* 403-284-8857. *Toll-free phone:* 877-284-SAIT. *Website:* http://www.sait.ca/.

INTERNATIONAL

MEXICO

Westhill University
Sante Fe, Mexico

- **Independent** primarily 2-year, founded 1996
- **Urban** campus with easy access to Mexico City
- **Coed**

Undergraduates 1,206 full-time. *Retention:* 86% of full-time freshmen returned.

Academics *Calendar:* trimesters. *Degrees:* associate, bachelor's, and master's. *Special study options:* accelerated degree program, adult/continuing education programs, distance learning, part-time degree program, study abroad.

Student Life *Campus security:* 24-hour patrols.

Costs (2015–16) *Tuition:* 178,200 Mexican pesos full-time. Full-time tuition and fees vary according to degree level, program, reciprocity agreements, and student level. *Payment plans:* tuition prepayment, installment, deferred payment.

Applying *Required:* high school transcript, interview, Local Test and Psychological Profile.

Freshman Application Contact Admissions, Westhill University, 56 Domingo Garcia Ramos, Zona Escolar, Prados de la Montana I, 05610 Sante Fe, Cuajimalpa, Mexico. *Phone:* 52-55 88517010. *Toll-free phone:* 800-838-7711. *E-mail:* admissions@westhill.edu.mx.
Website: http://www.westhill.edu.mx/.

PALAU

Palau Community College
Koror, Palau

- **Territory-supported** 2-year, founded 1969
- **Small-town** 30-acre campus
- **Endowment** $1.3 million
- **Coed,** 627 undergraduate students, 55% full-time, 54% women, 46% men

Undergraduates 347 full-time, 280 part-time. 0.3% transferred in; 20% live on campus. *Retention:* 58% of full-time freshmen returned.

Freshmen *Admission:* 180 enrolled.

Faculty *Total:* 46, 85% full-time. *Student/faculty ratio:* 10:1.

Majors Accounting; administrative assistant and secretarial science; agriculture; automobile/automotive mechanics technology; business teacher education; carpentry; construction engineering technology; criminal justice/police science; education; electrical, electronic and communications engineering technology; hotel/motel administration; liberal arts and sciences/liberal studies; natural resources and conservation related; registered nursing/registered nurse.

Academics *Calendar:* semesters. *Degree:* certificates and associate. *Special study options:* academic remediation for entering students, adult/continuing education programs, cooperative education, double majors, English as a second language, honors programs, internships, part-time degree program, summer session for credit.

Library Palau Community College Library.

Student Life *Housing Options:* coed, men-only. Campus housing is university owned. *Activities and Organizations:* Yapese Student Organization, Chuukes Student Organization, Palauans Student Organization, Environmental Club, Writing Club. *Campus security:* 24-hour emergency response devices and patrols, late-night transport/escort service, evening patrols by trained security personnel. *Student services:* health clinic, personal/psychological counseling, legal services.

Athletics *Intramural sports:* baseball M, basketball M, softball M/W, table tennis M/W, volleyball M/W, weight lifting M, wrestling M.

Costs (2015–16) *Tuition:* state resident $2640 full-time, $110 per credit part-time; nonresident $3000 full-time, $125 per credit part-time. Full-time tuition and fees vary according to course load. Part-time tuition and fees vary according to course load. *Required fees:* $610 full-time. *Room and board:* $3381; room only: $1176. *Payment plan:* installment.

Financial Aid *Financial aid deadline:* 6/30.

Applying *Options:* early admission, deferred entrance. *Application fee:* $10. *Required:* high school transcript, minimum 2.0 GPA. *Application deadlines:* 8/15 (freshmen), 8/15 (transfers). *Notification:* continuous (freshmen), continuous (transfers).

Freshman Application Contact Ms. Dahlia Katosang, Director of Admissions and Financial Aid, Palau Community College, PO Box 9, Koror, PW 96940-0009. *Phone:* 680-488-2471 Ext. 233. *Fax:* 680-488-4468.
E-mail: dahliapcc@palaunet.com.
Website: http://www.palau.edu/.

Institutional Changes Since *Peterson's® Two-Year Colleges 2016*

The following is an alphabetical listing of institutions that have closed, merged with other institutions, or changed their names or status since the release of *Peterson's® Two-Year Coleges 2016.*

Akron Institute of Herzing University (Akron, OH): *name changed to Herzing University.*

All-State Career School–Allied Health Campus (Essington, PA): *name changed to All-State Career School–Essington Campus.*

American Academy of Dramatic Arts (Hollywood, CA): *name changed to American Academy of Dramatic Arts–Los Angeles.*

American National University (Charlottesville, VA): *now classified as a 4-year college.*

American National University (Danville, VA): *now classified as a 4-year college.*

American National University (Harrisonburg, VA): *now classified as a 4-year college.*

American National University (Lynchburg, VA): *now classified as a 4-year college.*

American National University (Martinsville, VA): *now classified as a 4-year college.*

Anoka-Ramsey Community College, Cambridge Campus (Cambridge, MN): *merged into a single entry for Anoka-Ramsey Community College (Coon Rapids, MN) by request from the institution.*

Berkeley College–Westchester Campus (White Plains, NY): *name changed to Berkeley College–White Plains Campus.*

Bryant & Stratton College–North Campus (Liverpool, NY): *name changed to Bryant & Stratton College–Liverpool Campus.*

Bryant & Stratton College–Southtowns Campus (Orchard Park, NY): *name changed to Bryant & Stratton College–Orchard Park Campus.*

Burlington County College (Pemberton, NJ): *name changed to Rowan College at Burlington County.*

Business Informatics Center, Inc. (Valley Stream, NY): *closed.*

Camelot College (Baton Rouge, LA): *no longer degree granting.*

Career Technical College (Monroe, LA): *name changed to McCann School of Business & Technology.*

Career Technical College (Shreveport, LA): *name changed to McCann School of Business & Technology.*

Career Training Solutions (Fredericksburg, VA): *name changed to Eastern Virginia Career College.*

Carrington College–Phoenix (Phoenix, AZ): *name changed to Carrington College–Phoenix North.*

Carrington College–Phoenix Westside (Phoenix, AZ): *name changed to Carrington College–Phoenix West.*

Carrington College–Portland (Portland, OR): *no longer degree granting.*

Cascadia Community College (Bothell, WA): *name changed to Cascadia College.*

Cochise College (Douglas, AZ): *name changed to Cochise County Community College District.*

College of Business and Technology (Miami, FL): *name changed to College of Business and Technology–Main Campus.*

The Community College of Baltimore County (Baltimore, MD): *name changed to Community College of Baltimore County.*

Court Reporting Institute of Dallas (Dallas, TX): *closed.*

Daymar College (Jackson, OH): *closed.*

Daymar College (New Boston, OH): *closed.*

Daymar Institute (Nashville, TN): *name changed to Daymar College.*

Delta College of Arts and Technology (Baton Rouge, LA): *no longer degree granting.*

Eagle Gate College (Salt Lake City, UT): *closed.*

Everest College (Aurora, CO): *closed.*

Everest College (Portland, OR): *closed.*

Everest College (Dallas, TX): *closed.*

Everest College (Newport News, VA): *closed.*

Everest College (Bremerton, WA): *closed.*

Everest College (Vancouver, WA): *closed.*

Everest Institute (Pittsburgh, PA): *closed.*

FIDM/Fashion Institute of Design & Merchandising, Los Angeles Campus (Los Angeles, CA): *now classified as a 4-year college.*

FIDM/Fashion Institute of Design & Merchandising, San Francisco Campus (San Francisco, CA): *now classified as a 4-year college.*

Fort Berthold Community College (New Town, ND): *name changed to Nueta Hidatsa Sahnish College.*

Fortis Institute (Miami, FL): *closed.*

Four-D College (Colton, CA): *closed.*

Gem City College (Quincy, IL): *no longer degree granting.*

Georgia Perimeter College (Decatur, GA): *merged into Georgia State University (Atlanta, GA).*

H. Councill Trenholm State Technical College (Montgomery, AL): *name changed to H. Councill Trenholm State Community College.*

Helene Fuld College of Nursing of North General Hospital (New York, NY): *name changed to Helene Fuld College of Nursing.*

Henry Ford Community College (Dearborn, MI): *name changed to Henry Ford College.*

Hussian School of Art (Philadelphia, PA): *name changed to Hussian College, School of Art.*

Institute of Design and Construction (Brooklyn, NY): *closed.*

Institute of Technical Arts (Casselberry, FL): *closed.*

IntelliTec Medical Institute (Colorado Springs, CO): *name changed to IBMC College.*

ITT Technical Institute (Culver City, CA): *closed.*

ITT Technical Institute (Westminster, CO): *closed.*

ITT Technical Institute (Bradenton, FL): *closed.*

ITT Technical Institute (Orlando, FL): *closed.*

ITT Technical Institute (St. Petersburg, FL): *closed.*

ITT Technical Institute (Cedar Rapids, IA): *closed.*

ITT Technical Institute (Clive, IA): *closed.*

ITT Technical Institute (Eden Prairie, MN): *closed.*

ITT Technical Institute (Cary, NC): *closed.*

ITT Technical Institute (Dunmore, PA): *closed.*

ITT Technical Institute (Tarentum, PA): *closed.*

ITT Technical Institute (Myrtle Beach, SC): *closed.*

ITT Technical Institute (Johnson City, TN): *closed.*

ITT Technical Institute (Green Bay, WI): *closed.*

ITT Technical Institute (Madison, WI): *closed.*

ITT Technical Institute (Huntington, WV): *closed.*

Kaplan Career Institute, Broomall Campus (Broomall, PA): *name changed to Brightwood Career Institute, Broomall Campus.*

Kaplan Career Institute, Franklin Mills Campus (Philadelphia, PA): *name changed to Brightwood Career Institute, Philadelphia Mills Campus.*

Kaplan Career Institute, Harrisburg Campus (Harrisburg, PA): *name changed to Brightwood Career Institute, Harrisburg Campus.*

Kaplan Career Institute, Philadelphia Campus (Philadelphia, PA): *name changed to Brightwood Career Institute, Philadelphia Campus.*

Kaplan Career Institute, Pittsburgh Campus (Pittsburgh, PA): *name changed to Brightwood Career Institute, Pittsburgh Campus.*

Kaplan College, Arlington Campus (Arlington, TX): *name changed to Brightwood College, Arlington Campus.*

Kaplan College, Bakersfield Campus (Bakersfield, CA): *name changed to Brightwood College, Bakersfield Campus.*

Kaplan College, Beaumont Campus (Beaumont, TX): *name changed to Brightwood College, Beaumont Campus.*

Kaplan College, Brownsville Campus (Brownsville, TX): *name changed to Brightwood College, Brownsville Campus.*

Kaplan College, Charlotte Campus (Charlotte, NC): *name changed to Brightwood College, Charlotte Campus.*

Kaplan College, Chula Vista Campus (Chula Vista, CA): *name changed to Brightwood College, Chula Vista Campus.*

Kaplan College, Corpus Christi Campus (Corpus Christi, TX): *name changed to Brightwood College, Corpus Christi Campus.*

Kaplan College, Dallas Campus (Dallas, TX): *name changed to Brightwood College, Dallas Campus.*

Kaplan College, Dayton Campus (Dayton, OH): *name changed to Brightwood College, Dayton Campus.*

Kaplan College, El Paso Campus (El Paso, TX): *name changed to Brightwood College, El Paso Campus.*

Kaplan College, Fort Worth Campus (Fort Worth, TX): *name changed to Brightwood College, Fort Worth Campus.*

Kaplan College, Fresno Campus (Clovis, CA): *name changed to Brightwood College, Fresno Campus.*

Kaplan College, Hammond Campus (Hammond, IN): *name changed to Brightwood College, Hammond Campus.*

Kaplan College, Laredo Campus (Laredo, TX): *name changed to Brightwood College, Laredo Campus.*

Kaplan College, Las Vegas Campus (Las Vegas, NV): *name changed to Brightwood College, Las Vegas Campus.*

Kaplan College, Lubbock Campus (Lubbock, TX): *closed.*

Kaplan College, McAllen Campus (McAllen, TX): *name changed to Brightwood College, McAllen Campus.*

Kaplan College, Modesto Campus (Salida, CA): *name changed to Brightwood College, Modesto Campus.*

Kaplan College, Nashville Campus (Nashville, TN): *name changed to Brightwood College, Nashville Campus.*

Kaplan College, North Hollywood Campus (North Hollywood, CA): *name changed to Brightwood College, North Hollywood Campus.*

Kaplan College, Palm Springs Campus (Palm Springs, CA): *name changed to Brightwood College, Palm Springs Campus.*

Kaplan College, Riverside Campus (Riverside, CA): *name changed to Brightwood College, Riverside Campus.*

Kaplan College, Sacramento Campus (Sacramento, CA): *name changed to Brightwood College, Sacramento Campus.*

Kaplan College, San Antonio Campus (San Antonio, TX): *name changed to Brightwood College, San Antonio Ingram Campus.*

Kaplan College, San Antonio–San Pedro Area Campus (San Antonio, TX): *name changed to Brightwood College, San Antonio San Pedro Campus.*

Kaplan College, San Diego Campus (San Diego, CA): *name changed to Brightwood College, San Diego Campus.*

Kaplan College, Southeast Indianapolis Campus (Indianapolis, IN): *name changed to Brightwood College, Indianapolis Campus.*

Kaplan College, Vista Campus (Vista, CA): *name changed to Brightwood College, Vista Campus.*

Kilian Community College (Sioux Falls, SD): *closed.*

Le Cordon Bleu College of Culinary Arts in Atlanta (Tucker, GA): *closed.*

Le Cordon Bleu College of Culinary Arts in Austin (Austin, TX): *closed.*

Le Cordon Bleu College of Culinary Arts in Boston (Cambridge, MA): *closed.*

Le Cordon Bleu College of Culinary Arts in Chicago (Chicago, IL): *closed.*

Le Cordon Bleu College of Culinary Arts in Dallas (Dallas, TX): *closed.*

Le Cordon Bleu College of Culinary Arts in Las Vegas (Las Vegas, NV): *closed.*

Le Cordon Bleu College of Culinary Arts in Los Angeles (Pasadena, CA): *closed.*

Le Cordon Bleu College of Culinary Arts in Miami (Miramar, FL): *closed.*

Le Cordon Bleu College of Culinary Arts in Minneapolis/St. Paul (Mendota Heights, MN): *closed.*

Le Cordon Bleu College of Culinary Arts in Orlando (Orlando, FL): *closed.*

Le Cordon Bleu College of Culinary Arts in Portland (Portland, OR): *closed.*

Le Cordon Bleu College of Culinary Arts in San Francisco (San Francisco, CA): *closed.*

Le Cordon Bleu College of Culinary Arts in Scottsdale (Scottsdale, AZ): *closed.*

Marian Court College (Swampscott, MA): *closed.*

Metro Business College (Arnold, MO): *closed.*

Mid-South Community College (West Memphis, AR): *name changed to Arkansas State University Mid-South.*

Moultrie Technical College (Moultrie, GA): *merged into new Southern Regional Technical College (Thomasville, GA).*

Mount Washington College (Manchester, NH): *closed.*

National College (Danville, KY): *name changed to American National University and now classified as a 4-year college.*

National College (Florence, KY): *name changed to American National University and now classified as a 4-year college.*

National College (Lexington, KY): *name changed to American National University and now classified as a 4-year college.*

National College (Louisville, KY): *name changed to American National University and now classified as a 4-year college.*

National College (Pikeville, KY): *name changed to American National University and now classified as a 4-year college.*

National College (Richmond, KY): *name changed to American National University and now classified as a 4-year college.*

National College (Canton, OH): *name changed to American National University and now classified as a 4-year college.*

National College (Cincinnati, OH): *name changed to American National University and now classified as a 4-year college.*

National College (Cleveland, OH): *name changed to American National University and now classified as a 4-year college.*

National College (Columbus, OH): *name changed to American National University and now classified as a 4-year college.*

National College (Kettering, OH): *name changed to American National University and now classified as a 4-year college.*

National College (Stow, OH): name changed to American National University and now classified as a 4-year college.

National College (Youngstown, OH*): name changed to American National University and now classified as a 4-year college.*

National Park Community College (Hot Springs, AR): *name changed to National Park College.*

Northwestern College (Chicago, IL): *name changed to Northwestern College–Chicago Campus.*

Orleans Technical Institute (Philadelphia, PA): *no longer degree granting.*

The Paralegal Institute, Inc. (Scottsdale, AZ): *name changed to The Paralegal Institute at Brighton College.*

Professional Business College (New York, NY): *closed.*

Remington College–Houston Campus (Houston, TX): *closed.*

Remington College–Houston Southeast (Webster, TX): *name changed to Remington College–Houston Southeast Campus.*

Remington College–Orlando Campus (Heathrow, FL): *name changed to Remington College–Heathrow Campus.*

Remington College–Tampa Campus (Tampa, FL): *closed.*

SAE Institute of Technology (Nashville, TN): *name changed to SAE Institute Nashville.*

Southeastern College–Greenacres (Greenacres, FL): *name changed to Southeastern College–West Palm Beach.*

Southeastern College–Miami Lakes (Miami Lakes, FL): *merged into a single entry for Southeastern College–West Palm Beach (West Palm Beach, FL) by request from the institution.*

Southeastern College–St. Petersburg (St. Petersburg, FL): *closed.*

Southwest Georgia Technical College (Thomasville, GA): *name changed to Southern Regional Technical College.*

Stenotype Institute of Jacksonville (Jacksonville, FL): *closed.*

SUM Bible College & Theological Seminary (Oakland, CA): *now classified as a 4-year college.*

TCI–The College of Technology (New York, NY): *name changed to TCI–College of Technology.*

TESST College of Technology (Baltimore, MD): *name changed to Brightwood College, Baltimore Campus.*

TESST College of Technology (Beltsville, MD): *name changed to Brightwood College, Beltsville Campus.*

TESST College of Technology (Towson, MD): *name changed to Brightwood College, Towson Campus.*

Texas School of Business, Friendswood Campus (Friendswood, TX): *name changed to Brightwood College, Friendswood Campus.*

Texas School of Business, Houston North Campus (Houston, TX): *name changed to Brightwood College, Houston Campus.*

Texas State Technical College Harlingen (Harlingen, TX): *merged into a single entry for Texas State Technical College (Waco, TX) by request from the institution.*

Texas State Technical College–Marshall (Marshall, TX): *merged into a single entry for Texas State Technical College (Waco, TX) by request from the institution.*

Texas State Technical College Waco (Waco, TX): *name changed to Texas State Technical College.*

Texas State Technical College West Texas (Sweetwater, TX): *merged into a single entry for Texas State Technical College (Waco, TX) by request from the institution.*

Tribeca Flashpoint Media Arts Academy (Chicago, IL): *name changed to Tribeca Flashpoint College.*

University of Alaska, Prince William Sound Community.

Wright State University–Lake Campus (Celina, OH): *now classified as a 4-year college.*

Yorktowne Business Institute (York, PA): *closed.* College (Valdez, AK): *name changed to University of Alaska, Prince William Sound College.*

University of Cincinnati Blue Ash (Cincinnati, OH): *name changed to University of Cincinnati Blue Ash College.*

The Williamson Free School of Mechanical Trades (Media, PA): *name changed to Williamson College of the Trades.*

Wright Career College (Overland Park, KS): *closed.*

Wright Career College (Wichita, KS): *closed.*

Wright Career College (Omaha, NE): *closed.*

Wright Career College (Oklahoma City, OK): *closed.*

Wright Career College (Tulsa, OK): *closed.*

Wright State University–Lake Campus (Celina, OH): *now classified as a 4-year college.*

Yorktowne Business Institute (York, PA): *closed.*Orleans Technical Institute (Philadelphia, PA): *no longer degree granting.*

The Paralegal Institute, Inc. (Scottsdale, AZ): *name changed to The Paralegal Institute at Brighton College.*

Professional Business College (New York, NY): *closed.*

Remington College–Houston Campus (Houston, TX): *closed.*

Remington College–Houston Southeast (Webster, TX): *name changed to Remington College–Houston Southeast Campus.*

Remington College–Orlando Campus (Heathrow, FL): *name changed to Remington College–Heathrow Campus.*

Remington College–Tampa Campus (Tampa, FL): *closed.*

SAE Institute of Technology (Nashville, TN): *name changed to SAE Institute Nashville.*

Southeastern College–Greenacres (Greenacres, FL): *name changed to Southeastern College–West Palm Beach.*

Southeastern College–Miami Lakes (Miami Lakes, FL): *merged into a single entry for Southeastern College–West Palm Beach (West Palm Beach, FL) by request from the institution.*

Southeastern College–St. Petersburg (St. Petersburg, FL): *closed.*

Southwest Georgia Technical College (Thomasville, GA): *name changed to Southern Regional Technical College.*

Stenotype Institute of Jacksonville (Jacksonville, FL): *closed.*

SUM Bible College & Theological Seminary (Oakland, CA): *now classified as a 4-year college.*

TCI–The College of Technology (New York, NY): *name changed to TCI–College of Technology.*

TESST College of Technology (Baltimore, MD): *name changed to Brightwood College, Baltimore Campus.*

TESST College of Technology (Beltsville, MD): *name changed to Brightwood College, Beltsville Campus.*

TESST College of Technology (Towson, MD): *name changed to Brightwood College, Towson Campus.*

Texas School of Business, Friendswood Campus (Friendswood, TX): *name changed to Brightwood College, Friendswood Campus.*

Texas School of Business, Houston North Campus (Houston, TX): *name changed to Brightwood College, Houston Campus.*

Texas State Technical College Harlingen (Harlingen, TX): *merged into a single entry for Texas State Technical College (Waco, TX) by request from the institution.*

Texas State Technical College–Marshall (Marshall, TX): *merged into a single entry for Texas State Technical College (Waco, TX) by request from the institution.*

Texas State Technical College Waco (Waco, TX): *name changed to Texas State Technical College.*

Texas State Technical College West Texas (Sweetwater, TX): *merged into a single entry for Texas State Technical College (Waco, TX) by request from the institution.*

Tribeca Flashpoint Media Arts Academy (Chicago, IL): *name changed to Tribeca Flashpoint College.*

University of Alaska, Prince William Sound Community College (Valdez, AK): *name changed to University of Alaska, Prince William Sound College.*

University of Cincinnati Blue Ash (Cincinnati, OH): *name changed to University of Cincinnati Blue Ash College.*

The Williamson Free School of Mechanical Trades (Media, PA): *name changed to Williamson College of the Trades.*

Wright Career College (Overland Park, KS): *closed.*

Wright Career College (Wichita, KS): *closed.*

Wright Career College (Omaha, NE): *closed.*

Wright Career College (Oklahoma City, OK): *closed.*

Wright Career College (Tulsa, OK): *closed*

Featured Two-Year Colleges

BAY STATE COLLEGE
BOSTON, MASSACHUSETTS

The College and Its Mission

Founded in 1946, Bay State College is an independent, co-educational institution located in Boston's historic Back Bay. Since its founding, Bay State College has been preparing graduates for outstanding careers and continued education.

Bay State College is a small, private college focused on passionate students who want to turn their interests into rewarding careers. The College offers associate and bachelor's degrees in a number of rewarding fields. Everyone at Bay State—from admissions representatives and professors to the career services team—helps to assist, guide, and advise students, from the moment they step on campus. Located in Boston's Back Bay, the College offers the city of Boston as a campus, small classes, and one-on-one attention. For students seeking a career in one of the many professional opportunities offered by Bay State, a degree program at the College could be a strong first step on their career path.

The College offers day, evening, and online courses. Students can receive associate and bachelor's degrees, as well as a certificate in medical assisting. The educational experience offered through the variety of programs prepares students to excel in the careers of their choice. Personalized attention is the cornerstone of a Bay State College education. Through the transformative power of its core values of quality, respect, and support, Bay State College has, for the past seventy years, assisted students with setting and achieving goals that prepare them for careers and continued education.

Recognizing that one of the most important aspects of college is life outside the classroom, the Office of Student Affairs seeks to provide services from orientation through graduation. Special events throughout the year include an annual fashion show and a host of events produced by the Entertainment Management Association. Students also enjoy nearby professional sports teams such as the Boston Celtics and Boston Red Sox.

Bay State College's campus experience can be whatever the student chooses it to be. It's not the typical college campus—its residence halls are actually brownstones along Boston's trendy Commonwealth Avenue and Bay State's "quad" could be Boston Common, the banks of the Charles River by the Esplanade, or Copley Square. That's the advantage of being located in Boston's Back Bay, which is also one of the safest neighborhood in the city. Students can relax at a favorite coffee shop, bike along the Charles River, ice skate on the Frog Pond, check out the city's nightlife, or take in a ball game at Fenway Park.

Bay State College is accredited by the New England Association of Schools and Colleges and is authorized to award the Associate in Science, Associate in Applied Science, and three Bachelor of Science degrees by the Commonwealth of Massachusetts. Bay State is a member of several professional educational associations. Its medical assisting program is accredited by the Accrediting Bureau of Health Education Schools (ABHES). The physical therapist assistant program is accredited by the Commission on Accreditation in Physical Therapy Education (CAPTE) of the American Physical Therapy Association (APTA). Bay State College's Associate of Science in Nursing program is accredited by the Accreditation Commission for Education in Nursing (ACEN). ACEN is located at 3343 Peachtree Road NE, Suite 850, Atlanta, Georgia 30326. The Associate Degree in Nursing program was granted full approval status by the Massachusetts Board of Registration in Nursing on November 12, 2014.

Academic Programs

Bay State College's Day Division operates on a semester calendar. The fall semester typically runs from early September to mid-December. The spring semester runs from mid-January until mid-May.

Associate degrees are offered in business administration, criminal justice, entertainment management (with a concentration in audio production), fashion design, fashion merchandising, health studies, information technology, marketing, medical assisting, nursing, physical therapist assistant, retail business management, and hospitality management.

Bachelor's degrees are offered in criminal justice, entertainment management, fashion merchandising, information technology, management, and RN to B.S.N.

Bay State College's Evening and Online Division offers courses to working adults. The courses are offered in eight-week sessions and allow more flexibility for students who must balance work and family commitments while pursuing their education.

Bay State College's additional location in Taunton, Massachusetts, offers evening programs to working adults.

Bay State College reviews, enhances, and adds new programs to help graduates remain industry-current in their respective fields.

Off-Campus Programs

Many students cite Bay State's internship program as a turning point for them. Bay State internships allow students to gain hands-on experience and spend time working in their chosen fields. These valuable opportunities can give students an advantage when they apply for positions after they have completed their studies.

Bay State's Boston location allows the College to offer internships at many well-known companies and organizations. Students are able to apply what they've learned in the classroom and do meaningful work in their field of study. In addition, they build working relationships with people in their chosen profession. For more information on internships, prospective students may contact Career Services at 617-217-9000.

Costs

Tuition charges are assessed on a per-credit-hour basis and vary depending upon program of study. This provides students with maximum flexibility based on individual financial and academic needs, making a Bay State College education more accommodating and affordable. Rates quoted below by program are for the 2016–17 academic year. Charges are not prorated unless noted. Program flow sheets may require more or less than 30 credits per academic year.

Medical assisting certificate: $550 per credit, $15,950 (29 credits). Medical assisting, and health studies: $810 per credit, $24,300 (30 credits). Business, criminal justice, fashion merchandising, fashion design, entertainment management, and hospitality management: $905 per credit, $27,150 (30 credits). Nursing and physical therapy assistant: $905 per credit, $27,150 (30 credits).

Room and board are $13,000 per year, the student services fee is $400 (for day students only), and the student activity fee is $50. The cost of books and additional fees vary by major. A residence hall security deposit of $300 and a technology fee of $300 are required of all resident students.

The fall tuition payment due date is July 1; the spring tuition payment is due December 1.

Financial Aid

Each student works with a personal advocate to thoroughly explain financial options and guide them through the financial aid application process. Many options are available to those who qualify: aid, grants and scholarships, federal programs, and private loans. Bay State College's Financial Aid Department and tuition planners can help students determine what aid may apply. Approximately 85 percent of students receive some form of financial assistance. Bay State College requires a completed Free Application for Federal Student Aid (FAFSA) form and signed federal tax forms. The College's institutional financial aid priority deadline is March 31. Financial aid is granted on a rolling basis.

Faculty

There are approximately 100 faculty members, many holding advanced degrees and several holding doctoral degrees. The student-faculty ratio is 18:1.

Student Body Profile

There are approximately 1,100 students in degree programs in the day, evening, and online divisions.

Student Activities

Bay State College students participate in a number of activities offered by the College through existing student organizations. Students also have the opportunity to create clubs and organizations that meet their interests. Existing organizations include the Student Government Association, Entertainment Management Association, and the Justice Society. Fashion Design and Merchandising students produce an annual fashion show that showcases student work from the College's fashion design program. An annual literary magazine also features the work of students throughout the College.

Facilities and Resources

Advisement/Counseling: Trained staff members assist students in selecting courses and programs of study. A counseling center is available to provide mental and physical health referrals to all students in need of such services. Referral networks are extensive, within a wide range of geographic areas, and provide access to a variety of public and private health agencies.

Specialized Services: The Office of Academic Development at Bay State College is designed to meet and support the various academic needs of the student body and serve as a resource for supplemental instruction, academic plans, learning accommodations, and other types of support. The Office of Academic Development operates on the belief that all students can achieve success in their courses by accessing support services and creating individual academic plans.

The Center for Learning and Academic Success (CLAS) at Bay State College is a key component available to help students achieve academic success. Students come to CLAS to get support in specific subject areas as well as study skills such as note-taking, reading comprehension, writing research papers, time management, and coping with exam anxiety. They utilize CLAS to develop study plans and strategies that positively impact their grades in all subjects. Students can also take advantage of the tutoring and seminars CLAS offers. CLAS's goal is to ensure that students are provided with exceptional academic support in all areas of study.

Career Planning/Placement: For many college students, the transition from student life to professional life is filled with questions and uncharted realities. Bay State College's Career Services Department can help students learn to write a resume and cover letter, use social networks, practice interviewing skills, find the right job opportunity, and learn other career-related functions. The Career Services Department is determined to help each student succeed and offers valuable instruction that will serve students throughout their professional careers.

Library and Audiovisual Services: The library is staffed with trained librarians who are available to guide students in their research process. The library's resources include 7,500 books, eighty-five periodical subscriptions, and a dramatically increased reach through its online library resource databases that include ProQuest, InfoTrac, and LexisNexis. In addition, the library provides computer access and study space for students. The library catalog and databases are accessible from any Internet-ready terminal.

First-Year Experience: The First-Year Experience (FYE) is an orientation that is required of all first-year students. FYE combines social activities with an academic syllabus that is designed to ease the transition into the college experience. Through FYE, students have the opportunity to connect with their academic advisers as well as with other students in their academic programs. At the conclusion of FYE, students are on the road to mapping out their personal action plan for success. The plan, designed by students, guided by academic advisers, and revisited each semester, helps students set, monitor, and achieve academic and life goals.

Location

Located in the historic city of Boston, Massachusetts, and surrounded by dozens of colleges and universities, Bay State College is an ideal setting in which to pursue a college degree. Tree-lined streets around the school are mirrored in the skyscrapers of the Back Bay. The College is located within walking distance of several major league sport franchises, concert halls, museums, the Freedom Trail, Boston Symphony Hall, the Boston Public Library, and the Boston Public Garden. World-class shopping and major cultural and sporting events help make college life a memorable experience. The College is accessible by the MBTA and commuter rail and bus, and it is near Boston Logan International Airport.

Admission Requirements

Applicants must be a high school graduate, a current high school student working toward graduation, or a recipient of a GED certificate. The Office of Admissions requires that applicants to the associate degree programs have a minimum of a 2.0 GPA (on a 4.0 scale); if available, applicants may submit SAT and/or ACT scores. Applicants to bachelor's degree programs must have a minimum 2.3 GPA (on a 4.0 scale) and must also submit SAT or ACT scores. International applicants must also submit high school transcripts translated to English with an explanation of the grading system, financial documentation, and official TOEFL score of 183 or a 6.0 on the IELTS if native language is not English (or language school affiliate equivalent). The College also accepts iTEP test scores. If students are taking a different test, they need to check with the admissions team to ensure that test is accepted for admission.

The physical therapist assistant and nursing programs require a minimum 2.7 GPA (on a 4.0 scale) and the Evening Division has different or additional admission requirements. For more information about these programs, interested students should visit the website at http://www.baystate.edu.

A personal interview is required for all prospective students—parents are encouraged to attend. Applicants must receive the recommendation of a Bay State College Admissions Officer.

Application and Information

Applications are accepted on a rolling basis. Students are responsible for arranging for their official high school transcripts, test scores, and letters of recommendation to be submitted to Bay State College.

The Bay State College Admissions Office notifies applicants of a decision within one week of receipt of the transcript and other required documents. There is a $100 nonrefundable tuition deposit required upon acceptance to ensure a place in the class; the deposit is credited toward the tuition fee. Deposits are due within thirty days of acceptance. Once a student is accepted, a Bay State College representative creates a personalized financial plan that provides payment options for a Bay State College education.

Applications should be submitted to:

Admissions Office
Bay State College
122 Commonwealth Avenue
Boston, Massachusetts 02116
Phone: 800-81-LEARN (53276)
Fax: 617-249-0400 (eFax)
E-mail: admissions@baystate.edu
Website: http://www.baystate.edu
http://www.facebook.com/baystatecollege
http://twitter.com/baystatecollege

Giving students access is an essential part of a Bay State College education. Students have access to a community of support, experiential learning, faculty with real-world experience, and a dynamic location in the heart of the city.

CAMDEN COUNTY COLLEGE
BLACKWOOD, NEW JERSEY

The College and Its Mission

Camden County College (CCC) is a fully accredited comprehensive public community college located in New Jersey, near Philadelphia. CCC provides accessible and affordable education through 100-plus associate degree and occupational certificate programs along with noncredit development courses and job training. CCC is one of the largest community colleges in New Jersey and one of the most sophisticated in the nation. Recognized as a leader in technology programs, the College is also regionally acknowledged for nursing and healthcare education and as a vital resource for transfer education, customized training, and cultural events.

Although housing is not available on campus, students may reside at local apartment complexes within walking distance of the main campus in Blackwood and near the College's other locations in Camden and Cherry Hill.

More than 15 student clubs and service organizations, honor societies, and other activities are available. The College also has a student newspaper, *The Campus Press,* and a radio station, WDBK 91.5 FM.

Varsity sports teams compete against other two-year colleges in the Garden State Athletic Conference and Region XIX of the National Junior College Athletic Association. The athletic department at Camden County College offers 11 intercollegiate sports: men's and women's soccer, cross-country, basketball, golf, baseball/softball; women's tennis; and men's wrestling. Intramural sports are also offered, and students may use College athletic facilities, including an all-weather quarter-mile track; a fitness center; basketball/volleyball courts; and outdoor fields.

Academic Programs

http://camdencc.edu/academics/cataloginfo.cfm

Camden County College offers the following associate degrees: A.A., A.S., A.F.A., and A.A.S. The College also offers C.T., C.A., and C.P.S. certificates. Baccalaureate-completion programs are also offered on CCC's campuses, many of which allow students to earn Rutgers University degrees.

The College's fall and spring semesters include a 15-week session along with 13-week, 10-week, 7-week, 5-week, and weekend sessions. Summer sessions and a winter intersession are offered as well. On-campus, online, and hybrid courses are available. Classes are offered in arts, humanities, social sciences, business, computers, mathematics, healthcare, and the hard sciences. The College's academic calendar is available at **www.camdencc.edu**.

In general, approximately 60 credits are required to earn an associate degree and approximately 30 credits are required for a certificate. The total number of credits required varies by program.

Career Programs (A.A.S.) include accounting; addictions counseling; automotive technology (apprentice); automotive technology: GM/ASEP; biotechnology; biotechnology: cell and tissue culture option; biotechnology: forensic science option; CADD: computer-aided drafting and design; computer graphics; computer graphics: game design and development; computer information systems; computer integrated manufacturing/engineering technology; computer systems technology; dental assisting; dental hygiene; dietetic technology; engineering technology: electrical electronic engineering; engineering technology: electromechanical engineering; engineering technology: mechanical engineering; film and television production; finance; fire science technology; fire science technology: health information technology; health science; health science: certified medical assistant option; health science: surgical technology option; hospitality technology; management; management: business paraprofessional management option; management: small business management option; marketing; massage therapy; medical laboratory technology; office systems technology administrative assistant; office systems technology administrative assistant: information processing option; ophthalmic science technology; paralegal studies; paramedic sciences; paramedic sciences: paramedic educational management option; photonics: laser/electro-optic technology; photonics: laser/electro-optic technology fiber-optic option; preschool teacher education; respiratory therapy; sign language interpreter education; technical studies; veterinary technology; video imaging; and Web design and development.

Transfer Programs (A.A./ A.S. /A.F.A.) include business administration (A.S); computer science (A.A.) and (A.S.); criminal justice (A.S.); elementary/secondary education (A.S.); engineering science (A.S.); human services (A.S.); human services: developmental disabilities option (AS); human services: early childhood education option (A.S.); liberal arts and science (LAS) (A.A.); LAS: applied and fine arts option (A.A.); LAS: communications option (A.A.); LAS: public relations/advertising track (A.A.); LAS: computer graphics option (A.A.); LAS: electronic publishing track (A.A.); LAS: deaf studies option (A.A.); LAS English option (A.A.); LAS history option (A.A.); LAS: languages and international studies option (A.A.); LAS: law, government, and politics option (A.A.); LAS: music option (A.A.); LAS: photography option (A.A.); LAS: psychology option (A.A.); LAS: theatre option (A.A.); liberal arts and science (LAS) (A.S.); LAS: biology option (A.S.); LAS: chemistry option (A.S.); LAS: environmental science option (A.S.); LAS: food science option (A.S.); LAS: health and exercise science option (A.S.); LAS: mathematics option (A.S.); LAS: nursing, pre-nursing option; LAS: physics option (A.S.); LAS: pre-pharmacy option (A.S.); LAS: secondary education in biology option; LAS: secondary education in mathematics option (A.S.); management of information systems; nursing: Our Lady of Lourdes School of Nursing (A.S.); occupational therapy assistant (A.S.); psychosocial rehabilitation and treatment (A.S.); sport management (A.S.); and studio art (A.F.A).

Academic Certificate Programs (C.T.) offered are computer applications programming; computer graphics; computer integrated manufacturing technology; computer programming; computer systems technology; dental assisting; homeland security; medical coding; nutrition care manager; office assistant; photonics: fiber-optic technical specialist; practical nursing; and social services.

Certificate of Achievement Programs (C.A.) include ASL; ASL and English interpreting; addictions counseling; automotive general technician; CADD: computer-aided drafting and design; computer-aided manufacturing technician; culinary; educational interpreter training; emergency and disaster management; fundamentals of policing; industrial controls: precision machining technology; programmable logic controller; international healthcare; Linux/UNIX administration; massage therapy; meeting and event planning; multi-skilled technician; music recording; ophthalmic medical technician; ophthalmic science apprentice; paramedic sciences; personal trainer; relational database management system using ORACLE; SQL analyst; and surgical technology.

A Certificate of Postsecondary Study (C.P.S.) is offered in vocational skills.

Off-Campus Programs

Camden County College offers a cooperative program with Our Lady of Lourdes School of Nursing, through which associate degree students complete their nursing studies at Lourdes in Camden. Much of the training available through CCC's Camden County Career Institute is offered on the Sicklerville Campus of Camden County Technical Schools.

Credit for Nontraditional Learning Experiences

CCC offers a number of credit-earning opportunities including evaluating educational experiences approved by the American Council on Education and the Program on Non-Collegiate Sponsored Instruction and validating armed services training. Details are in the *Camden County College Catalog* at **www.camdencc.edu/academics/cataloginfo.cfm**.

Costs

For students who enter in September 2016, tuition costs are $107 per credit for in-county residents, $111 per credit for out-of-county residents, and $199 per credit for international students. The general service fee per credit is $30, and the facility fee per credit is $7. Other fees vary depending on courses taken.

The cost of books and supplies is estimated at $1,600 for one year for a full-time student. Actual costs depend on specific courses taken. Students who choose e-textbooks instead of new print books can reduce costs by up to 50 percent, and those who rent books or participate in buy-back programs can also save.

Financial Aid

Financial aid comes in the form of scholarships, grants, loans, and work-study employment. Students are required to file a Free Application for Federal Student Aid (FAFSA) as soon as possible after January 1 of each year using the College's school code of 006865, along with the College's authorization and certification form. Financial aid applications filed by May 1 and completed by June 1 of each year are given priority. Students must be admitted before an offer of financial aid can be made.

Faculty

The student-faculty ratio is 25:1. Faculty members are dedicated to teaching and supporting students throughout the academic year. In addition to the College's advisement staff, some faculty members may assist in providing academic advisement for their field of specialization. Most full-time and adjunct faculty members hold advanced degrees.

Student Body Profile

Of the College's 19,959 credit students served in fiscal year 2014, 73 percent were Camden County residents and 96 percent were New Jersey residents. Approximately 52.4 percent of the students were Caucasian, 21.5 percent African American, 5.7 percent Asian, 8.4 percent Hispanic, 1.3 percent American Indian/Alaskan native, 0.3 percent Native Hawaiian/Pacific Islander, 5.1 percent two or more, and 5.8 unknown/not reported. The mean student age is 28.

Academic Facilities

On the Blackwood Campus, the Kevin G. Halpern Hall for Science and Health Education houses state-of-the-art biology, chemistry, and physics labs; a dental hygiene clinic; a café and classroom kitchen; and a healthcare education suite with a laboratory, a surgical suite, and patient care areas for nursing, medical laboratory technology, veterinary technology, and surgical technology students. The library is located on the Blackwood Campus, and an e-library is available at the Cherry Hill location. Students on the Camden City Campus have access to the Rutgers University library and gym. CCC offers open-access computer labs, laser labs, an automotive facility, a vision care facility, and numerous other laboratories. The Otto R. Mauke Community Center houses a Barnes & Noble bookstore, a cyber café, student activities offices, a cafeteria, and student lounge areas. The Papiano Gymnasium hosts a fitness center and a variety of indoor and outdoor sports.

Location

The College has four primary locations: a 320-acre main campus in Blackwood, a branch campus in Camden in the University District, the William G. Rohrer Center in Cherry Hill, and the Regional Emergency Training Center (RETC) in Blackwood. The Blackwood Campus is accessible from many directions, particularly Route 42 via Exit 7B, which leads directly into the main entrance, and is easily reached from the interstate highway system, is located a short distance from the PATCO high-speed train line to and from Philadelphia, and is on NJ Transit bus routes.

A capital initiative has transformed many of the facilities and structural amenities of the Blackwood Campus: an all-in-one, fully networked Student Services Center was added during the renovation of Taft Hall; the Kevin G. Halpern Hall for Science and Health Education was constructed; and a traffic-flow-improving ring road, new athletic fields, and improved parking lots were completed. The Marlin Art Gallery, Dennis Flyer Memorial Theatre, Little Theatre, and Civic Hall, home to the Center for Civic Leadership and Responsibility, are venues for College, county, and community performances, presentations, and events. The Camden Conference Center on the Camden City Campus is used by College, business, community, and government groups. The RETC is home to the Camden County College Police Academy and the Camden County College Fire Academy.

Admission Requirements

Except for admission to selective programs, admission to credit programs and courses is open to all persons with a high school diploma or general equivalency diploma (GED), or other persons 18 years of age and older. In addition, high school students meeting the criteria under "Credit Programs for High School Students" and with the proper authorization are eligible for enrollment in credit courses but are considered non-matriculated students. Prospective students should apply online at **www.camdencc.edu**. There is no cost to apply to CCC.

Application and Information

Processing of admissions applications begins no later than February 15 for the fall semester and no later than October 1 for the spring semester. Rolling admission runs through the last day of a semester.

For more information, contact:

Office of Admissions, Records and Registration Services
Camden County College
P.O. Box 200
College Drive
Blackwood, New Jersey 08012
Phone: 856-227-7200 ext. 4200
Website: www.camdencc.edu

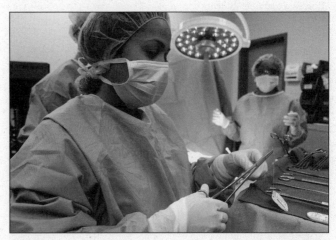

A student in Camden County College's surgical technology program practices her technique in one of the simulated operating rooms of the new Kevin G. Halpern Hall for Science & Health Education on the Blackwood Campus.

FASHION INSTITUTE OF TECHNOLOGY
State University of New York
NEW YORK, NEW YORK

 To read more about this school, visit http://petersons.to/fit

The College and Its Mission

The Fashion Institute of Technology, a college of the State University of New York, has been a leader in career education in art, design, business, and technology for more than 70 years. FIT infuses its nearly 50 majors with a comprehensive liberal arts education, providing a singular blend of practical experience and classroom study that prepares students for success and leadership in the competitive global marketplace. FIT offers a range of outstanding programs that are affordable and relevant to today's rapidly changing industries. Internationally renowned, FIT draws on its New York City location to provide a vibrant, creative community in which to learn. The schools of Art and Design, Business and Technology, and Liberal Arts offer Associate in Applied Science (A.A.S.), Bachelor of Fine Arts (B.F.A.), and Bachelor of Science (B.S.) degrees. The School of Graduate Studies offers Master of Arts (M.A.), Master of Fine Arts (M.F.A.), and Master of Professional Studies (M.P.S.) degrees. The college is accredited by the Middle States Commission on Higher Education, the National Association of Schools of Art and Design, and the Council for Interior Design Accreditation. FIT serves approximately 10,000 students from the greater metropolitan area, New York State, across the country, and around the world, providing full- and part-time study, evening/weekend degree programs, and online studies.

FIT's faculty members bring high-level industry experience to the classroom, working as corporate executives, entrepreneurs, consultants, designers, artists, and authors. Both practitioners and scholars, they connect students with real-world practice, fostering collaboration, innovation, and a global perspective. Academic departments consult with industry leaders to ensure that curricula and classroom technology reflect evolving professional practice.

FIT offers a complete college experience, with a vibrant campus life. Four residence halls house 2,300 students. Residential counselors and student staff members live in the residence halls, helping students adjust to college life and New York City.

Academic Programs

Each undergraduate program includes a core of traditional liberal arts courses, providing students with a global perspective, critical-thinking skills, and the ability to communicate effectively. All degree programs are designed to prepare students for creative and business careers and to provide them with the prerequisite studies to go on to baccalaureate, master's, or doctoral degrees, if they wish.

All students complete a two-year A.A.S. program in their major area and the liberal arts. They may then choose to go on to a related, two-year B.F.A. or B.S. program or begin their careers with their A.A.S. degree, which qualifies them for entry-level positions.

Associate Degree Programs: For the A.A.S. degree, FIT offers ten majors through the School of Art and Design, four through the Jay and Patty Baker School of Business and Technology, and one through the School of Liberal Arts. The A.A.S. programs are accessories design*, advertising and marketing communications*, communication design foundation*, fashion design*, fashion business management* (with an online option), film and media, fine arts, illustration, interior design, jewelry design, menswear, photography and related media, production management: fashion and related industries, textile development and marketing*, and textile/surface design*. Programs with an asterisk (*) are also available in a one-year format for students with sufficient transferable credits.

Bachelor's Degree Programs: Many A.A.S. graduates choose to pursue a related, two-year baccalaureate program at the college. FIT offers twenty-six baccalaureate programs—fourteen B.F.A. programs through the School of Art and Design, ten B.S. programs through the Baker School of Business and Technology, and two B.S. programs through the School of Liberal Arts. The B.F.A. programs are accessories design, advertising design, computer animation and interactive media, fabric styling, fashion design (with specializations in children's wear, intimate apparel, knitwear, special occasion, and sportswear), fine arts, graphic design, illustration, interior design, packaging design, photography and the digital image, textile/surface design, toy design, and visual

presentation and exhibition design. The B.S. programs are advertising and marketing communications, art history and museum professions, cosmetics and fragrance marketing, direct and interactive marketing, entrepreneurship for the fashion and design industries, fashion business management, film and media, home products development, international trade and marketing for the fashion industries, production management: fashion and related industries, technical design, and textile development and marketing.

Liberal Arts Minors: The School of Liberal Arts offers FIT students the opportunity to minor in a variety of liberal arts areas in two forms: traditional subject-based minors and interdisciplinary minors unique to the FIT liberal arts curriculum. Selected minors include economics, English literature, ethics and sustainability, international politics, Asian studies, and psychology.

Evening/Weekend Programs: FIT provides evening and weekend credit and noncredit classes to students and working professionals interested in pursuing a degree or furthering their knowledge of a particular industry, while balancing the demands of career or family. There are seven degree programs available through evening/weekend study: advertising and marketing communications (A.A.S.* and B.S.), communication design foundation (A.A.S.), fashion design (A.A.S.), fashion business management (A.A.S.* and B.S.), and international trade and marketing for the fashion industries (B.S.). Programs with an asterisk (*) are also available in a one-year format for students with sufficient transferable credits.

Certificate Programs: FIT's Center for Continuing and Professional Studies offers credit and noncredit certificates through its two divisions: Enterprise Studies and Digital Design and Professional Studies. Certificates available include leather apparel, millinery, retail management, fashion styling, pet product design and marketing, and sustainable design entrepreneurship. The center also provides career and personal development courses designed for adults with busy schedules.

Honors Program: The Presidential Scholars honors program, available to academically exceptional students in all majors, offers special courses, projects, colloquia, and off-campus activities that broaden horizons and stimulate discourse. Presidential Scholars receive priority course registration and an annual merit stipend.

Internships: Internships are a required element of most programs and are available to all matriculated students. Nearly one third of FIT student interns are offered employment on completion of their internships; past sponsors include American Eagle Outfitters, Bloomingdale's, Calvin Klein, Estée Lauder, Hearst Magazines, MTV, and Saatchi & Saatchi.

Precollege Programs: Precollege programs are available to middle and high school students during the fall, spring, and summer. More than 100 courses provide the chance to learn in an innovative environment, develop art and design portfolios, explore the business and technological sides of many creative careers, and discover natural talents and abilities.

Off-Campus Programs

The study-abroad experience lets students immerse themselves in diverse cultures and prepares them to live and work in a global community. FIT has two campuses in Italy—one in Milan, one in Florence—where students study fashion design or fashion business management and gain firsthand experience in the dynamics of European fashion. FIT also offers study-abroad options in countries like Australia, China, England, France, and Mexico. Students can study abroad during the winter or summer sessions, for a semester, or for a full academic year.

Costs

As a SUNY college, FIT offers affordable tuition for both New York State residents and nonresidents. The 2015–16 associate-level tuition per semester for in-state residents was $2,250; for nonresidents, $6,750. Baccalaureate-level tuition per semester was $3,235 for in-state residents and $9,796 for nonresidents. Per-semester housing costs were $6,693–$6,892 for traditional residence hall accommodations with mandatory meal plan and $6,175–$10,289 for apartment-style accommodations. Meal plans ranged from $1,797 to $2,300 per semester. Textbook costs and other nominal fees, such as locker rental or laboratory use, vary per program. All costs are subject to change.

Financial Aid

FIT offers scholarships, grants, loans, and work-study employment for students with financial need. Overall, two-thirds of full-time, matriculated undergraduate students who complete the federal financial aid application process receive some type of assistance through loans and/or grants. The college directly administers its own institutional grants and scholarships, which are provided by the FIT Foundation.

College-administered funding includes Federal Pell Grants, Federal Perkins Loans, Federal Supplemental Educational Opportunity Grants, Federal Work-Study, and the Federal Family Educational Loan Program, which includes student and parent loans. New York State residents who meet eligibility guidelines may also receive Tuition Assistance Program (TAP) and/or Educational Opportunity Program (EOP) grants. Financial aid applicants must file the Free Application for Federal Student Aid (FAFSA) and should also apply to all available outside sources of aid. Additional documentation may be requested by Financial Aid Services. Applications for financial aid should be completed prior to February 15 for fall admission or November 1 for spring admission.

Faculty

FIT's faculty is drawn from top professionals in academia, art, design, communications, and business, providing a curriculum rich in real-world experience and traditional educational values. Student-instructor interaction is encouraged, with a maximum class size of 25, and courses are structured to foster participation, independent thinking, and self-expression.

Student Body Profile

Fall 2014 enrollment was 9,764 with 8,455 students enrolled in degree programs. Thirty-six percent of degree-seeking students are enrolled in the School of Art and Design; 48 percent were in the Baker School of Business and Technology. The average age of full-time degree seekers was 23. Thirty-seven percent of FIT's students were New York City residents, 25 percent were New York State (non–New York City) residents, and 37 percent were out-of-state residents or international students. The ethnic/racial makeup of the student body was approximately 10 percent Asian; 10 percent black; 16 percent Hispanic; 3 percent multiracial; and 46 percent white. There were 1,211 international students.

Student Activities

Participation in campus life is encouraged, and the college is home to more than sixty student organizations, societies, athletic teams, major-related groups, and special-interest clubs. Each organization is open to all students who have paid their activity fee.

Student Government: The Student Council, the governing body of the FIT Student Association, grants all students the privileges and responsibilities of citizens in a self-governing college community. Faculty committees often include student representatives, and the president of the student government sits on FIT's Board of Trustees.

Athletics: FIT has intercollegiate teams in cross-country and half marathon, track and field, table tennis, women's tennis, women's soccer, swimming and diving, and women's volleyball; there is also a coed dance company. Athletics and Recreation offers a full array of group fitness classes, including aerobics, dance, spin, and yoga at no extra cost. Students can also work out on their own in a 5,000-square-foot fitness center. Open gym activities allow students to participate in both team and individual sports.

Events: Concerts, dances, field trips, films, flea markets, and other events are planned by the FIT Student Association and Programming Board and various clubs. Student-run publications include a campus newspaper, a fashion and beauty magazine, and a literary and art magazine.

Facilities and Resources

FIT's campus provides its students with classrooms, laboratories, and studios that reflect the most advanced educational and industry practices. The Fred P. Pomerantz Art and Design Center houses drawing, painting, photography, printmaking, and sculpture studios; display and exhibition design rooms; a model-making workshop; and a graphics printing service bureau. The Peter G. Scotese Computer-Aided Design and Communications Center provides the latest technology in computer graphics, design, photography, and animation. Other cutting-edge facilities include a professionally equipped fragrance-development laboratory—the only one of its kind on a U.S. college campus—cutting and sewing labs, a design/research lighting laboratory, knitting lab, broadcasting studio, multimedia foreign languages laboratory, and forty-six computer labs containing Mac and PC workstations.

The Museum at FIT, New York City's only museum dedicated to fashion, contains one of the most important collections of fashion and textiles in the world. The museum, which is accredited by the American Alliance of Museums, operates year-round, and its exhibitions are free and open to the public. The Gladys Marcus Library provides more than 300,000 volumes of print, nonprint, and electronic materials. The periodicals collection includes over 500 current subscriptions, with a specialization in international design and trade publications; online resources include more than 90 searchable databases.

The David Dubinsky Student Center offers student lounges, a game room, a student radio station, the Style Shop (a student-run boutique), a full-service dining hall and Starbucks, student government and club offices, disability services, comprehensive health services and a counseling center, two gyms, a state-of-the-art fitness center, and a dance studio.

Location

Occupying an entire block in Manhattan's Chelsea neighborhood, FIT makes extensive use of the city's creative, commercial, and cultural resources, providing students with unrivaled internship opportunities and professional connections. A wide range of cultural and entertainment options are available within a short walk of the campus, as is convenient access to several subway and bus lines and the city's major rail and bus transportation hubs.

Admission Requirements

Applicants for admission must be either candidates for or recipients of a high school diploma or a General Educational Development (GED) certificate. Admission is based on strength and performance in college-preparatory coursework and the student essay. A portfolio evaluation is required for art and design majors. Specific portfolio requirements are explained on FIT's website. SAT and ACT scores are required for placement in math and English classes and they are required for students applying to the Presidential Scholars honors program. International applicants whose native language is not English must submit scores from TOEFL, PTE, or IELTS examinations.

Transfer students must submit official transcripts for admission and credit evaluation. Students may qualify for the one-year A.A.S. option if they hold a bachelor's degree or if they have a minimum of 30 transferable college credits, including 24 credits equivalent to FIT's liberal arts requirements.

Students seeking admission to a B.F.A. or B.S. program must hold an A.A.S. degree from FIT or an equivalent college degree and must meet the prerequisites for the specific major. Further requirements may include an interview with a departmental committee, review of academic standing, and portfolio review for applicants to B.F.A. programs. Any student who applies for baccalaureate-level transfer to FIT from a four-year program must have completed a minimum of 60 credits, including the requisite art or technical courses and the liberal arts requirements.

Application and Information

Students wishing to visit FIT are encouraged to attend an admissions information session and take a tour of FIT's campus. The visit schedule is available online at fitnyc.edu/visitfit. A virtual tour of the campus can be found at fitnyc.edu/virtualtour. Candidates may apply online at fitnyc.edu/admissions. More information is available by contacting:

Office of Admissions

Fashion Institute of Technology
227 West 27 Street, Room C139
New York, New York 10001-5992
Phone: 212-217-3760
       800-GO-TO-FIT (toll-free)
E-mail: fitinfo@fitnyc.edu
Website: http://www.fitnyc.edu
       http://www.facebook.com/FashionInstituteofTechnology

FIDM/FASHION INSTITUTE OF DESIGN & MERCHANDISING
LOS ANGELES, CALIFORNIA

The Institute and Its Mission

For more than 46 years, FIDM/Fashion Institute of Design & Merchandising has been educating students for professional careers in fashion, interior design, digital arts, and entertainment, offering bachelor's and associate degrees in 25 creative majors. The talented and supportive faculty, dedicated staff, and renowned industry partners work together to create an academically rigorous, career-focused curriculum that results in skilled, marketable, and in-demand graduates. FIDM students complete more specialized and industry-driven classes in their major in two years than most four-year college students do throughout their education. FIDM's four vibrant campuses are strategically located in California's entertainment, fashion, action sports industry, and business hubs. FIDM's Career Center team has exceptional connections and offers one-on-one targeted career planning and placement services.

Established in 1969, FIDM is a private college of about 5,300 students with over 65,000 alumni. Graduates receive membership in the Alumni Association, which keeps them well connected while providing up-to-the-minute alumni news and information. FIDM alumni chapters can be found in 40 locations around the United States, Europe, and Asia.

FIDM offers two-year and four-year degree programs—Associate of Arts (A.A.), A.A. Professional Designation, A.A. Advanced Study, Bachelor of Science (B.S.), and Bachelor of Arts (B.A.).

Career Services: Career planning and job placement are among the most important services offered by the college. Career assistance includes job search techniques, preparation for employment interviews, resume preparation, virtual portfolios, and job adjustment assistance. FIDM's full-time advisors in the Career Center partner one-on-one with current students and graduates to help them move forward on their career paths, within their chosen major. Employers post over 20,000 jobs a year on FIDM's alumni job search site, which is available 24/7 exclusively to FIDM students and graduates. FIDM Career Advisors connect students to internships and directly to people in the industry. FIDM also offers job fairs, open portfolio days, and networking days to allow students to meet alumni and industry leaders face-to-face. Because of the college's long-standing industry relationships, many firms come to FIDM first to recruit its students. FIDM grads are highly marketable, and have a strong employment rate across all majors. Everything about FIDM's curriculum and resources is geared toward ensuring that its grads are highly sought-after in the marketplace. Some of FIDM's successful graduates include celebrity designers Nick Verreos, Monique Lhuillier, and a cofounder of Juicy Couture, Pamela Skaist-Levy, as well as Hollywood costume designers Trish Summerville, Marlene Stewart, and Mona May.

Student Life: FIDM's ethnically and culturally diverse student body attracts students from around the world. The current population includes students from more than 57 different countries. The Student Activities Department plans and coordinates social activities, cultural events, and community projects. Student organizations include the ASID student chapter, Cross-Cultural Student Alliance, Student Council, Phi Theta Kappa Honor Society, Student Veterans of America (SVA), and the Alumni Association. Students from all majors and campuses collaborate to produce *FIDM MODE*™, a glossy lifestyle magazine that promotes awareness about the design industry, current events, alumni news, and FIDM student life. The current issue can be viewed online at FIDMMODE.com.

FIDM's unique industry partnerships offer exciting opportunities for students through internships, job fair events, and informative guest speakers from companies such as Zara, JustFab, Gap Inc., Volcom, Oakley, Smashbox, and Stila.

Accreditation: FIDM is accredited by the Senior College and University Commission of the Western Association of Schools and Colleges (WASC) and the National Association of Schools of Art and Design (NASAD).

Academic Programs

FIDM offers Associate of Arts (A.A.), A.A. Advanced Study, A.A. Professional Designation, and Bachelor's (B.A. and B.S.) Degree programs. There are 25 specialized creative business and design majors to choose from.

FIDM's Admissions Advisors help students explore the career paths available and choose the right program.

Associate degree programs include:

Associate of Arts: A foundation of liberal arts combined with two years of specialized education in one of the following majors: Apparel Industry Management, Beauty Industry Merchandising & Marketing, Digital Media, Fashion Design, Fashion Knitwear Design, Graphic Design, Interior Design, Jewelry Design, Merchandising & Marketing, Merchandise Product Development, Social Media, Textile Design, and Visual Communications.

Associate of Arts Professional Designation: One-year programs designed for transfer students and college grads. Specialties include: Apparel Industry Management, Beauty Industry Merchandising & Marketing, Digital Media, Fashion Design, Fashion Knitwear Design, Graphic Design, Interior Design, Jewelry Design, Merchandising & Marketing, Merchandise Product Development, Social Media, Textile Design, and Visual Communications.

Associate of Arts Advanced Study: For students holding an A.A. degree from FIDM in a related discipline, programs include: Advanced Fashion Design, Beauty Industry Management, Entertainment Set Design & Decoration, Film & TV Costume Design, Footwear Design, International Manufacturing & Product Development, Menswear, and Theatre Costume Design.

Students who complete an A.A. degree at FIDM are qualified to apply for FIDM's specialized Bachelor's Degree programs including:

B.A. degrees in Design, Digital Media, Graphic Design, Interior Design, Professional Studies (both A.A. and A.A. Advanced Study required), and Social Media.

B.S. degrees in Apparel Technical Design and Business Management.

For specific information and requirements concerning the above programs, prospective students should contact an Admissions Advisor at any FIDM campus.

FIDM operates on a four-quarter academic calendar. New students may begin their studies at the start of any quarter throughout the year. Detailed information about FIDM majors and curriculum is also available online at http://fidm.edu/en/Majors/.

FIDM's eLearning program ensures that a student's educational experience can take place almost anywhere. The online courses are designed to replicate the experience of classes on campus. Students in the eLearning program are granted the same high-quality education as students on campus and have immediate access to valuable campus resources, including the FIDM Library, Career Advisors, and instructors.

Off-Campus Programs

Internships are available within each major. Paid and volunteer positions provide work experience for students to gain practical application of classroom skills. Some of the companies that recruit FIDM interns include Sephora, Zappos, Nordstrom, Inc., BCBG, GUESS?, Inc., Pottery Barn, Old Navy, Volcom, NBC Universal, Mattel, and Charlotte Russe.

FIDM provides the opportunity for students to participate in academic study tours in Europe, Asia, and New York. These tours are specifically designed to broaden and enhance the specialized education offered at FIDM. Participants may earn academic credit under faculty-supervised directed studies. Exchange programs are also available with Instituto Europeo de Design (IED), Milan, Turin, Rome, and Barcelona; Créapole, École de Création Management, Paris; Janette Klein Instituto de la Moda, Mexico

City; Universidad De La Salle Bajío, Guanajuato; Pearl Academy of Fashion, New Delhi; and RMIT University, Melbourne, Hanoi, and Ho Chi Minh City.

Costs

For the 2016–17 academic year, tuition, fees, books, and most supplies start at $32,260, depending on the selected major. First-year application fees range from $225 for California residents to $525 for international students.

Financial Aid

There are several sources of financial funding available, including federal financial aid and education loan programs, California state aid programs, institutional loan programs, and FIDM awards and scholarships. The FIDM Financial Services Department and FIDM Admissions Advisors work one-on-one with students and parents to help them find funding for their FIDM education. More information on FIDM scholarships and financial aid can be found at http://fidm.edu/go/fidmscholarships.

Faculty

FIDM faculty members are selected as specialists in their fields, working professionals with impressive resumes and invaluable industry connections. They bring daily exposure from their industries into the classroom for the benefit of the students. In pursuit of the best faculty members, consideration is given to both academic excellence and practical experience.

Facilities and Resources

FIDM's award-winning campuses feature design studios with computer labs and innovative study spaces, spacious classrooms, imaginative common areas, and state-of-the-industry technology. Computer labs support and enhance the educational programs of the Institute. Specialized labs offer computerized cutting and marking; graphic, interior, and textile design; word processing; and database management.

The FIDM Library goes beyond traditional sources of information. The collections include print and electronic resources encompassing all subject areas, with an emphasis on fashion, business, retail, and interior design. The library also subscribes to over 200 national and international periodicals, providing the latest information on art, design, graphics, business, fashion, beauty, and current trends. Rounding out the comprehensive collections are an international video collection, subscriptions to major trend forecasting services, a Textiles and Design Research Room, a materials workroom, and access to analog and digital technology tools.

The FIDM Museum & Galleries' permanent and study collections contain more than 15,000 fashion objects from the 18th century to present day, including film and theater costumes. One of the largest learning institution collections in the United States, it contains top designer holdings including Coco Chanel, Yves Saint Laurent, Christian Dior, and Thom Browne, which are exhibited in the 8,000 square-foot Galleries. In addition, the Museum houses the City of Los Angeles Hollywood Costume Collection, the Rudi Gernreich Archive, and the Versace Menswear Archive.

Location

FIDM's main campus is in the heart of the gentrified South Park neighborhood of downtown Los Angeles, between the Staples Center and the famed California Market Center and Fashion District. There are additional campuses in San Francisco, Orange County, and San Diego. A virtual tour of the campuses and their locations is available at http://fidm.edu/en/Visit+FIDM/Launch+Virtual+Tour.

FIDM Los Angeles is nestled at the center of an incredibly vibrant apparel and entertainment hub, surrounded by the fashion, entertainment, jewelry, and financial districts. It is situated next to beautiful Grand Hope Park, a tree-filled oasis amid the hustle and bustle of downtown LA. Renovated by acclaimed architect Clive Wilkinson, FIDM San Francisco stands in the heart of historic Union Square. The country's third-largest shopping area and stimulating atmosphere combined with the industry-based staff and faculty make this campus as incredible as the city in which it is located.

The FIDM Orange County campus is a dynamic visual experience with ultramodern lofts, an indoor/outdoor student lounge, eye-popping colors, and a one-of-a-kind audiovisual igloo. Also designed by world-renowned architect Clive Wilkinson, this campus has received several prestigious architectural awards and has been featured in numerous national magazines.

FIDM San Diego's gorgeous campus overlooks PETCO Park and is near the historic Gaslamp district and the San Diego harbor. FIDM's newest campus is sophisticated, stylish, and tech savvy, reflecting the importance of California's fastest-growing city and its appeal to the global industry.

Admission Requirements

Students are accepted into one of FIDM's specialized Associate of Arts degree programs packed with 15–30 challenging courses per major. Associate of Arts programs are designed for high school graduates or applicants with strong GED scores. They offer the highly specialized curriculum of a specific major, as well as a traditional liberal arts/general studies foundation. Official transcripts from high school/secondary schools and all colleges/universities attended are needed to apply. International students must send transcripts accompanied by official English translations. Three recommendations from teachers, counselors, or employers are also required for admission. FIDM provides a reference request form on its website in the Admissions section under "How to Apply." All references must be sealed and mailed to the school. An admissions essay portion and portfolio/entrance project requirement, specific to the student's selected major, are also available on the website's Admissions section under "How to Apply." For more information on the application process, prospective students can go online to www.fidm.edu. Admission to the Bachelor's Degree programs is contingent on completion of an A.A. degree from FIDM.

Application and Information

Applications are accepted on an ongoing basis. All prospective students should contact:

FIDM/Fashion Institute of Design & Merchandising
919 South Grand Avenue
Los Angeles, California 90015
Phone: 800-624-1200 (toll-free)
      213-624-1201 (outside the United States)
Fax: 213-624-4799
Website: www.fidm.edu
      facebook.com/fidmcollege
      instagram.com/fidm
      twitter.com/fidm
      snapchat.com/add/fidmcollege
      youtube.com/fidm
      fidm.tumblr.com

FIDM Los Angeles campus exterior.

MIAMI DADE COLLEGE
MIAMI, FLORIDA

 To read more about this school, visit http://petersons.to/miami-dade-college

The College and Its Mission

With approximately 165,000 currently enrolled students, and over 2 million students admitted, Miami Dade College (MDC) is the largest institution of higher education in the United States. MDC's seven campuses are located in and around Miami, Florida, and include the Hialeah Campus, Homestead Campus, InterAmerican Campus, Kendall Campus, Medical Campus, North Campus, and Wolfson Campus in Downtown Miami. In addition, MDC has two outreach centers: The Carrie P. Meek Entrepreneurial Education Center and MDC–West in Doral.

The College's multiple locations throughout Miami-Dade County allow it to offer students highly flexible scheduling options for its more than 300 study pathways. Students may pursue four-year bachelor's degrees and two-year associate degrees, as well as various vocational and college-credit certificates. MDC offers evening and weekend courses, many of which can be completed online through MDC's Virtual College at http://www.mdc.edu/virtual/.

Miami Dade College, its students, faculty, and staff have been recognized through numerous prestigious awards and honors. Recent examples include the 2014 Florida Professor of the Year from the Carnegie Foundation for the Advancement of Teaching; the Theodore M. Hesburgh Award for faculty development from the American Council on Education and TIAA-CREF, and the Chancellor's Best Practice Award for Academic Affairs from the Florida Department of Education.

In addition to being one of the foremost college's in the region, MDC also serves the community as the backbone of several of South Florida's most prominent cultural institutions. MDC's Department of Cultural Affairs presents and produces nationally acclaimed events including the Miami Book Fair and Miami Film Festival, and the MDC Museum of Art + Design, MDC Live Arts, Tower Theater, Koubek Center, the National Historic Landmark Freedom Tower, The Center for Writing and Literature at MDC, and Teatro Prometeo.

Graduates from MDC include many notable performers, political figures, and celebrities, including: Emilio Estefan; Sylvester Stallone; Pulitzer Prize–winning playwright Nilo Cruz; Andy García; U.S. Congresswoman Ileana Ros-Lehtinen; U.S. Senator Marco Rubio; Alex Fernandez, former Major League Baseball pitcher; former Major League Baseball catcher Mike Piazza; and Mireya Moscoso, former president of Panama.

Academic Programs

Associate Degree Programs: Two-year associate degree programs at Miami Dade College prepare students to enter into junior-year studies at universities or for immediate employment in certain career fields. MDC offers hundreds of associate degree pathways in areas such as architecture, biology, accounting, journalism, computer science, hospitality, education, criminal justice, theater and entertainment, translation, interior design, social work, dietetics, and fashion to name a few. MDC awards more associate degrees to Hispanics than any other institution of higher education in the United States.

A student graduating with an associate degree from MDC is guaranteed admission into any public university in Florida, as well as dozens of other universities nationwide with which MDC has articulation agreements. Graduates of Miami Dade College have transferred into such prestigious institutions as Harvard, Yale, Georgetown, Columbia, and Boston University among numerous others.

Specialized Training and Certificate Options: Miami Dade College offers several options for students looking to start new careers, improve their job skills, or learn a specialty. MDC's technical certification programs prepare students for specific vocations in over 40 areas, including real estate, practical nursing, massage therapy, firefighting, legal secretary, insurance marketing, and business computer programming.

For students who want to hone their knowledge in a specific area but are not seeking particular technical certifications or a degree, the College also offers college credit programs that focus on a unique industry or a specific job.

Noncredit options and alternative education options at MDC include courses open to accelerated high school students, GED preparation, and English as a second language (ESL) courses.

Bachelor's Degree Programs: Miami Dade College offers bachelor's degree programs in select majors, including biological sciences; education; electronics engineering technology; film, TV, and digital production; information systems technology; nursing; physician assistant studies; public safety management; supervision and management; and supply chain management. All bachelor's degree programs at MDC are workforce-driven and coursework is designed to prepare students for a specific career.

Students considering MDC have the option to apply to The Honors College, a division of Miami Dade College that is open to high school graduates with exceptionally high GPA and SAT scores. Benefits of admission to The Honors College include small classes, study-travel opportunities, and development of capstone projects for potential publication and personalized educational planning.

Study-Abroad Opportunities

Students at MDC can study abroad in other countries while earning credits toward an MDC degree. MDC sponsors study-abroad programs in Costa Rica and France, as well as numerous faculty-led programs to destinations around the world. As a member of the College Consortium for International Students (CCIS), MDC students also are able to participate in study-abroad programs sponsored by other CCIS partner institutions.

Costs

For the 2015–16 academic year, the full-time (12 credits) associate degree cost per term for in-state students was $1,418.64 and $4,830.12 for out-of-state students. Career and Technical Education Programs cost $1,092.96 per term for in-state students and $4,263.72 for out-of-state students. Up-to-date tuition and fees information can be found online at http://www.mdc.edu/about/tuition.aspx.

To pay in-state tuition rates, prospective students need to provide proof of Florida residency. More information is available at www.mdc.edu/main/flresidency/.

Financial Aid and Scholarships

Ample financial aid opportunities are awarded based on financial need and/or academic record, and include direct loan programs, scholarships, federal student aid, Pell Grants, the Florida Bright Futures Scholarship Program, and MDC's American Dream Scholarship, which covers two years of tuition for qualified high-achieving students.

Student Activities

Each MDC campus has a culture that is as diverse its student body. Each offers an opportunity for teamwork and leadership. All club and organization information can be found on SharkNet, MDC's virtual connection to Student Life (http://sharknet.mdc.edu). Here students can browse existing organizations, create a new organization, submit event requests, and more.

Miami Dade College is home to five intercollegiate athletic teams: women's basketball, softball, and volleyball; and men's basketball and baseball. Since 1961, the Miami Dade College Sharks have won multiple championship games and various recognitions and honors. MDC is a member of the National Junior College Athletic Association (NJCAA) and the Florida Community College Activities Association's (FCCAA) Southern Conference.

Facilities and Resources

Learning Resources at Miami Dade College provides a stimulating learning environment that enhances the classroom experience through a variety of services such as face-to-face tutoring, information literacy instruction, and informative workshops. Its facilities enable students to study collaboratively as well as individually and access MDC's specialized collections of print and electronic resources.

MDC's Learning Resources Labs and Courtyards offer students and faculty a wide array of supplemental assistance to ensure academic success, from state-of-the-art technology and software to knowledgeable tutors that can provide instruction in a variety of courses such as math, writing, reading, business, natural science, health sciences, speech and test preparation, and more.

Library liaisons work with discipline faculty to ensure that resources needed to support the curriculum are available college-wide. These resources may include such things as LibGuides, books, online databases, or eBooks. In addition, the library liaison can design instructional sessions or work with faculty to design assignments that teach students information literacy skills.

Location

Miami Dade College has nine Florida campuses: Hialeah, Homestead, InterAmerican (Miami), Kendall (Miami), Medical (Miami), North (Miami), West (Doral), Wolfson (Miami), and its Entrepreneurial Education Center (Miami).

Details on each of the campuses can be found at www.mdc.edu/about/campuses.aspx.

Application and Information

The online application is the fastest, easiest way to apply for admission to Miami Dade College, which has rolling admissions and an acceptance rate of 100 percent. There is a $30 application fee, and a transcript of the student's high school record is required.

Additional information, including the link to apply online, can be found at http://www.mdc.edu/admissions/.

For more information, prospective students should contact:

Ms. Ferne Creary, Interim College Registrar
Miami Dade College
300 Northeast Second Avenue
Miami, Florida 33132
United States
Phone: 305-237-2206
Fax: 305-237-2532
E-mail: fcreary@mdc.edu
Website: http://www.mdc.edu

Miami Dade College—North Campus, Science Complex Building
Photo credit: Cristian Lazzari

MIRACOSTA COLLEGE
OCEANSIDE, CALIFORNIA

The College and Its Mission

MiraCosta College offers a friendly and safe suburban environment within easy driving distance of world famous attractions in Southern California. The sunny climate and ocean views make the campus a great place to study. Facilities include library and technology center, student computer labs, free academic tutoring and writing center, cafeteria and patio, an outdoor amphitheater, tennis courts, track, gymnasium, and fitness center.

The MiraCosta Community College District is located in North San Diego County, along the Southern California coast between Orange County to the north and the metropolitan area of San Diego to the south. Classes and resources are available in four separate locations within the district.

The MiraCosta Community College District's mission is to provide superior educational opportunities and student support services to a diverse population of learners with a focus on their success. MiraCosta offers associate degrees, university transfer courses, career and technical education, certificate programs, basic skills education, and lifelong learning opportunities that strengthen the economic, cultural, social, and educational well-being of the communities it serves.

Academic Programs

MiraCosta Community College offers students a wide range of subjects to pursue. Most classes are also available online. Academic programs include:

Accounting
Administration of justice
American college English
Anthropology
Art
Astronomy
Athletics
Automotive technology
Biology
Biotechnology
Business administration
Business office technology
Career and life planning
Chemistry
Child development
Chinese
Communication
Computer studies and
    information technology
Computer science
Counseling
Dance
Design
Dramatic arts
Earth science
Economics
Education
English
English as a second
    language

Film
French
Geography
Geology
German
Gerontology
Health education
History
Horticulture
Hospitality management
Humanities
Internship studies and
    cooperative education
Italian
Japanese
Kinesiology
Learning skills
Library science
Linguistics
Literature
Mathematics
Media arts and technologies
Medical administrative
    professional
Massage therapy
Music
Nursing
Nutrition
Oceanography
Pharmacology

Philosophy
Physical science
Physics
Political science
Psychology
Reading

Real estate
Religious studies
Sociology
Spanish
Surgical technology

Costs

For the 2016–17 academic year, tuition at MiraCosta College is $46 per credit unit for California residents and $257 per credit unit for nonresident and international students.

Financial Aid

In fiscal year 2015, a total of $26,166,180 in financial aid was distributed to 9,997 students.

Faculty

The College has 178 full-time faculty members and 540 part-time faculty members.

Student Body Profile

There are approximately 15,300 students enrolled in credit classes at MiraCosta College. The diverse student body includes people from a variety of ages, ethnicities, and cultural backgrounds. Fifty-eight percent of the students are women and 42 percent are men; 59 percent are age 24 or younger, while 41 percent are 25 and older. Ethnicity of the student body is 43 percent white, 37 percent Hispanic, 8 percent Asian/Pacific Islander, 3 percent African American, and 8 percent multiethnic or other.

Student Activities

The Offices of Student Activities supports a wide range of activities and events, provides information and resources centers, and serves as a focal point for service and leadership development programs. MiraCosta has more than forty active student clubs including the Accounting and Business Club, the International Club, the Black Student Union, the Dance Club, the Martial Arts Club, the Performance Writers Club, and many others.

Facilities and Resources

Advisement/Counseling: The Counseling Center offers individualized academic, career, and personal counseling to assist both prospective and current students develop their educational programs; coordinate their career and academic goals; and understand graduation, major, certificate, and transfer requirements.

Specialized Services: With an average class size of about 30 to 45, MiraCosta students rave about their professors and the personal attention they receive. Both students and staff enjoy a friendly atmosphere and a shared belief in helping one another.

Career Planning/Placement: The mission of the Center for Career Studies and Services is to empower students to make informed, intentional career decisions. Career Center resources include a computer lab, resource library, workshops, and career counseling by appointment.

Library and Audiovisual Services: Maintaining thousands of academic research databases, periodicals, reference materials, and professional research guides, the Library and Information Hub is the center for learning and academic support for MiraCosta students. The Library is also home to the Academic Tutoring Center, the Math Learning Center, the Writing Center, and a large computer lab. All services are free to MiraCosta students.

Location

MiraCosta College's district is coastal North San Diego County, approximately 35 miles north of San Diego and 90 miles south of Los Angeles. The Oceanside Campus is a 121-acre hilltop location with coastal and mountain views; the San Elijo Campus is on 42 acres in Cardiff facing the San Elijo Lagoon and Nature Preserve; the Community Learning Center is a 7.6-acre urban facility in downtown Oceanside; and a Technical Career Institute is located in Carlsbad.

Admission Requirements

Adults and high school students (sophomore level and higher) are able to enroll. International students who are at least 18 years old with a high school diploma can apply with a written application to the International Office.

Application and Information

For more information, prospective students should contact:

Admissions Office
MiraCosta College
1 Barnard Drive
Oceanside, California 92056
Phone: 760-757-2121
Website: www.miracosta.edu
        www.facebook.com/MiraCostaCC
        www.twitter.com/MiraCosta

NORTHERN VIRGINIA COMMUNITY COLLEGE
ANNANDALE, VIRGINIA

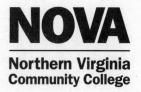

 To read more about this school, visit http://petersons.to/nvcc

The College and Its Mission

Since 1964, Northern Virginia Community College (NOVA) has provided high quality, convenient, and affordable academic programs. It's the largest public educational institution in the state of Virginia and the second-largest community college in the United States.

Diversity is an important component of the college's community. It has more than 75,000 students who represent 180-plus countries. It employs approximately 2,600 faculty and staff members, and it offers 77 two-year degree programs, 15 certificate programs, and 61 career studies certificate programs. It also has six campuses and an online learning center.

The college is committed to the values of access, excellence, opportunity, and student success. This commitment ensures that it fulfills its mission to deliver learning, teaching, and workforce development that cultivates an educated population and internationally competitive workforce.

Academic Programs

Healthcare: Healthcare programs include health information management, nursing, and physical therapist assistant.

The 72-credit Associate of Applied Science (A.A.S.) in Health Information Management trains students to collect, process, analyze, store, retrieve, and disseminate information related to healthcare services.

The 69-credit A.A.S. in Nursing trains students to deliver direct care to patients in diverse healthcare settings. It also prepares them for the National Council Licensure Examination for state licensure as registered nurses. The 69-credit A.A.S. in Physical Therapist Assistant trains students to use medical equipment and treatment procedures to identify, alleviate, correct, and prevent movement dysfunction.

Engineering: Engineering programs include the Associate of Science (A.S.) in Engineering and the A.A.S. in Engineering Technology.

The 67- to 68-credit A.S. in Engineering prepares students to transfer into baccalaureate programs in engineering fields such as aeronautical, chemical, civil, and mechanical engineering. The A.A.S. in Engineering Technology, which also has 67 to 68 credits, prepares students for positions in civil engineering, mechanical engineering, or drafting technology fields.

Business: Business programs include the A.S. in Business Administration and A.A.S. in Business Management.

The 61- to 65-credit A.S. in Business Administration prepares students to earn bachelor's degrees in business administration, with majors in accounting, finance, management, marketing, and other business-related fields. The 69-credit A.A.S. in Business Management prepares individuals to obtain entry-level positions in business management or advance their careers in the field.

Science: Northern Virginia Community College offers several programs in computer, social, and natural sciences.

The 61-credit A.S. in Social Sciences is designed for students who plan to earn bachelor's degrees in a social science discipline. It has five specializations: deaf studies, political science, social sciences psychology, teacher education, and geospatial systems.

The 60-credit A.S. in Computer Science prepares students to earn bachelor's degrees in computer science at other institutions. It focuses on the science of computing and the use of computing in scientific settings. The 60- to 64-credit A.S. in Science prepares students to earn bachelor's degrees in scientific and medical fields such as biology, chemistry, pre-medicine, and science education.

Arts: NOVA offers several arts and music programs.

The 60-credit Associate of Arts (A.A.) in Fine Arts prepares students to transfer to four-year programs and earn bachelor's degrees in fine arts fields. The 65- to 67-credit Associate of Applied Arts (A.A.A.) in Fine Arts trains students for positions in the applied arts. The program's photography specialization teaches students to use imagination and originality to solve a variety of visual problems.

The 60-credit A.A. in Music, which emphasizes fine arts, prepares students to complete Bachelor of Arts in Music degrees at four-year institutions. The 65-credit A.A.A. in Music prepares students for positions in the performing arts field. It includes a specialization in jazz/popular music and a certificate in music recording technology.

Costs

Northern Virginia Community College offers its students an exceptional educational value—among the lowest tuition of any college or university in the Washington, D.C. area, thanks to financial support from the Commonwealth of Virginia.

The total cost of enrollment is based upon a charge per credit hour. Tuition is the same for credit and audit courses.

For the 2016 fall semester, tuition and fees per credit hour total $177.25 for Virginia residents, $376.50 for out-of-state students, $197.25 for military contract students, and $257.25 for business contract students.

Tuition rates are subject to change. More information is available online at http://www.nvcc.edu/tuition/index.html.

Financial Aid

Northern Virginia Community College offers affordable tuition as well as grants, scholarships, loans, and work-study opportunities that help make college even more accessible. Financial aid programs include: federal grants, loans, and work study jobs; state grants, including the Commonwealth Grant, Virginia Guaranteed Assistance Program, and Part-Time Tuition Assistance Grant; and nearly 50 scholarships including the Biology Recognition Scholarship, Edward P. Myers Veterans Scholarship, and Intel High Technology Scholarship.

Faculty

The college's faculty members are excellent teachers and experts in their fields. They bring in-depth theoretical knowledge and real-world experience to their classrooms. Whether students earn their degrees at one of the college's campuses or online, faculty members are always accessible to help them meet their academic goals.

Professors include Mary A. Vander Maten (biology), Rujuta Panchal (accounting), and Michael Parker (information technology). Adjunct faculty members include Yasmin El Sawi (psychology), Gamal Abdel-Ghany (business and social science), and Mary Ebersole (biology).

Student Activities

Students are encouraged to take advantage of their time at NOVA. They can explore the arts by participating in a play, improve their health in a yoga class, join one of the college's many sport teams or intramural groups, attend guest lectures, or join in the many college-based organizations available.

Student Life at NOVA is building a community of learners and inspiring the growth of the whole student by facilitating extracurricular and co-curricular programs that support student civic engagement, leadership development, community involvement, teamwork, personal empowerment, and retention. The College maintains spaces and resources for students, focused on initiatives that enrich college culture. NOVA seeks to inspire students to become active members of the campus and community. The college creates programs and events that foster interactions between members of the college community and provides advising, training and mentoring to student leaders and advisors.

Campus Locations

Northern Virginia Community College's seven campuses provide a variety of academic programs, workforce development classes, events, facilities, and student activities.

The Alexandria campus, which is just minutes from Washington, D.C., provides a close-knit community and more than 70 programs. The Annandale campus, the college's largest campus with 15 buildings, has a cultural center, student services building, greenhouse, gymnasium, and theater. The Loudoun campus also has several amenities including an art gallery, computer and science labs, and a greenhouse. It also houses the Reston Center, which offers a variety of educational programs, personal interest courses, and workforce development programs.

The Manassas campus is located next to the historic Manassas National Battlefield Park. It has seven classroom buildings, an amphitheater, and a theater. Located in Springfield, the Medical Education Campus is a technologically advanced campus that provides education in the nursing and allied health professions. The Woodbridge campus has four academic buildings, sports fields, and a workforce education and training center.

Application and Information

Credit for prior learning is available. More information is available at http://www.nvcc.edu/prior-learning/index.html.

There are no application deadlines. Applications are accepted year round, and students are admitted on a rolling basis.

For more information, prospective students should contact:

Northern Virginia Community College
8333 Little River Turnpike
Annandale, Virginia 22003
United States
Phone: 703-323-3000
E-mail: information@nvcc.edu
Website: http://www.nvcc.edu/
https://apply.vccs.edu/oa/launch.action

Northern Virginia Community College's Annandale Campus.

WESTCHESTER COMMUNITY COLLEGE
VALHALLA, NEW YORK

The College and Its Mission

Westchester Community College is a public, 2-year college and one of the largest community colleges affiliated with the State University of New York (SUNY) system. It was founded in 1946, and in 1957 it relocated its main campus to 218 acres of the former John A. Harford estate in Valhalla, New York.

Today the college has an annual part- and full-time credit student enrollment of approximately 13,000 individuals who attend classes at the main campus in Valhalla or at extension sites or locations including Mount Vernon, Yonkers, Ossining, Peekskill, and White Plains. The college's Division of Workforce Development and Community Education is the largest in the SUNY system and raises the college's total student enrollment above 26,000.

Westchester Community College is recognized as a Veteran Friendly Campus with extensive services geared toward veterans. The college also has been recognized for its commitment to student diversity. The college has more than 60 associate degree and certificate programs.

Academic Programs

Westchester Community College is dedicated to the belief that growth and adaptation through educational experience are possible for individuals and organizations at all stages of development.

The college offers three types of associate degrees in more than thirty subject areas: the Associate in Arts (A.A.) degree for students transferring to 4-year institutions in the liberal arts; the Associate in Science (A.S.) degree for those transferring to 4-year institutions for business, math, science, or health careers; and the Associate in Applied Science (A.A.S) degree for students preparing to seek immediate employment, change careers, or transfer.

In addition, Westchester Community College offers certificate programs in approximately 20 career fields.

The college's Continuing Education Division offers programming for people of every age considering career choices, changes, or personal development. These programs include customized training for businesses, innovative programming for older adults, and an arts and culture series open to the public. The continuing education division is the largest in the state university of New York system.

Associate of Arts (A.A.) Degree Program: There are 4 A.A. degree programs at Westchester Community College: the Communications and Media Arts A.A. degree program; the Liberal Arts and Sciences/Childhood Education (Teacher Transfer) A.A. degree program; the Liberal Arts and Sciences/Humanities A.A.; and Liberal Arts and Sciences/Social Science A.A. Requirements for the A.A. degree at Westchester Community College are equivalent to the first two years at an accredited 4-year institution and emphasize the liberal arts and sciences. Graduates typically transfer to baccalaureate-granting institutions.

Associate of Science (A.S.) Degree Program: A.S. degrees are granted in a wide range of disciplines including various aspects of accounting, business, and computers; digital filmmaking; engineering; food service, food, and nutrition; human services; liberal arts, sciences/mathematics, and science; and individual studies. Requirements for the A.S. degree at the college are equivalent to the first two years at an accredited 4-year institution; they are designed to balance a professional orientation with the liberal arts and sciences. Graduates typically transfer to baccalaureate-granting institutions.

Associate of Applied Science (A.A.S.) Degree Program: The college offers 29 A.A.S. degree programs in a wide range of disciplines in business, criminal justice, education, energy, food service, healthcare, human services, technology, and veterinary technology. The curriculum for the A.A.S. degree prepares graduates for immediate employment within specific technical fields. The requirements combine specific career preparations with a firm foundation in the liberal arts and sciences. Although the A.A.S. is not intended as a transfer degree, graduates in some professions do transfer to baccalaureate-granting institutions.

Certificate Programs: The college offers 22 certificate programs covering virtually every sector of business, profession, and service that comprise today's economy. Certificate programs prepare students for immediate employment in a variety of skilled occupations. College credits earned in certificate programs can often be applied to parallel associate degrees offered at the college. Certificates provide a well-rounded course of study which may include English, mathematics, and science courses, in addition to occupational training.

Continuing Education: The Division of Workforce Development and Community Education at Westchester Community College offers a large variety of affordable, high-quality credit and non-credit classes for all ages at numerous locations and online. The division's commitment to lifelong learning and professional development is exemplified by its comprehensive offering of programs and support. Continuing education students at the college can not only improve career or language skills but also explore the creative side of life through a variety of workshops ranging from music, dance, and yoga to cooking, local history, and folklore.

Costs

For the 2015–16 academic year, tuition was $4,280 for in-state students and $11,770 for non-residents.

Fees for full-time students were $443.

Financial Aid

Westchester Community College participates in both federal and state financial aid programs. Most financial aid is based on income, and students are required to complete an application form and provide documentation of family income. Financial aid workshops are held to take students through the application process step by step.

The Westchester Community College Foundation provides many scholarships to students. In addition to monies given to incoming and graduating students, many scholarships are offered for continuing students who have demonstrated success while attending Westchester Community College.

Faculty

Westchester Community College's faculty members and professional staff members have received more SUNY Chancellors Awards for Excellence than those of any other community college in the SUNY system. More than 98 percent of faculty members hold master's or doctorate degrees in their fields. The student-faculty ratio is 16:1.

Student Activities

The Student Affairs Office is one of the busiest places on the main campus. This is where a student can access almost 80 different student clubs and organizations that cater to a wide variety of cultural, career, and personal interest fields. The office also is the hub for all student information on campus from bus schedules and voter registration forms to a variety of student services, athletics, scholarships, counseling, and employment services.

Westchester Community College is a member of the National Junior College Athletic Association (NJCAA). Intercollegiate sports include men's baseball, bowling, golf, and soccer and women's basketball, bowling, softball, and volleyball. Intra-mural sports include men's and women's badminton, basketball, softball, swimming, tennis, volleyball, and weightlifting.

For details on the various clubs and organizations, visit http://www.sunywcc.edu/student-services/getinvolved/clubs/.

Facilities and Resources

Advisement/Counseling:

The Center for Student provides a variety of services in order to aid student success. Personal, career, and educational goals are identified and discussed through one-on-one Counseling. Academic Counselors are available days and evenings, on campus and at extension sites. The goal is to increase student success and assist students in developing educational plans, selecting and scheduling courses, assessing abilities and interests, addressing personal concerns, career planning and job placement, attending to any special needs, and helping with available financial programs.

Specialized Services:

The professional staff of Westchester Community College's expanded Academic Support Center (ASC) offers students free tutoring and support in reading and math. An extensive series of academic workshops in test-taking, note taking and study skills are offered each semester to help sharpen students' academic skills. In addition to the ASC, tutoring centers for many other areas such as science and writing are available.

The Veterans Resource Office at Westchester Community College is committed to providing Veterans and Reserve component personnel, as well as active duty, family members, and dependents, the support they need through a variety of programs and services, intended to make a seamless transition into the college environment. Veterans are encouraged and supported to strengthen their existing foundation built through their military careers with additional career and internship opportunities, utilizing campus, community and national resources The College is devoted to assisting veterans and their dependents reach personal, professional, and academic goals, and is committed to guide each from admissions to graduation, and beyond.

Career Planning/Placement:

Counselors are available to help students with career and college decisions. Transfer Services include one-on-one college counseling, college searches, scholarship availability, and more. Career Services includes, one-on-one career counseling, on-campus recruitment, interviewing skill building, resume writing, and much more.

Location

The main campus of the college in Valhalla, New York, is located in Westchester County. The county is located 11 miles from Columbus Circle in New York City and has almost 1 million residents. Its geographical setting is beautiful, with the Long Island Sound on the southeast and the Hudson River on the west. Within the county's borders, the terrain is largely rolling hills, intersected by the Croton, Bronx, and Saw Mill rivers. It has retained much of its rural character, while adopting the urban and suburban lifestyles dictated by its proximity to New York City.

Application and Information

The Online Application may be used to apply as a matriculated student (for Admission to an Associate Degree/Certificate program) or for Non-matriculated/Summer Visiting Student Status. There is a $35 application fee.
Visit http://www.sunywcc.edu/admissions/apply/.

For more information, prospective students should contact:
Ms. Gloria Leon, Director of Admissions
Westchester Community College
75 Grasslands Road
Valhalla, New York 10595-1698
United States
Phone: 914-606-6735
Fax: 914-606-6540
E-mail: admissions@sunywcc.edu
Website: http://www.sunywcc.edu

Indexes

Associate Degree Programs at Two-Year Colleges

ACCOUNTING

Aiken Tech Coll (SC)
Albany Tech Coll (GA)
Alexandria Tech and Comm Coll (MN)
Allen Comm Coll (KS)
Alvin Comm Coll (TX)
Amarillo Coll (TX)
American River Coll (CA)
American Samoa Comm Coll (AS)
Anoka-Ramsey Comm Coll (MN)
Anoka Tech Coll (MN)
Arizona Western Coll (AZ)
Athens Tech Coll (GA)
Atlanta Tech Coll (GA)
Augusta Tech Coll (GA)
Bainbridge State Coll (GA)
Barton County Comm Coll (KS)
Beal Coll (ME)
Blackhawk Tech Coll (WI)
Blinn Coll (TX)
Blue Ridge Comm and Tech Coll (WV)
Borough of Manhattan Comm Coll of the City U of New York (NY)
Brookhaven Coll (TX)
Bunker Hill Comm Coll (MA)
Caldwell Comm Coll and Tech Inst (NC)
Casper Coll (WY)
Central Georgia Tech Coll (GA)
Central Lakes Coll (MN)
Central Maine Comm Coll (ME)
Central New Mexico Comm Coll (NM)
Central Ohio Tech Coll (OH)
Central Oregon Comm Coll (OR)
Central Wyoming Coll (WY)
Century Coll (MN)
Cerritos Coll (CA)
Chandler-Gilbert Comm Coll (AZ)
Chattahoochee Tech Coll (GA)
Chipola Coll (FL)
Chippewa Valley Tech Coll (WI)
Cincinnati State Tech and Comm Coll (OH)
City Colls of Chicago, Olive-Harvey College (IL)
Cleveland Comm Coll (NC)
Clinton Comm Coll (NY)
Coll of Business and Technology–Cutler Bay Campus (FL)
Coll of Business and Technology–Flagler Campus (FL)
Coll of Business and Technology–Main Campus (FL)
The Coll of Westchester (NY)
Colorado Northwestern Comm Coll (CO)
Columbus Tech Coll (GA)
Comm Coll of Philadelphia (PA)
Comm Coll of Rhode Island (RI)
Copiah-Lincoln Comm Coll (MS)
Corning Comm Coll (NY)
Craven Comm Coll (NC)
Daytona State Coll (FL)
Dodge City Comm Coll (KS)
Dutchess Comm Coll (NY)
Eastern Gateway Comm Coll (OH)
Eastern Idaho Tech Coll (ID)
Eastern Wyoming Coll (WY)
Edison Comm Coll (OH)
Elgin Comm Coll (IL)
Fayetteville Tech Comm Coll (NC)
Finger Lakes Comm Coll (NY)
Forrest (SC)
Fox Valley Tech Coll (WI)
Frederick Comm Coll (MD)
Gateway Tech Coll (WI)

Genesee Comm Coll (NY)
George C. Wallace Comm Coll (AL)
Georgia Northwestern Tech Coll (GA)
Georgia Piedmont Tech Coll (GA)
Greenville Tech Coll (SC)
Gwinnett Tech Coll (GA)
Harford Comm Coll (MD)
Hawkeye Comm Coll (IA)
Hennepin Tech Coll (MN)
Highland Comm Coll (IL)
Housatonic Comm Coll (CT)
Houston Comm Coll (TX)
Howard Comm Coll (MD)
Hudson County Comm Coll (NJ)
Illinois Central Coll (IL)
Illinois Eastern Comm Colls, Olney Central College (IL)
Iowa Central Comm Coll (IA)
Itawamba Comm Coll (MS)
Ivy Tech Comm Coll–Lafayette (IN)
James Sprunt Comm Coll (NC)
Jefferson Comm Coll (NY)
Johnston Comm Coll (NC)
Kaskaskia Coll (IL)
Kellogg Comm Coll (MI)
Lackawanna Coll (PA)
Lakeland Comm Coll (OH)
Lake Superior Coll (MN)
Lamar Comm Coll (CO)
Lanier Tech Coll (GA)
Laramie County Comm Coll (WY)
LDS Business Coll (UT)
Leeward Comm Coll (HI)
Lenoir Comm Coll (NC)
Lewis and Clark Comm Coll (IL)
Lone Star Coll–CyFair (TX)
Lone Star Coll–North Harris (TX)
Lone Star Coll–Tomball (TX)
Lone Star Coll–U Park (TX)
Long Island Business Inst (NY)
Lorain County Comm Coll (OH)
Los Angeles Trade-Tech Coll (CA)
Los Angeles Valley Coll (CA)
Luzerne County Comm Coll (PA)
Macomb Comm Coll (MI)
Manchester Comm Coll (CT)
Manor Coll (PA)
Martin Comm Coll (NC)
Massachusetts Bay Comm Coll (MA)
McHenry County Coll (IL)
Mercer County Comm Coll (NJ)
Middlesex County Coll (NJ)
Midlands Tech Coll (SC)
Minnesota State Coll–Southeast Tech (MN)
Minnesota State Comm and Tech Coll–Detroit Lakes (MN)
Minnesota State Comm and Tech Coll–Moorhead (MN)
Minnesota West Comm and Tech Coll (MN)
Mitchell Comm Coll (NC)
Mohave Comm Coll (AZ)
Monroe Comm Coll (NY)
Montgomery County Comm Coll (PA)
Mt. San Antonio Coll (CA)
Muskegon Comm Coll (MI)
Nashville State Comm Coll (TN)
Navarro Coll (TX)
New Mexico Jr Coll (NM)
New River Comm Coll (VA)
Niagara County Comm Coll (NY)
Norco Coll (CA)
Northcentral Tech Coll (WI)
Northeastern Jr Coll (CO)
Northeast Iowa Comm Coll (IA)
Northern Essex Comm Coll (MA)
North Hennepin Comm Coll (MN)

Northland Comm and Tech Coll (MN)
North Shore Comm Coll (MA)
NorthWest Arkansas Comm Coll (AR)
Northwest Coll (WY)
Northwest Tech Coll (MN)
Northwest Vista Coll (TX)
Norwalk Comm Coll (CT)
Oconee Fall Line Tech Coll (GA)
Odessa Coll (TX)
Ogeechee Tech Coll (GA)
Ohio Business Coll, Sheffield Village (OH)
Oklahoma State U, Oklahoma City (OK)
Onondaga Comm Coll (NY)
Orange Coast Coll (CA)
Ozarks Tech Comm Coll (MO)
Palau Comm Coll (Palau)
Paris Jr Coll (TX)
Pasadena City Coll (CA)
Penn Foster Coll (AZ)
Pennsylvania Highlands Comm Coll (PA)
Pensacola State Coll (FL)
Piedmont Comm Coll (NC)
Queensborough Comm Coll of the City U of New York (NY)
Quincy Coll (MA)
Randolph Comm Coll (NC)
Rappahannock Comm Coll (VA)
Reading Area Comm Coll (PA)
Richland Comm Coll (IL)
Richmond Comm Coll (NC)
Ridgewater Coll (MN)
River Valley Comm Coll (NH)
Rockingham Comm Coll (NC)
Rock Valley Coll (IL)
Rowan-Cabarrus Comm Coll (NC)
Rowan Coll at Burlington County (NJ)
St. Philip's Coll (TX)
San Jacinto Coll District (TX)
San Joaquin Delta Coll (CA)
Savannah Tech Coll (GA)
Scottsdale Comm Coll (AZ)
Seminole Coll (OK)
Seminole State Coll of Florida (FL)
Shawnee Comm Coll (IL)
Sierra Coll (CA)
Southeastern Comm Coll (IA)
Southeastern Tech Coll (GA)
Southeast Tech Inst (SD)
Southern Crescent Tech Coll (GA)
Southern Regional Tech Coll (GA)
Southern U at Shreveport (LA)
South Florida State Coll (FL)
South Georgia Tech Coll (GA)
South Suburban Coll (IL)
Southwestern Oregon Comm Coll (OR)
Southwest Tennessee Comm Coll (TN)
Spartanburg Comm Coll (SC)
Spoon River Coll (IL)
Springfield Tech Comm Coll (MA)
Stark State Coll (OH)
Sullivan County Comm Coll (NY)
Tarrant County Coll District (TX)
Three Rivers Comm Coll (CT)
Tidewater Comm Coll (VA)
Tri-County Tech Coll (SC)
Trumbull Business Coll (OH)
Tunxis Comm Coll (CT)
Tyler Jr Coll (TX)
U of New Mexico–Gallup (NM)
U of Pittsburgh at Titusville (PA)
Virginia Western Comm Coll (VA)
Waukesha County Tech Coll (WI)

Wayne Comm Coll (NC)
Wenatchee Valley Coll (WA)
Westchester Comm Coll (NY)
Western Iowa Tech Comm Coll (IA)
Western Nevada Coll (NV)
Western Piedmont Comm Coll (NC)
Western Texas Coll (TX)
Western Wyoming Comm Coll (WY)
West Georgia Tech Coll (GA)
White Mountains Comm Coll (NH)
Wiregrass Georgia Tech Coll (GA)
Wisconsin Indianhead Tech Coll (WI)
Wytheville Comm Coll (VA)
York County Comm Coll (ME)

ACCOUNTING AND BUSINESS/ MANAGEMENT

CollAmerica–Denver (CO)
LDS Business Coll (UT)
Lone Star Coll–Montgomery (TX)
Mitchell Tech Inst (SD)
Mountain State Coll (WV)
Reading Area Comm Coll (PA)
Renton Tech Coll (WA)

ACCOUNTING AND COMPUTER SCIENCE

Lone Star Coll–CyFair (TX)

ACCOUNTING RELATED

Central Virginia Comm Coll (VA)
Davis Coll (OH)
John Tyler Comm Coll (VA)
J. Sargeant Reynolds Comm Coll (VA)
Raritan Valley Comm Coll (NJ)
Southwest Virginia Comm Coll (VA)

ACCOUNTING TECHNOLOGY AND BOOKKEEPING

Alamance Comm Coll (NC)
Anne Arundel Comm Coll (MD)
Anoka-Ramsey Comm Coll (MN)
Antelope Valley Coll (CA)
Arapahoe Comm Coll (CO)
Asnuntuck Comm Coll (CT)
Austin Comm Coll District (TX)
Bellingham Tech Coll (WA)
Big Bend Comm Coll (WA)
Borough of Manhattan Comm Coll of the City U of New York (NY)
Bradford School (PA)
Bucks County Comm Coll (PA)
Camden County Coll (NJ)
Ca&nnada Coll (CA)
Cape Fear Comm Coll (NC)
Carrington Coll–Citrus Heights (CA)
Carroll Comm Coll (MD)
Casper Coll (WY)
Catawba Valley Comm Coll (NC)
Cayuga County Comm Coll (NY)
Central Wyoming Coll (WY)
Chandler-Gilbert Comm Coll (AZ)
Chesapeake Coll (MD)
Clark Coll (WA)
Coll of Central Florida (FL)
Coll of the Canyons (CA)
Columbia-Greene Comm Coll (NY)
Comm Care Coll (OK)
Comm Coll of Aurora (CO)
Comm Coll of Baltimore County (MD)
Danville Area Comm Coll (IL)
Delta Coll (MI)
Dutchess Comm Coll (NY)
East Central Coll (MO)
Feather River Coll (CA)
Fiorello H. LaGuardia Comm Coll of the City U of New York (NY)
Florida SouthWestern State Coll (FL)

Fox Coll (IL)
Front Range Comm Coll (CO)
Fullerton Coll (CA)
Gadsden State Comm Coll (AL)
Great Basin Coll (NV)
Great Falls Coll Montana State U (MT)
Gulf Coast State Coll (FL)
Hagerstown Comm Coll (MD)
Harrisburg Area Comm Coll (PA)
H. Councill Trenholm State Comm Coll (AL)
Herkimer County Comm Coll (NY)
Hillsborough Comm Coll (FL)
Hinds Comm Coll (MS)
Holyoke Comm Coll (MA)
Hudson County Comm Coll (NJ)
IBMC Coll, Fort Collins (CO)
Ilisagvik Coll (AK)
Illinois Central Coll (IL)
Interactive Coll of Technology, Chamblee (GA)
International Business Coll, Indianapolis (IN)
Ivy Tech Comm Coll–Bloomington (IN)
Ivy Tech Comm Coll–Central Indiana (IN)
Ivy Tech Comm Coll–Columbus (IN)
Ivy Tech Comm Coll–East Central (IN)
Ivy Tech Comm Coll–Kokomo (IN)
Ivy Tech Comm Coll–Lafayette (IN)
Ivy Tech Comm Coll–North Central (IN)
Ivy Tech Comm Coll–Northeast (IN)
Ivy Tech Comm Coll–Northwest (IN)
Ivy Tech Comm Coll–Richmond (IN)
Ivy Tech Comm Coll–Southeast (IN)
Ivy Tech Comm Coll–Southern Indiana (IN)
Ivy Tech Comm Coll–Southwest (IN)
Ivy Tech Comm Coll–Wabash Valley (IN)
Jamestown Comm Coll (NY)
Jefferson Coll (MO)
Jefferson Comm Coll (NY)
Jefferson State Comm Coll (AL)
Kellogg Comm Coll (MI)
Kennebec Valley Comm Coll (ME)
Kent State U at Ashtabula (OH)
Kent State U at East Liverpool (OH)
Kent State U at Salem (OH)
Kent State U at Trumbull (OH)
Kent State U at Tuscarawas (OH)
Kilgore Coll (TX)
King's Coll (NC)
Lackawanna Coll (PA)
Lake Land Coll (IL)
LDS Business Coll (UT)
Lehigh Carbon Comm Coll (PA)
Manhattan Area Tech Coll (KS)
Miami Dade Coll (FL)
Minneapolis Business Coll (MN)
Minnesota State Coll–Southeast Tech (MN)
Mohawk Valley Comm Coll (NY)
Montgomery Coll (MD)
Montgomery County Comm Coll (PA)
Mott Comm Coll (MI)
Naugatuck Valley Comm Coll (CT)
Northampton Comm Coll (PA)
North Hennepin Comm Coll (MN)
Northland Comm and Tech Coll (MN)
Northwest Vista Coll (TX)
Oakton Comm Coll (IL)
Olympic Coll (WA)
Onondaga Comm Coll (NY)
Orange Coast Coll (CA)

Palomar Coll (CA)
Pasadena City Coll (CA)
Pensacola State Coll (FL)
Pueblo Comm Coll (CO)
Queensborough Comm Coll of the City U of New York (NY)
Raritan Valley Comm Coll (NJ)
Rogue Comm Coll (OR)
St. Charles Comm Coll (MO)
St. Clair County Comm Coll (MI)
Salt Lake Comm Coll (UT)
San Juan Coll (NM)
Schenectady County Comm Coll (NY)
Schoolcraft Coll (MI)
Southern U at Shreveport (LA)
South Florida State Coll (FL)
South Suburban Coll (IL)
Southwestern Indian Polytechnic Inst (NM)
Southwestern Michigan Coll (MI)
Sowela Tech Comm Coll (LA)
State U of New York Coll of Technology at Alfred (NY)
Tallahassee Comm Coll (FL)
Three Rivers Comm Coll (CT)
Tompkins Cortland Comm Coll (NY)
Tulsa Comm Coll (OK)
U of Cincinnati Blue Ash Coll (OH)
Vincennes U (IN)
Wayne County Comm Coll District (MI)
Wenatchee Valley Coll (WA)
Western Iowa Tech Comm Coll (IA)
Western Piedmont Comm Coll (NC)
Westmoreland County Comm Coll (PA)
Williston State Coll (ND)
Wood Tobe–Coburn School (NY)
Wor-Wic Comm Coll (MD)

ACTING
Casper Coll (WY)
Central Wyoming Coll (WY)
Northampton Comm Coll (PA)

ACTUARIAL SCIENCE
South Florida State Coll (FL)

ADMINISTRATIVE ASSISTANT AND SECRETARIAL SCIENCE
Aiken Tech Coll (SC)
Allen Comm Coll (KS)
Alvin Comm Coll (TX)
Amarillo Coll (TX)
American River Coll (CA)
Anoka Tech Coll (MN)
Antelope Valley Coll (CA)
Athens Tech Coll (GA)
Augusta Tech Coll (GA)
Austin Comm Coll District (TX)
Bainbridge State Coll (GA)
Barton County Comm Coll (KS)
Beal Coll (ME)
Bevill State Comm Coll (AL)
Bismarck State Coll (ND)
Blackhawk Tech Coll (WI)
Blinn Coll (TX)
Borough of Manhattan Comm Coll of the City U of New York (NY)
Bossier Parish Comm Coll (LA)
Bradford School (PA)
Butler County Comm Coll (PA)
Camden County Coll (NJ)
Ca&nnada Coll (CA)
Carroll Comm Coll (MD)
Casper Coll (WY)
Cecil Coll (MD)
Central Georgia Tech Coll (GA)
Central Lakes Coll (MN)
Central Maine Comm Coll (ME)
Central New Mexico Comm Coll (NM)
Central Texas Coll (TX)
Central Wyoming Coll (WY)
Century Coll (MN)
Cerritos Coll (CA)
Chattahoochee Tech Coll (GA)
Chippewa Valley Tech Coll (WI)
Cincinnati State Tech and Comm Coll (OH)
Citrus Coll (CA)
Cleveland State Comm Coll (TN)
Cloud County Comm Coll (KS)
Coastal Pines Tech Coll (GA)
Cochise County Comm Coll District (AZ)
Coll of The Albemarle (NC)
Coll of the Canyons (CA)

Collin County Comm Coll District (TX)
Columbia Coll (CA)
Columbia-Greene Comm Coll (NY)
Columbus Tech Coll (GA)
Comm Coll of Baltimore County (MD)
Comm Coll of Rhode Island (RI)
Crowder Coll (MO)
Dabney S. Lancaster Comm Coll (VA)
Davis Coll (OH)
Daytona State Coll (FL)
Delta Coll (MI)
Denmark Tech Coll (SC)
Dodge City Comm Coll (KS)
East Central Coll (MO)
Eastern Gateway Comm Coll (OH)
Eastern Idaho Tech Coll (ID)
Eastern Wyoming Coll (WY)
Elgin Comm Coll (IL)
Feather River Coll (CA)
Finger Lakes Comm Coll (NY)
Fiorello H. LaGuardia Comm Coll of the City U of New York (NY)
Fox Coll (IL)
Fox Valley Tech Coll (WI)
Fullerton Coll (CA)
Gadsden State Comm Coll (AL)
Galveston Coll (TX)
Gateway Tech Coll (WI)
Genesee Comm Coll (NY)
George C. Wallace Comm Coll (AL)
Georgia Piedmont Tech Coll (GA)
Greenville Tech Coll (SC)
Gwinnett Tech Coll (GA)
Harford Comm Coll (MD)
Harrisburg Area Comm Coll (PA)
H. Councill Trenholm State Comm Coll (AL)
Hennepin Tech Coll (MN)
Highland Comm Coll (IL)
Hinds Comm Coll (MS)
Holyoke Comm Coll (MA)
Hopkinsville Comm Coll (KY)
Housatonic Comm Coll (CT)
Hutchinson Comm Coll (KS)
Illinois Central Coll (IL)
Interactive Coll of Technology, Chamblee (GA)
International Business Coll, Indianapolis (IN)
Iowa Central Comm Coll (IA)
Itawamba Comm Coll (MS)
Ivy Tech Comm Coll–Bloomington (IN)
Ivy Tech Comm Coll–Columbus (IN)
Ivy Tech Comm Coll–East Central (IN)
Ivy Tech Comm Coll–Kokomo (IN)
Ivy Tech Comm Coll–Southeast (IN)
Ivy Tech Comm Coll–Southern Indiana (IN)
Ivy Tech Comm Coll–Southwest (IN)
James H. Faulkner State Comm Coll (AL)
Jamestown Business Coll (NY)
Jamestown Comm Coll (NY)
Jefferson Comm Coll (MO)
Jefferson Comm Coll (NY)
Jefferson State Comm Coll (AL)
Johnston Comm Coll (NC)
Kankakee Comm Coll (IL)
Kellogg Comm Coll (MI)
Kent State U at Ashtabula (OH)
Kent State U at Salem (OH)
Kent State U at Trumbull (OH)
Kent State U at Tuscarawas (OH)
King's Coll (NC)
Kirtland Comm Coll (MI)
Lackawanna Coll (PA)
Lake Land Coll (IL)
Lakeland Comm Coll (OH)
Lake Region State Coll (ND)
Lanier Tech Coll (GA)
Leeward Comm Coll (HI)
Lewis and Clark Comm Coll (IL)
Lone Star Coll–Kingwood (TX)
Lone Star Coll–Tomball (TX)
Lorain County Comm Coll (OH)
Los Angeles Valley Coll (CA)
Lurleen B. Wallace Comm Coll (AL)
Luzerne County Comm Coll (PA)
Macomb Comm Coll (MI)
Manchester Comm Coll (CT)
Manhattan Area Tech Coll (KS)
Martin Comm Coll (NC)
McHenry County Coll (IL)
Mercer County Comm Coll (NJ)
Meridian Comm Coll (MS)

Mesabi Range Coll (MN)
Miami Dade Coll (FL)
Middlesex County Coll (NJ)
Midlands Tech Coll (SC)
Mid-Plains Comm Coll, North Platte (NE)
Minneapolis Business Coll (MN)
Minnesota State Coll–Southeast Tech (MN)
Minnesota State Comm and Tech Coll–Detroit Lakes (MN)
Minnesota State Comm and Tech Coll–Moorhead (MN)
Minnesota West Comm and Tech Coll (MN)
Mohawk Valley Comm Coll (NY)
Monroe Comm Coll (NY)
Montgomery County Comm Coll (PA)
Moraine Valley Comm Coll (IL)
Mountain State U (WV)
Mt. San Antonio Coll (CA)
Muskegon Comm Coll (MI)
Nashville State Comm Coll (TN)
Navarro Coll (TX)
New Mexico Jr Coll (NM)
New River Comm Coll (VA)
Niagara County Comm Coll (NY)
Northampton Comm Coll (PA)
Northcentral Tech Coll (WI)
North Central Texas Coll (TX)
Northeast Alabama Comm Coll (AL)
Northeast Iowa Comm Coll (IA)
Northern Essex Comm Coll (MA)
North Georgia Tech Coll (GA)
Northland Comm and Tech Coll (MN)
North Shore Comm Coll (MA)
Northwest Coll (WY)
Northwest-Shoals Comm Coll (AL)
Northwest Tech Coll (MN)
Northwest Vista Coll (TX)
Norwalk Comm Coll (CT)
Oakton Comm Coll (IL)
Oconee Fall Line Tech Coll (GA)
Odessa Coll (TX)
Ogeechee Tech Coll (GA)
Ohio Business Coll, Sheffield Village (OH)
Oklahoma City Comm Coll (OK)
Olympic Coll (WA)
Otero Jr Coll (CO)
Oxnard Coll (CA)
Ozarks Tech Comm Coll (MO)
Palau Comm Coll (Palau)
Palomar Coll (CA)
Panola Coll (TX)
Pasadena City Coll (CA)
Pensacola State Coll (FL)
Potomac State Coll of West Virginia U (WV)
Queensborough Comm Coll of the City U of New York (NY)
Rainy River Comm Coll (MN)
Rappahannock Comm Coll (VA)
Raritan Valley Comm Coll (NJ)
Reading Area Comm Coll (PA)
Reid State Tech Coll (AL)
Rend Lake Coll (IL)
Richland Comm Coll (IL)
Ridgewater Coll (MN)
Rock Valley Coll (IL)
St. Philip's Coll (TX)
San Jacinto Coll District (TX)
Savannah Tech Coll (GA)
Scottsdale Comm Coll (AZ)
Seminole State Coll of Florida (FL)
Shawnee Comm Coll (IL)
Sierra Coll (CA)
Southeast Comm Coll, Lincoln Campus (NE)
Southeastern Comm Coll (IA)
Southeastern Tech Coll (GA)
Southern Crescent Tech Coll (GA)
Southern Regional Tech Coll (GA)
South Georgia Tech Coll (GA)
Southwest Tennessee Comm Coll (TN)
Sowela Tech Comm Coll (LA)
Spartanburg Comm Coll (SC)
Spoon River Coll (IL)
Springfield Tech Comm Coll (MA)
Stark State Coll (OH)
Sullivan County Comm Coll (NY)
Tarrant County Coll District (TX)
Tech Coll of the Lowcountry (SC)
Texarkana Coll (TX)
Tidewater Comm Coll (VA)
Tompkins Cortland Comm Coll (NY)
Tri-County Tech Coll (SC)
Trumbull Business Coll (OH)
Tunxis Comm Coll (CT)

Tyler Jr Coll (TX)
U of Alaska, Prince William Sound Coll (AK)
U of New Mexico–Gallup (NM)
Victoria Coll (TX)
Victor Valley Coll (CA)
Vincennes U (IN)
Virginia Western Comm Coll (VA)
Waukesha County Tech Coll (WI)
Weatherford Coll (TX)
Wenatchee Valley Coll (WA)
Westchester Comm Coll (NY)
Western Iowa Tech Comm Coll (IA)
Western Texas Coll (TX)
Western Wyoming Comm Coll (WY)
West Georgia Tech Coll (GA)
Westmoreland County Comm Coll (PA)
Williamsburg Tech Coll (SC)
Wiregrass Georgia Tech Coll (GA)
Wisconsin Indianhead Tech Coll (WI)
Wood Tobe–Coburn School (NY)
Wor-Wic Comm Coll (MD)
Wytheville Comm Coll (VA)

ADULT AND CONTINUING EDUCATION
Cochise County Comm Coll District (AZ)

ADULT DEVELOPMENT AND AGING
Albany Tech Coll (GA)
American River Coll (CA)
Central Georgia Tech Coll (GA)
Comm Coll of Rhode Island (RI)
Fiorello H. LaGuardia Comm Coll of the City U of New York (NY)
Harrisburg Area Comm Coll (PA)

ADVERTISING
American River Coll (CA)
Central Ohio Tech Coll (OH)
Coll of Central Florida (FL)
Fashion Inst of Technology (NY)
Harford Comm Coll (MD)
Hussian Coll, School of Art (PA)
Mohawk Valley Comm Coll (NY)
Mt. San Antonio Coll (CA)
Muskegon Comm Coll (MI)
Palomar Coll (CA)
South Florida State Coll (FL)
Tidewater Comm Coll (VA)

AERONAUTICAL/AEROSPACE ENGINEERING TECHNOLOGY
Cincinnati State Tech and Comm Coll (OH)
Lenoir Comm Coll (NC)
Pittsburgh Inst of Aeronautics (PA)
Tulsa Comm Coll (OK)

AERONAUTICS/AVIATION/ AEROSPACE SCIENCE AND TECHNOLOGY
Alvin Comm Coll (TX)
Cecil Coll (MD)
Comm Coll of Baltimore County (MD)
Comm Coll of the Air Force (AL)
Hesston Coll (KS)
Hinds Comm Coll (MS)
Lehigh Carbon Comm Coll (PA)
Miami Dade Coll (FL)
Naugatuck Valley Comm Coll (CT)
Northland Comm and Tech Coll (MN)
Northwest Coll (WY)

AEROSPACE, AERONAUTICAL AND ASTRONAUTICAL/SPACE ENGINEERING
Kent State U at Ashtabula (OH)
Kilgore Coll (TX)
South Florida State Coll (FL)

AESTHETICIAN/ESTHETICIAN AND SKIN CARE
IBMC Coll, Fort Collins (CO)
Southeastern Coll–West Palm Beach (FL)

AGRIBUSINESS
Bainbridge State Coll (GA)
Coll of Central Florida (FL)
Copiah-Lincoln Comm Coll (MS)
Crowder Coll (MO)
Eastern Wyoming Coll (WY)
Harford Comm Coll (MD)
Hinds Comm Coll (MS)
James Sprunt Comm Coll (NC)
Laramie County Comm Coll (WY)

Minnesota West Comm and Tech Coll (MN)
Mitchell Comm Coll (NC)
Northcentral Tech Coll (WI)
Northeast Iowa Comm Coll (IA)
Northwest Coll (WY)
Ogeechee Tech Coll (GA)
Ridgewater Coll (MN)
Rowan Coll at Burlington County (NJ)
San Jacinto Coll District (TX)
South Florida State Coll (FL)
State U of New York Coll of Technology at Alfred (NY)
Wayne Comm Coll (NC)

AGRICULTURAL AND EXTENSION EDUCATION
Potomac State Coll of West Virginia U (WV)

AGRICULTURAL AND FOOD PRODUCTS PROCESSING
Minnesota West Comm and Tech Coll (MN)
Northeast Iowa Comm Coll (IA)
Rockingham Comm Coll (NC)

AGRICULTURAL BUSINESS AND MANAGEMENT
American Samoa Comm Coll (AS)
Arizona Western Coll (AZ)
Barton County Comm Coll (KS)
Bismarck State Coll (ND)
Casper Coll (WY)
Central Wyoming Coll (WY)
Cloud County Comm Coll (KS)
Cochise County Comm Coll District (AZ)
Copiah-Lincoln Comm Coll (MS)
County Coll of Morris (NJ)
Danville Area Comm Coll (IL)
Dawson Comm Coll (MT)
Dodge City Comm Coll (KS)
Illinois Central Coll (IL)
Illinois Eastern Comm Colls, Wabash Valley College (IL)
Itawamba Comm Coll (MS)
Lake Area Tech Inst (SD)
Lake Land Coll (IL)
Lake Region State Coll (ND)
Lamar Comm Coll (CO)
Mt. San Antonio Coll (CA)
Northeastern Jr Coll (CO)
Otero Jr Coll (CO)
Pensacola State Coll (FL)
Potomac State Coll of West Virginia U (WV)
Richland Comm Coll (IL)
San Joaquin Delta Coll (CA)
Shawnee Comm Coll (IL)
Southeastern Comm Coll (IA)
Spoon River Coll (IL)
Treasure Valley Comm Coll (OR)
Vincennes U (IN)

AGRICULTURAL BUSINESS AND MANAGEMENT RELATED
Chippewa Valley Tech Coll (WI)
Copiah-Lincoln Comm Coll (MS)
Penn State DuBois (PA)
Penn State Fayette, The Eberly Campus (PA)
Penn State Mont Alto (PA)
Penn State Shenango (PA)

AGRICULTURAL BUSINESS TECHNOLOGY
Laramie County Comm Coll (WY)

AGRICULTURAL COMMUNICATION/ JOURNALISM
Casper Coll (WY)
Northwest Coll (WY)

AGRICULTURAL ECONOMICS
Copiah-Lincoln Comm Coll (MS)
Dodge City Comm Coll (KS)
James H. Faulkner State Comm Coll (AL)
Northland Comm and Tech Coll (MN)
South Florida State Coll (FL)
Treasure Valley Comm Coll (OR)

AGRICULTURAL ENGINEERING
South Florida State Coll (FL)
Vincennes U (IN)

AGRICULTURAL/FARM SUPPLIES RETAILING AND WHOLESALING
Cloud County Comm Coll (KS)
Copiah-Lincoln Comm Coll (MS)
Fox Valley Tech Coll (WI)
Hawkeye Comm Coll (IA)
Illinois Central Coll (IL)
Minnesota West Comm and Tech Coll (MN)
Western Iowa Tech Comm Coll (IA)

AGRICULTURAL MECHANICS AND EQUIPMENT TECHNOLOGY
Hutchinson Comm Coll (KS)
Illinois Central Coll (IL)
Mitchell Tech Inst (SD)
Northland Comm and Tech Coll (MN)
Rend Lake Coll (IL)
Spoon River Coll (IL)

AGRICULTURAL MECHANIZATION
Crowder Coll (MO)
Dodge City Comm Coll (KS)
Fox Valley Tech Coll (WI)
Ivy Tech Comm Coll–Wabash Valley (IN)
Lake Land Coll (IL)
Navarro Coll (TX)
North Central Texas Coll (TX)
Paris Jr Coll (TX)
Rend Lake Coll (IL)
San Joaquin Delta Coll (CA)
Southern Regional Tech Coll (GA)
Southwest Texas Jr Coll (TX)
Spoon River Coll (IL)

AGRICULTURAL MECHANIZATION RELATED
Hinds Comm Coll (MS)

AGRICULTURAL POWER MACHINERY OPERATION
Hawkeye Comm Coll (IA)
Northeast Iowa Comm Coll (IA)

AGRICULTURAL PRODUCTION
Allen Comm Coll (KS)
Big Bend Comm Coll (WA)
Hopkinsville Comm Coll (KY)
Illinois Central Coll (IL)
Illinois Eastern Comm Colls, Wabash Valley College (IL)
Lake Land Coll (IL)
Laramie County Comm Coll (WY)
Minnesota West Comm and Tech Coll (MN)
Mitchell Tech Inst (SD)
Northeast Iowa Comm Coll (IA)
Northwest Coll (WY)
Owensboro Comm and Tech Coll (KY)
Rend Lake Coll (IL)
Ridgewater Coll (MN)
Southwestern Michigan Coll (MI)
Wenatchee Valley Coll (WA)

AGRICULTURAL TEACHER EDUCATION
Eastern Wyoming Coll (WY)
Northeastern Jr Coll (CO)
Northwest Coll (WY)
South Florida State Coll (FL)
Spoon River Coll (IL)
Victor Valley Coll (CA)
Western Texas Coll (TX)

AGRICULTURE
American Samoa Comm Coll (AS)
Ancilla Coll (IN)
Arizona Western Coll (AZ)
Bainbridge State Coll (GA)
Barton County Comm Coll (KS)
Blinn Coll (TX)
Casper Coll (WY)
Central Texas Coll (TX)
Chipola Coll (FL)
Coll of Central Florida (FL)
Copiah-Lincoln Comm Coll (MS)
Crowder Coll (MO)
Dyersburg State Comm Coll (TN)
Feather River Coll (CA)
Georgia Highlands Coll (GA)
Harford Comm Coll (MD)
Hutchinson Comm Coll (KS)
Ivy Tech Comm Coll–Columbus (IN)
Ivy Tech Comm Coll–East Central (IN)
Ivy Tech Comm Coll–Kokomo (IN)
Ivy Tech Comm Coll–Lafayette (IN)

Ivy Tech Comm Coll–Northeast (IN)
Ivy Tech Comm Coll–Richmond (IN)
Ivy Tech Comm Coll–Southwest (IN)
Ivy Tech Comm Coll–Wabash Valley (IN)
Kankakee Comm Coll (IL)
Kaskaskia Coll (IL)
Kilgore Coll (TX)
Lamar Comm Coll (CO)
Laramie County Comm Coll (WY)
Macomb Comm Coll (MI)
Miami Dade Coll (FL)
Minnesota West Comm and Tech Coll (MN)
Mt. San Antonio Coll (CA)
New Mexico Jr Coll (NM)
Northeastern Jr Coll (CO)
Northland Comm and Tech Coll (MN)
Odessa Coll (TX)
Palau Comm Coll (Palau)
Panola Coll (TX)
Paris Jr Coll (TX)
Pensacola State Coll (FL)
Potomac State Coll of West Virginia U (WV)
Ridgewater Coll (MN)
San Jacinto Coll District (TX)
San Joaquin Delta Coll (CA)
Shawnee Comm Coll (IL)
Sheridan Coll (WY)
Sierra Coll (CA)
South Florida State Coll (FL)
State U of New York Coll of Technology at Alfred (NY)
Texarkana Coll (TX)
Treasure Valley Comm Coll (OR)
Vincennes U (IN)
Western Texas Coll (TX)
Williston State Coll (ND)

AGRICULTURE AND AGRICULTURE OPERATIONS RELATED
Potomac State Coll of West Virginia U (WV)
Sheridan Coll (WY)

AGROECOLOGY AND SUSTAINABLE AGRICULTURE
Kennebec Valley Comm Coll (ME)
Lenoir Comm Coll (NC)
Southern Maine Comm Coll (ME)
Tompkins Cortland Comm Coll (NY)
Wayne Comm Coll (NC)
Western Piedmont Comm Coll (NC)

AGRONOMY AND CROP SCIENCE
Chipola Coll (FL)
Dodge City Comm Coll (KS)
Lamar Comm Coll (CO)
Minnesota West Comm and Tech Coll (MN)
Northcentral Tech Coll (WI)
Northeastern Jr Coll (CO)
Northland Comm and Tech Coll (MN)
Potomac State Coll of West Virginia U (WV)
Ridgewater Coll (MN)
Shawnee Comm Coll (IL)
Southeastern Comm Coll (IA)
Treasure Valley Comm Coll (OR)

AIR AND SPACE OPERATIONS TECHNOLOGY
Cochise County Comm Coll District (AZ)

AIRCRAFT POWERPLANT TECHNOLOGY
Antelope Valley Coll (CA)
Central Texas Coll (TX)
Colorado Northwestern Comm Coll (CO)
Lake Area Tech Inst (SD)
Orange Coast Coll (CA)
St. Philip's Coll (TX)
Somerset Comm Coll (KY)
Sowela Tech Comm Coll (LA)
Texas State Tech Coll (TX)
Vincennes U (IN)
Wayne County Comm Coll District (MI)

AIRFRAME MECHANICS AND AIRCRAFT MAINTENANCE TECHNOLOGY
Amarillo Coll (TX)
Antelope Valley Coll (CA)
Central New Mexico Comm Coll (NM)
Comm Coll of the Air Force (AL)

Craven Comm Coll (NC)
Hinds Comm Coll (MS)
Ivy Tech Comm Coll–Wabash Valley (IN)
Mohawk Valley Comm Coll (NY)
Mt. San Antonio Coll (CA)
Northland Comm and Tech Coll (MN)
Orange Coast Coll (CA)
Pittsburgh Inst of Aeronautics (PA)
St. Philip's Coll (TX)
San Joaquin Valley Coll–Fresno Aviation Campus (CA)
Texas State Tech Coll (TX)
Three Rivers Comm Coll (CT)
Wayne Comm Coll (NC)
Wayne County Comm Coll District (MI)

AIRLINE FLIGHT ATTENDANT
Mercer County Comm Coll (NJ)
Orange Coast Coll (CA)

AIRLINE PILOT AND FLIGHT CREW
Big Bend Comm Coll (WA)
Casper Coll (WY)
Central Oregon Comm Coll (OR)
Central Texas Coll (TX)
Chandler-Gilbert Comm Coll (AZ)
Cochise County Comm Coll District (AZ)
Colorado Northwestern Comm Coll (CO)
County Coll of Morris (NJ)
Dutchess Comm Coll (NY)
Fox Valley Tech Coll (WI)
Gateway Tech Coll (WI)
Hesston Coll (KS)
Iowa Central Comm Coll (IA)
Jamestown Comm Coll (NY)
Lake Superior Coll (MN)
Lehigh Carbon Comm Coll (PA)
Lenoir Comm Coll (NC)
Luzerne County Comm Coll (PA)
Mercer County Comm Coll (NJ)
Miami Dade Coll (FL)
Morgan Comm Coll (CO)
Mt. San Antonio Coll (CA)
North Shore Comm Coll (MA)
Palomar Coll (CA)
Pennsylvania Highlands Comm Coll (PA)
Salt Lake Comm Coll (UT)
San Jacinto Coll District (TX)
Texas State Tech Coll (TX)
Treasure Valley Comm Coll (OR)
Vincennes U (IN)

AIR TRAFFIC CONTROL
Cecil Coll (MD)
Comm Coll of the Air Force (AL)
Hesston Coll (KS)
Miami Dade Coll (FL)
Mt. San Antonio Coll (CA)
Texas State Tech Coll (TX)
Tulsa Comm Coll (OK)

AIR TRANSPORTATION RELATED
Cochise County Comm Coll District (AZ)

ALLIED HEALTH AND MEDICAL ASSISTING SERVICES RELATED
Blue Ridge Comm and Tech Coll (WV)
Bowling Green State U–Firelands Coll (OH)
Carrington Coll–San Jose (CA)
Cincinnati State Tech and Comm Coll (OH)
Mount Wachusett Comm Coll (MA)
Northwest Coll (WY)
Pennsylvania Inst of Technology (PA)

ALTERNATIVE AND COMPLEMENTARY MEDICAL SUPPORT SERVICES RELATED
Mount Wachusett Comm Coll (MA)

ALTERNATIVE AND COMPLEMENTARY MEDICINE RELATED
Quinsigamond Comm Coll (MA)

ALTERNATIVE FUEL VEHICLE TECHNOLOGY
Cerritos Coll (CA)

AMERICAN GOVERNMENT AND POLITICS
Oklahoma City Comm Coll (OK)

AMERICAN INDIAN/NATIVE AMERICAN STUDIES
Arizona Western Coll (AZ)
Central Wyoming Coll (WY)
Ilisagvik Coll (AK)
Keweenaw Bay Ojibwa Comm Coll (MI)
Leeward Comm Coll (HI)
Saginaw Chippewa Tribal Coll (MI)
San Juan Coll (NM)

AMERICAN SIGN LANGUAGE (ASL)
American River Coll (CA)
Antelope Valley Coll (CA)
Montgomery Coll (MD)
Oklahoma State U, Oklahoma City (OK)
Rowan Coll at Burlington County (NJ)
Sierra Coll (CA)
Vincennes U (IN)

AMERICAN STUDIES
Miami Dade Coll (FL)
South Florida State Coll (FL)

ANESTHESIOLOGIST ASSISTANT
Renton Tech Coll (WA)

ANIMAL/LIVESTOCK HUSBANDRY AND PRODUCTION
Hawkeye Comm Coll (IA)
Illinois Central Coll (IL)
Jefferson Comm Coll (NY)
North Central Texas Coll (TX)
Ridgewater Coll (MN)
Sierra Coll (CA)
Wayne Comm Coll (NC)

ANIMAL PHYSIOLOGY
Massachusetts Bay Comm Coll (MA)

ANIMAL SCIENCES
Alamance Comm Coll (NC)
Casper Coll (WY)
Coll of Central Florida (FL)
Dodge City Comm Coll (KS)
James Sprunt Comm Coll (NC)
Kaskaskia Coll (IL)
Lamar Comm Coll (CO)
Mt. San Antonio Coll (CA)
Niagara County Comm Coll (NY)
Northeastern Jr Coll (CO)
Northwest Coll (WY)
Potomac State Coll of West Virginia U (WV)
San Joaquin Delta Coll (CA)
Shawnee Comm Coll (IL)
Sheridan Coll (WY)
South Florida State Coll (FL)
Treasure Valley Comm Coll (OR)

ANIMAL TRAINING
Lamar Comm Coll (CO)

ANIMATION, INTERACTIVE TECHNOLOGY, VIDEO GRAPHICS AND SPECIAL EFFECTS
Antelope Valley Coll (CA)
Austin Comm Coll District (TX)
Borough of Manhattan Comm Coll of the City U of New York (NY)
Ca&nnada Coll (CA)
Cecil Coll (MD)
Century Coll (MN)
Cerritos Coll (CA)
Coll of the Canyons (CA)
Elgin Comm Coll (IL)
Finger Lakes Comm Coll (NY)
Front Range Comm Coll (CO)
Hagerstown Comm Coll (MD)
Houston Comm Coll (TX)
Illinois Central Coll (IL)
Kellogg Comm Coll (MI)
Lehigh Carbon Comm Coll (PA)
Lone Star Coll–CyFair (TX)
Lone Star Coll–Tomball (TX)
McHenry County Coll (IL)
Montgomery Coll (MD)
Morgan Comm Coll (CO)
Oklahoma City Comm Coll (OK)
Orange Coast Coll (CA)
Palomar Coll (CA)
Pasadena City Coll (CA)
Pueblo Comm Coll (CO)
Raritan Valley Comm Coll (NJ)
Rowan Coll at Burlington County (NJ)
Southeast Tech Inst (SD)
Springfield Tech Comm Coll (MA)

State U of New York Coll of Technology at Alfred (NY)
Western Iowa Tech Comm Coll (IA)
Western Piedmont Comm Coll (NC)
York County Comm Coll (ME)

ANTHROPOLOGY
American River Coll (CA)
Antelope Valley Coll (CA)
Austin Comm Coll District (TX)
Barton County Comm Coll (KS)
Ca&nnada Coll (CA)
Casper Coll (WY)
Central New Mexico Comm Coll (NM)
Cerritos Coll (CA)
Eastern Arizona Coll (AZ)
Feather River Coll (CA)
Fullerton Coll (CA)
Harford Comm Coll (MD)
Houston Comm Coll (TX)
Laramie County Comm Coll (WY)
Miami Dade Coll (FL)
Muskegon Comm Coll (MI)
Northeastern Jr Coll (CO)
Northwest Coll (WY)
Orange Coast Coll (CA)
Oxnard Coll (CA)
Pasadena City Coll (CA)
San Joaquin Delta Coll (CA)
South Florida State Coll (FL)
Truckee Meadows Comm Coll (NV)
Vincennes U (IN)
Western Wyoming Comm Coll (WY)

APPAREL AND TEXTILE MANUFACTURING
Academy of Couture Art (CA)
Ca&nnada Coll (CA)
Fashion Inst of Technology (NY)
Orange Coast Coll (CA)
Sierra Coll (CA)
Westchester Comm Coll (NY)

APPAREL AND TEXTILE MARKETING MANAGEMENT
American River Coll (CA)
Comm Coll of the Air Force (AL)
Fashion Inst of Design & Merchandising, LA Campus (CA)
FIDM/Fashion Inst of Design & Merchandising, Orange County Campus (CA)
Fullerton Coll (CA)
Orange Coast Coll (CA)
Palomar Coll (CA)
Sierra Coll (CA)

APPAREL AND TEXTILES
Antelope Valley Coll (CA)
Fullerton Coll (CA)
Mt. San Antonio Coll (CA)

APPLIANCE INSTALLATION AND REPAIR TECHNOLOGY
Renton Tech Coll (WA)

APPLIED HORTICULTURE/ HORTICULTURAL BUSINESS SERVICES RELATED
Chippewa Valley Tech Coll (WI)
Cincinnati State Tech and Comm Coll (OH)
Hinds Comm Coll (MS)
Southwest Tennessee Comm Coll (TN)

APPLIED HORTICULTURE/ HORTICULTURE OPERATIONS
Alamance Comm Coll (NC)
Antelope Valley Coll (CA)
Catawba Valley Comm Coll (NC)
Cecil Coll (MD)
Central Lakes Coll (MN)
Clark Coll (WA)
Comm Coll of Baltimore County (MD)
Fayetteville Tech Comm Coll (NC)
Front Range Comm Coll (CO)
Fullerton Coll (CA)
Gateway Tech Coll (WI)
Houston Comm Coll (TX)
Illinois Central Coll (IL)
J. Sargeant Reynolds Comm Coll (VA)
Kankakee Comm Coll (IL)
Kaskaskia Coll (IL)
Kent State U at Salem (OH)
Lenoir Comm Coll (NC)
McHenry County Coll (IL)
Montgomery Coll (MD)
Orange Coast Coll (CA)
Owensboro Comm and Tech Coll (KY)

Rend Lake Coll (IL)
Sierra Coll (CA)
Southeast Tech Inst (SD)
Spartanburg Comm Coll (SC)
Tulsa Comm Coll (OK)
Vincennes U (IN)
Western Piedmont Comm Coll (NC)
Western Texas Coll (TX)
Westmoreland County Comm Coll (PA)

APPLIED MATHEMATICS
Muskegon Comm Coll (MI)
South Florida State Coll (FL)

APPLIED PSYCHOLOGY
Northampton Comm Coll (PA)

AQUACULTURE
Hillsborough Comm Coll (FL)

ARABIC
Austin Comm Coll District (TX)

ARCHEOLOGY
Ca&nnada Coll (CA)
Northwest Coll (WY)
Palomar Coll (CA)
Western Wyoming Comm Coll (WY)

ARCHITECTURAL AND BUILDING SCIENCES
J. Sargeant Reynolds Comm Coll (VA)

ARCHITECTURAL DRAFTING AND CAD/CADD
American Samoa Comm Coll (AS)
Anne Arundel Comm Coll (MD)
Anoka Tech Coll (MN)
Butler County Comm Coll (PA)
Carroll Comm Coll (MD)
Central New Mexico Comm Coll (NM)
Central Ohio Tech Coll (OH)
Coll of the Canyons (CA)
Comm Coll of Baltimore County (MD)
Dunwoody Coll of Technology (MN)
Hennepin Tech Coll (MN)
Hutchinson Comm Coll (KS)
Island Drafting and Tech Inst (NY)
Kaskaskia Coll (IL)
Lake Superior Coll (MN)
Macomb Comm Coll (MI)
Miami Dade Coll (FL)
Montgomery Coll (MD)
Northland Comm and Tech Coll (MN)
Oakton Comm Coll (IL)
Oklahoma City Comm Coll (OK)
Oklahoma State U, Oklahoma City (OK)
Palomar Coll (CA)
Pennsylvania Highlands Comm Coll (PA)
Rend Lake Coll (IL)
Sierra Coll (CA)
South Suburban Coll (IL)
Three Rivers Comm Coll (CT)
Truckee Meadows Comm Coll (NV)
Vincennes U (IN)
Waukesha County Tech Coll (WI)
Westmoreland County Comm Coll (PA)
York County Comm Coll (ME)

ARCHITECTURAL ENGINEERING
Luzerne County Comm Coll (PA)
Nashville State Comm Coll (TN)
Springfield Tech Comm Coll (MA)

ARCHITECTURAL ENGINEERING TECHNOLOGY
Amarillo Coll (TX)
Arapahoe Comm Coll (CO)
Cape Fear Comm Coll (NC)
Catawba Valley Comm Coll (NC)
Cerritos Coll (CA)
Cincinnati State Tech and Comm Coll (OH)
Coll of The Albemarle (NC)
Comm Coll of Philadelphia (PA)
Daytona State Coll (FL)
Delta Coll (MI)
Dutchess Comm Coll (NY)
Erie Comm Coll, South Campus (NY)
Fayetteville Tech Comm Coll (NC)
Finger Lakes Comm Coll (NY)
Front Range Comm Coll (CO)

Gateway Tech Coll (WI)
Greenville Tech Coll (SC)
Harrisburg Area Comm Coll (PA)
Hillsborough Comm Coll (FL)
Hinds Comm Coll (MS)
Lake Land Coll (IL)
Los Angeles Trade-Tech Coll (CA)
Luzerne County Comm Coll (PA)
Mercer County Comm Coll (NJ)
Miami Dade Coll (FL)
Midlands Tech Coll (SC)
Mott Comm Coll (MI)
Mt. San Antonio Coll (CA)
Nashville State Comm Coll (TN)
New River Comm Coll (VA)
Northampton Comm Coll (PA)
Northcentral Tech Coll (WI)
Northland Comm and Tech Coll (MN)
Norwalk Comm Coll (CT)
Oklahoma State U, Oklahoma City (OK)
Onondaga Comm Coll (NY)
Penn State Fayette, The Eberly Campus (PA)
Ranken Tech Coll (MO)
Salt Lake Comm Coll (UT)
Seminole State Coll of Florida (FL)
Southeast Comm Coll, Milford Campus (NE)
Southeast Tech Inst (SD)
Southwest Tennessee Comm Coll (TN)
Stark State Coll (OH)
State U of New York Coll of Technology at Alfred (NY)
Tarrant County Coll District (TX)
Three Rivers Comm Coll (CT)
Western Iowa Tech Comm Coll (IA)
Wisconsin Indianhead Tech Coll (WI)

ARCHITECTURAL TECHNOLOGY
Arizona Western Coll (AZ)
Dunwoody Coll of Technology (MN)
Florida SouthWestern State Coll (FL)
Fullerton Coll (CA)
Grand Rapids Comm Coll (MI)
John Tyler Comm Coll (VA)
Miami Dade Coll (FL)
Minnesota State Comm and Tech Coll–Detroit Lakes (MN)
Onondaga Comm Coll (NY)
Orange Coast Coll (CA)
Palomar Coll (CA)
Thaddeus Stevens Coll of Technology (PA)

ARCHITECTURE
Allen Comm Coll (KS)
Barton County Comm Coll (KS)
Coll of Central Florida (FL)
Copiah-Lincoln Comm Coll (MS)
Grand Rapids Comm Coll (MI)
Harrisburg Area Comm Coll (PA)
Kilgore Coll (TX)
Panola Coll (TX)
Pasadena City Coll (CA)
South Florida State Coll (FL)
Truckee Meadows Comm Coll (NV)

ARCHITECTURE RELATED
LDS Business Coll (UT)

AREA STUDIES RELATED
Fullerton Coll (CA)

ART
Allen Comm Coll (KS)
Alvin Comm Coll (TX)
Amarillo Coll (TX)
American River Coll (CA)
American Samoa Comm Coll (AS)
Antelope Valley Coll (CA)
Austin Comm Coll District (TX)
Bainbridge State Coll (GA)
Barton County Comm Coll (KS)
Bunker Hill Comm Coll (MA)
Ca&nnada Coll (CA)
Carroll Comm Coll (MD)
Casper Coll (WY)
Cayuga County Comm Coll (NY)
Central New Mexico Comm Coll (NM)
Central Oregon Comm Coll (OR)
Central Wyoming Coll (WY)
Cerritos Coll (CA)
Chipola Coll (FL)
Citrus Coll (CA)
Cochise County Comm Coll District (AZ)

Coll of Central Florida (FL)
Coll of The Albemarle (NC)
Coll of the Canyons (CA)
Columbia Coll (CA)
Columbia-Greene Comm Coll (NY)
Comm Coll of Philadelphia (PA)
Comm Coll of Rhode Island (RI)
Corning Comm Coll (NY)
Crowder Coll (MO)
Dodge City Comm Coll (KS)
Dutchess Comm Coll (NY)
Eastern Arizona Coll (AZ)
Eastern Wyoming Coll (WY)
Edison Comm Coll (OH)
Frederick Comm Coll (MD)
Fullerton Coll (CA)
Georgia Highlands Coll (GA)
Gordon State Coll (GA)
Grand Rapids Comm Coll (MI)
Herkimer County Comm Coll (NY)
Holyoke Comm Coll (MA)
Housatonic Comm Coll (CT)
Howard Comm Coll (MD)
Itawamba Comm Coll (MS)
Kankakee Comm Coll (IL)
Kilgore Coll (TX)
Kirtland Comm Coll (MI)
Laramie County Comm Coll (WY)
Lehigh Carbon Comm Coll (PA)
Lewis and Clark Comm Coll (IL)
Lorain County Comm Coll (OH)
Los Angeles Valley Coll (CA)
Mercer County Comm Coll (NJ)
Miami Dade Coll (FL)
Mohave Comm Coll (AZ)
Mohawk Valley Comm Coll (NY)
Monroe Comm Coll (NY)
Montgomery Coll (MD)
Montgomery County Comm Coll (PA)
Mount Wachusett Comm Coll (MA)
Muskegon Comm Coll (MI)
Nashville State Comm Coll (TN)
Naugatuck Valley Comm Coll (CT)
Navarro Coll (TX)
New Mexico Jr Coll (NM)
Northeastern Jr Coll (CO)
Northwest Coll (WY)
Norwalk Comm Coll (CT)
Odessa Coll (TX)
Oklahoma City Comm Coll (OK)
Oklahoma State U, Oklahoma City (OK)
Onondaga Comm Coll (NY)
Orange Coast Coll (CA)
Oxnard Coll (CA)
Palomar Coll (CA)
Panola Coll (TX)
Paris Jr Coll (TX)
Pasadena City Coll (CA)
Pensacola State Coll (FL)
Reading Area Comm Coll (PA)
Rowan Coll at Burlington County (NJ)
St. Philip's Coll (TX)
San Jacinto Coll District (TX)
San Joaquin Delta Coll (CA)
Seminole State Coll (OK)
Sheridan Coll (WY)
Sierra Coll (CA)
South Florida State Coll (FL)
Spoon River Coll (IL)
Texarkana Coll (TX)
Tunxis Comm Coll (CT)
Tyler Jr Coll (TX)
U of New Mexico–Gallup (NM)
Victor Valley Coll (CA)
Vincennes U (IN)
Virginia Western Comm Coll (VA)
Western Texas Coll (TX)
Western Wyoming Comm Coll (WY)

ART HISTORY, CRITICISM AND CONSERVATION
Borough of Manhattan Comm Coll of the City U of New York (NY)
Bucks County Comm Coll (PA)
Mercer County Comm Coll (NJ)
Muskegon Comm Coll (MI)
Northeastern Jr Coll (CO)
South Florida State Coll (FL)

ARTIFICIAL INTELLIGENCE
Lorain County Comm Coll (OH)
Southeastern Comm Coll (IA)

ARTS, ENTERTAINMENT, AND MEDIA MANAGEMENT RELATED
Hinds Comm Coll (MS)

ART TEACHER EDUCATION
Casper Coll (WY)
Copiah-Lincoln Comm Coll (MS)
Eastern Arizona Coll (AZ)
Itawamba Comm Coll (MS)
Muskegon Comm Coll (MI)
New Mexico Jr Coll (NM)
Pensacola State Coll (FL)
South Florida State Coll (FL)
Vincennes U (IN)
Western Texas Coll (TX)

ART THERAPY
Vincennes U (IN)

ASIAN STUDIES
Miami Dade Coll (FL)

ASTRONOMY
Fullerton Coll (CA)
Gordon State Coll (GA)
Palomar Coll (CA)
South Florida State Coll (FL)

ATHLETIC TRAINING
Allen Comm Coll (KS)
Barton County Comm Coll (KS)
Casper Coll (WY)
Central Wyoming Coll (WY)
Coll of the Canyons (CA)
Dean Coll (MA)
Dodge City Comm Coll (KS)
Lorain County Comm Coll (OH)
New Mexico Jr Coll (NM)
Northampton Comm Coll (PA)
Northwest Coll (WY)
Odessa Coll (TX)
Tyler Jr Coll (TX)
Wenatchee Valley Coll (WA)

ATMOSPHERIC SCIENCES AND METEOROLOGY
Comm Coll of the Air Force (AL)
South Florida State Coll (FL)

AUDIOLOGY AND SPEECH-LANGUAGE PATHOLOGY
Cerritos Coll (CA)
Miami Dade Coll (FL)
Orange Coast Coll (CA)
Pasadena City Coll (CA)
South Florida State Coll (FL)

AUDIOVISUAL COMMUNICATIONS TECHNOLOGIES RELATED
Bossier Parish Comm Coll (LA)
Cincinnati State Tech and Comm Coll (OH)
International Coll of Broadcasting (OH)

AUTOBODY/COLLISION AND REPAIR TECHNOLOGY
American River Coll (CA)
American Samoa Comm Coll (AS)
Antelope Valley Coll (CA)
Bellingham Tech Coll (WA)
Bismarck State Coll (ND)
Casper Coll (WY)
Central Texas Coll (TX)
Cerritos Coll (CA)
Corning Comm Coll (NY)
Crowder Coll (MO)
Danville Area Comm Coll (IL)
Dunwoody Coll of Technology (MN)
Erie Comm Coll, South Campus (NY)
Fayetteville Tech Comm Coll (NC)
Fox Valley Tech Coll (WI)
George C. Wallace Comm Coll (AL)
Hawkeye Comm Coll (IA)
Hennepin Tech Coll (MN)
Highland Comm Coll (IL)
Hutchinson Comm Coll (KS)
Illinois Eastern Comm Colls, Olney Central College (IL)
Kaskaskia Coll (IL)
Kilgore Coll (TX)
Lake Area Tech Inst (SD)
Laramie County Comm Coll (WY)
Lenoir Comm Coll (NC)
Manhattan Area Tech Coll (KS)
Mid-Plains Comm Coll, North Platte (NE)
Minnesota State Coll–Southeast Tech (MN)
Minnesota State Comm and Tech Coll–Detroit Lakes (MN)
Morgan Comm Coll (CO)
Northland Comm and Tech Coll (MN)

Ohio Tech Coll (OH)
Oklahoma State U Inst of Technology (OK)
Oxnard Coll (CA)
Ozarks Tech Comm Coll (MO)
Palomar Coll (CA)
Pueblo Comm Coll (CO)
Randolph Comm Coll (NC)
Ranken Tech Coll (MO)
Renton Tech Coll (WA)
Ridgewater Coll (MN)
St. Philip's Coll (TX)
Salt Lake Comm Coll (UT)
San Jacinto Coll District (TX)
San Juan Coll (NM)
Southeast Comm Coll, Milford Campus (NE)
Southeast Tech Inst (SD)
State U of New York Coll of Technology at Alfred (NY)
Texas State Tech Coll (TX)
Thaddeus Stevens Coll of Technology (PA)
U of Arkansas Comm Coll at Morrilton (AR)
Vincennes U (IN)
Wayne Comm Coll (NC)
Wayne County Comm Coll District (MI)
Western Iowa Tech Comm Coll (IA)

AUTOMATION ENGINEER TECHNOLOGY
Alexandria Tech and Comm Coll (MN)
Blue Ridge Comm and Tech Coll (WV)
Dyersburg State Comm Coll (TN)
Fox Valley Tech Coll (WI)
Gateway Tech Coll (WI)
Gulf Coast State Coll (FL)
Hennepin Tech Coll (MN)
Miami Dade Coll (FL)
Mitchell Tech Inst (SD)
Mott Comm Coll (MI)
Northland Comm and Tech Coll (MN)
St. Clair County Comm Coll (MI)
Southwestern Michigan Coll (MI)
Waukesha County Tech Coll (WI)

AUTOMOBILE/AUTOMOTIVE MECHANICS TECHNOLOGY
Alamance Comm Coll (NC)
Alvin Comm Coll (TX)
Amarillo Coll (TX)
American River Coll (CA)
American Samoa Comm Coll (AS)
Anoka Tech Coll (MN)
Antelope Valley Coll (CA)
Arapahoe Comm Coll (CO)
Arizona Western Coll (AZ)
Austin Comm Coll District (TX)
Barton County Comm Coll (KS)
Bellingham Tech Coll (WA)
Big Bend Comm Coll (WA)
Bismarck State Coll (ND)
Brookhaven Coll (TX)
Caldwell Comm Coll and Tech Inst (NC)
Cape Fear Comm Coll (NC)
Casper Coll (WY)
Catawba Valley Comm Coll (NC)
Central Maine Comm Coll (ME)
Central New Mexico Comm Coll (NM)
Central Oregon Comm Coll (OR)
Central Texas Coll (TX)
Central Wyoming Coll (WY)
Cerritos Coll (CA)
Chattahoochee Tech Coll (GA)
Cincinnati State Tech and Comm Coll (OH)
Citrus Coll (CA)
Clark Coll (WA)
Cochise County Comm Coll District (AZ)
Coll of the Canyons (CA)
Columbia Coll (CA)
Columbia-Greene Comm Coll (NY)
Columbus Tech Coll (GA)
Comm Coll of Baltimore County (MD)
Comm Coll of Philadelphia (PA)
Comm Coll of the Air Force (AL)
Corning Comm Coll (NY)
Craven Comm Coll (NC)
Crowder Coll (MO)
Danville Area Comm Coll (IL)
Daytona State Coll (FL)
Delta Coll (MI)

Dodge City Comm Coll (KS)
Dunwoody Coll of Technology (MN)
East Central Coll (MO)
Eastern Arizona Coll (AZ)
Eastern Idaho Tech Coll (ID)
Elgin Comm Coll (IL)
Elizabethtown Comm and Tech Coll,
  Elizabethtown (KY)
Erie Comm Coll, South Campus (NY)
Fayetteville Tech Comm Coll (NC)
Fox Valley Tech Coll (WI)
Front Range Comm Coll (CO)
Fullerton Coll (CA)
Gateway Tech Coll (WI)
George C. Wallace Comm Coll (AL)
Georgia Piedmont Tech Coll (GA)
Grand Rapids Comm Coll (MI)
Greenville Tech Coll (SC)
Gwinnett Tech Coll (GA)
Harrisburg Area Comm Coll (PA)
Hawkeye Comm Coll (IA)
Hennepin Tech Coll (MN)
Highland Comm Coll (IL)
Houston Comm Coll (TX)
Hutchinson Comm Coll (KS)
Illinois Central Coll (IL)
Illinois Eastern Comm Colls, Frontier
  Community College (IL)
Illinois Eastern Comm Colls, Olney
  Central College (IL)
Iowa Central Comm Coll (IA)
Ivy Tech Comm Coll–Central Indiana
  (IN)
Ivy Tech Comm Coll–Columbus (IN)
Ivy Tech Comm Coll–East Central
  (IN)
Ivy Tech Comm Coll–Kokomo (IN)
Ivy Tech Comm Coll–Lafayette (IN)
Ivy Tech Comm Coll–North Central
  (IN)
Ivy Tech Comm Coll–Northeast (IN)
Ivy Tech Comm Coll–Northwest (IN)
Ivy Tech Comm Coll–Richmond (IN)
Ivy Tech Comm Coll–Southern
  Indiana (IN)
Ivy Tech Comm Coll–Southwest (IN)
Ivy Tech Comm Coll–Wabash Valley
  (IN)
Jefferson Coll (MO)
J. Sargeant Reynolds Comm Coll
  (VA)
Kankakee Comm Coll (IL)
Kaskaskia Coll (IL)
Kilgore Coll (TX)
Kirtland Comm Coll (MI)
Lake Area Tech Inst (SD)
Lake Land Coll (IL)
Lake Region State Coll (ND)
Lake Superior Coll (MN)
Laramie County Comm Coll (WY)
Leeward Comm Coll (HI)
Lenoir Comm Coll (NC)
Lewis and Clark Comm Coll (IL)
Lone Star Coll–Montgomery (TX)
Lone Star Coll–North Harris (TX)
Los Angeles Trade-Tech Coll (CA)
Luzerne County Comm Coll (PA)
Macomb Comm Coll (MI)
Manhattan Area Tech Coll (KS)
Martin Comm Coll (NC)
Massachusetts Bay Comm Coll (MA)
Midlands Tech Coll (SC)
Mid-Plains Comm Coll, North Platte
  (NE)
Minnesota West Comm and Tech
  Coll (MN)
Mohave Comm Coll (AZ)
Monroe Comm Coll (NY)
Montgomery Coll (MD)
Moraine Valley Comm Coll (IL)
Morgan Comm Coll (CO)
Mott Comm Coll (MI)
Mount Wachusett Comm Coll (MA)
Muskegon Comm Coll (MI)
Nashville State Comm Coll (TN)
Naugatuck Valley Comm Coll (CT)
New Mexico Jr Coll (NM)
New River Comm Coll (VA)
Northampton Comm Coll (PA)
Northcentral Tech Coll (WI)
North Central Texas Coll (TX)
Northeastern Jr Coll (CO)
Northeast Iowa Comm Coll (IA)
Northland Comm and Tech Coll (MN)
Northwest Tech Coll (MN)
Oakton Comm Coll (IL)
Odessa Coll (TX)
Ogeechee Tech Coll (GA)
Ohio Tech Coll (OH)
Oklahoma City Comm Coll (OK)
Oklahoma Tech Coll (OK)

Onondaga Comm Coll (NY)
Otero Jr Coll (CO)
Owensboro Comm and Tech Coll
  (KY)
Oxnard Coll (CA)
Ozarks Tech Comm Coll (MO)
Palau Comm Coll (Palau)
Palomar Coll (CA)
Pasadena City Coll (CA)
Pueblo Comm Coll (CO)
Quinsigamond Comm Coll (MA)
Randolph Comm Coll (NC)
Ranken Tech Coll (MO)
Rend Lake Coll (IL)
Renton Tech Coll (WA)
Richland Comm Coll (IL)
Ridgewater Coll (MN)
Rock Valley Coll (IL)
Rogue Comm Coll (OR)
Rowan-Cabarrus Comm Coll (NC)
St. Philip's Coll (TX)
San Jacinto Coll District (TX)
San Joaquin Delta Coll (CA)
San Juan Coll (NM)
Savannah Tech Coll (GA)
Seminole State Coll of Florida (FL)
Shawnee Comm Coll (IL)
Sierra Coll (CA)
Southeast Comm Coll, Lincoln
  Campus (NE)
Southeast Comm Coll, Milford
  Campus (NE)
Southeastern Comm Coll (IA)
Southeast Tech Inst (SD)
Southern Crescent Tech Coll (GA)
Southern Maine Comm Coll (ME)
Southwestern Michigan Coll (MI)
Southwest Tennessee Comm Coll
  (TN)
Southwest Texas Jr Coll (TX)
Spartanburg Comm Coll (SC)
Springfield Tech Comm Coll (MA)
Stark State Coll (OH)
State U of New York Coll of
  Technology at Alfred (NY)
Tarrant County Coll District (TX)
Texarkana Coll (TX)
Texas State Tech Coll (TX)
Tidewater Comm Coll (VA)
Truckee Meadows Comm Coll (NV)
Tyler Jr Coll (TX)
U of Arkansas Comm Coll at
  Morrilton (AR)
U of New Mexico–Gallup (NM)
Victor Valley Coll (CA)
Vincennes U (IN)
Virginia Western Comm Coll (VA)
Washington County Comm Coll (ME)
Waukesha County Tech Coll (WI)
Wayne Comm Coll (NC)
Wayne County Comm Coll District
  (MI)
Wenatchee Valley Coll (WA)
Western Iowa Tech Comm Coll (IA)
Western Nevada Coll (NV)
Western Texas Coll (TX)
Western Wyoming Comm Coll (WY)
West Georgia Tech Coll (GA)
White Mountains Comm Coll (NH)

AUTOMOTIVE ENGINEERING TECHNOLOGY
Arizona Western Coll (AZ)
Camden County Coll (NJ)
Cincinnati State Tech and Comm Coll
  (OH)
H. Councill Trenholm State Comm
  Coll (AL)
J. F. Drake State Comm and Tech
  Coll (AL)
Macomb Comm Coll (MI)
Mercer County Comm Coll (NJ)
Middlesex County Coll (NJ)
Minnesota State Comm and Tech
  Coll–Detroit Lakes (MN)
Minnesota State Comm and Tech
  Coll–Moorhead (MN)
New Castle School of Trades (PA)
Oklahoma City Comm Coll (OK)
Oklahoma State U Inst of Technology
  (OK)
Raritan Valley Comm Coll (NJ)
Rowan Coll at Burlington County (NJ)
Springfield Tech Comm Coll (MA)
Thaddeus Stevens Coll of
  Technology (PA)

AVIATION/AIRWAY MANAGEMENT
Dutchess Comm Coll (NY)
Hinds Comm Coll (MS)
Iowa Central Comm Coll (IA)

Luzerne County Comm Coll (PA)
Mercer County Comm Coll (NJ)
Miami Dade Coll (FL)
Orange Coast Coll (CA)
Palomar Coll (CA)
San Jacinto Coll District (TX)

AVIONICS MAINTENANCE TECHNOLOGY
Big Bend Comm Coll (WA)
Cochise County Comm Coll District
  (AZ)
Comm Coll of the Air Force (AL)
Fox Valley Tech Coll (WI)
Housatonic Comm Coll (CT)
Mt. San Antonio Coll (CA)
Northland Comm and Tech Coll (MN)
Pittsburgh Inst of Aeronautics (PA)
Rock Valley Coll (IL)
Salt Lake Comm Coll (UT)
Schenectady County Comm Coll
  (NY)
Southern U at Shreveport (LA)
Southwest Texas Jr Coll (TX)
Tarrant County Coll District (TX)
Texas State Tech Coll (TX)

BAKING AND PASTRY ARTS
Blue Ridge Comm and Tech Coll
  (WV)
Bucks County Comm Coll (PA)
Cape Fear Comm Coll (NC)
Cincinnati State Tech and Comm Coll
  (OH)
Clark Coll (WA)
Collin County Comm Coll District
  (TX)
Elgin Comm Coll (IL)
Hudson County Comm Coll (NJ)
J. Sargeant Reynolds Comm Coll
  (VA)
Luzerne County Comm Coll (PA)
Montgomery County Comm Coll (PA)
Moraine Valley Comm Coll (IL)
Mott Comm Coll (MI)
New England Culinary Inst (VT)
Niagara County Comm Coll (NY)
The Restaurant School at Walnut Hill
  Coll (PA)
Rowan Coll at Burlington County (NJ)
San Jacinto Coll District (TX)
Sullivan County Comm Coll (NY)
Waukesha County Tech Coll (WI)
Westmoreland County Comm Coll
  (PA)
White Mountains Comm Coll (NH)

BANKING AND FINANCIAL SUPPORT SERVICES
Alamance Comm Coll (NC)
Allen Comm Coll (KS)
Asnuntuck Comm Coll (CT)
Barton County Comm Coll (KS)
Central Georgia Tech Coll (GA)
Cleveland Comm Coll (NC)
Colorado Northwestern Comm Coll
  (CO)
Comm Coll of Rhode Island (RI)
Craven Comm Coll (NC)
Fayetteville Tech Comm Coll (NC)
Fox Valley Tech Coll (WI)
Harrisburg Area Comm Coll (PA)
Hinds Comm Coll (MS)
Houston Comm Coll (TX)
Illinois Central Coll (IL)
Lackawanna Coll (PA)
Lake Area Tech Inst (SD)
Lanier Tech Coll (GA)
Los Angeles Valley Coll (CA)
Luzerne County Comm Coll (PA)
Miami Dade Coll (FL)
Mohawk Valley Comm Coll (NY)
Oakton Comm Coll (IL)
Ogeechee Tech Coll (GA)
Ohio Business Coll, Sheffield Village
  (OH)
Oklahoma City Comm Coll (OK)
Rockingham Comm Coll (NC)
Seminole State Coll of Florida (FL)
Southeast Tech Inst (SD)
Southern U at Shreveport (LA)
South Florida State Coll (FL)
Three Rivers Comm Coll (CT)
Westmoreland County Comm Coll
  (PA)
Wiregrass Georgia Tech Coll (GA)

BARBERING
Rend Lake Coll (IL)

BEHAVIORAL SCIENCES
Amarillo Coll (TX)

Ancilla Coll (IN)
Citrus Coll (CA)
Dodge City Comm Coll (KS)
Galveston Coll (TX)
Miami Dade Coll (FL)
Monroe Comm Coll (NY)
Naugatuck Valley Comm Coll (CT)
San Jacinto Coll District (TX)
Seminole State Coll (OK)
Tyler Jr Coll (TX)
Vincennes U (IN)

BIBLICAL STUDIES
Amarillo Coll (TX)
Hesston Coll (KS)

BIOCHEMISTRY
Pasadena City Coll (CA)
Pensacola State Coll (FL)
South Florida State Coll (FL)
Vincennes U (IN)

BIOENGINEERING AND BIOMEDICAL ENGINEERING
Bunker Hill Comm Coll (MA)
Quinsigamond Comm Coll (MA)

BIOINFORMATICS
Massachusetts Bay Comm Coll (MA)

BIOLOGICAL AND BIOMEDICAL SCIENCES RELATED
Gordon State Coll (GA)
Massachusetts Bay Comm Coll (MA)
Seminole State Coll (OK)
Vincennes U (IN)

BIOLOGICAL AND PHYSICAL SCIENCES
American River Coll (CA)
Ancilla Coll (IN)
Antelope Valley Coll (CA)
Caldwell Comm Coll and Tech Inst
  (NC)
Ca&nnada Coll (CA)
Central Oregon Comm Coll (OR)
Cerritos Coll (CA)
Chipola Coll (FL)
Citrus Coll (CA)
City Colls of Chicago, Olive-Harvey
  College (IL)
Clinton Comm Coll (NY)
Coll of the Canyons (CA)
Columbia Coll (CA)
Comm Coll of Baltimore County (MD)
Comm Coll of Rhode Island (RI)
Copiah-Lincoln Comm Coll (MS)
Dabney S. Lancaster Comm Coll
  (VA)
Dodge City Comm Coll (KS)
Elgin Comm Coll (IL)
Finger Lakes Comm Coll (NY)
Fullerton Coll (CA)
Galveston Coll (TX)
Highland Comm Coll (IL)
Howard Comm Coll (MD)
Hudson County Comm Coll (NJ)
Illinois Eastern Comm Colls, Frontier
  Community College (IL)
Illinois Eastern Comm Colls, Lincoln
  Trail College (IL)
Illinois Eastern Comm Colls, Olney
  Central College (IL)
Illinois Eastern Comm Colls, Wabash
  Valley College (IL)
Iowa Central Comm Coll (IA)
Itawamba Comm Coll (MS)
J. Sargeant Reynolds Comm Coll
  (VA)
Kaskaskia Coll (IL)
Kilgore Coll (TX)
Lake Land Coll (IL)
Lamar Comm Coll (CO)
Laramie County Comm Coll (WY)
Lewis and Clark Comm Coll (IL)
Lorain County Comm Coll (OH)
Luzerne County Comm Coll (PA)
Marion Military Inst (AL)
McHenry County Coll (IL)
Monroe Comm Coll (NY)
Moraine Valley Comm Coll (IL)
Mt. San Antonio Coll (CA)
Navarro Coll (TX)
New Mexico Jr Coll (NM)
New River Comm Coll (VA)
Niagara County Comm Coll (NY)
North Central Texas Coll (TX)
Oakton Comm Coll (IL)
Otero Jr Coll (CO)
Palomar Coll (CA)
Paris Jr Coll (TX)
Pasadena City Coll (CA)

Penn State DuBois (PA)
Penn State Fayette, The Eberly
  Campus (PA)
Penn State Shenango (PA)
Rainy River Comm Coll (MN)
Rappahannock Comm Coll (VA)
Rend Lake Coll (IL)
Richland Comm Coll (IL)
Rowan Coll at Burlington County (NJ)
Shawnee Comm Coll (IL)
Sheridan Coll (WY)
Sierra Coll (CA)
South Florida State Coll (FL)
South Suburban Coll (IL)
Southwest Texas Jr Coll (TX)
Spoon River Coll (IL)
Tidewater Comm Coll (VA)
U of South Carolina Union (SC)
Victor Valley Coll (CA)
Vincennes U (IN)
Virginia Western Comm Coll (VA)
Weatherford Coll (TX)
Western Wyoming Comm Coll (WY)
Wor-Wic Comm Coll (MD)
Wytheville Comm Coll (VA)

BIOLOGY/BIOLOGICAL SCIENCES
Allen Comm Coll (KS)
Alvin Comm Coll (TX)
Amarillo Coll (TX)
Anoka-Ramsey Comm Coll (MN)
Arizona Western Coll (AZ)
Austin Comm Coll District (TX)
Bainbridge State Coll (GA)
Barton County Comm Coll (KS)
Blinn Coll (TX)
Bunker Hill Comm Coll (MA)
Butler County Comm Coll (PA)
Ca&nnada Coll (CA)
Carl Albert State Coll (OK)
Casper Coll (WY)
Cecil Coll (MD)
Central Maine Comm Coll (ME)
Central New Mexico Comm Coll (NM)
Central Oregon Comm Coll (OR)
Central Texas Coll (TX)
Central Wyoming Coll (WY)
Cerritos Coll (CA)
Cincinnati State Tech and Comm Coll
  (OH)
Citrus Coll (CA)
Cochise County Comm Coll District
  (AZ)
Coll of Central Florida (FL)
Columbia Coll (CA)
Copiah-Lincoln Comm Coll (MS)
Crowder Coll (MO)
Dean Coll (MA)
Dodge City Comm Coll (KS)
Eastern Arizona Coll (AZ)
Eastern Wyoming Coll (WY)
Edison Comm Coll (OH)
Feather River Coll (CA)
Finger Lakes Comm Coll (NY)
Fiorello H. LaGuardia Comm Coll of
  the City U of New York (NY)
Frederick Comm Coll (MD)
Fullerton Coll (CA)
Genesee Comm Coll (NY)
Georgia Highlands Coll (GA)
Georgia Military Coll (GA)
Great Basin Coll (NV)
Harford Comm Coll (MD)
Harrisburg Area Comm Coll (PA)
Holyoke Comm Coll (MA)
Houston Comm Coll (TX)
Hutchinson Comm Coll (KS)
Itawamba Comm Coll (MS)
Kankakee Comm Coll (IL)
Lackawanna Coll (PA)
Lamar Comm Coll (CO)
Laramie County Comm Coll (WY)
Lehigh Carbon Comm Coll (PA)
Lorain County Comm Coll (OH)
Los Angeles Valley Coll (CA)
Macomb Comm Coll (MI)
Mercer County Comm Coll (NJ)
Miami Dade Coll (FL)
Minnesota State Comm and Tech
  Coll–Moorhead (MN)
Monroe Comm Coll (NY)
Montgomery County Comm Coll (PA)
Moraine Valley Comm Coll (IL)
Mott Comm Coll (MI)
Nashville State Comm Coll (TN)
Navarro Coll (TX)
New Mexico Jr Coll (NM)
Northampton Comm Coll (PA)
Northeastern Jr Coll (CO)
Northern Essex Comm Coll (MA)

North Hennepin Comm Coll (MN)
Northwest Coll (WY)
Odessa Coll (TX)
Oklahoma City Comm Coll (OK)
Orange Coast Coll (CA)
Otero Jr Coll (CO)
Oxnard Coll (CA)
Palomar Coll (CA)
Panola Coll (TX)
Paris Jr Coll (TX)
Pasadena City Coll (CA)
Pensacola State Coll (FL)
Potomac State Coll of West Virginia U (WV)
Ridgewater Coll (MN)
Rowan Coll at Burlington County (NJ)
St. Charles Comm Coll (MO)
St. Philip's Coll (TX)
Salt Lake Comm Coll (UT)
San Jacinto Coll District (TX)
San Joaquin Delta Coll (CA)
San Juan Coll (NM)
Seminole State Coll (OK)
Sheridan Coll (WY)
Sierra Coll (CA)
Southern U at Shreveport (LA)
South Florida State Coll (FL)
Spoon River Coll (IL)
Springfield Tech Comm Coll (MA)
State U of New York Coll of Technology at Alfred (NY)
Texarkana Coll (TX)
Truckee Meadows Comm Coll (NV)
Tyler Jr Coll (TX)
U of Pittsburgh at Titusville (PA)
Victor Valley Coll (CA)
Vincennes U (IN)
Wenatchee Valley Coll (WA)
Western Texas Coll (TX)
Western Wyoming Comm Coll (WY)

BIOLOGY/BIOTECHNOLOGY LABORATORY TECHNICIAN
American River Coll (CA)
Athens Tech Coll (GA)
Austin Comm Coll District (TX)
Bucks County Comm Coll (PA)
Camden County Coll (NJ)
Collin County Comm Coll District (TX)
County Coll of Morris (NJ)
East Central Coll (MO)
Elgin Comm Coll (IL)
Erie Comm Coll, North Campus (NY)
Finger Lakes Comm Coll (NY)
Florida SouthWestern State Coll (FL)
Fox Valley Tech Coll (WI)
Genesee Comm Coll (NY)
Hagerstown Comm Coll (MD)
Hillsborough Comm Coll (FL)
Houston Comm Coll (TX)
Hutchinson Comm Coll (KS)
Jamestown Comm Coll (NY)
Kennebec Valley Comm Coll (ME)
Lone Star Coll–Montgomery (TX)
Manhattan Area Tech Coll (KS)
Massachusetts Bay Comm Coll (MA)
Mercer County Comm Coll (NJ)
Middlesex County Coll (NJ)
Minnesota West Comm and Tech Coll (MN)
Monroe Comm Coll (NY)
Montgomery Coll (MD)
Muskegon Comm Coll (MI)
North Shore Comm Coll (MA)
Northwest Vista Coll (TX)
Quincy Coll (MA)
Rockingham Comm Coll (NC)
Salt Lake Comm Coll (UT)
Tompkins Cortland Comm Coll (NY)
Wayne Comm Coll (NC)
Westmoreland County Comm Coll (PA)

BIOLOGY TEACHER EDUCATION
Bucks County Comm Coll (PA)

BIOMEDICAL SCIENCES
Ivy Tech Comm Coll–Wabash Valley (IN)

BIOMEDICAL TECHNOLOGY
Anoka-Ramsey Comm Coll (MN)
Anoka Tech Coll (MN)
Big Bend Comm Coll (WA)
Caldwell Comm Coll and Tech Inst (NC)
Cerritos Coll (CA)

Chattahoochee Tech Coll (GA)
Cincinnati State Tech and Comm Coll (OH)
Comm Coll of the Air Force (AL)
Fullerton Coll (CA)
Howard Comm Coll (MD)
Jefferson Coll (MO)
Los Angeles Valley Coll (CA)
Miami Dade Coll (FL)
Minnesota State Coll–Southeast Tech (MN)
Muskegon Comm Coll (MI)
Penn State DuBois (PA)
Penn State Fayette, The Eberly Campus (PA)
Penn State Shenango (PA)
Pennsylvania Inst of Technology (PA)
Quinsigamond Comm Coll (MA)
St. Philip's Coll (TX)
Schoolcraft Coll (MI)
Southeastern Comm Coll (IA)
Southeast Tech Inst (SD)
South Florida State Coll (FL)
Southwest Tennessee Comm Coll (TN)
Stark State Coll (OH)
Texas State Tech Coll (TX)
Waukesha County Tech Coll (WI)
Wayne County Comm Coll District (MI)
Western Iowa Tech Comm Coll (IA)

BIOTECHNOLOGY
Alamance Comm Coll (NC)
Augusta Tech Coll (GA)
Borough of Manhattan Comm Coll of the City U of New York (NY)
Bunker Hill Comm Coll (MA)
Caldwell Comm Coll and Tech Inst (NC)
Cecil Coll (MD)
Central New Mexico Comm Coll (NM)
Cleveland Comm Coll (NC)
Coll of The Albemarle (NC)
Genesee Comm Coll (NY)
Holyoke Comm Coll (MA)
Howard Comm Coll (MD)
Humacao Comm Coll (PR)
Ivy Tech Comm Coll–Bloomington (IN)
Ivy Tech Comm Coll–Central Indiana (IN)
Ivy Tech Comm Coll–Lafayette (IN)
Ivy Tech Comm Coll–North Central (IN)
Ivy Tech Comm Coll–Southwest (IN)
Lackawanna Coll (PA)
Lakeland Comm Coll (OH)
Lehigh Carbon Comm Coll (PA)
Miami Dade Coll (FL)
Middlesex County Coll (NJ)
Montgomery County Comm Coll (PA)
Mount Wachusett Comm Coll (MA)
Northampton Comm Coll (PA)
Oklahoma City Comm Coll (OK)
Queensborough Comm Coll of the City U of New York (NY)
Quinsigamond Comm Coll (MA)
Raritan Valley Comm Coll (NJ)
Rowan Coll at Burlington County (NJ)
Southern Maine Comm Coll (ME)
Springfield Tech Comm Coll (MA)
Tulsa Comm Coll (OK)
Vincennes U (IN)

BOILERMAKING
Ivy Tech Comm Coll–Southwest (IN)

BOTANY/PLANT BIOLOGY
Pensacola State Coll (FL)
South Florida State Coll (FL)
Spoon River Coll (IL)

BROADCAST JOURNALISM
Amarillo Coll (TX)
Cerritos Coll (CA)
Dodge City Comm Coll (KS)
Herkimer County Comm Coll (NY)
Iowa Central Comm Coll (IA)
Northwest Coll (WY)
Ocean County Coll (NJ)
Oklahoma City Comm Coll (OK)
Palomar Coll (CA)
Pasadena City Coll (CA)
San Joaquin Delta Coll (CA)

BUILDING/CONSTRUCTION FINISHING, MANAGEMENT, AND INSPECTION RELATED
Comm Coll of Baltimore County (MD)
Delta Coll (MI)
Fayetteville Tech Comm Coll (NC)
Frederick Comm Coll (MD)
Gwinnett Tech Coll (GA)
Ivy Tech Comm Coll–Northwest (IN)
Manhattan Area Tech Coll (KS)
Mid-Plains Comm Coll, North Platte (NE)
Mohave Comm Coll (AZ)
Montgomery Coll (MD)
Mt. San Antonio Coll (CA)
Oakton Comm Coll (IL)
St. Philip's Coll (TX)
Salt Lake Comm Coll (UT)
Seminole State Coll of Florida (FL)
Southeast Comm Coll, Milford Campus (NE)
Southeast Tech Inst (SD)
Springfield Tech Comm Coll (MA)
Victor Valley Coll (CA)
Western Piedmont Comm Coll (NC)

BUILDING/CONSTRUCTION SITE MANAGEMENT
Arapahoe Comm Coll (CO)
Coll of the Canyons (CA)
Comm Coll of Baltimore County (MD)
Dunwoody Coll of Technology (MN)
Erie Comm Coll, North Campus (NY)
Fox Valley Tech Coll (WI)
Fullerton Coll (CA)
Ivy Tech Comm Coll–Kokomo (IN)
J. Sargeant Reynolds Comm Coll (VA)
Lehigh Carbon Comm Coll (PA)

BUILDING CONSTRUCTION TECHNOLOGY
Central Maine Comm Coll (ME)
Cochise County Comm Coll District (AZ)
Kennebec Valley Comm Coll (ME)
Lake Area Tech Inst (SD)
Lake Superior Coll (MN)
Midlands Tech Coll (SC)
Mitchell Tech Inst (SD)
Penn Foster Coll (AZ)
Sheridan Coll (WY)
Western Nevada Coll (NV)

BUILDING/HOME/CONSTRUCTION INSPECTION
Bismarck State Coll (ND)
Bucks County Comm Coll (PA)
Fullerton Coll (CA)
Oklahoma State U, Oklahoma City (OK)
Palomar Coll (CA)
Pasadena City Coll (CA)
South Suburban Coll (IL)
Vincennes U (IN)

BUILDING/PROPERTY MAINTENANCE
Bellingham Tech Coll (WA)
Cape Fear Comm Coll (NC)
Central Texas Coll (TX)
Central Wyoming Coll (WY)
Century Coll (MN)
Delta Coll (MI)
Erie Comm Coll (NY)
Ivy Tech Comm Coll–Bloomington (IN)
Ivy Tech Comm Coll–Central Indiana (IN)
Ivy Tech Comm Coll–Columbus (IN)
Ivy Tech Comm Coll–East Central (IN)
Ivy Tech Comm Coll–Kokomo (IN)
Ivy Tech Comm Coll–Lafayette (IN)
Ivy Tech Comm Coll–North Central (IN)
Ivy Tech Comm Coll–Northeast (IN)
Ivy Tech Comm Coll–Northwest (IN)
Ivy Tech Comm Coll–Richmond (IN)
Ivy Tech Comm Coll–Southern Indiana (IN)
Ivy Tech Comm Coll–Southwest (IN)
Ivy Tech Comm Coll–Wabash Valley (IN)
Luzerne County Comm Coll (PA)
Manhattan Area Tech Coll (KS)
Mitchell Tech Inst (SD)
Pensacola State Coll (FL)

Renton Tech Coll (WA)
Rowan-Cabarrus Comm Coll (NC)
Wayne County Comm Coll District (MI)

BUSINESS ADMINISTRATION AND MANAGEMENT
Aiken Tech Coll (SC)
Alamance Comm Coll (NC)
Alaska Career Coll (AK)
Alexandria Tech and Comm Coll (MN)
Allen Comm Coll (KS)
Alvin Comm Coll (TX)
Amarillo Coll (TX)
American River Coll (CA)
American Samoa Comm Coll (AS)
Ancilla Coll (IN)
Anne Arundel Comm Coll (MD)
Anoka-Ramsey Comm Coll (MN)
Antelope Valley Coll (CA)
Arapahoe Comm Coll (CO)
Arizona Western Coll (AZ)
Augusta Tech Coll (GA)
Austin Comm Coll District (TX)
Barton County Comm Coll (KS)
Beal Coll (ME)
Beckfield Coll (KY)
Berkeley Coll–White Plains Campus (NY)
Berkshire Comm Coll (MA)
Blackhawk Tech Coll (WI)
Blinn Coll (TX)
Blue Ridge Comm and Tech Coll (WV)
Borough of Manhattan Comm Coll of the City U of New York (NY)
Bowling Green State U–Firelands Coll (OH)
Brookhaven Coll (TX)
Bucks County Comm Coll (PA)
Bunker Hill Comm Coll (MA)
Butler County Comm Coll (PA)
Caldwell Comm Coll and Tech Inst (NC)
Camden County Coll (NJ)
Ca&nnada Coll (CA)
Cape Fear Comm Coll (NC)
Carl Albert State Coll (OK)
Carrington Coll–Citrus Heights (CA)
Carroll Comm Coll (MD)
Casper Coll (WY)
Catawba Valley Comm Coll (NC)
Cayuga County Comm Coll (NY)
Cecil Coll (MD)
Central Georgia Tech Coll (GA)
Central Lakes Coll (MN)
Central Maine Comm Coll (ME)
Central New Mexico Comm Coll (NM)
Central Ohio Tech Coll (OH)
Central Oregon Comm Coll (OR)
Central Texas Coll (TX)
Central Virginia Comm Coll (VA)
Central Wyoming Coll (WY)
Century Coll (MN)
Cerritos Coll (CA)
Chandler-Gilbert Comm Coll (AZ)
Chattahoochee Tech Coll (GA)
Chesapeake Coll (MD)
Chipola Coll (FL)
Chippewa Valley Tech Coll (WI)
Cincinnati State Tech and Comm Coll (OH)
Citrus Coll (CA)
City Colls of Chicago, Olive-Harvey College (IL)
Clark Coll (WA)
Cleveland Comm Coll (NC)
Cleveland State Comm Coll (TN)
Clinton Comm Coll (NY)
Cloud County Comm Coll (KS)
Cochise County Comm Coll District (AZ)
Coll of Business and Technology– Cutler Bay Campus (FL)
Coll of Business and Technology– Flagler Campus (FL)
Coll of Business and Technology– Main Campus (FL)
Coll of Business and Technology– Miami Gardens (FL)
Coll of Central Florida (FL)
Coll of The Albemarle (NC)
Coll of the Canyons (CA)
The Coll of Westchester (NY)
Collin County Comm Coll District (TX)
Columbia Coll (CA)
Columbia-Greene Comm Coll (NY)

Comm Coll of Baltimore County (MD)
Comm Coll of Philadelphia (PA)
Comm Coll of Rhode Island (RI)
Copiah-Lincoln Comm Coll (MS)
Corning Comm Coll (NY)
County Coll of Morris (NJ)
Craven Comm Coll (NC)
Crowder Coll (MO)
Dabney S. Lancaster Comm Coll (VA)
Davis Coll (OH)
Daytona State Coll (FL)
Dean Coll (MA)
Delta Coll (MI)
Dodge City Comm Coll (KS)
Dutchess Comm Coll (NY)
Dyersburg State Comm Coll (TN)
Eastern Arizona Coll (AZ)
Eastern Gateway Comm Coll (OH)
Eastern Wyoming Coll (WY)
Edison Comm Coll (OH)
Elgin Comm Coll (IL)
Elizabethtown Comm and Tech Coll, Elizabethtown (KY)
Erie Comm Coll (NY)
Erie Comm Coll, North Campus (NY)
Erie Comm Coll, South Campus (NY)
Fayetteville Tech Comm Coll (NC)
Finger Lakes Comm Coll (NY)
Fiorello H. LaGuardia Comm Coll of the City U of New York (NY)
Florida SouthWestern State Coll (FL)
Forrest Coll (SC)
Fox Valley Tech Coll (WI)
Frederick Comm Coll (MD)
Front Range Comm Coll (CO)
Fullerton Coll (CA)
Galveston Coll (TX)
Garrett Coll (MD)
Gateway Comm and Tech Coll (KY)
Gateway Tech Coll (WI)
Genesee Comm Coll (NY)
George C. Wallace Comm Coll (AL)
Georgia Highlands Coll (GA)
Gordon State Coll (GA)
Grand Rapids Comm Coll (MI)
Great Basin Coll (NV)
Greenville Tech Coll (SC)
Gulf Coast State Coll (FL)
Gwinnett Tech Coll (GA)
Hagerstown Comm Coll (MD)
Halifax Comm Coll (NC)
Harford Comm Coll (MD)
Harrisburg Area Comm Coll (PA)
Hennepin Tech Coll (MN)
Herkimer County Comm Coll (NY)
Hesston Coll (KS)
Highland Comm Coll (IL)
Hillsborough Comm Coll (FL)
Holyoke Comm Coll (MA)
Hopkinsville Comm Coll (KY)
Housatonic Comm Coll (CT)
Houston Comm Coll (TX)
Howard Comm Coll (MD)
Hudson County Comm Coll (NJ)
IBMC Coll, Fort Collins (CO)
Ilisagvik Coll (AK)
Illinois Central Coll (IL)
Illinois Eastern Comm Colls, Olney Central College (IL)
Illinois Eastern Comm Colls, Wabash Valley College (IL)
Iowa Central Comm Coll (IA)
Itawamba Comm Coll (MS)
Ivy Tech Comm Coll–Bloomington (IN)
Ivy Tech Comm Coll–Central Indiana (IN)
Ivy Tech Comm Coll–Columbus (IN)
Ivy Tech Comm Coll–East Central (IN)
Ivy Tech Comm Coll–Kokomo (IN)
Ivy Tech Comm Coll–Lafayette (IN)
Ivy Tech Comm Coll–North Central (IN)
Ivy Tech Comm Coll–Northeast (IN)
Ivy Tech Comm Coll–Northwest (IN)
Ivy Tech Comm Coll–Richmond (IN)
Ivy Tech Comm Coll–Southeast (IN)
Ivy Tech Comm Coll–Southern Indiana (IN)
Ivy Tech Comm Coll–Southwest (IN)
Ivy Tech Comm Coll–Wabash Valley (IN)
James H. Faulkner State Comm Coll (AL)
James Sprunt Comm Coll (NC)
Jamestown Business Coll (NY)

Jamestown Comm Coll (NY)
Jefferson Coll (MO)
Jefferson Comm Coll (NY)
J. F. Drake State Comm and Tech Coll (AL)
Johnston Comm Coll (NC)
John Tyler Comm Coll (VA)
J. Sargeant Reynolds Comm Coll (VA)
Kankakee Comm Coll (IL)
Kellogg Comm Coll (MI)
Kilgore Coll (TX)
Kirtland Comm Coll (MI)
Lackawanna Coll (PA)
Lake Land Coll (IL)
Lakeland Comm Coll (OH)
Lake Region State Coll (ND)
Lake Superior Coll (MN)
Lamar Comm Coll (CO)
Laramie County Comm Coll (WY)
LDS Business Coll (UT)
Leeward Comm Coll (HI)
Lehigh Carbon Comm Coll (PA)
Lewis and Clark Comm Coll (IL)
Lone Star Coll–CyFair (TX)
Lone Star Coll–Kingwood (TX)
Lone Star Coll–Montgomery (TX)
Lone Star Coll–North Harris (TX)
Lone Star Coll–Tomball (TX)
Lone Star Coll–U Park (TX)
Long Island Business Inst (NY)
Lorain County Comm Coll (OH)
Los Angeles Trade-Tech Coll (CA)
Luzerne County Comm Coll (PA)
Macomb Comm Coll (MI)
Manchester Comm Coll (CT)
Manor Coll (PA)
Martin Comm Coll (NC)
Massachusetts Bay Comm Coll (MA)
McHenry County Coll (IL)
Mercer County Comm Coll (NJ)
Metro Business Coll, Jefferson City (MO)
Miami Dade Coll (FL)
Middlesex County Coll (NJ)
Midlands Tech Coll (SC)
Mid-Plains Comm Coll, North Platte (NE)
Minnesota State Coll–Southeast Tech (MN)
Minnesota State Comm and Tech Coll–Moorhead (MN)
Minnesota West Comm and Tech Coll (MN)
Mitchell Comm Coll (NC)
Mohave Comm Coll (AZ)
Mohawk Valley Comm Coll (NY)
Monroe Comm Coll (NY)
Montgomery Comm Coll (NC)
Montgomery County Comm Coll (PA)
Moraine Valley Comm Coll (IL)
Morgan Comm Coll (CO)
Mott Comm Coll (MI)
Mt. San Antonio Coll (CA)
Mount Wachusett Comm Coll (MA)
Muskegon Comm Coll (MI)
Nashville State Comm Coll (TN)
Naugatuck Valley Comm Coll (CT)
Navarro Coll (TX)
New Mexico Jr Coll (NM)
New River Comm Coll (VA)
Niagara County Comm Coll (NY)
Northampton Comm Coll (PA)
Northcentral Tech Coll (WI)
North Central Texas Coll (TX)
Northeast Alabama Comm Coll (AL)
Northeastern Jr Coll (CO)
Northeast Iowa Comm Coll (IA)
Northern Essex Comm Coll (MA)
North Hennepin Comm Coll (MN)
Northland Comm and Tech Coll (MN)
North Shore Comm Coll (MA)
NorthWest Arkansas Comm Coll (AR)
Northwest Coll (WY)
Northwest Tech Coll (MN)
Norwalk Comm Coll (CT)
Ocean County Coll (NJ)
Odessa Coll (TX)
Ohio Business Coll, Sheffield Village (OH)
Oklahoma City Comm Coll (OK)
Oklahoma State U, Oklahoma City (OK)
Olympic Coll (WA)
Onondaga Comm Coll (NY)
Orange Coast Coll (CA)
Otero Jr Coll (CO)
Owensboro Comm and Tech Coll (KY)
Oxnard Coll (CA)
Ozarks Tech Comm Coll (MO)
Palomar Coll (CA)
Panola Coll (TX)
Paris Jr Coll (TX)
Pasadena City Coll (CA)
Penn Foster Coll (AZ)
Pennsylvania Inst of Technology (PA)
Pensacola State Coll (FL)
Piedmont Comm Coll (NC)
Pittsburgh Tech Inst, Oakdale (PA)
Potomac State Coll of West Virginia U (WV)
Pueblo Comm Coll (CO)
Queensborough Comm Coll of the City U of New York (NY)
Quincy Coll (MA)
Quinsigamond Comm Coll (MA)
Rainy River Comm Coll (MN)
Randolph Comm Coll (NC)
Rappahannock Comm Coll (VA)
Raritan Valley Comm Coll (NJ)
Reading Area Comm Coll (PA)
Richland Comm Coll (IL)
Richmond Comm Coll (NC)
Ridgewater Coll (MN)
River Valley Comm Coll (NH)
Rockingham Comm Coll (NC)
Rock Valley Coll (IL)
Rogue Comm Coll (OR)
Rowan-Cabarrus Comm Coll (NC)
Rowan Coll at Burlington County (NJ)
St. Philip's Coll (TX)
Salt Lake Comm Coll (UT)
San Jacinto Coll District (TX)
San Joaquin Delta Coll (CA)
San Joaquin Valley Coll, Bakersfield (CA)
San Joaquin Valley Coll–Online (CA)
San Juan Coll (NM)
Schenectady County Comm Coll (NY)
Schoolcraft Coll (MI)
Scottsdale Comm Coll (AZ)
Seminole State Coll (OK)
Seminole State Coll of Florida (FL)
Shawnee Comm Coll (IL)
Sierra Coll (CA)
Somerset Comm Coll (KY)
Southeast Comm Coll, Lincoln Campus (NE)
Southeast Comm Coll, Milford Campus (NE)
Southeastern Comm Coll (IA)
Southeast Tech Inst (SD)
Southern Crescent Tech Coll (GA)
Southern Maine Comm Coll (ME)
South Florida State Coll (FL)
Southwestern Indian Polytechnic Inst (NM)
Southwestern Michigan Coll (MI)
Southwestern Oklahoma State U at Sayre (OK)
Southwestern Oregon Comm Coll (OR)
Southwest Tennessee Comm Coll (TN)
Southwest Texas Jr Coll (TX)
Spartanburg Comm Coll (SC)
Spoon River Coll (IL)
Springfield Tech Comm Coll (MA)
Stark State Coll (OH)
State U of New York Coll of Technology at Alfred (NY)
Sullivan County Comm Coll (NY)
Tarrant County Coll District (TX)
Texarkana Coll (TX)
Tidewater Comm Coll (VA)
Tohono O'odham Comm Coll (AZ)
Tompkins Cortland Comm Coll (NY)
Tri-County Tech Coll (SC)
Trocaire Coll (NY)
Trumbull Business Coll (OH)
Tulsa Comm Coll (OK)
Tunxis Comm Coll (CT)
Tyler Jr Coll (TX)
U of Alaska Anchorage, Kenai Peninsula Coll (AK)
U of Cincinnati Blue Ash Coll (OH)
U of New Mexico–Gallup (NM)
Victoria Coll (TX)
Victor Valley Coll (CA)
Vincennes U (IN)
Virginia Western Comm Coll (VA)
Volunteer State Comm Coll (TN)
Walters State Comm Coll (TN)
Washington County Comm Coll (ME)
Waukesha County Tech Coll (WI)
Wayne Comm Coll (NC)
Wayne County Comm Coll District (MI)
Weatherford Coll (TX)
Wenatchee Valley Coll (WA)
Westchester Comm Coll (NY)
Western Iowa Tech Comm Coll (IA)
Western Nevada Coll (NV)
Western Piedmont Comm Coll (NC)
Western Texas Coll (TX)
Western Wyoming Comm Coll (WY)
Westmoreland County Comm Coll (PA)
White Mountains Comm Coll (NH)
Wisconsin Indianhead Tech Coll (WI)
Wor-Wic Comm Coll (MD)
Wytheville Comm Coll (VA)
York County Comm Coll (ME)

BUSINESS ADMINISTRATION, MANAGEMENT AND OPERATIONS RELATED

Ancilla Coll (IN)
Anne Arundel Comm Coll (MD)
Blue Ridge Comm and Tech Coll (WV)
Bunker Hill Comm Coll (MA)
Chandler-Gilbert Comm Coll (AZ)
Cincinnati State Tech and Comm Coll (OH)
Coll of Central Florida (FL)
Comm Care Coll (OK)
Genesee Comm Coll (NY)
John Tyler Comm Coll (VA)
Lackawanna Coll (PA)
LDS Business Coll (UT)
Northwest Vista Coll (TX)
Pensacola State Coll (FL)
Rappahannock Comm Coll (VA)
Rowan-Cabarrus Comm Coll (NC)
Southwest Virginia Comm Coll (VA)
U of Cincinnati Blue Ash Coll (OH)
Waukesha County Tech Coll (WI)
Williston State Coll (ND)

BUSINESS AND PERSONAL/ FINANCIAL SERVICES MARKETING

Hutchinson Comm Coll (KS)
North Central Texas Coll (TX)

BUSINESS AUTOMATION/ TECHNOLOGY/DATA ENTRY

Berkshire Comm Coll (MA)
Bismarck State Coll (ND)
Casper Coll (WY)
Clark Coll (WA)
Crowder Coll (MO)
Danville Area Comm Coll (IL)
Garrett Coll (MD)
Houston Comm Coll (TX)
Illinois Eastern Comm Colls, Frontier Community College (IL)
Illinois Eastern Comm Colls, Lincoln Trail College (IL)
Illinois Eastern Comm Colls, Olney Central College (IL)
Illinois Eastern Comm Colls, Wabash Valley College (IL)
Ivy Tech Comm Coll–Bloomington (IN)
Ivy Tech Comm Coll–Central Indiana (IN)
Ivy Tech Comm Coll–Columbus (IN)
Ivy Tech Comm Coll–Lafayette (IN)
Ivy Tech Comm Coll–North Central (IN)
Ivy Tech Comm Coll–Northeast (IN)
Ivy Tech Comm Coll–Northwest (IN)
Ivy Tech Comm Coll–Richmond (IN)
Ivy Tech Comm Coll–Southeast (IN)
Ivy Tech Comm Coll–Southern Indiana (IN)
Ivy Tech Comm Coll–Southwest (IN)
Kaskaskia Coll (IL)
Lake Superior Coll (MN)
Macomb Comm Coll (MI)
Miami Dade Coll (FL)
Mitchell Tech Inst (SD)
Northeast Iowa Comm Coll (IA)
Panola Coll (TX)
Paris Jr Coll (TX)
Pasadena City Coll (CA)
Potomac State Coll of West Virginia U (WV)
Pueblo Comm Coll (CO)
Renton Tech Coll (WA)
Schoolcraft Coll (MI)
Shawnee Comm Coll (IL)
Western Iowa Tech Comm Coll (IA)

BUSINESS/COMMERCE

Allen Comm Coll (KS)
Alvin Comm Coll (TX)
American River Coll (CA)
Anne Arundel Comm Coll (MD)
Anoka-Ramsey Comm Coll (MN)
Antelope Valley Coll (CA)
Austin Comm Coll District (TX)
Berkshire Comm Coll (MA)
Bismarck State Coll (ND)
Bossier Parish Comm Coll (LA)
Brookhaven Coll (TX)
Butler County Comm Coll (PA)
Carl Albert State Coll (OK)
Cecil Coll (MD)
Central Virginia Comm Coll (VA)
Central Wyoming Coll (WY)
Chandler-Gilbert Comm Coll (AZ)
Chesapeake Coll (MD)
Citrus Coll (CA)
Coll of Central Florida (FL)
Collin County Comm Coll District (TX)
Columbia Coll (CA)
Columbia-Greene Comm Coll (NY)
Comm Coll of Baltimore County (MD)
Comm Coll of Rhode Island (RI)
Dawson Comm Coll (MT)
Denmark Tech Coll (SC)
East Central Coll (MO)
Feather River Coll (CA)
Garrett Coll (MD)
Georgia Military Coll (GA)
Georgia Piedmont Tech Coll (GA)
Great Basin Coll (NV)
Hagerstown Comm Coll (MD)
Harrisburg Area Comm Coll (PA)
Humacao Comm Coll (PR)
Hutchinson Comm Coll (KS)
Jefferson Coll (MO)
Kaskaskia Coll (IL)
Kent State U at Ashtabula (OH)
Kent State U at East Liverpool (OH)
Kent State U at Salem (OH)
Kent State U at Trumbull (OH)
Kent State U at Tuscarawas (OH)
Kilgore Coll (TX)
Lackawanna Coll (PA)
Laramie County Comm Coll (WY)
Lehigh Carbon Comm Coll (PA)
Macomb Comm Coll (MI)
Massachusetts Bay Comm Coll (MA)
Mesabi Range Coll (MN)
Midlands Tech Coll (SC)
Minnesota West Comm and Tech Coll (MN)
Montgomery Coll (MD)
Montgomery County Comm Coll (PA)
Moraine Valley Comm Coll (IL)
Mott Comm Coll (MI)
Mount Wachusett Comm Coll (MA)
Naugatuck Valley Comm Coll (CT)
Norco Coll (CA)
Northampton Comm Coll (PA)
Northeast Alabama Comm Coll (AL)
Northern Essex Comm Coll (MA)
Northwest Coll (WY)
Nunez Comm Coll (LA)
Ocean County Coll (NJ)
Oklahoma City Comm Coll (OK)
Oklahoma State U Inst of Technology (OK)
Onondaga Comm Coll (NY)
Orange Coast Coll (CA)
Palomar Coll (CA)
Paris Jr Coll (TX)
Penn State DuBois (PA)
Penn State Fayette, The Eberly Campus (PA)
Penn State Mont Alto (PA)
Penn State Shenango (PA)
Pennsylvania Highlands Comm Coll (PA)
Pensacola State Coll (FL)
Quinsigamond Comm Coll (MA)
Raritan Valley Comm Coll (NJ)
Rogue Comm Coll (OR)
Saginaw Chippewa Tribal Coll (MI)
St. Clair County Comm Coll (MI)
San Jacinto Coll District (TX)
San Joaquin Valley Coll, Visalia (CA)
Schoolcraft Coll (MI)
Seminole State Coll (OK)
Sheridan Coll (WY)
Sierra Coll (CA)
Southern U at Shreveport (LA)
South Florida State Coll (FL)
Southwestern Indian Polytechnic Inst (NM)
Southwest Tennessee Comm Coll (TN)
Spartanburg Methodist Coll (SC)
Springfield Tech Comm Coll (MA)
Tech Coll of the Lowcountry (SC)
Texarkana Coll (TX)
Three Rivers Comm Coll (CT)
Treasure Valley Comm Coll (OR)
Truckee Meadows Comm Coll (NV)
Tulsa Comm Coll (OK)
U of Arkansas Comm Coll at Morrilton (AR)
U of Cincinnati Blue Ash Coll (OH)
U of Pittsburgh at Titusville (PA)
Victor Valley Coll (CA)
Vincennes U (IN)
Western Nevada Coll (NV)
Westmoreland County Comm Coll (PA)
Williamsburg Tech Coll (SC)
Wor-Wic Comm Coll (MD)

BUSINESS/CORPORATE COMMUNICATIONS

Cecil Coll (MD)
Houston Comm Coll (TX)
Montgomery County Comm Coll (PA)

BUSINESS MACHINE REPAIR

Muskegon Comm Coll (MI)
Ozarks Tech Comm Coll (MO)

BUSINESS, MANAGEMENT, AND MARKETING RELATED

Bucks County Comm Coll (PA)
Butler County Comm Coll (PA)
Chandler-Gilbert Comm Coll (AZ)
Cloud County Comm Coll (KS)
County Coll of Morris (NJ)
Eastern Arizona Coll (AZ)
Genesee Comm Coll (NY)
LDS Business Coll (UT)
Long Island Business Inst (NY)
Manor Coll (PA)
Niagara County Comm Coll (NY)
Queensborough Comm Coll of the City U of New York (NY)
Schenectady County Comm Coll (NY)
Southeastern Coll–West Palm Beach (FL)
Tulsa Comm Coll (OK)

BUSINESS/MANAGERIAL ECONOMICS

South Florida State Coll (FL)

BUSINESS OPERATIONS SUPPORT AND SECRETARIAL SERVICES RELATED

Bunker Hill Comm Coll (MA)
Central Virginia Comm Coll (VA)
Davis Coll (OH)
Eastern Arizona Coll (AZ)
Genesee Comm Coll (NY)
Southwest Virginia Comm Coll (VA)

BUSINESS TEACHER EDUCATION

Allen Comm Coll (KS)
Amarillo Coll (TX)
Bainbridge State Coll (GA)
Eastern Arizona Coll (AZ)
Eastern Wyoming Coll (WY)
Iowa Central Comm Coll (IA)
Mt. San Antonio Coll (CA)
New Mexico Jr Coll (NM)
Northern Essex Comm Coll (MA)
Palau Comm Coll (Palau)
Paris Jr Coll (TX)
Rio Hondo Coll (CA)
South Florida State Coll (FL)
Spoon River Coll (IL)

CABINETMAKING AND MILLWORK

Bucks County Comm Coll (PA)
Central Georgia Tech Coll (GA)
Cerritos Coll (CA)
George C. Wallace Comm Coll (AL)
Ivy Tech Comm Coll–Bloomington (IN)
Ivy Tech Comm Coll–Central Indiana (IN)
Ivy Tech Comm Coll–Columbus (IN)
Ivy Tech Comm Coll–Lafayette (IN)
Ivy Tech Comm Coll–North Central (IN)
Ivy Tech Comm Coll–Northeast (IN)
Ivy Tech Comm Coll–Northwest (IN)
Ivy Tech Comm Coll–Richmond (IN)
Ivy Tech Comm Coll–Southern Indiana (IN)
Ivy Tech Comm Coll–Southwest (IN)
Ivy Tech Comm Coll–Wabash Valley (IN)
Macomb Comm Coll (MI)
Palomar Coll (CA)
Sierra Coll (CA)

Thaddeus Stevens Coll of Technology (PA)

CAD/CADD DRAFTING/DESIGN TECHNOLOGY
Arizona Western Coll (AZ)
Butler County Comm Coll (PA)
Central Ohio Tech Coll (OH)
Central Oregon Comm Coll (OR)
Century Coll (MN)
Corning Comm Coll (NY)
Danville Area Comm Coll (IL)
Dunwoody Coll of Technology (MN)
Elgin Comm Coll (IL)
Erie Comm Coll, South Campus (NY)
Front Range Comm Coll (CO)
Gateway Comm and Tech Coll (KY)
Gulf Coast State Coll (FL)
Hennepin Tech Coll (MN)
Jefferson Coll (MO)
Kellogg Comm Coll (MI)
Kent State U at Tuscarawas (OH)
Lake Superior Coll (MN)
Lewis and Clark Comm Coll (IL)
Manhattan Area Tech Coll (KS)
Miami Dade Coll (FL)
Minnesota State Coll–Southeast Tech (MN)
Mohawk Valley Comm Coll (NY)
Northampton Comm Coll (PA)
Northland Comm and Tech Coll (MN)
Northwest Coll (WY)
St. Philip's Coll (TX)
Sheridan Coll (WY)
South Suburban Coll (IL)
Tallahassee Comm Coll (FL)
Thaddeus Stevens Coll of Technology (PA)
Tyler Jr Coll (TX)
Wayne County Comm Coll District (MI)

CARDIOPULMONARY TECHNOLOGY
Lackawanna Coll (PA)

CARDIOVASCULAR TECHNOLOGY
Augusta Tech Coll (GA)
Bunker Hill Comm Coll (MA)
Central Georgia Tech Coll (GA)
Comm Coll of the Air Force (AL)
Florida SouthWestern State Coll (FL)
Harrisburg Area Comm Coll (PA)
Houston Comm Coll (TX)
Howard Comm Coll (MD)
Kirtland Comm Coll (MI)
Orange Coast Coll (CA)
Southeast Tech Inst (SD)
Southern Maine Comm Coll (ME)
Southern U at Shreveport (LA)

CARPENTRY
Alamance Comm Coll (NC)
American River Coll (CA)
Arizona Western Coll (AZ)
Austin Comm Coll District (TX)
Bismarck State Coll (ND)
Central Georgia Tech Coll (GA)
Central Wyoming Coll (WY)
Delta Coll (MI)
Fullerton Coll (CA)
George C. Wallace Comm Coll (AL)
Hawkeye Comm Coll (IA)
Hennepin Tech Coll (MN)
Hutchinson Comm Coll (KS)
Iowa Central Comm Coll (IA)
Ivy Tech Comm Coll–Central Indiana (IN)
Ivy Tech Comm Coll–East Central (IN)
Ivy Tech Comm Coll–Lafayette (IN)
Ivy Tech Comm Coll–North Central (IN)
Ivy Tech Comm Coll–Northwest (IN)
Ivy Tech Comm Coll–Southern Indiana (IN)
Ivy Tech Comm Coll–Southwest (IN)
Ivy Tech Comm Coll–Wabash Valley (IN)
Kaskaskia Coll (IL)
Los Angeles Trade-Tech Coll (CA)
Manhattan Area Tech Coll (KS)
Minnesota State Coll–Southeast Tech (MN)
Minnesota State Comm and Tech Coll–Moorhead (MN)
New Mexico Jr Coll (NM)
Northland Comm and Tech Coll (MN)

Palau Comm Coll (Palau)
Palomar Coll (CA)
Ranken Tech Coll (MO)
Ridgewater Coll (MN)
San Juan Coll (NM)
Southwestern Michigan Coll (MI)
Thaddeus Stevens Coll of Technology (PA)
Treasure Valley Comm Coll (OR)
Western Iowa Tech Comm Coll (IA)
Williamson Coll of the Trades (PA)

CASINO MANAGEMENT
Oklahoma State U Inst of Technology (OK)
Rowan Coll at Burlington County (NJ)
Wenatchee Valley Coll (WA)
Westmoreland County Comm Coll (PA)

CERAMIC ARTS AND CERAMICS
Mercer Comm Coll (NJ)
Palomar Coll (CA)

CHEMICAL ENGINEERING
Kilgore Coll (TX)
Los Angeles Trade-Tech Coll (CA)
Monroe Comm Coll (NY)
Muskegon Comm Coll (MI)
Olympic Coll (WA)
Rowan Coll at Burlington County (NJ)
South Florida State Coll (FL)

CHEMICAL PROCESS TECHNOLOGY
San Jacinto Coll District (TX)

CHEMICAL TECHNOLOGY
Alvin Comm Coll (TX)
Amarillo Coll (TX)
Bucks County Comm Coll (PA)
Cape Fear Comm Coll (NC)
Cincinnati State Tech and Comm Coll (OH)
Comm Coll of Philadelphia (PA)
Comm Coll of Rhode Island (RI)
Corning Comm Coll (NY)
County Coll of Morris (NJ)
Delta Coll (MI)
East Central Coll (MO)
Fullerton Coll (CA)
Houston Comm Coll (TX)
Humacao Comm Coll (PR)
Ivy Tech Comm Coll–Lafayette (IN)
Ivy Tech Comm Coll–Wabash Valley (IN)
Lehigh Carbon Comm Coll (PA)
Mohawk Valley Comm Coll (NY)
Niagara County Comm Coll (NY)
Pensacola State Coll (FL)
Raritan Valley Comm Coll (NJ)
San Jacinto Coll District (TX)
Texas State Tech Coll (TX)
U of Cincinnati Blue Ash Coll (OH)
Victoria Coll (TX)
Westmoreland County Comm Coll (PA)

CHEMISTRY
Allen Comm Coll (KS)
Amarillo Coll (TX)
Arizona Western Coll (AZ)
Austin Comm Coll District (TX)
Bainbridge State Coll (GA)
Barton County Comm Coll (KS)
Blinn Coll (TX)
Bunker Hill Comm Coll (MA)
Ca&nnada Coll (CA)
Casper Coll (WY)
Cecil Coll (MD)
Central New Mexico Comm Coll (NM)
Central Texas Coll (TX)
Cerritos Coll (CA)
Cochise County Comm Coll District (AZ)
Coll of Central Florida (FL)
Copiah-Lincoln Comm Coll (MS)
Dodge City Comm Coll (KS)
Eastern Arizona Coll (AZ)
Finger Lakes Comm Coll (NY)
Frederick Comm Coll (MD)
Fullerton Coll (CA)
Genesee Comm Coll (NY)
Georgia Highlands Coll (GA)
Gordon State Coll (GA)
Grand Rapids Comm Coll (MI)
Harford Comm Coll (MD)

Harrisburg Area Comm Coll (PA)
Holyoke Comm Coll (MA)
Houston Comm Coll (TX)
Itawamba Comm Coll (MS)
Kankakee Comm Coll (IL)
Kilgore Coll (TX)
Laramie County Comm Coll (WY)
Lehigh Carbon Comm Coll (PA)
Lorain County Comm Coll (OH)
Los Angeles Valley Coll (CA)
Macomb Comm Coll (MI)
Mercer County Comm Coll (NJ)
Miami Dade Coll (FL)
Monroe Comm Coll (NY)
Nashville State Comm Coll (TN)
Navarro Coll (TX)
New Mexico Jr Coll (NM)
Northampton Comm Coll (PA)
Northeastern Jr Coll (CO)
North Hennepin Comm Coll (MN)
Northwest Coll (WY)
Odessa Coll (TX)
Oklahoma City Comm Coll (OK)
Orange Coast Coll (CA)
Palomar Coll (CA)
Panola Coll (TX)
Paris Jr Coll (TX)
Pasadena City Coll (CA)
Pensacola State Coll (FL)
Potomac State Coll of West Virginia U (WV)
Queensborough Comm Coll of the City U of New York (NY)
Quinsigamond Comm Coll (MA)
Ridgewater Coll (MN)
Rowan Coll at Burlington County (NJ)
St. Charles Comm Coll (MO)
St. Philip's Coll (TX)
Salt Lake Comm Coll (UT)
San Jacinto Coll District (TX)
San Joaquin Delta Coll (CA)
San Juan Coll (NM)
Sierra Coll (CA)
Southern U at Shreveport (LA)
South Florida State Coll (FL)
Spoon River Coll (IL)
Springfield Tech Comm Coll (MA)
Texarkana Coll (TX)
Truckee Meadows Comm Coll (NV)
Tyler Jr Coll (TX)
Vincennes U (IN)
Wenatchee Valley Coll (WA)
Western Wyoming Comm Coll (WY)

CHEMISTRY RELATED
South Florida State Coll (FL)
Vincennes U (IN)

CHEMISTRY TEACHER EDUCATION
Anne Arundel Comm Coll (MD)
Carroll Comm Coll (MD)
Comm Coll of Baltimore County (MD)
Harford Comm Coll (MD)
Montgomery Coll (MD)
Vincennes U (IN)

CHILD-CARE AND SUPPORT SERVICES MANAGEMENT
Aiken Tech Coll (SC)
Anne Arundel Comm Coll (MD)
Barton County Comm Coll (KS)
Bevill State Comm Coll (AL)
Carroll Comm Coll (MD)
Cayuga County Comm Coll (NY)
Cecil Coll (MD)
Central Georgia Tech Coll (GA)
Central Lakes Coll (MN)
Central Oregon Comm Coll (OR)
Chesapeake Coll (MD)
Cloud County Comm Coll (KS)
Comm Coll of Baltimore County (MD)
Denmark Tech Coll (SC)
Dutchess Comm Coll (NY)
East Central Coll (MO)
Eastern Gateway Comm Coll (OH)
Erie Comm Coll (NY)
Forrest Coll (SC)
Gadsden State Comm Coll (AL)
Grand Rapids Comm Coll (MI)
Greenville Tech Coll (SC)
Hagerstown Comm Coll (MD)
H. Councill Trenholm State Comm Coll (AL)
Herkimer County Comm Coll (NY)
Hillsborough Comm Coll (FL)
Holyoke Comm Coll (MA)

Hutchinson Comm Coll (KS)
Ivy Tech Comm Coll–Bloomington (IN)
Ivy Tech Comm Coll–Central Indiana (IN)
Ivy Tech Comm Coll–Columbus (IN)
Ivy Tech Comm Coll–Lafayette (IN)
Ivy Tech Comm Coll–North Central (IN)
Ivy Tech Comm Coll–Northeast (IN)
Ivy Tech Comm Coll–Northwest (IN)
Ivy Tech Comm Coll–Richmond (IN)
Ivy Tech Comm Coll–Southeast (IN)
Ivy Tech Comm Coll–Southern Indiana (IN)
Ivy Tech Comm Coll–Southwest (IN)
Jefferson Coll (MO)
Jefferson Comm Coll (NY)
Jefferson State Comm Coll (AL)
Kellogg Comm Coll (MI)
Kilgore Coll (TX)
Lake Land Coll (IL)
Lurleen B. Wallace Comm Coll (AL)
Macomb Comm Coll (MI)
Midlands Tech Coll (SC)
Minnesota West Comm and Tech Coll (MN)
Mitchell Comm Coll (NC)
Montgomery County Comm Coll (PA)
Mount Wachusett Comm Coll (MA)
Northeast Alabama Comm Coll (AL)
Northwest-Shoals Comm Coll (AL)
Northwest Tech Coll (MN)
Orange Coast Coll (CA)
Palomar Coll (CA)
Pennsylvania Highlands Comm Coll (PA)
Pensacola State Coll (FL)
Piedmont Comm Coll (NC)
Reading Area Comm Coll (PA)
Reid State Tech Coll (AL)
Rogue Comm Coll (OR)
St. Charles Comm Coll (MO)
St. Clair County Comm Coll (MI)
Southeast Comm Coll, Lincoln Campus (NE)
Southeast Tech Inst (SD)
Texarkana Coll (TX)
Three Rivers Comm Coll (CT)
Tompkins Cortland Comm Coll (NY)
Victor Valley Coll (CA)
Vincennes U (IN)
Wayne County Comm Coll District (MI)
Western Piedmont Comm Coll (NC)
Williamsburg Tech Coll (SC)
Wor-Wic Comm Coll (MD)

CHILD-CARE PROVISION
Antelope Valley Coll (CA)
Bossier Parish Comm Coll (LA)
Bucks County Comm Coll (PA)
Ca&nnada Coll (CA)
Central Texas Coll (TX)
City Colls of Chicago, Olive-Harvey College (IL)
Coll of the Canyons (CA)
Collin County Comm Coll District (TX)
Columbia Coll (CA)
Danville Area Comm Coll (IL)
Dawson Comm Coll (MT)
Delta Coll (MI)
Elizabethtown Comm and Tech Coll, Elizabethtown (KY)
Feather River Coll (CA)
Florida SouthWestern State Coll (FL)
Fullerton Coll (CA)
Gulf Coast State Coll (FL)
Hawkeye Comm Coll (IA)
Highland Comm Coll (IL)
Hinds Comm Coll (MS)
Hopkinsville Comm Coll (KY)
Hudson County Comm Coll (NJ)
Illinois Central Coll (IL)
John Tyler Comm Coll (VA)
J. Sargeant Reynolds Comm Coll (VA)
Kaskaskia Coll (IL)
Kilgore Coll (TX)
Lakeland Comm Coll (OH)
Lake Region State Coll (ND)
Lewis and Clark Comm Coll (IL)
Luzerne County Comm Coll (PA)
McHenry County Coll (IL)
Meridian Comm Coll (MS)
Miami Dade Coll (FL)
Midlands Tech Coll (SC)
Montgomery Coll (MD)
Moraine Valley Comm Coll (IL)

Morgan Comm Coll (CO)
Mott Comm Coll (MI)
Northland Comm and Tech Coll (MN)
Nunez Comm Coll (LA)
Oakton Comm Coll (IL)
Orange Coast Coll (CA)
Owensboro Comm and Tech Coll (KY)
Palomar Coll (CA)
Pensacola State Coll (FL)
Raritan Valley Comm Coll (NJ)
Rend Lake Coll (IL)
St. Charles Comm Coll (MO)
San Juan Coll (NM)
Somerset Comm Coll (KY)
Southeast Tech Inst (SD)
South Suburban Coll (IL)
Southwestern Oregon Comm Coll (OR)
Southwest Virginia Comm Coll (VA)
Tech Coll of the Lowcountry (SC)
Vincennes U (IN)
Western Iowa Tech Comm Coll (IA)
Western Texas Coll (TX)
Westmoreland County Comm Coll (PA)

CHILD DEVELOPMENT
Albany Tech Coll (GA)
Allen Comm Coll (KS)
Alvin Comm Coll (TX)
Amarillo Coll (TX)
American River Coll (CA)
Athens Tech Coll (GA)
Atlanta Tech Coll (GA)
Augusta Tech Coll (GA)
Austin Comm Coll District (TX)
Blinn Coll (TX)
Brookhaven Coll (TX)
Carl Albert State Coll (OK)
Central Georgia Tech Coll (GA)
Chattahoochee Tech Coll (GA)
Citrus Coll (CA)
Cleveland State Comm Coll (TN)
Cloud County Comm Coll (KS)
Coastal Pines Tech Coll (GA)
Collin County Comm Coll District (TX)
Columbus Tech Coll (GA)
Comm Coll of Aurora (CO)
Copiah-Lincoln Comm Coll (MS)
Daytona State Coll (FL)
Dodge City Comm Coll (KS)
Dyersburg State Comm Coll (TN)
Edison Comm Coll (OH)
Frederick Comm Coll (MD)
Georgia Northwestern Tech Coll (GA)
Hennepin Tech Coll (MN)
Housatonic Comm Coll (CT)
Houston Comm Coll (TX)
Howard Comm Coll (MD)
Illinois Eastern Comm Colls, Wabash Valley College (IL)
Ivy Tech Comm Coll–Central Indiana (IN)
James Sprunt Comm Coll (NC)
Jefferson Comm Coll (NY)
Kennebec Valley Comm Coll (ME)
Lanier Tech Coll (GA)
Los Angeles Valley Coll (CA)
Miami Dade Coll (FL)
Mt. San Antonio Coll (CA)
Mount Wachusett Comm Coll (MA)
Muskegon Comm Coll (MI)
Nashville State Comm Coll (TN)
New River Comm Coll (VA)
Northeastern Jr Coll (CO)
North Shore Comm Coll (MA)
Northwest-Shoals Comm Coll (AL)
Oconee Fall Line Tech Coll (GA)
Odessa Coll (TX)
Ogeechee Tech Coll (GA)
Oklahoma City Comm Coll (OK)
Otero Jr Coll (CO)
Oxnard Coll (CA)
Pasadena City Coll (CA)
Reading Area Comm Coll (PA)
Richland Comm Coll (IL)
Rock Valley Coll (IL)
San Jacinto Coll District (TX)
Savannah Tech Coll (GA)
Schoolcraft Coll (MI)
Seminole State Coll (OK)
Seminole State Coll of Florida (FL)
Shawnee Comm Coll (IL)
Sierra Coll (CA)
Southeastern Comm Coll (IA)
Southeastern Tech Coll (GA)
Southern Crescent Tech Coll (GA)

Southern Regional Tech Coll (GA)
South Georgia Tech Coll (GA)
Spoon River Coll (IL)
Stark State Coll (OH)
Texarkana Coll (TX)
Tohono O'odham Comm Coll (AZ)
Tulsa Comm Coll (OK)
Tyler Jr Coll (TX)
U of Arkansas Comm Coll at Morrilton (AR)
Victor Valley Coll (CA)
Virginia Western Comm Coll (VA)
Volunteer State Comm Coll (TN)
Walters State Comm Coll (TN)
Washington County Comm Coll (ME)
Westchester Comm Coll (NY)
West Georgia Tech Coll (GA)
Wiregrass Georgia Tech Coll (GA)

CHINESE
Austin Comm Coll District (TX)

CHIROPRACTIC ASSISTANT
Barton County Comm Coll (KS)

CINEMATOGRAPHY AND FILM/ VIDEO PRODUCTION
Bucks County Comm Coll (PA)
Camden County Coll (NJ)
Cape Fear Comm Coll (NC)
Century Coll (MN)
Cerritos Coll (CA)
Coll of the Canyons (CA)
Comm Coll of Aurora (CO)
Fashion Inst of Design & Merchandising, LA Campus (CA)
Hillsborough Comm Coll (FL)
Houston Comm Coll (TX)
Los Angeles Valley Coll (CA)
Miami Dade Coll (FL)
Mott Comm Coll (MI)
Northcentral Tech Coll (WI)
Northwest Coll (WY)
Oklahoma City Comm Coll (OK)
Orange Coast Coll (CA)
Pasadena City Coll (CA)
Piedmont Comm Coll (NC)
Raritan Valley Comm Coll (NJ)
Western Iowa Tech Comm Coll (IA)
Western Piedmont Comm Coll (NC)

CITY/URBAN, COMMUNITY AND REGIONAL PLANNING
South Florida State Coll (FL)

CIVIL DRAFTING AND CAD/ CADD
Central Ohio Tech Coll (OH)
Genesee Comm Coll (NY)
Harford Comm Coll (MD)
Renton Tech Coll (WA)

CIVIL ENGINEERING
American Samoa Comm Coll (AS)
Fiorello H. LaGuardia Comm Coll of the City U of New York (NY)
Kilgore Coll (TX)
Nashville State Comm Coll (TN)
Potomac State Coll of West Virginia U (WV)
St. Charles Comm Coll (MO)
South Florida State Coll (FL)
Tidewater Comm Coll (VA)
Truckee Meadows Comm Coll (NV)
Vincennes U (IN)

CIVIL ENGINEERING TECHNOLOGY
Arizona Western Coll (AZ)
Bellingham Tech Coll (WA)
Butler County Comm Coll (PA)
Central Maine Comm Coll (ME)
Central Ohio Tech Coll (OH)
Chattahoochee Tech Coll (GA)
Chippewa Valley Tech Coll (WI)
Cincinnati State Tech and Comm Coll (OH)
Copiah-Lincoln Comm Coll (MS)
Eastern Arizona Coll (AZ)
Erie Comm Coll, North Campus (NY)
Fayetteville Tech Comm Coll (NC)
Florida SouthWestern State Coll (FL)
Gadsden State Comm Coll (AL)
Gulf Coast State Coll (FL)
Harrisburg Area Comm Coll (PA)
Hawkeye Comm Coll (IA)
Itawamba Comm Coll (MS)
Lake Land Coll (IL)
Lakeland Comm Coll (OH)
Lake Superior Coll (MN)
Lorain County Comm Coll (OH)
Macomb Comm Coll (MI)

Mercer County Comm Coll (NJ)
Miami Dade Coll (FL)
Middlesex County Coll (NJ)
Midlands Tech Coll (SC)
Mohawk Valley Comm Coll (NY)
Monroe Comm Coll (NY)
Mt. San Antonio Coll (CA)
Nashville State Comm Coll (TN)
Northern Essex Comm Coll (MA)
Oklahoma State U, Oklahoma City (OK)
Pensacola State Coll (FL)
San Joaquin Delta Coll (CA)
Seminole State Coll of Florida (FL)
Southeast Comm Coll, Milford Campus (NE)
Southeast Tech Inst (SD)
South Florida State Coll (FL)
Springfield Tech Comm Coll (MA)
Stark State Coll (OH)
Tech Coll of the Lowcountry (SC)
Three Rivers Comm Coll (CT)
Virginia Western Comm Coll (VA)
Westchester Comm Coll (NY)
Western Piedmont Comm Coll (NC)
Wytheville Comm Coll (VA)

CLASSICS AND CLASSICAL LANGUAGES
Pasadena City Coll (CA)

CLINICAL LABORATORY SCIENCE/MEDICAL TECHNOLOGY
Amarillo Coll (TX)
Athens Tech Coll (GA)
Casper Coll (WY)
Chipola Coll (FL)
Coll of Central Florida (FL)
Dodge City Comm Coll (KS)
Georgia Highlands Coll (GA)
Howard Comm Coll (MD)
Southeast Comm Coll, Lincoln Campus (NE)
South Florida State Coll (FL)
Tarrant County Coll District (TX)
Westchester Comm Coll (NY)
Westmoreland County Comm Coll (PA)

CLINICAL/MEDICAL LABORATORY ASSISTANT
Somerset Comm Coll (KY)
Wenatchee Valley Coll (WA)
Westmoreland County Comm Coll (PA)

CLINICAL/MEDICAL LABORATORY SCIENCE AND ALLIED PROFESSIONS RELATED
Houston Comm Coll (TX)
Southeast Tech Inst (SD)

CLINICAL/MEDICAL LABORATORY TECHNOLOGY
Alamance Comm Coll (NC)
Alexandria Tech and Comm Coll (MN)
Anne Arundel Comm Coll (MD)
Arapahoe Comm Coll (CO)
Austin Comm Coll District (TX)
Barton County Comm Coll (KS)
Bismarck State Coll (ND)
Blackhawk Tech Coll (WI)
Blue Ridge Comm and Tech Coll (WV)
Bunker Hill Comm Coll (MA)
Camden County Coll (NJ)
Carrington Coll–Phoenix West (AZ)
Carrington Coll–Tucson (AZ)
Central Georgia Tech Coll (GA)
Central New Mexico Comm Coll (NM)
Central Texas Coll (TX)
Chippewa Valley Tech Coll (WI)
Cincinnati State Tech and Comm Coll (OH)
Coastal Pines Tech Coll (GA)
Coll of the Canyons (CA)
Comm Coll of Baltimore County (MD)
Comm Coll of Philadelphia (PA)
Comm Coll of Rhode Island (RI)
Comm Coll of the Air Force (AL)
Copiah-Lincoln Comm Coll (MS)
County Coll of Morris (NJ)
Dutchess Comm Coll (NY)
Edison Comm Coll (OH)
Elgin Comm Coll (IL)
Erie Comm Coll, North Campus (NY)
Gadsden State Comm Coll (AL)
Genesee Comm Coll (NY)
George C. Wallace Comm Coll (AL)
Georgia Piedmont Tech Coll (GA)

Greenville Tech Coll (SC)
Halifax Comm Coll (NC)
Harrisburg Area Comm Coll (PA)
Hawkeye Comm Coll (IA)
Hinds Comm Coll (MS)
Housatonic Comm Coll (CT)
Houston Comm Coll (TX)
Hutchinson Comm Coll (KS)
Illinois Central Coll (IL)
Iowa Central Comm Coll (IA)
Ivy Tech Comm Coll–Lafayette (IN)
Ivy Tech Comm Coll–North Central (IN)
Ivy Tech Comm Coll–Southern Indiana (IN)
Ivy Tech Comm Coll–Wabash Valley (IN)
Jefferson State Comm Coll (AL)
J. Sargeant Reynolds Comm Coll (VA)
Kankakee Comm Coll (IL)
Kaskaskia Coll (IL)
Lake Area Tech Inst (SD)
Lakeland Comm Coll (OH)
Lake Superior Coll (MN)
Lorain County Comm Coll (OH)
Manchester Comm Coll (CT)
Manhattan Area Tech Coll (KS)
Mercer County Comm Coll (NJ)
Meridian Comm Coll (MS)
Miami Dade Coll (FL)
Middlesex County Coll (NJ)
Midlands Tech Coll (SC)
Mid-Plains Comm Coll, North Platte (NE)
Minnesota West Comm and Tech Coll (MN)
Mitchell Tech Inst (SD)
Montgomery County Comm Coll (PA)
Mount Wachusett Comm Coll (MA)
Navarro Coll (TX)
New Mexico Jr Coll (NM)
Northcentral Tech Coll (WI)
Northeast Iowa Comm Coll (IA)
North Hennepin Comm Coll (MN)
Oakton Comm Coll (IL)
Odessa Coll (TX)
Orange Coast Coll (CA)
Panola Coll (TX)
Queensborough Comm Coll of the City U of New York (NY)
Quincy Coll (MA)
Reading Area Comm Coll (PA)
Rend Lake Coll (IL)
River Valley Comm Coll (NH)
St. Philip's Coll (TX)
Salt Lake Comm Coll (UT)
San Jacinto Coll District (TX)
San Juan Coll (NM)
Seminole State Coll (OK)
Shawnee Comm Coll (IL)
Southeast Comm Coll, Lincoln Campus (NE)
Southeast Tech Inst (SD)
Southern U at Shreveport (LA)
Southwestern Oklahoma State U at Sayre (OK)
Southwest Tennessee Comm Coll (TN)
Spartanburg Comm Coll (SC)
Spencerian Coll (KY)
Spencerian Coll–Lexington (KY)
Springfield Tech Comm Coll (MA)
Stark State Coll (OH)
Tarrant County Coll District (TX)
Tri-County Tech Coll (SC)
Tulsa Comm Coll (OK)
Tyler Jr Coll (TX)
U of New Mexico–Gallup (NM)
Victoria Coll (TX)
Volunteer State Comm Coll (TN)
Waukesha County Tech Coll (WI)
Wenatchee Valley Coll (WA)
Westchester Comm Coll (NY)
Western Piedmont Comm Coll (NC)
Wytheville Comm Coll (VA)

CLINICAL/MEDICAL SOCIAL WORK
Central Texas Coll (TX)
Dawson Comm Coll (MT)
Southeast Comm Coll, Lincoln Campus (NE)

COMMERCIAL AND ADVERTISING ART
Alamance Comm Coll (NC)
Alexandria Tech and Comm Coll (MN)
Amarillo Coll (TX)
Austin Comm Coll District (TX)
Bismarck State Coll (ND)

Bucks County Comm Coll (PA)
Catawba Valley Comm Coll (NC)
Central Lakes Coll (MN)
Central Texas Coll (TX)
Cincinnati State Tech and Comm Coll (OH)
Collin County Comm Coll District (TX)
Comm Coll of Baltimore County (MD)
Comm Coll of the Air Force (AL)
Dutchess Comm Coll (NY)
East Central Coll (MO)
Eastern Arizona Coll (AZ)
Fashion Inst of Technology (NY)
Fayetteville Tech Comm Coll (NC)
Finger Lakes Comm Coll (NY)
Hagerstown Comm Coll (MD)
Halifax Comm Coll (NC)
Housatonic Comm Coll (CT)
Hussian Coll, School of Art (PA)
James H. Faulkner State Comm Coll (AL)
James Sprunt Comm Coll (NC)
Kilgore Coll (TX)
Lakeland Comm Coll (OH)
Los Angeles Trade-Tech Coll (CA)
Los Angeles Valley Coll (CA)
Luzerne County Comm Coll (PA)
Macomb Comm Coll (MI)
Manchester Comm Coll (CT)
Mercer County Comm Coll (NJ)
Miami Dade Coll (FL)
Midlands Tech Coll (SC)
Mid-Plains Comm Coll, North Platte (NE)
Mohawk Valley Comm Coll (NY)
Monroe Comm Coll (NY)
Montgomery Coll (MD)
Montgomery County Comm Coll (PA)
Mt. San Antonio Coll (CA)
Muskegon Comm Coll (MI)
Nashville State Comm Coll (TN)
Navarro Coll (TX)
New Mexico Jr Coll (NM)
Northern Essex Comm Coll (MA)
NorthWest Arkansas Comm Coll (AR)
Northwest Coll (WY)
Norwalk Comm Coll (CT)
Oklahoma City Comm Coll (OK)
Orange Coast Coll (CA)
Palomar Coll (CA)
Pensacola State Coll (FL)
Randolph Comm Coll (NC)
Rowan Coll at Burlington County (NJ)
St. Charles Comm Coll (MO)
St. Clair County Comm Coll (MI)
San Jacinto Coll District (TX)
San Joaquin Delta Coll (CA)
San Juan Coll (NM)
School of Advertising Art (OH)
Southeast Comm Coll, Lincoln Campus (NE)
Southeast Tech Inst (SD)
Southwest Tennessee Comm Coll (TN)
Sowela Tech Comm Coll (LA)
Springfield Tech Comm Coll (MA)
Sullivan County Comm Coll (NY)
Tallahassee Comm Coll (FL)
Tidewater Comm Coll (VA)
Tompkins Cortland Comm Coll (NY)
Truckee Meadows Comm Coll (NV)
Tunxis Comm Coll (CT)
Tyler Jr Coll (TX)
U of Arkansas Comm Coll at Morrilton (AR)
U of Cincinnati Blue Ash Coll (OH)
Vincennes U (IN)
Virginia Western Comm Coll (VA)
Western Nevada Coll (NV)

COMMERCIAL PHOTOGRAPHY
Austin Comm Coll District (TX)
Bucks County Comm Coll (PA)
Cecil Coll (MD)
Central Wyoming Coll (WY)
Century Coll (MN)
Fashion Inst of Technology (NY)
Fiorello H. LaGuardia Comm Coll of the City U of New York (NY)
Hawkeye Comm Coll (IA)
Houston Comm Coll (TX)
Kilgore Coll (TX)
Luzerne County Comm Coll (PA)
McHenry County Coll (IL)
Mohawk Valley Comm Coll (NY)
Montgomery Coll (MD)
Northwest Coll (WY)
Randolph Comm Coll (NC)
Ridgewater Coll (MN)

Sierra Coll (CA)
Springfield Tech Comm Coll (MA)
Tyler Jr Coll (TX)
Western Iowa Tech Comm Coll (IA)

COMMUNICATION
Arizona Western Coll (AZ)
Central New Mexico Comm Coll (NM)
Gordon State Coll (GA)
Northeastern Jr Coll (CO)
Pennsylvania Inst of Technology (PA)
Potomac State Coll of West Virginia U (WV)
Tulsa Comm Coll (OK)

COMMUNICATION AND JOURNALISM RELATED
Cayuga County Comm Coll (NY)
Gadsden State Comm Coll (AL)
Harrisburg Area Comm Coll (PA)
Ivy Tech Comm Coll–Kokomo (IN)
Queensborough Comm Coll of the City U of New York (NY)

COMMUNICATION AND MEDIA RELATED
County Coll of Morris (NJ)
Manor Coll (PA)
Raritan Valley Comm Coll (NJ)
Reading Area Comm Coll (PA)

COMMUNICATION DISORDERS SCIENCES AND SERVICES RELATED
Rowan Coll at Burlington County (NJ)

COMMUNICATIONS SYSTEMS INSTALLATION AND REPAIR TECHNOLOGY
Bellingham Tech Coll (WA)
Cayuga County Comm Coll (NY)
Dutchess Comm Coll (NY)
Erie Comm Coll, South Campus (NY)
Mohawk Valley Comm Coll (NY)
Ranken Tech Coll (MO)
Westmoreland County Comm Coll (PA)

COMMUNICATIONS TECHNOLOGIES AND SUPPORT SERVICES RELATED
Anne Arundel Comm Coll (MD)
Bowling Green State U–Firelands Coll (OH)
Middlesex County Coll (NJ)
Montgomery Coll (MD)
Montgomery County Comm Coll (PA)
Ocean County Coll (NJ)

COMMUNICATIONS TECHNOLOGY
Athens Tech Coll (GA)
Comm Coll of the Air Force (AL)
Daytona State Coll (FL)
Dodge City Comm Coll (KS)
Gulf Coast State Coll (FL)
Hutchinson Comm Coll (KS)
Lackawanna Coll (PA)
Mott Comm Coll (MI)
Pensacola State Coll (FL)
Pueblo Comm Coll (CO)
Vincennes U (IN)

COMMUNITY HEALTH AND PREVENTIVE MEDICINE
Anoka-Ramsey Comm Coll (MN)
Arizona Western Coll (AZ)
Massachusetts Bay Comm Coll (MA)
Northwest Vista Coll (TX)
Quinsigamond Comm Coll (MA)

COMMUNITY HEALTH SERVICES COUNSELING
Dutchess Comm Coll (NY)
Florida SouthWestern State Coll (FL)
Illinois Central Coll (IL)
Miami Dade Coll (FL)
Mott Comm Coll (MI)

COMMUNITY ORGANIZATION AND ADVOCACY
Berkshire Comm Coll (MA)
Borough of Manhattan Comm Coll of the City U of New York (NY)
Cleveland State Comm Coll (TN)
Clinton Comm Coll (NY)
Herkimer County Comm Coll (NY)
Iowa Central Comm Coll (IA)
Jefferson Comm Coll (NY)
Kellogg Comm Coll (MI)
Mercer County Comm Coll (NJ)
New River Comm Coll (VA)

Schenectady County Comm Coll (NY)
Sheridan Coll (WY)
U of New Mexico–Gallup (NM)
Westchester Comm Coll (NY)

COMMUNITY PSYCHOLOGY
Dawson Comm Coll (MT)

COMPARATIVE LITERATURE
Blinn Coll (TX)
Miami Dade Coll (FL)
Otero Jr Coll (CO)
San Joaquin Delta Coll (CA)

COMPUTER AND INFORMATION SCIENCES
Albany Tech Coll (GA)
Ancilla Coll (IN)
Anne Arundel Comm Coll (MD)
Arapahoe Comm Coll (CO)
Arizona Western Coll (AZ)
Austin Comm Coll District (TX)
Berkshire Comm Coll (MA)
Bevill State Comm Coll (AL)
Borough of Manhattan Comm Coll of the City U of New York (NY)
Bucks County Comm Coll (PA)
Butler County Comm Coll (PA)
Camden County Coll (NJ)
Carl Albert State Coll (OK)
Cayuga County Comm Coll (NY)
Central New Mexico Comm Coll (NM)
Central Virginia Comm Coll (VA)
Chandler-Gilbert Comm Coll (AZ)
Cincinnati State Tech and Comm Coll (OH)
Coll of Central Florida (FL)
Collin County Comm Coll District (TX)
Columbia-Greene Comm Coll (NY)
Comm Coll of Baltimore County (MD)
Comm Coll of Rhode Island (RI)
Corning Comm Coll (NY)
Dawson Comm Coll (MT)
Edison Comm Coll (OH)
Elizabethtown Comm and Tech Coll, Elizabethtown (KY)
Erie Comm Coll, North Campus (NY)
Finger Lakes Comm Coll (NY)
Front Range Comm Coll (CO)
Gadsden State Comm Coll (AL)
Gateway Comm and Tech Coll (KY)
George C. Wallace Comm Coll (AL)
Georgia Highlands Coll (GA)
Grand Rapids Comm Coll (MI)
Great Basin Coll (NV)
Hagerstown Comm Coll (MD)
Harford Comm Coll (MD)
Harrisburg Area Comm Coll (PA)
H. Councill Trenholm State Comm Coll (AL)
Herkimer County Comm Coll (NY)
Hopkinsville Comm Coll (KY)
Hudson County Comm Coll (NJ)
Hutchinson Comm Coll (KS)
Interactive Coll of Technology, Chamblee (GA)
Itawamba Comm Coll (MS)
Ivy Tech Comm Coll–Bloomington (IN)
Ivy Tech Comm Coll–Central Indiana (IN)
Ivy Tech Comm Coll–Columbus (IN)
Ivy Tech Comm Coll–East Central (IN)
Ivy Tech Comm Coll–Kokomo (IN)
Ivy Tech Comm Coll–Lafayette (IN)
Ivy Tech Comm Coll–North Central (IN)
Ivy Tech Comm Coll–Northeast (IN)
Ivy Tech Comm Coll–Northwest (IN)
Ivy Tech Comm Coll–Richmond (IN)
Ivy Tech Comm Coll–Southeast (IN)
Ivy Tech Comm Coll–Southern Indiana (IN)
Ivy Tech Comm Coll–Southwest (IN)
Ivy Tech Comm Coll–Wabash Valley (IN)
James H. Faulkner State Comm Coll (AL)
Jamestown Comm Coll (NY)
Jefferson Comm Coll (NY)
Jefferson State Comm Coll (AL)
J. F. Drake State Comm and Tech Coll (AL)
John Tyler Comm Coll (VA)

J. Sargeant Reynolds Comm Coll (VA)
Kilgore Coll (TX)
Lackawanna Coll (PA)
LDS Business Coll (UT)
Leeward Comm Coll (HI)
Lehigh Carbon Comm Coll (PA)
Lone Star Coll–CyFair (TX)
Lone Star Coll–Kingwood (TX)
Lurleen B. Wallace Comm Coll (AL)
Luzerne County Comm Coll (PA)
Middlesex County Coll (NJ)
Mid-Plains Comm Coll, North Platte (NE)
Mohawk Valley Comm Coll (NY)
Montgomery Coll (MD)
Montgomery County Comm Coll (PA)
Moraine Valley Comm Coll (IL)
Mountain State Coll (WV)
Mt. San Antonio Coll (CA)
Mount Wachusett Comm Coll (MA)
Northeast Alabama Comm Coll (AL)
Northern Essex Comm Coll (MA)
Northwest-Shoals Comm Coll (AL)
Northwest Vista Coll (TX)
Ocean County Coll (NJ)
Odessa Coll (TX)
Owensboro Comm and Tech Coll (KY)
Paris Jr Coll (TX)
Penn Foster Coll (AZ)
Pennsylvania Highlands Comm Coll (PA)
Pensacola State Coll (FL)
Potomac State Coll of West Virginia U (WV)
Pueblo Comm Coll (CO)
Quinsigamond Comm Coll (MA)
Reading Area Comm Coll (PA)
Reid State Tech Coll (AL)
Rogue Comm Coll (OR)
Salt Lake Comm Coll (UT)
San Jacinto Coll District (TX)
Sheridan Coll (WY)
Somerset Comm Coll (KY)
Southeast Comm Coll, Lincoln Campus (NE)
South Florida State Coll (FL)
Southwest Virginia Comm Coll (VA)
State U of New York Coll of Technology at Alfred (NY)
Texarkana Coll (TX)
Tompkins Cortland Comm Coll (NY)
Treasure Valley Comm Coll (OR)
Tyler Jr Coll (TX)
U of Arkansas Comm Coll at Morrilton (AR)
Victor Valley Coll (CA)
Vincennes U (IN)
Volunteer State Comm Coll (TN)
Walters State Comm Coll (TN)
Westchester Comm Coll (NY)
Western Nevada Coll (NV)
Western Texas Coll (TX)
Western Wyoming Comm Coll (WY)
White Mountains Comm Coll (NH)
Wor-Wic Comm Coll (MD)

COMPUTER AND INFORMATION SCIENCES AND SUPPORT SERVICES RELATED
Aiken Tech Coll (SC)
Bowling Green State U–Firelands Coll (OH)
Bunker Hill Comm Coll (MA)
Cayuga County Comm Coll (NY)
Chandler-Gilbert Comm Coll (AZ)
Chesapeake Coll (MD)
Corning Comm Coll (NY)
Fiorello H. LaGuardia Comm Coll of the City U of New York (NY)
Herkimer County Comm Coll (NY)
Interactive Coll of Technology, Chamblee (GA)
Island Drafting and Tech Inst (NY)
Jefferson Comm Coll (NY)
LDS Business Coll (UT)
Massachusetts Bay Comm Coll (MA)
Midlands Tech Coll (SC)
Mohawk Valley Comm Coll (NY)
Monroe Comm Coll (NY)
Northcentral Tech Coll (WI)
North Central Texas Coll (TX)
Northwest Vista Coll (TX)
Raritan Valley Comm Coll (NJ)
San Joaquin Valley Coll, Visalia (CA)
Seminole State Coll of Florida (FL)
Sierra Coll (CA)
Southeastern Coll–West Palm Beach (FL)

Southeast Tech Inst (SD)
Stark State Coll (OH)
Thaddeus Stevens Coll of Technology (PA)
Tulsa Comm Coll (OK)
Wayne County Comm Coll District (MI)
Westchester Comm Coll (NY)

COMPUTER AND INFORMATION SCIENCES RELATED
Central Oregon Comm Coll (OR)
Chipola Coll (FL)
Citrus Coll (CA)
Corning Comm Coll (NY)
Dawson Comm Coll (MT)
Daytona State Coll (FL)
Delta Coll (MI)
Genesee Comm Coll (NY)
Howard Comm Coll (MD)
LDS Business Coll (UT)
Lorain County Comm Coll (OH)
Luzerne County Comm Coll (PA)
Metro Business Coll, Jefferson City (MO)
Mohave Comm Coll (AZ)
Monroe Comm Coll (NY)
Nashville State Comm Coll (TN)
North Shore Comm Coll (MA)
Pensacola State Coll (FL)
Richland Comm Coll (IL)
Seminole State Coll of Florida (FL)
Stark State Coll (OH)
Tulsa Comm Coll (OK)
Tyler Jr Coll (TX)
Westchester Comm Coll (NY)

COMPUTER AND INFORMATION SYSTEMS SECURITY
Anne Arundel Comm Coll (MD)
Blue Ridge Comm and Tech Coll (WV)
Bunker Hill Comm Coll (MA)
Butler County Comm Coll (PA)
Casper Coll (WY)
Central Texas Coll (TX)
Century Coll (MN)
Chattahoochee Tech Coll (GA)
Chesapeake Coll (MD)
Cochise County Comm Coll District (AZ)
Collin County Comm Coll District (TX)
Comm Coll of Baltimore County (MD)
Craven Comm Coll (NC)
Delta Coll (MI)
Dyersburg State Comm Coll (TN)
Edison Comm Coll (OH)
Elgin Comm Coll (IL)
Fayetteville Tech Comm Coll (NC)
Georgia Military Coll (GA)
Grand Rapids Comm Coll (MI)
Hagerstown Comm Coll (MD)
Harrisburg Area Comm Coll (PA)
Hinds Comm Coll (MS)
Island Drafting and Tech Inst (NY)
Lanier Tech Coll (GA)
LDS Business Coll (UT)
Lehigh Carbon Comm Coll (PA)
Massachusetts Bay Comm Coll (MA)
Minnesota State Comm and Tech Coll–Detroit Lakes (MN)
Minnesota West Comm and Tech Coll (MN)
Mohawk Valley Comm Coll (NY)
Montgomery Coll (MD)
Moraine Valley Comm Coll (IL)
Northampton Comm Coll (PA)
Northwest Vista Coll (TX)
Norwalk Comm Coll (CT)
Oxnard Coll (CA)
Pensacola State Coll (FL)
Quinsigamond Comm Coll (MA)
Rowan-Cabarrus Comm Coll (NC)
St. Philip's Coll (TX)
Seminole State Coll of Florida (FL)
Sheridan Coll (WY)
Southeast Tech Inst (SD)
Southern Crescent Tech Coll (GA)
Spoon River Coll (IL)
Springfield Tech Comm Coll (MA)
Texas State Tech Coll (TX)
Westchester Comm Coll (NY)
Westmoreland County Comm Coll (PA)
Wiregrass Georgia Tech Coll (GA)

COMPUTER ENGINEERING
Carroll Comm Coll (MD)
Comm Coll of Baltimore County (MD)
Daytona State Coll (FL)
Pensacola State Coll (FL)
South Florida State Coll (FL)

COMPUTER ENGINEERING RELATED
Columbus Tech Coll (GA)
Daytona State Coll (FL)
Eastern Gateway Comm Coll (OH)
Monroe Comm Coll (NY)
Seminole State Coll of Florida (FL)
Stark State Coll (OH)

COMPUTER ENGINEERING TECHNOLOGIES RELATED
Catawba Valley Comm Coll (NC)

COMPUTER ENGINEERING TECHNOLOGY
Alvin Comm Coll (TX)
Amarillo Coll (TX)
Bowling Green State U–Firelands Coll (OH)
Brookhaven Coll (TX)
Catawba Valley Comm Coll (NC)
Cincinnati State Tech and Comm Coll (OH)
Coll of The Albemarle (NC)
Comm Coll of Rhode Island (RI)
Georgia Piedmont Tech Coll (GA)
Houston Comm Coll (TX)
Hudson County Comm Coll (NJ)
Iowa Central Comm Coll (IA)
Kellogg Comm Coll (MI)
Lakeland Comm Coll (OH)
Lenoir Comm Coll (NC)
Lorain County Comm Coll (OH)
Los Angeles Trade-Tech Coll (CA)
Miami Dade Coll (FL)
Minnesota West Comm and Tech Coll (MN)
Monroe Comm Coll (NY)
Mt. San Antonio Coll (CA)
Nashville State Comm Coll (TN)
Naugatuck Valley Comm Coll (CT)
New River Comm Coll (VA)
North Central Texas Coll (TX)
Northern Essex Comm Coll (MA)
North Shore Comm Coll (MA)
Oklahoma City Comm Coll (OK)
Onondaga Comm Coll (NY)
Paris Jr Coll (TX)
Queensborough Comm Coll of the City U of New York (NY)
Quinsigamond Comm Coll (MA)
Ranken Tech Coll (MO)
Richmond Comm Coll (NC)
Rock Valley Coll (IL)
Seminole State Coll of Florida (FL)
Southern Maine Comm Coll (ME)
South Florida State Coll (FL)
Southwest Tennessee Comm Coll (TN)
Southwest Texas Jr Coll (TX)
Springfield Tech Comm Coll (MA)
State U of New York Coll of Technology at Alfred (NY)
Three Rivers Comm Coll (CT)
Tyler Jr Coll (TX)
Western Piedmont Comm Coll (NC)
Western Texas Coll (TX)

COMPUTER GRAPHICS
Antelope Valley Coll (CA)
Arizona Western Coll (AZ)
Carroll Comm Coll (MD)
Central Ohio Tech Coll (OH)
Citrus Coll (CA)
Coll of Business and Technology–Main Campus (FL)
Daytona State Coll (FL)
Genesee Comm Coll (NY)
Great Basin Coll (NV)
Howard Comm Coll (MD)
Hudson County Comm Coll (NJ)
Kellogg Comm Coll (MI)
Lewis and Clark Comm Coll (IL)
Luzerne County Comm Coll (PA)
Mercer County Comm Coll (NJ)
Mesabi Range Coll (MN)
Miami Dade Coll (FL)
Moraine Valley Comm Coll (IL)
Mt. San Antonio Coll (CA)
Mount Wachusett Comm Coll (MA)
Navarro Coll (TX)
New Mexico Jr Coll (NM)

New River Comm Coll (VA)
North Central Texas Coll (TX)
Northern Essex Comm Coll (MA)
North Shore Comm Coll (MA)
Orange Coast Coll (CA)
Palomar Coll (CA)
Pittsburgh Tech Inst, Oakdale (PA)
Quinsigamond Comm Coll (MA)
Richland Comm Coll (IL)
Rowan Coll at Burlington County (NJ)
Schoolcraft Coll (MI)
Seminole State Coll of Florida (FL)
Shawnee Comm Coll (IL)
Sullivan County Comm Coll (NY)
Tallahassee Comm Coll (FL)
Tyler Jr Coll (TX)
Weatherford Coll (TX)

COMPUTER HARDWARE ENGINEERING
Seminole State Coll of Florida (FL)
Stark State Coll (OH)

COMPUTER/INFORMATION TECHNOLOGY SERVICES ADMINISTRATION RELATED
Barton County Comm Coll (KS)
Bossier Parish Comm Coll (LA)
Bunker Hill Comm Coll (MA)
Clinton Comm Coll (NY)
Corning Comm Coll (NY)
Daytona State Coll (FL)
Dutchess Comm Coll (NY)
ETI Tech Coll of Niles (OH)
Hawkeye Comm Coll (IA)
Hesston Coll (KS)
Howard Comm Coll (MD)
Jefferson Comm Coll (NY)
LDS Business Coll (UT)
Massachusetts Bay Comm Coll (MA)
Mesabi Range Coll (MN)
North Central Texas Coll (TX)
Northwest Vista Coll (TX)
Panola Coll (TX)
Pasadena City Coll (CA)
Schenectady County Comm Coll (NY)
Seminole State Coll of Florida (FL)
Southeast Tech Inst (SD)
Stark State Coll (OH)
Vincennes U (IN)
Western Iowa Tech Comm Coll (IA)

COMPUTER INSTALLATION AND REPAIR TECHNOLOGY
Delta Coll (MI)
Fiorello H. LaGuardia Comm Coll of the City U of New York (NY)
Forrest Coll (SC)
Genesee Comm Coll (NY)
Hinds Comm Coll (MS)
Lake Region State Coll (ND)
Los Angeles Valley Coll (CA)
Miami Dade Coll (FL)
Midlands Tech Coll (SC)
Northampton Comm Coll (PA)
Orange Coast Coll (CA)
Penn Foster Coll (AZ)
Queensborough Comm Coll of the City U of New York (NY)
Sierra Coll (CA)
Southeast Tech Inst (SD)
Tulsa Comm Coll (OK)
Washington County Comm Coll (ME)
Wisconsin Indianhead Tech Coll (WI)

COMPUTER NUMERICALLY CONTROLLED (CNC) MACHINIST TECHNOLOGY
Anoka Tech Coll (MN)
Corning Comm Coll (NY)
Hennepin Tech Coll (MN)
Lake Superior Coll (MN)
Wayne County Comm Coll District (MI)
Westmoreland County Comm Coll (PA)

COMPUTER PROGRAMMING
Aiken Tech Coll (SC)
Alvin Comm Coll (TX)
Amarillo Coll (TX)
American River Coll (CA)
Antelope Valley Coll (CA)
Athens Tech Coll (GA)
Atlanta Tech Coll (GA)
Augusta Tech Coll (GA)
Austin Comm Coll District (TX)
Big Bend Comm Coll (WA)

Bradford School (PA)
Brookhaven Coll (TX)
Bunker Hill Comm Coll (MA)
Caldwell Comm Coll and Tech Inst (NC)
Casper Coll (WY)
Catawba Valley Comm Coll (NC)
Central Georgia Tech Coll (GA)
Central Ohio Tech Coll (OH)
Cerritos Coll (CA)
Chandler-Gilbert Comm Coll (AZ)
Chattahoochee Tech Coll (GA)
Chippewa Valley Tech Coll (WI)
Clark Coll (WA)
Cochise County Comm Coll District (AZ)
Coll of The Albemarle (NC)
Copiah-Lincoln Comm Coll (MS)
Dabney S. Lancaster Comm Coll (VA)
Daytona State Coll (FL)
Delta Coll (MI)
Dodge City Comm Coll (KS)
Edison Comm Coll (OH)
Fayetteville Tech Comm Coll (NC)
Feather River Coll (CA)
Fiorello H. LaGuardia Comm Coll of the City U of New York (NY)
Florida SouthWestern State Coll (FL)
Fox Valley Tech Coll (WI)
Gateway Tech Coll (WI)
Georgia Northwestern Tech Coll (GA)
Georgia Piedmont Tech Coll (GA)
Grand Rapids Comm Coll (MI)
Gulf Coast State Coll (FL)
Gwinnett Tech Coll (GA)
Hennepin Tech Coll (MN)
Hinds Comm Coll (MS)
Houston Comm Coll (TX)
Illinois Central Coll (IL)
International Business Coll, Indianapolis (IN)
J. Sargeant Reynolds Comm Coll (VA)
Kellogg Comm Coll (MI)
Kilgore Coll (TX)
King's Coll (NC)
Lamar Comm Coll (CO)
Lanier Tech Coll (GA)
Laramie County Comm Coll (WY)
LDS Business Coll (UT)
Lehigh Carbon Comm Coll (PA)
Lewis and Clark Comm Coll (IL)
Lone Star Coll–Tomball (TX)
Lorain County Comm Coll (OH)
Los Angeles Trade-Tech Coll (CA)
Los Angeles Valley Coll (CA)
Macomb Comm Coll (MI)
Miami Dade Coll (FL)
Minneapolis Business Coll (MN)
Minnesota State Coll–Southeast Tech (MN)
Minnesota State Comm and Tech Coll–Moorhead (MN)
Mitchell Comm Coll (NC)
Mohawk Valley Comm Coll (NY)
Montgomery County Comm Coll (PA)
Mott Comm Coll (MI)
Navarro Coll (TX)
New Mexico Jr Coll (NM)
Norco Coll (CA)
Northampton Comm Coll (PA)
North Central Texas Coll (TX)
Northern Essex Comm Coll (MA)
North Shore Comm Coll (MA)
NorthWest Arkansas Comm Coll (AR)
Northwest Vista Coll (TX)
Oakton Comm Coll (IL)
Ohio Business Coll, Sheffield Village (OH)
Orange Coast Coll (CA)
Palomar Coll (CA)
Pensacola State Coll (FL)
Pittsburgh Tech Inst, Oakdale (PA)
Ridgewater Coll (MN)
Rowan-Cabarrus Comm Coll (NC)
St. Charles Comm Coll (MO)
St. Clair County Comm Coll (MI)
Schenectady County Comm Coll (NY)
Schoolcraft Coll (MI)
Seminole State Coll of Florida (FL)
Sierra Coll (CA)
Southeastern Comm Coll (IA)
Southeast Tech Inst (SD)
Southern Crescent Tech Coll (GA)
South Florida State Coll (FL)
Southwestern Michigan Coll (MI)
Sowela Tech Comm Coll (LA)
Stark State Coll (OH)

Tallahassee Comm Coll (FL)
Tarrant County Coll District (TX)
Texas State Tech Coll (TX)
Tidewater Comm Coll (VA)
Tyler Jr Coll (TX)
Vincennes U (IN)
Waukesha County Tech Coll (WI)
Wayne County Comm Coll District (MI)
Weatherford Coll (TX)
Westmoreland County Comm Coll (PA)
Wiregrass Georgia Tech Coll (GA)
Wisconsin Indianhead Tech Coll (WI)
Wood Tobe–Coburn School (NY)

COMPUTER PROGRAMMING RELATED

Genesee Comm Coll (NY)
LDS Business Coll (UT)
Lorain County Comm Coll (OH)
Luzerne County Comm Coll (PA)
Mesabi Range Coll (MN)
North Central Texas Coll (TX)
Northern Essex Comm Coll (MA)
Seminole State Coll of Florida (FL)
Southeast Tech Inst (SD)
Stark State Coll (OH)
Tyler Jr Coll (TX)

COMPUTER PROGRAMMING (SPECIFIC APPLICATIONS)

Barton County Comm Coll (KS)
Bunker Hill Comm Coll (MA)
Butler County Comm Coll (PA)
Cincinnati State Tech and Comm Coll (OH)
Coll of The Albemarle (NC)
Comm Coll of Rhode Island (RI)
Craven Comm Coll (NC)
Danville Area Comm Coll (IL)
Daytona State Coll (FL)
ETI Tech Coll of Niles (OH)
Grand Rapids Comm Coll (MI)
Hillsborough Comm Coll (FL)
Holyoke Comm Coll (MA)
Houston Comm Coll (TX)
Humacao Comm Coll (PR)
Kellogg Comm Coll (MI)
Kent State U at Ashtabula (OH)
Kent State U at East Liverpool (OH)
Kent State U at Salem (OH)
Kent State U at Trumbull (OH)
Kent State U at Tuscarawas (OH)
Lake Land Coll (IL)
Lakeland Comm Coll (OH)
LDS Business Coll (UT)
Lehigh Carbon Comm Coll (PA)
Lorain County Comm Coll (OH)
Macomb Comm Coll (MI)
Manor Coll (PA)
Mesabi Range Coll (MN)
Miami Dade Coll (FL)
Mitchell Comm Coll (NC)
Mohave Comm Coll (AZ)
Mott Comm Coll (MI)
North Central Texas Coll (TX)
Northeast Iowa Comm Coll (IA)
Northern Essex Comm Coll (MA)
North Shore Comm Coll (MA)
Pensacola State Coll (FL)
Quinsigamond Comm Coll (MA)
Richland Comm Coll (IL)
Schoolcraft Coll (MI)
Seminole State Coll of Florida (FL)
Spoon River Coll (IL)
Springfield Tech Comm Coll (MA)
Stark State Coll (OH)
Sullivan County Comm Coll (NY)
Tallahassee Comm Coll (FL)
Truckee Meadows Comm Coll (NV)
Victor Valley Coll (CA)
Western Iowa Tech Comm Coll (IA)
Western Wyoming Comm Coll (WY)
Westmoreland County Comm Coll (PA)

COMPUTER PROGRAMMING (VENDOR/PRODUCT CERTIFICATION)

Chandler-Gilbert Comm Coll (AZ)
Gulf Coast State Coll (FL)
Lorain County Comm Coll (OH)
Miami Dade Coll (FL)
North Central Texas Coll (TX)
Pensacola State Coll (FL)
Raritan Valley Comm Coll (NJ)
Seminole State Coll of Florida (FL)
Stark State Coll (OH)

COMPUTER SCIENCE

Allen Comm Coll (KS)

Amarillo Coll (TX)
American River Coll (CA)
Anoka-Ramsey Comm Coll (MN)
Barton County Comm Coll (KS)
Blinn Coll (TX)
Borough of Manhattan Comm Coll of the City U of New York (NY)
Bunker Hill Comm Coll (MA)
Ca&nnada Coll (CA)
Central New Mexico Comm Coll (NM)
Central Oregon Comm Coll (OR)
Central Wyoming Coll (WY)
Century Coll (MN)
Cerritos Coll (CA)
Chesapeake Coll (MD)
Chipola Coll (FL)
Citrus Coll (CA)
Cochise County Comm Coll District (AZ)
Coll of the Canyons (CA)
Collin County Comm Coll District (TX)
Columbia Coll (CA)
Comm Coll of Philadelphia (PA)
Corning Comm Coll (NY)
County Coll of Morris (NJ)
Daytona State Coll (FL)
Dodge City Comm Coll (KS)
Dutchess Comm Coll (NY)
Finger Lakes Comm Coll (NY)
Fiorello H. LaGuardia Comm Coll of the City U of New York (NY)
Frederick Comm Coll (MD)
Fullerton Coll (CA)
Galveston Coll (TX)
Genesee Comm Coll (NY)
George C. Wallace Comm Coll (AL)
Georgia Military Coll (GA)
Gordon State Coll (GA)
Gwinnett Tech Coll (GA)
Harford Comm Coll (MD)
Harrisburg Area Comm Coll (PA)
Houston Comm Coll (TX)
Howard Comm Coll (MD)
Itawamba Comm Coll (MS)
Ivy Tech Comm Coll–Bloomington (IN)
Ivy Tech Comm Coll–Central Indiana (IN)
Ivy Tech Comm Coll–Columbus (IN)
Ivy Tech Comm Coll–East Central (IN)
Ivy Tech Comm Coll–Kokomo (IN)
Ivy Tech Comm Coll–Lafayette (IN)
Ivy Tech Comm Coll–Northeast (IN)
Ivy Tech Comm Coll–Richmond (IN)
Ivy Tech Comm Coll–Southeast (IN)
Ivy Tech Comm Coll–Southern Indiana (IN)
Ivy Tech Comm Coll–Southwest (IN)
Ivy Tech Comm Coll–Wabash Valley (IN)
Jefferson Comm Coll (NY)
Lake Area Tech Inst (SD)
Lamar Comm Coll (CO)
Lanier Tech Coll (GA)
Laramie County Comm Coll (WY)
LDS Business Coll (UT)
Lone Star Coll–CyFair (TX)
Lone Star Coll–Kingwood (TX)
Lone Star Coll–Montgomery (TX)
Lone Star Coll–North Harris (TX)
Lone Star Coll–Tomball (TX)
Lorain County Comm Coll (OH)
Luzerne County Comm Coll (PA)
Massachusetts Bay Comm Coll (MA)
Mercer County Comm Coll (NJ)
Miami Dade Coll (FL)
Minnesota West Comm and Tech Coll (MN)
Mohave Comm Coll (AZ)
Monroe Comm Coll (NY)
Moraine Valley Comm Coll (IL)
Mt. San Antonio Coll (CA)
Nashville State Comm Coll (TN)
Navarro Coll (TX)
New Mexico Jr Coll (NM)
Niagara County Comm Coll (NY)
Northampton Comm Coll (PA)
North Central Texas Coll (TX)
Northern Essex Comm Coll (MA)
North Hennepin Comm Coll (MN)
North Shore Comm Coll (MA)
Northwest Vista Coll (TX)
Odessa Coll (TX)
Oklahoma City Comm Coll (OK)
Onondaga Comm Coll (NY)
Orange Coast Coll (CA)
Panola Coll (TX)
Pasadena City Coll (CA)

Pennsylvania Highlands Comm Coll (PA)
Pensacola State Coll (FL)
Quincy Coll (MA)
Quinsigamond Comm Coll (MA)
Renton Tech Coll (WA)
Ridgewater Coll (MN)
River Valley Comm Coll (NH)
Rock Valley Coll (IL)
Rogue Comm Coll (OR)
Rowan Coll at Burlington County (NJ)
Salt Lake Comm Coll (UT)
San Joaquin Delta Coll (CA)
Seminole State Coll (OK)
Southern Maine Comm Coll (ME)
Southern U at Shreveport (LA)
Southwestern Oklahoma State U at Sayre (OK)
Springfield Tech Comm Coll (MA)
Tarrant County Coll District (TX)
Tulsa Comm Coll (OK)
Tyler Jr Coll (TX)
Victor Valley Coll (CA)
Vincennes U (IN)
Virginia Western Comm Coll (VA)
Westchester Comm Coll (NY)
Western Texas Coll (TX)
Western Wyoming Comm Coll (WY)
York County Comm Coll (ME)

COMPUTER SOFTWARE AND MEDIA APPLICATIONS RELATED

The Coll of Westchester (NY)
ETI Tech Coll of Niles (OH)
Genesee Comm Coll (NY)
Kellogg Comm Coll (MI)
Mesabi Range Coll (MN)
Ohio Business Coll, Sheffield Village (OH)
Seminole State Coll of Florida (FL)
Stark State Coll (OH)

COMPUTER SOFTWARE ENGINEERING

LDS Business Coll (UT)
Seminole State Coll of Florida (FL)
Southeast Tech Inst (SD)
Stark State Coll (OH)

COMPUTER SOFTWARE TECHNOLOGY

Miami Dade Coll (FL)
Rogue Comm Coll (OR)

COMPUTER SUPPORT SPECIALIST

Central Ohio Tech Coll (OH)
Cincinnati State Tech and Comm Coll (OH)
Comm Coll of Rhode Island (RI)
Corning Comm Coll (NY)
Fox Valley Tech Coll (WI)
Gateway Tech Coll (WI)
Genesee Comm Coll (NY)
Grand Rapids Comm Coll (MI)
IBMC Coll, Fort Collins (CO)
Miami Dade Coll (FL)
Mitchell Tech Inst (SD)
Northland Comm and Tech Coll (MN)
Tompkins Cortland Comm Coll (NY)
Waukesha County Tech Coll (WI)
Westmoreland County Comm Coll (PA)
Wisconsin Indianhead Tech Coll (WI)

COMPUTER SYSTEMS ANALYSIS

Amarillo Coll (TX)
Cerritos Coll (CA)
Chandler-Gilbert Comm Coll (AZ)
Cincinnati State Tech and Comm Coll (OH)
Crowder Coll (MO)
Hillsborough Comm Coll (FL)
Hutchinson Comm Coll (KS)
Lakeland Comm Coll (OH)
Mitchell Comm Coll (NC)
Northcentral Tech Coll (WI)
Oklahoma City Comm Coll (OK)
Pensacola State Coll (FL)
Quinsigamond Comm Coll (MA)
Tohono O'odham Comm Coll (AZ)
Wor-Wic Comm Coll (MD)

COMPUTER SYSTEMS NETWORKING AND TELECOMMUNICATIONS

Aiken Tech Coll (SC)
Alexandria Tech and Comm Coll (MN)
Allen Comm Coll (KS)

American River Coll (CA)
Anne Arundel Comm Coll (MD)
Anoka-Ramsey Comm Coll (MN)
Antelope Valley Coll (CA)
Arapahoe Comm Coll (CO)
Athens Tech Coll (GA)
Augusta Tech Coll (GA)
Austin Comm Coll District (TX)
Barton County Comm Coll (KS)
Beckfield Coll (KY)
Bellingham Tech Coll (WA)
Big Bend Comm Coll (WA)
Bismarck State Coll (ND)
Blackhawk Tech Coll (WI)
Blinn Coll (TX)
Borough of Manhattan Comm Coll of the City U of New York (NY)
Bowling Green State U–Firelands Coll (OH)
Bradford School (PA)
Bucks County Comm Coll (PA)
Bunker Hill Comm Coll (MA)
Ca&nnada Coll (CA)
Cape Fear Comm Coll (NC)
Catawba Valley Comm Coll (NC)
Central Georgia Tech Coll (GA)
Central Lakes Coll (MN)
Central Oregon Comm Coll (OR)
Century Coll (MN)
Cerritos Coll (CA)
Chandler-Gilbert Comm Coll (AZ)
Chattahoochee Tech Coll (GA)
Chippewa Valley Tech Coll (WI)
Clark Coll (WA)
Coastal Pines Tech Coll (GA)
Cochise County Comm Coll District (AZ)
Coll of Business and Technology–Flagler Campus (FL)
Coll of Business and Technology–Main Campus (FL)
Coll of Business and Technology–Miami Gardens (FL)
Coll of the Canyons (CA)
Columbus Tech Coll (GA)
Comm Coll of Baltimore County (MD)
Comm Coll of Rhode Island (RI)
Craven Comm Coll (NC)
Crowder Coll (MO)
Danville Area Comm Coll (IL)
Davis Coll (OH)
Daytona State Coll (FL)
Delta Coll (MI)
Dunwoody Coll of Technology (MN)
East Central Coll (MO)
Eastern Idaho Tech Coll (ID)
Eastern Wyoming Coll (WY)
Edison Comm Coll (OH)
Fayetteville Tech Comm Coll (NC)
Fiorello H. LaGuardia Comm Coll of the City U of New York (NY)
Florida SouthWestern State Coll (FL)
Fox Valley Tech Coll (WI)
Front Range Comm Coll (CO)
Gateway Tech Coll (WI)
Genesee Comm Coll (NY)
Georgia Piedmont Tech Coll (GA)
Grand Rapids Comm Coll (MI)
Great Basin Coll (NV)
Great Falls Coll Montana State U (MT)
Gulf Coast State Coll (FL)
Gwinnett Tech Coll (GA)
Harrisburg Area Comm Coll (PA)
Hawkeye Comm Coll (IA)
Hennepin Tech Coll (MN)
Hinds Comm Coll (MS)
Houston Comm Coll (TX)
Howard Comm Coll (MD)
Hutchinson Comm Coll (KS)
Illinois Central Coll (IL)
Illinois Eastern Comm Colls, Lincoln Trail College (IL)
International Business Coll, Indianapolis (IN)
Island Drafting and Tech Inst (NY)
Ivy Tech Comm Coll–Bloomington (IN)
Ivy Tech Comm Coll–East Central (IN)
Ivy Tech Comm Coll–Kokomo (IN)
Ivy Tech Comm Coll–Lafayette (IN)
Ivy Tech Comm Coll–Southern Indiana (IN)
Ivy Tech Comm Coll–Wabash Valley (IN)
Jefferson Coll (MO)
J. Sargeant Reynolds Comm Coll (VA)
Kilgore Coll (TX)
King's Coll (NC)

Lake Land Coll (IL)
Lakeland Comm Coll (OH)
Lanier Tech Coll (GA)
Lehigh Carbon Comm Coll (PA)
Lenoir Comm Coll (NC)
Lewis and Clark Comm Coll (IL)
Lorain County Comm Coll (OH)
Luzerne County Comm Coll (PA)
Manhattan Area Tech Coll (KS)
McHenry County Coll (IL)
Mercer County Comm Coll (NJ)
Mesabi Range Coll (MN)
Miami Dade Coll (FL)
Midlands Tech Coll (SC)
Minneapolis Business Coll (MN)
Minnesota State Coll–Southeast Tech (MN)
Minnesota West Comm and Tech Coll (MN)
Montgomery County Comm Coll (PA)
Mott Comm Coll (MI)
Nashville State Comm Coll (TN)
Northampton Comm Coll (PA)
Northcentral Tech Coll (WI)
Northern Essex Comm Coll (MA)
North Georgia Tech Coll (GA)
Northland Comm and Tech Coll (MN)
Northwest Tech Coll (MN)
Norwalk Comm Coll (CT)
Oconee Fall Line Tech Coll (GA)
Odessa Coll (TX)
Ogeechee Tech Coll (GA)
Oklahoma City Comm Coll (OK)
Olympic Coll (WA)
Onondaga Comm Coll (NY)
Oxnard Coll (CA)
Ozarks Tech Comm Coll (MO)
Palomar Coll (CA)
Randolph Comm Coll (NC)
Raritan Valley Comm Coll (NJ)
Renton Tech Coll (WA)
Ridgewater Coll (MN)
River Valley Comm Coll (NH)
Rock Valley Coll (IL)
St. Clair County Comm Coll (MI)
St. Philip's Coll (TX)
Savannah Tech Coll (GA)
Seminole State Coll of Florida (FL)
Shawnee Comm Coll (IL)
Sierra Coll (CA)
Southeastern Coll–West Palm Beach (FL)
Southeastern Tech Coll (GA)
Southeast Tech Inst (SD)
Southern Crescent Tech Coll (GA)
Southern Regional Tech Coll (GA)
South Georgia Tech Coll (GA)
Southwestern Michigan Coll (MI)
Sowela Tech Comm Coll (LA)
Stark State Coll (OH)
Tallahassee Comm Coll (FL)
Trocaire Coll (NY)
Truckee Meadows Comm Coll (NV)
Tyler Jr Coll (TX)
Victoria Coll (TX)
Vincennes U (IN)
Waukesha County Tech Coll (WI)
Wenatchee Valley Coll (WA)
Westchester Comm Coll (NY)
West Georgia Tech Coll (GA)
Westmoreland County Comm Coll (PA)
Wiregrass Georgia Tech Coll (GA)
Wisconsin Indianhead Tech Coll (WI)
Wood Tobe–Coburn School (NY)

COMPUTER TECHNOLOGY/ COMPUTER SYSTEMS TECHNOLOGY
Anoka Tech Coll (MN)
Brookhaven Coll (TX)
Butler County Comm Coll (PA)
Cape Fear Comm Coll (NC)
Central Lakes Coll (MN)
Central Texas Coll (TX)
Central Wyoming Coll (WY)
Century Coll (MN)
Coastal Pines Tech Coll (GA)
CollAmerica–Denver (CO)
Corning Comm Coll (NY)
Daytona State Coll (FL)
Erie Comm Coll, South Campus (NY)
Forrest Coll (SC)
Hillsborough Comm Coll (FL)
Island Drafting and Tech Inst (NY)
ITI Tech Coll (LA)
Jefferson Comm Coll (NY)
Kellogg Comm Coll (MI)
Lakeland Comm Coll (OH)

Lake Superior Coll (MN)
Lorain County Comm Coll (OH)
Luzerne County Comm Coll (PA)
Manhattan Area Tech Coll (KS)
Miami Dade Coll (FL)
Minnesota State Coll–Southeast Tech (MN)
Minnesota West Comm and Tech Coll (MN)
Montgomery Coll (MD)
Nashville State Comm Coll (TN)
Ohio Business Coll, Sheffield Village (OH)
Pasadena City Coll (CA)
Pittsburgh Tech Inst, Oakdale (PA)
Reading Area Comm Coll (PA)
Rend Lake Coll (IL)
Ridgewater Coll (MN)
St. Philip's Coll (TX)
Southeast Tech Inst (SD)
Texas State Tech Coll (TX)
Tyler Jr Coll (TX)
U of Arkansas Comm Coll at Morrilton (AR)
U of Cincinnati Blue Ash Coll (OH)

COMPUTER TYPOGRAPHY AND COMPOSITION EQUIPMENT OPERATION
Housatonic Comm Coll (CT)
Lamar Comm Coll (CO)
New Mexico Jr Coll (NM)
Northern Essex Comm Coll (MA)
Paris Jr Coll (TX)

CONSERVATION BIOLOGY
Central Lakes Coll (MN)

CONSTRUCTION ENGINEERING
Bossier Parish Comm Coll (LA)

CONSTRUCTION ENGINEERING TECHNOLOGY
Arizona Western Coll (AZ)
Bossier Parish Comm Coll (LA)
Clark Coll (WA)
Coll of Central Florida (FL)
Comm Coll of Philadelphia (PA)
Comm Coll of the Air Force (AL)
Crowder Coll (MO)
Delta Coll (MI)
Dodge City Comm Coll (KS)
Greenville Tech Coll (SC)
Gulf Coast State Coll (FL)
Harrisburg Area Comm Coll (PA)
Houston Comm Coll (TX)
Illinois Central Coll (IL)
Itawamba Comm Coll (MS)
Jefferson State Comm Coll (AL)
Lake Area Tech Inst (SD)
Los Angeles Trade-Tech Coll (CA)
Macomb Comm Coll (MI)
Miami Dade Coll (FL)
Midlands Tech Coll (SC)
Mid-Plains Comm Coll, North Platte (NE)
Monroe Comm Coll (NY)
Nashville State Comm Coll (TN)
New Castle School of Trades (PA)
New Mexico Jr Coll (NM)
Norwalk Comm Coll (CT)
Odessa Coll (TX)
Oklahoma State U Inst of Technology (OK)
Oklahoma State U, Oklahoma City (OK)
Onondaga Comm Coll (NY)
Ozarks Tech Comm Coll (MO)
Palau Comm Coll (Palau)
Panola Coll (TX)
Pensacola State Coll (FL)
Raritan Valley Comm Coll (NJ)
Richland Comm Coll (IL)
Rock Valley Coll (IL)
Rogue Comm Coll (OR)
Rowan Coll at Burlington County (NJ)
St. Philip's Coll (TX)
San Jacinto Coll District (TX)
San Joaquin Delta Coll (CA)
Seminole State Coll of Florida (FL)
Southeastern Comm Coll (IA)
Southeast Tech Inst (SD)
South Florida State Coll (FL)
South Suburban Coll (IL)
State U of New York Coll of Technology at Alfred (NY)
Sullivan County Comm Coll (NY)
Tallahassee Comm Coll (FL)

Tarrant County Coll District (TX)
Tech Coll of the Lowcountry (SC)
Tompkins Cortland Comm Coll (NY)
U of New Mexico–Gallup (NM)
Victor Valley Coll (CA)
Washington County Comm Coll (ME)
Williamson Coll of the Trades (PA)

CONSTRUCTION/HEAVY EQUIPMENT/EARTHMOVING EQUIPMENT OPERATION
Ivy Tech Comm Coll–Southwest (IN)
Ivy Tech Comm Coll–Wabash Valley (IN)
Lake Area Tech Inst (SD)

CONSTRUCTION MANAGEMENT
Arizona Western Coll (AZ)
Caldwell Comm Coll and Tech Inst (NC)
Casper Coll (WY)
Central New Mexico Comm Coll (NM)
Dunwoody Coll of Technology (MN)
Kankakee Comm Coll (IL)
Kaskaskia Coll (IL)
McHenry County Coll (IL)
Minnesota State Comm and Tech Coll–Moorhead (MN)
Northampton Comm Coll (PA)
North Hennepin Comm Coll (MN)
Oklahoma State U, Oklahoma City (OK)
Renton Tech Coll (WA)
San Joaquin Valley Coll, Ontario (CA)
San Joaquin Valley Coll–Online (CA)
State U of New York Coll of Technology at Alfred (NY)
Three Rivers Comm Coll (CT)

CONSTRUCTION TRADES
American Samoa Comm Coll (AS)
Casper Coll (WY)
Coll of The Albemarle (NC)
Crowder Coll (MO)
East Central Coll (MO)
Harrisburg Area Comm Coll (PA)
Illinois Eastern Comm Colls, Frontier Community College (IL)
Illinois Eastern Comm Colls, Lincoln Trail College (IL)
Ivy Tech Comm Coll–East Central (IN)
Ivy Tech Comm Coll–Northeast (IN)
Ivy Tech Comm Coll–Northwest (IN)
Ivy Tech Comm Coll–Richmond (IN)
Lamar Comm Coll (CO)
Lehigh Carbon Comm Coll (PA)
Northeast Iowa Comm Coll (IA)
Ogeechee Tech Coll (GA)
Oklahoma State U, Oklahoma City (OK)
Orange Coast Coll (CA)
Owensboro Comm and Tech Coll (KY)
Pasadena City Coll (CA)
Rogue Comm Coll (OR)
Sierra Coll (CA)
Texas State Tech Coll (TX)
Vincennes U (IN)

CONSTRUCTION TRADES RELATED
Central Maine Comm Coll (ME)
Citrus Coll (CA)
Dutchess Comm Coll (NY)
East Central Coll (MO)
Fullerton Coll (CA)
Ivy Tech Comm Coll–East Central (IN)
Ivy Tech Comm Coll–Kokomo (IN)
Ivy Tech Comm Coll–Northeast (IN)
Ivy Tech Comm Coll–Richmond (IN)
Mitchell Tech Inst (SD)
Palomar Coll (CA)
State U of New York Coll of Technology at Alfred (NY)
York County Comm Coll (ME)

CONSUMER MERCHANDISING/ RETAILING MANAGEMENT
Clinton Comm Coll (NY)
J. Sargeant Reynolds Comm Coll (VA)
Lorain County Comm Coll (OH)
Monroe Comm Coll (NY)
Navarro Coll (TX)
Niagara County Comm Coll (NY)

Stark State Coll (OH)
Sullivan County Comm Coll (NY)
Tarrant County Coll District (TX)
Westchester Comm Coll (NY)

CONSUMER SERVICES AND ADVOCACY
Pensacola State Coll (FL)

COOKING AND RELATED CULINARY ARTS
Bradford School (OH)
Butler County Comm Coll (PA)
Central Oregon Comm Coll (OR)
Cerritos Coll (CA)
Columbia Coll (CA)
Columbus Culinary Inst at Bradford School (OH)
Culinary Inst of St. Louis at Hickey Coll (MO)
Feather River Coll (CA)
J. Sargeant Reynolds Comm Coll (VA)
Kennebec Valley Comm Coll (ME)
Leeward Comm Coll (HI)
Miami Dade Coll (FL)
Orange Coast Coll (CA)
Pensacola State Coll (FL)
Pueblo Comm Coll (CO)
Truckee Meadows Comm Coll (NV)

CORRECTIONS
Alvin Comm Coll (TX)
Amarillo Coll (TX)
Austin Comm Coll District (TX)
Barton County Comm Coll (KS)
Butler County Comm Coll (PA)
Cayuga County Comm Coll (NY)
Danville Area Comm Coll (IL)
Delta Coll (MI)
Eastern Gateway Comm Coll (OH)
Garrett Coll (MD)
Grand Rapids Comm Coll (MI)
Herkimer County Comm Coll (NY)
Illinois Central Coll (IL)
Illinois Eastern Comm Colls, Frontier Community College (IL)
Illinois Eastern Comm Colls, Lincoln Trail College (IL)
Kellogg Comm Coll (MI)
Lake Land Coll (IL)
Lakeland Comm Coll (OH)
Laramie County Comm Coll (WY)
Lorain County Comm Coll (OH)
Mercer County Comm Coll (NJ)
Miami Dade Coll (FL)
Monroe Comm Coll (NY)
Mott Comm Coll (MI)
Mt. San Antonio Coll (CA)
Mount Wachusett Comm Coll (MA)
Navarro Coll (TX)
Pennsylvania Highlands Comm Coll (PA)
Raritan Valley Comm Coll (NJ)
St. Clair County Comm Coll (MI)
San Joaquin Delta Coll (CA)
San Joaquin Valley Coll, Bakersfield (CA)
San Joaquin Valley Coll, Fresno (CA)
San Joaquin Valley Coll, Lancaster (CA)
San Joaquin Valley Coll, Ontario (CA)
San Joaquin Valley Coll, Visalia (CA)
Sierra Coll (CA)
Southwestern Oklahoma State U at Sayre (OK)
Tallahassee Comm Coll (FL)
Tunxis Comm Coll (CT)
U of New Mexico–Gallup (NM)
Wayne County Comm Coll District (MI)
Weatherford Coll (TX)
Westchester Comm Coll (NY)
Western Texas Coll (TX)
Westmoreland County Comm Coll (PA)
Wisconsin Indianhead Tech Coll (WI)
Wytheville Comm Coll (VA)

CORRECTIONS ADMINISTRATION
Eastern Wyoming Coll (WY)

CORRECTIONS AND CRIMINAL JUSTICE RELATED
Albany Tech Coll (GA)
Chesapeake Coll (MD)
Corning Comm Coll (NY)
Feather River Coll (CA)

Genesee Comm Coll (NY)
Hinds Comm Coll (MS)
Miami Dade Coll (FL)
Rockingham Comm Coll (NC)

COSMETOLOGY
Butler County Comm Coll (PA)
Caldwell Comm Coll and Tech Inst (NC)
Cape Fear Comm Coll (NC)
Central New Mexico Comm Coll (NM)
Century Coll (MN)
Cerritos Coll (CA)
Citrus Coll (CA)
Clary Sage Coll (OK)
Colorado Northwestern Comm Coll (CO)
Copiah-Lincoln Comm Coll (MS)
Dodge City Comm Coll (KS)
Eastern Arizona Coll (AZ)
Eastern Wyoming Coll (WY)
Fayetteville Tech Comm Coll (NC)
Fullerton Coll (CA)
Houston Comm Coll (TX)
Kaskaskia Coll (IL)
Kirtland Comm Coll (MI)
Lamar Comm Coll (CO)
Lenoir Comm Coll (NC)
Lone Star Coll–Kingwood (TX)
Lone Star Coll–North Harris (TX)
Lorain County Comm Coll (OH)
Los Angeles Trade-Tech Coll (CA)
Martin Comm Coll (NC)
Minnesota State Coll–Southeast Tech (MN)
New Mexico Jr Coll (NM)
Northeastern Jr Coll (CO)
Northeast Iowa Comm Coll (IA)
Odessa Coll (TX)
Olympic Coll (WA)
Paris Jr Coll (TX)
Pasadena City Coll (CA)
Pueblo Comm Coll (CO)
Randolph Comm Coll (NC)
Rend Lake Coll (IL)
Ridgewater Coll (MN)
Rowan-Cabarrus Comm Coll (NC)
Salt Lake Comm Coll (UT)
San Jacinto Coll District (TX)
San Juan Coll (NM)
Shawnee Comm Coll (IL)
Southeastern Comm Coll (IA)
Southwest Texas Jr Coll (TX)
Texarkana Coll (TX)
U of New Mexico–Gallup (NM)
Vincennes U (IN)
Weatherford Coll (TX)

COSMETOLOGY AND PERSONAL GROOMING ARTS RELATED
LDS Business Coll (UT)
Lorain County Comm Coll (OH)

COSMETOLOGY, BARBER/ STYLING, AND NAIL INSTRUCTION
IBMC Coll, Fort Collins (CO)
Pasadena City Coll (CA)
San Jacinto Coll District (TX)

COSTUME DESIGN
Fashion Inst of Design & Merchandising, LA Campus (CA)

COURT REPORTING
Alvin Comm Coll (TX)
Anoka Tech Coll (MN)
Cerritos Coll (CA)
Fox Valley Tech Coll (WI)
Gadsden State Comm Coll (AL)
Hinds Comm Coll (MS)
Houston Comm Coll (TX)
Long Island Business Inst (NY)
Luzerne County Comm Coll (PA)
Miami Dade Coll (FL)
Midlands Tech Coll (SC)
South Suburban Coll (IL)
Southwest Tennessee Comm Coll (TN)
Stark State Coll (OH)
State U of New York Coll of Technology at Alfred (NY)
Sumner Coll (OR)

CRAFTS, FOLK ART AND ARTISANRY
Coll of The Albemarle (NC)
Western Piedmont Comm Coll (NC)

CREATIVE WRITING
Anoka-Ramsey Comm Coll (MN)
Austin Comm Coll District (TX)
North Hennepin Comm Coll (MN)
Reading Area Comm Coll (PA)
Tompkins Cortland Comm Coll (NY)

CRIMINALISTICS AND CRIMINAL SCIENCE
Alvin Comm Coll (TX)
Central Lakes Coll (MN)
Tyler Jr Coll (TX)

CRIMINAL JUSTICE/LAW ENFORCEMENT ADMINISTRATION
Aiken Tech Coll (SC)
Allen Comm Coll (KS)
Amarillo Coll (TX)
Anne Arundel Comm Coll (MD)
Arapahoe Comm Coll (CO)
Arizona Western Coll (AZ)
Athens Tech Coll (GA)
Bainbridge State Coll (GA)
Beal Coll (ME)
Blinn Coll (TX)
Borough of Manhattan Comm Coll of the City U of New York (NY)
Brookhaven Coll (TX)
Bunker Hill Comm Coll (MA)
Butler County Comm Coll (PA)
Casper Coll (WY)
Central Maine Comm Coll (ME)
Central New Mexico Comm Coll (NM)
Central Ohio Tech Coll (OH)
Central Virginia Comm Coll (VA)
Central Wyoming Coll (WY)
Citrus Coll (CA)
Clinton Comm Coll (NY)
Coll of Central Florida (FL)
Coll of The Albemarle (NC)
Columbia-Greene Comm Coll (NY)
Comm Coll of Aurora (CO)
Comm Coll of Philadelphia (PA)
Comm Coll of the Air Force (AL)
Craven Comm Coll (NC)
Dabney S. Lancaster Comm Coll (VA)
Daytona State Coll (FL)
Dodge City Comm Coll (KS)
Eastern Arizona Coll (AZ)
Eastern Wyoming Coll (WY)
Elizabethtown Comm and Tech Coll, Elizabethtown (KY)
Erie Comm Coll, North Campus (NY)
Finger Lakes Comm Coll (NY)
Florida SouthWestern State Coll (FL)
Frederick Comm Coll (MD)
Gateway Comm and Tech Coll (KY)
Genesee Comm Coll (NY)
Georgia Military Coll (GA)
Grand Rapids Comm Coll (MI)
Gulf Coast State Coll (FL)
Harrisburg Area Comm Coll (PA)
Herkimer County Comm Coll (NY)
Hillsborough Comm Coll (FL)
Hopkinsville Comm Coll (KY)
Housatonic Comm Coll (CT)
Howard Comm Coll (MD)
James H. Faulkner State Comm Coll (AL)
Jamestown Comm Coll (NY)
Jefferson Coll (MO)
Jefferson Comm Coll (NY)
John Tyler Comm Coll (VA)
J. Sargeant Reynolds Comm Coll (VA)
Kankakee Comm Coll (IL)
Kaskaskia Coll (IL)
Kellogg Comm Coll (MI)
Kilgore Coll (TX)
Kirtland Comm Coll (MI)
Laramie County Comm Coll (WY)
Lehigh Carbon Comm Coll (PA)
Lewis and Clark Comm Coll (IL)
Lone Star Coll–CyFair (TX)
Lone Star Coll–Kingwood (TX)
Lone Star Coll–Montgomery (TX)
Lone Star Coll–North Harris (TX)
Lone Star Coll–Tomball (TX)
Lone Star Coll–U Park (TX)
Luzerne County Comm Coll (PA)
Macomb Comm Coll (MI)
Manchester Comm Coll (CT)
Manor Coll (PA)
Massachusetts Bay Comm Coll (MA)
Miami Dade Coll (FL)
Minnesota State Comm and Tech Coll–Moorhead (MN)
Mitchell Comm Coll (NC)
Mohawk Valley Comm Coll (NY)
Monroe Comm Coll (NY)

Moraine Valley Comm Coll (IL)
Mount Wachusett Comm Coll (MA)
Muskegon Comm Coll (MI)
Navarro Coll (TX)
New River Comm Coll (VA)
Niagara County Comm Coll (NY)
North Central Texas Coll (TX)
Northern Essex Comm Coll (MA)
North Shore Comm Coll (MA)
NorthWest Arkansas Comm Coll (AR)
Northwest Coll (WY)
Norwalk Comm Coll (CT)
Odessa Coll (TX)
Onondaga Comm Coll (NY)
Owensboro Comm and Tech Coll (KY)
Pasadena City Coll (CA)
Penn Foster Coll (AZ)
Pennsylvania Highlands Comm Coll (PA)
Pensacola State Coll (FL)
Pueblo Comm Coll (CO)
Queensborough Comm Coll of the City U of New York (NY)
Quincy Coll (MA)
Rappahannock Comm Coll (VA)
Raritan Valley Comm Coll (NJ)
Rio Hondo Coll (CA)
River Valley Comm Coll (NH)
Rock Valley Coll (IL)
Rowan-Cabarrus Comm Coll (NC)
St. Clair County Comm Coll (MI)
St. Philip's Coll (TX)
Salt Lake Comm Coll (UT)
San Joaquin Valley Coll, Hanford (CA)
San Joaquin Valley Coll, Hesperia (CA)
Schenectady County Comm Coll (NY)
Scottsdale Comm Coll (AZ)
Seminole State Coll (OK)
Seminole State Coll of Florida (FL)
Somerset Comm Coll (KY)
Southeastern Comm Coll (IA)
Southern U at Shreveport (LA)
South Florida State Coll (FL)
Southwest Texas Jr Coll (TX)
Southwest Virginia Comm Coll (VA)
Spartanburg Methodist Coll (SC)
Spoon River Coll (IL)
Tallahassee Comm Coll (FL)
Tarrant County Coll District (TX)
Texarkana Coll (TX)
Tompkins Cortland Comm Coll (NY)
Tunxis Comm Coll (CT)
Tyler Jr Coll (TX)
U of Arkansas Comm Coll at Morrilton (AR)
U of New Mexico–Gallup (NM)
U of Pittsburgh at Titusville (PA)
Virginia Western Comm Coll (VA)
Weatherford Coll (TX)
Western Nevada Coll (NV)
Western Piedmont Comm Coll (NC)
Western Texas Coll (TX)
Western Wyoming Comm Coll (WY)
Wytheville Comm Coll (VA)

CRIMINAL JUSTICE/POLICE SCIENCE
Alexandria Tech and Comm Coll (MN)
Alvin Comm Coll (TX)
Amarillo Coll (TX)
Anne Arundel Comm Coll (MD)
Antelope Valley Coll (CA)
Asnuntuck Comm Coll (CT)
Austin Comm Coll District (TX)
Barton County Comm Coll (KS)
Berkeley Coll–White Plains Campus (NY)
Blackhawk Tech Coll (WI)
Borough of Manhattan Comm Coll of the City U of New York (NY)
Bunker Hill Comm Coll (MA)
Butler County Comm Coll (PA)
Camden County Coll (NJ)
Cape Fear Comm Coll (NC)
Carrington Coll–Pleasant Hill (CA)
Carroll Comm Coll (MD)
Cayuga County Comm Coll (NY)
Cecil Coll (MD)
Central Lakes Coll (MN)
Central Ohio Tech Coll (OH)
Central Texas Coll (TX)
Century Coll (MN)
Cerritos Coll (CA)
Chippewa Valley Tech Coll (WI)
Citrus Coll (CA)

Cleveland State Comm Coll (TN)
Clinton Comm Coll (NY)
Cloud County Comm Coll (KS)
Coastal Pines Tech Coll (GA)
Cochise County Comm Coll District (AZ)
Coll of the Canyons (CA)
Collin County Comm Coll District (TX)
Comm Coll of Baltimore County (MD)
Comm Coll of Rhode Island (RI)
Copiah-Lincoln Comm Coll (MS)
Corning Comm Coll (NY)
County Coll of Morris (NJ)
Danville Area Comm Coll (IL)
Dawson Comm Coll (MT)
Daytona State Coll (FL)
Delta Coll (MI)
Dutchess Comm Coll (NY)
Dyersburg State Comm Coll (TN)
Eastern Arizona Coll (AZ)
Eastern Gateway Comm Coll (OH)
Eastern Wyoming Coll (WY)
Edison Comm Coll (OH)
Elgin Comm Coll (IL)
Erie Comm Coll (NY)
Erie Comm Coll, North Campus (NY)
Erie Comm Coll, South Campus (NY)
Finger Lakes Comm Coll (NY)
Fox Valley Tech Coll (WI)
Fullerton Coll (CA)
Gadsden State Comm Coll (AL)
Gateway Tech Coll (WI)
Genesee Comm Coll (NY)
George C. Wallace Comm Coll (AL)
Georgia Highlands Coll (GA)
Grand Rapids Comm Coll (MI)
Hagerstown Comm Coll (MD)
Harford Comm Coll (MD)
Harrisburg Area Comm Coll (PA)
Hawkeye Comm Coll (IA)
Houston Comm Coll (TX)
Hudson County Comm Coll (NJ)
Hutchinson Comm Coll (KS)
Illinois Central Coll (IL)
Iowa Central Comm Coll (IA)
Itawamba Comm Coll (MS)
Jamestown Comm Coll (NY)
Jefferson Coll (MO)
Jefferson State Comm Coll (AL)
Johnston Comm Coll (NC)
Kankakee Comm Coll (IL)
Kellogg Comm Coll (MI)
Kirtland Comm Coll (MI)
Lake Area Tech Inst (SD)
Lake Land Coll (IL)
Lakeland Comm Coll (OH)
Lake Region State Coll (ND)
Lorain County Comm Coll (OH)
Los Angeles Valley Coll (CA)
Macomb Comm Coll (MI)
McHenry County Coll (IL)
Mercer County Comm Coll (NJ)
Miami Dade Coll (FL)
Middlesex County Coll (NJ)
Minnesota West Comm and Tech Coll (MN)
Mohave Comm Coll (AZ)
Monroe Comm Coll (NY)
Montgomery Coll (MD)
Montgomery County Comm Coll (PA)
Moraine Valley Comm Coll (IL)
Mott Comm Coll (MI)
Mt. San Antonio Coll (CA)
Nashville State Comm Coll (TN)
Naugatuck Valley Comm Coll (CT)
Navarro Coll (TX)
New Mexico Jr Coll (NM)
New River Comm Coll (VA)
Northcentral Tech Coll (WI)
North Central Texas Coll (TX)
Northeastern Jr Coll (CO)
North Hennepin Comm Coll (MN)
Northland Comm and Tech Coll (MN)
Northwest-Shoals Comm Coll (AL)
Oakton Comm Coll (IL)
Ocean County Coll (NJ)
Odessa Coll (TX)
Oklahoma State U, Oklahoma City (OK)
Onondaga Comm Coll (NY)
Palau Comm Coll (Palau)
Quinsigamond Comm Coll (MA)
Rappahannock Comm Coll (VA)
Raritan Valley Comm Coll (NJ)
Reading Area Comm Coll (PA)
Rend Lake Coll (IL)
Richland Comm Coll (IL)
Ridgewater Coll (MN)
Rockingham Comm Coll (NC)
Rogue Comm Coll (OR)

Rowan Coll at Burlington County (NJ)
St. Charles Comm Coll (MO)
San Jacinto Coll District (TX)
San Joaquin Delta Coll (CA)
San Juan Coll (NM)
Schoolcraft Coll (MI)
Seminole State Coll (OK)
Shawnee Comm Coll (IL)
Sierra Coll (CA)
Southeast Tech Inst (SD)
Southwestern Oregon Comm Coll (OR)
Spoon River Coll (IL)
Springfield Tech Comm Coll (MA)
Sullivan County Comm Coll (NY)
Tallahassee Comm Coll (FL)
Three Rivers Comm Coll (CT)
Tompkins Cortland Comm Coll (NY)
Treasure Valley Comm Coll (OR)
Truckee Meadows Comm Coll (NV)
Tulsa Comm Coll (OK)
Tyler Jr Coll (TX)
Victoria Coll (TX)
Victor Valley Coll (CA)
Vincennes U (IN)
Volunteer State Comm Coll (TN)
Walters State Comm Coll (TN)
Waukesha County Tech Coll (WI)
Wayne Comm Coll (NC)
Wayne County Comm Coll District (MI)
Wenatchee Valley Coll (WA)
Western Iowa Tech Comm Coll (IA)
Western Piedmont Comm Coll (NC)
Western Texas Coll (TX)
Westmoreland County Comm Coll (PA)
Wisconsin Indianhead Tech Coll (WI)
Wor-Wic Comm Coll (MD)
Wytheville Comm Coll (VA)

CRIMINAL JUSTICE/SAFETY
Aiken Tech Coll (SC)
Alamance Comm Coll (NC)
Alvin Comm Coll (TX)
American Samoa Comm Coll (AS)
Ancilla Coll (IN)
Augusta Tech Coll (GA)
Berkshire Comm Coll (MA)
Bismarck State Coll (ND)
Blue Ridge Comm and Tech Coll (WV)
Bossier Parish Comm Coll (LA)
Bowling Green State U–Firelands Coll (OH)
Bucks County Comm Coll (PA)
Carrington Coll–Citrus Heights (CA)
Carrington Coll–San Jose (CA)
Catawba Valley Comm Coll (NC)
Central Georgia Tech Coll (GA)
Central Lakes Coll (MN)
Central Maine Comm Coll (ME)
Century Coll (MN)
Chandler-Gilbert Comm Coll (AZ)
Chattahoochee Tech Coll (GA)
Cleveland Comm Coll (NC)
Craven Comm Coll (NC)
Dean Coll (MA)
Denmark Tech Coll (SC)
Dyersburg State Comm Coll (TN)
Eastern Wyoming Coll (WY)
Fayetteville Tech Comm Coll (NC)
Fiorello H. LaGuardia Comm Coll of the City U of New York (NY)
Galveston Coll (TX)
Genesee Comm Coll (NY)
Georgia Northwestern Tech Coll (GA)
Georgia Piedmont Tech Coll (GA)
Gordon State Coll (GA)
Great Basin Coll (NV)
Greenville Tech Coll (SC)
Halifax Comm Coll (NC)
Holyoke Comm Coll (MA)
Ivy Tech Comm Coll–Bloomington (IN)
Ivy Tech Comm Coll–Central Indiana (IN)
Ivy Tech Comm Coll–Columbus (IN)
Ivy Tech Comm Coll–East Central (IN)
Ivy Tech Comm Coll–Kokomo (IN)
Ivy Tech Comm Coll–Lafayette (IN)
Ivy Tech Comm Coll–North Central (IN)
Ivy Tech Comm Coll–Northeast (IN)
Ivy Tech Comm Coll–Northwest (IN)
Ivy Tech Comm Coll–Richmond (IN)
Ivy Tech Comm Coll–Southeast (IN)
Ivy Tech Comm Coll–Southwest (IN)
Ivy Tech Comm Coll–Wabash Valley (IN)

James Sprunt Comm Coll (NC)
Kellogg Comm Coll (MI)
Kent State U at Ashtabula (OH)
Kent State U at East Liverpool (OH)
Kent State U at Salem (OH)
Kent State U at Trumbull (OH)
Kent State U at Tuscarawas (OH)
Lackawanna Coll (PA)
Lamar Comm Coll (CO)
Lanier Tech Coll (GA)
Lehigh Carbon Comm Coll (PA)
Lenoir Comm Coll (NC)
Midlands Tech Coll (SC)
Minnesota State Coll–Southeast Tech (MN)
Montgomery Comm Coll (NC)
Northampton Comm Coll (PA)
North Georgia Tech Coll (GA)
North Hennepin Comm Coll (MN)
NorthWest Arkansas Comm Coll (AR)
Northwest Vista Coll (TX)
Oregon Coast Comm Coll (OR)
Paris Jr Coll (TX)
Piedmont Comm Coll (NC)
Potomac State Coll of West Virginia U (WV)
Randolph Comm Coll (NC)
Richmond Comm Coll (NC)
Savannah Tech Coll (GA)
Sheridan Coll (WY)
Southeast Comm Coll, Lincoln Campus (NE)
Southeastern Tech Coll (GA)
Southern Crescent Tech Coll (GA)
Southern Regional Tech Coll (GA)
South Florida State Coll (FL)
South Georgia Tech Coll (GA)
South Suburban Coll (IL)
Southwestern Michigan Coll (MI)
Southwestern Oklahoma State U at Sayre (OK)
Southwestern Oregon Comm Coll (OR)
Southwest Tennessee Comm Coll (TN)
Sowela Tech Comm Coll (LA)
Texarkana Coll (TX)
Tri-County Tech Coll (SC)
Truckee Meadows Comm Coll (NV)
Tyler Jr Coll (TX)
U of Cincinnati Blue Ash Coll (OH)
Walters State Comm Coll (TN)
Wayne Comm Coll (NC)
West Georgia Tech Coll (GA)
Westmoreland County Comm Coll (PA)
White Mountains Comm Coll (NH)
Wiregrass Georgia Tech Coll (GA)
York County Comm Coll (ME)

CRIMINOLOGY
Central New Mexico Comm Coll (NM)
Coll of Central Florida (FL)
Genesee Comm Coll (NY)
Northland Comm and Tech Coll (MN)
Panola Coll (TX)
Paris Jr Coll (TX)
Potomac State Coll of West Virginia U (WV)
State U of New York Coll of Technology at Alfred (NY)
Western Wyoming Comm Coll (WY)

CRISIS/EMERGENCY/DISASTER MANAGEMENT
Cincinnati State Tech and Comm Coll (OH)
City Colls of Chicago, Olive-Harvey College (IL)
Comm Coll of Rhode Island (RI)
Erie Comm Coll (NY)
Fayetteville Tech Comm Coll (NC)
Montgomery Coll (MD)
Olympic Coll (WA)
Sullivan County Comm Coll (NY)
Wayne Comm Coll (NC)
Western Iowa Tech Comm Coll (IA)

CRITICAL INCIDENT RESPONSE/SPECIAL POLICE OPERATIONS
Raritan Valley Comm Coll (NJ)

CROP PRODUCTION
Arizona Western Coll (AZ)
Barton County Comm Coll (KS)
Illinois Central Coll (IL)
Northeast Iowa Comm Coll (IA)
Northwest Coll (WY)
Ridgewater Coll (MN)
San Joaquin Delta Coll (CA)

CULINARY ARTS

Alamance Comm Coll (NC)
Albany Tech Coll (GA)
Alvin Comm Coll (TX)
American River Coll (CA)
Arizona Western Coll (AZ)
Atlanta Tech Coll (GA)
Augusta Tech Coll (GA)
Austin Comm Coll District (TX)
Bellingham Tech Coll (WA)
Blackhawk Tech Coll (WI)
Blue Ridge Comm and Tech Coll (WV)
Bossier Parish Comm Coll (LA)
Bucks County Comm Coll (PA)
Bunker Hill Comm Coll (MA)
Caldwell Comm Coll and Tech Inst (NC)
Cape Fear Comm Coll (NC)
Central New Mexico Comm Coll (NM)
Central Ohio Tech Coll (OH)
Central Virginia Comm Coll (VA)
Central Wyoming Coll (WY)
Chattahoochee Tech Coll (GA)
Cincinnati State Tech and Comm Coll (OH)
Clark Coll (WA)
Cochise County Comm Coll District (AZ)
Coll of The Albemarle (NC)
Collin County Comm Coll District (TX)
Comm Coll of Philadelphia (PA)
County Coll of Morris (NJ)
Daytona State Coll (FL)
East Central Coll (MO)
Elgin Comm Coll (IL)
Erie Comm Coll (NY)
Erie Comm Coll, North Campus (NY)
Fayetteville Tech Comm Coll (NC)
Finger Lakes Comm Coll (NY)
Fox Valley Tech Coll (WI)
Galveston Coll (TX)
Gateway Tech Coll (WI)
Grand Rapids Comm Coll (MI)
Greenville Tech Coll (SC)
Harrisburg Area Comm Coll (PA)
H. Councill Trenholm State Comm Coll (AL)
Houston Comm Coll (TX)
Hudson County Comm Coll (NJ)
Illinois Central Coll (IL)
Illinois Eastern Comm Colls, Olney Central College (IL)
Jefferson Coll (MO)
J. F. Drake State Comm and Tech Coll (AL)
Kaskaskia Coll (IL)
Lenoir Comm Coll (NC)
Los Angeles Trade-Tech Coll (CA)
Luzerne County Comm Coll (PA)
Macomb Comm Coll (MI)
Mercer County Comm Coll (NJ)
Miami Dade Coll (FL)
Mitchell Tech Inst (SD)
Mohave Comm Coll (AZ)
Montgomery County Comm Coll (PA)
Mott Comm Coll (MI)
Nashville State Comm Coll (TN)
New England Culinary Inst (VT)
Niagara County Comm Coll (NY)
Northampton Comm Coll (PA)
Northcentral Tech Coll (WI)
North Georgia Tech Coll (GA)
North Shore Comm Coll (MA)
NorthWest Arkansas Comm Coll (AR)
Nunez Comm Coll (LA)
Odessa Coll (TX)
Ogeechee Tech Coll (GA)
Olympic Coll (WA)
Orange Coast Coll (CA)
Oxnard Coll (CA)
Ozarks Tech Comm Coll (MO)
Rend Lake Coll (IL)
Renton Tech Coll (WA)
The Restaurant School at Walnut Hill Coll (PA)
Rowan Coll at Burlington County (NJ)
St. Philip's Coll (TX)
Salt Lake Comm Coll (UT)
San Jacinto Coll District (TX)
San Joaquin Delta Coll (CA)
Savannah Tech Coll (GA)
Schoolcraft Coll (MI)
Scottsdale Comm Coll (AZ)
Sheridan Coll (WY)
Southern Maine Comm Coll (ME)
South Georgia Tech Coll (GA)
Sowela Tech Comm Coll (LA)
State U of New York Coll of Technology at Alfred (NY)
Sullivan County Comm Coll (NY)
Texarkana Coll (TX)
Texas State Tech Coll (TX)
Tompkins Cortland Comm Coll (NY)
Vincennes U (IN)
Westchester Comm Coll (NY)
Westmoreland County Comm Coll (PA)
White Mountains Comm Coll (NH)
York County Comm Coll (ME)

CULINARY ARTS RELATED

Ancilla Coll (IN)
Oklahoma State U Inst of Technology (OK)

CUSTOMER SERVICE MANAGEMENT

Central Oregon Comm Coll (OR)
Corning Comm Coll (NY)
Northland Comm and Tech Coll (MN)

CUSTOMER SERVICE SUPPORT/ CALL CENTER/TELESERVICE OPERATION

Central Wyoming Coll (WY)
Miami Dade Coll (FL)

CYBER/COMPUTER FORENSICS AND COUNTERTERRORISM

Catawba Valley Comm Coll (NC)
Century Coll (MN)
Columbia-Greene Comm Coll (NY)
Jefferson Coll (MO)
Pensacola State Coll (FL)

CYBER/ELECTRONIC OPERATIONS AND WARFARE

Oklahoma City Comm Coll (OK)

CYTOTECHNOLOGY

Barton County Comm Coll (KS)

DAIRY HUSBANDRY AND PRODUCTION

Northeast Iowa Comm Coll (IA)
Ridgewater Coll (MN)

DAIRY SCIENCE

Mt. San Antonio Coll (CA)

DANCE

Austin Comm Coll District (TX)
Barton County Comm Coll (KS)
Casper Coll (WY)
Cerritos Coll (CA)
Citrus Coll (CA)
Dean Coll (MA)
Fullerton Coll (CA)
Kilgore Coll (TX)
Lone Star Coll–CyFair (TX)
Mercer County Comm Coll (NJ)
Miami Dade Coll (FL)
Northern Essex Comm Coll (MA)
Orange Coast Coll (CA)
Palomar Coll (CA)
Pasadena City Coll (CA)
Raritan Valley Comm Coll (NJ)
San Jacinto Coll District (TX)
San Joaquin Delta Coll (CA)
Tyler Jr Coll (TX)
Westchester Comm Coll (NY)
Western Wyoming Comm Coll (WY)

DANCE RELATED

Citrus Coll (CA)
Orange Coast Coll (CA)

DATA ENTRY/ MICROCOMPUTER APPLICATIONS

American River Coll (CA)
Antelope Valley Coll (CA)
Arizona Western Coll (AZ)
Bellingham Tech Coll (WA)
Bunker Hill Comm Coll (MA)
Cerritos Coll (CA)
Chandler-Gilbert Comm Coll (AZ)
Clark Coll (WA)
Coll of The Albemarle (NC)
Elgin Comm Coll (IL)
Fiorello H. LaGuardia Comm Coll of the City U of New York (NY)
Galveston Coll (TX)
Illinois Central Coll (IL)
Kellogg Comm Coll (MI)
Lorain County Comm Coll (OH)

Luzerne County Comm Coll (PA)
Montgomery Coll (MD)
North Shore Comm Coll (MA)
Ohio Business Coll, Sheffield Village (OH)
Richland Comm Coll (IL)
St. Philip's Coll (TX)
Seminole State Coll of Florida (FL)
Sierra Coll (CA)
Stark State Coll (OH)
Sullivan County Comm Coll (NY)
Tyler Jr Coll (TX)
Western Wyoming Comm Coll (WY)
Westmoreland County Comm Coll (PA)

DATA ENTRY/ MICROCOMPUTER APPLICATIONS RELATED

Blue Ridge Comm and Tech Coll (WV)
ETI Tech Coll of Niles (OH)
Kellogg Comm Coll (MI)
Lorain County Comm Coll (OH)
Pasadena City Coll (CA)
Potomac State Coll of West Virginia U (WV)
Richland Comm Coll (IL)
Seminole State Coll of Florida (FL)
Stark State Coll (OH)

DATA MODELING/ WAREHOUSING AND DATABASE ADMINISTRATION

American River Coll (CA)
Chandler-Gilbert Comm Coll (AZ)
Ivy Tech Comm Coll–Bloomington (IN)
Ivy Tech Comm Coll–Central Indiana (IN)
Ivy Tech Comm Coll–Columbus (IN)
Ivy Tech Comm Coll–East Central (IN)
Ivy Tech Comm Coll–Kokomo (IN)
Ivy Tech Comm Coll–Lafayette (IN)
Ivy Tech Comm Coll–Northeast (IN)
Ivy Tech Comm Coll–Richmond (IN)
Ivy Tech Comm Coll–Southeast (IN)
Ivy Tech Comm Coll–Southern Indiana (IN)
Ivy Tech Comm Coll–Southwest (IN)
Ivy Tech Comm Coll–Wabash Valley (IN)
LDS Business Coll (UT)
Quinsigamond Comm Coll (MA)
Seminole State Coll of Florida (FL)
Wayne County Comm Coll District (MI)

DATA PROCESSING AND DATA PROCESSING TECHNOLOGY

Aiken Tech Coll (SC)
Allen Comm Coll (KS)
Ancilla Coll (IN)
Bainbridge State Coll (GA)
Citrus Coll (CA)
Copiah-Lincoln Comm Coll (MS)
Dabney S. Lancaster Comm Coll (VA)
Denmark Tech Coll (SC)
Dodge City Comm Coll (KS)
Eastern Gateway Comm Coll (OH)
Elizabethtown Comm and Tech Coll, Elizabethtown (KY)
Finger Lakes Comm Coll (NY)
Great Basin Coll (NV)
Greenville Tech Coll (SC)
Housatonic Comm Coll (CT)
Iowa Central Comm Coll (IA)
Itawamba Comm Coll (MS)
Lamar Comm Coll (CO)
Luzerne County Comm Coll (PA)
Midlands Tech Coll (SC)
Monroe Comm Coll (NY)
Mt. San Antonio Coll (CA)
Muskegon Comm Coll (MI)
Navarro Coll (TX)
New Mexico Jr Coll (NM)
North Central Texas Coll (TX)
Northern Essex Comm Coll (MA)
NorthWest Arkansas Comm Coll (AR)
Odessa Coll (TX)
Otero Jr Coll (CO)
Queensborough Comm Coll of the City U of New York (NY)
St. Clair County Comm Coll (MI)
San Juan Coll (NM)
Schenectady County Comm Coll (NY)

Seminole State Coll of Florida (FL)
Southwest Texas Jr Coll (TX)
Spartanburg Comm Coll (SC)
Tech Coll of the Lowcountry (SC)
Tri-County Tech Coll (SC)
Trumbull Business Coll (OH)
Tunxis Comm Coll (CT)
Virginia Western Comm Coll (VA)
Walters State Comm Coll (TN)
Westchester Comm Coll (NY)
Western Wyoming Comm Coll (WY)
Westmoreland County Comm Coll (PA)

DEAF STUDIES

Quinsigamond Comm Coll (MA)
Western Nevada Coll (NV)

DENTAL ASSISTING

Athens Tech Coll (GA)
Bradford School (PA)
Camden County Coll (NJ)
Carrington Coll–Boise (ID)
Carrington Coll–Citrus Heights (CA)
Carrington Coll–Pleasant Hill (CA)
Carrington Coll–Pomona (CA)
Carrington Coll–Sacramento (CA)
Carrington Coll–San Jose (CA)
Carrington Coll–San Leandro (CA)
Central Oregon Comm Coll (OR)
Century Coll (MN)
Citrus Coll (CA)
Coll of Central Florida (FL)
Comm Care Coll (OK)
Comm Coll of the Air Force (AL)
Delta Coll (MI)
Eastern Gateway Comm Coll (OH)
H. Councill Trenholm State Comm Coll (AL)
Hennepin Tech Coll (MN)
Hinds Comm Coll (MS)
Humacao Comm Coll (PR)
IBMC Coll, Fort Collins (CO)
International Business Coll, Indianapolis (IN)
Ivy Tech Comm Coll–Columbus (IN)
Ivy Tech Comm Coll–East Central (IN)
Ivy Tech Comm Coll–Kokomo (IN)
Ivy Tech Comm Coll–Lafayette (IN)
James H. Faulkner State Comm Coll (AL)
Kaskaskia Coll (IL)
Lake Area Tech Inst (SD)
Luzerne County Comm Coll (PA)
Manor Coll (PA)
Midlands Tech Coll (SC)
Mid-Plains Comm Coll, North Platte (NE)
Minnesota State Comm and Tech Coll–Detroit Lakes (MN)
Minnesota State Comm and Tech Coll–Moorhead (MN)
Minnesota West Comm and Tech Coll (MN)
Mohave Comm Coll (AZ)
Mott Comm Coll (MI)
Northern Essex Comm Coll (MA)
Northwest Tech Coll (MN)
Orange Coast Coll (CA)
Palomar Coll (CA)
Pasadena City Coll (CA)
Pueblo Comm Coll (CO)
Raritan Valley Comm Coll (NJ)
Renton Tech Coll (WA)
Tallahassee Comm Coll (FL)
Truckee Meadows Comm Coll (NV)
Western Iowa Tech Comm Coll (IA)
Westmoreland County Comm Coll (PA)

DENTAL HYGIENE

Amarillo Coll (TX)
Athens Tech Coll (GA)
Atlanta Tech Coll (GA)
Austin Comm Coll District (TX)
Barton County Comm Coll (KS)
Blinn Coll (TX)
Camden County Coll (NJ)
Cape Fear Comm Coll (NC)
Carrington Coll–Boise (ID)
Carrington Coll–Mesa (AZ)
Carrington Coll–Sacramento (CA)
Carrington Coll–San Jose (CA)
Catawba Valley Comm Coll (NC)
Central Georgia Tech Coll (GA)
Century Coll (MN)
Cerritos Coll (CA)
Chippewa Valley Tech Coll (WI)
Clark Coll (WA)

Collin County Comm Coll District (TX)
Colorado Northwestern Comm Coll (CO)
Columbus Tech Coll (GA)
Comm Coll of Baltimore County (MD)
Comm Coll of Philadelphia (PA)
Comm Coll of Rhode Island (RI)
Daytona State Coll (FL)
Delta Coll (MI)
Elizabethtown Comm and Tech Coll, Elizabethtown (KY)
Erie Comm Coll, North Campus (NY)
Fayetteville Tech Comm Coll (NC)
Florida SouthWestern State Coll (FL)
Fox Coll (IL)
Fox Valley Tech Coll (WI)
Georgia Highlands Coll (GA)
Grand Rapids Comm Coll (MI)
Great Falls Coll Montana State U (MT)
Greenville Tech Coll (SC)
Gulf Coast State Coll (FL)
Hagerstown Comm Coll (MD)
Halifax Comm Coll (NC)
Harrisburg Area Comm Coll (PA)
Hawkeye Comm Coll (IA)
Hillsborough Comm Coll (FL)
Illinois Central Coll (IL)
Ivy Tech Comm Coll–East Central (IN)
Ivy Tech Comm Coll–Kokomo (IN)
Kellogg Comm Coll (MI)
Lake Land Coll (IL)
Lakeland Comm Coll (OH)
Lake Superior Coll (MN)
Laramie County Comm Coll (WY)
Lewis and Clark Comm Coll (IL)
Lone Star Coll–Kingwood (TX)
Luzerne County Comm Coll (PA)
Manor Coll (PA)
Meridian Comm Coll (MS)
Miami Dade Coll (FL)
Middlesex County Coll (NJ)
Midlands Tech Coll (SC)
Minnesota State Comm and Tech Coll–Moorhead (MN)
Mohave Comm Coll (AZ)
Monroe Comm Coll (NY)
Montgomery County Comm Coll (PA)
Mott Comm Coll (MI)
Mount Wachusett Comm Coll (MA)
Northampton Comm Coll (PA)
Northcentral Tech Coll (WI)
Ogeechee Tech Coll (GA)
Oxnard Coll (CA)
Pasadena City Coll (CA)
Pensacola State Coll (FL)
Pueblo Comm Coll (CO)
Quinsigamond Comm Coll (MA)
Raritan Valley Comm Coll (NJ)
Rock Valley Coll (IL)
Rowan Coll at Burlington County (NJ)
Salt Lake Comm Coll (UT)
San Joaquin Valley Coll, Chula Vista (CA)
San Joaquin Valley Coll, Ontario (CA)
San Joaquin Valley Coll, Visalia (CA)
San Juan Coll (NM)
Sheridan Coll (WY)
Southeastern Tech Coll (GA)
Southern U at Shreveport (LA)
South Florida State Coll (FL)
Springfield Tech Comm Coll (MA)
Stark State Coll (OH)
Tallahassee Comm Coll (FL)
Tarrant County Coll District (TX)
Truckee Meadows Comm Coll (NV)
Tulsa Comm Coll (OK)
Tunxis Comm Coll (CT)
Tyler Jr Coll (TX)
U of Cincinnati Blue Ash Coll (OH)
Virginia Western Comm Coll (VA)
Waukesha County Tech Coll (WI)
Wayne Comm Coll (NC)
Wayne County Comm Coll District (MI)
Westmoreland County Comm Coll (PA)
Wytheville Comm Coll (VA)

DENTAL LABORATORY TECHNOLOGY

Comm Coll of the Air Force (AL)
Erie Comm Coll, South Campus (NY)

J. Sargeant Reynolds Comm Coll (VA)
Pasadena City Coll (CA)

DENTAL SERVICES AND ALLIED PROFESSIONS RELATED
Gordon State Coll (GA)
Quinsigamond Comm Coll (MA)

DESIGN AND APPLIED ARTS RELATED
County Coll of Morris (NJ)
Howard Comm Coll (MD)
LDS Business Coll (UT)
Muskegon Comm Coll (MI)
Niagara County Comm Coll (NY)
Odessa Coll (TX)
Oklahoma City Comm Coll (OK)
Onondaga Comm Coll (NY)
Raritan Valley Comm Coll (NJ)
Tunxis Comm Coll (CT)
Vincennes U (IN)
Wenatchee Valley Coll (WA)
Westchester Comm Coll (NY)

DESIGN AND VISUAL COMMUNICATIONS
Brookhaven Coll (TX)
Bunker Hill Comm Coll (MA)
Cecil Coll (MD)
Central Virginia Comm Coll (VA)
Elgin Comm Coll (IL)
Fashion Inst of Design & Merchandising, LA Campus (CA)
FIDM/Fashion Inst of Design & Merchandising, Orange County Campus (CA)
FIDM/Fashion Inst of Design & Merchandising, San Diego Campus (CA)
Harrisburg Area Comm Coll (PA)
Hutchinson Comm Coll (KS)
Ivy Tech Comm Coll–Central Indiana (IN)
Ivy Tech Comm Coll–Columbus (IN)
Ivy Tech Comm Coll–Kokomo (IN)
Ivy Tech Comm Coll–North Central (IN)
Ivy Tech Comm Coll–Southern Indiana (IN)
Ivy Tech Comm Coll–Southwest (IN)
Ivy Tech Comm Coll–Wabash Valley (IN)
Lone Star Coll–CyFair (TX)
Lone Star Coll–Kingwood (TX)
Lone Star Coll–North Harris (TX)
Moraine Valley Comm Coll (IL)
Nashville State Comm Coll (TN)
Oklahoma City Comm Coll (OK)
Palomar Coll (CA)
Salt Lake Comm Coll (UT)
Southeastern Tech Coll (GA)

DESKTOP PUBLISHING AND DIGITAL IMAGING DESIGN
Alvin Comm Coll (TX)
Antelope Valley Coll (CA)
Camden County Comm Coll (NJ)
Cincinnati State Tech and Comm Coll (OH)
Dunwoody Coll of Technology (MN)
Hawkeye Comm Coll (IA)
Hennepin Tech Coll (MN)
Houston Comm Coll (TX)
Kankakee Comm Coll (IL)
Lake Land Coll (IL)
Leeward Comm Coll (HI)
Northeast Iowa Comm Coll (IA)
Northwest Coll (WY)
Palomar Coll (CA)
Pasadena City Coll (CA)
Ridgewater Coll (MN)
Southeast Tech Inst (SD)
Western Iowa Tech Comm Coll (IA)

DEVELOPMENTAL AND CHILD PSYCHOLOGY
Central Lakes Coll (MN)
Itawamba Comm Coll (MS)
Muskegon Comm Coll (MI)
Navarro Coll (TX)
Tarrant County Coll District (TX)

DEVELOPMENTAL SERVICES WORKER
Anoka Tech Coll (MN)

DIAGNOSTIC MEDICAL SONOGRAPHY AND ULTRASOUND TECHNOLOGY
Alvin Comm Coll (TX)
Athens Tech Coll (GA)

Austin Comm Coll District (TX)
Blackhawk Tech Coll (WI)
Bowling Green State U–Firelands Coll (OH)
Bunker Hill Comm Coll (MA)
Caldwell Comm Coll and Tech Inst (NC)
Cape Fear Comm Coll (NC)
Central New Mexico Comm Coll (NM)
Central Ohio Tech Coll (OH)
Chippewa Valley Tech Coll (WI)
Cincinnati State Tech and Comm Coll (OH)
Columbus Tech Coll (GA)
Comm Coll of Rhode Island (RI)
Delta Coll (MI)
Greenville Tech Coll (SC)
Gulf Coast State Coll (FL)
Harrisburg Area Comm Coll (PA)
H. Councill Trenholm State Comm Coll (AL)
Hillsborough Comm Coll (FL)
Hinds Comm Coll (MS)
Howard Comm Coll (MD)
Kennebec Valley Comm Coll (ME)
Lackawanna Coll (PA)
Laramie County Comm Coll (WY)
Lone Star Coll–CyFair (TX)
Lorain County Comm Coll (OH)
Lurleen B. Wallace Comm Coll (AL)
Miami Dade Coll (FL)
Montgomery Coll (MD)
Northampton Comm Coll (PA)
Orange Coast Coll (CA)
Pensacola State Coll (FL)
San Jacinto Coll District (TX)
Southeast Tech Inst (SD)
Springfield Tech Comm Coll (MA)
Tallahassee Comm Coll (FL)
Tulsa Comm Coll (OK)
Tyler Jr Coll (TX)
Westmoreland County Comm Coll (PA)

DIESEL MECHANICS TECHNOLOGY
Alexandria Tech and Comm Coll (MN)
American River Coll (CA)
Bellingham Tech Coll (WA)
Casper Coll (WY)
Central Lakes Coll (MN)
Central Texas Coll (TX)
Citrus Coll (CA)
City Colls of Chicago, Olive-Harvey College (IL)
Clark Coll (WA)
Eastern Arizona Coll (AZ)
Eastern Idaho Tech Coll (ID)
Elizabethtown Comm and Tech Coll, Elizabethtown (KY)
Fox Valley Tech Coll (WI)
Gateway Tech Coll (WI)
Great Basin Coll (NV)
Hawkeye Comm Coll (IA)
Hinds Comm Coll (MS)
Illinois Central Coll (IL)
Illinois Eastern Comm Colls, Wabash Valley College (IL)
Johnston Comm Coll (NC)
Kilgore Coll (TX)
Lake Area Tech Inst (SD)
Laramie County Comm Coll (WY)
Mid-Plains Comm Coll, North Platte (NE)
Minnesota State Comm and Tech Coll–Moorhead (MN)
Minnesota West Comm and Tech Coll (MN)
New Castle School of Trades (PA)
Northcentral Tech Coll (WI)
Ohio Tech Coll (OH)
Oklahoma City Comm Coll (OK)
Oklahoma State U Inst of Technology (OK)
Oklahoma Tech Coll (OK)
Owensboro Comm and Tech Coll (KY)
Ozarks Tech Comm Coll (MO)
Palomar Coll (CA)
Raritan Valley Comm Coll (NJ)
Rogue Comm Coll (OR)
St. Philip's Coll (TX)
Salt Lake Comm Coll (UT)
San Jacinto Coll District (TX)
San Juan Coll (NM)
Sheridan Coll (WY)
Southeast Comm Coll, Milford Campus (NE)
Southeast Tech Inst (SD)

State U of New York Coll of Technology at Alfred (NY)
Texarkana Coll (TX)
Texas State Tech Coll (TX)
Truckee Meadows Comm Coll (NV)
Vincennes U (IN)
Western Wyoming Comm Coll (WY)
White Mountains Comm Coll (NH)
Williston State Coll (ND)

DIETETICS
Camden County Coll (NJ)
Central Oregon Comm Coll (OR)
Cincinnati State Tech and Comm Coll (OH)
Comm Coll of the Air Force (AL)
Harrisburg Area Comm Coll (PA)
Miami Dade Coll (FL)
Pensacola State Coll (FL)
South Florida State Coll (FL)
Tarrant County Coll District (TX)
Truckee Meadows Comm Coll (NV)
Vincennes U (IN)
Westchester Comm Coll (NY)

DIETETIC TECHNOLOGY
Camden County Coll (NJ)
Chandler-Gilbert Comm Coll (AZ)
Fiorello H. LaGuardia Comm Coll of the City U of New York (NY)
Hudson County Comm Coll (NJ)
Miami Dade Coll (FL)
Mohawk Valley Comm Coll (NY)
Northland Comm and Tech Coll (MN)
Orange Coast Coll (CA)
Southern Maine Comm Coll (ME)
Trocaire Coll (NY)
Westmoreland County Comm Coll (PA)

DIETITIAN ASSISTANT
Barton County Comm Coll (KS)
Chandler-Gilbert Comm Coll (AZ)
Erie Comm Coll, North Campus (NY)
Hillsborough Comm Coll (FL)
Martin Comm Coll (NC)
Middlesex County Coll (NJ)
Southwest Tennessee Comm Coll (TN)

DIGITAL ARTS
Corning Comm Coll (NY)
Fiorello H. LaGuardia Comm Coll of the City U of New York (NY)
Genesee Comm Coll (NY)
Gulf Coast State Coll (FL)
Harford Comm Coll (MD)
Mohawk Valley Comm Coll (NY)
Queensborough Comm Coll of the City U of New York (NY)
Volunteer State Comm Coll (TN)
Waukesha County Tech Coll (WI)

DIGITAL COMMUNICATION AND MEDIA/MULTIMEDIA
Butler County Comm Coll (PA)
Cochise County Comm Coll District (AZ)
Finger Lakes Comm Coll (NY)
Gulf Coast State Coll (FL)
Hawkeye Comm Coll (IA)
Hinds Comm Coll (MS)
Laramie County Comm Coll (WY)
Naugatuck Valley Comm Coll (CT)
Oklahoma City Comm Coll (OK)
Pasadena City Coll (CA)
Raritan Valley Comm Coll (NJ)
Ridgewater Coll (MN)
San Jacinto Coll District (TX)
Sierra Coll (CA)
Southern Maine Comm Coll (ME)
Tompkins Cortland Comm Coll (NY)
Tulsa Comm Coll (OK)
U of Alaska Anchorage, Kenai Peninsula Coll (AK)
Wayne County Comm Coll District (MI)

DIRECTING AND THEATRICAL PRODUCTION
Quinsigamond Comm Coll (MA)

DRAFTING AND DESIGN TECHNOLOGY
Albany Tech Coll (GA)
Allen Comm Coll (KS)
Alvin Comm Coll (TX)
Amarillo Coll (TX)
American River Coll (CA)
Antelope Valley Coll (CA)
Austin Comm Coll District (TX)
Bainbridge State Coll (GA)

Bevill State Comm Coll (AL)
Bossier Parish Comm Coll (LA)
Camden County Coll (NJ)
Casper Coll (WY)
Cayuga County Comm Coll (NY)
Central Georgia Tech Coll (GA)
Central Oregon Comm Coll (OR)
Central Texas Coll (TX)
Cerritos Coll (CA)
Chattahoochee Tech Coll (GA)
Citrus Coll (CA)
Coll of Central Florida (FL)
Collin County Comm Coll District (TX)
Columbus Tech Coll (GA)
Comm Coll of Philadelphia (PA)
Copiah-Lincoln Comm Coll (MS)
Crowder Coll (MO)
Dabney S. Lancaster Comm Coll (VA)
Daytona State Coll (FL)
East Central Coll (MO)
Eastern Arizona Coll (AZ)
Eastern Gateway Comm Coll (OH)
Finger Lakes Comm Coll (NY)
Florida SouthWestern State Coll (FL)
Frederick Comm Coll (MD)
Fullerton Coll (CA)
Gadsden State Comm Coll (AL)
Genesee Comm Coll (NY)
George C. Wallace Comm Coll (AL)
Georgia Piedmont Tech Coll (GA)
Gwinnett Tech Coll (GA)
H. Councill Trenholm State Comm Coll (AL)
Hinds Comm Coll (MS)
Houston Comm Coll (TX)
Hutchinson Comm Coll (KS)
Iowa Central Comm Coll (IA)
Itawamba Comm Coll (MS)
ITI Tech Coll (LA)
Ivy Tech Comm Coll–Bloomington (IN)
Ivy Tech Comm Coll–Central Indiana (IN)
Ivy Tech Comm Coll–Columbus (IN)
Ivy Tech Comm Coll–East Central (IN)
Ivy Tech Comm Coll–Kokomo (IN)
Ivy Tech Comm Coll–Lafayette (IN)
Ivy Tech Comm Coll–Northeast (IN)
Ivy Tech Comm Coll–Northwest (IN)
Ivy Tech Comm Coll–Southeast (IN)
Ivy Tech Comm Coll–Southern Indiana (IN)
Ivy Tech Comm Coll–Southwest (IN)
Ivy Tech Comm Coll–Wabash Valley (IN)
J. F. Drake State Comm and Tech Coll (AL)
Kankakee Comm Coll (IL)
Kellogg Comm Coll (MI)
Kilgore Coll (TX)
Lake Land Coll (IL)
Lanier Tech Coll (GA)
Laramie County Comm Coll (WY)
Lehigh Carbon Comm Coll (PA)
Lone Star Coll–North Harris (TX)
Lorain County Comm Coll (OH)
Los Angeles Trade-Tech Coll (CA)
Luzerne County Comm Coll (PA)
Macomb Comm Coll (MI)
Manhattan Area Tech Coll (KS)
Meridian Comm Coll (MS)
Miami Dade Coll (FL)
Mohave Comm Coll (AZ)
Mott Comm Coll (MI)
Mt. San Antonio Coll (CA)
Muskegon Comm Coll (MI)
Navarro Coll (TX)
New Mexico Jr Coll (NM)
New River Comm Coll (VA)
Niagara County Comm Coll (NY)
North Central Texas Coll (TX)
Northeast Alabama Comm Coll (AL)
NorthWest Arkansas Comm Coll (AR)
Northwest-Shoals Comm Coll (AL)
Odessa Coll (TX)
Oklahoma City Comm Coll (OK)
Oklahoma State U, Oklahoma City (OK)
Olympic Coll (WA)
Palomar Coll (CA)
Paris Jr Coll (TX)
Pasadena City Coll (CA)
Pensacola State Coll (FL)
Pittsburgh Tech Inst, Oakdale (PA)
Rend Lake Coll (IL)
Renton Tech Coll (WA)
Richland Comm Coll (IL)

Rowan Coll at Burlington County (NJ)
St. Charles Comm Coll (MO)
St. Clair County Comm Coll (MI)
Salt Lake Comm Coll (UT)
San Jacinto Coll District (TX)
San Juan Coll (NM)
Schoolcraft Coll (MI)
Seminole State Coll of Florida (FL)
Southeast Comm Coll, Lincoln Campus (NE)
Southeastern Comm Coll (IA)
Southern Crescent Tech Coll (GA)
Southern Maine Comm Coll (ME)
South Georgia Tech Coll (GA)
Sowela Tech Comm Coll (LA)
Stark State Coll (OH)
State U of New York Coll of Technology at Alfred (NY)
Tallahassee Comm Coll (FL)
Tarrant County Coll District (TX)
Texarkana Coll (TX)
Texas State Tech Coll (TX)
Tidewater Comm Coll (VA)
Treasure Valley Comm Coll (OR)
Truckee Meadows Comm Coll (NV)
Tyler Jr Coll (TX)
U of Arkansas Comm Coll at Morrilton (AR)
Wiregrass Georgia Tech Coll (GA)
Wytheville Comm Coll (VA)
York County Comm Coll (ME)

DRAFTING/DESIGN ENGINEERING TECHNOLOGIES RELATED
Coll of The Albemarle (NC)
Corning Comm Coll (NY)
Dabney S. Lancaster Comm Coll (VA)
Genesee Comm Coll (NY)
Hennepin Tech Coll (MN)
Kennebec Valley Comm Coll (ME)
Lorain County Comm Coll (OH)
Luzerne County Comm Coll (PA)
Macomb Comm Coll (MI)
Mt. San Antonio Coll (CA)
Niagara County Comm Coll (NY)
Rock Valley Coll (IL)

DRAMA AND DANCE TEACHER EDUCATION
Hutchinson Comm Coll (KS)

DRAMATIC/THEATER ARTS
Allen Comm Coll (KS)
Alvin Comm Coll (TX)
Amarillo Coll (TX)
American Academy of Dramatic Arts–New York (NY)
American River Coll (CA)
Anoka-Ramsey Comm Coll (MN)
Arizona Western Coll (AZ)
Austin Comm Coll District (TX)
Bainbridge State Coll (GA)
Barton County Comm Coll (KS)
Blinn Coll (TX)
Bossier Parish Comm Coll (LA)
Bunker Hill Comm Coll (MA)
Ca&nnada Coll (CA)
Central New Mexico Comm Coll (NM)
Central Texas Coll (TX)
Central Wyoming Coll (WY)
Cerritos Coll (CA)
Chandler-Gilbert Comm Coll (AZ)
Citrus Coll (CA)
Cochise County Comm Coll District (AZ)
Coll of Central Florida (FL)
Coll of The Albemarle (NC)
Coll of the Canyons (CA)
Comm Coll of Rhode Island (RI)
Crowder Coll (MO)
Dean Coll (MA)
Dodge City Comm Coll (KS)
Eastern Arizona Coll (AZ)
Edison Coll (OH)
Finger Lakes Comm Coll (NY)
Fiorello H. LaGuardia Comm Coll of the City U of New York (NY)
Fullerton Coll (CA)
Galveston Coll (TX)
Genesee Comm Coll (NY)
Gordon State Coll (GA)
Harrisburg Area Comm Coll (PA)
Howard Comm Coll (MD)
Kilgore Coll (TX)
Lorain County Comm Coll (OH)
Los Angeles Valley Coll (CA)
Manchester Comm Coll (CT)
Mercer County Comm Coll (NJ)
Miami Dade Coll (FL)
Navarro Coll (TX)

New Mexico Jr Coll (NM)
Niagara County Comm Coll (NY)
Northeastern Jr Coll (CO)
Northern Essex Comm Coll (MA)
North Hennepin Comm Coll (MN)
Oklahoma City Comm Coll (OK)
Orange Coast Coll (CA)
Otero Jr Coll (CO)
Owensboro Comm and Tech Coll (KY)
Palomar Coll (CA)
Panola Coll (TX)
Paris Jr Coll (TX)
Pasadena City Coll (CA)
Pensacola State Coll (FL)
Rowan Coll at Burlington County (NJ)
St. Charles Comm Coll (MO)
St. Philip's Coll (TX)
San Jacinto Coll District (TX)
San Joaquin Delta Coll (CA)
Scottsdale Comm Coll (AZ)
Sheridan Coll (WY)
South Florida State Coll (FL)
Spoon River Coll (IL)
Texarkana Coll (TX)
Tulsa Comm Coll (OK)
Tyler Jr Coll (TX)
Victor Valley Coll (CA)
Vincennes U (IN)
Western Texas Coll (TX)
Western Wyoming Comm Coll (WY)

DRAMATIC/THEATER ARTS AND STAGECRAFT RELATED
Genesee Comm Coll (NY)
St. Philip's Coll (TX)

DRAWING
Cecil Coll (MD)
Los Angeles Valley Coll (CA)
Luzerne County Comm Coll (PA)
Palomar Coll (CA)

DRYWALL INSTALLATION
American River Coll (CA)
Palomar Coll (CA)

EARLY CHILDHOOD EDUCATION
Aiken Tech Coll (SC)
Alexandria Tech and Comm Coll (MN)
Alvin Comm Coll (TX)
Ancilla Coll (IN)
Anne Arundel Comm Coll (MD)
Arizona Western Coll (AZ)
Austin Comm Coll District (TX)
Barton County Comm Coll (KS)
Big Bend Comm Coll (WA)
Blackhawk Tech Coll (WI)
Bucks County Comm Coll (PA)
Bunker Hill Comm Coll (MA)
Caldwell Comm Coll and Tech Inst (NC)
Camden County Coll (NJ)
Cape Fear Comm Coll (NC)
Carroll Comm Coll (MD)
Catawba Valley Comm Coll (NC)
Central Maine Comm Coll (ME)
Central New Mexico Comm Coll (NM)
Central Ohio Tech Coll (OH)
Central Oregon Comm Coll (OR)
Central Texas Coll (TX)
Central Wyoming Coll (WY)
Chesapeake Coll (MD)
Chippewa Valley Tech Coll (WI)
Cincinnati State Tech and Comm Coll (OH)
Clark Coll (WA)
Cleveland Comm Coll (NC)
Cochise County Comm Coll District (AZ)
Coll of Central Florida (FL)
Collin County Comm Coll District (TX)
Colorado Northwestern Comm Coll (CO)
Comm Care Coll (OK)
Comm Coll of Baltimore County (MD)
Corning Comm Coll (NY)
Craven Comm Coll (NC)
Davis Coll (OH)
Dean Coll (MA)
Eastern Arizona Coll (AZ)
Eastern Wyoming Coll (WY)
Fayetteville Tech Comm Coll (NC)
Finger Lakes Comm Coll (NY)

Florida SouthWestern State Coll (FL)
Fox Valley Tech Coll (WI)
Frederick Comm Coll (MD)
Front Range Comm Coll (CO)
Garrett Coll (MD)
Gateway Comm and Tech Coll (KY)
Gateway Tech Coll (WI)
Georgia Military Coll (GA)
Gordon State Coll (GA)
Great Basin Coll (NV)
Gulf Coast State Coll (FL)
Hagerstown Comm Coll (MD)
Halifax Comm Coll (NC)
Harford Comm Coll (MD)
Harrisburg Area Comm Coll (PA)
Hesston Coll (KS)
Highland Comm Coll (IL)
Houston Comm Coll (TX)
Ivy Tech Comm Coll–Bloomington (IN)
Ivy Tech Comm Coll–Central Indiana (IN)
Ivy Tech Comm Coll–Columbus (IN)
Ivy Tech Comm Coll–East Central (IN)
Ivy Tech Comm Coll–Kokomo (IN)
Ivy Tech Comm Coll–Lafayette (IN)
Ivy Tech Comm Coll–North Central (IN)
Ivy Tech Comm Coll–Northeast (IN)
Ivy Tech Comm Coll–Northwest (IN)
Ivy Tech Comm Coll–Richmond (IN)
Ivy Tech Comm Coll–Southeast (IN)
Ivy Tech Comm Coll–Southern Indiana (IN)
Ivy Tech Comm Coll–Southwest (IN)
Ivy Tech Comm Coll–Wabash Valley (IN)
James Sprunt Comm Coll (NC)
Jefferson Comm Coll (NY)
Johnston Comm Coll (NC)
Kankakee Comm Coll (IL)
Keweenaw Bay Ojibwa Comm Coll (MI)
Lackawanna Coll (PA)
Laramie County Comm Coll (WY)
Lehigh Carbon Comm Coll (PA)
Luzerne County Comm Coll (PA)
Massachusetts Bay Comm Coll (MA)
Miami Dade Coll (FL)
Minnesota State Coll–Southeast Tech (MN)
Minnesota State Comm and Tech Coll–Detroit Lakes (MN)
Mitchell Comm Coll (NC)
Montgomery Coll (MD)
Montgomery Comm Coll (NC)
Moraine Valley Comm Coll (IL)
Mott Comm Coll (MI)
Nashville State Comm Coll (TN)
Naugatuck Valley Comm Coll (CT)
Norco Coll (CA)
Northampton Comm Coll (PA)
Northcentral Tech Coll (WI)
NorthWest Arkansas Comm Coll (AR)
Norwalk Comm Coll (CT)
Oklahoma State U, Oklahoma City (OK)
Olympic Coll (WA)
Panola Coll (TX)
Paris Jr Coll (TX)
Penn Foster Coll (AZ)
Pennsylvania Highlands Comm Coll (PA)
Pensacola State Coll (FL)
Piedmont Comm Coll (NC)
Potomac State Coll of West Virginia U (WV)
Pueblo Comm Coll (CO)
Quincy Coll (MA)
Randolph Comm Coll (NC)
Renton Tech Coll (WA)
Richmond Comm Coll (NC)
Ridgewater Coll (MN)
River Valley Comm Coll (NH)
Rockingham Comm Coll (NC)
Rowan-Cabarrus Comm Coll (NC)
St. Philip's Coll (TX)
Sheridan Coll (WY)
Southern Maine Comm Coll (ME)
South Florida State Coll (FL)
Southwestern Indian Polytechnic Inst (NM)
Southwestern Michigan Coll (MI)
Springfield Tech Comm Coll (MA)
Tallahassee Comm Coll (FL)
Tech Coll of the Lowcountry (SC)
Tohono O'odham Comm Coll (AZ)

U of Alaska Anchorage, Kenai Peninsula Coll (AK)
Victoria Coll (TX)
Vincennes U (IN)
Waukesha County Tech Coll (WI)
Wayne Comm Coll (NC)
Wenatchee Valley Coll (WA)
Western Piedmont Comm Coll (NC)
Western Texas Coll (TX)
Western Wyoming Comm Coll (WY)
Westmoreland County Comm Coll (PA)
White Mountains Comm Coll (NH)
Wisconsin Indianhead Tech Coll (WI)
Wor-Wic Comm Coll (MD)
York County Comm Coll (ME)

E-COMMERCE
Augusta Tech Coll (GA)
Brookhaven Coll (TX)
Caldwell Comm Coll and Tech Inst (NC)
Central Georgia Tech Coll (GA)
Century Coll (MN)
Finger Lakes Comm Coll (NY)
Genesee Comm Coll (NY)
Rend Lake Coll (IL)
St. Philip's Coll (TX)
Three Rivers Comm Coll (CT)
Wayne County Comm Coll District (MI)
Wiregrass Georgia Tech Coll (GA)

ECONOMICS
Allen Comm Coll (KS)
Austin Comm Coll District (TX)
Barton County Comm Coll (KS)
Ca&nnada Coll (CA)
Casper Coll (WY)
Cerritos Coll (CA)
Cochise County Comm Coll District (AZ)
Coll of Central Florida (FL)
Copiah-Lincoln Comm Coll (MS)
Eastern Wyoming Coll (WY)
Edison Comm Coll (OH)
Fullerton Coll (CA)
Georgia Highlands Coll (GA)
Itawamba Comm Coll (MS)
Laramie County Comm Coll (WY)
Lone Star Coll–CyFair (TX)
Los Angeles Valley Coll (CA)
Miami Dade Coll (FL)
Muskegon Comm Coll (MI)
Nashville State Comm Coll (TN)
Northeastern Jr Coll (CO)
Oklahoma State U, Oklahoma City (OK)
Orange Coast Coll (CA)
Oxnard Coll (CA)
Palomar Coll (CA)
Potomac State Coll of West Virginia U (WV)
St. Charles Comm Coll (MO)
St. Philip's Coll (TX)
Salt Lake Comm Coll (UT)
San Joaquin Delta Coll (CA)
South Florida State Coll (FL)
Tyler Jr Coll (TX)
Vincennes U (IN)
Wenatchee Valley Coll (WA)
Western Wyoming Comm Coll (WY)

EDUCATION
American Samoa Comm Coll (AS)
Bainbridge State Coll (GA)
Bossier Parish Comm Coll (LA)
Bowling Green State U–Firelands Coll (OH)
Bunker Hill Comm Coll (MA)
Butler County Comm Coll (PA)
Caldwell Comm Coll and Tech Inst (NC)
Ca&nnada Coll (CA)
Carroll Comm Coll (MD)
Cecil Coll (MD)
Central Oregon Comm Coll (OR)
Central Virginia Comm Coll (VA)
Century Coll (MN)
Chesapeake Coll (MD)
Chipola Coll (FL)
Coll of The Albemarle (NC)
Comm Coll of Baltimore County (MD)
Comm Coll of Philadelphia (PA)
Copiah-Lincoln Comm Coll (MS)
Crowder Coll (MO)
Dabney S. Lancaster Comm Coll (VA)
Dodge City Comm Coll (KS)

Dyersburg State Comm Coll (TN)
East Central Coll (MO)
Edison Comm Coll (OH)
Frederick Comm Coll (MD)
Galveston Coll (TX)
Garrett Coll (MD)
Genesee Comm Coll (NY)
Georgia Highlands Coll (GA)
Hagerstown Comm Coll (MD)
Harford Comm Coll (MD)
Hutchinson Comm Coll (KS)
Iowa Central Comm Coll (IA)
Itawamba Comm Coll (MS)
Ivy Tech Comm Coll–Bloomington (IN)
Ivy Tech Comm Coll–Central Indiana (IN)
Ivy Tech Comm Coll–Columbus (IN)
Ivy Tech Comm Coll–East Central (IN)
Ivy Tech Comm Coll–Kokomo (IN)
Ivy Tech Comm Coll–Lafayette (IN)
Ivy Tech Comm Coll–Richmond (IN)
Ivy Tech Comm Coll–Southeast (IN)
Ivy Tech Comm Coll–Southern Indiana (IN)
Ivy Tech Comm Coll–Southwest (IN)
Ivy Tech Comm Coll–Wabash Valley (IN)
Jefferson Coll (MO)
Kankakee Comm Coll (IL)
Lackawanna Coll (PA)
Laramie County Comm Coll (WY)
Lehigh Carbon Comm Coll (PA)
Lone Star Coll–CyFair (TX)
Lone Star Coll–Kingwood (TX)
Lone Star Coll–Montgomery (TX)
Lone Star Coll–North Harris (TX)
Lone Star Coll–Tomball (TX)
Lorain County Comm Coll (OH)
Luzerne County Comm Coll (PA)
Miami Dade Coll (FL)
Mohave Comm Coll (AZ)
Muskegon Comm Coll (MI)
Navarro Coll (TX)
New Mexico Jr Coll (NM)
New River Comm Coll (VA)
Northern Essex Comm Coll (MA)
North Hennepin Comm Coll (MN)
NorthWest Arkansas Comm Coll (AR)
Nunez Comm Coll (LA)
Odessa Coll (TX)
Palau Comm Coll (Palau)
Palomar Coll (CA)
Panola Coll (TX)
Paris Jr Coll (TX)
Pennsylvania Highlands Comm Coll (PA)
Pensacola State Coll (FL)
Rowan Coll at Burlington County (NJ)
St. Philip's Coll (TX)
Schenectady County Comm Coll (NY)
Schoolcraft Coll (MI)
Southwest Texas Jr Coll (TX)
Spoon River Coll (IL)
Tech Coll of the Lowcountry (SC)
Three Rivers Comm Coll (CT)
Tidewater Comm Coll (VA)
Tulsa Comm Coll (OK)
U of Cincinnati Blue Ash Coll (OH)
U of New Mexico–Gallup (NM)
Vincennes U (IN)
Virginia Western Comm Coll (VA)
Volunteer State Comm Coll (TN)
Walters State Comm Coll (TN)
Wenatchee Valley Coll (WA)
Western Wyoming Comm Coll (WY)
White Mountains Comm Coll (NH)
Wor-Wic Comm Coll (MD)
Wytheville Comm Coll (VA)
York County Comm Coll (ME)

EDUCATIONAL/ INSTRUCTIONAL TECHNOLOGY
Bossier Parish Comm Coll (LA)
Comm Coll of the Air Force (AL)
Gateway Comm and Tech Coll (KY)
Ivy Tech Comm Coll–North Central (IN)
Lone Star Coll–North Harris (TX)
Tarrant County Coll District (TX)
Texas State Tech Coll (TX)

EDUCATIONAL LEADERSHIP AND ADMINISTRATION
Comm Coll of the Air Force (AL)

EDUCATION (MULTIPLE LEVELS)
Brookhaven Coll (TX)
Camden County Coll (NJ)
Cayuga County Comm Coll (NY)
Central New Mexico Comm Coll (NM)
Genesee Comm Coll (NY)
Houston Comm Coll (TX)
Oklahoma State U Inst of Technology (OK)
Onondaga Comm Coll (NY)
Paris Jr Coll (TX)
Tyler Jr Coll (TX)
U of Arkansas Comm Coll at Morrilton (AR)
Westchester Comm Coll (NY)
Western Wyoming Comm Coll (WY)

EDUCATION RELATED
Corning Comm Coll (NY)
Genesee Comm Coll (NY)
Kent State U at Salem (OH)
Kent State U at Tuscarawas (OH)
Miami Dade Coll (FL)

EDUCATION (SPECIFIC LEVELS AND METHODS) RELATED
Corning Comm Coll (NY)
Harford Comm Coll (MD)
Jefferson Coll (MO)
Leeward Comm Coll (HI)
Manor Coll (PA)
Miami Dade Coll (FL)

EDUCATION (SPECIFIC SUBJECT AREAS) RELATED
Harford Comm Coll (MD)
St. Charles Comm Coll (MO)

ELECTRICAL AND ELECTRONIC ENGINEERING TECHNOLOGIES RELATED
Albany Tech Coll (GA)
Blue Ridge Comm and Tech Coll (WV)
Corning Comm Coll (NY)
ETI Tech Coll of Niles (OH)
Fox Valley Tech Coll (WI)
Kent State U at Trumbull (OH)
Kent State U at Tuscarawas (OH)
Lake Region State Coll (ND)
Massachusetts Bay Comm Coll (MA)
Miami Dade Coll (FL)
Onondaga Comm Coll (NY)
Owensboro Comm and Tech Coll (KY)
Pasadena City Coll (CA)
Sheridan Coll (WY)
Thaddeus Stevens Coll of Technology (PA)
Wayne County Comm Coll District (MI)

ELECTRICAL AND ELECTRONICS ENGINEERING
Allen Comm Coll (KS)
Anne Arundel Comm Coll (MD)
Caldwell Comm Coll and Tech Inst (NC)
Carroll Comm Coll (MD)
Comm Coll of Baltimore County (MD)
Corning Comm Coll (NY)
Fiorello H. LaGuardia Comm Coll of the City U of New York (NY)
Garrett Coll (MD)
Humacao Comm Coll (PR)
Olympic Coll (WA)
Pasadena City Coll (CA)
Potomac State Coll of West Virginia U (WV)
South Florida State Coll (FL)

ELECTRICAL AND POWER TRANSMISSION INSTALLATION
Delta Coll (MI)
Ivy Tech Comm Coll–Columbus (IN)
Manhattan Area Tech Coll (KS)
Minnesota West Comm and Tech Coll (MN)
Oklahoma State U, Oklahoma City (OK)
Piedmont Comm Coll (NC)
Richmond Comm Coll (NC)
Rogue Comm Coll (OR)
San Jacinto Coll District (TX)
State U of New York Coll of Technology at Alfred (NY)

Westmoreland County Comm Coll (PA)

ELECTRICAL AND POWER TRANSMISSION INSTALLATION RELATED
Manhattan Area Tech Coll (KS)
Martin Comm Coll (NC)
Minnesota State Comm and Tech Coll–Wadena (MN)
Minnesota West Comm and Tech Coll (MN)

ELECTRICAL, ELECTRONIC AND COMMUNICATIONS ENGINEERING TECHNOLOGY
Aiken Tech Coll (SC)
Alamance Comm Coll (NC)
Allen Comm Coll (KS)
Alvin Comm Coll (TX)
Amarillo Coll (TX)
American River Coll (CA)
American Samoa Comm Coll (AS)
Anne Arundel Comm Coll (MD)
Anoka Tech Coll (MN)
Arizona Western Coll (AZ)
Athens Tech Coll (GA)
Augusta Tech Coll (GA)
Austin Comm Coll District (TX)
Bainbridge State Coll (GA)
Berkshire Comm Coll (MA)
Bismarck State Coll (ND)
Bowling Green State U–Firelands Coll (OH)
Butler County Comm Coll (PA)
Camden County Coll (NJ)
Cape Fear Comm Coll (NC)
Casper Coll (WY)
Catawba Valley Comm Coll (NC)
Cayuga County Comm Coll (NY)
Cecil Coll (MD)
Central Georgia Tech Coll (GA)
Central New Mexico Comm Coll (NM)
Central Ohio Tech Coll (OH)
Central Oregon Comm Coll (OR)
Cerritos Coll (CA)
Chattahoochee Tech Coll (GA)
Cincinnati State Tech and Comm Coll (OH)
Citrus Coll (CA)
Clark Coll (WA)
Cleveland Comm Coll (NC)
Clinton Comm Coll (NY)
Cochise County Comm Coll District (AZ)
Collin County Comm Coll District (TX)
Columbus Tech Coll (GA)
Comm Coll of the Air Force (AL)
Copiah-Lincoln Comm Coll (MS)
County Coll of Morris (NJ)
Craven Comm Coll (NC)
Crowder Coll (MO)
Dabney S. Lancaster Comm Coll (VA)
Daytona State Coll (FL)
Dodge City Comm Coll (KS)
Dunwoody Coll of Technology (MN)
Dutchess Comm Coll (NY)
Eastern Gateway Comm Coll (OH)
Edison Comm Coll (OH)
Erie Comm Coll, North Campus (NY)
ETI Tech Coll of Niles (OH)
Fayetteville Tech Comm Coll (NC)
Fox Valley Tech Coll (WI)
Gadsden State Comm Coll (AL)
Gateway Tech Coll (WI)
George C. Wallace Comm Coll (AL)
Georgia Piedmont Tech Coll (GA)
Grand Rapids Comm Coll (MI)
Great Basin Coll (NV)
Greenville Tech Coll (SC)
Gulf Coast State Coll (FL)
Gwinnett Tech Coll (GA)
Harrisburg Area Comm Coll (PA)
Hawkeye Comm Coll (IA)
Hennepin Tech Coll (MN)
Hillsborough Comm Coll (FL)
Hinds Comm Coll (MS)
Hopkinsville Comm Coll (KY)
Howard Comm Coll (MD)
Hudson County Comm Coll (NJ)
Hutchinson Comm Coll (KS)
Illinois Central Coll (IL)
Iowa Central Comm Coll (IA)
Island Drafting and Tech Inst (NY)
Itawamba Comm Coll (MS)
ITI Tech Coll (LA)
Ivy Tech Comm Coll–Bloomington (IN)
Ivy Tech Comm Coll–Central Indiana (IN)
Ivy Tech Comm Coll–Columbus (IN)
Ivy Tech Comm Coll–East Central (IN)
Ivy Tech Comm Coll–Kokomo (IN)
Ivy Tech Comm Coll–Lafayette (IN)
Ivy Tech Comm Coll–North Central (IN)
Ivy Tech Comm Coll–Northeast (IN)
Ivy Tech Comm Coll–Northwest (IN)
Ivy Tech Comm Coll–Richmond (IN)
Ivy Tech Comm Coll–Southeast (IN)
Ivy Tech Comm Coll–Southern Indiana (IN)
Ivy Tech Comm Coll–Southwest (IN)
Ivy Tech Comm Coll–Wabash Valley (IN)
Jefferson Coll (MO)
J. F. Drake State Comm and Tech Coll (AL)
Kaskaskia Coll (IL)
Kennebec Valley Comm Coll (ME)
Kilgore Coll (TX)
Kirtland Comm Coll (MI)
Lake Area Tech Inst (SD)
Lake Land Coll (IL)
Lakeland Comm Coll (OH)
Lake Superior Coll (MN)
Lanier Tech Coll (GA)
Lehigh Carbon Comm Coll (PA)
Lone Star Coll–CyFair (TX)
Lone Star Coll–North Harris (TX)
Lone Star Coll–Tomball (TX)
Lorain County Comm Coll (OH)
Los Angeles Trade-Tech Coll (CA)
Luzerne County Comm Coll (PA)
Macomb Comm Coll (MI)
Massachusetts Bay Comm Coll (MA)
Mercer County Comm Coll (NJ)
Meridian Comm Coll (MS)
Miami Dade Coll (FL)
Middlesex County Coll (NJ)
Midlands Tech Coll (SC)
Minnesota State Coll–Southeast Tech (MN)
Mitchell Comm Coll (NC)
Mohawk Valley Comm Coll (NY)
Monroe Comm Coll (NY)
Montgomery County Comm Coll (PA)
Mott Comm Coll (MI)
Mt. San Antonio Coll (CA)
Muskegon Comm Coll (MI)
Nashville State Comm Coll (TN)
Naugatuck Valley Comm Coll (CT)
New Castle School of Trades (PA)
New River Comm Coll (VA)
Northampton Comm Coll (PA)
North Central Texas Coll (TX)
Northeast Iowa Comm Coll (IA)
Northern Essex Comm Coll (MA)
NorthWest Arkansas Comm Coll (AR)
Oakton Comm Coll (IL)
Odessa Coll (TX)
Oklahoma State U, Oklahoma City (OK)
Olympic Coll (WA)
Onondaga Comm Coll (NY)
Ozarks Tech Comm Coll (MO)
Palau Comm Coll (Palau)
Paris Jr Coll (TX)
Penn State DuBois (PA)
Penn State Fayette, The Eberly Campus (PA)
Penn State Shenango (PA)
Pennsylvania Inst of Technology (PA)
Pensacola State Coll (FL)
Pittsburgh Inst of Aeronautics (PA)
Pittsburgh Tech Inst, Oakdale (PA)
Pueblo Comm Coll (CO)
Queensborough Comm Coll of the City U of New York (NY)
Quinsigamond Comm Coll (MA)
Reid State Tech Coll (AL)
Rend Lake Coll (IL)
Richland Comm Coll (IL)
Richmond Comm Coll (NC)
Ridgewater Coll (MN)
Rockingham Comm Coll (NC)
Rock Valley Coll (IL)
Rogue Comm Coll (OR)
Rowan-Cabarrus Comm Coll (NC)
Rowan Coll at Burlington County (NJ)
St. Clair County Comm Coll (MI)
Salt Lake Comm Coll (UT)
San Jacinto Coll District (TX)
San Joaquin Delta Coll (CA)
San Juan Coll (NM)
Savannah Tech Coll (GA)
Schenectady County Comm Coll (NY)
Schoolcraft Coll (MI)
Scottsdale Comm Coll (AZ)
Seminole State Coll of Florida (FL)
Shawnee Comm Coll (IL)
Southeast Comm Coll, Lincoln Campus (NE)
Southeast Comm Coll, Milford Campus (NE)
Southeastern Comm Coll (IA)
Southeastern Tech Coll (GA)
Southeast Tech Inst (SD)
Southern Crescent Tech Coll (GA)
Southern Maine Comm Coll (ME)
Southern U at Shreveport (LA)
South Florida State Coll (FL)
South Georgia Tech Coll (GA)
South Suburban Coll (IL)
Southwest Tennessee Comm Coll (TN)
Southwest Virginia Comm Coll (VA)
Spartanburg Comm Coll (SC)
Spoon River Coll (IL)
Springfield Tech Comm Coll (MA)
State U of New York Coll of Technology at Alfred (NY)
Sullivan County Comm Coll (NY)
Tarrant County Coll District (TX)
Texarkana Coll (TX)
Texas State Tech Coll (TX)
Thaddeus Stevens Coll of Technology (PA)
Three Rivers Comm Coll (CT)
Tidewater Comm Coll (VA)
Tri-County Tech Coll (SC)
Tulsa Comm Coll (OK)
Victoria Coll (TX)
Victor Valley Coll (CA)
Vincennes U (IN)
Virginia Western Comm Coll (VA)
Waukesha County Tech Coll (WI)
Wayne Comm Coll (NC)
Wayne County Comm Coll District (MI)
Westchester Comm Coll (NY)
Western Piedmont Comm Coll (NC)
Western Wyoming Comm Coll (WY)
West Georgia Tech Coll (GA)
Westmoreland County Comm Coll (PA)
Williamson Coll of the Trades (PA)
Wor-Wic Comm Coll (MD)
Wytheville Comm Coll (VA)

ELECTRICAL/ELECTRONICS DRAFTING AND CAD/CADD
Dunwoody Coll of Technology (MN)
Palomar Coll (CA)

ELECTRICAL/ELECTRONICS EQUIPMENT INSTALLATION AND REPAIR
Antelope Valley Coll (CA)
Cape Fear Comm Coll (NC)
Fullerton Coll (CA)
Hinds Comm Coll (MS)
Hutchinson Comm Coll (KS)
Los Angeles Valley Coll (CA)
Macomb Comm Coll (MI)
Mesabi Range Coll (MN)
Orange Coast Coll (CA)
Pittsburgh Tech Inst, Oakdale (PA)
St. Philip's Coll (TX)
Sierra Coll (CA)
Southeast Tech Inst (SD)
Southwest Tennessee Comm Coll (TN)
Wenatchee Valley Coll (WA)
Western Wyoming Comm Coll (WY)

ELECTRICAL/ELECTRONICS MAINTENANCE AND REPAIR TECHNOLOGY RELATED
Bunker Hill Comm Coll (MA)
Coll of Business and Technology–Cutler Bay Campus (FL)
Coll of Business and Technology–Flagler Campus (FL)
Coll of Business and Technology–Hialeah Campus (FL)
Coll of Business and Technology–Miami Gardens (FL)
Kennebec Valley Comm Coll (ME)
Mohawk Valley Comm Coll (NY)

ELECTRICIAN
American River Coll (CA)
Antelope Valley Coll (CA)
Bellingham Tech Coll (WA)
Bevill State Comm Coll (AL)
Central New Mexico Comm Coll (NM)
Cleveland Comm Coll (NC)
Danville Area Comm Coll (IL)
Delta Coll (MI)
Dunwoody Coll of Technology (MN)
Eastern Idaho Tech Coll (ID)
Elizabethtown Comm and Tech Coll, Elizabethtown (KY)
Fayetteville Tech Comm Coll (NC)
George C. Wallace Comm Coll (AL)
Harrisburg Area Comm Coll (PA)
H. Councill Trenholm State Comm Coll (AL)
Hinds Comm Coll (MS)
Ivy Tech Comm Coll–Bloomington (IN)
Ivy Tech Comm Coll–Central Indiana (IN)
Ivy Tech Comm Coll–East Central (IN)
Ivy Tech Comm Coll–Kokomo (IN)
Ivy Tech Comm Coll–Lafayette (IN)
Ivy Tech Comm Coll–North Central (IN)
Ivy Tech Comm Coll–Northeast (IN)
Ivy Tech Comm Coll–Northwest (IN)
Ivy Tech Comm Coll–Richmond (IN)
Ivy Tech Comm Coll–Southern Indiana (IN)
Ivy Tech Comm Coll–Southwest (IN)
Ivy Tech Comm Coll–Wabash Valley (IN)
J. F. Drake State Comm and Tech Coll (AL)
Kaskaskia Coll (IL)
Kennebec Valley Comm Coll (ME)
Lake Superior Coll (MN)
Luzerne County Comm Coll (PA)
Miami Dade Coll (FL)
Minnesota West Comm and Tech Coll (MN)
Mitchell Comm Coll (NC)
Mitchell Tech Inst (SD)
Montgomery Comm Coll (NC)
Northampton Comm Coll (PA)
Northeast Iowa Comm Coll (IA)
Northland Comm and Tech Coll (MN)
Owensboro Comm and Tech Coll (KY)
Palomar Coll (CA)
Panola Coll (TX)
Piedmont Comm Coll (NC)
Randolph Comm Coll (NC)
Rend Lake Coll (IL)
Ridgewater Coll (MN)
Rockingham Comm Coll (NC)
Rock Valley Coll (IL)
Rowan-Cabarrus Comm Coll (NC)
Southeast Tech Inst (SD)
Western Iowa Tech Comm Coll (IA)
Western Wyoming Comm Coll (WY)

ELECTROCARDIOGRAPH TECHNOLOGY
Oklahoma State U, Oklahoma City (OK)
Orange Coast Coll (CA)

ELECTROMECHANICAL AND INSTRUMENTATION AND MAINTENANCE TECHNOLOGIES RELATED
Cape Fear Comm Coll (NC)
Catawba Valley Comm Coll (NC)
Greenville Tech Coll (SC)
Halifax Comm Coll (NC)
Mitchell Comm Coll (NC)
Montgomery Comm Coll (NC)
Piedmont Comm Coll (NC)
Pueblo Comm Coll (CO)
Richmond Comm Coll (NC)
Wayne Comm Coll (NC)

ELECTROMECHANICAL TECHNOLOGY
Blackhawk Tech Coll (WI)
Bowling Green State U–Firelands Coll (OH)
Camden County Coll (NJ)
Central Maine Comm Coll (ME)
Chandler-Gilbert Comm Coll (AZ)
Chippewa Valley Tech Coll (WI)
Cincinnati State Tech and Comm Coll (OH)
Comm Coll of Rhode Island (RI)
Craven Comm Coll (NC)
Denmark Tech Coll (SC)
Edison Comm Coll (OH)
Fox Valley Tech Coll (WI)
Galveston Coll (TX)
Gateway Tech Coll (WI)
Georgia Piedmont Tech Coll (GA)
Hawkeye Comm Coll (IA)
Kirtland Comm Coll (MI)
Lake Land Coll (IL)
Macomb Comm Coll (MI)
Martin Comm Coll (NC)
Montgomery County Comm Coll (PA)
Muskegon Comm Coll (MI)
Northampton Comm Coll (PA)
Northcentral Tech Coll (WI)
Paris Jr Coll (TX)
Quincy Coll (MA)
Quinsigamond Comm Coll (MA)
Randolph Comm Coll (NC)
Richmond Comm Coll (NC)
Ridgewater Coll (MN)
St. Philip's Coll (TX)
Southeast Tech Inst (SD)
Springfield Tech Comm Coll (MA)
Tarrant County Coll District (TX)
Texas State Tech Coll (TX)
Tyler Jr Coll (TX)
Wayne County Comm Coll District (MI)
Westmoreland County Comm Coll (PA)

ELECTRONEURODIAGNOSTIC/ ELECTROENCEPHALOGRAPHIC TECHNOLOGY
Alvin Comm Coll (TX)
Catawba Valley Comm Coll (NC)
Collin County Comm Coll District (TX)
Harford Comm Coll (MD)
Lone Star Coll–Kingwood (TX)
Orange Coast Coll (CA)
Southeast Tech Inst (SD)

ELEMENTARY EDUCATION
Allen Comm Coll (KS)
Amarillo Coll (TX)
Ancilla Coll (IN)
Arizona Western Coll (AZ)
Bainbridge State Coll (GA)
Barton County Comm Coll (KS)
Butler County Comm Coll (PA)
Carl Albert State Coll (OK)
Carroll Comm Coll (MD)
Casper Coll (WY)
Cecil Coll (MD)
Central Wyoming Coll (WY)
Chandler-Gilbert Comm Coll (AZ)
Chesapeake Coll (MD)
Cleveland Comm Coll (NC)
Cochise County Comm Coll District (AZ)
Coll of Central Florida (FL)
Comm Coll of Baltimore County (MD)
Copiah-Lincoln Comm Coll (MS)
Craven Comm Coll (NC)
Crowder Coll (MO)
Dodge City Comm Coll (KS)
Eastern Arizona Coll (AZ)
Eastern Wyoming Coll (WY)
Fayetteville Tech Comm Coll (NC)
Frederick Comm Coll (MD)
Garrett Coll (MD)
Genesee Comm Coll (NY)
Grand Rapids Comm Coll (MI)
Great Basin Coll (NV)
Hagerstown Comm Coll (MD)
Harford Comm Coll (MD)
Howard Comm Coll (MD)
Itawamba Comm Coll (MS)
James Sprunt Comm Coll (NC)
Kankakee Comm Coll (IL)
Kellogg Comm Coll (MI)
Kilgore Coll (TX)
Lenoir Comm Coll (NC)
Lorain County Comm Coll (OH)
Manor Coll (PA)
Massachusetts Bay Comm Coll (MA)
Miami Dade Coll (FL)
Mitchell Comm Coll (NC)
Montgomery Coll (MD)
Montgomery County Comm Coll (PA)
Moraine Valley Comm Coll (IL)
Muskegon Comm Coll (MI)
Nashville State Comm Coll (TN)
Navarro Coll (TX)
New Mexico Jr Coll (NM)
Niagara County Comm Coll (NY)
Northeastern Jr Coll (CO)
Northern Essex Comm Coll (MA)
Northwest Coll (WY)
Oklahoma City Comm Coll (OK)
Orange Coast Coll (CA)
Otero Jr Coll (CO)
Paris Jr Coll (TX)
Pensacola State Coll (FL)
Potomac State Coll of West Virginia U (WV)
Quincy Coll (MA)
Quinsigamond Comm Coll (MA)
Reading Area Comm Coll (PA)
Richmond Comm Coll (NC)

Rowan-Cabarrus Comm Coll (NC)
San Juan Coll (NM)
Seminole State Coll (OK)
Sheridan Coll (WY)
South Florida State Coll (FL)
Springfield Tech Comm Coll (MA)
Sullivan County Comm Coll (NY)
Treasure Valley Comm Coll (OR)
Truckee Meadows Comm Coll (NV)
U of New Mexico–Gallup (NM)
Vincennes U (IN)
Wayne Comm Coll (NC)
Wayne County Comm Coll District (MI)
Western Wyoming Comm Coll (WY)
Wor-Wic Comm Coll (MD)

EMERGENCY CARE ATTENDANT (EMT AMBULANCE)
Barton County Comm Coll (KS)
Illinois Eastern Comm Colls, Frontier Community College (IL)
Mohawk Valley Comm Coll (NY)

EMERGENCY MEDICAL TECHNOLOGY (EMT PARAMEDIC)
Allen Comm Coll (KS)
Alvin Comm Coll (TX)
Amarillo Coll (TX)
American River Coll (CA)
Arapahoe Comm Coll (CO)
Arizona Western Coll (AZ)
Athens Tech Coll (GA)
Augusta Tech Coll (GA)
Austin Comm Coll District (TX)
Barton County Comm Coll (KS)
Bevill State Comm Coll (AL)
Bismarck State Coll (ND)
Blue Ridge Comm and Tech Coll (WV)
Borough of Manhattan Comm Coll of the City U of New York (NY)
Bossier Parish Comm Coll (LA)
Brookhaven Coll (TX)
Bunker Hill Comm Coll (MA)
Caldwell Comm Coll and Tech Inst (NC)
Camden County Coll (NJ)
Cape Fear Comm Coll (NC)
Carroll Comm Coll (MD)
Casper Coll (WY)
Catawba Valley Comm Coll (NC)
Cecil Coll (MD)
Central New Mexico Comm Coll (NM)
Central Ohio Tech Coll (OH)
Central Oregon Comm Coll (OR)
Central Texas Coll (TX)
Central Virginia Comm Coll (VA)
Century Coll (MN)
Chesapeake Coll (MD)
Chippewa Valley Tech Coll (WI)
Cincinnati State Tech and Comm Coll (OH)
Clark Coll (WA)
Cleveland Comm Coll (NC)
Cochise County Comm Coll District (AZ)
Coll of Central Florida (FL)
Collin County Comm Coll District (TX)
Colorado Northwestern Comm Coll (CO)
Columbia Coll (CA)
Columbus Tech Coll (GA)
Comm Coll of Aurora (CO)
Comm Coll of Baltimore County (MD)
Crowder Coll (MO)
Daytona State Coll (FL)
Dutchess Comm Coll (NY)
Dyersburg State Comm Coll (TN)
East Central Coll (MO)
Eastern Arizona Coll (AZ)
Eastern Gateway Comm Coll (OH)
Erie Comm Coll, South Campus (NY)
Fayetteville Tech Comm Coll (NC)
Finger Lakes Comm Coll (NY)
Fiorello H. LaGuardia Comm Coll of the City U of New York (NY)
Florida SouthWestern State Coll (FL)
Fox Valley Tech Coll (WI)
Frederick Comm Coll (MD)
Gadsden State Comm Coll (AL)
Galveston Coll (TX)
Gateway Tech Coll (WI)
George C. Wallace Comm Coll (AL)
Great Basin Coll (NV)
Great Falls Coll Montana State U (MT)
Greenville Tech Coll (SC)
Gulf Coast State Coll (FL)
Gwinnett Tech Coll (GA)
Hagerstown Comm Coll (MD)
Harrisburg Area Comm Coll (PA)
Hawkeye Comm Coll (IA)
H. Councill Trenholm State Comm Coll (AL)
Herkimer County Comm Coll (NY)
Highland Comm Coll (IL)
Hillsborough Comm Coll (FL)
Hinds Comm Coll (MS)
Houston Comm Coll (TX)
Howard Comm Coll (MD)
Hudson County Comm Coll (NJ)
Hutchinson Comm Coll (KS)
Illinois Central Coll (IL)
Ivy Tech Comm Coll–Bloomington (IN)
Ivy Tech Comm Coll–Columbus (IN)
Ivy Tech Comm Coll–Kokomo (IN)
Ivy Tech Comm Coll–North Central (IN)
Ivy Tech Comm Coll–Richmond (IN)
Ivy Tech Comm Coll–Southwest (IN)
Ivy Tech Comm Coll–Wabash Valley (IN)
Jefferson Coll (MO)
Jefferson Comm Coll (NY)
Jefferson State Comm Coll (AL)
John Tyler Comm Coll (VA)
J. Sargeant Reynolds Comm Coll (VA)
Kankakee Comm Coll (IL)
Kaskaskia Coll (IL)
Kellogg Comm Coll (MI)
Kennebec Valley Comm Coll (ME)
Kent State U at Trumbull (OH)
Kilgore Coll (TX)
Kirtland Comm Coll (MI)
Lackawanna Coll (PA)
Lake Area Tech Inst (SD)
Lamar Comm Coll (CO)
Laramie County Comm Coll (WY)
Lenoir Comm Coll (NC)
Lone Star Coll–CyFair (TX)
Lone Star Coll–Montgomery (TX)
Lone Star Coll–North Harris (TX)
Lurleen B. Wallace Comm Coll (AL)
Luzerne County Comm Coll (PA)
Macomb Comm Coll (MI)
McHenry County Coll (IL)
Meridian Comm Coll (MS)
Miami Dade Coll (FL)
Mohave Comm Coll (AZ)
Moraine Valley Comm Coll (IL)
Mott Comm Coll (MI)
Mt. San Antonio Coll (CA)
New Mexico Jr Coll (NM)
Northcentral Tech Coll (WI)
North Central Texas Coll (TX)
Northeast Alabama Comm Coll (AL)
Northeastern Jr Coll (CO)
Northeast Iowa Comm Coll (IA)
Northern Essex Comm Coll (MA)
Northland Comm and Tech Coll (MN)
NorthWest Arkansas Comm Coll (AR)
Northwest-Shoals Comm Coll (AL)
Odessa Coll (TX)
Oklahoma City Comm Coll (OK)
Oklahoma State U, Oklahoma City (OK)
Owensboro Comm and Tech Coll (KY)
Ozarks Tech Comm Coll (MO)
Palomar Coll (CA)
Paris Jr Coll (TX)
Pennsylvania Highlands Comm Coll (PA)
Pensacola State Coll (FL)
Pueblo Comm Coll (CO)
Quinsigamond Comm Coll (MA)
Rend Lake Coll (IL)
Rogue Comm Coll (OR)
St. Charles Comm Coll (MO)
St. Clair County Comm Coll (MI)
San Jacinto Coll District (TX)
San Juan Coll (NM)
Schoolcraft Coll (MI)
Seminole State Coll of Florida (FL)
Southeast Comm Coll, Lincoln Campus (NE)
Southeastern Coll–West Palm Beach (FL)
Southeastern Comm Coll (IA)
Southern Crescent Tech Coll (GA)
Southern Maine Comm Coll (ME)
South Florida State Coll (FL)
Southwest Virginia Comm Coll (VA)
Tallahassee Comm Coll (FL)
Tarrant County Coll District (TX)
Tech Coll of the Lowcountry (SC)
Texarkana Coll (TX)
Tyler Jr Coll (TX)
U of Alaska Anchorage, Kenai Peninsula Coll (AK)
U of Cincinnati Blue Ash Coll (OH)
Victoria Coll (TX)
Vincennes U (IN)
Waukesha County Tech Coll (WI)
Wayne County Comm Coll District (MI)
Weatherford Coll (TX)
Westchester Comm Coll (NY)
Western Iowa Tech Comm Coll (IA)
Wisconsin Indianhead Tech Coll (WI)
Wor-Wic Comm Coll (MD)

ENERGY MANAGEMENT AND SYSTEMS TECHNOLOGY
Casper Coll (WY)
Century Coll (MN)
Cincinnati State Tech and Comm Coll (OH)
Clinton Comm Coll (NY)
Corning Comm Coll (NY)
Crowder Coll (MO)
Danville Area Comm Coll (IL)
Delta Coll (MI)
Fox Valley Tech Coll (WI)
Front Range Comm Coll (CO)
Hawkeye Comm Coll (IA)
Houston Comm Coll (TX)
Illinois Central Coll (IL)
Illinois Eastern Comm Colls, Wabash Valley College (IL)
Ivy Tech Comm Coll–East Central (IN)
Ivy Tech Comm Coll–Southern Indiana (IN)
Ivy Tech Comm Coll–Southwest (IN)
Ivy Tech Comm Coll–Wabash Valley (IN)
Lakeland Comm Coll (OH)
Laramie County Comm Coll (WY)
Lenoir Comm Coll (NC)
Macomb Comm Coll (MI)
Middlesex County Coll (NJ)
Minnesota West Comm and Tech Coll (MN)
Mitchell Tech Inst (SD)
Mount Wachusett Comm Coll (MA)
Northeast Iowa Comm Coll (IA)
Northwest Tech Coll (MN)
Quinsigamond Comm Coll (MA)
Rock Valley Coll (IL)
Rowan Coll at Burlington County (NJ)
St. Clair County Comm Coll (MI)
St. Philip's Coll (TX)
Southeast Comm Coll, Milford Campus (NE)
Truckee Meadows Comm Coll (NV)
Walters State Comm Coll (TN)
Wayne Comm Coll (NC)
Westchester Comm Coll (NY)
Western Iowa Tech Comm Coll (IA)
Williamson Coll of the Trades (PA)

ENGINEERING
Allen Comm Coll (KS)
Amarillo Coll (TX)
American River Coll (CA)
Anne Arundel Comm Coll (MD)
Arizona Western Coll (AZ)
Austin Comm Coll District (TX)
Berkshire Comm Coll (MA)
Borough of Manhattan Comm Coll of the City U of New York (NY)
Bossier Parish Comm Coll (LA)
Bunker Hill Comm Coll (MA)
Butler County Comm Coll (PA)
Ca&nnada Coll (CA)
Carl Albert State Coll (OK)
Casper Coll (WY)
Central Lakes Coll (MN)
Central Oregon Comm Coll (OR)
Central Texas Coll (TX)
Central Virginia Comm Coll (VA)
Central Wyoming Coll (WY)
Citrus Coll (CA)
Cochise County Comm Coll District (AZ)
Coll of Central Florida (FL)
Collin County Comm Coll District (TX)
Comm Coll of Baltimore County (MD)
Comm Coll of Philadelphia (PA)
Comm Coll of Rhode Island (RI)
Copiah-Lincoln Comm Coll (MS)
Danville Area Comm Coll (IL)
Daytona State Coll (FL)
Dodge City Comm Coll (KS)
Dutchess Comm Coll (NY)
East Central Coll (MO)
Elgin Comm Coll (IL)
Erie Comm Coll, North Campus (NY)
Frederick Comm Coll (MD)
Fullerton Coll (CA)
Genesee Comm Coll (NY)
Grand Rapids Comm Coll (MI)
Hagerstown Comm Coll (MD)
Harford Comm Coll (MD)
Harrisburg Area Comm Coll (PA)
Highland Comm Coll (IL)
Holyoke Comm Coll (MA)
Howard Comm Coll (MD)
Hutchinson Comm Coll (KS)
Illinois Central Coll (IL)
Illinois Eastern Comm Colls, Frontier Community College (IL)
Illinois Eastern Comm Colls, Olney Central College (IL)
Illinois Eastern Comm Colls, Wabash Valley College (IL)
Jamestown Comm Coll (NY)
Jefferson Coll (MO)
Jefferson Comm Coll (NY)
John Tyler Comm Coll (VA)
J. Sargeant Reynolds Comm Coll (VA)
Kankakee Comm Coll (IL)
Kaskaskia Coll (IL)
Laramie County Comm Coll (WY)
Lehigh Carbon Comm Coll (PA)
Lewis and Clark Comm Coll (IL)
Lorain County Comm Coll (OH)
Los Angeles Trade-Tech Coll (CA)
Los Angeles Valley Coll (CA)
Marion Military Inst (AL)
McHenry County Coll (IL)
Miami Dade Coll (FL)
Minnesota State Comm and Tech Coll–Moorhead (MN)
Mohawk Valley Comm Coll (NY)
Montgomery Coll (MD)
Moraine Valley Comm Coll (IL)
Navarro Coll (TX)
New Mexico Jr Coll (NM)
New River Comm Coll (VA)
Northampton Comm Coll (PA)
Northwest Coll (WY)
Oakton Comm Coll (IL)
Ocean County Coll (NJ)
Paris Jr Coll (TX)
Pensacola State Coll (FL)
Queensborough Comm Coll of the City U of New York (NY)
Reading Area Comm Coll (PA)
Rend Lake Coll (IL)
Rowan Coll at Burlington County (NJ)
St. Charles Comm Coll (MO)
St. Clair County Comm Coll (MI)
Salt Lake Comm Coll (UT)
San Jacinto Coll District (TX)
San Joaquin Delta Coll (CA)
San Juan Coll (NM)
Schoolcraft Coll (MI)
Seminole State Coll (OK)
Sheridan Coll (WY)
Sierra Coll (CA)
South Florida State Coll (FL)
Southwestern Indian Polytechnic Inst (NM)
Southwest Texas Jr Coll (TX)
Springfield Tech Comm Coll (MA)
State U of New York Coll of Technology at Alfred (NY)
Texarkana Coll (TX)
Tidewater Comm Coll (VA)
Tompkins Cortland Comm Coll (NY)
Truckee Meadows Comm Coll (NV)
Tunxis Comm Coll (CT)
Tyler Jr Coll (TX)
Virginia Western Comm Coll (VA)
Western Texas Coll (TX)

ENGINEERING/INDUSTRIAL MANAGEMENT
LDS Business Coll (UT)
Mitchell Comm Coll (NC)

ENGINEERING RELATED
Macomb Comm Coll (MI)
Miami Dade Coll (FL)
San Joaquin Delta Coll (CA)
Southeastern Comm Coll (IA)

ENGINEERING-RELATED TECHNOLOGIES
Chesapeake Coll (MD)
Thaddeus Stevens Coll of Technology (PA)
Tulsa Comm Coll (OK)

ENGINEERING SCIENCE
Asnuntuck Comm Coll (CT)
Camden County Coll (NJ)
City Colls of Chicago, Olive-Harvey College (IL)
Corning Comm Coll (NY)
County Coll of Morris (NJ)
Finger Lakes Comm Coll (NY)
Genesee Comm Coll (NY)
Houston Comm Coll (TX)
Hudson County Comm Coll (NJ)
Jefferson Comm Coll (NY)
Manchester Comm Coll (CT)
Mercer County Comm Coll (NJ)
Middlesex County Coll (NJ)
Monroe Comm Coll (NY)
Montgomery County Comm Coll (PA)
Naugatuck Valley Comm Coll (CT)
Northern Essex Comm Coll (MA)
North Shore Comm Coll (MA)
Norwalk Comm Coll (CT)
Onondaga Comm Coll (NY)
Queensborough Comm Coll of the City U of New York (NY)
Raritan Valley Comm Coll (NJ)
South Florida State Coll (FL)
Three Rivers Comm Coll (CT)
Westchester Comm Coll (NY)

ENGINEERING TECHNOLOGIES AND ENGINEERING RELATED
Camden County Coll (NJ)
Carl Albert State Coll (OK)
Cincinnati State Tech and Comm Coll (OH)
Clinton Comm Coll (NY)
Comm Coll of Baltimore County (MD)
County Coll of Morris (NJ)
Hagerstown Comm Coll (MD)
Harrisburg Area Comm Coll (PA)
Hudson County Comm Coll (NJ)
Massachusetts Bay Comm Coll (MA)
Middlesex County Coll (NJ)
Montgomery County Comm Coll (PA)
Mott Comm Coll (MI)
Ocean County Coll (NJ)
Oklahoma City Comm Coll (OK)
Orange Coast Coll (CA)
Pennsylvania Highlands Comm Coll (PA)
Quinsigamond Comm Coll (MA)
Raritan Valley Comm Coll (NJ)
Rowan Coll at Burlington County (NJ)
Truckee Meadows Comm Coll (NV)
Western Piedmont Comm Coll (NC)
Wor-Wic Comm Coll (MD)

ENGINEERING TECHNOLOGY
Allen Comm Coll (KS)
American River Coll (CA)
Antelope Valley Coll (CA)
Arapahoe Comm Coll (CO)
Asnuntuck Comm Coll (CT)
Barton County Comm Coll (KS)
Bismarck State Coll (ND)
Bucks County Comm Coll (PA)
Central Virginia Comm Coll (VA)
Citrus Coll (CA)
Coll of Central Florida (FL)
Collin County Comm Coll District (TX)
Comm Coll of Philadelphia (PA)
Corning Comm Coll (NY)
Dodge City Comm Coll (KS)
Elizabethtown Comm and Tech Coll, Elizabethtown (KY)
Gateway Comm and Tech Coll (KY)
Georgia Piedmont Tech Coll (GA)
Gulf Coast State Coll (FL)
Harford Comm Coll (MD)
Hillsborough Comm Coll (FL)
Ivy Tech Comm Coll–Bloomington (IN)
Ivy Tech Comm Coll–Columbus (IN)
Ivy Tech Comm Coll–East Central (IN)
Ivy Tech Comm Coll–Kokomo (IN)

Ivy Tech Comm Coll–Richmond (IN)
Ivy Tech Comm Coll–Southern Indiana (IN)
Ivy Tech Comm Coll–Southwest (IN)
Ivy Tech Comm Coll–Wabash Valley (IN)
Jefferson State Comm Coll (AL)
Lorain County Comm Coll (OH)
Luzerne County Comm Coll (PA)
Massachusetts Bay Comm Coll (MA)
Miami Dade Coll (FL)
Midlands Tech Coll (SC)
Minnesota State Comm and Tech Coll–Detroit Lakes (MN)
Mt. San Antonio Coll (CA)
Muskegon Comm Coll (MI)
Naugatuck Valley Comm Coll (CT)
Norco Coll (CA)
North Central Texas Coll (TX)
Oklahoma State U Inst of Technology (OK)
Oklahoma State U, Oklahoma City (OK)
Olympic Coll (WA)
Pasadena City Coll (CA)
Penn Foster Coll (AZ)
Pennsylvania Inst of Technology (PA)
Pensacola State Coll (FL)
Pueblo Comm Coll (CO)
Rappahannock Comm Coll (VA)
Salt Lake Comm Coll (UT)
San Joaquin Delta Coll (CA)
San Juan Coll (NM)
Somerset Comm Coll (KY)
South Florida State Coll (FL)
Southwestern Michigan Coll (MI)
Three Rivers Comm Coll (CT)
Tri-County Tech Coll (SC)
Tunxis Comm Coll (CT)
Vincennes U (IN)
Washington County Comm Coll (ME)
Westchester Comm Coll (NY)
Western Wyoming Comm Coll (WY)

ENGINE MACHINIST
Lake Area Tech Inst (SD)
Northwest Tech Coll (MN)

ENGLISH
Amarillo Coll (TX)
American River Coll (CA)
Ancilla Coll (IN)
Antelope Valley Coll (CA)
Arizona Western Coll (AZ)
Bainbridge State Coll (GA)
Barton County Comm Coll (KS)
Blinn Coll (TX)
Borough of Manhattan Comm Coll of the City U of New York (NY)
Bucks County Comm Coll (PA)
Bunker Hill Comm Coll (MA)
Butler County Comm Coll (PA)
Ca&nnada Coll (CA)
Carl Albert State Coll (OK)
Casper Coll (WY)
Central New Mexico Comm Coll (NM)
Central Wyoming Coll (WY)
Cerritos Coll (CA)
Citrus Coll (CA)
Cochise County Comm Coll District (AZ)
Coll of Central Florida (FL)
Coll of the Canyons (CA)
Columbia Coll (CA)
Copiah-Lincoln Comm Coll (MS)
Dean Coll (MA)
Dodge City Comm Coll (KS)
Eastern Arizona Coll (AZ)
Eastern Wyoming Coll (WY)
Edison Comm Coll (OH)
Feather River Coll (CA)
Fiorello H. LaGuardia Comm Coll of the City U of New York (NY)
Fullerton Coll (CA)
Galveston Coll (TX)
Georgia Highlands Coll (GA)
Georgia Military Coll (GA)
Gordon State Coll (GA)
Grand Rapids Comm Coll (MI)
Harford Comm Coll (MD)
Houston Comm Coll (TX)
Hutchinson Comm Coll (KS)
Itawamba Comm Coll (MS)
Kankakee Comm Coll (IL)
Kilgore Coll (TX)
Laramie County Comm Coll (WY)
Los Angeles Valley Coll (CA)
Massachusetts Bay Comm Coll (MA)
Miami Dade Coll (FL)
Mohave Comm Coll (AZ)
Moraine Valley Comm Coll (IL)
Nashville State Comm Coll (TN)

Navarro Coll (TX)
New Mexico Jr Coll (NM)
Northeastern Jr Coll (CO)
Northwest Coll (WY)
Odessa Coll (TX)
Oxnard Coll (CA)
Palomar Coll (CA)
Panola Coll (TX)
Paris Jr Coll (TX)
Pensacola State Coll (FL)
Potomac State Coll of West Virginia U (WV)
Raritan Valley Comm Coll (NJ)
Rowan Coll at Burlington County (NJ)
St. Charles Comm Coll (MO)
St. Philip's Coll (TX)
Salt Lake Comm Coll (UT)
San Jacinto Coll District (TX)
San Joaquin Delta Coll (CA)
Seminole State Coll (OK)
Sheridan Coll (WY)
Sierra Coll (CA)
South Florida State Coll (FL)
Spoon River Coll (IL)
Truckee Meadows Comm Coll (NV)
Vincennes U (IN)
Western Wyoming Comm Coll (WY)

ENGLISH AS A SECOND/ FOREIGN LANGUAGE (TEACHING)
Gordon State Coll (GA)

ENGLISH LANGUAGE AND LITERATURE RELATED
Citrus Coll (CA)
Mt. San Antonio Coll (CA)

ENGLISH/LANGUAGE ARTS TEACHER EDUCATION
Anne Arundel Comm Coll (MD)
Carroll Comm Coll (MD)
Cecil Coll (MD)
Hagerstown Comm Coll (MD)
Harford Comm Coll (MD)
Montgomery Coll (MD)
South Florida State Coll (FL)
Vincennes U (IN)

ENGLISH LITERATURE (BRITISH AND COMMONWEALTH)
Tyler Jr Coll (TX)

ENTOMOLOGY
South Florida State Coll (FL)

ENTREPRENEURIAL AND SMALL BUSINESS RELATED
LDS Business Coll (UT)
Truckee Meadows Comm Coll (NV)

ENTREPRENEURSHIP
Anne Arundel Comm Coll (MD)
Bunker Hill Comm Coll (MA)
Casper Coll (WY)
Catawba Valley Comm Coll (NC)
Central Oregon Comm Coll (OR)
Central Wyoming Coll (WY)
Cincinnati State Tech and Comm Coll (OH)
Cleveland Comm Coll (NC)
Craven Comm Coll (NC)
Eastern Arizona Coll (AZ)
Elgin Comm Coll (IL)
Genesee Comm Coll (NY)
Great Falls Coll Montana State U (MT)
Harford Comm Coll (MD)
Herkimer County Comm Coll (NY)
Lamar Comm Coll (CO)
Laramie County Comm Coll (WY)
LDS Business Coll (UT)
Miami Dade Coll (FL)
Minnesota State Comm and Tech Coll–Detroit Lakes (MN)
Mott Comm Coll (MI)
Northcentral Tech Coll (WI)
North Hennepin Comm Coll (MN)
Northland Comm and Tech Coll (MN)
Richmond Comm Coll (NC)
Salt Lake Comm Coll (UT)
Tallahassee Comm Coll (FL)
Three Rivers Comm Coll (CT)
Tompkins Cortland Comm Coll (NY)

ENVIRONMENTAL BIOLOGY
Eastern Arizona Coll (AZ)
Eastern Wyoming Coll (WY)

ENVIRONMENTAL CONTROL TECHNOLOGIES RELATED
Bismarck State Coll (ND)

Cincinnati State Tech and Comm Coll (OH)
Hillsborough Comm Coll (FL)
Holyoke Comm Coll (MA)
Massachusetts Bay Comm Coll (MA)
Middlesex County Coll (NJ)
Westchester Comm Coll (NY)

ENVIRONMENTAL DESIGN/ ARCHITECTURE
Central New Mexico Comm Coll (NM)
Queensborough Comm Coll of the City U of New York (NY)
Scottsdale Comm Coll (AZ)

ENVIRONMENTAL EDUCATION
New Mexico Jr Coll (NM)

ENVIRONMENTAL ENGINEERING TECHNOLOGY
Austin Comm Coll District (TX)
Cincinnati State Tech and Comm Coll (OH)
Crowder Coll (MO)
Delta Coll (MI)
Erie Comm Coll, North Campus (NY)
Georgia Northwestern Tech Coll (GA)
Harford Comm Coll (MD)
James H. Faulkner State Comm Coll (AL)
Kent State U at Trumbull (OH)
Miami Dade Coll (FL)
Naugatuck Valley Comm Coll (CT)
Northwest-Shoals Comm Coll (AL)
Onondaga Comm Coll (NY)
Oxnard Coll (CA)
Queensborough Comm Coll of the City U of New York (NY)
Salt Lake Comm Coll (UT)
Schoolcraft Coll (MI)
Sheridan Coll (WY)
State U of New York Coll of Technology at Alfred (NY)
Texas State Tech Coll (TX)
Three Rivers Comm Coll (CT)
Wor-Wic Comm Coll (MD)

ENVIRONMENTAL/ ENVIRONMENTAL HEALTH ENGINEERING
Central Wyoming Coll (WY)
South Florida State Coll (FL)

ENVIRONMENTAL HEALTH
Amarillo Coll (TX)
Comm Coll of the Air Force (AL)
Queensborough Comm Coll of the City U of New York (NY)

ENVIRONMENTAL SCIENCE
Anoka-Ramsey Comm Coll (MN)
Arizona Western Coll (AZ)
Bucks County Comm Coll (PA)
Casper Coll (WY)
Central Texas Coll (TX)
Central Wyoming Coll (WY)
Columbia Coll (CA)
Corning Comm Coll (NY)
Erie Comm Coll, North Campus (NY)
Fiorello H. LaGuardia Comm Coll of the City U of New York (NY)
Gordon State Coll (GA)
Harford Comm Coll (MD)
Harrisburg Area Comm Coll (PA)
Humacao Comm Coll (PR)
Jamestown Comm Coll (NY)
Keweenaw Bay Ojibwa Comm Coll (MI)
Lake Area Tech Inst (SD)
Lehigh Carbon Comm Coll (PA)
Miami Dade Coll (FL)
Montgomery County Comm Coll (PA)
Northampton Comm Coll (PA)
NorthWest Arkansas Comm Coll (AR)
Ocean County Coll (NJ)
Pennsylvania Highlands Comm Coll (PA)
Quinsigamond Comm Coll (MA)
Rowan Coll at Burlington County (NJ)
St. Philip's Coll (TX)
San Jacinto Coll District (TX)
South Florida State Coll (FL)
State U of New York Coll of Technology at Alfred (NY)
Tallahassee Comm Coll (FL)
Truckee Meadows Comm Coll (NV)
Tulsa Comm Coll (OK)
Tyler Jr Coll (TX)
Westchester Comm Coll (NY)
Western Piedmont Comm Coll (NC)
Western Wyoming Comm Coll (WY)

ENVIRONMENTAL STUDIES
Ancilla Coll (IN)
Berkshire Comm Coll (MA)
Coll of Central Florida (FL)
Columbia-Greene Comm Coll (NY)
Comm Coll of the Air Force (AL)
Dean Coll (MA)
Feather River Coll (CA)
Finger Lakes Comm Coll (NY)
Fullerton Coll (CA)
Harrisburg Area Comm Coll (PA)
Housatonic Comm Coll (CT)
Howard Comm Coll (MD)
Hudson County Comm Coll (NJ)
Lackawanna Coll (PA)
Monroe Comm Coll (NY)
Mount Wachusett Comm Coll (MA)
New Mexico Jr Coll (NM)
Oxnard Coll (CA)
Stark State Coll (OH)
Sullivan County Comm Coll (NY)
Tompkins Cortland Comm Coll (NY)
Westchester Comm Coll (NY)
White Mountains Comm Coll (NH)

EQUESTRIAN STUDIES
Allen Comm Coll (KS)
Central Wyoming Coll (WY)
Cochise County Comm Coll District (AZ)
Coll of Central Florida (FL)
Colorado Northwestern Comm Coll (CO)
Dodge City Comm Coll (KS)
Highland Comm Coll (IL)
Lamar Comm Coll (CO)
Laramie County Comm Coll (WY)
Martin Comm Coll (NC)
North Central Texas Coll (TX)
Northeastern Jr Coll (CO)
Northwest Coll (WY)
Scottsdale Comm Coll (AZ)
Sierra Coll (CA)

ETHNIC, CULTURAL MINORITY, GENDER, AND GROUP STUDIES RELATED
Fullerton Coll (CA)
Los Angeles Valley Coll (CA)

EXECUTIVE ASSISTANT/ EXECUTIVE SECRETARY
Alamance Comm Coll (NC)
Alvin Comm Coll (TX)
Bellingham Tech Coll (WA)
Brookhaven Coll (TX)
Cape Fear Comm Coll (NC)
Cincinnati State Tech and Comm Coll (OH)
Clark Coll (WA)
Crowder Coll (MO)
Danville Area Comm Coll (IL)
Edison Comm Coll (OH)
Elgin Comm Coll (IL)
Elizabethtown Comm and Tech Coll, Elizabethtown (KY)
Hawkeye Comm Coll (IA)
Hillsborough Comm Coll (FL)
Hopkinsville Comm Coll (KY)
Humacao Comm Coll (PR)
Illinois Eastern Comm Colls, Frontier Community College (IL)
Illinois Eastern Comm Colls, Wabash Valley College (IL)
Ivy Tech Comm Coll–Bloomington (IN)
Ivy Tech Comm Coll–Central Indiana (IN)
Ivy Tech Comm Coll–Columbus (IN)
Ivy Tech Comm Coll–East Central (IN)
Ivy Tech Comm Coll–Kokomo (IN)
Ivy Tech Comm Coll–Lafayette (IN)
Ivy Tech Comm Coll–North Central (IN)
Ivy Tech Comm Coll–Northeast (IN)
Ivy Tech Comm Coll–Northwest (IN)
Ivy Tech Comm Coll–Richmond (IN)
Ivy Tech Comm Coll–Southeast (IN)
Ivy Tech Comm Coll–Southern Indiana (IN)
Ivy Tech Comm Coll–Southwest (IN)
Ivy Tech Comm Coll–Wabash Valley (IN)
Kaskaskia Coll (IL)
Kellogg Comm Coll (MI)
Kilgore Coll (TX)
Lake Land Coll (IL)
Luzerne County Comm Coll (PA)
Mitchell Comm Coll (NC)
Owensboro Comm and Tech Coll (KY)

ENVIRONMENTAL STUDIES
Pensacola State Coll (FL)
Quinsigamond Comm Coll (MA)
St. Clair County Comm Coll (MI)
Schoolcraft Coll (MI)
Somerset Comm Coll (KY)
South Suburban Coll (IL)
Thaddeus Stevens Coll of Technology (PA)
U of Cincinnati Blue Ash Coll (OH)
Western Piedmont Comm Coll (NC)
Westmoreland County Comm Coll (PA)

EXERCISE PHYSIOLOGY
Quincy Coll (MA)

FACILITIES PLANNING AND MANAGEMENT
Comm Coll of Philadelphia (PA)

FAMILY AND COMMUNITY SERVICES
Oxnard Coll (CA)
Palomar Coll (CA)
Rogue Comm Coll (OR)
Westmoreland County Comm Coll (PA)

FAMILY AND CONSUMER ECONOMICS RELATED
American Samoa Comm Coll (AS)

FAMILY AND CONSUMER SCIENCES/HOME ECONOMICS TEACHER EDUCATION
Copiah-Lincoln Comm Coll (MS)
Itawamba Comm Coll (MS)
South Florida State Coll (FL)
Vincennes U (IN)

FAMILY AND CONSUMER SCIENCES/HUMAN SCIENCES
Allen Comm Coll (KS)
Antelope Valley Coll (CA)
Arizona Western Coll (AZ)
Bainbridge State Coll (GA)
Coll of Central Florida (FL)
Hutchinson Comm Coll (KS)
Itawamba Comm Coll (MS)
Monroe Comm Coll (NY)
Mt. San Antonio Coll (CA)
Orange Coast Coll (CA)
Palomar Coll (CA)
San Joaquin Delta Coll (CA)
Tyler Jr Coll (TX)
Vincennes U (IN)

FAMILY SYSTEMS
American River Coll (CA)

FARM AND RANCH MANAGEMENT
Allen Comm Coll (KS)
Bismarck State Coll (ND)
Central Texas Coll (TX)
Copiah-Lincoln Comm Coll (MS)
Crowder Coll (MO)
Dodge City Comm Coll (KS)
Eastern Wyoming Coll (WY)
Hutchinson Comm Coll (KS)
Lamar Comm Coll (CO)
North Central Texas Coll (TX)
Northeastern Jr Coll (CO)
Northland Comm and Tech Coll (MN)
Northwest Coll (WY)
Southwest Texas Jr Coll (TX)
Treasure Valley Comm Coll (OR)

FASHION/APPAREL DESIGN
Academy of Couture Art (CA)
American River Coll (CA)
Ca&nnada Coll (CA)
Cerritos Coll (CA)
Clary Sage Coll (OK)
Fashion Inst of Technology (NY)
Fashion Inst of Design & Merchandising, LA Campus (CA)
FIDM/Fashion Inst of Design & Merchandising, Orange County Campus (CA)
FIDM/Fashion Inst of Design & Merchandising, San Diego Campus (CA)
Fullerton Coll (CA)
Genesee Comm Coll (NY)
Houston Comm Coll (TX)
Itawamba Comm Coll (MS)
Lehigh Carbon Comm Coll (PA)
Los Angeles Trade-Tech Coll (CA)
Monroe Comm Coll (NY)
Orange Coast Coll (CA)
Palomar Coll (CA)

Pasadena City Coll (CA)
Rowan Coll at Burlington County (NJ)
Wood Tobe–Coburn School (NY)

FASHION MERCHANDISING
Alexandria Tech and Comm Coll (MN)
Berkeley Coll–White Plains Campus (NY)
Fashion Inst of Technology (NY)
Fashion Inst of Design & Merchandising, LA Campus (CA)
FIDM/Fashion Inst of Design & Merchandising, Orange County Campus (CA)
FIDM/Fashion Inst of Design & Merchandising, San Diego Campus (CA)
Genesee Comm Coll (NY)
Grand Rapids Comm Coll (MI)
Herkimer County Comm Coll (NY)
Hinds Comm Coll (MS)
Houston Comm Coll (TX)
Los Angeles Trade-Tech Coll (CA)
Monroe Comm Coll (NY)
Mt. San Antonio Coll (CA)
Pasadena City Coll (CA)
Penn Foster Coll (AZ)
San Joaquin Delta Coll (CA)
Scottsdale Comm Coll (AZ)
Tarrant County Coll District (TX)
Vincennes U (IN)

FASHION MODELING
Fashion Inst of Technology (NY)

FILM/CINEMA/VIDEO STUDIES
Fashion Inst of Technology (NY)
Palomar Coll (CA)

FILM/VIDEO AND PHOTOGRAPHIC ARTS RELATED
Westchester Comm Coll (NY)

FINANCE
Bunker Hill Comm Coll (MA)
Chipola Coll (FL)
Comm Coll of Philadelphia (PA)
Comm Coll of the Air Force (AL)
Dodge City Comm Coll (KS)
Lorain County Comm Coll (OH)
Macomb Comm Coll (MI)
Miami Dade Coll (FL)
Mt. San Antonio Coll (CA)
Muskegon Comm Coll (MI)
Naugatuck Valley Comm Coll (CT)
New Mexico Jr Coll (NM)
Northern Essex Comm Coll (MA)
North Hennepin Comm Coll (MN)
NorthWest Arkansas Comm Coll (AR)
Norwalk Comm Coll (CT)
Penn Foster Coll (AZ)
Salt Lake Comm Coll (UT)
Scottsdale Comm Coll (AZ)
Seminole State Coll of Florida (FL)
Southeast Tech Inst (SD)
South Florida State Coll (FL)
Spoon River Coll (IL)
Stark State Coll (OH)
Tidewater Comm Coll (VA)
Vincennes U (IN)
Westchester Comm Coll (NY)
Western Iowa Tech Comm Coll (IA)
Wisconsin Indianhead Tech Coll (WI)

FINANCIAL PLANNING AND SERVICES
Barton County Comm Coll (KS)
Cecil Coll (MD)
Cincinnati State Tech and Comm Coll (OH)
Howard Comm Coll (MD)
Raritan Valley Comm Coll (NJ)

FINE ARTS RELATED
Bunker Hill Comm Coll (MA)
Butler County Comm Coll (PA)
Corning Comm Coll (NY)
County Coll of Morris (NJ)
Quincy Coll (MA)
Schoolcraft Coll (MI)
Seminole State Coll (OK)
Truckee Meadows Comm Coll (NV)

FINE/STUDIO ARTS
Amarillo Coll (TX)
Anoka-Ramsey Comm Coll (MN)
Arizona Western Coll (AZ)

Caldwell Comm Coll and Tech Inst (NC)
Camden County Coll (NJ)
Casper Coll (WY)
Cayuga County Comm Coll (NY)
Cecil Coll (MD)
Central Texas Coll (TX)
Century Coll (MN)
Chandler-Gilbert Comm Coll (AZ)
City Colls of Chicago, Olive-Harvey College (IL)
Corning Comm Coll (NY)
Delta Coll (MI)
East Central Coll (MO)
Elgin Comm Coll (IL)
Fashion Inst of Technology (NY)
Finger Lakes Comm Coll (NY)
Fiorello H. LaGuardia Comm Coll of the City U of New York (NY)
Genesee Comm Coll (NY)
Harford Comm Coll (MD)
Houston Comm Coll (TX)
Hudson County Comm Coll (NJ)
Ivy Tech Comm Coll–Bloomington (IN)
Jamestown Comm Coll (NY)
Lake Superior Coll (MN)
Manchester Comm Coll (CT)
McHenry County Coll (IL)
Niagara County Comm Coll (NY)
Northampton Comm Coll (PA)
Northeastern Jr Coll (CO)
North Hennepin Comm Coll (MN)
Norwalk Comm Coll (CT)
Oklahoma City Comm Coll (OK)
Owensboro Comm and Tech Coll (KY)
Oxnard Coll (CA)
Queensborough Comm Coll of the City U of New York (NY)
Raritan Valley Comm Coll (NJ)
Rend Lake Coll (IL)
South Florida State Coll (FL)
South Suburban Coll (IL)
Springfield Tech Comm Coll (MA)
Three Rivers Comm Coll (CT)
Tidewater Comm Coll (VA)
Tulsa Comm Coll (OK)
Westchester Comm Coll (NY)

FIRE PREVENTION AND SAFETY TECHNOLOGY
Anne Arundel Comm Coll (MD)
Antelope Valley Coll (CA)
Austin Comm Coll District (TX)
Bunker Hill Comm Coll (MA)
Camden County Coll (NJ)
Cape Fear Comm Coll (NC)
Catawba Valley Comm Coll (NC)
Cleveland Comm Coll (NC)
Coll of the Canyons (CA)
Collin County Comm Coll District (TX)
County Coll of Morris (NJ)
Delta Coll (MI)
Fayetteville Tech Comm Coll (NC)
Florida SouthWestern State Coll (FL)
Gulf Coast State Coll (FL)
Hillsborough Comm Coll (FL)
Houston Comm Coll (TX)
Jefferson Coll (MO)
Jefferson Comm Coll (NY)
Lakeland Comm Coll (OH)
Lake Superior Coll (MN)
Macomb Comm Coll (MI)
Middlesex County Coll (NJ)
Montgomery Coll (MD)
Montgomery County Comm Coll (PA)
Moraine Valley Comm Coll (IL)
Mott Comm Coll (MI)
Mount Wachusett Comm Coll (MA)
Northland Comm and Tech Coll (MN)
Oklahoma State U, Oklahoma City (OK)
Onondaga Comm Coll (NY)
Oxnard Coll (CA)
Palomar Coll (CA)
Pasadena City Coll (CA)
Rogue Comm Coll (OR)
South Florida State Coll (FL)
Springfield Tech Comm Coll (MA)
Sullivan County Comm Coll (NY)
Treasure Valley Comm Coll (OR)
Truckee Meadows Comm Coll (NV)
Victor Valley Coll (CA)
Wayne County Comm Coll District (MI)
Westmoreland County Comm Coll (PA)

FIRE PROTECTION RELATED
Fox Valley Tech Coll (WI)

FIRE SCIENCE/FIREFIGHTING
Amarillo Coll (TX)
American River Coll (CA)
Arizona Western Coll (AZ)
Augusta Tech Coll (GA)
Barton County Comm Coll (KS)
Berkshire Comm Coll (MA)
Blackhawk Tech Coll (WI)
Blinn Coll (TX)
Butler County Comm Coll (PA)
Casper Coll (WY)
Cecil Coll (MD)
Central New Mexico Comm Coll (NM)
Central Ohio Tech Coll (OH)
Central Oregon Comm Coll (OR)
Central Wyoming Coll (WY)
Chattahoochee Tech Coll (GA)
Cincinnati State Tech and Comm Coll (OH)
Cochise County Comm Coll District (AZ)
Coll of Central Florida (FL)
Collin County Comm Coll District (TX)
Columbia Coll (CA)
Comm Coll of Aurora (CO)
Comm Coll of Philadelphia (PA)
Comm Coll of Rhode Island (RI)
Comm Coll of the Air Force (AL)
Crowder Coll (MO)
Danville Area Comm Coll (IL)
Daytona State Coll (FL)
Delta Coll (MI)
Dodge City Comm Coll (KS)
East Central Coll (MO)
Eastern Arizona Coll (AZ)
Eastern Idaho Tech Coll (ID)
Elgin Comm Coll (IL)
Elizabethtown Comm and Tech Coll, Elizabethtown (KY)
Fox Valley Tech Coll (WI)
Frederick Comm Coll (MD)
Gateway Comm and Tech Coll (KY)
Georgia Northwestern Tech Coll (GA)
Greenville Tech Coll (SC)
Harrisburg Area Comm Coll (PA)
Hawkeye Comm Coll (IA)
Hennepin Tech Coll (MN)
Hutchinson Comm Coll (KS)
Ilisagvik Coll (AK)
Illinois Central Coll (IL)
Illinois Eastern Comm Colls, Frontier Community College (IL)
J. Sargeant Reynolds Comm Coll (VA)
Lanier Tech Coll (GA)
Laramie County Comm Coll (WY)
Lewis and Clark Comm Coll (IL)
Lone Star Coll–CyFair (TX)
Lone Star Coll–Kingwood (TX)
Lone Star Coll–Montgomery (TX)
Lorain County Comm Coll (OH)
Los Angeles Valley Coll (CA)
Luzerne County Comm Coll (PA)
McHenry County Coll (IL)
Mercer County Comm Coll (NJ)
Meridian Comm Coll (MS)
Miami Dade Coll (FL)
Mid-Plains Comm Coll, North Platte (NE)
Mohave Comm Coll (AZ)
Monroe Comm Coll (NY)
Moraine Valley Comm Coll (IL)
Mt. San Antonio Coll (CA)
Navarro Coll (TX)
New Mexico Jr Coll (NM)
Northampton Comm Coll (PA)
Northeast Iowa Comm Coll (IA)
Northland Comm and Tech Coll (MN)
North Shore Comm Coll (MA)
Norwalk Comm Coll (CT)
Oakton Comm Coll (IL)
Odessa Coll (TX)
Oklahoma State U, Oklahoma City (OK)
Owensboro Comm and Tech Coll (KY)
Oxnard Coll (CA)
Ozarks Tech Comm Coll (MO)
Pueblo Comm Coll (CO)
Richland Comm Coll (IL)
Rock Valley Coll (IL)
Rowan Coll at Burlington County (NJ)
St. Charles Comm Coll (MO)

St. Clair County Comm Coll (MI)
San Jacinto Coll District (TX)
San Joaquin Delta Coll (CA)
San Juan Coll (NM)
Savannah Tech Coll (GA)
Schenectady County Comm Coll (NY)
Schoolcraft Coll (MI)
Seminole State Coll of Florida (FL)
Sierra Coll (CA)
Southeast Comm Coll, Lincoln Campus (NE)
Southern Maine Comm Coll (ME)
Southwestern Michigan Coll (MI)
Southwestern Oregon Comm Coll (OR)
Southwest Tennessee Comm Coll (TN)
Stark State Coll (OH)
Tallahassee Comm Coll (FL)
Tarrant County Coll District (TX)
Treasure Valley Comm Coll (OR)
Tyler Jr Coll (TX)
Victoria Coll (TX)
Victor Valley Coll (CA)
Vincennes U (IN)
Volunteer State Comm Coll (TN)
Waukesha County Tech Coll (WI)
Weatherford Coll (TX)
Western Iowa Tech Comm Coll (IA)
West Georgia Tech Coll (GA)
Wiregrass Georgia Tech Coll (GA)

FIRE SERVICES ADMINISTRATION
Camden County Coll (NJ)
Central Texas Coll (TX)
Delta Coll (MI)
Dutchess Comm Coll (NY)
Erie Comm Coll, South Campus (NY)
Jefferson Comm Coll (NY)
Jefferson State Comm Coll (AL)
Mohawk Valley Comm Coll (NY)
Naugatuck Valley Comm Coll (CT)
Northampton Comm Coll (PA)
NorthWest Arkansas Comm Coll (AR)
Oxnard Coll (CA)
Quinsigamond Comm Coll (MA)
Tech Coll of the Lowcountry (SC)
Three Rivers Comm Coll (CT)
Tulsa Comm Coll (OK)

FISHING AND FISHERIES SCIENCES AND MANAGEMENT
Bellingham Tech Coll (WA)
Central Oregon Comm Coll (OR)
Finger Lakes Comm Coll (NY)

FLORICULTURE/FLORISTRY MANAGEMENT
Danville Area Comm Coll (IL)
J. Sargeant Reynolds Comm Coll (VA)
Westmoreland County Comm Coll (PA)

FOOD SCIENCE
Miami Dade Coll (FL)
South Florida State Coll (FL)
Vincennes U (IN)

FOOD SERVICE AND DINING ROOM MANAGEMENT
LDS Business Coll (UT)
Pasadena City Coll (CA)
Westmoreland County Comm Coll (PA)

FOOD SERVICE SYSTEMS ADMINISTRATION
American River Coll (CA)
Bucks County Comm Coll (PA)
Butler County Comm Coll (PA)
Mott Comm Coll (MI)
Pensacola State Coll (FL)
Rowan Coll at Burlington County (NJ)
San Jacinto Coll District (TX)
Wayne County Comm Coll District (MI)

FOODS, NUTRITION, AND WELLNESS
Bossier Parish Comm Coll (LA)
Carl Albert State Coll (OK)
Central New Mexico Comm Coll (NM)
Feather River Coll (CA)
Fullerton Coll (CA)

North Shore Comm Coll (MA)
Orange Coast Coll (CA)
Pensacola State Coll (FL)
Truckee Meadows Comm Coll (NV)

FOOD TECHNOLOGY AND PROCESSING
Butler County Comm Coll (PA)
Cerritos Coll (CA)
Copiah-Lincoln Comm Coll (MS)
Genesee Comm Coll (NY)
Luzerne County Comm Coll (PA)
Monroe Comm Coll (NY)
Richland Comm Coll (IL)
Stark State Coll (OH)
Tarrant County Coll District (TX)
Victor Valley Coll (CA)
Westchester Comm Coll (NY)

FOREIGN LANGUAGES AND LITERATURES
Borough of Manhattan Comm Coll of the City U of New York (NY)
Bunker Hill Comm Coll (MA)
Casper Coll (WY)
Central New Mexico Comm Coll (NM)
Central Oregon Comm Coll (OR)
Central Texas Coll (TX)
Coll of Central Florida (FL)
Eastern Arizona Coll (AZ)
Eastern Wyoming Coll (WY)
Fullerton Coll (CA)
Georgia Highlands Coll (GA)
Gordon State Coll (GA)
Grand Rapids Comm Coll (MI)
Hutchinson Comm Coll (KS)
Los Angeles Valley Coll (CA)
Oklahoma City Comm Coll (OK)
Orange Coast Coll (CA)
Palomar Coll (CA)
Panola Coll (TX)
Paris Jr Coll (TX)
St. Charles Comm Coll (MO)
San Jacinto Coll District (TX)
South Florida State Coll (FL)
Texarkana Coll (TX)
Tyler Jr Coll (TX)
Vincennes U (IN)

FOREIGN LANGUAGES RELATED
Genesee Comm Coll (NY)
Nashville State Comm Coll (TN)
Tulsa Comm Coll (OK)
Vincennes U (IN)

FOREIGN LANGUAGE TEACHER EDUCATION
South Florida State Coll (FL)

FORENSIC SCIENCE AND TECHNOLOGY
American Samoa Comm Coll (AS)
Borough of Manhattan Comm Coll of the City U of New York (NY)
Carroll Comm Coll (MD)
Casper Coll (WY)
Central Ohio Tech Coll (OH)
Comm Coll of Philadelphia (PA)
Fayetteville Tech Comm Coll (NC)
Florida SouthWestern State Coll (FL)
Fox Valley Tech Coll (WI)
Gulf Coast State Coll (FL)
Herkimer County Comm Coll (NY)
Illinois Central Coll (IL)
Macomb Comm Coll (MI)
Miami Dade Coll (FL)
New River Comm Coll (VA)
Palomar Coll (CA)
Pensacola State Coll (FL)
Potomac State Coll of West Virginia U (WV)
Queensborough Comm Coll of the City U of New York (NY)
South Florida State Coll (FL)
Sullivan County Comm Coll (NY)
Tunxis Comm Coll (CT)
U of Arkansas Comm Coll at Morrilton (AR)
Wayne Comm Coll (NC)

FOREST RESOURCES PRODUCTION AND MANAGEMENT
Potomac State Coll of West Virginia U (WV)

FORESTRY
Allen Comm Coll (KS)
Barton County Comm Coll (KS)

Central Oregon Comm Coll (OR)
Coll of Central Florida (FL)
Columbia Coll (CA)
Copiah-Lincoln Comm Coll (MS)
Dodge City Comm Coll (KS)
Eastern Arizona Coll (AZ)
Gordon State Coll (GA)
Grand Rapids Comm Coll (MI)
Miami Dade Coll (FL)
Monroe Comm Coll (NY)
Panola Coll (TX)
Sierra Coll (CA)
South Florida State Coll (FL)
Western Wyoming Comm Coll (WY)

FOREST TECHNOLOGY
Albany Tech Coll (GA)
Central Oregon Comm Coll (OR)
Coastal Pines Tech Coll (GA)
Dabney S. Lancaster Comm Coll (VA)
Itawamba Comm Coll (MS)
Lurleen B. Wallace Comm Coll (AL)
Montgomery Comm Coll (NC)
Mt. San Antonio Coll (CA)
Ogeechee Tech Coll (GA)
Penn State Mont Alto (PA)
Wayne Comm Coll (NC)

FRENCH
Austin Comm Coll District (TX)
Blinn Coll (TX)
Cerritos Coll (CA)
Citrus Coll (CA)
Coll of the Canyons (CA)
Los Angeles Valley Coll (CA)
Miami Dade Coll (FL)
Palomar Coll (CA)
St. Charles Comm Coll (MO)
South Florida State Coll (FL)

FUNERAL SERVICE AND MORTUARY SCIENCE
Amarillo Coll (TX)
American River Coll (CA)
Arapahoe Comm Coll (CO)
Barton County Comm Coll (KS)
Comm Coll of Baltimore County (MD)
Dallas Inst of Funeral Service (TX)
Fayetteville Tech Comm Coll (NC)
Fiorello H. LaGuardia Comm Coll of the City U of New York (NY)
Ivy Tech Comm Coll–Northwest (IN)
Jefferson State Comm Coll (AL)
John A. Gupton Coll (TN)
John Tyler Comm Coll (VA)
Luzerne County Comm Coll (PA)
Mercer County Comm Coll (NJ)
Miami Dade Coll (FL)
Northampton Comm Coll (PA)
Ogeechee Tech Coll (GA)
Randolph Comm Coll (NC)
Vincennes U (IN)

FURNITURE DESIGN AND MANUFACTURING
Northcentral Tech Coll (WI)

GAME AND INTERACTIVE MEDIA DESIGN
Arapahoe Comm Coll (CO)
Cayuga County Comm Coll (NY)
Collin County Comm Coll District (TX)
Fayetteville Tech Comm Coll (NC)
Hinds Comm Coll (MS)
Lehigh Carbon Comm Coll (PA)
Oklahoma City Comm Coll (OK)
Quinsigamond Comm Coll (MA)
Texas State Tech Coll (TX)
Wayne Comm Coll (NC)
Wayne County Comm Coll District (MI)
Western Iowa Tech Comm Coll (IA)
Western Piedmont Comm Coll (NC)

GENERAL STUDIES
Allen Comm Coll (KS)
Alvin Comm Coll (TX)
Amarillo Coll (TX)
Ancilla Coll (IN)
Arapahoe Comm Coll (CO)
Arizona Western Coll (AZ)
Asnuntuck Comm Coll (CT)
Austin Comm Coll District (TX)
Barton County Comm Coll (KS)
Bevill State Comm Coll (AL)
Blue Ridge Comm and Tech Coll (WV)
Borough of Manhattan Comm Coll of the City U of New York (NY)
Bossier Parish Comm Coll (LA)

Brookhaven Coll (TX)
Bunker Hill Comm Coll (MA)
Butler County Comm Coll (PA)
Carroll Comm Coll (MD)
Casper Coll (WY)
Catawba Valley Comm Coll (NC)
Cayuga County Comm Coll (NY)
Cecil Coll (MD)
Central New Mexico Comm Coll (NM)
Central Texas Coll (TX)
Central Wyoming Coll (WY)
Chandler-Gilbert Comm Coll (AZ)
Chesapeake Coll (MD)
Cincinnati State Tech and Comm Coll (OH)
City Colls of Chicago, Olive-Harvey College (IL)
Cleveland Comm Coll (NC)
Cleveland State Comm Coll (TN)
Cochise County Comm Coll District (AZ)
Colorado Northwestern Comm Coll (CO)
Columbia-Greene Comm Coll (NY)
Comm Coll of Aurora (CO)
Comm Coll of Rhode Island (RI)
Craven Comm Coll (NC)
Crowder Coll (MO)
Danville Area Comm Coll (IL)
Dean Coll (MA)
Delta Coll (MI)
Dutchess Comm Coll (NY)
Dyersburg State Comm Coll (TN)
East Central Coll (MO)
Eastern Wyoming Coll (WY)
Erie Comm Coll (NY)
Erie Comm Coll, North Campus (NY)
Erie Comm Coll, South Campus (NY)
Estrella Mountain Comm Coll (AZ)
Fayetteville Tech Comm Coll (NC)
Frederick Comm Coll (MD)
Front Range Comm Coll (CO)
Gadsden State Comm Coll (AL)
Galveston Coll (TX)
Gateway Comm and Tech Coll (KY)
Genesee Comm Coll (NY)
Georgia Highlands Coll (GA)
Georgia Military Coll (GA)
Gordon State Coll (GA)
Great Basin Coll (NV)
Harford Comm Coll (MD)
Harrisburg Area Comm Coll (PA)
Herkimer County Comm Coll (NY)
Hesston Coll (KS)
Highland Comm Coll (IL)
Hinds Comm Coll (MS)
Houston Comm Coll (TX)
Howard Comm Coll (MD)
Illinois Central Coll (IL)
Illinois Eastern Comm Colls, Frontier Community College (IL)
Illinois Eastern Comm Colls, Lincoln Trail College (IL)
Illinois Eastern Comm Colls, Olney Central College (IL)
Illinois Eastern Comm Colls, Wabash Valley College (IL)
Ivy Tech Comm Coll–Bloomington (IN)
Ivy Tech Comm Coll–Central Indiana (IN)
Ivy Tech Comm Coll–Columbus (IN)
Ivy Tech Comm Coll–East Central (IN)
Ivy Tech Comm Coll–Kokomo (IN)
Ivy Tech Comm Coll–Lafayette (IN)
Ivy Tech Comm Coll–North Central (IN)
Ivy Tech Comm Coll–Northwest (IN)
Ivy Tech Comm Coll–Richmond (IN)
Ivy Tech Comm Coll–Southeast (IN)
Ivy Tech Comm Coll–Southern Indiana (IN)
Ivy Tech Comm Coll–Southwest (IN)
Ivy Tech Comm Coll–Wabash Valley (IN)
James H. Faulkner State Comm Coll (AL)
James Sprunt Comm Coll (NC)
Jamestown Comm Coll (NY)
Jefferson State Comm Coll (AL)
John Tyler Comm Coll (VA)
Kankakee Comm Coll (IL)
Kaskaskia Coll (IL)
Kellogg Comm Coll (MI)
Kilgore Coll (TX)
Kirtland Comm Coll (MI)
Lackawanna Coll (PA)
Lake Land Coll (IL)
Laramie County Comm Coll (WY)
Lehigh Carbon Comm Coll (PA)

Lewis and Clark Comm Coll (IL)
Lurleen B. Wallace Comm Coll (AL)
Luzerne County Comm Coll (PA)
Macomb Comm Coll (MI)
Manchester Comm Coll (CT)
Marion Military Inst (AL)
Martin Comm Coll (NC)
Massachusetts Bay Comm Coll (MA)
McHenry County Coll (IL)
Miami Dade Coll (FL)
Mitchell Comm Coll (NC)
Mohawk Valley Comm Coll (NY)
Morgan Comm Coll (CO)
Mott Comm Coll (MI)
Mount Wachusett Comm Coll (MA)
Naugatuck Valley Comm Coll (CT)
New River Comm Coll (VA)
Niagara County Comm Coll (NY)
Northampton Comm Coll (PA)
Northcentral Tech Coll (WI)
Northern Essex Comm Coll (MA)
Northwest Coll (WY)
Northwest-Shoals Comm Coll (AL)
Norwalk Comm Coll (CT)
Nunez Comm Coll (LA)
Ocean County Coll (NJ)
Oklahoma City Comm Coll (OK)
Oklahoma State U, Oklahoma City (OK)
Onondaga Comm Coll (NY)
Oregon Coast Comm Coll (OR)
Panola Coll (TX)
Paris Jr Coll (TX)
Pennsylvania Highlands Comm Coll (PA)
Pennsylvania Inst of Technology (PA)
Piedmont Comm Coll (NC)
Pueblo Comm Coll (CO)
Queensborough Comm Coll of the City U of New York (NY)
Quincy Coll (MA)
Quinsigamond Comm Coll (MA)
Reading Area Comm Coll (PA)
River Valley Comm Coll (NH)
Rockingham Comm Coll (NC)
Rogue Comm Coll (OR)
Rowan-Cabarrus Comm Coll (NC)
St. Charles Comm Coll (MO)
St. Vincent's Coll (CT)
Salt Lake Comm Coll (UT)
San Jacinto Coll District (TX)
San Juan Coll (NM)
Schoolcraft Coll (MI)
Seminole State Coll (OK)
Sheridan Coll (WY)
Sierra Coll (CA)
Southern U at Shreveport (LA)
South Florida State Coll (FL)
Southwestern Michigan Coll (MI)
Southwestern Oklahoma State U at Sayre (OK)
Southwest Tennessee Comm Coll (TN)
Sowela Tech Comm Coll (LA)
Spoon River Coll (IL)
State U of New York Coll of Technology at Alfred (NY)
Three Rivers Comm Coll (CT)
Trocaire Coll (NY)
Truckee Meadows Comm Coll (NV)
Tulsa Comm Coll (OK)
Tyler Jr Coll (TX)
U of Arkansas Comm Coll at Morrilton (AR)
U of Cincinnati Blue Ash Coll (OH)
U of New Mexico–Gallup (NM)
Victoria Coll (TX)
Volunteer State Comm Coll (TN)
Walters State Comm Coll (TN)
Western Nevada Coll (NV)
Western Wyoming Comm Coll (WY)
White Mountains Comm Coll (NH)

GEOGRAPHIC INFORMATION SCIENCE AND CARTOGRAPHY
Austin Comm Coll District (TX)
Borough of Manhattan Comm Coll of the City U of New York (NY)
Brookhaven Coll (TX)
Casper Coll (WY)
Central New Mexico Comm Coll (NM)
Collin County Comm Coll District (TX)
Harrisburg Area Comm Coll (PA)
Hinds Comm Coll (MS)
Hudson County Comm Coll (NJ)
Lehigh Carbon Comm Coll (PA)
Lone Star Coll–CyFair (TX)
Mitchell Tech Inst (SD)
Oklahoma City Comm Coll (OK)

Southwestern Indian Polytechnic Inst (NM)
Southwest Tennessee Comm Coll (TN)

GEOGRAPHY
Allen Comm Coll (KS)
American River Coll (CA)
Antelope Valley Coll (CA)
Austin Comm Coll District (TX)
Ca&nnada Coll (CA)
Cayuga County Comm Coll (NY)
Cerritos Coll (CA)
Coll of the Canyons (CA)
Comm Coll of Baltimore County (MD)
Fullerton Coll (CA)
Los Angeles Valley Coll (CA)
Montgomery Coll (MD)
Nashville State Comm Coll (TN)
Northeastern Jr Coll (CO)
Orange Coast Coll (CA)
Palomar Coll (CA)
South Florida State Coll (FL)

GEOGRAPHY RELATED
American River Coll (CA)
Columbia Coll (CA)
Palomar Coll (CA)

GEOLOGICAL AND EARTH SCIENCES/GEOSCIENCES RELATED
Great Basin Coll (NV)
Potomac State Coll of West Virginia U (WV)
Rowan Coll at Burlington County (NJ)

GEOLOGY/EARTH SCIENCE
Amarillo Coll (TX)
Antelope Valley Coll (CA)
Arizona Western Coll (AZ)
Austin Comm Coll District (TX)
Barton County Comm Coll (KS)
Casper Coll (WY)
Central Texas Coll (TX)
Central Wyoming Coll (WY)
Cerritos Coll (CA)
Coll of the Canyons (CA)
Columbia Coll (CA)
Eastern Arizona Coll (AZ)
Edison Comm Coll (OH)
Fullerton Coll (CA)
Georgia Highlands Coll (GA)
Grand Rapids Comm Coll (MI)
Kilgore Coll (TX)
Los Angeles Valley Coll (CA)
Miami Dade Coll (FL)
Middlesex County Coll (NJ)
Northeastern Jr Coll (CO)
Odessa Coll (TX)
Orange Coast Coll (CA)
Palomar Coll (CA)
Panola Coll (TX)
Pensacola State Coll (FL)
Potomac State Coll of West Virginia U (WV)
St. Philip's Coll (TX)
Salt Lake Comm Coll (UT)
San Jacinto Coll District (TX)
San Joaquin Delta Coll (CA)
San Juan Coll (NM)
Sierra Coll (CA)
South Florida State Coll (FL)
Truckee Meadows Comm Coll (NV)
Tyler Jr Coll (TX)
Vincennes U (IN)
Western Wyoming Comm Coll (WY)

GERMAN
Austin Comm Coll District (TX)
Blinn Coll (TX)
Cerritos Coll (CA)
Citrus Coll (CA)
Los Angeles Valley Coll (CA)
Miami Dade Coll (FL)

GERONTOLOGY
Anne Arundel Comm Coll (MD)
Genesee Comm Coll (NY)
Midlands Tech Coll (SC)
North Shore Comm Coll (MA)
South Florida State Coll (FL)
Wisconsin Indianhead Tech Coll (WI)

GOLF COURSE OPERATION AND GROUNDS MANAGEMENT
Anoka Tech Coll (MN)
Hawkeye Comm Coll (IA)
Tech Coll of the Lowcountry (SC)

GRAPHIC AND PRINTING EQUIPMENT OPERATION/ PRODUCTION
Central Maine Comm Coll (ME)
Central Texas Coll (TX)
Erie Comm Coll, South Campus (NY)
Fullerton Coll (CA)
Lake Land Coll (IL)
Luzerne County Comm Coll (PA)
Macomb Comm Coll (MI)
Monroe Comm Coll (NY)
Northwest Coll (WY)
Ozarks Tech Comm Coll (MO)
Palomar Coll (CA)
Pasadena City Coll (CA)
Rock Valley Coll (IL)
Rowan Coll at Burlington County (NJ)
Tarrant County Coll District (TX)
Tulsa Comm Coll (OK)
Vincennes U (IN)

GRAPHIC COMMUNICATIONS
Central Maine Comm Coll (ME)
Clark Coll (WA)
Fox Valley Tech Coll (WI)
Hutchinson Comm Coll (KS)
Northcentral Tech Coll (WI)
Oklahoma City Comm Coll (OK)
Piedmont Comm Coll (NC)
Waukesha County Tech Coll (WI)

GRAPHIC COMMUNICATIONS RELATED
H. Councill Trenholm State Comm Coll (AL)
Middlesex County Coll (NJ)
Thaddeus Stevens Coll of Technology (PA)
Westmoreland County Comm Coll (PA)

GRAPHIC DESIGN
Anne Arundel Comm Coll (MD)
Antonelli Inst (PA)
Arapahoe Comm Coll (CO)
Barton County Comm Coll (KS)
Bradford School (OH)
Bradford School (PA)
Brookhaven Coll (TX)
Casper Coll (WY)
Cayuga County Comm Coll (NY)
Central Wyoming Coll (WY)
Century Coll (MN)
Cloud County Comm Coll (KS)
Coll of Business and Technology– Main Campus (FL)
Coll of Business and Technology– Miami Gardens (FL)
Coll of the Canyons (CA)
Collin County Comm Coll District (TX)
Corning Comm Coll (NY)
County Coll of Morris (NJ)
Davis Coll (OH)
Dunwoody Coll of Technology (MN)
Elgin Comm Coll (IL)
Fashion Inst of Design & Merchandising, LA Campus (CA)
FIDM/Fashion Inst of Design & Merchandising, Orange County Campus (CA)
Fullerton Coll (CA)
Gateway Tech Coll (WI)
Genesee Comm Coll (NY)
Harford Comm Coll (MD)
Harrisburg Area Comm Coll (PA)
Hennepin Tech Coll (MN)
Highland Comm Coll (IL)
Hinds Comm Coll (MS)
Illinois Central Coll (IL)
International Business Coll, Indianapolis (IN)
Ivy Tech Comm Coll–Southwest (IN)
King's Coll (NC)
Kirtland Comm Coll (MI)
Lehigh Carbon Comm Coll (PA)
Lenoir Comm Coll (NC)
Luzerne County Comm Coll (PA)
Minneapolis Business Coll (MN)
Minnesota State Comm and Tech Coll–Moorhead (MN)
Mott Comm Coll (MI)
Northampton Comm Coll (PA)
North Hennepin Comm Coll (MN)
Norwalk Comm Coll (CT)
Oakton Comm Coll (IL)
Oklahoma State U Inst of Technology (OK)
Palomar Coll (CA)
Pasadena City Coll (CA)
Penn Foster Coll (AZ)
Pensacola State Coll (FL)

Rend Lake Coll (IL)
Rowan Coll at Burlington County (NJ)
Salt Lake Comm Coll (UT)
Sierra Coll (CA)
South Florida State Coll (FL)
Southwestern Michigan Coll (MI)
Spoon River Coll (IL)
State U of New York Coll of Technology at Alfred (NY)
Texas State Tech Coll (TX)
Three Rivers Comm Coll (CT)
Tidewater Comm Coll (VA)
Waukesha County Tech Coll (WI)
Westmoreland County Comm Coll (PA)
Wood Tobe–Coburn School (NY)

GREENHOUSE MANAGEMENT
Century Coll (MN)
Hennepin Tech Coll (MN)

GUNSMITHING
Fayetteville Tech Comm Coll (NC)
Lenoir Comm Coll (NC)
Montgomery Comm Coll (NC)

HAIR STYLING AND HAIR DESIGN
IBMC Coll, Fort Collins (CO)

HAZARDOUS MATERIALS MANAGEMENT AND WASTE TECHNOLOGY
Barton County Comm Coll (KS)
Fullerton Coll (CA)
Odessa Coll (TX)
Pensacola State Coll (FL)
Sierra Coll (CA)

HEALTH AIDE
Allen Comm Coll (KS)
Ivy Tech Comm Coll–Kokomo (IN)
Ivy Tech Comm Coll–Lafayette (IN)
Ivy Tech Comm Coll–Wabash Valley (IN)
Texarkana Coll (TX)

HEALTH AIDES/ATTENDANTS/ORDERLIES RELATED
Barton County Comm Coll (KS)

HEALTH AND MEDICAL ADMINISTRATIVE SERVICES RELATED
Barton County Comm Coll (KS)
Butler County Comm Coll (PA)
Carrington Coll–Pleasant Hill (CA)
Carrington Coll–San Leandro (CA)
Hinds Comm Coll (MS)
Kent State U at Ashtabula (OH)
Kent State U at Salem (OH)
Owensboro Comm and Tech Coll (KY)
San Joaquin Valley Coll, Visalia (CA)
Westmoreland County Comm Coll (PA)

HEALTH AND PHYSICAL EDUCATION/FITNESS
Allen Comm Coll (KS)
Alvin Comm Coll (TX)
Anne Arundel Comm Coll (MD)
Antelope Valley Coll (CA)
Arapahoe Comm Coll (CO)
Arizona Western Coll (AZ)
Austin Comm Coll District (TX)
Ca&nnada Coll (CA)
Central New Mexico Comm Coll (NM)
Central Oregon Comm Coll (OR)
Central Texas Coll (TX)
Citrus Coll (CA)
Cochise County Comm Coll District (AZ)
Coll of the Canyons (CA)
Columbia Coll (CA)
Columbia-Greene Comm Coll (NY)
Comm Care Coll (OK)
Corning Comm Coll (NY)
Eastern Arizona Coll (AZ)
Elgin Comm Coll (IL)
Erie Comm Coll (NY)
Erie Comm Coll, North Campus (NY)
Erie Comm Coll, South Campus (NY)
Feather River Coll (CA)
Fullerton Coll (CA)
Genesee Comm Coll (NY)
Gordon State Coll (GA)
Holyoke Comm Coll (MA)

Houston Comm Coll (TX)
Illinois Central Coll (IL)
Jamestown Comm Coll (NY)
Los Angeles Valley Coll (CA)
Luzerne County Comm Coll (PA)
McHenry County Coll (IL)
Montgomery County Comm Coll (PA)
Mt. San Antonio Coll (CA)
North Hennepin Comm Coll (MN)
Northwest Coll (WY)
Orange Coast Coll (CA)
Paris Jr Coll (TX)
Raritan Valley Comm Coll (NJ)
San Jacinto Coll District (TX)
San Juan Coll (NM)
Sheridan Coll (WY)
Sierra Coll (CA)
Tyler Jr Coll (TX)
Vincennes U (IN)
Western Texas Coll (TX)

HEALTH AND PHYSICAL EDUCATION RELATED
Catawba Valley Comm Coll (NC)
Corning Comm Coll (NY)
Fayetteville Tech Comm Coll (NC)
Genesee Comm Coll (NY)
Herkimer County Comm Coll (NY)

HEALTH AND WELLNESS
Corning Comm Coll (NY)
Dean Coll (MA)
Erie Comm Coll (NY)
Erie Comm Coll, North Campus (NY)
Erie Comm Coll, South Campus (NY)

HEALTH/HEALTH-CARE ADMINISTRATION
Berkeley Coll–White Plains Campus (NY)
Butler County Comm Coll (PA)
Carrington Coll–Citrus Heights (CA)
Carrington Coll–Pleasant Hill (CA)
Carrington Coll–Sacramento (CA)
Carrington Coll–San Jose (CA)
Carrington Coll–San Leandro (CA)
Comm Care Coll (OK)
Comm Coll of the Air Force (AL)
Harrisburg Area Comm Coll (PA)
Kent State U at Trumbull (OH)
Luzerne County Comm Coll (PA)
Nashville State Comm Coll (TN)
Oklahoma State U, Oklahoma City (OK)
Penn Foster Coll (AZ)
Pennsylvania Inst of Technology (PA)
Pensacola State Coll (FL)
Rockingham Comm Coll (NC)
Southeast Comm Coll, Lincoln Campus (NE)
South Florida State Coll (FL)
Tyler Jr Coll (TX)
Ultimate Medical Academy Online (FL)

HEALTH INFORMATION/MEDICAL RECORDS ADMINISTRATION
Amarillo Coll (TX)
Barton County Comm Coll (KS)
Bowling Green State U–Firelands Coll (OH)
Bunker Hill Comm Coll (MA)
Camden County Coll (NJ)
Central New Mexico Comm Coll (NM)
The Coll of Westchester (NY)
Comm Coll of Philadelphia (PA)
Daytona State Coll (FL)
Dodge City Comm Coll (KS)
Georgia Highlands Coll (GA)
Humacao Comm Coll (PR)
Illinois Eastern Comm Colls, Lincoln Trail College (IL)
Itawamba Comm Coll (MS)
LDS Business Coll (UT)
Miami Dade Coll (FL)
Monroe Comm Coll (NY)
Mount Wachusett Comm Coll (MA)
Nashville State Comm Coll (TN)
North Central Texas Coll (TX)
Northern Essex Comm Coll (MA)
Oakton Comm Coll (IL)
Oklahoma City Comm Coll (OK)
Pensacola State Coll (FL)
Southern U at Shreveport (LA)
South Florida State Coll (FL)
Stark State Coll (OH)
Tarrant County Coll District (TX)

HEALTH INFORMATION/MEDICAL RECORDS TECHNOLOGY
Anne Arundel Comm Coll (MD)
Anoka Tech Coll (MN)
Arapahoe Comm Coll (CO)
Atlanta Tech Coll (GA)
Austin Comm Coll District (TX)
Bainbridge State Coll (GA)
Beal Coll (ME)
Berkeley Coll–White Plains Campus (NY)
Blinn Coll (TX)
Borough of Manhattan Comm Coll of the City U of New York (NY)
Carrington Coll–Pleasant Hill (CA)
Carroll Comm Coll (MD)
Catawba Valley Comm Coll (NC)
Central New Mexico Comm Coll (NM)
Central Oregon Comm Coll (OR)
Chippewa Valley Tech Coll (WI)
Cincinnati State Tech and Comm Coll (OH)
Coll of Business and Technology–Cutler Bay Campus (FL)
Coll of Central Florida (FL)
Collin County Comm Coll District (TX)
Columbus Tech Coll (GA)
Craven Comm Coll (NC)
Crowder Coll (MO)
Danville Area Comm Coll (IL)
Dyersburg State Comm Coll (TN)
East Central Coll (MO)
Erie Comm Coll, North Campus (NY)
Florida SouthWestern State Coll (FL)
Fox Valley Tech Coll (WI)
Front Range Comm Coll (CO)
Gateway Tech Coll (WI)
Great Falls Coll Montana State U (MT)
Greenville Tech Coll (SC)
Highland Comm Coll (IL)
Hinds Comm Coll (MS)
Houston Comm Coll (TX)
Hudson County Comm Coll (NJ)
Hutchinson Comm Coll (KS)
Illinois Eastern Comm Colls, Frontier Community College (IL)
Ivy Tech Comm Coll–Central Indiana (IN)
Ivy Tech Comm Coll–East Central (IN)
Ivy Tech Comm Coll–Kokomo (IN)
Ivy Tech Comm Coll–Lafayette (IN)
Ivy Tech Comm Coll–Wabash Valley (IN)
Jamestown Comm Coll (NY)
Jefferson Coll (MO)
Kaskaskia Coll (IL)
Kennebec Valley Comm Coll (ME)
Kirtland Comm Coll (MI)
Leeward Comm Coll (HI)
Lehigh Carbon Comm Coll (PA)
Lone Star Coll–CyFair (TX)
Lone Star Coll–North Harris (TX)
Miami Dade Coll (FL)
Midlands Tech Coll (SC)
Montgomery Coll (MD)
Moraine Valley Comm Coll (IL)
Northeast Iowa Comm Coll (IA)
NorthWest Arkansas Comm Coll (AR)
Ogeechee Tech Coll (GA)
Onondaga Comm Coll (NY)
Ozarks Tech Comm Coll (MO)
Panola Coll (TX)
Paris Jr Coll (TX)
Penn Foster Coll (AZ)
Pennsylvania Highlands Comm Coll (PA)
Pennsylvania Inst of Technology (PA)
Pensacola State Coll (FL)
Quinsigamond Comm Coll (MA)
Raritan Valley Comm Coll (NJ)
Reading Area Comm Coll (PA)
Rend Lake Coll (IL)
Richmond Comm Coll (NC)
Ridgewater Coll (MN)
Rowan Coll at Burlington County (NJ)
St. Charles Comm Coll (MO)
St. Clair County Comm Coll (MI)
St. Philip's Coll (TX)
San Jacinto Coll District (TX)
San Juan Coll (NM)
Schoolcraft Coll (MI)
Shawnee Comm Coll (IL)
Southern Maine Comm Coll (ME)

Southern U at Shreveport (LA)
Southwestern Michigan Coll (MI)
State U of New York Coll of Technology at Alfred (NY)
Tallahassee Comm Coll (FL)
Trocaire Coll (NY)
Tulsa Comm Coll (OK)
Tyler Jr Coll (TX)
Ultimate Medical Academy Online (FL)
Vincennes U (IN)
Volunteer State Comm Coll (TN)
Walters State Comm Coll (TN)
Waukesha County Tech Coll (WI)
West Georgia Tech Coll (GA)
Williston State Coll (ND)
Wisconsin Indianhead Tech Coll (WI)
York County Comm Coll (ME)

HEALTH/MEDICAL PREPARATORY PROGRAMS RELATED
Coll of Central Florida (FL)
Eastern Arizona Coll (AZ)
Eastern Wyoming Coll (WY)
Edison Comm Coll (OH)
Fullerton Coll (CA)
Gordon State Coll (GA)
Miami Dade Coll (FL)
Northwest Coll (WY)
Tulsa Comm Coll (OK)
U of Cincinnati Blue Ash Coll (OH)
Western Wyoming Comm Coll (WY)

HEALTH PROFESSIONS RELATED
Berkshire Comm Coll (MA)
Bowling Green State U–Firelands Coll (OH)
Bucks County Comm Coll (PA)
Carl Albert State Coll (OK)
Carroll Comm Coll (MD)
Comm Coll of Philadelphia (PA)
Corning Comm Coll (NY)
Gateway Comm and Tech Coll (KY)
Genesee Comm Coll (NY)
Harrisburg Area Comm Coll (PA)
Herkimer County Comm Coll (NY)
Lakeland Comm Coll (OH)
LDS Business Coll (UT)
Lanier Tech Coll (GA)
Manor Coll (PA)
Mercer County Comm Coll (NJ)
Miami Dade Coll (FL)
Middlesex County Coll (NJ)
Midlands Tech Coll (SC)
Mitchell Comm Coll (NC)
Nashville State Comm Coll (TN)
New Mexico Jr Coll (NM)
North Shore Comm Coll (MA)
Onondaga Comm Coll (NY)
Panola Coll (TX)
Pennsylvania Highlands Comm Coll (PA)
Phillips Beth Israel School of Nursing (NY)
Piedmont Comm Coll (NC)
Queensborough Comm Coll of the City U of New York (NY)
Richmond Comm Coll (NC)
Salt Lake Comm Coll (UT)
Southeastern Coll–West Palm Beach (FL)
Southwest Tennessee Comm Coll (TN)
Spoon River Coll (IL)
Volunteer State Comm Coll (TN)

HEALTH SERVICES ADMINISTRATION
Harrisburg Area Comm Coll (PA)
Quincy Coll (MA)

HEALTH SERVICES/ALLIED HEALTH/HEALTH SCIENCES
Alvin Comm Coll (TX)
American Samoa Comm Coll (AS)
Ancilla Coll (IN)
Anoka-Ramsey Comm Coll (MN)
Camden County Coll (NJ)
Carl Albert State Coll (OK)
Casper Coll (WY)
Cayuga County Comm Coll (NY)
Cecil Coll (MD)
Central New Mexico Comm Coll (NM)
Century Coll (MN)
Coll of Central Florida (FL)
Columbia Coll (CA)
Dyersburg State Comm Coll (TN)

Georgia Military Coll (GA)
Gulf Coast State Coll (FL)
Holyoke Comm Coll (MA)
Houston Comm Coll (TX)
Hudson County Comm Coll (NJ)
Ilisagvik Coll (AK)
Lake Superior Coll (MN)
Lehigh Carbon Comm Coll (PA)
Miami Dade Coll (FL)
Middlesex County Coll (NJ)
North Hennepin Comm Coll (MN)
Northland Comm and Tech Coll (MN)
Northwest Coll (WY)
Oklahoma State U Inst of Technology (OK)
Orange Coast Coll (CA)
Paris Jr Coll (TX)
Pennsylvania Inst of Technology (PA)
Queensborough Comm Coll of the City U of New York (NY)
Quinsigamond Comm Coll (MA)
Raritan Valley Comm Coll (NJ)
Reading Area Comm Coll (PA)
Rowan Coll at Burlington County (NJ)
Schoolcraft Coll (MI)
Sheridan Coll (WY)
South Florida State Coll (FL)
Ultimate Medical Academy Clearwater (FL)
Ultimate Medical Academy Online (FL)
Ultimate Medical Academy Tampa (FL)
Western Wyoming Comm Coll (WY)
White Mountains Comm Coll (NH)
York County Comm Coll (ME)

HEALTH TEACHER EDUCATION
Austin Comm Coll District (TX)
Bainbridge State Coll (GA)
Copiah-Lincoln Comm Coll (MS)
Georgia Military Coll (GA)
Howard Comm Coll (MD)
Kilgore Coll (TX)
South Florida State Coll (FL)

HEALTH UNIT COORDINATOR/WARD CLERK
Southeast Tech Inst (SD)

HEATING, AIR CONDITIONING, VENTILATION AND REFRIGERATION MAINTENANCE TECHNOLOGY
Amarillo Coll (TX)
Antelope Valley Coll (CA)
Arizona Western Coll (AZ)
Bellingham Tech Coll (WA)
Bismarck State Coll (ND)
Butler County Comm Coll (PA)
Catawba Valley Comm Coll (NC)
Central New Mexico Comm Coll (NM)
Central Texas Coll (TX)
Century Coll (MN)
Coll of Business and Technology–Main Campus (FL)
Craven Comm Coll (NC)
Delta Coll (MI)
Dunwoody Coll of Technology (MN)
East Central Coll (MO)
Elgin Comm Coll (IL)
Fayetteville Tech Comm Coll (NC)
Galveston Coll (TX)
Gateway Tech Coll (WI)
George C. Wallace Comm Coll (AL)
Grand Rapids Comm Coll (MI)
Harrisburg Area Comm Coll (PA)
Hennepin Tech Coll (MN)
Hinds Comm Coll (MS)
Illinois Central Coll (IL)
Ivy Tech Comm Coll–Bloomington (IN)
Ivy Tech Comm Coll–Central Indiana (IN)
Ivy Tech Comm Coll–Columbus (IN)
Ivy Tech Comm Coll–East Central (IN)
Ivy Tech Comm Coll–Kokomo (IN)
Ivy Tech Comm Coll–Lafayette (IN)
Ivy Tech Comm Coll–North Central (IN)
Ivy Tech Comm Coll–Northeast (IN)
Ivy Tech Comm Coll–Northwest (IN)
Ivy Tech Comm Coll–Richmond (IN)
Ivy Tech Comm Coll–Southern Indiana (IN)
Ivy Tech Comm Coll–Southwest (IN)

Ivy Tech Comm Coll–Wabash Valley (IN)
Jefferson Coll (MO)
Johnston Comm Coll (NC)
Kankakee Comm Coll (IL)
Kaskaskia Coll (IL)
Kellogg Comm Coll (MI)
Kilgore Coll (TX)
Kirtland Comm Coll (MI)
Laramie County Comm Coll (WY)
Lehigh Carbon Comm Coll (PA)
Lone Star Coll–North Harris (TX)
Los Angeles Trade-Tech Coll (CA)
Luzerne County Comm Coll (PA)
Macomb Comm Coll (MI)
Manhattan Area Tech Coll (KS)
Martin Comm Coll (NC)
Miami Dade Coll (FL)
Midlands Tech Coll (SC)
Mid-Plains Comm Coll, North Platte (NE)
Minnesota State Coll–Southeast Tech (MN)
Mitchell Tech Inst (SD)
Mohave Comm Coll (AZ)
Mohawk Valley Comm Coll (NY)
Monroe Comm Coll (NY)
Montgomery Comm Coll (NC)
Moraine Valley Comm Coll (IL)
Mt. San Antonio Coll (CA)
Northampton Comm Coll (PA)
Northland Comm and Tech Coll (MN)
Odessa Coll (TX)
Oklahoma State U Inst of Technology (OK)
Oxnard Coll (CA)
Ozarks Tech Comm Coll (MO)
Paris Jr Coll (TX)
Pittsburgh Tech Inst, Oakdale (PA)
Ranken Tech Coll (MO)
Renton Tech Coll (WA)
Richmond Comm Coll (NC)
St. Philip's Coll (TX)
Salt Lake Comm Coll (UT)
San Jacinto Coll District (TX)
San Joaquin Delta Coll (CA)
San Joaquin Valley Coll, Hesperia (CA)
San Joaquin Valley Coll, Lancaster (CA)
San Joaquin Valley Coll, Ontario (CA)
San Joaquin Valley Coll, Temecula (CA)
Southeast Comm Coll, Milford Campus (NE)
Southeast Tech Inst (SD)
Southern Maine Comm Coll (ME)
Spartanburg Comm Coll (SC)
State U of New York Coll of Technology at Alfred (NY)
Tarrant County Coll District (TX)
Texarkana Coll (TX)
Thaddeus Stevens Coll of Technology (PA)
Tri-County Tech Coll (SC)
Truckee Meadows Comm Coll (NV)
Tyler Jr Coll (TX)
U of Arkansas Comm Coll at Morrilton (AR)
Wayne County Comm Coll District (MI)
Wenatchee Valley Coll (WA)
Western Iowa Tech Comm Coll (IA)
Westmoreland County Comm Coll (PA)

HEATING, VENTILATION, AIR CONDITIONING AND REFRIGERATION ENGINEERING TECHNOLOGY
Alamance Comm Coll (NC)
Antelope Valley Coll (CA)
Arizona Western Coll (AZ)
Austin Comm Coll District (TX)
Bevill State Comm Coll (AL)
Chippewa Valley Tech Coll (WI)
Coll of Business and Technology–Flagler Campus (FL)
Coll of Business and Technology–Hialeah Campus (FL)
Comm Coll of Baltimore County (MD)
Dunwoody Coll of Technology (MN)
Front Range Comm Coll (CO)
Gadsden State Comm Coll (AL)
George C. Wallace Comm Coll (AL)
Georgia Piedmont Tech Coll (GA)
H. Councill Trenholm State Comm Coll (AL)
Humacao Comm Coll (PR)
J. F. Drake State Comm and Tech Coll (AL)

Kennebec Valley Comm Coll (ME)
Macomb Comm Coll (MI)
Manhattan Area Tech Coll (KS)
Martin Comm Coll (NC)
Mercer County Comm Coll (NJ)
Miami Dade Coll (FL)
Mott Comm Coll (MI)
New Castle School of Trades (PA)
North Georgia Tech Coll (GA)
Oakton Comm Coll (IL)
Oklahoma Tech Coll (OK)
Raritan Valley Comm Coll (NJ)
San Joaquin Valley Coll, Bakersfield (CA)
San Joaquin Valley Coll, Fresno (CA)
San Joaquin Valley Coll, Visalia (CA)
Savannah Tech Coll (GA)
Southern Crescent Tech Coll (GA)
South Georgia Tech Coll (GA)
Springfield Tech Comm Coll (MA)
Texas State Tech Coll (TX)

HEAVY EQUIPMENT MAINTENANCE TECHNOLOGY
Amarillo Coll (TX)
Comm Coll of Aurora (CO)
Highland Comm Coll (IL)
Los Angeles Trade-Tech Coll (CA)
Ozarks Tech Comm Coll (MO)
Rend Lake Coll (IL)
Southwest Tennessee Comm Coll (TN)
Western Wyoming Comm Coll (WY)

HEAVY/INDUSTRIAL EQUIPMENT MAINTENANCE TECHNOLOGIES RELATED
Bellingham Tech Coll (WA)
East Central Coll (MO)
Ranken Tech Coll (MO)
State U of New York Coll of Technology at Alfred (NY)
Wayne County Comm Coll District (MI)

HEBREW
Los Angeles Valley Coll (CA)

HEMATOLOGY TECHNOLOGY
Comm Coll of the Air Force (AL)

HIGH PERFORMANCE AND CUSTOM ENGINE TECHNOLOGY
Ohio Tech Coll (OH)

HISPANIC-AMERICAN, PUERTO RICAN, AND MEXICAN-AMERICAN/CHICANO STUDIES
Cerritos Coll (CA)
San Jacinto Coll District (TX)

HISTOLOGIC TECHNICIAN
Comm Coll of Rhode Island (RI)
Houston Comm Coll (TX)
Miami Dade Coll (FL)
Mott Comm Coll (MI)
North Hennepin Comm Coll (MN)
Pennsylvania Highlands Comm Coll (PA)

HISTOLOGIC TECHNOLOGY/HISTOTECHNOLOGIST
Miami Dade Coll (FL)

HISTORIC PRESERVATION AND CONSERVATION
Piedmont Comm Coll (NC)

HISTORY
Allen Comm Coll (KS)
Alvin Comm Coll (TX)
Amarillo Coll (TX)
Ancilla Coll (IN)
Antelope Valley Coll (CA)
Arizona Western Coll (AZ)
Austin Comm Coll District (TX)
Bainbridge State Coll (GA)
Barton County Comm Coll (KS)
Blinn Coll (TX)
Borough of Manhattan Comm Coll of the City U of New York (NY)
Bucks County Comm Coll (PA)
Bunker Hill Comm Coll (MA)
Ca&nnada Coll (CA)
Casper Coll (WY)
Central New Mexico Comm Coll (NM)
Cerritos Coll (CA)
Citrus Coll (CA)
Coll of Central Florida (FL)
Coll of the Canyons (CA)
Copiah-Lincoln Comm Coll (MS)

Dean Coll (MA)
Dodge City Comm Coll (KS)
Eastern Arizona Coll (AZ)
Edison Comm Coll (OH)
Feather River Coll (CA)
Fullerton Coll (CA)
Galveston Coll (TX)
Georgia Highlands Coll (GA)
Georgia Military Coll (GA)
Gordon State Coll (GA)
Harford Comm Coll (MD)
Itawamba Comm Coll (MS)
Kankakee Comm Coll (IL)
Lamar Comm Coll (CO)
Laramie County Comm Coll (WY)
Lorain County Comm Coll (OH)
Los Angeles Valley Coll (CA)
Miami Dade Coll (FL)
Mohave Comm Coll (AZ)
Monroe Comm Coll (NY)
Moraine Valley Comm Coll (IL)
Nashville State Comm Coll (TN)
New Mexico Jr Coll (NM)
Northeastern Jr Coll (CO)
Northern Essex Comm Coll (MA)
Northwest Coll (WY)
Odessa Coll (TX)
Oklahoma City Comm Coll (OK)
Oklahoma State U, Oklahoma City (OK)
Orange Coast Coll (CA)
Otero Jr Coll (CO)
Oxnard Coll (CA)
Panola Coll (TX)
Paris Jr Coll (TX)
Pasadena City Coll (CA)
Pensacola State Coll (FL)
Potomac State Coll of West Virginia U (WV)
Rowan Coll at Burlington County (NJ)
St. Charles Comm Coll (MO)
St. Philip's Coll (TX)
Salt Lake Comm Coll (UT)
San Jacinto Coll District (TX)
San Joaquin Delta Coll (CA)
Sheridan Coll (WY)
South Florida State Coll (FL)
Spoon River Coll (IL)
Texarkana Coll (TX)
Truckee Meadows Comm Coll (NV)
Tyler Jr Coll (TX)
Vincennes U (IN)
Wenatchee Valley Coll (WA)
Western Wyoming Comm Coll (WY)

HISTORY RELATED
U of Pittsburgh at Titusville (PA)

HISTORY TEACHER EDUCATION
Bucks County Comm Coll (PA)

HOLISTIC HEALTH
Anoka-Ramsey Comm Coll (MN)
Front Range Comm Coll (CO)

HOME HEALTH AIDE/HOME ATTENDANT
Allen Comm Coll (KS)
American River Coll (CA)
Barton County Comm Coll (KS)

HOMELAND SECURITY
Arizona Western Coll (AZ)
Butler County Comm Coll (PA)
City Colls of Chicago, Olive-Harvey College (IL)
Georgia Military Coll (GA)
Long Island Business Inst (NY)
Palomar Coll (CA)

HOMELAND SECURITY, LAW ENFORCEMENT, FIREFIGHTING AND PROTECTIVE SERVICES RELATED
Barton County Comm Coll (KS)
Butler County Comm Coll (PA)
Central Wyoming Coll (WY)
Century Coll (MN)
Lakeland Comm Coll (OH)
Laramie County Comm Coll (WY)
Northland Comm and Tech Coll (MN)
NorthWest Arkansas Comm Coll (AR)
Ocean County Coll (NJ)
Onondaga Comm Coll (NY)
Pittsburgh Tech Inst, Oakdale (PA)
San Joaquin Valley Coll, Bakersfield (CA)
Schoolcraft Coll (MI)
Westmoreland County Comm Coll (PA)

HOMELAND SECURITY RELATED
Fox Valley Tech Coll (WI)
Pensacola State Coll (FL)
Tallahassee Comm Coll (FL)

HORSE HUSBANDRY/EQUINE SCIENCE AND MANAGEMENT
Cecil Coll (MD)
Feather River Coll (CA)
Potomac State Coll of West Virginia U (WV)
Treasure Valley Comm Coll (OR)

HORTICULTURAL SCIENCE
Central Lakes Coll (MN)
Century Coll (MN)
Chattahoochee Tech Coll (GA)
Columbus Tech Coll (GA)
Gwinnett Tech Coll (GA)
Luzerne County Comm Coll (PA)
Miami Dade Coll (FL)
Mt. San Antonio Coll (CA)
Naugatuck Valley Comm Coll (CT)
North Georgia Tech Coll (GA)
Oklahoma State U, Oklahoma City (OK)
Potomac State Coll of West Virginia U (WV)
Sheridan Coll (WY)
Southeast Tech Inst (SD)
Southern Crescent Tech Coll (GA)
South Florida State Coll (FL)
South Georgia Tech Coll (GA)
Tarrant County Coll District (TX)
Tidewater Comm Coll (VA)
Treasure Valley Comm Coll (OR)
Victor Valley Coll (CA)
Williamson Coll of the Trades (PA)

HOSPITAL AND HEALTH-CARE FACILITIES ADMINISTRATION
Allen Comm Coll (KS)
Bossier Parish Comm Coll (LA)
Carrington Coll–Phoenix West (AZ)
Minnesota West Comm and Tech Coll (MN)

HOSPITALITY ADMINISTRATION
Arizona Western Coll (AZ)
Austin Comm Coll District (TX)
Berkshire Comm Coll (MA)
Bunker Hill Comm Coll (MA)
Casper Coll (WY)
Central New Mexico Comm Coll (NM)
Central Texas Coll (TX)
Chesapeake Coll (MD)
Cincinnati State Tech and Comm Coll (OH)
Coll of the Canyons (CA)
Collin County Comm Coll District (TX)
County Coll of Morris (NJ)
Daytona State Coll (FL)
Fox Valley Tech Coll (WI)
Front Range Comm Coll (CO)
Gateway Tech Coll (WI)
Genesee Comm Coll (NY)
Gulf Coast State Coll (FL)
Hawkeye Comm Coll (IA)
Highland Comm Coll (IL)
Hillsborough Comm Coll (FL)
Hinds Comm Coll (MS)
Hudson County Comm Coll (NJ)
Ivy Tech Comm Coll–Bloomington (IN)
Ivy Tech Comm Coll–Columbus (IN)
Ivy Tech Comm Coll–East Central (IN)
Ivy Tech Comm Coll–North Central (IN)
Ivy Tech Comm Coll–Northeast (IN)
Ivy Tech Comm Coll–Northwest (IN)
Ivy Tech Comm Coll–Southwest (IN)
James H. Faulkner State Comm Coll (AL)
Jefferson Comm Coll (NY)
Jefferson State Comm Coll (AL)
J. Sargeant Reynolds Comm Coll (VA)
Lakeland Comm Coll (OH)
Massachusetts Bay Comm Coll (MA)
Miami Dade Coll (FL)
Moraine Valley Comm Coll (IL)
Muskegon Comm Coll (MI)
Naugatuck Valley Comm Coll (CT)
Niagara County Comm Coll (NY)
North Shore Comm Coll (MA)
Onondaga Comm Coll (NY)
Pasadena City Coll (CA)
Penn Foster Coll (AZ)

Pensacola State Coll (FL)
Potomac State Coll of West Virginia U (WV)
Quinsigamond Comm Coll (MA)
Rowan Coll at Burlington County (NJ)
Scottsdale Comm Coll (AZ)
Sheridan Coll (WY)
Southern U at Shreveport (LA)
South Florida State Coll (FL)
Sullivan County Comm Coll (NY)
Tech Coll of the Lowcountry (SC)
Three Rivers Comm Coll (CT)
Trocaire Coll (NY)
Vincennes U (IN)
Wor-Wic Comm Coll (MD)

HOSPITALITY ADMINISTRATION RELATED
Ancilla Coll (IN)
Bunker Hill Comm Coll (MA)
Butler County Comm Coll (PA)
Corning Comm Coll (NY)
Holyoke Comm Coll (MA)
Ivy Tech Comm Coll–Central Indiana (IN)
Ivy Tech Comm Coll–East Central (IN)
Ivy Tech Comm Coll–Northeast (IN)
J. Sargeant Reynolds Comm Coll (VA)
Long Island Business Inst (NY)

HOSPITALITY AND RECREATION MARKETING
Iowa Central Comm Coll (IA)
Luzerne County Comm Coll (PA)
Montgomery County Comm Coll (PA)
Muskegon Comm Coll (MI)

HOTEL/MOTEL ADMINISTRATION
Albany Tech Coll (GA)
Anne Arundel Comm Coll (MD)
Athens Tech Coll (GA)
Atlanta Tech Coll (GA)
Bradford School (PA)
Cape Fear Comm Coll (NC)
Carl Albert State Coll (OK)
Central Georgia Tech Coll (GA)
Central Oregon Comm Coll (OR)
Central Wyoming Coll (WY)
Coll of the Canyons (CA)
Columbia Coll (CA)
Comm Coll of Baltimore County (MD)
Comm Coll of Philadelphia (PA)
Comm Coll of the Air Force (AL)
Daytona State Coll (FL)
Finger Lakes Comm Coll (NY)
Genesee Comm Coll (NY)
Gwinnett Tech Coll (GA)
Houston Comm Coll (TX)
International Business Coll, Indianapolis (IN)
J. Sargeant Reynolds Comm Coll (VA)
King's Coll (NC)
Luzerne County Comm Coll (PA)
Manchester Comm Coll (CT)
Mercer County Comm Coll (NJ)
Miami Dade Coll (FL)
Middlesex County Coll (NJ)
Minneapolis Business Coll (MN)
Mohawk Valley Comm Coll (NY)
Monroe Comm Coll (NY)
Montgomery Coll (MD)
Mt. San Antonio Coll (CA)
Muskegon Comm Coll (MI)
Naugatuck Valley Comm Coll (CT)
Northampton Comm Coll (PA)
Northern Essex Comm Coll (MA)
Norwalk Comm Coll (CT)
Ogeechee Tech Coll (GA)
Orange Coast Coll (CA)
Oxnard Coll (CA)
Ozarks Tech Comm Coll (MO)
Palau Comm Coll (Palau)
Pensacola State Coll (FL)
Pittsburgh Tech Inst, Oakdale (PA)
The Restaurant School at Walnut Hill Coll (PA)
St. Philip's Coll (TX)
Savannah Tech Coll (GA)
Schenectady County Comm Coll (NY)
Scottsdale Comm Coll (AZ)
Southern U at Shreveport (LA)
Vincennes U (IN)
Westmoreland County Comm Coll (PA)
Wood Tobe–Coburn School (NY)

HOTEL, MOTEL, AND RESTAURANT MANAGEMENT
Craven Comm Coll (NC)
Fayetteville Tech Comm Coll (NC)
Pensacola State Coll (FL)
Tompkins Cortland Comm Coll (NY)
Waukesha County Tech Coll (WI)

HUMAN DEVELOPMENT AND FAMILY STUDIES
Bucks County Comm Coll (PA)
Central New Mexico Comm Coll (NM)
City Colls of Chicago, Olive-Harvey College (IL)
Penn State DuBois (PA)
Penn State Fayette, The Eberly Campus (PA)
Penn State Mont Alto (PA)
Penn State Shenango (PA)
Salt Lake Comm Coll (UT)

HUMAN DEVELOPMENT AND FAMILY STUDIES RELATED
Albany Tech Coll (GA)

HUMANITIES
Allen Comm Coll (KS)
Antelope Valley Coll (CA)
Brookhaven Coll (TX)
Bucks County Comm Coll (PA)
Ca&nnada Coll (CA)
Cayuga County Comm Coll (NY)
Central Oregon Comm Coll (OR)
Clinton Comm Coll (NY)
Cochise County Comm Coll District (AZ)
Coll of Central Florida (FL)
Coll of the Canyons (CA)
Columbia Coll (CA)
Columbia-Greene Comm Coll (NY)
Corning Comm Coll (NY)
Dodge City Comm Coll (KS)
Dutchess Comm Coll (NY)
Erie Comm Coll (NY)
Erie Comm Coll, North Campus (NY)
Erie Comm Coll, South Campus (NY)
Feather River Coll (CA)
Finger Lakes Comm Coll (NY)
Fullerton Coll (CA)
Galveston Coll (TX)
Genesee Comm Coll (NY)
Herkimer County Comm Coll (NY)
Housatonic Comm Coll (CT)
Jamestown Comm Coll (NY)
Jefferson Comm Coll (NY)
John Tyler Comm Coll (VA)
Lackawanna Coll (PA)
Laramie County Comm Coll (WY)
Luzerne County Comm Coll (PA)
Mercer County Comm Coll (NJ)
Miami Dade Coll (FL)
Mohawk Valley Comm Coll (NY)
Montgomery County Comm Coll (PA)
Mt. San Antonio Coll (CA)
Niagara County Comm Coll (NY)
Oklahoma City Comm Coll (OK)
Oklahoma State U, Oklahoma City (OK)
Onondaga Comm Coll (NY)
Orange Coast Coll (CA)
Otero Jr Coll (CO)
Palomar Coll (CA)
Pasadena City Coll (CA)
Salt Lake Comm Coll (UT)
San Joaquin Delta Coll (CA)
Seminole State Coll (OK)
South Florida State Coll (FL)
State U of New York Coll of Technology at Alfred (NY)
Texarkana Coll (TX)
Tompkins Cortland Comm Coll (NY)
Victor Valley Coll (CA)
Westchester Comm Coll (NY)
Western Wyoming Comm Coll (WY)

HUMAN RESOURCES DEVELOPMENT
Minnesota State Comm and Tech Coll–Moorhead (MN)

HUMAN RESOURCES MANAGEMENT
Anoka-Ramsey Comm Coll (MN)
Barton County Comm Coll (KS)
Beal Coll (ME)
Blackhawk Tech Coll (WI)
Butler County Comm Coll (PA)
Cecil Coll (MD)

Chippewa Valley Tech Coll (WI)
Clark Coll (WA)
Comm Coll of the Air Force (AL)
Edison Comm Coll (OH)
Fayetteville Tech Comm Coll (NC)
Fox Valley Tech Coll (WI)
Harford Comm Coll (MD)
Hawkeye Comm Coll (IA)
Herkimer County Comm Coll (NY)
Illinois Eastern Comm Colls, Olney Central College (IL)
Lehigh Carbon Comm Coll (PA)
Moraine Valley Comm Coll (IL)
Ohio Business Coll, Sheffield Village (OH)
Penn Foster Coll (AZ)
San Joaquin Valley Coll, Visalia (CA)
San Joaquin Valley Coll–Online (CA)
South Florida State Coll (FL)
Trocaire Coll (NY)
Tulsa Comm Coll (OK)
Waukesha County Tech Coll (WI)
Western Iowa Tech Comm Coll (IA)
Westmoreland County Comm Coll (PA)
Wisconsin Indianhead Tech Coll (WI)

HUMAN RESOURCES MANAGEMENT AND SERVICES RELATED
Barton County Comm Coll (KS)

HUMAN SERVICES
Alexandria Tech and Comm Coll (MN)
American River Coll (CA)
American Samoa Comm Coll (AS)
Austin Comm Coll District (TX)
Beal Coll (ME)
Berkshire Comm Coll (MA)
Bismarck State Coll (ND)
Bowling Green State U–Firelands Coll (OH)
Bunker Hill Comm Coll (MA)
Ca&nnada Coll (CA)
Central Maine Comm Coll (ME)
Central Ohio Tech Coll (OH)
Century Coll (MN)
Cerritos Coll (CA)
Coll of Central Florida (FL)
Columbia Coll (CA)
Columbia-Greene Comm Coll (NY)
Comm Coll of Philadelphia (PA)
Corning Comm Coll (NY)
Daytona State Coll (FL)
Denmark Tech Coll (SC)
Dutchess Comm Coll (NY)
Finger Lakes Comm Coll (NY)
Frederick Comm Coll (MD)
Genesee Comm Coll (NY)
Georgia Highlands Coll (GA)
Great Basin Coll (NV)
Harrisburg Area Comm Coll (PA)
Hopkinsville Comm Coll (KY)
Housatonic Comm Coll (CT)
Itawamba Comm Coll (MS)
Ivy Tech Comm Coll–Bloomington (IN)
Ivy Tech Comm Coll–Central Indiana (IN)
Ivy Tech Comm Coll–Columbus (IN)
Ivy Tech Comm Coll–East Central (IN)
Ivy Tech Comm Coll–Kokomo (IN)
Ivy Tech Comm Coll–Lafayette (IN)
Ivy Tech Comm Coll–North Central (IN)
Ivy Tech Comm Coll–Northeast (IN)
Ivy Tech Comm Coll–Northwest (IN)
Ivy Tech Comm Coll–Richmond (IN)
Ivy Tech Comm Coll–Southeast (IN)
Ivy Tech Comm Coll–Southern Indiana (IN)
Ivy Tech Comm Coll–Southwest (IN)
Ivy Tech Comm Coll–Wabash Valley (IN)
Jamestown Comm Coll (NY)
Jefferson Comm Coll (NY)
Kellogg Comm Coll (MI)
Lackawanna Coll (PA)
Lake Area Tech Inst (SD)
Lake Land Coll (IL)
Laramie County Comm Coll (WY)
Lehigh Carbon Comm Coll (PA)
Lone Star Coll–Montgomery (TX)
Lorain County Comm Coll (OH)
Luzerne County Comm Coll (PA)
Manchester Comm Coll (CT)
Massachusetts Bay Comm Coll (MA)
Mesabi Range Coll (MN)

Miami Dade Coll (FL)
Midlands Tech Coll (SC)
Minnesota West Comm and Tech Coll (MN)
Mitchell Tech Inst (SD)
Mohawk Valley Comm Coll (NY)
Monroe Comm Coll (NY)
Mount Wachusett Comm Coll (MA)
Niagara County Comm Coll (NY)
Northern Essex Comm Coll (MA)
North Hennepin Comm Coll (MN)
Norwalk Comm Coll (CT)
Ocean County Coll (NJ)
Odessa Coll (TX)
Oklahoma State U, Oklahoma City (OK)
Owensboro Comm and Tech Coll (KY)
Pennsylvania Highlands Comm Coll (PA)
Quincy Coll (MA)
Quinsigamond Comm Coll (MA)
Randolph Comm Coll (NC)
River Valley Comm Coll (NH)
Rock Valley Coll (IL)
Rowan Coll at Burlington County (NJ)
St. Charles Comm Coll (MO)
Shawnee Comm Coll (IL)
Southern U at Shreveport (LA)
Stark State Coll (OH)
State U of New York Coll of Technology at Alfred (NY)
Sullivan County Comm Coll (NY)
Tohono O'odham Comm Coll (AZ)
Tompkins Cortland Comm Coll (NY)
Tunxis Comm Coll (CT)
Ultimate Medical Academy Online (FL)
U of Alaska Anchorage, Kenai Peninsula Coll (AK)
U of Pittsburgh at Titusville (PA)
Western Wyoming Comm Coll (WY)
White Mountains Comm Coll (NH)
York County Comm Coll (ME)

HYDRAULICS AND FLUID POWER TECHNOLOGY
Comm Coll of Baltimore County (MD)
Hennepin Tech Coll (MN)
Minnesota West Comm and Tech Coll (MN)

HYDROLOGY AND WATER RESOURCES SCIENCE
Citrus Coll (CA)
Dodge City Comm Coll (KS)
Los Angeles Trade-Tech Coll (CA)

ILLUSTRATION
Collin County Comm Coll District (TX)
Fashion Inst of Technology (NY)
Oklahoma State U, Oklahoma City (OK)

INDUSTRIAL AND PRODUCT DESIGN
Fiorello H. LaGuardia Comm Coll of the City U of New York (NY)
Luzerne County Comm Coll (PA)
Mt. San Antonio Coll (CA)
Rock Valley Coll (IL)

INDUSTRIAL ELECTRONICS TECHNOLOGY
American River Coll (CA)
Bevill State Comm Coll (AL)
Big Bend Comm Coll (WA)
Central Lakes Coll (MN)
Danville Area Comm Coll (IL)
Denmark Tech Coll (SC)
Dyersburg State Comm Coll (TN)
Eastern Arizona Coll (AZ)
Elizabethtown Comm and Tech Coll, Elizabethtown (KY)
J. F. Drake State Comm and Tech Coll (AL)
Kankakee Comm Coll (IL)
Lackawanna Coll (PA)
Lehigh Carbon Comm Coll (PA)
Lenoir Comm Coll (NC)
Los Angeles Valley Coll (CA)
Lurleen B. Wallace Comm Coll (AL)
Midlands Tech Coll (SC)
Moraine Valley Comm Coll (IL)
Northampton Comm Coll (PA)
Northeast Alabama Comm Coll (AL)
Northwest-Shoals Comm Coll (AL)

Pasadena City Coll (CA)
Penn Foster Coll (AZ)
Ranken Tech Coll (MO)
Sierra Coll (CA)
Spartanburg Comm Coll (SC)
Tech Coll of the Lowcountry (SC)
Tri-County Tech Coll (SC)
Tyler Jr Coll (TX)
Wenatchee Valley Coll (WA)
Western Wyoming Comm Coll (WY)

INDUSTRIAL ENGINEERING
Central Lakes Coll (MN)
Manchester Comm Coll (CT)
Nashville State Comm Coll (TN)
South Florida State Coll (FL)

INDUSTRIAL MECHANICS AND MAINTENANCE TECHNOLOGY
Aiken Tech Coll (SC)
Bellingham Tech Coll (WA)
Big Bend Comm Coll (WA)
Bismarck State Coll (ND)
Bossier Parish Comm Coll (LA)
Casper Coll (WY)
Catawba Valley Comm Coll (NC)
Chippewa Valley Tech Coll (WI)
Danville Area Comm Coll (IL)
Delta Coll (MI)
Dyersburg State Comm Coll (TN)
Eastern Arizona Coll (AZ)
Elgin Comm Coll (IL)
Elizabethtown Comm and Tech Coll, Elizabethtown (KY)
Gadsden State Comm Coll (AL)
Gateway Tech Coll (WI)
George C. Wallace Comm Coll (AL)
H. Councill Trenholm State Comm Coll (AL)
Illinois Eastern Comm Colls, Olney Central College (IL)
Ivy Tech Comm Coll–East Central (IN)
Jefferson Coll (MO)
Kaskaskia Coll (IL)
Kennebec Valley Comm Coll (ME)
Macomb Comm Coll (MI)
Midlands Tech Coll (SC)
Minnesota State Coll–Southeast Tech (MN)
New Castle School of Trades (PA)
North Central Texas Coll (TX)
Northeast Alabama Comm Coll (AL)
Northwest-Shoals Comm Coll (AL)
Reading Area Comm Coll (PA)
Rend Lake Coll (IL)
San Joaquin Valley Coll, Lancaster (CA)
San Joaquin Valley Coll, Ontario (CA)
San Juan Coll (NM)
Somerset Comm Coll (KY)
Southwestern Michigan Coll (MI)
Texarkana Coll (TX)
U of Arkansas Comm Coll at Morrilton (AR)
Western Iowa Tech Comm Coll (IA)
Western Wyoming Comm Coll (WY)
Westmoreland County Comm Coll (PA)

INDUSTRIAL PRODUCTION TECHNOLOGIES RELATED
Antelope Valley Coll (CA)
Barton County Comm Coll (KS)
Bismarck State Coll (ND)
Camden County Coll (NJ)
Ivy Tech Comm Coll–Central Indiana (IN)
Ivy Tech Comm Coll–East Central (IN)
Ivy Tech Comm Coll–Kokomo (IN)
Ivy Tech Comm Coll–Lafayette (IN)
Ivy Tech Comm Coll–North Central (IN)
Ivy Tech Comm Coll–Northeast (IN)
Ivy Tech Comm Coll–Richmond (IN)
Ivy Tech Comm Coll–Southwest (IN)
Ivy Tech Comm Coll–Wabash Valley (IN)
Kent State U at Trumbull (OH)
Middlesex County Coll (NJ)
Nashville State Comm Coll (TN)
Southwestern Michigan Coll (MI)
Tri-County Tech Coll (SC)

INDUSTRIAL RADIOLOGIC TECHNOLOGY
Amarillo Coll (TX)
Blinn Coll (TX)

Copiah-Lincoln Comm Coll (MS)
Daytona State Coll (FL)
Eastern Gateway Comm Coll (OH)
Iowa Central Comm Coll (IA)
Lorain County Comm Coll (OH)
Monroe Comm Coll (NY)
Mt. San Antonio Coll (CA)
Northern Essex Comm Coll (MA)
Odessa Coll (TX)
Salt Lake Comm Coll (UT)
Southeastern Comm Coll (IA)
Tarrant County Coll District (TX)
Tyler Jr Coll (TX)
Virginia Western Comm Coll (VA)

INDUSTRIAL SAFETY TECHNOLOGY
Fox Valley Tech Coll (WI)
Northwest Tech Coll (MN)

INDUSTRIAL TECHNOLOGY
Albany Tech Coll (GA)
Allen Comm Coll (KS)
Arizona Western Coll (AZ)
Bismarck State Coll (ND)
Bossier Parish Comm Coll (LA)
Bowling Green State U–Firelands Coll (OH)
Bucks County Comm Coll (PA)
Central Georgia Tech Coll (GA)
Central Oregon Comm Coll (OR)
Central Virginia Comm Coll (VA)
Cerritos Coll (CA)
Cincinnati State Tech and Comm Coll (OH)
Cleveland State Comm Coll (TN)
Clinton Comm Coll (NY)
Columbus Tech Coll (GA)
Comm Coll of the Air Force (AL)
Crowder Coll (MO)
Daytona State Coll (FL)
Dodge City Comm Coll (KS)
Eastern Gateway Comm Coll (OH)
Edison Comm Coll (OH)
Erie Comm Coll, North Campus (NY)
Gateway Comm and Tech Coll (KY)
Georgia Piedmont Tech Coll (GA)
Grand Rapids Comm Coll (MI)
Great Basin Coll (NV)
Hagerstown Comm Coll (MD)
Highland Comm Coll (IL)
Hopkinsville Comm Coll (KY)
Illinois Central Coll (IL)
Illinois Eastern Comm Colls, Wabash Valley College (IL)
Ivy Tech Comm Coll–Bloomington (IN)
Ivy Tech Comm Coll–Central Indiana (IN)
Ivy Tech Comm Coll–Columbus (IN)
Ivy Tech Comm Coll–East Central (IN)
Ivy Tech Comm Coll–Kokomo (IN)
Ivy Tech Comm Coll–Lafayette (IN)
Ivy Tech Comm Coll–North Central (IN)
Ivy Tech Comm Coll–Northeast (IN)
Ivy Tech Comm Coll–Northwest (IN)
Ivy Tech Comm Coll–Richmond (IN)
Ivy Tech Comm Coll–Southeast (IN)
Ivy Tech Comm Coll–Southern Indiana (IN)
Ivy Tech Comm Coll–Southwest (IN)
Ivy Tech Comm Coll–Wabash Valley (IN)
John Tyler Comm Coll (VA)
Kellogg Comm Coll (MI)
Kent State U at Trumbull (OH)
Kent State U at Tuscarawas (OH)
Lackawanna Coll (PA)
Lake Land Coll (IL)
Lanier Tech Coll (GA)
Lone Star Coll–CyFair (TX)
Lone Star Coll–North Harris (TX)
Lone Star Coll–Tomball (TX)
Lorain County Comm Coll (OH)
Los Angeles Trade-Tech Coll (CA)
Macomb Comm Coll (MI)
Manchester Comm Coll (CT)
Miami Dade Coll (FL)
Monroe Comm Coll (NY)
Muskegon Comm Coll (MI)
Nashville State Comm Coll (TN)
Navarro Coll (TX)
North Georgia Tech Coll (GA)
Northwest Tech Coll (MN)
Nunez Comm Coll (LA)
Olympic Coll (WA)
Ozarks Tech Comm Coll (MO)
Panola Coll (TX)

Piedmont Comm Coll (NC)
Richland Comm Coll (IL)
Rock Valley Coll (IL)
Rowan-Cabarrus Comm Coll (NC)
St. Charles Comm Coll (MO)
San Joaquin Valley Coll, Hesperia (CA)
San Joaquin Valley Coll, Salida (CA)
San Joaquin Valley Coll, Visalia (CA)
San Juan Coll (NM)
Savannah Tech Coll (GA)
Seminole State Coll of Florida (FL)
Southeast Tech Inst (SD)
Southern Crescent Tech Coll (GA)
South Georgia Tech Coll (GA)
Southwest Tennessee Comm Coll (TN)
Spoon River Coll (IL)
Stark State Coll (OH)
Walters State Comm Coll (TN)
Western Nevada Coll (NV)
West Georgia Tech Coll (GA)
Westmoreland County Comm Coll (PA)

INFORMATICS
Ivy Tech Comm Coll–Bloomington (IN)
Ivy Tech Comm Coll–Central Indiana (IN)
Ivy Tech Comm Coll–Columbus (IN)
Ivy Tech Comm Coll–East Central (IN)
Ivy Tech Comm Coll–Kokomo (IN)
Ivy Tech Comm Coll–Lafayette (IN)
Ivy Tech Comm Coll–Richmond (IN)
Ivy Tech Comm Coll–Southeast (IN)
Ivy Tech Comm Coll–Southern Indiana (IN)
Ivy Tech Comm Coll–Southwest (IN)
Ivy Tech Comm Coll–Wabash Valley (IN)

INFORMATION SCIENCE/ STUDIES
Alamance Comm Coll (NC)
Alexandria Tech and Comm Coll (MN)
Allen Comm Coll (KS)
Amarillo Coll (TX)
Athens Tech Coll (GA)
Augusta Tech Coll (GA)
Bainbridge State Coll (GA)
Barton County Comm Coll (KS)
Bossier Parish Comm Coll (LA)
Brookhaven Coll (TX)
Bucks County Comm Coll (PA)
Catawba Valley Comm Coll (NC)
Cayuga County Comm Coll (NY)
Central Georgia Tech Coll (GA)
Century Coll (MN)
Chattahoochee Tech Coll (GA)
Coastal Pines Tech Coll (GA)
Cochise County Comm Coll District (AZ)
Coll of The Albemarle (NC)
Columbus Tech Coll (GA)
Dabney S. Lancaster Comm Coll (VA)
Dodge City Comm Coll (KS)
Dutchess Comm Coll (NY)
Dyersburg State Comm Coll (TN)
Eastern Arizona Coll (AZ)
Fayetteville Tech Comm Coll (NC)
Genesee Comm Coll (NY)
Georgia Highlands Coll (GA)
Georgia Northwestern Tech Coll (GA)
Georgia Piedmont Tech Coll (GA)
Gwinnett Tech Coll (GA)
Harford Comm Coll (MD)
Howard Comm Coll (MD)
ITI Tech Coll (LA)
Ivy Tech Comm Coll–Bloomington (IN)
Ivy Tech Comm Coll–Central Indiana (IN)
Ivy Tech Comm Coll–Columbus (IN)
Ivy Tech Comm Coll–East Central (IN)
Ivy Tech Comm Coll–Kokomo (IN)
Ivy Tech Comm Coll–Lafayette (IN)
Ivy Tech Comm Coll–Richmond (IN)
Ivy Tech Comm Coll–Southeast (IN)
Ivy Tech Comm Coll–Southern Indiana (IN)
Ivy Tech Comm Coll–Southwest (IN)
Ivy Tech Comm Coll–Wabash Valley (IN)
Jamestown Comm Coll (NY)
Jefferson Comm Coll (NY)
Kaskaskia Coll (IL)
Kirtland Comm Coll (MI)

Lamar Comm Coll (CO)
Lanier Tech Coll (GA)
Lorain County Comm Coll (OH)
Los Angeles Trade-Tech Coll (CA)
Manchester Comm Coll (CT)
Martin Comm Coll (NC)
Miami Dade Coll (FL)
Mitchell Comm Coll (NC)
Monroe Comm Coll (NY)
Montgomery County Comm Coll (PA)
Muskegon Comm Coll (MI)
Nashville State Comm Coll (TN)
New River Comm Coll (VA)
Niagara County Comm Coll (NY)
North Central Texas Coll (TX)
North Shore Comm Coll (MA)
Norwalk Comm Coll (CT)
Oconee Fall Line Tech Coll (GA)
Odessa Coll (TX)
Ogeechee Tech Coll (GA)
Oklahoma State U, Oklahoma City (OK)
Ozarks Tech Comm Coll (MO)
Panola Coll (TX)
Paris Jr Coll (TX)
Penn State DuBois (PA)
Pensacola State Coll (FL)
Queensborough Comm Coll of the City U of New York (NY)
Rappahannock Comm Coll (VA)
Richland Comm Coll (IL)
Rowan-Cabarrus Comm Coll (NC)
Salt Lake Comm Coll (UT)
Scottsdale Comm Coll (AZ)
Seminole State Coll of Florida (FL)
Shawnee Comm Coll (IL)
Sheridan Coll (WY)
Southeastern Comm Coll (IA)
Southeastern Tech Coll (GA)
Southern Regional Tech Coll (GA)
South Florida State Coll (FL)
South Georgia Tech Coll (GA)
Spoon River Coll (IL)
State U of New York Coll of Technology at Alfred (NY)
Sullivan County Comm Coll (NY)
Tompkins Cortland Comm Coll (NY)
Tunxis Comm Coll (CT)
Victor Valley Coll (CA)
Weatherford Coll (TX)
Westchester Comm Coll (NY)
Western Wyoming Comm Coll (WY)
West Georgia Tech Coll (GA)
Wytheville Comm Coll (VA)

INFORMATION TECHNOLOGY
Antelope Valley Coll (CA)
Atlanta Tech Coll (GA)
Blue Ridge Comm and Tech Coll (WV)
Caldwell Comm Coll and Tech Inst (NC)
Catawba Valley Comm Coll (NC)
Chandler-Gilbert Comm Coll (AZ)
City Colls of Chicago, Olive-Harvey College (IL)
Cleveland Comm Coll (NC)
Coll of Central Florida (FL)
Coll of The Albemarle (NC)
Columbia Coll (CA)
Columbia-Greene Comm Coll (NY)
Corning Comm Coll (NY)
Craven Comm Coll (NC)
Daytona State Coll (FL)
Erie Comm Coll, South Campus (NY)
Fayetteville Tech Comm Coll (NC)
Florida SouthWestern State Coll (FL)
Frederick Comm Coll (MD)
Fullerton Coll (CA)
Galveston Coll (TX)
Georgia Military Coll (GA)
Gordon State Coll (GA)
Great Falls Coll Montana State U (MT)
Halifax Comm Coll (NC)
Highland Comm Coll (IL)
Howard Comm Coll (MD)
Illinois Eastern Comm Colls, Olney Central College (IL)
ITI Tech Coll (LA)
Ivy Tech Comm Coll–Bloomington (IN)
Ivy Tech Comm Coll–Central Indiana (IN)
Ivy Tech Comm Coll–Columbus (IN)
Ivy Tech Comm Coll–East Central (IN)
Ivy Tech Comm Coll–Kokomo (IN)
Ivy Tech Comm Coll–Lafayette (IN)
Ivy Tech Comm Coll–Richmond (IN)
Ivy Tech Comm Coll–Southeast (IN)

Ivy Tech Comm Coll–Southern Indiana (IN)
Ivy Tech Comm Coll–Southwest (IN)
Ivy Tech Comm Coll–Wabash Valley (IN)
James Sprunt Comm Coll (NC)
Jamestown Comm Coll (NY)
Jefferson Coll (MO)
John Tyler Comm Coll (VA)
Lake Land Coll (IL)
LDS Business Coll (UT)
Lenoir Comm Coll (NC)
Lone Star Coll–CyFair (TX)
Lone Star Coll–Montgomery (TX)
Lorain County Comm Coll (OH)
McHenry County Coll (IL)
Mesabi Range Coll (MN)
Miami Dade Coll (FL)
Minnesota State Comm and Tech Coll–Detroit Lakes (MN)
Minnesota State Comm and Tech Coll–Moorhead (MN)
Minnesota West Comm and Tech Coll (MN)
Mitchell Comm Coll (NC)
Mohave Comm Coll (AZ)
Monroe Comm Coll (NY)
Montgomery Comm Coll (NC)
Nashville State Comm Coll (TN)
Norwalk Comm Coll (CT)
Oakton Comm Coll (IL)
Oklahoma State U Inst of Technology (OK)
Oklahoma State U, Oklahoma City (OK)
Palomar Coll (CA)
Panola Coll (TX)
Piedmont Comm Coll (NC)
Queensborough Comm Coll of the City U of New York (NY)
Randolph Comm Coll (NC)
Raritan Valley Comm Coll (NJ)
Richmond Comm Coll (NC)
Rockingham Comm Coll (NC)
Rowan-Cabarrus Comm Coll (NC)
Rowan Coll at Burlington County (NJ)
Salt Lake Comm Coll (UT)
San Joaquin Valley Coll–Online (CA)
Savannah Tech Coll (GA)
Seminole State Coll of Florida (FL)
Sierra Coll (CA)
South Suburban Coll (IL)
Southwest Tennessee Comm Coll (TN)
Stark State Coll (OH)
Tallahassee Comm Coll (FL)
Tidewater Comm Coll (VA)
Tyler Jr Coll (TX)
U of Pittsburgh at Titusville (PA)
Wayne Comm Coll (NC)
Western Piedmont Comm Coll (NC)
Western Wyoming Comm Coll (WY)

INFORMATION TECHNOLOGY PROJECT MANAGEMENT
Cincinnati State Tech and Comm Coll (OH)

INSTITUTIONAL FOOD WORKERS
Hinds Comm Coll (MS)
James Sprunt Comm Coll (NC)
Southwestern Indian Polytechnic Inst (NM)

INSTRUMENTATION TECHNOLOGY
Amarillo Coll (TX)
Bellingham Tech Coll (WA)
Bismarck State Coll (ND)
Butler County Comm Coll (PA)
Cape Fear Comm Coll (NC)
Finger Lakes Comm Coll (NY)
Georgia Piedmont Tech Coll (GA)
Hagerstown Comm Coll (MD)
Houston Comm Coll (TX)
ITI Tech Coll (LA)
Lakeland Comm Coll (OH)
Mesabi Range Coll (MN)
Monroe Comm Coll (NY)
Moraine Valley Comm Coll (IL)
New River Comm Coll (VA)
Ozarks Tech Comm Coll (MO)
Ranken Tech Coll (MO)
Ridgewater Coll (MN)
Salt Lake Comm Coll (UT)
San Jacinto Coll District (TX)
San Juan Coll (NM)
Southwestern Indian Polytechnic Inst (NM)
Sowela Tech Comm Coll (LA)
Texas State Tech Coll (TX)

Western Wyoming Comm Coll (WY)

INSURANCE
Cerritos Coll (CA)
Palomar Coll (CA)
Richland Comm Coll (IL)
South Florida State Coll (FL)

INTEGRATED CIRCUIT DESIGN
Collin County Comm Coll District (TX)

INTELLIGENCE
Cochise County Comm Coll District (AZ)

INTERDISCIPLINARY STUDIES
Anoka-Ramsey Comm Coll (MN)
Blackhawk Tech Coll (WI)
Bowling Green State U–Firelands Coll (OH)
Elizabethtown Comm and Tech Coll, Elizabethtown (KY)
Gateway Tech Coll (WI)
Great Basin Coll (NV)
North Shore Comm Coll (MA)
Reading Area Comm Coll (PA)
Schenectady County Comm Coll (NY)
Williamsburg Tech Coll (SC)
Wisconsin Indianhead Tech Coll (WI)

INTERIOR ARCHITECTURE
Coll of Central Florida (FL)

INTERIOR DESIGN
Alexandria Tech and Comm Coll (MN)
Amarillo Coll (TX)
American River Coll (CA)
Antelope Valley Coll (CA)
Arapahoe Comm Coll (CO)
Ca&nnada Coll (CA)
Cape Fear Comm Coll (NC)
Century Coll (MN)
Clary Sage Coll (OK)
Coll of the Canyons (CA)
Collin County Comm Coll District (TX)
Davis Coll (OH)
Daytona State Coll (FL)
Fashion Inst of Technology (NY)
Fashion Inst of Design & Merchandising, LA Campus (CA)
FIDM/Fashion Inst of Design & Merchandising, Orange County Campus (CA)
Fox Valley Tech Coll (WI)
Front Range Comm Coll (CO)
Fullerton Coll (CA)
Gateway Tech Coll (WI)
Gwinnett Tech Coll (GA)
Harford Comm Coll (MD)
Hawkeye Comm Coll (IA)
Houston Comm Coll (TX)
Ivy Tech Comm Coll–Columbus (IN)
Ivy Tech Comm Coll–East Central (IN)
Ivy Tech Comm Coll–North Central (IN)
Ivy Tech Comm Coll–Southwest (IN)
Lanier Tech Coll (IN)
LDS Business Coll (UT)
Lehigh Carbon Comm Coll (PA)
Lone Star Coll–Kingwood (TX)
Miami Dade Coll (FL)
Monroe Comm Coll (NY)
Montgomery Coll (MD)
Mt. San Antonio Coll (CA)
Northampton Comm Coll (PA)
Norwalk Comm Coll (CT)
Ogeechee Tech Coll (GA)
Onondaga Comm Coll (NY)
Orange Coast Coll (CA)
Palomar Coll (CA)
Randolph Comm Coll (NC)
Raritan Valley Comm Coll (NJ)
San Jacinto Coll District (TX)
Scottsdale Comm Coll (AZ)
Seminole State Coll of Florida (FL)
State U of New York Coll of Technology at Alfred (NY)
Tidewater Comm Coll (VA)
Tulsa Comm Coll (OK)
Waukesha County Tech Coll (WI)
Western Iowa Tech Comm Coll (IA)

INTERMEDIA/MULTIMEDIA
Oklahoma State U Inst of Technology (OK)

Western Wyoming Comm Coll (WY)

INTERNATIONAL BUSINESS/ TRADE/COMMERCE
Austin Comm Coll District (TX)
Bunker Hill Comm Coll (MA)
Fullerton Coll (CA)
Herkimer County Comm Coll (NY)
Houston Comm Coll (TX)
Luzerne County Comm Coll (PA)
Massachusetts Bay Comm Coll (MA)
Monroe Comm Coll (NY)
Orange Coast Coll (CA)
Palomar Coll (CA)
Pasadena City Coll (CA)
Raritan Valley Comm Coll (NJ)
San Jacinto Coll District (TX)
South Florida State Coll (FL)
Stark State Coll (OH)
Tompkins Cortland Comm Coll (NY)
Tulsa Comm Coll (OK)
Westchester Comm Coll (NY)

INTERNATIONAL/GLOBAL STUDIES
Berkshire Comm Coll (MA)
Central Wyoming Coll (WY)
Jamestown Comm Coll (NY)
Macomb Comm Coll (MI)
Massachusetts Bay Comm Coll (MA)
Northampton Comm Coll (PA)
Northwest Vista Coll (TX)
Ocean County Coll (NJ)
Pasadena City Coll (CA)
Rowan Coll at Burlington County (NJ)
Salt Lake Comm Coll (UT)
Tompkins Cortland Comm Coll (NY)

INTERNATIONAL MARKETING
Waukesha County Tech Coll (WI)

INTERNATIONAL RELATIONS AND AFFAIRS
American River Coll (CA)
Ca&nnada Coll (CA)
Casper Coll (WY)
Cerritos Coll (CA)
Harford Comm Coll (MD)
Harrisburg Area Comm Coll (PA)
Miami Dade Coll (FL)
Northern Essex Comm Coll (MA)
Northwest Coll (WY)
Salt Lake Comm Coll (UT)
South Florida State Coll (FL)
Western Wyoming Comm Coll (WY)

IRONWORKING
Ivy Tech Comm Coll–Lafayette (IN)
Ivy Tech Comm Coll–North Central (IN)
Ivy Tech Comm Coll–Northeast (IN)
Ivy Tech Comm Coll–Northwest (IN)
Ivy Tech Comm Coll–Southwest (IN)
Ivy Tech Comm Coll–Wabash Valley (IN)

ITALIAN
Los Angeles Valley Coll (CA)
Miami Dade Coll (FL)

JAPANESE
Austin Comm Coll District (TX)
Citrus Coll (CA)

JAZZ/JAZZ STUDIES
Comm Coll of Rhode Island (RI)
South Florida State Coll (FL)

JOURNALISM
Allen Comm Coll (KS)
Amarillo Coll (TX)
American River Coll (CA)
Arapahoe Comm Coll (CO)
Austin Comm Coll District (TX)
Barton County Comm Coll (KS)
Bucks County Comm Coll (PA)
Casper Coll (WY)
Central Texas Coll (TX)
Cerritos Coll (CA)
Citrus Coll (CA)
Cloud County Comm Coll (KS)
Cochise County Comm Coll District (AZ)
Coll of Central Florida (FL)
Coll of the Canyons (CA)
Copiah-Lincoln Comm Coll (MS)
Delta Coll (MI)
Dodge City Comm Coll (KS)
Fullerton Coll (CA)
Georgia Highlands Coll (GA)
Grand Rapids Comm Coll (MI)
Housatonic Comm Coll (CT)
Iowa Central Comm Coll (IA)
Itawamba Comm Coll (MS)

Kilgore Coll (TX)
Lorain County Comm Coll (OH)
Los Angeles Valley Coll (CA)
Luzerne County Comm Coll (PA)
Manchester Comm Coll (CT)
Miami Dade Coll (FL)
Mt. San Antonio Coll (CA)
Northampton Comm Coll (PA)
Northeastern Jr Coll (CO)
Northern Essex Comm Coll (MA)
Northwest Coll (WY)
Orange Coast Coll (CA)
Palomar Coll (CA)
Panola Coll (TX)
Paris Jr Coll (TX)
Pensacola State Coll (FL)
Potomac State Coll of West Virginia U (WV)
Rowan Coll at Burlington County (NJ)
San Jacinto Coll District (TX)
San Joaquin Delta Coll (CA)
South Florida State Coll (FL)
Texarkana Coll (TX)
Vincennes U (IN)
Westchester Comm Coll (NY)
Western Wyoming Comm Coll (WY)

JUVENILE CORRECTIONS
Danville Area Comm Coll (IL)
Illinois Central Coll (IL)
Kaskaskia Coll (IL)

KEYBOARD INSTRUMENTS
Itawamba Comm Coll (MS)

KINDERGARTEN/PRESCHOOL EDUCATION
Alamance Comm Coll (NC)
Bainbridge State Coll (GA)
Butler County Comm Coll (PA)
Casper Coll (WY)
Central Lakes Coll (MN)
Cerritos Coll (CA)
Cleveland State Comm Coll (TN)
Comm Coll of Philadelphia (PA)
Comm Coll of Rhode Island (RI)
County Coll of Morris (NJ)
Daytona State Coll (FL)
Finger Lakes Comm Coll (NY)
Genesee Comm Coll (NY)
Hesston Coll (KS)
Howard Comm Coll (MD)
Itawamba Comm Coll (MS)
Lorain County Comm Coll (OH)
Los Angeles Valley Coll (CA)
Manchester Comm Coll (CT)
Miami Dade Coll (FL)
Mitchell Comm Coll (NC)
Mt. San Antonio Coll (CA)
Nashville State Comm Coll (TN)
Northern Essex Comm Coll (MA)
North Shore Comm Coll (MA)
Northwest Coll (WY)
Nunez Comm Coll (LA)
Odessa Coll (TX)
Otero Jr Coll (CO)
Ozarks Tech Comm Coll (MO)
Quinsigamond Comm Coll (MA)
Raritan Valley Comm Coll (NJ)
Southern U at Shreveport (LA)
Southwest Tennessee Comm Coll (TN)
Spoon River Coll (IL)
Sullivan County Comm Coll (NY)
Tidewater Comm Coll (VA)
Truckee Meadows Comm Coll (NV)
Tunxis Comm Coll (CT)
U of Cincinnati Blue Ash Coll (OH)
U of New Mexico–Gallup (NM)
Victor Valley Coll (CA)
Virginia Western Comm Coll (VA)
Wenatchee Valley Coll (WA)

KINESIOLOGY AND EXERCISE SCIENCE
Ancilla Coll (IN)
Antelope Valley Coll (CA)
Barton County Comm Coll (KS)
Bucks County Comm Coll (PA)
Carroll Comm Coll (MD)
Central Oregon Comm Coll (OR)
Cerritos Coll (CA)
Chandler-Gilbert Comm Coll (AZ)
County Coll of Morris (NJ)
Feather River Coll (CA)
Ivy Tech Comm Coll–East Central (IN)
Ivy Tech Comm Coll–Southern Indiana (IN)

Laramie County Comm Coll (WY)
Lehigh Carbon Comm Coll (PA)
Lewis and Clark Comm Coll (IL)
Nashville State Comm Coll (TN)
Norwalk Comm Coll (CT)
Orange Coast Coll (CA)
Palomar Coll (CA)
Raritan Valley Comm Coll (NJ)
St. Philip's Coll (TX)
Salt Lake Comm Coll (UT)
South Florida State Coll (FL)
South Suburban Coll (IL)
Three Rivers Comm Coll (CT)
Western Wyoming Comm Coll (WY)

LABOR AND INDUSTRIAL RELATIONS
Los Angeles Trade-Tech Coll (CA)

LANDSCAPE ARCHITECTURE
Caldwell Comm Coll and Tech Inst (NC)
Monroe Comm Coll (NY)
Mt. San Antonio Coll (CA)
Truckee Meadows Comm Coll (NV)
Western Texas Coll (TX)

LANDSCAPING AND GROUNDSKEEPING
American River Coll (CA)
Anoka Tech Coll (MN)
Antelope Valley Coll (CA)
Cape Fear Comm Coll (NC)
Century Coll (MN)
Cincinnati State Tech and Comm Coll (OH)
Clark Coll (WA)
Coll of Central Florida (FL)
Danville Area Comm Coll (IL)
Fullerton Coll (CA)
Grand Rapids Comm Coll (MI)
Hawkeye Comm Coll (IA)
Hennepin Tech Coll (MN)
Hinds Comm Coll (MS)
James H. Faulkner State Comm Coll (AL)
Miami Dade Coll (FL)
Pensacola State Coll (FL)
San Juan Coll (NM)
South Florida State Coll (FL)
Springfield Tech Comm Coll (MA)
Williamson Coll of the Trades (PA)

LANGUAGE INTERPRETATION AND TRANSLATION
Allen Comm Coll (KS)
Cape Fear Comm Coll (NC)
Century Coll (MN)
Cleveland Comm Coll (NC)
Lake Region State Coll (ND)
Oklahoma State U, Oklahoma City (OK)

LASER AND OPTICAL TECHNOLOGY
Amarillo Coll (TX)
Monroe Comm Coll (NY)
Queensborough Comm Coll of the City U of New York (NY)
Quinsigamond Comm Coll (MA)
Springfield Tech Comm Coll (MA)
Texas State Tech Coll (TX)
Three Rivers Comm Coll (CT)

LATIN
Austin Comm Coll District (TX)

LATIN AMERICAN STUDIES
Central New Mexico Comm Coll (NM)
Miami Dade Coll (FL)

LAW ENFORCEMENT INVESTIGATION AND INTERVIEWING
Arizona Western Coll (AZ)
Mohawk Valley Comm Coll (NY)

LEGAL ADMINISTRATIVE ASSISTANT/SECRETARY
Alamance Comm Coll (NC)
Alexandria Tech and Comm Coll (MN)
Alvin Comm Coll (TX)
Amarillo Coll (TX)
Anoka Tech Coll (MN)
Bismarck State Coll (ND)
Blackhawk Tech Coll (WI)
Blinn Coll (TX)
Bradford School (PA)
Butler County Comm Coll (PA)

Central Lakes Coll (MN)
Cerritos Coll (CA)
Clark Coll (WA)
Cleveland Comm Coll (NC)
Comm Coll of Rhode Island (RI)
Craven Comm Coll (NC)
Crowder Coll (MO)
Dabney S. Lancaster Comm Coll (VA)
Dodge City Comm Coll (KS)
Eastern Gateway Comm Coll (OH)
Forrest Coll (SC)
Fullerton Coll (CA)
Georgia Piedmont Tech Coll (GA)
Herkimer County Comm Coll (NY)
Howard Comm Coll (MD)
IBMC Coll, Fort Collins (CO)
International Business Coll, Indianapolis (IN)
Jefferson Coll (MO)
Kellogg Comm Coll (MI)
King's Coll (NC)
Lake Land Coll (IL)
Lake Superior Coll (MN)
Lewis and Clark Comm Coll (IL)
Manchester Comm Coll (CT)
Miami Dade Coll (FL)
Minneapolis Business Coll (MN)
Minnesota State Coll–Southeast Tech (MN)
Monroe Comm Coll (NY)
Mt. San Antonio Coll (CA)
Muskegon Comm Coll (MI)
Navarro Coll (TX)
New Mexico Jr Coll (NM)
North Central Texas Coll (TX)
North Shore Comm Coll (MA)
Odessa Coll (TX)
Ohio Business Coll, Sheffield Village (OH)
Oklahoma City Comm Coll (OK)
Otero Jr Coll (CO)
Pensacola State Coll (FL)
Renton Tech Coll (WA)
Richland Comm Coll (IL)
Ridgewater Coll (MN)
St. Philip's Coll (TX)
Shawnee Comm Coll (IL)
Spoon River Coll (IL)
Stark State Coll (OH)
Treasure Valley Comm Coll (OR)
Trumbull Business Coll (OH)
Tyler Jr Coll (TX)
Wenatchee Valley Coll (WA)
Western Wyoming Comm Coll (WY)

LEGAL ASSISTANT/PARALEGAL
Alexandria Tech and Comm Coll (MN)
Alvin Comm Coll (TX)
American River Coll (CA)
Anne Arundel Comm Coll (MD)
Arapahoe Comm Coll (CO)
Arizona Western Coll (AZ)
Athens Tech Coll (GA)
Atlanta Tech Coll (GA)
Austin Comm Coll District (TX)
Beckfield Coll (KY)
Bellingham Tech Coll (WA)
Bevill State Comm Coll (AL)
Blue Ridge Comm and Tech Coll (WV)
Bradford School (PA)
Bunker Hill Comm Coll (MA)
Caldwell Comm Coll and Tech Inst (NC)
Camden County Coll (NJ)
Ca&nnada Coll (CA)
Casper Coll (WY)
Central Georgia Tech Coll (GA)
Central New Mexico Comm Coll (NM)
Central Texas Coll (TX)
Cerritos Coll (CA)
Chesapeake Coll (MD)
Chippewa Valley Tech Coll (WI)
Clark Coll (WA)
Cloud County Comm Coll (KS)
Coll of Central Florida (FL)
Coll of the Canyons (CA)
Collin County Comm Coll District (TX)
Comm Care Coll (OK)
Comm Coll of Baltimore County (MD)
Comm Coll of Rhode Island (RI)
Comm Coll of the Air Force (AL)
Daytona State Coll (FL)
Delta Coll (MI)
Dutchess Comm Coll (NY)

Eastern Idaho Tech Coll (ID)
Edison Comm Coll (OH)
Elgin Comm Coll (IL)
Erie Comm Coll (NY)
ETI Tech Coll of Niles (OH)
Fayetteville Tech Comm Coll (NC)
Finger Lakes Comm Coll (NY)
Fiorello H. LaGuardia Comm Coll of the City U of New York (NY)
Florida SouthWestern State Coll (FL)
Forrest Coll (SC)
Fox Valley Tech Coll (WI)
Frederick Comm Coll (MD)
Front Range Comm Coll (CO)
Fullerton Coll (CA)
Gadsden State Comm Coll (AL)
Genesee Comm Coll (NY)
Georgia Military Coll (GA)
Georgia Northwestern Tech Coll (GA)
Georgia Piedmont Tech Coll (GA)
Greenville Tech Coll (SC)
Halifax Comm Coll (NC)
Harford Comm Coll (MD)
Harrisburg Area Comm Coll (PA)
Herkimer County Comm Coll (NY)
Hillsborough Comm Coll (FL)
Hinds Comm Coll (MS)
Houston Comm Coll (TX)
Hudson County Comm Coll (NJ)
Hutchinson Comm Coll (KS)
IBMC Coll, Fort Collins (CO)
Illinois Central Coll (IL)
Illinois Eastern Comm Colls, Wabash Valley College (IL)
International Business Coll, Indianapolis (IN)
Ivy Tech Comm Coll–Bloomington (IN)
Ivy Tech Comm Coll–Central Indiana (IN)
Ivy Tech Comm Coll–Columbus (IN)
Ivy Tech Comm Coll–East Central (IN)
Ivy Tech Comm Coll–Kokomo (IN)
Ivy Tech Comm Coll–Lafayette (IN)
Ivy Tech Comm Coll–North Central (IN)
Ivy Tech Comm Coll–Northeast (IN)
Ivy Tech Comm Coll–Northwest (IN)
Ivy Tech Comm Coll–Richmond (IN)
Ivy Tech Comm Coll–Southeast (IN)
Ivy Tech Comm Coll–Southern Indiana (IN)
Ivy Tech Comm Coll–Southwest (IN)
Ivy Tech Comm Coll–Wabash Valley (IN)
James H. Faulkner State Comm Coll (AL)
Jefferson Comm Coll (NY)
Johnston Comm Coll (NC)
J. Sargeant Reynolds Comm Coll (VA)
Kankakee Comm Coll (IL)
Kellogg Comm Coll (MI)
Kent State U at East Liverpool (OH)
Kent State U at Trumbull (OH)
Kilgore Coll (TX)
King's Coll (NC)
Lackawanna Coll (PA)
Lakeland Comm Coll (OH)
Lake Superior Coll (MN)
Laramie County Comm Coll (WY)
LDS Business Coll (UT)
Lehigh Carbon Comm Coll (PA)
Lewis and Clark Comm Coll (IL)
Lone Star Coll–North Harris (TX)
Luzerne County Comm Coll (PA)
Macomb Comm Coll (MI)
Manchester Comm Coll (CT)
Manor Coll (PA)
Massachusetts Bay Comm Coll (MA)
Mercer County Comm Coll (NJ)
Miami Dade Coll (FL)
Middlesex County Coll (NJ)
Midlands Tech Coll (SC)
Minneapolis Business Coll (MN)
Minnesota State Comm and Tech Coll–Detroit Lakes (MN)
Mohave Comm Coll (AZ)
Montgomery Coll (MD)
Mountain State Coll (WV)
Mt. San Antonio Coll (CA)
Mount Wachusett Comm Coll (MA)
Nashville State Comm Coll (TN)
Naugatuck Valley Comm Coll (CT)
Navarro Coll (TX)
New River Comm Coll (VA)
Northampton Comm Coll (PA)
North Central Texas Coll (TX)

Northern Essex Comm Coll (MA)
North Hennepin Comm Coll (MN)
North Shore Comm Coll (MA)
NorthWest Arkansas Comm Coll (AR)
Norwalk Comm Coll (CT)
Nunez Comm Coll (LA)
Ogeechee Tech Coll (GA)
Oxnard Coll (CA)
Pasadena City Coll (CA)
Penn Foster Coll (AZ)
Pensacola State Coll (FL)
Quincy Coll (MA)
Raritan Valley Comm Coll (NJ)
Rowan Coll at Burlington County (NJ)
Salt Lake Comm Coll (UT)
San Jacinto Coll District (TX)
San Juan Coll (NM)
Seminole State Coll of Florida (FL)
Southern Crescent Tech Coll (GA)
Southern U at Shreveport (LA)
South Florida State Coll (FL)
South Georgia Tech Coll (GA)
South Suburban Coll (IL)
Southwest Tennessee Comm Coll (TN)
Sullivan County Comm Coll (NY)
Sumner Coll (OR)
Tallahassee Comm Coll (FL)
Tarrant County Coll District (TX)
Tech Coll of the Lowcountry (SC)
Tidewater Comm Coll (VA)
Tompkins Cortland Comm Coll (NY)
Truckee Meadows Comm Coll (NV)
Tulsa Comm Coll (OK)
Tyler Jr Coll (TX)
Vincennes U (IN)
Volunteer State Comm Coll (TN)
Wayne County Comm Coll District (MI)
Westchester Comm Coll (NY)
Western Iowa Tech Comm Coll (IA)
Western Piedmont Comm Coll (NC)
Westmoreland County Comm Coll (PA)

LEGAL PROFESSIONS AND STUDIES RELATED
Bucks County Comm Coll (PA)

LEGAL STUDIES
Alvin Comm Coll (TX)
Carroll Comm Coll (MD)
Macomb Comm Coll (MI)
Navarro Coll (TX)
Palomar Coll (CA)

LIBERAL ARTS AND SCIENCES AND HUMANITIES RELATED
Anne Arundel Comm Coll (MD)
Arapahoe Comm Coll (CO)
Bossier Parish Comm Coll (LA)
Bucks County Comm Coll (PA)
Cascadia Coll (WA)
Chandler-Gilbert Comm Coll (AZ)
Chesapeake Coll (MD)
Cleveland Comm Coll (NC)
Cleveland State Comm Coll (TN)
Coll of Central Florida (FL)
Comm Coll of Aurora (CO)
Comm Coll of Baltimore County (MD)
Corning Comm Coll (NY)
Craven Comm Coll (NC)
Dutchess Comm Coll (NY)
Erie Comm Coll (NY)
Fayetteville Tech Comm Coll (NC)
Front Range Comm Coll (CO)
Garrett Coll (MD)
Genesee Comm Coll (NY)
Great Falls Coll Montana State U (MT)
Hagerstown Comm Coll (MD)
Halifax Comm Coll (NC)
Holyoke Comm Coll (MA)
Ivy Tech Comm Coll–Richmond (IN)
James Sprunt Comm Coll (NC)
Jamestown Comm Coll (NY)
J. Sargeant Reynolds Comm Coll (VA)
Kent State U at Ashtabula (OH)
Kent State U at East Liverpool (OH)
Kent State U at Salem (OH)
Kent State U at Trumbull (OH)
Kent State U at Tuscarawas (OH)
Lenoir Comm Coll (NC)
Luzerne County Comm Coll (PA)
Martin Comm Coll (NC)

Minnesota West Comm and Tech Coll (MN)
Mitchell Comm Coll (NC)
Mohawk Valley Comm Coll (NY)
Montgomery Coll (MD)
Morgan Comm Coll (CO)
Northampton Comm Coll (PA)
Nunez Comm Coll (LA)
Onondaga Comm Coll (NY)
Panola Coll (TX)
Piedmont Comm Coll (NC)
Pueblo Comm Coll (CO)
Randolph Comm Coll (NC)
Ridgewater Coll (MN)
Southern Maine Comm Coll (ME)
Southern U at Shreveport (LA)
South Florida State Coll (FL)
Sowela Tech Comm Coll (LA)
State U of New York Coll of Technology at Alfred (NY)
Tech Coll of the Lowcountry (SC)
Tompkins Cortland Comm Coll (NY)
Wayne Comm Coll (NC)
Western Piedmont Comm Coll (NC)
Wor-Wic Comm Coll (MD)

LIBERAL ARTS AND SCIENCES/ LIBERAL STUDIES

Aiken Tech Coll (SC)
Alamance Comm Coll (NC)
Alexandria Tech and Comm Coll (MN)
Alvin Comm Coll (TX)
Amarillo Coll (TX)
American River Coll (CA)
American Samoa Comm Coll (AS)
Anne Arundel Comm Coll (MD)
Anoka-Ramsey Comm Coll (MN)
Antelope Valley Coll (CA)
Arapahoe Comm Coll (CO)
Asnuntuck Comm Coll (CT)
Bainbridge State Coll (GA)
Barton County Comm Coll (KS)
Berkshire Comm Coll (MA)
Bevill State Comm Coll (AL)
Big Bend Comm Coll (WA)
Bismarck State Coll (ND)
Blue Ridge Comm and Tech Coll (WV)
Borough of Manhattan Comm Coll of the City U of New York (NY)
Bossier Parish Comm Coll (LA)
Bowling Green State U–Firelands Coll (OH)
Brookhaven Coll (TX)
Bucks County Comm Coll (PA)
Caldwell Comm Coll and Tech Inst (NC)
Camden County Coll (NJ)
Ca&nnada Coll (CA)
Cape Fear Comm Coll (NC)
Carroll Comm Coll (MD)
Cascadia Coll (WA)
Casper Coll (WY)
Catawba Valley Comm Coll (NC)
Cayuga County Comm Coll (NY)
Cecil Coll (MD)
Central Lakes Coll (MN)
Central Maine Comm Coll (ME)
Central New Mexico Comm Coll (NM)
Central Ohio Tech Coll (OH)
Central Oregon Comm Coll (OR)
Central Texas Coll (TX)
Central Virginia Comm Coll (VA)
Century Coll (MN)
Cerritos Coll (CA)
Chandler-Gilbert Comm Coll (AZ)
Chatfield Coll (OH)
Chesapeake Coll (MD)
Chipola Coll (FL)
Chippewa Valley Tech Coll (WI)
Cincinnati State Tech and Comm Coll (OH)
Citrus Coll (CA)
City Colls of Chicago, Olive-Harvey College (IL)
Clark Coll (WA)
Cleveland Comm Coll (NC)
Cleveland State Comm Coll (TN)
Clinton Comm Coll (NY)
Cloud County Comm Coll (KS)
Coastline Comm Coll (CA)
Coll of Central Florida (FL)
Coll of The Albemarle (NC)
Coll of the Canyons (CA)
Collin County Comm Coll District (TX)
Colorado Northwestern Comm Coll (CO)
Columbia Coll (CA)
Columbia-Greene Comm Coll (NY)

Comm Coll of Aurora (CO)
Comm Coll of Baltimore County (MD)
Comm Coll of Philadelphia (PA)
Comm Coll of Rhode Island (RI)
Copiah-Lincoln Comm Coll (MS)
Corning Comm Coll (NY)
County Coll of Morris (NJ)
Craven Comm Coll (NC)
Crowder Coll (MO)
Dabney S. Lancaster Comm Coll (VA)
Danville Area Comm Coll (IL)
Dawson Comm Coll (MT)
Delta Coll (MI)
Denmark Tech Coll (SC)
Dodge City Comm Coll (KS)
Donnelly Coll (KS)
Dutchess Comm Coll (NY)
Dyersburg State Comm Coll (TN)
Eastern Arizona Coll (AZ)
Eastern Wyoming Coll (WY)
Edison Comm Coll (OH)
Elgin Comm Coll (IL)
Elizabethtown Comm and Tech Coll, Elizabethtown (KY)
Emory U, Oxford Coll (GA)
Erie Comm Coll (NY)
Erie Comm Coll, North Campus (NY)
Erie Comm Coll, South Campus (NY)
Estrella Mountain Comm Coll (AZ)
Fayetteville Tech Comm Coll (NC)
Feather River Coll (CA)
Finger Lakes Comm Coll (NY)
Fiorello H. LaGuardia Comm Coll of the City U of New York (NY)
Florida SouthWestern State Coll (FL)
Frederick Comm Coll (MD)
Front Range Comm Coll (CO)
Fullerton Coll (CA)
Gadsden State Comm Coll (AL)
Galveston Coll (TX)
Garrett Coll (MD)
Genesee Comm Coll (NY)
Georgia Highlands Coll (GA)
Gordon State Coll (GA)
Grand Rapids Comm Coll (MI)
Great Basin Coll (NV)
Greenville Tech Coll (SC)
Gulf Coast State Coll (FL)
Hagerstown Comm Coll (MD)
Halifax Comm Coll (NC)
Hawaii Tokai International Coll (HI)
Hawkeye Comm Coll (IA)
Herkimer County Comm Coll (NY)
Hesston Coll (KS)
Highland Comm Coll (IL)
Hillsborough Comm Coll (FL)
Holyoke Comm Coll (MA)
Hopkinsville Comm Coll (KY)
Housatonic Comm Coll (CT)
Howard Comm Coll (MD)
Hudson County Comm Coll (NJ)
Hutchinson Comm Coll (KS)
Ilisagvik Coll (AK)
Illinois Central Coll (IL)
Illinois Eastern Comm Colls, Frontier Community College (IL)
Illinois Eastern Comm Colls, Lincoln Trail College (IL)
Illinois Eastern Comm Colls, Olney Central College (IL)
Illinois Eastern Comm Colls, Wabash Valley College (IL)
Iowa Central Comm Coll (IA)
Itawamba Comm Coll (MS)
Ivy Tech Comm Coll–Bloomington (IN)
Ivy Tech Comm Coll–Central Indiana (IN)
Ivy Tech Comm Coll–Columbus (IN)
Ivy Tech Comm Coll–East Central (IN)
Ivy Tech Comm Coll–Kokomo (IN)
Ivy Tech Comm Coll–Lafayette (IN)
Ivy Tech Comm Coll–North Central (IN)
Ivy Tech Comm Coll–Northeast (IN)
Ivy Tech Comm Coll–Northwest (IN)
Ivy Tech Comm Coll–Richmond (IN)
Ivy Tech Comm Coll–Southeast (IN)
Ivy Tech Comm Coll–Southern Indiana (IN)
Ivy Tech Comm Coll–Southwest (IN)
Ivy Tech Comm Coll–Wabash Valley (IN)
James H. Faulkner State Comm Coll (AL)
James Sprunt Comm Coll (NC)
Jamestown Comm Coll (NY)
Jefferson Coll (MO)
Jefferson Comm Coll (NY)

Jefferson State Comm Coll (AL)
Johnston Comm Coll (NC)
Kaskaskia Coll (IL)
Kellogg Comm Coll (MI)
Kennebec Valley Comm Coll (ME)
Kent State U at Salem (OH)
Keweenaw Bay Ojibwa Comm Coll (MI)
Kirtland Comm Coll (MI)
Lackawanna Coll (PA)
Lake Land Coll (IL)
Lakeland Comm Coll (OH)
Lake Region State Coll (ND)
Lake Superior Coll (MN)
Lamar Comm Coll (CO)
LDS Business Coll (UT)
Leeward Comm Coll (HI)
Lehigh Carbon Comm Coll (PA)
Lenoir Comm Coll (NC)
Lewis and Clark Comm Coll (IL)
Lone Star Coll–CyFair (TX)
Lorain County Comm Coll (OH)
Los Angeles Trade-Tech Coll (CA)
Los Angeles Valley Coll (CA)
Lurleen B. Wallace Comm Coll (AL)
Luzerne County Comm Coll (PA)
Macomb Comm Coll (MI)
Manchester Comm Coll (CT)
Manor Coll (PA)
Marion Military Inst (AL)
Martin Comm Coll (NC)
Massachusetts Bay Comm Coll (MA)
McHenry County Coll (IL)
Mercer County Comm Coll (NJ)
Mesabi Range Coll (MN)
Miami Dade Coll (FL)
Middlesex County Coll (NJ)
Midlands Tech Coll (SC)
Mid-Plains Comm Coll, North Platte (NE)
Minnesota West Comm and Tech Coll (MN)
Mitchell Comm Coll (NC)
Mohave Comm Coll (AZ)
Mohawk Valley Comm Coll (NY)
Monroe Comm Coll (NY)
Montgomery Coll (MD)
Montgomery Comm Coll (NC)
Montgomery County Comm Coll (PA)
Moraine Valley Comm Coll (IL)
Morgan Comm Coll (CO)
Mott Comm Coll (MI)
Mount Wachusett Comm Coll (MA)
Muskegon Comm Coll (MI)
Naugatuck Valley Comm Coll (CT)
New Mexico Jr Coll (NM)
New River Comm Coll (VA)
Niagara County Comm Coll (NY)
Northampton Comm Coll (PA)
North Central Texas Coll (TX)
Northeastern Jr Coll (CO)
Northeast Iowa Comm Coll (IA)
Northern Essex Comm Coll (MA)
North Hennepin Comm Coll (MN)
Northland Comm and Tech Coll (MN)
North Shore Comm Coll (MA)
NorthWest Arkansas Comm Coll (AR)
Northwest Coll (WY)
Northwest-Shoals Comm Coll (AL)
Northwest Vista Coll (TX)
Norwalk Comm Coll (CT)
Oakton Comm Coll (IL)
Ocean County Coll (NJ)
Odessa Coll (TX)
Oklahoma City Comm Coll (OK)
Olympic Coll (WA)
Orange Coast Coll (CA)
Oregon Coast Comm Coll (OR)
Otero Jr Coll (CO)
Owensboro Comm and Tech Coll (KY)
Ozarks Tech Comm Coll (MO)
Palau Comm Coll (Palau)
Palomar Coll (CA)
Paris Jr Coll (TX)
Pasadena City Coll (CA)
Penn State DuBois (PA)
Penn State Fayette, The Eberly Campus (PA)
Penn State Mont Alto (PA)
Penn State Shenango (PA)
Pensacola State Coll (FL)
Piedmont Comm Coll (NC)
Potomac State Coll of West Virginia U (WV)
Pueblo Comm Coll (CO)
Queensborough Comm Coll of the City U of New York (NY)
Quincy Coll (MA)
Quinsigamond Comm Coll (MA)

Rainy River Comm Coll (MN)
Randolph Comm Coll (NC)
Rappahannock Comm Coll (VA)
Raritan Valley Comm Coll (NJ)
Reading Area Comm Coll (PA)
Rend Lake Coll (IL)
Richland Comm Coll (IL)
Richmond Comm Coll (NC)
Ridgewater Coll (MN)
Rio Hondo Coll (CA)
River Valley Comm Coll (NH)
Rockingham Comm Coll (NC)
Rock Valley Coll (IL)
Rogue Comm Coll (OR)
Rowan-Cabarrus Comm Coll (NC)
Rowan Coll at Burlington County (NJ)
Saginaw Chippewa Tribal Coll (MI)
St. Charles Comm Coll (MO)
St. Clair County Comm Coll (MI)
St. Philip's Coll (TX)
San Joaquin Delta Coll (CA)
San Juan Coll (NM)
Schenectady County Comm Coll (NY)
Seminole State Coll (OK)
Seminole State Coll of Florida (FL)
Shawnee Comm Coll (IL)
Sierra Coll (CA)
Somerset Comm Coll (KY)
Southeast Comm Coll, Lincoln Campus (NE)
Southeastern Comm Coll (IA)
South Florida State Coll (FL)
South Suburban Coll (IL)
Southwestern Indian Polytechnic Inst (NM)
Southwestern Michigan Coll (MI)
Southwestern Oregon Comm Coll (OR)
Southwest Texas Jr Coll (TX)
Southwest Virginia Comm Coll (VA)
Spartanburg Comm Coll (SC)
Spartanburg Methodist Coll (SC)
Spoon River Coll (IL)
Springfield Tech Comm Coll (MA)
State U of New York Coll of Technology at Alfred (NY)
Sullivan County Comm Coll (NY)
Tallahassee Comm Coll (FL)
Tarrant County Coll District (TX)
Tech Coll of the Lowcountry (SC)
Texarkana Coll (TX)
Three Rivers Comm Coll (CT)
Tidewater Comm Coll (VA)
Tohono O'odham Comm Coll (AZ)
Tompkins Cortland Comm Coll (NY)
Tri-County Tech Coll (SC)
Trocaire Coll (NY)
Truckee Meadows Comm Coll (NV)
Tunxis Comm Coll (CT)
Tyler Jr Coll (TX)
U of Alaska Anchorage, Kenai Peninsula Coll (AK)
U of Alaska, Prince William Sound Coll (AK)
U of Arkansas Comm Coll at Morrilton (AR)
U of Cincinnati Blue Ash Coll (OH)
U of New Mexico–Gallup (NM)
U of Pittsburgh at Titusville (PA)
U of South Carolina Union (SC)
Victor Valley Coll (CA)
Vincennes U (IN)
Virginia Western Comm Coll (VA)
Volunteer State Comm Coll (TN)
Walters State Comm Coll (TN)
Wayne Comm Coll (NC)
Wayne County Comm Coll District (MI)
Weatherford Coll (TX)
Wenatchee Valley Coll (WA)
Westchester Comm Coll (NY)
Western Iowa Tech Comm Coll (IA)
Western Nevada Coll (NV)
Western Piedmont Comm Coll (NC)
Western Texas Coll (TX)
Western Wyoming Comm Coll (WY)
Westmoreland County Comm Coll (PA)
White Mountains Comm Coll (NH)
Williamsburg Tech Coll (SC)
Williston State Coll (ND)
Wor-Wic Comm Coll (MD)
Wytheville Comm Coll (VA)
York County Comm Coll (ME)

LIBRARY AND ARCHIVES ASSISTING

Citrus Coll (CA)
Illinois Central Coll (IL)

Ivy Tech Comm Coll–Bloomington (IN)
Ivy Tech Comm Coll–Columbus (IN)
Ivy Tech Comm Coll–East Central (IN)
Ivy Tech Comm Coll–Kokomo (IN)
Ivy Tech Comm Coll–Lafayette (IN)
Ivy Tech Comm Coll–North Central (IN)
Ivy Tech Comm Coll–Northeast (IN)
Ivy Tech Comm Coll–Northwest (IN)
Ivy Tech Comm Coll–Richmond (IN)
Ivy Tech Comm Coll–Southeast (IN)
Ivy Tech Comm Coll–Southern Indiana (IN)
Ivy Tech Comm Coll–Southwest (IN)
Ivy Tech Comm Coll–Wabash Valley (IN)
Lewis and Clark Comm Coll (IL)
Palomar Coll (CA)
Pueblo Comm Coll (CO)

LIBRARY AND INFORMATION SCIENCE

Allen Comm Coll (KS)
Citrus Coll (CA)
Coll of Central Florida (FL)
Copiah-Lincoln Comm Coll (MS)
Grand Rapids Comm Coll (MI)
Itawamba Comm Coll (MS)
U of Cincinnati Blue Ash Coll (OH)
Westmoreland County Comm Coll (PA)

LIBRARY SCIENCE RELATED

Pasadena City Coll (CA)

LICENSED PRACTICAL/ VOCATIONAL NURSE TRAINING

Alvin Comm Coll (TX)
Amarillo Coll (TX)
Athens Tech Coll (GA)
Bainbridge State Coll (GA)
Barton County Comm Coll (KS)
Carrington Coll–Sacramento (CA)
Carrington Coll–San Jose (CA)
Carroll Comm Coll (MD)
Central Maine Comm Coll (ME)
Central Ohio Tech Coll (OH)
Central Oregon Comm Coll (OR)
Central Texas Coll (TX)
Citrus Coll (CA)
Coll of The Albemarle (NC)
Comm Coll of Rhode Island (RI)
Dodge City Comm Coll (KS)
Eastern Gateway Comm Coll (OH)
Feather River Coll (CA)
Fiorello H. LaGuardia Comm Coll of the City U of New York (NY)
George C. Wallace Comm Coll (AL)
Grand Rapids Comm Coll (MI)
Great Falls Coll Montana State U (MT)
Hennepin Tech Coll (MN)
Howard Comm Coll (MD)
Hudson County Comm Coll (NJ)
Iowa Central Comm Coll (IA)
Ivy Tech Comm Coll–Southeast (IN)
James H. Faulkner State Comm Coll (AL)
Jefferson Coll (MO)
J. F. Drake State Comm and Tech Coll (AL)
J. Sargeant Reynolds Comm Coll (VA)
Kirtland Comm Coll (MI)
Lamar Comm Coll (CO)
Manhattan Area Tech Coll (KS)
Midlands Tech Coll (SC)
Mid-Plains Comm Coll, North Platte (NE)
Morgan Comm Coll (CO)
Navarro Coll (TX)
New Mexico Jr Coll (NM)
New River Comm Coll (VA)
Northeastern Jr Coll (CO)
Northland Comm and Tech Coll (MN)
Northwest Tech Coll (MN)
Pasadena City Coll (CA)
San Joaquin Delta Coll (CA)
San Joaquin Valley Coll, Visalia (CA)
Sierra Coll (CA)
Southeastern Coll–West Palm Beach (FL)
Southeastern Comm Coll (IA)
Southeast Tech Inst (SD)
Texarkana Coll (TX)
Tyler Jr Coll (TX)
Wenatchee Valley Coll (WA)
Western Iowa Tech Comm Coll (IA)
Western Texas Coll (TX)
Western Wyoming Comm Coll (WY)

Westmoreland County Comm Coll (PA)
Williston State Coll (ND)

LINEWORKER
Bismarck State Coll (ND)
Chandler-Gilbert Comm Coll (AZ)
Ivy Tech Comm Coll–Lafayette (IN)
Kennebec Valley Comm Coll (ME)
Minnesota West Comm and Tech Coll (MN)
Mitchell Tech Inst (SD)
Pennsylvania Highlands Comm Coll (PA)
Raritan Valley Comm Coll (NJ)

LINGUISTICS
Ca&nnada Coll (CA)
South Florida State Coll (FL)

LITERATURE
Oklahoma City Comm Coll (OK)

LITERATURE RELATED
Cayuga County Comm Coll (NY)

LIVESTOCK MANAGEMENT
Barton County Comm Coll (KS)

LOGISTICS, MATERIALS, AND SUPPLY CHAIN MANAGEMENT
Ancilla Coll (IN)
Arizona Western Coll (AZ)
Athens Tech Coll (GA)
Barton County Comm Coll (KS)
Cecil Coll (MD)
Chattahoochee Tech Coll (GA)
City Colls of Chicago, Olive-Harvey College (IL)
Cochise County Comm Coll District (AZ)
Comm Coll of the Air Force (AL)
Fayetteville Tech Comm Coll (NC)
Fashion Inst of Design & Merchandising, LA Campus (CA)
Fox Valley Tech Coll (WI)
Georgia Military Coll (GA)
Hinds Comm Coll (MS)
Houston Comm Coll (TX)
Ivy Tech Comm Coll–Bloomington (IN)
Ivy Tech Comm Coll–Central Indiana (IN)
Ivy Tech Comm Coll–Columbus (IN)
Ivy Tech Comm Coll–East Central (IN)
Ivy Tech Comm Coll–Richmond (IN)
Ivy Tech Comm Coll–Southeast (IN)
Ivy Tech Comm Coll–Southern Indiana (IN)
Ivy Tech Comm Coll–Southwest (IN)
Ivy Tech Comm Coll–Wabash Valley (IN)
LDS Business Coll (UT)
Lenoir Comm Coll (NC)
Lone Star Coll–CyFair (TX)
Miami Dade Coll (FL)
Northern Essex Comm Coll (MA)
Northland Comm and Tech Coll (MN)
Randolph Comm Coll (NC)
Rockingham Comm Coll (NC)
Truckee Meadows Comm Coll (NV)
Westmoreland County Comm Coll (PA)

MACHINE SHOP TECHNOLOGY
Butler County Comm Coll (PA)
Cape Fear Comm Coll (NC)
Catawba Valley Comm Coll (NC)
Craven Comm Coll (NC)
Daytona State Coll (FL)
Delta Coll (MI)
Eastern Arizona Coll (AZ)
Fayetteville Tech Comm Coll (NC)
Ivy Tech Comm Coll–Central Indiana (IN)
Ivy Tech Comm Coll–East Central (IN)
Ivy Tech Comm Coll–Kokomo (IN)
Ivy Tech Comm Coll–Richmond (IN)
Ivy Tech Comm Coll–Wabash Valley (IN)
Lenoir Comm Coll (NC)
Mitchell Comm Coll (NC)
North Central Texas Coll (TX)
Northland Comm and Tech Coll (MN)
Owensboro Comm and Tech Coll (KY)
Pasadena City Coll (CA)
Pueblo Comm Coll (CO)
Randolph Comm Coll (NC)

Rockingham Comm Coll (NC)
San Juan Coll (NM)
State U of New York Coll of Technology at Alfred (NY)
Thaddeus Stevens Coll of Technology (PA)
Wayne Comm Coll (NC)
Western Piedmont Comm Coll (NC)
Westmoreland County Comm Coll (PA)

MACHINE TOOL TECHNOLOGY
Alamance Comm Coll (NC)
Amarillo Coll (TX)
Bellingham Tech Coll (WA)
Butler County Comm Coll (PA)
Casper Coll (WY)
Central Lakes Coll (MN)
Central Maine Comm Coll (ME)
Central New Mexico Comm Coll (NM)
Cerritos Coll (CA)
Clark Coll (WA)
Columbus Tech Coll (GA)
Corning Comm Coll (NY)
East Central Coll (MO)
Elgin Comm Coll (IL)
George C. Wallace Comm Coll (AL)
Georgia Piedmont Tech Coll (GA)
Greenville Tech Coll (SC)
Gwinnett Tech Coll (GA)
Hawkeye Comm Coll (IA)
H. Councill Trenholm State Comm Coll (AL)
Hennepin Tech Coll (MN)
Hutchinson Comm Coll (KS)
Illinois Eastern Comm Colls, Wabash Valley College (IL)
Iowa Central Comm Coll (IA)
Ivy Tech Comm Coll–Bloomington (IN)
Ivy Tech Comm Coll–Central Indiana (IN)
Ivy Tech Comm Coll–Columbus (IN)
Ivy Tech Comm Coll–East Central (IN)
Ivy Tech Comm Coll–Kokomo (IN)
Ivy Tech Comm Coll–Lafayette (IN)
Ivy Tech Comm Coll–North Central (IN)
Ivy Tech Comm Coll–Northeast (IN)
Ivy Tech Comm Coll–Northwest (IN)
Ivy Tech Comm Coll–Richmond (IN)
Ivy Tech Comm Coll–Southern Indiana (IN)
Ivy Tech Comm Coll–Southwest (IN)
Ivy Tech Comm Coll–Wabash Valley (IN)
Jefferson Coll (MO)
Kellogg Comm Coll (MI)
Kennebec Valley Comm Coll (ME)
Lake Area Tech Inst (SD)
Lorain County Comm Coll (OH)
Los Angeles Valley Coll (CA)
Macomb Comm Coll (MI)
Meridian Comm Coll (MS)
Midlands Tech Coll (SC)
Mt. San Antonio Coll (CA)
Muskegon Comm Coll (MI)
New Castle School of Trades (PA)
New Mexico Jr Coll (NM)
New River Comm Coll (VA)
North Central Texas Coll (TX)
Northern Essex Comm Coll (MA)
Odessa Coll (TX)
Orange Coast Coll (CA)
Ozarks Tech Comm Coll (MO)
Ranken Tech Coll (MO)
Reading Area Comm Coll (PA)
Renton Tech Coll (WA)
Ridgewater Coll (MN)
San Joaquin Delta Coll (CA)
Sheridan Coll (WY)
Southeast Comm Coll, Milford Campus (NE)
Southeastern Comm Coll (IA)
Southern Maine Comm Coll (ME)
Southwestern Michigan Coll (MI)
Southwestern Oregon Comm Coll (OR)
Spartanburg Comm Coll (SC)
Tarrant County Coll District (TX)
Tri-County Tech Coll (SC)
Wayne County Comm Coll District (MI)
Western Nevada Coll (NV)
Westmoreland County Comm Coll (PA)
Williamson Coll of the Trades (PA)
Wiregrass Georgia Tech Coll (GA)

Wytheville Comm Coll (VA)
York County Comm Coll (ME)

MAGNETIC RESONANCE IMAGING (MRI) TECHNOLOGY
Mitchell Tech Inst (SD)

MANAGEMENT INFORMATION SYSTEMS
Anne Arundel Comm Coll (MD)
Asnuntuck Comm Coll (CT)
Camden County Coll (NJ)
Carl Albert State Coll (OK)
Carroll Comm Coll (MD)
Cecil Coll (MD)
Central Oregon Comm Coll (OR)
Comm Coll of Aurora (CO)
Comm Coll of Baltimore County (MD)
Comm Coll of the Air Force (AL)
County Coll of Morris (NJ)
Florida SouthWestern State Coll (FL)
Garrett Coll (MD)
Georgia Military Coll (GA)
Gulf Coast State Coll (FL)
Gwinnett Tech Coll (GA)
Hagerstown Comm Coll (MD)
Hennepin Tech Coll (MN)
Interactive Coll of Technology, Chamblee (GA)
Kennebec Valley Comm Coll (ME)
Kirtland Comm Coll (MI)
Lackawanna Coll (PA)
Lakeland Comm Coll (OH)
Lake Region State Coll (ND)
Lake Superior Coll (MN)
Lamar Comm Coll (CO)
Manchester Comm Coll (CT)
Manhattan Area Tech Coll (KS)
Martin Comm Coll (NC)
Mercer County Comm Coll (NJ)
Miami Dade Coll (FL)
Moraine Valley Comm Coll (IL)
North Hennepin Comm Coll (MN)
Ozarks Tech Comm Coll (MO)
Panola Coll (TX)
Pensacola State Coll (FL)
Raritan Valley Comm Coll (NJ)
River Valley Comm Coll (NH)
Rowan Coll at Burlington County (NJ)
San Jacinto Coll District (TX)
South Florida State Coll (FL)
Southwest Tennessee Comm Coll (TN)
Three Rivers Comm Coll (CT)
Treasure Valley Comm Coll (OR)
Trumbull Business Coll (OH)
U of Pittsburgh at Titusville (PA)
Victor Valley Coll (CA)
Western Nevada Coll (NV)

MANAGEMENT INFORMATION SYSTEMS AND SERVICES RELATED
Anne Arundel Comm Coll (MD)
Bowling Green State U–Firelands Coll (OH)
Hillsborough Comm Coll (FL)
Martin Comm Coll (NC)
Montgomery County Comm Coll (PA)
Pensacola State Coll (FL)
Seminole State Coll (OK)
Truckee Meadows Comm Coll (NV)

MANAGEMENT SCIENCE
Central Virginia Comm Coll (VA)
Pensacola State Coll (FL)
South Florida State Coll (FL)

MANUFACTURING ENGINEERING
Mitchell Comm Coll (NC)
Penn State Fayette, The Eberly Campus (PA)
Southeast Comm Coll, Milford Campus (NE)

MANUFACTURING ENGINEERING TECHNOLOGY
Albany Tech Coll (GA)
Arizona Western Coll (AZ)
Bowling Green State U–Firelands Coll (OH)
Butler County Comm Coll (PA)
Casper Coll (WY)
Central Ohio Tech Coll (OH)
Central Oregon Comm Coll (OR)
Cerritos Coll (CA)
Chippewa Valley Tech Coll (WI)

City Colls of Chicago, Olive-Harvey College (IL)
Clark Coll (WA)
Coll of the Canyons (CA)
Corning Comm Coll (NY)
Crowder Coll (MO)
Danville Area Comm Coll (IL)
Delta Coll (MI)
Edison Comm Coll (OH)
Fox Valley Tech Coll (WI)
Gadsden State Comm Coll (AL)
Gateway Comm and Tech Coll (KY)
Gulf Coast State Coll (FL)
H. Councill Trenholm State Comm Coll (AL)
Hennepin Tech Coll (MN)
Houston Comm Coll (TX)
Hutchinson Comm Coll (KS)
Illinois Central Coll (IL)
Illinois Eastern Comm Colls, Wabash Valley College (IL)
ITI Tech Coll (LA)
Ivy Tech Comm Coll–Bloomington (IN)
Ivy Tech Comm Coll–Central Indiana (IN)
Ivy Tech Comm Coll–Columbus (IN)
Ivy Tech Comm Coll–East Central (IN)
Ivy Tech Comm Coll–Kokomo (IN)
Ivy Tech Comm Coll–Lafayette (IN)
Ivy Tech Comm Coll–Northeast (IN)
Ivy Tech Comm Coll–Richmond (IN)
Ivy Tech Comm Coll–Southeast (IN)
Ivy Tech Comm Coll–Southern Indiana (IN)
Ivy Tech Comm Coll–Southwest (IN)
Ivy Tech Comm Coll–Wabash Valley (IN)
Jefferson Coll (MO)
Kellogg Comm Coll (MI)
Lake Area Tech Inst (SD)
Lehigh Carbon Comm Coll (PA)
Lewis and Clark Comm Coll (IL)
Los Angeles Valley Coll (CA)
Macomb Comm Coll (MI)
Miami Dade Coll (FL)
Minnesota West Comm and Tech Coll (MN)
Mitchell Comm Coll (NC)
Moraine Valley Comm Coll (IL)
Morgan Comm Coll (CO)
Northcentral Tech Coll (WI)
Northland Comm and Tech Coll (MN)
Northwest Tech Coll (MN)
Oakton Comm Coll (IL)
Pueblo Comm Coll (CO)
Quinsigamond Comm Coll (MA)
Raritan Valley Comm Coll (NJ)
Rend Lake Coll (IL)
Rogue Comm Coll (OR)
St. Clair County Comm Coll (MI)
Schoolcraft Coll (MI)
Sierra Coll (CA)
Southern Crescent Tech Coll (GA)
South Florida State Coll (FL)
South Georgia Tech Coll (GA)
Spartanburg Comm Coll (SC)
Tallahassee Comm Coll (FL)
Texas State Tech Coll (TX)
Three Rivers Comm Coll (CT)
Truckee Meadows Comm Coll (NV)
Vincennes U (IN)
Wayne County Comm Coll District (MI)
Western Nevada Coll (NV)
Westmoreland County Comm Coll (PA)

MARINE BIOLOGY AND BIOLOGICAL OCEANOGRAPHY
Oregon Coast Comm Coll (OR)
Southern Maine Comm Coll (ME)
South Florida State Coll (FL)

MARINE MAINTENANCE AND SHIP REPAIR TECHNOLOGY
Cape Fear Comm Coll (NC)
Coll of The Albemarle (NC)
Minnesota State Comm and Tech Coll–Detroit Lakes (MN)
Olympic Coll (WA)
Washington County Comm Coll (ME)

MARINE SCIENCE/MERCHANT MARINE OFFICER
American Samoa Comm Coll (AS)
San Jacinto Coll District (TX)

MARINE TRANSPORTATION RELATED
Orange Coast Coll (CA)

MARKETING/MARKETING MANAGEMENT
Albany Tech Coll (GA)
Alvin Comm Coll (TX)
Athens Tech Coll (GA)
Atlanta Tech Coll (GA)
Augusta Tech Coll (GA)
Austin Comm Coll District (TX)
Bainbridge State Coll (GA)
Barton County Comm Coll (KS)
Bellingham Tech Coll (WA)
Berkeley Coll–White Plains Campus (NY)
Blackhawk Tech Coll (WI)
Brookhaven Coll (TX)
Camden County Coll (NJ)
Casper Coll (WY)
Cecil Coll (MD)
Central Georgia Tech Coll (GA)
Central Lakes Coll (MN)
Central Oregon Comm Coll (OR)
Central Texas Coll (TX)
Century Coll (MN)
Cerritos Coll (CA)
Chattahoochee Tech Coll (GA)
Chippewa Valley Tech Coll (WI)
Cincinnati State Tech and Comm Coll (OH)
Cleveland Comm Coll (NC)
Coll of Central Florida (FL)
Comm Coll of Rhode Island (RI)
Davis Coll (OH)
Delta Coll (MI)
Dodge City Comm Coll (KS)
Eastern Idaho Tech Coll (ID)
Edison Comm Coll (OH)
Elgin Comm Coll (IL)
Fayetteville Tech Comm Coll (NC)
Fashion Inst of Design & Merchandising, LA Campus (CA)
Finger Lakes Comm Coll (NY)
Fox Valley Tech Coll (WI)
Gateway Tech Coll (WI)
Genesee Comm Coll (NY)
Georgia Northwestern Tech Coll (GA)
Georgia Piedmont Tech Coll (GA)
Gwinnett Tech Coll (GA)
Harford Comm Coll (MD)
Hinds Comm Coll (MS)
Houston Comm Coll (TX)
Itawamba Comm Coll (MS)
Kennebec Valley Comm Coll (ME)
Lake Area Tech Inst (SD)
Lake Land Coll (IL)
Lakeland Comm Coll (OH)
Lamar Comm Coll (CO)
Lanier Tech Coll (GA)
Lenoir Comm Coll (NC)
Lone Star Coll–CyFair (TX)
Lone Star Coll–Kingwood (TX)
Lorain County Comm Coll (OH)
Macomb Comm Coll (MI)
Manchester Comm Coll (CT)
Manor Coll (PA)
Meridian Comm Coll (MS)
Miami Dade Coll (FL)
Middlesex County Coll (NJ)
Minnesota State Comm and Tech Coll–Detroit Lakes (MN)
Monroe Comm Coll (NY)
Mott Comm Coll (MI)
Mt. San Antonio Coll (CA)
Muskegon Comm Coll (MI)
Naugatuck Valley Comm Coll (CT)
Navarro Coll (TX)
New Mexico Jr Coll (NM)
New River Comm Coll (VA)
Norco Coll (CA)
Northampton Comm Coll (PA)
Northcentral Tech Coll (WI)
Northeastern Jr Coll (CO)
Northern Essex Comm Coll (MA)
North Hennepin Comm Coll (MN)
Northland Comm and Tech Coll (MN)
North Shore Comm Coll (MA)
Norwalk Comm Coll (CT)
Oakton Comm Coll (IL)
Ogeechee Tech Coll (GA)
Oxnard Coll (CA)
Pasadena City Coll (CA)
Penn Foster Coll (AZ)
Raritan Valley Comm Coll (NJ)
Ridgewater Coll (MN)
Rock Valley Coll (IL)
Rogue Comm Coll (OR)

Rowan-Cabarrus Comm Coll (NC)
St. Charles Comm Coll (MO)
St. Clair County Comm Coll (MI)
Salt Lake Comm Coll (UT)
Savannah Tech Coll (GA)
Schoolcraft Coll (MI)
Seminole State Coll of Florida (FL)
Southeastern Tech Coll (GA)
Southeast Tech Inst (SD)
Southern Crescent Tech Coll (GA)
South Florida State Coll (FL)
South Georgia Tech Coll (GA)
Springfield Tech Comm Coll (MA)
Stark State Coll (OH)
Sullivan County Comm Coll (NY)
Tarrant County Coll District (TX)
Texarkana Coll (TX)
Three Rivers Comm Coll (CT)
Tidewater Comm Coll (VA)
Tulsa Comm Coll (OK)
Tunxis Comm Coll (CT)
U of New Mexico–Gallup (NM)
Vincennes U (IN)
Waukesha County Tech Coll (WI)
Westchester Comm Coll (NY)
Western Texas Coll (TX)
Western Wyoming Comm Coll (WY)
West Georgia Tech Coll (GA)
Wiregrass Georgia Tech Coll (GA)
Wisconsin Indianhead Tech Coll (WI)

MARKETING RELATED
LDS Business Coll (UT)

MARKETING RESEARCH
Penn Foster Coll (AZ)

MASONRY
Ivy Tech Comm Coll–Central Indiana (IN)
Ivy Tech Comm Coll–Columbus (IN)
Ivy Tech Comm Coll–East Central (IN)
Ivy Tech Comm Coll–Lafayette (IN)
Ivy Tech Comm Coll–North Central (IN)
Ivy Tech Comm Coll–Northeast (IN)
Ivy Tech Comm Coll–Northwest (IN)
Ivy Tech Comm Coll–Southern Indiana (IN)
Ivy Tech Comm Coll–Southwest (IN)
Ivy Tech Comm Coll–Wabash Valley (IN)
Palomar Coll (CA)
State U of New York Coll of Technology at Alfred (NY)
Tallahassee Comm Coll (FL)
Thaddeus Stevens Coll of Technology (PA)

MASSAGE THERAPY
Arizona Western Coll (AZ)
Butler County Comm Coll (PA)
Camden County Coll (NJ)
Career Training Academy, Lower Burrell (PA)
Carrington Coll–Boise (ID)
Carrington Coll–Phoenix North (AZ)
Carrington Coll–Pleasant Hill (CA)
Central Oregon Comm Coll (OR)
Chandler-Gilbert Comm Coll (AZ)
Clary Sage Coll (OK)
Comm Coll of Baltimore County (MD)
Comm Coll of Rhode Island (RI)
IBMC Coll, Fort Collins (CO)
Ivy Tech Comm Coll–Northeast (IN)
Lenoir Comm Coll (NC)
Lewis and Clark Comm Coll (IL)
Miami Dade Coll (FL)
Minnesota State Coll–Southeast Tech (MN)
Niagara County Comm Coll (NY)
Queensborough Comm Coll of the City U of New York (NY)
Renton Tech Coll (WA)
St. Clair County Comm Coll (MI)
San Joaquin Valley Coll, Salida (CA)
Schoolcraft Coll (MI)
Sheridan Coll (WY)
Southeastern Coll–West Palm Beach (FL)
Spencerian Coll (KY)
Springfield Tech Comm Coll (MA)
Trocaire Coll (NY)
Vincennes U (IN)
Williston State Coll (ND)

MASS COMMUNICATION/ MEDIA
Amarillo Coll (TX)
Ancilla Coll (IN)
Blinn Coll (TX)

Bunker Hill Comm Coll (MA)
Casper Coll (WY)
Chipola Coll (FL)
Crowder Coll (MO)
Dean Coll (MA)
Dodge City Comm Coll (KS)
Finger Lakes Comm Coll (NY)
Fullerton Coll (CA)
Genesee Comm Coll (NY)
Georgia Military Coll (GA)
Harford Comm Coll (MD)
Iowa Central Comm Coll (IA)
James H. Faulkner State Comm Coll (AL)
Lackawanna Coll (PA)
Laramie County Comm Coll (WY)
Lorain County Comm Coll (OH)
Los Angeles Valley Coll (CA)
Mercer County Comm Coll (NJ)
Miami Dade Coll (FL)
Monroe Comm Coll (NY)
Niagara County Comm Coll (NY)
Northland Comm and Tech Coll (MN)
Oklahoma City Comm Coll (OK)
Orange Coast Coll (CA)
Salt Lake Comm Coll (UT)
Spoon River Coll (IL)
Westchester Comm Coll (NY)
Western Texas Coll (TX)
Wytheville Comm Coll (VA)

MATERIALS ENGINEERING
Southern Maine Comm Coll (ME)
South Florida State Coll (FL)
Wisconsin Indianhead Tech Coll (WI)

MATERIALS SCIENCE
Mt. San Antonio Coll (CA)
Northern Essex Comm Coll (MA)

MATHEMATICS
Allen Comm Coll (KS)
Alvin Comm Coll (TX)
Amarillo Coll (TX)
American River Coll (CA)
Anne Arundel Comm Coll (MD)
Antelope Valley Coll (CA)
Arizona Western Coll (AZ)
Austin Comm Coll District (TX)
Bainbridge State Coll (GA)
Barton County Comm Coll (KS)
Blinn Coll (TX)
Borough of Manhattan Comm Coll of the City U of New York (NY)
Bucks County Comm Coll (PA)
Bunker Hill Comm Coll (MA)
Butler County Comm Coll (PA)
Ca&nnada Coll (CA)
Carl Albert State Coll (OK)
Casper Coll (WY)
Cecil Coll (MD)
Central New Mexico Comm Coll (NM)
Central Oregon Comm Coll (OR)
Central Texas Coll (TX)
Central Wyoming Coll (WY)
Cerritos Coll (CA)
Citrus Coll (CA)
Cochise County Comm Coll District (AZ)
Coll of Central Florida (FL)
Coll of the Canyons (CA)
Columbia Coll (CA)
Corning Comm Coll (NY)
Crowder Coll (MO)
Dean Coll (MA)
Dodge City Comm Coll (KS)
Eastern Arizona Coll (AZ)
Eastern Wyoming Coll (WY)
Edison Comm Coll (OH)
Feather River Coll (CA)
Finger Lakes Comm Coll (NY)
Frederick Comm Coll (MD)
Fullerton Coll (CA)
Galveston Coll (TX)
Genesee Comm Coll (NY)
Georgia Highlands Coll (GA)
Georgia Military Coll (GA)
Gordon State Coll (GA)
Harford Comm Coll (MD)
Harrisburg Area Comm Coll (PA)
Holyoke Comm Coll (MA)
Housatonic Comm Coll (CT)
Houston Comm Coll (TX)
Hutchinson Comm Coll (KS)
Itawamba Comm Coll (MS)
Jefferson Comm Coll (NY)
J. Sargeant Reynolds Comm Coll (VA)
Kankakee Comm Coll (IL)
Kilgore Coll (TX)
Laramie County Comm Coll (WY)
Lehigh Carbon Comm Coll (PA)

Lorain County Comm Coll (OH)
Los Angeles Valley Coll (CA)
Luzerne County Comm Coll (PA)
Macomb Comm Coll (MI)
Massachusetts Bay Comm Coll (MA)
Mercer County Comm Coll (NJ)
Miami Dade Coll (FL)
Mohave Comm Coll (AZ)
Monroe Comm Coll (NY)
Montgomery County Comm Coll (PA)
Moraine Valley Comm Coll (IL)
Mt. San Antonio Coll (CA)
Nashville State Comm Coll (TN)
Navarro Coll (TX)
New Mexico Jr Coll (NM)
Niagara County Comm Coll (NY)
Northampton Comm Coll (PA)
Northeastern Jr Coll (CO)
North Hennepin Comm Coll (MN)
Northwest Coll (WY)
Odessa Coll (TX)
Oklahoma City Comm Coll (OK)
Orange Coast Coll (CA)
Otero Jr Coll (CO)
Oxnard Coll (CA)
Palomar Coll (CA)
Panola Coll (TX)
Paris Jr Coll (TX)
Pasadena City Coll (CA)
Pensacola State Coll (FL)
Potomac State Coll of West Virginia U (WV)
Rowan Coll at Burlington County (NJ)
St. Charles Comm Coll (MO)
St. Philip's Coll (TX)
San Jacinto Coll District (TX)
San Joaquin Delta Coll (CA)
San Juan Coll (NM)
Scottsdale Comm Coll (AZ)
Seminole State Coll (OK)
Sheridan Coll (WY)
Sierra Coll (CA)
Southern U at Shreveport (LA)
South Florida State Coll (FL)
Spoon River Coll (IL)
Springfield Tech Comm Coll (MA)
Sullivan County Comm Coll (NY)
Texarkana Coll (TX)
Truckee Meadows Comm Coll (NV)
Tulsa Comm Coll (OK)
Tyler Jr Coll (TX)
Victor Valley Coll (CA)
Vincennes U (IN)
Wenatchee Valley Coll (WA)
Western Texas Coll (TX)
Western Wyoming Comm Coll (WY)

MATHEMATICS AND COMPUTER SCIENCE
Crowder Coll (MO)

MATHEMATICS RELATED
Cayuga County Comm Coll (NY)
Corning Comm Coll (NY)
Genesee Comm Coll (NY)

MATHEMATICS TEACHER EDUCATION
Anne Arundel Comm Coll (MD)
Bucks County Comm Coll (PA)
Carroll Comm Coll (MD)
Chesapeake Coll (MD)
Comm Coll of Baltimore County (MD)
Eastern Wyoming Coll (WY)
Frederick Comm Coll (MD)
Harford Comm Coll (MD)
Highland Comm Coll (IL)
Kankakee Comm Coll (IL)
Kaskaskia Coll (IL)
Montgomery Coll (MD)
Moraine Valley Comm Coll (IL)
South Florida State Coll (FL)
Vincennes U (IN)

MECHANICAL DRAFTING AND CAD/CADD
Alexandria Tech and Comm Coll (MN)
Anoka Tech Coll (MN)
Butler County Comm Coll (PA)
Central Lakes Coll (MN)
Cleveland Comm Coll (NC)
Corning Comm Coll (NY)
Edison Comm Coll (OH)
Fox Valley Tech Coll (WI)
Gateway Tech Coll (WI)
Greenville Tech Coll (SC)
Hutchinson Comm Coll (KS)
Island Drafting and Tech Inst (NY)
Lake Superior Coll (MN)
Los Angeles Valley Coll (CA)
Macomb Comm Coll (MI)

Midlands Tech Coll (SC)
Minnesota State Comm and Tech Coll–Moorhead (MN)
Mitchell Comm Coll (NC)
Northcentral Tech Coll (WI)
Ozarks Tech Comm Coll (MO)
Queensborough Comm Coll of the City U of New York (NY)
Ridgewater Coll (MN)
Sierra Coll (CA)
Tri-County Tech Coll (SC)
Vincennes U (IN)
Waukesha County Tech Coll (WI)
Western Iowa Tech Comm Coll (IA)
Westmoreland County Comm Coll (PA)

MECHANICAL ENGINEERING
Cayuga County Comm Coll (NY)
Fiorello H. LaGuardia Comm Coll of the City U of New York (NY)
Kilgore Coll (TX)
Lone Star Coll–North Harris (TX)
Nashville State Comm Coll (TN)
Olympic Coll (WA)
Pasadena City Coll (CA)
Potomac State Coll of West Virginia U (WV)
St. Charles Comm Coll (MO)
South Florida State Coll (FL)

MECHANICAL ENGINEERING/ MECHANICAL TECHNOLOGY
Alamance Comm Coll (NC)
Augusta Tech Coll (GA)
Bowling Green State U–Firelands Coll (OH)
Caldwell Comm Coll and Tech Inst (NC)
Camden County Coll (NJ)
Cape Fear Comm Coll (NC)
Catawba Valley Comm Coll (NC)
Cayuga County Comm Coll (NY)
Central Ohio Tech Coll (OH)
Cincinnati State Tech and Comm Coll (OH)
Citrus Coll (CA)
Columbus Tech Coll (GA)
Corning Comm Coll (NY)
County Coll of Morris (NJ)
Craven Comm Coll (NC)
Delta Coll (MI)
Eastern Gateway Comm Coll (OH)
Erie Comm Coll, North Campus (NY)
Finger Lakes Comm Coll (NY)
Fullerton Coll (CA)
Greenville Tech Coll (SC)
Hagerstown Comm Coll (MD)
Harrisburg Area Comm Coll (PA)
Illinois Central Coll (IL)
Illinois Eastern Comm Colls, Lincoln Trail College (IL)
Ivy Tech Comm Coll–Lafayette (IN)
Jamestown Comm Coll (NY)
Kent State U at Trumbull (OH)
Kent State U at Tuscarawas (OH)
Lakeland Comm Coll (OH)
Lehigh Carbon Comm Coll (PA)
Macomb Comm Coll (MI)
Massachusetts Bay Comm Coll (MA)
Middlesex County Coll (NJ)
Midlands Tech Coll (SC)
Mitchell Comm Coll (NC)
Mohawk Valley Comm Coll (NY)
Monroe Comm Coll (NY)
Montgomery County Comm Coll (PA)
Moraine Valley Comm Coll (IL)
Mott Comm Coll (MI)
Oakton Comm Coll (IL)
Oklahoma State U Inst of Technology (OK)
Onondaga Comm Coll (NY)
Penn State DuBois (PA)
Penn State Shenango (PA)
Queensborough Comm Coll of the City U of New York (NY)
Richmond Comm Coll (NC)
San Joaquin Delta Coll (CA)
Southeastern Comm Coll (IA)
Southeast Tech Inst (SD)
Southern U at Shreveport (LA)
Southwest Tennessee Comm Coll (TN)
Spartanburg Comm Coll (SC)
Springfield Tech Comm Coll (MA)
Stark State Coll (OH)
State U of New York Coll of Technology at Alfred (NY)
Tarrant County Coll District (TX)
Texas State Tech Coll (TX)
Three Rivers Comm Coll (CT)
Vincennes U (IN)

Virginia Western Comm Coll (VA)
Wayne Comm Coll (NC)
Westchester Comm Coll (NY)
Western Piedmont Comm Coll (NC)
Westmoreland County Comm Coll (PA)
Wytheville Comm Coll (VA)

MECHANICAL ENGINEERING TECHNOLOGIES RELATED
Camden County Coll (NJ)
Corning Comm Coll (NY)
Jefferson Comm Coll (NY)
John Tyler Comm Coll (VA)
Middlesex County Coll (NJ)
Mohawk Valley Comm Coll (NY)

MECHANIC AND REPAIR TECHNOLOGIES RELATED
Chandler-Gilbert Comm Coll (AZ)
Cloud County Comm Coll (KS)
Corning Comm Coll (NY)
Greenville Tech Coll (SC)
Ivy Tech Comm Coll–Bloomington (IN)
Ivy Tech Comm Coll–Columbus (IN)
Ivy Tech Comm Coll–Kokomo (IN)
Ivy Tech Comm Coll–Lafayette (IN)
Ivy Tech Comm Coll–North Central (IN)
Ivy Tech Comm Coll–Northwest (IN)
Ivy Tech Comm Coll–Southwest (IN)
Laramie County Comm Coll (WY)
Macomb Comm Coll (MI)
Ohio Tech Coll (OH)
Oklahoma State U Inst of Technology (OK)
Washington County Comm Coll (ME)

MECHANICS AND REPAIR
Corning Comm Coll (NY)
Ivy Tech Comm Coll–Bloomington (IN)
Ivy Tech Comm Coll–Central Indiana (IN)
Ivy Tech Comm Coll–Columbus (IN)
Ivy Tech Comm Coll–Kokomo (IN)
Ivy Tech Comm Coll–Lafayette (IN)
Ivy Tech Comm Coll–North Central (IN)
Ivy Tech Comm Coll–Northeast (IN)
Ivy Tech Comm Coll–Northwest (IN)
Ivy Tech Comm Coll–Richmond (IN)
Ivy Tech Comm Coll–Southern Indiana (IN)
Ivy Tech Comm Coll–Southwest (IN)
Ivy Tech Comm Coll–Wabash Valley (IN)
Owensboro Comm and Tech Coll (KY)
Rogue Comm Coll (OR)
Western Wyoming Comm Coll (WY)

MECHATRONICS, ROBOTICS, AND AUTOMATION ENGINEERING
Anne Arundel Comm Coll (MD)
Catawba Valley Comm Coll (NC)
Cochise County Comm Coll District (AZ)
Harrisburg Area Comm Coll (PA)
Mitchell Comm Coll (NC)
Randolph Comm Coll (NC)
Westmoreland County Comm Coll (PA)

MEDICAL ADMINISTRATIVE ASSISTANT AND MEDICAL SECRETARY
Alamance Comm Coll (NC)
Alexandria Tech and Comm Coll (MN)
Alvin Comm Coll (TX)
Amarillo Coll (TX)
Anne Arundel Comm Coll (MD)
Anoka Tech Coll (MN)
Barton County Comm Coll (KS)
Bismarck State Coll (ND)
Blackhawk Tech Coll (WI)
Bunker Hill Comm Coll (MA)
Carrington Coll–Sacramento (CA)
Carrington Coll–Spokane (WA)
Central Lakes Coll (MN)
Century Coll (MN)
Clark Coll (WA)
Coll of The Albemarle (NC)
Columbia Coll (CA)
Comm Coll of Baltimore County (MD)
Comm Coll of Rhode Island (RI)
Craven Comm Coll (NC)
Crowder Coll (MO)

Dabney S. Lancaster Comm Coll (VA)
Danville Area Comm Coll (IL)
Davis Coll (OH)
Daytona State Coll (FL)
Delta Coll (MI)
Dodge City Comm Coll (KS)
Eastern Gateway Comm Coll (OH)
Edison Comm Coll (OH)
Elizabethtown Comm and Tech Coll, Elizabethtown (KY)
Erie Comm Coll, North Campus (NY)
Frederick Comm Coll (MD)
Galveston Coll (TX)
Genesee Comm Coll (NY)
Grand Rapids Comm Coll (MI)
Gulf Coast State Coll (FL)
Halifax Comm Coll (NC)
Hawkeye Comm Coll (IA)
Hennepin Tech Coll (MN)
Howard Comm Coll (MD)
Humacao Comm Coll (PR)
IBMC Coll, Fort Collins (CO)
Illinois Eastern Comm Colls, Olney Central College (IL)
Jefferson Coll (MO)
Jefferson Comm Coll (NY)
Kellogg Comm Coll (MI)
Kennebec Valley Comm Coll (ME)
Kirtland Comm Coll (MI)
Lackawanna Coll (PA)
Lake Land Coll (IL)
Lake Superior Coll (MN)
Lewis and Clark Comm Coll (IL)
Luzerne County Comm Coll (PA)
Manchester Comm Coll (CT)
Martin Comm Coll (NC)
Metro Business Coll, Jefferson City (MO)
Minnesota State Coll–Southeast Tech (MN)
Minnesota State Comm and Tech Coll–Moorhead (MN)
Minnesota State Comm and Tech Coll–Wadena (MN)
Minnesota West Comm and Tech Coll (MN)
Mt. San Antonio Coll (CA)
Muskegon Comm Coll (MI)
New Mexico Jr Coll (NM)
New River Comm Coll (VA)
Northampton Comm Coll (PA)
Northern Essex Comm Coll (MA)
Northland Comm and Tech Coll (MN)
North Shore Comm Coll (MA)
Northwest Tech Coll (MN)
Ohio Business Coll, Sheffield Village (OH)
Otero Jr Coll (CO)
Owensboro Comm and Tech Coll (KY)
Palomar Coll (CA)
Piedmont Comm Coll (NC)
Quinsigamond Comm Coll (MA)
Reading Area Comm Coll (PA)
Renton Tech Coll (WA)
Richland Comm Coll (IL)
Ridgewater Coll (MN)
St. Philip's Coll (TX)
San Joaquin Valley Coll, Visalia (CA)
Scottsdale Comm Coll (AZ)
Shawnee Comm Coll (IL)
Somerset Comm Coll (KY)
Spoon River Coll (IL)
Springfield Tech Comm Coll (MA)
Treasure Valley Comm Coll (OR)
Trumbull Business Coll (OH)
Tunxis Comm Coll (CT)
Tyler Jr Coll (TX)
Ultimate Medical Academy Online (FL)
U of Cincinnati Blue Ash Coll (OH)
Wenatchee Valley Coll (WA)
Western Iowa Tech Comm Coll (IA)
Western Piedmont Comm Coll (NC)
Western Wyoming Comm Coll (WY)
Wisconsin Indianhead Tech Coll (WI)
Wytheville Comm Coll (VA)

MEDICAL/CLINICAL ASSISTANT
Alamance Comm Coll (NC)
Anoka Tech Coll (MN)
Antelope Valley Coll (CA)
Barton County Comm Coll (KS)
Beal Coll (ME)
Big Bend Comm Coll (WA)
Blue Ridge Comm and Tech Coll (WV)
Bossier Parish Comm Coll (LA)

Bradford School (OH)
Bradford School (PA)
Bucks County Comm Coll (PA)
Ca&nnada Coll (CA)
Career Training Academy, Lower Burrell (PA)
Carrington Coll–Boise (ID)
Carrington Coll–Citrus Heights (CA)
Carrington Coll–Pleasant Hill (CA)
Carrington Coll–Pomona (CA)
Carrington Coll–Sacramento (CA)
Carrington Coll–San Jose (CA)
Carrington Coll–San Leandro (CA)
Central Maine Comm Coll (ME)
Central Oregon Comm Coll (OR)
Central Virginia Comm Coll (VA)
Cerritos Coll (CA)
Clark Coll (WA)
Cleveland Comm Coll (NC)
Coll of Business and Technology–Cutler Bay Campus (FL)
Coll of Business and Technology–Main Campus (FL)
Coll of Business and Technology–Miami Gardens (FL)
The Coll of Westchester (NY)
Columbia-Greene Comm Coll (NY)
Comm Care Coll (OK)
Craven Comm Coll (NC)
Davis Coll (OH)
East Central Coll (MO)
Eastern Gateway Comm Coll (OH)
Eastern Idaho Tech Coll (ID)
Edison Comm Coll (OH)
ETI Tech Coll of Niles (OH)
Forrest Coll (SC)
Fox Coll (IL)
Frederick Comm Coll (MD)
George C. Wallace Comm Coll (AL)
Georgia Piedmont Tech Coll (GA)
Great Falls Coll Montana State U (MT)
Gwinnett Tech Coll (GA)
Harrisburg Area Comm Coll (PA)
H. Councill Trenholm State Comm Coll (AL)
Highland Comm Coll (IL)
Hinds Comm Coll (MS)
Hudson County Comm Coll (NJ)
IBMC Coll, Fort Collins (CO)
Illinois Eastern Comm Colls, Lincoln Trail College (IL)
International Business Coll, Indianapolis (IN)
Iowa Central Comm Coll (IA)
Ivy Tech Comm Coll–Central Indiana (IN)
Ivy Tech Comm Coll–Columbus (IN)
Ivy Tech Comm Coll–East Central (IN)
Ivy Tech Comm Coll–Kokomo (IN)
Ivy Tech Comm Coll–Lafayette (IN)
Ivy Tech Comm Coll–North Central (IN)
Ivy Tech Comm Coll–Northeast (IN)
Ivy Tech Comm Coll–Northwest (IN)
Ivy Tech Comm Coll–Richmond (IN)
Ivy Tech Comm Coll–Southeast (IN)
Ivy Tech Comm Coll–Southern Indiana (IN)
Ivy Tech Comm Coll–Southwest (IN)
Ivy Tech Comm Coll–Wabash Valley (IN)
James Sprunt Comm Coll (NC)
Jamestown Business Coll (NY)
J. F. Drake State Comm and Tech Coll (AL)
Johnston Comm Coll (NC)
Kankakee Comm Coll (IL)
Kennebec Valley Comm Coll (ME)
King's Coll (NC)
Kirtland Comm Coll (MI)
Lake Area Tech Inst (SD)
LDS Business Coll (UT)
Lehigh Carbon Comm Coll (PA)
Lenoir Comm Coll (NC)
Macomb Comm Coll (MI)
Martin Comm Coll (NC)
Miami Dade Coll (FL)
Midlands Tech Coll (SC)
Minneapolis Business Coll (MN)
Minnesota West Comm and Tech Coll (MN)
Mitchell Comm Coll (NC)
Mitchell Tech Inst (SD)
Mohave Comm Coll (AZ)
Mohawk Valley Comm Coll (NY)
Montgomery Comm Coll (NC)
Montgomery County Comm Coll (PA)
Morgan Comm Coll (CO)

Mountain State Coll (WV)
Mount Wachusett Comm Coll (MA)
New Mexico Jr Coll (NM)
Niagara County Comm Coll (NY)
Northeast Alabama Comm Coll (AL)
Northwest-Shoals Comm Coll (AL)
Oklahoma City Comm Coll (OK)
Olympic Coll (WA)
Orange Coast Coll (CA)
Panola Coll (TX)
Pasadena City Coll (CA)
Penn Foster Coll (AZ)
Pennsylvania Highlands Comm Coll (PA)
Piedmont Comm Coll (NC)
Potomac State Coll of West Virginia U (WV)
Queensborough Comm Coll of the City U of New York (NY)
Randolph Comm Coll (NC)
Raritan Valley Comm Coll (NJ)
Renton Tech Coll (WA)
Richmond Comm Coll (NC)
Ridgewater Coll (MN)
St. Vincent's Coll (CT)
Salt Lake Comm Coll (UT)
San Jacinto Coll District (TX)
San Joaquin Valley Coll, Bakersfield (CA)
San Joaquin Valley Coll, Fresno (CA)
San Joaquin Valley Coll, Hanford (CA)
San Joaquin Valley Coll, Hesperia (CA)
San Joaquin Valley Coll, Lancaster (CA)
San Joaquin Valley Coll, Ontario (CA)
San Joaquin Valley Coll, Salida (CA)
San Joaquin Valley Coll, Temecula (CA)
San Joaquin Valley Coll, Visalia (CA)
San Joaquin Valley Coll–Online (CA)
Southeastern Coll–West Palm Beach (FL)
Southeastern Comm Coll (IA)
Southern Maine Comm Coll (ME)
Southwestern Michigan Coll (MI)
Southwestern Oregon Comm Coll (OR)
Southwest Tennessee Comm Coll (TN)
Springfield Tech Comm Coll (MA)
Stark State Coll (OH)
Sullivan County Comm Coll (NY)
Trocaire Coll (NY)
U of Cincinnati Blue Ash Coll (OH)
Washington County Comm Coll (ME)
Wayne Comm Coll (NC)
Wenatchee Valley Coll (WA)
Western Iowa Tech Comm Coll (IA)
Western Piedmont Comm Coll (NC)
Western Wyoming Comm Coll (WY)
Westmoreland County Comm Coll (PA)
White Mountains Comm Coll (NH)
Wood Tobe–Coburn School (NY)
York County Comm Coll (ME)

MEDICAL/HEALTH MANAGEMENT AND CLINICAL ASSISTANT
CollAmerica–Denver (CO)
Ivy Tech Comm Coll–Bloomington (IN)
Ivy Tech Comm Coll–Central Indiana (IN)
Ivy Tech Comm Coll–Columbus (IN)
Ivy Tech Comm Coll–East Central (IN)
Ivy Tech Comm Coll–Lafayette (IN)
Ivy Tech Comm Coll–Richmond (IN)
Ivy Tech Comm Coll–Southeast (IN)
Ivy Tech Comm Coll–Southern Indiana (IN)
Ivy Tech Comm Coll–Southwest (IN)
Ivy Tech Comm Coll–Wabash Valley (IN)
Pittsburgh Tech Inst, Oakdale (PA)

MEDICAL INFORMATICS
Borough of Manhattan Comm Coll of the City U of New York (NY)
Comm Coll of Baltimore County (MD)
Dyersburg State Comm Coll (TN)
Harrisburg Area Comm Coll (PA)
Nashville State Comm Coll (TN)
Volunteer State Comm Coll (TN)

MEDICAL INSURANCE CODING
Barton County Comm Coll (KS)
Berkshire Comm Coll (MA)
Bucks County Comm Coll (PA)
Butler County Comm Coll (PA)
Career Training Academy, Lower Burrell (PA)
Collin County Comm Coll District (TX)
Comm Care Coll (OK)
Davis Coll (OH)
Hawkeye Comm Coll (IA)
Laramie County Comm Coll (WY)
LDS Business Coll (UT)
Metro Business Coll, Jefferson City (MO)
Minnesota West Comm and Tech Coll (MN)
Northland Comm and Tech Coll (MN)
Paris Jr Coll (TX)
Renton Tech Coll (WA)
San Joaquin Valley Coll–Online (CA)
Southeastern Coll–West Palm Beach (FL)
Southeast Tech Inst (SD)
Spencerian Coll (KY)
Springfield Tech Comm Coll (MA)

MEDICAL INSURANCE/ MEDICAL BILLING
Carrington Coll–Boise (ID)
Carrington Coll–Citrus Heights (CA)
Carrington Coll–Pleasant Hill (CA)
Carrington Coll–Pomona (CA)
Carrington Coll–Sacramento (CA)
Carrington Coll–San Jose (CA)
Carrington Coll–San Leandro (CA)
Northcentral Tech Coll (WI)
Pasadena City Coll (CA)
San Joaquin Valley Coll, Bakersfield (CA)
San Joaquin Valley Coll, Hanford (CA)
San Joaquin Valley Coll, Hesperia (CA)
Southeastern Coll–West Palm Beach (FL)
Ultimate Medical Academy Online (FL)

MEDICAL MICROBIOLOGY AND BACTERIOLOGY
South Florida State Coll (FL)

MEDICAL OFFICE ASSISTANT
Barton County Comm Coll (KS)
Beal Coll (ME)
Butler County Comm Coll (PA)
Central Wyoming Coll (WY)
Cincinnati State Tech and Comm Coll (OH)
Front Range Comm Coll (CO)
Harford Comm Coll (MD)
Kankakee Comm Coll (IL)
Manhattan Area Tech Coll (KS)
Metro Business Coll, Jefferson City (MO)
Mitchell Tech Inst (SD)
Northland Comm and Tech Coll (MN)
Pasadena City Coll (CA)
Pittsburgh Tech Inst, Oakdale (PA)
San Joaquin Valley Coll, Fresno (CA)
San Joaquin Valley Coll, Lancaster (CA)
San Joaquin Valley Coll, Ontario (CA)
San Joaquin Valley Coll, Salida (CA)
San Joaquin Valley Coll, Temecula (CA)
San Joaquin Valley Coll, Visalia (CA)
Western Wyoming Comm Coll (WY)
Westmoreland County Comm Coll (PA)
White Mountains Comm Coll (NH)

MEDICAL OFFICE COMPUTER SPECIALIST
Lamar Comm Coll (CO)
Richmond Comm Coll (NC)
Rogue Comm Coll (OR)
Western Wyoming Comm Coll (WY)

MEDICAL OFFICE MANAGEMENT
Beckfield Coll (KY)
Big Bend Comm Coll (WA)
Caldwell Comm Coll and Tech Inst (NC)
Cape Fear Comm Coll (NC)
Carrington Coll–Albuquerque (NM)

Carrington Coll–Boise (ID)
Carrington Coll–Mesa (AZ)
Carrington Coll–Phoenix North (AZ)
Carrington Coll–Sacramento (CA)
Carrington Coll–San Jose (CA)
Carrington Coll–Spokane (WA)
Carrington Coll–Tucson (AZ)
Catawba Valley Comm Coll (NC)
Cleveland Comm Coll (NC)
Columbus Tech Coll (GA)
Craven Comm Coll (NC)
Fayetteville Tech Comm Coll (NC)
Forrest Coll (SC)
Fox Valley Tech Coll (WI)
Georgia Northwestern Tech Coll (GA)
Halifax Comm Coll (NC)
Johnston Comm Coll (NC)
Lenoir Comm Coll (NC)
Long Island Business Inst (NY)
Norwalk Comm Coll (CT)
Pennsylvania Inst of Technology (PA)
Piedmont Comm Coll (NC)
Pueblo Comm Coll (CO)
Queensborough Comm Coll of the City U of New York (NY)
Randolph Comm Coll (NC)
Richmond Comm Coll (NC)
Rockingham Comm Coll (NC)
Rowan-Cabarrus Comm Coll (NC)
San Joaquin Valley Coll–Online (CA)
Spencerian Coll–Lexington (KY)
Wayne Comm Coll (NC)
Western Iowa Tech Comm Coll (IA)
Western Piedmont Comm Coll (NC)

MEDICAL RADIOLOGIC TECHNOLOGY
Aiken Tech Coll (SC)
Albany Tech Coll (GA)
Anne Arundel Comm Coll (MD)
Athens Tech Coll (GA)
Augusta Tech Coll (GA)
Bellingham Tech Coll (WA)
Bowling Green State U–Firelands Coll (OH)
Bunker Hill Comm Coll (MA)
Cape Fear Comm Coll (NC)
Carolinas Coll of Health Sciences (NC)
Carrington Coll–Phoenix West (AZ)
Carrington Coll–Spokane (WA)
Catawba Valley Comm Coll (NC)
Central Georgia Tech Coll (GA)
Chattahoochee Tech Coll (GA)
Chesapeake Coll (MD)
Chippewa Valley Tech Coll (WI)
Coll of Central Florida (FL)
Columbus Tech Coll (GA)
Comm Coll of Baltimore County (MD)
Comm Coll of Philadelphia (PA)
Comm Coll of the Air Force (AL)
Delta Coll (MI)
Dunwoody Coll of Technology (MN)
East Central Coll (MO)
Elizabethtown Comm and Tech Coll, Elizabethtown (KY)
Erie Comm Coll (NY)
Fiorello H. LaGuardia Comm Coll of the City U of New York (NY)
Florida SouthWestern State Coll (FL)
Galveston Coll (TX)
George C. Wallace Comm Coll (AL)
Greenville Tech Coll (SC)
Gulf Coast State Coll (FL)
Gwinnett Tech Coll (GA)
Hagerstown Comm Coll (MD)
Hillsborough Comm Coll (FL)
Holyoke Comm Coll (MA)
Hutchinson Comm Coll (KS)
Illinois Eastern Comm Colls, Olney Central College (IL)
Itawamba Comm Coll (MS)
Ivy Tech Comm Coll–Bloomington (IN)
Ivy Tech Comm Coll–Central Indiana (IN)
Ivy Tech Comm Coll–Columbus (IN)
Ivy Tech Comm Coll–East Central (IN)
Ivy Tech Comm Coll–Richmond (IN)
Ivy Tech Comm Coll–Southeast (IN)
Ivy Tech Comm Coll–Wabash Valley (IN)
Kellogg Comm Coll (MI)
Kent State U at Ashtabula (OH)
Kent State U at Salem (OH)
Kilgore Coll (TX)
Lakeland Comm Coll (OH)

Lanier Tech Coll (GA)
Lone Star Coll–CyFair (TX)
Mercer County Comm Coll (NJ)
Miami Dade Coll (FL)
Middlesex County Coll (NJ)
Midlands Tech Coll (SC)
Mitchell Tech Inst (SD)
Mohawk Valley Comm Coll (NY)
Montgomery Coll (MD)
Montgomery County Comm Coll (PA)
Mott Comm Coll (MI)
Naugatuck Valley Comm Coll (CT)
Niagara County Comm Coll (NY)
Northcentral Tech Coll (WI)
North Shore Comm Coll (MA)
Pensacola State Coll (FL)
Rend Lake Coll (IL)
Rowan Coll at Burlington County (NJ)
St. Clair County Comm Coll (MI)
St. Philip's Coll (TX)
Salt Lake Comm Coll (UT)
Somerset Comm Coll (KY)
Southeast Comm Coll, Lincoln
  Campus (NE)
Southeastern Tech Coll (GA)
Southern Crescent Tech Coll (GA)
Southern Regional Tech Coll (GA)
Southern U at Shreveport (LA)
South Florida State Coll (FL)
Southwestern Oklahoma State U at
  Sayre (OK)
Southwest Tennessee Comm Coll
  (TN)
Spartanburg Comm Coll (SC)
Tallahassee Comm Coll (FL)
Tech Coll of the Lowcountry (SC)
Truckee Meadows Comm Coll (NV)
Tulsa Comm Coll (OK)
U of Cincinnati Blue Ash Coll (OH)
Vincennes U (IN)
Volunteer State Comm Coll (TN)
Waukesha County Tech Coll (WI)
West Georgia Tech Coll (GA)
Wiregrass Georgia Tech Coll (GA)
Wor-Wic Comm Coll (MD)

**MEDICAL STAFF SERVICES
TECHNOLOGY**
Rend Lake Coll (IL)

MEDICAL TRANSCRIPTION
Barton County Comm Coll (KS)
Hudson County Comm Coll (NJ)
Mountain State Coll (WV)
Northern Essex Comm Coll (MA)
Treasure Valley Comm Coll (OR)
U of Cincinnati Blue Ash Coll (OH)

MEDICATION AIDE
Barton County Comm Coll (KS)

**MEDIUM/HEAVY VEHICLE AND
TRUCK TECHNOLOGY**
Edison Comm Coll (OH)
Hennepin Tech Coll (MN)

**MEETING AND EVENT
PLANNING**
Fox Valley Tech Coll (WI)
Northampton Comm Coll (PA)
Raritan Valley Comm Coll (NJ)

**MENTAL AND SOCIAL HEALTH
SERVICES AND ALLIED
PROFESSIONS RELATED**
Chesapeake Coll (MD)
Halifax Comm Coll (NC)
John Tyler Comm Coll (VA)
J. Sargeant Reynolds Comm Coll
  (VA)
Kennebec Valley Comm Coll (ME)
Lenoir Comm Coll (NC)
Montgomery Comm Coll (NC)
New River Comm Coll (VA)
Northcentral Tech Coll (WI)
Olympic Coll (WA)
Piedmont Comm Coll (NC)
Reading Area Comm Coll (PA)
Richmond Comm Coll (NC)
Southwest Virginia Comm Coll (VA)
Wayne Comm Coll (NC)
Western Piedmont Comm Coll (NC)

**MENTAL HEALTH
COUNSELING**
Alvin Comm Coll (TX)
Blinn Coll (TX)
Comm Coll of Rhode Island (RI)
Comm Coll of the Air Force (AL)
Housatonic Comm Coll (CT)
Illinois Central Coll (IL)
Lackawanna Coll (PA)

Macomb Comm Coll (MI)
Mt. San Antonio Coll (CA)
Northern Essex Comm Coll (MA)
North Shore Comm Coll (MA)
Orange Coast Coll (CA)
Southern U at Shreveport (LA)
Tarrant County Coll District (TX)
Truckee Meadows Comm Coll (NV)
U of Alaska, Prince William Sound
  Coll (AK)
Virginia Western Comm Coll (VA)

MERCHANDISING
Delta Coll (MI)
North Central Texas Coll (TX)

**MERCHANDISING, SALES, AND
MARKETING OPERATIONS
RELATED (GENERAL)**
Herkimer County Comm Coll (NY)
Lake Region State Coll (ND)
Northcentral Tech Coll (WI)
Orange Coast Coll (CA)
Southeast Tech Inst (SD)

**MERCHANDISING, SALES, AND
MARKETING OPERATIONS
RELATED (SPECIALIZED)**
Middlesex County Coll (NJ)

METAL AND JEWELRY ARTS
Coll of The Albemarle (NC)
Fashion Inst of Technology (NY)
Fashion Inst of Design &
  Merchandising, LA Campus (CA)
Palomar Coll (CA)
Paris Jr Coll (TX)

METAL FABRICATOR
Waukesha County Tech Coll (WI)

**METALLURGICAL
TECHNOLOGY**
Comm Coll of the Air Force (AL)
Kilgore Coll (TX)
Macomb Comm Coll (MI)
Penn State DuBois (PA)
Penn State Fayette, The Eberly
  Campus (PA)
Penn State Shenango (PA)
Schoolcraft Coll (MI)

MICROBIOLOGY
Fullerton Coll (CA)
Humacao Comm Coll (PR)

MIDDLE SCHOOL EDUCATION
Alvin Comm Coll (TX)
Austin Comm Coll District (TX)
Collin County Comm Coll District
  (TX)
Georgia Military Coll (GA)
Gordon State Coll (GA)
Miami Dade Coll (FL)
Nashville State Comm Coll (TN)
Northampton Comm Coll (PA)
Panola Coll (TX)
South Florida State Coll (FL)
Tyler Jr Coll (TX)

MILITARY STUDIES
Barton County Comm Coll (KS)

MINING TECHNOLOGY
Casper Coll (WY)
Eastern Arizona Coll (AZ)
Illinois Eastern Comm Colls, Wabash
  Valley College (IL)
Rend Lake Coll (IL)
Sheridan Coll (WY)
Western Wyoming Comm Coll (WY)

MODERN LANGUAGES
Amarillo Coll (TX)
Barton County Comm Coll (KS)
Citrus Coll (CA)
Itawamba Comm Coll (MS)
Odessa Coll (TX)
Otero Jr Coll (CO)
Potomac State Coll of West Virginia
  U (WV)
Tyler Jr Coll (TX)

**MORTUARY SCIENCE AND
EMBALMING**
Wayne County Comm Coll District
  (MI)

**MOTORCYCLE MAINTENANCE
AND REPAIR TECHNOLOGY**
Western Iowa Tech Comm Coll (IA)

**MOVEMENT AND MIND-BODY
THERAPIES AND EDUCATION
RELATED**
Moraine Valley Comm Coll (IL)

**MULTI/INTERDISCIPLINARY
STUDIES RELATED**
Aiken Tech Coll (SC)
Alexandria Tech and Comm Coll
  (MN)
Anne Arundel Comm Coll (MD)
Bismarck State Coll (ND)
Blue Ridge Comm and Tech Coll
  (WV)
Bucks County Comm Coll (PA)
Carroll Comm Coll (MD)
Central Maine Comm Coll (ME)
Century Coll (MN)
Chippewa Valley Tech Coll (WI)
Cincinnati State Tech and Comm Coll
  (OH)
County Coll of Morris (NJ)
Denmark Tech Coll (SC)
Eastern Arizona Coll (AZ)
Fox Valley Tech Coll (WI)
Greenville Tech Coll (SC)
Hawkeye Comm Coll (IA)
Hinds Comm Coll (MS)
Hopkinsville Comm Coll (KY)
Kennebec Valley Comm Coll (ME)
Lake Superior Coll (MN)
Manhattan Area Tech Coll (KS)
Midlands Tech Coll (SC)
Minnesota State Coll–Southeast
  Tech (MN)
Northcentral Tech Coll (WI)
North Hennepin Comm Coll (MN)
Northwest-Shoals Comm Coll (AL)
Oklahoma City Comm Coll (OK)
Oklahoma State U Inst of Technology
  (OK)
Owensboro Comm and Tech Coll
  (KY)
Raritan Valley Comm Coll (NJ)
Somerset Comm Coll (KY)
South Florida State Coll (FL)
Spartanburg Comm Coll (SC)
Tri-County Tech Coll (SC)
Tulsa Comm Coll (OK)
Washington County Comm Coll (ME)
Waukesha County Tech Coll (WI)
Western Iowa Tech Comm Coll (IA)
Williston State Coll (ND)
York County Comm Coll (ME)

MUSEUM STUDIES
Casper Coll (WY)
Queensborough Comm Coll of the
  City U of New York (NY)

MUSIC
Allen Comm Coll (KS)
Alvin Comm Coll (TX)
Amarillo Coll (TX)
American River Coll (CA)
American Samoa Comm Coll (AS)
Anoka-Ramsey Comm Coll (MN)
Antelope Valley Coll (CA)
Arizona Western Coll (AZ)
Austin Comm Coll District (TX)
Barton County Comm Coll (KS)
Blinn Coll (TX)
Bossier Parish Comm Coll (LA)
Brookhaven Coll (TX)
Bucks County Comm Coll (PA)
Bunker Hill Comm Coll (MA)
Ca&nnada Coll (CA)
Carroll Comm Coll (MD)
Casper Coll (WY)
Central Texas Coll (TX)
Central Wyoming Coll (WY)
Century Coll (MN)
Cerritos Coll (CA)
Citrus Coll (CA)
Cochise County Comm Coll District
  (AZ)
Coll of Central Florida (FL)
Coll of The Albemarle (NC)
Coll of the Canyons (CA)
Collin County Comm Coll District
  (TX)
Columbia Coll (CA)
Comm Coll of Philadelphia (PA)
Comm Coll of Rhode Island (RI)
Crowder Coll (MO)
Dawson Comm Coll (MT)
Dodge City Comm Coll (KS)
East Central Coll (MO)
Eastern Arizona Coll (AZ)
Eastern Wyoming Coll (WY)
Elgin Comm Coll (IL)
Finger Lakes Comm Coll (NY)

Fullerton Coll (CA)
Galveston Coll (TX)
Georgia Highlands Coll (GA)
Gordon State Coll (GA)
Grand Rapids Comm Coll (MI)
Harford Comm Coll (MD)
Holyoke Comm Coll (MA)
Howard Comm Coll (MD)
Itawamba Comm Coll (MS)
Jamestown Comm Coll (NY)
Kaskaskia Coll (IL)
Kilgore Coll (TX)
Laramie County Comm Coll (WY)
Lone Star Coll–CyFair (TX)
Lone Star Coll–Kingwood (TX)
Lone Star Coll–Montgomery (TX)
Lone Star Coll–North Harris (TX)
Lone Star Coll–Tomball (TX)
Lorain County Comm Coll (OH)
Los Angeles Valley Coll (CA)
Manchester Comm Coll (CT)
McHenry County Coll (IL)
Mercer County Comm Coll (NJ)
Miami Dade Coll (FL)
Monroe Comm Coll (NY)
Moraine Valley Comm Coll (IL)
Mt. San Antonio Coll (CA)
Nashville State Comm Coll (TN)
Navarro Coll (TX)
New Mexico Jr Coll (NM)
Niagara County Comm Coll (NY)
Northeastern Jr Coll (CO)
Northern Essex Comm Coll (MA)
North Hennepin Comm Coll (MN)
Northwest Coll (WY)
Oakton Comm Coll (IL)
Odessa Coll (TX)
Oklahoma City Comm Coll (OK)
Onondaga Comm Coll (NY)
Orange Coast Coll (CA)
Palomar Coll (CA)
Panola Coll (TX)
Paris Jr Coll (TX)
Pensacola State Coll (FL)
Quinsigamond Comm Coll (MA)
Raritan Valley Comm Coll (NJ)
Rowan Coll at Burlington County (NJ)
St. Philip's Coll (TX)
Salt Lake Comm Coll (UT)
San Jacinto Coll District (TX)
San Joaquin Delta Coll (CA)
Sheridan Coll (WY)
Sierra Coll (CA)
South Florida State Coll (FL)
Texarkana Coll (TX)
Tidewater Comm Coll (VA)
Truckee Meadows Comm Coll (NV)
Tulsa Comm Coll (OK)
Tyler Jr Coll (TX)
Victor Valley Coll (CA)
Vincennes U (IN)
Wenatchee Valley Coll (WA)
Western Wyoming Comm Coll (WY)

**MUSICAL INSTRUMENT
FABRICATION AND REPAIR**
Queensborough Comm Coll of the
  City U of New York (NY)
Renton Tech Coll (WA)
Western Iowa Tech Comm Coll (IA)

MUSICAL THEATER
Casper Coll (WY)
Coll of the Canyons (CA)

**MUSIC HISTORY, LITERATURE,
AND THEORY**
St. Charles Comm Coll (MO)
South Florida State Coll (FL)

MUSIC MANAGEMENT
American River Coll (CA)
Austin Comm Coll District (TX)
Chandler-Gilbert Comm Coll (AZ)
Collin County Comm Coll District
  (TX)
Harrisburg Area Comm Coll (PA)
Houston Comm Coll (TX)
Los Angeles Valley Coll (CA)

MUSIC PERFORMANCE
Casper Coll (WY)
Comm Coll of the Air Force (AL)
Dyersburg State Comm Coll (TN)
Houston Comm Coll (TX)
Macomb Comm Coll (MI)
Miami Dade Coll (FL)
South Florida State Coll (FL)
Truckee Meadows Comm Coll (NV)
Volunteer State Comm Coll (TN)
Walters State Comm Coll (TN)

MUSIC RELATED
Cayuga County Comm Coll (NY)
County Coll of Morris (NJ)

MUSIC TEACHER EDUCATION
Amarillo Coll (TX)
Casper Coll (WY)
Coll of Central Florida (FL)
Copiah-Lincoln Comm Coll (MS)
Dodge City Comm Coll (KS)
Eastern Wyoming Coll (WY)
Grand Rapids Comm Coll (MI)
Itawamba Comm Coll (MS)
Miami Dade Coll (FL)
Pensacola State Coll (FL)
South Florida State Coll (FL)
Vincennes U (IN)
Wenatchee Valley Coll (WA)

MUSIC TECHNOLOGY
Arapahoe Comm Coll (CO)
Gulf Coast State Coll (FL)
Miami Dade Coll (FL)
Mott Comm Coll (MI)

**MUSIC THEORY AND
COMPOSITION**
Houston Comm Coll (TX)
South Florida State Coll (FL)

MUSIC THERAPY
South Florida State Coll (FL)

**NAIL TECHNICIAN AND
MANICURIST**
IBMC Coll, Fort Collins (CO)

NANOTECHNOLOGY
Chippewa Valley Tech Coll (WI)
Erie Comm Coll, North Campus (NY)
Lehigh Carbon Comm Coll (PA)

**NATURAL RESOURCE
RECREATION AND TOURISM**
Wenatchee Valley Coll (WA)

**NATURAL RESOURCES AND
CONSERVATION RELATED**
Palau Comm Coll (Palau)
Southwestern Indian Polytechnic Inst
  (NM)

**NATURAL RESOURCES/
CONSERVATION**
American Samoa Comm Coll (AS)
Central Lakes Coll (MN)
Central Oregon Comm Coll (OR)
Colorado Northwestern Comm Coll
  (CO)
Columbia Coll (CA)
Feather River Coll (CA)
Finger Lakes Comm Coll (NY)
Fox Valley Tech Coll (WI)
Niagara County Comm Coll (NY)
St. Philip's Coll (TX)
Treasure Valley Comm Coll (OR)
Truckee Meadows Comm Coll (NV)
Vincennes U (IN)

**NATURAL RESOURCES LAW
ENFORCEMENT AND
PROTECTIVE SERVICES**
Finger Lakes Comm Coll (NY)

**NATURAL RESOURCES
MANAGEMENT AND POLICY**
American River Coll (CA)
Finger Lakes Comm Coll (NY)
Hawkeye Comm Coll (IA)
Hutchinson Comm Coll (KS)
Northwest Coll (WY)
Pensacola State Coll (FL)
San Joaquin Delta Coll (CA)

**NATURAL RESOURCES
MANAGEMENT AND POLICY
RELATED**
Finger Lakes Comm Coll (NY)
Great Basin Coll (NV)

NATURAL SCIENCES
Amarillo Coll (TX)
Bossier Parish Comm Coll (LA)
Citrus Coll (CA)
Galveston Coll (TX)
Leeward Comm Coll (HI)
Miami Dade Coll (FL)
Northeastern Jr Coll (CO)
Quincy Coll (MA)
San Joaquin Delta Coll (CA)
Tyler Jr Coll (TX)
U of Pittsburgh at Titusville (PA)
Victor Valley Coll (CA)

NETWORK AND SYSTEM ADMINISTRATION
American River Coll (CA)
Bucks County Comm Coll (PA)
Butler County Comm Coll (PA)
Ca&nnada Coll (CA)
Central Maine Comm Coll (ME)
Cincinnati State Tech and Comm Coll (OH)
The Coll of Westchester (NY)
Collin County Comm Coll District (TX)
Corning Comm Coll (NY)
Florida SouthWestern State Coll (FL)
Genesee Comm Coll (NY)
Gulf Coast State Coll (FL)
Houston Comm Coll (TX)
Island Drafting and Tech Inst (NY)
Ivy Tech Comm Coll–Bloomington (IN)
Ivy Tech Comm Coll–Central Indiana (IN)
Ivy Tech Comm Coll–East Central (IN)
Ivy Tech Comm Coll–Kokomo (IN)
Ivy Tech Comm Coll–Richmond (IN)
Ivy Tech Comm Coll–Southeast (IN)
Ivy Tech Comm Coll–Southern Indiana (IN)
Ivy Tech Comm Coll–Southwest (IN)
Ivy Tech Comm Coll–Wabash Valley (IN)
Kaskaskia Coll (IL)
Lake Superior Coll (MN)
Manhattan Area Tech Coll (KS)
Massachusetts Bay Comm Coll (MA)
Miami Dade Coll (FL)
Minnesota State Comm and Tech Coll–Wadena (MN)
Mitchell Tech Inst (SD)
Montgomery County Comm Coll (PA)
Pittsburgh Tech Inst, Oakdale (PA)
Ridgewater Coll (MN)
Seminole State Coll of Florida (FL)
Sierra Coll (CA)
Southeast Comm Coll, Lincoln Campus (NE)
Southeast Comm Coll, Milford Campus (NE)
South Florida State Coll (FL)
Texas State Tech Coll (TX)
Wayne County Comm Coll District (MI)
York County Comm Coll (ME)

NEUROSCIENCE
Bucks County Comm Coll (PA)

NONPROFIT MANAGEMENT
Miami Dade Coll (FL)

NUCLEAR ENGINEERING
South Florida State Coll (FL)

NUCLEAR ENGINEERING TECHNOLOGY
Bismarck State Coll (ND)

NUCLEAR MEDICAL TECHNOLOGY
Amarillo Coll (TX)
Caldwell Comm Coll and Tech Inst (NC)
Cincinnati State Tech and Comm Coll (OH)
Comm Coll of the Air Force (AL)
Frederick Comm Coll (MD)
Galveston Coll (TX)
Gulf Coast State Coll (FL)
Harrisburg Area Comm Coll (PA)
Hillsborough Comm Coll (FL)
Houston Comm Coll (TX)
Howard Comm Coll (MD)
Lakeland Comm Coll (OH)
Lorain County Comm Coll (OH)
Maine Coll of Health Professions (ME)
Miami Dade Coll (FL)
Midlands Tech Coll (SC)
Southeast Tech Inst (SD)
U of Cincinnati Blue Ash Coll (OH)
Vincennes U (IN)

NUCLEAR/NUCLEAR POWER TECHNOLOGY
Allen Comm Coll (KS)
Cape Fear Comm Coll (NC)
Texas State Tech Coll (TX)
Three Rivers Comm Coll (CT)

NURSING ADMINISTRATION
Paris Jr Coll (TX)
South Suburban Coll (IL)

NURSING ASSISTANT/AIDE AND PATIENT CARE ASSISTANT/AIDE
Allen Comm Coll (KS)
American River Coll (CA)
Barton County Comm Coll (KS)
Morgan Comm Coll (CO)
Northland Comm and Tech Coll (MN)
Pensacola State Coll (FL)
Tallahassee Comm Coll (FL)
Western Iowa Tech Comm Coll (IA)
Western Wyoming Comm Coll (WY)

NURSING PRACTICE
Genesee Comm Coll (NY)
Minnesota State Comm and Tech Coll–Detroit Lakes (MN)
Minnesota State Comm and Tech Coll–Moorhead (MN)
Minnesota State Comm and Tech Coll–Wadena (MN)
Nashville State Comm Coll (TN)

NURSING SCIENCE
Ultimate Medical Academy Tampa (FL)

NUTRITION SCIENCES
Casper Coll (WY)
Tulsa Comm Coll (OK)

OCCUPATIONAL HEALTH AND INDUSTRIAL HYGIENE
Niagara County Comm Coll (NY)

OCCUPATIONAL SAFETY AND HEALTH TECHNOLOGY
Anne Arundel Comm Coll (MD)
Central Wyoming Coll (WY)
Cincinnati State Tech and Comm Coll (OH)
Coastal Pines Tech Coll (GA)
Comm Coll of Baltimore County (MD)
Comm Coll of the Air Force (AL)
Houston Comm Coll (TX)
Ivy Tech Comm Coll–Central Indiana (IN)
Ivy Tech Comm Coll–Northeast (IN)
Ivy Tech Comm Coll–Northwest (IN)
Ivy Tech Comm Coll–Wabash Valley (IN)
Kilgore Coll (TX)
Lanier Tech Coll (GA)
Mt. San Antonio Coll (CA)
NorthWest Arkansas Comm Coll (AR)
Oklahoma State U, Oklahoma City (OK)
St. Philip's Coll (TX)
San Jacinto Coll District (TX)
San Juan Coll (NM)
Texas State Tech Coll (TX)
U of Alaska Anchorage, Kenai Peninsula Coll (AK)
Westmoreland County Comm Coll (PA)

OCCUPATIONAL THERAPIST ASSISTANT
Anoka Tech Coll (MN)
Augusta Tech Coll (GA)
Austin Comm Coll District (TX)
Bossier Parish Comm Coll (LA)
Cape Fear Comm Coll (NC)
Carrington Coll–Phoenix West (AZ)
Casper Coll (WY)
Cincinnati State Tech and Comm Coll (OH)
Comm Coll of Rhode Island (RI)
County Coll of Morris (NJ)
Crowder Coll (MO)
Daytona State Coll (FL)
East Central Coll (MO)
Erie Comm Coll, North Campus (NY)
Fiorello H. LaGuardia Comm Coll of the City U of New York (NY)
Fox Coll (IL)
Fox Valley Tech Coll (WI)
Greenville Tech Coll (SC)
Hawkeye Comm Coll (IA)
Houston Comm Coll (TX)
Illinois Central Coll (IL)
Ivy Tech Comm Coll–Central Indiana (IN)
Jamestown Comm Coll (NY)

Jefferson Coll (MO)
Kaskaskia Coll (IL)
Kennebec Valley Comm Coll (ME)
Kent State U at Ashtabula (OH)
Kent State U at East Liverpool (OH)
Lake Area Tech Inst (SD)
Lehigh Carbon Comm Coll (PA)
Lewis and Clark Comm Coll (IL)
Macomb Comm Coll (MI)
Manchester Comm Coll (CT)
McHenry County Coll (IL)
Midlands Tech Coll (SC)
Mott Comm Coll (MI)
Nashville State Comm Coll (TN)
Northland Comm and Tech Coll (MN)
Ocean County Coll (NJ)
Ozarks Tech Comm Coll (MO)
Panola Coll (TX)
Penn State DuBois (PA)
Penn State Mont Alto (PA)
Pueblo Comm Coll (CO)
Quinsigamond Comm Coll (MA)
Reading Area Comm Coll (PA)
Rend Lake Coll (IL)
River Valley Comm Coll (NH)
St. Charles Comm Coll (MO)
St. Philip's Coll (TX)
Salt Lake Comm Coll (UT)
San Juan Coll (NM)
Shawnee Comm Coll (IL)
South Suburban Coll (IL)
Springfield Tech Comm Coll (MA)
Tyler Jr Coll (TX)
Walters State Comm Coll (TN)
Weatherford Coll (TX)
Wisconsin Indianhead Tech Coll (WI)
Wor-Wic Comm Coll (MD)

OCCUPATIONAL THERAPY
Amarillo Coll (TX)
Barton County Comm Coll (KS)
Carrington Coll–Phoenix North (AZ)
Coll of Central Florida (FL)
Comm Coll of Baltimore County (MD)
Iowa Central Comm Coll (IA)
Lone Star Coll–Kingwood (TX)
Nashville State Comm Coll (TN)
Navarro Coll (TX)
North Central Texas Coll (TX)
North Shore Comm Coll (MA)
Ozarks Tech Comm Coll (MO)
South Florida State Coll (FL)
Stark State Coll (OH)
Tulsa Comm Coll (OK)

OCEAN ENGINEERING
South Florida State Coll (FL)

OCEANOGRAPHY (CHEMICAL AND PHYSICAL)
Cape Fear Comm Coll (NC)

OFFICE MANAGEMENT
Alexandria Tech and Comm Coll (MN)
Anoka Tech Coll (MN)
Big Bend Comm Coll (WA)
Brookhaven Coll (TX)
Catawba Valley Comm Coll (NC)
Cecil Coll (MD)
Cleveland Comm Coll (NC)
Coll of Central Florida (FL)
Comm Coll of Aurora (CO)
Comm Coll of the Air Force (AL)
Corning Comm Coll (NY)
Craven Comm Coll (NC)
Eastern Wyoming Coll (WY)
Erie Comm Coll, North Campus (NY)
Erie Comm Coll, South Campus (NY)
Fayetteville Tech Comm Coll (NC)
Forrest Coll (SC)
Fox Valley Tech Coll (WI)
Gulf Coast State Coll (FL)
Halifax Comm Coll (NC)
Howard Comm Coll (MD)
Ilisagvik Coll (AK)
Ivy Tech Comm Coll–Wabash Valley (IN)
Jamestown Business Coll (NY)
Jefferson Comm Coll (NY)
Jefferson State Comm Coll (AL)
Johnston Comm Coll (NC)
Lake Land Coll (IL)
Lake Superior Coll (MN)
Lenoir Comm Coll (NC)
Los Angeles Valley Coll (CA)
Miami Dade Coll (FL)
Mitchell Comm Coll (NC)

Montgomery Comm Coll (NC)
Northland Comm and Tech Coll (MN)
Piedmont Comm Coll (NC)
Renton Tech Coll (WA)
Richmond Comm Coll (NC)
Rockingham Comm Coll (NC)
Rowan-Cabarrus Comm Coll (NC)
St. Charles Comm Coll (MO)
St. Clair County Comm Coll (MI)
South Florida State Coll (FL)
South Suburban Coll (IL)
Tallahassee Comm Coll (FL)
Treasure Valley Comm Coll (OR)
Waukesha County Tech Coll (WI)
Wayne Comm Coll (NC)
Wayne County Comm Coll District (MI)
Wenatchee Valley Coll (WA)
Western Piedmont Comm Coll (NC)
White Mountains Comm Coll (NH)
Wisconsin Indianhead Tech Coll (WI)

OFFICE OCCUPATIONS AND CLERICAL SERVICES
Alamance Comm Coll (NC)
Alvin Comm Coll (TX)
American Samoa Comm Coll (AS)
Butler County Comm Coll (PA)
Caldwell Comm Coll and Tech Inst (NC)
Cloud County Comm Coll (KS)
Corning Comm Coll (NY)
Gateway Comm and Tech Coll (KY)
Great Basin Coll (NV)
IBMC Coll, Fort Collins (CO)
ITI Tech Coll (LA)
Jefferson Coll (MO)
Jefferson Comm Coll (NY)
Lone Star Coll–CyFair (TX)
Oklahoma State U Inst of Technology (OK)
San Joaquin Valley Coll, Fresno (CA)
San Joaquin Valley Coll, Hanford (CA)
San Joaquin Valley Coll, Hesperia (CA)
San Joaquin Valley Coll, Lancaster (CA)
San Joaquin Valley Coll, Ontario (CA)
San Joaquin Valley Coll, Salida (CA)
San Joaquin Valley Coll, Temecula (CA)
San Joaquin Valley Coll–Online (CA)
Southeast Tech Inst (SD)

OPERATIONS MANAGEMENT
Blue Ridge Comm and Tech Coll (WV)
Bunker Hill Comm Coll (MA)
Chippewa Valley Tech Coll (WI)
Cleveland Comm Coll (NC)
Fayetteville Tech Comm Coll (NC)
Georgia Piedmont Tech Coll (GA)
Great Basin Coll (NV)
Hillsborough Comm Coll (FL)
Kilgore Coll (TX)
Lenoir Comm Coll (NC)
Macomb Comm Coll (MI)
McHenry County Coll (IL)
Miami Dade Coll (FL)
Mitchell Comm Coll (NC)
Mohawk Valley Comm Coll (NY)
Northcentral Tech Coll (WI)
Northland Comm and Tech Coll (MN)
Oakton Comm Coll (IL)
Pennsylvania Highlands Comm Coll (PA)
South Florida State Coll (FL)
Stark State Coll (OH)
Wayne Comm Coll (NC)

OPHTHALMIC AND OPTOMETRIC SUPPORT SERVICES AND ALLIED PROFESSIONS RELATED
Vincennes U (IN)

OPHTHALMIC LABORATORY TECHNOLOGY
Comm Coll of the Air Force (AL)
Georgia Piedmont Tech Coll (GA)

OPHTHALMIC TECHNOLOGY
Lakeland Comm Coll (OH)
Miami Dade Coll (FL)
Renton Tech Coll (WA)
Volunteer State Comm Coll (TN)

OPTICIANRY
Camden County Coll (NJ)
Central New Mexico Comm Coll (NM)
Comm Coll of Rhode Island (RI)
Erie Comm Coll, North Campus (NY)
Florida SouthWestern State Coll (FL)
Georgia Piedmont Tech Coll (GA)
Hillsborough Comm Coll (FL)
J. Sargeant Reynolds Comm Coll (VA)
Miami Dade Coll (FL)
Ogeechee Tech Coll (GA)
Raritan Valley Comm Coll (NJ)
Southwestern Indian Polytechnic Inst (NM)

OPTOMETRIC TECHNICIAN
Barton County Comm Coll (KS)
Hillsborough Comm Coll (FL)
Raritan Valley Comm Coll (NJ)
San Jacinto Coll District (TX)

ORGANIZATIONAL BEHAVIOR
Chandler-Gilbert Comm Coll (AZ)

ORGANIZATIONAL COMMUNICATION
Butler County Comm Coll (PA)

ORGANIZATIONAL LEADERSHIP
Olympic Coll (WA)

ORNAMENTAL HORTICULTURE
Finger Lakes Comm Coll (NY)
Gwinnett Tech Coll (GA)
Mercer County Comm Coll (NJ)
Miami Dade Coll (FL)
Mt. San Antonio Coll (CA)
Pensacola State Coll (FL)
San Joaquin Delta Coll (CA)
Victor Valley Coll (CA)
Walters State Comm Coll (TN)

ORTHOTICS/PROSTHETICS
Century Coll (MN)
Oklahoma State U Inst of Technology (OK)

OUTDOOR EDUCATION
Corning Comm Coll (NY)

PAINTING
Luzerne County Comm Coll (PA)

PAINTING AND WALL COVERING
Ivy Tech Comm Coll–Central Indiana (IN)
Ivy Tech Comm Coll–East Central (IN)
Ivy Tech Comm Coll–Lafayette (IN)
Ivy Tech Comm Coll–North Central (IN)
Ivy Tech Comm Coll–Northeast (IN)
Ivy Tech Comm Coll–Northwest (IN)
Ivy Tech Comm Coll–Southwest (IN)
Ivy Tech Comm Coll–Wabash Valley (IN)

PARKS, RECREATION AND LEISURE
American River Coll (CA)
Central Wyoming Coll (WY)
Coll of Central Florida (FL)
Coll of the Canyons (CA)
Comm Coll of Baltimore County (MD)
Comm Coll of the Air Force (AL)
Corning Comm Coll (NY)
Feather River Coll (CA)
Fullerton Coll (CA)
Miami Dade Coll (FL)
Monroe Comm Coll (NY)
Mt. San Antonio Coll (CA)
Muskegon Comm Coll (MI)
New Mexico Jr Coll (NM)
Niagara County Comm Coll (NY)
Northern Essex Comm Coll (MA)
Northwest Coll (WY)
Norwalk Comm Coll (CT)
Onondaga Comm Coll (NY)
Palomar Coll (CA)
San Juan Coll (NM)
Sierra Coll (CA)
Sullivan County Comm Coll (NY)
Tompkins Cortland Comm Coll (NY)
Vincennes U (IN)

PARKS, RECREATION AND LEISURE FACILITIES MANAGEMENT

Allen Comm Coll (KS)
Arizona Western Coll (AZ)
Augusta Tech Coll (GA)
Butler County Comm Coll (PA)
Central Wyoming Coll (WY)
Chattahoochee Tech Coll (GA)
Herkimer County Comm Coll (NY)
James H. Faulkner State Comm Coll (AL)
Mohawk Valley Comm Coll (NY)
Moraine Valley Comm Coll (IL)
Mt. San Antonio Coll (CA)
North Georgia Tech Coll (GA)
Potomac State Coll of West Virginia U (WV)
Southeastern Coll–West Palm Beach (FL)
South Florida State Coll (FL)
Tompkins Cortland Comm Coll (NY)
Western Texas Coll (TX)

PARKS, RECREATION, LEISURE, AND FITNESS STUDIES RELATED

Cincinnati State Tech and Comm Coll (OH)
Comm Coll of Baltimore County (MD)
Corning Comm Coll (NY)
Genesee Comm Coll (NY)
Washington County Comm Coll (ME)

PASTORAL STUDIES/ COUNSELING

Hesston Coll (KS)

PEACE STUDIES AND CONFLICT RESOLUTION

Delta Coll (MI)

PERCUSSION INSTRUMENTS

Itawamba Comm Coll (MS)

PERSONAL AND CULINARY SERVICES RELATED

Mohave Comm Coll (AZ)
U of Cincinnati Blue Ash Coll (OH)

PETROLEUM ENGINEERING

Kilgore Coll (TX)

PETROLEUM TECHNOLOGY

Bismarck State Coll (ND)
Bossier Parish Comm Coll (LA)
Houston Comm Coll (TX)
Lackawanna Coll (PA)
New Mexico Jr Coll (NM)
Oklahoma State U Inst of Technology (OK)
Panola Coll (TX)
Rend Lake Coll (IL)
U of Arkansas Comm Coll at Morrilton (AR)
Western Texas Coll (TX)
Williston State Coll (ND)

PHARMACY

Barton County Comm Coll (KS)
Cerritos Coll (CA)
Lorain County Comm Coll (OH)
Navarro Coll (TX)
South Florida State Coll (FL)

PHARMACY TECHNICIAN

Albany Tech Coll (GA)
Alvin Comm Coll (TX)
Anoka-Ramsey Comm Coll (MN)
Augusta Tech Coll (GA)
Austin Comm Coll District (TX)
Barton County Comm Coll (KS)
Bossier Parish Comm Coll (LA)
Carrington Coll–Boise (ID)
Carrington Coll–Citrus Heights (CA)
Carrington Coll–Pleasant Hill (CA)
Carrington Coll–Pomona (CA)
Carrington Coll–Sacramento (CA)
Carrington Coll–San Jose (CA)
Carrington Coll–San Leandro (CA)
Casper Coll (WY)
Columbus Tech Coll (GA)
Comm Care Coll (OK)
Comm Coll of the Air Force (AL)
Eastern Arizona Coll (AZ)
Fayetteville Tech Comm Coll (NC)
Humacao Comm Coll (PR)
Hutchinson Comm Coll (KS)
J. Sargeant Reynolds Comm Coll (VA)
Kirtland Comm Coll (MI)
Lone Star Coll–North Harris (TX)

Miami Dade Coll (FL)
Midlands Tech Coll (SC)
Mohave Comm Coll (AZ)
Northland Comm and Tech Coll (MN)
Pennsylvania Inst of Technology (PA)
Pensacola State Coll (FL)
Renton Tech Coll (WA)
San Jacinto Coll District (TX)
San Joaquin Valley Coll, Bakersfield (CA)
San Joaquin Valley Coll, Fresno (CA)
San Joaquin Valley Coll, Hesperia (CA)
San Joaquin Valley Coll, Lancaster (CA)
San Joaquin Valley Coll, Ontario (CA)
San Joaquin Valley Coll, Salida (CA)
San Joaquin Valley Coll, Temecula (CA)
San Joaquin Valley Coll, Visalia (CA)
Southeastern Coll–West Palm Beach (FL)
Southern Crescent Tech Coll (GA)
Tallahassee Comm Coll (FL)
Texarkana Coll (TX)
Ultimate Medical Academy Online (FL)
Vincennes U (IN)
Wayne County Comm Coll District (MI)
Weatherford Coll (TX)
Western Iowa Tech Comm Coll (IA)
West Georgia Tech Coll (GA)

PHILOSOPHY

Allen Comm Coll (KS)
Antelope Valley Coll (CA)
Arizona Western Coll (AZ)
Austin Comm Coll District (TX)
Barton County Comm Coll (KS)
Blinn Coll (TX)
Ca&nnada Coll (CA)
Cerritos Coll (CA)
Cochise County Comm Coll District (AZ)
Coll of Central Florida (FL)
Coll of the Canyons (CA)
Fiorello H. LaGuardia Comm Coll of the City U of New York (NY)
Fullerton Coll (CA)
Georgia Highlands Coll (GA)
Harford Comm Coll (MD)
Harrisburg Area Comm Coll (PA)
Los Angeles Valley Coll (CA)
Miami Dade Coll (FL)
Nashville State Comm Coll (TN)
Northeastern Jr Coll (CO)
Oklahoma City Comm Coll (OK)
Orange Coast Coll (CA)
Oxnard Coll (CA)
Pensacola State Coll (FL)
Rowan Coll at Burlington County (NJ)
St. Charles Comm Coll (MO)
St. Philip's Coll (TX)
San Jacinto Coll District (TX)
San Joaquin Delta Coll (CA)
Sierra Coll (CA)
South Florida State Coll (FL)
Truckee Meadows Comm Coll (NV)
Vincennes U (IN)

PHILOSOPHY AND RELIGIOUS STUDIES RELATED

Edison Comm Coll (OH)
South Florida State Coll (FL)

PHLEBOTOMY TECHNOLOGY

Barton County Comm Coll (KS)
Miami Dade Coll (FL)
Northland Comm and Tech Coll (MN)
Westmoreland County Comm Coll (PA)

PHOTOGRAPHIC AND FILM/ VIDEO TECHNOLOGY

Antelope Valley Coll (CA)
Catawba Valley Comm Coll (NC)
Central Lakes Coll (MN)
Daytona State Coll (FL)
Herkimer County Comm Coll (NY)
Hinds Comm Coll (MS)
Miami Dade Coll (FL)
Oklahoma City Comm Coll (OK)
Olympic Coll (WA)
Orange Coast Coll (CA)
Palomar Coll (CA)
Randolph Comm Coll (NC)
Salt Lake Comm Coll (UT)
Tompkins Cortland Comm Coll (NY)
U of Cincinnati Blue Ash Coll (OH)

PHOTOGRAPHY

Amarillo Coll (TX)
American River Coll (CA)
Antelope Valley Coll (CA)
Antonelli Inst (PA)
Butler County Comm Coll (PA)
Casper Coll (WY)
Cecil Coll (MD)
Cerritos Coll (CA)
Citrus Coll (CA)
Coll of the Canyons (CA)
Columbia Coll (CA)
Comm Coll of Philadelphia (PA)
County Coll of Morris (NJ)
Gwinnett Tech Coll (GA)
Harford Comm Coll (MD)
Harrisburg Area Comm Coll (PA)
Hennepin Tech Coll (MN)
Howard Comm Coll (MD)
Luzerne County Comm Coll (PA)
Mercer County Comm Coll (NJ)
Miami Dade Coll (FL)
Mott Comm Coll (MI)
Mt. San Antonio Coll (CA)
Nashville State Comm Coll (TN)
Odessa Coll (TX)
Oklahoma State U Inst of Technology (OK)
Orange Coast Coll (CA)
Pasadena City Coll (CA)
Pensacola State Coll (FL)
San Joaquin Delta Coll (CA)
Scottsdale Comm Coll (AZ)
Sullivan County Comm Coll (NY)
Tyler Jr Coll (TX)
Western Wyoming Comm Coll (WY)

PHOTOJOURNALISM

Pasadena City Coll (CA)
Randolph Comm Coll (NC)
Vincennes U (IN)

PHYSICAL EDUCATION TEACHING AND COACHING

Alvin Comm Coll (TX)
Amarillo Coll (TX)
Barton County Comm Coll (KS)
Blinn Coll (TX)
Bucks County Comm Coll (PA)
Carl Albert State Coll (OK)
Casper Coll (WY)
Cerritos Coll (CA)
Citrus Coll (CA)
Clinton Comm Coll (NY)
Coll of Central Florida (FL)
Copiah-Lincoln Comm Coll (MS)
Crowder Coll (MO)
Dodge City Comm Coll (KS)
Dutchess Comm Coll (NY)
Eastern Wyoming Coll (WY)
Finger Lakes Comm Coll (NY)
Galveston Coll (TX)
Genesee Comm Coll (NY)
Grand Rapids Comm Coll (MI)
Itawamba Comm Coll (MS)
Kilgore Coll (TX)
Laramie County Comm Coll (WY)
Lorain County Comm Coll (OH)
Luzerne County Comm Coll (PA)
Miami Dade Coll (FL)
Monroe Comm Coll (NY)
Montgomery County Comm Coll (PA)
Navarro Coll (TX)
New Mexico Jr Coll (NM)
Niagara County Comm Coll (NY)
Northeastern Jr Coll (CO)
Northern Essex Comm Coll (MA)
North Hennepin Comm Coll (MN)
Odessa Coll (TX)
Panola Coll (TX)
Potomac State Coll of West Virginia U (WV)
San Joaquin Delta Coll (CA)
Seminole State Coll (OK)
Spoon River Coll (IL)
Tyler Jr Coll (TX)
Vincennes U (IN)

PHYSICAL FITNESS TECHNICIAN

Alexandria Tech and Comm Coll (MN)
Anoka-Ramsey Comm Coll (MN)
Central Maine Comm Coll (ME)
Lake Region State Coll (ND)
Orange Coast Coll (CA)
Sheridan Coll (WY)
Tallahassee Comm Coll (FL)
Western Iowa Tech Comm Coll (IA)

PHYSICAL SCIENCES

Alvin Comm Coll (TX)

Amarillo Coll (TX)
American River Coll (CA)
Antelope Valley Coll (CA)
Austin Comm Coll District (TX)
Barton County Comm Coll (KS)
Borough of Manhattan Comm Coll of the City U of New York (NY)
Butler County Comm Coll (PA)
Carl Albert State Coll (OK)
Central Oregon Comm Coll (OR)
Central Wyoming Coll (WY)
Chandler-Gilbert Comm Coll (AZ)
Citrus Coll (CA)
Columbia Coll (CA)
Crowder Coll (MO)
Dodge City Comm Coll (KS)
Feather River Coll (CA)
Harrisburg Area Comm Coll (PA)
Howard Comm Coll (MD)
Hutchinson Comm Coll (KS)
Lehigh Carbon Comm Coll (PA)
Miami Dade Coll (FL)
Middlesex County Coll (NJ)
Montgomery County Comm Coll (PA)
Navarro Coll (TX)
Northeastern Jr Coll (CO)
Olympic Coll (WA)
Ozarks Tech Comm Coll (MO)
Paris Jr Coll (TX)
Queensborough Comm Coll of the City U of New York (NY)
Reading Area Comm Coll (PA)
Salt Lake Comm Coll (UT)
San Jacinto Coll District (TX)
San Joaquin Delta Coll (CA)
San Juan Coll (NM)
Seminole State Coll (OK)
Spoon River Coll (IL)
Tulsa Comm Coll (OK)
U of New Mexico–Gallup (NM)
Victor Valley Coll (CA)
Vincennes U (IN)
Wenatchee Valley Coll (WA)
Western Nevada Coll (NV)

PHYSICAL SCIENCES RELATED

Cerritos Coll (CA)
Mt. San Antonio Coll (CA)
Naugatuck Valley Comm Coll (CT)

PHYSICAL SCIENCE TECHNOLOGIES RELATED

Westmoreland County Comm Coll (PA)

PHYSICAL THERAPY

Allen Comm Coll (KS)
Amarillo Coll (TX)
Athens Tech Coll (GA)
Barton County Comm Coll (KS)
Bossier Parish Comm Coll (LA)
Central Oregon Comm Coll (OR)
Cerritos Coll (CA)
Chesapeake Coll (MD)
Coll of Central Florida (FL)
Daytona State Coll (FL)
Dodge City Comm Coll (KS)
Genesee Comm Coll (NY)
Gwinnett Tech Coll (GA)
Herkimer County Comm Coll (NY)
Housatonic Comm Coll (CT)
Iowa Central Comm Coll (IA)
Kilgore Coll (TX)
NorthWest Arkansas Comm Coll (AR)
Odessa Coll (TX)
Seminole State Coll of Florida (FL)
Stark State Coll (OH)
Tarrant County Coll District (TX)
Wytheville Comm Coll (VA)

PHYSICAL THERAPY TECHNOLOGY

Anne Arundel Comm Coll (MD)
Anoka-Ramsey Comm Coll (MN)
Arapahoe Comm Coll (CO)
Austin Comm Coll District (TX)
Barton County Comm Coll (KS)
Berkshire Comm Coll (MA)
Blackhawk Tech Coll (WI)
Blinn Coll (TX)
Blue Ridge Comm and Tech Coll (WV)
Bossier Parish Comm Coll (LA)
Bradford School (OH)
Butler County Comm Coll (PA)
Caldwell Comm Coll and Tech Inst (NC)
Carl Albert State Coll (OK)
Carrington Coll–Albuquerque (NM)
Carrington Coll–Boise (ID)
Carrington Coll–Las Vegas (NV)

Carrington Coll–Mesa (AZ)
Carrington Coll–Pleasant Hill (CA)
Carroll Comm Coll (MD)
Chippewa Valley Tech Coll (WI)
Coll of Central Florida (FL)
Comm Coll of Rhode Island (RI)
Comm Coll of the Air Force (AL)
Craven Comm Coll (NC)
Delta Coll (MI)
Edison Comm Coll (OH)
Elgin Comm Coll (IL)
Fayetteville Tech Comm Coll (NC)
Fiorello H. LaGuardia Comm Coll of the City U of New York (NY)
Florida SouthWestern State Coll (FL)
Fox Coll (IL)
Gateway Tech Coll (WI)
Genesee Comm Coll (NY)
George C. Wallace Comm Coll (AL)
Great Falls Coll Montana State U (MT)
Greenville Tech Coll (SC)
Gulf Coast State Coll (FL)
Gwinnett Tech Coll (GA)
Hawkeye Comm Coll (IA)
Hinds Comm Coll (MS)
Houston Comm Coll (TX)
Howard Comm Coll (MD)
Hutchinson Comm Coll (KS)
Illinois Central Coll (IL)
Ivy Tech Comm Coll–East Central (IN)
Ivy Tech Comm Coll–Kokomo (IN)
Ivy Tech Comm Coll–Southern Indiana (IN)
Jefferson Coll (MO)
Jefferson State Comm Coll (AL)
Kankakee Comm Coll (IL)
Kaskaskia Coll (IL)
Kellogg Comm Coll (MI)
Kennebec Valley Comm Coll (ME)
Kent State U at Ashtabula (OH)
Kent State U at East Liverpool (OH)
Kilgore Coll (TX)
Lake Area Tech Inst (SD)
Lake Land Coll (IL)
Lake Superior Coll (MN)
Laramie County Comm Coll (WY)
Lehigh Carbon Comm Coll (PA)
Lone Star Coll–Montgomery (TX)
Lorain County Comm Coll (OH)
Macomb Comm Coll (MI)
Manchester Comm Coll (CT)
Martin Comm Coll (NC)
Mercer County Comm Coll (NJ)
Miami Dade Coll (FL)
Midlands Tech Coll (SC)
Mohave Comm Coll (AZ)
Montgomery Coll (MD)
Morgan Comm Coll (CO)
Mott Comm Coll (MI)
Mount Wachusett Comm Coll (MA)
Naugatuck Valley Comm Coll (CT)
Niagara County Comm Coll (NY)
Northland Comm and Tech Coll (MN)
North Shore Comm Coll (MA)
Oakton Comm Coll (IL)
Olympic Coll (WA)
Onondaga Comm Coll (NY)
Ozarks Tech Comm Coll (MO)
Penn State DuBois (PA)
Penn State Mont Alto (PA)
Penn State Shenango (PA)
Pennsylvania Inst of Technology (PA)
Pensacola State Coll (FL)
Pueblo Comm Coll (CO)
Quincy Coll (MA)
Randolph Comm Coll (NC)
Reading Area Comm Coll (PA)
River Valley Comm Coll (NH)
St. Philip's Coll (TX)
Salt Lake Comm Coll (UT)
San Jacinto Coll District (TX)
San Juan Coll (NM)
Somerset Comm Coll (KY)
Southeast Comm Coll, Lincoln Campus (NE)
Southern U at Shreveport (LA)
Southwest Tennessee Comm Coll (TN)
Springfield Tech Comm Coll (MA)
Tech Coll of the Lowcountry (SC)
Tulsa Comm Coll (OK)
Tyler Jr Coll (TX)
U of Pittsburgh at Titusville (PA)
Victoria Coll (TX)
Vincennes U (IN)
Volunteer State Comm Coll (TN)
Walters State Comm Coll (TN)
Waukesha County Tech Coll (WI)
Weatherford Coll (TX)

Western Iowa Tech Comm Coll (IA)
Wor-Wic Comm Coll (MD)

PHYSICIAN ASSISTANT
Barton County Comm Coll (KS)
Georgia Highlands Coll (GA)
Miami Dade Coll (FL)
San Joaquin Valley Coll, Visalia (CA)
Wayne County Comm Coll District (MI)

PHYSICS
Allen Comm Coll (KS)
Amarillo Coll (TX)
Antelope Valley Coll (CA)
Arizona Western Coll (AZ)
Austin Comm Coll District (TX)
Barton County Comm Coll (KS)
Blinn Coll (TX)
Bunker Hill Comm Coll (MA)
Ca&nnada Coll (CA)
Casper Coll (WY)
Cecil Coll (MD)
Central New Mexico Comm Coll (NM)
Cerritos Coll (CA)
Cochise County Comm Coll District (AZ)
Coll of Central Florida (FL)
Coll of the Canyons (CA)
Dodge City Comm Coll (KS)
Eastern Arizona Coll (AZ)
Finger Lakes Comm Coll (NY)
Fullerton Coll (CA)
Georgia Highlands Coll (GA)
Gordon State Coll (GA)
Harford Comm Coll (MD)
Holyoke Comm Coll (MA)
Houston Comm Coll (TX)
Kankakee Comm Coll (IL)
Kilgore Coll (TX)
Lorain County Comm Coll (OH)
Los Angeles Valley Coll (CA)
Mercer County Comm Coll (NJ)
Miami Dade Coll (FL)
Monroe Comm Coll (NY)
Moraine Valley Comm Coll (IL)
Nashville State Comm Coll (TN)
Navarro Coll (TX)
Northampton Comm Coll (PA)
Northwest Coll (WY)
Odessa Coll (TX)
Oklahoma City Comm Coll (OK)
Oklahoma State U, Oklahoma City (OK)
Orange Coast Coll (CA)
Panola Coll (TX)
Paris Jr Coll (TX)
Pensacola State Coll (FL)
Potomac State Coll of West Virginia U (WV)
Rowan Coll at Burlington County (NJ)
Salt Lake Comm Coll (UT)
San Jacinto Coll District (TX)
San Juan Coll (NM)
Sierra Coll (CA)
South Florida State Coll (FL)
Spoon River Coll (IL)
Springfield Tech Comm Coll (MA)
Texarkana Coll (TX)
Truckee Meadows Comm Coll (NV)
Tyler Jr Coll (TX)

PHYSICS RELATED
South Florida State Coll (FL)

PHYSICS TEACHER EDUCATION
Anne Arundel Comm Coll (MD)
Chesapeake Coll (MD)
Comm Coll of Baltimore County (MD)
Harford Comm Coll (MD)
Montgomery Coll (MD)

PHYSIOLOGY
Comm Coll of the Air Force (AL)

PIPEFITTING AND SPRINKLER FITTING
Delta Coll (MI)
Ivy Tech Comm Coll–Bloomington (IN)
Ivy Tech Comm Coll–Central Indiana (IN)
Ivy Tech Comm Coll–Columbus (IN)
Ivy Tech Comm Coll–East Central (IN)
Ivy Tech Comm Coll–Lafayette (IN)

Ivy Tech Comm Coll–North Central (IN)
Ivy Tech Comm Coll–Northeast (IN)
Ivy Tech Comm Coll–Northwest (IN)
Ivy Tech Comm Coll–Richmond (IN)
Ivy Tech Comm Coll–Southern Indiana (IN)
Ivy Tech Comm Coll–Southwest (IN)
Ivy Tech Comm Coll–Wabash Valley (IN)
Kellogg Comm Coll (MI)
Los Angeles Trade-Tech Coll (CA)
Miami Dade Coll (FL)

PLANT NURSERY MANAGEMENT
American River Coll (CA)
Fullerton Coll (CA)
Miami Dade Coll (FL)

PLANT PROTECTION AND INTEGRATED PEST MANAGEMENT
Hinds Comm Coll (MS)

PLANT SCIENCES
Leeward Comm Coll (HI)
Mercer County Comm Coll (NJ)
Rend Lake Coll (IL)
South Florida State Coll (FL)

PLASTICS AND POLYMER ENGINEERING TECHNOLOGY
Cerritos Coll (CA)
Cincinnati State Tech and Comm Coll (OH)
Daytona State Coll (FL)
Grand Rapids Comm Coll (MI)
Hennepin Tech Coll (MN)
Lorain County Comm Coll (OH)
Macomb Comm Coll (MI)
Mount Wachusett Comm Coll (MA)
West Georgia Tech Coll (GA)

PLATEMAKING/IMAGING
Illinois Central Coll (IL)

PLAYWRITING AND SCREENWRITING
Northwest Coll (WY)

PLUMBING TECHNOLOGY
Arizona Western Coll (AZ)
Central New Mexico Comm Coll (NM)
Delta Coll (MI)
Hinds Comm Coll (MS)
Luzerne County Comm Coll (PA)
Macomb Comm Coll (MI)
Miami Dade Coll (FL)
Minnesota State Comm and Tech Coll–Moorhead (MN)
Minnesota West Comm and Tech Coll (MN)
Northeast Iowa Comm Coll (IA)
Northland Comm and Tech Coll (MN)
Southeast Tech Inst (SD)
Southern Maine Comm Coll (ME)
Thaddeus Stevens Coll of Technology (PA)

POLITICAL SCIENCE AND GOVERNMENT
Allen Comm Coll (KS)
American Samoa Comm Coll (AS)
Antelope Valley Coll (CA)
Arizona Western Coll (AZ)
Austin Comm Coll District (TX)
Bainbridge State Coll (GA)
Barton County Comm Coll (KS)
Ca&nnada Coll (CA)
Casper Coll (WY)
Central New Mexico Comm Coll (NM)
Cerritos Coll (CA)
Coll of the Canyons (CA)
Dodge City Comm Coll (KS)
Eastern Arizona Coll (AZ)
Feather River Coll (CA)
Finger Lakes Comm Coll (NY)
Frederick Comm Coll (MD)
Fullerton Coll (CA)
Georgia Highlands Coll (GA)
Georgia Military Coll (GA)
Gordon State Coll (GA)
Harford Comm Coll (MD)
Itawamba Comm Coll (MS)
Kankakee Comm Coll (IL)
Laramie County Comm Coll (WY)
Lorain County Comm Coll (OH)
Los Angeles Valley Coll (CA)

Miami Dade Coll (FL)
Monroe Comm Coll (NY)
Moraine Valley Comm Coll (IL)
Nashville State Comm Coll (TN)
Northeastern Jr Coll (CO)
Northern Essex Comm Coll (MA)
Northwest Coll (WY)
Odessa Coll (TX)
Oklahoma City Comm Coll (OK)
Orange Coast Coll (CA)
Otero Jr Coll (CO)
Oxnard Coll (CA)
Paris Jr Coll (TX)
Potomac State Coll of West Virginia U (WV)
St. Charles Comm Coll (MO)
St. Philip's Coll (TX)
Salt Lake Comm Coll (UT)
San Jacinto Coll District (TX)
San Joaquin Delta Coll (CA)
South Florida State Coll (FL)
Spoon River Coll (IL)
Texarkana Coll (TX)
Tyler Jr Coll (TX)
Vincennes U (IN)
Western Wyoming Comm Coll (WY)

POLYMER/PLASTICS ENGINEERING
Central Oregon Comm Coll (OR)

POLYSOMNOGRAPHY
Catawba Valley Comm Coll (NC)
Genesee Comm Coll (NY)
Lenoir Comm Coll (NC)
Moraine Valley Comm Coll (IL)

PORTUGUESE
Miami Dade Coll (FL)

POULTRY SCIENCE
Hinds Comm Coll (MS)

PRACTICAL NURSING, VOCATIONAL NURSING AND NURSING ASSISTANTS RELATED
Pennsylvania Inst of Technology (PA)

PRECISION METAL WORKING RELATED
Delta Coll (MI)

PRECISION PRODUCTION RELATED
Delta Coll (MI)
East Central Coll (MO)
Jefferson Coll (MO)
Midlands Tech Coll (SC)
Mott Comm Coll (MI)
St. Charles Comm Coll (MO)
Sheridan Coll (WY)
Western Piedmont Comm Coll (NC)

PRECISION PRODUCTION TRADES
Butler County Comm Coll (PA)
Midlands Tech Coll (SC)
Owensboro Comm and Tech Coll (KY)

PRE-DENTISTRY STUDIES
Allen Comm Coll (KS)
Austin Comm Coll District (TX)
Barton County Comm Coll (KS)
Casper Coll (WY)
Eastern Wyoming Coll (WY)
Kilgore Coll (TX)
Panola Coll (TX)
Pensacola State Coll (FL)
Potomac State Coll of West Virginia U (WV)
St. Philip's Coll (TX)
Vincennes U (IN)
Western Wyoming Comm Coll (WY)

PRE-ENGINEERING
Alexandria Tech and Comm Coll (MN)
Amarillo Coll (TX)
Anoka-Ramsey Comm Coll (MN)
Antelope Valley Coll (CA)
Barton County Comm Coll (KS)
Central New Mexico Comm Coll (NM)
Century Coll (MN)
Cerritos Coll (CA)
Chipola Coll (FL)
Coll of the Canyons (CA)
Comm Coll of Philadelphia (PA)
Corning Comm Coll (NY)

Craven Comm Coll (NC)
Crowder Coll (MO)
Dodge City Comm Coll (KS)
Fayetteville Tech Comm Coll (NC)
Finger Lakes Comm Coll (NY)
Georgia Highlands Coll (GA)
Gordon State Coll (GA)
Housatonic Comm Coll (CT)
Itawamba Comm Coll (MS)
Ivy Tech Comm Coll–Columbus (IN)
Ivy Tech Comm Coll–Lafayette (IN)
Ivy Tech Comm Coll–Southwest (IN)
Lamar Comm Coll (CO)
Lorain County Comm Coll (OH)
Macomb Comm Coll (MI)
Mesabi Range Coll (MN)
Miami Dade Coll (FL)
Mt. San Antonio Coll (CA)
Nashville State Comm Coll (TN)
Navarro Coll (TX)
North Central Texas Coll (TX)
Northeastern Jr Coll (CO)
North Hennepin Comm Coll (MN)
North Shore Comm Coll (MA)
Northwest Vista Coll (TX)
Odessa Coll (TX)
Oklahoma City Comm Coll (OK)
Oklahoma State U, Oklahoma City (OK)
Orange Coast Coll (CA)
Otero Jr Coll (CO)
Palomar Coll (CA)
Rainy River Comm Coll (MN)
Richland Comm Coll (IL)
Rock Valley Coll (IL)
St. Philip's Coll (TX)
Seminole State Coll (OK)
Southern Maine Comm Coll (ME)
Spoon River Coll (IL)
Tulsa Comm Coll (OK)
Virginia Western Comm Coll (VA)
Wayne County Comm Coll District (MI)
Wenatchee Valley Coll (WA)
Western Wyoming Comm Coll (WY)
Westmoreland County Comm Coll (PA)

PRE-LAW STUDIES
Allen Comm Coll (KS)
American Samoa Comm Coll (AS)
Anne Arundel Comm Coll (MD)
Barton County Comm Coll (KS)
Carl Albert State Coll (OK)
Casper Coll (WY)
Central New Mexico Comm Coll (NM)
Central Oregon Comm Coll (OR)
Central Wyoming Coll (WY)
Coll of Central Florida (FL)
Kilgore Coll (TX)
Laramie County Comm Coll (WY)
Nashville State Comm Coll (TN)
Panola Coll (TX)
Paris Jr Coll (TX)
Pensacola State Coll (FL)
Potomac State Coll of West Virginia U (WV)
St. Philip's Coll (TX)
U of Cincinnati Blue Ash Coll (OH)
Western Texas Coll (TX)
Western Wyoming Comm Coll (WY)

PREMEDICAL STUDIES
Allen Comm Coll (KS)
Austin Comm Coll District (TX)
Barton County Comm Coll (KS)
Casper Coll (WY)
Central Oregon Comm Coll (OR)
Coll of Central Florida (FL)
Eastern Arizona Coll (AZ)
Eastern Wyoming Coll (WY)
Howard Comm Coll (MD)
Kilgore Coll (TX)
Nashville State Comm Coll (TN)
Paris Jr Coll (TX)
Pensacola State Coll (FL)
Potomac State Coll of West Virginia U (WV)
St. Philip's Coll (TX)
San Juan Coll (NM)
Springfield Tech Comm Coll (MA)
Vincennes U (IN)
Western Texas Coll (TX)
Western Wyoming Comm Coll (WY)

PRENURSING STUDIES
Arizona Western Coll (AZ)
Edison Comm Coll (OH)
Georgia Military Coll (GA)

Nashville State Comm Coll (TN)
Oklahoma State U, Oklahoma City (OK)
Paris Jr Coll (TX)
Pensacola State Coll (FL)
Potomac State Coll of West Virginia U (WV)
St. Philip's Coll (TX)
Southwestern Michigan Coll (MI)
Tulsa Comm Coll (OK)
Tyler Jr Coll (TX)
Western Wyoming Comm Coll (WY)

PRE-OCCUPATIONAL THERAPY
Casper Coll (WY)
Gordon State Coll (GA)
Nashville State Comm Coll (TN)
Potomac State Coll of West Virginia U (WV)

PRE-OPTOMETRY
Casper Coll (WY)

PRE-PHARMACY STUDIES
Allen Comm Coll (KS)
Amarillo Coll (TX)
Austin Comm Coll District (TX)
Casper Coll (WY)
Central Oregon Comm Coll (OR)
Coll of Central Florida (FL)
Dodge City Comm Coll (KS)
Eastern Arizona Coll (AZ)
Eastern Wyoming Coll (WY)
Georgia Highlands Coll (GA)
Gordon State Coll (GA)
Howard Comm Coll (MD)
Kilgore Coll (TX)
Laramie County Comm Coll (WY)
Luzerne County Comm Coll (PA)
Monroe Comm Coll (NY)
Northwest Coll (WY)
Panola Coll (TX)
Paris Jr Coll (TX)
Pensacola State Coll (FL)
Potomac State Coll of West Virginia U (WV)
Quinsigamond Comm Coll (MA)
St. Charles Comm Coll (MO)
St. Philip's Coll (TX)
Schoolcraft Coll (MI)
Tulsa Comm Coll (OK)
U of Cincinnati Blue Ash Coll (OH)
Vincennes U (IN)
Western Wyoming Comm Coll (WY)

PRE-PHYSICAL THERAPY
Casper Coll (WY)
Georgia Highlands Coll (GA)
Gordon State Coll (GA)
Nashville State Comm Coll (TN)
Potomac State Coll of West Virginia U (WV)

PRE-VETERINARY STUDIES
Allen Comm Coll (KS)
Austin Comm Coll District (TX)
Barton County Comm Coll (KS)
Casper Coll (WY)
Coll of Central Florida (FL)
Eastern Wyoming Coll (WY)
Kilgore Coll (TX)
Panola Coll (TX)
Pensacola State Coll (FL)
Potomac State Coll of West Virginia U (WV)
Vincennes U (IN)
Western Wyoming Comm Coll (WY)

PRINTING PRESS OPERATION
Dunwoody Coll of Technology (MN)
Lake Land Coll (IL)

PROFESSIONAL, TECHNICAL, BUSINESS, AND SCIENTIFIC WRITING
Austin Comm Coll District (TX)
Fox Valley Tech Coll (WI)
Gateway Tech Coll (WI)
Oklahoma State U, Oklahoma City (OK)
Southwestern Michigan Coll (MI)

PSYCHIATRIC/MENTAL HEALTH SERVICES TECHNOLOGY
Alvin Comm Coll (TX)
Anne Arundel Comm Coll (MD)
Asnuntuck Comm Coll (CT)
Comm Coll of Baltimore County (MD)

Fiorello H. LaGuardia Comm Coll of the City U of New York (NY)
Gateway Tech Coll (WI)
Hagerstown Comm Coll (MD)
Hillsborough Comm Coll (FL)
Houston Comm Coll (TX)
Illinois Central Coll (IL)
Ivy Tech Comm Coll–Bloomington (IN)
Ivy Tech Comm Coll–Central Indiana (IN)
Ivy Tech Comm Coll–Columbus (IN)
Ivy Tech Comm Coll–Lafayette (IN)
Ivy Tech Comm Coll–Northeast (IN)
Ivy Tech Comm Coll–Northwest (IN)
Ivy Tech Comm Coll–Richmond (IN)
Ivy Tech Comm Coll–Southeast (IN)
Ivy Tech Comm Coll–Southern Indiana (IN)
Ivy Tech Comm Coll–Southwest (IN)
Montgomery Coll (MD)
Montgomery County Comm Coll (PA)
Naugatuck Valley Comm Coll (CT)
Pueblo Comm Coll (CO)
Three Rivers Comm Coll (CT)
Waukesha County Tech Coll (WI)
Wayne County Comm Coll District (MI)
Western Piedmont Comm Coll (NC)
Williston State Coll (ND)
Wisconsin Indianhead Tech Coll (WI)

PSYCHOLOGY
Allen Comm Coll (KS)
Alvin Comm Coll (TX)
Amarillo Coll (TX)
American River Coll (CA)
Arizona Western Coll (AZ)
Austin Comm Coll District (TX)
Bainbridge State Coll (GA)
Barton County Comm Coll (KS)
Blinn Coll (TX)
Bucks County Comm Coll (PA)
Bunker Hill Comm Coll (MA)
Butler County Comm Coll (PA)
Ca&nnada Coll (CA)
Carroll Comm Coll (MD)
Casper Coll (WY)
Central New Mexico Comm Coll (NM)
Central Wyoming Coll (WY)
Cerritos Coll (CA)
Chandler-Gilbert Comm Coll (AZ)
Citrus Coll (CA)
Cochise County Comm Coll District (AZ)
Coll of Central Florida (FL)
Coll of the Canyons (CA)
Comm Coll of Philadelphia (PA)
Crowder Coll (MO)
Dean Coll (MA)
Dodge City Comm Coll (KS)
Eastern Arizona Coll (AZ)
Edison Comm Coll (OH)
Finger Lakes Comm Coll (NY)
Fiorello H. LaGuardia Comm Coll of the City U of New York (NY)
Frederick Comm Coll (MD)
Fullerton Coll (CA)
Genesee Comm Coll (NY)
Georgia Highlands Coll (GA)
Georgia Military Coll (GA)
Gordon State Coll (GA)
Harford Comm Coll (MD)
Harrisburg Area Comm Coll (PA)
Hutchinson Comm Coll (KS)
Itawamba Comm Coll (MS)
Kankakee Comm Coll (IL)
Kilgore Coll (TX)
Laramie County Comm Coll (WY)
Lehigh Carbon Comm Coll (PA)
Lorain County Comm Coll (OH)
Los Angeles Valley Coll (CA)
Manor Coll (PA)
Miami Dade Coll (FL)
Mohave Comm Coll (AZ)
Montgomery County Comm Coll (PA)
Moraine Valley Comm Coll (IL)
Nashville State Comm Coll (TN)
Navarro Coll (TX)
Northeastern Jr Coll (CO)
Northern Essex Comm Coll (MA)
Northwest Coll (WY)
Norwalk Comm Coll (CT)
Odessa Coll (TX)
Oklahoma City Comm Coll (OK)
Oklahoma State U, Oklahoma City (OK)
Orange Coast Coll (CA)
Otero Jr Coll (CO)
Oxnard Coll (CA)
Palomar Coll (CA)

Panola Coll (TX)
Paris Jr Coll (TX)
Pasadena City Coll (CA)
Pennsylvania Highlands Comm Coll (PA)
Pensacola State Coll (FL)
Potomac State Coll of West Virginia U (WV)
Quinsigamond Comm Coll (MA)
Reading Area Comm Coll (PA)
Rowan Coll at Burlington County (NJ)
St. Charles Comm Coll (MO)
St. Philip's Coll (TX)
Salt Lake Comm Coll (UT)
San Jacinto Coll District (TX)
San Joaquin Delta Coll (CA)
San Juan Coll (NM)
Sheridan Coll (WY)
Sierra Coll (CA)
South Florida State Coll (FL)
Spoon River Coll (IL)
Sullivan County Comm Coll (NY)
Truckee Meadows Comm Coll (NV)
Tyler Jr Coll (TX)
U of Cincinnati Blue Ash Coll (OH)
Vincennes U (IN)
Western Wyoming Comm Coll (WY)

PSYCHOLOGY RELATED
Cayuga County Comm Coll (NY)
Genesee Comm Coll (NY)
Seminole State Coll (OK)
U of Pittsburgh at Titusville (PA)

PUBLIC ADMINISTRATION
Barton County Comm Coll (KS)
Central Texas Coll (TX)
Citrus Coll (CA)
County Coll of Morris (NJ)
Fayetteville Tech Comm Coll (NC)
Housatonic Comm Coll (CT)
Houston Comm Coll (TX)
Itawamba Comm Coll (MS)
Laramie County Comm Coll (WY)
Lehigh Carbon Comm Coll (PA)
Lenoir Comm Coll (NC)
Miami Dade Coll (FL)
Palomar Coll (CA)
Scottsdale Comm Coll (AZ)
Southern U at Shreveport (LA)
South Florida State Coll (FL)
Tyler Jr Coll (TX)
Westchester Comm Coll (NY)

PUBLIC ADMINISTRATION AND SOCIAL SERVICE PROFESSIONS RELATED
Cleveland State Comm Coll (TN)
Oklahoma State U, Oklahoma City (OK)
Onondaga Comm Coll (NY)
Schenectady County Comm Coll (NY)

PUBLIC HEALTH
Anne Arundel Comm Coll (MD)
County Coll of Morris (NJ)
Northern Essex Comm Coll (MA)

PUBLIC HEALTH EDUCATION AND PROMOTION
Borough of Manhattan Comm Coll of the City U of New York (NY)
Northampton Comm Coll (PA)
U of Cincinnati Blue Ash Coll (OH)

PUBLIC HEALTH RELATED
Salt Lake Comm Coll (UT)

PUBLIC RELATIONS, ADVERTISING, AND APPLIED COMMUNICATION
Oklahoma City Comm Coll (OK)

PUBLIC RELATIONS, ADVERTISING, AND APPLIED COMMUNICATION RELATED
LDS Business Coll (UT)

PUBLIC RELATIONS/IMAGE MANAGEMENT
Amarillo Coll (TX)
Bismarck State Coll (ND)
Comm Coll of the Air Force (AL)
Crowder Coll (MO)
South Florida State Coll (FL)
Vincennes U (IN)

PURCHASING, PROCUREMENT/ACQUISITIONS AND CONTRACTS MANAGEMENT
Cecil Coll (MD)

Comm Coll of the Air Force (AL)
Greenville Tech Coll (SC)

QUALITY CONTROL AND SAFETY TECHNOLOGIES RELATED
Elizabethtown Comm and Tech Coll, Elizabethtown (KY)
Ivy Tech Comm Coll–Lafayette (IN)
Ivy Tech Comm Coll–Wabash Valley (IN)
Macomb Comm Coll (MI)

QUALITY CONTROL TECHNOLOGY
Aiken Tech Coll (SC)
Grand Rapids Comm Coll (MI)
Illinois Eastern Comm Colls, Frontier Community College (IL)
Illinois Eastern Comm Colls, Lincoln Trail College (IL)
Ivy Tech Comm Coll–Lafayette (IN)
Lakeland Comm Coll (OH)
Lorain County Comm Coll (OH)
Macomb Comm Coll (MI)
Monroe Comm Coll (NY)
Mt. San Antonio Coll (CA)
Northampton Comm Coll (PA)
Rock Valley Coll (IL)
Salt Lake Comm Coll (UT)
Southeast Comm Coll, Milford Campus (NE)
Tarrant County Coll District (TX)

RADIATION PROTECTION/HEALTH PHYSICS TECHNOLOGY
Aiken Tech Coll (SC)
Lone Star Coll–CyFair (TX)
Spartanburg Comm Coll (SC)

RADIO AND TELEVISION
Alvin Comm Coll (TX)
Amarillo Coll (TX)
Austin Comm Coll District (TX)
Central Texas Coll (TX)
Central Wyoming Coll (WY)
Daytona State Coll (FL)
Delta Coll (MI)
Dodge City Comm Coll (KS)
Fullerton Coll (CA)
Genesee Comm Coll (NY)
Illinois Eastern Comm Colls, Wabash Valley College (IL)
Iowa Central Comm Coll (IA)
Lake Land Coll (IL)
Lewis and Clark Comm Coll (IL)
Los Angeles Valley Coll (CA)
Miami Dade Coll (FL)
Mt. San Antonio Coll (CA)
Northwest Coll (WY)
Onondaga Comm Coll (NY)
Oxnard Coll (CA)
Palomar Coll (CA)
Pasadena City Coll (CA)
South Florida State Coll (FL)
Sullivan County Comm Coll (NY)
Tyler Jr Coll (TX)
Virginia Western Comm Coll (VA)
Western Texas Coll (TX)

RADIO AND TELEVISION BROADCASTING TECHNOLOGY
Arizona Western Coll (AZ)
Borough of Manhattan Comm Coll of the City U of New York (NY)
Camden County Coll (NJ)
Cleveland Comm Coll (NC)
Cloud County Comm Coll (KS)
Genesee Comm Coll (NY)
Hinds Comm Coll (MS)
Houston Comm Coll (TX)
Hutchinson Comm Coll (KS)
International Coll of Broadcasting (OH)
Leeward Comm Coll (HI)
Lehigh Carbon Comm Coll (PA)
Luzerne County Comm Coll (PA)
Mercer County Comm Coll (NJ)
Miami Dade Coll (FL)
Mount Wachusett Comm Coll (MA)
Northampton Comm Coll (PA)
Northwest Coll (WY)
Ozarks Tech Comm Coll (MO)
Pasadena City Coll (CA)
Salt Lake Comm Coll (UT)
San Jacinto Coll District (TX)
Schoolcraft Coll (MI)
Springfield Tech Comm Coll (MA)
Tompkins Cortland Comm Coll (NY)
Tri-County Tech Coll (SC)
Vincennes U (IN)

Westmoreland County Comm Coll (PA)

RADIOLOGIC TECHNOLOGY/SCIENCE
Amarillo Coll (TX)
Antelope Valley Coll (CA)
Arizona Western Coll (AZ)
Austin Comm Coll District (TX)
Barton County Comm Coll (KS)
Brookhaven Coll (TX)
Butler County Comm Coll (PA)
Caldwell Comm Coll and Tech Inst (NC)
Ca&nnada Coll (CA)
Carolinas Coll of Health Sciences (NC)
Carrington Coll–Phoenix North (AZ)
Casper Coll (WY)
Catawba Valley Comm Coll (NC)
Central New Mexico Comm Coll (NM)
Central Ohio Tech Coll (OH)
Central Oregon Comm Coll (OR)
Central Virginia Comm Coll (VA)
Century Coll (MN)
Clark Coll (WA)
Cleveland Comm Coll (NC)
Comm Coll of Rhode Island (RI)
County Coll of Morris (NJ)
Danville Area Comm Coll (IL)
Elgin Comm Coll (IL)
Fayetteville Tech Comm Coll (NC)
Gadsden State Comm Coll (AL)
Galveston Coll (TX)
George C. Wallace Comm Coll (AL)
Gordon State Coll (GA)
Great Basin Coll (NV)
Great Falls Coll Montana State U (MT)
Harrisburg Area Comm Coll (PA)
H. Councill Trenholm State Comm Coll (AL)
Hinds Comm Coll (MS)
Houston Comm Coll (TX)
Hudson County Comm Coll (NJ)
Hutchinson Comm Coll (KS)
Illinois Central Coll (IL)
Jefferson Coll (MO)
Jefferson State Comm Coll (AL)
Kankakee Comm Coll (IL)
Kaskaskia Coll (IL)
Kennebec Valley Comm Coll (ME)
Kilgore Coll (TX)
Lake Superior Coll (MN)
Laramie County Comm Coll (WY)
Lenoir Comm Coll (NC)
Maine Coll of Health Professions (ME)
Massachusetts Bay Comm Coll (MA)
Miami Dade Coll (FL)
Minnesota State Coll–Southeast Tech (MN)
Minnesota State Comm and Tech Coll–Detroit Lakes (MN)
Minnesota West Comm and Tech Coll (MN)
Mitchell Tech Inst (SD)
Montgomery County Comm Coll (PA)
Moraine Valley Comm Coll (IL)
Northampton Comm Coll (PA)
Northeast Iowa Comm Coll (IA)
Northern Essex Comm Coll (MA)
Northland Comm and Tech Coll (MN)
Oklahoma State U, Oklahoma City (OK)
Owensboro Comm and Tech Coll (KY)
Paris Jr Coll (TX)
Pasadena City Coll (CA)
Pennsylvania Highlands Comm Coll (PA)
Pueblo Comm Coll (CO)
Quinsigamond Comm Coll (MA)
Randolph Comm Coll (NC)
Ridgewater Coll (MN)
Rowan-Cabarrus Comm Coll (NC)
St. Luke's Coll (IA)
St. Vincent's Coll (CT)
San Jacinto Coll District (TX)
Southern Maine Comm Coll (ME)
Southern U at Shreveport (LA)
South Suburban Coll (IL)
Southwest Virginia Comm Coll (VA)
Spencerian Coll (KY)
Spencerian Coll–Lexington (KY)
Springfield Tech Comm Coll (MA)
State U of New York Coll of Technology at Alfred (NY)
Tyler Jr Coll (TX)
Virginia Western Comm Coll (VA)
Weatherford Coll (TX)

Wenatchee Valley Coll (WA)
Westmoreland County Comm Coll (PA)

RADIOLOGIST ASSISTANT
Blackhawk Tech Coll (WI)

RADIO, TELEVISION, AND DIGITAL COMMUNICATION RELATED
American River Coll (CA)
Cayuga County Comm Coll (NY)
Fox Valley Tech Coll (WI)
Genesee Comm Coll (NY)
Mitchell Tech Inst (SD)
Montgomery County Comm Coll (PA)
Pennsylvania Highlands Comm Coll (PA)
Sullivan County Comm Coll (NY)

RANGE SCIENCE AND MANAGEMENT
Casper Coll (WY)
Central Wyoming Coll (WY)
Eastern Wyoming Coll (WY)
Northwest Coll (WY)
Sheridan Coll (WY)
Treasure Valley Comm Coll (OR)

REAL ESTATE
Amarillo Coll (TX)
American River Coll (CA)
Antelope Valley Coll (CA)
Austin Comm Coll District (TX)
Blinn Coll (TX)
Cerritos Coll (CA)
Cincinnati State Tech and Comm Coll (OH)
Citrus Coll (CA)
Coll of the Canyons (CA)
Collin County Comm Coll District (TX)
Dodge City Comm Coll (KS)
Eastern Gateway Comm Coll (OH)
Fullerton Coll (CA)
Harrisburg Area Comm Coll (PA)
Hinds Comm Coll (MS)
Houston Comm Coll (TX)
Illinois Central Coll (IL)
Lorain County Comm Coll (OH)
Los Angeles Trade-Tech Coll (CA)
Los Angeles Valley Coll (CA)
Luzerne County Comm Coll (PA)
Miami Dade Coll (FL)
Montgomery County Comm Coll (PA)
Mt. San Antonio Coll (CA)
New Mexico Jr Coll (NM)
Norco Coll (CA)
North Central Texas Coll (TX)
Northern Essex Comm Coll (MA)
Oakton Comm Coll (IL)
Orange Coast Coll (CA)
Palomar Coll (CA)
San Jacinto Coll District (TX)
Scottsdale Comm Coll (AZ)
Sierra Coll (CA)
South Florida State Coll (FL)
Texarkana Coll (TX)
Tidewater Comm Coll (VA)
U of Cincinnati Blue Ash Coll (OH)
Victor Valley Coll (CA)
Waukesha County Tech Coll (WI)
Westmoreland County Comm Coll (PA)

RECORDING ARTS TECHNOLOGY
Bismarck State Coll (ND)
Bossier Parish Comm Coll (LA)
Citrus Coll (CA)
Comm Coll of Philadelphia (PA)
Finger Lakes Comm Coll (NY)
Fiorello H. LaGuardia Comm Coll of the City U of New York (NY)
Fullerton Coll (CA)
Grand Rapids Comm Coll (MI)
Hennepin Tech Coll (MN)
Lehigh Carbon Comm Coll (PA)
Miami Dade Coll (FL)
Montgomery County Comm Coll (PA)
Northwest Vista Coll (TX)
Orange Coast Coll (CA)
Queensborough Comm Coll of the City U of New York (NY)
Ridgewater Coll (MN)
Schoolcraft Coll (MI)
Springfield Tech Comm Coll (MA)
Vincennes U (IN)
Western Iowa Tech Comm Coll (IA)

REGISTERED NURSING, NURSING ADMINISTRATION,

NURSING RESEARCH AND CLINICAL NURSING RELATED
Genesee Comm Coll (NY)
Harford Comm Coll (MD)
St. Joseph School of Nursing (NH)

REGISTERED NURSING/ REGISTERED NURSE
Aiken Tech Coll (SC)
Alamance Comm Coll (NC)
Alexandria Tech and Comm Coll (MN)
Alvin Comm Coll (TX)
Amarillo Coll (TX)
American River Coll (CA)
Ancilla Coll (IN)
Anne Arundel Comm Coll (MD)
Anoka-Ramsey Comm Coll (MN)
Antelope Valley Coll (CA)
Arapahoe Comm Coll (CO)
Arizona Western Coll (AZ)
Athens Tech Coll (GA)
Austin Comm Coll District (TX)
Bainbridge State Coll (GA)
Barton County Comm Coll (KS)
Beckfield Coll (KY)
The Belanger School of Nursing (NY)
Bellingham Tech Coll (WA)
Berkshire Comm Coll (MA)
Bevill State Comm Coll (AL)
Big Bend Comm Coll (WA)
Bismarck State Coll (ND)
Blackhawk Tech Coll (WI)
Blinn Coll (TX)
Blue Ridge Comm and Tech Coll (WV)
Borough of Manhattan Comm Coll of the City U of New York (NY)
Bossier Parish Comm Coll (LA)
Bowling Green State U–Firelands Coll (OH)
Brookhaven Coll (TX)
Bucks County Comm Coll (PA)
Bunker Hill Comm Coll (MA)
Butler County Comm Coll (PA)
Caldwell Comm Coll and Tech Inst (NC)
Camden County Coll (NJ)
Cape Fear Comm Coll (NC)
Carl Albert State Coll (OK)
Carolinas Coll of Health Sciences (NC)
Carrington Coll–Albuquerque (NM)
Carrington Coll–Boise (ID)
Carrington Coll–Phoenix North (AZ)
Carrington Coll–Phoenix West (AZ)
Carrington Coll–Reno (NV)
Carrington Coll–Sacramento (CA)
Carroll Comm Coll (MD)
Casper Coll (WY)
Catawba Valley Comm Coll (NC)
Cayuga County Comm Coll (NY)
Cecil Coll (MD)
Central Lakes Coll (MN)
Central Maine Comm Coll (ME)
Central New Mexico Comm Coll (NM)
Central Ohio Tech Coll (OH)
Central Oregon Comm Coll (OR)
Central Texas Coll (TX)
Central Wyoming Coll (WY)
Century Coll (MN)
Cerritos Coll (CA)
Chandler-Gilbert Comm Coll (AZ)
Chesapeake Coll (MD)
Chipola Coll (FL)
Chippewa Valley Tech Coll (WI)
Cincinnati State Tech and Comm Coll (OH)
Citrus Coll (CA)
City Colls of Chicago, Olive-Harvey College (IL)
Clark Coll (WA)
Cleveland Comm Coll (NC)
Cleveland State Comm Coll (TN)
Clinton Comm Coll (NY)
Cloud County Comm Coll (KS)
Cochise County Comm Coll District (AZ)
Cochran School of Nursing (NY)
Coll of Central Florida (FL)
Coll of The Albemarle (NC)
Coll of the Canyons (CA)
Collin County Comm Coll District (TX)
Colorado Northwestern Comm Coll (CO)
Columbia-Greene Comm Coll (NY)
Columbus Tech Coll (GA)

Comm Coll of Baltimore County (MD)
Comm Coll of Philadelphia (PA)
Comm Coll of Rhode Island (RI)
Copiah-Lincoln Comm Coll (MS)
Corning Comm Coll (NY)
County Coll of Morris (NJ)
Craven Comm Coll (NC)
Crowder Coll (MO)
Dabney S. Lancaster Comm Coll (VA)
Danville Area Comm Coll (IL)
Daytona State Coll (FL)
Delta Coll (MI)
Dodge City Comm Coll (KS)
Dutchess Comm Coll (NY)
Dyersburg State Comm Coll (TN)
East Central Coll (MO)
Eastern Arizona Coll (AZ)
Eastern Idaho Tech Coll (ID)
Edison Comm Coll (OH)
Elgin Comm Coll (IL)
Elizabethtown Comm and Tech Coll, Elizabethtown (KY)
Erie Comm Coll (NY)
Erie Comm Coll, North Campus (NY)
Fayetteville Tech Comm Coll (NC)
Finger Lakes Comm Coll (NY)
Fiorello H. LaGuardia Comm Coll of the City U of New York (NY)
Florida SouthWestern State Coll (FL)
Fox Valley Tech Coll (WI)
Frederick Comm Coll (MD)
Front Range Comm Coll (CO)
Gadsden State Comm Coll (AL)
Galveston Coll (TX)
Gateway Comm and Tech Coll (KY)
Gateway Tech Coll (WI)
Genesee Comm Coll (NY)
George C. Wallace Comm Coll (AL)
Georgia Highlands Coll (GA)
Gordon State Coll (GA)
Grand Rapids Comm Coll (MI)
Great Basin Coll (NV)
Greenville Tech Coll (SC)
Gulf Coast State Coll (FL)
Hagerstown Comm Coll (MD)
Halifax Comm Coll (NC)
Harrisburg Area Comm Coll (PA)
Hawkeye Comm Coll (IA)
Helene Fuld Coll of Nursing (NY)
Hesston Coll (KS)
Highland Comm Coll (IL)
Hillsborough Comm Coll (FL)
Hinds Comm Coll (MS)
Holyoke Comm Coll (MA)
Hopkinsville Comm Coll (KY)
Houston Comm Coll (TX)
Howard Comm Coll (MD)
Hudson County Comm Coll (NJ)
Hutchinson Comm Coll (KS)
Illinois Central Coll (IL)
Illinois Eastern Comm Colls, Frontier Community College (IL)
Illinois Eastern Comm Colls, Olney Central College (IL)
Iowa Central Comm Coll (IA)
Itawamba Comm Coll (MS)
Ivy Tech Comm Coll–Bloomington (IN)
Ivy Tech Comm Coll–Central Indiana (IN)
Ivy Tech Comm Coll–East Central (IN)
Ivy Tech Comm Coll–Kokomo (IN)
Ivy Tech Comm Coll–Lafayette (IN)
Ivy Tech Comm Coll–North Central (IN)
Ivy Tech Comm Coll–Northeast (IN)
Ivy Tech Comm Coll–Northwest (IN)
Ivy Tech Comm Coll–Richmond (IN)
Ivy Tech Comm Coll–Southeast (IN)
Ivy Tech Comm Coll–Southern Indiana (IN)
Ivy Tech Comm Coll–Southwest (IN)
Ivy Tech Comm Coll–Wabash Valley (IN)
James H. Faulkner State Comm Coll (AL)
James Sprunt Comm Coll (NC)
Jamestown Comm Coll (NY)
Jefferson Coll (MO)
Jefferson Comm Coll (NY)
Jefferson State Comm Coll (AL)
Johnston Comm Coll (NC)
John Tyler Comm Coll (VA)
Kankakee Comm Coll (IL)
Kaskaskia Coll (IL)
Kellogg Comm Coll (MI)
Kennebec Valley Comm Coll (ME)

Kent State U at Ashtabula (OH)
Kent State U at East Liverpool (OH)
Kent State U at Tuscarawas (OH)
Kilgore Coll (TX)
Kirtland Comm Coll (MI)
Lake Land Coll (IL)
Lakeland Comm Coll (OH)
Lake Region State Coll (ND)
Lake Superior Coll (MN)
Lamar Comm Coll (CO)
Laramie County Comm Coll (WY)
Lehigh Carbon Comm Coll (PA)
Lenoir Comm Coll (NC)
Lewis and Clark Comm Coll (IL)
Lone Star Coll–CyFair (TX)
Lone Star Coll–Kingwood (TX)
Lone Star Coll–Montgomery (TX)
Lone Star Coll–North Harris (TX)
Lone Star Coll–Tomball (TX)
Lorain County Comm Coll (OH)
Los Angeles Trade-Tech Coll (CA)
Los Angeles Valley Coll (CA)
Lurleen B. Wallace Comm Coll (AL)
Luzerne County Comm Coll (PA)
Macomb Comm Coll (MI)
Maine Coll of Health Professions (ME)
Manhattan Area Tech Coll (KS)
Massachusetts Bay Comm Coll (MA)
McHenry County Coll (IL)
Mercer County Comm Coll (NJ)
Meridian Comm Coll (MS)
Miami Dade Coll (FL)
Middlesex County Coll (NJ)
Midlands Tech Coll (SC)
Mid-Plains Comm Coll, North Platte (NE)
Minnesota State Coll–Southeast Tech (MN)
Minnesota West Comm and Tech Coll (MN)
Mitchell Comm Coll (NC)
Mohave Comm Coll (AZ)
Mohawk Valley Comm Coll (NY)
Monroe Comm Coll (NY)
Montgomery Coll (MD)
Montgomery County Comm Coll (PA)
Moraine Valley Comm Coll (IL)
Mott Comm Coll (MI)
Mt. San Antonio Coll (CA)
Mount Wachusett Comm Coll (MA)
Muskegon Comm Coll (MI)
Naugatuck Valley Comm Coll (CT)
Navarro Coll (TX)
New Mexico Jr Coll (NM)
New River Comm Coll (VA)
Niagara County Comm Coll (NY)
Northampton Comm Coll (PA)
Northcentral Tech Coll (WI)
North Central Texas Coll (TX)
Northeast Alabama Comm Coll (AL)
Northeastern Jr Coll (CO)
Northeast Iowa Comm Coll (IA)
Northern Essex Comm Coll (MA)
North Hennepin Comm Coll (MN)
Northland Comm and Tech Coll (MN)
North Shore Comm Coll (MA)
NorthWest Arkansas Comm Coll (AR)
Northwest Coll (WY)
Northwest-Shoals Comm Coll (AL)
Northwest Tech Coll (MN)
Norwalk Comm Coll (CT)
Oakton Comm Coll (IL)
Ocean County Coll (NJ)
Odessa Coll (TX)
Oklahoma City Comm Coll (OK)
Oklahoma State U Inst of Technology (OK)
Oklahoma State U, Oklahoma City (OK)
Olympic Coll (WA)
Onondaga Comm Coll (NY)
Oregon Coast Comm Coll (OR)
Otero Jr Coll (CO)
Owensboro Comm and Tech Coll (KY)
Palau Comm Coll (Palau)
Palomar Coll (CA)
Panola Coll (TX)
Paris Jr Coll (TX)
Pasadena City Coll (CA)
Penn State Fayette, The Eberly Campus (PA)
Penn State Mont Alto (PA)
Pensacola State Coll (FL)
Phillips Beth Israel School of Nursing (NY)
Piedmont Comm Coll (NC)
Pittsburgh Tech Inst, Oakdale (PA)

Pueblo Comm Coll (CO)
Queensborough Comm Coll of the City U of New York (NY)
Quincy Coll (MA)
Quinsigamond Comm Coll (MA)
Randolph Comm Coll (NC)
Rappahannock Comm Coll (VA)
Raritan Valley Comm Coll (NJ)
Reading Area Comm Coll (PA)
Renton Tech Coll (WA)
Richland Comm Coll (IL)
Richmond Comm Coll (NC)
Ridgewater Coll (MN)
Rio Hondo Coll (CA)
River Valley Comm Coll (NH)
Rockingham Comm Coll (NC)
Rock Valley Coll (IL)
Rogue Comm Coll (OR)
Rowan-Cabarrus Comm Coll (NC)
Rowan Coll at Burlington County (NJ)
St. Charles Comm Coll (MO)
St. Clair County Comm Coll (MI)
St. Joseph's Coll of Nursing (NY)
St. Luke's Coll (IA)
St. Vincent's Coll (CT)
Salt Lake Comm Coll (UT)
San Jacinto Coll District (TX)
San Joaquin Delta Coll (CA)
San Joaquin Valley Coll, Visalia (CA)
San Juan Coll (NM)
Schoolcraft Coll (MI)
Scottsdale Comm Coll (AZ)
Seminole State Coll (OK)
Seminole State Coll of Florida (FL)
Shawnee Comm Coll (IL)
Sheridan Coll (WY)
Sierra Coll (CA)
Somerset Comm Coll (KY)
Southeast Comm Coll, Lincoln Campus (NE)
Southeastern Comm Coll (IA)
Southeast Tech Inst (SD)
Southern Maine Comm Coll (ME)
Southern Regional Tech Coll (GA)
Southern U at Shreveport (LA)
South Florida State Coll (FL)
Southwestern Michigan Coll (MI)
Southwestern Oklahoma State U at Sayre (OK)
Southwestern Oregon Comm Coll (OR)
Southwest Tennessee Comm Coll (TN)
Southwest Virginia Comm Coll (VA)
Spartanburg Comm Coll (SC)
Spencerian Coll (KY)
Spoon River Coll (IL)
Springfield Tech Comm Coll (MA)
Stark State Coll (OH)
State U of New York Coll of Technology at Alfred (NY)
Sullivan County Comm Coll (NY)
Sumner Coll (OR)
Tallahassee Comm Coll (FL)
Tarrant County Coll District (TX)
Tech Coll of the Lowcountry (SC)
Texarkana Coll (TX)
Three Rivers Comm Coll (CT)
Tidewater Comm Coll (VA)
Tompkins Cortland Comm Coll (NY)
Treasure Valley Comm Coll (OR)
Tri-County Tech Coll (SC)
Trocaire Coll (NY)
Truckee Meadows Comm Coll (NV)
Tulsa Comm Coll (OK)
Tyler Jr Coll (TX)
U of Arkansas Comm Coll at Morrilton (AR)
U of Cincinnati Blue Ash Coll (OH)
U of New Mexico–Gallup (NM)
U of Pittsburgh at Titusville (PA)
Victoria Coll (TX)
Victor Valley Coll (CA)
Vincennes U (IN)
Virginia Western Comm Coll (VA)
Walters State Comm Coll (TN)
Waukesha County Tech Coll (WI)
Wayne Comm Coll (NC)
Wayne County Comm Coll District (MI)
Weatherford Coll (TX)
Wenatchee Valley Coll (WA)
Westchester Comm Coll (NY)
Western Iowa Tech Comm Coll (IA)
Western Nevada Coll (NV)
Western Piedmont Comm Coll (NC)
Western Texas Coll (TX)
Westmoreland County Comm Coll (PA)

White Mountains Comm Coll (NH)
Williston State Coll (ND)
Wisconsin Indianhead Tech Coll (WI)
Wor-Wic Comm Coll (MD)
Wytheville Comm Coll (VA)

REHABILITATION AND THERAPEUTIC PROFESSIONS RELATED
Camden County Coll (NJ)
Central Wyoming Coll (WY)
Middlesex County Coll (NJ)
Ocean County Coll (NJ)

RELIGIOUS STUDIES
Allen Comm Coll (KS)
Amarillo Coll (TX)
Barton County Comm Coll (KS)
Cerritos Coll (CA)
Coll of Central Florida (FL)
Fullerton Coll (CA)
Kilgore Coll (TX)
Laramie County Comm Coll (WY)
Orange Coast Coll (CA)
San Joaquin Delta Coll (CA)
South Florida State Coll (FL)

RELIGIOUS STUDIES RELATED
Ancilla Coll (IN)
Spartanburg Methodist Coll (SC)

RESORT MANAGEMENT
Finger Lakes Comm Coll (NY)
Lehigh Carbon Comm Coll (PA)
White Mountains Comm Coll (NH)

RESPIRATORY CARE THERAPY
Alvin Comm Coll (TX)
Amarillo Coll (TX)
American River Coll (CA)
Antelope Valley Coll (CA)
Athens Tech Coll (GA)
Augusta Tech Coll (GA)
Barton County Comm Coll (KS)
Berkshire Comm Coll (MA)
Bossier Parish Comm Coll (LA)
Bowling Green State U–Firelands Coll (OH)
Carrington Coll–Mesa (AZ)
Carrington Coll–Phoenix North (AZ)
Casper Coll (WY)
Catawba Valley Comm Coll (NC)
Central New Mexico Comm Coll (NM)
Central Virginia Comm Coll (VA)
Chippewa Valley Tech Coll (WI)
City Colls of Chicago, Olive-Harvey College (IL)
Cochise County Comm Coll District (AZ)
Collin County Comm Coll District (TX)
Comm Coll of Baltimore County (MD)
Comm Coll of Philadelphia (PA)
Comm Coll of Rhode Island (RI)
County Coll of Morris (NJ)
Daytona State Coll (FL)
Delta Coll (MI)
Dodge City Comm Coll (KS)
East Central Coll (MO)
Eastern Gateway Comm Coll (OH)
Elizabethtown Comm and Tech Coll, Elizabethtown (KY)
Erie Comm Coll, North Campus (NY)
Fayetteville Tech Comm Coll (NC)
Florida SouthWestern State Coll (FL)
Frederick Comm Coll (MD)
Genesee Comm Coll (NY)
George C. Wallace Comm Coll (AL)
Great Falls Coll Montana State U (MT)
Greenville Tech Coll (SC)
Gulf Coast State Coll (FL)
Gwinnett Tech Coll (GA)
Harrisburg Area Comm Coll (PA)
Hawkeye Comm Coll (IA)
Hillsborough Comm Coll (FL)
Hinds Comm Coll (MS)
Houston Comm Coll (TX)
Hudson County Comm Coll (NJ)
Hutchinson Comm Coll (KS)
Illinois Central Coll (IL)
Itawamba Comm Coll (MS)
Ivy Tech Comm Coll–Bloomington (IN)
Ivy Tech Comm Coll–Central Indiana (IN)
Ivy Tech Comm Coll–Lafayette (IN)
Ivy Tech Comm Coll–Northeast (IN)

Ivy Tech Comm Coll–Northwest (IN)
Ivy Tech Comm Coll–Richmond (IN)
Ivy Tech Comm Coll–Southern Indiana (IN)
Ivy Tech Comm Coll–Wabash Valley (IN)
J. Sargeant Reynolds Comm Coll (VA)
Kankakee Comm Coll (IL)
Kaskaskia Coll (IL)
Kennebec Valley Comm Coll (ME)
Kent State U at Ashtabula (OH)
Lakeland Comm Coll (OH)
Lake Superior Coll (MN)
Lone Star Coll–Kingwood (TX)
Los Angeles Valley Coll (CA)
Luzerne County Comm Coll (PA)
Macomb Comm Coll (MI)
Manchester Comm Coll (CT)
Mercer County Comm Coll (NJ)
Meridian Comm Coll (MS)
Miami Dade Coll (FL)
Middlesex County Coll (NJ)
Midlands Tech Coll (SC)
Mohawk Valley Comm Coll (NY)
Moraine Valley Comm Coll (IL)
Mott Comm Coll (MI)
Mt. San Antonio Coll (CA)
Naugatuck Valley Comm Coll (CT)
Northeast Iowa Comm Coll (IA)
Northern Essex Comm Coll (MA)
Northland Comm and Tech Coll (MN)
North Shore Comm Coll (MA)
NorthWest Arkansas Comm Coll (AR)
Norwalk Comm Coll (CT)
Ocean County Coll (NJ)
Oklahoma City Comm Coll (OK)
Orange Coast Coll (CA)
Ozarks Tech Comm Coll (MO)
Pueblo Comm Coll (CO)
Quinsigamond Comm Coll (MA)
Raritan Valley Comm Coll (NJ)
Reading Area Comm Coll (PA)
River Valley Comm Coll (NH)
Rockingham Comm Coll (NC)
Rock Valley Coll (IL)
Rowan Coll at Burlington County (NJ)
St. Luke's Coll (IA)
St. Philip's Coll (TX)
San Jacinto Coll District (TX)
San Joaquin Valley Coll, Bakersfield (CA)
San Joaquin Valley Coll, Ontario (CA)
San Joaquin Valley Coll, Temecula (CA)
San Joaquin Valley Coll, Visalia (CA)
San Juan Coll (NM)
Seminole State Coll of Florida (FL)
Somerset Comm Coll (KY)
Southeast Comm Coll, Lincoln Campus (NE)
Southeastern Comm Coll (IA)
Southern Maine Comm Coll (ME)
Southern Regional Tech Coll (GA)
Southern U at Shreveport (LA)
South Florida State Coll (FL)
Spartanburg Comm Coll (SC)
Spencerian Coll (KY)
Springfield Tech Comm Coll (MA)
Stark State Coll (OH)
Sullivan County Comm Coll (NY)
Tallahassee Comm Coll (FL)
Tarrant County Coll District (TX)
Thaddeus Stevens Coll of Technology (PA)
Tulsa Comm Coll (OK)
Tyler Jr Coll (TX)
Victoria Coll (TX)
Victor Valley Coll (CA)
Volunteer State Comm Coll (TN)
Walters State Comm Coll (TN)
Weatherford Coll (TX)
Westchester Comm Coll (NY)

RESPIRATORY THERAPY TECHNICIAN
Augusta Tech Coll (GA)
Borough of Manhattan Comm Coll of the City U of New York (NY)
Bunker Hill Comm Coll (MA)
Carrington Coll–Las Vegas (NV)
Carrington Coll–Mesa (AZ)
Carrington Coll–Phoenix West (AZ)
Carrington Coll–Pleasant Hill (CA)
Coastal Pines Tech Coll (GA)
Columbus Tech Coll (GA)
Florida SouthWestern State Coll (FL)
Georgia Highlands Coll (GA)
Georgia Northwestern Tech Coll (GA)
Hutchinson Comm Coll (KS)

Miami Dade Coll (FL)
Northern Essex Comm Coll (MA)
San Joaquin Valley Coll, Rancho Cordova (CA)
Southeastern Tech Coll (GA)
Southern Crescent Tech Coll (GA)
Tri-County Tech Coll (SC)

RESTAURANT, CULINARY, AND CATERING MANAGEMENT
American River Coll (CA)
Blue Ridge Comm and Tech Coll (WV)
Cincinnati State Tech and Comm Coll (OH)
Coll of Central Florida (FL)
Coll of the Canyons (CA)
Columbia Coll (CA)
Elgin Comm Coll (IL)
Grand Rapids Comm Coll (MI)
Gulf Coast State Coll (FL)
Hillsborough Comm Coll (FL)
Lakeland Comm Coll (OH)
LDS Business Coll (UT)
McHenry County Coll (IL)
Miami Dade Coll (FL)
Mohawk Valley Comm Coll (NY)
Moraine Valley Comm Coll (IL)
New England Culinary Inst (VT)
Orange Coast Coll (CA)
Pensacola State Coll (FL)
Raritan Valley Comm Coll (NJ)
Reading Area Comm Coll (PA)
San Jacinto Coll District (TX)
Southeast Comm Coll, Lincoln Campus (NE)
Southwestern Oregon Comm Coll (OR)
Vincennes U (IN)
Waukesha County Tech Coll (WI)
Westmoreland County Comm Coll (PA)

RESTAURANT/FOOD SERVICES MANAGEMENT
Central Texas Coll (TX)
Erie Comm Coll, North Campus (NY)
Fiorello H. LaGuardia Comm Coll of the City U of New York (NY)
Hillsborough Comm Coll (FL)
J. Sargeant Reynolds Comm Coll (VA)
LDS Business Coll (UT)
Miami Dade Coll (FL)
Naugatuck Valley Comm Coll (CT)
Northampton Comm Coll (PA)
Norwalk Comm Coll (CT)
Oxnard Coll (CA)
Quinsigamond Comm Coll (MA)
The Restaurant School at Walnut Hill Coll (PA)
Rowan Coll at Burlington County (NJ)
St. Philip's Coll (TX)
Schenectady County Comm Coll (NY)

RETAILING
Alamance Comm Coll (NC)
American River Coll (CA)
Arapahoe Comm Coll (CO)
Bradford School (PA)
Bucks County Comm Coll (PA)
Ca&nnada Coll (CA)
Casper Coll (WY)
Central Oregon Comm Coll (OR)
Clark Coll (WA)
Delta Coll (MI)
Elgin Comm Coll (IL)
Hutchinson Comm Coll (KS)
Illinois Central Coll (IL)
Minnesota State Coll–Southeast Tech (MN)
Moraine Valley Comm Coll (IL)
North Central Texas Coll (TX)
Rowan Coll at Burlington County (NJ)
U of Cincinnati Blue Ash Coll (OH)
Western Iowa Tech Comm Coll (IA)
Wood Tobe–Coburn School (NY)

RETAIL MANAGEMENT
Collin County Comm Coll District (TX)
Orange Coast Coll (CA)
Penn Foster Coll (AZ)

RHETORIC AND COMPOSITION
Allen Comm Coll (KS)
Amarillo Coll (TX)
Austin Comm Coll District (TX)
Bainbridge State Coll (GA)
Blinn Coll (TX)
Carl Albert State Coll (OK)

Dodge City Comm Coll (KS)
Itawamba Comm Coll (MS)
Los Angeles Valley Coll (CA)
Navarro Coll (TX)
Odessa Coll (TX)
Paris Jr Coll (TX)
St. Charles Comm Coll (MO)
St. Philip's Coll (TX)
San Jacinto Coll District (TX)
San Joaquin Delta Coll (CA)
Sierra Coll (CA)
South Florida State Coll (FL)
Spoon River Coll (IL)

ROBOTICS TECHNOLOGY
Butler County Comm Coll (PA)
Casper Coll (WY)
Central Lakes Coll (MN)
Daytona State Coll (FL)
Dunwoody Coll of Technology (MN)
Illinois Central Coll (IL)
Ivy Tech Comm Coll–Columbus (IN)
Ivy Tech Comm Coll–Lafayette (IN)
Ivy Tech Comm Coll–North Central (IN)
Ivy Tech Comm Coll–Northeast (IN)
Ivy Tech Comm Coll–Richmond (IN)
Ivy Tech Comm Coll–Southwest (IN)
Kaskaskia Coll (IL)
Kirtland Comm Coll (MI)
Lake Area Tech Inst (SD)
Macomb Comm Coll (MI)
McHenry County Coll (IL)
Minnesota West Comm and Tech Coll (MN)
Southern U at Shreveport (LA)
Texas State Tech Coll (TX)
Vincennes U (IN)

ROOFING
Penn Foster Coll (AZ)

RUSSIAN
Austin Comm Coll District (TX)

SALES, DISTRIBUTION, AND MARKETING OPERATIONS
Aiken Tech Coll (SC)
Alexandria Tech and Comm Coll (MN)
American River Coll (CA)
Anoka-Ramsey Comm Coll (MN)
Antelope Valley Coll (CA)
Coll of the Canyons (CA)
Fullerton Coll (CA)
Gadsden State Comm Coll (AL)
Greenville Tech Coll (SC)
Harrisburg Area Comm Coll (PA)
Hawkeye Comm Coll (IA)
Los Angeles Valley Coll (CA)
Midlands Tech Coll (SC)
Minnesota State Coll–Southeast Tech (MN)
Montgomery County Comm Coll (PA)
North Central Texas Coll (TX)
Northeast Iowa Comm Coll (IA)
Northland Comm and Tech Coll (MN)
Northwest Tech Coll (MN)
Oakton Comm Coll (IL)
Orange Coast Coll (CA)
Ridgewater Coll (MN)
Rowan Coll at Burlington County (NJ)
Sierra Coll (CA)
State U of New York Coll of Technology at Alfred (NY)
Western Iowa Tech Comm Coll (IA)
Westmoreland County Comm Coll (PA)

SALON/BEAUTY SALON MANAGEMENT
Delta Coll (MI)
J. F. Drake State Comm and Tech Coll (AL)
LDS Business Coll (UT)
Mott Comm Coll (MI)
Northwest-Shoals Comm Coll (AL)
Schoolcraft Coll (MI)
Southeastern Coll–West Palm Beach (FL)

SCIENCE TEACHER EDUCATION
Iowa Central Comm Coll (IA)
Itawamba Comm Coll (MS)
Moraine Valley Comm Coll (IL)
San Jacinto Coll District (TX)
South Florida State Coll (FL)
Vincennes U (IN)

SCIENCE TECHNOLOGIES
Central Virginia Comm Coll (VA)

Great Basin Coll (NV)
Northern Essex Comm Coll (MA)

SCIENCE TECHNOLOGIES RELATED
Arapahoe Comm Coll (CO)
Blue Ridge Comm and Tech Coll (WV)
Cascadia Coll (WA)
Cayuga County Comm Coll (NY)
Cleveland State Comm Coll (TN)
Comm Coll of Aurora (CO)
Front Range Comm Coll (CO)
Morgan Comm Coll (CO)
Pueblo Comm Coll (CO)
Reading Area Comm Coll (PA)
Schenectady County Comm Coll (NY)
Sullivan County Comm Coll (NY)
U of Cincinnati Blue Ash Coll (OH)
Victor Valley Coll (CA)

SCIENCE, TECHNOLOGY AND SOCIETY
Truckee Meadows Comm Coll (NV)

SCULPTURE
Los Angeles Valley Coll (CA)
Mercer County Comm Coll (NJ)
Palomar Coll (CA)

SECONDARY EDUCATION
Allen Comm Coll (KS)
Alvin Comm Coll (TX)
Ancilla Coll (IN)
Arizona Western Coll (AZ)
Austin Comm Coll District (TX)
Barton County Comm Coll (KS)
Brookhaven Coll (TX)
Carl Albert State Coll (OK)
Cecil Coll (MD)
Central Wyoming Coll (WY)
Coll of Central Florida (FL)
Collin County Comm Coll District (TX)
Eastern Arizona Coll (AZ)
Eastern Wyoming Coll (WY)
Georgia Military Coll (GA)
Gordon State Coll (GA)
Grand Rapids Comm Coll (MI)
Harrisburg Area Comm Coll (PA)
Houston Comm Coll (TX)
Howard Comm Coll (MD)
Kankakee Comm Coll (IL)
Montgomery County Comm Coll (PA)
Nashville State Comm Coll (TN)
Northampton Comm Coll (PA)
Northwest Coll (WY)
Paris Jr Coll (TX)
Potomac State Coll of West Virginia U (WV)
Reading Area Comm Coll (PA)
San Jacinto Coll District (TX)
San Juan Coll (NM)
Sheridan Coll (WY)
South Florida State Coll (FL)
Springfield Tech Comm Coll (MA)
Tyler Jr Coll (TX)
U of Cincinnati Blue Ash Coll (OH)
Vincennes U (IN)
Western Texas Coll (TX)
Western Wyoming Coll (WY)

SECURITIES SERVICES ADMINISTRATION
Quincy Coll (MA)
Vincennes U (IN)
Western Iowa Tech Comm Coll (IA)

SECURITY AND LOSS PREVENTION
Carrington Coll–Pleasant Hill (CA)
Carrington Coll–San Jose (CA)
Carrington Coll–San Leandro (CA)
Citrus Coll (CA)
Comm Coll of the Air Force (AL)
Delta Coll (MI)
Illinois Central Coll (IL)
Miami Dade Coll (FL)
Tallahassee Comm Coll (FL)
Vincennes U (IN)

SELLING SKILLS AND SALES
Butler County Comm Coll (PA)
Clark Coll (WA)
Danville Area Comm Coll (IL)
McHenry County Coll (IL)
Minnesota State Coll–Southeast Tech (MN)
Ridgewater Coll (MN)

SEMICONDUCTOR MANUFACTURING TECHNOLOGY
Mohawk Valley Comm Coll (NY)

SHEET METAL TECHNOLOGY
American River Coll (CA)
Delta Coll (MI)
Ivy Tech Comm Coll–Central Indiana (IN)
Ivy Tech Comm Coll–Lafayette (IN)
Ivy Tech Comm Coll–North Central (IN)
Ivy Tech Comm Coll–Northeast (IN)
Ivy Tech Comm Coll–Northwest (IN)
Ivy Tech Comm Coll–Southern Indiana (IN)
Ivy Tech Comm Coll–Southwest (IN)
Ivy Tech Comm Coll–Wabash Valley (IN)
Lake Superior Coll (MN)
Macomb Comm Coll (MI)
Miami Dade Coll (FL)
Palomar Coll (CA)
Rock Valley Coll (IL)
Shawnee Comm Coll (IL)
Thaddeus Stevens Coll of Technology (PA)
Vincennes U (IN)

SIGNAL/GEOSPATIAL INTELLIGENCE
Northland Comm and Tech Coll (MN)

SIGN LANGUAGE INTERPRETATION AND TRANSLATION
American River Coll (CA)
Antelope Valley Coll (CA)
Austin Comm Coll District (TX)
Camden County Coll (NJ)
Cincinnati State Tech and Comm Coll (OH)
Coll of the Canyons (CA)
Collin County Comm Coll District (TX)
Comm Coll of Baltimore County (MD)
Comm Coll of Philadelphia (PA)
Front Range Comm Coll (CO)
Hinds Comm Coll (MS)
Houston Comm Coll (TX)
Illinois Central Coll (IL)
J. Sargeant Reynolds Comm Coll (VA)
Lakeland Comm Coll (OH)
Lone Star Coll–CyFair (TX)
Lone Star Coll–North Harris (TX)
Miami Dade Coll (FL)
Minnesota State Comm and Tech Coll–Moorhead (MN)
Mohawk Valley Comm Coll (NY)
Mott Comm Coll (MI)
Mt. San Antonio Coll (CA)
Nashville State Comm Coll (TN)
Northcentral Tech Coll (WI)
Northern Essex Comm Coll (MA)
Ocean County Coll (NJ)
Oklahoma State U, Oklahoma City (OK)
Palomar Coll (CA)
Rowan Coll at Burlington County (NJ)
Salt Lake Comm Coll (UT)
Tarrant County Coll District (TX)
Tulsa Comm Coll (OK)
Tyler Jr Coll (TX)
Western Piedmont Comm Coll (NC)

SMALL BUSINESS ADMINISTRATION
American River Coll (CA)
Antelope Valley Coll (CA)
Borough of Manhattan Comm Coll of the City U of New York (NY)
Bucks County Comm Coll (PA)
Ca&nnada Coll (CA)
Cerritos Coll (CA)
Coll of the Canyons (CA)
Colorado Northwestern Comm Coll (CO)
Delta Coll (MI)
Fullerton Coll (CA)
J. Sargeant Reynolds Comm Coll (VA)
Middlesex County Coll (NJ)
Moraine Valley Comm Coll (IL)
Raritan Valley Comm Coll (NJ)
Schoolcraft Coll (MI)
Sierra Coll (CA)
South Suburban Coll (IL)
Springfield Tech Comm Coll (MA)

SMALL ENGINE MECHANICS AND REPAIR TECHNOLOGY
Mitchell Tech Inst (SD)

SOCIAL PSYCHOLOGY
Macomb Comm Coll (MI)
South Florida State Coll (FL)

SOCIAL SCIENCES
Amarillo Coll (TX)
American River Coll (CA)
Antelope Valley Coll (CA)
Arizona Western Coll (AZ)
Carl Albert State Coll (OK)
Central Oregon Comm Coll (OR)
Central Texas Coll (TX)
Central Wyoming Coll (WY)
Citrus Coll (CA)
Clinton Comm Coll (NY)
Cochise County Comm Coll District (AZ)
Coll of Central Florida (FL)
Coll of the Canyons (CA)
Corning Comm Coll (NY)
Dodge City Comm Coll (KS)
Eastern Wyoming Coll (WY)
Feather River Coll (CA)
Finger Lakes Comm Coll (NY)
Galveston Coll (TX)
Genesee Comm Coll (NY)
Harrisburg Area Comm Coll (PA)
Housatonic Comm Coll (CT)
Howard Comm Coll (MD)
Hutchinson Comm Coll (KS)
Itawamba Comm Coll (MS)
J. Sargeant Reynolds Comm Coll (VA)
Kilgore Coll (TX)
Laramie County Comm Coll (WY)
Lorain County Comm Coll (OH)
Luzerne County Comm Coll (PA)
Massachusetts Bay Comm Coll (MA)
Miami Dade Coll (FL)
Monroe Comm Coll (NY)
Montgomery County Comm Coll (PA)
Mt. San Antonio Coll (CA)
Navarro Coll (TX)
Niagara County Comm Coll (NY)
Northeastern Jr Coll (CO)
Northwest Coll (WY)
Odessa Coll (TX)
Orange Coast Coll (CA)
Otero Jr Coll (CO)
Palomar Coll (CA)
Paris Jr Coll (TX)
Reading Area Comm Coll (PA)
Rowan Coll at Burlington County (NJ)
San Jacinto Coll District (TX)
San Joaquin Delta Coll (CA)
Seminole State Coll (OK)
Sierra Coll (CA)
South Florida State Coll (FL)
Spoon River Coll (IL)
Texarkana Coll (TX)
Tulsa Comm Coll (OK)
Tyler Jr Coll (TX)
Victor Valley Coll (CA)
Westchester Comm Coll (NY)
Western Texas Coll (TX)
Western Wyoming Comm Coll (WY)

SOCIAL SCIENCES RELATED
Genesee Comm Coll (NY)

SOCIAL SCIENCE TEACHER EDUCATION
South Florida State Coll (FL)

SOCIAL STUDIES TEACHER EDUCATION
Casper Coll (WY)

SOCIAL WORK
Allen Comm Coll (KS)
Amarillo Coll (TX)
Austin Comm Coll District (TX)
Barton County Comm Coll (KS)
Bowling Green State U–Firelands Coll (OH)
Camden County Coll (NJ)
Casper Coll (WY)
Chandler-Gilbert Comm Coll (AZ)
Chipola Coll (FL)
Cochise County Comm Coll District (AZ)
Coll of Central Florida (FL)
Comm Coll of Rhode Island (RI)
Comm Coll of the Air Force (AL)
Dodge City Comm Coll (KS)

Edison Comm Coll (OH)
Elgin Comm Coll (IL)
Elizabethtown Comm and Tech Coll, Elizabethtown (KY)
Galveston Coll (TX)
Genesee Comm Coll (NY)
Georgia Military Coll (GA)
Gordon State Coll (GA)
Harford Comm Coll (MD)
Harrisburg Area Comm Coll (PA)
Holyoke Comm Coll (MA)
Hopkinsville Comm Coll (KY)
Hudson County Comm Coll (NJ)
Illinois Eastern Comm Colls, Wabash Valley College (IL)
Iowa Central Comm Coll (IA)
Itawamba Comm Coll (MS)
Lake Land Coll (IL)
Lakeland Comm Coll (OH)
Lehigh Carbon Comm Coll (PA)
Lorain County Comm Coll (OH)
Manchester Comm Coll (CT)
Miami Dade Coll (FL)
Nashville State Comm Coll (TN)
Northampton Comm Coll (PA)
Northeast Iowa Comm Coll (IA)
Oakton Comm Coll (IL)
Paris Jr Coll (TX)
Potomac State Coll of West Virginia U (WV)
Reading Area Comm Coll (PA)
Rogue Comm Coll (OR)
St. Charles Comm Coll (MO)
St. Philip's Coll (TX)
Salt Lake Comm Coll (UT)
San Juan Coll (NM)
Shawnee Comm Coll (IL)
South Florida State Coll (FL)
South Suburban Coll (IL)
Southwestern Michigan Coll (MI)
Tulsa Comm Coll (OK)
Tyler Jr Coll (TX)
U of Cincinnati Blue Ash Coll (OH)
Vincennes U (IN)
Wayne County Comm Coll District (MI)
Western Wyoming Comm Coll (WY)
West Georgia Tech Coll (GA)

SOCIAL WORK RELATED
Butler County Comm Coll (PA)
Genesee Comm Coll (NY)

SOCIOLOGY
Allen Comm Coll (KS)
Alvin Comm Coll (TX)
Antelope Valley Coll (CA)
Austin Comm Coll District (TX)
Bainbridge State Coll (GA)
Barton County Comm Coll (KS)
Borough of Manhattan Comm Coll of the City U of New York (NY)
Bunker Hill Comm Coll (MA)
Ca&nnada Coll (CA)
Casper Coll (WY)
Central New Mexico Comm Coll (NM)
Cerritos Coll (CA)
Citrus Coll (CA)
Coll of Central Florida (FL)
Coll of the Canyons (CA)
Dean Coll (MA)
Eastern Arizona Coll (AZ)
Feather River Coll (CA)
Finger Lakes Comm Coll (NY)
Fullerton Coll (CA)
Georgia Highlands Coll (GA)
Georgia Military Coll (GA)
Gordon State Coll (GA)
Harford Comm Coll (MD)
Iowa Central Comm Coll (IA)
Itawamba Comm Coll (MS)
Kankakee Comm Coll (IL)
Laramie County Comm Coll (WY)
Lorain County Comm Coll (OH)
Los Angeles Valley Coll (CA)
Miami Dade Coll (FL)
Mohave Comm Coll (AZ)
Moraine Valley Comm Coll (IL)
Nashville State Comm Coll (TN)
Navarro Coll (TX)
Northeastern Jr Coll (CO)
Northwest Coll (WY)
Odessa Coll (TX)
Oklahoma City Comm Coll (OK)
Orange Coast Coll (CA)
Oxnard Coll (CA)
Palomar Coll (CA)
Panola Coll (TX)

Paris Jr Coll (TX)
Pasadena City Coll (CA)
Pensacola State Coll (FL)
Potomac State Coll of West Virginia U (WV)
Rowan Coll at Burlington County (NJ)
St. Charles Comm Coll (MO)
St. Philip's Coll (TX)
Salt Lake Comm Coll (UT)
San Jacinto Coll District (TX)
San Joaquin Delta Coll (CA)
Southern U at Shreveport (LA)
South Florida State Coll (FL)
Spoon River Coll (IL)
Tyler Jr Coll (TX)
Vincennes U (IN)
Wenatchee Valley Coll (WA)
Western Wyoming Comm Coll (WY)

SOIL SCIENCE AND AGRONOMY
South Florida State Coll (FL)
Treasure Valley Comm Coll (OR)

SOLAR ENERGY TECHNOLOGY
Arizona Western Coll (AZ)
Crowder Coll (MO)
San Juan Coll (NM)
Texas State Tech Coll (TX)
Treasure Valley Comm Coll (OR)

SPANISH
Arizona Western Coll (AZ)
Austin Comm Coll District (TX)
Blinn Coll (TX)
Ca&nnada Coll (CA)
Cerritos Coll (CA)
Citrus Coll (CA)
Coll of the Canyons (CA)
Fiorello H. LaGuardia Comm Coll of the City U of New York (NY)
Laramie County Comm Coll (WY)
Los Angeles Valley Coll (CA)
Miami Dade Coll (FL)
Northwest Coll (WY)
Orange Coast Coll (CA)
Oxnard Coll (CA)
Pasadena City Coll (CA)
St. Charles Comm Coll (MO)
St. Philip's Coll (TX)
South Florida State Coll (FL)
Western Wyoming Comm Coll (WY)

SPANISH LANGUAGE TEACHER EDUCATION
Anne Arundel Comm Coll (MD)
Carroll Comm Coll (MD)
Comm Coll of Baltimore County (MD)
Frederick Comm Coll (MD)
Harford Comm Coll (MD)
Montgomery Coll (MD)

SPECIAL EDUCATION
Coll of Central Florida (FL)
Comm Coll of Rhode Island (RI)
Craven Comm Coll (NC)
Harford Comm Coll (MD)
Highland Comm Coll (IL)
Kankakee Comm Coll (IL)
Lehigh Carbon Comm Coll (PA)
McHenry County Coll (IL)
Miami Dade Coll (FL)
Moraine Valley Comm Coll (IL)
Nashville State Comm Coll (TN)
Pensacola State Coll (FL)
Rend Lake Coll (IL)
San Juan Coll (NM)
South Florida State Coll (FL)
Vincennes U (IN)

SPECIAL EDUCATION–EARLY CHILDHOOD
Harford Comm Coll (MD)
Los Angeles Valley Coll (CA)
Mitchell Comm Coll (NC)
Orange Coast Coll (CA)
Palomar Coll (CA)

SPECIAL EDUCATION–ELEMENTARY SCHOOL
Harford Comm Coll (MD)
Westmoreland County Comm Coll (PA)

SPECIAL EDUCATION–INDIVIDUALS WITH EMOTIONAL DISTURBANCES
South Florida State Coll (FL)

SPECIAL EDUCATION–INDIVIDUALS WITH HEARING IMPAIRMENTS
Hillsborough Comm Coll (FL)
Miami Dade Coll (FL)

SPECIAL EDUCATION–INDIVIDUALS WITH INTELLECTUAL DISABILITIES
South Florida State Coll (FL)

SPECIAL EDUCATION–INDIVIDUALS WITH SPECIFIC LEARNING DISABILITIES
South Florida State Coll (FL)

SPECIAL EDUCATION–INDIVIDUALS WITH VISION IMPAIRMENTS
South Florida State Coll (FL)

SPECIAL PRODUCTS MARKETING
Copiah-Lincoln Comm Coll (MS)
Monroe Comm Coll (NY)
Muskegon Comm Coll (MI)
Northland Comm and Tech Coll (MN)
Scottsdale Comm Coll (AZ)
Tompkins Cortland Comm Coll (NY)

SPEECH COMMUNICATION AND RHETORIC
Ancilla Coll (IN)
Antelope Valley Coll (CA)
Barton County Comm Coll (KS)
Brookhaven Coll (TX)
Bucks County Comm Coll (PA)
Bunker Hill Comm Coll (MA)
Camden County Coll (NJ)
Ca&nnada Coll (CA)
Casper Coll (WY)
Central Oregon Comm Coll (OR)
Cerritos Coll (CA)
Citrus Coll (CA)
Cochise County Comm Coll District (AZ)
Coll of the Canyons (CA)
Collin County Comm Coll District (TX)
Columbia Coll (CA)
Dutchess Comm Coll (NY)
Eastern Wyoming Coll (WY)
Edison Comm Coll (OH)
Erie Comm Coll, South Campus (NY)
Fiorello H. LaGuardia Comm Coll of the City U of New York (NY)
Fullerton Coll (CA)
Georgia Highlands Coll (GA)
Houston Comm Coll (TX)
Hutchinson Comm Coll (KS)
Jamestown Comm Coll (NY)
Lackawanna Coll (PA)
Laramie County Comm Coll (WY)
Lehigh Carbon Comm Coll (PA)
Lone Star Coll–CyFair (TX)
Lone Star Coll–U Park (TX)
Macomb Comm Coll (MI)
Manchester Comm Coll (CT)
Montgomery Coll (MD)
Montgomery County Comm Coll (PA)
Nashville State Comm Coll (TN)
Northampton Comm Coll (PA)
Northwest Coll (WY)
Norwalk Comm Coll (CT)
Onondaga Comm Coll (NY)
Orange Coast Coll (CA)
Oxnard Coll (CA)
Palomar Coll (CA)
Panola Coll (TX)
Pasadena City Coll (CA)
Salt Lake Comm Coll (UT)
South Florida State Coll (FL)
Tompkins Cortland Comm Coll (NY)
Tyler Jr Coll (TX)
U of Cincinnati Blue Ash Coll (OH)
Western Wyoming Comm Coll (WY)

SPEECH-LANGUAGE PATHOLOGY
Lake Region State Coll (ND)
Williston State Coll (ND)

SPEECH-LANGUAGE PATHOLOGY ASSISTANT
Alexandria Tech and Comm Coll (MN)
Fayetteville Tech Comm Coll (NC)
Mitchell Tech Inst (SD)
Oklahoma City Comm Coll (OK)

SPORT AND FITNESS ADMINISTRATION/ MANAGEMENT
American River Coll (CA)
Arizona Western Coll (AZ)
Barton County Comm Coll (KS)
Bucks County Comm Coll (PA)
Bunker Hill Comm Coll (MA)
Butler County Comm Coll (PA)
Camden County Coll (NJ)
Ca&nnada Coll (CA)
Cayuga County Comm Coll (NY)
Central Oregon Comm Coll (OR)
Cerritos Coll (CA)
Clark Coll (WA)
Dean Coll (MA)
Delta Coll (MI)
Fullerton Coll (CA)
Garrett Coll (MD)
Holyoke Comm Coll (MA)
Howard Comm Coll (MD)
Hutchinson Comm Coll (KS)
Illinois Eastern Comm Colls, Frontier Community College (IL)
Illinois Eastern Comm Colls, Lincoln Trail College (IL)
Illinois Eastern Comm Colls, Wabash Valley College (IL)
Jefferson Comm Coll (NY)
Lehigh Carbon Comm Coll (PA)
Lorain County Comm Coll (OH)
Manor Coll (PA)
Niagara County Comm Coll (NY)
Northampton Comm Coll (PA)
Northern Essex Comm Coll (MA)
Rock Valley Coll (IL)
Salt Lake Comm Coll (UT)
Southwestern Michigan Coll (MI)
Springfield Tech Comm Coll (MA)
State U of New York Coll of Technology at Alfred (NY)
Sullivan County Comm Coll (NY)
Three Rivers Comm Coll (CT)
Tompkins Cortland Comm Coll (NY)
Tulsa Comm Coll (OK)
Vincennes U (IN)

SPORTS STUDIES
Finger Lakes Comm Coll (NY)
Genesee Comm Coll (NY)

STATISTICS
Coll of Central Florida (FL)
Eastern Wyoming Coll (WY)
South Florida State Coll (FL)

STATISTICS RELATED
Casper Coll (WY)

STRUCTURAL ENGINEERING
Harrisburg Area Comm Coll (PA)

SUBSTANCE ABUSE/ ADDICTION COUNSELING
Alvin Comm Coll (TX)
Amarillo Coll (TX)
American River Coll (CA)
Anne Arundel Comm Coll (MD)
Austin Comm Coll District (TX)
Beal Coll (ME)
Camden County Coll (NJ)
Casper Coll (WY)
Central Oregon Comm Coll (OR)
Century Coll (MN)
Chippewa Valley Tech Coll (WI)
Clark Coll (WA)
Comm Coll of Baltimore County (MD)
Comm Coll of Rhode Island (RI)
Corning Comm Coll (NY)
Dawson Comm Coll (MT)
Erie Comm Coll (NY)
Finger Lakes Comm Coll (NY)
Florida SouthWestern State Coll (FL)
Fox Valley Tech Coll (WI)
Gadsden State Comm Coll (AL)
Genesee Comm Coll (NY)
Housatonic Comm Coll (CT)
Howard Comm Coll (MD)
Illinois Central Coll (IL)
J. Sargeant Reynolds Comm Coll (VA)
Mesabi Range Coll (MN)
Miami Dade Coll (FL)
Mohave Comm Coll (AZ)
Mohawk Valley Comm Coll (NY)
Moraine Valley Comm Coll (IL)
Mountain State Coll (WV)
Naugatuck Valley Comm Coll (CT)
Northcentral Tech Coll (WI)

North Shore Comm Coll (MA)
Oakton Comm Coll (IL)
Odessa Coll (TX)
Oklahoma State U, Oklahoma City (OK)
Olympic Coll (WA)
Oxnard Coll (CA)
Palomar Coll (CA)
Southeastern Comm Coll (IA)
Texarkana Coll (TX)
Tompkins Cortland Comm Coll (NY)
Treasure Valley Comm Coll (OR)
Tyler Jr Coll (TX)
Wenatchee Valley Comm Coll (WA)
Westchester Comm Coll (NY)
Western Piedmont Comm Coll (NC)
Wor-Wic Comm Coll (MD)

SURGICAL TECHNOLOGY

Anne Arundel Comm Coll (MD)
Anoka Tech Coll (MN)
Athens Tech Coll (GA)
Augusta Tech Coll (GA)
Austin Comm Coll District (TX)
Bellingham Tech Coll (WA)
Bismarck State Coll (ND)
Cape Fear Comm Coll (NC)
Carrington Coll–Citrus Heights (CA)
Carrington Coll–San Jose (CA)
Central New Mexico Comm Coll (NM)
Central Ohio Tech Coll (OH)
Cincinnati State Tech and Comm Coll (OH)
Coastal Pines Tech Coll (GA)
Collin County Comm Coll District (TX)
Columbus Tech Coll (GA)
Comm Care Coll (OK)
Comm Coll of the Air Force (AL)
Delta Coll (MI)
Eastern Idaho Tech Coll (ID)
Fayetteville Tech Comm Coll (NC)
Frederick Comm Coll (MD)
Gateway Tech Coll (WI)
Georgia Northwestern Tech Coll (GA)
Georgia Piedmont Tech Coll (GA)
Great Falls Coll Montana State U (MT)
Gulf Coast State Coll (FL)
Harrisburg Area Comm Coll (PA)
Hinds Comm Coll (MS)
Hutchinson Comm Coll (KS)
Illinois Central Coll (IL)
Ivy Tech Comm Coll–Central Indiana (IN)
Ivy Tech Comm Coll–Columbus (IN)
Ivy Tech Comm Coll–East Central (IN)
Ivy Tech Comm Coll–Kokomo (IN)
Ivy Tech Comm Coll–Lafayette (IN)
Ivy Tech Comm Coll–Northwest (IN)
Ivy Tech Comm Coll–Southwest (IN)
Ivy Tech Comm Coll–Wabash Valley (IN)
James H. Faulkner State Comm Coll (AL)
Kilgore Coll (TX)
Kirtland Comm Coll (MI)
Lackawanna Coll (PA)
Lakeland Comm Coll (OH)
Lake Superior Coll (MN)
Lanier Tech Coll (GA)
Laramie County Comm Coll (WY)
Lone Star Coll–Tomball (TX)
Lorain County Comm Coll (OH)
Luzerne County Comm Coll (PA)
Macomb Comm Coll (MI)
Manchester Comm Coll (CT)
Midlands Tech Coll (SC)
Minnesota West Comm and Tech Coll (MN)
Mohave Comm Coll (AZ)
Montgomery Coll (MD)
Montgomery County Comm Coll (PA)
Niagara County Comm Coll (NY)
Northland Comm and Tech Coll (MN)
Oklahoma City Comm Coll (OK)
Owensboro Comm and Tech Coll (KY)
Paris Jr Coll (TX)
Pittsburgh Tech Inst, Oakdale (PA)
Pueblo Comm Coll (CO)
Renton Tech Coll (WA)
Richland Comm Coll (IL)
Rock Valley Coll (IL)
San Jacinto Coll District (TX)
San Joaquin Valley Coll, Bakersfield (CA)
San Joaquin Valley Coll, Fresno (CA)
San Juan Coll (NM)
Savannah Tech Coll (GA)

Somerset Comm Coll (KY)
Southeast Comm Coll, Lincoln Campus (NE)
Southeastern Coll–West Palm Beach (FL)
Southeast Tech Inst (SD)
Southern Crescent Tech Coll (GA)
Southern Maine Comm Coll (ME)
Southern Regional Tech Coll (GA)
Southern U at Shreveport (LA)
Spencerian Coll (KY)
Springfield Tech Comm Coll (MA)
Tallahassee Comm Coll (FL)
Tarrant County Coll District (TX)
Trocaire Coll (NY)
Tulsa Comm Coll (OK)
Tyler Jr Coll (TX)
Vincennes U (IN)
Walters State Comm Coll (TN)
Waukesha County Tech Coll (WI)
Wayne County Comm Coll District (MI)
Western Iowa Tech Comm Coll (IA)

SURVEYING ENGINEERING

Central New Mexico Comm Coll (NM)
Comm Coll of Rhode Island (RI)

SURVEYING TECHNOLOGY

Austin Comm Coll District (TX)
Bellingham Tech Coll (WA)
Bismarck State Coll (ND)
Clark Coll (WA)
Coll of the Canyons (CA)
Comm Coll of Baltimore County (MD)
Fayetteville Tech Comm Coll (NC)
Gateway Tech Coll (WI)
Macomb Comm Coll (MI)
Middlesex County Coll (NJ)
Mohawk Valley Comm Coll (NY)
Moraine Valley Comm Coll (IL)
Mt. San Antonio Coll (CA)
Oklahoma State U, Oklahoma City (OK)
Renton Tech Coll (WA)
Salt Lake Comm Coll (UT)
Sheridan Coll (WY)
Southeast Tech Inst (SD)
South Florida State Coll (FL)
Stark State Coll (OH)
State U of New York Coll of Technology at Alfred (NY)
Texas State Tech Coll (TX)
Tyler Jr Coll (TX)
U of Arkansas Comm Coll at Morrilton (AR)
Vincennes U (IN)
Western Piedmont Comm Coll (NC)

SUSTAINABILITY STUDIES

Rowan Coll at Burlington County (NJ)

SYSTEM, NETWORKING, AND LAN/WAN MANAGEMENT

Blue Ridge Comm and Tech Coll (WV)
Central Texas Coll (TX)
Cloud County Comm Coll (KS)
Coll of Business and Technology–Main Campus (FL)
Collin County Comm Coll District (TX)
Craven Comm Coll (NC)
LDS Business Coll (UT)
Lone Star Coll–Tomball (TX)
Moraine Valley Comm Coll (IL)
Oklahoma City Comm Coll (OK)
Paris Jr Coll (TX)
Rowan-Cabarrus Comm Coll (NC)
St. Philip's Coll (TX)
Southwestern Indian Polytechnic Inst (NM)
Texas State Tech Coll (TX)
Tyler Jr Coll (TX)
Wayne County Comm Coll District (MI)
Williston State Coll (ND)

SYSTEMS ENGINEERING

South Florida State Coll (FL)

TEACHER ASSISTANT/AIDE

Alamance Comm Coll (NC)
Antelope Valley Coll (CA)
Borough of Manhattan Comm Coll of the City U of New York (NY)
Central Wyoming Coll (WY)
Century Coll (MN)
Cloud County Comm Coll (KS)
Coll of The Albemarle (NC)
Danville Area Comm Coll (IL)

Elizabethtown Comm and Tech Coll, Elizabethtown (KY)
Fiorello H. LaGuardia Comm Coll of the City U of New York (NY)
Gateway Comm and Tech Coll (KY)
Gateway Tech Coll (WI)
Genesee Comm Coll (NY)
Harford Comm Coll (MD)
Highland Comm Coll (IL)
Illinois Central Coll (IL)
Illinois Eastern Comm Colls, Lincoln Trail College (IL)
Jamestown Comm Coll (NY)
Jefferson Comm Coll (NY)
Kankakee Comm Coll (IL)
Kaskaskia Coll (IL)
Lehigh Carbon Comm Coll (PA)
Manchester Comm Coll (CT)
Mercer County Comm Coll (NJ)
Miami Dade Coll (FL)
Middlesex County Coll (NJ)
Mitchell Comm Coll (NC)
Montgomery County Comm Coll (PA)
Moraine Valley Comm Coll (IL)
Northampton Comm Coll (PA)
Northcentral Tech Coll (WI)
Northland Comm and Tech Coll (MN)
Odessa Coll (TX)
Ridgewater Coll (MN)
St. Charles Comm Coll (MO)
St. Philip's Coll (TX)
Salt Lake Comm Coll (UT)
Schenectady County Comm Coll (NY)
Somerset Comm Coll (KY)
Southern U at Shreveport (LA)
Southwest Texas Jr Coll (TX)
Victor Valley Coll (CA)
Vincennes U (IN)
Washington County Comm Coll (ME)
Waukesha County Tech Coll (WI)
Western Iowa Tech Comm Coll (IA)

TECHNICAL TEACHER EDUCATION

East Central Coll (MO)
Tri-County Tech Coll (SC)

TECHNOLOGY/INDUSTRIAL ARTS TEACHER EDUCATION

Allen Comm Coll (KS)
Casper Coll (WY)
Central New Mexico Comm Coll (NM)
Cerritos Coll (CA)
Delta Coll (MI)
Eastern Arizona Coll (AZ)
Fullerton Coll (CA)

TELECOMMUNICATIONS TECHNOLOGY

Amarillo Coll (TX)
Arapahoe Comm Coll (CO)
Carl Albert State Coll (OK)
Cayuga County Comm Coll (NY)
Central Texas Coll (TX)
Clark Coll (WA)
Collin County Comm Coll District (TX)
County Coll of Morris (NJ)
Erie Comm Coll, South Campus (NY)
Georgia Piedmont Tech Coll (GA)
Hinds Comm Coll (MS)
Howard Comm Coll (MD)
Illinois Eastern Comm Colls, Lincoln Trail College (IL)
Iowa Central Comm Coll (IA)
Ivy Tech Comm Coll–Lafayette (IN)
Ivy Tech Comm Coll–North Central (IN)
Ivy Tech Comm Coll–Northwest (IN)
Ivy Tech Comm Coll–Southern Indiana (IN)
Ivy Tech Comm Coll–Southwest (IN)
Lake Land Coll (IL)
Meridian Comm Coll (MS)
Miami Dade Coll (FL)
Mitchell Tech Inst (SD)
Monroe Comm Coll (NY)
Northern Essex Comm Coll (MA)
Penn State DuBois (PA)
Penn State Fayette, The Eberly Campus (PA)
Penn State Shenango (PA)
Pensacola State Coll (FL)
Queensborough Comm Coll of the City U of New York (NY)
Quinsigamond Comm Coll (MA)
Ridgewater Coll (MN)
St. Philip's Coll (TX)
Salt Lake Comm Coll (UT)
Seminole State Coll of Florida (FL)
Springfield Tech Comm Coll (MA)

Texas State Tech Coll (TX)
Western Iowa Tech Comm Coll (IA)

THEATER DESIGN AND TECHNOLOGY

American River Coll (CA)
Carroll Comm Coll (MD)
Casper Coll (WY)
Central Wyoming Coll (WY)
Genesee Comm Coll (NY)
Harford Comm Coll (MD)
Howard Comm Coll (MD)
Los Angeles Valley Coll (CA)
Miami Dade Coll (FL)
Pasadena City Coll (CA)
San Juan Coll (NM)
Vincennes U (IN)
Western Wyoming Comm Coll (WY)

THEATER/THEATER ARTS MANAGEMENT

Genesee Comm Coll (NY)

THEOLOGY AND RELIGIOUS VOCATIONS RELATED

Ancilla Coll (IN)

THERAPEUTIC RECREATION

Austin Comm Coll District (TX)
Ridgewater Coll (MN)
Western Piedmont Comm Coll (NC)

TOOL AND DIE TECHNOLOGY

Bevill State Comm Coll (AL)
Craven Comm Coll (NC)
Delta Coll (MI)
Dunwoody Coll of Technology (MN)
Gadsden State Comm Coll (AL)
George C. Wallace Comm Coll (AL)
Hennepin Tech Coll (MN)
Ivy Tech Comm Coll–Bloomington (IN)
Ivy Tech Comm Coll–Central Indiana (IN)
Ivy Tech Comm Coll–Columbus (IN)
Ivy Tech Comm Coll–East Central (IN)
Ivy Tech Comm Coll–Kokomo (IN)
Ivy Tech Comm Coll–Lafayette (IN)
Ivy Tech Comm Coll–North Central (IN)
Ivy Tech Comm Coll–Northeast (IN)
Ivy Tech Comm Coll–Northwest (IN)
Ivy Tech Comm Coll–Richmond (IN)
Ivy Tech Comm Coll–Southern Indiana (IN)
Ivy Tech Comm Coll–Southwest (IN)
Ivy Tech Comm Coll–Wabash Valley (IN)
J. F. Drake State Comm and Tech Coll (AL)
Macomb Comm Coll (MI)
Ridgewater Coll (MN)
Rock Valley Coll (IL)
Vincennes U (IN)

TOURISM AND TRAVEL SERVICES MANAGEMENT

Albany Tech Coll (GA)
Amarillo Coll (TX)
Athens Tech Coll (GA)
Atlanta Tech Coll (GA)
Austin Comm Coll District (TX)
Bucks County Comm Coll (PA)
Bunker Hill Comm Coll (MA)
Central Georgia Tech Coll (GA)
Daytona State Coll (FL)
Finger Lakes Comm Coll (NY)
Fiorello H. LaGuardia Comm Coll of the City U of New York (NY)
Genesee Comm Coll (NY)
Gwinnett Tech Coll (GA)
Hinds Comm Coll (MS)
Houston Comm Coll (TX)
Lakeland Comm Coll (OH)
Lorain County Comm Coll (OH)
Luzerne County Comm Coll (PA)
Miami Dade Coll (FL)
Monroe Comm Coll (NY)
Moraine Valley Comm Coll (IL)
Niagara County Comm Coll (NY)
Northern Essex Comm Coll (MA)
North Shore Comm Coll (MA)
Ogeechee Tech Coll (GA)
Savannah Tech Coll (GA)
Southern U at Shreveport (LA)
Sullivan County Comm Coll (NY)
Westmoreland County Comm Coll (PA)

TOURISM AND TRAVEL SERVICES MARKETING

Herkimer County Comm Coll (NY)
Luzerne County Comm Coll (PA)
Montgomery County Comm Coll (PA)
Orange Coast Coll (CA)

TOURISM PROMOTION

Genesee Comm Coll (NY)
Jefferson Comm Coll (NY)

TRADE AND INDUSTRIAL TEACHER EDUCATION

Copiah-Lincoln Comm Coll (MS)
Itawamba Comm Coll (MS)
Lenoir Comm Coll (NC)
New Mexico Jr Coll (NM)
Quinsigamond Comm Coll (MA)
Southeastern Comm Coll (IA)
South Florida State Coll (FL)
Victor Valley Coll (CA)

TRANSPORTATION AND HIGHWAY ENGINEERING

Gateway Tech Coll (WI)

TRANSPORTATION AND MATERIALS MOVING RELATED

Cecil Coll (MD)
Cochise County Comm Coll District (AZ)
Los Angeles Trade-Tech Coll (CA)
Mid-Plains Comm Coll, North Platte (NE)
Mt. San Antonio Coll (CA)
Muskegon Comm Coll (MI)
Schenectady County Comm Coll (NY)

TRANSPORTATION/MOBILITY MANAGEMENT

Cecil Coll (MD)
Gulf Coast State Coll (FL)
Hagerstown Comm Coll (MD)
Ivy Tech Comm Coll–Central Indiana (IN)
South Florida State Coll (FL)

TRUCK AND BUS DRIVER/COMMERCIAL VEHICLE OPERATION/INSTRUCTION

Mohave Comm Coll (AZ)
Northland Comm and Tech Coll (MN)
Spoon River Coll (IL)

TURF AND TURFGRASS MANAGEMENT

Catawba Valley Comm Coll (NC)
Cincinnati State Tech and Comm Coll (OH)
Danville Area Comm Coll (IL)
Florida SouthWestern State Coll (FL)
Houston Comm Coll (TX)
North Georgia Tech Coll (GA)
Oklahoma State U, Oklahoma City (OK)
Ozarks Tech Comm Coll (MO)
Southeast Tech Inst (SD)
Texas State Tech Coll (TX)
Wayne Comm Coll (NC)
Western Texas Coll (TX)
Westmoreland County Comm Coll (PA)
Williamson Coll of the Trades (PA)

URBAN FORESTRY

Hennepin Tech Coll (MN)
Kent State U at Trumbull (OH)

URBAN STUDIES/AFFAIRS

Lorain County Comm Coll (OH)

VEHICLE MAINTENANCE AND REPAIR TECHNOLOGIES

Corning Comm Coll (NY)
Ohio Tech Coll (OH)

VEHICLE MAINTENANCE AND REPAIR TECHNOLOGIES RELATED

Central New Mexico Comm Coll (NM)
Corning Comm Coll (NY)
LDS Business Coll (UT)
Northland Comm and Tech Coll (MN)
State U of New York Coll of Technology at Alfred (NY)
Victor Valley Coll (CA)

VETERINARY/ANIMAL HEALTH TECHNOLOGY

Athens Tech Coll (GA)
Austin Comm Coll District (TX)
Bradford School (OH)

Camden County Coll (NJ)
Carrington Coll–Citrus Heights (CA)
Carrington Coll–Pleasant Hill (CA)
Carrington Coll–Pomona (CA)
Carrington Coll–Sacramento (CA)
Carrington Coll–San Jose (CA)
Carrington Coll–San Leandro (CA)
Carrington Coll–Stockton (CA)
Central Georgia Tech Coll (GA)
Central New Mexico Comm Coll (NM)
Coll of Central Florida (FL)
Comm Care Coll (OK)
Comm Coll of Baltimore County (MD)
Crowder Coll (MO)
Eastern Wyoming Coll (WY)
Fiorello H. LaGuardia Comm Coll of the City U of New York (NY)
Fox Coll (IL)
Front Range Comm Coll (CO)
Gateway Tech Coll (WI)
Genesee Comm Coll (NY)
Gwinnett Tech Coll (GA)
Hillsborough Comm Coll (FL)
Hinds Comm Coll (MS)
Holyoke Comm Coll (MA)
International Business Coll, Indianapolis (IN)
Jefferson Coll (MO)
Jefferson State Comm Coll (AL)
Kaskaskia Coll (IL)
Kent State U at Tuscarawas (OH)
Lehigh Carbon Comm Coll (PA)
Lone Star Coll–Tomball (TX)
Macomb Comm Coll (MI)
Manor Coll (PA)
Miami Dade Coll (FL)
Northampton Comm Coll (PA)
North Shore Comm Coll (MA)
Northwest Coll (WY)
Ogeechee Tech Coll (GA)
Oklahoma State U, Oklahoma City (OK)
Owensboro Comm and Tech Coll (KY)
Penn Foster Coll (AZ)
Pensacola State Coll (FL)
Rend Lake Coll (IL)
Ridgewater Coll (MN)
San Joaquin Valley Coll, Fresno (CA)
San Juan Coll (NM)
Shawnee Comm Coll (IL)
State U of New York Coll of Technology at Alfred (NY)
Tri-County Tech Coll (SC)
Truckee Meadows Comm Coll (NV)
Tulsa Comm Coll (OK)
U of Cincinnati Blue Ash Coll (OH)
Vet Tech Inst (PA)
Vet Tech Inst at Bradford School (OH)
Vet Tech Inst at Fox Coll (IL)
Vet Tech Inst at Hickey Coll (MO)
Vet Tech Inst at International Business Coll, Fort Wayne (IN)
Vet Tech Inst at International Business Coll, Indianapolis (IN)
Vet Tech Inst of Houston (TX)
Volunteer State Comm Coll (TN)
Wayne County Comm Coll District (MI)
Westchester Comm Coll (NY)
Western Iowa Tech Comm Coll (IA)
York County Comm Coll (ME)

VISUAL AND PERFORMING ARTS
Amarillo Coll (TX)
Antelope Valley Coll (CA)
Berkshire Comm Coll (MA)
Borough of Manhattan Comm Coll of the City U of New York (NY)
Bucks County Comm Coll (PA)
Cerritos Coll (CA)
Chandler-Gilbert Comm Coll (AZ)
Citrus Coll (CA)
Comm Coll of Baltimore County (MD)
Dutchess Comm Coll (NY)
Feather River Coll (CA)
Fiorello H. LaGuardia Comm Coll of the City U of New York (NY)
Harrisburg Area Comm Coll (PA)
Herkimer County Comm Coll (NY)
Hutchinson Comm Coll (KS)
Kankakee Comm Coll (IL)
Middlesex County Coll (NJ)
Moraine Valley Comm Coll (IL)
Mott Comm Coll (MI)

Mt. San Antonio Coll (CA)
Ocean County Coll (NJ)
Queensborough Comm Coll of the City U of New York (NY)
Rogue Comm Coll (OR)
Schenectady County Comm Coll (NY)
Sierra Coll (CA)
Spartanburg Methodist Coll (SC)
Western Wyoming Comm Coll (WY)

VISUAL AND PERFORMING ARTS RELATED
Bossier Parish Comm Coll (LA)
John Tyler Comm Coll (VA)
Northwest Coll (WY)

VITICULTURE AND ENOLOGY
Finger Lakes Comm Coll (NY)
Harrisburg Area Comm Coll (PA)
James Sprunt Comm Coll (NC)
Kent State U at Ashtabula (OH)
Texas State Tech Coll (TX)

VOCATIONAL REHABILITATION COUNSELING
South Florida State Coll (FL)

VOICE AND OPERA
Alvin Comm Coll (TX)
Navarro Coll (TX)

WATCHMAKING AND JEWELRYMAKING
Austin Comm Coll District (TX)
Paris Jr Coll (TX)

WATER QUALITY AND WASTEWATER TREATMENT MANAGEMENT AND RECYCLING TECHNOLOGY
Arizona Western Coll (AZ)
Citrus Coll (CA)
Coll of the Canyons (CA)
Delta Coll (MI)
Northwest Vista Coll (TX)
Ogeechee Tech Coll (GA)
Palomar Coll (CA)
Thaddeus Stevens Coll of Technology (PA)

WATER RESOURCES ENGINEERING
Gateway Tech Coll (WI)

WATER, WETLANDS, AND MARINE RESOURCES MANAGEMENT
South Florida State Coll (FL)

WEB/MULTIMEDIA MANAGEMENT AND WEBMASTER
Casper Coll (WY)
Clark Coll (WA)
Comm Coll of Rhode Island (RI)
Delta Coll (MI)
Fox Valley Tech Coll (WI)
Gateway Tech Coll (WI)
Illinois Central Coll (IL)
Kaskaskia Coll (IL)
Montgomery County Comm Coll (PA)
Moraine Valley Comm Coll (IL)
Northern Essex Comm Coll (MA)
River Valley Comm Coll (NH)
St. Clair County Comm Coll (MI)
Seminole State Coll of Florida (FL)
Stark State Coll (OH)
Vincennes U (IN)
Wayne County Comm Coll District (MI)
Western Wyoming Comm Coll (WY)

WEB PAGE, DIGITAL/ MULTIMEDIA AND INFORMATION RESOURCES DESIGN
Bismarck State Coll (ND)
Blackhawk Tech Coll (WI)
Borough of Manhattan Comm Coll of the City U of New York (NY)
Bucks County Comm Coll (PA)
Bunker Hill Comm Coll (MA)
Butler County Comm Coll (PA)
Casper Coll (WY)
Cecil Coll (MD)
Central Georgia Tech Coll (GA)
Central Ohio Tech Coll (OH)
Century Coll (MN)
Chattahoochee Tech Coll (GA)

City Colls of Chicago, Olive-Harvey College (IL)
Cloud County Comm Coll (KS)
The Coll of Westchester (NY)
Collin County Comm Coll District (TX)
Columbus Tech Coll (GA)
Corning Comm Coll (NY)
County Coll of Morris (NJ)
Dunwoody Coll of Technology (MN)
Dyersburg State Comm Coll (TN)
Eastern Idaho Tech Coll (ID)
Florida SouthWestern State Coll (FL)
Genesee Comm Coll (NY)
Georgia Northwestern Tech Coll (GA)
Gulf Coast State Coll (FL)
Hagerstown Comm Coll (MD)
Harrisburg Area Comm Coll (PA)
Hawkeye Comm Coll (IA)
Hennepin Tech Coll (MN)
Highland Comm Coll (IL)
Hutchinson Comm Coll (KS)
Illinois Central Coll (IL)
J. Sargeant Reynolds Comm Coll (VA)
Kellogg Comm Coll (MI)
Lake Superior Coll (MN)
Lanier Tech Coll (GA)
LDS Business Coll (UT)
Lehigh Carbon Comm Coll (PA)
Lewis and Clark Comm Coll (IL)
Mesabi Range Coll (MN)
Miami Dade Coll (FL)
Minnesota State Coll–Southeast Tech (MN)
Minnesota State Comm and Tech Coll–Detroit Lakes (MN)
Mohawk Valley Comm Coll (NY)
Montgomery Coll (MD)
Mount Wachusett Comm Coll (MA)
Niagara County Comm Coll (NY)
Northampton Comm Coll (PA)
Northern Essex Comm Coll (MA)
North Georgia Tech Coll (GA)
North Shore Comm Coll (MA)
Northwest Vista Coll (TX)
Norwalk Comm Coll (CT)
Ohio Business Coll, Sheffield Village (OH)
Oklahoma State U, Oklahoma City (OK)
Oxnard Coll (CA)
Palomar Coll (CA)
Pittsburgh Tech Inst, Oakdale (PA)
Pueblo Comm Coll (CO)
Quinsigamond Comm Coll (MA)
Raritan Valley Comm Coll (NJ)
Reading Area Comm Coll (PA)
Ridgewater Coll (MN)
Schoolcraft Coll (MI)
Seminole State Coll of Florida (FL)
Sierra Coll (CA)
Southeastern Tech Coll (GA)
Southern Crescent Tech Coll (GA)
Spoon River Coll (IL)
Stark State Coll (OH)
Tallahassee Comm Coll (FL)
Texas State Tech Coll (TX)
Walters State Comm Coll (TN)
Western Iowa Tech Comm Coll (IA)
Western Wyoming Comm Coll (WY)
West Georgia Tech Coll (GA)
Westmoreland County Comm Coll (PA)
Wiregrass Georgia Tech Coll (GA)
Wisconsin Indianhead Tech Coll (WI)

WELDING ENGINEERING TECHNOLOGY
Arizona Western Coll (AZ)
Mitchell Tech Inst (SD)
St. Clair County Comm Coll (MI)

WELDING TECHNOLOGY
Alamance Comm Coll (NC)
American River Coll (CA)
American Samoa Comm Coll (AS)
Anoka Tech Coll (MN)
Antelope Valley Coll (CA)
Austin Comm Coll District (TX)
Bainbridge State Coll (GA)
Beal Coll (ME)
Bellingham Tech Coll (WA)
Big Bend Comm Coll (WA)
Bismarck State Coll (ND)
Casper Coll (WY)
Catawba Valley Comm Coll (NC)
Central Lakes Coll (MN)
Central New Mexico Comm Coll (NM)

Central Texas Coll (TX)
Central Wyoming Coll (WY)
Cerritos Coll (CA)
Clark Coll (WA)
Cochise County Comm Coll District (AZ)
Coll of the Canyons (CA)
Craven Comm Coll (NC)
Crowder Coll (MO)
Dawson Comm Coll (MT)
Delta Coll (MI)
Dodge City Comm Coll (KS)
Dunwoody Coll of Technology (MN)
East Central Coll (MO)
Eastern Arizona Coll (AZ)
Eastern Idaho Tech Coll (ID)
Eastern Wyoming Coll (WY)
Elizabethtown Comm and Tech Coll, Elizabethtown (KY)
Fox Valley Tech Coll (WI)
Front Range Comm Coll (CO)
Galveston Coll (TX)
George C. Wallace Comm Coll (AL)
Grand Rapids Comm Coll (MI)
Great Basin Coll (NV)
Great Falls Coll Montana State U (MT)
Halifax Comm Coll (NC)
Highland Comm Coll (IL)
Hutchinson Comm Coll (KS)
Illinois Central Coll (IL)
Iowa Central Comm Coll (IA)
Jamestown Comm Coll (NY)
Jefferson Coll (MO)
Kankakee Comm Coll (IL)
Kaskaskia Coll (IL)
Kellogg Comm Coll (MI)
Kennebec Valley Comm Coll (ME)
Kilgore Coll (TX)
Kirtland Comm Coll (MI)
Lake Area Tech Inst (SD)
Lenoir Comm Coll (NC)
Lone Star Coll–CyFair (TX)
Lone Star Coll–North Harris (TX)
Los Angeles Trade-Tech Coll (CA)
Macomb Comm Coll (MI)
Manhattan Area Tech Coll (KS)
Mid-Plains Comm Coll, North Platte (NE)
Mohave Comm Coll (AZ)
Mohawk Valley Comm Coll (NY)
Morgan Comm Coll (CO)
Mt. San Antonio Coll (CA)
Muskegon Comm Coll (MI)
New Mexico Jr Coll (NM)
New River Comm Coll (VA)
North Central Texas Coll (TX)
Northland Comm and Tech Coll (MN)
Northwest Coll (WY)
Odessa Coll (TX)
Ohio Tech Coll (OH)
Oklahoma Tech Coll (OK)
Olympic Coll (WA)
Orange Coast Coll (CA)
Ozarks Tech Comm Coll (MO)
Palomar Coll (CA)
Panola Coll (TX)
Paris Jr Coll (TX)
Pasadena City Coll (CA)
Pennsylvania Highlands Comm Coll (PA)
Pittsburgh Tech Inst, Oakdale (PA)
Pueblo Comm Coll (CO)
Rend Lake Coll (IL)
Renton Tech Coll (WA)
Ridgewater Coll (MN)
Rock Valley Coll (IL)
Rogue Comm Coll (OR)
St. Charles Comm Coll (MO)
St. Philip's Coll (TX)
Salt Lake Comm Coll (UT)
San Jacinto Coll District (TX)
San Juan Coll (NM)
Schoolcraft Coll (MI)
Shawnee Comm Coll (IL)
Sheridan Coll (WY)
Southeast Comm Coll, Lincoln Campus (NE)
Southeastern Comm Coll (IA)
Southeast Tech Inst (SD)
Southwestern Oregon Comm Coll (OR)
State U of New York Coll of Technology at Alfred (NY)
Tallahassee Comm Coll (FL)
Tarrant County Coll District (TX)
Texarkana Coll (TX)
Thaddeus Stevens Coll of Technology (PA)
Treasure Valley Comm Coll (OR)

Truckee Meadows Comm Coll (NV)
Tyler Jr Coll (TX)
U of New Mexico–Gallup (NM)
Victor Valley Coll (CA)
Wayne County Comm Coll District (MI)
Western Iowa Tech Comm Coll (IA)
Western Nevada Coll (NV)
Western Piedmont Comm Coll (NC)
Western Texas Coll (TX)
Western Wyoming Comm Coll (WY)
Westmoreland County Comm Coll (PA)
White Mountains Comm Coll (NH)
Williston State Coll (ND)

WELL DRILLING
Westmoreland County Comm Coll (PA)

WILDLAND/FOREST FIREFIGHTING AND INVESTIGATION
Antelope Valley Coll (CA)
Fox Valley Tech Coll (WI)

WILDLIFE BIOLOGY
Dodge City Comm Coll (KS)
Eastern Arizona Coll (AZ)

WILDLIFE, FISH AND WILDLANDS SCIENCE AND MANAGEMENT
Barton County Comm Coll (KS)
Casper Coll (WY)
Eastern Wyoming Coll (WY)
Feather River Coll (CA)
Front Range Comm Coll (CO)
Garrett Coll (MD)
Laramie County Comm Coll (WY)
Mt. San Antonio Coll (CA)
Ogeechee Tech Coll (GA)
Penn State DuBois (PA)
Potomac State Coll of West Virginia U (WV)
Shawnee Comm Coll (IL)
Treasure Valley Comm Coll (OR)
Western Wyoming Comm Coll (WY)

WINE STEWARD/SOMMELIER
Cayuga County Comm Coll (NY)
Niagara County Comm Coll (NY)

WOMEN'S STUDIES
Casper Coll (WY)
Cerritos Coll (CA)
Palomar Coll (CA)
Sierra Coll (CA)

WOOD SCIENCE AND WOOD PRODUCTS/PULP AND PAPER TECHNOLOGY
Dabney S. Lancaster Comm Coll (VA)
Kennebec Valley Comm Coll (ME)
Ogeechee Tech Coll (GA)
Potomac State Coll of West Virginia U (WV)

WOODWIND INSTRUMENTS
Itawamba Comm Coll (MS)

WOODWORKING
Vincennes U (IN)

WORD PROCESSING
ETI Tech Coll of Niles (OH)
Galveston Coll (TX)
Kellogg Comm Coll (MI)
Lorain County Comm Coll (OH)
North Central Texas Coll (TX)
Richland Comm Coll (IL)
Seminole State Coll of Florida (FL)
Stark State Coll (OH)
Western Wyoming Comm Coll (WY)

WRITING
Allen Comm Coll (KS)
Austin Comm Coll District (TX)
Cayuga County Comm Coll (NY)

YOUTH MINISTRY
Hesston Coll (KS)

YOUTH SERVICES
Midlands Tech Coll (SC)

ZOOLOGY/ANIMAL BIOLOGY
Cerritos Coll (CA)
South Florida State Coll (FL)

Associate Degree Programs at Four-Year Colleges

ACCOUNTING
Baker Coll (MI)
Berkeley Coll–New York City
  Campus (NY)
California U of Pennsylvania (PA)
Calumet Coll of Saint Joseph (IN)
Caribbean U (PR)
Champlain Coll (VT)
Cleary U (MI)
Colorado Mountain Coll, Glenwood
  Springs (CO)
Colorado Mountain Coll, Steamboat
  Springs (CO)
Davenport U, Grand Rapids (MI)
Franciscan U of Steubenville (OH)
Hawai`i Pacific U (HI)
Hobe Sound Bible Coll (FL)
Humphreys Coll (CA)
Husson U (ME)
Immaculata U (PA)
Indiana Wesleyan U (IN)
Inter American U of Puerto Rico,
  Aguadilla Campus (PR)
Inter American U of Puerto Rico,
  Barranquitas Campus (PR)
Inter American U of Puerto Rico,
  Bayamón Campus (PR)
Inter American U of Puerto Rico,
  Fajardo Campus (PR)
Inter American U of Puerto Rico,
  Guayama Campus (PR)
Inter American U of Puerto Rico,
  Metropolitan Campus (PR)
Inter American U of Puerto Rico,
  Ponce Campus (PR)
Inter American U of Puerto Rico, San
  Germán Campus (PR)
Johnson State Coll (VT)
Maria Coll (NY)
Monroe Coll, Bronx (NY)
Mount Aloysius Coll (PA)
Mount Marty Coll (SD)
Mount St. Joseph U (OH)
Muhlenberg Coll (PA)
Oakland City U (IN)
Palm Beach State Coll (FL)
Post U (CT)
Rasmussen Coll Appleton (WI)
Rasmussen Coll Aurora (IL)
Rasmussen Coll Blaine (MN)
Rasmussen Coll Bloomington (MN)
Rasmussen Coll Brooklyn Park (MN)
Rasmussen Coll Eagan (MN)
Rasmussen Coll Fort Myers (FL)
Rasmussen Coll Green Bay (WI)
Rasmussen Coll Kansas City/
  Overland Park (KS)
Rasmussen Coll Lake Elmo/
  Woodbury (MN)
Rasmussen Coll Land O' Lakes (FL)
Rasmussen Coll Mankato (MN)
Rasmussen Coll Mokena/Tinley Park
  (IL)
Rasmussen Coll Moorhead (MN)
Rasmussen Coll New Port Richey
  (FL)
Rasmussen Coll Ocala (FL)
Rasmussen Coll Romeoville/Joliet
  (IL)
Rasmussen Coll St. Cloud (MN)
Rasmussen Coll Tampa/Brandon
  (FL)
Rasmussen Coll Topeka (KS)
Rasmussen Coll Wausau (WI)
Rogers State U (OK)
Saint Francis U (PA)
Shawnee State U (OH)
Southern Adventist U (TN)
Southern New Hampshire U (NH)
State Coll of Florida Manatee-
  Sarasota (FL)
Stratford U, Newport News (VA)
Thiel Coll (PA)
Thomas Coll (ME)
Thomas More Coll (KY)
Tiffin U (OH)
Trine U (IN)
Union Coll (NE)
Universidad del Turabo (PR)
The U of Findlay (OH)
U of Rio Grande (OH)
U of the Potomac (DC)
U of the Virgin Islands (VI)
Utah Valley U (UT)
Walsh U (OH)
Webber International U (FL)
Wright State U–Lake Campus (OH)
Youngstown State U (OH)

ACCOUNTING AND BUSINESS/
MANAGEMENT
Kansas State U (KS)
Stevens-Henager Coll, Boise (ID)

ACCOUNTING AND FINANCE
Ohio Christian U (OH)

ACCOUNTING RELATED
Florida National U (FL)
Montana State U Billings (MT)

ACCOUNTING TECHNOLOGY
AND BOOKKEEPING
American Public U System (WV)
Ferris State U (MI)
Florida National U (FL)
Hickey Coll (MO)
Hilbert Coll (NY)
International Business Coll, Fort
  Wayne (IN)
Kent State U at Geauga (OH)
Lewis-Clark State Coll (ID)
Miami U (OH)
Montana State U Billings (MT)
Montana Tech of The U of Montana
  (MT)
New York City Coll of Technology of
  the City U of New York (NY)
Pennsylvania Coll of Technology
  (PA)
Polk State Coll (FL)
State U of New York Coll of
  Agriculture and Technology at
  Cobleskill (NY)
State U of New York Coll of
  Technology at Canton (NY)
State U of New York Coll of
  Technology at Delhi (NY)
Sullivan U (KY)
The U of Akron (OH)
U of Montana (MT)
U of Rio Grande (OH)
The U of Toledo (OH)
Valencia Coll (FL)

ACTING
Academy of Art U (CA)
Pacific Union Coll (CA)

ADMINISTRATIVE ASSISTANT
AND SECRETARIAL SCIENCE
Arkansas Tech U (AR)
Baker Coll (MI)
Ball State U (IN)
Campbellsville U (KY)
Clayton State U (GA)
Concordia Coll–New York (NY)
Dickinson State U (ND)
Eastern Kentucky U (KY)

EDP U of Puerto Rico (PR)
EDP U of Puerto Rico–San
  Sebastian (PR)
Faith Baptist Bible Coll and
  Theological Seminary (IA)
Fort Hays State U (KS)
Hickey Coll (MO)
Hobe Sound Bible Coll (FL)
Humphreys Coll (CA)
Idaho State U (ID)
Inter American U of Puerto Rico, San
  Germán Campus (PR)
International Business Coll, Fort
  Wayne (IN)
Kuyper Coll (MI)
Lewis-Clark State Coll (ID)
Miami U (OH)
Montana State U Billings (MT)
Montana Tech of The U of Montana
  (MT)
Ohio U–Chillicothe (OH)
Palm Beach State Coll (FL)
Rider U (NJ)
State Coll of Florida Manatee-
  Sarasota (FL)
Tennessee State U (TN)
Universidad Adventista de las
  Antillas (PR)
The U of Akron (OH)
U of Rio Grande (OH)
Washburn U (KS)
Weber State U (UT)
Welch Coll (TN)
Williams Baptist Coll (AR)
Wright State U–Lake Campus (OH)

ADULT AND CONTINUING
EDUCATION
ADMINISTRATION
Concordia Coll–New York (NY)

ADULT DEVELOPMENT AND
AGING
Madonna U (MI)

ADVERTISING
Academy of Art U (CA)
Fashion Inst of Technology (NY)
State Coll of Florida Manatee-
  Sarasota (FL)

AERONAUTICAL/AEROSPACE
ENGINEERING TECHNOLOGY
Vaughn Coll of Aeronautics and
  Technology (NY)

AERONAUTICS/AVIATION/
AEROSPACE SCIENCE AND
TECHNOLOGY
Embry-Riddle Aeronautical U–
  Worldwide (FL)
Liberty U (VA)
Montana State U (MT)
Ohio U (OH)
Pacific Union Coll (CA)
Purdue U (IN)
Vaughn Coll of Aeronautics and
  Technology (NY)

AEROSPACE, AERONAUTICAL
AND ASTRONAUTICAL/SPACE
ENGINEERING
Embry-Riddle Aeronautical U–
  Worldwide (FL)

AFRICAN AMERICAN/BLACK
STUDIES
State Coll of Florida Manatee-
  Sarasota (FL)

AGRIBUSINESS
Southern Arkansas U–Magnolia
  (AR)
State U of New York Coll of
  Agriculture and Technology at
  Cobleskill (NY)
Vermont Tech Coll (VT)
Wright State U–Lake Campus (OH)

AGRICULTURAL BUSINESS
AND MANAGEMENT
Coll of Coastal Georgia (GA)
Colorado Mesa U (CO)
Dickinson State U (ND)
North Carolina State U (NC)
State U of New York Coll of
  Agriculture and Technology at
  Cobleskill (NY)
U of New Hampshire (NH)

AGRICULTURAL BUSINESS
AND MANAGEMENT RELATED
Penn State Abington (PA)
Penn State Altoona (PA)
Penn State Beaver (PA)
Penn State Berks (PA)
Penn State Brandywine (PA)
Penn State Erie, The Behrend Coll
  (PA)
Penn State Greater Allegheny (PA)
Penn State Hazleton (PA)
Penn State Lehigh Valley (PA)
Penn State New Kensington (PA)
Penn State Schuylkill (PA)
Penn State Wilkes-Barre (PA)
Penn State Worthington Scranton
  (PA)
Penn State York (PA)

AGRICULTURAL BUSINESS
TECHNOLOGY
Wright State U (OH)

AGRICULTURAL PRODUCTION
U of the Fraser Valley (BC, Canada)
Western Kentucky U (KY)

AGRICULTURE
North Carolina State U (NC)
South Dakota State U (SD)
State U of New York Coll of
  Agriculture and Technology at
  Cobleskill (NY)
U of Delaware (DE)

AGRICULTURE AND
AGRICULTURE OPERATIONS
RELATED
Murray State U (KY)

AGRONOMY AND CROP
SCIENCE
State U of New York Coll of
  Agriculture and Technology at
  Cobleskill (NY)

AIRCRAFT POWERPLANT
TECHNOLOGY
Embry-Riddle Aeronautical U–
  Daytona (FL)
Embry-Riddle Aeronautical U–
  Worldwide (FL)
Hallmark U (TX)
Idaho State U (ID)
Middle Georgia State U (GA)
Pennsylvania Coll of Technology
  (PA)

AIRFRAME MECHANICS AND
AIRCRAFT MAINTENANCE
TECHNOLOGY
Hallmark U (TX)
Lewis U (IL)
St. Petersburg Coll (FL)

AIRLINE FLIGHT ATTENDANT
Liberty U (VA)

AIRLINE PILOT AND FLIGHT
CREW
Lewis U (IL)
Middle Georgia State U (GA)
Palm Beach State Coll (FL)
Polk State Coll (FL)
Southern Illinois U Carbondale (IL)
Southern Utah U (UT)
Utah Valley U (UT)

AIR TRAFFIC CONTROL
LeTourneau U (TX)
Lewis U (IL)
Middle Georgia State U (GA)

ALLIED HEALTH AND MEDICAL
ASSISTING SERVICES RELATED
Florida National U (FL)
Jones Coll, Jacksonville (FL)
National U (CA)
Nebraska Methodist Coll (NE)
Stratford U, Falls Church (VA)
Widener U (PA)

ALLIED HEALTH DIAGNOSTIC,
INTERVENTION, AND
TREATMENT PROFESSIONS
RELATED
Ball State U (IN)
Cameron U (OK)
Cox Coll (MO)
Gwynedd Mercy U (PA)
Pennsylvania Coll of Technology
  (PA)

AMERICAN GOVERNMENT AND
POLITICS
State Coll of Florida Manatee-
  Sarasota (FL)

AMERICAN INDIAN/NATIVE
AMERICAN STUDIES
Inst of American Indian Arts (NM)
Southwestern Oklahoma State U
  (OK)

AMERICAN NATIVE/NATIVE
AMERICAN LANGUAGES
Idaho State U (ID)

AMERICAN SIGN LANGUAGE
(ASL)
Bethel Coll (IN)
Idaho State U (ID)
Madonna U (MI)
Weber State U (UT)

AMERICAN STUDIES
State Coll of Florida Manatee-
  Sarasota (FL)

ANIMAL/LIVESTOCK
HUSBANDRY AND
PRODUCTION
North Carolina State U (NC)
Southern Utah U (UT)
U of the Fraser Valley (BC, Canada)

ANIMAL SCIENCES
Becker Coll (MA)

State U of New York Coll of Agriculture and Technology at Cobleskill (NY)
U of New Hampshire (NH)

ANIMAL TRAINING
Becker Coll (MA)

ANIMATION, INTERACTIVE TECHNOLOGY, VIDEO GRAPHICS AND SPECIAL EFFECTS
Academy of Art U (CA)
Colorado Mesa U (CO)
Ferris State U (MI)
New England Inst of Technology (RI)

APPAREL AND ACCESSORIES MARKETING
U of Montana (MT)

APPAREL AND TEXTILE MANUFACTURING
Academy of Art U (CA)
Fashion Inst of Technology (NY)

APPAREL AND TEXTILE MARKETING MANAGEMENT
Academy of Art U (CA)
FIDM/Fashion Inst of Design & Merchandising, Los Angeles Campus (CA)
FIDM/Fashion Inst of Design & Merchandising, San Francisco Campus (CA)
U of the Incarnate Word (TX)

APPAREL AND TEXTILES
Palm Beach State Coll (FL)

APPLIED HORTICULTURE/ HORTICULTURAL BUSINESS SERVICES RELATED
U of Massachusetts Amherst (MA)

APPLIED HORTICULTURE/ HORTICULTURE OPERATIONS
Pennsylvania Coll of Technology (PA)
State U of New York Coll of Technology at Delhi (NY)
U of Massachusetts Amherst (MA)
U of New Hampshire (NH)
U of the Fraser Valley (BC, Canada)

APPLIED MATHEMATICS
Central Methodist U (MO)

APPLIED PSYCHOLOGY
Christian Brothers U (TN)

ARCHEOLOGY
Weber State U (UT)

ARCHITECTURAL DRAFTING AND CAD/CADD
New York City Coll of Technology of the City U of New York (NY)
Universidad del Turabo (PR)

ARCHITECTURAL ENGINEERING TECHNOLOGY
Baker Coll (MI)
Bluefield State Coll (WV)
Ferris State U (MI)
New England Inst of Technology (RI)
Penn State Worthington Scranton (PA)
State U of New York Coll of Technology at Delhi (NY)
Vermont Tech Coll (VT)

ARCHITECTURAL TECHNOLOGY
New York Inst of Technology (NY)
Pennsylvania Coll of Technology (PA)

ARCHITECTURE RELATED
Abilene Christian U (TX)

ART
Coll of Coastal Georgia (GA)
Felician U (NJ)
Hannibal-LaGrange U (MO)
Indiana Wesleyan U (IN)
Lourdes U (OH)
Middle Georgia State U (GA)
Mount St. Joseph U (OH)
Oakland City U (IN)
Palm Beach State Coll (FL)

State Coll of Florida Manatee-Sarasota (FL)
State U of New York Empire State Coll (NY)
U of Rio Grande (OH)

ART HISTORY, CRITICISM AND CONSERVATION
John Cabot U (Italy)
Palm Beach State Coll (FL)
State Coll of Florida Manatee-Sarasota (FL)
Thomas More Coll (KY)

ASIAN STUDIES
State Coll of Florida Manatee-Sarasota (FL)

ASTRONOMY
State Coll of Florida Manatee-Sarasota (FL)

ATHLETIC TRAINING
Shawnee State U (OH)
The U of Akron (OH)

AUTOBODY/COLLISION AND REPAIR TECHNOLOGY
Academy of Art U (CA)
Idaho State U (ID)
Lewis-Clark State Coll (ID)
Montana State U Billings (MT)
New England Inst of Technology (RI)
Pennsylvania Coll of Technology (PA)
Utah Valley U (UT)

AUTOMOBILE/AUTOMOTIVE MECHANICS TECHNOLOGY
Baker Coll (MI)
Colorado Mesa U (CO)
Dixie State U (UT)
Ferris State U (MI)
Idaho State U (ID)
Lewis-Clark State Coll (ID)
Midland Coll (TX)
Montana State U Billings (MT)
Montana Tech of The U of Montana (MT)
New England Inst of Technology (RI)
Pennsylvania Coll of Technology (PA)
Pittsburg State U (KS)
Southern Adventist U (TN)
State U of New York Coll of Technology at Canton (NY)
State U of New York Coll of Technology at Delhi (NY)
Utah Valley U (UT)
Weber State U (UT)

AUTOMOTIVE ENGINEERING TECHNOLOGY
Farmingdale State Coll (NY)
Vermont Tech Coll (VT)

AVIATION/AIRWAY MANAGEMENT
Embry-Riddle Aeronautical U–Worldwide (FL)
Polk State Coll (FL)
Vaughn Coll of Aeronautics and Technology (NY)

AVIONICS MAINTENANCE TECHNOLOGY
Excelsior Coll (NY)
Hallmark U (TX)
Middle Georgia State U (GA)
Universidad del Este (PR)
Vaughn Coll of Aeronautics and Technology (NY)

BAKING AND PASTRY ARTS
Colorado Mesa U (CO)
The Culinary Inst of America (NY)
Johnson & Wales U (FL)
Johnson & Wales U (RI)
Kendall Coll (IL)
Monroe Coll, Bronx (NY)
Newbury Coll (MA)
Pennsylvania Coll of Technology (PA)
Southern New Hampshire U (NH)
Stratford U (MD)
Stratford U, Alexandria (VA)
Stratford U, Falls Church (VA)
Stratford U, Glen Allen (VA)
Stratford U, Newport News (VA)
Stratford U, Virginia Beach (VA)
Stratford U, Woodbridge (VA)

Sullivan U (KY)
Valencia Coll (FL)

BANKING AND FINANCIAL SUPPORT SERVICES
Brescia U (KY)
Hilbert Coll (NY)
St. Petersburg Coll (FL)
Touro Coll (NY)
Universidad Metropolitana (PR)

BEHAVIORAL SCIENCES
Colorado Mountain Coll, Glenwood Springs (CO)
Colorado Mountain Coll, Steamboat Springs (CO)
Granite State Coll (NH)
Lewis-Clark State Coll (ID)
Loyola U Chicago (IL)

BIBLICAL STUDIES
Appalachian Bible Coll (WV)
Barclay Coll (KS)
Bethel Coll (IN)
Beulah Heights U (GA)
Calvary Bible Coll and Theological Seminary (MO)
Campbellsville U (KY)
Carver Coll (GA)
Coll of Biblical Studies–Houston (TX)
Corban U (OR)
Covenant Coll (GA)
Dallas Baptist U (TX)
Faith Baptist Bible Coll and Theological Seminary (IA)
Grace Coll (IN)
Houghton Coll (NY)
Kentucky Mountain Bible Coll (KY)
Kuyper Coll (MI)
Laurel U (NC)
Lincoln Christian U (IL)
Mid-Atlantic Christian U (NC)
Nyack Coll (NY)
Point U (GA)
Simpson U (CA)
Southeastern Bible Coll (AL)
Southern Adventist U (TN)
Southern California Seminary (CA)
Trinity Bible Coll (ND)
Trinity Coll of Florida (FL)
U of Valley Forge (PA)
Welch Coll (TN)

BIOLOGICAL AND BIOMEDICAL SCIENCES RELATED
Gwynedd Mercy U (PA)
Roberts Wesleyan Coll (NY)

BIOLOGICAL AND PHYSICAL SCIENCES
Colorado Mountain Coll, Glenwood Springs (CO)
Colorado Mountain Coll, Steamboat Springs (CO)
Ferris State U (MI)
Jefferson Coll of Health Sciences (VA)
Oklahoma Wesleyan U (OK)
Penn State Altoona (PA)
Penn State Beaver (PA)
Penn State Greater Allegheny (PA)
Penn State New Kensington (PA)
Penn State Schuylkill (PA)
Trine U (IN)
Valparaiso U (IN)
Welch Coll (TN)

BIOLOGY/BIOLOGICAL SCIENCES
Cleveland U–Kansas City (KS)
Coll of Coastal Georgia (GA)
Colorado Mountain Coll, Glenwood Springs (CO)
Colorado Mountain Coll, Steamboat Springs (CO)
Dallas Baptist U (TX)
Dalton State Coll (GA)
Immaculata U (PA)
Indiana Wesleyan U (IN)
Lourdes U (OH)
Oklahoma Wesleyan U (OK)
Palm Beach State Coll (FL)
Pine Manor Coll (MA)
Rogers State U (OK)
Shawnee State U (OH)
State Coll of Florida Manatee-Sarasota (FL)

State U of New York Coll of Agriculture and Technology at Cobleskill (NY)
Thomas More Coll (KY)
U of New Hampshire at Manchester (NH)
U of Rio Grande (OH)
Utah Valley U (UT)
Welch Coll (TN)
Wright State U (OH)
Wright State U–Lake Campus (OH)
York Coll of Pennsylvania (PA)

BIOLOGY/BIOTECHNOLOGY LABORATORY TECHNICIAN
State U of New York Coll of Agriculture and Technology at Cobleskill (NY)
Weber State U (UT)

BIOLOGY TEACHER EDUCATION
State Coll of Florida Manatee-Sarasota (FL)

BIOMEDICAL TECHNOLOGY
Indiana U–Purdue U Indianapolis (IN)
Penn State Altoona (PA)
Penn State Berks (PA)
Penn State Erie, The Behrend Coll (PA)
Penn State Hazleton (PA)
Penn State New Kensington (PA)
Penn State Schuylkill (PA)
Penn State York (PA)
U of Arkansas for Medical Sciences (AR)

BIOTECHNOLOGY
EDP U of Puerto Rico (PR)
Inter American U of Puerto Rico, Barranquitas Campus (PR)
Universidad del Turabo (PR)

BLOOD BANK TECHNOLOGY
Rasmussen Coll St. Cloud (MN)

BOTANY/PLANT BIOLOGY
Palm Beach State Coll (FL)

BROADCAST JOURNALISM
Evangel U (MO)

BUILDING/CONSTRUCTION FINISHING, MANAGEMENT, AND INSPECTION RELATED
Baker Coll (MI)
John Brown U (AR)
Palm Beach State Coll (FL)
Pratt Inst (NY)
Weber State U (UT)

BUILDING/CONSTRUCTION SITE MANAGEMENT
State U of New York Coll of Technology at Canton (NY)
Wentworth Inst of Technology (MA)

BUILDING CONSTRUCTION TECHNOLOGY
Southern Utah U (UT)
Wentworth Inst of Technology (MA)

BUILDING/HOME/ CONSTRUCTION INSPECTION
Utah Valley U (UT)

BUILDING/PROPERTY MAINTENANCE
Southern Adventist U (TN)
Utah Valley U (UT)

BUSINESS ADMINISTRATION AND MANAGEMENT
Anderson U (IN)
Austin Peay State U (TN)
Baker Coll (MI)
Bay Path U (MA)
Beacon Coll (FL)
Berkeley Coll–New York City Campus (NY)
Berkeley Coll–Woodland Park Campus (NJ)
Bethel Coll (TN)
Beulah Heights U (GA)
Bryan Coll (TN)
California U of Pennsylvania (PA)
Calumet Coll of Saint Joseph (IN)
Cameron U (OK)
Campbellsville U (KY)

Caribbean U (PR)
Carroll Coll (MT)
Central Baptist Coll (AR)
Chaminade U of Honolulu (HI)
City Vision U (MO)
Cleary U (MI)
Coll of Coastal Georgia (GA)
Coll of Saint Mary (NE)
Colorado Mountain Coll, Glenwood Springs (CO)
Colorado Mountain Coll, Steamboat Springs (CO)
Columbia Southern U (AL)
Concordia Coll–New York (NY)
Corban U (OR)
Cornerstone U (MI)
Dakota State U (SD)
Dallas Baptist U (TX)
Dalton State Coll (GA)
Davenport U, Grand Rapids (MI)
Defiance Coll (OH)
Dixie State U (UT)
EDP U of Puerto Rico (PR)
EDP U of Puerto Rico–San Sebastian (PR)
Elmira Coll (NY)
Embry-Riddle Aeronautical U–Worldwide (FL)
Excelsior Coll (NY)
Farmingdale State Coll (NY)
Faulkner U (AL)
Felician U (NJ)
Fisher Coll (MA)
Five Towns Coll (NY)
Florida National U (FL)
Franciscan U of Steubenville (OH)
Geneva Coll (PA)
Hallmark U (TX)
Hampton U (VA)
Hawai`i Pacific U (HI)
Hilbert Coll (NY)
Humphreys Coll (CA)
Husson U (ME)
Immaculata U (PA)
Indiana Wesleyan U (IN)
Inter American U of Puerto Rico, Aguadilla Campus (PR)
Inter American U of Puerto Rico, Barranquitas Campus (PR)
Inter American U of Puerto Rico, Bayamón Campus (PR)
Inter American U of Puerto Rico, Fajardo Campus (PR)
Inter American U of Puerto Rico, Guayama Campus (PR)
Inter American U of Puerto Rico, Ponce Campus (PR)
Inter American U of Puerto Rico, San Germán Campus (PR)
Jarvis Christian Coll (TX)
John Cabot U (Italy)
Johnson State Coll (VT)
Jones Coll, Jacksonville (FL)
Kansas Wesleyan U (KS)
Lincoln Coll of New England, Southington (CT)
Lock Haven U of Pennsylvania (PA)
Long Island U–LIU Brooklyn (NY)
Loyola U Chicago (IL)
Madonna U (MI)
Maria Coll (NY)
Marian U (IN)
Marietta Coll (OH)
McKendree U (IL)
Medgar Evers Coll of the City U of New York (NY)
Missouri Baptist U (MO)
Monroe Coll, Bronx (NY)
Montana State U Billings (MT)
Montreat Coll, Montreat (NC)
Mount Aloysius Coll (PA)
Mount Marty Coll (SD)
Mount St. Joseph U (OH)
Mount Saint Mary's U (CA)
Muhlenberg Coll (PA)
National U (CA)
Newbury Coll (MA)
New England Coll (NH)
New England Inst of Technology (RI)
Newman U (KS)
New Mexico Inst of Mining and Technology (NM)
New York Inst of Technology (NY)
Niagara U (NY)
Nichols Coll (MA)
Nyack Coll (NY)
Oakland City U (IN)
Ohio Christian U (OH)
Ohio Dominican U (OH)
Ohio U–Chillicothe (OH)

Oklahoma Wesleyan U (OK)
Peirce Coll (PA)
Pennsylvania Coll of Technology (PA)
Pine Manor Coll (MA)
Point U (GA)
Post U (CT)
Providence Coll (RI)
Rasmussen Coll Appleton (WI)
Rasmussen Coll Aurora (IL)
Rasmussen Coll Blaine (MN)
Rasmussen Coll Bloomington (MN)
Rasmussen Coll Brooklyn Park (MN)
Rasmussen Coll Eagan (MN)
Rasmussen Coll Fort Myers (FL)
Rasmussen Coll Green Bay (WI)
Rasmussen Coll Kansas City/
  Overland Park (KS)
Rasmussen Coll Lake Elmo/
  Woodbury (MN)
Rasmussen Coll Land O' Lakes (FL)
Rasmussen Coll Mankato (MN)
Rasmussen Coll Mokena/Tinley Park
  (IL)
Rasmussen Coll Moorhead (MN)
Rasmussen Coll New Port Richey
  (FL)
Rasmussen Coll Ocala (FL)
Rasmussen Coll Romeoville/Joliet
  (IL)
Rasmussen Coll St. Cloud (MN)
Rasmussen Coll Tampa/Brandon
  (FL)
Rasmussen Coll Topeka (KS)
Rasmussen Coll Wausau (WI)
Regent U (VA)
Robert Morris U Illinois (IL)
Rogers State U (OK)
Rust Coll (MS)
St. Francis Coll (NY)
Saint Francis U (PA)
St. Gregory's U, Shawnee (OK)
St. John's U (NY)
Saint Joseph's U (PA)
Saint Leo U (FL)
St. Petersburg Coll (FL)
Saint Peter's U (NJ)
St. Thomas Aquinas Coll (NY)
Shawnee State U (OH)
Shorter U (GA)
Southern Adventist U (TN)
Southern New Hampshire U (NH)
Southwestern Oklahoma State U
  (OK)
State Coll of Florida Manatee-
  Sarasota (FL)
State U of New York Coll of
  Agriculture and Technology at
  Cobleskill (NY)
State U of New York Coll of
  Technology at Canton (NY)
State U of New York Coll of
  Technology at Delhi (NY)
Sullivan U (KY)
Taylor U (IN)
Thomas Coll (ME)
Thomas More Coll (KY)
Tiffin U (OH)
Toccoa Falls Coll (GA)
Touro Coll (NY)
Trevecca Nazarene U (TN)
Trine U (IN)
Trinity Bible Coll (ND)
Tulane U (LA)
Union Coll (NE)
Universidad Adventista de las Antillas
  (PR)
Universidad del Turabo (PR)
The U of Akron (OH)
The U of Findlay (OH)
U of Maine at Augusta (ME)
U of Maine at Fort Kent (ME)
U of Maine at Presque Isle (ME)
U of Management and Technology
  (VA)
The U of Montana Western (MT)
U of New Hampshire at Manchester
  (NH)
U of New Haven (CT)
U of Pennsylvania (PA)
U of Pikeville (KY)
U of Rio Grande (OH)
The U of Scranton (PA)
U of the Cumberlands (KY)
U of the Fraser Valley (BC, Canada)
U of the Incarnate Word (TX)
U of the Potomac (DC)
U of the Virgin Islands (VI)
Utah Valley U (UT)
Valencia Coll (FL)
Vermont Tech Coll (VT)
Villa Maria Coll (NY)

Walsh U (OH)
Wayland Baptist U (TX)
Webber International U (FL)
Welch Coll (TN)
Western Kentucky U (KY)
Williams Baptist Coll (AR)
Wright State U (OH)
Wright State U–Lake Campus (OH)
York Coll of Pennsylvania (PA)
Youngstown State U (OH)

**BUSINESS ADMINISTRATION,
MANAGEMENT AND
OPERATIONS RELATED**
Bay Path U (MA)
Dixie State U (UT)
Eastern Oregon U (OR)
Embry-Riddle Aeronautical U–
  Worldwide (FL)

**BUSINESS AND PERSONAL/
FINANCIAL SERVICES
MARKETING**
Dixie State U (UT)

**BUSINESS AUTOMATION/
TECHNOLOGY/DATA ENTRY**
Colorado Mesa U (CO)
Hallmark U (TX)
Montana State U Billings (MT)
The U of Akron (OH)
U of Rio Grande (OH)
Utah Valley U (UT)

BUSINESS/COMMERCE
Adams State U (CO)
Alderson Broaddus U (WV)
Alvernia U (PA)
American Public U System (WV)
Bethel Coll (IN)
Brescia U (KY)
Champlain Coll (VT)
Christian Brothers U (TN)
Coll of Staten Island of the City U of
  New York (NY)
Columbia Coll (MO)
Delaware Valley U (PA)
Ferris State U (MI)
Gannon U (PA)
Glenville State Coll (WV)
Granite State Coll (NH)
Idaho State U (ID)
Kent State U at Geauga (OH)
Limestone Coll (SC)
Lourdes U (OH)
Mayville State U (ND)
Metropolitan Coll of New York (NY)
Miami U (OH)
Midland Coll (TX)
Montana State U Billings (MT)
Mount Vernon Nazarene U (OH)
Murray State U (KY)
New Mexico State U (NM)
Olivet Nazarene U (IL)
Pacific Union Coll (CA)
Penn State Abington (PA)
Penn State Altoona (PA)
Penn State Beaver (PA)
Penn State Berks (PA)
Penn State Brandywine (PA)
Penn State Erie, The Behrend Coll
  (PA)
Penn State Greater Allegheny (PA)
Penn State Harrisburg (PA)
Penn State Hazleton (PA)
Penn State Lehigh Valley (PA)
Penn State New Kensington (PA)
Penn State Schuylkill (PA)
Penn State Wilkes-Barre (PA)
Penn State Worthington Scranton
  (PA)
Penn State York (PA)
Southern Arkansas U–Magnolia (AR)
Southern Nazarene U (OK)
Southern Utah U (UT)
Southwest Baptist U (MO)
Spalding U (KY)
State Coll of Florida Manatee-
  Sarasota (FL)
State U of New York Empire State
  Coll (NY)
Stratford U, Falls Church (VA)
Stratford U, Glen Allen (VA)
Stratford U, Newport News (VA)
Stratford U, Woodbridge (VA)
Thomas Coll (ME)
Thomas More Coll (KY)
Tulane U (LA)
U of Bridgeport (CT)
U of Maine at Fort Kent (ME)
U of Massachusetts Lowell (MA)

U of New Hampshire (NH)
U of Southern Indiana (IN)
The U of Toledo (OH)
Wright State U (OH)
Youngstown State U (OH)

**BUSINESS, MANAGEMENT, AND
MARKETING RELATED**
Ball State U (IN)
Five Towns Coll (NY)
Florida National U (FL)
Oklahoma Wesleyan U (OK)

**BUSINESS/MANAGERIAL
ECONOMICS**
Campbellsville U (KY)
Hawai'i Pacific U (HI)
Saint Peter's U (NJ)
State Coll of Florida Manatee-
  Sarasota (FL)

**BUSINESS TEACHER
EDUCATION**
Wright State U (OH)

**CABINETMAKING AND
MILLWORK**
Utah Valley U (UT)

**CAD/CADD DRAFTING/DESIGN
TECHNOLOGY**
Ferris State U (MI)
Idaho State U (ID)
Missouri Southern State U (MO)
Montana Tech of The U of Montana
  (MT)
Shawnee State U (OH)
Southern Utah U (UT)
State U of New York Coll of
  Technology at Delhi (NY)

**CARDIOPULMONARY
TECHNOLOGY**
Inter American U of Puerto Rico,
  Barranquitas Campus (PR)

**CARDIOVASCULAR
TECHNOLOGY**
Arkansas Tech U (AR)
Mercy Coll of Ohio (OH)
Molloy Coll (NY)
Nebraska Methodist Coll (NE)
Pennsylvania Coll of Health Sciences
  (PA)
Polk State Coll (FL)
Sentara Coll of Health Sciences (VA)
Valencia Coll (FL)

CARPENTRY
Liberty U (VA)
Montana State U Billings (MT)
Montana Tech of The U of Montana
  (MT)
New England Inst of Technology (RI)
Southern Utah U (UT)

CASINO MANAGEMENT
National U (CA)

**CELL BIOLOGY AND
ANATOMICAL SCIENCES
RELATED**
National U (CA)

CERAMIC ARTS AND CERAMICS
Palm Beach State Coll (FL)

CHEMICAL TECHNOLOGY
Ball State U (IN)
Inter American U of Puerto Rico,
  Guayama Campus (PR)
Lawrence Technological U (MI)
New York City Coll of Technology of
  the City U of New York (NY)
State U of New York Coll of
  Agriculture and Technology at
  Cobleskill (NY)
Weber State U (UT)

CHEMISTRY
Central Methodist U (MO)
Coll of Coastal Georgia (GA)
Dalton State Coll (GA)
Immaculata U (PA)
Indiana Wesleyan U (IN)
Lindsey Wilson Coll (KY)
Ohio Dominican U (OH)
Oklahoma Wesleyan U (OK)
Palm Beach State Coll (FL)
Southern Arkansas U–Magnolia (AR)
State Coll of Florida Manatee-
  Sarasota (FL)
Thomas More Coll (KY)

U of Rio Grande (OH)
U of Saint Francis (IN)
U of the Incarnate Word (TX)
Utah Valley U (UT)
Wright State U (OH)
Wright State U–Lake Campus (OH)
York Coll of Pennsylvania (PA)

**CHEMISTRY TEACHER
EDUCATION**
State Coll of Florida Manatee-
  Sarasota (FL)

**CHILD-CARE AND SUPPORT
SERVICES MANAGEMENT**
Ferris State U (MI)
Polk State Coll (FL)
Post U (CT)
Southeast Missouri State U (MO)
State U of New York Coll of
  Agriculture and Technology at
  Cobleskill (NY)
State U of New York Coll of
  Technology at Canton (NY)
U of the Fraser Valley (BC, Canada)
Youngstown State U (OH)

CHILD-CARE PROVISION
American Public U System (WV)
Eastern Kentucky U (KY)
Louisiana State U at Alexandria (LA)
Mayville State U (ND)
Pennsylvania Coll of Technology (PA)

CHILD DEVELOPMENT
Arkansas Tech U (AR)
Evangel U (MO)
Franciscan U of Steubenville (OH)
Kuyper Coll (MI)
Lewis-Clark State Coll (ID)
Madonna U (MI)
Midland Coll (TX)
Ohio U (OH)
Ohio U–Chillicothe (OH)
Point U (GA)
Polk State Coll (FL)
Southern Utah U (UT)
State Coll of Florida Manatee-
  Sarasota (FL)
Weber State U (UT)
Youngstown State U (OH)

CHRISTIAN STUDIES
Inter American U of Puerto Rico,
  Metropolitan Campus (PR)
Oklahoma Baptist U (OK)
Oklahoma Wesleyan U (OK)
Ouachita Baptist U (AR)
Regent U (VA)

**CINEMATOGRAPHY AND FILM/
VIDEO PRODUCTION**
Academy of Art U (CA)
Clayton State U (GA)
FIDM/Fashion Inst of Design &
  Merchandising, Los Angeles
  Campus (CA)
Inst of American Indian Arts (NM)
New England Inst of Technology (RI)
Pacific Union Coll (CA)
Valencia Coll (FL)

**CIVIL ENGINEERING
TECHNOLOGY**
Bluefield State Coll (WV)
Fairmont State U (WV)
Ferris State U (MI)
Idaho State U (ID)
Montana Tech of The U of Montana
  (MT)
Murray State U (KY)
New England Inst of Technology (RI)
New York City Coll of Technology of
  the City U of New York (NY)
Pennsylvania Coll of Technology (PA)
State Coll of Florida Manatee-
  Sarasota (FL)
State U of New York Coll of
  Technology at Canton (NY)
U of Massachusetts Lowell (MA)
U of New Hampshire (NH)
U of Puerto Rico in Bayamón (PR)
Valencia Coll (FL)
Vermont Tech Coll (VT)
Youngstown State U (OH)

**CLASSICS AND CLASSICAL
LANGUAGES**
John Cabot U (Italy)

**CLINICAL LABORATORY
SCIENCE/MEDICAL
TECHNOLOGY**
Arkansas State U (AR)
Dalton State Coll (GA)
Dixie State U (UT)
New England Inst of Technology (RI)
Shawnee State U (OH)
U of Wisconsin–Parkside (WI)

**CLINICAL/MEDICAL
LABORATORY ASSISTANT**
New England Inst of Technology (RI)
U of Maine at Augusta (ME)
U of Maine at Presque Isle (ME)

**CLINICAL/MEDICAL
LABORATORY SCIENCE AND
ALLIED PROFESSIONS RELATED**
State U of New York Coll of
  Agriculture and Technology at
  Cobleskill (NY)
Youngstown State U (OH)

**CLINICAL/MEDICAL
LABORATORY TECHNOLOGY**
Baker Coll (MI)
Coll of Coastal Georgia (GA)
Colorado Mesa U (CO)
Dalton State Coll (GA)
Eastern Kentucky U (KY)
Farmingdale State Coll (NY)
Ferris State U (MI)
The George Washington U (DC)
Louisiana State U at Alexandria (LA)
Marshall U (WV)
Mount Aloysius Coll (PA)
Our Lady of the Lake Coll (LA)
Penn State Hazleton (PA)
Penn State Schuylkill (PA)
Rasmussen Coll Green Bay (WI)
Rasmussen Coll Lake Elmo/
  Woodbury (MN)
Rasmussen Coll Mankato (MN)
Rasmussen Coll Moorhead (MN)
Rasmussen Coll St. Cloud (MN)
St. Petersburg Coll (FL)
Southwestern Oklahoma State U (OK)
Tarleton State U (TX)
U of Maine at Presque Isle (ME)
U of Rio Grande (OH)
U of Saint Francis (IN)
Weber State U (UT)
Youngstown State U (OH)

**COMMERCIAL AND
ADVERTISING ART**
Academy of Art U (CA)
Baker Coll (MI)
California U of Pennsylvania (PA)
Colorado Mountain Coll, Glenwood
  Springs (CO)
Fashion Inst of Technology (NY)
Mitchell Coll (CT)
Mount Saint Mary's U (CA)
New York City Coll of Technology of
  the City U of New York (NY)
Nossi Coll of Art (TN)
Palm Beach State Coll (FL)
Pennsylvania Coll of Technology (PA)
Pratt Inst (NY)
Robert Morris U Illinois (IL)
Southern Adventist U (TN)
State Coll of Florida Manatee-
  Sarasota (FL)
State U of New York Coll of
  Agriculture and Technology at
  Cobleskill (NY)

COMMERCIAL PHOTOGRAPHY
Fashion Inst of Technology (NY)
Nossi Coll of Art (TN)

COMMUNICATION
Inter American U of Puerto Rico,
  Ponce Campus (PR)
John Cabot U (Italy)
National U (CA)
Thomas More Coll (KY)

**COMMUNICATION AND
JOURNALISM RELATED**
Immaculata U (PA)
Madonna U (MI)
Tulane U (LA)
Valparaiso U (IN)

**COMMUNICATION DISORDERS
SCIENCES AND SERVICES
RELATED**
Granite State Coll (NH)

COMMUNICATION SCIENCES AND DISORDERS
Ohio U–Chillicothe (OH)

COMMUNICATIONS TECHNOLOGIES AND SUPPORT SERVICES RELATED
Southern Adventist U (TN)

COMMUNICATIONS TECHNOLOGY
Colorado Mesa U (CO)
East Stroudsburg U of Pennsylvania (PA)

COMMUNITY HEALTH AND PREVENTIVE MEDICINE
National U (CA)
Utah Valley U (UT)

COMMUNITY HEALTH SERVICES COUNSELING
State Coll of Florida Manatee-Sarasota (FL)

COMMUNITY ORGANIZATION AND ADVOCACY
Elmira Coll (NY)
Metropolitan Coll of New York (NY)
State U of New York Empire State Coll (NY)
Touro Coll (NY)
The U of Akron (OH)
U of New Hampshire (NH)

COMPARATIVE LITERATURE
John Cabot U (Italy)
Palm Beach State Coll (FL)

COMPUTER AND INFORMATION SCIENCES
Beacon Coll (FL)
California U of Pennsylvania (PA)
Calumet Coll of Saint Joseph (IN)
Columbia Coll (MO)
Excelsior Coll (NY)
Husson U (ME)
Indiana Wesleyan U (IN)
Inter American U of Puerto Rico, Barranquitas Campus (PR)
Inter American U of Puerto Rico, Fajardo Campus (PR)
Inter American U of Puerto Rico, Ponce Campus (PR)
Jones Coll, Jacksonville (FL)
Lewis-Clark State Coll (ID)
Lincoln U (MO)
Manchester U (IN)
Montana State U Billings (MT)
National U (CA)
New England Inst of Technology (RI)
New York City Coll of Technology of the City U of New York (NY)
Penn State Schuylkill (PA)
Rogers State U (OK)
Southern New Hampshire U (NH)
State Coll of Florida Manatee-Sarasota (FL)
State U of New York Coll of Agriculture and Technology at Cobleskill (NY)
Troy U (AL)
Tulane U (LA)
Union Coll (NE)
Universidad del Turabo (PR)
The U of Findlay (OH)
The U of Toledo (OH)
Utah Valley U (UT)
Washburn U (KS)
Webber International U (FL)
Youngstown State U (OH)

COMPUTER AND INFORMATION SCIENCES AND SUPPORT SERVICES RELATED
Colorado Mountain Coll, Glenwood Springs (CO)
Inter American U of Puerto Rico, Guayama Campus (PR)
Montana State U Billings (MT)
Pace U (NY)
Pace U, Pleasantville Campus (NY)
Palm Beach State Coll (FL)
Universidad del Este (PR)
U of the Potomac (DC)

COMPUTER AND INFORMATION SCIENCES RELATED
Limestone Coll (SC)

Lindsey Wilson Coll (KY)
Madonna U (MI)
State Coll of Florida Manatee-Sarasota (FL)

COMPUTER AND INFORMATION SYSTEMS SECURITY
Davenport U, Grand Rapids (MI)
St. John's U (NY)
Stratford U, Falls Church (VA)
Stratford U, Glen Allen (VA)
Stratford U, Woodbridge (VA)
U of Maine at Fort Kent (ME)
U of the Potomac (DC)

COMPUTER ENGINEERING
Johnson & Wales U (RI)
New England Inst of Technology (RI)
The U of Scranton (PA)

COMPUTER ENGINEERING TECHNOLOGIES RELATED
Universidad del Turabo (PR)

COMPUTER ENGINEERING TECHNOLOGY
California U of Pennsylvania (PA)
Colorado Mountain Coll, Glenwood Springs (CO)
Colorado Mountain Coll, Steamboat Springs (CO)
Dalton State Coll (GA)
Eastern Kentucky U (KY)
Penn State New Kensington (PA)
Polk State Coll (FL)
St. Petersburg Coll (FL)
State Coll of Florida Manatee-Sarasota (FL)
U of Hartford (CT)
Valencia Coll (FL)
Vermont Tech Coll (VT)
Weber State U (UT)

COMPUTER GRAPHICS
EDP U of Puerto Rico (PR)
Purdue U (IN)
State Coll of Florida Manatee-Sarasota (FL)

COMPUTER/INFORMATION TECHNOLOGY SERVICES ADMINISTRATION RELATED
Berkeley Coll–New York City Campus (NY)
Berkeley Coll–Woodland Park Campus (NJ)
Limestone Coll (SC)
Maria Coll (NY)
Pennsylvania Coll of Technology (PA)
St. Petersburg Coll (FL)

COMPUTER INSTALLATION AND REPAIR TECHNOLOGY
Dalton State Coll (GA)
Inter American U of Puerto Rico, Aguadilla Campus (PR)
Inter American U of Puerto Rico, Bayamón Campus (PR)
Inter American U of Puerto Rico, Fajardo Campus (PR)
Universidad Metropolitana (PR)

COMPUTER PROGRAMMING
Baker Coll (MI)
Caribbean U (PR)
Champlain Coll (VT)
Coll of Staten Island of the City U of New York (NY)
EDP U of Puerto Rico (PR)
EDP U of Puerto Rico–San Sebastian (PR)
Humphreys Coll (CA)
International Business Coll, Fort Wayne (IN)
Johnson & Wales U (RI)
Limestone Coll (SC)
Medgar Evers Coll of the City U of New York (NY)
Missouri Southern State U (MO)
New England Inst of Technology (RI)
Palm Beach State Coll (FL)
Polk State Coll (FL)
Rasmussen Coll Fargo (ND)
Saint Francis U (PA)
St. Petersburg Coll (FL)
State Coll of Florida Manatee-Sarasota (FL)
Stevens-Henager Coll, Boise (ID)

Stratford U, Falls Church (VA)
The U of Toledo (OH)
Youngstown State U (OH)

COMPUTER PROGRAMMING RELATED
State Coll of Florida Manatee-Sarasota (FL)
Stratford U, Falls Church (VA)

COMPUTER PROGRAMMING (SPECIFIC APPLICATIONS)
Academy of Art U (CA)
Indiana U South Bend (IN)
Kent State U at Geauga (OH)
Palm Beach State Coll (FL)
Universidad del Este (PR)
Valencia Coll (FL)

COMPUTER SCIENCE
Baker Coll (MI)
Carroll Coll (MT)
Central Methodist U (MO)
Coll of Coastal Georgia (GA)
Creighton U (NE)
Dalton State Coll (GA)
Felician U (NJ)
Florida National U (FL)
Hawai'i Pacific U (HI)
Humphreys Coll (CA)
Inter American U of Puerto Rico, Aguadilla Campus (PR)
Inter American U of Puerto Rico, Barranquitas Campus (PR)
Inter American U of Puerto Rico, Bayamón Campus (PR)
Inter American U of Puerto Rico, Ponce Campus (PR)
Inter American U of Puerto Rico, San Germán Campus (PR)
Madonna U (MI)
Monroe Coll, Bronx (NY)
New England Inst of Technology (RI)
New York City Coll of Technology of the City U of New York (NY)
Palm Beach State Coll (FL)
Southwest Baptist U (MO)
Southwestern Oklahoma State U (OK)
Universidad Adventista de las Antillas (PR)
Universidad Metropolitana (PR)
The U of Findlay (OH)
U of Maine at Fort Kent (ME)
U of Management and Technology (VA)
U of New Haven (CT)
U of Rio Grande (OH)
U of the Virgin Islands (VI)
Utah Valley U (UT)
Walsh U (OH)
Weber State U (UT)

COMPUTER SOFTWARE AND MEDIA APPLICATIONS RELATED
American Public U System (WV)
Champlain Coll (VT)
Hobe Sound Bible Coll (FL)
Pace U (NY)
Pace U, Pleasantville Campus (NY)
Polytechnic U of Puerto Rico (PR)

COMPUTER SOFTWARE ENGINEERING
Rasmussen Coll Appleton (WI)
Rasmussen Coll Blaine (MN)
Rasmussen Coll Bloomington (MN)
Rasmussen Coll Brooklyn Park (MN)
Rasmussen Coll Eagan (MN)
Rasmussen Coll Fargo (ND)
Rasmussen Coll Fort Myers (FL)
Rasmussen Coll Green Bay (WI)
Rasmussen Coll Kansas City/Overland Park (KS)
Rasmussen Coll Lake Elmo/Woodbury (MN)
Rasmussen Coll Land O' Lakes (FL)
Rasmussen Coll Mankato (MN)
Rasmussen Coll Moorhead (MN)
Rasmussen Coll New Port Richey (FL)
Rasmussen Coll Ocala (FL)
Rasmussen Coll St. Cloud (MN)
Rasmussen Coll Tampa/Brandon (FL)
Rasmussen Coll Topeka (KS)
Rasmussen Coll Wausau (WI)
Vermont Tech Coll (VT)

COMPUTER SOFTWARE TECHNOLOGY
Universidad del Este (PR)

COMPUTER SUPPORT SPECIALIST
Sullivan U (KY)

COMPUTER SYSTEMS ANALYSIS
Caribbean U (PR)
Davenport U, Grand Rapids (MI)
Johnson & Wales U (RI)
The U of Akron (OH)

COMPUTER SYSTEMS NETWORKING AND TELECOMMUNICATIONS
Baker Coll (MI)
Clayton State U (GA)
Colorado Mesa U (CO)
Colorado Mountain Coll, Glenwood Springs (CO)
DeVry Coll of New York (NY)
Florida National U (FL)
Hickey Coll (MO)
Idaho State U (ID)
International Business Coll, Fort Wayne (IN)
Montana Tech of The U of Montana (MT)
Pace U (NY)
Pace U, Pleasantville Campus (NY)
Robert Morris U Illinois (IL)
Stevens-Henager Coll, Boise (ID)
Stratford U, Falls Church (VA)
The U of Akron (OH)
Weber State U (UT)

COMPUTER TECHNOLOGY/COMPUTER SYSTEMS TECHNOLOGY
Dalton State Coll (GA)
New England Inst of Technology (RI)
Southeast Missouri State U (MO)

CONSTRUCTION ENGINEERING TECHNOLOGY
Baker Coll (MI)
Ferris State U (MI)
Lawrence Technological U (MI)
New York City Coll of Technology of the City U of New York (NY)
Pennsylvania Coll of Technology (PA)
Southern Utah U (UT)
State Coll of Florida Manatee-Sarasota (FL)
State U of New York Coll of Technology at Delhi (NY)
The U of Akron (OH)
Valencia Coll (FL)
Vermont Tech Coll (VT)

CONSTRUCTION MANAGEMENT
Utah Valley U (UT)
Vermont Tech Coll (VT)
Wentworth Inst of Technology (MA)

CONSTRUCTION TRADES
Colorado Mesa U (CO)
Liberty U (VA)

CONSTRUCTION TRADES RELATED
John Brown U (AR)

CONSUMER MERCHANDISING/RETAILING MANAGEMENT
Academy of Art U (CA)
Colorado Mountain Coll, Steamboat Springs (CO)

COOKING AND RELATED CULINARY ARTS
Colorado Mesa U (CO)
Hickey Coll (MO)

CORRECTIONS
Baker Coll (MI)
California U of Pennsylvania (PA)
Langston U (OK)
Mount Aloysius Coll (PA)
Youngstown State U (OH)

CORRECTIONS ADMINISTRATION
John Jay Coll of Criminal Justice of the City U of New York (NY)

CORRECTIONS AND CRIMINAL JUSTICE RELATED
Cameron U (OK)
EDP U of Puerto Rico (PR)
EDP U of Puerto Rico–San Sebastian (PR)
Inter American U of Puerto Rico, Aguadilla Campus (PR)
Inter American U of Puerto Rico, Fajardo Campus (PR)
Inter American U of Puerto Rico, Metropolitan Campus (PR)
Rasmussen Coll Appleton (WI)
Rasmussen Coll Aurora (IL)
Rasmussen Coll Blaine (MN)
Rasmussen Coll Bloomington (MN)
Rasmussen Coll Brooklyn Park (MN)
Rasmussen Coll Eagan (MN)
Rasmussen Coll Fort Myers (FL)
Rasmussen Coll Green Bay (WI)
Rasmussen Coll Kansas City/Overland Park (KS)
Rasmussen Coll Lake Elmo/Woodbury (MN)
Rasmussen Coll Land O' Lakes (FL)
Rasmussen Coll Mankato (MN)
Rasmussen Coll Mokena/Tinley Park (IL)
Rasmussen Coll Moorhead (MN)
Rasmussen Coll New Port Richey (FL)
Rasmussen Coll Ocala (FL)
Rasmussen Coll Rockford (IL)
Rasmussen Coll Romeoville/Joliet (IL)
Rasmussen Coll St. Cloud (MN)
Rasmussen Coll Tampa/Brandon (FL)
Rasmussen Coll Topeka (KS)
Rasmussen Coll Wausau (WI)

COSMETOLOGY
Midland Coll (TX)

COSTUME DESIGN
FIDM/Fashion Inst of Design & Merchandising, Los Angeles Campus (CA)

COUNSELING PSYCHOLOGY
Hobe Sound Bible Coll (FL)

COURT REPORTING
Humphreys Coll (CA)

CREATIVE WRITING
Inst of American Indian Arts (NM)
John Cabot U (Italy)
National U (CA)
Trevecca Nazarene U (TN)

CRIMINAL JUSTICE/LAW ENFORCEMENT ADMINISTRATION
American Public U System (WV)
Anderson U (IN)
Arkansas State U (AR)
Bemidji State U (MN)
Boise State U (ID)
Campbellsville U (KY)
Coll of Coastal Georgia (GA)
Colorado Mesa U (CO)
Colorado Mountain Coll, Glenwood Springs (CO)
Columbia Coll (MO)
Dalton State Coll (GA)
Glenville State Coll (WV)
Hannibal-LaGrange U (MO)
Hawai'i Pacific U (HI)
Husson U (ME)
Lincoln Coll of New England, Southington (CT)
Lincoln U (MO)
Lock Haven U of Pennsylvania (PA)
MacMurray Coll (IL)
Mansfield U of Pennsylvania (PA)
Miami U (OH)
Middle Georgia State U (GA)
Monroe Coll, Bronx (NY)
New England Inst of Technology (RI)
Palm Beach State Coll (FL)
Peirce Coll (PA)
Polk State Coll (FL)
Regent U (VA)
Roger Williams U (RI)
St. John's U (NY)
St. Petersburg Coll (FL)
Salve Regina U (RI)
Tiffin U (OH)
Trevecca Nazarene U (TN)
Trine U (IN)

Universidad del Este (PR)
U of Arkansas at Pine Bluff (AR)
U of Maine at Fort Kent (ME)
U of Maine at Presque Isle (ME)
U of Management and Technology (VA)
Utah Valley U (UT)
Valencia Coll (FL)
Washburn U (KS)
Wayland Baptist U (TX)
Webber International U (FL)
Wright State U (OH)
York Coll of Pennsylvania (PA)
Youngstown State U (OH)

CRIMINAL JUSTICE/POLICE SCIENCE
Arkansas State U (AR)
Armstrong State U (GA)
Berkeley Coll–New York City Campus (NY)
Berkeley Coll–Woodland Park Campus (NJ)
Caribbean U (PR)
Columbia Southern U (AL)
Dalton State Coll (GA)
Eastern Kentucky U (KY)
Farmingdale State Coll (NY)
Ferris State U (MI)
Hilbert Coll (NY)
Idaho State U (ID)
Inter American U of Puerto Rico, Guayama Campus (PR)
Inter American U of Puerto Rico, Ponce Campus (PR)
John Jay Coll of Criminal Justice of the City U of New York (NY)
MacMurray Coll (IL)
Midland Coll (TX)
Missouri Southern State U (MO)
Missouri Western State U (MO)
Monroe Coll, Bronx (NY)
Ohio U–Chillicothe (OH)
Palm Beach State Coll (FL)
Rasmussen Coll Blaine (MN)
Rasmussen Coll Bloomington (MN)
Rasmussen Coll Brooklyn Park (MN)
Rasmussen Coll Eagan (MN)
Rasmussen Coll Lake Elmo/Woodbury (MN)
Rasmussen Coll Mankato (MN)
Rasmussen Coll St. Cloud (MN)
Rogers State U (OK)
Southern Utah U (UT)
State U of New York Coll of Technology at Canton (NY)
Sullivan U (KY)
Universidad del Este (PR)
Universidad del Turabo (PR)
Universidad Metropolitana (PR)
The U of Akron (OH)
U of Arkansas at Pine Bluff (AR)
U of New Haven (CT)
U of the Virgin Islands (VI)
Youngstown State U (OH)

CRIMINAL JUSTICE/SAFETY
American Public U System (WV)
Arkansas Tech U (AR)
Ball State U (IN)
Bethel Coll (IN)
Calumet Coll of Saint Joseph (IN)
Chaminade U of Honolulu (HI)
Columbus State U (GA)
Defiance Coll (OH)
Dixie State U (UT)
Fisher Coll (MA)
Florida National U (FL)
Gannon U (PA)
Hilbert Coll (NY)
Husson U (ME)
Idaho State U (ID)
Indiana Wesleyan U (IN)
Inter American U of Puerto Rico, Aguadilla Campus (PR)
Inter American U of Puerto Rico, Barranquitas Campus (PR)
Jarvis Christian Coll (TX)
Kent State U at Stark (OH)
Liberty U (VA)
Lourdes U (OH)
Madonna U (MI)
Manchester U (IN)
Oakland City U (IN)
Penn State Altoona (PA)
Point U (GA)
Post U (CT)
St. Francis Coll (NY)
Southwestern Oklahoma State U (OK)
State Coll of Florida Manatee-Sarasota (FL)

Thomas More Coll (KY)
Universidad Metropolitana (PR)
U of Maine at Augusta (ME)
U of Pikeville (KY)
U of Saint Francis (IN)
The U of Scranton (PA)
U of the Cumberlands (KY)
U of the Fraser Valley (BC, Canada)
Weber State U (UT)
Youngstown State U (OH)

CRIMINOLOGY
LeTourneau U (TX)

CRISIS/EMERGENCY/DISASTER MANAGEMENT
Arkansas State U (AR)
Universidad del Turabo (PR)

CROP PRODUCTION
North Carolina State U (NC)
U of Massachusetts Amherst (MA)

CULINARY ARTS
Baker Coll (MI)
The Culinary Inst of America (NY)
Johnson & Wales U (CO)
Johnson & Wales U (FL)
Johnson & Wales U (RI)
Kendall Coll (IL)
Monroe Coll, Bronx (NY)
Newbury Coll (MA)
Pennsylvania Coll of Technology (PA)
Robert Morris U Illinois (IL)
Southern Adventist U (TN)
Southern New Hampshire U (NH)
State U of New York Coll of Agriculture and Technology at Cobleskill (NY)
State U of New York Coll of Technology at Delhi (NY)
Stratford U (MD)
Stratford U, Alexandria (VA)
Stratford U, Falls Church (VA)
Stratford U, Glen Allen (VA)
Stratford U, Newport News (VA)
Stratford U, Virginia Beach (VA)
Stratford U, Woodbridge (VA)
Sullivan U (KY)
Universidad del Este (PR)
The U of Akron (OH)
U of Montana (MT)
Utah Valley U (UT)
Valencia Coll (FL)

CULINARY ARTS RELATED
Johnson & Wales U (CO)
Johnson & Wales U (FL)
Johnson & Wales U (RI)
U of New Hampshire (NH)

CULINARY SCIENCE
Wright State U (OH)

CURRICULUM AND INSTRUCTION
State U of New York Coll of Technology at Delhi (NY)

DAIRY SCIENCE
Vermont Tech Coll (VT)

DANCE
Dixie State U (UT)
U of Saint Francis (IN)
Utah Valley U (UT)

DATA ENTRY/MICROCOMPUTER APPLICATIONS RELATED
Colorado Mountain Coll, Glenwood Springs (CO)
Colorado Mountain Coll, Steamboat Springs (CO)

DATA MODELING/WAREHOUSING AND DATABASE ADMINISTRATION
American Public U System (WV)
Limestone Coll (SC)

DATA PROCESSING AND DATA PROCESSING TECHNOLOGY
American Public U System (WV)
Baker Coll (MI)
Campbellsville U (KY)
Hallmark U (TX)
Humphreys Coll (CA)
Miami U (OH)
Montana State U Billings (MT)
Pace U, Pleasantville Campus (NY)
Palm Beach State Coll (FL)
Youngstown State U (OH)

DENTAL ASSISTING
Lincoln Coll of New England, Southington (CT)
U of Maine at Augusta (ME)
U of Southern Indiana (IN)

DENTAL HYGIENE
Baker Coll (MI)
Coll of Coastal Georgia (GA)
Dalton State Coll (GA)
Dixie State U (UT)
Farmingdale State Coll (NY)
Ferris State U (MI)
Florida National U (FL)
Indiana U–Purdue U Indianapolis (IN)
Indiana U South Bend (IN)
Missouri Southern State U (MO)
New York City Coll of Technology of the City U of New York (NY)
Palm Beach State Coll (FL)
Pennsylvania Coll of Technology (PA)
Rutgers U–New Brunswick (NJ)
St. Petersburg Coll (FL)
Shawnee State U (OH)
Southern Adventist U (TN)
State U of New York Coll of Technology at Canton (NY)
Tennessee State U (TN)
U of Arkansas for Medical Sciences (AR)
U of Bridgeport (CT)
U of Maine at Augusta (ME)
U of New Haven (CT)
Utah Valley U (UT)
Valencia Coll (FL)
Vermont Tech Coll (VT)
Weber State U (UT)
Western Kentucky U (KY)
West Liberty U (WV)

DENTAL LABORATORY TECHNOLOGY
Florida National U (FL)
Louisiana State U Health Sciences Center (LA)
New York City Coll of Technology of the City U of New York (NY)

DENTAL SERVICES AND ALLIED PROFESSIONS RELATED
Valdosta State U (GA)

DESIGN AND APPLIED ARTS RELATED
U of Maine at Presque Isle (ME)
Washburn U (KS)

DESIGN AND VISUAL COMMUNICATIONS
FIDM/Fashion Inst of Design & Merchandising, Los Angeles Campus (CA)
FIDM/Fashion Inst of Design & Merchandising, San Francisco Campus (CA)
U of Saint Francis (IN)
Utah Valley U (UT)

DESKTOP PUBLISHING AND DIGITAL IMAGING DESIGN
New England Inst of Technology (RI)

DIAGNOSTIC MEDICAL SONOGRAPHY AND ULTRASOUND TECHNOLOGY
Adventist U of Health Sciences (FL)
Baker Coll (MI)
Ferris State U (MI)
Florida National U (FL)
Lincoln U (CA)
Mercy Coll of Health Sciences (IA)
Midland Coll (TX)
Nebraska Methodist Coll (NE)
Pennsylvania Coll of Health Sciences (PA)
Polk State Coll (FL)
St. Catherine U (MN)
Universidad del Este (PR)
Universidad Metropolitana (PR)
U of Arkansas for Medical Sciences (AR)
The U of Findlay (OH)
Valencia Coll (FL)

DIESEL MECHANICS TECHNOLOGY
Idaho State U (ID)
Lewis-Clark State Coll (ID)
Midland Coll (TX)
Montana State U Billings (MT)
Pennsylvania Coll of Technology (PA)

State U of New York Coll of Agriculture and Technology at Cobleskill (NY)
Utah Valley U (UT)
Vermont Tech Coll (VT)
Weber State U (UT)

DIETETICS
Ferris State U (MI)
State Coll of Florida Manatee-Sarasota (FL)

DIETETIC TECHNOLOGY
Youngstown State U (OH)

DIETITIAN ASSISTANT
Youngstown State U (OH)

DIGITAL ARTS
Academy of Art U (CA)
Oakland City U (IN)

DIGITAL COMMUNICATION AND MEDIA/MULTIMEDIA
Colorado Mountain Coll, Glenwood Springs (CO)
Florida National U (FL)
Indiana U–Purdue U Indianapolis (IN)
National U (CA)
Vaughn Coll of Aeronautics and Technology (NY)

DIVINITY/MINISTRY
Bethel Coll (VA)
Carson-Newman U (TN)
Nebraska Christian Coll (NE)
Ohio Christian U (OH)
Providence Coll (RI)

DOG/PET/ANIMAL GROOMING
Becker Coll (MA)

DRAFTING AND DESIGN TECHNOLOGY
Baker Coll (MI)
California U of Pennsylvania (PA)
Caribbean U (PR)
Dalton State Coll (GA)
Johnson & Wales U (RI)
Langston U (OK)
LeTourneau U (TX)
Lewis-Clark State Coll (ID)
Lincoln U (MO)
Montana State U (MT)
Montana State U Billings (MT)
Palm Beach State Coll (FL)
State Coll of Florida Manatee-Sarasota (FL)
Universidad Metropolitana (PR)
The U of Akron (OH)
U of Rio Grande (OH)
Utah Valley U (UT)
Valencia Coll (FL)
Weber State U (UT)
Wright State U (OH)
Youngstown State U (OH)

DRAFTING/DESIGN ENGINEERING TECHNOLOGIES RELATED
Pennsylvania Coll of Technology (PA)

DRAMATIC/THEATER ARTS
Adams State U (CO)
Colorado Mountain Coll, Glenwood Springs (CO)
Palm Beach State Coll (FL)
Pine Manor Coll (MA)
State Coll of Florida Manatee-Sarasota (FL)
Thomas More Coll (KY)
U of the Fraser Valley (BC, Canada)
Utah Valley U (UT)

DRAWING
Pratt Inst (NY)

EARLY CHILDHOOD EDUCATION
Adams State U (CO)
Becker Coll (MA)
Bethel Coll (IN)
Boise State U (ID)
Chaminade U of Honolulu (HI)
Coll of Saint Mary (NE)
Colorado Mountain Coll, Steamboat Springs (CO)
Cornerstone U (MI)
Dixie State U (UT)
Fisher Coll (MA)
Gannon U (PA)
Granite State Coll (NH)
Lincoln U (MO)

Lindsey Wilson Coll (KY)
Manchester U (IN)
Maranatha Baptist U (WI)
Mount Aloysius Coll (PA)
Mount Saint Mary's U (CA)
National U (CA)
Nazarene Bible Coll (CO)
Nova Southeastern U (FL)
Oakland City U (IN)
Oklahoma Wesleyan U (OK)
Pacific Union Coll (CA)
Pine Manor Coll (MA)
Rasmussen Coll Appleton (WI)
Rasmussen Coll Aurora (IL)
Rasmussen Coll Blaine (MN)
Rasmussen Coll Bloomington (MN)
Rasmussen Coll Brooklyn Park (MN)
Rasmussen Coll Eagan (MN)
Rasmussen Coll Fargo (ND)
Rasmussen Coll Fort Myers (FL)
Rasmussen Coll Green Bay (WI)
Rasmussen Coll Kansas City/Overland Park (KS)
Rasmussen Coll Lake Elmo/Woodbury (MN)
Rasmussen Coll Land O' Lakes (FL)
Rasmussen Coll Mankato (MN)
Rasmussen Coll Mokena/Tinley Park (IL)
Rasmussen Coll Moorhead (MN)
Rasmussen Coll New Port Richey (FL)
Rasmussen Coll Ocala (FL)
Rasmussen Coll Rockford (IL)
Rasmussen Coll Romeoville/Joliet (IL)
Rasmussen Coll St. Cloud (MN)
Rasmussen Coll Tampa/Brandon (FL)
Rasmussen Coll Topeka (KS)
Rasmussen Coll Wausau (WI)
Rust Coll (MS)
St. Gregory's U, Shawnee (OK)
St. Petersburg Coll (FL)
Sullivan U (KY)
Taylor U (IN)
U of Cincinnati (OH)
U of Great Falls (MT)
The U of Montana Western (MT)
U of Southern Indiana (IN)
U of the Virgin Islands (VI)
Utah Valley U (UT)
Washburn U (KS)
Wayland Baptist U (TX)
Weber State U (UT)
Western Kentucky U (KY)
Wilmington U (DE)

E-COMMERCE
Colorado Mountain Coll, Steamboat Springs (CO)
Limestone Coll (SC)

ECONOMICS
John Cabot U (Italy)
Palm Beach State Coll (FL)
State Coll of Florida Manatee-Sarasota (FL)
Thomas More Coll (KY)
U of Wisconsin–Parkside (WI)

EDUCATION
Alderson Broaddus U (WV)
Baker Coll (MI)
Central Baptist Coll (AR)
Corban U (OR)
Dalton State Coll (GA)
Eastern Oregon U (OR)
Florida National U (FL)
Lincoln Christian U (IL)
Montana State U Billings (MT)
Montreat Coll, Montreat (NC)
National U (CA)
Ohio Christian U (OH)
Palm Beach State Coll (FL)
Saint Francis U (PA)
State U of New York Empire State Coll (NY)

EDUCATIONAL/INSTRUCTIONAL TECHNOLOGY
Cameron U (OK)

EDUCATION (MULTIPLE LEVELS)
Coll of Coastal Georgia (GA)
Midland Coll (TX)

EDUCATION RELATED
Colorado Christian U (CO)

The U of Akron (OH)
Weber State U (UT)

EDUCATION (SPECIFIC SUBJECT AREAS) RELATED
National U (CA)
Penn State U Park (PA)

ELECTRICAL AND ELECTRONIC ENGINEERING TECHNOLOGIES RELATED
Lawrence Technological U (MI)
Rochester Inst of Technology (NY)
Vaughn Coll of Aeronautics and Technology (NY)
Youngstown State U (OH)

ELECTRICAL AND ELECTRONICS ENGINEERING
New England Inst of Technology (RI)
The U of Scranton (PA)

ELECTRICAL AND POWER TRANSMISSION INSTALLATION
Polk State Coll (FL)
State U of New York Coll of Technology at Delhi (NY)

ELECTRICAL, ELECTRONIC AND COMMUNICATIONS ENGINEERING TECHNOLOGY
Baker Coll (MI)
Bluefield State Coll (WV)
California U of Pennsylvania (PA)
Coll of Staten Island of the City U of New York (NY)
Dalton State Coll (GA)
DeVry Coll of New York (NY)
Fairmont State U (WV)
Hallmark U (TX)
Idaho State U (ID)
Inter American U of Puerto Rico, Aguadilla Campus (PR)
Inter American U of Puerto Rico, San Germán Campus (PR)
Langston U (OK)
Lawrence Technological U (MI)
New York City Coll of Technology of the City U of New York (NY)
Palm Beach State Coll (FL)
Penn State Altoona (PA)
Penn State Berks (PA)
Penn State Brandywine (PA)
Penn State Erie, The Behrend Coll (PA)
Penn State Hazleton (PA)
Penn State New Kensington (PA)
Penn State Schuylkill (PA)
Penn State Wilkes-Barre (PA)
Penn State Worthington Scranton (PA)
Penn State York (PA)
Pennsylvania Coll of Technology (PA)
Purdue U (IN)
State Coll of Florida Manatee-Sarasota (FL)
State U of New York Coll of Technology at Canton (NY)
State U of New York Coll of Technology at Delhi (NY)
Universidad del Este (PR)
Universidad del Turabo (PR)
The U of Akron (OH)
U of Hartford (CT)
U of Massachusetts Lowell (MA)
U of Montana (MT)
Vermont Tech Coll (VT)
Weber State U (UT)
Youngstown State U (OH)

ELECTRICAL/ELECTRONICS EQUIPMENT INSTALLATION AND REPAIR
Lewis-Clark State Coll (ID)
New England Inst of Technology (RI)
Pittsburg State U (KS)

ELECTRICIAN
Liberty U (VA)
Pennsylvania Coll of Technology (PA)
Universidad del Turabo (PR)
Weber State U (UT)

ELECTROCARDIOGRAPH TECHNOLOGY
Pennsylvania Coll of Health Sciences (PA)

ELECTROMECHANICAL AND INSTRUMENTATION AND MAINTENANCE TECHNOLOGIES RELATED
Excelsior Coll (NY)

ELECTROMECHANICAL TECHNOLOGY
Excelsior Coll (NY)
John Brown U (AR)
Midland Coll (TX)
New York City Coll of Technology of the City U of New York (NY)
Pennsylvania Coll of Technology (PA)
Shawnee State U (OH)
State U of New York Coll of Technology at Delhi (NY)

ELEMENTARY EDUCATION
Adams State U (CO)
Dalton State Coll (GA)
Ferris State U (MI)
New Mexico Highlands U (NM)
Palm Beach State Coll (FL)
Rogers State U (OK)

EMERGENCY MEDICAL TECHNOLOGY (EMT PARAMEDIC)
Arkansas Tech U (AR)
Baker Coll (MI)
Colorado Mesa U (CO)
Creighton U (NE)
Dixie State U (UT)
Eastern Kentucky U (KY)
EDP U of Puerto Rico (PR)
EDP U of Puerto Rico–San Sebastian (PR)
Idaho State U (ID)
Indiana U–Purdue U Indianapolis (IN)
Mercy Coll of Health Sciences (IA)
Midland Coll (TX)
Montana State U Billings (MT)
New England Inst of Technology (RI)
Pacific Union Coll (CA)
Pennsylvania Coll of Technology (PA)
Polk State Coll (FL)
Purdue U Northwest, Hammond (IN)
Rogers State U (OK)
St. Petersburg Coll (FL)
Shawnee State U (OH)
Southwest Baptist U (MO)
Spalding U (KY)
State U of New York Coll of Agriculture and Technology at Cobleskill (NY)
The U of Akron (OH)
U of Arkansas for Medical Sciences (AR)
U of New Haven (CT)
The U of West Alabama (AL)
Valencia Coll (FL)
Weber State U (UT)
Western Kentucky U (KY)
Youngstown State U (OH)

ENERGY MANAGEMENT AND SYSTEMS TECHNOLOGY
Idaho State U (ID)
Montana State U Billings (MT)
U of Rio Grande (OH)

ENGINEERING
Brescia U (KY)
Cameron U (OK)
Coll of Staten Island of the City U of New York (NY)
Dixie State U (UT)
Ferris State U (MI)
Geneva Coll (PA)
Lindsey Wilson Coll (KY)
St. Thomas U (FL)
Southern Adventist U (TN)
State Coll of Florida Manatee-Sarasota (FL)
State U of New York Coll of Technology at Canton (NY)
Union Coll (NE)
Weber State U (UT)

ENGINEERING/INDUSTRIAL MANAGEMENT
U of Management and Technology (VA)

ENGINEERING RELATED
Eastern Kentucky U (KY)

ENGINEERING SCIENCE
National U (CA)
Rochester Inst of Technology (NY)
U of Pittsburgh at Bradford (PA)

ENGINEERING TECHNOLOGIES AND ENGINEERING RELATED
Arkansas State U (AR)
Excelsior Coll (NY)
Missouri Southern State U (MO)
Rogers State U (OK)
State U of New York Coll of Agriculture and Technology at Cobleskill (NY)
State U of New York Coll of Technology at Canton (NY)
State U of New York Maritime Coll (NY)
U of Puerto Rico in Bayamón (PR)

ENGINEERING TECHNOLOGY
Austin Peay State U (TN)
Brescia U (KY)
Fairmont State U (WV)
Kansas State U (KS)
Lincoln U (MO)
Miami U (OH)
Michigan Technological U (MI)
Morehead State U (KY)
National U (CA)
Polk State Coll (FL)
St. Petersburg Coll (FL)
The U of Toledo (OH)
Wentworth Inst of Technology (MA)
Wright State U (OH)
Wright State U–Lake Campus (OH)
Youngstown State U (OH)

ENGLISH
Calumet Coll of Saint Joseph (IN)
Carroll Coll (MT)
Central Methodist U (MO)
Coll of Coastal Georgia (GA)
Colorado Mountain Coll, Glenwood Springs (CO)
Colorado Mountain Coll, Steamboat Springs (CO)
Dalton State Coll (GA)
Felician U (NJ)
Hannibal-LaGrange U (MO)
Immaculata U (PA)
Indiana Wesleyan U (IN)
John Cabot U (Italy)
Liberty U (VA)
Lourdes U (OH)
Madonna U (MI)
Palm Beach State Coll (FL)
Pine Manor Coll (MA)
State Coll of Florida Manatee-Sarasota (FL)
Thomas More Coll (KY)
Utah Valley U (UT)

ENGLISH AS A SECOND/FOREIGN LANGUAGE (TEACHING)
Cornerstone U (MI)
Union Coll (NE)

ENGLISH LANGUAGE AND LITERATURE RELATED
John Cabot U (Italy)
State U of New York Empire State Coll (NY)

ENGLISH/LANGUAGE ARTS TEACHER EDUCATION
State Coll of Florida Manatee-Sarasota (FL)

ENTREPRENEURSHIP
Baker Coll (MI)
Cogswell Polytechnical Coll (CA)
Inter American U of Puerto Rico, Barranquitas Campus (PR)
John Cabot U (Italy)

ENVIRONMENTAL CONTROL TECHNOLOGIES RELATED
Montana Tech of The U of Montana (MT)

ENVIRONMENTAL ENGINEERING TECHNOLOGY
Baker Coll (MI)
New York City Coll of Technology of the City U of New York (NY)
Ohio U–Chillicothe (OH)

ENVIRONMENTAL SCIENCE
Georgia Gwinnett Coll (GA)

Madonna U (MI)
U of Saint Francis (IN)

ENVIRONMENTAL STUDIES
Columbia Coll (MO)
Dickinson State U (ND)
State U of New York Coll of Agriculture and Technology at Cobleskill (NY)

EQUESTRIAN STUDIES
The U of Findlay (OH)
U of Massachusetts Amherst (MA)
The U of Montana Western (MT)

EXECUTIVE ASSISTANT/EXECUTIVE SECRETARY
Sullivan U (KY)
Universidad del Este (PR)
U of Montana (MT)

FAMILY AND COMMUNITY SERVICES
Baker Coll (MI)

FAMILY AND CONSUMER SCIENCES/HOME ECONOMICS TEACHER EDUCATION
State Coll of Florida Manatee-Sarasota (FL)

FAMILY AND CONSUMER SCIENCES/HUMAN SCIENCES
Palm Beach State Coll (FL)

FASHION AND FABRIC CONSULTING
Academy of Art U (CA)

FASHION/APPAREL DESIGN
Academy of Art U (CA)
EDP U of Puerto Rico (PR)
EDP U of Puerto Rico–San Sebastian (PR)
Fashion Inst of Technology (NY)
FIDM/Fashion Inst of Design & Merchandising, Los Angeles Campus (CA)
FIDM/Fashion Inst of Design & Merchandising, San Francisco Campus (CA)
Palm Beach State Coll (FL)
Parsons School of Design (NY)
Universidad del Turabo (PR)

FASHION MERCHANDISING
Academy of Art U (CA)
Berkeley Coll–New York City Campus (NY)
Berkeley Coll–Woodland Park Campus (NJ)
Fashion Inst of Technology (NY)
FIDM/Fashion Inst of Design & Merchandising, Los Angeles Campus (CA)
FIDM/Fashion Inst of Design & Merchandising, San Francisco Campus (CA)
Fisher Coll (MA)
Immaculata U (PA)
LIM Coll (NY)
New York City Coll of Technology of the City U of New York (NY)
Palm Beach State Coll (FL)
Parsons School of Design (NY)
Southern New Hampshire U (NH)
The U of Akron (OH)
U of Bridgeport (CT)

FASHION MODELING
Fashion Inst of Technology (NY)

FILM/CINEMA/VIDEO STUDIES
Fashion Inst of Technology (NY)
Los Angeles Film School (CA)

FINANCE
Davenport U, Grand Rapids (MI)
Hawai'i Pacific U (HI)
Indiana Wesleyan U (IN)
John Cabot U (Italy)
Palm Beach State Coll (FL)
Saint Peter's U (NJ)
State Coll of Florida Manatee-Sarasota (FL)
The U of Findlay (OH)
Youngstown State U (OH)

FINANCIAL PLANNING AND SERVICES
Berkeley Coll–New York City Campus (NY)
Berkeley Coll–Woodland Park Campus (NJ)

FINE ARTS RELATED
Academy of Art U (CA)
Madonna U (MI)
Pennsylvania Coll of Technology (PA)
Saint Francis U (PA)

FINE/STUDIO ARTS
Academy of Art U (CA)
Adams State U (CO)
Beacon Coll (FL)
Colorado Mountain Coll, Steamboat Springs (CO)
Fashion Inst of Technology (NY)
Inst of American Indian Arts (NM)
Lindsey Wilson Coll (KY)
Pratt Inst (NY)
State Coll of Florida Manatee-Sarasota (FL)
Thomas More Coll (KY)
U of Maine at Augusta (ME)
U of Saint Francis (IN)
Villa Maria Coll (NY)
York Coll of Pennsylvania (PA)

FIRE PREVENTION AND SAFETY TECHNOLOGY
Montana State U Billings (MT)
Polk State Coll (FL)
The U of Akron (OH)
U of New Haven (CT)

FIRE SCIENCE/FIREFIGHTING
American Public U System (WV)
Columbia Southern U (AL)
Idaho State U (ID)
Lewis-Clark State Coll (ID)
Madonna U (MI)
Midland Coll (TX)
Palm Beach State Coll (FL)
Polk State Coll (FL)
St. Petersburg Coll (FL)
Southwestern Adventist U (TX)
Southwestern Oklahoma State U (OK)
State Coll of Florida Manatee-Sarasota (FL)
U of Cincinnati (OH)
U of New Haven (CT)
Utah Valley U (UT)
Vermont Tech Coll (VT)

FIRE SERVICES ADMINISTRATION
American Public U System (WV)
Columbia Coll (MO)

FISHING AND FISHERIES SCIENCES AND MANAGEMENT
State U of New York Coll of Agriculture and Technology at Cobleskill (NY)

FOOD PREPARATION
Washburn U (KS)

FOOD SERVICE SYSTEMS ADMINISTRATION
Inter American U of Puerto Rico, Aguadilla Campus (PR)
Lincoln Coll of New England, Southington (CT)
U of New Hampshire (NH)
Wright State U–Lake Campus (OH)

FOODS, NUTRITION, AND WELLNESS
Madonna U (MI)
Palm Beach State Coll (FL)
Southern Adventist U (TN)
Youngstown State U (OH)

FOREIGN LANGUAGE TEACHER EDUCATION
State Coll of Florida Manatee-Sarasota (FL)

FORENSIC SCIENCE AND TECHNOLOGY
Arkansas State U (AR)
St. Petersburg Coll (FL)

FORESTRY
Coll of Coastal Georgia (GA)

FOREST TECHNOLOGY
Glenville State Coll (WV)
Pennsylvania Coll of Technology (PA)
State U of New York Coll of
Environmental Science and
Forestry (NY)
U of Maine at Fort Kent (ME)
U of New Hampshire (NH)

FRENCH
State Coll of Florida Manatee-
Sarasota (FL)
Thomas More Coll (KY)
Weber State U (UT)

FUNERAL SERVICE AND
MORTUARY SCIENCE
Cincinnati Coll of Mortuary Science
(OH)
Ferris State U (MI)
Lincoln Coll of New England,
Southington (CT)
St. Petersburg Coll (FL)

GAME AND INTERACTIVE
MEDIA DESIGN
Academy of Art U (CA)
National U (CA)

GENERAL STUDIES
Adventist U of Health Sciences (FL)
Alderson Broaddus U (WV)
Alverno Coll (WI)
American Baptist Coll (TN)
American Public U System (WV)
Arkansas State U (AR)
Arkansas Tech U (AR)
Asbury U (KY)
Austin Peay State U (TN)
Ball State U (IN)
Barclay Coll (KS)
Belhaven U (MS)
Bethel Coll (IN)
Brandman U (CA)
Cabarrus Coll of Health Sciences
(NC)
California Christian Coll (CA)
Calumet Coll of Saint Joseph (IN)
Cameron U (OK)
Cardinal Stritch U (WI)
Central Baptist Coll (AR)
Chaminade U of Honolulu (HI)
Christian Brothers U (TN)
Colorado Christian U (CO)
Columbia Coll (MO)
Columbia Southern U (AL)
Concordia Coll Alabama (AL)
Concordia U, St. Paul (MN)
Dakota State U (SD)
Dalton State Coll (GA)
Dixie State U (UT)
Eastern Connecticut State U (CT)
Eastern Kentucky U (KY)
Ferris State U (MI)
Fisher Coll (MA)
Fort Hays State U (KS)
Franciscan U of Steubenville (OH)
Granite State Coll (NH)
Hampton U (VA)
Hawai`i Pacific U (HI)
Hope International U (CA)
Idaho State U (ID)
Indiana U South Bend (IN)
Indiana Wesleyan U (IN)
Jarvis Christian Coll (TX)
John Brown U (AR)
Johnson State Coll (VT)
La Salle U (PA)
Lawrence Technological U (MI)
Liberty U (VA)
Lincoln Christian U (IL)
Lipscomb U (TN)
Louisiana Tech U (LA)
McNeese State U (LA)
Mercy Coll of Ohio (OH)
Miami U (OH)
Midland Coll (TX)
Monmouth U (NJ)
Montana State U Billings (MT)
Morehead State U (KY)
Mount Aloysius Coll (PA)
Mount Marty Coll (SD)
Mount St. Joseph U (OH)
Mount Vernon Nazarene U (OH)
National U (CA)
Newbury Coll (MA)
New Mexico Inst of Mining and
Technology (NM)
Northern Kentucky U (KY)
Northwest Christian U (OR)
Northwest U (WA)

Oakland City U (IN)
Ohio Dominican U (OH)
The Ohio State U (OH)
The Ohio State U at Lima (OH)
The Ohio State U at Marion (OH)
The Ohio State U–Mansfield Campus
(OH)
The Ohio State U–Newark Campus
(OH)
Oklahoma Wesleyan U (OK)
Ouachita Baptist U (AR)
Our Lady of the Lake Coll (LA)
Pace U (NY)
Pace U, Pleasantville Campus (NY)
Pacific Union Coll (CA)
Peirce Coll (PA)
Point U (GA)
Regent U (VA)
Rider U (NJ)
Sacred Heart U (CT)
Shawnee State U (OH)
Simpson U (CA)
South Dakota School of Mines and
Technology (SD)
South Dakota State U (SD)
Southern Arkansas U–Magnolia (AR)
Southern Nazarene U (OK)
Southern Utah U (UT)
Southwest Baptist U (MO)
Southwestern Adventist U (TX)
Southwestern Coll (KS)
Southwestern Oklahoma State U
(OK)
State U of New York Coll of
Technology at Canton (NY)
State U of New York Coll of
Technology at Delhi (NY)
Temple U (PA)
Tiffin U (OH)
Toccoa Falls Coll (GA)
Trevecca Nazarene U (TN)
Trinity Coll of Florida (FL)
U of Bridgeport (CT)
U of Central Arkansas (AR)
U of Hartford (CT)
U of Louisiana at Monroe (LA)
U of Maine at Fort Kent (ME)
U of Management and Technology
(VA)
U of Mobile (AL)
U of Rio Grande (OH)
U of Saint Francis (IN)
U of South Florida Sarasota-Manatee
(FL)
U of the Fraser Valley (BC, Canada)
The U of Toledo (OH)
U of Wisconsin–Superior (WI)
Utah State U (UT)
Utah Valley U (UT)
Viterbo U (WI)
Wayland Baptist U (TX)
Weber State U (UT)
Western Kentucky U (KY)
Widener U (PA)
Wilmington U (DE)
York Coll of Pennsylvania (PA)

GEOGRAPHIC INFORMATION
SCIENCE AND CARTOGRAPHY
The U of Akron (OH)

GEOGRAPHY
Wright State U (OH)

GEOGRAPHY RELATED
Adams State U (CO)

GEOLOGY/EARTH SCIENCE
Coll of Coastal Georgia (GA)
Colorado Mountain Coll, Steamboat
Springs (CO)
Wright State U (OH)
Wright State U–Lake Campus (OH)

GERMAN
State Coll of Florida Manatee-
Sarasota (FL)
Weber State U (UT)

GERONTOLOGY
Holy Cross Coll (IN)
Madonna U (MI)
Manchester U (IN)
Ohio Dominican U (OH)
Thomas More Coll (KY)

GRAPHIC AND PRINTING
EQUIPMENT OPERATION/
PRODUCTION
Chowan U (NC)
Dixie State U (UT)
Lewis-Clark State Coll (ID)

GRAPHIC COMMUNICATIONS
New England Inst of Technology (RI)

GRAPHIC COMMUNICATIONS
RELATED
Rasmussen Coll Moorhead (MN)
Wright State U–Lake Campus (OH)

GRAPHIC DESIGN
Academy of Art U (CA)
California U of Pennsylvania (PA)
Creative Center (NE)
Defiance Coll (OH)
Ferris State U (MI)
FIDM/Fashion Inst of Design &
Merchandising, Los Angeles
Campus (CA)
FIDM/Fashion Inst of Design &
Merchandising, San Francisco
Campus (CA)
Hickey Coll (MO)
Inter American U of Puerto Rico, San
Germán Campus (PR)
International Business Coll, Fort
Wayne (IN)
Madonna U (MI)
Mount St. Joseph U (OH)
Pacific Union Coll (CA)
Parsons School of Design (NY)
Pratt Inst (NY)
State U of New York Coll of
Agriculture and Technology at
Cobleskill (NY)
Stevens-Henager Coll, Boise (ID)
Union Coll (NE)
U of the Fraser Valley (BC, Canada)
Villa Maria Coll (NY)
Wright State U (OH)
Wright State U–Lake Campus (OH)

HAZARDOUS MATERIALS
MANAGEMENT AND WASTE
TECHNOLOGY
Ohio U–Chillicothe (OH)

HEALTH AIDE
National U (CA)

HEALTH AND MEDICAL
ADMINISTRATIVE SERVICES
RELATED
National U (CA)

HEALTH AND PHYSICAL
EDUCATION/FITNESS
Coll of Coastal Georgia (GA)
Robert Morris U Illinois (IL)
State U of New York Coll of
Technology at Delhi (NY)
Universidad del Turabo (PR)
Universidad Metropolitana (PR)
Utah Valley U (UT)

HEALTH AND PHYSICAL
EDUCATION RELATED
Pennsylvania Coll of Technology (PA)

HEALTH AND WELLNESS
Northwest U (WA)

HEALTH/HEALTH-CARE
ADMINISTRATION
Baker Coll (MI)
Berkeley Coll–New York City Campus
(NY)
Berkeley Coll–Woodland Park
Campus (NJ)
LeTourneau U (TX)
Mount Saint Mary's U (CA)
National U (CA)
State Coll of Florida Manatee-
Sarasota (FL)
The U of Scranton (PA)
Washburn U (KS)

HEALTH INFORMATION/
MEDICAL RECORDS
ADMINISTRATION
Dalton State Coll (GA)
Lincoln Coll of New England,
Southington (CT)
Montana State U Billings (MT)
St. Petersburg Coll (FL)

HEALTH INFORMATION/
MEDICAL RECORDS
TECHNOLOGY
Baker Coll (MI)
Berkeley Coll–New York City Campus
(NY)
Berkeley Coll–Woodland Park
Campus (NJ)

Boise State U (ID)
Dakota State U (SD)
Davenport U, Grand Rapids (MI)
Ferris State U (MI)
Fisher Coll (MA)
Hodges U (FL)
Idaho State U (ID)
Indiana U Northwest (IN)
Lincoln Coll of New England,
Southington (CT)
Louisiana Tech U (LA)
Mercy Coll of Ohio (OH)
Middle Georgia State U (GA)
Midland Coll (TX)
National U (CA)
New England Inst of Technology (RI)
Peirce Coll (PA)
Pennsylvania Coll of Technology (PA)
Rasmussen Coll Appleton (WI)
Rasmussen Coll Aurora (IL)
Rasmussen Coll Blaine (MN)
Rasmussen Coll Bloomington (MN)
Rasmussen Coll Brooklyn Park (MN)
Rasmussen Coll Eagan (MN)
Rasmussen Coll Fort Myers (FL)
Rasmussen Coll Green Bay (WI)
Rasmussen Coll Kansas City/
Overland Park (KS)
Rasmussen Coll Lake Elmo/
Woodbury (MN)
Rasmussen Coll Land O' Lakes (FL)
Rasmussen Coll Mankato (MN)
Rasmussen Coll Mokena/Tinley Park
(IL)
Rasmussen Coll Moorhead (MN)
Rasmussen Coll New Port Richey
(FL)
Rasmussen Coll Ocala (FL)
Rasmussen Coll Rockford (IL)
Rasmussen Coll Romeoville/Joliet
(IL)
Rasmussen Coll St. Cloud (MN)
Rasmussen Coll Tampa/Brandon
(FL)
Rasmussen Coll Topeka (KS)
Rasmussen Coll Wausau (WI)
St. Catherine U (MN)
Sullivan U (KY)
U of Arkansas for Medical Sciences
(AR)
Washburn U (KS)
Weber State U (UT)
Western Kentucky U (KY)

HEALTH/MEDICAL
PREPARATORY PROGRAMS
RELATED
Immaculata U (PA)
Mount Saint Mary's U (CA)
Ohio Valley U (WV)

HEALTH PROFESSIONS
RELATED
American Public U System (WV)
Caribbean U (PR)
Ferris State U (MI)
Fisher Coll (MA)
Lock Haven U of Pennsylvania (PA)
Newman U (KS)
Northwest U (WA)
Ohio U–Chillicothe (OH)
Saint Peter's U (NJ)
U of Hartford (CT)
Villa Maria Coll (NY)

HEALTH SERVICES
ADMINISTRATION
Florida National U (FL)

HEALTH SERVICES/ALLIED
HEALTH/HEALTH SCIENCES
Aultman Coll of Nursing and Health
Sciences (OH)
Berkeley Coll–Woodland Park
Campus (NJ)
Cameron U (OK)
Fisher Coll (MA)
Lindsey Wilson Coll (KY)
Ohio Dominican U (OH)
Pine Manor Coll (MA)
State U of New York Coll of
Agriculture and Technology at
Cobleskill (NY)
U of Hartford (CT)
U of Maine at Fort Kent (ME)
U of the Incarnate Word (TX)
Weber State U (UT)

HEALTH TEACHER EDUCATION
Palm Beach State Coll (FL)
State Coll of Florida Manatee-
Sarasota (FL)

HEATING, AIR CONDITIONING,
VENTILATION AND
REFRIGERATION
MAINTENANCE TECHNOLOGY
Lewis-Clark State Coll (ID)
Montana State U Billings (MT)
New England Inst of Technology (RI)
State U of New York Coll of
Technology at Delhi (NY)

HEATING, VENTILATION, AIR
CONDITIONING AND
REFRIGERATION ENGINEERING
TECHNOLOGY
Ferris State U (MI)
Midland Coll (TX)
Pennsylvania Coll of Technology (PA)
State U of New York Coll of
Technology at Canton (NY)

HEAVY EQUIPMENT
MAINTENANCE TECHNOLOGY
Ferris State U (MI)
Pennsylvania Coll of Technology (PA)
U of Montana (MT)

HEBREW
Yeshiva U (NY)

HISTOLOGIC TECHNICIAN
Indiana U–Purdue U Indianapolis (IN)
Tarleton State U (TX)

HISTOLOGIC TECHNOLOGY/
HISTOTECHNOLOGIST
Tarleton State U (TX)

HISTORIC PRESERVATION AND
CONSERVATION
Montana Tech of The U of Montana
(MT)

HISTORY
American Public U System (WV)
Coll of Coastal Georgia (GA)
Dalton State Coll (GA)
Immaculata U (PA)
Indiana Wesleyan U (IN)
John Cabot U (Italy)
Lindsey Wilson Coll (KY)
Lourdes U (OH)
Oklahoma Wesleyan U (OK)
Palm Beach State Coll (FL)
Regent U (VA)
Rogers State U (OK)
State Coll of Florida Manatee-
Sarasota (FL)
State U of New York Empire State
Coll (NY)
Thomas More Coll (KY)
U of Rio Grande (OH)
Utah Valley U (UT)
Wright State U (OH)
Wright State U–Lake Campus (OH)

HOMELAND SECURITY
National U (CA)
U of Management and Technology
(VA)

HOMELAND SECURITY, LAW
ENFORCEMENT, FIREFIGHTING
AND PROTECTIVE SERVICES
RELATED
Idaho State U (ID)
St. Petersburg Coll (FL)

HORSE HUSBANDRY/EQUINE
SCIENCE AND MANAGEMENT
Delaware Valley U (PA)
Southern Utah U (UT)

HORTICULTURAL SCIENCE
Andrews U (MI)
Temple U (PA)

HOSPITAL AND HEALTH-CARE
FACILITIES ADMINISTRATION
State Coll of Florida Manatee-
Sarasota (FL)

HOSPITALITY
ADMINISTRATION
Colorado Mesa U (CO)
Colorado Mountain Coll, Steamboat
Springs (CO)
Florida National U (FL)
Lewis-Clark State Coll (ID)
Monroe Coll, Bronx (NY)
National U (CA)
New York City Coll of Technology of
the City U of New York (NY)
St. Petersburg Coll (FL)

Stratford U (MD)
The U of Akron (OH)
Utah Valley U (UT)
Valencia Coll (FL)
Webber International U (FL)
Youngstown State U (OH)

HOSPITALITY ADMINISTRATION RELATED
Penn State Beaver (PA)
Penn State Berks (PA)

HOSPITALITY AND RECREATION MARKETING
Ferris State U (MI)

HOTEL/MOTEL ADMINISTRATION
Baker Coll (MI)
Colorado Mountain Coll, Steamboat Springs (CO)
Ferris State U (MI)
Inter American U of Puerto Rico, Fajardo Campus (PR)
International Business Coll, Fort Wayne (IN)
Palm Beach State Coll (FL)
State U of New York Coll of Agriculture and Technology at Cobleskill (NY)
Stratford U, Falls Church (VA)
Stratford U, Woodbridge (VA)
Universidad del Este (PR)
The U of Akron (OH)
Valencia Coll (FL)

HOTEL, MOTEL, AND RESTAURANT MANAGEMENT
Stratford U, Glen Allen (VA)
Stratford U, Newport News (VA)
Sullivan U (KY)

HUMAN DEVELOPMENT AND FAMILY STUDIES
Penn State Abington (PA)
Penn State Altoona (PA)
Penn State Berks (PA)
Penn State Brandywine (PA)
Penn State Erie, The Behrend Coll (PA)
Penn State New Kensington (PA)
Penn State Schuylkill (PA)
Penn State Worthington Scranton (PA)
Penn State York (PA)

HUMAN DEVELOPMENT AND FAMILY STUDIES RELATED
Utah State U (UT)

HUMANITIES
Aquinas Coll (TN)
Colorado Mountain Coll, Glenwood Springs (CO)
Colorado Mountain Coll, Steamboat Springs (CO)
Fisher Coll (MA)
Harrison Middleton U (AZ)
John Cabot U (Italy)
Long Island U–LIU Brooklyn (NY)
Michigan Technological U (MI)
Ohio U (OH)
Ohio U–Chillicothe (OH)
Saint Peter's U (NJ)
State Coll of Florida Manatee-Sarasota (FL)
State U of New York Coll of Agriculture and Technology at Cobleskill (NY)
State U of New York Coll of Technology at Delhi (NY)
Thomas More Coll (KY)
Utah Valley U (UT)
Valparaiso U (IN)
Washburn U (KS)

HUMAN RESOURCES MANAGEMENT
Baker Coll (MI)
Montana State U Billings (MT)
Rasmussen Coll Appleton (WI)
Rasmussen Coll Blaine (MN)
Rasmussen Coll Bloomington (MN)
Rasmussen Coll Brooklyn Park (MN)
Rasmussen Coll Eagan (MN)
Rasmussen Coll Fargo (ND)
Rasmussen Coll Fort Myers (FL)
Rasmussen Coll Green Bay (WI)
Rasmussen Coll Kansas City/Overland Park (KS)

Rasmussen Coll Lake Elmo/Woodbury (MN)
Rasmussen Coll Land O' Lakes (FL)
Rasmussen Coll Mankato (MN)
Rasmussen Coll Moorhead (MN)
Rasmussen Coll New Port Richey (FL)
Rasmussen Coll Ocala (FL)
Rasmussen Coll Tampa/Brandon (FL)
Rasmussen Coll Topeka (KS)
Rasmussen Coll Wausau (WI)
The U of Findlay (OH)
The U of Scranton (PA)

HUMAN RESOURCES MANAGEMENT AND SERVICES RELATED
American Public U System (WV)
Oakland City U (IN)

HUMAN SERVICES
Arkansas Tech U (AR)
Baker Coll (MI)
Beacon Coll (FL)
Bethel Coll (IN)
Brescia U (KY)
Calumet Coll of Saint Joseph (IN)
Caribbean U (PR)
The Catholic U of America (DC)
Columbia Coll (MO)
Cornerstone U (MI)
Hilbert Coll (NY)
Lincoln Coll of New England, Southington (CT)
Mount Saint Mary's U (CA)
New York City Coll of Technology of the City U of New York (NY)
Ohio Christian U (OH)
Rasmussen Coll Appleton (WI)
Rasmussen Coll Blaine (MN)
Rasmussen Coll Bloomington (MN)
Rasmussen Coll Brooklyn Park (MN)
Rasmussen Coll Eagan (MN)
Rasmussen Coll Fargo (ND)
Rasmussen Coll Fort Myers (FL)
Rasmussen Coll Green Bay (WI)
Rasmussen Coll Kansas City/Overland Park (KS)
Rasmussen Coll Lake Elmo/Woodbury (MN)
Rasmussen Coll Land O' Lakes (FL)
Rasmussen Coll Mankato (MN)
Rasmussen Coll Moorhead (MN)
Rasmussen Coll New Port Richey (FL)
Rasmussen Coll Ocala (FL)
Rasmussen Coll St. Cloud (MN)
Rasmussen Coll Tampa/Brandon (FL)
Rasmussen Coll Topeka (KS)
Rasmussen Coll Wausau (WI)
U of Great Falls (MT)
U of Maine at Fort Kent (ME)
The U of Scranton (PA)
U of the Cumberlands (KY)
U of Valley Forge (PA)
Walsh U (OH)
Wayland Baptist U (TX)

ILLUSTRATION
Academy of Art U (CA)
Fashion Inst of Technology (NY)
Pratt Inst (NY)

INDUSTRIAL AND PRODUCT DESIGN
Academy of Art U (CA)

INDUSTRIAL ELECTRONICS TECHNOLOGY
Dalton State Coll (GA)
Ferris State U (MI)
Lewis-Clark State Coll (ID)
Pennsylvania Coll of Technology (PA)

INDUSTRIAL MECHANICS AND MAINTENANCE TECHNOLOGY
Pennsylvania Coll of Technology (PA)
The U of West Alabama (AL)

INDUSTRIAL PRODUCTION TECHNOLOGIES RELATED
California U of Pennsylvania (PA)

INDUSTRIAL RADIOLOGIC TECHNOLOGY
The George Washington U (DC)
Our Lady of the Lake Coll (LA)

Palm Beach State Coll (FL)
Widener U (PA)

INDUSTRIAL TECHNOLOGY
Arkansas Tech U (AR)
Dalton State Coll (GA)
Eastern Kentucky U (KY)
Millersville U of Pennsylvania (PA)
Murray State U (KY)
Penn State York (PA)
Pittsburg State U (KS)
St. Petersburg Coll (FL)
Southeastern Louisiana U (LA)
Southern Arkansas U–Magnolia (AR)
U of Arkansas at Pine Bluff (AR)
U of Puerto Rico in Bayamón (PR)
U of Rio Grande (OH)
Washburn U (KS)

INFORMATION RESOURCES MANAGEMENT
Rasmussen Coll Fort Myers (FL)
Rasmussen Coll Land O' Lakes (FL)
Rasmussen Coll New Port Richey (FL)
Rasmussen Coll Ocala (FL)
Rasmussen Coll Tampa/Brandon (FL)

INFORMATION SCIENCE/STUDIES
Campbellsville U (KY)
Humphreys Coll (CA)
Immaculata U (PA)
Johnson State Coll (VT)
Mansfield U of Pennsylvania (PA)
Monroe Coll, Bronx (NY)
Newman U (KS)
Penn State Abington (PA)
Penn State Altoona (PA)
Penn State Berks (PA)
Penn State Erie, The Behrend Coll (PA)
Penn State Hazleton (PA)
Penn State Lehigh Valley (PA)
Penn State New Kensington (PA)
Penn State Schuylkill (PA)
Penn State U Park (PA)
Saint Peter's U (NJ)
State Coll of Florida Manatee-Sarasota (FL)
State U of New York Coll of Agriculture and Technology at Cobleskill (NY)
State U of New York Coll of Technology at Canton (NY)
State U of New York Coll of Technology at Delhi (NY)
Touro Coll (NY)
Tulane U (LA)
U of Management and Technology (VA)
U of Massachusetts Lowell (MA)
U of Pittsburgh at Bradford (PA)
The U of Scranton (PA)

INFORMATION TECHNOLOGY
Arkansas Tech U (AR)
Cameron U (OK)
EDP U of Puerto Rico–San Sebastian (PR)
Ferris State U (MI)
Florida National U (FL)
Hallmark U (TX)
Life U (GA)
Limestone Coll (SC)
Monroe Coll, Bronx (NY)
New England Inst of Technology (RI)
Peirce Coll (PA)
Purdue U (IN)
Regent U (VA)
Southern Utah U (UT)
Thomas More Coll (KY)
Tiffin U (OH)
Trevecca Nazarene U (TN)
U of Maine at Augusta (ME)
U of Management and Technology (VA)
Vermont Tech Coll (VT)
Youngstown State U (OH)

INSTRUMENTATION TECHNOLOGY
Idaho State U (ID)
U of Puerto Rico in Bayamón (PR)

INSURANCE
Inter American U of Puerto Rico, Metropolitan Campus (PR)

INTERCULTURAL/MULTICULTURAL AND DIVERSITY STUDIES
Baptist U of the Americas (TX)
Nyack Coll (NY)

INTERDISCIPLINARY STUDIES
Central Methodist U (MO)
Coll of Coastal Georgia (GA)
John Brown U (AR)
Lesley U (MA)
Ohio Christian U (OH)
U of North Florida (FL)

INTERIOR DESIGN
Academy of Art U (CA)
Baker Coll (MI)
Bay Path U (MA)
Berkeley Coll–Woodland Park Campus (NJ)
Chaminade U of Honolulu (HI)
EDP U of Puerto Rico (PR)
EDP U of Puerto Rico–San Sebastian (PR)
Fashion Inst of Technology (NY)
FIDM/Fashion Inst of Design & Merchandising, Los Angeles Campus (CA)
FIDM/Fashion Inst of Design & Merchandising, San Francisco Campus (CA)
Indiana U–Purdue U Indianapolis (IN)
Montana State U (MT)
New England Inst of Technology (RI)
New York School of Interior Design (NY)
Palm Beach State Coll (FL)
Parsons School of Design (NY)
Robert Morris U Illinois (IL)
Villa Maria Coll (NY)
Weber State U (UT)

INTERNATIONAL BUSINESS/TRADE/COMMERCE
Berkeley Coll–New York City Campus (NY)
Berkeley Coll–Woodland Park Campus (NJ)
John Cabot U (Italy)
Saint Peter's U (NJ)
U of the Potomac (DC)

INTERNATIONAL/GLOBAL STUDIES
Holy Cross Coll (IN)
Sacred Heart U (CT)
Thomas More Coll (KY)

INTERNATIONAL RELATIONS AND AFFAIRS
John Cabot U (Italy)

ITALIAN STUDIES
John Cabot U (Italy)

JAPANESE
Weber State U (UT)

JAZZ/JAZZ STUDIES
Five Towns Coll (NY)
State Coll of Florida Manatee-Sarasota (FL)
U of Maine at Augusta (ME)

JEWISH/JUDAIC STUDIES
State Coll of Florida Manatee-Sarasota (FL)

JOURNALISM
Academy of Art U (CA)
John Brown U (AR)
Madonna U (MI)
Manchester U (IN)
Palm Beach State Coll (FL)
State Coll of Florida Manatee-Sarasota (FL)

JOURNALISM RELATED
Adams State U (CO)
National U (CA)

KINDERGARTEN/PRESCHOOL EDUCATION
Baker Coll (MI)
California U of Pennsylvania (PA)
Fisher Coll (MA)
Maria Coll (NY)
Miami U (OH)
Mitchell Coll (CT)
Mount Saint Mary's U (CA)

Palm Beach State Coll (FL)
Shawnee State U (OH)
State Coll of Florida Manatee-Sarasota (FL)
Tennessee State U (TN)
U of Great Falls (MT)
U of Rio Grande (OH)

KINESIOLOGY AND EXERCISE SCIENCE
Southwestern Adventist U (TX)

LABOR AND INDUSTRIAL RELATIONS
State U of New York Empire State Coll (NY)
Youngstown State U (OH)

LABOR STUDIES
Indiana U Bloomington (IN)
Indiana U Northwest (IN)
Indiana U–Purdue U Indianapolis (IN)

LANDSCAPE ARCHITECTURE
Academy of Art U (CA)

LANDSCAPING AND GROUNDSKEEPING
North Carolina State U (NC)
Pennsylvania Coll of Technology (PA)
State U of New York Coll of Technology at Delhi (NY)
U of Massachusetts Amherst (MA)
Valencia Coll (FL)
Vermont Tech Coll (VT)

LATIN AMERICAN STUDIES
State Coll of Florida Manatee-Sarasota (FL)

LAW ENFORCEMENT INVESTIGATION AND INTERVIEWING
Universidad del Turabo (PR)

LAY MINISTRY
Maranatha Baptist U (WI)
Southeastern Bible Coll (AL)
U of Saint Francis (IN)

LEGAL ADMINISTRATIVE ASSISTANT/SECRETARY
Baker Coll (MI)
Hickey Coll (MO)
International Business Coll, Fort Wayne (IN)
Lewis-Clark State Coll (ID)
Palm Beach State Coll (FL)
Shawnee State U (OH)
Sullivan U (KY)
Universidad del Este (PR)
U of Montana (MT)
U of Rio Grande (OH)
Washburn U (KS)
Youngstown State U (OH)

LEGAL ASSISTANT/PARALEGAL
American Public U System (WV)
Bay Path U (MA)
Calumet Coll of Saint Joseph (IN)
Champlain Coll (VT)
Clayton State U (GA)
Coll of Saint Mary (NE)
Davenport U, Grand Rapids (MI)
Eastern Kentucky U (KY)
Elms Coll (MA)
Ferris State U (MI)
Florida National U (FL)
Gannon U (PA)
Hickey Coll (MO)
Hilbert Coll (NY)
Hodges U (FL)
Husson U (ME)
Idaho State U (ID)
International Business Coll, Fort Wayne (IN)
Jones Coll, Jacksonville (FL)
Lewis-Clark State Coll (ID)
Madonna U (MI)
Maria Coll (NY)
Marian U (IN)
McNeese State U (LA)
Midland Coll (TX)
Missouri Western State U (MO)
Mount Aloysius Coll (PA)
Mount St. Joseph U (OH)
National Paralegal Coll (AZ)
National U (CA)
Newman U (KS)

New York City Coll of Technology of the City U of New York (NY)
Peirce Coll (PA)
Pennsylvania Coll of Technology (PA)
Rasmussen Coll Appleton (WI)
Rasmussen Coll Aurora (IL)
Rasmussen Coll Blaine (MN)
Rasmussen Coll Bloomington (MN)
Rasmussen Coll Brooklyn Park (MN)
Rasmussen Coll Eagan (MN)
Rasmussen Coll Fargo (ND)
Rasmussen Coll Fort Myers (FL)
Rasmussen Coll Green Bay (WI)
Rasmussen Coll Kansas City/Overland Park (KS)
Rasmussen Coll Lake Elmo/Woodbury (MN)
Rasmussen Coll Land O' Lakes (FL)
Rasmussen Coll Mankato (MN)
Rasmussen Coll Mokena/Tinley Park (IL)
Rasmussen Coll Moorhead (MN)
Rasmussen Coll New Port Richey (FL)
Rasmussen Coll Ocala (FL)
Rasmussen Coll Rockford (IL)
Rasmussen Coll Romeoville/Joliet (IL)
Rasmussen Coll St. Cloud (MN)
Rasmussen Coll Tampa/Brandon (FL)
Rasmussen Coll Topeka (KS)
Rasmussen Coll Wausau (WI)
Robert Morris U Illinois (IL)
St. Petersburg Coll (FL)
Shawnee State U (OH)
Southern Utah U (UT)
State Coll of Florida Manatee-Sarasota (FL)
Suffolk U (MA)
Sullivan U (KY)
Tulane U (LA)
Universidad del Este (PR)
The U of Akron (OH)
U of Great Falls (MT)
U of Hartford (CT)
U of Louisville (KY)
U of Montana (MT)
The U of Toledo (OH)
Utah Valley U (UT)
Valencia Coll (FL)
Washburn U (KS)
Western Kentucky U (KY)
Widener U (PA)

LEGAL PROFESSIONS AND STUDIES RELATED
Berkeley Coll–New York City Campus (NY)
Berkeley Coll–Woodland Park Campus (NJ)

LEGAL STUDIES
Maria Coll (NY)
Post U (CT)
St. John's U (NY)
U of Hartford (CT)
U of Montana (MT)
U of New Haven (CT)

LIBERAL ARTS AND SCIENCES AND HUMANITIES RELATED
Adams State U (CO)
Anderson U (IN)
Ball State U (IN)
Calumet Coll of Saint Joseph (IN)
Colorado Mesa U (CO)
Ferris State U (MI)
Kent State U at Geauga (OH)
Kent State U at Stark (OH)
Long Island U–LIU Post (NY)
Marymount California U (CA)
Mount Aloysius Coll (PA)
Pennsylvania Coll of Technology (PA)
State U of New York Coll of Technology at Delhi (NY)
Taylor U (IN)
U of Maryland U Coll (MD)
U of Wisconsin–Green Bay (WI)
U of Wisconsin–La Crosse (WI)
Walsh U (OH)
Wayland Baptist U (TX)
William Penn U (IA)

LIBERAL ARTS AND SCIENCES/LIBERAL STUDIES
Adams State U (CO)
Adelphi U (NY)
Alverno Coll (WI)
American International Coll (MA)
American U (DC)
Amridge U (AL)

Aquinas Coll (MI)
Arizona Christian U (AZ)
Arkansas State U (AR)
Armstrong State U (GA)
Averett U (VA)
Bard Coll (NY)
Bard Coll at Simon's Rock (MA)
Bay Path U (MA)
Beacon Coll (FL)
Bemidji State U (MN)
Bethel Coll (IN)
Bethel U (MN)
Boise State U (ID)
Brescia U (KY)
Briar Cliff U (IA)
Bryan Coll (TN)
Bryn Athyn Coll of the New Church (PA)
California U of Pennsylvania (PA)
Central Baptist Coll (AR)
Charter Oak State Coll (CT)
Chestnut Hill Coll (PA)
Christendom Coll (VA)
Clarke U (IA)
Clayton State U (GA)
Coll of Staten Island of the City U of New York (NY)
Colorado Mesa U (CO)
Colorado Mountain Coll, Glenwood Springs (CO)
Colorado Mountain Coll, Steamboat Springs (CO)
Columbia Coll (MO)
Columbus State U (GA)
Concordia Coll–New York (NY)
Concordia U Irvine (CA)
Dallas Baptist U (TX)
Dalton State Coll (GA)
Dickinson State U (ND)
Dominican Coll (NY)
Elmira Coll (NY)
Emmanuel Coll (GA)
Endicott Coll (MA)
Excelsior Coll (NY)
Farmingdale State Coll (NY)
Faulkner U (AL)
Felician U (NJ)
Ferris State U (MI)
Fisher Coll (MA)
Five Towns Coll (NY)
Florida A&M U (FL)
Florida Coll (FL)
Gannon U (PA)
Glenville State Coll (WV)
Gwynedd Mercy U (PA)
Hilbert Coll (NY)
Hobe Sound Bible Coll (FL)
Holy Cross Coll (IN)
Houghton Coll (NY)
Humphreys Coll (CA)
Huston-Tillotson U (TX)
Indiana U of Pennsylvania (PA)
Johnson State Coll (VT)
Judson U (IL)
Kentucky State U (KY)
Kuyper Coll (MI)
Lewis-Clark State Coll (ID)
Limestone Coll (SC)
Long Island U–LIU Brooklyn (NY)
Loras Coll (IA)
Louisiana State U at Alexandria (LA)
Lourdes U (OH)
Loyola U Chicago (IL)
Mansfield U of Pennsylvania (PA)
Maria Coll (NY)
Marian U (IN)
Marietta Coll (OH)
Marymount California U (CA)
Medgar Evers Coll of the City U of New York (NY)
Mercy Coll (NY)
Mercy Coll of Health Sciences (IA)
MidAmerica Nazarene U (KS)
Middle Georgia State U (GA)
Midwestern State U (TX)
Minnesota State U Mankato (MN)
Minnesota State U Moorhead (MN)
Mitchell Coll (CT)
Molloy Coll (NY)
Montana State U (MT)
Montana State U Billings (MT)
Montreat Coll, Montreat (NC)
Mount Aloysius Coll (PA)
Mount Marty Coll (SD)
Mount Saint Mary's U (CA)
Murray State U (KY)
Neumann U (PA)
New England Coll (NH)
Newman U (KS)
New Saint Andrews Coll (ID)

New York City Coll of Technology of the City U of New York (NY)
Niagara U (NY)
Northern Kentucky U (KY)
Northwest U (WA)
Nyack Coll (NY)
The Ohio State U at Marion (OH)
The Ohio State U–Mansfield Campus (OH)
The Ohio State U–Newark Campus (OH)
Ohio U (OH)
Ohio U–Chillicothe (OH)
Ohio Valley U (WV)
Palm Beach State Coll (FL)
Penn State Abington (PA)
Penn State Altoona (PA)
Penn State Beaver (PA)
Penn State Berks (PA)
Penn State Brandywine (PA)
Penn State Erie, The Behrend Coll (PA)
Penn State Greater Allegheny (PA)
Penn State Harrisburg (PA)
Penn State Hazleton (PA)
Penn State Lehigh Valley (PA)
Penn State New Kensington (PA)
Penn State Schuylkill (PA)
Penn State U Park (PA)
Penn State Wilkes-Barre (PA)
Penn State Worthington Scranton (PA)
Penn State York (PA)
Pine Manor Coll (MA)
Polk State Coll (FL)
Providence Coll (RI)
Quincy U (IL)
Rocky Mountain Coll (MT)
Rogers State U (OK)
St. Catherine U (MN)
St. Francis Coll (NY)
St. Gregory's U, Shawnee (OK)
St. John's U (NY)
Saint Joseph's U (PA)
Saint Leo U (FL)
Saint Louis Christian Coll (MO)
St. Petersburg Coll (FL)
St. Thomas Aquinas Coll (NY)
Salve Regina U (RI)
San Diego Christian Coll (CA)
Savannah State U (GA)
Schreiner U (TX)
Shiloh U (IA)
Southern Adventist U (TN)
Southern Vermont Coll (VT)
Spring Arbor U (MI)
State Coll of Florida Manatee-Sarasota (FL)
State U of New York Coll of Agriculture and Technology at Cobleskill (NY)
State U of New York Coll of Technology at Delhi (NY)
Suffolk U (MA)
Syracuse U (NY)
Tabor Coll (KS)
Thiel Coll (PA)
Thomas Coll (ME)
Thomas More Coll (KY)
Touro Coll (NY)
Trine U (IN)
Trinity Bible Coll (ND)
Troy U (AL)
Unity Coll (ME)
The U of Akron (OH)
U of Delaware (DE)
U of Hartford (CT)
U of Maine at Augusta (ME)
U of Maine at Fort Kent (ME)
U of Maine at Presque Isle (ME)
The U of Montana Western (MT)
U of New Hampshire at Manchester (NH)
U of North Georgia (GA)
U of Pittsburgh at Bradford (PA)
U of Saint Francis (IN)
U of South Carolina Beaufort (SC)
U of South Florida, St. Petersburg (FL)
U of the Fraser Valley (BC, Canada)
U of the Incarnate Word (TX)
U of West Florida (FL)
U of Wisconsin–Eau Claire (WI)
U of Wisconsin–Parkside (WI)
U of Wisconsin–Stevens Point (WI)
U of Wisconsin–Superior (WI)
U of Wisconsin–Whitewater (WI)
Valdosta State U (GA)
Valencia Coll (FL)
Villa Maria Coll (NY)
Washburn U (KS)

Western Connecticut State U (CT)
Western New England U (MA)
Wichita State U (KS)
Williams Baptist Coll (AR)
William Woods U (MO)
Winona State U (MN)
Wright State U–Lake Campus (OH)
Youngstown State U (OH)

LIBRARY AND ARCHIVES ASSISTING
U of Maine at Augusta (ME)
U of the Fraser Valley (BC, Canada)

LICENSED PRACTICAL/VOCATIONAL NURSE TRAINING
Arkansas Tech U (AR)
Campbellsville U (KY)
Colorado Mountain Coll, Glenwood Springs (CO)
Dickinson State U (ND)
Inter American U of Puerto Rico, Aguadilla Campus (PR)
Inter American U of Puerto Rico, Bayamón Campus (PR)
Inter American U of Puerto Rico, Metropolitan Campus (PR)
Inter American U of Puerto Rico, Ponce Campus (PR)
Inter American U of Puerto Rico, San Germán Campus (PR)
Lewis-Clark State Coll (ID)
Maria Coll (NY)
Medgar Evers Coll of the City U of New York (NY)
Monroe Coll, Bronx (NY)
Montana State U Billings (MT)
National U (CA)
Ohio U–Chillicothe (OH)
U of Montana (MT)
U of the Fraser Valley (BC, Canada)
Virginia State U (VA)

LINGUISTIC AND COMPARATIVE LANGUAGE STUDIES RELATED
Northwest U (WA)

LOGISTICS, MATERIALS, AND SUPPLY CHAIN MANAGEMENT
Arkansas Tech U (AR)
Embry-Riddle Aeronautical U–Worldwide (FL)
FIDM/Fashion Inst of Design & Merchandising, Los Angeles Campus (CA)
Polytechnic U of Puerto Rico (PR)
Sullivan U (KY)

MACHINE TOOL TECHNOLOGY
Colorado Mesa U (CO)
Idaho State U (ID)
Pennsylvania Coll of Technology (PA)

MANAGEMENT INFORMATION SYSTEMS
Arkansas State U (AR)
Inter American U of Puerto Rico, Ponce Campus (PR)
Johnson State Coll (VT)
Lindsey Wilson Coll (KY)
Morehead State U (KY)
Ohio U–Chillicothe (OH)
Shawnee State U (OH)
Thiel Coll (PA)
U of the Virgin Islands (VI)
Weber State U (UT)
Wright State U (OH)

MANAGEMENT INFORMATION SYSTEMS AND SERVICES RELATED
Mount Aloysius Coll (PA)
Rasmussen Coll Appleton (WI)
Rasmussen Coll Aurora (IL)
Rasmussen Coll Blaine (MN)
Rasmussen Coll Bloomington (MN)
Rasmussen Coll Brooklyn Park (MN)
Rasmussen Coll Eagan (MN)
Rasmussen Coll Fargo (ND)
Rasmussen Coll Fort Myers (FL)
Rasmussen Coll Green Bay (WI)
Rasmussen Coll Kansas City/Overland Park (KS)
Rasmussen Coll Lake Elmo/Woodbury (MN)
Rasmussen Coll Land O' Lakes (FL)
Rasmussen Coll Mankato (MN)
Rasmussen Coll Mokena/Tinley Park (IL)
Rasmussen Coll Moorhead (MN)

Rasmussen Coll New Port Richey (FL)
Rasmussen Coll Ocala (FL)
Rasmussen Coll Rockford (IL)
Rasmussen Coll Romeoville/Joliet (IL)
Rasmussen Coll St. Cloud (MN)
Rasmussen Coll Tampa/Brandon (FL)
Rasmussen Coll Wausau (WI)

MANUFACTURING ENGINEERING
Penn State Greater Allegheny (PA)
Penn State Hazleton (PA)
Penn State Wilkes-Barre (PA)
Penn State York (PA)

MANUFACTURING ENGINEERING TECHNOLOGY
Colorado Mesa U (CO)
Excelsior Coll (NY)
Lawrence Technological U (MI)
Lewis-Clark State Coll (ID)
Missouri Southern State U (MO)
Missouri Western State U (MO)
Morehead State U (KY)
New England Inst of Technology (RI)
Pennsylvania Coll of Technology (PA)
Purdue U (IN)
The U of Akron (OH)
Weber State U (UT)
Wright State U (OH)

MARINE BIOLOGY AND BIOLOGICAL OCEANOGRAPHY
Savannah State U (GA)

MARINE MAINTENANCE AND SHIP REPAIR TECHNOLOGY
New England Inst of Technology (RI)

MARKETING/MARKETING MANAGEMENT
Baker Coll (MI)
Berkeley Coll–New York City Campus (NY)
Cleary U (MI)
Colorado Mountain Coll, Steamboat Springs (CO)
Dalton State Coll (GA)
Ferris State U (MI)
FIDM/Fashion Inst of Design & Merchandising, Los Angeles Campus (CA)
Idaho State U (ID)
John Cabot U (Italy)
Madonna U (MI)
Miami U (OH)
New York City Coll of Technology of the City U of New York (NY)
Palm Beach State Coll (FL)
Post U (CT)
Rasmussen Coll Appleton (WI)
Rasmussen Coll Blaine (MN)
Rasmussen Coll Bloomington (MN)
Rasmussen Coll Brooklyn Park (MN)
Rasmussen Coll Eagan (MN)
Rasmussen Coll Fargo (ND)
Rasmussen Coll Fort Myers (FL)
Rasmussen Coll Green Bay (WI)
Rasmussen Coll Kansas City/Overland Park (KS)
Rasmussen Coll Lake Elmo/Woodbury (MN)
Rasmussen Coll Land O' Lakes (FL)
Rasmussen Coll Mankato (MN)
Rasmussen Coll Moorhead (MN)
Rasmussen Coll New Port Richey (FL)
Rasmussen Coll Ocala (FL)
Rasmussen Coll St. Cloud (MN)
Rasmussen Coll Tampa/Brandon (FL)
Rasmussen Coll Topeka (KS)
Rasmussen Coll Wausau (WI)
Saint Peter's U (NJ)
Southern New Hampshire U (NH)
Tulane U (LA)
Universidad Metropolitana (PR)
The U of Akron (OH)
Walsh U (OH)
Webber International U (FL)
Wright State U (OH)
Youngstown State U (OH)

MASONRY
Pennsylvania Coll of Technology (PA)

MASSAGE THERAPY
Idaho State U (ID)

MASS COMMUNICATION/ MEDIA
Adams State U (CO)
John Cabot U (Italy)
Palm Beach State Coll (FL)
Southern Adventist U (TN)
State Coll of Florida Manatee-
    Sarasota (FL)
U of Rio Grande (OH)
U of the Incarnate Word (TX)
Wright State U–Lake Campus (OH)
York Coll of Pennsylvania (PA)

MATHEMATICS
Coll of Coastal Georgia (GA)
Colorado Mountain Coll, Glenwood
    Springs (CO)
Colorado Mountain Coll, Steamboat
    Springs (CO)
Creighton U (NE)
Dalton State Coll (GA)
Hawai'i Pacific U (HI)
Idaho State U (ID)
Indiana Wesleyan U (IN)
Oklahoma Wesleyan U (OK)
Palm Beach State Coll (FL)
Shawnee State U (OH)
State U of New York Coll of
    Agriculture and Technology at
    Cobleskill (NY)
Thomas More Coll (KY)
Trevecca Nazarene U (TN)
Trine U (IN)
U of Great Falls (MT)
U of Rio Grande (OH)
Utah Valley U (UT)

MATHEMATICS TEACHER EDUCATION
State Coll of Florida Manatee-
    Sarasota (FL)

MECHANICAL DRAFTING AND CAD/CADD
Baker Coll (MI)
Midland Coll (TX)
New York City Coll of Technology of
    the City U of New York (NY)

MECHANICAL ENGINEERING
New England Inst of Technology (RI)

MECHANICAL ENGINEERING/ MECHANICAL TECHNOLOGY
Baker Coll (MI)
Bluefield State Coll (WV)
Fairmont State U (WV)
Farmingdale State Coll (NY)
Ferris State U (MI)
Idaho State U (ID)
Lawrence Technological U (MI)
Miami U (OH)
New York City Coll of Technology of
    the City U of New York (NY)
Penn State Altoona (PA)
Penn State Berks (PA)
Penn State Erie, The Behrend Coll
    (PA)
Penn State Hazleton (PA)
Penn State New Kensington (PA)
Penn State York (PA)
Purdue U (IN)
State U of New York Coll of
    Agriculture and Technology at
    Cobleskill (NY)
State U of New York Coll of
    Technology at Canton (NY)
Syracuse U (NY)
Universidad del Turabo (PR)
The U of Akron (OH)
U of Rio Grande (OH)
Vermont Tech Coll (VT)
Weber State U (UT)
Youngstown State U (OH)

MECHANICAL ENGINEERING TECHNOLOGIES RELATED
Polytechnic U of Puerto Rico (PR)
U of Massachusetts Lowell (MA)

MECHANIC AND REPAIR TECHNOLOGIES RELATED
Inter American U of Puerto Rico,
    Guayama Campus (PR)
Pennsylvania Coll of Technology
    (PA)
Washburn U (KS)

MECHANICS AND REPAIR
Idaho State U (ID)
Lewis-Clark State Coll (ID)

Utah Valley U (UT)
Weber State U (UT)

MECHATRONICS, ROBOTICS, AND AUTOMATION ENGINEERING
Johnson & Wales U (RI)
U of the Fraser Valley (BC, Canada)
Utah Valley U (UT)

MEDICAL ADMINISTRATIVE ASSISTANT AND MEDICAL SECRETARY
Arkansas Tech U (AR)
Baker Coll (MI)
Dickinson State U (ND)
Florida National U (FL)
Hallmark U (TX)
Lincoln Coll of New England,
    Southington (CT)
Monroe Coll, Bronx (NY)
Montana State U Billings (MT)
Rasmussen Coll Appleton (WI)
Rasmussen Coll Aurora (IL)
Rasmussen Coll Blaine (MN)
Rasmussen Coll Bloomington (MN)
Rasmussen Coll Brooklyn Park (MN)
Rasmussen Coll Eagan (MN)
Rasmussen Coll Fargo (ND)
Rasmussen Coll Fort Myers (FL)
Rasmussen Coll Green Bay (WI)
Rasmussen Coll Kansas City/
    Overland Park (KS)
Rasmussen Coll Lake Elmo/
    Woodbury (MN)
Rasmussen Coll Land O' Lakes (FL)
Rasmussen Coll Mankato (MN)
Rasmussen Coll Mokena/Tinley Park
    (IL)
Rasmussen Coll Moorhead (MN)
Rasmussen Coll New Port Richey
    (FL)
Rasmussen Coll Ocala (FL)
Rasmussen Coll Rockford (IL)
Rasmussen Coll Romeoville/Joliet
    (IL)
Rasmussen Coll St. Cloud (MN)
Rasmussen Coll Tampa/Brandon
    (FL)
Rasmussen Coll Wausau (WI)
Universidad del Este (PR)
U of Montana (MT)
U of Rio Grande (OH)

MEDICAL/CLINICAL ASSISTANT
Arkansas Tech U (AR)
Baker Coll (MI)
Berkeley Coll–Woodland Park
    Campus (NJ)
Cabarrus Coll of Health Sciences
    (NC)
Colorado Mesa U (CO)
Cox Coll (MO)
Davenport U, Grand Rapids (MI)
Florida National U (FL)
Hallmark U (TX)
Hodges U (FL)
Idaho State U (ID)
International Business Coll, Fort
    Wayne (IN)
Lincoln Coll of New England,
    Southington (CT)
Mercy Coll of Health Sciences (IA)
Monroe Coll, Bronx (NY)
Montana State U Billings (MT)
Montana Tech of The U of Montana
    (MT)
Mount Aloysius Coll (PA)
New England Inst of Technology (RI)
Ohio U–Chillicothe (OH)
Rasmussen Coll Appleton (WI)
Rasmussen Coll Aurora (IL)
Rasmussen Coll Blaine (MN)
Rasmussen Coll Bloomington (MN)
Rasmussen Coll Brooklyn Park (MN)
Rasmussen Coll Eagan (MN)
Rasmussen Coll Fort Myers (FL)
Rasmussen Coll Green Bay (WI)
Rasmussen Coll Kansas City/
    Overland Park (KS)
Rasmussen Coll Lake Elmo/
    Woodbury (MN)
Rasmussen Coll Land O' Lakes (FL)
Rasmussen Coll Mankato (MN)
Rasmussen Coll Mokena/Tinley Park
    (IL)
Rasmussen Coll Moorhead (MN)
Rasmussen Coll New Port Richey
    (FL)

Rasmussen Coll Ocala (FL)
Rasmussen Coll Rockford (IL)
Rasmussen Coll Romeoville/Joliet
    (IL)
Rasmussen Coll St. Cloud (MN)
Rasmussen Coll Tampa/Brandon
    (FL)
Rasmussen Coll Topeka (KS)
Rasmussen Coll Wausau (WI)
Robert Morris U Illinois (IL)
Stratford U, Alexandria (VA)
Stratford U, Falls Church (VA)
Stratford U, Glen Allen (VA)
Stratford U, Newport News (VA)
Stratford U, Virginia Beach (VA)
Stratford U, Woodbridge (VA)
Sullivan U (KY)
Universidad del Este (PR)
The U of Akron (OH)
Youngstown State U (OH)

MEDICAL/HEALTH MANAGEMENT AND CLINICAL ASSISTANT
Florida National U (FL)
Lewis-Clark State Coll (ID)
Stratford U, Woodbridge (VA)

MEDICAL INFORMATICS
Champlain Coll (VT)
Montana Tech of The U of Montana
    (MT)
National U (CA)

MEDICAL INSURANCE CODING
Columbia Southern U (AL)
National U (CA)
Stratford U, Woodbridge (VA)

MEDICAL INSURANCE/ MEDICAL BILLING
Cox Coll (MO)
Stratford U, Falls Church (VA)
Stratford U, Glen Allen (VA)
Stratford U, Newport News (VA)
Stratford U, Woodbridge (VA)

MEDICAL MICROBIOLOGY AND BACTERIOLOGY
Florida National U (FL)

MEDICAL OFFICE ASSISTANT
Hickey Coll (MO)
Lewis-Clark State Coll (ID)
Sullivan U (KY)

MEDICAL OFFICE MANAGEMENT
Dalton State Coll (GA)
The U of Akron (OH)

MEDICAL RADIOLOGIC TECHNOLOGY
Ball State U (IN)
Bluefield State Coll (WV)
Coll of Coastal Georgia (GA)
Ferris State U (MI)
Idaho State U (ID)
Inter American U of Puerto Rico,
    Aguadilla Campus (PR)
Inter American U of Puerto Rico,
    Ponce Campus (PR)
Inter American U of Puerto Rico, San
    Germán Campus (PR)
La Roche Coll (PA)
Mercy Coll of Ohio (OH)
Missouri Southern State U (MO)
Morehead State U (KY)
Mount Aloysius Coll (PA)
Newman U (KS)
New York City Coll of Technology of
    the City U of New York (NY)
Penn State New Kensington (PA)
Penn State Schuylkill (PA)
Pennsylvania Coll of Health
    Sciences (PA)
Pennsylvania Coll of Technology
    (PA)
Polk State Coll (FL)
St. Catherine U (MN)
Shawnee State U (OH)
Southwestern Oklahoma State U
    (OK)
State Coll of Florida Manatee-
    Sarasota (FL)
The U of Akron (OH)
U of Arkansas for Medical Sciences
    (AR)
U of Charleston (WV)
U of New Mexico (NM)
Valencia Coll (FL)

Weber State U (UT)

MEETING AND EVENT PLANNING
Sullivan U (KY)

MENTAL AND SOCIAL HEALTH SERVICES AND ALLIED PROFESSIONS RELATED
U of Maine at Augusta (ME)
Washburn U (KS)

MERCHANDISING
The U of Akron (OH)

MERCHANDISING, SALES, AND MARKETING OPERATIONS RELATED (GENERAL)
Inter American U of Puerto Rico,
    Aguadilla Campus (PR)
Inter American U of Puerto Rico,
    Ponce Campus (PR)
State U of New York Coll of
    Technology at Delhi (NY)

METAL AND JEWELRY ARTS
Academy of Art U (CA)
Fashion Inst of Technology (NY)
FIDM/Fashion Inst of Design &
    Merchandising, Los Angeles
    Campus (CA)

METALLURGICAL TECHNOLOGY
Penn State Altoona (PA)
Penn State Berks (PA)
Penn State Erie, The Behrend Coll
    (PA)
Penn State Hazleton (PA)
Penn State New Kensington (PA)
Penn State Schuylkill (PA)
Penn State Wilkes-Barre (PA)
Penn State York (PA)

MICROBIOLOGY
Weber State U (UT)

MIDDLE SCHOOL EDUCATION
Wright State U (OH)

MILITARY HISTORY
American Public U System (WV)

MILITARY TECHNOLOGIES AND APPLIED SCIENCES RELATED
Central Baptist Coll (AR)

MINING AND PETROLEUM TECHNOLOGIES RELATED
U of the Virgin Islands (VI)

MISSIONARY STUDIES AND MISSIOLOGY
Faith Baptist Bible Coll and
    Theological Seminary (IA)
Hobe Sound Bible Coll (FL)
Ohio Christian U (OH)
U of the Cumberlands (KY)

MULTI/INTERDISCIPLINARY STUDIES RELATED
Arkansas Tech U (AR)
Liberty U (VA)
Miami U (OH)
Montana Tech of The U of Montana
    (MT)
Northwest Missouri State U (MO)
Ohio U–Chillicothe (OH)
Pennsylvania Coll of Technology
    (PA)
State U of New York Empire State
    Coll (NY)
The U of Akron (OH)
The U of Montana Western (MT)
Utah Valley U (UT)
Washburn U (KS)

MUSEUM STUDIES
Inst of American Indian Arts (NM)

MUSIC
Clayton State U (GA)
Five Towns Coll (NY)
Hannibal-LaGrange U (MO)
Marian U (IN)
Middle Georgia State U (GA)
Mount Vernon Nazarene U (OH)
Nyack Coll (NY)
Pacific Union Coll (CA)
Palm Beach State Coll (FL)

St. Petersburg Coll (FL)
State Coll of Florida Manatee-
    Sarasota (FL)
Thomas More Coll (KY)
U of Rio Grande (OH)
Utah Valley U (UT)
Williams Baptist Coll (AR)
York Coll of Pennsylvania (PA)

MUSICAL INSTRUMENT FABRICATION AND REPAIR
Indiana U Bloomington (IN)

MUSIC MANAGEMENT
Five Towns Coll (NY)
U of Central Oklahoma (OK)

MUSIC PERFORMANCE
Five Towns Coll (NY)
Inter American U of Puerto Rico,
    Metropolitan Campus (PR)
State Coll of Florida Manatee-
    Sarasota (FL)
Trevecca Nazarene U (TN)
U of Central Oklahoma (OK)

MUSIC RELATED
Academy of Art U (CA)
Alverno Coll (WI)
Five Towns Coll (NY)
Hobe Sound Bible Coll (FL)

MUSIC TEACHER EDUCATION
State Coll of Florida Manatee-
    Sarasota (FL)
Wright State U (OH)

MUSIC TECHNOLOGY
U of Central Oklahoma (OK)
U of Saint Francis (IN)

MUSIC THEORY AND COMPOSITION
State Coll of Florida Manatee-
    Sarasota (FL)

NANOTECHNOLOGY
Lock Haven U of Pennsylvania (PA)

NATURAL RESOURCES/ CONSERVATION
State U of New York Coll of
    Environmental Science and
    Forestry (NY)

NATURAL RESOURCES MANAGEMENT AND POLICY RELATED
State U of New York Coll of
    Technology at Delhi (NY)

NATURAL SCIENCES
Colorado Mountain Coll, Glenwood
    Springs (CO)
Lourdes U (OH)
Madonna U (MI)
Roberts Wesleyan Coll (NY)
St. Petersburg Coll (FL)
Universidad del Este (PR)
Washburn U (KS)

NETWORK AND SYSTEM ADMINISTRATION
Florida National U (FL)
Palm Beach State Coll (FL)
Polk State Coll (FL)

NUCLEAR ENGINEERING TECHNOLOGY
Arkansas Tech U (AR)
Idaho State U (ID)

NUCLEAR MEDICAL TECHNOLOGY
Ball State U (IN)
The George Washington U (DC)
Molloy Coll (NY)
Pennsylvania Coll of Health
    Sciences (PA)
The U of Findlay (OH)

NUCLEAR/NUCLEAR POWER TECHNOLOGY
Excelsior Coll (NY)

NURSING ASSISTANT/AIDE AND PATIENT CARE ASSISTANT/AIDE
Universidad del Turabo (PR)

NURSING EDUCATION
Middle Georgia State U (GA)

NURSING SCIENCE
Baker Coll (MI)
Dixie State U (UT)
EDP U of Puerto Rico (PR)
EDP U of Puerto Rico–San Sebastian (PR)
Inter American U of Puerto Rico, Barranquitas Campus (PR)

OCCUPATIONAL SAFETY AND HEALTH TECHNOLOGY
Columbia Southern U (AL)
Fairmont State U (WV)

OCCUPATIONAL THERAPIST ASSISTANT
Adventist U of Health Sciences (FL)
Arkansas State U (AR)
Arkansas Tech U (AR)
Baker Coll (MI)
Cabarrus Coll of Health Sciences (NC)
California U of Pennsylvania (PA)
Inter American U of Puerto Rico, Ponce Campus (PR)
Jefferson Coll of Health Sciences (VA)
Lincoln Coll of New England, Southington (CT)
Maria Coll (NY)
Mercy Coll (NY)
Middle Georgia State U (GA)
New England Inst of Technology (RI)
Newman U (KS)
Penn State Berks (PA)
Pennsylvania Coll of Technology (PA)
Polk State Coll (FL)
Rutgers U–New Brunswick (NJ)
St. Catherine U (MN)
Southwestern Oklahoma State U (OK)
State Coll of Florida Manatee-Sarasota (FL)
U of Charleston (WV)
U of Louisiana at Monroe (LA)
U of Southern Indiana (IN)
Washburn U (KS)

OCCUPATIONAL THERAPY
Coll of Coastal Georgia (GA)
Palm Beach State Coll (FL)
Shawnee State U (OH)
Southern Adventist U (TN)
State Coll of Florida Manatee-Sarasota (FL)
Touro Coll (NY)

OFFICE MANAGEMENT
Dalton State Coll (GA)
Emmanuel Coll (GA)
Inter American U of Puerto Rico, Aguadilla Campus (PR)
Inter American U of Puerto Rico, Barranquitas Campus (PR)
Inter American U of Puerto Rico, Bayamón Campus (PR)
Inter American U of Puerto Rico, Fajardo Campus (PR)
Inter American U of Puerto Rico, Guayama Campus (PR)
Inter American U of Puerto Rico, Ponce Campus (PR)
Inter American U of Puerto Rico, San Germán Campus (PR)
Maranatha Baptist U (WI)
Miami U (OH)
Shawnee State U (OH)
Universidad del Turabo (PR)
Universidad Metropolitana (PR)
The U of Akron (OH)

OFFICE OCCUPATIONS AND CLERICAL SERVICES
Midland Coll (TX)

OPERATIONS MANAGEMENT
Polk State Coll (FL)

OPTICAL SCIENCES
Indiana U of Pennsylvania (PA)

OPTICIANRY
New York City Coll of Technology of the City U of New York (NY)

OPTOMETRIC TECHNICIAN
Indiana U Bloomington (IN)
Inter American U of Puerto Rico, Ponce Campus (PR)

ORGANIZATIONAL COMMUNICATION
Creighton U (NE)

ORGANIZATIONAL LEADERSHIP
Beulah Heights U (GA)
Grace Coll (IN)
Hawai`i Pacific U (HI)
Point U (GA)
Purdue U (IN)

ORNAMENTAL HORTICULTURE
Farmingdale State Coll (NY)
State U of New York Coll of Agriculture and Technology at Cobleskill (NY)
U of the Fraser Valley (BC, Canada)
Vermont Tech Coll (VT)

ORTHOTICS/PROSTHETICS
Baker Coll (MI)

PAINTING
Pratt Inst (NY)

PALLIATIVE CARE NURSING
Madonna U (MI)

PARKS, RECREATION AND LEISURE
St. Petersburg Coll (FL)

PARKS, RECREATION AND LEISURE FACILITIES MANAGEMENT
Coll of Coastal Georgia (GA)
Colorado Mountain Coll, Steamboat Springs (CO)
Webber International U (FL)

PARKS, RECREATION, LEISURE, AND FITNESS STUDIES RELATED
Southern Nazarene U (OK)

PASTORAL COUNSELING AND SPECIALIZED MINISTRIES RELATED
Brescia U (KY)

PASTORAL STUDIES/COUNSELING
Indiana Wesleyan U (IN)
Marian U (IN)
William Jessup U (CA)

PETROLEUM TECHNOLOGY
Mansfield U of Pennsylvania (PA)
Montana State U Billings (MT)
U of Pittsburgh at Bradford (PA)

PHARMACEUTICAL SCIENCES
Universidad del Turabo (PR)

PHARMACOLOGY
Universidad del Turabo (PR)

PHARMACY, PHARMACEUTICAL SCIENCES, AND ADMINISTRATION RELATED
EDP U of Puerto Rico (PR)
EDP U of Puerto Rico–San Sebastian (PR)
Universidad del Turabo (PR)

PHARMACY TECHNICIAN
Baker Coll (MI)
Cabarrus Coll of Health Sciences (NC)
Inter American U of Puerto Rico, Aguadilla Campus (PR)
Inter American U of Puerto Rico, Guayama Campus (PR)
Rasmussen Coll Appleton (WI)
Rasmussen Coll Aurora (IL)
Rasmussen Coll Blaine (MN)
Rasmussen Coll Bloomington (MN)
Rasmussen Coll Brooklyn Park (MN)
Rasmussen Coll Eagan (MN)
Rasmussen Coll Fort Myers (FL)
Rasmussen Coll Green Bay (WI)
Rasmussen Coll Kansas City/Overland Park (KS)
Rasmussen Coll Lake Elmo/Woodbury (MN)
Rasmussen Coll Land O' Lakes (FL)
Rasmussen Coll Mankato (MN)
Rasmussen Coll Mokena/Tinley Park (IL)
Rasmussen Coll Moorhead (MN)
Rasmussen Coll New Port Richey (FL)
Rasmussen Coll Ocala (FL)
Rasmussen Coll Rockford (IL)
Rasmussen Coll Romeoville/Joliet (IL)
Rasmussen Coll St. Cloud (MN)
Rasmussen Coll Tampa/Brandon (FL)
Rasmussen Coll Topeka (KS)
Rasmussen Coll Wausau (WI)
Robert Morris U Illinois (IL)
Stratford U, Falls Church (VA)
Stratford U, Glen Allen (VA)
Stratford U, Newport News (VA)
Stratford U, Virginia Beach (VA)
Stratford U, Woodbridge (VA)
Sullivan U (KY)
Universidad del Este (PR)
Universidad del Turabo (PR)

PHILOSOPHY
Carroll Coll (MT)
Coll of Coastal Georgia (GA)
John Cabot U (Italy)
Palm Beach State Coll (FL)
State Coll of Florida Manatee-Sarasota (FL)
Thomas More Coll (KY)
Utah Valley U (UT)

PHLEBOTOMY TECHNOLOGY
Stratford U, Glen Allen (VA)
Stratford U, Newport News (VA)
Stratford U, Woodbridge (VA)

PHOTOGRAPHIC AND FILM/VIDEO TECHNOLOGY
St. John's U (NY)

PHOTOGRAPHY
Colorado Mountain Coll, Glenwood Springs (CO)
Pacific Union Coll (CA)
Paier Coll of Art, Inc. (CT)
Palm Beach State Coll (FL)
St. Petersburg Coll (FL)
Villa Maria Coll (NY)

PHYSICAL EDUCATION TEACHING AND COACHING
Palm Beach State Coll (FL)
State Coll of Florida Manatee-Sarasota (FL)
U of Rio Grande (OH)

PHYSICAL SCIENCES
Coll of Staten Island of the City U of New York (NY)
Colorado Mountain Coll, Steamboat Springs (CO)
New York City Coll of Technology of the City U of New York (NY)
Oklahoma Wesleyan U (OK)
Palm Beach State Coll (FL)
Roberts Wesleyan Coll (NY)
U of the Fraser Valley (BC, Canada)
Utah Valley U (UT)

PHYSICAL SCIENCES RELATED
State U of New York Empire State Coll (NY)

PHYSICAL THERAPY
Coll of Coastal Georgia (GA)
Palm Beach State Coll (FL)
Southern Adventist U (TN)
State Coll of Florida Manatee-Sarasota (FL)
Touro Coll (NY)

PHYSICAL THERAPY TECHNOLOGY
Arkansas State U (AR)
Arkansas Tech U (AR)
Baker Coll (MI)
California U of Pennsylvania (PA)
Dixie State U (UT)
EDP U of Puerto Rico (PR)
EDP U of Puerto Rico–San Sebastian (PR)
Idaho State U (ID)
Inter American U of Puerto Rico, Ponce Campus (PR)
Jefferson Coll of Health Sciences (VA)
Louisiana Coll (LA)
Mercy Coll of Health Sciences (IA)
Missouri Western State U (MO)
Mount Aloysius Coll (PA)
Nebraska Methodist Coll (NE)
New England Inst of Technology (RI)
Our Lady of the Lake Coll (LA)
Penn State Hazleton (PA)
Polk State Coll (FL)
St. Catherine U (MN)

PHYSICIAN ASSISTANT
Coll of Coastal Georgia (GA)
State Coll of Florida Manatee-Sarasota (FL)

PHYSICS
Coll of Coastal Georgia (GA)
Dalton State Coll (GA)
Idaho State U (ID)
Rogers State U (OK)
State Coll of Florida Manatee-Sarasota (FL)
Thomas More Coll (KY)
U of the Virgin Islands (VI)
U of Wisconsin–Parkside (WI)
Utah Valley U (UT)
York Coll of Pennsylvania (PA)

PHYSICS TEACHER EDUCATION
State Coll of Florida Manatee-Sarasota (FL)

PIPEFITTING AND SPRINKLER FITTING
New England Inst of Technology (RI)
State U of New York Coll of Technology at Delhi (NY)

PLANT NURSERY MANAGEMENT
Dalhousie U (NS, Canada)

PLANT PROTECTION AND INTEGRATED PEST MANAGEMENT
Dalhousie U (NS, Canada)

PLANT SCIENCES
State U of New York Coll of Agriculture and Technology at Cobleskill (NY)

PLASTICS AND POLYMER ENGINEERING TECHNOLOGY
Ferris State U (MI)
Penn State Erie, The Behrend Coll (PA)
Pennsylvania Coll of Technology (PA)
Shawnee State U (OH)

PLAYWRITING AND SCREENWRITING
Pacific Union Coll (CA)

POLITICAL SCIENCE AND GOVERNMENT
Adams State U (CO)
Coll of Coastal Georgia (GA)
Dalton State Coll (GA)
Holy Cross Coll (IN)
Immaculata U (PA)
John Cabot U (Italy)
Liberty U (VA)
Middle Georgia State U (GA)
Palm Beach State Coll (FL)
Thomas More Coll (KY)

POLITICAL SCIENCE AND GOVERNMENT RELATED
Inter American U of Puerto Rico, Fajardo Campus (PR)

POULTRY SCIENCE
State U of New York Coll of Agriculture and Technology at Cobleskill (NY)

PRACTICAL NURSING, VOCATIONAL NURSING AND NURSING ASSISTANTS RELATED
Caribbean U (PR)
Rasmussen Coll Ocala School of Nursing (FL)

St. Petersburg Coll (FL)
Shawnee State U (OH)
Southern Illinois U Carbondale (IL)
Southwestern Oklahoma State U (OK)
State Coll of Florida Manatee-Sarasota (FL)
State U of New York Coll of Technology at Canton (NY)
U of Evansville (IN)
U of Maine at Presque Isle (ME)
U of Saint Francis (IN)
Villa Maria Coll (NY)
Washburn U (KS)

PRECISION METAL WORKING RELATED
Montana Tech of The U of Montana (MT)

PRE-DENTISTRY STUDIES
Coll of Coastal Georgia (GA)
Concordia U Wisconsin (WI)

PRE-ENGINEERING
Coll of Coastal Georgia (GA)
Colorado Mountain Coll, Steamboat Springs (CO)
Columbia Coll (MO)
Dixie State U (UT)
Newman U (KS)
Palm Beach State Coll (FL)
Southern Utah U (UT)
Utah Valley U (UT)
Weber State U (UT)

PRE-LAW STUDIES
Ferris State U (MI)
Florida National U (FL)
Thomas More Coll (KY)
Wayland Baptist U (TX)

PREMEDICAL STUDIES
Coll of Coastal Georgia (GA)
Concordia U Wisconsin (WI)

PRENURSING STUDIES
Concordia U Wisconsin (WI)
Lincoln Christian U (IL)
National U (CA)

PRE-PHARMACY STUDIES
Coll of Coastal Georgia (GA)
Dalton State Coll (GA)
Ferris State U (MI)
Madonna U (MI)
State Coll of Florida Manatee-Sarasota (FL)

PRE-THEOLOGY/PRE-MINISTERIAL STUDIES
Nazarene Bible Coll (CO)
Theological U of the Caribbean (PR)

PRE-VETERINARY STUDIES
Coll of Coastal Georgia (GA)

PROFESSIONAL, TECHNICAL, BUSINESS, AND SCIENTIFIC WRITING
Ferris State U (MI)
Florida National U (FL)

PSYCHIATRIC/MENTAL HEALTH SERVICES TECHNOLOGY
Pennsylvania Coll of Technology (PA)
U of Maine at Augusta (ME)

PSYCHOLOGY
Beacon Coll (FL)
Calumet Coll of Saint Joseph (IN)
Central Methodist U (MO)
Coll of Coastal Georgia (GA)
Colorado Mountain Coll, Glenwood Springs (CO)
Dalton State Coll (GA)
Ferris State U (MI)
Fisher Coll (MA)
John Cabot U (Italy)
Liberty U (VA)
Life U (CA)
Montana State U Billings (MT)
Muhlenberg Coll (PA)
New England Coll (NH)
Palm Beach State Coll (FL)
Point U (GA)
Regent U (VA)
State Coll of Florida Manatee-Sarasota (FL)
State U of New York Empire State Coll (NY)
Thomas More Coll (KY)
U of Rio Grande (OH)
U of the Cumberlands (KY)
Utah Valley U (UT)
Wright State U (OH)
Wright State U–Lake Campus (OH)

PUBLIC ADMINISTRATION
Central Methodist U (MO)
Ferris State U (MI)
Florida National U (FL)
State Coll of Florida Manatee-Sarasota (FL)
Universidad del Turabo (PR)
U of Maine at Augusta (ME)

PUBLIC ADMINISTRATION AND SOCIAL SERVICE PROFESSIONS RELATED
Metropolitan Coll of New York (NY)
Thomas More Coll (KY)
The U of Akron (OH)

PUBLIC HEALTH
American Public U System (WV)

PUBLIC POLICY ANALYSIS
Saint Peter's U (NJ)

PUBLIC RELATIONS, ADVERTISING, AND APPLIED COMMUNICATION RELATED
John Brown U (AR)
U of Maine at Presque Isle (ME)

PUBLIC RELATIONS/IMAGE MANAGEMENT
John Brown U (AR)

PURCHASING, PROCUREMENT/ ACQUISITIONS AND CONTRACTS MANAGEMENT
Trevecca Nazarene U (TN)

QUALITY CONTROL AND SAFETY TECHNOLOGIES RELATED
Madonna U (MI)

QUALITY CONTROL TECHNOLOGY
Universidad del Turabo (PR)
Weber State U (UT)

RADIO AND TELEVISION
Lawrence Technological U (MI)
State Coll of Florida Manatee-Sarasota (FL)

RADIO AND TELEVISION BROADCASTING TECHNOLOGY
Lincoln Coll of New England, Southington (CT)
New England Inst of Technology (RI)
State Coll of Florida Manatee-Sarasota (FL)

RADIOLOGIC TECHNOLOGY/ SCIENCE
Adventist U of Health Sciences (FL)
Allen Coll (IA)
Alvernia U (PA)
Aultman Coll of Nursing and Health Sciences (OH)
Baker Coll (MI)
Champlain Coll (VT)
Colorado Mesa U (CO)
Cox Coll (MO)
Dalton State Coll (GA)
Dixie State U (UT)
Florida National U (FL)
Fort Hays State U (KS)
Gannon U (PA)
Holy Family U (PA)
Indiana U Kokomo (IN)
Indiana U Northwest (IN)
Indiana U–Purdue U Indianapolis (IN)
Indiana U South Bend (IN)
Inter American U of Puerto Rico, Barranquitas Campus (PR)
Lewis-Clark State Coll (ID)
Louisiana State U at Alexandria (LA)
Mansfield U of Pennsylvania (PA)
Mercy Coll of Health Sciences (IA)
Montana Tech of The U of Montana (MT)
Nebraska Methodist Coll (NE)
Newman U (KS)
Pennsylvania Coll of Health Sciences (PA)
Regis Coll (MA)
St. Petersburg Coll (FL)
State Coll of Florida Manatee-Sarasota (FL)
Universidad del Este (PR)
U of Montana (MT)
U of Rio Grande (OH)
U of Saint Francis (IN)
Washburn U (KS)
Weber State U (UT)
Widener U (PA)

RADIO, TELEVISION, AND DIGITAL COMMUNICATION RELATED
Lawrence Technological U (MI)
Madonna U (MI)

REAL ESTATE
American Public U System (WV)
Colorado Mountain Coll, Steamboat Springs (CO)
National U (CA)
Saint Francis U (PA)

RECEPTIONIST
U of Montana (MT)

RECORDING ARTS TECHNOLOGY
Indiana U Bloomington (IN)
Los Angeles Film School (CA)

REGIONAL STUDIES
Arkansas Tech U (AR)

REGISTERED NURSING, NURSING ADMINISTRATION, NURSING RESEARCH AND CLINICAL NURSING RELATED
Rasmussen Coll Ocala School of Nursing (FL)
Universidad del Este (PR)

REGISTERED NURSING/ REGISTERED NURSE
Alcorn State U (MS)
Aquinas Coll (TN)
Arkansas State U (AR)
Arkansas Tech U (AR)
Aultman Coll of Nursing and Health Sciences (OH)
Becker Coll (MA)
Bethel Coll (IN)
Bluefield State Coll (WV)
Cabarrus Coll of Health Sciences (NC)
California U of Pennsylvania (PA)
Campbellsville U (KY)
Coll of Coastal Georgia (GA)
Coll of Staten Island of the City U of New York (NY)
Colorado Mesa U (CO)
Colorado Mountain Coll, Glenwood Springs (CO)
Columbia Coll (MO)
Cox Coll (MO)
Dalton State Coll (GA)
Dixie State U (UT)
Eastern Kentucky U (KY)
Excelsior Coll (NY)
Fairmont State U (WV)
Florida National U (FL)
Gardner-Webb U (NC)
Hallmark U (TX)
Hannibal-LaGrange U (MO)
Idaho State U (ID)
Inter American U of Puerto Rico, Barranquitas Campus (PR)
Inter American U of Puerto Rico, Guayama Campus (PR)
Judson Coll (AL)
Kent State U at Geauga (OH)
Kentucky State U (KY)
La Roche Coll (PA)
Lincoln U (MO)
Lock Haven U of Pennsylvania (PA)
Louisiana State U at Alexandria (LA)
Louisiana Tech U (LA)
Maria Coll (NY)
Marshall U (WV)
Mercy Coll of Health Sciences (IA)
Mercy Coll of Ohio (OH)
Miami U (OH)
Middle Georgia State U (GA)
Midland Coll (TX)
Mississippi U for Women (MS)
Montana State U Billings (MT)
Montana Tech of The U of Montana (MT)
Morehead State U (KY)
Mount Aloysius Coll (PA)
Mount Saint Mary's U (CA)
National U (CA)
New England Inst of Technology (RI)
New York City Coll of Technology of the City U of New York (NY)
Our Lady of the Lake Coll (LA)
Pacific Union Coll (CA)
Palm Beach State Coll (FL)
Penn State Altoona (PA)
Penn State Berks (PA)

Penn State Erie, The Behrend Coll (PA)
Penn State Worthington Scranton (PA)
Pennsylvania Coll of Health Sciences (PA)
Pennsylvania Coll of Technology (PA)
Polk State Coll (FL)
Regis Coll (MA)
Robert Morris U Illinois (IL)
Rogers State U (OK)
St. Petersburg Coll (FL)
Shawnee State U (OH)
Southern Adventist U (TN)
Southern Arkansas U–Magnolia (AR)
Southwest Baptist U (MO)
State Coll of Florida Manatee-Sarasota (FL)
State U of New York Coll of Technology at Canton (NY)
State U of New York Coll of Technology at Delhi (NY)
Stevens-Henager Coll, Boise (ID)
Stratford U, Glen Allen (VA)
Sul Ross State U (TX)
Tennessee State U (TN)
Troy U (AL)
Universidad Adventista de las Antillas (PR)
Universidad del Turabo (PR)
Universidad Metropolitana (PR)
U of Charleston (WV)
U of North Georgia (GA)
U of Pikeville (KY)
U of Pittsburgh at Bradford (PA)
U of Rio Grande (OH)
U of Saint Francis (IN)
U of the Virgin Islands (VI)
The U of West Alabama (AL)
Utah Valley U (UT)
Valencia Coll (FL)
Vermont Tech Coll (VT)
Weber State U (UT)
Western Kentucky U (KY)

REHABILITATION AIDE
U of Maine at Augusta (ME)

REHABILITATION AND THERAPEUTIC PROFESSIONS RELATED
National U (CA)
Rutgers U–Newark (NJ)
Rutgers U–New Brunswick (NJ)

RELIGIOUS EDUCATION
Dallas Baptist U (TX)
Kuyper Coll (MI)
Marian U (IN)
Nazarene Bible Coll (CO)

RELIGIOUS/SACRED MUSIC
Calvary Bible Coll and Theological Seminary (MO)
Dallas Baptist U (TX)
Indiana Wesleyan U (IN)
Mount Vernon Nazarene U (OH)
Nazarene Bible Coll (CO)
Nebraska Christian Coll (NE)
Ohio Christian U (OH)
Trevecca Nazarene U (TN)

RELIGIOUS STUDIES
Beulah Heights U (GA)
Calumet Coll of Saint Joseph (IN)
Concordia Coll–New York (NY)
Corban U (OR)
Holy Apostles Coll and Seminary (CT)
Jarvis Christian Coll (TX)
Liberty U (VA)
Lourdes U (OH)
Madonna U (MI)
Mount Marty Coll (SD)
Mount Vernon Nazarene U (OH)
Northwest U (WA)
Oakland City U (IN)
Palm Beach State Coll (FL)
Southern Adventist U (TN)
State Coll of Florida Manatee-Sarasota (FL)
Thomas More Coll (KY)

RESORT MANAGEMENT
State U of New York Coll of Technology at Delhi (NY)

RESPIRATORY CARE THERAPY
Boise State U (ID)

Coll of Coastal Georgia (GA)
Dakota State U (SD)
Dixie State U (UT)
Ferris State U (MI)
Gannon U (PA)
Gwynedd Mercy U (PA)
Idaho State U (ID)
Inter American U of Puerto Rico, Guayama Campus (PR)
Jefferson Coll of Health Sciences (VA)
Mansfield U of Pennsylvania (PA)
Middle Georgia State U (GA)
Midland Coll (TX)
Missouri Southern State U (MO)
Molloy Coll (NY)
Morehead State U (KY)
Nebraska Methodist Coll (NE)
Newman U (KS)
Pennsylvania Coll of Health Sciences (PA)
Polk State Coll (FL)
Rutgers U–New Brunswick (NJ)
St. Petersburg Coll (FL)
Shawnee State U (OH)
State Coll of Florida Manatee-Sarasota (FL)
Stevens-Henager Coll, Boise (ID)
Universidad Adventista de las Antillas (PR)
Universidad del Turabo (PR)
Universidad Metropolitana (PR)
U of Arkansas for Medical Sciences (AR)
U of Montana (MT)
U of Southern Indiana (IN)
Valencia Coll (FL)
Vermont Tech Coll (VT)
Washburn U (KS)
Weber State U (UT)
York Coll of Pennsylvania (PA)

RESPIRATORY THERAPY TECHNICIAN
Dalton State Coll (GA)
Florida National U (FL)

RESTAURANT, CULINARY, AND CATERING MANAGEMENT
Arkansas Tech U (AR)
Colorado Mountain Coll, Steamboat Springs (CO)
Ferris State U (MI)
St. Petersburg Coll (FL)
State U of New York Coll of Agriculture and Technology at Cobleskill (NY)
State U of New York Coll of Technology at Delhi (NY)
Stratford U (MD)

RESTAURANT/FOOD SERVICES MANAGEMENT
Pennsylvania Coll of Technology (PA)
Stratford U (MD)
Stratford U, Falls Church (VA)
Stratford U, Newport News (VA)
Stratford U, Woodbridge (VA)
The U of Akron (OH)
Valencia Coll (FL)

RETAILING
American Public U System (WV)
International Business Coll, Fort Wayne (IN)
Weber State U (UT)

RHETORIC AND COMPOSITION
Ferris State U (MI)
State Coll of Florida Manatee-Sarasota (FL)

ROBOTICS TECHNOLOGY
California U of Pennsylvania (PA)
Idaho State U (ID)
Pennsylvania Coll of Technology (PA)
U of Rio Grande (OH)
Utah Valley U (UT)

RUSSIAN
Idaho State U (ID)

RUSSIAN, CENTRAL EUROPEAN, EAST EUROPEAN AND EURASIAN STUDIES
State Coll of Florida Manatee-Sarasota (FL)

RUSSIAN STUDIES
State Coll of Florida Manatee-Sarasota (FL)

SALES AND MARKETING/ MARKETING AND DISTRIBUTION TEACHER EDUCATION
Wright State U (OH)

SALES, DISTRIBUTION, AND MARKETING OPERATIONS
Baker Coll (MI)
Dalton State Coll (GA)
Inter American U of Puerto Rico, Aguadilla Campus (PR)
Southern Adventist U (TN)
Sullivan U (KY)
Universidad Metropolitana (PR)
The U of Findlay (OH)

SCIENCE TEACHER EDUCATION
State Coll of Florida Manatee-Sarasota (FL)
Wright State U (OH)

SCIENCE TECHNOLOGIES
Washburn U (KS)

SCIENCE TECHNOLOGIES RELATED
Madonna U (MI)
Maria Coll (NY)
Ohio Valley U (WV)
State U of New York Coll of Agriculture and Technology at Cobleskill (NY)

SECONDARY EDUCATION
Ferris State U (MI)
Ohio U–Chillicothe (OH)
Rogers State U (OK)

SECURITY AND LOSS PREVENTION
John Jay Coll of Criminal Justice of the City U of New York (NY)

SELLING SKILLS AND SALES
Inter American U of Puerto Rico, San Germán Campus (PR)
The U of Akron (OH)

SHEET METAL TECHNOLOGY
Montana State U Billings (MT)

SIGN LANGUAGE INTERPRETATION AND TRANSLATION
Mount Aloysius Coll (PA)
St. Catherine U (MN)

SMALL BUSINESS ADMINISTRATION
Lewis-Clark State Coll (ID)
The U of Akron (OH)

SMALL ENGINE MECHANICS AND REPAIR TECHNOLOGY
U of Montana (MT)

SOCIAL PSYCHOLOGY
State Coll of Florida Manatee-Sarasota (FL)

SOCIAL SCIENCES
Campbellsville U (KY)
Colorado Mountain Coll, Glenwood Springs (CO)
Colorado Mountain Coll, Steamboat Springs (CO)
Long Island U–LIU Brooklyn (NY)
Marymount Manhattan Coll (NY)
Palm Beach State Coll (FL)
Rogers State U (OK)
St. Gregory's U, Shawnee (OK)
Saint Peter's U (NJ)
Shawnee State U (OH)
State Coll of Florida Manatee-Sarasota (FL)
State U of New York Empire State Coll (NY)
Trine U (IN)
Universidad del Turabo (PR)
U of Southern Indiana (IN)
Valparaiso U (IN)
Wayland Baptist U (TX)

SOCIAL SCIENCES RELATED
U of Wisconsin–Parkside (WI)

SOCIAL SCIENCE TEACHER EDUCATION
Montana State U (MT)

SOCIAL STUDIES TEACHER EDUCATION
State Coll of Florida Manatee-Sarasota (FL)

SOCIAL WORK
Ferris State U (MI)
Palm Beach State Coll (FL)
State Coll of Florida Manatee-Sarasota (FL)
State U of New York Coll of Agriculture and Technology at Cobleskill (NY)
U of Rio Grande (OH)
U of the Fraser Valley (BC, Canada)
Wright State U (OH)
Wright State U–Lake Campus (OH)
Youngstown State U (OH)

SOCIAL WORK RELATED
Middle Georgia State U (GA)
The U of Akron (OH)

SOCIOLOGY
Coll of Coastal Georgia (GA)
Holy Cross Coll (IN)
Lourdes U (OH)
Middle Georgia State U (GA)
Montana State U Billings (MT)
New England Coll (NH)
Thomas More Coll (KY)
U of Rio Grande (OH)
The U of Scranton (PA)
Wright State U (OH)
Wright State U–Lake Campus (OH)

SOLAR ENERGY TECHNOLOGY
Pennsylvania Coll of Technology (PA)

SPANISH
Holy Cross Coll (IN)
Immaculata U (PA)
State Coll of Florida Manatee-Sarasota (FL)
Thomas More Coll (KY)
Weber State U (UT)

SPECIAL EDUCATION
Inter American U of Puerto Rico, Barranquitas Campus (PR)
Montana State U Billings (MT)
U of Maine at Presque Isle (ME)

SPECIAL EDUCATION RELATED
Minot State U (ND)

SPECIAL PRODUCTS MARKETING
Palm Beach State Coll (FL)

SPEECH COMMUNICATION AND RHETORIC
American Public U System (WV)
Indiana Wesleyan U (IN)
Lincoln Coll of New England, Southington (CT)
Mount St. Joseph U (OH)
State U of New York Coll of Agriculture and Technology at Cobleskill (NY)
Trevecca Nazarene U (TN)
Trine U (IN)
Tulane U (LA)
U of Rio Grande (OH)
Utah Valley U (UT)
Wright State U (OH)
Wright State U–Lake Campus (OH)

SPEECH-LANGUAGE PATHOLOGY
Elms Coll (MA)
Southern Adventist U (TN)

SPORT AND FITNESS ADMINISTRATION/MANAGEMENT
Mount Vernon Nazarene U (OH)
National U (CA)
Southwestern Adventist U (TX)
State U of New York Coll of Technology at Delhi (NY)
Webber International U (FL)

STATISTICS
State Coll of Florida Manatee-Sarasota (FL)

SUBSTANCE ABUSE/ADDICTION COUNSELING
Indiana Wesleyan U (IN)
Midland Coll (TX)
National U (CA)
St. Petersburg Coll (FL)
U of Great Falls (MT)
Washburn U (KS)

SURGICAL TECHNOLOGY
Baker Coll (MI)
Berkeley Coll–Woodland Park Campus (NJ)
Cabarrus Coll of Health Sciences (NC)
Lincoln U (MO)
Mercy Coll of Health Sciences (IA)
Montana State U Billings (MT)
Mount Aloysius Coll (PA)
Nebraska Methodist Coll (NE)
New England Inst of Technology (RI)
Pennsylvania Coll of Health Sciences (PA)
Pennsylvania Coll of Technology (PA)
Rasmussen Coll Brooklyn Park (MN)
Rasmussen Coll St. Cloud (MN)
Robert Morris U Illinois (IL)
Sentara Coll of Health Sciences (VA)
Stevens-Henager Coll, Boise (ID)
The U of Akron (OH)
U of Arkansas for Medical Sciences (AR)
U of Montana (MT)
U of Saint Francis (IN)
Washburn U (KS)

SURVEYING TECHNOLOGY
Ferris State U (MI)
Glenville State Coll (WV)
Palm Beach State Coll (FL)
Penn State Wilkes-Barre (PA)
Pennsylvania Coll of Technology (PA)
Polytechnic U of Puerto Rico (PR)
State U of New York Coll of Environmental Science and Forestry (NY)
The U of Akron (OH)
Utah Valley U (UT)

SUSTAINABILITY STUDIES
Lock Haven U of Pennsylvania (PA)

SYSTEM, NETWORKING, AND LAN/WAN MANAGEMENT
Baker Coll (MI)
Dakota State U (SD)
Midland Coll (TX)
Stratford U, Falls Church (VA)

TEACHER ASSISTANT/AIDE
Alverno Coll (WI)
National U (CA)
State U of New York Coll of Agriculture and Technology at Cobleskill (NY)
U of Maine at Presque Isle (ME)
The U of Montana Western (MT)
Valparaiso U (IN)

TECHNICAL TEACHER EDUCATION
Western Kentucky U (KY)

TECHNOLOGY/INDUSTRIAL ARTS TEACHER EDUCATION
State Coll of Florida Manatee-Sarasota (FL)

TELECOMMUNICATIONS TECHNOLOGY
New York City Coll of Technology of the City U of New York (NY)
Pace U (NY)
Penn State Hazleton (PA)
Penn State New Kensington (PA)
Penn State Schuylkill (PA)
Penn State Wilkes-Barre (PA)
Penn State York (PA)

TERRORISM AND COUNTERTERRORISM OPERATIONS
American Public U System (WV)

THEATER DESIGN AND TECHNOLOGY
Johnson State Coll (VT)
U of Rio Grande (OH)
Utah Valley U (UT)

THEOLOGICAL AND MINISTERIAL STUDIES RELATED
California Christian Coll (CA)
Lincoln Christian U (IL)

THEOLOGY
Appalachian Bible Coll (WV)
Briar Cliff U (IA)
Calvary Bible Coll and Theological Seminary (MO)
Creighton U (NE)
Franciscan U of Steubenville (OH)
Immaculata U (PA)
Marian U (IN)
Missouri Baptist U (MO)
Ohio Dominican U (OH)
William Jessup U (CA)
Williams Baptist Coll (AR)

THEOLOGY AND RELIGIOUS VOCATIONS RELATED
Anderson U (IN)
Southeastern U (FL)
Trevecca Nazarene U (TN)
U of Valley Forge (PA)

THERAPEUTIC RECREATION
Colorado Mountain Coll, Glenwood Springs (CO)

TOOL AND DIE TECHNOLOGY
Ferris State U (MI)

TOURISM AND TRAVEL SERVICES MANAGEMENT
Colorado Mountain Coll, Steamboat Springs (CO)

TOURISM AND TRAVEL SERVICES MARKETING
State U of New York Coll of Agriculture and Technology at Cobleskill (NY)
State U of New York Coll of Technology at Delhi (NY)

TRADE AND INDUSTRIAL TEACHER EDUCATION
Eastern Kentucky U (KY)
Murray State U (KY)
State Coll of Florida Manatee-Sarasota (FL)

TRANSPORTATION AND HIGHWAY ENGINEERING
The U of Toledo (OH)

TRANSPORTATION AND MATERIALS MOVING RELATED
Baker Coll (MI)

TRANSPORTATION/MOBILITY MANAGEMENT
Polk State Coll (FL)

TURF AND TURFGRASS MANAGEMENT
North Carolina State U (NC)
U of Massachusetts Amherst (MA)

URBAN MINISTRY
Tabor Coll (KS)

URBAN STUDIES/AFFAIRS
Saint Peter's U (NJ)

VEHICLE AND VEHICLE PARTS AND ACCESSORIES MARKETING
Pennsylvania Coll of Technology (PA)

VETERINARY/ANIMAL HEALTH TECHNOLOGY
Baker Coll (MI)
Becker Coll (MA)
Colorado Mountain Coll, Glenwood Springs (CO)
Dalhousie U (NS, Canada)
Hickey Coll (MO)
International Business Coll, Fort Wayne (IN)
Morehead State U (KY)
New England Inst of Technology (RI)
Purdue U (IN)
St. Petersburg Coll (FL)
State U of New York Coll of Technology at Canton (NY)
State U of New York Coll of Technology at Delhi (NY)
Universidad del Turabo (PR)
U of Maine at Augusta (ME)
U of New Hampshire (NH)
Vermont Tech Coll (VT)

VISUAL AND PERFORMING ARTS
Pine Manor Coll (MA)

VOCATIONAL REHABILITATION COUNSELING
State Coll of Florida Manatee-Sarasota (FL)

WATER QUALITY AND WASTEWATER TREATMENT MANAGEMENT AND RECYCLING TECHNOLOGY
Colorado Mesa U (CO)
Western Kentucky U (KY)

WEAPONS OF MASS DESTRUCTION
American Public U System (WV)

WEB/MULTIMEDIA MANAGEMENT AND WEBMASTER
American Public U System (WV)
Lewis-Clark State Coll (ID)
Montana Tech of The U of Montana (MT)
St. Petersburg Coll (FL)

WEB PAGE, DIGITAL/MULTIMEDIA AND INFORMATION RESOURCES DESIGN
Academy of Art U (CA)
Baker Coll (MI)
Champlain Coll (VT)
Florida National U (FL)
Limestone Coll (SC)

New England Inst of Technology (RI)
Palm Beach State Coll (FL)
Polk State Coll (FL)
Rasmussen Coll Appleton (WI)
Rasmussen Coll Aurora (IL)
Rasmussen Coll Blaine (MN)
Rasmussen Coll Bloomington (MN)
Rasmussen Coll Brooklyn Park (MN)
Rasmussen Coll Eagan (MN)
Rasmussen Coll Fargo (ND)
Rasmussen Coll Fort Myers (FL)
Rasmussen Coll Green Bay (WI)
Rasmussen Coll Kansas City/Overland Park (KS)
Rasmussen Coll Lake Elmo/Woodbury (MN)
Rasmussen Coll Land O' Lakes (FL)
Rasmussen Coll Mankato (MN)
Rasmussen Coll Mokena/Tinley Park (IL)
Rasmussen Coll Moorhead (MN)
Rasmussen Coll New Port Richey (FL)
Rasmussen Coll Ocala (FL)
Rasmussen Coll Romeoville/Joliet (IL)
Rasmussen Coll St. Cloud (MN)
Rasmussen Coll Tampa/Brandon (FL)
Rasmussen Coll Topeka (KS)
Rasmussen Coll Wausau (WI)
St. Petersburg Coll (FL)
Stratford U, Woodbridge (VA)
Thomas More Coll (KY)
Universidad del Turabo (PR)
Utah Valley U (UT)
Wilmington U (DE)

WELDING ENGINEERING TECHNOLOGY
New England Inst of Technology (RI)

WELDING TECHNOLOGY
Ferris State U (MI)
Idaho State U (ID)
Lewis-Clark State Coll (ID)
Liberty U (VA)
Midland Coll (TX)
Pennsylvania Coll of Technology (PA)
State U of New York Coll of Technology at Delhi (NY)
U of Montana (MT)
Weber State U (UT)

WILDLAND/FOREST FIREFIGHTING AND INVESTIGATION
Colorado Mesa U (CO)

WILDLIFE, FISH AND WILDLANDS SCIENCE AND MANAGEMENT
Coll of Coastal Georgia (GA)
State U of New York Coll of Agriculture and Technology at Cobleskill (NY)

WOMEN'S STUDIES
State Coll of Florida Manatee-Sarasota (FL)

WORD PROCESSING
Palm Beach State Coll (FL)

WRITING
Carroll Coll (MT)

YOUTH MINISTRY
Calvary Bible Coll and Theological Seminary (MO)
U of Valley Forge (PA)

ZOOLOGY/ANIMAL BIOLOGY
Palm Beach State Coll (FL)

Alphabetical Listing of Two-Year Colleges

In this index, the page numbers of the profiles are printed in regular type, the displays are in *italic*, and the Close-Ups are in **bold**.

NOTES

NOTES

NOTES